Economic Indicators Handbook

Second Edition

Economic Indicators Handbook

TIME SERIES • CONVERSIONS • DOCUMENTATION

Second Edition

Compiled and Edited by
Arsen J. Darnay

Gale Research Inc. • DETROIT • WASHINGTON, D.C. • LONDON

Arsen J. Darnay, *Editor*

Editorial Code & Data Inc. Staff

Marlita A. Reddy, *Research*
Nancy Ratliff, *Data Entry*
Ken Muth, *Data Processing*

Gale Research Staff

Jane Hoehner, *Developmental Editor*
Lawrence W. Baker, *Senior Developmental Editor*
Mary Beth Trimper, *Production Director*
Shanna P. Heilveil, *Production Assistant*
Cynthia Baldwin, *Art Director*
Pursuit Studios, *Cover Designers*

Library of Congress Cataloging-in-Publication Data

Economic indicators handbook: time series, conversions, documentation / compiled and edited
by Arsen J. Darnay. - 2d ed.
p. cm.
Includes index.
ISBN 0-8103-9064-7
1. Economic indicators - United States 2. United States - Economic conditions. I. Darnay,
Arsen
HC103.E26 1994
330.973 - dc20   92-13545
                                                                                        CIP

∞™ This book is printed on acid-free paper that meets the minimum requirements of American National Standard for Information Sciences - Permanence
Paper for Printed Library Materials, ANSI Z39.48-1984.

♻ This book is printed on recycled paper that meets Environmental Protection
Agency standards.

Gale Research Inc.
835 Penobscot Building
Detroit, Mi 48226-4094
ISBN 0-8103-9064-7
Printed in the United States of America
Published simultaneously in the United Kingdom
by Gale Research International Limited
(An affiliated company of Gale Research Inc.)

I(T)P

The trademark **ITP** is used under license.

TABLE OF CONTENTS

Chapter 6 - Consumer Price Index - continued

Chapter 6 - Consumer Price Index - continued

INTRODUCTION

SUMMARY

Economic Indicators Handbook (EIH), now in its second edition, presents a wide range of statistical series commonly used for measuring the economy of the United States. Featured are national income and production accounts, including Gross National Product (GNP) and Gross Domestic Product (GDP); the composite indexes of leading, lagging, and coincident indicators and their subcomponents; other cyclic indicators; selected economic series; a comprehensive presentation of the Consumer Price Index (CPI) in the aggregate and for 27 cities; a substantial selection from Producer Price Index (PPI); and selected stock market indexes. *EIH* covers 254 series; most are shown with detailed subdivisions or in constant and actual dollars so that, in total, 792 tables are presented. In all cases where data were available, series begin with the earliest date for which statistics were collected or estimated by the government or other sources, ranging from 1864-67 for GNP, 1913 for the CPI, and the 1940s for most business cycle indicators. *EIH* also features descriptive text; each major category is introduced and brief explanations, including an indication of significance, are provided for each series. Texts and tables are thoroughly indexed.

NEW IN THE SECOND EDITION

The second edition of *EIH* updates all series from their beginning to 1993. Some series were dropped because they have become obsolete. Others were added. Specific changes include the following:

- Detailed tables showing Gross National Product (GNP) subcomponents have been dropped in the second edition. The federal government has completed its shift to reporting Gross Domestic Product (GDP) instead of GNP. GDP data, including detailed subcomponent tables, have been issued back to 1929. These now replace the GNP details. However, GNP data are still reported in the aggregate in actual and in constant dollars.

- The reporting basis of GNP, GDP, cyclic indicators, business indicators, and economic indicator data has changed from a 1982 base year to a 1987 base year. The second edition presents these series in 1987 dollars.

- A chart has been added showing GDP and the major economic indicators from 1956 to 1993 in order to show visually how the series perform relative to periods of recession.

- A new section, *Implicit Price Deflators for Gross Domestic Product Sectors*, has been added in the chapter on Economic Series. This addition will make it easier for individuals, farmers, business analysts, and government analysts to calculate changes in prices due to inflation.

- Two Consumer Price Index (CPI) tables with a base year of 1967 have been dropped. All CPI data are now shown with a 1982-1984 index basis.

SCOPE

EIH presents statistical series grouped by major categories.

GNP and GDP. The fundamental measure of the U.S. economy—at least until the fall of 1991—has been GNP. For that reason, *EIH* begins with a presentation of aggregate GNP beginning with data for the 1869-1828 period and ending with data for the second quarter of 1993.

Late in 1991, the U.S. Department of Commerce, through its Bureau of Economic Analysis (BEA), announced that the government would henceforth feature Gross Domestic Product as the principal measure. The difference between GNP and GDP is subtle: GNP represents all income produced by U.S. residents and by their investments anywhere in the world; GDP represents all income produced on U.S. soil, by residents or foreigners. GNP is only slightly larger than GDP and is a better measure of total *resources* available to Americans; GDP is a better measure of the domestic economy's *performance*.

Although GNP-GDP differences are small, the manner in which income is calculated is different (see Chapter 2). Along with the shift from GNP to GDP, BEA also introduced a new base year for calculating the size of the economy in constant (inflation-adjusted) dollars; the base was moved from 1982 to 1987 dollars.

In this edition of *EIH*, GNP data are presented in aggregate form in actual and in 1987 dollars. GDP data are presented in aggregate form and by subcomponents in actual and in 1987 dollars.

Business Cycle Indicators. The federal government attempts to predict business cycles—recurring brief periods of decline in GNP/GDP followed by recovery and periods of growth—by using a number of economic series that lead the economy, coincide with it, or lag it (see Chapter 3). The composite indexes of leading, coincident, and lagging indicators are presented in full from the earliest period for which they are available; the series that make up these composite indexes are also presented.

Cyclic Indicators. Not all series classified as cyclic in behavior are included in the leading, coincident, and lagging indexes. A selection of others is presented under headings of Employment; Production and Income; Consumption, Trade, Orders, and Deliveries; Fixed Capital Investment; Inventories and Inventory Investment; Prices, Costs, and Profits; and Money and Credit. The selection was based in part on a review of series normally published in the business press (hence indicating usage by the public) and editorial judgment.

Economic Series. Many statistical measures of the economy are not classified as cyclic in nature and are not used to *predict* but to *measure* economic activity. The series included in *EIH* were, again, selected because they are commonly reported in the press or, in the editor's opinion, provide interesting insight into the functioning of the economy. Series on GDP implicit deflators were added in the second edition.

Prices. Chapters 6 and 7 present consumer and producer price indexes in considerable detail. The CPI is shown for both "all urban consumers" and the "urban wage earners" categories. Furthermore, major subcomponents categories (food, apparel, housing, etc.) are shown. Data for 27 cities/metro areas are then presented in the same detail. All CPI data are shown back to the earliest year for which they were collected or estimated by the Department of Labor.

The Producer Price Index is presented in Chapter 7 for 119 major categories and subcategories in monthly format; annual average data are also shown.

Selected Stock Market Indexes. The final chapter shows selected index data from the American Stock Exchange, NASDAQ (National Association of Securities Dealers Automated Equation system), and the New York Stock Exchange. Another stock index series, the Standard & Poor's 500 index—which is used by the BEA as a leading indicator—is presented in Chapter 3.

SOURCES

The information included in *EIH* came from the U.S. Department of Commerce, the U.S. Department of Labor, the American Stock Exchanged, the National Association of Securities Dealers, and the New York Stock Exchange. With a few exceptions, data were obtained by special arrangement rather than being extracted from published sources.

Most federal data series, of course, are built from multiple sources, public and private. The majority rely on surveys, some of which are voluntary and some of which, such as the quadrennial censuses of business, are mandated by law. GNP and GDP data; the indicator series built into the leading, coincident, and lagging indexes; and the CPI and PPI all require substantial statistical work by the federal agencies that prepare them. They are, in a very real sense, statistical "products" of the agencies (or consortia of agencies): they are built from a diverse number of statistical "raw materials" and the methods of constructing the final series are continuously being refined.

ORGANIZATION AND PRESENTATION

EIH is organized into eight chapters as follows:

Chapter 1 - Gross National Product
Chapter 2 - Gross Domestic Product
Chapter 3 - Business Cycle Indicators
Chapter 4 - Cyclic Indicators
Chapter 5 - Economic Series
Chapter 6 - Consumer Price Index
Chapter 7 - Producer Price Index
Chapter 8 - Selected Stock Market Indexes

A keyword index holds references to text and table contents.

Each chapter begins with an introductory text. The subject to be covered in the chapter is outlined in general terms. A bibliography is provided. Chapters 1, 3, 4, and 5 are further subdivided. Each subdivision is separately introduced. Each series covered is separately discussed under its own heading in the chapter or section introductions.

STATISTICAL CONVENTIONS

Many statistical series presented in *EIH* make use of conventions which may be unfamiliar to the casual user. While most of these are discussed in context in the chapter and section notes, a general discussion of *Indexing, Base Periods, Constant and Current Dollars, Annualized Rates,* and *Seasonal Adjustments* is presented here.

Indexing. Statistical information in *EIH* is presented in the form of raw information (dollars, hours, weeks, etc.) or in the form of indexes. Index numbers are used to present information relative to a data obtained for a specific period. A typical example is an index defined to have the value of 100 for the average outcome of a series in the year 1982. The following example illustrates the method used.

Year	Raw Value in Dollar	Index Value
1985	345	83.7
1986	356	86.4
1987	412	100.0
1988	436	105.8
1990	489	118.7

In the illustration above, 1987 is "the base period," discussed further below. It is assigned an arbitrary index value. In this case the value is 100, but it can be any number. Indexes of 10 or 50 are also commonly used, but 100 is the usual index base. The index for any year is calculated by the following formula:

(Current Year Raw Data / Base Year Raw Data) x 100.

Changes from one period to another may be calculated in index points or as a percent change. In the example above, the index point change between 1989 and 1990 is 12.9. The percentage change is 12.2, obtained by the formula:

((Current Index / Previous Index) - 1) x 100.

Measuring the percentage change between two index values produces the same result as measuring the percentage change in the raw data for the same periods.

Base Periods. Statistical series expressed as indexes or in constant dollars (see below) have base periods. A base period can be a day, a month, a year, or a range of years. The Consumer Price Index, for instances, is based on the 1982-1984 period; the average prices for these years are defined as 100.

The government periodically changes the base periods of indexes. The year chosen is typically the year of one of the quadrennial business censuses. The most recent such census was held in 1992. Many series are still expressed with a base of 1982 or 1987. Rebasing of a series (shifting to a more recent base period) is usually associated with a significant reworking of the statistical machinery which produces the numbers; hence there tends to be a lag time between the most recent business census and the base period in use. For example, the Gross National Product began to be reported (in November 1991) in 1987 dollars—four years after the last quadrennial business census.

Constant and Current Dollars. The measurement of dollar-denominated values from one period of the next can produce inaccurate results, for some purposes, if changes due only to increasing or dropping prices are not taken into account. For this reason, many series are reported both in current dollars (also called "actual" dollars) and in constant dollars (also called "real" dollars). Constant dollars are current dollars that have been adjusted for the effects of inflation relative to a base period. Because a base period is used, people sometimes use phrases like "1982 dollars" or "1987 dollars." They mean constant dollars with a 1982 or a 1987 base year. The purchasing power of the dollar in the base year is arbitrarily defined as "real." And today's dollars are adjusted to that value by using series such as the Consumer Price Index and the Producer's Price Index. These indexes record changes in prices by surveying the actual prices charged for identical products and services two periods apart. If the same loaf of bread costs 89 cents in 1991 and 92 cents in 1992, inflation accounts for 3 cents: it took 3 cents more to get the same loaf in the second period. Constant dollar calculations, of course, use a wide range of representative products and services measured in a systematic manner across the nation.

Annualized Rates. National production and income data—as well as some other series—report some figures quarterly at "annualized rates." This means that data developed for the quarter are multiplied by four to show what the year would be like if results in this quarter continued. The data, typically, are seasonally adjusted (see below) before they are expressed at annualized rates.

Seasonal Adjustments. Economic activity is by nature seasonal. More heating oil will be used in the winter, more people seek employment in the summer as college students come home. Retailers sell proportionally more goods in December than in other months. Many series are seasonally adjusted to take such fluctuations into account. Other series are shown as "not seasonally adjusted." Seasonal adjustments are made by statisticians in and out of government by using experience factors developed over time. Data are recalculated using these experience factors so that heavy fuel oil sales in the fall and winter are "distributed" evenly across the entire year.

ACKNOWLEDGMENTS

Economic Indicators Handbook is based on the hard work and intellectual rigor of many individuals in government, academia, associations, and industry. Some of them took of their valuable time to help in the preparation of this book by providing data and patient explanations of sometimes very difficult concepts. In particular, the editor is indebted to the staff of the Bureau of Economic Analysis, U.S. Department of Commerce and staff of the Bureau of Labor Statistics, U.S. Department of Labor.

COMMENTS AND SUGGESTIONS

Comments on *EIH* or suggestion for its improvement are always welcome. Although every effort is made to maintain accuracy, errors may occasionally occur; the editor will be grateful if these are called to his attention. Please contact:

> Editor
> *Economic Indicators Handbook*
> Gale Research Inc.
> 835 Penobscot Building
> Detroit, MI 48226-4094
> Phone: (313) 961-2242 or (800) 347-GALE
> Fax: (313) 961-6741

Economic Indicators Handbook

Second Edition

CHAPTER 1

GROSS NATIONAL PRODUCT

GROSS NATIONAL PRODUCT

The Gross National Product (GNP) is the sum of all purchases of goods and services by individuals and government; the value of gross domestic investment, including changes in business inventories; and exports less imports (net exports). GNP is thus a measure of the productivity of the nation. GNP can be summarized by the following formula:

GNP = Consumption + Investment + Government + Exports - Imports.

Only final purchases are measured to avoid double counting. The value of unfinished goods purchased by companies and not resold as finished product is reflected in changed business inventories.

GNP measures goods and services *produced by labor and property supplied by U.S. residents*. The labor and property may be located *in* the U.S. or abroad. Conversely, goods and services produced by foreign labor and property are excluded, even if located on U.S. soil. The next chapter covers Gross Domestic Product (GDP) which measures goods and services *produced by labor and property located in the U.S.* GDP has been selected by the U.S. Department of Commerce as the new measure of U.S. production, displacing GNP. However, since GNP accounting has been the dominant method until very recently (November 1991), a full historical treatment of GNP is provided first.

Modern GNP reporting began in 1929 and is the product of a comprehensive statistical system (the National Income and Product Accounts, NIPA) managed by the Department of Commerce, Bureau of Economic Analysis (BEA). GNP estimates were extended back to 1909 based on limited statistical sources by the government; and estimates based on even less information have been made back to colonial times. Data in *EIH* are reported from 1929 forward.

GNP data are *estimates* based on a large number of surveys conducted by the federal government for other purposes or obtained from private industry or association sources. Precise measurement of economic activity on a scale such as that of the United States is virtually impossible; hence partial data, estimates, and statistical methods are necessary to approximate actual economic activity. During the years of the economic censuses, which recur at 5-year intervals, detailed data are collected for many GNP components which serve as "benchmarks" for estimates.

Presentation of Data

The first table is a summary of GNP for the period 1869-1928. Data were obtained, courtesy of the Bureau of Economic Analysis, for aggregate GNP for this period, in actual and in constant (1982) dollars.

Two tables for the GNP, one in actual and one in 1987 constant dollars, are presented for the 1929 through 1993 period. Detailed component tables are not included in this edition because the government has now completely shifted emphasis to Gross Domestic Product (GDP) and all data have been restated using GDP definitions.

Historical Data. The historical data are presented in decade averages for the 1869-1878 and the 1879-1888 periods and the annually thereafter to 1928. Data are shown in actual and in constant dollars, permitting the calculation of growth and decline rates year to year and the implicit price deflator. The implicit price deflator shows the relationship of prices, in a given year, as they compare to those of a base year—in this case 1982. The deflator is calculated by the formula:

(Actual Dollar Value / Constant Dollar Value) x 100.

With the implicit price deflator known, constant dollar value can be calculated, if unknown, by the formula:

(Current Dollar Value x 100) / Implicit Price Deflator.

And current value, if unknown, can be calculated from constant dollar value by the formula:

(Constant Dollar Value / 100) x Implicit Price Deflator.

Quarterly Data. Data for quarters, when available, represent seasonally adjusted, annualized quarterly estimates. This means that the results for the quarter are projected for the entire year; for example, if 2 million cars were sold in the quarter, the annual rate would be 8 million cars; therefore, the production value of 8 million cars is reflected in that quarter's estimate. Seasonal adjustments are made to reflect conditions that are due to well known, recurring, seasonal phenomena. For example, fuel oil consumption is known to be much higher in winter than in summer; fuel consumption, therefore, is increased in summer quarters and decreased in winter quarters to "smooth" the data. Each quarter, in other words, shows what GNP would be for the entire year if the conditions in that quarter, as adjusted, were to continue for the balance of the year.

Growth or decline between any two quarters is also annualized, showing a compounded growth rate reached by the formula:

(This Quarter / Last Quarter)^4 - 1 x 100 = percent growth rate of GNP.

If this quarter is \$4,118.9 billion and last quarter was \$4,124.1 billion, the formula results in - 0.503 percent because the quarterly growth rate was compounded and annualized—rather than a rate of - 0.12 percent, which is the simple percentile difference between the two numbers.

Annual Data. Annual figures show final estimates for GNP. Since GNP estimates are revised as better and better data become available, data for recent years are subject to revision and results for the most recent year tend to be preliminary estimates. Annual growth or decline figures show simple percentile changes between the two years reached by the formula:

(This Year / Last Year) - 1 x 100.

If this year is \$4,157.3 billion and last year was \$4,117.7 billion, the growth is 0.96 percent.

GNP in Constant Dollars. Constant dollars (also referred to as "real" dollars) are used to measure GNP in order to account for inflationary or deflationary price changes; inflation is believed to come about because prices are raised in response to unusually high demand; deflation (a much rarer phenomenon) results when prices drop because demand is soft; in both cases, products or services sold remain unchanged; only prices change; constant dollar expression of GNP permits direct comparison of one period with another. In the 20-year period 1970 to 1989, for instance, GNP showed positive growth in every year in actual dollars; measured in constant dollars, the years 1970, 1974-75, 1980, and 1982 showed negative growth.

GNP Revisions

Changes in GNP methodologies and allocation of items to national accounts are continuous. These changes typically involve (1) changes in the classification of certain items from one GNP account to another; for example, in 1985, railroad track replacement costs were shifted from business expenditures to investment; (2) the inclusion or exclusion of areas (e.g., Puerto Rico and U.S. territories were excluded from GNP in 1985); and (3) changes in methodology, especially for estimating categories not fully covered by surveys; for example, in 1985, improved adjustments were made for misreporting on tax returns, the so-called "underground economy adjustments." Major changes in recent decades were introduced in 1976, 1980, 1985, and 1991. For a bibliography of major and annual changes, see p. 23-30, reference 3, below, and July issues of the *Survey of Current Business* (reference 4).

Bibliography

1. Carnes, W. Stansbury and Stephen D. Slifer. *The Atlas of Economic Indicators*. Harper Collins, 1991.

2. U.S. Department of Commerce, Bureau of Economic Analysis. *GNP: An Overview of Source Data and Estimating Methods*. Methodology Paper Series MP-4. Washington, DC: U.S. Government Printing Office, September 1987.

3. U.S. Department of Commerce, Bureau of Economic Analysis. *An Introduction to National Economic Accounting*. Methodology Paper Series MP-1. Washington, DC: U.S. Government Printing Office, March 1985.

4. U.S. Department of Commerce, Bureau of Economic Analysis. *Survey of Current Business*. Superintendent of Documents, U.S. Government Printing Office, Washington, DC 20302.

Historical Gross National Product
1869-1928

Historial GNP estimates, 1869-1928, shown in billions of actual and constant 1982 dollars. 1869-78 and 1879-88 values are decade averages.

Year	Current Dollars (Billions)	Change from Previous Year - %	Constant 82 Dol. (Billions)	Change from Previous Year - %	Implicit Price Deflator 82=100	Year	Current Dollars (Billions)	Change from Previous Year - %	Constant 82 Dol. (Billions)	Change from Previous Year - %	Implicit Price Deflator 82=100
1869-78	7.7	-	84.6	-	9.102	1908	29.0	-8.8	366.4	-8.3	7.915
1879-88	11.7	-	154.5	-	7.573	1909	33.7	16.2	411.3	12.3	8.194
1889	13.1	-	179.5	-	7.298	1910	35.7	5.9	423.3	2.9	8.434
1890	13.7	4.6	192.8	7.4	7.106	1911	36.1	1.1	436.3	3.1	8.274
1891	14.1	2.9	201.6	4.6	6.994	1912	39.7	10.0	457.2	4.8	8.683
1892	15.0	6.4	220.7	9.5	6.797	1913	39.9	0.5	462.4	1.1	8.629
1893	14.4	-4.0	210.4	-4.7	6.844	1914	38.9	-2.5	444.4	-3.9	8.753
1894	13.2	-8.3	204.5	-2.8	6.455	1915	40.3	3.6	439.6	-1.1	9.167
1895	14.5	9.8	228.8	11.9	6.337	1916	48.6	20.6	472.8	7.6	10.279
1896	13.9	-4.1	223.7	-2.2	6.214	1917	60.7	24.9	481.7	1.9	12.601
1897	15.3	10.1	245.0	9.5	6.245	1918	76.8	26.5	570.0	18.3	13.474
1898	16.1	5.2	250.9	2.4	6.417	1919	84.7	10.3	528.3	-7.3	16.033
1899	18.2	13.0	273.7	9.1	6.650	1920	92.2	8.9	487.1	-7.8	18.928
1900	19.6	7.7	281.1	2.7	6.973	1921	70.2	-23.9	452.8	-7.0	15.504
1901	21.7	10.7	313.4	11.5	6.924	1922	74.8	6.6	519.6	14.8	14.396
1902	22.6	4.1	316.4	1.0	7.143	1923	85.9	14.8	576.9	11.0	14.890
1903	24.0	6.2	331.8	4.9	7.233	1924	85.5	-0.5	582.7	1.0	14.673
1904	24.0	0.0	328.2	-1.1	7.313	1925	94.0	9.9	625.0	7.3	15.040
1905	26.3	9.6	352.4	7.4	7.463	1926	97.9	4.1	662.3	6.0	14.782
1906	30.0	14.1	392.9	11.5	7.636	1927	95.8	-2.1	661.2	-0.2	14.489
1907	31.8	6.0	399.5	1.7	7.960	1928	97.7	2.0	667.7	1.0	14.632

Sources: National Bureau of Economic Research and U.S. Department of Commerce. Obtained as handwritten communication from Bureau of Economic Analysis.

Gross National Product - Actual Dollars

In billions of actual dollars and percent. Quarterly data are seasonally adjusted and annualized. Growth rates for quarters are compound annual growth rates; changes from year to year are percentage changes.

Year	1st Quarter	% Change	2nd Quarter	% Change	3rd Quarter	% Change	4th Quarter	% Change	TOTAL	% Change
1929	-	-	-	-	-	-	-	-	103.9	-
1930	-	-	-	-	-	-	-	-	91.1	-12.3
1931	-	-	-	-	-	-	-	-	76.3	-16.2
1932	-	-	-	-	-	-	-	-	58.3	-23.6
1933	-	-	-	-	-	-	-	-	55.9	-4.1
1934	-	-	-	-	-	-	-	-	65.4	17.0
1935	-	-	-	-	-	-	-	-	72.7	11.2
1936	-	-	-	-	-	-	-	-	83.0	14.2
1937	-	-	-	-	-	-	-	-	91.2	9.9
1938	-	-	-	-	-	-	-	-	85.3	-6.5
1939	-	-	-	-	-	-	-	-	91.3	7.0
1940	-	-	-	-	-	-	-	-	100.4	10.0
1941	-	-	-	-	-	-	-	-	125.5	25.0
1942	-	-	-	-	-	-	-	-	159.0	26.7
1943	-	-	-	-	-	-	-	-	192.8	21.3
1944	-	-	-	-	-	-	-	-	211.5	9.7
1945	-	-	-	-	-	-	-	-	213.5	0.9
1946	200.3	-	208.4	17.2	218.6	21.1	223.0	8.3	212.6	-0.4
1947	227.8	8.9	231.7	7.0	236.1	7.8	246.3	18.4	235.5	10.8
1948	252.6	10.6	259.9	12.1	266.8	11.0	268.1	2.0	261.8	11.2
1949	263.0	-7.4	259.5	-5.2	261.2	2.6	258.9	-3.5	260.7	-0.4
1950	269.6	17.6	279.3	15.2	296.9	27.7	308.4	16.4	288.5	10.7
1951	323.2	20.6	331.1	10.1	337.9	8.5	342.3	5.3	333.6	15.6
1952	345.3	3.6	345.9	0.7	351.7	6.9	364.2	15.0	351.8	5.5
1953	371.0	7.7	374.5	3.8	373.7	-0.9	368.7	-5.2	372.0	5.7
1954	368.4	-0.3	368.7	0.3	373.4	5.2	381.9	9.4	373.1	0.3
1955	394.8	14.2	403.1	8.7	411.4	8.5	417.8	6.4	406.8	9.0
1956	420.5	2.6	426.0	5.3	430.8	4.6	439.2	8.0	429.1	5.5
1957	448.1	8.4	450.1	1.8	457.2	6.5	451.7	-4.7	451.8	5.3
1958	444.4	-6.3	448.6	3.8	461.8	12.3	475.0	11.9	457.5	1.3
1959	486.2	9.8	498.9	10.9	499.3	0.3	503.6	3.5	497.0	8.6
1960	517.0	11.1	516.0	-0.8	519.0	2.3	514.2	-3.6	516.6	3.9
1961	518.8	3.6	529.4	8.4	540.2	8.4	553.2	10.0	535.4	3.6
1962	565.7	9.3	573.5	5.6	580.3	4.8	583.7	2.4	575.8	7.5
1963	592.7	6.3	601.1	5.8	613.9	8.8	623.0	6.1	607.7	5.5
1964	639.9	11.3	648.5	5.5	659.2	6.8	664.5	3.3	653.0	7.5
1965	685.3	13.1	697.7	7.4	713.7	9.5	735.6	12.9	708.1	8.4
1966	758.2	12.9	767.3	4.9	780.3	7.0	793.9	7.2	774.9	9.4
1967	803.0	4.7	809.0	3.0	826.2	8.8	841.0	7.4	819.8	5.8
1968	865.5	12.2	889.8	11.7	906.6	7.8	920.0	6.0	895.5	9.2
1969	943.7	10.7	957.3	5.9	976.7	8.4	984.8	3.4	965.6	7.8
1970	996.0	4.6	1,010.4	5.9	1,029.4	7.7	1,032.5	1.2	1,017.1	5.3
1971	1,077.3	18.5	1,096.2	7.2	1,115.7	7.3	1,130.2	5.3	1,104.9	8.6
1972	1,169.2	14.5	1,200.8	11.3	1,226.8	8.9	1,265.9	13.4	1,215.7	10.0
1973	1,315.1	16.5	1,346.2	9.8	1,372.3	8.0	1,415.6	13.2	1,362.3	12.1
1974	1,428.1	3.6	1,460.7	9.4	1,490.2	8.3	1,518.3	7.8	1,474.3	8.2
1975	1,525.2	1.8	1,564.0	10.6	1,627.6	17.3	1,679.5	13.4	1,599.1	8.5
1976	1,733.7	13.5	1,763.3	7.0	1,797.2	7.9	1,847.7	11.7	1,785.5	11.7
1977	1,902.7	12.4	1,973.8	15.8	2,036.2	13.3	2,065.8	5.9	1,994.6	11.7
1978	2,112.4	9.3	2,232.8	24.8	2,295.9	11.8	2,377.1	14.9	2,254.5	13.0
1979	2,425.2	8.3	2,483.0	9.9	2,559.6	12.9	2,615.3	9.0	2,520.8	11.8
1980	2,687.7	11.5	2,679.4	-1.2	2,739.8	9.3	2,861.5	19.0	2,742.1	8.8
1981	2,985.5	18.5	3,023.5	5.2	3,112.4	12.3	3,133.7	2.8	3,063.8	11.7
1982	3,123.7	-1.3	3,179.2	7.3	3,193.8	1.8	3,222.6	3.7	3,179.8	3.8
1983	3,283.8	7.8	3,394.0	14.1	3,481.6	10.7	3,578.4	11.6	3,434.4	8.0
1984	3,694.2	13.6	3,778.3	9.4	3,843.3	7.1	3,890.2	5.0	3,801.5	10.7
1985	3,955.7	6.9	4,012.9	5.9	4,089.5	7.9	4,156.2	6.7	4,053.6	6.6
1986	4,231.4	7.4	4,239.1	0.7	4,300.0	5.9	4,340.5	3.8	4,277.7	5.5
1987	4,412.4	6.8	4,497.5	7.9	4,577.7	7.3	4,690.5	10.2	4,544.5	6.2
1988	4,764.3	6.4	4,862.7	8.5	4,951.6	7.5	5,054.3	8.6	4,908.2	8.0
1989	5,164.0	9.0	5,243.3	6.3	5,294.7	4.0	5,365.0	5.4	5,266.8	7.3
1990	5,482.1	9.0	5,559.3	5.8	5,599.9	3.0	5,630.0	2.2	5,567.8	5.7
1991	5,656.1	1.9	5,710.6	3.9	5,766.2	4.0	5,815.5	3.5	5,737.1	3.0
1992	5,927.6	7.9	5,996.3	4.7	6,067.3	4.8	6,191.9	8.5	6,045.8	5.4
1993	6,262.1	4.6	6,327.1	4.2	-	-	-	-	-	-

Source: "The National Income and Product Accounts of the United States, 1929-82: Statistical Tables," and subsequent July issues of the *Survey of Current Business*. - indicates that data are unavailable or zero.

Gross National Product - 1987 Dollars

In billions of 1987 dollars and percent. Quarterly data are seasonally adjusted and annualized. Growth rates for quarters are compound annual growth rates; changes from year to year are percentage changes.

Year	1st Quarter	% Change	2nd Quarter	% Change	3rd Quarter	% Change	4th Quarter	% Change	TOTAL	% Change
1929	-	-	-	-	-	-	-	-	827.4	-
1930	-	-	-	-	-	-	-	-	754.2	-8.8
1931	-	-	-	-	-	-	-	-	695.5	-7.8
1932	-	-	-	-	-	-	-	-	603.0	-13.3
1933	-	-	-	-	-	-	-	-	589.9	-2.2
1934	-	-	-	-	-	-	-	-	634.8	7.6
1935	-	-	-	-	-	-	-	-	684.1	7.8
1936	-	-	-	-	-	-	-	-	780.0	14.0
1937	-	-	-	-	-	-	-	-	814.5	4.4
1938	-	-	-	-	-	-	-	-	782.2	-4.0
1939	-	-	-	-	-	-	-	-	844.2	7.9
1940	-	-	-	-	-	-	-	-	908.8	7.7
1941	-	-	-	-	-	-	-	-	1,074.4	18.2
1942	-	-	-	-	-	-	-	-	1,288.4	19.9
1943	-	-	-	-	-	-	-	-	1,543.6	19.8
1944	-	-	-	-	-	-	-	-	1,673.3	8.4
1945	-	-	-	-	-	-	-	-	1,605.0	-4.1
1946	-	-	-	-	-	-	-	-	1,276.0	-20.5
1947	1,244.9	-	1,252.9	2.6	1,260.7	2.5	1,275.6	4.8	1,258.5	-1.4
1948	1,290.9	4.9	1,302.9	3.8	1,310.9	2.5	1,323.5	3.9	1,307.0	3.9
1949	1,312.1	-3.4	1,308.6	-1.1	1,318.9	3.2	1,307.6	-3.4	1,311.8	0.4
1950	1,357.0	16.0	1,400.1	13.3	1,451.7	15.6	1,490.3	11.1	1,425.6	8.7
1951	1,509.2	5.2	1,557.1	13.3	1,594.9	10.1	1,606.2	2.9	1,567.4	9.9
1952	1,617.3	2.8	1,621.8	1.1	1,631.3	2.4	1,666.8	9.0	1,634.3	4.3
1953	1,696.2	7.2	1,704.8	2.0	1,696.2	-2.0	1,679.6	-3.9	1,694.2	3.7
1954	1,669.9	-2.3	1,667.5	-0.6	1,686.9	4.7	1,708.8	5.3	1,683.3	-0.6
1955	1,753.3	10.8	1,769.1	3.7	1,788.8	4.5	1,804.8	3.6	1,779.0	5.7
1956	1,799.2	-1.2	1,810.6	2.6	1,814.6	0.9	1,837.4	5.1	1,815.5	2.1
1957	1,849.3	2.6	1,848.8	-0.1	1,864.6	3.5	1,841.0	-5.0	1,850.9	1.9
1958	1,800.8	-8.5	1,815.4	3.3	1,851.4	8.2	1,891.2	8.9	1,839.7	-0.6
1959	1,915.1	5.2	1,947.7	7.0	1,941.8	-1.2	1,953.6	2.5	1,939.6	5.4
1960	1,988.1	7.3	1,983.3	-1.0	1,985.8	0.5	1,974.0	-2.4	1,982.8	2.2
1961	1,991.1	3.5	2,018.9	5.7	2,048.4	6.0	2,090.1	8.4	2,037.1	2.7
1962	2,117.3	5.3	2,140.6	4.5	2,157.7	3.2	2,157.6	-0.0	2,143.3	5.2
1963	2,187.4	5.6	2,215.3	5.2	2,253.6	7.1	2,271.0	3.1	2,231.8	4.1
1964	2,329.3	10.7	2,347.3	3.1	2,375.4	4.9	2,380.6	0.9	2,358.1	5.7
1965	2,429.1	8.4	2,462.5	5.6	2,503.8	6.9	2,560.3	9.3	2,488.9	5.5
1966	2,613.8	8.6	2,618.5	0.7	2,642.7	3.7	2,657.8	2.3	2,633.2	5.8
1967	2,674.2	2.5	2,685.5	1.7	2,717.9	4.9	2,732.8	2.2	2,702.6	2.6
1968	2,770.3	5.6	2,815.6	6.7	2,836.0	2.9	2,840.6	0.7	2,815.6	4.2
1969	2,883.6	6.2	2,886.0	0.3	2,901.7	2.2	2,892.2	-1.3	2,890.9	2.7
1970	2,885.5	-0.9	2,877.9	-1.0	2,913.0	5.0	2,889.7	-3.2	2,891.5	0.0
1971	2,959.7	10.0	2,965.4	0.8	2,981.2	2.1	2,997.4	2.2	2,975.9	2.9
1972	3,058.4	8.4	3,110.5	7.0	3,148.4	5.0	3,197.8	6.4	3,128.8	5.1
1973	3,279.4	10.6	3,295.6	2.0	3,297.2	0.2	3,322.1	3.1	3,298.6	5.4
1974	3,298.4	-2.8	3,304.3	0.7	3,272.2	-3.8	3,254.6	-2.1	3,282.4	-0.5
1975	3,177.3	-9.2	3,213.9	4.7	3,275.5	7.9	3,323.6	6.0	3,247.6	-1.1
1976	3,386.8	7.8	3,400.5	1.6	3,412.7	1.4	3,448.9	4.3	3,412.2	5.1
1977	3,503.9	6.5	3,561.7	6.8	3,610.8	5.6	3,599.3	-1.3	3,569.0	4.6
1978	3,629.1	3.4	3,737.9	12.5	3,769.8	3.5	3,819.3	5.4	3,739.0	4.8
1979	3,821.2	0.2	3,829.8	0.9	3,862.0	3.4	3,868.3	0.7	3,845.3	2.8
1980	3,884.6	1.7	3,782.3	-10.1	3,780.5	-0.2	3,846.2	7.1	3,823.4	-0.6
1981	3,901.6	5.9	3,882.8	-1.9	3,904.9	2.3	3,848.5	-5.7	3,884.4	1.6
1982	3,793.0	-5.6	3,810.3	1.8	3,789.4	-2.2	3,791.7	0.2	3,796.1	-2.3
1983	3,816.5	2.6	3,916.7	10.9	3,978.8	6.5	4,046.6	7.0	3,939.6	3.8
1984	4,119.1	7.4	4,169.4	5.0	4,193.0	2.3	4,216.4	2.3	4,174.5	6.0
1985	4,238.1	2.1	4,270.5	3.1	4,321.8	4.9	4,349.5	2.6	4,295.0	2.9
1986	4,406.4	5.3	4,394.6	-1.1	4,422.3	2.5	4,430.8	0.8	4,413.5	2.8
1987	4,463.9	3.0	4,517.8	4.9	4,563.6	4.1	4,633.0	6.2	4,544.5	3.0
1988	4,667.1	3.0	4,710.3	3.8	4,738.7	2.4	4,789.0	4.3	4,726.3	4.0
1989	4,830.7	3.5	4,851.6	1.7	4,853.4	0.1	4,875.1	1.8	4,852.7	2.7
1990	4,916.4	3.4	4,933.4	1.4	4,920.9	-1.0	4,895.4	-2.1	4,916.5	1.3
1991	4,859.3	-2.9	4,867.5	0.7	4,880.3	1.1	4,890.9	0.9	4,874.5	-0.9
1992	4,939.0	4.0	4,962.2	1.9	5,006.4	3.6	5,068.4	5.0	4,994.0	2.5
1993	5,080.7	1.0	5,104.1	1.9	-	-	-	-	-	-

Source: "The National Income and Product Accounts of the United States, 1929-82: Statistical Tables," and subsequent July issues of the *Survey of Current Business*. - indicates that data are unavailable or zero.

8

CHAPTER 2

GROSS DOMESTIC PRODUCT

GROSS DOMESTIC PRODUCT

In November 1991, the U.S. Department of Commerce's Bureau of Economic Analysis (BEA) introduced revisions to the National Income and Product Accounts (NIPA) which (1) changed the NIPA basing year from 1982 constant dollars to 1987 constant dollars, (2) introduced a variety of statistical revisions in the NIPA series, and (3) shifted emphasis from Gross National Product (GNP) to Gross Domestic Product (GDP) as the principal measure of U.S. production.

This chapter provides a brief explanation of the changes and presents GDP and its components in 44 tables.

GDP versus GNP

The GDP and GNP differ in the following manner:

GNP measures goods and services produced by labor and property *supplied* by U.S. residents—wherever the goods and services are produced.

GDP measures goods and services produced by labor and property *located* in the U.S.—regardless of the nationality of the persons supplying the labor and property.

The difference between the two measures is *net factor income*; this is income produced by U.S. residents abroad less income produced by foreign residents in the United States. GNP is a better measure of *income* available to U.S. citizens by reason of their contribution to production. Savings are naturally expressed in relation to GNP; and estimating the availability of total resources (e.g., for education) is more appropriately made by looking at GNP.

GDP is a better measurement of *production* within the borders of the United States. Nonetheless, BEA's shift in emphasis from GNP to GDP is a dramatic departure: GNP has been the accepted measure of the U.S. economy for more than 60 years. Econometric models, textbooks, and other indicators still feature GNP; some time will pass before GDP will be as widely accepted and understood as GNP.

BEA's reasons for the shift may be summarized as follows:

1. GDP is the "appropriate measure for much of the short-term monitoring and analysis of the U.S. economy." It is "consistent in coverage with indicators such as employment, productivity, industry output, and investment in equipment and structures."

2. GDP is the measuring unit used by other countries; hence country-to-country comparisons will be easier. The U.S., in fact, is late in adopting the international System of National Accounts, the set of international guidelines for economic accounting.

3. The GDP measure makes quarterly estimates more accurate because BEA need not estimate factor income (which is received late and requires many adjustments for exchange rates, inflation, etc.) to obtain measures of the economy.

The 1991 Benchmark Revision

In November 1991, BEA released a comprehensive revision to the National Income and Product Accounts. The 1991 revision is the ninth comprehensive "benchmark" revision of NIPA. These revisions involve changes in definitions and classifications to reflect better the character of the U.S. economy and its evolving structure of law as well as statistical changes to incorporate new and revised data. A full discussion of the changes is beyond the scope of this book. Readers are referred to the August, September, October, and November 1991 editions of *Survey of Current Business*, reference 3 in the Bibliography. Highlights follow:

> With emphasis shifting to GDP, NIPA accounts heretofore constructed to reflect net factor income exclude factor income.

> Constant dollar tables are shown in 1987 constant dollars.

> Indexes are now shown with 1987 as the base year (1987 = 100) rather than 1982.

Presentation of Data

BEA has issued recalculated data for the GDP and its components back to 1929. All tables, therefore, show data for the 1929-1991 period.

The chapter consists of 22 series shown in current and in 1987 constant dollars—a total of 44 tables. Explanatory texts are provided for subsections on Personal Consumption Expenditures, Gross Private Domestic Investment, Net Exports of Goods and Services, and Government Purchases.

Uses of GDP

Since 1991, the GDP is used as the instrument for measuring the output of the U.S. economy as a whole (its magnitude, growth, or decline) and to determine the economic processes or mechanisms which accounts for the national product (what proportion of it is accounted for by government spending, investment in structures and capital goods, by personal consumption expenditures—and subcategories of these such as durable goods, nondurable goods, services, etc.).

GDP, Business Cycles, and Markets. The best-known use of GDP is as an indicator of economic growth or decline. A sustained period of decline in real GDP is defined as a recession. A sustained period of growth is called an expansion. The period from the trough of a recession to the peak of an expansion is a business cycle. Various economic indicators, covered in this part of *EIH*, have in the past proved capable of predicting the onset of recessions and recoveries.

Since recession invariably means increased unemployment, dropping demand, and slowing production . . . and rapid expansions can result in shortages and inflation, GDP is closely watched by government and private sector alike. Stock and bond market behavior is closely correlated with GDP's behavior as well: the stock market tends to rise and decline with GDP; the bond market behaves "counter cyclically," meaning that it rises when GDP drops and drops when GDP rises.

Bibliography

1. U.S. Department of Commerce. Bureau of Economic Analysis. *An Introduction to National Economic*

Accounting. Methodology Paper Series MP-1. Washington, DC: U.S. Government Printing Office, March 1985.

2. U.S. Department of Commerce. Bureau of Economic Analysis. *GNP: An Overview of Source Data and Estimating Methods.* Methodology Paper Series MP-4. Washington, DC: U.S. Government Printing Office, September 1987.

3. U.S. Department of Commerce. Bureau of Economic Analysis. *Survey of Current Business.* Superintendent of Documents, U.S. Government Printing Office, Washington, DC 20302.

Gross Domestic Product - Actual Dollars

In billions of actual dollars and percent. Quarterly data are seasonally adjusted and annualized. Growth rates for quarters are compound annual growth rates; changes from year to year are percentage changes.

Year	1st Quarter	% Change	2nd Quarter	% Change	3rd Quarter	% Change	4th Quarter	% Change	TOTAL	% Change
1929	-	-	-	-	-	-	-	-	103.1	-
1930	-	-	-	-	-	-	-	-	90.4	-12.3
1931	-	-	-	-	-	-	-	-	75.8	-16.2
1932	-	-	-	-	-	-	-	-	58.0	-23.5
1933	-	-	-	-	-	-	-	-	55.6	-4.1
1934	-	-	-	-	-	-	-	-	65.1	17.1
1935	-	-	-	-	-	-	-	-	72.3	11.1
1936	-	-	-	-	-	-	-	-	82.7	14.4
1937	-	-	-	-	-	-	-	-	90.8	9.8
1938	-	-	-	-	-	-	-	-	84.9	-6.5
1939	-	-	-	-	-	-	-	-	90.8	6.9
1940	-	-	-	-	-	-	-	-	100.0	10.1
1941	-	-	-	-	-	-	-	-	125.0	25.0
1942	-	-	-	-	-	-	-	-	158.5	26.8
1943	-	-	-	-	-	-	-	-	192.4	21.4
1944	-	-	-	-	-	-	-	-	211.0	9.7
1945	-	-	-	-	-	-	-	-	213.1	1.0
1946	199.7	-	207.7	17.0	217.9	21.1	222.2	8.1	211.9	-0.6
1947	226.7	8.4	230.6	7.1	234.9	7.7	245.0	18.3	234.3	10.6
1948	251.1	10.3	258.3	12.0	265.3	11.3	266.6	2.0	260.3	11.1
1949	261.6	-7.3	258.1	-5.2	259.9	2.8	257.7	-3.3	259.3	-0.4
1950	268.3	17.5	277.9	15.1	295.3	27.5	306.7	16.4	287.0	10.7
1951	321.6	20.9	329.1	9.7	335.8	8.4	340.0	5.1	331.6	15.5
1952	343.2	3.8	343.7	0.6	349.6	7.0	362.2	15.2	349.7	5.5
1953	369.0	7.7	372.4	3.7	371.8	-0.6	366.8	-5.3	370.0	5.8
1954	366.3	-0.5	366.6	0.3	371.2	5.1	379.4	9.1	370.9	0.2
1955	392.3	14.3	400.6	8.7	408.9	8.5	415.2	6.3	404.3	9.0
1956	417.6	2.3	423.1	5.4	427.8	4.5	436.5	8.4	426.2	5.4
1957	444.9	7.9	446.6	1.5	453.9	6.7	449.0	-4.2	448.6	5.3
1958	441.6	-6.4	445.8	3.9	459.1	12.5	472.3	12.0	454.7	1.4
1959	483.5	9.8	496.2	10.9	496.4	0.2	500.5	3.3	494.2	8.7
1960	514.0	11.2	512.9	-0.9	515.8	2.3	510.8	-3.8	513.3	3.9
1961	515.1	3.4	525.9	8.7	536.6	8.4	549.5	10.0	531.8	3.6
1962	561.9	9.3	569.4	5.4	576.2	4.9	578.9	1.9	571.6	7.5
1963	588.1	6.5	596.7	6.0	609.4	8.8	618.3	6.0	603.1	5.5
1964	634.8	11.1	643.6	5.7	654.1	6.7	659.7	3.5	648.0	7.4
1965	679.8	12.8	691.9	7.3	708.3	9.8	730.7	13.3	702.7	8.4
1966	753.1	12.8	762.2	4.9	775.3	7.1	788.5	7.0	769.8	9.5
1967	797.7	4.7	803.8	3.1	820.5	8.6	835.3	7.4	814.3	5.8
1968	859.6	12.2	883.7	11.7	900.3	7.7	913.7	6.1	889.3	9.2
1969	937.3	10.7	951.1	6.0	970.7	8.5	978.8	3.4	959.5	7.9
1970	989.7	4.5	1,003.8	5.8	1,022.8	7.8	1,026.4	1.4	1,010.7	5.3
1971	1,069.8	18.0	1,088.2	7.1	1,108.4	7.6	1,122.3	5.1	1,097.2	8.6
1972	1,160.9	14.5	1,192.5	11.3	1,217.7	8.7	1,256.8	13.5	1,207.0	10.0
1973	1,304.4	16.0	1,334.5	9.6	1,358.4	7.4	1,401.2	13.2	1,349.6	11.8
1974	1,410.9	2.8	1,444.1	9.7	1,474.7	8.7	1,504.8	8.4	1,458.6	8.1
1975	1,513.6	2.4	1,552.1	10.6	1,614.4	17.0	1,663.3	12.7	1,585.9	8.7
1976	1,717.8	13.8	1,746.4	6.8	1,779.9	7.9	1,829.6	11.6	1,768.4	11.5
1977	1,881.7	11.9	1,952.9	16.0	2,015.1	13.4	2,046.8	6.4	1,974.1	11.6
1978	2,090.2	8.8	2,213.9	25.9	2,274.7	11.4	2,352.0	14.3	2,232.7	13.1
1979	2,399.2	8.3	2,453.3	9.3	2,523.3	11.9	2,578.8	9.1	2,488.6	11.5
1980	2,650.1	11.5	2,643.9	-0.9	2,705.3	9.6	2,832.9	20.2	2,708.0	8.8
1981	2,953.5	18.1	2,993.0	5.5	3,079.6	12.1	3,096.3	2.2	3,030.6	11.9
1982	3,092.9	-0.4	3,146.2	7.1	3,164.2	2.3	3,195.1	4.0	3,149.6	3.9
1983	3,254.9	7.7	3,367.1	14.5	3,450.9	10.3	3,547.3	11.7	3,405.0	8.1
1984	3,666.9	14.2	3,754.6	9.9	3,818.2	6.9	3,869.1	5.4	3,777.2	10.9
1985	3,940.0	7.5	3,997.5	6.0	4,076.9	8.2	4,140.5	6.4	4,038.7	6.9
1986	4,215.7	7.5	4,232.0	1.6	4,290.2	5.6	4,336.6	4.4	4,268.6	5.7
1987	4,408.3	6.8	4,494.9	8.1	4,573.5	7.2	4,683.0	9.9	4,539.9	6.4
1988	4,752.4	6.1	4,857.2	9.1	4,947.3	7.6	5,044.6	8.1	4,900.4	7.9
1989	5,150.0	8.6	5,229.5	6.3	5,278.9	3.8	5,344.8	5.1	5,250.8	7.2
1990	5,461.9	9.1	5,540.9	5.9	5,583.8	3.1	5,597.9	1.0	5,546.1	5.6
1991	5,631.7	2.4	5,697.7	4.8	5,758.6	4.3	5,803.7	3.2	5,722.9	3.2
1992	5,908.7	7.4	5,991.4	5.7	6,059.5	4.6	6,194.4	9.2	6,038.5	5.5
1993	6,261.6	4.4	6,327.6	4.3	-	-	-	-	-	-

Source: "National Income and Product Account Tables: Selected NIPA Tables," *Survey of Current Business*, November 1991, U.S. Department of Commerce, Bureau of Economic Analysis, National Income and Wealth Division. - indicates that no data are available.

Gross Domestic Product - 1987 Dollars

In billions of constant 1987 dollars and percent. Quarterly data are seasonally adjusted and annualized. Growth rates for quarters are compound annual growth rates; changes from year to year are percentage changes.

Year	1st Quarter	% Change	2nd Quarter	% Change	3rd Quarter	% Change	4th Quarter	% Change	TOTAL	% Change
1929	-	-	-	-	-	-	-	-	821.8	-
1930	-	-	-	-	-	-	-	-	748.9	-8.9
1931	-	-	-	-	-	-	-	-	691.3	-7.7
1932	-	-	-	-	-	-	-	-	599.7	-13.3
1933	-	-	-	-	-	-	-	-	587.1	-2.1
1934	-	-	-	-	-	-	-	-	632.6	7.7
1935	-	-	-	-	-	-	-	-	681.3	7.7
1936	-	-	-	-	-	-	-	-	777.9	14.2
1937	-	-	-	-	-	-	-	-	811.4	4.3
1938	-	-	-	-	-	-	-	-	778.9	-4.0
1939	-	-	-	-	-	-	-	-	840.7	7.9
1940	-	-	-	-	-	-	-	-	906.0	7.8
1941	-	-	-	-	-	-	-	-	1,070.6	18.2
1942	-	-	-	-	-	-	-	-	1,284.9	20.0
1943	-	-	-	-	-	-	-	-	1,540.5	19.9
1944	-	-	-	-	-	-	-	-	1,670.0	8.4
1945	-	-	-	-	-	-	-	-	1,602.6	-4.0
1946	-	-	-	-	-	-	-	-	1,272.1	-20.6
1947	1,239.5	-	1,247.2	2.5	1,255.0	2.5	1,269.5	4.7	1,252.8	-1.5
1948	1,284.0	4.6	1,295.7	3.7	1,303.8	2.5	1,316.4	3.9	1,300.0	3.8
1949	1,305.3	-3.3	1,302.0	-1.0	1,312.6	3.3	1,301.9	-3.2	1,305.5	0.4
1950	1,350.9	15.9	1,393.5	13.2	1,443.9	15.3	1,482.6	11.2	1,418.5	8.7
1951	1,502.0	5.3	1,548.3	12.9	1,585.4	9.9	1,596.0	2.7	1,558.4	9.9
1952	1,607.7	3.0	1,612.1	1.1	1,621.9	2.5	1,657.8	9.2	1,624.9	4.3
1953	1,687.3	7.3	1,695.3	1.9	1,687.9	-1.7	1,671.2	-3.9	1,685.5	3.7
1954	1,660.8	-2.5	1,658.4	-0.6	1,677.7	4.7	1,698.3	5.0	1,673.8	-0.7
1955	1,742.5	10.8	1,758.6	3.7	1,778.2	4.5	1,793.9	3.6	1,768.3	5.6
1956	1,787.0	-1.5	1,798.5	2.6	1,802.2	0.8	1,826.6	5.5	1,803.6	2.0
1957	1,836.4	2.2	1,834.8	-0.3	1,851.2	3.6	1,830.5	-4.4	1,838.2	1.9
1958	1,790.1	-8.5	1,804.4	3.2	1,840.9	8.3	1,880.9	9.0	1,829.1	-0.5
1959	1,904.9	5.2	1,937.5	7.0	1,930.8	-1.4	1,941.9	2.3	1,928.8	5.5
1960	1,976.9	7.4	1,971.7	-1.0	1,973.7	0.4	1,961.1	-2.5	1,970.8	2.2
1961	1,977.4	3.4	2,006.0	5.9	2,035.2	6.0	2,076.5	8.4	2,023.8	2.7
1962	2,103.8	5.4	2,125.7	4.2	2,142.6	3.2	2,140.2	-0.4	2,128.1	5.2
1963	2,170.9	5.9	2,199.5	5.4	2,237.6	7.1	2,254.5	3.1	2,215.6	4.1
1964	2,311.1	10.4	2,329.9	3.3	2,357.4	4.8	2,364.0	1.1	2,340.6	5.6
1965	2,410.1	8.0	2,442.8	5.5	2,485.5	7.2	2,543.8	9.7	2,470.5	5.5
1966	2,596.8	8.6	2,601.4	0.7	2,626.1	3.9	2,640.5	2.2	2,616.2	5.9
1967	2,657.2	2.6	2,669.0	1.8	2,699.5	4.6	2,715.1	2.3	2,685.2	2.6
1968	2,752.1	5.6	2,796.9	6.7	2,816.8	2.9	2,821.7	0.7	2,796.9	4.2
1969	2,864.6	6.2	2,867.8	0.4	2,884.5	2.3	2,875.1	-1.3	2,873.0	2.7
1970	2,867.8	-1.0	2,859.5	-1.2	2,895.0	5.1	2,873.3	-3.0	2,873.9	0.0
1971	2,939.9	9.6	2,944.2	0.6	2,962.3	2.5	2,977.3	2.0	2,955.9	2.9
1972	3,037.3	8.3	3,089.7	7.1	3,125.8	4.8	3,175.5	6.5	3,107.1	5.1
1973	3,253.3	10.2	3,267.6	1.8	3,264.3	-0.4	3,289.1	3.1	3,268.6	5.2
1974	3,259.4	-3.6	3,267.6	1.0	3,239.1	-3.4	3,226.4	-1.6	3,248.1	-0.6
1975	3,154.0	-8.7	3,190.4	4.7	3,249.9	7.7	3,292.5	5.3	3,221.7	-0.8
1976	3,356.7	8.0	3,369.2	1.5	3,381.0	1.4	3,416.3	4.2	3,380.8	4.9
1977	3,466.4	6.0	3,525.0	6.9	3,574.4	5.7	3,567.2	-0.8	3,533.3	4.5
1978	3,591.8	2.8	3,707.0	13.5	3,735.6	3.1	3,779.6	4.8	3,703.5	4.8
1979	3,780.8	0.1	3,784.3	0.4	3,807.5	2.5	3,814.6	0.7	3,796.8	2.5
1980	3,830.8	1.7	3,732.6	-9.9	3,733.5	0.1	3,808.5	8.3	3,776.3	-0.5
1981	3,860.5	5.6	3,844.4	-1.7	3,864.5	2.1	3,803.1	-6.2	3,843.1	1.8
1982	3,756.1	-4.9	3,771.1	1.6	3,754.4	-1.8	3,759.6	0.6	3,760.3	-2.2
1983	3,783.5	2.6	3,886.5	11.3	3,944.4	6.1	4,012.1	7.0	3,906.6	3.9
1984	4,089.5	7.9	4,144.0	5.4	4,166.4	2.2	4,194.2	2.7	4,148.5	6.2
1985	4,221.8	2.7	4,254.8	3.2	4,309.0	5.2	4,333.5	2.3	4,279.8	3.2
1986	4,390.5	5.4	4,387.7	-0.3	4,412.6	2.3	4,427.1	1.3	4,404.5	2.9
1987	4,460.0	3.0	4,515.3	5.1	4,559.3	4.0	4,625.5	5.9	4,539.9	3.1
1988	4,655.3	2.6	4,704.8	4.3	4,734.5	2.5	4,779.7	3.9	4,718.6	3.9
1989	4,817.6	3.2	4,839.0	1.8	4,839.0	-	4,856.7	1.5	4,838.0	2.5
1990	4,898.3	3.5	4,917.1	1.5	4,906.5	-0.9	4,867.2	-3.2	4,897.3	1.2
1991	4,837.8	-2.4	4,855.6	1.5	4,872.6	1.4	4,879.6	0.6	4,861.4	-0.7
1992	4,922.0	3.5	4,956.5	2.8	4,998.2	3.4	5,068.3	5.7	4,986.3	2.6
1993	5,078.2	0.8	5,102.1	1.9	-	-	-	-	-	-

Source: "National Income and Product Account Tables: Selected NIPA Tables," *Survey of Current Business*, November 1991, U.S. Department of Commerce, Bureau of Economic Analysis, National Income and Wealth Division. - indicates that no data are available.

PERSONAL CONSUMPTION EXPENDITURES
Component of Gross Domestic Product

Personal Consumption Expenditures is the largest component of Gross Domestic Product (GDP). In 1992, it accounted for 67 percent of real GDP. The measure includes all expenditures by individuals on goods and services; goods are divided into durable and nondurable goods; services are reported as a single category.

The category is labeled "personal" consumption because it reflects all purchases by individuals. The category also incorporates goods and services that the private sector purchases in order to make final products. Paper clips purchased by an automobile producers, for instance, are accounted for in the ultimate price of cars sold to consumers. The measure excludes government purchases of goods and services and private purchases of goods (such as tooling) which are considered to be capital investments.

Note that Personal Consumption Expenditures do *not* include imported goods; these are measured as a separate category in the national accounts.

Sources for the data included in Personal Consumption Expenditures are many and varied. Typically, different sources are used for "benchmark" years (the years of the economic censuses), for other years, and for the most recent period in order to obtain the best and most accurate information. Where partial data only are available, estimates are made using a variety of procedures, including judgement based on trends.

All explanations are provided in this section, followed by tables showing Personal Consumption Expenditure totals and tables showing the subcomponents of the measure. Each item is shown in actual and in constant 1987 dollars.

Durable and Nondurable Goods

The Bureau of Economic Affairs bases its estimates on six distinct categories, each handled in a different way (reference 1). Most goods are based on census surveys in benchmark years and on annual and monthly retail surveys conducted in other years by the Census Bureau. Other distinct categories, using distinct estimating methodologies, are new trucks, new and used autos, gasoline and oil, and food furnished employees (including the military).

In 1992, durable goods accounted for 9.2 percent and nondurable goods for 21.3 percent of real GDP. Durable goods are products expected to last three years or longer; nondurables for a lesser time period.

Services

The category measures expenditures on services by individuals. The grouping of categories includes (1) rent paid for housing; (2) medical services; (3) expenditures on education from whatever sources; (4) financial, banking, brokerage services; (5) insurance, hospital expenses, religious activities, cable TV, utilities, and local transportation; (6) water and sanitary services; lotteries, (7) foreign travel by U.S. citizens less foreign visitors' spending in the U.S., and (8) a variety of other services, including repairs, tools, club memberships, etc. Estimating methods differ for each of these groupings.

The Services category of Personal Consumption Expenditures should not be viewed as equivalent to the "services" sector of the economy. The category includes rentals, insurance, banking, and financial services, which are classified elsewhere in the Standard Industrial Classification (SIC) system. And the category excludes services purchased by corporations and by government; services purchased by the private sector are "hidden" in the price of goods sold or services rendered; those purchased by government appear under the governmental category.

Presentation of Data

Data are shown from 1929 to 1993 in quarterly and in annual increments. Changes from one period to the next are shown. Changes from quarter to quarter are annualized, compounded growth rates as explained in the previous section on Gross National Product. Changes from year to year are simple percentile changes.

Analytical Uses

Personal consumption expenditures measure the allocation of individual resources between consumable products (food, clothing, etc.), durable goods (automobiles, appliances, etc.), and services (medical, entertainment, etc.) over time. As in all GDP series, significance appears when results for different periods are compared. Nondurable goods are the most essential; durable goods purchases can be deferred. Growth in one and decline in the other can thus signal a lack of consumer confidence. Strong growth in durables output, conversely, shows confidence in the future. The shift of expenditures from goods to services or from services to goods indicates, over time, changes in economic structure.

Gross Domestic Product
Personal consumption expenditures: Total - Actual Dollars

In billions of actual dollars and percent. Quarterly data are seasonally adjusted and annualized. Growth rates for quarters are compound annual growth rates; changes from year to year are percentage changes.

Year	1st Quarter	% Change	2nd Quarter	% Change	3rd Quarter	% Change	4th Quarter	% Change	TOTAL	% Change
1929	-	-	-	-	-	-	-	-	77.5	-
1930	-	-	-	-	-	-	-	-	70.2	-9.4
1931	-	-	-	-	-	-	-	-	60.7	-13.5
1932	-	-	-	-	-	-	-	-	48.7	-19.8
1933	-	-	-	-	-	-	-	-	45.9	-5.7
1934	-	-	-	-	-	-	-	-	51.4	12.0
1935	-	-	-	-	-	-	-	-	55.9	8.8
1936	-	-	-	-	-	-	-	-	62.2	11.3
1937	-	-	-	-	-	-	-	-	66.8	7.4
1938	-	-	-	-	-	-	-	-	64.2	-3.9
1939	-	-	-	-	-	-	-	-	67.2	4.7
1940	-	-	-	-	-	-	-	-	71.2	6.0
1941	-	-	-	-	-	-	-	-	81.0	13.8
1942	-	-	-	-	-	-	-	-	88.9	9.8
1943	-	-	-	-	-	-	-	-	99.7	12.1
1944	-	-	-	-	-	-	-	-	108.5	8.8
1945	-	-	-	-	-	-	-	-	119.9	10.5
1946	134.9	-	140.1	16.3	148.9	27.6	153.2	12.1	144.3	20.4
1947	156.6	9.2	160.5	10.3	164.1	9.3	168.2	10.4	162.3	12.5
1948	170.9	6.6	174.7	9.2	177.6	6.8	178.5	2.0	175.4	8.1
1949	177.4	-2.4	179.0	3.7	178.3	-1.6	180.8	5.7	178.9	2.0
1950	183.6	6.3	187.5	8.8	201.2	32.6	198.6	-5.1	192.7	7.7
1951	209.7	24.3	205.3	-8.1	207.9	5.2	211.9	7.9	208.7	8.3
1952	213.3	2.7	217.4	7.9	219.9	4.7	228.0	15.6	219.7	5.3
1953	231.6	6.5	233.5	3.3	234.5	1.7	234.2	-0.5	233.5	6.3
1954	236.4	3.8	239.1	4.6	241.4	3.9	246.0	7.8	240.7	3.1
1955	252.2	10.5	257.2	8.2	261.5	6.9	265.6	6.4	259.1	7.6
1956	267.2	2.4	269.7	3.8	272.8	4.7	278.0	7.8	271.9	4.9
1957	282.3	6.3	284.5	3.2	289.1	6.6	290.9	2.5	286.7	5.4
1958	290.5	-0.5	293.5	4.2	298.6	7.1	302.5	5.3	296.3	3.3
1959	310.5	11.0	316.4	7.8	321.7	6.9	323.8	2.6	318.1	7.4
1960	327.3	4.4	333.4	7.7	333.4	-	335.5	2.5	332.4	4.5
1961	336.4	1.1	341.4	6.1	344.4	3.6	351.7	8.8	343.5	3.3
1962	356.2	5.2	362.2	6.9	366.4	4.7	372.7	7.1	364.4	6.1
1963	376.3	3.9	380.6	4.6	387.7	7.7	392.3	4.8	384.2	5.4
1964	401.7	9.9	409.4	7.9	418.1	8.8	420.6	2.4	412.5	7.4
1965	431.2	10.5	438.2	6.7	447.4	8.7	461.5	13.2	444.6	7.8
1966	471.8	9.2	476.8	4.3	486.1	8.0	491.7	4.7	481.6	8.3
1967	496.6	4.0	506.1	7.9	513.5	6.0	521.0	6.0	509.3	5.8
1968	539.0	14.6	552.6	10.5	568.3	11.9	576.6	6.0	559.1	9.8
1969	587.9	8.1	598.5	7.4	608.3	6.7	620.0	7.9	603.7	8.0
1970	631.0	7.3	641.1	6.6	653.5	8.0	660.3	4.2	646.5	7.1
1971	679.6	12.2	693.6	8.5	706.0	7.3	722.1	9.4	700.3	8.3
1972	739.2	9.8	757.1	10.0	775.1	9.9	799.7	13.3	767.8	9.6
1973	824.0	12.7	838.8	7.4	857.3	9.1	872.6	7.3	848.1	10.5
1974	891.0	8.7	919.0	13.2	946.7	12.6	954.2	3.2	927.7	9.4
1975	978.9	10.8	1,008.3	12.6	1,042.1	14.1	1,070.3	11.3	1,024.9	10.5
1976	1,104.8	13.5	1,124.5	7.3	1,153.9	10.9	1,189.1	12.8	1,143.1	11.5
1977	1,225.5	12.8	1,253.5	9.5	1,284.7	10.3	1,322.4	12.3	1,271.5	11.2
1978	1,351.7	9.2	1,410.1	18.4	1,442.7	9.6	1,480.3	10.8	1,421.2	11.8
1979	1,520.4	11.3	1,554.8	9.4	1,607.1	14.1	1,652.5	11.8	1,583.7	11.4
1980	1,701.5	12.4	1,704.9	0.8	1,762.3	14.2	1,823.6	14.7	1,748.1	10.4
1981	1,876.0	12.0	1,908.9	7.2	1,952.1	9.4	1,968.0	3.3	1,926.2	10.2
1982	2,005.4	7.8	2,029.4	4.9	2,073.1	8.9	2,128.7	11.2	2,059.2	6.9
1983	2,162.9	6.6	2,231.9	13.4	2,288.7	10.6	2,346.8	10.5	2,257.5	9.6
1984	2,392.4	8.0	2,444.5	9.0	2,477.8	5.6	2,526.4	8.1	2,460.3	9.0
1985	2,589.2	10.3	2,636.4	7.5	2,704.2	10.7	2,739.8	5.4	2,667.4	8.4
1986	2,784.8	6.7	2,812.3	4.0	2,882.0	10.3	2,923.1	5.8	2,850.6	6.9
1987	2,962.8	5.5	3,030.1	9.4	3,091.4	8.3	3,124.6	4.4	3,052.2	7.1
1988	3,199.1	9.9	3,260.5	7.9	3,326.6	8.4	3,398.2	8.9	3,296.1	8.0
1989	3,440.8	5.1	3,499.1	7.0	3,553.3	6.3	3,599.1	5.3	3,523.1	6.9
1990	3,679.3	9.2	3,727.0	5.3	3,801.7	8.3	3,836.6	3.7	3,761.2	6.8
1991	3,843.6	0.7	3,887.8	4.7	3,929.8	4.4	3,964.1	3.5	3,906.4	3.9
1992	4,046.5	8.6	4,099.9	5.4	4,157.1	5.7	4,256.2	9.9	4,139.9	6.0
1993	4,296.2	3.8	4,359.9	6.1	-	-	-	-	-	-

Source: "National Income and Product Account Tables: Selected NIPA Tables," *Survey of Current Business*, November 1991, U.S. Department of Commerce, Bureau of Economic Analysis, National Income and Wealth Division. - indicates that no data are available.

Gross Domestic Product
Personal consumption expenditures: Total - 1987 Dollars

In billions of constant 1987 dollars and percent. Quarterly data are seasonally adjusted and annualized. Growth rates for quarters are compound annual growth rates; changes from year to year are percentage changes.

Year	1st Quarter	% Change	2nd Quarter	% Change	3rd Quarter	% Change	4th Quarter	% Change	TOTAL	% Change
1929	-	-	-	-	-	-	-	-	554.5	-
1930	-	-	-	-	-	-	-	-	520.0	-6.2
1931	-	-	-	-	-	-	-	-	501.0	-3.7
1932	-	-	-	-	-	-	-	-	456.6	-8.9
1933	-	-	-	-	-	-	-	-	447.4	-2.0
1934	-	-	-	-	-	-	-	-	461.1	3.1
1935	-	-	-	-	-	-	-	-	487.6	5.7
1936	-	-	-	-	-	-	-	-	534.4	9.6
1937	-	-	-	-	-	-	-	-	554.6	3.8
1938	-	-	-	-	-	-	-	-	542.2	-2.2
1939	-	-	-	-	-	-	-	-	568.7	4.9
1940	-	-	-	-	-	-	-	-	595.2	4.7
1941	-	-	-	-	-	-	-	-	629.3	5.7
1942	-	-	-	-	-	-	-	-	628.7	-0.1
1943	-	-	-	-	-	-	-	-	647.3	3.0
1944	-	-	-	-	-	-	-	-	671.2	3.7
1945	-	-	-	-	-	-	-	-	714.6	6.5
1946	-	-	-	-	-	-	-	-	779.1	9.0
1947	784.0	-	796.8	6.7	796.7	-0.1	795.7	-0.5	793.3	1.8
1948	803.3	3.9	811.6	4.2	814.5	1.4	822.6	4.0	813.0	2.5
1949	823.9	0.6	834.3	5.1	831.3	-1.4	836.2	2.4	831.4	2.3
1950	848.8	6.2	865.0	7.9	899.3	16.8	884.3	-6.5	874.3	5.2
1951	899.8	7.2	884.9	-6.5	894.2	4.3	899.9	2.6	894.7	2.3
1952	903.4	1.6	919.7	7.4	925.4	2.5	945.2	8.8	923.4	3.2
1953	958.0	5.5	963.4	2.3	963.2	-0.1	965.3	0.9	962.5	4.2
1954	969.1	1.6	976.9	3.3	992.9	6.7	1,010.4	7.2	987.3	2.6
1955	1,025.1	5.9	1,041.3	6.5	1,051.3	3.9	1,070.2	7.4	1,047.0	6.0
1956	1,072.7	0.9	1,074.0	0.5	1,078.8	1.8	1,089.2	3.9	1,078.7	3.0
1957	1,097.1	2.9	1,100.3	1.2	1,107.4	2.6	1,113.0	2.0	1,104.4	2.4
1958	1,102.2	-3.8	1,114.3	4.5	1,130.6	6.0	1,141.7	4.0	1,122.2	1.6
1959	1,159.5	6.4	1,175.5	5.6	1,188.0	4.3	1,192.7	1.6	1,178.9	5.1
1960	1,201.7	3.1	1,216.4	5.0	1,210.8	-1.8	1,214.1	1.1	1,210.8	2.7
1961	1,218.1	1.3	1,235.6	5.9	1,238.8	1.0	1,261.0	7.4	1,238.4	2.3
1962	1,273.5	4.0	1,287.0	4.3	1,298.2	3.5	1,314.3	5.1	1,293.3	4.4
1963	1,322.5	2.5	1,332.3	3.0	1,350.7	5.6	1,362.0	3.4	1,341.9	3.8
1964	1,388.0	7.9	1,409.3	6.3	1,433.8	7.1	1,437.6	1.1	1,417.2	5.6
1965	1,463.4	7.4	1,480.9	4.9	1,503.1	6.1	1,540.6	10.4	1,497.0	5.6
1966	1,559.6	5.0	1,566.1	1.7	1,582.0	4.1	1,587.6	1.4	1,573.8	5.1
1967	1,600.2	3.2	1,620.8	5.2	1,629.4	2.1	1,639.0	2.4	1,622.4	3.1
1968	1,672.9	8.5	1,696.8	5.8	1,725.2	6.9	1,735.0	2.3	1,707.5	5.2
1969	1,754.7	4.6	1,765.1	2.4	1,775.0	2.3	1,790.1	3.4	1,771.2	3.7
1970	1,800.5	2.3	1,807.5	1.6	1,824.7	3.9	1,821.2	-0.8	1,813.5	2.4
1971	1,849.9	6.5	1,863.5	3.0	1,876.9	2.9	1,904.6	6.0	1,873.7	3.3
1972	1,929.3	5.3	1,963.6	7.2	1,989.1	5.4	2,032.1	8.9	1,978.4	5.6
1973	2,063.9	6.4	2,062.0	-0.4	2,073.7	2.3	2,067.4	-1.2	2,066.7	4.5
1974	2,050.8	-3.2	2,059.0	1.6	2,065.5	1.3	2,039.9	-4.9	2,053.8	-0.6
1975	2,051.8	2.4	2,086.9	7.0	2,114.4	5.4	2,137.0	4.3	2,097.5	2.1
1976	2,179.3	8.2	2,194.7	2.9	2,213.0	3.4	2,242.0	5.3	2,207.3	5.2
1977	2,271.3	5.3	2,280.8	1.7	2,302.6	3.9	2,331.6	5.1	2,296.6	4.0
1978	2,347.1	2.7	2,394.0	8.2	2,404.5	1.8	2,421.6	2.9	2,391.8	4.1
1979	2,437.9	2.7	2,435.4	-0.4	2,454.7	3.2	2,465.4	1.8	2,448.4	2.4
1980	2,464.6	-0.1	2,414.2	-7.9	2,440.3	4.4	2,469.2	4.8	2,447.1	-0.1
1981	2,475.5	1.0	2,476.1	0.1	2,487.4	1.8	2,468.6	-3.0	2,476.9	1.2
1982	2,484.0	2.5	2,488.9	0.8	2,502.5	2.2	2,539.3	6.0	2,503.7	1.1
1983	2,556.5	2.7	2,604.0	7.6	2,639.0	5.5	2,678.2	6.1	2,619.4	4.6
1984	2,703.8	3.9	2,741.1	5.6	2,754.6	2.0	2,784.8	4.5	2,746.1	4.8
1985	2,824.9	5.9	2,849.7	3.6	2,893.3	6.3	2,895.3	0.3	2,865.8	4.4
1986	2,922.4	3.8	2,947.9	3.5	2,993.7	6.4	3,012.5	2.5	2,969.1	3.6
1987	3,011.5	-0.1	3,046.8	4.8	3,075.8	3.9	3,074.7	-0.1	3,052.2	2.8
1988	3,128.2	7.1	3,147.8	2.5	3,170.6	2.9	3,202.9	4.1	3,162.4	3.6
1989	3,203.6	0.1	3,212.2	1.1	3,235.3	2.9	3,242.0	0.8	3,223.3	1.9
1990	3,264.4	2.8	3,271.6	0.9	3,288.4	2.1	3,265.9	-2.7	3,272.6	1.5
1991	3,242.7	-2.8	3,256.9	1.8	3,267.1	1.3	3,267.5	0.0	3,258.6	-0.4
1992	3,302.3	4.3	3,316.8	1.8	3,350.9	4.2	3,397.2	5.6	3,341.8	2.6
1993	3,403.8	0.8	3,432.7	3.4	-	-	-	-	-	-

Source: "National Income and Product Account Tables: Selected NIPA Tables," *Survey of Current Business*, November 1991, U.S. Department of Commerce, Bureau of Economic Analysis, National Income and Wealth Division. - indicates that no data are available.

Gross Domestic Product
Personal consumption expenditures
Durable goods - Actual Dollars

In billions of actual dollars and percent. Quarterly data are seasonally adjusted and annualized. Growth rates for quarters are compound annual growth rates; changes from year to year are percentage changes.

Year	1st Quarter	% Change	2nd Quarter	% Change	3rd Quarter	% Change	4th Quarter	% Change	TOTAL	% Change
1929	-	-	-	-	-	-	-	-	9.2	-
1930	-	-	-	-	-	-	-	-	7.2	-21.7
1931	-	-	-	-	-	-	-	-	5.5	-23.6
1932	-	-	-	-	-	-	-	-	3.6	-34.5
1933	-	-	-	-	-	-	-	-	3.5	-2.8
1934	-	-	-	-	-	-	-	-	4.2	20.0
1935	-	-	-	-	-	-	-	-	5.1	21.4
1936	-	-	-	-	-	-	-	-	6.3	23.5
1937	-	-	-	-	-	-	-	-	6.9	9.5
1938	-	-	-	-	-	-	-	-	5.7	-17.4
1939	-	-	-	-	-	-	-	-	6.7	17.5
1940	-	-	-	-	-	-	-	-	7.8	16.4
1941	-	-	-	-	-	-	-	-	9.7	24.4
1942	-	-	-	-	-	-	-	-	6.9	-28.9
1943	-	-	-	-	-	-	-	-	6.5	-5.8
1944	-	-	-	-	-	-	-	-	6.7	3.1
1945	-	-	-	-	-	-	-	-	8.0	19.4
1946	12.6	-	14.7	85.3	17.1	83.1	18.7	43.0	15.8	97.5
1947	19.4	15.8	20.0	13.0	20.3	6.1	22.0	37.9	20.4	29.1
1948	22.0	-	22.4	7.5	23.7	25.3	23.3	-6.6	22.9	12.3
1949	22.8	-8.3	24.8	40.0	25.8	17.1	26.8	16.4	25.0	9.2
1950	27.7	14.1	28.1	5.9	35.6	157.6	31.5	-38.7	30.8	23.2
1951	33.8	32.6	28.9	-46.6	28.3	-8.0	28.4	1.4	29.9	-2.9
1952	28.9	7.2	29.1	2.8	27.4	-21.4	31.5	74.7	29.3	-2.0
1953	33.0	20.5	32.9	-1.2	32.7	-2.4	32.1	-7.1	32.7	11.6
1954	31.4	-8.4	32.1	9.2	31.6	-6.1	33.3	23.3	32.1	-1.8
1955	36.5	44.3	38.8	27.7	40.6	19.9	39.6	-9.5	38.9	21.2
1956	37.9	-16.1	38.0	1.1	37.6	-4.1	39.3	19.3	38.2	-1.8
1957	40.3	10.6	39.8	-4.9	39.4	-4.0	39.1	-3.0	39.7	3.9
1958	37.1	-18.9	36.3	-8.4	37.0	7.9	38.3	14.8	37.2	-6.3
1959	41.6	39.2	43.4	18.5	44.2	7.6	42.0	-18.5	42.8	15.1
1960	43.3	13.0	44.2	8.6	43.7	-4.4	42.5	-10.5	43.5	1.6
1961	40.0	-21.5	41.0	10.4	42.3	13.3	44.3	20.3	41.9	-3.7
1962	45.3	9.3	46.6	12.0	47.1	4.4	49.1	18.1	47.0	12.2
1963	50.2	9.3	51.5	10.8	52.2	5.5	53.3	8.7	51.8	10.2
1964	55.4	16.7	56.8	10.5	58.6	13.3	56.6	-13.0	56.8	9.7
1965	62.1	44.9	61.9	-1.3	63.8	12.9	66.1	15.2	63.5	11.8
1966	69.2	20.1	66.5	-14.7	69.1	16.6	69.3	1.2	68.5	7.9
1967	67.8	-8.4	71.2	21.6	71.3	0.6	72.2	5.1	70.6	3.1
1968	77.3	31.4	79.3	10.8	83.6	23.5	83.8	1.0	81.0	14.7
1969	85.8	9.9	86.2	1.9	86.4	0.9	86.5	0.5	86.2	6.4
1970	85.2	-5.9	86.4	5.8	87.3	4.2	82.5	-20.2	85.3	-1.0
1971	93.1	62.2	95.9	12.6	98.1	9.5	101.9	16.4	97.2	14.0
1972	105.3	14.0	108.5	12.7	111.8	12.7	117.4	21.6	110.7	13.9
1973	125.7	31.4	124.6	-3.5	124.3	-1.0	121.7	-8.1	124.1	12.1
1974	119.5	-7.0	123.6	14.4	129.5	20.5	119.3	-28.0	123.0	-0.9
1975	124.0	16.7	129.1	17.5	138.9	34.0	145.4	20.1	134.3	9.2
1976	155.2	29.8	157.5	6.1	160.8	8.6	166.6	15.2	160.0	19.1
1977	175.2	22.3	180.3	12.2	184.6	9.9	190.5	13.4	182.6	14.1
1978	187.9	-5.3	205.3	42.5	205.5	0.4	210.4	9.9	202.3	10.8
1979	211.8	2.7	210.6	-2.2	218.3	15.4	216.0	-4.1	214.2	5.9
1980	218.7	5.1	198.2	-32.5	211.3	29.2	221.8	21.4	212.5	-0.8
1981	230.8	17.2	225.5	-8.9	236.3	20.6	221.4	-22.9	228.5	7.5
1982	230.9	18.3	232.9	3.5	235.2	4.0	246.9	21.4	236.5	3.5
1983	251.2	7.2	270.1	33.7	281.0	17.1	297.7	26.0	275.0	16.3
1984	307.6	14.0	317.9	14.1	318.0	0.1	328.2	13.5	317.9	15.6
1985	342.2	18.2	347.0	5.7	368.2	26.8	354.4	-14.2	352.9	11.0
1986	363.8	11.0	376.1	14.2	411.6	43.4	406.8	-4.6	389.6	10.4
1987	384.9	-19.9	401.4	18.3	419.7	19.5	408.8	-10.0	403.7	3.6
1988	428.8	21.1	433.1	4.1	433.5	0.4	452.9	19.1	437.1	8.3
1989	450.8	-1.8	457.6	6.2	470.8	12.0	458.3	-10.2	459.4	5.1
1990	479.8	20.1	466.0	-11.0	467.3	1.1	459.5	-6.5	468.2	1.9
1991	448.9	-8.9	452.0	2.8	465.1	12.1	465.2	0.1	457.8	-2.2
1992	484.0	17.2	487.8	3.2	500.9	11.2	516.6	13.1	497.3	8.6
1993	515.3	-1.0	531.6	13.3	-	-	-	-	-	-

Source: "National Income and Product Account Tables: Selected NIPA Tables," *Survey of Current Business*, November 1991, U.S. Department of Commerce, Bureau of Economic Analysis, National Income and Wealth Division. - indicates that no data are available.

Gross Domestic Product
Personal consumption expenditures
Durable goods - 1987 Dollars

In billions of constant 1987 dollars and percent. Quarterly data are seasonally adjusted and annualized. Growth rates for quarters are compound annual growth rates; changes from year to year are percentage changes.

Year	1st Quarter	% Change	2nd Quarter	% Change	3rd Quarter	% Change	4th Quarter	% Change	TOTAL	% Change
1929	-	-	-	-	-	-	-	-	48.1	-
1930	-	-	-	-	-	-	-	-	38.1	-20.8
1931	-	-	-	-	-	-	-	-	32.4	-15.0
1932	-	-	-	-	-	-	-	-	24.5	-24.4
1933	-	-	-	-	-	-	-	-	24.4	-0.4
1934	-	-	-	-	-	-	-	-	27.8	13.9
1935	-	-	-	-	-	-	-	-	34.6	24.5
1936	-	-	-	-	-	-	-	-	43.1	24.6
1937	-	-	-	-	-	-	-	-	45.2	4.9
1938	-	-	-	-	-	-	-	-	36.2	-19.9
1939	-	-	-	-	-	-	-	-	42.6	17.7
1940	-	-	-	-	-	-	-	-	48.3	13.4
1941	-	-	-	-	-	-	-	-	54.6	13.0
1942	-	-	-	-	-	-	-	-	37.8	-30.8
1943	-	-	-	-	-	-	-	-	34.2	-9.5
1944	-	-	-	-	-	-	-	-	32.2	-5.8
1945	-	-	-	-	-	-	-	-	34.8	8.1
1946	-	-	-	-	-	-	-	-	55.2	58.6
1947	63.2	-	64.1	5.8	65.0	5.7	70.7	40.0	65.7	19.0
1948	70.9	1.1	70.5	-2.2	73.1	15.6	74.3	6.7	72.2	9.9
1949	73.2	-5.8	81.1	50.7	82.7	8.1	83.3	2.9	80.1	10.9
1950	85.5	11.0	86.6	5.2	108.9	150.1	99.0	-31.7	95.0	18.6
1951	98.8	-0.8	86.3	-41.8	84.0	-10.2	83.8	-0.9	88.2	-7.2
1952	85.7	9.4	88.1	11.7	82.2	-24.2	89.7	41.8	86.4	-2.0
1953	94.9	25.3	93.3	-6.6	93.5	0.9	98.1	21.2	95.0	10.0
1954	94.2	-15.0	94.0	-0.8	96.3	10.2	102.7	29.4	96.8	1.9
1955	108.2	23.2	115.2	28.5	117.6	8.6	118.2	2.1	114.8	18.6
1956	111.2	-21.7	109.2	-7.0	108.5	-2.5	108.1	-1.5	109.2	-4.9
1957	111.6	13.6	109.3	-8.0	106.8	-8.8	107.5	2.6	108.8	-0.4
1958	102.0	-18.9	101.2	-3.1	101.7	2.0	105.1	14.1	102.5	-5.8
1959	111.9	28.5	116.2	16.3	117.6	4.9	112.0	-17.7	114.4	11.6
1960	114.5	9.2	117.6	11.3	116.2	-4.7	113.2	-9.9	115.4	0.9
1961	106.7	-21.1	107.2	1.9	109.3	8.1	114.4	20.0	109.4	-5.2
1962	116.7	8.3	119.1	8.5	120.1	3.4	125.0	17.3	120.2	9.9
1963	127.3	7.6	129.7	7.8	131.3	5.0	133.0	5.3	130.3	8.4
1964	137.8	15.2	140.6	8.4	144.8	12.5	139.4	-14.1	140.7	8.0
1965	152.2	42.1	152.4	0.5	157.3	13.5	162.8	14.7	156.2	11.0
1966	169.9	18.6	162.0	-17.3	166.3	11.0	166.0	-0.7	166.0	6.3
1967	162.8	-7.5	170.0	18.9	168.1	-4.4	167.8	-0.7	167.2	0.7
1968	178.2	27.2	182.0	8.8	189.4	17.3	188.5	-1.9	184.5	10.3
1969	192.0	7.6	190.9	-2.3	190.6	-0.6	189.7	-1.9	190.8	3.4
1970	185.2	-9.2	187.3	4.6	188.2	1.9	174.2	-26.6	183.7	-3.7
1971	193.0	50.7	197.8	10.3	203.3	11.6	211.5	17.1	201.4	9.6
1972	215.9	8.6	220.9	9.6	225.7	9.0	238.3	24.3	225.2	11.8
1973	253.4	27.9	248.2	-8.0	245.9	-3.7	239.0	-10.8	246.6	9.5
1974	230.9	-12.9	233.5	4.6	235.3	3.1	209.1	-37.6	227.2	-7.9
1975	214.6	10.9	218.5	7.5	233.3	30.0	240.7	13.3	226.8	-0.2
1976	254.0	24.0	254.4	0.6	256.2	2.9	261.0	7.7	256.4	13.1
1977	272.3	18.5	278.1	8.8	282.1	5.9	287.3	7.6	280.0	9.2
1978	279.0	-11.1	300.4	34.4	295.2	-6.7	297.0	2.5	292.9	4.6
1979	293.8	-4.2	285.9	-10.3	292.4	9.4	283.8	-11.3	289.0	-1.3
1980	279.7	-5.7	246.3	-39.9	258.4	21.1	266.6	13.3	262.7	-9.1
1981	274.4	12.2	262.6	-16.1	271.3	13.9	250.0	-27.9	264.6	0.7
1982	259.3	15.7	258.6	-1.1	260.0	2.2	272.3	20.3	262.5	-0.8
1983	274.3	3.0	294.0	32.0	303.3	13.3	319.1	22.5	297.7	13.4
1984	329.6	13.8	339.0	11.9	337.6	-1.6	347.7	12.5	338.5	13.7
1985	360.1	15.0	364.4	4.9	386.4	26.4	369.6	-16.3	370.1	9.3
1986	378.9	10.5	390.2	12.5	423.1	38.2	415.7	-6.8	402.0	8.6
1987	389.4	-23.0	403.1	14.8	417.7	15.3	404.7	-11.9	403.7	0.4
1988	425.1	21.7	426.9	1.7	423.8	-2.9	439.2	15.3	428.7	6.2
1989	435.2	-3.6	440.2	4.7	450.6	9.8	436.8	-11.7	440.7	2.8
1990	454.8	17.5	441.8	-11.0	442.4	0.5	433.2	-8.1	443.1	0.5
1991	420.3	-11.4	422.0	1.6	432.6	10.4	431.5	-1.0	426.6	-3.7
1992	446.6	14.7	447.5	0.8	459.0	10.7	473.4	13.2	456.6	7.0
1993	471.9	-1.3	484.2	10.8	-	-	-	-	-	-

Source: "National Income and Product Account Tables: Selected NIPA Tables," *Survey of Current Business*, November 1991, U.S. Department of Commerce, Bureau of Economic Analysis, National Income and Wealth Division. - indicates that no data are available.

Gross Domestic Product

Personal consumption expenditures
Nondurable goods - Actual Dollars

In billions of actual dollars and percent. Quarterly data are seasonally adjusted and annualized. Growth rates for quarters are compound annual growth rates; changes from year to year are percentage changes.

Year	1st Quarter	% Change	2nd Quarter	% Change	3rd Quarter	% Change	4th Quarter	% Change	TOTAL	% Change
1929	-	-	-	-	-	-	-	-	37.7	-
1930	-	-	-	-	-	-	-	-	34.0	-9.8
1931	-	-	-	-	-	-	-	-	29.0	-14.7
1932	-	-	-	-	-	-	-	-	22.7	-21.7
1933	-	-	-	-	-	-	-	-	22.3	-1.8
1934	-	-	-	-	-	-	-	-	26.7	19.7
1935	-	-	-	-	-	-	-	-	29.3	9.7
1936	-	-	-	-	-	-	-	-	32.9	12.3
1937	-	-	-	-	-	-	-	-	35.2	7.0
1938	-	-	-	-	-	-	-	-	34.0	-3.4
1939	-	-	-	-	-	-	-	-	35.1	3.2
1940	-	-	-	-	-	-	-	-	37.0	5.4
1941	-	-	-	-	-	-	-	-	42.9	15.9
1942	-	-	-	-	-	-	-	-	50.8	18.4
1943	-	-	-	-	-	-	-	-	58.6	15.4
1944	-	-	-	-	-	-	-	-	64.3	9.7
1945	-	-	-	-	-	-	-	-	71.9	11.8
1946	78.9	-	80.6	8.9	85.1	24.3	86.3	5.8	82.7	15.0
1947	87.7	6.6	90.1	11.4	92.1	9.2	93.6	6.7	90.9	9.9
1948	95.1	6.6	97.0	8.2	97.0	-	97.3	1.2	96.6	6.3
1949	96.3	-4.0	95.3	-4.1	93.5	-7.3	94.3	3.5	94.9	-1.8
1950	94.8	2.1	96.3	6.5	100.9	20.5	100.9	-	98.2	3.5
1951	107.8	30.3	107.4	-1.5	109.4	7.7	112.0	9.9	109.2	11.2
1952	111.4	-2.1	113.7	8.5	115.9	8.0	117.9	7.1	114.7	5.0
1953	118.1	0.7	118.1	-	117.6	-1.7	117.5	-0.3	117.8	2.7
1954	118.7	4.1	118.8	0.3	119.9	3.8	121.3	4.8	119.7	1.6
1955	122.3	3.3	124.0	5.7	125.0	3.3	127.5	8.2	124.7	4.2
1956	129.1	5.1	130.0	2.8	131.3	4.1	132.7	4.3	130.8	4.9
1957	134.5	5.5	135.8	3.9	139.2	10.4	138.9	-0.9	137.1	4.8
1958	139.5	1.7	140.8	3.8	142.8	5.8	143.9	3.1	141.7	3.4
1959	146.2	6.5	147.6	3.9	149.2	4.4	150.8	4.4	148.5	4.8
1960	150.9	0.3	153.8	7.9	153.4	-1.0	154.4	2.6	153.1	3.1
1961	155.9	3.9	156.8	2.3	157.4	1.5	159.6	5.7	157.4	2.8
1962	161.5	4.8	162.9	3.5	164.4	3.7	166.3	4.7	163.8	4.1
1963	167.5	2.9	168.2	1.7	170.7	6.1	171.2	1.2	169.4	3.4
1964	175.3	9.9	178.5	7.5	182.0	8.1	183.1	2.4	179.7	6.1
1965	185.6	5.6	189.1	7.8	192.8	8.1	200.0	15.8	191.9	6.8
1966	204.2	8.7	207.7	7.0	210.7	5.9	211.4	1.3	208.5	8.7
1967	213.7	4.4	215.5	3.4	217.8	4.3	220.6	5.2	216.9	4.0
1968	227.6	13.3	232.6	9.1	238.6	10.7	241.1	4.3	235.0	8.3
1969	245.5	7.5	250.2	7.9	254.2	6.5	258.8	7.4	252.2	7.3
1970	264.7	9.4	268.2	5.4	271.9	5.6	276.5	6.9	270.4	7.2
1971	278.3	2.6	282.0	5.4	284.4	3.4	288.5	5.9	283.3	4.8
1972	293.2	6.7	301.5	11.8	308.5	9.6	317.4	12.0	305.2	7.7
1973	327.0	12.7	333.6	8.3	344.0	13.1	353.7	11.8	339.6	11.3
1974	365.6	14.2	376.7	12.7	388.0	12.5	392.9	5.1	380.8	12.1
1975	400.3	7.7	411.1	11.2	423.0	12.1	429.8	6.6	416.0	9.2
1976	439.4	9.2	446.3	6.4	455.8	8.8	465.8	9.1	451.8	8.6
1977	477.4	10.3	485.6	7.0	492.0	5.4	506.9	12.7	490.4	8.5
1978	516.7	8.0	534.5	14.5	549.4	11.6	565.5	12.2	541.5	10.4
1979	583.6	13.4	599.8	11.6	624.5	17.5	645.5	14.1	613.3	13.3
1980	667.1	14.1	673.8	4.1	686.2	7.6	704.6	11.2	682.9	11.3
1981	731.3	16.0	741.6	5.8	748.5	3.8	755.5	3.8	744.2	9.0
1982	761.2	3.1	763.3	1.1	777.5	7.7	787.3	5.1	772.3	3.8
1983	791.7	2.3	810.4	9.8	829.4	9.7	839.8	5.1	817.8	5.9
1984	854.1	7.0	872.0	8.7	878.2	2.9	887.8	4.4	873.0	6.7
1985	899.9	5.6	914.3	6.6	923.8	4.2	939.5	7.0	919.4	5.3
1986	950.1	4.6	943.9	-2.6	951.0	3.0	963.7	5.4	952.2	3.6
1987	989.0	10.9	1,007.6	7.7	1,018.4	4.4	1,029.4	4.4	1,011.1	6.2
1988	1,041.5	4.8	1,062.0	8.1	1,085.8	9.3	1,105.8	7.6	1,073.8	6.2
1989	1,121.1	5.7	1,146.5	9.4	1,157.1	3.7	1,173.5	5.8	1,149.5	7.0
1990	1,201.7	10.0	1,213.6	4.0	1,241.0	9.3	1,260.7	6.5	1,229.2	6.9
1991	1,252.3	-2.6	1,259.2	2.2	1,260.0	0.3	1,260.0	-	1,257.9	2.3
1992	1,278.2	5.9	1,288.2	3.2	1,305.7	5.5	1,331.7	8.2	1,300.9	3.4
1993	1,335.3	1.1	1,344.8	2.9	-	-	-	-	-	-

Source: "National Income and Product Account Tables: Selected NIPA Tables," *Survey of Current Business*, November 1991, U.S. Department of Commerce, Bureau of Economic Analysis, National Income and Wealth Division. - indicates that no data are available.

Gross Domestic Product
Personal consumption expenditures
Nondurable goods - 1987 Dollars

In billions of constant 1987 dollars and percent. Quarterly data are seasonally adjusted and annualized. Growth rates for quarters are compound annual growth rates; changes from year to year are percentage changes.

Year	1st Quarter	% Change	2nd Quarter	% Change	3rd Quarter	% Change	4th Quarter	% Change	TOTAL	% Change
1929	-	-	-	-	-	-	-	-	238.5	-
1930	-	-	-	-	-	-	-	-	229.2	-3.9
1931	-	-	-	-	-	-	-	-	228.3	-0.4
1932	-	-	-	-	-	-	-	-	211.7	-7.3
1933	-	-	-	-	-	-	-	-	205.0	-3.2
1934	-	-	-	-	-	-	-	-	215.7	5.2
1935	-	-	-	-	-	-	-	-	226.2	4.9
1936	-	-	-	-	-	-	-	-	252.4	11.6
1937	-	-	-	-	-	-	-	-	262.8	4.1
1938	-	-	-	-	-	-	-	-	266.6	1.4
1939	-	-	-	-	-	-	-	-	279.7	4.9
1940	-	-	-	-	-	-	-	-	293.0	4.8
1941	-	-	-	-	-	-	-	-	311.5	6.3
1942	-	-	-	-	-	-	-	-	317.9	2.1
1943	-	-	-	-	-	-	-	-	327.6	3.1
1944	-	-	-	-	-	-	-	-	346.2	5.7
1945	-	-	-	-	-	-	-	-	377.3	9.0
1946	-	-	-	-	-	-	-	-	391.7	3.8
1947	377.1	-	385.1	8.8	386.2	1.1	381.0	-5.3	382.3	-2.4
1948	381.8	0.8	385.7	4.1	381.9	-3.9	386.6	5.0	384.0	0.4
1949	388.5	2.0	389.5	1.0	387.2	-2.3	391.6	4.6	389.2	1.4
1950	396.1	4.7	400.0	4.0	406.7	6.9	398.8	-7.5	400.4	2.9
1951	409.5	11.2	405.7	-3.7	415.1	9.6	420.4	5.2	412.7	3.1
1952	417.4	-2.8	426.7	9.2	433.1	6.1	438.8	5.4	429.0	3.9
1953	444.0	4.8	445.2	1.1	442.5	-2.4	443.0	0.5	443.7	3.4
1954	445.9	2.6	444.1	-1.6	450.2	5.6	457.4	6.6	449.4	1.3
1955	460.5	2.7	467.8	6.5	472.0	3.6	481.6	8.4	470.5	4.7
1956	486.5	4.1	484.6	-1.6	484.6	-	488.2	3.0	486.0	3.3
1957	490.4	1.8	493.1	2.2	500.0	5.7	498.3	-1.4	495.5	2.0
1958	492.2	-4.8	495.3	2.5	503.5	6.8	509.1	4.5	500.0	0.9
1959	514.9	4.6	516.9	1.6	519.9	2.3	522.4	1.9	518.5	3.7
1960	522.8	0.3	529.6	5.3	527.0	-1.9	528.0	0.8	526.9	1.6
1961	532.1	3.1	537.7	4.3	536.9	-0.6	543.9	5.3	537.7	2.0
1962	548.9	3.7	550.6	1.2	554.5	2.9	558.2	2.7	553.0	2.8
1963	561.0	2.0	561.8	0.6	565.4	2.6	566.1	0.5	563.6	1.9
1964	575.7	7.0	584.9	6.5	595.9	7.7	596.3	0.3	588.2	4.4
1965	602.8	4.4	609.5	4.5	617.6	5.4	637.2	13.3	616.7	4.8
1966	641.9	3.0	647.2	3.3	651.7	2.8	649.4	-1.4	647.6	5.0
1967	655.4	3.7	659.0	2.2	658.8	-0.1	662.7	2.4	659.0	1.8
1968	675.5	8.0	683.0	4.5	692.9	5.9	692.7	-0.1	686.0	4.1
1969	698.7	3.5	702.3	2.1	703.8	0.9	708.0	2.4	703.2	2.5
1970	714.6	3.8	714.0	-0.3	718.0	2.3	722.3	2.4	717.2	2.0
1971	724.0	0.9	724.9	0.5	724.2	-0.4	729.4	2.9	725.6	1.2
1972	734.9	3.1	752.7	10.0	761.7	4.9	774.0	6.6	755.8	4.2
1973	780.7	3.5	773.7	-3.5	780.5	3.6	776.7	-1.9	777.9	2.9
1974	766.3	-5.2	761.2	-2.6	760.7	-0.3	750.9	-5.1	759.8	-2.3
1975	752.1	0.6	767.1	8.2	773.5	3.4	775.6	1.1	767.1	1.0
1976	789.2	7.2	799.3	5.2	805.2	3.0	811.6	3.2	801.3	4.5
1977	817.8	3.1	815.7	-1.0	816.7	0.5	829.2	6.3	819.8	2.3
1978	833.5	2.1	840.9	3.6	848.0	3.4	856.9	4.3	844.8	3.0
1979	860.5	1.7	856.6	-1.8	863.5	3.3	870.8	3.4	862.8	2.1
1980	869.2	-0.7	857.4	-5.3	855.3	-1.0	859.9	2.2	860.5	-0.3
1981	867.3	3.5	868.6	0.6	867.9	-0.3	868.1	0.1	867.9	0.9
1982	867.6	-0.2	867.7	0.0	872.7	2.3	880.7	3.7	872.2	0.5
1983	885.2	2.1	893.8	3.9	907.1	6.1	915.2	3.6	900.3	3.2
1984	920.6	2.4	936.2	7.0	938.5	1.0	942.9	1.9	934.6	3.8
1985	949.2	2.7	955.6	2.7	961.3	2.4	968.7	3.1	958.7	2.6
1986	980.8	5.1	990.2	3.9	992.3	0.9	1,000.9	3.5	991.0	3.4
1987	1,005.6	1.9	1,011.3	2.3	1,012.9	0.6	1,014.6	0.7	1,011.1	2.0
1988	1,023.5	3.6	1,031.0	3.0	1,039.3	3.3	1,046.8	2.9	1,035.1	2.4
1989	1,048.1	0.5	1,047.0	-0.4	1,052.6	2.2	1,058.9	2.4	1,051.6	1.6
1990	1,059.8	0.3	1,060.6	0.3	1,065.0	1.7	1,057.5	-2.8	1,060.7	0.9
1991	1,048.2	-3.5	1,051.1	1.1	1,049.3	-0.7	1,044.0	-2.0	1,048.2	-1.2
1992	1,052.0	3.1	1,055.0	1.1	1,062.9	3.0	1,081.8	7.3	1,062.9	1.4
1993	1,076.0	-2.1	1,083.1	2.7	-	-	-	-	-	-

Source: "National Income and Product Account Tables: Selected NIPA Tables," *Survey of Current Business*, November 1991, U.S. Department of Commerce, Bureau of Economic Analysis, National Income and Wealth Division. - indicates that no data are available.

Gross Domestic Product
Personal consumption expenditures
Services - Actual Dollars

In billions of actual dollars and percent. Quarterly data are seasonally adjusted and annualized. Growth rates for quarters are compound annual growth rates; changes from year to year are percentage changes.

Year	1st Quarter	% Change	2nd Quarter	% Change	3rd Quarter	% Change	4th Quarter	% Change	TOTAL	% Change
1929	-	-	-	-	-	-	-	-	30.5	-
1930	-	-	-	-	-	-	-	-	29.0	-4.9
1931	-	-	-	-	-	-	-	-	26.2	-9.7
1932	-	-	-	-	-	-	-	-	22.3	-14.9
1933	-	-	-	-	-	-	-	-	20.2	-9.4
1934	-	-	-	-	-	-	-	-	20.5	1.5
1935	-	-	-	-	-	-	-	-	21.5	4.9
1936	-	-	-	-	-	-	-	-	23.0	7.0
1937	-	-	-	-	-	-	-	-	24.7	7.4
1938	-	-	-	-	-	-	-	-	24.6	-0.4
1939	-	-	-	-	-	-	-	-	25.4	3.3
1940	-	-	-	-	-	-	-	-	26.4	3.9
1941	-	-	-	-	-	-	-	-	28.5	8.0
1942	-	-	-	-	-	-	-	-	31.3	9.8
1943	-	-	-	-	-	-	-	-	34.6	10.5
1944	-	-	-	-	-	-	-	-	37.4	8.1
1945	-	-	-	-	-	-	-	-	40.0	7.0
1946	43.5	-	44.9	13.5	46.7	17.0	48.2	13.5	45.8	14.5
1947	49.4	10.3	50.5	9.2	51.7	9.8	52.6	7.1	51.0	11.4
1948	53.9	10.3	55.3	10.8	56.9	12.1	57.9	7.2	56.0	9.8
1949	58.3	2.8	58.9	4.2	59.0	0.7	59.8	5.5	59.0	5.4
1950	61.1	9.0	63.0	13.0	64.7	11.2	66.2	9.6	63.7	8.0
1951	68.0	11.3	69.0	6.0	70.2	7.1	71.4	7.0	69.7	9.4
1952	72.9	8.7	74.6	9.7	76.5	10.6	78.6	11.4	75.7	8.6
1953	80.5	10.0	82.5	10.3	84.2	8.5	84.7	2.4	83.0	9.6
1954	86.3	7.8	88.2	9.1	90.0	8.4	91.4	6.4	89.0	7.2
1955	93.4	9.0	94.4	4.4	95.8	6.1	98.4	11.3	95.5	7.3
1956	100.2	7.5	101.8	6.5	103.9	8.5	106.0	8.3	103.0	7.9
1957	107.5	5.8	108.9	5.3	110.5	6.0	112.9	9.0	109.9	6.7
1958	113.9	3.6	116.4	9.1	118.9	8.9	120.3	4.8	117.4	6.8
1959	122.7	8.2	125.4	9.1	128.2	9.2	131.0	9.0	126.8	8.0
1960	133.1	6.6	135.4	7.1	136.3	2.7	138.6	6.9	135.9	7.2
1961	140.5	5.6	143.5	8.8	144.8	3.7	147.8	8.5	144.1	6.0
1962	149.4	4.4	152.7	9.1	154.8	5.6	157.3	6.6	153.6	6.6
1963	158.6	3.3	161.0	6.2	164.8	9.8	167.9	7.7	163.1	6.2
1964	171.1	7.8	174.2	7.4	177.5	7.8	180.9	7.9	175.9	7.8
1965	183.5	5.9	187.1	8.1	190.8	8.1	195.5	10.2	189.2	7.6
1966	198.5	6.3	202.6	8.5	206.4	7.7	210.9	9.0	204.6	8.1
1967	215.1	8.2	219.4	8.2	224.3	9.2	228.2	7.1	221.7	8.4
1968	234.1	10.7	240.6	11.6	246.1	9.5	251.6	9.2	243.1	9.7
1969	256.6	8.2	262.1	8.9	267.6	8.7	274.7	11.0	265.3	9.1
1970	281.1	9.7	286.5	7.9	294.3	11.3	301.3	9.9	290.8	9.6
1971	308.2	9.5	315.8	10.2	323.4	10.0	331.7	10.7	319.8	10.0
1972	340.8	11.4	347.2	7.7	354.8	9.0	364.9	11.9	351.9	10.0
1973	371.3	7.2	380.6	10.4	388.9	9.0	397.2	8.8	384.5	9.3
1974	405.9	9.1	418.6	13.1	429.2	10.5	442.0	12.5	423.9	10.2
1975	454.6	11.9	468.1	12.4	480.1	10.7	495.1	13.1	474.5	11.9
1976	510.3	12.9	520.8	8.5	537.2	13.2	556.7	15.3	531.2	11.9
1977	572.9	12.2	587.6	10.7	608.2	14.8	625.0	11.5	598.4	12.7
1978	647.1	14.9	670.2	15.1	687.8	10.9	704.4	10.0	677.4	13.2
1979	725.0	12.2	744.4	11.1	764.3	11.1	791.0	14.7	756.2	11.6
1980	815.7	13.1	832.9	8.7	864.9	16.3	897.2	15.8	852.7	12.8
1981	913.9	7.7	941.7	12.7	967.2	11.3	991.1	10.3	953.5	11.8
1982	1,013.3	9.3	1,033.2	8.1	1,060.4	11.0	1,094.6	13.5	1,050.4	10.2
1983	1,120.0	9.6	1,151.4	11.7	1,178.3	9.7	1,209.3	10.9	1,164.7	10.9
1984	1,230.8	7.3	1,254.6	8.0	1,281.7	8.9	1,310.4	9.3	1,269.4	9.0
1985	1,347.1	11.7	1,375.2	8.6	1,412.2	11.2	1,446.0	9.9	1,395.1	9.9
1986	1,470.9	7.1	1,492.3	5.9	1,519.4	7.5	1,552.6	9.0	1,508.8	8.1
1987	1,588.8	9.7	1,621.2	8.4	1,653.3	8.2	1,686.4	8.3	1,637.4	8.5
1988	1,728.8	10.4	1,765.4	8.7	1,807.3	9.8	1,839.5	7.3	1,785.2	9.0
1989	1,868.8	6.5	1,895.1	5.7	1,925.4	6.6	1,967.3	9.0	1,914.2	7.2
1990	1,997.8	6.3	2,047.5	10.3	2,093.4	9.3	2,116.4	4.5	2,063.8	7.8
1991	2,142.4	5.0	2,176.6	6.5	2,204.8	5.3	2,239.0	6.4	2,190.7	6.1
1992	2,284.4	8.4	2,323.8	7.1	2,350.5	4.7	2,407.9	10.1	2,341.6	6.9
1993	2,445.5	6.4	2,483.4	6.3	-	-	-	-	-	-

Source: "National Income and Product Account Tables: Selected NIPA Tables," *Survey of Current Business*, November 1991, U.S. Department of Commerce, Bureau of Economic Analysis, National Income and Wealth Division. - indicates that no data are available.

Gross Domestic Product
Personal consumption expenditures
Services - 1987 Dollars

In billions of constant 1987 dollars and percent. Quarterly data are seasonally adjusted and annualized. Growth rates for quarters are compound annual growth rates; changes from year to year are percentage changes.

Year	1st Quarter	% Change	2nd Quarter	% Change	3rd Quarter	% Change	4th Quarter	% Change	TOTAL	% Change
1929	-	-	-	-	-	-	-	-	267.9	-
1930	-	-	-	-	-	-	-	-	252.6	-5.7
1931	-	-	-	-	-	-	-	-	240.2	-4.9
1932	-	-	-	-	-	-	-	-	220.4	-8.2
1933	-	-	-	-	-	-	-	-	218.1	-1.0
1934	-	-	-	-	-	-	-	-	217.6	-0.2
1935	-	-	-	-	-	-	-	-	226.8	4.2
1936	-	-	-	-	-	-	-	-	238.9	5.3
1937	-	-	-	-	-	-	-	-	246.6	3.2
1938	-	-	-	-	-	-	-	-	239.4	-2.9
1939	-	-	-	-	-	-	-	-	246.4	2.9
1940	-	-	-	-	-	-	-	-	253.9	3.0
1941	-	-	-	-	-	-	-	-	263.1	3.6
1942	-	-	-	-	-	-	-	-	273.1	3.8
1943	-	-	-	-	-	-	-	-	285.6	4.6
1944	-	-	-	-	-	-	-	-	292.7	2.5
1945	-	-	-	-	-	-	-	-	302.4	3.3
1946	-	-	-	-	-	-	-	-	332.2	9.9
1947	343.7	-	347.6	4.6	345.5	-2.4	344.0	-1.7	345.2	3.9
1948	350.6	7.9	355.5	5.7	359.5	4.6	361.6	2.4	356.8	3.4
1949	362.2	0.7	363.7	1.7	361.4	-2.5	361.3	-0.1	362.2	1.5
1950	367.2	6.7	378.4	12.8	383.7	5.7	386.5	3.0	378.9	4.6
1951	391.5	5.3	392.9	1.4	395.2	2.4	395.8	0.6	393.8	3.9
1952	400.2	4.5	404.9	4.8	410.0	5.1	416.7	6.7	407.9	3.6
1953	419.2	2.4	424.9	5.6	427.1	2.1	424.1	-2.8	423.8	3.9
1954	429.1	4.8	438.8	9.4	446.4	7.1	450.3	3.5	441.2	4.1
1955	456.4	5.5	458.3	1.7	461.7	3.0	470.5	7.8	461.7	4.6
1956	475.0	3.9	480.2	4.5	485.7	4.7	492.9	6.1	483.5	4.7
1957	495.1	1.8	497.9	2.3	500.6	2.2	507.2	5.4	500.2	3.5
1958	508.0	0.6	517.9	8.0	525.3	5.8	527.5	1.7	519.7	3.9
1959	532.7	4.0	542.4	7.5	550.6	6.2	558.2	5.6	546.0	5.1
1960	564.4	4.5	569.1	3.4	567.6	-1.1	572.9	3.8	568.5	4.1
1961	579.3	4.5	590.6	8.0	592.6	1.4	602.7	7.0	591.3	4.0
1962	608.0	3.6	617.4	6.3	623.5	4.0	631.1	5.0	620.0	4.9
1963	634.2	2.0	640.8	4.2	654.1	8.6	663.0	5.6	648.0	4.5
1964	674.5	7.1	683.7	5.6	693.2	5.7	701.9	5.1	688.3	6.2
1965	708.4	3.8	719.0	6.1	728.2	5.2	740.7	7.0	724.1	5.2
1966	747.9	3.9	756.9	4.9	764.0	3.8	772.2	4.4	760.2	5.0
1967	781.9	5.1	791.8	5.2	802.5	5.5	808.6	3.1	796.2	4.7
1968	819.2	5.3	831.9	6.3	842.9	5.4	853.8	5.3	837.0	5.1
1969	863.9	4.8	871.8	3.7	880.6	4.1	892.4	5.5	877.2	4.8
1970	900.7	3.8	906.2	2.5	918.5	5.5	924.7	2.7	912.5	4.0
1971	932.9	3.6	940.8	3.4	949.4	3.7	963.7	6.2	946.7	3.7
1972	978.5	6.3	989.6	4.6	1,001.6	4.9	1,019.8	7.5	997.4	5.4
1973	1,029.7	3.9	1,040.1	4.1	1,047.3	2.8	1,051.6	1.7	1,042.2	4.5
1974	1,053.6	0.8	1,064.3	4.1	1,069.5	2.0	1,079.9	3.9	1,066.8	2.4
1975	1,085.0	1.9	1,101.3	6.1	1,107.6	2.3	1,120.6	4.8	1,103.6	3.4
1976	1,136.1	5.6	1,141.0	1.7	1,151.6	3.8	1,169.4	6.3	1,149.5	4.2
1977	1,181.2	4.1	1,187.0	2.0	1,203.8	5.8	1,215.1	3.8	1,196.8	4.1
1978	1,234.6	6.6	1,252.8	6.0	1,261.3	2.7	1,267.7	2.0	1,254.1	4.8
1979	1,283.6	5.1	1,292.8	2.9	1,298.7	1.8	1,310.9	3.8	1,296.5	3.4
1980	1,315.6	1.4	1,310.4	-1.6	1,326.6	5.0	1,342.8	5.0	1,323.9	2.1
1981	1,333.8	-2.7	1,344.9	3.4	1,348.2	1.0	1,350.6	0.7	1,344.4	1.5
1982	1,357.1	1.9	1,362.6	1.6	1,369.8	2.1	1,386.2	4.9	1,368.9	1.8
1983	1,396.9	3.1	1,416.1	5.6	1,428.6	3.6	1,443.9	4.4	1,421.4	3.8
1984	1,453.6	2.7	1,465.8	3.4	1,478.6	3.5	1,494.2	4.3	1,473.0	3.6
1985	1,515.5	5.8	1,529.8	3.8	1,545.6	4.2	1,557.1	3.0	1,537.0	4.3
1986	1,562.8	1.5	1,567.5	1.2	1,578.3	2.8	1,595.8	4.5	1,576.1	2.5
1987	1,616.5	5.3	1,632.4	4.0	1,645.2	3.2	1,655.5	2.5	1,637.4	3.9
1988	1,679.6	6.0	1,690.0	2.5	1,707.5	4.2	1,716.9	2.2	1,698.5	3.7
1989	1,720.3	0.8	1,725.1	1.1	1,732.2	1.7	1,746.3	3.3	1,731.0	1.9
1990	1,749.8	0.8	1,769.2	4.5	1,781.1	2.7	1,775.2	-1.3	1,768.8	2.2
1991	1,774.2	-0.2	1,783.8	2.2	1,785.2	0.3	1,792.0	1.5	1,783.8	0.8
1992	1,803.7	2.6	1,814.3	2.4	1,829.0	3.3	1,842.0	2.9	1,822.3	2.2
1993	1,855.9	3.1	1,865.4	2.1	-	-	-	-	-	-

Source: "National Income and Product Account Tables: Selected NIPA Tables," *Survey of Current Business*, November 1991, U.S. Department of Commerce, Bureau of Economic Analysis, National Income and Wealth Division. - indicates that no data are available.

GROSS PRIVATE DOMESTIC INVESTMENT
Component of Gross Domestic Product

Gross Private Domestic Investment (GPDI) accounts for all expenditures on building and structures by corporations and individuals, all durable equipment ("capital goods") used in the production of goods and services (e.g., tooling, refineries, power plants, transmission lines, etc.), and change in business inventories. Excluded from this category are investments made by government (accounted for under *Government Purchases of Goods and Services*) and capital goods exports less imports (accounted for under *Net Exports of Goods and Services*).

The category is subdivided into Fixed Investment and Change in Business Inventories as follows:

> *Fixed Investment*
>   Nonresidential
>   Structures
>   Producers' durable equipment
>   Residential
> *Change in business inventories*
>   Nonfarm
>   Farm

GPDI represented 14.7 percent of real GDP in 1992.

Fixed Investment

Nonresidential. Nonresidential fixed investment represents expenditures on permanent production facilities and equipment used by the private sector—the engine of economic activity. The category includes farm structures and farm machinery but excludes all investments made by government at all level, e.g., highways and bridges or government owned and operated production facilities. BEA estimates for the category are obtained under the headings of nonfarm buildings, public utilities, mining, other nonfarm structures, farm buildings, equipment except autos, and new and used autos; autos included in this category are used for business purposes; trucks are included under "equipment except autos." Each category has different sources of data and methods for obtaining estimates.

Residential. Residential fixed investments include permanent-site single-family housing units; multifamily housing units; mobile homes; and additions, alterations, and major replacements. Brokers commissions are also included under this category, as are purchases of capital equipment, used in production in a residential environment (e.g. a small printing press, apartment laundromat equipment, etc.).

Change in Business Inventories

Inventories are universally treated as capital investment—although not as fixed investment. Inventories "turn," meaning that stocks are withdrawn for use or sale while new stocks are added from purchases or production. For this reason, inventories, viewed as investments, are measured by comparing inventory levels at two points in time and measuring the change. The value can well be (1) negative if inventory levels have dropped from the first to the second period, (2) zero if no change took place, or (3) positive if inventory level has increased. Inventories may include finished goods (an automobile), work in process (an engine block), and raw materials in various stages (sheet steel, ingots). They may also be commodities like oil or gasoline stocks, grains or potatoes, or livestock.

The BEA subdivides the category into manufacturing and trade, other nonfarm industries, and farm; for each, different sources and estimating methods are used to arrive at quarterly and annual GDP estimates.

Presentation of Data

Data are shown from 1929 to 1993 in quarterly and in annual increments. Changes from one period to the next are shown for each category except Change in Business Inventories, which is already a change from one period to another. Changes from quarter to quarter are annualized, compounded growth rates as explained in the section on Gross National Product. Changes from year to year are simple percentile changes.

Analytical Uses

At the highest level of abstraction, GPDI is a measure, over time, of the relative proportion of national income that is reinvested to provide future productivity. A long-term decline in GPDI as a percentage of GDP indicates erosion of the nation's productive tooling and private infrastructure. A long-term growth in this measure may herald strong investment with benefits to be reaped in the future. The measure's chief limitation, for such analysis, is that it excludes public investment in infrastructure.

Change in business inventories can be used to evaluate the confidence of producers (signaled by inventory build-ups) or their vulnerability (unusually high inventories as the economy begins to decline). The measure will also reflect the likelihood of economic overheating (when inventories are low and demand is showing strong, sustained growth).

Gross Domestic Product

Gross private domestic investment: Total - Actual Dollars

In billions of actual dollars and percent. Quarterly data are seasonally adjusted and annualized. Growth rates for quarters are compound annual growth rates; changes from year to year are percentage changes.

Year	1st Quarter	% Change	2nd Quarter	% Change	3rd Quarter	% Change	4th Quarter	% Change	TOTAL	% Change
1929	-	-	-	-	-	-	-	-	16.7	-
1930	-	-	-	-	-	-	-	-	10.6	-36.5
1931	-	-	-	-	-	-	-	-	5.9	-44.3
1932	-	-	-	-	-	-	-	-	1.1	-81.4
1933	-	-	-	-	-	-	-	-	1.7	54.5
1934	-	-	-	-	-	-	-	-	3.7	117.6
1935	-	-	-	-	-	-	-	-	6.7	81.1
1936	-	-	-	-	-	-	-	-	8.7	29.9
1937	-	-	-	-	-	-	-	-	12.2	40.2
1938	-	-	-	-	-	-	-	-	7.1	-41.8
1939	-	-	-	-	-	-	-	-	9.3	31.0
1940	-	-	-	-	-	-	-	-	13.6	46.2
1941	-	-	-	-	-	-	-	-	18.2	33.8
1942	-	-	-	-	-	-	-	-	10.5	-42.3
1943	-	-	-	-	-	-	-	-	6.1	-41.9
1944	-	-	-	-	-	-	-	-	7.8	27.9
1945	-	-	-	-	-	-	-	-	10.9	39.7
1946	25.1	-	32.2	170.8	33.3	14.4	34.6	16.6	31.3	187.2
1947	33.6	-11.1	32.4	-13.5	32.9	6.3	41.2	145.9	35.0	11.8
1948	44.9	41.1	48.0	30.6	50.4	21.6	49.0	-10.7	48.1	37.4
1949	40.9	-51.5	33.9	-52.8	37.2	45.0	35.0	-21.6	36.7	-23.7
1950	44.4	159.0	49.9	59.5	56.2	60.9	66.3	93.7	54.2	47.7
1951	62.1	-23.0	65.0	20.0	59.5	-29.8	54.6	-29.1	60.3	11.3
1952	55.4	6.0	49.9	-34.2	53.9	36.1	57.0	25.1	54.0	-10.4
1953	57.8	5.7	57.9	0.7	57.2	-4.7	52.2	-30.6	56.3	4.3
1954	51.6	-4.5	51.2	-3.1	54.7	30.3	57.8	24.7	53.8	-4.4
1955	64.2	52.2	68.1	26.6	69.9	11.0	73.7	23.6	69.0	28.3
1956	73.1	-3.2	71.5	-8.5	72.6	6.3	71.5	-5.9	72.2	4.6
1957	71.9	2.3	71.9	-	73.4	8.6	65.1	-38.1	70.6	-2.2
1958	60.5	-25.4	58.7	-11.4	65.5	55.0	73.2	56.0	64.5	-8.6
1959	76.7	20.5	82.7	35.2	76.3	-27.5	79.4	17.3	78.8	22.2
1960	89.1	58.6	79.4	-36.9	78.4	-4.9	68.1	-43.1	78.7	-0.1
1961	70.2	12.9	75.4	33.1	82.2	41.3	84.0	9.1	77.9	-1.0
1962	89.3	27.7	87.9	-6.1	89.1	5.6	85.4	-15.6	87.9	12.8
1963	90.3	25.0	91.8	6.8	94.7	13.2	96.6	8.3	93.4	6.3
1964	100.6	17.6	100.4	-0.8	101.5	4.5	104.4	11.9	101.7	8.9
1965	115.8	51.4	115.8	-	119.1	11.9	121.3	7.6	118.0	16.0
1966	130.5	34.0	129.9	-1.8	129.4	-1.5	131.9	8.0	130.4	10.5
1967	126.6	-15.1	122.5	-12.3	129.5	24.9	133.5	12.9	128.0	-1.8
1968	135.3	5.5	141.7	20.3	140.3	-3.9	142.4	6.1	139.9	9.3
1969	154.3	37.9	154.1	-0.5	159.1	13.6	153.3	-13.8	155.2	10.9
1970	148.6	-11.7	150.2	4.4	154.0	10.5	148.5	-13.5	150.3	-3.2
1971	169.2	68.5	175.2	15.0	180.1	11.7	177.7	-5.2	175.5	16.8
1972	192.2	36.9	203.3	25.2	209.4	12.6	217.6	16.6	205.6	17.2
1973	232.1	29.4	241.4	17.0	240.1	-2.1	258.7	34.8	243.1	18.2
1974	241.8	-23.7	247.7	10.1	244.4	-5.2	249.3	8.3	245.8	1.1
1975	211.0	-48.7	210.6	-0.8	236.3	58.5	246.2	17.8	226.0	-8.1
1976	271.3	47.5	284.6	21.1	289.7	7.4	299.8	14.7	286.4	26.7
1977	321.6	32.4	355.2	48.8	380.3	31.4	376.0	-4.4	358.3	25.1
1978	391.9	18.0	429.4	44.1	447.3	17.7	467.4	19.2	434.0	21.1
1979	470.9	3.0	481.7	9.5	485.5	3.2	482.9	-2.1	480.2	10.6
1980	495.3	10.7	451.5	-31.0	432.1	-16.1	491.5	67.4	467.6	-2.6
1981	548.5	55.1	543.3	-3.7	575.4	25.8	564.7	-7.2	558.0	19.3
1982	517.9	-29.3	522.1	3.3	509.4	-9.4	464.2	-31.0	503.4	-9.8
1983	478.3	12.7	532.5	53.6	561.2	23.4	614.8	44.0	546.7	8.6
1984	693.6	62.0	719.2	15.6	739.9	12.0	722.8	-8.9	718.9	31.5
1985	700.5	-11.8	714.8	8.4	706.0	-4.8	737.0	18.8	714.5	-0.6
1986	752.8	8.9	724.1	-14.4	696.4	-14.4	697.1	0.4	717.6	0.4
1987	725.2	17.1	733.9	4.9	737.9	2.2	800.2	38.3	749.3	4.4
1988	770.6	-14.0	788.4	9.6	800.7	6.4	814.8	7.2	793.6	5.9
1989	843.9	15.1	840.3	-1.7	819.6	-9.5	825.2	2.8	832.3	4.9
1990	828.9	1.8	837.8	4.4	812.5	-11.5	756.4	-24.9	808.9	-2.8
1991	729.1	-13.7	721.5	-4.1	744.5	13.4	752.4	4.3	736.9	-8.9
1992	750.8	-0.8	799.7	28.7	802.2	1.3	833.3	16.4	796.5	8.1
1993	874.1	21.1	874.1	-	-	-	-	-	-	-

Source: "National Income and Product Account Tables: Selected NIPA Tables," *Survey of Current Business*, November 1991, U.S. Department of Commerce, Bureau of Economic Analysis, National Income and Wealth Division. - indicates that no data are available.

Gross Domestic Product

Gross private domestic investment: Total - 1987 Dollars

In billions of constant 1987 dollars and percent. Quarterly data are seasonally adjusted and annualized. Growth rates for quarters are compound annual growth rates; changes from year to year are percentage changes.

Year	1st Quarter	% Change	2nd Quarter	% Change	3rd Quarter	% Change	4th Quarter	% Change	TOTAL	% Change
1929	-	-	-	-	-	-	-	-	152.8	-
1930	-	-	-	-	-	-	-	-	107.2	-29.8
1931	-	-	-	-	-	-	-	-	67.2	-37.3
1932	-	-	-	-	-	-	-	-	25.0	-62.8
1933	-	-	-	-	-	-	-	-	26.6	6.4
1934	-	-	-	-	-	-	-	-	41.1	54.5
1935	-	-	-	-	-	-	-	-	65.2	58.6
1936	-	-	-	-	-	-	-	-	89.9	37.9
1937	-	-	-	-	-	-	-	-	106.4	18.4
1938	-	-	-	-	-	-	-	-	69.9	-34.3
1939	-	-	-	-	-	-	-	-	93.4	33.6
1940	-	-	-	-	-	-	-	-	121.8	30.4
1941	-	-	-	-	-	-	-	-	149.4	22.7
1942	-	-	-	-	-	-	-	-	81.4	-45.5
1943	-	-	-	-	-	-	-	-	53.5	-34.3
1944	-	-	-	-	-	-	-	-	59.8	11.8
1945	-	-	-	-	-	-	-	-	82.6	38.1
1946	-	-	-	-	-	-	-	-	195.5	136.7
1947	194.9	-	189.3	-11.0	191.7	5.2	219.1	70.6	198.8	1.7
1948	227.0	15.2	232.6	10.2	232.7	0.2	226.9	-9.6	229.8	15.6
1949	200.9	-38.5	176.3	-40.7	187.8	28.8	184.5	-6.8	187.4	-18.5
1950	222.6	111.9	245.7	48.4	262.9	31.1	291.3	50.7	256.4	36.8
1951	262.8	-33.8	270.1	11.6	252.6	-23.5	234.9	-25.2	255.6	-0.3
1952	237.9	5.2	219.7	-27.3	227.3	14.6	241.4	27.2	231.6	-9.4
1953	247.1	9.8	246.6	-0.8	241.2	-8.5	226.3	-22.5	240.3	3.8
1954	226.3	-	226.5	0.4	237.0	19.9	246.4	16.8	234.1	-2.6
1955	269.1	42.3	285.2	26.2	289.3	5.9	295.6	9.0	284.8	21.7
1956	286.2	-12.1	283.9	-3.2	281.6	-3.2	277.0	-6.4	282.2	-0.9
1957	272.2	-6.8	269.3	-4.2	273.8	6.9	252.3	-27.9	266.9	-5.4
1958	234.4	-25.5	229.4	-8.3	247.3	35.1	271.9	46.1	245.7	-7.9
1959	290.7	30.7	308.9	27.5	288.1	-24.3	297.8	14.2	296.4	20.6
1960	321.8	36.3	292.0	-32.2	288.5	-4.7	261.0	-33.0	290.8	-1.9
1961	266.4	8.5	279.9	21.9	302.4	36.2	308.9	8.9	289.4	-0.5
1962	321.4	17.2	322.0	0.7	327.3	6.7	314.1	-15.2	321.2	11.0
1963	330.8	23.0	339.5	10.9	349.3	12.1	353.5	4.9	343.3	6.9
1964	372.1	22.8	367.9	-4.4	371.3	3.7	376.0	5.2	371.8	8.3
1965	407.6	38.1	407.5	-0.1	418.1	10.8	418.9	0.8	413.0	11.1
1966	449.5	32.6	435.9	-11.6	435.1	-0.7	431.4	-3.4	438.0	6.1
1967	411.7	-17.1	406.1	-5.3	424.9	19.8	431.8	6.7	418.6	-4.4
1968	433.0	1.1	447.0	13.6	442.3	-4.1	438.0	-3.8	440.1	5.1
1969	466.2	28.3	460.6	-4.7	471.0	9.3	447.4	-18.6	461.3	4.8
1970	431.8	-13.2	423.6	-7.4	439.4	15.8	424.1	-13.2	429.7	-6.9
1971	467.8	48.0	476.2	7.4	482.0	5.0	476.8	-4.2	475.7	10.7
1972	511.3	32.2	527.4	13.2	542.1	11.6	547.8	4.3	532.2	11.9
1973	586.8	31.7	596.3	6.6	580.0	-10.5	603.6	17.3	591.7	11.2
1974	565.1	-23.2	554.6	-7.2	528.5	-17.5	523.7	-3.6	543.0	-8.2
1975	419.8	-58.7	411.3	-7.9	451.7	45.5	467.7	14.9	437.6	-19.4
1976	509.4	40.7	521.8	10.1	519.2	-2.0	532.1	10.3	520.6	19.0
1977	563.6	25.9	602.7	30.8	628.3	18.1	607.1	-12.8	600.4	15.3
1978	625.4	12.6	663.6	26.8	676.2	7.8	693.1	10.4	664.6	10.7
1979	679.0	-7.9	682.3	2.0	666.5	-8.9	651.1	-8.9	669.7	0.8
1980	650.4	-0.4	577.5	-37.8	544.3	-21.1	605.5	53.1	594.4	-11.2
1981	643.8	27.8	627.0	-10.0	644.5	11.6	609.1	-20.2	631.1	6.2
1982	553.9	-31.6	559.5	4.1	545.0	-10.0	503.5	-27.2	540.5	-14.4
1983	519.7	13.5	588.0	63.9	620.8	24.3	669.5	35.3	599.5	10.9
1984	739.9	49.2	760.6	11.7	773.1	6.7	756.4	-8.4	757.5	26.4
1985	732.6	-12.0	748.4	8.9	739.6	-4.6	763.1	13.3	745.9	-1.5
1986	776.4	7.2	746.3	-14.6	711.7	-17.3	705.9	-3.2	735.1	-1.4
1987	729.3	13.9	735.7	3.6	738.4	1.5	793.8	33.6	749.3	1.9
1988	756.9	-17.3	769.4	6.8	782.2	6.8	785.0	1.4	773.4	3.2
1989	802.9	9.4	794.5	-4.1	769.0	-12.2	769.5	0.3	784.0	1.4
1990	766.5	-1.6	773.9	3.9	751.0	-11.3	695.7	-26.4	746.8	-4.7
1991	667.8	-15.1	659.8	-4.7	682.8	14.7	692.3	5.7	675.7	-9.5
1992	691.7	-0.3	737.0	28.9	739.6	1.4	763.0	13.3	732.9	8.5
1993	803.0	22.7	803.6	0.3	-	-	-	-	-	-

Source: "National Income and Product Account Tables: Selected NIPA Tables," *Survey of Current Business*, November 1991, U.S. Department of Commerce, Bureau of Economic Analysis, National Income and Wealth Division. - indicates that no data are available.

Gross Domestic Product
Gross private domestic investment
Fixed investment - Actual Dollars

In billions of actual dollars and percent. Quarterly data are seasonally adjusted and annualized. Growth rates for quarters are compound annual growth rates; changes from year to year are percentage changes.

Year	1st Quarter	% Change	2nd Quarter	% Change	3rd Quarter	% Change	4th Quarter	% Change	TOTAL	% Change
1929	-	-	-	-	-	-	-	-	14.9	-
1930	-	-	-	-	-	-	-	-	11.0	-26.2
1931	-	-	-	-	-	-	-	-	7.0	-36.4
1932	-	-	-	-	-	-	-	-	3.6	-48.6
1933	-	-	-	-	-	-	-	-	3.1	-13.9
1934	-	-	-	-	-	-	-	-	4.3	38.7
1935	-	-	-	-	-	-	-	-	5.6	30.2
1936	-	-	-	-	-	-	-	-	7.5	33.9
1937	-	-	-	-	-	-	-	-	9.5	26.7
1938	-	-	-	-	-	-	-	-	7.7	-18.9
1939	-	-	-	-	-	-	-	-	9.1	18.2
1940	-	-	-	-	-	-	-	-	11.2	23.1
1941	-	-	-	-	-	-	-	-	13.8	23.2
1942	-	-	-	-	-	-	-	-	8.5	-38.4
1943	-	-	-	-	-	-	-	-	6.9	-18.8
1944	-	-	-	-	-	-	-	-	8.7	26.1
1945	-	-	-	-	-	-	-	-	12.3	41.4
1946	19.4	-	23.5	115.3	27.4	84.8	30.2	47.6	25.1	104.1
1947	33.2	46.1	33.6	4.9	35.6	26.0	39.6	53.1	35.5	41.4
1948	41.3	18.3	42.2	9.0	43.1	8.8	43.1	-	42.4	19.4
1949	40.5	-22.0	39.2	-12.2	38.6	-6.0	39.9	14.2	39.6	-6.6
1950	42.3	26.3	47.0	52.4	52.0	49.8	51.8	-1.5	48.3	22.0
1951	51.7	-0.8	50.0	-12.5	49.6	-3.2	49.6	-	50.3	4.1
1952	50.5	7.5	51.4	7.3	48.3	-22.0	51.9	33.3	50.5	0.4
1953	54.0	17.2	54.6	4.5	55.1	3.7	54.3	-5.7	54.5	7.9
1954	53.5	-5.8	54.6	8.5	56.8	17.1	58.1	9.5	55.8	2.4
1955	60.4	16.8	63.5	22.2	65.7	14.6	66.6	5.6	64.0	14.7
1956	66.6	-	67.8	7.4	68.9	6.6	69.0	0.6	68.1	6.4
1957	69.6	3.5	69.3	-1.7	70.4	6.5	69.4	-5.6	69.7	2.3
1958	64.6	-24.9	63.0	-9.5	63.9	5.8	68.0	28.2	64.9	-6.9
1959	72.3	27.8	74.9	15.2	76.1	6.6	75.1	-5.2	74.6	14.9
1960	77.8	15.2	76.3	-7.5	74.2	-10.6	73.8	-2.1	75.5	1.2
1961	72.7	-5.8	73.8	6.2	75.5	9.5	78.0	13.9	75.0	-0.7
1962	79.8	9.6	82.2	12.6	82.9	3.5	82.4	-2.4	81.8	9.1
1963	83.3	4.4	86.9	18.4	88.8	9.0	91.8	14.2	87.7	7.2
1964	95.0	14.7	95.6	2.6	97.2	6.9	99.0	7.6	96.7	10.3
1965	103.5	19.5	106.6	12.5	109.6	11.7	113.4	14.6	108.3	12.0
1966	117.0	13.3	117.4	1.4	117.2	-0.7	114.9	-7.6	116.7	7.8
1967	112.7	-7.4	116.2	13.0	118.1	6.7	123.3	18.8	117.6	0.8
1968	127.5	14.3	128.0	1.6	130.7	8.7	137.0	20.7	130.8	11.2
1969	142.7	17.7	144.8	6.0	148.3	10.0	146.2	-5.5	145.5	11.2
1970	146.5	0.8	146.5	-	148.6	5.9	150.6	5.5	148.1	1.8
1971	156.8	17.5	165.7	24.7	170.7	12.6	176.8	15.1	167.5	13.1
1972	187.2	25.7	191.7	10.0	195.8	8.8	208.1	27.6	195.7	16.8
1973	219.0	22.7	224.7	10.8	228.7	7.3	229.1	0.7	225.4	15.2
1974	228.0	-1.9	231.2	5.7	235.9	8.4	231.0	-8.1	231.5	2.7
1975	223.9	-11.7	225.9	3.6	234.4	15.9	242.6	14.7	231.7	0.1
1976	255.2	22.5	264.0	14.5	270.4	10.1	288.9	30.3	269.6	16.4
1977	306.4	26.5	330.2	34.9	341.8	14.8	355.7	17.3	333.5	23.7
1978	366.7	13.0	400.7	42.6	419.8	20.5	437.2	17.6	406.1	21.8
1979	450.4	12.6	458.5	7.4	478.2	18.3	482.7	3.8	467.5	15.1
1980	488.2	4.6	453.8	-25.3	468.0	13.1	498.4	28.6	477.1	2.1
1981	515.6	14.5	529.5	11.2	538.5	7.0	546.6	6.2	532.5	11.6
1982	537.3	-6.6	522.2	-10.8	507.4	-10.9	510.5	2.5	519.3	-2.5
1983	515.6	4.1	535.3	16.2	563.3	22.6	594.6	24.1	552.2	6.3
1984	615.7	15.0	644.5	20.1	659.2	9.4	671.8	7.9	647.8	17.3
1985	681.2	5.7	688.1	4.1	686.1	-1.2	704.4	11.1	689.9	6.5
1986	704.7	0.2	706.8	1.2	708.4	0.9	715.9	4.3	709.0	2.8
1987	702.1	-7.5	716.1	8.2	733.0	9.8	740.9	4.4	723.0	2.0
1988	753.8	7.1	774.6	11.5	783.6	4.7	797.5	7.3	777.4	7.5
1989	800.2	1.4	800.5	0.2	800.0	-0.2	795.0	-2.5	798.9	2.8
1990	819.3	12.8	804.5	-7.0	804.1	-0.2	780.3	-11.3	802.0	0.4
1991	749.0	-15.1	744.5	-2.4	745.0	0.3	743.5	-0.8	745.5	-7.0
1992	755.9	6.8	786.8	17.4	792.5	2.9	821.3	15.3	789.1	5.8
1993	839.5	9.2	861.0	10.6	-	-	-	-	-	-

Source: "National Income and Product Account Tables: Selected NIPA Tables," *Survey of Current Business*, November 1991, U.S. Department of Commerce, Bureau of Economic Analysis, National Income and Wealth Division. - indicates that no data are available.

Gross Domestic Product
Gross private domestic investment
Fixed investment - 1987 Dollars

In billions of constant 1987 dollars and percent. Quarterly data are seasonally adjusted and annualized. Growth rates for quarters are compound annual growth rates; changes from year to year are percentage changes.

Year	1st Quarter	% Change	2nd Quarter	% Change	3rd Quarter	% Change	4th Quarter	% Change	TOTAL	% Change
1929	-	-	-	-	-	-	-	-	142.1	-
1930	-	-	-	-	-	-	-	-	108.0	-24.0
1931	-	-	-	-	-	-	-	-	75.0	-30.6
1932	-	-	-	-	-	-	-	-	42.5	-43.3
1933	-	-	-	-	-	-	-	-	36.8	-13.4
1934	-	-	-	-	-	-	-	-	46.9	27.4
1935	-	-	-	-	-	-	-	-	59.8	27.5
1936	-	-	-	-	-	-	-	-	79.9	33.6
1937	-	-	-	-	-	-	-	-	92.9	16.3
1938	-	-	-	-	-	-	-	-	75.3	-18.9
1939	-	-	-	-	-	-	-	-	90.4	20.1
1940	-	-	-	-	-	-	-	-	107.1	18.5
1941	-	-	-	-	-	-	-	-	122.0	13.9
1942	-	-	-	-	-	-	-	-	70.0	-42.6
1943	-	-	-	-	-	-	-	-	53.6	-23.4
1944	-	-	-	-	-	-	-	-	65.4	22.0
1945	-	-	-	-	-	-	-	-	91.3	39.6
1946	-	-	-	-	-	-	-	-	167.5	83.5
1947	195.4	-	189.7	-11.2	196.9	16.1	212.0	34.4	198.5	18.5
1948	217.2	10.2	218.4	2.2	215.5	-5.2	213.3	-4.0	216.1	8.9
1949	201.2	-20.8	192.8	-15.7	192.5	-0.6	199.2	14.7	196.4	-9.1
1950	211.9	28.0	231.7	42.9	248.2	31.7	243.9	-6.8	233.9	19.1
1951	234.4	-14.7	225.1	-15.0	222.3	-4.9	220.6	-3.0	225.6	-3.5
1952	223.1	4.6	225.6	4.6	212.8	-20.8	226.5	28.3	222.0	-1.6
1953	235.5	16.9	235.9	0.7	235.4	-0.8	234.1	-2.2	235.2	5.9
1954	231.5	-4.4	235.8	7.6	243.6	13.9	247.8	7.1	239.7	1.9
1955	257.8	17.1	268.5	17.7	273.6	7.8	275.0	2.1	268.7	12.1
1956	269.7	-7.5	270.9	1.8	271.4	0.7	268.1	-4.8	270.0	0.5
1957	267.4	-1.0	264.0	-5.0	266.0	3.1	261.9	-6.0	264.8	-1.9
1958	247.7	-20.0	241.2	-10.1	244.3	5.2	259.1	26.5	248.1	-6.3
1959	275.2	27.3	284.4	14.1	287.6	4.6	284.0	-4.9	282.8	14.0
1960	292.2	12.1	284.8	-9.8	277.0	-10.5	276.9	-0.1	282.7	-0.0
1961	274.9	-2.9	277.3	3.5	283.9	9.9	292.6	12.8	282.2	-0.2
1962	298.1	7.7	307.8	13.7	309.8	2.6	306.7	-3.9	305.6	8.3
1963	309.5	3.7	324.6	21.0	332.6	10.2	342.3	12.2	327.3	7.1
1964	355.2	15.9	352.5	-3.0	357.3	5.6	359.6	2.6	356.2	8.8
1965	373.6	16.5	384.1	11.7	393.5	10.2	400.3	7.1	387.9	8.9
1966	413.4	13.7	403.8	-9.0	402.1	-1.7	385.7	-15.3	401.3	3.5
1967	377.4	-8.3	388.3	12.1	393.2	5.1	405.0	12.6	391.0	-2.6
1968	413.0	8.1	411.1	-1.8	415.8	4.7	425.9	10.1	416.5	6.5
1969	437.4	11.2	437.0	-0.4	442.8	5.4	428.9	-12.0	436.5	4.8
1970	426.8	-1.9	415.3	-10.4	425.0	9.7	428.1	2.9	423.8	-2.9
1971	436.0	7.6	452.4	15.9	460.1	7.0	471.3	10.1	454.9	7.3
1972	492.8	19.5	503.2	8.7	509.0	4.7	533.4	20.6	509.6	12.0
1973	555.5	17.6	558.2	2.0	555.2	-2.1	547.0	-5.8	554.0	8.7
1974	533.2	-9.7	524.8	-6.2	510.9	-10.2	479.3	-22.5	512.0	-7.6
1975	447.7	-23.9	441.8	-5.2	453.7	11.2	462.8	8.3	451.5	-11.8
1976	482.5	18.1	488.5	5.1	492.0	2.9	517.5	22.4	495.1	9.7
1977	538.7	17.4	568.4	23.9	574.3	4.2	583.4	6.5	566.2	14.4
1978	589.4	4.2	626.6	27.7	640.9	9.4	652.5	7.4	627.4	10.8
1979	657.3	3.0	652.6	-2.8	661.5	5.6	653.1	-5.0	656.1	4.6
1980	643.4	-5.8	581.1	-33.5	581.5	0.3	604.7	16.9	602.7	-8.1
1981	611.2	4.4	611.1	-0.1	608.8	-1.5	594.9	-8.8	606.5	0.6
1982	578.3	-10.7	561.0	-11.4	544.3	-11.4	548.4	3.0	558.0	-8.0
1983	553.2	3.5	578.1	19.3	608.7	22.9	640.2	22.4	595.1	6.6
1984	660.1	13.0	689.6	19.1	700.1	6.2	708.4	4.8	689.6	15.9
1985	717.8	5.4	724.6	3.8	719.9	-2.6	732.9	7.4	723.8	5.0
1986	728.2	-2.5	728.1	-0.1	723.8	-2.3	725.9	1.2	726.5	0.4
1987	706.8	-10.1	718.3	6.7	733.0	8.4	733.9	0.5	723.0	-0.5
1988	737.7	2.1	753.3	8.7	758.6	2.8	764.1	2.9	753.4	4.2
1989	761.7	-1.3	757.5	-2.2	753.1	-2.3	744.6	-4.4	754.2	0.1
1990	761.8	9.6	745.8	-8.1	740.1	-3.0	716.6	-12.1	741.1	-1.7
1991	685.2	-16.4	682.1	-1.8	683.8	1.0	685.2	0.8	684.1	-7.7
1992	696.7	6.9	724.4	16.9	730.0	3.1	754.3	14.0	726.4	6.2
1993	773.7	10.7	790.6	9.0	-	-	-	-	-	-

Source: "National Income and Product Account Tables: Selected NIPA Tables," *Survey of Current Business*, November 1991, U.S. Department of Commerce, Bureau of Economic Analysis, National Income and Wealth Division. - indicates that no data are available.

Gross Domestic Product
Gross private domestic investment
Fixed investment - Nonresidential - Actual Dollars

In billions of actual dollars and percent. Quarterly data are seasonally adjusted and annualized. Growth rates for quarters are compound annual growth rates; changes from year to year are percentage changes.

Year	1st Quarter	% Change	2nd Quarter	% Change	3rd Quarter	% Change	4th Quarter	% Change	TOTAL	% Change
1929	-	-	-	-	-	-	-	-	11.0	-
1930	-	-	-	-	-	-	-	-	8.6	-21.8
1931	-	-	-	-	-	-	-	-	5.3	-38.4
1932	-	-	-	-	-	-	-	-	2.9	-45.3
1933	-	-	-	-	-	-	-	-	2.5	-13.8
1934	-	-	-	-	-	-	-	-	3.3	32.0
1935	-	-	-	-	-	-	-	-	4.3	30.3
1936	-	-	-	-	-	-	-	-	5.8	34.9
1937	-	-	-	-	-	-	-	-	7.5	29.3
1938	-	-	-	-	-	-	-	-	5.5	-26.7
1939	-	-	-	-	-	-	-	-	6.1	10.9
1940	-	-	-	-	-	-	-	-	7.7	26.2
1941	-	-	-	-	-	-	-	-	9.7	26.0
1942	-	-	-	-	-	-	-	-	6.3	-35.1
1943	-	-	-	-	-	-	-	-	5.4	-14.3
1944	-	-	-	-	-	-	-	-	7.4	37.0
1945	-	-	-	-	-	-	-	-	10.6	43.2
1946	13.6	-	16.1	96.4	18.7	82.0	20.9	56.0	17.3	63.2
1947	22.8	41.6	23.2	7.2	23.3	1.7	24.5	22.2	23.5	35.8
1948	26.2	30.8	26.0	-3.0	27.0	16.3	28.1	17.3	26.8	14.0
1949	26.6	-19.7	25.5	-15.5	24.1	-20.2	23.5	-9.6	24.9	-7.1
1950	24.2	12.5	26.6	46.0	29.6	53.3	30.6	14.2	27.8	11.6
1951	30.9	4.0	31.8	12.2	32.5	9.1	32.2	-3.6	31.8	14.4
1952	32.4	2.5	32.9	6.3	29.8	-32.7	32.5	41.5	31.9	0.3
1953	34.3	24.1	34.8	6.0	35.9	13.3	35.4	-5.5	35.1	10.0
1954	34.5	-9.8	34.3	-2.3	35.0	8.4	34.9	-1.1	34.7	-1.1
1955	35.4	5.9	37.9	31.4	40.4	29.1	42.5	22.5	39.0	12.4
1956	42.8	2.9	43.9	10.7	45.4	14.4	45.9	4.5	44.5	14.1
1957	47.0	9.9	47.1	0.9	48.4	11.5	47.5	-7.2	47.5	6.7
1958	43.6	-29.0	42.0	-13.9	41.4	-5.6	43.0	16.4	42.5	-10.5
1959	44.5	14.7	46.1	15.2	47.8	15.6	47.6	-1.7	46.5	9.4
1960	49.4	16.0	50.2	6.6	48.9	-10.0	48.5	-3.2	49.2	5.8
1961	47.4	-8.8	48.3	7.8	48.6	2.5	50.2	13.8	48.6	-1.2
1962	51.4	9.9	53.0	13.0	53.7	5.4	53.2	-3.7	52.8	8.6
1963	53.1	-0.7	54.7	12.6	56.3	12.2	58.1	13.4	55.6	5.3
1964	59.6	10.7	61.4	12.6	63.5	14.4	65.2	11.1	62.4	12.2
1965	69.7	30.6	72.4	16.4	75.3	17.0	78.9	20.5	74.1	18.8
1966	82.2	17.8	84.2	10.1	85.3	5.3	85.7	1.9	84.4	13.9
1967	84.3	-6.4	84.5	1.0	84.7	1.0	87.2	12.3	85.2	0.9
1968	90.6	16.5	89.9	-3.1	91.8	8.7	96.0	19.6	92.1	8.1
1969	99.5	15.4	101.4	7.9	105.1	15.4	105.6	1.9	102.9	11.7
1970	105.8	0.8	107.1	5.0	108.2	4.2	105.7	-8.9	106.7	3.7
1971	108.2	9.8	111.1	11.2	112.4	4.8	115.3	10.7	111.7	4.7
1972	120.6	19.7	123.5	10.0	126.3	9.4	133.8	26.0	126.1	12.9
1973	141.2	24.0	149.0	24.0	153.7	13.2	156.4	7.2	150.0	19.0
1974	159.0	6.8	163.7	12.4	168.5	12.3	171.0	6.1	165.6	10.4
1975	166.3	-10.5	166.0	-0.7	169.7	9.2	173.9	10.3	169.0	2.1
1976	179.1	12.5	183.4	10.0	189.8	14.7	196.4	14.7	187.2	10.8
1977	208.8	27.7	218.5	19.9	226.8	16.1	238.8	22.9	223.2	19.2
1978	245.7	12.1	270.1	46.0	284.0	22.2	298.2	21.6	274.5	23.0
1979	311.9	19.7	317.7	7.6	334.7	23.2	341.5	8.4	326.4	18.9
1980	353.6	14.9	342.5	-12.0	352.1	11.7	367.1	18.2	353.8	8.4
1981	383.7	19.4	400.7	18.9	418.4	18.9	437.1	19.1	410.0	15.9
1982	432.6	-4.1	419.4	-11.7	405.0	-13.0	397.7	-7.0	413.7	0.9
1983	385.3	-11.9	387.2	2.0	401.3	15.4	426.9	28.1	400.2	-3.3
1984	441.0	13.9	463.9	22.4	479.3	14.0	491.5	10.6	468.9	17.2
1985	499.1	6.3	506.1	5.7	499.6	-5.0	511.3	9.7	504.0	7.5
1986	501.6	-7.4	490.1	-8.9	486.0	-3.3	491.7	4.8	492.4	-2.3
1987	479.3	-9.7	489.7	9.0	507.8	15.6	514.3	5.2	497.8	1.1
1988	526.8	10.1	544.1	13.8	550.3	4.6	560.2	7.4	545.4	9.6
1989	563.4	2.3	568.4	3.6	571.5	2.2	568.8	-1.9	568.1	4.2
1990	586.2	12.8	582.1	-2.8	594.1	8.5	584.4	-6.4	586.7	3.3
1991	566.8	-11.5	561.0	-4.0	552.6	-5.9	543.3	-6.6	555.9	-5.2
1992	547.0	2.8	566.3	14.9	569.2	2.1	579.5	7.4	565.5	1.7
1993	594.7	10.9	619.1	17.4	-	-	-	-	-	-

Source: "National Income and Product Account Tables: Selected NIPA Tables," *Survey of Current Business*, November 1991, U.S. Department of Commerce, Bureau of Economic Analysis, National Income and Wealth Division. - indicates that no data are available.

Gross Domestic Product
Gross private domestic investment
Fixed investment - Nonresidential - 1987 Dollars

In billions of constant 1987 dollars and percent. Quarterly data are seasonally adjusted and annualized. Growth rates for quarters are compound annual growth rates; changes from year to year are percentage changes.

Year	1st Quarter	% Change	2nd Quarter	% Change	3rd Quarter	% Change	4th Quarter	% Change	TOTAL	% Change
1929	-	-	-	-	-	-	-	-	100.6	-
1930	-	-	-	-	-	-	-	-	82.7	-17.8
1931	-	-	-	-	-	-	-	-	54.0	-34.7
1932	-	-	-	-	-	-	-	-	31.4	-41.9
1933	-	-	-	-	-	-	-	-	27.7	-11.8
1934	-	-	-	-	-	-	-	-	34.2	23.5
1935	-	-	-	-	-	-	-	-	42.4	24.0
1936	-	-	-	-	-	-	-	-	57.9	36.6
1937	-	-	-	-	-	-	-	-	69.1	19.3
1938	-	-	-	-	-	-	-	-	51.3	-25.8
1939	-	-	-	-	-	-	-	-	56.5	10.1
1940	-	-	-	-	-	-	-	-	69.0	22.1
1941	-	-	-	-	-	-	-	-	81.6	18.3
1942	-	-	-	-	-	-	-	-	49.6	-39.2
1943	-	-	-	-	-	-	-	-	41.3	-16.7
1944	-	-	-	-	-	-	-	-	54.6	32.2
1945	-	-	-	-	-	-	-	-	78.5	43.8
1946	-	-	-	-	-	-	-	-	114.9	46.4
1947	133.8	-	131.3	-7.3	129.6	-5.1	131.4	5.7	131.5	14.4
1948	137.8	21.0	134.2	-10.0	134.0	-0.6	138.0	12.5	136.0	3.4
1949	131.4	-17.8	124.1	-20.4	117.7	-19.1	115.2	-8.2	122.1	-10.2
1950	118.6	12.3	129.6	42.6	140.5	38.1	141.4	2.6	132.5	8.5
1951	137.0	-11.9	140.8	11.6	143.6	8.2	141.1	-6.8	140.6	6.1
1952	141.5	1.1	142.5	2.9	130.4	-29.9	139.9	32.5	138.6	-1.4
1953	147.5	23.6	147.7	0.5	150.5	7.8	149.8	-1.8	148.9	7.4
1954	146.3	-9.0	145.2	-3.0	147.5	6.5	145.8	-4.5	146.2	-1.8
1955	148.3	7.0	157.5	27.2	165.1	20.7	171.3	15.9	160.5	9.8
1956	169.0	-5.3	170.9	4.6	173.4	6.0	171.5	-4.3	171.2	6.7
1957	172.3	1.9	171.2	-2.5	174.5	7.9	170.4	-9.1	172.1	0.5
1958	159.5	-23.2	153.1	-15.1	149.9	-8.1	154.8	13.7	154.3	-10.3
1959	158.8	10.7	163.8	13.2	169.1	13.6	169.0	-0.2	165.2	7.1
1960	173.8	11.9	176.1	5.4	171.7	-9.6	171.4	-0.7	173.3	4.9
1961	169.0	-5.5	171.0	4.8	171.8	1.9	176.8	12.2	172.1	-0.7
1962	180.0	7.4	186.1	14.3	188.3	4.8	185.4	-6.0	185.0	7.5
1963	183.7	-3.6	189.7	13.7	195.1	11.9	200.7	12.0	192.3	3.9
1964	205.2	9.3	210.4	10.5	217.8	14.8	222.7	9.3	214.0	11.3
1965	236.4	27.0	245.9	17.1	255.0	15.6	265.0	16.6	250.6	17.1
1966	275.0	16.0	276.8	2.6	279.2	3.5	275.8	-4.8	276.7	10.4
1967	271.0	-6.8	269.7	-1.9	268.8	-1.3	273.4	7.0	270.8	-2.1
1968	280.9	11.4	275.5	-7.5	277.7	3.2	286.4	13.1	280.1	3.4
1969	293.1	9.7	293.8	1.0	300.9	10.0	297.7	-4.2	296.4	5.8
1970	294.9	-3.7	292.5	-3.2	295.5	4.2	284.9	-13.6	292.0	-1.5
1971	284.9	-	286.2	1.8	285.8	-0.6	290.3	6.4	286.8	-1.8
1972	299.7	13.6	306.1	8.8	311.4	7.1	329.1	24.7	311.6	8.6
1973	344.3	19.8	357.7	16.5	363.1	6.2	364.3	1.3	357.4	14.7
1974	364.0	-0.3	363.3	-0.8	354.9	-8.9	343.7	-12.0	356.5	-0.3
1975	320.7	-24.2	312.4	-10.0	315.5	4.0	318.5	3.9	316.8	-11.1
1976	323.6	6.6	324.9	1.6	330.8	7.5	335.7	6.1	328.7	3.8
1977	351.6	20.3	360.5	10.5	366.6	6.9	378.5	13.6	364.3	10.8
1978	383.1	5.0	411.0	32.5	423.0	12.2	434.3	11.1	412.9	13.3
1979	444.1	9.3	442.9	-1.1	454.7	11.1	453.4	-1.1	448.8	8.7
1980	457.7	3.8	430.7	-21.6	428.2	-2.3	434.7	6.2	437.8	-2.5
1981	444.9	9.7	450.9	5.5	461.6	9.8	462.5	0.8	455.0	3.9
1982	453.6	-7.5	440.1	-11.4	424.8	-13.2	417.2	-7.0	433.9	-4.6
1983	403.1	-12.8	407.6	4.5	423.0	16.0	449.6	27.6	420.8	-3.0
1984	463.7	13.1	487.2	21.9	500.4	11.3	509.6	7.6	490.2	16.5
1985	518.8	7.4	525.8	5.5	517.2	-6.4	525.5	6.6	521.8	6.4
1986	513.2	-9.0	500.1	-9.8	492.5	-5.9	495.5	2.5	500.3	-4.1
1987	481.1	-11.1	490.7	8.2	508.6	15.4	510.6	1.6	497.8	-0.5
1988	517.7	5.7	531.4	11.0	535.2	2.9	538.8	2.7	530.8	6.6
1989	539.5	0.5	542.2	2.0	541.8	-0.3	536.7	-3.7	540.0	1.7
1990	550.2	10.4	544.5	-4.1	551.2	5.0	540.2	-7.7	546.5	1.2
1991	521.4	-13.2	517.8	-2.7	512.8	-3.8	506.1	-5.1	514.5	-5.9
1992	510.5	3.5	528.8	15.1	533.8	3.8	543.7	7.6	529.2	2.9
1993	562.3	14.4	584.3	16.6	-	-	-	-	-	-

Source: "National Income and Product Account Tables: Selected NIPA Tables," *Survey of Current Business*, November 1991, U.S. Department of Commerce, Bureau of Economic Analysis, National Income and Wealth Division. - indicates that no data are available.

Gross Domestic Product

Gross private domestic investment
Fixed investment - Nonresidential - Structures - Actual Dollars

In billions of actual dollars and percent. Quarterly data are seasonally adjusted and annualized. Growth rates for quarters are compound annual growth rates; changes from year to year are percentage changes.

Year	1st Quarter	% Change	2nd Quarter	% Change	3rd Quarter	% Change	4th Quarter	% Change	TOTAL	% Change
1929	-	-	-	-	-	-	-	-	5.5	-
1930	-	-	-	-	-	-	-	-	4.4	-20.0
1931	-	-	-	-	-	-	-	-	2.6	-40.9
1932	-	-	-	-	-	-	-	-	1.4	-46.2
1933	-	-	-	-	-	-	-	-	1.1	-21.4
1934	-	-	-	-	-	-	-	-	1.2	9.1
1935	-	-	-	-	-	-	-	-	1.4	16.7
1936	-	-	-	-	-	-	-	-	1.9	35.7
1937	-	-	-	-	-	-	-	-	2.7	42.1
1938	-	-	-	-	-	-	-	-	2.1	-22.2
1939	-	-	-	-	-	-	-	-	2.2	4.8
1940	-	-	-	-	-	-	-	-	2.6	18.2
1941	-	-	-	-	-	-	-	-	3.3	26.9
1942	-	-	-	-	-	-	-	-	2.2	-33.3
1943	-	-	-	-	-	-	-	-	1.8	-18.2
1944	-	-	-	-	-	-	-	-	2.4	33.3
1945	-	-	-	-	-	-	-	-	3.3	37.5
1946	6.2	-	7.4	102.9	7.9	29.9	7.9	-	7.4	124.2
1947	7.9	-	7.9	-	8.3	21.8	8.4	4.9	8.1	9.5
1948	8.8	20.5	9.3	24.7	9.9	28.4	10.1	8.3	9.5	17.3
1949	9.7	-14.9	9.4	-11.8	8.9	-19.6	8.7	-8.7	9.2	-3.2
1950	9.1	19.7	9.5	18.8	10.3	38.2	11.0	30.1	10.0	8.7
1951	11.5	19.5	12.2	26.7	12.3	3.3	11.9	-12.4	12.0	20.0
1952	12.0	3.4	12.1	3.4	12.2	3.3	12.6	13.8	12.2	1.7
1953	13.1	16.8	13.5	12.8	13.7	6.1	14.0	9.1	13.6	11.5
1954	13.9	-2.8	13.9	-	13.9	-	13.8	-2.8	13.9	2.2
1955	14.3	15.3	14.7	11.7	15.4	20.5	16.2	22.5	15.2	9.4
1956	17.4	33.1	18.0	14.5	18.6	14.0	18.7	2.2	18.2	19.7
1957	18.8	2.2	19.0	4.3	19.1	2.1	18.9	-4.1	19.0	4.4
1958	18.1	-15.9	17.6	-10.6	17.3	-6.6	17.6	7.1	17.6	-7.4
1959	17.4	-4.5	18.0	14.5	18.6	14.0	18.5	-2.1	18.1	2.8
1960	19.4	20.9	19.5	2.1	19.4	-2.0	20.0	13.0	19.6	8.3
1961	19.9	-2.0	19.6	-5.9	19.7	2.1	19.6	-2.0	19.7	0.5
1962	20.0	8.4	20.8	17.0	21.4	12.0	20.9	-9.0	20.8	5.6
1963	20.2	-12.7	21.2	21.3	21.4	3.8	21.9	9.7	21.2	1.9
1964	22.4	9.4	23.4	19.1	24.3	16.3	24.8	8.5	23.7	11.8
1965	26.1	22.7	28.2	36.3	28.5	4.3	30.4	29.5	28.3	19.4
1966	31.1	9.5	31.2	1.3	31.9	9.3	31.2	-8.5	31.3	10.6
1967	31.7	6.6	30.9	-9.7	31.5	8.0	32.0	6.5	31.5	0.6
1968	33.1	14.5	33.2	1.2	33.2	-	34.8	20.7	33.6	6.7
1969	35.8	12.0	36.7	10.4	38.9	26.2	39.4	5.2	37.7	12.2
1970	39.5	1.0	40.3	8.4	40.6	3.0	40.8	2.0	40.3	6.9
1971	41.5	7.0	42.3	7.9	43.1	7.8	43.8	6.7	42.7	6.0
1972	45.8	19.6	46.6	7.2	47.3	6.1	49.0	15.2	47.2	10.5
1973	51.3	20.1	54.1	23.7	56.8	21.5	57.7	6.5	55.0	16.5
1974	59.0	9.3	61.3	16.5	61.4	0.7	63.2	12.3	61.2	11.3
1975	61.7	-9.2	60.4	-8.2	61.3	6.1	62.0	4.6	61.4	0.3
1976	64.1	14.3	65.1	6.4	66.7	10.2	67.8	6.8	65.9	7.3
1977	69.7	11.7	73.6	24.3	76.4	16.1	78.5	11.5	74.6	13.2
1978	81.2	14.5	90.5	54.3	98.5	40.3	105.4	31.1	93.9	25.9
1979	108.5	12.3	113.4	19.3	122.5	36.2	129.2	23.7	118.4	26.1
1980	133.9	15.4	133.5	-1.2	137.0	10.9	145.4	26.9	137.5	16.1
1981	151.6	18.2	162.6	32.3	171.8	24.6	190.6	51.5	169.1	23.0
1982	189.6	-2.1	184.0	-11.3	172.8	-22.2	168.9	-8.7	178.8	5.7
1983	158.0	-23.4	148.5	-22.0	151.2	7.5	154.6	9.3	153.1	-14.4
1984	163.8	26.0	173.8	26.7	180.8	17.1	184.1	7.5	175.6	14.7
1985	193.9	23.1	194.3	0.8	190.0	-8.6	195.4	11.9	193.4	10.1
1986	189.4	-11.7	171.8	-32.3	166.1	-12.6	168.4	5.7	174.0	-10.0
1987	164.1	-9.8	166.4	5.7	174.8	21.8	180.0	12.4	171.3	-1.6
1988	176.6	-7.3	181.4	11.3	183.1	3.8	186.8	8.3	182.0	6.2
1989	190.2	7.5	189.6	-1.3	195.5	13.0	198.0	5.2	193.3	6.2
1990	203.6	11.8	203.2	-0.8	203.8	1.2	195.7	-15.0	201.6	4.3
1991	192.2	-7.0	188.4	-7.7	178.0	-20.3	171.7	-13.4	182.6	-9.4
1992	173.9	5.2	174.5	1.4	170.8	-8.2	171.1	0.7	172.6	-5.5
1993	172.4	3.1	177.6	12.6	-	-	-	-	-	-

Source: "National Income and Product Account Tables: Selected NIPA Tables," *Survey of Current Business*, November 1991, U.S. Department of Commerce, Bureau of Economic Analysis, National Income and Wealth Division. - indicates that no data are available.

Gross Domestic Product
Gross private domestic investment
Fixed investment - Nonresidential - Structures - 1987 Dollars

In billions of constant 1987 dollars and percent. Quarterly data are seasonally adjusted and annualized. Growth rates for quarters are compound annual growth rates; changes from year to year are percentage changes.

Year	1st Quarter	% Change	2nd Quarter	% Change	3rd Quarter	% Change	4th Quarter	% Change	TOTAL	% Change
1929	-	-	-	-	-	-	-	-	58.9	-
1930	-	-	-	-	-	-	-	-	49.7	-15.6
1931	-	-	-	-	-	-	-	-	32.1	-35.4
1932	-	-	-	-	-	-	-	-	18.8	-41.4
1933	-	-	-	-	-	-	-	-	14.8	-21.3
1934	-	-	-	-	-	-	-	-	16.3	10.1
1935	-	-	-	-	-	-	-	-	18.1	11.0
1936	-	-	-	-	-	-	-	-	24.0	32.6
1937	-	-	-	-	-	-	-	-	30.3	26.2
1938	-	-	-	-	-	-	-	-	24.1	-20.5
1939	-	-	-	-	-	-	-	-	25.6	6.2
1940	-	-	-	-	-	-	-	-	28.9	12.9
1941	-	-	-	-	-	-	-	-	34.4	19.0
1942	-	-	-	-	-	-	-	-	20.9	-39.2
1943	-	-	-	-	-	-	-	-	15.3	-26.8
1944	-	-	-	-	-	-	-	-	19.9	30.1
1945	-	-	-	-	-	-	-	-	27.2	36.7
1946	-	-	-	-	-	-	-	-	54.5	100.4
1947	49.9	-	49.5	-3.2	49.8	2.4	49.0	-6.3	49.5	-9.2
1948	49.8	6.7	51.2	11.7	52.9	14.0	53.9	7.8	51.9	4.8
1949	53.1	-5.8	52.0	-8.0	49.8	-15.9	48.4	-10.8	50.8	-2.1
1950	50.5	18.5	53.0	21.3	55.9	23.7	57.3	10.4	54.2	6.7
1951	57.5	1.4	59.4	13.9	59.1	-2.0	56.9	-14.1	58.2	7.4
1952	57.0	0.7	57.5	3.6	58.0	3.5	60.2	16.1	58.2	-
1953	61.9	11.8	63.0	7.3	63.3	1.9	64.4	7.1	63.2	8.6
1954	65.2	5.1	65.6	2.5	65.4	-1.2	65.1	-1.8	65.3	3.3
1955	67.1	12.9	68.7	9.9	70.8	12.8	72.5	10.0	69.8	6.9
1956	74.7	12.7	77.4	15.3	77.9	2.6	77.8	-0.5	77.0	10.3
1957	77.2	-3.0	77.2	-	77.2	-	76.7	-2.6	77.1	0.1
1958	75.0	-8.6	72.6	-12.2	71.0	-8.5	72.1	6.3	72.6	-5.8
1959	71.7	-2.2	73.9	12.8	76.3	13.6	75.8	-2.6	74.4	2.5
1960	79.1	18.6	80.0	4.6	80.3	1.5	83.6	17.5	80.8	8.6
1961	83.5	-0.5	82.1	-6.5	82.0	-0.5	81.6	-1.9	82.3	1.9
1962	83.1	7.6	86.3	16.3	88.7	11.6	86.4	-10.0	86.1	4.6
1963	83.3	-13.6	87.1	19.5	87.8	3.3	89.4	7.5	86.9	0.9
1964	91.8	11.2	94.9	14.2	98.2	14.7	98.9	2.9	95.9	10.4
1965	104.1	22.7	111.4	31.1	112.6	4.4	117.9	20.2	111.5	16.3
1966	120.7	9.8	118.2	-8.0	120.8	9.1	116.7	-12.9	119.1	6.8
1967	117.9	4.2	114.4	-11.4	115.7	4.6	115.8	0.3	116.0	-2.6
1968	118.0	7.8	117.1	-3.0	116.0	-3.7	118.4	8.5	117.4	1.2
1969	120.1	5.9	121.1	3.4	126.8	20.2	125.8	-3.1	123.5	5.2
1970	124.8	-3.1	123.1	-5.3	123.4	1.0	121.9	-4.8	123.3	-0.2
1971	121.6	-1.0	121.2	-1.3	121.1	-0.3	120.8	-1.0	121.2	-1.7
1972	123.7	10.0	124.5	2.6	124.6	0.3	126.5	6.2	124.8	3.0
1973	130.7	14.0	134.7	12.8	137.7	9.2	136.6	-3.2	134.9	8.1
1974	135.9	-2.0	135.5	-1.2	129.6	-16.3	128.1	-4.5	132.3	-1.9
1975	121.2	-19.9	116.5	-14.6	117.2	2.4	117.1	-0.3	118.0	-10.8
1976	120.5	12.1	119.8	-2.3	120.8	3.4	121.0	0.7	120.5	2.1
1977	122.1	3.7	125.9	13.0	127.7	5.8	128.6	2.8	126.1	4.6
1978	130.6	6.4	141.2	36.6	149.5	25.7	155.0	15.5	144.1	14.3
1979	155.7	1.8	159.6	10.4	166.3	17.9	171.7	13.6	163.3	13.3
1980	173.5	4.3	169.3	-9.3	167.4	-4.4	170.7	8.1	170.2	4.2
1981	174.8	10.0	179.8	11.9	185.0	12.1	192.1	16.3	182.9	7.5
1982	190.4	-3.5	185.6	-9.7	175.9	-19.3	173.2	-6.0	181.3	-0.9
1983	163.0	-21.6	156.1	-15.9	159.5	9.0	162.6	8.0	160.3	-11.6
1984	172.1	25.5	182.0	25.1	187.6	12.9	189.5	4.1	182.8	14.0
1985	198.1	19.4	199.1	2.0	193.9	-10.0	198.3	9.4	197.4	8.0
1986	191.9	-12.3	175.1	-30.7	169.0	-13.2	170.4	3.4	176.6	-10.5
1987	165.4	-11.2	167.3	4.7	174.7	18.9	177.9	7.5	171.3	-3.0
1988	171.6	-13.4	174.4	6.7	174.1	-0.7	175.7	3.7	174.0	1.6
1989	177.0	3.0	174.7	-5.1	178.8	9.7	179.8	2.3	177.6	2.1
1990	182.9	7.1	181.6	-2.8	180.9	-1.5	172.8	-16.7	179.5	1.1
1991	169.0	-8.5	165.2	-8.7	155.6	-21.3	151.0	-11.3	160.2	-10.8
1992	152.8	4.9	152.9	0.3	148.8	-10.3	148.0	-2.1	150.6	-6.0
1993	148.2	0.5	151.1	8.1	-		-		-	

Source: "National Income and Product Account Tables: Selected NIPA Tables," *Survey of Current Business*, November 1991, U.S. Department of Commerce, Bureau of Economic Analysis, National Income and Wealth Division. - indicates that no data are available.

Gross Domestic Product
Gross private domestic investment
Fixed investment - Nonresidential - Producers' durable equipment - Actual Dollars

In billions of actual dollars and percent. Quarterly data are seasonally adjusted and annualized. Growth rates for quarters are compound annual growth rates; changes from year to year are percentage changes.

Year	1st Quarter	% Change	2nd Quarter	% Change	3rd Quarter	% Change	4th Quarter	% Change	TOTAL	% Change
1929	-	-	-	-	-	-	-	-	5.5	-
1930	-	-	-	-	-	-	-	-	4.2	-23.6
1931	-	-	-	-	-	-	-	-	2.6	-38.1
1932	-	-	-	-	-	-	-	-	1.5	-42.3
1933	-	-	-	-	-	-	-	-	1.4	-6.7
1934	-	-	-	-	-	-	-	-	2.1	50.0
1935	-	-	-	-	-	-	-	-	2.8	33.3
1936	-	-	-	-	-	-	-	-	3.9	39.3
1937	-	-	-	-	-	-	-	-	4.8	23.1
1938	-	-	-	-	-	-	-	-	3.4	-29.2
1939	-	-	-	-	-	-	-	-	3.9	14.7
1940	-	-	-	-	-	-	-	-	5.2	33.3
1941	-	-	-	-	-	-	-	-	6.4	23.1
1942	-	-	-	-	-	-	-	-	4.1	-35.9
1943	-	-	-	-	-	-	-	-	3.7	-9.8
1944	-	-	-	-	-	-	-	-	5.0	35.1
1945	-	-	-	-	-	-	-	-	7.3	46.0
1946	7.3	-	8.6	92.6	10.8	148.7	13.0	109.9	9.9	35.6
1947	14.9	72.6	15.2	8.3	15.0	-5.2	16.1	32.7	15.3	54.5
1948	17.3	33.3	16.7	-13.2	17.1	9.9	18.0	22.8	17.3	13.1
1949	16.8	-24.1	16.1	-15.7	15.2	-20.6	14.9	-7.7	15.7	-9.2
1950	15.1	5.5	17.1	64.5	19.4	65.7	19.6	4.2	17.8	13.4
1951	19.4	-4.0	19.7	6.3	20.2	10.5	20.2	-	19.9	11.8
1952	20.4	4.0	20.8	8.1	17.7	-47.6	19.9	59.8	19.7	-1.0
1953	21.3	31.3	21.3	-	22.1	15.9	21.4	-12.1	21.5	9.1
1954	20.6	-14.1	20.4	-3.8	21.1	14.4	21.1	-	20.8	-3.3
1955	21.1	-	23.1	43.7	25.0	37.2	26.3	22.5	23.9	14.9
1956	25.4	-13.0	25.9	8.1	26.8	14.6	27.2	6.1	26.3	10.0
1957	28.2	15.5	28.1	-1.4	29.3	18.2	28.6	-9.2	28.6	8.7
1958	25.5	-36.8	24.4	-16.2	24.1	-4.8	25.5	25.3	24.9	-12.9
1959	27.1	27.6	28.1	15.6	29.1	15.0	29.1	-	28.3	13.7
1960	30.1	14.5	30.7	8.2	29.5	-14.7	28.4	-14.1	29.7	4.9
1961	27.5	-12.1	28.7	18.6	28.9	2.8	30.6	25.7	28.9	-2.7
1962	31.4	10.9	32.2	10.6	32.3	1.2	32.3	-	32.1	11.1
1963	32.9	7.6	33.5	7.5	34.9	17.8	36.2	15.8	34.4	7.2
1964	37.2	11.5	38.0	8.9	39.3	14.4	40.3	10.6	38.7	12.5
1965	43.5	35.7	44.3	7.6	46.8	24.6	48.5	15.3	45.8	18.3
1966	51.1	23.2	53.0	15.7	53.4	3.1	54.5	8.5	53.0	15.7
1967	52.7	-12.6	53.6	7.0	53.2	-3.0	55.3	16.7	53.7	1.3
1968	57.6	17.7	56.7	-6.1	58.6	14.1	61.3	19.7	58.5	8.9
1969	63.7	16.6	64.7	6.4	66.1	8.9	66.2	0.6	65.2	11.5
1970	66.4	1.2	66.8	2.4	67.6	4.9	64.9	-15.0	66.4	1.8
1971	66.7	11.6	68.8	13.2	69.3	2.9	71.5	13.3	69.1	4.1
1972	74.8	19.8	76.9	11.7	78.9	10.8	84.9	34.1	78.9	14.2
1973	89.9	25.7	94.9	24.2	96.8	8.3	98.6	7.6	95.1	20.5
1974	100.0	5.8	102.3	9.5	107.1	20.1	107.8	2.6	104.3	9.7
1975	104.6	-11.4	105.6	3.9	108.4	11.0	111.8	13.1	107.6	3.2
1976	115.0	12.0	118.3	12.0	123.1	17.2	128.6	19.1	121.2	12.6
1977	139.1	36.9	144.8	17.4	150.4	16.4	160.3	29.0	148.7	22.7
1978	164.5	10.9	179.6	42.1	185.6	14.0	192.8	16.4	180.6	21.5
1979	203.4	23.9	204.3	1.8	212.2	16.4	212.3	0.2	208.1	15.2
1980	219.7	14.7	209.1	-17.9	215.1	12.0	221.6	12.6	216.4	4.0
1981	232.1	20.3	238.1	10.7	246.6	15.1	246.5	-0.2	240.9	11.3
1982	243.0	-5.6	235.5	-11.8	232.2	-5.5	228.8	-5.7	234.9	-2.5
1983	227.3	-2.6	238.7	21.6	250.1	20.5	272.3	40.5	247.1	5.2
1984	277.1	7.2	290.1	20.1	298.5	12.1	307.3	12.3	293.3	18.7
1985	305.1	-2.8	311.8	9.1	309.6	-2.8	315.9	8.4	310.6	5.9
1986	312.2	-4.6	318.2	7.9	319.9	2.2	323.3	4.3	318.4	2.5
1987	315.2	-9.7	323.2	10.5	333.0	12.7	334.3	1.6	326.5	2.5
1988	350.2	20.4	362.6	14.9	367.3	5.3	373.4	6.8	363.4	11.3
1989	373.3	-0.1	378.8	6.0	376.1	-2.8	370.8	-5.5	374.8	3.1
1990	382.5	13.2	378.9	-3.7	390.3	12.6	388.7	-1.6	385.1	2.7
1991	374.6	-13.7	372.6	-2.1	374.6	2.2	371.5	-3.3	373.3	-3.1
1992	373.1	1.7	391.7	21.5	398.4	7.0	408.3	10.3	392.9	5.3
1993	422.2	14.3	441.6	19.7	-	-	-	-	-	-

Source: "National Income and Product Account Tables: Selected NIPA Tables," *Survey of Current Business*, November 1991, U.S. Department of Commerce, Bureau of Economic Analysis, National Income and Wealth Division. - indicates that no data are available.

Gross Domestic Product
Gross private domestic investment
Fixed investment - Nonresidential - Producers' durable equipment - 1987 Dollars

In billions of constant 1987 dollars and percent. Quarterly data are seasonally adjusted and annualized. Growth rates for quarters are compound annual growth rates; changes from year to year are percentage changes.

Year	1st Quarter	% Change	2nd Quarter	% Change	3rd Quarter	% Change	4th Quarter	% Change	TOTAL	% Change
1929	-	-	-	-	-	-	-	-	41.7	-
1930	-	-	-	-	-	-	-	-	33.0	-20.9
1931	-	-	-	-	-	-	-	-	21.9	-33.6
1932	-	-	-	-	-	-	-	-	12.6	-42.5
1933	-	-	-	-	-	-	-	-	12.9	2.4
1934	-	-	-	-	-	-	-	-	17.9	38.8
1935	-	-	-	-	-	-	-	-	24.3	35.8
1936	-	-	-	-	-	-	-	-	33.9	39.5
1937	-	-	-	-	-	-	-	-	38.7	14.2
1938	-	-	-	-	-	-	-	-	27.2	-29.7
1939	-	-	-	-	-	-	-	-	30.9	13.6
1940	-	-	-	-	-	-	-	-	40.1	29.8
1941	-	-	-	-	-	-	-	-	47.2	17.7
1942	-	-	-	-	-	-	-	-	28.6	-39.4
1943	-	-	-	-	-	-	-	-	26.0	-9.1
1944	-	-	-	-	-	-	-	-	34.7	33.5
1945	-	-	-	-	-	-	-	-	51.3	47.8
1946	-	-	-	-	-	-	-	-	60.4	17.7
1947	83.9	-	81.8	-9.6	79.8	-9.4	82.4	13.7	82.0	35.8
1948	88.0	30.1	83.0	-20.9	81.2	-8.4	84.1	15.1	84.1	2.6
1949	78.3	-24.9	72.2	-27.7	67.9	-21.8	66.8	-6.3	71.3	-15.2
1950	68.0	7.4	76.6	61.0	84.6	48.8	84.1	-2.3	78.3	9.8
1951	79.6	-19.7	81.4	9.4	84.5	16.1	84.2	-1.4	82.4	5.2
1952	84.5	1.4	85.1	2.9	72.5	-47.3	79.7	46.0	80.4	-2.4
1953	85.6	33.1	84.7	-4.1	87.2	12.3	85.4	-8.0	85.7	6.6
1954	81.1	-18.7	79.6	-7.2	82.1	13.2	80.7	-6.6	80.9	-5.6
1955	81.1	2.0	88.8	43.7	94.3	27.2	98.8	20.5	90.8	12.2
1956	94.2	-17.4	93.5	-2.9	95.5	8.8	93.8	-6.9	94.3	3.9
1957	95.0	5.2	94.0	-4.1	97.3	14.8	93.8	-13.6	95.0	0.7
1958	84.5	-34.1	80.6	-17.2	79.0	-7.7	82.7	20.1	81.7	-14.0
1959	87.1	23.0	89.8	13.0	92.8	14.0	93.2	1.7	90.8	11.1
1960	94.7	6.6	96.1	6.0	91.4	-18.2	87.8	-14.8	92.5	1.9
1961	85.5	-10.1	88.9	16.9	89.8	4.1	95.2	26.3	89.8	-2.9
1962	97.0	7.8	99.9	12.5	99.6	-1.2	98.9	-2.8	98.9	10.1
1963	100.4	6.2	102.5	8.6	107.3	20.1	111.3	15.8	105.4	6.6
1964	113.4	7.8	115.5	7.6	119.6	15.0	123.8	14.8	118.1	12.0
1965	132.3	30.4	134.5	6.8	142.4	25.6	147.2	14.2	139.1	17.8
1966	154.4	21.0	158.6	11.3	158.4	-0.5	159.0	1.5	157.6	13.3
1967	153.1	-14.0	155.3	5.9	153.2	-5.3	157.6	12.0	154.8	-1.8
1968	162.9	14.1	158.3	-10.8	161.7	8.9	168.0	16.5	162.7	5.1
1969	173.0	12.4	172.7	-0.7	174.0	3.0	171.9	-4.7	172.9	6.3
1970	170.2	-3.9	169.4	-1.9	172.2	6.8	163.0	-19.7	168.7	-2.4
1971	163.3	0.7	165.0	4.2	164.7	-0.7	169.5	12.2	165.6	-1.8
1972	176.0	16.2	181.6	13.3	186.8	12.0	202.6	38.4	186.8	12.8
1973	213.6	23.6	223.0	18.8	225.4	4.4	227.8	4.3	222.4	19.1
1974	228.0	0.4	227.8	-0.4	225.3	-4.3	215.7	-16.0	224.2	0.8
1975	199.5	-26.8	195.9	-7.0	198.4	5.2	201.4	6.2	198.8	-11.3
1976	203.1	3.4	205.1	4.0	210.0	9.9	214.6	9.1	208.2	4.7
1977	229.5	30.8	234.6	9.2	239.0	7.7	249.9	19.5	238.2	14.4
1978	252.5	4.2	269.9	30.5	273.5	5.4	279.3	8.8	268.8	12.8
1979	288.4	13.7	283.3	-6.9	288.5	7.5	281.7	-9.1	285.5	6.2
1980	284.3	3.7	261.4	-28.5	260.8	-0.9	264.1	5.2	267.6	-6.3
1981	270.2	9.6	271.1	1.3	276.5	8.2	270.3	-8.7	272.0	1.6
1982	263.2	-10.1	254.5	-12.6	248.9	-8.5	244.0	-7.6	252.6	-7.1
1983	240.1	-6.2	251.5	20.4	263.5	20.5	287.0	40.7	260.5	3.1
1984	291.6	6.6	305.2	20.0	312.8	10.3	320.1	9.7	307.4	18.0
1985	320.7	0.8	326.6	7.6	323.3	-4.0	327.2	4.9	324.4	5.5
1986	321.4	-6.9	325.0	4.6	323.4	-2.0	325.0	2.0	323.7	-0.2
1987	315.7	-11.0	323.4	10.1	333.9	13.6	332.7	-1.4	326.5	0.9
1988	346.1	17.1	356.9	13.1	361.0	4.7	363.1	2.3	356.8	9.3
1989	362.4	-0.8	367.5	5.7	363.0	-4.8	356.9	-6.6	362.5	1.6
1990	367.3	12.2	363.0	-4.6	370.3	8.3	367.4	-3.1	367.0	1.2
1991	352.5	-15.3	352.6	0.1	357.2	5.3	355.2	-2.2	354.3	-3.5
1992	357.7	2.8	375.9	22.0	385.1	10.2	395.7	11.5	378.6	6.9
1993	414.1	19.9	433.2	19.8	-	-	-	-	-	-

Source: "National Income and Product Account Tables: Selected NIPA Tables," *Survey of Current Business*, November 1991, U.S. Department of Commerce, Bureau of Economic Analysis, National Income and Wealth Division. - indicates that no data are available.

Gross Domestic Product
Gross private domestic investment
Fixed investment - Residential - Actual Dollars

In billions of actual dollars and percent. Quarterly data are seasonally adjusted and annualized. Growth rates for quarters are compound annual growth rates; changes from year to year are percentage changes.

Year	1st Quarter	% Change	2nd Quarter	% Change	3rd Quarter	% Change	4th Quarter	% Change	TOTAL	% Change
1929	-	-	-	-	-	-	-	-	4.0	-
1930	-	-	-	-	-	-	-	-	2.4	-40.0
1931	-	-	-	-	-	-	-	-	1.8	-25.0
1932	-	-	-	-	-	-	-	-	0.8	-55.6
1933	-	-	-	-	-	-	-	-	0.6	-25.0
1934	-	-	-	-	-	-	-	-	0.9	50.0
1935	-	-	-	-	-	-	-	-	1.3	44.4
1936	-	-	-	-	-	-	-	-	1.7	30.8
1937	-	-	-	-	-	-	-	-	2.1	23.5
1938	-	-	-	-	-	-	-	-	2.1	-
1939	-	-	-	-	-	-	-	-	3.0	42.9
1940	-	-	-	-	-	-	-	-	3.5	16.7
1941	-	-	-	-	-	-	-	-	4.1	17.1
1942	-	-	-	-	-	-	-	-	2.2	-46.3
1943	-	-	-	-	-	-	-	-	1.4	-36.4
1944	-	-	-	-	-	-	-	-	1.4	-
1945	-	-	-	-	-	-	-	-	1.7	21.4
1946	5.9	-	7.4	147.5	8.7	91.1	9.3	30.6	7.8	358.8
1947	10.4	56.4	10.4	-	12.3	95.7	15.1	127.1	12.1	55.1
1948	15.2	2.7	16.3	32.2	16.1	-4.8	15.0	-24.7	15.6	28.9
1949	14.0	-24.1	13.7	-8.3	14.5	25.5	16.3	59.7	14.6	-6.4
1950	18.1	52.0	20.4	61.4	22.3	42.8	21.3	-16.8	20.5	40.4
1951	20.8	-9.1	18.2	-41.4	17.2	-20.2	17.5	7.2	18.4	-10.2
1952	18.0	11.9	18.5	11.6	18.5	-	19.4	20.9	18.6	1.1
1953	19.7	6.3	19.8	2.0	19.2	-11.6	18.9	-6.1	19.4	4.3
1954	19.0	2.1	20.3	30.3	21.8	33.0	23.2	28.3	21.1	8.8
1955	25.0	34.8	25.6	10.0	25.2	-6.1	24.2	-15.0	25.0	18.5
1956	23.7	-8.0	23.9	3.4	23.5	-6.5	23.0	-8.2	23.6	-5.6
1957	22.6	-6.8	22.2	-6.9	22.0	-3.6	21.9	-1.8	22.2	-5.9
1958	20.9	-17.1	21.0	1.9	22.5	31.8	24.9	50.0	22.3	0.5
1959	27.8	55.4	28.8	15.2	28.3	-6.8	27.5	-10.8	28.1	26.0
1960	28.4	13.7	26.1	-28.7	25.3	-11.7	25.3	-	26.3	-6.4
1961	25.3	-	25.5	3.2	26.9	23.8	27.8	14.1	26.4	0.4
1962	28.4	8.9	29.2	11.8	29.2	-	29.1	-1.4	29.0	9.8
1963	30.2	16.0	32.2	29.2	32.5	3.8	33.7	15.6	32.1	10.7
1964	35.4	21.8	34.2	-12.9	33.7	-5.7	33.8	1.2	34.3	6.9
1965	33.9	1.2	34.2	3.6	34.3	1.2	34.5	2.4	34.2	-0.3
1966	34.8	3.5	33.2	-17.2	31.9	-14.8	29.2	-29.8	32.3	-5.6
1967	28.3	-11.8	31.6	55.5	33.4	24.8	36.0	35.0	32.4	0.3
1968	36.9	10.4	38.2	14.9	38.9	7.5	40.9	22.2	38.7	19.4
1969	43.2	24.5	43.4	1.9	43.2	-1.8	40.7	-21.2	42.6	10.1
1970	40.7	-	39.4	-12.2	40.4	10.5	45.0	53.9	41.4	-2.8
1971	48.6	36.0	54.6	59.3	58.3	30.0	61.5	23.8	55.8	34.8
1972	66.6	37.5	68.2	10.0	69.6	8.5	74.3	29.9	69.7	24.9
1973	77.9	20.8	75.8	-10.4	75.0	-4.2	72.7	-11.7	75.3	8.0
1974	69.0	-18.9	67.5	-8.4	67.4	-0.6	60.0	-37.2	66.0	-12.4
1975	57.7	-14.5	59.9	16.1	64.6	35.3	68.7	27.9	62.7	-5.0
1976	76.2	51.4	80.7	25.8	80.6	-0.5	92.5	73.5	82.5	31.6
1977	97.6	23.9	111.7	71.6	115.0	12.4	116.9	6.8	110.3	33.7
1978	121.0	14.8	130.5	35.3	135.8	17.3	139.0	9.8	131.6	19.3
1979	138.6	-1.1	140.9	6.8	143.5	7.6	141.2	-6.3	141.0	7.1
1980	134.6	-17.4	111.2	-53.4	115.9	18.0	131.3	64.7	123.3	-12.6
1981	131.9	1.8	128.7	-9.4	120.1	-24.2	109.5	-30.9	122.5	-0.6
1982	104.7	-16.4	102.8	-7.1	102.4	-1.5	112.8	47.2	105.7	-13.7
1983	130.3	78.0	148.1	66.9	162.0	43.2	167.7	14.8	152.0	43.8
1984	174.7	17.8	180.6	14.2	179.8	-1.8	180.4	1.3	178.9	17.7
1985	182.1	3.8	182.0	-0.2	186.5	10.3	193.1	14.9	185.9	3.9
1986	203.1	22.4	216.7	29.6	222.4	10.9	224.2	3.3	216.6	16.5
1987	222.8	-2.5	226.4	6.6	225.2	-2.1	226.5	2.3	225.2	4.0
1988	227.0	0.9	230.5	6.3	233.3	4.9	237.3	7.0	232.0	3.0
1989	236.8	-0.8	232.1	-7.7	228.5	-6.1	226.2	-4.0	230.9	-0.5
1990	233.2	13.0	222.4	-17.3	209.9	-20.7	195.8	-24.3	215.3	-6.8
1991	182.2	-25.0	183.6	3.1	192.4	20.6	200.3	17.5	189.6	-11.9
1992	208.9	18.3	220.6	24.4	223.3	5.0	241.8	37.5	223.6	17.9
1993	244.9	5.2	241.9	-4.8	-	-	-	-	-	-

Source: "National Income and Product Account Tables: Selected NIPA Tables," *Survey of Current Business*, November 1991, U.S. Department of Commerce, Bureau of Economic Analysis, National Income and Wealth Division. - indicates that no data are available.

Gross Domestic Product
Gross private domestic investment
Fixed investment - Residential - 1987 Dollars

In billions of constant 1987 dollars and percent. Quarterly data are seasonally adjusted and annualized. Growth rates for quarters are compound annual growth rates; changes from year to year are percentage changes.

Year	1st Quarter	% Change	2nd Quarter	% Change	3rd Quarter	% Change	4th Quarter	% Change	TOTAL	% Change
1929	-	-	-	-	-	-	-	-	41.6	-
1930	-	-	-	-	-	-	-	-	25.3	-39.2
1931	-	-	-	-	-	-	-	-	21.0	-17.0
1932	-	-	-	-	-	-	-	-	11.1	-47.1
1933	-	-	-	-	-	-	-	-	9.1	-18.0
1934	-	-	-	-	-	-	-	-	12.7	39.6
1935	-	-	-	-	-	-	-	-	17.5	37.8
1936	-	-	-	-	-	-	-	-	22.0	25.7
1937	-	-	-	-	-	-	-	-	23.8	8.2
1938	-	-	-	-	-	-	-	-	24.0	0.8
1939	-	-	-	-	-	-	-	-	33.9	41.3
1940	-	-	-	-	-	-	-	-	38.1	12.4
1941	-	-	-	-	-	-	-	-	40.4	6.0
1942	-	-	-	-	-	-	-	-	20.4	-49.5
1943	-	-	-	-	-	-	-	-	12.4	-39.2
1944	-	-	-	-	-	-	-	-	10.9	-12.1
1945	-	-	-	-	-	-	-	-	12.8	17.4
1946	-	-	-	-	-	-	-	-	52.5	310.2
1947	61.6	-	58.4	-19.2	67.4	77.4	80.6	104.5	67.0	27.6
1948	79.5	-5.3	84.2	25.8	81.5	-12.2	75.4	-26.7	80.1	19.6
1949	69.9	-26.1	68.7	-6.7	74.8	40.5	84.0	59.0	74.3	-7.2
1950	93.3	52.2	102.1	43.4	107.7	23.8	102.5	-18.0	101.4	36.5
1951	97.4	-18.5	84.2	-44.2	78.8	-23.3	79.5	3.6	85.0	-16.2
1952	81.6	11.0	83.0	7.0	82.3	-3.3	86.6	22.6	83.4	-1.9
1953	88.0	6.6	88.2	0.9	84.9	-14.1	84.2	-3.3	86.3	3.5
1954	85.1	4.3	90.6	28.5	96.1	26.6	102.0	26.9	93.5	8.3
1955	109.6	33.3	111.0	5.2	108.5	-8.7	103.7	-16.6	108.2	15.7
1956	100.7	-11.1	100.0	-2.8	98.0	-7.8	96.6	-5.6	98.8	-8.7
1957	95.1	-6.1	92.8	-9.3	91.6	-5.1	91.5	-0.4	92.7	-6.2
1958	88.2	-13.7	88.1	-0.5	94.3	31.3	104.3	49.7	93.7	1.1
1959	116.4	55.1	120.7	15.6	118.5	-7.1	115.0	-11.3	117.6	25.5
1960	118.4	12.4	108.6	-29.2	105.3	-11.6	105.4	0.4	109.4	-7.0
1961	105.9	1.9	106.3	1.5	112.2	24.1	115.8	13.5	110.1	0.6
1962	118.0	7.8	121.6	12.8	121.5	-0.3	121.3	-0.7	120.6	9.5
1963	125.8	15.7	135.0	32.6	137.5	7.6	141.6	12.5	135.0	11.9
1964	150.0	25.9	142.1	-19.5	139.5	-7.1	136.9	-7.2	142.1	5.3
1965	137.2	0.9	138.3	3.2	138.5	0.6	135.2	-9.2	137.3	-3.4
1966	138.4	9.8	127.0	-29.1	122.9	-12.3	109.9	-36.1	124.5	-9.3
1967	106.4	-12.1	118.6	54.4	124.4	21.0	131.6	25.2	120.2	-3.5
1968	132.2	1.8	135.6	10.7	138.1	7.6	139.6	4.4	136.4	13.5
1969	144.3	14.2	143.2	-3.0	141.9	-3.6	131.3	-26.7	140.1	2.7
1970	131.9	1.8	122.8	-24.9	129.5	23.7	143.2	49.5	131.8	-5.9
1971	151.1	24.0	166.1	46.0	174.2	21.0	181.0	16.6	168.1	27.5
1972	193.1	29.5	197.1	8.5	197.6	1.0	204.2	14.0	198.0	17.8
1973	211.2	14.4	200.5	-18.8	192.1	-15.7	182.6	-18.4	196.6	-0.7
1974	169.3	-26.1	161.5	-17.2	156.0	-12.9	135.6	-42.9	155.6	-20.9
1975	127.0	-23.1	129.4	7.8	138.2	30.1	144.3	18.9	134.7	-13.4
1976	159.0	47.4	163.6	12.1	161.2	-5.7	181.8	61.8	166.4	23.5
1977	187.1	12.2	207.9	52.4	207.7	-0.4	204.8	-5.5	201.9	21.3
1978	206.3	3.0	215.6	19.3	217.9	4.3	218.2	0.6	214.5	6.2
1979	213.2	-8.9	209.8	-6.2	206.7	-5.8	199.7	-12.9	207.4	-3.3
1980	185.6	-25.4	150.4	-56.9	153.4	8.2	170.0	50.8	164.8	-20.5
1981	166.2	-8.6	160.2	-13.7	147.3	-28.5	132.5	-34.5	151.6	-8.0
1982	124.8	-21.3	120.8	-12.2	119.5	-4.2	131.2	45.3	124.1	-18.1
1983	150.1	71.3	170.5	66.5	185.7	40.7	190.6	11.0	174.2	40.4
1984	196.4	12.7	202.4	12.8	199.7	-5.2	198.8	-1.8	199.3	14.4
1985	199.0	0.4	198.9	-0.2	202.7	7.9	207.4	9.6	202.0	1.4
1986	215.0	15.5	228.0	26.5	231.3	5.9	230.5	-1.4	226.2	12.0
1987	225.7	-8.1	227.7	3.6	224.3	-5.8	223.3	-1.8	225.2	-0.4
1988	220.0	-5.8	222.0	3.7	223.5	2.7	225.3	3.3	222.7	-1.1
1989	222.2	-5.4	215.4	-11.7	211.2	-7.6	208.0	-5.9	214.2	-3.8
1990	211.6	7.1	201.2	-18.3	189.0	-22.1	176.3	-24.3	194.5	-9.2
1991	163.8	-25.5	164.3	1.2	171.0	17.3	179.1	20.3	169.5	-12.9
1992	186.2	16.8	195.6	21.8	196.2	1.2	210.6	32.8	197.1	16.3
1993	211.4	1.5	206.2	-9.5	-	-	-	-	-	-

Source: "National Income and Product Account Tables: Selected NIPA Tables," *Survey of Current Business*, November 1991, U.S. Department of Commerce, Bureau of Economic Analysis, National Income and Wealth Division. - indicates that no data are available.

Gross Domestic Product
Gross private domestic investment
Change in business inventories - Actual Dollars

In billions of actual dollars. Quarterly data are seasonally adjusted and annualized.

Year	1st Quarter	2nd Quarter	3rd Quarter	4th Quarter	TOTAL
1929	-	-	-	-	1.7
1930	-	-	-	-	-0.4
1931	-	-	-	-	-1.1
1932		-	-	-	-2.5
1933			-	-	-1.5
1934	-	-	-	-	-0.6
1935	-	-	-	-	1.1
1936	-	-	-	-	1.2
1937	-	-	-	-	2.7
1938	-	-	-	-	-0.6
1939	-	-	-	-	0.2
1940	-	-	-	-	2.4
1941	-	-	-	-	4.4
1942	-		-	-	1.9
1943	-	-	-	-	-0.8
1944	-	-	-	-	-0.9
1945	-	-	-		-1.4
1946	5.7	8.6	5.9	4.5	6.2
1947	0.4	-1.2	-2.8	1.6	-0.5
1948	3.5	5.7	7.3	5.9	5.6
1949	0.4	-5.3	-1.5	-4.9	-2.8
1950	2.0	2.9	4.3	14.5	5.9
1951	10.4	15.0	9.9	4.9	10.1
1952	4.9	-1.5	5.6	5.1	3.5
1953	3.8	3.4	2.2	-2.2	1.8
1954	-1.9	-3.4	-2.1	-0.3	-1.9
1955	3.7	4.6	4.2	7.1	4.9
1956	6.6	3.7	3.7	2.5	4.1
1957	2.3	2.6	3.0	-4.3	0.9
1958	-4.0	-4.2	1.5	5.2	-0.4
1959	4.4	7.8	0.2	4.3	4.2
1960	11.3	3.0	4.2	-5.7	3.2
1961	-2.6	1.6	6.7	6.0	2.9
1962	9.5	5.6	6.2	3.1	6.1
1963	7.0	4.9	5.9	4.8	5.7
1964	5.6	4.8	4.3	5.4	5.0
1965	12.3	9.2	9.5	7.8	9.7
1966	13.5	12.5	12.2	17.0	13.8
1967	14.0	6.4	11.4	10.2	10.5
1968	7.8	13.7	9.6	5.4	9.1
1969	11.6	9.3	10.9	7.1	9.7
1970	2.1	3.7	5.4	-2.2	2.3
1971	12.4	9.5	9.4	0.9	8.0
1972	5.0	11.6	13.6	9.4	9.9
1973	13.1	16.7	11.4	29.6	17.7
1974	13.8	16.5	8.5	18.3	14.3
1975	-12.9	-15.4	1.9	3.7	-5.7
1976	16.1	20.6	19.2	10.9	16.7
1977	15.2	25.0	38.4	20.3	24.7
1978	25.2	28.7	27.5	30.2	27.9
1979	20.4	23.2	7.3	0.2	12.8
1980	7.1	-2.2	-35.9	-6.8	-9.5
1981	32.9	13.9	36.9	18.1	25.4
1982	-19.3	-0.2	2.0	-46.3	-15.9
1983	-37.3	-2.8	-2.1	20.2	-5.5
1984	77.9	74.7	80.7	51.0	71.1
1985	19.3	26.7	19.9	32.6	24.6
1986	48.1	17.4	-12.0	-18.8	8.6
1987	23.1	17.8	4.9	59.3	26.3
1988	16.8	13.8	17.1	17.3	16.2
1989	43.7	39.8	19.6	30.2	33.3
1990	9.6	33.3	8.4	-23.9	6.9
1991	-19.9	-23.0	-0.5	8.9	-8.6
1992	-5.1	12.9	9.7	12.0	7.3
1993	34.6	13.1	-	-	-

Source: "National Income and Product Account Tables: Selected NIPA Tables," *Survey of Current Business*, November 1991, U.S. Department of Commerce, Bureau of Economic Analysis, National Income and Wealth Division. - indicates that no data are available.

Gross Domestic Product
Gross private domestic investment
Change in business inventories - 1987 Dollars

In billions of constant 1987 dollars. Quarterly data are seasonally adjusted and annualized.

Year	1st Quarter	2nd Quarter	3rd Quarter	4th Quarter	TOTAL
1929	-	-	-	-	10.6
1930	-	-	-	-	-0.8
1931	-	-	-	-	-7.8
1932	-	-	-	-	-17.5
1933	-	-	-	-	-10.2
1934	-	-	-	-	-5.8
1935	-	-	-	-	5.4
1936	-	-	-	-	10.0
1937	-	-	-	-	13.6
1938	-	-	-	-	-5.4
1939	-	-	-	-	3.0
1940	-	-	-	-	14.7
1941	-	-	-	-	27.4
1942	-	-	-	-	11.3
1943	-	-	-	-	-0.1
1944	-	-	-	-	-5.6
1945	-	-	-	-	-8.7
1946	-	-	-	-	28.0
1947	-0.5	-0.4	-5.2	7.1	0.3
1948	9.7	14.2	17.2	13.5	13.7
1949	-0.3	-16.5	-4.7	-14.8	-9.1
1950	10.8	13.9	14.6	47.5	22.5
1951	28.4	45.1	30.3	14.3	30.0
1952	14.7	-5.9	14.5	14.9	9.6
1953	11.6	10.7	5.7	-7.8	5.1
1954	-5.2	-9.3	-6.6	-1.4	-5.6
1955	11.3	16.8	15.7	20.6	16.1
1956	16.5	12.9	10.2	8.9	12.1
1957	4.9	5.3	7.8	-9.6	2.1
1958	-13.3	-11.8	3.1	12.8	-2.3
1959	15.5	24.4	0.5	13.9	13.6
1960	29.6	7.2	11.6	-15.9	8.1
1961	-8.5	2.6	18.5	16.3	7.2
1962	23.3	14.2	17.5	7.4	15.6
1963	21.3	14.9	16.7	11.2	16.0
1964	16.9	15.4	13.9	16.4	15.7
1965	34.0	23.4	24.6	18.6	25.1
1966	36.1	32.1	32.9	45.7	36.7
1967	34.3	17.8	31.6	26.8	27.6
1968	20.0	36.0	26.5	12.1	23.6
1969	28.9	23.7	28.2	18.5	24.8
1970	5.1	8.4	14.4	-4.0	5.9
1971	31.9	23.8	21.9	5.4	20.8
1972	18.4	24.2	33.1	14.4	22.5
1973	31.3	38.1	24.8	56.7	37.7
1974	31.9	29.8	17.6	44.4	30.9
1975	-28.0	-30.6	-2.0	4.9	-13.9
1976	26.9	33.3	27.2	14.7	25.5
1977	24.9	34.3	54.0	23.8	34.3
1978	36.0	36.9	35.3	40.6	37.2
1979	21.7	29.7	5.0	-2.0	13.6
1980	7.1	-3.6	-37.2	0.8	-8.3
1981	32.6	15.8	35.7	14.1	24.6
1982	-24.4	-1.5	0.7	-44.9	-17.5
1983	-33.5	9.9	12.1	29.3	4.4
1984	79.9	71.0	73.0	47.9	67.9
1985	14.8	23.7	19.8	30.2	22.1
1986	48.1	18.2	-12.0	-20.1	8.5
1987	22.5	17.3	5.4	59.9	26.3
1988	19.2	16.1	23.5	20.9	19.9
1989	41.2	36.9	16.0	24.9	29.8
1990	4.7	28.1	10.9	-20.9	5.7
1991	-17.4	-22.3	-0.9	7.1	-8.4
1992	-5.0	12.6	9.6	8.7	6.5
1993	29.3	13.0	-	-	-

Source: "National Income and Product Account Tables: Selected NIPA Tables," *Survey of Current Business*, November 1991, U.S. Department of Commerce, Bureau of Economic Analysis, National Income and Wealth Division. - indicates that no data are available.

Gross Domestic Product

Gross private domestic investment
Change in business inventories - Nonfarm - Actual Dollars

In billions of actual dollars. Quarterly data are seasonally adjusted and annualized.

Year	1st Quarter	2nd Quarter	3rd Quarter	4th Quarter	TOTAL
1929	-	-	-	-	1.8
1930	-	-	-	-	-0.1
1931	-	-	-	-	-1.6
1932	-	-	-	-	-2.6
1933	-	-	-	-	-1.4
1934	-	-	-	-	0.2
1935	-	-	-	-	0.4
1936	-	-	-	-	2.1
1937	-	-	-	-	1.7
1938	-	-	-	-	-1.0
1939	-	-	-	-	0.3
1940	-	-	-	-	1.9
1941	-	-	-	-	4.0
1942	-	-	-	-	0.7
1943	-	-	-	-	-0.6
1944	-	-	-	-	-0.6
1945	-	-	-	-	-0.6
1946	6.0	8.7	5.9	4.8	6.4
1947	1.5	1.5	-0.3	2.4	1.3
1948	2.3	2.9	3.9	2.8	3.0
1949	0.6	-4.1	-0.6	-4.7	-2.2
1950	2.2	4.2	3.8	13.8	6.0
1951	9.3	14.0	9.1	3.8	9.1
1952	4.0	-3.3	3.3	4.6	2.1
1953	3.0	4.1	1.5	-4.3	1.1
1954	-2.8	-3.2	-2.8	0.2	-2.1
1955	3.8	5.7	5.5	6.8	5.5
1956	6.6	5.2	4.4	4.1	5.1
1957	2.0	2.0	2.5	-3.3	0.8
1958	-6.3	-5.8	-0.7	3.4	-2.3
1959	4.7	9.7	2.5	6.1	5.7
1960	10.7	2.2	3.2	-5.4	2.7
1961	-3.1	1.0	5.7	4.6	2.0
1962	8.0	5.4	5.9	2.7	5.5
1963	5.1	4.8	6.6	4.2	5.2
1964	6.2	6.1	6.1	6.5	6.2
1965	11.9	8.0	8.7	6.8	8.9
1966	12.8	14.1	12.7	17.4	14.3
1967	12.9	4.5	10.8	10.2	9.6
1968	4.7	9.6	9.8	7.0	7.8
1969	10.0	8.4	12.3	8.0	9.7
1970	0.4	3.9	7.8	0.3	3.1
1971	9.9	6.2	7.3	2.0	6.4
1972	5.5	10.4	12.8	9.8	9.6
1973	17.6	13.5	9.7	23.9	16.2
1974	17.0	17.8	9.4	24.1	17.0
1975	-19.3	-17.1	0.9	-0.6	-9.0
1976	16.5	23.2	17.1	13.4	17.6
1977	17.5	19.5	29.8	14.0	20.2
1978	29.1	27.5	19.4	30.2	26.5
1979	15.9	19.9	0.8	0.2	9.2
1980	7.1	3.0	-23.2	-0.5	-3.4
1981	23.0	1.0	29.5	13.2	16.7
1982	-25.4	-7.7	-6.4	-47.4	-21.7
1983	-28.5	9.9	29.7	28.2	9.8
1984	70.7	69.7	72.8	48.3	65.4
1985	12.3	21.8	12.9	28.5	18.9
1986	45.5	19.7	-8.0	-16.8	10.1
1987	31.9	26.9	9.7	62.4	32.7
1988	23.8	26.0	28.2	32.0	27.5
1989	35.8	33.3	23.4	34.8	31.8
1990	6.0	28.9	1.0	-20.8	3.8
1991	-20.0	-27.3	0.2	12.8	-8.6
1992	-10.8	6.2	4.4	9.5	2.3
1993	33.0	16.8	-	-	

Source: "National Income and Product Account Tables: Selected NIPA Tables," *Survey of Current Business*, November 1991, U.S. Department of Commerce, Bureau of Economic Analysis, National Income and Wealth Division. - indicates that no data are available.

Gross Domestic Product
Gross private domestic investment
Change in business inventories - Nonfarm - 1987 Dollars

In billions of constant 1987 dollars. Quarterly data are seasonally adjusted and annualized.

Year	1st Quarter	2nd Quarter	3rd Quarter	4th Quarter	TOTAL
1929	-	-	-	-	10.2
1930	-	-	-	-	-1.3
1931	-	-	-	-	-11.2
1932	-	-	-	-	-20.0
1933	-	-	-	-	-10.9
1934	-	-	-	-	1.0
1935	-	-	-	-	2.9
1936	-	-	-	-	13.5
1937	-	-	-	-	10.6
1938	-	-	-	-	-7.3
1939	-	-	-	-	1.9
1940	-	-	-	-	12.1
1941	-	-	-	-	24.4
1942	-	-	-	-	5.8
1943	-	-	-	-	-1.2
1944	-	-	-	-	-3.9
1945	-	-	-	-	-5.9
1946	-	-	-	-	29.2
1947	2.3	4.3	-0.6	9.6	3.9
1948	8.5	10.2	13.5	10.4	10.6
1949	-0.1	-14.5	-4.1	-16.4	-8.8
1950	9.9	15.4	14.2	46.8	21.6
1951	27.3	41.7	27.8	11.7	27.1
1952	12.3	-9.4	10.0	13.7	6.6
1953	9.1	11.4	4.2	-11.7	3.3
1954	-7.7	-10.1	-8.0	-0.1	-6.5
1955	12.2	18.1	16.5	20.3	16.8
1956	18.9	16.2	13.1	12.0	15.0
1957	5.5	5.6	6.8	-9.2	2.2
1958	-17.4	-15.4	-1.2	10.1	-6.0
1959	15.3	27.7	4.0	16.5	15.9
1960	28.7	5.9	10.0	-15.7	7.2
1961	-9.6	1.4	16.6	14.1	5.6
1962	20.6	13.4	16.1	5.4	13.9
1963	14.6	14.5	18.4	10.6	14.5
1964	18.8	17.7	16.3	17.5	17.6
1965	33.4	21.9	23.4	17.0	23.9
1966	34.9	35.6	34.1	46.7	37.8
1967	31.1	13.5	31.7	30.5	26.7
1968	12.6	27.3	27.6	17.4	21.2
1969	24.9	21.1	31.6	21.6	24.8
1970	0.4	7.4	17.9	0.2	6.5
1971	27.7	17.4	19.5	7.0	17.9
1972	11.5	23.8	28.5	20.6	21.1
1973	38.0	30.9	23.7	49.5	35.5
1974	33.8	31.7	16.1	43.5	31.3
1975	-32.1	-28.0	0.2	2.6	-14.3
1976	28.9	36.8	26.2	18.5	27.6
1977	28.4	29.6	47.2	20.4	31.4
1978	41.3	37.6	29.0	43.4	37.8
1979	18.4	26.5	0.1	-1.3	10.9
1980	6.7	-0.8	-28.8	3.4	-4.9
1981	24.3	6.7	31.2	12.1	18.6
1982	-26.7	-5.0	-4.8	-46.2	-20.7
1983	-29.7	15.1	33.3	32.3	12.8
1984	73.9	68.8	71.3	50.8	66.2
1985	12.8	23.0	15.2	28.0	19.8
1986	46.8	22.1	-7.9	-18.6	10.6
1987	31.9	26.9	9.9	62.1	32.7
1988	23.7	24.1	29.4	30.5	26.9
1989	35.5	31.4	21.5	31.2	29.9
1990	3.1	24.5	4.0	-18.7	3.2
1991	-18.7	-26.2	-	10.3	-8.6
1992	-9.6	7.0	5.8	7.5	2.7
1993	29.3	17.1	-	-	-

Source: "National Income and Product Account Tables: Selected NIPA Tables," *Survey of Current Business*, November 1991, U.S. Department of Commerce, Bureau of Economic Analysis, National Income and Wealth Division. - indicates that no data are available.

Gross Domestic Product
Gross private domestic investment
Change in business inventories - Farm - Actual Dollars

In billions of actual dollars. Quarterly data are seasonally adjusted and annualized.

Year	1st Quarter	2nd Quarter	3rd Quarter	4th Quarter	TOTAL
1929	-	-	-	-	-0.1
1930	-	-	-	-	-0.3
1931	-	-	-	-	0.5
1932	-	-	-	-	0.1
1933	-	-	-	-	-0.1
1934	-	-	-	-	-0.8
1935	-	-	-	-	0.7
1936	-	-	-	-	-0.9
1937	-	-	-	-	0.9
1938	-	-	-	-	0.4
1939	-	-	-	-	-0.1
1940	-	-	-	-	0.5
1941	-	-	-	-	0.4
1942	-	-	-	-	1.3
1943	-	-	-	-	-0.2
1944	-	-	-	-	-0.3
1945	-	-	-	-	-0.9
1946	-0.3	-0.1	-	-0.4	-0.2
1947	-1.1	-2.7	-2.5	-0.8	-1.8
1948	1.3	2.8	3.4	3.1	2.7
1949	-0.2	-1.2	-0.9	-0.2	-0.6
1950	-0.1	-1.3	0.5	0.7	-0.1
1951	1.2	0.9	0.8	1.1	1.0
1952	1.0	1.9	2.2	0.5	1.4
1953	0.8	-0.7	0.7	2.1	0.7
1954	0.8	-0.2	0.7	-0.5	0.2
1955	-0.1	-1.1	-1.3	0.3	-0.6
1956	-	-1.5	-0.8	-1.6	-1.0
1957	0.3	0.7	0.5	-1.0	0.1
1958	2.2	1.6	2.2	1.8	2.0
1959	-0.3	-1.9	-2.3	-1.8	-1.6
1960	0.6	0.9	1.0	-0.2	0.6
1961	0.6	0.6	0.9	1.4	0.9
1962	1.5	0.2	0.2	0.4	0.6
1963	1.9	0.1	-0.6	0.6	0.5
1964	-0.6	-1.2	-1.8	-1.1	-1.2
1965	0.3	1.1	0.8	1.0	0.8
1966	0.6	-1.7	-0.6	-0.4	-0.5
1967	1.1	1.9	0.6	-	0.9
1968	3.1	4.1	-0.2	-1.6	1.4
1969	1.6	0.9	-1.5	-1.0	-
1970	1.7	-0.2	-2.4	-2.5	-0.8
1971	2.5	3.2	2.1	-1.1	1.7
1972	-0.5	1.2	0.8	-0.3	0.3
1973	-4.6	3.3	1.7	5.7	1.5
1974	-3.2	-1.3	-0.9	-5.8	-2.8
1975	6.4	1.7	1.0	4.3	3.4
1976	-0.3	-2.6	2.1	-2.5	-0.8
1977	-2.3	5.5	8.6	6.3	4.5
1978	-3.9	1.3	8.1	-	1.4
1979	4.6	3.3	6.4	-	3.6
1980	-0.1	-5.3	-12.7	-6.4	-6.1
1981	9.8	12.9	7.4	4.9	8.8
1982	6.0	7.5	8.4	1.1	5.8
1983	-8.8	-12.8	-31.9	-8.0	-15.4
1984	7.2	5.1	7.9	2.7	5.7
1985	7.0	4.9	7.0	4.1	5.8
1986	2.6	-2.3	-4.0	-2.0	-1.5
1987	-8.7	-9.1	-4.8	-3.1	-6.4
1988	-7.0	-12.3	-11.2	-14.7	-11.3
1989	7.9	6.5	-3.8	-4.6	1.5
1990	3.6	4.5	7.4	-3.1	3.1
1991	0.1	4.3	-0.7	-3.9	-
1992	5.6	6.7	5.3	2.4	5.0
1993	1.5	-3.7	-	-	-

Source: "National Income and Product Account Tables: Selected NIPA Tables," *Survey of Current Business*, November 1991, U.S. Department of Commerce, Bureau of Economic Analysis, National Income and Wealth Division. - indicates that no data are available.

Gross Domestic Product
Gross private domestic investment
Change in business inventories - Farm - 1987 Dollars

In billions of constant 1987 dollars. Quarterly data are seasonally adjusted and annualized.

Year	1st Quarter	2nd Quarter	3rd Quarter	4th Quarter	TOTAL
1929	-	-	-	-	0.4
1930	-	-	-	-	0.4
1931	-	-	-	-	3.4
1932	-	-	-	-	2.4
1933	-	-	-	-	0.8
1934	-	-	-	-	-6.8
1935	-	-	-	-	2.5
1936	-	-	-	-	-3.5
1937	-	-	-	-	3.0
1938	-	-	-	-	1.9
1939	-	-	-	-	1.1
1940	-	-	-	-	2.6
1941	-	-	-	-	3.0
1942					5.5
1943	-	-	-		1.1
1944	-	-	-	-	-1.7
1945	-	-	-	-	-2.9
1946	-	-	-	-	-1.2
1947	-2.8	-4.7	-4.6	-2.5	-3.7
1948	1.3	4.0	3.7	3.2	3.1
1949	-0.2	-2.0	-0.6	1.7	-0.3
1950	0.9	-1.4	0.5	0.7	1.0
1951	1.2	3.4	2.5	2.6	2.9
1952	2.4	3.5	4.5	1.2	2.9
1953	2.6	-0.7	1.6	3.9	1.8
1954	2.6	0.8	1.4	-1.3	0.9
1955	-1.0	-1.3	-0.8	0.3	-0.7
1956	-2.4	-3.3	-2.9	-3.1	-2.9
1957	-0.6	-0.3	1.0	-0.3	-0.1
1958	4.1	3.6	4.3	2.7	3.7
1959	0.1	-3.2	-3.5	-2.6	-2.3
1960	0.9	1.2	1.6	-0.2	0.9
1961	1.1	1.2	1.8	2.3	1.6
1962	2.7	0.8	1.4	2.0	1.7
1963	6.7	0.5	-1.7	0.6	1.5
1964	-1.9	-2.3	-2.4	-1.1	-1.9
1965	0.6	1.5	1.2	1.6	1.2
1966	1.2	-3.5	-1.1	-1.0	-1.1
1967	3.2	4.3	-0.1	-3.7	0.9
1968	7.4	8.7	-1.1	-5.3	2.4
1969	4.0	2.5	-3.4	-3.1	-
1970	4.7	1.0	-3.5	-4.2	-0.5
1971	4.1	6.3	2.5	-1.5	2.9
1972	6.9	0.4	4.6	-6.1	1.5
1973	-6.6	7.2	1.1	7.2	2.2
1974	-1.9	-1.9	1.5	0.8	-0.4
1975	4.2	-2.6	-2.2	2.3	0.4
1976	-2.0	-3.5	1.0	-3.8	-2.1
1977	-3.5	4.7	6.8	3.4	2.8
1978	-5.3	-0.6	6.3	-2.9	-0.6
1979	3.3	3.2	4.9	-0.8	2.7
1980	0.4	-2.8	-8.5	-2.6	-3.4
1981	8.3	9.1	4.5	2.0	6.0
1982	2.3	3.5	5.5	1.3	3.1
1983	-3.8	-5.2	-21.2	-3.1	-8.3
1984	5.9	2.2	1.7	-2.8	1.7
1985	1.9	0.7	4.6	2.2	2.4
1986	1.3	-3.9	-4.2	-1.5	-2.1
1987	-9.4	-9.5	-4.5	-2.2	-6.4
1988	-4.5	-8.1	-5.8	-9.6	-7.0
1989	5.8	5.6	-5.6	-6.3	-0.1
1990	1.6	3.6	6.9	-2.1	2.5
1991	1.3	3.8	-0.9	-3.2	0.2
1992	4.6	5.6	3.8	1.2	3.8
1993	-	-4.1	-	-	-

Source: "National Income and Product Account Tables: Selected NIPA Tables," *Survey of Current Business*, November 1991, U.S. Department of Commerce, Bureau of Economic Analysis, National Income and Wealth Division. - indicates that no data are available.

NET EXPORTS OF GOODS AND SERVICES
Component of Gross Domestic Product

Net exports of goods and services—the trade balance—account for the United States' trade with the rest of the world. This measure presents exports less imports of all goods and services; hence it can be a negative value. The category is subdivided into Exports and Imports. BEA estimates are developed from three categories: (1) merchandise exports and imports, (2) receipts from abroad and payments made abroad, including investment earnings, and (3) receipts and payments for other services; federal purchases and sales abroad are included in this category.

Presentation of Data

Data are shown from 1929 to 1993 in quarterly and in annual increments. Changes from one period to the next are shown for Exports and Imports but not for Net Exports, which can and do exhibit negative values. Changes from quarter to quarter are annualized, compounded growth rates as explained in the section on Gross National Product. Changes from year to year are simple percentile changes.

Analytical Uses

Net exports are, generally, an indicator of the national vigor in trading with the rest of the world. The category measures the U.S. trade balance directly; the trade balance, in turn, has a direct impact on GDP. Indirectly, net exports reflect (1) the strength of the dollar, (2) U.S. vulnerability in commodity categories, and (3) U.S. competitiveness in manufacturing and services.

A positive net exports figure adds to GDP; a negative figure subtracts from GDP and, consequently, can contribute to or even cause negative GDP growth rate. In national product accounting, exports, manufactured domestically, are part of GDP; imports, manufactured elsewhere, and therefore in another nation's GDP, are taken from GDP.

The trade balance is significantly influenced by the strength of the dollar as measured against other currencies. When the dollar is strong relative to other currencies, it can buy more abroad; at the same time, dollar-denominated goods are more expensive abroad and discourage sales. The value of the dollar, however, is controlled in part by national and international policies and the relative performance of other economies rather than by pure market forces. A negative trade balance, therefore, does not invariably signal economic weakness.

The trade balance was negative in 36 of the 51 years in the 1929-1989 period. As an indicator of economic prospects, the fact that net exports are negative is not as meaningful as the trend: is the trade deficit growing or decreasing. A growing deficit may signal problems; a shrinking deficit may signal a stronger economy because the ratio of exports to imports is changing favorably.

Net exports indicate, indirectly, U.S. dependence on important commodities, e.g. petroleum. An artificial increase in the price of crude oil can produce large trade deficits and also increase prices domestically. Similarly, net exports are influenced by the competitiveness of other economies in selling their goods to us. In recent years attention has focused on Japan, for instance.

Gross Domestic Product

Net exports of goods and services - Actual Dollars

In billions of actual dollars. Quarterly data are seasonally adjusted and annualized.

Year	1st Quarter	2nd Quarter	3rd Quarter	4th Quarter	TOTAL
1929	-	-	-	-	0.4
1930	-	-	-	-	0.3
1931	-	-	-	-	-
1932	-	-	-	-	-
1933	-	-	-	-	0.1
1934	-	-	-	-	0.3
1935	-	-	-	-	-0.2
1936	-	-	-	-	-0.2
1937	-	-	-	-	-
1938	-	-	-	-	0.9
1939	-	-	-	-	0.8
1940	-	-	-	-	1.4
1941	-	-	-	-	1.0
1942	-	-	-	-	-0.3
1943	-	-	-	-	-2.4
1944	-	-	-	-	-2.2
1945	-	-	-	-	-0.9
1946	6.5	7.3	8.4	6.3	7.1
1947	10.8	11.2	11.7	9.2	10.8
1948	7.2	5.2	4.9	4.4	5.4
1949	6.4	6.2	5.1	2.9	5.2
1950	2.1	1.6	-0.8	-0.2	0.7
1951	0.1	1.9	3.7	4.1	2.4
1952	3.6	1.8	-0.1	-1.1	1.0
1953	-0.8	-1.4	-0.7	-0.4	-0.8
1954	-0.4	0.2	0.5	1.1	0.3
1955	1.0	-0.3	0.6	0.1	0.4
1956	0.3	1.8	2.5	4.4	2.3
1957	4.7	4.0	3.9	3.3	4.0
1958	1.0	0.4	0.7	-0.4	0.4
1959	-1.7	-2.5	-1.1	-1.4	-1.7
1960	0.9	1.7	3.0	4.0	2.4
1961	4.4	3.3	2.8	2.9	3.4
1962	2.3	3.2	2.9	1.5	2.4
1963	2.0	3.7	3.1	4.4	3.3
1964	5.9	4.9	5.4	5.7	5.5
1965	3.0	4.7	3.7	4.1	3.9
1966	3.2	2.0	0.8	1.5	1.9
1967	2.3	2.1	1.1	0.2	1.4
1968	-1.2	-0.6	-1.3	-1.9	-1.3
1969	-1.9	-1.8	-1.3	0.1	-1.2
1970	1.1	2.4	0.9	0.4	1.2
1971	0.8	-3.8	-3.1	-6.0	-3.0
1972	-8.6	-8.3	-7.9	-7.1	-8.0
1973	-4.4	-1.1	3.2	4.7	0.6
1974	4.3	-5.6	-9.1	-2.1	-3.1
1975	13.1	16.6	11.6	12.9	13.6
1976	4.2	-1.1	-5.0	-7.2	-2.3
1977	-21.2	-21.5	-21.2	-30.8	-23.7
1978	-39.3	-23.3	-24.6	-17.3	-26.1
1979	-19.2	-23.3	-24.2	-28.6	-23.8
1980	-37.1	-16.6	3.5	-8.6	-14.7
1981	-16.3	-16.0	-10.0	-16.4	-14.7
1982	-17.5	-5.1	-30.3	-29.5	-20.6
1983	-23.7	-44.9	-65.2	-71.8	-51.4
1984	-95.5	-104.5	-103.8	-107.1	-102.7
1985	-91.8	-116.0	-118.9	-135.5	-115.6
1986	-127.8	-129.7	-139.4	-133.2	-132.5
1987	-140.3	-145.1	-143.8	-143.2	-143.1
1988	-122.0	-105.6	-98.5	-106.0	-108.0
1989	-85.1	-80.1	-79.7	-73.9	-79.7
1990	-73.9	-61.3	-78.7	-71.6	-71.4
1991	-34.0	-11.5	-19.8	-13.0	-19.6
1992	-7.0	-33.9	-38.8	-38.8	-29.6
1993	-48.3	-65.1	-	-	-

Source: "National Income and Product Account Tables: Selected NIPA Tables," *Survey of Current Business*, November 1991, U.S. Department of Commerce, Bureau of Economic Analysis, National Income and Wealth Division. - indicates that no data are available.

Gross Domestic Product

Net exports of goods and services - 1987 Dollars

In billions of constant 1987 dollars. Quarterly data are seasonally adjusted and annualized.

Year	1st Quarter	2nd Quarter	3rd Quarter	4th Quarter	TOTAL
1929	-	-	-	-	1.9
1930	-	-	-	-	-0.3
1931	-	-	-	-	-2.3
1932	-	-	-	-	-2.4
1933	-	-	-	-	-3.0
1934	-	-	-	-	-1.0
1935	-	-	-	-	-7.2
1936	-	-	-	-	-5.1
1937	-	-	-	-	-1.9
1938	-	-	-	-	4.2
1939	-	-	-	-	4.6
1940	-	-	-	-	8.2
1941	-	-	-	-	2.8
1942	-	-	-	-	-11.1
1943	-	-	-	-	-28.1
1944	-	-	-	-	-29.0
1945	-	-	-	-	-23.9
1946	-	-	-	-	26.5
1947	43.1	43.9	45.2	35.4	41.9
1948	24.1	15.7	14.2	12.4	16.6
1949	21.2	21.2	17.7	9.3	17.3
1950	7.9	6.3	-2.6	1.4	3.2
1951	3.3	10.4	15.3	15.3	11.1
1952	12.7	5.9	-2.3	-7.0	2.3
1953	-6.7	-9.1	-6.7	-6.0	-7.1
1954	-5.0	-2.7	-1.5	0.1	-2.3
1955	-1.0	-7.5	-5.2	-7.0	-5.2
1956	-6.8	-2.7	-1.7	6.4	-1.2
1957	5.4	2.3	1.3	-2.6	1.6
1958	-13.0	-16.3	-13.4	-16.8	-14.9
1959	-21.4	-25.0	-20.3	-20.5	-21.8
1960	-13.4	-10.4	-5.6	-1.2	-7.6
1961	-0.9	-6.0	-6.7	-8.4	-5.5
1962	-11.9	-7.8	-8.9	-13.5	-10.5
1963	-10.4	-5.2	-6.1	-1.6	-5.8
1964	4.6	1.1	2.5	1.9	2.5
1965	-7.5	-5.0	-7.8	-5.3	-6.4
1966	-11.4	-16.0	-22.8	-21.7	-18.0
1967	-20.5	-21.1	-23.5	-29.7	-23.7
1968	-36.8	-35.7	-37.4	-40.1	-37.5
1969	-38.9	-44.1	-43.3	-39.8	-41.5
1970	-36.0	-33.9	-34.4	-36.4	-35.2
1971	-34.0	-48.8	-47.0	-53.8	-45.9
1972	-61.2	-57.0	-53.9	-54.0	-56.5
1973	-49.7	-36.6	-26.1	-23.9	-34.1
1974	-5.3	-4.5	-9.2	2.6	-4.1
1975	23.3	32.7	18.4	18.2	23.1
1976	2.8	-6.2	-8.3	-13.7	-6.4
1977	-27.8	-25.2	-22.5	-35.9	-27.8
1978	-46.8	-26.5	-26.9	-19.2	-29.9
1979	-17.3	-20.4	-7.3	2.8	-10.6
1980	11.1	33.1	47.0	31.5	30.7
1981	29.0	27.9	20.9	10.0	22.0
1982	3.5	3.5	-17.7	-19.0	-7.4
1983	-28.0	-45.9	-67.0	-83.7	-56.1
1984	-108.4	-121.0	-127.2	-131.4	-122.0
1985	-127.1	-149.2	-149.6	-155.4	-145.3
1986	-143.1	-157.1	-164.3	-156.0	-155.1
1987	-150.0	-146.3	-139.8	-136.0	-143.1
1988	-113.4	-98.1	-101.9	-102.7	-104.0
1989	-79.8	-70.0	-77.5	-67.4	-73.7
1990	-60.8	-58.9	-62.2	-36.8	-54.7
1991	-21.6	-13.3	-25.0	-16.4	-19.1
1992	-15.2	-38.0	-42.5	-38.8	-33.6
1993	-59.9	-75.2	-	-	-

Source: "National Income and Product Account Tables: Selected NIPA Tables," *Survey of Current Business*, November 1991, U.S. Department of Commerce, Bureau of Economic Analysis, National Income and Wealth Division. - indicates that no data are available.

Gross Domestic Product
Net exports of goods and services
Exports - Actual Dollars

In billions of actual dollars and percent. Quarterly data are seasonally adjusted and annualized. Growth rates for quarters are compound annual growth rates; changes from year to year are percentage changes.

Year	1st Quarter	% Change	2nd Quarter	% Change	3rd Quarter	% Change	4th Quarter	% Change	TOTAL	% Change
1929	-	-	-	-	-	-	-	-	5.9	-
1930	-	-	-	-	-	-	-	-	4.4	-25.4
1931	-	-	-	-	-	-	-	-	2.9	-34.1
1932	-	-	-	-	-	-	-	-	2.0	-31.0
1933	-	-	-	-	-	-	-	-	2.0	-
1934	-	-	-	-	-	-	-	-	2.6	30.0
1935	-	-	-	-	-	-	-	-	2.8	7.7
1936	-	-	-	-	-	-	-	-	3.0	7.1
1937	-	-	-	-	-	-	-	-	4.0	33.3
1938	-	-	-	-	-	-	-	-	3.8	-5.0
1939	-	-	-	-	-	-	-	-	3.9	2.6
1940	-	-	-	-	-	-	-	-	4.8	23.1
1941	-	-	-	-	-	-	-	-	5.4	12.5
1942	-	-	-	-	-	-	-	-	4.3	-20.4
1943	-	-	-	-	-	-	-	-	3.9	-9.3
1944	-	-	-	-	-	-	-	-	4.8	23.1
1945	-	-	-	-	-	-	-	-	6.7	39.6
1946	13.0	-	14.2	42.4	15.4	38.3	13.6	-39.2	14.1	110.4
1947	18.3	227.8	19.4	26.3	19.4	-	17.6	-32.3	18.7	32.6
1948	16.9	-15.0	15.2	-34.6	15.4	5.4	14.6	-19.2	15.5	-17.1
1949	16.0	44.2	15.6	-9.6	14.0	-35.1	12.0	-46.0	14.4	-7.1
1950	11.6	-12.7	11.8	7.1	12.2	14.3	13.5	49.9	12.3	-14.6
1951	15.0	52.4	17.0	65.0	18.0	25.7	18.1	2.2	17.0	38.2
1952	18.6	11.5	16.5	-38.1	15.1	-29.9	15.2	2.7	16.3	-4.1
1953	15.0	-5.2	15.1	2.7	15.7	16.9	15.1	-14.4	15.2	-6.7
1954	14.3	-19.6	16.3	68.8	15.8	-11.7	16.5	18.9	15.7	3.3
1955	17.2	18.1	16.8	-9.0	18.1	34.7	18.3	4.5	17.6	12.1
1956	19.3	23.7	20.8	34.9	21.7	18.5	23.0	26.2	21.2	20.5
1957	24.8	35.2	24.3	-7.8	23.6	-11.0	22.9	-11.3	23.9	12.7
1958	20.4	-37.0	20.4	-	20.5	2.0	20.5	-	20.4	-14.6
1959	19.7	-14.7	20.0	6.2	21.8	41.2	21.1	-12.2	20.6	1.0
1960	24.2	73.0	25.2	17.6	25.9	11.6	25.8	-1.5	25.3	22.8
1961	26.1	4.7	25.2	-13.1	26.1	15.1	26.8	11.2	26.0	2.8
1962	26.6	-3.0	28.1	24.5	28.0	-1.4	27.0	-13.5	27.4	5.4
1963	27.2	3.0	29.6	40.2	29.8	2.7	31.1	18.6	29.4	7.3
1964	32.9	25.2	32.6	-3.6	33.9	16.9	35.0	13.6	33.6	14.3
1965	31.5	-34.4	36.3	76.4	35.7	-6.4	38.0	28.4	35.4	5.4
1966	38.2	2.1	38.2	-	39.0	8.6	40.4	15.2	38.9	9.9
1967	41.7	13.5	41.1	-5.6	40.7	-3.8	41.9	12.3	41.4	6.4
1968	43.2	13.0	44.8	15.7	47.0	21.1	46.2	-6.6	45.3	9.4
1969	41.9	-32.3	50.9	117.8	51.0	0.8	53.2	18.4	49.3	8.8
1970	54.7	11.8	57.6	23.0	57.3	-2.1	58.3	7.2	57.0	15.6
1971	59.5	8.5	59.5	-	62.4	21.0	55.9	-35.6	59.3	4.0
1972	63.5	66.5	63.1	-2.5	66.2	21.1	72.1	40.7	66.2	11.6
1973	81.0	59.3	88.3	41.2	94.3	30.1	103.4	44.6	91.8	38.7
1974	114.6	50.9	123.7	35.8	124.5	2.6	134.4	35.8	124.3	35.4
1975	138.0	11.2	131.8	-16.8	133.7	5.9	141.7	26.2	136.3	9.7
1976	143.1	4.0	146.0	8.4	150.9	14.1	155.4	12.5	148.9	9.2
1977	154.8	-1.5	161.3	17.9	161.8	1.2	157.1	-11.1	158.8	6.6
1978	164.0	18.8	185.6	64.0	190.5	11.0	204.5	32.8	186.1	17.2
1979	210.7	12.7	219.9	18.6	233.1	26.3	251.9	36.4	228.9	23.0
1980	267.5	27.2	276.2	13.7	282.7	9.8	290.4	11.3	279.2	22.0
1981	303.0	18.5	305.8	3.7	299.9	-7.5	303.4	4.8	303.0	8.5
1982	291.9	-14.3	293.9	2.8	279.0	-18.8	265.6	-17.9	282.6	-6.7
1983	270.6	7.7	272.3	2.5	277.7	8.2	286.2	12.8	276.7	-2.1
1984	293.1	10.0	302.1	12.9	305.7	4.9	308.7	4.0	302.4	9.3
1985	305.0	-4.7	302.7	-3.0	295.8	-8.8	304.7	12.6	302.1	-0.1
1986	311.5	9.2	313.0	1.9	318.4	7.1	333.9	20.9	319.2	5.7
1987	336.3	2.9	355.7	25.1	371.5	19.0	392.4	24.5	364.0	14.0
1988	418.5	29.4	438.8	20.9	452.4	13.0	467.0	13.5	444.2	22.0
1989	489.7	20.9	509.5	17.2	509.0	-0.4	523.8	12.1	508.0	14.4
1990	542.0	14.6	553.5	8.8	555.3	1.3	577.6	17.1	557.1	9.7
1991	576.5	-0.8	600.7	17.9	603.0	1.5	625.7	15.9	601.5	8.0
1992	633.7	5.2	632.4	-0.8	641.1	5.6	654.7	8.8	640.5	6.5
1993	651.3	-2.1	660.0	5.5	-	-	-	-	-	-

Source: "National Income and Product Account Tables: Selected NIPA Tables," *Survey of Current Business*, November 1991, U.S. Department of Commerce, Bureau of Economic Analysis, National Income and Wealth Division. - indicates that no data are available.

Gross Domestic Product

Net exports of goods and services
Exports - 1987 Dollars

In billions of constant 1987 dollars and percent. Quarterly data are seasonally adjusted and annualized. Growth rates for quarters are compound annual growth rates; changes from year to year are percentage changes.

Year	1st Quarter	% Change	2nd Quarter	% Change	3rd Quarter	% Change	4th Quarter	% Change	TOTAL	% Change
1929	-	-	-	-	-	-	-	-	36.0	-
1930	-	-	-	-	-	-	-	-	29.8	-17.2
1931	-	-	-	-	-	-	-	-	24.7	-17.1
1932	-	-	-	-	-	-	-	-	19.6	-20.6
1933	-	-	-	-	-	-	-	-	19.9	1.5
1934	-	-	-	-	-	-	-	-	22.3	12.1
1935	-	-	-	-	-	-	-	-	23.9	7.2
1936	-	-	-	-	-	-	-	-	25.3	5.9
1937	-	-	-	-	-	-	-	-	31.9	26.1
1938	-	-	-	-	-	-	-	-	30.7	-3.8
1939	-	-	-	-	-	-	-	-	32.7	6.5
1940	-	-	-	-	-	-	-	-	37.5	14.7
1941	-	-	-	-	-	-	-	-	39.1	4.3
1942	-	-	-	-	-	-	-	-	26.3	-32.7
1943	-	-	-	-	-	-	-	-	22.3	-15.2
1944	-	-	-	-	-	-	-	-	24.6	10.3
1945	-	-	-	-	-	-	-	-	32.8	33.3
1946	-	-	-	-	-	-	-	-	66.7	103.4
1947	80.1	-	82.9	14.7	80.7	-10.2	72.5	-34.9	79.1	18.6
1948	65.6	-33.0	59.1	-34.1	60.1	6.9	57.9	-13.9	60.7	-23.3
1949	64.8	56.9	64.3	-3.1	59.1	-28.6	51.3	-43.2	59.9	-1.3
1950	50.7	-4.6	51.4	5.6	52.8	11.3	57.1	36.8	53.0	-11.5
1951	59.5	17.9	65.1	43.3	66.5	8.9	66.0	-3.0	64.3	21.3
1952	69.8	25.1	62.5	-35.7	58.0	-25.8	58.7	4.9	62.3	-3.1
1953	58.4	-2.0	58.9	3.5	61.4	18.1	59.4	-12.4	59.5	-4.5
1954	56.6	-17.6	64.6	69.7	62.4	-12.9	65.0	17.7	62.2	4.5
1955	67.0	12.9	65.3	-9.8	69.3	26.8	69.4	0.6	67.7	8.8
1956	72.3	17.8	77.0	28.6	79.5	13.6	83.2	20.0	78.0	15.2
1957	88.7	29.2	86.3	-10.4	84.0	-10.2	81.0	-13.5	85.0	9.0
1958	72.7	-35.1	73.2	2.8	74.0	4.4	74.6	3.3	73.7	-13.3
1959	70.9	-18.4	72.0	6.4	77.5	34.2	74.7	-13.7	73.8	0.1
1960	84.9	66.9	88.3	17.0	90.5	10.3	90.2	-1.3	88.4	19.8
1961	90.7	2.2	86.5	-17.3	90.7	20.9	91.4	3.1	89.9	1.7
1962	91.1	-1.3	97.3	30.1	97.5	0.8	94.2	-12.9	95.0	5.7
1963	94.4	0.9	102.1	36.8	103.4	5.2	107.3	16.0	101.8	7.2
1964	113.6	25.6	112.6	-3.5	116.8	15.8	118.7	6.7	115.4	13.4
1965	105.2	-38.3	121.0	75.0	119.0	-6.4	127.1	30.1	118.1	2.3
1966	125.2	-5.8	124.3	-2.8	125.5	3.9	127.9	7.9	125.7	6.4
1967	131.0	10.1	129.5	-4.5	128.3	-3.7	131.3	9.7	130.0	3.4
1968	134.2	9.1	137.6	10.5	146.2	27.4	142.9	-8.7	140.2	7.8
1969	128.4	-34.8	154.5	109.6	153.1	-3.6	155.0	5.1	147.8	5.4
1970	157.3	6.1	163.3	16.2	161.3	-4.8	163.2	4.8	161.3	9.1
1971	162.5	-1.7	162.7	0.5	171.0	22.0	151.4	-38.6	161.9	0.4
1972	169.5	57.1	166.5	-6.9	173.9	19.0	185.0	28.1	173.7	7.3
1973	200.7	38.5	209.2	18.0	212.4	6.3	219.0	13.0	210.3	21.1
1974	229.0	19.6	240.2	21.0	230.4	-15.3	237.8	13.5	234.4	11.5
1975	233.9	-6.4	227.7	-10.2	229.7	3.6	240.2	19.6	232.9	-0.6
1976	238.9	-2.1	239.9	1.7	246.4	11.3	248.4	3.3	243.4	4.5
1977	244.0	-6.9	250.8	11.6	250.5	-0.5	242.1	-12.8	246.9	1.4
1978	248.7	11.4	271.6	42.2	274.5	4.3	286.0	17.8	270.2	9.4
1979	286.5	0.7	284.9	-2.2	292.9	11.7	309.9	25.3	293.5	8.6
1980	319.6	13.1	323.0	4.3	320.1	-3.5	319.5	-0.7	320.5	9.2
1981	328.1	11.2	332.0	4.8	323.3	-10.1	321.1	-2.7	326.1	1.7
1982	306.1	-17.4	306.5	0.5	293.9	-15.5	280.4	-17.1	296.7	-9.0
1983	282.5	3.0	283.7	1.7	286.1	3.4	291.5	7.8	285.9	-3.6
1984	298.0	9.2	303.9	8.2	308.2	5.8	312.8	6.1	305.7	6.9
1985	310.9	-2.4	309.8	-1.4	304.3	-6.9	312.0	10.5	309.2	1.1
1986	320.9	11.9	323.9	3.8	330.6	8.5	342.9	15.7	329.6	6.6
1987	342.1	-0.9	356.5	17.9	371.5	17.9	386.1	16.7	364.0	10.4
1988	407.1	23.6	417.2	10.3	424.1	6.8	438.2	14.0	421.6	15.8
1989	454.5	15.7	472.0	16.3	472.9	0.8	487.7	13.1	471.8	11.9
1990	501.8	12.1	511.1	7.6	508.6	-1.9	520.4	9.6	510.5	8.2
1991	519.4	-0.8	542.9	19.4	546.9	3.0	564.2	13.3	543.4	6.4
1992	571.0	4.9	570.2	-0.6	579.3	6.5	591.6	8.8	578.0	6.4
1993	588.0	-2.4	593.2	3.6	-	-	-	-	-	-

Source: "National Income and Product Account Tables: Selected NIPA Tables," *Survey of Current Business*, November 1991, U.S. Department of Commerce, Bureau of Economic Analysis, National Income and Wealth Division. - indicates that no data are available.

Gross Domestic Product
Net exports of goods and services
Imports - Actual Dollars

In billions of actual dollars and percent. Quarterly data are seasonally adjusted and annualized. Growth rates for quarters are compound annual growth rates; changes from year to year are percentage changes.

Year	1st Quarter	% Change	2nd Quarter	% Change	3rd Quarter	% Change	4th Quarter	% Change	TOTAL	% Change
1929	-	-	-	-	-	-	-	-	5.6	-
1930	-	-	-	-	-	-	-	-	4.1	-26.8
1931	-	-	-	-	-	-	-	-	2.9	-29.3
1932	-	-	-	-	-	-	-	-	1.9	-34.5
1933	-	-	-	-	-	-	-	-	1.9	-
1934	-	-	-	-	-	-	-	-	2.2	15.8
1935	-	-	-	-	-	-	-	-	3.0	36.4
1936	-	-	-	-	-	-	-	-	3.2	6.7
1937	-	-	-	-	-	-	-	-	4.0	25.0
1938	-	-	-	-	-	-	-	-	2.8	-30.0
1939	-	-	-	-	-	-	-	-	3.1	10.7
1940	-	-	-	-	-	-	-	-	3.4	9.7
1941	-	-	-	-	-	-	-	-	4.4	29.4
1942	-	-	-	-	-	-	-	-	4.6	4.5
1943	-	-	-	-	-	-	-	-	6.3	37.0
1944	-	-	-	-	-	-	-	-	6.9	9.5
1945	-	-	-	-	-	-	-	-	7.5	8.7
1946	6.6	-	7.0	26.5	7.0	-	7.3	18.3	7.0	-6.7
1947	7.5	11.4	8.2	42.9	7.7	-22.2	8.3	35.0	7.9	12.9
1948	9.6	79.0	10.0	17.7	10.5	21.6	10.1	-14.4	10.1	27.8
1949	9.6	-18.4	9.4	-8.1	8.9	-19.6	9.1	9.3	9.2	-8.9
1950	9.5	18.8	10.2	32.9	13.0	163.9	13.7	23.3	11.6	26.1
1951	14.9	39.9	15.2	8.3	14.3	-21.7	14.0	-8.1	14.6	25.9
1952	15.0	31.8	14.6	-10.2	15.3	20.6	16.3	28.8	15.3	4.8
1953	15.8	-11.7	16.4	16.1	16.3	-2.4	15.5	-18.2	16.0	4.6
1954	14.8	-16.9	16.2	43.6	15.3	-20.4	15.5	5.3	15.4	-3.8
1955	16.2	19.3	17.1	24.1	17.4	7.2	18.1	17.1	17.2	11.7
1956	18.9	18.9	19.0	2.1	19.3	6.5	18.5	-15.6	18.9	9.9
1957	20.1	39.3	20.3	4.0	19.8	-9.5	19.6	-4.0	19.9	5.3
1958	19.5	-2.0	20.1	12.9	19.7	-7.7	20.8	24.3	20.0	0.5
1959	21.4	12.0	22.5	22.2	22.9	7.3	22.5	-6.8	22.3	11.5
1960	23.3	15.0	23.5	3.5	22.9	-9.8	21.7	-19.4	22.8	2.2
1961	21.7	-	21.9	3.7	23.3	28.1	23.9	10.7	22.7	-0.4
1962	24.3	6.9	24.9	10.2	25.1	3.3	25.5	6.5	25.0	10.1
1963	25.2	-4.6	25.9	11.6	26.7	12.9	26.8	1.5	26.1	4.4
1964	27.0	3.0	27.7	10.8	28.4	10.5	29.3	13.3	28.1	7.7
1965	28.5	-10.5	31.7	53.1	32.0	3.8	33.9	26.0	31.5	12.1
1966	35.0	13.6	36.2	14.4	38.2	24.0	38.8	6.4	37.1	17.8
1967	39.4	6.3	39.0	-4.0	39.5	5.2	41.7	24.2	39.9	7.5
1968	44.4	28.5	45.4	9.3	48.2	27.0	48.2	-	46.6	16.8
1969	43.8	-31.8	52.7	109.6	52.4	-2.3	53.1	5.5	50.5	8.4
1970	53.5	3.0	55.2	13.3	56.4	9.0	57.9	11.1	55.8	10.5
1971	58.7	5.6	63.3	35.2	65.5	14.6	61.9	-20.2	62.3	11.6
1972	72.2	85.1	71.4	-4.4	74.1	16.0	79.2	30.5	74.2	19.1
1973	85.4	35.2	89.5	20.6	91.1	7.3	98.7	37.8	91.2	22.9
1974	110.3	56.0	129.4	89.4	133.6	13.6	136.6	9.3	127.5	39.8
1975	124.9	-30.1	115.2	-27.6	122.1	26.2	128.7	23.4	122.7	-3.8
1976	138.9	35.7	147.1	25.8	155.9	26.2	162.7	18.6	151.1	23.1
1977	176.1	37.2	182.8	16.1	183.0	0.4	187.9	11.1	182.4	20.7
1978	203.3	37.0	208.9	11.5	215.1	12.4	221.8	13.1	212.3	16.4
1979	229.9	15.4	243.2	25.2	257.3	25.3	280.4	41.0	252.7	19.0
1980	304.6	39.3	292.8	-14.6	279.2	-17.3	299.0	31.5	293.9	16.3
1981	319.3	30.1	321.7	3.0	310.0	-13.8	319.7	13.1	317.7	8.1
1982	309.4	-12.3	299.0	-12.8	309.3	14.5	295.1	-17.1	303.2	-4.6
1983	294.3	-1.1	317.2	34.9	342.9	36.6	358.0	18.8	328.1	8.2
1984	388.5	38.7	406.7	20.1	409.5	2.8	415.7	6.2	405.1	23.5
1985	396.8	-17.0	418.7	24.0	414.7	-3.8	440.2	27.0	417.6	3.1
1986	439.2	-0.9	442.7	3.2	457.8	14.4	467.1	8.4	451.7	8.2
1987	476.5	8.3	500.8	22.0	515.3	12.1	535.6	16.7	507.1	12.3
1988	540.5	3.7	544.3	2.8	550.9	4.9	573.1	17.1	552.2	8.9
1989	574.9	1.3	589.6	10.6	588.7	-0.6	597.7	6.3	587.7	6.4
1990	615.9	12.7	614.8	-0.7	634.0	13.1	649.2	9.9	628.5	6.9
1991	610.6	-21.7	612.2	1.1	622.8	7.1	638.8	10.7	621.1	-1.2
1992	640.7	1.2	666.3	17.0	679.9	8.4	693.5	8.2	670.1	7.9
1993	699.6	3.6	725.0	15.3	-	-	-	-	-	-

Source: "National Income and Product Account Tables: Selected NIPA Tables," *Survey of Current Business*, November 1991, U.S. Department of Commerce, Bureau of Economic Analysis, National Income and Wealth Division. - indicates that no data are available.

Gross Domestic Product
Net exports of goods and services
Imports - 1987 Dollars

In billions of constant 1987 dollars and percent. Quarterly data are seasonally adjusted and annualized. Growth rates for quarters are compound annual growth rates; changes from year to year are percentage changes.

Year	1st Quarter	% Change	2nd Quarter	% Change	3rd Quarter	% Change	4th Quarter	% Change	TOTAL	% Change
1929	-	-	-	-	-	-	-	-	34.1	-
1930	-	-	-	-	-	-	-	-	30.1	-11.7
1931	-	-	-	-	-	-	-	-	27.0	-10.3
1932	-	-	-	-	-	-	-	-	22.0	-18.5
1933	-	-	-	-	-	-	-	-	22.9	4.1
1934	-	-	-	-	-	-	-	-	23.4	2.2
1935	-	-	-	-	-	-	-	-	31.1	32.9
1936	-	-	-	-	-	-	-	-	30.4	-2.3
1937	-	-	-	-	-	-	-	-	33.8	11.2
1938	-	-	-	-	-	-	-	-	26.5	-21.6
1939	-	-	-	-	-	-	-	-	28.1	6.0
1940	-	-	-	-	-	-	-	-	29.2	3.9
1941	-	-	-	-	-	-	-	-	36.3	24.3
1942	-	-	-	-	-	-	-	-	37.4	3.0
1943	-	-	-	-	-	-	-	-	50.4	34.8
1944	-	-	-	-	-	-	-	-	53.5	6.2
1945	-	-	-	-	-	-	-	-	56.7	6.0
1946	-	-	-	-	-	-	-	-	40.2	-29.1
1947	37.0	-	39.0	23.4	35.4	-32.1	37.2	21.9	37.1	-7.7
1948	41.6	56.4	43.3	17.4	45.9	26.3	45.4	-4.3	44.1	18.9
1949	43.6	-14.9	43.1	-4.5	41.4	-14.9	42.0	5.9	42.5	-3.6
1950	42.8	7.8	45.1	23.3	55.4	127.7	55.7	2.2	49.7	16.9
1951	56.2	3.6	54.7	-10.3	51.2	-23.2	50.7	-3.8	53.2	7.0
1952	57.1	60.9	56.6	-3.5	60.3	28.8	65.8	41.8	59.9	12.6
1953	65.0	-4.8	68.0	19.8	68.1	0.6	65.4	-14.9	66.6	11.2
1954	61.7	-20.8	67.3	41.6	63.9	-18.7	64.9	6.4	64.4	-3.3
1955	68.0	20.5	72.8	31.4	74.5	9.7	76.4	10.6	72.9	13.2
1956	79.1	14.9	79.7	3.1	81.2	7.7	76.8	-20.0	79.2	8.6
1957	83.3	38.4	84.0	3.4	82.7	-6.0	83.6	4.4	83.4	5.3
1958	85.8	10.9	89.5	18.4	87.4	-9.1	91.4	19.6	88.5	6.1
1959	92.3	4.0	97.0	22.0	97.8	3.3	95.3	-9.8	95.6	8.0
1960	98.3	13.2	98.7	1.6	96.1	-10.1	91.4	-18.2	96.1	0.5
1961	91.6	0.9	92.6	4.4	97.4	22.4	99.8	10.2	95.3	-0.8
1962	103.1	13.9	105.0	7.6	106.3	5.0	107.6	5.0	105.5	10.7
1963	104.8	-10.0	107.3	9.9	109.5	8.5	109.0	-1.8	107.7	2.1
1964	109.0	-	111.5	9.5	114.3	10.4	116.8	9.0	112.9	4.8
1965	112.7	-13.3	125.9	55.7	126.8	2.9	132.4	18.9	124.5	10.3
1966	136.5	13.0	140.3	11.6	148.3	24.8	149.6	3.6	143.7	15.4
1967	151.6	5.5	150.6	-2.6	151.8	3.2	161.0	26.5	153.7	7.0
1968	170.9	27.0	173.2	5.5	183.6	26.3	183.1	-1.1	177.7	15.6
1969	167.3	-30.3	198.6	98.6	196.3	-4.6	194.8	-3.0	189.2	6.5
1970	193.3	-3.0	197.1	8.1	195.7	-2.8	199.6	8.2	196.4	3.8
1971	196.5	-6.1	211.5	34.2	218.0	12.9	205.2	-21.5	207.8	5.8
1972	230.7	59.8	223.5	-11.9	227.8	7.9	239.0	21.2	230.2	10.8
1973	250.3	20.3	245.9	-6.8	238.5	-11.5	242.9	7.6	244.4	6.2
1974	234.3	-13.4	244.7	19.0	239.6	-8.1	235.1	-7.3	238.4	-2.5
1975	210.7	-35.5	195.0	-26.6	211.4	38.1	222.0	21.6	209.8	-12.0
1976	236.0	27.7	246.1	18.2	254.7	14.7	262.1	12.1	249.7	19.0
1977	271.8	15.6	276.0	6.3	273.0	-4.3	277.9	7.4	274.7	10.0
1978	295.6	28.0	298.1	3.4	301.4	4.5	305.2	5.1	300.1	9.2
1979	303.8	-1.8	305.3	2.0	300.2	-6.5	307.1	9.5	304.1	1.3
1980	308.5	1.8	290.0	-21.9	273.1	-21.4	287.9	23.5	289.9	-4.7
1981	299.0	16.3	304.1	7.0	302.3	-2.3	311.1	12.2	304.1	4.9
1982	302.6	-10.5	302.9	0.4	311.5	11.8	299.4	-14.7	304.1	-
1983	310.5	15.7	329.5	26.8	353.1	31.9	375.1	27.3	342.1	12.5
1984	406.3	37.7	424.9	19.6	435.4	10.3	444.2	8.3	427.7	25.0
1985	438.1	-5.4	459.0	20.5	454.0	-4.3	467.4	12.3	454.6	6.3
1986	464.0	-2.9	480.9	15.4	494.9	12.2	498.9	3.3	484.7	6.6
1987	492.1	-5.3	502.7	8.9	511.3	7.0	522.1	8.7	507.1	4.6
1988	520.5	-1.2	515.2	-4.0	526.1	8.7	540.9	11.7	525.7	3.7
1989	534.3	-4.8	541.9	5.8	550.5	6.5	555.0	3.3	545.4	3.7
1990	562.6	5.6	570.0	5.4	570.7	0.5	557.2	-9.1	565.1	3.6
1991	541.0	-11.1	556.2	11.7	571.9	11.8	580.7	6.3	562.5	-0.5
1992	586.2	3.8	608.2	15.9	621.8	9.2	630.3	5.6	611.6	8.7
1993	647.9	11.6	668.4	13.3	-	-	-	-	-	-

Source: "National Income and Product Account Tables: Selected NIPA Tables," *Survey of Current Business*, November 1991, U.S. Department of Commerce, Bureau of Economic Analysis, National Income and Wealth Division. - indicates that no data are available.

GOVERNMENT PURCHASES OF GOODS AND SERVICES
Component of Gross Domestic Product

Government—federal, state, and local—represented nearly 19 percent of real GDP in 1992. The category includes purchases of durable and nondurable goods, expenditures on structures (such as highways and bridges), purchases of services, and compensation of government employees. This category *excludes* transfer payments such as entitlements, transactions in land, grants-in-aid, and financial transactions. The effect of these excluded budgetary items are accounted for in purchases made by those who receive the money. In constant dollars, state and local purchases account for well over half of the total (60 percent), the federal government for the rest.

The category is divided as follows:

> *Federal*
> National defense
> Nondefense
> *State and local*

Estimates are prepared by BEA under four categories: (1) federal expenditures, derived from the *Budget of the United States* and other sources, with categories such as transfer payments removed; (2) state and local compensation, (3) state and local expenditures for structures, and (4) state and local purchases other than compensation and structures. Each category is governed by its own estimating procedures and analytical methodologies.

Presentation of Data

Data are shown from 1929 to 1993 in quarterly and in annual increments. Changes from one period to the next are shown for each category covered. Changes from quarter to quarter are annualized, compounded growth rates as explained in the section on Gross National Product. Changes from year to year are simple percentile changes.

Analytical Uses

The total category best depicts the importance of government as a customer and employer—in that it includes what governmental bodies purchase and what they pay. It is not a good measure of total governmental activity because it excludes money the government collects for redistribution in transfer payments. Government activity has shown sharp rise during periods of war.

Gross Domestic Product

Government purchases of goods and services: Total - Actual Dollars

In billions of actual dollars and percent. Quarterly data are seasonally adjusted and annualized. Growth rates for quarters are compound annual growth rates; changes from year to year are percentage changes.

Year	1st Quarter	% Change	2nd Quarter	% Change	3rd Quarter	% Change	4th Quarter	% Change	TOTAL	% Change
1929	-	-	-	-	-	-	-	-	8.6	-
1930	-	-	-	-	-	-	-	-	9.2	7.0
1931	-	-	-	-	-	-	-	-	9.2	-
1932	-	-	-	-	-	-	-	-	8.1	-12.0
1933	-	-	-	-	-	-	-	-	7.9	-2.5
1934	-	-	-	-	-	-	-	-	9.7	22.8
1935	-	-	-	-	-	-	-	-	10.0	3.1
1936	-	-	-	-	-	-	-	-	12.1	21.0
1937	-	-	-	-	-	-	-	-	11.7	-3.3
1938	-	-	-	-	-	-	-	-	12.7	8.5
1939	-	-	-	-	-	-	-	-	13.5	6.3
1940	-	-	-	-	-	-	-	-	13.8	2.2
1941	-	-	-	-	-	-	-	-	24.8	79.7
1942	-	-	-	-	-	-	-	-	59.5	139.9
1943	-	-	-	-	-	-	-	-	88.9	49.4
1944	-	-	-	-	-	-	-	-	96.9	9.0
1945	-	-	-	-	-	-	-	-	83.3	-14.0
1946	33.1	-	28.2	-47.3	27.3	-12.2	28.1	12.2	29.2	-64.9
1947	25.8	-28.9	26.4	9.6	26.2	-3.0	26.3	1.5	26.2	-10.3
1948	28.1	30.3	30.5	38.8	32.3	25.8	34.7	33.2	31.4	19.8
1949	36.8	26.5	39.0	26.1	39.3	3.1	39.0	-3.0	38.5	22.6
1950	38.2	-8.0	38.9	7.5	38.7	-2.0	42.0	38.7	39.5	2.6
1951	49.7	96.1	57.0	73.0	64.7	66.0	69.5	33.1	60.2	52.4
1952	70.9	8.3	74.5	21.9	76.0	8.3	78.3	12.7	74.9	24.4
1953	80.4	11.2	82.3	9.8	80.7	-7.6	80.8	0.5	81.0	8.1
1954	78.8	-9.5	76.1	-13.0	74.6	-7.7	74.6	-	76.0	-6.2
1955	75.0	2.2	75.5	2.7	76.9	7.6	75.8	-5.6	75.8	-0.3
1956	76.9	5.9	80.0	17.1	79.9	-0.5	82.6	14.2	79.8	5.3
1957	86.0	17.5	86.2	0.9	87.5	6.2	89.8	10.9	87.4	9.5
1958	89.6	-0.9	93.2	17.1	94.3	4.8	97.0	12.0	93.5	7.0
1959	98.0	4.2	99.6	6.7	99.5	-0.4	98.7	-3.2	99.0	5.9
1960	96.7	-7.9	98.4	7.2	100.9	10.6	103.1	9.0	99.8	0.8
1961	104.2	4.3	105.9	6.7	107.1	4.6	110.8	14.6	107.0	7.2
1962	114.1	12.5	116.1	7.2	117.9	6.3	119.2	4.5	116.8	9.2
1963	119.5	1.0	120.5	3.4	124.0	12.1	125.0	3.3	122.3	4.7
1964	126.6	5.2	128.8	7.1	129.0	0.6	129.1	0.3	128.3	4.9
1965	129.8	2.2	133.3	11.2	138.2	15.5	143.8	17.2	136.3	6.2
1966	147.5	10.7	153.5	17.3	159.0	15.1	163.4	11.5	155.9	14.4
1967	172.2	23.3	173.1	2.1	176.3	7.6	180.6	10.1	175.6	12.6
1968	186.5	13.7	190.0	7.7	192.9	6.2	196.7	8.1	191.5	9.1
1969	196.9	0.4	200.2	6.9	204.6	9.1	205.4	1.6	201.8	5.4
1970	208.9	7.0	210.0	2.1	214.5	8.9	217.3	5.3	212.7	5.4
1971	220.2	5.4	223.2	5.6	225.5	4.2	228.5	5.4	224.3	5.5
1972	238.1	17.9	240.4	3.9	241.1	1.2	246.5	9.3	241.5	7.7
1973	252.7	10.4	255.4	4.3	257.7	3.7	265.1	12.0	257.7	6.7
1974	273.8	13.8	283.1	14.3	292.8	14.4	303.4	15.3	288.3	11.9
1975	310.5	9.7	316.7	8.2	324.5	10.2	333.8	12.0	321.4	11.5
1976	337.4	4.4	338.4	1.2	341.3	3.5	347.9	8.0	341.3	6.2
1977	355.9	9.5	365.7	11.5	371.3	6.3	379.2	8.8	368.0	7.8
1978	385.8	7.1	397.7	12.9	409.3	12.2	421.5	12.5	403.6	9.7
1979	427.1	5.4	440.1	12.7	454.9	14.1	471.9	15.8	448.5	11.1
1980	490.5	16.7	504.1	11.6	507.4	2.6	526.4	15.8	507.1	13.1
1981	545.4	15.2	556.8	8.6	562.2	3.9	579.9	13.2	561.1	10.6
1982	587.1	5.1	599.8	8.9	612.0	8.4	631.6	13.4	607.6	8.3
1983	637.5	3.8	647.7	6.6	666.3	12.0	657.6	-5.1	652.3	7.4
1984	676.3	11.9	695.4	11.8	704.4	5.3	727.0	13.5	700.8	7.4
1985	742.2	8.6	762.4	11.3	785.6	12.7	799.2	7.1	772.3	10.2
1986	805.9	3.4	825.3	10.0	851.2	13.2	849.7	-0.7	833.0	7.9
1987	860.6	5.2	876.0	7.4	888.0	5.6	901.4	6.2	881.5	5.8
1988	904.7	1.5	913.8	4.1	918.5	2.1	937.6	8.6	918.7	4.2
1989	950.4	5.6	970.2	8.6	985.6	6.5	994.5	3.7	975.2	6.1
1990	1,027.7	14.0	1,037.3	3.8	1,048.3	4.3	1,076.5	11.2	1,047.4	7.4
1991	1,093.0	6.3	1,099.9	2.5	1,104.0	1.5	1,100.2	-1.4	1,099.3	5.0
1992	1,118.5	6.8	1,125.8	2.6	1,139.1	4.8	1,143.8	1.7	1,131.8	3.0
1993	1,139.7	-1.4	1,158.6	6.8	-	-	-	-	-	-

Source: "National Income and Product Account Tables: Selected NIPA Tables," *Survey of Current Business*, November 1991, U.S. Department of Commerce, Bureau of Economic Analysis, National Income and Wealth Division. - indicates that no data are available.

Gross Domestic Product

Government purchases of goods and services: Total - 1987 Dollars

In billions of constant 1987 dollars and percent. Quarterly data are seasonally adjusted and annualized. Growth rates for quarters are compound annual growth rates; changes from year to year are percentage changes.

Year	1st Quarter	% Change	2nd Quarter	% Change	3rd Quarter	% Change	4th Quarter	% Change	TOTAL	% Change
1929	-	-	-	-	-	-	-	-	112.6	-
1930	-	-	-	-	-	-	-	-	122.0	8.3
1931	-	-	-	-	-	-	-	-	125.5	2.9
1932	-	-	-	-	-	-	-	-	120.5	-4.0
1933	-	-	-	-	-	-	-	-	116.1	-3.7
1934	-	-	-	-	-	-	-	-	131.4	13.2
1935	-	-	-	-	-	-	-	-	135.7	3.3
1936	-	-	-	-	-	-	-	-	158.6	16.9
1937	-	-	-	-	-	-	-	-	152.2	-4.0
1938	-	-	-	-	-	-	-	-	162.5	6.8
1939	-	-	-	-	-	-	-	-	174.0	7.1
1940	-	-	-	-	-	-	-	-	180.7	3.9
1941	-	-	-	-	-	-	-	-	289.1	60.0
1942	-	-	-	-	-	-	-	-	586.0	102.7
1943	-	-	-	-	-	-	-	-	867.7	48.1
1944	-	-	-	-	-	-	-	-	968.0	11.6
1945	-	-	-	-	-	-	-	-	829.4	-14.3
1946	-	-	-	-	-	-	-	-	271.0	-67.3
1947	217.5	-	217.2	-0.6	221.3	7.8	219.4	-3.4	218.8	-19.3
1948	229.7	20.1	235.7	10.9	242.3	11.7	254.5	21.7	240.6	10.0
1949	259.2	7.6	270.2	18.1	275.9	8.7	272.0	-5.5	269.3	11.9
1950	271.5	-0.7	276.6	7.7	284.3	11.6	305.5	33.3	284.5	5.6
1951	336.1	46.5	382.8	68.3	423.3	49.5	445.8	23.0	397.0	39.5
1952	453.7	7.3	466.8	12.1	471.6	4.2	478.2	5.7	467.6	17.8
1953	488.9	9.3	494.4	4.6	490.2	-3.4	485.6	-3.7	489.8	4.7
1954	470.4	-11.9	457.6	-10.4	449.3	-7.1	441.4	-6.8	454.7	-7.2
1955	449.3	7.4	439.6	-8.4	442.7	2.9	435.1	-6.7	441.7	-2.9
1956	434.9	-0.2	443.3	8.0	443.5	0.2	454.1	9.9	444.0	0.5
1957	461.7	6.9	462.9	1.0	468.7	5.1	467.8	-0.8	465.3	4.8
1958	466.5	-1.1	476.9	9.2	476.3	-0.5	484.1	6.7	476.0	2.3
1959	476.1	-6.4	478.2	1.8	474.9	-2.7	471.9	-2.5	475.3	-0.1
1960	466.8	-4.3	473.7	6.0	479.9	5.3	487.2	6.2	476.9	0.3
1961	493.7	5.4	496.6	2.4	500.7	3.3	515.1	12.0	501.5	5.2
1962	520.8	4.5	524.4	2.8	526.0	1.2	525.3	-0.5	524.2	4.5
1963	528.1	2.1	532.9	3.7	543.6	8.3	540.6	-2.2	536.3	2.3
1964	546.4	4.4	551.6	3.9	549.8	-1.3	548.4	-1.0	549.1	2.4
1965	546.6	-1.3	559.3	9.6	572.1	9.5	589.6	12.8	566.9	3.2
1966	599.0	6.5	615.4	11.4	631.8	11.1	643.2	7.4	622.4	9.8
1967	665.8	14.8	663.2	-1.6	668.7	3.4	673.9	3.1	667.9	7.3
1968	682.9	5.5	688.7	3.4	686.7	-1.2	688.8	1.2	686.8	2.8
1969	682.6	-3.6	686.3	2.2	681.7	-2.7	677.3	-2.6	682.0	-0.7
1970	671.5	-3.4	662.2	-5.4	665.3	1.9	664.4	-0.5	665.8	-2.4
1971	656.1	-4.9	653.3	-1.7	650.4	-1.8	649.7	-0.4	652.4	-2.0
1972	657.9	5.1	656.0	-1.2	648.5	-4.5	649.5	0.6	653.0	0.1
1973	652.3	1.7	645.9	-3.9	636.8	-5.5	642.0	3.3	644.2	-1.3
1974	648.8	4.3	658.6	6.2	654.2	-2.6	660.1	3.7	655.4	1.7
1975	659.2	-0.5	659.5	0.2	665.4	3.6	669.7	2.6	663.5	1.2
1976	665.1	-2.7	658.9	-3.7	657.0	-1.1	655.9	-0.7	659.2	-0.6
1977	659.2	2.0	666.7	4.6	666.0	-0.4	664.3	-1.0	664.1	0.7
1978	666.1	1.1	675.9	6.0	681.8	3.5	684.1	1.4	677.0	1.9
1979	681.2	-1.7	687.0	3.4	693.6	3.9	695.3	1.0	689.3	1.8
1980	704.7	5.5	707.9	1.8	701.9	-3.3	702.2	0.2	704.2	2.2
1981	712.2	5.8	713.4	0.7	711.7	-0.9	715.5	2.2	713.2	1.3
1982	714.7	-0.4	719.2	2.5	724.6	3.0	735.9	6.4	723.6	1.5
1983	735.3	-0.3	740.4	2.8	751.5	6.1	748.1	-1.8	743.8	2.8
1984	754.1	3.2	763.3	5.0	766.0	1.4	784.3	9.9	766.9	3.1
1985	791.5	3.7	805.8	7.4	825.7	10.3	830.5	2.3	813.4	6.1
1986	834.9	2.1	850.6	7.7	871.6	10.2	864.8	-3.1	855.4	5.2
1987	869.1	2.0	879.0	4.6	884.9	2.7	893.0	3.7	881.5	3.1
1988	883.7	-4.1	885.6	0.9	883.7	-0.9	894.5	5.0	886.8	0.6
1989	890.8	-1.6	902.3	5.3	912.2	4.5	912.6	0.2	904.4	2.0
1990	928.1	7.0	930.6	1.1	929.2	-0.6	942.4	5.8	932.6	3.1
1991	948.9	2.8	952.3	1.4	947.6	-2.0	936.2	-4.7	946.3	1.5
1992	943.1	3.0	940.7	-1.0	950.2	4.1	946.9	-1.4	945.2	-0.1
1993	931.3	-6.4	941.1	4.3	-	-	-	-	-	-

Source: "National Income and Product Account Tables: Selected NIPA Tables," *Survey of Current Business*, November 1991, U.S. Department of Commerce, Bureau of Economic Analysis, National Income and Wealth Division. - indicates that no data are available.

Gross Domestic Product
Government purchases of goods and services
Federal: Total - Actual Dollars

In billions of actual dollars and percent. Quarterly data are seasonally adjusted and annualized. Growth rates for quarters are compound annual growth rates; changes from year to year are percentage changes.

Year	1st Quarter	% Change	2nd Quarter	% Change	3rd Quarter	% Change	4th Quarter	% Change	TOTAL	% Change
1929	-	-	-	-	-	-	-	-	1.5	-
1930	-	-	-	-	-	-	-	-	1.6	6.7
1931	-	-	-	-	-	-	-	-	1.7	6.3
1932	-	-	-	-	-	-	-	-	1.6	-5.9
1933	-	-	-	-	-	-	-	-	2.1	31.2
1934	-	-	-	-	-	-	-	-	3.0	42.9
1935	-	-	-	-	-	-	-	-	3.0	-
1936	-	-	-	-	-	-	-	-	5.2	73.3
1937	-	-	-	-	-	-	-	-	4.7	-9.6
1938	-	-	-	-	-	-	-	-	5.2	10.6
1939	-	-	-	-	-	-	-	-	5.5	5.8
1940	-	-	-	-	-	-	-	-	6.0	9.1
1941	-	-	-	-	-	-	-	-	17.1	185.0
1942	-	-	-	-	-	-	-	-	52.0	204.1
1943	-	-	-	-	-	-	-	-	81.7	57.1
1944	-	-	-	-	-	-	-	-	89.5	9.5
1945	-	-	-	-	-	-	-	-	75.4	-15.8
1946	24.4	-	19.1	-62.5	17.4	-31.1	17.3	-2.3	19.6	-74.0
1947	14.0	-57.1	14.3	8.9	13.6	-18.2	13.1	-13.9	13.8	-29.6
1948	14.3	42.0	16.1	60.7	17.0	24.3	18.7	46.4	16.5	19.6
1949	20.4	41.6	21.7	28.0	21.3	-7.2	20.7	-10.8	21.0	27.3
1950	19.6	-19.6	19.9	6.3	19.2	-13.3	22.0	72.4	20.2	-3.8
1951	29.2	210.3	35.8	125.9	43.1	110.1	47.7	50.0	39.0	93.1
1952	48.9	10.4	51.8	25.9	53.5	13.8	55.2	13.3	52.4	34.4
1953	56.5	9.8	58.6	15.7	56.3	-14.8	55.7	-4.2	56.8	8.4
1954	52.8	-19.3	49.5	-22.8	47.0	-18.7	46.7	-2.5	49.0	-13.7
1955	46.1	-5.0	46.2	0.9	47.1	8.0	45.5	-12.9	46.2	-5.7
1956	45.7	1.8	48.0	21.7	47.2	-6.5	49.2	18.1	47.5	2.8
1957	51.4	19.1	50.8	-4.6	51.4	4.8	52.8	11.3	51.6	8.6
1958	51.5	-9.5	54.2	22.7	54.3	0.7	56.0	13.1	54.0	4.7
1959	56.3	2.2	57.7	10.3	57.6	-0.7	56.9	-4.8	57.1	5.7
1960	53.7	-20.7	54.2	3.8	55.8	12.3	57.3	11.2	55.3	-3.2
1961	56.7	-4.1	58.2	11.0	58.7	3.5	60.6	13.6	58.6	6.0
1962	63.7	22.1	65.1	9.1	66.2	6.9	66.7	3.1	65.4	11.6
1963	65.4	-7.6	65.6	1.2	67.4	11.4	67.2	-1.2	66.4	1.5
1964	67.6	2.4	68.2	3.6	67.4	-4.6	66.6	-4.7	67.5	1.7
1965	66.1	-3.0	67.6	9.4	70.0	15.0	74.1	25.6	69.5	3.0
1966	75.9	10.1	80.2	24.7	83.8	19.2	85.3	7.4	81.3	17.0
1967	91.8	34.1	91.4	-1.7	93.2	8.1	95.0	8.0	92.8	14.1
1968	98.0	13.2	98.6	2.5	99.4	3.3	100.6	4.9	99.2	6.9
1969	99.0	-6.2	99.6	2.4	102.2	10.9	101.3	-3.5	100.5	1.3
1970	101.4	0.4	99.6	-6.9	99.6	-	99.8	0.8	100.1	-0.4
1971	99.5	-1.2	99.7	0.8	100.2	2.0	100.5	1.2	100.0	-0.1
1972	107.0	28.5	108.1	4.2	105.6	-8.9	106.7	4.2	106.9	6.9
1973	108.9	8.5	108.5	-1.5	107.0	-5.4	109.8	10.9	108.5	1.5
1974	112.3	9.4	114.3	7.3	118.8	16.7	124.9	22.2	117.6	8.4
1975	126.1	3.9	127.7	5.2	129.8	6.7	134.1	13.9	129.4	10.0
1976	133.2	-2.7	134.0	2.4	135.7	5.2	140.1	13.6	135.8	4.9
1977	142.7	7.6	146.8	12.0	148.8	5.6	153.3	12.7	147.9	8.9
1978	154.9	4.2	160.7	15.8	163.7	7.7	169.4	14.7	162.2	9.7
1979	172.5	7.5	175.2	6.4	180.4	12.4	189.2	21.0	179.3	10.5
1980	198.6	21.4	208.5	21.5	208.8	0.6	220.6	24.6	209.1	16.6
1981	229.0	16.1	239.8	20.2	241.8	3.4	252.6	19.1	240.8	15.2
1982	255.8	5.2	261.0	8.4	268.0	11.2	281.4	21.6	266.6	10.7
1983	284.6	4.6	291.0	9.3	302.6	16.9	289.7	-16.0	292.0	9.5
1984	297.9	11.8	309.6	16.7	311.2	2.1	324.7	18.5	310.9	6.5
1985	330.0	6.7	338.2	10.3	352.1	17.5	356.9	5.6	344.3	10.7
1986	352.2	-5.2	364.2	14.3	381.5	20.4	373.1	-8.5	367.8	6.8
1987	375.6	2.7	384.5	9.8	387.1	2.7	392.5	5.7	384.9	4.6
1988	386.6	-5.9	386.0	-0.6	383.5	-2.6	392.0	9.2	387.0	0.5
1989	392.3	0.3	401.6	9.8	407.3	5.8	405.1	-2.1	401.6	3.8
1990	422.7	18.5	423.6	0.9	423.2	-0.4	436.5	13.2	426.5	6.2
1991	450.2	13.2	449.4	-0.7	446.8	-2.3	437.4	-8.2	445.9	4.5
1992	445.5	7.6	444.6	-0.8	452.8	7.6	452.4	-0.4	448.8	0.7
1993	442.7	-8.3	447.5	4.4	-	-	-	-	-	-

Source: "National Income and Product Account Tables: Selected NIPA Tables," *Survey of Current Business*, November 1991, U.S. Department of Commerce, Bureau of Economic Analysis, National Income and Wealth Division. - indicates that no data are available.

Gross Domestic Product

Government purchases of goods and services
Federal: Total - 1987 Dollars

In billions of constant 1987 dollars and percent. Quarterly data are seasonally adjusted and annualized. Growth rates for quarters are compound annual growth rates; changes from year to year are percentage changes.

Year	1st Quarter	% Change	2nd Quarter	% Change	3rd Quarter	% Change	4th Quarter	% Change	TOTAL	% Change
1929	-	-	-	-	-	-	-	-	21.9	-
1930	-	-	-	-	-	-	-	-	24.4	11.4
1931	-	-	-	-	-	-	-	-	24.9	2.0
1932	-	-	-	-	-	-	-	-	25.9	4.0
1933	-	-	-	-	-	-	-	-	30.9	19.3
1934	-	-	-	-	-	-	-	-	40.0	29.4
1935	-	-	-	-	-	-	-	-	40.2	0.5
1936	-	-	-	-	-	-	-	-	63.5	58.0
1937	-	-	-	-	-	-	-	-	56.8	-10.6
1938	-	-	-	-	-	-	-	-	62.3	9.7
1939	-	-	-	-	-	-	-	-	65.1	4.5
1940	-	-	-	-	-	-	-	-	76.2	17.1
1941	-	-	-	-	-	-	-	-	189.0	148.0
1942	-	-	-	-	-	-	-	-	492.5	160.6
1943	-	-	-	-	-	-	-	-	781.1	58.6
1944	-	-	-	-	-	-	-	-	884.3	13.2
1945	-	-	-	-	-	-	-	-	742.9	-16.0
1946	-	-	-	-	-	-	-	-	175.4	-76.4
1947	112.6	-	110.0	-8.9	111.9	7.1	108.3	-12.3	110.7	-36.9
1948	118.7	44.3	122.4	13.1	127.3	17.0	136.8	33.4	126.3	14.1
1949	137.1	0.9	142.3	16.1	143.1	2.3	136.8	-16.5	139.8	10.7
1950	133.7	-8.8	137.7	12.5	145.1	23.3	165.9	70.9	145.6	4.1
1951	197.3	100.0	242.0	126.3	281.7	83.6	304.2	36.0	256.3	76.0
1952	311.9	10.5	322.6	14.4	330.1	9.6	333.7	4.4	324.6	26.6
1953	341.4	9.6	346.9	6.6	339.2	-8.6	331.3	-9.0	339.7	4.7
1954	311.2	-22.1	297.7	-16.3	285.4	-15.5	276.5	-11.9	292.7	-13.8
1955	278.3	2.6	266.6	-15.8	269.4	4.3	260.4	-12.7	268.7	-8.2
1956	258.7	-2.6	264.6	9.4	263.6	-1.5	272.3	13.9	264.8	-1.5
1957	276.1	5.7	275.7	-0.6	278.8	4.6	273.8	-7.0	276.1	4.3
1958	267.8	-8.5	274.9	11.0	270.5	-6.3	274.9	6.7	272.0	-1.5
1959	266.4	-11.8	268.4	3.0	265.0	-5.0	262.8	-3.3	265.7	-2.3
1960	254.9	-11.5	257.3	3.8	259.5	3.5	264.3	7.6	259.0	-2.5
1961	263.8	-0.8	268.3	7.0	269.7	2.1	278.6	13.9	270.1	4.3
1962	286.8	12.3	289.1	3.2	288.1	-1.4	285.1	-4.1	287.3	6.4
1963	283.4	-2.4	285.9	3.6	290.0	5.9	283.4	-8.8	285.7	-0.6
1964	285.3	2.7	285.1	-0.3	280.5	-6.3	276.2	-6.0	281.8	-1.4
1965	272.3	-5.5	277.8	8.3	282.7	7.2	295.8	19.9	282.1	0.1
1966	301.1	7.4	315.3	20.2	328.5	17.8	332.3	4.7	319.3	13.2
1967	351.8	25.6	347.7	-4.6	352.0	5.0	352.2	0.2	350.9	9.9
1968	356.4	4.9	355.9	-0.6	350.3	-6.1	349.7	-0.7	353.1	0.6
1969	342.2	-8.3	343.5	1.5	339.3	-4.8	335.4	-4.5	340.1	-3.7
1970	326.3	-10.4	315.1	-13.0	310.9	-5.2	307.5	-4.3	315.0	-7.4
1971	297.7	-12.2	292.7	-6.6	289.3	-4.6	283.6	-7.7	290.8	-7.7
1972	290.7	10.4	290.6	-0.1	280.3	-13.4	275.8	-6.3	284.4	-2.2
1973	276.9	1.6	270.0	-9.6	256.8	-18.2	257.7	1.4	265.3	-6.7
1974	260.0	3.6	264.0	6.3	260.1	-5.8	266.2	9.7	262.6	-1.0
1975	262.0	-6.2	261.5	-0.8	262.6	1.7	264.6	3.1	262.7	0.0
1976	258.6	-8.8	258.1	-0.8	257.7	-0.6	258.2	0.8	258.2	-1.7
1977	259.4	1.9	264.2	7.6	264.3	0.2	264.3	-	263.1	1.9
1978	263.5	-1.2	270.4	10.9	270.3	-0.1	270.1	-0.3	268.6	2.1
1979	270.4	0.4	269.9	-0.7	273.5	5.4	272.9	-0.9	271.7	1.2
1980	281.0	12.4	288.2	10.6	285.6	-3.6	284.4	-1.7	284.8	4.8
1981	290.6	9.0	297.3	9.5	297.5	0.3	297.9	0.5	295.8	3.9
1982	299.5	2.2	301.6	2.8	307.0	7.4	316.0	12.3	306.0	3.4
1983	315.5	-0.6	319.2	4.8	326.3	9.2	322.2	-4.9	320.8	4.8
1984	323.8	2.0	329.6	7.4	328.7	-1.1	341.7	16.8	331.0	3.2
1985	343.4	2.0	350.0	7.9	363.5	16.3	363.7	0.2	355.2	7.3
1986	359.4	-4.6	369.7	12.0	385.5	18.2	377.5	-8.0	373.0	5.0
1987	376.8	-0.7	384.5	8.4	386.8	2.4	391.6	5.1	384.9	3.2
1988	379.7	-11.6	377.2	-2.6	373.7	-3.7	378.4	5.1	377.3	-2.0
1989	370.1	-8.5	376.9	7.6	381.5	5.0	376.1	-5.5	376.1	-0.3
1990	385.4	10.3	384.7	-0.7	379.6	-5.2	386.5	7.5	384.1	2.1
1991	393.8	7.8	393.6	-0.2	386.6	-6.9	372.1	-14.2	386.5	0.6
1992	372.1	-	369.2	-3.1	377.0	8.7	373.7	-3.5	373.0	-3.5
1993	357.6	-16.2	359.4	2.0	-	-	-	-	-	-

Source: "National Income and Product Account Tables: Selected NIPA Tables," *Survey of Current Business*, November 1991, U.S. Department of Commerce, Bureau of Economic Analysis, National Income and Wealth Division. - indicates that no data are available.

Gross Domestic Product
Government purchases of goods and services
Federal - National defense - Actual Dollars

In billions of actual dollars and percent. Quarterly data are seasonally adjusted and annualized. Growth rates for quarters are compound annual growth rates; changes from year to year are percentage changes.

Year	1st Quarter	% Change	2nd Quarter	% Change	3rd Quarter	% Change	4th Quarter	% Change	TOTAL	% Change
1929	-	-	-	-	-	-	-	-	-	-
1930	-	-	-	-	-	-	-	-	-	-
1931	-	-	-	-	-	-	-	-	-	-
1932	-	-	-	-	-	-	-	-	-	-
1933	-	-	-	-	-	-	-	-	-	-
1934	-	-	-	-	-	-	-	-	-	-
1935	-	-	-	-	-	-	-	-	-	-
1936	-	-	-	-	-	-	-	-	-	-
1937	-	-	-	-	-	-	-	-	-	-
1938	-	-	-	-	-	-	-	-	-	-
1939	-	-	-	-	-	-	-	-	1.3	-
1940	-	-	-	-	-	-	-	-	2.3	76.9
1941	-	-	-	-	-	-	-	-	13.8	500.0
1942	-	-	-	-	-	-	-	-	49.4	258.0
1943	-	-	-	-	-	-	-	-	79.8	61.5
1944	-	-	-	-	-	-	-	-	87.5	9.6
1945	-	-	-	-	-	-	-	-	73.7	-15.8
1946	21.9	-	16.4	-68.6	13.8	-49.9	13.5	-8.4	16.4	-77.7
1947	10.7	-60.5	9.8	-29.6	9.5	-11.7	9.9	17.9	10.0	-39.0
1948	10.6	31.4	10.9	11.8	11.2	11.5	12.5	55.2	11.3	13.0
1949	13.6	40.1	14.2	18.8	14.2	-	13.4	-20.7	13.9	23.0
1950	12.8	-16.7	12.9	3.2	14.4	55.3	17.3	108.3	14.3	2.9
1951	24.3	289.3	30.6	151.5	38.0	137.8	42.4	55.0	33.8	136.4
1952	42.7	2.9	45.9	33.5	47.3	12.8	48.9	14.2	46.2	36.7
1953	49.5	5.0	49.9	3.3	48.7	-9.3	47.9	-6.4	49.0	6.1
1954	44.8	-23.5	42.4	-19.8	40.3	-18.4	38.9	-13.2	41.6	-15.1
1955	39.1	2.1	38.6	-5.0	39.7	11.9	38.5	-11.6	39.0	-6.2
1956	38.8	3.2	40.8	22.3	40.8	-	42.4	16.6	40.7	4.4
1957	43.8	13.9	44.4	5.6	45.2	7.4	44.9	-2.6	44.6	9.6
1958	45.1	1.8	46.1	9.2	46.6	4.4	47.2	5.3	46.3	3.8
1959	46.9	-2.5	46.3	-5.0	46.3	-	45.9	-3.4	46.4	0.2
1960	44.7	-10.1	44.6	-0.9	45.6	9.3	46.2	5.4	45.3	-2.4
1961	46.9	6.2	47.6	6.1	47.8	1.7	49.4	14.1	47.9	5.7
1962	51.9	21.8	52.3	3.1	52.1	-1.5	52.0	-0.8	52.1	8.8
1963	51.3	-5.3	51.6	2.4	51.4	-1.5	51.6	1.6	51.5	-1.2
1964	51.2	-3.1	50.9	-2.3	50.3	-4.6	49.4	-7.0	50.4	-2.1
1965	48.6	-6.3	49.7	9.4	50.9	10.0	54.7	33.4	51.0	1.2
1966	56.8	16.3	60.1	25.3	64.4	31.8	66.8	15.8	62.0	21.6
1967	71.3	29.8	72.4	6.3	74.5	12.1	75.5	5.5	73.4	18.4
1968	78.3	15.7	79.4	5.7	79.1	-1.5	79.8	3.6	79.1	7.8
1969	77.8	-9.7	78.2	2.1	79.9	9.0	79.9	-	78.9	-0.3
1970	78.8	-5.4	76.0	-13.5	76.1	0.5	76.2	0.5	76.8	-2.7
1971	75.6	-3.1	73.8	-9.2	72.9	-4.8	74.0	6.2	74.1	-3.5
1972	78.3	25.3	78.6	1.5	76.1	-12.1	76.7	3.2	77.4	4.5
1973	78.0	7.0	77.6	-2.0	75.8	-9.0	78.5	15.0	77.5	0.1
1974	79.1	3.1	82.0	15.5	82.9	4.5	86.5	18.5	82.6	6.6
1975	87.7	5.7	88.3	2.8	89.9	7.4	92.5	12.1	89.6	8.5
1976	91.4	-4.7	92.3	4.0	93.8	6.7	96.2	10.6	93.4	4.2
1977	98.1	8.1	100.7	11.0	101.7	4.0	103.0	5.2	100.9	8.0
1978	104.3	5.1	108.1	15.4	110.1	7.6	113.0	11.0	108.9	7.9
1979	116.0	11.0	118.5	8.9	122.9	15.7	130.0	25.2	121.9	11.9
1980	136.3	20.8	139.8	10.7	142.5	8.0	152.2	30.1	142.7	17.1
1981	157.3	14.1	165.4	22.2	169.0	9.0	178.1	23.3	167.5	17.4
1982	182.5	10.3	190.7	19.2	196.6	13.0	205.5	19.4	193.8	15.7
1983	206.3	1.6	212.9	13.4	215.8	5.6	222.8	13.6	214.4	10.6
1984	227.2	8.1	231.0	6.9	231.4	0.7	242.9	21.4	233.1	8.7
1985	246.3	5.7	253.5	12.2	265.9	21.0	268.6	4.1	258.6	10.9
1986	264.6	-5.8	275.1	16.8	288.5	21.0	278.6	-13.0	276.7	7.0
1987	283.8	7.7	291.6	11.5	296.9	7.5	295.8	-1.5	292.1	5.6
1988	296.7	1.2	294.8	-2.5	294.0	-1.1	296.8	3.9	295.6	1.2
1989	293.5	-4.4	298.2	6.6	305.3	9.9	302.5	-3.6	299.9	1.5
1990	312.1	13.3	312.5	0.5	309.1	-4.3	322.5	18.5	314.0	4.7
1991	331.4	11.5	326.3	-6.0	321.2	-6.1	311.2	-11.9	322.5	2.7
1992	312.3	1.4	310.4	-2.4	316.7	8.4	315.7	-1.3	313.8	-2.7
1993	304.8	-13.1	307.6	3.7	-	-	-	-	-	-

Source: "National Income and Product Account Tables: Selected NIPA Tables," *Survey of Current Business*, November 1991, U.S. Department of Commerce, Bureau of Economic Analysis, National Income and Wealth Division. - indicates that no data are available.

Gross Domestic Product
Government purchases of goods and services
Federal - National defense - 1987 Dollars

In billions of constant 1987 dollars and percent. Quarterly data are seasonally adjusted and annualized. Growth rates for quarters are compound annual growth rates; changes from year to year are percentage changes.

Year	1st Quarter	% Change	2nd Quarter	% Change	3rd Quarter	% Change	4th Quarter	% Change	TOTAL	% Change
1929	-	-	-	-	-	-	-	-	-	-
1930	-	-	-	-	-	-	-	-	-	-
1931	-	-	-	-	-	-	-	-	-	-
1932	-	-	-	-	-	-	-	-	-	-
1933	-	-	-	-	-	-	-	-	-	-
1934	-	-	-	-	-	-	-	-	-	-
1935	-	-	-	-	-	-	-	-	-	-
1936	-	-	-	-	-	-	-	-	-	-
1937	-	-	-	-	-	-	-	-	-	-
1938	-	-	-	-	-	-	-	-	-	-
1939	-	-	-	-	-	-	-	-	-	-
1940	-	-	-	-	-	-	-	-	-	-
1941	-	-	-	-	-	-	-	-	-	-
1942	-	-	-	-	-	-	-	-	-	-
1943	-	-	-	-	-	-	-	-	-	-
1944	-	-	-	-	-	-	-	-	-	-
1945	-	-	-	-	-	-	-	-	-	-
1946	-	-	-	-	-	-	-	-	-	-
1947	-	-	-	-	-	-	-	-	-	-
1948	-	-	-	-	-	-	-	-	-	-
1949	-	-	-	-	-	-	-	-	-	-
1950	-	-	-	-	-	-	-	-	-	-
1951	-	-	-	-	-	-	-	-	-	-
1952	-	-	-	-	-	-	-	-	-	-
1953	-	-	-	-	-	-	-	-	-	-
1954	-	-	-	-	-	-	-	-	-	-
1955	-	-	-	-	-	-	-	-	-	-
1956	-	-	-	-	-	-	-	-	-	-
1957	-	-	-	-	-	-	-	-	-	-
1958	-	-	-	-	-	-	-	-	-	-
1959	-	-	-	-	-	-	-	-	-	-
1960	-	-	-	-	-	-	-	-	-	-
1961	-	-	-	-	-	-	-	-	-	-
1962	-	-	-	-	-	-	-	-	-	-
1963	-	-	-	-	-	-	-	-	-	-
1964	-	-	-	-	-	-	-	-	-	-
1965	-	-	-	-	-	-	-	-	-	-
1966	-	-	-	-	-	-	-	-	-	-
1967	-	-	-	-	-	-	-	-	-	-
1968	-	-	-	-	-	-	-	-	-	-
1969	-	-	-	-	-	-	-	-	-	-
1970	-	-	-	-	-	-	-	-	-	-
1971	-	-	-	-	-	-	-	-	-	-
1972	216.8	-	215.1	-3.1	205.0	-17.5	201.5	-6.7	209.6	-
1973	201.1	-0.8	194.6	-12.3	183.3	-21.3	186.0	6.0	191.3	-8.7
1974	184.3	-3.6	188.9	10.4	182.8	-12.3	187.1	9.7	185.8	-2.9
1975	185.1	-4.2	183.9	-2.6	185.0	2.4	185.7	1.5	184.9	-0.5
1976	180.2	-11.3	180.3	0.2	179.7	-1.3	179.3	-0.9	179.9	-2.7
1977	180.4	2.5	183.7	7.5	182.3	-3.0	179.9	-5.2	181.6	0.9
1978	179.3	-1.3	184.0	10.9	183.2	-1.7	182.0	-2.6	182.1	0.3
1979	183.2	2.7	182.8	-0.9	186.3	7.9	188.0	3.7	185.1	1.6
1980	192.2	9.2	194.2	4.2	194.1	-0.2	196.4	4.8	194.2	4.9
1981	200.1	7.8	206.6	13.6	208.9	4.5	210.2	2.5	206.4	6.3
1982	213.3	6.0	219.1	11.3	223.6	8.5	229.4	10.8	221.4	7.3
1983	227.6	-3.1	232.4	8.7	233.9	2.6	242.9	16.3	234.2	5.8
1984	241.7	-2.0	244.3	4.4	243.0	-2.1	254.3	19.9	245.8	5.0
1985	255.0	1.1	261.7	10.9	273.7	19.6	272.1	-2.3	265.6	8.1
1986	269.2	-4.2	279.1	15.5	292.1	20.0	282.2	-12.9	280.6	5.6
1987	284.9	3.9	291.6	9.7	296.8	7.3	295.0	-2.4	292.1	4.1
1988	290.8	-5.6	287.1	-5.0	284.6	-3.4	285.7	1.6	287.0	-1.7
1989	276.7	-12.0	280.4	5.5	286.9	9.6	281.5	-7.3	281.4	-2.0
1990	285.3	5.5	285.0	-0.4	278.5	-8.8	285.7	10.7	283.6	0.8
1991	292.0	9.1	288.7	-4.4	279.4	-12.3	264.9	-19.2	281.3	-0.8
1992	261.2	-5.5	257.9	-5.0	264.4	10.5	261.3	-4.6	261.2	-7.1
1993	246.0	-21.4	246.4	0.7	-	-	-	-	-	-

Source: "National Income and Product Account Tables: Selected NIPA Tables," *Survey of Current Business*, November 1991, U.S. Department of Commerce, Bureau of Economic Analysis, National Income and Wealth Division. - indicates that no data are available.

Gross Domestic Product
Government purchases of goods and services
Federal - Nondefense - Actual Dollars

In billions of actual dollars and percent. Quarterly data are seasonally adjusted and annualized. Growth rates for quarters are compound annual growth rates; changes from year to year are percentage changes.

Year	1st Quarter	% Change	2nd Quarter	% Change	3rd Quarter	% Change	4th Quarter	% Change	TOTAL	% Change
1929	-	-	-	-	-	-	-	-	-	-
1930	-	-	-	-	-	-	-	-	-	-
1931	-	-	-	-	-	-	-	-	-	-
1932	-	-	-	-	-	-	-	-	-	-
1933	-	-	-	-	-	-	-	-	-	-
1934	-	-	-	-	-	-	-	-	-	-
1935	-	-	-	-	-	-	-	-	-	-
1936	-	-	-	-	-	-	-	-	-	-
1937	-	-	-	-	-	-	-	-	-	-
1938	-	-	-	-	-	-	-	-	-	-
1939	-	-	-	-	-	-	-	-	4.2	-
1940	-	-	-	-	-	-	-	-	3.7	-11.9
1941	-	-	-	-	-	-	-	-	3.3	-10.8
1942	-	-	-	-	-	-	-	-	2.5	-24.2
1943	-	-	-	-	-	-	-	-	1.9	-24.0
1944	-	-	-	-	-	-	-	-	2.0	5.3
1945	-	-	-	-	-	-	-	-	1.7	-15.0
1946	2.6	-	2.7	16.3	3.7	252.7	3.8	11.3	3.2	88.2
1947	3.4	-35.9	4.5	206.9	4.1	-31.1	3.2	-62.9	3.8	18.8
1948	3.7	78.7	5.1	261.0	5.8	67.3	6.2	30.6	5.2	36.8
1949	6.8	44.7	7.5	48.0	7.0	-24.1	7.3	18.3	7.2	38.5
1950	6.8	-24.7	7.1	18.8	4.8	-79.1	4.7	-8.1	5.8	-19.4
1951	5.0	28.1	5.2	17.0	5.1	-7.5	5.3	16.6	5.1	-12.1
1952	6.2	87.3	5.9	-18.0	6.3	30.0	6.4	6.5	6.2	21.6
1953	7.1	51.5	8.7	125.4	7.6	-41.8	7.8	10.9	7.8	25.8
1954	8.0	10.7	7.1	-38.0	6.7	-20.7	7.8	83.7	7.4	-5.1
1955	6.9	-38.8	7.5	39.6	7.5	-	7.0	-24.1	7.2	-2.7
1956	6.8	-10.9	7.1	18.8	6.4	-34.0	6.8	27.4	6.8	-5.6
1957	7.6	56.0	6.3	-52.8	6.2	-6.2	7.8	150.5	7.0	2.9
1958	6.4	-54.7	8.1	156.6	7.7	-18.3	8.8	70.6	7.7	10.0
1959	9.4	30.2	11.5	124.0	11.3	-6.8	11.0	-10.2	10.8	40.3
1960	9.1	-53.2	9.6	23.9	10.2	27.4	11.1	40.2	10.0	-7.4
1961	9.7	-41.7	10.6	42.6	10.9	11.8	11.2	11.5	10.6	6.0
1962	11.8	23.2	12.8	38.5	14.1	47.2	14.7	18.1	13.3	25.5
1963	14.1	-15.4	14.0	-2.8	16.0	70.6	15.6	-9.6	14.9	12.0
1964	16.4	22.1	17.3	23.8	17.1	-4.5	17.2	2.4	17.0	14.1
1965	17.6	9.6	17.9	7.0	19.1	29.6	19.3	4.3	18.5	8.8
1966	19.1	-4.1	20.1	22.6	19.4	-13.2	18.4	-19.1	19.3	4.3
1967	20.4	51.1	19.0	-24.8	18.7	-6.2	19.5	18.2	19.4	0.5
1968	19.8	6.3	19.2	-11.6	20.4	27.4	20.8	8.1	20.0	3.1
1969	21.1	5.9	21.5	7.8	22.4	17.8	21.4	-16.7	21.6	8.0
1970	22.6	24.4	23.6	18.9	23.5	-1.7	23.6	1.7	23.3	7.9
1971	23.9	5.2	25.9	37.9	27.4	25.3	26.5	-12.5	25.9	11.2
1972	28.7	37.6	29.5	11.6	29.6	1.4	29.9	4.1	29.4	13.5
1973	30.9	14.1	30.9	-	31.2	3.9	31.3	1.3	31.1	5.8
1974	33.2	26.6	32.3	-10.4	35.9	52.6	38.4	30.9	35.0	12.5
1975	38.4	-	39.3	9.7	39.9	6.2	41.6	18.2	39.8	13.7
1976	41.8	1.9	41.7	-1.0	41.9	1.9	44.0	21.6	42.4	6.5
1977	44.6	5.6	46.0	13.2	47.1	9.9	50.2	29.0	47.0	10.8
1978	50.6	3.2	52.6	16.8	53.6	7.8	56.4	22.6	53.3	13.4
1979	56.4	-	56.7	2.1	57.5	5.8	59.2	12.4	57.5	7.9
1980	62.4	23.4	68.7	46.9	66.2	-13.8	68.4	14.0	66.4	15.5
1981	71.7	20.7	74.4	15.9	72.8	-8.3	74.4	9.1	73.3	10.4
1982	73.2	-6.3	70.3	-14.9	71.4	6.4	75.9	27.7	72.7	-0.8
1983	78.3	13.3	78.1	-1.0	86.8	52.6	66.9	-64.7	77.5	6.6
1984	70.7	24.7	78.6	52.8	79.8	6.2	81.9	10.9	77.8	0.4
1985	83.7	9.1	84.7	4.9	86.2	7.3	88.3	10.1	85.7	10.2
1986	87.6	-3.1	89.1	7.0	93.1	19.2	94.5	6.2	91.1	6.3
1987	91.8	-10.9	92.9	4.9	90.1	-11.5	96.7	32.7	92.9	2.0
1988	89.9	-25.3	91.2	5.9	89.5	-7.3	95.2	28.0	91.4	-1.6
1989	98.7	15.5	103.4	20.5	101.9	-5.7	102.6	2.8	101.7	11.3
1990	110.6	35.0	111.2	2.2	114.1	10.8	114.0	-0.4	112.5	10.6
1991	118.7	17.5	123.0	15.3	125.6	8.7	126.2	1.9	123.4	9.7
1992	133.1	23.7	134.2	3.3	136.1	5.8	136.7	1.8	135.0	9.4
1993	137.9	3.6	140.0	6.2	-	-	-	-	-	-

Source: "National Income and Product Account Tables: Selected NIPA Tables," *Survey of Current Business*, November 1991, U.S. Department of Commerce, Bureau of Economic Analysis, National Income and Wealth Division. - indicates that no data are available.

Gross Domestic Product
Government purchases of goods and services
Federal - Nondefense - 1987 Dollars

In billions of constant 1987 dollars and percent. Quarterly data are seasonally adjusted and annualized. Growth rates for quarters are compound annual growth rates; changes from year to year are percentage changes.

Year	1st Quarter	% Change	2nd Quarter	% Change	3rd Quarter	% Change	4th Quarter	% Change	TOTAL	% Change
1929	-	-	-	-	-	-	-	-	-	-
1930	-	-	-	-	-	-	-	-	-	-
1931	-	-	-	-	-	-	-	-	-	-
1932	-	-	-	-	-	-	-	-	-	-
1933	-	-	-	-	-	-	-	-	-	-
1934	-	-	-	-	-	-	-	-	-	-
1935	-	-	-	-	-	-	-	-	-	-
1936	-	-	-	-	-	-	-	-	-	-
1937	-	-	-	-	-	-	-	-	-	-
1938	-	-	-	-	-	-	-	-	-	-
1939	-	-	-	-	-	-	-	-	-	-
1940	-	-	-	-	-	-	-	-	-	-
1941	-	-	-	-	-	-	-	-	-	-
1942	-	-	-	-	-	-	-	-	-	-
1943	-	-	-	-	-	-	-	-	-	-
1944	-	-	-	-	-	-	-	-	-	-
1945	-	-	-	-	-	-	-	-	-	-
1946	-	-	-	-	-	-	-	-	-	-
1947	-	-	-	-	-	-	-	-	-	-
1948	-	-	-	-	-	-	-	-	-	-
1949	-	-	-	-	-	-	-	-	-	-
1950	-	-	-	-	-	-	-	-	-	-
1951	-	-	-	-	-	-	-	-	-	-
1952	-	-	-	-	-	-	-	-	-	-
1953	-	-	-	-	-	-	-	-	-	-
1954	-	-	-	-	-	-	-	-	-	-
1955	-	-	-	-	-	-	-	-	-	-
1956	-	-	-	-	-	-	-	-	-	-
1957	-	-	-	-	-	-	-	-	-	-
1958	-	-	-	-	-	-	-	-	-	-
1959	-	-	-	-	-	-	-	-	-	-
1960	-	-	-	-	-	-	-	-	-	-
1961	-	-	-	-	-	-	-	-	-	-
1962	-	-	-	-	-	-	-	-	-	-
1963	-	-	-	-	-	-	-	-	-	-
1964	-	-	-	-	-	-	-	-	-	-
1965	-	-	-	-	-	-	-	-	-	-
1966	-	-	-	-	-	-	-	-	-	-
1967	-	-	-	-	-	-	-	-	-	-
1968	-	-	-	-	-	-	-	-	-	-
1969	-	-	-	-	-	-	-	-	-	-
1970	-	-	-	-	-	-	-	-	-	-
1971	-	-	-	-	-	-	-	-	-	-
1972	74.0	-	75.5	8.4	75.4	-0.5	74.3	-5.7	74.8	-
1973	75.8	8.3	75.3	-2.6	73.4	-9.7	71.8	-8.4	74.1	-0.9
1974	75.7	23.6	75.0	-3.6	77.4	13.4	79.2	9.6	76.8	3.6
1975	76.9	-11.1	77.6	3.7	77.6	-	78.9	6.9	77.8	1.3
1976	78.4	-2.5	77.8	-3.0	78.0	1.0	78.9	4.7	78.3	0.6
1977	78.9	-	80.5	8.4	81.9	7.1	84.4	12.8	81.4	4.0
1978	84.2	-0.9	86.5	11.4	87.1	2.8	88.1	4.7	86.5	6.3
1979	87.2	-4.0	87.1	-0.5	87.1	-	85.0	-9.3	86.6	0.1
1980	88.8	19.1	94.0	25.6	91.5	-10.2	88.1	-14.1	90.6	4.6
1981	90.5	11.4	90.7	0.9	88.6	-8.9	87.7	-4.0	89.4	-1.3
1982	86.2	-6.7	82.5	-16.1	83.4	4.4	86.6	16.3	84.7	-5.3
1983	87.9	6.1	86.8	-4.9	92.3	27.9	79.3	-45.5	86.6	2.2
1984	82.1	14.9	85.3	16.5	85.7	1.9	87.4	8.2	85.1	-1.7
1985	88.4	4.7	88.4	-	89.8	6.5	91.6	8.3	89.5	5.2
1986	90.3	-5.6	90.6	1.3	93.4	12.9	95.3	8.4	92.4	3.2
1987	92.0	-13.1	92.9	4.0	90.0	-11.9	96.6	32.7	92.9	0.5
1988	88.9	-28.3	90.1	5.5	89.1	-4.4	92.7	17.2	90.2	-2.9
1989	93.4	3.1	96.5	14.0	94.5	-8.0	94.7	0.8	94.8	5.1
1990	100.1	24.8	99.8	-1.2	101.1	5.3	100.8	-1.2	100.4	5.9
1991	101.8	4.0	104.9	12.7	107.2	9.1	107.2	-	105.3	4.9
1992	110.9	14.5	111.3	1.5	112.5	4.4	112.4	-0.4	111.8	6.2
1993	111.5	-3.2	113.0	5.5	-	-	-	-	-	-

Source: "National Income and Product Account Tables: Selected NIPA Tables," *Survey of Current Business*, November 1991, U.S. Department of Commerce, Bureau of Economic Analysis, National Income and Wealth Division. - indicates that no data are available.

Gross Domestic Product

Government purchases of goods and services
State and local - Actual Dollars

In billions of actual dollars and percent. Quarterly data are seasonally adjusted and annualized. Growth rates for quarters are compound annual growth rates; changes from year to year are percentage changes.

Year	1st Quarter	% Change	2nd Quarter	% Change	3rd Quarter	% Change	4th Quarter	% Change	TOTAL	% Change
1929	-	-	-	-	-	-	-	-	7.1	-
1930	-	-	-	-	-	-	-	-	7.6	7.0
1931	-	-	-	-	-	-	-	-	7.5	-1.3
1932	-	-	-	-	-	-	-	-	6.4	-14.7
1933	-	-	-	-	-	-	-	-	5.9	-7.8
1934	-	-	-	-	-	-	-	-	6.6	11.9
1935	-	-	-	-	-	-	-	-	6.9	4.5
1936	-	-	-	-	-	-	-	-	6.9	-
1937	-	-	-	-	-	-	-	-	7.1	2.9
1938	-	-	-	-	-	-	-	-	7.4	4.2
1939	-	-	-	-	-	-	-	-	8.1	9.5
1940	-	-	-	-	-	-	-	-	7.8	-3.7
1941	-	-	-	-	-	-	-	-	7.7	-1.3
1942	-	-	-	-	-	-	-	-	7.6	-1.3
1943	-	-	-	-	-	-	-	-	7.3	-3.9
1944	-	-	-	-	-	-	-	-	7.4	1.4
1945	-	-	-	-	-	-	-	-	7.9	6.8
1946	8.7	-	9.2	25.0	9.9	34.1	10.8	41.6	9.6	21.5
1947	11.7	37.7	12.1	14.4	12.6	17.6	13.3	24.1	12.4	29.2
1948	13.7	12.6	14.4	22.1	15.3	27.4	15.9	16.6	14.8	19.4
1949	16.5	16.0	17.2	18.1	18.0	19.9	18.3	6.8	17.5	18.2
1950	18.6	6.7	19.0	8.9	19.5	10.9	20.0	10.7	19.3	10.3
1951	20.4	8.2	21.1	14.4	21.6	9.8	21.9	5.7	21.3	10.4
1952	22.0	1.8	22.7	13.3	22.5	-3.5	23.1	11.1	22.6	6.1
1953	23.8	12.7	23.7	-1.7	24.4	12.3	25.0	10.2	24.2	7.1
1954	26.0	17.0	26.6	9.6	27.6	15.9	27.8	2.9	27.0	11.6
1955	28.9	16.8	29.4	7.1	29.7	4.1	30.2	6.9	29.6	9.6
1956	31.2	13.9	32.0	10.7	32.7	9.0	33.4	8.8	32.3	9.1
1957	34.6	15.2	35.4	9.6	36.1	8.1	37.0	10.4	35.8	10.8
1958	38.1	12.4	39.0	9.8	40.0	10.7	40.9	9.3	39.5	10.3
1959	41.7	8.1	41.9	1.9	41.9	-	41.7	-1.9	41.8	5.8
1960	42.9	12.0	44.2	12.7	45.1	8.4	45.8	6.4	44.5	6.5
1961	47.5	15.7	47.6	0.8	48.4	6.9	50.2	15.7	48.4	8.8
1962	50.4	1.6	51.0	4.8	51.7	5.6	52.6	7.1	51.4	6.2
1963	54.1	11.9	54.9	6.0	56.5	12.2	57.8	9.5	55.8	8.6
1964	59.0	8.6	60.6	11.3	61.5	6.1	62.5	6.7	60.9	9.1
1965	63.6	7.2	65.6	13.2	68.2	16.8	69.7	9.1	66.8	9.7
1966	71.6	11.4	73.3	9.8	75.2	10.8	78.1	16.3	74.6	11.7
1967	80.4	12.3	81.7	6.6	83.1	7.0	85.6	12.6	82.7	10.9
1968	88.5	14.3	91.4	13.8	93.5	9.5	96.1	11.6	92.3	11.6
1969	98.0	8.1	100.6	11.0	102.4	7.4	104.1	6.8	101.3	9.8
1970	107.5	13.7	110.4	11.2	114.8	16.9	117.5	9.7	112.6	11.2
1971	120.6	11.0	123.5	10.0	125.2	5.6	128.1	9.6	124.3	10.4
1972	131.0	9.4	132.3	4.0	135.5	10.0	139.9	13.6	134.7	8.4
1973	143.7	11.3	146.9	9.2	150.7	10.8	155.4	13.1	149.2	10.8
1974	161.5	16.7	168.8	19.3	174.0	12.9	178.5	10.8	170.7	14.4
1975	184.4	13.9	189.1	10.6	194.7	12.4	199.7	10.7	192.0	12.5
1976	204.2	9.3	204.3	0.2	205.6	2.6	207.8	4.3	205.5	7.0
1977	213.1	10.6	218.9	11.3	222.5	6.7	225.9	6.3	220.1	7.1
1978	230.9	9.2	237.0	11.0	245.6	15.3	252.1	11.0	241.4	9.7
1979	254.6	4.0	264.8	17.0	274.5	15.5	282.7	12.5	269.2	11.5
1980	291.9	13.7	295.5	5.0	298.6	4.3	305.8	10.0	298.0	10.7
1981	316.4	14.6	317.0	0.8	320.3	4.2	327.4	9.2	320.3	7.5
1982	331.3	4.9	338.8	9.4	344.0	6.3	350.3	7.5	341.1	6.5
1983	352.9	3.0	356.7	4.4	363.7	8.1	367.9	4.7	360.3	5.6
1984	378.4	11.9	385.8	8.1	393.1	7.8	402.2	9.6	389.9	8.2
1985	412.2	10.3	424.2	12.2	433.4	9.0	442.4	8.6	428.1	9.8
1986	453.7	10.6	461.2	6.8	469.7	7.6	476.6	6.0	465.3	8.7
1987	485.0	7.2	491.5	5.5	501.0	8.0	509.0	6.5	496.6	6.7
1988	518.1	7.3	527.8	7.7	535.1	5.6	545.7	8.2	531.7	7.1
1989	558.1	9.4	568.6	7.7	578.4	7.1	589.3	7.8	573.6	7.9
1990	605.0	11.1	613.7	5.9	625.1	7.6	640.0	9.9	620.9	8.2
1991	642.9	1.8	650.5	4.8	657.3	4.2	662.8	3.4	653.4	5.2
1992	673.0	6.3	681.2	5.0	686.2	3.0	691.4	3.1	683.0	4.5
1993	697.0	3.3	711.1	8.3	-	-	-	-	-	-

Source: "National Income and Product Account Tables: Selected NIPA Tables," *Survey of Current Business*, November 1991, U.S. Department of Commerce, Bureau of Economic Analysis, National Income and Wealth Division. - indicates that no data are available.

Gross Domestic Product

Government purchases of goods and services
State and local - 1987 Dollars

In billions of constant 1987 dollars and percent. Quarterly data are seasonally adjusted and annualized. Growth rates for quarters are compound annual growth rates; changes from year to year are percentage changes.

Year	1st Quarter	% Change	2nd Quarter	% Change	3rd Quarter	% Change	4th Quarter	% Change	TOTAL	% Change
1929	-	-	-	-	-	-	-	-	90.7	-
1930	-	-	-	-	-	-	-	-	97.6	7.6
1931	-	-	-	-	-	-	-	-	100.7	3.2
1932	-	-	-	-	-	-	-	-	94.6	-6.1
1933	-	-	-	-	-	-	-	-	85.2	-9.9
1934	-	-	-	-	-	-	-	-	91.4	7.3
1935	-	-	-	-	-	-	-	-	95.6	4.6
1936	-	-	-	-	-	-	-	-	95.1	-0.5
1937	-	-	-	-	-	-	-	-	95.4	0.3
1938	-	-	-	-	-	-	-	-	100.2	5.0
1939	-	-	-	-	-	-	-	-	108.9	8.7
1940	-	-	-	-	-	-	-	-	104.5	-4.0
1941	-	-	-	-	-	-	-	-	100.2	-4.1
1942	-	-	-	-	-	-	-	-	93.5	-6.7
1943	-	-	-	-	-	-	-	-	86.7	-7.3
1944	-	-	-	-	-	-	-	-	83.7	-3.5
1945	-	-	-	-	-	-	-	-	86.5	3.3
1946	-	-	-	-	-	-	-	-	95.6	10.5
1947	104.9	-	107.1	8.7	109.4	8.9	111.2	6.7	108.1	13.1
1948	111.0	-0.7	113.3	8.5	115.1	6.5	117.7	9.3	114.3	5.7
1949	122.2	16.2	127.9	20.0	132.7	15.9	135.2	7.8	129.5	13.3
1950	137.9	8.2	138.9	2.9	139.2	0.9	139.6	1.2	138.9	7.3
1951	138.7	-2.6	140.8	6.2	141.6	2.3	141.6	-	140.7	1.3
1952	141.8	0.6	144.3	7.2	141.5	-7.5	144.5	8.8	143.0	1.6
1953	147.5	8.6	147.5	-	151.0	9.8	154.3	9.0	150.1	5.0
1954	159.2	13.3	159.9	1.8	163.9	10.4	164.8	2.2	162.0	7.9
1955	170.9	15.6	173.0	5.0	173.3	0.7	174.6	3.0	173.0	6.8
1956	176.3	4.0	178.7	5.6	180.0	2.9	181.8	4.1	179.2	3.6
1957	185.7	8.9	187.2	3.3	189.9	5.9	194.0	8.9	189.2	5.6
1958	198.8	10.3	202.0	6.6	205.9	7.9	209.2	6.6	204.0	7.8
1959	209.7	1.0	209.8	0.2	210.0	0.4	209.1	-1.7	209.6	2.7
1960	211.9	5.5	216.4	8.8	220.4	7.6	222.9	4.6	217.9	4.0
1961	229.9	13.2	228.3	-2.8	231.0	4.8	236.5	9.9	231.4	6.2
1962	234.0	-4.2	235.3	2.2	238.0	4.7	240.2	3.7	236.9	2.4
1963	244.7	7.7	247.0	3.8	253.6	11.1	257.1	5.6	250.6	5.8
1964	261.1	6.4	266.5	8.5	269.3	4.3	272.2	4.4	267.3	6.7
1965	274.4	3.3	281.5	10.8	289.5	11.9	293.8	6.1	284.8	6.5
1966	297.9	5.7	300.2	3.1	303.3	4.2	310.9	10.4	303.1	6.4
1967	313.9	3.9	315.5	2.1	316.7	1.5	321.7	6.5	317.0	4.6
1968	326.5	6.1	332.8	7.9	336.4	4.4	339.1	3.2	333.7	5.3
1969	340.4	1.5	342.7	2.7	342.4	-0.3	342.0	-0.5	341.9	2.5
1970	345.2	3.8	347.1	2.2	354.3	8.6	356.9	3.0	350.9	2.6
1971	358.4	1.7	360.7	2.6	361.1	0.4	366.1	5.7	361.6	3.0
1972	367.2	1.2	365.4	-1.9	368.2	3.1	373.7	6.1	368.6	1.9
1973	375.3	1.7	375.9	0.6	380.0	4.4	384.2	4.5	378.9	2.8
1974	388.8	4.9	394.6	6.1	394.1	-0.5	393.9	-0.2	392.9	3.7
1975	397.1	3.3	398.0	0.9	402.8	4.9	405.1	2.3	400.8	2.0
1976	406.5	1.4	400.8	-5.5	399.3	-1.5	397.7	-1.6	401.1	0.1
1977	399.9	2.2	402.5	2.6	401.7	-0.8	400.0	-1.7	401.0	-0.0
1978	402.6	2.6	405.4	2.8	411.5	6.2	414.0	2.5	408.4	1.8
1979	410.8	-3.1	417.1	6.3	420.1	2.9	422.4	2.2	417.6	2.3
1980	423.7	1.2	419.7	-3.7	416.2	-3.3	417.8	1.5	419.4	0.4
1981	421.6	3.7	416.2	-5.0	414.2	-1.9	417.5	3.2	417.4	-0.5
1982	415.2	-2.2	417.6	2.3	417.6	-	419.9	2.2	417.6	0.0
1983	419.8	-0.1	421.2	1.3	425.3	4.0	425.9	0.6	423.0	1.3
1984	430.4	4.3	433.7	3.1	437.3	3.4	442.6	4.9	436.0	3.1
1985	448.1	5.1	455.8	7.1	462.2	5.7	466.7	4.0	458.2	5.1
1986	475.4	7.7	480.9	4.7	486.0	4.3	487.3	1.1	482.4	5.3
1987	492.3	4.2	494.6	1.9	498.1	2.9	501.4	2.7	496.6	2.9
1988	503.9	2.0	508.3	3.5	510.0	1.3	516.1	4.9	509.6	2.6
1989	520.7	3.6	525.4	3.7	530.7	4.1	536.5	4.4	528.3	3.7
1990	542.8	4.8	545.9	2.3	549.6	2.7	555.8	4.6	548.5	3.8
1991	555.1	-0.5	558.7	2.6	561.0	1.7	564.1	2.2	559.7	2.0
1992	571.0	5.0	571.5	0.4	573.2	1.2	573.2	-	572.2	2.2
1993	573.7	0.3	581.6	5.6	-	-	-	-	-	-

Source: "National Income and Product Account Tables: Selected NIPA Tables," *Survey of Current Business*, November 1991, U.S. Department of Commerce, Bureau of Economic Analysis, National Income and Wealth Division. - indicates that no data are available.

CHAPTER 3

BUSINESS CYCLE INDICATORS

BUSINESS CYCLE INDICATORS

The indexes of economic indicators, also called business cycle indicators, are used by government, industry, and other institutions to forecast tendencies in the national economy. They are composites of several statistical series which tend to signal *changes* in the economy's general direction. They are "business cycle indicators" because they can predict the beginnings and ends of periods of sustained growth; each such period is a single business cycle; each ends when economic growth stops, as measured by Gross Domestic Product (GDP), or shows negative growth.

Arthur F. Burns and Wesley C. Mitchell have described business cycles as follows:

> Business cycles are a type of fluctuation found in the aggregate economic activity of nations that organize their work mainly in business enterprises; a cycle consists of expansions occurring at about the same time in many economic activities, followed by similarly general recessions, contractions, and revivals which merge into the expansion phase of the next cycle; this sequence of changes is recurrent but not periodic; in duration business cycles vary from more than one year to ten or twelve years; they are not divisible into shorter cycles of similar character with amplitudes approximating their own. (Reference 2.)

History

Business cycle indicators were developed by the National Bureau of Economic Research, Inc. (NBER). The first list of cyclic indicators was published by Burns and Mitchell in 1938. Publication of the NBER's indicators by the U.S. Department of Commerce began in 1961. Commerce began to publish composite indexes of leading, coincident, and lagging indicators in 1968. The series are available from 1948 to the present time. The series have been revised from time to time. Significant changes were made in 1983, 1987, and in 1989. After changes are made, the indexes are restated in the new format for past years.

Characteristics of the Indexes

Three composite indexes are used to predict the peaks and troughs of business cycles—the highest points of growth and the bottoms of periods of decline. The composite index of *Leading Indicators* tends to signal a change (downturn or upturn) before the economy actually turns down or resumes growth. The composite index of *Coincident Indicators* tends to turn up or down at the same time as the economy. And the composite index of *Lagging Indicators* shows changes after they have already become visible.

A graphic presentation following this introductory text illustrates the relationships between the indicator series and Gross Domestic Product (GDP) for the period 1956-1993. The vertical rectangular areas indicate periods of recession as commonly defined.

Each composite index combines several component indexes which behave in the appropriate manner. For example, the composite index of leading indicators is formed of several other leading indicators. A composite of selected leading, coincident, or lagging indicators is used because, over time, it has been found that the composite index predicts more accurately than any one of the components taken alone. Revisions of the business cycle indicators have typically taken the form of removing and adding components and changing the relative weight assigned to each component in calculating the composite index. Components will be discussed in separate sections.

Presentation

Data for each of the composite indexes are presented in sequence. Each section begins with a discussion of the composite index and its components. Tables with the indexes follow. The composite indexes are shown in two formats: the actual index and change from previous month.

Format and Calculation

Data are presented, in most cases, for the years 1948 to 1993 and for each month of the year.

The composite indexes relate to a base year. The base year at present (1994) is 1987, with the value of 100. All other data points are calibrated to 1987. The 1987 base value, in turn, is produced by averaging the 1987 monthly values; for this reason, monthly values in 1987 will be very near 100. The significance of the composite indexes lies in month-to-month changes rather than in absolute value. A change is signalled when the index increases or decreases over a period of three or more months.

Values for the component indexes are shown in various formats (hours, weeks, dollars, percentages, index values). The formats are noted at the top of each component table.

Month-to-month percentage changes in the component series are used to construct the composite index. Calculation of each component's contribution is made by applying mathematical methods to minimize the tendency of volatile series to dominate the average and to standardize each series. These technical methods are described in References 1 and 2. At present, each component contributes equally to the composite index; that is to say, the weighting factor for each is 1. Before the 1989 revisions, different weights were assigned to each component to reflect its perceived relative importance; for example, in the composite index of leading indicators, the weighting for Stock Prices was 1.149 but that for Manufacturers' New Orders was .973. A change in Stock Prices of .10 would contribute .1149 to the index; a change of .10 in Manufacturers' New Orders would contribute .0973.

Bibliography

1. Hertzberg, Marie P. and Barry A. Beckman, "Business Cycle Indicators: Revised Composite Indexes." U.S. Department of Commerce, Bureau of Economic Analysis. *Survey of Current Business*. January 1989, Superintendent of Documents, U.S. Government Printing Office, Washington, DC 20302.

2. *Measuring Business Cycles*. National Bureau of Economic Research, Inc., 1946.

3. U.S. Department of Commerce, Bureau of Economic Analysis. "Composite Indexes of Leading, Coincident, and Lagging Indicators," *Survey of Current Business*. November 1987, Superintendent of Documents, U.S. Government Printing Office, Washington, DC 20302.

GDP and Economic Indicators: 1956-1993
[In bil. 87$ (GDP) and Indices]

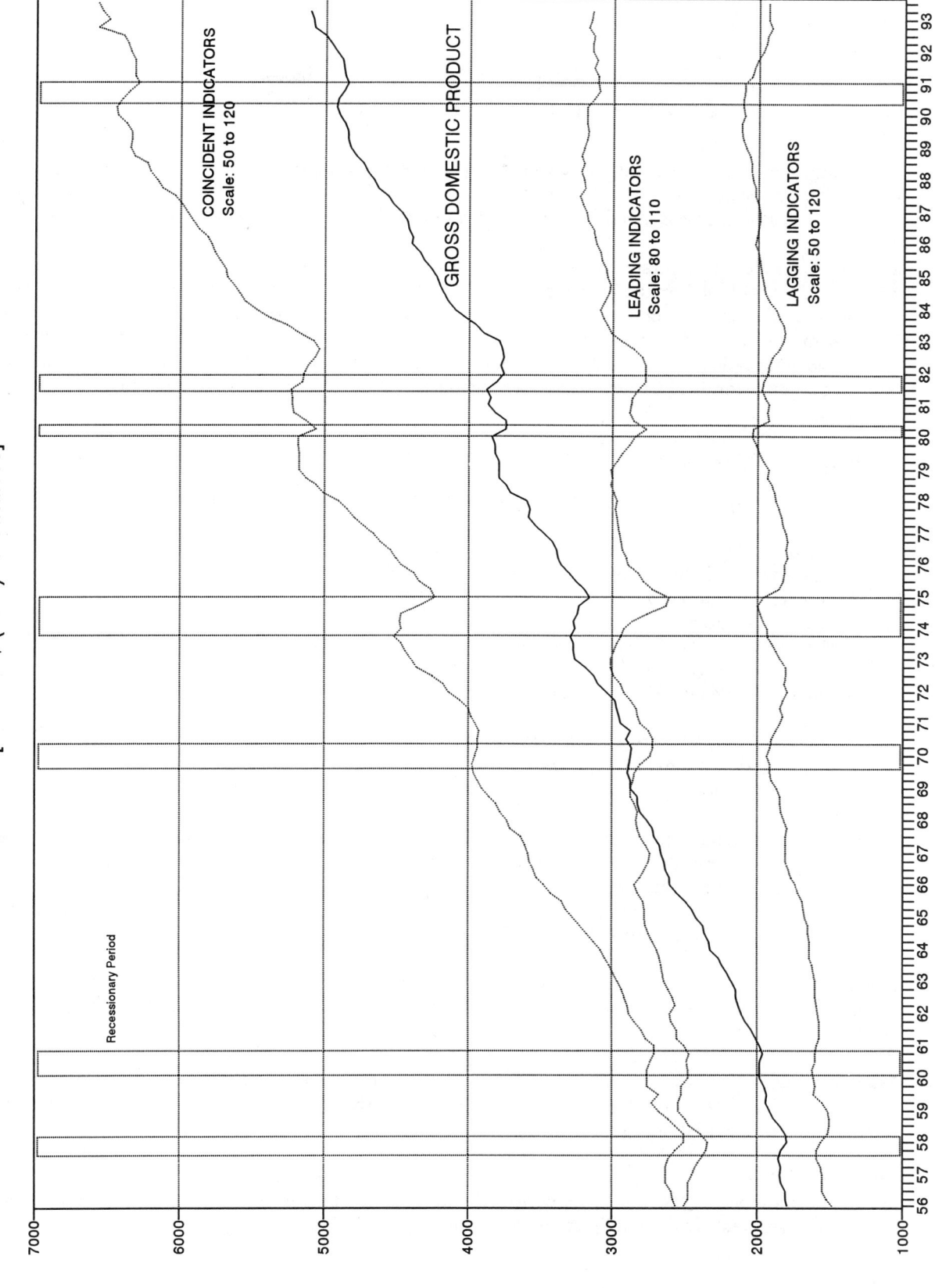

COMPOSITE INDEX OF LEADING INDICATORS

The composite index of leading indicators tends to signal the onset of a recession or a recovery some months before the economy actually registers the change. It is generally held that a change in the direction of the indicator must be sustained for at least three months before the indicator becomes predictive.

The "leading index" is accurate but fallible. All recessions have been accurately predicted by the index. But not all predictions based on the index have actually resulted in downturns or upturns. In 1950-51, 1966, and in 1984, the index showed obvious downturns which did not materialize. These "false signals" reflect the fact that the index components do not always measure economic factors completely; for example, service sector and international activity are not reflected in the index—although these sectors are increasingly important. The theoretical framework behind the index is also still in the process of development.

Components of the Leading Index

The index is a composite of 11 indicators, each of which is further discussed below:

> Average weekly hours in manufacturing
> Average weekly initial claims for unemployment insurance
> Manufacturers' new orders
> Index of stock prices, 500 common stocks
> Contracts and orders for plant and equipment
> Building permits for new private housing units
> Vendor performance, slow deliveries
> Consumer expectations
> Change in manufacturers' unfilled orders
> Change in sensitive materials prices
> Money supply M2

Average Weekly Hours in Manufacturing. The index is shown in hours worked by production or nonsupervisory workers. A decline in hours worked, if sustained over some period, signals a lower level of production; conversely, a sustained increase in hours shows pick-up in production. Data are always close to 40 hours per week because unemployed labor forces are drawn into the labor pool when demand increases—unless there is a labor shortage, as in the early months of 1945.

Average Weekly Initial Claims for Unemployment Insurance. Data are drawn from state unemployment program files and are a signal of increasing or decreasing layoffs—therefore an early signal of economic change.

Manufacturers' New Orders. The series covers new orders in the consumer goods and materials industries. Since new orders represent future economic activity, the values (in constant 1987 dollars, to remove inflationary bias) indicate future trends.

Index of Stock Prices, 500 Common Stocks. This indicator is the Standard & Poor's 500 stock average index; it is an index to the 1941-1943 period, the average of which is expressed as 10. The index reflects stock price averages and is an indirect measure of investor confidence.

Contracts and Orders for Plant and Equipment. The indicator, in constant 1987 dollars, shows future spending on capital goods. It is both an indicator of confidence and a direct commitment to spend money in the future; hence it is predictive of future economic activity.

Building Permits for New Private Housing Units. The data are based on local building permits issued. The indicator is an index with a base of 100 for the year 1967. Since permits must be obtained before building begins, this series predicts future housing starts and is thus a leading indicator. Increases in this index imply confidence that the economy will be strong, that money will be available for construction financing and house purchases.

Vendor Performance. The index charts the percent of companies reporting late deliveries by vendors. Late deliveries are common when vendors are overbooked and have difficulty obtaining raw materials—a situation typically encountered in a strong economy. If late delivery percentages begin to rise in a recessionary economy, it signals the onset of an upturn—again only if the trend is sustained.

Consumer Expectations. The index, based on surveys conducted by the University of Michigan, Survey Research Center, was added to the leading index in 1989. It is based on a monthly telephone survey of approximately 500 people in 48 states and the District of Columbia and combines the respondents' answers to questions about their expectations for the economy. The index is pegged to the year 1966, which is expressed as 100. The indicator, of course, measures consumer confidence. The index values, in themselves—while showing how attitudes have changed since 1966—are less valuable than changes month to month indicating a trend in consumer attitudes.

Change in Manufacturers' Unfilled Orders. The indicator is for durable goods industries and is shown in billions of 1987 dollars. The data shown are *changes* from the previous month rather than total unfilled orders. Positive values mean an increase since the month before, negative values mean a decrease. The series gives an indication of durable goods "backlogs." Increasing backlogs signal increasing demand—before it is actually met; declining backlogs indicate that production in the future will be lower.

Change in Sensitive Materials Prices. "Sensitive materials" are those most vital to a modern economy: metals, fibers, and minerals. Being raw materials (rather than finished components), they are purchased early in the production cycle and therefore can predict future economic behavior. The prices of sensitive materials will reflect their scarcity. When the economy is beginning to slow, purchases of materials will be cut back; these cutbacks will reflect in a drop in commodity prices. In a sluggish economy which is on the brink of turning around, sensitive materials prices will tend to signal the turn-around by increasing in price. The index shows a percent *change* from the previous month. Negative values indicate a decline in price.

Money Supply M2. M2 is one of four monetary aggregates used by the Federal Reserve System to measure money supply. M1 is all currency, checking accounts, and other types of checkable deposits that can be turned into cash easily. M2 includes M1 and adds other liquid assets in the economy, including money market funds, money market deposit accounts, savings accounts, and small time deposits. M3 includes M2 plus large time deposits, institutional money market funds, and other less liquid assets. The fourth measure, labeled L (because it is *L*east under Federal Reserve control and *L*east liquid) includes M3 plus short-term Treasury securities, commercial paper, savings bonds, and bankers' acceptances. M2 is thus a measure of the money supply which includes some funds that are typically held for investment but not assets that are difficult to "liquefy."

M2 is used as a leading indicator because it tends to reach low points in its cycle approximately 12 months before Gross Domestic Product (GDP) reaches the bottom of its cycle. M2 thus serves as an early indicator of future GNP behavior.

Money supply, generally, affects the economy by influencing interest rates; these, in turn, can stimulate housing purchases and investments in capital goods. An increase in money supply usually results in low interest rates: there is more money to lend; a decline in money supply pushes interest rates up. In periods of high inflation, however, interest rates may not respond as just stated because lenders anticipate an inflationary devaluation of their funds and hence compensate by keeping interest rates high.

Sources and Revisions

Sources for the component series are largely drawn from federal sources, including the U.S. Department of Commerce, Bureau of Economic Analysis and Bureau of the Census; and U.S. Department of Labor, Bureau of Labor Statistics and Employment and Training Administration. Other sources are Standard & Poor's Corporation (Stock Index), McGraw-Hill Information Systems Company (contributor to Contracts and Orders for Plant and Equipment), National Association of Purchasing Management and Purchasing Management Association of Chicago (Vendor Performance), University of Michigan (Consumer Expectations), and Commodity Research Bureau, Inc. (contributor to Change in Sensitive Materials Prices).

The composite index itself is constructed by the Bureau of Economic Analysis. In the process, mathematical operations are performed on the component data series to ensure that volatile series do not dominate the index. A volatile series may be one that fluctuates wildly month to month but shows less volatility when averaged over several months. Other smoothing and standardization methods are used as well.

The index was last revised in 1993 to reflect comprehensive revisions of the National Income and Product Accounts which were made in 1991 and to incorporate improvements in methodology.

Bibliography

1. Frumkin, Norman. *Guide to Economic Indicators*. M.E. Sharpe, Inc., 1990.

2. Green, George R. and Barry A. Beckman. "Business Cycle Indicators: Upcoming Revision of the Composite Indexes." U.S. Department of Commerce, Bureau of Economic Analysis. *Survey of Current Business*, October 1993. Superintendent of Documents, U.S. Government Printing Office, Washington, DC 20302.

3. Hertzberg, Marie P. and Barry A. Beckman. "Business Cycle Indicators: Revised Composite Indexes." U.S. Department of Commerce, Bureau of Economic Analysis. *Survey of Current Business*, January 1989. Superintendent of Documents, U.S. Government Printing Office, Washington, DC 20302.

4. U.S. Department of Commerce, Bureau of Economic Analysis. "Composite Indexes of Leading, Coincident, and Lagging Indicators." In *Survey of Current Business*, November 1987. Superintendent of Documents, U.S. Government Printing Office, Washington, DC 20302.

5. U.S. Department of Commerce, Bureau of Economic Analysis. *Survey of Current Business*. Superintendent of Documents, U.S. Government Printing Office, Washington, DC 20302.

Composite Index of 11 Leading Indicators
(1987 = 100)

Year	Jan	Feb	Mar	Apr	May	Jun	Jul	Aug	Sep	Oct	Nov	Dec
1948	72.1	71.4	71.7	72.3	71.5	72.2	71.9	71.5	70.9	70.9	70.6	69.9
1949	69.3	68.9	68.6	68.2	68.2	68.0	68.8	69.6	70.7	70.8	71.4	71.9
1950	72.7	73.0	73.3	73.7	74.5	74.8	76.0	77.4	76.9	77.0	76.8	76.9
1951	77.8	77.2	76.9	76.0	75.6	74.5	73.7	73.0	73.0	72.9	72.7	72.8
1952	72.9	73.1	72.9	72.9	72.9	73.7	73.7	74.4	75.5	75.0	74.9	75.0
1953	75.3	75.3	75.1	74.9	74.5	73.9	73.7	72.7	71.8	71.6	71.2	71.2
1954	71.2	71.6	71.7	72.0	72.5	73.0	73.4	73.6	74.1	74.8	75.5	76.0
1955	76.7	77.3	77.7	77.9	78.1	78.2	78.5	78.3	78.5	78.3	78.6	78.6
1956	78.4	78.1	78.2	78.3	77.6	77.3	77.5	77.5	77.3	77.3	77.4	77.2
1957	76.8	76.6	76.3	75.9	75.8	75.6	75.3	75.1	74.5	74.1	73.6	73.2
1958	73.1	72.7	73.0	73.2	73.9	74.6	75.5	76.2	76.8	77.3	77.9	77.8
1959	78.4	78.8	79.4	79.4	79.5	79.4	79.2	78.8	78.6	78.4	78.0	78.8
1960	78.7	78.1	77.3	77.3	77.4	77.3	77.4	77.5	77.5	77.2	77.1	77.0
1961	77.4	77.6	78.2	78.7	79.1	79.5	79.5	80.2	79.7	80.3	80.7	80.9
1962	80.9	81.3	81.3	81.0	80.5	80.0	80.2	80.2	80.5	80.6	81.2	81.4
1963	81.8	82.1	82.4	82.6	82.9	82.8	82.7	82.7	83.1	83.2	83.3	83.3
1964	83.6	83.9	84.0	84.4	84.6	84.7	85.1	85.3	85.6	85.7	86.0	86.2
1965	86.5	86.4	86.6	86.5	86.8	86.7	86.9	86.8	87.0	87.6	88.0	88.2
1966	88.3	88.3	88.7	88.5	88.0	87.6	87.3	86.7	86.5	86.0	85.8	85.7
1967	86.0	85.7	85.4	85.5	85.8	86.3	86.8	87.4	87.5	87.6	87.7	88.2
1968	88.0	88.4	88.5	88.0	88.2	88.2	88.4	88.2	88.7	89.4	89.5	89.7
1969	90.1	90.0	89.7	89.8	89.6	89.1	88.7	88.6	88.7	88.2	87.7	87.4
1970	86.7	86.0	85.4	84.8	84.8	84.9	84.8	84.9	84.7	84.6	84.7	85.7
1971	86.3	86.9	87.5	87.9	88.0	88.0	88.0	88.1	88.3	88.5	88.8	89.8
1972	90.4	90.9	91.3	91.4	91.5	91.8	92.3	93.0	93.3	93.3	93.7	93.9
1973	93.9	94.1	93.9	93.6	93.5	93.3	93.2	92.7	92.8	92.8	92.8	91.9
1974	91.5	90.7	91.1	90.4	90.3	89.3	88.6	87.4	85.9	84.8	83.3	82.0
1975	81.2	81.0	81.6	83.3	84.4	85.0	85.7	86.4	87.0	87.5	87.9	88.2
1976	89.5	90.0	90.2	90.1	90.4	90.7	91.3	91.4	91.5	91.3	91.4	91.8
1977	91.5	91.8	92.1	92.2	92.4	92.5	92.3	92.5	92.6	92.4	92.5	92.9
1978	92.2	92.6	92.8	93.2	93.2	93.3	93.2	93.4	93.8	94.3	93.9	93.6
1979	93.5	93.4	93.8	92.9	93.0	92.7	91.9	91.5	91.5	90.8	90.3	90.0
1980	90.1	90.4	88.6	87.0	85.6	86.3	87.2	88.2	89.1	89.9	90.4	90.1
1981	89.9	89.4	89.6	90.2	90.1	89.5	89.1	89.0	88.0	87.2	86.7	86.6
1982	86.1	86.9	86.5	86.7	86.8	86.6	87.0	86.6	87.3	87.7	88.2	89.0
1983	90.1	91.0	91.7	92.3	93.0	93.8	94.3	94.4	94.9	95.7	96.0	95.8
1984	96.4	96.4	96.3	96.1	96.0	95.4	95.1	94.8	94.4	93.9	94.1	94.2
1985	94.7	94.6	94.8	94.5	94.7	95.1	95.2	95.6	95.9	95.9	95.8	96.4
1986	96.6	96.8	97.1	97.5	97.4	97.6	97.7	97.7	97.7	98.2	98.5	99.2
1987	99.0	99.3	99.4	99.5	99.7	100.2	100.9	101.0	101.0	100.6	99.8	99.6
1988	99.4	100.0	100.0	100.0	99.9	100.6	100.0	100.2	100.1	100.1	100.0	100.5
1989	100.9	100.7	100.1	100.4	99.6	99.4	99.2	99.1	99.2	98.9	99.0	99.4
1990	99.4	98.9	99.4	99.2	99.4	99.3	99.1	98.4	97.8	97.2	96.5	96.5
1991	96.0	96.4	96.8	96.8	97.0	97.0	97.9	97.7	97.7	97.6	97.4	97.2
1992	97.5	97.8	98.1	98.1	98.3	98.2	98.1	97.9	97.8	98.0	98.2	99.2
1993	98.9	99.1	98.4	98.4	98.1	98.1	97.9	98.4	98.6	99.1	-	-

Source: U.S. Department of Commerce, Bureau of Economic Analysis. - indicates data not available or zero.

Composite Index of 11 Leading Indicators
Change in Index from Previous Month

Year	Jan	Feb	Mar	Apr	May	Jun	Jul	Aug	Sep	Oct	Nov	Dec
1948	-	-0.7	+0.3	+0.6	-0.8	+0.7	-0.3	-0.4	-0.6	-	-0.3	-0.7
1949	-0.6	-0.4	-0.3	-0.4	-	-0.2	+0.8	+0.8	+1.1	+0.1	+0.6	+0.5
1950	+0.8	+0.3	+0.3	+0.4	+0.8	+0.3	+1.2	+1.4	-0.5	+0.1	-0.2	+0.1
1951	+0.9	-0.6	-0.3	-0.9	-0.4	-1.1	-0.8	-0.7	-	-0.1	-0.2	+0.1
1952	+0.1	+0.2	-0.2	-	-	+0.8	-	+0.7	+1.1	-0.5	-0.1	+0.1
1953	+0.3	-	-0.2	-0.2	-0.4	-0.6	-0.2	-1.0	-0.9	-0.2	-0.4	-
1954	-	+0.4	+0.1	+0.3	+0.5	+0.5	+0.4	+0.2	+0.5	+0.7	+0.7	+0.5
1955	+0.7	+0.6	+0.4	+0.2	+0.2	+0.1	+0.3	-0.2	+0.2	-0.2	+0.3	-
1956	-0.2	-0.3	+0.1	+0.1	-0.7	-0.3	+0.2	-	-0.2	-	+0.1	-0.2
1957	-0.4	-0.2	-0.3	-0.4	-0.1	-0.2	-0.3	-0.2	-0.6	-0.4	-0.5	-0.4
1958	-0.1	-0.4	+0.3	+0.2	+0.7	+0.7	+0.9	+0.7	+0.6	+0.5	+0.6	-0.1
1959	+0.6	+0.4	+0.6	-	+0.1	-0.1	-0.2	-0.4	-0.2	-0.2	-0.4	+0.8
1960	-0.1	-0.6	-0.8	-	+0.1	-0.1	+0.1	+0.1	-	-0.3	-0.1	-0.1
1961	+0.4	+0.2	+0.6	+0.5	+0.4	+0.4	-	+0.7	-0.5	+0.6	+0.4	+0.2
1962	-	+0.4	-	-0.3	-0.5	-0.5	+0.2	-	+0.3	+0.1	+0.6	+0.2
1963	+0.4	+0.3	+0.3	+0.2	+0.3	-0.1	-0.1	-	+0.4	+0.1	+0.1	-
1964	+0.3	+0.3	+0.1	+0.4	+0.2	+0.1	+0.4	+0.2	+0.3	+0.1	+0.3	+0.2
1965	+0.3	-0.1	+0.2	-0.1	+0.3	-0.1	+0.2	-0.1	+0.2	+0.6	+0.4	+0.2
1966	+0.1	-	+0.4	-0.2	-0.5	-0.4	-0.3	-0.6	-0.2	-0.5	-0.2	-0.1
1967	+0.3	-0.3	-0.3	+0.1	+0.3	+0.5	+0.5	+0.6	+0.1	+0.1	+0.1	+0.5
1968	-0.2	+0.4	+0.1	-0.5	+0.2	-	+0.2	-0.2	+0.5	+0.7	+0.1	+0.2
1969	+0.4	-0.1	-0.3	+0.1	-0.2	-0.5	-0.4	-0.1	+0.1	-0.5	-0.5	-0.3
1970	-0.7	-0.7	-0.6	-0.6	-	+0.1	-0.1	+0.1	-0.2	-0.1	+0.1	+1.0
1971	+0.6	+0.6	+0.6	+0.4	+0.1	-	-	+0.1	+0.2	+0.2	+0.3	+1.0
1972	+0.6	+0.5	+0.4	+0.1	+0.1	+0.3	+0.5	+0.7	+0.3	-	+0.4	+0.2
1973	-	+0.2	-0.2	-0.3	-0.1	-0.2	-0.1	-0.5	+0.1	-	-	-0.9
1974	-0.4	-0.8	+0.4	-0.7	-0.1	-1.0	-0.7	-1.2	-1.5	-1.1	-1.5	-1.3
1975	-0.8	-0.2	+0.6	+1.7	+1.1	+0.6	+0.7	+0.7	+0.6	+0.5	+0.4	+0.3
1976	+1.3	+0.5	+0.2	-0.1	+0.3	+0.3	+0.6	+0.1	+0.1	-0.2	+0.1	+0.4
1977	-0.3	+0.3	+0.3	+0.1	+0.2	+0.1	-0.2	+0.2	+0.1	-0.2	+0.1	+0.4
1978	-0.7	+0.4	+0.2	+0.4	-	+0.1	-0.1	+0.2	+0.4	+0.5	-0.4	-0.3
1979	-0.1	-0.1	+0.4	-0.9	+0.1	-0.3	-0.8	-0.4	-	-0.7	-0.5	-0.3
1980	+0.1	+0.3	-1.8	-1.6	-1.4	+0.7	+0.9	+1.0	+0.9	+0.8	+0.5	-0.3
1981	-0.2	-0.5	+0.2	+0.6	-0.1	-0.6	-0.4	-0.1	-1.0	-0.8	-0.5	-0.1
1982	-0.5	+0.8	-0.4	+0.2	+0.1	-0.2	+0.4	-0.4	+0.7	+0.4	+0.5	+0.8
1983	+1.1	+0.9	+0.7	+0.6	+0.7	+0.8	+0.5	+0.1	+0.5	+0.8	+0.3	-0.2
1984	+0.6	-	-0.1	-0.2	-0.1	-0.6	-0.3	-0.3	-0.4	-0.5	+0.2	+0.1
1985	+0.5	-0.1	+0.2	-0.3	+0.2	+0.4	+0.1	+0.4	+0.3	-	-0.1	+0.6
1986	+0.2	+0.2	+0.3	+0.4	-0.1	+0.2	+0.1	-	-	+0.5	+0.3	+0.7
1987	-0.2	+0.3	+0.1	+0.1	+0.2	+0.5	+0.7	+0.1	-	-0.4	-0.8	-0.2
1988	-0.2	+0.6	-	-	-0.1	+0.7	-0.6	+0.2	-0.1	-	-0.1	+0.5
1989	+0.4	-0.2	-0.6	+0.3	-0.8	-0.2	-0.2	-0.1	+0.1	-0.3	+0.1	+0.4
1990	-	-0.5	+0.5	-0.2	+0.2	-0.1	-0.2	-0.7	-0.6	-0.6	-0.7	-
1991	-0.5	+0.4	+0.4	-	+0.2	-	+0.9	-0.2	-	-0.1	-0.2	-0.2
1992	+0.3	+0.3	+0.3	-	+0.2	-0.1	-0.1	-0.2	-0.1	+0.2	+0.2	+1.0
1993	-0.3	+0.2	-0.7	-	-0.3	-	-0.2	+0.5	+0.2	+0.5	-	-

Source: U.S. Department of Commerce, Bureau of Economic Analysis. - indicates data not available or zero.

Average Weekly Hours, Manufacturing
(Hours)

Year	Jan	Feb	Mar	Apr	May	Jun	Jul	Aug	Sep	Oct	Nov	Dec
1945	45.3	45.4	45.2	45.1	44.3	44.5	44.3	40.8	41.7	41.4	41.1	41.1
1946	40.8	40.4	40.5	40.4	39.9	39.8	39.8	40.5	40.5	40.3	40.2	40.5
1947	40.5	40.5	40.4	40.5	40.5	40.4	40.2	39.8	40.3	40.3	40.4	40.7
1948	40.4	40.2	40.4	40.4	40.2	40.2	40.1	40.0	39.6	39.7	39.7	39.5
1949	39.4	39.4	39.1	38.8	38.9	38.9	39.1	39.0	39.4	39.4	39.0	39.3
1950	39.6	39.7	39.7	40.1	40.2	40.5	40.8	41.1	40.8	40.9	40.9	40.8
1951	40.8	40.8	41.0	41.2	40.9	40.7	40.5	40.2	40.4	40.2	40.3	40.6
1952	40.7	40.7	40.6	40.1	40.4	40.5	40.1	40.5	41.0	41.1	41.0	41.1
1953	41.0	41.0	41.1	41.1	40.9	40.7	40.6	40.4	39.8	40.0	39.8	39.6
1954	39.5	39.7	39.5	39.4	39.5	39.6	39.6	39.7	39.5	39.6	40.1	40.0
1955	40.3	40.5	40.7	40.6	40.9	40.6	40.6	40.6	40.7	40.9	41.0	40.8
1956	40.8	40.6	40.4	40.6	40.2	40.1	40.2	40.2	40.4	40.5	40.4	40.5
1957	40.3	40.4	40.2	40.1	39.8	39.9	39.9	39.8	39.7	39.3	39.2	39.0
1958	38.8	38.6	38.7	38.6	38.8	39.0	39.2	39.4	39.6	39.5	39.8	39.8
1959	40.1	40.2	40.4	40.5	40.6	40.5	40.2	40.3	40.1	40.1	39.8	40.2
1960	40.5	40.1	39.9	39.7	40.0	39.8	39.8	39.7	39.4	39.6	39.2	38.4
1961	39.2	39.3	39.4	39.6	39.6	39.9	40.0	40.1	39.5	40.2	40.5	40.3
1962	40.0	40.3	40.5	40.7	40.5	40.4	40.4	40.3	40.5	40.2	40.3	40.2
1963	40.4	40.3	40.4	40.2	40.5	40.6	40.5	40.4	40.6	40.6	40.5	40.6
1964	40.1	40.6	40.6	40.8	40.7	40.7	40.8	40.9	40.5	40.6	40.8	41.1
1965	41.2	41.2	41.4	41.0	41.2	41.1	41.1	41.0	40.8	41.2	41.3	41.4
1966	41.4	41.6	41.5	41.5	41.4	41.4	41.2	41.4	41.3	41.3	41.2	40.9
1967	41.0	40.4	40.4	40.5	40.4	40.4	40.5	40.6	40.7	40.6	40.6	40.7
1968	40.3	40.9	40.7	40.0	40.9	40.9	40.8	40.7	40.9	40.9	40.8	40.7
1969	40.7	40.4	40.8	40.7	40.7	40.7	40.6	40.6	40.7	40.6	40.4	40.5
1970	40.4	40.2	40.1	39.9	39.8	39.9	40.0	39.8	39.3	39.5	39.5	39.5
1971	39.9	39.7	39.8	39.7	39.9	40.0	39.9	39.8	39.4	39.9	40.0	40.2
1972	40.2	40.4	40.4	40.7	40.5	40.6	40.5	40.6	40.6	40.7	40.8	40.5
1973	40.4	40.9	40.8	40.9	40.7	40.6	40.7	40.5	40.7	40.6	40.7	40.6
1974	40.5	40.4	40.4	39.3	40.3	40.2	40.2	40.2	40.0	40.0	39.5	39.3
1975	39.2	38.9	38.8	39.2	39.0	39.2	39.4	39.7	39.9	39.8	39.9	40.2
1976	40.5	40.3	40.2	39.6	40.3	40.2	40.3	40.1	39.8	40.0	40.1	40.0
1977	39.7	40.3	40.2	40.4	40.4	40.5	40.3	40.4	40.4	40.5	40.4	40.4
1978	39.6	39.9	40.5	40.8	40.4	40.5	40.6	40.5	40.6	40.5	40.6	40.6
1979	40.5	40.5	40.6	39.2	40.2	40.2	40.2	40.1	40.2	40.2	40.1	40.2
1980	40.0	40.1	39.8	39.5	39.3	39.2	39.1	39.4	39.6	39.8	40.0	40.3
1981	40.1	40.0	40.0	40.1	40.1	39.9	39.9	39.9	39.7	39.7	39.5	39.4
1982	38.0	39.6	39.1	38.9	39.0	39.1	39.2	39.0	39.0	38.9	39.1	39.1
1983	39.4	39.3	39.6	39.8	40.0	40.1	40.3	40.3	40.6	40.7	40.7	40.6
1984	40.7	41.1	40.7	40.9	40.7	40.7	40.6	40.5	40.5	40.5	40.5	40.6
1985	40.4	40.1	40.5	40.3	40.4	40.5	40.4	40.6	40.6	40.7	40.7	41.0
1986	40.8	40.6	40.8	40.6	40.7	40.6	40.6	40.8	40.7	40.6	40.8	40.9
1987	40.9	41.2	41.0	40.9	41.0	41.0	41.0	41.0	40.9	41.1	41.1	41.1
1988	41.1	41.0	41.0	41.1	41.1	41.1	41.1	40.9	41.1	41.1	41.2	41.0
1989	41.2	41.2	41.1	41.2	41.0	41.0	41.0	40.9	40.9	40.7	40.7	40.6
1990	40.8	40.8	40.9	40.8	41.0	40.9	40.9	40.9	40.9	40.7	40.5	40.6
1991	40.4	40.3	40.3	40.3	40.4	40.7	40.7	40.9	41.0	40.9	40.9	41.0
1992	40.8	41.0	41.1	41.1	41.2	41.1	41.1	41.1	41.0	41.1	41.2	41.2
1993	41.4	41.4	41.2	41.5	41.4	41.2	41.4	41.4	41.5	41.6	-	-

Source: U.S. Department of Labor, Bureau of Labor Statistics. - indicates data not available or zero.

Average Weekly Initial Claims, for Unemployment Insurance
(Thousands)

Year	Jan	Feb	Mar	Apr	May	Jun	Jul	Aug	Sep	Oct	Nov	Dec
1945	16	26	28	34	43	70	72	360	375	248	220	185
1946	134	225	192	205	220	206	171	163	191	181	178	211
1947	121	174	185	207	235	219	229	193	179	163	172	172
1948	166	206	201	210	239	219	194	202	218	203	211	234
1949	285	305	333	379	377	359	340	385	320	386	344	298
1950	294	288	276	263	250	252	223	170	182	194	200	197
1951	174	181	166	199	199	209	236	254	242	234	210	213
1952	221	201	209	219	213	242	315	207	168	175	169	190
1953	175	177	188	179	198	195	207	229	238	251	298	280
1954	303	318	320	313	313	314	294	319	322	315	276	253
1955	256	240	228	228	222	222	223	233	204	224	215	214
1956	218	226	221	223	236	227	245	224	236	214	223	230
1957	242	225	219	239	244	246	267	235	305	302	320	355
1958	354	407	436	438	400	410	350	363	338	314	311	320
1959	292	284	258	244	246	258	264	291	271	311	351	275
1960	281	271	303	294	316	322	335	363	351	373	385	381
1961	393	429	379	381	358	334	348	316	329	304	305	296
1962	301	295	287	283	301	304	303	305	300	304	299	310
1963	310	301	288	293	288	284	282	290	285	282	276	301
1964	283	270	277	265	262	257	260	244	245	249	262	251
1965	243	248	237	237	224	224	231	248	218	209	212	206
1966	222	219	182	179	192	194	199	195	197	203	208	219
1967	196	231	256	259	236	231	231	212	217	220	209	204
1968	206	196	194	193	195	194	192	199	194	188	190	190
1969	179	186	185	181	182	197	195	196	195	202	211	210
1970	240	256	262	326	302	291	273	287	319	329	322	299
1971	292	286	294	281	290	289	285	325	307	294	283	265
1972	264	262	258	260	262	286	272	246	245	250	241	236
1973	226	223	227	238	234	233	232	247	241	244	251	284
1974	294	315	302	289	294	314	294	350	374	419	473	494
1975	522	532	536	521	496	491	442	449	447	420	393	364
1976	360	340	358	371	392	394	393	389	410	409	390	361
1977	394	427	346	371	378	358	370	368	363	357	347	342
1978	343	381	335	322	324	331	347	339	321	326	340	347
1979	353	352	346	411	341	358	377	383	378	400	420	428
1980	416	397	438	532	616	581	510	495	488	447	422	420
1981	424	410	413	395	401	405	395	421	483	517	539	551
1982	563	514	566	566	585	551	533	605	653	651	616	531
1983	507	478	479	470	453	406	380	408	387	386	381	378
1984	364	345	348	360	348	350	365	358	368	405	397	386
1985	378	402	389	387	383	392	381	375	381	367	371	391
1986	375	373	395	371	370	374	363	376	380	361	351	350
1987	355	348	326	318	321	320	286	299	294	289	303	308
1988	345	310	302	299	304	295	323	299	290	291	298	304
1989	291	299	317	304	320	334	340	329	337	359	338	351
1990	360	346	345	356	354	362	377	384	397	423	447	442
1991	440	472	499	467	443	434	411	431	435	422	436	435
1992	424	423	425	413	418	429	417	436	455	396	373	333
1993	364	343	376	374	390	386	399	378	381	356	-	-

Source: U.S. Department of Labor, Employment and Training Administration; seasonal adjustment by Bureau of Economic Analysis. - indicates data not available or zero.

Manufacturers' New Orders, Consumer Goods and Materials

(Billions of 1987 $)

Year	Jan	Feb	Mar	Apr	May	Jun	Jul	Aug	Sep	Oct	Nov	Dec
1948	31.29	31.00	32.66	31.76	32.72	35.21	34.63	34.15	32.24	31.20	30.22	28.92
1949	27.93	27.05	26.49	25.31	25.43	24.27	25.98	30.08	30.34	28.33	29.58	29.05
1950	31.31	31.44	31.22	32.68	36.45	36.76	45.79	51.27	40.49	40.87	37.25	39.44
1951	51.43	46.00	47.23	43.00	41.29	39.98	39.76	36.30	34.83	38.59	37.19	36.00
1952	36.60	36.82	41.15	42.46	37.39	43.43	40.81	39.86	42.05	39.88	40.03	43.26
1953	47.00	45.03	45.66	47.23	46.00	45.16	44.70	39.04	34.93	33.79	34.40	34.71
1954	34.67	36.50	36.62	36.78	36.78	38.66	36.97	38.06	40.03	40.51	42.93	46.02
1955	48.27	47.89	51.27	49.90	49.52	50.51	51.45	49.90	49.10	48.54	50.36	49.37
1956	47.89	46.50	46.20	46.88	45.41	44.35	44.63	45.26	44.09	45.54	45.72	46.14
1957	45.11	46.98	46.02	44.55	44.35	44.73	42.95	43.46	43.61	41.75	40.11	37.83
1958	39.82	36.70	37.78	37.66	39.25	41.00	41.93	44.08	43.38	44.40	46.63	46.10
1959	47.87	51.40	51.67	50.73	49.37	49.32	47.79	45.65	45.26	45.25	44.81	48.35
1960	47.08	45.98	44.93	45.15	45.18	45.94	45.54	46.86	46.80	45.18	44.78	44.52
1961	42.54	42.46	45.38	47.02	48.61	49.55	47.71	50.08	49.56	49.51	52.17	53.91
1962	52.50	51.35	51.24	48.94	50.11	49.55	50.94	51.80	52.29	53.03	52.87	51.56
1963	52.97	54.70	55.14	56.84	55.36	53.71	55.93	53.19	54.38	56.40	56.21	55.75
1964	58.36	56.98	56.57	59.54	58.41	59.09	61.09	58.59	62.52	58.95	60.45	62.56
1965	64.00	64.04	64.24	64.43	63.98	64.61	66.59	66.38	62.19	65.16	67.60	69.12
1966	68.48	69.43	72.07	70.43	69.35	70.12	68.43	68.60	70.14	70.26	68.38	67.87
1967	66.96	66.71	66.32	67.01	68.17	68.57	67.98	71.23	69.01	67.80	69.99	75.37
1968	71.80	72.47	72.47	71.90	73.37	73.36	72.62	69.11	76.47	76.97	77.60	75.53
1969	76.42	76.24	76.37	76.27	76.16	75.76	76.34	76.22	77.46	77.31	74.31	74.60
1970	70.74	70.12	69.72	69.39	70.53	71.82	70.12	69.92	69.59	65.26	64.87	71.68
1971	73.05	73.07	73.49	71.80	71.16	70.56	71.44	73.36	72.98	72.61	74.22	75.79
1972	76.70	78.74	78.28	78.56	79.42	81.02	79.11	83.05	86.12	85.31	86.87	89.14
1973	91.46	92.91	93.18	89.94	92.00	90.75	90.85	90.49	89.54	90.82	91.64	88.32
1974	89.58	88.91	86.72	87.67	90.09	88.41	85.72	85.37	82.01	79.42	77.04	69.96
1975	69.06	69.00	66.03	69.00	69.70	70.60	74.27	76.12	76.17	76.01	75.44	76.42
1976	78.80	80.65	82.32	81.65	82.91	83.47	82.73	83.19	82.89	80.91	84.48	87.87
1977	88.15	88.61	92.42	89.44	90.44	91.49	91.59	92.52	91.95	91.89	93.96	94.66
1978	90.17	92.62	94.22	98.30	97.90	98.50	96.80	98.14	96.84	98.70	97.86	101.98
1979	99.35	97.20	99.68	95.79	97.17	97.42	94.47	92.06	92.81	90.96	90.17	89.47
1980	89.76	92.05	86.46	79.57	76.19	77.17	79.25	81.48	86.32	89.44	88.79	89.04
1981	83.77	87.76	87.20	88.68	89.59	89.55	88.14	85.10	83.32	80.65	79.07	78.28
1982	76.99	77.91	80.53	79.18	80.53	79.83	80.29	77.76	78.85	75.53	75.88	75.95
1983	80.51	81.72	81.98	83.34	85.68	88.32	89.35	90.73	90.59	94.07	94.76	96.17
1984	97.67	97.48	95.25	95.41	94.79	92.95	95.95	95.49	91.38	93.63	93.89	94.40
1985	96.95	93.70	94.03	93.80	95.63	94.87	95.01	96.03	96.73	95.94	95.73	95.58
1986	99.96	97.22	94.73	97.05	94.88	97.36	96.09	96.46	99.01	98.14	95.43	100.61
1987	97.25	102.50	102.65	101.18	100.63	102.65	103.59	100.64	102.98	104.07	103.33	104.11
1988	102.46	103.99	104.54	104.22	105.56	106.17	104.75	104.04	105.85	105.53	106.34	111.00
1989	109.85	107.66	104.55	106.40	103.82	103.49	98.21	104.04	104.08	101.43	103.75	103.00
1990	99.13	103.58	106.08	103.09	106.12	104.70	102.82	105.00	101.86	102.55	98.23	94.23
1991	95.67	95.35	92.43	97.97	99.80	96.75	102.44	101.23	102.52	101.74	102.10	97.94
1992	98.67	100.24	100.62	102.17	101.08	102.92	102.33	101.79	101.69	104.34	105.60	110.03
1993	109.30	109.79	107.23	106.72	105.54	106.58	105.35	106.54	109.15	111.82	-	-

Source: U.S. Department of Commerce, Bureau of Economic Analysis, U.S. Department of Commerce, Bureau of the Census. - indicates data not available or zero.

Index of Stock Prices, 500 Common Stocks

Not seasonally adjusted
(1941-43 = 10)

Year	Jan	Feb	Mar	Apr	May	Jun	Jul	Aug	Sep	Oct	Nov	Dec
1945	13.49	13.94	13.93	14.28	14.82	15.09	14.78	14.83	15.84	16.50	17.04	17.33
1946	18.02	18.07	17.53	18.66	18.70	18.58	18.05	17.70	15.09	14.75	14.69	15.13
1947	15.21	15.80	15.16	14.60	14.34	14.84	15.77	15.46	15.06	15.45	15.27	15.03
1948	14.83	14.10	14.30	15.40	16.15	16.82	16.42	15.94	15.76	16.19	15.29	15.19
1949	15.36	14.77	14.91	14.89	14.78	13.97	14.76	15.29	15.49	15.89	16.11	16.54
1950	16.88	17.21	17.35	17.84	18.44	18.74	17.38	18.43	19.08	19.87	19.83	19.75
1951	21.21	22.00	21.63	21.92	21.93	21.55	21.93	22.89	23.48	23.36	22.71	23.41
1952	24.19	23.75	23.81	23.74	23.73	24.38	25.08	25.18	24.78	24.26	25.03	26.04
1953	26.18	25.86	25.99	24.71	24.84	23.95	24.29	24.39	23.27	23.97	24.50	24.83
1954	25.46	26.02	26.57	27.63	28.73	28.96	30.13	30.73	31.45	32.18	33.44	34.97
1955	35.60	36.79	36.50	37.76	37.60	39.78	42.69	42.43	44.34	42.11	44.95	45.37
1956	44.15	44.43	47.49	48.05	46.54	46.27	48.78	48.49	46.84	46.24	45.76	46.44
1957	45.43	43.47	44.03	45.05	46.78	47.55	48.51	45.84	43.98	41.24	40.35	40.33
1958	41.12	41.26	42.11	42.34	43.70	44.75	45.98	47.70	48.96	50.95	52.50	53.49
1959	55.62	54.77	56.15	57.10	57.96	57.46	59.74	59.40	57.05	57.00	57.23	59.06
1960	58.03	55.78	55.02	55.73	55.22	57.26	55.84	56.51	54.81	53.73	55.47	56.80
1961	59.72	62.17	64.12	65.83	66.50	65.62	65.44	67.79	67.26	68.00	71.08	71.74
1962	69.07	70.22	70.29	68.05	62.99	55.63	56.97	58.52	58.00	56.17	60.04	62.64
1963	65.06	65.92	65.67	68.76	70.14	70.11	69.07	70.98	72.85	73.03	72.62	74.17
1964	76.45	77.39	78.80	79.94	80.72	80.24	83.22	82.00	83.41	84.85	85.44	83.96
1965	86.12	86.75	86.83	87.97	89.28	85.04	84.91	86.49	89.38	91.39	92.15	91.73
1966	93.32	92.69	88.88	91.60	86.78	86.06	85.84	80.65	77.81	77.13	80.99	81.33
1967	84.45	87.36	89.42	90.96	92.59	91.43	93.01	94.49	95.81	95.66	92.66	95.30
1968	95.04	90.75	89.09	95.67	97.87	100.53	100.30	98.11	101.34	103.76	105.40	106.48
1969	102.04	101.46	99.30	101.26	104.62	99.14	94.71	94.18	94.51	95.52	96.21	91.11
1970	90.31	87.16	88.65	85.95	76.06	75.59	75.72	77.92	82.58	84.37	84.28	90.05
1971	93.49	97.11	99.60	103.04	101.64	99.72	99.00	97.24	99.40	97.29	92.78	99.17
1972	103.30	105.24	107.69	108.81	107.65	108.01	107.21	111.01	109.39	109.56	115.05	117.50
1973	118.42	114.16	112.42	110.27	107.22	104.75	105.83	103.80	105.61	109.84	102.03	94.78
1974	96.11	93.45	97.44	92.46	89.67	89.79	82.82	76.03	68.12	69.44	71.74	67.07
1975	72.56	80.10	83.78	84.72	90.10	92.40	92.49	85.71	84.67	88.57	90.07	88.70
1976	96.86	100.64	101.08	101.93	101.16	101.77	104.20	103.29	105.45	101.89	101.19	104.66
1977	103.81	100.96	100.57	99.05	98.76	99.29	100.18	97.75	96.23	93.74	94.28	93.82
1978	90.25	88.98	88.82	92.71	97.41	97.66	97.19	103.92	103.86	100.58	94.71	96.11
1979	99.71	98.23	100.11	102.07	99.73	101.73	102.71	107.36	108.60	104.47	103.66	107.78
1980	110.87	115.34	104.69	102.97	107.69	114.55	119.83	123.50	126.51	130.22	135.65	133.48
1981	132.97	128.40	133.19	134.43	131.73	132.28	129.13	129.63	118.27	119.80	122.92	123.79
1982	117.28	114.50	110.84	116.31	116.35	109.70	109.38	109.65	122.43	132.66	138.10	139.37
1983	144.27	146.80	151.88	157.71	164.10	166.39	166.96	162.42	167.16	167.65	165.23	164.36
1984	166.39	157.25	157.44	157.60	156.55	153.12	151.08	164.42	166.11	164.82	166.27	164.48
1985	171.61	180.88	179.42	180.62	184.90	188.89	192.54	188.31	184.06	186.18	197.45	207.26
1986	208.19	219.37	232.33	237.98	238.46	245.30	240.18	245.00	238.27	237.36	245.09	248.61
1987	264.51	280.93	292.47	289.32	289.12	301.38	310.09	329.36	318.66	280.16	245.01	240.96
1988	250.48	258.13	265.74	262.61	256.12	270.68	269.05	263.73	267.97	277.40	271.02	276.51
1989	285.41	294.01	292.71	302.25	313.93	323.73	331.93	346.61	347.33	347.40	340.22	348.57
1990	339.97	330.45	338.47	338.18	350.25	360.39	360.03	330.75	315.41	307.12	315.29	328.75
1991	325.49	362.26	372.28	379.68	377.99	378.29	380.23	389.40	387.20	386.88	385.92	388.51
1992	416.08	412.56	407.36	407.41	414.81	408.27	415.05	417.93	418.48	412.50	422.84	435.64
1993	435.23	441.70	450.16	443.08	445.25	448.06	447.29	454.13	459.24	463.90	462.89	-

Source: Standard & Poor's Corporation. - indicates data not available or zero.

Contracts and Orders for Plant and Equipment
(Billions of 1987 $)

Year	Jan	Feb	Mar	Apr	May	Jun	Jul	Aug	Sep	Oct	Nov	Dec
1948	8.04	9.26	8.78	9.72	8.40	9.65	8.71	8.12	7.93	8.06	7.88	7.81
1949	6.46	7.01	6.94	6.00	6.18	6.83	6.25	6.79	7.46	7.21	8.17	7.38
1950	8.05	7.95	8.72	8.67	10.65	10.28	12.31	15.18	14.07	12.48	12.43	13.19
1951	14.82	15.15	13.62	13.71	19.62	12.76	12.17	11.72	10.05	11.14	11.18	12.15
1952	10.70	10.85	11.00	10.92	10.19	11.56	11.81	10.66	14.84	10.71	10.16	12.30
1953	12.09	12.39	11.22	12.24	11.69	8.98	11.22	9.29	10.85	11.67	9.87	8.90
1954	9.20	9.32	7.96	8.12	8.37	8.60	8.97	9.01	9.63	10.24	9.44	10.02
1955	10.37	11.23	12.98	12.20	11.54	12.20	12.09	12.72	13.42	12.67	13.66	13.48
1956	13.06	12.71	12.62	12.95	13.42	13.55	12.95	12.72	12.16	12.09	13.63	12.81
1957	13.16	12.67	12.59	11.16	11.70	11.09	10.78	11.00	9.80	10.11	10.10	9.63
1958	9.55	9.22	9.16	9.23	9.32	9.84	9.43	10.86	10.82	10.48	10.20	9.89
1959	10.50	10.81	12.74	11.40	11.69	11.91	12.13	10.74	12.22	11.79	11.09	11.70
1960	10.98	11.22	10.90	11.85	11.86	11.45	11.56	11.53	11.69	11.34	10.88	11.82
1961	11.90	11.53	10.86	11.04	10.90	11.51	11.70	12.34	11.51	11.79	12.59	11.53
1962	12.16	13.28	12.39	12.92	12.39	12.15	12.30	12.34	12.21	12.48	13.40	13.87
1963	12.68	13.08	12.94	13.30	14.72	13.34	13.18	13.53	13.95	14.25	15.20	15.31
1964	15.67	14.15	14.69	14.84	15.94	16.38	15.40	15.57	15.80	15.89	17.04	17.27
1965	16.10	16.31	17.17	17.30	17.08	16.59	17.20	16.53	18.01	17.94	17.58	18.75
1966	18.90	20.31	19.76	20.53	20.10	19.59	20.97	19.63	21.56	19.30	19.12	19.01
1967	16.42	17.66	18.08	17.59	18.13	18.85	18.52	19.19	18.72	19.00	18.96	19.32
1968	23.13	22.39	26.82	21.58	19.25	19.36	23.26	24.30	20.71	25.52	21.02	22.93
1969	26.49	26.02	23.00	26.39	24.60	23.06	23.49	23.73	26.01	23.26	22.50	22.46
1970	25.50	23.46	20.77	20.27	19.77	19.24	20.64	19.87	19.50	17.38	19.71	21.51
1971	20.88	22.59	22.30	21.89	20.49	23.51	18.87	22.10	22.40	19.89	21.45	21.94
1972	20.69	21.24	22.79	22.36	24.69	21.08	24.46	23.34	25.96	24.83	25.30	25.90
1973	26.08	28.03	27.72	28.10	28.73	28.65	29.66	30.69	29.10	32.47	32.06	30.38
1974	30.47	31.09	31.51	30.09	31.06	28.25	33.48	29.98	29.31	27.68	24.05	26.70
1975	23.47	21.70	20.02	23.83	23.82	23.51	22.39	25.21	20.72	20.59	20.11	19.24
1976	23.74	22.85	24.38	23.90	21.12	25.23	27.55	24.45	26.44	26.87	24.44	25.36
1977	25.10	25.20	24.04	26.38	28.63	28.59	25.02	27.52	30.55	26.40	26.56	30.33
1978	29.64	32.46	29.04	28.54	31.72	29.28	31.32	32.79	34.14	39.58	33.12	29.21
1979	34.53	36.67	37.84	36.22	32.27	33.43	34.38	32.56	33.69	34.33	33.22	33.67
1980	34.73	31.00	31.69	31.66	26.18	27.70	28.89	29.44	29.16	30.39	28.05	29.41
1981	32.25	27.56	30.60	32.39	29.03	29.28	29.47	27.98	26.71	27.87	25.42	24.09
1982	28.19	29.45	26.94	24.83	22.47	22.56	23.42	22.25	23.12	23.52	22.08	22.79
1983	22.47	21.55	21.33	22.94	24.25	23.99	22.21	24.44	25.31	26.91	24.92	23.66
1984	27.22	27.31	27.82	26.69	30.30	28.10	29.38	27.50	27.02	28.21	27.53	26.94
1985	27.41	29.78	29.73	27.53	27.77	29.08	28.77	28.82	30.99	30.94	27.51	31.20
1986	28.76	30.39	28.55	27.82	27.27	27.98	27.50	27.09	28.31	29.02	28.51	30.28
1987	29.06	28.83	28.52	29.85	30.92	32.48	33.63	30.77	30.68	32.16	31.72	34.44
1988	35.36	35.81	32.96	34.30	31.72	34.87	36.00	39.01	35.30	33.81	34.60	37.84
1989	39.01	35.92	35.77	37.52	34.94	37.33	38.61	33.58	34.09	33.51	35.53	41.56
1990	36.57	33.76	37.60	34.10	34.12	33.50	36.56	31.86	34.58	37.56	32.46	37.65
1991	33.95	33.83	32.36	30.13	29.31	28.48	36.42	31.21	30.14	31.20	34.04	28.96
1992	32.17	31.97	34.29	33.31	32.52	33.23	32.59	31.51	33.33	33.60	30.55	35.33
1993	32.95	35.87	33.61	33.68	33.89	37.90	34.75	36.40	35.87	37.25	-	-

Source: U.S. Department of Commerce, Bureau of Economic Analysis, U.S. Department of Commerce, Bureau of the Census, McGraw-Hill Information Systems Company. - indicates data not available or zero.

Building Permits for New Private Housing Units

(1967 = 100)

Year	Jan	Feb	Mar	Apr	May	Jun	Jul	Aug	Sep	Oct	Nov	Dec
1946	86.6	91.4	114.7	82.7	82.4	79.6	77.6	77.7	78.3	74.3	77.1	72.9
1947	80.1	85.8	83.9	77.5	80.5	91.6	96.6	108.1	111.2	118.2	117.5	117.4
1948	109.4	100.4	104.0	116.5	106.7	103.1	102.2	94.9	84.8	89.4	86.2	82.8
1949	80.4	81.9	86.8	96.7	104.2	106.4	110.2	112.3	136.2	135.6	141.9	146.7
1950	157.4	159.2	159.1	161.9	161.3	160.7	182.8	158.2	133.8	126.2	123.6	158.6
1951	146.3	114.9	104.5	96.9	99.3	96.9	92.9	94.8	122.2	93.2	90.9	94.2
1952	99.6	115.3	105.6	103.5	101.2	101.6	107.9	107.7	115.5	116.8	117.2	108.3
1953	105.0	110.7	111.6	106.3	106.4	103.5	100.0	98.4	94.6	99.6	100.1	102.4
1954	101.9	100.4	105.8	106.9	108.8	116.9	119.9	118.9	121.9	126.2	135.9	132.1
1955	136.4	151.0	129.3	132.9	133.6	126.2	126.7	122.2	120.4	117.9	107.5	107.0
1956	109.8	106.8	109.8	109.5	101.9	100.1	99.4	97.0	94.5	93.1	93.7	92.8
1957	86.5	90.9	91.7	86.7	90.5	92.5	86.2	92.1	92.4	91.1	88.5	89.3
1958	91.5	78.7	87.2	91.9	96.2	102.7	111.9	111.7	114.5	118.2	134.1	115.8
1959	114.7	119.6	125.0	119.4	117.4	115.5	112.6	113.7	109.5	105.3	100.7	108.2
1960	102.8	102.4	89.8	95.6	99.0	90.1	93.9	93.5	92.6	91.4	92.1	89.3
1961	91.2	90.4	94.0	94.2	96.6	100.7	101.9	109.0	103.2	105.6	108.3	109.2
1962	105.5	112.3	106.7	116.2	107.4	108.5	111.9	112.9	115.0	111.1	116.2	116.2
1963	113.0	109.7	113.9	116.6	122.2	121.8	119.6	118.6	128.0	128.1	122.9	128.8
1964	117.4	130.6	118.8	114.5	117.6	115.8	118.1	118.3	114.5	111.5	113.5	105.3
1965	114.5	107.3	109.6	105.2	109.3	112.4	112.0	113.1	111.1	115.8	118.3	119.1
1966	120.0	104.9	111.8	103.7	97.7	86.6	84.4	79.4	70.2	66.9	66.6	67.2
1967	87.2	79.5	83.7	90.8	94.3	102.5	103.2	107.8	112.1	112.2	113.7	115.3
1968	103.3	117.6	120.0	112.8	113.7	114.0	117.9	118.9	128.4	124.6	125.9	121.8
1969	127.9	131.0	126.0	126.3	116.5	118.3	112.0	115.4	110.7	106.6	104.4	101.3
1970	93.1	98.0	99.2	107.3	116.5	115.8	116.1	122.2	125.0	137.2	131.7	154.9
1971	144.0	139.2	154.2	153.0	172.9	166.8	181.4	175.7	175.0	177.6	182.2	186.9
1972	192.9	186.9	181.4	184.3	178.1	188.1	189.2	195.1	206.2	202.9	192.6	208.5
1973	195.7	191.9	177.7	164.5	166.4	176.7	156.8	155.9	146.9	121.7	120.8	111.0
1974	114.7	117.2	124.1	108.1	98.1	93.6	86.4	79.0	72.4	71.0	67.5	74.9
1975	62.6	62.8	61.2	74.6	78.8	81.5	87.9	85.7	91.7	94.4	95.6	94.0
1976	103.0	102.6	100.3	97.6	102.9	102.4	107.3	112.9	127.6	122.8	132.0	130.2
1977	124.6	134.5	143.1	143.1	143.8	151.0	145.4	153.4	144.3	151.5	152.7	151.2
1978	140.6	140.2	145.3	157.4	142.7	160.2	144.3	136.6	141.4	143.9	145.0	146.9
1979	118.0	120.5	138.9	129.0	136.0	132.5	123.9	128.5	132.3	119.6	103.1	101.3
1980	103.4	96.9	79.8	65.3	69.6	90.3	101.7	110.4	119.9	110.3	111.7	100.9
1981	98.6	96.9	95.6	96.1	94.8	78.8	75.5	71.8	68.4	59.1	60.4	64.3
1982	64.1	65.3	72.0	71.7	77.0	73.8	84.3	74.8	84.2	92.8	99.3	109.1
1983	115.2	118.8	119.2	126.5	134.8	142.9	145.0	138.4	128.0	138.6	134.7	131.4
1984	144.8	158.5	137.6	141.6	138.8	144.7	128.0	122.0	121.5	118.8	131.0	129.7
1985	132.4	132.5	137.7	132.7	136.3	136.8	135.3	144.2	152.8	139.0	134.9	143.1
1986	147.3	140.9	141.9	148.2	143.3	142.7	141.9	137.6	134.4	133.6	131.1	151.8
1987	134.8	134.7	135.9	127.7	119.6	121.4	120.9	120.5	120.7	115.4	116.2	107.3
1988	99.2	114.7	121.6	114.0	115.2	118.4	114.8	116.4	114.5	120.9	120.3	119.7
1989	116.9	110.3	96.8	109.7	110.1	105.4	102.3	106.4	104.8	108.9	107.2	113.4
1990	139.4	106.0	99.4	90.6	85.1	88.4	86.0	85.2	77.8	73.8	75.0	68.7
1991	62.7	68.0	72.6	73.0	79.0	76.9	77.6	75.3	77.7	79.0	78.5	84.6
1992	85.9	90.5	86.3	82.9	84.0	83.6	86.4	86.2	89.3	91.0	90.6	95.4
1993	92.3	91.0	82.5	87.8	89.4	88.9	92.7	99.0	101.4	104.0	-	-

Source: U.S. Department of Commerce, Bureau of the Census. - indicates data not available or zero.

Vendor Performance, Slower Deliveries Diffusion Index
(Percent)

Year	Jan	Feb	Mar	Apr	May	Jun	Jul	Aug	Sep	Oct	Nov	Dec
1948	36.3	37.1	32.7	41.6	40.4	38.4	36.8	31.2	28.3	28.7	28.0	17.7
1949	16.6	13.1	12.4	16.2	15.5	15.0	22.4	33.0	39.9	46.1	51.5	52.2
1950	56.3	68.0	72.0	68.8	82.9	76.5	89.4	81.7	73.7	70.3	79.1	87.5
1951	88.7	93.3	85.1	65.7	45.0	36.7	32.2	32.0	46.4	47.2	34.9	33.6
1952	31.3	24.9	18.8	19.4	22.4	33.0	47.4	41.2	42.7	43.3	45.0	43.5
1953	41.5	41.8	41.8	38.6	35.1	33.3	28.5	26.5	23.2	20.7	20.2	21.8
1954	23.6	26.9	28.0	30.3	34.3	35.8	38.1	36.4	43.6	49.5	51.9	54.5
1955	60.6	67.2	68.5	71.9	68.7	65.7	67.0	64.3	66.3	66.5	64.9	61.4
1956	53.5	51.3	51.0	51.0	38.6	41.0	53.9	46.8	42.8	40.1	44.6	39.5
1957	36.3	31.2	26.3	28.9	30.0	30.0	36.8	30.8	28.8	32.6	27.8	27.3
1958	30.3	31.0	34.0	35.5	38.5	39.2	43.0	44.7	51.1	52.4	55.8	56.4
1959	61.8	67.3	66.3	64.8	63.0	63.7	59.1	57.4	57.5	58.5	54.6	53.7
1960	46.2	31.7	28.8	28.9	32.3	34.8	35.8	38.0	37.3	36.2	37.6	40.4
1961	39.2	41.1	42.1	47.5	47.9	49.3	49.4	50.6	50.7	52.4	51.1	55.8
1962	57.1	56.2	57.0	47.4	45.2	43.3	45.1	43.7	45.1	46.7	48.7	50.1
1963	50.4	51.0	54.9	58.2	56.4	56.3	43.6	48.5	49.7	47.4	48.7	47.6
1964	55.3	51.9	60.3	57.7	61.4	57.6	61.8	66.2	71.9	71.2	70.3	67.8
1965	68.5	68.1	65.9	69.4	68.9	69.3	65.1	65.4	61.2	59.1	65.1	73.5
1966	74.9	80.1	86.4	79.3	74.6	71.6	73.1	74.3	72.4	68.7	62.6	57.9
1967	48.2	49.9	38.0	36.9	34.4	36.5	40.9	44.8	46.5	51.1	51.4	49.9
1968	50.6	53.9	54.0	49.0	49.4	49.9	55.9	47.8	48.4	53.3	61.0	58.3
1969	63.6	60.1	60.5	63.9	64.9	67.0	65.7	70.3	68.9	66.8	64.1	66.8
1970	57.9	57.7	49.3	48.7	67.2	66.1	49.8	46.1	46.5	39.0	37.8	37.5
1971	39.8	44.2	45.0	48.9	49.4	47.9	47.4	49.7	48.9	50.9	50.9	53.3
1972	55.2	52.6	57.1	55.0	56.1	57.7	61.7	62.9	65.5	73.0	74.5	80.7
1973	83.7	85.2	87.5	86.7	86.6	85.6	85.2	86.7	90.1	88.7	96.8	92.8
1974	91.8	88.8	88.9	82.1	74.5	73.1	69.2	66.3	51.8	45.3	34.0	23.2
1975	19.5	15.9	17.3	21.7	22.7	24.9	28.7	35.1	43.8	44.8	46.8	41.2
1976	54.0	56.1	56.7	57.3	58.3	58.6	54.0	55.2	52.6	49.0	47.2	53.3
1977	55.3	65.1	49.6	54.6	55.4	53.3	58.3	53.5	56.7	53.6	56.3	57.1
1978	55.6	63.4	58.9	57.1	57.4	61.1	59.4	60.6	60.0	64.7	64.5	63.5
1979	66.4	64.0	66.7	75.6	63.7	61.4	57.4	52.9	50.7	46.9	46.8	42.2
1980	42.1	46.0	39.1	36.9	29.8	32.4	36.3	40.1	41.2	46.5	46.8	50.1
1981	49.7	48.5	48.7	51.2	50.2	47.9	44.9	49.6	45.9	37.7	40.5	41.2
1982	40.1	40.8	36.4	38.2	42.1	45.2	45.8	45.3	45.9	46.5	46.9	48.6
1983	46.7	49.9	50.8	52.7	51.9	56.8	58.9	60.2	60.7	62.8	67.5	62.1
1984	64.4	61.5	65.5	64.6	62.5	56.2	59.1	55.2	52.8	49.3	48.1	48.8
1985	50.4	48.6	46.7	46.1	48.0	47.1	45.7	46.6	49.5	50.0	48.5	49.3
1986	50.1	49.8	50.5	50.7	50.2	49.9	49.9	50.8	49.6	51.3	52.0	52.8
1987	51.5	51.2	51.9	52.8	54.0	56.8	58.9	60.3	61.5	62.2	64.9	62.7
1988	62.0	61.2	57.3	58.6	56.9	65.6	58.4	57.4	55.2	54.8	52.1	53.0
1989	53.9	54.0	52.5	52.2	49.1	46.5	46.1	44.0	43.9	43.3	42.5	43.5
1990	47.5	44.0	46.9	47.1	48.0	49.7	47.0	50.4	49.4	48.3	49.0	47.3
1991	44.7	44.9	44.0	45.5	46.2	47.1	49.3	48.3	48.5	50.2	49.6	49.1
1992	49.5	49.8	50.1	48.1	50.2	50.5	51.1	50.2	50.9	48.8	51.0	51.7
1993	53.2	53.1	52.1	53.6	51.7	49.9	49.6	51.6	50.9	50.8	50.5	-

Source: National Association of Purchasing Management and Purchasing Management Association of Chicago. - indicates data not available or zero.

Consumer Expectations

Not seasonally adjusted
(1966:I = 100)

Year	Jan	Feb	Mar	Apr	May	Jun	Jul	Aug	Sep	Oct	Nov	Dec
1952	-	-	-	-	-	-	-	-	-	-	92.4	93.4
1953	94.5	95.5	94.2	92.9	91.6	90.3	89.1	87.8	86.5	85.2	83.9	84.4
1954	84.8	85.3	85.6	85.8	86.1	86.7	87.3	87.9	88.5	89.1	89.7	91.4
1955	93.1	94.8	96.5	98.2	99.9	100.6	101.2	101.9	102.5	103.2	103.8	103.7
1956	103.6	103.6	103.5	103.4	103.3	103.9	104.6	105.2	105.2	105.2	105.2	103.7
1957	102.2	100.7	99.2	97.7	96.2	94.6	92.9	91.3	89.6	88.0	86.3	85.7
1958	85.2	84.6	84.0	83.5	82.9	84.8	86.6	88.5	90.4	92.2	94.1	94.7
1959	95.2	95.8	96.4	96.9	97.5	97.2	96.9	96.7	96.4	96.1	95.8	98.7
1960	101.7	104.6	102.6	100.6	98.6	98.2	97.9	97.5	96.1	94.8	93.4	93.9
1961	94.4	94.9	96.0	97.0	98.1	98.2	98.4	98.5	97.9	97.4	96.8	99.0
1962	101.2	103.4	101.1	98.8	96.5	95.5	94.4	93.4	95.3	97.3	99.2	99.4
1963	99.7	99.9	98.0	96.0	94.1	95.1	96.0	97.0	97.0	97.0	97.0	97.8
1964	98.6	99.4	98.7	97.9	97.2	97.8	98.5	99.1	99.8	100.4	101.1	101.7
1965	102.4	103.0	103.2	103.4	103.7	103.9	104.1	104.3	105.3	106.3	107.3	104.9
1966	102.4	100.0	98.7	97.3	96.0	94.2	92.5	90.7	90.5	90.4	90.2	92.3
1967	94.3	96.4	95.7	95.0	94.3	94.7	95.1	95.5	94.0	92.6	91.1	92.2
1968	93.2	94.3	92.8	91.4	89.9	89.8	89.7	89.6	90.3	90.9	91.6	93.7
1969	95.9	98.0	95.7	93.4	91.1	89.6	88.1	86.6	84.3	81.9	79.6	78.3
1970	77.1	75.8	74.3	72.7	71.2	72.7	74.2	75.7	74.2	72.8	71.3	72.8
1971	74.4	75.9	75.9	75.9	75.9	76.7	77.6	78.4	78.0	77.6	77.2	81.8
1972	86.3	90.9	88.0	85.1	82.2	85.2	88.3	91.3	90.1	89.0	87.8	83.0
1973	78.1	73.3	71.3	69.3	67.3	65.9	64.4	63.0	64.4	65.7	67.1	61.2
1974	55.3	49.4	54.2	59.1	63.9	61.8	59.7	57.6	55.5	53.3	51.2	50.8
1975	50.4	50.0	56.6	63.2	69.8	70.1	70.4	70.7	70.4	70.2	69.9	73.7
1976	77.4	81.2	80.6	80.1	79.5	81.5	83.5	85.5	85.6	85.8	85.9	85.3
1977	84.8	84.2	84.0	83.8	83.6	82.9	82.2	81.5	79.6	77.8	75.9	75.8
1978	75.7	77.2	69.5	71.1	73.0	68.1	72.0	67.0	69.8	71.7	62.8	53.8
1979	58.4	62.2	53.7	53.3	54.9	51.4	44.2	49.3	53.6	49.5	52.0	51.5
1980	54.1	54.9	44.3	44.4	45.3	53.0	53.4	59.6	67.2	68.9	76.2	59.7
1981	67.2	61.4	61.4	68.1	72.9	70.5	66.4	70.1	68.3	61.5	55.6	56.8
1982	62.9	58.7	53.1	61.1	62.0	60.1	57.6	60.9	66.9	70.4	71.0	67.9
1983	65.2	71.2	80.9	86.9	93.4	89.2	91.1	88.2	85.8	86.1	87.9	91.0
1984	97.0	93.2	97.7	91.4	90.6	89.8	91.9	93.7	96.4	91.6	91.5	87.9
1985	90.3	86.5	87.3	87.0	84.2	91.1	87.4	86.3	84.2	80.8	84.5	88.1
1986	85.3	87.8	86.9	88.5	87.5	90.3	88.5	85.9	81.3	87.1	81.6	78.3
1987	80.9	81.6	83.3	84.7	80.6	80.8	83.3	85.8	84.2	80.4	72.7	76.7
1988	80.9	81.9	85.2	82.4	87.3	85.7	82.3	88.8	89.5	87.0	86.3	85.5
1989	89.9	88.8	87.6	83.2	80.1	82.0	85.5	80.3	88.6	87.2	84.3	85.5
1990	83.4	81.3	81.3	83.9	79.3	76.6	77.3	62.9	58.8	50.9	52.8	53.7
1991	55.2	62.0	84.5	74.7	71.5	75.9	74.4	75.3	76.4	70.5	61.9	61.5
1992	59.1	61.8	70.3	70.5	71.2	70.7	67.6	69.5	67.4	67.5	78.2	89.5
1993	83.4	80.6	75.8	76.4	68.5	70.4	64.7	65.8	66.8	72.5	-	-

Source: University of Michigan, Survey Research Center. Used by permission. - indicates data not available or zero.

Change in Manufacturers' Unfilled Orders, Durables
(Billions of 1987 $)

Year	Jan	Feb	Mar	Apr	May	Jun	Jul	Aug	Sep	Oct	Nov	Dec
1947	-	-	-	-	-	-	-5.59	-2.58	-0.81	-4.04	-0.93	-0.45
1948	-2.36	-2.20	-2.10	-0.61	-2.33	1.59	1.08	-0.94	-2.54	-6.27	-3.32	-4.44
1949	-4.99	-3.82	-4.30	-5.82	-4.95	-5.14	-3.58	-1.45	-0.96	1.93	2.38	1.63
1950	2.69	1.23	1.88	1.65	1.50	3.06	9.58	16.46	8.52	6.80	2.95	3.61
1951	20.82	11.02	13.60	12.54	8.89	9.52	8.99	3.86	3.21	7.30	3.27	0.78
1952	2.38	-0.02	7.92	8.75	-0.26	10.89	7.21	2.61	2.21	-3.41	-1.41	-0.74
1953	6.91	1.71	-4.41	-3.21	-1.51	-3.22	-9.71	-10.91	-15.53	-8.85	-6.27	-7.56
1954	-9.55	-6.57	-9.71	-7.10	-6.98	-7.21	-4.60	-4.52	1.14	5.06	-3.15	-0.24
1955	2.32	1.70	4.56	0.66	1.32	0.68	2.36	2.48	2.26	4.00	2.07	5.37
1956	4.00	0.84	0.71	2.87	0.43	-0.58	4.46	5.92	1.18	-2.11	-1.45	-1.27
1957	-1.62	-0.06	-3.70	-3.67	-2.88	-4.24	-6.52	-5.74	-5.40	-6.43	-4.88	-4.85
1958	-15.37	-5.03	-0.91	-2.37	-0.33	1.19	-0.34	-0.48	-1.87	-0.39	1.96	-0.54
1959	2.42	3.16	3.81	2.04	-0.48	0.68	-1.76	-0.05	2.34	2.05	-0.33	-1.40
1960	-4.36	-3.52	-3.82	-2.70	-1.58	-0.64	-1.61	1.08	0.37	-2.56	-0.60	-1.51
1961	-0.27	0.33	-0.80	1.20	0.85	0.36	0.57	1.40	0.30	-0.20	0.88	2.16
1962	1.73	1.85	-1.26	-1.70	-1.19	-0.64	-0.09	-1.48	1.23	2.08	-	4.67
1963	3.80	3.02	4.88	2.59	2.77	-0.70	-0.21	-0.27	0.80	0.56	0.30	-1.64
1964	3.89	1.70	2.24	2.82	3.27	2.84	4.93	1.65	2.94	4.49	1.33	1.69
1965	4.31	3.24	2.79	2.71	3.04	2.77	2.06	2.47	3.26	5.09	3.86	4.49
1966	6.06	5.50	6.84	5.72	3.95	5.60	4.17	3.44	5.89	2.55	1.04	1.08
1967	-0.16	-0.23	-1.16	0.32	3.36	4.08	1.44	0.02	-0.39	2.71	0.19	4.16
1968	-2.34	0.28	3.24	0.02	-2.83	-1.19	-3.80	2.40	2.14	4.14	-0.15	0.16
1969	0.36	1.20	0.67	4.85	0.74	0.20	0.43	0.45	1.74	-1.25	-2.32	-2.88
1970	-3.64	-3.92	-2.99	-3.73	-4.71	-2.63	-4.07	-4.34	-2.00	-4.59	-2.00	-1.06
1971	2.67	2.85	-1.16	-3.12	-5.17	-4.72	-3.46	0.77	0.07	-1.47	0.98	0.75
1972	0.39	0.74	0.53	-0.44	2.18	2.26	2.05	2.10	5.32	2.28	1.61	6.05
1973	4.64	6.80	9.40	6.70	3.24	4.85	2.72	7.24	6.45	6.98	6.12	4.55
1974	6.56	4.38	1.54	4.23	3.70	0.68	-1.28	4.42	-3.10	-9.01	-6.76	-8.67
1975	-7.75	-6.61	-8.48	-7.28	-5.59	-5.45	0.68	-1.70	-2.42	-3.31	-3.35	-4.28
1976	-3.78	-2.34	1.66	0.33	-1.81	-0.18	1.67	-2.91	-0.20	1.67	-0.65	1.36
1977	-0.11	-1.71	0.27	1.75	0.30	2.99	1.00	2.56	1.62	2.98	1.31	4.52
1978	1.28	2.18	5.76	3.64	5.19	4.30	2.98	4.18	6.72	7.68	7.59	3.64
1979	2.37	8.21	6.28	3.10	0.12	2.41	-0.76	-1.14	1.91	1.16	-2.14	-1.69
1980	3.34	0.64	-5.85	-4.02	-4.62	-1.83	3.79	-1.42	1.64	1.27	-0.68	0.62
1981	-0.35	-3.09	-0.19	-0.05	0.11	-2.99	-0.11	-2.90	-1.26	-4.29	-3.69	-5.24
1982	-1.28	-1.92	0.09	-0.51	-5.07	-4.63	-3.82	-4.97	-2.37	-0.06	-2.97	3.19
1983	3.38	-2.09	0.75	-0.55	0.99	3.51	1.58	1.12	3.15	7.22	4.99	2.26
1984	3.74	4.79	9.45	0.78	2.40	-1.16	3.42	-0.10	-0.04	-2.92	1.36	-0.72
1985	3.47	0.48	-1.75	-2.13	-0.73	3.91	-0.08	1.42	3.11	0.23	-2.88	1.89
1986	3.67	1.64	4.64	-2.54	-2.60	-2.63	-0.53	-2.26	1.71	-1.02	0.81	-0.46
1987	-1.90	-1.24	1.17	4.03	3.96	4.71	5.53	2.49	0.02	1.59	1.22	0.99
1988	4.33	3.38	-1.40	0.88	0.93	1.16	1.43	2.97	0.05	1.84	-0.47	7.69
1989	3.96	0.80	2.63	2.93	-1.72	2.60	2.74	-3.51	1.53	-0.65	2.85	7.74
1990	2.59	-0.78	4.85	1.07	-0.01	-2.60	1.87	-1.85	0.29	1.92	-5.76	3.05
1991	-0.78	0.67	-2.92	-4.08	-2.40	-4.89	6.71	0.38	-4.29	-2.26	-2.42	-2.38
1992	-1.82	-4.39	-3.61	-1.66	-2.67	-2.88	-4.99	-4.10	-4.64	-1.39	-5.30	0.10
1993	-0.29	-0.69	-5.96	-4.24	-4.80	-4.07	-0.96	-2.07	-4.11	-2.52	-	-

Source: U.S. Department of Commerce, Bureau of Economic Analysis, U.S. Department of Commerce, Bureau of the Census, U.S. Department of Labor, Bureau of Labor Statistics. - indicates data not available or zero.

Change in Sensitive Materials Prices
(Percent)

Year	Jan	Feb	Mar	Apr	May	Jun	Jul	Aug	Sep	Oct	Nov	Dec
1948	-	1.28	-1.18	-0.06	1.51	0.42	-0.20	-0.17	-0.79	-0.40	0.54	-0.31
1949	-0.51	-1.54	-1.65	-3.65	-1.59	-1.68	0.47	1.16	1.27	-1.53	1.18	0.12
1950	-	-0.15	0.74	0.21	2.17	2.48	4.66	5.87	4.57	2.24	2.66	2.11
1951	4.34	1.30	-0.11	-1.42	-0.74	-2.18	-3.95	-4.23	-2.62	1.06	-1.08	-0.70
1952	-0.91	-1.45	-2.62	-0.66	-1.13	-1.23	0.17	1.13	1.17	-0.83	-1.09	0.62
1953	-0.76	0.08	0.42	-0.64	0.56	-0.03	-0.51	-0.42	-0.74	-0.37	-0.83	-0.66
1954	-0.79	-0.09	0.62	0.87	0.20	0.81	0.57	-0.60	0.46	0.37	-0.37	-0.37
1955	0.63	0.82	0.14	0.48	0.45	0.42	1.00	-0.36	0.08	-0.25	0.72	1.15
1956	0.38	0.51	0.19	-0.43	-0.49	-0.98	-0.36	0.14	0.38	0.05	0.44	0.35
1957	-0.30	-0.90	-0.22	-0.55	-0.55	-0.86	-0.31	-0.17	-0.53	-1.13	-0.57	-0.63
1958	-0.49	0.09	-1.05	-1.12	0.39	0.15	1.15	0.53	0.67	1.59	0.74	-0.76
1959	0.37	-0.09	0.77	0.76	0.70	0.39	-0.06	0.17	0.36	0.55	0.22	0.66
1960	0.14	-0.68	-0.57	0.14	-0.14	-0.69	-0.25	0.06	-0.22	-0.53	-0.11	-0.73
1961	-0.59	0.96	-0.17	-0.17	0.39	-0.45	0.82	0.28	0.06	0.86	-1.38	1.06
1962	0.22	-0.36	0.03	-0.91	0.42	-0.61	-0.25	-0.31	0.03	0.17	0.25	-0.42
1963	0.14	-0.03	0.08	-0.37	0.11	0.28	0.76	0.25	-0.25	0.50	0.61	0.94
1964	-0.05	-	0.19	0.68	-0.38	0.30	0.22	0.89	0.78	1.36	0.37	0.34
1965	-0.89	-0.37	0.37	0.74	1.07	-0.10	0.18	0.80	0.18	0.61	0.18	-0.08
1966	0.48	0.33	0.63	0.25	-0.42	-0.20	-0.10	-2.36	-0.77	-0.70	-0.71	-0.45
1967	-0.82	-0.72	-1.05	-1.00	-0.19	0.71	-0.08	-0.05	0.35	0.24	0.49	1.11
1968	-0.53	0.56	0.83	0.40	-0.74	0.74	0.76	0.71	0.55	1.11	1.18	0.73
1969	0.98	0.77	0.07	0.25	0.07	0.20	0.34	0.66	1.09	0.12	0.70	0.38
1970	-0.31	-0.64	-0.53	-0.10	-0.34	-0.97	-0.90	-0.17	-0.76	0.32	0.35	-1.01
1971	-0.40	0.05	0.65	1.19	-0.91	0.55	0.62	0.64	0.63	0.39	0.39	1.23
1972	0.47	0.78	2.41	1.21	3.12	0.81	0.61	0.22	0.11	1.08	2.43	1.37
1973	1.48	2.65	1.81	1.70	1.03	2.20	1.57	2.47	2.73	2.03	2.30	4.76
1974	1.70	2.47	1.89	0.10	-1.94	-0.12	1.33	-1.17	-0.56	-3.95	-2.91	-4.55
1975	-1.16	-0.16	-0.52	0.56	0.61	-2.79	-0.39	1.95	3.09	0.88	0.65	0.97
1976	0.56	0.93	0.39	2.10	1.57	1.14	3.46	0.25	0.21	-0.70	-0.40	0.60
1977	0.25	0.98	2.02	-0.55	-0.16	-0.87	0.26	0.82	-0.04	0.77	0.84	1.46
1978	0.99	0.66	-0.39	-0.74	0.36	1.82	0.44	1.65	1.18	2.14	1.63	-0.38
1979	0.92	1.76	1.94	1.93	1.50	1.09	0.70	-0.05	0.02	3.30	1.86	1.06
1980	1.45	1.52	1.27	-1.99	-3.05	-1.50	0.36	1.92	1.17	1.05	0.64	-0.38
1981	-0.95	-1.22	1.24	0.82	-0.05	-0.20	0.16	0.35	-0.90	-1.11	-1.59	-1.31
1982	-0.69	-0.33	-1.03	-2.16	-0.25	-1.67	0.54	-0.52	0.51	-0.10	-0.64	-0.23
1983	0.50	1.56	-0.11	-0.04	0.89	1.00	2.57	2.78	1.67	2.35	1.58	0.63
1984	0.07	0.95	0.81	0.43	-0.23	-0.32	-0.50	-1.18	-0.24	-1.56	0.03	-0.59
1985	-0.87	-0.72	-0.38	-0.81	-0.77	-0.96	-0.39	-0.49	-1.45	0.10	-0.03	0.07
1986	0.24	-0.47	-1.11	-0.27	0.78	1.33	1.57	-2.42	1.73	3.13	2.03	-0.12
1987	0.81	-0.48	0.55	2.06	2.19	0.93	1.38	1.21	0.60	0.45	-0.67	0.47
1988	0.52	0.06	0.87	0.84	0.44	1.21	-0.01	0.32	-0.31	-0.11	2.13	0.82
1989	1.09	0.99	0.26	-0.56	-0.83	-0.72	-0.82	-0.32	0.23	0.21	-1.47	-2.08
1990	-0.75	-1.15	1.00	1.31	0.04	-0.04	0.14	0.36	-0.27	-0.69	-1.61	-0.48
1991	-0.39	-0.65	-0.76	-0.28	-0.11	-0.71	-0.27	-1.23	-1.26	-0.42	0.32	-0.02
1992	-0.28	0.31	1.63	1.28	0.78	0.07	-0.19	-0.18	1.17	-1.32	-1.24	0.61
1993	0.55	0.07	-0.55	-1.10	-0.43	-0.15	-0.32	-0.24	-0.67	0.77	-	-

Source: U.S. Department of Commerce, Bureau of Economic Analysis, U.S. Department of Labor, Bureau of Labor Statistics, Commodity Research Bureau, Inc. - indicates data not available or zero.

Money Supply M2
(Billions of 1987 $)

Year	Jan	Feb	Mar	Apr	May	Jun	Jul	Aug	Sep	Oct	Nov	Dec
1947	1,039.2	1,030.9	1,025.4	1,031.6	1,036.8	1,040.4	1,030.8	1,025.9	1,015.5	1,011.9	1,010.9	991.3
1948	984.1	984.1	985.0	973.7	963.0	958.5	946.5	947.9	947.0	950.9	958.5	956.6
1949	959.7	964.3	964.3	965.7	967.6	967.1	976.0	974.5	968.9	973.6	974.5	976.0
1950	982.6	983.2	985.6	990.9	990.9	993.3	982.1	979.3	975.2	973.5	970.8	955.5
1951	945.7	930.8	929.8	931.6	930.6	937.7	942.5	951.1	949.3	949.6	952.4	949.4
1952	953.2	962.1	964.2	963.1	970.7	970.8	965.5	973.5	979.5	982.5	987.2	986.0
1953	991.5	993.2	994.0	997.0	1,000.0	997.0	1,003.4	1,001.7	1,002.5	1,001.3	1,007.2	1,005.5
1954	1,008.4	1,011.4	1,014.3	1,013.5	1,022.4	1,025.3	1,034.7	1,039.8	1,041.9	1,051.1	1,050.4	1,056.6
1955	1,062.1	1,064.0	1,062.7	1,065.7	1,074.5	1,074.5	1,077.0	1,077.0	1,070.9	1,077.1	1,072.2	1,079.2
1956	1,080.1	1,075.5	1,078.1	1,081.0	1,080.2	1,074.1	1,070.8	1,070.8	1,071.0	1,067.8	1,070.7	1,068.3
1957	1,072.4	1,070.1	1,069.8	1,071.4	1,070.3	1,067.2	1,066.1	1,064.7	1,065.1	1,066.3	1,063.2	1,063.2
1958	1,053.6	1,066.3	1,070.8	1,074.4	1,081.5	1,091.3	1,095.7	1,102.8	1,105.9	1,109.8	1,111.4	1,117.7
1959	1,124.3	1,128.6	1,138.2	1,137.6	1,146.3	1,148.0	1,153.5	1,153.3	1,149.2	1,145.2	1,147.5	1,149.8
1960	1,156.2	1,152.5	1,155.2	1,158.7	1,162.2	1,162.3	1,174.5	1,180.0	1,185.4	1,181.7	1,187.0	1,192.0
1961	1,199.2	1,208.4	1,214.1	1,221.0	1,230.2	1,237.0	1,238.4	1,245.6	1,247.3	1,254.5	1,263.3	1,270.8
1962	1,278.8	1,283.8	1,294.0	1,299.2	1,306.4	1,312.4	1,319.2	1,326.3	1,328.1	1,338.2	1,347.9	1,358.4
1963	1,368.5	1,378.3	1,382.5	1,392.9	1,403.4	1,405.9	1,417.1	1,420.7	1,428.5	1,433.2	1,445.0	1,445.6
1964	1,454.0	1,462.1	1,469.1	1,477.2	1,486.4	1,490.1	1,502.6	1,514.3	1,526.0	1,535.5	1,540.9	1,550.4
1965	1,561.3	1,570.8	1,574.5	1,577.9	1,583.7	1,582.0	1,598.9	1,603.2	1,615.8	1,622.9	1,634.4	1,640.4
1966	1,651.4	1,653.0	1,655.7	1,652.8	1,654.9	1,652.3	1,652.3	1,641.0	1,650.3	1,647.1	1,652.2	1,660.9
1967	1,667.5	1,672.1	1,687.2	1,691.4	1,702.4	1,713.0	1,728.7	1,732.2	1,744.7	1,751.7	1,754.5	1,759.4
1968	1,757.7	1,755.3	1,763.9	1,768.3	1,778.5	1,778.7	1,778.2	1,785.1	1,791.9	1,800.0	1,807.7	1,815.1
1969	1,818.8	1,808.9	1,810.4	1,805.6	1,801.9	1,796.3	1,789.5	1,786.2	1,786.2	1,779.9	1,778.5	1,775.6
1970	1,776.0	1,756.4	1,753.6	1,743.1	1,751.9	1,756.2	1,755.3	1,766.8	1,774.8	1,784.7	1,787.9	1,794.3
1971	1,807.1	1,825.0	1,850.0	1,872.5	1,890.1	1,895.2	1,902.8	1,914.8	1,934.0	1,945.3	1,963.3	1,974.0
1972	1,988.7	1,999.7	2,021.2	2,031.8	2,039.1	2,050.7	2,071.5	2,091.6	2,110.3	2,122.0	2,135.7	2,152.7
1973	2,169.9	2,163.2	2,148.8	2,150.1	2,151.8	2,152.2	2,162.5	2,130.3	2,127.2	2,115.7	2,114.9	2,120.4
1974	2,106.1	2,092.1	2,086.7	2,083.4	2,064.4	2,057.4	2,046.8	2,029.6	2,016.0	2,004.7	1,998.7	1,987.7
1975	1,983.0	1,987.3	2,007.1	2,024.3	2,039.1	2,062.3	2,061.6	2,074.6	2,080.0	2,079.9	2,088.1	2,092.2
1976	2,105.5	2,129.5	2,148.2	2,166.5	2,181.2	2,176.8	2,186.6	2,200.0	2,210.7	2,231.8	2,247.7	2,263.6
1977	2,280.8	2,280.6	2,288.7	2,293.4	2,309.3	2,312.0	2,315.3	2,327.9	2,338.0	2,343.2	2,345.1	2,347.4
1978	2,352.1	2,348.4	2,344.8	2,343.1	2,342.8	2,330.8	2,329.3	2,327.2	2,334.2	2,326.4	2,322.1	2,325.8
1979	2,321.1	2,301.0	2,295.8	2,296.5	2,279.5	2,280.6	2,274.9	2,269.6	2,263.4	2,251.6	2,230.7	2,216.9
1980	2,196.8	2,189.9	2,165.7	2,139.9	2,134.0	2,137.9	2,166.5	2,171.9	2,173.6	2,167.2	2,163.1	2,143.7
1981	2,137.5	2,132.4	2,143.5	2,156.5	2,149.7	2,142.0	2,133.9	2,138.3	2,133.3	2,145.9	2,153.0	2,167.6
1982	2,182.8	2,178.0	2,193.3	2,204.3	2,200.2	2,184.9	2,188.1	2,207.2	2,222.7	2,230.2	2,248.5	2,273.2
1983	2,331.9	2,372.3	2,392.2	2,396.8	2,404.0	2,413.7	2,417.0	2,421.5	2,427.2	2,442.4	2,448.0	2,454.0
1984	2,451.3	2,462.1	2,470.3	2,478.7	2,489.7	2,498.4	2,501.1	2,503.4	2,512.3	2,518.1	2,538.8	2,560.3
1985	2,582.3	2,594.7	2,594.7	2,591.5	2,600.6	2,624.2	2,636.3	2,648.9	2,662.4	2,661.8	2,664.3	2,671.2
1986	2,668.3	2,682.2	2,719.3	2,753.8	2,772.9	2,787.0	2,812.1	2,832.7	2,844.2	2,863.0	2,873.4	2,891.2
1987	2,889.9	2,881.9	2,874.2	2,875.2	2,871.2	2,862.9	2,860.4	2,862.8	2,866.7	2,876.7	2,867.7	2,868.4
1988	2,881.2	2,896.8	2,905.6	2,910.0	2,918.3	2,917.4	2,913.9	2,909.3	2,895.7	2,895.9	2,899.5	2,898.6
1989	2,886.2	2,877.2	2,870.4	2,852.7	2,838.8	2,852.2	2,864.1	2,880.0	2,893.2	2,892.5	2,902.0	2,910.3
1990	2,893.6	2,893.0	2,888.0	2,892.3	2,889.5	2,887.1	2,880.6	2,871.7	2,865.1	2,848.0	2,837.0	2,837.6
1991	2,827.7	2,835.9	2,852.7	2,851.4	2,853.6	2,856.4	2,849.0	2,845.1	2,836.6	2,835.5	2,834.8	2,838.4
1992	2,833.3	2,840.0	2,830.9	2,821.5	2,819.1	2,807.8	2,801.9	2,801.8	2,803.4	2,801.0	2,799.2	2,795.8
1993	2,773.0	2,755.0	2,748.6	2,739.1	2,758.8	2,764.5	2,766.6	2,763.7	2,772.9	2,764.2	-	-

Source: U.S. Department of Commerce, Bureau of Economic Analysis, Board of Governors of the Federal Reserve System. - indicates data not available or zero.

COMPOSITE INDEX OF COINCIDENT INDICATORS

The composite index of coincident indicators tends to *confirm* what the composite index of leading indicators has foreshadowed. In other words, the "coincident index" tends to decline just as the economy does (rather than before) and turns up as the economy turns up. As with the other composite indicators, a tendency signaled by this index must be sustained for at least three months before the indicator "confirms" a change in the economy's direction of growth or decline.

The coincident index is a fairly reliable indicator. In the 1948 to 1988 period, for instance, more than half of the turning points in the economy were marked exactly by the coincident index. With the exception of the 1957 peak, which the index showed six months too early, the rest of the turning points were indicated within three months of the actual turn.

Components of the Coincident Index

The index is a composite of 4 indicators, each of which is further discussed below:

> Employees on nonagricultural payrolls
> Index of industrial production
> Personal income less transfer payments
> Manufacturing and trade sales

Employees on Nonagricultural Payrolls. The index is shown in thousands of employees. Employment tends to drop during recessionary periods and increase with expansions. Before a recession or upturn takes place, producers tend to decrease or increase hours worked (hence Average Weekly Hours is part of the leading index). As the trend is confirmed, layoffs or hirings are reflected in actual employment totals. Total employment, of course, tends to grow over time. The significance of the index lies in month-to-month changes that show a pattern.

Index of Industrial Production. This indicator, expressed as an index with 1987 as its base (1987 = 100), measures changes in the physical goods and power (rather than dollar sales) produced in mining, manufacturing, and utilities. Other sectors of the economy (construction, services, communications, trade, government, etc.) are, of course, indirectly reflected in this measure. Components of this index are measured and indexed; next, these indexes are weighted by their relative importance to the economy as measured by value added—the amount of value added to raw materials purchased by an industry through its own efforts. Industrial production reflects actual output; it does not signal future intent; therefore it serves well as a coincident indicator.

Personal Income Less Transfer Payments. Expressed in billions of 1987 dollars, this index measures all income except that derived from such sources as welfare, unemployment benefits, social security, medicaid, and the like, which are transfer payments. It includes dividends, rents, interest, and wages (the bulk). It is thus a good indicator of money now available to individuals from economic activities—which tends to shrink in recessions (while transfer payments may increase) and grow in periods of economic expansion.

Manufacturing and Trade Sales. The index is reported in millions of 1987 dollars. It represents sales at all levels—production, wholesale, and retail. New orders signal future sales and are therefore indicators of future activity. The actual sales, as they are made, are an indicator of current activity; they drop or increase in cycle with the economy.

Sources and Revisions

The component series are drawn from federal sources, including the U.S. Department of Commerce, Bureau of Economic Analysis and Bureau of the Census; the U.S. Department of Labor, Bureau of Labor Statistics; and the Federal Reserve System.

The composite index itself is constructed by the Bureau of Economic Analysis. In the process, mathematical operations are performed on the component data series to ensure that volatile series do not dominate the index. A volatile series may be one that fluctuates wildly month to month but shows less volatility when averaged over several months. Other smoothing and standardization methods are used as well.

The coincident index was last revised late in 1993. The 1993 revisions transcended the usual annual revisions but were smaller in scope than the comprehensive revisions of 1989 (see reference 2).

Bibliography

1. Frumkin, Norman. *Guide to Economic Indicators*. M.E. Sharpe, Inc., 1990.

2. Green, George R. and Barry A. Beckman. "Business Cycle Indicators: Upcoming Revision of the Composite Indexes." U.S. Department of Commerce, Bureau of Economic Analysis. *Survey of Current Business*, October 1993. Superintendent of Documents, U.S. Government Printing Office, Washington, DC 20302.

3. Hertzberg, Marie P. and Barry A. Beckman. "Business Cycle Indicators: Revised Composite Indexes." U.S. Department of Commerce, Bureau of Economic Analysis. *Survey of Current Business*, January 1989. Superintendent of Documents, U.S. Government Printing Office, Washington, DC 20302.

4. U.S. Department of Commerce, Bureau of Economic Analysis. "Composite Indexes of Leading, Coincident, and Lagging Indicators." In *Survey of Current Business*, November 1987. Superintendent of Documents, U.S. Government Printing Office, Washington, DC 20302.

5. U.S. Department of Commerce, Bureau of Economic Analysis. *Survey of Current Business*. Superintendent of Documents, U.S. Government Printing Office, Washington, DC 20302.

Composite Index of 4 Coincident Indicators
(1987 = 100)

Year	Jan	Feb	Mar	Apr	May	Jun	Jul	Aug	Sep	Oct	Nov	Dec
1948	32.8	32.7	32.8	32.8	33.0	33.3	33.4	33.5	33.5	33.5	33.4	33.3
1949	32.9	32.7	32.6	32.5	32.3	32.2	31.9	32.2	32.5	31.7	32.1	32.3
1950	32.6	32.6	33.2	33.6	34.1	34.6	35.4	36.0	35.8	35.9	35.9	36.4
1951	36.6	36.6	36.8	36.9	36.9	37.0	36.7	36.9	36.9	37.0	37.1	37.2
1952	37.2	37.6	37.6	37.6	37.7	37.5	37.2	38.2	38.8	39.1	39.2	39.5
1953	39.6	39.9	40.1	40.1	40.2	40.1	40.3	40.1	39.9	39.8	39.4	39.0
1954	38.9	38.9	38.7	38.6	38.6	38.7	38.6	38.7	38.8	39.0	39.4	39.7
1955	40.0	40.2	40.6	40.9	41.3	41.4	41.7	41.7	41.9	42.2	42.4	42.6
1956	42.6	42.6	42.7	43.0	42.9	43.0	42.1	42.9	43.2	43.5	43.5	43.7
1957	43.6	43.8	43.8	43.6	43.6	43.7	43.7	43.7	43.5	43.3	43.0	42.6
1958	42.3	41.8	41.6	41.2	41.3	41.7	42.1	42.4	42.7	42.8	43.4	43.4
1959	43.8	44.2	44.6	45.0	45.3	45.4	45.3	44.6	44.5	44.5	44.8	45.8
1960	46.2	46.1	45.9	46.0	45.9	45.8	45.7	45.7	45.6	45.5	45.3	45.0
1961	45.0	44.9	45.1	45.3	45.6	46.0	46.1	46.4	46.5	46.8	47.2	47.4
1962	47.3	47.6	47.9	48.1	48.1	48.2	48.4	48.5	48.5	48.6	48.8	48.8
1963	48.8	49.1	49.2	49.5	49.6	49.8	49.9	50.0	50.2	50.5	50.5	50.8
1964	50.9	51.2	51.2	51.6	51.9	52.0	52.3	52.5	52.8	52.5	53.2	53.7
1965	53.8	54.0	54.4	54.6	54.9	55.2	55.5	55.7	55.8	56.2	56.7	57.0
1966	57.3	57.5	57.9	58.0	58.3	58.6	58.8	58.9	59.0	59.3	59.4	59.5
1967	59.8	59.7	59.7	59.8	59.9	60.0	60.1	60.5	60.5	60.6	61.2	61.7
1968	61.6	61.9	62.1	62.3	62.6	62.9	63.1	63.1	63.4	63.7	64.0	64.2
1969	64.3	64.6	64.9	65.0	65.1	65.4	65.7	65.9	66.0	66.2	66.0	66.1
1970	65.7	65.7	65.7	65.7	65.6	65.5	65.6	65.5	65.5	64.9	64.6	65.3
1971	65.6	65.6	65.7	65.9	66.1	66.3	66.2	66.2	66.6	66.8	67.2	67.6
1972	68.2	68.3	68.8	69.2	69.4	69.5	69.8	70.4	70.8	71.5	72.1	72.6
1973	72.9	73.2	73.3	73.3	73.5	73.8	74.0	74.1	74.3	75.0	75.4	75.1
1974	74.7	74.5	74.4	74.2	74.5	74.5	74.6	74.4	74.3	74.2	73.4	72.2
1975	71.5	71.0	70.4	70.6	70.7	70.9	71.2	71.8	72.2	72.5	72.6	72.9
1976	73.6	74.1	74.3	74.7	74.9	75.0	75.2	75.4	75.6	75.5	76.2	76.7
1977	76.8	77.2	77.6	78.0	78.4	78.8	79.2	79.4	79.8	80.0	80.3	80.6
1978	80.4	80.9	81.6	82.7	82.9	83.4	83.5	83.9	84.2	84.6	85.0	85.3
1979	85.3	85.5	86.2	85.5	86.1	86.1	86.1	86.1	86.1	86.4	86.4	86.4
1980	86.8	86.7	86.3	85.5	84.6	84.2	84.2	84.7	85.3	86.0	86.5	86.8
1981	86.8	86.8	86.9	86.8	86.7	86.9	87.3	87.3	87.1	86.7	86.3	85.9
1982	85.3	85.8	85.7	85.7	85.7	85.2	84.9	84.6	84.4	84.0	84.0	83.9
1983	84.4	84.3	84.6	85.0	85.6	86.2	86.8	86.7	87.7	88.4	88.9	89.5
1984	90.2	90.7	91.2	91.5	91.8	92.4	92.6	92.8	93.2	93.1	93.5	93.8
1985	93.8	94.1	94.5	94.8	94.9	94.8	94.8	95.2	95.4	95.4	95.6	96.1
1986	96.2	96.3	96.4	97.1	96.9	96.8	97.1	97.2	97.8	97.7	97.9	98.5
1987	98.1	99.0	99.1	99.3	99.5	99.7	100.1	100.3	100.5	101.3	101.2	102.0
1988	101.8	102.3	102.7	102.9	103.0	103.4	103.5	103.7	103.8	104.5	104.6	105.3
1989	105.6	105.6	105.8	106.0	105.7	105.6	105.4	105.8	105.6	105.6	106.1	106.3
1990	106.2	106.8	107.2	106.9	107.2	107.3	107.1	107.0	106.7	106.3	105.9	105.9
1991	105.1	104.9	104.7	104.8	105.0	105.3	105.2	105.2	105.3	105.4	105.2	105.3
1992	105.1	105.6	105.8	106.0	106.1	106.1	106.4	106.4	106.5	107.1	107.4	109.5
1993	107.6	107.9	108.1	108.6	108.8	108.9	108.6	109.2	109.5	109.8	-	-

Source: U.S. Department of Commerce, Bureau of Economic Analysis. - indicates data not available or zero.

Composite Index of 4 Coincident Indicators
Change in Index from Previous Month

Year	Jan	Feb	Mar	Apr	May	Jun	Jul	Aug	Sep	Oct	Nov	Dec
1948	-	-0.1	+0.1	-	+0.2	+0.3	+0.1	+0.1	-	-	-0.1	-0.1
1949	-0.4	-0.2	-0.1	-0.1	-0.2	-0.1	-0.3	+0.3	+0.3	-0.8	+0.4	+0.2
1950	+0.3	-	+0.6	+0.4	+0.5	+0.5	+0.8	+0.6	-0.2	+0.1	-	+0.5
1951	+0.2	-	+0.2	+0.1	-	+0.1	-0.3	+0.2	-	+0.1	+0.1	+0.1
1952	-	+0.4	-	-	+0.1	-0.2	-0.3	+1.0	+0.6	+0.3	+0.1	+0.3
1953	+0.1	+0.3	+0.2	-	+0.1	-0.1	+0.2	-0.2	-0.2	-0.1	-0.4	-0.4
1954	-0.1	-	-0.2	-0.1	-	+0.1	-0.1	+0.1	+0.1	+0.2	+0.4	+0.3
1955	+0.3	+0.2	+0.4	+0.3	+0.4	+0.1	+0.3	-	+0.2	+0.3	+0.2	+0.2
1956	-	-	+0.1	+0.3	-0.1	+0.1	-0.9	+0.8	+0.3	+0.3	-	+0.2
1957	-0.1	+0.2	-	-0.2	-	+0.1	-	-	-0.2	-0.2	-0.3	-0.4
1958	-0.3	-0.5	-0.2	-0.4	+0.1	+0.4	+0.4	+0.3	+0.3	+0.1	+0.6	-
1959	+0.4	+0.4	+0.4	+0.4	+0.3	+0.1	-0.1	-0.7	-0.1	-	+0.3	+1.0
1960	+0.4	-0.1	-0.2	+0.1	-0.1	-0.1	-0.1	-	-0.1	-0.1	-0.2	-0.3
1961	-	-0.1	+0.2	+0.2	+0.3	+0.4	+0.1	+0.3	+0.1	+0.3	+0.4	+0.2
1962	-0.1	+0.3	+0.3	+0.2	-	+0.1	+0.2	+0.1	-	+0.1	+0.2	-
1963	-	+0.3	+0.1	+0.3	+0.1	+0.2	+0.1	+0.1	+0.2	+0.3	-	+0.3
1964	+0.1	+0.3	-	+0.4	+0.3	+0.1	+0.3	+0.2	+0.3	-0.3	+0.7	+0.5
1965	+0.1	+0.2	+0.4	+0.2	+0.3	+0.3	+0.3	+0.2	+0.1	+0.4	+0.5	+0.3
1966	+0.3	+0.2	+0.4	+0.1	+0.3	+0.3	+0.2	+0.1	+0.1	+0.3	+0.1	+0.1
1967	+0.3	-0.1	-	+0.1	+0.1	+0.1	+0.1	+0.4	-	+0.1	+0.6	+0.5
1968	-0.1	+0.3	+0.2	+0.2	+0.3	+0.3	+0.2	-	+0.3	+0.3	+0.3	+0.2
1969	+0.1	+0.3	+0.3	+0.1	+0.1	+0.3	+0.3	+0.2	+0.1	+0.2	-0.2	+0.1
1970	-0.4	-	-	-	-0.1	-0.1	+0.1	-0.1	-	-0.6	-0.3	+0.7
1971	+0.3	-	+0.1	+0.2	+0.2	+0.2	-0.1	-	+0.4	+0.2	+0.4	+0.4
1972	+0.6	+0.1	+0.5	+0.4	+0.2	+0.1	+0.3	+0.6	+0.4	+0.7	+0.6	+0.5
1973	+0.3	+0.3	+0.1	-	+0.2	+0.3	+0.2	+0.1	+0.2	+0.7	+0.4	-0.3
1974	-0.4	-0.2	-0.1	-0.2	+0.3	-	+0.1	-0.2	-0.1	-0.1	-0.8	-1.2
1975	-0.7	-0.5	-0.6	+0.2	+0.1	+0.2	+0.3	+0.6	+0.4	+0.3	+0.1	+0.3
1976	+0.7	+0.5	+0.2	+0.4	+0.2	+0.1	+0.2	+0.2	+0.2	-0.1	+0.7	+0.5
1977	+0.1	+0.4	+0.4	+0.4	+0.4	+0.4	+0.4	+0.2	+0.4	+0.2	+0.3	+0.3
1978	-0.2	+0.5	+0.7	+1.1	+0.2	+0.5	+0.1	+0.4	+0.3	+0.4	+0.4	+0.3
1979	-	+0.2	+0.7	-0.7	+0.6	-	-	-	-	+0.3	-	-
1980	+0.4	-0.1	-0.4	-0.8	-0.9	-0.4	-	+0.5	+0.6	+0.7	+0.5	+0.3
1981	-	-	+0.1	-0.1	-0.1	+0.2	+0.4	-	-0.2	-0.4	-0.4	-0.4
1982	-0.6	+0.5	-0.1	-	-	-0.5	-0.3	-0.3	-0.2	-0.4	-	-0.1
1983	+0.5	-0.1	+0.3	+0.4	+0.6	+0.6	+0.6	-0.1	+1.0	+0.7	+0.5	+0.6
1984	+0.7	+0.5	+0.5	+0.3	+0.3	+0.6	+0.2	+0.2	+0.4	-0.1	+0.4	+0.3
1985	-	+0.3	+0.4	+0.3	+0.1	-0.1	-	+0.4	+0.2	-	+0.2	+0.5
1986	+0.1	+0.1	+0.1	+0.7	-0.2	-0.1	+0.3	+0.1	+0.6	-0.1	+0.2	+0.6
1987	-0.4	+0.9	+0.1	+0.2	+0.2	+0.2	+0.4	+0.2	+0.2	+0.8	-0.1	+0.8
1988	-0.2	+0.5	+0.4	+0.2	+0.1	+0.4	+0.1	+0.2	+0.1	+0.7	+0.1	+0.7
1989	+0.3	-	+0.2	+0.2	-0.3	-0.1	-0.2	+0.4	-0.2	-	+0.5	+0.2
1990	-0.1	+0.6	+0.4	-0.3	+0.3	+0.1	-0.2	-0.1	-0.3	-0.4	-0.4	-
1991	-0.8	-0.2	-0.2	+0.1	+0.2	+0.3	-0.1	-	+0.1	+0.1	-0.2	+0.1
1992	-0.2	+0.5	+0.2	+0.2	+0.1	-	+0.3	-	+0.1	+0.6	+0.3	+2.1
1993	-1.9	+0.3	+0.2	+0.5	+0.2	+0.1	-0.3	+0.6	+0.3	+0.3	-	-

Source: U.S. Department of Commerce, Bureau of Economic Analysis. - indicates data not available or zero.

Employees On Nonagricultural Payrolls

(Thousands)

Year	Jan	Feb	Mar	Apr	May	Jun	Jul	Aug	Sep	Oct	Nov	Dec
1945	41,784	41,783	41,678	41,364	41,085	40,888	40,599	40,290	38,345	38,427	38,807	39,000
1946	39,740	39,209	40,202	40,831	41,263	41,534	41,943	42,462	42,744	42,957	43,238	43,322
1947	43,524	43,584	43,630	43,510	43,529	43,669	43,669	43,783	44,003	44,184	44,324	44,529
1948	44,680	44,492	44,615	44,334	44,615	44,863	45,059	45,052	45,167	45,084	45,083	45,032
1949	44,631	44,399	44,169	44,057	43,806	43,582	43,415	43,490	43,708	42,823	43,148	43,497
1950	43,472	43,175	43,816	44,238	44,589	44,953	45,361	46,035	46,304	46,530	46,654	46,756
1951	47,227	47,519	47,700	47,849	47,803	47,915	47,923	47,806	47,743	47,833	48,026	48,119
1952	48,229	48,491	48,450	48,476	48,478	48,130	47,992	48,687	49,076	49,436	49,710	49,933
1953	50,043	50,271	50,360	50,367	50,343	50,386	50,385	50,272	50,216	50,114	49,824	49,627
1954	49,340	49,270	49,081	48,984	48,857	48,810	48,689	48,644	48,752	48,828	49,102	49,242
1955	49,363	49,523	49,867	50,106	50,414	50,705	50,823	50,905	51,085	51,308	51,491	51,721
1956	51,880	52,096	52,141	52,302	52,387	52,454	51,764	52,396	52,446	52,667	52,722	52,865
1957	52,808	53,000	53,052	53,029	52,999	52,961	52,970	52,918	52,825	52,673	52,458	52,281
1958	52,002	51,448	51,131	50,787	50,760	50,822	50,915	51,118	51,359	51,379	51,831	51,968
1959	52,410	52,558	52,863	53,190	53,382	53,603	53,683	53,230	53,265	53,203	53,503	54,033
1960	54,184	54,406	54,348	54,561	54,366	54,292	54,230	54,198	54,069	53,982	53,843	53,571
1961	53,524	53,373	53,462	53,485	53,664	53,922	54,052	54,232	54,303	54,375	54,636	54,739
1962	54,703	54,996	55,109	55,384	55,514	55,563	55,663	55,796	55,860	55,919	55,943	55,915
1963	55,927	56,039	56,157	56,398	56,534	56,571	56,705	56,832	56,971	57,148	57,125	57,251
1964	57,281	57,621	57,686	57,846	57,974	58,128	58,309	58,510	58,777	58,658	59,080	59,320
1965	59,419	59,710	59,921	60,080	60,389	60,590	60,868	61,072	61,333	61,538	61,859	62,209
1966	62,415	62,766	63,129	63,318	63,595	63,989	64,166	64,306	64,367	64,614	64,839	65,042
1967	65,240	65,224	65,305	65,373	65,478	65,642	65,816	65,933	66,074	66,091	66,570	66,767
1968	66,656	67,026	67,156	67,422	67,519	67,779	67,979	68,189	68,333	68,569	68,837	69,151
1969	69,297	69,575	69,803	69,980	70,197	70,478	70,629	70,742	70,800	70,957	70,921	71,119
1970	71,059	71,201	71,363	71,283	70,998	70,888	70,927	70,750	70,815	70,383	70,264	70,661
1971	70,752	70,689	70,766	70,969	71,129	71,136	71,169	71,168	71,499	71,485	71,723	71,977
1972	72,357	72,542	72,850	73,079	73,346	73,639	73,576	73,908	74,107	74,537	74,904	75,164
1973	75,521	75,923	76,168	76,308	76,473	76,743	76,713	77,009	77,170	77,506	77,867	77,933
1974	78,020	78,181	78,184	78,239	78,381	78,443	78,492	78,511	78,542	78,599	78,234	77,531
1975	77,153	76,743	76,429	76,333	76,470	76,400	76,640	77,034	77,216	77,479	77,582	77,878
1976	78,317	78,614	78,828	79,142	79,188	79,264	79,469	79,591	79,857	79,847	80,122	80,310
1977	80,527	80,783	81,228	81,615	81,984	82,392	82,743	82,954	83,460	83,659	84,012	84,260
1978	84,478	84,800	85,339	86,064	86,396	86,833	87,060	87,319	87,470	87,788	88,233	88,534
1979	88,711	88,955	89,406	89,356	89,671	89,985	90,088	90,148	90,166	90,356	90,449	90,595
1980	90,784	90,889	90,970	90,747	90,269	89,931	89,670	89,933	90,058	90,350	90,583	90,818
1981	91,021	91,080	91,184	91,214	91,132	91,292	91,394	91,299	91,206	91,185	91,039	90,834
1982	90,466	90,467	90,331	90,028	89,965	89,710	89,371	89,163	89,011	88,759	88,664	88,666
1983	88,841	88,754	88,936	89,209	89,496	89,894	90,318	89,966	91,099	91,382	91,735	92,104
1984	92,537	93,045	93,307	93,651	93,950	94,331	94,646	94,861	95,185	95,485	95,843	95,992
1985	96,271	96,406	96,739	96,903	97,160	97,288	97,458	97,666	97,871	98,085	98,289	98,491
1986	98,628	98,731	98,805	98,978	99,095	98,977	99,264	99,416	99,740	99,974	100,142	100,386
1987	100,576	100,788	101,015	101,369	101,564	101,719	102,034	102,252	102,420	102,976	103,191	103,537
1988	103,641	104,076	104,354	104,604	104,789	105,162	105,377	105,534	105,780	106,067	106,382	106,694
1989	107,076	107,294	107,471	107,633	107,731	107,865	107,924	108,003	108,175	108,287	108,566	108,701
1990	109,019	109,307	109,497	109,485	109,783	109,905	109,701	109,534	109,470	109,296	109,106	108,977
1991	108,808	108,517	108,364	108,133	108,186	108,169	108,111	108,172	108,221	108,215	108,099	108,117
1992	108,051	108,045	108,164	108,347	108,470	108,454	108,605	108,615	108,674	108,789	108,921	109,079
1993	109,235	109,539	109,565	109,820	110,058	110,101	110,338	110,305	110,467	110,644	-	-

Source: U.S. Department of Labor, Bureau of Labor Statistics. - indicates data not available or zero.

Index of Industrial Production
(1987 = 100)

Year	Jan	Feb	Mar	Apr	May	Jun	Jul	Aug	Sep	Oct	Nov	Dec
1945	26.8	26.7	26.5	26.0	25.3	24.8	24.2	21.7	19.7	18.9	19.6	19.7
1946	18.6	17.7	19.6	19.2	18.5	19.6	20.3	21.1	21.5	21.8	22.0	22.1
1947	22.4	22.5	22.6	22.5	22.6	22.6	22.4	22.6	22.7	22.9	23.3	23.3
1948	23.5	23.5	23.3	23.3	23.7	24.0	24.0	23.9	23.7	23.9	23.6	23.4
1949	23.2	22.9	22.5	22.4	22.1	22.0	22.0	22.2	22.4	21.6	22.2	22.6
1950	22.9	23.0	23.8	24.6	25.2	25.9	26.7	27.6	27.4	27.6	27.5	28.0
1951	28.1	28.3	28.4	28.5	28.4	28.2	27.8	27.5	27.7	27.7	27.9	28.1
1952	28.4	28.5	28.6	28.4	28.1	27.8	27.4	29.2	30.2	30.5	31.1	31.3
1953	31.4	31.6	31.8	32.0	32.2	32.0	32.4	32.2	31.6	31.3	30.6	29.8
1954	29.6	29.7	29.5	29.3	29.5	29.6	29.6	29.6	29.6	30.0	30.5	30.9
1955	31.6	32.0	32.7	33.1	33.7	33.7	34.0	33.9	34.1	34.7	34.8	34.9
1956	35.1	34.8	34.8	35.1	34.8	34.5	33.4	34.8	35.6	35.9	35.6	36.1
1957	36.0	36.3	36.3	35.8	35.7	35.8	36.0	36.0	35.7	35.1	34.3	33.7
1958	33.0	32.3	31.9	31.4	31.7	32.6	33.0	33.7	34.0	34.4	35.4	35.5
1959	36.0	36.7	37.2	38.0	38.6	38.6	37.7	36.4	36.4	36.1	36.3	38.6
1960	39.6	39.2	38.9	38.6	38.5	38.1	37.9	37.9	37.5	37.4	36.9	36.2
1961	36.3	36.2	36.4	37.2	37.7	38.3	38.7	39.1	39.0	39.8	40.4	40.7
1962	40.4	41.1	41.3	41.4	41.3	41.2	41.6	41.7	41.9	42.0	42.2	42.2
1963	42.5	42.9	43.2	43.6	44.1	44.3	44.1	44.2	44.6	44.9	45.1	45.1
1964	45.5	45.8	45.8	46.5	46.8	46.9	47.2	47.5	47.7	47.0	48.5	49.1
1965	49.6	49.9	50.6	50.8	51.2	51.6	52.1	52.3	52.4	52.9	53.2	53.8
1966	54.4	54.7	55.5	55.5	56.1	56.3	56.6	56.7	57.2	57.6	57.2	57.3
1967	57.6	57.0	56.6	57.2	56.7	56.7	56.5	57.6	57.5	58.0	58.8	59.5
1968	59.4	59.6	59.8	59.9	60.6	60.8	60.7	60.9	61.1	61.2	62.0	62.2
1969	62.6	63.0	63.5	63.2	63.0	63.6	63.9	64.1	64.1	64.1	63.5	63.3
1970	62.1	62.1	62.0	61.9	61.8	61.6	61.7	61.6	61.2	60.0	59.6	61.0
1971	61.5	61.3	61.3	61.6	61.9	62.2	62.0	61.7	62.7	63.1	63.4	64.1
1972	65.6	66.0	66.5	67.6	67.5	67.7	67.6	68.5	69.2	70.2	71.1	71.7
1973	71.8	72.8	72.8	73.0	73.4	73.9	74.4	74.3	74.9	75.2	75.2	74.0
1974	73.0	72.7	73.0	72.9	73.8	74.0	73.6	73.4	73.7	73.2	71.1	68.1
1975	66.3	65.3	64.1	64.7	64.5	65.3	65.7	66.9	67.6	67.9	68.6	69.1
1976	69.9	71.1	70.9	71.2	72.0	72.1	72.5	72.9	73.1	73.4	74.6	75.2
1977	75.5	75.9	76.6	77.7	78.3	78.9	78.9	79.0	79.4	79.4	79.5	79.1
1978	78.8	79.0	80.0	82.0	82.3	83.1	83.3	83.6	84.1	84.5	85.2	85.4
1979	85.1	85.8	86.1	85.2	86.2	86.1	85.6	85.3	85.5	86.0	85.7	85.6
1980	85.9	86.2	86.2	84.5	82.5	81.5	81.2	82.4	83.5	84.0	85.5	85.9
1981	85.2	85.4	85.7	85.0	85.6	86.1	87.1	86.9	86.5	85.8	84.8	84.1
1982	82.4	84.2	83.7	83.2	82.7	82.4	82.0	81.6	81.0	80.3	80.0	79.3
1983	80.8	80.7	81.3	82.3	83.2	83.7	85.3	86.5	87.9	88.6	88.8	89.2
1984	91.0	90.9	91.9	92.4	93.0	93.5	93.9	94.0	93.9	93.2	93.3	92.8
1985	93.1	93.8	94.1	94.5	94.7	94.4	94.1	94.5	95.0	94.2	94.6	95.6
1986	96.1	95.5	94.6	94.8	94.7	94.3	94.8	94.9	95.0	95.6	96.3	96.8
1987	96.5	97.9	98.2	98.8	99.4	100.3	100.6	100.9	100.7	102.1	102.2	102.8
1988	103.2	103.4	103.4	104.3	104.0	104.0	104.6	105.2	104.7	105.0	105.6	106.3
1989	106.6	106.2	107.1	107.1	106.7	106.4	105.3	105.8	105.4	105.0	105.4	106.1
1990	105.5	106.1	106.4	105.7	106.5	106.7	106.5	106.8	106.8	106.3	105.0	104.5
1991	104.4	103.2	102.5	102.6	103.3	104.4	104.5	104.6	105.3	105.1	105.0	104.7
1992	104.5	105.3	105.6	106.3	106.7	106.0	106.8	106.6	106.2	107.5	108.4	108.9
1993	109.3	109.9	110.1	110.4	110.2	110.5	110.8	110.9	111.4	112.2	-	-

Source: Board of Governors of the Federal Reserve System. - indicates data not available or zero.

Personal Income Less Transfer Payments

(Annual Rate, Billions of 1987 $)

Year	Jan	Feb	Mar	Apr	May	Jun	Jul	Aug	Sep	Oct	Nov	Dec
1947	888.9	886.4	880.5	865.5	864.7	873.8	867.5	867.3	878.3	876.1	875.8	880.7
1948	897.6	891.1	902.3	903.7	911.2	925.5	923.5	930.3	932.6	937.2	931.2	921.7
1949	906.0	904.6	905.1	906.0	903.7	895.3	887.0	894.0	907.9	887.5	898.1	902.8
1950	919.9	915.7	931.9	937.8	954.4	953.4	969.7	981.6	993.3	1,000.0	1,011.6	1,023.3
1951	1,014.3	1,014.2	1,026.2	1,042.2	1,046.1	1,053.0	1,047.2	1,060.5	1,058.1	1,065.1	1,065.7	1,072.0
1952	1,058.2	1,075.5	1,077.6	1,075.5	1,086.1	1,087.8	1,082.4	1,105.4	1,118.4	1,114.9	1,107.9	1,115.7
1953	1,115.6	1,124.7	1,135.4	1,132.4	1,138.5	1,141.4	1,139.8	1,136.1	1,136.1	1,140.2	1,136.1	1,131.1
1954	1,131.1	1,129.0	1,123.3	1,113.0	1,115.9	1,121.2	1,121.2	1,132.4	1,138.5	1,143.9	1,156.6	1,155.9
1955	1,159.3	1,161.9	1,170.0	1,177.8	1,187.9	1,191.1	1,206.0	1,206.8	1,215.7	1,220.9	1,230.5	1,238.6
1956	1,236.0	1,243.6	1,248.8	1,262.4	1,259.8	1,263.5	1,254.2	1,265.4	1,269.8	1,283.1	1,278.5	1,280.2
1957	1,278.2	1,284.5	1,283.8	1,284.6	1,283.1	1,293.5	1,294.3	1,295.0	1,291.2	1,282.9	1,283.7	1,273.9
1958	1,270.5	1,264.5	1,268.3	1,261.9	1,265.3	1,274.3	1,297.4	1,295.5	1,303.0	1,301.1	1,320.3	1,322.1
1959	1,318.7	1,326.1	1,338.1	1,349.3	1,354.6	1,359.3	1,360.7	1,346.1	1,344.1	1,346.7	1,366.1	1,381.6
1960	1,387.1	1,379.9	1,378.0	1,380.7	1,390.9	1,390.5	1,388.0	1,388.4	1,385.1	1,385.6	1,383.0	1,377.9
1961	1,389.5	1,390.9	1,391.3	1,400.4	1,408.7	1,415.9	1,417.6	1,425.5	1,425.8	1,439.8	1,454.8	1,462.4
1962	1,459.1	1,464.3	1,475.7	1,481.9	1,480.9	1,491.1	1,497.5	1,495.7	1,494.4	1,500.7	1,505.3	1,512.3
1963	1,505.6	1,515.5	1,515.1	1,520.7	1,529.1	1,530.7	1,533.4	1,541.5	1,552.3	1,564.1	1,564.9	1,573.7
1964	1,576.5	1,586.2	1,593.8	1,604.5	1,609.6	1,618.2	1,628.2	1,636.3	1,646.2	1,649.7	1,663.7	1,677.1
1965	1,676.5	1,678.3	1,686.4	1,691.9	1,708.8	1,722.0	1,726.3	1,735.0	1,738.8	1,759.5	1,775.6	1,784.3
1966	1,783.1	1,786.1	1,791.1	1,798.7	1,806.6	1,817.4	1,822.9	1,830.0	1,829.1	1,841.4	1,846.5	1,848.4
1967	1,863.9	1,863.2	1,865.3	1,864.4	1,872.1	1,880.5	1,889.2	1,897.1	1,893.7	1,897.8	1,909.1	1,923.2
1968	1,922.1	1,937.9	1,941.0	1,948.3	1,961.7	1,971.6	1,982.3	1,984.5	2,000.3	2,002.1	2,011.4	2,022.2
1969	2,020.1	2,025.1	2,037.2	2,040.2	2,051.0	2,056.0	2,074.2	2,079.9	2,086.9	2,093.0	2,098.3	2,097.4
1970	2,092.0	2,087.2	2,090.6	2,098.3	2,093.0	2,087.6	2,096.6	2,101.7	2,101.1	2,091.7	2,091.7	2,093.1
1971	2,104.6	2,103.8	2,105.4	2,107.0	2,116.7	2,114.4	2,117.3	2,130.3	2,130.2	2,134.9	2,147.2	2,166.6
1972	2,177.2	2,188.3	2,195.1	2,208.1	2,215.8	2,199.2	2,232.7	2,256.6	2,267.8	2,289.8	2,314.0	2,327.8
1973	2,331.1	2,331.6	2,330.8	2,324.0	2,346.6	2,355.5	2,355.0	2,368.6	2,379.6	2,409.3	2,428.2	2,421.8
1974	2,390.7	2,364.1	2,334.9	2,322.9	2,324.4	2,330.2	2,334.8	2,327.5	2,330.3	2,337.2	2,314.7	2,305.3
1975	2,276.6	2,255.9	2,259.0	2,256.5	2,264.0	2,271.2	2,273.5	2,294.9	2,309.9	2,326.6	2,328.9	2,328.0
1976	2,349.0	2,362.5	2,370.7	2,380.6	2,391.0	2,388.2	2,392.3	2,398.1	2,402.1	2,401.9	2,424.9	2,432.3
1977	2,432.8	2,439.8	2,447.1	2,452.7	2,469.9	2,473.8	2,496.8	2,510.8	2,524.5	2,527.7	2,534.5	2,546.8
1978	2,550.0	2,562.3	2,590.8	2,620.4	2,623.4	2,640.0	2,642.0	2,654.8	2,668.7	2,685.4	2,692.5	2,702.8
1979	2,701.6	2,714.6	2,726.6	2,712.6	2,711.3	2,717.9	2,725.7	2,727.0	2,728.8	2,737.0	2,744.2	2,749.7
1980	2,753.7	2,744.1	2,731.4	2,706.4	2,686.5	2,684.0	2,676.4	2,692.2	2,706.6	2,741.9	2,760.9	2,781.2
1981	2,776.2	2,772.6	2,775.7	2,775.9	2,772.4	2,781.5	2,799.9	2,814.3	2,813.5	2,805.3	2,793.9	2,781.9
1982	2,768.6	2,776.1	2,781.7	2,800.5	2,806.1	2,788.1	2,776.4	2,771.7	2,762.0	2,758.7	2,756.5	2,767.6
1983	2,767.8	2,760.2	2,764.4	2,778.0	2,791.7	2,800.3	2,814.1	2,804.3	2,826.3	2,862.2	2,879.3	2,900.7
1984	2,922.4	2,963.6	2,982.9	2,987.2	2,986.8	3,007.7	3,023.7	3,038.6	3,064.3	3,046.0	3,060.1	3,098.8
1985	3,081.3	3,092.9	3,103.6	3,118.7	3,098.2	3,109.9	3,104.1	3,104.5	3,105.1	3,123.6	3,118.7	3,154.3
1986	3,139.7	3,158.7	3,187.4	3,227.7	3,212.3	3,199.5	3,198.3	3,211.0	3,216.3	3,206.7	3,209.9	3,233.1
1987	3,220.2	3,240.1	3,240.6	3,242.8	3,233.5	3,232.3	3,242.1	3,255.8	3,258.5	3,309.4	3,292.7	3,345.5
1988	3,307.9	3,322.3	3,335.3	3,342.1	3,341.6	3,350.7	3,355.2	3,357.6	3,362.6	3,410.6	3,386.5	3,411.5
1989	3,427.6	3,445.5	3,455.2	3,448.3	3,429.0	3,422.5	3,429.0	3,424.8	3,414.2	3,432.1	3,447.5	3,457.2
1990	3,457.4	3,476.7	3,487.8	3,495.0	3,481.5	3,482.6	3,485.1	3,464.3	3,461.2	3,429.0	3,439.3	3,467.5
1991	3,409.1	3,402.6	3,413.4	3,408.0	3,411.1	3,417.6	3,397.4	3,391.3	3,394.3	3,398.7	3,387.6	3,425.1
1992	3,394.8	3,418.1	3,423.9	3,426.8	3,433.8	3,434.1	3,432.8	3,450.0	3,451.2	3,484.7	3,484.5	3,689.9
1993	3,441.9	3,449.3	3,471.1	3,517.7	3,524.3	3,511.7	3,497.8	3,540.6	3,543.1	3,552.3	-	-

Source: U.S. Department of Commerce, Bureau of Economic Analysis. - indicates data not available or zero.

Manufacturing and Trade Sales
(Million 1987 $)

Year	Jan	Feb	Mar	Apr	May	Jun	Jul	Aug	Sep	Oct	Nov	Dec
1948	124,835	124,910	125,800	126,345	124,888	126,436	127,564	127,824	127,782	127,893	127,342	128,259
1949	127,027	126,820	126,345	125,777	123,840	126,928	123,456	126,132	128,607	123,746	125,394	124,324
1950	126,685	129,318	131,057	132,663	135,960	141,587	152,196	154,455	144,882	141,946	137,578	145,307
1951	149,265	145,359	143,047	140,585	141,818	140,754	137,926	141,418	141,361	142,330	141,980	140,607
1952	142,908	144,424	143,663	145,420	146,916	147,175	144,070	147,275	152,374	157,262	156,711	159,538
1953	160,423	162,734	164,495	164,552	163,828	161,834	164,136	160,742	159,321	158,526	154,589	151,918
1954	152,719	154,444	153,588	154,895	152,195	154,137	153,682	152,696	153,460	154,055	158,685	162,435
1955	164,854	166,234	169,611	171,379	172,115	172,131	172,682	171,979	174,807	174,073	175,542	175,829
1956	174,810	173,428	174,077	174,579	173,984	174,808	167,114	172,717	174,330	175,829	176,662	178,391
1957	178,898	179,508	178,270	175,438	174,779	175,789	175,082	176,271	173,898	173,046	170,731	166,862
1958	166,580	163,715	161,262	160,504	161,136	164,147	165,833	168,752	169,723	172,518	175,180	170,372
1959	177,579	180,295	182,424	185,177	187,213	187,464	186,905	180,702	180,205	180,599	181,001	186,020
1960	189,271	188,409	187,454	187,916	185,445	185,299	184,402	183,416	185,475	184,494	182,100	182,475
1961	178,627	179,133	182,209	181,214	183,946	187,282	185,026	189,399	190,051	192,566	194,393	195,194
1962	195,352	195,537	198,194	198,356	198,124	197,286	198,071	199,471	198,952	200,913	203,713	200,284
1963	201,169	204,347	204,465	206,370	204,950	206,727	209,795	208,574	208,791	211,015	208,723	213,334
1964	214,560	214,575	214,008	217,537	219,879	219,279	222,959	222,257	224,339	220,983	223,310	230,443
1965	229,885	230,640	235,579	236,142	233,649	234,691	238,911	237,557	237,547	239,786	243,138	243,988
1966	246,684	246,953	250,964	249,027	248,149	250,815	249,321	250,896	250,438	251,112	250,109	251,214
1967	252,621	252,020	253,265	253,761	253,796	254,250	254,249	257,298	256,699	254,730	261,763	267,141
1968	265,864	264,932	267,361	267,119	268,528	271,129	274,384	270,066	271,294	275,450	277,670	275,368
1969	275,855	276,373	277,968	279,301	278,781	278,746	280,072	281,564	283,152	285,865	282,135	281,792
1970	279,400	279,282	276,126	274,134	277,364	278,207	278,441	277,112	276,793	272,273	267,731	276,499
1971	279,715	281,661	282,908	284,258	286,259	289,727	288,174	286,277	289,563	290,422	295,093	297,156
1972	300,201	297,396	302,716	305,077	306,605	307,938	308,992	314,304	317,743	321,720	326,386	331,125
1973	335,572	336,568	334,362	332,728	331,496	330,711	335,267	330,662	330,325	337,743	342,034	337,065
1974	338,234	337,134	340,708	339,270	340,309	338,974	340,112	335,795	332,271	327,459	323,059	312,343
1975	314,166	312,571	303,419	308,306	307,936	310,588	313,554	315,628	316,972	317,251	315,777	319,167
1976	327,307	329,157	331,645	334,615	333,800	337,423	338,535	337,677	338,062	334,574	340,175	350,306
1977	348,170	352,455	356,339	357,357	356,424	359,677	360,474	360,774	361,351	362,999	365,148	369,826
1978	361,385	368,449	371,288	381,447	380,766	381,737	379,394	385,200	383,969	388,325	390,207	391,501
1979	390,311	386,651	397,051	384,979	395,454	389,307	389,666	389,991	388,185	388,053	387,094	385,697
1980	392,835	387,465	378,012	370,276	363,974	362,525	368,215	369,349	377,120	384,277	383,965	384,437
1981	386,997	385,511	383,406	384,070	380,834	380,509	380,508	378,832	376,090	370,117	367,217	362,912
1982	360,956	367,357	366,724	366,034	368,412	363,473	363,756	360,466	360,457	357,085	358,425	355,895
1983	364,244	362,022	367,358	367,559	373,644	383,026	383,113	382,368	388,192	392,992	397,711	404,330
1984	406,597	406,454	406,443	409,273	412,897	416,925	414,612	413,394	413,473	415,489	419,077	419,995
1985	419,796	420,338	423,347	423,752	428,318	422,405	423,369	430,477	431,734	426,741	430,444	428,476
1986	434,221	432,399	432,011	440,859	436,751	440,049	443,290	442,924	453,686	447,725	447,543	455,846
1987	442,494	457,538	456,914	455,945	456,686	457,448	461,671	459,995	464,493	463,462	462,103	465,943
1988	464,759	469,853	476,647	474,281	475,544	480,081	477,144	478,297	479,231	483,578	484,896	492,175
1989	491,465	484,744	481,604	487,372	484,550	482,601	478,519	491,646	486,981	482,179	486,347	487,416
1990	482,078	489,852	493,772	488,218	491,123	492,767	488,253	493,080	485,166	483,540	477,368	473,562
1991	467,635	471,153	469,197	477,019	479,121	478,991	482,728	481,862	483,043	484,360	482,731	477,382
1992	482,744	486,586	489,051	489,073	485,303	490,092	493,312	489,482	494,155	495,838	499,906	509,751
1993	509,095	510,542	509,156	507,532	510,649	514,996	506,078	513,187	517,220	-	-	-

Source: U.S. Department of Commerce, Bureau of Economic Analysis, U.S. Department of Commerce, Bureau of the Census. - indicates data not available or zero.

COMPOSITE INDEX OF LAGGING INDICATORS

The composite index of lagging indicators turns down about 10 months after the economy turns down and turns up about six months after the economy has turned up. Thus it lags behind the economy. It is made up of components that have inertial tendencies—they change more slowly than the economy. The "lagging index," of course, also confirms the cyclical behaviour of the economy by moving in tandem with the leading and coincident indicators—at a lag in time.

The lagging index is also a somewhat uncertain indicator. At business cycle peaks, the lags range from 2 to 13 months; at business cycle troughs, the range is 4 to 15 months.

Components of the Lagging Index

The index is a composite of 7 indicators, each of which is further discussed below:

> Index of labor cost per unit of output in manufacturing
> Ratio, manufacturing and trade inventories to sales
> Average duration of unemployment in weeks
> Ratio, consumer installment credit outstanding to personal income
> Commercial and industrial loans outstanding
> Average prime rate charged by banks
> Change in consumer price index for services

Index of Labor Cost per Unit of Output in Manufacturing. The indicator is an index with a 1987 base (1987 = 100). Labor cost in manufacturing is in part a reflection of longer-term contractual arrangements between manufacturers and labor unions which are not subject to rapid adjustment as the economy changes. Even the compensation of non-union labor forces tends to lag behind economic events: managements avoid downward adjustments in wages to maintain morale and productivity and resist demands for increased pay in periods of growth. For these reasons, the index lags economic events. Recessionary forces cause the cost of labor to decline—slowly. In periods of upturn, labor cost rises slowly as well. Thus it is normal to have high wages at the start and during recessions and relatively low wages as the economy begins climbing to a new peak.

Ratio, Manufacturing and Trade Inventories to Sales. The indicator is expressed as a ratio based on inventory and sales measures expressed in 1987 constant dollars. A ratio of 1.0 means that inventories and sales are identical. A high ratio indicates high inventories relative to sales. A low indicator tends to mean that inventories are depleted. A dropping ratio means that inventories are "selling out" while a climbing ratio means that sales are slowing. Manufacturers and merchants caught at the beginning of a recession with high inventories will be unable to sell them; therefore, the ratio will increase as the economy slumps. Conversely, in an expansionary period, the ratio will be dropping because producers cannot keep up with demand. In both cases, the indicator tends to move in the opposite direction of the economy—or in the same direction, but with a lag in time.

Average Duration of Unemployment. The indicator is shown as number of weeks of unemployment. A recession is a sustained downturn in production after a sustained period of growth. The average duration of unemployment, therefore, will tend to be low at the start of a recession. The shrinking of the economy will cause this average to grow. As the economy turns up again, the average will be high; time has to pass until laid-off people are employed again and the average duration of unemployment drops. In this case, also, the indicator grows as the economy shrinks and declines as the economy grows.

Ratio, Consumer Installment Credit Outstanding to Personal Income. The indicator is expressed as a percent. A high percentage indicates that consumer debt relative to income is high. A decline in personal income or an increase in consumer debt will cause the indicator to rise and, of course, an increase in personal income or decrease in debt will cause the ratio to decline. At the start of a recession, personal income tends to drop more rapidly than debt outstanding; this indicator, therefore, will increase as the economy decreases. Later, as debt is paid off and less is borrowed (because times are uncertain), the ratio will decrease just as the economy begins to expand again—the signature of a lagging indicator.

Commercial and Industrial Loans Outstanding. The indicator is shown in millions of constant 1987 dollars. Business and industry assume debt in periods of growth and minimize debt in periods of decline. The total debt outstanding, however, reflects the business cycle at a lag in time; borrowers pay off debt over time and may be late in paying during economic turn-downs; they also contract new obligations later than the economy's upturn because both lenders and borrowers are more cautious after a recessionary period.

Average Prime Rate Charged by Banks. The indicator is shown as a percent of interest charged by major banks to their largest customers. Historically, the prime rate has tended to increase during recessions and to decrease during periods of expansion. At the onset of an economic downturn, the rate reflects the conditions of the previous expansion; as the recession deepens and demand for money slackens, the prime rate drops. The prime rate is strongly influenced by actions of the Federal Reserve System. The Federal Reserve's discount rate (interest charged to member banks for short-term borrowings) has an immediate effect on the prime rate; therefore, the behavior of this indicator is indirectly subject to alteration by government action.

Change in Consumer Price Index for Services. The index is expressed as a percent; the data are "smoothed," meaning that data are arithmetically transformed to remove irregular short-term movements. Prices for services are less volatile than prices for food, fuel, and products. Hence this series is a good lagging indicator: it changes more slowly than the economy. More detailed presentations of the Consumer Price Index are provided later in this book.

Sources and Revisions

The component series are drawn from federal sources, including the U.S. Department of Commerce, Bureau of Economic Analysis and Bureau of the Census; the U.S. Department of Labor, Bureau of Labor Statistics; the Federal Reserve System; and the Federal Reserve Bank of New York.

The composite index itself is constructed by the Bureau of Economic Analysis. In the process, mathematical operations are performed on the component data series to ensure that volatile series do not dominate the index. A volatile series may be one that fluctuates wildly month to month but shows less volatility when averaged over several months. Other smoothing and standardization methods are used as well.

The lagging index was last revised in 1993 to reflect comprehensive revisions of the National Income and Product Accounts which were made in 1991 and to incorporate improvements in methodology.

Bibliography

1. Frumkin, Norman. *Guide to Economic Indicators*. M.E. Sharpe, Inc., 1990.

2. Green, George R. and Barry A. Beckman. "Business Cycle Indicators: Upcoming Revision of the

Composite Indexes." U.S. Department of Commerce, Bureau of Economic Analysis. *Survey of Current Business*, October 1993. Superintendent of Documents, U.S. Government Printing Office, Washington, DC 20302.

3. Hertzberg, Marie P. and Barry A. Beckman. "Business Cycle Indicators: Revised Composite Indexes." U.S. Department of Commerce, Bureau of Economic Analysis. *Survey of Current Business*, January 1989. Superintendent of Documents, U.S. Government Printing Office, Washington, DC 20302.

4. U.S. Department of Commerce, Bureau of Economic Analysis. "Composite Indexes of Leading, Coincident, and Lagging Indicators." In *Survey of Current Business*, November 1987. Superintendent of Documents, U.S. Government Printing Office, Washington, DC 20302.

5. U.S. Department of Commerce, Bureau of Economic Analysis. *Survey of Current Business*. Superintendent of Documents, U.S. Government Printing Office, Washington, DC 20302.

Composite Index of 7 Lagging Indicators
(1987 = 100)

Year	Jan	Feb	Mar	Apr	May	Jun	Jul	Aug	Sep	Oct	Nov	Dec
1948	49.4	49.9	50.2	50.4	50.5	50.5	51.0	52.6	53.0	52.9	53.3	53.4
1949	53.8	54.0	53.8	53.7	54.0	53.9	53.8	53.5	53.2	54.1	53.9	54.0
1950	54.0	54.0	53.9	54.2	54.3	54.2	53.8	54.1	55.7	57.2	58.5	58.1
1951	59.2	60.0	60.6	61.0	61.3	62.0	62.1	62.0	62.1	62.5	62.8	63.5
1952	64.3	64.3	64.5	64.4	65.0	65.9	66.3	65.8	65.8	65.8	66.3	66.9
1953	67.2	67.6	67.8	68.8	69.8	70.0	70.0	70.3	70.7	70.8	71.2	71.3
1954	70.9	70.6	69.6	68.6	68.2	67.7	67.4	66.7	66.6	66.5	66.5	66.7
1955	66.5	66.4	66.7	66.5	66.9	67.7	68.1	70.0	70.4	71.5	72.5	72.6
1956	73.0	73.1	73.8	74.7	75.7	76.0	77.0	76.8	77.2	77.1	77.3	77.2
1957	77.4	77.1	77.4	77.7	77.9	78.0	77.9	78.7	79.2	79.1	79.5	79.6
1958	79.1	78.3	78.1	77.4	76.1	75.3	74.9	74.4	75.1	75.2	74.9	75.2
1959	75.0	75.2	75.4	75.6	76.4	77.2	77.7	78.7	80.1	80.5	80.4	80.0
1960	79.5	79.8	80.1	80.3	80.7	80.9	80.9	80.6	79.9	79.7	79.9	80.0
1961	80.0	79.8	79.4	79.2	78.8	78.4	78.1	78.0	78.2	78.3	78.2	78.5
1962	78.8	78.7	78.9	79.2	79.4	79.6	79.7	79.7	79.7	79.6	79.7	79.9
1963	80.0	80.1	79.9	80.0	80.1	80.3	80.4	80.8	80.9	80.9	81.3	81.6
1964	81.4	81.6	81.7	81.8	81.7	81.9	81.7	82.0	82.1	82.4	82.3	82.4
1965	82.8	83.1	83.3	83.6	83.8	83.7	83.7	84.0	84.2	84.5	84.9	85.9
1966	86.0	86.5	86.7	87.3	88.0	88.3	88.8	89.1	89.1	89.2	89.8	89.9
1967	89.9	89.9	90.1	90.0	89.8	90.1	90.1	89.7	89.9	89.9	89.6	89.8
1968	89.6	90.1	90.4	90.8	91.1	91.4	91.3	91.8	91.8	91.7	91.9	92.2
1969	92.7	93.0	93.1	93.7	94.2	94.8	94.8	95.0	95.2	95.4	95.4	95.6
1970	96.0	96.1	96.4	95.9	95.6	95.5	95.2	95.2	94.8	94.6	94.2	93.4
1971	93.0	92.7	92.2	91.5	91.4	90.8	91.4	92.0	91.9	91.4	90.9	90.9
1972	89.6	89.2	89.5	89.7	90.0	90.3	90.3	90.1	90.1	90.1	90.0	89.9
1973	90.8	91.5	91.9	92.8	93.0	93.5	94.2	94.3	95.1	95.2	95.5	96.3
1974	96.6	96.8	96.5	97.2	97.7	98.0	98.0	98.2	98.9	98.8	99.1	99.8
1975	99.2	98.3	97.6	96.0	94.7	92.5	91.9	91.3	90.8	90.8	90.7	90.6
1976	90.5	90.4	90.3	90.1	90.0	89.6	89.7	89.7	89.9	90.1	89.8	89.5
1977	89.6	89.9	90.0	90.2	90.3	90.8	91.0	91.4	91.7	92.1	92.3	92.4
1978	93.0	93.1	93.4	93.0	93.4	93.8	94.2	94.4	94.8	94.9	95.7	96.2
1979	96.4	96.6	96.1	97.4	97.3	98.0	98.3	98.8	99.5	99.8	100.1	100.1
1980	100.4	100.6	101.7	102.5	102.2	101.4	99.2	97.2	95.8	95.1	95.3	96.3
1981	96.2	95.9	95.7	95.8	96.9	97.4	97.5	97.6	98.4	98.4	98.3	97.9
1982	98.0	96.9	96.3	96.1	95.9	96.1	95.9	95.5	95.0	94.4	93.5	92.6
1983	91.7	91.6	91.2	91.2	90.6	90.5	90.7	91.3	91.2	91.2	91.8	92.3
1984	92.4	93.1	93.6	94.4	95.2	95.7	96.4	97.0	97.5	98.0	97.9	98.0
1985	98.2	98.1	98.5	98.2	98.6	98.7	98.9	99.0	99.2	99.8	99.8	100.0
1986	100.1	100.3	100.8	100.4	100.4	100.4	100.2	100.1	99.6	100.1	100.0	99.4
1987	100.1	99.4	99.3	99.5	99.5	99.6	99.7	99.9	100.6	100.8	100.9	100.7
1988	101.2	101.2	101.5	101.8	101.8	102.2	102.3	102.4	102.4	102.6	103.0	102.8
1989	103.3	103.9	104.3	104.0	104.6	105.1	105.4	105.5	105.5	105.8	105.7	105.6
1990	104.8	104.8	104.8	105.2	105.1	105.1	105.2	104.9	104.9	104.7	104.5	104.6
1991	104.9	104.6	104.6	103.7	103.0	102.1	101.9	101.3	101.0	100.8	100.4	100.2
1992	99.4	98.8	98.4	98.1	97.6	97.3	97.0	97.1	96.8	96.5	96.7	95.6
1993	96.6	96.6	96.4	96.4	96.3	96.3	96.8	96.5	96.5	96.3	-	-

Source: U.S. Department of Commerce, Bureau of Economic Analysis. - indicates data not available or zero.

Composite Index of 7 Lagging Indicators
Change in Index from Previous Month

Year	Jan	Feb	Mar	Apr	May	Jun	Jul	Aug	Sep	Oct	Nov	Dec
1948	-	+0.5	+0.3	+0.2	+0.1	-	+0.5	+1.6	+0.4	-0.1	+0.4	+0.1
1949	+0.4	+0.2	-0.2	-0.1	+0.3	-0.1	-0.1	-0.3	-0.3	+0.9	-0.2	+0.1
1950	-	-	-0.1	+0.3	+0.1	-0.1	-0.4	+0.3	+1.6	+1.5	+1.3	-0.4
1951	+1.1	+0.8	+0.6	+0.4	+0.3	+0.7	+0.1	-0.1	+0.1	+0.4	+0.3	+0.7
1952	+0.8	-	+0.2	-0.1	+0.6	+0.9	+0.4	-0.5	-	-	+0.5	+0.6
1953	+0.3	+0.4	+0.2	+1.0	+1.0	+0.2	-	+0.3	+0.4	+0.1	+0.4	+0.1
1954	-0.4	-0.3	-1.0	-1.0	-0.4	-0.5	-0.3	-0.7	-0.1	-0.1	-	+0.2
1955	-0.2	-0.1	+0.3	-0.2	+0.4	+0.8	+0.4	+1.9	+0.4	+1.1	+1.0	+0.1
1956	+0.4	+0.1	+0.7	+0.9	+1.0	+0.3	+1.0	-0.2	+0.4	-0.1	+0.2	-0.1
1957	+0.2	-0.3	+0.3	+0.3	+0.2	+0.1	-0.1	+0.8	+0.5	-0.1	+0.4	+0.1
1958	-0.5	-0.8	-0.2	-0.7	-1.3	-0.8	-0.4	-0.5	+0.7	+0.1	-0.3	+0.3
1959	-0.2	+0.2	+0.2	+0.2	+0.8	+0.8	+0.5	+1.0	+1.4	+0.4	-0.1	-0.4
1960	-0.5	+0.3	+0.3	+0.2	+0.4	+0.2	-	-0.3	-0.7	-0.2	+0.2	+0.1
1961	-	-0.2	-0.4	-0.2	-0.4	-0.4	-0.3	-0.1	+0.2	+0.1	-0.1	+0.3
1962	+0.3	-0.1	+0.2	+0.3	+0.2	+0.2	+0.1	-	-	-0.1	+0.1	+0.2
1963	+0.1	+0.1	-0.2	+0.1	+0.1	+0.2	+0.1	+0.4	+0.1	-	+0.4	+0.3
1964	-0.2	+0.2	+0.1	+0.1	-0.1	+0.2	-0.2	+0.3	+0.1	+0.3	-0.1	+0.1
1965	+0.4	+0.3	+0.2	+0.3	+0.2	-0.1	-	+0.3	+0.2	+0.3	+0.4	+1.0
1966	+0.1	+0.5	+0.2	+0.6	+0.7	+0.3	+0.5	+0.3	-	+0.1	+0.6	+0.1
1967	-	-	+0.2	-0.1	-0.2	+0.3	-	-0.4	+0.2	-	-0.3	+0.2
1968	-0.2	+0.5	+0.3	+0.4	+0.3	+0.3	-0.1	+0.5	-	-0.1	+0.2	+0.3
1969	+0.5	+0.3	+0.1	+0.6	+0.5	+0.6	-	+0.2	+0.2	+0.2	-	+0.2
1970	+0.4	+0.1	+0.3	-0.5	-0.3	-0.1	-0.3	-	-0.4	-0.2	-0.4	-0.8
1971	-0.4	-0.3	-0.5	-0.7	-0.1	-0.6	+0.6	+0.6	-0.1	-0.5	-0.5	-
1972	-1.3	-0.4	+0.3	+0.2	+0.3	+0.3	-	-0.2	-	-	-0.1	-0.1
1973	+0.9	+0.7	+0.4	+0.9	+0.2	+0.5	+0.7	+0.1	+0.8	+0.1	+0.3	+0.8
1974	+0.3	+0.2	-0.3	+0.7	+0.5	+0.3	-	+0.2	+0.7	-0.1	+0.3	+0.7
1975	-0.6	-0.9	-0.7	-1.6	-1.3	-2.2	-0.6	-0.6	-0.5	-	-0.1	-0.1
1976	-0.1	-0.1	-0.1	-0.2	-0.1	-0.4	+0.1	-	+0.2	+0.2	-0.3	-0.3
1977	+0.1	+0.3	+0.1	+0.2	+0.1	+0.5	+0.2	+0.4	+0.3	+0.4	+0.2	+0.1
1978	+0.6	+0.1	+0.3	-0.4	+0.4	+0.4	+0.4	+0.2	+0.4	+0.1	+0.8	+0.5
1979	+0.2	+0.2	-0.5	+1.3	-0.1	+0.7	+0.3	+0.5	+0.7	+0.3	+0.3	-
1980	+0.3	+0.2	+1.1	+0.8	-0.3	-0.8	-2.2	-2.0	-1.4	-0.7	+0.2	+1.0
1981	-0.1	-0.3	-0.2	+0.1	+1.1	+0.5	+0.1	+0.1	+0.8	-	-0.1	-0.4
1982	+0.1	-1.1	-0.6	-0.2	-0.2	+0.2	-0.2	-0.4	-0.5	-0.6	-0.9	-0.9
1983	-0.9	-0.1	-0.4	-	-0.6	-0.1	+0.2	+0.6	-0.1	-	+0.6	+0.5
1984	+0.1	+0.7	+0.5	+0.8	+0.8	+0.5	+0.7	+0.6	+0.5	+0.5	-0.1	+0.1
1985	+0.2	-0.1	+0.4	-0.3	+0.4	+0.1	+0.2	+0.1	+0.2	+0.6	-	+0.2
1986	+0.1	+0.2	+0.5	-0.4	-	-	-0.2	-0.1	-0.5	+0.5	-0.1	-0.6
1987	+0.7	-0.7	-0.1	+0.2	-	+0.1	+0.1	+0.2	+0.7	+0.2	+0.1	-0.2
1988	+0.5	-	+0.3	+0.3	-	+0.4	+0.1	+0.1	-	+0.2	+0.4	-0.2
1989	+0.5	+0.6	+0.4	-0.3	+0.6	+0.5	+0.3	+0.1	-	+0.3	-0.1	-0.1
1990	-0.8	-	-	+0.4	-0.1	-	+0.1	-0.3	-	-0.2	-0.2	+0.1
1991	+0.3	-0.3	-	-0.9	-0.7	-0.9	-0.2	-0.6	-0.3	-0.2	-0.4	-0.2
1992	-0.8	-0.6	-0.4	-0.3	-0.5	-0.3	-0.3	+0.1	-0.3	-0.3	+0.2	-1.1
1993	+1.0	-	-0.2	-	-0.1	-	+0.5	-0.3	-	-0.2	-	-

Source: U.S. Department of Commerce, Bureau of Economic Analysis. - indicates data not available or zero.

Index of Labor Cost per Unit of Output, Manufacturing
(1987 = 100)

Year	Jan	Feb	Mar	Apr	May	Jun	Jul	Aug	Sep	Oct	Nov	Dec
1947	34.3	34.8	34.6	34.9	35.2	35.2	35.4	35.2	36.0	36.0	35.9	36.9
1948	37.0	37.0	37.6	37.2	36.8	36.9	37.7	38.3	38.2	38.5	38.8	38.7
1949	38.8	38.7	38.1	38.3	38.7	38.2	38.0	37.7	37.4	37.4	37.1	37.1
1950	37.2	37.3	37.3	36.7	37.0	36.4	36.4	36.3	36.6	37.5	38.4	38.5
1951	38.6	39.2	39.5	40.2	40.4	41.1	41.3	41.8	42.0	41.8	41.7	42.1
1952	42.2	42.3	42.1	42.2	42.6	43.1	42.1	42.3	42.6	42.7	42.1	42.9
1953	42.7	43.0	43.0	43.2	42.9	43.3	43.0	42.7	42.9	43.3	43.9	44.6
1954	44.6	44.7	44.5	44.5	44.2	44.0	43.8	44.0	43.6	43.9	44.2	43.9
1955	42.9	43.1	42.8	42.5	42.5	42.7	42.9	42.9	42.9	43.0	43.8	43.3
1956	43.5	43.7	44.1	44.0	44.3	44.7	46.3	45.0	45.0	45.5	45.6	45.5
1957	45.3	45.4	45.2	45.9	45.9	45.8	45.8	46.1	45.9	46.4	47.5	47.4
1958	47.9	48.3	48.5	48.6	47.9	47.3	47.2	47.2	47.1	46.5	46.6	46.8
1959	46.4	46.2	46.2	45.9	45.8	46.1	46.9	47.3	47.8	47.9	48.1	46.5
1960	46.0	46.7	47.2	47.3	47.6	47.9	47.7	47.6	47.8	48.0	48.2	48.2
1961	48.6	48.6	48.6	47.8	47.7	47.4	47.2	46.8	46.6	46.7	46.8	46.4
1962	47.0	46.8	47.0	47.4	47.5	47.6	47.4	47.0	47.2	47.0	46.9	46.9
1963	46.8	46.7	46.4	45.8	45.8	46.0	46.4	46.2	46.1	45.9	46.0	46.5
1964	45.8	46.1	46.6	46.2	46.1	46.2	46.2	46.4	46.4	46.4	46.0	45.8
1965	45.5	45.4	45.3	45.0	44.9	45.0	44.6	44.8	44.8	45.0	45.3	45.2
1966	45.2	45.6	45.5	45.8	45.8	46.0	45.9	46.4	46.3	46.2	46.8	46.6
1967	46.7	46.8	47.3	47.0	47.3	47.5	47.9	47.8	47.6	47.2	47.3	47.3
1968	47.8	48.3	48.4	48.7	48.7	48.9	49.2	49.2	49.5	49.9	49.6	49.8
1969	49.7	49.7	49.8	50.3	50.8	50.9	50.9	51.3	51.6	51.7	52.0	52.6
1970	53.5	53.3	53.8	53.7	53.6	53.8	54.0	54.0	53.8	54.0	53.9	54.0
1971	54.1	54.3	54.4	54.2	54.4	54.3	54.2	54.9	53.7	53.5	53.5	54.0
1972	53.2	53.8	54.1	53.6	54.1	54.2	54.1	54.1	54.2	54.0	54.0	54.2
1973	54.8	55.1	55.3	55.7	55.8	55.7	56.0	56.1	56.2	56.6	57.1	58.5
1974	59.3	59.9	59.9	60.4	60.8	61.1	61.9	62.3	62.5	63.5	64.6	66.7
1975	67.5	68.2	69.7	69.1	69.8	69.2	69.0	69.4	69.3	69.6	69.7	70.0
1976	70.7	69.9	70.8	71.1	71.0	71.3	71.3	71.9	72.0	71.8	72.0	72.0
1977	72.0	72.8	72.9	72.9	73.2	73.8	74.4	74.4	75.0	75.8	76.1	76.5
1978	77.0	77.9	78.7	77.7	78.0	77.9	78.5	78.5	79.0	79.5	79.4	80.8
1979	81.6	81.8	82.3	83.5	83.2	84.0	85.1	85.7	86.5	86.3	86.9	88.1
1980	88.1	88.4	89.3	90.8	92.7	94.1	94.3	94.4	94.4	94.7	94.6	95.6
1981	96.9	96.1	97.1	98.4	98.5	99.1	98.7	99.8	100.1	101.5	102.0	102.8
1982	104.7	102.4	102.8	103.4	103.8	103.9	104.0	104.2	104.3	104.5	104.7	105.5
1983	103.8	103.8	103.0	102.8	102.3	102.2	101.8	101.0	100.4	100.6	101.2	101.8
1984	100.7	101.1	100.9	101.4	101.1	101.1	101.3	101.7	102.0	102.4	102.9	103.9
1985	104.1	103.1	104.4	102.5	102.2	103.2	103.5	103.0	102.8	104.8	103.3	103.8
1986	102.4	102.6	104.7	102.9	103.1	103.3	102.9	102.9	102.6	103.0	101.9	101.2
1987	102.3	100.8	101.0	100.1	99.3	98.5	98.6	99.3	100.5	99.5	99.9	99.9
1988	100.4	101.0	102.4	101.4	102.1	102.8	102.9	102.5	103.2	104.8	103.6	103.0
1989	102.6	103.7	104.3	102.9	103.2	103.7	105.2	104.9	105.2	106.9	106.1	106.1
1990	106.0	106.5	106.8	108.2	107.4	107.8	108.1	107.4	107.8	108.4	108.8	110.5
1991	110.2	110.9	111.9	111.4	111.4	110.9	111.2	111.4	110.9	112.3	111.8	113.1
1992	111.9	111.8	111.5	111.5	111.5	112.1	111.8	111.9	112.3	111.9	110.6	112.0
1993	109.9	109.5	109.3	109.2	109.2	109.0	109.0	109.0	108.8	108.0	-	-

Source: U.S. Department of Commerce, Bureau of Economic Analysis, Board of Governors of the Federal Reserve System. - indicates data not available or zero.

Ratio, Manufacturing and Trade Inventories to Sales in 1987 $
(Ratio)

Year	Jan	Feb	Mar	Apr	May	Jun	Jul	Aug	Sep	Oct	Nov	Dec
1948	1.41	1.42	1.42	1.42	1.44	1.44	1.45	1.44	1.45	1.45	1.45	1.44
1949	1.48	1.48	1.49	1.49	1.51	1.48	1.52	1.49	1.47	1.51	1.48	1.47
1950	1.45	1.42	1.41	1.40	1.38	1.33	1.22	1.23	1.33	1.37	1.44	1.37
1951	1.37	1.41	1.45	1.50	1.51	1.55	1.59	1.57	1.58	1.58	1.59	1.61
1952	1.60	1.58	1.59	1.57	1.55	1.56	1.59	1.56	1.53	1.49	1.51	1.49
1953	1.51	1.49	1.48	1.50	1.51	1.53	1.52	1.55	1.57	1.57	1.60	1.62
1954	1.60	1.58	1.58	1.56	1.58	1.55	1.55	1.55	1.54	1.53	1.49	1.46
1955	1.44	1.43	1.41	1.39	1.39	1.41	1.41	1.42	1.40	1.41	1.40	1.40
1956	1.42	1.45	1.44	1.45	1.47	1.47	1.54	1.50	1.49	1.48	1.48	1.46
1957	1.46	1.45	1.46	1.49	1.50	1.49	1.50	1.50	1.52	1.52	1.53	1.57
1958	1.55	1.57	1.59	1.59	1.58	1.54	1.53	1.50	1.50	1.48	1.46	1.51
1959	1.45	1.43	1.42	1.42	1.41	1.42	1.43	1.48	1.48	1.48	1.47	1.45
1960	1.44	1.46	1.47	1.47	1.49	1.50	1.51	1.52	1.51	1.51	1.53	1.51
1961	1.54	1.53	1.50	1.51	1.48	1.46	1.48	1.45	1.45	1.44	1.43	1.43
1962	1.44	1.44	1.43	1.43	1.44	1.45	1.45	1.45	1.46	1.45	1.43	1.46
1963	1.46	1.44	1.44	1.43	1.44	1.44	1.42	1.44	1.44	1.43	1.45	1.42
1964	1.42	1.43	1.44	1.42	1.41	1.42	1.39	1.41	1.40	1.42	1.42	1.38
1965	1.40	1.40	1.38	1.38	1.40	1.40	1.39	1.41	1.41	1.40	1.39	1.39
1966	1.38	1.40	1.38	1.40	1.42	1.42	1.44	1.45	1.45	1.46	1.48	1.49
1967	1.50	1.51	1.51	1.51	1.51	1.51	1.51	1.51	1.52	1.53	1.50	1.48
1968	1.49	1.50	1.49	1.50	1.50	1.49	1.48	1.51	1.51	1.49	1.49	1.50
1969	1.50	1.51	1.50	1.50	1.51	1.51	1.51	1.52	1.51	1.51	1.53	1.54
1970	1.55	1.55	1.57	1.59	1.57	1.57	1.58	1.59	1.59	1.62	1.64	1.59
1971	1.58	1.57	1.57	1.57	1.57	1.55	1.56	1.58	1.56	1.56	1.53	1.53
1972	1.52	1.53	1.50	1.50	1.50	1.49	1.49	1.47	1.47	1.45	1.44	1.42
1973	1.41	1.41	1.43	1.44	1.45	1.46	1.45	1.47	1.48	1.45	1.44	1.48
1974	1.47	1.48	1.48	1.49	1.50	1.52	1.51	1.53	1.56	1.59	1.62	1.69
1975	1.68	1.67	1.71	1.69	1.68	1.65	1.63	1.62	1.61	1.61	1.62	1.60
1976	1.56	1.56	1.55	1.55	1.56	1.55	1.55	1.56	1.57	1.59	1.57	1.53
1977	1.54	1.53	1.52	1.52	1.53	1.52	1.52	1.53	1.54	1.53	1.53	1.52
1978	1.56	1.54	1.54	1.51	1.52	1.52	1.53	1.51	1.52	1.51	1.51	1.52
1979	1.53	1.55	1.51	1.57	1.53	1.56	1.57	1.56	1.56	1.57	1.57	1.57
1980	1.55	1.57	1.61	1.66	1.68	1.68	1.65	1.64	1.60	1.57	1.57	1.57
1981	1.57	1.58	1.59	1.58	1.60	1.61	1.61	1.62	1.64	1.66	1.69	1.70
1982	1.70	1.66	1.66	1.67	1.65	1.68	1.68	1.69	1.69	1.70	1.68	1.69
1983	1.64	1.65	1.61	1.61	1.59	1.55	1.56	1.57	1.55	1.54	1.53	1.51
1984	1.51	1.53	1.54	1.55	1.55	1.54	1.57	1.59	1.60	1.60	1.60	1.60
1985	1.60	1.60	1.59	1.59	1.58	1.61	1.60	1.58	1.58	1.60	1.59	1.60
1986	1.58	1.60	1.61	1.59	1.60	1.59	1.58	1.58	1.54	1.56	1.56	1.52
1987	1.58	1.53	1.54	1.54	1.55	1.55	1.53	1.54	1.53	1.55	1.56	1.55
1988	1.56	1.55	1.53	1.54	1.54	1.53	1.55	1.55	1.55	1.54	1.54	1.53
1989	1.54	1.57	1.58	1.56	1.58	1.59	1.62	1.58	1.59	1.62	1.61	1.61
1990	1.62	1.60	1.59	1.61	1.61	1.60	1.62	1.61	1.64	1.64	1.66	1.67
1991	1.70	1.69	1.68	1.65	1.64	1.64	1.62	1.62	1.63	1.62	1.63	1.65
1992	1.63	1.62	1.61	1.61	1.62	1.61	1.61	1.62	1.61	1.60	1.59	1.56
1993	1.57	1.57	1.57	1.58	1.58	1.56	1.59	1.57	1.56	-	-	-

Source: U.S. Department of Commerce, Bureau of Economic Analysis, U.S. Department of Commerce, Bureau of the Census. - indicates data not available or zero.

Average Duration of Unemployment in Weeks

Year	Jan	Feb	Mar	Apr	May	Jun	Jul	Aug	Sep	Oct	Nov	Dec
1948	8.9	8.4	8.7	8.5	9.1	8.8	8.6	8.8	8.5	9.5	7.8	8.1
1949	8.2	8.3	8.3	8.8	9.1	10.0	10.8	11.0	11.7	10.9	11.6	11.8
1950	11.3	11.8	12.4	12.6	12.7	13.1	12.5	12.2	12.2	12.3	10.7	10.7
1951	10.6	10.8	10.1	10.6	9.9	8.7	9.2	9.1	9.1	8.9	9.7	9.3
1952	9.3	8.8	8.4	9.0	7.8	7.3	7.5	7.6	8.1	9.1	9.5	8.8
1953	9.3	8.4	8.5	7.8	7.9	8.2	7.9	8.0	7.1	7.2	7.9	8.0
1954	8.7	9.5	10.6	10.9	11.6	12.3	12.5	12.8	12.9	13.3	13.2	13.4
1955	13.4	14.2	13.4	14.3	14.4	13.4	13.8	12.3	11.7	11.5	11.3	12.0
1956	11.7	12.5	11.6	11.0	10.4	10.1	10.5	12.0	11.8	11.6	10.9	11.4
1957	10.4	10.7	10.8	10.6	10.4	10.2	10.1	10.5	9.8	11.1	10.4	10.4
1958	10.5	11.0	11.2	12.1	13.1	14.4	14.6	15.7	16.5	16.5	16.4	15.7
1959	16.3	15.5	15.3	14.9	14.7	14.9	14.3	13.7	13.7	12.9	13.1	13.1
1960	13.5	13.1	13.0	12.6	11.9	11.9	12.6	12.2	12.9	13.5	13.9	12.4
1961	13.7	13.6	14.1	15.5	15.6	16.2	17.3	17.0	16.1	15.9	17.0	15.8
1962	15.3	16.0	15.0	14.9	15.5	15.1	14.6	14.5	14.1	14.1	13.3	13.6
1963	13.8	14.1	14.5	14.5	14.5	14.0	14.0	13.9	14.2	13.9	13.3	13.3
1964	13.5	13.2	13.5	12.4	13.6	13.6	14.7	13.0	12.7	12.6	14.0	12.7
1965	12.2	12.6	12.0	11.4	11.1	11.6	11.6	11.9	11.9	12.1	11.7	11.4
1966	11.9	11.2	11.1	10.8	10.2	9.7	9.7	9.8	10.1	10.3	9.7	9.5
1967	9.3	9.2	8.9	8.8	8.7	8.3	8.3	8.9	8.4	8.7	8.9	8.6
1968	9.4	8.7	8.5	8.7	8.2	7.9	8.4	8.3	8.2	8.4	8.1	8.2
1969	8.1	7.9	7.9	7.9	7.9	7.7	7.8	7.9	8.0	7.6	8.0	8.0
1970	7.9	8.0	8.3	8.2	8.6	8.6	8.9	8.8	8.9	8.7	9.3	9.8
1971	10.5	10.4	10.6	10.9	11.2	11.6	11.5	11.5	11.9	12.6	12.0	11.5
1972	12.1	12.4	12.3	12.4	12.3	12.4	11.8	11.8	12.1	11.7	11.4	11.4
1973	11.0	10.5	10.6	10.0	10.1	9.6	9.6	9.8	9.4	10.2	9.9	9.5
1974	9.5	9.6	9.7	9.8	9.6	9.7	9.9	9.8	9.6	9.9	9.6	10.1
1975	10.7	11.7	11.8	12.9	13.4	15.3	15.0	15.6	16.1	15.4	16.6	16.5
1976	16.6	16.3	16.5	15.9	15.0	16.9	15.7	15.6	15.2	15.2	15.3	15.1
1977	15.2	14.7	14.5	14.4	14.9	14.4	14.3	13.9	14.0	13.7	13.6	13.6
1978	12.9	12.5	12.4	12.3	12.1	12.1	12.0	11.4	11.4	11.7	11.1	10.6
1979	11.1	11.2	11.7	11.0	11.1	10.4	10.3	10.6	10.5	10.5	10.6	10.8
1980	10.4	10.6	11.0	11.4	10.9	11.3	11.8	12.4	12.9	13.1	13.6	13.7
1981	14.3	14.1	14.0	13.9	13.6	13.7	13.8	14.4	13.6	13.5	13.1	13.1
1982	13.4	14.1	14.1	14.5	14.9	15.7	15.4	16.2	16.6	17.2	17.1	18.1
1983	19.4	19.2	19.4	19.5	20.5	20.8	21.2	20.0	20.2	20.2	19.7	19.2
1984	20.4	19.0	19.1	18.9	18.8	18.1	18.0	17.3	17.0	16.7	17.0	16.8
1985	15.9	15.9	16.1	16.4	15.3	15.5	15.5	15.3	15.3	15.3	15.7	15.1
1986	14.8	15.2	14.6	14.7	14.7	15.2	15.2	15.5	15.4	15.2	15.0	15.0
1987	14.9	14.7	14.9	14.8	14.9	14.9	14.2	14.4	14.2	14.0	14.0	14.2
1988	14.2	14.4	13.7	13.3	13.8	13.1	13.4	13.6	13.6	13.4	12.6	12.9
1989	12.6	12.4	12.3	12.4	11.9	11.0	11.8	11.4	11.5	11.9	11.8	11.6
1990	12.0	11.7	11.9	11.9	11.7	11.7	12.0	12.3	12.5	12.1	12.6	12.6
1991	12.4	12.8	13.0	13.5	12.9	13.8	13.9	14.2	14.3	14.4	15.1	15.5
1992	16.3	16.8	17.0	17.2	17.9	18.2	18.3	18.3	18.5	19.2	18.4	19.2
1993	18.7	18.3	17.5	17.4	17.6	17.6	17.9	18.3	18.5	18.6	-	-

Source: U.S. Department of Labor, Bureau of Labor Statistics. - indicates data not available or zero.

Ratio, Consumer Installment Credit to Personal Income
(Percent)

Year	Jan	Feb	Mar	Apr	May	Jun	Jul	Aug	Sep	Oct	Nov	Dec
1946	1.53	1.60	1.63	1.71	1.77	1.83	1.86	1.95	2.08	2.13	2.23	2.31
1947	2.42	2.54	2.66	2.82	2.93	3.00	3.09	3.16	3.02	3.25	3.39	3.49
1948	3.56	3.65	3.78	3.89	3.96	3.97	4.06	4.11	4.22	4.22	4.29	4.40
1949	4.52	4.61	4.65	4.77	4.91	5.07	5.21	5.28	5.31	5.57	5.65	5.74
1950	5.65	5.71	5.69	5.91	6.04	6.20	6.32	6.35	6.46	6.43	6.35	6.21
1951	6.27	6.25	6.19	6.08	6.03	5.98	5.93	5.90	5.94	5.91	5.95	5.98
1952	6.06	6.01	6.04	6.12	6.25	6.45	6.63	6.56	6.63	6.80	6.96	7.09
1953	7.22	7.31	7.45	7.56	7.66	7.73	7.86	7.97	8.04	8.07	8.19	8.21
1954	8.19	8.16	8.16	8.20	8.17	8.18	8.19	8.16	8.15	8.14	8.10	8.15
1955	8.21	8.28	8.40	8.48	8.59	8.74	8.74	8.90	9.01	9.06	9.09	9.14
1956	9.20	9.24	9.32	9.30	9.35	9.34	9.40	9.35	9.33	9.30	9.38	9.38
1957	9.42	9.41	9.42	9.44	9.47	9.45	9.48	9.50	9.58	9.63	9.66	9.71
1958	9.72	9.70	9.61	9.58	9.52	9.43	9.27	9.26	9.24	9.21	9.13	9.17
1959	9.25	9.29	9.32	9.35	9.41	9.48	9.61	9.84	9.96	10.08	10.08	10.02
1960	10.10	10.21	10.35	10.38	10.43	10.51	10.56	10.60	10.64	10.64	10.70	10.79
1961	10.76	10.72	10.65	10.59	10.50	10.40	10.35	10.36	10.38	10.33	10.28	10.30
1962	10.35	10.37	10.33	10.37	10.45	10.51	10.56	10.63	10.66	10.72	10.79	10.85
1963	10.87	11.06	11.10	11.19	11.24	11.26	11.38	11.44	11.48	11.53	11.60	11.60
1964	11.68	11.67	11.84	11.87	11.94	12.00	12.05	12.07	12.14	12.23	12.21	12.20
1965	12.25	12.42	12.44	12.53	12.56	12.58	12.63	12.70	12.48	12.61	12.60	12.60
1966	12.67	12.69	12.68	12.69	12.69	12.65	12.66	12.61	12.55	12.52	12.48	12.53
1967	12.48	12.53	12.45	12.43	12.39	12.35	12.28	12.24	12.26	12.25	12.22	12.20
1968	12.12	12.01	12.08	12.08	12.06	12.07	12.07	12.06	12.06	12.10	12.12	12.18
1969	12.26	12.38	12.33	12.36	12.39	12.40	12.39	12.36	12.38	12.39	12.41	12.37
1970	12.43	12.43	12.38	12.10	12.19	12.25	12.26	12.25	12.23	12.23	12.18	12.17
1971	12.38	12.41	12.39	12.38	12.36	12.15	12.38	12.39	12.46	12.52	12.54	12.55
1972	12.48	12.34	12.50	12.57	12.63	12.88	12.75	12.73	12.75	12.63	12.56	12.61
1973	12.91	13.00	13.05	13.15	13.18	13.21	13.33	13.28	13.28	13.21	13.13	13.12
1974	13.22	13.32	13.34	13.35	13.30	13.29	13.20	13.19	13.15	13.03	13.03	12.97
1975	12.79	12.83	12.74	12.65	12.52	12.21	12.36	12.24	12.18	12.14	12.13	12.16
1976	12.11	12.09	12.15	12.20	12.22	12.27	12.26	12.27	12.32	12.36	12.31	12.41
1977	12.51	12.53	12.64	12.73	12.79	12.89	12.84	12.90	12.96	13.04	13.07	13.15
1978	13.22	13.23	13.24	13.21	13.32	13.44	13.49	13.54	13.58	13.54	13.63	13.69
1979	13.75	13.78	13.77	13.89	13.96	13.98	13.87	13.88	13.91	13.91	13.90	13.80
1980	13.83	13.75	13.76	13.67	13.54	13.36	13.13	12.98	12.77	12.59	12.44	12.35
1981	12.25	12.13	12.16	12.16	12.18	12.13	11.98	11.85	11.93	11.94	11.91	11.93
1982	12.01	11.87	11.91	11.84	11.79	11.81	11.75	11.76	11.78	11.73	11.72	11.80
1983	11.80	11.76	11.88	11.83	11.77	11.87	11.95	12.11	12.10	12.14	12.21	12.32
1984	12.34	12.39	12.51	12.61	12.88	13.01	13.08	13.15	13.17	13.38	13.45	13.53
1985	13.62	13.63	13.89	14.01	14.22	14.28	14.39	14.48	14.69	14.74	14.87	14.82
1986	14.99	15.05	15.03	15.04	15.19	15.27	15.37	15.42	15.52	15.71	15.72	15.57
1987	15.47	15.34	15.33	15.40	15.41	15.53	15.65	15.62	15.63	15.41	15.49	15.39
1988	15.61	15.62	15.60	15.61	15.65	15.70	15.67	15.74	15.72	15.56	15.75	15.71
1989	16.10	16.03	15.98	16.03	16.13	16.17	16.14	16.21	16.23	16.19	16.15	16.11
1990	15.96	15.88	15.77	15.73	15.80	15.73	15.76	15.75	15.68	15.68	15.62	15.39
1991	15.45	15.41	15.40	15.35	15.27	15.16	15.17	15.11	15.04	15.01	14.97	14.74
1992	14.79	14.60	14.53	14.42	14.33	14.30	14.24	14.28	14.17	14.01	14.05	13.46
1993	14.23	14.24	14.18	14.02	13.94	14.00	14.12	14.04	14.15	-	-	-

Source: U.S. Department of Commerce, Bureau of Economic Analysis, Board of Governors of the Federal Reserve System. - indicates data not available or zero.

Commercial and Industrial Loans Outstanding
(Million 1987 $)

Year	Jan	Feb	Mar	Apr	May	Jun	Jul	Aug	Sep	Oct	Nov	Dec
1945	34,369	33,720	33,166	32,899	32,652	33,456	33,685	33,771	34,243	34,107	34,852	37,094
1946	38,221	38,349	38,690	39,492	40,193	40,361	38,291	39,028	42,178	40,726	40,235	40,390
1947	40,890	41,471	42,105	43,810	44,319	44,498	44,451	44,844	44,806	45,361	46,109	46,130
1948	46,338	46,831	46,877	46,880	48,137	48,576	49,133	49,188	49,212	49,397	48,847	48,833
1949	49,089	49,759	49,339	48,991	48,662	48,336	47,124	46,489	46,237	46,526	46,283	46,353
1950	46,736	46,686	46,683	46,997	46,763	47,499	47,566	48,190	49,468	50,218	50,939	51,390
1951	51,623	52,829	54,258	55,987	57,337	58,326	59,071	59,817	60,143	60,597	60,861	61,548
1952	62,462	62,922	63,306	63,685	63,901	64,641	64,972	64,681	65,746	66,846	68,557	69,376
1953	69,685	69,849	70,104	71,408	71,618	71,645	70,744	71,500	70,877	70,790	70,421	68,887
1954	68,217	68,665	68,574	68,109	67,603	67,552	67,318	64,557	64,618	64,731	65,278	66,924
1955	67,156	67,452	68,422	68,615	70,305	71,050	72,511	73,622	74,120	75,553	76,949	78,046
1956	78,808	79,084	81,136	82,225	83,292	84,398	85,779	86,055	86,601	86,850	87,619	87,934
1957	88,275	88,351	89,772	90,461	91,213	92,086	92,430	92,249	92,824	91,890	90,377	89,910
1958	88,566	87,546	86,655	86,410	84,966	84,973	84,851	84,555	85,103	85,663	85,768	86,235
1959	86,169	86,217	86,931	87,468	88,915	90,618	90,570	92,166	92,440	93,555	94,350	94,993
1960	95,123	96,445	96,491	97,092	98,307	99,574	99,519	99,381	99,732	99,528	99,896	99,594
1961	99,215	99,116	99,552	100,103	100,251	100,713	100,227	100,588	100,840	100,844	101,041	101,163
1962	101,295	101,688	102,276	103,257	104,044	104,773	105,131	106,032	105,845	107,488	108,405	108,901
1963	109,061	109,682	110,061	111,052	111,200	111,182	111,219	112,111	113,001	114,453	116,368	118,158
1964	117,050	118,612	118,630	119,698	121,085	121,860	122,343	123,587	124,932	125,556	126,892	128,910
1965	130,974	133,716	136,548	138,021	140,574	140,737	141,781	144,928	147,883	149,387	151,373	152,317
1966	154,439	155,524	157,635	159,281	161,472	164,097	165,925	168,648	170,324	173,168	175,035	175,864
1967	176,879	178,387	180,934	183,494	183,509	184,332	185,475	185,414	186,252	187,650	189,127	189,967
1968	189,914	189,219	189,536	192,740	192,691	194,173	195,527	199,086	200,557	202,872	205,645	207,174
1969	211,778	212,704	214,850	219,752	221,562	223,565	224,009	227,953	230,669	232,548	233,108	234,390
1970	231,662	234,272	237,448	237,017	238,395	239,232	237,879	240,857	240,458	235,941	234,402	234,369
1971	232,757	231,944	232,018	228,839	229,536	226,531	224,043	227,608	232,726	230,305	229,897	227,400
1972	224,080	223,780	226,234	228,644	228,922	228,674	227,324	227,692	226,581	232,056	233,184	230,278
1973	232,788	237,947	237,261	240,019	238,046	237,395	243,892	234,859	238,894	243,698	245,303	242,438
1974	238,925	239,346	239,305	247,696	248,236	250,073	248,964	245,044	252,627	250,184	250,419	251,118
1975	252,065	251,088	249,823	244,301	237,567	232,973	228,919	225,747	221,706	218,211	217,843	217,289
1976	215,007	215,708	211,455	205,075	204,854	205,072	202,551	202,819	200,849	202,276	204,506	204,317
1977	203,682	203,599	202,535	201,149	201,483	204,098	203,570	206,035	206,060	207,169	208,238	208,652
1978	207,935	206,481	209,269	209,568	211,581	213,725	214,507	215,755	215,295	215,617	217,526	216,223
1979	217,235	217,203	217,551	221,648	223,115	226,117	227,688	231,288	233,532	230,787	228,386	229,893
1980	232,893	233,477	235,495	234,875	231,381	234,593	228,827	226,665	228,046	226,719	230,709	231,375
1981	230,039	228,226	224,233	226,213	231,463	235,402	238,488	243,836	248,540	250,912	254,760	257,912
1982	262,570	267,697	269,688	275,220	279,116	280,472	279,591	280,266	282,513	281,904	276,880	270,653
1983	275,439	274,624	275,793	271,857	266,801	266,903	265,688	265,530	264,866	263,409	265,042	268,712
1984	274,494	278,251	284,243	290,731	296,668	306,360	310,035	314,251	319,520	323,706	325,684	327,169
1985	327,702	330,758	333,669	333,491	335,758	335,200	338,026	341,081	341,993	343,513	344,958	346,090
1986	349,702	353,278	356,443	353,604	354,627	355,944	359,322	364,318	362,987	363,679	363,805	369,877
1987	374,734	371,625	369,357	366,515	363,445	363,040	360,147	356,425	360,018	361,306	359,781	362,348
1988	364,212	369,215	370,688	374,172	372,820	373,261	374,240	375,619	374,780	378,545	380,468	382,694
1989	382,138	389,498	389,149	390,289	396,162	399,578	403,648	412,784	410,823	411,120	412,091	410,034
1990	404,311	410,559	419,123	419,712	416,481	418,605	420,791	416,318	415,168	406,100	402,470	406,115
1991	404,731	407,059	412,928	407,872	401,440	398,722	399,847	389,822	387,071	383,337	381,813	381,227
1992	378,469	378,938	377,645	375,676	370,186	365,110	366,078	366,421	364,842	369,680	374,896	375,465
1993	369,012	369,503	363,038	364,190	365,859	366,923	372,577	372,333	371,886	372,008	-	-

Source: U.S. Department of Commerce, Bureau of Economic Analysis, Board of Governors of the Federal Reserve System, The Federal Reserve Bank of New York. - indicates data not available or zero.

Average Prime Rate Charged By Banks
Not seasonally adjusted
(Percent)

Year	Jan	Feb	Mar	Apr	May	Jun	Jul	Aug	Sep	Oct	Nov	Dec
1945	1.50	1.50	1.50	1.50	1.50	1.50	1.50	1.50	1.50	1.50	1.50	1.50
1946	1.50	1.50	1.50	1.50	1.50	1.50	1.50	1.50	1.50	1.50	1.50	1.50
1947	1.50	1.50	1.50	1.50	1.50	1.50	1.50	1.50	1.50	1.50	1.50	1.75
1948	1.75	1.75	1.75	1.75	1.75	1.75	1.75	2.00	2.00	2.00	2.00	2.00
1949	2.00	2.00	2.00	2.00	2.00	2.00	2.00	2.00	2.00	2.00	2.00	2.00
1950	2.00	2.00	2.00	2.00	2.00	2.00	2.00	2.00	2.08	2.25	2.25	2.25
1951	2.44	2.50	2.50	2.50	2.50	2.50	2.50	2.50	2.50	2.62	2.75	2.85
1952	3.00	3.00	3.00	3.00	3.00	3.00	3.00	3.00	3.00	3.00	3.00	3.00
1953	3.00	3.00	3.00	3.03	3.25	3.25	3.25	3.25	3.25	3.25	3.25	3.25
1954	3.25	3.25	3.13	3.00	3.00	3.00	3.00	3.00	3.00	3.00	3.00	3.00
1955	3.00	3.00	3.00	3.00	3.00	3.00	3.00	3.23	3.25	3.40	3.50	3.50
1956	3.50	3.50	3.50	3.65	3.75	3.75	3.75	3.84	4.00	4.00	4.00	4.00
1957	4.00	4.00	4.00	4.00	4.00	4.00	4.00	4.42	4.50	4.50	4.50	4.50
1958	4.34	4.00	4.00	3.83	3.50	3.50	3.50	3.50	3.83	4.00	4.00	4.00
1959	4.00	4.00	4.00	4.00	4.23	4.50	4.50	4.50	5.00	5.00	5.00	5.00
1960	5.00	5.00	5.00	5.00	5.00	5.00	5.00	4.85	4.50	4.50	4.50	4.50
1961	4.50	4.50	4.50	4.50	4.50	4.50	4.50	4.50	4.50	4.50	4.50	4.50
1962	4.50	4.50	4.50	4.50	4.50	4.50	4.50	4.50	4.50	4.50	4.50	4.50
1963	4.50	4.50	4.50	4.50	4.50	4.50	4.50	4.50	4.50	4.50	4.50	4.50
1964	4.50	4.50	4.50	4.50	4.50	4.50	4.50	4.50	4.50	4.50	4.50	4.50
1965	4.50	4.50	4.50	4.50	4.50	4.50	4.50	4.50	4.50	4.50	4.50	4.92
1966	5.00	5.00	5.35	5.50	5.50	5.52	5.75	5.88	6.00	6.00	6.00	6.00
1967	5.96	5.75	5.71	5.50	5.50	5.50	5.50	5.50	5.50	5.50	5.68	6.00
1968	6.00	6.00	6.00	6.20	6.50	6.50	6.50	6.50	6.40	6.00	6.20	6.60
1969	6.95	7.00	7.24	7.50	7.50	8.23	8.50	8.50	8.50	8.50	8.50	8.50
1970	8.50	8.50	8.39	8.00	8.00	8.00	8.00	8.00	7.83	7.50	7.28	6.92
1971	6.29	5.88	5.48	5.25	5.42	5.50	5.90	6.00	6.00	5.91	5.47	5.25
1972	5.18	4.75	4.75	4.98	5.00	5.04	5.25	5.27	5.50	5.73	5.75	5.79
1973	6.00	6.02	6.30	6.60	7.01	7.49	8.30	9.23	9.86	9.94	9.75	9.75
1974	9.73	9.21	8.83	10.02	11.25	11.54	11.98	12.00	12.00	11.68	10.83	10.50
1975	10.05	8.96	7.93	7.50	7.40	7.07	7.15	7.66	7.88	7.96	7.53	7.26
1976	7.00	6.75	6.75	6.75	6.75	7.20	7.25	7.01	7.00	6.78	6.50	6.35
1977	6.25	6.25	6.25	6.25	6.41	6.75	6.75	6.83	7.13	7.52	7.75	7.75
1978	7.93	8.00	8.00	8.00	8.27	8.63	9.00	9.01	9.41	9.94	10.94	11.55
1979	11.75	11.75	11.75	11.75	11.75	11.65	11.54	11.91	12.90	14.39	15.55	15.30
1980	15.25	15.63	18.31	19.77	16.57	12.63	11.48	11.12	12.23	13.79	16.06	20.35
1981	20.16	19.43	18.05	17.15	19.61	20.03	20.39	20.50	20.08	18.45	16.84	15.75
1982	15.75	16.56	16.50	16.50	16.50	16.50	16.26	14.39	13.50	12.52	11.85	11.50
1983	11.16	10.98	10.50	10.50	10.50	10.50	10.50	10.89	11.00	11.00	11.00	11.00
1984	11.00	11.00	11.21	11.93	12.39	12.60	13.00	13.00	12.97	12.58	11.77	11.06
1985	10.61	10.50	10.50	10.50	10.31	9.78	9.50	9.50	9.50	9.50	9.50	9.50
1986	9.50	9.50	9.10	8.83	8.50	8.50	8.16	7.90	7.50	7.50	7.50	7.50
1987	7.50	7.50	7.50	7.75	8.14	8.25	8.25	8.25	8.70	9.07	8.78	8.75
1988	8.75	8.51	8.50	8.50	8.84	9.00	9.29	9.84	10.00	10.00	10.05	10.50
1989	10.50	10.93	11.50	11.50	11.50	11.07	10.98	10.50	10.50	10.50	10.50	10.50
1990	10.11	10.00	10.00	10.00	10.00	10.00	10.00	10.00	10.00	10.00	10.00	10.00
1991	9.52	9.05	9.00	9.00	8.50	8.50	8.50	8.50	8.20	8.00	7.58	7.21
1992	6.50	6.50	6.50	6.50	6.50	6.50	6.02	6.00	6.00	6.00	6.00	6.00
1993	6.00	6.00	6.00	6.00	6.00	6.00	6.00	6.00	6.00	6.00	6.00	-

Source: Board of Governors of the Federal Reserve System. - indicates data not available or zero.

Smoothed Change in CPI for Services
(Annual Rate, Percent)

Year	Jan	Feb	Mar	Apr	May	Jun	Jul	Aug	Sep	Oct	Nov	Dec
1956	-	-	-	-	-	2.3	3.0	3.4	3.9	3.7	3.9	4.3
1957	4.7	4.3	5.1	4.8	4.8	4.9	4.3	4.2	4.2	4.5	4.8	4.3
1958	4.2	4.3	3.8	3.7	3.9	3.5	3.5	3.1	3.1	2.7	2.1	1.5
1959	1.6	2.2	2.3	2.7	3.3	3.2	3.4	3.8	4.2	4.6	4.2	4.1
1960	3.5	3.4	3.5	3.2	3.2	2.8	2.9	2.5	2.7	2.4	2.6	2.4
1961	2.6	2.4	1.9	2.1	1.9	1.5	1.1	1.4	1.4	1.8	1.9	2.3
1962	2.3	1.9	2.1	2.0	2.3	2.1	2.4	2.3	1.9	1.4	1.6	1.5
1963	1.9	1.9	1.6	1.9	1.8	2.1	2.1	2.4	2.2	1.9	2.0	2.5
1964	2.5	2.1	1.6	1.7	1.6	1.9	1.9	1.6	1.2	1.4	2.0	2.1
1965	2.5	3.0	2.9	3.1	2.8	2.2	2.2	1.9	2.1	2.5	3.1	3.0
1966	3.1	2.8	2.8	3.7	4.3	4.7	5.5	5.3	5.6	5.7	6.1	5.6
1967	5.1	4.7	4.4	4.2	3.5	3.8	3.5	3.4	3.4	4.2	4.0	4.5
1968	4.8	4.9	5.4	5.5	5.4	5.7	6.2	6.8	6.8	6.9	6.6	6.6
1969	6.8	6.5	7.1	7.5	7.8	7.4	7.3	7.2	7.8	7.5	7.4	7.3
1970	7.8	8.0	9.1	9.5	9.4	9.0	8.6	8.1	7.6	7.3	7.1	6.9
1971	6.8	6.2	5.1	4.2	3.5	4.1	4.3	4.7	4.8	4.6	4.3	4.0
1972	4.2	4.1	4.0	3.8	3.6	3.4	3.3	3.2	3.2	3.1	3.1	3.1
1973	3.1	3.1	3.5	3.7	3.7	4.1	4.2	4.9	5.9	7.9	9.2	9.5
1974	9.6	9.2	9.3	8.9	9.5	10.1	11.1	12.2	13.0	13.3	13.2	12.8
1975	12.0	11.3	9.7	8.6	7.5	6.8	6.2	6.1	6.6	7.0	8.4	9.1
1976	10.4	10.7	10.5	9.5	8.0	7.1	6.8	6.7	7.1	7.2	7.3	7.3
1977	7.6	7.7	7.9	8.2	7.9	7.8	8.3	8.3	8.1	7.7	7.7	7.5
1978	7.5	7.7	7.9	8.4	8.6	9.1	9.5	9.9	10.4	10.7	10.8	9.9
1979	9.4	9.4	9.5	9.8	10.5	11.0	11.9	13.2	13.9	14.7	15.7	16.3
1980	17.2	17.8	18.9	19.8	19.9	20.5	17.1	12.8	9.7	8.7	9.4	10.8
1981	11.9	12.3	12.4	12.5	13.2	14.0	15.4	16.1	16.9	16.0	14.8	13.0
1982	11.1	9.2	7.0	6.4	6.6	7.3	7.5	7.7	6.8	5.8	4.2	1.4
1983	0.6	0.7	1.0	2.1	2.8	3.3	3.8	3.9	4.1	4.5	5.1	5.3
1984	5.5	5.7	5.7	5.7	5.6	5.2	5.5	5.6	5.8	5.7	5.5	5.3
1985	4.9	4.8	4.8	4.7	5.0	5.2	5.3	5.3	5.0	4.9	5.1	5.1
1986	5.3	5.3	5.5	5.5	5.1	5.2	4.9	4.5	4.3	4.2	3.9	3.7
1987	3.6	3.6	3.6	3.9	4.1	4.2	4.1	4.4	4.6	4.6	4.6	4.5
1988	4.5	4.4	4.3	4.5	4.5	4.7	4.6	4.7	4.9	5.0	5.0	5.0
1989	5.0	5.0	5.0	4.9	4.9	4.9	5.1	5.1	4.8	4.8	4.9	5.0
1990	5.1	5.3	5.6	5.8	5.7	5.9	6.1	6.6	6.7	6.3	6.0	5.6
1991	5.9	6.0	5.6	5.0	4.5	3.9	3.8	3.8	4.0	4.1	4.0	4.2
1992	4.3	4.2	4.2	4.2	3.9	3.7	3.5	3.3	3.1	3.4	3.7	3.9
1993	4.1	4.2	4.2	4.3	4.3	4.2	3.8	3.7	3.5	3.3	-	-

Source: U.S. Department of Commerce, Bureau of Economic Analysis, U.S. Department of Commerce, Bureau of the Census. - indicates data not available or zero.

RATIO, COINCIDENT TO LAGGING INDEX

The composite indexes of coincident and the lagging indicators are used to create what is sometimes referred to as the "second" or the "best" leading indicator—the ratio of the coincident to the lagging index. The "coincident to lagging ratio" tends to signal changes in the economy's turning points (especially downturns) *sooner* than the leading index.

For example, in the 1970 recession the leading index signaled the downturn 8 months ahead of time, the ratio 13 months earlier. In other recessionary periods, similar results were noted: 1974-75, leading was 8, the ratio 11 months in advance of actual events; in 1980, leading was 15, the ratio 21; in 1982, leading was 2, the ratio was 9.

The ratio has been less predictive of turn-arounds. In 1970 it turned up as the economy turned up (acting as a coincident indicator), whereas the leading index gave a one-month warning; in 1974-1975, this pattern repeated; in 1980 and 1982, both the leading index and the ratio turned up 10 months ahead of the economy's actual turn-around.

The coincident to lagging ratio tends to work because of the manner in which its components—the coincident and the lagging indexes—behave. The lagging index tends to reflect the *past* of a business cycle, the coincident index its *present*. As the coincident index reaches a turning point, its rate of change tends to be smaller than that of the lagging indicator. If, for example, the economy is approaching a peak, monthly growth reflected in the coincident indicator will be small; meanwhile, the lagging indicator, which reflects events a few months back, will still be growing rapidly. The ratio between the two will, therefore, turn down, signaling a future decline in the economy as the peak is reached and passed. The process works in the same manner as a trough is reached: the composite index will decline less than the lagging index (which is still mirroring the earlier period of the recession); the consequence is an upturn in the ratio promising the start of an expansion soon.

Components of the Ratio

The ratio is expressed as an index with a 1987 base (1987 = 100) and is constructed by dividing the composite index value for a month by the lagging index value for the same month.

Bibliography

1. Carnes, W. Stansbury and Stephen D. Slifer. *The Atlas of Economic Indicators*. HarperCollins, 1991.

2. Frumkin, Norman. *Guide to Economic Indicators*. M.E. Sharpe, Inc., 1990.

Ratio, Coincident Index to Lagging Index
(1987 = 100)

Year	Jan	Feb	Mar	Apr	May	Jun	Jul	Aug	Sep	Oct	Nov	Dec
1948	66.4	65.5	65.3	65.1	65.3	65.9	65.5	63.7	63.2	63.3	62.7	62.4
1949	61.2	60.6	60.6	60.5	59.8	59.7	59.3	60.2	61.1	58.6	59.6	59.8
1950	60.4	60.4	61.6	62.0	62.8	63.8	65.8	66.5	64.3	62.8	61.4	62.7
1951	61.8	61.0	60.7	60.5	60.2	59.7	59.1	59.5	59.4	59.2	59.1	58.6
1952	57.9	58.5	58.3	58.4	58.0	56.9	56.1	58.1	59.0	59.4	59.1	59.0
1953	58.9	59.0	59.1	58.3	57.6	57.3	57.6	57.0	56.4	56.2	55.3	54.7
1954	54.9	55.1	55.6	56.3	56.6	57.2	57.3	58.0	58.3	58.6	59.2	59.5
1955	60.2	60.5	60.9	61.5	61.7	61.2	61.2	59.6	59.5	59.0	58.5	58.7
1956	58.4	58.3	57.9	57.6	56.7	56.6	54.7	55.9	56.0	56.4	56.3	56.6
1957	56.3	56.8	56.6	56.1	56.0	56.0	56.1	55.5	54.9	54.7	54.1	53.5
1958	53.5	53.4	53.3	53.2	54.3	55.4	56.2	57.0	56.9	56.9	57.9	57.7
1959	58.4	58.8	59.2	59.5	59.3	58.8	58.3	56.7	55.6	55.3	55.7	57.2
1960	58.1	57.8	57.3	57.3	56.9	56.6	56.5	56.7	57.1	57.1	56.7	56.2
1961	56.2	56.3	56.8	57.2	57.9	58.7	59.0	59.5	59.5	59.8	60.4	60.4
1962	60.0	60.5	60.7	60.7	60.6	60.6	60.7	60.9	60.9	61.1	61.2	61.1
1963	61.0	61.3	61.6	61.9	61.9	62.0	62.1	61.9	62.1	62.4	62.1	62.3
1964	62.5	62.7	62.7	63.1	63.5	63.5	64.0	64.0	64.3	63.7	64.6	65.2
1965	65.0	65.0	65.3	65.3	65.5	65.9	66.3	66.3	66.3	66.5	66.8	66.4
1966	66.6	66.5	66.8	66.4	66.2	66.4	66.2	66.1	66.2	66.5	66.1	66.2
1967	66.5	66.4	66.3	66.4	66.7	66.6	66.7	67.4	67.3	67.4	68.3	68.7
1968	68.8	68.7	68.7	68.6	68.7	68.8	69.1	68.7	69.1	69.5	69.6	69.6
1969	69.4	69.5	69.7	69.4	69.1	69.0	69.3	69.4	69.3	69.4	69.2	69.1
1970	68.4	68.4	68.2	68.5	68.6	68.6	68.9	68.8	69.1	68.6	68.6	69.9
1971	70.5	70.8	71.3	72.0	72.3	73.0	72.4	72.0	72.5	73.1	73.9	74.4
1972	76.1	76.6	76.9	77.1	77.1	77.0	77.3	78.1	78.6	79.4	80.1	80.8
1973	80.3	80.0	79.8	79.0	79.0	78.9	78.6	78.6	78.1	78.8	79.0	78.0
1974	77.3	77.0	77.1	76.3	76.3	76.0	76.1	75.8	75.1	75.1	74.1	72.3
1975	72.1	72.2	72.1	73.5	74.7	76.6	77.5	78.6	79.5	79.8	80.0	80.5
1976	81.3	82.0	82.3	82.9	83.2	83.7	83.8	84.1	84.1	83.8	84.9	85.7
1977	85.7	85.9	86.2	86.5	86.8	86.8	87.0	86.9	87.0	86.9	87.0	87.2
1978	86.5	86.9	87.4	88.9	88.8	88.9	88.6	88.9	88.8	89.1	88.8	88.7
1979	88.5	88.5	89.7	87.8	88.5	87.9	87.6	87.1	86.5	86.6	86.3	86.3
1980	86.5	86.2	84.9	83.4	82.8	83.0	84.9	87.1	89.0	90.4	90.8	90.1
1981	90.2	90.5	90.8	90.6	89.5	89.2	89.5	89.4	88.5	88.1	87.8	87.7
1982	87.0	88.5	89.0	89.2	89.4	88.7	88.5	88.6	88.8	89.0	89.8	90.6
1983	92.0	92.0	92.8	93.2	94.5	95.2	95.7	95.0	96.2	96.9	96.8	97.0
1984	97.6	97.4	97.4	96.9	96.4	96.6	96.1	95.7	95.6	95.0	95.5	95.7
1985	95.5	95.9	95.9	96.5	96.2	96.0	95.9	96.2	96.2	95.6	95.8	96.1
1986	96.1	96.0	95.6	96.7	96.5	96.4	96.9	97.1	98.2	97.6	97.9	99.1
1987	98.0	99.6	99.8	99.8	100.0	100.1	100.4	100.4	99.9	100.5	100.3	101.3
1988	100.6	101.1	101.2	101.1	101.2	101.2	101.2	101.3	101.4	101.9	101.6	102.4
1989	102.2	101.6	101.4	101.9	101.1	100.5	100.0	100.3	100.1	99.8	100.4	100.7
1990	101.3	101.9	102.3	101.6	102.0	102.1	101.8	102.0	101.7	101.5	101.3	101.2
1991	100.2	100.3	100.1	101.1	101.9	103.1	103.2	103.8	104.3	104.6	104.8	105.1
1992	105.7	106.9	107.5	108.1	108.7	109.0	109.7	109.6	110.0	111.0	111.1	114.5
1993	111.4	111.7	112.1	112.7	113.0	113.1	112.2	113.2	113.5	114.0	-	-

Source: U.S. Department of Commerce, Bureau of Economic Analysis. - indicates data not available or zero.

CHAPTER 4

CYCLIC INDICATORS

CYCLIC INDICATORS

The Business Cycle Indicators include, all told, 22 economic series which have been found, over time, to work well as indicators of cyclic change in the economy. In this section are presented 49 other economic series which are also considered cyclic indicators but are not part of the composite indexes of leading, coincident, and lagging indicators. They are grouped under seven headings:

Employment
Production and Income
Consumption, Trade, Orders, and Deliveries
Fixed Capital Investment
Inventories and Inventory Investment
Prices, Costs, and Profits
Money and Credit

A brief introduction to each of these sections provides a description of each series covered, the principal analytical uses of each series, and a listing of related series which are included under the Business Cycle Indicators heading.

All of the series shown are reported regularly in the *Survey of Current Business*, a monthly publication of the U.S. Department of Commerce.

Bibliography

1. Fischer, Stanley, Rudiger Dornbusch, and Richard Schmalensee. *Introduction to Macroeconomics*. McGraw-Hill Book Company, New York, 1988.

2. Fitch, Thomas P. *Dictionary of Banking Terms*. Barron's, New York, 1990.

3. Siegel, Barry N. *Money, Banking, and the Economy*. Academic Press, New York, 1982.

3. U.S. Department of Commerce, Bureau of Economic Analysis. *Survey of Current Business*. Superintendent of Documents, U.S. Government Printing Office, Washington, DC 20302.

INDICATORS OF EMPLOYMENT

In modern industrial economies, employment is the single most important indicator of economic well-being—and decline in employment a signal of economic woes. This section presents two series:

> Unemployment rate
> Number of persons unemployed

Related series, reported under Business Cycle Indicators, are:

> Average weekly hours in manufacturing (Leading Index)
> Average weekly initial claims for unemployment insurance (Leading Index)
> Employment on nonagricultural payrolls (Coincident Index)
> Average duration of unemployment in weeks (Lagging Index)

Unemployment Rate. Data are presented for persons unemployed 15 weeks and over as a percent of the work force. Data are shown from 1948 to 1993. The series behaves as a lagging indicator but is not part of the composite index of lagging indicators.

Number of Persons Unemployed. Data show total number of people unemployed in thousands from 1948 to 1993. The series is classified as a leading indicator at business cycle peaks, as a lagging indicator of business cycle troughs, and is unclassified overall.

Unemployment Rate, 15 Weeks and Over
(Percent)

Year	Jan	Feb	Mar	Apr	May	Jun	Jul	Aug	Sep	Oct	Nov	Dec
1948	0.5	0.5	0.5	0.5	0.5	0.5	0.5	0.5	0.5	0.5	0.5	0.5
1949	0.5	0.6	0.7	0.8	1.0	1.2	1.4	1.5	1.6	1.6	1.7	1.6
1950	1.5	1.5	1.5	1.5	1.4	1.4	1.2	1.0	1.0	0.9	0.8	0.8
1951	0.7	0.6	0.6	0.5	0.4	0.4	0.4	0.4	0.4	0.4	0.5	0.4
1952	0.5	0.4	0.4	0.4	0.4	0.3	0.3	0.3	0.4	0.4	0.3	0.4
1953	0.4	0.3	0.3	0.3	0.3	0.3	0.3	0.3	0.3	0.3	0.4	0.5
1954	0.6	0.8	1.2	1.2	1.4	1.4	1.5	1.6	1.6	1.6	1.5	1.3
1955	1.4	1.3	1.3	1.3	1.1	1.0	1.0	0.8	0.9	0.9	0.9	0.9
1956	0.8	0.8	0.8	0.7	0.8	0.8	0.8	0.8	0.9	0.8	0.9	0.9
1957	0.8	0.8	0.8	0.8	0.8	0.8	0.8	0.8	0.8	1.0	1.0	1.1
1958	1.3	1.5	1.7	2.1	2.2	2.5	2.6	2.8	2.6	2.5	2.3	2.2
1959	2.1	1.9	1.8	1.5	1.4	1.4	1.3	1.3	1.3	1.3	1.4	1.3
1960	1.3	1.2	1.4	1.3	1.1	1.2	1.3	1.3	1.4	1.7	1.7	1.6
1961	1.9	2.0	2.1	2.3	2.4	2.3	2.6	2.3	2.2	2.1	2.0	1.9
1962	1.8	1.8	1.7	1.6	1.6	1.5	1.5	1.5	1.5	1.4	1.5	1.5
1963	1.6	1.6	1.5	1.5	1.6	1.5	1.5	1.6	1.5	1.5	1.5	1.4
1964	1.5	1.4	1.4	1.3	1.3	1.4	1.4	1.3	1.3	1.2	1.3	1.2
1965	1.1	1.2	1.1	1.1	1.0	1.1	0.9	1.0	1.0	0.9	0.9	0.9
1966	0.8	0.8	0.8	0.8	0.7	0.6	0.6	0.6	0.6	0.6	0.6	0.6
1967	0.6	0.6	0.6	0.6	0.5	0.5	0.5	0.6	0.6	0.6	0.6	0.6
1968	0.6	0.6	0.6	0.5	0.5	0.5	0.5	0.5	0.5	0.5	0.5	0.4
1969	0.4	0.4	0.4	0.5	0.5	0.5	0.5	0.5	0.5	0.5	0.5	0.5
1970	0.5	0.6	0.6	0.7	0.7	0.8	0.8	0.9	0.9	0.9	1.0	1.3
1971	1.3	1.3	1.3	1.4	1.4	1.4	1.5	1.5	1.5	1.5	1.5	1.5
1972	1.5	1.5	1.4	1.4	1.3	1.3	1.3	1.3	1.3	1.3	1.2	1.1
1973	1.1	1.0	1.0	0.9	0.9	0.9	0.8	0.9	0.9	0.9	0.9	0.8
1974	0.9	0.9	0.9	1.0	1.0	1.0	1.0	1.0	1.1	1.2	1.2	1.4
1975	1.7	2.0	2.2	2.6	2.8	3.0	3.1	3.0	3.1	2.9	3.0	3.0
1976	2.9	2.7	2.6	2.3	2.2	2.4	2.4	2.5	2.4	2.4	2.4	2.4
1977	2.3	2.2	2.1	2.0	2.0	1.9	1.9	1.8	1.9	1.8	1.8	1.7
1978	1.6	1.6	1.5	1.5	1.4	1.3	1.3	1.2	1.3	1.3	1.2	1.2
1979	1.2	1.2	1.3	1.2	1.2	1.1	1.1	1.1	1.1	1.2	1.2	1.2
1980	1.3	1.3	1.4	1.6	1.6	1.6	1.9	2.0	2.2	2.1	2.2	2.2
1981	2.2	2.2	2.1	2.0	2.0	2.1	2.0	2.1	2.1	2.1	2.1	2.2
1982	2.2	2.5	2.7	2.8	3.0	3.1	3.2	3.3	3.5	3.8	4.0	4.2
1983	4.2	4.2	4.2	3.9	4.1	4.0	3.9	3.6	3.4	3.3	3.1	3.0
1984	2.9	2.7	2.6	2.5	2.5	2.3	2.3	2.3	2.2	2.2	2.1	2.1
1985	2.0	2.1	2.1	2.1	2.0	2.0	2.0	2.0	1.9	2.0	1.9	1.9
1986	1.8	2.0	1.9	1.8	1.9	2.0	1.9	1.9	2.0	1.8	1.9	1.8
1987	1.8	1.8	1.7	1.8	1.8	1.7	1.6	1.6	1.6	1.5	1.5	1.5
1988	1.4	1.4	1.4	1.3	1.4	1.3	1.3	1.3	1.3	1.3	1.2	1.2
1989	1.2	1.1	1.1	1.1	1.1	1.0	1.2	1.1	1.1	1.1	1.1	1.1
1990	1.1	1.1	1.1	1.1	1.1	1.1	1.2	1.3	1.3	1.3	1.5	1.4
1991	1.5	1.6	1.7	1.8	1.8	1.9	1.9	1.9	2.0	2.1	2.2	2.3
1992	2.4	2.5	2.5	2.4	2.6	2.7	2.8	2.8	2.8	2.8	2.7	2.8
1993	2.6	2.5	2.4	2.3	2.3	2.2	2.4	2.4	2.4	2.4	-	-

Source: U.S. Department of Labor, Bureau of Labor Statistics. - indicates data not available or zero.

Number of Persons Unemployed
(Thousands)

Year	Jan	Feb	Mar	Apr	May	Jun	Jul	Aug	Sep	Oct	Nov	Dec
1948	2,034	2,328	2,399	2,386	2,118	2,214	2,213	2,350	2,302	2,259	2,285	2,429
1949	2,596	2,849	3,030	3,260	3,707	3,776	4,111	4,193	4,049	4,916	3,996	4,063
1950	4,026	3,936	3,876	3,575	3,434	3,367	3,120	2,799	2,774	2,625	2,589	2,639
1951	2,305	2,117	2,125	1,919	1,856	1,995	1,950	1,933	2,067	2,194	2,178	1,960
1952	1,972	1,957	1,813	1,811	1,863	1,884	1,991	2,087	1,936	1,839	1,743	1,667
1953	1,839	1,636	1,647	1,723	1,596	1,607	1,660	1,665	1,821	1,974	2,211	2,818
1954	3,077	3,331	3,607	3,749	3,767	3,551	3,659	3,854	3,927	3,666	3,402	3,196
1955	3,157	2,969	2,918	3,049	2,747	2,701	2,632	2,784	2,678	2,830	2,780	2,761
1956	2,666	2,606	2,764	2,650	2,861	2,882	2,952	2,701	2,635	2,571	2,861	2,790
1957	2,796	2,622	2,509	2,600	2,710	2,856	2,796	2,747	2,943	3,020	3,454	3,476
1958	3,875	4,303	4,492	5,016	5,021	4,944	5,079	5,025	4,821	4,570	4,188	4,191
1959	4,068	3,965	3,801	3,571	3,479	3,429	3,528	3,588	3,775	3,910	4,003	3,653
1960	3,615	3,329	3,726	3,620	3,569	3,766	3,836	3,946	3,884	4,252	4,330	4,617
1961	4,671	4,832	4,853	4,893	5,003	4,885	4,928	4,682	4,676	4,573	4,295	4,177
1962	4,081	3,871	3,921	3,906	3,863	3,844	3,819	4,013	3,961	3,803	4,024	3,907
1963	4,074	4,238	4,072	4,055	4,217	3,977	4,051	3,878	3,957	3,987	4,151	3,975
1964	4,029	3,932	3,950	3,918	3,764	3,814	3,608	3,655	3,712	3,726	3,551	3,651
1965	3,572	3,730	3,510	3,595	3,432	3,387	3,301	3,254	3,216	3,143	3,073	3,031
1966	2,988	2,820	2,887	2,828	2,950	2,872	2,876	2,900	2,798	2,798	2,770	2,912
1967	2,968	2,915	2,889	2,895	2,929	2,992	2,944	2,945	2,958	3,143	3,066	3,018
1968	2,878	3,001	2,877	2,709	2,740	2,938	2,883	2,768	2,686	2,689	2,715	2,685
1969	2,718	2,692	2,712	2,758	2,713	2,816	2,868	2,856	3,040	3,049	2,856	2,884
1970	3,201	3,453	3,635	3,797	3,919	4,071	4,175	4,256	4,456	4,591	4,898	5,076
1971	4,986	4,903	4,987	4,959	4,996	4,949	5,035	5,134	5,042	4,954	5,161	5,154
1972	5,019	4,928	5,038	4,959	4,922	4,923	4,913	4,939	4,849	4,875	4,602	4,543
1973	4,326	4,452	4,394	4,459	4,329	4,363	4,305	4,305	4,350	4,144	4,396	4,489
1974	4,644	4,731	4,634	4,618	4,705	4,927	5,063	5,022	5,437	5,523	6,140	6,636
1975	7,501	7,520	7,978	8,210	8,433	8,220	8,127	7,928	7,923	7,897	7,794	7,744
1976	7,534	7,326	7,230	7,330	7,053	7,322	7,490	7,518	7,380	7,430	7,620	7,545
1977	7,280	7,443	7,307	7,059	6,911	7,134	6,829	6,925	6,751	6,763	6,815	6,386
1978	6,489	6,318	6,337	6,180	6,127	6,028	6,309	6,080	6,125	5,947	6,077	6,228
1979	6,109	6,173	6,109	6,069	5,840	5,959	5,996	6,320	6,190	6,296	6,238	6,325
1980	6,683	6,702	6,729	7,358	7,984	8,098	8,363	8,281	8,021	8,088	8,023	7,718
1981	8,071	8,051	7,982	7,869	8,174	8,098	7,863	8,036	8,230	8,646	9,029	9,267
1982	9,397	9,705	9,895	10,244	10,335	10,538	10,849	10,881	11,217	11,529	11,938	12,051
1983	11,534	11,545	11,408	11,268	11,154	11,246	10,548	10,623	10,282	9,887	9,499	9,331
1984	9,008	8,791	8,746	8,762	8,456	8,226	8,537	8,519	8,367	8,381	8,198	8,358
1985	8,423	8,321	8,339	8,395	8,302	8,460	8,513	8,196	8,248	8,298	8,128	8,138
1986	7,795	8,402	8,383	8,364	8,439	8,508	8,319	8,135	8,310	8,243	8,159	7,883
1987	7,892	7,865	7,862	7,542	7,574	7,398	7,268	7,261	7,102	7,227	7,035	6,936
1988	6,953	6,929	6,876	6,601	6,779	6,546	6,605	6,843	6,604	6,568	6,537	6,518
1989	6,684	6,355	6,204	6,475	6,370	6,567	6,498	6,501	6,596	6,655	6,724	6,667
1990	6,606	6,573	6,491	6,711	6,583	6,403	6,712	7,012	7,121	7,255	7,502	7,726
1991	7,806	8,123	8,462	8,306	8,507	8,487	8,378	8,460	8,479	8,695	8,670	8,984
1992	8,992	9,223	9,284	9,225	9,459	9,788	9,628	9,624	9,550	9,379	9,301	9,280
1993	9,013	8,876	8,864	8,925	8,858	8,908	8,769	8,661	8,517	8,786	-	-

Source: U.S. Department of Labor, Bureau of Labor Statistics. - indicates data not available or zero.

INDICATORS OF PRODUCTION AND INCOME

Production and personal income are indicators of overall economic performance. They are cyclic indicators which tend to be coincident: they turn up or down as the economy does. This section presents four series:

     Personal income
     Wages and salaries
     Capacity utilization rate, all industry
     Capacity utilization rate, manufacturing

Related series, reported under Business Cycle Indicators, are:

     Index of industrial production (Coincident Index)
     Personal income less transfer payments (Coincident Index)

Personal Income. Data are reported for 1947 to 1993 in billions of constant 1987 dollars. Monthly data are annualized, meaning that monthly survey results are multiplied by 12 months. Although not part of any composite index of economic indicators, personal income is viewed as a coincident cyclic indicator. The category includes all income received by individuals from any source, including dividends, rents, and transfer payments (welfare, social security, unemployment benefits, medicaid, etc.).

Wages and Salaries. Data are for wages and salaries in mining, manufacturing, and construction and are reported in billions of constant 1987 dollars. Monthly data are annualized, showing what would be annual results if the month's results were applied to the year as a whole. The series behaves as a coincident indicator overall but is not a component of a composite index.

Capacity Utilization Rate, All Industry. Data, for 1967 through 1993, are shown as percent of total capacity. The series can be used as a cyclic indicator (it is leading at the peak of the business cycle and coincident at the trough) and as an indicator of inflation. High rates of capacity utilization signal high rates of production and hence upward pressure on prices.

Capacity Utilization Rate, Manufacturing. Data are shown for 1948 through 1993 in percent. The series is a leading indicator at the peak and a coincident indicator at the trough of a cycle.

Personal Income
(Annual Rate, Billions of 1987 $)

Year	Jan	Feb	Mar	Apr	May	Jun	Jul	Aug	Sep	Oct	Nov	Dec
1947	942.4	938.2	933.0	918.0	915.4	924.8	921.7	918.5	980.7	933.5	927.5	932.5
1948	950.0	943.7	958.7	958.4	962.3	976.4	974.7	981.2	982.1	985.8	979.4	971.4
1949	956.2	956.5	961.6	961.9	959.5	951.6	944.2	952.1	967.4	945.8	957.4	963.4
1950	1,002.8	1,017.1	1,041.2	1,015.7	1,018.4	1,014.2	1,024.4	1,034.1	1,043.9	1,054.5	1,064.7	1,075.3
1951	1,067.4	1,065.2	1,076.8	1,093.5	1,099.6	1,107.3	1,100.9	1,114.2	1,111.5	1,119.6	1,118.6	1,123.3
1952	1,111.0	1,127.4	1,129.5	1,127.4	1,139.7	1,141.2	1,136.6	1,163.2	1,175.3	1,171.0	1,163.6	1,172.7
1953	1,172.0	1,180.7	1,192.2	1,188.9	1,194.7	1,198.0	1,196.3	1,193.9	1,194.7	1,200.8	1,193.9	1,191.0
1954	1,191.4	1,191.0	1,187.3	1,177.2	1,180.5	1,186.1	1,187.8	1,198.8	1,205.7	1,213.9	1,225.4	1,224.9
1955	1,227.2	1,230.0	1,240.1	1,247.2	1,257.3	1,261.3	1,275.9	1,277.1	1,285.9	1,291.6	1,300.8	1,309.6
1956	1,308.0	1,315.6	1,321.6	1,334.8	1,332.7	1,336.5	1,327.3	1,339.8	1,343.9	1,357.6	1,352.7	1,354.9
1957	1,354.9	1,362.0	1,362.2	1,364.5	1,366.2	1,376.5	1,377.0	1,377.5	1,373.7	1,368.8	1,370.3	1,362.1
1958	1,361.7	1,355.1	1,362.3	1,360.0	1,365.3	1,372.8	1,397.0	1,396.2	1,403.8	1,401.1	1,418.0	1,419.5
1959	1,416.8	1,425.7	1,437.3	1,448.5	1,453.2	1,458.1	1,460.4	1,445.0	1,444.1	1,447.4	1,469.0	1,483.8
1960	1,487.5	1,480.6	1,480.6	1,482.9	1,493.8	1,495.3	1,492.4	1,494.2	1,492.4	1,492.4	1,492.1	1,489.1
1961	1,501.8	1,509.4	1,508.7	1,516.7	1,528.3	1,538.6	1,541.4	1,543.9	1,543.0	1,557.0	1,572.8	1,581.7
1962	1,579.2	1,583.9	1,596.8	1,601.4	1,600.0	1,611.0	1,618.5	1,617.4	1,614.4	1,624.7	1,627.8	1,634.5
1963	1,641.8	1,639.1	1,638.9	1,644.9	1,654.0	1,655.7	1,658.2	1,666.9	1,678.0	1,690.9	1,691.3	1,702.4
1964	1,711.8	1,713.8	1,722.1	1,733.8	1,738.5	1,747.4	1,758.1	1,766.1	1,776.7	1,780.1	1,793.8	1,808.9
1965	1,816.7	1,809.5	1,818.6	1,825.0	1,841.6	1,855.4	1,860.3	1,867.7	1,906.0	1,898.7	1,916.7	1,926.3
1966	1,926.2	1,930.0	1,935.5	1,942.8	1,951.3	1,961.0	1,966.3	1,978.8	1,984.5	1,997.7	2,007.7	2,011.9
1967	2,029.7	2,031.9	2,038.9	2,035.6	2,044.6	2,053.7	2,064.3	2,073.7	2,068.1	2,075.1	2,087.4	2,101.9
1968	2,102.5	2,118.6	2,129.9	2,141.2	2,154.3	2,164.8	2,176.5	2,181.2	2,197.6	2,200.0	2,209.9	2,221.9
1969	2,221.9	2,229.0	2,241.7	2,245.3	2,256.6	2,260.4	2,280.9	2,286.6	2,294.2	2,302.0	2,307.8	2,308.9
1970	2,304.9	2,302.0	2,306.5	2,352.1	2,327.6	2,323.0	2,334.7	2,342.5	2,346.9	2,342.4	2,341.7	2,345.6
1971	2,356.0	2,358.0	2,360.7	2,362.8	2,373.4	2,416.8	2,386.7	2,399.7	2,404.8	2,407.1	2,423.0	2,441.8
1972	2,451.8	2,471.0	2,478.9	2,487.5	2,496.6	2,481.1	2,514.9	2,541.4	2,550.9	2,593.1	2,626.7	2,635.4
1973	2,640.7	2,640.9	2,641.5	2,632.8	2,658.9	2,665.0	2,663.5	2,681.6	2,693.5	2,724.9	2,743.4	2,735.0
1974	2,710.9	2,685.0	2,654.7	2,653.2	2,655.0	2,660.4	2,674.4	2,666.0	2,670.6	2,681.3	2,661.8	2,660.9
1975	2,635.8	2,625.7	2,632.2	2,635.6	2,646.2	2,697.1	2,669.0	2,690.9	2,706.9	2,727.2	2,723.4	2,725.6
1976	2,751.2	2,765.1	2,771.7	2,780.0	2,786.5	2,786.0	2,799.4	2,803.6	2,806.5	2,802.5	2,830.6	2,838.6
1977	2,835.6	2,843.1	2,852.1	2,857.6	2,869.4	2,869.1	2,898.7	2,917.7	2,929.8	2,928.4	2,941.9	2,953.7
1978	2,957.2	2,968.2	2,997.9	3,022.6	3,027.5	3,039.3	3,051.4	3,065.7	3,076.9	3,093.6	3,102.6	3,112.0
1979	3,114.7	3,123.4	3,136.8	3,126.5	3,122.1	3,123.1	3,151.6	3,152.5	3,153.2	3,163.5	3,171.5	3,178.0
1980	3,189.5	3,176.4	3,158.2	3,135.9	3,119.1	3,118.8	3,145.4	3,157.6	3,178.2	3,210.6	3,224.0	3,248.6
1981	3,239.8	3,235.5	3,240.8	3,238.6	3,235.3	3,244.0	3,281.5	3,293.1	3,290.1	3,280.5	3,271.1	3,257.9
1982	3,243.6	3,254.3	3,262.5	3,289.5	3,294.1	3,277.0	3,276.4	3,272.7	3,267.3	3,267.0	3,275.3	3,287.1
1983	3,278.9	3,274.3	3,281.1	3,291.9	3,309.5	3,314.8	3,322.0	3,309.8	3,327.8	3,360.6	3,385.3	3,407.1
1984	3,427.9	3,468.2	3,487.7	3,493.7	3,491.7	3,513.6	3,529.6	3,545.8	3,568.9	3,553.6	3,568.2	3,599.1
1985	3,601.5	3,614.7	3,626.3	3,641.0	3,619.1	3,630.7	3,631.8	3,625.6	3,627.6	3,645.4	3,640.5	3,676.0
1986	3,669.0	3,689.3	3,723.0	3,765.2	3,751.5	3,739.5	3,745.2	3,752.6	3,758.3	3,749.2	3,752.3	3,776.4
1987	3,762.8	3,783.1	3,782.7	3,785.4	3,781.8	3,775.6	3,785.7	3,797.3	3,798.7	3,849.6	3,831.2	3,885.7
1988	3,861.8	3,877.5	3,895.9	3,898.4	3,895.4	3,902.9	3,907.4	3,909.8	3,912.7	3,961.4	3,937.6	3,963.1
1989	3,990.3	4,008.9	4,026.3	4,014.0	3,995.0	3,991.2	3,999.7	3,999.3	3,989.8	4,010.2	4,030.3	4,038.8
1990	4,053.6	4,071.3	4,081.5	4,088.5	4,075.7	4,079.6	4,082.3	4,060.3	4,059.8	4,031.4	4,043.6	4,079.3
1991	4,035.2	4,030.7	4,045.4	4,043.4	4,049.3	4,058.2	4,039.7	4,036.2	4,040.8	4,054.5	4,039.3	4,089.6
1992	4,076.1	4,104.1	4,108.2	4,114.4	4,123.8	4,125.3	4,126.0	4,151.2	4,151.2	4,187.9	4,180.8	4,391.8
1993	4,150.7	4,156.1	4,181.2	4,228.2	4,236.5	4,227.9	4,216.3	4,261.8	4,264.7	4,274.0	-	-

Source: U.S. Department of Commerce, Bureau of Economic Analysis. - indicates data not available or zero.

Wages & Salaries in Mining, Manufacturing, Construction
(Annual Rate, Billions of 1987 $)

Year	Jan	Feb	Mar	Apr	May	Jun	Jul	Aug	Sep	Oct	Nov	Dec
1947	260.3	259.2	259.1	259.1	262.7	264.2	260.5	260.9	262.5	264.7	267.3	267.5
1948	271.6	270.2	275.4	267.9	271.1	274.1	274.0	278.1	276.7	278.5	281.6	278.3
1949	276.8	275.7	269.0	265.2	263.3	258.6	262.0	259.6	262.2	252.4	255.3	260.1
1950	266.2	263.0	273.6	280.8	287.1	291.9	296.7	304.7	304.7	313.5	317.1	315.0
1951	314.3	313.7	317.5	323.2	321.4	325.0	325.0	325.6	323.6	321.3	323.4	325.8
1952	328.3	332.3	334.5	329.2	333.2	328.8	314.9	340.2	352.6	356.4	361.5	365.5
1953	367.9	371.4	373.6	374.0	374.9	372.5	375.7	372.5	366.1	365.8	362.3	357.0
1954	352.7	354.0	351.5	348.9	350.2	348.9	347.9	348.3	347.0	354.0	360.2	363.4
1955	365.5	368.2	373.3	377.1	384.7	386.0	389.4	388.9	388.6	394.9	399.2	401.7
1956	403.0	402.5	404.6	411.8	409.3	408.8	400.8	411.2	414.9	418.6	417.8	422.6
1957	419.3	421.3	418.8	417.1	413.4	414.6	412.1	412.0	408.4	405.2	402.0	396.4
1958	388.9	380.6	378.7	371.3	371.3	375.6	379.5	385.4	389.8	387.8	400.4	403.9
1959	405.9	408.6	416.9	420.8	426.3	427.7	426.6	413.6	412.0	408.9	413.5	426.3
1960	433.7	433.2	430.9	430.9	432.4	427.7	427.4	423.5	420.4	418.3	414.1	406.5
1961	410.3	409.2	411.1	414.1	418.3	424.0	424.0	427.0	421.2	429.2	435.6	438.3
1962	436.4	439.6	444.2	448.5	447.4	447.7	449.6	449.6	451.3	449.8	452.1	452.4
1963	454.3	454.3	453.7	456.0	460.4	461.7	463.2	461.9	465.2	465.7	467.2	469.9
1964	466.9	475.4	478.7	482.0	483.8	484.2	487.5	491.9	496.0	489.4	496.0	504.7
1965	505.8	510.6	510.5	507.2	513.0	512.9	516.2	517.3	519.8	524.4	530.1	534.6
1966	537.5	543.8	547.2	549.6	552.1	556.8	558.2	558.0	560.8	561.9	563.3	563.0
1967	567.5	560.7	562.1	560.5	558.2	560.1	563.8	566.8	564.7	562.8	571.4	575.5
1968	574.0	580.5	583.1	585.1	591.7	590.2	589.6	589.6	593.9	597.7	601.6	603.2
1969	604.5	600.6	607.6	607.2	609.7	610.9	611.4	614.2	615.3	614.0	608.8	608.7
1970	603.9	601.2	603.0	593.2	588.2	589.4	589.2	586.3	575.7	565.6	560.9	569.7
1971	572.6	571.0	573.0	575.1	579.9	577.0	574.0	572.7	574.7	575.3	577.8	586.4
1972	591.7	596.4	602.7	604.9	606.3	606.5	603.8	610.6	615.4	620.7	625.5	628.9
1973	636.5	642.1	639.9	642.6	642.0	642.7	649.6	639.1	644.1	644.1	647.3	648.5
1974	641.1	638.0	633.1	632.2	633.5	633.7	629.3	628.2	624.5	620.3	600.4	591.7
1975	584.3	570.0	567.2	564.9	566.5	567.4	562.8	572.5	576.0	578.3	579.8	585.1
1976	594.3	597.2	601.2	604.3	605.2	602.6	606.4	608.7	607.5	606.7	614.9	615.8
1977	612.0	616.9	622.9	627.3	634.6	640.6	640.1	641.9	647.7	650.0	651.2	647.8
1978	644.3	649.3	658.4	672.4	672.3	674.1	676.2	675.9	679.1	680.5	686.0	690.3
1979	689.5	686.9	690.7	682.6	684.6	684.6	681.9	676.9	676.9	673.7	669.5	671.9
1980	662.8	660.1	652.9	642.1	633.4	625.9	622.3	630.3	633.5	636.6	641.3	643.6
1981	642.1	633.9	637.2	636.7	636.1	637.3	635.2	635.5	629.0	630.1	624.4	619.0
1982	616.6	616.7	614.5	608.6	605.6	595.8	590.1	586.2	581.6	574.7	572.9	576.4
1983	580.0	577.3	578.1	579.4	581.2	585.1	588.8	591.1	598.6	603.3	607.1	610.3
1984	612.8	617.3	618.2	623.1	624.4	629.4	630.4	632.4	631.3	630.6	633.3	636.2
1985	638.0	633.7	643.7	635.0	635.6	636.8	635.5	637.9	638.9	642.5	639.2	641.2
1986	639.3	637.6	647.9	645.4	643.9	641.0	641.5	644.6	642.3	648.2	644.2	645.1
1987	642.3	641.5	644.3	639.0	639.0	637.4	638.2	641.3	646.2	647.4	650.5	652.4
1988	653.1	657.0	666.0	662.6	663.1	664.7	665.9	663.0	663.8	671.8	665.9	664.3
1989	664.1	662.2	666.3	656.5	651.1	651.1	650.2	652.4	651.6	655.3	651.9	649.2
1990	642.8	649.7	650.3	649.2	647.1	646.8	642.9	636.6	634.2	626.9	619.6	624.5
1991	614.2	609.8	606.8	604.4	604.9	606.4	605.9	606.8	606.9	610.0	601.8	606.9
1992	597.2	598.4	600.2	600.7	602.6	600.7	599.9	598.8	597.3	600.9	596.9	660.2
1993	579.6	580.8	578.4	595.3	595.5	592.8	595.2	595.7	597.6	597.2	-	-

Source: U.S. Department of Commerce, Bureau of Economic Analysis. - indicates data not available or zero.

Capacity Utilization Rate
Total industry
(Percent)

Year	Jan	Feb	Mar	Apr	May	Jun	Jul	Aug	Sep	Oct	Nov	Dec
1967	88.7	87.3	86.4	86.8	85.7	85.3	84.8	86.0	85.5	85.8	86.7	87.3
1968	86.8	86.8	86.7	86.5	87.1	87.1	86.6	86.5	86.5	86.4	87.2	87.1
1969	87.3	87.6	87.9	87.3	86.7	87.2	87.4	87.3	86.9	86.7	85.6	85.0
1970	83.2	82.9	82.5	82.1	81.7	81.2	81.1	80.8	80.0	78.1	77.4	79.0
1971	79.3	79.0	78.7	79.0	79.2	79.3	78.9	78.2	79.3	79.7	79.8	80.6
1972	82.1	82.5	83.0	84.1	83.7	83.7	83.4	84.3	85.0	86.0	86.8	87.4
1973	87.3	88.2	88.0	88.0	88.2	88.6	88.9	88.6	89.1	89.2	89.0	87.3
1974	85.9	85.3	85.4	85.0	85.8	85.8	85.2	84.6	84.7	83.9	81.2	77.6
1975	75.4	74.1	72.6	73.1	72.7	73.5	73.8	75.0	75.6	75.8	76.4	76.8
1976	77.5	78.7	78.3	78.4	79.2	79.0	79.3	79.6	79.7	79.8	80.9	81.4
1977	81.5	81.7	82.3	83.3	83.8	84.2	84.0	83.9	84.2	83.9	83.8	83.2
1978	82.7	82.6	83.5	85.4	85.5	86.1	86.1	86.2	86.5	86.7	87.1	87.1
1979	86.6	87.2	87.3	86.2	87.0	86.7	86.0	85.4	85.5	85.8	85.3	85.0
1980	85.1	85.1	84.9	83.0	80.8	79.6	79.1	80.0	80.9	81.2	82.4	82.5
1981	81.6	81.7	81.7	80.7	81.1	81.3	82.1	81.7	81.1	80.2	79.1	78.2
1982	76.4	77.9	77.3	76.7	76.0	75.6	75.0	74.5	73.8	73.0	72.6	71.8
1983	73.0	72.8	73.2	73.9	74.6	74.9	76.1	77.1	78.2	78.7	78.7	78.9
1984	80.4	80.1	80.8	81.1	81.5	81.8	81.9	81.8	81.6	80.9	80.8	80.2
1985	80.3	80.7	80.7	80.9	80.9	80.5	80.0	80.2	80.4	79.6	79.7	80.4
1986	80.6	79.9	79.1	79.1	78.9	78.4	78.7	78.7	78.7	79.1	79.4	79.8
1987	79.3	80.3	80.5	80.8	81.2	81.8	81.9	82.0	81.8	82.7	82.7	83.1
1988	83.2	83.3	83.2	83.8	83.5	83.4	83.8	84.2	83.6	83.8	84.2	84.6
1989	84.8	84.3	84.8	84.7	84.3	83.9	82.9	83.2	82.7	82.3	82.4	82.8
1990	82.3	82.6	82.8	82.1	82.5	82.6	82.3	82.4	82.3	81.8	80.7	80.2
1991	80.0	78.9	78.3	78.3	78.8	79.5	79.5	79.4	79.9	79.6	79.4	79.1
1992	78.8	79.3	79.5	79.9	80.1	79.5	80.0	79.7	79.3	80.2	80.8	81.0
1993	81.2	81.5	81.6	81.7	81.5	81.5	81.7	81.6	81.9	82.4	-	-

Source: Board of Governors of the Federal Reserve System. - indicates data not available or zero.

Capacity Utilization Rate
Manufacturing
(Percent)

Year	Jan	Feb	Mar	Apr	May	Jun	Jul	Aug	Sep	Oct	Nov	Dec
1948	84.4	84.0	83.4	82.8	83.3	83.6	83.4	82.7	81.5	81.7	80.2	79.3
1949	77.9	76.9	75.9	74.2	73.2	73.1	73.1	73.6	74.8	71.7	72.0	73.6
1950	74.9	75.4	76.4	79.2	81.0	83.1	85.5	88.4	87.2	87.5	87.0	88.1
1951	88.3	88.3	88.4	88.2	87.4	86.6	84.9	83.6	83.7	83.1	83.6	83.9
1952	84.4	84.6	84.7	83.6	83.1	81.9	79.8	85.1	87.7	88.8	90.2	90.5
1953	90.5	91.1	91.4	91.5	91.7	90.7	91.0	90.6	88.3	87.2	84.7	82.3
1954	81.3	80.8	80.2	79.4	79.8	79.9	79.4	78.8	79.2	79.7	80.9	81.8
1955	83.5	84.1	85.8	86.7	87.9	87.6	87.7	87.3	87.5	88.4	88.3	89.0
1956	88.2	87.4	87.0	87.8	86.3	85.3	81.5	84.9	86.0	86.5	85.8	86.8
1957	86.2	87.0	86.4	85.0	84.2	84.6	84.3	84.2	83.2	81.4	79.4	77.5
1958	75.7	73.8	72.7	71.3	71.9	73.9	74.3	75.7	76.2	76.4	79.1	79.0
1959	80.2	81.4	82.5	84.0	84.9	84.8	83.0	79.5	79.0	78.2	78.5	83.6
1960	85.6	84.6	83.2	82.3	81.5	80.2	79.7	79.1	77.9	77.5	75.8	74.3
1961	74.1	73.5	73.9	75.4	76.4	77.3	78.1	79.0	78.2	79.6	80.8	81.6
1962	80.2	81.4	81.9	81.7	81.3	80.9	81.5	81.4	81.8	81.4	81.8	81.7
1963	81.9	82.4	82.6	83.5	84.0	83.9	83.3	83.5	83.8	84.3	84.3	84.0
1964	84.5	84.7	84.4	85.6	85.6	85.4	85.9	86.1	86.2	84.6	86.8	88.0
1965	88.6	88.7	89.3	89.3	89.4	89.5	90.3	89.9	89.6	89.8	89.6	90.5
1966	90.9	90.9	91.6	91.5	91.6	91.5	91.4	91.1	91.2	91.6	90.1	90.0
1967	89.8	88.4	87.5	87.7	86.6	86.1	85.3	86.5	86.1	86.4	87.6	88.1
1968	87.5	87.5	87.2	87.0	87.7	87.5	86.8	86.9	86.6	86.8	87.6	87.3
1969	87.4	87.8	88.2	87.5	86.8	87.0	87.3	87.1	86.6	86.4	85.2	84.4
1970	82.3	82.1	81.6	81.1	80.7	80.2	80.2	79.4	78.5	76.5	75.8	77.5
1971	78.0	77.8	77.5	77.7	78.0	78.0	78.0	76.8	78.2	79.2	79.3	79.8
1972	81.5	81.8	82.3	83.4	83.0	83.1	82.9	83.7	84.3	85.4	86.3	87.0
1973	87.0	87.9	87.9	87.9	87.9	88.3	88.5	88.4	88.6	88.9	88.8	86.9
1974	85.7	85.1	85.1	84.6	85.3	85.4	84.7	84.4	84.3	83.3	80.7	76.6
1975	74.2	72.5	70.8	71.4	71.1	72.0	72.6	73.6	74.4	74.8	75.2	75.8
1976	76.4	78.0	77.5	77.5	78.4	78.1	78.6	78.8	78.8	79.0	79.9	80.5
1977	80.9	81.1	81.8	82.5	83.3	83.4	83.3	83.6	83.6	83.3	83.3	83.6
1978	82.9	82.8	83.1	84.9	84.8	85.4	85.4	85.6	85.9	86.1	87.3	86.9
1979	86.5	86.9	86.9	85.2	86.4	86.0	85.4	84.5	84.4	84.7	84.1	83.9
1980	84.0	84.0	83.5	81.3	78.9	77.4	76.9	77.9	78.7	79.4	80.5	80.5
1981	79.8	80.0	79.9	79.6	79.8	79.5	79.9	79.1	78.5	77.4	76.4	75.1
1982	73.7	75.6	74.9	74.0	73.7	73.5	72.9	72.3	71.7	70.9	70.5	70.0
1983	71.4	71.5	72.4	73.0	73.8	74.2	75.2	76.0	77.5	77.9	78.1	78.0
1984	79.6	79.9	80.3	80.4	80.6	80.9	81.0	80.9	80.7	80.5	80.3	79.7
1985	79.5	79.7	80.0	80.0	80.3	79.6	79.2	79.5	79.5	78.6	79.4	79.2
1986	80.0	79.4	78.5	79.0	78.8	78.4	78.7	78.9	78.9	79.3	79.5	80.0
1987	79.3	80.5	80.7	81.0	81.3	81.9	82.1	81.9	81.9	82.6	82.8	83.1
1988	83.1	83.1	83.1	83.7	83.4	83.2	83.5	83.7	83.6	83.6	84.2	84.5
1989	85.1	84.1	84.5	84.6	83.9	83.5	82.4	82.6	82.1	81.5	81.6	81.6
1990	81.4	82.0	82.3	81.4	81.6	81.5	81.2	81.5	81.3	80.7	79.6	79.0
1991	78.5	77.5	76.6	77.0	77.2	77.9	77.9	78.0	78.6	78.4	78.0	77.9
1992	77.6	78.2	78.6	78.8	79.1	78.6	78.9	78.7	78.4	79.2	79.7	79.8
1993	80.3	80.5	80.6	80.9	80.7	80.6	80.7	80.7	81.1	81.7	-	-

Source: Board of Governors of the Federal Reserve System. - indicates data not available or zero.

INDICATORS OF CONSUMPTION, TRADE, ORDERS, AND DELIVERIES

Consumption, trade, orders, and deliveries are indicators of the economy's general performance. They tend, on the whole, to be leading indicators. Included are two series:

> Manufacturers' new orders, durable goods
> Sales of retail stores

Related series, reported under Business Cycle Indicators, are:

> Manufacturers' new orders, consumer goods and materials (Leading Index)
> Vendor performance (Leading Index)
> Consumer expectations (Leading Index)
> Change in manufacturers unfilled orders, durables (Leading Index)
> Manufacturing and trade sales (Coincident Index)

Manufacturers' New Orders, Durable Goods. Orders are reported in billions of constant 1987 dollars from 1947 to 1993. New orders for consumer goods and materials are part of the leading index. This series is also considered to be a leading indicator overall but is not part of the composite index of leading indicators—most likely because orders for durable goods are less predictive than those for consumer goods and materials.

Sales of Retail Stores. The series shows data from 1948 to 1993 in millions of constant 1987 dollars. Retail sales are classified as leading indicators of the trough of business cycles but produce uncertain results at the peak of cycles. In other words, retail sales tend to grow somewhat earlier than the economy as a whole.

Manufacturers' New Orders

Durable goods industries
(Billions of 1987 $)

Year	Jan	Feb	Mar	Apr	May	Jun	Jul	Aug	Sep	Oct	Nov	Dec
1947	-	-	-	29.76	31.04	29.56	29.57	30.47	33.46	34.05	35.69	37.23
1948	35.62	35.62	36.98	37.28	37.38	40.44	40.08	39.12	36.57	36.24	34.36	33.38
1949	30.87	30.62	28.84	26.77	26.28	25.21	26.11	30.32	30.75	30.25	31.77	31.10
1950	33.60	33.69	34.60	36.60	40.10	40.44	49.18	59.86	49.02	49.26	44.37	46.93
1951	60.35	54.77	56.69	53.37	51.12	49.68	48.65	44.38	41.82	46.41	44.72	43.30
1952	42.83	42.84	49.42	49.92	41.88	50.14	46.26	45.01	48.64	45.72	46.09	49.72
1953	55.51	54.38	50.85	51.99	51.38	49.55	45.98	40.72	36.43	37.49	37.31	37.39
1954	37.50	38.68	36.49	38.00	36.45	38.32	39.11	38.92	43.52	47.07	41.34	46.57
1955	49.80	51.25	55.06	52.02	52.81	54.02	53.91	53.74	55.60	55.21	54.99	57.38
1956	54.74	50.50	51.62	53.48	51.46	50.94	50.08	59.78	49.33	49.16	52.10	51.95
1957	49.91	51.31	49.51	46.12	47.50	46.35	43.62	45.57	44.29	42.09	43.94	40.44
1958	43.29	40.22	42.24	39.59	41.40	44.81	43.72	45.94	44.27	47.12	50.95	48.43
1959	51.47	53.69	54.89	55.31	52.81	55.28	51.06	48.65	49.97	50.92	48.06	52.52
1960	50.35	50.18	49.62	49.09	49.85	50.80	49.07	52.06	52.03	48.05	48.30	48.93
1961	46.20	47.35	47.46	50.28	50.73	51.90	51.24	54.09	53.25	53.87	55.71	57.50
1962	57.28	57.61	55.92	55.17	55.40	55.07	55.84	55.50	58.02	59.17	57.68	60.61
1963	60.37	61.04	62.12	61.58	62.30	59.69	61.69	59.80	61.47	62.36	61.23	60.08
1964	66.77	64.34	63.90	66.24	66.25	66.72	69.81	64.16	67.96	66.72	66.33	69.89
1965	72.31	71.40	73.16	74.17	71.94	72.96	75.06	75.73	73.57	77.36	77.93	79.71
1966	81.88	81.53	84.79	82.90	81.39	83.55	81.32	79.23	85.13	82.44	79.43	78.95
1967	77.16	76.70	75.55	76.10	80.15	81.31	78.23	79.64	77.97	79.43	80.04	87.21
1968	81.18	82.35	85.77	82.10	80.32	81.15	80.52	80.10	84.51	88.01	84.53	83.67
1969	85.52	87.32	85.50	90.07	84.77	83.33	83.49	85.10	87.90	85.19	82.83	81.46
1970	78.25	77.75	75.46	73.64	75.56	76.57	75.69	75.01	75.11	68.64	69.75	77.55
1971	79.73	80.79	78.79	76.41	75.09	77.06	75.53	79.16	79.32	77.65	79.82	81.40
1972	82.90	84.44	84.60	85.27	86.87	87.09	85.10	89.31	94.16	92.52	94.05	98.01
1973	100.28	102.47	104.06	102.06	102.29	102.43	103.04	102.82	101.13	104.68	106.71	100.27
1974	103.93	103.14	100.26	100.02	102.38	100.12	100.80	102.84	95.60	88.95	86.84	79.21
1975	78.06	76.42	71.81	75.82	74.52	74.53	81.37	81.65	80.87	79.07	79.29	79.42
1976	82.40	86.07	89.15	88.60	88.44	89.35	91.67	90.53	90.29	89.85	92.15	96.71
1977	94.03	94.57	99.17	97.90	97.91	101.03	99.27	99.85	101.39	103.02	101.75	105.15
1978	98.10	101.21	105.50	108.39	108.58	109.20	106.64	109.21	111.23	114.83	113.60	111.94
1979	111.24	113.77	117.64	108.30	109.84	109.80	106.74	103.74	106.24	104.13	101.54	101.86
1980	104.87	104.23	100.45	93.69	85.80	87.97	94.47	92.19	100.07	102.01	98.32	101.43
1981	96.80	96.55	98.62	100.30	99.77	99.20	98.73	95.79	94.35	89.80	87.79	84.32
1982	88.13	88.08	90.93	88.60	85.23	84.90	85.91	81.86	84.01	82.74	79.94	85.88
1983	89.88	83.52	86.83	89.55	89.06	95.00	93.93	94.16	98.35	103.27	102.90	103.27
1984	105.31	106.35	110.71	102.19	105.03	101.60	105.75	104.59	100.92	101.77	106.27	103.11
1985	108.41	103.36	103.00	101.40	103.74	107.53	104.95	107.30	107.77	105.94	101.83	107.23
1986	110.90	107.57	106.77	104.26	102.49	103.61	105.37	101.77	107.17	104.41	104.10	108.42
1987	103.86	107.15	109.73	110.91	111.10	112.39	114.46	108.74	110.63	112.79	112.36	113.82
1988	115.12	115.19	114.28	114.00	114.61	117.11	115.67	117.08	116.18	117.32	115.38	126.95
1989	123.29	117.82	118.12	118.66	112.03	114.48	112.04	111.76	113.04	109.87	116.49	119.67
1990	109.92	111.70	119.34	111.84	115.12	112.61	114.22	112.23	111.57	115.02	103.01	107.78
1991	105.05	104.63	98.99	102.57	104.59	101.25	114.51	109.26	105.08	107.94	108.15	102.20
1992	105.59	104.84	107.86	108.85	106.37	109.12	105.68	105.64	106.08	110.52	108.07	117.64
1993	114.64	116.99	112.96	112.41	109.67	114.50	111.18	113.68	114.98	117.27	-	-

Source: U.S. Department of Commerce, Bureau of Economic Analysis. - indicates data not available or zero.

Sales of Retail Stores
(Million 1987 $)

Year	Jan	Feb	Mar	Apr	May	Jun	Jul	Aug	Sep	Oct	Nov	Dec
1948	37,985	37,879	38,518	38,785	37,312	38,034	38,179	38,288	37,946	38,168	38,129	39,113
1949	37,788	38,398	38,963	39,406	39,223	41,521	38,715	39,264	39,971	39,759	40,134	39,632
1950	40,660	41,504	41,862	41,849	42,290	43,643	46,661	46,535	43,973	42,226	40,785	43,154
1951	45,685	44,438	41,648	40,828	41,166	41,060	40,561	41,472	41,214	41,691	41,491	40,629
1952	41,105	42,019	40,897	41,907	43,494	44,056	42,822	41,821	42,513	44,466	44,022	45,213
1953	45,536	45,502	45,851	45,215	45,000	44,933	44,755	44,474	44,440	44,662	44,111	43,679
1954	43,656	44,750	44,637	44,597	44,539	45,597	44,856	44,976	45,435	45,517	46,564	47,421
1955	47,669	48,091	48,444	49,310	49,443	49,123	50,026	50,013	50,794	50,917	50,771	50,320
1956	50,320	49,974	50,869	50,273	50,857	50,704	50,185	50,503	50,641	50,437	50,984	51,142
1957	51,452	52,119	51,549	51,557	51,626	52,342	52,100	52,382	52,053	51,928	51,499	51,223
1958	50,919	49,633	49,102	49,538	49,584	49,821	50,586	50,977	50,514	50,331	51,223	52,757
1959	53,444	53,673	54,121	53,991	54,414	54,580	54,726	54,910	54,192	54,425	53,310	53,063
1960	54,330	54,368	54,636	55,567	55,066	54,826	54,438	54,461	54,574	54,889	54,105	53,710
1961	53,751	53,560	54,126	53,327	53,967	54,368	54,003	54,761	54,531	55,679	56,071	56,092
1962	56,574	56,412	57,192	57,333	57,723	56,982	58,228	58,417	58,076	58,988	59,471	59,459
1963	59,534	59,259	59,557	59,640	59,437	59,531	60,047	59,971	59,997	60,687	60,177	61,322
1964	60,827	60,756	61,372	61,879	62,715	62,764	63,075	63,963	64,379	62,429	62,832	65,189
1965	65,668	66,083	65,427	65,789	66,618	66,219	67,299	67,706	67,692	69,439	70,276	70,127
1966	70,592	70,403	71,433	70,263	69,056	70,453	70,749	71,153	71,100	70,599	70,430	69,928
1967	66,545	65,873	66,354	66,522	66,038	67,646	67,177	66,829	68,541	67,315	68,528	70,496
1968	68,856	69,484	70,971	70,622	70,700	71,858	72,380	73,138	71,210	72,829	74,438	73,369
1969	73,779	74,125	73,155	73,203	73,904	73,068	72,927	73,596	74,422	75,050	74,615	74,928
1970	74,973	74,953	74,252	74,766	75,650	76,131	76,583	76,373	76,241	76,501	74,629	76,450
1971	77,910	78,520	78,259	79,526	78,874	79,793	80,224	80,297	81,872	82,668	83,433	82,995
1972	82,554	83,051	85,000	85,406	85,938	86,499	86,565	87,191	88,235	89,479	89,878	91,703
1973	92,652	93,168	93,053	91,567	91,171	91,415	91,247	90,165	91,376	91,113	90,698	87,436
1974	87,457	86,922	87,128	87,600	87,742	87,446	88,172	89,820	86,522	85,074	84,006	82,268
1975	85,132	86,055	83,650	84,654	88,090	87,363	87,941	88,264	88,281	88,555	88,458	89,218
1976	91,443	90,799	91,244	92,876	91,809	93,390	93,605	92,784	92,167	92,925	93,312	95,649
1977	94,656	96,036	96,353	97,368	96,468	96,666	97,302	97,061	97,330	98,789	98,938	98,919
1978	96,661	98,477	100,433	102,143	101,851	102,823	101,541	102,262	102,276	103,321	104,129	104,888
1979	103,634	103,451	104,479	103,059	103,105	102,541	101,257	104,287	104,602	103,152	103,829	103,159
1980	104,102	102,166	99,341	97,276	96,720	97,558	98,975	98,970	98,317	100,118	100,206	99,605
1981	101,344	101,571	101,589	100,345	99,260	99,822	100,020	101,256	100,261	98,681	98,077	98,274
1982	96,663	99,217	98,314	98,880	99,518	97,057	98,340	97,967	99,192	100,124	101,677	101,582
1983	101,240	101,520	103,994	103,709	104,986	107,173	107,450	105,392	107,288	108,716	110,013	110,348
1984	112,489	112,116	110,972	112,792	113,528	115,030	113,102	112,118	113,350	113,659	115,707	115,098
1985	115,603	116,355	116,462	117,723	118,583	117,800	117,884	119,451	122,818	118,765	118,971	119,844
1986	120,759	120,369	120,896	122,556	123,948	123,693	124,244	125,385	132,340	126,933	126,083	131,236
1987	121,618	127,045	127,364	128,033	127,892	128,543	129,265	131,707	129,467	128,597	128,538	130,724
1988	130,668	131,193	133,482	132,156	132,856	133,309	133,074	133,359	131,791	134,899	135,946	136,415
1989	136,574	134,444	134,500	136,738	136,280	135,859	136,744	139,490	138,591	136,829	137,943	138,296
1990	139,945	138,782	138,547	138,037	137,543	138,379	138,366	138,039	137,945	136,740	136,898	134,895
1991	131,832	134,420	135,907	135,119	135,897	136,395	136,030	135,367	135,457	135,240	134,834	135,354
1992	137,039	138,608	137,380	137,437	137,933	137,926	138,317	139,215	140,416	142,271	142,497	144,207
1993	143,782	143,076	141,496	143,793	145,047	146,144	146,713	147,577	147,931	149,387	-	-

Source: U.S. Department of Commerce, Bureau of Economic Analysis, U.S. Department of Commerce, Bureau of the Census. - indicates data not available or zero.

INDICATORS OF FIXED CAPITAL INVESTMENT

Indicators of fixed capital investment cover business formations as well as expenditures on tooling and equipment and on buildings and housing. In the context of business cycles, the series reflect relative confidence in the future and hence tend to be leading indicators. Five series are presented:

> New business incorporations
> Contracts and orders for plant and equipment, current dollars
> Manufacturers' new orders, capital goods, nondefense
> New plant and equipment expenditures by business
> New private housing units started

Related series, reported under Business Cycle Indicators, are:

> Contracts and orders for plant and equipment, Constant Dollars (Leading Index)
> Index of new private housing units (Leading Index)

New Business Incorporations. Data show total incorporations from 1947 to 1993. New businesses are formed when entrepreneurs anticipate a strong economy and can obtain financing. The series, therefore, is classified as a leading indicator—although not included in the composite index of leading indicators.

Contracts and Orders for Plant and Equipment, Current Dollars. Data are shown in billions of current dollars from 1947 to 1993. The same series, in constant 1987 dollars, is included as one of the components of the composite index of leading indicators. The series shows commitments to spend money on capital goods in the future—because payment will be made at a later date. The series, therefore, tends to predict future economic activity.

Manufacturers' New Orders, Capital Goods, Nondefense. Data are reported in billions of constant 1987 dollars. The defense category is excluded because government procurement is less responsive to short-term changes in the economy than is private sector procurement; defense procurement, also, tends to be staged over multiples of budget cycles; for these reasons, inclusion of defense would make the series less predictive of economic activity in the future. The series is classified as a leading indicator but is not part of the composite index.

New Plant and Equipment Expenditures by Business. In billions of current dollars, data are available from 1945 to 1993 by quarter. Quarterly data are annualized. Since these are expenditures, the series is classified as coincident at the peak of business cycles, as a lagging indicator in the trough, and as a lagging indicator overall. Spending grows as the economy reaches for a peak; as the economy begins to move out of a slump, however, businesses tend to hold back on new expenditures on capital goods out of caution; therefore the indicator lags in a trough.

New Private Housing Units Started. Data are in thousands of units, by month, for 1946 through 1993. The composite index of leading indicators measures building permits issued—the first step in a cycle of construction. This series measures actual starts. Both series are leading indicators. Since the construction sector tends to be the first to slump and the first to revive, "housing starts" is a closely watched indicator series.

Number of New Business Incorporations
(Number)

Year	Jan	Feb	Mar	Apr	May	Jun	Jul	Aug	Sep	Oct	Nov	Dec
1947	9,922	9,800	9,743	9,057	8,699	8,748	9,308	9,244	9,316	9,806	9,453	9,690
1948	9,380	8,329	8,349	8,396	8,064	8,210	8,168	7,439	7,483	7,349	7,241	7,054
1949	7,012	6,826	6,791	6,879	7,006	6,879	7,057	7,330	7,403	7,532	7,659	7,788
1950	7,830	8,275	8,078	8,132	8,403	8,394	7,898	7,684	7,092	7,176	7,059	7,007
1951	7,214	7,016	6,937	7,082	6,848	6,759	6,796	6,880	6,952	6,995	7,119	7,181
1952	7,080	7,214	7,348	7,499	7,441	7,700	7,683	8,065	8,259	8,341	8,265	8,096
1953	8,304	8,351	8,634	8,534	8,785	8,605	8,757	8,515	8,185	8,698	8,556	8,696
1954	8,638	8,937	9,155	9,276	9,158	9,436	9,772	9,882	10,085	10,730	11,212	11,604
1955	11,902	11,843	11,679	11,215	11,521	12,072	11,655	11,572	11,968	11,668	11,761	11,560
1956	11,620	12,449	11,591	11,888	12,245	11,999	11,851	11,707	11,193	11,925	11,186	11,139
1957	11,250	11,359	11,367	11,507	11,109	11,739	11,686	11,593	11,318	11,251	10,788	10,791
1958	11,042	11,049	11,042	10,636	11,752	12,032	12,504	13,644	13,933	13,669	14,599	15,577
1959	16,346	16,255	16,548	16,604	16,296	15,204	15,658	15,813	15,728	15,383	15,695	15,959
1960	16,561	15,274	15,233	15,280	15,176	15,630	15,828	15,114	15,112	15,035	14,264	14,097
1961	13,607	14,570	14,658	15,327	15,298	15,431	15,492	15,277	15,402	16,035	16,149	15,881
1962	15,599	15,758	15,670	15,372	15,245	14,947	15,171	15,056	15,249	14,892	14,951	14,985
1963	14,924	15,390	15,563	15,305	15,682	15,536	15,431	16,093	15,689	16,275	15,759	15,867
1964	15,993	16,326	15,917	16,132	16,473	16,282	16,550	15,692	16,948	16,728	16,804	17,021
1965	16,784	16,854	17,131	16,664	16,580	17,017	16,844	16,901	17,136	16,994	17,606	17,625
1966	18,087	17,451	17,266	17,057	16,644	16,577	16,074	16,343	15,764	16,233	16,206	16,583
1967	16,703	15,987	16,244	16,760	17,627	17,799	16,300	17,674	17,818	17,654	17,958	18,238
1968	18,061	18,041	18,538	18,663	18,723	18,839	19,407	19,947	20,582	21,093	20,890	20,619
1969	21,364	22,105	22,083	23,262	23,118	23,439	23,366	22,871	22,594	24,263	23,125	22,404
1970	22,196	22,968	21,346	21,829	21,874	21,796	21,614	21,796	22,181	21,712	22,217	22,272
1971	22,563	21,034	22,883	22,814	23,960	24,481	24,677	25,012	23,623	25,356	25,510	25,634
1972	25,270	25,084	26,231	26,630	26,270	26,175	26,789	26,365	27,168	27,529	26,234	27,699
1973	27,796	28,752	28,964	28,522	28,286	27,999	27,477	26,689	26,240	26,809	26,718	24,881
1974	26,511	27,056	26,458	29,071	27,562	25,785	27,790	26,495	26,313	25,404	25,555	25,003
1975	24,809	24,931	25,076	26,708	26,632	26,307	28,655	27,810	28,359	29,079	28,634	29,282
1976	29,613	29,772	31,000	30,808	28,784	31,420	31,037	31,301	31,921	32,160	33,183	33,124
1977	34,311	33,844	35,018	34,529	35,256	36,694	36,874	38,180	37,271	38,213	38,308	38,900
1978	36,414	39,434	37,847	39,585	39,059	39,860	40,152	41,007	41,553	41,437	41,423	42,179
1979	42,043	42,014	43,299	43,401	44,317	43,504	44,513	43,634	44,173	45,295	44,540	43,563
1980	44,230	44,175	43,359	42,240	42,710	40,648	43,621	44,255	45,746	45,945	46,750	47,840
1981	46,039	48,588	47,972	49,413	48,866	49,172	49,038	48,631	48,450	47,947	49,413	47,556
1982	43,330	47,234	46,899	46,876	46,995	45,936	44,525	46,981	45,552	45,530	48,474	57,507
1983	49,999	48,296	48,032	48,903	50,211	50,992	48,601	52,828	50,445	50,441	51,642	51,557
1984	52,674	53,535	53,075	53,298	50,736	53,884	53,211	52,025	52,646	52,587	53,838	53,558
1985	53,674	53,479	55,335	55,133	55,545	55,339	54,507	56,159	56,662	58,307	57,308	58,074
1986	57,636	59,114	58,870	59,156	57,747	57,446	57,717	56,299	57,942	57,120	56,652	65,691
1987	55,348	58,495	60,248	57,537	56,178	57,612	57,330	57,650	57,568	55,504	56,681	55,226
1988	56,108	56,475	60,655	54,670	58,046	55,620	56,915	59,730	55,915	56,529	54,553	58,592
1989	58,253	58,560	57,383	57,631	57,326	56,950	54,948	55,500	55,390	54,651	55,116	56,945
1990	59,141	56,325	56,172	55,000	53,616	53,784	52,142	52,958	52,176	51,899	51,429	52,060
1991	51,991	50,384	51,536	52,235	52,327	52,071	52,767	53,313	52,284	53,892	54,163	52,923
1992	58,141	55,092	57,449	54,474	48,688	58,730	56,942	51,245	59,179	52,492	55,392	61,695
1993	55,689	59,691	61,002	59,648	51,765	60,422	-	-	-	-	-	-

Source: Dun & Bradstreet, Inc; seasonal adjustment by Bureau of Economic Analysis. - indicates data not available or zero.

Contracts and Orders for Plant and Equipment
(Billions of $)

Year	Jan	Feb	Mar	Apr	May	Jun	Jul	Aug	Sep	Oct	Nov	Dec
1948	1.50	1.72	1.66	1.84	1.59	1.84	1.68	1.60	1.59	1.62	1.60	1.59
1949	1.31	1.42	1.41	1.21	1.25	1.37	1.26	1.36	1.49	1.43	1.61	1.46
1950	1.60	1.60	1.74	1.74	2.16	2.09	2.53	3.20	3.01	2.71	2.72	3.00
1951	3.43	3.51	3.19	3.21	4.36	2.98	2.84	2.73	2.36	2.63	2.63	2.83
1952	2.51	2.55	2.59	2.56	2.39	2.69	2.76	2.48	3.34	2.50	2.36	2.83
1953	2.84	2.88	2.64	2.88	2.76	2.16	2.66	2.23	2.57	2.72	2.34	2.14
1954	2.20	2.24	1.91	1.96	2.00	2.05	2.15	2.15	2.31	2.43	2.25	2.40
1955	2.50	2.72	3.15	2.93	2.80	2.99	2.97	3.15	3.33	3.20	3.45	3.45
1956	3.35	3.26	3.28	3.40	3.56	3.60	3.43	3.41	3.33	3.34	3.79	3.58
1957	3.65	3.55	3.52	3.15	3.29	3.13	3.06	3.13	2.83	2.89	2.89	2.74
1958	2.77	2.67	2.66	2.69	2.72	2.85	2.75	3.13	3.14	3.04	3.00	2.91
1959	3.09	3.19	3.73	3.35	3.46	3.54	3.61	3.22	3.63	3.50	3.30	3.49
1960	3.27	3.35	3.27	3.52	3.51	3.41	3.41	3.41	3.44	3.34	3.20	3.49
1961	3.48	3.40	3.25	3.27	3.22	3.41	3.49	3.67	3.43	3.51	3.72	3.43
1962	3.62	3.94	3.65	3.85	3.68	3.61	3.65	3.66	3.64	3.73	4.00	4.08
1963	3.80	3.91	3.88	3.98	4.36	3.99	3.96	4.07	4.20	4.28	4.50	4.56
1964	4.70	4.24	4.43	4.46	4.82	4.95	4.64	4.69	4.75	4.79	5.10	5.17
1965	4.89	4.93	5.22	5.25	5.18	5.10	5.27	5.08	5.49	5.51	5.45	5.82
1966	5.81	6.28	6.14	6.41	6.34	6.21	6.64	6.22	6.79	6.20	6.14	6.14
1967	5.30	5.69	5.81	5.70	5.88	6.11	6.05	6.26	6.09	6.19	6.22	6.40
1968	7.74	7.48	9.02	7.35	6.43	6.47	7.85	8.14	6.99	8.66	7.19	7.84
1969	8.99	9.00	7.96	9.24	8.51	8.05	8.24	8.36	9.24	8.24	8.06	8.01
1970	9.08	8.40	7.57	7.35	7.20	7.04	7.53	7.36	7.16	6.45	7.30	8.01
1971	7.80	8.41	8.28	8.19	7.77	8.88	7.24	8.46	8.56	7.66	8.25	8.46
1972	8.09	8.43	9.06	8.88	9.72	8.43	9.68	9.15	10.19	9.78	9.97	10.17
1973	10.35	11.06	11.00	11.14	11.53	11.69	12.06	12.53	11.96	13.29	13.28	12.58
1974	12.82	13.19	13.39	12.95	13.88	12.92	15.66	14.45	14.49	14.00	12.39	13.71
1975	12.42	11.57	10.89	12.82	12.91	12.83	12.21	13.74	11.46	11.40	11.26	10.84
1976	13.38	13.14	13.65	13.71	12.09	14.42	15.84	14.08	15.37	15.80	14.40	15.06
1977	14.98	15.12	14.57	15.87	17.44	17.41	15.55	17.50	18.96	16.75	16.73	19.10
1978	18.53	20.73	18.87	18.79	21.19	19.61	21.16	22.26	23.00	26.76	22.60	20.30
1979	23.78	25.42	27.94	25.41	22.73	23.97	24.62	23.31	24.15	25.20	25.15	24.95
1980	26.66	23.94	24.37	23.95	20.92	22.87	24.64	24.14	24.30	25.54	24.03	25.70
1981	27.48	24.30	26.67	28.22	25.74	26.39	26.43	25.67	24.82	25.74	24.42	23.04
1982	26.34	27.87	25.48	24.24	21.56	21.46	22.42	21.32	22.26	22.89	21.46	22.75
1983	21.94	21.06	21.46	22.90	23.84	24.01	22.32	24.12	25.45	26.79	24.75	23.87
1984	27.28	27.37	27.87	26.82	30.36	28.24	29.40	27.69	27.22	28.39	28.09	27.03
1985	27.49	30.78	30.11	27.57	28.06	29.35	28.95	29.09	31.14	31.14	27.64	31.29
1986	28.73	30.53	28.64	27.87	27.43	28.18	27.68	27.32	28.50	29.18	28.75	30.46
1987	29.18	28.95	28.60	29.88	30.93	32.41	33.52	30.65	30.55	32.07	31.70	34.47
1988	35.51	36.06	33.27	34.66	32.06	35.34	36.56	39.74	36.16	34.66	35.52	39.08
1989	40.49	37.40	37.21	39.11	36.39	39.02	40.63	35.13	35.69	35.21	37.34	43.94
1990	38.60	35.39	39.70	35.78	35.86	35.37	38.65	33.81	36.42	40.16	34.40	40.40
1991	36.05	36.07	34.39	31.88	30.63	29.78	39.01	32.95	31.75	32.68	36.08	30.26
1992	33.59	33.38	35.86	34.65	33.66	34.05	33.14	31.74	33.83	34.44	30.23	35.77
1993	32.84	35.91	33.13	33.35	33.17	38.19	33.84	35.60	34.90	36.06	-	-

Source: U.S. Department of Commerce, Bureau of Economic Analysis, U.S. Department of Commerce, Bureau of the Census, McGraw-Hill Information Systems Company. - indicates data not available or zero.

Manufacturers' New Orders
Nondefense capital goods
(Billions of 1987 $)

Year	Jan	Feb	Mar	Apr	May	Jun	Jul	Aug	Sep	Oct	Nov	Dec
1948	6.75	7.56	7.59	8.43	6.82	8.08	7.03	6.77	6.76	6.74	6.78	6.87
1949	5.42	5.88	5.80	4.88	5.19	5.47	5.10	5.47	6.13	5.80	6.10	5.87
1950	6.44	6.94	6.93	7.20	9.08	8.70	10.54	13.02	12.05	10.75	10.51	11.46
1951	12.88	12.99	12.24	12.04	11.44	10.68	10.25	9.83	8.81	10.01	9.92	9.86
1952	9.10	9.39	9.56	9.25	8.47	9.31	9.87	8.65	9.20	9.18	8.24	9.16
1953	10.75	10.14	9.53	9.95	9.43	7.70	8.46	7.43	7.59	7.24	7.16	7.06
1954	7.16	7.48	6.25	6.60	6.46	6.61	7.03	7.00	7.81	7.78	7.34	7.82
1955	8.36	9.14	10.39	9.11	9.14	9.72	9.51	10.04	9.80	10.04	10.47	10.79
1956	10.20	9.48	9.96	10.34	10.85	10.92	10.02	10.18	10.02	10.09	11.13	10.60
1957	10.16	10.11	9.62	8.86	8.91	8.55	8.50	8.57	8.05	7.82	7.70	7.15
1958	7.54	7.14	7.31	7.40	7.45	7.49	7.55	8.10	8.46	8.18	8.48	8.08
1959	8.58	8.82	9.98	9.07	9.46	9.66	9.71	8.94	9.73	9.39	8.78	9.48
1960	8.74	9.03	8.89	9.24	9.25	9.20	8.89	8.91	8.81	8.63	8.36	9.18
1961	8.77	8.81	8.81	8.76	8.53	9.01	9.43	9.89	9.34	9.43	9.75	9.25
1962	9.82	10.49	9.34	10.22	9.65	9.52	9.59	9.58	9.81	9.94	10.70	10.09
1963	10.27	10.56	10.74	10.76	11.19	10.63	10.73	11.09	11.26	11.29	10.99	11.47
1964	12.56	11.19	11.99	11.78	13.06	13.43	12.36	12.48	12.42	12.72	12.84	13.14
1965	13.04	12.81	13.87	13.68	13.30	13.73	13.99	13.60	14.08	14.49	14.75	15.76
1966	14.92	16.26	15.97	16.39	16.44	16.19	16.94	15.76	16.50	16.11	15.40	15.48
1967	13.17	13.90	14.01	14.15	14.42	14.85	15.12	15.42	14.68	14.78	14.96	15.70
1968	19.53	18.46	22.59	19.13	14.79	14.74	18.62	18.21	15.83	19.91	16.75	17.95
1969	19.31	21.52	18.82	22.91	19.00	18.66	18.91	19.61	21.56	18.34	18.84	16.94
1970	19.15	17.89	15.81	15.02	15.84	14.95	16.25	15.82	15.59	14.90	15.82	17.36
1971	16.79	18.06	17.66	17.17	16.43	19.17	15.20	17.28	18.64	16.55	17.41	18.18
1972	16.77	18.08	18.60	18.06	20.25	17.22	20.30	19.70	21.44	20.61	21.14	21.72
1973	21.62	23.23	23.70	24.74	24.07	23.25	24.68	25.00	24.64	26.88	26.83	26.20
1974	26.78	27.18	27.90	27.23	25.21	24.66	28.83	26.52	24.97	21.87	20.82	20.66
1975	20.71	18.55	16.67	18.79	17.09	16.72	18.83	18.40	17.51	17.83	17.63	16.77
1976	17.70	18.10	18.36	19.37	18.92	18.85	21.93	19.93	20.60	21.33	19.16	21.05
1977	20.67	20.18	20.40	21.24	21.10	23.46	21.43	21.09	23.61	23.29	22.52	24.00
1978	23.60	24.74	23.98	25.24	25.50	25.35	25.26	26.74	28.38	31.15	28.53	25.11
1979	28.40	31.68	31.95	28.46	29.16	29.22	28.73	29.05	29.60	29.94	27.70	28.92
1980	30.76	27.70	27.98	28.48	23.24	23.79	25.39	24.06	25.26	26.19	23.32	25.21
1981	27.90	22.91	26.15	27.01	24.24	24.18	24.83	24.02	22.50	22.75	21.36	18.88
1982	22.57	21.47	22.09	20.89	18.28	18.64	19.47	17.62	18.51	19.77	17.92	17.57
1983	19.36	16.05	17.17	18.63	18.58	19.75	18.22	19.52	20.92	22.58	20.20	19.93
1984	23.08	22.94	23.26	22.38	24.86	23.37	24.17	22.77	22.40	23.15	22.60	22.03
1985	22.70	25.08	24.40	22.44	22.42	24.26	23.27	23.95	25.50	25.18	22.45	26.45
1986	24.11	25.06	24.12	22.90	22.72	23.18	22.82	22.50	23.52	24.48	23.70	25.06
1987	24.43	24.08	23.37	24.92	26.62	26.74	28.43	25.63	25.57	26.81	27.00	29.26
1988	31.02	30.25	28.22	29.26	27.12	29.84	31.24	33.68	30.58	29.34	30.19	33.14
1989	33.49	31.21	31.08	32.46	30.29	32.51	33.93	28.79	28.34	28.17	30.92	35.81
1990	31.46	29.18	33.18	29.83	28.89	28.96	32.44	28.25	30.95	33.18	27.41	34.33
1991	30.44	30.00	28.61	25.92	25.47	25.72	32.85	27.61	26.87	27.71	30.88	25.62
1992	28.44	27.92	30.50	28.82	29.03	29.76	28.66	27.72	29.75	29.80	27.52	32.26
1993	29.26	33.09	30.13	31.18	31.08	34.11	31.47	33.25	32.44	34.01	-	-

Source: U.S. Department of Commerce, Bureau of Economic Analysis, U.S. Department of Commerce, Bureau of the Census. - indicates data not available or zero.

New Plant & Equipment Expenditures By Business
(Annual Rate, Billions of $)

Year	1st Quarter	2nd Quarter	3rd Quarter	4th Quarter
1947	18.70	19.71	20.68	21.36
1948	22.68	22.53	22.55	23.37
1949	21.84	20.68	19.75	18.84
1950	19.25	20.13	22.44	24.42
1951	25.10	26.88	27.57	27.69
1952	29.23	28.54	26.91	27.97
1953	29.41	30.19	30.26	29.98
1954	29.51	29.16	28.67	28.08
1955	28.06	29.57	32.03	34.08
1956	36.11	37.63	38.48	39.40
1957	40.62	41.37	41.07	39.11
1958	36.36	33.25	32.71	33.03
1959	34.11	35.38	36.94	37.10
1960	39.22	40.63	38.94	38.97
1961	37.57	37.80	38.43	39.54
1962	40.03	40.75	41.51	41.15
1963	40.87	42.66	44.81	46.34
1964	49.02	50.37	52.00	53.67
1965	55.57	58.34	60.67	63.52
1966	66.42	69.82	71.72	73.63
1967	72.37	72.38	72.60	73.63
1968	76.27	74.73	76.02	78.63
1969	82.04	84.21	87.91	88.80
1970	90.30	92.37	93.72	91.27
1971	90.59	92.90	92.75	95.41
1972	98.97	100.86	103.27	110.50
1973	113.09	118.57	122.69	125.77
1974	130.12	138.81	143.00	146.79
1975	144.12	141.56	141.04	142.93
1976	150.18	154.60	161.20	167.76
1977	176.64	181.74	190.46	190.46
1978	199.75	212.35	218.61	232.89
1979	238.27	249.12	259.22	270.02
1980	279.63	284.82	287.96	291.20
1981	308.68	319.65	333.00	333.77
1982	338.20	332.91	322.18	313.40
1983	306.65	310.77	323.37	338.91
1984	357.38	368.50	380.93	382.95
1985	397.21	412.34	414.35	413.23
1986	404.17	397.65	394.28	401.13
1987	395.63	399.44	414.30	427.41
1988	436.52	452.03	459.98	468.42
1989	487.21	501.87	513.71	521.06
1990	531.15	535.62	533.38	530.47
1991	534.02	525.74	526.76	529.51
1992	534.85	541.41	547.40	559.24
1993	564.13	579.79	598.91	597.98

Source: U.S. Department of Commerce, Bureau of the Census. - indicates data not available or zero.

New Private Housing Units Started

(Annual Rate, Thousands)

Year	Jan	Feb	Mar	Apr	May	Jun	Jul	Aug	Sep	Oct	Nov	Dec
1946	1,040	1,085	1,167	1,057	1,028	985	972	1,007	958	974	957	991
1947	1,052	1,074	1,032	1,039	1,090	1,174	1,252	1,355	1,532	1,571	1,557	1,447
1948	1,385	1,200	1,379	1,501	1,450	1,441	1,419	1,329	1,303	1,190	1,196	1,218
1949	1,196	1,137	1,171	1,292	1,319	1,341	1,384	1,500	1,603	1,662	1,785	1,824
1950	1,883	1,834	1,976	1,945	2,052	2,042	2,051	2,121	1,821	1,605	1,561	1,900
1951	1,928	1,638	1,481	1,352	1,359	1,419	1,257	1,334	1,456	1,386	1,324	1,330
1952	1,388	1,516	1,483	1,412	1,408	1,353	1,438	1,443	1,483	1,513	1,475	1,476
1953	1,484	1,460	1,506	1,498	1,425	1,380	1,346	1,324	1,348	1,342	1,383	1,343
1954	1,358	1,417	1,411	1,433	1,412	1,498	1,559	1,563	1,618	1,610	1,730	1,807
1955	1,757	1,664	1,684	1,708	1,730	1,704	1,632	1,625	1,580	1,490	1,434	1,431
1956	1,441	1,444	1,401	1,408	1,375	1,325	1,289	1,313	1,234	1,266	1,212	1,184
1957	1,151	1,168	1,173	1,147	1,174	1,175	1,191	1,193	1,191	1,204	1,162	1,146
1958	1,170	1,107	1,108	1,154	1,191	1,236	1,337	1,374	1,451	1,472	1,593	1,598
1959	1,657	1,667	1,620	1,590	1,498	1,503	1,547	1,430	1,540	1,355	1,416	1,601
1960	1,460	1,503	1,109	1,289	1,271	1,247	1,197	1,344	1,097	1,246	1,246	1,063
1961	1,183	1,226	1,312	1,166	1,228	1,382	1,335	1,312	1,429	1,415	1,385	1,365
1962	1,361	1,278	1,443	1,524	1,483	1,404	1,450	1,517	1,324	1,533	1,622	1,564
1963	1,244	1,456	1,534	1,689	1,641	1,588	1,614	1,639	1,763	1,779	1,622	1,491
1964	1,603	1,820	1,517	1,448	1,467	1,550	1,562	1,569	1,455	1,524	1,486	1,484
1965	1,361	1,433	1,423	1,438	1,478	1,488	1,529	1,432	1,482	1,452	1,460	1,656
1966	1,370	1,378	1,394	1,352	1,265	1,194	1,086	1,119	1,046	843	961	990
1967	1,067	1,123	1,056	1,091	1,304	1,248	1,364	1,407	1,421	1,491	1,538	1,308
1968	1,380	1,520	1,466	1,554	1,408	1,405	1,512	1,495	1,556	1,569	1,630	1,548
1969	1,769	1,705	1,561	1,524	1,583	1,528	1,368	1,358	1,507	1,381	1,229	1,327
1970	1,085	1,305	1,319	1,264	1,290	1,385	1,517	1,399	1,534	1,580	1,647	1,893
1971	1,828	1,741	1,910	1,986	2,049	2,026	2,083	2,158	2,041	2,128	2,182	2,295
1972	2,494	2,390	2,334	2,249	2,221	2,254	2,252	2,382	2,481	2,485	2,421	2,366
1973	2,481	2,289	2,365	2,084	2,266	2,067	2,123	2,051	1,874	1,677	1,724	1,526
1974	1,451	1,752	1,555	1,607	1,426	1,513	1,316	1,142	1,150	1,070	1,026	975
1975	1,032	904	993	1,005	1,121	1,087	1,226	1,260	1,264	1,344	1,360	1,321
1976	1,367	1,538	1,421	1,395	1,459	1,495	1,401	1,550	1,720	1,629	1,641	1,804
1977	1,527	1,943	2,063	1,892	1,971	1,893	2,058	2,020	1,949	2,042	2,042	2,142
1978	1,718	1,738	2,032	2,197	2,075	2,070	2,092	1,996	1,970	1,981	2,094	2,044
1979	1,630	1,520	1,847	1,748	1,876	1,913	1,760	1,778	1,832	1,681	1,524	1,498
1980	1,341	1,350	1,047	1,051	927	1,196	1,269	1,436	1,471	1,523	1,510	1,482
1981	1,547	1,246	1,306	1,360	1,140	1,045	1,041	940	911	873	837	910
1982	843	866	931	917	1,025	902	1,166	1,046	1,144	1,173	1,372	1,303
1983	1,586	1,699	1,606	1,472	1,776	1,733	1,785	1,910	1,710	1,715	1,785	1,688
1984	1,897	2,260	1,663	1,851	1,774	1,843	1,732	1,586	1,698	1,590	1,689	1,612
1985	1,711	1,632	1,800	1,821	1,680	1,676	1,684	1,743	1,676	1,834	1,698	1,942
1986	1,972	1,848	1,876	1,933	1,854	1,847	1,782	1,807	1,687	1,681	1,623	1,833
1987	1,774	1,784	1,726	1,614	1,628	1,594	1,575	1,605	1,695	1,515	1,656	1,400
1988	1,271	1,473	1,532	1,573	1,421	1,478	1,467	1,493	1,492	1,522	1,569	1,563
1989	1,621	1,425	1,422	1,339	1,331	1,397	1,427	1,332	1,279	1,410	1,351	1,251
1990	1,551	1,437	1,289	1,248	1,212	1,177	1,171	1,115	1,110	1,014	1,145	969
1991	819	985	898	1,000	982	1,048	1,068	1,037	1,022	1,093	1,083	1,094
1992	1,164	1,285	1,318	1,095	1,197	1,141	1,106	1,229	1,218	1,226	1,226	1,286
1993	1,171	1,180	1,124	1,206	1,248	1,248	1,232	1,328	1,359	1,396	-	-

Source: U.S. Department of Commerce, Bureau of the Census. - indicates data not available or zero.

INDICATORS OF INVENTORIES AND INVENTORY INVESTMENT

Inventory levels tend to be leading indicators of economic activity. Inventories are built up in anticipation of sales; they stay high when sales do not materialize; are are depleted when the economy is growing rapidly, signaling overheating and the potential for inflation; they are "worked down" in anticipation of recession and built up in expectation of turn-arounds. One series is shown:

Change in business inventories

One related series, reported under Business Cycle Indicators, is:

Ratio, manufacturing and trade inventories to sales

Change in Business Inventories. The changes are reported quarterly for the 1947-1993 period in billions of constant 1987 dollars. The series is considered a leading indicator but is excluded from the composite index.

Change in Business Inventories
(Annual Rate, Billions of 1987 $)

Year	1st Quarter	2nd Quarter	3rd Quarter	4th Quarter
1947	-0.5	-0.4	-5.2	7.1
1948	9.7	14.2	17.2	13.5
1949	-0.3	-16.5	-4.7	-14.8
1950	10.8	13.9	15.9	49.4
1951	30.5	45.1	30.3	14.3
1952	14.7	-5.9	14.5	14.9
1953	11.6	10.7	5.7	-7.8
1954	-5.2	-9.3	-6.6	-1.4
1955	11.3	16.8	15.7	20.6
1956	16.5	12.9	10.2	8.9
1957	4.9	5.3	7.8	-9.6
1958	-13.3	-11.8	3.1	12.8
1959	15.5	24.4	0.5	13.9
1960	29.6	7.2	11.6	-15.9
1961	-8.5	2.6	18.5	16.3
1962	23.3	14.2	17.5	7.4
1963	21.3	14.9	16.7	11.2
1964	16.9	15.4	13.9	16.4
1965	34.0	23.4	24.6	18.6
1966	36.1	32.1	32.9	45.7
1967	34.3	17.8	31.6	26.8
1968	20.0	36.0	26.5	12.1
1969	28.9	23.7	28.2	18.5
1970	5.1	8.4	14.4	-4.0
1971	31.9	23.8	21.9	5.4
1972	18.4	24.2	33.1	14.4
1973	31.3	38.1	24.8	56.7
1974	31.9	29.8	17.6	44.4
1975	-28.0	-30.6	-2.0	4.9
1976	26.9	33.3	27.2	14.7
1977	24.9	34.3	54.0	23.8
1978	36.0	36.9	35.3	40.6
1979	21.7	29.7	5.0	-2.0
1980	7.1	-3.6	-37.2	0.8
1981	32.6	15.8	35.7	14.1
1982	-24.4	-1.5	0.7	-44.9
1983	-33.5	9.9	12.1	29.3
1984	79.9	71.0	73.0	47.9
1985	14.8	23.7	19.8	30.2
1986	48.1	18.2	-12.0	-20.1
1987	22.5	17.3	5.4	59.9
1988	19.2	16.1	23.5	20.9
1989	41.2	36.9	16.0	24.9
1990	4.7	28.1	10.9	-20.9
1991	-17.4	-22.3	-0.9	7.1
1992	-5.0	12.6	9.6	8.7
1993	29.3	13.0	5.5	-

Source: U.S. Department of Commerce, Bureau of Economic Analysis. - indicates data not available or zero.

INDICATORS OF PRICES, COSTS, AND PROFITS

Prices, profits, and certain kinds of costs tend to react rapidly to changes in the economy—or anticipated changes. They tend, therefore, to be leading indicators. Some costs, however, most notably wages, are lagging indicators because institutional factors work against rapid response to changing circumstances. Four series are presented:

> Index of sensitive materials prices
> Index of producer prices, sensitive crude and intermediate materials
> Corporate profits after tax
> Index of unit labor costs, all persons, business

Three related series, reported under Business Cycle Indicators, are:

> Index of stock prices (Leading Index)
> Change in sensitive materials (Leading Index)
> Index of labor cost per unit of output, manufacturing (Lagging Index)
> Change in consumer price index for services (Lagging Index)

Index of Sensitive Materials Prices. The index is based on 1987 (1987 = 100) and is available for 1948 through 1993. "Sensitive materials" are those most vital to a modern economy: metals, fibers, and minerals. Being raw materials (rather than finished components), they are purchased early in the production cycle and therefore can predict future economic behavior. A series showing *changes* in these prices is included in the composite index of leading indicators.

Index of Producer Prices, Sensitive Crude and Intermediate Materials. This index, based on 1982 (1982 = 100), is available from 1947 to 1993. Subcomponents of the index include cattle hides, lumber and wood products, waste paper, ferrous and non-ferrous metal scrap, sand, gravel, and crushed stone, raw cotton, and domestic apparel wool. These openly traded commodities are early indicators of slacking demand (as an economy slows) or of the pick-up of the economy's pace (in a turn-around). The series is considered to be a leading indicator but is not part of the composite index of leading indicators.

Corporate Profits after Tax. Data are available from 1947 to 1993 in billions of 1987 constant dollars, on a quarterly, annualized basis. The series is classified as a leading indicator. The leading character of this series is explained by the fact that corporate profits tend to decline even as the economy is still reaching for a peak; the *rate* of economic growth slows before the economy turns around. Similarly, the rate of decline slows before a turn-around, with the consequence that profits improve before the economy as a whole reflects the shift.

Index of Unit Labor Costs, All Persons, Business. This lagging indicator is available in quarterly increments from 1947 to 1993; it is based on 1987 (1987 = 100). A similar index, for manufacturing only, is included in the composite index of lagging indicators. The lagging character of the index is explained by the fact that wage costs respond more slowly to economic cycles than do prices.

Index of Sensitive Materials Prices
(1987 = 100)

Year	Jan	Feb	Mar	Apr	May	Jun	Jul	Aug	Sep	Oct	Nov	Dec
1948	35.05	35.50	35.08	35.06	35.59	35.74	35.67	35.61	35.33	35.19	35.38	35.27
1949	35.09	34.55	33.98	32.74	32.22	31.68	31.83	32.20	32.61	32.11	32.49	32.53
1950	32.53	32.48	32.72	32.79	33.50	34.33	35.93	38.04	39.78	40.67	41.75	42.63
1951	44.48	45.06	45.01	44.37	44.04	43.08	41.38	39.63	38.59	39.00	38.58	38.31
1952	37.96	37.41	36.43	36.19	35.78	35.34	35.40	35.80	36.22	35.92	35.53	35.75
1953	35.48	35.51	35.66	35.43	35.63	35.62	35.44	35.29	35.03	34.90	34.61	34.38
1954	34.11	34.08	34.29	34.59	34.66	34.94	35.14	34.93	35.09	35.22	35.09	34.96
1955	35.18	35.47	35.52	35.69	35.85	36.00	36.36	36.23	36.26	36.17	36.43	36.85
1956	36.99	37.18	37.25	37.09	36.91	36.55	36.42	36.47	36.61	36.63	36.79	36.92
1957	36.81	36.48	36.40	36.20	36.00	35.69	35.58	35.52	35.33	34.93	34.73	34.51
1958	34.34	34.37	34.01	33.63	33.76	33.81	34.20	34.38	34.61	35.16	35.42	35.15
1959	35.28	35.25	35.52	35.79	36.04	36.18	36.16	36.22	36.35	36.55	36.63	36.87
1960	36.92	36.67	36.46	36.51	36.46	36.21	36.12	36.14	36.06	35.87	35.83	35.57
1961	35.36	35.70	35.64	35.58	35.72	35.56	35.85	35.95	35.97	36.28	35.78	36.16
1962	36.24	36.11	36.12	35.79	35.94	35.72	35.63	35.52	35.53	35.59	35.68	35.53
1963	35.58	35.57	35.60	35.47	35.51	35.61	35.88	35.97	35.88	36.06	36.28	36.62
1964	36.60	36.60	36.67	36.92	36.78	36.89	36.97	37.30	37.59	38.10	38.24	38.37
1965	38.03	37.89	38.03	38.31	38.72	38.68	38.75	39.06	39.13	39.37	39.44	39.41
1966	39.60	39.73	39.98	40.08	39.91	39.83	39.79	38.85	38.55	38.28	38.01	37.84
1967	37.53	37.26	36.87	36.50	36.43	36.69	36.66	36.64	36.77	36.86	37.04	37.45
1968	37.25	37.46	37.77	37.92	37.64	37.92	38.21	38.48	38.69	39.12	39.58	39.87
1969	40.26	40.57	40.60	40.70	40.73	40.81	40.95	41.22	41.67	41.72	42.01	42.17
1970	42.04	41.77	41.55	41.51	41.37	40.97	40.60	40.53	40.22	40.35	40.49	40.08
1971	39.92	39.94	40.20	40.68	40.31	40.53	40.78	41.04	41.30	41.46	41.62	42.13
1972	42.33	42.66	43.69	44.22	45.60	45.97	46.25	46.35	46.40	46.90	48.04	48.70
1973	49.42	50.73	51.65	52.53	53.07	54.24	55.09	56.45	57.99	59.17	60.53	63.41
1974	64.49	66.08	67.33	67.40	66.09	66.01	66.89	66.11	65.74	63.14	61.30	58.51
1975	57.83	57.74	57.44	57.76	58.11	56.49	56.27	57.37	59.14	59.66	60.05	60.63
1976	60.97	61.54	61.78	63.08	64.07	64.80	67.04	67.21	67.35	66.88	66.61	67.01
1977	67.18	67.84	69.21	68.83	68.72	68.12	68.30	68.86	68.83	69.36	69.94	70.96
1978	71.66	72.13	71.85	71.32	71.58	72.88	73.20	74.41	75.29	76.90	78.15	77.85
1979	78.57	79.95	81.50	83.07	84.32	85.24	85.84	85.80	85.82	88.65	90.30	91.26
1980	92.58	93.99	95.18	93.29	90.44	89.08	89.40	91.12	92.19	93.16	93.76	93.40
1981	92.51	91.38	92.51	93.27	93.22	93.03	93.18	93.51	92.67	91.64	90.18	89.00
1982	88.39	88.10	87.19	85.31	85.10	83.68	84.13	83.69	84.12	84.04	83.50	83.31
1983	83.73	85.04	84.95	84.92	85.68	86.54	88.76	91.23	92.75	94.93	96.43	97.04
1984	97.11	98.03	98.82	99.24	99.01	98.69	98.20	97.04	96.81	95.30	95.33	94.77
1985	93.95	93.27	92.92	92.17	91.46	90.58	90.23	89.79	88.49	88.58	88.55	88.61
1986	88.82	88.40	87.42	87.18	87.86	89.03	90.43	88.24	89.77	92.58	94.46	94.35
1987	95.11	94.65	95.17	97.13	99.26	100.18	101.56	102.79	103.41	103.88	103.18	103.67
1988	104.21	104.27	105.18	106.06	106.53	107.82	107.81	108.15	107.82	107.70	109.99	110.89
1989	112.10	113.21	113.50	112.86	111.92	111.11	110.20	109.85	110.10	110.33	108.71	106.45
1990	105.65	104.44	105.48	106.86	106.90	106.86	107.01	107.39	107.10	106.36	104.65	104.15
1991	103.74	103.07	102.29	102.00	101.89	101.17	100.90	99.66	98.40	97.99	98.30	98.28
1992	98.00	98.30	99.90	101.18	101.97	102.04	101.85	101.67	102.86	101.50	100.24	100.85
1993	101.40	101.47	100.91	99.80	99.37	99.22	98.90	98.66	98.00	98.75	-	-

Source: U.S. Department of Commerce, Bureau of Economic Analysis, U.S. Department of Labor, Bureau of Labor Statistics, Commodity Research Bureau, Inc. - indicates data not available or zero.

Index of Producer Prices

Sensitive crude and intermediate materials

(1982 = 100)

Year	Jan	Feb	Mar	Apr	May	Jun	Jul	Aug	Sep	Oct	Nov	Dec
1947	38.50	39.90	42.10	43.40	42.20	42.10	42.60	42.60	42.30	43.40	42.80	42.80
1948	43.90	45.20	44.80	46.10	47.50	47.20	46.60	45.10	44.80	44.10	43.70	43.00
1949	42.40	40.80	40.10	37.70	36.20	35.80	35.10	35.30	37.30	37.30	38.10	38.40
1950	38.40	39.20	39.90	41.00	43.20	45.80	46.90	49.60	51.20	51.60	52.90	54.80
1951	57.40	57.80	58.10	56.60	57.30	58.50	57.40	50.50	49.40	48.20	47.20	46.80
1952	46.30	46.30	45.90	45.90	45.50	45.40	45.00	45.60	46.30	45.70	45.20	45.80
1953	45.30	45.90	46.50	46.60	46.50	46.30	46.60	46.10	45.10	44.30	43.50	42.40
1954	41.60	41.50	41.30	41.40	42.10	42.10	42.50	41.90	42.30	43.40	44.20	43.60
1955	44.40	44.90	45.30	45.30	45.70	46.40	47.70	48.00	48.20	48.10	48.80	50.00
1956	50.60	50.50	51.00	51.90	51.60	49.60	48.30	48.90	49.20	48.50	49.10	49.80
1957	46.90	45.20	44.70	43.00	43.80	45.70	44.70	44.30	43.60	42.20	41.20	41.20
1958	40.70	41.40	41.00	40.40	40.70	41.10	41.50	42.40	43.20	44.10	44.40	43.50
1959	44.00	44.80	45.40	45.20	44.90	45.60	45.20	44.80	45.00	45.70	45.70	45.30
1960	42.80	41.60	40.50	40.50	40.20	39.20	38.90	38.10	37.90	37.30	37.20	37.30
1961	37.20	37.50	37.90	38.70	38.80	39.20	39.30	39.30	39.50	39.80	38.80	39.10
1962	39.50	39.40	39.00	38.50	38.20	37.80	37.70	37.80	37.70	37.60	37.40	37.60
1963	37.60	37.80	37.90	37.70	37.90	37.90	38.50	38.70	38.30	38.50	38.60	38.70
1964	38.80	38.70	39.00	39.60	39.60	39.90	40.20	40.70	40.50	41.00	41.20	41.60
1965	41.10	40.70	40.80	40.80	41.30	41.00	41.10	41.60	41.40	41.70	42.00	42.10
1966	42.70	43.00	43.90	44.10	44.20	44.30	44.30	42.20	41.80	41.60	41.10	40.40
1967	39.90	39.20	38.80	38.50	38.80	39.50	39.80	40.00	40.60	40.50	41.10	41.60
1968	41.50	41.60	42.10	42.00	41.80	42.60	43.30	43.60	44.10	45.10	45.60	46.70
1969	47.70	48.30	49.40	48.70	48.30	47.50	47.00	47.50	47.80	47.80	48.60	48.60
1970	48.40	47.80	47.50	47.30	47.60	47.50	46.90	46.60	46.40	46.50	45.10	44.70
1971	45.00	45.40	45.70	46.30	46.10	46.60	47.80	48.60	48.70	48.90	49.10	49.80
1972	50.50	50.70	51.20	51.40	51.80	52.70	53.60	54.20	54.10	55.60	56.60	57.30
1973	58.30	60.50	62.10	64.80	67.20	68.60	68.10	70.50	74.00	77.30	82.50	84.90
1974	83.70	85.70	88.90	92.40	84.90	85.40	86.60	85.20	83.60	79.90	77.60	70.80
1975	68.10	67.90	66.50	66.90	68.90	67.10	65.50	67.60	71.30	71.10	71.40	73.00
1976	75.50	76.50	78.30	80.30	81.10	82.40	86.20	86.00	86.30	84.80	85.00	86.30
1977	85.80	85.70	87.90	87.30	86.70	85.60	86.80	89.00	90.40	89.50	88.90	92.00
1978	94.30	95.30	95.30	95.70	97.30	100.60	101.60	103.20	104.10	106.40	109.70	109.40
1979	110.30	112.50	118.20	118.10	118.50	121.80	119.60	118.50	118.50	120.40	120.00	118.20
1980	119.20	121.20	120.30	113.20	108.50	107.00	109.80	113.80	115.20	117.20	119.70	120.20
1981	116.50	112.90	113.60	114.90	114.90	114.40	113.30	113.10	110.50	109.10	106.20	105.30
1982	105.20	103.50	102.40	101.20	100.80	99.30	99.50	97.90	97.80	97.60	97.10	97.70
1983	99.90	103.00	105.20	104.70	106.80	109.90	113.80	116.70	116.60	117.80	119.40	120.70
1984	120.40	122.10	122.50	121.90	121.30	119.70	117.10	115.00	115.20	113.80	113.20	112.70
1985	112.90	111.40	110.60	109.90	109.60	109.20	109.10	108.70	107.70	108.20	107.80	107.80
1986	108.09	107.39	108.25	110.07	110.56	111.04	112.15	109.90	111.12	112.51	113.67	113.48
1987	113.72	114.31	115.14	115.61	117.60	119.89	122.07	123.90	127.87	131.45	133.29	133.79
1988	134.05	135.73	137.22	136.27	135.47	135.74	137.69	137.32	137.08	137.02	138.04	138.91
1989	140.33	141.28	142.14	141.28	141.84	141.22	140.51	139.76	140.22	142.03	140.64	138.99
1990	138.24	137.70	138.82	140.72	141.88	141.38	141.50	142.21	141.80	141.14	139.88	139.42
1991	139.10	137.90	137.00	135.68	136.25	136.47	136.57	134.60	134.48	135.03	135.47	135.78
1992	136.43	139.63	141.83	141.33	141.73	141.40	141.21	141.28	142.97	142.96	144.17	148.80
1993	154.09	159.15	162.94	161.85	160.98	160.05	159.46	157.97	159.89	163.53	-	-

Source: U.S. Department of Commerce, Bureau of Economic Analysis, U.S. Department of Labor, Bureau of Labor Statistics. - indicates data not available or zero.

Corporate Profits After Tax
(Annual Rate, Billions of 1987 $)

Year	1st Quarter	2nd Quarter	3rd Quarter	4th Quarter
1947	119.2	109.2	105.3	111.8
1948	116.5	120.9	115.4	110.4
1949	101.7	88.7	92.0	90.3
1950	92.6	110.6	130.7	141.3
1951	112.5	95.3	86.8	93.4
1952	90.1	85.7	86.4	93.9
1953	96.5	95.3	92.5	72.5
1954	83.4	86.2	91.9	98.3
1955	111.2	112.3	112.9	116.5
1956	111.4	112.9	106.1	110.5
1957	110.0	104.5	101.3	92.6
1958	79.8	81.3	90.0	101.7
1959	107.7	116.5	104.0	102.4
1960	111.0	102.7	98.2	95.0
1961	92.9	97.7	102.9	110.5
1962	112.1	112.1	115.1	116.8
1963	114.4	120.9	123.8	126.7
1964	137.1	136.0	138.9	137.1
1965	154.6	160.5	162.0	170.0
1966	172.0	171.1	168.2	162.3
1967	154.8	153.5	155.6	161.3
1968	154.8	156.6	155.2	157.8
1969	153.5	146.4	139.6	134.8
1970	127.2	123.5	124.0	115.0
1971	131.3	135.0	142.7	145.2
1972	151.7	152.4	157.5	170.0
1973	195.0	197.2	194.6	199.8
1974	204.7	203.3	207.2	178.8
1975	151.7	158.8	188.2	195.8
1976	202.3	200.9	198.8	196.0
1977	211.0	220.5	225.6	221.1
1978	222.0	242.2	243.7	253.4
1979	248.6	251.7	250.6	239.0
1980	234.3	190.8	193.3	192.8
1981	194.7	172.9	174.6	162.4
1982	133.2	131.8	131.3	125.8
1983	129.4	149.2	161.7	156.4
1984	169.6	166.0	153.5	146.8
1985	134.6	133.5	137.6	140.9
1986	114.5	111.2	115.2	122.8
1987	142.2	158.6	168.7	173.7
1988	191.5	201.1	205.4	215.1
1989	201.8	188.0	175.4	182.6
1990	195.9	205.5	204.1	203.0
1991	201.5	200.1	200.0	209.3
1992	224.0	221.3	193.3	216.3
1993	219.2	230.7	232.8	-

Source: U.S. Department of Commerce, Bureau of Economic Analysis. - indicates data not available or zero.

Unit Labor Cost, All Persons, Business Sector
(1982 = 100)

Year	1st Quarter	2nd Quarter	3rd Quarter	4th Quarter
1947	23.3	23.7	24.0	24.8
1948	24.5	24.3	25.4	25.5
1949	25.1	24.8	24.7	25.1
1950	24.9	24.6	24.6	24.8
1951	26.0	26.5	26.2	26.2
1952	26.5	26.6	26.9	27.4
1953	27.5	27.7	28.1	28.0
1954	28.1	28.2	27.8	28.0
1955	27.5	27.7	27.9	28.2
1956	28.9	29.3	29.5	29.6
1957	30.1	30.3	30.4	30.6
1958	30.9	30.7	30.9	30.7
1959	30.9	31.0	31.6	31.7
1960	31.9	32.2	32.3	32.3
1961	32.4	32.2	32.2	32.1
1962	32.5	32.7	32.6	32.5
1963	32.6	32.3	32.4	32.6
1964	32.5	32.7	32.8	33.0
1965	33.0	33.2	33.2	33.1
1966	33.6	34.4	34.8	35.2
1967	35.4	35.4	35.6	35.8
1968	36.6	37.0	37.5	38.1
1969	38.6	39.5	40.2	40.9
1970	41.8	42.2	42.2	42.7
1971	42.8	43.4	43.8	43.9
1972	44.7	44.7	44.9	45.0
1973	45.9	47.1	48.2	48.8
1974	50.5	52.5	54.3	55.3
1975	57.0	56.8	56.8	57.9
1976	58.7	59.9	61.2	62.3
1977	62.8	63.9	64.4	66.2
1978	67.8	68.5	70.1	71.9
1979	74.2	76.2	78.4	80.2
1980	82.4	86.2	87.7	88.4
1981	90.2	92.0	93.5	96.6
1982	98.8	99.6	100.7	101.0
1983	101.6	100.7	101.5	102.1
1984	102.5	102.7	104.1	104.3
1985	105.6	105.9	106.4	108.0
1986	107.6	108.6	110.1	111.6
1987	112.0	111.4	111.9	113.7
1988	113.6	115.7	117.0	117.9
1989	119.4	120.1	121.5	123.0
1990	124.6	125.9	127.9	129.8
1991	130.6	131.4	132.6	133.1
1992	133.4	133.9	134.5	134.8
1993	136.4	137.3	137.4	-

Source: U.S. Department of Labor, Bureau of Labor Statistics. - indicates data not available or zero.

INDICATORS OF MONEY AND CREDIT

This section presents 10 series commonly used to measure the relationships between the economy and money, expressed in measures of money supply, interest and other yields on investments, and credit. These indicators are leading, coincident, or lagging depending on the nature of the series. The series presented are:

   Ratio, gross domestic product to money supply M1
   Free reserves
   Member bank borrowings from the Federal Reserve
   Federal funds rate
   Discount rate on new issues of 91-day Treasury bills
   Yield on new issues of high-grade corporate bonds
   Yield on long-term Treasury bonds
   Yield on municipal bonds, 20-bond average
   Secondary market yields on FHA mortgages
   Commercial and industrial loans outstanding, current dollars

Three related series, reported under Business Cycle Indicators, are:

   Money supply M2 (Leading Index)
   Commercial and industrial loans outstanding, 1987 dollars (Lagging Index)
   Average prime rate charged by banks (Lagging Index)
   Change in consumer price index for services (Lagging Index)

Ratio, Gross Domestic Product to Money Supply M1. This indicator is a ratio calculated by dividing the GDP by M1. The ratio is calculated in current dollars and is also referred to as the ratio of "nominal GDP" to "nominal" money supply. GDP is the sum of all productive economic activities; M1 is that portion of the money supply which is most liquid (cash, checking accounts). The ratio of GDP to M1 is a measure of the "velocity of money." If GDP is $5,557.7 billion and M1 is $835.0 billion (in current dollars) then the ratio will be 6.66—meaning that the money supply turned over nearly 7 times to finance the nation's economic activities in one year.

The velocity of money is a coincident indicator, but not part of the composite index of coincident indicators. The velocity of money is used in many kinds of analysis. Velocity tends to increase in inflationary times because holding money (in savings accounts, for instance) decreases the value of the money; people prefer to spend. In periods of low inflation, money is held more and velocity drops. The use of alternatives to money, such as credit cards, decreases the need for money and increase velocity; and the velocity of money has tended to rise, historically, with higher levels of income. In countries with very high rates of inflation, velocities 20 to 50 are not uncommon.

Free Reserves. Data are for 1945 to 1991 in millions of dollars; data are not seasonally adjusted. Free reserves are funds held by banks that may be loaned out. Banks are required by the Federal Reserve System to hold reserves in a fixed ratio to their total deposits (the "reserve ratio"). Deposits in excess of the required reserve less borrowings from the Federal Reserve System, are "free" to be lent.

The series is a leading indicator at business cycle peaks. It is an "inverted" indicator: for cyclical analysis, changes from period to period are inverted; a growth is depicted as negative growth, a decline as a growth.

A pattern of decreasing free reserves signals an increasing demand for money for purchases, that is, increasing economic activity; a pattern of increasing free reserves indicates the opposite—no demand for money. Thus by "inverting the sign" of this indicator, the right message is obtained. The series is undefined at cycle troughs and overall.

Member Bank Borrowings from the Federal Reserve. To some extent this series is the inverse of the previous series. Both are shown in millions of current dollars. Members of the Federal Reserve System may borrow from the Fed for short-term purposes paying the prevailing "discount rate" charged by each Federal Reserve bank. Banks borrow to satisfy immediate needs for cash, to maintain required reserve ratios, and to meet contingencies (such as, for instance, sudden withdrawals which exceed the bank's cash reserves). Member borrowings and free reserves move in tandem. With high free reserves on hand, banks borrow less.

The series is classified as a leading indicator of cycle peaks and as a lagging indicator of troughs. Before a business cycle peaks, growth will tend to slow and member borrowings therefore fall before the economy stops growing. On a resumption of growth, member borrowings will tend to lag because members have high levels of free reserves.

Federal Funds Rate. Shown for 1954 through 1991 as a percent. This is the interest rate charged in the interbank market for bank purchases of excess reserve balances. Excess reserves are bank money holdings that exceed minimum deposit requirements; excess reserves minus loans outstanding to the Fed are "free reserves" (see above). Therefore excess reserves are free reserves plus obligations outstanding to the Fed. These assets may be bought and sold in the federal funds market at an interest rate called the federal funds rate. Unlike the discount rate, the funds rate changes with each transaction.

The series is a leading indicator of cycle peaks and a lagging indicator of troughs; slowing demand for reserves as a business cycle draws to its close causes a drop in the funds rate; as the economy turns around, some time passes before bank demand for reserves causes the funds rate to rise again.

Discount Rate on New Issues of 91-Day Treasury Bills. Data are shown for 1945 through 1991 as a percent. Treasury bills are short-term securities issued by the Treasury; 91-day Treasury bills have the shortest maturities. The bills are purchased at prices below the face value (minimum $10,0000); the difference between face value and purchase price is the discount rate. The bills are sold at auction; hence the discount rate is set by market forces. The Federal Reserve usually buys or sells treasury bills to carry out its open market operations; purchases act to decrease money supply; sales act to increase money supply. The series acts as a coincident indicator of the peak of business cycles and as a lagging indicator of troughs.

Yield on New Issues of High-Grade Corporate Bonds. Data for 1946 through 1991 are shown as percent. Bonds are long-term debt instruments issued by corporations; high-grade "corporates" are bonds with high ratings for security based on the financial strength of the issuer. The yield percentage will tend to decline *after* a recessionary trend is well established and turn up *after* a recovery is clearly under way; hence the series is regarded as a lagging indicator of the business cycle.

Yield on Long-Term Treasury Bonds. Data for 1945 through 1991 are shown in percent. Long-term Treasury bonds are debt instruments sold by the U.S. Treasury with maturities of 10 years or more in denominations of $1,000. The series is a coincident indicator of business cycle peaks and a lagging indictor of troughs.

Yield on Municipal Bonds, 20-Bond Average. These instruments are governmental debt instruments sold by municipalities. Data are shown in percent from 1948 through 1991. The series is classified as a lagging indicator of the trough of business cycles; it is unclassified at the peak, indicating behavior that does not follow any discernible pattern. Since most municipal bond yields ("public purpose bonds") are tax exempt, yields will tend to rise in an expanding economy where tax shelters are more valuable than in a declining economy.

Secondary Market Yields on FHA Mortgages. Data are shown in percent from 1949 to 1991. The primary market for Federal Housing Administration (FHA) or other mortgages is that defined by the home buyer and the original mortgage lender. The lender can then sell the loan—at a discount, of course—to investors. This second transaction is the secondary market for mortgages. The original lender receives cash for lending (increases his/her liquidity); the investor obtains an asset. Government agencies buy the original mortgages, assemble them into mortgage pools, and sell them as collateralized mortgage obligations.

The series is a lagging indicator. Before mortgages can be resold, people have to buy homes and take out mortgages. The secondary market, therefore, will tend to "soften" after a downturn in the economy; although housing starts tend to lead an expansion, housing purchases come later and secondary mortgage operations even later than that—explaining the lagging character of this series.

Commercial and Industrial Loans Outstanding, Current Dollars. This series is shown for 1945 through 1991 in millions of current dollars. The same series, in constant 1987 dollars, is a lagging indicator—as is this series. Business and industry assume debt in periods of growth and minimize debt in periods of decline. The total debt outstanding, however, reflects the business cycle at a lag in time; borrowers pay off debt over time and may be late in paying during economic turn-downs; they also contract new obligations later than the economy's upturn because both lenders and borrowers are more cautious after a recessionary period.

Ratio, Gross Domestic Product to Money Supply M1
(Ratio)

Year	1st Quarter	2nd Quarter	3rd Quarter	4th Quarter
1947	2.113	2.116	2.135	2.217
1948	2.272	2.359	2.421	2.441
1949	2.409	2.372	2.398	2.377
1950	2.452	2.501	2.632	2.709
1951	2.811	2.849	2.873	2.855
1952	2.846	2.826	2.845	2.919
1953	2.961	2.970	2.960	2.918
1954	2.905	2.900	2.909	2.943
1955	3.008	3.053	3.102	3.145
1956	3.152	3.188	3.221	3.272
1957	3.328	3.340	3.392	3.376
1958	3.323	3.317	3.381	3.437
1959	3.471	3.532	3.508	3.567
1960	3.674	3.674	3.661	3.628
1961	3.640	3.688	3.742	3.798
1962	3.859	3.884	3.933	3.930
1963	3.952	3.973	4.017	4.036
1964	4.117	4.147	4.145	4.128
1965	4.222	4.271	4.322	4.378
1966	4.438	4.442	4.534	4.598
1967	4.606	4.577	4.571	4.577
1968	4.654	4.701	4.696	4.666
1969	4.703	4.734	4.810	4.810
1970	4.811	4.847	4.873	4.805
1971	4.923	4.906	4.911	4.927
1972	4.997	5.053	5.055	5.090
1973	5.180	5.239	5.271	5.371
1974	5.318	5.394	5.458	5.502
1975	5.502	5.561	5.675	5.802
1976	5.911	5.914	5.963	6.014
1977	6.043	6.163	6.254	6.217
1978	6.226	6.453	6.499	6.605
1979	6.657	6.641	6.665	6.751
1980	6.827	6.867	6.773	6.903
1981	7.117	7.042	7.210	7.157
1982	6.991	7.043	6.999	6.788
1983	6.729	6.750	6.762	6.828
1984	6.949	6.993	7.046	7.062
1985	7.012	6.939	6.835	6.749
1986	6.730	6.496	6.317	6.119
1987	6.027	6.037	6.133	6.215
1988	6.261	6.280	6.314	6.419
1989	6.563	6.736	6.764	6.762
1990	6.837	6.868	6.836	6.794
1991	6.757	6.709	6.639	6.522
1992	6.393	6.316	6.207	6.090
1993	6.057	5.964	5.839	-

Source: U.S. Department of Commerce, Bureau of Economic Analysis, Board of Governors of the Federal Reserve System. - indicates data not available or zero.

Free Reserves

Not seasonally adjusted

(Million $)

Year	Jan	Feb	Mar	Apr	May	Jun	Jul	Aug	Sep	Oct	Nov	Dec
1945	996	720	766	571	373	749	1,056	701	675	699	575	1,157
1946	1,126	807	505	631	806	816	807	765	736	756	643	743
1947	744	602	698	707	677	650	689	673	798	783	576	762
1948	938	560	552	700	599	752	722	750	756	706	655	663
1949	669	600	546	608	601	658	910	861	847	816	677	685
1950	900	614	655	593	624	700	623	483	669	775	586	885
1951	613	298	471	672	152	664	562	412	383	821	389	169
1952	723	330	578	283	65	130	-468	-383	95	-400	-875	-870
1953	-640	-672	-614	-631	-353	365	366	-7	250	390	198	252
1954	836	339	503	626	561	711	770	725	708	638	650	457
1955	369	270	122	95	212	168	92	-189	-286	-359	-492	-245
1956	-255	-267	-409	-533	-504	-195	-139	-339	-214	-195	-154	-36
1957	116	-126	-316	-504	-444	-508	-383	-471	-466	-344	-293	-133
1958	122	324	495	492	547	484	547	382	95	96	20	-41
1959	-54	-51	-139	-261	-320	-523	-545	-542	-484	-466	-415	-435
1960	-373	-356	-218	-180	-51	46	122	246	412	495	610	669
1961	706	516	476	559	461	527	562	514	542	461	493	451
1962	536	434	383	420	456	371	442	405	409	414	437	312
1963	359	295	286	327	220	158	156	116	109	77	92	158
1964	166	111	108	141	94	107	113	106	86	77	8	142
1965	115	7	-45	-130	-161	-175	-175	-151	-144	-130	-80	-21
1966	-41	-135	-218	-282	-346	-351	-363	-368	-398	-401	-222	-193
1967	-7	5	214	204	276	246	303	284	253	206	226	147
1968	141	13	-322	-350	-381	-366	-176	-236	-142	-198	-237	-320
1969	-490	-581	-683	-836	-1,119	-1,081	-1,027	-982	-805	-987	-974	-833
1970	-785	-872	-735	-693	-811	-691	-1,194	-663	-356	-258	-181	-83
1971	-130	-78	-124	15	-65	-291	-639	-613	-306	-194	-147	56
1972	185	119	92	39	28	103	-45	-200	-329	-344	-254	-766
1973	-902	-1,396	-1,615	-1,488	-1,704	-1,626	-1,638	-1,968	-1,595	-1,208	-1,168	-994
1974	-886	-1,007	-1,180	-1,554	-1,772	-1,582	-1,709	-1,611	-1,472	-1,208	-887	-322
1975	-115	100	131	59	93	-10	-93	-4	-192	28	228	148
1976	173	147	172	111	95	88	101	107	139	125	185	221
1977	198	127	112	119	2	-115	-48	-861	-417	-1,096	-611	-379
1978	-217	-165	-129	-409	-993	-916	-1,120	-972	-867	-1,115	-481	-636
1979	-789	-764	-833	-742	-1,624	-1,197	-960	-863	-1,149	-1,750	-1,661	-1,031
1980	-990	-1,444	-2,538	-1,706	-97	131	142	-115	-964	-1,104	-1,538	-1,173
1981	-951	-932	-705	-1,161	-1,960	-1,692	-1,336	-1,048	-741	-465	-154	-169
1982	-902	-1,253	-886	-1,050	-582	-793	-327	-109	-430	68	-31	52
1983	176	132	-42	-128	10	-198	-368	-609	-428	-83	-370	-211
1984	-98	356	-246	-701	-2,381	-659	-287	-289	-153	-365	-73	273
1985	364	378	139	296	-48	376	222	320	30	176	-295	218
1986	848	688	635	497	557	642	507	319	252	366	596	846
1987	728	925	652	124	327	712	328	527	257	622	719	752
1988	592	957	642	496	583	367	116	382	220	545	610	575
1989	533	700	427	217	513	333	378	250	266	486	617	678
1990	603	76	687	672	503	238	385	68	291	455	741	1,361
1991	1,662	1,590	991	886	815	676	345	622	586	834	785	788
1992	771	990	939	1,049	845	684	681	684	707	931	939	1,032
1993	1,096	1,059	1,122	1,023	875	730	845	600	662	801	-	-

Source: Board of Governors of the Federal Reserve System. - indicates data not available or zero.

Member Bank Borrowings From Federal Reserve
Not seasonally adjusted
(Million $)

Year	Jan	Feb	Mar	Apr	May	Jun	Jul	Aug	Sep	Oct	Nov	Dec
1947	106	203	173	126	107	135	92	127	133	171	274	224
1948	143	244	270	111	144	100	95	87	128	111	118	134
1949	169	110	148	98	176	100	109	94	75	46	134	118
1950	35	123	128	101	80	68	123	164	96	67	145	142
1951	212	330	242	161	438	170	194	292	338	95	340	657
1952	210	365	307	367	563	579	1,077	1,032	683	1,048	1,532	1,593
1953	1,347	1,310	1,202	1,166	944	423	418	651	468	362	486	441
1954	100	293	189	139	155	146	65	115	67	82	164	246
1955	313	354	463	495	368	401	527	765	849	884	1,016	839
1956	807	799	993	1,060	971	769	738	898	792	715	744	688
1957	406	640	834	1,011	909	1,005	917	1,005	988	811	804	710
1958	451	242	138	130	119	142	109	252	476	425	486	557
1959	552	505	599	692	741	930	961	990	927	907	859	941
1960	887	810	641	606	496	434	379	296	215	167	133	74
1961	66	133	70	57	95	63	54	65	38	71	98	133
1962	87	68	89	72	61	102	92	125	81	63	120	260
1963	146	166	148	130	210	259	298	329	319	320	349	332
1964	274	286	278	211	260	268	263	315	345	321	400	264
1965	300	405	411	471	495	537	528	547	554	488	432	444
1966	420	482	560	637	687	707	741	735	769	734	607	532
1967	410	364	200	146	89	106	115	81	89	129	132	228
1968	246	373	659	685	741	694	527	565	503	443	545	746
1969	736	835	902	1,003	1,374	1,385	1,252	1,219	1,079	1,150	1,203	1,119
1970	959	1,080	898	845	968	881	1,360	837	600	463	415	332
1971	364	332	319	153	284	492	823	809	495	357	384	126
1972	21	33	98	117	111	100	238	388	541	555	608	1,050
1973	1,160	1,593	1,824	1,711	1,843	1,851	1,953	2,165	1,852	1,476	1,393	1,298
1974	1,051	1,191	1,314	1,736	2,590	3,006	3,301	3,336	3,282	1,813	1,252	727
1975	398	147	106	110	66	227	301	211	397	190	60	130
1976	78	81	54	44	115	126	133	100	62	94	72	53
1977	68	71	103	73	206	262	323	1,061	626	1,306	862	569
1978	484	406	328	557	1,212	1,094	1,317	1,140	1,060	1,277	703	868
1979	1,003	973	991	918	1,765	1,418	1,171	1,085	1,340	2,022	1,906	1,473
1980	1,241	1,655	2,823	2,455	1,018	379	395	658	1,311	1,310	2,059	1,690
1981	1,395	1,303	1,000	1,338	2,223	2,037	1,679	1,420	1,456	1,181	663	636
1982	1,517	1,789	1,555	1,568	1,117	1,205	691	515	933	477	621	634
1983	529	582	792	1,009	952	1,636	1,453	1,546	1,441	844	905	774
1984	715	567	952	1,234	2,988	3,300	5,924	8,017	7,242	6,017	4,617	3,186
1985	1,395	1,289	1,593	1,323	1,334	1,205	1,107	1,073	1,289	1,187	1,741	1,318
1986	770	884	761	893	876	803	741	872	1,008	841	752	827
1987	580	556	527	993	1,035	776	672	647	940	943	625	777
1988	1,082	396	1,752	2,993	2,578	3,083	3,440	3,241	2,839	2,299	2,861	1,716
1989	1,662	1,487	1,813	2,289	1,720	1,490	694	675	693	555	349	265
1990	440	1,448	2,124	1,628	1,335	881	757	927	624	410	230	326
1991	534	252	241	231	303	340	607	764	645	261	108	192
1992	233	77	91	90	155	229	284	251	287	143	104	124
1993	165	45	91	73	121	181	244	352	428	285	-	-

Source: Board of Governors of the Federal Reserve System. - indicates data not available or zero.

Federal Funds Rate
Not seasonally adjusted
(Percent)

Year	Jan	Feb	Mar	Apr	May	Jun	Jul	Aug	Sep	Oct	Nov	Dec
1954	-	-	-	-	-	-	-	1.21	1.07	0.90	0.91	1.26
1955	1.37	1.29	1.35	1.43	1.43	1.62	1.68	1.90	2.18	2.24	2.35	2.48
1956	2.44	2.50	2.50	2.62	2.75	2.71	2.74	2.74	2.95	2.96	2.88	2.94
1957	2.93	3.00	2.96	3.00	3.00	3.00	2.99	3.24	3.50	3.50	3.22	2.98
1958	2.72	1.67	1.20	1.26	0.63	0.93	0.68	1.53	1.76	1.80	2.27	2.42
1959	2.48	2.40	2.80	2.96	2.90	3.39	3.44	3.50	3.76	3.98	4.00	3.99
1960	3.99	3.97	3.84	3.92	3.85	3.32	3.23	2.98	2.60	2.47	2.44	1.98
1961	1.45	2.54	2.02	1.50	1.98	1.73	1.16	2.00	1.88	2.26	2.62	2.33
1962	2.14	2.37	2.70	2.69	2.29	2.68	2.71	2.93	2.90	2.90	2.94	2.93
1963	2.91	3.00	2.98	2.90	3.00	2.99	3.02	3.49	3.48	3.50	3.48	3.38
1964	3.48	3.48	3.43	3.47	3.50	3.50	3.42	3.50	3.45	3.36	3.52	3.85
1965	3.90	3.98	4.04	4.09	4.10	4.04	4.09	4.12	4.01	4.08	4.10	4.32
1966	4.42	4.60	4.65	4.67	4.90	5.17	5.30	5.53	5.40	5.53	5.77	5.40
1967	4.94	5.00	4.53	4.05	3.94	3.98	3.79	3.89	4.00	3.88	4.12	4.51
1968	4.60	4.72	5.05	5.76	6.12	6.07	6.02	6.03	5.78	5.92	5.81	6.02
1969	6.30	6.64	6.79	7.41	8.67	8.90	8.61	9.19	9.15	9.00	8.85	8.97
1970	8.98	8.98	7.76	8.10	7.94	7.60	7.21	6.61	6.29	6.20	5.60	4.90
1971	4.14	3.72	3.71	4.15	4.63	4.91	5.31	5.57	5.55	5.20	4.91	4.14
1972	3.50	3.29	3.83	4.17	4.27	4.46	4.55	4.80	4.87	5.04	5.06	5.33
1973	5.94	6.58	7.09	7.12	7.84	8.49	10.40	10.50	10.78	10.01	10.03	9.95
1974	9.65	8.97	9.35	10.51	11.31	11.93	12.92	12.01	11.34	10.06	9.45	8.53
1975	7.13	6.24	5.54	5.49	5.22	5.55	6.10	6.14	6.24	5.82	5.22	5.20
1976	4.87	4.77	4.84	4.82	5.29	5.48	5.31	5.29	5.25	5.03	4.95	4.65
1977	4.61	4.68	4.69	4.73	5.35	5.39	5.42	5.90	6.14	6.47	6.51	6.56
1978	6.70	6.78	6.79	6.89	7.36	7.60	7.81	8.04	8.45	8.96	9.76	10.03
1979	10.07	10.06	10.09	10.01	10.24	10.29	10.47	10.94	11.43	13.77	13.18	13.78
1980	13.82	14.13	17.19	17.61	10.98	9.47	9.03	9.61	10.87	12.81	15.85	18.90
1981	19.08	15.93	14.70	15.72	18.52	19.10	19.04	17.82	15.87	15.08	13.31	12.37
1982	13.22	14.78	14.68	14.94	14.45	14.15	12.59	10.12	10.31	9.71	9.20	8.95
1983	8.68	8.51	8.77	8.80	8.63	8.98	9.37	9.56	9.45	9.48	9.34	9.47
1984	9.56	9.59	9.91	10.29	10.32	11.06	11.23	11.64	11.30	9.99	9.43	8.38
1985	8.35	8.50	8.58	8.27	7.97	7.53	7.88	7.90	7.92	7.99	8.05	8.27
1986	8.14	7.86	7.48	6.99	6.85	6.92	6.56	6.17	5.89	5.85	6.04	6.91
1987	6.43	6.10	6.13	6.37	6.85	6.73	6.58	6.73	7.22	7.29	6.69	6.77
1988	6.83	6.58	6.58	6.87	7.09	7.51	7.75	8.01	8.19	8.30	8.35	8.76
1989	9.12	9.36	9.85	9.84	9.81	9.53	9.24	8.99	9.02	8.84	8.55	8.45
1990	8.23	8.24	8.28	8.26	8.18	8.29	8.15	8.13	8.20	8.11	7.81	7.31
1991	6.91	6.25	6.12	5.91	5.78	5.90	5.82	5.66	5.45	5.21	4.81	4.43
1992	4.03	4.06	3.98	3.73	3.82	3.76	3.25	3.30	3.22	3.10	3.09	2.92
1993	3.02	3.03	3.07	2.96	3.00	3.04	3.06	3.03	3.09	2.99	3.00	-

Source: Board of Governors of the Federal Reserve System. - indicates data not available or zero.

Discount Rate On New 91-Day Treasury Bills
Not seasonally adjusted
(Percent)

Year	Jan	Feb	Mar	Apr	May	Jun	Jul	Aug	Sep	Oct	Nov	Dec
1945	0.38	0.38	0.38	0.38	0.38	0.38	0.38	0.38	0.38	0.38	0.38	0.38
1946	0.38	0.38	0.38	0.38	0.38	0.38	0.38	0.38	0.38	0.38	0.38	0.38
1947	0.38	0.38	0.38	0.38	0.38	0.38	0.64	0.74	0.79	0.84	0.92	0.95
1948	0.97	0.99	1.00	1.00	1.00	1.00	1.00	1.03	1.09	1.12	1.14	1.15
1949	1.16	1.16	1.16	1.16	1.15	1.16	0.98	1.02	1.06	1.04	1.06	1.10
1950	1.09	1.12	1.14	1.16	1.17	1.17	1.17	1.21	1.32	1.33	1.36	1.37
1951	1.39	1.39	1.42	1.52	1.58	1.50	1.59	1.64	1.65	1.61	1.61	1.73
1952	1.69	1.57	1.66	1.62	1.71	1.70	1.82	1.88	1.79	1.78	1.86	2.13
1953	2.04	2.02	2.08	2.18	2.20	2.23	2.10	2.09	1.88	1.40	1.43	1.63
1954	1.21	0.98	1.05	1.01	0.78	0.65	0.71	0.89	1.01	0.99	0.95	1.17
1955	1.26	1.18	1.34	1.62	1.49	1.43	1.62	1.88	2.09	2.26	2.22	2.56
1956	2.46	2.37	2.31	2.61	2.65	2.53	2.33	2.61	2.85	2.96	3.00	3.23
1957	3.21	3.16	3.14	3.11	3.04	3.32	3.16	3.40	3.58	3.59	3.34	3.10
1958	2.60	1.56	1.35	1.13	1.05	0.88	0.96	1.69	2.48	2.79	2.76	2.81
1959	2.84	2.71	2.85	2.96	2.85	3.25	3.24	3.36	4.00	4.12	4.21	4.57
1960	4.44	3.95	3.44	3.24	3.39	2.64	2.40	2.29	2.49	2.43	2.38	2.27
1961	2.30	2.41	2.42	2.33	2.29	2.36	2.27	2.40	2.30	2.35	2.46	2.62
1962	2.75	2.75	2.72	2.74	2.69	2.72	2.94	2.84	2.79	2.75	2.80	2.86
1963	2.91	2.92	2.90	2.91	2.92	3.00	3.14	3.32	3.38	3.45	3.52	3.52
1964	3.53	3.53	3.55	3.48	3.48	3.48	3.48	3.51	3.53	3.58	3.62	3.86
1965	3.83	3.93	3.94	3.93	3.90	3.81	3.83	3.84	3.91	4.03	4.08	4.36
1966	4.60	4.67	4.63	4.61	4.64	4.54	4.86	4.93	5.36	5.39	5.34	5.01
1967	4.76	4.55	4.29	3.85	3.64	3.48	4.31	4.28	4.45	4.59	4.76	5.01
1968	5.08	4.97	5.14	5.36	5.62	5.54	5.38	5.10	5.20	5.33	5.49	5.92
1969	6.18	6.16	6.08	6.15	6.08	6.49	7.00	7.01	7.13	7.04	7.19	7.72
1970	7.91	7.16	6.71	6.48	7.04	6.74	6.50	6.41	6.24	5.93	5.29	4.86
1971	4.49	3.77	3.32	3.78	4.14	4.70	5.40	5.08	4.67	4.49	4.19	4.02
1972	3.40	3.18	3.72	3.72	3.65	3.87	4.06	4.01	4.65	4.72	4.77	5.06
1973	5.31	5.56	6.05	6.29	6.35	7.19	8.02	8.67	8.48	7.16	7.87	7.36
1974	7.76	7.06	7.99	8.23	8.43	8.14	7.75	8.74	8.36	7.24	7.58	7.18
1975	6.49	5.58	5.54	5.69	5.32	5.19	6.16	6.46	6.38	6.08	5.47	5.50
1976	4.96	4.85	5.05	4.88	5.18	5.44	5.28	5.15	5.08	4.93	4.81	4.35
1977	4.60	4.66	4.61	4.54	4.94	5.00	5.15	5.50	5.77	6.19	6.16	6.06
1978	6.45	6.46	6.32	6.31	6.43	6.71	7.07	7.04	7.84	8.13	8.79	9.12
1979	9.35	9.27	9.46	9.49	9.58	9.05	9.26	9.45	10.18	11.47	11.87	12.07
1980	12.04	12.81	15.53	14.00	9.15	7.00	8.13	9.26	10.32	11.58	13.89	15.66
1981	14.72	14.90	13.48	13.63	16.30	14.56	14.70	15.61	14.95	13.87	11.27	10.93
1982	12.41	13.78	12.49	12.82	12.15	12.11	11.91	9.01	8.20	7.75	8.04	8.01
1983	7.81	8.13	8.30	8.25	8.19	8.82	9.12	9.39	9.05	8.71	8.71	8.96
1984	8.93	9.03	9.44	9.69	9.90	9.94	10.13	10.49	10.41	9.97	8.79	8.16
1985	7.76	8.22	8.57	8.00	7.56	7.01	7.05	7.18	7.08	7.17	7.20	7.07
1986	7.04	7.03	6.59	6.06	6.12	6.21	5.84	5.57	5.19	5.18	5.35	5.49
1987	5.45	5.59	5.56	5.76	5.75	5.69	5.78	6.00	6.32	6.40	5.81	5.80
1988	5.90	5.69	5.69	5.92	6.27	6.50	6.73	7.02	7.23	7.34	7.68	8.09
1989	8.29	8.48	8.83	8.70	8.40	8.22	7.92	7.91	7.72	7.63	7.65	7.64
1990	7.64	7.76	7.87	7.78	7.78	7.74	7.66	7.44	7.38	7.19	7.07	6.81
1991	6.30	5.95	5.91	5.67	5.51	5.60	5.58	5.39	5.25	5.03	4.60	4.12
1992	3.84	3.84	4.05	3.81	3.66	3.70	3.28	3.14	2.97	2.84	3.14	3.25
1993	3.06	2.95	2.97	2.89	2.96	3.10	3.05	3.05	2.96	3.04	3.12	-

Source: Board of Governors of the Federal Reserve System. - indicates data not available or zero.

Yield On New High-Grade Corporate Bonds
Not seasonally adjusted
(Percent)

Year	Jan	Feb	Mar	Apr	May	Jun	Jul	Aug	Sep	Oct	Nov	Dec
1946	2.56	2.38	2.46	2.27	2.47	2.45	2.48	2.06	2.75	2.70	2.49	2.70
1947	2.46	2.53	2.60	2.43	2.47	2.60	2.57	2.62	2.66	2.91	2.69	2.88
1948	2.97	2.85	2.99	2.81	2.86	2.93	2.80	2.83	2.86	2.99	2.96	3.15
1949	2.66	2.77	2.75	2.74	2.69	2.77	2.68	2.60	2.40	2.50	2.54	2.53
1950	2.60	2.58	2.57	2.40	2.58	2.63	2.55	2.61	2.70	2.64	2.63	2.75
1951	2.74	2.78	2.90	3.06	2.98	3.24	3.20	3.01	2.91	3.09	3.36	3.22
1952	3.08	2.94	3.14	3.09	3.25	3.09	3.11	3.08	3.14	3.16	3.07	3.04
1953	3.17	3.26	3.41	3.53	3.80	3.82	3.59	3.46	3.60	3.09	3.13	3.23
1954	3.00	2.88	2.74	2.88	2.90	2.91	2.94	2.94	3.01	2.84	2.94	2.87
1955	2.99	3.09	3.14	3.11	3.15	3.11	3.14	3.41	3.27	3.15	3.17	3.27
1956	3.20	3.07	3.25	3.55	3.48	3.56	3.56	4.02	3.96	3.94	4.29	4.26
1957	4.28	4.13	4.18	4.23	4.41	4.81	4.59	4.78	4.68	4.71	4.56	4.04
1958	3.62	3.73	3.88	3.67	3.66	3.61	3.85	4.39	4.56	4.48	4.35	4.44
1959	4.58	4.60	4.53	4.60	4.92	5.00	4.95	4.90	5.28	5.37	5.14	5.27
1960	5.34	5.24	4.98	4.97	4.95	4.91	4.79	4.65	4.64	4.75	4.82	4.94
1961	4.63	4.43	4.37	4.57	4.67	4.82	4.81	4.79	4.72	4.60	4.52	4.58
1962	4.56	4.53	4.41	4.37	4.32	4.30	4.41	4.39	4.28	4.26	4.23	4.28
1963	4.22	4.25	4.28	4.35	4.36	4.32	4.34	4.34	4.40	4.37	4.42	4.49
1964	4.50	4.39	4.45	4.48	4.48	4.50	4.44	4.44	4.49	4.49	4.48	4.49
1965	4.45	4.45	4.49	4.48	4.52	4.57	4.57	4.66	4.71	4.70	4.75	4.92
1966	4.93	5.09	5.33	5.38	5.55	5.67	5.81	6.04	6.14	6.04	6.11	5.98
1967	5.53	5.35	5.55	5.59	5.90	6.06	6.06	6.30	6.33	6.53	6.87	6.93
1968	6.57	6.57	6.80	6.79	7.00	7.02	6.91	6.54	6.69	6.88	7.00	7.28
1969	7.29	7.33	7.76	7.54	7.62	8.04	8.06	8.05	8.36	8.46	8.94	9.22
1970	9.00	8.84	9.00	9.09	9.53	9.70	9.09	9.08	9.00	9.14	8.97	8.13
1971	7.63	7.54	7.62	7.76	8.25	8.15	8.24	8.14	7.90	7.72	7.67	7.54
1972	7.36	7.57	7.53	7.77	7.61	7.63	7.72	7.59	7.72	7.66	7.46	7.50
1973	7.61	7.67	7.75	7.70	7.69	7.73	7.97	8.45	8.10	7.97	7.95	8.09
1974	8.32	8.21	8.60	9.04	9.39	9.59	10.18	10.30	10.44	10.29	9.22	9.47
1975	9.17	8.84	9.48	9.81	9.76	9.27	9.56	9.71	9.89	9.54	9.48	9.59
1976	8.97	8.71	8.73	8.68	9.00	8.90	8.76	8.59	8.37	8.25	8.17	7.90
1977	7.96	8.18	8.33	8.30	8.38	8.08	8.12	8.06	8.11	8.21	8.26	8.39
1978	8.70	8.70	8.70	8.88	9.00	9.15	9.27	8.83	8.78	9.14	9.30	9.30
1979	9.47	9.52	9.65	9.69	9.82	9.51	9.47	9.57	9.87	11.17	11.52	11.30
1980	11.65	13.23	14.08	13.36	11.61	11.12	11.48	12.31	12.74	13.17	14.10	14.38
1981	14.01	14.60	14.49	15.00	15.68	14.97	15.67	16.34	16.97	16.96	15.53	15.55
1982	16.34	16.35	15.72	15.62	15.37	15.96	15.75	14.64	13.78	12.63	11.89	12.15
1983	12.04	12.11	11.81	11.58	11.24	11.90	12.46	12.89	12.68	12.54	12.86	12.87
1984	12.65	12.80	13.36	13.64	14.41	14.49	14.25	13.54	13.37	13.02	12.40	12.47
1985	12.46	12.39	12.85	12.45	11.85	11.33	11.28	11.61	11.66	11.51	11.19	10.42
1986	10.33	9.76	8.95	8.71	9.09	9.39	9.11	9.03	9.28	9.29	8.99	8.87
1987	8.59	8.58	8.68	9.36	9.95	9.64	9.70	10.09	10.63	10.80	10.09	10.22
1988	9.81	9.43	9.68	9.92	10.25	10.08	10.12	10.27	10.03	9.86	9.98	10.05
1989	9.92	10.11	10.33	10.11	9.82	9.24	9.20	9.09	9.29	9.04	9.20	9.23
1990	9.56	9.68	9.79	10.02	9.97	9.69	9.72	10.05	10.17	10.09	9.79	9.55
1991	9.60	9.14	9.14	9.07	9.13	9.37	9.38	8.88	8.79	8.81	8.72	8.55
1992	8.36	8.63	8.62	8.59	8.57	8.45	8.19	7.96	7.99	8.17	8.25	8.12
1993	7.91	7.73	7.39	7.48	7.52	7.48	7.35	7.04	6.88	6.88	7.18	-

Source: Citibank and U.S. Department of the Treasury. - indicates data not available or zero.

Yield On Long-Term Treasury Bonds
Not seasonally adjusted
(Percent)

Year	Jan	Feb	Mar	Apr	May	Jun	Jul	Aug	Sep	Oct	Nov	Dec
1945	2.44	2.38	2.40	2.39	2.39	2.35	2.34	2.36	2.37	2.35	2.33	2.33
1946	2.21	2.12	2.09	2.08	2.19	2.16	2.18	2.23	2.28	2.26	2.25	2.24
1947	2.21	2.21	2.19	2.19	2.19	2.22	2.25	2.24	2.24	2.27	2.36	2.39
1948	2.45	2.45	2.44	2.44	2.42	2.41	2.44	2.45	2.45	2.45	2.44	2.44
1949	2.42	2.39	2.38	2.38	2.38	2.38	2.27	2.24	2.22	2.22	2.20	2.19
1950	2.20	2.24	2.27	2.30	2.31	2.33	2.34	2.33	2.36	2.38	2.38	2.39
1951	2.39	2.40	2.47	2.56	2.63	2.65	2.63	2.57	2.56	2.61	2.66	2.70
1952	2.74	2.71	2.70	2.64	2.57	2.61	2.61	2.70	2.71	2.74	2.71	2.75
1953	2.80	2.83	2.89	2.97	3.11	3.13	3.02	3.02	2.98	2.83	2.86	2.79
1954	2.69	2.62	2.53	2.48	2.54	2.55	2.47	2.48	2.52	2.54	2.57	2.59
1955	2.68	2.78	2.78	2.82	2.81	2.82	2.91	2.95	2.92	2.87	2.89	2.91
1956	2.88	2.85	2.93	3.07	2.97	2.93	3.00	3.17	3.21	3.20	3.30	3.40
1957	3.34	3.22	3.26	3.32	3.40	3.58	3.60	3.63	3.66	3.73	3.57	3.30
1958	3.24	3.28	3.25	3.12	3.14	3.20	3.36	3.60	3.75	3.76	3.70	3.80
1959	3.91	3.92	3.92	4.01	4.08	4.09	4.11	4.10	4.26	4.11	4.12	4.27
1960	4.37	4.22	4.08	4.18	4.16	3.98	3.86	3.79	3.84	3.91	3.93	3.88
1961	3.89	3.81	3.78	3.80	3.73	3.88	3.90	4.00	4.02	3.98	3.98	4.06
1962	4.08	4.09	4.01	3.89	3.88	3.90	4.02	3.98	3.94	3.89	3.87	3.87
1963	3.89	3.92	3.93	3.97	3.97	4.00	4.01	3.99	4.04	4.07	4.11	4.14
1964	4.15	4.14	4.18	4.20	4.16	4.13	4.13	4.14	4.16	4.16	4.12	4.14
1965	4.14	4.16	4.15	4.15	4.14	4.14	4.15	4.19	4.25	4.28	4.34	4.43
1966	4.43	4.61	4.63	4.55	4.57	4.63	4.75	4.80	4.79	4.70	4.74	4.65
1967	4.40	4.47	4.45	4.51	4.76	4.86	4.86	4.95	4.99	5.19	5.44	5.36
1968	5.18	5.16	5.39	5.28	5.40	5.23	5.09	5.04	5.09	5.24	5.36	5.66
1969	5.74	5.86	6.05	5.84	5.85	6.05	6.07	6.02	6.32	6.27	6.52	6.81
1970	6.86	6.44	6.39	6.53	6.94	6.99	6.57	6.75	6.63	6.59	6.24	5.97
1971	5.92	5.84	5.71	5.75	5.96	5.94	5.91	5.78	5.56	5.46	5.48	5.62
1972	5.62	5.67	5.66	5.74	5.64	5.59	5.59	5.59	5.70	5.69	5.51	5.63
1973	5.96	6.14	6.20	6.11	6.25	6.32	6.53	6.85	6.41	6.25	6.30	6.35
1974	6.56	6.54	6.81	7.04	7.09	7.02	7.18	7.33	7.30	7.22	6.93	6.77
1975	6.68	6.66	6.77	7.05	7.01	6.86	6.89	7.11	7.28	7.29	7.21	7.17
1976	6.93	6.92	6.88	6.73	7.01	6.92	6.85	6.82	6.70	6.65	6.62	6.38
1977	6.68	7.16	7.20	7.13	7.17	6.99	6.98	7.01	6.94	7.08	7.16	7.24
1978	7.51	7.60	7.63	7.74	7.87	7.94	8.10	7.88	7.82	8.07	8.16	8.36
1979	8.43	8.43	8.45	8.44	8.55	8.32	8.35	8.42	8.68	9.44	9.80	9.58
1980	10.03	11.55	11.87	10.83	9.82	9.40	9.83	10.53	10.94	11.20	11.83	11.89
1981	11.65	12.23	12.15	12.62	12.96	12.39	13.05	13.61	14.14	14.13	12.68	12.88
1982	13.73	13.63	12.98	12.84	12.67	13.32	12.97	12.15	11.48	10.51	10.18	10.33
1983	10.37	10.60	10.34	10.19	10.21	10.64	11.10	11.42	11.26	11.21	11.32	11.44
1984	11.29	11.44	11.90	12.17	12.89	13.00	12.82	12.23	11.97	11.66	11.25	11.21
1985	11.15	11.35	11.78	11.42	10.96	10.36	10.51	10.59	10.67	10.56	10.08	9.60
1986	9.51	9.07	8.13	7.59	8.02	8.23	7.86	7.72	8.08	8.04	7.81	7.67
1987	7.60	7.69	7.62	8.31	8.79	8.63	8.70	8.97	9.58	9.61	8.99	9.12
1988	8.82	8.41	8.61	8.91	9.24	9.04	9.20	9.33	9.06	8.89	9.07	9.13
1989	9.07	9.16	9.33	9.18	8.95	8.40	8.19	8.26	8.31	8.15	8.03	8.02
1990	8.39	8.66	8.74	8.92	8.90	8.62	8.64	8.97	9.11	8.93	8.60	8.31
1991	8.33	8.12	8.38	8.29	8.33	8.54	8.50	8.17	7.96	7.88	7.83	7.58
1992	7.48	7.78	7.93	7.88	7.80	7.72	7.40	7.19	7.08	7.26	7.43	7.30
1993	7.17	6.89	6.65	6.64	6.68	6.55	6.34	6.18	5.94	5.90	6.24	-

Source: U.S. Department of the Treasury. - indicates data not available or zero.

Yield On Municipal Bonds, 20-Bond Average
Not seasonally adjusted
(Percent)

Year	Jan	Feb	Mar	Apr	May	Jun	Jul	Aug	Sep	Oct	Nov	Dec
1948	-	2.47	2.45	2.37	2.31	2.24	2.27	2.37	2.41	2.42	2.38	2.26
1949	2.16	2.20	2.18	2.14	2.14	2.20	2.16	2.12	2.14	2.16	2.12	2.09
1950	2.06	2.03	2.01	2.03	2.00	1.99	2.01	1.83	1.84	1.79	1.74	1.72
1951	1.61	1.58	1.74	1.94	2.00	2.19	2.15	2.02	2.01	2.06	2.05	2.09
1952	2.09	2.07	2.08	2.04	2.06	2.13	2.15	2.24	2.30	2.38	2.38	2.38
1953	2.43	2.55	2.65	2.65	2.78	2.99	2.98	2.90	2.90	2.75	2.62	2.60
1954	2.50	2.42	2.40	2.47	2.50	2.48	2.32	2.26	2.31	2.34	2.32	2.36
1955	2.40	2.44	2.44	2.41	2.38	2.41	2.54	2.60	2.58	2.51	2.46	2.57
1956	2.50	2.44	2.57	2.70	2.68	2.54	2.65	2.80	2.94	2.95	3.16	3.22
1957	3.18	3.00	3.10	3.13	3.27	3.41	3.40	3.54	3.54	3.42	3.37	3.04
1958	2.91	3.02	3.06	2.96	2.92	2.97	3.09	3.36	3.54	3.45	3.32	3.34
1959	3.42	3.36	3.30	3.39	3.58	3.72	3.71	3.58	3.78	3.62	3.55	3.68
1960	3.72	3.60	3.56	3.56	3.60	3.55	3.50	3.34	3.42	3.53	3.40	3.40
1961	3.40	3.31	3.45	3.50	3.43	3.52	3.52	3.52	3.53	3.42	3.41	3.47
1962	3.34	3.21	3.14	3.06	3.11	3.26	3.28	3.23	3.11	3.02	3.04	3.07
1963	3.10	3.15	3.05	3.10	3.11	3.21	3.22	3.13	3.20	3.20	3.30	3.27
1964	3.22	3.14	3.28	3.28	3.20	3.20	3.18	3.19	3.23	3.25	3.18	3.13
1965	3.06	3.09	3.18	3.15	3.17	3.24	3.27	3.24	3.35	3.40	3.46	3.54
1966	3.52	3.64	3.72	3.56	3.65	3.77	3.95	4.12	4.12	3.94	3.86	3.86
1967	3.54	3.52	3.55	3.60	3.89	3.96	4.02	3.99	4.12	4.30	4.34	4.43
1968	4.29	4.31	4.54	4.34	4.54	4.50	4.33	4.21	4.38	4.49	4.60	4.82
1969	4.85	4.98	5.26	5.19	5.33	5.76	5.75	6.00	6.26	6.09	6.30	6.82
1970	6.65	6.36	6.03	6.49	7.00	6.96	6.53	6.20	6.25	6.39	5.93	5.46
1971	5.36	5.23	5.17	5.37	5.90	5.95	6.06	5.82	5.37	5.06	5.20	5.21
1972	5.12	5.28	5.31	5.43	5.30	5.34	5.41	5.30	5.36	5.18	5.02	5.05
1973	5.05	5.13	5.29	5.15	5.14	5.18	5.40	5.48	5.10	5.05	5.18	5.12
1974	5.22	5.20	5.40	5.73	6.02	6.13	6.68	6.71	6.76	6.57	6.61	7.05
1975	6.82	6.39	6.74	6.95	6.97	6.95	7.07	7.17	7.44	7.39	7.43	7.31
1976	7.07	6.94	6.92	6.60	6.87	6.87	6.79	6.61	6.51	6.30	6.29	5.94
1977	5.87	5.89	5.89	5.73	5.75	5.62	5.63	5.62	5.51	5.64	5.49	5.57
1978	5.71	5.62	5.61	5.80	6.03	6.22	6.28	6.12	6.09	6.13	6.19	6.50
1979	6.47	6.31	6.33	6.29	6.25	6.13	6.13	6.20	6.52	7.08	7.30	7.22
1980	7.35	8.16	9.17	8.63	7.59	7.63	8.13	8.67	8.94	9.11	9.56	10.20
1981	9.68	10.10	10.16	10.62	10.78	10.67	11.14	12.26	12.92	12.83	11.89	12.91
1982	13.28	12.97	12.82	12.59	11.95	12.45	12.28	11.23	10.66	9.69	10.06	9.96
1983	9.50	9.58	9.20	9.05	9.11	9.52	9.53	9.72	9.58	9.66	9.75	9.89
1984	9.63	9.64	9.93	9.96	10.49	10.67	10.42	9.99	10.10	10.25	10.17	9.95
1985	9.51	9.65	9.77	9.42	9.01	8.69	8.81	9.08	9.27	9.08	8.54	8.43
1986	8.08	7.44	7.08	7.20	7.54	7.87	7.51	7.21	7.11	7.08	6.85	6.86
1987	6.61	6.61	6.66	7.55	8.00	7.79	7.72	7.82	8.26	8.70	7.95	7.96
1988	7.69	7.49	7.74	7.81	7.91	7.78	7.76	7.79	7.66	7.47	7.46	7.61
1989	7.35	7.44	7.59	7.49	7.25	7.02	6.96	7.06	7.26	7.22	7.14	6.98
1990	7.10	7.22	7.29	7.39	7.35	7.24	7.19	7.32	7.43	7.49	7.18	7.09
1991	7.08	6.91	7.10	7.02	6.95	7.13	7.05	6.90	6.80	6.68	6.73	6.69
1992	6.54	6.74	6.76	6.67	6.57	6.49	6.13	6.16	6.25	6.41	6.36	6.22
1993	6.16	5.87	5.64	5.76	5.73	5.63	5.57	5.45	5.29	5.25	5.46	-

Source: The Bond Buyer. - indicates data not available or zero.

Secondary Market Yields On FHA Mortgages
Not seasonally adjusted
(Percent)

Year	Jan	Feb	Mar	Apr	May	Jun	Jul	Aug	Sep	Oct	Nov	Dec
1949	4.35	4.35	4.35	4.35	4.34	4.35	4.34	4.34	4.32	4.32	4.32	4.32
1950	4.31	4.31	4.30	-	-	4.09	4.07	4.07	4.07	4.07	4.07	4.07
1951	4.07	4.07	4.12	4.19	4.27	4.29	4.31	4.31	4.30	4.27	4.27	4.26
1952	4.26	4.27	4.29	4.29	4.29	4.30	4.30	4.30	4.30	4.31	4.32	4.32
1953	4.34	4.34	4.34	-	-	4.67	4.74	4.82	4.86	4.82	4.81	4.78
1954	4.75	4.69	4.64	4.62	4.59	4.57	4.56	4.56	4.56	4.56	4.56	4.56
1955	4.56	4.56	4.59	4.60	4.63	4.63	4.64	4.67	4.70	4.73	4.75	4.73
1956	4.73	4.70	4.68	4.71	4.78	4.81	4.81	4.87	4.92	4.95	-	-
1957	-	5.36	5.35	5.35	5.32	5.35	5.38	-	-	5.63	5.63	5.62
1958	5.59	5.57	5.51	5.44	5.39	5.37	5.35	5.37	5.50	5.58	5.60	5.60
1959	5.60	5.59	5.58	5.59	5.64	5.71	5.75	5.81	-	-	6.23	6.23
1960	6.25	6.23	6.22	6.21	6.20	6.19	6.17	6.14	6.11	6.09	6.07	6.04
1961	6.02	5.86	5.80	5.77	-	-	5.68	5.68	5.69	5.70	5.70	5.69
1962	5.69	5.68	5.65	5.64	5.60	5.59	5.58	5.57	5.56	5.55	5.54	5.53
1963	5.52	5.48	5.47	5.46	5.45	5.45	5.45	5.45	5.45	5.45	5.45	5.45
1964	5.45	5.45	5.45	5.45	5.45	5.45	5.46	5.46	5.45	5.45	5.45	5.45
1965	5.45	5.45	5.45	5.45	5.45	5.44	5.44	5.45	5.46	5.49	5.51	5.62
1966	5.70	-	6.00	-	6.32	6.45	6.51	6.58	6.63	-	6.81	6.77
1967	6.62	6.46	6.35	6.29	6.44	6.51	6.53	6.60	6.63	6.65	6.77	6.81
1968	6.81	6.78	6.83	6.94	-	7.52	7.42	7.35	7.28	7.29	7.36	7.50
1969	-	7.99	8.05	8.06	8.06	8.35	8.36	8.36	8.40	8.48	8.48	8.62
1970	-	9.29	9.20	9.10	9.11	9.16	9.11	9.07	9.01	8.97	8.90	8.40
1971	-	-	7.32	7.37	7.75	7.89	7.97	7.92	7.84	7.75	7.62	7.59
1972	7.49	7.46	7.45	7.50	7.53	7.54	7.54	7.55	7.56	7.57	7.57	7.56
1973	7.55	7.56	7.63	7.73	7.79	7.89	8.19	-	9.18	8.97	8.86	8.78
1974	-	8.54	8.66	9.17	9.46	9.46	9.85	10.30	10.38	10.13	-	9.51
1975	8.99	8.84	8.69	-	9.16	9.06	9.13	9.32	9.74	9.53	9.41	9.32
1976	9.06	9.04	-	8.82	9.03	9.05	8.99	8.93	8.82	8.55	8.45	8.28
1977	8.45	8.55	8.65	8.64	-	8.77	8.77	8.77	8.74	8.81	8.81	8.96
1978	9.18	-	9.35	9.44	9.74	-	9.96	9.81	9.81	9.98	10.04	10.23
1979	10.24	10.24	10.26	-	10.61	10.49	10.46	10.58	11.37	-	12.41	12.24
1980	12.60	-	14.63	13.45	11.99	11.85	12.39	13.54	14.26	14.38	14.47	14.08
1981	14.23	14.79	15.04	15.91	16.33	16.31	16.76	17.96	18.55	17.43	15.98	16.43
1982	17.38	17.10	16.41	16.31	16.19	16.73	16.29	14.61	14.03	12.99	12.82	12.80
1983	12.87	12.65	12.68	12.50	12.41	12.96	14.23	13.78	13.55	13.23	13.23	13.25
1984	13.08	13.20	13.68	13.80	15.01	14.91	14.58	14.21	13.99	13.43	12.90	12.99
1985	13.01	13.27	13.43	12.97	12.28	11.89	12.12	11.99	12.04	11.87	11.28	10.70
1986	10.78	10.59	9.77	9.80	10.07	9.98	10.01	9.80	9.90	9.80	9.26	9.21
1987	8.79	8.81	8.94	10.02	10.61	10.33	10.38	10.55	11.22	10.90	10.76	10.63
1988	10.17	9.86	10.28	10.46	10.84	10.65	10.66	10.74	10.58	10.23	10.63	10.81
1989	10.69	10.88	11.16	10.88	10.55	10.08	9.61	9.95	9.94	9.73	9.69	9.72
1990	10.01	10.22	10.30	10.75	10.23	10.18	10.11	10.28	10.24	10.23	9.81	9.66
1991	9.58	9.57	9.61	9.61	9.62	9.71	9.59	9.14	9.06	8.71	8.69	8.10
1992	8.72	8.74	8.85	8.79	8.66	8.56	8.12	8.08	8.06	8.29	8.54	8.12
1993	8.04	7.55	7.57	7.56	7.59	7.52	7.51	7.02	7.03	7.08	-	-

Source: U.S. Department of Housing and Urban Development, Federal Housing Administration. - indicates data not available or zero.

Commercial and Industrial Loans Outstanding
(Million $)

Year	Jan	Feb	Mar	Apr	May	Jun	Jul	Aug	Sep	Oct	Nov	Dec
1945	6,511	6,388	6,283	6,268	6,256	6,410	6,454	6,434	6,487	6,498	6,715	7,147
1946	7,364	7,430	7,621	7,864	8,047	8,211	8,614	9,074	9,443	9,863	10,134	10,260
1947	10,475	10,713	11,149	11,506	11,592	11,639	11,770	12,019	12,250	12,548	12,904	13,158
1948	13,417	13,358	13,371	13,473	13,834	14,065	14,385	14,507	14,461	14,356	14,196	14,087
1949	14,055	13,979	13,861	13,605	13,409	13,163	12,833	12,660	12,641	12,670	12,604	12,573
1950	12,677	12,764	12,763	12,849	12,936	13,242	13,619	14,057	14,696	15,027	15,462	15,986
1951	16,503	17,116	17,579	18,079	18,453	18,646	18,757	18,865	18,968	19,111	19,194	19,411
1952	19,632	19,641	19,761	19,742	19,809	19,969	20,141	20,190	20,381	20,650	21,031	21,133
1953	21,227	21,277	21,430	21,675	21,816	21,747	21,778	21,934	21,819	21,640	21,451	21,058
1954	21,000	21,064	21,036	20,967	20,811	20,650	20,651	19,804	19,753	19,718	19,955	20,314
1955	20,529	20,692	20,916	21,049	21,416	21,796	22,244	22,664	22,977	23,421	23,771	24,110
1956	24,515	24,686	25,414	25,932	26,448	26,799	27,145	27,418	27,778	27,858	28,199	28,395
1957	28,695	28,720	29,182	29,503	29,650	30,033	30,245	30,285	30,374	29,969	29,573	29,517
1958	29,171	28,835	28,728	28,554	28,168	28,079	28,039	27,941	28,122	28,215	28,342	28,496
1959	28,567	28,583	28,820	29,092	29,573	30,042	30,026	30,456	30,646	30,915	31,076	31,288
1960	31,433	31,870	32,093	32,293	32,591	33,011	32,993	32,840	32,956	32,996	33,118	33,018
1961	32,999	32,966	33,111	33,079	33,020	32,955	33,012	33,131	33,214	33,215	33,280	33,429
1962	33,582	33,712	33,907	34,121	34,269	34,509	34,740	35,038	35,318	35,635	35,939	35,986
1963	36,039	36,126	36,251	36,458	36,626	36,740	36,872	37,047	37,341	37,821	38,579	39,045
1964	38,931	39,195	39,201	39,554	39,882	40,137	40,428	40,839	41,418	41,625	42,068	42,737
1965	43,562	44,618	45,563	46,203	47,209	47,718	48,072	49,139	50,141	50,812	51,650	52,300
1966	53,195	54,071	54,805	55,377	56,139	57,228	58,223	59,360	59,950	60,578	61,043	61,332
1967	61,876	62,404	63,100	63,598	63,998	64,682	65,083	64,862	65,155	65,644	66,161	67,068
1968	67,254	67,415	67,732	68,877	69,067	69,598	70,294	71,359	72,318	73,153	74,374	75,150
1969	77,048	77,843	79,091	81,132	82,277	83,502	83,909	85,141	86,404	87,358	88,070	89,059
1970	88,521	90,023	91,243	91,333	91,864	92,444	92,433	93,072	93,435	91,680	91,082	91,069
1971	90,944	91,625	91,904	90,891	91,662	90,706	89,951	91,627	93,437	92,465	92,301	91,788
1972	84,478	85,260	86,195	87,342	87,906	88,268	88,429	88,800	88,593	90,502	91,408	92,111
1973	94,279	98,034	100,124	101,768	103,074	105,166	106,581	108,505	108,458	109,664	110,877	111,764
1974	113,967	116,322	117,738	122,857	125,111	126,537	130,706	133,304	137,429	138,352	139,734	139,873
1975	140,652	139,605	138,152	136,564	133,750	131,397	130,713	129,579	128,146	126,999	126,131	126,245
1976	125,349	125,758	123,490	120,789	121,069	122,018	121,328	121,083	120,710	121,770	123,317	124,225
1977	124,450	125,824	126,179	126,925	127,740	128,990	128,860	130,214	130,848	132,174	133,272	134,372
1978	135,158	135,658	138,536	140,620	143,029	145,547	146,937	147,792	148,769	150,501	152,486	152,870
1979	155,975	158,341	160,335	165,793	168,229	171,623	175,320	179,017	183,790	184,399	183,394	186,443
1980	193,068	197,288	200,406	200,583	198,756	202,454	200,910	201,732	203,417	204,727	209,253	211,014
1981	213,016	213,391	211,676	215,581	221,279	225,515	229,664	234,814	238,847	241,377	244,824	247,853
1982	254,693	259,934	261,328	266,688	271,022	272,899	273,160	273,540	274,885	274,856	270,235	264,699
1983	268,553	268,582	269,450	265,604	261,465	262,099	261,703	262,875	262,747	261,829	263,187	267,368
1984	274,768	279,364	287,370	294,220	300,525	310,036	314,375	317,394	321,437	325,648	328,615	329,459
1985	329,668	332,412	334,670	335,158	338,108	336,876	339,378	340,740	339,599	343,857	347,028	348,859
1986	351,101	349,392	347,888	342,642	345,052	345,978	347,464	351,931	351,008	352,769	353,255	358,781
1987	366,490	364,936	363,447	363,216	362,718	363,766	362,668	359,989	363,258	366,003	364,818	367,421
1988	370,404	376,230	378,102	385,023	386,242	389,311	392,952	394,400	393,894	398,229	400,633	405,656
1989	410,798	419,879	422,227	426,196	436,174	438,737	442,802	449,522	449,030	450,999	451,652	450,627
1990	452,020	456,952	465,646	465,880	464,376	465,489	468,761	471,688	478,273	477,168	470,085	469,063
1991	468,274	464,047	466,609	460,080	454,832	451,353	451,427	440,499	437,003	433,938	432,212	429,643
1992	425,399	427,442	426,361	424,890	422,012	419,146	419,892	419,552	418,839	424,762	429,631	429,532
1993	423,626	425,667	419,309	422,460	425,860	426,364	432,189	430,417	429,528	430,785	-	-

Source: U.S. Department of Commerce, Bureau of Economic Analysis, Board of Governors of the Federal Reserve System, Citibank and U.S. Department of the Treasury. - indicates data not available or zero.

CHAPTER 5

ECONOMIC SERIES

ECONOMIC SERIES

The 21 series in this chapter are classified as "important economic measures" by the Department of Commerce. They are not cyclic indicators but measure other aspects of the economy. The series are grouped under four headings:

Savings
Producer Prices, Wages, and Productivity
Implicit Price Deflators for Gross Domestic Product Sectors
Labor and Employment
International Transactions

The section on implicit price deflators for GDP is a new feature of this edition aimed at providing better data to the user for calculating inflationary pressures on personal or institutional income.

A brief introduction to each of these sections provides a description of each series covered and some discussion of the analytical uses of each series.

All of the series shown are reported regularly in the *Survey of Current Business*, a monthly publication of the U.S. Department of Commerce.

Bibliography

1. Fischer, Stanley, Rudiger Dornbusch, and Richard Schmalensee. *Introduction to Macroeconomics*. McGraw-Hill Book Company, New York, 1988.

2. Fitch, Thomas P. *Dictionary of Banking Terms*. Barron's, New York, 1990.

3. Siegel, Barry N. *Money, Banking, and the Economy*. Academic Press, New York, 1982.

3. U.S. Department of Commerce, Bureau of Economic Analysis. *Survey of Current Business*. Superintendent of Documents, U.S. Government Printing Office, Washington, DC 20302.

INDICATORS OF SAVINGS

This section presents 5 series used to measure the nation's savings rate. The series presented are:

    Gross saving
    Personal saving
    Personal saving rate
    Government surplus or deficit

In the aggregate, savings taken as a total are an indirect indicator of the nation's capacity to invest in future productive facilities. Business and personal savings create the pool of capital available for new housing, infrastructure, tooling, factories, etc.—investment. These private sources of savings are diminished by government deficits and increased by foreign investment in the United States.

Gross Saving. Data for 1946 through 1993 are shown on a quarterly, annualized basis in billions of current dollars. The series is made up of personal savings plus business savings plus less (currently) government deficits at the federal, state, and local levels.

Business Saving. Presented as billions of current dollars for 1946 through 1993 in quarterly, annualized values, business savings is a complex category made up of the following components:

    Undistributed corporate profits
    Corporate capital consumption allowances
    Noncorporate capital consumption allowances
    Wage accruals less disbursements

Corporate profits are adjusted for inventory valuation changes and capital consumption adjustments. Noncorporate capital consumption allowances are also adjusted. The sum of these values combines into savings carried by the business sector from one period into another.

Personal Saving and **Personal Saving Rate**. Data for Personal saving are presented in the same format as Gross and Business saving; Personal saving rate is shown in percent. Personal saving is derived by deducting taxes from personal income, yielding disposable personal income (DPI); personal expenditures are deducted from DPI to obtain personal saving. Personal saving as a percent of DPI is the Personal saving rate. In the first quarter of 1993, this value was 3.9 percent; the highest rate shown in the data was the 2nd quarter of 1975 (10.5%—after a recession) and, before that, in the first quarter of 1946 (11.0%). The saving rate rarely reaches double digits in the United States; in Japan and some European countries, a high double-digit saving rate is the rule rather than the exception.

Government Surplus or Deficit. Data show quarterly values, in billions of current dollars, for 1946 through 1993. In recent years, the government has run large deficits; since deficits are financed from savings, deficits reduce total resources available for investment; the government competes with private users of capital for funds. However, if government deficits were erased by higher taxes, the net result would be largely the same: personal and business savings are income *net* of taxes; therefore higher taxes would also reduce gross savings.

Gross Saving
(Annual Rate, Billions of $)

Year	1st Quarter	2nd Quarter	3rd Quarter	4th Quarter
1946	27.3	36.0	38.6	40.0
1947	42.9	40.3	40.8	46.0
1948	50.4	53.2	52.0	51.3
1949	43.2	35.2	36.2	31.8
1950	40.1	47.7	53.4	64.5
1951	58.7	61.8	57.4	55.2
1952	56.3	49.7	51.6	53.7
1953	54.0	53.9	53.7	47.1
1954	48.7	49.1	51.7	57.1
1955	62.2	67.1	69.5	74.0
1956	75.5	76.7	78.9	79.7
1957	79.3	79.9	79.5	70.4
1958	65.3	60.7	66.0	73.9
1959	77.5	84.2	75.8	80.1
1960	92.6	85.3	84.1	78.5
1961	78.2	81.5	87.3	90.5
1962	92.6	92.3	93.3	93.1
1963	96.3	101.0	99.5	104.7
1964	106.5	106.4	110.2	116.8
1965	124.5	125.9	124.4	125.1
1966	130.6	131.4	129.7	134.5
1967	127.4	125.0	131.9	138.7
1968	136.1	140.8	141.5	148.5
1969	154.2	157.0	163.7	163.1
1970	155.4	157.7	156.2	151.5
1971	167.2	170.8	176.0	180.9
1972	187.3	194.0	203.7	221.7
1973	234.9	241.9	253.5	278.9
1974	255.5	246.5	246.0	249.9
1975	224.1	225.6	252.4	263.6
1976	279.7	287.6	284.9	286.9
1977	299.7	332.3	364.2	356.6
1978	370.3	413.7	426.6	452.3
1979	463.9	470.7	470.8	468.4
1980	465.1	443.0	453.4	500.3
1981	541.1	539.9	579.3	566.2
1982	519.6	542.0	513.4	458.5
1983	476.1	493.3	494.4	542.4
1984	611.0	635.4	652.3	637.0
1985	625.7	619.9	592.1	603.8
1986	625.8	584.4	538.2	550.1
1987	588.2	600.1	619.7	667.9
1988	678.0	701.5	716.5	720.1
1989	760.6	749.4	728.9	728.4
1990	735.5	765.9	705.5	683.8
1991	780.3	734.3	694.4	726.0
1992	709.9	715.5	727.0	718.8
1993	762.0	766.7	774.0	-

Source: U.S. Department of Commerce, Bureau of Economic Analysis. - indicates data not available or zero.

Business Saving
(Annual Rate, Billions of $)

Year	1st Quarter	2nd Quarter	3rd Quarter	4th Quarter
1946	15.6	17.1	16.3	17.9
1947	19.0	23.6	24.2	25.7
1948	29.4	31.4	31.5	33.7
1949	33.7	33.1	34.1	30.9
1950	30.1	31.4	32.5	34.3
1951	31.1	35.5	38.8	39.2
1952	39.3	38.1	38.3	40.9
1953	41.2	40.1	40.1	38.1
1954	40.4	42.1	42.9	45.4
1955	48.2	49.5	49.6	50.4
1956	50.1	50.4	51.9	51.8
1957	53.7	54.0	54.5	53.3
1958	50.6	51.4	53.9	57.5
1959	59.4	62.2	59.6	60.6
1960	62.3	60.7	60.9	59.9
1961	59.4	62.4	63.3	64.9
1962	69.2	68.7	69.6	72.0
1963	72.1	73.8	74.9	75.7
1964	79.5	79.5	80.5	80.4
1965	87.2	88.4	89.4	91.7
1966	94.6	95.5	95.3	99.1
1967	97.3	96.8	98.6	102.1
1968	98.8	102.4	103.3	105.5
1969	106.8	106.4	107.2	104.5
1970	103.5	110.0	110.3	109.2
1971	120.5	123.6	128.2	133.3
1972	137.7	146.7	146.0	151.3
1973	156.3	157.5	160.5	163.1
1974	160.2	161.8	158.8	169.4
1975	186.0	200.5	214.5	223.2
1976	228.9	227.5	230.2	233.7
1977	244.0	265.4	280.1	278.9
1978	282.3	302.0	311.9	323.9
1979	321.7	331.6	340.5	344.3
1980	338.0	337.1	346.3	361.7
1981	374.9	383.6	404.4	413.4
1982	400.8	413.7	423.6	431.7
1983	447.8	463.9	476.7	502.4
1984	501.0	514.9	524.9	542.1
1985	528.5	542.4	559.2	555.5
1986	551.5	531.0	527.9	525.3
1987	557.7	582.4	600.7	613.9
1988	638.4	645.1	644.6	658.4
1989	644.7	662.5	682.1	679.8
1990	690.9	712.9	673.9	686.9
1991	717.9	728.9	719.8	746.9
1992	756.6	749.8	796.9	769.7
1993	766.9	779.6	808.1	-

Source: U.S. Department of Commerce, Bureau of Economic Analysis. - indicates data not available or zero.

Personal Saving

(Annual Rate, Billions of $)

Year	1st Quarter	2nd Quarter	3rd Quarter	4th Quarter
1946	16.8	15.2	11.7	10.6
1947	8.0	2.0	6.0	4.1
1948	6.6	10.3	13.8	12.7
1949	8.7	6.4	6.9	6.0
1950	16.5	12.2	5.8	14.5
1951	9.9	19.4	18.8	18.2
1952	17.4	15.7	19.4	16.4
1953	16.7	18.8	18.1	18.6
1954	18.6	15.3	15.0	16.0
1955	14.2	15.3	17.1	17.0
1956	18.8	21.2	22.1	23.1
1957	21.8	23.6	23.3	21.9
1958	22.7	22.4	25.0	26.1
1959	22.8	24.0	19.6	21.7
1960	22.2	19.5	20.9	19.8
1961	22.6	23.2	26.6	27.3
1962	27.1	26.6	26.0	23.7
1963	24.1	24.1	23.1	27.3
1964	27.8	32.1	30.7	35.5
1965	31.2	32.4	38.4	36.4
1966	34.0	34.2	36.0	41.2
1967	45.3	43.0	46.4	48.6
1968	46.1	48.2	39.1	42.0
1969	35.5	38.5	49.0	50.3
1970	48.9	57.4	60.9	62.9
1971	63.8	68.4	67.1	62.3
1972	56.7	51.0	58.7	72.6
1973	72.1	79.7	85.3	107.3
1974	98.3	84.2	88.7	102.4
1975	84.5	121.3	95.0	100.3
1976	97.4	95.7	92.6	86.4
1977	73.4	83.9	100.7	93.7
1978	102.6	102.3	109.4	116.7
1979	119.7	122.5	123.9	127.2
1980	141.8	145.8	152.8	175.0
1981	179.7	176.1	199.1	212.3
1982	191.3	213.5	209.3	183.8
1983	179.2	159.2	160.0	176.3
1984	217.4	213.1	234.8	222.6
1985	190.5	228.8	158.6	179.2
1986	199.3	225.1	174.4	151.1
1987	184.5	98.5	115.2	169.8
1988	162.0	151.8	152.4	156.4
1989	182.0	148.5	129.0	148.8
1990	176.5	175.7	151.6	176.2
1991	201.5	206.0	186.8	211.7
1992	217.5	237.9	219.6	279.7
1993	177.9	208.7	176.4	-

Source: U.S. Department of Commerce, Bureau of Economic Analysis. - indicates data not available or zero.

Personal Saving Rate
(Percent)

Year	1st Quarter	2nd Quarter	3rd Quarter	4th Quarter
1946	11.0	9.7	7.2	6.4
1947	4.8	1.2	3.5	2.4
1948	3.7	5.5	7.1	6.6
1949	4.6	3.4	3.7	3.2
1950	8.2	6.0	2.8	6.7
1951	4.4	8.5	8.2	7.8
1952	7.5	6.7	8.0	6.6
1953	6.6	7.3	7.1	7.2
1954	7.2	5.9	5.8	6.0
1955	5.3	5.5	6.0	5.9
1956	6.4	7.1	7.3	7.5
1957	7.0	7.5	7.3	6.9
1958	7.1	7.0	7.6	7.8
1959	6.7	6.9	5.6	6.2
1960	6.2	5.4	5.8	5.5
1961	6.2	6.2	7.0	7.0
1962	6.9	6.7	6.5	5.9
1963	5.9	5.8	5.5	6.4
1964	6.3	7.1	6.7	7.6
1965	6.6	6.7	7.7	7.1
1966	6.6	6.5	6.7	7.6
1967	8.2	7.6	8.1	8.3
1968	7.7	7.8	6.3	6.6
1969	5.6	5.9	7.3	7.3
1970	7.0	8.0	8.3	8.5
1971	8.4	8.8	8.5	7.7
1972	6.9	6.1	6.9	8.1
1973	7.9	8.5	8.8	10.7
1974	9.7	8.2	8.4	9.5
1975	7.8	10.5	8.2	8.4
1976	7.9	7.7	7.3	6.6
1977	5.5	6.1	7.1	6.5
1978	6.9	6.6	6.9	7.1
1979	7.1	7.1	7.0	7.0
1980	7.5	7.7	7.8	8.5
1981	8.5	8.2	9.0	9.5
1982	8.5	9.3	8.9	7.7
1983	7.4	6.5	6.4	6.8
1984	8.1	7.8	8.4	7.9
1985	6.7	7.8	5.4	6.0
1986	6.5	7.2	5.5	4.8
1987	5.7	3.1	3.5	5.0
1988	4.7	4.3	4.3	4.3
1989	4.9	4.0	3.4	3.9
1990	4.4	4.4	3.7	4.3
1991	4.8	4.9	4.4	4.9
1992	5.0	5.3	4.9	6.0
1993	3.9	4.4	3.7	-

Source: U.S. Department of Commerce, Bureau of Economic Analysis. - indicates data not available or zero.

Government Surplus or Deficit
(Annual Rate, Billions of $)

Year	1st Quarter	2nd Quarter	3rd Quarter	4th Quarter
1946	-5.8	4.6	10.6	11.5
1947	16.0	14.7	10.6	16.2
1948	14.3	11.3	7.0	4.9
1949	0.7	-3.9	-4.8	-5.1
1950	-6.5	4.0	15.0	15.7
1951	17.6	7.0	-0.2	-2.2
1952	-0.5	-4.2	-5.7	-3.5
1953	-3.8	-5.0	-4.5	-9.6
1954	-10.3	-8.3	-6.2	-4.2
1955	-0.1	2.3	2.8	6.6
1956	6.6	5.1	5.0	4.8
1957	3.9	2.4	1.8	-4.9
1958	-8.0	-13.2	-12.8	-9.7
1959	-4.8	-2.0	-3.3	-2.2
1960	8.1	5.1	2.3	-1.2
1961	-3.8	-4.0	-2.6	-1.7
1962	-3.7	-3.0	-2.3	-2.7
1963	0.2	3.0	1.5	1.7
1964	-0.9	-5.3	-1.0	0.9
1965	6.1	5.1	-3.3	-2.9
1966	2.0	1.9	-1.7	-5.9
1967	-15.2	-14.8	-13.0	-12.0
1968	-8.9	-9.7	-0.8	1.0
1969	12.0	12.1	7.5	8.4
1970	2.1	-10.6	-15.8	-21.5
1971	-17.9	-22.2	-20.4	-16.4
1972	-7.0	-4.2	-1.4	-2.9
1973	6.5	4.8	7.7	8.5
1974	5.0	0.6	-1.5	-21.9
1975	-46.3	-96.2	-57.0	-59.8
1976	-46.6	-35.5	-37.9	-33.2
1977	-17.7	-16.9	-16.5	-16.0
1978	-14.5	9.4	5.3	11.6
1979	21.3	15.5	5.3	-4.3
1980	-15.9	-41.1	-47.3	-36.9
1981	-14.6	-20.9	-25.1	-60.7
1982	-72.6	-85.2	-119.6	-156.9
1983	-150.8	-129.8	-142.3	-136.3
1984	-107.5	-92.6	-107.4	-127.8
1985	-93.4	-151.2	-125.7	-130.9
1986	-125.0	-171.7	-164.2	-126.2
1987	-154.0	-80.7	-96.2	-115.8
1988	-122.4	-95.5	-80.5	-94.7
1989	-66.1	-61.5	-82.3	-100.2
1990	-131.9	-122.7	-119.9	-179.3
1991	-139.1	-200.7	-212.2	-232.6
1992	-264.2	-272.2	-289.5	-250.6
1993	-262.8	-221.5	-210.6	-

Source: U.S. Department of Commerce, Bureau of Economic Analysis. - indicates data not available or zero.

INDICATORS OF PRODUCER PRICES, WAGES, AND PRODUCTIVITY

This section presents 8 series used to measure the nation's inflation rate, prices, and output. The series presented are:

Producer Price Index, crude materials for further processing
Producer Price Index, intermediate materials, supplies, and components
Producer Price Index, capital equipment
Producer Price Index, finished consumer goods
Producer Price Index, finished goods
Producer Price Index, finished goods less food and energy
Index of output per hour, all persons, business sector

Conspicuous by absence, perhaps, is the *Consumer Price Index*. It is presented in the next chapter in considerable detail. Similarly, much more detailed statistics are presented on the *Producer Price Index*, a summary of which is presented later in this section.

Producer Price Index Series. All six tables are indexes based on 1987 (1987 = 100). Detailed PPI tables are presented in the next chapter. The tables included in this section are summary series showing broad categories. Production processes refine crude raw materials (ores, logs, crude oil) into intermediate products (steel, pulp, engine blocks); intermediate products are transformed into finished products (autos, writing paper, gasoline). The tables included follow price trends at each of these levels. The data are used in a variety of ways in macroeconomic analysis and in business planning. For example, note that the inflation rate shown by the PPI for crude and intermediate materials is substantially less than it is for finished goods; at lower levels of refinement and product differentiation, competitive forces are greater (the "stuff" handled is more of a commodity); as raw materials are formed into products, differentiation increases and opportunities for aggressive pricing are greater.

Index of Output Per Hour, All Persons, Business Sector. Data are shown from 1947 to 1993 in quarterly increments as an index based on 1987 (1987 = 100). This is an indicator of national productivity. Output per hour reflects all inputs to the production process, including tooling, fuels, improved raw materials, degree of capacity utilization . . . *and* human effort, measured in time. The indicator, therefore, is influenced by the personal productivity of employees but also, more importantly in today's environment, by technology and therefore by the level of investment. Rising productivity means that more is produced, in absolute terms, by one hour of labor. It does not mean that employment is increasing; it may be decreasing as better machines take over human tasks. Rising productivity may also mean that the capital required per workplace is on the increase. The series, therefore, yields best results when viewed in concert with other series on wages, employment, capacity utilization, and investment.

Producer Price Index
Crude materials
(1982 = 100)

Year	Jan	Feb	Mar	Apr	May	Jun	Jul	Aug	Sep	Oct	Nov	Dec
1947	-	-	-	30.7	30.5	30.6	31.1	31.6	32.4	33.6	33.8	35.3
1948	36.3	34.4	33.5	34.2	35.3	36.2	36.0	35.5	34.8	33.8	33.5	33.0
1949	32.0	31.0	30.7	30.2	30.1	29.7	29.2	29.2	29.5	29.5	29.7	29.7
1950	29.6	30.5	30.3	30.5	31.6	32.1	33.3	34.0	34.5	34.5	35.4	36.7
1951	38.1	39.6	39.1	39.1	38.5	38.1	36.7	36.2	35.9	36.7	36.4	36.5
1952	35.8	35.5	35.0	34.9	34.8	34.7	34.6	34.7	33.9	33.7	33.7	32.9
1953	32.6	32.4	32.5	31.6	31.9	31.4	32.4	31.7	32.0	31.4	31.2	31.7
1954	32.1	32.0	32.1	32.2	32.1	31.5	31.4	31.3	31.0	31.2	31.4	30.9
1955	31.1	31.0	30.7	30.9	30.1	30.7	30.4	30.1	30.5	30.4	29.4	29.5
1956	29.5	29.9	29.8	30.3	30.7	30.5	30.5	31.0	31.0	31.0	31.1	31.6
1957	31.3	31.0	30.8	30.8	30.7	31.5	32.0	32.1	31.2	31.0	31.1	31.5
1958	31.4	31.9	32.3	31.9	32.4	32.0	32.1	31.9	31.7	31.9	32.1	31.6
1959	31.6	31.4	31.5	31.7	31.5	31.3	31.0	30.7	30.9	30.7	30.5	30.4
1960	30.4	30.4	30.7	30.7	30.8	30.5	30.4	29.8	30.0	30.2	30.2	30.3
1961	30.4	30.5	30.3	30.2	29.9	29.4	29.7	30.5	30.2	30.3	30.2	30.6
1962	30.6	30.6	30.5	30.1	30.1	30.0	30.2	30.5	31.2	30.8	31.0	30.7
1963	30.3	30.0	29.5	29.7	29.6	29.9	30.0	29.9	29.8	30.0	30.2	29.4
1964	29.8	29.4	29.5	29.5	29.4	29.1	29.2	29.4	30.1	29.8	29.9	29.8
1965	29.5	29.9	30.0	30.4	30.8	31.6	31.2	31.5	31.4	31.7	32.1	32.7
1966	33.0	33.7	33.5	33.3	33.1	33.0	33.4	33.6	33.4	32.9	32.3	32.0
1967	32.2	31.5	31.1	30.7	31.1	31.4	31.3	31.3	31.2	31.3	31.1	31.5
1968	31.4	31.5	31.6	31.7	31.5	31.3	31.6	31.7	31.9	32.1	32.8	32.4
1969	32.6	32.3	32.7	33.1	34.0	34.5	34.1	34.4	34.4	34.8	35.2	35.1
1970	35.1	35.2	35.6	35.5	35.0	35.0	35.1	34.7	35.5	35.5	35.1	34.5
1971	34.8	35.9	35.4	36.0	36.0	36.2	35.9	35.8	35.7	36.4	37.0	37.2
1972	37.8	38.1	38.1	38.7	39.3	39.4	40.0	40.3	40.5	40.9	42.0	43.8
1973	45.0	47.1	49.3	50.1	52.5	55.0	52.5	64.1	60.9	58.5	59.0	59.1
1974	63.3	64.3	62.3	60.6	58.3	55.4	59.8	62.9	60.9	63.2	64.2	61.5
1975	59.6	57.9	57.1	59.5	61.2	61.5	62.4	63.0	64.5	65.1	64.4	64.0
1976	63.0	62.1	61.5	63.9	63.6	65.2	64.8	63.6	63.4	63.0	63.4	64.5
1977	64.3	65.7	66.6	68.3	67.6	65.5	64.7	63.9	63.7	64.0	65.4	66.4
1978	67.3	68.4	69.8	72.1	72.8	74.6	74.2	73.7	75.1	77.0	77.4	78.0
1979	80.1	82.1	83.8	84.4	84.7	85.6	86.5	85.5	87.9	88.8	90.0	91.2
1980	90.9	92.6	90.8	88.3	89.5	90.1	94.6	99.0	100.4	102.2	103.5	102.7
1981	103.4	104.2	103.8	104.2	103.8	104.9	105.0	104.0	102.7	101.2	99.7	98.8
1982	99.7	100.0	99.7	100.2	101.9	101.8	100.7	99.8	99.2	98.7	99.2	98.8
1983	98.8	100.0	100.5	101.2	100.9	100.5	99.5	102.2	103.3	103.2	102.3	103.5
1984	104.6	103.8	105.7	105.2	104.5	103.3	104.0	103.3	102.8	101.5	101.9	101.4
1985	99.9	99.4	97.6	96.7	95.8	95.2	94.9	92.9	91.8	94.1	95.7	95.5
1986	94.2	90.5	88.2	85.6	86.5	86.2	86.4	86.7	86.6	87.4	87.6	86.9
1987	89.3	90.2	90.5	92.5	93.8	94.5	95.6	96.5	96.0	95.8	95.1	94.9
1988	94.2	95.2	94.1	95.4	95.8	97.0	96.7	97.0	97.0	96.6	95.2	98.1
1989	102.0	101.7	102.9	104.1	104.6	103.3	103.5	101.3	102.5	102.7	103.5	104.9
1990	107.1	107.0	105.1	102.6	103.2	100.4	100.9	110.3	115.7	125.5	117.7	111.3
1991	113.3	104.4	100.6	100.3	100.9	99.1	99.2	99.2	98.3	100.5	100.6	98.4
1992	97.3	98.8	97.1	98.1	100.1	101.5	101.6	100.9	103.0	102.7	102.6	101.5
1993	101.8	101.6	101.8	103.3	105.4	103.7	102.5	102.0	101.6	103.0	-	-

Source: U.S. Department of Labor, Bureau of Labor Statistics. - indicates data not available or zero.

Producer Price Index
Intermediate materials
(1982 = 100)

Year	Jan	Feb	Mar	Apr	May	Jun	Jul	Aug	Sep	Oct	Nov	Dec
1947	-	-	-	23.1	23.0	23.1	23.2	23.3	23.7	23.9	24.2	24.5
1948	25.0	24.7	24.8	25.0	25.2	25.4	25.4	25.5	25.5	25.4	25.4	25.2
1949	25.1	24.9	24.7	24.4	24.3	24.1	24.1	23.9	23.8	23.8	23.7	23.7
1950	23.8	24.0	24.1	24.2	24.6	24.7	25.2	25.6	26.2	26.6	26.9	27.7
1951	28.5	28.7	28.8	28.8	28.8	28.7	28.4	28.0	27.9	27.9	27.9	27.8
1952	27.8	27.7	27.5	27.5	27.4	27.5	27.5	27.5	27.6	27.5	27.4	27.3
1953	27.4	27.4	27.5	27.5	27.7	27.8	28.0	27.9	27.8	27.8	27.8	27.8
1954	27.9	27.8	27.8	27.9	27.9	27.8	27.9	27.8	27.8	27.8	27.9	27.8
1955	27.9	28.0	28.0	28.0	28.1	28.2	28.4	28.5	28.7	28.9	28.9	29.0
1956	29.1	29.1	29.4	29.5	29.6	29.7	29.4	29.7	29.8	30.0	30.0	30.1
1957	30.2	30.3	30.3	30.3	30.2	30.3	30.3	30.4	30.4	30.3	30.4	30.4
1958	30.4	30.3	30.3	30.3	30.3	30.3	30.3	30.4	30.4	30.4	30.5	30.6
1959	30.6	30.7	30.7	30.8	30.9	30.9	30.9	30.8	30.8	30.8	30.9	30.8
1960	30.9	30.9	30.9	30.9	30.8	30.9	30.8	30.8	30.8	30.8	30.7	30.6
1961	30.7	30.7	30.7	30.7	30.6	30.5	30.5	30.5	30.5	30.4	30.5	30.6
1962	30.5	30.5	30.6	30.6	30.6	30.6	30.6	30.6	30.6	30.6	30.5	30.5
1963	30.5	30.5	30.5	30.4	30.7	30.7	30.7	30.7	30.7	30.8	30.8	30.8
1964	30.8	30.8	30.7	30.7	30.7	30.6	30.7	30.7	30.7	30.9	30.9	30.9
1965	30.9	30.9	31.0	31.0	31.1	31.2	31.2	31.3	31.3	31.3	31.4	31.4
1966	31.5	31.6	31.7	31.8	32.0	32.0	32.2	32.3	32.3	32.2	32.2	32.2
1967	32.2	32.1	32.1	32.1	32.1	32.2	32.2	32.2	32.3	32.3	32.4	32.6
1968	32.6	32.7	32.8	32.8	32.8	32.9	33.0	33.0	33.1	33.2	33.2	33.4
1969	33.6	33.7	33.9	33.8	33.9	34.0	34.0	34.2	34.2	34.4	34.6	34.7
1970	35.0	35.0	34.9	35.1	35.2	35.3	35.5	35.5	35.6	35.8	35.9	35.9
1971	36.0	36.1	36.3	36.3	36.5	36.7	36.9	37.2	37.2	37.1	37.2	37.4
1972	37.5	37.7	37.8	37.9	38.0	38.0	38.1	38.2	38.5	38.7	39.0	39.6
1973	39.8	40.4	41.1	41.3	42.2	43.0	42.3	43.5	43.0	43.4	43.8	44.8
1974	45.9	46.8	48.1	49.0	50.6	51.5	53.4	55.8	55.9	57.2	57.8	57.8
1975	58.0	57.8	57.4	57.5	57.3	57.3	57.5	58.0	58.2	58.8	59.0	59.2
1976	59.4	59.6	59.8	60.0	60.3	60.8	61.1	61.3	61.9	62.0	62.4	62.8
1977	63.0	63.3	63.9	64.4	64.9	64.9	65.1	65.4	65.7	65.8	66.3	66.6
1978	66.9	67.4	67.8	68.1	68.7	69.2	69.4	69.9	70.5	71.3	71.9	72.4
1979	73.1	73.7	74.6	75.7	76.6	77.5	78.7	79.8	81.1	82.4	83.2	84.0
1980	86.0	87.6	88.2	88.5	89.0	89.8	90.5	91.5	91.9	92.8	93.5	94.4
1981	95.6	96.1	97.1	98.3	98.7	99.0	99.2	99.7	99.7	99.8	99.9	100.0
1982	100.4	100.3	99.9	99.7	99.7	99.8	100.0	99.9	100.0	99.9	100.1	100.1
1983	99.8	100.0	99.7	99.5	99.8	100.2	100.5	100.9	101.6	101.7	101.8	101.9
1984	102.1	102.5	103.0	103.2	103.4	103.6	103.4	103.2	103.1	103.2	103.3	103.2
1985	103.1	102.8	102.7	102.9	103.2	102.6	102.3	102.3	102.2	102.3	102.5	102.9
1986	102.4	101.2	99.9	98.9	98.7	98.6	98.0	98.0	98.5	98.3	98.3	98.5
1987	99.0	99.8	99.9	100.3	100.8	101.4	101.9	102.4	102.6	103.1	103.5	103.8
1988	104.1	104.4	104.8	105.5	106.2	107.4	108.3	108.5	108.7	108.6	108.8	109.4
1989	110.5	111.1	111.7	112.3	112.6	112.7	112.6	112.2	112.4	112.2	111.8	111.9
1990	113.2	112.6	112.6	112.7	112.9	113.2	113.3	114.6	116.3	117.5	117.5	116.5
1991	116.5	115.8	114.6	114.2	114.0	114.1	113.8	114.1	114.2	113.9	113.9	113.7
1992	113.2	113.8	113.9	114.1	114.5	115.3	115.3	115.3	115.5	115.2	114.9	114.9
1993	115.3	115.9	116.3	116.6	116.3	116.5	116.4	116.4	116.5	116.4	-	-

Source: U.S. Department of Labor, Bureau of Labor Statistics. - indicates data not available or zero.

Producer Price Index

Capital equipment

(1982 = 100)

Year	Jan	Feb	Mar	Apr	May	Jun	Jul	Aug	Sep	Oct	Nov	Dec
1947	-	-	-	19.5	19.8	19.9	19.9	20.0	20.1	20.3	20.4	20.5
1948	20.6	20.7	20.8	20.9	21.0	21.3	21.7	22.1	22.3	22.5	22.5	22.6
1949	22.6	22.8	22.8	22.9	22.8	22.8	22.8	22.7	22.5	22.5	22.5	22.5
1950	22.5	22.5	22.5	22.7	22.8	22.8	23.0	23.4	23.7	23.9	24.1	24.8
1951	25.1	25.2	25.4	25.5	25.6	25.6	25.6	25.5	25.6	25.7	25.7	25.7
1952	25.7	25.9	25.9	25.9	26.0	26.0	26.1	25.9	25.9	25.9	25.9	25.9
1953	25.9	25.9	26.0	26.1	26.2	26.4	26.6	26.5	26.6	26.6	26.4	26.5
1954	26.6	26.6	26.6	26.7	26.7	26.7	26.7	26.7	26.6	26.6	26.4	26.5
1955	26.8	26.9	26.9	27.0	27.1	27.2	27.3	27.6	27.9	28.2	28.1	28.3
1956	28.4	28.6	28.8	29.1	29.2	29.3	29.4	29.6	30.1	30.3	30.6	30.6
1957	30.7	30.9	31.0	31.1	31.1	31.2	31.4	31.5	31.6	31.7	31.9	32.0
1958	32.0	32.0	32.0	32.1	32.1	32.1	32.1	32.1	32.1	32.1	32.3	32.4
1959	32.5	32.5	32.6	32.7	32.8	32.9	32.9	32.9	32.9	32.9	32.7	32.7
1960	32.8	32.8	32.9	32.8	32.8	32.8	32.9	32.9	32.9	32.9	32.7	32.7
1961	32.9	32.8	32.9	32.9	32.9	32.9	32.9	32.9	32.9	32.6	32.8	32.8
1962	32.9	32.9	33.0	33.0	33.0	33.0	33.0	33.0	33.0	33.0	32.9	32.9
1963	33.0	33.0	33.0	33.0	33.0	33.0	33.0	33.0	33.0	33.0	33.0	33.0
1964	33.1	33.2	33.3	33.3	33.4	33.4	33.5	33.5	33.5	33.5	33.5	33.5
1965	33.6	33.6	33.7	33.8	33.7	33.8	33.8	33.9	33.9	33.9	33.9	34.0
1966	34.0	34.1	34.2	34.3	34.5	34.6	34.7	34.8	34.9	35.0	35.2	35.3
1967	35.4	35.5	35.5	35.6	35.7	35.7	35.8	35.9	35.9	36.1	36.2	36.4
1968	36.5	36.6	36.6	36.8	37.0	37.0	37.1	37.2	37.3	37.4	37.5	37.5
1969	37.6	37.7	37.8	37.9	38.0	38.1	38.3	38.4	38.5	38.7	39.0	39.2
1970	39.3	39.4	39.6	39.7	39.8	39.9	40.0	40.2	40.3	40.8	41.0	41.1
1971	41.3	41.4	41.5	41.6	41.7	41.7	41.9	42.0	41.9	41.8	41.8	42.1
1972	42.3	42.5	42.6	42.7	42.8	42.8	42.9	42.9	43.0	42.8	42.9	43.0
1973	43.0	43.3	43.6	43.8	44.1	44.2	44.3	44.4	44.6	44.7	44.9	45.3
1974	45.8	46.2	46.8	47.4	48.7	49.7	50.7	52.1	53.1	54.2	55.0	55.5
1975	56.2	56.7	57.2	57.5	57.8	58.0	58.4	58.5	58.9	59.3	59.7	60.0
1976	60.4	60.7	61.1	61.3	61.5	61.8	62.1	62.5	62.9	63.1	63.4	64.0
1977	64.0	64.3	64.7	65.0	65.3	65.7	66.0	66.6	67.0	67.6	68.1	68.6
1978	68.8	69.1	69.6	69.9	70.5	71.0	71.5	72.0	72.6	72.8	73.5	74.0
1979	74.5	75.2	75.7	76.4	76.8	77.3	77.8	77.8	78.7	79.2	79.8	80.6
1980	81.7	82.3	83.1	84.4	84.6	85.1	86.2	87.0	87.5	88.8	89.3	89.7
1981	90.8	91.7	92.4	93.1	93.8	94.4	95.0	95.4	96.1	96.9	97.5	98.1
1982	98.6	98.2	98.7	99.0	99.5	100.0	100.3	100.7	101.0	101.1	101.3	101.9
1983	101.8	102.1	102.2	102.3	102.5	102.6	102.8	103.1	103.3	103.4	103.5	103.8
1984	104.1	104.5	104.6	105.3	105.1	105.2	105.5	105.6	105.9	105.6	105.8	105.6
1985	106.3	106.9	107.1	107.1	107.4	107.6	107.7	107.9	107.2	108.3	108.5	108.6
1986	108.6	108.7	108.9	109.2	109.3	109.6	109.7	109.8	109.7	110.6	110.8	110.9
1987	111.3	111.1	111.1	111.6	111.6	111.5	111.7	112.0	112.0	112.0	112.1	112.2
1988	112.8	113.0	113.2	113.5	113.8	114.0	114.4	114.9	115.2	115.5	115.7	116.1
1989	116.9	117.3	117.5	117.6	118.3	118.9	118.9	119.3	119.8	120.0	120.4	120.6
1990	121.0	121.4	121.8	122.2	122.3	122.6	123.0	123.4	123.8	124.0	124.3	124.6
1991	125.7	125.9	126.1	126.2	126.6	126.7	126.8	126.9	127.1	127.3	127.5	127.7
1992	128.3	128.4	128.8	129.1	129.2	129.1	129.2	129.5	129.5	129.3	129.5	129.7
1993	130.4	130.8	131.1	131.3	131.4	131.2	131.6	131.9	131.9	131.4	-	-

Source: U.S. Department of Labor, Bureau of Labor Statistics. - indicates data not available or zero.

Producer Price Index
Finished consumer goods
(1982 = 100)

Year	Jan	Feb	Mar	Apr	May	Jun	Jul	Aug	Sep	Oct	Nov	Dec
1947	-	-	-	28.4	28.3	28.3	28.3	28.5	28.9	29.2	29.6	30.1
1948	30.7	30.5	30.5	30.7	30.9	31.0	31.1	31.2	31.0	30.9	30.6	30.4
1949	30.2	29.9	29.8	29.6	29.5	29.5	29.2	29.1	29.0	29.0	28.9	28.8
1950	28.8	28.9	28.9	28.9	29.1	29.2	29.8	30.4	30.7	30.8	31.1	31.7
1951	32.3	32.8	32.8	32.9	33.0	32.8	32.5	32.5	32.4	32.6	32.6	32.7
1952	32.5	32.5	32.5	32.4	32.3	32.2	32.4	32.4	32.2	32.1	32.0	31.7
1953	31.8	31.7	31.7	31.6	31.6	31.7	31.7	31.7	31.9	31.8	31.6	31.7
1954	31.9	31.7	31.7	31.9	31.9	31.7	31.8	31.7	31.5	31.5	31.6	31.5
1955	31.6	31.7	31.5	31.6	31.4	31.6	31.3	31.4	31.5	31.4	31.5	31.5
1956	31.5	31.5	31.7	31.7	32.0	32.1	32.0	32.0	32.2	32.2	32.4	32.5
1957	32.5	32.6	32.6	32.7	32.7	32.8	33.0	33.0	33.0	33.1	33.2	33.4
1958	33.5	33.5	33.9	33.7	33.8	33.7	33.6	33.6	33.6	33.5	33.5	33.5
1959	33.4	33.4	33.3	33.4	33.3	33.3	33.2	33.1	33.5	33.2	33.1	33.2
1960	33.2	33.2	33.5	33.6	33.6	33.6	33.7	33.7	33.7	33.9	34.0	33.9
1961	33.8	34.0	33.8	33.6	33.4	33.4	33.5	33.6	33.5	33.4	33.5	33.6
1962	33.7	33.8	33.7	33.6	33.6	33.5	33.5	33.7	34.0	33.7	33.7	33.6
1963	33.6	33.5	33.3	33.3	33.5	33.6	33.6	33.5	33.5	33.5	33.6	33.5
1964	33.7	33.5	33.5	33.5	33.5	33.5	33.6	33.6	33.6	33.6	33.6	33.6
1965	33.6	33.6	33.8	34.0	34.1	34.3	34.2	34.3	34.3	34.5	34.6	34.9
1966	34.9	35.2	35.3	35.4	35.2	35.1	35.2	35.7	35.8	35.7	35.6	35.5
1967	35.4	35.3	35.2	35.3	35.4	35.7	35.6	35.7	35.8	35.8	35.9	35.9
1968	35.9	36.1	36.2	36.4	36.4	36.5	36.6	36.7	36.9	37.0	37.0	37.0
1969	37.2	37.1	37.3	37.5	37.8	38.0	38.0	38.1	38.2	38.5	38.8	38.8
1970	39.0	38.9	39.0	39.0	38.9	39.0	39.0	39.0	39.4	39.3	39.5	39.4
1971	39.5	39.7	39.8	40.0	40.1	40.3	40.1	40.4	40.3	40.4	40.6	40.9
1972	40.7	40.9	40.9	40.9	41.1	41.4	41.6	41.7	42.0	41.9	42.1	42.6
1973	43.0	43.5	44.7	45.0	45.3	45.9	45.7	47.7	47.5	47.4	47.9	48.3
1974	49.6	50.7	51.1	51.5	52.0	51.8	53.2	54.1	54.6	55.6	56.7	56.6
1975	56.8	56.6	56.4	56.9	57.3	57.8	58.4	59.0	59.4	59.9	60.1	60.1
1976	59.9	59.6	59.6	60.0	60.0	60.1	60.3	60.4	60.5	60.9	61.4	61.9
1977	62.1	62.8	63.4	63.7	64.2	64.2	64.5	64.8	65.0	65.3	65.8	66.1
1978	66.4	66.9	67.3	68.2	68.6	69.3	69.9	69.9	70.6	71.0	71.5	72.5
1979	73.3	74.2	74.8	75.6	75.9	76.4	77.3	78.3	79.8	80.6	81.8	82.6
1980	83.9	85.2	86.1	86.7	87.1	87.9	89.4	90.5	90.8	91.3	92.0	92.4
1981	93.3	94.1	95.3	96.4	96.6	97.0	97.1	97.1	97.5	97.8	98.0	98.4
1982	99.0	99.0	98.8	98.9	98.8	99.8	100.1	100.5	100.7	101.0	101.4	101.7
1983	100.8	100.8	100.7	100.7	101.0	101.3	101.3	101.6	101.8	101.9	101.5	101.9
1984	102.7	103.1	103.6	103.5	103.5	103.4	103.6	103.3	103.2	103.1	103.4	103.5
1985	103.4	103.4	103.3	103.9	104.2	103.8	103.8	103.6	102.9	103.9	104.6	105.3
1986	104.6	102.8	101.0	100.3	101.0	101.2	100.2	100.7	100.9	101.5	101.4	101.5
1987	102.1	102.5	102.6	103.3	103.4	103.8	104.0	104.2	104.5	104.4	104.3	104.1
1988	104.6	104.4	104.7	105.2	105.4	105.7	106.6	107.1	107.3	107.5	107.9	108.3
1989	109.5	110.4	110.9	111.9	112.9	112.8	112.5	111.8	112.5	113.2	113.2	114.0
1990	116.8	116.6	116.2	115.9	116.2	116.2	116.8	118.3	120.1	121.7	122.2	121.5
1991	121.7	120.7	120.1	120.2	120.5	120.1	119.9	120.1	120.3	120.6	120.8	120.4
1992	120.2	120.6	120.9	121.1	121.6	122.1	122.1	122.1	122.5	122.6	122.3	122.3
1993	122.6	123.1	123.6	124.4	124.4	123.6	123.5	122.4	122.6	122.4	-	-

Source: U.S. Department of Labor, Bureau of Labor Statistics. - indicates data not available or zero.

Producer Price Index
Finished goods
(1982 = 100)

Year	Jan	Feb	Mar	Apr	May	Jun	Jul	Aug	Sep	Oct	Nov	Dec
1947	-	-	-	26.0	26.1	26.2	26.2	26.3	26.7	26.8	27.1	27.7
1948	28.1	27.9	28.0	28.1	28.4	28.6	28.8	28.9	28.8	28.7	28.5	28.5
1949	28.3	28.0	28.0	27.9	27.8	27.7	27.5	27.4	27.4	27.3	27.2	27.2
1950	27.2	27.2	27.3	27.3	27.5	27.6	28.0	28.6	28.9	29.0	29.4	30.0
1951	30.5	30.8	30.9	30.9	31.1	31.0	30.8	30.7	30.6	30.8	30.9	30.9
1952	30.8	30.7	30.9	30.7	30.7	30.7	30.8	30.7	30.6	30.5	30.4	30.2
1953	30.3	30.2	30.3	30.2	30.3	30.4	30.5	30.4	30.4	30.4	30.3	30.4
1954	30.5	30.4	30.4	30.6	30.6	30.4	30.5	30.4	30.4	30.4	30.3	30.3
1955	30.4	30.5	30.3	30.4	30.4	30.5	30.4	30.4	30.5	30.6	30.6	30.7
1956	30.7	30.8	30.9	31.0	31.2	31.4	31.3	31.4	31.6	31.8	31.9	31.9
1957	32.1	32.2	32.1	32.3	32.3	32.5	32.6	32.6	32.6	32.7	32.9	33.0
1958	33.2	33.2	33.4	33.2	33.2	33.3	33.2	33.2	33.2	33.2	32.9	33.0
1959	33.1	33.2	33.2	33.2	33.3	33.2	33.1	33.0	33.4	33.1	33.0	33.1
1960	33.1	33.1	33.4	33.4	33.4	33.4	33.5	33.4	33.4	33.7	33.7	33.6
1961	33.6	33.7	33.6	33.4	33.3	33.3	33.3	33.4	33.3	33.3	33.4	33.4
1962	33.5	33.6	33.5	33.5	33.4	33.4	33.4	33.5	33.8	33.6	33.6	33.5
1963	33.4	33.4	33.3	33.3	33.4	33.5	33.4	33.4	33.4	33.5	33.5	33.4
1964	33.5	33.5	33.4	33.5	33.5	33.5	33.5	33.6	33.6	33.6	33.6	33.6
1965	33.6	33.7	33.7	34.0	34.1	34.2	34.1	34.2	34.3	34.4	34.5	34.7
1966	34.7	35.0	35.0	35.1	35.1	34.9	35.1	35.4	35.6	35.5	35.5	35.4
1967	35.4	35.3	35.3	35.3	35.4	35.7	35.7	35.8	35.8	35.9	35.9	36.0
1968	36.1	36.2	36.3	36.5	36.5	36.6	36.7	36.8	37.0	37.0	37.1	37.1
1969	37.2	37.2	37.4	37.6	37.8	38.0	38.1	38.2	38.3	38.5	38.8	38.9
1970	39.1	39.0	39.1	39.1	39.1	39.2	39.2	39.2	39.6	39.6	39.8	39.8
1971	39.9	40.1	40.2	40.3	40.5	40.6	40.4	40.7	40.7	40.7	40.8	41.1
1972	41.0	41.3	41.3	41.3	41.5	41.7	41.8	42.0	42.2	42.0	42.3	42.7
1973	43.0	43.5	44.4	44.7	45.0	45.5	45.4	47.0	46.9	46.8	47.2	47.6
1974	48.8	49.7	50.2	50.7	51.3	51.3	52.7	53.7	54.3	55.3	56.4	56.4
1975	56.7	56.6	56.6	57.1	57.4	57.9	58.4	58.9	59.3	59.8	60.0	60.1
1976	60.0	59.9	60.0	60.3	60.4	60.5	60.7	60.9	61.1	61.4	61.9	62.4
1977	62.5	63.2	63.7	64.0	64.4	64.6	64.8	65.2	65.5	65.9	66.4	66.7
1978	67.0	67.5	67.8	68.6	69.1	69.7	70.3	70.4	71.1	71.4	72.0	72.8
1979	73.7	74.4	75.0	75.8	76.2	76.6	77.4	78.2	79.5	80.4	81.4	82.2
1980	83.4	84.6	85.5	86.2	86.6	87.3	88.7	89.7	90.1	90.8	91.4	91.8
1981	92.8	93.6	94.7	95.7	96.0	96.5	96.7	96.8	97.2	97.6	97.9	98.3
1982	98.9	98.8	98.8	99.0	99.0	99.8	100.2	100.6	100.7	101.0	101.4	101.8
1983	101.0	101.1	101.0	101.1	101.4	101.6	101.6	101.9	102.2	102.2	102.0	102.3
1984	103.0	103.4	103.8	103.9	103.8	103.8	104.0	103.8	103.8	103.6	104.0	104.0
1985	104.0	104.1	104.1	104.6	104.9	104.6	104.7	104.5	103.8	104.9	105.5	106.0
1986	105.5	104.1	102.8	102.3	102.8	103.1	102.3	102.7	102.9	103.5	103.4	103.6
1987	104.1	104.4	104.5	105.1	105.2	105.5	105.7	105.9	106.2	106.0	106.0	105.8
1988	106.4	106.3	106.6	107.0	107.2	107.5	108.4	108.8	109.0	109.2	109.6	110.0
1989	111.1	111.9	112.3	113.1	114.0	114.0	113.9	113.5	114.1	114.6	114.7	115.4
1990	117.6	117.6	117.4	117.3	117.5	117.6	118.1	119.3	120.8	122.0	122.5	122.0
1991	122.4	121.7	121.3	121.4	121.7	121.4	121.3	121.5	121.7	122.0	122.2	121.9
1992	121.9	122.2	122.5	122.8	123.2	123.5	123.5	123.6	123.9	124.0	123.8	123.8
1993	124.2	124.7	125.1	125.8	125.8	125.1	125.1	124.3	124.5	124.2	-	-

Source: U.S. Department of Labor, Bureau of Labor Statistics. - indicates data not available or zero.

Producer Price Index
Finished goods less foods and energy
(1982 = 100)

Year	Jan	Feb	Mar	Apr	May	Jun	Jul	Aug	Sep	Oct	Nov	Dec
1974	49.7	50.0	50.5	51.1	52.2	53.1	54.0	55.0	55.7	56.7	57.4	57.9
1975	58.3	58.7	59.0	59.2	59.3	59.5	59.8	59.9	60.2	60.6	61.0	61.4
1976	61.7	61.9	62.2	62.3	62.4	62.8	63.1	63.5	63.9	64.1	64.6	64.9
1977	65.1	65.4	65.7	65.9	66.1	66.5	66.8	67.3	67.8	68.2	68.8	69.0
1978	69.2	69.5	69.9	70.6	71.1	71.7	72.3	72.8	73.5	73.4	74.1	74.7
1979	75.3	75.9	76.4	77.0	77.4	78.0	78.5	78.8	79.7	80.4	81.0	81.7
1980	83.3	84.2	84.7	85.5	85.7	86.6	87.7	88.4	88.8	89.6	90.1	90.4
1981	91.4	92.0	92.6	93.5	94.0	94.6	94.8	95.3	95.9	96.5	97.0	97.6
1982	98.1	98.1	98.7	99.0	99.4	99.9	100.1	100.6	100.8	101.3	101.6	102.2
1983	101.8	102.2	102.5	102.4	102.6	102.8	103.1	103.5	103.5	103.6	103.8	104.1
1984	104.5	104.7	105.2	105.3	105.3	105.5	105.7	105.9	106.2	105.9	106.2	106.3
1985	106.9	107.3	107.6	107.6	107.8	108.2	108.4	108.5	107.9	108.9	109.1	109.1
1986	109.3	109.5	109.6	110.1	110.2	110.5	110.7	110.8	110.7	111.8	112.0	112.1
1987	112.5	112.3	112.4	112.9	113.0	113.1	113.3	113.6	113.9	114.0	114.2	114.3
1988	115.0	115.3	115.6	115.9	116.2	116.6	117.2	117.7	118.1	118.4	118.7	119.2
1989	119.9	120.5	120.7	120.8	121.6	122.1	122.2	122.7	123.2	123.5	123.8	124.2
1990	124.5	125.0	125.3	125.6	126.0	126.4	126.8	127.1	127.7	127.8	128.3	128.5
1991	129.6	130.0	130.2	130.5	130.7	130.7	131.1	131.4	131.7	132.0	132.2	132.4
1992	133.1	133.2	133.6	134.0	134.5	134.2	134.4	134.4	134.6	134.5	134.8	135.0
1993	135.6	135.9	136.2	136.7	136.8	136.3	136.7	135.3	135.3	134.6	-	-

Source: U.S. Department of Labor, Bureau of Labor Statistics. - indicates data not available or zero.

Output per Hour, Business Sector
(1982 = 100)

Year	1st Quarter	2nd Quarter	3rd Quarter	4th Quarter
1947	43.2	43.5	43.3	43.4
1948	44.7	45.8	45.0	45.7
1949	45.5	45.5	46.5	46.5
1950	48.4	49.5	50.5	51.0
1951	50.4	51.0	52.4	52.9
1952	52.7	53.7	53.9	54.0
1953	54.8	55.3	55.5	55.5
1954	55.6	56.2	57.2	57.7
1955	58.6	58.9	58.5	58.4
1956	58.6	59.1	59.3	60.4
1957	60.5	60.9	61.1	61.7
1958	61.8	62.6	63.3	64.1
1959	64.6	64.5	64.2	64.8
1960	66.2	65.3	65.1	65.7
1961	66.2	68.1	68.5	69.5
1962	69.5	69.8	70.8	71.7
1963	72.1	73.0	73.8	74.4
1964	76.0	76.0	77.0	77.1
1965	77.7	77.8	79.0	79.9
1966	80.6	80.5	80.7	81.1
1967	81.4	82.8	83.3	83.8
1968	84.5	85.2	85.6	85.9
1969	85.2	85.5	85.8	86.2
1970	85.8	86.2	88.1	88.0
1971	89.4	89.2	90.3	90.6
1972	91.1	92.1	93.0	94.7
1973	95.7	94.8	94.5	95.3
1974	93.7	93.2	92.9	93.2
1975	93.2	95.3	96.7	96.9
1976	98.2	98.2	98.3	98.6
1977	99.6	99.5	100.9	100.0
1978	100.0	100.9	100.6	100.6
1979	100.0	99.7	99.0	99.1
1980	99.2	97.6	98.2	99.6
1981	100.1	100.0	100.7	98.8
1982	98.7	99.8	100.5	101.1
1983	101.0	102.9	102.5	103.1
1984	104.1	104.9	104.8	105.4
1985	105.1	106.0	107.0	107.0
1986	108.6	108.8	108.4	108.3
1987	108.4	109.5	110.1	110.6
1988	110.9	110.4	110.8	110.9
1989	110.1	110.1	109.7	109.7
1990	110.2	111.1	110.8	110.5
1991	110.9	111.6	111.8	112.8
1992	114.1	114.8	116.0	117.1
1993	116.6	116.6	117.6	-

Source: U.S. Department of Labor, Bureau of Labor Statistics. - indicates data not available or zero.

IMPLICIT PRICE DEFLATORS FOR GROSS DOMESTIC PRODUCT

The 12 series in this section show the functioning of inflation in the U.S. economy from 1947 through 1993.

Implicit price deflators are presented for:

Gross domestic product as a whole
Busines sector
 Nonfarm business sector
  Nonfarm less housing
  Housing sector only
 Farms
Households and institutions
 Private households
 Nonprofit institutions
 General government
 Federal government
 State and local government

What is the Implicit Price Deflator?

The series of indexes shown below are based on 1987 prices (1987 = 100) and indicate the level of inflation from that base year for GDP as a whole and for sectors of GDP.

The simplest explanation for these indicators is that they shows how inflation or deflation influence Gross Domestic Product and its major sectors. Using artificially simple numbers, if GDP in actual, current dollars was $1,000 in 1987 and $2,000 in 1993 and *no inflation in prices* had taken place in the 1987-1993 period, the Implicit Price Deflator for GDP in 1993 would be 100, i.e. the *same* as in the base year. Therefore, the change between 1987 and 1993 was *real growth*.

Assume, however, that cumulative inflation in the period was 30%; this would mean that, in 1993, a person would have to spend $1.30 to have the same purchasing power as in 1987. The constant value of the $2,000 GDP in 1993 would therefore be $1,538.46 (2000 / 1.30). The implicit deflator would be calculated as follows:

(2000 / 1538.46) x 100

This would produce a deflator of 130.0. The deflator, in other words, can be read as an indicator of inflation relative to the base year—in this case 1987. The difference between any two years is the increase or decrease in prices between those years. In the example above, the *real growth* between 1987 and 1993 is only $538.46 rather than the apparent $1,000.

The implicit deflator for GDP is an indicator of *overall* inflation or deflation. Deflators are also provided for major sectors of GDP. Thus the user who whishes to calculate how she or he is doing relative to inflation would consult the table for private households; the business owner would consult the table for busines or for nonfarm business less housing.

An example showing the use of the Private Household table is presented below.

An Example. A person who got a job in January of 1989 paying $39,500 a year would like to calculate how he is doing in January 1993. The person now makes $42,300 a year, an increase of $2,800. Has this person gained or lost purchasing power?

The implicit price deflator for the Private Households sector of GDP was 100.4 in the first quarter of 1989; it was 117.9 in the first quarter of 1993. The following formula provides the percent increase in prices between 1989 and 1993 in the index:

((Current Index / Previous Index) - 1) x 100.

The result is 17.4 percent. Multiplying the 1989 salary by 1.174 produces $46,373. Therefore the person has not kept up with inflation. On the contrary, he has lost real purchasing power since 1989 despite a 7 percent increase in pay.

Implicit Price Deflator for Gross Domestic Product
(1987 = 100)

Year	1st Quarter	2nd Quarter	3rd Quarter	4th Quarter
1946	-	-	-	-
1947	18.3	18.5	18.7	19.3
1948	19.6	19.9	20.3	20.3
1949	20.0	19.8	19.8	19.8
1950	19.9	19.9	20.5	20.7
1951	21.4	21.3	21.2	21.3
1952	21.3	21.3	21.6	21.8
1953	21.9	22.0	22.0	21.9
1954	22.1	22.1	22.1	22.3
1955	22.5	22.8	23.0	23.1
1956	23.4	23.5	23.7	23.9
1957	24.2	24.3	24.5	24.5
1958	24.7	24.7	24.9	25.1
1959	25.4	25.6	25.7	25.8
1960	26.0	26.0	26.1	26.0
1961	26.1	26.2	26.4	26.5
1962	26.7	26.8	26.9	27.0
1963	27.1	27.1	27.2	27.4
1964	27.5	27.6	27.7	27.9
1965	28.2	28.3	28.5	28.7
1966	29.0	29.3	29.5	29.9
1967	30.0	30.1	30.4	30.8
1968	31.2	31.6	32.0	32.4
1969	32.7	33.2	33.7	34.0
1970	34.5	35.1	35.3	35.7
1971	36.4	37.0	37.4	37.7
1972	38.2	38.6	39.0	39.6
1973	40.1	40.8	41.6	42.6
1974	43.3	44.2	45.5	46.6
1975	48.0	48.7	49.7	50.5
1976	51.2	51.8	52.6	53.6
1977	54.3	55.4	56.4	57.4
1978	58.2	59.7	60.9	62.2
1979	63.5	64.8	66.3	67.6
1980	69.2	70.8	72.5	74.4
1981	76.5	77.9	79.7	81.4
1982	82.3	83.4	84.3	85.0
1983	86.0	86.6	87.5	88.4
1984	89.7	90.6	91.6	92.3
1985	93.3	94.0	94.6	95.5
1986	96.0	96.5	97.2	98.0
1987	98.8	99.5	100.3	101.2
1988	102.1	103.2	104.5	105.5
1989	106.9	108.1	109.1	110.1
1990	111.5	112.7	113.8	115.0
1991	116.4	117.3	118.2	118.9
1992	120.0	120.9	121.2	122.2
1993	123.3	124.0	-	-

Source: U.S. Department of Commerce, Bureau of Economic Analysis. - indicates data not available or zero.

Implicit Price Deflator for GDP
Business Sector
(1987 = 100)

Year	1st Quarter	2nd Quarter	3rd Quarter	4th Quarter
1946	-	-	-	-
1947	19.9	20.0	20.4	21.1
1948	21.4	21.8	22.3	22.2
1949	21.9	21.7	21.7	21.6
1950	21.6	21.7	22.3	22.7
1951	23.6	23.6	23.5	23.6
1952	23.7	23.6	23.9	24.1
1953	24.1	24.2	24.3	24.1
1954	24.3	24.3	24.2	24.5
1955	24.6	24.8	25.0	25.2
1956	25.4	25.6	25.8	26.0
1957	26.3	26.5	26.6	26.6
1958	26.8	26.8	27.0	27.1
1959	27.4	27.6	27.7	27.8
1960	28.0	28.0	28.1	28.0
1961	28.0	28.1	28.3	28.4
1962	28.6	28.7	28.8	28.9
1963	28.9	28.9	29.0	29.1
1964	29.1	29.3	29.3	29.5
1965	29.8	29.9	30.1	30.2
1966	30.5	30.9	31.1	31.5
1967	31.6	31.7	31.9	32.2
1968	32.7	33.1	33.4	33.8
1969	34.1	34.6	35.0	35.3
1970	35.7	36.2	36.4	36.8
1971	37.3	37.9	38.4	38.6
1972	38.9	39.3	39.6	40.2
1973	40.6	41.4	42.2	43.2
1974	44.0	44.9	46.4	47.5
1975	49.0	49.6	50.6	51.4
1976	52.0	52.6	53.4	54.3
1977	55.0	56.1	57.1	58.1
1978	58.9	60.5	61.8	63.1
1979	64.4	65.9	67.4	68.6
1980	70.3	72.1	73.8	75.6
1981	77.8	79.2	81.2	82.9
1982	83.7	84.7	85.5	86.0
1983	87.1	87.6	88.4	89.3
1984	90.4	91.4	92.4	92.9
1985	94.0	94.5	95.2	96.1
1986	96.5	96.8	97.6	98.2
1987	98.9	99.5	100.3	101.2
1988	101.9	103.1	104.4	105.4
1989	106.7	107.9	108.9	109.8
1990	111.1	112.2	113.3	114.5
1991	115.8	116.7	117.4	118.0
1992	118.9	119.6	119.9	120.9
1993	121.8	122.5	-	-

Source: U.S. Department of Commerce, Bureau of Economic Analysis. - indicates data not available or zero.

Implicit Price Deflator for GDP
Business Sector - Nonfarm
(1987 = 100)

Year	1st Quarter	2nd Quarter	3rd Quarter	4th Quarter
1946	-	-	-	-
1947	18.6	18.9	19.4	19.8
1948	20.2	20.4	20.9	21.0
1949	21.0	20.8	20.8	20.8
1950	20.9	20.9	20.9	21.3
1951	22.1	22.5	22.5	22.6
1952	22.8	22.7	22.9	23.3
1953	23.4	23.5	23.7	23.5
1954	23.6	23.7	23.6	24.0
1955	24.0	24.3	24.6	24.8
1956	25.0	25.1	25.4	25.6
1957	26.0	26.0	26.2	26.2
1958	26.2	26.2	26.4	26.6
1959	26.9	27.2	27.3	27.4
1960	27.6	27.6	27.7	27.6
1961	27.6	27.8	27.9	27.9
1962	28.2	28.3	28.4	28.5
1963	28.5	28.5	28.6	28.8
1964	28.8	29.0	29.1	29.2
1965	29.5	29.5	29.7	29.8
1966	30.0	30.4	30.6	31.1
1967	31.3	31.3	31.6	31.9
1968	32.4	32.7	33.0	33.4
1969	33.8	34.2	34.6	34.9
1970	35.3	35.9	36.0	36.4
1971	37.0	37.5	38.0	38.2
1972	38.7	38.8	39.2	39.5
1973	39.9	40.5	41.0	41.9
1974	42.8	44.2	45.6	46.6
1975	48.2	48.8	49.7	50.4
1976	51.3	51.9	52.8	53.7
1977	54.4	55.6	56.6	57.5
1978	58.2	59.7	60.9	62.2
1979	63.3	64.9	66.4	67.8
1980	69.7	71.8	73.2	74.7
1981	77.0	78.5	80.5	82.4
1982	83.2	84.2	85.0	85.8
1983	86.9	87.5	88.5	89.2
1984	89.9	90.8	91.8	92.5
1985	93.5	94.3	95.2	96.0
1986	96.5	96.8	97.5	98.2
1987	99.0	99.5	100.3	101.2
1988	102.0	103.1	104.2	105.3
1989	106.4	107.7	108.7	109.6
1990	110.8	112.1	113.2	114.6
1991	115.9	116.7	117.5	118.2
1992	119.1	119.9	120.2	121.2
1993	122.1	122.8	-	-

Source: U.S. Department of Commerce, Bureau of Economic Analysis. - indicates data not available or zero.

Implicit Price Deflator for GDP
Business Sector - Nonfarm Less Housing
(1987 = 100)

Year	1st Quarter	2nd Quarter	3rd Quarter	4th Quarter
1946	-	-	-	-
1947	18.5	18.9	19.4	19.8
1948	20.2	20.4	20.9	21.0
1949	20.9	20.7	20.8	20.8
1950	20.8	20.8	20.8	21.2
1951	22.1	22.5	22.5	22.5
1952	22.7	22.6	22.8	23.2
1953	23.3	23.4	23.5	23.3
1954	23.4	23.5	23.4	23.8
1955	23.8	24.1	24.4	24.7
1956	24.9	25.0	25.2	25.4
1957	25.8	25.9	26.1	26.0
1958	26.0	26.0	26.3	26.4
1959	26.8	27.1	27.2	27.2
1960	27.5	27.5	27.5	27.4
1961	27.4	27.6	27.7	27.8
1962	28.0	28.1	28.3	28.4
1963	28.4	28.4	28.5	28.6
1964	28.6	28.8	28.9	29.1
1965	29.4	29.4	29.6	29.7
1966	29.9	30.4	30.6	31.1
1967	31.3	31.3	31.6	31.9
1968	32.4	32.8	33.1	33.5
1969	33.9	34.3	34.7	35.0
1970	35.3	36.0	36.1	36.5
1971	37.1	37.6	38.1	38.3
1972	38.8	38.9	39.3	39.6
1973	40.0	40.6	41.1	42.0
1974	43.0	44.6	46.1	47.1
1975	48.9	49.4	50.3	51.0
1976	51.9	52.5	53.4	54.3
1977	55.0	56.1	57.1	58.1
1978	58.8	60.3	61.6	62.9
1979	64.0	65.7	67.2	68.5
1980	70.6	72.8	74.2	75.7
1981	78.1	79.6	81.6	83.5
1982	84.3	85.3	86.1	86.8
1983	87.9	88.4	89.3	90.0
1984	90.7	91.5	92.5	93.2
1985	94.2	94.9	95.7	96.4
1986	96.9	97.0	97.7	98.3
1987	99.1	99.5	100.3	101.1
1988	101.8	103.0	104.1	105.2
1989	106.2	107.6	108.4	109.3
1990	110.6	111.8	112.9	114.3
1991	115.7	116.4	117.2	117.8
1992	118.7	119.6	118.9	120.8
1993	121.6	122.3	-	-

Source: U.S. Department of Commerce, Bureau of Economic Analysis. - indicates data not available or zero.

Implicit Price Deflator for GDP

Business Sector - Nonfarm Housing

(1987 = 100)

Year	1st Quarter	2nd Quarter	3rd Quarter	4th Quarter
1946	-	-	-	-
1947	19.0	19.2	19.5	19.8
1948	20.2	20.5	20.8	21.1
1949	21.3	21.5	21.7	21.8
1950	22.0	22.2	22.4	22.7
1951	22.9	23.2	23.4	23.6
1952	23.8	24.0	24.3	24.7
1953	25.0	25.4	25.7	26.0
1954	26.2	26.4	26.5	26.6
1955	26.7	26.7	26.8	27.0
1956	27.1	27.2	27.4	27.5
1957	27.6	27.7	27.8	28.0
1958	28.1	28.3	28.4	28.5
1959	28.5	28.7	28.7	28.9
1960	29.0	29.1	29.2	29.3
1961	29.4	29.5	29.6	29.6
1962	29.8	29.8	29.9	30.0
1963	30.1	30.1	30.2	30.3
1964	30.4	30.4	30.5	30.6
1965	30.7	30.7	30.8	30.9
1966	31.0	31.1	31.2	31.4
1967	31.6	31.7	31.8	32.0
1968	32.2	32.4	32.7	32.9
1969	33.1	33.4	33.7	34.1
1970	34.4	34.8	35.1	35.6
1971	36.0	36.4	36.8	37.1
1972	37.4	37.7	38.0	38.3
1973	38.9	39.3	39.7	40.2
1974	40.4	40.6	41.1	41.8
1975	42.7	43.4	44.0	44.8
1976	45.5	46.2	47.0	47.9
1977	49.1	50.2	51.1	52.1
1978	52.8	53.6	54.4	55.5
1979	56.4	57.4	58.9	60.5
1980	61.5	62.8	64.3	66.2
1981	67.8	69.4	71.2	72.9
1982	74.2	74.9	76.4	77.8
1983	78.9	79.9	81.0	82.0
1984	82.9	84.2	85.5	86.6
1985	87.7	89.1	90.8	92.3
1986	93.5	95.0	96.1	97.3
1987	98.2	99.2	100.4	102.1
1988	103.3	104.1	105.4	106.5
1989	107.7	108.9	111.8	112.0
1990	112.8	114.4	116.3	117.1
1991	118.0	119.0	120.0	122.0
1992	122.2	122.9	132.5	124.5
1993	126.9	126.8	-	-

Source: U.S. Department of Commerce, Bureau of Economic Analysis. - indicates data not available or zero.

Implicit Price Deflator for GDP
Business Sector - Farms
(1987 = 100)

Year	1st Quarter	2nd Quarter	3rd Quarter	4th Quarter
1946	-	-	-	-
1947	50.6	49.7	42.2	56.5
1948	53.4	53.0	55.1	48.3
1949	45.2	44.0	40.8	39.5
1950	38.7	40.7	100.0	100.0
1951	100.0	52.2	48.8	52.0
1952	50.1	50.3	50.1	47.0
1953	43.9	42.0	42.4	41.8
1954	42.2	40.5	40.3	38.8
1955	39.8	38.5	36.8	36.3
1956	38.0	38.2	39.2	37.8
1957	38.6	39.9	40.4	39.1
1958	43.6	43.9	44.1	44.0
1959	42.2	42.2	42.0	40.8
1960	41.6	43.8	42.6	42.7
1961	42.6	41.5	42.4	44.6
1962	44.7	43.1	43.0	43.6
1963	41.8	43.1	44.6	43.7
1964	42.7	42.2	40.6	42.0
1965	43.8	49.1	47.3	49.7
1966	52.7	51.5	52.5	49.0
1967	47.4	47.6	47.5	48.6
1968	47.2	50.5	50.3	53.5
1969	50.4	54.1	53.9	56.6
1970	54.7	53.0	53.1	51.2
1971	54.4	56.7	55.8	55.6
1972	52.4	66.3	62.4	76.3
1973	86.1	94.2	131.0	102.9
1974	114.0	85.5	88.7	87.9
1975	84.6	89.1	99.5	93.8
1976	86.2	92.3	92.4	83.7
1977	86.1	88.5	88.9	87.3
1978	100.6	114.4	113.9	126.5
1979	134.4	128.9	126.8	121.7
1980	108.7	91.3	114.0	125.4
1981	122.6	117.3	114.6	106.1
1982	109.8	113.7	111.2	98.2
1983	92.8	90.6	85.2	97.6
1984	121.4	126.8	128.8	120.5
1985	118.3	106.7	94.7	100.4
1986	94.4	97.3	99.9	99.9
1987	95.7	102.3	99.6	102.3
1988	99.0	102.2	116.2	113.0
1989	126.1	120.0	120.7	123.3
1990	126.1	121.3	117.6	110.9
1991	110.7	116.8	113.7	106.8
1992	109.8	105.5	104.3	104.9
1993	107.1	109.3	-	-

Source: U.S. Department of Commerce, Bureau of Economic Analysis. - indicates data not available or zero.

Implicit Price Deflator for GDP
Households and Institutions
(1987 = 100)

Year	1st Quarter	2nd Quarter	3rd Quarter	4th Quarter
1946	-	-	-	-
1947	10.2	11.4	11.5	11.4
1948	10.6	10.9	11.3	11.3
1949	11.3	11.3	11.2	11.4
1950	11.4	11.4	11.8	11.9
1951	12.0	12.0	12.2	12.3
1952	12.2	12.5	12.8	12.8
1953	12.8	13.0	13.2	13.3
1954	13.2	13.3	13.3	13.4
1955	13.7	13.6	13.7	13.7
1956	13.8	13.9	14.1	14.3
1957	14.2	14.4	14.7	14.9
1958	14.8	15.1	15.2	15.2
1959	15.2	15.3	15.5	15.9
1960	15.7	16.0	16.2	16.3
1961	16.4	16.5	16.5	16.7
1962	17.0	17.1	17.1	17.4
1963	17.6	17.8	17.8	17.9
1964	18.3	18.4	18.7	18.7
1965	18.5	19.0	19.4	19.9
1966	19.7	20.1	20.6	20.9
1967	21.2	21.4	21.7	22.1
1968	22.9	23.1	23.4	24.0
1969	24.5	25.1	25.7	26.7
1970	27.3	28.0	29.0	29.3
1971	29.9	30.3	30.6	31.2
1972	31.8	32.3	32.6	33.2
1973	33.8	34.6	35.2	36.1
1974	36.8	37.6	38.2	39.2
1975	39.8	40.2	40.7	41.9
1976	43.0	43.9	44.6	46.1
1977	46.9	47.7	48.5	49.4
1978	50.9	51.7	53.3	54.2
1979	55.3	56.1	57.6	59.1
1980	60.3	62.0	63.3	64.8
1981	66.7	68.2	69.8	71.1
1982	72.9	74.1	75.8	77.2
1983	78.2	79.5	81.1	82.5
1984	83.5	84.8	86.0	86.5
1985	87.4	88.1	89.2	89.8
1986	90.3	91.0	92.9	94.6
1987	97.1	99.4	100.8	102.5
1988	102.6	103.6	104.2	105.2
1989	106.3	107.2	108.7	110.4
1990	112.9	114.7	116.3	118.0
1991	119.0	120.2	122.1	123.5
1992	125.3	127.3	128.2	129.8
1993	131.3	131.3	-	-

Source: U.S. Department of Commerce, Bureau of Economic Analysis. - indicates data not available or zero.

Implicit Price Deflator for GDP
Private Households
(1987 = 100)

Year	1st Quarter	2nd Quarter	3rd Quarter	4th Quarter
1946	-	-	-	-
1947	16.7	16.6	16.7	16.8
1948	17.0	17.1	17.2	17.2
1949	17.2	17.1	17.1	17.1
1950	17.0	17.0	17.2	17.4
1951	17.6	17.8	18.2	18.6
1952	18.8	19.1	19.4	19.7
1953	19.9	20.1	20.3	20.4
1954	20.4	20.4	20.5	20.5
1955	20.4	20.4	20.5	20.6
1956	20.7	20.8	21.1	21.3
1957	21.5	21.7	21.9	22.1
1958	22.2	22.4	22.5	22.6
1959	21.6	21.6	22.6	23.1
1960	23.3	23.6	23.7	23.8
1961	23.8	23.9	23.9	24.1
1962	24.3	24.4	24.6	24.8
1963	24.9	25.0	25.0	25.1
1964	25.4	25.9	26.1	26.3
1965	26.5	26.9	27.4	27.7
1966	28.1	28.2	28.8	29.3
1967	29.3	29.5	29.7	30.4
1968	31.6	32.5	32.8	33.6
1969	34.2	34.6	35.2	36.1
1970	36.8	37.5	38.2	39.0
1971	39.5	39.9	40.4	40.7
1972	41.5	41.9	42.2	42.8
1973	44.0	44.9	45.3	46.2
1974	46.2	48.6	51.9	52.3
1975	52.5	52.4	53.3	55.1
1976	57.9	59.9	60.9	63.1
1977	64.5	65.1	65.7	65.9
1978	67.0	69.2	71.5	74.1
1979	76.2	77.9	79.5	81.1
1980	82.6	84.2	85.8	87.3
1981	89.0	90.6	92.5	94.1
1982	95.0	95.3	95.3	95.3
1983	95.3	95.8	95.8	95.9
1984	96.4	96.4	96.6	96.9
1985	97.4	97.8	97.9	98.2
1986	98.5	98.6	99.0	99.4
1987	99.8	99.7	100.2	100.3
1988	100.4	101.1	101.5	101.7
1989	102.3	102.7	102.8	102.9
1990	103.8	105.1	106.6	108.6
1991	109.9	111.0	111.9	113.3
1992	113.9	115.0	116.4	117.4
1993	117.9	118.7	-	-

Source: U.S. Department of Commerce, Bureau of Economic Analysis. - indicates data not available or zero.

Implicit Price Deflator for GDP
Nonprofit Institutions
(1987 = 100)

Year	1st Quarter	2nd Quarter	3rd Quarter	4th Quarter
1946	-	-	-	-
1947	7.5	9.1	9.0	9.0
1948	8.2	8.6	9.0	9.2
1949	9.3	9.3	9.2	9.2
1950	9.2	9.3	9.7	10.0
1951	9.9	10.0	10.0	10.4
1952	10.4	10.4	10.5	10.7
1953	10.8	10.9	11.1	11.2
1954	11.3	11.4	11.5	11.5
1955	11.8	11.7	11.7	11.7
1956	11.8	11.9	12.2	12.3
1957	12.3	12.5	12.8	13.0
1958	13.0	13.1	13.2	13.4
1959	13.6	13.7	13.8	14.1
1960	14.0	14.2	14.5	14.6
1961	14.7	14.9	15.0	15.2
1962	15.4	15.6	15.6	15.9
1963	16.2	16.4	16.4	16.6
1964	17.0	16.9	17.3	17.4
1965	17.2	17.7	18.1	18.6
1966	18.3	18.8	19.3	19.6
1967	19.9	20.2	20.5	20.9
1968	21.7	21.8	22.1	22.7
1969	23.3	23.9	24.6	25.6
1970	26.1	26.9	27.9	28.2
1971	28.8	29.3	29.5	30.2
1972	30.8	31.3	31.6	32.2
1973	32.9	33.6	34.2	35.2
1974	35.9	36.7	37.2	38.3
1975	38.9	39.3	39.8	41.0
1976	41.9	42.7	43.4	44.8
1977	45.6	46.3	47.1	48.2
1978	49.6	50.4	51.9	52.8
1979	53.9	54.8	56.2	57.8
1980	59.1	60.8	62.1	63.6
1981	65.6	67.1	68.7	70.0
1982	71.9	73.1	74.9	76.4
1983	77.4	78.8	80.4	81.8
1984	82.9	84.2	85.4	85.9
1985	86.9	87.6	88.7	89.3
1986	89.9	90.6	92.6	94.3
1987	97.0	99.4	100.8	102.6
1988	102.7	103.7	104.3	105.4
1989	106.5	107.4	109.0	110.8
1990	113.4	115.2	116.8	118.4
1991	119.4	120.6	122.5	123.9
1992	125.8	127.8	128.7	130.4
1993	131.9	131.9	-	-

Source: U.S. Department of Commerce, Bureau of Economic Analysis. - indicates data not available or zero.

Implicit Price Deflator for GDP
General Government
(1987 = 100)

Year	1st Quarter	2nd Quarter	3rd Quarter	4th Quarter
1946	-	-	-	-
1947	11.0	10.9	10.0	10.1
1948	10.3	10.5	10.6	10.8
1949	11.1	11.2	11.2	11.4
1950	11.3	11.2	11.4	11.1
1951	11.7	11.4	11.4	11.6
1952	11.8	11.9	12.1	12.3
1953	12.3	12.4	12.3	12.5
1954	12.6	12.9	13.0	13.1
1955	13.3	13.8	13.8	13.9
1956	14.1	14.4	14.6	14.6
1957	14.8	15.0	15.2	15.4
1958	15.9	16.1	16.4	16.4
1959	16.7	16.8	16.9	16.9
1960	17.2	17.3	17.7	17.8
1961	17.8	18.0	18.1	18.2
1962	18.5	18.6	18.7	19.1
1963	19.4	19.4	19.5	20.0
1964	20.3	20.4	20.7	20.8
1965	21.0	21.1	21.4	21.8
1966	22.1	22.3	22.7	22.8
1967	23.0	23.5	23.8	24.5
1968	24.9	25.2	25.9	26.3
1969	26.6	26.9	28.0	28.4
1970	29.7	30.3	30.8	31.3
1971	32.4	33.0	33.5	34.1
1972	35.5	36.0	36.5	37.5
1973	38.2	38.8	39.5	40.2
1974	40.7	41.2	42.0	43.2
1975	44.3	45.4	46.3	47.6
1976	48.4	49.2	49.7	50.8
1977	51.7	52.5	53.2	54.9
1978	55.5	56.2	56.9	58.3
1979	59.1	59.8	60.8	62.5
1980	63.7	64.8	65.9	68.9
1981	69.9	70.9	71.8	74.3
1982	75.8	77.2	78.4	80.1
1983	81.3	82.1	82.8	83.7
1984	85.7	86.7	87.7	88.7
1985	90.4	91.3	91.9	93.2
1986	94.2	95.2	96.0	97.3
1987	98.7	99.6	100.4	101.3
1988	103.4	104.5	105.5	106.6
1989	108.9	109.9	110.9	112.0
1990	114.5	115.8	117.0	118.1
1991	120.2	121.5	123.0	124.7
1992	127.4	128.9	129.4	130.3
1993	132.8	133.8	-	-

Source: U.S. Department of Commerce, Bureau of Economic Analysis. - indicates data not available or zero.

Implicit Price Deflator for GDP

Federal Government

(1987 = 100)

Year	1st Quarter	2nd Quarter	3rd Quarter	4th Quarter
1946	-	-	-	-
1947	12.8	12.8	10.9	10.8
1948	10.8	10.9	10.8	10.8
1949	11.5	11.7	11.7	12.1
1950	11.9	11.4	11.5	10.9
1951	11.7	11.2	11.1	11.2
1952	11.4	11.6	11.7	11.8
1953	11.8	11.9	11.8	11.9
1954	12.0	12.2	12.1	12.3
1955	12.5	13.3	13.4	13.4
1956	13.6	13.9	14.1	14.0
1957	14.2	14.4	14.5	14.7
1958	15.4	15.8	16.2	16.2
1959	16.6	16.7	16.7	16.7
1960	16.8	16.8	17.4	17.5
1961	17.5	17.5	17.5	17.4
1962	17.5	17.6	17.8	18.3
1963	18.6	18.6	18.6	19.4
1964	19.8	19.9	20.3	20.5
1965	20.6	20.7	21.1	21.8
1966	21.9	22.0	22.3	22.1
1967	21.9	22.3	22.4	23.5
1968	23.8	24.0	25.0	25.3
1969	25.3	25.4	27.0	27.2
1970	29.2	29.8	30.3	30.7
1971	32.5	33.2	33.7	34.9
1972	37.3	37.8	38.1	39.7
1973	40.3	40.8	41.6	43.0
1974	43.1	43.4	44.3	46.4
1975	47.3	47.9	48.6	50.6
1976	50.9	51.3	51.5	53.5
1977	54.1	54.5	54.6	57.6
1978	57.9	58.3	58.8	61.4
1979	61.9	62.4	62.8	66.3
1980	66.9	67.5	68.0	74.3
1981	74.7	75.3	75.3	80.2
1982	81.0	81.8	82.1	84.6
1983	85.5	86.3	86.6	86.9
1984	89.6	90.0	90.5	91.1
1985	93.8	94.1	94.1	95.8
1986	96.1	96.4	96.5	96.7
1987	99.6	100.2	100.0	100.2
1988	103.4	104.0	104.2	104.7
1989	109.0	109.5	109.7	110.2
1990	114.6	115.3	115.5	115.8
1991	119.8	121.3	123.4	125.7
1992	131.6	132.8	133.3	133.5
1993	138.6	139.5	-	-

Source: U.S. Department of Commerce, Bureau of Economic Analysis. - indicates data not available or zero.

Implicit Price Deflator for GDP

State and Local Government

(1987 = 100)

Year	1st Quarter	2nd Quarter	3rd Quarter	4th Quarter
1946	-	-	-	-
1947	8.9	9.0	9.1	9.4
1948	9.8	10.1	10.5	10.8
1949	10.7	10.6	10.7	10.6
1950	10.8	10.9	11.2	11.4
1951	11.6	11.7	12.0	12.2
1952	12.4	12.5	12.8	13.0
1953	13.1	13.2	13.2	13.4
1954	13.6	13.9	14.1	14.2
1955	14.3	14.4	14.4	14.5
1956	14.8	14.9	15.1	15.3
1957	15.5	15.8	15.9	16.1
1958	16.3	16.5	16.5	16.6
1959	16.8	17.0	17.0	17.2
1960	17.6	17.8	17.9	18.1
1961	18.2	18.5	18.7	19.0
1962	19.4	19.5	19.6	19.8
1963	20.0	20.2	20.3	20.5
1964	20.6	20.8	20.9	21.1
1965	21.3	21.4	21.6	21.8
1966	22.2	22.6	23.0	23.4
1967	24.0	24.5	24.9	25.3
1968	25.8	26.2	26.7	27.1
1969	27.6	28.1	28.8	29.3
1970	30.1	30.7	31.2	31.6
1971	32.4	33.0	33.4	33.6
1972	34.4	34.9	35.6	36.2
1973	37.0	37.8	38.4	38.8
1974	39.4	40.0	40.8	41.6
1975	42.7	44.1	45.2	46.1
1976	47.1	48.1	48.7	49.4
1977	50.4	51.5	52.6	53.6
1978	54.4	55.1	56.0	56.8
1979	57.7	58.6	59.8	60.8
1980	62.2	63.5	65.0	66.4
1981	67.7	68.9	70.2	71.5
1982	73.4	75.0	76.6	78.0
1983	79.3	80.1	81.0	82.1
1984	83.8	85.1	86.4	87.6
1985	88.8	90.0	90.9	92.0
1986	93.3	94.7	95.8	97.5
1987	98.2	99.3	100.6	101.9
1988	103.5	104.7	106.0	107.4
1989	108.8	110.1	111.4	112.8
1990	114.4	116.1	117.6	119.1
1991	120.4	121.6	122.9	124.2
1992	125.6	127.2	127.7	129.0
1993	130.4	131.4	-	-

Source: U.S. Department of Commerce, Bureau of Economic Analysis. - indicates data not available or zero.

INDICATORS OF LABOR AND EMPLOYMENT

This section presents 3 indicators of employment and labor:

    Civilian labor force
    Civilian employment
    Civilian labor force participation
      Males, 20 years and over
      Females, 20 years and over
      Both sexes, 16 to 19 years of age

Civilian Labor Force and **Civilian Employment**. The series are available from 1948 through 1993 and are shown in thousands. The two series are the source of unemployment data (number and rate) shown in the section on Other Cyclic Indicators. The labor force is defined as individuals working or actively seeking work. Civilian employment is that portion of the labor force which is now employed. The unemployment rate is calculated by the following formula:

(1-(Civilian Employment / Civilian Labor Force)) x 100

For January 1991, the labor force was 124,638,000 employment was 116,922,000, indicating unemployment of 7,716,000. This number represents 6.19 percent of the labor force.

A certain level of unemployment is a "natural" phenomenon in a healthy economy. Some economists equate 3-4 percent unemployment with "full employment," on the basis that a certain small fraction of the labor force is, of necessity, in transition between jobs. At the peak of the 1961-1969 expansion (12/69), unemployment was at 3.5 percent; at the peak of the 1971-1973 expansion (10/73), unemployment stood at 4.6 percent. By contrast, at the trough of the 1970 recession, unemployment stood at 6.1 percent; at the trough of the 1974-1975 recession, unemployment stood at 8.6 percent.

Civilian Labor Force Participation. The three tables showing labor force participation extend from 1948 to 1993 and show participation in percent. In January 1991, for instance, 77.3 percent of males 20 years or older participated in the labor force. Base data—the number of people of the gender and age group overall—are derived from the censuses of population and estimates based on them. The participation values are based on estimates of the total labor force.

The values show interesting general patterns. Labor force participation for males has declined gradually from nearly 90 percent in the late 1940s to under 80 percent in recent times. Female labor force participation, however, which was just over 30 percent in the 1940s and 1950s, has reached nearly 60 percent in the 1990s. The participation of young people (16 to 19 years of age) has remained virtually unchanged since the 1940s—although it dipped somewhat in the 1950s and 1960s.

Underlying the labor participation numbers are complex economic and demographic forces, including efforts to maintain family income levels, the rise in the skill level demanded in the work place, the reduced role of manufacturing and the corresponding rise in the services sectors of the economy, and others.

Civilian Labor Force
(Thousands)

Year	Jan	Feb	Mar	Apr	May	Jun	Jul	Aug	Sep	Oct	Nov	Dec
1948	60,095	60,524	60,070	60,677	59,972	60,957	61,181	60,806	60,815	60,646	60,702	61,169
1949	60,771	61,057	61,073	61,007	61,259	60,948	61,301	61,590	61,633	62,185	62,005	61,908
1950	61,661	61,687	61,604	62,158	62,083	62,419	62,121	62,596	62,349	62,428	62,286	62,068
1951	61,941	61,778	62,526	61,808	62,044	61,615	62,106	61,927	61,780	62,204	62,014	62,457
1952	62,432	62,419	61,721	61,720	62,058	62,103	61,962	61,877	62,457	61,971	62,491	62,621
1953	63,439	63,520	63,657	63,167	62,615	63,063	63,057	62,816	62,727	62,867	62,949	62,795
1954	63,101	63,994	63,793	63,934	63,675	63,343	63,302	63,707	64,209	63,936	63,759	63,312
1955	63,910	63,696	63,882	64,564	64,381	64,482	65,145	65,581	65,628	65,821	66,037	66,445
1956	66,419	66,124	66,175	66,264	66,722	66,702	66,752	66,673	66,714	66,546	66,657	66,700
1957	66,428	66,879	66,913	66,647	66,695	67,052	67,336	66,706	67,064	67,066	67,123	67,398
1958	67,095	67,201	67,223	67,647	67,895	67,674	67,824	68,037	68,002	68,045	67,658	67,740
1959	67,936	67,649	68,068	68,339	68,178	68,278	68,539	68,432	68,545	68,821	68,533	68,994
1960	68,962	68,949	68,399	69,579	69,626	69,934	69,745	69,841	70,151	69,884	70,439	70,395
1961	70,447	70,420	70,703	70,267	70,452	70,878	70,536	70,534	70,217	70,492	70,376	70,077
1962	70,189	70,409	70,414	70,278	70,551	70,514	70,302	70,981	71,153	70,917	70,871	70,854
1963	71,146	71,262	71,423	71,697	71,832	71,626	71,956	71,786	72,131	72,281	72,418	72,188
1964	72,356	72,683	72,713	73,274	73,395	73,032	73,007	73,118	73,290	73,308	73,286	73,465
1965	73,569	73,857	73,949	74,228	74,466	74,412	74,761	74,616	74,502	74,838	74,797	75,093
1966	75,186	74,954	75,075	75,338	75,447	75,647	75,736	76,046	76,056	76,199	76,610	76,641
1967	76,639	76,521	76,328	76,777	76,773	77,270	77,464	77,712	77,812	78,194	78,191	78,491
1968	77,578	78,230	78,256	78,270	78,847	79,120	78,970	78,811	78,858	78,913	79,209	79,463
1969	79,523	80,019	80,079	80,281	80,125	80,696	80,827	81,106	81,290	81,494	81,397	81,624
1970	81,981	82,151	82,498	82,727	82,483	82,484	82,901	82,880	82,954	83,276	83,548	83,670
1971	83,850	83,603	83,575	83,946	84,135	83,706	84,340	84,673	84,731	84,872	85,458	85,625
1972	85,978	86,036	86,611	86,614	86,809	87,006	87,143	87,517	87,392	87,491	87,592	87,943
1973	87,487	88,364	88,846	89,018	88,977	89,548	89,604	89,509	89,838	90,131	90,716	90,890
1974	91,199	91,485	91,453	91,287	91,596	91,868	92,212	92,059	92,488	92,518	92,766	92,780
1975	93,128	92,776	93,165	93,399	93,884	93,575	94,021	94,162	94,202	94,267	94,250	94,409
1976	94,934	94,998	95,215	95,746	95,847	95,885	96,583	96,741	96,553	96,704	97,254	97,348
1977	97,208	97,785	98,115	98,330	98,665	99,093	98,913	99,366	99,453	99,815	100,576	100,491
1978	100,873	100,837	101,092	101,574	101,896	102,371	102,399	102,511	102,795	103,080	103,562	103,809
1979	104,057	104,502	104,589	104,172	104,171	104,638	105,002	105,096	105,530	105,700	105,812	106,258
1980	106,562	106,697	106,442	106,591	106,929	106,780	107,159	107,105	107,098	107,405	107,568	107,352
1981	108,026	108,242	108,553	108,925	109,222	108,396	108,556	108,725	108,294	109,024	109,236	108,912
1982	109,089	109,467	109,567	109,820	110,451	110,081	110,342	110,514	110,721	110,744	111,050	111,083
1983	110,695	110,634	110,587	110,828	110,796	111,879	111,756	112,231	112,298	111,926	112,228	112,327
1984	112,209	112,615	112,713	113,098	113,649	113,817	113,972	113,682	113,857	114,019	114,170	114,581
1985	114,725	114,876	115,328	115,331	115,234	114,965	115,320	115,291	115,905	116,145	116,135	116,354
1986	116,682	116,882	117,220	117,316	117,528	118,084	118,129	118,150	118,395	118,516	118,634	118,611
1987	118,845	119,122	119,270	119,336	120,008	119,644	119,902	120,318	120,011	120,509	120,540	120,729
1988	120,969	121,156	120,913	121,251	121,071	121,473	121,665	122,125	121,960	122,206	122,637	122,622
1989	123,375	123,132	123,218	123,546	123,485	123,980	123,965	124,152	123,939	124,237	124,689	124,536
1990	124,549	124,623	124,760	124,749	124,920	124,645	124,647	124,821	124,892	124,965	124,930	125,218
1991	124,700	125,019	125,258	125,613	125,186	125,371	125,089	124,982	125,587	125,675	125,602	125,736
1992	126,028	126,185	126,548	126,743	127,039	127,298	127,350	127,404	127,274	127,066	127,365	127,591
1993	127,083	127,327	127,429	127,341	128,131	128,127	128,070	128,370	127,975	128,714	-	-

Source: U.S. Department of Labor, Bureau of Labor Statistics. - indicates data not available or zero.

Civilian Employment
(Thousands)

Year	Jan	Feb	Mar	Apr	May	Jun	Jul	Aug	Sep	Oct	Nov	Dec
1948	58,061	58,196	57,671	58,291	57,854	58,743	58,968	58,456	58,513	58,387	58,417	58,740
1949	58,175	58,208	58,043	57,747	57,552	57,172	57,190	57,397	57,584	57,269	58,009	57,845
1950	57,635	57,751	57,728	58,583	58,649	59,052	59,001	59,797	59,575	59,803	59,697	59,429
1951	59,636	59,661	60,401	59,889	60,188	59,620	60,156	59,994	59,713	60,010	59,836	60,497
1952	60,460	60,462	59,908	59,909	60,195	60,219	59,971	59,790	60,521	60,132	60,748	60,954
1953	61,600	61,884	62,010	61,444	61,019	61,456	61,397	61,151	60,906	60,893	60,738	59,977
1954	60,024	60,663	60,186	60,185	59,908	59,792	59,643	59,853	60,282	60,270	60,357	60,116
1955	60,753	60,727	60,964	61,515	61,634	61,781	62,513	62,797	62,950	62,991	63,257	63,684
1956	63,753	63,518	63,411	63,614	63,861	63,820	63,800	63,972	64,079	63,975	63,796	63,910
1957	63,632	64,257	64,404	64,047	63,985	64,196	64,540	63,959	64,121	64,046	63,669	63,922
1958	63,220	62,898	62,731	62,631	62,874	62,730	62,745	63,012	63,181	63,475	63,470	63,549
1959	63,868	63,684	64,267	64,768	64,699	64,849	65,011	64,844	64,770	64,911	64,530	65,341
1960	65,347	65,620	64,673	65,959	66,057	66,168	65,909	65,895	66,267	65,632	66,109	65,778
1961	65,776	65,588	65,850	65,374	65,449	65,993	65,608	65,852	65,541	65,919	66,081	65,900
1962	66,108	66,538	66,493	66,372	66,688	66,670	66,483	66,968	67,192	67,114	66,847	66,947
1963	67,072	67,024	67,351	67,642	67,615	67,649	67,905	67,908	68,174	68,294	68,267	68,213
1964	68,327	68,751	68,763	69,356	69,631	69,218	69,399	69,463	69,578	69,582	69,735	69,814
1965	69,997	70,127	70,439	70,633	71,034	71,025	71,460	71,362	71,286	71,695	71,724	72,062
1966	72,198	72,134	72,188	72,510	72,497	72,775	72,860	73,146	73,258	73,401	73,840	73,729
1967	73,671	73,606	73,439	73,882	73,844	74,278	74,520	74,767	74,854	75,051	75,125	75,473
1968	74,700	75,229	75,379	75,561	76,107	76,182	76,087	76,043	76,172	76,224	76,494	76,778
1969	76,805	77,327	77,367	77,523	77,412	77,880	77,959	78,250	78,250	78,445	78,541	78,740
1970	78,780	78,698	78,863	78,930	78,564	78,413	78,726	78,624	78,498	78,685	78,650	78,594
1971	78,864	78,700	78,588	78,987	79,139	78,757	79,305	79,539	79,689	79,918	80,297	80,471
1972	80,959	81,108	81,573	81,655	81,887	82,083	82,230	82,578	82,543	82,616	82,990	83,400
1973	83,161	83,912	84,452	84,559	84,648	85,185	85,299	85,204	85,488	85,987	86,320	86,401
1974	86,555	86,754	86,819	86,669	86,891	86,941	87,149	87,037	87,051	86,995	86,626	86,144
1975	85,627	85,256	85,187	85,189	85,451	85,355	85,894	86,234	86,279	86,370	86,456	86,665
1976	87,400	87,672	87,985	88,416	88,794	88,563	89,093	89,223	89,173	89,274	89,634	89,803
1977	89,928	90,342	90,808	91,271	91,754	91,959	92,084	92,441	92,702	93,052	93,761	94,105
1978	94,384	94,519	94,755	95,394	95,769	96,343	96,090	96,431	96,670	97,133	97,485	97,581
1979	97,948	98,329	98,480	98,103	98,331	98,679	99,006	98,776	99,340	99,404	99,574	99,933
1980	99,879	99,995	99,713	99,233	98,945	98,682	98,796	98,824	99,077	99,317	99,545	99,634
1981	99,955	100,191	100,571	101,056	101,048	100,298	100,693	100,689	100,064	100,378	100,207	99,645
1982	99,692	99,762	99,672	99,576	100,116	99,543	99,493	99,633	99,504	99,215	99,112	99,032
1983	99,161	99,089	99,179	99,560	99,642	100,633	101,208	101,608	102,016	102,039	102,729	102,996
1984	103,201	103,824	103,967	104,336	105,193	105,591	105,435	105,163	105,490	105,638	105,972	106,223
1985	106,302	106,555	106,989	106,936	106,932	106,505	106,807	107,095	107,657	107,847	108,007	108,216
1986	108,887	108,480	108,837	108,952	109,089	109,576	109,810	110,015	110,085	110,273	110,475	110,728
1987	110,953	111,257	111,408	111,794	112,434	112,246	112,634	113,057	112,909	113,282	113,505	113,793
1988	114,016	114,227	114,037	114,650	114,292	114,927	115,060	115,282	115,356	115,638	116,100	116,104
1989	116,691	116,777	117,014	117,071	117,115	117,413	117,467	117,651	117,343	117,582	117,965	117,869
1990	117,943	118,050	118,269	118,038	118,337	118,242	117,935	117,809	117,771	117,710	117,428	117,492
1991	116,894	116,896	116,796	117,307	116,679	116,884	116,711	116,522	117,108	116,980	116,932	116,752
1992	117,036	116,962	117,264	117,518	117,580	117,510	117,722	117,780	117,724	117,687	118,064	118,311
1993	118,071	118,451	118,565	118,416	119,273	119,219	119,301	119,710	119,457	119,928	-	-

Source: U.S. Department of Labor, Bureau of Labor Statistics. - indicates data not available or zero.

Labor Force Participation Rate
Males 20 and over
(Percent)

Year	Jan	Feb	Mar	Apr	May	Jun	Jul	Aug	Sep	Oct	Nov	Dec
1948	88.7	89.0	88.2	88.3	88.1	88.5	88.7	88.8	88.5	88.8	88.7	89.0
1949	88.5	88.5	88.5	88.4	88.4	88.4	88.2	88.7	88.6	89.5	88.7	88.7
1950	88.1	88.0	88.0	88.2	88.4	88.3	88.1	88.5	88.4	88.2	88.2	88.2
1951	88.0	88.4	88.8	88.3	88.4	88.4	88.2	88.4	88.2	88.6	88.4	88.7
1952	88.8	89.0	88.6	88.5	88.4	88.4	88.3	88.0	88.0	87.6	87.6	88.5
1953	88.3	88.6	88.7	88.2	88.0	88.0	88.1	87.9	87.6	87.6	88.0	87.8
1954	87.8	88.1	87.7	88.2	87.9	87.8	87.7	88.2	88.4	88.0	87.6	87.3
1955	87.4	87.2	87.4	87.5	87.4	87.2	87.6	87.6	87.6	87.6	87.7	87.8
1956	88.1	87.9	87.9	87.8	87.6	87.6	87.5	87.5	87.3	87.2	87.3	87.3
1957	87.0	87.2	87.2	87.1	87.0	87.3	87.1	86.7	86.9	86.6	86.5	86.6
1958	86.4	86.2	86.2	86.6	86.9	86.8	87.0	87.1	87.1	87.0	86.5	86.3
1959	86.2	86.0	86.3	86.4	86.2	86.1	86.6	86.3	86.5	86.4	86.3	86.5
1960	86.2	86.0	85.6	86.1	86.0	85.9	85.9	86.0	86.2	86.1	86.3	86.3
1961	86.1	85.8	85.9	85.8	85.9	85.8	85.6	85.6	85.5	85.5	85.5	85.3
1962	85.1	85.3	85.3	84.7	85.0	84.8	84.4	84.9	84.8	84.6	84.6	84.4
1963	84.3	84.3	84.4	84.4	84.3	84.3	84.5	84.3	84.3	84.2	84.3	84.2
1964	84.2	84.1	84.0	84.5	84.5	84.0	84.3	84.1	84.2	84.2	84.0	83.9
1965	84.1	84.1	84.1	84.1	84.3	83.8	83.9	83.8	83.6	83.6	83.5	83.6
1966	83.6	83.5	83.6	83.7	83.6	83.6	83.4	83.5	83.5	83.4	83.5	83.6
1967	83.7	83.5	83.3	83.5	83.4	83.5	83.5	83.4	83.2	83.4	83.3	83.4
1968	83.1	83.1	83.0	83.1	83.2	83.4	83.3	83.2	83.0	82.9	82.9	83.1
1969	82.9	83.1	83.0	82.8	82.7	82.7	82.7	82.9	82.9	82.8	82.5	82.6
1970	82.8	82.8	82.9	83.0	82.9	82.6	82.6	82.5	82.5	82.4	82.5	82.5
1971	82.3	82.0	81.9	82.2	82.3	82.0	82.1	82.1	82.0	81.7	81.9	81.9
1972	81.6	81.5	81.8	81.7	81.6	81.7	81.7	81.6	81.6	81.4	81.4	81.5
1973	81.2	81.4	81.6	81.4	81.2	81.2	81.3	81.1	81.0	81.1	81.3	81.4
1974	81.8	81.7	81.3	81.0	81.1	80.9	80.7	80.9	80.8	80.8	80.9	80.7
1975	80.6	80.4	80.4	80.5	80.7	80.2	80.4	80.4	80.2	80.0	79.9	79.6
1976	79.7	79.6	79.6	79.9	79.8	79.7	79.9	79.9	79.9	79.8	80.0	79.8
1977	79.6	79.8	79.7	79.6	79.6	79.8	79.6	79.7	79.4	79.8	79.9	80.0
1978	79.9	79.8	79.7	79.8	79.8	79.8	79.7	79.6	79.5	79.6	80.0	80.0
1979	80.1	80.3	79.9	79.8	79.5	79.7	79.8	79.7	79.8	79.7	79.5	79.5
1980	79.7	79.9	79.4	79.5	79.6	79.3	79.4	79.4	79.3	79.2	79.2	79.0
1981	79.1	79.1	79.3	79.3	79.5	78.9	78.9	78.9	78.7	78.7	78.7	78.6
1982	78.6	78.7	78.7	78.8	78.9	78.8	78.8	78.7	78.9	78.8	78.8	78.7
1983	78.2	78.2	78.2	78.3	78.3	78.7	78.7	78.7	78.6	78.4	78.5	78.3
1984	78.3	78.3	78.2	78.3	78.3	78.4	78.4	78.3	78.4	78.3	78.3	78.3
1985	78.1	78.0	78.1	78.2	78.1	78.0	77.9	78.0	78.2	78.3	78.1	78.0
1986	78.3	78.1	78.1	78.0	78.0	78.1	78.1	78.0	78.1	78.0	78.2	78.4
1987	78.2	78.1	78.1	78.0	78.2	78.0	78.0	78.0	77.9	78.0	78.0	77.8
1988	77.9	78.0	77.8	78.1	78.0	77.8	77.9	78.1	77.8	77.9	77.9	77.8
1989	78.1	78.1	78.1	78.1	77.9	78.3	78.0	78.0	77.9	78.0	78.0	78.0
1990	78.0	78.0	77.9	77.8	77.8	77.8	77.7	77.8	77.7	77.8	77.9	77.9
1991	77.4	77.4	77.6	77.7	77.3	77.4	77.3	77.2	77.5	77.2	77.1	77.1
1992	77.1	77.1	77.4	77.4	77.7	77.6	77.4	77.5	77.3	77.3	77.1	77.1
1993	76.8	76.8	76.9	76.8	77.1	77.0	76.9	77.1	76.7	77.1	-	-

Source: U.S. Department of Labor, Bureau of Labor Statistics. - indicates data not available or zero.

Labor Force Participation Rate

Females 20 and over

(Percent)

Year	Jan	Feb	Mar	Apr	May	Jun	Jul	Aug	Sep	Oct	Nov	Dec
1948	31.0	31.4	31.1	32.1	31.3	32.5	32.7	32.0	32.3	31.7	31.8	32.1
1949	31.7	32.1	31.9	31.9	32.3	32.2	32.9	32.7	32.5	32.7	32.9	32.7
1950	32.7	32.8	32.7	33.4	33.0	33.8	33.2	33.6	33.1	33.6	33.7	33.5
1951	33.7	33.6	34.3	33.8	34.1	33.6	34.5	33.9	33.8	34.2	34.1	34.5
1952	34.4	34.3	33.5	33.6	34.0	33.8	33.7	33.9	34.9	34.2	34.8	34.2
1953	34.6	34.2	34.5	34.0	33.4	34.1	34.1	33.7	33.7	34.0	33.6	33.2
1954	33.4	34.5	34.5	34.4	34.3	34.1	33.8	33.9	34.5	34.4	34.4	34.0
1955	34.5	34.4	34.3	35.1	34.7	35.0	35.5	36.0	35.9	36.0	36.0	36.4
1956	36.3	36.0	36.0	36.2	36.7	36.4	36.6	36.6	36.8	36.6	36.4	36.4
1957	36.2	36.7	36.5	36.2	36.3	36.4	36.9	36.4	36.5	36.6	36.6	36.9
1958	36.7	36.8	36.8	37.1	37.0	37.0	37.0	37.2	36.8	36.8	36.6	36.7
1959	37.0	36.7	37.0	37.1	37.1	37.2	37.1	36.9	36.9	37.3	37.0	37.2
1960	36.9	36.9	36.3	37.6	37.7	37.9	37.9	37.9	38.1	37.6	38.2	38.2
1961	38.1	38.4	38.5	37.9	38.1	38.4	38.0	37.7	37.5	37.9	37.6	37.5
1962	37.9	38.0	37.7	37.6	37.6	37.5	37.6	38.1	38.3	37.9	37.8	37.8
1963	38.0	38.2	38.2	38.4	38.4	38.2	38.3	38.1	38.4	38.6	38.7	38.5
1964	38.5	38.8	38.8	39.5	39.3	39.0	38.7	38.9	38.6	38.8	38.7	38.9
1965	39.0	39.2	39.2	39.2	39.2	39.7	39.7	39.6	39.3	39.4	39.5	39.6
1966	39.8	39.6	39.6	39.8	40.0	39.9	40.0	40.3	40.6	40.6	40.9	40.8
1967	40.7	40.5	40.4	40.8	40.8	40.9	41.0	41.1	41.4	41.7	41.6	41.8
1968	40.9	41.3	41.4	41.4	42.0	41.9	41.7	41.3	41.6	41.6	41.9	41.9
1969	42.0	42.4	42.4	42.6	42.5	42.8	42.7	42.8	42.8	42.9	42.8	42.9
1970	43.1	43.1	43.4	43.5	43.0	43.2	43.5	43.3	43.0	43.4	43.4	43.4
1971	43.6	43.3	43.2	43.2	43.2	43.0	43.0	43.2	43.4	43.5	43.8	43.8
1972	43.6	43.4	43.7	43.6	43.8	43.6	43.7	43.8	43.7	43.7	43.6	43.7
1973	43.6	44.0	44.1	44.3	44.3	44.5	44.5	44.5	44.6	44.6	44.9	44.8
1974	44.7	45.0	45.1	45.1	45.1	45.3	45.8	45.5	45.5	45.3	45.5	45.6
1975	45.9	45.6	45.9	46.0	46.0	46.0	46.1	46.2	46.1	46.3	46.2	46.3
1976	46.6	46.6	46.7	46.8	46.8	47.0	47.3	47.3	47.1	47.1	47.5	47.6
1977	47.4	47.6	47.9	48.0	48.2	48.1	48.0	48.1	48.5	48.3	48.8	48.7
1978	48.9	48.9	49.1	49.4	49.4	49.6	49.6	49.5	49.9	50.0	50.1	50.2
1979	50.1	50.3	50.5	50.2	50.2	50.3	50.6	50.8	50.8	50.9	51.0	51.2
1980	51.3	51.3	51.2	51.4	51.3	51.2	51.3	51.4	51.2	51.4	51.6	51.4
1981	51.8	51.9	52.1	52.2	52.4	52.2	52.2	52.1	51.7	52.3	52.4	52.2
1982	52.2	52.4	52.5	52.5	52.8	52.9	52.9	52.9	52.9	52.7	52.9	53.1
1983	53.0	53.0	52.9	52.8	52.8	53.1	53.0	53.3	53.5	53.2	53.3	53.3
1984	53.0	53.3	53.4	53.6	54.1	53.8	54.0	53.8	53.6	53.9	53.9	54.1
1985	54.3	54.5	54.8	54.7	54.5	54.5	54.4	54.5	54.8	54.8	54.9	55.1
1986	54.9	55.0	55.1	55.2	55.4	55.7	55.7	55.8	55.8	55.8	55.8	55.6
1987	55.7	55.8	56.0	56.0	56.2	56.2	56.3	56.4	56.3	56.5	56.5	56.6
1988	56.6	56.7	56.7	56.7	56.4	56.5	56.6	56.8	56.8	57.1	57.5	57.4
1989	57.7	57.5	57.5	57.6	57.6	57.5	57.7	57.6	57.7	57.7	58.0	57.8
1990	57.9	57.9	57.9	57.9	58.1	57.9	57.9	58.1	57.9	57.9	57.7	57.8
1991	57.6	57.8	57.8	58.0	57.9	58.0	57.7	57.8	57.9	58.0	57.9	58.0
1992	58.1	58.2	58.4	58.4	58.3	58.5	58.6	58.5	58.3	58.2	58.4	58.5
1993	58.2	58.2	58.2	58.1	58.4	58.5	58.3	58.5	58.3	58.6	-	-

Source: U.S. Department of Labor, Bureau of Labor Statistics. - indicates data not available or zero.

Labor Force Participation Rate
16-19 years of age
(Percent)

Year	Jan	Feb	Mar	Apr	May	Jun	Jul	Aug	Sep	Oct	Nov	Dec
1948	53.2	53.7	54.1	54.2	50.9	53.8	52.6	51.5	51.5	50.6	51.0	53.1
1949	52.8	53.7	54.5	53.0	53.4	49.8	50.3	51.7	53.1	52.5	52.9	52.6
1950	51.9	51.7	50.2	50.8	50.9	50.4	50.8	52.0	52.5	53.5	52.6	52.5
1951	51.4	51.0	53.3	50.9	52.6	51.3	52.6	53.0	52.7	52.4	51.9	52.9
1952	52.2	51.8	50.9	50.7	52.3	52.8	51.2	50.0	50.5	50.2	51.4	51.1
1953	52.4	54.0	53.1	51.8	49.5	50.9	49.5	49.6	49.1	48.2	48.9	49.2
1954	50.9	51.4	51.7	50.1	48.6	46.3	47.1	48.0	48.5	47.3	46.3	44.6
1955	46.8	45.4	46.3	47.3	47.6	46.7	48.4	49.6	50.5	51.1	52.7	53.4
1956	51.4	50.5	50.0	49.4	52.1	52.5	51.7	50.6	50.3	49.7	50.4	50.3
1957	49.5	49.8	50.6	49.5	49.4	50.2	50.2	48.4	49.3	49.3	49.4	49.3
1958	47.4	48.0	47.5	48.1	48.9	46.5	46.8	47.1	47.9	47.9	46.8	47.1
1959	47.5	46.7	46.7	47.7	46.2	46.0	46.3	46.6	46.9	46.6	46.3	47.4
1960	47.2	47.4	46.7	48.5	48.1	49.7	47.3	46.9	47.4	47.3	47.4	46.5
1961	47.4	46.7	47.6	46.0	45.8	47.8	47.1	48.0	46.4	46.4	47.4	45.6
1962	45.6	45.9	46.8	46.5	47.4	47.8	46.5	46.4	45.8	45.3	44.9	44.8
1963	45.4	45.1	44.8	45.3	46.2	44.6	45.0	44.8	45.7	45.8	44.8	43.9
1964	44.4	45.3	45.0	44.0	44.8	44.4	44.0	44.2	45.5	44.1	44.1	44.3
1965	43.0	43.7	44.1	45.3	45.6	44.0	46.3	45.5	46.5	47.8	47.1	48.1
1966	48.0	46.7	46.9	47.4	46.9	48.5	49.1	49.3	47.5	48.2	49.1	49.3
1967	48.3	48.2	47.5	47.6	47.2	48.8	49.0	49.5	48.3	48.7	48.3	48.3
1968	46.6	48.5	48.2	47.9	48.2	49.3	49.1	49.0	47.9	48.0	47.7	47.8
1969	47.7	47.8	48.3	48.7	47.5	49.6	50.0	50.0	50.5	50.9	50.9	50.4
1970	50.4	50.3	50.4	49.9	49.7	49.0	49.4	49.7	50.4	50.1	50.1	49.8
1971	50.0	49.9	49.3	49.7	49.4	47.5	50.5	50.5	49.3	49.7	50.5	50.6
1972	51.1	51.4	51.9	51.8	51.5	51.9	51.6	52.9	51.6	51.9	52.4	52.8
1973	50.8	52.9	53.5	53.7	53.2	54.5	53.3	53.2	54.3	54.8	55.1	55.1
1974	55.1	55.2	55.0	53.8	54.3	55.3	54.9	53.8	55.7	55.5	55.1	54.4
1975	54.9	54.1	54.1	53.6	54.7	53.8	54.1	53.8	54.1	53.5	53.2	53.8
1976	54.2	54.2	54.4	55.2	55.1	53.8	55.3	55.1	53.9	54.4	54.4	54.1
1977	54.2	55.2	55.5	55.7	55.6	57.0	56.1	57.2	55.9	56.5	57.2	56.3
1978	56.7	56.6	56.5	57.0	57.9	58.5	58.4	59.3	58.1	58.3	58.2	58.2
1979	58.5	58.6	58.4	57.9	57.3	58.0	57.7	56.8	57.8	57.5	57.7	58.3
1980	57.7	57.2	57.2	55.9	57.0	57.0	57.3	55.9	56.3	56.6	56.2	55.9
1981	56.7	56.6	56.4	57.0	56.3	54.0	54.5	55.2	54.8	55.0	55.2	53.8
1982	54.4	54.7	53.8	54.3	55.3	52.5	53.2	54.2	54.0	54.4	54.7	53.9
1983	53.7	52.7	52.5	52.6	52.2	55.2	53.8	55.1	53.8	53.0	53.6	53.8
1984	53.2	53.3	53.3	53.9	53.8	55.2	54.8	53.3	54.4	53.9	53.8	54.5
1985	55.0	54.9	55.3	54.7	55.0	53.0	55.5	53.4	54.1	54.5	54.3	54.1
1986	53.3	54.6	55.1	55.6	55.2	55.4	54.7	54.6	54.8	54.9	54.2	53.4
1987	54.0	54.8	54.4	54.4	55.3	53.7	54.1	56.2	54.3	55.1	54.6	55.4
1988	55.6	55.0	53.8	54.4	54.2	56.4	56.4	56.6	56.1	55.1	54.8	55.1
1989	55.6	54.8	54.5	55.5	55.5	56.9	56.1	57.4	55.6	56.4	56.5	55.8
1990	55.1	54.7	55.6	55.2	54.5	53.4	53.2	52.3	52.9	53.0	52.2	52.7
1991	52.8	52.7	52.9	52.7	52.0	51.5	50.7	49.7	51.0	51.8	51.3	51.0
1992	51.4	51.7	50.5	50.4	51.2	51.8	51.3	51.5	52.1	50.6	51.4	51.6
1993	51.0	52.1	51.3	51.7	52.7	51.4	51.9	51.6	51.0	51.3	-	-

Source: U.S. Department of Labor, Bureau of Labor Statistics. - indicates data not available or zero.

INDICATORS OF INTERNATIONAL TRANSACTIONS

International trade has been a subject of concern and debate since the mid-1970s, when the U.S. trade balance turned negative and has continued negative since. As a percent of GDP, foreign trade has also grown. And with the rise of new industrial economies on the Asian rim of the Pacific, a world-wide competition for trade has intensified concerns. Negative trade balances have a direct impact on GDP; they are also, indirectly, a measure of U.S. competitiveness in world markets. The three tables included in this section present the basic facts about this phenomenon as seen from the U.S. vantage point. The tables are:

    Merchandise exports, adjusted, excluding military
    Merchandise imports, adjusted, excluding military
    Balance on merchandise trade

Merchandise Exports, Excluding Military. Data from 1960 to 1993 are shown in millions of current dollars. Data exclude Department of Defense sales contracts (exports) and military grants. Military aid shipments and exports are excluded because, arising from government policy, such shipments would distort the market-based nature of the overall export business.

Merchandise Imports, Excluding Military. Data are also for 1960 to 1993 in millions of current dollars. Data exclude Department of Defense purchases (imports).

Balance on Merchandise Trade. Data are in millions of current dollars for 1960 to 1993. The values shown are merchandise exports less merchandise imports from the earlier tables, indicating to what extent the U.S. enjoyed a trade surplus (positive numbers) or a deficit (negative values).

Surplus or deficit in foreign trade has always played an important role in international relations. In pre-modern times, when gold was the standard of exchange, a trade deficit meant that a country lost some of its gold stock to another country; a surplus meant a gain in gold; for this reason, countries tried to maintain surpluses or, failing that, a balance between imports and exports. International trade has become much more complex since, but underlying concepts remain in force. Thus the purchasing power of the dollar has a direct influence on the trade deficit. A strong dollar (meaning a dollar expensive relative to other currencies) acts to diminish exports—because dollar-denominated goods are expensive elsewhere; importers are aided because their goods are relatively cheap in the U.S. market. Conversely, a weak dollar helps exports and impedes imports. The strong and weak dollar have other consequences as well: a strong dollar tends to reduce production but curbs inflation; a weak dollar is associated with high production but also with inflation.

A strong dollar in the 1980-1985 period was one of the causes of a dramatically increasing trade deficit in that period. A weaker dollar since has reduced the deficit. The value of the dollar, in turn, reflects the strength of an economy relative to other economies and *perceptions* of this strength; perceptions are translated into policy and trading actions by others—which cause the value of the dollar to rise or fall. Public policy can influence—but cannot set—the value of the dollar.

The trade deficit has a negative impact on GDP growth because trade balance is part of GDP. The change from period to period is more important, in this context, than the absolute magnitude of the trade balance or its arithmetic sign. A shrinking deficit or a growing surplus will both translate into a positive signal for GDP.

Exports, imports, and the trade balance are subject to trade policies followed in the U.S. and in foreign countries. Therefore, ultimately, foreign trade data reflect pure market forces only indirectly.

Merchandise Exports
Adjusted, excluding military
(Million $)

Year	1st Quarter	2nd Quarter	3rd Quarter	4th Quarter
1960	4,685	4,916	5,031	5,018
1961	5,095	4,806	5,038	5,169
1962	5,077	5,336	5,331	5,037
1963	5,063	5,599	5,671	5,939
1964	6,242	6,199	6,423	6,637
1965	5,768	6,876	6,643	7,174
1966	7,242	7,169	7,290	7,609
1967	7,751	7,693	7,530	7,692
1968	7,998	8,324	8,745	8,559
1969	7,468	9,536	9,400	10,010
1970	10,258	10,744	10,665	10,802
1971	10,920	10,878	11,548	9,973
1972	11,833	11,618	12,351	13,579
1973	15,474	17,112	18,271	20,553
1974	22,614	24,500	24,629	26,563
1975	27,480	25,866	26,109	27,633
1976	27,575	28,256	29,056	29,858
1977	29,668	30,852	30,752	29,544
1978	30,470	35,674	36,523	39,408
1979	41,475	43,885	47,104	51,975
1980	54,237	55,967	55,830	58,216
1981	60,317	60,141	58,031	58,555
1982	55,163	55,344	52,089	48,561
1983	49,198	49,340	50,324	52,937
1984	52,991	54,626	55,893	56,416
1985	54,866	54,154	52,836	54,059
1986	53,536	56,828	55,645	57,335
1987	56,696	60,202	64,217	69,093
1988	75,655	79,542	80,941	84,092
1989	87,522	92,041	90,074	92,479
1990	95,286	97,337	96,431	100,249
1991	101,333	104,206	103,764	107,634
1992	108,347	108,306	109,493	113,992
1993	111,530	113,118	111,912	-

Source: U.S. Department of Commerce, Bureau of the Census. - indicates data not available or zero.

Merchandise Imports
Adjusted, excluding military
(Million $)

Year	1st Quarter	2nd Quarter	3rd Quarter	4th Quarter
1960	3,812	3,858	3,648	3,440
1961	3,394	3,438	3,809	3,896
1962	3,966	4,080	4,116	4,098
1963	4,064	4,226	4,372	4,386
1964	4,416	4,598	4,756	4,930
1965	4,711	5,428	5,516	5,855
1966	6,012	6,195	6,576	6,710
1967	6,708	6,475	6,526	7,157
1968	7,796	8,051	8,612	8,532
1969	7,444	9,527	9,380	9,456
1970	9,587	9,766	10,049	10,464
1971	10,600	11,614	12,171	11,194
1972	13,501	13,254	14,022	15,020
1973	16,285	17,168	17,683	19,363
1974	21,952	26,346	27,368	28,145
1975	24,980	22,832	24,487	25,886
1976	28,176	30,182	32,213	33,657
1977	36,585	38,063	38,005	39,254
1978	42,487	43,419	44,422	45,674
1979	47,582	50,778	54,002	59,645
1980	65,815	62,274	59,010	62,651
1981	67,004	67,181	64,407	66,475
1982	63,502	60,580	63,696	59,864
1983	59,757	64,783	70,370	73,991
1984	79,740	83,798	83,918	84,962
1985	80,319	84,565	83,909	89,295
1986	89,220	91,743	92,801	94,661
1987	96,023	100,648	104,412	108,682
1988	109,963	110,836	110,901	115,489
1989	116,600	120,803	118,768	121,194
1990	122,508	122,084	125,385	128,359
1991	120,123	120,525	123,404	126,687
1992	126,110	133,107	137,105	139,954
1993	140,839	147,502	148,191	-

Source: U.S. Department of Commerce, Bureau of the Census. - indicates data not available or zero.

Balance On Merchandise Trade
(Million $)

Year	1st Quarter	2nd Quarter	3rd Quarter	4th Quarter
1960	873	1,058	1,383	1,578
1961	1,701	1,368	1,229	1,273
1962	1,111	1,256	1,215	939
1963	999	1,373	1,299	1,553
1964	1,826	1,601	1,667	1,707
1965	1,057	1,448	1,127	1,319
1966	1,230	974	714	899
1967	1,043	1,218	1,004	535
1968	202	273	133	27
1969	24	9	20	554
1970	671	978	616	338
1971	320	-736	-623	-1,221
1972	-1,668	-1,636	-1,671	-1,441
1973	-811	-56	588	1,190
1974	662	-1,846	-2,739	-1,582
1975	2,500	3,034	1,622	1,747
1976	-601	-1,926	-3,157	-3,799
1977	-6,917	-7,211	-7,253	-9,710
1978	-12,017	-7,745	-7,899	-6,266
1979	-6,107	-6,893	-6,898	-7,670
1980	-11,578	-6,307	-3,180	-4,435
1981	-6,687	-7,040	-6,376	-7,920
1982	-8,339	-5,236	-11,607	-11,303
1983	-10,559	-15,443	-20,046	-21,054
1984	-26,749	-29,172	-28,025	-28,546
1985	-25,453	-30,411	-31,073	-35,236
1986	-35,684	-34,915	-37,156	-37,326
1987	-39,327	-40,446	-40,195	-39,589
1988	-34,308	-31,294	-29,960	-31,397
1989	-29,078	-28,762	-28,694	-28,715
1990	-27,222	-24,747	-28,954	-28,110
1991	-18,790	-16,319	-19,640	-19,053
1992	-17,763	-24,801	-27,612	-25,962
1993	-29,309	-34,384	-36,279	-

Source: U.S. Department of Commerce, Bureau of Economic Analysis. - indicates data not available or zero.

CHAPTER 6

CONSUMER PRICE INDEX

CONSUMER PRICE INDEX

The Consumer Price Index (CPI) is the primary system for measuring price change in the United States in a consistent manner. The CPI, therefore, is the chief measure of inflation and the source of data for converting "current dollar" measurements and estimates into "constant" or "real dollar" values used in National Income and Product Accounts and in cyclic indicators of the economy. It is produced by the U.S. Department of Labor, Bureau of Labor Statistics (BLS), Division of Consumer Prices and Price Indexes.

General Concept

The CPI is based on obtaining the price of an *identical* "basket" of goods at two different points in time and measuring the difference. By way of illustration, consider the following simple case:

> A basket of goods is purchased in January 1975 containing a loaf of bread, a quart of milk, a pound of potatoes, a package of bacon, five pounds of flour and of sugar. The price is noted. It is $15.00.

> A year later, exactly the same items are purchased. This time the price is $18.00.

In this situation, inflation has been $3.00. Only the price has changed. It has increased by 20%.

Rather than dealing with actual dollar figures, we can express these relationships as an index. If 1975 is chosen as the base year and set to a value of 100, the 1976 value would be 120—showing a 20% inflation rate.

The system works in the same way if prices decrease. Assume that in 1977 the same basket of goods cost $12.00. This price is 20% lower than the price in the base year. The new 1977 index, therefore, would be 80. The change between 1976 and 1977 would be a 33.3% decrease:

$$((80 / 120) - 1) \times 100 = -33.3$$

These concepts underlie the CPI. The index measures the price of a "fixed market basket of goods and services" at monthly intervals. This is a hypothetical basket because it includes not only items one ordinarily buys in a store but also the costs of fuel, housing, transportation, and other services. A base period is selected; currently (1994) it is the average of 1982-1984. The price index is shown with reference to the base period, which is defined as 100.

Implementation of the Concept

In order to implement this concept in a useful manner, it is necessary, first, to determine the make-up of the "fixed market basket": what proportion of a family's budget is devoted to food, clothing, housing, etc. Since consumption patterns differ somewhat from region to region, it is also necessary to know how the market basket's contents change from place to place; fuel costs, typically, will be a lesser proportion of budgets in mild climates, for instance. BLS conducts surveys at regular intervals in selected urban areas to answer these questions. Consumer surveys are then used to change how the index is constructed and what weight or importance to give to each major component in the basket. From the beginning of the CPI, surveys of spending patterns have been followed by comprehensive revisions of the index.

The modern index is built by pricing goods and services in 94 primary sampling units in 91 geographical areas. Sampling units and geographical areas are selected using population census data to arrive at a representative sampling.

Raw data collected from sampling units are processed into geographical indexes and into a U.S. City average. Major components (food, apparel, housing, etc.) are combined by applying appropriate weights to produce a final consumer price index.

History and Revisions

The CPI was initiated during World War I as a tool for calculating cost-of-living adjustments in wages. The first surveys of consumption patterns were carried out by the Department of Labor from 1917-1919; periodic collection of prices began in 1919 by the Department's Bureau of Labor Statistics. Regular publication began in 1921, with indexes estimated back to 1913. The cycle of surveys and revisions began in 1934-36 (survey) and 1940 (index revision). Thereafter, major changes were introduced as follows:

    1951 - adjustments to reflect immediate postwar changes
    1953 - comprehensive postwar revisions, statistical overhaul
    1964 - new expenditure weights reflecting single persons as well as families
    1978 - changes in sample, data collection, inclusion of all urban consumers
    1983 - changes in home ownership cost calculations for all urban consumers
    1985 - changes in home ownership cost calculationsfor urban wage earners
    1987 - improvements of sampling, data collection, processing, and estimation

The CPI was originally designed to measure the cost of living of urban wage earners and clerical workers (usually called CPI-W). A more encompassing category including all urban families (CPI-U) was introduced in 1978; CPI-U includes, in addition to CPI-W, professional and salaried workers, part-time workers, the self-employed, the unemployed, and retired people.

Sampling, Components, and Methods

Sampling Universe. CPI pricing data are collected in 91 urban areas; 21,000 retail and service establishments are sampled; these include supermarkets, department stores, filling stations, hospitals, and other establishments. Housing costs are collected from 40,000 tenants and on 20,000 owner-occupied housing units.

Product/Service Categories. Items/services to be priced are subdivided into 7 major product groups: food and beverages, fuels and utilities, household services and furnishings, apparel and upkeep, transportation, medical care, entertainment, and other commodities and services. These major groupings are made up of 69 expenditure classes (e.g. furniture and bedding) which, in turn, are divided into 207 item strata (bedroom furniture) and finally into 364 "entry level items" (mattresses and springs). Pricing on approximately 100,000 entry level items is conducted for the CPI on a regular basis.

Sampling Frequency. Food, fuel, and selected other items are priced monthly in all of the sample geographies. Most other goods and services are surveyed monthly in the five largest urban areas and bimonthly in all the others.

Basing Years. BLS provides data calculated with a base of 1967 and 1982-1984—in which data are expressed with 1967 values as 100 and the 1982-1984 averages as 100. The annual average index for 1982 is 95.6, for 1983 99.6 and for 1984 103.9. The sum of these index values is 300; divided by 3, we get the basing value of 100.

Measurement of Changes. Index movements from one month to the next are expressed as percent changes rather than as changes in index points. The following formula is used in the tables to show change from period to period:

((Current Index / Previous Index) - 1) x 100.

This formula can be used to calculate, for example, how the cost of living has changed between January 1990 and January 1991 without reference to the base year of the series. The U.S. average data for base 1982-1984 were as follows:

> January 1990 - 127.4
> January 1991 - 134.6

By applying the formula to these values, we get a percent change of 5.7.

The data for the same series but with a 1967 base are:

> January 1990 - 381.5
> January 1991 - 403.1

These values *also* produce a 5.7% change.

The meaning of the change for a person with a fixed income of $30,000 a year would be that his or her income in 1991 was 5.7% less than in 1990 due to inflation. The purchasing power of the income would be $28,290 in 1991.

Uses of the CPI

The CPI is the most widely used measure of inflation; consequently, it plays a role in economic measurement and in the setting of monetary and fiscal policy and is used widely as an indicator in all manner of institutions, public and private, for a range of activities, including wage settlements.

The CPI is used as a deflator of other economic series. Throughout *Economic Indicators Handbook*, references are made to current dollar and constant dollar presentations of data; the latter are also referred to as "real" dollars, meaning that inflation has been removed by use of a deflator. In the example above, the person with a fixed income of $30,000 had an income in 1991 of $30,000 in *current* dollars but only an income of $28,290 in *constant* or "real" dollars (in this case 1990 dollars).

The CPI is used for income adjustments. More than 3 million union workers are covered by contracts tied to CPI. The income of more than 60 million other people is affected by changes in CPI, including 38 million Social Security recipients, 3 million military and federal retirees and survivors, and about 19 million people receiving food stamps. Federal income tax indexing uses the CPI. There are also many uses of the CPI by the private sector.

Presentation and Limitations of Data

In the following tables, data are presented as follows:

U.S. City Average Data. These data are the overall CPI, calculated for all cities. *EIH* presents the following subsets of the data:

> Annual Averages for all items and 7 subcategories, 1982-1984 basis
> > For all urban consumers
> > For urban wage earners and clerical workers

> U.S. City Average for all items, monthly, 1982-1984 basis
> > All urban consumers
> > Urban wage earners and clerical workers

> U.S. City Average for each of 7 subcategories of expenditure, 1982-1984 basis
> > Monthly for all urban consumers
> > Monthly for urban wage earners and clerical workers

Index values are shown from 1913 to 1993 as available. Percent change from one period to the next is precalculated and shown. In tables of annual averages, the comparison is between two rows in the same column; in monthly tables, the comparison is between two columns of the same row.

Limitations of the U.S. City Average Data. The CPI measures cost changes in urban areas and should not be applied to situations in other contexts. The index is based on a sample of consumer purchases rather than all consumer purchases; hence sampling errors are inherent in the series. The CPI cannot be used for demographic subgroups of the population, such as the elderly.

City/Urban Area Data. Following the U.S. City Average tables, data are presented for 27 cities/urban areas. The cities are ordered alphabetically. For each city, the following tables are presented:

> Annual averages for all items and 7 subcategories, 1982-1984 basis
> > For all urban consumers
> > For urban wage earners and clerical workers

> All items, monthly, 1982-1984 basis
> > All urban consumers
> > Urban wage earners and clerical workers

> Seven tables of subcategories, 1982-1984 basis
> > Monthly for all urban consumers
> > Monthly for urban wage earners and clerical workers

Years and months of coverage for cities varies. For some, categories data are available back to 1913. In other cases, data start at a later date and are shown for the months in which data were collected. The tables, in fact, show how the frequency and timing of collections have changed over time.

Limitations of City/Urban Area Data. Is it more expensive to live in New York than in Los Angeles? *The CPI cannot be used to answer this question*. Cost of living comparisons *between* cities are not a legitimate use of the index. The CPI, in other words, cannot be used to determine "relative" cost of living. The index measures only changes in the cost of living *in* one urban area. The CPI is suitable for determining whether or not prices are rising faster in one city than in another; they do not measure absolute price levels between cities.

Bibliography

1. U.S. Department of Labor, Bureau of Labor Statistics. *BLS Handbook of Methods*, Bulletin 2285, 1987. Washington, DC.

U.S. CITY AVERAGE
Consumer Price Index - All Urban Consumers
Base 1982-1984 = 100
Annual Averages

For 1913-1993. Columns headed % show percentile change in the index from the previous period for which an index is available.

Year	All Items		Food & Beverage		Housing		Apparel & Upkeep		Trans-portation		Medical Care		Entertain-ment		Other Goods & Services	
	Index	%	Index	%	Index	%	Index	%	Index	%	Index	%	Index	%	Index	%
1913	9.9	-	-	-	-	-	14.9	-	-	-	-	-	-	-	-	-
1914	10.0	1.0	-	-	-	-	15.0	0.7	-	-	-	-	-	-	-	-
1915	10.1	1.0	-	-	-	-	15.3	2.0	-	-	-	-	-	-	-	-
1916	10.9	7.9	-	-	-	-	16.8	9.8	-	-	-	-	-	-	-	-
1917	12.8	17.4	-	-	-	-	20.2	20.2	-	-	-	-	-	-	-	-
1918	15.1	18.0	-	-	-	-	27.3	35.1	-	-	-	-	-	-	-	-
1919	17.3	14.6	-	-	-	-	36.2	32.6	-	-	-	-	-	-	-	-
1920	20.0	15.6	-	-	-	-	43.1	19.1	-	-	-	-	-	-	-	-
1921	17.9	-10.5	-	-	-	-	33.2	-23.0	-	-	-	-	-	-	-	-
1922	16.8	-6.1	-	-	-	-	27.0	-18.7	-	-	-	-	-	-	-	-
1923	17.1	1.8	-	-	-	-	27.1	0.4	-	-	-	-	-	-	-	-
1924	17.1	0.0	-	-	-	-	26.8	-1.1	-	-	-	-	-	-	-	-
1925	17.5	2.3	-	-	-	-	26.3	-1.9	-	-	-	-	-	-	-	-
1926	17.7	1.1	-	-	-	-	25.9	-1.5	-	-	-	-	-	-	-	-
1927	17.4	-1.7	-	-	-	-	25.3	-2.3	-	-	-	-	-	-	-	-
1928	17.1	-1.7	-	-	-	-	25.0	-1.2	-	-	-	-	-	-	-	-
1929	17.1	0.0	-	-	-	-	24.7	-1.2	-	-	-	-	-	-	-	-
1930	16.7	-2.3	-	-	-	-	24.2	-2.0	-	-	-	-	-	-	-	-
1931	15.2	-9.0	-	-	-	-	22.0	-9.1	-	-	-	-	-	-	-	-
1932	13.7	-9.9	-	-	-	-	19.5	-11.4	-	-	-	-	-	-	-	-
1933	13.0	-5.1	-	-	-	-	18.8	-3.6	-	-	-	-	-	-	-	-
1934	13.4	3.1	-	-	-	-	20.6	9.6	-	-	-	-	-	-	-	-
1935	13.7	2.2	-	-	-	-	20.8	1.0	14.2	-	10.2	-	-	-	-	-
1936	13.9	1.5	-	-	-	-	21.0	1.0	14.3	0.7	10.2	0.0	-	-	-	-
1937	14.4	3.6	-	-	-	-	22.0	4.8	14.5	1.4	10.3	1.0	-	-	-	-
1938	14.1	-2.1	-	-	-	-	21.9	-0.5	14.6	0.7	10.3	0.0	-	-	-	-
1939	13.9	-1.4	-	-	-	-	21.6	-1.4	14.3	-2.1	10.3	0.0	-	-	-	-
1940	14.0	0.7	-	-	-	-	21.8	0.9	14.2	-0.7	10.4	1.0	-	-	-	-
1941	14.7	5.0	-	-	-	-	22.8	4.6	14.7	3.5	10.4	0.0	-	-	-	-
1942	16.3	10.9	-	-	-	-	26.7	17.1	16.0	8.8	10.7	2.9	-	-	-	-
1943	17.3	6.1	-	-	-	-	27.8	4.1	15.9	-0.6	11.2	4.7	-	-	-	-
1944	17.6	1.7	-	-	-	-	29.8	7.2	15.9	0.0	11.6	3.6	-	-	-	-
1945	18.0	2.3	-	-	-	-	31.4	5.4	15.9	0.0	11.9	2.6	-	-	-	-
1946	19.5	8.3	-	-	-	-	34.4	9.6	16.7	5.0	12.5	5.0	-	-	-	-
1947	22.3	14.4	-	-	-	-	39.9	16.0	18.5	10.8	13.5	8.0	-	-	-	-
1948	24.1	8.1	-	-	-	-	42.5	6.5	20.6	11.4	14.4	6.7	-	-	-	-
1949	23.8	-1.2	-	-	-	-	40.8	-4.0	22.1	7.3	14.8	2.8	-	-	-	-
1950	24.1	1.3	-	-	-	-	40.3	-1.2	22.7	2.7	15.1	2.0	-	-	-	-
1951	26.0	7.9	-	-	-	-	43.9	8.9	24.1	6.2	15.9	5.3	-	-	-	-
1952	26.5	1.9	-	-	-	-	43.5	-0.9	25.7	6.6	16.7	5.0	-	-	-	-
1953	26.7	0.8	-	-	-	-	43.1	-0.9	26.5	3.1	17.3	3.6	-	-	-	-
1954	26.9	0.7	-	-	-	-	43.1	0.0	26.1	-1.5	17.8	2.9	-	-	-	-
1955	26.8	-0.4	-	-	-	-	42.9	-0.5	25.8	-1.1	18.2	2.2	-	-	-	-
1956	27.2	1.5	-	-	-	-	43.7	1.9	26.2	1.6	18.9	3.8	-	-	-	-
1957	28.1	3.3	-	-	-	-	44.5	1.8	27.7	5.7	19.7	4.2	-	-	-	-

[Continued]

U.S. City Average

Consumer Price Index - All Urban Consumers
Base 1982-1984 = 100
Annual Averages
[Continued]

For 1913-1993. Columns headed % show percentile change in the index from the previous period for which an index is available.

Year	All Items		Food & Beverage		Housing		Apparel & Upkeep		Trans- portation		Medical Care		Entertain- ment		Other Goods & Services	
	Index	%	Index	%	Index	%	Index	%	Index	%	Index	%	Index	%	Index	%
1958	28.9	2.8	-	-	-	-	44.6	0.2	28.6	3.2	20.6	4.6	-	-	-	-
1959	29.1	0.7	-	-	-	-	45.0	0.9	29.8	4.2	21.5	4.4	-	-	-	-
1960	29.6	1.7	-	-	-	-	45.7	1.6	29.8	0.0	22.3	3.7	-	-	-	-
1961	29.9	1.0	-	-	-	-	46.1	0.9	30.1	1.0	22.9	2.7	-	-	-	-
1962	30.2	1.0	-	-	-	-	46.3	0.4	30.8	2.3	23.5	2.6	-		-	
1963	30.6	1.3	-	-	-	-	46.9	1.3	30.9	0.3	24.1	2.6				
1964	31.0	1.3	-	-	-	-	47.3	0.9	31.4	1.6	24.6	2.1	-		-	
1965	31.5	1.6	-	-	-	-	47.8	1.1	31.9	1.6	25.2	2.4	-	-	-	-
1966	32.4	2.9	-	-	-	-	49.0	2.5	32.3	1.3	26.3	4.4	-		-	
1967	33.4	3.1	35.0	-	30.8	-	51.0	4.1	33.3	3.1	28.2	7.2	40.7	-	35.1	-
1968	34.8	4.2	36.2	3.4	32.0	3.9	53.7	5.3	34.3	3.0	29.9	6.0	43.0	5.7	36.9	5.1
1969	36.7	5.5	38.1	5.2	34.0	6.3	56.8	5.8	35.7	4.1	31.9	6.7	45.2	5.1	38.7	4.9
1970	38.8	5.7	40.1	5.2	36.4	7.1	59.2	4.2	37.5	5.0	34.0	6.6	47.5	5.1	40.9	5.7
1971	40.5	4.4	41.4	3.2	38.0	4.4	61.1	3.2	39.5	5.3	36.1	6.2	50.0	5.3	42.9	4.9
1972	41.8	3.2	43.1	4.1	39.4	3.7	62.3	2.0	39.9	1.0	37.3	3.3	51.5	3.0	44.7	4.2
1973	44.4	6.2	48.8	13.2	41.2	4.6	64.6	3.7	41.2	3.3	38.8	4.0	52.9	2.7	46.4	3.8
1974	49.3	11.0	55.5	13.7	45.8	11.2	69.4	7.4	45.8	11.2	42.4	9.3	56.9	7.6	49.8	7.3
1975	53.8	9.1	60.2	8.5	50.7	10.7	72.5	4.5	50.1	9.4	47.5	12.0	62.0	9.0	53.9	8.2
1976	56.9	5.8	62.1	3.2	53.8	6.1	75.2	3.7	55.1	10.0	52.0	9.5	65.1	5.0	57.0	5.8
1977	60.6	6.5	65.8	6.0	57.4	6.7	78.6	4.5	59.0	7.1	57.0	9.6	68.3	4.9	60.4	6.0
1978	65.2	7.6	72.2	9.7	62.4	8.7	81.4	3.6	61.7	4.6	61.8	8.4	71.9	5.3	64.3	6.5
1979	72.6	11.3	79.9	10.7	70.1	12.3	84.9	4.3	70.5	14.3	67.5	9.2	76.7	6.7	68.9	7.2
1980	82.4	13.5	86.7	8.5	81.1	15.7	90.9	7.1	83.1	17.9	74.9	11.0	83.6	9.0	75.2	9.1
1981	90.9	10.3	93.5	7.8	90.4	11.5	95.3	4.8	93.2	12.2	82.9	10.7	90.1	7.8	82.6	9.8
1982	96.5	6.2	97.3	4.1	96.9	7.2	97.8	2.6	97.0	4.1	92.5	11.6	96.0	6.5	91.1	10.3
1983	99.6	3.2	99.5	2.3	99.5	2.7	100.2	2.5	99.3	2.4	100.6	8.8	100.1	4.3	101.1	11.0
1984	103.9	4.3	103.2	3.7	103.6	4.1	102.1	1.9	103.7	4.4	106.8	6.2	103.8	3.7	107.9	6.7
1985	107.6	3.6	105.6	2.3	107.7	4.0	105.0	2.8	106.4	2.6	113.5	6.3	107.9	3.9	114.5	6.1
1986	109.6	1.9	109.1	3.3	110.9	3.0	105.9	0.9	102.3	-3.9	122.0	7.5	111.6	3.4	121.4	6.0
1987	113.6	3.6	113.5	4.0	114.2	3.0	110.6	4.4	105.4	3.0	130.1	6.6	115.3	3.3	128.5	5.8
1988	118.3	4.1	118.2	4.1	118.5	3.8	115.4	4.3	108.7	3.1	138.6	6.5	120.3	4.3	137.0	6.6
1989	124.0	4.8	124.9	5.7	123.0	3.8	118.6	2.8	114.1	5.0	149.3	7.7	126.5	5.2	147.7	7.8
1990	130.7	5.4	132.1	5.8	128.5	4.5	124.1	4.6	120.5	5.6	162.8	9.0	132.4	4.7	159.0	7.7
1991	136.2	4.2	136.8	3.6	133.6	4.0	128.7	3.7	123.8	2.7	177.0	8.7	138.4	4.5	171.6	7.9
1992	140.3	3.0	138.7	1.4	137.5	2.9	131.9	2.5	126.5	2.2	190.1	7.4	142.3	2.8	183.3	6.8
1993	144.5	3.0	141.6	2.1	141.2	2.7	133.7	1.4	130.4	3.1	201.4	5.9	145.8	2.5	192.9	5.2

Source: U.S. Department of Labor, Bureau of Labor Statistics, Division of Consumer Prices and Price Indexes.

U.S. CITY AVERAGE
Consumer Price Index - Urban Wage Earners
Base 1982-1984 = 100
Annual Averages

For 1913-1993. Columns headed % show percentile change in the index from the previous period for which an index is available.

Year	All Items		Food & Beverage		Housing		Apparel & Upkeep		Trans-portation		Medical Care		Entertain-ment		Other Goods & Services	
	Index	%	Index	%	Index	%	Index	%	Index	%	Index	%	Index	%	Index	%
1913	10.0	-	-	-	-	-	15.0	-	-	-	-	-	-	-	-	-
1914	10.1	1.0	-	-	-	-	15.1	0.7	-	-	-	-	-	-	-	-
1915	10.2	1.0	-	-	-	-	15.4	2.0	-	-	-	-	-	-	-	-
1916	11.0	7.8	-	-	-	-	16.9	9.7	-	-	-	-	-	-	-	-
1917	12.9	17.3	-	-	-	-	20.3	20.1	-	-	-	-	-	-	-	-
1918	15.1	17.1	-	-	-	-	27.5	35.5	-	-	-	-	-	-	-	-
1919	17.4	15.2	-	-	-	-	36.4	32.4	-	-	-	-	-	-	-	-
1920	20.1	15.5	-	-	-	-	43.3	19.0	-	-	-	-	-	-	-	-
1921	18.0	-10.4	-	-	-	-	33.4	-22.9	-	-	-	-	-	-	-	-
1922	16.9	-6.1	-	-	-	-	27.2	-18.6	-	-	-	-	-	-	-	-
1923	17.2	1.8	-	-	-	-	27.2	0.0	-	-	-	-	-	-	-	-
1924	17.2	0.0	-	-	-	-	26.9	-1.1	-	-	-	-	-	-	-	-
1925	17.6	2.3	-	-	-	-	26.4	-1.9	-	-	-	-	-	-	-	-
1926	17.8	1.1	-	-	-	-	26.0	-1.5	-	-	-	-	-	-	-	-
1927	17.5	-1.7	-	-	-	-	25.5	-1.9	-	-	-	-	-	-	-	-
1928	17.2	-1.7	-	-	-	-	25.1	-1.6	-	-	-	-	-	-	-	-
1929	17.2	0.0	-	-	-	-	24.8	-1.2	-	-	-	-	-	-	-	-
1930	16.8	-2.3	-	-	-	-	24.3	-2.0	-	-	-	-	-	-	-	-
1931	15.3	-8.9	-	-	-	-	22.1	-9.1	-	-	-	-	-	-	-	-
1932	13.7	-10.5	-	-	-	-	19.6	-11.3	-	-	-	-	-	-	-	-
1933	13.0	-5.1	-	-	-	-	18.9	-3.6	-	-	-	-	-	-	-	-
1934	13.5	3.8	-	-	-	-	20.7	9.5	-	-	-	-	-	-	-	-
1935	13.8	2.2	-	-	-	-	20.9	1.0	14.1	-	10.2	-	-	-	-	-
1936	13.9	0.7	-	-	-	-	21.1	1.0	14.2	0.7	10.3	1.0	-	-	-	-
1937	14.4	3.6	-	-	-	-	22.1	4.7	14.5	2.1	10.4	1.0	-	-	-	-
1938	14.2	-1.4	-	-	-	-	22.0	-0.5	14.6	0.7	10.4	0.0	-	-	-	-
1939	14.0	-1.4	-	-	-	-	21.7	-1.4	14.2	-2.7	10.4	0.0	-	-	-	-
1940	14.1	0.7	-	-	-	-	21.9	0.9	14.1	-0.7	10.4	0.0	-	-	-	-
1941	14.8	5.0	-	-	-	-	23.0	5.0	14.6	3.5	10.5	1.0	-	-	-	-
1942	16.4	10.8	-	-	-	-	26.8	16.5	15.9	8.9	10.8	2.9	-	-	-	-
1943	17.4	6.1	-	-	-	-	28.0	4.5	15.8	-0.6	11.3	4.6	-	-	-	-
1944	17.7	1.7	-	-	-	-	30.0	7.1	15.8	0.0	11.6	2.7	-	-	-	-
1945	18.1	2.3	-	-	-	-	31.5	5.0	15.8	0.0	11.9	2.6	-	-	-	-
1946	19.6	8.3	-	-	-	-	34.6	9.8	16.6	5.1	12.6	5.9	-	-	-	-
1947	22.5	14.8	-	-	-	-	40.1	15.9	18.4	10.8	13.6	7.9	-	-	-	-
1948	24.2	7.6	-	-	-	-	42.7	6.5	20.4	10.9	14.5	6.6	-	-	-	-
1949	24.0	-0.8	-	-	-	-	41.0	-4.0	22.0	7.8	14.9	2.8	-	-	-	-
1950	24.2	0.8	-	-	-	-	40.5	-1.2	22.6	2.7	15.2	2.0	-	-	-	-
1951	26.1	7.9	-	-	-	-	44.1	8.9	24.0	6.2	15.9	4.6	-	-	-	-
1952	26.7	2.3	-	-	-	-	43.7	-0.9	25.6	6.7	16.8	5.7	-	-	-	-
1953	26.9	0.7	-	-	-	-	43.3	-0.9	26.3	2.7	17.4	3.6	-	-	-	-
1954	27.0	0.4	-	-	-	-	43.3	0.0	25.9	-1.5	17.9	2.9	-	-	-	-
1955	26.9	-0.4	-	-	-	-	43.1	-0.5	25.6	-1.2	18.3	2.2	-	-	-	-
1956	27.3	1.5	-	-	-	-	44.0	2.1	26.1	2.0	19.0	3.8	-	-	-	-
1957	28.3	3.7	-	-	-	-	44.7	1.6	27.6	5.7	19.8	4.2	-	-	-	-

[Continued]

U.S. City Average
Consumer Price Index - Urban Wage Earners
Base 1982-1984 = 100
Annual Averages
[Continued]

For 1913-1993. Columns headed % show percentile change in the index from the previous period for which an index is available.

Year	All Items		Food & Beverage		Housing		Apparel & Upkeep		Trans-portation		Medical Care		Entertain-ment		Other Goods & Services	
	Index	%	Index	%	Index	%	Index	%	Index	%	Index	%	Index	%	Index	%
1958	29.1	2.8	-	-	-	-	44.8	0.2	28.4	2.9	20.7	4.5	-	-	-	-
1959	29.3	0.7	-	-	-	-	45.2	0.9	29.6	4.2	21.6	4.3	-	-	-	-
1960	29.8	1.7	-	-	-	-	45.9	1.5	29.6	0.0	22.4	3.7	-	-	-	-
1961	30.1	1.0	-	-	-	-	46.3	0.9	30.0	1.4	23.0	2.7	-	-	-	-
1962	30.4	1.0	-	-	-	-	46.6	0.6	30.6	2.0	23.6	2.6	-	-	-	-
1963	30.8	1.3	-	-	-	-	47.1	1.1	30.8	0.7	24.2	2.5	-	-	-	-
1964	31.2	1.3	-	-	-	-	47.5	0.8	31.2	1.3	24.7	2.1	-	-	-	-
1965	31.7	1.6	-	-	-	-	48.0	1.1	31.7	1.6	25.3	2.4	-	-	-	-
1966	32.6	2.8	-	-	-	-	49.2	2.5	32.2	1.6	26.4	4.3	-	-	-	-
1967	33.6	3.1	35.0	-	31.1	-	51.2	4.1	33.1	2.8	28.3	7.2	41.3	-	35.4	-
1968	35.0	4.2	36.2	3.4	32.3	3.9	54.0	5.5	34.1	3.0	30.0	6.0	43.7	5.8	37.2	5.1
1969	36.9	5.4	38.0	5.0	34.3	6.2	57.1	5.7	35.5	4.1	32.1	7.0	45.9	5.0	39.1	5.1
1970	39.0	5.7	40.1	5.5	36.7	7.0	59.5	4.2	37.3	5.1	34.1	6.2	48.2	5.0	41.3	5.6
1971	40.7	4.4	41.3	3.0	38.3	4.4	61.4	3.2	39.2	5.1	36.3	6.5	50.8	5.4	43.3	4.8
1972	42.1	3.4	43.1	4.4	39.8	3.9	62.7	2.1	39.7	1.3	37.5	3.3	52.3	3.0	45.1	4.2
1973	44.7	6.2	48.8	13.2	41.5	4.3	65.0	3.7	41.0	3.3	39.0	4.0	53.7	2.7	46.9	4.0
1974	49.6	11.0	55.5	13.7	46.2	11.3	69.8	7.4	45.5	11.0	42.6	9.2	57.8	7.6	50.2	7.0
1975	54.1	9.1	60.2	8.5	51.1	10.6	72.9	4.4	49.8	9.5	47.7	12.0	62.9	8.8	54.4	8.4
1976	57.2	5.7	62.0	3.0	54.2	6.1	75.6	3.7	54.7	9.8	52.3	9.6	66.0	4.9	57.6	5.9
1977	60.9	6.5	65.7	6.0	57.9	6.8	79.0	4.5	58.6	7.1	57.3	9.6	69.3	5.0	60.9	5.7
1978	65.6	7.7	72.1	9.7	62.9	8.6	81.7	3.4	61.5	4.9	62.1	8.4	72.8	5.1	64.8	6.4
1979	73.1	11.4	79.9	10.8	70.7	12.4	85.2	4.3	70.4	14.5	68.0	9.5	77.6	6.6	69.4	7.1
1980	82.9	13.4	86.9	8.8	81.7	15.6	90.9	6.7	82.9	17.8	75.6	11.2	84.2	8.5	75.6	8.9
1981	91.4	10.3	93.6	7.7	91.1	11.5	95.6	5.2	93.0	12.2	83.5	10.4	90.5	7.5	82.5	9.1
1982	96.9	6.0	97.3	4.0	97.7	7.2	97.8	2.3	97.0	4.3	92.5	10.8	96.0	6.1	90.9	10.2
1983	99.8	3.0	99.5	2.3	100.0	2.4	100.2	2.5	99.2	2.3	100.5	8.6	100.2	4.4	101.3	11.4
1984	103.3	3.5	103.2	3.7	102.2	2.2	102.0	1.8	103.8	4.6	106.9	6.4	103.8	3.6	107.9	6.5
1985	106.9	3.5	105.5	2.2	106.6	4.3	105.0	2.9	106.4	2.5	113.6	6.3	107.5	3.6	114.2	5.8
1986	108.6	1.6	108.9	3.2	109.7	2.9	105.8	0.8	101.7	-4.4	122.0	7.4	111.0	3.3	120.9	5.9
1987	112.5	3.6	113.3	4.0	112.8	2.8	110.4	4.3	105.1	3.3	130.2	6.7	114.8	3.4	127.8	5.7
1988	117.0	4.0	117.9	4.1	116.8	3.5	114.9	4.1	108.3	3.0	139.0	6.8	119.7	4.3	136.5	6.8
1989	122.6	4.8	124.6	5.7	121.2	3.8	117.9	2.6	113.9	5.2	149.6	7.6	125.8	5.1	147.4	8.0
1990	129.0	5.2	131.8	5.8	126.4	4.3	123.1	4.4	120.1	5.4	162.7	8.8	131.4	4.5	158.9	7.8
1991	134.3	4.1	136.5	3.6	131.2	3.8	127.4	3.5	123.1	2.5	176.5	8.5	136.9	4.2	171.7	8.1
1992	138.2	2.9	138.3	1.3	135.0	2.9	130.7	2.6	125.8	2.2	189.6	7.4	140.8	2.8	183.3	6.8
1993	142.1	2.8	141.2	2.1	138.5	2.6	132.4	1.3	129.4	2.9	200.9	6.0	144.1	2.3	192.2	4.9

Source: U.S. Department of Labor, Bureau of Labor Statistics, Division of Consumer Prices and Price Indexes.

U.S. CITY AVERAGE
Consumer Price Index - All Urban Consumers
Base 1982-1984 = 100
All Items

For 1913-1993. Columns headed % show percentile change in the index from the previous period for which an index is available.

Year	Jan Index	%	Feb Index	%	Mar Index	%	Apr Index	%	May Index	%	Jun Index	%	Jul Index	%	Aug Index	%	Sep Index	%	Oct Index	%	Nov Index	%	Dec Index	%
1913	9.8	-	9.8	0.0	9.8	0.0	9.8	0.0	9.7	-1.0	9.8	1.0	9.9	1.0	9.9	0.0	10.0	1.0	10.0	0.0	10.1	1.0	10.0	-1.0
1914	10.0	0.0	9.9	-1.0	9.9	0.0	9.8	-1.0	9.9	1.0	9.9	0.0	10.0	1.0	10.2	2.0	10.2	0.0	10.1	-1.0	10.2	1.0	10.1	-1.0
1915	10.1	0.0	10.0	-1.0	9.9	-1.0	10.0	1.0	10.1	1.0	10.1	0.0	10.1	0.0	10.1	0.0	10.1	0.0	10.2	1.0	10.3	1.0	10.3	0.0
1916	10.4	1.0	10.4	0.0	10.5	1.0	10.6	1.0	10.7	0.9	10.8	0.9	10.8	0.0	10.9	0.9	11.1	1.8	11.3	1.8	11.5	1.8	11.6	0.9
1917	11.7	0.9	12.0	2.6	12.0	0.0	12.6	5.0	12.8	1.6	13.0	1.6	12.8	-1.5	13.0	1.6	13.3	2.3	13.5	1.5	13.5	0.0	13.7	1.5
1918	14.0	2.2	14.1	0.7	14.0	-0.7	14.2	1.4	14.5	2.1	14.7	1.4	15.1	2.7	15.4	2.0	15.7	1.9	16.0	1.9	16.3	1.9	16.5	1.2
1919	16.5	0.0	16.2	-1.8	16.4	1.2	16.7	1.8	16.9	1.2	16.9	0.0	17.4	3.0	17.7	1.7	17.8	0.6	18.1	1.7	18.5	2.2	18.9	2.2
1920	19.3	2.1	19.5	1.0	19.7	1.0	20.3	3.0	20.6	1.5	20.9	1.5	20.8	-0.5	20.3	-2.4	20.0	-1.5	19.9	-0.5	19.8	-0.5	19.4	-2.0
1921	19.0	-2.1	18.4	-3.2	18.3	-0.5	18.1	-1.1	17.7	-2.2	17.6	-0.6	17.7	0.6	17.7	0.0	17.5	-1.1	17.5	0.0	17.4	-0.6	17.3	-0.6
1922	16.9	-2.3	16.9	0.0	16.7	-1.2	16.7	0.0	16.7	0.0	16.7	0.0	16.8	0.6	16.6	-1.2	16.6	0.0	16.7	0.6	16.8	0.6	16.9	0.6
1923	16.8	-0.6	16.8	0.0	16.8	0.0	16.9	0.6	16.9	0.0	17.0	0.6	17.2	1.2	17.1	-0.6	17.2	0.6	17.3	0.6	17.3	0.0	17.3	0.0
1924	17.3	0.0	17.2	-0.6	17.1	-0.6	17.0	-0.6	17.0	0.0	17.0	0.0	17.1	0.6	17.0	-0.6	17.1	0.6	17.2	0.6	17.2	0.0	17.3	0.6
1925	17.3	0.0	17.2	-0.6	17.3	0.6	17.2	-0.6	17.3	0.6	17.5	1.2	17.7	1.1	17.7	0.0	17.7	0.0	17.7	0.0	18.0	1.7	17.9	-0.6
1926	17.9	0.0	17.9	0.0	17.8	-0.6	17.9	0.6	17.8	-0.6	17.7	-0.6	17.5	-1.1	17.4	-0.6	17.5	0.6	17.6	0.6	17.7	0.6	17.7	0.0
1927	17.5	-1.1	17.4	-0.6	17.3	-0.6	17.3	0.0	17.4	0.6	17.6	1.1	17.3	-1.7	17.2	-0.6	17.3	0.6	17.4	0.6	17.3	-0.6	17.3	0.0
1928	17.3	0.0	17.1	-1.2	17.1	0.0	17.1	0.0	17.2	0.6	17.1	-0.6	17.1	0.0	17.1	0.0	17.3	1.2	17.2	-0.6	17.2	0.0	17.1	-0.6
1929	17.1	0.0	17.1	0.0	17.0	-0.6	16.9	-0.6	17.0	0.6	17.1	0.6	17.3	1.2	17.3	0.0	17.3	0.0	17.3	0.0	17.3	0.0	17.2	-0.6
1930	17.1	-0.6	17.0	-0.6	16.9	-0.6	17.0	0.6	16.9	-0.6	16.8	-0.6	16.6	-1.2	16.5	-0.6	16.6	0.6	16.5	-0.6	16.4	-0.6	16.1	-1.8
1931	15.9	-1.2	15.7	-1.3	15.6	-0.6	15.5	-0.6	15.3	-1.3	15.1	-1.3	15.1	0.0	15.1	0.0	15.0	-0.7	14.9	-0.7	14.7	-1.3	14.6	-0.7
1932	14.3	-2.1	14.1	-1.4	14.0	-0.7	13.9	-0.7	13.7	-1.4	13.6	-0.7	13.6	0.0	13.5	-0.7	13.4	-0.7	13.3	-0.7	13.2	-0.8	13.1	-0.8
1933	12.9	-1.5	12.7	-1.6	12.6	-0.8	12.6	0.0	12.6	0.0	12.7	0.8	13.1	3.1	13.2	0.8	13.2	0.0	13.2	0.0	13.2	0.0	13.2	0.0
1934	13.2	0.0	13.3	0.8	13.3	0.0	13.3	0.0	13.3	0.0	13.4	0.8	13.4	0.0	13.4	0.0	13.6	1.5	13.5	-0.7	13.5	0.0	13.4	-0.7
1935	13.6	1.5	13.7	0.7	13.7	0.0	13.8	0.7	13.8	0.0	13.7	-0.7	13.7	0.0	13.7	0.0	13.7	0.0	13.7	0.0	13.8	0.7	13.8	0.0
1936	13.8	0.0	13.8	0.0	13.7	-0.7	13.7	0.0	13.7	0.0	13.8	0.7	13.9	0.7	14.0	0.7	14.0	0.0	14.0	0.0	14.0	0.0	14.0	0.0
1937	14.1	0.7	14.1	0.0	14.2	0.7	14.3	0.7	14.4	0.7	14.4	0.0	14.5	0.7	14.5	0.0	14.6	0.7	14.6	0.0	14.5	-0.7	14.4	-0.7
1938	14.2	-1.4	14.1	-0.7	14.1	0.0	14.2	0.7	14.1	-0.7	14.1	0.0	14.1	0.0	14.1	0.0	14.1	0.0	14.0	-0.7	14.0	0.0	14.0	0.0
1939	14.0	0.0	13.9	-0.7	13.9	0.0	13.8	-0.7	13.8	0.0	13.8	0.0	13.8	0.0	13.8	0.0	14.1	2.2	14.0	-0.7	14.0	0.0	14.0	0.0
1940	13.9	-0.7	14.0	0.7	14.0	0.0	14.0	0.0	14.0	0.0	14.1	0.7	14.0	-0.7	14.0	0.0	14.0	0.0	14.0	0.0	14.0	0.0	14.1	0.7
1941	14.1	0.0	14.1	0.0	14.2	0.7	14.3	0.7	14.4	0.7	14.7	2.1	14.7	0.0	14.9	1.4	15.1	1.3	15.3	1.3	15.4	0.7	15.5	0.6
1942	15.7	1.3	15.8	0.6	16.0	1.3	16.1	0.6	16.3	1.2	16.3	0.0	16.4	0.6	16.5	0.6	16.5	0.0	16.7	1.2	16.8	0.6	16.9	0.6
1943	16.9	0.0	16.9	0.0	17.2	1.8	17.4	1.2	17.5	0.6	17.5	0.0	17.4	-0.6	17.3	-0.6	17.4	0.6	17.4	0.0	17.4	0.0	17.4	0.0
1944	17.4	0.0	17.4	0.0	17.4	0.0	17.5	0.6	17.5	0.0	17.6	0.6	17.7	0.6	17.7	0.0	17.7	0.0	17.7	0.0	17.7	0.0	17.8	0.6
1945	17.8	0.0	17.8	0.0	17.8	0.0	17.8	0.0	17.9	0.6	18.1	1.1	18.1	0.0	18.1	0.0	18.1	0.0	18.1	0.0	18.1	0.0	18.2	0.6
1946	18.2	0.0	18.1	-0.5	18.3	1.1	18.4	0.5	18.5	0.5	18.7	1.1	19.8	5.9	20.2	2.0	20.4	1.0	20.8	2.0	21.3	2.4	21.5	0.9
1947	21.5	0.0	21.5	0.0	21.9	1.9	21.9	0.0	21.9	0.0	22.0	0.5	22.2	0.9	22.5	1.4	23.0	2.2	23.0	0.0	23.1	0.4	23.4	1.3
1948	23.7	1.3	23.5	-0.8	23.4	-0.4	23.8	1.7	23.9	0.4	24.1	0.8	24.4	1.2	24.5	0.4	24.5	0.0	24.4	-0.4	24.2	-0.8	24.1	-0.4
1949	24.0	-0.4	23.8	-0.8	23.8	0.0	23.9	0.4	23.8	-0.4	23.9	0.4	23.7	-0.8	23.8	0.4	23.9	0.4	23.7	-0.8	23.8	0.4	23.6	-0.8
1950	23.5	-0.4	23.5	0.0	23.6	0.4	23.6	0.0	23.7	0.4	23.8	0.4	24.1	1.3	24.3	0.8	24.4	0.4	24.6	0.8	24.7	0.4	25.0	1.2
1951	25.4	1.6	25.7	1.2	25.8	0.4	25.8	0.0	25.9	0.4	25.9	0.0	25.9	0.0	25.9	0.0	26.1	0.8	26.2	0.4	26.4	0.8	26.5	0.4
1952	26.5	0.0	26.3	-0.8	26.3	0.0	26.4	0.4	26.4	0.0	26.5	0.4	26.7	0.8	26.7	0.0	26.7	0.0	26.7	0.0	26.7	0.0	26.7	0.0
1953	26.6	-0.4	26.5	-0.4	26.6	0.4	26.6	0.0	26.7	0.4	26.8	0.4	26.8	0.0	26.9	0.4	26.9	0.0	27.0	0.4	26.9	-0.4	26.9	0.0
1954	26.9	0.0	26.9	0.0	26.9	0.0	26.8	-0.4	26.9	0.4	26.9	0.0	26.9	0.0	26.9	0.0	26.8	-0.4	26.8	0.0	26.8	0.0	26.7	-0.4
1955	26.7	0.0	26.7	0.0	26.7	0.0	26.7	0.0	26.7	0.0	26.7	0.0	26.8	0.4	26.8	0.0	26.9	0.4	26.9	0.0	26.9	0.0	26.8	-0.4
1956	26.8	0.0	26.8	0.0	26.8	0.0	26.9	0.4	27.0	0.4	27.2	0.7	27.4	0.7	27.3	-0.4	27.4	0.4	27.5	0.4	27.5	0.0	27.6	0.4
1957	27.6	0.0	27.7	0.4	27.8	0.4	27.9	0.4	28.0	0.4	28.1	0.4	28.3	0.7	28.3	0.0	28.3	0.0	28.3	0.0	28.4	0.4	28.4	0.0

[Continued]

U.S. City Average
Consumer Price Index - All Urban Consumers
Base 1982-1984 = 100
All Items
[Continued]

For 1913-1993. Columns headed % show percentile change in the index from the previous period for which an index is available.

Year	Jan Index	%	Feb Index	%	Mar Index	%	Apr Index	%	May Index	%	Jun Index	%	Jul Index	%	Aug Index	%	Sep Index	%	Oct Index	%	Nov Index	%	Dec Index	%
1958	28.6	0.7	28.6	0.0	28.8	0.7	28.9	0.3	28.9	0.0	28.9	0.0	29.0	0.3	28.9	-0.3	28.9	0.0	28.9	0.0	29.0	0.3	28.9	-0.3
1959	29.0	0.3	28.9	-0.3	28.9	0.0	29.0	0.3	29.0	0.0	29.1	0.3	29.2	0.3	29.2	0.0	29.3	0.3	29.4	0.3	29.4	0.0	29.4	0.0
1960	29.3	-0.3	29.4	0.3	29.4	0.0	29.5	0.3	29.5	0.0	29.6	0.3	29.6	0.0	29.6	0.0	29.6	0.0	29.8	0.7	29.8	0.0	29.8	0.0
1961	29.8	0.0	29.8	0.0	29.8	0.0	29.8	0.0	29.8	0.0	29.8	0.0	30.0	0.7	29.9	-0.3	30.0	0.3	30.0	0.0	30.0	0.0	30.0	0.0
1962	30.0	0.0	30.1	0.3	30.1	0.0	30.2	0.3	30.2	0.0	30.2	0.0	30.3	0.3	30.3	0.0	30.4	0.3	30.4	0.0	30.4	0.0	30.4	0.0
1963	30.4	0.0	30.4	0.0	30.5	0.3	30.5	0.0	30.5	0.0	30.6	0.3	30.7	0.3	30.7	0.0	30.7	0.0	30.8	0.3	30.8	0.0	30.9	0.3
1964	30.9	0.0	30.9	0.0	30.9	0.0	30.9	0.0	30.9	0.0	31.0	0.3	31.1	0.3	31.0	-0.3	31.1	0.3	31.1	0.0	31.2	0.3	31.2	0.0
1965	31.2	0.0	31.2	0.0	31.3	0.3	31.4	0.3	31.4	0.0	31.6	0.6	31.6	0.0	31.6	0.0	31.6	0.0	31.7	0.3	31.7	0.0	31.8	0.3
1966	31.8	0.0	32.0	0.6	32.1	0.3	32.3	0.6	32.3	0.0	32.4	0.3	32.5	0.3	32.7	0.6	32.7	0.0	32.9	0.6	32.9	0.0	32.9	0.0
1967	32.9	0.0	32.9	0.0	33.0	0.3	33.1	0.3	33.2	0.3	33.3	0.3	33.4	0.3	33.5	0.3	33.6	0.3	33.7	0.3	33.8	0.3	33.9	0.3
1968	34.1	0.6	34.2	0.3	34.3	0.3	34.4	0.3	34.5	0.3	34.7	0.6	34.9	0.6	35.0	0.3	35.1	0.3	35.3	0.6	35.4	0.3	35.5	0.3
1969	35.6	0.3	35.8	0.6	36.1	0.8	36.3	0.6	36.4	0.3	36.6	0.5	36.8	0.5	37.0	0.5	37.1	0.3	37.3	0.5	37.5	0.5	37.7	0.5
1970	37.8	0.3	38.0	0.5	38.2	0.5	38.5	0.8	38.6	0.3	38.8	0.5	39.0	0.5	39.0	0.0	39.2	0.5	39.4	0.5	39.6	0.5	39.8	0.5
1971	39.8	0.0	39.9	0.3	40.0	0.3	40.1	0.2	40.3	0.5	40.6	0.7	40.7	0.2	40.8	0.2	40.8	0.0	40.9	0.2	40.9	0.0	41.1	0.5
1972	41.1	0.0	41.3	0.5	41.4	0.2	41.5	0.2	41.6	0.2	41.7	0.2	41.9	0.5	42.0	0.2	42.1	0.2	42.3	0.5	42.4	0.2	42.5	0.2
1973	42.6	0.2	42.9	0.7	43.3	0.9	43.6	0.7	43.9	0.7	44.2	0.7	44.3	0.2	45.1	1.8	45.2	0.2	45.6	0.9	45.9	0.7	46.2	0.7
1974	46.6	0.9	47.2	1.3	47.8	1.3	48.0	0.4	48.6	1.2	49.0	0.8	49.4	0.8	50.0	1.2	50.6	1.2	51.1	1.0	51.5	0.8	51.9	0.8
1975	52.1	0.4	52.5	0.8	52.7	0.4	52.9	0.4	53.2	0.6	53.6	0.8	54.2	1.1	54.3	0.2	54.6	0.6	54.9	0.5	55.3	0.7	55.5	0.4
1976	55.6	0.2	55.8	0.4	55.9	0.2	56.1	0.4	56.5	0.7	56.8	0.5	57.1	0.5	57.4	0.5	57.6	0.3	57.9	0.5	58.0	0.2	58.2	0.3
1977	58.5	0.5	59.1	1.0	59.5	0.7	60.0	0.8	60.3	0.5	60.7	0.7	61.0	0.5	61.2	0.3	61.4	0.3	61.6	0.3	61.9	0.5	62.1	0.3
1978	62.5	0.6	62.9	0.6	63.4	0.8	63.9	0.8	64.5	0.9	65.2	1.1	65.7	0.8	66.0	0.5	66.5	0.8	67.1	0.9	67.4	0.4	67.7	0.4
1979	68.3	0.9	69.1	1.2	69.8	1.0	70.6	1.1	71.5	1.3	72.3	1.1	73.1	1.1	73.8	1.0	74.6	1.1	75.2	0.8	75.9	0.9	76.7	1.1
1980	77.8	1.4	78.9	1.4	80.1	1.5	81.0	1.1	81.8	1.0	82.7	1.1	82.7	0.0	83.3	0.7	84.0	0.8	84.8	1.0	85.5	0.8	86.3	0.9
1981	87.0	0.8	87.9	1.0	88.5	0.7	89.1	0.7	89.8	0.8	90.6	0.9	91.6	1.1	92.3	0.8	93.2	1.0	93.4	0.2	93.7	0.3	94.0	0.3
1982	94.3	0.3	94.6	0.3	94.5	-0.1	94.9	0.4	95.8	0.9	97.0	1.3	97.5	0.5	97.7	0.2	97.9	0.2	98.2	0.3	98.0	-0.2	97.6	-0.4
1983	97.8	0.2	97.9	0.1	97.9	0.0	98.6	0.7	99.2	0.6	99.5	0.3	99.9	0.4	100.2	0.3	100.7	0.5	101.0	0.3	101.2	0.2	101.3	0.1
1984	101.9	0.6	102.4	0.5	102.6	0.2	103.1	0.5	103.4	0.3	103.7	0.3	104.1	0.4	104.5	0.4	105.0	0.5	105.3	0.3	105.3	0.0	105.3	0.0
1985	105.5	0.2	106.0	0.5	106.4	0.4	106.9	0.5	107.3	0.4	107.6	0.3	107.8	0.2	108.0	0.2	108.3	0.3	108.7	0.4	109.0	0.3	109.3	0.3
1986	109.6	0.3	109.3	-0.3	108.8	-0.5	108.6	-0.2	108.9	0.3	109.5	0.6	109.5	0.0	109.7	0.2	110.2	0.5	110.3	0.1	110.4	0.1	110.5	0.1
1987	111.2	0.6	111.6	0.4	112.1	0.4	112.7	0.5	113.1	0.4	113.5	0.4	113.8	0.3	114.4	0.5	115.0	0.5	115.3	0.3	115.4	0.1	115.4	0.0
1988	115.7	0.3	116.0	0.3	116.5	0.4	117.1	0.5	117.5	0.3	118.0	0.4	118.5	0.4	119.0	0.4	119.8	0.7	120.2	0.3	120.3	0.1	120.5	0.2
1989	121.1	0.5	121.6	0.4	122.3	0.6	123.1	0.7	123.8	0.6	124.1	0.2	124.4	0.2	124.6	0.2	125.0	0.3	125.6	0.5	125.9	0.2	126.1	0.2
1990	127.4	1.0	128.0	0.5	128.7	0.5	128.9	0.2	129.2	0.2	129.9	0.5	130.4	0.4	131.6	0.9	132.7	0.8	133.5	0.6	133.8	0.2	133.8	0.0
1991	134.6	0.6	134.8	0.1	135.0	0.1	135.2	0.1	135.6	0.3	136.0	0.3	136.2	0.1	136.6	0.3	137.2	0.4	137.4	0.1	137.8	0.3	137.9	0.1
1992	138.1	0.1	138.6	0.4	139.3	0.5	139.5	0.1	139.7	0.1	140.2	0.4	140.5	0.2	140.9	0.3	141.3	0.3	141.8	0.4	142.0	0.1	141.9	-0.1
1993	142.6	0.5	143.1	0.4	143.6	0.3	144.0	0.3	144.2	0.1	144.4	0.1	144.4	0.0	144.8	0.3	145.1	0.2	145.7	0.4	145.8	0.1	145.8	0.0

Source: U.S. Department of Labor, Bureau of Labor Statistics, Division of Consumer Prices and Price Indexes.

U.S. CITY AVERAGE
Consumer Price Index - Urban Wage Earners
Base 1982-1984 = 100
All Items

For 1913-1993. Columns headed % show percentile change in the index from the previous period for which an index is available.

Year	Jan Index	%	Feb Index	%	Mar Index	%	Apr Index	%	May Index	%	Jun Index	%	Jul Index	%	Aug Index	%	Sep Index	%	Oct Index	%	Nov Index	%	Dec Index	%
1913	9.9	-	9.8	-1.0	9.8	0.0	9.9	1.0	9.8	-1.0	9.8	0.0	9.9	1.0	10.0	1.0	10.0	0.0	10.1	1.0	10.1	0.0	10.1	0.0
1914	10.1	0.0	10.0	-1.0	10.0	0.0	9.9	-1.0	9.9	0.0	10.0	1.0	10.1	1.0	10.2	1.0	10.3	1.0	10.2	-1.0	10.2	0.0	10.2	0.0
1915	10.2	0.0	10.1	-1.0	10.0	-1.0	10.1	1.0	10.1	0.0	10.2	1.0	10.2	0.0	10.2	0.0	10.2	0.0	10.3	1.0	10.4	1.0	10.4	0.0
1916	10.5	1.0	10.5	0.0	10.6	1.0	10.7	0.9	10.7	0.0	10.9	1.9	10.9	0.0	11.0	0.9	11.2	1.8	11.3	0.9	11.5	1.8	11.6	0.9
1917	11.8	1.7	12.0	1.7	12.1	0.8	12.6	4.1	12.9	2.4	13.0	0.8	12.9	-0.8	13.1	1.6	13.3	1.5	13.6	2.3	13.6	0.0	13.8	1.5
1918	14.0	1.4	14.2	1.4	14.1	-0.7	14.3	1.4	14.5	1.4	14.8	2.1	15.2	2.7	15.4	1.3	15.8	2.6	16.1	1.9	16.3	1.2	16.6	1.8
1919	16.6	0.0	16.2	-2.4	16.5	1.9	16.8	1.8	17.0	1.2	17.0	0.0	17.5	2.9	17.8	1.7	17.9	0.6	18.2	1.7	18.6	2.2	19.0	2.2
1920	19.4	2.1	19.6	1.0	19.8	1.0	20.4	3.0	20.7	1.5	21.0	1.4	20.9	-0.5	20.4	-2.4	20.1	-1.5	20.0	-0.5	19.9	-0.5	19.5	-2.0
1921	19.1	-2.1	18.5	-3.1	18.4	-0.5	18.2	-1.1	17.8	-2.2	17.7	-0.6	17.8	0.6	17.8	0.0	17.6	-1.1	17.6	0.0	17.5	-0.6	17.4	-0.6
1922	17.0	-2.3	17.0	0.0	16.8	-1.2	16.8	0.0	16.8	0.0	16.8	0.0	16.9	0.6	16.7	-1.2	16.7	0.0	16.8	0.6	16.9	0.6	17.0	0.6
1923	16.9	-0.6	16.9	0.0	16.9	0.0	17.0	0.6	17.0	0.0	17.1	0.6	17.3	1.2	17.2	-0.6	17.3	0.6	17.4	0.6	17.4	0.0	17.4	0.0
1924	17.4	0.0	17.3	-0.6	17.2	-0.6	17.1	-0.6	17.1	0.0	17.1	0.0	17.2	0.6	17.1	-0.6	17.2	0.6	17.3	0.6	17.3	0.0	17.4	0.6
1925	17.4	0.0	17.3	-0.6	17.4	0.6	17.3	-0.6	17.4	0.6	17.6	1.1	17.8	1.1	17.8	0.0	17.8	0.0	17.8	0.0	18.1	1.7	18.0	-0.6
1926	18.0	0.0	18.0	0.0	17.9	-0.6	18.0	0.6	17.9	-0.6	17.8	-0.6	17.6	-1.1	17.5	-0.6	17.6	0.6	17.7	0.6	17.8	0.6	17.8	0.0
1927	17.6	-1.1	17.5	-0.6	17.4	-0.6	17.4	0.0	17.5	0.6	17.7	1.1	17.4	-1.7	17.3	-0.6	17.4	0.6	17.5	0.6	17.4	-0.6	17.4	0.0
1928	17.4	0.0	17.2	-1.1	17.2	0.0	17.2	0.0	17.3	0.6	17.2	-0.6	17.2	0.0	17.2	0.0	17.4	1.2	17.3	-0.6	17.3	0.0	17.2	-0.6
1929	17.2	0.0	17.2	0.0	17.1	-0.6	17.0	-0.6	17.1	0.6	17.2	0.6	17.4	1.2	17.4	0.0	17.4	0.0	17.4	0.0	17.4	0.0	17.3	-0.6
1930	17.2	-0.6	17.1	-0.6	17.0	-0.6	17.1	0.6	17.0	-0.6	16.9	-0.6	16.7	-1.2	16.6	-0.6	16.7	0.6	16.6	-0.6	16.5	-0.6	16.2	-1.8
1931	16.0	-1.2	15.7	-1.9	15.6	-0.6	15.5	-0.6	15.4	-0.6	15.2	-1.3	15.2	0.0	15.1	-0.7	15.1	0.0	15.0	-0.7	14.8	-1.3	14.7	-0.7
1932	14.4	-2.0	14.2	-1.4	14.1	-0.7	14.0	-0.7	13.8	-1.4	13.7	-0.7	13.7	0.0	13.5	-1.5	13.5	0.0	13.4	-0.7	13.3	-0.7	13.2	-0.8
1933	13.0	-1.5	12.8	-1.5	12.7	-0.8	12.6	-0.8	12.7	0.8	12.8	0.8	13.2	3.1	13.3	0.8	13.3	0.0	13.3	0.0	13.3	0.0	13.2	-0.8
1934	13.3	0.8	13.4	0.8	13.4	0.0	13.4	0.0	13.4	0.0	13.4	0.0	13.4	0.0	13.5	0.7	13.7	1.5	13.6	-0.7	13.5	-0.7	13.5	0.0
1935	13.7	1.5	13.8	0.7	13.8	0.0	13.9	0.7	13.8	-0.7	13.8	0.0	13.7	-0.7	13.7	0.0	13.8	0.7	13.8	0.0	13.9	0.7	13.9	0.0
1936	13.9	0.0	13.8	-0.7	13.8	0.0	13.8	0.0	13.8	0.0	13.9	0.7	14.0	0.7	14.1	0.7	14.1	0.0	14.1	0.0	14.1	0.0	14.1	0.0
1937	14.2	0.7	14.2	0.0	14.3	0.7	14.4	0.7	14.4	0.0	14.5	0.7	14.5	0.0	14.6	0.7	14.7	0.7	14.6	-0.7	14.5	-0.7	14.5	0.0
1938	14.3	-1.4	14.2	-0.7	14.2	0.0	14.2	0.0	14.2	0.0	14.2	0.0	14.2	0.0	14.2	0.0	14.2	0.0	14.1	-0.7	14.1	0.0	14.1	0.0
1939	14.0	-0.7	14.0	0.0	13.9	-0.7	13.9	0.0	13.9	0.0	13.9	0.0	13.9	0.0	13.9	0.0	14.2	2.2	14.1	-0.7	14.1	0.0	14.0	-0.7
1940	14.0	0.0	14.1	0.7	14.1	0.0	14.1	0.0	14.1	0.0	14.1	0.0	14.1	0.0	14.1	0.0	14.1	0.0	14.1	0.0	14.1	0.0	14.2	0.7
1941	14.2	0.0	14.2	0.0	14.2	0.0	14.4	1.4	14.5	0.7	14.7	1.4	14.8	0.7	14.9	0.7	15.2	2.0	15.4	1.3	15.5	0.6	15.5	0.0
1942	15.7	1.3	15.9	1.3	16.1	1.3	16.2	0.6	16.3	0.6	16.4	0.6	16.5	0.6	16.6	0.6	16.6	0.0	16.8	1.2	16.9	0.6	17.0	0.6
1943	17.0	0.0	17.0	0.0	17.3	1.8	17.5	1.2	17.6	0.6	17.6	0.0	17.5	-0.6	17.4	-0.6	17.5	0.6	17.5	0.0	17.5	0.0	17.5	0.0
1944	17.5	0.0	17.5	0.0	17.5	0.0	17.6	0.6	17.6	0.0	17.7	0.6	17.8	0.6	17.8	0.0	17.8	0.0	17.8	0.0	17.8	0.0	17.9	0.6
1945	17.9	0.0	17.9	0.0	17.9	0.0	17.9	0.0	18.0	0.6	18.2	1.1	18.2	0.0	18.2	0.0	18.2	0.0	18.2	0.0	18.2	0.0	18.3	0.5
1946	18.3	0.0	18.2	-0.5	18.4	1.1	18.5	0.5	18.6	0.5	18.8	1.1	19.9	5.9	20.3	2.0	20.5	1.0	20.9	2.0	21.5	2.9	21.6	0.5
1947	21.6	0.0	21.6	0.0	22.1	2.3	22.1	0.0	22.0	-0.5	22.2	0.9	22.4	0.9	22.6	0.9	23.1	2.2	23.1	0.0	23.3	0.9	23.6	1.3
1948	23.8	0.8	23.6	-0.8	23.6	0.0	23.9	1.3	24.1	0.8	24.2	0.4	24.5	1.2	24.6	0.4	24.6	0.0	24.5	-0.4	24.4	-0.4	24.2	-0.8
1949	24.2	0.0	23.9	-1.2	24.0	0.4	24.0	0.0	24.0	0.0	24.0	0.0	23.8	-0.8	23.9	0.4	24.0	0.4	23.9	-0.4	23.9	0.0	23.8	-0.4
1950	23.7	-0.4	23.6	-0.4	23.7	0.4	23.7	0.0	23.8	0.4	24.0	0.8	24.2	0.8	24.4	0.8	24.6	0.8	24.7	0.4	24.8	0.4	25.1	1.2
1951	25.5	1.6	25.9	1.6	26.0	0.4	26.0	0.0	26.1	0.4	26.1	0.0	26.1	0.0	26.1	0.0	26.3	0.8	26.4	0.4	26.5	0.4	26.6	0.4
1952	26.6	0.0	26.5	-0.4	26.5	0.0	26.6	0.4	26.6	0.0	26.7	0.4	26.9	0.7	26.9	0.0	26.9	0.0	26.9	0.0	26.9	0.0	26.9	0.0
1953	26.8	-0.4	26.7	-0.4	26.7	0.0	26.8	0.4	26.8	0.0	26.9	0.4	27.0	0.4	27.1	0.4	27.1	0.0	27.2	0.4	27.1	-0.4	27.0	-0.4
1954	27.1	0.4	27.1	0.0	27.0	-0.4	27.0	0.0	27.1	0.4	27.1	0.0	27.1	0.0	27.1	0.0	27.0	-0.4	26.9	-0.4	27.0	0.4	26.9	-0.4
1955	26.9	0.0	26.9	0.0	26.9	0.0	26.9	0.0	26.9	0.0	26.9	0.0	27.0	0.4	26.9	-0.4	27.0	0.4	27.0	0.0	27.1	0.4	27.0	-0.4
1956	27.0	0.0	27.0	0.0	27.0	0.0	27.0	0.0	27.2	0.7	27.3	0.4	27.5	0.7	27.5	0.0	27.5	0.0	27.7	0.7	27.7	0.0	27.8	0.4
1957	27.8	0.0	27.9	0.4	28.0	0.4	28.1	0.4	28.1	0.0	28.3	0.7	28.4	0.4	28.5	0.4	28.5	0.0	28.5	0.0	28.6	0.4	28.6	0.0

[Continued]

U.S. City Average
Consumer Price Index - Urban Wage Earners
Base 1982-1984 = 100
All Items
[Continued]

For 1913-1993. Columns headed % show percentile change in the index from the previous period for which an index is available.

Year	Jan Index	%	Feb Index	%	Mar Index	%	Apr Index	%	May Index	%	Jun Index	%	Jul Index	%	Aug Index	%	Sep Index	%	Oct Index	%	Nov Index	%	Dec Index	%
1958	28.8	0.7	28.8	0.0	29.0	0.7	29.1	0.3	29.1	0.0	29.1	0.0	29.1	0.0	29.1	0.0	29.1	0.0	29.1	0.0	29.1	0.0	29.1	0.0
1959	29.1	0.0	29.1	0.0	29.1	0.0	29.1	0.0	29.2	0.3	29.3	0.3	29.4	0.3	29.3	-0.3	29.4	0.3	29.5	0.3	29.5	0.0	29.5	0.0
1960	29.5	0.0	29.5	0.0	29.5	0.0	29.7	0.7	29.7	0.0	29.8	0.3	29.8	0.0	29.8	0.0	29.8	0.0	29.9	0.3	30.0	0.3	30.0	0.0
1961	30.0	0.0	30.0	0.0	30.0	0.0	30.0	0.0	30.0	0.0	30.0	0.0	30.1	0.3	30.1	0.0	30.2	0.3	30.2	0.0	30.2	0.0	30.2	0.0
1962	30.2	0.0	30.2	0.0	30.3	0.3	30.4	0.3	30.4	0.0	30.4	0.0	30.4	0.0	30.4	0.0	30.6	0.7	30.6	0.0	30.6	0.0	30.6	0.0
1963	30.6	0.0	30.6	0.0	30.7	0.3	30.7	0.0	30.7	0.0	30.8	0.3	30.9	0.3	30.9	0.0	30.9	0.0	31.0	0.3	31.0	0.0	31.1	0.3
1964	31.1	0.0	31.1	0.0	31.1	0.0	31.1	0.0	31.1	0.0	31.2	0.3	31.3	0.3	31.2	-0.3	31.3	0.3	31.3	0.0	31.4	0.3	31.4	0.0
1965	31.4	0.0	31.4	0.0	31.5	0.3	31.6	0.3	31.6	0.0	31.8	0.6	31.8	0.0	31.8	0.0	31.8	0.0	31.9	0.3	31.9	0.0	32.0	0.3
1966	32.0	0.0	32.2	0.6	32.3	0.3	32.5	0.6	32.5	0.0	32.6	0.3	32.7	0.3	32.9	0.6	32.9	0.0	33.1	0.6	33.1	0.0	33.1	0.0
1967	33.1	0.0	33.1	0.0	33.2	0.3	33.3	0.3	33.4	0.3	33.5	0.3	33.6	0.3	33.7	0.3	33.8	0.3	33.9	0.3	34.0	0.3	34.1	0.3
1968	34.2	0.3	34.3	0.3	34.5	0.6	34.6	0.3	34.7	0.3	34.9	0.6	35.1	0.6	35.2	0.3	35.3	0.3	35.5	0.6	35.6	0.3	35.7	0.3
1969	35.8	0.3	36.0	0.6	36.3	0.8	36.5	0.6	36.6	0.3	36.8	0.5	37.0	0.5	37.2	0.5	37.3	0.3	37.5	0.5	37.7	0.5	37.9	0.5
1970	38.0	0.3	38.2	0.5	38.4	0.5	38.7	0.8	38.8	0.3	39.0	0.5	39.2	0.5	39.2	0.0	39.4	0.5	39.6	0.5	39.8	0.5	40.0	0.5
1971	40.0	0.0	40.1	0.2	40.2	0.2	40.4	0.5	40.6	0.5	40.8	0.5	40.9	0.2	41.0	0.2	41.0	0.0	41.1	0.2	41.2	0.2	41.3	0.2
1972	41.4	0.2	41.6	0.5	41.6	0.0	41.7	0.2	41.9	0.5	42.0	0.2	42.1	0.2	42.2	0.2	42.4	0.5	42.5	0.2	42.6	0.2	42.7	0.2
1973	42.9	0.5	43.2	0.7	43.6	0.9	43.9	0.7	44.1	0.5	44.4	0.7	44.5	0.2	45.4	2.0	45.5	0.2	45.9	0.9	46.2	0.7	46.5	0.6
1974	46.9	0.9	47.5	1.3	48.0	1.1	48.3	0.6	48.8	1.0	49.3	1.0	49.7	0.8	50.3	1.2	50.9	1.2	51.4	1.0	51.8	0.8	52.2	0.8
1975	52.4	0.4	52.8	0.8	53.0	0.4	53.2	0.4	53.5	0.6	53.9	0.7	54.5	1.1	54.7	0.4	54.9	0.4	55.3	0.7	55.6	0.5	55.8	0.4
1976	56.0	0.4	56.1	0.2	56.2	0.2	56.5	0.5	56.8	0.5	57.1	0.5	57.4	0.5	57.7	0.5	57.9	0.3	58.2	0.5	58.3	0.2	58.5	0.3
1977	58.9	0.7	59.5	1.0	59.8	0.5	60.3	0.8	60.6	0.5	61.0	0.7	61.3	0.5	61.5	0.3	61.8	0.5	61.9	0.2	62.2	0.5	62.5	0.5
1978	62.8	0.5	63.2	0.6	63.7	0.8	64.3	0.9	64.9	0.9	65.6	1.1	66.0	0.6	66.4	0.6	66.8	0.6	67.4	0.9	67.7	0.4	68.1	0.6
1979	68.7	0.9	69.5	1.2	70.3	1.2	71.1	1.1	71.9	1.1	72.8	1.3	73.7	1.2	74.4	0.9	75.1	0.9	75.7	0.8	76.4	0.9	77.2	1.0
1980	78.3	1.4	79.4	1.4	80.5	1.4	81.4	1.1	82.3	1.1	83.2	1.1	83.3	0.1	83.8	0.6	84.6	1.0	85.3	0.8	86.1	0.9	86.9	0.9
1981	87.5	0.7	88.5	1.1	89.0	0.6	89.6	0.7	90.3	0.8	91.1	0.9	92.2	1.2	92.8	0.7	93.7	1.0	93.9	0.2	94.1	0.2	94.4	0.3
1982	94.7	0.3	95.0	0.3	94.8	-0.2	95.2	0.4	96.2	1.1	97.4	1.2	98.0	0.6	98.2	0.2	98.3	0.1	98.6	0.3	98.4	-0.2	98.0	-0.4
1983	98.1	0.1	98.1	0.0	98.4	0.3	99.0	0.6	99.5	0.5	99.8	0.3	100.1	0.3	100.5	0.4	101.0	0.5	101.2	0.2	101.2	0.0	101.2	0.0
1984	101.6	0.4	101.8	0.2	101.8	0.0	102.1	0.3	102.5	0.4	102.8	0.3	103.2	0.4	104.2	1.0	104.8	0.6	104.8	0.0	104.7	-0.1	104.8	0.1
1985	104.9	0.1	105.4	0.5	105.9	0.5	106.3	0.4	106.7	0.4	107.0	0.3	107.1	0.1	107.3	0.2	107.6	0.3	107.9	0.3	108.3	0.4	108.6	0.3
1986	108.9	0.3	108.5	-0.4	107.9	-0.6	107.6	-0.3	107.9	0.3	108.4	0.5	108.4	0.0	108.6	0.2	109.1	0.5	109.1	0.0	109.2	0.1	109.3	0.1
1987	110.0	0.6	110.5	0.5	111.0	0.5	111.6	0.5	111.9	0.3	112.4	0.4	112.7	0.3	113.3	0.5	113.8	0.4	114.1	0.3	114.3	0.2	114.2	-0.1
1988	114.5	0.3	114.7	0.2	115.1	0.3	115.7	0.5	116.2	0.4	116.7	0.4	117.2	0.4	117.7	0.4	118.5	0.7	118.9	0.3	119.0	0.1	119.2	0.2
1989	119.7	0.4	120.2	0.4	120.8	0.5	121.8	0.8	122.5	0.6	122.8	0.2	123.2	0.3	123.2	0.0	123.6	0.3	124.2	0.5	124.4	0.2	124.6	0.2
1990	125.9	1.0	126.4	0.4	127.1	0.6	127.3	0.2	127.5	0.2	128.3	0.6	128.7	0.3	129.9	0.9	131.1	0.9	131.9	0.6	132.2	0.2	132.2	0.0
1991	132.8	0.5	132.8	0.0	133.0	0.2	133.3	0.2	133.8	0.4	134.1	0.2	134.3	0.1	134.6	0.2	135.2	0.4	135.4	0.1	135.8	0.3	135.9	0.1
1992	136.0	0.1	136.4	0.3	137.0	0.4	137.3	0.2	137.6	0.2	138.1	0.4	138.4	0.2	138.8	0.3	139.1	0.2	139.6	0.4	139.8	0.1	139.8	0.0
1993	140.3	0.4	140.7	0.3	141.1	0.3	141.6	0.4	141.9	0.2	142.0	0.1	142.1	0.1	142.4	0.2	142.6	0.1	143.3	0.5	143.4	0.1	143.3	-0.1

Source: U.S. Department of Labor, Bureau of Labor Statistics, Division of Consumer Prices and Price Indexes.

U.S. City Average
Consumer Price Index - All Urban Consumers
Base 1982-1984 = 100
Food and Beverages

For 1967-1993. Columns headed % show percentile change in the index from the previous period for which an index is available.

Year	Jan Index	%	Feb Index	%	Mar Index	%	Apr Index	%	May Index	%	Jun Index	%	Jul Index	%	Aug Index	%	Sep Index	%	Oct Index	%	Nov Index	%	Dec Index	%
1967	34.8	-	34.7	-0.3	34.7	0.0	34.6	-0.3	34.6	0.0	34.9	0.9	35.2	0.9	35.4	0.6	35.2	-0.6	35.2	0.0	35.2	0.0	35.3	0.3
1968	35.6	0.8	35.7	0.3	35.8	0.3	36.0	0.6	36.1	0.3	36.2	0.3	36.4	0.6	36.6	0.5	36.6	0.0	36.7	0.3	36.6	-0.3	36.8	0.5
1969	37.0	0.5	37.0	0.0	37.2	0.5	37.4	0.5	37.5	0.3	38.0	1.3	38.4	1.1	38.6	0.5	38.7	0.3	38.6	-0.3	38.9	0.8	39.4	1.3
1970	39.6	0.5	39.8	0.5	39.8	0.0	40.0	0.5	40.1	0.2	40.2	0.2	40.4	0.5	40.4	0.0	40.4	0.0	40.4	0.0	40.2	-0.5	40.3	0.2
1971	40.4	0.2	40.5	0.2	40.9	1.0	41.2	0.7	41.3	0.2	41.6	0.7	41.8	0.5	41.9	0.2	41.6	-0.7	41.6	0.0	41.6	0.0	42.0	1.0
1972	42.0	0.0	42.6	1.4	42.7	0.2	42.7	0.0	42.7	0.0	42.9	0.5	43.3	0.9	43.4	0.2	43.5	0.2	43.5	0.0	43.7	0.5	43.9	0.5
1973	44.7	1.8	45.5	1.8	46.6	2.4	47.2	1.3	47.7	1.1	48.3	1.3	48.7	0.8	51.3	5.3	51.0	-0.6	51.0	0.0	51.6	1.2	52.0	0.8
1974	52.8	1.5	54.0	2.3	54.5	0.9	54.4	-0.2	54.8	0.7	55.0	0.4	55.1	0.2	55.9	1.5	56.7	1.4	57.1	0.7	57.6	0.9	58.3	1.2
1975	58.7	0.7	58.9	0.3	58.9	0.0	58.8	-0.2	59.0	0.3	59.9	1.5	61.2	2.2	61.1	-0.2	61.0	-0.2	61.4	0.7	61.6	0.3	61.9	0.5
1976	61.9	0.0	61.7	-0.3	61.3	-0.6	61.5	0.3	61.8	0.5	62.1	0.5	62.5	0.6	62.6	0.2	62.3	-0.5	62.4	0.2	62.2	-0.3	62.4	0.3
1977	62.9	0.8	64.3	2.2	64.6	0.5	65.3	1.1	65.6	0.5	66.2	0.9	66.5	0.5	66.7	0.3	66.5	-0.3	66.5	0.0	66.9	0.6	67.1	0.3
1978	68.1	1.5	69.0	1.3	69.8	1.2	70.9	1.6	71.8	1.3	72.9	1.5	73.4	0.7	73.5	0.1	73.6	0.1	74.0	0.5	74.3	0.4	74.9	0.8
1979	76.4	2.0	77.8	1.8	78.5	0.9	79.2	0.9	79.8	0.8	80.2	0.5	80.7	0.6	80.5	-0.2	80.8	0.4	81.2	0.5	81.5	0.4	82.4	1.1
1980	83.1	0.8	83.5	0.5	84.3	1.0	84.9	0.7	85.4	0.6	85.9	0.6	86.9	1.2	88.1	1.4	88.9	0.9	89.4	0.6	90.0	0.7	90.7	0.8
1981	91.4	0.8	92.2	0.9	92.7	0.5	92.9	0.2	92.8	-0.1	93.2	0.4	94.1	1.0	94.5	0.4	94.7	0.2	94.5	-0.2	94.4	-0.1	94.6	0.2
1982	95.7	1.2	96.5	0.8	96.4	-0.1	96.7	0.3	97.3	0.6	98.0	0.7	98.2	0.2	97.9	-0.3	98.0	0.1	97.8	-0.2	97.6	-0.2	97.6	0.0
1983	98.2	0.6	98.5	0.3	99.1	0.6	99.6	0.5	99.7	0.1	99.6	-0.1	99.6	0.0	99.7	0.1	99.8	0.1	99.9	0.1	99.8	-0.1	100.2	0.4
1984	102.0	1.8	102.9	0.9	102.9	0.0	103.0	0.1	102.7	-0.3	102.9	0.2	103.3	0.4	103.9	0.6	103.7	-0.2	103.7	0.0	103.6	-0.1	104.0	0.4
1985	104.7	0.7	105.4	0.7	105.5	0.1	105.5	0.0	105.3	-0.2	105.4	0.1	105.5	0.1	105.6	0.1	105.7	0.1	105.8	0.1	106.2	0.4	106.9	0.7
1986	107.7	0.7	107.6	-0.1	107.7	0.1	107.9	0.2	108.2	0.3	108.3	0.1	109.2	0.8	110.0	0.7	110.2	0.2	110.4	0.2	110.7	0.3	110.9	0.2
1987	112.1	1.1	112.5	0.4	112.5	0.0	112.8	0.3	113.3	0.4	113.8	0.4	113.7	-0.1	113.8	0.1	114.2	0.4	114.3	0.1	114.3	0.0	114.8	0.4
1988	115.7	0.8	115.8	0.1	116.0	0.2	116.7	0.6	117.1	0.3	117.6	0.4	118.8	1.0	119.4	0.5	120.1	0.6	120.3	0.2	120.2	-0.1	120.6	0.3
1989	122.0	1.2	122.7	0.6	123.3	0.5	124.0	0.6	124.7	0.6	124.9	0.2	125.4	0.4	125.6	0.2	125.9	0.2	126.3	0.3	126.7	0.3	127.2	0.4
1990	130.0	2.2	130.9	0.7	131.2	0.2	131.0	-0.2	131.1	0.1	131.7	0.5	132.4	0.5	132.7	0.2	133.0	0.2	133.4	0.3	133.7	0.2	133.9	0.1
1991	135.9	1.5	136.0	0.1	136.3	0.2	137.2	0.7	137.3	0.1	137.7	0.3	137.1	-0.4	136.6	-0.4	136.7	0.1	136.5	-0.1	136.9	0.3	137.3	0.3
1992	137.9	0.4	138.1	0.1	138.8	0.5	138.8	0.0	138.3	-0.4	138.3	0.0	138.1	-0.1	138.8	0.5	139.3	0.4	139.2	-0.1	139.1	-0.1	139.5	0.3
1993	140.5	0.7	140.7	0.1	140.9	0.1	141.4	0.4	141.8	0.3	141.1	-0.5	141.1	0.0	141.5	0.3	141.8	0.2	142.3	0.4	142.6	0.2	143.3	0.5

Source: U.S. Department of Labor, Bureau of Labor Statistics, Division of Consumer Prices and Price Indexes.

U.S. City Average
Consumer Price Index - Urban Wage Earners
Base 1982-1984 = 100
Food and Beverages

For 1967-1993. Columns headed % show percentile change in the index from the previous period for which an index is available.

Year	Jan Index	%	Feb Index	%	Mar Index	%	Apr Index	%	May Index	%	Jun Index	%	Jul Index	%	Aug Index	%	Sep Index	%	Oct Index	%	Nov Index	%	Dec Index	%
1967	34.8	-	34.6	-0.6	34.6	0.0	34.5	-0.3	34.6	0.3	34.9	0.9	35.2	0.9	35.4	0.6	35.2	-0.6	35.1	-0.3	35.1	0.0	35.3	0.6
1968	35.5	0.6	35.7	0.6	35.8	0.3	35.9	0.3	36.0	0.3	36.1	0.3	36.4	0.8	36.6	0.5	36.5	-0.3	36.7	0.5	36.6	-0.3	36.8	0.5
1969	37.0	0.5	37.0	0.0	37.2	0.5	37.4	0.5	37.5	0.3	38.0	1.3	38.3	0.8	38.6	0.8	38.6	0.0	38.6	0.0	38.8	0.5	39.3	1.3
1970	39.6	0.8	39.8	0.5	39.8	0.0	39.9	0.3	40.1	0.5	40.2	0.2	40.4	0.5	40.4	0.0	40.4	0.0	40.3	-0.2	40.2	-0.2	40.3	0.2
1971	40.4	0.2	40.5	0.2	40.9	1.0	41.1	0.5	41.3	0.5	41.6	0.7	41.8	0.5	41.9	0.2	41.6	-0.7	41.5	-0.2	41.6	0.2	42.0	1.0
1972	42.0	0.0	42.6	1.4	42.7	0.2	42.7	0.0	42.7	0.0	42.9	0.5	43.3	0.9	43.4	0.2	43.5	0.2	43.5	0.0	43.7	0.5	43.9	0.5
1973	44.7	1.8	45.5	1.8	46.6	2.4	47.2	1.3	47.6	0.8	48.3	1.5	48.6	0.6	51.3	5.6	51.0	-0.6	51.0	0.0	51.5	1.0	52.0	1.0
1974	52.7	1.3	54.0	2.5	54.5	0.9	54.4	-0.2	54.7	0.6	55.0	0.5	55.1	0.2	55.9	1.5	56.7	1.4	57.0	0.5	57.6	1.1	58.2	1.0
1975	58.6	0.7	58.9	0.5	58.8	-0.2	58.8	0.0	59.0	0.3	59.8	1.4	61.1	2.2	61.0	-0.2	60.9	-0.2	61.3	0.7	61.5	0.3	61.9	0.7
1976	61.9	0.0	61.7	-0.3	61.3	-0.6	61.5	0.3	61.7	0.3	62.0	0.5	62.4	0.6	62.5	0.2	62.3	-0.3	62.3	0.0	62.1	-0.3	62.4	0.5
1977	62.9	0.8	64.2	2.1	64.5	0.5	65.3	1.2	65.5	0.3	66.2	1.1	66.5	0.5	66.7	0.3	66.5	-0.3	66.4	-0.2	66.8	0.6	67.1	0.4
1978	68.0	1.3	68.9	1.3	69.6	1.0	70.7	1.6	71.7	1.4	72.8	1.5	73.2	0.5	73.4	0.3	73.4	0.0	73.9	0.7	74.2	0.4	74.8	0.8
1979	76.3	2.0	77.8	2.0	78.7	1.2	79.2	0.6	79.8	0.8	80.1	0.4	80.7	0.7	80.5	-0.2	80.8	0.4	81.2	0.5	81.5	0.4	82.4	1.1
1980	83.1	0.8	83.5	0.5	84.3	1.0	85.0	0.8	85.5	0.6	86.1	0.7	87.1	1.2	88.3	1.4	89.2	1.0	89.7	0.6	90.4	0.8	91.0	0.7
1981	91.6	0.7	92.4	0.9	92.8	0.4	93.0	0.2	92.9	-0.1	93.3	0.4	94.2	1.0	94.6	0.4	94.7	0.1	94.6	-0.1	94.5	-0.1	94.6	0.1
1982	95.7	1.2	96.5	0.8	96.4	-0.1	96.7	0.3	97.3	0.6	98.0	0.7	98.3	0.3	97.9	-0.4	98.0	0.1	97.8	-0.2	97.7	-0.1	97.7	0.0
1983	98.2	0.5	98.6	0.4	99.1	0.5	99.6	0.5	99.8	0.2	99.6	-0.2	99.6	0.0	99.6	0.0	99.8	0.2	99.9	0.1	99.8	-0.1	100.2	0.4
1984	102.0	1.8	102.9	0.9	102.9	0.0	103.0	0.1	102.7	-0.3	102.9	0.2	103.2	0.3	103.8	0.6	103.6	-0.2	103.6	0.0	103.5	-0.1	103.8	0.3
1985	104.5	0.7	105.3	0.8	105.4	0.1	105.3	-0.1	105.1	-0.2	105.3	0.2	105.3	0.0	105.4	0.1	105.5	0.1	105.6	0.1	106.0	0.4	106.7	0.7
1986	107.5	0.7	107.5	0.0	107.5	0.0	107.8	0.3	108.0	0.2	108.1	0.1	109.0	0.8	109.9	0.8	110.1	0.2	110.2	0.1	110.5	0.3	110.7	0.2
1987	111.9	1.1	112.3	0.4	112.3	0.0	112.6	0.3	113.1	0.4	113.6	0.4	113.5	-0.1	113.6	0.1	114.0	0.4	114.1	0.1	114.1	0.0	114.5	0.4
1988	115.4	0.8	115.5	0.1	115.7	0.2	116.3	0.5	116.8	0.4	117.4	0.5	118.5	0.9	119.1	0.5	119.8	0.6	120.0	0.2	119.9	-0.1	120.3	0.3
1989	121.7	1.2	122.4	0.6	123.1	0.6	123.7	0.5	124.4	0.6	124.6	0.2	125.1	0.4	125.3	0.2	125.6	0.2	126.0	0.3	126.4	0.3	126.9	0.4
1990	129.7	2.2	130.6	0.7	130.9	0.2	130.7	-0.2	130.7	0.0	131.5	0.6	132.1	0.5	132.4	0.2	132.7	0.2	133.1	0.3	133.5	0.3	133.6	0.1
1991	135.6	1.5	135.7	0.1	136.1	0.3	136.9	0.6	137.0	0.1	137.4	0.3	136.8	-0.4	136.4	-0.3	136.5	0.1	136.2	-0.2	136.5	0.2	136.9	0.3
1992	137.4	0.4	137.8	0.3	138.4	0.4	138.5	0.1	137.9	-0.4	137.9	0.0	137.8	-0.1	138.5	0.5	138.9	0.3	138.8	-0.1	138.8	0.0	139.1	0.2
1993	140.1	0.7	140.2	0.1	140.5	0.2	140.9	0.3	141.4	0.4	140.8	-0.4	140.8	0.0	141.2	0.3	141.5	0.2	142.0	0.4	142.2	0.1	142.9	0.5

Source: U.S. Department of Labor, Bureau of Labor Statistics, Division of Consumer Prices and Price Indexes.

U.S. City Average
Consumer Price Index - All Urban Consumers
Base 1982-1984 = 100
Housing

For 1967-1993. Columns headed % show percentile change in the index from the previous period for which an index is available.

Year	Jan Index	%	Feb Index	%	Mar Index	%	Apr Index	%	May Index	%	Jun Index	%	Jul Index	%	Aug Index	%	Sep Index	%	Oct Index	%	Nov Index	%	Dec Index	%
1967	30.5	-	30.5	0.0	30.5	0.0	30.6	0.3	30.7	0.3	30.7	0.0	30.8	0.3	30.9	0.3	30.9	0.0	31.0	0.3	31.1	0.3	31.2	0.3
1968	31.3	0.3	31.5	0.6	31.5	0.0	31.6	0.3	31.7	0.3	31.9	0.6	32.1	0.6	32.3	0.6	32.4	0.3	32.5	0.3	32.7	0.6	32.9	0.6
1969	32.9	0.0	33.1	0.6	33.4	0.9	33.6	0.6	33.8	0.6	33.9	0.3	34.1	0.6	34.3	0.6	34.5	0.6	34.6	0.3	34.8	0.6	35.0	0.6
1970	35.1	0.3	35.4	0.9	35.8	1.1	36.0	0.6	36.2	0.6	36.3	0.3	36.5	0.6	36.7	0.5	36.9	0.5	37.1	0.5	37.3	0.5	37.5	0.5
1971	37.5	0.0	37.5	0.0	37.4	-0.3	37.4	0.0	37.7	0.8	37.9	0.5	38.1	0.5	38.2	0.3	38.3	0.3	38.5	0.5	38.6	0.3	38.7	0.3
1972	38.9	0.5	39.0	0.3	39.1	0.3	39.2	0.3	39.3	0.3	39.4	0.3	39.5	0.3	39.7	0.5	39.8	0.3	39.8	0.0	39.9	0.3	40.1	0.5
1973	40.1	0.0	40.3	0.5	40.4	0.2	40.5	0.2	40.7	0.5	40.8	0.2	40.9	0.2	41.2	0.7	41.6	1.0	42.1	1.2	42.5	1.0	42.8	0.7
1974	43.3	1.2	43.7	0.9	44.1	0.9	44.5	0.9	44.9	0.9	45.4	1.1	45.9	1.1	46.5	1.3	47.1	1.3	47.6	1.1	48.1	1.1	48.6	1.0
1975	49.0	0.8	49.5	1.0	49.7	0.4	50.0	0.6	50.2	0.4	50.5	0.6	50.7	0.4	50.9	0.4	51.3	0.8	51.5	0.4	52.0	1.0	52.3	0.6
1976	52.6	0.6	52.7	0.2	53.0	0.6	53.1	0.2	53.3	0.4	53.5	0.4	53.9	0.7	54.1	0.4	54.4	0.6	54.6	0.4	54.8	0.4	55.1	0.5
1977	55.5	0.7	55.9	0.7	56.2	0.5	56.6	0.7	56.8	0.4	57.3	0.9	57.7	0.7	58.0	0.5	58.4	0.7	58.6	0.3	58.9	0.5	59.2	0.5
1978	59.7	0.8	60.0	0.5	60.6	1.0	61.1	0.8	61.6	0.8	62.2	1.0	62.8	1.0	63.2	0.6	63.9	1.1	64.5	0.9	64.9	0.6	65.1	0.3
1979	65.6	0.8	66.4	1.2	67.0	0.9	67.7	1.0	68.5	1.2	69.4	1.3	70.3	1.3	71.3	1.4	72.2	1.3	73.2	1.4	74.1	1.2	75.0	1.2
1980	76.2	1.6	77.1	1.2	78.4	1.7	79.4	1.3	80.6	1.5	82.1	1.9	81.6	-0.6	81.8	0.2	82.4	0.7	83.5	1.3	84.3	1.0	85.3	1.2
1981	85.9	0.7	86.5	0.7	87.0	0.6	87.7	0.8	88.8	1.3	90.0	1.4	91.5	1.7	92.3	0.9	93.5	1.3	93.5	0.0	93.7	0.2	94.0	0.3
1982	94.3	0.3	94.6	0.3	94.4	-0.2	95.3	1.0	96.6	1.4	97.8	1.2	98.3	0.5	98.6	0.3	98.4	-0.2	98.8	0.4	98.2	-0.6	97.4	-0.8
1983	97.9	0.5	98.1	0.2	98.1	0.0	98.6	0.5	99.1	0.5	99.5	0.4	99.9	0.4	100.0	0.1	100.5	0.5	100.6	0.1	100.7	0.1	100.8	0.1
1984	101.4	0.6	101.9	0.5	102.1	0.2	102.6	0.5	103.0	0.4	103.5	0.5	104.1	0.6	104.5	0.4	105.1	0.6	105.1	0.0	105.0	-0.1	105.1	0.1
1985	105.3	0.2	105.8	0.5	106.1	0.3	106.5	0.4	107.3	0.8	107.9	0.6	108.3	0.4	108.7	0.4	108.9	0.2	109.1	0.2	109.3	0.2	109.6	0.3
1986	109.9	0.3	109.8	-0.1	109.9	0.1	110.2	0.3	110.4	0.2	111.2	0.7	111.3	0.1	111.6	0.3	112.0	0.4	111.8	-0.2	111.4	-0.4	111.5	0.1
1987	112.0	0.4	112.4	0.4	112.8	0.4	113.2	0.4	113.6	0.4	114.3	0.6	114.7	0.3	115.4	0.6	115.6	0.2	115.5	-0.1	115.5	0.0	115.6	0.1
1988	116.2	0.5	116.6	0.3	117.0	0.3	117.3	0.3	117.7	0.3	118.6	0.8	119.1	0.4	119.5	0.3	119.9	0.3	119.9	0.0	119.9	0.0	120.2	0.3
1989	120.7	0.4	121.1	0.3	121.5	0.3	121.6	0.1	122.1	0.4	122.9	0.7	123.9	0.8	124.2	0.2	124.3	0.1	124.4	0.1	124.5	0.1	124.9	0.3
1990	125.9	0.8	126.1	0.2	126.8	0.6	126.8	0.0	127.1	0.2	128.3	0.9	129.2	0.7	130.2	0.8	130.5	0.2	130.6	0.1	130.4	-0.2	130.5	0.1
1991	131.8	1.0	132.4	0.5	132.6	0.2	132.5	-0.1	132.8	0.2	133.4	0.5	134.2	0.6	134.5	0.2	134.7	0.1	134.7	0.0	134.7	0.0	135.0	0.2
1992	135.7	0.5	136.1	0.3	136.6	0.4	136.5	-0.1	136.7	0.1	137.7	0.7	138.3	0.4	138.6	0.2	138.4	-0.1	138.5	0.1	138.5	0.0	138.5	0.0
1993	139.3	0.6	139.7	0.3	140.2	0.4	140.4	0.1	140.5	0.1	141.5	0.7	141.9	0.3	142.3	0.3	142.3	0.0	142.2	-0.1	142.0	-0.1	142.3	0.2

Source: U.S. Department of Labor, Bureau of Labor Statistics, Division of Consumer Prices and Price Indexes.

U.S. City Average
Consumer Price Index - Urban Wage Earners
Base 1982-1984 = 100
Housing

For 1967-1993. Columns headed % show percentile change in the index from the previous period for which an index is available.

Year	Jan Index	%	Feb Index	%	Mar Index	%	Apr Index	%	May Index	%	Jun Index	%	Jul Index	%	Aug Index	%	Sep Index	%	Oct Index	%	Nov Index	%	Dec Index	%
1967	30.7	-	30.8	0.3	30.8	0.0	30.9	0.3	31.0	0.3	31.0	0.0	31.1	0.3	31.1	0.0	31.2	0.3	31.3	0.3	31.3	0.0	31.5	0.6
1968	31.6	0.3	31.7	0.3	31.8	0.3	31.9	0.3	32.0	0.3	32.2	0.6	32.4	0.6	32.6	0.6	32.6	0.0	32.8	0.6	33.0	0.6	33.1	0.3
1969	33.2	0.3	33.4	0.6	33.7	0.9	33.9	0.6	34.1	0.6	34.2	0.3	34.4	0.6	34.6	0.6	34.8	0.6	34.9	0.3	35.1	0.6	35.3	0.6
1970	35.4	0.3	35.7	0.8	36.1	1.1	36.3	0.6	36.5	0.6	36.6	0.3	36.8	0.5	37.0	0.5	37.2	0.5	37.4	0.5	37.6	0.5	37.8	0.5
1971	37.8	0.0	37.8	0.0	37.7	-0.3	37.8	0.3	38.0	0.5	38.2	0.5	38.4	0.5	38.5	0.3	38.7	0.5	38.8	0.3	38.9	0.3	39.1	0.5
1972	39.2	0.3	39.3	0.3	39.4	0.3	39.5	0.3	39.6	0.3	39.7	0.3	39.9	0.5	40.0	0.3	40.1	0.2	40.2	0.2	40.3	0.2	40.4	0.2
1973	40.5	0.2	40.6	0.2	40.7	0.2	40.9	0.5	41.0	0.2	41.2	0.5	41.3	0.2	41.6	0.7	42.0	1.0	42.5	1.2	42.8	0.7	43.2	0.9
1974	43.7	1.2	44.1	0.9	44.5	0.9	44.8	0.7	45.3	1.1	45.8	1.1	46.3	1.1	46.9	1.3	47.5	1.3	48.0	1.1	48.5	1.0	49.0	1.0
1975	49.4	0.8	49.9	1.0	50.1	0.4	50.5	0.8	50.7	0.4	51.0	0.6	51.2	0.4	51.4	0.4	51.7	0.6	52.0	0.6	52.5	1.0	52.7	0.4
1976	53.0	0.6	53.2	0.4	53.4	0.4	53.5	0.2	53.7	0.4	54.0	0.6	54.3	0.6	54.6	0.6	54.9	0.5	55.1	0.4	55.3	0.4	55.5	0.4
1977	56.0	0.9	56.3	0.5	56.7	0.7	57.1	0.7	57.3	0.4	57.8	0.9	58.2	0.7	58.5	0.5	58.9	0.7	59.1	0.3	59.4	0.5	59.8	0.7
1978	60.2	0.7	60.6	0.7	61.1	0.8	61.5	0.7	62.1	1.0	62.7	1.0	63.2	0.8	63.6	0.6	64.3	1.1	64.9	0.9	65.3	0.6	65.6	0.5
1979	66.1	0.8	66.9	1.2	67.6	1.0	68.2	0.9	69.0	1.2	70.0	1.4	70.9	1.3	71.9	1.4	72.8	1.3	73.8	1.4	74.8	1.4	75.7	1.2
1980	76.8	1.5	77.8	1.3	79.0	1.5	80.1	1.4	81.3	1.5	82.9	2.0	82.3	-0.7	82.6	0.4	83.1	0.6	84.2	1.3	85.0	1.0	86.1	1.3
1981	86.7	0.7	87.2	0.6	87.6	0.5	88.3	0.8	89.5	1.4	90.7	1.3	92.2	1.7	93.1	1.0	94.3	1.3	94.2	-0.1	94.4	0.2	94.6	0.2
1982	94.9	0.3	95.3	0.4	95.1	-0.2	96.0	0.9	97.4	1.5	98.6	1.2	99.2	0.6	99.5	0.3	99.4	-0.1	99.8	0.4	99.3	-0.5	98.4	-0.9
1983	98.5	0.1	98.6	0.1	99.1	0.5	99.5	0.4	99.8	0.3	100.1	0.3	100.3	0.2	100.7	0.4	101.0	0.3	101.0	0.0	100.8	-0.2	100.7	-0.1
1984	100.8	0.1	100.7	-0.1	100.3	-0.4	100.2	-0.1	101.0	0.8	101.3	0.3	102.1	0.8	103.8	1.7	104.6	0.8	104.2	-0.4	103.9	-0.3	104.0	0.1
1985	104.3	0.3	104.7	0.4	105.0	0.3	105.4	0.4	106.3	0.9	106.8	0.5	107.2	0.4	107.5	0.3	107.8	0.3	107.9	0.1	108.2	0.3	108.4	0.2
1986	108.7	0.3	108.6	-0.1	108.7	0.1	109.0	0.3	109.2	0.2	110.0	0.7	110.1	0.1	110.4	0.3	110.8	0.4	110.4	-0.4	110.0	-0.4	110.2	0.2
1987	110.7	0.5	111.0	0.3	111.4	0.4	111.8	0.4	112.2	0.4	112.9	0.6	113.2	0.3	114.0	0.7	114.1	0.1	114.0	-0.1	113.9	-0.1	114.1	0.2
1988	114.6	0.4	115.0	0.3	115.4	0.3	115.6	0.2	116.0	0.3	116.9	0.8	117.4	0.4	117.8	0.3	118.2	0.3	118.2	0.0	118.3	0.1	118.5	0.2
1989	119.0	0.4	119.3	0.3	119.6	0.3	119.8	0.2	120.3	0.4	121.1	0.7	122.1	0.8	122.4	0.2	122.5	0.1	122.5	0.0	122.7	0.2	123.1	0.3
1990	123.9	0.6	124.1	0.2	124.7	0.5	124.7	0.0	125.1	0.3	126.2	0.9	127.0	0.6	127.9	0.7	128.3	0.3	128.3	0.0	128.2	-0.1	128.3	0.1
1991	129.4	0.9	130.0	0.5	130.2	0.2	130.1	-0.1	130.5	0.3	131.1	0.5	131.8	0.5	132.0	0.2	132.4	0.3	132.3	-0.1	132.4	0.1	132.7	0.2
1992	133.3	0.5	133.6	0.2	134.0	0.3	133.9	-0.1	134.1	0.1	135.1	0.7	135.7	0.4	135.9	0.1	135.8	-0.1	135.9	0.1	136.0	0.1	136.1	0.1
1993	136.7	0.4	137.0	0.2	137.4	0.3	137.7	0.2	137.9	0.1	138.8	0.7	139.1	0.2	139.5	0.3	139.7	0.1	139.6	-0.1	139.4	-0.1	139.7	0.2

Source: U.S. Department of Labor, Bureau of Labor Statistics, Division of Consumer Prices and Price Indexes.

U.S. City Average
Consumer Price Index - All Urban Consumers
Base 1982-1984 = 100
Apparel and Upkeep

For 1913-1993. Columns headed % show percentile change in the index from the previous period for which an index is available.

Year	Jan Index	%	Feb Index	%	Mar Index	%	Apr Index	%	May Index	%	Jun Index	%	Jul Index	%	Aug Index	%	Sep Index	%	Oct Index	%	Nov Index	%	Dec Index	%
1913	-	-	-	-	-	-	-	-	-	-	-	-	-	-	-	-	-	-	-	-	-	-	-	-
1914	-	-	-	-	-	-	-	-	-	-	-	-	-	-	-	-	-	-	-	-	-	-	15.0	-
1915	-	-	-	-	-	-	-	-	-	-	-	-	-	-	-	-	-	-	-	-	-	-	15.6	4.0
1916	-	-	-	-	-	-	-	-	-	-	-	-	-	-	-	-	-	-	-	-	-	-	17.9	14.7
1917	-	-	-	-	-	-	-	-	-	-	-	-	-	-	-	-	-	-	-	-	-	-	22.2	24.0
1918	-	-	-	-	-	-	-	-	-	-	-	-	-	-	-	-	-	-	-	-	-	-	31.8	43.2
1919	-	-	-	-	-	-	-	-	-	-	34.4	8.2	-	-	-	-	-	-	-	-	-	-	42.6	23.8
1920	-	-	-	-	-	-	-	-	-	-	45.0	5.6	-	-	-	-	-	-	-	-	-	-	40.3	-10.4
1921	-	-	-	-	-	-	-	-	34.7	-13.9	-	-	-	-	-	-	30.0	-13.5	-	-	-	-	28.6	-4.7
1922	-	-	-	-	27.3	-4.5	-	-	-	-	26.8	-1.8	-	-	-	-	26.6	-0.7	-	-	-	-	26.6	0.0
1923	-	-	-	-	27.0	1.5	-	-	-	-	27.0	0.0	-	-	-	-	27.2	0.7	-	-	-	-	27.2	0.0
1924	-	-	-	-	27.1	-0.4	-	-	-	-	26.9	-0.7	-	-	-	-	26.6	-1.1	-	-	-	-	26.4	-0.8
1925	-	-	-	-	-	-	-	-	-	-	26.4	0.0	-	-	-	-	-	-	-	-	-	-	26.2	-0.8
1926	-	-	-	-	-	-	-	-	-	-	25.9	-1.1	-	-	-	-	-	-	-	-	-	-	25.7	-0.8
1927	-	-	-	-	-	-	-	-	-	-	25.4	-1.2	-	-	-	-	-	-	-	-	-	-	25.1	-1.2
1928	-	-	-	-	-	-	-	-	-	-	25.0	-0.4	-	-	-	-	-	-	-	-	-	-	24.9	-0.4
1929	-	-	-	-	-	-	-	-	-	-	24.7	-0.8	-	-	-	-	-	-	-	-	-	-	24.6	-0.4
1930	-	-	-	-	-	-	-	-	-	-	24.5	-0.4	-	-	-	-	-	-	-	-	-	-	23.5	-4.1
1931	-	-	-	-	-	-	-	-	-	-	22.2	-5.5	-	-	-	-	-	-	-	-	-	-	20.6	-7.2
1932	-	-	-	-	-	-	-	-	-	-	19.5	-5.3	-	-	-	-	-	-	-	-	-	-	18.6	-4.6
1933	-	-	-	-	-	-	-	-	-	-	18.2	-2.2	-	-	-	-	-	-	-	-	-	-	20.2	11.0
1934	-	-	-	-	-	-	-	-	-	-	20.7	2.5	-	-	-	-	-	-	-	-	20.7	0.0	-	-
1935	-	-	-	-	20.8	0.5	-	-	-	-	-	-	20.7	-0.5	-	-	-	-	20.9	1.0	-	-	-	-
1936	21.0	0.5	-	-	-	-	21.0	0.0	-	-	-	-	20.9	-0.5	-	-	21.0	0.5	-	-	-	-	21.3	1.4
1937	-	-	-	-	21.7	1.9	-	-	-	-	22.0	1.4	-	-	-	-	22.5	2.3	-	-	-	-	22.5	0.0
1938	-	-	-	-	22.1	-1.8	-	-	-	-	21.9	-0.9	-	-	-	-	21.7	-0.9	-	-	-	-	21.7	0.0
1939	-	-	-	-	21.6	-0.5	-	-	-	-	21.6	0.0	-	-	-	-	21.6	0.0	-	-	-	-	21.7	0.5
1940	-	-	-	-	21.9	0.9	-	-	-	-	21.8	-0.5	-	-	-	-	21.8	0.0	21.8	0.0	21.8	0.0	21.8	0.0
1941	21.6	-0.9	21.6	0.0	21.9	1.4	22.0	0.5	22.0	0.0	22.2	0.9	22.5	1.4	22.9	1.8	23.8	3.9	24.2	1.7	24.5	1.2	24.6	0.4
1942	24.9	1.2	25.5	2.4	26.6	4.3	27.2	2.3	27.1	-0.4	26.9	-0.7	26.9	0.0	26.9	0.0	27.1	0.7	27.1	0.0	27.1	0.0	27.1	0.0
1943	27.1	0.0	27.1	0.0	27.4	1.1	27.5	0.4	27.5	0.0	27.5	0.0	27.7	0.7	27.8	0.4	28.4	2.2	28.6	0.7	28.7	0.3	29.0	1.0
1944	29.0	0.0	29.1	0.3	29.4	1.0	29.5	0.3	29.5	0.0	29.7	0.7	29.7	0.0	30.0	1.0	30.3	1.0	30.4	0.3	30.5	0.3	30.6	0.3
1945	30.7	0.3	30.8	0.3	30.8	0.0	30.9	0.3	31.0	0.3	31.2	0.6	31.4	0.6	31.5	0.3	31.9	1.3	31.9	0.0	31.9	0.0	32.1	0.6
1946	32.2	0.3	32.3	0.3	32.9	1.9	33.2	0.9	33.4	0.6	33.7	0.9	34.1	1.2	34.6	1.5	35.6	2.9	36.1	1.4	36.7	1.7	37.9	3.3
1947	38.4	1.3	38.9	1.3	39.5	1.5	39.7	0.5	39.7	0.0	39.9	0.5	39.6	-0.8	39.9	0.8	40.3	1.0	40.6	0.7	40.8	0.5	41.0	0.5
1948	41.3	0.7	41.9	1.5	42.1	0.5	42.2	0.2	42.4	0.5	42.3	-0.2	42.3	0.0	42.9	1.4	43.1	0.5	43.3	0.5	43.2	-0.2	43.1	-0.2
1949	42.2	-2.1	41.9	-0.7	41.7	-0.5	41.3	-1.0	41.1	-0.5	40.9	-0.5	40.5	-1.0	40.2	-0.7	40.2	0.0	40.1	-0.2	40.0	-0.2	39.9	-0.2
1950	39.7	-0.5	39.7	0.0	39.8	0.3	39.7	-0.3	39.6	-0.3	39.6	0.0	39.6	0.0	39.9	0.8	40.7	2.0	41.4	1.7	41.7	0.7	42.0	0.7
1951	42.6	1.4	43.4	1.9	43.6	0.5	43.7	0.2	43.8	0.2	43.8	0.0	43.7	-0.2	43.7	0.0	44.9	2.7	44.9	0.0	44.6	-0.7	44.4	-0.4
1952	43.9	-1.1	43.9	0.0	43.7	-0.5	43.5	-0.5	43.5	0.0	43.4	-0.2	43.2	-0.5	43.1	-0.2	43.5	0.9	43.4	-0.2	43.2	-0.5	43.1	-0.2
1953	43.0	-0.2	43.0	0.0	43.0	0.0	43.0	0.0	43.1	0.2	43.1	0.0	43.1	0.0	43.0	-0.2	43.4	0.9	43.5	0.2	43.5	0.0	43.4	-0.2
1954	43.2	-0.5	43.1	-0.2	43.0	-0.2	42.9	-0.2	43.0	0.2	43.0	0.0	42.9	-0.2	42.8	-0.2	43.0	0.5	43.1	0.2	43.1	0.0	43.1	0.0
1955	42.7	-0.9	42.7	0.0	42.7	0.0	42.6	-0.2	42.7	0.2	42.7	0.0	42.7	0.0	42.8	0.2	43.2	0.9	43.2	0.0	43.3	0.2	43.3	0.0
1956	43.2	-0.2	43.4	0.5	43.4	0.0	43.5	0.2	43.5	0.0	43.5	0.0	43.6	0.2	43.7	0.2	44.1	0.9	44.3	0.5	44.4	0.2	44.4	0.0
1957	44.2	-0.5	44.1	-0.2	44.4	0.7	44.3	-0.2	44.4	0.2	44.4	0.0	44.4	0.0	44.4	0.0	44.7	0.7	44.9	0.4	45.0	0.2	44.8	-0.4

[Continued]

U.S. City Average
Consumer Price Index - All Urban Consumers
Base 1982-1984 = 100
Apparel and Upkeep
[Continued]

For 1913-1993. Columns headed % show percentile change in the index from the previous period for which an index is available.

Year	Jan Index	%	Feb Index	%	Mar Index	%	Apr Index	%	May Index	%	Jun Index	%	Jul Index	%	Aug Index	%	Sep Index	%	Oct Index	%	Nov Index	%	Dec Index	%
1958	44.6	-0.4	44.6	0.0	44.6	0.0	44.6	0.0	44.6	0.0	44.6	0.0	44.6	0.0	44.5	-0.2	44.7	0.4	44.8	0.2	45.0	0.4	44.9	-0.2
1959	44.6	-0.7	44.6	0.0	44.6	0.0	44.7	0.2	44.8	0.2	44.8	0.0	44.9	0.2	45.1	0.4	45.5	0.9	45.6	0.2	45.6	0.0	45.5	-0.2
1960	45.1	-0.9	45.3	0.4	45.4	0.2	45.5	0.2	45.5	0.0	45.5	0.0	45.6	0.2	45.7	0.2	46.1	0.9	46.3	0.4	46.2	-0.2	46.2	0.0
1961	45.8	-0.9	45.8	0.0	45.9	0.2	45.8	-0.2	45.9	0.2	45.8	-0.2	46.0	0.4	46.0	0.0	46.4	0.9	46.5	0.2	46.4	-0.2	46.4	0.0
1962	45.7	-1.5	45.9	0.4	46.1	0.4	46.1	0.0	46.1	0.0	46.2	0.2	46.2	0.0	46.1	-0.2	46.9	1.7	47.0	0.2	46.8	-0.4	46.7	-0.2
1963	46.4	-0.6	46.5	0.2	46.6	0.2	46.7	0.2	46.6	-0.2	46.7	0.2	46.7	0.0	46.8	0.2	47.2	0.9	47.4	0.4	47.5	0.2	47.5	0.0
1964	47.0	-1.1	47.0	0.0	47.1	0.2	47.2	0.2	47.3	0.2	47.3	0.0	47.2	-0.2	47.1	-0.2	47.4	0.6	47.5	0.2	47.6	0.2	47.7	0.2
1965	47.2	-1.0	47.3	0.2	47.4	0.2	47.5	0.2	47.8	0.6	47.8	0.0	47.5	-0.6	47.6	0.2	47.9	0.6	48.2	0.6	48.3	0.2	48.3	0.0
1966	48.0	-0.6	48.1	0.2	48.4	0.6	48.6	0.4	48.9	0.6	48.9	0.0	48.8	-0.2	48.8	0.0	49.5	1.4	49.9	0.8	50.1	0.4	50.2	0.2
1967	49.8	-0.8	50.1	0.6	50.4	0.6	50.5	0.2	50.9	0.8	50.9	0.0	50.8	-0.2	50.9	0.2	51.5	1.2	51.9	0.8	52.2	0.6	52.3	0.2
1968	51.8	-1.0	52.2	0.8	52.6	0.8	53.0	0.8	53.4	0.8	53.6	0.4	53.5	-0.2	53.8	0.6	54.7	1.7	55.2	0.9	55.5	0.5	55.6	0.2
1969	55.2	-0.7	55.4	0.4	55.9	0.9	56.2	0.5	56.6	0.7	56.8	0.4	56.7	-0.2	56.6	-0.2	57.6	1.8	58.1	0.9	58.4	0.5	58.5	0.2
1970	57.8	-1.2	58.1	0.5	58.4	0.5	58.6	0.3	59.0	0.7	59.1	0.2	58.8	-0.5	58.8	0.0	59.7	1.5	60.3	1.0	60.7	0.7	60.8	0.2
1971	60.0	-1.3	60.2	0.3	60.5	0.5	60.7	0.3	61.3	1.0	61.2	-0.2	60.8	-0.7	60.7	-0.2	61.5	1.3	62.0	0.8	62.1	0.2	62.1	0.0
1972	61.3	-1.3	61.5	0.3	61.8	0.5	62.1	0.5	62.5	0.6	62.2	-0.5	61.7	-0.8	61.6	-0.2	62.8	1.9	63.4	1.0	63.7	0.5	63.7	0.0
1973	62.7	-1.6	63.0	0.5	63.6	1.0	64.1	0.8	64.6	0.8	64.6	0.0	64.1	-0.8	64.5	0.6	65.4	1.4	66.1	1.1	66.5	0.6	66.5	0.0
1974	65.7	-1.2	66.5	1.2	67.4	1.4	68.1	1.0	68.8	1.0	69.2	0.6	69.0	-0.3	70.4	2.0	71.3	1.3	71.9	0.8	72.6	1.0	72.3	-0.4
1975	71.1	-1.7	71.5	0.6	71.8	0.4	72.0	0.3	72.3	0.4	72.1	-0.3	71.9	-0.3	72.5	0.8	73.2	1.0	73.7	0.7	74.2	0.7	74.0	-0.3
1976	73.1	-1.2	73.4	0.4	73.9	0.7	74.3	0.5	74.8	0.7	74.9	0.1	74.7	-0.3	75.5	1.1	76.6	1.5	76.9	0.4	77.4	0.7	77.4	0.0
1977	76.5	-1.2	76.9	0.5	77.3	0.5	77.6	0.4	78.2	0.8	78.5	0.4	78.2	-0.4	78.9	0.9	79.6	0.9	80.1	0.6	80.8	0.9	80.7	-0.1
1978	79.4	-1.6	78.8	-0.8	79.8	1.3	80.8	1.3	81.5	0.9	81.5	0.0	80.5	-1.2	81.4	1.1	82.5	1.4	83.3	1.0	83.7	0.5	83.2	-0.6
1979	81.9	-1.6	82.3	0.5	83.8	1.8	84.3	0.6	84.7	0.5	84.5	-0.2	83.8	-0.8	84.8	1.2	86.6	2.1	87.2	0.7	87.5	0.3	87.8	0.3
1980	87.2	-0.7	87.6	0.5	89.7	2.4	90.4	0.8	90.5	0.1	90.3	-0.2	89.8	-0.6	91.1	1.4	92.9	2.0	93.8	1.0	94.2	0.4	93.8	-0.4
1981	92.3	-1.6	92.8	0.5	94.4	1.7	95.0	0.6	95.0	0.0	94.7	-0.3	94.2	-0.5	95.5	1.4	97.2	1.8	97.6	0.4	97.5	-0.1	97.1	-0.4
1982	95.5	-1.6	95.8	0.3	97.4	1.7	97.8	0.4	97.6	-0.2	97.3	-0.3	96.7	-0.6	97.8	1.1	99.4	1.6	99.7	0.3	99.6	-0.1	98.7	-0.9
1983	97.4	-1.3	97.9	0.5	99.2	1.3	99.7	0.5	100.0	0.3	99.7	-0.3	99.4	-0.3	100.6	1.2	102.2	1.6	102.3	0.1	102.3	0.0	101.6	-0.7
1984	100.1	-1.5	100.0	-0.1	101.3	1.3	101.6	0.3	101.4	-0.2	100.6	-0.8	100.2	-0.4	102.0	1.8	104.1	2.1	104.9	0.8	104.6	-0.3	103.6	-1.0
1985	101.9	-1.6	102.9	1.0	104.7	1.7	105.0	0.3	104.7	-0.3	104.3	-0.4	103.4	-0.9	104.7	1.3	106.9	2.1	107.6	0.7	107.7	0.1	106.5	-1.1
1986	104.5	-1.9	104.1	-0.4	105.2	1.1	105.7	0.5	105.2	-0.5	104.3	-0.9	103.6	-0.7	105.5	1.8	108.1	2.5	108.7	0.6	108.6	-0.1	107.5	-1.0
1987	105.6	-1.8	106.2	0.6	109.7	3.3	111.5	1.6	111.1	-0.4	109.3	-1.6	107.3	-1.8	109.4	2.0	113.3	3.6	115.4	1.9	115.4	0.0	112.7	-2.3
1988	110.4	-2.0	110.2	-0.2	114.3	3.7	117.0	2.4	116.3	-0.6	114.6	-1.5	112.7	-1.7	112.6	-0.1	117.8	4.6	120.7	2.5	119.9	-0.7	118.0	-1.6
1989	115.3	-2.3	115.3	0.0	119.3	3.5	120.9	1.3	120.4	-0.4	117.8	-2.2	115.0	-2.4	115.0	0.0	120.0	4.3	122.7	2.2	122.1	-0.5	119.2	-2.4
1990	116.7	-2.1	120.4	3.2	125.4	4.2	126.7	1.0	125.5	-0.9	123.3	-1.8	120.8	-2.0	122.2	1.2	126.8	3.8	128.4	1.3	127.5	-0.7	125.3	-1.7
1991	123.8	-1.2	126.2	1.9	128.8	2.1	130.1	1.0	129.4	-0.5	126.9	-1.9	125.2	-1.3	127.6	1.9	131.3	2.9	132.7	1.1	132.9	0.2	129.6	-2.5
1992	127.9	-1.3	130.2	1.8	133.4	2.5	133.3	-0.1	133.1	-0.2	131.0	-1.6	129.2	-1.4	130.2	0.8	133.3	2.4	135.0	1.3	134.5	-0.4	131.4	-2.3
1993	129.7	-1.3	133.4	2.9	136.2	2.1	136.9	0.5	135.0	-1.4	131.9	-2.3	129.4	-1.9	131.9	1.9	134.6	2.0	136.1	1.1	136.2	0.1	132.6	-2.6

Source: U.S. Department of Labor, Bureau of Labor Statistics, Division of Consumer Prices and Price Indexes.

U.S. City Average
Consumer Price Index - Urban Wage Earners
Base 1982-1984 = 100
Apparel and Upkeep

For 1913-1993. Columns headed % show percentile change in the index from the previous period for which an index is available.

Year	Jan Index	%	Feb Index	%	Mar Index	%	Apr Index	%	May Index	%	Jun Index	%	Jul Index	%	Aug Index	%	Sep Index	%	Oct Index	%	Nov Index	%	Dec Index	%
1913	-	-	-	-	-	-	-	-	-	-	-	-	-	-	-	-	-	-	-	-	-	-	-	-
1914	-	-	-	-	-	-	-	-	-	-	-	-	-	-	-	-	-	-	-	-	-	-	15.1	-
1915	-	-	-	-	-	-	-	-	-	-	-	-	-	-	-	-	-	-	-	-	-	-	15.7	4.0
1916	-	-	-	-	-	-	-	-	-	-	-	-	-	-	-	-	-	-	-	-	-	-	18.0	14.6
1917	-	-	-	-	-	-	-	-	-	-	-	-	-	-	-	-	-	-	-	-	-	-	22.3	23.9
1918	-	-	-	-	-	-	-	-	-	-	-	-	-	-	-	-	-	-	-	-	-	-	31.9	43.0
1919	-	-	-	-	-	-	-	-	-	-	34.6	8.5	-	-	-	-	-	-	-	-	-	-	42.8	23.7
1920	-	-	-	-	-	-	-	-	-	-	45.2	5.6	-	-	-	-	-	-	-	-	-	-	40.5	-10.4
1921	-	-	-	-	-	-	-	-	34.8	-14.1	-	-	-	-	-	-	30.1	-13.5	-	-	-	-	28.7	-4.7
1922	-	-	-	-	27.5	-4.2	-	-	-	-	26.9	-2.2	-	-	-	-	26.7	-0.7	-	-	-	-	26.7	0.0
1923	-	-	-	-	27.1	1.5	-	-	-	-	27.2	0.4	-	-	-	-	27.4	0.7	-	-	-	-	27.4	0.0
1924	-	-	-	-	27.3	-0.4	-	-	-	-	27.0	-1.1	-	-	-	-	26.7	-1.1	-	-	-	-	26.5	-0.7
1925	-	-	-	-	-	-	-	-	-	-	26.5	0.0	-	-	-	-	-	-	-	-	-	-	26.3	-0.8
1926	-	-	-	-	-	-	-	-	-	-	26.1	-0.8	-	-	-	-	-	-	-	-	-	-	25.8	-1.1
1927	-	-	-	-	-	-	-	-	-	-	25.5	-1.2	-	-	-	-	-	-	-	-	-	-	25.2	-1.2
1928	-	-	-	-	-	-	-	-	-	-	25.2	0.0	-	-	-	-	-	-	-	-	-	-	25.0	-0.8
1929	-	-	-	-	-	-	-	-	-	-	24.8	-0.8	-	-	-	-	-	-	-	-	-	-	24.7	-0.4
1930	-	-	-	-	-	-	-	-	-	-	24.6	-0.4	-	-	-	-	-	-	-	-	-	-	23.6	-4.1
1931	-	-	-	-	-	-	-	-	-	-	22.3	-5.5	-	-	-	-	-	-	-	-	-	-	20.7	-7.2
1932	-	-	-	-	-	-	-	-	-	-	19.6	-5.3	-	-	-	-	-	-	-	-	-	-	18.6	-5.1
1933	-	-	-	-	-	-	-	-	-	-	18.3	-1.6	-	-	-	-	-	-	-	-	-	-	20.3	10.9
1934	-	-	-	-	-	-	-	-	-	-	20.8	2.5	-	-	-	-	-	-	-	-	20.8	0.0	-	-
1935	-	-	-	-	20.9	0.5	-	-	-	-	-	-	20.8	-0.5	-	-	-	-	21.0	1.0	-	-	-	-
1936	21.1	0.5	-	-	-	-	21.1	0.0	-	-	-	-	21.0	-0.5	-	-	21.1	0.5	-	-	-	-	21.4	1.4
1937	-	-	-	-	21.8	1.9	-	-	-	-	22.1	1.4	-	-	-	-	22.6	2.3	-	-	-	-	22.6	0.0
1938	-	-	-	-	22.2	-1.8	-	-	-	-	22.0	-0.9	-	-	-	-	21.8	-0.9	-	-	-	-	21.8	0.0
1939	-	-	-	-	21.7	-0.5	-	-	-	-	21.7	0.0	-	-	-	-	21.7	0.0	-	-	-	-	21.8	0.5
1940	-	-	-	-	22.0	0.9	-	-	-	-	21.9	-0.5	-	-	-	-	21.9	0.0	21.9	0.0	21.9	0.0	21.9	0.0
1941	21.7	-0.9	21.7	0.0	22.0	1.4	22.1	0.5	22.1	0.0	22.3	0.9	22.6	1.3	23.1	2.2	23.9	3.5	24.3	1.7	24.6	1.2	24.7	0.4
1942	25.1	1.6	25.7	2.4	26.7	3.9	27.3	2.2	27.3	0.0	27.0	-1.1	27.0	0.0	27.0	0.0	27.2	0.7	27.2	0.0	27.2	0.0	27.2	0.0
1943	27.3	0.4	27.3	0.0	27.5	0.7	27.6	0.4	27.6	0.0	27.6	0.0	27.9	1.1	28.0	0.4	28.6	2.1	28.7	0.3	28.8	0.3	29.1	1.0
1944	29.1	0.0	29.2	0.3	29.5	1.0	29.6	0.3	29.7	0.3	29.8	0.3	29.8	0.0	30.1	1.0	30.5	1.3	30.6	0.3	30.6	0.0	30.8	0.7
1945	30.9	0.3	30.9	0.0	31.0	0.3	31.0	0.0	31.2	0.6	31.4	0.6	31.5	0.3	31.6	0.3	32.0	1.3	32.0	0.0	32.1	0.3	32.3	0.6
1946	32.3	0.0	32.5	0.6	33.0	1.5	33.3	0.9	33.6	0.9	33.9	0.9	34.2	0.9	34.8	1.8	35.8	2.9	36.3	1.4	36.9	1.7	38.1	3.3
1947	38.6	1.3	39.1	1.3	39.7	1.5	39.9	0.5	39.9	0.0	40.1	0.5	39.8	-0.7	40.1	0.8	40.5	1.0	40.8	0.7	41.0	0.5	41.2	0.5
1948	41.5	0.7	42.1	1.4	42.3	0.5	42.4	0.2	42.6	0.5	42.5	-0.2	42.5	0.0	43.1	1.4	43.3	0.5	43.5	0.5	43.4	-0.2	43.3	-0.2
1949	42.4	-2.1	42.1	-0.7	41.9	-0.5	41.5	-1.0	41.3	-0.5	41.1	-0.5	40.7	-1.0	40.4	-0.7	40.4	0.0	40.3	-0.2	40.2	-0.2	40.1	-0.2
1950	39.9	-0.5	39.9	0.0	40.0	0.3	39.9	-0.2	39.8	-0.3	39.8	0.0	39.8	0.0	40.1	0.8	40.9	2.0	41.6	1.7	41.9	0.7	42.2	0.7
1951	42.8	1.4	43.6	1.9	43.9	0.7	44.0	0.2	44.0	0.0	44.0	0.0	43.9	-0.2	44.0	0.2	45.1	2.5	45.1	0.0	44.8	-0.7	44.6	-0.4
1952	44.2	-0.9	44.1	-0.2	44.0	-0.2	43.7	-0.7	43.7	0.0	43.6	-0.2	43.4	-0.5	43.3	-0.2	43.7	0.9	43.6	-0.2	43.4	-0.5	43.3	-0.2
1953	43.2	-0.2	43.2	0.0	43.2	0.0	43.2	0.0	43.3	0.2	43.3	0.0	43.3	0.0	43.2	-0.2	43.6	0.9	43.7	0.2	43.7	0.0	43.6	-0.2
1954	43.4	-0.5	43.3	-0.2	43.2	-0.2	43.1	-0.2	43.2	0.2	43.2	0.0	43.1	-0.2	43.0	-0.2	43.2	0.5	43.3	0.2	43.3	0.0	43.3	0.0
1955	42.9	-0.9	42.9	0.0	42.9	0.0	42.8	-0.2	42.9	0.2	42.9	0.0	42.9	0.0	43.0	0.2	43.4	0.9	43.4	0.0	43.5	0.2	43.5	0.0
1956	43.4	-0.2	43.6	0.5	43.6	0.0	43.7	0.2	43.7	0.0	43.7	0.0	43.9	0.5	44.0	0.2	44.4	0.9	44.5	0.2	44.6	0.2	44.6	0.0
1957	44.4	-0.4	44.4	0.0	44.6	0.5	44.5	-0.2	44.6	0.2	44.6	0.0	44.6	0.0	44.6	0.0	44.9	0.7	45.1	0.4	45.2	0.2	45.0	-0.4

[Continued]

U.S. City Average
Consumer Price Index - Urban Wage Earners
Base 1982-1984 = 100
Apparel and Upkeep
[Continued]

For 1913-1993. Columns headed % show percentile change in the index from the previous period for which an index is available.

Year	Jan Index	%	Feb Index	%	Mar Index	%	Apr Index	%	May Index	%	Jun Index	%	Jul Index	%	Aug Index	%	Sep Index	%	Oct Index	%	Nov Index	%	Dec Index	%
1958	44.8	-0.4	44.8	0.0	44.8	0.0	44.8	0.0	44.8	0.0	44.8	0.0	44.8	0.0	44.7	-0.2	44.9	0.4	45.0	0.2	45.2	0.4	45.1	-0.2
1959	44.8	-0.7	44.8	0.0	44.8	0.0	44.9	0.2	45.0	0.2	45.0	0.0	45.1	0.2	45.3	0.4	45.7	0.9	45.8	0.2	45.8	0.0	45.7	-0.2
1960	45.3	-0.9	45.5	0.4	45.6	0.2	45.7	0.2	45.7	0.0	45.7	0.0	45.8	0.2	45.9	0.2	46.4	1.1	46.6	0.4	46.5	-0.2	46.4	-0.2
1961	46.0	-0.9	46.1	0.2	46.1	0.0	46.1	0.0	46.1	0.0	46.1	0.0	46.2	0.2	46.2	0.0	46.7	1.1	46.7	0.0	46.7	0.0	46.6	-0.2
1962	46.0	-1.3	46.1	0.2	46.4	0.7	46.4	0.0	46.4	0.0	46.5	0.2	46.5	0.0	46.3	-0.4	47.1	1.7	47.2	0.2	47.0	-0.4	46.9	-0.2
1963	46.6	-0.6	46.7	0.2	46.8	0.2	46.9	0.2	46.9	0.0	47.0	0.2	47.0	0.0	47.0	0.0	47.4	0.9	47.6	0.4	47.7	0.2	47.7	0.0
1964	47.2	-1.0	47.2	0.0	47.3	0.2	47.4	0.2	47.5	0.2	47.5	0.0	47.4	-0.2	47.3	-0.2	47.6	0.6	47.7	0.2	47.8	0.2	47.9	0.2
1965	47.4	-1.0	47.5	0.2	47.6	0.2	47.7	0.2	48.0	0.6	48.1	0.2	47.7	-0.8	47.8	0.2	48.2	0.8	48.5	0.6	48.6	0.2	48.6	0.0
1966	48.2	-0.8	48.4	0.4	48.6	0.4	48.9	0.6	49.1	0.4	49.2	0.2	49.1	-0.2	49.1	0.0	49.7	1.2	50.1	0.8	50.3	0.4	50.5	0.4
1967	50.0	-1.0	50.3	0.6	50.6	0.6	50.8	0.4	51.1	0.6	51.2	0.2	51.1	-0.2	51.1	0.0	51.7	1.2	52.2	1.0	52.4	0.4	52.5	0.2
1968	52.1	-0.8	52.4	0.6	52.9	1.0	53.2	0.6	53.7	0.9	53.9	0.4	53.8	-0.2	54.0	0.4	54.9	1.7	55.4	0.9	55.7	0.5	55.8	0.2
1969	55.4	-0.7	55.7	0.5	56.1	0.7	56.5	0.7	56.9	0.7	57.1	0.4	57.0	-0.2	56.9	-0.2	57.8	1.6	58.3	0.9	58.7	0.7	58.8	0.2
1970	58.1	-1.2	58.4	0.5	58.7	0.5	58.9	0.3	59.3	0.7	59.4	0.2	59.1	-0.5	59.1	0.0	60.0	1.5	60.6	1.0	61.0	0.7	61.1	0.2
1971	60.2	-1.5	60.5	0.5	60.8	0.5	61.0	0.3	61.6	1.0	61.5	-0.2	61.1	-0.7	61.0	-0.2	61.8	1.3	62.3	0.8	62.4	0.2	62.4	0.0
1972	61.6	-1.3	61.8	0.3	62.1	0.5	62.4	0.5	62.8	0.6	62.5	-0.5	62.0	-0.8	61.9	-0.2	63.1	1.9	63.7	1.0	64.0	0.5	64.0	0.0
1973	63.0	-1.6	63.3	0.5	63.9	0.9	64.4	0.8	64.9	0.8	65.0	0.2	64.4	-0.9	64.8	0.6	65.7	1.4	66.4	1.1	66.9	0.8	66.9	0.0
1974	66.0	-1.3	66.8	1.2	67.7	1.3	68.4	1.0	69.2	1.2	69.5	0.4	69.3	-0.3	70.7	2.0	71.7	1.4	72.3	0.8	72.9	0.8	72.7	-0.3
1975	71.4	-1.8	71.8	0.6	72.2	0.6	72.4	0.3	72.6	0.3	72.4	-0.3	72.3	-0.1	72.9	0.8	73.5	0.8	74.1	0.8	74.5	0.5	74.4	-0.1
1976	73.4	-1.3	73.8	0.5	74.3	0.7	74.6	0.4	75.2	0.8	75.3	0.1	75.0	-0.4	75.9	1.2	76.9	1.3	77.3	0.5	77.8	0.6	77.8	0.0
1977	76.8	-1.3	77.3	0.7	77.7	0.5	78.0	0.4	78.6	0.8	78.8	0.3	78.6	-0.3	79.3	0.9	80.0	0.9	80.5	0.6	81.2	0.9	81.0	-0.2
1978	79.6	-1.7	79.1	-0.6	79.9	1.0	81.0	1.4	81.8	1.0	81.9	0.1	81.0	-1.1	81.8	1.0	82.9	1.3	83.8	1.1	84.0	0.2	83.7	-0.4
1979	82.5	-1.4	82.8	0.4	84.1	1.6	84.7	0.7	84.9	0.2	84.7	-0.2	84.3	-0.5	85.1	0.9	86.7	1.9	87.5	0.9	87.8	0.3	87.8	0.0
1980	87.0	-0.9	87.9	1.0	89.7	2.0	90.2	0.6	90.6	0.4	90.2	-0.4	89.9	-0.3	91.1	1.3	92.9	2.0	93.6	0.8	93.9	0.3	93.7	-0.2
1981	92.6	-1.2	93.1	0.5	94.4	1.4	95.3	1.0	95.4	0.1	95.2	-0.2	95.0	-0.2	96.3	1.4	97.6	1.3	97.6	0.0	97.6	0.0	97.0	-0.6
1982	95.5	-1.5	96.0	0.5	97.6	1.7	97.9	0.3	97.6	-0.3	97.1	-0.5	96.7	-0.4	97.7	1.0	99.4	1.7	99.7	0.3	99.6	-0.1	98.8	-0.8
1983	97.3	-1.5	97.8	0.5	99.4	1.6	99.8	0.4	100.0	0.2	99.7	-0.3	99.4	-0.3	100.6	1.2	102.1	1.5	102.4	0.3	102.3	-0.1	101.5	-0.8
1984	100.0	-1.5	100.1	0.1	101.4	1.3	101.5	0.1	101.3	-0.2	100.5	-0.8	100.0	-0.5	101.9	1.9	104.1	2.2	104.9	0.8	104.6	-0.3	103.5	-1.1
1985	101.7	-1.7	102.8	1.1	104.6	1.8	105.0	0.4	104.6	-0.4	104.4	-0.2	103.4	-1.0	104.7	1.3	106.9	2.1	107.7	0.7	107.7	0.0	106.6	-1.0
1986	104.6	-1.9	104.0	-0.6	105.1	1.1	105.6	0.5	105.1	-0.5	104.0	-1.0	103.4	-0.6	105.5	2.0	108.1	2.5	108.6	0.5	108.3	-0.3	107.4	-0.8
1987	105.4	-1.9	106.0	0.6	109.5	3.3	111.4	1.7	110.9	-0.4	109.1	-1.6	107.1	-1.8	109.1	1.9	112.9	3.5	115.2	2.0	115.2	0.0	112.6	-2.3
1988	110.3	-2.0	110.0	-0.3	113.9	3.5	116.3	2.1	115.7	-0.5	114.1	-1.4	112.4	-1.5	112.2	-0.2	117.2	4.5	120.1	2.5	119.5	-0.5	117.6	-1.6
1989	114.8	-2.4	114.7	-0.1	118.4	3.2	120.0	1.4	119.4	-0.5	116.9	-2.1	114.4	-2.1	114.5	0.1	119.3	4.2	122.0	2.3	121.4	-0.5	118.5	-2.4
1990	116.1	-2.0	119.3	2.8	124.4	4.3	125.8	1.1	124.7	-0.9	122.4	-1.8	119.8	-2.1	121.3	1.3	125.7	3.6	127.1	1.1	126.5	-0.5	124.5	-1.6
1991	122.9	-1.3	124.8	1.5	127.5	2.2	128.8	1.0	127.9	-0.7	125.7	-1.7	124.1	-1.3	126.4	1.9	129.7	2.6	131.1	1.1	131.4	0.2	128.4	-2.3
1992	126.8	-1.2	128.8	1.6	132.1	2.6	132.1	0.0	131.8	-0.2	129.8	-1.5	128.1	-1.3	129.5	1.1	132.1	2.0	133.8	1.3	133.4	-0.3	130.4	-2.2
1993	128.4	-1.5	132.0	2.8	134.8	2.1	135.2	0.3	133.6	-1.2	130.7	-2.2	128.4	-1.8	130.5	1.6	133.3	2.1	135.1	1.4	135.0	-0.1	131.3	-2.7

Source: U.S. Department of Labor, Bureau of Labor Statistics, Division of Consumer Prices and Price Indexes.

U.S. City Average
Consumer Price Index - All Urban Consumers
Base 1982-1984 = 100
Transportation

For 1935-1993. Columns headed % show percentile change in the index from the previous period for which an index is available.

Year	Jan Index	%	Feb Index	%	Mar Index	%	Apr Index	%	May Index	%	Jun Index	%	Jul Index	%	Aug Index	%	Sep Index	%	Oct Index	%	Nov Index	%	Dec Index	%
1935	-	-	-	-	14.2	-	-	-	-	-	-	-	14.3	0.7	-	-	-	-	14.1	-1.4	-	-	-	-
1936	14.1	0.0	-	-	-	-	14.3	1.4	-	-	-	-	14.3	0.0	-	-	14.3	0.0	-	-	-	-	14.3	0.0
1937	-	-	-	-	14.5	1.4	-	-	-	-	14.5	0.0	-	-	-	-	14.6	0.7	-	-	-	-	14.7	0.7
1938	-	-	-	-	14.7	0.0	-	-	-	-	14.7	0.0	-	-	-	-	14.7	0.0	-	-	-	-	14.4	-2.0
1939	-	-	-	-	14.3	-0.7	-	-	-	-	14.3	0.0	-	-	-	-	14.3	0.0	-	-	-	-	14.3	0.0
1940	-	-	-	-	14.3	0.0	-	-	-	-	14.1	-1.4	-	-	-	-	14.2	0.7	-	-	-	-	14.3	0.7
1941	-	-	-	-	14.3	0.0	-	-	-	-	14.6	2.1	-	-	-	-	14.8	1.4	-	-	-	-	15.4	4.1
1942	-	-	-	-	16.0	3.9	-	-	-	-	16.1	0.6	-	-	-	-	16.0	-0.6	-	-	-	-	16.0	0.0
1943	-	-	-	-	16.0	0.0	-	-	-	-	15.9	-0.6	-	-	-	-	15.9	0.0	-	-	-	-	15.9	0.0
1944	-	-	-	-	15.9	0.0	-	-	-	-	15.9	0.0	-	-	-	-	15.9	0.0	-	-	-	-	15.9	0.0
1945	-	-	-	-	15.9	0.0	-	-	-	-	15.9	0.0	-	-	-	-	15.9	0.0	-	-	-	-	15.9	0.0
1946	-	-	-	-	16.0	0.6	-	-	-	-	16.2	1.3	-	-	-	-	17.5	8.0	-	-	-	-	17.9	2.3
1947	17.9	0.0	17.9	0.0	18.1	1.1	18.2	0.6	18.3	0.5	18.3	0.0	18.4	0.5	18.5	0.5	18.7	1.1	18.9	1.1	19.0	0.5	19.2	1.1
1948	19.5	1.6	19.6	0.5	19.6	0.0	19.8	1.0	19.8	0.0	19.9	0.5	21.0	5.5	21.4	1.9	21.5	0.5	21.6	0.5	21.6	0.0	21.6	0.0
1949	21.6	0.0	21.8	0.9	21.9	0.5	22.0	0.5	22.1	0.5	22.0	-0.5	22.1	0.5	22.3	0.9	22.3	0.0	22.4	0.4	22.4	0.0	22.5	0.4
1950	22.5	0.0	22.4	-0.4	22.4	0.0	22.3	-0.4	22.4	0.4	22.4	0.0	22.7	1.3	22.9	0.9	23.0	0.4	22.9	-0.4	23.0	0.4	23.3	1.3
1951	23.4	0.4	23.6	0.9	23.8	0.8	23.9	0.4	24.0	0.4	24.0	0.0	24.0	0.0	24.2	0.8	24.4	0.8	24.6	0.8	24.9	1.2	24.9	0.0
1952	25.0	0.4	25.2	0.8	25.4	0.8	25.4	0.0	25.5	0.4	25.7	0.8	25.9	0.8	25.9	0.0	26.0	0.4	26.2	0.8	26.3	0.4	26.3	0.0
1953	26.4	0.4	26.3	-0.4	26.4	0.4	26.4	0.0	26.4	0.0	26.4	0.0	26.5	0.4	26.6	0.4	26.7	0.4	26.7	0.0	26.5	-0.7	26.3	-0.8
1954	26.6	1.1	26.4	-0.8	26.3	-0.4	26.3	0.0	26.3	0.0	26.3	0.0	25.8	-1.9	25.8	0.0	25.8	0.0	25.5	-1.2	26.0	2.0	25.9	-0.4
1955	26.0	0.4	26.0	0.0	25.9	-0.4	25.5	-1.5	25.6	0.4	25.6	0.0	25.6	0.0	25.6	0.0	25.5	-0.4	25.8	1.2	26.2	1.6	25.9	-1.1
1956	25.9	0.0	25.9	0.0	25.8	-0.4	25.8	0.0	25.9	0.4	25.9	0.0	26.0	0.4	26.2	0.8	26.2	0.0	27.0	3.1	27.1	0.4	27.1	0.0
1957	27.2	0.4	27.4	0.7	27.5	0.4	27.6	0.4	27.5	-0.4	27.5	0.0	27.7	0.7	27.7	0.0	27.7	0.0	27.7	0.0	28.5	2.9	28.3	-0.7
1958	28.2	-0.4	28.2	0.0	28.2	0.0	28.2	0.0	28.2	0.0	28.3	0.4	28.6	1.1	28.7	0.3	28.8	0.3	29.1	1.0	29.4	1.0	29.4	0.0
1959	29.4	0.0	29.4	0.0	29.5	0.3	29.6	0.3	29.6	0.0	29.7	0.3	29.8	0.3	29.9	0.3	29.8	-0.3	30.2	1.3	30.3	0.3	30.3	0.0
1960	30.1	-0.7	30.0	-0.3	29.8	-0.7	29.8	0.0	29.6	-0.7	29.7	0.3	29.7	0.0	29.8	0.3	29.5	-1.0	29.8	1.0	29.8	0.0	29.8	0.0
1961	29.8	0.0	29.8	0.0	29.7	-0.3	29.7	0.0	29.8	0.3	30.1	1.0	30.2	0.3	30.4	0.7	30.4	0.0	30.6	0.7	30.6	0.0	30.4	-0.7
1962	30.4	0.0	30.4	0.0	30.4	0.0	30.8	1.3	30.8	0.0	30.8	0.0	30.6	-0.6	30.8	0.7	30.9	0.3	31.0	0.3	31.1	0.3	31.0	-0.3
1963	30.6	-1.3	30.6	0.0	30.7	0.3	30.7	0.0	30.8	0.3	30.8	0.0	30.9	0.3	31.1	0.6	31.0	-0.3	31.3	1.0	31.3	0.0	31.3	0.0
1964	31.4	0.3	31.2	-0.6	31.3	0.3	31.3	0.0	31.3	0.0	31.3	0.0	31.4	0.3	31.4	0.0	31.3	-0.3	31.4	0.3	31.6	0.6	31.7	0.3
1965	31.9	0.6	31.7	-0.6	31.7	0.0	31.9	0.6	32.0	0.3	31.9	-0.3	32.0	0.3	31.9	-0.3	31.9	0.0	31.9	0.0	32.0	0.3	32.0	0.0
1966	31.9	-0.3	31.9	0.0	32.0	0.3	32.1	0.3	32.1	0.0	32.2	0.3	32.6	1.2	32.6	0.0	32.5	-0.3	32.8	0.9	32.9	0.3	32.7	-0.6
1967	32.5	-0.6	32.7	0.6	32.8	0.3	33.0	0.6	33.2	0.6	33.2	0.0	33.4	0.6	33.4	0.0	33.5	0.3	33.8	0.9	34.0	0.6	33.8	-0.6
1968	34.1	0.9	34.0	-0.3	34.2	0.6	34.2	0.0	34.2	0.0	34.4	0.6	34.4	0.0	34.4	0.0	34.3	-0.3	34.6	0.9	34.8	0.6	34.5	-0.9
1969	34.6	0.3	35.0	1.2	35.7	2.0	35.8	0.3	35.6	-0.6	35.8	0.6	35.7	-0.3	35.7	0.0	35.5	-0.6	36.1	1.7	36.1	0.0	36.3	0.6
1970	36.5	0.6	36.5	0.0	36.5	0.0	37.0	1.4	37.3	0.8	37.5	0.5	37.7	0.5	37.5	-0.5	37.6	0.3	38.3	1.9	38.6	0.8	38.9	0.8
1971	39.1	0.5	39.1	0.0	39.2	0.3	39.3	0.3	39.5	0.5	39.8	0.8	39.7	-0.3	39.7	0.0	39.5	-0.5	39.7	0.5	39.5	-0.5	39.4	-0.3
1972	39.6	0.5	39.4	-0.5	39.4	0.0	39.5	0.3	39.8	0.8	39.9	0.3	40.0	0.3	40.1	0.2	40.3	0.5	40.3	0.0	40.4	0.2	40.4	0.0
1973	40.3	-0.2	40.3	0.0	40.4	0.2	40.8	1.0	41.1	0.7	41.5	1.0	41.5	0.0	41.4	-0.2	41.2	-0.5	41.6	1.0	41.9	0.7	42.2	0.7
1974	42.6	0.9	43.0	0.9	43.9	2.1	44.5	1.4	45.4	2.0	46.2	1.8	46.8	1.3	47.0	0.4	47.3	0.6	47.5	0.4	47.7	0.4	47.7	0.0
1975	47.6	-0.2	47.7	0.2	48.2	1.0	48.6	0.8	49.0	0.8	49.8	1.6	50.8	2.0	51.1	0.6	51.7	1.2	51.9	0.4	52.4	1.0	52.4	0.0
1976	52.6	0.4	52.7	0.2	53.2	0.9	53.7	0.9	54.4	1.3	55.2	1.5	55.8	1.1	56.1	0.5	56.4	0.5	56.9	0.9	57.0	0.2	57.0	0.0
1977	57.3	0.5	57.6	0.5	58.1	0.9	58.8	1.2	59.3	0.9	59.6	0.5	59.6	0.0	59.5	-0.2	59.4	-0.2	59.4	0.0	59.5	0.2	59.5	0.0
1978	59.6	0.2	59.7	0.2	59.9	0.3	60.3	0.7	61.0	1.2	61.7	1.1	62.3	1.0	62.6	0.5	62.8	0.3	63.1	0.5	63.7	1.0	64.1	0.6
1979	64.5	0.6	65.1	0.9	65.9	1.2	67.5	2.4	69.1	2.4	70.7	2.3	72.1	2.0	73.1	1.4	73.7	0.8	74.1	0.5	74.8	0.9	75.8	1.3

[Continued]

U.S. City Average
Consumer Price Index - All Urban Consumers
Base 1982-1984 = 100
Transportation
[Continued]

For 1935-1993. Columns headed % show percentile change in the index from the previous period for which an index is available.

Year	Jan Index	%	Feb Index	%	Mar Index	%	Apr Index	%	May Index	%	Jun Index	%	Jul Index	%	Aug Index	%	Sep Index	%	Oct Index	%	Nov Index	%	Dec Index	%
1980	77.7	2.5	79.7	2.6	81.1	1.8	82.1	1.2	82.8	0.9	83.1	0.4	83.5	0.5	84.1	0.7	84.7	0.7	85.2	0.6	86.2	1.2	86.9	0.8
1981	88.1	1.4	90.1	2.3	91.0	1.0	91.6	0.7	92.4	0.9	93.1	0.8	94.0	1.0	94.4	0.4	94.9	0.5	95.6	0.7	96.2	0.6	96.4	0.2
1982	96.5	0.1	95.8	-0.7	94.9	-0.9	94.1	-0.8	95.0	1.0	97.4	2.5	98.5	1.1	98.6	0.1	98.3	-0.3	98.3	0.0	98.4	0.1	98.1	-0.3
1983	97.5	-0.6	96.5	-1.0	95.6	-0.9	97.3	1.8	98.6	1.3	99.3	0.7	100.0	0.7	100.6	0.6	101.0	0.4	101.5	0.5	101.9	0.4	101.9	0.0
1984	101.8	-0.1	101.7	-0.1	102.1	0.4	103.0	0.9	103.9	0.9	104.2	0.3	104.1	-0.1	104.1	0.0	104.4	0.3	105.0	0.6	105.2	0.2	105.1	-0.1
1985	104.7	-0.4	104.6	-0.1	105.4	0.8	106.5	1.0	106.9	0.4	107.1	0.2	107.1	0.0	106.7	-0.4	106.4	-0.3	106.8	0.4	107.5	0.7	107.8	0.3
1986	107.8	0.0	106.2	-1.5	103.0	-3.0	100.9	-2.0	101.7	0.8	102.7	1.0	101.4	-1.3	100.3	-1.1	100.5	0.2	100.7	0.2	101.2	0.5	101.4	0.2
1987	102.6	1.2	103.1	0.5	103.3	0.2	104.2	0.9	104.7	0.5	105.4	0.7	106.0	0.6	106.5	0.5	106.6	0.1	107.1	0.5	107.8	0.7	107.6	-0.2
1988	107.1	-0.5	106.8	-0.3	106.5	-0.3	107.2	0.7	108.1	0.8	108.5	0.4	108.9	0.4	109.6	0.6	109.7	0.1	110.0	0.3	110.7	0.6	110.8	0.1
1989	111.1	0.3	111.6	0.5	111.9	0.3	114.6	2.4	116.0	1.2	115.9	-0.1	115.4	-0.4	114.3	-1.0	113.7	-0.5	114.5	0.7	115.0	0.4	115.2	0.2
1990	117.2	1.7	117.1	-0.1	116.8	-0.3	117.3	0.4	117.7	0.3	118.2	0.4	118.4	0.2	120.6	1.9	123.0	2.0	125.8	2.3	126.9	0.9	127.2	0.2
1991	125.5	-1.3	123.7	-1.4	122.3	-1.1	122.2	-0.1	123.3	0.9	123.7	0.3	123.4	-0.2	123.8	0.3	123.8	0.0	124.0	0.2	125.0	0.8	125.3	0.2
1992	124.5	-0.6	124.1	-0.3	124.4	0.2	125.2	0.6	126.3	0.9	126.9	0.5	127.2	0.2	126.9	-0.2	126.8	-0.1	128.0	0.9	129.2	0.9	129.0	-0.2
1993	129.1	0.1	129.2	0.1	129.0	-0.2	129.4	0.3	130.2	0.6	130.3	0.1	130.3	0.0	130.2	-0.1	130.1	-0.1	131.8	1.3	132.6	0.6	132.1	-0.4

Source: U.S. Department of Labor, Bureau of Labor Statistics, Division of Consumer Prices and Price Indexes.

U.S. City Average
Consumer Price Index - Urban Wage Earners
Base 1982-1984 = 100
Transportation

For 1935-1993. Columns headed % show percentile change in the index from the previous period for which an index is available.

Year	Jan Index	%	Feb Index	%	Mar Index	%	Apr Index	%	May Index	%	Jun Index	%	Jul Index	%	Aug Index	%	Sep Index	%	Oct Index	%	Nov Index	%	Dec Index	%
1935	-	-	-	-	14.1	-	-	-	-	-	-	-	14.2	0.7	-	-	-	-	14.0	-1.4	-	-	-	-
1936	14.1	0.7	-	-	-	-	14.2	0.7	-	-	-	-	14.3	0.7	-	-	14.3	0.0	-	-	-	-	14.3	0.0
1937	-	-	-	-	14.4	0.7	-	-	-	-	14.4	0.0	-	-	-	-	14.5	0.7	-	-	-	-	14.6	0.7
1938	-	-	-	-	14.6	0.0	-	-	-	-	14.6	0.0	-	-	-	-	14.6	0.0	-	-	-	-	14.3	-2.1
1939	-	-	-	-	14.2	-0.7	-	-	-	-	14.2	0.0	-	-	-	-	14.3	0.7	-	-	-	-	14.2	-0.7
1940	-	-	-	-	14.2	0.0	-	-	-	-	14.1	-0.7	-	-	-	-	14.1	0.0	-	-	-	-	14.2	0.7
1941	-	-	-	-	14.3	0.7	-	-	-	-	14.6	2.1	-	-	-	-	14.7	0.7	-	-	-	-	15.3	4.1
1942	-	-	-	-	15.9	3.9	-	-	-	-	16.0	0.6	-	-	-	-	15.9	-0.6	-	-	-	-	15.9	0.0
1943	-	-	-	-	15.9	0.0	-	-	-	-	15.8	-0.6	-	-	-	-	15.8	0.0	-	-	-	-	15.8	0.0
1944	-	-	-	-	15.8	0.0	-	-	-	-	15.8	0.0	-	-	-	-	15.8	0.0	-	-	-	-	15.8	0.0
1945	-	-	-	-	15.8	0.0	-	-	-	-	15.8	0.0	-	-	-	-	15.8	0.0	-	-	-	-	15.8	0.0
1946	-	-	-	-	15.9	0.6	-	-	-	-	16.1	1.3	-	-	-	-	17.4	8.1	-	-	-	-	17.8	2.3
1947	17.8	0.0	17.8	0.0	18.0	1.1	18.1	0.6	18.2	0.6	18.2	0.0	18.3	0.5	18.4	0.5	18.6	1.1	18.8	1.1	18.9	0.5	19.1	1.1
1948	19.4	1.6	19.4	0.0	19.4	0.0	19.7	1.5	19.7	0.0	19.8	0.5	20.8	5.1	21.2	1.9	21.3	0.5	21.5	0.9	21.5	0.0	21.5	0.0
1949	21.5	0.0	21.7	0.9	21.8	0.5	21.9	0.5	22.0	0.5	21.9	-0.5	22.0	0.5	22.2	0.9	22.2	0.0	22.3	0.5	22.2	-0.4	22.4	0.9
1950	22.3	-0.4	22.3	0.0	22.2	-0.4	22.2	0.0	22.3	0.5	22.3	0.0	22.5	0.9	22.8	1.3	22.8	0.0	22.8	0.0	22.9	0.4	23.1	0.9
1951	23.2	0.4	23.5	1.3	23.7	0.9	23.7	0.0	23.8	0.4	23.8	0.0	23.8	0.0	24.0	0.8	24.2	0.8	24.4	0.8	24.7	1.2	24.7	0.0
1952	24.9	0.8	25.1	0.8	25.2	0.4	25.3	0.4	25.3	0.0	25.6	1.2	25.7	0.4	25.7	0.0	25.9	0.8	26.0	0.4	26.1	0.4	26.1	0.0
1953	26.2	0.4	26.1	-0.4	26.2	0.4	26.2	0.0	26.2	0.0	26.2	0.0	26.3	0.4	26.5	0.8	26.5	0.0	26.5	0.0	26.3	-0.8	26.1	-0.8
1954	26.4	1.1	26.2	-0.8	26.1	-0.4	26.1	0.0	26.1	0.0	26.1	0.0	25.7	-1.5	25.7	0.0	25.6	-0.4	25.3	-1.2	25.9	2.4	25.8	-0.4
1955	25.9	0.4	25.8	-0.4	25.8	0.0	25.4	-1.6	25.4	0.0	25.5	0.4	25.4	-0.4	25.4	0.0	25.4	0.0	25.7	1.2	26.0	1.2	25.8	-0.8
1956	25.7	-0.4	25.7	0.0	25.7	0.0	25.6	-0.4	25.7	0.4	25.7	0.0	25.9	0.8	26.0	0.4	26.1	0.4	26.9	3.1	27.0	0.4	27.0	0.0
1957	27.1	0.4	27.2	0.4	27.4	0.7	27.5	0.4	27.4	-0.4	27.4	0.0	27.5	0.4	27.6	0.4	27.6	0.0	27.5	-0.4	28.4	3.3	28.1	-1.1
1958	28.1	0.0	28.1	0.0	28.1	0.0	28.0	-0.4	28.1	0.4	28.1	0.0	28.4	1.1	28.6	0.7	28.6	0.0	28.9	1.0	29.3	1.4	29.2	-0.3
1959	29.2	0.0	29.2	0.0	29.3	0.3	29.4	0.3	29.4	0.0	29.5	0.3	29.6	0.3	29.7	0.3	29.6	-0.3	30.1	1.7	30.2	0.3	30.1	-0.3
1960	29.9	-0.7	29.9	0.0	29.7	-0.7	29.6	-0.3	29.5	-0.3	29.5	0.0	29.5	0.0	29.6	0.3	29.3	-1.0	29.6	1.0	29.7	0.3	29.7	0.0
1961	29.6	-0.3	29.6	0.0	29.5	-0.3	29.5	0.0	29.7	0.7	29.9	0.7	30.1	0.7	30.3	0.7	30.3	0.0	30.5	0.7	30.5	0.0	30.3	-0.7
1962	30.3	0.0	30.3	0.0	30.2	-0.3	30.6	1.3	30.6	0.0	30.6	0.0	30.5	-0.3	30.7	0.7	30.8	0.3	30.9	0.3	30.9	0.0	30.8	-0.3
1963	30.4	-1.3	30.5	0.3	30.5	0.0	30.5	0.0	30.7	0.7	30.7	0.0	30.8	0.3	30.9	0.3	30.8	-0.3	31.1	1.0	31.1	0.0	31.1	0.0
1964	31.2	0.3	31.0	-0.6	31.1	0.3	31.1	0.0	31.1	0.0	31.2	0.3	31.2	0.0	31.2	0.0	31.1	-0.3	31.2	0.3	31.4	0.6	31.5	0.3
1965	31.7	0.6	31.6	-0.3	31.6	0.0	31.7	0.3	31.8	0.3	31.7	-0.3	31.8	0.3	31.7	-0.3	31.7	0.0	31.7	0.0	31.8	0.3	31.9	0.3
1966	31.7	-0.6	31.7	0.0	31.8	0.3	32.0	0.6	32.0	0.0	32.0	0.0	32.4	1.3	32.4	0.0	32.4	0.0	32.6	0.6	32.7	0.3	32.5	-0.6
1967	32.4	-0.3	32.5	0.3	32.6	0.3	32.8	0.6	33.0	0.6	33.0	0.0	33.2	0.6	33.2	0.0	33.3	0.3	33.6	0.9	33.8	0.6	33.6	-0.6
1968	33.9	0.9	33.8	-0.3	34.0	0.6	34.0	0.0	34.0	0.0	34.2	0.6	34.2	0.0	34.2	0.0	34.1	-0.3	34.4	0.9	34.6	0.6	34.3	-0.9
1969	34.4	0.3	34.8	1.2	35.5	2.0	35.6	0.3	35.4	-0.6	35.6	0.6	35.5	-0.3	35.5	0.0	35.3	-0.6	35.9	1.7	35.9	0.0	36.1	0.6
1970	36.3	0.6	36.3	0.0	36.3	0.0	36.8	1.4	37.1	0.8	37.3	0.5	37.5	0.5	37.3	-0.5	37.4	0.3	38.1	1.9	38.4	0.8	38.7	0.8
1971	38.9	0.5	38.9	0.0	39.0	0.3	39.1	0.3	39.3	0.5	39.6	0.8	39.5	-0.3	39.5	0.0	39.2	-0.8	39.5	0.8	39.3	-0.5	39.2	-0.3
1972	39.3	0.3	39.1	-0.5	39.2	0.3	39.2	0.0	39.5	0.8	39.6	0.3	39.8	0.5	39.9	0.3	40.0	0.3	40.1	0.2	40.2	0.2	41.9	0.7
1973	40.0	-0.2	40.1	0.2	40.2	0.2	40.6	1.0	40.9	0.7	41.2	0.7	41.3	0.2	41.2	-0.2	41.0	-0.5	41.3	0.7	41.6	0.7	41.9	0.7
1974	42.4	1.2	42.8	0.9	43.7	2.1	44.2	1.1	45.1	2.0	45.9	1.8	46.5	1.3	46.7	0.4	47.0	0.6	47.3	0.6	47.4	0.2	47.5	0.2
1975	47.4	-0.2	47.5	0.2	47.9	0.8	48.4	1.0	48.8	0.8	49.6	1.6	50.5	1.8	50.8	0.6	51.4	1.2	51.6	0.4	52.1	1.0	52.1	0.0
1976	52.3	0.4	52.4	0.2	52.9	1.0	53.4	0.9	54.1	1.3	54.9	1.5	55.4	0.9	55.7	0.5	56.1	0.7	56.5	0.7	56.7	0.4	56.7	0.0
1977	57.0	0.5	57.3	0.5	57.8	0.9	58.4	1.0	58.9	0.9	59.2	0.5	59.3	0.2	59.1	-0.3	59.0	-0.2	59.1	0.2	59.1	0.0	59.1	0.0
1978	59.2	0.2	59.4	0.3	59.5	0.2	60.0	0.8	60.7	1.2	61.5	1.3	62.1	1.0	62.4	0.5	62.6	0.3	62.9	0.5	63.5	1.0	63.9	0.6
1979	64.3	0.6	64.9	0.9	65.7	1.2	67.4	2.6	69.0	2.4	70.7	2.5	72.0	1.8	73.0	1.4	73.6	0.8	73.9	0.4	74.7	1.1	75.5	1.1

[Continued]

U.S. City Average
Consumer Price Index - Urban Wage Earners
Base 1982-1984 = 100
Transportation
[Continued]

For 1935-1993. Columns headed % show percentile change in the index from the previous period for which an index is available.

Year	Jan Index	%	Feb Index	%	Mar Index	%	Apr Index	%	May Index	%	Jun Index	%	Jul Index	%	Aug Index	%	Sep Index	%	Oct Index	%	Nov Index	%	Dec Index	%
1980	77.4	2.5	79.5	2.7	80.8	1.6	81.9	1.4	82.7	1.0	82.9	0.2	83.3	0.5	83.9	0.7	84.4	0.6	84.9	0.6	85.9	1.2	86.6	0.8
1981	87.9	1.5	90.0	2.4	90.8	0.9	91.4	0.7	92.3	1.0	92.9	0.7	93.9	1.1	94.3	0.4	94.8	0.5	95.6	0.8	96.2	0.6	96.4	0.2
1982	96.5	0.1	95.8	-0.7	94.8	-1.0	94.0	-0.8	95.0	1.1	97.4	2.5	98.5	1.1	98.6	0.1	98.2	-0.4	98.2	0.0	98.3	0.1	98.0	-0.3
1983	97.3	-0.7	96.3	-1.0	95.5	-0.8	97.1	1.7	98.4	1.3	99.1	0.7	99.9	0.8	100.6	0.7	101.1	0.5	101.5	0.4	101.9	0.4	101.9	0.0
1984	101.8	-0.1	101.8	0.0	102.2	0.4	103.2	1.0	104.1	0.9	104.4	0.3	104.3	-0.1	104.3	0.0	104.5	0.2	105.1	0.6	105.3	0.2	105.2	-0.1
1985	104.8	-0.4	104.6	-0.2	105.4	0.8	106.5	1.0	106.9	0.4	107.0	0.1	107.0	0.0	106.6	-0.4	106.2	-0.4	106.6	0.4	107.4	0.8	107.6	0.2
1986	107.5	-0.1	105.9	-1.5	102.6	-3.1	100.4	-2.1	101.2	0.8	102.1	0.9	100.8	-1.3	99.5	-1.3	99.8	0.3	100.0	0.2	100.6	0.6	100.6	0.0
1987	101.9	1.3	102.5	0.6	102.8	0.3	103.8	1.0	104.4	0.6	105.1	0.7	105.8	0.7	106.3	0.5	106.4	0.1	106.9	0.5	107.6	0.7	107.3	-0.3
1988	106.8	-0.5	106.4	-0.4	106.2	-0.2	106.8	0.6	107.8	0.9	108.2	0.4	108.6	0.4	109.4	0.7	109.4	0.0	109.8	0.4	110.3	0.5	110.4	0.1
1989	110.7	0.3	111.2	0.5	111.6	0.4	114.5	2.6	116.0	1.3	116.0	0.0	115.4	-0.5	114.2	-1.0	113.5	-0.6	114.3	0.7	114.6	0.3	114.8	0.2
1990	116.8	1.7	116.6	-0.2	116.2	-0.3	116.6	0.3	117.1	0.4	117.7	0.5	117.8	0.1	120.3	2.1	122.9	2.2	125.7	2.3	126.6	0.7	126.7	0.1
1991	124.7	-1.6	122.6	-1.7	121.2	-1.1	121.3	0.1	122.7	1.2	123.1	0.3	122.9	-0.2	123.2	0.2	123.3	0.1	123.4	0.1	124.5	0.9	124.5	0.0
1992	123.5	-0.8	122.9	-0.5	123.2	0.2	124.1	0.7	125.5	1.1	126.5	0.8	126.7	0.2	126.5	-0.2	126.5	0.0	127.5	0.8	128.5	0.8	128.2	-0.2
1993	128.0	-0.2	128.0	0.0	127.8	-0.2	128.4	0.5	129.2	0.6	129.5	0.2	129.4	-0.1	129.4	0.0	129.2	-0.2	131.0	1.4	131.6	0.5	130.8	-0.6

Source: U.S. Department of Labor, Bureau of Labor Statistics, Division of Consumer Prices and Price Indexes.

217

U.S. City Average

Consumer Price Index - All Urban Consumers
Base 1982-1984 = 100
Medical Care

For 1935-1993. Columns headed % show percentile change in the index from the previous period for which an index is available.

Year	Jan		Feb		Mar		Apr		May		Jun		Jul		Aug		Sep		Oct		Nov		Dec	
	Index	%	Index	%	Index	%	Index	%	Index	%	Index	%	Index	%	Index	%	Index	%	Index	%	Index	%	Index	%
1935	-		-		10.2		-		-		-		10.2	0.0	-		-		10.2	0.0	-		-	
1936	10.2	0.0	-		-		10.2	0.0	-		-		10.2	0.0	-		10.2	0.0	-		-		10.2	0.0
1937	-		-		10.3	1.0	-		-		10.3	0.0	-		-		10.3	0.0	-		-		10.3	0.0
1938	-		-		10.3	0.0	-		-		10.3	0.0	-		-		10.3	0.0	-		-		10.3	0.0
1939	-		-		10.3	0.0	-		-		10.4	1.0	-		-		10.4	0.0	-		-		10.4	0.0
1940	-		-		10.4	0.0	-		-		10.3	-1.0	-		-		10.3	0.0	-		-		10.4	1.0
1941	-		-		10.4	0.0	-		-		10.4	0.0	-		-		10.4	0.0	-		-		10.5	1.0
1942	-		-		10.6	1.0	-		-		10.7	0.9	-		-		10.8	0.9	-		-		10.9	0.9
1943	-		-		11.1	1.8	-		-		11.2	0.9	-		-		11.4	1.8	-		-		11.4	0.0
1944	-		-		11.5	0.9	-		-		11.5	0.0	-		-		11.6	0.9	-		-		11.7	0.9
1945	-		-		11.8	0.9	-		-		11.9	0.8	-		-		11.9	0.0	-		-		12.0	0.8
1946	-		-		12.2	1.7	-		-		12.4	1.6	-		-		12.7	2.4	-		-		13.0	2.4
1947	13.2	1.5	13.3	0.8	13.3	0.0	13.4	0.8	13.5	0.7	13.5	0.0	13.5	0.0	13.6	0.7	13.7	0.7	13.8	0.7	13.8	0.0	13.9	0.7
1948	14.0	0.7	14.0	0.0	14.1	0.7	14.3	1.4	14.3	0.0	14.3	0.0	14.5	1.4	14.5	0.0	14.5	0.0	14.6	0.7	14.7	0.7	14.7	0.0
1949	14.8	0.7	14.8	0.0	14.8	0.0	14.8	0.0	14.8	0.0	14.8	0.0	14.8	0.0	14.9	0.7	14.9	0.0	14.9	0.0	14.9	0.0	14.9	0.0
1950	15.0	0.7	15.0	0.0	15.0	0.0	15.0	0.0	15.0	0.0	15.0	0.0	15.1	0.7	15.1	0.0	15.2	0.7	15.3	0.7	15.3	0.0	15.4	0.7
1951	15.5	0.6	15.5	0.0	15.7	1.3	15.7	0.0	15.8	0.6	15.8	0.0	15.8	0.0	15.9	0.6	15.9	0.0	16.0	0.6	16.1	0.6	16.3	1.2
1952	16.4	0.6	16.4	0.0	16.5	0.6	16.5	0.0	16.5	0.0	16.8	1.8	16.8	0.0	16.8	0.0	16.9	0.6	16.9	0.0	16.9	0.0	17.0	0.6
1953	17.0	0.0	17.0	0.0	17.0	0.0	17.1	0.6	17.2	0.6	17.3	0.6	17.3	0.0	17.4	0.6	17.5	0.6	17.5	0.0	17.6	0.6	17.6	0.0
1954	17.6	0.0	17.7	0.6	17.7	0.0	17.8	0.6	17.8	0.0	17.8	0.0	17.8	0.0	17.9	0.6	17.9	0.0	17.9	0.0	18.0	0.6	18.0	0.0
1955	18.0	0.0	18.1	0.6	18.1	0.0	18.1	0.0	18.2	0.6	18.2	0.0	18.2	0.0	18.2	0.0	18.3	0.5	18.4	0.5	18.5	0.5	18.6	0.5
1956	18.6	0.0	18.7	0.5	18.7	0.0	18.8	0.5	18.8	0.0	18.8	0.0	18.8	0.0	18.9	0.5	19.0	0.5	19.1	0.5	19.2	0.5	19.2	0.0
1957	19.3	0.5	19.3	0.0	19.5	1.0	19.5	0.0	19.6	0.5	19.7	0.5	19.7	0.0	19.8	0.5	19.8	0.0	19.9	0.5	20.0	0.5	20.1	0.5
1958	20.2	0.5	20.2	0.0	20.3	0.5	20.4	0.5	20.5	0.5	20.6	0.5	20.7	0.5	20.7	0.0	20.9	1.0	21.0	0.5	21.0	0.0	21.0	0.0
1959	21.1	0.5	21.2	0.5	21.3	0.5	21.3	0.0	21.4	0.5	21.5	0.5	21.5	0.0	21.6	0.5	21.7	0.5	21.7	0.0	21.8	0.5	21.8	0.0
1960	21.9	0.5	22.0	0.5	22.1	0.5	22.2	0.5	22.2	0.0	22.2	0.0	22.3	0.5	22.3	0.0	22.4	0.4	22.4	0.0	22.5	0.4	22.5	0.0
1961	22.6	0.4	22.7	0.4	22.7	0.0	22.8	0.4	22.9	0.4	22.9	0.0	23.0	0.4	23.0	0.0	23.1	0.4	23.1	0.0	23.1	0.0	23.2	0.4
1962	23.2	0.0	23.3	0.4	23.4	0.4	23.5	0.4	23.5	0.0	23.6	0.4	23.6	0.0	23.6	0.0	23.6	0.0	23.7	0.4	23.7	0.0	23.7	0.0
1963	23.8	0.4	23.9	0.4	23.9	0.0	24.0	0.4	24.0	0.0	24.1	0.4	24.2	0.4	24.2	0.0	24.2	0.0	24.2	0.0	24.3	0.4	24.3	0.0
1964	24.4	0.4	24.4	0.0	24.4	0.0	24.5	0.4	24.5	0.0	24.6	0.4	24.6	0.0	24.7	0.4	24.7	0.0	24.7	0.0	24.7	0.0	24.8	0.4
1965	24.8	0.0	24.9	0.4	25.0	0.4	25.1	0.4	25.1	0.0	25.2	0.4	25.3	0.4	25.3	0.0	25.3	0.0	25.3	0.0	25.4	0.4	25.5	0.4
1966	25.6	0.4	25.6	0.0	25.8	0.8	25.9	0.4	26.0	0.4	26.2	0.8	26.3	0.4	26.4	0.4	26.7	1.1	26.9	0.7	27.0	0.4	27.2	0.7
1967	27.4	0.7	27.5	0.4	27.7	0.7	27.8	0.4	28.0	0.7	28.1	0.4	28.2	0.4	28.3	0.4	28.5	0.7	28.6	0.7	28.8	0.7	28.9	0.3
1968	29.1	0.7	29.2	0.3	29.4	0.7	29.6	0.7	29.6	0.0	29.7	0.3	29.9	0.7	30.0	0.3	30.2	0.7	30.4	0.7	30.5	0.3	30.7	0.7
1969	30.9	0.7	31.2	1.0	31.4	0.6	31.6	0.6	31.8	0.6	32.0	0.6	32.1	0.3	32.3	0.6	32.5	0.6	32.3	-0.6	32.4	0.3	32.6	0.6
1970	32.7	0.3	33.0	0.9	33.3	0.9	33.5	0.6	33.7	0.6	33.9	0.6	34.2	0.9	34.3	0.3	34.5	0.6	34.6	0.3	34.7	0.3	35.0	0.9
1971	35.2	0.6	35.4	0.6	35.7	0.8	35.9	0.6	36.1	0.6	36.2	0.3	36.4	0.6	36.6	0.5	36.7	0.3	36.5	-0.5	36.5	0.0	36.6	0.3
1972	36.7	0.3	36.9	0.5	37.0	0.3	37.1	0.3	37.2	0.3	37.3	0.3	37.4	0.3	37.4	0.0	37.5	0.3	37.7	0.5	37.8	0.3	37.8	0.0
1973	38.0	0.5	38.1	0.3	38.2	0.3	38.3	0.3	38.5	0.5	38.6	0.3	38.7	0.3	38.7	0.0	38.9	0.5	39.6	1.8	39.7	0.3	39.8	0.3
1974	40.0	0.5	40.4	1.0	40.8	1.0	41.0	0.5	41.4	1.0	42.1	1.7	42.6	1.2	43.3	1.6	43.7	0.9	44.0	0.7	44.3	0.7	44.8	1.1
1975	45.3	1.1	45.9	1.3	46.3	0.9	46.7	0.9	47.0	0.6	47.3	0.6	47.8	1.1	48.1	0.6	48.5	0.8	48.8	0.6	48.8	0.0	49.2	0.8
1976	49.7	1.0	50.3	1.2	50.8	1.0	51.1	0.6	51.4	0.6	51.7	0.6	52.2	1.0	52.6	0.8	52.9	0.6	53.2	0.6	53.9	1.3	54.1	0.4
1977	54.6	0.9	55.1	0.9	55.6	0.9	56.1	0.9	56.4	0.5	56.8	0.7	57.3	0.9	57.7	0.7	58.1	0.7	58.3	0.3	58.6	0.5	58.9	0.5
1978	59.5	1.0	60.1	1.0	60.4	0.5	60.7	0.5	61.1	0.7	61.3	0.3	61.8	0.8	62.3	0.8	62.7	0.6	63.3	1.0	63.9	0.9	64.1	0.3
1979	65.0	1.4	65.5	0.8	65.9	0.6	66.2	0.5	66.5	0.5	66.9	0.6	67.5	0.9	68.1	0.9	68.6	0.7	69.2	0.9	69.8	0.9	70.6	1.1

[Continued]

U.S. City Average
Consumer Price Index - All Urban Consumers
Base 1982-1984 = 100
Medical Care
[Continued]

For 1935-1993. Columns headed % show percentile change in the index from the previous period for which an index is available.

Year	Jan Index	%	Feb Index	%	Mar Index	%	Apr Index	%	May Index	%	Jun Index	%	Jul Index	%	Aug Index	%	Sep Index	%	Oct Index	%	Nov Index	%	Dec Index	%
1980	71.5	1.3	72.6	1.5	73.3	1.0	73.8	0.7	74.2	0.5	74.5	0.4	75.1	0.8	75.6	0.7	76.2	0.8	76.8	0.8	77.3	0.7	77.6	0.4
1981	78.7	1.4	79.6	1.1	80.2	0.8	80.8	0.7	81.4	0.7	82.1	0.9	83.2	1.3	84.3	1.3	84.9	0.7	85.8	1.1	86.8	1.2	87.3	0.6
1982	88.2	1.0	89.0	0.9	89.8	0.9	90.6	0.9	91.2	0.7	91.9	0.8	92.9	1.1	93.8	1.0	94.6	0.9	95.4	0.8	96.3	0.9	96.9	0.6
1983	97.9	1.0	98.9	1.0	99.2	0.3	99.5	0.3	99.7	0.2	100.1	0.4	100.7	0.6	101.4	0.7	101.7	0.3	102.2	0.5	102.7	0.5	103.1	0.4
1984	104.0	0.9	105.1	1.1	105.4	0.3	105.8	0.4	106.1	0.3	106.4	0.3	107.1	0.7	107.5	0.4	107.9	0.4	108.5	0.6	109.1	0.6	109.4	0.3
1985	110.1	0.6	110.9	0.7	111.6	0.6	112.1	0.4	112.5	0.4	113.1	0.5	113.7	0.5	114.5	0.7	115.0	0.4	115.6	0.5	116.3	0.6	116.8	0.4
1986	117.7	0.8	118.9	1.0	119.9	0.8	120.5	0.5	121.0	0.4	121.6	0.5	122.4	0.7	123.2	0.7	123.8	0.5	124.5	0.6	125.2	0.6	125.8	0.5
1987	126.6	0.6	127.4	0.6	128.1	0.5	128.7	0.5	129.2	0.4	129.9	0.5	130.7	0.6	131.2	0.4	131.7	0.4	132.3	0.5	132.8	0.4	133.1	0.2
1988	134.4	1.0	135.5	0.8	136.3	0.6	136.9	0.4	137.5	0.4	138.2	0.5	139.3	0.8	139.9	0.4	140.4	0.4	141.2	0.6	141.8	0.4	142.3	0.4
1989	143.8	1.1	145.2	1.0	146.1	0.6	146.8	0.5	147.5	0.5	148.5	0.7	149.7	0.8	150.7	0.7	151.7	0.7	152.7	0.7	153.9	0.8	154.4	0.3
1990	155.9	1.0	157.5	1.0	158.7	0.8	159.8	0.7	160.8	0.6	161.9	0.7	163.5	1.0	165.0	0.9	165.8	0.5	167.1	0.8	168.4	0.8	169.2	0.5
1991	171.0	1.1	172.5	0.9	173.7	0.7	174.4	0.4	175.2	0.5	176.2	0.6	177.5	0.7	178.9	0.8	179.7	0.4	180.7	0.6	181.8	0.6	182.6	0.4
1992	184.3	0.9	186.2	1.0	187.3	0.6	188.1	0.4	188.7	0.3	189.4	0.4	190.7	0.7	191.5	0.4	192.3	0.4	193.3	0.5	194.3	0.5	194.7	0.2
1993	196.4	0.9	198.0	0.8	198.6	0.3	199.4	0.4	200.5	0.6	201.1	0.3	202.2	0.5	202.9	0.3	203.3	0.2	204.4	0.5	204.9	0.2	205.2	0.1

Source: U.S. Department of Labor, Bureau of Labor Statistics, Division of Consumer Prices and Price Indexes.

U.S. City Average
Consumer Price Index - Urban Wage Earners
Base 1982-1984 = 100
Medical Care

For 1935-1993. Columns headed % show percentile change in the index from the previous period for which an index is available.

Year	Jan Index	%	Feb Index	%	Mar Index	%	Apr Index	%	May Index	%	Jun Index	%	Jul Index	%	Aug Index	%	Sep Index	%	Oct Index	%	Nov Index	%	Dec Index	%
1935	-	-	-	-	10.2	-	-	-	-	-	-	-	10.2	0.0	-	-	-	-	10.2	0.0	-	-	-	-
1936	10.2	0.0	-	-	-	-	10.2	0.0	-	-	-	-	10.2	0.0	-	-	10.3	1.0	-	-	-	-	10.3	0.0
1937	-	-	-	-	10.4	1.0	-	-	-	-	10.4	0.0	-	-	-	-	10.4	0.0	-	-	-	-	10.4	0.0
1938	-	-	-	-	10.4	0.0	-	-	-	-	10.4	0.0	-	-	-	-	10.4	0.0	-	-	-	-	10.4	0.0
1939	-	-	-	-	10.4	0.0	-	-	-	-	10.4	0.0	-	-	-	-	10.4	0.0	-	-	-	-	10.4	0.0
1940	-	-	-	-	10.4	0.0	-	-	-	-	10.4	0.0	-	-	-	-	10.4	0.0	-	-	-	-	10.4	0.0
1941	-	-	-	-	10.4	0.0	-	-	-	-	10.4	0.0	-	-	-	-	10.5	1.0	-	-	-	-	10.6	1.0
1942	-	-	-	-	10.6	0.0	-	-	-	-	10.8	1.9	-	-	-	-	10.9	0.9	-	-	-	-	11.0	0.9
1943	-	-	-	-	11.2	1.8	-	-	-	-	11.3	0.9	-	-	-	-	11.4	0.9	-	-	-	-	11.5	0.9
1944	-	-	-	-	11.5	0.0	-	-	-	-	11.6	0.9	-	-	-	-	11.7	0.9	-	-	-	-	11.8	0.9
1945	-	-	-	-	11.8	0.0	-	-	-	-	11.9	0.8	-	-	-	-	11.9	0.0	-	-	-	-	12.1	1.7
1946	-	-	-	-	12.3	1.7	-	-	-	-	12.5	1.6	-	-	-	-	12.8	2.4	-	-	-	-	13.1	2.3
1947	13.3	1.5	13.3	0.0	13.4	0.8	13.5	0.7	13.5	0.0	13.6	0.7	13.6	0.0	13.6	0.0	13.8	1.5	13.8	0.0	13.9	0.7	13.9	0.0
1948	14.1	1.4	14.1	0.0	14.2	0.7	14.4	1.4	14.4	0.0	14.4	0.0	14.6	1.4	14.6	0.0	14.6	0.0	14.7	0.7	14.7	0.0	14.7	0.0
1949	14.8	0.7	14.8	0.0	14.9	0.7	14.9	0.0	14.9	0.0	14.9	0.0	14.9	0.0	14.9	0.0	15.0	0.7	14.9	-0.7	14.9	0.0	15.0	0.7
1950	15.1	0.7	15.1	0.0	15.1	0.0	15.1	0.0	15.1	0.0	15.1	0.0	15.1	0.0	15.2	0.7	15.3	0.7	15.3	0.0	15.4	0.7	15.5	0.6
1951	15.5	0.0	15.6	0.6	15.8	1.3	15.8	0.0	15.9	0.6	15.9	0.0	15.9	0.0	15.9	0.0	16.0	0.6	16.1	0.6	16.2	0.6	16.4	1.2
1952	16.4	0.0	16.4	0.0	16.6	1.2	16.6	0.0	16.6	0.0	16.9	1.8	16.9	0.0	16.9	0.0	17.0	0.6	17.0	0.0	17.0	0.0	17.1	0.6
1953	17.1	0.0	17.1	0.0	17.1	0.0	17.2	0.6	17.3	0.6	17.4	0.6	17.4	0.0	17.5	0.6	17.6	0.6	17.6	0.0	17.7	0.6	17.7	0.0
1954	17.7	0.0	17.8	0.6	17.8	0.0	17.9	0.6	17.9	0.0	17.9	0.0	17.9	0.0	18.0	0.6	18.0	0.0	18.0	0.0	18.1	0.6	18.1	0.0
1955	18.1	0.0	18.2	0.6	18.2	0.0	18.2	0.0	18.3	0.5	18.3	0.0	18.3	0.0	18.3	0.0	18.4	0.5	18.5	0.5	18.6	0.5	18.7	0.5
1956	18.7	0.0	18.8	0.5	18.8	0.0	18.9	0.5	18.9	0.0	18.9	0.0	19.0	0.5	19.1	0.5	19.2	0.5	19.2	0.0	19.3	0.5	19.3	0.0
1957	19.4	0.5	19.4	0.0	19.6	1.0	19.6	0.0	19.7	0.5	19.8	0.5	19.8	0.0	19.9	0.5	19.9	0.0	20.0	0.5	20.1	0.5	20.2	0.5
1958	20.3	0.5	20.3	0.0	20.4	0.5	20.5	0.5	20.6	0.5	20.7	0.5	20.8	0.5	20.8	0.0	21.0	1.0	21.1	0.5	21.1	0.0	21.1	0.0
1959	21.2	0.5	21.3	0.5	21.4	0.5	21.4	0.0	21.5	0.5	21.6	0.5	21.6	0.0	21.7	0.5	21.8	0.5	21.9	0.5	21.9	0.0	21.9	0.0
1960	22.0	0.5	22.2	0.9	22.2	0.0	22.3	0.5	22.3	0.0	22.4	0.4	22.4	0.0	22.4	0.0	22.5	0.4	22.6	0.4	22.6	0.0	22.6	0.0
1961	22.7	0.4	22.8	0.4	22.9	0.4	22.9	0.0	23.0	0.4	23.0	0.0	23.1	0.4	23.1	0.0	23.2	0.4	23.3	0.4	23.3	0.0	23.3	0.0
1962	23.3	0.0	23.4	0.4	23.5	0.4	23.6	0.4	23.6	0.0	23.7	0.4	23.7	0.0	23.7	0.0	23.8	0.4	23.8	0.0	23.8	0.0	23.9	0.4
1963	24.0	0.4	24.0	0.0	24.0	0.0	24.1	0.4	24.2	0.4	24.3	0.4	24.3	0.0	24.3	0.0	24.3	0.0	24.4	0.4	24.4	0.0	24.4	0.0
1964	24.5	0.4	24.5	0.0	24.6	0.4	24.7	0.4	24.7	0.0	24.7	0.0	24.7	0.0	24.8	0.4	24.8	0.0	24.8	0.0	24.9	0.4	24.9	0.0
1965	25.0	0.4	25.1	0.4	25.1	0.0	25.2	0.4	25.2	0.0	25.3	0.4	25.4	0.4	25.4	0.0	25.4	0.0	25.5	0.4	25.6	0.4	25.6	0.0
1966	25.7	0.4	25.8	0.4	26.0	0.8	26.0	0.0	26.2	0.8	26.3	0.4	26.4	0.4	26.6	0.8	26.8	0.8	27.0	0.7	27.2	0.7	27.3	0.4
1967	27.5	0.7	27.7	0.7	27.9	0.7	28.0	0.4	28.1	0.4	28.2	0.4	28.3	0.4	28.5	0.7	28.7	0.7	28.8	0.3	28.9	0.3	29.1	0.7
1968	29.2	0.3	29.4	0.7	29.6	0.7	29.7	0.3	29.8	0.3	29.9	0.3	30.0	0.3	30.1	0.3	30.3	0.7	30.5	0.7	30.7	0.7	30.9	0.7
1969	31.1	0.6	31.3	0.6	31.6	1.0	31.8	0.6	32.0	0.6	32.1	0.3	32.3	0.6	32.5	0.6	32.6	0.3	32.5	-0.3	32.6	0.3	32.8	0.6
1970	32.9	0.3	33.1	0.6	33.5	1.2	33.7	0.6	33.9	0.6	34.1	0.6	34.3	0.6	34.5	0.6	34.7	0.6	34.8	0.3	34.9	0.3	35.2	0.9
1971	35.4	0.6	35.6	0.6	35.9	0.8	36.1	0.6	36.3	0.6	36.4	0.3	36.6	0.5	36.8	0.5	36.9	0.3	36.7	-0.5	36.7	0.0	36.8	0.3
1972	36.9	0.3	37.1	0.5	37.2	0.3	37.3	0.3	37.4	0.3	37.5	0.3	37.6	0.3	37.6	0.0	37.7	0.3	37.9	0.5	38.0	0.3	38.0	0.0
1973	38.2	0.5	38.3	0.3	38.4	0.3	38.6	0.5	38.7	0.3	38.8	0.3	38.9	0.3	39.0	0.3	39.2	0.5	39.8	1.5	39.9	0.3	40.0	0.3
1974	40.3	0.7	40.6	0.7	41.0	1.0	41.2	0.5	41.7	1.2	42.3	1.4	42.9	1.4	43.5	1.4	43.9	0.9	44.2	0.7	44.6	0.9	45.0	0.9
1975	45.6	1.3	46.1	1.1	46.6	1.1	46.9	0.6	47.2	0.6	47.6	0.8	48.1	1.1	48.4	0.6	48.7	0.6	49.1	0.8	49.1	0.0	49.5	0.8
1976	50.0	1.0	50.6	1.2	51.1	1.0	51.4	0.6	51.7	0.6	52.0	0.6	52.5	1.0	52.9	0.8	53.2	0.6	53.5	0.6	54.2	1.3	54.4	0.4
1977	54.9	0.9	55.4	0.9	55.9	0.9	56.4	0.9	56.8	0.7	57.1	0.5	57.6	0.9	58.0	0.7	58.4	0.7	58.7	0.5	58.9	0.3	59.2	0.5
1978	59.8	1.0	60.4	1.0	60.7	0.5	61.0	0.5	61.4	0.7	61.7	0.5	62.1	0.6	62.6	0.8	63.1	0.8	63.7	1.0	64.2	0.8	64.5	0.5
1979	65.2	1.1	65.7	0.8	66.2	0.8	66.6	0.6	66.9	0.5	67.4	0.7	68.1	1.0	68.7	0.9	69.3	0.9	70.0	1.0	70.5	0.7	71.3	1.1

[Continued]

U.S. City Average
Consumer Price Index - Urban Wage Earners
Base 1982-1984 = 100
Medical Care
[Continued]

For 1935-1993. Columns headed % show percentile change in the index from the previous period for which an index is available.

Year	Jan Index	%	Feb Index	%	Mar Index	%	Apr Index	%	May Index	%	Jun Index	%	Jul Index	%	Aug Index	%	Sep Index	%	Oct Index	%	Nov Index	%	Dec Index	%
1980	72.2	1.3	73.2	1.4	73.9	1.0	74.5	0.8	75.0	0.7	75.3	0.4	75.8	0.7	76.4	0.8	77.1	0.9	77.7	0.8	78.2	0.6	78.6	0.5
1981	79.7	1.4	80.5	1.0	81.2	0.9	81.8	0.7	82.3	0.6	82.9	0.7	83.6	0.8	84.5	1.1	85.2	0.8	86.1	1.1	86.9	0.9	87.5	0.7
1982	88.3	0.9	89.1	0.9	89.9	0.9	90.6	0.8	91.2	0.7	91.9	0.8	92.9	1.1	93.8	1.0	94.5	0.7	95.3	0.8	96.2	0.9	96.8	0.6
1983	97.7	0.9	98.8	1.1	99.1	0.3	99.4	0.3	99.7	0.3	100.0	0.3	100.7	0.7	101.3	0.6	101.7	0.4	102.2	0.5	102.7	0.5	103.1	0.4
1984	104.0	0.9	105.1	1.1	105.5	0.4	105.8	0.3	106.2	0.4	106.5	0.3	107.1	0.6	107.6	0.5	107.9	0.3	108.6	0.6	109.2	0.6	109.5	0.3
1985	110.2	0.6	111.0	0.7	111.7	0.6	112.1	0.4	112.6	0.4	113.2	0.5	113.8	0.5	114.5	0.6	115.0	0.4	115.6	0.5	116.3	0.6	116.8	0.4
1986	117.8	0.9	118.9	0.9	119.9	0.8	120.5	0.5	121.0	0.4	121.6	0.5	122.4	0.7	123.1	0.6	123.7	0.5	124.5	0.6	125.0	0.4	125.7	0.6
1987	126.5	0.6	127.3	0.6	128.1	0.6	128.8	0.5	129.3	0.4	130.0	0.5	130.8	0.6	131.4	0.5	132.0	0.5	132.6	0.5	133.0	0.3	133.4	0.3
1988	134.6	0.9	135.8	0.9	136.5	0.5	137.1	0.4	137.8	0.5	138.5	0.5	139.6	0.8	140.3	0.5	140.8	0.4	141.7	0.6	142.2	0.4	142.8	0.4
1989	144.2	1.0	145.6	1.0	146.5	0.6	147.2	0.5	147.9	0.5	148.8	0.6	150.1	0.9	151.1	0.7	152.1	0.7	153.0	0.6	154.2	0.8	154.7	0.3
1990	156.1	0.9	157.6	1.0	158.8	0.8	159.8	0.6	160.8	0.6	161.8	0.6	163.3	0.9	164.7	0.9	165.5	0.5	166.8	0.8	168.1	0.8	168.8	0.4
1991	170.5	1.0	172.1	0.9	173.2	0.6	173.9	0.4	174.6	0.4	175.6	0.6	176.9	0.7	178.3	0.8	179.2	0.5	180.2	0.6	181.2	0.6	182.0	0.4
1992	183.7	0.9	185.7	1.1	186.8	0.6	187.6	0.4	188.2	0.3	188.9	0.4	190.2	0.7	191.2	0.5	191.9	0.4	193.0	0.6	193.8	0.4	194.3	0.3
1993	196.0	0.9	197.6	0.8	198.2	0.3	199.0	0.4	200.1	0.6	200.7	0.3	201.7	0.5	202.4	0.3	202.8	0.2	203.8	0.5	204.2	0.2	204.5	0.1

Source: U.S. Department of Labor, Bureau of Labor Statistics, Division of Consumer Prices and Price Indexes.

U.S. City Average

Consumer Price Index - All Urban Consumers
Base 1982-1984 = 100
Entertainment

For 1967-1993. Columns headed % show percentile change in the index from the previous period for which an index is available.

Year	Jan Index	%	Feb Index	%	Mar Index	%	Apr Index	%	May Index	%	Jun Index	%	Jul Index	%	Aug Index	%	Sep Index	%	Oct Index	%	Nov Index	%	Dec Index	%
1967	39.9	-	40.0	0.3	40.1	0.2	40.4	0.7	40.5	0.2	40.6	0.2	40.7	0.2	40.7	0.0	41.0	0.7	41.3	0.7	41.6	0.7	41.6	0.0
1968	41.9	0.7	42.1	0.5	42.3	0.5	42.7	0.9	42.8	0.2	43.0	0.5	43.1	0.2	43.3	0.5	43.5	0.5	43.7	0.5	43.9	0.5	44.0	0.2
1969	44.2	0.5	44.2	0.0	44.3	0.2	44.7	0.9	45.0	0.7	45.1	0.2	45.3	0.4	45.5	0.4	45.7	0.4	45.8	0.2	46.0	0.4	46.2	0.4
1970	46.4	0.4	46.5	0.2	46.7	0.4	46.9	0.4	47.1	0.4	47.3	0.4	47.6	0.6	47.9	0.6	48.1	0.4	48.4	0.6	48.6	0.4	48.8	0.4
1971	49.1	0.6	49.2	0.2	49.3	0.2	49.7	0.8	50.0	0.6	50.2	0.4	50.4	0.4	50.4	0.0	50.5	0.2	50.5	0.0	50.6	0.2	50.6	0.0
1972	50.8	0.4	50.9	0.2	51.0	0.2	51.3	0.6	51.4	0.2	51.6	0.4	51.7	0.2	51.7	0.0	51.8	0.2	51.9	0.2	51.9	0.0	51.9	0.0
1973	52.0	0.2	52.1	0.2	52.2	0.2	52.6	0.8	52.8	0.4	53.0	0.4	53.2	0.4	53.2	0.0	53.2	0.0	53.4	0.4	53.6	0.4	53.7	0.2
1974	54.1	0.7	54.4	0.6	54.7	0.6	55.2	0.9	56.1	1.6	57.0	1.6	57.5	0.9	57.8	0.5	58.5	1.2	58.7	0.3	59.2	0.9	59.7	0.8
1975	60.3	1.0	60.8	0.8	60.9	0.2	61.7	1.3	61.8	0.2	62.0	0.3	62.2	0.3	62.3	0.2	62.7	0.6	62.7	0.0	62.9	0.3	63.2	0.5
1976	63.6	0.6	63.7	0.2	64.0	0.5	64.3	0.5	64.8	0.8	65.1	0.5	65.3	0.3	65.4	0.2	65.7	0.5	66.0	0.5	66.3	0.5	66.5	0.3
1977	66.8	0.5	67.1	0.4	67.3	0.3	67.4	0.1	67.8	0.6	68.3	0.7	68.4	0.1	68.6	0.3	69.1	0.7	69.3	0.3	69.4	0.1	69.6	0.3
1978	70.0	0.6	70.4	0.6	70.9	0.7	71.5	0.8	71.7	0.3	71.7	0.0	72.1	0.6	72.2	0.1	72.6	0.6	73.0	0.6	73.1	0.1	73.6	0.7
1979	74.2	0.8	74.6	0.5	75.2	0.8	75.9	0.9	76.5	0.8	76.6	0.1	77.0	0.5	77.4	0.5	77.8	0.5	78.2	0.5	78.5	0.4	78.7	0.3
1980	79.5	1.0	80.5	1.3	81.7	1.5	82.4	0.9	83.0	0.7	83.6	0.7	84.1	0.6	84.7	0.7	85.4	0.8	85.9	0.6	86.0	0.1	86.3	0.3
1981	87.3	1.2	88.2	1.0	88.8	0.7	89.2	0.5	89.7	0.6	89.9	0.2	90.0	0.1	90.5	0.6	91.2	0.8	91.8	0.7	92.3	0.5	92.5	0.2
1982	93.3	0.9	94.1	0.9	94.8	0.7	95.2	0.4	95.4	0.2	95.9	0.5	96.3	0.4	96.6	0.3	97.0	0.4	97.8	0.8	97.7	-0.1	97.7	0.0
1983	98.3	0.6	99.0	0.7	99.6	0.6	99.6	0.0	99.7	0.1	99.9	0.2	100.1	0.2	100.4	0.3	100.8	0.4	101.4	0.6	101.6	0.2	101.6	0.0
1984	101.7	0.1	102.4	0.7	102.5	0.1	103.3	0.8	103.2	-0.1	103.6	0.4	103.9	0.3	104.4	0.5	104.7	0.3	105.2	0.5	105.4	0.2	105.9	0.5
1985	106.3	0.4	106.4	0.1	106.7	0.3	107.2	0.5	107.3	0.1	107.8	0.5	108.2	0.4	108.2	0.0	108.6	0.4	109.3	0.6	109.5	0.2	109.2	-0.3
1986	110.2	0.9	110.7	0.5	110.7	0.0	110.9	0.2	111.1	0.2	111.5	0.4	111.7	0.2	111.8	0.1	112.1	0.3	112.6	0.4	112.9	0.3	112.9	0.0
1987	113.3	0.4	113.5	0.2	113.9	0.4	114.5	0.5	114.8	0.3	114.9	0.1	115.4	0.4	115.6	0.2	116.1	0.4	116.9	0.7	117.3	0.3	117.4	0.1
1988	118.1	0.6	118.3	0.2	119.0	0.6	119.6	0.5	119.7	0.1	120.1	0.3	120.5	0.3	120.7	0.2	121.3	0.5	121.8	0.4	122.2	0.3	122.8	0.5
1989	123.8	0.8	124.3	0.4	124.7	0.3	125.4	0.6	125.5	0.1	126.2	0.6	126.9	0.6	127.3	0.3	127.8	0.4	128.4	0.5	128.6	0.2	129.1	0.4
1990	129.9	0.6	130.4	0.4	130.9	0.4	131.4	0.4	131.7	0.2	131.9	0.2	132.7	0.6	133.0	0.2	134.1	0.8	134.3	0.1	134.4	0.1	134.6	0.1
1991	135.5	0.7	136.2	0.5	136.7	0.4	137.7	0.7	137.8	0.1	138.1	0.2	138.6	0.4	139.2	0.4	140.2	0.7	140.5	0.2	140.4	-0.1	139.9	-0.4
1992	140.1	0.1	140.7	0.4	141.2	0.4	142.0	0.6	142.0	0.0	142.0	0.0	142.4	0.3	142.6	0.1	143.2	0.4	143.5	0.2	143.7	0.1	143.8	0.1
1993	144.3	0.3	144.5	0.1	144.8	0.2	145.3	0.3	145.0	-0.2	145.5	0.3	145.3	-0.1	145.8	0.3	146.6	0.5	147.3	0.5	147.7	0.3	147.8	0.1

Source: U.S. Department of Labor, Bureau of Labor Statistics, Division of Consumer Prices and Price Indexes.

U.S. City Average

Consumer Price Index - Urban Wage Earners
Base 1982-1984 = 100
Entertainment

For 1967-1993. Columns headed % show percentile change in the index from the previous period for which an index is available.

Year	Jan Index	%	Feb Index	%	Mar Index	%	Apr Index	%	May Index	%	Jun Index	%	Jul Index	%	Aug Index	%	Sep Index	%	Oct Index	%	Nov Index	%	Dec Index	%
1967	40.5	-	40.6	0.2	40.7	0.2	41.0	0.7	41.1	0.2	41.2	0.2	41.3	0.2	41.3	0.0	41.6	0.7	41.9	0.7	42.2	0.7	42.3	0.2
1968	42.6	0.7	42.7	0.2	42.9	0.5	43.3	0.9	43.4	0.2	43.6	0.5	43.7	0.2	44.0	0.7	44.1	0.2	44.4	0.7	44.6	0.5	44.7	0.2
1969	44.8	0.2	44.8	0.0	45.0	0.4	45.4	0.9	45.7	0.7	45.8	0.2	46.0	0.4	46.2	0.4	46.4	0.4	46.5	0.2	46.7	0.4	46.9	0.4
1970	47.1	0.4	47.2	0.2	47.4	0.4	47.6	0.4	47.8	0.4	48.1	0.6	48.3	0.4	48.6	0.6	48.8	0.4	49.1	0.6	49.4	0.6	49.5	0.2
1971	49.8	0.6	49.9	0.2	50.0	0.2	50.5	1.0	50.7	0.4	51.0	0.6	51.1	0.2	51.2	0.2	51.3	0.2	51.3	0.0	51.4	0.2	51.4	0.0
1972	51.6	0.4	51.7	0.2	51.7	0.0	52.1	0.8	52.2	0.2	52.4	0.4	52.5	0.2	52.4	-0.2	52.6	0.4	52.7	0.2	52.7	0.0	52.7	0.0
1973	52.8	0.2	52.9	0.2	53.0	0.2	53.4	0.8	53.6	0.4	53.8	0.4	54.0	0.4	54.0	0.0	54.1	0.2	54.2	0.2	54.4	0.4	54.5	0.2
1974	54.9	0.7	55.2	0.5	55.5	0.5	56.0	0.9	56.9	1.6	57.8	1.6	58.4	1.0	58.7	0.5	59.4	1.2	59.6	0.3	60.1	0.8	60.6	0.8
1975	61.2	1.0	61.7	0.8	61.8	0.2	62.6	1.3	62.8	0.3	63.0	0.3	63.1	0.2	63.3	0.3	63.6	0.5	63.7	0.2	63.9	0.3	64.2	0.5
1976	64.5	0.5	64.7	0.3	65.0	0.5	65.2	0.3	65.7	0.8	66.1	0.6	66.3	0.3	66.4	0.2	66.7	0.5	67.0	0.4	67.3	0.4	67.5	0.3
1977	67.8	0.4	68.1	0.4	68.3	0.3	68.4	0.1	68.8	0.6	69.3	0.7	69.4	0.1	69.7	0.4	70.1	0.6	70.4	0.4	70.4	0.0	70.7	0.4
1978	71.0	0.4	71.8	1.1	71.9	0.1	72.4	0.7	72.6	0.3	72.5	-0.1	72.8	0.4	72.9	0.1	73.3	0.5	73.7	0.5	73.9	0.3	74.8	1.2
1979	75.2	0.5	75.4	0.3	76.0	0.8	76.7	0.9	77.3	0.8	77.5	0.3	77.9	0.5	78.1	0.3	78.6	0.6	79.1	0.6	79.3	0.3	79.5	0.3
1980	80.1	0.8	81.1	1.2	82.4	1.6	83.2	1.0	83.6	0.5	84.3	0.8	84.5	0.2	85.0	0.6	86.0	1.2	86.4	0.5	86.7	0.3	86.8	0.1
1981	87.7	1.0	88.8	1.3	89.3	0.6	89.7	0.4	90.0	0.3	90.2	0.2	90.4	0.2	90.9	0.6	91.5	0.7	92.3	0.9	92.7	0.4	92.7	0.0
1982	93.4	0.8	94.3	1.0	94.8	0.5	95.2	0.4	95.5	0.3	96.0	0.5	96.5	0.5	96.7	0.2	97.0	0.3	97.7	0.7	97.6	-0.1	97.7	0.1
1983	98.2	0.5	99.0	0.8	99.5	0.5	99.6	0.1	99.7	0.1	100.0	0.3	100.2	0.2	100.5	0.3	100.9	0.4	101.4	0.5	101.5	0.1	101.6	0.1
1984	101.7	0.1	102.4	0.7	102.5	0.1	103.2	0.7	103.1	-0.1	103.6	0.5	103.9	0.3	104.3	0.4	104.7	0.4	105.0	0.3	105.3	0.3	105.7	0.4
1985	106.0	0.3	106.2	0.2	106.3	0.1	106.9	0.6	107.0	0.1	107.5	0.5	107.8	0.3	107.8	0.0	108.1	0.3	108.7	0.6	109.0	0.3	108.7	-0.3
1986	109.7	0.9	110.1	0.4	110.1	0.0	110.3	0.2	110.5	0.2	110.9	0.4	111.2	0.3	111.2	0.0	111.6	0.4	112.0	0.4	112.4	0.4	112.5	0.1
1987	112.8	0.3	113.0	0.2	113.4	0.4	114.0	0.5	114.4	0.4	114.5	0.1	115.0	0.4	115.1	0.1	115.6	0.4	116.3	0.6	116.7	0.3	116.9	0.2
1988	117.4	0.4	117.6	0.2	118.2	0.5	118.9	0.6	119.0	0.1	119.4	0.3	119.8	0.3	120.1	0.3	120.6	0.4	121.2	0.5	121.7	0.4	122.2	0.4
1989	123.1	0.7	123.6	0.4	124.1	0.4	124.8	0.6	124.9	0.1	125.5	0.5	126.1	0.5	126.5	0.3	127.0	0.4	127.7	0.6	127.9	0.2	128.4	0.4
1990	129.1	0.5	129.5	0.3	130.0	0.4	130.6	0.5	130.8	0.2	131.0	0.2	131.7	0.5	132.1	0.3	132.9	0.6	133.1	0.2	133.2	0.1	133.3	0.1
1991	134.2	0.7	134.9	0.5	135.4	0.4	136.4	0.7	136.4	0.0	136.7	0.2	137.1	0.3	137.6	0.4	138.7	0.8	138.8	0.1	138.7	-0.1	138.4	-0.2
1992	138.6	0.1	139.1	0.4	139.7	0.4	140.5	0.6	140.5	0.0	140.5	0.0	141.0	0.4	141.2	0.1	141.6	0.3	141.9	0.2	142.2	0.2	142.2	0.0
1993	142.7	0.4	142.8	0.1	143.1	0.2	143.5	0.3	143.3	-0.1	143.8	0.3	143.7	-0.1	144.1	0.3	144.8	0.5	145.5	0.5	145.8	0.2	146.1	0.2

Source: U.S. Department of Labor, Bureau of Labor Statistics, Division of Consumer Prices and Price Indexes.

U.S. City Average
Consumer Price Index - All Urban Consumers
Base 1982-1984 = 100
Other Goods and Services

For 1967-1993. Columns headed % show percentile change in the index from the previous period for which an index is available.

Year	Jan Index	%	Feb Index	%	Mar Index	%	Apr Index	%	May Index	%	Jun Index	%	Jul Index	%	Aug Index	%	Sep Index	%	Oct Index	%	Nov Index	%	Dec Index	%
1967	34.4	-	34.5	0.3	34.5	0.0	34.6	0.3	34.7	0.3	34.8	0.3	35.0	0.6	35.3	0.9	35.5	0.6	35.6	0.3	35.8	0.6	35.9	0.3
1968	36.1	0.6	36.1	0.0	36.5	1.1	36.5	0.0	36.6	0.3	36.9	0.8	36.9	0.0	37.1	0.5	37.2	0.3	37.4	0.5	37.6	0.5	37.7	0.3
1969	37.8	0.3	37.8	0.0	38.0	0.5	38.1	0.3	38.2	0.3	38.5	0.8	38.8	0.8	39.0	0.5	39.3	0.8	39.4	0.3	39.7	0.8	39.8	0.3
1970	39.9	0.3	40.0	0.3	40.2	0.5	40.5	0.7	40.6	0.2	40.9	0.7	41.2	0.7	41.3	0.2	41.5	0.5	41.6	0.2	41.8	0.5	41.9	0.2
1971	42.2	0.7	42.2	0.0	42.3	0.2	42.4	0.2	42.5	0.2	42.6	0.2	42.9	0.7	43.1	0.5	43.5	0.9	43.6	0.2	43.6	0.0	43.7	0.2
1972	43.9	0.5	44.2	0.7	44.3	0.2	44.4	0.2	44.6	0.5	44.8	0.4	44.8	0.0	44.8	0.0	45.0	0.4	45.2	0.4	45.2	0.0	45.3	0.2
1973	45.4	0.2	45.5	0.2	45.8	0.7	46.0	0.4	46.2	0.4	46.4	0.4	46.5	0.2	46.6	0.2	46.9	0.6	47.1	0.4	47.4	0.6	47.5	0.2
1974	47.7	0.4	47.9	0.4	48.2	0.6	48.4	0.4	48.9	1.0	49.4	1.0	50.0	1.2	50.3	0.6	50.9	1.2	51.4	1.0	51.9	1.0	52.4	1.0
1975	52.7	0.6	53.1	0.8	53.3	0.4	53.5	0.4	53.6	0.2	53.7	0.2	53.9	0.4	54.0	0.2	54.4	0.7	54.7	0.6	54.9	0.4	55.3	0.7
1976	55.7	0.7	56.1	0.7	56.2	0.2	56.4	0.4	56.6	0.4	56.8	0.4	56.9	0.2	57.1	0.4	57.6	0.9	58.0	0.7	58.4	0.7	58.6	0.3
1977	59.0	0.7	59.2	0.3	59.3	0.2	59.5	0.3	59.7	0.3	60.0	0.5	60.2	0.3	60.4	0.3	61.1	1.2	61.7	1.0	62.1	0.6	62.3	0.3
1978	62.6	0.5	62.7	0.2	62.9	0.3	63.0	0.2	63.2	0.3	63.4	0.3	64.2	1.3	64.5	0.5	65.8	2.0	66.0	0.3	66.2	0.3	66.3	0.2
1979	66.8	0.8	67.3	0.7	67.6	0.4	67.7	0.1	68.0	0.4	68.2	0.3	68.4	0.3	69.1	1.0	70.7	2.3	70.9	0.3	71.1	0.3	71.5	0.6
1980	72.3	1.1	72.9	0.8	73.2	0.4	73.5	0.4	74.0	0.7	74.5	0.7	74.8	0.4	75.2	0.5	77.3	2.8	77.6	0.4	78.1	0.6	78.7	0.8
1981	79.3	0.8	79.7	0.5	80.2	0.6	80.6	0.5	81.4	1.0	81.8	0.5	82.2	0.5	82.6	0.5	85.2	3.1	86.0	0.9	86.2	0.2	86.5	0.3
1982	87.1	0.7	87.7	0.7	88.4	0.8	89.0	0.7	89.4	0.4	89.7	0.3	90.2	0.6	90.5	0.3	93.5	3.3	95.1	1.7	96.0	0.9	97.0	1.0
1983	98.1	1.1	98.7	0.6	98.8	0.1	99.3	0.5	99.4	0.1	99.7	0.3	100.8	1.1	101.3	0.5	103.2	1.9	104.0	0.8	104.5	0.5	104.7	0.2
1984	105.3	0.6	105.7	0.4	105.9	0.2	106.1	0.2	106.3	0.2	106.7	0.4	107.4	0.7	107.7	0.3	110.3	2.4	110.7	0.4	110.9	0.2	111.0	0.1
1985	111.9	0.8	112.3	0.4	112.6	0.3	112.8	0.2	113.0	0.2	113.2	0.2	113.9	0.6	114.3	0.4	116.8	2.2	117.4	0.5	117.5	0.1	118.0	0.4
1986	118.9	0.8	119.3	0.3	119.6	0.3	119.8	0.2	119.9	0.1	120.1	0.2	120.9	0.7	121.4	0.4	123.8	2.0	124.3	0.4	124.4	0.1	124.5	0.1
1987	125.5	0.8	126.1	0.5	126.3	0.2	126.6	0.2	126.9	0.2	127.2	0.2	128.0	0.6	128.5	0.4	131.1	2.0	131.6	0.4	131.8	0.2	132.1	0.2
1988	133.4	1.0	134.2	0.6	134.6	0.3	134.8	0.1	135.1	0.2	135.5	0.3	136.5	0.7	137.5	0.7	140.0	1.8	140.6	0.4	141.0	0.3	141.3	0.2
1989	143.4	1.5	144.1	0.5	144.4	0.2	144.7	0.2	145.4	0.5	146.3	0.6	147.3	0.7	148.7	1.0	151.2	1.7	151.8	0.4	151.9	0.1	152.9	0.7
1990	154.0	0.7	154.7	0.5	155.2	0.3	155.8	0.4	156.6	0.5	157.8	0.8	159.2	0.9	160.4	0.8	162.6	1.4	163.2	0.4	163.6	0.2	164.5	0.6
1991	166.5	1.2	167.4	0.5	167.9	0.3	168.8	0.5	169.1	0.2	170.0	0.5	170.8	0.5	172.2	0.8	175.8	2.1	176.2	0.2	176.9	0.4	177.6	0.4
1992	178.6	0.6	179.4	0.4	179.8	0.2	180.3	0.3	181.3	0.6	181.5	0.1	182.3	0.4	183.9	0.9	187.0	1.7	187.9	0.5	188.0	0.1	189.1	0.6
1993	191.0	1.0	191.5	0.3	192.0	0.3	192.4	0.2	193.2	0.4	193.1	-0.1	193.7	0.3	193.4	-0.2	193.1	-0.2	193.4	0.2	193.8	0.2	194.2	0.2

Source: U.S. Department of Labor, Bureau of Labor Statistics, Division of Consumer Prices and Price Indexes.

U.S. City Average
Consumer Price Index - Urban Wage Earners
Base 1982-1984 = 100
Other Goods and Services

For 1967-1993. Columns headed % show percentile change in the index from the previous period for which an index is available.

Year	Jan Index	%	Feb Index	%	Mar Index	%	Apr Index	%	May Index	%	Jun Index	%	Jul Index	%	Aug Index	%	Sep Index	%	Oct Index	%	Nov Index	%	Dec Index	%
1967	34.7	-	34.8	0.3	34.8	0.0	34.9	0.3	35.0	0.3	35.1	0.3	35.3	0.6	35.6	0.8	35.8	0.6	36.0	0.6	36.1	0.3	36.3	0.6
1968	36.4	0.3	36.4	0.0	36.8	1.1	36.8	0.0	36.9	0.3	37.2	0.8	37.3	0.3	37.4	0.3	37.6	0.5	37.8	0.5	37.9	0.3	38.1	0.5
1969	38.1	0.0	38.2	0.3	38.3	0.3	38.5	0.5	38.6	0.3	38.8	0.5	39.1	0.8	39.4	0.8	39.6	0.5	39.8	0.5	40.0	0.5	40.1	0.2
1970	40.3	0.5	40.4	0.2	40.5	0.2	40.8	0.7	41.0	0.5	41.3	0.7	41.5	0.5	41.7	0.5	41.8	0.2	42.0	0.5	42.2	0.5	42.3	0.2
1971	42.6	0.7	42.6	0.0	42.7	0.2	42.8	0.2	42.9	0.2	43.0	0.2	43.3	0.7	43.5	0.5	43.9	0.9	44.0	0.2	44.0	0.0	44.1	0.2
1972	44.3	0.5	44.6	0.7	44.7	0.2	44.8	0.2	45.0	0.4	45.2	0.4	45.2	0.0	45.2	0.0	45.5	0.7	45.6	0.2	45.6	0.0	45.7	0.2
1973	45.8	0.2	46.0	0.4	46.2	0.4	46.4	0.4	46.6	0.4	46.8	0.4	46.9	0.2	47.0	0.2	47.3	0.6	47.6	0.6	47.8	0.4	48.0	0.4
1974	48.1	0.2	48.4	0.6	48.6	0.4	48.9	0.6	49.3	0.8	49.9	1.2	50.4	1.0	50.8	0.8	51.4	1.2	51.9	1.0	52.4	1.0	52.8	0.8
1975	53.2	0.8	53.6	0.8	53.8	0.4	53.9	0.2	54.1	0.4	54.2	0.2	54.4	0.4	54.5	0.2	54.9	0.7	55.2	0.5	55.4	0.4	55.9	0.9
1976	56.2	0.5	56.6	0.7	56.7	0.2	57.0	0.5	57.1	0.2	57.3	0.4	57.4	0.2	57.7	0.5	58.2	0.9	58.5	0.5	58.9	0.7	59.1	0.3
1977	59.5	0.7	59.7	0.3	59.9	0.3	60.1	0.3	60.3	0.3	60.5	0.3	60.7	0.3	60.9	0.3	61.7	1.3	62.3	1.0	62.7	0.6	62.9	0.3
1978	63.1	0.3	63.4	0.5	63.5	0.2	63.7	0.3	63.9	0.3	64.2	0.5	65.0	1.2	65.2	0.3	66.2	1.5	66.4	0.3	66.6	0.3	66.6	0.0
1979	67.3	1.1	67.9	0.9	68.1	0.3	68.3	0.3	68.6	0.4	68.7	0.1	69.0	0.4	69.8	1.2	71.0	1.7	71.2	0.3	71.5	0.4	71.8	0.4
1980	72.9	1.5	73.5	0.8	73.7	0.3	74.0	0.4	74.5	0.7	75.0	0.7	75.3	0.4	75.7	0.5	77.5	2.4	77.8	0.4	78.2	0.5	78.9	0.9
1981	79.4	0.6	79.8	0.5	80.2	0.5	80.6	0.5	81.5	1.1	81.9	0.5	82.2	0.4	82.6	0.5	84.6	2.4	85.4	0.9	85.8	0.5	86.1	0.3
1982	86.7	0.7	87.4	0.8	88.2	0.9	88.8	0.7	89.3	0.6	89.5	0.2	90.0	0.6	90.5	0.6	93.0	2.8	94.7	1.8	95.8	1.2	96.9	1.1
1983	98.3	1.4	98.9	0.6	99.0	0.1	99.5	0.5	99.7	0.2	100.0	0.3	101.3	1.3	101.9	0.6	103.3	1.4	104.0	0.7	104.5	0.5	104.7	0.2
1984	105.4	0.7	105.8	0.4	106.0	0.2	106.3	0.3	106.4	0.1	106.9	0.5	107.7	0.7	108.0	0.3	110.0	1.9	110.3	0.3	110.6	0.3	110.6	0.0
1985	111.6	0.9	112.2	0.5	112.3	0.1	112.6	0.3	112.8	0.2	113.0	0.2	113.8	0.7	114.2	0.4	116.3	1.8	116.8	0.4	116.9	0.1	117.4	0.4
1986	118.5	0.9	118.9	0.3	119.2	0.3	119.4	0.2	119.6	0.2	119.7	0.1	120.7	0.8	121.2	0.4	122.9	1.4	123.4	0.4	123.5	0.1	123.6	0.1
1987	124.8	1.0	125.4	0.5	125.6	0.2	125.9	0.2	126.2	0.2	126.6	0.3	127.5	0.7	128.0	0.4	130.3	1.8	130.8	0.4	131.0	0.2	131.3	0.2
1988	132.7	1.1	133.6	0.7	134.0	0.3	134.2	0.1	134.5	0.2	135.0	0.4	136.3	1.0	137.2	0.7	139.3	1.5	139.9	0.4	140.3	0.3	140.6	0.2
1989	143.0	1.7	143.7	0.5	144.0	0.2	144.4	0.3	145.2	0.6	146.3	0.8	147.5	0.8	148.8	0.9	150.8	1.3	151.4	0.4	151.5	0.1	152.7	0.8
1990	153.9	0.8	154.6	0.5	155.1	0.3	155.7	0.4	156.3	0.4	157.8	1.0	159.4	1.0	160.5	0.7	162.4	1.2	162.8	0.2	163.4	0.4	164.4	0.6
1991	166.6	1.3	167.5	0.5	168.1	0.4	169.1	0.6	169.4	0.2	170.5	0.6	171.2	0.4	172.6	0.8	175.5	1.7	175.9	0.2	176.8	0.5	177.7	0.5
1992	178.6	0.5	179.4	0.4	179.7	0.2	180.3	0.3	181.6	0.7	181.8	0.1	182.7	0.5	184.2	0.8	186.7	1.4	187.7	0.5	187.7	0.0	189.0	0.7
1993	191.2	1.2	191.6	0.2	192.2	0.3	192.8	0.3	193.6	0.4	193.3	-0.2	193.8	0.3	192.7	-0.6	190.9	-0.9	191.1	0.1	191.6	0.3	192.0	0.2

Source: U.S. Department of Labor, Bureau of Labor Statistics, Division of Consumer Prices and Price Indexes.

Anchorage, AK
Consumer Price Index - All Urban Consumers
Base 1982-1984 = 100
Annual Averages

For 1960-1993. Columns headed % show percentile change in the index from the previous period for which an index is available.

Year	All Items		Food & Beverage		Housing		Apparel & Upkeep		Trans-portation		Medical Care		Entertain-ment		Other Goods & Services	
	Index	%	Index	%	Index	%	Index	%	Index	%	Index	%	Index	%	Index	%
1960	-	-	-	-	-	-	-	-	-	-	-	-	-	-	-	-
1961	34.5	-	-	-	-	-	-	-	-	-	-	-	-	-	-	-
1962	34.7	0.6	-	-	-	-	-	-	-	-	-	-	-	-	-	-
1963	34.8	0.3	-	-	-	-	-	-	-	-	-	-	-	-	-	-
1964	35.0	0.6	-	-	-	-	-	-	-	-	-	-	-	-	-	-
1965	35.3	0.9	-	-	-	-	-	-	-	-	-	-	-	-	-	-
1966	36.3	2.8	-	-	-	-	-	-	-	-	-	-	-	-	-	-
1967	37.2	2.5	-	-	-	-	-	-	-	-	-	-	-	-	-	-
1968	38.1	2.4	-	-	-	-	-	-	-	-	-	-	-	-	-	-
1969	39.6	3.9	-	-	-	-	-	-	-	-	-	-	-	-	-	-
1970	41.1	3.8	-	-	-	-	-	-	-	-	-	-	-	-	-	-
1971	42.3	2.9	-	-	-	-	56.5	-	40.8	-	35.2	-	-	-	-	-
1972	43.4	2.6	-	-	-	-	58.3	3.2	40.9	0.2	35.8	1.7	-	-	-	-
1973	45.3	4.4	-	-	-	-	60.7	4.1	41.4	1.2	37.3	4.2	-	-	-	-
1974	50.2	10.8	-	-	-	-	64.7	6.6	44.9	8.5	41.5	11.3	-	-	-	-
1975	57.1	13.7	-	-	-	-	69.8	7.9	49.3	9.8	46.9	13.0	-	-	-	-
1976	61.5	7.7	64.2	-	62.6	-	74.1	6.2	54.9	11.4	52.6	12.2	64.4	-	63.8	-
1977	65.6	6.7	68.9	7.3	65.5	4.6	79.2	6.9	60.2	9.7	57.9	10.1	69.4	7.8	68.1	6.7
1978	70.2	7.0	75.9	10.2	69.7	6.4	79.7	0.6	64.5	7.1	63.4	9.5	72.6	4.6	71.7	5.3
1979	77.6	10.5	84.0	10.7	78.0	11.9	81.7	2.5	71.3	10.5	69.1	9.0	74.5	2.6	76.9	7.3
1980	85.5	10.2	89.7	6.8	85.9	10.1	89.7	9.8	82.2	15.3	78.8	14.0	79.0	6.0	83.1	8.1
1981	92.4	8.1	94.3	5.1	92.5	7.7	94.1	4.9	92.7	12.8	86.9	10.3	85.9	8.7	88.1	6.0
1982	97.4	5.4	97.2	3.1	98.2	6.2	96.6	2.7	96.8	4.4	94.8	9.1	94.7	10.2	93.2	5.8
1983	99.2	1.8	99.7	2.6	99.0	0.8	101.6	5.2	98.5	1.8	99.7	5.2	100.6	6.2	101.5	8.9
1984	103.3	4.1	103.2	3.5	102.7	3.7	101.7	0.1	104.6	6.2	105.5	5.8	104.6	4.0	105.3	3.7
1985	105.8	2.4	106.2	2.9	103.0	0.3	105.8	4.0	108.2	3.4	110.9	5.1	108.9	4.1	114.2	8.5
1986	107.8	1.9	110.8	4.3	102.6	-0.4	109.0	3.0	107.8	-0.4	127.8	15.2	112.4	3.2	123.2	7.9
1987	108.2	0.4	113.1	2.1	97.5	-5.0	116.6	7.0	111.3	3.2	137.0	7.2	116.4	3.6	132.2	7.3
1988	108.6	0.4	113.8	0.6	95.4	-2.2	119.1	2.1	113.0	1.5	145.8	6.4	120.1	3.2	138.1	4.5
1989	111.7	2.9	117.2	3.0	96.3	0.9	125.0	5.0	116.7	3.3	154.4	5.9	128.2	6.7	143.7	4.1
1990	118.6	6.2	123.7	5.5	103.9	7.9	127.7	2.2	120.7	3.4	161.2	4.4	141.9	10.7	155.7	8.4
1991	124.0	4.6	127.7	3.2	111.2	7.0	126.6	-0.9	121.7	0.8	173.5	7.6	148.8	4.9	166.9	7.2
1992	128.2	3.4	130.3	2.0	116.6	4.9	130.2	2.8	123.3	1.3	183.0	5.5	151.0	1.5	175.2	5.0
1993	132.2	3.1	131.2	0.7	121.1	3.9	131.2	0.8	128.7	4.4	189.6	3.6	157.9	4.6	177.8	1.5

Source: U.S. Department of Labor, Bureau of Labor Statistics, Division of Consumer Prices and Price Indexes. - indicates no data collected for period.

Anchorage, AK
Consumer Price Index - Urban Wage Earners
Base 1982-1984 = 100
Annual Averages

For 1960-1993. Columns headed % show percentile change in the index from the previous period for which an index is available.

Year	All Items		Food & Beverage		Housing		Apparel & Upkeep		Trans- portation		Medical Care		Entertain- ment		Other Goods & Services	
	Index	%	Index	%	Index	%	Index	%	Index	%	Index	%	Index	%	Index	%
1960	-	-	-	-	-	-	-	-	-	-	-	-	-	-	-	-
1961	35.4	-	-	-	-	-	-	-	-	-	-	-	-	-	-	-
1962	35.5	0.3	-	-	-	-	-	-	-	-	-	-	-	-	-	-
1963	35.7	0.6	-	-	-	-	-	-	-	-	-	-	-	-	-	-
1964	35.9	0.6	-	-	-	-	-	-	-	-	-	-	-	-	-	-
1965	36.2	0.8	-	-	-	-	-	-	-	-	-	-	-	-	-	-
1966	37.2	2.8	-	-	-	-	-	-	-	-	-	-	-	-	-	-
1967	38.2	2.7	-	-	-	-	-	-	-	-	-	-	-	-	-	-
1968	39.1	2.4	-	-	-	-	-	-	-	-	-	-	-	-	-	-
1969	40.7	4.1	-	-	-	-	-	-	-	-	-	-	-	-	-	-
1970	42.1	3.4	-	-	-	-	-	-	-	-	-	-	-	-	-	-
1971	43.4	3.1	-	-	-	-	57.1	-	40.4	-	36.2	-	-	-	-	-
1972	44.5	2.5	-	-	-	-	58.9	3.2	40.5	0.2	36.9	1.9	-	-	-	-
1973	46.4	4.3	-	-	-	-	61.4	4.2	41.0	1.2	38.4	4.1	-	-	-	-
1974	51.4	10.8	-	-	-	-	65.4	6.5	44.4	8.3	42.7	11.2	-	-	-	-
1975	58.5	13.8	-	-	-	-	70.5	7.8	48.8	9.9	48.3	13.1	-	-	-	-
1976	63.1	7.9	64.5	-	65.7	-	74.9	6.2	54.3	11.3	54.1	12.0	70.5	-	62.6	-
1977	67.2	6.5	69.3	7.4	68.8	4.7	80.0	6.8	59.6	9.8	59.7	10.4	76.0	7.8	66.9	6.9
1978	72.0	7.1	76.9	11.0	73.0	6.1	80.3	0.4	64.1	7.6	67.1	12.4	76.0	0.0	70.1	4.8
1979	79.0	9.7	86.1	12.0	80.5	10.3	81.6	1.6	71.2	11.1	72.8	8.5	77.0	1.3	75.0	7.0
1980	86.3	9.2	90.3	4.9	87.6	8.8	86.5	6.0	82.9	16.4	79.3	8.9	79.9	3.8	81.9	9.2
1981	92.9	7.6	94.2	4.3	93.9	7.2	92.6	7.1	93.4	12.7	86.8	9.5	86.2	7.9	86.4	5.5
1982	98.2	5.7	97.2	3.2	100.1	6.6	96.3	4.0	97.3	4.2	94.9	9.3	94.6	9.7	92.4	6.9
1983	98.9	0.7	99.7	2.6	98.2	-1.9	101.6	5.5	98.4	1.1	99.8	5.2	100.5	6.2	101.9	10.3
1984	102.9	4.0	103.2	3.5	101.6	3.5	102.1	0.5	104.3	6.0	105.3	5.5	105.0	4.5	105.7	3.7
1985	105.8	2.8	106.2	2.9	103.4	1.8	105.5	3.3	107.6	3.2	110.5	4.9	108.7	3.5	114.1	7.9
1986	107.7	1.8	110.9	4.4	103.1	-0.3	108.1	2.5	106.5	-1.0	125.3	13.4	112.5	3.5	123.2	8.0
1987	107.9	0.2	113.2	2.1	97.8	-5.1	115.9	7.2	109.5	2.8	133.6	6.6	118.1	5.0	131.1	6.4
1988	108.3	0.4	113.9	0.6	95.8	-2.0	116.3	0.3	111.0	1.4	142.1	6.4	121.7	3.0	137.3	4.7
1989	111.3	2.8	117.4	3.1	96.6	0.8	120.3	3.4	114.6	3.2	150.9	6.2	131.5	8.1	143.9	4.8
1990	118.4	6.4	124.1	5.7	104.1	7.8	125.7	4.5	118.5	3.4	157.9	4.6	146.4	11.3	158.4	10.1
1991	123.8	4.6	128.1	3.2	111.4	7.0	125.5	-0.2	119.4	0.8	169.7	7.5	154.8	5.7	170.8	7.8
1992	128.0	3.4	130.7	2.0	116.6	4.7	129.8	3.4	121.6	1.8	178.5	5.2	158.1	2.1	179.7	5.2
1993	132.0	3.1	131.7	0.8	121.1	3.9	131.4	1.2	126.8	4.3	185.6	4.0	164.0	3.7	182.0	1.3

Source: U.S. Department of Labor, Bureau of Labor Statistics, Division of Consumer Prices and Price Indexes. - indicates no data collected for period.

Anchorage, AK
Consumer Price Index - All Urban Consumers
Base 1982-1984 = 100
All Items

For 1960-1993. Columns headed % show percentile change in the index from the previous period for which an index is available.

Year	Jan Index	%	Feb Index	%	Mar Index	%	Apr Index	%	May Index	%	Jun Index	%	Jul Index	%	Aug Index	%	Sep Index	%	Oct Index	%	Nov Index	%	Dec Index	%
1960	-	-	-	-	-	-	-	-	34.2	-	-	-	-	-	-	-	-	-	34.4	0.6	-	-	-	-
1961	-	-	-	-	-	-	-	-	34.4	0.0	-	-	-	-	-	-	-	-	34.8	1.2	-	-	-	-
1962	-	-	-	-	-	-	-	-	34.6	-0.6	-	-	-	-	-	-	-	-	34.7	0.3	-	-	-	-
1963	-	-	-	-	-	-	34.8	0.3	-	-	-	-	-	-	-	-	-	-	34.9	0.3	-	-	-	-
1964	-	-	-	-	-	-	34.8	-0.3	-	-	-	-	-	-	-	-	-	-	35.2	1.1	-	-	-	-
1965	-	-	-	-	-	-	35.3	0.3	-	-	-	-	-	-	-	-	-	-	35.3	0.0	-	-	-	-
1966	-	-	-	-	-	-	-	-	-	-	-	-	-	-	-	-	-	-	36.7	4.0	-	-	-	-
1967	-	-	-	-	-	-	-	-	-	-	-	-	-	-	-	-	-	-	37.5	2.2	-	-	-	-
1968	-	-	-	-	-	-	-	-	-	-	-	-	-	-	-	-	-	-	38.4	2.4	-	-	-	-
1969	38.9	1.3	-	-	-	-	39.5	1.5	-	-	-	-	39.6	0.3	-	-	-	-	40.2	1.5	-	-	-	-
1970	40.4	0.5	-	-	-	-	40.5	0.2	-	-	-	-	41.1	1.5	-	-	-	-	41.8	1.7	-	-	-	-
1971	41.8	0.0	-	-	-	-	41.8	0.0	-	-	-	-	42.3	1.2	-	-	-	-	42.8	1.2	-	-	-	-
1972	42.8	0.0	-	-	-	-	43.4	1.4	-	-	-	-	43.4	0.0	-	-	-	-	43.8	0.9	-	-	-	-
1973	43.6	-0.5	-	-	-	-	44.7	2.5	-	-	-	-	45.1	0.9	-	-	-	-	46.4	2.9	-	-	-	-
1974	47.1	1.5	-	-	-	-	48.7	3.4	-	-	-	-	50.3	3.3	-	-	-	-	52.5	4.4	-	-	-	-
1975	53.5	1.9	-	-	-	-	56.2	5.0	-	-	-	-	57.6	2.5	-	-	-	-	59.0	2.4	-	-	-	-
1976	59.5	0.8	-	-	-	-	60.6	1.8	-	-	-	-	61.8	2.0	-	-	-	-	62.8	1.6	-	-	-	-
1977	63.5	1.1	-	-	-	-	64.7	1.9	-	-	-	-	66.5	2.8	-	-	-	-	66.4	-0.2	-	-	-	-
1978	67.1	1.1	-	-	67.7	0.9	-	-	69.0	1.9	-	-	70.6	2.3	-	-	72.4	2.5	-	-	72.9	0.7	-	-
1979	74.2	1.8	-	-	75.3	1.5	-	-	76.2	1.2	-	-	77.7	2.0	-	-	79.9	2.8	-	-	80.1	0.3	-	-
1980	81.7	2.0	-	-	83.7	2.4	-	-	84.9	1.4	-	-	85.6	0.8	-	-	86.5	1.1	-	-	88.6	2.4	-	-
1981	90.0	1.6	-	-	90.3	0.3	-	-	91.6	1.4	-	-	92.2	0.7	-	-	93.9	1.8	-	-	95.0	1.2	-	-
1982	94.8	-0.2	-	-	97.4	2.7	-	-	98.8	1.4	-	-	98.8	0.0	-	-	98.7	-0.1	-	-	96.4	-2.3	-	-
1983	96.5	0.1	-	-	97.8	1.3	-	-	98.3	0.5	-	-	99.6	1.3	-	-	100.4	0.8	-	-	101.3	0.9	-	-
1984	101.7	0.4	-	-	102.8	1.1	-	-	103.1	0.3	-	-	103.2	0.1	-	-	104.1	0.9	-	-	104.0	-0.1	-	-
1985	104.3	0.3	-	-	104.9	0.6	-	-	104.5	-0.4	-	-	106.1	1.5	-	-	106.6	0.5	-	-	107.5	0.8	-	-
1986	107.6	0.1	-	-	109.1	1.4	-	-	108.2	-0.8	-	-	107.3	-0.8	-	-	107.2	-0.1	-	-	107.8	0.6	107.4	-0.4
1987	-	-	-	-	-	-	-	-	-	-	108.3	0.8	-	-	-	-	-	-	-	-	-	-	108.1	-0.2
1988	-	-	-	-	-	-	-	-	-	-	108.4	0.3	-	-	-	-	-	-	-	-	-	-	108.9	0.5
1989	-	-	-	-	-	-	-	-	-	-	110.9	1.8	-	-	-	-	-	-	-	-	-	-	112.5	1.4
1990	-	-	-	-	-	-	-	-	-	-	116.9	3.9	-	-	-	-	-	-	-	-	-	-	120.4	3.0
1991	-	-	-	-	-	-	-	-	-	-	123.3	2.4	-	-	-	-	-	-	-	-	-	-	124.7	1.1
1992	-	-	-	-	-	-	-	-	-	-	127.3	2.1	-	-	-	-	-	-	-	-	-	-	129.1	1.4
1993	-	-	-	-	-	-	-	-	-	-	131.5	1.9	-	-	-	-	-	-	-	-	-	-	-	-

Source: U.S. Department of Labor, Bureau of Labor Statistics, Division of Consumer Prices and Price Indexes. - indicates no data collected for period.

Anchorage, AK
Consumer Price Index - Urban Wage Earners
Base 1982-1984 = 100
All Items

For 1960-1993. Columns headed % show percentile change in the index from the previous period for which an index is available.

Year	Jan Index	%	Feb Index	%	Mar Index	%	Apr Index	%	May Index	%	Jun Index	%	Jul Index	%	Aug Index	%	Sep Index	%	Oct Index	%	Nov Index	%	Dec Index	%
1960	-	-	-	-	-	-	-	-	35.1	-	-	-	-	-	-	-	-	-	35.3	0.6	-	-	-	-
1961	-	-	-	-	-	-	-	-	35.2	-0.3	-	-	-	-	-	-	-	-	35.7	1.4	-	-	-	-
1962	-	-	-	-	-	-	-	-	35.5	-0.6	-	-	-	-	-	-	-	-	35.5	0.0	-	-	-	-
1963	-	-	-	-	-	-	35.7	0.6	-	-	-	-	-	-	-	-	-	-	35.8	0.3	-	-	-	-
1964	-	-	-	-	-	-	35.7	-0.3	-	-	-	-	-	-	-	-	-	-	36.1	1.1	-	-	-	-
1965	-	-	-	-	-	-	36.2	0.3	-	-	-	-	-	-	-	-	-	-	36.2	0.0	-	-	-	-
1966	-	-	-	-	-	-	-	-	-	-	-	-	-	-	-	-	-	-	37.6	3.9	-	-	-	-
1967	-	-	-	-	-	-	-	-	-	-	-	-	-	-	-	-	-	-	38.4	2.1	-	-	-	-
1968	-	-	-	-	-	-	-	-	-	-	-	-	-	-	-	-	-	-	39.4	2.6	-	-	-	-
1969	39.8	1.0	-	-	-	-	40.5	1.8	-	-	-	-	40.6	0.2	-	-	-	-	41.2	1.5	-	-	-	-
1970	41.4	0.5	-	-	-	-	41.6	0.5	-	-	-	-	42.1	1.2	-	-	-	-	42.8	1.7	-	-	-	-
1971	42.8	0.0	-	-	-	-	42.9	0.2	-	-	-	-	43.4	1.2	-	-	-	-	43.9	1.2	-	-	-	-
1972	43.9	0.0	-	-	-	-	44.5	1.4	-	-	-	-	44.5	0.0	-	-	-	-	44.9	0.9	-	-	-	-
1973	44.7	-0.4	-	-	-	-	45.9	2.7	-	-	-	-	46.3	0.9	-	-	-	-	47.6	2.8	-	-	-	-
1974	48.3	1.5	-	-	-	-	49.9	3.3	-	-	-	-	51.6	3.4	-	-	-	-	53.9	4.5	-	-	-	-
1975	54.9	1.9	-	-	-	-	57.6	4.9	-	-	-	-	59.1	2.6	-	-	-	-	60.5	2.4	-	-	-	-
1976	61.0	0.8	-	-	-	-	62.1	1.8	-	-	-	-	63.4	2.1	-	-	-	-	64.4	1.6	-	-	-	-
1977	65.1	1.1	-	-	-	-	66.3	1.8	-	-	-	-	68.2	2.9	-	-	-	-	68.1	-0.1	-	-	-	-
1978	68.9	1.2	-	-	69.5	0.9	-	-	70.7	1.7	-	-	72.5	2.5	-	-	74.1	2.2	-	-	74.8	0.9	-	-
1979	75.8	1.3	-	-	77.0	1.6	-	-	77.8	1.0	-	-	79.3	1.9	-	-	81.0	2.1	-	-	81.4	0.5	-	-
1980	83.0	2.0	-	-	84.6	1.9	-	-	85.7	1.3	-	-	86.4	0.8	-	-	87.1	0.8	-	-	89.1	2.3	-	-
1981	90.3	1.3	-	-	90.8	0.6	-	-	92.3	1.7	-	-	92.9	0.7	-	-	94.5	1.7	-	-	95.8	1.4	-	-
1982	95.5	-0.3	-	-	97.8	2.4	-	-	99.1	1.3	-	-	99.6	0.5	-	-	99.5	-0.1	-	-	97.7	-1.8	-	-
1983	96.3	-1.4	-	-	97.6	1.3	-	-	97.9	0.3	-	-	98.9	1.0	-	-	100.2	1.3	-	-	101.4	1.2	-	-
1984	101.4	0.0	-	-	102.2	0.8	-	-	102.1	-0.1	-	-	102.5	0.4	-	-	104.1	1.6	-	-	104.1	0.0	-	-
1985	104.4	0.3	-	-	104.9	0.5	-	-	104.5	-0.4	-	-	106.0	1.4	-	-	106.5	0.5	-	-	107.6	1.0	-	-
1986	107.7	0.1	-	-	109.3	1.5	-	-	108.3	-0.9	-	-	107.0	-1.2	-	-	106.8	-0.2	-	-	107.5	0.7	107.2	-0.3
1987	-	-	-	-	-	-	-	-	-	-	108.0	0.7	-	-	-	-	-	-	-	-	-	-	107.9	-0.1
1988	-	-	-	-	-	-	-	-	-	-	108.1	0.2	-	-	-	-	-	-	-	-	-	-	108.5	0.4
1989	-	-	-	-	-	-	-	-	-	-	110.5	1.8	-	-	-	-	-	-	-	-	-	-	112.1	1.4
1990	-	-	-	-	-	-	-	-	-	-	116.6	4.0	-	-	-	-	-	-	-	-	-	-	120.2	3.1
1991	-	-	-	-	-	-	-	-	-	-	123.0	2.3	-	-	-	-	-	-	-	-	-	-	124.5	1.2
1992	-	-	-	-	-	-	-	-	-	-	127.0	2.0	-	-	-	-	-	-	-	-	-	-	129.1	1.7
1993	-	-	-	-	-	-	-	-	-	-	131.4	1.8	-	-	-	-	-	-	-	-	-	-	-	-

Source: U.S. Department of Labor, Bureau of Labor Statistics, Division of Consumer Prices and Price Indexes. - indicates no data collected for period.

Anchorage, AK
Consumer Price Index - All Urban Consumers
Base 1982-1984 = 100
Food and Beverages

For 1976-1993. Columns headed % show percentile change in the index from the previous period for which an index is available.

Year	Jan Index	%	Feb Index	%	Mar Index	%	Apr Index	%	May Index	%	Jun Index	%	Jul Index	%	Aug Index	%	Sep Index	%	Oct Index	%	Nov Index	%	Dec Index	%
1976	63.2	-	-	-	-	-	63.4	0.3	-	-	-	-	64.4	1.6	-	-	-	-	64.8	0.6	-	-	-	-
1977	65.4	0.9	-	-	-	-	67.3	2.9	-	-	-	-	70.9	5.3	-	-	-	-	69.8	-1.6	-	-	-	-
1978	71.6	2.6	-	-	73.2	2.2	-	-	76.2	4.1	-	-	76.2	0.0	-	-	77.7	2.0	-	-	78.2	0.6	-	-
1979	80.6	3.1	-	-	82.7	2.6	-	-	82.7	0.0	-	-	84.5	2.2	-	-	85.7	1.4	-	-	86.2	0.6	-	-
1980	86.8	0.7	-	-	87.3	0.6	-	-	88.6	1.5	-	-	89.9	1.5	-	-	91.0	1.2	-	-	93.0	2.2	-	-
1981	92.9	-0.1	-	-	92.6	-0.3	-	-	93.1	0.5	-	-	94.6	1.6	-	-	95.7	1.2	-	-	96.0	0.3	-	-
1982	96.5	0.5	-	-	95.6	-0.9	-	-	96.7	1.2	-	-	98.2	1.6	-	-	97.8	-0.4	-	-	97.9	0.1	-	-
1983	97.8	-0.1	-	-	98.4	0.6	-	-	99.2	0.8	-	-	100.2	1.0	-	-	100.3	0.1	-	-	101.0	0.7	-	-
1984	102.2	1.2	-	-	102.9	0.7	-	-	103.3	0.4	-	-	103.2	-0.1	-	-	103.2	0.0	-	-	103.7	0.5	-	-
1985	103.8	0.1	-	-	104.5	0.7	-	-	105.1	0.6	-	-	106.5	1.3	-	-	107.1	0.6	-	-	108.6	1.4	-	-
1986	109.7	1.0	-	-	109.8	0.1	-	-	110.5	0.6	-	-	111.1	0.5	-	-	111.5	0.4	-	-	111.6	0.1	111.9	0.3
1987	-	-	-	-	-	-	-	-	-	-	113.6	1.5	-	-	-	-	-	-	-	-	-	-	112.7	-0.8
1988	-	-	-	-	-	-	-	-	-	-	113.5	0.7	-	-	-	-	-	-	-	-	-	-	114.2	0.6
1989	-	-	-	-	-	-	-	-	-	-	116.4	1.9	-	-	-	-	-	-	-	-	-	-	118.0	1.4
1990	-	-	-	-	-	-	-	-	-	-	122.5	3.8	-	-	-	-	-	-	-	-	-	-	125.0	2.0
1991	-	-	-	-	-	-	-	-	-	-	128.2	2.6	-	-	-	-	-	-	-	-	-	-	127.2	-0.8
1992	-	-	-	-	-	-	-	-	-	-	129.9	2.1	-	-	-	-	-	-	-	-	-	-	130.7	0.6
1993	-	-	-	-	-	-	-	-	-	-	131.6	0.7	-	-	-	-	-	-	-	-	-	-	-	-

Source: U.S. Department of Labor, Bureau of Labor Statistics, Division of Consumer Prices and Price Indexes. - indicates no data collected for period.

Anchorage, AK
Consumer Price Index - Urban Wage Earners
Base 1982-1984 = 100
Food and Beverages

For 1976-1993. Columns headed % show percentile change in the index from the previous period for which an index is available.

Year	Jan Index	%	Feb Index	%	Mar Index	%	Apr Index	%	May Index	%	Jun Index	%	Jul Index	%	Aug Index	%	Sep Index	%	Oct Index	%	Nov Index	%	Dec Index	%
1976	63.6	-	-	-	-	-	63.7	0.2	-	-	-	-	64.8	1.7	-	-	-	-	65.2	0.6	-	-	-	-
1977	65.8	0.9	-	-	-	-	67.7	2.9	-	-	-	-	71.3	5.3	-	-	-	-	70.2	-1.5	-	-	-	-
1978	72.0	2.6	-	-	73.3	1.8	-	-	76.0	3.7	-	-	78.0	2.6	-	-	79.5	1.9	-	-	80.4	1.1	-	-
1979	81.6	1.5	-	-	84.9	4.0	-	-	85.5	0.7	-	-	86.8	1.5	-	-	88.0	1.4	-	-	88.3	0.3	-	-
1980	88.8	0.6	-	-	88.1	-0.8	-	-	89.2	1.2	-	-	90.6	1.6	-	-	91.3	0.8	-	-	93.0	1.9	-	-
1981	92.4	-0.6	-	-	92.2	-0.2	-	-	93.2	1.1	-	-	94.2	1.1	-	-	95.9	1.8	-	-	96.0	0.1	-	-
1982	96.4	0.4	-	-	95.6	-0.8	-	-	96.6	1.0	-	-	98.1	1.6	-	-	97.8	-0.3	-	-	97.9	0.1	-	-
1983	98.1	0.2	-	-	98.5	0.4	-	-	99.1	0.6	-	-	100.2	1.1	-	-	100.4	0.2	-	-	100.9	0.5	-	-
1984	102.1	1.2	-	-	102.9	0.8	-	-	103.3	0.4	-	-	103.3	0.0	-	-	103.3	0.0	-	-	103.8	0.5	-	-
1985	103.8	0.0	-	-	104.6	0.8	-	-	105.2	0.6	-	-	106.6	1.3	-	-	107.0	0.4	-	-	108.5	1.4	-	-
1986	109.6	1.0	-	-	110.0	0.4	-	-	110.5	0.5	-	-	111.1	0.5	-	-	111.6	0.5	-	-	111.8	0.2	111.9	0.1
1987	-	-	-	-	-	-	-	-	-	-	113.6	1.5	-	-	-	-	-	-	-	-	-	-	112.8	-0.7
1988	-	-	-	-	-	-	-	-	-	-	113.5	0.6	-	-	-	-	-	-	-	-	-	-	114.3	0.7
1989	-	-	-	-	-	-	-	-	-	-	116.5	1.9	-	-	-	-	-	-	-	-	-	-	118.2	1.5
1990	-	-	-	-	-	-	-	-	-	-	122.9	4.0	-	-	-	-	-	-	-	-	-	-	125.3	2.0
1991	-	-	-	-	-	-	-	-	-	-	128.7	2.7	-	-	-	-	-	-	-	-	-	-	127.4	-1.0
1992	-	-	-	-	-	-	-	-	-	-	130.3	2.3	-	-	-	-	-	-	-	-	-	-	131.1	0.6
1993	-	-	-	-	-	-	-	-	-	-	132.2	0.8	-	-	-	-	-	-	-	-	-	-	-	-

Source: U.S. Department of Labor, Bureau of Labor Statistics, Division of Consumer Prices and Price Indexes. - indicates no data collected for period.

Anchorage, AK
Consumer Price Index - All Urban Consumers
Base 1982-1984 = 100
Housing

For 1976-1993. Columns headed % show percentile change in the index from the previous period for which an index is available.

Year	Jan Index	%	Feb Index	%	Mar Index	%	Apr Index	%	May Index	%	Jun Index	%	Jul Index	%	Aug Index	%	Sep Index	%	Oct Index	%	Nov Index	%	Dec Index	%
1976	61.0	-	-	-	-	-	61.7	1.1	-	-	-	-	62.8	1.8	-	-	-	-	63.7	1.4	-	-	-	-
1977	64.3	0.9	-	-	-	-	64.6	0.5	-	-	-	-	66.0	2.2	-	-	-	-	66.4	0.6	-	-	-	-
1978	66.6	0.3	-	-	66.9	0.5	-	-	67.5	0.9	-	-	70.1	3.9	-	-	72.5	3.4	-	-	73.0	0.7	-	-
1979	74.4	1.9	-	-	75.7	1.7	-	-	76.7	1.3	-	-	78.3	2.1	-	-	80.5	2.8	-	-	80.4	-0.1	-	-
1980	82.4	2.5	-	-	84.6	2.7	-	-	85.4	0.9	-	-	85.9	0.6	-	-	86.4	0.6	-	-	88.8	2.8	-	-
1981	90.8	2.3	-	-	90.7	-0.1	-	-	91.6	1.0	-	-	91.9	0.3	-	-	93.7	2.0	-	-	95.2	1.6	-	-
1982	94.4	-0.8	-	-	99.4	5.3	-	-	101.4	2.0	-	-	100.1	-1.3	-	-	99.6	-0.5	-	-	94.8	-4.8	-	-
1983	95.2	0.4	-	-	97.8	2.7	-	-	98.1	0.3	-	-	99.7	1.6	-	-	100.7	1.0	-	-	100.9	0.2	-	-
1984	101.7	0.8	-	-	102.9	1.2	-	-	103.0	0.1	-	-	102.2	-0.8	-	-	103.2	1.0	-	-	102.7	-0.5	-	-
1985	103.0	0.3	-	-	102.7	-0.3	-	-	101.4	-1.3	-	-	104.2	2.8	-	-	103.8	-0.4	-	-	103.2	-0.6	-	-
1986	103.3	0.1	-	-	105.8	2.4	-	-	105.5	-0.3	-	-	101.1	-4.2	-	-	100.2	-0.9	-	-	100.1	-0.1	100.1	0.0
1987	-	-	-	-	-	-	-	-	-	-	99.0	-1.1	-	-	-	-	-	-	-	-	-	-	96.1	-2.9
1988	-	-	-	-	-	-	-	-	-	-	95.8	-0.3	-	-	-	-	-	-	-	-	-	-	94.9	-0.9
1989	-	-	-	-	-	-	-	-	-	-	95.8	0.9	-	-	-	-	-	-	-	-	-	-	96.8	1.0
1990	-	-	-	-	-	-	-	-	-	-	102.2	5.6	-	-	-	-	-	-	-	-	-	-	105.7	3.4
1991	-	-	-	-	-	-	-	-	-	-	109.5	3.6	-	-	-	-	-	-	-	-	-	-	113.0	3.2
1992	-	-	-	-	-	-	-	-	-	-	115.5	2.2	-	-	-	-	-	-	-	-	-	-	117.8	2.0
1993	-	-	-	-	-	-	-	-	-	-	120.6	2.4	-	-	-	-	-	-	-	-	-	-	-	-

Source: U.S. Department of Labor, Bureau of Labor Statistics, Division of Consumer Prices and Price Indexes. - indicates no data collected for period.

Anchorage, AK
Consumer Price Index - Urban Wage Earners
Base 1982-1984 = 100
Housing

For 1976-1993. Columns headed % show percentile change in the index from the previous period for which an index is available.

Year	Jan Index	%	Feb Index	%	Mar Index	%	Apr Index	%	May Index	%	Jun Index	%	Jul Index	%	Aug Index	%	Sep Index	%	Oct Index	%	Nov Index	%	Dec Index	%
1976	64.1	-	-	-	-	-	64.8	1.1	-	-	-	-	66.0	1.9	-	-	-	-	66.9	1.4	-	-	-	-
1977	67.5	0.9	-	-	-	-	67.8	0.4	-	-	-	-	69.3	2.2	-	-	-	-	69.7	0.6	-	-	-	-
1978	69.9	0.3	-	-	70.3	0.6	-	-	70.9	0.9	-	-	73.3	3.4	-	-	75.6	3.1	-	-	76.2	0.8	-	-
1979	77.4	1.6	-	-	78.7	1.7	-	-	79.2	0.6	-	-	80.7	1.9	-	-	82.6	2.4	-	-	82.6	0.0	-	-
1980	84.3	2.1	-	-	86.3	2.4	-	-	87.3	1.2	-	-	87.6	0.3	-	-	87.9	0.3	-	-	90.3	2.7	-	-
1981	92.1	2.0	-	-	92.0	-0.1	-	-	93.1	1.2	-	-	93.3	0.2	-	-	95.0	1.8	-	-	96.8	1.9	-	-
1982	96.0	-0.8	-	-	100.8	5.0	-	-	103.0	2.2	-	-	102.3	-0.7	-	-	101.7	-0.6	-	-	97.6	-4.0	-	-
1983	94.5	-3.2	-	-	97.1	2.8	-	-	97.0	-0.1	-	-	98.1	1.1	-	-	99.9	1.8	-	-	102.9	-0.1	-	-
1984	100.8	-0.3	-	-	101.4	0.6	-	-	100.4	-1.0	-	-	100.6	0.2	-	-	103.0	2.4	-	-	103.8	-0.4	-	-
1985	103.3	0.4	-	-	102.9	-0.4	-	-	101.5	-1.4	-	-	104.4	2.9	-	-	104.2	-0.2	-	-	100.4	-0.5	-	-
1986	103.6	-0.2	-	-	106.6	2.9	-	-	106.3	-0.3	-	-	101.7	-4.3	-	-	100.9	-0.8	-	-	100.4	-0.5	100.6	0.2
1987	-	-	-	-	-	-	-	-	-	-	99.1	-1.5	-	-	-	-	-	-	-	-	-	-	96.4	-2.7
1988	-	-	-	-	-	-	-	-	-	-	96.3	-0.1	-	-	-	-	-	-	-	-	-	-	95.3	-1.0
1989	-	-	-	-	-	-	-	-	-	-	96.1	0.8	-	-	-	-	-	-	-	-	-	-	97.2	1.1
1990	-	-	-	-	-	-	-	-	-	-	102.4	5.3	-	-	-	-	-	-	-	-	-	-	105.8	3.3
1991	-	-	-	-	-	-	-	-	-	-	109.7	3.7	-	-	-	-	-	-	-	-	-	-	113.1	3.1
1992	-	-	-	-	-	-	-	-	-	-	115.4	2.0	-	-	-	-	-	-	-	-	-	-	117.9	2.2
1993	-	-	-	-	-	-	-	-	-	-	120.7	2.4	-	-	-	-	-	-	-	-	-	-	-	-

Source: U.S. Department of Labor, Bureau of Labor Statistics, Division of Consumer Prices and Price Indexes. - indicates no data collected for period.

Anchorage, AK
Consumer Price Index - All Urban Consumers
Base 1982-1984 = 100
Apparel and Upkeep

For 1971-1993. Columns headed % show percentile change in the index from the previous period for which an index is available.

Year	Jan Index	%	Feb Index	%	Mar Index	%	Apr Index	%	May Index	%	Jun Index	%	Jul Index	%	Aug Index	%	Sep Index	%	Oct Index	%	Nov Index	%	Dec Index	%
1971	55.3	-	-	-	-	-	56.1	1.4	-	-	-	-	56.8	1.2	-	-	-	-	57.0	0.4	-	-	-	-
1972	56.7	-0.5	-	-	-	-	58.5	3.2	-	-	-	-	58.3	-0.3	-	-	-	-	59.0	1.2	-	-	-	-
1973	58.9	-0.2	-	-	-	-	59.9	1.7	-	-	-	-	61.1	2.0	-	-	-	-	62.1	1.6	-	-	-	-
1974	61.7	-0.6	-	-	-	-	62.8	1.8	-	-	-	-	64.9	3.3	-	-	-	-	67.4	3.9	-	-	-	-
1975	67.6	0.3	-	-	-	-	70.1	3.7	-	-	-	-	69.6	-0.7	-	-	-	-	71.2	2.3	-	-	-	-
1976	70.3	-1.3	-	-	-	-	72.3	2.8	-	-	-	-	73.5	1.7	-	-	-	-	77.4	5.3	-	-	-	-
1977	78.7	1.7	-	-	-	-	79.1	0.5	-	-	-	-	79.0	-0.1	-	-	-	-	80.3	1.6	-	-	-	-
1978	77.5	-3.5	-	-	78.2	0.9	-	-	80.1	2.4	-	-	79.1	-1.2	-	-	81.4	2.9	-	-	81.5	0.1	-	-
1979	79.6	-2.3	-	-	79.3	-0.4	-	-	79.7	0.5	-	-	78.9	-1.0	-	-	86.5	9.6	-	-	85.0	-1.7	-	-
1980	83.8	-1.4	-	-	86.4	3.1	-	-	88.4	2.3	-	-	91.7	3.7	-	-	92.1	0.4	-	-	93.5	1.5	-	-
1981	92.7	-0.9	-	-	94.3	1.7	-	-	95.0	0.7	-	-	91.5	-3.7	-	-	95.7	4.6	-	-	95.0	-0.7	-	-
1982	93.9	-1.2	-	-	93.9	0.0	-	-	96.3	2.6	-	-	96.7	0.4	-	-	99.0	2.4	-	-	99.4	0.4	-	-
1983	95.7	-3.7	-	-	101.5	6.1	-	-	101.9	0.4	-	-	102.4	0.5	-	-	102.3	-0.1	-	-	104.8	2.4	-	-
1984	100.8	-3.8	-	-	102.3	1.5	-	-	99.9	-2.3	-	-	101.5	1.6	-	-	104.7	3.2	-	-	101.6	-3.0	-	-
1985	100.4	-1.2	-	-	107.3	6.9	-	-	106.1	-1.1	-	-	103.2	-2.7	-	-	108.7	5.3	-	-	107.6	-1.0	-	-
1986	105.5	-2.0	-	-	110.2	4.5	-	-	107.7	-2.3	-	-	109.0	1.2	-	-	110.3	1.2	-	-	110.7	0.4	108.9	-1.6
1987	-	-	-	-	-	-	-	-	-	-	115.4	6.0	-	-	-	-	-	-	-	-	-	-	117.8	2.1
1988	-	-	-	-	-	-	-	-	-	-	118.6	0.7	-	-	-	-	-	-	-	-	-	-	119.6	0.8
1989	-	-	-	-	-	-	-	-	-	-	124.4	4.0	-	-	-	-	-	-	-	-	-	-	125.6	1.0
1990	-	-	-	-	-	-	-	-	-	-	127.8	1.8	-	-	-	-	-	-	-	-	-	-	127.6	-0.2
1991	-	-	-	-	-	-	-	-	-	-	124.4	-2.5	-	-	-	-	-	-	-	-	-	-	128.9	3.6
1992	-	-	-	-	-	-	-	-	-	-	131.1	1.7	-	-	-	-	-	-	-	-	-	-	129.4	-1.3
1993	-	-	-	-	-	-	-	-	-	-	128.5	-0.7	-	-	-	-	-	-	-	-	-	-	-	-

Source: U.S. Department of Labor, Bureau of Labor Statistics, Division of Consumer Prices and Price Indexes. - indicates no data collected for period.

Anchorage, AK
Consumer Price Index - Urban Wage Earners
Base 1982-1984 = 100
Apparel and Upkeep

For 1971-1993. Columns headed % show percentile change in the index from the previous period for which an index is available.

Year	Jan Index	%	Feb Index	%	Mar Index	%	Apr Index	%	May Index	%	Jun Index	%	Jul Index	%	Aug Index	%	Sep Index	%	Oct Index	%	Nov Index	%	Dec Index	%
1971	55.9	-	-	-	-	-	56.7	1.4	-	-	-	-	57.4	1.2	-	-	-	-	57.6	0.3	-	-	-	-
1972	57.3	-0.5	-	-	-	-	59.1	3.1	-	-	-	-	58.9	-0.3	-	-	-	-	59.7	1.4	-	-	-	-
1973	59.6	-0.2	-	-	-	-	60.5	1.5	-	-	-	-	61.8	2.1	-	-	-	-	62.8	1.6	-	-	-	-
1974	62.4	-0.6	-	-	-	-	63.5	1.8	-	-	-	-	65.6	3.3	-	-	-	-	68.2	4.0	-	-	-	-
1975	68.4	0.3	-	-	-	-	70.8	3.5	-	-	-	-	70.3	-0.7	-	-	-	-	71.9	2.3	-	-	-	-
1976	71.1	-1.1	-	-	-	-	73.0	2.7	-	-	-	-	74.3	1.8	-	-	-	-	78.2	5.2	-	-	-	-
1977	79.6	1.8	-	-	-	-	80.0	0.5	-	-	-	-	79.8	-0.2	-	-	-	-	81.2	1.8	-	-	-	-
1978	78.3	-3.6	-	-	78.9	0.8	-	-	80.5	2.0	-	-	80.0	-0.6	-	-	81.6	2.0	-	-	82.0	0.5	-	-
1979	81.1	-1.1	-	-	80.0	-1.4	-	-	80.0	0.0	-	-	80.7	0.9	-	-	84.0	4.1	-	-	83.5	-0.6	-	-
1980	83.1	-0.5	-	-	84.1	1.2	-	-	84.6	0.6	-	-	87.2	3.1	-	-	88.4	1.4	-	-	89.6	1.4	-	-
1981	91.6	2.2	-	-	92.3	0.8	-	-	92.3	0.0	-	-	90.9	-1.5	-	-	93.9	3.3	-	-	94.3	0.4	-	-
1982	92.7	-1.7	-	-	93.5	0.9	-	-	95.0	1.6	-	-	96.9	2.0	-	-	99.3	2.5	-	-	99.8	0.5	-	-
1983	95.7	-4.1	-	-	101.7	6.3	-	-	102.2	0.5	-	-	102.1	-0.1	-	-	102.6	0.5	-	-	104.2	1.6	-	-
1984	100.6	-3.5	-	-	101.8	1.2	-	-	100.2	-1.6	-	-	102.1	1.9	-	-	105.4	3.2	-	-	102.4	-2.8	-	-
1985	101.2	-1.2	-	-	106.5	5.2	-	-	105.8	-0.7	-	-	103.3	-2.4	-	-	108.4	4.9	-	-	106.9	-1.4	-	-
1986	105.0	-1.8	-	-	109.6	4.4	-	-	107.0	-2.4	-	-	108.2	1.1	-	-	108.9	0.6	-	-	109.4	0.5	108.2	-1.1
1987	-	-	-	-	-	-	-	-	-	-	114.6	5.9	-	-	-	-	-	-	-	-	-	-	117.3	2.4
1988	-	-	-	-	-	-	-	-	-	-	116.3	-0.9	-	-	-	-	-	-	-	-	-	-	116.3	0.0
1989	-	-	-	-	-	-	-	-	-	-	119.6	2.8	-	-	-	-	-	-	-	-	-	-	121.0	1.2
1990	-	-	-	-	-	-	-	-	-	-	125.5	3.7	-	-	-	-	-	-	-	-	-	-	126.0	0.4
1991	-	-	-	-	-	-	-	-	-	-	122.3	-2.9	-	-	-	-	-	-	-	-	-	-	128.7	5.2
1992	-	-	-	-	-	-	-	-	-	-	131.1	1.9	-	-	-	-	-	-	-	-	-	-	128.6	-1.9
1993	-	-	-	-	-	-	-	-	-	-	127.9	-0.5	-	-	-	-	-	-	-	-	-	-	-	-

Source: U.S. Department of Labor, Bureau of Labor Statistics, Division of Consumer Prices and Price Indexes. - indicates no data collected for period.

Anchorage, AK
Consumer Price Index - All Urban Consumers
Base 1982-1984 = 100
Transportation

For 1971-1993. Columns headed % show percentile change in the index from the previous period for which an index is available.

Year	Jan Index	%	Feb Index	%	Mar Index	%	Apr Index	%	May Index	%	Jun Index	%	Jul Index	%	Aug Index	%	Sep Index	%	Oct Index	%	Nov Index	%	Dec Index	%
1971	40.3	-	-	-	-	-	40.6	0.7	-	-	-	-	41.2	1.5	-	-	-	-	40.8	-1.0	-	-	-	-
1972	40.7	-0.2	-	-	-	-	40.6	-0.2	-	-	-	-	41.0	1.0	-	-	-	-	41.2	0.5	-	-	-	-
1973	41.0	-0.5	-	-	-	-	41.1	0.2	-	-	-	-	41.6	1.2	-	-	-	-	41.5	-0.2	-	-	-	-
1974	42.0	1.2	-	-	-	-	43.3	3.1	-	-	-	-	45.6	5.3	-	-	-	-	46.9	2.9	-	-	-	-
1975	46.8	-0.2	-	-	-	-	48.0	2.6	-	-	-	-	50.1	4.4	-	-	-	-	50.7	1.2	-	-	-	-
1976	51.5	1.6	-	-	-	-	53.8	4.5	-	-	-	-	55.4	3.0	-	-	-	-	57.0	2.9	-	-	-	-
1977	57.1	0.2	-	-	-	-	59.8	4.7	-	-	-	-	61.6	3.0	-	-	-	-	60.9	-1.1	-	-	-	-
1978	61.6	1.1	-	-	61.9	0.5	-	-	64.2	3.7	-	-	65.5	2.0	-	-	65.7	0.3	-	-	66.8	1.7	-	-
1979	67.3	0.7	-	-	67.7	0.6	-	-	69.7	3.0	-	-	72.1	3.4	-	-	73.9	2.5	-	-	74.9	1.4	-	-
1980	77.1	2.9	-	-	79.6	3.2	-	-	80.8	1.5	-	-	82.3	1.9	-	-	84.0	2.1	-	-	86.7	3.2	-	-
1981	87.7	1.2	-	-	89.7	2.3	-	-	92.1	2.7	-	-	93.6	1.6	-	-	95.0	1.5	-	-	96.0	1.1	-	-
1982	95.7	-0.3	-	-	95.8	0.1	-	-	95.8	0.0	-	-	97.3	1.6	-	-	97.8	0.5	-	-	98.1	0.3	-	-
1983	97.6	-0.5	-	-	95.8	-1.8	-	-	97.1	1.4	-	-	98.3	1.2	-	-	99.4	1.1	-	-	101.9	2.5	-	-
1984	101.6	-0.3	-	-	102.6	1.0	-	-	104.3	1.7	-	-	105.0	0.7	-	-	106.0	1.0	-	-	107.0	0.9	-	-
1985	107.2	0.2	-	-	107.4	0.2	-	-	107.6	0.2	-	-	107.5	-0.1	-	-	107.9	0.4	-	-	110.6	2.5	-	-
1986	111.1	0.5	-	-	110.8	-0.3	-	-	107.1	-3.3	-	-	105.5	-1.5	-	-	105.0	-0.5	-	-	108.1	3.0	107.9	-0.2
1987	-	-	-	-	-	-	-	-	-	-	109.8	1.8	-	-	-	-	-	-	-	-	-	-	112.8	2.7
1988	-	-	-	-	-	-	-	-	-	-	112.2	-0.5	-	-	-	-	-	-	-	-	-	-	113.8	1.4
1989	-	-	-	-	-	-	-	-	-	-	116.3	2.2	-	-	-	-	-	-	-	-	-	-	117.1	0.7
1990	-	-	-	-	-	-	-	-	-	-	118.4	1.1	-	-	-	-	-	-	-	-	-	-	123.1	4.0
1991	-	-	-	-	-	-	-	-	-	-	123.4	0.2	-	-	-	-	-	-	-	-	-	-	120.0	-2.8
1992	-	-	-	-	-	-	-	-	-	-	122.7	2.2	-	-	-	-	-	-	-	-	-	-	123.8	0.9
1993	-	-	-	-	-	-	-	-	-	-	126.7	2.3	-	-	-	-	-	-	-	-	-	-	-	-

Source: U.S. Department of Labor, Bureau of Labor Statistics, Division of Consumer Prices and Price Indexes. - indicates no data collected for period.

Anchorage, AK
Consumer Price Index - Urban Wage Earners
Base 1982-1984 = 100
Transportation

For 1971-1993. Columns headed % show percentile change in the index from the previous period for which an index is available.

Year	Jan Index	%	Feb Index	%	Mar Index	%	Apr Index	%	May Index	%	Jun Index	%	Jul Index	%	Aug Index	%	Sep Index	%	Oct Index	%	Nov Index	%	Dec Index	%
1971	39.9	-	-	-	-	-	40.2	0.8	-	-	-	-	40.8	1.5	-	-	-	-	40.4	-1.0	-	-	-	-
1972	40.3	-0.2	-	-	-	-	40.2	-0.2	-	-	-	-	40.6	1.0	-	-	-	-	40.8	0.5	-	-	-	-
1973	40.6	-0.5	-	-	-	-	40.7	0.2	-	-	-	-	41.2	1.2	-	-	-	-	41.1	-0.2	-	-	-	-
1974	41.6	1.2	-	-	-	-	42.9	3.1	-	-	-	-	45.1	5.1	-	-	-	-	46.4	2.9	-	-	-	-
1975	46.3	-0.2	-	-	-	-	47.5	2.6	-	-	-	-	49.6	4.4	-	-	-	-	50.1	1.0	-	-	-	-
1976	51.0	1.8	-	-	-	-	53.2	4.3	-	-	-	-	54.8	3.0	-	-	-	-	56.4	2.9	-	-	-	-
1977	56.5	0.2	-	-	-	-	59.2	4.8	-	-	-	-	60.9	2.9	-	-	-	-	60.2	-1.1	-	-	-	-
1978	61.0	1.3	-	-	61.3	0.5	-	-	63.8	4.1	-	-	65.2	2.2	-	-	65.3	0.2	-	-	66.5	1.8	-	-
1979	66.9	0.6	-	-	67.4	0.7	-	-	69.5	3.1	-	-	72.0	3.6	-	-	73.8	2.5	-	-	74.7	1.2	-	-
1980	77.4	3.6	-	-	80.2	3.6	-	-	81.7	1.9	-	-	83.2	1.8	-	-	84.8	1.9	-	-	87.4	3.1	-	-
1981	88.3	1.0	-	-	90.3	2.3	-	-	92.9	2.9	-	-	94.5	1.7	-	-	95.8	1.4	-	-	96.8	1.0	-	-
1982	96.5	-0.3	-	-	96.5	0.0	-	-	96.2	-0.3	-	-	97.9	1.8	-	-	98.1	0.2	-	-	98.5	0.4	-	-
1983	97.7	-0.8	-	-	95.7	-2.0	-	-	96.8	1.1	-	-	98.2	1.4	-	-	99.3	1.1	-	-	101.7	2.4	-	-
1984	101.6	-0.1	-	-	102.3	0.7	-	-	104.0	1.7	-	-	104.7	0.7	-	-	105.5	0.8	-	-	106.5	0.9	-	-
1985	106.6	0.1	-	-	106.7	0.1	-	-	107.0	0.3	-	-	106.8	-0.2	-	-	107.2	0.4	-	-	110.1	2.7	-	-
1986	110.5	0.4	-	-	109.8	-0.6	-	-	105.7	-3.7	-	-	104.0	-1.6	-	-	103.5	-0.5	-	-	106.8	3.2	106.6	-0.2
1987	-	-	-	-	-	-	-	-	-	-	108.0	1.3	-	-	-	-	-	-	-	-	-	-	111.1	2.9
1988	-	-	-	-	-	-	-	-	-	-	110.4	-0.6	-	-	-	-	-	-	-	-	-	-	111.7	1.2
1989	-	-	-	-	-	-	-	-	-	-	114.1	2.1	-	-	-	-	-	-	-	-	-	-	115.0	0.8
1990	-	-	-	-	-	-	-	-	-	-	116.1	1.0	-	-	-	-	-	-	-	-	-	-	120.9	4.1
1991	-	-	-	-	-	-	-	-	-	-	120.8	-0.1	-	-	-	-	-	-	-	-	-	-	118.0	-2.3
1992	-	-	-	-	-	-	-	-	-	-	120.4	2.0	-	-	-	-	-	-	-	-	-	-	122.8	2.0
1993	-	-	-	-	-	-	-	-	-	-	125.2	2.0	-	-	-	-	-	-	-	-	-	-	-	-

Source: U.S. Department of Labor, Bureau of Labor Statistics, Division of Consumer Prices and Price Indexes. - indicates no data collected for period.

237

Anchorage, AK
Consumer Price Index - All Urban Consumers
Base 1982-1984 = 100
Medical Care

For 1971-1993. Columns headed % show percentile change in the index from the previous period for which an index is available.

Year	Jan Index	%	Feb Index	%	Mar Index	%	Apr Index	%	May Index	%	Jun Index	%	Jul Index	%	Aug Index	%	Sep Index	%	Oct Index	%	Nov Index	%	Dec Index	%
1971	34.4	-	-	-	-	-	35.0	1.7	-	-	-	-	35.1	0.3	-	-	-	-	35.5	1.1	-	-	-	-
1972	35.7	0.6	-	-	-	-	35.7	0.0	-	-	-	-	35.7	0.0	-	-	-	-	36.1	1.1	-	-	-	-
1973	36.2	0.3	-	-	-	-	36.5	0.8	-	-	-	-	37.3	2.2	-	-	-	-	38.3	2.7	-	-	-	-
1974	38.7	1.0	-	-	-	-	39.7	2.6	-	-	-	-	41.9	5.5	-	-	-	-	43.6	4.1	-	-	-	-
1975	44.7	2.5	-	-	-	-	45.6	2.0	-	-	-	-	47.0	3.1	-	-	-	-	48.3	2.8	-	-	-	-
1976	49.9	3.3	-	-	-	-	51.1	2.4	-	-	-	-	53.3	4.3	-	-	-	-	54.1	1.5	-	-	-	-
1977	55.4	2.4	-	-	-	-	57.0	2.9	-	-	-	-	58.1	1.9	-	-	-	-	59.0	1.5	-	-	-	-
1978	62.0	5.1	-	-	62.1	0.2	-	-	-	-	62.2	0.2	63.5	2.1	-	-	64.7	1.9	-	-	64.8	0.2	-	-
1979	67.9	4.8	-	-	67.6	-0.4	-	-	69.4	2.7	-	-	69.2	-0.3	-	-	69.4	0.3	-	-	69.8	0.6	-	-
1980	73.4	5.2	-	-	77.4	5.4	-	-	79.0	2.1	-	-	79.8	1.0	-	-	80.2	0.5	-	-	80.9	0.9	-	-
1981	82.7	2.2	-	-	84.7	2.4	-	-	87.2	3.0	-	-	87.7	0.6	-	-	87.5	-0.2	-	-	89.0	1.7	-	-
1982	92.9	4.4	-	-	92.9	0.0	-	-	93.6	0.8	-	-	95.2	1.7	-	-	96.1	0.9	-	-	96.7	0.6	-	-
1983	99.0	2.4	-	-	99.2	0.2	-	-	99.0	-0.2	-	-	99.6	0.6	-	-	100.0	0.4	-	-	100.0	0.0	-	-
1984	103.7	3.7	-	-	104.7	1.0	-	-	104.8	0.1	-	-	105.6	0.8	-	-	106.7	1.0	-	-	106.7	0.0	-	-
1985	107.2	0.5	-	-	108.5	1.2	-	-	108.8	0.3	-	-	112.8	3.7	-	-	112.9	0.1	-	-	113.5	0.5	-	-
1986	115.0	1.3	-	-	118.2	2.8	-	-	119.1	0.8	-	-	137.2	15.2	-	-	137.3	0.1	-	-	137.7	0.3	131.5	-4.5
1987	-	-	-	-	-	-	-	-	-	-	135.0	2.7	-	-	-	-	-	-	-	-	-	-	139.1	3.0
1988	-	-	-	-	-	-	-	-	-	-	143.0	2.8	-	-	-	-	-	-	-	-	-	-	148.6	3.9
1989	-	-	-	-	-	-	-	-	-	-	153.1	3.0	-	-	-	-	-	-	-	-	-	-	155.7	1.7
1990	-	-	-	-	-	-	-	-	-	-	160.1	2.8	-	-	-	-	-	-	-	-	-	-	162.3	1.4
1991	-	-	-	-	-	-	-	-	-	-	170.1	4.8	-	-	-	-	-	-	-	-	-	-	176.9	4.0
1992	-	-	-	-	-	-	-	-	-	-	181.5	2.6	-	-	-	-	-	-	-	-	-	-	184.6	1.7
1993	-	-	-	-	-	-	-	-	-	-	188.5	2.1	-	-	-	-	-	-	-	-	-	-	-	-

Source: U.S. Department of Labor, Bureau of Labor Statistics, Division of Consumer Prices and Price Indexes. - indicates no data collected for period.

Anchorage, AK
Consumer Price Index - Urban Wage Earners
Base 1982-1984 = 100
Medical Care

For 1971-1993. Columns headed % show percentile change in the index from the previous period for which an index is available.

Year	Jan Index	%	Feb Index	%	Mar Index	%	Apr Index	%	May Index	%	Jun Index	%	Jul Index	%	Aug Index	%	Sep Index	%	Oct Index	%	Nov Index	%	Dec Index	%
1971	35.4	-	-	-	-	-	36.1	2.0	-	-	-	-	36.1	0.0	-	-	-	-	36.6	1.4	-	-	-	-
1972	36.8	0.5	-	-	-	-	36.8	0.0	-	-	-	-	36.8	0.0	-	-	-	-	37.2	1.1	-	-	-	-
1973	37.3	0.3	-	-	-	-	37.6	0.8	-	-	-	-	38.4	2.1	-	-	-	-	39.5	2.9	-	-	-	-
1974	39.8	0.8	-	-	-	-	40.9	2.8	-	-	-	-	43.2	5.6	-	-	-	-	44.9	3.9	-	-	-	-
1975	46.1	2.7	-	-	-	-	47.0	2.0	-	-	-	-	48.4	3.0	-	-	-	-	49.8	2.9	-	-	-	-
1976	51.4	3.2	-	-	-	-	52.6	2.3	-	-	-	-	54.9	4.4	-	-	-	-	55.7	1.5	-	-	-	-
1977	57.0	2.3	-	-	-	-	58.8	3.2	-	-	-	-	59.9	1.9	-	-	-	-	60.7	1.3	-	-	-	-
1978	63.9	5.3	-	-	66.0	3.3	-	-	66.1	0.2	-	-	66.4	0.5	-	-	67.6	1.8	-	-	70.5	4.3	-	-
1979	72.7	3.1	-	-	72.3	-0.6	-	-	72.4	0.1	-	-	72.8	0.6	-	-	72.9	0.1	-	-	73.3	0.5	-	-
1980	75.0	2.3	-	-	77.5	3.3	-	-	79.0	1.9	-	-	80.4	1.8	-	-	80.9	0.6	-	-	80.9	0.0	-	-
1981	82.9	2.5	-	-	84.6	2.1	-	-	86.6	2.4	-	-	87.4	0.9	-	-	87.6	0.2	-	-	89.3	1.9	-	-
1982	92.7	3.8	-	-	92.8	0.1	-	-	93.7	1.0	-	-	95.3	1.7	-	-	96.4	1.2	-	-	97.0	0.6	-	-
1983	99.1	2.2	-	-	99.3	0.2	-	-	99.0	-0.3	-	-	99.8	0.8	-	-	100.3	0.5	-	-	100.3	0.0	-	-
1984	103.3	3.0	-	-	104.5	1.2	-	-	104.6	0.1	-	-	105.4	0.8	-	-	106.6	1.1	-	-	106.4	-0.2	-	-
1985	106.8	0.4	-	-	108.2	1.3	-	-	108.5	0.3	-	-	112.3	3.5	-	-	112.4	0.1	-	-	113.1	0.6	-	-
1986	114.4	1.1	-	-	117.8	3.0	-	-	118.7	0.8	-	-	132.8	11.9	-	-	132.8	0.0	-	-	133.3	0.4	128.4	-3.7
1987	-	-	-	-	-	-	-	-	-	-	131.8	2.6	-	-	-	-	-	-	-	-	-	-	135.6	2.9
1988	-	-	-	-	-	-	-	-	-	-	139.7	3.0	-	-	-	-	-	-	-	-	-	-	144.6	3.5
1989	-	-	-	-	-	-	-	-	-	-	149.4	3.3	-	-	-	-	-	-	-	-	-	-	152.4	2.0
1990	-	-	-	-	-	-	-	-	-	-	156.9	3.0	-	-	-	-	-	-	-	-	-	-	158.9	1.3
1991	-	-	-	-	-	-	-	-	-	-	166.6	4.8	-	-	-	-	-	-	-	-	-	-	172.8	3.7
1992	-	-	-	-	-	-	-	-	-	-	177.1	2.5	-	-	-	-	-	-	-	-	-	-	179.9	1.6
1993	-	-	-	-	-	-	-	-	-	-	184.5	2.6	-	-	-	-	-	-	-	-	-	-	-	-

Source: U.S. Department of Labor, Bureau of Labor Statistics, Division of Consumer Prices and Price Indexes. - indicates no data collected for period.

Anchorage, AK
Consumer Price Index - All Urban Consumers
Base 1982-1984 = 100
Entertainment

For 1976-1993. Columns headed % show percentile change in the index from the previous period for which an index is available.

Year	Jan Index	%	Feb Index	%	Mar Index	%	Apr Index	%	May Index	%	Jun Index	%	Jul Index	%	Aug Index	%	Sep Index	%	Oct Index	%	Nov Index	%	Dec Index	%
1976	60.6	-	-	-	-	-	64.3	6.1	-	-	-	-	64.6	0.5	-	-	-	-	66.0	2.2	-	-	-	-
1977	66.5	0.8	-	-	-	-	69.0	3.8	-	-	-	-	70.0	1.4	-	-	-	-	70.6	0.9	-	-	-	-
1978	70.2	-0.6	-	-	72.2	2.8	-	-	72.9	1.0	-	-	71.9	-1.4	-	-	74.1	3.1	-	-	73.6	-0.7	-	-
1979	73.7	0.1	-	-	73.8	0.1	-	-	73.3	-0.7	-	-	73.5	0.3	-	-	75.8	3.1	-	-	76.3	0.7	-	-
1980	77.5	1.6	-	-	78.8	1.7	-	-	81.7	3.7	-	-	76.4	-6.5	-	-	79.6	4.2	-	-	79.3	-0.4	-	-
1981	80.5	1.5	-	-	82.0	1.9	-	-	85.2	3.9	-	-	85.6	0.5	-	-	87.2	1.9	-	-	91.6	5.0	-	-
1982	92.8	1.3	-	-	92.6	-0.2	-	-	94.1	1.6	-	-	94.9	0.9	-	-	94.5	-0.4	-	-	97.8	3.5	-	-
1983	99.1	1.3	-	-	101.0	1.9	-	-	99.3	-1.7	-	-	99.7	0.4	-	-	101.4	1.7	-	-	102.6	1.2	-	-
1984	102.0	-0.6	-	-	103.4	1.4	-	-	103.4	0.0	-	-	105.5	2.0	-	-	106.5	0.9	-	-	106.0	-0.5	-	-
1985	106.4	0.4	-	-	108.6	2.1	-	-	106.9	-1.6	-	-	109.5	2.4	-	-	109.1	-0.4	-	-	112.2	2.8	-	-
1986	109.5	-2.4	-	-	111.4	1.7	-	-	110.2	-1.1	-	-	113.4	2.9	-	-	114.5	1.0	-	-	114.8	0.3	113.1	-1.5
1987	-	-	-	-	-	-	-	-	-	-	115.2	1.9	-	-	-	-	-	-	-	-	-	-	117.7	2.2
1988	-	-	-	-	-	-	-	-	-	-	119.8	1.8	-	-	-	-	-	-	-	-	-	-	120.4	0.5
1989	-	-	-	-	-	-	-	-	-	-	126.4	5.0	-	-	-	-	-	-	-	-	-	-	130.0	2.8
1990	-	-	-	-	-	-	-	-	-	-	136.9	5.3	-	-	-	-	-	-	-	-	-	-	146.8	7.2
1991	-	-	-	-	-	-	-	-	-	-	148.1	0.9	-	-	-	-	-	-	-	-	-	-	149.4	0.9
1992	-	-	-	-	-	-	-	-	-	-	150.0	0.4	-	-	-	-	-	-	-	-	-	-	152.0	1.3
1993	-	-	-	-	-	-	-	-	-	-	157.1	3.4	-	-	-	-	-	-	-	-	-	-	-	-

Source: U.S. Department of Labor, Bureau of Labor Statistics, Division of Consumer Prices and Price Indexes. - indicates no data collected for period.

Anchorage, AK
Consumer Price Index - Urban Wage Earners
Base 1982-1984 = 100
Entertainment

For 1976-1993. Columns headed % show percentile change in the index from the previous period for which an index is available.

Year	Jan Index	%	Feb Index	%	Mar Index	%	Apr Index	%	May Index	%	Jun Index	%	Jul Index	%	Aug Index	%	Sep Index	%	Oct Index	%	Nov Index	%	Dec Index	%
1976	66.4	-	-	-	-	-	70.4	6.0	-	-	-	-	70.7	0.4	-	-	-	-	72.3	2.3	-	-	-	-
1977	72.8	0.7	-	-	-	-	75.6	3.8	-	-	-	-	76.7	1.5	-	-	-	-	77.3	0.8	-	-	-	-
1978	76.9	-0.5	-	-	77.2	0.4	-	-	74.7	-3.2	-	-	74.9	0.3	-	-	76.2	1.7	-	-	76.1	-0.1	-	-
1979	76.6	0.7	-	-	76.6	0.0	-	-	76.1	-0.7	-	-	75.8	-0.4	-	-	77.6	2.4	-	-	78.6	1.3	-	-
1980	80.0	1.8	-	-	81.5	1.9	-	-	82.7	1.5	-	-	76.9	-7.0	-	-	78.9	2.6	-	-	79.6	0.9	-	-
1981	79.7	0.1	-	-	82.0	2.9	-	-	85.6	4.4	-	-	86.7	1.3	-	-	88.6	2.2	-	-	91.4	3.2	-	-
1982	92.8	1.5	-	-	92.4	-0.4	-	-	94.0	1.7	-	-	95.0	1.1	-	-	94.3	-0.7	-	-	97.5	3.4	-	-
1983	99.1	1.6	-	-	100.7	1.6	-	-	99.2	-1.5	-	-	99.7	0.5	-	-	101.1	1.4	-	-	102.3	1.2	-	-
1984	102.2	-0.1	-	-	103.4	1.2	-	-	103.6	0.2	-	-	106.2	2.5	-	-	107.0	0.8	-	-	106.3	-0.7	-	-
1985	106.4	0.1	-	-	108.3	1.8	-	-	106.9	-1.3	-	-	109.2	2.2	-	-	108.7	-0.5	-	-	111.9	2.9	-	-
1986	109.7	-2.0	-	-	110.8	1.0	-	-	110.1	-0.6	-	-	113.9	3.5	-	-	114.8	0.8	-	-	115.2	0.3	113.7	-1.3
1987	-	-	-	-	-	-	-	-	-	-	116.7	2.6	-	-	-	-	-	-	-	-	-	-	119.6	2.5
1988	-	-	-	-	-	-	-	-	-	-	121.2	1.3	-	-	-	-	-	-	-	-	-	-	122.3	0.9
1989	-	-	-	-	-	-	-	-	-	-	129.2	5.6	-	-	-	-	-	-	-	-	-	-	133.8	3.6
1990	-	-	-	-	-	-	-	-	-	-	141.1	5.5	-	-	-	-	-	-	-	-	-	-	151.7	7.5
1991	-	-	-	-	-	-	-	-	-	-	154.4	1.8	-	-	-	-	-	-	-	-	-	-	155.2	0.5
1992	-	-	-	-	-	-	-	-	-	-	157.2	1.3	-	-	-	-	-	-	-	-	-	-	158.9	1.1
1993	-	-	-	-	-	-	-	-	-	-	163.1	2.6	-	-	-	-	-	-	-	-	-	-	-	-

Source: U.S. Department of Labor, Bureau of Labor Statistics, Division of Consumer Prices and Price Indexes. - indicates no data collected for period.

Anchorage, AK
Consumer Price Index - All Urban Consumers
Base 1982-1984 = 100
Other Goods and Services

For 1976-1993. Columns headed % show percentile change in the index from the previous period for which an index is available.

Year	Jan Index	%	Feb Index	%	Mar Index	%	Apr Index	%	May Index	%	Jun Index	%	Jul Index	%	Aug Index	%	Sep Index	%	Oct Index	%	Nov Index	%	Dec Index	%
1976	60.9	-	-	-	-	-	63.2	3.8	-	-	-	-	63.8	0.9	-	-	-	-	65.0	1.9	-	-	-	-
1977	67.3	3.5	-	-	-	-	67.5	0.3	-	-	-	-	68.2	1.0	-	-	-	-	68.8	0.9	-	-	-	-
1978	69.5	1.0	-	-	70.0	0.7	-	-	71.1	1.6	-	-	71.5	0.6	-	-	73.3	2.5	-	-	73.5	0.3	-	-
1979	74.1	0.8	-	-	75.4	1.8	-	-	76.2	1.1	-	-	76.1	-0.1	-	-	78.8	3.5	-	-	78.9	0.1	-	-
1980	80.5	2.0	-	-	80.9	0.5	-	-	82.7	2.2	-	-	83.3	0.7	-	-	84.7	1.7	-	-	85.0	0.4	-	-
1981	86.3	1.5	-	-	85.9	-0.5	-	-	87.7	2.1	-	-	88.0	0.3	-	-	89.5	1.7	-	-	90.4	1.0	-	-
1982	89.9	-0.6	-	-	92.1	2.4	-	-	92.5	0.4	-	-	92.9	0.4	-	-	94.6	1.8	-	-	95.3	0.7	-	-
1983	98.1	2.9	-	-	99.3	1.2	-	-	100.9	1.6	-	-	102.5	1.6	-	-	103.2	0.7	-	-	103.8	0.6	-	-
1984	103.2	-0.6	-	-	104.6	1.4	-	-	105.1	0.5	-	-	105.5	0.4	-	-	106.7	1.1	-	-	105.4	-1.2	-	-
1985	108.4	2.8	-	-	110.9	2.3	-	-	111.3	0.4	-	-	112.0	0.6	-	-	118.0	5.4	-	-	121.8	3.2	-	-
1986	119.6	-1.8	-	-	121.0	1.2	-	-	121.7	0.6	-	-	121.9	0.2	-	-	126.5	3.8	-	-	126.6	0.1	126.9	0.2
1987	-	-	-	-	-	-	-	-	-	-	130.7	3.0	-	-	-	-	-	-	-	-	-	-	133.7	2.3
1988	-	-	-	-	-	-	-	-	-	-	136.4	2.0	-	-	-	-	-	-	-	-	-	-	139.9	2.6
1989	-	-	-	-	-	-	-	-	-	-	141.0	0.8	-	-	-	-	-	-	-	-	-	-	146.3	3.8
1990	-	-	-	-	-	-	-	-	-	-	154.9	5.9	-	-	-	-	-	-	-	-	-	-	156.5	1.0
1991	-	-	-	-	-	-	-	-	-	-	164.6	5.2	-	-	-	-	-	-	-	-	-	-	169.2	2.8
1992	-	-	-	-	-	-	-	-	-	-	172.5	2.0	-	-	-	-	-	-	-	-	-	-	177.9	3.1
1993	-	-	-	-	-	-	-	-	-	-	180.5	1.5	-	-	-	-	-	-	-	-	-	-	-	-

Source: U.S. Department of Labor, Bureau of Labor Statistics, Division of Consumer Prices and Price Indexes. - indicates no data collected for period.

Anchorage, AK
Consumer Price Index - Urban Wage Earners
Base 1982-1984 = 100
Other Goods and Services

For 1976-1993. Columns headed % show percentile change in the index from the previous period for which an index is available.

Year	Jan Index	%	Feb Index	%	Mar Index	%	Apr Index	%	May Index	%	Jun Index	%	Jul Index	%	Aug Index	%	Sep Index	%	Oct Index	%	Nov Index	%	Dec Index	%
1976	59.8	-	-	-	-	-	62.1	3.8	-	-	-	-	62.6	0.8	-	-	-	-	63.8	1.9	-	-	-	-
1977	66.0	3.4	-	-	-	-	66.3	0.5	-	-	-	-	67.0	1.1	-	-	-	-	67.5	0.7	-	-	-	-
1978	68.2	1.0	-	-	68.7	0.7	-	-	69.5	1.2	-	-	70.4	1.3	-	-	71.5	1.6	-	-	71.4	-0.1	-	-
1979	72.1	1.0	-	-	73.5	1.9	-	-	73.6	0.1	-	-	75.0	1.9	-	-	76.5	2.0	-	-	77.7	1.6	-	-
1980	78.8	1.4	-	-	80.3	1.9	-	-	82.1	2.2	-	-	82.6	0.6	-	-	82.5	-0.1	-	-	83.4	1.1	-	-
1981	84.8	1.7	-	-	83.9	-1.1	-	-	85.5	1.9	-	-	85.8	0.4	-	-	88.0	2.6	-	-	89.2	1.4	-	-
1982	88.7	-0.6	-	-	91.4	3.0	-	-	91.5	0.1	-	-	92.0	0.5	-	-	93.8	2.0	-	-	94.7	1.0	-	-
1983	98.0	3.5	-	-	99.2	1.2	-	-	101.2	2.0	-	-	103.1	1.9	-	-	104.0	0.9	-	-	104.5	0.5	-	-
1984	104.0	-0.5	-	-	105.4	1.3	-	-	106.0	0.6	-	-	106.5	0.5	-	-	106.4	-0.1	-	-	104.9	-1.4	-	-
1985	108.4	3.3	-	-	111.4	2.8	-	-	111.8	0.4	-	-	112.7	0.8	-	-	116.4	3.3	-	-	120.9	3.9	-	-
1986	120.0	-0.7	-	-	121.8	1.5	-	-	122.5	0.6	-	-	122.6	0.1	-	-	125.2	2.1	-	-	125.4	0.2	125.8	0.3
1987	-	-	-	-	-	-	-	-	-	-	129.6	3.0	-	-	-	-	-	-	-	-	-	-	132.5	2.2
1988	-	-	-	-	-	-	-	-	-	-	135.4	2.2	-	-	-	-	-	-	-	-	-	-	139.2	2.8
1989	-	-	-	-	-	-	-	-	-	-	140.7	1.1	-	-	-	-	-	-	-	-	-	-	147.1	4.5
1990	-	-	-	-	-	-	-	-	-	-	157.4	7.0	-	-	-	-	-	-	-	-	-	-	159.3	1.2
1991	-	-	-	-	-	-	-	-	-	-	168.3	5.6	-	-	-	-	-	-	-	-	-	-	173.3	3.0
1992	-	-	-	-	-	-	-	-	-	-	176.5	1.8	-	-	-	-	-	-	-	-	-	-	182.9	3.6
1993	-	-	-	-	-	-	-	-	-	-	185.7	1.5	-	-	-	-	-	-	-	-	-	-	-	-

Source: U.S. Department of Labor, Bureau of Labor Statistics, Division of Consumer Prices and Price Indexes. - indicates no data collected for period.

Atlanta, GA
Consumer Price Index - All Urban Consumers
Base 1982-1984 = 100
Annual Averages

For 1917-1993. Columns headed % show percentile change in the index from the previous period for which an index is available.

Year	All Items		Food & Beverage		Housing		Apparel & Upkeep		Trans-portation		Medical Care		Entertain-ment		Other Goods & Services	
	Index	%	Index	%	Index	%	Index	%	Index	%	Index	%	Index	%	Index	%
1917	-	-	-	-	-	-	-	-	-	-	-	-	-	-	-	-
1918	16.6	-	-	-	-	-	-	-	-	-	-	-	-	-	-	-
1919	19.3	16.3	-	-	-	-	-	-	-	-	-	-	-	-	-	-
1920	21.9	13.5	-	-	-	-	-	-	-	-	-	-	-	-	-	-
1921	19.0	-13.2	-	-	-	-	-	-	-	-	-	-	-	-	-	-
1922	17.5	-7.9	-	-	-	-	-	-	-	-	-	-	-	-	-	-
1923	17.6	0.6	-	-	-	-	-	-	-	-	-	-	-	-	-	-
1924	17.3	-1.7	-	-	-	-	-	-	-	-	-	-	-	-	-	-
1925	17.9	3.5	-	-	-	-	-	-	-	-	-	-	-	-	-	-
1926	18.1	1.1	-	-	-	-	-	-	-	-	-	-	-	-	-	-
1927	17.5	-3.3	-	-	-	-	-	-	-	-	-	-	-	-	-	-
1928	17.3	-1.1	-	-	-	-	-	-	-	-	-	-	-	-	-	-
1929	17.2	-0.6	-	-	-	-	-	-	-	-	-	-	-	-	-	-
1930	16.5	-4.1	-	-	-	-	-	-	-	-	-	-	-	-	-	-
1931	14.9	-9.7	-	-	-	-	-	-	-	-	-	-	-	-	-	-
1932	13.3	-10.7	-	-	-	-	-	-	-	-	-	-	-	-	-	-
1933	12.6	-5.3	-	-	-	-	-	-	-	-	-	-	-	-	-	-
1934	13.2	4.8	-	-	-	-	-	-	-	-	-	-	-	-	-	-
1935	13.5	2.3	-	-	-	-	-	-	-	-	-	-	-	-	-	-
1936	13.7	1.5	-	-	-	-	-	-	-	-	-	-	-	-	-	-
1937	14.1	2.9	-	-	-	-	-	-	-	-	-	-	-	-	-	-
1938	13.7	-2.8	-	-	-	-	-	-	-	-	-	-	-	-	-	-
1939	13.6	-0.7	-	-	-	-	-	-	-	-	-	-	-	-	-	-
1940	13.6	0.0	-	-	-	-	-	-	-	-	-	-	-	-	-	-
1941	14.4	5.9	-	-	-	-	-	-	-	-	-	-	-	-	-	-
1942	15.9	10.4	-	-	-	-	-	-	-	-	-	-	-	-	-	-
1943	17.0	6.9	-	-	-	-	-	-	-	-	-	-	-	-	-	-
1944	17.3	1.8	-	-	-	-	-	-	-	-	-	-	-	-	-	-
1945	17.9	3.5	-	-	-	-	-	-	-	-	-	-	-	-	-	-
1946	19.3	7.8	-	-	-	-	-	-	-	-	15.2	-	-	-	-	-
1947	22.3	15.5	-	-	-	-	-	-	20.4	-	15.7	3.3	-	-	-	-
1948	23.8	6.7	-	-	-	-	-	-	22.4	9.8	16.1	2.5	-	-	-	-
1949	23.8	0.0	-	-	-	-	-	-	24.1	7.6	16.1	0.0	-	-	-	-
1950	24.1	1.3	-	-	-	-	-	-	24.6	2.1	16.9	5.0	-	-	-	-
1951	26.4	9.5	-	-	-	-	-	-	26.4	7.3	16.9	5.0	-	-	-	-
1952	27.0	2.3	-	-	-	-	-	-	28.1	6.4	18.1	7.1	-	-	-	-
1953	27.3	1.1	-	-	-	-	42.2	-	28.9	2.8	18.5	2.2	-	-	-	-
1954	27.2	-0.4	-	-	-	-	42.4	0.5	28.0	-3.1	18.9	2.2	-	-	-	-
1955	27.1	-0.4	-	-	-	-	42.1	-0.7	27.5	-1.8	19.6	3.7	-	-	-	-
1956	27.5	1.5	-	-	-	-	42.9	1.9	28.2	2.5	20.2	3.1	-	-	-	-
1957	28.3	2.9	-	-	-	-	43.7	1.9	30.0	6.4	20.7	2.5	-	-	-	-
1958	29.0	2.5	-	-	-	-	44.3	1.4	31.3	4.3	21.4	3.4	-	-	-	-
1959	29.2	0.7	-	-	-	-	44.3	0.0	32.4	3.5	22.3	4.2	-	-	-	-
1960	29.6	1.4	-	-	-	-	45.0	1.6	32.0	-1.2	23.0	3.1	-	-	-	-
1961	29.7	0.3	-	-	-	-	45.1	0.2	32.4	1.3	23.2	0.9	-	-	-	-

[Continued]

Atlanta, GA
Consumer Price Index - All Urban Consumers
Base 1982-1984 = 100
Annual Averages
[Continued]

For 1917-1993. Columns headed % show percentile change in the index from the previous period for which an index is available.

Year	All Items		Food & Beverage		Housing		Apparel & Upkeep		Trans- portation		Medical Care		Entertain- ment		Other Goods & Services	
	Index	%	Index	%	Index	%	Index	%	Index	%	Index	%	Index	%	Index	%
1962	30.0	1.0	-	-	-	-	45.1	0.0	33.1	2.2	23.9	3.0	-	-	-	-
1963	30.3	1.0	-	-	-	-	46.1	2.2	33.8	2.1	24.2	1.3	-	-	-	-
1964	30.8	1.7	-	-	-	-	46.2	0.2	34.7	2.7	24.8	2.5	-	-	-	-
1965	31.2	1.3	-	-	-	-	46.7	1.1	34.6	-0.3	25.4	2.4	-	-	-	-
1966	32.2	3.2	-	-	-	-	48.9	4.7	34.6	0.0	26.7	5.1	-	-	-	-
1967	33.2	3.1	-	-	-	-	51.6	5.5	35.2	1.7	28.4	6.4	-	-	-	-
1968	34.5	3.9	-	-	-	-	53.8	4.3	36.1	2.6	30.3	6.7	-	-	-	-
1969	36.5	5.8	-	-	-	-	56.0	4.1	37.3	3.3	33.3	9.9	-	-	-	-
1970	38.6	5.8	-	-	-	-	58.4	4.3	38.2	2.4	35.8	7.5	-	-	-	-
1971	40.4	4.7	-	-	-	-	59.9	2.6	40.6	6.3	38.6	7.8	-	-	-	-
1972	41.6	3.0	-	-	-	-	61.3	2.3	39.8	-2.0	39.6	2.6	-	-	-	-
1973	44.3	6.5	-	-	-	-	63.8	4.1	41.1	3.3	41.5	4.8	-	-	-	-
1974	49.2	11.1	-	-	-	-	69.1	8.3	46.5	13.1	46.1	11.1	-	-	-	-
1975	53.6	8.9	-	-	-	-	71.6	3.6	50.4	8.4	52.1	13.0	-	-	-	-
1976	56.1	4.7	62.5	-	51.9	-	74.3	3.8	54.2	7.5	56.0	7.5	77.2	-	55.4	-
1977	59.6	6.2	65.9	5.4	55.2	6.4	79.5	7.0	57.3	5.7	60.7	8.4	80.3	4.0	58.5	5.6
1978	63.9	7.2	72.2	9.6	59.8	8.3	84.0	5.7	59.6	4.0	63.8	5.1	83.8	4.4	62.7	7.2
1979	70.5	10.3	79.5	10.1	65.9	10.2	87.6	4.3	69.5	16.6	68.1	6.7	85.6	2.1	68.9	9.9
1980	80.3	13.9	85.8	7.9	76.1	15.5	93.1	6.3	84.8	22.0	74.7	9.7	88.7	3.6	75.6	9.7
1981	90.2	12.3	93.1	8.5	87.7	15.2	96.2	3.3	94.9	11.9	82.3	10.2	94.6	6.7	84.1	11.2
1982	96.0	6.4	97.1	4.3	95.4	8.8	96.8	0.6	97.5	2.7	92.6	12.5	97.8	3.4	91.7	9.0
1983	99.9	4.1	99.8	2.8	100.0	4.8	100.5	3.8	99.4	1.9	101.2	9.3	98.0	0.2	100.5	9.6
1984	104.1	4.2	103.1	3.3	104.6	4.6	102.7	2.2	103.0	3.6	106.2	4.9	104.1	6.2	107.9	7.4
1985	108.9	4.6	106.1	2.9	109.9	5.1	111.7	8.8	106.7	3.6	112.9	6.3	111.4	7.0	113.0	4.7
1986	112.2	3.0	111.2	4.8	115.2	4.8	110.4	-1.2	102.9	-3.6	123.7	9.6	118.7	6.6	119.8	6.0
1987	116.5	3.8	112.3	1.0	119.5	3.7	125.8	13.9	103.7	0.8	136.5	10.3	124.5	4.9	125.4	4.7
1988	120.4	3.3	117.4	4.5	122.6	2.6	129.2	2.7	105.6	1.8	150.1	10.0	128.8	3.5	129.3	3.1
1989	126.1	4.7	123.7	5.4	125.8	2.6	137.1	6.1	110.9	5.0	165.7	10.4	138.9	7.8	138.9	7.4
1990	131.7	4.4	131.9	6.6	128.8	2.4	133.8	-2.4	117.7	6.1	177.6	7.2	149.8	7.8	155.1	11.7
1991	135.9	3.2	135.3	2.6	130.6	1.4	148.4	10.9	118.7	0.8	191.6	7.9	156.7	4.6	166.5	7.4
1992	138.5	1.9	135.7	0.3	132.7	1.6	152.6	2.8	119.5	0.7	202.7	5.8	163.3	4.2	173.1	4.0
1993	143.4	3.5	139.6	2.9	136.6	2.9	158.0	3.5	124.2	3.9	213.0	5.1	172.1	5.4	181.3	4.7

Source: U.S. Department of Labor, Bureau of Labor Statistics, Division of Consumer Prices and Price Indexes. - indicates no data collected for period.

Atlanta, GA
Consumer Price Index - Urban Wage Earners
Base 1982-1984 = 100
Annual Averages

For 1917-1993. Columns headed % show percentile change in the index from the previous period for which an index is available.

Year	All Items		Food & Beverage		Housing		Apparel & Upkeep		Trans-portation		Medical Care		Entertain-ment		Other Goods & Services	
	Index	%	Index	%	Index	%	Index	%	Index	%	Index	%	Index	%	Index	%
1917	-	-	-	-	-	-	-	-	-	-	-	-	-	-	-	-
1918	16.6	-	-	-	-	-	-	-	-	-	-	-	-	-	-	-
1919	19.3	16.3	-	-	-	-	-	-	-	-	-	-	-	-	-	-
1920	21.8	13.0	-	-	-	-	-	-	-	-	-	-	-	-	-	-
1921	18.9	-13.3	-	-	-	-	-	-	-	-	-	-	-	-	-	-
1922	17.5	-7.4	-	-	-	-	-	-	-	-	-	-	-	-	-	-
1923	17.5	0.0	-	-	-	-	-	-	-	-	-	-	-	-	-	-
1924	17.3	-1.1	-	-	-	-	-	-	-	-	-	-	-	-	-	-
1925	17.8	2.9	-	-	-	-	-	-	-	-	-	-	-	-	-	-
1926	18.0	1.1	-	-	-	-	-	-	-	-	-	-	-	-	-	-
1927	17.5	-2.8	-	-	-	-	-	-	-	-	-	-	-	-	-	-
1928	17.3	-1.1	-	-	-	-	-	-	-	-	-	-	-	-	-	-
1929	17.2	-0.6	-	-	-	-	-	-	-	-	-	-	-	-	-	-
1930	16.5	-4.1	-	-	-	-	-	-	-	-	-	-	-	-	-	-
1931	14.8	-10.3	-	-	-	-	-	-	-	-	-	-	-	-	-	-
1932	13.2	-10.8	-	-	-	-	-	-	-	-	-	-	-	-	-	-
1933	12.6	-4.5	-	-	-	-	-	-	-	-	-	-	-	-	-	-
1934	13.2	4.8	-	-	-	-	-	-	-	-	-	-	-	-	-	-
1935	13.5	2.3	-	-	-	-	-	-	-	-	-	-	-	-	-	-
1936	13.7	1.5	-	-	-	-	-	-	-	-	-	-	-	-	-	-
1937	14.1	2.9	-	-	-	-	-	-	-	-	-	-	-	-	-	-
1938	13.7	-2.8	-	-	-	-	-	-	-	-	-	-	-	-	-	-
1939	13.6	-0.7	-	-	-	-	-	-	-	-	-	-	-	-	-	-
1940	13.6	0.0	-	-	-	-	-	-	-	-	-	-	-	-	-	-
1941	14.3	5.1	-	-	-	-	-	-	-	-	-	-	-	-	-	-
1942	15.9	11.2	-	-	-	-	-	-	-	-	-	-	-	-	-	-
1943	17.0	6.9	-	-	-	-	-	-	-	-	-	-	-	-	-	-
1944	17.3	1.8	-	-	-	-	-	-	-	-	-	-	-	-	-	-
1945	17.9	3.5	-	-	-	-	-	-	-	-	-	-	-	-	-	-
1946	19.2	7.3	-	-	-	-	-	-	-	-	-	-	-	-	-	-
1947	22.3	16.1	-	-	-	-	-	-	19.8	-	14.6	-	-	-	-	-
1948	23.7	6.3	-	-	-	-	-	-	21.8	10.1	15.1	3.4	-	-	-	-
1949	23.7	0.0	-	-	-	-	-	-	23.5	7.8	15.5	2.6	-	-	-	-
1950	24.0	1.3	-	-	-	-	-	-	24.0	2.1	15.5	0.0	-	-	-	-
1951	26.3	9.6	-	-	-	-	-	-	25.7	7.1	16.3	5.2	-	-	-	-
1952	27.0	2.7	-	-	-	-	-	-	27.4	6.6	17.4	6.7	-	-	-	-
1953	27.2	0.7	-	-	-	-	40.0	-	28.1	2.6	17.8	2.3	-	-	-	-
1954	27.1	-0.4	-	-	-	-	40.1	0.2	27.2	-3.2	18.2	2.2	-	-	-	-
1955	27.0	-0.4	-	-	-	-	39.9	-0.5	26.8	-1.5	18.8	3.3	-	-	-	-
1956	27.5	1.9	-	-	-	-	40.7	2.0	27.5	2.6	19.5	3.7	-	-	-	-
1957	28.2	2.5	-	-	-	-	41.5	2.0	29.2	6.2	19.9	2.1	-	-	-	-
1958	28.9	2.5	-	-	-	-	42.0	1.2	30.5	4.5	20.6	3.5	-	-	-	-
1959	29.1	0.7	-	-	-	-	42.0	0.0	31.5	3.3	21.5	4.4	-	-	-	-
1960	29.5	1.4	-	-	-	-	42.7	1.7	31.2	-1.0	22.1	2.8	-	-	-	-
1961	29.7	0.7	-	-	-	-	42.7	0.0	31.6	1.3	22.3	0.9	-	-	-	-

[Continued]

Atlanta, GA
Consumer Price Index - Urban Wage Earners
Base 1982-1984 = 100
Annual Averages
[Continued]

For 1917-1993. Columns headed % show percentile change in the index from the previous period for which an index is available.

Year	All Items		Food & Beverage		Housing		Apparel & Upkeep		Trans- portation		Medical Care		Entertain- ment		Other Goods & Services	
	Index	%	Index	%	Index	%	Index	%	Index	%	Index	%	Index	%	Index	%
1962	29.9	0.7	-	-	-	-	42.7	0.0	32.2	1.9	23.0	3.1	-	-	-	-
1963	30.2	1.0	-	-	-	-	43.7	2.3	32.9	2.2	23.3	1.3	-	-	-	-
1964	30.7	1.7	-	-	-	-	43.8	0.2	33.8	2.7	23.9	2.6	-	-	-	-
1965	31.1	1.3	-	-	-	-	44.3	1.1	33.7	-0.3	24.4	2.1	-	-	-	-
1966	32.1	3.2	-	-	-	-	46.4	4.7	33.7	0.0	25.7	5.3	-	-	-	-
1967	33.1	3.1	-	-	-	-	49.0	5.6	34.3	1.8	27.3	6.2	-	-	-	-
1968	34.4	3.9	-	-	-	-	51.0	4.1	35.1	2.3	29.1	6.6	-	-	-	-
1969	36.4	5.8	-	-	-	-	53.1	4.1	36.3	3.4	32.1	10.3	-	-	-	-
1970	38.5	5.8	-	-	-	-	55.3	4.1	37.2	2.5	34.5	7.5	-	-	-	-
1971	40.2	4.4	-	-	-	-	56.8	2.7	39.5	6.2	37.2	7.8	-	-	-	-
1972	41.5	3.2	-	-	-	-	58.1	2.3	38.8	-1.8	38.1	2.4	-	-	-	-
1973	44.2	6.5	-	-	-	-	60.5	4.1	40.0	3.1	40.0	5.0	-	-	-	-
1974	49.1	11.1	-	-	-	-	65.5	8.3	45.3	13.2	44.3	10.8	-	-	-	-
1975	53.5	9.0	-	-	-	-	67.9	3.7	49.0	8.2	50.2	13.3	-	-	-	-
1976	56.0	4.7	61.8	-	52.6	-	70.4	3.7	52.8	7.8	53.9	7.4	69.9	-	58.1	-
1977	59.4	6.1	65.2	5.5	56.0	6.5	75.3	7.0	55.8	5.7	58.4	8.3	72.6	3.9	61.3	5.5
1978	63.8	7.4	71.9	10.3	60.6	8.2	78.2	3.9	58.3	4.5	62.4	6.8	74.6	2.8	65.2	6.4
1979	71.0	11.3	79.4	10.4	67.0	10.6	84.4	7.9	69.0	18.4	68.1	9.1	75.6	1.3	70.2	7.7
1980	81.1	14.2	85.7	7.9	76.7	14.5	89.9	6.5	86.1	24.8	73.0	7.2	89.1	17.9	75.7	7.8
1981	90.8	12.0	93.2	8.8	87.9	14.6	95.9	6.7	96.0	11.5	81.8	12.1	98.9	11.0	83.6	10.4
1982	96.4	6.2	97.1	4.2	95.8	9.0	97.9	2.1	98.2	2.3	92.5	13.1	99.6	0.7	91.4	9.3
1983	100.1	3.8	99.9	2.9	100.7	5.1	100.0	2.1	99.5	1.3	101.3	9.5	94.9	-4.7	100.7	10.2
1984	103.5	3.4	103.0	3.1	103.6	2.9	102.1	2.1	102.3	2.8	106.3	4.9	105.5	11.2	107.9	7.1
1985	107.9	4.3	105.9	2.8	108.4	4.6	109.4	7.1	106.0	3.6	113.0	6.3	110.3	4.5	112.8	4.5
1986	110.8	2.7	111.0	4.8	113.1	4.3	108.2	-1.1	101.9	-3.9	124.0	9.7	118.2	7.2	119.7	6.1
1987	114.8	3.6	111.9	0.8	117.5	3.9	122.3	13.0	102.7	0.8	136.7	10.2	123.1	4.1	126.4	5.6
1988	118.6	3.3	117.0	4.6	120.6	2.6	126.0	3.0	104.5	1.8	150.4	10.0	127.7	3.7	130.5	3.2
1989	124.4	4.9	123.3	5.4	123.9	2.7	134.2	6.5	109.7	5.0	165.6	10.1	137.4	7.6	141.2	8.2
1990	130.0	4.5	131.4	6.6	126.6	2.2	131.5	-2.0	115.8	5.6	177.1	6.9	149.3	8.7	158.0	11.9
1991	133.9	3.0	135.1	2.8	128.4	1.4	143.8	9.4	116.7	0.8	191.4	8.1	156.5	4.8	169.4	7.2
1992	136.6	2.0	135.4	0.2	130.5	1.6	148.4	3.2	117.5	0.7	202.3	5.7	163.4	4.4	178.1	5.1
1993	141.4	3.5	139.1	2.7	134.5	3.1	153.0	3.1	122.0	3.8	212.2	4.9	172.6	5.6	185.5	4.2

Source: U.S. Department of Labor, Bureau of Labor Statistics, Division of Consumer Prices and Price Indexes. - indicates no data collected for period.

Atlanta, GA
Consumer Price Index - All Urban Consumers
Base 1982-1984 = 100
All Items

For 1917-1993. Columns headed % show percentile change in the index from the previous period for which an index is available.

Year	Jan Index	Jan %	Feb Index	Feb %	Mar Index	Mar %	Apr Index	Apr %	May Index	May %	Jun Index	Jun %	Jul Index	Jul %	Aug Index	Aug %	Sep Index	Sep %	Oct Index	Oct %	Nov Index	Nov %	Dec Index	Dec %
1917	-	-	-	-	-	-	-	-	-	-	-	-	-	-	-	-	-	-	-	-	-	-	15.2	-
1918	-	-	-	-	-	-	-	-	-	-	-	-	-	-	-	-	-	-	-	-	-	-	18.2	19.7
1919	-	-	-	-	-	-	-	-	-	-	18.9	3.8	-	-	-	-	-	-	-	-	-	-	20.8	10.1
1920	-	-	-	-	-	-	-	-	-	-	23.0	10.6	-	-	-	-	-	-	-	-	-	-	20.8	-9.6
1921	-	-	-	-	-	-	-	-	19.0	-8.7	-	-	-	-	-	-	18.5	-2.6	-	-	-	-	18.0	-2.7
1922	-	-	-	-	17.4	-3.3	-	-	-	-	17.5	0.6	-	-	-	-	17.4	-0.6	-	-	-	-	17.3	-0.6
1923	-	-	-	-	17.4	0.6	-	-	-	-	17.6	1.1	-	-	-	-	17.8	1.1	-	-	-	-	17.5	-1.7
1924	-	-	-	-	17.3	-1.1	-	-	-	-	17.3	0.0	-	-	-	-	17.3	0.0	-	-	-	-	17.3	0.0
1925	-	-	-	-	-	-	-	-	-	-	17.9	3.5	-	-	-	-	-	-	-	-	-	-	18.3	2.2
1926	-	-	-	-	-	-	-	-	-	-	18.0	-1.6	-	-	-	-	-	-	-	-	-	-	17.8	-1.1
1927	-	-	-	-	-	-	-	-	-	-	18.1	1.7	-	-	-	-	-	-	-	-	-	-	17.2	-5.0
1928	-	-	-	-	-	-	-	-	-	-	17.4	1.2	-	-	-	-	-	-	-	-	-	-	17.3	-0.6
1929	-	-	-	-	-	-	-	-	-	-	17.1	-1.2	-	-	-	-	-	-	-	-	-	-	17.1	0.0
1930	-	-	-	-	-	-	-	-	-	-	16.5	-3.5	-	-	-	-	-	-	-	-	-	-	15.8	-4.2
1931	-	-	-	-	-	-	-	-	-	-	14.8	-6.3	-	-	-	-	-	-	-	-	-	-	14.0	-5.4
1932	-	-	-	-	-	-	-	-	-	-	13.4	-4.3	-	-	-	-	-	-	-	-	-	-	12.6	-6.0
1933	-	-	-	-	-	-	-	-	-	-	12.5	-0.8	-	-	-	-	-	-	-	-	-	-	12.9	3.2
1934	-	-	-	-	-	-	-	-	-	-	13.1	1.6	-	-	-	-	-	-	-	-	13.4	2.3	-	-
1935	-	-	-	-	13.4	0.0	-	-	-	-	-	-	13.4	0.0	-	-	-	-	13.7	2.2	-	-	-	-
1936	13.8	0.7	-	-	-	-	13.5	-2.2	-	-	-	-	13.7	1.5	-	-	13.9	1.5	-	-	-	-	13.9	0.0
1937	-	-	-	-	14.0	0.7	-	-	-	-	14.1	0.7	-	-	-	-	14.3	1.4	-	-	-	-	14.1	-1.4
1938	-	-	-	-	13.8	-2.1	-	-	-	-	13.6	-1.4	-	-	-	-	13.8	1.5	-	-	-	-	13.8	0.0
1939	-	-	-	-	13.6	-1.4	-	-	-	-	13.5	-0.7	-	-	-	-	13.8	2.2	-	-	-	-	13.6	-1.4
1940	-	-	-	-	13.7	0.7	-	-	-	-	13.5	-1.5	-	-	-	-	13.6	0.7	-	-	-	-	13.8	1.5
1941	-	-	-	-	13.8	0.0	-	-	-	-	14.2	2.9	-	-	-	-	14.8	4.2	-	-	-	-	15.2	2.7
1942	-	-	-	-	15.7	3.3	-	-	-	-	15.9	1.3	-	-	-	-	16.1	1.3	-	-	-	-	16.4	1.9
1943	-	-	-	-	16.9	3.0	-	-	-	-	17.2	1.8	-	-	-	-	17.1	-0.6	-	-	-	-	17.1	0.0
1944	-	-	-	-	17.0	-0.6	-	-	-	-	17.3	1.8	-	-	-	-	17.5	1.2	-	-	-	-	17.7	1.1
1945	-	-	-	-	17.7	0.0	-	-	-	-	17.9	1.1	-	-	-	-	18.1	1.1	-	-	-	-	18.1	0.0
1946	-	-	-	-	18.1	0.0	-	-	-	-	18.4	1.7	-	-	-	-	20.2	9.8	-	-	-	-	21.4	5.9
1947	-	-	-	-	22.2	3.7	-	-	-	-	21.9	-1.4	-	-	22.3	1.8	-	-	-	-	23.1	3.6	-	-
1948	-	-	23.3	0.9	-	-	-	-	23.6	1.3	-	-	-	-	24.4	3.4	-	-	-	-	24.0	-1.6	-	-
1949	-	-	23.6	-1.7	-	-	-	-	23.7	0.4	-	-	-	-	24.0	1.3	-	-	-	-	23.8	-0.8	-	-
1950	-	-	23.4	-1.7	-	-	-	-	23.6	0.9	-	-	-	-	24.4	3.4	-	-	-	-	24.8	1.6	-	-
1951	-	-	25.8	4.0	-	-	-	-	26.5	2.7	-	-	-	-	26.5	0.0	-	-	-	-	26.9	1.5	-	-
1952	-	-	26.8	-0.4	-	-	-	-	26.7	-0.4	-	-	-	-	27.3	2.2	-	-	-	-	27.3	0.0	27.2	-0.4
1953	-	-	-	-	27.2	0.0	-	-	-	-	27.3	0.4	-	-	-	-	27.4	0.4	-	-	-	-	27.3	-0.4
1954	-	-	-	-	27.3	0.0	-	-	-	-	27.4	0.4	-	-	-	-	27.1	-1.1	-	-	-	-	27.0	-0.4
1955	-	-	-	-	26.9	-0.4	-	-	-	-	27.0	0.4	-	-	-	-	27.3	1.1	-	-	-	-	27.3	0.0
1956	-	-	-	-	27.2	-0.4	-	-	-	-	27.5	1.1	-	-	-	-	27.7	0.7	-	-	-	-	27.8	0.4
1957	-	-	-	-	28.1	1.1	-	-	-	-	28.2	0.4	-	-	-	-	28.5	1.1	-	-	-	-	28.5	0.0
1958	-	-	-	-	29.1	2.1	-	-	-	-	29.1	0.0	-	-	-	-	29.0	-0.3	-	-	-	-	29.0	0.0
1959	-	-	-	-	28.9	-0.3	-	-	-	-	29.2	1.0	-	-	-	-	29.3	0.3	-	-	-	-	29.4	0.3
1960	-	-	-	-	29.5	0.3	-	-	-	-	29.6	0.3	-	-	-	-	29.8	0.7	-	-	-	-	29.7	-0.3
1961	-	-	-	-	29.7	0.0	-	-	-	-	29.7	0.0	-	-	-	-	29.9	0.7	-	-	-	-	29.8	-0.3

[Continued]

Atlanta, GA
Consumer Price Index - All Urban Consumers
Base 1982-1984 = 100
All Items
[Continued]

For 1917-1993. Columns headed % show percentile change in the index from the previous period for which an index is available.

Year	Jan Index	%	Feb Index	%	Mar Index	%	Apr Index	%	May Index	%	Jun Index	%	Jul Index	%	Aug Index	%	Sep Index	%	Oct Index	%	Nov Index	%	Dec Index	%
1962	-	-	-	-	29.9	0.3	-	-	-	-	30.0	0.3	-	-	-	-	30.2	0.7	-	-	-	-	30.1	-0.3
1963	-	-	-	-	30.2	0.3	-	-	-	-	30.2	0.0	-	-	-	-	30.3	0.3	-	-	-	-	30.5	0.7
1964	-	-	-	-	30.7	0.7	-	-	-	-	30.6	-0.3	-	-	-	-	30.9	1.0	-	-	-	-	31.0	0.3
1965	-	-	-	-	31.0	0.0	-	-	-	-	31.1	0.3	-	-	-	-	31.2	0.3	-	-	-	-	31.5	1.0
1966	-	-	-	-	31.8	1.0	-	-	-	-	32.0	0.6	-	-	-	-	32.5	1.6	-	-	-	-	32.7	0.6
1967	-	-	-	-	32.9	0.6	-	-	-	-	33.1	0.6	-	-	-	-	33.3	0.6	-	-	-	-	33.7	1.2
1968	-	-	-	-	34.0	0.9	-	-	-	-	34.3	0.9	-	-	-	-	35.0	2.0	-	-	-	-	35.2	0.6
1969	-	-	-	-	36.0	2.3	-	-	-	-	36.4	1.1	-	-	-	-	37.1	1.9	-	-	-	-	37.5	1.1
1970	-	-	-	-	38.0	1.3	-	-	-	-	38.6	1.6	-	-	-	-	39.0	1.0	-	-	-	-	39.6	1.5
1971	-	-	-	-	39.9	0.8	-	-	-	-	40.6	1.8	-	-	-	-	40.5	-0.2	-	-	-	-	41.0	1.2
1972	-	-	-	-	41.1	0.2	-	-	-	-	41.4	0.7	-	-	-	-	42.1	1.7	-	-	-	-	42.3	0.5
1973	-	-	-	-	43.1	1.9	-	-	-	-	44.0	2.1	-	-	-	-	45.4	3.2	-	-	-	-	46.1	1.5
1974	-	-	-	-	47.8	3.7	-	-	-	-	48.8	2.1	-	-	-	-	50.6	3.7	-	-	-	-	51.7	2.2
1975	-	-	-	-	52.6	1.7	-	-	-	-	53.4	1.5	-	-	-	-	54.6	2.2	-	-	-	-	55.1	0.9
1976	-	-	-	-	55.2	0.2	-	-	-	-	55.9	1.3	-	-	-	-	56.9	1.8	-	-	-	-	57.0	0.2
1977	-	-	-	-	58.4	2.5	-	-	-	-	59.4	1.7	-	-	-	-	60.7	2.2	-	-	-	-	61.2	0.8
1978	-	-	61.7	0.8	-	-	62.5	1.3	-	-	63.6	1.8	-	-	64.7	1.7	-	-	65.9	1.9	-	-	65.9	0.0
1979	-	-	66.9	1.5	-	-	68.5	2.4	-	-	70.5	2.9	-	-	71.9	2.0	-	-	73.2	1.8	-	-	74.0	1.1
1980	-	-	76.4	3.2	-	-	78.0	2.1	-	-	80.3	2.9	-	-	81.7	1.7	-	-	83.0	1.6	-	-	85.7	3.3
1981	-	-	87.2	1.8	-	-	88.2	1.1	-	-	89.3	1.2	-	-	91.6	2.6	-	-	93.3	1.9	-	-	93.6	0.3
1982	-	-	92.8	-0.9	-	-	92.9	0.1	-	-	96.5	3.9	-	-	98.0	1.6	-	-	98.8	0.8	-	-	98.2	-0.6
1983	-	-	97.9	-0.3	-	-	98.7	0.8	-	-	100.2	1.5	-	-	100.8	0.6	-	-	100.9	0.1	-	-	101.9	1.0
1984	-	-	102.6	0.7	-	-	103.2	0.6	-	-	104.1	0.9	-	-	104.8	0.7	-	-	105.4	0.6	-	-	105.5	0.1
1985	-	-	107.0	1.4	-	-	107.6	0.6	-	-	108.8	1.1	-	-	109.9	1.0	-	-	110.4	0.5	-	-	111.2	0.7
1986	-	-	111.7	0.4	-	-	111.1	-0.5	-	-	112.2	1.0	-	-	112.4	0.2	-	-	112.7	0.3	-	-	113.5	0.7
1987	-	-	-	-	-	-	-	-	-	-	115.5	1.8	-	-	-	-	-	-	-	-	-	-	117.5	1.7
1988	-	-	-	-	-	-	-	-	-	-	119.1	1.4	-	-	-	-	-	-	-	-	-	-	121.7	2.2
1989	-	-	-	-	-	-	-	-	-	-	124.9	2.6	-	-	-	-	-	-	-	-	-	-	127.3	1.9
1990	-	-	-	-	-	-	-	-	-	-	130.8	2.7	-	-	-	-	-	-	-	-	-	-	132.6	1.4
1991	-	-	-	-	-	-	-	-	-	-	135.5	2.2	-	-	-	-	-	-	-	-	-	-	136.2	0.5
1992	-	-	-	-	-	-	-	-	-	-	138.6	1.8	-	-	-	-	-	-	-	-	-	-	138.5	-0.1
1993	-	-	-	-	-	-	-	-	-	-	142.2	2.7	-	-	-	-	-	-	-	-	-	-		

Source: U.S. Department of Labor, Bureau of Labor Statistics, Division of Consumer Prices and Price Indexes. - indicates no data collected for period.

Atlanta, GA
Consumer Price Index - Urban Wage Earners
Base 1982-1984 = 100
All Items

For 1917-1993. Columns headed % show percentile change in the index from the previous period for which an index is available.

Year	Jan Index	%	Feb Index	%	Mar Index	%	Apr Index	%	May Index	%	Jun Index	%	Jul Index	%	Aug Index	%	Sep Index	%	Oct Index	%	Nov Index	%	Dec Index	%
1917	-		-		-		-		-		-		-		-		-		-		-		15.1	-
1918	-		-		-		-		-		-		-		-		-		-		-		18.1	19.9
1919	-		-		-		-		-		18.9	4.4	-		-		-		-		-		20.7	9.5
1920	-		-		-		-		-		23.0	11.1	-		-		-		-		-		20.8	-9.6
1921	-		-		-		-		18.9	-9.1	-		-		-		18.4	-2.6	-		-		17.9	-2.7
1922	-		-		17.4	-2.8	-		-		17.5	0.6	-		-		17.3	-1.1	-		-		17.3	0.0
1923	-		-		17.3	0.0	-		-		17.5	1.2	-		-		17.8	1.7	-		-		17.5	-1.7
1924	-		-		17.2	-1.7	-		-		17.3	0.6	-		-		17.3	0.0	-		-		17.3	0.0
1925	-		-		-		-		-		17.8	2.9	-		-		-		-		-		18.2	2.2
1926	-		-		-		-		-		18.0	-1.1	-		-		-		-		-		17.7	-1.7
1927	-		-		-		-		-		18.1	2.3	-		-		-		-		-		17.2	-5.0
1928	-		-		-		-		-		17.3	0.6	-		-		-		-		-		17.3	0.0
1929	-		-		-		-		-		17.1	-1.2	-		-		-		-		-		17.1	0.0
1930	-		-		-		-		-		16.4	-4.1	-		-		-		-		-		15.7	-4.3
1931	-		-		-		-		-		14.8	-5.7	-		-		-		-		-		14.0	-5.4
1932	-		-		-		-		-		13.3	-5.0	-		-		-		-		-		12.6	-5.3
1933	-		-		-		-		-		12.5	-0.8	-		-		-		-		-		12.9	3.2
1934	-		-		-		-		-		13.1	1.6	-		-		-		-		13.3	1.5	-	
1935	-		-		13.3	0.0	-		-		-		13.3	0.0	-		-		13.7	3.0	-		-	
1936	13.7	0.0	-		-		13.5	-1.5	-		-		13.7	1.5	-		13.8	0.7	-		-		13.8	0.0
1937	-		-		14.0	1.4	-		-		14.1	0.7	-		-		14.3	1.4	-		-		14.1	-1.4
1938	-		-		13.7	-2.8	-		-		13.6	-0.7	-		-		13.7	0.7	-		-		13.7	0.0
1939	-		-		13.6	-0.7	-		-		13.4	-1.5	-		-		13.7	2.2	-		-		13.5	-1.5
1940	-		-		13.6	0.7	-		-		13.5	-0.7	-		-		13.6	0.7	-		-		13.7	0.7
1941	-		-		13.8	0.7	-		-		14.2	2.9	-		-		14.7	3.5	-		-		15.1	2.7
1942	-		-		15.6	3.3	-		-		15.8	1.3	-		-		16.1	1.9	-		-		16.3	1.2
1943	-		-		16.9	3.7	-		-		17.2	1.8	-		-		17.1	-0.6	-		-		17.0	-0.6
1944	-		-		16.9	-0.6	-		-		17.2	1.8	-		-		17.5	1.7	-		-		17.7	1.1
1945	-		-		17.7	0.0	-		-		17.8	0.6	-		-		18.1	1.7	-		-		18.0	-0.6
1946	-		-		18.1	0.6	-		-		18.4	1.7	-		-		20.1	9.2	-		-		21.4	6.5
1947	-		-		22.1	3.3	-		-		21.8	-1.4	-		22.3	2.3	-		-		23.0	3.1	-	
1948	-		23.3	1.3	-		-		23.5	0.9	-		-		24.3	3.4	-		-		24.0	-1.2	-	
1949	-		23.5	-2.1	-		-		23.6	0.4	-		-		23.9	1.3	-		-		23.7	-0.8	-	
1950	-		23.4	-1.3	-		-		23.5	0.4	-		-		24.4	3.8	-		-		24.7	1.2	-	
1951	-		25.7	4.0	-		-		26.4	2.7	-		-		26.5	0.4	-		-		26.9	1.5	-	
1952	-		26.8	-0.4	-		-		26.6	-0.7	-		-		27.2	2.3	-		-		27.2	0.0	27.1	-0.4
1953	-		-		27.1	0.0	-		-		27.2	0.4	-		-		27.3	0.4	-		-		27.2	-0.4
1954	-		-		27.2	0.0	-		-		27.3	0.4	-		-		27.0	-1.1	-		-		26.9	-0.4
1955	-		-		26.8	-0.4	-		-		27.0	0.7	-		-		27.2	0.7	-		-		27.2	0.0
1956	-		-		27.1	-0.4	-		-		27.4	1.1	-		-		27.6	0.7	-		-		27.7	0.4
1957	-		-		28.0	1.1	-		-		28.1	0.4	-		-		28.4	1.1	-		-		28.4	0.0
1958	-		-		29.0	2.1	-		-		29.0	0.0	-		-		28.9	-0.3	-		-		28.9	0.0
1959	-		-		28.9	0.0	-		-		29.2	1.0	-		-		29.3	0.3	-		-		29.4	0.3
1960	-		-		29.4	0.0	-		-		29.5	0.3	-		-		29.7	0.7	-		-		29.7	0.0
1961	-		-		29.7	0.0	-		-		29.6	-0.3	-		-		29.8	0.7	-		-		29.7	-0.3

[Continued]

Atlanta, GA
Consumer Price Index - Urban Wage Earners
Base 1982-1984 = 100
All Items
[Continued]

For 1917-1993. Columns headed % show percentile change in the index from the previous period for which an index is available.

Year	Jan Index	%	Feb Index	%	Mar Index	%	Apr Index	%	May Index	%	Jun Index	%	Jul Index	%	Aug Index	%	Sep Index	%	Oct Index	%	Nov Index	%	Dec Index	%
1962	-		-		29.8	0.3	-		-		29.9	0.3	-		-		30.1	0.7	-		-		30.1	0.0
1963	-		-		30.2	0.3	-		-		30.2	0.0	-		-		30.3	0.3	-		-		30.4	0.3
1964	-		-		30.7	1.0	-		-		30.6	-0.3	-		-		30.8	0.7	-		-		30.9	0.3
1965	-		-		31.0	0.3	-		-		31.0	0.0	-		-		31.1	0.3	-		-		31.4	1.0
1966	-		-		31.7	1.0	-		-		31.9	0.6	-		-		32.4	1.6	-		-		32.6	0.6
1967	-		-		32.8	0.6	-		-		33.0	0.6	-		-		33.2	0.6	-		-		33.6	1.2
1968	-		-		33.9	0.9	-		-		34.2	0.9	-		-		34.9	2.0	-		-		35.1	0.6
1969	-		-		35.9	2.3	-		-		36.3	1.1	-		-		37.0	1.9	-		-		37.4	1.1
1970	-		-		37.9	1.3	-		-		38.5	1.6	-		-		38.9	1.0	-		-		39.5	1.5
1971	-		-		39.8	0.8	-		-		40.4	1.5	-		-		40.3	-0.2	-		-		40.8	1.2
1972	-		-		40.9	0.2	-		-		41.3	1.0	-		-		42.0	1.7	-		-		42.2	0.5
1973	-		-		43.0	1.9	-		-		43.9	2.1	-		-		45.3	3.2	-		-		45.9	1.3
1974	-		-		47.7	3.9	-		-		48.7	2.1	-		-		50.5	3.7	-		-		51.6	2.2
1975	-		-		52.4	1.6	-		-		53.2	1.5	-		-		54.5	2.4	-		-		55.0	0.9
1976	-		-		55.1	0.2	-		-		55.7	1.1	-		-		56.8	2.0	-		-		56.9	0.2
1977	-		-		58.2	2.3	-		-		59.2	1.7	-		-		60.5	2.2	-		-		61.0	0.8
1978	-		61.7	1.1	-		62.5	1.3	-		63.7	1.9	-		64.6	1.4	-		65.6	1.5	-		65.9	0.5
1979	-		67.0	1.7	-		68.9	2.8	-		70.9	2.9	-		72.4	2.1	-		73.9	2.1	-		75.1	1.6
1980	-		77.2	2.8	-		79.1	2.5	-		80.9	2.3	-		82.6	2.1	-		83.5	1.1	-		86.1	3.1
1981	-		88.1	2.3	-		88.9	0.9	-		90.2	1.5	-		92.0	2.0	-		93.6	1.7	-		94.0	0.4
1982	-		93.5	-0.5	-		93.6	0.1	-		96.9	3.5	-		98.3	1.4	-		98.8	0.5	-		98.5	-0.3
1983	-		98.2	-0.3	-		99.3	1.1	-		99.9	0.6	-		100.6	0.7	-		101.3	0.7	-		102.4	1.1
1984	-		102.4	0.0	-		102.3	-0.1	-		102.8	0.5	-		104.2	1.4	-		105.2	1.0	-		104.5	-0.7
1985	-		105.9	1.3	-		106.6	0.7	-		107.8	1.1	-		108.9	1.0	-		109.1	0.2	-		110.0	0.8
1986	-		110.6	0.5	-		109.7	-0.8	-		111.0	1.2	-		110.9	-0.1	-		111.1	0.2	-		111.7	0.5
1987	-		-		-		-		-		113.7	1.8	-		-		-		-		-		115.8	1.8
1988	-		-		-		-		-		117.2	1.2	-		-		-		-		-		120.1	2.5
1989	-		-		-		-		-		123.2	2.6	-		-		-		-		-		125.5	1.9
1990	-		-		-		-		-		128.9	2.7	-		-		-		-		-		131.1	1.7
1991	-		-		-		-		-		133.5	1.8	-		-		-		-		-		134.4	0.7
1992	-		-		-		-		-		136.3	1.4	-		-		-		-		-		136.9	0.4
1993	-		-		-		-		-		140.2	2.4	-		-		-		-		-		-	

Source: U.S. Department of Labor, Bureau of Labor Statistics, Division of Consumer Prices and Price Indexes. - indicates no data collected for period.

Atlanta, GA
Consumer Price Index - All Urban Consumers
Base 1982-1984 = 100
Food and Beverages

For 1975-1993. Columns headed % show percentile change in the index from the previous period for which an index is available.

Year	Jan Index	%	Feb Index	%	Mar Index	%	Apr Index	%	May Index	%	Jun Index	%	Jul Index	%	Aug Index	%	Sep Index	%	Oct Index	%	Nov Index	%	Dec Index	%
1975	-		-		-		-		-		-		-		-		-		-		-		63.2	-
1976	-		-		62.1	-1.7	-		-		62.2	0.2	-		-		63.0	1.3	-		-		62.4	-1.0
1977	-		-		64.9	4.0	-		-		65.9	1.5	-		-		67.2	2.0	-		-		67.6	0.6
1978	-		69.0	2.1	-		70.2	1.7	-		73.1	4.1	-		73.8	1.0	-		74.0	0.3	-		74.9	1.2
1979	-		77.7	3.7	-		78.8	1.4	-		79.1	0.4	-		80.8	2.1	-		80.7	-0.1	-		81.6	1.1
1980	-		82.4	1.0	-		82.9	0.6	-		84.4	1.8	-		87.6	3.8	-		88.6	1.1	-		91.4	3.2
1981	-		92.2	0.9	-		92.2	0.0	-		92.5	0.3	-		93.5	1.1	-		94.1	0.6	-		95.0	1.0
1982	-		96.1	1.2	-		96.3	0.2	-		97.5	1.2	-		97.4	-0.1	-		97.7	0.3	-		98.2	0.5
1983	-		98.8	0.6	-		100.2	1.4	-		100.0	-0.2	-		99.9	-0.1	-		100.1	0.2	-		100.4	0.3
1984	-		103.4	3.0	-		102.7	-0.7	-		102.2	-0.5	-		103.8	1.6	-		103.5	-0.3	-		104.3	0.8
1985	-		106.2	1.8	-		105.5	-0.7	-		105.5	0.0	-		105.3	-0.2	-		106.3	0.9	-		108.6	2.2
1986	-		109.4	0.7	-		110.5	1.0	-		110.6	0.1	-		113.0	2.2	-		112.5	-0.4	-		112.1	-0.4
1987	-		-		-		-		-		112.2	0.1	-		-		-		-		-		112.3	0.1
1988	-		-		-		-		-		115.6	2.9	-		-		-		-		-		119.2	3.1
1989	-		-		-		-		-		121.4	1.8	-		-		-		-		-		125.9	3.7
1990	-		-		-		-		-		130.5	3.7	-		-		-		-		-		133.3	2.1
1991	-		-		-		-		-		135.3	1.5	-		-		-		-		-		135.3	0.0
1992	-		-		-		-		-		135.8	0.4	-		-		-		-		-		135.7	-0.1
1993	-		-		-		-		-		138.4	2.0	-		-		-		-		-		-	

Source: U.S. Department of Labor, Bureau of Labor Statistics, Division of Consumer Prices and Price Indexes. - indicates no data collected for period.

Atlanta, GA
Consumer Price Index - Urban Wage Earners
Base 1982-1984 = 100
Food and Beverages

For 1975-1993. Columns headed % show percentile change in the index from the previous period for which an index is available.

Year	Jan Index	%	Feb Index	%	Mar Index	%	Apr Index	%	May Index	%	Jun Index	%	Jul Index	%	Aug Index	%	Sep Index	%	Oct Index	%	Nov Index	%	Dec Index	%
1975	-	-	-	-	-	-	-	-	-	-	-	-	-	-	-	-	-	-	-	-	-	-	-	-
1976	-	-	-	-	61.4	-1.8	-	-	-	-	61.5	0.2	-	-	-	-	-	-	-	-	-	-	62.5	-
1977	-	-	-	-	64.1	3.9	-	-	-	-	65.1	1.6	-	-	-	-	62.3	1.3	-	-	-	-	61.7	-1.0
1978	-	-	68.3	2.2	-	-	70.1	2.6	-	-	72.8	3.9	-	-	73.8	1.4	66.5	2.2	73.7	-0.1	-	-	66.8	0.5
1979	-	-	77.4	4.0	-	-	78.7	1.7	-	-	79.1	0.5	-	-	80.5	1.8	-	-	80.7	0.2	-	-	74.4	0.9
1980	-	-	82.4	1.0	-	-	83.6	1.5	-	-	84.3	0.8	-	-	87.1	3.3	-	-	88.4	1.5	-	-	81.6	1.1
1981	-	-	91.9	1.2	-	-	92.6	0.8	-	-	93.1	0.5	-	-	93.7	0.6	-	-	94.2	0.5	-	-	90.8	2.7
1982	-	-	95.9	1.2	-	-	96.3	0.4	-	-	97.5	1.2	-	-	97.5	0.0	-	-	97.9	0.4	-	-	94.8	0.6
1983	-	-	98.9	0.5	-	-	100.3	1.4	-	-	100.1	-0.2	-	-	99.9	-0.2	-	-	100.1	0.2	-	-	98.4	0.5
1984	-	-	103.1	2.7	-	-	102.5	-0.6	-	-	102.3	-0.2	-	-	103.6	1.3	-	-	103.4	-0.2	-	-	100.4	0.3
1985	-	-	106.0	1.7	-	-	105.3	-0.7	-	-	105.4	0.1	-	-	105.2	-0.2	-	-	106.1	0.9	-	-	104.2	0.8
1986	-	-	109.2	0.7	-	-	110.3	1.0	-	-	110.3	0.0	-	-	112.9	2.4	-	-	112.5	-0.4	-	-	108.4	2.2
1987	-	-	-	-	-	-	-	-	-	-	111.9	0.1	-	-	-	-	-	-	-	-	-	-	111.8	-0.6
1988	-	-	-	-	-	-	-	-	-	-	115.0	2.8	-	-	-	-	-	-	-	-	-	-	111.9	0.0
1989	-	-	-	-	-	-	-	-	-	-	121.1	1.8	-	-	-	-	-	-	-	-	-	-	119.0	3.5
1990	-	-	-	-	-	-	-	-	-	-	129.9	3.6	-	-	-	-	-	-	-	-	-	-	125.4	3.6
1991	-	-	-	-	-	-	-	-	-	-	135.1	1.7	-	-	-	-	-	-	-	-	-	-	132.9	2.3
1992	-	-	-	-	-	-	-	-	-	-	135.4	0.2	-	-	-	-	-	-	-	-	-	-	135.1	0.0
1993	-	-	-	-	-	-	-	-	-	-	137.8	1.8	-	-	-	-	-	-	-	-	-	-	135.4	0.0

Source: U.S. Department of Labor, Bureau of Labor Statistics, Division of Consumer Prices and Price Indexes. - indicates no data collected for period.

Atlanta, GA
Consumer Price Index - All Urban Consumers
Base 1982-1984 = 100
Housing

For 1975-1993. Columns headed % show percentile change in the index from the previous period for which an index is available.

Year	Jan Index	%	Feb Index	%	Mar Index	%	Apr Index	%	May Index	%	Jun Index	%	Jul Index	%	Aug Index	%	Sep Index	%	Oct Index	%	Nov Index	%	Dec Index	%
1975	-	-	-	-	-	-	-	-	-	-	-	-	-	-	-	-	-	-	-	-	-	-	50.7	-
1976	-	-	-	-	51.2	1.0	-	-	-	-	51.8	1.2	-	-	-	-	52.5	1.4	-	-	-	-	52.8	0.6
1977	-	-	-	-	53.7	1.7	-	-	-	-	55.1	2.6	-	-	-	-	56.4	2.4	-	-	-	-	57.2	1.4
1978	-	-	57.6	0.7	-	-	58.5	1.6	-	-	59.2	1.2	-	-	60.4	2.0	-	-	62.2	3.0	-	-	62.0	-0.3
1979	-	-	62.3	0.5	-	-	63.5	1.9	-	-	66.0	3.9	-	-	66.9	1.4	-	-	68.9	3.0	-	-	69.6	1.0
1980	-	-	71.5	2.7	-	-	73.6	2.9	-	-	77.0	4.6	-	-	76.8	-0.3	-	-	78.4	2.1	-	-	82.4	5.1
1981	-	-	83.6	1.5	-	-	84.3	0.8	-	-	86.4	2.5	-	-	90.0	4.2	-	-	92.3	2.6	-	-	92.4	0.1
1982	-	-	90.7	-1.8	-	-	91.7	1.1	-	-	96.4	5.1	-	-	98.5	2.2	-	-	98.7	0.2	-	-	97.7	-1.0
1983	-	-	98.0	0.3	-	-	98.9	0.9	-	-	101.1	2.2	-	-	100.5	-0.6	-	-	100.2	-0.3	-	-	102.5	2.3
1984	-	-	102.7	0.2	-	-	103.4	0.7	-	-	105.3	1.8	-	-	106.0	0.7	-	-	105.4	-0.6	-	-	105.7	0.3
1985	-	-	107.4	1.6	-	-	108.4	0.9	-	-	110.2	1.7	-	-	111.6	1.3	-	-	111.2	-0.4	-	-	112.3	1.0
1986	-	-	112.7	0.4	-	-	114.1	1.2	-	-	116.1	1.8	-	-	116.3	0.2	-	-	115.9	-0.3	-	-	117.4	1.3
1987	-	-	-	-	-	-	-	-	-	-	118.2	0.7	-	-	-	-	-	-	-	-	-	-	120.8	2.2
1988	-	-	-	-	-	-	-	-	-	-	122.0	1.0	-	-	-	-	-	-	-	-	-	-	123.2	1.0
1989	-	-	-	-	-	-	-	-	-	-	124.7	1.2	-	-	-	-	-	-	-	-	-	-	126.9	1.8
1990	-	-	-	-	-	-	-	-	-	-	129.0	1.7	-	-	-	-	-	-	-	-	-	-	128.7	-0.2
1991	-	-	-	-	-	-	-	-	-	-	129.3	0.5	-	-	-	-	-	-	-	-	-	-	131.8	1.9
1992	-	-	-	-	-	-	-	-	-	-	132.4	0.5	-	-	-	-	-	-	-	-	-	-	133.0	0.5
1993	-	-	-	-	-	-	-	-	-	-	135.7	2.0	-	-	-	-	-	-	-	-	-	-	-	-

Source: U.S. Department of Labor, Bureau of Labor Statistics, Division of Consumer Prices and Price Indexes. - indicates no data collected for period.

Atlanta, GA
Consumer Price Index - Urban Wage Earners
Base 1982-1984 = 100
Housing

For 1975-1993. Columns headed % show percentile change in the index from the previous period for which an index is available.

Year	Jan Index	%	Feb Index	%	Mar Index	%	Apr Index	%	May Index	%	Jun Index	%	Jul Index	%	Aug Index	%	Sep Index	%	Oct Index	%	Nov Index	%	Dec Index	%
1975	-	-	-	-	-	-	-	-	-	-	-	-	-	-	-	-	-	-	-	-	-	-	-	-
1976	-	-	-	-	51.9	1.2	-	-	-	-	52.5	1.2	-	-	-	-	53.2	1.3	-	-	-	-	51.3	-
1977	-	-	-	-	54.5	1.9	-	-	-	-	55.8	2.4	-	-	-	-	57.2	2.5	-	-	-	-	53.5	0.6
1978	-	-	58.6	1.0	-	-	59.3	1.2	-	-	60.1	1.3	-	-	61.1	1.7	-	-	62.6	2.5	-	-	58.0	1.4
1979	-	-	63.3	0.6	-	-	64.6	2.1	-	-	67.3	4.2	-	-	68.0	1.0	-	-	69.8	2.6	-	-	62.9	0.5
1980	-	-	72.4	2.4	-	-	74.6	3.0	-	-	77.8	4.3	-	-	77.6	-0.3	-	-	78.4	1.0	-	-	70.7	1.3
1981	-	-	83.6	1.5	-	-	84.4	1.0	-	-	86.8	2.8	-	-	90.2	3.9	-	-	92.3	2.3	-	-	82.4	5.1
1982	-	-	91.2	-1.5	-	-	92.4	1.3	-	-	96.8	4.8	-	-	98.8	2.1	-	-	98.7	-0.1	-	-	92.6	0.3
1983	-	-	99.0	1.0	-	-	100.2	1.2	-	-	100.3	0.1	-	-	100.7	0.4	-	-	101.7	1.0	-	-	98.0	-0.7
1984	-	-	102.5	-1.3	-	-	101.7	-0.8	-	-	102.4	0.7	-	-	104.8	2.3	-	-	105.7	0.9	-	-	103.8	2.1
1985	-	-	106.1	1.6	-	-	107.0	0.8	-	-	108.8	1.7	-	-	110.2	1.3	-	-	109.4	-0.7	-	-	104.4	-1.2
1986	-	-	110.7	0.3	-	-	111.9	1.1	-	-	114.2	2.1	-	-	114.2	0.0	-	-	113.7	-0.4	-	-	110.4	0.9
1987	-	-	-	-	-	-	-	-	-	-	116.2	0.8	-	-	-	-	-	-	-	-	-	-	115.3	1.4
1988	-	-	-	-	-	-	-	-	-	-	120.0	1.0	-	-	-	-	-	-	-	-	-	-	118.8	2.2
1989	-	-	-	-	-	-	-	-	-	-	122.9	1.3	-	-	-	-	-	-	-	-	-	-	121.3	1.1
1990	-	-	-	-	-	-	-	-	-	-	126.7	1.5	-	-	-	-	-	-	-	-	-	-	124.8	1.5
1991	-	-	-	-	-	-	-	-	-	-	127.1	0.6	-	-	-	-	-	-	-	-	-	-	126.4	-0.2
1992	-	-	-	-	-	-	-	-	-	-	130.2	0.4	-	-	-	-	-	-	-	-	-	-	129.7	2.0
1993	-	-	-	-	-	-	-	-	-	-	133.6	2.1	-	-	-	-	-	-	-	-	-	-	130.9	0.5

Source: U.S. Department of Labor, Bureau of Labor Statistics, Division of Consumer Prices and Price Indexes. - indicates no data collected for period.

Atlanta, GA
Consumer Price Index - All Urban Consumers
Base 1982-1984 = 100
Apparel and Upkeep

For 1952-1993. Columns headed % show percentile change in the index from the previous period for which an index is available.

Year	Jan Index	%	Feb Index	%	Mar Index	%	Apr Index	%	May Index	%	Jun Index	%	Jul Index	%	Aug Index	%	Sep Index	%	Oct Index	%	Nov Index	%	Dec Index	%
1952	-	-	-	-	-	-	-	-	-	-	42.1	-0.2	-	-	-	-	42.5	1.0	-	-	42.1	-	42.2	-0.7
1953	-	-	-	-	42.2	0.2	-	-	-	-	42.6	0.2	-	-	-	-	42.2	-0.9	-	-	-	-	42.1	-0.2
1954	-	-	-	-	42.5	0.7	-	-	-	-	42.1	1.4	-	-	-	-	42.5	1.0	-	-	-	-	42.5	0.0
1955	-	-	-	-	41.5	-1.4	-	-	-	-	42.8	0.5	-	-	-	-	43.4	1.4	-	-	-	-	43.2	-0.5
1956	-	-	-	-	42.6	0.2	-	-	-	-	43.6	-0.2	-	-	-	-	44.1	1.1	-	-	-	-	44.1	0.0
1957	-	-	-	-	43.7	1.2	-	-	-	-	44.1	-0.5	-	-	-	-	44.3	0.5	-	-	-	-	44.3	0.0
1958	-	-	-	-	44.3	0.5	-	-	-	-	44.0	0.0	-	-	-	-	44.4	0.9	-	-	-	-	44.7	0.7
1959	-	-	-	-	44.0	-0.7	-	-	-	-	44.7	0.0	-	-	-	-	45.5	1.8	-	-	-	-	45.3	-0.4
1960	-	-	-	-	44.7	0.0	-	-	-	-	45.1	0.0	-	-	-	-	45.0	-0.2	-	-	-	-	44.9	-0.2
1961	-	-	-	-	45.1	-0.4	-	-	-	-	44.9	-0.2	-	-	-	-	45.2	0.7	-	-	-	-	45.5	0.7
1962	-	-	-	-	45.0	0.2	-	-	-	-	46.0	0.2	-	-	-	-	46.5	1.1	-	-	-	-	46.2	-0.6
1963	-	-	-	-	45.9	0.9	-	-	-	-	46.0	-0.4	-	-	-	-	46.2	0.4	-	-	-	-	46.3	0.2
1964	-	-	-	-	46.2	0.0	-	-	-	-	46.4	0.0	-	-	-	-	47.0	1.3	-	-	-	-	47.1	0.2
1965	-	-	-	-	46.4	0.2	-	-	-	-	48.4	1.3	-	-	-	-	50.0	3.3	-	-	-	-	50.8	1.6
1966	-	-	-	-	47.8	1.5	-	-	-	-	51.4	0.2	-	-	-	-	52.0	1.2	-	-	-	-	52.3	0.6
1967	-	-	-	-	51.3	1.0	-	-	-	-	53.4	0.2	-	-	-	-	54.3	1.7	-	-	-	-	55.0	1.3
1968	-	-	-	-	53.3	1.9	-	-	-	-	55.8	1.5	-	-	-	-	56.7	1.6	-	-	-	-	57.1	0.7
1969	-	-	-	-	55.0	0.0	-	-	-	-	57.9	0.2	-	-	-	-	59.0	1.9	-	-	-	-	59.4	0.7
1970	-	-	-	-	57.8	1.2	-	-	-	-	59.3	-1.3	-	-	-	-	60.2	1.5	-	-	-	-	60.2	0.0
1971	-	-	-	-	60.1	1.2	-	-	-	-	60.3	-0.2	-	-	-	-	62.6	3.8	-	-	-	-	62.6	0.0
1972	-	-	-	-	60.4	0.3	-	-	-	-	62.7	-0.5	-	-	-	-	65.0	3.7	-	-	-	-	65.4	0.6
1973	-	-	-	-	63.0	0.6	-	-	-	-	69.1	2.7	-	-	-	-	71.1	2.9	-	-	-	-	70.3	-1.1
1974	-	-	-	-	67.3	2.9	-	-	-	-	70.5	-1.5	-	-	-	-	72.7	3.1	-	-	-	-	72.4	-0.4
1975	-	-	-	-	71.6	1.8	-	-	-	-	72.8	-0.4	-	-	-	-	76.3	4.8	-	-	-	-	76.4	0.1
1976	-	-	-	-	73.1	1.0	-	-	-	-	77.0	-2.2	-	-	-	-	82.2	6.8	-	-	-	-	82.0	-0.2
1977	-	-	-	-	78.7	3.0	-	-	-	-	-	-	-	-	-	-	-	-	-	-	-	-	84.4	-0.8
1978	-	-	81.7	-0.4	-	-	83.8	2.6	-	-	83.6	-0.2	-	-	85.9	2.8	-	-	85.1	-0.9	-	-	89.4	0.4
1979	-	-	85.0	0.7	-	-	86.8	2.1	-	-	88.0	1.4	-	-	88.8	0.9	-	-	89.0	0.2	-	-	95.0	-1.0
1980	-	-	92.1	3.0	-	-	90.8	-1.4	-	-	92.1	1.4	-	-	94.1	2.2	-	-	96.0	2.0	-	-	96.4	-0.1
1981	-	-	94.1	-0.9	-	-	96.9	3.0	-	-	94.1	-2.9	-	-	99.6	5.8	-	-	96.5	-3.1	-	-	99.3	-3.1
1982	-	-	94.9	-1.6	-	-	93.9	-1.1	-	-	93.9	0.0	-	-	96.9	3.2	-	-	102.5	5.8	-	-	101.0	-3.9
1983	-	-	97.7	-1.6	-	-	93.8	-4.0	-	-	99.1	5.7	-	-	107.0	8.0	-	-	105.1	-1.8	-	-	106.7	-2.5
1984	-	-	98.4	-2.6	-	-	101.0	2.6	-	-	101.0	0.0	-	-	101.1	0.1	-	-	109.4	8.2	-	-	109.5	-6.3
1985	-	-	113.3	6.2	-	-	107.9	-4.8	-	-	109.1	1.1	-	-	114.0	4.5	-	-	116.9	2.5	-	-	114.4	-1.2
1986	-	-	108.0	-1.4	-	-	110.4	2.2	-	-	107.0	-3.1	-	-	107.9	0.8	-	-	115.8	7.3	-	-	126.6	1.4
1987	-	-	-	-	-	-	-	-	-	-	124.9	9.2	-	-	-	-	-	-	-	-	-	-	129.4	0.3
1988	-	-	-	-	-	-	-	-	-	-	129.0	1.9	-	-	-	-	-	-	-	-	-	-	135.9	-1.8
1989	-	-	-	-	-	-	-	-	-	-	138.4	7.0	-	-	-	-	-	-	-	-	-	-	130.3	-5.1
1990	-	-	-	-	-	-	-	-	-	-	137.3	1.0	-	-	-	-	-	-	-	-	-	-	142.5	-7.6
1991	-	-	-	-	-	-	-	-	-	-	154.3	18.4	-	-	-	-	-	-	-	-	-	-	143.7	-11.0
1992	-	-	-	-	-	-	-	-	-	-	161.4	13.3	-	-	-	-	-	-	-	-	-	-	-	-
1993	-	-	-	-	-	-	-	-	-	-	153.8	7.0	-	-	-	-	-	-	-	-	-	-	-	-

Source: U.S. Department of Labor, Bureau of Labor Statistics, Division of Consumer Prices and Price Indexes. - indicates no data collected for period.

Atlanta, GA
Consumer Price Index - Urban Wage Earners
Base 1982-1984 = 100
Apparel and Upkeep

For 1952-1993. Columns headed % show percentile change in the index from the previous period for which an index is available.

Year	Jan Index	Jan %	Feb Index	Feb %	Mar Index	Mar %	Apr Index	Apr %	May Index	May %	Jun Index	Jun %	Jul Index	Jul %	Aug Index	Aug %	Sep Index	Sep %	Oct Index	Oct %	Nov Index	Nov %	Dec Index	Dec %
1952	-		-		-		-		-		-		-		-		-		-		-		-	
1953	-		-		40.0	0.3	-		-		39.9	-0.2	-		-		40.2	0.8	-		39.9		-	
1954	-		-		40.3	0.7	-		-		40.3	0.0	-		-		40.0	-0.7	-		-		40.0	-0.5
1955	-		-		39.3	-1.5	-		-		39.9	1.5	-		-		40.3	1.0	-		-		39.9	-0.2
1956	-		-		40.4	0.5	-		-		40.5	0.2	-		-		41.1	1.5	-		-		40.2	-0.2
1957	-		-		41.4	1.0	-		-		41.3	-0.2	-		-		41.8	1.2	-		-		41.0	-0.2
1958	-		-		42.0	0.5	-		-		41.8	-0.5	-		-		42.0	0.5	-		-		41.8	0.0
1959	-		-		41.7	-0.7	-		-		41.7	0.0	-		-		42.1	1.0	-		-		42.0	0.0
1960	-		-		42.3	-0.2	-		-		42.4	0.2	-		-		43.1	1.7	-		-		42.4	0.7
1961	-		-		42.8	-0.5	-		-		42.8	0.0	-		-		42.6	-0.5	-		-		43.0	-0.2
1962	-		-		42.6	0.2	-		-		42.5	-0.2	-		-		42.8	0.7	-		-		42.5	-0.2
1963	-		-		43.5	0.9	-		-		43.6	0.2	-		-		44.1	1.1	-		-		43.1	0.7
1964	-		-		43.8	0.0	-		-		43.6	-0.5	-		-		43.8	0.5	-		-		43.8	-0.7
1965	-		-		44.0	0.2	-		-		44.0	0.0	-		-		44.5	1.1	-		-		43.9	0.2
1966	-		-		45.3	1.6	-		-		45.9	1.3	-		-		47.4	3.3	-		-		44.6	0.2
1967	-		-		48.7	1.2	-		-		48.8	0.2	-		-		49.3	1.0	-		-		48.1	1.5
1968	-		-		50.5	1.8	-		-		50.6	0.2	-		-		51.5	1.8	-		-		49.6	0.6
1969	-		-		52.1	0.0	-		-		52.9	1.5	-		-		53.8	1.7	-		-		52.1	1.2
1970	-		-		54.8	1.3	-		-		54.9	0.2	-		-		56.0	2.0	-		-		54.1	0.6
1971	-		-		57.0	1.2	-		-		56.2	-1.4	-		-		57.0	1.4	-		-		56.3	0.5
1972	-		-		57.3	0.4	-		-		57.2	-0.2	-		-		59.3	3.7	-		-		57.1	0.2
1973	-		-		59.7	0.7	-		-		59.4	-0.5	-		-		61.6	3.7	-		-		59.3	0.0
1974	-		-		63.8	2.9	-		-		65.5	2.7	-		-		67.4	2.9	-		-		62.0	0.6
1975	-		-		67.9	1.8	-		-		66.8	-1.6	-		-		68.9	3.1	-		-		66.7	-1.0
1976	-		-		69.3	1.0	-		-		69.0	-0.4	-		-		72.4	4.9	-		-		68.6	-0.4
1977	-		-		74.6	2.9	-		-		72.9	-2.3	-		-		77.9	6.9	-		-		72.5	0.1
1978	-		77.3	-0.5	-		77.5	0.3	-		77.5	0.0	-		78.1	0.8	-		79.7	2.0	-		77.7	-0.3
1979	-		79.3	-0.5	-		82.5	4.0	-		84.1	1.9	-		86.7	3.1	-		87.1	0.5	-		79.7	0.0
1980	-		86.5	-2.4	-		86.5	0.0	-		87.9	1.6	-		92.3	5.0	-		92.9	0.7	-		88.6	1.7
1981	-		93.4	-1.8	-		94.6	1.3	-		94.7	0.1	-		95.9	1.3	-		99.5	3.8	-		95.1	2.4
1982	-		96.8	-0.9	-		95.5	-1.3	-		95.2	-0.3	-		98.4	3.4	-		102.6	4.3	-		97.7	-1.8
1983	-		97.5	-2.3	-		94.4	-3.2	-		98.5	4.3	-		105.3	6.9	-		104.4	-0.9	-		99.8	-2.7
1984	-		97.6	-2.5	-		100.6	3.1	-		101.2	0.6	-		101.4	0.2	-		108.6	7.1	-		100.1	-4.1
1985	-		110.8	6.4	-		106.0	-4.3	-		108.2	2.1	-		111.9	3.4	-		113.1	1.1	-		104.1	-4.1
1986	-		106.1	-1.3	-		108.9	2.6	-		105.6	-3.0	-		105.5	-0.1	-		112.7	6.8	-		107.5	-5.0
1987	-		-		-		-		-		121.3	9.1	-		-		-		-		-		111.2	-1.3
1988	-		-		-		-		-		125.5	1.7	-		-		-		-		-		123.4	1.7
1989	-		-		-		-		-		135.4	7.0	-		-		-		-		-		126.5	0.8
1990	-		-		-		-		-		134.6	1.2	-		-		-		-		-		133.0	-1.8
1991	-		-		-		-		-		148.4	15.7	-		-		-		-		-		128.3	-4.7
1992	-		-		-		-		-		155.7	11.9	-		-		-		-		-		139.2	-6.2
1993	-		-		-		-		-		148.9	5.5	-		-		-		-		-		141.2	-9.3

Source: U.S. Department of Labor, Bureau of Labor Statistics, Division of Consumer Prices and Price Indexes. - indicates no data collected for period.

Atlanta, GA
Consumer Price Index - All Urban Consumers
Base 1982-1984 = 100
Transportation

For 1947-1993. Columns headed % show percentile change in the index from the previous period for which an index is available.

Year	Jan Index	%	Feb Index	%	Mar Index	%	Apr Index	%	May Index	%	Jun Index	%	Jul Index	%	Aug Index	%	Sep Index	%	Oct Index	%	Nov Index	%	Dec Index	%
1947	-	-	-	-	20.0	-	-	-	-	-	20.2	1.0	-	-	20.4	1.0	-	-	-	-	21.0	2.9	-	-
1948	-	-	21.5	2.4	-	-	-	-	22.0	2.3	-	-	-	-	23.1	5.0	-	-	-	-	23.1	0.0	-	-
1949	-	-	23.5	1.7	-	-	-	-	24.1	2.6	-	-	-	-	24.4	1.2	-	-	-	-	24.4	0.0	-	-
1950	-	-	24.4	0.0	-	-	-	-	24.4	0.0	-	-	-	-	24.8	1.6	-	-	-	-	25.0	0.8	-	-
1951	-	-	24.9	-0.4	-	-	-	-	26.6	6.8	-	-	-	-	26.6	0.0	-	-	-	-	27.2	2.3	-	-
1952	-	-	27.7	1.8	-	-	-	-	27.7	0.0	-	-	-	-	28.0	1.1	-	-	-	-	29.2	4.3	-	-
1953	-	-	-	-	29.1	-0.3	-	-	-	-	28.8	-1.0	-	-	-	-	28.8	0.0	-	-	-	-	28.8	0.0
1954	-	-	-	-	28.4	-1.4	-	-	-	-	28.4	0.0	-	-	-	-	26.8	-5.6	-	-	-	-	28.0	4.5
1955	-	-	-	-	27.5	-1.8	-	-	-	-	27.7	0.7	-	-	-	-	27.2	-1.8	-	-	-	-	27.7	1.8
1956	-	-	-	-	27.7	0.0	-	-	-	-	27.7	0.0	-	-	-	-	28.7	3.6	-	-	-	-	29.1	1.4
1957	-	-	-	-	30.2	3.8	-	-	-	-	29.8	-1.3	-	-	-	-	29.5	-1.0	-	-	-	-	31.0	5.1
1958	-	-	-	-	31.2	0.6	-	-	-	-	31.1	-0.3	-	-	-	-	31.2	0.3	-	-	-	-	32.2	3.2
1959	-	-	-	-	32.3	0.3	-	-	-	-	31.9	-1.2	-	-	-	-	32.5	1.9	-	-	-	-	33.1	1.8
1960	-	-	-	-	32.2	-2.7	-	-	-	-	32.0	-0.6	-	-	-	-	31.8	-0.6	-	-	-	-	31.4	-1.3
1961	-	-	-	-	32.1	2.2	-	-	-	-	32.6	1.6	-	-	-	-	32.5	-0.3	-	-	-	-	32.9	1.2
1962	-	-	-	-	32.4	-1.5	-	-	-	-	33.0	1.9	-	-	-	-	33.4	1.2	-	-	-	-	33.8	1.2
1963	-	-	-	-	33.5	-0.9	-	-	-	-	33.8	0.9	-	-	-	-	33.4	-1.2	-	-	-	-	34.8	4.2
1964	-	-	-	-	34.6	-0.6	-	-	-	-	34.5	-0.3	-	-	-	-	34.7	0.6	-	-	-	-	35.0	0.9
1965	-	-	-	-	35.0	0.0	-	-	-	-	34.0	-2.9	-	-	-	-	34.5	1.5	-	-	-	-	34.8	0.9
1966	-	-	-	-	34.4	-1.1	-	-	-	-	34.5	0.3	-	-	-	-	34.6	0.3	-	-	-	-	34.7	0.3
1967	-	-	-	-	34.7	0.0	-	-	-	-	35.2	1.4	-	-	-	-	35.5	0.9	-	-	-	-	35.9	1.1
1968	-	-	-	-	35.9	0.0	-	-	-	-	36.1	0.6	-	-	-	-	36.0	-0.3	-	-	-	-	36.5	1.4
1969	-	-	-	-	37.3	2.2	-	-	-	-	37.3	0.0	-	-	-	-	37.1	-0.5	-	-	-	-	37.6	1.3
1970	-	-	-	-	37.2	-1.1	-	-	-	-	38.1	2.4	-	-	-	-	38.4	0.8	-	-	-	-	40.1	4.4
1971	-	-	-	-	40.3	0.5	-	-	-	-	41.2	2.2	-	-	-	-	40.4	-1.9	-	-	-	-	40.7	0.7
1972	-	-	-	-	39.2	-3.7	-	-	-	-	39.5	0.8	-	-	-	-	40.1	1.5	-	-	-	-	40.4	0.7
1973	-	-	-	-	40.4	0.0	-	-	-	-	41.3	2.2	-	-	-	-	41.1	-0.5	-	-	-	-	42.2	2.7
1974	-	-	-	-	44.2	4.7	-	-	-	-	47.0	6.3	-	-	-	-	48.5	3.2	-	-	-	-	48.5	0.0
1975	-	-	-	-	48.6	0.2	-	-	-	-	50.4	3.7	-	-	-	-	51.5	2.2	-	-	-	-	52.2	1.4
1976	-	-	-	-	52.4	0.4	-	-	-	-	54.4	3.8	-	-	-	-	55.5	2.0	-	-	-	-	56.0	0.9
1977	-	-	-	-	56.5	0.9	-	-	-	-	57.9	2.5	-	-	-	-	57.5	-0.7	-	-	-	-	58.0	0.9
1978	-	-	57.9	-0.2	-	-	58.1	0.3	-	-	59.5	2.4	-	-	60.3	1.3	-	-	61.3	1.7	-	-	61.8	0.8
1979	-	-	63.0	1.9	-	-	66.3	5.2	-	-	69.4	4.7	-	-	72.3	4.2	-	-	73.8	2.1	-	-	75.6	2.4
1980	-	-	80.4	6.3	-	-	83.4	3.7	-	-	84.0	0.7	-	-	87.3	3.9	-	-	88.2	1.0	-	-	89.3	1.2
1981	-	-	92.5	3.6	-	-	94.4	2.1	-	-	95.2	0.8	-	-	95.1	-0.1	-	-	97.0	2.0	-	-	97.5	0.5
1982	-	-	96.4	-1.1	-	-	94.4	-2.1	-	-	98.3	4.1	-	-	99.2	0.9	-	-	98.7	-0.5	-	-	98.6	-0.1
1983	-	-	96.4	-2.2	-	-	97.9	1.6	-	-	99.5	1.6	-	-	100.6	1.1	-	-	101.3	0.7	-	-	101.8	0.5
1984	-	-	101.6	-0.2	-	-	102.7	1.1	-	-	103.3	0.6	-	-	103.1	-0.2	-	-	103.9	0.8	-	-	104.0	0.1
1985	-	-	103.3	-0.7	-	-	106.1	2.7	-	-	106.6	0.5	-	-	107.5	0.8	-	-	108.2	0.7	-	-	109.7	1.4
1986	-	-	108.4	-1.2	-	-	101.5	-6.4	-	-	103.3	1.8	-	-	100.6	-2.6	-	-	100.1	-0.5	-	-	101.0	0.9
1987	-	-	-	-	-	-	-	-	-	-	102.8	1.8	-	-	-	-	-	-	-	-	-	-	104.7	1.8
1988	-	-	-	-	-	-	-	-	-	-	104.5	-0.2	-	-	-	-	-	-	-	-	-	-	106.7	2.1
1989	-	-	-	-	-	-	-	-	-	-	110.7	3.7	-	-	-	-	-	-	-	-	-	-	111.2	0.5
1990	-	-	-	-	-	-	-	-	-	-	114.4	2.9	-	-	-	-	-	-	-	-	-	-	120.9	5.7
1991	-	-	-	-	-	-	-	-	-	-	119.0	-1.6	-	-	-	-	-	-	-	-	-	-	118.4	-0.5

[Continued]

Atlanta, GA
Consumer Price Index - All Urban Consumers
Base 1982-1984 = 100
Transportation
[Continued]

For 1947-1993. Columns headed % show percentile change in the index from the previous period for which an index is available.

Year	Jan		Feb		Mar		Apr		May		Jun		Jul		Aug		Sep		Oct		Nov		Dec	
	Index	%	Index	%	Index	%	Index	%	Index	%	Index	%	Index	%	Index	%	Index	%	Index	%	Index	%	Index	%
1992	-	-	-	-	-	-	-	-	-	-	117.8	-0.5	-	-	-	-	-	-	-	-	-	-	121.2	2.9
1993	-	-	-	-	-	-	-	-	-	-	123.1	1.6	-	-	-	-	-	-	-	-	-	-	-	-

Source: U.S. Department of Labor, Bureau of Labor Statistics, Division of Consumer Prices and Price Indexes. - indicates no data collected for period.

Atlanta, GA
Consumer Price Index - Urban Wage Earners
Base 1982-1984 = 100
Transportation

For 1947-1993. Columns headed % show percentile change in the index from the previous period for which an index is available.

Year	Jan Index	%	Feb Index	%	Mar Index	%	Apr Index	%	May Index	%	Jun Index	%	Jul Index	%	Aug Index	%	Sep Index	%	Oct Index	%	Nov Index	%	Dec Index	%
1947	-	-	-	-	19.5	-	-	-	-	-	19.6	0.5	-	-	19.9	1.5	-	-	-	-	20.4	2.5	-	-
1948	-	-	20.9	2.5	-	-	-	-	21.4	2.4	-	-	-	-	22.5	5.1	-	-	-	-	22.5	0.0	-	-
1949	-	-	22.9	1.8	-	-	-	-	23.5	2.6	-	-	-	-	23.8	1.3	-	-	-	-	23.8	0.0	-	-
1950	-	-	23.8	0.0	-	-	-	-	23.8	0.0	-	-	-	-	24.1	1.3	-	-	-	-	24.3	0.8	-	-
1951	-	-	24.3	0.0	-	-	-	-	25.9	6.6	-	-	-	-	25.9	0.0	-	-	-	-	26.5	2.3	-	-
1952	-	-	27.0	1.9	-	-	-	-	27.0	0.0	-	-	-	-	27.3	1.1	-	-	-	-	28.4	4.0	-	-
1953	-	-	-	-	28.3	-0.4	-	-	-	-	28.0	-1.1	-	-	-	-	28.0	0.0	-	-	-	-	28.0	0.0
1954	-	-	-	-	27.6	-1.4	-	-	-	-	27.6	0.0	-	-	-	-	26.0	-5.8	-	-	-	-	27.3	5.0
1955	-	-	-	-	26.8	-1.8	-	-	-	-	26.9	0.4	-	-	-	-	26.5	-1.5	-	-	-	-	27.0	1.9
1956	-	-	-	-	27.0	0.0	-	-	-	-	27.0	0.0	-	-	-	-	28.0	3.7	-	-	-	-	28.3	1.1
1957	-	-	-	-	29.4	3.9	-	-	-	-	29.0	-1.4	-	-	-	-	28.7	-1.0	-	-	-	-	30.2	5.2
1958	-	-	-	-	30.3	0.3	-	-	-	-	30.2	-0.3	-	-	-	-	30.4	0.7	-	-	-	-	31.3	3.0
1959	-	-	-	-	31.4	0.3	-	-	-	-	31.1	-1.0	-	-	-	-	31.6	1.6	-	-	-	-	32.2	1.9
1960	-	-	-	-	31.4	-2.5	-	-	-	-	31.2	-0.6	-	-	-	-	31.0	-0.6	-	-	-	-	30.6	-1.3
1961	-	-	-	-	31.3	2.3	-	-	-	-	31.7	1.3	-	-	-	-	31.7	0.0	-	-	-	-	32.0	0.9
1962	-	-	-	-	31.6	-1.2	-	-	-	-	32.1	1.6	-	-	-	-	32.5	1.2	-	-	-	-	32.9	1.2
1963	-	-	-	-	32.6	-0.9	-	-	-	-	32.9	0.9	-	-	-	-	32.5	-1.2	-	-	-	-	33.9	4.3
1964	-	-	-	-	33.7	-0.6	-	-	-	-	33.6	-0.3	-	-	-	-	33.8	0.6	-	-	-	-	34.1	0.9
1965	-	-	-	-	34.1	0.0	-	-	-	-	33.1	-2.9	-	-	-	-	33.6	1.5	-	-	-	-	33.9	0.9
1966	-	-	-	-	33.5	-1.2	-	-	-	-	33.6	0.3	-	-	-	-	33.7	0.3	-	-	-	-	33.8	0.3
1967	-	-	-	-	33.8	0.0	-	-	-	-	34.3	1.5	-	-	-	-	34.6	0.9	-	-	-	-	35.0	1.2
1968	-	-	-	-	34.9	-0.3	-	-	-	-	35.2	0.9	-	-	-	-	35.1	-0.3	-	-	-	-	35.5	1.1
1969	-	-	-	-	36.3	2.3	-	-	-	-	36.3	0.0	-	-	-	-	36.1	-0.6	-	-	-	-	36.6	1.4
1970	-	-	-	-	36.2	-1.1	-	-	-	-	37.1	2.5	-	-	-	-	37.4	0.8	-	-	-	-	39.0	4.3
1971	-	-	-	-	39.2	0.5	-	-	-	-	40.1	2.3	-	-	-	-	39.4	-1.7	-	-	-	-	39.7	0.8
1972	-	-	-	-	38.2	-3.8	-	-	-	-	38.5	0.8	-	-	-	-	39.0	1.3	-	-	-	-	39.3	0.8
1973	-	-	-	-	39.3	0.0	-	-	-	-	40.2	2.3	-	-	-	-	40.0	-0.5	-	-	-	-	41.1	2.8
1974	-	-	-	-	43.1	4.9	-	-	-	-	45.7	6.0	-	-	-	-	47.2	3.3	-	-	-	-	47.2	0.0
1975	-	-	-	-	47.3	0.2	-	-	-	-	49.1	3.8	-	-	-	-	50.1	2.0	-	-	-	-	50.8	1.4
1976	-	-	-	-	51.0	0.4	-	-	-	-	53.0	3.9	-	-	-	-	54.0	1.9	-	-	-	-	54.5	0.9
1977	-	-	-	-	55.0	0.9	-	-	-	-	56.3	2.4	-	-	-	-	56.0	-0.5	-	-	-	-	56.5	0.9
1978	-	-	56.6	0.2	-	-	56.8	0.4	-	-	58.0	2.1	-	-	58.9	1.6	-	-	59.9	1.7	-	-	60.5	1.0
1979	-	-	61.8	2.1	-	-	65.5	6.0	-	-	68.5	4.6	-	-	71.6	4.5	-	-	74.3	3.8	-	-	76.5	3.0
1980	-	-	81.0	5.9	-	-	84.5	4.3	-	-	84.7	0.2	-	-	89.3	5.4	-	-	89.9	0.7	-	-	90.8	1.0
1981	-	-	94.5	4.1	-	-	95.7	1.3	-	-	96.0	0.3	-	-	95.9	-0.1	-	-	97.5	1.7	-	-	98.5	1.0
1982	-	-	97.5	-1.0	-	-	95.1	-2.5	-	-	99.0	4.1	-	-	99.8	0.8	-	-	99.1	-0.7	-	-	98.9	-0.2
1983	-	-	96.5	-2.4	-	-	98.1	1.7	-	-	99.7	1.6	-	-	100.6	0.9	-	-	101.1	0.5	-	-	101.4	0.3
1984	-	-	101.2	-0.2	-	-	102.2	1.0	-	-	102.6	0.4	-	-	102.3	-0.3	-	-	103.0	0.7	-	-	103.1	0.1
1985	-	-	102.3	-0.8	-	-	105.2	2.8	-	-	105.9	0.7	-	-	107.1	1.1	-	-	107.7	0.6	-	-	109.4	1.6
1986	-	-	108.1	-1.2	-	-	100.6	-6.9	-	-	102.5	1.9	-	-	99.6	-2.8	-	-	98.7	-0.9	-	-	99.6	0.9
1987	-	-	-	-	-	-	-	-	-	-	101.5	1.9	-	-	-	-	-	-	-	-	-	-	103.8	2.3
1988	-	-	-	-	-	-	-	-	-	-	103.5	-0.3	-	-	-	-	-	-	-	-	-	-	105.6	2.0
1989	-	-	-	-	-	-	-	-	-	-	109.6	3.8	-	-	-	-	-	-	-	-	-	-	109.7	0.1
1990	-	-	-	-	-	-	-	-	-	-	112.6	2.6	-	-	-	-	-	-	-	-	-	-	118.9	5.6
1991	-	-	-	-	-	-	-	-	-	-	116.9	-1.7	-	-	-	-	-	-	-	-	-	-	116.5	-0.3

[Continued]

Atlanta, GA
Consumer Price Index - Urban Wage Earners
Base 1982-1984 = 100
Transportation
[Continued]

For 1947-1993. Columns headed % show percentile change in the index from the previous period for which an index is available.

Year	Jan		Feb		Mar		Apr		May		Jun		Jul		Aug		Sep		Oct		Nov		Dec	
	Index	%	Index	%	Index	%	Index	%	Index	%	Index	%	Index	%	Index	%	Index	%	Index	%	Index	%	Index	%
1992	-	-	-	-	-	-	-	-	-	-	115.8	-0.6	-	-	-	-	-	-	-	-	-	-	119.1	2.8
1993	-	-	-	-	-	-	-	-	-	-	120.9	1.5	-	-	-	-	-	-	-	-	-	-	-	-

Source: U.S. Department of Labor, Bureau of Labor Statistics, Division of Consumer Prices and Price Indexes. - indicates no data collected for period.

Atlanta, GA
Consumer Price Index - All Urban Consumers
Base 1982-1984 = 100
Medical Care

For 1947-1993. Columns headed % show percentile change in the index from the previous period for which an index is available.

Year	Jan Index	%	Feb Index	%	Mar Index	%	Apr Index	%	May Index	%	Jun Index	%	Jul Index	%	Aug Index	%	Sep Index	%	Oct Index	%	Nov Index	%	Dec Index	%
1947	-	-	-	-	15.1	-	-	-	-	-	15.1	0.0	-	-	15.3	1.3	-	-	-	-	15.3	0.0	-	-
1948	-	-	15.5	1.3	-	-	-	-	15.6	0.6	-	-	-	-	15.8	1.3	-	-	-	-	16.0	1.3	-	-
1949	-	-	16.1	0.6	-	-	-	-	16.1	0.0	-	-	-	-	16.1	0.0	-	-	-	-	16.1	0.0	-	-
1950	-	-	16.1	0.0	-	-	-	-	16.1	0.0	-	-	-	-	16.1	0.0	-	-	-	-	16.3	1.2	-	-
1951	-	-	16.6	1.8	-	-	-	-	17.0	2.4	-	-	-	-	17.0	0.0	-	-	-	-	17.1	0.6	-	-
1952	-	-	17.5	2.3	-	-	-	-	18.2	4.0	-	-	-	-	18.2	0.0	-	-	-	-	18.5	1.6	-	-
1953	-	-	-	-	18.5	0.0	-	-	-	-	18.6	0.5	-	-	-	-	18.4	-1.1	-	-	-	-	18.7	1.6
1954	-	-	-	-	18.9	1.1	-	-	-	-	18.9	0.0	-	-	-	-	19.0	0.5	-	-	-	-	19.0	0.0
1955	-	-	-	-	19.2	1.1	-	-	-	-	19.2	0.0	-	-	-	-	20.0	4.2	-	-	-	-	20.1	0.5
1956	-	-	-	-	20.1	0.0	-	-	-	-	20.3	1.0	-	-	-	-	20.2	-0.5	-	-	-	-	20.3	0.5
1957	-	-	-	-	20.7	2.0	-	-	-	-	20.7	0.0	-	-	-	-	20.8	0.5	-	-	-	-	20.9	0.5
1958	-	-	-	-	21.3	1.9	-	-	-	-	21.4	0.5	-	-	-	-	21.4	0.0	-	-	-	-	21.6	0.9
1959	-	-	-	-	21.6	0.0	-	-	-	-	22.6	4.6	-	-	-	-	22.6	0.0	-	-	-	-	22.8	0.9
1960	-	-	-	-	23.0	0.9	-	-	-	-	23.0	0.0	-	-	-	-	23.0	0.0	-	-	-	-	22.8	-0.9
1961	-	-	-	-	22.8	0.0	-	-	-	-	23.0	0.9	-	-	-	-	23.4	1.7	-	-	-	-	23.6	0.9
1962	-	-	-	-	23.8	0.8	-	-	-	-	23.9	0.4	-	-	-	-	23.9	0.0	-	-	-	-	23.9	0.0
1963	-	-	-	-	23.9	0.0	-	-	-	-	24.4	2.1	-	-	-	-	24.4	0.0	-	-	-	-	24.4	0.0
1964	-	-	-	-	24.6	0.8	-	-	-	-	24.7	0.4	-	-	-	-	25.0	1.2	-	-	-	-	25.1	0.4
1965	-	-	-	-	25.3	0.8	-	-	-	-	25.3	0.0	-	-	-	-	25.5	0.8	-	-	-	-	25.6	0.4
1966	-	-	-	-	26.1	2.0	-	-	-	-	26.6	1.9	-	-	-	-	27.3	2.6	-	-	-	-	27.4	0.4
1967	-	-	-	-	28.1	2.6	-	-	-	-	28.3	0.7	-	-	-	-	28.8	1.8	-	-	-	-	28.9	0.3
1968	-	-	-	-	29.7	2.8	-	-	-	-	30.0	1.0	-	-	-	-	30.8	2.7	-	-	-	-	31.4	1.9
1969	-	-	-	-	32.7	4.1	-	-	-	-	33.3	1.8	-	-	-	-	34.0	2.1	-	-	-	-	34.2	0.6
1970	-	-	-	-	35.1	2.6	-	-	-	-	35.9	2.3	-	-	-	-	36.2	0.8	-	-	-	-	36.9	1.9
1971	-	-	-	-	38.3	3.8	-	-	-	-	38.8	1.3	-	-	-	-	39.1	0.8	-	-	-	-	38.9	-0.5
1972	-	-	-	-	39.2	0.8	-	-	-	-	39.8	1.5	-	-	-	-	39.8	0.0	-	-	-	-	40.1	0.8
1973	-	-	-	-	40.4	0.7	-	-	-	-	41.5	2.7	-	-	-	-	42.3	1.9	-	-	-	-	42.9	1.4
1974	-	-	-	-	43.9	2.3	-	-	-	-	46.4	5.7	-	-	-	-	47.6	2.6	-	-	-	-	48.3	1.5
1975	-	-	-	-	51.3	6.2	-	-	-	-	51.8	1.0	-	-	-	-	53.5	3.3	-	-	-	-	53.7	0.4
1976	-	-	-	-	55.0	2.4	-	-	-	-	55.3	0.5	-	-	-	-	57.0	3.1	-	-	-	-	58.0	1.8
1977	-	-	-	-	59.9	3.3	-	-	-	-	60.9	1.7	-	-	-	-	61.7	1.3	-	-	-	-	61.7	0.0
1978	-	-	62.9	1.9	-	-	63.3	0.6	-	-	63.8	0.8	-	-	64.3	0.8	-	-	64.7	0.6	-	-	64.6	-0.2
1979	-	-	65.9	2.0	-	-	67.2	2.0	-	-	68.0	1.2	-	-	68.8	1.2	-	-	69.4	0.9	-	-	70.5	1.6
1980	-	-	71.5	1.4	-	-	72.1	0.8	-	-	75.0	4.0	-	-	76.4	1.9	-	-	77.0	0.8	-	-	78.3	1.7
1981	-	-	80.6	2.9	-	-	80.9	0.4	-	-	81.6	0.9	-	-	82.9	1.6	-	-	84.9	2.4	-	-	84.5	-0.5
1982	-	-	85.2	0.8	-	-	87.0	2.1	-	-	92.7	6.6	-	-	95.7	3.2	-	-	99.2	3.7	-	-	100.0	0.8
1983	-	-	100.9	0.9	-	-	101.1	0.2	-	-	101.2	0.1	-	-	101.1	-0.1	-	-	101.5	0.4	-	-	101.8	0.3
1984	-	-	103.5	1.7	-	-	104.6	1.1	-	-	106.0	1.3	-	-	107.3	1.2	-	-	108.8	1.4	-	-	109.0	0.2
1985	-	-	110.9	1.7	-	-	111.6	0.6	-	-	113.1	1.3	-	-	113.5	0.4	-	-	115.0	1.3	-	-	114.7	-0.3
1986	-	-	120.4	5.0	-	-	120.9	0.4	-	-	123.2	1.9	-	-	125.3	1.7	-	-	127.2	1.5	-	-	128.6	1.1
1987	-	-	-	-	-	-	-	-	-	-	133.4	3.7	-	-	-	-	-	-	-	-	-	-	139.5	4.6
1988	-	-	-	-	-	-	-	-	-	-	143.8	3.1	-	-	-	-	-	-	-	-	-	-	156.5	8.8
1989	-	-	-	-	-	-	-	-	-	-	162.4	3.8	-	-	-	-	-	-	-	-	-	-	169.1	4.1
1990	-	-	-	-	-	-	-	-	-	-	174.7	3.3	-	-	-	-	-	-	-	-	-	-	180.4	3.3
1991	-	-	-	-	-	-	-	-	-	-	187.8	4.1	-	-	-	-	-	-	-	-	-	-	195.5	4.1

[Continued]

Atlanta, GA
Consumer Price Index - All Urban Consumers
Base 1982-1984 = 100
Medical Care
[Continued]

For 1947-1993. Columns headed % show percentile change in the index from the previous period for which an index is available.

Year	Jan Index	%	Feb Index	%	Mar Index	%	Apr Index	%	May Index	%	Jun Index	%	Jul Index	%	Aug Index	%	Sep Index	%	Oct Index	%	Nov Index	%	Dec Index	%
1992	-	-	-	-	-	-	-	-	-	-	202.1	3.4	-	-	-	-	-	-	-	-	-	-	203.3	0.6
1993	-	-	-	-	-	-	-	-	-	-	210.9	3.7	-	-	-	-	-	-	-	-	-	-	-	-

Source: U.S. Department of Labor, Bureau of Labor Statistics, Division of Consumer Prices and Price Indexes. - indicates no data collected for period.

Atlanta, GA
Consumer Price Index - Urban Wage Earners
Base 1982-1984 = 100
Medical Care

For 1947-1993. Columns headed % show percentile change in the index from the previous period for which an index is available.

Year	Jan Index	%	Feb Index	%	Mar Index	%	Apr Index	%	May Index	%	Jun Index	%	Jul Index	%	Aug Index	%	Sep Index	%	Oct Index	%	Nov Index	%	Dec Index	%
1947	-	-	-	-	14.6	-	-	-	-	-	14.6	0.0	-	-	14.7	0.7	-	-	-	-	14.7	0.0	-	-
1948	-	-	14.9	1.4	-	-	-	-	15.0	0.7	-	-	-	-	15.2	1.3	-	-	-	-	15.4	1.3	-	-
1949	-	-	15.5	0.6	-	-	-	-	15.5	0.0	-	-	-	-	15.5	0.0	-	-	-	-	15.5	0.0	-	-
1950	-	-	15.5	0.0	-	-	-	-	15.5	0.0		-	-	-	15.5	0.0	-	-	-	-	15.6	0.6	-	-
1951	-	-	16.0	2.6	-	-	-	-	16.4	2.5	-	-	-	-	16.3	-0.6	-	-	-	-	16.4	0.6	-	-
1952	-	-	16.8	2.4	-	-	-	-	17.6	4.8	-	-	-	-	17.5	-0.6	-	-	-	-	17.8	1.7	-	-
1953	-	-	-	-	17.8	0.0	-	-	-	-	17.9	0.6	-	-	-	-	17.7	-1.1	-	-	-	-	18.0	1.7
1954	-	-	-	-	18.2	1.1	-	-	-	-	18.2	0.0	-	-	-	-	18.2	0.0	-	-	-	-	18.3	0.5
1955	-	-	-	-	18.5	1.1	-	-	-	-	18.5	0.0	-	-	-	-	19.2	3.8	-	-	-	-	19.4	1.0
1956	-	-	-	-	19.4	0.0	-	-	-	-	19.6	1.0	-	-	-	-	19.5	-0.5	-	-	-	-	19.6	0.5
1957	-	-	-	-	19.9	1.5	-	-	-	-	19.9	0.0	-	-	-	-	20.0	0.5	-	-	-	-	20.1	0.5
1958	-	-	-	-	20.5	2.0	-	-	-	-	20.6	0.5	-	-	-	-	20.6	0.0	-	-	-	-	20.8	1.0
1959	-	-	-	-	20.8	0.0	-	-	-	-	21.8	4.8	-	-	-	-	21.8	0.0	-	-	-	-	22.0	0.9
1960	-	-	-	-	22.1	0.5	-	-	-	-	22.1	0.0	-	-	-	-	22.2	0.5	-	-	-	-	21.9	-1.4
1961	-	-	-	-	21.9	0.0	-	-	-	-	22.2	1.4	-	-	-	-	22.6	1.8	-	-	-	-	22.7	0.4
1962	-	-	-	-	22.9	0.9	-	-	-	-	23.0	0.4	-	-	-	-	23.0	0.0	-	-	-	-	23.0	0.0
1963	-	-	-	-	23.0	0.0	-	-	-	-	23.5	2.2	-	-	-	-	23.5	0.0	-	-	-	-	23.5	0.0
1964	-	-	-	-	23.7	0.9	-	-	-	-	23.7	0.0	-	-	-	-	24.1	1.7	-	-	-	-	24.1	0.0
1965	-	-	-	-	24.3	0.8	-	-	-	-	24.4	0.4	-	-	-	-	24.5	0.4	-	-	-	-	24.6	0.4
1966	-	-	-	-	25.2	2.4	-	-	-	-	25.6	1.6	-	-	-	-	26.2	2.3	-	-	-	-	26.3	0.4
1967	-	-	-	-	27.0	2.7	-	-	-	-	27.2	0.7	-	-	-	-	27.7	1.8	-	-	-	-	27.9	0.7
1968	-	-	-	-	28.6	2.5	-	-	-	-	28.8	0.7	-	-	-	-	29.6	2.8	-	-	-	-	30.2	2.0
1969	-	-	-	-	31.5	4.3	-	-	-	-	32.0	1.6	-	-	-	-	32.7	2.2	-	-	-	-	32.9	0.6
1970	-	-	-	-	33.8	2.7	-	-	-	-	34.5	2.1	-	-	-	-	34.8	0.9	-	-	-	-	35.6	2.3
1971	-	-	-	-	36.9	3.7	-	-	-	-	37.3	1.1	-	-	-	-	37.6	0.8	-	-	-	-	37.5	-0.3
1972	-	-	-	-	37.7	0.5	-	-	-	-	38.3	1.6	-	-	-	-	38.3	0.0	-	-	-	-	38.6	0.8
1973	-	-	-	-	38.8	0.5	-	-	-	-	40.0	3.1	-	-	-	-	40.7	1.7	-	-	-	-	41.3	1.5
1974	-	-	-	-	42.2	2.2	-	-	-	-	44.6	5.7	-	-	-	-	45.8	2.7	-	-	-	-	46.5	1.5
1975	-	-	-	-	49.4	6.2	-	-	-	-	49.8	0.8	-	-	-	-	51.5	3.4	-	-	-	-	51.7	0.4
1976	-	-	-	-	52.9	2.3	-	-	-	-	53.2	0.6	-	-	-	-	54.8	3.0	-	-	-	-	55.8	1.8
1977	-	-	-	-	57.7	3.4	-	-	-	-	58.6	1.6	-	-	-	-	59.3	1.2	-	-	-	-	59.3	0.0
1978	-	-	60.4	1.9	-	-	61.8	2.3	-	-	62.3	0.8	-	-	63.1	1.3	-	-	63.6	0.8	-	-	64.4	1.3
1979	-	-	66.0	2.5	-	-	67.1	1.7	-	-	68.2	1.6	-	-	69.3	1.6	-	-	69.6	0.4	-	-	70.0	0.6
1980	-	-	70.7	1.0	-	-	70.8	0.1	-	-	72.3	2.1	-	-	74.1	2.5	-	-	75.0	1.2	-	-	76.5	2.0
1981	-	-	80.6	5.4	-	-	80.8	0.2	-	-	81.0	0.2	-	-	82.2	1.5	-	-	83.9	2.1	-	-	84.1	0.2
1982	-	-	84.8	0.8	-	-	86.6	2.1	-	-	92.7	7.0	-	-	95.5	3.0	-	-	99.2	3.9	-	-	100.0	0.8
1983	-	-	101.0	1.0	-	-	101.2	0.2	-	-	101.2	0.0	-	-	101.3	0.1	-	-	101.7	0.4	-	-	102.0	0.3
1984	-	-	103.6	1.6	-	-	104.7	1.1	-	-	106.0	1.2	-	-	107.3	1.2	-	-	108.7	1.3	-	-	109.0	0.3
1985	-	-	111.0	1.8	-	-	111.6	0.5	-	-	113.2	1.4	-	-	113.7	0.4	-	-	115.1	1.2	-	-	114.6	-0.4
1986	-	-	120.6	5.2	-	-	121.1	0.4	-	-	123.6	2.1	-	-	125.8	1.8	-	-	127.6	1.4	-	-	128.8	0.9
1987	-	-	-	-	-	-	-	-	-	-	133.5	3.6	-	-	-	-	-	-	-	-	-	-	139.8	4.7
1988	-	-	-	-	-	-	-	-	-	-	144.1	3.1	-	-	-	-	-	-	-	-	-	-	156.7	8.7
1989	-	-	-	-	-	-	-	-	-	-	162.3	3.6	-	-	-	-	-	-	-	-	-	-	168.8	4.0
1990	-	-	-	-	-	-	-	-	-	-	174.0	3.1	-	-	-	-	-	-	-	-	-	-	180.2	3.6
1991	-	-	-	-	-	-	-	-	-	-	187.6	4.1	-	-	-	-	-	-	-	-	-	-	195.2	4.1

[Continued]

Atlanta, GA
Consumer Price Index - Urban Wage Earners
Base 1982-1984 = 100
Medical Care
[Continued]

For 1947-1993. Columns headed % show percentile change in the index from the previous period for which an index is available.

Year	Jan		Feb		Mar		Apr		May		Jun		Jul		Aug		Sep		Oct		Nov		Dec	
	Index	%	Index	%	Index	%	Index	%	Index	%	Index	%	Index	%	Index	%	Index	%	Index	%	Index	%	Index	%
1992	-	-	-	-	-	-	-	-	-	-	202.0	3.5	-	-	-	-	-	-	-	-	-	-	202.7	0.3
1993	-	-	-	-	-	-	-	-	-	-	210.2	3.7	-	-	-	-	-	-	-	-	-	-	-	-

Source: U.S. Department of Labor, Bureau of Labor Statistics, Division of Consumer Prices and Price Indexes. - indicates no data collected for period.

Atlanta, GA
Consumer Price Index - All Urban Consumers
Base 1982-1984 = 100
Entertainment

For 1975-1993. Columns headed % show percentile change in the index from the previous period for which an index is available.

Year	Jan Index	%	Feb Index	%	Mar Index	%	Apr Index	%	May Index	%	Jun Index	%	Jul Index	%	Aug Index	%	Sep Index	%	Oct Index	%	Nov Index	%	Dec Index	%
1975	-		-		-		-		-		-		-		-		-		-		-		76.6	-
1976	-		-		76.2	-0.5	-		-		77.7	2.0	-		-		77.6	-0.1	-		-		77.8	0.3
1977	-		-		78.8	1.3	-		-		80.7	2.4	-		-		81.4	0.9	-		-		81.3	-0.1
1978	-		83.2	2.3	-		83.7	0.6	-		84.4	0.8	-		83.9	-0.6	-		85.2	1.5	-		82.5	-3.2
1979	-		84.7	2.7	-		87.2	3.0	-		86.3	-1.0	-		87.3	1.2	-		85.7	-1.8	-		82.0	-4.3
1980	-		85.1	3.8	-		85.5	0.5	-		86.1	0.7	-		94.3	9.5	-		92.3	-2.1	-		91.0	-1.4
1981	-		93.7	3.0	-		94.1	0.4	-		92.7	-1.5	-		94.8	2.3	-		97.8	3.2	-		95.8	-2.0
1982	-		101.0	5.4	-		94.3	-6.6	-		96.6	2.4	-		96.2	-0.4	-		101.3	5.3	-		98.1	-3.2
1983	-		95.4	-2.8	-		96.5	1.2	-		98.3	1.9	-		98.7	0.4	-		98.6	-0.1	-		101.9	3.3
1984	-		102.8	0.9	-		103.4	0.6	-		103.6	0.2	-		104.6	1.0	-		106.1	1.4	-		105.2	-0.8
1985	-		106.1	0.9	-		109.1	2.8	-		113.5	4.0	-		114.7	1.1	-		114.4	-0.3	-		113.0	-1.2
1986	-		116.8	3.4	-		117.7	0.8	-		120.0	2.0	-		119.5	-0.4	-		120.0	0.4	-		120.1	0.1
1987	-		-		-		-		-		123.3	2.7	-		-		-		-		-		125.9	2.1
1988	-		-		-		-		-		127.5	1.3	-		-		-		-		-		130.1	2.0
1989	-		-		-		-		-		136.1	4.6	-		-		-		-		-		141.6	4.0
1990	-		-		-		-		-		147.0	3.8	-		-		-		-		-		152.6	3.8
1991	-		-		-		-		-		155.7	2.0	-		-		-		-		-		157.7	1.3
1992	-		-		-		-		-		160.2	1.6	-		-		-		-		-		166.5	3.9
1993	-		-		-		-		-		170.3	2.3	-		-		-		-		-		-	

Source: U.S. Department of Labor, Bureau of Labor Statistics, Division of Consumer Prices and Price Indexes. - indicates no data collected for period.

Atlanta, GA
Consumer Price Index - Urban Wage Earners
Base 1982-1984 = 100
Entertainment

For 1975-1993. Columns headed % show percentile change in the index from the previous period for which an index is available.

Year	Jan Index	%	Feb Index	%	Mar Index	%	Apr Index	%	May Index	%	Jun Index	%	Jul Index	%	Aug Index	%	Sep Index	%	Oct Index	%	Nov Index	%	Dec Index	%
1975	-	-	-	-	-	-	-	-	-	-	-	-	-	-	-	-	-	-	-	-	-	-	69.3	-
1976	-	-	-	-	69.0	-0.4	-	-	-	-	70.3	1.9	-	-	-	-	70.2	-0.1	-	-	-	-	70.4	0.3
1977	-	-	-	-	71.3	1.3	-	-	-	-	73.0	2.4	-	-	-	-	73.6	0.8	-	-	-	-	73.6	0.0
1978	-	-	74.7	1.5	-	-	74.3	-0.5	-	-	75.0	0.9	-	-	74.9	-0.1	-	-	75.1	0.3	-	-	73.5	-2.1
1979	-	-	72.7	-1.1	-	-	75.3	3.6	-	-	75.4	0.1	-	-	76.7	1.7	-	-	76.8	0.1	-	-	77.7	1.2
1980	-	-	89.6	15.3	-	-	89.8	0.2	-	-	90.9	1.2	-	-	90.0	-1.0	-	-	88.8	-1.3	-	-	88.5	-0.3
1981	-	-	99.9	12.9	-	-	99.5	-0.4	-	-	100.5	1.0	-	-	100.5	0.0	-	-	97.8	-2.7	-	-	97.4	-0.4
1982	-	-	102.1	4.8	-	-	96.9	-5.1	-	-	99.0	2.2	-	-	98.3	-0.7	-	-	101.0	2.7	-	-	101.5	0.5
1983	-	-	89.5	-11.8	-	-	90.8	1.5	-	-	95.1	4.7	-	-	95.6	0.5	-	-	95.1	-0.5	-	-	104.0	9.4
1984	-	-	104.9	0.9	-	-	104.9	0.0	-	-	105.0	0.1	-	-	105.7	0.7	-	-	108.0	2.2	-	-	104.8	-3.0
1985	-	-	105.4	0.6	-	-	109.0	3.4	-	-	112.5	3.2	-	-	113.5	0.9	-	-	113.4	-0.1	-	-	109.6	-3.4
1986	-	-	116.9	6.7	-	-	117.3	0.3	-	-	120.9	3.1	-	-	118.0	-2.4	-	-	119.3	1.1	-	-	119.3	0.0
1987	-	-	-	-	-	-	-	-	-	-	122.0	2.3	-	-	-	-	-	-	-	-	-	-	124.3	1.9
1988	-	-	-	-	-	-	-	-	-	-	126.4	1.7	-	-	-	-	-	-	-	-	-	-	129.0	2.1
1989	-	-	-	-	-	-	-	-	-	-	134.4	4.2	-	-	-	-	-	-	-	-	-	-	140.5	4.5
1990	-	-	-	-	-	-	-	-	-	-	146.2	4.1	-	-	-	-	-	-	-	-	-	-	152.4	4.2
1991	-	-	-	-	-	-	-	-	-	-	155.6	2.1	-	-	-	-	-	-	-	-	-	-	157.5	1.2
1992	-	-	-	-	-	-	-	-	-	-	160.2	1.7	-	-	-	-	-	-	-	-	-	-	166.6	4.0
1993	-	-	-	-	-	-	-	-	-	-	170.4	2.3	-	-	-	-	-	-	-	-	-	-	-	-

Source: U.S. Department of Labor, Bureau of Labor Statistics, Division of Consumer Prices and Price Indexes. - indicates no data collected for period.

Atlanta, GA
Consumer Price Index - All Urban Consumers
Base 1982-1984 = 100
Other Goods and Services

For 1975-1993. Columns headed % show percentile change in the index from the previous period for which an index is available.

Year	Jan Index	%	Feb Index	%	Mar Index	%	Apr Index	%	May Index	%	Jun Index	%	Jul Index	%	Aug Index	%	Sep Index	%	Oct Index	%	Nov Index	%	Dec Index	%
1975	-	-	-	-	-	-	-	-	-	-	-	-	-	-	-	-	-	-	-	-	-	-	54.7	-
1976	-	-	-	-	54.8	0.2	-	-	-	-	55.4	1.1	-	-	-	-	55.7	0.5	-	-	-	-	56.5	1.4
1977	-	-	-	-	57.1	1.1	-	-	-	-	58.1	1.8	-	-	-	-	59.5	2.4	-	-	-	-	60.5	1.7
1978	-	-	60.4	-0.2	-	-	61.1	1.2	-	-	61.8	1.1	-	-	63.8	3.2	-	-	65.2	2.2	-	-	65.3	0.2
1979	-	-	67.3	3.1	-	-	67.8	0.7	-	-	67.9	0.1	-	-	69.1	1.8	-	-	71.1	2.9	-	-	72.0	1.3
1980	-	-	73.8	2.5	-	-	74.1	0.4	-	-	75.3	1.6	-	-	75.6	0.4	-	-	77.8	2.9	-	-	79.2	1.8
1981	-	-	81.5	2.9	-	-	83.3	2.2	-	-	83.9	0.7	-	-	84.1	0.2	-	-	86.6	3.0	-	-	87.6	1.2
1982	-	-	87.9	0.3	-	-	90.0	2.4	-	-	91.0	1.1	-	-	91.9	1.0	-	-	95.2	3.6	-	-	96.6	1.5
1983	-	-	98.5	2.0	-	-	98.9	0.4	-	-	98.9	0.0	-	-	100.6	1.7	-	-	103.4	2.8	-	-	104.2	0.8
1984	-	-	106.2	1.9	-	-	106.0	-0.2	-	-	107.7	1.6	-	-	108.3	0.6	-	-	110.2	1.8	-	-	110.3	0.1
1985	-	-	111.7	1.3	-	-	111.3	-0.4	-	-	112.0	0.6	-	-	113.2	1.1	-	-	115.1	1.7	-	-	116.2	1.0
1986	-	-	118.3	1.8	-	-	119.0	0.6	-	-	118.5	-0.4	-	-	120.0	1.3	-	-	121.6	1.3	-	-	122.9	1.1
1987	-	-	-	-	-	-	-	-	-	-	126.0	2.5	-	-	-	-	-	-	-	-	-	-	124.7	-1.0
1988	-	-	-	-	-	-	-	-	-	-	126.2	1.2	-	-	-	-	-	-	-	-	-	-	132.4	4.9
1989	-	-	-	-	-	-	-	-	-	-	135.5	2.3	-	-	-	-	-	-	-	-	-	-	142.3	5.0
1990	-	-	-	-	-	-	-	-	-	-	151.9	6.7	-	-	-	-	-	-	-	-	-	-	158.4	4.3
1991	-	-	-	-	-	-	-	-	-	-	165.7	4.6	-	-	-	-	-	-	-	-	-	-	167.3	1.0
1992	-	-	-	-	-	-	-	-	-	-	171.7	2.6	-	-	-	-	-	-	-	-	-	-	174.4	1.6
1993	-	-	-	-	-	-	-	-	-	-	182.7	4.8	-	-	-	-	-	-	-	-	-	-	-	-

Source: U.S. Department of Labor, Bureau of Labor Statistics, Division of Consumer Prices and Price Indexes. - indicates no data collected for period.

Atlanta, GA
Consumer Price Index - Urban Wage Earners
Base 1982-1984 = 100
Other Goods and Services

For 1975-1993. Columns headed % show percentile change in the index from the previous period for which an index is available.

Year	Jan Index	%	Feb Index	%	Mar Index	%	Apr Index	%	May Index	%	Jun Index	%	Jul Index	%	Aug Index	%	Sep Index	%	Oct Index	%	Nov Index	%	Dec Index	%
1975	-	-	-	-	-	-	-	-	-	-	-	-	-	-	-	-	-	-	-	-	-	-	57.3	-
1976	-	-	-	-	57.4	0.2	-	-	-	-	58.1	1.2	-	-	-	-	58.4	0.5	-	-	-	-	59.2	1.4
1977	-	-	-	-	59.8	1.0	-	-	-	-	60.9	1.8	-	-	-	-	62.4	2.5	-	-	-	-	63.3	1.4
1978	-	-	64.0	1.1	-	-	64.4	0.6	-	-	65.2	1.2	-	-	65.3	0.2	-	-	66.7	2.1	-	-	66.4	-0.4
1979	-	-	68.5	3.2	-	-	68.9	0.6	-	-	69.9	1.5	-	-	70.5	0.9	-	-	72.2	2.4	-	-	72.6	0.6
1980	-	-	74.1	2.1	-	-	74.4	0.4	-	-	75.1	0.9	-	-	75.5	0.5	-	-	77.7	2.9	-	-	79.0	1.7
1981	-	-	81.1	2.7	-	-	81.6	0.6	-	-	83.4	2.2	-	-	84.2	1.0	-	-	86.1	2.3	-	-	87.1	1.2
1982	-	-	87.4	0.3	-	-	89.6	2.5	-	-	90.9	1.5	-	-	91.7	0.9	-	-	94.9	3.5	-	-	96.5	1.7
1983	-	-	98.7	2.3	-	-	99.2	0.5	-	-	99.3	0.1	-	-	101.1	1.8	-	-	103.5	2.4	-	-	104.3	0.8
1984	-	-	106.7	2.3	-	-	106.3	-0.4	-	-	107.9	1.5	-	-	108.5	0.6	-	-	109.7	1.1	-	-	109.8	0.1
1985	-	-	111.4	1.5	-	-	111.3	-0.1	-	-	111.9	0.5	-	-	113.3	1.3	-	-	114.6	1.1	-	-	115.9	1.1
1986	-	-	118.5	2.2	-	-	119.5	0.8	-	-	118.6	-0.8	-	-	119.8	1.0	-	-	121.2	1.2	-	-	122.5	1.1
1987	-	-	-	-	-	-	-	-	-	-	127.1	3.8	-	-	-	-	-	-	-	-	-	-	125.7	-1.1
1988	-	-	-	-	-	-	-	-	-	-	127.3	1.3	-	-	-	-	-	-	-	-	-	-	133.7	5.0
1989	-	-	-	-	-	-	-	-	-	-	137.5	2.8	-	-	-	-	-	-	-	-	-	-	144.9	5.4
1990	-	-	-	-	-	-	-	-	-	-	155.2	7.1	-	-	-	-	-	-	-	-	-	-	160.9	3.7
1991	-	-	-	-	-	-	-	-	-	-	168.1	4.5	-	-	-	-	-	-	-	-	-	-	170.7	1.5
1992	-	-	-	-	-	-	-	-	-	-	176.7	3.5	-	-	-	-	-	-	-	-	-	-	179.4	1.5
1993	-	-	-	-	-	-	-	-	-	-	187.3	4.4	-	-	-	-	-	-	-	-	-	-	-	-

Source: U.S. Department of Labor, Bureau of Labor Statistics, Division of Consumer Prices and Price Indexes. - indicates no data collected for period.

Baltimore, MD
Consumer Price Index - All Urban Consumers
Base 1982-1984 = 100
Annual Averages

For 1914-1993. Columns headed % show percentile change in the index from the previous period for which an index is available.

Year	All Items		Food & Beverage		Housing		Apparel & Upkeep		Trans-portation		Medical Care		Entertain-ment		Other Goods & Services	
	Index	%	Index	%	Index	%	Index	%	Index	%	Index	%	Index	%	Index	%
1914	-	-	-	-	-	-	-	-	-	-	-	-	-	-	-	-
1915	8.9	-	-	-	-	-	-	-	-	-	-	-	-	-	-	-
1916	9.7	9.0	-	-	-	-	-	-	-	-	-	-	-	-	-	-
1917	11.9	22.7	-	-	-	-	-	-	-	-	-	-	-	-	-	-
1918	14.3	20.2	-	-	-	-	-	-	-	-	-	-	-	-	-	-
1919	16.3	14.0	-	-	-	-	-	-	-	-	-	-	-	-	-	-
1920	18.3	12.3	-	-	-	-	-	-	-	-	-	-	-	-	-	-
1921	16.2	-11.5	-	-	-	-	-	-	-	-	-	-	-	-	-	-
1922	15.4	-4.9	-	-	-	-	-	-	-	-	-	-	-	-	-	-
1923	15.7	1.9	-	-	-	-	-	-	-	-	-	-	-	-	-	-
1924	15.7	0.0	-	-	-	-	-	-	-	-	-	-	-	-	-	-
1925	16.2	3.2	-	-	-	-	-	-	-	-	-	-	-	-	-	-
1926	16.4	1.2	-	-	-	-	-	-	-	-	-	-	-	-	-	-
1927	16.0	-2.4	-	-	-	-	-	-	-	-	-	-	-	-	-	-
1928	15.9	-0.6	-	-	-	-	-	-	-	-	-	-	-	-	-	-
1929	15.9	0.0	-	-	-	-	-	-	-	-	-	-	-	-	-	-
1930	15.6	-1.9	-	-	-	-	-	-	-	-	-	-	-	-	-	-
1931	14.4	-7.7	-	-	-	-	-	-	-	-	-	-	-	-	-	-
1932	13.1	-9.0	-	-	-	-	-	-	-	-	-	-	-	-	-	-
1933	12.5	-4.6	-	-	-	-	-	-	-	-	-	-	-	-	-	-
1934	13.0	4.0	-	-	-	-	-	-	-	-	-	-	-	-	-	-
1935	13.3	2.3	-	-	-	-	-	-	-	-	-	-	-	-	-	-
1936	13.4	0.8	-	-	-	-	-	-	-	-	-	-	-	-	-	-
1937	13.8	3.0	-	-	-	-	-	-	-	-	-	-	-	-	-	-
1938	13.5	-2.2	-	-	-	-	-	-	-	-	-	-	-	-	-	-
1939	13.4	-0.7	-	-	-	-	-	-	-	-	-	-	-	-	-	-
1940	13.5	0.7	-	-	-	-	-	-	-	-	-	-	-	-	-	-
1941	14.3	5.9	-	-	-	-	-	-	-	-	-	-	-	-	-	-
1942	16.0	11.9	-	-	-	-	-	-	-	-	-	-	-	-	-	-
1943	17.0	6.3	-	-	-	-	-	-	-	-	-	-	-	-	-	-
1944	17.3	1.8	-	-	-	-	-	-	-	-	-	-	-	-	-	-
1945	17.8	2.9	-	-	-	-	-	-	-	-	-	-	-	-	-	-
1946	19.2	7.9	-	-	-	-	-	-	-	-	-	-	-	-	-	-
1947	22.1	15.1	-	-	-	-	-	-	17.3	-	12.8	-	-	-	-	-
1948	23.8	7.7	-	-	-	-	-	-	18.8	8.7	13.3	3.9	-	-	-	-
1949	23.7	-0.4	-	-	-	-	-	-	21.8	16.0	13.4	0.8	-	-	-	-
1950	23.9	0.8	-	-	-	-	-	-	22.7	4.1	13.6	1.5	-	-	-	-
1951	25.6	7.1	-	-	-	-	-	-	24.2	6.6	14.8	8.8	-	-	-	-
1952	26.3	2.7	-	-	-	-	-	-	25.6	5.8	16.4	10.8	-	-	-	-
1953	26.6	1.1	-	-	-	-	38.1	-	26.9	5.1	17.4	6.1	-	-	-	-
1954	26.7	0.4	-	-	-	-	38.0	-0.3	26.6	-1.1	17.6	1.1	-	-	-	-
1955	26.7	0.0	-	-	-	-	37.9	-0.3	26.4	-0.8	17.8	1.1	-	-	-	-
1956	27.1	1.5	-	-	-	-	39.3	3.7	26.9	1.9	18.6	4.5	-	-	-	-
1957	28.1	3.7	-	-	-	-	40.1	2.0	28.5	5.9	19.1	2.7	-	-	-	-
1958	28.9	2.8	-	-	-	-	40.7	1.5	29.3	2.8	19.7	3.1	-	-	-	-

[Continued]

Baltimore, MD
Consumer Price Index - All Urban Consumers
Base 1982-1984 = 100
Annual Averages
[Continued]

For 1914-1993. Columns headed % show percentile change in the index from the previous period for which an index is available.

Year	All Items		Food & Beverage		Housing		Apparel & Upkeep		Trans- portation		Medical Care		Entertain- ment		Other Goods & Services	
	Index	%	Index	%	Index	%	Index	%	Index	%	Index	%	Index	%	Index	%
1959	29.4	1.7	-	-	-	-	41.6	2.2	31.1	6.1	21.0	6.6	-	-	-	-
1960	29.8	1.4	-	-	-	-	42.2	1.4	30.9	-0.6	22.2	5.7	-	-	-	-
1961	30.1	1.0	-	-	-	-	42.9	1.7	31.4	1.6	23.2	4.5	-	-	-	-
1962	30.3	0.7	-	-	-	-	43.2	0.7	31.4	0.0	23.7	2.2	-	-	-	-
1963	30.8	1.7	-	-	-	-	43.6	0.9	32.0	1.9	25.2	6.3	-	-	-	-
1964	31.1	1.0	-	-	-	-	43.5	-0.2	32.8	2.5	25.8	2.4	-	-	-	-
1965	31.6	1.6	-	-	-	-	44.1	1.4	33.3	1.5	26.4	2.3	-	-	-	-
1966	32.7	3.5	-	-	-	-	45.4	2.9	33.6	0.9	27.5	4.2	-	-	-	-
1967	33.4	2.1	-	-	-	-	47.5	4.6	34.3	2.1	29.8	8.4	-	-	-	-
1968	34.8	4.2	-	-	-	-	49.7	4.6	35.5	3.5	31.5	5.7	-	-	-	-
1969	36.9	6.0	-	-	-	-	53.7	8.0	37.4	5.4	33.6	6.7	-	-	-	-
1970	39.1	6.0	-	-	-	-	56.6	5.4	38.5	2.9	36.7	9.2	-	-	-	-
1971	41.3	5.6	-	-	-	-	58.6	3.5	40.3	4.7	40.5	10.4	-	-	-	-
1972	42.2	2.2	-	-	-	-	58.8	0.3	40.0	-0.7	42.5	4.9	-	-	-	-
1973	45.1	6.9	-	-	-	-	62.0	5.4	41.3	3.2	44.4	4.5	-	-	-	-
1974	51.0	13.1	-	-	-	-	67.1	8.2	46.1	11.6	49.2	10.8	-	-	-	-
1975	55.2	8.2	-	-	-	-	70.1	4.5	50.2	8.9	53.8	9.3	-	-	-	-
1976	58.1	5.3	63.9	-	55.1	-	73.2	4.4	54.5	8.6	57.5	6.9	66.9	-	57.2	-
1977	62.2	7.1	67.9	6.3	59.8	8.5	77.2	5.5	57.7	5.9	61.9	7.7	69.7	4.2	60.3	5.4
1978	66.7	7.2	74.3	9.4	64.9	8.5	80.6	4.4	60.1	4.2	65.7	6.1	72.5	4.0	64.4	6.8
1979	73.0	9.4	81.2	9.3	70.4	8.5	83.2	3.2	68.9	14.6	72.2	9.9	76.6	5.7	69.5	7.9
1980	83.7	14.7	87.9	8.3	82.8	17.6	93.3	12.1	82.3	19.4	79.2	9.7	83.5	9.0	75.8	9.1
1981	91.5	9.3	94.0	6.9	91.2	10.1	96.7	3.6	92.0	11.8	85.0	7.3	90.0	7.8	82.5	8.8
1982	95.6	4.5	96.5	2.7	95.5	4.7	98.2	1.6	96.0	4.3	94.0	10.6	94.4	4.9	89.6	8.6
1983	99.9	4.5	99.5	3.1	99.6	4.3	100.5	2.3	99.8	4.0	100.6	7.0	101.5	7.5	101.2	12.9
1984	104.5	4.6	104.0	4.5	104.8	5.2	101.3	0.8	104.3	4.5	105.4	4.8	104.2	2.7	109.2	7.9
1985	108.2	3.5	107.1	3.0	108.3	3.3	106.3	4.9	107.3	2.9	111.9	6.2	109.3	4.9	114.1	4.5
1986	110.9	2.5	112.0	4.6	111.1	2.6	110.8	4.2	104.5	-2.6	121.8	8.8	113.9	4.2	120.3	5.4
1987	114.2	3.0	116.8	4.3	112.6	1.4	119.7	8.0	106.9	2.3	127.9	5.0	118.9	4.4	127.1	5.7
1988	119.3	4.5	121.8	4.3	116.2	3.2	130.1	8.7	111.5	4.3	134.7	5.3	122.8	3.3	138.9	9.3
1989	124.5	4.4	129.2	6.1	120.0	3.3	127.8	-1.8	116.9	4.8	145.6	8.1	128.7	4.8	149.2	7.4
1990	130.8	5.1	136.9	6.0	125.2	4.3	128.1	0.2	122.8	5.0	158.4	8.8	138.3	7.5	158.5	6.2
1991	136.4	4.3	140.6	2.7	131.0	4.6	132.9	3.7	125.5	2.2	171.9	8.5	143.8	4.0	172.8	9.0
1992	140.1	2.7	142.4	1.3	133.3	1.8	135.2	1.7	128.5	2.4	184.4	7.3	149.3	3.8	188.2	8.9
1993	-	-	-	-	-	-	-	-	-	-	-	-	-	-	-	-

Source: U.S. Department of Labor, Bureau of Labor Statistics, Division of Consumer Prices and Price Indexes. - indicates no data collected for period.

Baltimore, MD
Consumer Price Index - Urban Wage Earners
Base 1982-1984 = 100
Annual Averages

For 1914-1993. Columns headed % show percentile change in the index from the previous period for which an index is available.

Year	All Items		Food & Beverage		Housing		Apparel & Upkeep		Trans-portation		Medical Care		Entertain-ment		Other Goods & Services	
	Index	%	Index	%	Index	%	Index	%	Index	%	Index	%	Index	%	Index	%
1914	-	-	-	-	-	-	-	-	-	-	-	-	-	-	-	-
1915	8.9	-	-	-	-	-	-	-	-	-	-	-	-	-	-	-
1916	9.7	9.0	-	-	-	-	-	-	-	-	-	-	-	-	-	-
1917	11.9	22.7	-	-	-	-	-	-	-	-	-	-	-	-	-	-
1918	14.4	21.0	-	-	-	-	-	-	-	-	-	-	-	-	-	-
1919	16.3	13.2	-	-	-	-	-	-	-	-	-	-	-	-	-	-
1920	18.3	12.3	-	-	-	-	-	-	-	-	-	-	-	-	-	-
1921	16.3	-10.9	-	-	-	-	-	-	-	-	-	-	-	-	-	-
1922	15.4	-5.5	-	-	-	-	-	-	-	-	-	-	-	-	-	-
1923	15.8	2.6	-	-	-	-	-	-	-	-	-	-	-	-	-	-
1924	15.8	0.0	-	-	-	-	-	-	-	-	-	-	-	-	-	-
1925	16.2	2.5	-	-	-	-	-	-	-	-	-	-	-	-	-	-
1926	16.4	1.2	-	-	-	-	-	-	-	-	-	-	-	-	-	-
1927	16.0	-2.4	-	-	-	-	-	-	-	-	-	-	-	-	-	-
1928	15.9	-0.6	-	-	-	-	-	-	-	-	-	-	-	-	-	-
1929	15.9	0.0	-	-	-	-	-	-	-	-	-	-	-	-	-	-
1930	15.7	-1.3	-	-	-	-	-	-	-	-	-	-	-	-	-	-
1931	14.5	-7.6	-	-	-	-	-	-	-	-	-	-	-	-	-	-
1932	13.1	-9.7	-	-	-	-	-	-	-	-	-	-	-	-	-	-
1933	12.5	-4.6	-	-	-	-	-	-	-	-	-	-	-	-	-	-
1934	13.0	4.0	-	-	-	-	-	-	-	-	-	-	-	-	-	-
1935	13.4	3.1	-	-	-	-	-	-	-	-	-	-	-	-	-	-
1936	13.5	0.7	-	-	-	-	-	-	-	-	-	-	-	-	-	-
1937	13.8	2.2	-	-	-	-	-	-	-	-	-	-	-	-	-	-
1938	13.6	-1.4	-	-	-	-	-	-	-	-	-	-	-	-	-	-
1939	13.5	-0.7	-	-	-	-	-	-	-	-	-	-	-	-	-	-
1940	13.5	0.0	-	-	-	-	-	-	-	-	-	-	-	-	-	-
1941	14.4	6.7	-	-	-	-	-	-	-	-	-	-	-	-	-	-
1942	16.0	11.1	-	-	-	-	-	-	-	-	-	-	-	-	-	-
1943	17.1	6.9	-	-	-	-	-	-	-	-	-	-	-	-	-	-
1944	17.3	1.2	-	-	-	-	-	-	-	-	-	-	-	-	-	-
1945	17.9	3.5	-	-	-	-	-	-	-	-	-	-	-	-	-	-
1946	19.3	7.8	-	-	-	-	-	-	-	-	-	-	-	-	-	-
1947	22.2	15.0	-	-	-	-	-	-	17.2	-	13.7	-	-	-	-	-
1948	23.9	7.7	-	-	-	-	-	-	18.7	8.7	14.2	3.6	-	-	-	-
1949	23.8	-0.4	-	-	-	-	-	-	21.7	16.0	14.3	0.7	-	-	-	-
1950	24.0	0.8	-	-	-	-	-	-	22.5	3.7	14.5	1.4	-	-	-	-
1951	25.7	7.1	-	-	-	-	-	-	24.0	6.7	15.7	8.3	-	-	-	-
1952	26.4	2.7	-	-	-	-	-	-	25.5	6.3	17.5	11.5	-	-	-	-
1953	26.7	1.1	-	-	-	-	39.0	-	26.7	4.7	18.5	5.7	-	-	-	-
1954	26.8	0.4	-	-	-	-	38.9	-0.3	26.5	-0.7	18.7	1.1	-	-	-	-
1955	26.8	0.0	-	-	-	-	38.8	-0.3	26.2	-1.1	18.9	1.1	-	-	-	-
1956	27.2	1.5	-	-	-	-	40.2	3.6	26.7	1.9	19.7	4.2	-	-	-	-
1957	28.2	3.7	-	-	-	-	41.1	2.2	28.4	6.4	20.3	3.0	-	-	-	-
1958	29.0	2.8	-	-	-	-	41.6	1.2	29.1	2.5	20.9	3.0				

[Continued]

Baltimore, MD
Consumer Price Index - Urban Wage Earners
Base 1982-1984 = 100
Annual Averages
[Continued]

For 1914-1993. Columns headed % show percentile change in the index from the previous period for which an index is available.

Year	All Items		Food & Beverage		Housing		Apparel & Upkeep		Trans- portation		Medical Care		Entertain- ment		Other Goods & Services	
	Index	%	Index	%	Index	%	Index	%	Index	%	Index	%	Index	%	Index	%
1959	29.5	1.7	-	-	-	-	42.5	2.2	30.9	6.2	22.3	6.7	-	-	-	-
1960	29.9	1.4	-	-	-	-	43.2	1.6	30.7	-0.6	23.6	5.8	-	-	-	-
1961	30.2	1.0	-	-	-	-	43.9	1.6	31.2	1.6	24.7	4.7	-	-	-	-
1962	30.4	0.7	-	-	-	-	44.2	0.7	31.2	0.0	25.2	2.0	-	-	-	-
1963	30.9	1.6	-	-	-	-	44.6	0.9	31.8	1.9	26.7	6.0	-	-	-	-
1964	31.2	1.0	-	-	-	-	44.6	0.0	32.6	2.5	27.4	2.6	-	-	-	-
1965	31.7	1.6	-	-	-	-	45.1	1.1	33.1	1.5	28.1	2.6	-	-	-	-
1966	32.8	3.5	-	-	-	-	46.5	3.1	33.4	0.9	29.3	4.3	-	-	-	-
1967	33.5	2.1	-	-	-	-	48.6	4.5	34.1	2.1	31.7	8.2	-	-	-	-
1968	34.9	4.2	-	-	-	-	50.8	4.5	35.2	3.2	33.4	5.4	-	-	-	-
1969	37.1	6.3	-	-	-	-	54.9	8.1	37.1	5.4	35.7	6.9	-	-	-	-
1970	39.2	5.7	-	-	-	-	57.9	5.5	38.3	3.2	39.0	9.2	-	-	-	-
1971	41.4	5.6	-	-	-	-	60.0	3.6	40.0	4.4	43.0	10.3	-	-	-	-
1972	42.4	2.4	-	-	-	-	60.2	0.3	39.7	-0.7	45.1	4.9	-	-	-	-
1973	45.3	6.8	-	-	-	-	63.4	5.3	41.1	3.5	47.2	4.7	-	-	-	-
1974	51.1	12.8	-	-	-	-	68.7	8.4	45.8	11.4	52.3	10.8	-	-	-	-
1975	55.4	8.4	-	-	-	-	71.7	4.4	49.9	9.0	57.1	9.2	-	-	-	-
1976	58.3	5.2	63.8	-	55.5	-	74.9	4.5	54.1	8.4	61.1	7.0	66.5	-	58.7	-
1977	62.4	7.0	67.8	6.3	60.2	8.5	79.0	5.5	57.3	5.9	65.8	7.7	69.3	4.2	61.9	5.5
1978	67.0	7.4	73.9	9.0	65.5	8.8	82.4	4.3	59.8	4.4	70.0	6.4	72.0	3.9	65.2	5.3
1979	73.4	9.6	80.4	8.8	71.9	9.8	83.9	1.8	68.0	13.7	76.0	8.6	76.6	6.4	69.2	6.1
1980	83.6	13.9	87.7	9.1	83.5	16.1	91.3	8.8	80.6	18.5	81.1	6.7	83.1	8.5	75.8	9.5
1981	91.8	9.8	93.7	6.8	92.6	10.9	95.9	5.0	91.0	12.9	85.7	5.7	89.1	7.2	83.0	9.5
1982	95.9	4.5	96.5	3.0	96.5	4.2	97.6	1.8	95.5	4.9	94.0	9.7	95.7	7.4	89.5	7.8
1983	99.8	4.1	99.5	3.1	99.4	3.0	100.7	3.2	99.7	4.4	100.6	7.0	101.2	5.7	101.3	13.2
1984	104.3	4.5	104.0	4.5	104.0	4.6	101.7	1.0	104.8	5.1	105.4	4.8	103.1	1.9	109.2	7.8
1985	108.3	3.8	107.1	3.0	108.7	4.5	106.6	4.8	107.6	2.7	111.9	6.2	108.2	4.9	114.1	4.5
1986	110.5	2.0	111.9	4.5	111.3	2.4	110.1	3.3	104.2	-3.2	122.0	9.0	112.8	4.3	120.2	5.3
1987	113.8	3.0	116.6	4.2	112.5	1.1	119.1	8.2	107.2	2.9	127.6	4.6	118.1	4.7	126.7	5.4
1988	118.9	4.5	121.7	4.4	116.0	3.1	128.9	8.2	112.3	4.8	134.1	5.1	123.0	4.1	138.1	9.0
1989	124.1	4.4	128.8	5.8	120.0	3.4	126.0	-2.2	117.7	4.8	143.9	7.3	129.2	5.0	148.2	7.3
1990	130.1	4.8	136.4	5.9	124.9	4.1	125.5	-0.4	123.6	5.0	156.1	8.5	139.0	7.6	157.2	6.1
1991	135.6	4.2	140.2	2.8	130.5	4.5	130.9	4.3	125.9	1.9	169.4	8.5	145.9	5.0	172.1	9.5
1992	139.5	2.9	142.1	1.4	132.6	1.6	135.5	3.5	129.1	2.5	181.3	7.0	151.6	3.9	189.7	10.2
1993	-	-	-	-	-	-	-	-	-	-	-	-	-	-	-	-

Source: U.S. Department of Labor, Bureau of Labor Statistics, Division of Consumer Prices and Price Indexes. - indicates no data collected for period.

Baltimore, MD
Consumer Price Index - All Urban Consumers
Base 1982-1984 = 100
All Items

For 1914-1993. Columns headed % show percentile change in the index from the previous period for which an index is available.

Year	Jan Index	%	Feb Index	%	Mar Index	%	Apr Index	%	May Index	%	Jun Index	%	Jul Index	%	Aug Index	%	Sep Index	%	Oct Index	%	Nov Index	%	Dec Index	%
1914	-	-	-	-	-	-	-	-	-	-	-	-	-	-	-	-	-	-	-	-	-	-	9.0	-
1915	-	-	-	-	-	-	-	-	-	-	-	-	-	-	-	-	-	-	-	-	-	-	9.0	0.0
1916	-	-	-	-	-	-	-	-	-	-	-	-	-	-	-	-	-	-	-	-	-	-	10.4	15.6
1917	-	-	-	-	-	-	-	-	-	-	-	-	-	-	-	-	-	-	-	-	-	-	12.9	24.0
1918	-	-	-	-	-	-	-	-	-	-	-	-	-	-	-	-	-	-	-	-	-	-	15.7	21.7
1919	-	-	-	-	-	-	-	-	-	-	15.9	1.3	-	-	-	-	-	-	-	-	-	-	17.3	8.8
1920	-	-	-	-	-	-	-	-	-	-	19.2	11.0	-	-	-	-	-	-	-	-	-	-	17.5	-8.9
1921	-	-	-	-	-	-	-	-	16.1	-8.0	-	-	-	-	-	-	16.1	0.0	-	-	-	-	15.7	-2.5
1922	-	-	-	-	15.4	-1.9	-	-	-	-	15.4	0.0	-	-	-	-	15.2	-1.3	-	-	-	-	15.5	2.0
1923	-	-	-	-	15.5	0.0	-	-	-	-	15.8	1.9	-	-	-	-	16.0	1.3	-	-	-	-	15.9	-0.6
1924	-	-	-	-	15.7	-1.3	-	-	-	-	15.8	0.6	-	-	-	-	15.7	-0.6	-	-	-	-	15.8	0.6
1925	-	-	-	-	-	-	-	-	-	-	16.2	2.5	-	-	-	-	-	-	-	-	-	-	16.6	2.5
1926	-	-	-	-	-	-	-	-	-	-	16.4	-1.2	-	-	-	-	-	-	-	-	-	-	16.3	-0.6
1927	-	-	-	-	-	-	-	-	-	-	16.2	-0.6	-	-	-	-	-	-	-	-	-	-	15.9	-1.9
1928	-	-	-	-	-	-	-	-	-	-	15.9	0.0	-	-	-	-	-	-	-	-	-	-	15.7	-1.3
1929	-	-	-	-	-	-	-	-	-	-	15.8	0.6	-	-	-	-	-	-	-	-	-	-	15.9	0.6
1930	-	-	-	-	-	-	-	-	-	-	15.8	-0.6	-	-	-	-	-	-	-	-	-	-	15.2	-3.8
1931	-	-	-	-	-	-	-	-	-	-	14.3	-5.9	-	-	-	-	-	-	-	-	-	-	13.9	-2.8
1932	-	-	-	-	-	-	-	-	-	-	13.0	-6.5	-	-	-	-	-	-	-	-	-	-	12.6	-3.1
1933	-	-	-	-	-	-	-	-	-	-	12.2	-3.2	-	-	-	-	-	-	-	-	-	-	12.8	4.9
1934	-	-	-	-	-	-	-	-	-	-	12.9	0.8	-	-	-	-	-	-	-	-	13.1	1.6	-	-
1935	-	-	-	-	13.2	0.8	-	-	-	-	-	-	13.3	0.8	-	-	-	-	13.3	0.0	-	-	-	-
1936	13.5	1.5	-	-	-	-	13.4	-0.7	-	-	-	-	13.4	0.0	-	-	13.6	1.5	-	-	-	-	13.4	-1.5
1937	-	-	-	-	13.7	2.2	-	-	-	-	13.7	0.0	-	-	-	-	13.9	1.5	-	-	-	-	13.8	-0.7
1938	-	-	-	-	13.5	-2.2	-	-	-	-	13.5	0.0	-	-	-	-	13.5	0.0	-	-	-	-	13.5	0.0
1939	-	-	-	-	13.4	-0.7	-	-	-	-	13.4	0.0	-	-	-	-	13.6	1.5	-	-	-	-	13.3	-2.2
1940	-	-	-	-	13.4	0.8	-	-	-	-	13.6	1.5	-	-	-	-	13.5	-0.7	13.5	0.0	13.5	0.0	13.6	0.7
1941	13.6	0.0	13.6	0.0	13.7	0.7	13.8	0.7	14.0	1.4	14.3	2.1	14.4	0.7	14.5	0.7	14.8	2.1	14.9	0.7	15.0	0.7	15.2	1.3
1942	15.4	1.3	15.5	0.6	15.7	1.3	15.8	0.6	15.9	0.6	16.1	1.3	16.0	-0.6	16.1	0.6	16.2	0.6	16.3	0.6	16.3	0.0	16.5	1.2
1943	16.6	0.6	16.6	0.0	16.9	1.8	17.1	1.2	17.4	1.8	17.4	0.0	17.1	-1.7	17.0	-0.6	17.1	0.6	17.2	0.6	17.0	-1.2	17.1	0.6
1944	17.1	0.0	17.0	-0.6	17.1	0.6	17.1	0.0	17.2	0.6	17.3	0.6	17.4	0.6	17.4	0.0	17.3	-0.6	17.4	0.6	17.5	0.6	17.5	0.0
1945	17.6	0.6	17.6	0.0	17.6	0.0	17.6	0.0	17.8	1.1	18.0	1.1	18.0	0.0	18.0	0.0	18.0	0.0	17.9	-0.6	17.9	0.0	18.0	0.6
1946	18.0	0.0	17.8	-1.1	17.9	0.6	18.1	1.1	18.1	0.0	18.4	1.7	19.4	5.4	19.9	2.6	20.1	1.0	20.5	2.0	21.0	2.4	21.1	0.5
1947	21.2	0.5	21.1	-0.5	21.7	2.8	21.7	0.0	21.6	-0.5	21.8	0.9	-	-	-	-	22.8	4.6	-	-	-	-	23.3	2.2
1948	-	-	-	-	23.2	-0.4	-	-	-	-	23.9	3.0	-	-	-	-	24.4	2.1	-	-	-	-	23.7	-2.9
1949	-	-	-	-	23.7	0.0	-	-	-	-	23.8	0.4	-	-	-	-	23.8	0.0	-	-	-	-	23.4	-1.7
1950	-	-	-	-	23.4	0.0	-	-	-	-	23.6	0.9	-	-	-	-	24.4	3.4	-	-	-	-	24.7	1.2
1951	-	-	-	-	25.4	2.8	-	-	-	-	25.6	0.8	-	-	-	-	25.7	0.4	-	-	-	-	26.1	1.6
1952	-	-	-	-	26.1	0.0	-	-	-	-	26.2	0.4	-	-	-	-	26.7	1.9	-	-	-	-	26.5	-0.7
1953	-	-	-	-	26.5	0.0	-	-	-	-	26.7	0.8	-	-	-	-	26.7	0.0	-	-	-	-	26.6	-0.4
1954	-	-	-	-	26.6	0.0	-	-	-	-	26.8	0.8	-	-	-	-	26.7	-0.4	-	-	-	-	26.6	-0.4
1955	-	-	-	-	26.7	0.4	-	-	-	-	26.7	0.0	-	-	-	-	26.8	0.4	-	-	-	-	26.9	0.4
1956	-	-	-	-	26.7	-0.7	-	-	-	-	27.1	1.5	-	-	-	-	27.3	0.7	-	-	-	-	27.7	1.5
1957	-	-	-	-	27.8	0.4	-	-	-	-	28.2	1.4	-	-	-	-	28.3	0.4	-	-	-	-	28.4	0.4
1958	-	-	-	-	28.8	1.4	-	-	-	-	29.0	0.7	-	-	-	-	29.0	0.0	-	-	-	-	29.1	0.3

[Continued]

Baltimore, MD
Consumer Price Index - All Urban Consumers
Base 1982-1984 = 100
All Items
[Continued]

For 1914-1993. Columns headed % show percentile change in the index from the previous period for which an index is available.

Year	Jan Index	%	Feb Index	%	Mar Index	%	Apr Index	%	May Index	%	Jun Index	%	Jul Index	%	Aug Index	%	Sep Index	%	Oct Index	%	Nov Index	%	Dec Index	%
1959	-	-	-	-	29.4	1.0	-	-	-	-	29.4	0.0	-	-	-	-	29.6	0.7	-	-	-	-	29.5	-0.3
1960	-	-	-	-	29.6	0.3	-	-	-	-	29.8	0.7	-	-	-	-	29.9	0.3	-	-	-	-	30.0	0.3
1961	-	-	-	-	30.1	0.3	-	-	-	-	30.1	0.0	-	-	-	-	30.1	0.0	-	-	-	-	30.1	0.0
1962	-	-	-	-	30.1	0.0	-	-	-	-	30.2	0.3	-	-	-	-	30.5	1.0	-	-	-	-	30.4	-0.3
1963	-	-	-	-	30.6	0.7	-	-	-	-	30.8	0.7	-	-	-	-	30.8	0.0	-	-	-	-	31.0	0.6
1964	-	-	-	-	31.0	0.0	-	-	-	-	31.1	0.3	-	-	-	-	31.1	0.0	-	-	-	-	31.3	0.6
1965	-	-	-	-	31.2	-0.3	-	-	-	-	31.7	1.6	-	-	-	-	31.7	0.0	-	-	-	-	31.9	0.6
1966	-	-	-	-	32.4	1.6	-	-	-	-	32.7	0.9	-	-	-	-	32.9	0.6	-	-	-	-	33.0	0.3
1967	-	-	-	-	33.1	0.3	-	-	-	-	33.3	0.6	-	-	-	-	33.9	1.8	-	-	-	-	33.8	-0.3
1968	-	-	-	-	34.2	1.2	-	-	-	-	34.7	1.5	-	-	-	-	35.2	1.4	-	-	-	-	35.7	1.4
1969	-	-	-	-	36.2	1.4	-	-	-	-	36.8	1.7	-	-	-	-	37.5	1.9	-	-	-	-	38.0	1.3
1970	-	-	-	-	38.4	1.1	-	-	-	-	39.0	1.6	-	-	-	-	39.5	1.3	-	-	-	-	40.4	2.3
1971	-	-	-	-	40.8	1.0	-	-	-	-	41.3	1.2	-	-	-	-	41.6	0.7	-	-	-	-	41.8	0.5
1972	-	-	-	-	41.8	0.0	-	-	-	-	42.0	0.5	-	-	-	-	42.7	1.7	-	-	-	-	42.8	0.2
1973	-	-	-	-	44.1	3.0	-	-	-	-	44.7	1.4	-	-	-	-	46.0	2.9	-	-	-	-	47.0	2.2
1974	-	-	-	-	49.2	4.7	-	-	-	-	50.6	2.8	-	-	-	-	52.6	4.0	-	-	-	-	53.5	1.7
1975	-	-	-	-	54.5	1.9	-	-	-	-	55.1	1.1	-	-	-	-	56.0	1.6	-	-	-	-	56.3	0.5
1976	-	-	-	-	57.0	1.2	-	-	-	-	58.1	1.9	-	-	-	-	59.0	1.5	-	-	-	-	59.6	1.0
1977	-	-	-	-	60.9	2.2	-	-	-	-	62.1	2.0	-	-	-	-	63.1	1.6	-	-	-	-	63.8	1.1
1978	-	-	-	-	65.4	2.5	-	-	66.2	1.2	-	-	67.5	2.0	-	-	68.0	0.7	-	-	67.9	-0.1	-	-
1979	68.3	0.6	-	-	69.9	2.3	-	-	72.0	3.0	-	-	73.9	2.6	-	-	75.2	1.8	-	-	76.0	1.1	-	-
1980	78.4	3.2	-	-	81.9	4.5	-	-	83.3	1.7	-	-	84.4	1.3	-	-	85.3	1.1	-	-	86.4	1.3	-	-
1981	88.4	2.3	-	-	90.4	2.3	-	-	90.0	-0.4	-	-	91.1	1.2	-	-	93.6	2.7	-	-	93.9	0.3	-	-
1982	94.3	0.4	-	-	94.3	0.0	-	-	94.8	0.5	-	-	95.7	0.9	-	-	96.7	1.0	-	-	97.0	0.3	-	-
1983	97.4	0.4	-	-	97.9	0.5	-	-	99.1	1.2	-	-	100.4	1.3	-	-	101.3	0.9	-	-	101.9	0.6	-	-
1984	102.8	0.9	-	-	103.8	1.0	-	-	104.1	0.3	-	-	104.7	0.6	-	-	105.8	1.1	-	-	105.4	-0.4	-	-
1985	105.4	0.0	-	-	107.2	1.7	-	-	108.0	0.7	-	-	108.3	0.3	-	-	109.5	1.1	-	-	109.4	-0.1	-	-
1986	111.0	1.5	-	-	110.7	-0.3	-	-	110.0	-0.6	-	-	110.4	0.4	-	-	111.7	1.2	-	-	111.5	-0.2	-	-
1987	111.7	0.2	-	-	112.3	0.5	-	-	113.7	1.2	-	-	115.0	1.1	-	-	115.7	0.6	-	-	115.7	0.0	-	-
1988	116.8	1.0	-	-	117.7	0.8	-	-	117.8	0.1	-	-	119.9	1.8	-	-	121.3	1.2	-	-	121.2	-0.1	-	-
1989	121.3	0.1	-	-	122.8	1.2	-	-	124.1	1.1	-	-	124.9	0.6	-	-	125.9	0.8	-	-	126.6	0.6	-	-
1990	127.9	1.0	-	-	129.3	1.1	-	-	129.0	-0.2	-	-	130.2	0.9	-	-	132.9	2.1	-	-	133.9	0.8	-	-
1991	134.3	0.3	-	-	135.1	0.6	-	-	135.4	0.2	-	-	136.5	0.8	-	-	138.2	1.2	-	-	137.8	-0.3	-	-
1992	138.0	0.1	-	-	138.7	0.5	-	-	139.5	0.6	-	-	140.6	0.8	-	-	141.9	0.9	-	-	141.1	-0.6	-	-
1993	142.0	0.6	-	-	142.6	0.4	-	-	142.8	0.1	-	-	143.7	0.6	-	-	143.6	-0.1	-	-	143.4	-0.1	-	-

Source: U.S. Department of Labor, Bureau of Labor Statistics, Division of Consumer Prices and Price Indexes. - indicates no data collected for period.

Baltimore, MD
Consumer Price Index - Urban Wage Earners
Base 1982-1984 = 100
All Items

For 1914-1993. Columns headed % show percentile change in the index from the previous period for which an index is available.

Year	Jan Index	%	Feb Index	%	Mar Index	%	Apr Index	%	May Index	%	Jun Index	%	Jul Index	%	Aug Index	%	Sep Index	%	Oct Index	%	Nov Index	%	Dec Index	%
1914	-	-	-	-	-	-	-	-	-	-	-	-	-	-	-	-	-	-	-	-	-	-	9.0	-
1915	-	-	-	-	-	-	-	-	-	-	-	-	-	-	-	-	-	-	-	-	-	-	9.0	0.0
1916	-	-	-	-	-	-	-	-	-	-	-	-	-	-	-	-	-	-	-	-	-	-	10.4	15.6
1917	-	-	-	-	-	-	-	-	-	-	-	-	-	-	-	-	-	-	-	-	-	-	12.9	24.0
1918	-	-	-	-	-	-	-	-	-	-	-	-	-	-	-	-	-	-	-	-	-	-	15.8	22.5
1919	-	-	-	-	-	-	-	-	-	-	16.0	1.3	-	-	-	-	-	-	-	-	-	-	17.3	8.1
1920	-	-	-	-	-	-	-	-	-	-	19.3	11.6	-	-	-	-	-	-	-	-	-	-	17.5	-9.3
1921	-	-	-	-	-	-	-	-	16.1	-8.0	-	-	-	-	-	-	16.1	0.0	-	-	-	-	15.8	-1.9
1922	-	-	-	-	15.4	-2.5	-	-	-	-	15.4	0.0	-	-	-	-	15.3	-0.6	-	-	-	-	15.5	1.3
1923	-	-	-	-	15.5	0.0	-	-	-	-	15.9	2.6	-	-	-	-	16.0	0.6	-	-	-	-	15.9	-0.6
1924	-	-	-	-	15.8	-0.6	-	-	-	-	15.8	0.0	-	-	-	-	15.8	0.0	-	-	-	-	15.9	0.6
1925	-	-	-	-	-	-	-	-	-	-	16.2	1.9	-	-	-	-	-	-	-	-	-	-	16.6	2.5
1926	-	-	-	-	-	-	-	-	-	-	16.5	-0.6	-	-	-	-	-	-	-	-	-	-	16.4	-0.6
1927	-	-	-	-	-	-	-	-	-	-	16.3	-0.6	-	-	-	-	-	-	-	-	-	-	15.9	-2.5
1928	-	-	-	-	-	-	-	-	-	-	15.9	0.0	-	-	-	-	-	-	-	-	-	-	15.8	-0.6
1929	-	-	-	-	-	-	-	-	-	-	15.9	0.6	-	-	-	-	-	-	-	-	-	-	16.0	0.6
1930	-	-	-	-	-	-	-	-	-	-	15.8	-1.2	-	-	-	-	-	-	-	-	-	-	15.2	-3.8
1931	-	-	-	-	-	-	-	-	-	-	14.4	-5.3	-	-	-	-	-	-	-	-	-	-	14.0	-2.8
1932	-	-	-	-	-	-	-	-	-	-	13.0	-7.1	-	-	-	-	-	-	-	-	-	-	12.6	-3.1
1933	-	-	-	-	-	-	-	-	-	-	12.3	-2.4	-	-	-	-	-	-	-	-	-	-	12.9	4.9
1934	-	-	-	-	-	-	-	-	-	-	13.0	0.8	-	-	-	-	-	-	-	-	13.1	0.8	-	-
1935	-	-	-	-	13.3	1.5	-	-	-	-	-	-	13.3	0.0	-	-	-	-	13.4	0.8	-	-	-	-
1936	13.5	0.7	-	-	-	-	13.4	-0.7	-	-	-	-	13.5	0.7	-	-	13.6	0.7	-	-	-	-	13.5	-0.7
1937	-	-	-	-	13.7	1.5	-	-	-	-	13.8	0.7	-	-	-	-	14.0	1.4	-	-	-	-	13.8	-1.4
1938	-	-	-	-	13.6	-1.4	-	-	-	-	13.6	0.0	-	-	-	-	13.6	0.0	-	-	-	-	13.6	0.0
1939	-	-	-	-	13.5	-0.7	-	-	-	-	13.5	0.0	-	-	-	-	13.6	0.7	-	-	-	-	13.4	-1.5
1940	-	-	-	-	13.5	0.7	-	-	-	-	13.6	0.7	-	-	-	-	13.6	0.0	13.5	-0.7	13.5	0.0	13.6	0.7
1941	13.7	0.7	13.7	0.0	13.7	0.0	13.9	1.5	14.1	1.4	14.3	1.4	14.5	1.4	14.6	0.7	14.9	2.1	15.0	0.7	15.1	0.7	15.2	0.7
1942	15.4	1.3	15.6	1.3	15.8	1.3	15.9	0.6	16.0	0.6	16.1	0.6	16.1	0.0	16.1	0.0	16.2	0.6	16.4	1.2	16.4	0.0	16.5	0.6
1943	16.6	0.6	16.6	0.0	17.0	2.4	17.2	1.2	17.4	1.2	17.4	0.0	17.1	-1.7	17.0	-0.6	17.1	0.6	17.2	0.6	17.0	-1.2	17.1	0.6
1944	17.1	0.0	17.0	-0.6	17.1	0.6	17.2	0.6	17.2	0.0	17.3	0.6	17.4	0.6	17.5	0.6	17.4	-0.6	17.4	0.0	17.6	1.1	17.6	0.0
1945	17.6	0.0	17.7	0.6	17.6	-0.6	17.7	0.6	17.8	0.6	18.0	1.1	18.1	0.6	18.0	-0.6	18.0	0.0	18.0	0.0	17.9	-0.6	18.0	0.6
1946	18.0	0.0	17.9	-0.6	18.0	0.6	18.2	1.1	18.2	0.0	18.5	1.6	19.5	5.4	20.0	2.6	20.1	0.5	20.5	2.0	21.1	2.9	21.1	0.0
1947	21.2	0.5	21.2	0.0	21.7	2.4	21.8	0.5	21.7	-0.5	21.9	0.9	-	-	-	-	22.8	4.1	-	-	-	-	23.3	2.2
1948	-	-	-	-	23.3	0.0	-	-	-	-	24.0	3.0	-	-	-	-	24.5	2.1	-	-	-	-	23.8	-2.9
1949	-	-	-	-	23.8	0.0	-	-	-	-	23.9	0.4	-	-	-	-	23.9	0.0	-	-	-	-	23.5	-1.7
1950	-	-	-	-	23.4	-0.4	-	-	-	-	23.6	0.9	-	-	-	-	24.5	3.8	-	-	-	-	24.8	1.2
1951	-	-	-	-	25.5	2.8	-	-	-	-	25.7	0.8	-	-	-	-	25.8	0.4	-	-	-	-	26.2	1.6
1952	-	-	-	-	26.2	0.0	-	-	-	-	26.3	0.4	-	-	-	-	26.8	1.9	-	-	-	-	26.6	-0.7
1953	-	-	-	-	26.6	0.0	-	-	-	-	26.8	0.8	-	-	-	-	26.8	0.0	-	-	-	-	26.7	-0.4
1954	-	-	-	-	26.7	0.0	-	-	-	-	26.9	0.7	-	-	-	-	26.8	-0.4	-	-	-	-	26.7	-0.4
1955	-	-	-	-	26.8	0.4	-	-	-	-	26.8	0.0	-	-	-	-	26.9	0.4	-	-	-	-	27.0	0.4
1956	-	-	-	-	26.8	-0.7	-	-	-	-	27.2	1.5	-	-	-	-	27.4	0.7	-	-	-	-	27.8	1.5
1957	-	-	-	-	27.9	0.4	-	-	-	-	28.2	1.1	-	-	-	-	28.3	0.4	-	-	-	-	28.4	0.4
1958	-	-	-	-	28.9	1.8	-	-	-	-	29.1	0.7	-	-	-	-	29.1	0.0	-	-	-	-	29.2	0.3

[Continued]

Baltimore, MD
Consumer Price Index - Urban Wage Earners
Base 1982-1984 = 100
All Items
[Continued]

For 1914-1993. Columns headed % show percentile change in the index from the previous period for which an index is available.

Year	Jan Index	%	Feb Index	%	Mar Index	%	Apr Index	%	May Index	%	Jun Index	%	Jul Index	%	Aug Index	%	Sep Index	%	Oct Index	%	Nov Index	%	Dec Index	%
1959	-	-	-	-	29.5	1.0	-	-	-	-	29.5	0.0	-	-	-	-	29.7	0.7	-	-	-	-	29.6	-0.3
1960	-	-	-	-	29.7	0.3	-	-	-	-	29.9	0.7	-	-	-	-	30.0	0.3	-	-	-	-	30.1	0.3
1961	-	-	-	-	30.2	0.3	-	-	-	-	30.2	0.0	-	-	-	-	30.2	0.0	-	-	-	-	30.2	0.0
1962	-	-	-	-	30.2	0.0	-	-	-	-	30.3	0.3	-	-	-	-	30.6	1.0	-	-	-	-	30.5	-0.3
1963	-	-	-	-	30.7	0.7	-	-	-	-	30.9	0.7	-	-	-	-	30.9	0.0	-	-	-	-	31.1	0.6
1964	-	-	-	-	31.1	0.0	-	-	-	-	31.2	0.3	-	-	-	-	31.2	0.0	-	-	-	-	31.4	0.6
1965	-	-	-	-	31.3	-0.3	-	-	-	-	31.8	1.6	-	-	-	-	31.8	0.0	-	-	-	-	32.0	0.6
1966	-	-	-	-	32.5	1.6	-	-	-	-	32.8	0.9	-	-	-	-	33.0	0.6	-	-	-	-	33.1	0.3
1967	-	-	-	-	33.2	0.3	-	-	-	-	33.4	0.6	-	-	-	-	34.0	1.8	-	-	-	-	33.9	-0.3
1968	-	-	-	-	34.3	1.2	-	-	-	-	34.9	1.7	-	-	-	-	35.4	1.4	-	-	-	-	35.8	1.1
1969	-	-	-	-	36.3	1.4	-	-	-	-	37.0	1.9	-	-	-	-	37.7	1.9	-	-	-	-	38.1	1.1
1970	-	-	-	-	38.6	1.3	-	-	-	-	39.1	1.3	-	-	-	-	39.7	1.5	-	-	-	-	40.5	2.0
1971	-	-	-	-	41.0	1.2	-	-	-	-	41.4	1.0	-	-	-	-	41.7	0.7	-	-	-	-	42.0	0.7
1972	-	-	-	-	41.9	-0.2	-	-	-	-	42.1	0.5	-	-	-	-	42.8	1.7	-	-	-	-	42.9	0.2
1973	-	-	-	-	44.2	3.0	-	-	-	-	44.8	1.4	-	-	-	-	46.1	2.9	-	-	-	-	47.2	2.4
1974	-	-	-	-	49.4	4.7	-	-	-	-	50.8	2.8	-	-	-	-	52.8	3.9	-	-	-	-	53.7	1.7
1975	-	-	-	-	54.6	1.7	-	-	-	-	55.2	1.1	-	-	-	-	56.2	1.8	-	-	-	-	56.5	0.5
1976	-	-	-	-	57.2	1.2	-	-	-	-	58.3	1.9	-	-	-	-	59.2	1.5	-	-	-	-	59.8	1.0
1977	-	-	-	-	61.1	2.2	-	-	-	-	62.3	2.0	-	-	-	-	63.3	1.6	-	-	-	-	64.0	1.1
1978	-	-	-	-	65.6	2.5	-	-	66.6	1.5	-	-	67.7	1.7	-	-	68.2	0.7	-	-	68.1	-0.1	-	-
1979	68.8	1.0	-	-	70.6	2.6	-	-	72.5	2.7	-	-	74.3	2.5	-	-	75.4	1.5	-	-	76.5	1.5	-	-
1980	78.7	2.9	-	-	81.8	3.9	-	-	83.1	1.6	-	-	84.1	1.2	-	-	84.9	1.0	-	-	86.3	1.6	-	-
1981	88.1	2.1	-	-	90.3	2.5	-	-	90.1	-0.2	-	-	91.8	1.9	-	-	94.5	2.9	-	-	94.2	-0.3	-	-
1982	94.7	0.5	-	-	94.7	0.0	-	-	95.2	0.5	-	-	96.3	1.2	-	-	96.9	0.6	-	-	97.2	0.3	-	-
1983	97.2	0.0	-	-	99.0	1.9	-	-	99.5	0.5	-	-	99.8	0.3	-	-	100.5	0.7	-	-	101.4	0.9	-	-
1984	101.9	0.5	-	-	103.1	1.2	-	-	103.8	0.7	-	-	104.5	0.7	-	-	106.1	1.5	-	-	105.7	-0.4	-	-
1985	105.7	0.0	-	-	107.4	1.6	-	-	108.1	0.7	-	-	108.5	0.4	-	-	109.5	0.9	-	-	109.5	0.0	-	-
1986	111.1	1.5	-	-	110.5	-0.5	-	-	109.6	-0.8	-	-	110.0	0.4	-	-	111.0	0.9	-	-	110.8	-0.2	-	-
1987	111.1	0.3	-	-	111.8	0.6	-	-	113.2	1.3	-	-	114.7	1.3	-	-	115.5	0.7	-	-	115.3	-0.2	-	-
1988	116.2	0.8	-	-	117.3	0.9	-	-	117.4	0.1	-	-	119.7	2.0	-	-	121.0	1.1	-	-	120.8	-0.2	-	-
1989	120.9	0.1	-	-	122.3	1.2	-	-	123.7	1.1	-	-	124.6	0.7	-	-	125.4	0.6	-	-	126.0	0.5	-	-
1990	127.2	1.0	-	-	128.6	1.1	-	-	128.3	-0.2	-	-	129.5	0.9	-	-	132.3	2.2	-	-	133.2	0.7	-	-
1991	133.7	0.4	-	-	134.1	0.3	-	-	134.4	0.2	-	-	135.8	1.0	-	-	137.5	1.3	-	-	137.0	-0.4	-	-
1992	137.3	0.2	-	-	137.9	0.4	-	-	138.9	0.7	-	-	140.2	0.9	-	-	141.4	0.9	-	-	140.6	-0.6	-	-
1993	141.3	0.5	-	-	141.8	0.4	-	-	142.1	0.2	-	-	143.0	0.6	-	-	142.8	-0.1	-	-	142.5	-0.2	-	-

Source: U.S. Department of Labor, Bureau of Labor Statistics, Division of Consumer Prices and Price Indexes. - indicates no data collected for period.

Baltimore, MD

Consumer Price Index - All Urban Consumers
Base 1982-1984 = 100

Food and Beverages

For 1975-1993. Columns headed % show percentile change in the index from the previous period for which an index is available.

Year	Jan Index	%	Feb Index	%	Mar Index	%	Apr Index	%	May Index	%	Jun Index	%	Jul Index	%	Aug Index	%	Sep Index	%	Oct Index	%	Nov Index	%	Dec Index	%
1975	-	-	-	-	-	-	-	-	-	-	-	-	-	-	-	-	-	-	-	-	-	-	63.2	-
1976	-	-	-	-	63.0	-0.3	-	-	-	-	64.1	1.7	-	-	-	-	64.6	0.8	-	-	-	-	64.3	-0.5
1977	-	-	-	-	66.6	3.6	-	-	-	-	68.4	2.7	-	-	-	-	69.1	1.0	-	-	-	-	69.2	0.1
1978	-	-	-	-	72.0	4.0	-	-	74.0	2.8	-	-	76.6	3.5	-	-	75.5	-1.4	-	-	75.8	0.4	-	-
1979	78.4	3.4	-	-	80.1	2.2	-	-	80.7	0.7	-	-	81.9	1.5	-	-	82.4	0.6	-	-	82.3	-0.1	-	-
1980	84.3	2.4	-	-	85.2	1.1	-	-	86.2	1.2	-	-	87.8	1.9	-	-	90.1	2.6	-	-	91.3	1.3	-	-
1981	93.1	2.0	-	-	94.8	1.8	-	-	93.2	-1.7	-	-	93.5	0.3	-	-	94.2	0.7	-	-	94.3	0.1	-	-
1982	95.2	1.0	-	-	95.3	0.1	-	-	96.5	1.3	-	-	97.6	1.1	-	-	97.5	-0.1	-	-	96.3	-1.2	-	-
1983	96.9	0.6	-	-	98.3	1.4	-	-	100.3	2.0	-	-	99.9	-0.4	-	-	99.7	-0.2	-	-	100.6	0.9	-	-
1984	102.9	2.3	-	-	103.6	0.7	-	-	104.2	0.6	-	-	104.2	0.0	-	-	104.3	0.1	-	-	104.2	-0.1	-	-
1985	105.2	1.0	-	-	107.3	2.0	-	-	106.7	-0.6	-	-	107.5	0.7	-	-	106.9	-0.6	-	-	107.8	0.8	-	-
1986	110.5	2.5	-	-	110.2	-0.3	-	-	110.1	-0.1	-	-	112.1	1.8	-	-	113.9	1.6	-	-	114.1	0.2	-	-
1987	115.6	1.3	-	-	115.1	-0.4	-	-	116.2	1.0	-	-	117.0	0.7	-	-	118.0	0.9	-	-	118.0	0.0	-	-
1988	118.8	0.7	-	-	119.7	0.8	-	-	121.1	1.2	-	-	123.1	1.7	-	-	123.2	0.1	-	-	123.5	0.2	-	-
1989	125.5	1.6	-	-	127.4	1.5	-	-	129.0	1.3	-	-	129.7	0.5	-	-	129.3	-0.3	-	-	131.5	1.7	-	-
1990	135.7	3.2	-	-	135.8	0.1	-	-	134.9	-0.7	-	-	137.3	1.8	-	-	137.6	0.2	-	-	138.9	0.9	-	-
1991	140.2	0.9	-	-	140.9	0.5	-	-	140.5	-0.3	-	-	141.3	0.6	-	-	140.3	-0.7	-	-	139.8	-0.4	-	-
1992	141.6	1.3	-	-	142.5	0.6	-	-	141.9	-0.4	-	-	141.8	-0.1	-	-	143.5	1.2	-	-	142.8	-0.5	-	-
1993	143.6	0.6	-	-	144.3	0.5	-	-	143.9	-0.3	-	-	144.0	0.1	-	-	143.8	-0.1	-	-	145.2	1.0	-	-

Source: U.S. Department of Labor, Bureau of Labor Statistics, Division of Consumer Prices and Price Indexes. - indicates no data collected for period.

Baltimore, MD

Consumer Price Index - Urban Wage Earners
Base 1982-1984 = 100
Food and Beverages

For 1975-1993. Columns headed % show percentile change in the index from the previous period for which an index is available.

Year	Jan		Feb		Mar		Apr		May		Jun		Jul		Aug		Sep		Oct		Nov		Dec	
	Index	%	Index	%	Index	%	Index	%	Index	%	Index	%	Index	%	Index	%	Index	%	Index	%	Index	%	Index	%
1975	-	-	-	-	-	-	-	-	-	-	-	-	-	-	-	-	-	-	-	-	-	-	63.1	-
1976	-	-	-	-	63.0	-0.2	-	-	-	-	64.0	1.6	-	-	-	-	64.5	0.8	-	-	-	-	64.2	-0.5
1977	-	-	-	-	66.5	3.6	-	-	-	-	68.3	2.7	-	-	-	-	69.0	1.0	-	-	-	-	69.1	0.1
1978	-	-	-	-	71.9	4.1	-	-	73.9	2.8	-	-	75.5	2.2	-	-	74.9	-0.8	-	-	75.3	0.5	-	-
1979	77.7	3.2	-	-	79.8	2.7	-	-	80.0	0.3	-	-	80.8	1.0	-	-	80.9	0.1	-	-	82.0	1.4	-	-
1980	83.8	2.2	-	-	85.3	1.8	-	-	85.9	0.7	-	-	87.0	1.3	-	-	90.4	3.9	-	-	91.5	1.2	-	-
1981	92.7	1.3	-	-	94.3	1.7	-	-	92.9	-1.5	-	-	92.9	0.0	-	-	94.5	1.7	-	-	94.5	0.0	-	-
1982	95.1	0.6	-	-	95.3	0.2	-	-	96.5	1.3	-	-	97.7	1.2	-	-	97.4	-0.3	-	-	96.4	-1.0	-	-
1983	97.0	0.6	-	-	98.3	1.3	-	-	100.4	2.1	-	-	99.9	-0.5	-	-	99.7	-0.2	-	-	100.5	0.8	-	-
1984	102.9	2.4	-	-	103.6	0.7	-	-	104.3	0.7	-	-	104.3	0.0	-	-	104.4	0.1	-	-	104.2	-0.2	-	-
1985	105.3	1.1	-	-	107.3	1.9	-	-	106.8	-0.5	-	-	107.4	0.6	-	-	106.9	-0.5	-	-	107.7	0.7	-	-
1986	110.5	2.6	-	-	110.3	-0.2	-	-	110.1	-0.2	-	-	111.8	1.5	-	-	113.7	1.7	-	-	113.9	0.2	-	-
1987	115.5	1.4	-	-	114.8	-0.6	-	-	115.9	1.0	-	-	116.7	0.7	-	-	118.0	1.1	-	-	118.0	0.0	-	-
1988	118.8	0.7	-	-	119.7	0.8	-	-	121.1	1.2	-	-	122.9	1.5	-	-	123.0	0.1	-	-	123.2	0.2	-	-
1989	125.2	1.6	-	-	127.0	1.4	-	-	128.6	1.3	-	-	129.4	0.6	-	-	128.9	-0.4	-	-	131.0	1.6	-	-
1990	135.2	3.2	-	-	135.3	0.1	-	-	134.6	-0.5	-	-	136.9	1.7	-	-	137.2	0.2	-	-	138.4	0.9	-	-
1991	139.9	1.1	-	-	140.5	0.4	-	-	139.9	-0.4	-	-	141.0	0.8	-	-	140.1	-0.6	-	-	139.5	-0.4	-	-
1992	141.2	1.2	-	-	142.3	0.8	-	-	141.5	-0.6	-	-	141.5	0.0	-	-	143.0	1.1	-	-	142.5	-0.3	-	-
1993	143.2	0.5	-	-	143.8	0.4	-	-	143.4	-0.3	-	-	143.5	0.1	-	-	143.4	-0.1	-	-	144.6	0.8	-	-

Source: U.S. Department of Labor, Bureau of Labor Statistics, Division of Consumer Prices and Price Indexes. - indicates no data collected for period.

Baltimore, MD
Consumer Price Index - All Urban Consumers
Base 1982-1984 = 100
Housing

For 1975-1993. Columns headed % show percentile change in the index from the previous period for which an index is available.

Year	Jan Index	%	Feb Index	%	Mar Index	%	Apr Index	%	May Index	%	Jun Index	%	Jul Index	%	Aug Index	%	Sep Index	%	Oct Index	%	Nov Index	%	Dec Index	%
1975	-	-	-	-	-	-	-	-	-	-	-	-	-	-	-	-	-	-	-	-	-	-	52.8	-
1976	-	-	-	-	53.7	1.7	-	-	-	-	54.6	1.7	-	-	-	-	56.1	2.7	-	-	-	-	57.3	2.1
1977	-	-	-	-	58.2	1.6	-	-	-	-	59.0	1.4	-	-	-	-	61.0	3.4	-	-	-	-	62.4	2.3
1978	-	-	-	-	64.1	2.7	-	-	64.0	-0.2	-	-	65.9	3.0	-	-	66.5	0.9	-	-	65.2	-2.0	-	-
1979	65.2	0.0	-	-	66.3	1.7	-	-	69.3	4.5	-	-	72.1	4.0	-	-	73.3	1.7	-	-	73.7	0.5	-	-
1980	76.5	3.8	-	-	81.2	6.1	-	-	82.8	2.0	-	-	84.0	1.4	-	-	83.9	-0.1	-	-	85.3	1.7	-	-
1981	87.9	3.0	-	-	89.6	1.9	-	-	88.5	-1.2	-	-	90.1	1.8	-	-	94.9	5.3	-	-	94.6	-0.3	-	-
1982	95.2	0.6	-	-	94.2	-1.1	-	-	95.2	1.1	-	-	95.4	0.2	-	-	95.9	0.5	-	-	96.9	1.0	-	-
1983	97.4	0.5	-	-	97.7	0.3	-	-	98.3	0.6	-	-	100.6	2.3	-	-	101.4	0.8	-	-	100.9	-0.5	-	-
1984	103.3	2.4	-	-	104.0	0.7	-	-	104.1	0.1	-	-	105.2	1.1	-	-	106.7	1.4	-	-	105.1	-1.5	-	-
1985	105.5	0.4	-	-	107.1	1.5	-	-	108.0	0.8	-	-	108.6	0.6	-	-	110.3	1.6	-	-	109.0	-1.2	-	-
1986	110.7	1.6	-	-	110.8	0.1	-	-	110.3	-0.5	-	-	111.0	0.6	-	-	112.6	1.4	-	-	111.5	-1.0	-	-
1987	111.4	-0.1	-	-	110.9	-0.4	-	-	113.1	2.0	-	-	113.5	0.4	-	-	113.0	-0.4	-	-	112.8	-0.2	-	-
1988	114.9	1.9	-	-	115.1	0.2	-	-	115.0	-0.1	-	-	117.1	1.8	-	-	117.5	0.3	-	-	116.8	-0.6	-	-
1989	117.4	0.5	-	-	117.8	0.3	-	-	118.9	0.9	-	-	121.3	2.0	-	-	122.1	0.7	-	-	121.4	-0.6	-	-
1990	123.1	1.4	-	-	123.6	0.4	-	-	123.8	0.2	-	-	126.1	1.9	-	-	127.1	0.8	-	-	126.7	-0.3	-	-
1991	127.6	0.7	-	-	130.2	2.0	-	-	129.6	-0.5	-	-	131.9	1.8	-	-	134.0	1.6	-	-	131.9	-1.6	-	-
1992	131.9	0.0	-	-	131.7	-0.2	-	-	132.4	0.5	-	-	135.3	2.2	-	-	135.1	-0.1	-	-	132.8	-1.7	-	-
1993	134.1	1.0	-	-	134.5	0.3	-	-	134.2	-0.2	-	-	137.1	2.2	-	-	137.3	0.1	-	-	135.6	-1.2	-	-

Source: U.S. Department of Labor, Bureau of Labor Statistics, Division of Consumer Prices and Price Indexes. - indicates no data collected for period.

Baltimore, MD
Consumer Price Index - Urban Wage Earners
Base 1982-1984 = 100
Housing

For 1975-1993. Columns headed % show percentile change in the index from the previous period for which an index is available.

Year	Jan Index	%	Feb Index	%	Mar Index	%	Apr Index	%	May Index	%	Jun Index	%	Jul Index	%	Aug Index	%	Sep Index	%	Oct Index	%	Nov Index	%	Dec Index	%
1975	-	-	-	-	-	-	-	-	-	-	-	-	-	-	-	-	-	-	-	-	-	-	-	-
1976	-	-	-	-	54.2	1.9	-	-	-	-	55.0	1.5	-	-	-	-	56.6	2.9	-	-	-	-	53.2	-
1977	-	-	-	-	58.7	1.7	-	-	-	-	59.5	1.4	-	-	-	-	61.5	3.4	-	-	-	-	57.7	1.9
1978	-	-	-	-	64.6	2.7	-	-	64.9	0.5	-	-	66.4	2.3	-	-	67.1	1.1	-	-	66.0	-1.6	62.9	2.3
1979	66.3	0.5	-	-	68.1	2.7	-	-	70.8	4.0	-	-	73.5	3.8	-	-	74.7	1.6	-	-	75.3	0.8	-	-
1980	78.0	3.6	-	-	81.9	5.0	-	-	83.7	2.2	-	-	84.9	1.4	-	-	84.1	-0.9	-	-	85.6	1.8	-	-
1981	88.1	2.9	-	-	90.4	2.6	-	-	89.4	-1.1	-	-	92.4	3.4	-	-	97.4	5.4	-	-	95.7	-1.7	-	-
1982	96.2	0.5	-	-	95.4	-0.8	-	-	96.3	0.9	-	-	96.7	0.4	-	-	96.7	0.0	-	-	97.7	1.0	-	-
1983	97.0	-0.7	-	-	100.5	3.6	-	-	99.5	-1.0	-	-	99.1	-0.4	-	-	99.5	0.4	-	-	99.9	0.4	-	-
1984	100.8	0.9	-	-	102.2	1.4	-	-	103.0	0.8	-	-	104.4	1.4	-	-	107.1	2.6	-	-	105.6	-1.4	-	-
1985	105.9	0.3	-	-	107.5	1.5	-	-	108.2	0.7	-	-	108.9	0.6	-	-	110.8	1.7	-	-	109.6	-1.1	-	-
1986	111.3	1.6	-	-	111.1	-0.2	-	-	110.5	-0.5	-	-	111.2	0.6	-	-	112.7	1.3	-	-	111.4	-1.2	-	-
1987	111.3	-0.1	-	-	110.7	-0.5	-	-	113.0	2.1	-	-	113.5	0.4	-	-	113.1	-0.4	-	-	112.6	-0.4	-	-
1988	114.5	1.7	-	-	114.8	0.3	-	-	114.7	-0.1	-	-	117.0	2.0	-	-	117.4	0.3	-	-	116.7	-0.6	-	-
1989	117.3	0.5	-	-	117.6	0.3	-	-	118.8	1.0	-	-	121.5	2.3	-	-	122.1	0.5	-	-	121.3	-0.7	-	-
1990	122.8	1.2	-	-	123.3	0.4	-	-	123.5	0.2	-	-	126.0	2.0	-	-	126.8	0.6	-	-	126.2	-0.5	-	-
1991	127.2	0.8	-	-	129.5	1.8	-	-	128.8	-0.5	-	-	131.4	2.0	-	-	133.6	1.7	-	-	131.2	-1.8	-	-
1992	131.4	0.2	-	-	131.2	-0.2	-	-	131.6	0.3	-	-	134.8	2.4	-	-	134.3	-0.4	-	-	131.8	-1.9	-	-
1993	133.0	0.9	-	-	133.2	0.2	-	-	133.2	0.0	-	-	136.5	2.5	-	-	136.8	0.2	-	-	134.8	-1.5	-	-

Source: U.S. Department of Labor, Bureau of Labor Statistics, Division of Consumer Prices and Price Indexes. - indicates no data collected for period.

Baltimore, MD
Consumer Price Index - All Urban Consumers
Base 1982-1984 = 100
Apparel and Upkeep

For 1952-1993. Columns headed % show percentile change in the index from the previous period for which an index is available.

Year	Jan Index	Jan %	Feb Index	Feb %	Mar Index	Mar %	Apr Index	Apr %	May Index	May %	Jun Index	Jun %	Jul Index	Jul %	Aug Index	Aug %	Sep Index	Sep %	Oct Index	Oct %	Nov Index	Nov %	Dec Index	Dec %
1952	-	-	-	-	-	-	-	-	-	-	-	-	-	-	-	-	-	-	-	-	-	-	37.9	-
1953	-	-	-	-	38.0	0.3	-	-	-	-	38.4	1.1	-	-	-	-	38.2	-0.5	-	-	-	-	37.8	-1.0
1954	-	-	-	-	37.8	0.0	-	-	-	-	37.8	0.0	-	-	-	-	38.2	1.1	-	-	-	-	38.0	-0.5
1955	-	-	-	-	37.8	-0.5	-	-	-	-	37.9	0.3	-	-	-	-	37.8	-0.3	-	-	-	-	38.3	1.3
1956	-	-	-	-	38.8	1.3	-	-	-	-	39.3	1.3	-	-	-	-	39.8	1.3	-	-	-	-	39.7	-0.3
1957	-	-	-	-	39.6	-0.3	-	-	-	-	40.0	1.0	-	-	-	-	40.8	2.0	-	-	-	-	40.5	-0.7
1958	-	-	-	-	40.7	0.5	-	-	-	-	40.7	0.0	-	-	-	-	40.8	0.2	-	-	-	-	40.3	-1.2
1959	-	-	-	-	41.3	2.5	-	-	-	-	41.4	0.2	-	-	-	-	42.1	1.7	-	-	-	-	41.9	-0.5
1960	-	-	-	-	42.1	0.5	-	-	-	-	41.9	-0.5	-	-	-	-	42.6	1.7	-	-	-	-	42.4	-0.5
1961	-	-	-	-	43.0	1.4	-	-	-	-	42.9	-0.2	-	-	-	-	43.0	0.2	-	-	-	-	42.8	-0.5
1962	-	-	-	-	42.9	0.2	-	-	-	-	42.9	0.0	-	-	-	-	43.5	1.4	-	-	-	-	43.5	0.0
1963	-	-	-	-	43.5	0.0	-	-	-	-	43.6	0.2	-	-	-	-	43.6	0.0	-	-	-	-	43.6	0.0
1964	-	-	-	-	43.3	-0.7	-	-	-	-	43.5	0.5	-	-	-	-	43.6	0.2	-	-	-	-	43.8	0.5
1965	-	-	-	-	43.6	-0.5	-	-	-	-	44.1	1.1	-	-	-	-	44.4	0.7	-	-	-	-	44.5	0.2
1966	-	-	-	-	45.1	1.3	-	-	-	-	45.4	0.7	-	-	-	-	45.6	0.4	-	-	-	-	46.0	0.9
1967	-	-	-	-	46.9	2.0	-	-	-	-	47.4	1.1	-	-	-	-	48.2	1.7	-	-	-	-	48.0	-0.4
1968	-	-	-	-	48.6	1.2	-	-	-	-	49.5	1.9	-	-	-	-	50.5	2.0	-	-	-	-	51.0	1.0
1969	-	-	-	-	52.3	2.5	-	-	-	-	53.5	2.3	-	-	-	-	54.9	2.6	-	-	-	-	55.3	0.7
1970	-	-	-	-	55.7	0.7	-	-	-	-	56.3	1.1	-	-	-	-	57.1	1.4	-	-	-	-	58.3	2.1
1971	-	-	-	-	58.6	0.5	-	-	-	-	57.8	-1.4	-	-	-	-	59.2	2.4	-	-	-	-	59.0	-0.3
1972	-	-	-	-	59.0	0.0	-	-	-	-	58.1	-1.5	-	-	-	-	59.1	1.7	-	-	-	-	58.9	-0.3
1973	-	-	-	-	60.5	2.7	-	-	-	-	61.4	1.5	-	-	-	-	63.4	3.3	-	-	-	-	64.3	1.4
1974	-	-	-	-	65.6	2.0	-	-	-	-	66.7	1.7	-	-	-	-	68.4	2.5	-	-	-	-	69.3	1.3
1975	-	-	-	-	70.0	1.0	-	-	-	-	69.7	-0.4	-	-	-	-	70.7	1.4	-	-	-	-	70.4	-0.4
1976	-	-	-	-	72.0	2.3	-	-	-	-	73.0	1.4	-	-	-	-	74.3	1.8	-	-	-	-	75.0	0.9
1977	-	-	-	-	75.9	1.2	-	-	-	-	77.3	1.8	-	-	-	-	78.3	1.3	-	-	-	-	78.3	0.0
1978	-	-	-	-	81.0	3.4	-	-	83.4	3.0	-	-	76.5	-8.3	-	-	82.1	7.3	-	-	81.9	-0.2	-	-
1979	77.5	-5.4	-	-	83.2	7.4	-	-	84.2	1.2	-	-	80.4	-4.5	-	-	85.1	5.8	-	-	86.9	2.1	-	-
1980	85.0	-2.2	-	-	92.5	8.8	-	-	94.2	1.8	-	-	93.3	-1.0	-	-	95.3	2.1	-	-	97.2	2.0	-	-
1981	94.6	-2.7	-	-	98.5	4.1	-	-	98.2	-0.3	-	-	96.2	-2.0	-	-	96.5	0.3	-	-	96.5	0.0	-	-
1982	92.4	-4.2	-	-	98.7	6.8	-	-	99.1	0.4	-	-	95.5	-3.6	-	-	100.9	5.7	-	-	101.2	0.3	-	-
1983	98.4	-2.8	-	-	99.0	0.6	-	-	101.6	2.6	-	-	101.4	-0.2	-	-	99.3	-2.1	-	-	103.2	3.9	-	-
1984	99.4	-3.7	-	-	101.7	2.3	-	-	101.5	-0.2	-	-	98.5	-3.0	-	-	103.6	5.2	-	-	103.2	-0.4	-	-
1985	98.2	-4.8	-	-	106.5	8.5	-	-	106.6	0.1	-	-	103.9	-2.5	-	-	111.2	7.0	-	-	109.3	-1.7	-	-
1986	106.9	-2.2	-	-	111.5	4.3	-	-	112.3	0.7	-	-	108.5	-3.4	-	-	112.6	3.8	-	-	112.9	0.3	-	-
1987	106.2	-5.9	-	-	120.4	13.4	-	-	120.2	-0.2	-	-	123.0	2.3	-	-	124.4	1.1	-	-	121.2	-2.6	-	-
1988	118.0	-2.6	-	-	129.2	9.5	-	-	123.0	-4.8	-	-	133.1	8.2	-	-	140.1	5.3	-	-	136.0	-2.9	-	-
1989	124.2	-8.7	-	-	136.1	9.6	-	-	130.1	-4.4	-	-	123.1	-5.4	-	-	129.4	5.1	-	-	127.2	-1.7	-	-
1990	112.2	-11.8	-	-	136.6	21.7	-	-	130.9	-4.2	-	-	118.1	-9.8	-	-	137.3	16.3	-	-	130.0	-5.3	-	-
1991	129.2	-0.6	-	-	135.6	5.0	-	-	134.4	-0.9	-	-	129.7	-3.5	-	-	134.4	3.6	-	-	133.8	-0.4	-	-
1992	129.9	-2.9	-	-	142.4	9.6	-	-	140.3	-1.5	-	-	128.4	-8.5	-	-	136.7	6.5	-	-	133.7	-2.2	-	-
1993	130.7	-2.2	-	-	140.3	7.3	-	-	141.9	1.1	-	-	133.6	-5.8	-	-	137.4	2.8	-	-	133.1	-3.1	-	-

Source: U.S. Department of Labor, Bureau of Labor Statistics, Division of Consumer Prices and Price Indexes. - indicates no data collected for period.

Baltimore, MD
Consumer Price Index - Urban Wage Earners
Base 1982-1984 = 100
Apparel and Upkeep

For 1952-1993. Columns headed % show percentile change in the index from the previous period for which an index is available.

Year	Jan Index	%	Feb Index	%	Mar Index	%	Apr Index	%	May Index	%	Jun Index	%	Jul Index	%	Aug Index	%	Sep Index	%	Oct Index	%	Nov Index	%	Dec Index	%
1952	-	-	-	-	-	-	-	-	-	-	-	-	-	-	-	-	-	-	-	-	-	-	-	-
1953	-	-	-	-	38.9	0.3	-	-	-	-	39.3	1.0	-	-	-	-	39.1	-0.5	-	-	-	-	38.8	-
1954	-	-	-	-	38.7	0.0	-	-	-	-	38.7	0.0	-	-	-	-	39.1	1.0	-	-	-	-	38.7	-1.0
1955	-	-	-	-	38.7	-0.5	-	-	-	-	38.8	0.3	-	-	-	-	38.7	-0.3	-	-	-	-	38.9	-0.5
1956	-	-	-	-	39.6	1.0	-	-	-	-	40.2	1.5	-	-	-	-	40.8	1.5	-	-	-	-	39.2	1.3
1957	-	-	-	-	40.5	-0.5	-	-	-	-	40.9	1.0	-	-	-	-	41.8	2.2	-	-	-	-	40.7	-0.2
1958	-	-	-	-	41.6	0.5	-	-	-	-	41.6	0.0	-	-	-	-	41.8	0.5	-	-	-	-	41.4	-1.0
1959	-	-	-	-	42.2	2.2	-	-	-	-	42.3	0.2	-	-	-	-	43.0	1.7	-	-	-	-	41.3	-1.2
1960	-	-	-	-	43.0	0.2	-	-	-	-	42.9	-0.2	-	-	-	-	43.6	1.6	-	-	-	-	42.9	-0.2
1961	-	-	-	-	44.0	1.4	-	-	-	-	43.9	-0.2	-	-	-	-	44.0	0.2	-	-	-	-	43.4	-0.5
1962	-	-	-	-	43.9	0.2	-	-	-	-	43.9	0.0	-	-	-	-	44.6	1.6	-	-	-	-	43.8	-0.5
1963	-	-	-	-	44.6	0.2	-	-	-	-	44.6	0.0	-	-	-	-	44.6	0.0	-	-	-	-	44.5	-0.2
1964	-	-	-	-	44.3	-0.7	-	-	-	-	44.5	0.5	-	-	-	-	44.7	0.4	-	-	-	-	44.6	0.0
1965	-	-	-	-	44.7	-0.2	-	-	-	-	45.1	0.9	-	-	-	-	45.4	0.7	-	-	-	-	44.8	0.2
1966	-	-	-	-	46.1	1.3	-	-	-	-	46.5	0.9	-	-	-	-	46.7	0.4	-	-	-	-	45.5	0.2
1967	-	-	-	-	48.0	2.1	-	-	-	-	48.5	1.0	-	-	-	-	49.3	1.6	-	-	-	-	47.0	0.6
1968	-	-	-	-	49.8	1.4	-	-	-	-	50.7	1.8	-	-	-	-	51.7	2.0	-	-	-	-	49.1	-0.4
1969	-	-	-	-	53.5	2.5	-	-	-	-	54.8	2.4	-	-	-	-	56.1	2.4	-	-	-	-	52.2	1.0
1970	-	-	-	-	57.0	0.7	-	-	-	-	57.6	1.1	-	-	-	-	58.5	1.6	-	-	-	-	56.6	0.9
1971	-	-	-	-	60.0	0.5	-	-	-	-	59.2	-1.3	-	-	-	-	60.5	2.2	-	-	-	-	59.7	2.1
1972	-	-	-	-	60.4	0.2	-	-	-	-	59.5	-1.5	-	-	-	-	60.4	1.5	-	-	-	-	60.3	-0.3
1973	-	-	-	-	62.0	2.8	-	-	-	-	62.8	1.3	-	-	-	-	64.9	3.3	-	-	-	-	60.3	-0.2
1974	-	-	-	-	67.1	2.1	-	-	-	-	68.3	1.8	-	-	-	-	70.0	2.5	-	-	-	-	65.7	1.2
1975	-	-	-	-	71.6	1.0	-	-	-	-	71.3	-0.4	-	-	-	-	72.3	1.4	-	-	-	-	70.9	1.3
1976	-	-	-	-	73.7	2.2	-	-	-	-	74.7	1.4	-	-	-	-	76.0	1.7	-	-	-	-	72.1	-0.3
1977	-	-	-	-	77.6	1.0	-	-	-	-	79.1	1.9	-	-	-	-	80.1	1.3	-	-	-	-	76.8	1.1
1978	-	-	-	-	82.9	3.5	-	-	83.8	1.1	-	-	80.5	-3.9	-	-	82.9	3.0	-	-	83.2	0.4	80.1	0.0
1979	80.2	-3.6	-	-	83.9	4.6	-	-	85.6	2.0	-	-	81.9	-4.3	-	-	85.2	4.0	-	-	85.5	0.4	-	-
1980	85.4	-0.1	-	-	90.9	6.4	-	-	91.3	0.4	-	-	90.4	-1.0	-	-	92.9	2.8	-	-	94.4	1.6	-	-
1981	95.0	0.6	-	-	96.7	1.8	-	-	97.0	0.3	-	-	94.9	-2.2	-	-	96.4	1.6	-	-	95.9	-0.5	-	-
1982	92.5	-3.5	-	-	98.4	6.4	-	-	98.9	0.5	-	-	95.5	-3.4	-	-	99.4	4.1	-	-	99.7	0.3	-	-
1983	98.0	-1.7	-	-	99.5	1.5	-	-	102.0	2.5	-	-	101.1	-0.9	-	-	99.1	-2.0	-	-	103.5	4.4	-	-
1984	100.8	-2.6	-	-	101.7	0.9	-	-	102.1	0.4	-	-	99.0	-3.0	-	-	103.7	4.7	-	-	103.5	-0.2	-	-
1985	99.0	-4.3	-	-	107.1	8.2	-	-	106.9	-0.2	-	-	105.2	-1.6	-	-	110.5	5.0	-	-	109.0	-1.4	-	-
1986	106.8	-2.0	-	-	111.0	3.9	-	-	111.6	0.5	-	-	107.8	-3.4	-	-	110.8	2.8	-	-	112.0	1.1	-	-
1987	105.9	-5.4	-	-	120.2	13.5	-	-	119.5	-0.6	-	-	122.7	2.7	-	-	124.3	1.3	-	-	119.5	-3.9	-	-
1988	116.0	-2.9	-	-	128.2	10.5	-	-	120.6	-5.9	-	-	133.0	10.3	-	-	139.0	4.5	-	-	135.4	-2.6	-	-
1989	122.0	-9.9	-	-	135.1	10.7	-	-	127.8	-5.4	-	-	120.5	-5.7	-	-	127.7	6.0	-	-	135.4	-2.6	-	-
1990	110.6	-12.2	-	-	133.6	20.8	-	-	128.3	-4.0	-	-	115.8	-9.7	-	-	134.6	16.2	-	-	126.7	-5.9	-	-
1991	126.1	-0.5	-	-	133.3	5.7	-	-	131.6	-1.3	-	-	127.0	-3.5	-	-	133.8	5.4	-	-	132.6	-0.9	-	-
1992	129.0	-2.7	-	-	141.9	10.0	-	-	140.2	-1.2	-	-	128.3	-8.5	-	-	137.4	7.1	-	-	135.8	-1.2	-	-
1993	131.6	-3.1	-	-	141.0	7.1	-	-	142.3	0.9	-	-	133.2	-6.4	-	-	138.3	3.8	-	-	131.7	-4.8	-	-

Source: U.S. Department of Labor, Bureau of Labor Statistics, Division of Consumer Prices and Price Indexes. - indicates no data collected for period.

Baltimore, MD
Consumer Price Index - All Urban Consumers
Base 1982-1984 = 100
Transportation

For 1947-1993. Columns headed % show percentile change in the index from the previous period for which an index is available.

Year	Jan Index	%	Feb Index	%	Mar Index	%	Apr Index	%	May Index	%	Jun Index	%	Jul Index	%	Aug Index	%	Sep Index	%	Oct Index	%	Nov Index	%	Dec Index	%
1947	16.9		16.8	-0.6	16.8	0.0	17.0	1.2	17.0	0.0	17.0	0.0	-		-		17.8	4.7	-		-		17.9	0.6
1948	-		-		18.4	2.8	-		-		18.4	0.0	-		-		19.5	6.0	-		-		19.6	0.5
1949	-		-		22.0	12.2	-		-		22.1	0.5	-		-		22.1	0.0	-		-		22.0	-0.5
1950	-		-		22.0	0.0	-		-		21.9	-0.5	-		-		23.7	8.2	-		-		23.7	0.0
1951	-		-		23.9	0.8	-		-		23.9	0.0	-		-		24.5	2.5	-		-		24.7	0.8
1952	-		-		24.9	0.8	-		-		24.9	0.0	-		-		26.7	7.2	-		-		26.7	0.0
1953	-		-		26.7	0.0	-		-		26.8	0.4	-		-		27.1	1.1	-		-		27.0	-0.4
1954	-		-		26.7	-1.1	-		-		26.7	0.0	-		-		26.2	-1.9	-		-		26.9	2.7
1955	-		-		26.4	-1.9	-		-		26.5	0.4	-		-		26.2	-1.1	-		-		26.2	0.0
1956	-		-		26.4	0.8	-		-		26.5	0.4	-		-		27.1	2.3	-		-		28.1	3.7
1957	-		-		28.5	1.4	-		-		28.4	-0.4	-		-		28.6	0.7	-		-		29.1	1.7
1958	-		-		28.9	-0.7	-		-		28.6	-1.0	-		-		29.4	2.8	-		-		30.8	4.8
1959	-		-		30.8	0.0	-		-		30.9	0.3	-		-		31.2	1.0	-		-		31.5	1.0
1960	-		-		31.3	-0.6	-		-		30.9	-1.3	-		-		30.5	-1.3	-		-		30.8	1.0
1961	-		-		31.0	0.6	-		-		31.4	1.3	-		-		31.8	1.3	-		-		31.7	-0.3
1962	-		-		31.5	-0.6	-		-		30.9	-1.9	-		-		31.5	1.9	-		-		31.6	0.3
1963	-		-		31.7	0.3	-		-		32.0	0.9	-		-		32.2	0.6	-		-		32.6	1.2
1964	-		-		32.5	-0.3	-		-		32.9	1.2	-		-		32.8	-0.3	-		-		33.2	1.2
1965	-		-		33.3	0.3	-		-		33.2	-0.3	-		-		33.3	0.3	-		-		33.6	0.9
1966	-		-		33.5	-0.3	-		-		33.7	0.6	-		-		33.7	0.0	-		-		33.7	0.0
1967	-		-		33.9	0.6	-		-		34.2	0.9	-		-		34.4	0.6	-		-		34.9	1.5
1968	-		-		34.9	0.0	-		-		35.4	1.4	-		-		35.5	0.3	-		-		36.4	2.5
1969	-		-		37.2	2.2	-		-		37.6	1.1	-		-		37.3	-0.8	-		-		37.8	1.3
1970	-		-		37.7	-0.3	-		-		38.6	2.4	-		-		38.5	-0.3	-		-		39.8	3.4
1971	-		-		39.8	0.0	-		-		40.7	2.3	-		-		40.4	-0.7	-		-		40.3	-0.2
1972	-		-		39.5	-2.0	-		-		39.8	0.8	-		-		40.3	1.3	-		-		40.4	0.2
1973	-		-		40.7	0.7	-		-		41.5	2.0	-		-		41.4	-0.2	-		-		42.3	2.2
1974	-		-		44.3	4.7	-		-		46.3	4.5	-		-		47.7	3.0	-		-		48.2	1.0
1975	-		-		48.7	1.0	-		-		50.1	2.9	-		-		51.2	2.2	-		-		51.6	0.8
1976	-		-		52.8	2.3	-		-		54.9	4.0	-		-		55.6	1.3	-		-		56.0	0.7
1977	-		-		56.9	1.6	-		-		58.5	2.8	-		-		58.1	-0.7	-		-		58.0	-0.2
1978	-		-		58.2	0.3	-		59.4	2.1	-		60.5	1.9	-		60.9	0.7	-		62.3	2.3	-	
1979	63.0	1.1	-		64.3	2.1	-		66.9	4.0	-		70.2	4.9	-		71.6	2.0	-		73.8	3.1	-	
1980	76.8	4.1	-		80.6	4.9	-		81.7	1.4	-		83.1	1.7	-		84.0	1.1	-		85.0	1.2	-	
1981	87.1	2.5	-		90.1	3.4	-		91.6	1.7	-		93.1	1.6	-		93.3	0.2	-		94.6	1.4	-	
1982	95.5	1.0	-		94.4	-1.2	-		94.1	-0.3	-		97.3	3.4	-		97.3	0.0	-		96.9	-0.4	-	
1983	97.4	0.5	-		96.4	-1.0	-		98.1	1.8	-		99.8	1.7	-		102.4	2.6	-		103.2	0.8	-	
1984	102.7	-0.5	-		103.2	0.5	-		103.8	0.6	-		104.8	1.0	-		105.1	0.3	-		105.5	0.4	-	
1985	105.2	-0.3	-		105.9	0.7	-		107.7	1.7	-		107.7	0.0	-		107.5	-0.2	-		108.7	1.1	-	
1986	110.0	1.2	-		106.8	-2.9	-		103.5	-3.1	-		103.0	-0.5	-		102.5	-0.5	-		102.8	0.3	-	
1987	104.1	1.3	-		104.5	0.4	-		105.3	0.8	-		108.2	2.8	-		108.5	0.3	-		109.3	0.7	-	
1988	110.1	0.7	-		109.5	-0.5	-		110.6	1.0	-		111.3	0.6	-		112.4	1.0	-		113.9	1.3	-	
1989	114.1	0.2	-		114.8	0.6	-		117.9	2.7	-		117.5	-0.3	-		117.0	-0.4	-		118.6	1.4	-	
1990	121.2	2.2	-		119.9	-1.1	-		119.5	-0.3	-		120.4	0.8	-		124.6	3.5	-		129.8	4.2	-	
1991	128.0	-1.4	-		123.1	-3.8	-		124.4	1.1	-		124.5	0.1	-		125.7	1.0	-		127.4	1.4	-	

[Continued]

Baltimore, MD
Consumer Price Index - All Urban Consumers
Base 1982-1984 = 100
Transportation
[Continued]

For 1947-1993. Columns headed % show percentile change in the index from the previous period for which an index is available.

Year	Jan Index	Jan %	Feb Index	Feb %	Mar Index	Mar %	Apr Index	Apr %	May Index	May %	Jun Index	Jun %	Jul Index	Jul %	Aug Index	Aug %	Sep Index	Sep %	Oct Index	Oct %	Nov Index	Nov %	Dec Index	Dec %
1992	127.1	-0.2	-	-	126.7	-0.3	-	-	127.7	0.8	-	-	129.0	1.0	-	-	129.0	0.0	-	-	130.8	1.4	-	-
1993	130.2	-0.5	-	-	129.0	-0.9	-	-	129.8	0.6	-	-	129.5	-0.2	-	-	128.6	-0.7	-	-	131.0	1.9	-	-

Source: U.S. Department of Labor, Bureau of Labor Statistics, Division of Consumer Prices and Price Indexes. - indicates no data collected for period.

Baltimore, MD
Consumer Price Index - Urban Wage Earners
Base 1982-1984 = 100
Transportation

For 1947-1993. Columns headed % show percentile change in the index from the previous period for which an index is available.

Year	Jan Index	%	Feb Index	%	Mar Index	%	Apr Index	%	May Index	%	Jun Index	%	Jul Index	%	Aug Index	%	Sep Index	%	Oct Index	%	Nov Index	%	Dec Index	%
1947	16.8	-	16.7	-0.6	16.7	0.0	16.9	1.2	16.9	0.0	16.9	0.0	-	-	-	-	17.7	4.7	-	-	-	-	17.8	0.6
1948	-	-	-	-	18.3	2.8	-	-	-	-	18.3	0.0	-	-	-	-	19.4	6.0	-	-	-	-	19.5	0.5
1949	-	-	-	-	21.9	12.3	-	-	-	-	21.9	0.0	-	-	-	-	21.9	0.0	-	-	-	-	21.9	0.0
1950	-	-	-	-	21.9	0.0	-	-	-	-	21.7	-0.9	-	-	-	-	23.5	8.3	-	-	-	-	23.6	0.4
1951	-	-	-	-	23.7	0.4	-	-	-	-	23.8	0.4	-	-	-	-	24.3	2.1	-	-	-	-	24.6	1.2
1952	-	-	-	-	24.8	0.8	-	-	-	-	24.8	0.0	-	-	-	-	26.6	7.3	-	-	-	-	26.6	0.0
1953	-	-	-	-	26.5	-0.4	-	-	-	-	26.7	0.8	-	-	-	-	26.9	0.7	-	-	-	-	26.8	-0.4
1954	-	-	-	-	26.6	-0.7	-	-	-	-	26.5	-0.4	-	-	-	-	26.0	-1.9	-	-	-	-	26.7	2.7
1955	-	-	-	-	26.3	-1.5	-	-	-	-	26.3	0.0	-	-	-	-	26.1	-0.8	-	-	-	-	26.0	-0.4
1956	-	-	-	-	26.3	1.2	-	-	-	-	26.4	0.4	-	-	-	-	26.9	1.9	-	-	-	-	27.9	3.7
1957	-	-	-	-	28.3	1.4	-	-	-	-	28.2	-0.4	-	-	-	-	28.4	0.7	-	-	-	-	28.9	1.8
1958	-	-	-	-	28.8	-0.3	-	-	-	-	28.5	-1.0	-	-	-	-	29.3	2.8	-	-	-	-	30.6	4.4
1959	-	-	-	-	30.6	0.0	-	-	-	-	30.7	0.3	-	-	-	-	31.0	1.0	-	-	-	-	31.3	1.0
1960	-	-	-	-	31.1	-0.6	-	-	-	-	30.7	-1.3	-	-	-	-	30.3	-1.3	-	-	-	-	30.6	1.0
1961	-	-	-	-	30.8	0.7	-	-	-	-	31.2	1.3	-	-	-	-	31.6	1.3	-	-	-	-	31.5	-0.3
1962	-	-	-	-	31.3	-0.6	-	-	-	-	30.7	-1.9	-	-	-	-	31.3	2.0	-	-	-	-	31.4	0.3
1963	-	-	-	-	31.5	0.3	-	-	-	-	31.8	1.0	-	-	-	-	32.0	0.6	-	-	-	-	32.4	1.3
1964	-	-	-	-	32.3	-0.3	-	-	-	-	32.7	1.2	-	-	-	-	32.6	-0.3	-	-	-	-	33.0	1.2
1965	-	-	-	-	33.1	0.3	-	-	-	-	33.0	-0.3	-	-	-	-	33.1	0.3	-	-	-	-	33.4	0.9
1966	-	-	-	-	33.3	-0.3	-	-	-	-	33.5	0.6	-	-	-	-	33.5	0.0	-	-	-	-	33.5	0.0
1967	-	-	-	-	33.7	0.6	-	-	-	-	34.0	0.9	-	-	-	-	34.2	0.6	-	-	-	-	34.7	1.5
1968	-	-	-	-	34.7	0.0	-	-	-	-	35.2	1.4	-	-	-	-	35.3	0.3	-	-	-	-	36.2	2.5
1969	-	-	-	-	37.0	2.2	-	-	-	-	37.4	1.1	-	-	-	-	37.1	-0.8	-	-	-	-	37.5	1.1
1970	-	-	-	-	37.5	0.0	-	-	-	-	38.4	2.4	-	-	-	-	38.3	-0.3	-	-	-	-	39.6	3.4
1971	-	-	-	-	39.6	0.0	-	-	-	-	40.4	2.0	-	-	-	-	40.1	-0.7	-	-	-	-	40.0	-0.2
1972	-	-	-	-	39.3	-1.7	-	-	-	-	39.5	0.5	-	-	-	-	40.0	1.3	-	-	-	-	40.1	0.2
1973	-	-	-	-	40.5	1.0	-	-	-	-	41.3	2.0	-	-	-	-	41.2	-0.2	-	-	-	-	42.1	2.2
1974	-	-	-	-	44.0	4.5	-	-	-	-	46.0	4.5	-	-	-	-	47.4	3.0	-	-	-	-	47.9	1.1
1975	-	-	-	-	48.5	1.3	-	-	-	-	49.8	2.7	-	-	-	-	50.9	2.2	-	-	-	-	51.3	0.8
1976	-	-	-	-	52.5	2.3	-	-	-	-	54.6	4.0	-	-	-	-	55.2	1.1	-	-	-	-	55.6	0.7
1977	-	-	-	-	56.6	1.8	-	-	-	-	58.2	2.8	-	-	-	-	57.8	-0.7	-	-	-	-	57.6	-0.3
1978	-	-	-	-	57.9	0.5	-	-	59.1	2.1	-	-	60.4	2.2	-	-	60.8	0.7	-	-	61.5	1.2	-	-
1979	62.2	1.1	-	-	63.5	2.1	-	-	66.2	4.3	-	-	69.2	4.5	-	-	70.7	2.2	-	-	72.7	2.8	-	-
1980	75.2	3.4	-	-	78.7	4.7	-	-	79.8	1.4	-	-	81.2	1.8	-	-	82.1	1.1	-	-	84.1	2.4	-	-
1981	86.0	2.3	-	-	89.0	3.5	-	-	90.1	1.2	-	-	92.1	2.2	-	-	92.6	0.5	-	-	94.0	1.5	-	-
1982	94.7	0.7	-	-	93.7	-1.1	-	-	93.4	-0.3	-	-	96.9	3.7	-	-	97.0	0.1	-	-	96.7	-0.3	-	-
1983	97.1	0.4	-	-	96.1	-1.0	-	-	97.9	1.9	-	-	99.9	2.0	-	-	102.4	2.5	-	-	103.4	1.0	-	-
1984	102.9	-0.5	-	-	103.4	0.5	-	-	104.5	1.1	-	-	105.4	0.9	-	-	105.7	0.3	-	-	106.0	0.3	-	-
1985	105.8	-0.2	-	-	106.3	0.5	-	-	107.9	1.5	-	-	107.9	0.0	-	-	107.7	-0.2	-	-	108.7	0.9	-	-
1986	109.8	1.0	-	-	106.8	-2.7	-	-	103.2	-3.4	-	-	102.8	-0.4	-	-	102.2	-0.6	-	-	102.4	0.2	-	-
1987	103.7	1.3	-	-	104.4	0.7	-	-	105.5	1.1	-	-	108.9	3.2	-	-	109.4	0.5	-	-	109.9	0.5	-	-
1988	110.8	0.8	-	-	110.5	-0.3	-	-	111.3	0.7	-	-	112.3	0.9	-	-	113.4	1.0	-	-	114.5	1.0	-	-
1989	114.7	0.2	-	-	115.3	0.5	-	-	118.9	3.1	-	-	118.5	-0.3	-	-	117.8	-0.6	-	-	119.4	1.4	-	-
1990	122.0	2.2	-	-	120.5	-1.2	-	-	120.2	-0.2	-	-	120.9	0.6	-	-	125.6	3.9	-	-	131.0	4.3	-	-
1991	128.6	-1.8	-	-	123.2	-4.2	-	-	124.7	1.2	-	-	125.0	0.2	-	-	126.4	1.1	-	-	127.9	1.2	-	-

[Continued]

286

Baltimore, MD
Consumer Price Index - Urban Wage Earners
Base 1982-1984 = 100
Transportation
[Continued]

For 1947-1993. Columns headed % show percentile change in the index from the previous period for which an index is available.

Year	Jan Index	%	Feb Index	%	Mar Index	%	Apr Index	%	May Index	%	Jun Index	%	Jul Index	%	Aug Index	%	Sep Index	%	Oct Index	%	Nov Index	%	Dec Index	%
1992	127.3	-0.5	-	-	126.6	-0.5	-	-	128.2	1.3	-	-	130.1	1.5	-	-	130.1	0.0	-	-	131.7	1.2	-	-
1993	130.9	-0.6	-	-	129.3	-1.2	-	-	130.2	0.7	-	-	129.8	-0.3	-	-	128.8	-0.8	-	-	131.4	2.0	-	-

Source: U.S. Department of Labor, Bureau of Labor Statistics, Division of Consumer Prices and Price Indexes. - indicates no data collected for period.

Baltimore, MD
Consumer Price Index - All Urban Consumers
Base 1982-1984 = 100
Medical Care

For 1947-1993. Columns headed % show percentile change in the index from the previous period for which an index is available.

Year	Jan Index	%	Feb Index	%	Mar Index	%	Apr Index	%	May Index	%	Jun Index	%	Jul Index	%	Aug Index	%	Sep Index	%	Oct Index	%	Nov Index	%	Dec Index	%
1947	12.5	-	12.6	0.8	12.6	0.0	12.6	0.0	12.7	0.8	12.8	0.8	-	-	-	-	13.1	2.3	-	-	-	-	13.2	0.8
1948	-	-	-	-	13.2	0.0	-	-	-	-	13.4	1.5	-	-	-	-	13.4	0.0	-	-	-	-	13.4	0.0
1949	-	-	-	-	13.4	0.0	-	-	-	-	13.4	0.0	-	-	-	-	13.4	0.0	-	-	-	-	13.5	0.7
1950	-	-	-	-	13.6	0.7	-	-	-	-	13.6	0.0	-	-	-	-	13.7	0.7	-	-	-	-	13.8	0.7
1951	-	-	-	-	14.3	3.6	-	-	-	-	14.9	4.2	-	-	-	-	14.9	0.0	-	-	-	-	15.9	6.7
1952	-	-	-	-	16.4	3.1	-	-	-	-	16.5	0.6	-	-	-	-	16.5	0.0	-	-	-	-	16.5	0.0
1953	-	-	-	-	17.4	5.5	-	-	-	-	17.4	0.0	-	-	-	-	17.5	0.6	-	-	-	-	17.5	0.0
1954	-	-	-	-	17.6	0.6	-	-	-	-	17.6	0.0	-	-	-	-	17.6	0.0	-	-	-	-	17.6	0.0
1955	-	-	-	-	17.7	0.6	-	-	-	-	17.7	0.0	-	-	-	-	17.8	0.6	-	-	-	-	18.0	1.1
1956	-	-	-	-	18.0	0.0	-	-	-	-	18.8	4.4	-	-	-	-	18.9	0.5	-	-	-	-	19.0	0.5
1957	-	-	-	-	19.1	0.5	-	-	-	-	19.1	0.0	-	-	-	-	19.1	0.0	-	-	-	-	19.1	0.0
1958	-	-	-	-	19.3	1.0	-	-	-	-	19.6	1.6	-	-	-	-	19.7	0.5	-	-	-	-	20.6	4.6
1959	-	-	-	-	20.7	0.5	-	-	-	-	20.9	1.0	-	-	-	-	21.0	0.5	-	-	-	-	21.8	3.8
1960	-	-	-	-	22.0	0.9	-	-	-	-	22.1	0.5	-	-	-	-	22.3	0.9	-	-	-	-	23.0	3.1
1961	-	-	-	-	23.2	0.9	-	-	-	-	23.2	0.0	-	-	-	-	23.3	0.4	-	-	-	-	23.4	0.4
1962	-	-	-	-	23.6	0.9	-	-	-	-	23.7	0.4	-	-	-	-	23.9	0.8	-	-	-	-	23.9	0.0
1963	-	-	-	-	25.0	4.6	-	-	-	-	25.3	1.2	-	-	-	-	25.4	0.4	-	-	-	-	25.5	0.4
1964	-	-	-	-	25.6	0.4	-	-	-	-	25.8	0.8	-	-	-	-	25.9	0.4	-	-	-	-	26.1	0.8
1965	-	-	-	-	26.2	0.4	-	-	-	-	26.3	0.4	-	-	-	-	26.6	1.1	-	-	-	-	26.8	0.8
1966	-	-	-	-	27.0	0.7	-	-	-	-	27.5	1.9	-	-	-	-	27.9	1.5	-	-	-	-	28.2	1.1
1967	-	-	-	-	29.5	4.6	-	-	-	-	29.7	0.7	-	-	-	-	30.3	2.0	-	-	-	-	30.5	0.7
1968	-	-	-	-	31.3	2.6	-	-	-	-	31.4	0.3	-	-	-	-	31.9	1.6	-	-	-	-	32.0	0.3
1969	-	-	-	-	33.0	3.1	-	-	-	-	33.2	0.6	-	-	-	-	34.5	3.9	-	-	-	-	34.5	0.0
1970	-	-	-	-	35.8	3.8	-	-	-	-	36.4	1.7	-	-	-	-	37.3	2.5	-	-	-	-	38.5	3.2
1971	-	-	-	-	39.5	2.6	-	-	-	-	40.3	2.0	-	-	-	-	41.7	3.5	-	-	-	-	41.6	-0.2
1972	-	-	-	-	41.8	0.5	-	-	-	-	42.4	1.4	-	-	-	-	43.1	1.7	-	-	-	-	43.4	0.7
1973	-	-	-	-	43.7	0.7	-	-	-	-	43.9	0.5	-	-	-	-	44.6	1.6	-	-	-	-	46.3	3.8
1974	-	-	-	-	46.9	1.3	-	-	-	-	49.5	5.5	-	-	-	-	50.7	2.4	-	-	-	-	51.4	1.4
1975	-	-	-	-	53.1	3.3	-	-	-	-	53.8	1.3	-	-	-	-	54.6	1.5	-	-	-	-	54.7	0.2
1976	-	-	-	-	56.0	2.4	-	-	-	-	58.0	3.6	-	-	-	-	58.1	0.2	-	-	-	-	59.4	2.2
1977	-	-	-	-	61.3	3.2	-	-	-	-	61.9	1.0	-	-	-	-	62.5	1.0	-	-	-	-	63.1	1.0
1978	-	-	-	-	64.3	1.9	-	-	65.0	1.1	-	-	66.1	1.7	-	-	66.7	0.9	-	-	67.6	1.3	-	-
1979	68.5	1.3	-	-	70.4	2.8	-	-	70.8	0.6	-	-	72.0	1.7	-	-	74.3	3.2	-	-	75.3	1.3	-	-
1980	76.1	1.1	-	-	77.5	1.8	-	-	79.6	2.7	-	-	79.0	-0.8	-	-	80.3	1.6	-	-	81.0	0.9	-	-
1981	81.4	0.5	-	-	83.2	2.2	-	-	84.3	1.3	-	-	85.1	0.9	-	-	87.1	2.4	-	-	86.8	-0.3	-	-
1982	89.3	2.9	-	-	91.4	2.4	-	-	92.7	1.4	-	-	94.0	1.4	-	-	96.8	3.0	-	-	97.5	0.7	-	-
1983	98.7	1.2	-	-	99.2	0.5	-	-	99.5	0.3	-	-	101.2	1.7	-	-	101.6	0.4	-	-	102.9	1.3	-	-
1984	102.7	-0.2	-	-	103.5	0.8	-	-	104.2	0.7	-	-	106.8	2.5	-	-	106.3	-0.5	-	-	107.3	0.9	-	-
1985	108.1	0.7	-	-	109.0	0.8	-	-	110.5	1.4	-	-	111.6	1.0	-	-	113.7	1.9	-	-	115.6	1.7	-	-
1986	118.2	2.2	-	-	119.7	1.3	-	-	121.3	1.3	-	-	122.6	1.1	-	-	123.7	0.9	-	-	123.5	-0.2	-	-
1987	125.4	1.5	-	-	124.5	-0.7	-	-	126.0	1.2	-	-	127.9	1.5	-	-	130.6	2.1	-	-	131.7	0.8	-	-
1988	130.8	-0.7	-	-	133.3	1.9	-	-	134.2	0.7	-	-	133.9	-0.2	-	-	136.8	2.2	-	-	137.1	0.2	-	-
1989	139.8	2.0	-	-	140.9	0.8	-	-	142.3	1.0	-	-	143.4	0.8	-	-	151.0	5.3	-	-	153.5	1.7	-	-
1990	150.3	-2.1	-	-	152.3	1.3	-	-	157.1	3.2	-	-	159.8	1.7	-	-	161.2	0.9	-	-	165.2	2.5	-	-
1991	167.4	1.3	-	-	167.2	-0.1	-	-	170.7	2.1	-	-	172.7	1.2	-	-	172.7	0.0	-	-	177.5	2.8	-	-

[Continued]

Baltimore, MD
Consumer Price Index - All Urban Consumers
Base 1982-1984 = 100
Medical Care
[Continued]

For 1947-1993. Columns headed % show percentile change in the index from the previous period for which an index is available.

Year	Jan		Feb		Mar		Apr		May		Jun		Jul		Aug		Sep		Oct		Nov		Dec	
	Index	%	Index	%	Index	%	Index	%	Index	%	Index	%	Index	%	Index	%	Index	%	Index	%	Index	%	Index	%
1992	181.2	2.1	-	-	179.9	-0.7	-	-	178.8	-0.6	-	-	185.2	3.6	-	-	187.4	1.2	-	-	190.6	1.7	-	-
1993	193.8	1.7	-	-	194.3	0.3	-	-	196.0	0.9	-	-	197.7	0.9	-	-	203.0	2.7	-	-	204.5	0.7	-	-

Source: U.S. Department of Labor, Bureau of Labor Statistics, Division of Consumer Prices and Price Indexes. - indicates no data collected for period.

Baltimore, MD
Consumer Price Index - Urban Wage Earners
Base 1982-1984 = 100
Medical Care

For 1947-1993. Columns headed % show percentile change in the index from the previous period for which an index is available.

Year	Jan Index	%	Feb Index	%	Mar Index	%	Apr Index	%	May Index	%	Jun Index	%	Jul Index	%	Aug Index	%	Sep Index	%	Oct Index	%	Nov Index	%	Dec Index	%
1947	13.3	-	13.3	0.0	13.4	0.8	13.4	0.0	13.5	0.7	13.6	0.7	-	-	-	-	13.9	2.2	-	-	-	-	14.0	0.7
1948	-	-	-	-	14.1	0.7	-	-	-	-	14.2	0.7	-	-	-	-	14.2	0.0	-	-	-	-	14.2	0.0
1949	-	-	-	-	14.3	0.7	-	-	-	-	14.3	0.0	-	-	-	-	14.3	0.0	-	-	-	-	14.3	0.0
1950	-	-	-	-	14.4	0.7	-	-	-	-	14.5	0.7	-	-	-	-	14.5	0.0	-	-	-	-	14.6	0.7
1951	-	-	-	-	15.1	3.4	-	-	-	-	15.8	4.6	-	-	-	-	15.8	0.0	-	-	-	-	16.9	7.0
1952	-	-	-	-	17.4	3.0	-	-	-	-	17.5	0.6	-	-	-	-	17.5	0.0	-	-	-	-	17.6	0.6
1953	-	-	-	-	18.5	5.1	-	-	-	-	18.5	0.0	-	-	-	-	18.6	0.5	-	-	-	-	18.6	0.0
1954	-	-	-	-	18.7	0.5	-	-	-	-	18.7	0.0	-	-	-	-	18.7	0.0	-	-	-	-	18.7	0.0
1955	-	-	-	-	18.8	0.5	-	-	-	-	18.8	0.0	-	-	-	-	18.9	0.5	-	-	-	-	19.1	1.1
1956	-	-	-	-	19.1	0.0	-	-	-	-	20.0	4.7	-	-	-	-	20.1	0.5	-	-	-	-	20.2	0.5
1957	-	-	-	-	20.3	0.5	-	-	-	-	20.3	0.0	-	-	-	-	20.3	0.0	-	-	-	-	20.3	0.0
1958	-	-	-	-	20.5	1.0	-	-	-	-	20.8	1.5	-	-	-	-	20.9	0.5	-	-	-	-	21.9	4.8
1959	-	-	-	-	22.0	0.5	-	-	-	-	22.2	0.9	-	-	-	-	22.3	0.5	-	-	-	-	23.2	4.0
1960	-	-	-	-	23.3	0.4	-	-	-	-	23.4	0.4	-	-	-	-	23.7	1.3	-	-	-	-	24.5	3.4
1961	-	-	-	-	24.6	0.4	-	-	-	-	24.7	0.4	-	-	-	-	24.7	0.0	-	-	-	-	24.9	0.8
1962	-	-	-	-	25.1	0.8	-	-	-	-	25.2	0.4	-	-	-	-	25.4	0.8	-	-	-	-	25.4	0.0
1963	-	-	-	-	26.5	4.3	-	-	-	-	26.9	1.5	-	-	-	-	27.0	0.4	-	-	-	-	27.1	0.4
1964	-	-	-	-	27.2	0.4	-	-	-	-	27.4	0.7	-	-	-	-	27.5	0.4	-	-	-	-	27.7	0.7
1965	-	-	-	-	27.9	0.7	-	-	-	-	27.9	0.0	-	-	-	-	28.3	1.4	-	-	-	-	28.5	0.7
1966	-	-	-	-	28.7	0.7	-	-	-	-	29.2	1.7	-	-	-	-	29.6	1.4	-	-	-	-	29.9	1.0
1967	-	-	-	-	31.3	4.7	-	-	-	-	31.6	1.0	-	-	-	-	32.2	1.9	-	-	-	-	32.4	0.6
1968	-	-	-	-	33.2	2.5	-	-	-	-	33.4	0.6	-	-	-	-	33.9	1.5	-	-	-	-	34.0	0.3
1969	-	-	-	-	35.0	2.9	-	-	-	-	35.3	0.9	-	-	-	-	36.6	3.7	-	-	-	-	36.7	0.3
1970	-	-	-	-	38.0	3.5	-	-	-	-	38.7	1.8	-	-	-	-	39.6	2.3	-	-	-	-	40.9	3.3
1971	-	-	-	-	42.0	2.7	-	-	-	-	42.8	1.9	-	-	-	-	44.3	3.5	-	-	-	-	44.2	-0.2
1972	-	-	-	-	44.4	0.5	-	-	-	-	45.0	1.4	-	-	-	-	45.7	1.6	-	-	-	-	46.1	0.9
1973	-	-	-	-	46.5	0.9	-	-	-	-	46.6	0.2	-	-	-	-	47.4	1.7	-	-	-	-	49.2	3.8
1974	-	-	-	-	49.8	1.2	-	-	-	-	52.6	5.6	-	-	-	-	53.9	2.5	-	-	-	-	54.6	1.3
1975	-	-	-	-	56.4	3.3	-	-	-	-	57.2	1.4	-	-	-	-	58.0	1.4	-	-	-	-	58.1	0.2
1976	-	-	-	-	59.5	2.4	-	-	-	-	61.6	3.5	-	-	-	-	61.7	0.2	-	-	-	-	63.1	2.3
1977	-	-	-	-	65.2	3.3	-	-	-	-	65.8	0.9	-	-	-	-	66.4	0.9	-	-	-	-	67.0	0.9
1978	-	-	-	-	68.4	2.1	-	-	69.6	1.8	-	-	70.1	0.7	-	-	71.3	1.7	-	-	71.9	0.8	-	-
1979	72.4	0.7	-	-	74.7	3.2	-	-	74.3	-0.5	-	-	75.9	2.2	-	-	78.2	3.0	-	-	78.7	0.6	-	-
1980	79.3	0.8	-	-	80.5	1.5	-	-	82.2	2.1	-	-	81.0	-1.5	-	-	81.4	0.5	-	-	81.6	0.2	-	-
1981	81.8	0.2	-	-	84.4	3.2	-	-	85.3	1.1	-	-	85.6	0.4	-	-	87.4	2.1	-	-	87.8	0.5	-	-
1982	89.6	2.1	-	-	91.5	2.1	-	-	92.6	1.2	-	-	93.9	1.4	-	-	96.8	3.1	-	-	97.5	0.7	-	-
1983	98.7	1.2	-	-	99.2	0.5	-	-	99.3	0.1	-	-	101.1	1.8	-	-	101.6	0.5	-	-	102.8	1.2	-	-
1984	102.6	-0.2	-	-	103.5	0.9	-	-	104.2	0.7	-	-	106.9	2.6	-	-	106.4	-0.5	-	-	107.4	0.9	-	-
1985	108.2	0.7	-	-	109.0	0.7	-	-	110.7	1.6	-	-	111.7	0.9	-	-	113.9	2.0	-	-	115.6	1.5	-	-
1986	118.5	2.5	-	-	120.0	1.3	-	-	121.6	1.3	-	-	122.7	0.9	-	-	123.7	0.8	-	-	123.5	-0.2	-	-
1987	124.7	1.0	-	-	124.4	-0.2	-	-	125.8	1.1	-	-	127.5	1.4	-	-	130.3	2.2	-	-	131.4	0.8	-	-
1988	130.6	-0.6	-	-	132.5	1.5	-	-	133.6	0.8	-	-	133.4	-0.1	-	-	135.9	1.9	-	-	136.5	0.4	-	-
1989	139.1	1.9	-	-	140.0	0.6	-	-	141.1	0.8	-	-	142.4	0.9	-	-	148.2	4.1	-	-	150.4	1.5	-	-
1990	148.1	-1.5	-	-	150.3	1.5	-	-	155.2	3.3	-	-	157.5	1.5	-	-	158.7	0.8	-	-	162.9	2.6	-	-
1991	164.8	1.2	-	-	165.3	0.3	-	-	168.0	1.6	-	-	170.1	1.3	-	-	170.1	0.0	-	-	174.9	2.8	-	-

[Continued]

Baltimore, MD
Consumer Price Index - Urban Wage Earners
Base 1982-1984 = 100
Medical Care
[Continued]

For 1947-1993. Columns headed % show percentile change in the index from the previous period for which an index is available.

Year	Jan		Feb		Mar		Apr		May		Jun		Jul		Aug		Sep		Oct		Nov		Dec	
	Index	%	Index	%	Index	%	Index	%	Index	%	Index	%	Index	%	Index	%	Index	%	Index	%	Index	%	Index	%
1992	178.2	*1.9*	-	-	176.3	*-1.1*	-	-	175.8	*-0.3*	-	-	182.2	*3.6*	-	-	184.3	*1.2*	-	-	187.8	*1.9*	-	-
1993	191.0	*1.7*	-	-	191.6	*0.3*	-	-	193.0	*0.7*	-	-	195.0	*1.0*	-	-	200.3	*2.7*	-	-	201.8	*0.7*	-	-

Source: U.S. Department of Labor, Bureau of Labor Statistics, Division of Consumer Prices and Price Indexes. - indicates no data collected for period.

Baltimore, MD
Consumer Price Index - All Urban Consumers
Base 1982-1984 = 100
Entertainment

For 1975-1993. Columns headed % show percentile change in the index from the previous period for which an index is available.

Year	Jan Index	%	Feb Index	%	Mar Index	%	Apr Index	%	May Index	%	Jun Index	%	Jul Index	%	Aug Index	%	Sep Index	%	Oct Index	%	Nov Index	%	Dec Index	%
1975	-	-	-	-	-	-	-	-	-	-	-	-	-	-	-	-	-	-	-	-	-	-	65.5	-
1976	-	-	-	-	65.7	0.3	-	-	-	-	66.8	1.7	-	-	-	-	67.6	1.2	-	-	-	-	68.0	0.6
1977	-	-	-	-	68.8	1.2	-	-	-	-	69.6	1.2	-	-	-	-	70.5	1.3	-	-	-	-	70.9	0.6
1978	-	-	-	-	71.5	0.8	-	-	72.6	1.5	-	-	72.5	-0.1	-	-	73.0	0.7	-	-	73.8	1.1	-	-
1979	74.5	0.9	-	-	76.5	2.7	-	-	77.0	0.7	-	-	75.9	-1.4	-	-	76.2	0.4	-	-	77.8	2.1	-	-
1980	81.4	4.6	-	-	82.2	1.0	-	-	82.4	0.2	-	-	83.5	1.3	-	-	85.1	1.9	-	-	84.7	-0.5	-	-
1981	87.7	3.5	-	-	89.4	1.9	-	-	89.8	0.4	-	-	89.9	0.1	-	-	90.5	0.7	-	-	91.8	1.4	-	-
1982	91.5	-0.3	-	-	94.3	3.1	-	-	91.8	-2.7	-	-	92.6	0.9	-	-	97.1	4.9	-	-	97.2	0.1	-	-
1983	98.5	1.3	-	-	101.8	3.4	-	-	102.2	0.4	-	-	101.1	-1.1	-	-	102.5	1.4	-	-	102.5	0.0	-	-
1984	99.2	-3.2	-	-	103.4	4.2	-	-	104.3	0.9	-	-	104.5	0.2	-	-	105.1	0.6	-	-	106.8	1.6	-	-
1985	106.1	-0.7	-	-	107.6	1.4	-	-	109.8	2.0	-	-	109.6	-0.2	-	-	110.8	1.1	-	-	110.4	-0.4	-	-
1986	111.9	1.4	-	-	112.4	0.4	-	-	114.1	1.5	-	-	113.1	-0.9	-	-	114.8	1.5	-	-	115.8	0.9	-	-
1987	117.1	1.1	-	-	118.4	1.1	-	-	118.9	0.4	-	-	118.8	-0.1	-	-	119.0	0.2	-	-	119.9	0.8	-	-
1988	121.7	1.5	-	-	120.0	-1.4	-	-	121.1	0.9	-	-	122.8	1.4	-	-	125.5	2.2	-	-	124.7	-0.6	-	-
1989	125.3	0.5	-	-	126.7	1.1	-	-	128.4	1.3	-	-	129.0	0.5	-	-	126.5	-1.9	-	-	133.1	5.2	-	-
1990	137.9	3.6	-	-	138.1	0.1	-	-	137.2	-0.7	-	-	137.6	0.3	-	-	138.0	0.3	-	-	140.5	1.8	-	-
1991	140.2	-0.2	-	-	142.3	1.5	-	-	142.6	0.2	-	-	142.3	-0.2	-	-	145.9	2.5	-	-	147.6	1.2	-	-
1992	147.7	0.1	-	-	148.6	0.6	-	-	149.4	0.5	-	-	150.3	0.6	-	-	150.4	0.1	-	-	148.3	-1.4	-	-
1993	152.1	2.6	-	-	152.5	0.3	-	-	151.9	-0.4	-	-	152.7	0.5	-	-	154.4	1.1	-	-	152.1	-1.5	-	-

Source: U.S. Department of Labor, Bureau of Labor Statistics, Division of Consumer Prices and Price Indexes. - indicates no data collected for period.

Baltimore, MD
Consumer Price Index - Urban Wage Earners
Base 1982-1984 = 100
Entertainment

For 1975-1993. Columns headed % show percentile change in the index from the previous period for which an index is available.

Year	Jan Index	%	Feb Index	%	Mar Index	%	Apr Index	%	May Index	%	Jun Index	%	Jul Index	%	Aug Index	%	Sep Index	%	Oct Index	%	Nov Index	%	Dec Index	%
1975	-	-	-	-	-	-	-	-	-	-	-	-	-	-	-	-	-	-	-	-	-	-	65.1	-
1976	-	-	-	-	65.3	0.3	-	-	-	-	66.4	1.7	-	-	-	-	67.2	1.2	-	-	-	-	67.6	0.6
1977	-	-	-	-	68.4	1.2	-	-	-	-	69.2	1.2	-	-	-	-	70.1	1.3	-	-	-	-	70.4	0.4
1978	-	-	-	-	71.1	1.0	-	-	72.7	2.3	-	-	71.4	-1.8	-	-	72.8	2.0	-	-	72.5	-0.4	-	-
1979	75.4	4.0	-	-	76.3	1.2	-	-	76.4	0.1	-	-	76.8	0.5	-	-	76.3	-0.7	-	-	77.6	1.7	-	-
1980	79.8	2.8	-	-	81.9	2.6	-	-	83.0	1.3	-	-	83.4	0.5	-	-	85.0	1.9	-	-	84.4	-0.7	-	-
1981	85.0	0.7	-	-	87.2	2.6	-	-	87.3	0.1	-	-	89.2	2.2	-	-	90.2	1.1	-	-	93.6	3.8	-	-
1982	93.3	-0.3	-	-	96.3	3.2	-	-	93.6	-2.8	-	-	94.2	0.6	-	-	97.8	3.8	-	-	97.7	-0.1	-	-
1983	98.6	0.9	-	-	101.8	3.2	-	-	102.5	0.7	-	-	100.7	-1.8	-	-	101.8	1.1	-	-	101.9	0.1	-	-
1984	98.2	-3.6	-	-	102.5	4.4	-	-	103.0	0.5	-	-	103.1	0.1	-	-	104.2	1.1	-	-	106.1	1.8	-	-
1985	105.6	-0.5	-	-	106.8	1.1	-	-	108.8	1.9	-	-	108.4	-0.4	-	-	109.5	1.0	-	-	109.0	-0.5	-	-
1986	110.9	1.7	-	-	110.9	0.0	-	-	113.1	2.0	-	-	112.6	-0.4	-	-	113.4	0.7	-	-	114.6	1.1	-	-
1987	115.5	0.8	-	-	117.0	1.3	-	-	118.1	0.9	-	-	118.2	0.1	-	-	118.6	0.3	-	-	119.6	0.8	-	-
1988	121.3	1.4	-	-	120.4	-0.7	-	-	121.7	1.1	-	-	122.4	0.6	-	-	125.4	2.5	-	-	125.4	0.0	-	-
1989	126.0	0.5	-	-	127.3	1.0	-	-	129.0	1.3	-	-	129.9	0.7	-	-	126.5	-2.6	-	-	133.8	5.8	-	-
1990	138.1	3.2	-	-	138.6	0.4	-	-	137.6	-0.7	-	-	138.0	0.3	-	-	138.7	0.5	-	-	142.1	2.5	-	-
1991	142.0	-0.1	-	-	144.1	1.5	-	-	144.6	0.3	-	-	144.7	0.1	-	-	147.8	2.1	-	-	150.3	1.7	-	-
1992	150.1	-0.1	-	-	151.1	0.7	-	-	151.9	0.5	-	-	152.5	0.4	-	-	152.7	0.1	-	-	150.6	-1.4	-	-
1993	153.9	2.2	-	-	154.6	0.5	-	-	154.1	-0.3	-	-	154.9	0.5	-	-	156.9	1.3	-	-	154.9	-1.3	-	-

Source: U.S. Department of Labor, Bureau of Labor Statistics, Division of Consumer Prices and Price Indexes. - indicates no data collected for period.

Baltimore, MD
Consumer Price Index - All Urban Consumers
Base 1982-1984 = 100
Other Goods and Services

For 1975-1993. Columns headed % show percentile change in the index from the previous period for which an index is available.

Year	Jan		Feb		Mar		Apr		May		Jun		Jul		Aug		Sep		Oct		Nov		Dec	
	Index	%	Index	%	Index	%	Index	%	Index	%	Index	%	Index	%	Index	%	Index	%	Index	%	Index	%	Index	%
1975	-	-	-	-	-	-	-	-	-	-	-	-	-	-	-	-	-	-	-	-	-	-	56.2	-
1976	-	-	-	-	56.7	0.9	-	-	-	-	57.0	0.5	-	-	-	-	57.4	0.7	-	-	-	-	58.7	2.3
1977	-	-	-	-	59.1	0.7	-	-	-	-	60.4	2.2	-	-	-	-	61.2	1.3	-	-	-	-	61.8	1.0
1978	-	-	-	-	62.2	0.6	-	-	62.8	1.0	-	-	65.0	3.5	-	-	66.2	1.8	-	-	67.2	1.5	-	-
1979	66.7	-0.7	-	-	69.2	3.7	-	-	69.3	0.1	-	-	68.9	-0.6	-	-	70.5	2.3	-	-	70.7	0.3	-	-
1980	72.1	2.0	-	-	73.2	1.5	-	-	75.0	2.5	-	-	75.6	0.8	-	-	78.2	3.4	-	-	78.5	0.4	-	-
1981	79.3	1.0	-	-	79.7	0.5	-	-	82.1	3.0	-	-	83.2	1.3	-	-	83.1	-0.1	-	-	85.9	3.4	-	-
1982	86.3	0.5	-	-	86.8	0.6	-	-	87.1	0.3	-	-	87.2	0.1	-	-	92.7	6.3	-	-	94.9	2.4	-	-
1983	96.8	2.0	-	-	98.5	1.8	-	-	99.4	0.9	-	-	101.9	2.5	-	-	102.7	0.8	-	-	105.6	2.8	-	-
1984	107.3	1.6	-	-	108.6	1.2	-	-	107.7	-0.8	-	-	107.7	0.0	-	-	110.6	2.7	-	-	112.0	1.3	-	-
1985	112.0	0.0	-	-	112.7	0.6	-	-	112.9	0.2	-	-	113.9	0.9	-	-	115.6	1.5	-	-	116.2	0.5	-	-
1986	117.0	0.7	-	-	118.2	1.0	-	-	119.8	1.4	-	-	120.6	0.7	-	-	121.7	0.9	-	-	122.8	0.9	-	-
1987	122.7	-0.1	-	-	122.5	-0.2	-	-	122.7	0.2	-	-	125.2	2.0	-	-	132.4	5.8	-	-	134.0	1.2	-	-
1988	134.4	0.3	-	-	136.0	1.2	-	-	136.0	0.0	-	-	137.3	1.0	-	-	142.7	3.9	-	-	144.2	1.1	-	-
1989	144.7	0.3	-	-	144.9	0.1	-	-	147.6	1.9	-	-	148.8	0.8	-	-	153.3	3.0	-	-	153.2	-0.1	-	-
1990	155.7	1.6	-	-	155.7	0.0	-	-	154.8	-0.6	-	-	158.7	2.5	-	-	161.8	2.0	-	-	161.8	0.0	-	-
1991	165.3	2.2	-	-	166.2	0.5	-	-	170.5	2.6	-	-	174.2	2.2	-	-	178.5	2.5	-	-	178.5	0.0	-	-
1992	178.9	0.2	-	-	179.0	0.1	-	-	187.5	4.7	-	-	187.8	0.2	-	-	195.0	3.8	-	-	196.3	0.7	-	-
1993	199.2	1.5	-	-	199.0	-0.1	-	-	199.9	0.5	-	-	201.6	0.9	-	-	194.2	-3.7	-	-	195.3	0.6	-	-

Source: U.S. Department of Labor, Bureau of Labor Statistics, Division of Consumer Prices and Price Indexes. - indicates no data collected for period.

Baltimore, MD
Consumer Price Index - Urban Wage Earners
Base 1982-1984 = 100
Other Goods and Services

For 1975-1993. Columns headed % show percentile change in the index from the previous period for which an index is available.

Year	Jan Index	%	Feb Index	%	Mar Index	%	Apr Index	%	May Index	%	Jun Index	%	Jul Index	%	Aug Index	%	Sep Index	%	Oct Index	%	Nov Index	%	Dec Index	%
1975	-	-	-	-	-	-	-	-	-	-	-	-	-	-	-	-	-	-	-	-	-	-	57.7	-
1976	-	-	-	-	58.1	0.7	-	-	-	-	58.5	0.7	-	-	-	-	58.9	0.7	-	-	-	-	60.3	2.4
1977	-	-	-	-	60.6	0.5	-	-	-	-	61.9	2.1	-	-	-	-	62.8	1.5	-	-	-	-	63.4	1.0
1978	-	-	-	-	63.8	0.6	-	-	63.6	-0.3	-	-	65.6	3.1	-	-	66.5	1.4	-	-	67.4	1.4	-	-
1979	67.2	-0.3	-	-	69.2	3.0	-	-	69.1	-0.1	-	-	68.3	-1.2	-	-	69.9	2.3	-	-	70.4	0.7	-	-
1980	72.0	2.3	-	-	73.1	1.5	-	-	74.1	1.4	-	-	76.5	3.2	-	-	78.2	2.2	-	-	79.2	1.3	-	-
1981	79.0	-0.3	-	-	80.7	2.2	-	-	83.4	3.3	-	-	84.0	0.7	-	-	83.7	-0.4	-	-	85.1	1.7	-	-
1982	86.2	1.3	-	-	87.0	0.9	-	-	87.3	0.3	-	-	87.3	0.0	-	-	92.1	5.5	-	-	94.5	2.6	-	-
1983	97.0	2.6	-	-	98.5	1.5	-	-	99.4	0.9	-	-	102.0	2.6	-	-	102.7	0.7	-	-	105.6	2.8	-	-
1984	107.4	1.7	-	-	108.6	1.1	-	-	107.8	-0.7	-	-	108.0	0.2	-	-	110.6	2.4	-	-	111.7	1.0	-	-
1985	111.8	0.1	-	-	112.8	0.9	-	-	112.9	0.1	-	-	114.1	1.1	-	-	115.7	1.4	-	-	116.0	0.3	-	-
1986	117.1	0.9	-	-	118.2	0.9	-	-	119.6	1.2	-	-	120.7	0.9	-	-	121.5	0.7	-	-	122.4	0.7	-	-
1987	122.4	0.0	-	-	122.4	0.0	-	-	122.8	0.3	-	-	125.5	2.2	-	-	131.8	5.0	-	-	132.8	0.8	-	-
1988	133.5	0.5	-	-	135.2	1.3	-	-	135.2	0.0	-	-	137.0	1.3	-	-	142.2	3.8	-	-	143.1	0.6	-	-
1989	143.9	0.6	-	-	144.3	0.3	-	-	146.7	1.7	-	-	148.2	1.0	-	-	151.8	2.4	-	-	151.6	-0.1	-	-
1990	154.3	1.8	-	-	154.3	0.0	-	-	153.5	-0.5	-	-	157.7	2.7	-	-	160.5	1.8	-	-	160.5	0.0	-	-
1991	164.6	2.6	-	-	165.5	0.5	-	-	169.6	2.5	-	-	174.0	2.6	-	-	177.8	2.2	-	-	177.8	0.0	-	-
1992	178.9	0.6	-	-	179.0	0.1	-	-	189.8	6.0	-	-	190.2	0.2	-	-	196.9	3.5	-	-	197.7	0.4	-	-
1993	201.8	2.1	-	-	201.5	-0.1	-	-	202.6	0.5	-	-	203.9	0.6	-	-	193.5	-5.1	-	-	194.5	0.5	-	-

Source: U.S. Department of Labor, Bureau of Labor Statistics, Division of Consumer Prices and Price Indexes. - indicates no data collected for period.

Boston, MA
Consumer Price Index - All Urban Consumers
Base 1982-1984 = 100
Annual Averages

For 1914-1993. Columns headed % show percentile change in the index from the previous period for which an index is available.

Year	All Items		Food & Beverage		Housing		Apparel & Upkeep		Trans-portation		Medical Care		Entertain-ment		Other Goods & Services	
	Index	%	Index	%	Index	%	Index	%	Index	%	Index	%	Index	%	Index	%
1914	-		-	-	-	-	-	-	-	-	-	-	-	-	-	-
1915	10.5	-	-	-	-	-	-	-	-	-	-	-	-	-	-	-
1916	11.3	7.6	-	-	-	-	-	-	-	-	-	-	-	-	-	-
1917	13.3	17.7	-	-	-	-	-	-	-	-	-	-	-	-	-	-
1918	15.7	18.0	-	-	-	-	-	-	-	-	-	-	-	-	-	-
1919	18.0	14.6	-	-	-	-	-	-	-	-	-	-	-	-	-	-
1920	20.6	14.4	-	-	-	-	-	-	-	-	-	-	-	-	-	-
1921	18.3	-11.2	-	-	-	-	-	-	-	-	-	-	-	-	-	-
1922	17.0	-7.1	-	-	-	-	-	-	-	-	-	-	-	-	-	-
1923	17.4	2.4	-	-	-	-	-	-	-	-	-	-	-	-	-	-
1924	17.4	0.0	-	-	-	-	-	-	-	-	-	-	-	-	-	-
1925	17.9	2.9	-	-	-	-	-	-	-	-	-	-	-	-	-	-
1926	18.2	1.7	-	-	-	-	-	-	-	-	-	-	-	-	-	-
1927	17.9	-1.6	-	-	-	-	-	-	-	-	-	-	-	-	-	-
1928	17.7	-1.1	-	-	-	-	-	-	-	-	-	-	-	-	-	-
1929	17.8	0.6	-	-	-	-	-	-	-	-	-	-	-	-	-	-
1930	17.3	-2.8	-	-	-	-	-	-	-	-	-	-	-	-	-	-
1931	15.8	-8.7	-	-	-	-	-	-	-	-	-	-	-	-	-	-
1932	14.2	-10.1	-	-	-	-	-	-	-	-	-	-	-	-	-	-
1933	13.6	-4.2	-	-	-	-	-	-	-	-	-	-	-	-	-	-
1934	14.1	3.7	-	-	-	-	-	-	-	-	-	-	-	-	-	-
1935	14.3	1.4	-	-	-	-	-	-	-	-	-	-	-	-	-	-
1936	14.3	0.0	-	-	-	-	-	-	-	-	-	-	-	-	-	-
1937	14.8	3.5	-	-	-	-	-	-	-	-	-	-	-	-	-	-
1938	14.3	-3.4	-	-	-	-	-	-	-	-	-	-	-	-	-	-
1939	14.1	-1.4	-	-	-	-	-	-	-	-	-	-	-	-	-	-
1940	14.3	1.4	-	-	-	-	-	-	-	-	-	-	-	-	-	-
1941	14.9	4.2	-	-	-	-	-	-	-	-	-	-	-	-	-	-
1942	16.5	10.7	-	-	-	-	-	-	-	-	-	-	-	-	-	-
1943	17.4	5.5	-	-	-	-	-	-	-	-	-	-	-	-	-	-
1944	17.6	1.1	-	-	-	-	-	-	-	-	-	-	-	-	-	-
1945	17.9	1.7	-	-	-	-	-	-	-	-	-	-	-	-	-	-
1946	19.4	8.4	-	-	-	-	-	-	-	-	-	-	-	-	-	-
1947	22.1	13.9	-	-	-	-	-	-	16.4	-	13.4	-	-	-	-	-
1948	23.9	8.1	-	-	-	-	-	-	16.9	3.0	14.3	6.7	-	-	-	-
1949	23.6	-1.3	-	-	-	-	-	-	18.6	10.1	15.1	5.6	-	-	-	-
1950	23.9	1.3	-	-	-	-	-	-	20.6	10.8	15.7	4.0	-	-	-	-
1951	25.5	6.7	-	-	-	-	-	-	21.2	2.9	16.3	3.8	-	-	-	-
1952	26.0	2.0	-	-	-	-	-	-	22.6	6.6	17.2	5.5	-	-	-	-
1953	26.1	0.4	-	-	-	-	39.4	-	23.5	4.0	17.6	2.3	-	-	-	-
1954	26.3	0.8	-	-	-	-	39.1	-0.8	23.6	0.4	17.7	0.6	-	-	-	-
1955	26.4	0.4	-	-	-	-	39.2	0.3	23.2	-1.7	17.9	1.1	-	-	-	-
1956	27.1	2.7	-	-	-	-	39.8	1.5	24.0	3.4	19.0	6.1	-	-	-	-
1957	28.1	3.7	-	-	-	-	40.5	1.8	25.0	4.2	20.8	9.5	-	-	-	-
1958	28.9	2.8	-	-	-	-	41.1	1.5	25.8	3.2	22.2	6.7	-	-	-	-

[Continued]

Boston, MA
Consumer Price Index - All Urban Consumers
Base 1982-1984 = 100
Annual Averages
[Continued]

For 1914-1993. Columns headed % show percentile change in the index from the previous period for which an index is available.

Year	All Items		Food & Beverage		Housing		Apparel & Upkeep		Trans- portation		Medical Care		Entertain- ment		Other Goods & Services	
	Index	%	Index	%	Index	%	Index	%	Index	%	Index	%	Index	%	Index	%
1959	29.1	0.7	-	-	-	-	40.8	-0.7	26.4	2.3	22.8	2.7	-	-	-	-
1960	29.8	2.4	-	-	-	-	42.0	2.9	25.8	-2.3	23.2	1.8	-	-	-	-
1961	30.2	1.3	-	-	-	-	42.4	1.0	26.2	1.6	23.9	3.0	-	-	-	-
1962	30.8	2.0	-	-	-	-	43.0	1.4	28.2	7.6	24.8	3.8	-	-	-	-
1963	31.4	1.9	-	-	-	-	43.3	0.7	28.3	0.4	25.3	2.0	-	-	-	-
1964	31.9	1.6	-	-	-	-	43.6	0.7	28.5	0.7	26.1	3.2	-	-	-	-
1965	32.5	1.9	-	-	-	-	43.9	0.7	29.2	2.5	27.1	3.8	-	-	-	-
1966	33.6	3.4	-	-	-	-	45.0	2.5	29.9	2.4	28.2	4.1	-	-	-	-
1967	34.4	2.4	-	-	-	-	46.5	3.3	30.6	2.3	30.1	6.7	-	-	-	-
1968	35.8	4.1	-	-	-	-	49.3	6.0	31.6	3.3	32.5	8.0	-	-	-	-
1969	37.8	5.6	-	-	-	-	52.1	5.7	33.5	6.0	35.1	8.0	-	-	-	-
1970	40.2	6.3	-	-	-	-	54.6	4.8	34.9	4.2	37.4	6.6	-	-	-	-
1971	42.2	5.0	-	-	-	-	56.6	3.7	36.6	4.9	39.2	4.8	-	-	-	-
1972	43.7	3.6	-	-	-	-	57.8	2.1	36.6	0.0	40.5	3.3	-	-	-	-
1973	46.3	5.9	-	-	-	-	59.8	3.5	37.6	2.7	41.8	3.2	-	-	-	-
1974	51.2	10.6	-	-	-	-	64.1	7.2	41.0	9.0	44.8	7.2	-	-	-	-
1975	55.8	9.0	-	-	-	-	68.3	6.6	47.0	14.6	50.1	11.8	-	-	-	-
1976	60.0	7.5	67.0	-	56.3	-	71.5	4.7	59.3	26.2	53.4	6.6	64.6	-	56.4	-
1977	63.1	5.2	69.7	4.0	59.5	5.7	73.2	2.4	63.4	6.9	57.8	8.2	66.2	2.5	59.4	5.3
1978	66.4	5.2	75.3	8.0	63.1	6.1	78.7	7.5	63.0	-0.6	62.0	7.3	69.2	4.5	62.5	5.2
1979	73.2	10.2	83.2	10.5	69.9	10.8	84.9	7.9	69.4	10.2	69.5	12.1	75.6	9.2	67.4	7.8
1980	82.6	12.8	89.1	7.1	80.5	15.2	89.5	5.4	82.7	19.2	76.9	10.6	83.3	10.2	73.6	9.2
1981	91.8	11.1	94.3	5.8	92.0	14.3	93.8	4.8	94.1	13.8	83.7	8.8	89.9	7.9	81.0	10.1
1982	95.5	4.0	96.6	2.4	94.6	2.8	97.4	3.8	98.3	4.5	92.6	10.6	96.3	7.1	90.5	11.7
1983	99.8	4.5	99.1	2.6	100.3	6.0	99.8	2.5	99.2	0.9	98.8	6.7	100.2	4.0	100.1	10.6
1984	104.7	4.9	104.2	5.1	105.0	4.7	102.7	2.9	102.5	3.3	108.6	9.9	103.5	3.3	109.4	9.3
1985	109.4	4.5	108.6	4.2	109.1	3.9	106.1	3.3	105.3	2.7	120.5	11.0	109.8	6.1	118.9	8.7
1986	112.2	2.6	113.7	4.7	111.6	2.3	108.3	2.1	101.6	-3.5	131.8	9.4	114.6	4.4	128.8	8.3
1987	117.1	4.4	119.4	5.0	116.8	4.7	115.8	6.9	103.3	1.7	139.2	5.6	119.4	4.2	136.0	5.6
1988	124.2	6.1	124.4	4.2	123.7	5.9	125.8	8.6	108.3	4.8	152.1	9.3	127.0	6.4	147.1	8.2
1989	131.3	5.7	132.2	6.3	131.3	6.1	125.1	-0.6	113.7	5.0	165.3	8.7	133.6	5.2	157.9	7.3
1990	138.9	5.8	138.6	4.8	137.0	4.3	138.2	10.5	119.7	5.3	181.6	9.9	144.2	7.9	173.4	9.8
1991	145.0	4.4	142.5	2.8	140.9	2.8	144.6	4.6	125.5	4.8	202.7	11.6	152.2	5.5	188.4	8.7
1992	148.6	2.5	143.3	0.6	143.5	1.8	145.1	0.3	129.1	2.9	224.2	10.6	155.0	1.8	197.9	5.0
1993	-	-	-	-	-	-	-	-	-	-	-	-	-	-	-	-

Source: U.S. Department of Labor, Bureau of Labor Statistics, Division of Consumer Prices and Price Indexes. - indicates no data collected for period.

Boston, MA
Consumer Price Index - Urban Wage Earners
Base 1982-1984 = 100
Annual Averages

For 1914-1993. Columns headed % show percentile change in the index from the previous period for which an index is available.

Year	All Items		Food & Beverage		Housing		Apparel & Upkeep		Trans-portation		Medical Care		Entertain-ment		Other Goods & Services	
	Index	%	Index	%	Index	%	Index	%	Index	%	Index	%	Index	%	Index	%
1914	-	-	-	-	-	-	-	-	-	-	-	-	-	-	-	-
1915	10.5	-	-	-	-	-	-	-	-	-	-	-	-	-	-	-
1916	11.3	7.6	-	-	-	-	-	-	-	-	-	-	-	-	-	-
1917	13.4	18.6	-	-	-	-	-	-	-	-	-	-	-	-	-	-
1918	15.8	17.9	-	-	-	-	-	-	-	-	-	-	-	-	-	-
1919	18.1	14.6	-	-	-	-	-	-	-	-	-	-	-	-	-	-
1920	20.8	14.9	-	-	-	-	-	-	-	-	-	-	-	-	-	-
1921	18.4	-11.5	-	-	-	-	-	-	-	-	-	-	-	-	-	-
1922	17.1	-7.1	-	-	-	-	-	-	-	-	-	-	-	-	-	-
1923	17.5	2.3	-	-	-	-	-	-	-	-	-	-	-	-	-	-
1924	17.5	0.0	-	-	-	-	-	-	-	-	-	-	-	-	-	-
1925	18.0	2.9	-	-	-	-	-	-	-	-	-	-	-	-	-	-
1926	18.3	1.7	-	-	-	-	-	-	-	-	-	-	-	-	-	-
1927	18.0	-1.6	-	-	-	-	-	-	-	-	-	-	-	-	-	-
1928	17.8	-1.1	-	-	-	-	-	-	-	-	-	-	-	-	-	-
1929	17.9	0.6	-	-	-	-	-	-	-	-	-	-	-	-	-	-
1930	17.4	-2.8	-	-	-	-	-	-	-	-	-	-	-	-	-	-
1931	15.9	-8.6	-	-	-	-	-	-	-	-	-	-	-	-	-	-
1932	14.3	-10.1	-	-	-	-	-	-	-	-	-	-	-	-	-	-
1933	13.7	-4.2	-	-	-	-	-	-	-	-	-	-	-	-	-	-
1934	14.2	3.6	-	-	-	-	-	-	-	-	-	-	-	-	-	-
1935	14.4	1.4	-	-	-	-	-	-	-	-	-	-	-	-	-	-
1936	14.4	0.0	-	-	-	-	-	-	-	-	-	-	-	-	-	-
1937	14.8	2.8	-	-	-	-	-	-	-	-	-	-	-	-	-	-
1938	14.4	-2.7	-	-	-	-	-	-	-	-	-	-	-	-	-	-
1939	14.2	-1.4	-	-	-	-	-	-	-	-	-	-	-	-	-	-
1940	14.4	1.4	-	-	-	-	-	-	-	-	-	-	-	-	-	-
1941	15.0	4.2	-	-	-	-	-	-	-	-	-	-	-	-	-	-
1942	16.6	10.7	-	-	-	-	-	-	-	-	-	-	-	-	-	-
1943	17.5	5.4	-	-	-	-	-	-	-	-	-	-	-	-	-	-
1944	17.7	1.1	-	-	-	-	-	-	-	-	-	-	-	-	-	-
1945	18.0	1.7	-	-	-	-	-	-	-	-	-	-	-	-	-	-
1946	19.5	8.3	-	-	-	-	-	-	-	-	-	-	-	-	-	-
1947	22.2	13.8	-	-	-	-	-	-	16.4	-	13.6	-	-	-	-	-
1948	24.0	8.1	-	-	-	-	-	-	16.9	3.0	14.5	6.6	-	-	-	-
1949	23.7	-1.2	-	-	-	-	-	-	18.5	9.5	15.3	5.5	-	-	-	-
1950	24.0	1.3	-	-	-	-	-	-	20.5	10.8	16.0	4.6	-	-	-	-
1951	25.6	6.7	-	-	-	-	-	-	21.2	3.4	16.5	3.1	-	-	-	-
1952	26.2	2.3	-	-	-	-	-	-	22.6	6.6	17.4	5.5	-	-	-	-
1953	26.3	0.4	-	-	-	-	39.7	-	23.4	3.5	17.9	2.9	-	-	-	-
1954	26.4	0.4	-	-	-	-	39.4	-0.8	23.6	0.9	18.0	0.6	-	-	-	-
1955	26.5	0.4	-	-	-	-	39.5	0.3	23.1	-2.1	18.1	0.6	-	-	-	-
1956	27.3	3.0	-	-	-	-	40.1	1.5	24.0	3.9	19.3	6.6	-	-	-	-
1957	28.2	3.3	-	-	-	-	40.8	1.7	24.9	3.8	21.1	9.3	-	-	-	-
1958	29.1	3.2	-	-	-	-	41.4	1.5	25.7	3.2	22.6	7.1	-	-	-	-

[Continued]

298

Boston, MA
Consumer Price Index - Urban Wage Earners
Base 1982-1984 = 100
Annual Averages
[Continued]

For 1914-1993. Columns headed % show percentile change in the index from the previous period for which an index is available.

Year	All Items		Food & Beverage		Housing		Apparel & Upkeep		Trans-portation		Medical Care		Entertain-ment		Other Goods & Services	
	Index	%	Index	%	Index	%	Index	%	Index	%	Index	%	Index	%	Index	%
1959	29.3	0.7	-	-	-	-	41.1	-0.7	26.3	2.3	23.1	2.2	-	-	-	-
1960	29.9	2.0	-	-	-	-	42.4	3.2	25.7	-2.3	23.5	1.7	-	-	-	-
1961	30.3	1.3	-	-	-	-	42.7	0.7	26.2	1.9	24.3	3.4	-	-	-	-
1962	31.0	2.3	-	-	-	-	43.3	1.4	28.1	7.3	25.1	3.3	-	-	-	-
1963	31.6	1.9	-	-	-	-	43.7	0.9	28.2	0.4	25.7	2.4	-	-	-	-
1964	32.1	1.6	-	-	-	-	43.9	0.5	28.4	0.7	26.5	3.1	-	-	-	-
1965	32.7	1.9	-	-	-	-	44.3	0.9	29.1	2.5	27.5	3.8	-	-	-	-
1966	33.8	3.4	-	-	-	-	45.3	2.3	29.8	2.4	28.6	4.0	-	-	-	-
1967	34.6	2.4	-	-	-	-	46.8	3.3	30.6	2.7	30.5	6.6	-	-	-	-
1968	36.0	4.0	-	-	-	-	49.7	6.2	31.5	2.9	33.0	8.2	-	-	-	-
1969	38.1	5.8	-	-	-	-	52.5	5.6	33.4	6.0	35.6	7.9	-	-	-	-
1970	40.4	6.0	-	-	-	-	55.0	4.8	34.8	4.2	38.0	6.7	-	-	-	-
1971	42.5	5.2	-	-	-	-	57.1	3.8	36.5	4.9	39.8	4.7	-	-	-	-
1972	44.0	3.5	-	-	-	-	58.2	1.9	36.5	0.0	41.1	3.3	-	-	-	-
1973	46.6	5.9	-	-	-	-	60.2	3.4	37.5	2.7	42.4	3.2	-	-	-	-
1974	51.4	10.3	-	-	-	-	64.6	7.3	40.9	9.1	45.4	7.1	-	-	-	-
1975	56.1	9.1	-	-	-	-	68.8	6.5	46.9	14.7	50.8	11.9	-	-	-	-
1976	60.4	7.7	67.6	-	56.2	-	72.0	4.7	59.2	26.2	54.2	6.7	67.0	-	57.1	-
1977	63.5	5.1	70.3	4.0	59.4	5.7	73.7	2.4	63.2	6.8	58.7	8.3	68.5	2.2	60.2	5.4
1978	66.7	5.0	75.8	7.8	63.0	6.1	78.2	6.1	62.9	-0.5	62.8	7.0	70.7	3.2	63.3	5.1
1979	73.5	10.2	83.3	9.9	70.1	11.3	82.6	5.6	70.0	11.3	69.4	10.5	77.0	8.9	68.1	7.6
1980	83.0	12.9	89.6	7.6	81.3	16.0	86.8	5.1	83.4	19.1	76.4	10.1	83.4	8.3	73.7	8.2
1981	92.2	11.1	94.6	5.6	93.2	14.6	92.9	7.0	94.0	12.7	83.8	9.7	89.6	7.4	81.1	10.0
1982	95.9	4.0	96.5	2.0	95.4	2.4	98.0	5.5	98.4	4.7	92.3	10.1	96.2	7.4	90.3	11.3
1983	99.7	4.0	99.1	2.7	100.2	5.0	100.2	2.2	99.1	0.7	98.8	7.0	100.3	4.3	100.1	10.9
1984	104.3	4.6	104.4	5.3	104.2	4.0	101.8	1.6	102.5	3.4	108.9	10.2	103.6	3.3	109.6	9.5
1985	109.3	4.8	108.4	3.8	109.6	5.2	104.8	2.9	105.1	2.5	119.3	9.6	109.2	5.4	119.1	8.7
1986	111.8	2.3	113.1	4.3	111.9	2.1	107.0	2.1	101.1	-3.8	130.6	9.5	114.1	4.5	128.8	8.1
1987	117.1	4.7	118.9	5.1	116.8	4.4	121.3	13.4	103.7	2.6	138.8	6.3	117.8	3.2	136.0	5.6
1988	124.1	6.0	123.8	4.1	123.5	5.7	132.6	9.3	109.2	5.3	151.4	9.1	125.3	6.4	147.0	8.1
1989	131.5	6.0	131.5	6.2	131.0	6.1	134.0	1.1	115.6	5.9	163.9	8.3	133.0	6.1	158.6	7.9
1990	138.8	5.6	137.9	4.9	136.0	3.8	146.9	9.6	122.0	5.5	179.7	9.6	144.5	8.6	174.3	9.9
1991	144.6	4.2	141.6	2.7	139.6	2.6	153.1	4.2	128.3	5.2	199.7	11.1	152.8	5.7	189.6	8.8
1992	148.0	2.4	142.4	0.6	142.0	1.7	153.2	0.1	131.9	2.8	219.9	10.1	155.5	1.8	200.0	5.5
1993	-	-	-	-	-	-	-	-	-	-	-	-	-	-	-	-

Source: U.S. Department of Labor, Bureau of Labor Statistics, Division of Consumer Prices and Price Indexes. - indicates no data collected for period.

Boston, MA
Consumer Price Index - All Urban Consumers
Base 1982-1984 = 100
All Items

For 1914-1993. Columns headed % show percentile change in the index from the previous period for which an index is available.

Year	Jan		Feb		Mar		Apr		May		Jun		Jul		Aug		Sep		Oct		Nov		Dec	
	Index	%	Index	%	Index	%	Index	%	Index	%	Index	%	Index	%	Index	%	Index	%	Index	%	Index	%	Index	%
1914	-	-	-	-	-	-	-	-	-	-	-	-	-	-	-	-	-	-	-	-	-	-	10.5	-
1915	-	-	-	-	-	-	-	-	-	-	-	-	-	-	-	-	-	-	-	-	-	-	10.7	1.9
1916	-	-	-	-	-	-	-	-	-	-	-	-	-	-	-	-	-	-	-	-	-	-	12.1	13.1
1917	-	-	-	-	-	-	-	-	-	-	-	-	-	-	-	-	-	-	-	-	-	-	14.2	17.4
1918	-	-	-	-	-	-	-	-	-	-	-	-	-	-	-	-	-	-	-	-	-	-	17.3	21.8
1919	-	-	-	-	-	-	-	-	-	-	17.4	0.6	-	-	-	-	-	-	-	-	-	-	19.5	12.1
1920	-	-	-	-	-	-	-	-	-	-	21.5	10.3	-	-	-	-	-	-	-	-	-	-	20.2	-6.0
1921	-	-	-	-	-	-	-	-	18.0	-10.9	-	-	-	-	-	-	18.0	0.0	-	-	-	-	17.8	-1.1
1922	-	-	-	-	16.9	-5.1	-	-	-	-	16.8	-0.6	-	-	-	-	16.9	0.6	-	-	-	-	17.3	2.4
1923	-	-	-	-	17.1	-1.2	-	-	-	-	17.1	0.0	-	-	-	-	17.6	2.9	-	-	-	-	17.8	1.1
1924	-	-	-	-	17.3	-2.8	-	-	-	-	17.2	-0.6	-	-	-	-	17.5	1.7	-	-	-	-	17.6	0.6
1925	-	-	-	-	-	-	-	-	-	-	17.5	-0.6	-	-	-	-	-	-	-	-	-	-	18.5	5.7
1926	-	-	-	-	-	-	-	-	-	-	18.1	-2.2	-	-	-	-	-	-	-	-	-	-	18.2	0.6
1927	-	-	-	-	-	-	-	-	-	-	18.0	-1.1	-	-	-	-	-	-	-	-	-	-	18.0	0.0
1928	-	-	-	-	-	-	-	-	-	-	17.5	-2.8	-	-	-	-	-	-	-	-	-	-	17.8	1.7
1929	-	-	-	-	-	-	-	-	-	-	17.5	-1.7	-	-	-	-	-	-	-	-	-	-	17.8	1.7
1930	-	-	-	-	-	-	-	-	-	-	17.4	-2.2	-	-	-	-	-	-	-	-	-	-	16.9	-2.9
1931	-	-	-	-	-	-	-	-	-	-	15.7	-7.1	-	-	-	-	-	-	-	-	-	-	15.3	-2.5
1932	-	-	-	-	-	-	-	-	-	-	14.1	-7.8	-	-	-	-	-	-	-	-	-	-	13.8	-2.1
1933	-	-	-	-	-	-	-	-	-	-	13.4	-2.9	-	-	-	-	-	-	-	-	-	-	13.9	3.7
1934	-	-	-	-	-	-	-	-	-	-	14.1	1.4	-	-	-	-	-	-	-	-	14.2	0.7	-	-
1935	-	-	-	-	14.5	2.1	-	-	-	-	-	-	14.2	-2.1	-	-	-	-	14.3	0.7	-	-	-	-
1936	14.4	0.7	-	-	-	-	14.3	-0.7	-	-	-	-	14.5	1.4	-	-	14.5	0.0	-	-	-	-	14.3	-1.4
1937	-	-	-	-	14.6	2.1	-	-	-	-	14.8	1.4	-	-	-	-	15.1	2.0	-	-	-	-	14.7	-2.6
1938	-	-	-	-	14.3	-2.7	-	-	-	-	14.3	0.0	-	-	-	-	14.3	0.0	-	-	-	-	14.2	-0.7
1939	-	-	-	-	14.1	-0.7	-	-	-	-	14.0	-0.7	-	-	-	-	14.3	2.1	-	-	-	-	14.1	-1.4
1940	-	-	-	-	14.3	1.4	-	-	-	-	14.4	0.7	-	-	-	-	14.3	-0.7	14.2	-0.7	14.2	0.0	14.3	0.7
1941	14.3	0.0	14.3	0.0	14.3	0.0	14.5	1.4	14.6	0.7	14.8	1.4	15.0	1.4	15.1	0.7	15.3	1.3	15.4	0.7	15.7	1.9	15.6	-0.6
1942	15.8	1.3	16.0	1.3	16.1	0.6	16.1	0.0	16.3	1.2	16.4	0.6	16.7	1.8	16.6	-0.6	16.8	1.2	17.0	1.2	17.1	0.6	17.1	0.0
1943	17.1	0.0	17.1	0.0	17.4	1.8	17.5	0.6	17.6	0.6	17.5	-0.6	17.3	-1.1	17.3	0.0	17.3	0.0	17.6	-1.1	17.7	0.6	17.8	0.6
1944	17.4	0.0	17.3	-0.6	17.3	0.0	17.5	1.2	17.5	0.0	17.5	0.0	17.6	0.6	17.7	0.6	18.0	-0.6	17.9	-0.6	18.0	0.6	18.0	0.0
1945	17.8	0.0	17.8	0.0	17.7	-0.6	17.7	0.0	17.8	0.6	18.1	1.7	18.1	0.0	18.1	0.0	18.1	0.0	17.9	-0.6	18.0	0.6	18.0	0.0
1946	18.1	0.6	18.0	-0.6	18.1	0.6	18.2	0.6	18.2	0.0	18.4	1.1	19.8	7.6	20.2	2.0	20.4	1.0	20.8	2.0	21.1	1.4	21.3	0.9
1947	21.4	0.5	21.3	-0.5	21.7	1.9	21.5	-0.9	21.4	-0.5	21.7	1.4	21.9	0.9	22.3	1.8	22.9	2.7	22.7	-0.9	22.8	0.4	23.2	1.8
1948	23.5	1.3	23.3	-0.9	23.2	-0.4	23.6	1.7	23.7	0.4	24.0	1.3	24.3	1.2	24.4	0.4	24.4	0.0	24.3	-0.4	24.1	-0.8	23.8	-1.2
1949	23.7	-0.4	23.3	-1.7	23.5	0.9	23.5	0.0	23.5	0.0	23.6	0.4	23.5	-0.4	23.7	0.9	23.9	0.8	23.7	-0.8	23.7	0.0	23.5	-0.8
1950	23.4	-0.4	23.3	-0.4	23.5	0.9	23.5	0.0	23.5	0.0	23.8	1.3	24.0	0.8	24.2	0.8	24.2	0.0	24.4	0.8	24.4	0.0	24.6	0.8
1951	25.0	1.6	25.3	1.2	25.3	0.0	25.3	0.0	25.4	0.4	25.4	0.0	25.5	0.4	25.5	0.0	25.6	0.4	25.8	0.8	25.9	0.4	26.0	0.4
1952	25.9	-0.4	25.8	-0.4	25.8	0.0	25.8	0.0	25.9	0.4	26.0	0.4	26.4	1.5	26.4	0.0	26.3	-0.4	26.3	0.0	26.1	-0.8	26.0	-0.4
1953	26.0	0.0	-	-	-	-	-	-	25.9	-0.4	-	-	26.2	1.2	-	-	-	-	26.4	0.8	-	-	-	-
1954	26.1	-1.1	-	-	-	-	-	-	26.1	0.0	-	-	26.4	1.1	-	-	-	-	26.3	-0.4	-	-	-	-
1955	26.2	-0.4	-	-	-	-	-	-	26.3	0.4	-	-	26.4	0.4	-	-	-	-	26.5	0.4	-	-	-	-
1956	26.6	0.4	-	-	-	-	-	-	26.7	0.4	-	-	27.3	2.2	-	-	-	-	27.7	1.5	-	-	-	-
1957	27.6	-0.4	-	-	-	-	-	-	27.9	1.1	-	-	28.3	1.4	-	-	-	-	28.3	0.0	-	-	-	-
1958	28.6	1.1	-	-	-	-	-	-	28.9	1.0	-	-	29.1	0.7	-	-	-	-	29.1	0.0	-	-	-	-

[Continued]

Boston, MA
Consumer Price Index - All Urban Consumers
Base 1982-1984 = 100
All Items
[Continued]

For 1914-1993. Columns headed % show percentile change in the index from the previous period for which an index is available.

Year	Jan Index	%	Feb Index	%	Mar Index	%	Apr Index	%	May Index	%	Jun Index	%	Jul Index	%	Aug Index	%	Sep Index	%	Oct Index	%	Nov Index	%	Dec Index	%
1959	29.1	0.0	-	-	-	-	29.0	-0.3	-	-	-	-	29.1	0.3	-	-	-	-	29.4	1.0	-	-	-	-
1960	29.3	-0.3	-	-	-	-	29.8	1.7	-	-	-	-	29.8	0.0	-	-	-	-	29.9	0.3	-	-	-	-
1961	30.0	0.3	-	-	-	-	30.1	0.3	-	-	-	-	30.2	0.3	-	-	-	-	30.3	0.3	-	-	-	-
1962	30.5	0.7	-	-	-	-	30.8	1.0	-	-	-	-	30.8	0.0	-	-	-	-	31.1	1.0	-	-	-	-
1963	31.2	0.3	-	-	-	-	31.4	0.6	-	-	-	-	31.5	0.3	-	-	-	-	31.6	0.3	-	-	-	-
1964	31.6	0.0	-	-	-	-	31.8	0.6	-	-	-	-	31.9	0.3	-	-	-	-	32.1	0.6	-	-	-	-
1965	32.2	0.3	-	-	-	-	32.4	0.6	-	-	-	-	32.6	0.6	-	-	-	-	32.6	0.0	-	-	-	-
1966	32.7	0.3	-	-	-	-	33.5	2.4	-	-	-	-	33.6	0.3	-	-	-	-	34.0	1.2	-	-	-	-
1967	34.1	0.3	-	-	-	-	34.1	0.0	-	-	-	-	34.4	0.9	-	-	-	-	34.7	0.9	-	-	-	-
1968	35.0	0.9	-	-	-	-	35.5	1.4	-	-	-	-	35.8	0.8	-	-	-	-	36.4	1.7	-	-	-	-
1969	36.7	0.8	-	-	-	-	37.3	1.6	-	-	-	-	37.9	1.6	-	-	-	-	38.7	2.1	-	-	-	-
1970	39.1	1.0	-	-	-	-	39.6	1.3	-	-	-	-	40.0	1.0	-	-	-	-	41.1	2.8	-	-	-	-
1971	41.5	1.0	-	-	-	-	41.8	0.7	-	-	-	-	42.2	1.0	-	-	-	-	42.8	1.4	-	-	-	-
1972	42.9	0.2	-	-	-	-	43.4	1.2	-	-	-	-	43.7	0.7	-	-	-	-	44.3	1.4	-	-	-	-
1973	44.6	0.7	-	-	-	-	45.6	2.2	-	-	-	-	46.1	1.1	-	-	-	-	47.7	3.5	-	-	-	-
1974	48.9	2.5	-	-	-	-	50.0	2.2	-	-	-	-	51.5	3.0	-	-	-	-	52.6	2.1	-	-	-	-
1975	53.8	2.3	-	-	-	-	54.7	1.7	-	-	-	-	56.1	2.6	-	-	-	-	56.7	1.1	-	-	-	-
1976	59.1	4.2	-	-	-	-	59.3	0.3	-	-	-	-	60.3	1.7	-	-	-	-	60.6	0.5	-	-	-	-
1977	61.6	1.7	-	-	-	-	62.5	1.5	-	-	-	-	63.5	1.6	-	-	-	-	63.9	0.6	-	-	-	-
1978	64.5	0.9	-	-	64.8	0.5	-	-	65.6	1.2	-	-	66.4	1.2	-	-	67.4	1.5	-	-	68.7	1.9	-	-
1979	69.4	1.0	-	-	70.6	1.7	-	-	72.1	2.1	-	-	73.7	2.2	-	-	75.0	1.8	-	-	76.6	2.1	-	-
1980	78.2	2.1	-	-	80.6	3.1	-	-	81.5	1.1	-	-	82.9	1.7	-	-	84.1	1.4	-	-	85.6	1.8	-	-
1981	88.2	3.0	-	-	90.2	2.3	-	-	90.7	0.6	-	-	91.6	1.0	-	-	93.9	2.5	-	-	94.3	0.4	-	-
1982	94.3	0.0	-	-	92.8	-1.6	-	-	93.8	1.1	-	-	96.1	2.5	-	-	97.3	1.2	-	-	98.1	0.8	-	-
1983	98.7	0.6	-	-	98.6	-0.1	-	-	99.1	0.5	-	-	99.7	0.6	-	-	100.2	0.5	-	-	101.4	1.2	-	-
1984	102.3	0.9	-	-	103.9	1.6	-	-	104.3	0.4	-	-	104.9	0.6	-	-	105.8	0.9	-	-	105.9	0.1	-	-
1985	106.5	0.6	-	-	108.2	1.6	-	-	108.4	0.2	-	-	109.3	0.8	-	-	110.5	1.1	-	-	112.0	1.4	-	-
1986	112.5	0.4	-	-	111.8	-0.6	-	-	111.0	-0.7	-	-	111.3	0.3	-	-	112.9	1.4	-	-	113.3	0.4	-	-
1987	114.6	1.1	-	-	115.9	1.1	-	-	115.3	-0.5	-	-	116.3	0.9	-	-	119.5	2.8	-	-	119.9	0.3	-	-
1988	120.1	0.2	-	-	122.1	1.7	-	-	123.1	0.8	-	-	123.8	0.6	-	-	126.2	1.9	-	-	127.4	1.0	-	-
1989	129.0	1.3	-	-	129.7	0.5	-	-	130.5	0.6	-	-	130.3	-0.2	-	-	132.2	1.5	-	-	134.3	1.6	-	-
1990	136.0	1.3	-	-	136.3	0.2	-	-	136.6	0.2	-	-	137.6	0.7	-	-	141.3	2.7	-	-	143.7	1.7	-	-
1991	143.8	0.1	-	-	143.9	0.1	-	-	143.5	-0.3	-	-	145.1	1.1	-	-	146.3	0.8	-	-	146.6	0.2	-	-
1992	146.3	-0.2	-	-	147.9	1.1	-	-	147.5	-0.3	-	-	148.9	0.9	-	-	149.4	0.3	-	-	150.4	0.7	-	-
1993	151.9	1.0	-	-	154.1	1.4	-	-	151.9	-1.4	-	-	152.5	0.4	-	-	152.0	-0.3	-	-	154.5	1.6	-	-

Source: U.S. Department of Labor, Bureau of Labor Statistics, Division of Consumer Prices and Price Indexes. - indicates no data collected for period.

Boston, MA
Consumer Price Index - Urban Wage Earners
Base 1982-1984 = 100
All Items

For 1914-1993. Columns headed % show percentile change in the index from the previous period for which an index is available.

Year	Jan Index	%	Feb Index	%	Mar Index	%	Apr Index	%	May Index	%	Jun Index	%	Jul Index	%	Aug Index	%	Sep Index	%	Oct Index	%	Nov Index	%	Dec Index	%
1914	-	-	-	-	-	-	-	-	-	-	-	-	-	-	-	-	-	-	-	-	-	-	10.6	-
1915	-	-	-	-	-	-	-	-	-	-	-	-	-	-	-	-	-	-	-	-	-	-	10.7	0.9
1916	-	-	-	-	-	-	-	-	-	-	-	-	-	-	-	-	-	-	-	-	-	-	12.1	13.1
1917	-	-	-	-	-	-	-	-	-	-	-	-	-	-	-	-	-	-	-	-	-	-	14.3	18.2
1918	-	-	-	-	-	-	-	-	-	-	-	-	-	-	-	-	-	-	-	-	-	-	17.4	21.7
1919	-	-	-	-	-	-	-	-	-	-	17.5	0.6	-	-	-	-	-	-	-	-	-	-	19.6	12.0
1920	-	-	-	-	-	-	-	-	-	-	21.6	10.2	-	-	-	-	-	-	-	-	-	-	20.3	-6.0
1921	-	-	-	-	-	-	-	-	18.1	-10.8	-	-	-	-	-	-	18.1	0.0	-	-	-	-	17.9	-1.1
1922	-	-	-	-	17.0	-5.0	-	-	-	-	16.8	-1.2	-	-	-	-	17.0	1.2	-	-	-	-	17.4	2.4
1923	-	-	-	-	17.2	-1.1	-	-	-	-	17.2	0.0	-	-	-	-	17.7	2.9	-	-	-	-	17.9	1.1
1924	-	-	-	-	17.4	-2.8	-	-	-	-	17.3	-0.6	-	-	-	-	17.6	1.7	-	-	-	-	17.7	0.6
1925	-	-	-	-	-	-	-	-	-	-	17.6	-0.6	-	-	-	-	-	-	-	-	-	-	18.6	5.7
1926	-	-	-	-	-	-	-	-	-	-	18.2	-2.2	-	-	-	-	-	-	-	-	-	-	18.3	0.5
1927	-	-	-	-	-	-	-	-	-	-	18.1	-1.1	-	-	-	-	-	-	-	-	-	-	18.1	0.0
1928	-	-	-	-	-	-	-	-	-	-	17.6	-2.8	-	-	-	-	-	-	-	-	-	-	17.9	1.7
1929	-	-	-	-	-	-	-	-	-	-	17.6	-1.7	-	-	-	-	-	-	-	-	-	-	17.9	1.7
1930	-	-	-	-	-	-	-	-	-	-	17.5	-2.2	-	-	-	-	-	-	-	-	-	-	17.0	-2.9
1931	-	-	-	-	-	-	-	-	-	-	15.8	-7.1	-	-	-	-	-	-	-	-	-	-	15.4	-2.5
1932	-	-	-	-	-	-	-	-	-	-	14.2	-7.8	-	-	-	-	-	-	-	-	-	-	13.9	-2.1
1933	-	-	-	-	-	-	-	-	-	-	13.5	-2.9	-	-	-	-	-	-	-	-	-	-	13.9	3.0
1934	-	-	-	-	-	-	-	-	-	-	14.2	2.2	-	-	-	-	-	-	-	-	14.3	0.7	-	-
1935	-	-	-	-	14.5	1.4	-	-	-	-	-	-	14.3	-1.4	-	-	-	-	14.4	0.7	-	-	-	-
1936	14.5	0.7	-	-	-	-	14.4	-0.7	-	-	-	-	14.6	1.4	-	-	14.5	-0.7	-	-	-	-	14.4	-0.7
1937	-	-	-	-	14.7	2.1	-	-	-	-	14.8	0.7	-	-	-	-	15.2	2.7	-	-	-	-	14.8	-2.6
1938	-	-	-	-	14.4	-2.7	-	-	-	-	14.4	0.0	-	-	-	-	14.4	0.0	-	-	-	-	14.3	-0.7
1939	-	-	-	-	14.2	-0.7	-	-	-	-	14.1	-0.7	-	-	-	-	14.4	2.1	-	-	-	-	14.2	-1.4
1940	-	-	-	-	14.4	1.4	-	-	-	-	14.5	0.7	-	-	-	-	14.4	-0.7	14.3	-0.7	14.3	0.0	14.4	0.7
1941	14.4	0.0	14.4	0.0	14.4	0.0	14.6	1.4	14.7	0.7	14.8	0.7	15.1	2.0	15.2	0.7	15.4	1.3	15.5	0.6	15.7	1.3	15.6	-0.6
1942	15.8	1.3	16.1	1.9	16.2	0.6	16.2	0.0	16.4	1.2	16.5	0.6	16.7	1.2	16.7	0.0	16.8	0.6	17.1	1.8	17.2	0.6	17.2	0.0
1943	17.2	0.0	17.2	0.0	17.5	1.7	17.6	0.6	17.6	0.0	17.6	0.0	17.7	0.6	17.8	0.6	17.9	0.6	17.7	-1.1	17.8	0.6	17.9	0.6
1944	17.5	0.0	17.4	-0.6	17.4	0.0	17.6	1.1	17.6	0.0	17.6	0.0	17.7	0.6	18.2	0.0	18.1	-0.5	18.0	-0.6	18.1	0.6	18.1	0.0
1945	17.9	0.0	17.9	0.0	17.8	-0.6	17.8	0.0	17.9	0.6	18.2	1.7	18.2	0.0	18.2	0.0	18.1	-0.5	18.0	-0.6	18.1	0.6	18.1	0.0
1946	18.2	0.6	18.1	-0.5	18.2	0.6	18.3	0.5	18.3	0.0	18.5	1.1	19.9	7.6	20.3	2.0	20.5	1.0	21.0	2.4	21.2	1.0	21.5	1.4
1947	21.6	0.5	21.4	-0.9	21.8	1.9	21.7	-0.5	21.6	-0.5	21.8	0.9	22.0	0.9	22.4	1.8	23.0	2.7	22.8	-0.9	23.0	0.9	23.3	1.3
1948	23.7	1.7	23.4	-1.3	23.4	0.0	23.7	1.3	23.8	0.4	24.1	1.3	24.5	1.7	24.5	0.0	24.6	0.4	24.4	-0.8	24.2	-0.8	23.9	-1.2
1949	23.8	-0.4	23.5	-1.3	23.6	0.4	23.6	0.0	23.6	0.0	23.7	0.4	23.7	0.0	23.8	0.4	24.0	0.8	23.8	-0.8	23.8	0.0	23.7	-0.4
1950	23.5	-0.8	23.5	0.0	23.6	0.4	23.6	0.0	23.7	0.4	24.0	1.3	24.2	0.8	24.4	0.8	24.4	0.0	24.6	0.8	24.6	0.0	24.8	0.8
1951	25.1	1.2	25.4	1.2	25.4	0.0	25.4	0.0	25.5	0.4	25.6	0.4	25.6	0.0	25.7	0.4	25.7	0.0	25.9	0.8	26.1	0.8	26.2	0.4
1952	26.1	-0.4	25.9	-0.8	25.9	0.0	25.9	0.0	26.1	0.8	26.1	0.0	26.5	1.5	26.5	0.0	26.4	-0.4	26.4	0.0	26.3	-0.4	26.2	-0.4
1953	26.1	-0.4	-	-	-	-	26.1	0.0	-	-	-	-	26.4	1.1	-	-	-	-	26.5	0.4	-	-	-	-
1954	26.3	-0.8	-	-	-	-	26.3	0.0	-	-	-	-	26.5	0.8	-	-	-	-	26.5	0.0	-	-	-	-
1955	26.3	-0.8	-	-	-	-	26.4	0.4	-	-	-	-	26.5	0.4	-	-	-	-	26.7	0.8	-	-	-	-
1956	26.7	0.0	-	-	-	-	26.8	0.4	-	-	-	-	27.5	2.6	-	-	-	-	27.8	1.1	-	-	-	-
1957	27.7	-0.4	-	-	-	-	28.0	1.1	-	-	-	-	28.4	1.4	-	-	-	-	28.4	0.0	-	-	-	-
1958	28.8	1.4	-	-	-	-	29.0	0.7	-	-	-	-	29.2	0.7	-	-	-	-	29.2	0.0	-	-	-	-

[Continued]

Boston, MA
Consumer Price Index - Urban Wage Earners
Base 1982-1984 = 100
All Items
[Continued]

For 1914-1993. Columns headed % show percentile change in the index from the previous period for which an index is available.

Year	Jan Index	%	Feb Index	%	Mar Index	%	Apr Index	%	May Index	%	Jun Index	%	Jul Index	%	Aug Index	%	Sep Index	%	Oct Index	%	Nov Index	%	Dec Index	%
1959	29.2	0.0	-	-	-	-	29.2	0.0	-	-	-	-	29.3	0.3	-	-	-	-	29.5	0.7	-	-	-	-
1960	29.4	-0.3	-	-	-	-	29.9	1.7	-	-	-	-	30.0	0.3	-	-	-	-	30.1	0.3	-	-	-	-
1961	30.1	0.0	-	-	-	-	30.3	0.7	-	-	-	-	30.4	0.3	-	-	-	-	30.4	0.0	-	-	-	-
1962	30.7	1.0	-	-	-	-	30.9	0.7	-	-	-	-	31.0	0.3	-	-	-	-	31.2	0.6	-	-	-	-
1963	31.4	0.6	-	-	-	-	31.6	0.6	-	-	-	-	31.7	0.3	-	-	-	-	31.8	0.3	-	-	-	-
1964	31.8	0.0	-	-	-	-	31.9	0.3	-	-	-	-	32.1	0.6	-	-	-	-	32.2	0.3	-	-	-	-
1965	32.4	0.6	-	-	-	-	32.6	0.6	-	-	-	-	32.8	0.6	-	-	-	-	32.8	0.0	-	-	-	-
1966	32.9	0.3	-	-	-	-	33.7	2.4	-	-	-	-	33.8	0.3	-	-	-	-	34.2	1.2	-	-	-	-
1967	34.3	0.3	-	-	-	-	34.3	0.0	-	-	-	-	34.6	0.9	-	-	-	-	34.9	0.9	-	-	-	-
1968	35.2	0.9	-	-	-	-	35.7	1.4	-	-	-	-	36.0	0.8	-	-	-	-	36.6	1.7	-	-	-	-
1969	37.0	1.1	-	-	-	-	37.5	1.4	-	-	-	-	38.2	1.9	-	-	-	-	38.9	1.8	-	-	-	-
1970	39.3	1.0	-	-	-	-	39.8	1.3	-	-	-	-	40.3	1.3	-	-	-	-	41.3	2.5	-	-	-	-
1971	41.8	1.2	-	-	-	-	42.1	0.7	-	-	-	-	42.5	1.0	-	-	-	-	43.0	1.2	-	-	-	-
1972	43.2	0.5	-	-	-	-	43.7	1.2	-	-	-	-	43.9	0.5	-	-	-	-	44.6	1.6	-	-	-	-
1973	44.9	0.7	-	-	-	-	45.8	2.0	-	-	-	-	46.4	1.3	-	-	-	-	48.0	3.4	-	-	-	-
1974	49.1	2.3	-	-	-	-	50.2	2.2	-	-	-	-	51.8	3.2	-	-	-	-	52.9	2.1	-	-	-	-
1975	54.1	2.3	-	-	-	-	55.0	1.7	-	-	-	-	56.4	2.5	-	-	-	-	57.0	1.1	-	-	-	-
1976	59.5	4.4	-	-	-	-	59.7	0.3	-	-	-	-	60.6	1.5	-	-	-	-	60.9	0.5	-	-	-	-
1977	61.9	1.6	-	-	-	-	62.8	1.5	-	-	-	-	63.8	1.6	-	-	-	-	64.2	0.6	-	-	-	-
1978	64.9	1.1	-	-	65.0	0.2	-	-	65.8	1.2	-	-	66.7	1.4	-	-	67.6	1.3	-	-	68.9	1.9	-	-
1979	69.4	0.7	-	-	70.7	1.9	-	-	72.2	2.1	-	-	73.9	2.4	-	-	75.4	2.0	-	-	77.0	2.1	-	-
1980	78.5	1.9	-	-	81.0	3.2	-	-	81.9	1.1	-	-	83.3	1.7	-	-	84.6	1.6	-	-	86.2	1.9	-	-
1981	88.5	2.7	-	-	90.6	2.4	-	-	91.2	0.7	-	-	92.2	1.1	-	-	94.7	2.7	-	-	94.9	0.2	-	-
1982	94.6	-0.3	-	-	93.3	-1.4	-	-	94.1	0.9	-	-	96.4	2.4	-	-	97.8	1.5	-	-	98.4	0.6	-	-
1983	98.4	0.0	-	-	98.6	0.2	-	-	98.9	0.3	-	-	99.9	1.0	-	-	100.1	0.2	-	-	101.4	1.3	-	-
1984	102.1	0.7	-	-	103.2	1.1	-	-	104.1	0.9	-	-	104.1	0.0	-	-	105.6	1.4	-	-	106.0	0.4	-	-
1985	106.5	0.5	-	-	108.0	1.4	-	-	108.4	0.4	-	-	109.2	0.7	-	-	110.5	1.2	-	-	111.8	1.2	-	-
1986	112.3	0.4	-	-	111.5	-0.7	-	-	110.5	-0.9	-	-	111.0	0.5	-	-	112.5	1.4	-	-	112.8	0.3	-	-
1987	114.5	1.5	-	-	115.8	1.1	-	-	115.2	-0.5	-	-	116.4	1.0	-	-	119.5	2.7	-	-	119.9	0.3	-	-
1988	120.2	0.3	-	-	121.8	1.3	-	-	123.1	1.1	-	-	123.7	0.5	-	-	126.1	1.9	-	-	127.4	1.0	-	-
1989	128.9	1.2	-	-	129.7	0.6	-	-	130.6	0.7	-	-	130.8	0.2	-	-	132.6	1.4	-	-	134.7	1.6	-	-
1990	136.0	1.0	-	-	136.5	0.4	-	-	136.8	0.2	-	-	137.4	0.4	-	-	140.9	2.5	-	-	143.5	1.8	-	-
1991	143.3	-0.1	-	-	143.3	0.0	-	-	143.4	0.1	-	-	144.7	0.9	-	-	145.8	0.8	-	-	146.2	0.3	-	-
1992	146.1	-0.1	-	-	147.2	0.8	-	-	146.8	-0.3	-	-	148.2	1.0	-	-	148.7	0.3	-	-	150.0	0.9	-	-
1993	151.1	0.7	-	-	154.0	1.9	-	-	151.4	-1.7	-	-	151.6	0.1	-	-	151.0	-0.4	-	-	153.4	1.6	-	-

Source: U.S. Department of Labor, Bureau of Labor Statistics, Division of Consumer Prices and Price Indexes. - indicates no data collected for period.

Boston, MA
Consumer Price Index - All Urban Consumers
Base 1982-1984 = 100
Food and Beverages

For 1976-1993. Columns headed % show percentile change in the index from the previous period for which an index is available.

Year	Jan Index	%	Feb Index	%	Mar Index	%	Apr Index	%	May Index	%	Jun Index	%	Jul Index	%	Aug Index	%	Sep Index	%	Oct Index	%	Nov Index	%	Dec Index	%
1976	66.9	-	-	-	-	-	66.6	-0.4	-	-	-	-	67.6	1.5	-	-	-	-	67.0	-0.9	-	-	-	-
1977	66.8	-0.3	-	-	-	-	69.0	3.3	-	-	-	-	70.8	2.6	-	-	-	-	70.6	-0.3	-	-	-	-
1978	71.5	1.3	-	-	72.7	1.7	-	-	74.6	2.6	-	-	76.5	2.5	-	-	77.1	0.8	-	-	77.4	0.4	-	-
1979	78.7	1.7	-	-	81.0	2.9	-	-	83.7	3.3	-	-	85.7	2.4	-	-	84.1	-1.9	-	-	84.1	0.0	-	-
1980	86.2	2.5	-	-	87.4	1.4	-	-	87.6	0.2	-	-	89.6	2.3	-	-	90.2	0.7	-	-	91.6	1.6	-	-
1981	94.4	3.1	-	-	94.6	0.2	-	-	94.2	-0.4	-	-	94.4	0.2	-	-	93.8	-0.6	-	-	94.1	0.3	-	-
1982	95.9	1.9	-	-	95.9	0.0	-	-	96.5	0.6	-	-	97.2	0.7	-	-	97.1	-0.1	-	-	96.8	-0.3	-	-
1983	97.4	0.6	-	-	99.1	1.7	-	-	98.6	-0.5	-	-	99.5	0.9	-	-	99.2	-0.3	-	-	100.0	0.8	-	-
1984	102.2	2.2	-	-	103.8	1.6	-	-	104.0	0.2	-	-	104.4	0.4	-	-	105.0	0.6	-	-	104.9	-0.1	-	-
1985	106.6	1.6	-	-	107.7	1.0	-	-	107.8	0.1	-	-	109.2	1.3	-	-	109.0	-0.2	-	-	110.1	1.0	-	-
1986	111.9	1.6	-	-	110.8	-1.0	-	-	112.2	1.3	-	-	114.1	1.7	-	-	116.2	1.8	-	-	115.4	-0.7	-	-
1987	119.3	3.4	-	-	118.4	-0.8	-	-	119.0	0.5	-	-	119.4	0.3	-	-	120.2	0.7	-	-	119.7	-0.4	-	-
1988	122.0	1.9	-	-	120.8	-1.0	-	-	123.5	2.2	-	-	124.8	1.1	-	-	127.3	2.0	-	-	126.4	-0.7	-	-
1989	128.1	1.3	-	-	130.2	1.6	-	-	131.5	1.0	-	-	133.5	1.5	-	-	133.8	0.2	-	-	133.9	0.1	-	-
1990	137.1	2.4	-	-	138.3	0.9	-	-	138.0	-0.2	-	-	138.3	0.2	-	-	139.4	0.8	-	-	139.5	0.1	-	-
1991	142.2	1.9	-	-	141.3	-0.6	-	-	143.2	1.3	-	-	143.0	-0.1	-	-	141.9	-0.8	-	-	142.9	0.7	-	-
1992	143.5	0.4	-	-	143.7	0.1	-	-	142.4	-0.9	-	-	143.1	0.5	-	-	143.3	0.1	-	-	143.5	0.1	-	-
1993	145.4	1.3	-	-	145.2	-0.1	-	-	146.3	0.8	-	-	146.7	0.3	-	-	146.6	-0.1	-	-	146.9	0.2	-	-

Source: U.S. Department of Labor, Bureau of Labor Statistics, Division of Consumer Prices and Price Indexes. - indicates no data collected for period.

Boston, MA
Consumer Price Index - Urban Wage Earners
Base 1982-1984 = 100
Food and Beverages

For 1976-1993. Columns headed % show percentile change in the index from the previous period for which an index is available.

Year	Jan Index	%	Feb Index	%	Mar Index	%	Apr Index	%	May Index	%	Jun Index	%	Jul Index	%	Aug Index	%	Sep Index	%	Oct Index	%	Nov Index	%	Dec Index	%
1976	67.5	-	-	-	-	-	67.2	-0.4	-	-	-	-	68.1	1.3	-	-	-	-	67.5	-0.9	-	-	-	-
1977	67.4	-0.1	-	-	-	-	69.7	3.4	-	-	-	-	71.4	2.4	-	-	-	-	71.2	-0.3	-	-	-	-
1978	72.1	1.3	-	-	73.3	1.7	-	-	74.9	2.2	-	-	77.6	3.6	-	-	77.5	-0.1	-	-	78.0	0.6	-	-
1979	78.6	0.8	-	-	81.3	3.4	-	-	83.5	2.7	-	-	85.8	2.8	-	-	84.0	-2.1	-	-	84.6	0.7	-	-
1980	86.1	1.8	-	-	87.7	1.9	-	-	88.6	1.0	-	-	90.1	1.7	-	-	90.9	0.9	-	-	92.2	1.4	-	-
1981	94.3	2.3	-	-	95.2	1.0	-	-	94.7	-0.5	-	-	94.7	0.0	-	-	94.4	-0.3	-	-	94.2	-0.2	-	-
1982	95.6	1.5	-	-	95.7	0.1	-	-	96.3	0.6	-	-	97.3	1.0	-	-	97.2	-0.1	-	-	96.7	-0.5	-	-
1983	97.2	0.5	-	-	99.0	1.9	-	-	98.6	-0.4	-	-	99.6	1.0	-	-	99.2	-0.4	-	-	99.9	0.7	-	-
1984	102.3	2.4	-	-	104.1	1.8	-	-	104.2	0.1	-	-	104.8	0.6	-	-	104.9	0.1	-	-	104.7	-0.2	-	-
1985	106.5	1.7	-	-	107.7	1.1	-	-	107.6	-0.1	-	-	109.1	1.4	-	-	108.7	-0.4	-	-	109.4	0.6	-	-
1986	111.3	1.7	-	-	110.3	-0.9	-	-	111.4	1.0	-	-	113.8	2.2	-	-	115.9	1.8	-	-	114.7	-1.0	-	-
1987	119.1	3.8	-	-	117.9	-1.0	-	-	118.2	0.3	-	-	118.8	0.5	-	-	119.6	0.7	-	-	119.0	-0.5	-	-
1988	121.3	1.9	-	-	120.1	-1.0	-	-	123.0	2.4	-	-	124.4	1.1	-	-	126.9	2.0	-	-	125.7	-0.9	-	-
1989	127.5	1.4	-	-	129.5	1.6	-	-	130.8	1.0	-	-	133.0	1.7	-	-	133.1	0.1	-	-	132.9	-0.2	-	-
1990	136.2	2.5	-	-	137.4	0.9	-	-	137.2	-0.1	-	-	137.7	0.4	-	-	138.9	0.9	-	-	138.8	-0.1	-	-
1991	141.3	1.8	-	-	140.4	-0.6	-	-	142.5	1.5	-	-	142.1	-0.3	-	-	141.2	-0.6	-	-	142.1	0.6	-	-
1992	142.6	0.4	-	-	142.8	0.1	-	-	141.6	-0.8	-	-	142.0	0.3	-	-	142.4	0.3	-	-	142.5	0.1	-	-
1993	144.6	1.5	-	-	144.4	-0.1	-	-	145.3	0.6	-	-	145.9	0.4	-	-	145.7	-0.1	-	-	145.9	0.1	-	-

Source: U.S. Department of Labor, Bureau of Labor Statistics, Division of Consumer Prices and Price Indexes. - indicates no data collected for period.

Boston, MA
Consumer Price Index - All Urban Consumers
Base 1982-1984 = 100
Housing

For 1976-1993. Columns headed % show percentile change in the index from the previous period for which an index is available.

Year	Jan Index	%	Feb Index	%	Mar Index	%	Apr Index	%	May Index	%	Jun Index	%	Jul Index	%	Aug Index	%	Sep Index	%	Oct Index	%	Nov Index	%	Dec Index	%
1976	55.2	-	-	-	-	-	55.6	0.7	-	-	-	-	56.4	1.4	-	-	-	-	56.7	0.5	-	-	-	-
1977	58.7	3.5	-	-	-	-	58.9	0.3	-	-	-	-	59.8	1.5	-	-	-	-	60.0	0.3	-	-	-	-
1978	61.2	2.0	-	-	61.9	1.1	-	-	62.1	0.3	-	-	62.9	1.3	-	-	63.6	1.1	-	-	65.4	2.8	-	-
1979	67.1	2.6	-	-	67.4	0.4	-	-	67.9	0.7	-	-	69.2	1.9	-	-	71.7	3.6	-	-	74.1	3.3	-	-
1980	75.6	2.0	-	-	78.4	3.7	-	-	79.3	1.1	-	-	81.0	2.1	-	-	82.0	1.2	-	-	83.4	1.7	-	-
1981	87.8	5.3	-	-	90.0	2.5	-	-	90.1	0.1	-	-	91.7	1.8	-	-	95.5	4.1	-	-	95.2	-0.3	-	-
1982	94.1	-1.2	-	-	89.6	-4.8	-	-	91.7	2.3	-	-	95.2	3.8	-	-	97.1	2.0	-	-	98.6	1.5	-	-
1983	100.1	1.5	-	-	98.8	-1.3	-	-	99.3	0.5	-	-	99.7	0.4	-	-	100.8	1.1	-	-	102.5	1.7	-	-
1984	103.1	0.6	-	-	104.0	0.9	-	-	104.3	0.3	-	-	105.5	1.2	-	-	106.1	0.6	-	-	106.4	0.3	-	-
1985	106.9	0.5	-	-	107.6	0.7	-	-	107.6	0.0	-	-	109.4	1.7	-	-	110.1	0.6	-	-	112.2	1.9	-	-
1986	111.8	-0.4	-	-	111.4	-0.4	-	-	110.1	-1.2	-	-	110.2	0.1	-	-	112.4	2.0	-	-	113.5	1.0	-	-
1987	114.2	0.6	-	-	115.3	1.0	-	-	114.7	-0.5	-	-	116.1	1.2	-	-	119.1	2.6	-	-	119.9	0.7	-	-
1988	119.8	-0.1	-	-	121.0	1.0	-	-	122.9	1.6	-	-	123.9	0.8	-	-	125.5	1.3	-	-	126.6	0.9	-	-
1989	130.0	2.7	-	-	130.5	0.4	-	-	129.2	-1.0	-	-	129.7	0.4	-	-	132.8	2.4	-	-	134.1	1.0	-	-
1990	136.0	1.4	-	-	135.4	-0.4	-	-	134.4	-0.7	-	-	136.4	1.5	-	-	137.4	0.7	-	-	140.9	2.5	-	-
1991	142.3	1.0	-	-	142.3	0.0	-	-	139.4	-2.0	-	-	140.6	0.9	-	-	140.7	0.1	-	-	140.7	0.0	-	-
1992	140.9	0.1	-	-	143.9	2.1	-	-	142.0	-1.3	-	-	144.1	1.5	-	-	143.7	-0.3	-	-	145.5	1.3	-	-
1993	146.7	0.8	-	-	147.1	0.3	-	-	144.8	-1.6	-	-	146.0	0.8	-	-	145.4	-0.4	-	-	148.1	1.9	-	-

Source: U.S. Department of Labor, Bureau of Labor Statistics, Division of Consumer Prices and Price Indexes. - indicates no data collected for period.

Boston, MA
Consumer Price Index - Urban Wage Earners
Base 1982-1984 = 100
Housing

For 1976-1993. Columns headed % show percentile change in the index from the previous period for which an index is available.

Year	Jan Index	%	Feb Index	%	Mar Index	%	Apr Index	%	May Index	%	Jun Index	%	Jul Index	%	Aug Index	%	Sep Index	%	Oct Index	%	Nov Index	%	Dec Index	%
1976	55.1	-	-	-	-	-	55.5	0.7	-	-	-	-	56.3	1.4	-	-	-	-	56.6	0.5	-	-	-	-
1977	58.6	3.5	-	-	-	-	58.8	0.3	-	-	-	-	59.7	1.5	-	-	-	-	59.9	0.3	-	-	-	-
1978	61.1	2.0	-	-	61.8	1.1	-	-	61.9	0.2	-	-	62.8	1.5	-	-	63.7	1.4	-	-	65.5	2.8	-	-
1979	67.1	2.4	-	-	67.4	0.4	-	-	68.1	1.0	-	-	69.5	2.1	-	-	71.9	3.5	-	-	74.4	3.5	-	-
1980	76.2	2.4	-	-	79.2	3.9	-	-	80.1	1.1	-	-	81.7	2.0	-	-	82.7	1.2	-	-	84.6	2.3	-	-
1981	88.9	5.1	-	-	91.0	2.4	-	-	91.3	0.3	-	-	93.5	2.4	-	-	97.1	3.9	-	-	96.2	-0.9	-	-
1982	95.1	-1.1	-	-	90.2	-5.2	-	-	92.5	2.5	-	-	96.1	3.9	-	-	98.0	2.0	-	-	99.6	1.6	-	-
1983	99.8	0.2	-	-	98.7	-1.1	-	-	98.8	0.1	-	-	100.3	1.5	-	-	100.5	0.2	-	-	102.6	2.1	-	-
1984	102.6	0.0	-	-	102.3	-0.3	-	-	103.8	1.5	-	-	103.3	-0.5	-	-	105.9	2.5	-	-	106.9	0.9	-	-
1985	107.4	0.5	-	-	108.0	0.6	-	-	108.1	0.1	-	-	109.9	1.7	-	-	110.5	0.5	-	-	112.6	1.9	-	-
1986	112.4	-0.2	-	-	111.8	-0.5	-	-	110.3	-1.3	-	-	110.4	0.1	-	-	112.5	1.9	-	-	113.6	1.0	-	-
1987	114.0	0.4	-	-	115.4	1.2	-	-	114.8	-0.5	-	-	116.1	1.1	-	-	119.1	2.6	-	-	120.1	0.8	-	-
1988	119.7	-0.3	-	-	120.8	0.9	-	-	122.8	1.7	-	-	123.6	0.7	-	-	125.2	1.3	-	-	126.6	1.1	-	-
1989	129.6	2.4	-	-	130.1	0.4	-	-	128.7	-1.1	-	-	129.5	0.6	-	-	132.5	2.3	-	-	134.1	1.2	-	-
1990	135.3	0.9	-	-	134.8	-0.4	-	-	133.6	-0.9	-	-	135.2	1.2	-	-	136.1	0.7	-	-	140.0	2.9	-	-
1991	140.6	0.4	-	-	140.5	-0.1	-	-	138.1	-1.7	-	-	139.1	0.7	-	-	139.5	0.3	-	-	139.9	0.3	-	-
1992	139.6	-0.2	-	-	142.2	1.9	-	-	140.4	-1.3	-	-	142.5	1.5	-	-	142.1	-0.3	-	-	144.5	1.7	-	-
1993	145.4	0.6	-	-	145.5	0.1	-	-	143.5	-1.4	-	-	144.2	0.5	-	-	143.9	-0.2	-	-	147.2	2.3	-	-

Source: U.S. Department of Labor, Bureau of Labor Statistics, Division of Consumer Prices and Price Indexes. - indicates no data collected for period.

Boston, MA
Consumer Price Index - All Urban Consumers
Base 1982-1984 = 100
Apparel and Upkeep

For 1952-1993. Columns headed % show percentile change in the index from the previous period for which an index is available.

Year	Jan Index	%	Feb Index	%	Mar Index	%	Apr Index	%	May Index	%	Jun Index	%	Jul Index	%	Aug Index	%	Sep Index	%	Oct Index	%	Nov Index	%	Dec Index	%
1952	-		-		-		-		-		-		-		-		-		39.6	-	-		-	
1953	39.2	-1.0	-		-		39.5	0.8	-		-		39.5	0.0	-		-		39.6	0.3	-		-	
1954	38.6	-2.5	-		-		38.8	0.5	-		-		39.1	0.8	-		-		39.9	2.0	-		-	
1955	39.0	-2.3	-		-		39.3	0.8	-		-		39.1	-0.5	-		-		39.5	1.0	-		-	
1956	39.0	-1.3	-		-		39.6	1.5	-		-		39.7	0.3	-		-		40.6	2.3	-		-	
1957	39.7	-2.2	-		-		40.5	2.0	-		-		40.3	-0.5	-		-		41.1	2.0	-		-	
1958	40.8	-0.7	-		-		40.9	0.2	-		-		41.2	0.7	-		-		41.8	1.5	-		-	
1959	40.3	-3.6	-		-		40.3	0.0	-		-		40.7	1.0	-		-		41.7	2.5	-		-	
1960	41.3	-1.0	-		-		41.9	1.5	-		-		42.3	1.0	-		-		42.6	0.7	-		-	
1961	42.1	-1.2	-		-		42.0	-0.2	-		-		42.3	0.7	-		-		43.0	1.7	-		-	
1962	41.9	-2.6	-		-		43.0	2.6	-		-		43.1	0.2	-		-		43.7	1.4	-		-	
1963	43.0	-1.6	-		-		43.3	0.7	-		-		43.0	-0.7	-		-		44.1	2.6	-		-	
1964	43.0	-2.5	-		-		43.8	1.9	-		-		43.5	-0.7	-		-		44.1	1.4	-		-	
1965	43.2	-2.0	-		-		43.7	1.2	-		-		44.0	0.7	-		-		44.5	1.1	-		-	
1966	44.4	-0.2	-		-		44.9	1.1	-		-		44.6	-0.7	-		-		45.9	2.9	-		-	
1967	45.3	-1.3	-		-		46.3	2.2	-		-		46.3	0.0	-		-		47.5	2.6	-		-	
1968	46.9	-1.3	-		-		49.3	5.1	-		-		48.8	-1.0	-		-		51.0	4.5	-		-	
1969	50.4	-1.2	-		-		51.4	2.0	-		-		51.4	0.0	-		-		54.4	5.8	-		-	
1970	52.6	-3.3	-		-		54.9	4.4	-		-		53.7	-2.2	-		-		56.5	5.2	-		-	
1971	55.4	-1.9	-		-		56.6	2.2	-		-		56.2	-0.7	-		-		57.9	3.0	-		-	
1972	56.7	-2.1	-		-		57.2	0.9	-		-		57.3	0.2	-		-		59.5	3.8	-		-	
1973	58.1	-2.4	-		-		59.6	2.6	-		-		59.2	-0.7	-		-		61.3	3.5	-		-	
1974	60.7	-1.0	-		-		63.4	4.4	-		-		63.8	0.6	-		-		66.6	4.4	-		-	
1975	66.0	-0.9	-		-		67.5	2.3	-		-		67.6	0.1	-		-		70.4	4.1	-		-	
1976	70.6	0.3	-		-		71.2	0.8	-		-		71.1	-0.1	-		-		72.7	2.3	-		-	
1977	71.4	-1.8	-		-		72.5	1.5	-		-		72.0	-0.7	-		-		75.6	5.0	-		-	
1978	74.8	-1.1	-		76.9	2.8	-		79.4	3.3	-		76.2	-4.0	-		81.2	6.6	-		83.0	2.2	-	
1979	78.7	-5.2	-		84.6	7.5	-		84.6	0.0	-		83.7	-1.1	-		88.0	5.1	-		88.1	0.1	-	
1980	85.7	-2.7	-		88.4	3.2	-		88.8	0.5	-		87.2	-1.8	-		92.5	6.1	-		93.2	0.8	-	
1981	90.6	-2.8	-		95.3	5.2	-		93.4	-2.0	-		92.3	-1.2	-		95.6	3.6	-		95.6	0.0	-	
1982	92.5	-3.2	-		97.0	4.9	-		95.8	-1.2	-		95.9	0.1	-		101.0	5.3	-		100.6	-0.4	-	
1983	99.3	-1.3	-		101.3	2.0	-		100.8	-0.5	-		99.8	-1.0	-		98.4	-1.4	-		99.8	1.4	-	
1984	98.7	-1.1	-		103.3	4.7	-		102.9	-0.4	-		101.0	-1.8	-		106.2	5.1	-		103.8	-2.3	-	
1985	100.7	-3.0	-		106.8	6.1	-		107.1	0.3	-		101.7	-5.0	-		110.4	8.6	-		108.8	-1.4	-	
1986	106.2	-2.4	-		108.4	2.1	-		107.8	-0.6	-		106.6	-1.1	-		111.2	4.3	-		108.5	-2.4	-	
1987	107.4	-1.0	-		122.6	14.2	-		112.4	-8.3	-		110.3	-1.9	-		123.4	11.9	-		117.8	-4.5	-	
1988	112.6	-4.4	-		134.7	19.6	-		128.4	-4.7	-		118.9	-7.4	-		126.7	6.6	-		130.8	3.2	-	
1989	124.6	-4.7	-		121.4	-2.6	-		126.3	4.0	-		117.6	-6.9	-		121.5	3.3	-		137.5	13.2	-	
1990	132.0	-4.0	-		129.7	-1.7	-		135.2	4.2	-		124.7	-7.8	-		154.6	24.0	-		152.5	-1.4	-	
1991	135.6	-11.1	-		139.3	2.7	-		140.8	1.1	-		138.1	-1.9	-		157.9	14.3	-		154.1	-2.4	-	
1992	144.5	-6.2	-		142.5	-1.4	-		142.7	0.1	-		141.4	-0.9	-		152.7	8.0	-		145.8	-4.5	-	
1993	148.6	1.9	-		182.1	22.5	-		155.8	-14.4	-		150.1	-3.7	-		151.4	0.9	-		158.0	4.4	-	

Source: U.S. Department of Labor, Bureau of Labor Statistics, Division of Consumer Prices and Price Indexes. - indicates no data collected for period.

Boston, MA
Consumer Price Index - Urban Wage Earners
Base 1982-1984 = 100
Apparel and Upkeep

For 1952-1993. Columns headed % show percentile change in the index from the previous period for which an index is available.

Year	Jan Index	%	Feb Index	%	Mar Index	%	Apr Index	%	May Index	%	Jun Index	%	Jul Index	%	Aug Index	%	Sep Index	%	Oct Index	%	Nov Index	%	Dec Index	%
1952	-	-	-	-	-	-	-	-	-	-	-	-	-	-	-	-	-	-	39.9	-	-	-	-	-
1953	39.4	-1.3	-	-	-	-	39.8	1.0	-	-	-	-	39.8	0.0	-	-	-	-	39.9	0.3	-	-	-	-
1954	38.9	-2.5	-	-	-	-	39.1	0.5	-	-	-	-	39.4	0.8	-	-	-	-	40.1	1.8	-	-	-	-
1955	39.3	-2.0	-	-	-	-	39.6	0.8	-	-	-	-	39.4	-0.5	-	-	-	-	39.8	1.0	-	-	-	-
1956	39.3	-1.3	-	-	-	-	39.9	1.5	-	-	-	-	40.0	0.3	-	-	-	-	40.9	2.3	-	-	-	-
1957	40.0	-2.2	-	-	-	-	40.8	2.0	-	-	-	-	40.6	-0.5	-	-	-	-	41.4	2.0	-	-	-	-
1958	41.1	-0.7	-	-	-	-	41.2	0.2	-	-	-	-	41.5	0.7	-	-	-	-	42.1	1.4	-	-	-	-
1959	40.6	-3.6	-	-	-	-	40.6	0.0	-	-	-	-	41.0	1.0	-	-	-	-	42.0	2.4	-	-	-	-
1960	41.6	-1.0	-	-	-	-	42.2	1.4	-	-	-	-	42.6	0.9	-	-	-	-	42.9	0.7	-	-	-	-
1961	42.4	-1.2	-	-	-	-	42.4	0.0	-	-	-	-	42.6	0.5	-	-	-	-	43.3	1.6	-	-	-	-
1962	42.3	-2.3	-	-	-	-	43.3	2.4	-	-	-	-	43.4	0.2	-	-	-	-	44.0	1.4	-	-	-	-
1963	43.3	-1.6	-	-	-	-	43.6	0.7	-	-	-	-	43.3	-0.7	-	-	-	-	44.4	2.5	-	-	-	-
1964	43.3	-2.5	-	-	-	-	44.1	1.8	-	-	-	-	43.8	-0.7	-	-	-	-	44.4	1.4	-	-	-	-
1965	43.6	-1.8	-	-	-	-	44.0	0.9	-	-	-	-	44.3	0.7	-	-	-	-	44.8	1.1	-	-	-	-
1966	44.7	-0.2	-	-	-	-	45.3	1.3	-	-	-	-	44.9	-0.9	-	-	-	-	46.2	2.9	-	-	-	-
1967	45.7	-1.1	-	-	-	-	46.7	2.2	-	-	-	-	46.7	0.0	-	-	-	-	47.9	2.6	-	-	-	-
1968	47.2	-1.5	-	-	-	-	49.7	5.3	-	-	-	-	49.1	-1.2	-	-	-	-	51.3	4.5	-	-	-	-
1969	50.7	-1.2	-	-	-	-	51.8	2.2	-	-	-	-	51.8	0.0	-	-	-	-	54.8	5.8	-	-	-	-
1970	53.0	-3.3	-	-	-	-	55.3	4.3	-	-	-	-	54.1	-2.2	-	-	-	-	57.0	5.4	-	-	-	-
1971	55.8	-2.1	-	-	-	-	57.0	2.2	-	-	-	-	56.6	-0.7	-	-	-	-	58.4	3.2	-	-	-	-
1972	57.2	-2.1	-	-	-	-	57.7	0.9	-	-	-	-	57.7	0.0	-	-	-	-	59.9	3.8	-	-	-	-
1973	58.5	-2.3	-	-	-	-	60.0	2.6	-	-	-	-	59.6	-0.7	-	-	-	-	61.8	3.7	-	-	-	-
1974	61.1	-1.1	-	-	-	-	63.9	4.6	-	-	-	-	64.3	0.6	-	-	-	-	67.1	4.4	-	-	-	-
1975	66.5	-0.9	-	-	-	-	68.0	2.3	-	-	-	-	68.1	0.1	-	-	-	-	70.9	4.1	-	-	-	-
1976	71.2	0.4	-	-	-	-	71.7	0.7	-	-	-	-	71.6	-0.1	-	-	-	-	73.3	2.4	-	-	-	-
1977	72.0	-1.8	-	-	-	-	73.0	1.4	-	-	-	-	72.5	-0.7	-	-	-	-	76.1	5.0	-	-	-	-
1978	75.4	-0.9	-	-	76.3	1.2	-	-	79.2	3.8	-	-	75.9	-4.2	-	-	81.4	7.2	-	-	80.9	-0.6	-	-
1979	77.2	-4.6	-	-	80.8	4.7	-	-	82.0	1.5	-	-	79.7	-2.8	-	-	87.7	10.0	-	-	86.8	-1.0	-	-
1980	83.0	-4.4	-	-	85.5	3.0	-	-	85.2	-0.4	-	-	84.4	-0.9	-	-	90.3	7.0	-	-	91.4	1.2	-	-
1981	87.6	-4.2	-	-	93.9	7.2	-	-	93.1	-0.9	-	-	89.6	-3.8	-	-	95.9	7.0	-	-	96.3	0.4	-	-
1982	92.2	-4.3	-	-	99.4	7.8	-	-	95.8	-3.6	-	-	95.9	0.1	-	-	102.3	6.7	-	-	101.0	-1.3	-	-
1983	98.5	-2.5	-	-	103.9	5.5	-	-	102.2	-1.6	-	-	99.2	-2.9	-	-	98.4	-0.8	-	-	99.0	0.6	-	-
1984	97.7	-1.3	-	-	101.9	4.3	-	-	101.6	-0.3	-	-	100.3	-1.3	-	-	105.8	5.5	-	-	103.4	-2.3	-	-
1985	99.6	-3.7	-	-	105.4	5.8	-	-	104.8	-0.6	-	-	100.0	-4.6	-	-	110.0	10.0	-	-	107.9	-1.9	-	-
1986	104.4	-3.2	-	-	107.8	3.3	-	-	106.2	-1.5	-	-	105.2	-0.9	-	-	110.1	4.7	-	-	107.2	-2.6	-	-
1987	112.2	4.7	-	-	127.6	13.7	-	-	115.9	-9.2	-	-	115.7	-0.2	-	-	130.1	12.4	-	-	124.3	-4.5	-	-
1988	120.9	-2.7	-	-	139.3	15.2	-	-	134.6	-3.4	-	-	125.9	-6.5	-	-	134.1	6.5	-	-	138.4	3.2	-	-
1989	130.5	-5.7	-	-	128.6	-1.5	-	-	134.9	4.9	-	-	126.8	-6.0	-	-	132.6	4.6	-	-	148.3	11.8	-	-
1990	141.4	-4.7	-	-	139.5	-1.3	-	-	147.3	5.6	-	-	134.5	-8.7	-	-	158.8	18.1	-	-	159.7	0.6	-	-
1991	143.7	-10.0	-	-	151.4	5.4	-	-	151.5	0.1	-	-	149.4	-1.4	-	-	162.6	8.8	-	-	157.7	-3.0	-	-
1992	154.2	-2.2	-	-	149.8	-2.9	-	-	150.1	0.2	-	-	149.1	-0.7	-	-	161.3	8.2	-	-	155.1	-3.8	-	-
1993	153.9	-0.8	-	-	202.4	31.5	-	-	164.3	-18.8	-	-	155.2	-5.5	-	-	157.8	1.7	-	-	163.1	3.4	-	-

Source: U.S. Department of Labor, Bureau of Labor Statistics, Division of Consumer Prices and Price Indexes. - indicates no data collected for period.

Boston, MA
Consumer Price Index - All Urban Consumers
Base 1982-1984 = 100
Transportation

For 1947-1993. Columns headed % show percentile change in the index from the previous period for which an index is available.

Year	Jan Index	%	Feb Index	%	Mar Index	%	Apr Index	%	May Index	%	Jun Index	%	Jul Index	%	Aug Index	%	Sep Index	%	Oct Index	%	Nov Index	%	Dec Index	%
1947	16.2	-	16.2	0.0	16.3	0.6	16.3	0.0	16.3	0.0	16.4	0.6	16.4	0.0	16.5	0.6	16.6	0.6	16.6	0.0	16.6	0.0	16.6	0.0
1948	16.7	0.6	16.8	0.6	16.8	0.0	16.8	0.0	16.8	0.0	16.8	0.0	16.9	0.6	17.1	1.2	17.1	0.0	17.1	0.0	17.1	0.0	17.1	0.0
1949	17.1	0.0	17.2	0.6	17.2	0.0	17.3	0.6	17.3	0.0	17.3	0.0	17.3	0.0	20.4	17.9	20.4	0.0	20.4	0.0	20.4	0.0	20.5	0.5
1950	20.5	0.0	20.4	-0.5	20.4	0.0	20.4	0.0	20.5	0.5	20.5	0.0	20.6	0.5	20.6	0.0	20.7	0.5	20.7	0.0	20.7	0.0	20.8	0.5
1951	20.8	0.0	20.8	0.0	20.8	0.0	20.8	0.0	20.8	0.0	20.8	0.0	20.8	0.0	21.6	3.8	21.6	0.0	21.8	0.9	21.9	0.5	21.9	0.0
1952	22.0	0.5	22.3	1.4	22.3	0.0	22.3	0.0	22.3	0.0	22.3	0.0	23.0	3.1	23.0	0.0	23.1	0.4	23.1	0.0	23.1	0.0	23.1	0.0
1953	23.2	0.4	-		-		23.5	1.3	-		-		23.7	0.9	-		-		23.7	0.0	-		-	
1954	23.4	-1.3	-		-		24.4	4.3	-		-		23.7	-2.9	-		-		23.0	-3.0	-		-	
1955	23.2	0.9	-		-		23.2	0.0	-		-		22.9	-1.3	-		-		23.5	2.6	-		-	
1956	23.5	0.0	-		-		23.6	0.4	-		-		23.5	-0.4	-		-		25.1	6.8	-		-	
1957	24.7	-1.6	-		-		24.9	0.8	-		-		25.0	0.4	-		-		25.2	0.8	-		-	
1958	25.4	0.8	-		-		25.9	2.0	-		-		25.8	-0.4	-		-		25.7	-0.4	-		-	
1959	26.5	3.1	-		-		26.4	-0.4	-		-		26.4	0.0	-		-		26.4	0.0	-		-	
1960	25.7	-2.7	-		-		25.7	0.0	-		-		25.9	0.8	-		-		25.9	0.0	-		-	
1961	25.6	-1.2	-		-		26.0	1.6	-		-		26.4	1.5	-		-		26.2	-0.8	-		-	
1962	28.1	7.3	-		-		28.3	0.7	-		-		28.0	-1.1	-		-		28.3	1.1	-		-	
1963	28.0	-1.1	-		-		28.3	1.1	-		-		28.5	0.7	-		-		28.3	-0.7	-		-	
1964	28.4	0.4	-		-		28.3	-0.4	-		-		28.6	1.1	-		-		28.3	-1.0	-		-	
1965	28.9	2.1	-		-		29.0	0.3	-		-		29.2	0.7	-		-		29.5	1.0	-		-	
1966	29.3	-0.7	-		-		29.9	2.0	-		-		30.1	0.7	-		-		30.1	0.0	-		-	
1967	30.1	0.0	-		-		30.4	1.0	-		-		30.7	1.0	-		-		30.9	0.7	-		-	
1968	31.2	1.0	-		-		31.5	1.0	-		-		31.5	0.0	-		-		31.7	0.6	-		-	
1969	32.9	3.8	-		-		33.6	2.1	-		-		33.6	0.0	-		-		33.6	0.0	-		-	
1970	33.7	0.3	-		-		34.0	0.9	-		-		34.5	1.5	-		-		36.3	5.2	-		-	
1971	36.6	0.8	-		-		36.2	-1.1	-		-		36.9	1.9	-		-		36.7	-0.5	-		-	
1972	36.5	-0.5	-		-		36.3	-0.5	-		-		36.5	0.6	-		-		37.0	1.4	-		-	
1973	37.0	0.0	-		-		37.1	0.3	-		-		37.8	1.9	-		-		37.8	0.0	-		-	
1974	38.6	2.1	-		-		39.8	3.1	-		-		42.0	5.5	-		-		42.3	0.7	-		-	
1975	42.8	1.2	-		-		45.1	5.4	-		-		47.0	4.2	-		-		47.6	1.3	-		-	
1976	57.8	21.4	-		-		58.1	0.5	-		-		59.8	2.9	-		-		60.2	0.7	-		-	
1977	62.2	3.3	-		-		63.3	1.8	-		-		63.9	0.9	-		-		63.6	-0.5	-		-	
1978	63.7	0.2	-		61.2	-3.9	-		62.2	1.6	-		63.3	1.8	-		63.6	0.5	-		64.2	0.9	-	
1979	63.6	-0.9	-		64.8	1.9	-		68.0	4.9	-		70.9	4.3	-		72.1	1.7	-		74.0	2.6	-	
1980	76.6	3.5	-		80.5	5.1	-		81.8	1.6	-		83.5	2.1	-		84.7	1.4	-		86.3	1.9	-	
1981	87.6	1.5	-		91.3	4.2	-		94.0	3.0	-		94.5	0.5	-		96.6	2.2	-		98.0	1.4	-	
1982	97.6	-0.4	-		97.0	-0.6	-		96.1	-0.9	-		99.3	3.3	-		99.8	0.5	-		99.7	-0.1	-	
1983	98.7	-1.0	-		97.2	-1.5	-		98.5	1.3	-		99.6	1.1	-		100.1	0.5	-		100.5	0.4	-	
1984	100.7	0.2	-		101.8	1.1	-		102.9	1.1	-		103.0	0.1	-		103.0	0.0	-		103.1	0.1	-	
1985	102.9	-0.2	-		104.3	1.4	-		105.4	1.1	-		105.7	0.3	-		105.7	0.0	-		106.8	1.0	-	
1986	106.9	0.1	-		103.8	-2.9	-		100.5	-3.2	-		100.5	0.0	-		99.4	-1.1	-		100.1	0.7	-	
1987	101.4	1.3	-		100.6	-0.8	-		101.8	1.2	-		103.4	1.6	-		104.9	1.5	-		106.8	1.8	-	
1988	106.1	-0.7	-		105.5	-0.6	-		106.2	0.7	-		107.9	1.6	-		109.6	1.6	-		112.8	2.9	-	
1989	112.5	-0.3	-		113.5	0.9	-		115.8	2.0	-		112.6	-2.8	-		112.6	0.0	-		114.6	1.8	-	
1990	115.7	1.0	-		116.1	0.3	-		117.1	0.9	-		117.3	0.2	-		122.3	4.3	-		127.4	4.2	-	
1991	125.3	-1.6	-		123.0	-1.8	-		124.3	1.1	-		125.7	1.1	-		126.2	0.4	-		127.8	1.3	-	

[Continued]

Boston, MA
Consumer Price Index - All Urban Consumers
Base 1982-1984 = 100
Transportation
[Continued]

For 1947-1993. Columns headed % show percentile change in the index from the previous period for which an index is available.

Year	Jan		Feb		Mar		Apr		May		Jun		Jul		Aug		Sep		Oct		Nov		Dec	
	Index	%	Index	%	Index	%	Index	%	Index	%	Index	%	Index	%	Index	%	Index	%	Index	%	Index	%	Index	%
1992	127.2	-0.5	-	-	128.6	1.1	-	-	129.1	0.4	-	-	129.9	0.6	-	-	128.9	-0.8	-	-	129.8	0.7	-	-
1993	131.9	1.6	-	-	132.4	0.4	-	-	132.1	-0.2	-	-	132.2	0.1	-	-	131.4	-0.6	-	-	134.4	2.3	-	-

Source: U.S. Department of Labor, Bureau of Labor Statistics, Division of Consumer Prices and Price Indexes. - indicates no data collected for period.

Boston, MA
Consumer Price Index - Urban Wage Earners
Base 1982-1984 = 100
Transportation

For 1947-1993. Columns headed % show percentile change in the index from the previous period for which an index is available.

Year	Jan Index	%	Feb Index	%	Mar Index	%	Apr Index	%	May Index	%	Jun Index	%	Jul Index	%	Aug Index	%	Sep Index	%	Oct Index	%	Nov Index	%	Dec Index	%
1947	16.2	-	16.2	0.0	16.2	0.0	16.3	0.6	16.3	0.0	16.3	0.0	16.4	0.6	16.4	0.0	16.5	0.6	16.5	0.0	16.5	0.0	16.6	0.6
1948	16.7	0.6	16.7	0.0	16.8	0.6	16.7	-0.6	16.8	0.6	16.8	0.0	16.9	0.6	17.0	0.6	17.1	0.6	17.1	0.0	17.1	0.0	17.1	0.0
1949	17.1	0.0	17.2	0.6	17.2	0.0	17.2	0.0	17.2	0.0	17.2	0.0	17.2	0.0	20.4	18.6	20.4	0.0	20.4	0.0	20.4	0.0	20.4	0.0
1950	20.4	0.0	20.4	0.0	20.4	0.0	20.4	0.0	20.4	0.0	20.5	0.5	20.5	0.0	20.6	0.5	20.6	0.0	20.6	0.0	20.6	0.0	20.7	0.5
1951	20.7	0.0	20.7	0.0	20.8	0.5	20.8	0.0	20.8	0.0	20.8	0.0	20.7	-0.5	21.5	3.9	21.5	0.0	21.8	1.4	21.9	0.5	21.9	0.0
1952	21.9	0.0	22.2	1.4	22.3	0.5	22.3	0.0	22.3	0.0	22.2	-0.4	23.0	3.6	23.0	0.0	23.0	0.0	23.0	0.0	23.0	0.0	23.0	0.0
1953	23.1	0.4	-	-	-	-	23.4	1.3	-	-	-	-	23.6	0.9	-	-	-	-	23.6	0.0	-	-	-	-
1954	23.4	-0.8	-	-	-	-	24.3	3.8	-	-	-	-	23.7	-2.5	-	-	-	-	22.9	-3.4	-	-	-	-
1955	23.1	0.9	-	-	-	-	23.1	0.0	-	-	-	-	22.9	-0.9	-	-	-	-	23.4	2.2	-	-	-	-
1956	23.4	0.0	-	-	-	-	23.5	0.4	-	-	-	-	23.4	-0.4	-	-	-	-	25.1	7.3	-	-	-	-
1957	24.7	-1.6	-	-	-	-	24.8	0.4	-	-	-	-	24.9	0.4	-	-	-	-	25.2	1.2	-	-	-	-
1958	25.4	0.8	-	-	-	-	25.8	1.6	-	-	-	-	25.7	-0.4	-	-	-	-	25.6	-0.4	-	-	-	-
1959	26.4	3.1	-	-	-	-	26.4	0.0	-	-	-	-	26.4	0.0	-	-	-	-	26.3	-0.4	-	-	-	-
1960	25.6	-2.7	-	-	-	-	25.7	0.4	-	-	-	-	25.8	0.4	-	-	-	-	25.8	0.0	-	-	-	-
1961	25.5	-1.2	-	-	-	-	25.9	1.6	-	-	-	-	26.3	1.5	-	-	-	-	26.1	-0.8	-	-	-	-
1962	28.0	7.3	-	-	-	-	28.3	1.1	-	-	-	-	27.9	-1.4	-	-	-	-	28.2	1.1	-	-	-	-
1963	27.9	-1.1	-	-	-	-	28.2	1.1	-	-	-	-	28.4	0.7	-	-	-	-	28.2	-0.7	-	-	-	-
1964	28.3	0.4	-	-	-	-	28.2	-0.4	-	-	-	-	28.6	1.4	-	-	-	-	28.2	-1.4	-	-	-	-
1965	28.9	2.5	-	-	-	-	28.9	0.0	-	-	-	-	29.1	0.7	-	-	-	-	29.4	1.0	-	-	-	-
1966	29.2	-0.7	-	-	-	-	29.9	2.4	-	-	-	-	30.0	0.3	-	-	-	-	30.0	0.0	-	-	-	-
1967	30.1	0.3	-	-	-	-	30.3	0.7	-	-	-	-	30.7	1.3	-	-	-	-	30.9	0.7	-	-	-	-
1968	31.2	1.0	-	-	-	-	31.4	0.6	-	-	-	-	31.4	0.0	-	-	-	-	31.6	0.6	-	-	-	-
1969	32.8	3.8	-	-	-	-	33.6	2.4	-	-	-	-	33.5	-0.3	-	-	-	-	33.5	0.0	-	-	-	-
1970	33.6	0.3	-	-	-	-	33.9	0.9	-	-	-	-	34.5	1.8	-	-	-	-	36.2	4.9	-	-	-	-
1971	36.6	1.1	-	-	-	-	36.1	-1.4	-	-	-	-	36.8	1.9	-	-	-	-	36.6	-0.5	-	-	-	-
1972	36.4	-0.5	-	-	-	-	36.2	-0.5	-	-	-	-	36.4	0.6	-	-	-	-	36.9	1.4	-	-	-	-
1973	36.9	0.0	-	-	-	-	37.1	0.5	-	-	-	-	37.7	1.6	-	-	-	-	37.8	0.3	-	-	-	-
1974	38.5	1.9	-	-	-	-	39.7	3.1	-	-	-	-	41.9	5.5	-	-	-	-	42.2	0.7	-	-	-	-
1975	42.7	1.2	-	-	-	-	45.0	5.4	-	-	-	-	46.9	4.2	-	-	-	-	47.5	1.3	-	-	-	-
1976	57.6	21.3	-	-	-	-	57.9	0.5	-	-	-	-	59.7	3.1	-	-	-	-	60.1	0.7	-	-	-	-
1977	62.1	3.3	-	-	-	-	63.2	1.8	-	-	-	-	63.7	0.8	-	-	-	-	63.4	-0.5	-	-	-	-
1978	63.6	0.3	-	-	60.9	-4.2	-	-	62.1	2.0	-	-	63.0	1.4	-	-	63.4	0.6	-	-	64.3	1.4	-	-
1979	63.8	-0.8	-	-	65.2	2.2	-	-	68.4	4.9	-	-	71.6	4.7	-	-	72.9	1.8	-	-	74.6	2.3	-	-
1980	77.3	3.6	-	-	81.1	4.9	-	-	82.3	1.5	-	-	84.6	2.8	-	-	85.4	0.9	-	-	86.7	1.5	-	-
1981	88.0	1.5	-	-	90.8	3.2	-	-	93.0	2.4	-	-	94.3	1.4	-	-	96.9	2.8	-	-	98.4	1.5	-	-
1982	97.9	-0.5	-	-	97.3	-0.6	-	-	96.2	-1.1	-	-	99.3	3.2	-	-	99.8	0.5	-	-	99.6	-0.2	-	-
1983	98.6	-1.0	-	-	97.1	-1.5	-	-	98.4	1.3	-	-	99.5	1.1	-	-	100.1	0.6	-	-	100.6	0.5	-	-
1984	100.6	0.0	-	-	101.8	1.2	-	-	103.0	1.2	-	-	102.9	-0.1	-	-	102.9	0.0	-	-	103.2	0.3	-	-
1985	103.0	-0.2	-	-	104.2	1.2	-	-	105.3	1.1	-	-	105.5	0.2	-	-	105.3	-0.2	-	-	106.4	1.0	-	-
1986	106.6	0.2	-	-	103.3	-3.1	-	-	100.0	-3.2	-	-	100.0	0.0	-	-	98.9	-1.1	-	-	99.5	0.6	-	-
1987	100.8	1.3	-	-	100.4	-0.4	-	-	101.9	1.5	-	-	103.8	1.9	-	-	105.9	2.0	-	-	107.7	1.7	-	-
1988	107.3	-0.4	-	-	106.4	-0.8	-	-	107.0	0.6	-	-	108.7	1.6	-	-	110.6	1.7	-	-	113.9	3.0	-	-
1989	113.6	-0.3	-	-	115.3	1.5	-	-	117.9	2.3	-	-	114.8	-2.6	-	-	114.6	-0.2	-	-	116.5	1.7	-	-
1990	117.4	0.8	-	-	117.8	0.3	-	-	118.7	0.8	-	-	119.1	0.3	-	-	125.6	5.5	-	-	131.0	4.3	-	-
1991	127.9	-2.4	-	-	124.9	-2.3	-	-	127.4	2.0	-	-	128.7	1.0	-	-	129.6	0.7	-	-	130.7	0.8	-	-

[Continued]

Boston, MA
Consumer Price Index - Urban Wage Earners
Base 1982-1984 = 100
Transportation
[Continued]

For 1947-1993. Columns headed % show percentile change in the index from the previous period for which an index is available.

Year	Jan		Feb		Mar		Apr		May		Jun		Jul		Aug		Sep		Oct		Nov		Dec	
	Index	%	Index	%	Index	%	Index	%	Index	%	Index	%	Index	%	Index	%	Index	%	Index	%	Index	%	Index	%
1992	130.5	-0.2	-	-	130.8	0.2	-	-	131.5	0.5	-	-	133.0	1.1	-	-	132.2	-0.6	-	-	132.7	0.4	-	-
1993	134.6	1.4	-	-	134.9	0.2	-	-	134.6	-0.2	-	-	134.7	0.1	-	-	133.7	-0.7	-	-	136.5	2.1	-	-

Source: U.S. Department of Labor, Bureau of Labor Statistics, Division of Consumer Prices and Price Indexes. - indicates no data collected for period.

Boston, MA
Consumer Price Index - All Urban Consumers
Base 1982-1984 = 100
Medical Care

For 1947-1993. Columns headed % show percentile change in the index from the previous period for which an index is available.

Year	Jan Index	%	Feb Index	%	Mar Index	%	Apr Index	%	May Index	%	Jun Index	%	Jul Index	%	Aug Index	%	Sep Index	%	Oct Index	%	Nov Index	%	Dec Index	%
1947	13.3	-	13.3	0.0	13.4	0.8	13.4	0.0	13.4	0.0	13.4	0.0	13.3	-0.7	13.3	0.0	13.4	0.8	13.4	0.0	13.4	0.0	13.4	0.0
1948	13.8	3.0	13.8	0.0	14.3	3.6	14.4	0.7	14.5	0.7	14.3	-1.4	14.3	0.0	14.3	0.0	14.4	0.7	14.4	0.0	14.4	0.0	14.4	0.0
1949	14.8	2.8	14.8	0.0	14.9	0.7	14.9	0.0	14.9	0.0	15.0	0.7	15.3	2.0	15.3	0.0	15.4	0.7	15.4	0.0	15.4	0.0	15.4	0.0
1950	15.6	1.3	15.6	0.0	15.7	0.6	15.7	0.0	15.7	0.0	15.7	0.0	15.7	0.0	15.7	0.0	15.7	0.0	15.7	0.0	15.8	0.6	16.0	1.3
1951	16.1	0.6	16.1	0.0	16.2	0.6	16.2	0.0	16.2	0.0	16.3	0.6	16.3	0.0	16.3	0.0	16.2	-0.6	16.3	0.6	16.3	0.0	16.7	2.5
1952	16.8	0.6	16.8	0.0	16.8	0.0	16.9	0.6	16.9	0.0	17.1	1.2	17.2	0.6	17.2	0.0	17.5	1.7	17.5	0.0	17.5	0.0	17.5	0.0
1953	17.6	0.6	-	-	-	-	17.6	0.0	-	-	-	-	17.6	0.0	-	-	-	-	17.7	0.6	-	-	-	-
1954	17.7	0.0					17.7	0.0					17.7	0.0					17.7	0.0				
1955	17.7	0.0					17.7	0.0					17.8	0.6					18.0	1.1				
1956	18.3	1.7					18.3	0.0					19.5	6.6					19.6	0.5				
1957	19.7	0.5					20.1	2.0					21.2	5.5					21.2	0.0				
1958	22.0	3.8					22.1	0.5					22.3	0.9					22.4	0.4				
1959	22.6	0.9					22.7	0.4					22.7	0.0					22.9	0.9				
1960	23.0	0.4					23.1	0.4					23.2	0.4					23.3	0.4				
1961	23.7	1.7					23.8	0.4					23.9	0.4					24.1	0.8				
1962	24.5	1.7					24.8	1.2					24.8	0.0					24.9	0.4				
1963	24.9	0.0					25.3	1.6					25.3	0.0					25.5	0.8				
1964	25.6	0.4					25.9	1.2					25.9	0.0					26.5	2.3				
1965	26.8	1.1					26.8	0.0					27.1	1.1					27.3	0.7				
1966	27.4	0.4					27.9	1.8					28.0	0.4					28.8	2.9				
1967	29.3	1.7					29.3	0.0					29.9	2.0					31.0	3.7				
1968	31.7	2.3					31.8	0.3					32.2	1.3					33.6	4.3				
1969	34.2	1.8					34.5	0.9					34.9	1.2					36.0	3.2				
1970	36.5	1.4					36.8	0.8					37.2	1.1					38.5	3.5				
1971	38.8	0.8			-	-	39.2	1.0					39.4	0.5					39.2	-0.5				
1972	40.0	2.0			-	-	40.4	1.0					40.5	0.2					40.9	1.0				
1973	41.2	0.7			-	-	41.4	0.5					41.6	0.5					42.5	2.2				
1974	42.8	0.7			-	-	43.3	1.2					44.7	3.2					46.6	4.3				
1975	47.9	2.8			-	-	49.2	2.7					50.2	2.0					51.9	3.4				
1976	51.6	-0.6			-	-	51.8	0.4					53.9	4.1					54.9	1.9				
1977	56.2	2.4			-	-	56.9	1.2					57.9	1.8					59.2	2.2				
1978	59.4	0.3	-	-	59.8	0.7	-	-	60.6	1.3	-	-	61.5	1.5	-	-	62.8	2.1	-	-	66.1	5.3	-	-
1979	66.9	1.2	-	-	67.7	1.2	-	-	68.2	0.7	-	-	69.8	2.3	-	-	70.2	0.6	-	-	72.1	2.7	-	-
1980	74.3	3.1	-	-	74.9	0.8	-	-	76.6	2.3	-	-	76.4	-0.3	-	-	76.5	0.1	-	-	80.9	5.8	-	-
1981	81.6	0.9	-	-	82.0	0.5	-	-	82.3	0.4	-	-	82.7	0.5	-	-	83.4	0.8	-	-	88.0	5.5	-	-
1982	90.3	2.6	-	-	90.6	0.3	-	-	91.4	0.9	-	-	93.2	2.0	-	-	93.4	0.2	-	-	95.1	1.8	-	-
1983	96.9	1.9	-	-	96.6	-0.3	-	-	96.9	0.3	-	-	98.3	1.4	-	-	100.3	2.0	-	-	102.1	1.8	-	-
1984	104.2	2.1	-	-	106.7	2.4	-	-	107.8	1.0	-	-	109.4	1.5	-	-	109.1	-0.3	-	-	112.2	2.8	-	-
1985	112.2	0.0	-	-	119.7	6.7	-	-	121.5	1.5	-	-	121.6	0.1	-	-	120.9	-0.6	-	-	123.5	2.2	-	-
1986	126.5	2.4	-	-	130.2	2.9	-	-	131.9	1.3	-	-	132.9	0.8	-	-	133.8	0.7	-	-	133.5	-0.2	-	-
1987	135.0	1.1	-	-	137.7	2.0	-	-	138.5	0.6	-	-	138.7	0.1	-	-	139.4	0.5	-	-	143.3	2.8	-	-
1988	146.2	2.0	-	-	149.3	2.1	-	-	150.7	0.9	-	-	153.4	1.8	-	-	155.0	1.0	-	-	154.9	-0.1	-	-
1989	157.7	1.8	-	-	160.3	1.6	-	-	164.3	2.5	-	-	166.4	1.3	-	-	169.3	1.7	-	-	170.1	0.5	-	-
1990	173.2	1.8	-	-	177.9	2.7	-	-	181.7	2.1	-	-	182.3	0.3	-	-	182.7	0.2	-	-	187.5	2.6	-	-
1991	189.7	1.2	-	-	198.4	4.6	-	-	201.8	1.7	-	-	205.4	1.8	-	-	204.6	-0.4	-	-	210.4	2.8	-	-

[Continued]

Boston, MA
Consumer Price Index - All Urban Consumers
Base 1982-1984 = 100
Medical Care
[Continued]

For 1947-1993. Columns headed % show percentile change in the index from the previous period for which an index is available.

Year	Jan Index	%	Feb Index	%	Mar Index	%	Apr Index	%	May Index	%	Jun Index	%	Jul Index	%	Aug Index	%	Sep Index	%	Oct Index	%	Nov Index	%	Dec Index	%
1992	213.8	1.6	-	-	218.6	2.2	-	-	223.9	2.4	-	-	223.9	0.0	-	-	227.4	1.6	-	-	232.5	2.2	-	-
1993	233.9	0.6	-	-	232.7	-0.5	-	-	237.7	2.1	-	-	240.1	1.0	-	-	240.2	0.0	-	-	246.1	2.5	-	-

Source: U.S. Department of Labor, Bureau of Labor Statistics, Division of Consumer Prices and Price Indexes. - indicates no data collected for period.

Boston, MA
Consumer Price Index - Urban Wage Earners
Base 1982-1984 = 100
Medical Care

For 1947-1993. Columns headed % show percentile change in the index from the previous period for which an index is available.

Year	Jan Index	%	Feb Index	%	Mar Index	%	Apr Index	%	May Index	%	Jun Index	%	Jul Index	%	Aug Index	%	Sep Index	%	Oct Index	%	Nov Index	%	Dec Index	%
1947	13.5	-	13.5	0.0	13.6	0.7	13.6	0.0	13.6	0.0	13.6	0.0	13.5	-0.7	13.5	0.0	13.6	0.7	13.6	0.0	13.6	0.0	13.6	0.0
1948	14.0	2.9	14.0	0.0	14.5	3.6	14.7	1.4	14.7	0.0	14.5	-1.4	14.5	0.0	14.6	0.7	14.6	0.0	14.6	0.0	14.6	0.0	14.6	0.0
1949	15.0	2.7	15.0	0.0	15.1	0.7	15.1	0.0	15.1	0.0	15.2	0.7	15.5	2.0	15.6	0.6	15.6	0.0	15.6	0.0	15.6	0.0	15.6	0.0
1950	15.8	1.3	15.8	0.0	15.9	0.6	15.9	0.0	15.9	0.0	16.0	0.6	16.0	0.0	16.0	0.0	16.0	0.0	16.0	0.0	16.0	0.0	16.2	1.3
1951	16.3	0.6	16.3	0.0	16.5	1.2	16.5	0.0	16.5	0.0	16.5	0.0	16.5	0.0	16.5	0.0	16.5	0.0	16.5	0.0	16.6	0.6	17.0	2.4
1952	17.1	0.6	17.1	0.0	17.1	0.0	17.1	0.0	17.1	0.0	17.3	1.2	17.4	0.6	17.4	0.0	17.7	1.7	17.7	0.0	17.7	0.0	17.8	0.6
1953	17.8	0.0	-	-	-	-	17.8	0.0	-	-	-	-	17.9	0.6	-	-	-	-	18.0	0.6	-	-	-	-
1954	18.0	0.0	-	-	-	-	18.0	0.0	-	-	-	-	18.0	0.0	-	-	-	-	18.0	0.0	-	-	-	-
1955	18.0	0.0	-	-	-	-	18.0	0.0	-	-	-	-	18.1	0.6	-	-	-	-	18.3	1.1	-	-	-	-
1956	18.6	1.6	-	-	-	-	18.6	0.0	-	-	-	-	19.8	6.5	-	-	-	-	19.9	0.5	-	-	-	-
1957	20.0	0.5	-	-	-	-	20.4	2.0	-	-	-	-	21.5	5.4	-	-	-	-	21.6	0.5	-	-	-	-
1958	22.3	3.2	-	-	-	-	22.4	0.4	-	-	-	-	22.6	0.9	-	-	-	-	22.7	0.4	-	-	-	-
1959	23.0	1.3	-	-	-	-	23.0	0.0	-	-	-	-	23.1	0.4	-	-	-	-	23.2	0.4	-	-	-	-
1960	23.3	0.4	-	-	-	-	23.4	0.4	-	-	-	-	23.5	0.4	-	-	-	-	23.6	0.4	-	-	-	-
1961	24.1	2.1	-	-	-	-	24.1	0.0	-	-	-	-	24.3	0.8	-	-	-	-	24.4	0.4	-	-	-	-
1962	24.9	2.0	-	-	-	-	25.1	0.8	-	-	-	-	25.1	0.0	-	-	-	-	25.2	0.4	-	-	-	-
1963	25.3	0.4	-	-	-	-	25.7	1.6	-	-	-	-	25.7	0.0	-	-	-	-	25.9	0.8	-	-	-	-
1964	26.0	0.4	-	-	-	-	26.3	1.2	-	-	-	-	26.3	0.0	-	-	-	-	26.9	2.3	-	-	-	-
1965	27.2	1.1	-	-	-	-	27.2	0.0	-	-	-	-	27.5	1.1	-	-	-	-	27.7	0.7	-	-	-	-
1966	27.8	0.4	-	-	-	-	28.3	1.8	-	-	-	-	28.4	0.4	-	-	-	-	29.2	2.8	-	-	-	-
1967	29.8	2.1	-	-	-	-	29.8	0.0	-	-	-	-	30.4	2.0	-	-	-	-	31.4	3.3	-	-	-	-
1968	32.1	2.2	-	-	-	-	32.3	0.6	-	-	-	-	32.7	1.2	-	-	-	-	34.1	4.3	-	-	-	-
1969	34.7	1.8	-	-	-	-	35.0	0.9	-	-	-	-	35.4	1.1	-	-	-	-	36.5	3.1	-	-	-	-
1970	37.0	1.4	-	-	-	-	37.4	1.1	-	-	-	-	37.8	1.1	-	-	-	-	39.0	3.2	-	-	-	-
1971	39.4	1.0	-	-	-	-	39.7	0.8	-	-	-	-	40.0	0.8	-	-	-	-	39.8	-0.5	-	-	-	-
1972	40.6	2.0	-	-	-	-	41.0	1.0	-	-	-	-	41.1	0.2	-	-	-	-	41.5	1.0	-	-	-	-
1973	41.8	0.7	-	-	-	-	42.0	0.5	-	-	-	-	42.2	0.5	-	-	-	-	43.2	2.4	-	-	-	-
1974	43.4	0.5	-	-	-	-	44.0	1.4	-	-	-	-	45.3	3.0	-	-	-	-	47.3	4.4	-	-	-	-
1975	48.6	2.7	-	-	-	-	49.9	2.7	-	-	-	-	50.9	2.0	-	-	-	-	52.7	3.5	-	-	-	-
1976	52.4	-0.6	-	-	-	-	52.6	0.4	-	-	-	-	54.7	4.0	-	-	-	-	55.7	1.8	-	-	-	-
1977	57.0	2.3	-	-	-	-	57.8	1.4	-	-	-	-	58.7	1.6	-	-	-	-	60.1	2.4	-	-	-	-
1978	60.3	0.3	-	-	61.2	1.5	-	-	61.9	1.1	-	-	62.0	0.2	-	-	63.9	3.1	-	-	65.8	3.0	-	-
1979	66.7	1.4	-	-	67.3	0.9	-	-	68.2	1.3	-	-	69.8	2.3	-	-	69.9	0.1	-	-	72.5	3.7	-	-
1980	73.6	1.5	-	-	74.4	1.1	-	-	77.0	3.5	-	-	75.6	-1.8	-	-	76.1	0.7	-	-	79.7	5.0	-	-
1981	80.5	1.0	-	-	81.9	1.7	-	-	83.9	2.4	-	-	82.8	-1.3	-	-	83.5	0.1	-	-	94.6	1.6	-	-
1982	89.8	2.4	-	-	90.3	0.6	-	-	91.2	1.0	-	-	93.0	2.0	-	-	100.5	2.1	-	-	102.3	1.8	-	-
1983	96.6	2.1	-	-	96.4	-0.2	-	-	96.7	0.3	-	-	98.4	1.8	-	-	109.5	-0.3	-	-	112.0	2.3	-	-
1984	104.9	2.5	-	-	107.2	2.2	-	-	108.3	1.0	-	-	109.8	1.4	-	-	120.0	-0.4	-	-	122.4	2.0	-	-
1985	111.8	-0.2	-	-	118.1	5.6	-	-	119.9	1.5	-	-	120.5	0.5	-	-	132.8	0.8	-	-	132.7	-0.1	-	-
1986	125.1	2.2	-	-	128.8	3.0	-	-	130.6	1.4	-	-	131.7	0.8	-	-	139.3	0.8	-	-	142.8	2.5	-	-
1987	134.6	1.4	-	-	137.1	1.9	-	-	138.2	0.8	-	-	138.2	0.0	-	-	154.0	0.9	-	-	154.5	0.3	-	-
1988	145.7	2.0	-	-	148.5	1.9	-	-	150.2	1.1	-	-	152.6	1.6	-	-	167.7	1.9	-	-	168.4	0.4	-	-
1989	157.1	1.7	-	-	159.5	1.5	-	-	162.7	2.0	-	-	164.5	1.1	-	-	181.1	0.2	-	-	185.3	2.3	-	-
1990	171.3	1.7	-	-	175.8	2.6	-	-	180.0	2.4	-	-	180.7	0.4	-	-	201.9	-0.3	-	-	207.1	2.6	-	-
1991	187.4	1.1	-	-	194.9	4.0	-	-	198.9	2.1	-	-	202.5	1.8	-	-	-	-	-	-	-	-	-	-

[Continued]

Boston, MA
Consumer Price Index - Urban Wage Earners
Base 1982-1984 = 100
Medical Care
[Continued]

For 1947-1993. Columns headed % show percentile change in the index from the previous period for which an index is available.

Year	Jan Index	%	Feb Index	%	Mar Index	%	Apr Index	%	May Index	%	Jun Index	%	Jul Index	%	Aug Index	%	Sep Index	%	Oct Index	%	Nov Index	%	Dec Index	%
1992	210.2	1.5	-	-	214.4	2.0	-	-	219.1	2.2	-	-	219.1	0.0	-	-	223.7	2.1	-	-	228.4	2.1	-	-
1993	229.5	0.5	-	-	228.7	-0.3	-	-	233.8	2.2	-	-	236.1	1.0	-	-	236.1	0.0	-	-	240.4	1.8	-	-

Source: U.S. Department of Labor, Bureau of Labor Statistics, Division of Consumer Prices and Price Indexes. - indicates no data collected for period.

317

Boston, MA

Consumer Price Index - All Urban Consumers
Base 1982-1984 = 100
Entertainment

For 1976-1993. Columns headed % show percentile change in the index from the previous period for which an index is available.

Year	Jan		Feb		Mar		Apr		May		Jun		Jul		Aug		Sep		Oct		Nov		Dec	
	Index	%	Index	%	Index	%	Index	%	Index	%	Index	%	Index	%	Index	%	Index	%	Index	%	Index	%	Index	%
1976	63.7	-	-	-	-	-	64.0	0.5	-	-	-	-	64.8	1.3	-	-	-	-	65.4	0.9	-	-	-	-
1977	65.5	0.2	-	-	-	-	65.4	-0.2	-	-	-	-	66.6	1.8	-	-	-	-	66.7	0.2	-	-	-	-
1978	67.1	0.6	-	-	68.3	1.8	-	-	69.0	1.0	-	-	68.4	-0.9	-	-	68.7	0.4	-	-	72.6	5.7	-	-
1979	72.4	-0.3	-	-	73.5	1.5	-	-	75.6	2.9	-	-	76.0	0.5	-	-	76.5	0.7	-	-	78.1	2.1	-	-
1980	79.9	2.3	-	-	80.7	1.0	-	-	83.3	3.2	-	-	83.7	0.5	-	-	84.4	0.8	-	-	85.7	1.5	-	-
1981	87.0	1.5	-	-	88.7	2.0	-	-	88.8	0.1	-	-	90.1	1.5	-	-	91.1	1.1	-	-	91.9	0.9	-	-
1982	92.9	1.1	-	-	93.8	1.0	-	-	96.4	2.8	-	-	96.6	0.2	-	-	97.9	1.3	-	-	98.4	0.5	-	-
1983	99.0	0.6	-	-	99.3	0.3	-	-	100.8	1.5	-	-	101.3	0.5	-	-	100.5	-0.8	-	-	100.0	-0.5	-	-
1984	101.8	1.8	-	-	103.8	2.0	-	-	103.2	-0.6	-	-	103.6	0.4	-	-	104.1	0.5	-	-	103.0	-1.1	-	-
1985	107.4	4.3	-	-	110.1	2.5	-	-	107.4	-2.5	-	-	109.4	1.9	-	-	111.0	1.5	-	-	111.0	0.0	-	-
1986	117.0	5.4	-	-	114.0	-2.6	-	-	114.7	0.6	-	-	112.9	-1.6	-	-	113.4	0.4	-	-	115.2	1.6	-	-
1987	118.5	2.9	-	-	118.1	-0.3	-	-	116.9	-1.0	-	-	119.4	2.1	-	-	121.5	1.8	-	-	120.7	-0.7	-	-
1988	122.9	1.8	-	-	127.9	4.1	-	-	125.9	-1.6	-	-	127.5	1.3	-	-	127.9	0.3	-	-	128.2	0.2	-	-
1989	128.9	0.5	-	-	128.9	0.0	-	-	132.5	2.8	-	-	135.4	2.2	-	-	137.0	1.2	-	-	136.7	-0.2	-	-
1990	137.7	0.7	-	-	141.2	2.5	-	-	143.7	1.8	-	-	145.4	1.2	-	-	148.4	2.1	-	-	146.3	-1.4	-	-
1991	147.5	0.8	-	-	148.5	0.7	-	-	150.7	1.5	-	-	156.3	3.7	-	-	156.7	0.3	-	-	152.3	-2.8	-	-
1992	152.8	0.3	-	-	152.8	0.0	-	-	154.0	0.8	-	-	155.9	1.2	-	-	156.3	0.3	-	-	156.9	0.4	-	-
1993	156.9	0.0	-	-	157.7	0.5	-	-	159.5	1.1	-	-	159.5	0.0	-	-	161.9	1.5	-	-	163.5	1.0	-	-

Source: U.S. Department of Labor, Bureau of Labor Statistics, Division of Consumer Prices and Price Indexes. - indicates no data collected for period.

Boston, MA
Consumer Price Index - Urban Wage Earners
Base 1982-1984 = 100
Entertainment

For 1976-1993. Columns headed % show percentile change in the index from the previous period for which an index is available.

Year	Jan Index	%	Feb Index	%	Mar Index	%	Apr Index	%	May Index	%	Jun Index	%	Jul Index	%	Aug Index	%	Sep Index	%	Oct Index	%	Nov Index	%	Dec Index	%
1976	66.0	-	-	-	-	-	66.3	0.5	-	-	-	-	67.1	1.2	-	-	-	-	67.8	1.0	-	-	-	-
1977	67.8	0.0	-	-	-	-	67.7	-0.1	-	-	-	-	69.0	1.9	-	-	-	-	69.1	0.1	-	-	-	-
1978	69.5	0.6	-	-	70.2	1.0	-	-	70.8	0.9	-	-	68.8	-2.8	-	-	69.0	0.3	-	-	74.6	8.1	-	-
1979	74.9	0.4	-	-	75.6	0.9	-	-	76.4	1.1	-	-	77.3	1.2	-	-	77.8	0.6	-	-	79.1	1.7	-	-
1980	79.6	0.6	-	-	81.8	2.8	-	-	83.2	1.7	-	-	83.5	0.4	-	-	84.4	1.1	-	-	86.1	2.0	-	-
1981	86.6	0.6	-	-	88.3	2.0	-	-	89.0	0.8	-	-	89.4	0.4	-	-	90.7	1.5	-	-	92.2	1.7	-	-
1982	93.0	0.9	-	-	93.7	0.8	-	-	96.5	3.0	-	-	96.1	-0.4	-	-	97.8	1.8	-	-	98.5	0.7	-	-
1983	98.9	0.4	-	-	99.2	0.3	-	-	100.8	1.6	-	-	101.2	0.4	-	-	100.4	-0.8	-	-	100.3	-0.1	-	-
1984	102.1	1.8	-	-	103.2	1.1	-	-	103.4	0.2	-	-	103.9	0.5	-	-	104.1	0.2	-	-	103.4	-0.7	-	-
1985	107.3	3.8	-	-	109.0	1.6	-	-	107.5	-1.4	-	-	109.0	1.4	-	-	109.9	0.8	-	-	110.6	0.6	-	-
1986	116.0	4.9	-	-	113.7	-2.0	-	-	114.4	0.6	-	-	112.4	-1.7	-	-	112.9	0.4	-	-	114.4	1.3	-	-
1987	117.2	2.4	-	-	116.8	-0.3	-	-	115.1	-1.5	-	-	118.3	2.8	-	-	120.0	1.4	-	-	118.9	-0.9	-	-
1988	120.5	1.3	-	-	125.2	3.9	-	-	124.8	-0.3	-	-	126.2	1.1	-	-	125.8	-0.3	-	-	127.4	1.3	-	-
1989	127.8	0.3	-	-	127.7	-0.1	-	-	131.6	3.1	-	-	135.1	2.7	-	-	136.7	1.2	-	-	136.5	-0.1	-	-
1990	137.6	0.8	-	-	140.8	2.3	-	-	144.1	2.3	-	-	146.6	1.7	-	-	149.0	1.6	-	-	146.2	-1.9	-	-
1991	148.1	1.3	-	-	150.0	1.3	-	-	152.2	1.5	-	-	155.7	2.3	-	-	156.1	0.3	-	-	153.4	-1.7	-	-
1992	153.3	-0.1	-	-	153.3	0.0	-	-	154.9	1.0	-	-	156.7	1.2	-	-	156.6	-0.1	-	-	157.1	0.3	-	-
1993	157.1	0.0	-	-	158.4	0.8	-	-	160.3	1.2	-	-	161.9	1.0	-	-	164.0	1.3	-	-	164.3	0.2	-	-

Source: U.S. Department of Labor, Bureau of Labor Statistics, Division of Consumer Prices and Price Indexes. - indicates no data collected for period.

Boston, MA
Consumer Price Index - All Urban Consumers
Base 1982-1984 = 100
Other Goods and Services

For 1976-1993. Columns headed % show percentile change in the index from the previous period for which an index is available.

Year	Jan Index	%	Feb Index	%	Mar Index	%	Apr Index	%	May Index	%	Jun Index	%	Jul Index	%	Aug Index	%	Sep Index	%	Oct Index	%	Nov Index	%	Dec Index	%
1976	55.1	-	-	-	-	-	55.6	0.9	-	-	-	-	56.3	1.3	-	-	-	-	57.2	1.6	-	-	-	-
1977	58.3	1.9	-	-	-	-	58.6	0.5	-	-	-	-	59.1	0.9	-	-	64.3	3.5	60.7	2.7	-	-	-	-
1978	60.8	0.2	-	-	60.9	0.2	-	-	61.1	0.3	-	-	62.1	1.6	-	-	64.3	3.5	-	-	64.6	0.5	-	-
1979	64.6	0.0	-	-	65.3	1.1	-	-	65.9	0.9	-	-	66.7	1.2	-	-	69.8	4.6	-	-	70.4	0.9	-	-
1980	71.0	0.9	-	-	71.5	0.7	-	-	72.1	0.8	-	-	72.9	1.1	-	-	75.9	4.1	-	-	76.5	0.8	-	-
1981	77.4	1.2	-	-	78.4	1.3	-	-	79.3	1.1	-	-	81.0	2.1	-	-	83.5	3.1	-	-	84.7	1.4	-	-
1982	85.4	0.8	-	-	89.5	4.8	-	-	89.9	0.4	-	-	89.9	0.0	-	-	92.2	2.6	-	-	93.7	1.6	-	-
1983	94.7	1.1	-	-	99.0	4.5	-	-	99.5	0.5	-	-	100.4	0.9	-	-	101.4	1.0	-	-	103.4	2.0	-	-
1984	104.3	0.9	-	-	107.7	3.3	-	-	108.0	0.3	-	-	108.4	0.4	-	-	112.7	4.0	-	-	113.1	0.4	-	-
1985	113.2	0.1	-	-	114.7	1.3	-	-	115.7	0.9	-	-	116.0	0.3	-	-	124.4	7.2	-	-	126.1	1.4	-	-
1986	126.7	0.5	-	-	127.4	0.6	-	-	126.8	-0.5	-	-	127.3	0.4	-	-	131.0	2.9	-	-	132.1	0.8	-	-
1987	132.3	0.2	-	-	132.7	0.3	-	-	132.7	0.0	-	-	133.2	0.4	-	-	141.3	6.1	-	-	141.6	0.2	-	-
1988	142.3	0.5	-	-	144.0	1.2	-	-	144.2	0.1	-	-	145.1	0.6	-	-	152.0	4.8	-	-	152.3	0.2	-	-
1989	153.9	1.1	-	-	154.8	0.6	-	-	156.2	0.9	-	-	159.2	1.9	-	-	159.2	0.0	-	-	161.1	1.2	-	-
1990	166.3	3.2	-	-	167.8	0.9	-	-	168.4	0.4	-	-	175.4	4.2	-	-	180.1	2.7	-	-	178.0	-1.2	-	-
1991	183.1	2.9	-	-	182.3	-0.4	-	-	182.7	0.2	-	-	191.9	5.0	-	-	194.0	1.1	-	-	193.5	-0.3	-	-
1992	194.5	0.5	-	-	192.9	-0.8	-	-	196.1	1.7	-	-	200.4	2.2	-	-	199.8	-0.3	-	-	201.5	0.9	-	-
1993	202.7	0.6	-	-	202.2	-0.2	-	-	202.1	-0.0	-	-	205.5	1.7	-	-	202.2	-1.6	-	-	200.6	-0.8	-	-

Source: U.S. Department of Labor, Bureau of Labor Statistics, Division of Consumer Prices and Price Indexes. - indicates no data collected for period.

Boston, MA
Consumer Price Index - Urban Wage Earners
Base 1982-1984 = 100
Other Goods and Services

For 1976-1993. Columns headed % show percentile change in the index from the previous period for which an index is available.

Year	Jan Index	%	Feb Index	%	Mar Index	%	Apr Index	%	May Index	%	Jun Index	.%	Jul Index	%	Aug Index	%	Sep Index	%	Oct Index	%	Nov Index	%	Dec Index	%
1976	55.9	-	-	-	-	-	56.4	0.9	-	-	-	-	57.1	1.2	-	-	-	-	58.0	1.6	-	-	-	-
1977	59.1	1.9	-	-	-	-	59.4	0.5	-	-	-	-	59.9	0.8	-	-	-	-	61.5	2.7	-	-	-	-
1978	61.6	0.2	-	-	61.7	0.2	-	-	61.9	0.3	-	-	62.9	1.6	-	-	65.0	3.3	-	-	-	-	-	-
1979	65.3	-0.3	-	-	66.3	1.5	-	-	66.6	0.5	-	-	67.6	1.5	-	-	70.3	4.0	-	-	65.5	0.8	-	-
1980	71.6	1.1	-	-	72.0	0.6	-	-	71.9	-0.1	-	-	73.1	1.7	-	-	75.8	3.7	-	-	70.8	0.7	-	-
1981	77.1	0.8	-	-	78.8	2.2	-	-	79.5	0.9	-	-	81.2	2.1	-	-	83.4	2.7	-	-	76.5	0.9	-	-
1982	85.1	0.5	-	-	89.4	5.1	-	-	89.7	0.3	-	-	89.7	0.0	-	-	92.0	2.6	-	-	84.7	1.6	-	-
1983	94.6	1.1	-	-	99.0	4.7	-	-	99.5	0.5	-	-	100.4	0.9	-	-	101.3	0.9	-	-	93.6	1.7	-	-
1984	104.4	0.9	-	-	107.9	3.4	-	-	108.2	0.3	-	-	108.7	0.5	-	-	112.8	3.8	-	-	103.5	2.2	-	-
1985	113.3	0.1	-	-	114.9	1.4	-	-	116.0	1.0	-	-	116.3	0.3	-	-	124.6	7.1	-	-	113.2	0.4	-	-
1986	126.8	0.5	-	-	127.5	0.6	-	-	126.9	-0.5	-	-	127.4	0.4	-	-	130.9	2.7	-	-	126.2	1.3	-	-
1987	132.5	0.3	-	-	133.0	0.4	-	-	133.0	0.0	-	-	133.9	0.7	-	-	140.5	4.9	-	-	132.1	0.9	-	-
1988	141.6	0.6	-	-	143.6	1.4	-	-	144.1	0.3	-	-	145.2	0.8	-	-	151.9	4.6	-	-	140.7	0.1	-	-
1989	154.1	1.2	-	-	154.7	0.4	-	-	156.4	1.1	-	-	160.6	2.7	-	-	160.3	-0.2	-	-	152.3	0.3	-	-
1990	167.5	3.2	-	-	170.1	1.6	-	-	170.2	0.1	-	-	176.9	3.9	-	-	180.3	1.9	-	-	162.3	1.2	-	-
1991	183.7	4.0	-	-	182.4	-0.7	-	-	183.0	0.3	-	-	193.0	5.5	-	-	195.4	1.2	-	-	176.7	-2.0	-	-
1992	197.7	0.7	-	-	195.0	-1.4	-	-	199.1	2.1	-	-	203.2	2.1	-	-	200.3	-1.4	-	-	196.4	0.5	-	-
1993	205.0	0.9	-	-	205.8	0.4	-	-	205.6	-0.1	-	-	208.3	1.3	-	-	200.6	-3.7	-	-	203.2	1.4	-	-

Source: U.S. Department of Labor, Bureau of Labor Statistics, Division of Consumer Prices and Price Indexes. - indicates no data collected for period.

Buffalo, NY
Consumer Price Index - All Urban Consumers
Base 1982-1984 = 100
Annual Averages

For 1963-1993. Columns headed % show percentile change in the index from the previous period for which an index is available.

Year	All Items		Food & Beverage		Housing		Apparel & Upkeep		Transportation		Medical Care		Entertainment		Other Goods & Services	
	Index	%	Index	%	Index	%	Index	%	Index	%	Index	%	Index	%	Index	%
1963	-	-	-	-	-	-	40.4	-	32.8	-	29.9	-	-	-	-	-
1964	32.6	-	-	-	-	-	41.8	3.5	34.1	4.0	30.7	2.7	-	-	-	-
1965	33.4	2.5	-	-	-	-	43.2	3.3	34.9	2.3	32.4	5.5	-	-	-	-
1966	34.5	3.3	-	-	-	-	45.3	4.9	35.8	2.6	34.4	6.2	-	-	-	-
1967	35.5	2.9	-	-	-	-	48.3	6.6	36.7	2.5	35.7	3.8	-	-	-	-
1968	37.1	4.5	-	-	-	-	51.6	6.8	38.1	3.8	37.5	5.0	-	-	-	-
1969	38.9	4.9	-	-	-	-	53.3	3.3	40.0	5.0	39.7	5.9	-	-	-	-
1970	41.2	5.9	-	-	-	-	55.8	4.7	41.8	4.5	42.1	6.0	-	-	-	-
1971	43.2	4.9	-	-	-	-	57.1	2.3	42.2	1.0	43.4	3.1	-	-	-	-
1972	44.9	3.9	-	-	-	-	61.0	6.8	43.9	4.0	44.8	3.2	-	-	-	-
1973	47.8	6.5	-	-	-	-	66.0	8.2	48.7	10.9	48.9	9.2	-	-	-	-
1974	53.0	10.9	-	-	-	-	69.8	5.8	52.7	8.2	53.4	9.2	-	-	-	-
1975	57.4	8.3	-	-	59.5	-	73.2	4.9	57.7	9.5	57.9	8.4	62.9	-	58.1	-
1976	60.5	5.4	63.4	-	59.5	-	79.0	7.9	61.3	6.2	62.6	8.1	66.3	5.4	60.7	4.5
1977	64.4	6.4	66.9	5.5	63.5	6.7	82.2	4.1	64.3	4.9	68.2	8.9	70.5	6.3	63.4	4.4
1978	68.4	6.2	72.8	8.8	67.0	5.5	86.1	4.7	73.8	14.8	73.1	7.2	72.1	2.3	66.9	5.5
1979	74.9	9.5	80.0	9.9	73.0	9.0	91.1	5.8	86.5	17.2	78.4	7.3	78.8	9.3	72.6	8.5
1980	83.5	11.5	86.8	8.5	81.7	11.9	93.8	3.0	95.6	10.5	85.7	9.3	88.1	11.8	81.7	12.5
1981	91.3	9.3	94.2	8.5	89.5	9.5	97.7	4.2	97.5	2.0	91.5	6.8	94.0	6.7	90.7	11.0
1982	94.7	3.7	97.5	3.5	92.5	3.4	100.4	2.8	99.5	2.1	100.9	10.3	100.6	7.0	101.0	11.4
1983	100.9	6.5	99.8	2.4	102.2	10.5	101.9	1.5	103.0	3.5	107.6	6.6	105.5	4.9	108.3	7.2
1984	104.4	3.5	102.6	2.8	105.3	3.0	108.3	6.3	105.2	2.1	113.0	5.0	111.5	5.7	116.6	7.7
1985	108.6	4.0	105.8	3.1	110.2	4.7	111.4	2.9	98.4	-6.5	119.8	6.0	114.6	2.8	125.5	7.6
1986	109.6	0.9	108.5	2.6	112.4	2.0	117.9	5.8	99.8	1.4	127.6	6.5	122.7	7.1	132.3	5.4
1987	113.0	3.1	112.1	3.3	114.8	2.1	125.8	6.7	101.0	1.2	131.9	3.4	125.1	2.0	139.5	5.4
1988	117.4	3.9	116.7	4.1	120.1	4.6	109.4	-13.0	103.2	2.2	141.9	7.6	132.2	5.7	147.7	5.9
1989	121.6	3.6	125.8	7.8	125.0	4.1	107.6	-1.6	109.1	5.7	151.7	6.9	142.8	8.0	155.0	4.9
1990	127.7	5.0	131.5	4.5	132.0	5.6	112.0	4.1	112.2	2.8	159.0	4.8	148.2	3.8	164.6	6.2
1991	133.4	4.5	136.0	3.4	139.4	5.6	111.3	-0.6	114.0	1.6	166.5	4.7	155.7	5.1	180.0	9.4
1992	137.9	3.4	137.1	0.8	146.2	4.9	112.6	1.2	117.5	3.1	172.4	3.5	167.4	7.5	190.9	6.1
1993	142.7	3.5	139.3	1.6	152.1	4.0										

Source: U.S. Department of Labor, Bureau of Labor Statistics, Division of Consumer Prices and Price Indexes. - indicates no data collected for period.

Buffalo, NY
Consumer Price Index - Urban Wage Earners
Base 1982-1984 = 100
Annual Averages

For 1963-1993. Columns headed % show percentile change in the index from the previous period for which an index is available.

Year	All Items		Food & Beverage		Housing		Apparel & Upkeep		Trans- portation		Medical Care		Entertain- ment		Other Goods & Services	
	Index	%	Index	%	Index	%	Index	%	Index	%	Index	%	Index	%	Index	%
1963	-	-	-	-	-	-	-	-	-	-	-	-	-	-	-	-
1964	33.0	-	-	-	-	-	41.8	-	32.6	-	29.4	-	-	-	-	-
1965	33.8	2.4	-	-	-	-	43.2	3.3	33.8	3.7	30.2	2.7	-	-	-	-
1966	35.0	3.6	-	-	-	-	44.7	3.5	34.7	2.7	31.8	5.3	-	-	-	-
1967	35.9	2.6	-	-	-	-	46.9	4.9	35.5	2.3	33.8	6.3	-	-	-	-
1968	37.5	4.5	-	-	-	-	50.0	6.6	36.5	2.8	35.1	3.8	-	-	-	-
1969	39.4	5.1	-	-	-	-	53.4	6.8	37.8	3.6	36.8	4.8	-	-	-	-
1970	41.7	5.8	-	-	-	-	55.2	3.4	39.7	5.0	39.0	6.0	-	-	-	-
1971	43.7	4.8	-	-	-	-	57.8	4.7	41.5	4.5	41.3	5.9	-	-	-	-
1972	45.5	4.1	-	-	-	-	59.1	2.2	41.9	1.0	42.6	3.1	-	-	-	-
1973	48.4	6.4	-	-	-	-	63.2	6.9	43.6	4.1	44.0	3.3	-	-	-	-
1974	53.7	11.0	-	-	-	-	68.3	8.1	48.4	11.0	48.0	9.1	-	-	-	-
1975	58.1	8.2	-	-	-	-	72.3	5.9	52.3	8.1	52.5	9.4	-	-	-	-
1976	61.3	5.5	64.3	-	60.3	-	75.7	4.7	57.3	9.6	56.9	8.4	67.2	-	61.0	-
1977	65.3	6.5	68.0	5.8	64.4	6.8	81.7	7.9	60.8	6.1	61.5	8.1	70.9	5.5	63.7	4.4
1978	69.3	6.1	73.9	8.7	68.1	5.7	84.8	3.8	64.0	5.3	67.0	8.9	72.3	2.0	66.7	4.7
1979	76.0	9.7	81.3	10.0	73.9	8.5	87.3	2.9	73.8	15.3	72.2	7.8	72.6	0.4	70.9	6.3
1980	84.3	10.9	87.8	8.0	82.4	11.5	90.0	3.1	86.0	16.5	79.0	9.4	79.3	9.2	76.7	8.2
1981	92.0	9.1	94.5	7.6	90.3	9.6	93.4	3.8	95.5	11.0	85.6	8.4	87.4	10.2	83.8	9.3
1982	95.2	3.5	97.6	3.3	93.0	3.0	97.6	4.5	97.4	2.0	91.7	7.1	94.3	7.9	90.7	8.2
1983	101.3	6.4	99.7	2.2	103.8	11.6	100.3	2.8	99.4	2.1	100.7	9.8	100.6	6.7	101.3	11.7
1984	103.5	2.2	102.7	3.0	103.2	-0.6	102.0	1.7	103.1	3.7	107.6	6.9	105.2	4.6	107.9	6.5
1985	105.1	1.5	106.0	3.2	101.4	-1.7	107.9	5.8	105.0	1.8	112.9	4.9	110.3	4.8	115.2	6.8
1986	105.7	0.6	108.7	2.5	103.5	2.1	111.0	2.9	97.3	-7.3	119.3	5.7	113.8	3.2	123.7	7.4
1987	109.0	3.1	112.1	3.1	105.8	2.2	118.1	6.4	99.3	2.1	126.8	6.3	122.0	7.2	130.4	5.4
1988	113.2	3.9	116.7	4.1	110.5	4.4	126.3	6.9	100.5	1.2	131.0	3.3	124.6	2.1	137.8	5.7
1989	117.3	3.6	125.7	7.7	115.1	4.2	109.9	-13.0	103.0	2.5	141.3	7.9	131.1	5.2	146.3	6.2
1990	123.2	5.0	131.4	4.5	121.6	5.6	107.7	-2.0	109.2	6.0	150.4	6.4	141.7	8.1	154.1	5.3
1991	128.8	4.5	135.7	3.3	128.7	5.8	112.0	4.0	112.3	2.8	158.1	5.1	146.8	3.6	164.5	6.7
1992	133.1	3.3	137.0	1.0	135.1	5.0	111.5	-0.4	113.9	1.4	165.9	4.9	154.3	5.1	180.4	9.7
1993	137.6	3.4	139.1	1.5	140.4	3.9	112.0	0.4	116.9	2.6	172.6	4.0	165.8	7.5	192.4	6.7

Source: U.S. Department of Labor, Bureau of Labor Statistics, Division of Consumer Prices and Price Indexes. - indicates no data collected for period.

Buffalo, NY
Consumer Price Index - All Urban Consumers
Base 1982-1984 = 100
All Items

For 1963-1993. Columns headed % show percentile change in the index from the previous period for which an index is available.

Year	Jan Index	%	Feb Index	%	Mar Index	%	Apr Index	%	May Index	%	Jun Index	%	Jul Index	%	Aug Index	%	Sep Index	%	Oct Index	%	Nov Index	%	Dec Index	%
1963	-		-		-		-		-		-		-		-		-		-		32.3		-	-
1964	-	-	32.3	0.0	-	-	-	-	32.5	0.6	-	-	-	-	32.7	0.6	-	-	-	-	32.9	0.6	-	-
1965	-	-	33.0	0.3	-	-	-	-	33.2	0.6	-	-	-	-	33.5	0.9	-	-	-	-	33.8	0.9	-	-
1966	-	-	34.1	0.9	-	-	-	-	34.4	0.9	-	-	-	-	34.7	0.9	-	-	-	-	34.9	0.6	-	-
1967	-	-	35.0	0.3	-	-	-	-	35.3	0.9	-	-	-	-	35.6	0.8	-	-	-	-	35.9	0.8	-	-
1968	-	-	36.2	0.8	-	-	-	-	36.9	1.9	-	-	-	-	37.3	1.1	-	-	-	-	37.7	1.1	-	-
1969	-	-	37.8	0.3	-	-	-	-	38.8	2.6	-	-	-	-	39.1	0.8	-	-	-	-	39.7	1.5	-	-
1970	-	-	40.4	1.8	-	-	-	-	41.0	1.5	-	-	-	-	41.3	0.7	-	-	-	-	42.1	1.9	-	-
1971	-	-	42.4	0.7	-	-	-	-	43.0	1.4	-	-	-	-	43.5	1.2	-	-	-	-	43.6	0.2	-	-
1972	-	-	44.3	1.6	-	-	-	-	44.7	0.9	-	-	-	-	45.0	0.7	-	-	-	-	45.6	1.3	-	-
1973	-	-	46.2	1.3	-	-	-	-	47.2	2.2	-	-	-	-	48.4	2.5	-	-	-	-	49.1	1.4	-	-
1974	-	-	51.1	4.1	-	-	-	-	52.3	2.3	-	-	-	-	53.7	2.7	-	-	-	-	55.0	2.4	-	-
1975	-	-	55.9	1.6	-	-	-	-	56.9	1.8	-	-	-	-	58.0	1.9	-	-	-	-	58.8	1.4	-	-
1976	-	-	59.3	0.9	-	-	-	-	60.0	1.2	-	-	-	-	61.0	1.7	-	-	-	-	61.6	1.0	-	-
1977	-	-	62.9	2.1	-	-	-	-	64.3	2.2	-	-	-	-	64.8	0.8	-	-	-	-	65.7	1.4	-	-
1978	-	-	66.5	1.2	-	-	67.0	0.8	-	-	68.3	1.9	-	-	69.0	1.0	-	-	70.2	1.7	-	-	70.8	0.9
1979	-	-	72.0	1.7	-	-	73.3	1.8	-	-	74.2	1.2	-	-	76.1	2.6	-	-	77.5	1.8	-	-	78.4	1.2
1980	-	-	80.8	3.1	-	-	82.9	2.6	-	-	83.5	0.7	-	-	84.0	0.6	-	-	85.0	1.2	-	-	87.4	2.8
1981	-	-	89.1	1.9	-	-	90.3	1.3	-	-	91.2	1.0	-	-	92.3	1.2	-	-	93.1	0.9	-	-	93.7	0.6
1982	-	-	92.2	-1.6	-	-	91.6	-0.7	-	-	94.2	2.8	-	-	94.9	0.7	-	-	98.3	3.6	-	-	98.5	0.2
1983	-	-	99.4	0.9	-	-	100.2	0.8	-	-	100.8	0.6	-	-	101.4	0.6	-	-	102.3	0.9	-	-	102.2	-0.1
1984	-	-	103.0	0.8	-	-	103.9	0.9	-	-	103.7	-0.2	-	-	104.4	0.7	-	-	105.0	0.6	-	-	107.6	2.5
1985	-	-	106.8	-0.7	-	-	108.3	1.4	-	-	109.0	0.6	-	-	108.7	-0.3	-	-	109.7	0.9	-	-	109.9	0.2
1986	-	-	110.0	0.1	-	-	109.2	-0.7	-	-	109.5	0.3	-	-	109.0	-0.5	-	-	109.7	0.6	-	-	110.4	0.6
1987	-	-	-	-	-	-	-	-	-	-	111.8	1.3	-	-	-	-	-	-	-	-	-	-	114.2	2.1
1988	-	-	-	-	-	-	-	-	-	-	115.9	1.5	-	-	-	-	-	-	-	-	-	-	118.9	2.6
1989	-	-	-	-	-	-	-	-	-	-	120.7	1.5	-	-	-	-	-	-	-	-	-	-	122.4	1.4
1990	-	-	-	-	-	-	-	-	-	-	125.8	2.8	-	-	-	-	-	-	-	-	-	-	129.7	3.1
1991	-	-	-	-	-	-	-	-	-	-	132.7	2.3	-	-	-	-	-	-	-	-	-	-	134.1	1.1
1992	-	-	-	-	-	-	-	-	-	-	136.0	1.4	-	-	-	-	-	-	-	-	-	-	139.8	2.8
1993	-	-	-	-	-	-	-	-	-	-	141.2	1.0	-	-	-	-	-	-	-	-	-	-	-	-

Source: U.S. Department of Labor, Bureau of Labor Statistics, Division of Consumer Prices and Price Indexes. - indicates no data collected for period.

Buffalo, NY
Consumer Price Index - Urban Wage Earners
Base 1982-1984 = 100
All Items

For 1963-1993. Columns headed % show percentile change in the index from the previous period for which an index is available.

Year	Jan Index	%	Feb Index	%	Mar Index	%	Apr Index	%	May Index	%	Jun Index	%	Jul Index	%	Aug Index	%	Sep Index	%	Oct Index	%	Nov Index	%	Dec Index	%
1963	-	-	-	-	-	-	-	-	-	-	-	-	-	-	-	-	-	-	-	-	32.7	-	-	-
1964	-	-	32.7	0.0	-	-	-	-	32.9	0.6	-	-	-	-	33.1	0.6	-	-	-	-	33.4	0.9	-	-
1965	-	-	33.5	0.3	-	-	-	-	33.7	0.6	-	-	-	-	34.0	0.9	-	-	-	-	34.2	0.6	-	-
1966	-	-	34.6	1.2	-	-	-	-	34.8	0.6	-	-	-	-	35.2	1.1	-	-	-	-	35.3	0.3	-	-
1967	-	-	35.4	0.3	-	-	-	-	35.8	1.1	-	-	-	-	36.1	0.8	-	-	-	-	36.3	0.6	-	-
1968	-	-	36.7	1.1	-	-	-	-	37.3	1.6	-	-	-	-	37.8	1.3	-	-	-	-	38.2	1.1	-	-
1969	-	-	38.3	0.3	-	-	-	-	39.3	2.6	-	-	-	-	39.6	0.8	-	-	-	-	40.3	1.8	-	-
1970	-	-	40.9	1.5	-	-	-	-	41.5	1.5	-	-	-	-	41.8	0.7	-	-	-	-	42.6	1.9	-	-
1971	-	-	43.0	0.9	-	-	-	-	43.6	1.4	-	-	-	-	44.1	1.1	-	-	-	-	44.2	0.2	-	-
1972	-	-	44.9	1.6	-	-	-	-	45.3	0.9	-	-	-	-	45.5	0.4	-	-	-	-	46.2	1.5	-	-
1973	-	-	46.8	1.3	-	-	-	-	47.8	2.1	-	-	-	-	49.1	2.7	-	-	-	-	49.8	1.4	-	-
1974	-	-	51.8	4.0	-	-	-	-	53.0	2.3	-	-	-	-	54.4	2.6	-	-	-	-	55.7	2.4	-	-
1975	-	-	56.6	1.6	-	-	-	-	57.6	1.8	-	-	-	-	58.7	1.9	-	-	-	-	59.5	1.4	-	-
1976	-	-	60.0	0.8	-	-	-	-	60.7	1.2	-	-	-	-	61.8	1.8	-	-	-	-	62.4	1.0	-	-
1977	-	-	63.7	2.1	-	-	-	-	65.1	2.2	-	-	-	-	65.6	0.8	-	-	-	-	66.5	1.4	-	-
1978	-	-	67.3	1.2	-	-	67.9	0.9	-	-	69.3	2.1	-	-	69.9	0.9	-	-	71.0	1.6	-	-	71.6	0.8
1979	-	-	72.9	1.8	-	-	74.4	2.1	-	-	75.3	1.2	-	-	77.3	2.7	-	-	78.5	1.6	-	-	79.3	1.0
1980	-	-	81.8	3.2	-	-	83.8	2.4	-	-	84.3	0.6	-	-	84.6	0.4	-	-	85.5	1.1	-	-	88.1	3.0
1981	-	-	89.7	1.8	-	-	90.8	1.2	-	-	92.0	1.3	-	-	93.2	1.3	-	-	93.8	0.6	-	-	94.3	0.5
1982	-	-	92.7	-1.7	-	-	92.1	-0.6	-	-	94.8	2.9	-	-	95.3	0.5	-	-	98.5	3.4	-	-	98.8	0.3
1983	-	-	99.3	0.5	-	-	100.0	0.7	-	-	101.7	1.7	-	-	102.4	0.7	-	-	103.0	0.6	-	-	102.6	-0.4
1984	-	-	102.7	0.1	-	-	102.9	0.2	-	-	103.2	0.3	-	-	103.6	0.4	-	-	104.9	1.3	-	-	104.1	-0.8
1985	-	-	103.5	-0.6	-	-	104.8	1.3	-	-	105.5	0.7	-	-	105.2	-0.3	-	-	106.1	0.9	-	-	106.3	0.2
1986	-	-	106.2	-0.1	-	-	105.1	-1.0	-	-	105.6	0.5	-	-	105.0	-0.6	-	-	105.7	0.7	-	-	106.3	0.6
1987	-	-	-	-	-	-	-	-	-	-	107.8	1.4	-	-	-	-	-	-	-	-	-	-	110.2	2.2
1988	-	-	-	-	-	-	-	-	-	-	111.7	1.4	-	-	-	-	-	-	-	-	-	-	114.6	2.6
1989	-	-	-	-	-	-	-	-	-	-	116.5	1.7	-	-	-	-	-	-	-	-	-	-	118.2	1.5
1990	-	-	-	-	-	-	-	-	-	-	121.2	2.5	-	-	-	-	-	-	-	-	-	-	125.2	3.3
1991	-	-	-	-	-	-	-	-	-	-	128.0	2.2	-	-	-	-	-	-	-	-	-	-	129.6	1.3
1992	-	-	-	-	-	-	-	-	-	-	131.2	1.2	-	-	-	-	-	-	-	-	-	-	135.0	2.9
1993	-	-	-	-	-	-	-	-	-	-	136.1	0.8	-	-	-	-	-	-	-	-	-	-	-	-

Source: U.S. Department of Labor, Bureau of Labor Statistics, Division of Consumer Prices and Price Indexes. - indicates no data collected for period.

Buffalo, NY
Consumer Price Index - All Urban Consumers
Base 1982-1984 = 100
Food and Beverages

For 1975-1993. Columns headed % show percentile change in the index from the previous period for which an index is available.

Year	Jan Index	%	Feb Index	%	Mar Index	%	Apr Index	%	May Index	%	Jun Index	%	Jul Index	%	Aug Index	%	Sep Index	%	Oct Index	%	Nov Index	%	Dec Index	%
1975	-	-	-	-	-	-	-	-	-	-	-	-	-	-	-	-	-	-	-	-	62.5	-	-	-
1976	-	-	63.3	1.3	-	-	-	-	62.7	-0.9	-	-	-	-	63.7	1.6	-	-	-	-	63.4	-0.5	-	-
1977	-	-	66.0	4.1	-	-	-	-	66.7	1.1	-	-	-	-	67.4	1.0	-	-	-	-	67.8	0.6	-	-
1978	-	-	69.8	2.9	-	-	71.3	2.1	-	-	74.3	4.2	-	-	73.8	-0.7	-	-	74.2	0.5	-	-	75.1	1.2
1979	-	-	77.6	3.3	-	-	79.8	2.8	-	-	80.7	1.1	-	-	80.1	-0.7	-	-	81.1	1.2	-	-	82.5	1.7
1980	-	-	83.7	1.5	-	-	84.3	0.7	-	-	86.2	2.3	-	-	87.6	1.6	-	-	89.8	2.5	-	-	91.6	2.0
1981	-	-	93.4	2.0	-	-	94.1	0.7	-	-	94.1	0.0	-	-	94.9	0.9	-	-	94.4	-0.5	-	-	94.9	0.5
1982	-	-	96.5	1.7	-	-	96.6	0.1	-	-	99.0	2.5	-	-	98.0	-1.0	-	-	97.9	-0.1	-	-	97.8	-0.1
1983	-	-	99.2	1.4	-	-	99.6	0.4	-	-	100.5	0.9	-	-	100.0	-0.5	-	-	99.7	-0.3	-	-	100.9	1.2
1984	-	-	103.2	2.3	-	-	103.3	0.1	-	-	102.4	-0.9	-	-	102.7	0.3	-	-	102.4	-0.3	-	-	102.2	-0.2
1985	-	-	104.9	2.6	-	-	106.9	1.9	-	-	106.2	-0.7	-	-	105.5	-0.7	-	-	105.8	0.3	-	-	106.7	0.9
1986	-	-	107.3	0.6	-	-	106.9	-0.4	-	-	107.6	0.7	-	-	109.9	2.1	-	-	110.1	0.2	-	-	110.2	0.1
1987	-	-	-	-	-	-	-	-	-	-	111.7	1.4	-	-	-	-	-	-	-	-	-	-	112.6	0.8
1988	-	-	-	-	-	-	-	-	-	-	114.7	1.9	-	-	-	-	-	-	-	-	-	-	118.8	3.6
1989	-	-	-	-	-	-	-	-	-	-	123.7	4.1	-	-	-	-	-	-	-	-	-	-	127.9	3.4
1990	-	-	-	-	-	-	-	-	-	-	130.9	2.3	-	-	-	-	-	-	-	-	-	-	132.2	1.0
1991	-	-	-	-	-	-	-	-	-	-	136.2	3.0	-	-	-	-	-	-	-	-	-	-	135.9	-0.2
1992	-	-	-	-	-	-	-	-	-	-	136.3	0.3	-	-	-	-	-	-	-	-	-	-	138.0	1.2
1993	-	-	-	-	-	-	-	-	-	-	137.6	-0.3	-	-	-	-	-	-	-	-	-	-	-	-

Source: U.S. Department of Labor, Bureau of Labor Statistics, Division of Consumer Prices and Price Indexes. - indicates no data collected for period.

Buffalo, NY
Consumer Price Index - Urban Wage Earners
Base 1982-1984 = 100
Food and Beverages

For 1975-1993. Columns headed % show percentile change in the index from the previous period for which an index is available.

Year	Jan Index	%	Feb Index	%	Mar Index	%	Apr Index	%	May Index	%	Jun Index	%	Jul Index	%	Aug Index	%	Sep Index	%	Oct Index	%	Nov Index	%	Dec Index	%
1975	-	-	-	-	-	-	-	-	-	-	-	-	-	-	-	-	-	-	-	-	63.5	-	-	-
1976	-	-	64.3	1.3	-	-	-	-	63.7	-0.9	-	-	-	-	64.7	1.6	-	-	-	-	64.4	-0.5	-	-
1977	-	-	67.0	4.0	-	-	-	-	67.7	1.0	-	-	-	-	68.5	1.2	-	-	-	-	68.8	0.4	-	-
1978	-	-	70.9	3.1	-	-	72.4	2.1	-	-	75.2	3.9	-	-	75.1	-0.1	-	-	75.4	0.4	-	-	76.1	0.9
1979	-	-	78.5	3.2	-	-	81.5	3.8	-	-	82.2	0.9	-	-	82.1	-0.1	-	-	82.4	0.4	-	-	83.0	0.7
1980	-	-	84.5	1.8	-	-	85.5	1.2	-	-	87.2	2.0	-	-	88.6	1.6	-	-	90.8	2.5	-	-	92.6	2.0
1981	-	-	94.0	1.5	-	-	94.0	0.0	-	-	94.5	0.5	-	-	95.4	1.0	-	-	94.6	-0.8	-	-	95.2	0.6
1982	-	-	96.5	1.4	-	-	96.8	0.3	-	-	99.3	2.6	-	-	98.0	-1.3	-	-	97.9	-0.1	-	-	97.9	0.0
1983	-	-	99.2	1.3	-	-	99.3	0.1	-	-	100.5	1.2	-	-	99.9	-0.6	-	-	99.6	-0.3	-	-	100.7	1.1
1984	-	-	103.3	2.6	-	-	103.5	0.2	-	-	102.3	-1.2	-	-	102.6	0.3	-	-	102.4	-0.2	-	-	102.3	-0.1
1985	-	-	105.0	2.6	-	-	107.1	2.0	-	-	106.4	-0.7	-	-	105.6	-0.8	-	-	106.1	0.5	-	-	106.9	0.8
1986	-	-	107.5	0.6	-	-	107.0	-0.5	-	-	107.6	0.6	-	-	110.5	2.7	-	-	110.3	-0.2	-	-	110.0	-0.3
1987	-	-	-	-	-	-	-	-	-	-	111.7	1.5	-	-	-	-	-	-	-	-	-	-	112.6	0.8
1988	-	-	-	-	-	-	-	-	-	-	114.7	1.9	-	-	-	-	-	-	-	-	-	-	118.7	3.5
1989	-	-	-	-	-	-	-	-	-	-	123.6	4.1	-	-	-	-	-	-	-	-	-	-	127.7	3.3
1990	-	-	-	-	-	-	-	-	-	-	130.7	2.3	-	-	-	-	-	-	-	-	-	-	132.1	1.1
1991	-	-	-	-	-	-	-	-	-	-	135.7	2.7	-	-	-	-	-	-	-	-	-	-	135.6	-0.1
1992	-	-	-	-	-	-	-	-	-	-	136.1	0.4	-	-	-	-	-	-	-	-	-	-	137.8	1.2
1993	-	-	-	-	-	-	-	-	-	-	137.4	-0.3	-	-	-	-	-	-	-	-	-	-	-	-

Source: U.S. Department of Labor, Bureau of Labor Statistics, Division of Consumer Prices and Price Indexes. - indicates no data collected for period.

Buffalo, NY
Consumer Price Index - All Urban Consumers
Base 1982-1984 = 100
Housing

For 1975-1993. Columns headed % show percentile change in the index from the previous period for which an index is available.

Year	Jan Index	%	Feb Index	%	Mar Index	%	Apr Index	%	May Index	%	Jun Index	%	Jul Index	%	Aug Index	%	Sep Index	%	Oct Index	%	Nov Index	%	Dec Index	%
1975	-	-	-	-	-	-	-	-	-	-	-	-	-	-	-	-	-	-	-	-	57.8	-	-	-
1976	-	-	58.1	0.5	-	-	-	-	58.7	1.0	-	-	-	-	60.1	2.4	-	-	-	-	60.7	1.0	-	-
1977	-	-	62.0	2.1	-	-	-	-	63.5	2.4	-	-	-	-	63.8	0.5	-	-	-	-	65.0	1.9	-	-
1978	-	-	65.4	0.6	-	-	65.7	0.5	-	-	66.2	0.8	-	-	67.3	1.7	-	-	69.1	2.7	-	-	69.7	0.9
1979	-	-	70.9	1.7	-	-	71.2	0.4	-	-	71.4	0.3	-	-	73.8	3.4	-	-	75.7	2.6	-	-	76.6	1.2
1980	-	-	79.0	3.1	-	-	82.2	4.1	-	-	82.3	0.1	-	-	81.4	-1.1	-	-	81.7	0.4	-	-	86.0	5.3
1981	-	-	86.9	1.0	-	-	87.4	0.6	-	-	89.4	2.3	-	-	91.1	1.9	-	-	91.7	0.7	-	-	92.5	0.9
1982	-	-	87.9	-5.0	-	-	87.0	-1.0	-	-	91.0	4.6	-	-	92.5	1.6	-	-	99.1	7.1	-	-	99.4	0.3
1983	-	-	101.5	2.1	-	-	102.0	0.5	-	-	102.0	0.0	-	-	102.7	0.7	-	-	103.5	0.8	-	-	102.5	-1.0
1984	-	-	102.7	0.2	-	-	104.0	1.3	-	-	104.1	0.1	-	-	105.3	1.2	-	-	105.5	0.2	-	-	112.6	6.7
1985	-	-	108.7	-3.5	-	-	109.3	0.6	-	-	110.4	1.0	-	-	110.1	-0.3	-	-	111.3	1.1	-	-	110.9	-0.4
1986	-	-	111.9	0.9	-	-	113.3	1.3	-	-	113.2	-0.1	-	-	111.7	-1.3	-	-	112.0	0.3	-	-	112.7	0.6
1987	-	-	-	-	-	-	-	-	-	-	113.1	0.4	-	-	-	-	-	-	-	-	-	-	116.5	3.0
1988	-	-	-	-	-	-	-	-	-	-	118.4	1.6	-	-	-	-	-	-	-	-	-	-	121.8	2.9
1989	-	-	-	-	-	-	-	-	-	-	123.6	1.5	-	-	-	-	-	-	-	-	-	-	126.4	2.3
1990	-	-	-	-	-	-	-	-	-	-	130.2	3.0	-	-	-	-	-	-	-	-	-	-	133.8	2.8
1991	-	-	-	-	-	-	-	-	-	-	138.2	3.3	-	-	-	-	-	-	-	-	-	-	140.7	1.8
1992	-	-	-	-	-	-	-	-	-	-	144.2	2.5	-	-	-	-	-	-	-	-	-	-	148.1	2.7
1993	-	-	-	-	-	-	-	-	-	-	150.6	1.7	-	-	-	-	-	-	-	-	-	-	-	-

Source: U.S. Department of Labor, Bureau of Labor Statistics, Division of Consumer Prices and Price Indexes. - indicates no data collected for period.

Buffalo, NY
Consumer Price Index - Urban Wage Earners
Base 1982-1984 = 100
Housing

For 1975-1993. Columns headed % show percentile change in the index from the previous period for which an index is available.

Year	Jan Index	%	Feb Index	%	Mar Index	%	Apr Index	%	May Index	%	Jun Index	%	Jul Index	%	Aug Index	%	Sep Index	%	Oct Index	%	Nov Index	%	Dec Index	%
1975	-	-	-	-	-	-	-	-	-	-	-	-	-	-	-	-	-	-	-	-	58.6	-	-	-
1976	-	-	58.9	0.5	-	-	-	-	59.5	1.0	-	-	-	-	61.0	2.5	-	-	-	-	61.6	1.0	-	-
1977	-	-	62.8	1.9	-	-	-	-	64.3	2.4	-	-	-	-	64.7	0.6	-	-	-	-	65.9	1.9	-	-
1978	-	-	66.3	0.6	-	-	66.5	0.3	-	-	67.2	1.1	-	-	68.4	1.8	-	-	70.3	2.8	-	-	71.0	1.0
1979	-	-	72.1	1.5	-	-	72.1	0.0	-	-	72.0	-0.1	-	-	74.6	3.6	-	-	76.6	2.7	-	-	77.6	1.3
1980	-	-	80.2	3.4	-	-	83.0	3.5	-	-	82.7	-0.4	-	-	81.9	-1.0	-	-	82.1	0.2	-	-	86.7	5.6
1981	-	-	87.4	0.8	-	-	88.0	0.7	-	-	90.1	2.4	-	-	92.2	2.3	-	-	92.6	0.4	-	-	93.5	1.0
1982	-	-	88.2	-5.7	-	-	87.2	-1.1	-	-	91.5	4.9	-	-	92.9	1.5	-	-	99.9	7.5	-	-	100.2	0.3
1983	-	-	101.7	1.5	-	-	102.0	0.3	-	-	104.8	2.7	-	-	105.5	0.7	-	-	105.6	0.1	-	-	103.7	-1.8
1984	-	-	102.2	-1.4	-	-	101.5	-0.7	-	-	103.0	1.5	-	-	103.6	0.6	-	-	105.7	2.0	-	-	103.6	-2.0
1985	-	-	100.1	-3.4	-	-	100.7	0.6	-	-	101.6	0.9	-	-	101.4	-0.2	-	-	102.4	1.0	-	-	102.2	-0.2
1986	-	-	103.0	0.8	-	-	104.3	1.3	-	-	104.2	-0.1	-	-	102.8	-1.3	-	-	103.1	0.3	-	-	104.0	0.9
1987	-	-	-	-	-	-	-	-	-	-	104.4	0.4	-	-	-	-	-	-	-	-	-	-	107.4	2.9
1988	-	-	-	-	-	-	-	-	-	-	108.9	1.4	-	-	-	-	-	-	-	-	-	-	112.1	2.9
1989	-	-	-	-	-	-	-	-	-	-	113.9	1.6	-	-	-	-	-	-	-	-	-	-	116.4	2.2
1990	-	-	-	-	-	-	-	-	-	-	120.0	3.1	-	-	-	-	-	-	-	-	-	-	123.2	2.7
1991	-	-	-	-	-	-	-	-	-	-	127.5	3.5	-	-	-	-	-	-	-	-	-	-	129.9	1.9
1992	-	-	-	-	-	-	-	-	-	-	133.4	2.7	-	-	-	-	-	-	-	-	-	-	136.9	2.6
1993	-	-	-	-	-	-	-	-	-	-	139.0	1.5	-	-	-	-	-	-	-	-	-	-	-	-

Source: U.S. Department of Labor, Bureau of Labor Statistics, Division of Consumer Prices and Price Indexes. - indicates no data collected for period.

Buffalo, NY
Consumer Price Index - All Urban Consumers
Base 1982-1984 = 100
Apparel and Upkeep

For 1963-1993. Columns headed % show percentile change in the index from the previous period for which an index is available.

Year	Jan Index	%	Feb Index	%	Mar Index	%	Apr Index	%	May Index	%	Jun Index	%	Jul Index	%	Aug Index	%	Sep Index	%	Oct Index	%	Nov Index	%	Dec Index	%
1963	-		-		-		-		-		-		-		-		-		-		40.0		-	
1964	-		40.1	0.2	-		-		40.0	-0.2	-		-		40.4	1.0	-		-		40.9	1.2	-	
1965	-		41.2	0.7	-		-		41.6	1.0	-		-		41.9	0.7	-		-		42.4	1.2	-	
1966	-		42.8	0.9	-		-		43.3	1.2	-		-		43.1	-0.5	-		-		43.8	1.6	-	
1967	-		44.4	1.4	-		-		45.4	2.3	-		-		45.2	-0.4	-		-		46.1	2.0	-	
1968	-		46.8	1.5	-		-		48.2	3.0	-		-		48.9	1.5	-		-		49.5	1.2	-	
1969	-		48.9	-1.2	-		-		51.9	6.1	-		-		52.0	0.2	-		-		53.9	3.7	-	
1970	-		52.5	-2.6	-		-		53.1	1.1	-		-		52.5	-1.1	-		-		55.1	5.0	-	
1971	-		54.7	-0.7	-		-		56.6	3.5	-		-		55.5	-1.9	-		-		56.5	1.8	-	
1972	-		55.4	-1.9	-		-		57.8	4.3	-		-		56.2	-2.8	-		-		58.9	4.8	-	
1973	-		60.1	2.0	-		-		60.5	0.7	-		-		61.6	1.8	-		-		61.9	0.5	-	
1974	-		63.1	1.9	-		-		65.0	3.0	-		-		67.0	3.1	-		-		68.9	2.8	-	
1975	-		68.5	-0.6	-		-		68.9	0.6	-		-		70.1	1.7	-		-		71.8	2.4	-	
1976	-		70.6	-1.7	-		-		73.8	4.5	-		-		73.0	-1.1	-		-		75.1	2.9	-	
1977	-		75.1	0.0	-		-		79.2	5.5	-		-		80.0	1.0	-		-		81.8	2.3	-	
1978	-		80.3	-1.8	-		81.1	1.0	-		81.0	-0.1	-		83.2	2.7	-		84.4	1.4	-		84.0	-0.5
1979	-		82.2	-2.1	-		84.8	3.2	-		83.8	-1.2	-		88.6	5.7	-		90.3	1.9	-		88.0	-2.5
1980	-		88.1	0.1	-		89.1	1.1	-		90.0	1.0	-		94.2	4.7	-		94.4	0.2	-		91.7	-2.9
1981	-		91.1	-0.7	-		93.7	2.9	-		93.6	-0.1	-		93.9	0.3	-		95.5	1.7	-		96.0	0.5
1982	-		95.8	-0.2	-		97.3	1.6	-		97.3	0.0	-		98.2	0.9	-		99.7	1.5	-		98.2	-1.5
1983	-		96.3	-1.9	-		100.9	4.8	-		100.4	-0.5	-		100.5	0.1	-		103.4	2.9	-		102.1	-1.3
1984	-		101.5	-0.6	-		101.1	-0.4	-		99.9	-1.2	-		101.1	1.2	-		103.9	2.8	-		104.8	0.9
1985	-		103.5	-1.2	-		110.0	6.3	-		109.6	-0.4	-		107.1	-2.3	-		111.1	3.7	-		109.3	-1.6
1986	-		108.2	-1.0	-		113.6	5.0	-		109.2	-3.9	-		112.6	3.1	-		111.5	-1.0	-		115.0	3.1
1987	-		-		-		-		-		116.7	1.5	-		-		-		-		-		119.1	2.1
1988	-		-		-		-		-		123.5	3.7	-		-		-		-		-		128.1	3.7
1989	-		-		-		-		-		113.8	-11.2	-		-		-		-		-		105.1	-7.6
1990	-		-		-		-		-		106.1	1.0	-		-		-		-		-		109.1	2.8
1991	-		-		-		-		-		109.5	0.4	-		-		-		-		-		114.5	4.6
1992	-		-		-		-		-		106.0	-7.4	-		-		-		-		-		116.7	10.1
1993	-		-		-		-		-		111.3	-4.6	-		-		-		-		-		-	

Source: U.S. Department of Labor, Bureau of Labor Statistics, Division of Consumer Prices and Price Indexes. - indicates no data collected for period.

Buffalo, NY
Consumer Price Index - Urban Wage Earners
Base 1982-1984 = 100
Apparel and Upkeep

For 1963-1993. Columns headed % show percentile change in the index from the previous period for which an index is available.

Year	Jan Index	%	Feb Index	%	Mar Index	%	Apr Index	%	May Index	%	Jun Index	%	Jul Index	%	Aug Index	%	Sep Index	%	Oct Index	%	Nov Index	%	Dec Index	%
1963	-		-		-		-		-		-		-		-		-		-		41.4		-	
1964	-		41.5	0.2	-		-		41.4	-0.2	-		-		41.8	1.0	-		-		42.4	1.4	-	
1965	-		42.6	0.5	-		-		43.0	0.9	-		-		43.4	0.9	-		-		43.9	1.2	-	
1966	-		44.3	0.9	-		-		44.8	1.1	-		-		44.6	-0.4	-		-		45.3	1.6	-	
1967	-		46.0	1.5	-		-		47.0	2.2	-		-		46.8	-0.4	-		-		47.7	1.9	-	
1968	-		48.5	1.7	-		-		49.9	2.9	-		-		50.6	1.4	-		-		51.2	1.2	-	
1969	-		50.6	-1.2	-		-		53.7	6.1	-		-		53.8	0.2	-		-		55.8	3.7	-	
1970	-		54.3	-2.7	-		-		55.0	1.3	-		-		54.3	-1.3	-		-		57.1	5.2	-	
1971	-		56.6	-0.9	-		-		58.6	3.5	-		-		57.4	-2.0	-		-		58.5	1.9	-	
1972	-		57.4	-1.9	-		-		59.8	4.2	-		-		58.1	-2.8	-		-		61.0	5.0	-	
1973	-		62.2	2.0	-		-		62.6	0.6	-		-		63.7	1.8	-		-		64.1	0.6	-	
1974	-		65.4	2.0	-		-		67.3	2.9	-		-		69.4	3.1	-		-		71.3	2.7	-	
1975	-		70.9	-0.6	-		-		71.4	0.7	-		-		72.5	1.5	-		-		74.4	2.6	-	
1976	-		73.1	-1.7	-		-		76.4	4.5	-		-		75.6	-1.0	-		-		77.8	2.9	-	
1977	-		77.7	-0.1	-		-		82.0	5.5	-		-		82.8	1.0	-		-		84.6	2.2	-	
1978	-		83.1	-1.8	-		85.6	3.0	-		85.4	-0.2	-		84.5	-1.1	-		85.2	0.8	-		85.3	0.1
1979	-		84.4	-1.1	-		86.9	3.0	-		85.1	-2.1	-		89.1	4.7	-		90.5	1.6	-		88.9	-1.8
1980	-		88.6	-0.3	-		89.4	0.9	-		90.5	1.2	-		90.7	0.2	-		90.5	-0.2	-		90.8	0.3
1981	-		88.1	-3.0	-		92.8	5.3	-		93.8	1.1	-		95.0	1.3	-		96.4	1.5	-		95.4	-1.0
1982	-		95.6	0.2	-		97.3	1.8	-		96.9	-0.4	-		98.1	1.2	-		100.0	1.9	-		98.8	-1.2
1983	-		96.8	-2.0	-		100.2	3.5	-		100.1	-0.1	-		99.6	-0.5	-		104.0	4.4	-		102.2	-1.7
1984	-		101.5	-0.7	-		101.7	0.2	-		99.5	-2.2	-		100.7	1.2	-		104.6	3.9	-		105.1	0.5
1985	-		104.6	-0.5	-		108.4	3.6	-		108.7	0.3	-		107.5	-1.1	-		110.2	2.5	-		109.0	-1.1
1986	-		107.9	-1.0	-		112.6	4.4	-		109.0	-3.2	-		111.9	2.7	-		110.9	-0.9	-		115.6	4.2
1987	-		-		-		-		-		117.0	1.2	-		-		-		-		-		119.3	2.0
1988	-		-		-		-		-		124.4	4.3	-		-		-		-		-		128.1	3.0
1989	-		-		-		-		-		114.4	-10.7	-		-		-		-		-		105.5	-7.8
1990	-		-		-		-		-		105.9	0.4	-		-		-		-		-		109.5	3.4
1991	-		-		-		-		-		109.2	-0.3	-		-		-		-		-		114.8	5.1
1992	-		-		-		-		-		106.2	-7.5	-		-		-		-		-		116.8	10.0
1993	-		-		-		-		-		110.0	-5.8	-		-		-		-		-		-	

Source: U.S. Department of Labor, Bureau of Labor Statistics, Division of Consumer Prices and Price Indexes. - indicates no data collected for period.

Buffalo, NY
Consumer Price Index - All Urban Consumers
Base 1982-1984 = 100
Transportation

For 1963-1993. Columns headed % show percentile change in the index from the previous period for which an index is available.

Year	Jan Index	%	Feb Index	%	Mar Index	%	Apr Index	%	May Index	%	Jun Index	%	Jul Index	%	Aug Index	%	Sep Index	%	Oct Index	%	Nov Index	%	Dec Index	%
1963	-	-	-	-	-	-	-	-	-	-	-	-	-	-	-	-	-	-	-	-	32.9	-	-	-
1964	-	-	32.5	-1.2	-	-	-	-	33.0	1.5	-	-	-	-	32.6	-1.2	-	-	-	-	33.1	1.5	-	-
1965	-	-	33.6	1.5	-	-	-	-	34.1	1.5	-	-	-	-	34.3	0.6	-	-	-	-	34.3	0.0	-	-
1966	-	-	34.5	0.6	-	-	-	-	34.8	0.9	-	-	-	-	35.1	0.9	-	-	-	-	35.2	0.3	-	-
1967	-	-	35.4	0.6	-	-	-	-	35.7	0.8	-	-	-	-	35.7	0.0	-	-	-	-	36.3	1.7	-	-
1968	-	-	36.4	0.3	-	-	-	-	36.6	0.5	-	-	-	-	36.8	0.5	-	-	-	-	37.1	0.8	-	-
1969	-	-	37.4	0.8	-	-	-	-	38.0	1.6	-	-	-	-	38.1	0.3	-	-	-	-	38.8	1.8	-	-
1970	-	-	39.3	1.3	-	-	-	-	39.8	1.3	-	-	-	-	39.8	0.0	-	-	-	-	40.9	2.8	-	-
1971	-	-	41.8	2.2	-	-	-	-	41.8	0.0	-	-	-	-	42.3	1.2	-	-	-	-	41.3	-2.4	-	-
1972	-	-	41.2	-0.2	-	-	-	-	42.3	2.7	-	-	-	-	42.3	0.0	-	-	-	-	42.8	1.2	-	-
1973	-	-	43.1	0.7	-	-	-	-	43.7	1.4	-	-	-	-	44.2	1.1	-	-	-	-	44.7	1.1	-	-
1974	-	-	46.1	3.1	-	-	-	-	48.6	5.4	-	-	-	-	50.0	2.9	-	-	-	-	50.3	0.6	-	-
1975	-	-	50.7	0.8	-	-	-	-	51.8	2.2	-	-	-	-	53.5	3.3	-	-	-	-	54.7	2.2	-	-
1976	-	-	55.2	0.9	-	-	-	-	57.2	3.6	-	-	-	-	58.7	2.6	-	-	-	-	59.7	1.7	-	-
1977	-	-	59.9	0.3	-	-	-	-	61.3	2.3	-	-	-	-	61.6	0.5	-	-	-	-	62.1	0.8	-	-
1978	-	-	62.1	0.0	-	-	62.5	0.6	-	-	64.3	2.9	-	-	65.2	1.4	-	-	66.0	1.2	-	-	66.4	0.6
1979	-	-	67.4	1.5	-	-	69.9	3.7	-	-	73.7	5.4	-	-	77.2	4.7	-	-	78.3	1.4	-	-	79.6	1.7
1980	-	-	84.3	5.9	-	-	86.1	2.1	-	-	86.4	0.3	-	-	87.4	1.2	-	-	88.4	1.1	-	-	89.1	0.8
1981	-	-	93.0	4.4	-	-	95.4	2.6	-	-	95.7	0.3	-	-	96.3	0.6	-	-	97.5	1.2	-	-	97.9	0.4
1982	-	-	96.9	-1.0	-	-	94.8	-2.2	-	-	97.5	2.8	-	-	98.2	0.7	-	-	99.0	0.8	-	-	99.0	0.0
1983	-	-	96.6	-2.4	-	-	97.2	0.6	-	-	99.1	2.0	-	-	100.8	1.7	-	-	101.9	1.1	-	-	102.0	0.1
1984	-	-	101.6	-0.4	-	-	102.6	1.0	-	-	103.5	0.9	-	-	103.1	-0.4	-	-	103.8	0.7	-	-	103.9	0.1
1985	-	-	103.1	-0.8	-	-	104.6	1.5	-	-	105.9	1.2	-	-	105.6	-0.3	-	-	105.9	0.3	-	-	106.5	0.6
1986	-	-	104.4	-2.0	-	-	97.4	-6.7	-	-	99.2	1.8	-	-	95.0	-4.2	-	-	95.9	0.9	-	-	96.5	0.6
1987	-	-	-	-	-	-	-	-	-	-	98.4	2.0	-	-	-	-	-	-	-	-	-	-	101.1	2.7
1988	-	-	-	-	-	-	-	-	-	-	100.9	-0.2	-	-	-	-	-	-	-	-	-	-	101.2	0.3
1989	-	-	-	-	-	-	-	-	-	-	103.1	1.9	-	-	-	-	-	-	-	-	-	-	103.4	0.3
1990	-	-	-	-	-	-	-	-	-	-	105.8	2.3	-	-	-	-	-	-	-	-	-	-	112.4	6.2
1991	-	-	-	-	-	-	-	-	-	-	112.6	0.2	-	-	-	-	-	-	-	-	-	-	111.9	-0.6
1992	-	-	-	-	-	-	-	-	-	-	112.7	0.7	-	-	-	-	-	-	-	-	-	-	115.2	2.2
1993	-	-	-	-	-	-	-	-	-	-	116.7	1.3	-	-	-	-	-	-	-	-	-	-	-	-

Source: U.S. Department of Labor, Bureau of Labor Statistics, Division of Consumer Prices and Price Indexes. - indicates no data collected for period.

Buffalo, NY
Consumer Price Index - Urban Wage Earners
Base 1982-1984 = 100
Transportation

For 1963-1993. Columns headed % show percentile change in the index from the previous period for which an index is available.

Year	Jan Index	%	Feb Index	%	Mar Index	%	Apr Index	%	May Index	%	Jun Index	%	Jul Index	%	Aug Index	%	Sep Index	%	Oct Index	%	Nov Index	%	Dec Index	%
1963	-		-		-		-		-				-		-		-		-		32.7		-	
1964	-		32.3	-1.2	-		-		32.8	1.5	-		-		32.4	-1.2	-		-		32.8	1.2	-	
1965	-		33.4	1.8	-		-		33.8	1.2	-		-		34.0	0.6	-		-		34.1	0.3	-	
1966	-		34.3	0.6	-		-		34.5	0.6	-		-		34.9	1.2	-		-		34.9	0.0	-	
1967	-		35.2	0.9	-		-		35.5	0.9	-		-		35.4	-0.3	-		-		36.0	1.7	-	
1968	-		36.1	0.3	-		-		36.3	0.6	-		-		36.5	0.6	-		-		36.8	0.8	-	
1969	-		37.2	1.1	-		-		37.7	1.3	-		-		37.8	0.3	-		-		38.5	1.9	-	
1970	-		39.0	1.3	-		-		39.5	1.3	-		-		39.5	0.0	-		-		40.6	2.8	-	
1971	-		41.5	2.2	-		-		41.5	0.0	-		-		42.0	1.2	-		-		41.0	-2.4	-	
1972	-		40.9	-0.2	-		-		42.0	2.7	-		-		42.0	0.0	-		-		42.5	1.2	-	
1973	-		42.8	0.7	-		-		43.4	1.4	-		-		43.9	1.2	-		-		44.3	0.9	-	
1974	-		45.8	3.4	-		-		48.2	5.2	-		-		49.7	3.1	-		-		50.0	0.6	-	
1975	-		50.3	0.6	-		-		51.5	2.4	-		-		53.1	3.1	-		-		54.3	2.3	-	
1976	-		54.8	0.9	-		-		56.8	3.6	-		-		58.3	2.6	-		-		59.2	1.5	-	
1977	-		59.5	0.5	-		-		60.9	2.4	-		-		61.2	0.5	-		-		61.7	0.8	-	
1978	-		61.7	0.0	-		62.1	0.6	-		64.1	3.2	-		65.2	1.7	-		65.7	0.8	-		66.0	0.5
1979	-		67.3	2.0	-		69.9	3.9	-		73.9	5.7	-		77.5	4.9	-		78.1	0.8	-		79.3	1.5
1980	-		83.7	5.5	-		86.1	2.9	-		85.8	-0.3	-		86.8	1.2	-		87.8	1.2	-		88.6	0.9
1981	-		92.9	4.9	-		95.1	2.4	-		95.8	0.7	-		96.0	0.2	-		97.6	1.7	-		98.0	0.4
1982	-		96.8	-1.2	-		94.6	-2.3	-		97.4	3.0	-		98.2	0.8	-		98.9	0.7	-		98.9	0.0
1983	-		96.4	-2.5	-		96.9	0.5	-		99.1	2.3	-		100.9	1.8	-		102.0	1.1	-		102.2	0.2
1984	-		101.7	-0.5	-		102.8	1.1	-		103.7	0.9	-		103.3	-0.4	-		103.8	0.5	-		103.9	0.1
1985	-		103.0	-0.9	-		104.4	1.4	-		105.8	1.3	-		105.4	-0.4	-		105.7	0.3	-		106.3	0.6
1986	-		103.9	-2.3	-		96.3	-7.3	-		98.1	1.9	-		93.4	-4.8	-		94.4	1.1	-		94.9	0.5
1987	-		-		-		-		-		97.8	3.1	-		-		-		-		-		100.9	3.2
1988	-		-		-		-		-		100.4	-0.5	-		-		-		-		-		100.7	0.3
1989	-		-		-		-		-		102.7	2.0	-		-		-		-		-		103.3	0.6
1990	-		-		-		-		-		105.4	2.0	-		-		-		-		-		113.0	7.2
1991	-		-		-		-		-		112.6	-0.4	-		-		-		-		-		112.0	-0.5
1992	-		-		-		-		-		112.5	0.4	-		-		-		-		-		115.2	2.4
1993	-		-		-		-		-		115.9	0.6	-		-		-		-		-		-	

Source: U.S. Department of Labor, Bureau of Labor Statistics, Division of Consumer Prices and Price Indexes. - indicates no data collected for period.

Buffalo, NY
Consumer Price Index - All Urban Consumers
Base 1982-1984 = 100
Medical Care

For 1963-1993. Columns headed % show percentile change in the index from the previous period for which an index is available.

Year	Jan Index	%	Feb Index	%	Mar Index	%	Apr Index	%	May Index	%	Jun Index	%	Jul Index	%	Aug Index	%	Sep Index	%	Oct Index	%	Nov Index	%	Dec Index	%
1963	-		-		-		-		-		-		-		-		-		-		29.5	-	-	
1964	-		29.6	0.3	-		-		29.7	0.3	-		-		29.9	0.7	-		-		30.5	2.0	-	
1965	-		30.5	0.0	-		-		30.5	0.0	-		-		30.7	0.7	-		-		31.0	1.0	-	
1966	-		31.4	1.3	-		-		32.0	1.9	-		-		32.8	2.5	-		-		33.3	1.5	-	
1967	-		33.8	1.5	-		-		34.1	0.9	-		-		34.6	1.5	-		-		35.1	1.4	-	
1968	-		35.4	0.9	-		-		35.4	0.0	-		-		35.9	1.4	-		-		36.3	1.1	-	
1969	-		36.8	1.4	-		-		37.4	1.6	-		-		37.7	0.8	-		-		38.0	0.8	-	
1970	-		38.8	2.1	-		-		39.6	2.1	-		-		40.0	1.0	-		-		40.6	1.5	-	
1971	-		41.2	1.5	-		-		41.8	1.5	-		-		42.6	1.9	-		-		42.6	0.0	-	
1972	-		43.1	1.2	-		-		43.3	0.5	-		-		43.4	0.2	-		-		43.6	0.5	-	
1973	-		44.2	1.4	-		-		44.6	0.9	-		-		44.8	0.4	-		-		45.5	1.6	-	
1974	-		47.3	4.0	-		-		48.1	1.7	-		-		49.6	3.1	-		-		50.5	1.8	-	
1975	-		52.1	3.2	-		-		53.0	1.7	-		-		53.9	1.7	-		-		54.6	1.3	-	
1976	-		56.6	3.7	-		-		57.3	1.2	-		-		58.5	2.1	-		-		59.0	0.9	-	
1977	-		61.9	4.9	-		-		62.2	0.5	-		-		63.1	1.4	-		-		64.0	1.4	-	
1978	-		67.2	5.0	-		67.5	0.4	-		68.2	1.0	-		68.4	0.3	-		69.0	0.9	-		70.1	1.6
1979	-		71.9	2.6	-		72.0	0.1	-		73.2	1.7	-		73.9	1.0	-		74.3	0.5	-		74.8	0.7
1980	-		76.7	2.5	-		77.5	1.0	-		77.8	0.4	-		78.8	1.3	-		79.7	1.1	-		81.3	2.0
1981	-		83.5	2.7	-		84.7	1.4	-		85.6	1.1	-		86.5	1.1	-		87.5	1.2	-		87.8	0.3
1982	-		89.9	2.4	-		90.8	1.0	-		91.3	0.6	-		91.5	0.2	-		92.2	0.8	-		94.9	2.9
1983	-		99.2	4.5	-		100.3	1.1	-		100.5	0.2	-		101.7	1.2	-		102.6	0.9	-		103.0	0.4
1984	-		106.4	3.3	-		107.6	1.1	-		107.8	0.2	-		107.9	0.1	-		108.5	0.6	-		109.2	0.6
1985	-		111.1	1.7	-		111.6	0.5	-		112.7	1.0	-		114.2	1.3	-		114.9	0.6	-		115.2	0.3
1986	-		116.6	1.2	-		117.3	0.6	-		119.2	1.6	-		121.5	1.9	-		122.6	0.9	-		123.4	0.7
1987	-		-		-		-		-		126.7	2.7	-		-		-		-		-		128.6	1.5
1988	-		-		-		-		-		129.9	1.0	-		-		-		-		-		134.0	3.2
1989	-		-		-		-		-		140.4	4.8	-		-		-		-		-		143.4	2.1
1990	-		-		-		-		-		150.0	4.6	-		-		-		-		-		153.4	2.3
1991	-		-		-		-		-		157.7	2.8	-		-		-		-		-		160.4	1.7
1992	-		-		-		-		-		165.5	3.2	-		-		-		-		-		167.4	1.1
1993	-		-		-		-		-		171.8	2.6	-		-		-		-		-		-	

Source: U.S. Department of Labor, Bureau of Labor Statistics, Division of Consumer Prices and Price Indexes. - indicates no data collected for period.

Buffalo, NY
Consumer Price Index - Urban Wage Earners
Base 1982-1984 = 100
Medical Care

For 1963-1993. Columns headed % show percentile change in the index from the previous period for which an index is available.

Year	Jan Index	%	Feb Index	%	Mar Index	%	Apr Index	%	May Index	%	Jun Index	%	Jul Index	%	Aug Index	%	Sep Index	%	Oct Index	%	Nov Index	%	Dec Index	%
1963	-	-	-	-	-	-	-	-	-	-	-	-	-	-	-	-	-	-	-	-	29.0	-	-	-
1964	-	-	29.1	0.3	-	-	-	-	29.2	0.3	-	-	-	-	29.4	0.7	-	-	-	-	30.0	2.0	-	-
1965	-	-	30.0	0.0	-	-	-	-	30.0	0.0	-	-	-	-	30.1	0.3	-	-	-	-	30.5	1.3	-	-
1966	-	-	30.8	1.0	-	-	-	-	31.5	2.3	-	-	-	-	32.2	2.2	-	-	-	-	32.7	1.6	-	-
1967	-	-	33.2	1.5	-	-	-	-	33.5	0.9	-	-	-	-	34.0	1.5	-	-	-	-	34.5	1.5	-	-
1968	-	-	34.8	0.9	-	-	-	-	34.8	0.0	-	-	-	-	35.2	1.1	-	-	-	-	35.7	1.4	-	-
1969	-	-	36.1	1.1	-	-	-	-	36.8	1.9	-	-	-	-	37.1	0.8	-	-	-	-	37.3	0.5	-	-
1970	-	-	38.1	2.1	-	-	-	-	38.9	2.1	-	-	-	-	39.3	1.0	-	-	-	-	39.9	1.5	-	-
1971	-	-	40.4	1.3	-	-	-	-	41.1	1.7	-	-	-	-	41.9	1.9	-	-	-	-	41.8	-0.2	-	-
1972	-	-	42.4	1.4	-	-	-	-	42.5	0.2	-	-	-	-	42.6	0.2	-	-	-	-	42.8	0.5	-	-
1973	-	-	43.4	1.4	-	-	-	-	43.8	0.9	-	-	-	-	44.0	0.5	-	-	-	-	44.7	1.6	-	-
1974	-	-	46.4	3.8	-	-	-	-	47.3	1.9	-	-	-	-	48.7	3.0	-	-	-	-	49.6	1.8	-	-
1975	-	-	51.2	3.2	-	-	-	-	52.1	1.8	-	-	-	-	52.9	1.5	-	-	-	-	53.6	1.3	-	-
1976	-	-	55.6	3.7	-	-	-	-	56.3	1.3	-	-	-	-	57.5	2.1	-	-	-	-	58.0	0.9	-	-
1977	-	-	60.8	4.8	-	-	-	-	61.1	0.5	-	-	-	-	62.0	1.5	-	-	-	-	62.9	1.5	-	-
1978	-	-	66.0	4.9	-	-	66.2	0.3	-	-	67.1	1.4	-	-	67.4	0.4	-	-	67.5	0.1	-	-	69.2	2.5
1979	-	-	71.1	2.7	-	-	71.1	0.0	-	-	72.2	1.5	-	-	72.9	1.0	-	-	73.2	0.4	-	-	73.6	0.5
1980	-	-	76.8	4.3	-	-	77.9	1.4	-	-	79.0	1.4	-	-	79.4	0.5	-	-	81.2	2.3	-	-	81.8	0.7
1981	-	-	83.1	1.6	-	-	84.6	1.8	-	-	85.2	0.7	-	-	86.2	1.2	-	-	87.7	1.7	-	-	88.3	0.7
1982	-	-	90.3	2.3	-	-	91.1	0.9	-	-	91.6	0.5	-	-	91.8	0.2	-	-	92.5	0.8	-	-	94.8	2.5
1983	-	-	99.0	4.4	-	-	100.1	1.1	-	-	100.4	0.3	-	-	101.6	1.2	-	-	102.5	0.9	-	-	103.0	0.5
1984	-	-	106.3	3.2	-	-	107.5	1.1	-	-	107.7	0.2	-	-	107.8	0.1	-	-	108.4	0.6	-	-	109.1	0.6
1985	-	-	111.1	1.8	-	-	111.5	0.4	-	-	112.5	0.9	-	-	114.1	1.4	-	-	114.8	0.6	-	-	115.0	0.2
1986	-	-	116.2	1.0	-	-	116.9	0.6	-	-	118.8	1.6	-	-	120.9	1.8	-	-	121.9	0.8	-	-	122.7	0.7
1987	-	-	-	-	-	-	-	-	-	-	125.9	2.6	-	-	-	-	-	-	-	-	-	-	127.8	1.5
1988	-	-	-	-	-	-	-	-	-	-	128.6	0.6	-	-	-	-	-	-	-	-	-	-	133.4	3.7
1989	-	-	-	-	-	-	-	-	-	-	140.0	4.9	-	-	-	-	-	-	-	-	-	-	142.6	1.9
1990	-	-	-	-	-	-	-	-	-	-	148.8	4.3	-	-	-	-	-	-	-	-	-	-	152.0	2.2
1991	-	-	-	-	-	-	-	-	-	-	156.7	3.1	-	-	-	-	-	-	-	-	-	-	159.6	1.9
1992	-	-	-	-	-	-	-	-	-	-	164.9	3.3	-	-	-	-	-	-	-	-	-	-	167.0	1.3
1993	-	-	-	-	-	-	-	-	-	-	171.7	2.8	-	-	-	-	-	-	-	-	-	-	-	-

Source: U.S. Department of Labor, Bureau of Labor Statistics, Division of Consumer Prices and Price Indexes. - indicates no data collected for period.

Buffalo, NY
Consumer Price Index - All Urban Consumers
Base 1982-1984 = 100
Entertainment

For 1975-1993. Columns headed % show percentile change in the index from the previous period for which an index is available.

Year	Jan Index	%	Feb Index	%	Mar Index	%	Apr Index	%	May Index	%	Jun Index	%	Jul Index	%	Aug Index	%	Sep Index	%	Oct Index	%	Nov Index	%	Dec Index	%
1975	-	-	-	-	-	-	-	-	-	-	-	-	-	-	-	-	-	-	-	-	62.4	-	-	-
1976	-	-	62.3	-0.2	-	-	-	-	62.6	0.5	-	-	-	-	62.5	-0.2	-	-	-	-	64.2	2.7	-	-
1977	-	-	64.8	0.9	-	-	-	-	66.5	2.6	-	-	-	-	66.3	-0.3	-	-	-	-	67.7	2.1	-	-
1978	-	-	68.9	1.8	-	-	68.7	-0.3	-	-	70.6	2.8	-	-	69.8	-1.1	-	-	72.8	4.3	-	-	73.8	1.4
1979	-	-	72.8	-1.4	-	-	73.3	0.7	-	-	70.0	-4.5	-	-	70.2	0.3	-	-	72.8	3.7	-	-	73.1	0.4
1980	-	-	73.7	0.8	-	-	77.6	5.3	-	-	77.5	-0.1	-	-	78.9	1.8	-	-	82.6	4.7	-	-	85.5	3.5
1981	-	-	87.7	2.6	-	-	88.5	0.9	-	-	86.5	-2.3	-	-	86.6	0.1	-	-	90.0	3.9	-	-	90.6	0.7
1982	-	-	92.5	2.1	-	-	93.1	0.6	-	-	91.4	-1.8	-	-	93.5	2.3	-	-	97.7	4.5	-	-	97.5	-0.2
1983	-	-	99.6	2.2	-	-	100.0	0.4	-	-	100.6	0.6	-	-	99.4	-1.2	-	-	102.4	3.0	-	-	102.6	0.2
1984	-	-	103.7	1.1	-	-	105.8	2.0	-	-	101.9	-3.7	-	-	105.0	3.0	-	-	109.2	4.0	-	-	108.8	-0.4
1985	-	-	109.7	0.8	-	-	111.1	1.3	-	-	111.7	0.5	-	-	112.6	0.8	-	-	112.3	-0.3	-	-	112.8	0.4
1986	-	-	113.2	0.4	-	-	114.1	0.8	-	-	111.6	-2.2	-	-	112.4	0.7	-	-	118.6	5.5	-	-	119.2	0.5
1987	-	-	-	-	-	-	-	-	-	-	121.9	2.3	-	-	-	-	-	-	-	-	-	-	123.5	1.3
1988	-	-	-	-	-	-	-	-	-	-	123.5	0.0	-	-	-	-	-	-	-	-	-	-	126.7	2.6
1989	-	-	-	-	-	-	-	-	-	-	130.8	3.2	-	-	-	-	-	-	-	-	-	-	133.7	2.2
1990	-	-	-	-	-	-	-	-	-	-	140.5	5.1	-	-	-	-	-	-	-	-	-	-	145.1	3.3
1991	-	-	-	-	-	-	-	-	-	-	146.8	1.2	-	-	-	-	-	-	-	-	-	-	149.5	1.8
1992	-	-	-	-	-	-	-	-	-	-	152.9	2.3	-	-	-	-	-	-	-	-	-	-	158.5	3.7
1993	-	-	-	-	-	-	-	-	-	-	162.9	2.8	-	-	-	-	-	-	-	-	-	-	-	-

Source: U.S. Department of Labor, Bureau of Labor Statistics, Division of Consumer Prices and Price Indexes. - indicates no data collected for period.

Buffalo, NY
Consumer Price Index - Urban Wage Earners
Base 1982-1984 = 100
Entertainment

For 1975-1993. Columns headed % show percentile change in the index from the previous period for which an index is available.

Year	Jan Index	%	Feb Index	%	Mar Index	%	Apr Index	%	May Index	%	Jun Index	%	Jul Index	%	Aug Index	%	Sep Index	%	Oct Index	%	Nov Index	%	Dec Index	%
1975	-		-	-	-	-	-	-	-	-	-	-	-	-	-	-	-	-	-	-	66.7	-	-	-
1976	-	-	66.6	-0.1	-	-	-	-	66.9	0.5	-	-	-	-	66.8	-0.1	-	-	-	-	68.6	2.7	-	-
1977	-	-	69.2	0.9	-	-	-	-	71.0	2.6	-	-	-	-	70.9	-0.1	-	-	-	-	72.3	2.0	-	-
1978	-	-	73.6	1.8	-	-	72.6	-1.4	-	-	70.7	-2.6	-	-	69.5	-1.7	-	-	73.7	6.0	-	-	74.3	0.8
1979	-	-	73.2	-1.5	-	-	73.8	0.8	-	-	70.3	-4.7	-	-	70.3	0.0	-	-	73.5	4.6	-	-	74.4	1.2
1980	-	-	75.8	1.9	-	-	78.2	3.2	-	-	78.9	0.9	-	-	79.4	0.6	-	-	82.0	3.3	-	-	83.6	2.0
1981	-	-	85.2	1.9	-	-	86.6	1.6	-	-	86.8	0.2	-	-	87.4	0.7	-	-	89.9	2.9	-	-	90.4	0.6
1982	-	-	92.4	2.2	-	-	93.1	0.8	-	-	92.1	-1.1	-	-	94.5	2.6	-	-	97.6	3.3	-	-	97.4	-0.2
1983	-	-	99.6	2.3	-	-	100.1	0.5	-	-	100.3	0.2	-	-	100.5	0.2	-	-	101.9	1.4	-	-	102.4	0.5
1984	-	-	103.6	1.2	-	-	105.5	1.8	-	-	101.9	-3.4	-	-	105.3	3.3	-	-	108.4	2.9	-	-	107.7	-0.6
1985	-	-	108.5	0.7	-	-	109.9	1.3	-	-	110.6	0.6	-	-	111.4	0.7	-	-	110.9	-0.4	-	-	111.3	0.4
1986	-	-	111.8	0.4	-	-	112.7	0.8	-	-	110.9	-1.6	-	-	111.9	0.9	-	-	118.4	5.8	-	-	118.9	0.4
1987	-	-	-	-	-	-	-	-	-	-	121.2	1.9	-	-	-	-	-	-	-	-	-	-	122.9	1.4
1988	-	-	-	-	-	-	-	-	-	-	123.0	0.1	-	-	-	-	-	-	-	-	-	-	126.1	2.5
1989	-	-	-	-	-	-	-	-	-	-	129.8	2.9	-	-	-	-	-	-	-	-	-	-	132.4	2.0
1990	-	-	-	-	-	-	-	-	-	-	139.4	5.3	-	-	-	-	-	-	-	-	-	-	144.0	3.3
1991	-	-	-	-	-	-	-	-	-	-	145.5	1.0	-	-	-	-	-	-	-	-	-	-	148.0	1.7
1992	-	-	-	-	-	-	-	-	-	-	151.6	2.4	-	-	-	-	-	-	-	-	-	-	157.1	3.6
1993	-	-	-	-	-	-	-	-	-	-	161.5	2.8	-	-	-	-	-	-	-	-	-	-	-	-

Source: U.S. Department of Labor, Bureau of Labor Statistics, Division of Consumer Prices and Price Indexes. - indicates no data collected for period.

Buffalo, NY
Consumer Price Index - All Urban Consumers
Base 1982-1984 = 100
Other Goods and Services

For 1975-1993. Columns headed % show percentile change in the index from the previous period for which an index is available.

Year	Jan Index	%	Feb Index	%	Mar Index	%	Apr Index	%	May Index	%	Jun Index	%	Jul Index	%	Aug Index	%	Sep Index	%	Oct Index	%	Nov Index	%	Dec Index	%
1975	-	-	-	-	-	-	-	-	-	-	-	-	-	-	-	-	-	-	-	-	55.9	-	-	-
1976	-	-	56.9	1.8	-	-	-	-	57.6	1.2	-	-	-	-	58.3	1.2	-	-	-	-	59.6	2.2	-	-
1977	-	-	60.1	0.8	-	-	-	-	60.1	0.0	-	-	-	-	60.4	0.5	-	-	-	-	62.1	2.8	-	-
1978	-	-	62.3	0.3	-	-	62.5	0.3	-	-	62.8	0.5	-	-	63.9	1.8	-	-	64.7	1.3	-	-	64.8	0.2
1979	-	-	65.5	1.1	-	-	65.9	0.6	-	-	66.3	0.6	-	-	67.5	1.8	-	-	68.3	1.2	-	-	69.0	1.0
1980	-	-	70.4	2.0	-	-	70.7	0.4	-	-	72.3	2.3	-	-	73.2	1.2	-	-	74.7	2.0	-	-	76.3	2.1
1981	-	-	77.6	1.7	-	-	79.4	2.3	-	-	81.6	2.8	-	-	82.1	0.6	-	-	86.1	4.9	-	-	86.2	0.1
1982	-	-	88.7	2.9	-	-	90.2	1.7	-	-	90.0	-0.2	-	-	89.0	-1.1	-	-	93.1	4.6	-	-	95.9	3.0
1983	-	-	97.7	1.9	-	-	100.2	2.6	-	-	100.5	0.3	-	-	101.7	1.2	-	-	103.8	2.1	-	-	104.3	0.5
1984	-	-	105.9	1.5	-	-	107.8	1.8	-	-	107.5	-0.3	-	-	109.8	2.1	-	-	110.3	0.5	-	-	109.7	-0.5
1985	-	-	113.0	3.0	-	-	114.2	1.1	-	-	116.0	1.6	-	-	116.7	0.6	-	-	121.0	3.7	-	-	121.6	0.5
1986	-	-	122.6	0.8	-	-	123.3	0.6	-	-	124.7	1.1	-	-	126.7	1.6	-	-	128.7	1.6	-	-	129.1	0.3
1987	-	-	-	-	-	-	-	-	-	-	130.7	1.2	-	-	-	-	-	-	-	-	-	-	134.0	2.5
1988	-	-	-	-	-	-	-	-	-	-	137.5	2.6	-	-	-	-	-	-	-	-	-	-	141.5	2.9
1989	-	-	-	-	-	-	-	-	-	-	144.8	2.3	-	-	-	-	-	-	-	-	-	-	150.7	4.1
1990	-	-	-	-	-	-	-	-	-	-	151.8	0.7	-	-	-	-	-	-	-	-	-	-	158.2	4.2
1991	-	-	-	-	-	-	-	-	-	-	163.5	3.4	-	-	-	-	-	-	-	-	-	-	165.7	1.3
1992	-	-	-	-	-	-	-	-	-	-	175.6	6.0	-	-	-	-	-	-	-	-	-	-	184.5	5.1
1993	-	-	-	-	-	-	-	-	-	-	189.1	2.5	-	-	-	-	-	-	-	-	-	-	-	-

Source: U.S. Department of Labor, Bureau of Labor Statistics, Division of Consumer Prices and Price Indexes. - indicates no data collected for period.

Buffalo, NY
Consumer Price Index - Urban Wage Earners
Base 1982-1984 = 100
Other Goods and Services

For 1975-1993. Columns headed % show percentile change in the index from the previous period for which an index is available.

Year	Jan Index	%	Feb Index	%	Mar Index	%	Apr Index	%	May Index	%	Jun Index	%	Jul Index	%	Aug Index	%	Sep Index	%	Oct Index	%	Nov Index	%	Dec Index	%
1975	-	-	-	-	-	-	-	-	-	-	-	-	-	-	-	-	-	-	-	-	58.7	-	-	-
1976	-	-	59.8	1.9	-	-	-	-	60.5	1.2	-	-	-	-	61.2	1.2	-	-	-	-	58.7	-	-	-
1977	-	-	63.0	0.8	-	-	-	-	63.1	0.2	-	-	-	-	63.4	0.5	-	-	-	-	62.5	2.1	-	-
1978	-	-	65.4	0.3	-	-	66.2	1.2	-	-	65.9	-0.5	-	-	67.3	2.1	-	-	67.7	0.6	65.2	2.8	68.2	0.7
1979	-	-	69.1	1.3	-	-	70.2	1.6	-	-	70.4	0.3	-	-	71.4	1.4	-	-	72.2	1.1	-	-	73.0	1.1
1980	-	-	74.9	2.6	-	-	74.5	-0.5	-	-	76.8	3.1	-	-	77.8	1.3	-	-	77.6	-0.3	-	-	80.0	3.1
1981	-	-	81.1	1.4	-	-	81.9	1.0	-	-	83.5	2.0	-	-	84.0	0.6	-	-	87.5	4.2	-	-	86.5	-1.1
1982	-	-	88.7	2.5	-	-	90.2	1.7	-	-	90.1	-0.1	-	-	89.2	-1.0	-	-	92.8	4.0	-	-	95.9	3.3
1983	-	-	97.8	2.0	-	-	100.7	3.0	-	-	100.8	0.1	-	-	102.3	1.5	-	-	103.9	1.6	-	-	104.4	0.5
1984	-	-	106.0	1.5	-	-	107.3	1.2	-	-	107.1	-0.2	-	-	109.2	2.0	-	-	110.1	0.8	-	-	109.3	-0.7
1985	-	-	112.3	2.7	-	-	113.0	0.6	-	-	114.6	1.4	-	-	115.2	0.5	-	-	119.3	3.6	-	-	119.6	0.3
1986	-	-	120.7	0.9	-	-	121.5	0.7	-	-	123.0	1.2	-	-	125.1	1.7	-	-	126.9	1.4	-	-	127.2	0.2
1987	-	-	-	-	-	-	-	-	-	-	128.7	1.2	-	-	-	-	-	-	-	-	-	-	132.2	2.7
1988	-	-	-	-	-	-	-	-	-	-	135.7	2.6	-	-	-	-	-	-	-	-	-	-	139.9	3.1
1989	-	-	-	-	-	-	-	-	-	-	142.9	2.1	-	-	-	-	-	-	-	-	-	-	149.6	4.7
1990	-	-	-	-	-	-	-	-	-	-	151.1	1.0	-	-	-	-	-	-	-	-	-	-	157.0	3.9
1991	-	-	-	-	-	-	-	-	-	-	163.0	3.8	-	-	-	-	-	-	-	-	-	-	166.0	1.8
1992	-	-	-	-	-	-	-	-	-	-	175.3	5.6	-	-	-	-	-	-	-	-	-	-	185.5	5.8
1993	-	-	-	-	-	-	-	-	-	-	190.7	2.8	-	-	-	-	-	-	-	-	-	-	-	-

Source: U.S. Department of Labor, Bureau of Labor Statistics, Division of Consumer Prices and Price Indexes. - indicates no data collected for period.

Chicago, IL-NW IN
Consumer Price Index - All Urban Consumers
Base 1982-1984 = 100
Annual Averages

For 1914-1993. Columns headed % show percentile change in the index from the previous period for which an index is available.

Year	All Items Index	%	Food & Beverage Index	%	Housing Index	%	Apparel & Upkeep Index	%	Trans-portation Index	%	Medical Care Index	%	Entertain-ment Index	%	Other Goods & Services Index	%
1914	-	-	-	-	-	-	-	-	-	-	-	-	-	-	-	-
1915	10.1	-	-	-	-	-	-	-	-	-	-	-	-	-	-	-
1916	10.9	7.9	-	-	-	-	-	-	-	-	-	-	-	-	-	-
1917	12.9	18.3	-	-	-	-	-	-	-	-	-	-	-	-	-	-
1918	14.9	15.5	-	-	-	-	-	-	-	-	-	-	-	-	-	-
1919	17.3	16.1	-	-	-	-	-	-	-	-	-	-	-	-	-	-
1920	19.8	14.5	-	-	-	-	-	-	-	-	-	-	-	-	-	-
1921	18.0	-9.1	-	-	-	-	-	-	-	-	-	-	-	-	-	-
1922	17.0	-5.6	-	-	-	-	-	-	-	-	-	-	-	-	-	-
1923	17.4	2.4	-	-	-	-	-	-	-	-	-	-	-	-	-	-
1924	17.7	1.7	-	-	-	-	-	-	-	-	-	-	-	-	-	-
1925	18.2	2.8	-	-	-	-	-	-	-	-	-	-	-	-	-	-
1926	18.3	0.5	-	-	-	-	-	-	-	-	-	-	-	-	-	-
1927	17.9	-2.2	-	-	-	-	-	-	-	-	-	-	-	-	-	-
1928	17.7	-1.1	-	-	-	-	-	-	-	-	-	-	-	-	-	-
1929	17.6	-0.6	-	-	-	-	-	-	-	-	-	-	-	-	-	-
1930	17.2	-2.3	-	-	-	-	-	-	-	-	-	-	-	-	-	-
1931	15.6	-9.3	-	-	-	-	-	-	-	-	-	-	-	-	-	-
1932	13.7	-12.2	-	-	-	-	-	-	-	-	-	-	-	-	-	-
1933	12.6	-8.0	-	-	-	-	-	-	-	-	-	-	-	-	-	-
1934	12.8	1.6	-	-	-	-	-	-	-	-	-	-	-	-	-	-
1935	13.4	4.7	-	-	-	-	-	-	-	-	-	-	-	-	-	-
1936	13.5	0.7	-	-	-	-	-	-	-	-	-	-	-	-	-	-
1937	14.2	5.2	-	-	-	-	-	-	-	-	-	-	-	-	-	-
1938	13.9	-2.1	-	-	-	-	-	-	-	-	-	-	-	-	-	-
1939	13.7	-1.4	-	-	-	-	-	-	-	-	-	-	-	-	-	-
1940	13.8	0.7	-	-	-	-	-	-	-	-	-	-	-	-	-	-
1941	14.5	5.1	-	-	-	-	-	-	-	-	-	-	-	-	-	-
1942	16.0	10.3	-	-	-	-	-	-	-	-	-	-	-	-	-	-
1943	16.9	5.6	-	-	-	-	-	-	-	-	-	-	-	-	-	-
1944	17.1	1.2	-	-	-	-	-	-	-	-	-	-	-	-	-	-
1945	17.5	2.3	-	-	-	-	-	-	-	-	-	-	-	-	-	-
1946	19.0	8.6	-	-	-	-	-	-	-	-	-	-	-	-	-	-
1947	22.1	16.3	-	-	-	-	-	-	17.5	-	12.1	-	-	-	-	-
1948	24.0	8.6	-	-	-	-	.-	-	20.2	15.4	12.9	6.6	-	-	-	-
1949	24.0	0.0	-	-	-	-	-	-	22.0	8.9	13.5	4.7	-	-	-	-
1950	24.2	0.8	-	-	-	-	-	-	22.6	2.7	13.7	1.5	-	-	-	-
1951	26.1	7.9	-	-	-	-	-	-	23.9	5.8	14.5	5.8	-	-	-	-
1952	26.7	2.3	-	-	-	-	-	-	26.0	8.8	14.9	2.8	-	-	-	-
1953	26.9	0.7	-	-	-	-	52.4	-	26.6	2.3	15.5	4.0	-	-	-	-
1954	27.4	1.9	-	-	-	-	52.7	0.6	26.4	-0.8	15.9	2.6	-	-	-	-
1955	27.5	0.4	-	-	-	-	52.3	-0.8	26.2	-0.8	16.6	4.4	-	-	-	-
1956	27.9	1.5	-	-	-	-	54.0	3.3	26.7	1.9	17.6	6.0	-	-	-	-
1957	28.8	3.2	-	-	-	-	54.8	1.5	28.4	6.4	18.3	4.0	-	-	-	-
1958	29.7	3.1	-	-	-	-	55.0	0.4	30.0	5.6	19.4	6.0	-	-	-	-

[Continued]

340

Chicago, IL-NW IN
Consumer Price Index - All Urban Consumers
Base 1982-1984 = 100
Annual Averages
[Continued]

For 1914-1993. Columns headed % show percentile change in the index from the previous period for which an index is available.

Year	All Items		Food & Beverage		Housing		Apparel & Upkeep		Trans- portation		Medical Care		Entertain- ment		Other Goods & Services	
	Index	%	Index	%	Index	%	Index	%	Index	%	Index	%	Index	%	Index	%
1959	29.9	0.7	-	-	-	-	55.5	0.9	31.0	3.3	20.3	4.6	-	-	-	-
1960	30.4	1.7	-	-	-	-	56.4	1.6	31.1	0.3	21.5	5.9	-	-	-	-
1961	30.5	0.3	-	-	-	-	56.0	-0.7	30.9	-0.6	22.0	2.3	-	-	-	-
1962	30.8	1.0	-	-	-	-	55.8	-0.4	31.5	1.9	22.7	3.2	-	-	-	-
1963	31.1	1.0	-	-	-	-	56.0	0.4	31.7	0.6	24.3	7.0	-	-	-	-
1964	31.3	0.6	-	-	-	-	56.2	0.4	31.8	0.3	24.7	1.6	-	-	-	-
1965	31.7	1.3	-	-	-	-	56.8	1.1	32.6	2.5	25.1	1.6	-	-	-	-
1966	32.6	2.8	-	-	-	-	58.3	2.6	32.6	0.0	25.9	3.2	-	-	-	-
1967	33.5	2.8	-	-	-	-	60.6	3.9	33.5	2.8	28.0	8.1	-	-	-	-
1968	34.9	4.2	-	-	-	-	63.8	5.3	35.0	4.5	29.6	5.7	-	-	-	-
1969	36.8	5.4	-	-	-	-	66.9	4.9	37.2	6.3	31.4	6.1	-	-	-	-
1970	38.9	5.7	-	-	-	-	68.6	2.5	39.7	6.7	33.5	6.7	-	-	-	-
1971	40.4	3.9	-	-	-	-	71.1	3.6	42.1	6.0	35.9	7.2			-	-
1972	41.6	3.0	-	-	-	-	72.5	2.0	41.7	-1.0	36.8	2.5			-	-
1973	44.2	6.3	-	-	-	-	76.0	4.8	42.9	2.9	38.3	4.1			-	-
1974	48.9	10.6	-	-	-	-	80.4	5.8	47.2	10.0	42.0	9.7			-	-
1975	52.8	8.0	-	-	-	-	82.7	2.9	50.9	7.8	47.3	12.6	-	-	-	-
1976	55.3	4.7	64.2	-	48.5	-	83.7	1.2	56.1	10.2	52.8	11.6	61.7	-	58.0	-
1977	58.8	6.3	67.9	5.8	51.5	6.2	86.2	3.0	60.8	8.4	58.0	9.8	64.6	4.7	62.2	7.2
1978	63.8	8.5	75.8	11.6	57.3	11.3	88.0	2.1	63.1	3.8	62.1	7.1	68.0	5.3	65.8	5.8
1979	71.8	12.5	83.8	10.6	66.1	15.4	90.5	2.8	71.7	13.6	67.6	8.9	75.7	11.3	69.7	5.9
1980	82.2	14.5	91.2	8.8	77.4	17.1	95.6	5.6	85.0	18.5	76.3	12.9	84.9	12.2	76.1	9.2
1981	90.0	9.5	96.4	5.7	85.6	10.6	96.4	0.8	95.6	12.5	84.3	10.5	92.4	8.8	84.5	11.0
1982	96.2	6.9	98.7	2.4	94.7	10.6	97.7	1.3	98.3	2.8	92.1	9.3	98.4	6.5	91.9	8.8
1983	100.0	4.0	99.4	0.7	100.6	6.2	100.2	2.6	99.0	0.7	101.1	9.8	99.6	1.2	100.5	9.4
1984	103.8	3.8	102.0	2.6	104.7	4.1	102.1	1.9	102.7	3.7	106.8	5.6	102.1	2.5	107.6	7.1
1985	107.7	3.8	104.2	2.2	109.6	4.7	106.0	3.8	105.3	2.5	112.8	5.6	105.1	2.9	115.1	7.0
1986	110.0	2.1	108.9	4.5	112.9	3.0	103.9	-2.0	101.2	-3.9	120.1	6.5	109.9	4.6	124.2	7.9
1987	114.5	4.1	113.2	3.9	116.3	3.0	109.2	5.1	106.1	4.8	129.2	7.6	116.0	5.6	129.6	4.3
1988	119.0	3.9	117.1	3.4	120.7	3.8	116.6	6.8	107.6	1.4	138.0	6.8	122.3	5.4	138.0	6.5
1989	125.0	5.0	122.5	4.6	126.4	4.7	118.1	1.3	112.1	4.2	149.2	8.1	131.6	7.6	153.1	10.9
1990	131.7	5.4	130.3	6.4	131.4	4.0	124.3	5.2	118.7	5.9	163.0	9.2	139.2	5.8	164.3	7.3
1991	137.0	4.0	135.5	4.0	136.4	3.8	125.3	0.8	121.2	2.1	177.9	9.1	145.9	4.8	179.0	8.9
1992	141.1	3.0	139.2	2.7	139.9	2.6	126.2	0.7	123.2	1.7	190.7	7.2	149.4	2.4	192.0	7.3
1993	145.4	3.0	143.1	2.8	143.3	2.4	131.1	3.9	126.2	2.4	203.1	6.5	153.9	3.0	202.5	5.5

Source: U.S. Department of Labor, Bureau of Labor Statistics, Division of Consumer Prices and Price Indexes. - indicates no data collected for period.

Chicago, IL-NW IN
Consumer Price Index - Urban Wage Earners
Base 1982-1984 = 100
Annual Averages

For 1914-1993. Columns headed % show percentile change in the index from the previous period for which an index is available.

Year	All Items		Food & Beverage		Housing		Apparel & Upkeep		Trans- portation		Medical Care		Entertain- ment		Other Goods & Services	
	Index	%	Index	%	Index	%	Index	%	Index	%	Index	%	Index	%	Index	%
1914	-		-	-	-	-	-	-	-	-	-	-	-	-	-	-
1915	10.2	-	-	-	-	-	-	-	-	-	-	-	-	-	-	-
1916	11.1	*8.8*	-	-	-	-	-	-	-	-	-	-	-	-	-	-
1917	13.1	*18.0*	-	-	-	-	-	-	-	-	-	-	-	-	-	-
1918	15.2	*16.0*	-	-	-	-	-	-	-	-	-	-	-	-	-	-
1919	17.6	*15.8*	-	-	-	-	-	-	-	-	-	-	-	-	-	-
1920	20.2	*14.8*	-	-	-	-	-	-	-	-	-	-	-	-	-	-
1921	18.3	*-9.4*	-	-	-	-	-	-	-	-	-	-	-	-	-	-
1922	17.3	*-5.5*	-	-	-	-	-	-	-	-	-	-	-	-	-	-
1923	17.7	*2.3*	-	-	-	-	-	-	-	-	-	-	-	-	-	-
1924	18.0	*1.7*	-	-	-	-	-	-	-	-	-	-	-	-	-	-
1925	18.5	*2.8*	-	-	-	-	-	-	-	-	-	-	-	-	-	-
1926	18.6	*0.5*	-	-	-	-	-	-	-	-	-	-	-	-	-	-
1927	18.2	*-2.2*	-	-	-	-	-	-	-	-	-	-	-	-	-	-
1928	18.0	*-1.1*	-	-	-	-	-	-	-	-	-	-	-	-	-	-
1929	17.9	*-0.6*	-	-	-	-	-	-	-	-	-	-	-	-	-	-
1930	17.5	*-2.2*	-	-	-	-	-	-	-	-	-	-	-	-	-	-
1931	15.9	*-9.1*	-	-	-	-	-	-	-	-	-	-	-	-	-	-
1932	13.9	*-12.6*	-	-	-	-	-	-	-	-	-	-	-	-	-	-
1933	12.8	*-7.9*	-	-	-	-	-	-	-	-	-	-	-	-	-	-
1934	13.0	*1.6*	-	-	-	-	-	-	-	-	-	-	-	-	-	-
1935	13.6	*4.6*	-	-	-	-	-	-	-	-	-	-	-	-	-	-
1936	13.7	*0.7*	-	-	-	-	-	-	-	-	-	-	-	-	-	-
1937	14.4	*5.1*	-	-	-	-	-	-	-	-	-	-	-	-	-	-
1938	14.2	*-1.4*	-	-	-	-	-	-	-	-	-	-	-	-	-	-
1939	13.9	*-2.1*	-	-	-	-	-	-	-	-	-	-	-	-	-	-
1940	14.1	*1.4*	-	-	-	-	-	-	-	-	-	-	-	-	-	-
1941	14.7	*4.3*	-	-	-	-	-	-	-	-	-	-	-	-	-	-
1942	16.2	*10.2*	-	-	-	-	-	-	-	-	-	-	-	-	-	-
1943	17.2	*6.2*	-	-	-	-	-	-	-	-	-	-	-	-	-	-
1944	17.4	*1.2*	-	-	-	-	-	-	-	-	-	-	-	-	-	-
1945	17.8	*2.3*	-	-	-	-	-	-	-	-	-	-	-	-	-	-
1946	19.4	*9.0*	-	-	-	-	-	-	-	-	-	-	-	-	-	-
1947	22.4	*15.5*	-	-	-	-	-	-	17.2	-	11.9	-	-	-	-	-
1948	24.4	*8.9*	-	-	-	-	-	-	19.9	*15.7*	12.7	*6.7*	-	-	-	-
1949	24.4	*0.0*	-	-	-	-	-	-	21.6	*8.5*	13.3	*4.7*	-	-	-	-
1950	24.7	*1.2*	-	-	-	-	-	-	22.3	*3.2*	13.5	*1.5*	-	-	-	-
1951	26.6	*7.7*	-	-	-	-	-	-	23.5	*5.4*	14.3	*5.9*	-	-	-	-
1952	27.2	*2.3*	-	-	-	-	-	-	25.6	*8.9*	14.7	*2.8*	-	-	-	-
1953	27.4	*0.7*	-	-	-	-	50.8	-	26.2	*2.3*	15.2	*3.4*	-	-	-	-
1954	27.9	*1.8*	-	-	-	-	51.1	*0.6*	26.0	*-0.8*	15.6	*2.6*	-	-	-	-
1955	28.0	*0.4*	-	-	-	-	50.7	*-0.8*	25.7	*-1.2*	16.3	*4.5*	-	-	-	-
1956	28.4	*1.4*	-	-	-	-	52.3	*3.2*	26.2	*1.9*	17.3	*6.1*	-	-	-	-
1957	29.3	*3.2*	-	-	-	-	53.1	*1.5*	27.9	*6.5*	18.0	*4.0*	-	-	-	-
1958	30.2	*3.1*	-	-	-	-	53.3	*0.4*	29.5	*5.7*	19.1	*6.1*	-	-	-	-

[Continued]

342

Chicago, IL-NW IN
Consumer Price Index - Urban Wage Earners
Base 1982-1984 = 100
Annual Averages
[Continued]

For 1914-1993. Columns headed % show percentile change in the index from the previous period for which an index is available.

Year	All Items		Food & Beverage		Housing		Apparel & Upkeep		Trans- portation		Medical Care		Entertain- ment		Other Goods & Services	
	Index	%	Index	%	Index	%	Index	%	Index	%	Index	%	Index	%	Index	%
1959	30.4	0.7	-	-	-	-	53.8	0.9	30.5	3.4	20.0	4.7	-	-	-	-
1960	30.9	1.6	-	-	-	-	54.7	1.7	30.6	0.3	21.1	5.5	-	-	-	-
1961	31.1	0.6	-	-	-	-	54.3	-0.7	30.4	-0.7	21.6	2.4	-	-	-	-
1962	31.4	1.0	-	-	-	-	54.1	-0.4	31.0	2.0	22.4	3.7	-	-	-	-
1963	31.7	1.0	-	-	-	-	54.3	0.4	31.2	0.6	23.9	6.7	-	-	-	-
1964	31.8	0.3	-	-	-	-	54.5	0.4	31.3	0.3	24.3	1.7	-	-	-	-
1965	32.2	1.3	-	-	-	-	55.1	1.1	32.0	2.2	24.7	1.6	-	-	-	-
1966	33.2	3.1	-	-	-	-	56.5	2.5	32.1	0.3	25.5	3.2	-	-	-	-
1967	34.0	2.4	-	-	-	-	58.7	3.9	33.0	2.8	27.5	7.8	-	-	-	-
1968	35.5	4.4	-	-	-	-	61.8	5.3	34.5	4.5	29.1	5.8	-	-	-	-
1969	37.4	5.4	-	-	-	-	64.8	4.9	36.6	6.1	30.9	6.2	-	-	-	-
1970	39.6	5.9	-	-	-	-	66.5	2.6	39.1	6.8	33.0	6.8	-	-	-	-
1971	41.1	3.8	-	-	-	-	68.9	3.6	41.4	5.9	35.3	7.0	-	-	-	-
1972	42.3	2.9	-	-	-	-	70.3	2.0	41.0	-1.0	36.2	2.5	-	-	-	-
1973	44.9	6.1	-	-	-	-	73.7	4.8	42.2	2.9	37.7	4.1	-	-	-	-
1974	49.7	10.7	-	-	-	-	77.9	5.7	46.4	10.0	41.3	9.5	-	-	-	-
1975	53.7	8.0	-	-	-	-	80.2	3.0	50.1	8.0	46.5	12.6	-	-	-	-
1976	56.2	4.7	65.2	-	50.7	-	81.1	1.1	55.2	10.2	51.9	11.6	54.6	-	59.6	-
1977	59.8	6.4	69.0	5.8	53.8	6.1	83.5	3.0	59.8	8.3	57.1	10.0	57.2	4.8	63.9	7.2
1978	64.8	8.4	76.3	10.6	59.6	10.8	86.8	4.0	62.1	3.8	61.3	7.4	59.7	4.4	68.1	6.6
1979	72.9	12.5	84.5	10.7	68.4	14.8	89.7	3.3	71.1	14.5	67.5	10.1	67.1	12.4	71.8	5.4
1980	83.5	14.5	92.3	9.2	79.8	16.7	94.9	5.8	84.5	18.8	76.9	13.9	77.4	15.4	78.1	8.8
1981	91.4	9.5	96.3	4.3	88.3	10.7	95.9	1.1	95.5	13.0	84.4	9.8	88.1	13.8	84.9	8.7
1982	97.7	6.9	98.7	2.5	97.9	10.9	97.9	2.1	98.7	3.4	92.1	9.1	97.4	10.6	91.9	8.2
1983	100.4	2.8	99.4	0.7	101.6	3.8	100.0	2.1	98.8	0.1	101.0	9.7	99.9	2.6	100.6	9.5
1984	101.9	1.5	102.0	2.6	100.6	-1.0	102.2	2.2	102.4	3.6	106.8	5.7	102.8	2.9	107.5	6.9
1985	105.1	3.1	104.2	2.2	103.9	3.3	105.6	3.3	104.8	2.3	112.7	5.5	105.8	2.9	115.2	7.2
1986	106.8	1.6	109.0	4.6	106.9	2.9	104.1	-1.4	99.8	-4.8	119.9	6.4	110.9	4.8	124.8	8.3
1987	111.1	4.0	113.3	3.9	109.7	2.6	109.4	5.1	104.3	4.5	128.9	7.5	118.0	6.4	130.3	4.4
1988	115.3	3.8	117.2	3.4	113.6	3.6	116.1	6.1	106.3	1.9	138.4	7.4	124.2	5.3	138.5	6.3
1989	121.2	5.1	122.6	4.6	118.9	4.7	117.6	1.3	111.0	4.4	150.4	8.7	132.9	7.0	153.6	10.9
1990	127.8	5.4	130.4	6.4	123.8	4.1	124.5	5.9	117.2	5.6	164.3	9.2	140.0	5.3	166.2	8.2
1991	132.9	4.0	135.7	4.1	128.4	3.7	125.6	0.9	119.3	1.8	179.4	9.2	146.0	4.3	182.4	9.7
1992	136.7	2.9	139.2	2.6	131.7	2.6	125.9	0.2	121.2	1.6	192.4	7.2	149.5	2.4	195.9	7.4
1993	140.9	3.1	143.3	2.9	135.0	2.5	130.5	3.7	124.0	2.3	205.6	6.9	153.7	2.8	207.0	5.7

Source: U.S. Department of Labor, Bureau of Labor Statistics, Division of Consumer Prices and Price Indexes. - indicates no data collected for period.

Chicago, IL-NW IN
Consumer Price Index - All Urban Consumers
Base 1982-1984 = 100
All Items

For 1914-1993. Columns headed % show percentile change in the index from the previous period for which an index is available.

Year	Jan Index	%	Feb Index	%	Mar Index	%	Apr Index	%	May Index	%	Jun Index	%	Jul Index	%	Aug Index	%	Sep Index	%	Oct Index	%	Nov Index	%	Dec Index	%
1914	-	-	-	-	-	-	-	-	-	-	-	-	-	-	-	-	-	-	-	-	-	-	10.0	-
1915	-	-	-	-	-	-	-	-	-	-	-	-	-	-	-	-	-	-	-	-	-	-	10.2	2.0
1916	-	-	-	-	-	-	-	-	-	-	-	-	-	-	-	-	-	-	-	-	-	-	11.6	13.7
1917	-	-	-	-	-	-	-	-	-	-	-	-	-	-	-	-	-	-	-	-	-	-	13.5	16.4
1918	-	-	-	-	-	-	-	-	-	-	-	-	-	-	-	-	-	-	-	-	-	-	16.3	20.7
1919	-	-	-	-	-	-	-	-	-	-	16.6	1.8	-	-	-	-	-	-	-	-	-	-	18.9	13.9
1920	-	-	-	-	-	-	-	-	-	-	20.8	10.1	-	-	-	-	-	-	-	-	-	-	18.9	-9.1
1921	-	-	-	-	-	-	-	-	17.9	-5.3	-	-	-	-	-	-	17.8	-0.6	-	-	-	-	17.5	-1.7
1922	-	-	-	-	-	-	-	-	16.9	-3.4	17.0	0.6	-	-	-	-	17.0	0.0	-	-	-	-	17.1	0.6
1923	-	-	-	-	17.2	0.6	-	-	-	-	17.3	0.6	-	-	-	-	17.7	2.3	-	-	-	-	17.7	0.0
1924	-	-	-	-	17.6	-0.6	-	-	-	-	17.7	0.6	-	-	-	-	17.8	0.6	-	-	-	-	17.9	0.6
1925	-	-	-	-	-	-	-	-	-	-	18.2	1.7	-	-	-	-	-	-	-	-	-	-	18.6	2.2
1926	-	-	-	-	-	-	-	-	-	-	18.3	-1.6	-	-	-	-	-	-	-	-	-	-	18.3	0.0
1927	-	-	-	-	-	-	-	-	-	-	18.3	0.0	-	-	-	-	-	-	-	-	-	-	17.8	-2.7
1928	-	-	-	-	-	-	-	-	-	-	17.6	-1.1	-	-	-	-	-	-	-	-	-	-	17.7	0.6
1929	-	-	-	-	-	-	-	-	-	-	17.6	-0.6	-	-	-	-	-	-	-	-	-	-	17.7	0.6
1930	-	-	-	-	-	-	-	-	-	-	17.4	-1.7	-	-	-	-	-	-	-	-	-	-	16.6	-4.6
1931	-	-	-	-	-	-	-	-	-	-	15.6	-6.0	-	-	-	-	-	-	-	-	-	-	14.9	-4.5
1932	-	-	-	-	-	-	-	-	-	-	13.6	-8.7	-	-	-	-	-	-	-	-	-	-	12.9	-5.1
1933	-	-	-	-	-	-	-	-	-	-	12.4	-3.9	-	-	-	-	-	-	-	-	-	-	12.7	2.4
1934	-	-	-	-	-	-	-	-	-	-	12.7	0.0	-	-	-	-	-	-	-	-	12.8	0.8	-	-
1935	-	-	-	-	13.3	3.9	-	-	-	-	-	-	13.4	0.8	-	-	-	-	13.4	0.0	-	-	-	-
1936	13.4	0.0	-	-	-	-	13.3	-0.7	-	-	-	-	13.6	2.3	-	-	13.8	1.5	-	-	-	-	13.7	-0.7
1937	-	-	-	-	13.9	1.5	-	-	-	-	14.2	2.2	-	-	-	-	14.4	1.4	-	-	-	-	14.2	-1.4
1938	-	-	-	-	13.9	-2.1	-	-	-	-	14.0	0.7	-	-	-	-	14.0	0.0	-	-	-	-	13.8	-1.4
1939	-	-	-	-	13.7	-0.7	-	-	-	-	13.6	-0.7	-	-	-	-	13.8	1.5	-	-	-	-	13.7	-0.7
1940	-	-	-	-	13.7	0.0	-	-	-	-	13.9	1.5	-	-	-	-	13.8	-0.7	13.8	0.0	13.8	0.0	13.9	0.7
1941	13.9	0.0	13.9	0.0	13.9	0.0	14.1	1.4	14.2	0.7	14.4	1.4	14.6	1.4	14.7	0.7	15.0	2.0	15.1	0.7	15.2	0.7	15.2	0.0
1942	15.4	1.3	15.4	0.0	15.6	1.3	15.8	1.3	16.0	1.3	16.0	0.0	16.0	0.0	16.1	0.6	16.1	0.0	16.3	1.2	16.4	0.6	16.4	0.0
1943	16.4	0.0	16.5	0.6	16.8	1.8	16.9	0.6	17.1	1.2	17.0	-0.6	16.8	-1.2	16.9	0.6	17.0	0.6	17.0	0.0	16.9	-0.6	16.9	0.0
1944	16.8	-0.6	16.8	0.0	16.8	0.0	17.0	1.2	17.0	0.0	17.1	0.6	17.3	1.2	17.3	0.0	17.3	0.0	17.3	0.0	17.3	0.0	17.3	0.0
1945	17.3	0.0	17.3	0.0	17.3	0.0	17.3	0.0	17.6	1.7	17.6	0.0	17.6	0.0	17.6	0.0	17.5	-0.6	17.5	0.0	17.5	0.0	17.6	0.6
1946	17.6	0.0	17.6	0.0	17.6	0.0	17.8	1.1	17.9	0.6	18.0	0.6	19.4	7.8	19.8	2.1	20.0	1.0	20.6	3.0	21.0	1.9	21.1	0.5
1947	21.1	0.0	21.0	-0.5	21.5	2.4	21.4	-0.5	21.5	0.5	21.8	1.4	22.0	0.9	22.4	1.8	23.1	3.1	23.0	-0.4	23.1	0.4	23.4	1.3
1948	23.5	0.4	23.2	-1.3	23.2	0.0	23.7	2.2	24.0	1.3	24.2	0.8	24.5	1.2	24.6	0.4	24.7	0.4	24.5	-0.8	24.2	-1.2	24.1	-0.4
1949	24.0	-0.4	23.8	-0.8	24.0	0.8	24.1	0.4	24.0	-0.4	24.2	0.8	23.9	-1.2	24.0	0.4	24.2	0.8	24.0	-0.8	24.1	0.4	23.8	-1.2
1950	23.7	-0.4	23.7	0.0	23.8	0.4	23.7	-0.4	24.0	1.3	24.0	0.0	24.3	1.2	24.5	0.8	24.6	0.4	24.7	0.4	24.8	0.4	25.2	1.6
1951	25.5	1.2	25.9	1.6	25.9	0.0	26.0	0.4	26.0	0.0	26.1	0.4	26.2	0.4	26.2	0.0	26.3	0.4	26.5	0.8	26.7	0.8	26.6	-0.4
1952	26.6	0.0	26.3	-1.1	26.4	0.4	26.5	0.4	26.7	0.8	26.8	0.4	26.9	0.4	27.0	0.4	26.9	-0.4	26.9	0.0	26.9	0.0	26.8	-0.4
1953	26.7	-0.4	26.6	-0.4	26.6	0.0	26.7	0.4	26.8	0.4	26.9	0.4	27.0	0.4	27.2	0.7	27.2	0.0	27.4	0.7	27.2	-0.7	27.2	0.0
1954	27.2	0.0	27.2	0.0	27.2	0.0	27.2	0.0	27.4	0.7	27.4	0.0	27.6	0.7	27.5	-0.4	27.4	-0.4	27.4	0.0	27.5	0.4	27.3	-0.7
1955	27.3	0.0	27.4	0.4	27.3	-0.4	27.3	0.0	27.4	0.4	27.4	0.0	27.6	0.7	27.7	0.4	27.8	0.4	27.8	0.0	27.8	0.0	27.7	-0.4
1956	27.6	-0.4	27.6	0.0	27.5	-0.4	27.6	0.4	27.7	0.4	27.9	0.7	28.2	1.1	28.0	-0.7	28.1	0.4	28.3	0.7	28.3	0.0	28.3	0.0
1957	28.3	0.0	28.4	0.4	28.4	0.0	28.5	0.4	28.6	0.4	28.7	0.3	29.0	1.0	29.0	0.0	29.1	0.3	29.2	0.3	29.4	0.7	29.4	0.0
1958	29.5	0.3	29.5	0.0	29.7	0.7	29.7	0.0	29.7	0.0	29.8	0.3	29.8	0.0	29.7	-0.3	29.8	0.3	29.8	0.0	29.8	0.0	29.7	-0.3

[Continued]

Chicago, IL-NW IN
Consumer Price Index - All Urban Consumers
Base 1982-1984 = 100
All Items
[Continued]

For 1914-1993. Columns headed % show percentile change in the index from the previous period for which an index is available.

Year	Jan Index	%	Feb Index	%	Mar Index	%	Apr Index	%	May Index	%	Jun Index	%	Jul Index	%	Aug Index	%	Sep Index	%	Oct Index	%	Nov Index	%	Dec Index	%
1959	29.7	0.0	29.7	0.0	29.7	0.0	29.8	0.3	29.8	0.0	29.9	0.3	30.0	0.3	30.0	0.0	30.2	0.7	30.2	0.0	30.2	0.0	30.2	0.0
1960	30.1	-0.3	30.2	0.3	30.2	0.0	30.3	0.3	30.3	0.0	30.4	0.3	30.5	0.3	30.4	-0.3	30.5	0.3	30.5	0.0	30.5	0.0	30.5	0.0
1961	30.5	0.0	30.5	0.0	30.4	-0.3	30.4	0.0	30.4	0.0	30.3	-0.3	30.6	1.0	30.6	0.0	30.6	0.0	30.7	0.3	30.6	-0.3	30.6	0.0
1962	30.6	0.0	30.8	0.7	30.8	0.0	30.9	0.3	30.8	-0.3	30.8	0.0	30.8	0.0	30.8	0.0	31.0	0.6	30.9	-0.3	30.9	0.0	30.9	0.0
1963	31.0	0.3	31.0	0.0	31.1	0.3	31.1	0.0	31.0	-0.3	31.1	0.3	31.3	0.6	31.2	-0.3	31.2	0.0	31.2	0.0	31.2	0.0	31.3	0.3
1964	31.2	-0.3	31.1	-0.3	31.1	0.0	31.1	0.0	31.2	0.3	31.3	0.3	31.4	0.3	31.3	-0.3	31.3	0.0	31.4	0.3	31.4	0.0	31.4	0.0
1965	31.4	0.0	31.4	0.0	31.4	0.0	31.5	0.3	31.6	0.3	31.8	0.6	31.7	-0.3	31.7	0.0	31.8	0.3	31.9	0.3	31.9	0.0	32.1	0.6
1966	32.0	-0.3	32.2	0.6	32.4	0.6	32.4	0.0	32.5	0.3	32.6	0.3	32.6	0.0	32.8	0.6	33.0	0.6	33.0	0.0	33.0	0.0	33.1	0.3
1967	32.9	-0.6	33.1	0.6	33.1	0.0	33.1	0.0	33.2	0.3	33.3	0.3	33.5	0.6	33.7	0.6	33.9	0.6	33.9	0.0	34.0	0.3	34.1	0.3
1968	34.1	0.0	34.3	0.6	34.5	0.6	34.6	0.3	34.7	0.3	34.8	0.3	35.0	0.6	35.1	0.3	35.3	0.6	35.4	0.3	35.4	0.0	35.6	0.6
1969	35.8	0.6	35.9	0.3	36.2	0.8	36.3	0.3	36.4	0.3	36.7	0.8	36.9	0.5	37.2	0.8	37.5	0.8	37.4	-0.3	37.6	0.5	37.8	0.5
1970	38.0	0.5	38.1	0.3	38.3	0.5	38.4	0.3	38.6	0.5	38.8	0.5	39.0	0.5	39.2	0.5	39.4	0.5	39.6	0.5	39.7	0.3	39.9	0.5
1971	39.9	0.0	40.0	0.3	40.1	0.2	40.2	0.2	40.4	0.5	40.5	0.2	40.5	0.0	40.7	0.5	40.7	0.0	40.7	0.0	40.8	0.2	40.9	0.2
1972	40.9	0.0	41.2	0.7	41.2	0.0	41.3	0.2	41.4	0.2	41.6	0.5	41.6	0.0	41.8	0.5	41.9	0.2	42.0	0.2	42.1	0.2	42.2	0.2
1973	42.3	0.2	42.7	0.9	43.2	1.2	43.5	0.7	43.8	0.7	44.1	0.7	44.0	-0.2	45.0	2.3	45.1	0.2	45.4	0.7	45.6	0.4	45.8	0.4
1974	46.4	1.3	47.1	1.5	47.6	1.1	47.8	0.4	48.2	0.8	48.7	1.0	48.9	0.4	49.5	1.2	49.9	0.8	50.4	1.0	50.8	0.8	51.3	1.0
1975	51.3	0.0	51.7	0.8	52.1	0.8	52.2	0.2	52.0	-0.4	52.4	0.8	53.0	1.1	53.3	0.6	53.4	0.2	53.7	0.6	53.8	0.2	54.0	0.4
1976	53.7	-0.6	54.1	0.7	54.2	0.2	54.5	0.6	54.8	0.6	55.2	0.7	55.5	0.5	55.8	0.5	56.1	0.5	56.3	0.4	56.4	0.2	56.6	0.4
1977	56.7	0.2	57.3	1.1	57.7	0.7	58.2	0.9	58.4	0.3	58.6	0.3	59.0	0.7	59.3	0.5	59.7	0.7	59.8	0.2	60.0	0.3	60.2	0.3
1978	61.1	1.5	61.7	1.0	62.4	1.1	62.7	0.5	63.3	1.0	63.7	0.6	64.1	0.6	64.1	0.0	64.9	1.2	65.4	0.8	66.3	1.4	66.5	0.3
1979	66.8	0.5	67.8	1.5	69.2	2.1	69.9	1.0	70.3	0.6	71.5	1.7	72.8	1.8	73.2	0.5	74.1	1.2	74.2	0.1	75.6	1.9	76.4	1.1
1980	77.1	0.9	77.9	1.0	78.8	1.2	80.4	2.0	81.4	1.2	83.1	2.1	82.6	-0.6	82.1	-0.6	83.7	1.9	84.9	1.4	87.0	2.5	87.1	0.1
1981	86.7	-0.5	86.9	0.2	86.9	0.0	88.3	1.6	88.5	0.2	90.1	1.8	91.3	1.3	92.3	1.1	92.7	0.4	92.4	-0.3	92.7	0.3	91.7	-1.1
1982	92.2	0.5	92.0	-0.2	92.5	0.5	93.8	1.4	96.3	2.7	97.7	1.5	98.1	0.4	98.1	0.0	98.4	0.3	98.5	0.1	98.5	0.0	98.1	-0.4
1983	98.4	0.3	98.3	-0.1	98.3	0.0	98.8	0.5	99.2	0.4	99.9	0.7	100.3	0.4	101.0	0.7	101.4	0.4	101.2	-0.2	101.7	0.5	101.7	0.0
1984	102.2	0.5	102.1	-0.1	102.3	0.2	102.7	0.4	102.8	0.1	103.7	0.9	104.0	0.3	104.9	0.9	105.5	0.6	105.1	-0.4	105.1	0.0	105.1	0.0
1985	105.5	0.4	106.0	0.5	106.2	0.2	106.8	0.6	107.0	0.2	108.5	1.4	108.6	0.1	109.1	0.5	109.2	0.1	108.0	-1.1	108.5	0.5	109.1	0.6
1986	109.2	0.1	109.3	0.1	108.4	-0.8	108.3	-0.1	108.5	0.2	110.6	1.9	110.8	0.2	110.9	0.1	111.8	0.8	110.0	-1.6	110.9	0.8	110.8	-0.1
1987	111.9	1.0	111.9	0.0	112.3	0.4	112.8	0.4	113.3	0.4	115.5	1.9	115.9	0.3	116.7	0.7	117.1	0.3	115.1	-1.7	115.7	0.5	115.7	0.0
1988	115.3	-0.3	116.6	1.1	116.9	0.3	117.1	0.2	117.0	-0.1	118.9	1.6	119.8	0.8	120.1	0.3	122.0	1.6	121.6	-0.3	121.0	-0.5	121.3	0.2
1989	121.5	0.2	122.2	0.6	123.0	0.7	123.6	0.5	123.9	0.2	125.7	1.5	126.4	0.6	126.4	0.0	127.1	0.6	126.8	-0.2	126.7	-0.1	126.5	-0.2
1990	128.1	1.3	129.2	0.9	129.5	0.2	130.4	0.7	130.4	0.0	131.7	1.0	132.0	0.2	133.2	0.9	133.8	0.5	133.3	-0.4	134.2	0.7	134.6	0.3
1991	135.1	0.4	135.5	0.3	136.2	0.5	136.1	-0.1	136.8	0.5	137.3	0.4	137.3	0.0	137.6	0.2	138.3	0.5	138.0	-0.2	138.0	0.0	138.3	0.2
1992	138.9	0.4	139.2	0.2	139.7	0.4	139.8	0.1	140.5	0.5	141.2	0.5	141.4	0.1	141.9	0.4	142.7	0.6	142.1	-0.4	142.4	0.2	142.9	0.4
1993	143.2	0.2	143.6	0.3	144.1	0.3	144.7	0.4	145.7	0.7	145.6	-0.1	145.5	-0.1	146.1	0.4	146.7	0.4	147.2	0.3	146.4	-0.5	146.1	-0.2

Source: U.S. Department of Labor, Bureau of Labor Statistics, Division of Consumer Prices and Price Indexes. - indicates no data collected for period.

Chicago, IL-NW IN
Consumer Price Index - Urban Wage Earners
Base 1982-1984 = 100
All Items

For 1914-1993. Columns headed % show percentile change in the index from the previous period for which an index is available.

Year	Jan Index	%	Feb Index	%	Mar Index	%	Apr Index	%	May Index	%	Jun Index	%	Jul Index	%	Aug Index	%	Sep Index	%	Oct Index	%	Nov Index	%	Dec Index	%
1914	-	-	-	-	-	-	-	-	-	-	-	-	-	-	-	-	-	-	-	-	-	-	10.1	-
1915	-	-	-	-	-	-	-	-	-	-	-	-	-	-	-	-	-	-	-	-	-	-	10.4	3.0
1916	-	-	-	-	-	-	-	-	-	-	-	-	-	-	-	-	-	-	-	-	-	-	11.8	13.5
1917	-	-	-	-	-	-	-	-	-	-	-	-	-	-	-	-	-	-	-	-	-	-	13.7	16.1
1918	-	-	-	-	-	-	-	-	-	-	-	-	-	-	-	-	-	-	-	-	-	-	16.6	21.2
1919	-	-	-	-	-	-	-	-	-	-	16.9	1.8	-	-	-	-	-	-	-	-	-	-	19.2	13.6
1920	-	-	-	-	-	-	-	-	-	-	21.2	10.4	-	-	-	-	-	-	-	-	-	-	19.2	-9.4
1921	-	-	-	-	-	-	-	-	18.2	-5.2	-	-	-	-	-	-	18.1	-0.5	-	-	-	-	17.8	-1.7
1922	-	-	-	-	-	-	-	-	17.2	-3.4	17.3	0.6	-	-	-	-	17.3	0.0	-	-	-	-	17.4	0.6
1923	-	-	-	-	17.5	0.6	-	-	-	-	17.6	0.6	-	-	-	-	18.0	2.3	-	-	-	-	18.0	0.0
1924	-	-	-	-	17.9	-0.6	-	-	-	-	18.0	0.6	-	-	-	-	18.1	0.6	-	-	-	-	18.2	0.6
1925	-	-	-	-	-	-	-	-	-	-	18.5	1.6	-	-	-	-	-	-	-	-	-	-	18.9	2.2
1926	-	-	-	-	-	-	-	-	-	-	18.7	-1.1	-	-	-	-	-	-	-	-	-	-	18.6	-0.5
1927	-	-	-	-	-	-	-	-	-	-	18.6	0.0	-	-	-	-	-	-	-	-	-	-	18.1	-2.7
1928	-	-	-	-	-	-	-	-	-	-	17.9	-1.1	-	-	-	-	-	-	-	-	-	-	18.0	0.6
1929	-	-	-	-	-	-	-	-	-	-	17.9	-0.6	-	-	-	-	-	-	-	-	-	-	18.0	0.6
1930	-	-	-	-	-	-	-	-	-	-	17.7	-1.7	-	-	-	-	-	-	-	-	-	-	16.9	-4.5
1931	-	-	-	-	-	-	-	-	-	-	15.8	-6.5	-	-	-	-	-	-	-	-	-	-	15.2	-3.8
1932	-	-	-	-	-	-	-	-	-	-	13.8	-9.2	-	-	-	-	-	-	-	-	-	-	13.1	-5.1
1933	-	-	-	-	-	-	-	-	-	-	12.6	-3.8	-	-	-	-	-	-	-	-	-	-	12.9	2.4
1934	-	-	-	-	-	-	-	-	-	-	12.9	0.0	-	-	-	-	-	-	-	-	13.0	0.8	-	-
1935	-	-	-	-	13.6	4.6	-	-	-	-	-	-	13.6	0.0	-	-	-	-	13.6	0.0	-	-	-	-
1936	13.7	0.7	-	-	-	-	13.5	-1.5	-	-	-	-	13.8	2.2	-	-	14.0	1.4	-	-	-	-	13.9	-0.7
1937	-	-	-	-	14.1	1.4	-	-	-	-	14.4	2.1	-	-	-	-	14.6	1.4	-	-	-	-	14.4	-1.4
1938	-	-	-	-	14.1	-2.1	-	-	-	-	14.3	1.4	-	-	-	-	14.3	0.0	-	-	-	-	14.1	-1.4
1939	-	-	-	-	13.9	-1.4	-	-	-	-	13.8	-0.7	-	-	-	-	14.1	2.2	-	-	-	-	13.9	-1.4
1940	-	-	-	-	13.9	0.0	-	-	-	-	14.1	1.4	-	-	-	-	14.1	0.0	14.1	0.0	14.0	-0.7	14.1	0.7
1941	14.1	0.0	14.1	0.0	14.2	0.7	14.3	0.7	14.4	0.7	14.6	1.4	14.8	1.4	14.9	0.7	15.3	2.7	15.4	0.7	15.5	0.6	15.4	-0.6
1942	15.7	1.9	15.7	0.0	15.9	1.3	16.1	1.3	16.2	0.6	16.2	0.0	16.2	0.0	16.4	1.2	16.4	0.0	16.6	1.2	16.7	0.6	16.7	0.0
1943	16.7	0.0	16.8	0.6	17.1	1.8	17.2	0.6	17.4	1.2	17.3	-0.6	17.1	-1.2	17.2	0.6	17.3	0.6	17.3	0.0	17.2	-0.6	17.2	0.0
1944	17.1	-0.6	17.1	0.0	17.1	0.0	17.3	1.2	17.3	0.0	17.4	0.6	17.6	1.1	17.6	0.0	17.6	0.0	17.6	0.0	17.6	0.0	17.6	0.0
1945	17.6	0.0	17.6	0.0	17.6	0.0	17.6	0.0	17.9	1.7	17.9	0.0	17.9	0.0	17.9	0.0	17.8	-0.6	17.8	0.0	17.8	0.0	17.9	0.6
1946	17.9	0.0	17.9	0.0	17.9	0.0	18.1	1.1	18.2	0.6	18.3	0.5	19.7	7.7	20.2	2.5	20.4	1.0	20.9	2.5	21.3	1.9	21.4	0.5
1947	21.4	0.0	21.3	-0.5	21.8	2.3	21.8	0.0	21.9	0.5	22.1	0.9	22.4	1.4	22.7	1.3	23.5	3.5	23.4	-0.4	23.5	0.4	23.8	1.3
1948	23.9	0.4	23.6	-1.3	23.6	0.0	24.1	2.1	24.4	1.2	24.7	1.2	25.0	1.2	25.0	0.0	25.1	0.4	24.9	-0.8	24.6	-1.2	24.5	-0.4
1949	24.4	-0.4	24.2	-0.8	24.4	0.8	24.5	0.4	24.4	-0.4	24.6	0.8	24.3	-1.2	24.4	0.4	24.6	0.8	24.4	-0.8	24.5	0.4	24.2	-1.2
1950	24.1	-0.4	24.1	0.0	24.2	0.4	24.1	-0.4	24.4	1.2	24.4	0.0	24.8	1.6	25.0	0.8	25.1	0.4	25.2	0.4	25.2	0.0	25.6	1.6
1951	25.9	1.2	26.3	1.5	26.4	0.4	26.4	0.0	26.5	0.4	26.5	0.0	26.7	0.8	26.7	0.0	26.8	0.4	27.0	0.7	27.1	0.4	27.1	0.0
1952	27.1	0.0	26.8	-1.1	26.9	0.4	26.9	0.0	27.2	1.1	27.3	0.4	27.3	0.0	27.4	0.4	27.3	-0.4	27.3	0.0	27.4	0.4	27.2	-0.7
1953	27.2	0.0	27.1	-0.4	27.0	-0.4	27.2	0.7	27.2	0.0	27.4	0.7	27.5	0.4	27.6	0.4	27.7	0.4	27.9	0.7	27.7	-0.7	27.7	0.0
1954	27.7	0.0	27.7	0.0	27.7	0.0	27.7	0.0	27.9	0.7	27.9	0.0	28.1	0.7	28.0	-0.4	27.9	-0.4	27.9	0.0	28.0	0.4	27.8	-0.7
1955	27.8	0.0	27.9	0.4	27.8	-0.4	27.8	0.0	27.9	0.4	27.9	0.0	28.1	0.7	28.2	0.4	28.3	0.4	28.3	0.0	28.3	0.0	28.2	-0.4
1956	28.1	-0.4	28.1	0.0	28.0	-0.4	28.1	0.4	28.2	0.4	28.4	0.7	28.7	1.1	28.5	-0.7	28.6	0.4	28.8	0.7	28.8	0.0	28.8	0.0
1957	28.8	0.0	28.9	0.3	28.9	0.0	29.0	0.3	29.0	0.0	29.2	0.7	29.5	1.0	29.5	0.0	29.6	0.3	29.7	0.3	29.9	0.7	29.9	0.0
1958	30.0	0.3	30.0	0.0	30.2	0.7	30.2	0.0	30.2	0.0	30.3	0.3	30.3	0.0	30.2	-0.3	30.3	0.3	30.3	0.0	30.3	0.0	30.2	-0.3

[Continued]

Chicago, IL-NW IN
Consumer Price Index - Urban Wage Earners
Base 1982-1984 = 100
All Items
[Continued]

For 1914-1993. Columns headed % show percentile change in the index from the previous period for which an index is available.

Year	Jan Index	%	Feb Index	%	Mar Index	%	Apr Index	%	May Index	%	Jun Index	%	Jul Index	%	Aug Index	%	Sep Index	%	Oct Index	%	Nov Index	%	Dec Index	%
1959	30.2	0.0	30.2	0.0	30.2	0.0	30.3	0.3	30.3	0.0	30.4	0.3	30.5	0.3	30.5	0.0	30.7	0.7	30.7	0.0	30.7	0.0	30.7	0.0
1960	30.6	-0.3	30.7	0.3	30.7	0.0	30.8	0.3	30.8	0.0	30.9	0.3	31.0	0.3	31.0	0.0	31.0	0.0	31.1	0.3	31.0	-0.3	31.1	0.3
1961	31.0	-0.3	31.0	0.0	31.0	0.0	30.9	-0.3	30.9	0.0	30.8	-0.3	31.1	1.0	31.1	0.0	31.2	0.3	31.2	0.0	31.1	-0.3	31.1	0.0
1962	31.2	0.3	31.3	0.3	31.3	0.0	31.4	0.3	31.4	0.0	31.3	-0.3	31.3	0.0	31.3	0.0	31.5	0.6	31.5	0.0	31.5	0.0	31.4	-0.3
1963	31.5	0.3	31.5	0.0	31.6	0.3	31.6	0.0	31.6	0.0	31.6	0.0	31.9	0.9	31.8	-0.3	31.8	0.0	31.8	0.0	31.7	-0.3	31.8	0.3
1964	31.7	-0.3	31.7	0.0	31.7	0.0	31.7	0.0	31.7	0.0	31.8	0.3	31.9	0.3	31.9	0.0	31.9	0.0	31.9	0.0	31.9	0.0	31.9	0.0
1965	31.9	0.0	31.9	0.0	32.0	0.3	32.0	0.0	32.1	0.3	32.3	0.6	32.3	0.0	32.3	0.0	32.4	0.3	32.4	0.0	32.5	0.3	32.6	0.3
1966	32.6	0.0	32.8	0.6	32.9	0.3	32.9	0.0	33.0	0.3	33.2	0.6	33.1	-0.3	33.4	0.9	33.5	0.3	33.6	0.3	33.5	-0.3	33.6	0.3
1967	33.5	-0.3	33.6	0.3	33.7	0.3	33.6	-0.3	33.7	0.3	33.8	0.3	34.1	0.9	34.3	0.6	34.5	0.6	34.5	0.0	34.6	0.3	34.7	0.3
1968	34.7	0.0	34.9	0.6	35.1	0.6	35.2	0.3	35.3	0.3	35.4	0.3	35.7	0.8	35.8	0.3	35.9	0.3	36.0	0.3	36.1	0.3	36.3	0.6
1969	36.4	0.3	36.5	0.3	36.8	0.8	36.9	0.3	37.0	0.3	37.4	1.1	37.6	0.5	37.8	0.5	38.1	0.8	38.0	-0.3	38.3	0.8	38.4	0.3
1970	38.7	0.8	38.7	0.0	38.9	0.5	39.0	0.3	39.3	0.8	39.4	0.3	39.7	0.8	39.9	0.5	40.1	0.5	40.3	0.5	40.4	0.2	40.6	0.5
1971	40.6	0.0	40.7	0.2	40.8	0.2	40.9	0.2	41.1	0.5	41.2	0.2	41.2	0.0	41.4	0.5	41.4	0.0	41.4	0.0	41.5	0.2	41.6	0.2
1972	41.6	0.0	41.9	0.7	41.9	0.0	42.0	0.2	42.1	0.2	42.3	0.5	42.4	0.2	42.6	0.5	42.7	0.2	42.7	0.0	42.8	0.2	42.9	0.2
1973	43.0	0.2	43.4	0.9	43.9	1.2	44.2	0.7	44.5	0.7	44.8	0.7	44.7	-0.2	45.8	2.5	45.8	0.0	46.2	0.9	46.3	0.2	46.6	0.6
1974	47.2	1.3	47.9	1.5	48.4	1.0	48.7	0.6	49.0	0.6	49.6	1.2	49.8	0.4	50.4	1.2	50.7	0.6	51.3	1.2	51.7	0.8	52.2	1.0
1975	52.2	0.0	52.6	0.8	53.0	0.8	53.1	0.2	52.9	-0.4	53.3	0.8	53.9	1.1	54.2	0.6	54.3	0.2	54.7	0.7	54.7	0.0	54.9	0.4
1976	54.7	-0.4	55.0	0.5	55.2	0.4	55.5	0.5	55.7	0.4	56.1	0.7	56.4	0.5	56.8	0.7	57.0	0.4	57.3	0.5	57.4	0.2	57.6	0.3
1977	57.7	0.2	58.3	1.0	58.7	0.7	59.2	0.9	59.4	0.3	59.6	0.3	60.1	0.8	60.4	0.5	60.8	0.7	60.9	0.2	61.1	0.3	61.3	0.3
1978	62.1	1.3	62.6	0.8	63.2	1.0	63.5	0.5	64.1	0.9	64.7	0.9	65.2	0.8	65.0	-0.3	65.7	1.1	66.5	1.2	67.3	1.2	67.6	0.4
1979	68.0	0.6	68.9	1.3	70.2	1.9	70.9	1.0	71.4	0.7	72.6	1.7	73.8	1.7	74.3	0.7	75.1	1.1	75.5	0.5	76.8	1.7	77.6	1.0
1980	78.3	0.9	79.2	1.1	80.1	1.1	81.7	2.0	82.7	1.2	84.4	2.1	84.1	-0.4	83.6	-0.6	85.0	1.7	86.1	1.3	88.2	2.4	88.2	0.0
1981	87.9	-0.3	88.1	0.2	88.2	0.1	89.6	1.6	89.9	0.3	91.2	1.4	92.5	1.4	93.5	1.1	93.9	0.4	94.1	0.2	94.4	0.3	93.4	-1.1
1982	93.9	0.5	93.8	-0.1	94.1	0.3	95.3	1.3	97.7	2.5	99.3	1.6	99.7	0.4	99.6	-0.1	99.7	0.1	99.8	0.1	99.8	0.0	99.4	-0.4
1983	99.7	0.3	99.2	-0.5	99.2	0.0	100.0	0.8	100.4	0.4	100.7	0.3	100.9	0.2	101.3	0.4	101.8	0.5	100.3	-1.5	100.7	0.4	100.2	-0.5
1984	101.6	1.4	101.1	-0.5	100.9	-0.2	100.9	0.0	101.0	0.1	101.5	0.5	101.8	0.3	102.6	0.8	103.6	1.0	102.8	-0.8	103.0	0.2	102.7	-0.3
1985	103.0	0.3	103.5	0.5	103.8	0.3	104.3	0.5	104.5	0.2	105.9	1.3	105.9	0.0	106.3	0.4	106.3	0.0	105.2	-1.0	105.9	0.7	106.4	0.5
1986	106.5	0.1	106.5	0.0	105.5	-0.9	105.2	-0.3	105.4	0.2	107.5	2.0	107.6	0.1	107.7	0.1	108.4	0.6	106.7	-1.6	107.6	0.8	107.5	-0.1
1987	108.7	1.1	108.6	-0.1	109.0	0.4	109.5	0.5	109.9	0.4	112.0	1.9	112.4	0.4	113.2	0.7	113.6	0.4	111.7	-1.7	112.2	0.4	112.2	0.0
1988	111.9	-0.3	112.9	0.9	113.2	0.3	113.3	0.1	113.3	0.0	115.2	1.7	116.2	0.9	116.4	0.2	118.2	1.5	117.8	-0.3	117.4	-0.3	117.7	0.3
1989	117.9	0.2	118.4	0.4	119.1	0.6	119.8	0.6	120.1	0.3	121.8	1.4	122.6	0.7	122.5	-0.1	123.1	0.5	122.9	-0.2	122.9	0.0	122.8	-0.1
1990	124.4	1.3	125.4	0.8	125.6	0.2	126.5	0.7	126.5	0.0	127.9	1.1	128.0	0.1	129.3	1.0	129.9	0.5	129.4	-0.4	130.3	0.7	130.7	0.3
1991	131.1	0.3	131.5	0.3	132.0	0.4	132.1	0.1	132.7	0.5	133.1	0.3	133.2	0.1	133.4	0.2	133.9	0.4	133.6	-0.2	133.8	0.1	134.1	0.2
1992	134.4	0.2	134.7	0.2	135.2	0.4	135.4	0.1	136.2	0.6	136.9	0.5	137.0	0.1	137.5	0.4	138.3	0.6	137.7	-0.4	138.2	0.4	138.5	0.2
1993	138.9	0.3	139.1	0.1	139.5	0.3	140.3	0.6	141.4	0.8	141.2	-0.1	141.1	-0.1	141.6	0.4	142.1	0.4	142.6	0.4	141.8	-0.6	141.7	-0.1

Source: U.S. Department of Labor, Bureau of Labor Statistics, Division of Consumer Prices and Price Indexes. - indicates no data collected for period.

Chicago, IL-NW IN
Consumer Price Index - All Urban Consumers
Base 1982-1984 = 100
Food and Beverages

For 1976-1993. Columns headed % show percentile change in the index from the previous period for which an index is available.

Year	Jan Index	%	Feb Index	%	Mar Index	%	Apr Index	%	May Index	%	Jun Index	%	Jul Index	%	Aug Index	%	Sep Index	%	Oct Index	%	Nov Index	%	Dec Index	%
1976	63.6	-	63.7	0.2	63.3	-0.6	64.0	1.1	63.7	-0.5	64.4	1.1	64.9	0.8	65.0	0.2	64.7	-0.5	64.9	0.3	64.5	-0.6	64.4	-0.2
1977	64.7	0.5	65.9	1.9	66.5	0.9	67.3	1.2	67.3	0.0	67.9	0.9	68.6	1.0	69.0	0.6	69.4	0.6	69.5	0.1	69.4	-0.1	70.0	0.9
1978	71.8	2.6	72.8	1.4	73.5	1.0	74.4	1.2	75.1	0.9	76.0	1.2	76.4	0.5	77.0	0.8	77.4	0.5	77.5	0.1	78.4	1.2	78.6	0.3
1979	80.0	1.8	81.2	1.5	82.3	1.4	82.9	0.7	83.7	1.0	83.9	0.2	84.7	1.0	84.1	-0.7	84.3	0.2	85.0	0.8	86.1	1.3	87.0	1.0
1980	86.8	-0.2	87.6	0.9	88.8	1.4	89.5	0.8	90.1	0.7	90.2	0.1	91.4	1.3	92.7	1.4	93.5	0.9	94.1	0.6	94.5	0.4	95.0	0.5
1981	95.6	0.6	96.2	0.6	96.3	0.1	95.9	-0.4	95.4	-0.5	96.2	0.8	96.5	0.3	97.1	0.6	96.9	-0.2	97.1	0.2	96.7	-0.4	96.7	0.0
1982	97.5	0.8	97.6	0.1	97.4	-0.2	98.5	1.1	99.4	0.9	99.9	0.5	99.5	-0.4	99.1	-0.4	98.9	-0.2	98.9	0.0	98.7	-0.2	98.8	0.1
1983	99.7	0.9	99.7	0.0	99.6	-0.1	99.8	0.2	99.4	-0.4	99.3	-0.1	98.5	-0.8	98.4	-0.1	99.3	0.9	99.3	0.0	99.8	0.5	99.5	-0.3
1984	101.8	2.3	102.7	0.9	102.2	-0.5	102.0	-0.2	101.7	-0.3	101.4	-0.3	102.0	0.6	102.5	0.5	102.1	-0.4	102.0	-0.1	101.2	-0.8	101.9	0.7
1985	102.6	0.7	104.0	1.4	104.1	0.1	103.5	-0.6	103.2	-0.3	104.1	0.9	103.8	-0.3	104.0	0.2	104.3	0.3	104.4	0.1	105.6	1.1	107.0	1.3
1986	106.9	-0.1	107.9	0.9	107.7	-0.2	107.8	0.1	107.4	-0.4	108.5	1.0	109.3	0.7	110.4	1.0	110.1	-0.3	109.1	-0.9	111.1	1.8	110.9	-0.2
1987	113.1	2.0	112.7	-0.4	112.0	-0.6	112.9	0.8	112.7	-0.2	113.6	0.8	113.2	-0.4	113.5	0.3	113.7	0.2	113.5	-0.2	113.7	0.2	113.7	0.0
1988	114.4	0.6	114.9	0.4	115.0	0.1	115.2	0.2	115.8	0.5	116.1	0.3	117.9	1.6	118.8	0.8	119.3	0.4	119.2	-0.1	118.9	-0.3	119.3	0.3
1989	120.7	1.2	121.5	0.7	121.5	0.0	122.7	1.0	122.3	-0.3	122.3	0.0	122.7	0.3	122.4	-0.2	122.9	0.4	123.2	0.2	123.6	0.3	124.2	0.5
1990	128.0	3.1	128.7	0.5	129.0	0.2	128.9	-0.1	129.1	0.2	129.8	0.5	131.3	1.2	131.0	-0.2	131.3	0.2	131.1	-0.2	132.2	0.8	132.9	0.5
1991	134.7	1.4	134.8	0.1	135.3	0.4	136.0	0.5	136.5	0.4	136.2	-0.2	136.0	-0.1	134.8	-0.9	135.5	0.5	134.6	-0.7	135.6	0.7	135.9	0.2
1992	136.6	0.5	137.7	0.8	138.8	0.8	139.1	0.2	139.8	0.5	138.9	-0.6	138.8	-0.1	139.2	0.3	140.4	0.9	139.6	-0.6	140.2	0.4	140.8	0.4
1993	142.5	1.2	140.8	-1.2	142.2	1.0	141.9	-0.2	143.3	1.0	142.7	-0.4	142.9	0.1	143.1	0.1	143.3	0.1	144.3	0.7	144.4	0.1	145.6	0.8

Source: U.S. Department of Labor, Bureau of Labor Statistics, Division of Consumer Prices and Price Indexes. - indicates no data collected for period.

Chicago, IL-NW IN

Consumer Price Index - Urban Wage Earners
Base 1982-1984 = 100

Food and Beverages

For 1976-1993. Columns headed % show percentile change in the index from the previous period for which an index is available.

Year	Jan Index	%	Feb Index	%	Mar Index	%	Apr Index	%	May Index	%	Jun Index	%	Jul Index	%	Aug Index	%	Sep Index	%	Oct Index	%	Nov Index	%	Dec Index	%
1976	64.6	-	64.6	0.0	64.2	-0.6	64.9	1.1	64.7	-0.3	65.3	0.9	65.9	0.9	66.0	0.2	65.6	-0.6	65.9	0.5	65.5	-0.6	65.4	-0.2
1977	65.7	0.5	66.9	1.8	67.5	0.9	68.3	1.2	68.3	0.0	68.9	0.9	69.6	1.0	70.1	0.7	70.4	0.4	70.6	0.3	70.5	-0.1	71.1	0.9
1978	72.6	2.1	73.1	0.7	73.6	0.7	74.7	1.5	75.5	1.1	76.5	1.3	77.1	0.8	77.5	0.5	78.0	0.6	78.4	0.5	79.1	0.9	79.3	0.3
1979	81.1	2.3	81.9	1.0	83.3	1.7	83.7	0.5	84.4	0.8	84.6	0.2	85.2	0.7	84.4	-0.9	84.7	0.4	85.9	1.4	86.8	1.0	87.6	0.9
1980	87.9	0.3	88.4	0.6	89.7	1.5	90.5	0.9	91.5	1.1	91.7	0.2	93.0	1.4	93.6	0.6	94.8	1.3	95.0	0.2	95.8	0.8	95.4	-0.4
1981	95.5	0.1	95.9	0.4	95.9	0.0	96.0	0.1	95.4	-0.6	96.2	0.8	96.5	0.3	96.9	0.4	96.8	-0.1	97.1	0.3	96.6	-0.5	96.7	0.1
1982	97.5	0.8	97.6	0.1	97.3	-0.3	98.5	1.2	99.4	0.9	99.8	0.4	99.5	-0.3	99.1	-0.4	98.8	-0.3	98.7	-0.1	98.7	0.0	98.8	0.1
1983	99.6	0.8	99.7	0.1	99.6	-0.1	99.7	0.1	99.4	-0.3	99.3	-0.1	98.5	-0.8	98.4	-0.1	99.3	0.9	99.5	0.2	99.8	0.3	99.7	-0.1
1984	101.9	2.2	102.7	0.8	102.2	-0.5	102.1	-0.1	101.8	-0.3	101.5	-0.3	101.9	0.4	102.5	0.6	102.0	-0.5	101.9	-0.1	101.3	-0.6	102.0	0.7
1985	102.6	0.6	104.0	1.4	104.1	0.1	103.6	-0.5	103.2	-0.4	104.1	0.9	103.7	-0.4	103.9	0.2	104.3	0.4	104.5	0.2	105.7	1.1	106.9	1.1
1986	107.0	0.1	107.9	0.8	107.8	-0.1	107.9	0.1	107.5	-0.4	108.6	1.0	109.4	0.7	110.5	1.0	110.2	-0.3	109.2	-0.9	111.3	1.9	110.9	-0.4
1987	113.2	2.1	112.8	-0.4	112.1	-0.6	113.0	0.8	112.8	-0.2	113.7	0.8	113.3	-0.4	113.6	0.3	113.8	0.2	113.6	-0.2	113.8	0.2	113.8	0.0
1988	114.5	0.6	114.9	0.3	115.1	0.2	115.3	0.2	115.9	0.5	116.1	0.2	118.0	1.6	118.9	0.8	119.4	0.4	119.3	-0.1	119.0	-0.3	119.4	0.3
1989	120.8	1.2	121.5	0.6	121.5	0.0	122.7	1.0	122.3	-0.3	122.4	0.1	122.8	0.3	122.5	-0.2	123.1	0.5	123.3	0.2	123.7	0.3	124.3	0.5
1990	128.3	3.2	128.8	0.4	129.1	0.2	129.1	0.0	129.2	0.1	130.0	0.6	131.4	1.1	131.2	-0.2	131.5	0.2	131.2	-0.2	132.4	0.9	133.0	0.5
1991	134.8	1.4	134.9	0.1	135.5	0.4	136.2	0.5	136.7	0.4	136.4	-0.2	136.2	-0.1	135.0	-0.9	135.7	0.5	134.7	-0.7	135.8	0.8	135.9	0.1
1992	136.6	0.5	137.7	0.8	138.9	0.9	139.2	0.2	139.8	0.4	139.0	-0.6	138.8	-0.1	139.2	0.3	140.4	0.9	139.7	-0.5	140.3	0.4	140.9	0.4
1993	142.6	1.2	140.9	-1.2	142.3	1.0	142.1	-0.1	143.4	0.9	142.8	-0.4	143.1	0.2	143.3	0.1	143.5	0.1	144.5	0.7	144.7	0.1	145.9	0.8

Source: U.S. Department of Labor, Bureau of Labor Statistics, Division of Consumer Prices and Price Indexes. - indicates no data collected for period.

Chicago, IL-NW IN

Consumer Price Index - All Urban Consumers
Base 1982-1984 = 100
Housing

For 1976-1993. Columns headed % show percentile change in the index from the previous period for which an index is available.

Year	Jan Index	%	Feb Index	%	Mar Index	%	Apr Index	%	May Index	%	Jun Index	%	Jul Index	%	Aug Index	%	Sep Index	%	Oct Index	%	Nov Index	%	Dec Index	%
1976	47.5	-	47.6	0.2	47.8	0.4	47.9	0.2	48.1	0.4	48.3	0.4	48.6	0.6	48.8	0.4	49.1	0.6	49.3	0.4	49.3	0.0	49.9	1.2
1977	50.0	0.2	50.4	0.8	50.5	0.2	50.9	0.8	51.0	0.2	51.0	0.0	51.6	1.2	51.9	0.6	52.4	1.0	52.6	0.4	52.9	0.6	53.0	0.2
1978	54.2	2.3	55.0	1.5	56.1	2.0	56.2	0.2	56.6	0.7	57.0	0.7	57.5	0.9	57.0	-0.9	58.2	2.1	58.9	1.2	60.1	2.0	60.3	0.3
1979	60.3	0.0	61.5	2.0	63.3	2.9	64.1	1.3	63.8	-0.5	65.6	2.8	67.2	2.4	68.0	1.2	68.9	1.3	68.6	-0.4	70.6	2.9	71.1	0.7
1980	71.5	0.6	72.0	0.7	72.3	0.4	74.6	3.2	76.2	2.1	79.6	4.5	78.1	-1.9	76.2	-2.4	78.7	3.3	80.7	2.5	84.3	4.5	84.1	-0.2
1981	81.8	-2.7	81.4	-0.5	81.0	-0.5	83.3	2.8	83.6	0.4	86.3	3.2	88.0	2.0	89.3	1.5	89.4	0.1	88.5	-1.0	88.8	0.3	86.3	-2.8
1982	87.5	1.4	87.2	-0.3	88.8	1.8	91.0	2.5	95.6	5.1	97.1	1.6	98.0	0.9	97.9	-0.1	98.5	0.6	98.5	0.0	98.5	0.0	97.8	-0.7
1983	98.2	0.4	98.6	0.4	98.8	0.2	99.1	0.3	99.4	0.3	101.5	2.1	102.1	0.6	102.4	0.3	102.2	-0.2	100.8	-1.4	101.8	1.0	102.3	0.5
1984	102.5	0.2	102.1	-0.4	102.5	0.4	103.0	0.5	103.0	0.0	105.1	2.0	105.0	-0.1	106.7	1.6	107.8	1.0	106.1	-1.6	106.2	0.1	106.3	0.1
1985	107.1	0.8	107.2	0.1	106.8	-0.4	107.6	0.7	108.1	0.5	111.6	3.2	111.7	0.1	113.2	1.3	113.3	0.1	109.4	-3.4	109.2	-0.2	109.6	0.4
1986	110.3	0.6	110.5	0.2	110.4	-0.1	111.3	0.8	111.0	-0.3	115.5	4.1	116.0	0.4	116.1	0.1	117.1	0.9	112.1	-4.3	112.7	0.5	112.1	-0.5
1987	113.1	0.9	113.3	0.2	113.3	0.0	113.9	0.5	114.1	0.2	118.7	4.0	119.6	0.8	120.3	0.6	120.6	0.2	115.4	-4.3	116.6	1.0	117.0	0.3
1988	115.7	-1.1	118.0	2.0	118.0	0.0	118.1	0.1	118.1	0.0	121.9	3.2	122.7	0.7	122.1	-0.5	124.6	2.0	123.7	-0.7	122.3	-1.1	123.1	0.7
1989	123.1	0.0	123.8	0.6	124.2	0.3	124.2	0.0	124.5	0.2	128.2	3.0	128.9	0.5	128.8	-0.1	129.9	0.9	126.9	-2.3	126.9	0.0	127.2	0.2
1990	128.0	0.6	129.2	0.9	129.3	0.1	130.2	0.7	129.6	-0.5	133.2	2.8	133.4	0.2	134.3	0.7	134.2	-0.1	130.8	-2.5	131.7	0.7	132.5	0.6
1991	134.2	1.3	134.3	0.1	135.8	1.1	134.9	-0.7	136.1	0.9	137.6	1.1	138.3	0.5	137.9	-0.3	137.7	-0.1	137.0	-0.5	135.6	-1.0	137.4	1.3
1992	138.9	1.1	138.3	-0.4	138.2	-0.1	138.2	0.0	139.1	0.7	141.4	1.7	140.7	-0.5	140.6	-0.1	141.6	0.7	139.5	-1.5	140.5	0.7	141.8	0.9
1993	141.8	0.0	141.3	-0.4	141.0	-0.2	142.5	1.1	142.9	0.3	144.3	1.0	143.3	-0.7	144.3	0.7	145.2	0.6	145.6	0.3	143.4	-1.5	143.4	0.0

Source: U.S. Department of Labor, Bureau of Labor Statistics, Division of Consumer Prices and Price Indexes. - indicates no data collected for period.

Chicago, IL-NW IN
Consumer Price Index - Urban Wage Earners
Base 1982-1984 = 100
Housing

For 1976-1993. Columns headed % show percentile change in the index from the previous period for which an index is available.

Year	Jan Index	%	Feb Index	%	Mar Index	%	Apr Index	%	May Index	%	Jun Index	%	Jul Index	%	Aug Index	%	Sep Index	%	Oct Index	%	Nov Index	%	Dec Index	%
1976	49.6	-	49.7	0.2	50.0	0.6	50.1	0.2	50.3	0.4	50.5	0.4	50.7	0.4	51.0	0.6	51.3	0.6	51.5	0.4	51.5	0.0	52.1	1.2
1977	52.3	0.4	52.7	0.8	52.8	0.2	53.2	0.8	53.3	0.2	53.3	0.0	53.9	1.1	54.2	0.6	54.7	0.9	54.9	0.4	55.3	0.7	55.4	0.2
1978	56.6	2.2	57.4	1.4	58.5	1.9	58.5	0.0	59.0	0.9	59.4	0.7	60.0	1.0	59.1	-1.5	60.3	2.0	61.3	1.7	62.4	1.8	62.9	0.8
1979	62.8	-0.2	63.9	1.8	65.7	2.8	66.3	0.9	66.1	-0.3	67.9	2.7	69.5	2.4	70.3	1.2	71.2	1.3	71.0	-0.3	73.0	2.8	73.4	0.5
1980	73.8	0.5	74.3	0.7	74.9	0.8	77.0	2.8	78.6	2.1	82.1	4.5	80.6	-1.8	78.7	-2.4	81.1	3.0	82.9	2.2	86.4	4.2	86.5	0.1
1981	84.3	-2.5	83.8	-0.6	83.4	-0.5	85.8	2.9	86.2	0.5	88.9	3.1	90.7	2.0	92.1	1.5	92.3	0.2	91.4	-1.0	91.8	0.4	89.2	-2.8
1982	90.4	1.3	90.2	-0.2	91.8	1.8	94.0	2.4	98.8	5.1	100.5	1.7	101.4	0.9	101.2	-0.2	101.8	0.6	101.8	0.0	101.7	-0.1	101.0	-0.7
1983	101.6	0.6	101.1	-0.5	101.3	0.2	102.1	0.8	102.5	0.4	103.2	0.7	103.4	0.2	103.0	-0.4	103.3	0.3	99.1	-4.1	99.6	0.5	98.8	-0.8
1984	101.4	2.6	100.1	-1.3	99.4	-0.7	99.0	-0.4	98.9	-0.1	99.9	1.0	100.0	0.1	101.3	1.3	103.3	2.0	100.7	-2.5	101.6	0.9	100.9	-0.7
1985	101.5	0.6	101.7	0.2	101.3	-0.4	102.0	0.7	102.4	0.4	106.0	3.5	106.1	0.1	107.4	1.2	107.5	0.1	103.6	-3.6	103.5	-0.1	103.9	0.4
1986	104.5	0.6	104.7	0.2	104.4	-0.3	105.3	0.9	105.0	-0.3	109.4	4.2	110.1	0.6	110.3	0.2	111.0	0.6	105.9	-4.6	106.5	0.6	105.9	-0.6
1987	106.8	0.8	107.0	0.2	106.9	-0.1	107.3	0.4	107.5	0.2	112.0	4.2	112.8	0.7	113.6	0.7	113.8	0.2	108.7	-4.5	109.8	1.0	110.3	0.5
1988	109.1	-1.1	111.2	1.9	110.9	-0.3	111.0	0.1	111.0	0.0	114.7	3.3	115.6	0.8	114.8	-0.7	117.2	2.1	116.4	-0.7	115.3	-0.9	116.1	0.7
1989	116.0	-0.1	116.6	0.5	116.7	0.1	116.7	0.0	117.0	0.3	120.7	3.2	121.3	0.5	121.3	0.0	122.3	0.8	119.3	-2.5	119.6	0.3	119.8	0.2
1990	120.6	0.7	121.7	0.9	121.7	0.0	122.7	0.8	122.1	-0.5	125.5	2.8	125.7	0.2	126.6	0.7	126.7	0.1	123.2	-2.8	124.1	0.7	125.0	0.7
1991	126.4	1.1	126.5	0.1	127.8	1.0	127.0	-0.6	128.0	0.8	129.4	1.1	130.2	0.6	129.7	-0.4	129.6	-0.1	128.8	-0.6	127.6	-0.9	129.5	1.5
1992	130.7	0.9	130.1	-0.5	129.9	-0.2	130.0	0.1	130.9	0.7	133.0	1.6	132.4	-0.5	132.2	-0.2	133.3	0.8	131.4	-1.4	132.5	0.8	133.7	0.9
1993	133.8	0.1	133.3	-0.4	132.8	-0.4	134.3	1.1	134.7	0.3	135.9	0.9	135.0	-0.7	135.9	0.7	136.7	0.6	137.2	0.4	135.1	-1.5	135.3	0.1

Source: U.S. Department of Labor, Bureau of Labor Statistics, Division of Consumer Prices and Price Indexes. - indicates no data collected for period.

Chicago, IL-NW IN

Consumer Price Index - All Urban Consumers
Base 1982-1984 = 100
Apparel and Upkeep

For 1952-1993. Columns headed % show percentile change in the index from the previous period for which an index is available.

Year	Jan Index	%	Feb Index	%	Mar Index	%	Apr Index	%	May Index	%	Jun Index	%	Jul Index	%	Aug Index	%	Sep Index	%	Oct Index	%	Nov Index	%	Dec Index	%
1952	-	-	-	-	-	-	-	-	-	-	-	-	-	-	-	-	-	-	-	-	-	-	52.2	-
1953	51.8	-0.8	51.9	0.2	52.0	0.2	52.1	0.2	52.3	0.4	52.4	0.2	52.4	0.0	52.6	0.4	53.1	1.0	53.1	0.0	53.1	0.0	52.9	-0.4
1954	52.9	0.0	52.9	0.0	53.0	0.2	52.9	-0.2	52.9	0.0	52.9	0.0	52.9	0.0	52.4	-0.9	52.5	0.2	52.4	-0.2	52.3	-0.2	52.2	-0.2
1955	51.4	-1.5	51.6	0.4	51.7	0.2	51.3	-0.8	51.4	0.2	51.5	0.2	52.1	1.2	52.3	0.4	53.3	1.9	53.4	0.2	53.7	0.6	53.4	-0.6
1956	53.4	0.0	53.4	0.0	53.5	0.2	53.6	0.2	53.5	-0.2	53.5	0.0	53.8	0.6	54.1	0.6	54.5	0.7	54.8	0.6	54.6	-0.4	54.8	0.4
1957	53.9	-1.6	54.1	0.4	54.7	1.1	54.6	-0.2	54.6	0.0	54.8	0.4	54.7	-0.2	54.8	0.2	55.7	1.6	55.6	-0.2	55.4	-0.4	55.4	0.0
1958	54.9	-0.9	54.8	-0.2	54.8	0.0	54.7	-0.2	54.7	0.0	54.9	0.4	55.2	0.5	54.8	-0.7	55.4	1.1	55.3	-0.2	55.4	0.2	55.1	-0.5
1959	54.8	-0.5	54.6	-0.4	54.5	-0.2	54.9	0.7	55.1	0.4	54.9	-0.4	55.4	0.9	55.6	0.4	56.6	1.8	56.6	0.0	56.6	0.0	56.6	0.0
1960	56.0	-1.1	56.1	0.2	56.2	0.2	55.7	-0.9	56.0	0.5	56.0	0.0	56.4	0.7	56.6	0.4	56.7	0.2	56.8	0.2	56.7	-0.2	56.9	0.4
1961	56.0	-1.6	56.0	0.0	56.0	0.0	56.0	0.0	55.8	-0.4	55.5	-0.5	55.8	0.5	55.5	-0.5	56.7	2.2	56.6	-0.2	56.4	-0.4	56.4	0.0
1962	55.4	-1.8	55.3	-0.2	55.6	0.5	55.5	-0.2	55.6	0.2	55.5	-0.2	55.7	0.4	55.4	-0.5	56.3	1.6	56.3	0.0	56.3	0.0	56.4	0.2
1963	55.6	-1.4	55.7	0.2	55.8	0.2	55.9	0.2	55.8	-0.2	55.4	-0.7	55.7	0.5	55.5	-0.4	56.9	2.5	57.0	0.2	56.6	-0.7	56.8	0.4
1964	55.4	-2.5	55.8	0.7	56.4	1.1	56.4	0.0	56.4	0.0	56.3	-0.2	56.1	-0.4	55.7	-0.7	56.7	1.8	56.6	-0.2	56.4	-0.4	56.5	0.2
1965	56.0	-0.9	55.8	-0.4	56.3	0.9	56.4	0.2	56.9	0.9	57.0	0.2	56.1	-1.6	56.4	0.5	57.5	2.0	57.7	0.3	57.7	0.0	57.9	0.3
1966	56.8	-1.9	56.7	-0.2	58.0	2.3	57.8	-0.3	58.1	0.5	58.3	0.3	57.4	-1.5	57.9	0.9	59.7	3.1	59.7	0.0	59.4	-0.5	59.7	0.5
1967	59.1	-1.0	59.2	0.2	59.7	0.8	59.8	0.2	60.3	0.8	60.4	0.2	59.8	-1.0	60.3	0.8	61.7	2.3	61.9	0.3	62.1	0.3	62.3	0.3
1968	60.5	-2.9	61.2	1.2	62.8	2.6	63.2	0.6	63.9	1.1	64.0	0.2	63.2	-1.2	63.4	0.3	65.2	2.8	65.7	0.8	65.8	0.2	65.9	0.2
1969	64.1	-2.7	65.7	2.5	66.3	0.9	66.0	-0.5	66.6	0.9	67.0	0.6	66.6	-0.6	65.2	-2.1	68.6	5.2	68.5	-0.1	68.9	0.6	68.8	-0.1
1970	66.2	-3.8	66.8	0.9	68.2	2.1	67.6	-0.9	68.7	1.6	68.3	-0.6	67.1	-1.8	67.9	1.2	71.0	4.6	70.7	-0.4	70.7	0.0	70.4	-0.4
1971	68.1	-3.3	69.8	2.5	70.7	1.3	70.5	-0.3	71.1	0.9	71.3	0.3	69.7	-2.2	70.3	0.9	72.9	3.7	72.8	-0.1	73.0	0.3	73.0	0.0
1972	70.4	-3.6	72.0	2.3	72.4	0.6	72.1	-0.4	72.2	0.1	72.1	-0.1	70.2	-2.6	70.4	0.3	74.3	5.5	74.3	0.0	74.7	0.5	74.7	0.0
1973	73.0	-2.3	74.1	1.5	76.1	2.7	76.1	0.0	76.5	0.5	76.2	-0.4	74.7	-2.0	75.5	1.1	77.5	2.6	77.3	-0.3	77.8	0.6	77.5	-0.4
1974	75.5	-2.6	77.2	2.3	78.4	1.6	79.3	1.1	79.6	0.4	80.1	0.6	79.0	-1.4	82.3	4.2	82.6	0.4	82.9	0.4	83.7	1.0	83.7	0.0
1975	81.0	-3.2	81.5	0.6	82.7	1.5	82.9	0.2	82.6	-0.4	82.1	-0.6	81.6	-0.6	82.7	1.3	84.3	1.9	84.1	-0.2	84.1	0.0	83.5	-0.7
1976	80.9	-3.1	82.0	1.4	82.6	0.7	82.2	-0.5	83.0	1.0	83.6	0.7	82.7	-1.1	84.2	1.8	86.0	2.1	85.6	-0.5	85.9	0.4	85.7	-0.2
1977	83.0	-3.2	84.1	1.3	85.4	1.5	85.3	-0.1	85.3	0.0	86.4	1.3	85.9	-0.6	87.0	1.3	88.7	2.0	87.3	-1.6	88.0	0.8	87.8	-0.2
1978	85.2	-3.0	85.0	-0.2	86.4	1.6	87.9	1.7	88.6	0.8	88.4	-0.2	87.7	-0.8	88.8	1.3	89.5	0.8	89.5	0.0	90.2	0.8	88.8	-1.6
1979	87.5	-1.5	88.2	0.8	90.4	2.5	89.6	-0.9	90.2	0.7	89.4	-0.9	89.9	0.6	89.3	-0.7	91.9	2.9	91.9	0.0	93.5	1.7	93.8	0.3
1980	93.7	-0.1	93.0	-0.7	95.1	2.3	94.8	-0.3	94.2	-0.6	95.2	1.1	95.5	0.3	96.2	0.7	97.4	1.2	97.9	0.5	98.3	0.4	95.8	-2.5
1981	93.1	-2.8	93.0	-0.1	94.4	1.5	94.9	0.5	95.1	0.2	94.0	-1.2	94.1	0.1	99.0	5.2	100.8	1.8	99.9	-0.9	100.8	0.9	98.1	-2.7
1982	95.6	-2.5	96.9	1.4	95.7	-1.2	97.2	1.6	98.7	1.5	97.8	-0.9	94.3	-3.6	99.3	5.3	100.5	1.2	99.8	-0.7	99.2	-0.6	97.4	-1.8
1983	96.4	-1.0	95.6	-0.8	98.6	3.1	97.9	-0.7	99.0	1.1	96.8	-2.2	97.4	0.6	102.2	4.9	104.7	2.4	104.7	0.0	106.0	1.2	103.5	-2.4
1984	99.0	-4.3	96.5	-2.5	98.7	2.3	99.7	1.0	100.4	0.7	98.8	-1.6	102.4	3.6	104.9	2.4	106.1	1.1	106.1	0.0	107.8	1.6	104.7	-2.9
1985	100.7	-3.8	103.8	3.1	105.7	1.8	106.7	0.9	105.7	-0.9	104.9	-0.8	105.6	0.7	106.4	0.8	108.4	1.9	108.3	-0.1	108.6	0.3	106.9	-1.6
1986	102.5	-4.1	102.4	-0.1	101.1	-1.3	100.2	-0.9	100.3	0.1	99.3	-1.0	101.1	1.8	105.0	3.9	109.4	4.2	109.4	0.0	108.6	-0.7	107.0	-1.5
1987	104.4	-2.4	102.7	-1.6	108.0	5.2	107.6	-0.4	108.6	0.9	106.7	-1.7	105.1	-1.5	112.7	7.2	114.3	1.4	114.2	-0.1	114.5	0.3	112.0	-2.2
1988	111.1	-0.8	112.2	1.0	115.8	3.2	115.3	-0.4	113.6	-1.5	115.6	1.8	114.7	-0.8	116.8	1.8	122.8	5.1	121.1	-1.4	120.4	-0.6	119.8	-0.5
1989	114.1	-4.8	112.3	-1.6	119.3	6.2	117.8	-1.3	116.0	-1.5	113.5	-2.2	118.1	4.1	119.6	1.3	120.5	0.8	124.8	3.6	123.2	-1.3	117.5	-4.6
1990	114.5	-2.6	121.4	6.0	126.1	3.9	129.4	2.6	129.4	0.0	123.0	-4.9	119.8	-2.6	123.5	3.1	126.7	2.6	126.6	-0.1	127.9	1.0	122.8	-4.0
1991	116.5	-5.1	124.1	6.5	127.1	2.4	128.9	1.4	125.2	-2.9	122.3	-2.3	119.6	-2.2	127.1	6.3	128.8	1.3	129.5	0.5	130.0	0.4	124.0	-4.6
1992	120.8	-2.6	126.5	4.7	129.3	2.2	124.7	-3.6	124.5	-0.2	123.5	-0.8	124.7	1.0	132.3	6.1	130.8	-1.1	129.4	-1.1	125.2	-3.2	123.1	-1.7
1993	121.2	-1.5	133.3	10.0	137.0	2.8	133.4	-2.6	133.9	0.4	126.6	-5.5	128.2	1.3	134.0	4.5	134.3	0.2	133.9	-0.3	131.9	-1.5	125.8	-4.6

Source: U.S. Department of Labor, Bureau of Labor Statistics, Division of Consumer Prices and Price Indexes. - indicates no data collected for period.

Chicago, IL-NW IN
Consumer Price Index - Urban Wage Earners
Base 1982-1984 = 100
Apparel and Upkeep

For 1952-1993. Columns headed % show percentile change in the index from the previous period for which an index is available.

Year	Jan Index	%	Feb Index	%	Mar Index	%	Apr Index	%	May Index	%	Jun Index	%	Jul Index	%	Aug Index	%	Sep Index	%	Oct Index	%	Nov Index	%	Dec Index	%
1952	-		-		-		-		-		-		-		-		-		-		-		50.6	-
1953	50.2	-0.8	50.3	0.2	50.4	0.2	50.5	0.2	50.7	0.4	50.8	0.2	50.8	0.0	51.0	0.4	51.4	0.8	51.4	0.0	51.5	0.2	51.3	-0.4
1954	51.2	-0.2	51.3	0.2	51.4	0.2	51.3	-0.2	51.3	0.0	51.3	0.0	51.3	0.0	50.8	-1.0	50.9	0.2	50.8	-0.2	50.7	-0.2	50.6	-0.2
1955	49.8	-1.6	50.0	0.4	50.1	0.2	49.7	-0.8	49.8	0.2	50.0	0.4	50.5	1.0	50.7	0.4	51.7	2.0	51.7	0.0	52.0	0.6	51.8	-0.4
1956	51.8	0.0	51.7	-0.2	51.9	0.4	52.0	0.2	51.8	-0.4	51.8	0.0	52.2	0.8	52.4	0.4	52.8	0.8	53.1	0.6	52.9	-0.4	53.1	0.4
1957	52.2	-1.7	52.4	0.4	53.0	1.1	52.9	-0.2	52.9	0.0	53.1	0.4	53.0	-0.2	53.1	0.2	54.0	1.7	53.9	-0.2	53.7	-0.4	53.7	0.0
1958	53.2	-0.9	53.1	-0.2	53.1	0.0	53.0	-0.2	53.0	0.0	53.2	0.4	53.5	0.6	53.1	-0.7	53.7	1.1	53.6	-0.2	53.7	0.2	53.4	-0.6
1959	53.1	-0.6	52.9	-0.4	52.8	-0.2	53.2	0.8	53.4	0.4	53.2	-0.4	53.7	0.9	53.9	0.4	54.8	1.7	54.8	0.0	54.8	0.0	54.8	0.0
1960	54.2	-1.1	54.4	0.4	54.5	0.2	54.0	-0.9	54.3	0.6	54.2	-0.2	54.7	0.9	54.8	0.2	55.0	0.4	55.1	0.2	55.0	-0.2	55.1	0.2
1961	54.3	-1.5	54.2	-0.2	54.2	0.0	54.2	0.0	54.1	-0.2	53.8	-0.6	54.1	0.6	53.8	-0.6	54.9	2.0	54.8	-0.2	54.7	-0.2	54.7	0.0
1962	53.7	-1.8	53.6	-0.2	53.9	0.6	53.8	-0.2	53.9	0.2	53.8	-0.2	53.9	0.2	53.7	-0.4	54.6	1.7	54.6	0.0	54.5	-0.2	54.7	0.4
1963	53.9	-1.5	53.9	0.0	54.1	0.4	54.2	0.2	54.1	-0.2	53.7	-0.7	54.0	0.6	53.8	-0.4	55.1	2.4	55.2	0.2	54.9	-0.5	55.1	0.4
1964	53.7	-2.5	54.1	0.7	54.7	1.1	54.7	0.0	54.7	0.0	54.5	-0.4	54.4	-0.2	54.0	-0.7	54.9	1.7	54.9	0.0	54.7	-0.4	54.8	0.2
1965	54.2	-1.1	54.1	-0.2	54.5	0.7	54.7	0.4	55.1	0.7	55.2	0.2	54.4	-1.4	54.7	0.6	55.7	1.8	55.9	0.4	55.9	0.0	56.1	0.4
1966	55.1	-1.8	55.0	-0.2	56.2	2.2	56.1	-0.2	56.3	0.4	56.5	0.4	55.6	-1.6	56.1	0.9	57.8	3.0	57.8	0.0	57.6	-0.3	57.9	0.5
1967	57.2	-1.2	57.4	0.3	57.8	0.7	57.9	0.2	58.4	0.9	58.6	0.3	58.0	-1.0	58.5	0.9	59.8	2.2	60.0	0.3	60.2	0.3	60.3	0.2
1968	58.6	-2.8	59.3	1.2	60.9	2.7	61.3	0.7	61.9	1.0	62.0	0.2	61.2	-1.3	61.5	0.5	63.2	2.8	63.7	0.8	63.8	0.2	63.9	0.2
1969	62.2	-2.7	63.6	2.3	64.2	0.9	64.0	-0.3	64.5	0.8	65.0	0.8	64.6	-0.6	63.2	-2.2	66.5	5.2	66.4	-0.2	66.7	0.5	66.7	0.0
1970	64.2	-3.7	64.7	0.8	66.1	2.2	65.5	-0.9	66.6	1.7	66.2	-0.6	65.0	-1.8	65.8	1.2	68.8	4.6	68.6	-0.3	68.5	-0.1	68.3	-0.3
1971	66.0	-3.4	67.6	2.4	68.5	1.3	68.3	-0.3	68.9	0.9	69.1	0.3	67.5	-2.3	68.1	0.9	70.7	3.8	70.6	-0.1	70.8	0.3	70.7	-0.1
1972	68.3	-3.4	69.7	2.0	70.2	0.7	69.9	-0.4	70.0	0.1	69.9	-0.1	68.0	-2.7	68.2	0.3	72.0	5.6	72.0	0.0	72.4	0.6	72.4	0.0
1973	70.8	-2.2	71.9	1.6	73.7	2.5	73.8	0.1	74.1	0.4	73.8	-0.4	72.4	-1.9	73.2	1.1	75.1	2.6	74.9	-0.3	75.4	0.7	75.1	-0.4
1974	73.1	-2.7	74.8	2.3	76.0	1.6	76.9	1.2	77.1	0.3	77.7	0.8	76.5	-1.5	79.8	4.3	80.1	0.4	80.3	0.2	81.1	1.0	81.1	0.0
1975	78.5	-3.2	79.0	0.6	80.2	1.5	80.4	0.2	80.1	-0.4	79.6	-0.6	79.1	-0.6	80.2	1.4	81.7	1.9	81.5	-0.2	81.5	0.0	80.9	-0.7
1976	78.4	-3.1	79.5	1.4	80.1	0.8	79.7	-0.5	80.4	0.9	81.0	0.7	80.1	-1.1	81.6	1.9	83.4	2.2	82.9	-0.6	83.2	0.4	83.1	-0.1
1977	80.5	-3.1	81.5	1.2	82.8	1.6	82.7	-0.1	82.7	0.0	83.8	1.3	83.3	-0.6	84.3	1.2	85.9	1.9	84.6	-1.5	85.3	0.8	85.1	-0.2
1978	84.4	-0.8	84.6	0.2	84.5	-0.1	86.4	2.2	86.2	-0.2	86.9	0.8	86.9	0.0	86.6	-0.3	87.9	1.5	89.3	1.6	89.6	0.3	88.2	-1.6
1979	85.7	-2.8	87.9	2.6	89.4	1.7	88.8	-0.7	88.9	0.1	88.2	-0.8	88.5	0.3	88.6	0.1	91.8	3.6	91.9	0.1	93.6	1.8	93.3	-0.3
1980	91.5	-1.9	93.0	1.6	93.6	0.6	93.3	-0.3	94.4	1.2	95.7	1.4	95.5	-0.2	96.1	0.6	95.9	-0.2	97.6	1.8	97.0	-0.6	95.1	-2.0
1981	92.2	-3.0	90.8	-1.5	91.8	1.1	93.2	1.5	94.0	0.9	93.2	-0.9	94.9	1.8	99.0	4.3	101.4	2.4	100.7	-0.7	100.7	0.0	98.5	-2.2
1982	96.0	-2.5	97.2	1.2	95.4	-1.9	97.2	1.9	99.1	2.0	98.1	-1.0	95.0	-3.2	98.7	3.9	100.4	1.7	100.0	-0.4	99.3	-0.7	97.6	-1.7
1983	96.2	-1.4	94.9	-1.4	98.1	3.4	97.5	-0.6	98.7	1.2	96.6	-2.1	97.2	0.6	101.8	4.7	104.6	2.8	104.6	0.0	106.0	1.3	103.6	-2.3
1984	98.6	-4.8	96.4	-2.2	99.0	2.7	99.5	0.5	100.4	0.9	99.4	-1.0	101.9	2.5	105.0	3.0	106.5	1.4	106.3	-0.2	108.2	1.8	105.0	-3.0
1985	100.5	-4.3	103.3	2.8	105.4	2.0	106.2	0.8	105.6	-0.6	104.5	-1.0	104.5	0.0	105.3	0.8	108.5	3.0	108.1	-0.4	108.2	0.1	107.0	-1.1
1986	102.9	-3.8	103.1	0.2	101.4	-1.6	100.6	-0.8	100.8	0.2	99.9	-0.9	101.2	1.3	104.7	3.5	109.4	4.5	109.4	0.0	108.7	-0.6	107.3	-1.3
1987	104.5	-2.6	102.9	-1.5	108.4	5.3	108.8	0.4	109.1	0.3	107.2	-1.7	105.5	-1.6	112.3	6.4	113.9	1.4	114.8	0.8	114.0	-0.7	111.9	-1.8
1988	110.5	-1.3	110.8	0.3	115.0	3.8	114.7	-0.3	112.1	-2.3	115.2	2.8	114.6	-0.5	115.8	1.0	122.9	6.1	121.2	-1.4	120.3	-0.7	119.8	-0.4
1989	114.0	-4.8	112.0	-1.8	118.8	6.1	117.9	-0.8	115.1	-2.4	113.2	-1.7	117.4	3.7	118.2	0.7	119.3	0.9	124.5	4.4	122.8	-1.4	117.7	-4.2
1990	114.3	-2.9	121.4	6.2	126.4	4.1	130.4	3.2	130.0	-0.3	123.8	-4.8	120.1	-3.0	123.6	2.9	126.9	2.7	126.6	-0.2	127.8	0.9	123.1	-3.7
1991	117.1	-4.9	125.6	7.3	128.0	1.9	130.2	1.7	126.0	-3.2	122.7	-2.6	120.3	-2.0	126.8	5.4	128.1	1.0	129.1	0.8	130.2	0.9	123.6	-5.1
1992	120.0	-2.9	125.6	4.7	129.2	2.9	125.8	-2.6	125.2	-0.5	123.9	-1.0	124.4	0.4	132.3	6.4	130.2	-1.6	128.7	-1.2	124.1	-3.6	121.3	-2.3
1993	119.3	-1.6	131.1	9.9	135.4	3.3	133.0	-1.8	134.1	0.8	126.9	-5.4	128.5	1.3	133.2	3.7	134.2	0.8	133.7	-0.4	131.6	-1.6	125.5	-4.6

Source: U.S. Department of Labor, Bureau of Labor Statistics, Division of Consumer Prices and Price Indexes. - indicates no data collected for period.

Chicago, IL-NW IN
Consumer Price Index - All Urban Consumers
Base 1982-1984 = 100
Transportation

For 1947-1993. Columns headed % show percentile change in the index from the previous period for which an index is available.

Year	Jan Index	%	Feb Index	%	Mar Index	%	Apr Index	%	May Index	%	Jun Index	%	Jul Index	%	Aug Index	%	Sep Index	%	Oct Index	%	Nov Index	%	Dec Index	%
1947	16.8	-	16.8	0.0	16.8	0.0	17.1	1.8	17.4	1.8	17.4	0.0	17.4	0.0	17.5	0.6	17.7	1.1	18.1	2.3	18.2	0.6	18.3	0.5
1948	18.6	1.6	18.6	0.0	18.6	0.0	18.6	0.0	19.3	3.8	19.3	0.0	21.2	9.8	21.5	1.4	21.6	0.5	21.6	0.0	21.6	0.0	21.6	0.0
1949	21.6	0.0	21.7	0.5	21.7	0.0	21.7	0.0	21.7	0.0	21.7	0.0	21.7	0.0	21.7	0.0	21.7	0.0	22.9	5.5	22.9	0.0	22.8	-0.4
1950	22.8	0.0	22.7	-0.4	22.6	-0.4	22.4	-0.9	22.4	0.0	22.4	0.0	22.5	0.4	22.8	1.3	22.6	-0.9	22.6	0.0	22.7	0.4	22.9	0.9
1951	22.9	0.0	23.0	0.4	23.3	1.3	23.3	0.0	23.3	0.0	23.3	0.0	23.8	2.1	24.6	3.4	24.8	0.8	24.9	0.4	25.1	0.8	24.4	-2.8
1952	25.2	3.3	25.3	0.4	25.3	0.0	25.3	0.0	25.4	0.4	26.5	4.3	26.5	0.0	26.6	0.4	26.6	0.0	26.6	0.0	26.6	0.0	26.6	0.0
1953	26.8	0.8	26.7	-0.4	26.7	0.0	26.6	-0.4	26.5	-0.4	26.6	0.4	26.7	0.4	26.7	0.0	26.6	-0.4	26.5	-0.4	26.4	-0.4	26.4	0.0
1954	26.6	0.8	26.4	-0.8	26.4	0.0	26.3	-0.4	26.6	1.1	26.7	0.4	26.6	-0.4	26.5	-0.4	26.5	0.0	25.4	-4.2	26.7	5.1	26.5	-0.7
1955	26.6	0.4	26.4	-0.8	26.5	0.4	25.8	-2.6	25.9	0.4	25.9	0.0	25.9	0.0	26.0	0.4	26.0	0.0	26.3	1.2	26.5	0.8	26.1	-1.5
1956	26.0	-0.4	26.1	0.4	26.0	-0.4	26.1	0.4	26.2	0.4	26.2	0.0	26.6	1.5	26.6	0.0	26.6	0.0	27.8	4.5	27.8	0.0	27.7	-0.4
1957	28.0	1.1	27.7	-1.1	27.8	0.4	27.8	0.0	27.7	-0.4	27.7	0.0	28.7	3.6	28.9	0.7	28.6	-1.0	28.5	-0.3	29.6	3.9	30.0	1.4
1958	30.1	0.3	29.7	-1.3	29.5	-0.7	29.4	-0.3	29.5	0.3	29.7	0.7	29.6	-0.3	29.8	0.7	29.8	0.0	30.4	2.0	30.6	0.7	30.9	1.0
1959	30.8	-0.3	30.7	-0.3	30.8	0.3	30.8	0.0	30.7	-0.3	30.6	-0.3	30.9	1.0	30.9	0.0	30.9	0.0	31.5	1.9	31.7	0.6	31.9	0.6
1960	31.5	-1.3	31.4	-0.3	31.2	-0.6	31.0	-0.6	30.8	-0.6	30.9	0.3	31.0	0.3	31.1	0.3	31.0	-0.3	31.4	1.3	31.2	-0.6	31.0	-0.6
1961	30.8	-0.6	30.7	-0.3	30.3	-1.3	30.5	0.7	30.5	0.0	30.2	-1.0	31.2	3.3	31.4	0.6	31.3	-0.3	31.8	1.6	31.3	-1.6	31.1	-0.6
1962	31.2	0.3	31.4	0.6	31.4	0.0	31.8	1.3	31.8	0.0	31.3	-1.6	31.0	-1.0	30.8	-0.6	31.8	3.2	31.8	0.0	31.8	0.0	31.7	-0.3
1963	31.4	-0.9	31.5	0.3	31.8	1.0	31.7	-0.3	32.0	0.9	31.9	-0.3	31.9	0.0	31.8	-0.3	31.5	-0.9	31.9	1.3	31.6	-0.9	31.9	0.9
1964	31.5	-1.3	31.4	-0.3	31.3	-0.3	31.3	0.0	31.8	1.6	31.9	0.3	32.1	0.6	32.0	-0.3	31.7	-0.9	31.9	0.6	32.2	0.9	32.2	0.0
1965	32.4	0.6	32.3	-0.3	32.4	0.3	32.7	0.9	32.8	0.3	32.7	-0.3	32.7	0.0	32.5	-0.6	32.3	-0.6	32.6	0.9	32.6	0.0	32.7	0.3
1966	32.4	-0.9	32.4	0.0	32.4	0.0	32.5	0.3	32.5	0.0	32.6	0.3	32.6	0.0	32.8	0.6	32.8	0.0	32.9	0.3	32.9	0.0	32.7	-0.6
1967	32.6	-0.3	33.0	1.2	33.0	0.0	33.1	0.3	33.3	0.6	33.3	0.0	33.5	0.6	33.5	0.0	33.8	0.9	33.9	0.3	34.8	2.7	34.6	-0.6
1968	34.7	0.3	34.7	0.0	34.9	0.6	35.0	0.3	34.9	-0.3	35.0	0.3	35.0	0.0	35.0	0.0	34.9	-0.3	35.2	0.9	35.3	0.3	36.0	2.0
1969	36.2	0.6	36.5	0.8	37.2	1.9	37.4	0.5	37.1	-0.8	37.3	0.5	37.3	0.0	37.3	0.0	37.2	-0.3	37.7	1.3	37.8	0.3	38.0	0.5
1970	38.4	1.1	38.1	-0.8	38.1	0.0	38.7	1.6	38.9	0.5	39.1	0.5	40.3	3.1	40.3	0.0	40.0	-0.7	41.2	3.0	41.7	1.2	42.0	0.7
1971	41.9	-0.2	42.2	0.7	42.0	-0.5	42.0	0.0	42.5	1.2	42.0	-1.2	42.3	0.7	42.5	0.5	42.2	-0.7	41.9	-0.7	41.8	-0.2	42.0	0.5
1972	41.5	-1.2	40.9	-1.4	40.9	0.0	41.2	0.7	41.6	1.0	41.5	-0.2	41.9	1.0	42.1	0.5	42.1	0.0	42.0	-0.2	42.1	0.2	42.1	0.0
1973	41.8	-0.7	41.8	0.0	42.0	0.5	42.4	1.0	42.9	1.2	43.2	0.7	43.2	0.0	43.0	-0.5	42.9	-0.2	43.5	1.4	43.6	0.2	44.0	0.9
1974	44.5	1.1	44.6	0.2	45.3	1.6	45.7	0.9	46.7	2.2	47.4	1.5	48.1	1.5	48.4	0.6	48.6	0.4	48.8	0.4	49.0	0.4	49.0	0.0
1975	48.5	-1.0	48.5	0.0	49.0	1.0	49.4	0.8	49.8	0.8	50.5	1.4	51.6	2.2	52.4	1.6	52.6	0.4	52.7	0.2	52.9	0.4	52.8	-0.2
1976	52.6	-0.4	53.4	1.5	53.8	0.7	54.3	0.9	55.4	2.0	56.2	1.4	56.7	0.9	57.2	0.9	57.8	1.0	58.3	0.9	58.9	1.0	58.8	-0.2
1977	59.0	0.3	59.6	1.0	60.0	0.7	60.9	1.5	61.4	0.8	61.6	0.3	61.5	-0.2	61.4	-0.2	61.0	-0.7	61.1	0.2	61.0	-0.2	61.2	0.3
1978	61.3	0.2	61.3	0.0	61.3	0.0	61.5	0.3	62.4	1.5	63.2	1.3	63.5	0.5	63.9	0.6	63.9	0.0	64.6	1.1	65.0	0.6	65.4	0.6
1979	66.0	0.9	66.5	0.8	67.2	1.1	68.6	2.1	69.9	1.9	71.5	2.3	72.7	1.7	73.8	1.5	74.7	1.2	75.7	1.3	76.3	0.8	77.4	1.4
1980	79.8	3.1	81.2	1.8	83.1	2.3	84.7	1.9	85.5	0.9	85.4	-0.1	85.2	-0.2	85.7	0.6	86.2	0.6	86.6	0.5	88.1	1.7	88.8	0.8
1981	91.1	2.6	92.5	1.5	93.4	1.0	93.6	0.2	94.4	0.9	95.0	0.6	96.6	1.7	96.7	0.1	97.3	0.6	98.3	1.0	98.9	0.6	99.2	0.3
1982	98.7	-0.5	97.7	-1.0	96.7	-1.0	96.3	-0.4	96.9	0.6	99.6	2.8	100.1	0.5	99.8	-0.3	98.6	-1.2	98.9	0.3	98.8	-0.1	98.0	-0.8
1983	97.4	-0.6	96.4	-1.0	95.4	-1.0	97.0	1.7	98.2	1.2	98.4	0.2	99.3	0.9	100.7	1.4	100.6	-0.1	101.6	1.0	101.8	0.2	101.3	-0.5
1984	101.3	0.0	100.9	-0.4	101.5	0.6	102.2	0.7	102.6	0.4	103.0	0.4	103.2	0.2	103.0	-0.2	103.0	0.0	103.8	0.8	103.8	0.0	103.6	-0.2
1985	103.6	0.0	103.3	-0.3	104.2	0.9	105.3	1.1	106.1	0.8	106.0	-0.1	106.3	0.3	105.7	-0.6	104.7	-0.9	105.3	0.6	106.6	1.2	106.6	0.0
1986	106.1	-0.5	104.8	-1.2	101.3	-3.3	99.2	-2.1	100.8	1.6	101.9	1.1	99.9	-2.0	98.9	-1.0	99.0	0.1	99.7	0.7	100.7	1.0	101.9	1.2
1987	103.4	1.5	103.3	-0.1	104.0	0.7	104.6	0.6	105.9	1.2	106.5	0.6	107.2	0.7	107.2	0.0	107.1	-0.1	108.1	0.9	108.1	0.0	107.7	-0.4
1988	107.0	-0.6	107.1	0.1	107.0	-0.1	107.5	0.5	106.6	-0.8	107.1	0.5	107.1	0.0	108.1	0.9	108.3	0.2	108.1	-0.2	109.0	0.8	108.6	-0.4
1989	109.3	0.6	109.5	0.2	109.9	0.4	112.1	2.0	113.7	1.4	114.0	0.3	112.8	-1.1	111.9	-0.8	111.6	-0.3	113.9	2.1	113.1	-0.7	113.1	0.0
1990	116.6	3.1	115.4	-1.0	114.3	-1.0	115.5	1.0	115.9	0.3	116.6	0.6	116.1	-0.4	118.9	2.4	119.8	0.8	124.5	3.9	125.3	0.6	125.5	0.2
1991	123.5	-1.6	121.7	-1.5	120.0	-1.4	119.3	-0.6	121.1	1.5	121.1	0.0	120.4	-0.6	120.4	0.0	120.6	0.2	121.1	0.4	122.5	1.2	122.1	-0.3

[Continued]

Chicago, IL-NW IN
Consumer Price Index - All Urban Consumers
Base 1982-1984 = 100
Transportation
[Continued]

For 1947-1993. Columns headed % show percentile change in the index from the previous period for which an index is available.

Year	Jan Index	%	Feb Index	%	Mar Index	%	Apr Index	%	May Index	%	Jun Index	%	Jul Index	%	Aug Index	%	Sep Index	%	Oct Index	%	Nov Index	%	Dec Index	%
1992	121.9	-0.2	120.7	-1.0	120.6	-0.1	121.9	1.1	123.1	1.0	123.2	0.1	123.6	0.3	122.6	-0.8	122.8	0.2	125.6	2.3	126.3	0.6	125.6	-0.6
1993	124.9	-0.6	125.0	0.1	124.8	-0.2	126.2	1.1	127.4	1.0	126.8	-0.5	126.6	-0.2	125.4	-0.9	125.6	0.2	127.0	1.1	127.7	0.6	126.6	-0.9

Source: U.S. Department of Labor, Bureau of Labor Statistics, Division of Consumer Prices and Price Indexes. - indicates no data collected for period.

Chicago, IL-NW IN
Consumer Price Index - Urban Wage Earners
Base 1982-1984 = 100
Transportation

For 1947-1993. Columns headed % show percentile change in the index from the previous period for which an index is available.

Year	Jan Index	%	Feb Index	%	Mar Index	%	Apr Index	%	May Index	%	Jun Index	%	Jul Index	%	Aug Index	%	Sep Index	%	Oct Index	%	Nov Index	%	Dec Index	%
1947	16.5	-	16.5	0.0	16.6	0.6	16.8	1.2	17.2	2.4	17.2	0.0	17.2	0.0	17.3	0.6	17.5	1.2	17.8	1.7	17.9	0.6	18.0	0.6
1948	18.3	1.7	18.3	0.0	18.3	0.0	18.3	0.0	19.0	3.8	19.0	0.0	20.9	10.0	21.1	1.0	21.2	0.5	21.2	0.0	21.2	0.0	21.2	0.0
1949	21.2	0.0	21.3	0.5	21.3	0.0	21.4	0.5	21.4	0.0	21.3	-0.5	21.3	0.0	21.3	0.0	21.3	0.0	22.5	5.6	22.5	0.0	22.4	-0.4
1950	22.4	0.0	22.4	0.0	22.3	-0.4	22.0	-1.3	22.0	0.0	22.1	0.5	22.1	0.0	22.4	1.4	22.3	-0.4	22.3	0.0	22.3	0.0	22.5	0.9
1951	22.5	0.0	22.6	0.4	23.0	1.8	23.0	0.0	23.0	0.0	23.0	0.0	23.4	1.7	24.2	3.4	24.4	0.8	24.5	0.4	24.7	0.8	24.0	-2.8
1952	24.7	2.9	24.9	0.8	24.9	0.0	24.9	0.0	24.9	0.0	26.1	4.8	26.1	0.0	26.1	0.0	26.1	0.0	26.1	0.0	26.1	0.0	26.1	0.0
1953	26.3	0.8	26.3	0.0	26.2	-0.4	26.2	0.0	26.1	-0.4	26.2	0.4	26.3	0.4	26.3	0.0	26.2	-0.4	26.1	-0.4	26.0	-0.4	26.0	0.0
1954	26.2	0.8	26.0	-0.8	26.0	0.0	25.9	-0.4	26.2	1.2	26.3	0.4	26.2	-0.4	26.1	-0.4	26.1	0.0	25.0	-4.2	26.2	4.8	26.1	-0.4
1955	26.2	0.4	26.0	-0.8	26.0	0.0	25.3	-2.7	25.5	0.8	25.5	0.0	25.4	-0.4	25.5	0.4	25.5	0.0	25.9	1.6	26.1	0.8	25.7	-1.5
1956	25.6	-0.4	25.6	0.0	25.5	-0.4	25.6	0.4	25.8	0.8	25.8	0.0	26.1	1.2	26.2	0.4	26.2	0.0	27.3	4.2	27.3	0.0	27.3	0.0
1957	27.5	0.7	27.3	-0.7	27.4	0.4	27.3	-0.4	27.2	-0.4	27.2	0.0	28.3	4.0	28.4	0.4	28.1	-1.1	28.0	-0.4	29.2	4.3	29.5	1.0
1958	29.6	0.3	29.2	-1.4	29.0	-0.7	29.0	0.0	29.0	0.0	29.2	0.7	29.1	-0.3	29.3	0.7	29.4	0.3	29.9	1.7	30.1	0.7	30.4	1.0
1959	30.3	-0.3	30.2	-0.3	30.3	0.3	30.3	0.0	30.2	-0.3	30.1	-0.3	30.4	1.0	30.4	0.0	30.4	0.0	31.0	2.0	31.2	0.6	31.3	0.3
1960	30.9	-1.3	30.9	0.0	30.7	-0.6	30.5	-0.7	30.3	-0.7	30.4	0.3	30.5	0.3	30.6	0.3	30.5	-0.3	30.8	1.0	30.7	-0.3	30.5	-0.7
1961	30.3	-0.7	30.2	-0.3	29.8	-1.3	30.0	0.7	30.0	0.0	29.7	-1.0	30.7	3.4	30.8	0.3	30.8	0.0	31.3	1.6	30.8	-1.6	30.5	-1.0
1962	30.7	0.7	30.8	0.3	30.9	0.3	31.3	1.3	31.3	0.0	30.8	-1.6	30.5	-1.0	30.3	-0.7	31.2	3.0	31.3	0.3	31.2	-0.3	31.2	0.0
1963	30.8	-1.3	30.9	0.3	31.3	1.3	31.2	-0.3	31.5	1.0	31.4	-0.3	31.4	0.0	31.3	-0.3	31.0	-1.0	31.4	1.3	31.0	-1.3	31.3	1.0
1964	31.0	-1.0	30.8	-0.6	30.8	0.0	30.7	-0.3	31.3	2.0	31.4	0.3	31.6	0.6	31.4	-0.6	31.2	-0.6	31.4	0.6	31.6	0.6	31.6	0.0
1965	31.9	0.9	31.8	-0.3	31.8	0.0	32.2	1.3	32.2	0.0	32.2	0.0	32.2	0.0	32.0	-0.6	31.8	-0.6	32.1	0.9	32.1	0.0	32.2	0.3
1966	31.9	-0.9	31.9	0.0	31.8	-0.3	31.9	0.3	32.0	0.3	32.1	0.3	32.1	0.0	32.3	0.6	32.2	-0.3	32.3	0.3	32.3	0.0	32.2	-0.3
1967	32.1	-0.3	32.4	0.9	32.5	0.3	32.6	0.3	32.7	0.3	32.8	0.3	32.9	0.3	33.0	0.3	33.3	0.9	33.3	0.0	34.2	2.7	34.1	-0.3
1968	34.2	0.3	34.2	0.0	34.3	0.3	34.4	0.3	34.3	-0.3	34.4	0.3	34.5	0.3	34.4	-0.3	34.4	0.0	34.6	0.6	34.7	0.3	35.4	2.0
1969	35.6	0.6	35.9	0.8	36.6	1.9	36.8	0.5	36.5	-0.8	36.7	0.5	36.7	0.0	36.7	0.0	36.6	-0.3	37.1	1.4	37.1	0.0	37.4	0.8
1970	37.8	1.1	37.5	-0.8	37.4	-0.3	38.0	1.6	38.2	0.5	38.4	0.5	39.6	3.1	39.6	0.0	39.4	-0.5	40.5	2.8	41.0	1.2	41.3	0.7
1971	41.2	-0.2	41.5	0.7	41.3	-0.5	41.3	0.0	41.8	1.2	41.3	-1.2	41.6	0.7	41.8	0.5	41.5	-0.7	41.2	-0.7	41.1	-0.2	41.3	0.5
1972	40.8	-1.2	40.2	-1.5	40.2	0.0	40.5	0.7	40.9	1.0	40.8	-0.2	41.2	1.0	41.4	0.5	41.4	0.0	41.3	-0.2	41.4	0.2	41.4	0.0
1973	41.1	-0.7	41.1	0.0	41.3	0.5	41.7	1.0	42.2	1.2	42.5	0.7	42.5	0.0	42.3	-0.5	42.2	-0.2	42.8	1.4	42.9	0.2	43.3	0.9
1974	43.8	1.2	43.8	0.0	44.6	1.8	45.0	0.9	45.9	2.0	46.6	1.5	47.3	1.5	47.6	0.6	47.8	0.4	48.0	0.4	48.2	0.4	48.2	0.0
1975	47.7	-1.0	47.7	0.0	48.2	1.0	48.6	0.8	49.0	0.8	49.7	1.4	50.8	2.2	51.6	1.6	51.8	0.4	51.8	0.0	52.1	0.6	52.0	-0.2
1976	51.7	-0.6	52.6	1.7	52.9	0.6	53.4	0.9	54.5	2.1	55.3	1.5	55.8	0.9	56.2	0.7	56.9	1.2	57.3	0.7	57.9	1.0	57.8	-0.2
1977	58.1	0.5	58.6	0.9	59.0	0.7	59.9	1.5	60.4	0.8	60.6	0.3	60.5	-0.2	60.4	-0.2	60.0	-0.7	60.1	0.2	60.0	-0.2	60.2	0.3
1978	60.3	0.2	60.3	0.0	60.4	0.2	60.5	0.2	61.2	1.2	62.0	1.3	62.4	0.6	62.7	0.5	62.8	0.2	63.6	1.3	63.9	0.5	64.4	0.8
1979	65.0	0.9	65.6	0.9	66.4	1.2	67.8	2.1	69.3	2.2	71.0	2.5	72.4	2.0	73.6	1.7	74.4	1.1	75.1	0.9	76.0	1.2	77.0	1.3
1980	79.1	2.7	80.6	1.9	82.3	2.1	84.2	2.3	84.8	0.7	84.9	0.1	85.0	0.1	85.3	0.4	85.5	0.2	85.8	0.4	87.6	2.1	88.0	0.5
1981	90.7	3.1	92.2	1.7	93.0	0.9	93.9	1.0	94.5	0.6	94.9	0.4	96.4	1.6	96.6	0.2	97.2	0.6	98.4	1.2	98.9	0.5	99.7	0.8
1982	99.3	-0.4	98.1	-1.2	97.2	-0.9	96.5	-0.7	97.3	0.8	100.1	2.9	100.6	0.5	100.3	-0.3	98.9	-1.4	99.2	0.3	99.0	-0.2	98.0	-1.0
1983	97.3	-0.7	96.1	-1.2	95.2	-0.9	96.8	1.7	98.0	1.2	98.2	0.2	99.1	0.9	100.7	1.6	100.5	-0.2	101.5	1.0	101.7	0.2	101.2	-0.5
1984	101.1	-0.1	100.8	-0.3	101.2	0.4	102.1	0.9	102.4	0.3	102.8	0.4	103.0	0.2	102.7	-0.3	102.8	0.1	103.6	0.8	103.6	0.0	103.3	-0.3
1985	103.2	-0.1	102.9	-0.3	103.9	1.0	104.8	0.9	105.6	0.8	105.5	-0.1	105.7	0.2	105.1	-0.6	103.9	-1.1	104.6	0.7	106.0	1.3	106.0	0.0
1986	105.3	-0.7	103.9	-1.3	100.0	-3.8	97.8	-2.2	99.4	1.6	100.5	1.1	98.3	-2.2	97.3	-1.0	97.3	0.0	98.1	0.8	99.2	1.1	100.1	0.9
1987	101.9	1.8	101.7	-0.2	102.4	0.7	102.9	0.5	104.0	1.1	104.7	0.7	105.3	0.6	105.3	0.0	105.3	0.0	106.3	0.9	106.0	-0.3	105.7	-0.3
1988	105.2	-0.5	105.3	0.1	105.1	-0.2	105.3	0.2	105.4	0.1	105.9	0.5	106.1	0.2	107.2	1.0	107.4	0.2	107.2	-0.2	107.9	0.7	107.6	-0.3
1989	108.1	0.5	108.3	0.2	108.6	0.3	111.0	2.2	112.7	1.5	113.1	0.4	111.9	-1.1	110.9	-0.9	110.4	-0.5	112.8	2.2	112.0	-0.7	112.0	0.0
1990	115.4	3.0	114.4	-0.9	112.9	-1.3	114.0	1.0	114.4	0.4	115.1	0.6	114.5	-0.5	117.5	2.6	118.3	0.7	122.8	3.8	123.4	0.5	123.5	0.1
1991	121.4	-1.7	119.6	-1.5	117.8	-1.5	117.5	-0.3	119.3	1.5	119.4	0.1	118.6	-0.7	118.8	0.2	118.8	0.0	119.4	0.5	120.6	1.0	120.1	-0.4

[Continued]

Chicago, IL-NW IN
Consumer Price Index - Urban Wage Earners
Base 1982-1984 = 100
Transportation
[Continued]

For 1947-1993. Columns headed % show percentile change in the index from the previous period for which an index is available.

Year	Jan Index	%	Feb Index	%	Mar Index	%	Apr Index	%	May Index	%	Jun Index	%	Jul Index	%	Aug Index	%	Sep Index	%	Oct Index	%	Nov Index	%	Dec Index	%
1992	119.6	-0.4	118.5	-0.9	118.3	-0.2	119.5	1.0	121.2	1.4	121.8	0.5	121.8	0.0	121.0	-0.7	121.4	0.3	123.6	1.8	124.3	0.6	123.6	-0.6
1993	122.8	-0.6	122.9	0.1	122.6	-0.2	123.9	1.1	125.3	1.1	124.9	-0.3	124.4	-0.4	123.4	-0.8	123.4	0.0	124.9	1.2	125.4	0.4	124.4	-0.8

Source: U.S. Department of Labor, Bureau of Labor Statistics, Division of Consumer Prices and Price Indexes. - indicates no data collected for period.

Chicago, IL-NW IN
Consumer Price Index - All Urban Consumers
Base 1982-1984 = 100
Medical Care

For 1947-1993. Columns headed % show percentile change in the index from the previous period for which an index is available.

Year	Jan Index	%	Feb Index	%	Mar Index	%	Apr Index	%	May Index	%	Jun Index	%	Jul Index	%	Aug Index	%	Sep Index	%	Oct Index	%	Nov Index	%	Dec Index	%
1947	11.7	-	11.7	0.0	11.9	1.7	12.0	0.8	12.1	0.8	12.2	0.8	12.2	0.0	12.4	1.6	12.4	0.0	12.4	0.0	12.4	0.0	12.5	0.8
1948	12.7	1.6	12.7	0.0	12.7	0.0	12.8	0.8	12.9	0.8	12.9	0.0	12.9	0.0	13.0	0.8	13.0	0.0	13.0	0.0	13.3	2.3	13.3	0.0
1949	13.4	0.8	13.4	0.0	13.6	1.5	13.6	0.0	13.6	0.0	13.6	0.0	13.6	0.0	13.6	0.0	13.5	-0.7	13.5	0.0	13.5	0.0	13.5	0.0
1950	13.5	0.0	13.5	0.0	13.5	0.0	13.5	0.0	13.5	0.0	13.5	0.0	13.5	0.0	13.6	0.7	14.2	4.4	14.2	0.0	14.2	0.0	14.3	0.7
1951	14.3	0.0	14.3	0.0	14.4	0.7	14.5	0.7	14.5	0.0	14.5	0.0	14.5	0.0	14.5	0.0	14.7	1.4	14.7	0.0	14.8	0.7	14.8	0.0
1952	14.8	0.0	14.8	0.0	14.9	0.7	14.9	0.0	14.9	0.0	14.9	0.0	14.9	0.0	14.9	0.0	14.9	0.0	14.9	0.0	14.9	0.0	15.0	0.7
1953	15.0	0.0	15.0	0.0	15.0	0.0	15.4	2.7	15.4	0.0	15.4	0.0	15.6	1.3	15.6	0.0	15.6	0.0	15.7	0.6	15.8	0.6	15.8	0.0
1954	15.8	0.0	15.8	0.0	15.8	0.0	15.8	0.0	15.8	0.0	15.8	0.0	15.8	0.0	15.8	0.0	15.8	0.0	16.2	2.5	16.2	0.0	16.2	0.0
1955	16.4	1.2	16.4	0.0	16.4	0.0	16.5	0.6	16.5	0.0	16.5	0.0	16.5	0.0	16.5	0.0	16.5	0.0	16.6	0.6	17.2	3.6	17.2	0.0
1956	17.4	1.2	17.4	0.0	17.4	0.0	17.6	1.1	17.6	0.0	17.5	-0.6	17.6	0.6	17.6	0.0	17.6	0.0	17.7	0.6	17.8	0.6	17.8	0.0
1957	17.9	0.6	17.9	0.0	18.0	0.6	18.2	1.1	18.2	0.0	18.2	0.0	18.2	0.0	18.2	0.0	18.2	0.0	18.8	3.3	18.9	0.5	18.9	0.0
1958	19.3	2.1	19.3	0.0	19.3	0.0	19.4	0.5	19.4	0.0	19.4	0.0	19.4	0.0	19.4	0.0	19.4	0.0	19.5	0.5	19.5	0.0	19.5	0.0
1959	19.5	0.0	20.1	3.1	20.1	0.0	20.4	1.5	20.4	0.0	20.4	0.0	20.4	0.0	20.4	0.0	20.4	0.0	20.5	0.5	20.5	0.0	20.6	0.5
1960	20.7	0.5	21.5	3.9	21.5	0.0	21.6	0.5	21.6	0.0	21.6	0.0	21.4	-0.9	21.4	0.0	21.4	0.0	21.7	1.4	21.7	0.0	21.7	0.0
1961	21.9	0.9	21.9	0.0	21.9	0.0	21.9	0.0	21.9	0.0	21.9	0.0	21.9	0.0	21.9	0.0	21.9	0.0	22.3	1.8	22.3	0.0	22.3	0.0
1962	22.6	1.3	22.6	0.0	22.6	0.0	22.7	0.4	22.7	0.0	22.7	0.0	22.7	0.0	22.7	0.0	22.7	0.0	22.9	0.9	22.9	0.0	22.9	0.0
1963	24.1	5.2	24.1	0.0	24.1	0.0	24.2	0.4	24.3	0.4	24.3	0.0	24.4	0.4	24.4	0.0	24.4	0.0	24.5	0.4	24.5	0.0	24.5	0.0
1964	24.6	0.4	24.6	0.0	24.6	0.0	24.6	0.0	24.6	0.0	24.6	0.0	24.8	0.8	24.8	0.0	24.7	-0.4	24.8	0.4	24.9	0.4	24.9	0.0
1965	24.9	0.0	25.0	0.4	25.0	0.0	25.0	0.0	25.0	0.0	25.0	0.0	25.1	0.4	25.2	0.4	25.2	0.0	25.2	0.0	25.3	0.4	25.3	0.0	25.4	0.4
1966	25.5	0.4	25.6	0.4	25.6	0.0	25.6	0.0	25.6	0.0	25.7	0.4	25.8	0.4	25.9	0.4	26.0	0.4	26.3	1.2	26.4	0.4	26.5	0.4	26.7	0.8
1967	26.9	0.7	27.0	0.4	27.5	1.9	27.5	0.0	27.7	0.7	27.8	0.4	28.1	1.1	28.3	0.7	28.6	1.1	28.6	0.0	28.7	0.3	28.8	0.3
1968	29.0	0.7	29.3	1.0	29.4	0.3	29.6	0.7	29.5	-0.3	29.5	0.0	29.5	0.0	29.6	0.3	29.7	0.3	29.8	0.3	30.1	1.0	30.3	0.7
1969	30.4	0.3	30.6	0.7	30.7	0.3	31.3	2.0	31.4	0.3	31.5	0.3	31.5	0.0	31.6	0.3	32.0	1.3	31.9	-0.3	32.1	0.6	32.1	0.0
1970	32.3	0.6	32.5	0.6	33.0	1.5	33.1	0.3	33.2	0.3	33.2	0.0	33.3	0.3	33.8	1.5	34.2	1.2	34.5	0.9	34.6	0.3	34.8	0.6
1971	35.2	1.1	35.6	1.1	35.7	0.3	35.7	0.0	35.9	0.6	36.0	0.3	36.1	0.3	36.3	0.6	36.3	0.0	36.0	-0.8	36.0	0.0	36.1	0.3
1972	36.2	0.3	36.4	0.6	36.4	0.0	36.5	0.3	36.7	0.5	36.7	0.0	36.8	0.3	36.9	0.3	36.9	0.0	37.2	0.8	37.4	0.5	37.4	0.0
1973	37.6	0.5	37.6	0.0	37.8	0.5	37.8	0.0	38.0	0.5	38.0	0.0	38.2	0.5	38.2	0.0	38.6	1.0	39.2	1.6	39.3	0.3	39.3	0.0
1974	39.7	1.0	40.1	1.0	40.4	0.7	40.4	0.0	41.0	1.5	42.1	2.7	42.3	0.5	42.7	0.9	43.2	1.2	43.5	0.7	43.9	0.9	44.4	1.1
1975	45.0	1.4	45.3	0.7	45.8	1.1	45.9	0.2	46.2	0.7	47.0	1.7	47.7	1.5	48.3	1.3	48.7	0.8	49.2	1.0	48.8	-0.8	49.3	1.0
1976	49.7	0.8	50.6	1.8	51.5	1.8	51.8	0.6	52.2	0.8	52.5	0.6	53.2	1.3	53.5	0.6	54.0	0.9	54.3	0.6	54.8	0.9	55.1	0.5
1977	55.7	1.1	56.5	1.4	56.7	0.4	57.1	0.7	57.4	0.5	57.9	0.9	58.3	0.7	58.6	0.5	59.1	0.9	59.5	0.7	59.6	0.2	59.7	0.2
1978	60.4	1.2	60.7	0.5	60.9	0.3	61.3	0.7	61.5	0.3	61.6	0.2	62.2	1.0	62.1	-0.2	62.3	0.3	63.6	2.1	64.4	1.3	64.5	0.2
1979	65.4	1.4	65.4	0.0	65.5	0.2	65.9	0.6	67.1	1.8	67.1	0.0	68.4	1.9	68.5	0.1	68.6	0.1	68.7	0.1	69.0	0.4	71.5	3.6
1980	72.8	1.8	73.8	1.4	74.3	0.7	75.8	2.0	76.3	0.7	76.5	0.3	77.2	0.9	77.5	0.4	77.6	0.1	77.8	0.3	77.8	0.0	78.6	1.0
1981	80.1	1.9	80.7	0.7	81.2	0.6	82.8	2.0	83.1	0.4	84.6	1.8	84.9	0.4	86.1	1.4	86.2	0.1	86.6	0.5	87.0	0.5	88.0	1.1
1982	87.9	-0.1	88.8	1.0	89.3	0.6	90.2	1.0	90.6	0.4	91.8	1.3	93.0	1.3	93.3	0.3	93.5	0.2	94.3	0.9	95.7	1.5	97.2	1.6
1983	98.7	1.5	99.4	0.7	99.8	0.4	100.2	0.4	100.3	0.1	100.8	0.5	101.4	0.6	101.4	0.0	102.4	1.0	102.6	0.2	102.7	0.1	103.1	0.4
1984	104.6	1.5	105.1	0.5	105.1	0.0	105.1	0.0	105.0	-0.1	106.8	1.7	107.8	0.9	107.6	-0.2	107.7	0.1	108.8	1.0	108.9	0.1	109.3	0.4
1985	109.9	0.5	110.0	0.1	111.4	1.3	111.7	0.3	112.3	0.5	112.6	0.3	112.7	0.1	113.3	0.5	114.6	1.1	114.7	0.1	115.1	0.3	115.2	0.1
1986	116.3	1.0	117.1	0.7	118.0	0.8	118.7	0.6	119.2	0.4	119.5	0.3	121.0	1.3	121.1	0.1	122.0	0.7	122.6	0.5	122.7	0.1	123.1	0.3
1987	124.4	1.1	125.7	1.0	125.9	0.2	126.3	0.3	127.6	1.0	129.4	1.4	130.6	0.9	130.9	0.2	132.0	0.8	132.3	0.2	132.7	0.3	132.9	0.2
1988	134.2	1.0	134.8	0.4	135.6	0.6	135.9	0.2	136.4	0.4	137.4	0.7	139.9	1.8	139.5	-0.3	140.4	0.6	140.9	0.4	140.5	-0.3	140.8	0.2
1989	142.1	0.9	143.7	1.1	144.7	0.7	144.9	0.1	146.0	0.8	147.2	0.8	150.2	2.0	152.1	1.3	153.9	1.2	155.2	0.8	155.3	0.1	155.6	0.2
1990	156.2	0.4	157.6	0.9	158.9	0.8	160.2	0.8	161.5	0.8	162.0	0.3	164.3	1.4	165.3	0.6	166.8	0.9	167.4	0.4	168.0	0.4	168.2	0.1
1991	170.2	1.2	172.9	1.6	175.0	1.2	175.7	0.4	176.4	0.4	176.9	0.3	179.2	1.3	179.7	0.3	181.3	0.9	181.3	0.0	183.0	0.9	183.7	0.4

[Continued]

358

Chicago, IL-NW IN
Consumer Price Index - All Urban Consumers
Base 1982-1984 = 100
Medical Care
[Continued]

For 1947-1993. Columns headed % show percentile change in the index from the previous period for which an index is available.

Year	Jan		Feb		Mar		Apr		May		Jun		Jul		Aug		Sep		Oct		Nov		Dec	
	Index	%	Index	%	Index	%	Index	%	Index	%	Index	%	Index	%	Index	%	Index	%	Index	%	Index	%	Index	%
1992	185.1	0.8	186.9	1.0	189.4	1.3	189.5	0.1	189.9	0.2	190.2	0.2	191.3	0.6	191.7	0.2	193.1	0.7	192.9	-0.1	194.0	0.6	194.7	0.4
1993	198.4	1.9	199.3	0.5	200.5	0.6	201.0	0.2	202.1	0.5	203.1	0.5	204.8	0.8	205.3	0.2	205.3	0.0	205.4	0.0	205.7	0.1	206.2	0.2

Source: U.S. Department of Labor, Bureau of Labor Statistics, Division of Consumer Prices and Price Indexes. - indicates no data collected for period.

Chicago, IL-NW IN
Consumer Price Index - Urban Wage Earners
Base 1982-1984 = 100
Medical Care

For 1947-1993. Columns headed % show percentile change in the index from the previous period for which an index is available.

Year	Jan Index	%	Feb Index	%	Mar Index	%	Apr Index	%	May Index	%	Jun Index	%	Jul Index	%	Aug Index	%	Sep Index	%	Oct Index	%	Nov Index	%	Dec Index	%
1947	11.5	-	11.5	0.0	11.7	1.7	11.8	0.9	11.9	0.8	12.0	0.8	12.0	0.0	12.2	1.7	12.2	0.0	12.2	0.0	12.2	0.0	12.3	0.8
1948	12.5	1.6	12.5	0.0	12.5	0.0	12.6	0.8	12.7	0.8	12.7	0.0	12.7	0.0	12.8	0.8	12.8	0.0	12.8	0.0	13.1	2.3	13.1	0.0
1949	13.2	0.8	13.2	0.0	13.4	1.5	13.4	0.0	13.4	0.0	13.3	-0.7	13.3	0.0	13.3	0.0	13.3	0.0	13.3	0.0	13.2	-0.8	13.2	0.0
1950	13.2	0.0	13.2	0.0	13.3	0.8	13.3	0.0	13.3	0.0	13.3	0.0	13.3	0.0	13.3	0.0	14.0	5.3	14.0	0.0	14.0	0.0	14.1	0.7
1951	14.1	0.0	14.1	0.0	14.2	0.7	14.3	0.7	14.3	0.0	14.3	0.0	14.3	0.0	14.3	0.0	14.4	0.7	14.4	0.0	14.6	1.4	14.6	0.0
1952	14.6	0.0	14.6	0.0	14.6	0.0	14.7	0.7	14.7		14.7	0.0	14.7	0.0	14.7	0.0	14.7	0.0	14.7	0.0	14.7	0.0	14.8	0.7
1953	14.8	0.0	14.8	0.0	14.8	0.0	15.1	2.0	15.2	0.7	15.2	0.0	15.3	0.7	15.3	0.0	15.3	0.0	15.5	1.3	15.5	0.0	15.5	0.0
1954	15.5	0.0	15.5	0.0	15.5	0.0	15.5	0.0	15.5	0.0	15.5	0.0	15.5	0.0	15.5	0.0	15.5	0.0	16.0	3.2	16.0	0.0	16.0	0.0
1955	16.1	0.6	16.1	0.0	16.1	0.0	16.2	0.6	16.2	0.0	16.3	0.6	16.3	0.0	16.3	0.0	16.3	0.0	16.3	0.0	16.9	3.7	16.9	0.0
1956	17.1	1.2	17.1	0.0	17.1	0.0	17.3	1.2	17.3	0.0	17.3	0.0	17.3	0.0	17.3	0.0	17.3	0.0	17.4	0.6	17.5	0.6	17.5	0.0
1957	17.6	0.6	17.6	0.0	17.7	0.6	17.9	1.1	17.9	0.0	17.9	0.0	17.9	0.0	17.9	0.0	17.9	0.0	18.5	3.4	18.6	0.5	18.6	0.0
1958	19.0	2.2	19.0	0.0	19.0	0.0	19.0	0.0	19.0	0.0	19.0	0.0	19.0	0.0	19.0	0.0	19.1	0.5	19.2	0.5	19.2	0.0	19.2	0.0
1959	19.2	0.0	19.7	2.6	19.7	0.0	20.1	2.0	20.1	0.0	20.1	0.0	20.1	0.0	20.1	0.0	20.1	0.0	20.1	0.0	20.1	0.0	20.2	0.5
1960	20.3	0.5	21.2	4.4	21.2	0.0	21.3	0.5	21.3	0.0	21.3	0.0	21.1	-0.9	21.1	0.0	21.1	0.0	21.3	0.9	21.3	0.0	21.3	0.0
1961	21.5	0.9	21.5	0.0	21.5	0.0	21.5	0.0	21.6	0.5	21.6	0.0	21.5	-0.5	21.5	0.0	21.5	0.0	21.9	1.9	21.9	0.0	21.9	0.0
1962	22.2	1.4	22.2	0.0	22.2	0.0	22.3	0.5	22.3	0.0	22.3	0.0	22.4	0.4	22.4	0.0	22.4	0.0	22.6	0.9	22.6	0.0	22.6	0.0
1963	23.7	4.9	23.7	0.0	23.7	0.0	23.9	0.8	23.9	0.0	23.9	0.0	24.0	0.4	24.0	0.0	24.0	0.0	24.1	0.4	24.1	0.0	24.1	0.0
1964	24.2	0.4	24.2	0.0	24.2	0.0	24.2	0.0	24.2	0.0	24.2	0.0	24.4	0.8	24.4	0.0	24.3	-0.4	24.4	0.4	24.5	0.4	24.5	0.0
1965	24.5	0.0	24.6	0.4	24.6	0.0	24.6	0.0	24.6	0.0	24.7	0.4	24.8	0.4	24.8	0.0	24.8	0.0	24.9	0.4	24.9	0.0	25.0	0.4
1966	25.1	0.4	25.1	0.0	25.1	0.0	25.2	0.4	25.3	0.4	25.3	0.0	25.5	0.8	25.5	0.0	25.8	1.2	25.9	0.4	26.1	0.8	26.3	0.8
1967	26.4	0.4	26.6	0.8	27.0	1.5	27.1	0.4	27.2	0.4	27.4	0.7	27.6	0.7	27.8	0.7	28.1	1.1	28.1	0.0	28.2	0.4	28.4	0.7
1968	28.5	0.4	28.8	1.1	29.0	0.7	29.1	0.3	29.0	-0.3	29.0	0.0	29.1	0.3	29.1	0.0	29.2	0.3	29.3	0.3	29.6	1.0	29.9	1.0
1969	29.9	0.0	30.1	0.7	30.2	0.3	30.8	2.0	30.9	0.3	31.0	0.3	31.0	0.0	31.1	0.3	31.5	1.3	31.4	-0.3	31.6	0.6	31.6	0.0
1970	31.8	0.6	32.0	0.6	32.5	1.6	32.6	0.3	32.7	0.3	32.7	0.0	32.8	0.3	33.2	1.2	33.7	1.5	33.9	0.6	34.0	0.3	34.3	0.9
1971	34.6	0.9	35.0	1.2	35.2	0.6	35.2	0.0	35.4	0.6	35.4	0.0	35.6	0.6	35.7	0.3	35.7	0.0	35.4	-0.8	35.4	0.0	35.5	0.3
1972	35.7	0.6	35.8	0.3	35.9	0.3	35.9	0.0	36.1	0.6	36.1	0.0	36.2	0.3	36.3	0.3	36.3	0.0	36.6	0.8	36.8	0.5	36.8	0.0
1973	37.0	0.5	37.0	0.0	37.2	0.5	37.2	0.0	37.4	0.5	37.4	0.0	37.6	0.5	37.6	0.0	37.9	0.8	38.6	1.8	38.7	0.3	38.7	0.0
1974	39.0	0.8	39.4	1.0	39.8	1.0	39.8	0.0	40.3	1.3	41.5	3.0	41.6	0.2	42.0	1.0	42.5	1.2	42.8	0.7	43.2	0.9	43.7	1.2
1975	44.3	1.4	44.6	0.7	45.1	1.1	45.2	0.2	45.5	0.7	46.3	1.8	46.9	1.3	47.5	1.3	47.9	0.8	48.4	1.0	48.0	-0.8	48.5	1.0
1976	48.9	0.8	49.8	1.8	50.7	1.8	51.0	0.6	51.4	0.8	51.7	0.6	52.4	1.4	52.6	0.4	53.2	1.1	53.4	0.4	53.9	0.9	54.2	0.6
1977	54.8	1.1	55.6	1.5	55.7	0.2	56.2	0.9	56.5	0.5	57.0	0.9	57.4	0.7	57.7	0.5	58.1	0.7	58.5	0.7	58.6	0.2	58.8	0.3
1978	59.2	0.7	59.5	0.5	59.8	0.5	60.3	0.8	60.6	0.5	60.8	0.3	61.5	1.2	61.5	0.0	61.6	0.2	62.9	2.1	63.9	1.6	64.2	0.5
1979	65.3	1.7	65.4	0.2	65.7	0.5	66.0	0.5	66.7	1.1	66.7	0.0	67.7	1.5	67.9	0.3	68.4	0.7	69.2	1.2	69.4	0.3	72.1	3.9
1980	73.9	2.5	74.6	0.9	74.7	0.1	76.1	1.9	76.7	0.8	76.5	-0.3	77.7	1.6	77.9	0.3	78.3	0.5	78.6	0.4	78.8	0.3	79.2	0.5
1981	80.6	1.8	81.5	1.1	81.9	0.5	82.9	1.2	83.6	0.8	84.4	1.0	84.8	0.5	84.8	0.0	85.8	1.2	86.3	0.6	87.6	1.5	88.1	0.6
1982	87.9	-0.2	88.8	1.0	89.3	0.6	90.1	0.9	90.6	0.6	91.8	1.3	93.0	1.3	93.3	0.3	93.4	0.1	94.3	1.0	95.6	1.4	97.1	1.6
1983	98.6	1.5	99.3	0.7	99.8	0.5	100.1	0.3	100.3	0.2	100.8	0.5	101.4	0.6	101.4	0.0	102.4	1.0	102.6	0.2	102.7	0.1	103.2	0.5
1984	104.7	1.5	105.2	0.5	105.2	0.0	105.2	0.0	105.1	-0.1	106.8	1.6	107.8	0.9	107.5	-0.3	107.7	0.2	108.7	0.9	108.9	0.2	109.2	0.3
1985	109.8	0.5	109.9	0.1	111.3	1.3	111.5	0.2	112.2	0.6	112.5	0.3	112.6	0.1	113.2	0.5	114.5	1.1	114.6	0.1	115.0	0.3	115.2	0.2
1986	116.2	0.9	117.0	0.7	117.8	0.7	118.5	0.6	119.1	0.5	119.3	0.2	120.8	1.3	120.8	0.0	121.8	0.8	122.3	0.4	122.4	0.1	122.8	0.3
1987	124.0	1.0	125.3	1.0	125.5	0.2	125.9	0.3	127.2	1.0	128.8	1.3	130.3	1.2	130.6	0.2	131.8	0.9	132.1	0.2	132.4	0.2	132.7	0.2
1988	134.1	1.1	134.9	0.6	135.5	0.4	136.1	0.4	136.6	0.4	137.4	0.6	140.4	2.2	140.1	-0.2	141.0	0.6	141.5	0.4	141.2	-0.2	141.5	0.2
1989	142.9	1.0	144.8	1.3	145.7	0.6	145.8	0.1	147.1	0.9	148.2	0.7	151.6	2.3	153.2	1.1	155.5	1.5	156.7	0.8	156.7	0.0	157.0	0.2
1990	157.5	0.3	158.8	0.8	159.8	0.6	161.4	1.0	162.7	0.8	163.1	0.2	165.8	1.7	166.6	0.5	168.2	1.0	168.6	0.2	169.2	0.4	169.3	0.1
1991	171.6	1.4	174.6	1.7	176.5	1.1	176.8	0.2	177.7	0.5	178.1	0.2	180.6	1.4	181.2	0.3	182.9	0.9	182.8	-0.1	184.8	1.1	185.5	0.4

[Continued]

Chicago, IL-NW IN
Consumer Price Index - Urban Wage Earners
Base 1982-1984 = 100
Medical Care
[Continued]

For 1947-1993. Columns headed % show percentile change in the index from the previous period for which an index is available.

Year	Jan Index	%	Feb Index	%	Mar Index	%	Apr Index	%	May Index	%	Jun Index	%	Jul Index	%	Aug Index	%	Sep Index	%	Oct Index	%	Nov Index	%	Dec Index	%
1992	186.9	0.8	188.6	0.9	190.7	1.1	190.8	0.1	191.2	0.2	191.7	0.3	193.0	0.7	193.5	0.3	195.2	0.9	194.9	-0.2	195.8	0.5	196.7	0.5
1993	200.7	2.0	201.7	0.5	202.9	0.6	203.4	0.2	204.4	0.5	205.3	0.4	207.4	1.0	207.9	0.2	207.9	0.0	208.0	0.0	208.3	0.1	208.7	0.2

Source: U.S. Department of Labor, Bureau of Labor Statistics, Division of Consumer Prices and Price Indexes. - indicates no data collected for period.

Chicago, IL-NW IN
Consumer Price Index - All Urban Consumers
Base 1982-1984 = 100
Entertainment

For 1976-1993. Columns headed % show percentile change in the index from the previous period for which an index is available.

Year	Jan Index	%	Feb Index	%	Mar Index	%	Apr Index	%	May Index	%	Jun Index	%	Jul Index	%	Aug Index	%	Sep Index	%	Oct Index	%	Nov Index	%	Dec Index	%
1976	60.3	-	60.5	0.3	61.3	1.3	61.6	0.5	61.8	0.3	61.6	-0.3	61.8	0.3	61.9	0.2	62.0	0.2	62.5	0.8	62.8	0.5	62.8	0.0
1977	63.8	1.6	63.8	0.0	64.5	1.1	63.9	-0.9	64.3	0.6	64.3	0.0	64.2	-0.2	64.6	0.6	64.6	0.0	65.2	0.9	65.7	0.8	66.0	0.5
1978	66.7	1.1	67.0	0.4	67.2	0.3	67.4	0.3	67.4	0.0	67.2	-0.3	67.7	0.7	67.9	0.3	68.7	1.2	69.2	0.7	69.6	0.6	69.7	0.1
1979	70.4	1.0	71.8	2.0	73.1	1.8	72.9	-0.3	75.7	3.8	75.7	0.0	77.0	1.7	77.2	0.3	77.6	0.5	78.3	0.9	79.0	0.9	80.3	1.6
1980	80.2	-0.1	82.8	3.2	83.8	1.2	84.0	0.2	84.0	0.0	84.3	0.4	84.9	0.7	85.6	0.8	87.1	1.8	87.5	0.5	87.2	-0.3	87.6	0.5
1981	90.3	3.1	90.4	0.1	89.6	-0.9	91.6	2.2	91.7	0.1	92.1	0.4	92.2	0.1	93.1	1.0	94.4	1.4	93.2	-1.3	94.2	1.1	96.0	1.9
1982	97.1	1.1	97.5	0.4	97.0	-0.5	98.2	1.2	97.3	-0.9	98.0	0.7	98.8	0.8	98.7	-0.1	99.8	1.1	100.6	0.8	97.9	-2.7	99.6	1.7
1983	100.0	0.4	98.8	-1.2	98.6	-0.2	99.3	0.7	99.0	-0.3	99.3	0.3	99.7	0.4	99.2	-0.5	100.4	1.2	100.0	-0.4	100.2	0.2	100.2	0.0
1984	100.5	0.3	100.7	0.2	100.7	0.0	100.7	0.0	100.8	0.1	101.8	1.0	101.3	-0.5	102.0	0.7	104.3	2.3	104.4	0.1	103.1	-1.2	104.3	1.2
1985	104.5	0.2	105.7	1.1	105.2	-0.5	106.7	1.4	106.3	-0.4	105.5	-0.8	105.8	0.3	105.5	-0.3	103.2	-2.2	103.5	0.3	104.5	1.0	104.9	0.4
1986	107.6	2.6	108.2	0.6	108.5	0.3	108.6	0.1	108.2	-0.4	108.2	0.0	109.7	1.4	107.9	-1.6	111.4	3.2	112.8	1.3	113.8	0.9	113.3	-0.4
1987	114.1	0.7	113.9	-0.2	115.6	1.5	116.0	0.3	115.6	-0.3	115.6	0.0	116.3	0.6	115.3	-0.9	116.6	1.1	117.4	0.7	117.5	0.1	118.1	0.5
1988	118.9	0.7	119.0	0.1	120.3	1.1	121.1	0.7	120.3	-0.7	121.3	0.8	122.0	0.6	123.1	0.9	124.0	0.7	125.5	1.2	126.2	0.6	125.8	-0.3
1989	126.9	0.9	128.7	1.4	130.3	1.2	130.5	0.2	130.3	-0.2	132.4	1.6	133.3	0.7	131.3	-1.5	132.7	1.1	134.3	1.2	135.2	0.7	133.2	-1.5
1990	136.0	2.1	136.8	0.6	137.7	0.7	137.8	0.1	139.2	1.0	138.3	-0.6	139.0	0.5	139.9	0.6	140.3	0.3	141.2	0.6	141.3	0.1	142.5	0.8
1991	144.8	1.6	144.6	-0.1	144.4	-0.1	144.7	0.2	145.8	0.8	147.0	0.8	144.4	-1.8	146.5	1.5	148.4	1.3	147.1	-0.9	147.0	-0.1	146.2	-0.5
1992	147.3	0.8	146.9	-0.3	148.0	0.7	148.7	0.5	148.3	-0.3	148.1	-0.1	151.5	2.3	150.7	-0.5	151.3	0.4	151.2	-0.1	150.7	-0.3	150.3	-0.3
1993	151.0	0.5	152.7	1.1	152.9	0.1	153.9	0.7	152.4	-1.0	155.2	1.8	153.9	-0.8	153.4	-0.3	155.2	1.2	154.7	-0.3	154.8	0.1	156.6	1.2

Source: U.S. Department of Labor, Bureau of Labor Statistics, Division of Consumer Prices and Price Indexes. - indicates no data collected for period.

Chicago, IL-NW IN
Consumer Price Index - Urban Wage Earners
Base 1982-1984 = 100
Entertainment

For 1976-1993. Columns headed % show percentile change in the index from the previous period for which an index is available.

Year	Jan Index	%	Feb Index	%	Mar Index	%	Apr Index	%	May Index	%	Jun Index	%	Jul Index	%	Aug Index	%	Sep Index	%	Oct Index	%	Nov Index	%	Dec Index	%
1976	53.4	-	53.5	0.2	54.3	1.5	54.6	0.6	54.7	0.2	54.5	-0.4	54.7	0.4	54.8	0.2	54.9	0.2	55.3	0.7	55.6	0.5	55.6	0.0
1977	56.5	1.6	56.5	0.0	57.1	1.1	56.6	-0.9	56.9	0.5	56.9	0.0	56.9	0.0	57.2	0.5	57.2	0.0	57.8	1.0	58.2	0.7	58.4	0.3
1978	58.8	0.7	59.4	1.0	59.4	0.0	59.3	-0.2	59.4	0.2	59.0	-0.7	59.6	1.0	59.7	0.2	60.1	0.7	60.4	0.5	60.9	0.8	60.8	-0.2
1979	60.9	0.2	61.8	1.5	63.3	2.4	63.3	0.0	66.5	5.1	68.3	2.7	69.3	1.5	69.5	0.3	69.5	0.0	70.3	1.2	71.0	1.0	72.3	1.8
1980	71.8	-0.7	74.1	3.2	74.7	0.8	75.0	0.4	75.3	0.4	76.9	2.1	76.8	-0.1	77.4	0.8	78.3	1.2	82.2	5.0	82.8	0.7	83.1	0.4
1981	84.9	2.2	85.4	0.6	84.6	-0.9	86.1	1.8	86.6	0.6	85.9	-0.8	86.4	0.6	87.5	1.3	86.8	-0.8	93.2	7.4	94.8	1.7	95.0	0.2
1982	96.4	1.5	96.4	0.0	96.0	-0.4	97.0	1.0	95.9	-1.1	96.8	0.9	97.7	0.9	97.6	-0.1	98.9	1.3	99.5	0.6	97.4	-2.1	98.9	1.5
1983	99.3	0.4	99.0	-0.3	98.9	-0.1	99.7	0.8	99.3	-0.4	99.8	0.5	100.0	0.2	99.5	-0.5	100.9	1.4	100.5	-0.4	100.7	0.2	100.8	0.1
1984	101.1	0.3	101.2	0.1	101.0	-0.2	101.4	0.4	101.5	0.1	102.4	0.9	101.8	-0.6	102.6	0.8	105.4	2.7	105.4	0.0	104.0	-1.3	105.3	1.3
1985	106.2	0.9	106.7	0.5	105.9	-0.7	107.5	1.5	107.2	-0.3	106.1	-1.0	106.4	0.3	106.1	-0.3	103.0	-2.9	103.5	0.5	105.0	1.4	105.5	0.5
1986	108.9	3.2	109.2	0.3	109.5	0.3	109.7	0.2	109.0	-0.6	109.0	0.0	110.5	1.4	108.4	-1.9	112.6	3.9	114.4	1.6	115.4	0.9	114.7	-0.6
1987	115.6	0.8	115.4	-0.2	117.5	1.8	118.0	0.4	117.9	-0.1	117.6	-0.3	118.3	0.6	117.4	-0.8	118.7	1.1	119.5	0.7	119.6	0.1	120.3	0.6
1988	120.9	0.5	121.1	0.2	122.4	1.1	123.2	0.7	122.6	-0.5	123.6	0.8	123.9	0.2	124.9	0.8	125.4	0.4	127.0	1.3	127.9	0.7	127.5	-0.3
1989	128.5	0.8	130.4	1.5	132.0	1.2	132.2	0.2	132.2	0.0	133.3	0.8	134.1	0.6	132.5	-1.2	134.0	1.1	135.3	1.0	136.2	0.7	134.3	-1.4
1990	137.0	2.0	137.6	0.4	138.6	0.7	139.0	0.3	140.1	0.8	139.1	-0.7	139.6	0.4	140.8	0.9	141.1	0.2	142.1	0.7	142.1	0.0	143.3	0.8
1991	145.1	1.3	144.9	-0.1	144.5	-0.3	145.2	0.5	146.0	0.6	147.0	0.7	143.8	-2.2	146.4	1.8	148.5	1.4	147.0	-1.0	147.0	0.0	146.2	-0.5
1992	147.3	0.8	146.9	-0.3	147.9	0.7	148.9	0.7	148.4	-0.3	148.2	-0.1	151.8	2.4	151.0	-0.5	151.6	0.4	151.1	-0.3	150.4	-0.5	150.0	-0.3
1993	150.9	0.6	152.4	1.0	152.6	0.1	153.7	0.7	152.2	-1.0	155.2	2.0	153.9	-0.8	153.3	-0.4	155.0	1.1	154.3	-0.5	154.4	0.1	156.2	1.2

Source: U.S. Department of Labor, Bureau of Labor Statistics, Division of Consumer Prices and Price Indexes. - indicates no data collected for period.

Chicago, IL-NW IN
Consumer Price Index - All Urban Consumers
Base 1982-1984 = 100
Other Goods and Services

For 1976-1993. Columns headed % show percentile change in the index from the previous period for which an index is available.

Year	Jan Index	%	Feb Index	%	Mar Index	%	Apr Index	%	May Index	%	Jun Index	%	Jul Index	%	Aug Index	%	Sep Index	%	Oct Index	%	Nov Index	%	Dec Index	%
1976	56.7	-	56.9	0.4	57.2	0.5	57.3	0.2	57.4	0.2	57.8	0.7	57.8	0.0	57.9	0.2	58.6	1.2	59.0	0.7	59.8	1.4	59.9	0.2
1977	60.5	1.0	60.2	-0.5	60.8	1.0	61.0	0.3	61.2	0.3	61.4	0.3	62.0	1.0	62.2	0.3	63.5	2.1	64.3	1.3	64.3	0.0	64.4	0.2
1978	64.7	0.5	64.6	-0.2	64.3	-0.5	64.4	0.2	65.3	1.4	65.1	-0.3	65.7	0.9	65.4	-0.5	67.8	3.7	67.5	-0.4	67.4	-0.1	67.1	-0.4
1979	68.1	1.5	68.2	0.1	69.1	1.3	68.2	-1.3	69.0	1.2	68.5	-0.7	69.2	1.0	68.5	-1.0	71.5	4.4	71.3	-0.3	72.0	1.0	72.8	1.1
1980	72.8	0.0	73.6	1.1	74.1	0.7	74.4	0.4	74.7	0.4	75.8	1.5	75.6	-0.3	75.8	0.3	78.0	2.9	78.6	0.8	79.7	1.4	80.1	0.5
1981	80.5	0.5	81.1	0.7	81.5	0.5	82.8	1.6	84.0	1.4	84.2	0.2	84.4	0.2	84.9	0.6	87.2	2.7	87.7	0.6	87.8	0.1	88.4	0.7
1982	88.5	0.1	89.2	0.8	89.6	0.4	90.0	0.4	89.9	-0.1	90.4	0.6	90.6	0.2	90.7	0.1	94.7	4.4	95.3	0.6	96.5	1.3	97.0	0.5
1983	98.3	1.3	98.6	0.3	98.8	0.2	98.8	0.0	98.8	0.0	99.3	0.5	99.5	0.2	100.0	0.5	102.9	2.9	103.6	0.7	103.6	0.0	104.1	0.5
1984	104.9	0.8	105.8	0.9	105.8	0.0	105.6	-0.2	105.9	0.3	106.8	0.8	107.3	0.5	107.8	0.5	109.6	1.7	110.5	0.8	110.6	0.1	110.6	0.0
1985	112.2	1.4	113.3	1.0	113.1	-0.2	113.1	0.0	113.5	0.4	113.7	0.2	113.9	0.2	113.5	-0.4	117.5	3.5	117.8	0.3	118.1	0.3	121.4	2.8
1986	122.2	0.7	122.8	0.5	123.1	0.2	123.2	0.1	122.8	-0.3	123.1	0.2	124.5	1.1	124.0	-0.4	125.7	1.4	126.5	0.6	126.3	-0.2	126.4	0.1
1987	127.7	1.0	128.2	0.4	128.2	0.0	128.4	0.2	129.2	0.6	129.4	0.2	129.9	0.4	130.5	0.5	130.7	0.2	131.0	0.2	131.2	0.2	131.2	0.0
1988	132.6	1.1	134.9	1.7	135.4	0.4	135.6	0.1	135.6	0.0	135.8	0.1	136.8	0.7	137.7	0.7	142.7	3.6	143.1	0.3	143.2	0.1	143.0	-0.1
1989	144.7	1.2	147.2	1.7	147.9	0.5	148.0	0.1	148.6	0.4	152.5	2.6	155.1	1.7	156.8	1.1	157.9	0.7	158.7	0.5	159.0	0.2	160.3	0.8
1990	159.7	-0.4	160.7	0.6	161.1	0.2	161.5	0.2	162.2	0.4	162.8	0.4	163.1	0.2	164.3	0.7	167.0	1.6	167.8	0.5	170.2	1.4	171.3	0.6
1991	172.8	0.9	174.1	0.8	174.6	0.3	175.9	0.7	175.4	-0.3	175.5	0.1	177.3	1.0	178.3	0.6	184.9	3.7	185.5	0.3	187.0	0.8	186.8	-0.1
1992	186.7	-0.1	188.0	0.7	187.7	-0.2	188.7	0.5	189.9	0.6	189.4	-0.3	191.3	1.0	194.4	1.6	196.2	0.9	196.7	0.3	196.8	0.1	197.6	0.4
1993	198.2	0.3	196.4	-0.9	198.5	1.1	198.5	0.0	204.0	2.8	201.8	-1.1	204.5	1.3	204.8	0.1	206.6	0.9	204.9	-0.8	205.7	0.4	206.1	0.2

Source: U.S. Department of Labor, Bureau of Labor Statistics, Division of Consumer Prices and Price Indexes. - indicates no data collected for period.

Chicago, IL-NW IN
Consumer Price Index - Urban Wage Earners
Base 1982-1984 = 100
Other Goods and Services

For 1976-1993. Columns headed % show percentile change in the index from the previous period for which an index is available.

Year	Jan Index	%	Feb Index	%	Mar Index	%	Apr Index	%	May Index	%	Jun Index	%	Jul Index	%	Aug Index	%	Sep Index	%	Oct Index	%	Nov Index	%	Dec Index	%
1976	58.2	-	58.5	0.5	58.8	0.5	58.9	0.2	59.0	0.2	59.4	0.7	59.3	-0.2	59.5	0.3	60.2	1.2	60.6	0.7	61.5	1.5	61.6	0.2
1977	62.2	1.0	61.9	-0.5	62.4	0.8	62.7	0.5	62.9	0.3	63.1	0.3	63.7	1.0	63.9	0.3	65.2	2.0	66.0	1.2	66.1	0.2	66.2	0.2
1978	66.3	0.2	66.5	0.3	66.5	0.0	67.2	1.1	67.2	0.0	67.7	0.7	68.5	1.2	68.7	0.3	69.6	1.3	69.8	0.3	69.9	0.1	70.0	0.1
1979	70.6	0.9	71.1	0.7	71.3	0.3	71.2	-0.1	71.2	0.0	70.9	-0.4	71.0	0.1	71.1	0.1	72.5	2.0	72.6	0.1	73.3	1.0	74.0	1.0
1980	74.9	1.2	75.7	1.1	76.0	0.4	76.4	0.5	77.0	0.8	78.2	1.6	78.3	0.1	78.4	0.1	80.0	2.0	80.2	0.2	80.9	0.9	81.2	0.4
1981	81.7	0.6	82.1	0.5	82.4	0.4	82.8	0.5	83.7	1.1	83.3	-0.5	84.1	1.0	85.4	1.5	87.7	2.7	88.2	0.6	88.3	0.1	88.4	0.1
1982	88.5	0.1	89.3	0.9	89.8	0.6	90.3	0.6	90.1	-0.2	90.6	0.6	90.8	0.2	90.9	0.1	94.1	3.5	94.9	0.9	96.3	1.5	96.9	0.6
1983	98.6	1.8	99.0	0.4	99.2	0.2	99.2	0.0	99.2	0.0	99.8	0.6	100.0	0.2	100.6	0.6	102.2	1.6	103.1	0.9	103.0	-0.1	103.6	0.6
1984	104.6	1.0	105.6	1.0	105.6	0.0	105.5	-0.1	105.9	0.4	106.7	0.8	107.4	0.7	108.0	0.6	109.4	1.3	110.4	0.9	110.5	0.1	110.5	0.0
1985	112.5	1.8	113.7	1.1	113.4	-0.3	113.5	0.1	113.8	0.3	114.1	0.3	114.3	0.2	114.0	-0.3	116.8	2.5	117.1	0.3	117.5	0.3	121.5	3.4
1986	122.7	1.0	123.3	0.5	123.8	0.4	123.9	0.1	123.4	-0.4	123.8	0.3	125.6	1.5	125.1	-0.4	126.0	0.7	126.8	0.6	126.6	-0.2	126.7	0.1
1987	128.1	1.1	128.6	0.4	128.5	-0.1	128.8	0.2	129.7	0.7	129.9	0.2	130.6	0.5	131.3	0.5	131.7	0.3	132.0	0.2	132.3	0.2	132.4	0.1
1988	134.5	1.6	135.6	0.8	136.1	0.4	136.4	0.2	136.5	0.1	136.7	0.1	138.2	1.1	138.9	0.5	141.9	2.2	142.4	0.4	142.6	0.1	142.5	-0.1
1989	144.8	1.6	146.6	1.2	147.5	0.6	147.6	0.1	148.1	0.3	152.3	2.8	156.2	2.6	158.6	1.5	158.7	0.1	159.9	0.8	160.2	0.2	162.2	1.2
1990	161.0	-0.7	162.5	0.9	163.0	0.3	163.3	0.2	164.3	0.6	165.3	0.6	165.6	0.2	166.7	0.7	168.5	1.1	169.3	0.5	171.9	1.5	173.5	0.9
1991	175.5	1.2	177.2	1.0	177.8	0.3	179.6	1.0	179.0	-0.3	179.8	0.4	181.7	1.1	182.6	0.5	187.4	2.6	187.7	0.2	190.1	1.3	189.9	-0.1
1992	189.8	-0.1	191.1	0.7	190.7	-0.2	192.6	1.0	194.0	0.7	193.4	-0.3	196.1	1.4	199.4	1.7	200.2	0.4	200.7	0.2	201.0	0.1	202.1	0.5
1993	203.1	0.5	200.5	-1.3	202.4	0.9	202.8	0.2	210.6	3.8	207.6	-1.4	210.8	1.5	210.7	-0.0	209.9	-0.4	207.6	-1.1	208.7	0.5	209.2	0.2

Source: U.S. Department of Labor, Bureau of Labor Statistics, Division of Consumer Prices and Price Indexes. - indicates no data collected for period.

Cincinnati, OH-KY-IN
Consumer Price Index - All Urban Consumers
Base 1982-1984 = 100
Annual Averages

For 1917-1993. Columns headed % show percentile change in the index from the previous period for which an index is available.

Year	All Items		Food & Beverage		Housing		Apparel & Upkeep		Trans-portation		Medical Care		Entertain-ment		Other Goods & Services	
	Index	%	Index	%	Index	%	Index	%	Index	%	Index	%	Index	%	Index	%
1917	-	-	-	-	-	-	-	-	-	-	-	-	-	-	-	-
1918	14.5	-	-	-	-	-	-	-	-	-	-	-	-	-	-	-
1919	16.9	16.6	-	-	-	-	-	-	-	-	-	-	-	-	-	-
1920	19.3	14.2	-	-	-	-	-	-	-	-	-	-	-	-	-	-
1921	16.5	-14.5	-	-	-	-	-	-	-	-	-	-	-	-	-	-
1922	15.5	-6.1	-	-	-	-	-	-	-	-	-	-	-	-	-	-
1923	15.9	2.6	-	-	-	-	-	-	-	-	-	-	-	-	-	-
1924	16.0	0.6	-	-	-	-	-	-	-	-	-	-	-	-	-	-
1925	16.8	5.0	-	-	-	-	-	-	-	-	-	-	-	-	-	-
1926	17.1	1.8	-	-	-	-	-	-	-	-	-	-	-	-	-	-
1927	16.8	-1.8	-	-	-	-	-	-	-	-	-	-	-	-	-	-
1928	16.7	-0.6	-	-	-	-	-	-	-	-	-	-	-	-	-	-
1929	16.9	1.2	-	-	-	-	-	-	-	-	-	-	-	-	-	-
1930	16.7	-1.2	-	-	-	-	-	-	-	-	-	-	-	-	-	-
1931	15.1	-9.6	-	-	-	-	-	-	-	-	-	-	-	-	-	-
1932	13.3	-11.9	-	-	-	-	-	-	-	-	-	-	-	-	-	-
1933	12.8	-3.8	-	-	-	-	-	-	-	-	-	-	-	-	-	-
1934	13.3	3.9	-	-	-	-	-	-	-	-	-	-	-	-	-	-
1935	13.7	3.0	-	-	-	-	-	-	-	-	-	-	-	-	-	-
1936	13.9	1.5	-	-	-	-	-	-	-	-	-	-	-	-	-	-
1937	14.3	2.9	-	-	-	-	-	-	-	-	-	-	-	-	-	-
1938	14.0	-2.1	-	-	-	-	-	-	-	-	-	-	-	-	-	-
1939	13.7	-2.1	-	-	-	-	-	-	-	-	-	-	-	-	-	-
1940	13.8	0.7	-	-	-	-	-	-	-	-	-	-	-	-	-	-
1941	14.5	5.1	-	-	-	-	-	-	-	-	-	-	-	-	-	-
1942	16.2	11.7	-	-	-	-	-	-	-	-	-	-	-	-	-	-
1943	17.1	5.6	-	-	-	-	-	-	-	-	-	-	-	-	-	-
1944	17.5	2.3	-	-	-	-	-	-	-	-	-	-	-	-	-	-
1945	17.8	1.7	-	-	-	-	-	-	-	-	-	-	-	-	-	-
1946	19.3	8.4	-	-	-	-	-	-	-	-	-	-	-	-	-	-
1947	22.4	16.1	-	-	-	-	-	-	20.6	-	11.8	-	-	-	-	-
1948	24.1	7.6	-	-	-	-	-	-	23.3	13.1	13.1	11.0	-	-	-	-
1949	23.7	-1.7	-	-	-	-	-	-	25.1	7.7	13.4	2.3	-	-	-	-
1950	23.9	0.8	-	-	-	-	-	-	25.6	2.0	13.5	0.7	-	-	-	-
1951	25.8	7.9	-	-	-	-	-	-	27.5	7.4	13.8	2.2	-	-	-	-
1952	26.3	1.9	-	-	-	-	-	-	29.2	6.2	14.9	8.0	-	-	-	-
1953	26.7	1.5	-	-	-	-	37.5	-	30.0	2.7	15.6	4.7	-	-	-	-
1954	26.7	0.0	-	-	-	-	37.2	-0.8	29.2	-2.7	16.0	2.6	-	-	-	-
1955	26.6	-0.4	-	-	-	-	37.6	1.1	28.2	-3.4	16.5	3.1	-	-	-	-
1956	27.1	1.9	-	-	-	-	38.5	2.4	28.4	0.7	17.5	6.1	-	-	-	-
1957	28.0	3.3	-	-	-	-	38.8	0.8	30.1	6.0	18.0	2.9	-	-	-	-
1958	28.6	2.1	-	-	-	-	39.1	0.8	30.8	2.3	19.1	6.1	-	-	-	-
1959	28.8	0.7	-	-	-	-	39.5	1.0	32.8	6.5	19.6	2.6	-	-	-	-
1960	29.1	1.0	-	-	-	-	40.1	1.5	33.1	0.9	20.0	2.0	-	-	-	-
1961	29.2	0.3	-	-	-	-	40.3	0.5	33.1	0.0	20.6	3.0	-	-	-	-

[Continued]

366

Cincinnati, OH-KY-IN

Consumer Price Index - All Urban Consumers
Base 1982-1984 = 100
Annual Averages
[Continued]

For 1917-1993. Columns headed % show percentile change in the index from the previous period for which an index is available.

Year	All Items		Food & Beverage		Housing		Apparel & Upkeep		Trans-portation		Medical Care		Entertain-ment		Other Goods & Services	
	Index	%	Index	%	Index	%	Index	%	Index	%	Index	%	Index	%	Index	%
1962	29.5	1.0	-	-	-	-	40.6	0.7	33.8	2.1	21.1	2.4	-	-	-	-
1963	29.8	1.0	-	-	-	-	41.0	1.0	34.0	0.6	21.8	3.3	-	-	-	-
1964	30.3	1.7	-	-	-	-	41.5	1.2	34.5	1.5	22.4	2.8	-	-	-	-
1965	30.5	0.7	-	-	-	-	41.8	0.7	34.5	0.0	23.9	6.7	-	-	-	-
1966	31.4	3.0	-	-	-	-	43.3	3.6	35.1	1.7	24.9	4.2	-	-	-	-
1967	32.3	2.9	-	-	-	-	45.0	3.9	35.9	2.3	26.7	7.2	-	-	-	-
1968	33.9	5.0	-	-	-	-	48.1	6.9	37.7	5.0	28.7	7.5	-	-	-	-
1969	35.5	4.7	-	-	-	-	51.2	6.4	38.8	2.9	31.1	8.4	-	-	-	-
1970	37.4	5.4	-	-	-	-	53.5	4.5	40.7	4.9	32.7	5.1	-	-	-	-
1971	39.0	4.3	-	-	-	-	55.0	2.8	43.0	5.7	35.2	7.6	-	-	-	-
1972	40.3	3.3	-	-	-	-	55.3	0.5	44.4	3.3	36.4	3.4	-	-	-	-
1973	42.7	6.0	-	-	-	-	57.6	4.2	44.3	-0.2	38.4	5.5	-	-	-	-
1974	47.3	10.8	-	-	-	-	61.6	6.9	47.7	7.7	42.4	10.4	-	-	-	-
1975	51.8	9.5	-	-	-	-	64.6	4.9	51.7	8.4	47.2	11.3	-	-	-	-
1976	55.0	6.2	60.1	-	50.8	-	68.8	6.5	56.0	8.3	52.6	11.4	67.1	-	55.8	-
1977	58.9	7.1	64.3	7.0	54.5	7.3	72.3	5.1	60.0	7.1	58.9	12.0	68.9	2.7	59.2	6.1
1978	64.3	9.2	71.1	10.6	60.4	10.8	77.7	7.5	62.5	4.2	65.5	11.2	72.5	5.2	62.7	5.9
1979	72.3	12.4	79.1	11.3	69.1	14.4	82.1	5.7	71.5	14.4	72.6	10.8	77.1	6.3	67.6	7.8
1980	82.1	13.6	85.9	8.6	80.1	15.9	89.1	8.5	84.1	17.6	79.2	9.1	83.7	8.6	74.2	9.8
1981	87.9	7.1	93.2	8.5	84.2	5.1	93.4	4.8	93.8	11.5	85.9	8.5	87.5	4.5	81.6	10.0
1982	94.9	8.0	97.0	4.1	93.6	11.2	97.6	4.5	97.3	3.7	93.6	9.0	94.8	8.3	90.1	10.4
1983	100.8	6.2	99.2	2.3	102.1	9.1	100.6	3.1	99.7	2.5	100.2	7.1	100.7	6.2	101.5	12.7
1984	104.3	3.5	103.8	4.6	104.2	2.1	101.7	1.1	103.0	3.3	106.3	6.1	104.5	3.8	108.4	6.8
1985	106.6	2.2	104.6	0.8	106.8	2.5	103.4	1.7	106.0	2.9	112.0	5.4	99.8	-4.5	115.5	6.5
1986	107.6	0.9	107.2	2.5	108.6	1.7	105.5	2.0	99.7	-5.9	117.7	5.1	103.8	4.0	120.9	4.7
1987	111.9	4.0	110.7	3.3	112.0	3.1	115.8	9.8	102.8	3.1	125.7	6.8	107.7	3.8	128.3	6.1
1988	116.1	3.8	114.6	3.5	114.8	2.5	125.1	8.0	104.8	1.9	136.8	8.8	112.4	4.4	141.3	10.1
1989	120.9	4.1	119.6	4.4	119.2	3.8	119.7	-4.3	111.2	6.1	144.3	5.5	119.1	6.0	149.9	6.1
1990	126.5	4.6	128.3	7.3	121.1	1.6	121.2	1.3	117.7	5.8	157.4	9.1	129.7	8.9	165.8	10.6
1991	131.4	3.9	131.7	2.7	126.5	4.5	121.6	0.3	120.1	2.0	175.5	11.5	134.6	3.8	174.4	5.2
1992	134.1	2.1	129.6	-1.6	129.6	2.5	131.9	8.5	118.8	-1.1	188.0	7.1	140.0	4.0	185.3	6.3
1993	-	-	-	-	-	-	-	-	-	-	-	-	-	-	-	-

Source: U.S. Department of Labor, Bureau of Labor Statistics, Division of Consumer Prices and Price Indexes. - indicates no data collected for period.

Cincinnati, OH-KY-IN
Consumer Price Index - Urban Wage Earners
Base 1982-1984 = 100
Annual Averages

For 1917-1993. Columns headed % show percentile change in the index from the previous period for which an index is available.

Year	All Items		Food & Beverage		Housing		Apparel & Upkeep		Trans-portation		Medical Care		Entertain-ment		Other Goods & Services	
	Index	%	Index	%	Index	%	Index	%	Index	%	Index	%	Index	%	Index	%
1917	-	-	-	-	-	-	-	-	-	-	-	-	-	-	-	-
1918	14.6	-	-	-	-	-	-	-	-	-	-	-	-	-	-	-
1919	17.0	16.4	-	-	-	-	-	-	-	-	-	-	-	-	-	-
1920	19.5	14.7	-	-	-	-	-	-	-	-	-	-	-	-	-	-
1921	16.7	-14.4	-	-	-	-	-	-	-	-	-	-	-	-	-	-
1922	15.7	-6.0	-	-	-	-	-	-	-	-	-	-	-	-	-	-
1923	16.0	1.9	-	-	-	-	-	-	-	-	-	-	-	-	-	-
1924	16.1	0.6	-	-	-	-	-	-	-	-	-	-	-	-	-	-
1925	17.0	5.6	-	-	-	-	-	-	-	-	-	-	-	-	-	-
1926	17.2	1.2	-	-	-	-	-	-	-	-	-	-	-	-	-	-
1927	16.9	-1.7	-	-	-	-	-	-	-	-	-	-	-	-	-	-
1928	16.8	-0.6	-	-	-	-	-	-	-	-	-	-	-	-	-	-
1929	17.0	1.2	-	-	-	-	-	-	-	-	-	-	-	-	-	-
1930	16.8	-1.2	-	-	-	-	-	-	-	-	-	-	-	-	-	-
1931	15.2	-9.5	-	-	-	-	-	-	-	-	-	-	-	-	-	-
1932	13.4	-11.8	-	-	-	-	-	-	-	-	-	-	-	-	-	-
1933	12.9	-3.7	-	-	-	-	-	-	-	-	-	-	-	-	-	-
1934	13.4	3.9	-	-	-	-	-	-	-	-	-	-	-	-	-	-
1935	13.8	3.0	-	-	-	-	-	-	-	-	-	-	-	-	-	-
1936	14.0	1.4	-	-	-	-	-	-	-	-	-	-	-	-	-	-
1937	14.4	2.9	-	-	-	-	-	-	-	-	-	-	-	-	-	-
1938	14.1	-2.1	-	-	-	-	-	-	-	-	-	-	-	-	-	-
1939	13.8	-2.1	-	-	-	-	-	-	-	-	-	-	-	-	-	-
1940	13.9	0.7	-	-	-	-	-	-	-	-	-	-	-	-	-	-
1941	14.6	5.0	-	-	-	-	-	-	-	-	-	-	-	-	-	-
1942	16.3	11.6	-	-	-	-	-	-	-	-	-	-	-	-	-	-
1943	17.2	5.5	-	-	-	-	-	-	-	-	-	-	-	-	-	-
1944	17.6	2.3	-	-	-	-	-	-	-	-	-	-	-	-	-	-
1945	18.0	2.3	-	-	-	-	-	-	-	-	-	-	-	-	-	-
1946	19.4	7.8	-	-	-	-	-	-	-	-	-	-	-	-	-	-
1947	22.6	16.5	-	-	-	-	-	-	20.8	-	11.3	-	-	-	-	-
1948	24.3	7.5	-	-	-	-	-	-	23.5	13.0	12.4	9.7	-	-	-	-
1949	23.9	-1.6	-	-	-	-	-	-	25.4	8.1	12.8	3.2	-	-	-	-
1950	24.1	0.8	-	-	-	-	-	-	25.9	2.0	12.8	0.0	-	-	-	-
1951	25.9	7.5	-	-	-	-	-	-	27.7	6.9	13.2	3.1	-	-	-	-
1952	26.5	2.3	-	-	-	-	-	-	29.5	6.5	14.2	7.6	-	-	-	-
1953	26.9	1.5	-	-	-	-	36.4	-	30.3	2.7	14.9	4.9	-	-	-	-
1954	26.9	0.0	-	-	-	-	36.2	-0.5	29.5	-2.6	15.2	2.0	-	-	-	-
1955	26.8	-0.4	-	-	-	-	36.5	0.8	28.5	-3.4	15.7	3.3	-	-	-	-
1956	27.3	1.9	-	-	-	-	37.4	2.5	28.7	0.7	16.7	6.4	-	-	-	-
1957	28.2	3.3	-	-	-	-	37.7	0.8	30.4	5.9	17.2	3.0	-	-	-	-
1958	28.8	2.1	-	-	-	-	37.9	0.5	31.1	2.3	18.2	5.8	-	-	-	-
1959	29.0	0.7	-	-	-	-	38.3	1.1	33.2	6.8	18.7	2.7	-	-	-	-
1960	29.3	1.0	-	-	-	-	38.9	1.6	33.4	0.6	19.0	1.6	-	-	-	-
1961	29.4	0.3	-	-	-	-	39.1	0.5	33.5	0.3	19.6	3.2	-	-	-	-

[Continued]

368

Cincinnati, OH-KY-IN
Consumer Price Index - Urban Wage Earners
Base 1982-1984 = 100
Annual Averages
[Continued]

For 1917-1993. Columns headed % show percentile change in the index from the previous period for which an index is available.

Year	All Items		Food & Beverage		Housing		Apparel & Upkeep		Trans- portation		Medical Care		Entertain- ment		Other Goods & Services	
	Index	%	Index	%	Index	%	Index	%	Index	%	Index	%	Index	%	Index	%
1962	29.7	1.0	-	-	-	-	39.4	0.8	34.1	1.8	20.1	2.6	-	-	-	-
1963	30.0	1.0	-	-	-	-	39.8	1.0	34.3	0.6	20.8	3.5	-	-	-	-
1964	30.5	1.7	-	-	-	-	40.3	1.3	34.8	1.5	21.4	2.9	-	-	-	-
1965	30.7	0.7	-	-	-	-	40.6	0.7	34.9	0.3	22.7	6.1	-	-	-	-
1966	31.6	2.9	-	-	-	-	42.0	3.4	35.5	1.7	23.8	4.8	-	-	-	-
1967	32.5	2.8	-	-	-	-	43.7	4.0	36.2	2.0	25.4	6.7	-	-	-	-
1968	34.1	4.9	-	-	-	-	46.7	6.9	38.1	5.2	27.4	7.9	-	-	-	-
1969	35.7	4.7	-	-	-	-	49.7	6.4	39.2	2.9	29.7	8.4	-	-	-	-
1970	37.6	5.3	-	-	-	-	52.0	4.6	41.1	4.8	31.2	5.1	-	-	-	-
1971	39.3	4.5	-	-	-	-	53.4	2.7	43.5	5.8	33.5	7.4	-	-	-	-
1972	40.6	3.3	-	-	-	-	53.7	0.6	44.8	3.0	34.7	3.6	-	-	-	-
1973	43.0	5.9	-	-	-	-	55.9	4.1	44.7	-0.2	36.6	5.5	-	-	-	-
1974	47.6	10.7	-	-	-	-	59.8	7.0	48.2	7.8	40.4	10.4	-	-	-	-
1975	52.2	9.7	-	-	-	-	62.7	4.8	52.2	8.3	45.0	11.4	-	-	-	-
1976	55.4	6.1	59.8	-	51.7	-	66.8	6.5	56.5	8.2	50.1	11.3	69.7	-	55.6	-
1977	59.3	7.0	64.1	7.2	55.5	7.4	70.2	5.1	60.6	7.3	56.1	12.0	71.6	2.7	59.0	6.1
1978	64.9	9.4	71.1	10.9	61.7	11.2	75.8	8.0	63.0	4.0	62.0	10.5	75.5	5.4	63.1	6.9
1979	73.3	12.9	79.7	12.1	70.8	14.7	81.0	6.9	72.0	14.3	70.2	13.2	78.3	3.7	68.3	8.2
1980	83.2	13.5	86.3	8.3	82.4	16.4	86.6	6.9	84.5	17.4	78.2	11.4	83.9	7.2	74.6	9.2
1981	89.2	7.2	92.9	7.6	86.3	4.7	93.1	7.5	94.0	11.2	85.6	9.5	88.5	5.5	82.3	10.3
1982	96.4	8.1	97.2	4.6	96.5	11.8	97.5	4.7	97.4	3.6	93.5	9.2	95.2	7.6	90.2	9.6
1983	100.8	4.6	99.2	2.1	102.0	5.7	100.9	3.5	99.7	2.4	100.2	7.2	100.7	5.8	101.7	12.7
1984	102.8	2.0	103.6	4.4	101.5	-0.5	101.6	0.7	102.9	3.2	106.3	6.1	104.0	3.3	108.2	6.4
1985	105.2	2.3	104.3	0.7	104.6	3.1	102.5	0.9	105.7	2.7	112.0	5.4	96.8	-6.9	114.7	6.0
1986	105.8	0.6	106.8	2.4	106.3	1.6	104.5	2.0	99.7	-5.7	117.4	4.8	100.3	3.6	119.9	4.5
1987	109.8	3.8	110.2	3.2	109.6	3.1	111.5	6.7	103.1	3.4	125.5	6.9	104.6	4.3	127.2	6.1
1988	114.0	3.8	114.1	3.5	112.2	2.4	121.4	8.9	105.6	2.4	137.5	9.6	108.4	3.6	139.6	9.7
1989	118.6	4.0	119.1	4.4	116.4	3.7	115.7	-4.7	112.2	6.3	145.1	5.5	114.9	6.0	147.5	5.7
1990	124.3	4.8	128.0	7.5	118.5	1.8	118.3	2.2	118.9	6.0	157.8	8.8	124.7	8.5	161.7	9.6
1991	128.8	3.6	131.3	2.6	123.7	4.4	118.1	-0.2	121.2	1.9	175.2	11.0	129.0	3.4	170.3	5.3
1992	131.4	2.0	129.3	-1.5	126.8	2.5	128.3	8.6	120.2	-0.8	187.8	7.2	133.8	3.7	181.7	6.7
1993	-	-	-	-	-	-	-	-	-	-	-	-	-	-	-	-

Source: U.S. Department of Labor, Bureau of Labor Statistics, Division of Consumer Prices and Price Indexes. - indicates no data collected for period.

Cincinnati, OH-KY-IN
Consumer Price Index - All Urban Consumers
Base 1982-1984 = 100
All Items

For 1917-1993. Columns headed % show percentile change in the index from the previous period for which an index is available.

Year	Jan Index	%	Feb Index	%	Mar Index	%	Apr Index	%	May Index	%	Jun Index	%	Jul Index	%	Aug Index	%	Sep Index	%	Oct Index	%	Nov Index	%	Dec Index	%
1917	-		-		-		-		-		-		-		-		-		-		-		13.5	-
1918	-		-		-		-		-		-		-		-		-		-		-		15.7	16.3
1919	-		-		-		-		-		16.5	5.1	-		-		-		-		-		18.2	10.3
1920	-		-		-		-		-		20.4	12.1	-		-		-		-		-		18.3	-10.3
1921	-		-		-		-		16.6	-9.3	-		-		-		16.4	-1.2	-		-		15.8	-3.7
1922	-		-		15.4	-2.5	-		-		15.7	1.9	-		-		15.4	-1.9	-		-		15.5	0.6
1923	-		-		15.7	1.3	-		-		16.0	1.9	-		-		16.1	0.6	-		-		16.0	-0.6
1924	-		-		16.1	0.6	-		-		16.1	0.0	-		-		16.1	0.0	-		-		16.1	0.0
1925	-		-		-		-		-		17.0	5.6	-		-		-		-		-		17.1	0.6
1926	-		-		-		-		-		17.1	0.0	-		-		-		-		-		17.0	-0.6
1927	-		-		-		-		-		17.4	2.4	-		-		-		-		-		16.6	-4.6
1928	-		-		-		-		-		16.7	0.6	-		-		-		-		-		16.6	-0.6
1929	-		-		-		-		-		16.8	1.2	-		-		-		-		-		17.0	1.2
1930	-		-		-		-		-		16.7	-1.8	-		-		-		-		-		16.0	-4.2
1931	-		-		-		-		-		15.0	-6.3	-		-		-		-		-		14.4	-4.0
1932	-		-		-		-		-		13.3	-7.6	-		-		-		-		-		12.8	-3.8
1933	-		-		-		-		-		12.6	-1.6	-		-		-		-		-		12.9	2.4
1934	-		-		-		-		-		13.2	2.3	-		-		-		-		13.3	0.8	-	-
1935	-		-		13.7	3.0	-		-		-		13.7	0.0	-		-		13.8	0.7	-		-	-
1936	13.8	0.0	-		-		13.6	-1.4	-		-		14.0	2.9	-		14.1	0.7	-		-		13.9	-1.4
1937	-		-		14.3	2.9	-		-		14.3	0.0	-		-		14.5	1.4	-		-		14.3	-1.4
1938	-		-		14.0	-2.1	-		-		14.0	0.0	-		-		14.0	0.0	-		-		13.8	-1.4
1939	-		-		13.6	-1.4	-		-		13.5	-0.7	-		-		13.8	2.2	-		-		13.6	-1.4
1940	-		-		13.7	0.7	-		-		13.7	0.0	-		-		13.9	1.5	13.8	-0.7	13.8	0.0	13.8	0.0
1941	13.8	0.0	13.8	0.0	14.0	1.4	14.1	0.7	14.2	0.7	14.4	1.4	14.5	0.7	14.8	2.1	15.0	1.4	15.3	2.0	15.4	0.7	15.3	-0.6
1942	15.5	1.3	15.7	1.3	15.9	1.3	16.0	0.6	16.1	0.6	16.2	0.6	16.2	0.0	16.3	0.6	16.4	0.6	16.6	1.2	16.6	0.0	16.7	0.6
1943	16.6	-0.6	16.7	0.6	16.9	1.2	17.1	1.2	17.2	0.6	17.3	0.6	17.3	0.0	17.3	0.0	17.2	-0.6	17.3	0.6	17.2	-0.6	17.3	0.6
1944	17.2	-0.6	17.1	-0.6	17.1	0.0	17.4	1.8	17.3	-0.6	17.6	1.7	17.6	0.0	17.6	0.0	17.6	0.0	17.5	-0.6	17.6	0.6	17.6	0.0
1945	17.6	0.0	17.6	0.0	17.6	0.0	17.6	0.0	17.8	1.1	18.0	1.1	18.0	0.0	18.0	0.0	17.9	-0.6	18.0	0.6	-		18.0	0.0
1946	18.0	0.0	17.9	-0.6	18.0	0.6	18.1	0.6	18.2	0.6	18.4	1.1	19.5	6.0	20.0	2.6	20.2	1.0	20.4	1.0	21.3	4.4	21.2	-0.5
1947	21.2	0.0	21.3	0.5	21.8	2.3	21.9	0.5	21.8	-0.5	22.1	1.4	22.4	1.4	22.6	0.9	23.1	2.2	23.3	0.9	23.3	0.0	23.7	1.7
1948	23.9	0.8	23.7	-0.8	23.6	-0.4	23.8	0.8	24.0	0.8	24.2	0.8	24.5	1.2	24.5	0.0	24.6	0.4	24.5	-0.4	24.2	-1.2	24.0	-0.8
1949	24.0	0.0	23.7	-1.2	23.8	0.4	23.8	0.0	23.6	-0.8	23.8	0.8	23.6	-0.8	23.6	0.0	23.8	0.8	23.6	-0.8	23.5	-0.4	23.4	-0.4
1950	23.4	0.0	23.3	-0.4	23.4	0.4	23.3	-0.4	23.6	1.3	23.7	0.4	23.9	0.8	24.2	1.3	24.4	0.8	24.5	0.4	24.5	0.0	24.8	1.2
1951	25.3	2.0	25.5	0.8	25.6	0.4	25.7	0.4	25.7	0.0	25.7	0.0	25.8	0.4	25.7	-0.4	26.0	1.2	26.0	0.0	26.1	0.4	26.1	0.0
1952	26.2	0.4	26.0	-0.8	26.0	0.0	26.2	0.8	26.3	0.4	26.4	0.4	26.5	0.4	26.5	0.0	26.5	0.0	26.5	0.0	26.3	-0.8	26.3	0.0
1953	-		-		26.3	0.0	-		-		26.8	1.9	-		-		27.0	0.7	-		-		26.8	-0.7
1954	-		-		26.7	-0.4	-		-		26.7	0.0	-		-		26.7	0.0	-		-		26.5	-0.7
1955	-		-		26.5	0.0	-		-		26.6	0.4	-		-		26.6	0.0	-		-		26.7	0.4
1956	-		-		26.7	0.0	-		-		27.2	1.9	-		-		27.4	0.7	-		-		27.5	0.4
1957	-		-		27.6	0.4	-		-		28.0	1.4	-		-		28.3	1.1	-		-		28.3	0.0
1958	-		-		28.6	1.1	-		-		28.7	0.3	-		-		28.7	0.0	-		-		28.6	-0.3
1959	-		-		28.6	0.0	-		-		28.8	0.7	-		-		28.9	0.3	-		-		29.0	0.3
1960	-		-		28.9	-0.3	-		-		29.2	1.0	-		-		29.2	0.0	-		-		29.2	0.0
1961	-		-		29.2	0.0	-		-		29.2	0.0	-		-		29.3	0.3	-		-		29.2	-0.3

[Continued]

Cincinnati, OH-KY-IN

Consumer Price Index - All Urban Consumers
Base 1982-1984 = 100
All Items
[Continued]

For 1917-1993. Columns headed % show percentile change in the index from the previous period for which an index is available.

Year	Jan		Feb		Mar		Apr		May		Jun		Jul		Aug		Sep		Oct		Nov		Dec	
	Index	%	Index	%	Index	%	Index	%	Index	%	Index	%	Index	%	Index	%	Index	%	Index	%	Index	%	Index	%
1962	-	-	-	-	29.4	0.7	-	-	-	-	29.4	0.0	-	-	-	-	29.7	1.0	-	-	-	-	29.6	-0.3
1963	-	-	-	-	29.8	0.7	-	-	-	-	29.8	0.0	-	-	-	-	29.9	0.3	-	-	-	-	29.9	0.0
1964	-	-	-	-	30.1	0.7	-	-	-	-	30.2	0.3	-	-	-	-	30.5	1.0	-	-	-	-	30.4	-0.3
1965	-	-	-	-	30.4	0.0	-	-	-	-	30.6	0.7	-	-	-	-	30.5	-0.3	-	-	-	-	30.7	0.7
1966	-	-	-	-	31.1	1.3	-	-	-	-	31.4	1.0	-	-	-	-	31.8	1.3	-	-	-	-	31.7	-0.3
1967	-	-	-	-	31.8	0.3	-	-	-	-	32.2	1.3	-	-	-	-	32.7	1.6	-	-	-	-	33.0	0.9
1968	-	-	-	-	33.4	1.2	-	-	-	-	33.8	1.2	-	-	-	-	34.3	1.5	-	-	-	-	34.5	0.6
1969	-	-	-	-	34.9	1.2	-	-	-	-	35.5	1.7	-	-	-	-	35.7	0.6	-	-	-	-	36.4	2.0
1970	-	-	-	-	36.8	1.1	-	-	-	-	37.4	1.6	-	-	-	-	37.7	0.8	-	-	-	-	38.3	1.6
1971	-	-	-	-	38.7	1.0	-	-	-	-	39.0	0.8	-	-	-	-	39.2	0.5	-	-	-	-	39.4	0.5
1972	-	-	-	-	39.8	1.0	-	-	-	-	40.3	1.3	-	-	-	-	40.8	1.2	-	-	-	-	40.9	0.2
1973	-	-	-	-	41.9	2.4	-	-	-	-	42.3	1.0	-	-	-	-	43.4	2.6	-	-	-	-	44.1	1.6
1974	-	-	-	-	45.7	3.6	-	-	-	-	47.1	3.1	-	-	-	-	48.6	3.2	-	-	-	-	49.7	2.3
1975	-	-	-	-	50.4	1.4	-	-	-	-	51.9	3.0	-	-	-	-	53.0	2.1	-	-	-	-	53.2	0.4
1976	-	-	-	-	54.0	1.5	-	-	-	-	54.9	1.7	-	-	-	-	55.6	1.3	-	-	-	-	56.4	1.4
1977	-	-	-	-	57.8	2.5	-	-	-	-	58.8	1.7	-	-	-	-	59.9	1.9	-	-	-	-	60.3	0.7
1978	-	-	-	-	62.1	3.0	-	-	63.8	2.7	-	-	64.7	1.4	-	-	65.8	1.7	-	-	66.9	1.7	-	-
1979	68.3	2.1	-	-	69.7	2.0	-	-	71.6	2.7	-	-	72.7	1.5	-	-	74.0	1.8	-	-	75.4	1.9	-	-
1980	77.4	2.7	-	-	80.1	3.5	-	-	81.3	1.5	-	-	83.0	2.1	-	-	84.0	1.2	-	-	84.7	0.8	-	-
1981	85.5	0.9	-	-	86.0	0.6	-	-	87.8	2.1	-	-	88.3	0.6	-	-	88.9	0.7	-	-	89.4	0.6	-	-
1982	92.3	3.2	-	-	92.1	-0.2	-	-	93.3	1.3	-	-	94.8	1.6	-	-	97.0	2.3	-	-	98.3	1.3	-	-
1983	98.9	0.6	-	-	99.4	0.5	-	-	100.6	1.2	-	-	101.0	0.4	-	-	101.7	0.7	-	-	102.4	0.7	-	-
1984	102.9	0.5	-	-	103.4	0.5	-	-	104.0	0.6	-	-	104.5	0.5	-	-	105.1	0.6	-	-	105.2	0.1	-	-
1985	105.1	-0.1	-	-	106.1	1.0	-	-	106.8	0.7	-	-	106.7	-0.1	-	-	106.6	-0.1	-	-	107.7	1.0	-	-
1986	107.7	0.0	-	-	106.5	-1.1	-	-	107.3	0.8	-	-	107.4	0.1	-	-	107.6	0.2	-	-	108.4	0.7	-	-
1987	-	-	-	-	-	-	-	-	-	-	110.6	2.0	-	-	-	-	-	-	-	-	-	-	113.2	2.4
1988	-	-	-	-	-	-	-	-	-	-	114.3	1.0	-	-	-	-	-	-	-	-	-	-	118.0	3.2
1989	-	-	-	-	-	-	-	-	-	-	119.9	1.6	-	-	-	-	-	-	-	-	-	-	121.8	1.6
1990	-	-	-	-	-	-	-	-	-	-	125.0	2.6	-	-	-	-	-	-	-	-	-	-	128.1	2.5
1991	-	-	-	-	-	-	-	-	-	-	130.5	1.9	-	-	-	-	-	-	-	-	-	-	132.3	1.4
1992	-	-	-	-	-	-	-	-	-	-	133.2	0.7	-	-	-	-	-	-	-	-	-	-	134.9	1.3
1993	-	-	-	-	-	-	-	-	-	-	137.0	1.6	-	-	-	-	-	-	-	-	-	-	-	-

Source: U.S. Department of Labor, Bureau of Labor Statistics, Division of Consumer Prices and Price Indexes. - indicates no data collected for period.

Cincinnati, OH-KY-IN
Consumer Price Index - Urban Wage Earners
Base 1982-1984 = 100
All Items

For 1917-1993. Columns headed % show percentile change in the index from the previous period for which an index is available.

Year	Jan Index	%	Feb Index	%	Mar Index	%	Apr Index	%	May Index	%	Jun Index	%	Jul Index	%	Aug Index	%	Sep Index	%	Oct Index	%	Nov Index	%	Dec Index	%
1917	-	-	-	-	-	-	-	-	-	-	-	-	-	-	-	-	-	-	-	-	-	-	13.6	-
1918	-	-	-	-	-	-	-	-	-	-	-	-	-	-	-	-	-	-	-	-	-	-	15.8	16.2
1919	-	-	-	-	-	-	-	-	-	-	16.6	5.1	-	-	-	-	-	-	-	-	-	-	18.4	10.8
1920	-	-	-	-	-	-	-	-	-	-	20.6	12.0	-	-	-	-	-	-	-	-	-	-	18.4	-10.7
1921	-	-	-	-	-	-	-	-	16.8	-8.7	-	-	-	-	-	-	16.5	-1.8	-	-	-	-	15.9	-3.6
1922	-	-	-	-	15.6	-1.9	-	-	-	-	15.8	1.3	-	-	-	-	15.6	-1.3	-	-	-	-	15.6	0.0
1923	-	-	-	-	15.8	1.3	-	-	-	-	16.1	1.9	-	-	-	-	16.2	0.6	-	-	-	-	16.1	-0.6
1924	-	-	-	-	16.2	0.6	-	-	-	-	16.2	0.0	-	-	-	-	16.2	0.0	-	-	-	-	16.2	0.0
1925	-	-	-	-	-	-	-	-	-	-	17.1	5.6	-	-	-	-	-	-	-	-	-	-	17.2	0.6
1926	-	-	-	-	-	-	-	-	-	-	17.2	0.0	-	-	-	-	-	-	-	-	-	-	17.1	-0.6
1927	-	-	-	-	-	-	-	-	-	-	17.5	2.3	-	-	-	-	-	-	-	-	-	-	16.7	-4.6
1928	-	-	-	-	-	-	-	-	-	-	16.8	0.6	-	-	-	-	-	-	-	-	-	-	16.7	-0.6
1929	-	-	-	-	-	-	-	-	-	-	17.0	1.8	-	-	-	-	-	-	-	-	-	-	17.1	0.6
1930	-	-	-	-	-	-	-	-	-	-	16.9	-1.2	-	-	-	-	-	-	-	-	-	-	16.1	-4.7
1931	-	-	-	-	-	-	-	-	-	-	15.1	-6.2	-	-	-	-	-	-	-	-	-	-	14.5	-4.0
1932	-	-	-	-	-	-	-	-	-	-	13.4	-7.6	-	-	-	-	-	-	-	-	-	-	12.9	-3.7
1933	-	-	-	-	-	-	-	-	-	-	12.7	-1.6	-	-	-	-	-	-	-	-	-	-	13.0	2.4
1934	-	-	-	-	-	-	-	-	-	-	13.3	2.3	-	-	-	-	-	-	-	-	13.4	0.8	-	-
1935	-	-	-	-	13.8	3.0	-	-	-	-	-	-	13.8	0.0	-	-	-	-	13.9	0.7	-	-	-	-
1936	13.9	0.0	-	-	-	-	13.7	-1.4	-	-	-	-	14.1	2.9	-	-	14.2	0.7	-	-	-	-	14.0	-1.4
1937	-	-	-	-	14.4	2.9	-	-	-	-	14.4	0.0	-	-	-	-	14.6	1.4	-	-	-	-	14.4	-1.4
1938	-	-	-	-	14.1	-2.1	-	-	-	-	14.1	0.0	-	-	-	-	14.1	0.0	-	-	-	-	13.9	-1.4
1939	-	-	-	-	13.7	-1.4	-	-	-	-	13.6	-0.7	-	-	-	-	13.9	2.2	-	-	-	-	13.7	-1.4
1940	-	-	-	-	13.8	0.7	-	-	-	-	13.8	0.0	-	-	-	-	14.0	1.4	13.9	-0.7	13.9	0.0	13.9	0.0
1941	13.9	0.0	13.9	0.0	14.1	1.4	14.2	0.7	14.3	0.7	14.5	1.4	14.6	0.7	14.9	2.1	15.1	1.3	15.4	2.0	15.5	0.6	15.4	-0.6
1942	15.7	1.9	15.8	0.6	16.0	1.3	16.1	0.6	16.2	0.6	16.3	0.6	16.3	0.0	16.4	0.6	16.5	0.6	16.7	1.2	16.7	0.0	16.8	0.6
1943	16.8	0.0	16.8	0.0	17.1	1.8	17.2	0.6	17.3	0.6	17.4	0.6	17.4	0.0	17.4	0.0	17.3	-0.6	17.4	0.6	17.3	-0.6	17.4	0.6
1944	17.3	-0.6	17.2	-0.6	17.2	0.0	17.5	1.7	17.4	-0.6	17.7	1.7	17.8	0.6	17.7	-0.6	17.7	0.0	17.6	-0.6	17.7	0.6	17.7	0.0
1945	17.8	0.6	17.7	-0.6	17.7	0.0	17.8	0.6	17.9	0.6	18.1	1.1	18.2	0.6	18.1	-0.5	18.0	-0.6	18.1	0.6	-	-	18.2	0.6
1946	18.2	0.0	18.1	-0.5	18.1	0.0	18.2	0.6	18.4	1.1	18.5	0.5	19.7	6.5	20.1	2.0	20.4	1.5	20.5	0.5	21.4	4.4	21.4	0.0
1947	21.3	-0.5	21.5	0.9	22.0	2.3	22.0	0.0	22.0	0.0	22.2	0.9	22.5	1.4	22.8	1.3	23.3	2.2	23.5	0.9	23.5	0.0	23.9	1.7
1948	24.0	0.4	23.9	-0.4	23.8	-0.4	24.0	0.8	24.2	0.8	24.4	0.8	24.7	1.2	24.7	0.0	24.8	0.4	24.6	-0.8	24.4	-0.8	24.2	-0.8
1949	24.2	0.0	23.9	-1.2	24.0	0.4	24.0	0.0	23.8	-0.8	24.0	0.8	23.7	-1.2	23.7	0.0	24.0	1.3	23.7	-1.2	23.7	0.0	23.6	-0.4
1950	23.6	0.0	23.5	-0.4	23.6	0.4	23.5	-0.4	23.8	1.3	23.9	0.4	24.0	0.4	24.3	1.2	24.5	0.8	24.6	0.4	24.6	0.0	25.0	1.6
1951	25.5	2.0	25.7	0.8	25.8	0.4	25.8	0.0	25.8	0.0	25.9	0.4	26.0	0.4	25.9	-0.4	26.1	0.8	26.2	0.4	26.3	0.4	26.3	0.0
1952	26.4	0.4	26.2	-0.8	26.2	0.0	26.4	0.8	26.5	0.4	26.6	0.4	26.7	0.4	26.7	0.0	26.7	0.0	26.7	0.0	26.5	-0.7	26.5	0.0
1953	-	-	-	-	26.5	0.0	-	-	-	-	27.0	1.9	-	-	-	-	27.1	0.4	-	-	-	-	27.0	-0.4
1954	-	-	-	-	26.9	-0.4	-	-	-	-	26.9	0.0	-	-	-	-	26.9	0.0	-	-	-	-	26.7	-0.7
1955	-	-	-	-	26.7	0.0	-	-	-	-	26.8	0.4	-	-	-	-	26.8	0.0	-	-	-	-	26.9	0.4
1956	-	-	-	-	26.9	0.0	-	-	-	-	27.4	1.9	-	-	-	-	27.6	0.7	-	-	-	-	27.7	0.4
1957	-	-	-	-	27.8	0.4	-	-	-	-	28.2	1.4	-	-	-	-	28.5	1.1	-	-	-	-	28.5	0.0
1958	-	-	-	-	28.8	1.1	-	-	-	-	28.9	0.3	-	-	-	-	28.9	0.0	-	-	-	-	28.8	-0.3
1959	-	-	-	-	28.8	0.0	-	-	-	-	29.0	0.7	-	-	-	-	29.1	0.3	-	-	-	-	29.2	0.3
1960	-	-	-	-	29.1	-0.3	-	-	-	-	29.4	1.0	-	-	-	-	29.4	0.0	-	-	-	-	29.4	0.0
1961	-	-	-	-	29.4	0.0	-	-	-	-	29.4	0.0	-	-	-	-	29.5	0.3	-	-	-	-	29.4	-0.3

[Continued]

Cincinnati, OH-KY-IN

Consumer Price Index - Urban Wage Earners
Base 1982-1984 = 100
All Items
[Continued]

For 1917-1993. Columns headed % show percentile change in the index from the previous period for which an index is available.

Year	Jan Index	%	Feb Index	%	Mar Index	%	Apr Index	%	May Index	%	Jun Index	%	Jul Index	%	Aug Index	%	Sep Index	%	Oct Index	%	Nov Index	%	Dec Index	%
1962	-	-	-	-	29.6	0.7	-	-	-	-	29.6	0.0	-	-	-	-	29.9	1.0	-	-	-	-	29.8	-0.3
1963	-	-	-	-	30.0	0.7	-	-	-	-	30.0	0.0	-	-	-	-	30.1	0.3	-	-	-	-	30.1	0.0
1964	-	-	-	-	30.3	0.7	-	-	-	-	30.4	0.3	-	-	-	-	30.7	1.0	-	-	-	-	30.7	0.0
1965	-	-	-	-	30.6	-0.3	-	-	-	-	30.8	0.7	-	-	-	-	30.7	-0.3	-	-	-	-	30.9	0.7
1966	-	-	-	-	31.3	1.3	-	-	-	-	31.6	1.0	-	-	-	-	32.0	1.3	-	-	-	-	31.9	-0.3
1967	-	-	-	-	32.0	0.3	-	-	-	-	32.4	1.3	-	-	-	-	32.9	1.5	-	-	-	-	33.3	1.2
1968	-	-	-	-	33.6	0.9	-	-	-	-	34.0	1.2	-	-	-	-	34.5	1.5	-	-	-	-	34.7	0.6
1969	-	-	-	-	35.2	1.4	-	-	-	-	35.7	1.4	-	-	-	-	36.0	0.8	-	-	-	-	36.6	1.7
1970	-	-	-	-	37.0	1.1	-	-	-	-	37.6	1.6	-	-	-	-	38.0	1.1	-	-	-	-	38.6	1.6
1971	-	-	-	-	39.0	1.0	-	-	-	-	39.3	0.8	-	-	-	-	39.5	0.5	-	-	-	-	39.7	0.5
1972	-	-	-	-	40.0	0.8	-	-	-	-	40.5	1.3	-	-	-	-	41.1	1.5	-	-	-	-	41.2	0.2
1973	-	-	-	-	42.2	2.4	-	-	-	-	42.6	0.9	-	-	-	-	43.7	2.6	-	-	-	-	44.5	1.8
1974	-	-	-	-	46.0	3.4	-	-	-	-	47.4	3.0	-	-	-	-	48.9	3.2	-	-	-	-	50.0	2.2
1975	-	-	-	-	50.7	1.4	-	-	-	-	52.3	3.2	-	-	-	-	53.3	1.9	-	-	-	-	53.6	0.6
1976	-	-	-	-	54.4	1.5	-	-	-	-	55.3	1.7	-	-	-	-	56.0	1.3	-	-	-	-	56.8	1.4
1977	-	-	-	-	58.2	2.5	-	-	-	-	59.2	1.7	-	-	-	-	60.3	1.9	-	-	-	-	60.8	0.8
1978	-	-	-	-	62.6	3.0	-	-	64.3	2.7	-	-	65.4	1.7	-	-	66.3	1.4	-	-	67.5	1.8	-	-
1979	69.1	2.4	-	-	70.5	2.0	-	-	72.6	3.0	-	-	73.7	1.5	-	-	75.1	1.9	-	-	76.7	2.1	-	-
1980	78.4	2.2	-	-	81.3	3.7	-	-	82.3	1.2	-	-	84.3	2.4	-	-	85.2	1.1	-	-	85.7	0.6	-	-
1981	86.7	1.2	-	-	87.1	0.5	-	-	88.9	2.1	-	-	89.9	1.1	-	-	90.2	0.3	-	-	90.8	0.7	-	-
1982	93.8	3.3	-	-	93.5	-0.3	-	-	94.8	1.4	-	-	96.3	1.6	-	-	98.5	2.3	-	-	99.9	1.4	-	-
1983	99.3	-0.6	-	-	100.1	0.8	-	-	100.7	0.6	-	-	100.2	-0.5	-	-	101.3	1.1	-	-	102.8	1.5	-	-
1984	102.0	-0.8	-	-	102.1	0.1	-	-	101.6	-0.5	-	-	102.3	0.7	-	-	104.4	2.1	-	-	103.9	-0.5	-	-
1985	103.8	-0.1	-	-	104.8	1.0	-	-	105.4	0.6	-	-	105.2	-0.2	-	-	105.0	-0.2	-	-	106.1	1.0	-	-
1986	106.1	0.0	-	-	104.7	-1.3	-	-	105.7	1.0	-	-	105.7	0.0	-	-	105.7	0.0	-	-	106.6	0.9	-	-
1987	-	-	-	-	-	-	-	-	-	-	108.6	1.9	-	-	-	-	-	-	-	-	-	-	111.1	2.3
1988	-	-	-	-	-	-	-	-	-	-	112.1	0.9	-	-	-	-	-	-	-	-	-	-	115.9	3.4
1989	-	-	-	-	-	-	-	-	-	-	117.7	1.6	-	-	-	-	-	-	-	-	-	-	119.6	1.6
1990	-	-	-	-	-	-	-	-	-	-	122.7	2.6	-	-	-	-	-	-	-	-	-	-	125.9	2.6
1991	-	-	-	-	-	-	-	-	-	-	127.9	1.6	-	-	-	-	-	-	-	-	-	-	129.7	1.4
1992	-	-	-	-	-	-	-	-	-	-	130.4	0.5	-	-	-	-	-	-	-	-	-	-	132.4	1.5
1993	-	-	-	-	-	-	-	-	-	-	134.1	1.3	-	-	-	-	-	-	-	-	-	-	-	-

Source: U.S. Department of Labor, Bureau of Labor Statistics, Division of Consumer Prices and Price Indexes. - indicates no data collected for period.

Cincinnati, OH-KY-IN
Consumer Price Index - All Urban Consumers
Base 1982-1984 = 100
Food and Beverages

For 1975-1993. Columns headed % show percentile change in the index from the previous period for which an index is available.

Year	Jan Index	%	Feb Index	%	Mar Index	%	Apr Index	%	May Index	%	Jun Index	%	Jul Index	%	Aug Index	%	Sep Index	%	Oct Index	%	Nov Index	%	Dec Index	%
1975	-	-	-	-	-	-	-	-	-	-	-	-	-	-	-	-	-	-	-	-	-	-	59.1	-
1976	-	-	-	-	59.2	0.2	-	-	-	-	60.2	1.7	-	-	-	-	60.7	0.8	-	-	-	-	60.7	0.0
1977	-	-	-	-	63.0	3.8	-	-	-	-	64.5	2.4	-	-	-	-	65.5	1.6	-	-	-	-	66.0	0.8
1978	-	-	-	-	68.5	3.8	-	-	70.4	2.8	-	-	72.7	3.3	-	-	72.4	-0.4	-	-	73.5	1.5	-	-
1979	75.6	2.9	-	-	77.5	2.5	-	-	79.5	2.6	-	-	79.7	0.3	-	-	79.9	0.3	-	-	80.8	1.1	-	-
1980	82.2	1.7	-	-	83.5	1.6	-	-	84.7	1.4	-	-	85.8	1.3	-	-	87.9	2.4	-	-	89.1	1.4	-	-
1981	91.4	2.6	-	-	92.5	1.2	-	-	93.1	0.6	-	-	93.2	0.1	-	-	94.0	0.9	-	-	93.8	-0.2	-	-
1982	95.2	1.5	-	-	95.3	0.1	-	-	96.6	1.4	-	-	98.4	1.9	-	-	98.1	-0.3	-	-	97.7	-0.4	-	-
1983	97.7	0.0	-	-	99.0	1.3	-	-	99.5	0.5	-	-	99.2	-0.3	-	-	98.8	-0.4	-	-	99.7	0.9	-	-
1984	102.4	2.7	-	-	103.5	1.1	-	-	103.9	0.4	-	-	103.7	-0.2	-	-	104.7	1.0	-	-	104.5	-0.2	-	-
1985	104.1	-0.4	-	-	105.4	1.2	-	-	105.1	-0.3	-	-	104.4	-0.7	-	-	104.1	-0.3	-	-	104.4	0.3	-	-
1986	105.0	0.6	-	-	105.2	0.2	-	-	106.0	0.8	-	-	107.8	1.7	-	-	109.0	1.1	-	-	109.2	0.2	-	-
1987	-	-	-	-	-	-	-	-	-	-	110.1	0.8	-	-	-	-	-	-	-	-	-	-	111.4	1.2
1988	-	-	-	-	-	-	-	-	-	-	112.8	1.3	-	-	-	-	-	-	-	-	-	-	116.3	3.1
1989	-	-	-	-	-	-	-	-	-	-	118.0	1.5	-	-	-	-	-	-	-	-	-	-	121.3	2.8
1990	-	-	-	-	-	-	-	-	-	-	127.2	4.9	-	-	-	-	-	-	-	-	-	-	129.4	1.7
1991	-	-	-	-	-	-	-	-	-	-	132.0	2.0	-	-	-	-	-	-	-	-	-	-	131.4	-0.5
1992	-	-	-	-	-	-	-	-	-	-	130.8	-0.5	-	-	-	-	-	-	-	-	-	-	128.5	-1.8
1993	-	-	-	-	-	-	-	-	-	-	131.5	2.3	-	-	-	-	-	-	-	-	-	-	-	-

Source: U.S. Department of Labor, Bureau of Labor Statistics, Division of Consumer Prices and Price Indexes. - indicates no data collected for period.

Cincinnati, OH-KY-IN
Consumer Price Index - Urban Wage Earners
Base 1982-1984 = 100
Food and Beverages

For 1975-1993. Columns headed % show percentile change in the index from the previous period for which an index is available.

Year	Jan Index	Jan %	Feb Index	Feb %	Mar Index	Mar %	Apr Index	Apr %	May Index	May %	Jun Index	Jun %	Jul Index	Jul %	Aug Index	Aug %	Sep Index	Sep %	Oct Index	Oct %	Nov Index	Nov %	Dec Index	Dec %
1975	-	-	-	-	-	-	-	-	-	-	-	-	-	-	-	-	-	-	-	-	-	-	58.9	-
1976	-	-	-	-	59.0	0.2	-	-	-	-	60.0	1.7	-	-	-	-	60.4	0.7	-	-	-	-	60.4	0.0
1977	-	-	-	-	62.7	3.8	-	-	-	-	64.3	2.6	-	-	-	-	65.3	1.6	-	-	-	-	65.8	0.8
1978	-	-	-	-	68.3	3.8	-	-	70.6	3.4	-	-	72.6	2.8	-	-	72.3	-0.4	-	-	73.7	1.9	-	-
1979	76.1	3.3	-	-	77.8	2.2	-	-	80.3	3.2	-	-	80.5	0.2	-	-	80.8	0.4	-	-	81.5	0.9	-	-
1980	82.2	0.9	-	-	83.8	1.9	-	-	85.0	1.4	-	-	86.4	1.6	-	-	88.6	2.5	-	-	89.3	0.8	-	-
1981	91.5	2.5	-	-	92.2	0.8	-	-	92.6	0.4	-	-	92.9	0.3	-	-	93.7	0.9	-	-	93.8	0.1	-	-
1982	95.6	1.9	-	-	95.7	0.1	-	-	96.9	1.3	-	-	98.4	1.5	-	-	98.2	-0.2	-	-	97.8	-0.4	-	-
1983	97.8	0.0	-	-	99.2	1.4	-	-	99.7	0.5	-	-	99.2	-0.5	-	-	98.8	-0.4	-	-	99.7	0.9	-	-
1984	102.3	2.6	-	-	103.3	1.0	-	-	103.7	0.4	-	-	103.3	-0.4	-	-	104.4	1.1	-	-	104.1	-0.3	-	-
1985	104.0	-0.1	-	-	105.3	1.3	-	-	104.8	-0.5	-	-	104.0	-0.8	-	-	103.8	-0.2	-	-	104.1	0.3	-	-
1986	104.7	0.6	-	-	105.0	0.3	-	-	105.7	0.7	-	-	107.4	1.6	-	-	108.4	0.9	-	-	108.8	0.4	-	-
1987	-	-	-	-	-	-	-	-	-	-	109.6	0.7	-	-	-	-	-	-	-	-	-	-	110.9	1.2
1988	-	-	-	-	-	-	-	-	-	-	112.4	1.4	-	-	-	-	-	-	-	-	-	-	115.8	3.0
1989	-	-	-	-	-	-	-	-	-	-	117.4	1.4	-	-	-	-	-	-	-	-	-	-	120.8	2.9
1990	-	-	-	-	-	-	-	-	-	-	126.9	5.0	-	-	-	-	-	-	-	-	-	-	129.1	1.7
1991	-	-	-	-	-	-	-	-	-	-	131.6	1.9	-	-	-	-	-	-	-	-	-	-	131.1	-0.4
1992	-	-	-	-	-	-	-	-	-	-	130.4	-0.5	-	-	-	-	-	-	-	-	-	-	128.3	-1.6
1993	-	-	-	-	-	-	-	-	-	-	131.2	2.3	-	-	-	-	-	-	-	-	-	-	-	-

Source: U.S. Department of Labor, Bureau of Labor Statistics, Division of Consumer Prices and Price Indexes. - indicates no data collected for period.

Cincinnati, OH-KY-IN
Consumer Price Index - All Urban Consumers
Base 1982-1984 = 100
Housing

For 1975-1993. Columns headed % show percentile change in the index from the previous period for which an index is available.

Year	Jan Index	%	Feb Index	%	Mar Index	%	Apr Index	%	May Index	%	Jun Index	%	Jul Index	%	Aug Index	%	Sep Index	%	Oct Index	%	Nov Index	%	Dec Index	%
1975	-	-	-	-	-	-	-	-	-	-	-	-	-	-	-	-	-	-	-	-	-	-	49.3	-
1976	-	-	-	-	50.2	1.8	-	-	-	-	50.6	0.8	-	-	-	-	51.0	0.8	-	-	-	-	52.5	2.9
1977	-	-	-	-	53.3	1.5	-	-	-	-	54.2	1.7	-	-	-	-	55.4	2.2	-	-	-	-	56.2	1.4
1978	-	-	-	-	58.0	3.2	-	-	59.9	3.3	-	-	60.4	0.8	-	-	62.2	3.0	-	-	63.5	2.1	-	-
1979	64.7	1.9	-	-	66.6	2.9	-	-	68.1	2.3	-	-	69.2	1.6	-	-	70.5	1.9	-	-	72.7	3.1	-	-
1980	74.7	2.8	-	-	78.1	4.6	-	-	79.3	1.5	-	-	82.2	3.7	-	-	82.1	-0.1	-	-	82.5	0.5	-	-
1981	82.2	-0.4	-	-	81.2	-1.2	-	-	84.7	4.3	-	-	85.4	0.8	-	-	84.6	-0.9	-	-	85.2	0.7	-	-
1982	90.0	5.6	-	-	89.4	-0.7	-	-	91.6	2.5	-	-	92.7	1.2	-	-	96.6	4.2	-	-	99.3	2.8	-	-
1983	99.6	0.3	-	-	101.1	1.5	-	-	102.4	1.3	-	-	102.6	0.2	-	-	103.1	0.5	-	-	103.0	-0.1	-	-
1984	103.3	0.3	-	-	103.6	0.3	-	-	104.0	0.4	-	-	104.6	0.6	-	-	104.6	0.0	-	-	104.7	0.1	-	-
1985	105.7	1.0	-	-	106.2	0.5	-	-	106.7	0.5	-	-	107.4	0.7	-	-	106.7	-0.7	-	-	107.4	0.7	-	-
1986	107.8	0.4	-	-	108.5	0.6	-	-	109.1	0.6	-	-	109.3	0.2	-	-	107.3	-1.8	-	-	109.1	1.7	113.3	2.3
1987	-	-	-	-	-	-	-	-	-	-	110.8	1.6	-	-	-	-	-	-	-	-	-	-	116.3	2.6
1988	-	-	-	-	-	-	-	-	-	-	113.3	0.0	-	-	-	-	-	-	-	-	-	-	119.8	1.1
1989	-	-	-	-	-	-	-	-	-	-	118.5	1.9	-	-	-	-	-	-	-	-	-	-	122.0	1.5
1990	-	-	-	-	-	-	-	-	-	-	120.2	0.3	-	-	-	-	-	-	-	-	-	-	127.4	1.5
1991	-	-	-	-	-	-	-	-	-	-	125.5	2.9	-	-	-	-	-	-	-	-	-	-	130.5	1.4
1992	-	-	-	-	-	-	-	-	-	-	128.7	1.0	-	-	-	-	-	-	-	-	-	-	-	-
1993	-	-	-	-	-	-	-	-	-	-	130.1	-0.3	-	-	-	-	-	-	-	-	-	-	-	-

Source: U.S. Department of Labor, Bureau of Labor Statistics, Division of Consumer Prices and Price Indexes. - indicates no data collected for period.

Cincinnati, OH-KY-IN
Consumer Price Index - Urban Wage Earners
Base 1982-1984 = 100
Housing

For 1975-1993. Columns headed % show percentile change in the index from the previous period for which an index is available.

Year	Jan Index	%	Feb Index	%	Mar Index	%	Apr Index	%	May Index	%	Jun Index	%	Jul Index	%	Aug Index	%	Sep Index	%	Oct Index	%	Nov Index	%	Dec Index	%
1975	-	-	-	-	-	-	-	-	-	-	-	-	-	-	-	-	-	-	-	-	-	-	-	-
1976	-	-	-	-	51.1	1.8	-	-	-	-	51.5	0.8	-	-	-	-	51.9	0.8	-	-	-	-	50.2	-
1977	-	-	-	-	54.3	1.5	-	-	-	-	55.2	1.7	-	-	-	-	56.5	2.4	-	-	-	-	53.5	3.1
1978	-	-	-	-	59.1	3.3	-	-	61.0	3.2	-	-	61.7	1.1	-	-	63.3	2.6	-	-	65.0	2.7	57.2	1.2
1979	66.2	1.8	-	-	68.3	3.2	-	-	69.9	2.3	-	-	71.0	1.6	-	-	72.3	1.8	-	-	74.8	3.5	-	-
1980	76.9	2.8	-	-	80.5	4.7	-	-	81.5	1.2	-	-	84.5	3.7	-	-	84.3	-0.2	-	-	84.7	0.5	-	-
1981	84.4	-0.4	-	-	83.2	-1.4	-	-	86.6	4.1	-	-	87.7	1.3	-	-	86.7	-1.1	-	-	87.5	0.9	-	-
1982	92.7	5.9	-	-	91.9	-0.9	-	-	94.3	2.6	-	-	95.5	1.3	-	-	99.7	4.4	-	-	102.7	3.0	-	-
1983	100.5	-2.1	-	-	102.3	1.8	-	-	102.3	0.0	-	-	100.7	-1.6	-	-	102.0	1.3	-	-	104.1	2.1	-	-
1984	101.4	-2.6	-	-	101.0	-0.4	-	-	99.1	-1.9	-	-	100.4	1.3	-	-	103.9	3.5	-	-	102.7	-1.2	-	-
1985	103.7	1.0	-	-	104.2	0.5	-	-	104.5	0.3	-	-	105.2	0.7	-	-	104.4	-0.8	-	-	105.2	0.8	-	-
1986	105.6	0.4	-	-	106.3	0.7	-	-	107.0	0.7	-	-	107.0	0.0	-	-	104.8	-2.1	-	-	106.8	1.9	-	-
1987	-	-	-	-	-	-	-	-	-	-	108.4	1.5	-	-	-	-	-	-	-	-	-	-	110.9	2.3
1988	-	-	-	-	-	-	-	-	-	-	110.8	-0.1	-	-	-	-	-	-	-	-	-	-	113.7	2.6
1989	-	-	-	-	-	-	-	-	-	-	115.7	1.8	-	-	-	-	-	-	-	-	-	-	117.1	1.2
1990	-	-	-	-	-	-	-	-	-	-	117.5	0.3	-	-	-	-	-	-	-	-	-	-	119.4	1.6
1991	-	-	-	-	-	-	-	-	-	-	122.7	2.8	-	-	-	-	-	-	-	-	-	-	124.7	1.6
1992	-	-	-	-	-	-	-	-	-	-	125.9	1.0	-	-	-	-	-	-	-	-	-	-	127.7	1.4
1993	-	-	-	-	-	-	-	-	-	-	127.3	-0.3	-	-	-	-	-	-	-	-	-	-	-	-

Source: U.S. Department of Labor, Bureau of Labor Statistics, Division of Consumer Prices and Price Indexes. - indicates no data collected for period.

Cincinnati, OH-KY-IN
Consumer Price Index - All Urban Consumers
Base 1982-1984 = 100
Apparel and Upkeep

For 1952-1993. Columns headed % show percentile change in the index from the previous period for which an index is available.

Year	Jan Index	%	Feb Index	%	Mar Index	%	Apr Index	%	May Index	%	Jun Index	%	Jul Index	%	Aug Index	%	Sep Index	%	Oct Index	%	Nov Index	%	Dec Index	%
1952	-	-	-	-	-	-	-	-	-	-	-	-	-	-	-	-	-	-	-	-	-	-	36.9	-
1953	-	-	-	-	37.1	0.5	-	-	-	-	37.7	1.6	-	-	-	-	37.8	0.3	-	-	-	-	37.4	-1.1
1954	-	-	-	-	37.1	-0.8	-	-	-	-	37.0	-0.3	-	-	-	-	37.5	1.4	-	-	-	-	37.2	-0.8
1955	-	-	-	-	37.3	0.3	-	-	-	-	37.2	-0.3	-	-	-	-	38.0	2.2	-	-	-	-	38.1	0.3
1956	-	-	-	-	38.6	1.3	-	-	-	-	38.4	-0.5	-	-	-	-	38.8	1.0	-	-	-	-	38.7	-0.3
1957	-	-	-	-	38.6	-0.3	-	-	-	-	38.6	0.0	-	-	-	-	39.4	2.1	-	-	-	-	38.9	-1.3
1958	-	-	-	-	39.0	0.3	-	-	-	-	38.7	-0.8	-	-	-	-	39.3	1.6	-	-	-	-	39.3	0.0
1959	-	-	-	-	39.3	0.0	-	-	-	-	39.3	0.0	-	-	-	-	39.7	1.0	-	-	-	-	39.7	0.0
1960	-	-	-	-	39.8	0.3	-	-	-	-	40.1	0.8	-	-	-	-	40.6	1.2	-	-	-	-	40.2	-1.0
1961	-	-	-	-	40.2	0.0	-	-	-	-	39.9	-0.7	-	-	-	-	40.6	1.8	-	-	-	-	40.5	-0.2
1962	-	-	-	-	40.5	0.0	-	-	-	-	40.5	0.0	-	-	-	-	40.9	1.0	-	-	-	-	40.8	-0.2
1963	-	-	-	-	40.9	0.2	-	-	-	-	40.7	-0.5	-	-	-	-	41.3	1.5	-	-	-	-	41.2	-0.2
1964	-	-	-	-	41.3	0.2	-	-	-	-	41.4	0.2	-	-	-	-	41.9	1.2	-	-	-	-	41.4	-1.2
1965	-	-	-	-	41.5	0.2	-	-	-	-	41.5	0.0	-	-	-	-	42.1	1.4	-	-	-	-	42.1	0.0
1966	-	-	-	-	42.7	1.4	-	-	-	-	43.3	1.4	-	-	-	-	44.0	1.6	-	-	-	-	44.0	0.0
1967	-	-	-	-	44.4	0.9	-	-	-	-	44.3	-0.2	-	-	-	-	45.7	3.2	-	-	-	-	46.0	0.7
1968	-	-	-	-	46.9	2.0	-	-	-	-	47.3	0.9	-	-	-	-	49.8	5.3	-	-	-	-	49.9	0.2
1969	-	-	-	-	50.3	0.8	-	-	-	-	50.9	1.2	-	-	-	-	52.3	2.8	-	-	-	-	52.3	0.0
1970	-	-	-	-	52.8	1.0	-	-	-	-	53.1	0.6	-	-	-	-	54.1	1.9	-	-	-	-	54.9	1.5
1971	-	-	-	-	55.2	0.5	-	-	-	-	54.7	-0.9	-	-	-	-	55.2	0.9	-	-	-	-	54.9	-0.5
1972	-	-	-	-	54.6	-0.5	-	-	-	-	54.7	0.2	-	-	-	-	55.9	2.2	-	-	-	-	56.2	0.5
1973	-	-	-	-	56.7	0.9	-	-	-	-	56.8	0.2	-	-	-	-	58.5	3.0	-	-	-	-	59.1	1.0
1974	-	-	-	-	59.8	1.2	-	-	-	-	60.8	1.7	-	-	-	-	63.5	4.4	-	-	-	-	63.7	0.3
1975	-	-	-	-	64.0	0.5	-	-	-	-	63.3	-1.1	-	-	-	-	65.6	3.6	-	-	-	-	66.1	0.8
1976	-	-	-	-	68.0	2.9	-	-	-	-	67.9	-0.1	-	-	-	-	70.6	4.0	-	-	-	-	70.0	-0.8
1977	-	-	-	-	71.1	1.6	-	-	-	-	71.1	0.0	-	-	-	-	73.9	3.9	-	-	-	-	74.7	1.1
1978	-	-	-	-	75.8	1.5	-	-	78.7	3.8	-	-	76.7	-2.5	-	-	78.9	2.9	-	-	80.0	1.4	-	-
1979	80.3	0.4	-	-	78.0	-2.9	-	-	83.1	6.5	-	-	81.5	-1.9	-	-	84.4	3.6	-	-	83.5	-1.1	-	-
1980	86.2	3.2	-	-	88.8	3.0	-	-	88.5	-0.3	-	-	85.2	-3.7	-	-	92.9	9.0	-	-	92.4	-0.5	-	-
1981	89.5	-3.1	-	-	94.7	5.8	-	-	91.5	-3.4	-	-	88.8	-3.0	-	-	97.7	10.0	-	-	96.9	-0.8	-	-
1982	94.3	-2.7	-	-	98.4	4.3	-	-	96.7	-1.7	-	-	95.5	-1.2	-	-	100.4	5.1	-	-	98.9	-1.5	-	-
1983	101.1	2.2	-	-	100.9	-0.2	-	-	98.6	-2.3	-	-	99.5	0.9	-	-	102.6	3.1	-	-	102.1	-0.5	-	-
1984	97.3	-4.7	-	-	101.5	4.3	-	-	102.7	1.2	-	-	101.8	-0.9	-	-	104.4	2.6	-	-	101.6	-2.7	-	-
1985	101.7	0.1	-	-	103.6	1.9	-	-	102.7	-0.9	-	-	98.0	-4.6	-	-	105.4	7.6	-	-	108.6	3.0	-	-
1986	103.3	-4.9	-	-	103.8	0.5	-	-	102.7	-1.1	-	-	101.7	-1.0	-	-	111.3	9.4	-	-	109.3	-1.8	-	-
1987	-	-	-	-	-	-	-	-	-	-	112.9	3.3	-	-	-	-	-	-	-	-	-	-	118.7	5.1
1988	-	-	-	-	-	-	-	-	-	-	120.9	1.9	-	-	-	-	-	-	-	-	-	-	129.4	7.0
1989	-	-	-	-	-	-	-	-	-	-	124.4	-3.9	-	-	-	-	-	-	-	-	-	-	114.9	-7.6
1990	-	-	-	-	-	-	-	-	-	-	121.5	5.7	-	-	-	-	-	-	-	-	-	-	121.0	-0.4
1991	-	-	-	-	-	-	-	-	-	-	120.1	-0.7	-	-	-	-	-	-	-	-	-	-	123.1	2.5
1992	-	-	-	-	-	-	-	-	-	-	127.1	3.2	-	-	-	-	-	-	-	-	-	-	136.6	7.5
1993	-	-	-	-	-	-	-	-	-	-	143.6	5.1	-	-	-	-	-	-	-	-	-	-	-	-

Source: U.S. Department of Labor, Bureau of Labor Statistics, Division of Consumer Prices and Price Indexes. - indicates no data collected for period.

Cincinnati, OH-KY-IN
Consumer Price Index - Urban Wage Earners
Base 1982-1984 = 100
Apparel and Upkeep

For 1952-1993. Columns headed % show percentile change in the index from the previous period for which an index is available.

Year	Jan Index	%	Feb Index	%	Mar Index	%	Apr Index	%	May Index	%	Jun Index	%	Jul Index	%	Aug Index	%	Sep Index	%	Oct Index	%	Nov Index	%	Dec Index	%
1952	-	-	-	-	-	-	-	-	-	-	-	-	-	-	-	-	-	-	-	-	-	-	35.8	-
1953	-	-	-	-	36.1	0.8	-	-	-	-	36.6	1.4	-	-	-	-	36.7	0.3	-	-	-	-	36.3	-1.1
1954	-	-	-	-	36.1	-0.6	-	-	-	-	35.9	-0.6	-	-	-	-	36.4	1.4	-	-	-	-	36.1	-0.8
1955	-	-	-	-	36.2	0.3	-	-	-	-	36.1	-0.3	-	-	-	-	36.9	2.2	-	-	-	-	37.0	0.3
1956	-	-	-	-	37.5	1.4	-	-	-	-	37.2	-0.8	-	-	-	-	37.6	1.1	-	-	-	-	37.6	0.0
1957	-	-	-	-	37.5	-0.3	-	-	-	-	37.5	0.0	-	-	-	-	38.2	1.9	-	-	-	-	37.8	-1.0
1958	-	-	-	-	37.9	0.3	-	-	-	-	37.5	-1.1	-	-	-	-	38.2	1.9	-	-	-	-	38.2	0.0
1959	-	-	-	-	38.2	0.0	-	-	-	-	38.2	0.0	-	-	-	-	38.6	1.0	-	-	-	-	38.5	-0.3
1960	-	-	-	-	38.7	0.5	-	-	-	-	38.9	0.5	-	-	-	-	39.4	1.3	-	-	-	-	39.0	-1.0
1961	-	-	-	-	39.0	0.0	-	-	-	-	38.8	-0.5	-	-	-	-	39.4	1.5	-	-	-	-	39.3	-0.3
1962	-	-	-	-	39.3	0.0	-	-	-	-	39.3	0.0	-	-	-	-	39.7	1.0	-	-	-	-	39.6	-0.3
1963	-	-	-	-	39.7	0.3	-	-	-	-	39.6	-0.3	-	-	-	-	40.1	1.3	-	-	-	-	40.0	-0.2
1964	-	-	-	-	40.1	0.2	-	-	-	-	40.2	0.2	-	-	-	-	40.6	1.0	-	-	-	-	40.2	-1.0
1965	-	-	-	-	40.3	0.2	-	-	-	-	40.3	0.0	-	-	-	-	40.9	1.5	-	-	-	-	40.9	0.0
1966	-	-	-	-	41.4	1.2	-	-	-	-	42.0	1.4	-	-	-	-	42.7	1.7	-	-	-	-	42.7	0.0
1967	-	-	-	-	43.1	0.9	-	-	-	-	43.1	0.0	-	-	-	-	44.4	3.0	-	-	-	-	44.7	0.7
1968	-	-	-	-	45.5	1.8	-	-	-	-	46.0	1.1	-	-	-	-	48.4	5.2	-	-	-	-	48.4	0.0
1969	-	-	-	-	48.9	1.0	-	-	-	-	49.4	1.0	-	-	-	-	50.8	2.8	-	-	-	-	50.8	0.0
1970	-	-	-	-	51.3	1.0	-	-	-	-	51.5	0.4	-	-	-	-	52.6	2.1	-	-	-	-	53.3	1.3
1971	-	-	-	-	53.6	0.6	-	-	-	-	53.1	-0.9	-	-	-	-	53.6	0.9	-	-	-	-	53.3	-0.6
1972	-	-	-	-	53.0	-0.6	-	-	-	-	53.1	0.2	-	-	-	-	54.3	2.3	-	-	-	-	54.6	0.6
1973	-	-	-	-	55.1	0.9	-	-	-	-	55.1	0.0	-	-	-	-	56.8	3.1	-	-	-	-	57.4	1.1
1974	-	-	-	-	58.0	1.0	-	-	-	-	59.1	1.9	-	-	-	-	61.7	4.4	-	-	-	-	61.9	0.3
1975	-	-	-	-	62.1	0.3	-	-	-	-	61.5	-1.0	-	-	-	-	63.7	3.6	-	-	-	-	64.2	0.8
1976	-	-	-	-	66.0	2.8	-	-	-	-	66.0	0.0	-	-	-	-	68.5	3.8	-	-	-	-	67.9	-0.9
1977	-	-	-	-	69.1	1.8	-	-	-	-	69.1	0.0	-	-	-	-	71.7	3.8	-	-	-	-	72.5	1.1
1978	-	-	-	-	73.6	1.5	-	-	76.3	3.7	-	-	74.8	-2.0	-	-	77.7	3.9	-	-	77.6	-0.1	-	-
1979	79.5	2.4	-	-	76.6	-3.6	-	-	82.2	7.3	-	-	80.2	-2.4	-	-	83.6	4.2	-	-	83.4	-0.2	-	-
1980	81.9	-1.8	-	-	84.7	3.4	-	-	83.9	-0.9	-	-	85.5	1.9	-	-	90.9	6.3	-	-	91.1	0.2	-	-
1981	88.1	-3.3	-	-	92.7	5.2	-	-	91.2	-1.6	-	-	92.0	0.9	-	-	97.2	5.7	-	-	96.2	-1.0	-	-
1982	93.6	-2.7	-	-	97.7	4.4	-	-	96.8	-0.9	-	-	95.8	-1.0	-	-	100.9	5.3	-	-	99.1	-1.8	-	-
1983	100.2	1.1	-	-	101.7	1.5	-	-	98.6	-3.0	-	-	99.2	0.6	-	-	103.5	4.3	-	-	102.5	-1.0	-	-
1984	98.6	-3.8	-	-	101.7	3.1	-	-	102.3	0.6	-	-	100.8	-1.5	-	-	104.2	3.4	-	-	101.2	-2.9	-	-
1985	101.3	0.1	-	-	103.2	1.9	-	-	101.7	-1.5	-	-	97.2	-4.4	-	-	104.9	7.9	-	-	106.6	1.6	-	-
1986	101.9	-4.4	-	-	102.6	0.7	-	-	101.7	-0.9	-	-	102.6	0.9	-	-	109.5	6.7	-	-	108.2	-1.2	-	-
1987	-	-	-	-	-	-	-	-	-	-	109.2	0.9	-	-	-	-	-	-	-	-	-	-	113.8	4.2
1988	-	-	-	-	-	-	-	-	-	-	116.7	2.5	-	-	-	-	-	-	-	-	-	-	126.2	8.1
1989	-	-	-	-	-	-	-	-	-	-	119.8	-5.1	-	-	-	-	-	-	-	-	-	-	111.7	-6.8
1990	-	-	-	-	-	-	-	-	-	-	118.3	5.9	-	-	-	-	-	-	-	-	-	-	118.4	0.1
1991	-	-	-	-	-	-	-	-	-	-	116.9	-1.3	-	-	-	-	-	-	-	-	-	-	119.3	2.1
1992	-	-	-	-	-	-	-	-	-	-	123.5	3.5	-	-	-	-	-	-	-	-	-	-	133.1	7.8
1993	-	-	-	-	-	-	-	-	-	-	136.9	2.9	-	-	-	-	-	-	-	-	-	-	-	-

Source: U.S. Department of Labor, Bureau of Labor Statistics, Division of Consumer Prices and Price Indexes. - indicates no data collected for period.

Cincinnati, OH-KY-IN
Consumer Price Index - All Urban Consumers
Base 1982-1984 = 100
Transportation

For 1947-1993. Columns headed % show percentile change in the index from the previous period for which an index is available.

Year	Jan Index	%	Feb Index	%	Mar Index	%	Apr Index	%	May Index	%	Jun Index	%	Jul Index	%	Aug Index	%	Sep Index	%	Oct Index	%	Nov Index	%	Dec Index	%
1947	19.8		19.8	0.0	20.2	2.0	20.2	0.0	20.2	0.0	20.2	0.0	20.5	1.5	20.5	0.0	21.0	2.4	21.0	0.0	21.9	4.3	22.1	0.9
1948	22.2	0.5	22.2	0.0	22.2	0.0	22.2	0.0	22.2	0.0	22.7	2.3	23.8	4.8	24.2	1.7	24.3	0.4	24.3	0.0	24.3	0.0	24.3	0.0
1949	24.3	0.0	24.6	1.2	25.2	2.4	25.3	0.4	25.3	0.0	25.2	-0.4	25.2	0.0	25.2	0.0	25.2	0.0	25.2	0.0	25.2	0.0	25.1	-0.4
1950	25.1	0.0	25.1	0.0	25.1	0.0	24.9	-0.8	25.6	2.8	25.6	0.0	25.7	0.4	26.0	1.2	26.0	0.0	26.0	0.0	26.0	0.0	26.1	0.4
1951	26.7	2.3	26.7	0.0	27.0	1.1	27.0	0.0	27.0	0.0	27.0	0.0	27.0	0.0	27.4	1.5	28.1	2.6	28.3	0.7	28.6	1.1	28.6	0.0
1952	28.6	0.0	28.9	1.0	28.9	0.0	28.8	-0.3	29.4	2.1	29.4	0.0	29.4	0.0	29.4	0.0	29.4	0.0	29.4	0.0	29.4	0.0	29.4	0.0
1953	-		-		30.0	2.0	-		-		29.9	-0.3	-		-		30.2	1.0	-		-		30.0	-0.7
1954	-		-		29.4	-2.0	-		-		29.1	-1.0	-		-		29.2	0.3	-		-		28.4	-2.7
1955	-		-		28.5	0.4	-		-		28.3	-0.7	-		-		27.7	-2.1	-		-		28.1	1.4
1956	-		-		27.8	-1.1	-		-		28.1	1.1	-		-		28.5	1.4	-		-		29.5	3.5
1957	-		-		29.7	0.7	-		-		29.9	0.7	-		-		30.4	1.7	-		-		30.7	1.0
1958	-		-		30.4	-1.0	-		-		30.4	0.0	-		-		30.6	0.7	-		-		32.1	4.9
1959	-		-		32.5	1.2	-		-		32.8	0.9	-		-		32.7	-0.3	-		-		34.1	4.3
1960	-		-		33.5	-1.8	-		-		32.9	-1.8	-		-		32.8	-0.3	-		-		32.8	0.0
1961	-		-		32.8	0.0	-		-		33.3	1.5	-		-		33.6	0.9	-		-		32.9	-2.1
1962	-		-		33.8	2.7	-		-		33.8	0.0	-		-		33.9	0.3	-		-		33.8	-0.3
1963	-		-		33.9	0.3	-		-		33.8	-0.3	-		-		34.0	0.6	-		-		34.2	0.6
1964	-		-		34.4	0.6	-		-		34.4	0.0	-		-		34.5	0.3	-		-		34.5	0.0
1965	-		-		34.3	-0.6	-		-		34.5	0.6	-		-		34.6	0.3	-		-		34.8	0.6
1966	-		-		34.7	-0.3	-		-		35.1	1.2	-		-		35.5	1.1	-		-		35.3	-0.6
1967	-		-		35.1	-0.6	-		-		35.6	1.4	-		-		36.2	1.7	-		-		37.2	2.8
1968	-		-		37.4	0.5	-		-		37.9	1.3	-		-		37.9	0.0	-		-		37.6	-0.8
1969	-		-		38.9	3.5	-		-		38.9	0.0	-		-		38.5	-1.0	-		-		39.4	2.3
1970	-		-		39.0	-1.0	-		-		40.8	4.6	-		-		41.1	0.7	-		-		42.9	4.4
1971	-		-		42.3	-1.4	-		-		43.3	2.4	-		-		43.1	-0.5	-		-		43.6	1.2
1972	-		-		42.7	-2.1	-		-		44.5	4.2	-		-		45.6	2.5	-		-		45.2	-0.9
1973	-		-		45.5	0.7	-		-		43.8	-3.7	-		-		43.6	-0.5	-		-		43.8	0.5
1974	-		-		45.1	3.0	-		-		48.4	7.3	-		-		49.6	2.5	-		-		49.6	0.0
1975	-		-		49.7	0.2	-		-		51.7	4.0	-		-		53.3	3.1	-		-		53.2	-0.2
1976	-		-		53.2	0.0	-		-		56.5	6.2	-		-		57.5	1.8	-		-		58.2	1.2
1977	-		-		59.4	2.1	-		-		60.9	2.5	-		-		60.2	-1.1	-		-		60.1	-0.2
1978	-		-		60.7	1.0	-		61.7	1.6	-		62.9	1.9	-		63.5	1.0	-		64.5	1.6	-	
1979	65.2	1.1	-		66.4	1.8	-		69.6	4.8	-		72.6	4.3	-		75.1	3.4	-		76.5	1.9	-	
1980	79.0	3.3	-		81.3	2.9	-		83.6	2.8	-		85.0	1.7	-		86.1	1.3	-		87.2	1.3	-	
1981	89.8	3.0	-		92.2	2.7	-		93.5	1.4	-		94.0	0.5	-		95.0	1.1	-		96.3	1.4	-	
1982	97.2	0.9	-		95.4	-1.9	-		95.2	-0.2	-		98.8	3.8	-		98.5	-0.3	-		98.4	-0.1	-	
1983	98.0	-0.4	-		95.8	-2.2	-		99.1	3.4	-		100.0	0.9	-		101.4	1.4	-		102.6	1.2	-	
1984	101.8	-0.8	-		101.7	-0.1	-		102.9	1.2	-		103.2	0.3	-		103.7	0.5	-		104.8	1.1	-	
1985	103.3	-1.4	-		104.8	1.5	-		107.2	2.3	-		107.1	-0.1	-		105.4	-1.6	-		107.6	2.1	-	
1986	106.8	-0.7	-		98.4	-7.9	-		100.4	2.0	-		97.8	-2.6	-		98.0	0.2	-		98.7	0.7	104.0	2.3
1987	-		-		-		-		-		101.7	3.0	-		-		-		-		-		106.3	2.9
1988	-		-		-		-		-		103.3	-0.7	-		-		-		-		-		112.5	2.4
1989	-		-		-		-		-		109.9	3.4	-		-		-		-		-		120.4	4.7
1990	-		-		-		-		-		115.0	2.2	-		-		-		-		-		120.7	0.9
1991	-		-		-		-		-		119.6	-0.7	-		-		-		-		-		-	

[Continued]

Cincinnati, OH-KY-IN
Consumer Price Index - All Urban Consumers
Base 1982-1984 = 100
Transportation
[Continued]

For 1947-1993. Columns headed % show percentile change in the index from the previous period for which an index is available.

Year	Jan Index	%	Feb Index	%	Mar Index	%	Apr Index	%	May Index	%	Jun Index	%	Jul Index	%	Aug Index	%	Sep Index	%	Oct Index	%	Nov Index	%	Dec Index	%
1992	-	-	-	-	-	-	-	-	-	-	118.5	-1.8	-	-	-	-	-	-	-	-	-	-	119.1	0.5
1993	-	-	-	-	-	-	-	-	-	-	120.6	1.3	-	-	-	-	-	-	-	-	-	-	-	-

Source: U.S. Department of Labor, Bureau of Labor Statistics, Division of Consumer Prices and Price Indexes. - indicates no data collected for period.

Cincinnati, OH-KY-IN
Consumer Price Index - Urban Wage Earners
Base 1982-1984 = 100
Transportation

For 1947-1993. Columns headed % show percentile change in the index from the previous period for which an index is available.

Year	Jan Index	%	Feb Index	%	Mar Index	%	Apr Index	%	May Index	%	Jun Index	%	Jul Index	%	Aug Index	%	Sep Index	%	Oct Index	%	Nov Index	%	Dec Index	%
1947	20.0	-	20.0	0.0	20.4	2.0	20.4	0.0	20.4	0.0	20.4	0.0	20.7	1.5	20.8	0.5	21.2	1.9	21.2	0.0	22.1	4.2	22.3	0.9
1948	22.5	0.9	22.5	0.0	22.5	0.0	22.5	0.0	22.5	0.0	22.9	1.8	24.0	4.8	24.4	1.7	24.6	0.8	24.6	0.0	24.6	0.0	24.6	0.0
1949	24.6	0.0	24.8	0.8	25.4	2.4	25.5	0.4	25.5	0.0	25.5	0.0	25.4	-0.4	25.5	0.4	25.5	0.0	25.5	0.0	25.5	0.0	25.4	-0.4
1950	25.3	-0.4	25.3	0.0	25.3	0.0	25.2	-0.4	25.8	2.4	25.9	0.4	26.0	0.4	26.3	1.2	26.3	0.0	26.3	0.0	26.3	0.0	26.3	0.0
1951	26.9	2.3	27.0	0.4	27.3	1.1	27.3	0.0	27.3	0.0	27.3	0.0	27.3	0.0	27.6	1.1	28.4	2.9	28.6	0.7	28.9	1.0	28.9	0.0
1952	28.9	0.0	29.2	1.0	29.2	0.0	29.1	-0.3	29.7	2.1	29.7	0.0	29.7	0.0	29.7	0.0	29.7	0.0	29.7	0.0	29.7	0.0	29.7	0.0
1953	-	-	-	-	30.3	2.0	-	-	-	-	30.2	-0.3	-	-	-	-	30.5	1.0	-	-	-	-	30.3	-0.7
1954	-	-	-	-	29.7	-2.0	-	-	-	-	29.4	-1.0	-	-	-	-	29.5	0.3	-	-	-	-	28.7	-2.7
1955	-	-	-	-	28.8	0.3	-	-	-	-	28.6	-0.7	-	-	-	-	28.0	-2.1	-	-	-	-	28.4	1.4
1956	-	-	-	-	28.1	-1.1	-	-	-	-	28.4	1.1	-	-	-	-	28.8	1.4	-	-	-	-	29.8	3.5
1957	-	-	-	-	30.0	0.7	-	-	-	-	30.2	0.7	-	-	-	-	30.7	1.7	-	-	-	-	31.0	1.0
1958	-	-	-	-	30.7	-1.0	-	-	-	-	30.7	0.0	-	-	-	-	30.9	0.7	-	-	-	-	32.4	4.9
1959	-	-	-	-	32.8	1.2	-	-	-	-	33.2	1.2	-	-	-	-	33.0	-0.6	-	-	-	-	34.4	4.2
1960	-	-	-	-	33.8	-1.7	-	-	-	-	33.3	-1.5	-	-	-	-	33.1	-0.6	-	-	-	-	33.2	0.3
1961	-	-	-	-	33.2	0.0	-	-	-	-	33.6	1.2	-	-	-	-	33.9	0.9	-	-	-	-	33.2	-2.1
1962	-	-	-	-	34.1	2.7	-	-	-	-	34.2	0.3	-	-	-	-	34.2	0.0	-	-	-	-	34.2	0.0
1963	-	-	-	-	34.2	0.0	-	-	-	-	34.2	0.0	-	-	-	-	34.3	0.3	-	-	-	-	34.5	0.6
1964	-	-	-	-	34.7	0.6	-	-	-	-	34.8	0.3	-	-	-	-	34.9	0.3	-	-	-	-	34.8	-0.3
1965	-	-	-	-	34.6	-0.6	-	-	-	-	34.8	0.6	-	-	-	-	35.0	0.6	-	-	-	-	35.1	0.3
1966	-	-	-	-	35.1	0.0	-	-	-	-	35.5	1.1	-	-	-	-	35.8	0.8	-	-	-	-	35.6	-0.6
1967	-	-	-	-	35.4	-0.6	-	-	-	-	36.0	1.7	-	-	-	-	36.6	1.7	-	-	-	-	37.6	2.7
1968	-	-	-	-	37.8	0.5	-	-	-	-	38.3	1.3	-	-	-	-	38.3	0.0	-	-	-	-	38.0	-0.8
1969	-	-	-	-	39.3	3.4	-	-	-	-	39.3	0.0	-	-	-	-	38.9	-1.0	-	-	-	-	39.8	2.3
1970	-	-	-	-	39.4	-1.0	-	-	-	-	41.2	4.6	-	-	-	-	41.5	0.7	-	-	-	-	43.3	4.3
1971	-	-	-	-	42.8	-1.2	-	-	-	-	43.7	2.1	-	-	-	-	43.5	-0.5	-	-	-	-	44.1	1.4
1972	-	-	-	-	43.2	-2.0	-	-	-	-	45.0	4.2	-	-	-	-	46.1	2.4	-	-	-	-	45.6	-1.1
1973	-	-	-	-	46.0	0.9	-	-	-	-	44.3	-3.7	-	-	-	-	44.0	-0.7	-	-	-	-	44.2	0.5
1974	-	-	-	-	45.6	3.2	-	-	-	-	48.9	7.2	-	-	-	-	50.1	2.5	-	-	-	-	50.1	0.0
1975	-	-	-	-	50.2	0.2	-	-	-	-	52.2	4.0	-	-	-	-	53.8	3.1	-	-	-	-	53.8	0.0
1976	-	-	-	-	53.7	-0.2	-	-	-	-	57.1	6.3	-	-	-	-	58.1	1.8	-	-	-	-	58.8	1.2
1977	-	-	-	-	60.0	2.0	-	-	-	-	61.5	2.5	-	-	-	-	60.8	-1.1	-	-	-	-	60.7	-0.2
1978	-	-	-	-	61.3	1.0	-	-	62.3	1.6	-	-	63.7	2.2	-	-	63.9	0.3	-	-	65.1	1.9	-	-
1979	65.8	1.1	-	-	67.0	1.8	-	-	70.2	4.8	-	-	73.1	4.1	-	-	75.5	3.3	-	-	77.0	2.0	-	-
1980	79.6	3.4	-	-	82.2	3.3	-	-	83.9	2.1	-	-	85.6	2.0	-	-	86.0	0.5	-	-	87.0	1.2	-	-
1981	89.7	3.1	-	-	92.6	3.2	-	-	93.6	1.1	-	-	94.6	1.1	-	-	95.3	0.7	-	-	96.4	1.2	-	-
1982	97.3	0.9	-	-	95.6	-1.7	-	-	95.4	-0.2	-	-	98.9	3.7	-	-	98.5	-0.4	-	-	98.5	0.0	-	-
1983	98.2	-0.3	-	-	96.1	-2.1	-	-	99.1	3.1	-	-	99.9	0.8	-	-	101.3	1.4	-	-	102.6	1.3	-	-
1984	101.7	-0.9	-	-	101.6	-0.1	-	-	102.8	1.2	-	-	103.0	0.2	-	-	103.5	0.5	-	-	104.6	1.1	-	-
1985	103.1	-1.4	-	-	104.6	1.5	-	-	106.9	2.2	-	-	106.7	-0.2	-	-	105.0	-1.6	-	-	107.3	2.2	-	-
1986	106.5	-0.7	-	-	98.4	-7.6	-	-	100.4	2.0	-	-	97.7	-2.7	-	-	97.9	0.2	-	-	98.7	0.8	-	-
1987	-	-	-	-	-	-	-	-	-	-	101.9	3.2	-	-	-	-	-	-	-	-	-	-	104.4	2.5
1988	-	-	-	-	-	-	-	-	-	-	104.0	-0.4	-	-	-	-	-	-	-	-	-	-	107.1	3.0
1989	-	-	-	-	-	-	-	-	-	-	110.8	3.5	-	-	-	-	-	-	-	-	-	-	113.6	2.5
1990	-	-	-	-	-	-	-	-	-	-	116.1	2.2	-	-	-	-	-	-	-	-	-	-	121.7	4.8
1991	-	-	-	-	-	-	-	-	-	-	120.5	-1.0	-	-	-	-	-	-	-	-	-	-	121.8	1.1

[Continued]

Cincinnati, OH-KY-IN
Consumer Price Index - Urban Wage Earners
Base 1982-1984 = 100
Transportation
[Continued]

For 1947-1993. Columns headed % show percentile change in the index from the previous period for which an index is available.

Year	Jan		Feb		Mar		Apr		May		Jun		Jul		Aug		Sep		Oct		Nov		Dec	
	Index	%	Index	%	Index	%	Index	%	Index	%	Index	%	Index	%	Index	%	Index	%	Index	%	Index	%	Index	%
1992	-	-	-	-	-	-	-	-	-	-	119.5	-1.9	-	-	-	-	-	-	-	-	-	-	120.9	1.2
1993	-	-	-	-	-	-	-	-	-	-	122.1	1.0	-	-	-	-	-	-	-	-	-	-	-	-

Source: U.S. Department of Labor, Bureau of Labor Statistics, Division of Consumer Prices and Price Indexes. - indicates no data collected for period.

Cincinnati, OH-KY-IN
Consumer Price Index - All Urban Consumers
Base 1982-1984 = 100
Medical Care

For 1947-1993. Columns headed % show percentile change in the index from the previous period for which an index is available.

Year	Jan Index	%	Feb Index	%	Mar Index	%	Apr Index	%	May Index	%	Jun Index	%	Jul Index	%	Aug Index	%	Sep Index	%	Oct Index	%	Nov Index	%	Dec Index	%
1947	11.3	-	11.3	0.0	11.3	0.0	11.4	0.9	11.6	1.8	11.7	0.9	12.1	3.4	12.2	0.8	12.2	0.0	12.3	0.8	12.3	0.0	12.4	0.8
1948	12.8	3.2	12.7	-0.8	12.7	0.0	13.1	3.1	13.1	0.0	13.1	0.0	13.2	0.8	13.2	0.0	13.2	0.0	13.2	0.0	13.2	0.0	13.2	0.0
1949	13.2	0.0	13.2	0.0	13.4	1.5	13.4	0.0	13.4	0.0	13.5	0.7	13.5	0.0	13.5	0.0	13.5	0.0	13.5	0.0	13.5	0.0	13.5	0.0
1950	13.5	0.0	13.5	0.0	13.5	0.0	13.5	0.0	13.5	0.0	13.5	0.0	13.5	0.0	13.5	0.0	13.5	0.0	13.5	0.0	13.5	0.0	13.6	0.7
1951	13.6	0.0	13.6	0.0	13.7	0.7	13.7	0.0	13.7	0.0	13.8	0.7	13.8	0.0	13.8	0.0	13.9	0.7	13.9	0.0	13.9	0.0	14.6	5.0
1952	14.6	0.0	14.7	0.7	14.9	1.4	14.9	0.0	14.9	0.0	14.9	0.0	15.0	0.7	15.0	0.0	15.0	0.0	15.0	0.0	15.0	0.0	15.0	0.0
1953	-	-	-	-	15.5	3.3	-	-	-	-	15.5	0.0	-	-	-	-	15.7	1.3	-	-	-	-	15.9	1.3
1954	-	-	-	-	15.9	0.0	-	-	-	-	15.9	0.0	-	-	-	-	15.9	0.0	-	-	-	-	16.1	1.3
1955	-	-	-	-	16.3	1.2	-	-	-	-	16.3	0.0	-	-	-	-	16.3	0.0	-	-	-	-	17.5	7.4
1956	-	-	-	-	17.5	0.0	-	-	-	-	17.5	0.0	-	-	-	-	17.5	0.0	-	-	-	-	17.6	0.6
1957	-	-	-	-	17.8	1.1	-	-	-	-	17.9	0.6	-	-	-	-	17.9	0.0	-	-	-	-	19.0	6.1
1958	-	-	-	-	19.0	0.0	-	-	-	-	19.0	0.0	-	-	-	-	19.0	0.0	-	-	-	-	19.4	2.1
1959	-	-	-	-	19.3	-0.5	-	-	-	-	19.7	2.1	-	-	-	-	19.7	0.0	-	-	-	-	19.7	0.0
1960	-	-	-	-	19.8	0.5	-	-	-	-	19.8	0.0	-	-	-	-	20.0	1.0	-	-	-	-	20.4	2.0
1961	-	-	-	-	20.5	0.5	-	-	-	-	20.6	0.5	-	-	-	-	20.7	0.5	-	-	-	-	20.7	0.0
1962	-	-	-	-	20.7	0.0	-	-	-	-	20.8	0.5	-	-	-	-	21.5	3.4	-	-	-	-	21.5	0.0
1963	-	-	-	-	21.7	0.9	-	-	-	-	21.9	0.9	-	-	-	-	21.9	0.0	-	-	-	-	21.9	0.0
1964	-	-	-	-	22.2	1.4	-	-	-	-	22.3	0.5	-	-	-	-	22.3	0.0	-	-	-	-	23.5	5.4
1965	-	-	-	-	23.6	0.4	-	-	-	-	23.9	1.3	-	-	-	-	23.9	0.0	-	-	-	-	24.2	1.3
1966	-	-	-	-	24.6	1.7	-	-	-	-	24.9	1.2	-	-	-	-	25.1	0.8	-	-	-	-	25.6	2.0
1967	-	-	-	-	26.5	3.5	-	-	-	-	26.6	0.4	-	-	-	-	27.0	1.5	-	-	-	-	27.4	1.5
1968	-	-	-	-	28.5	4.0	-	-	-	-	28.7	0.7	-	-	-	-	29.0	1.0	-	-	-	-	29.4	1.4
1969	-	-	-	-	30.8	4.8	-	-	-	-	31.2	1.3	-	-	-	-	31.7	1.6	-	-	-	-	31.7	0.0
1970	-	-	-	-	32.3	1.9	-	-	-	-	32.6	0.9	-	-	-	-	32.9	0.9	-	-	-	-	33.6	2.1
1971	-	-	-	-	35.0	4.2	-	-	-	-	35.4	1.1	-	-	-	-	35.6	0.6	-	-	-	-	35.4	-0.6
1972	-	-	-	-	36.4	2.8	-	-	-	-	36.5	0.3	-	-	-	-	36.5	0.0	-	-	-	-	36.9	1.1
1973	-	-	-	-	38.0	3.0	-	-	-	-	38.3	0.8	-	-	-	-	38.5	0.5	-	-	-	-	39.7	3.1
1974	-	-	-	-	41.4	4.3	-	-	-	-	42.0	1.4	-	-	-	-	43.3	3.1	-	-	-	-	44.4	2.5
1975	-	-	-	-	46.5	4.7	-	-	-	-	47.1	1.3	-	-	-	-	48.0	1.9	-	-	-	-	48.4	0.8
1976	-	-	-	-	51.6	6.6	-	-	-	-	52.3	1.4	-	-	-	-	53.6	2.5	-	-	-	-	55.1	2.8
1977	-	-	-	-	58.2	5.6	-	-	-	-	58.8	1.0	-	-	-	-	60.0	2.0	-	-	-	-	60.2	0.3
1978	-	-	-	-	63.3	5.1	-	-	64.5	1.9	-	-	65.4	1.4	-	-	68.1	4.1	-	-	68.2	0.1	-	-
1979	71.6	5.0	-	-	72.1	0.7	-	-	71.8	-0.4	-	-	72.1	0.4	-	-	73.0	1.2	-	-	73.9	1.2	-	-
1980	76.6	3.7	-	-	78.5	2.5	-	-	78.6	0.1	-	-	79.6	1.3	-	-	80.1	0.6	-	-	80.6	0.6	-	-
1981	82.0	1.7	-	-	83.2	1.5	-	-	83.9	0.8	-	-	87.3	4.1	-	-	88.1	0.9	-	-	88.7	0.7	-	-
1982	91.4	3.0	-	-	91.8	0.4	-	-	92.7	1.0	-	-	93.8	1.2	-	-	95.0	1.3	-	-	94.9	-0.1	-	-
1983	98.5	3.8	-	-	98.9	0.4	-	-	99.4	0.5	-	-	100.6	1.2	-	-	100.5	-0.1	-	-	101.7	1.2	-	-
1984	104.2	2.5	-	-	104.5	0.3	-	-	105.1	0.6	-	-	107.1	1.9	-	-	107.8	0.7	-	-	107.7	-0.1	-	-
1985	109.2	1.4	-	-	110.4	1.1	-	-	111.5	1.0	-	-	112.2	0.6	-	-	113.2	0.9	-	-	114.3	1.0	-	-
1986	115.1	0.7	-	-	115.8	0.6	-	-	116.3	0.4	-	-	119.0	2.3	-	-	118.8	-0.2	-	-	119.1	0.3	-	-
1987	-	-	-	-	-	-	-	-	-	-	124.4	4.5	-	-	-	-	-	-	-	-	-	-	126.9	2.0
1988	-	-	-	-	-	-	-	-	-	-	135.3	6.6	-	-	-	-	-	-	-	-	-	-	138.2	2.1
1989	-	-	-	-	-	-	-	-	-	-	142.5	3.1	-	-	-	-	-	-	-	-	-	-	146.2	2.6
1990	-	-	-	-	-	-	-	-	-	-	153.9	5.3	-	-	-	-	-	-	-	-	-	-	161.0	4.6
1991	-	-	-	-	-	-	-	-	-	-	172.0	6.8	-	-	-	-	-	-	-	-	-	-	178.9	4.0

[Continued]

Cincinnati, OH-KY-IN

Consumer Price Index - All Urban Consumers
Base 1982-1984 = 100

Medical Care

[Continued]

For 1947-1993. Columns headed % show percentile change in the index from the previous period for which an index is available.

Year	Jan		Feb		Mar		Apr		May		Jun		Jul		Aug		Sep		Oct		Nov		Dec	
	Index	%	Index	%	Index	%	Index	%	Index	%	Index	%	Index	%	Index	%	Index	%	Index	%	Index	%	Index	%
1992	-	-	-	-	-	-	-	-	-	-	185.4	3.6	-	-	-	-	-	-	-	-	-	-	190.6	2.8
1993	-	-	-	-	-	-	-	-	-	-	197.9	3.8	-	-	-	-	-	-	-	-	-	-	-	-

Source: U.S. Department of Labor, Bureau of Labor Statistics, Division of Consumer Prices and Price Indexes. - indicates no data collected for period.

Cincinnati, OH-KY-IN
Consumer Price Index - Urban Wage Earners
Base 1982-1984 = 100
Medical Care

For 1947-1993. Columns headed % show percentile change in the index from the previous period for which an index is available.

Year	Jan Index	%	Feb Index	%	Mar Index	%	Apr Index	%	May Index	%	Jun Index	%	Jul Index	%	Aug Index	%	Sep Index	%	Oct Index	%	Nov Index	%	Dec Index	%
1947	10.8	-	10.8	0.0	10.8	0.0	10.9	0.9	11.0	0.9	11.2	1.8	11.5	2.7	11.6	0.9	11.7	0.9	11.7	0.0	11.7	0.0	11.8	0.9
1948	12.2	3.4	12.1	-0.8	12.1	0.0	12.4	2.5	12.4	0.0	12.5	0.8	12.5	0.0	12.5	0.0	12.6	0.8	12.6	0.0	12.6	0.0	12.6	0.0
1949	12.6	0.0	12.6	0.0	12.7	0.8	12.8	0.8	12.8	0.0	12.8	0.0	12.8	0.0	12.8	0.0	12.8	0.0	12.8	0.0	12.8	0.0	13.0	1.6
1950	12.8	0.0	12.8	0.0	12.8	0.0	12.8	0.0	12.8	0.0	12.8	0.0	12.8	0.0	12.8	0.0	12.8	0.0	12.8	0.0	12.8	0.0	13.9	4.5
1951	13.0	0.0	13.0	0.0	13.0	0.0	13.1	0.8	13.1	0.0	13.1	0.0	13.1	0.0	13.1	0.0	13.3	1.5	13.3	0.0	13.3	0.0	14.3	0.0
1952	13.9	0.0	14.0	0.7	14.2	1.4	14.2	0.0	14.2	0.0	14.2	0.0	14.3	0.7	14.3	0.0	14.3	0.0	14.3	0.0	14.3	0.0	15.2	1.3
1953	-	-	-	-	14.7	2.8	-	-	-	-	14.8	0.7	-	-	-	-	15.0	1.4	-	-	-	-	15.4	1.3
1954	-	-	-	-	15.2	0.0	-	-	-	-	15.2	0.0	-	-	-	-	15.2	0.0	-	-	-	-	16.7	7.7
1955	-	-	-	-	15.5	0.6	-	-	-	-	15.5	0.0	-	-	-	-	15.5	0.0	-	-	-	-	16.7	0.0
1956	-	-	-	-	16.7	0.0	-	-	-	-	16.7	0.0	-	-	-	-	16.7	0.0	-	-	-	-	18.1	5.8
1957	-	-	-	-	17.0	1.8	-	-	-	-	17.0	0.0	-	-	-	-	17.1	0.6	-	-	-	-	18.5	2.2
1958	-	-	-	-	18.1	0.0	-	-	-	-	18.1	0.0	-	-	-	-	18.1	0.0	-	-	-	-	18.8	0.0
1959	-	-	-	-	18.4	-0.5	-	-	-	-	18.7	1.6	-	-	-	-	18.8	0.5	-	-	-	-	19.5	2.1
1960	-	-	-	-	18.9	0.5	-	-	-	-	18.9	0.0	-	-	-	-	19.1	1.1	-	-	-	-	19.7	0.0
1961	-	-	-	-	19.6	0.5	-	-	-	-	19.7	0.5	-	-	-	-	19.7	0.0	-	-	-	-	20.5	0.0
1962	-	-	-	-	19.7	0.0	-	-	-	-	19.8	0.5	-	-	-	-	20.5	3.5	-	-	-	-	20.9	0.0
1963	-	-	-	-	20.7	1.0	-	-	-	-	20.9	1.0	-	-	-	-	20.9	0.0	-	-	-	-	22.4	5.7
1964	-	-	-	-	21.2	1.4	-	-	-	-	21.2	0.0	-	-	-	-	21.2	0.0	-	-	-	-	23.1	1.3
1965	-	-	-	-	22.5	0.4	-	-	-	-	22.7	0.9	-	-	-	-	22.8	0.4	-	-	-	-	24.4	2.1
1966	-	-	-	-	23.5	1.7	-	-	-	-	23.7	0.9	-	-	-	-	23.9	0.8	-	-	-	-	26.1	1.6
1967	-	-	-	-	25.2	3.3	-	-	-	-	25.3	0.4	-	-	-	-	25.7	1.6	-	-	-	-	28.0	1.4
1968	-	-	-	-	27.2	4.2	-	-	-	-	27.3	0.4	-	-	-	-	27.6	1.1	-	-	-	-	30.2	0.0
1969	-	-	-	-	29.4	5.0	-	-	-	-	29.8	1.4	-	-	-	-	30.2	1.3	-	-	-	-	32.1	2.6
1970	-	-	-	-	30.8	2.0	-	-	-	-	31.0	0.6	-	-	-	-	31.3	1.0	-	-	-	-	33.7	-0.6
1971	-	-	-	-	33.4	4.0	-	-	-	-	33.7	0.9	-	-	-	-	33.9	0.6	-	-	-	-	35.1	0.9
1972	-	-	-	-	34.7	3.0	-	-	-	-	34.8	0.3	-	-	-	-	34.8	0.0	-	-	-	-	37.8	3.0
1973	-	-	-	-	36.2	3.1	-	-	-	-	36.5	0.8	-	-	-	-	36.7	0.5	-	-	-	-	42.3	2.4
1974	-	-	-	-	39.5	4.5	-	-	-	-	40.0	1.3	-	-	-	-	41.3	3.2	-	-	-	-	46.1	0.7
1975	-	-	-	-	44.3	4.7	-	-	-	-	44.8	1.1	-	-	-	-	45.8	2.2	-	-	-	-	52.5	2.7
1976	-	-	-	-	49.2	6.7	-	-	-	-	49.9	1.4	-	-	-	-	51.1	2.4	-	-	-	-	57.4	0.3
1977	-	-	-	-	55.4	5.5	-	-	-	-	56.1	1.3	-	-	-	-	57.2	2.0	-	-	-	-	-	-
1978	-	-	-	-	60.3	5.1	-	-	60.6	0.5	-	-	63.3	4.5	-	-	63.4	0.2	-	-	63.9	0.8	-	-
1979	68.2	6.7	-	-	68.5	0.4	-	-	69.8	1.9	-	-	70.5	1.0	-	-	71.2	1.0	-	-	71.5	0.4	-	-
1980	75.0	4.9	-	-	77.1	2.8	-	-	77.6	0.6	-	-	78.8	1.5	-	-	79.2	0.5	-	-	79.7	0.6	-	-
1981	82.0	2.9	-	-	82.6	0.7	-	-	83.4	1.0	-	-	86.6	3.8	-	-	87.8	1.4	-	-	88.8	1.1	-	-
1982	91.4	2.9	-	-	91.7	0.3	-	-	92.7	1.1	-	-	93.8	1.2	-	-	95.0	1.3	-	-	94.9	-0.1	-	-
1983	98.3	3.6	-	-	98.8	0.5	-	-	99.4	0.6	-	-	100.7	1.3	-	-	100.5	-0.2	-	-	101.8	1.3	-	-
1984	104.3	2.5	-	-	104.6	0.3	-	-	105.2	0.6	-	-	107.1	1.8	-	-	107.8	0.7	-	-	107.6	-0.2	-	-
1985	109.2	1.5	-	-	110.4	1.1	-	-	111.5	1.0	-	-	112.2	0.6	-	-	113.1	0.8	-	-	114.2	1.0	-	-
1986	114.9	0.6	-	-	115.6	0.6	-	-	116.0	0.3	-	-	118.7	2.3	-	-	118.5	-0.2	-	-	118.8	0.3	-	-
1987	-	-	-	-	-	-	-	-	-	-	124.1	4.5	-	-	-	-	-	-	-	-	-	-	127.0	2.3
1988	-	-	-	-	-	-	-	-	-	-	135.7	6.9	-	-	-	-	-	-	-	-	-	-	139.2	2.6
1989	-	-	-	-	-	-	-	-	-	-	143.3	2.9	-	-	-	-	-	-	-	-	-	-	146.9	2.5
1990	-	-	-	-	-	-	-	-	-	-	154.6	5.2	-	-	-	-	-	-	-	-	-	-	161.0	4.1
1991	-	-	-	-	-	-	-	-	-	-	171.7	6.6	-	-	-	-	-	-	-	-	-	-	178.7	4.1

[Continued]

Cincinnati, OH-KY-IN
Consumer Price Index - Urban Wage Earners
Base 1982-1984 = 100
Medical Care
[Continued]

For 1947-1993. Columns headed % show percentile change in the index from the previous period for which an index is available.

Year	Jan Index	%	Feb Index	%	Mar Index	%	Apr Index	%	May Index	%	Jun Index	%	Jul Index	%	Aug Index	%	Sep Index	%	Oct Index	%	Nov Index	%	Dec Index	%
1992	-	-	-	-	-	-	-	-	-	-	185.2	3.6	-	-	-	-	-	-	-	-	-	-	190.4	2.8
1993	-	-	-	-	-	-	-	-	-	-	197.0	3.5	-	-	-	-	-	-	-	-	-	-	-	-

Source: U.S. Department of Labor, Bureau of Labor Statistics, Division of Consumer Prices and Price Indexes. - indicates no data collected for period.

Cincinnati, OH-KY-IN
Consumer Price Index - All Urban Consumers
Base 1982-1984 = 100
Entertainment

For 1975-1993. Columns headed % show percentile change in the index from the previous period for which an index is available.

Year	Jan Index	%	Feb Index	%	Mar Index	%	Apr Index	%	May Index	%	Jun Index	%	Jul Index	%	Aug Index	%	Sep Index	%	Oct Index	%	Nov Index	%	Dec Index	%
1975	-	-	-	-	-	-	-	-	-	-	-	-	-	-	-	-	-	-	-	-	-	-	65.3	-
1976	-	-	-	-	66.5	1.8	-	-	-	-	67.1	0.9	-	-	-	-	67.7	0.9	-	-	-	-	67.6	-0.1
1977	-	-	-	-	68.4	1.2	-	-	-	-	68.6	0.3	-	-	-	-	69.6	1.5	-	-	-	-	69.8	0.3
1978	-	-	-	-	71.7	2.7	-	-	73.1	2.0	-	-	72.7	-0.5	-	-	73.0	0.4	-	-	73.2	0.3	-	-
1979	74.2	1.4	-	-	76.1	2.6	-	-	77.1	1.3	-	-	78.1	1.3	-	-	78.3	0.3	-	-	77.4	-1.1	-	-
1980	78.0	0.8	-	-	83.6	7.2	-	-	84.6	1.2	-	-	83.1	-1.8	-	-	84.8	2.0	-	-	86.1	1.5	-	-
1981	86.6	0.6	-	-	88.1	1.7	-	-	86.1	-2.3	-	-	86.4	0.3	-	-	88.0	1.9	-	-	88.0	0.0	-	-
1982	93.2	5.9	-	-	93.5	0.3	-	-	93.5	0.0	-	-	94.4	1.0	-	-	95.6	1.3	-	-	97.3	1.8	-	-
1983	99.7	2.5	-	-	100.1	0.4	-	-	99.7	-0.4	-	-	99.7	0.0	-	-	101.2	1.5	-	-	102.8	1.6	-	-
1984	103.3	0.5	-	-	102.6	-0.7	-	-	103.4	0.8	-	-	105.5	2.0	-	-	106.2	0.7	-	-	106.7	0.5	-	-
1985	99.8	-6.5	-	-	100.4	0.6	-	-	100.0	-0.4	-	-	98.0	-2.0	-	-	98.7	0.7	-	-	101.6	2.9	-	-
1986	101.7	0.1	-	-	102.1	0.4	-	-	104.3	2.2	-	-	104.2	-0.1	-	-	104.7	0.5	-	-	104.7	0.0	-	-
1987	-	-	-	-	-	-	-	-	-	-	107.0	2.2	-	-	-	-	-	-	-	-	-	-	108.5	1.4
1988	-	-	-	-	-	-	-	-	-	-	109.8	1.2	-	-	-	-	-	-	-	-	-	-	115.0	4.7
1989	-	-	-	-	-	-	-	-	-	-	117.8	2.4	-	-	-	-	-	-	-	-	-	-	120.4	2.2
1990	-	-	-	-	-	-	-	-	-	-	127.6	6.0	-	-	-	-	-	-	-	-	-	-	131.7	3.2
1991	-	-	-	-	-	-	-	-	-	-	133.8	1.6	-	-	-	-	-	-	-	-	-	-	135.5	1.3
1992	-	-	-	-	-	-	-	-	-	-	137.2	1.3	-	-	-	-	-	-	-	-	-	-	142.7	4.0
1993	-	-	-	-	-	-	-	-	-	-	141.6	-0.8	-	-	-	-	-	-	-	-	-	-	-	-

Source: U.S. Department of Labor, Bureau of Labor Statistics, Division of Consumer Prices and Price Indexes. - indicates no data collected for period.

Cincinnati, OH-KY-IN
Consumer Price Index - Urban Wage Earners
Base 1982-1984 = 100
Entertainment

For 1975-1993. Columns headed % show percentile change in the index from the previous period for which an index is available.

Year	Jan Index	%	Feb Index	%	Mar Index	%	Apr Index	%	May Index	%	Jun Index	%	Jul Index	%	Aug Index	%	Sep Index	%	Oct Index	%	Nov Index	%	Dec Index	%
1975	-	-	-	-	-	-	-	-	-	-	-	-	-	-	-	-	-	-	-	-	-	-	67.8	-
1976	-	-	-	-	69.1	1.9	-	-	-	-	69.8	1.0	-	-	-	-	70.4	0.9	-	-	-	-	70.2	-0.3
1977	-	-	-	-	71.1	1.3	-	-	-	-	71.2	0.1	-	-	-	-	72.3	1.5	-	-	-	-	72.6	0.4
1978	-	-	-	-	74.5	2.6	-	-	75.2	0.9	-	-	76.1	1.2	-	-	76.6	0.7	-	-	76.7	0.1	-	-
1979	77.1	0.5	-	-	77.6	0.6	-	-	78.3	0.9	-	-	78.8	0.6	-	-	79.0	0.3	-	-	78.4	-0.8	-	-
1980	79.4	1.3	-	-	83.5	5.2	-	-	85.1	1.9	-	-	83.3	-2.1	-	-	84.7	1.7	-	-	85.7	1.2	-	-
1981	86.7	1.2	-	-	88.0	1.5	-	-	87.8	-0.2	-	-	88.0	0.2	-	-	89.5	1.7	-	-	89.4	-0.1	-	-
1982	93.8	4.9	-	-	94.0	0.2	-	-	94.0	0.0	-	-	94.6	0.6	-	-	96.0	1.5	-	-	97.6	1.7	-	-
1983	99.7	2.2	-	-	100.0	0.3	-	-	99.9	-0.1	-	-	100.0	0.1	-	-	101.3	1.3	-	-	102.6	1.3	-	-
1984	103.2	0.6	-	-	102.6	-0.6	-	-	103.0	0.4	-	-	105.1	2.0	-	-	105.7	0.6	-	-	106.1	0.4	-	-
1985	97.7	-7.9	-	-	98.2	0.5	-	-	97.9	-0.3	-	-	94.5	-3.5	-	-	95.2	0.7	-	-	97.7	2.6	-	-
1986	97.7	0.0	-	-	97.8	0.1	-	-	101.4	3.7	-	-	101.2	-0.2	-	-	101.2	0.0	-	-	101.3	0.1	-	-
1987	-	-	-	-	-	-	-	-	-	-	104.5	3.2	-	-	-	-	-	-	-	-	-	-	104.8	0.3
1988	-	-	-	-	-	-	-	-	-	-	105.9	1.0	-	-	-	-	-	-	-	-	-	-	110.9	4.7
1989	-	-	-	-	-	-	-	-	-	-	113.7	2.5	-	-	-	-	-	-	-	-	-	-	116.1	2.1
1990	-	-	-	-	-	-	-	-	-	-	122.7	5.7	-	-	-	-	-	-	-	-	-	-	126.7	3.3
1991	-	-	-	-	-	-	-	-	-	-	128.3	1.3	-	-	-	-	-	-	-	-	-	-	129.7	1.1
1992	-	-	-	-	-	-	-	-	-	-	130.7	0.8	-	-	-	-	-	-	-	-	-	-	136.9	4.7
1993	-	-	-	-	-	-	-	-	-	-	135.8	-0.8	-	-	-	-	-	-	-	-	-	-	-	-

Source: U.S. Department of Labor, Bureau of Labor Statistics, Division of Consumer Prices and Price Indexes. - indicates no data collected for period.

Cincinnati, OH-KY-IN
Consumer Price Index - All Urban Consumers
Base 1982-1984 = 100
Other Goods and Services

For 1975-1993. Columns headed % show percentile change in the index from the previous period for which an index is available.

Year	Jan Index	%	Feb Index	%	Mar Index	%	Apr Index	%	May Index	%	Jun Index	%	Jul Index	%	Aug Index	%	Sep Index	%	Oct Index	%	Nov Index	%	Dec Index	%
1975	-	-	-	-	-	-	-	-	-	-	-	-	-	-	-	-	-	-	-	-	-	-	54.7	-
1976	-	-	-	-	55.4	1.3	-	-	-	-	55.3	-0.2	-	-	-	-	56.0	1.3	-	-	-	-	57.7	3.0
1977	-	-	-	-	57.9	0.3	-	-	-	-	58.6	1.2	-	-	-	-	60.6	3.4	-	-	-	-	60.8	0.3
1978	-	-	-	-	61.7	1.5	-	-	61.8	0.2	-	-	62.8	1.6	-	-	64.2	2.2	-	-	63.6	-0.9	-	-
1979	65.2	2.5	-	-	65.7	0.8	-	-	66.3	0.9	-	-	66.9	0.9	-	-	69.6	4.0	-	-	70.3	1.0	-	-
1980	71.5	1.7	-	-	72.4	1.3	-	-	73.3	1.2	-	-	73.8	0.7	-	-	75.6	2.4	-	-	77.0	1.9	-	-
1981	78.9	2.5	-	-	79.0	0.1	-	-	80.3	1.6	-	-	80.8	0.6	-	-	84.1	4.1	-	-	84.9	1.0	-	-
1982	86.3	1.6	-	-	87.6	1.5	-	-	88.1	0.6	-	-	87.8	-0.3	-	-	92.1	4.9	-	-	96.0	4.2	-	-
1983	98.0	2.1	-	-	99.1	1.1	-	-	100.0	0.9	-	-	101.5	1.5	-	-	102.3	0.8	-	-	105.7	3.3	-	-
1984	107.0	1.2	-	-	107.5	0.5	-	-	106.7	-0.7	-	-	108.5	1.7	-	-	109.5	0.9	-	-	109.8	0.3	-	-
1985	111.3	1.4	-	-	113.6	2.1	-	-	114.5	0.8	-	-	115.9	1.2	-	-	117.6	1.5	-	-	118.1	0.4	-	-
1986	119.0	0.8	-	-	119.2	0.2	-	-	119.7	0.4	-	-	120.4	0.6	-	-	122.7	1.9	-	-	123.0	0.2	-	-
1987	-	-	-	-	-	-	-	-	-	-	125.1	1.7	-	-	-	-	-	-	-	-	-	-	131.5	5.1
1988	-	-	-	-	-	-	-	-	-	-	137.3	4.4	-	-	-	-	-	-	-	-	-	-	145.4	5.9
1989	-	-	-	-	-	-	-	-	-	-	144.5	-0.6	-	-	-	-	-	-	-	-	-	-	155.2	7.4
1990	-	-	-	-	-	-	-	-	-	-	161.6	4.1	-	-	-	-	-	-	-	-	-	-	170.0	5.2
1991	-	-	-	-	-	-	-	-	-	-	171.1	0.6	-	-	-	-	-	-	-	-	-	-	177.8	3.9
1992	-	-	-	-	-	-	-	-	-	-	183.1	3.0	-	-	-	-	-	-	-	-	-	-	187.5	2.4
1993	-	-	-	-	-	-	-	-	-	-	199.0	6.1	-	-	-	-	-	-	-	-	-	-	-	-

Source: U.S. Department of Labor, Bureau of Labor Statistics, Division of Consumer Prices and Price Indexes. - indicates no data collected for period.

Cincinnati, OH-KY-IN
Consumer Price Index - Urban Wage Earners
Base 1982-1984 = 100
Other Goods and Services

For 1975-1993. Columns headed % show percentile change in the index from the previous period for which an index is available.

Year	Jan Index	%	Feb Index	%	Mar Index	%	Apr Index	%	May Index	%	Jun Index	%	Jul Index	%	Aug Index	%	Sep Index	%	Oct Index	%	Nov Index	%	Dec Index	%
1975	-	-	-	-	-	-	-	-	-	-	-	-	-	-	-	-	-	-	-	-	-	-	54.5	-
1976	-	-	-	-	55.2	1.3	-	-	-	-	55.1	-0.2	-	-	-	-	55.8	1.3	-	-	-	-	57.5	3.0
1977	-	-	-	-	57.7	0.3	-	-	-	-	58.4	1.2	-	-	-	-	60.4	3.4	-	-	-	-	60.6	0.3
1978	-	-	-	-	61.5	1.5	-	-	62.5	1.6	-	-	63.4	1.4	-	-	64.4	1.6	-	-	64.4	0.0	-	-
1979	66.4	3.1	-	-	67.3	1.4	-	-	66.4	-1.3	-	-	67.4	1.5	-	-	69.9	3.7	-	-	71.0	1.6	-	-
1980	72.1	1.5	-	-	73.0	1.2	-	-	73.7	1.0	-	-	74.5	1.1	-	-	75.7	1.6	-	-	76.9	1.6	-	-
1981	79.5	3.4	-	-	80.0	0.6	-	-	81.2	1.5	-	-	81.7	0.6	-	-	84.5	3.4	-	-	85.1	0.7	-	-
1982	86.2	1.3	-	-	87.7	1.7	-	-	88.2	0.6	-	-	87.9	-0.3	-	-	92.1	4.8	-	-	95.9	4.1	-	-
1983	98.2	2.4	-	-	99.3	1.1	-	-	100.2	0.9	-	-	102.1	1.9	-	-	102.4	0.3	-	-	105.6	3.1	-	-
1984	107.0	1.3	-	-	107.5	0.5	-	-	106.6	-0.8	-	-	108.6	1.9	-	-	109.1	0.5	-	-	109.2	0.1	-	-
1985	110.9	1.6	-	-	112.7	1.6	-	-	113.7	0.9	-	-	115.3	1.4	-	-	116.8	1.3	-	-	117.2	0.3	-	-
1986	118.2	0.9	-	-	118.3	0.1	-	-	118.9	0.5	-	-	119.6	0.6	-	-	121.5	1.6	-	-	121.6	0.1	-	-
1987	-	-	-	-	-	-	-	-	-	-	124.1	2.1	-	-	-	-	-	-	-	-	-	-	130.3	5.0
1988	-	-	-	-	-	-	-	-	-	-	135.9	4.3	-	-	-	-	-	-	-	-	-	-	143.4	5.5
1989	-	-	-	-	-	-	-	-	-	-	143.5	0.1	-	-	-	-	-	-	-	-	-	-	151.5	5.6
1990	-	-	-	-	-	-	-	-	-	-	157.6	4.0	-	-	-	-	-	-	-	-	-	-	165.8	5.2
1991	-	-	-	-	-	-	-	-	-	-	166.9	0.7	-	-	-	-	-	-	-	-	-	-	173.8	4.1
1992	-	-	-	-	-	-	-	-	-	-	179.6	3.3	-	-	-	-	-	-	-	-	-	-	183.7	2.3
1993	-	-	-	-	-	-	-	-	-	-	197.3	7.4	-	-	-	-	-	-	-	-	-	-	-	-

Source: U.S. Department of Labor, Bureau of Labor Statistics, Division of Consumer Prices and Price Indexes. - indicates no data collected for period.

Cleveland, OH
Consumer Price Index - All Urban Consumers
Base 1982-1984 = 100
Annual Averages

For 1914-1993. Columns headed % show percentile change in the index from the previous period for which an index is available.

Year	All Items		Food & Beverage		Housing		Apparel & Upkeep		Trans- portation		Medical Care		Entertain- ment		Other Goods & Services	
	Index	%	Index	%	Index	%	Index	%	Index	%	Index	%	Index	%	Index	%
1914	-	-	-	-	-	-	-	-	-	-	-	-	-	-	-	-
1915	8.7	-	-	-	-	-	-	-	-	-	-	-	-	-	-	-
1916	9.4	8.0	-	-	-	-	-	-	-	-	-	-	-	-	-	-
1917	11.4	21.3	-	-	-	-	-	-	-	-	-	-	-	-	-	-
1918	13.2	15.8	-	-	-	-	-	-	-	-	-	-	-	-	-	-
1919	15.5	17.4	-	-	-	-	-	-	-	-	-	-	-	-	-	-
1920	18.3	18.1	-	-	-	-	-	-	-	-	-	-	-	-	-	-
1921	16.6	-9.3	-	-	-	-	-	-	-	-	-	-	-	-	-	-
1922	15.1	-9.0	-	-	-	-	-	-	-	-	-	-	-	-	-	-
1923	15.7	4.0	-	-	-	-	-	-	-	-	-	-	-	-	-	-
1924	15.7	0.0	-	-	-	-	-	-	-	-	-	-	-	-	-	-
1925	16.0	1.9	-	-	-	-	-	-	-	-	-	-	-	-	-	-
1926	16.1	0.6	-	-	-	-	-	-	-	-	-	-	-	-	-	-
1927	15.8	-1.9	-	-	-	-	-	-	-	-	-	-	-	-	-	-
1928	15.6	-1.3	-	-	-	-	-	-	-	-	-	-	-	-	-	-
1929	15.5	-0.6	-	-	-	-	-	-	-	-	-	-	-	-	-	-
1930	15.2	-1.9	-	-	-	-	-	-	-	-	-	-	-	-	-	-
1931	13.7	-9.9	-	-	-	-	-	-	-	-	-	-	-	-	-	-
1932	12.4	-9.5	-	-	-	-	-	-	-	-	-	-	-	-	-	-
1933	11.8	-4.8	-	-	-	-	-	-	-	-	-	-	-	-	-	-
1934	12.2	3.4	-	-	-	-	-	-	-	-	-	-	-	-	-	-
1935	12.7	4.1	-	-	-	-	-	-	-	-	-	-	-	-	-	-
1936	12.8	0.8	-	-	-	-	-	-	-	-	-	-	-	-	-	-
1937	13.4	4.7	-	-	-	-	-	-	-	-	-	-	-	-	-	-
1938	13.3	-0.7	-	-	-	-	-	-	-	-	-	-	-	-	-	-
1939	13.2	-0.8	-	-	-	-	-	-	-	-	-	-	-	-	-	-
1940	13.2	0.0	-	-	-	-	-	-	-	-	-	-	-	-	-	-
1941	14.0	6.1	-	-	-	-	-	-	-	-	-	-	-	-	-	-
1942	15.5	10.7	-	-	-	-	-	-	-	-	-	-	-	-	-	-
1943	16.6	7.1	-	-	-	-	-	-	-	-	-	-	-	-	-	-
1944	16.9	1.8	-	-	-	-	-	-	-	-	-	-	-	-	-	-
1945	17.2	1.8	-	-	-	-	-	-	-	-	-	-	-	-	-	-
1946	18.5	7.6	-	-	-	-	-	-	-	-	-	-	-	-	-	-
1947	21.2	14.6	-	-	-	-	-	-	18.9	-	10.6	-	-	-	-	-
1948	23.0	8.5	-	-	-	-	-	-	21.8	15.3	11.2	5.7	-	-	-	-
1949	22.6	-1.7	-	-	-	-	-	-	23.1	6.0	11.7	4.5	-	-	-	-
1950	22.8	0.9	-	-	-	-	-	-	23.1	0.0	11.8	0.9	-	-	-	-
1951	24.6	7.9	-	-	-	-	-	-	24.6	6.5	12.6	6.8	-	-	-	-
1952	25.2	2.4	-	-	-	-	-	-	26.0	5.7	13.3	5.6	-	-	-	-
1953	25.4	0.8	-	-	-	-	44.1	-	26.3	1.2	13.8	3.8	-	-	-	-
1954	25.7	1.2	-	-	-	-	44.1	0.0	25.8	-1.9	14.5	5.1	-	-	-	-
1955	25.7	0.0	-	-	-	-	43.8	-0.7	25.6	-0.8	15.1	4.1	-	-	-	-
1956	26.2	1.9	-	-	-	-	44.8	2.3	26.7	4.3	16.1	6.6	-	-	-	-
1957	27.2	3.8	-	-	-	-	45.5	1.6	28.5	6.7	16.7	3.7	-	-	-	-
1958	27.8	2.2	-	-	-	-	45.9	0.9	29.0	1.8	17.1	2.4	-	-	-	-

[Continued]

Cleveland, OH
Consumer Price Index - All Urban Consumers
Base 1982-1984 = 100
Annual Averages
[Continued]

For 1914-1993. Columns headed % show percentile change in the index from the previous period for which an index is available.

Year	All Items		Food & Beverage		Housing		Apparel & Upkeep		Trans-portation		Medical Care		Entertain-ment		Other Goods & Services	
	Index	%	Index	%	Index	%	Index	%	Index	%	Index	%	Index	%	Index	%
1959	27.9	0.4	-	-	-	-	46.2	0.7	30.1	3.8	18.7	9.4	-	-	-	-
1960	28.3	1.4	-	-	-	-	46.4	0.4	30.3	0.7	19.3	3.2	-	-	-	-
1961	28.5	0.7	-	-	-	-	46.8	0.9	31.0	2.3	20.7	7.3	-	-	-	-
1962	28.6	0.4	-	-	-	-	47.0	0.4	31.4	1.3	20.8	0.5	-	-	-	-
1963	28.9	1.0	-	-	-	-	47.7	1.5	31.5	0.3	21.9	5.3	-	-	-	-
1964	29.1	0.7	-	-	-	-	47.9	0.4	32.1	1.9	22.5	2.7	-	-	-	-
1965	29.6	1.7	-	-	-	-	48.3	0.8	32.6	1.6	23.2	3.1	-	-	-	-
1966	30.3	2.4	-	-	-	-	49.8	3.1	32.9	0.9	23.7	2.2	-	-	-	-
1967	31.2	3.0	-	-	-	-	51.3	3.0	33.9	3.0	25.2	6.3	-	-	-	-
1968	33.0	5.8	-	-	-	-	54.4	6.0	35.5	4.7	27.3	8.3	-	-	-	-
1969	34.9	5.8	-	-	-	-	57.6	5.9	37.0	4.2	30.5	11.7	-	-	-	-
1970	37.2	6.6	-	-	-	-	60.4	4.9	39.5	6.8	32.9	7.9	-	-	-	-
1971	38.3	3.0			-	-	62.4	3.3	42.2	6.8	35.2	7.0	-	-	-	-
1972	39.5	3.1			-	-	63.5	1.8	42.7	1.2	36.2	2.8	-	-	-	-
1973	41.8	5.8	-	-	-	-	66.5	4.7	44.1	3.3	38.0	5.0	-	-	-	-
1974	46.1	10.3	-	-	-	-	72.6	9.2	49.4	12.0	41.3	8.7	-	-	-	-
1975	50.2	8.9	-	-	-	-	74.4	2.5	52.1	5.5	46.0	11.4	-	-	-	-
1976	52.7	5.0	63.1	-	46.2	-	76.2	2.4	54.4	4.4	50.6	10.0	67.3	-	58.3	-
1977	56.3	6.8	66.4	5.2	49.7	7.6	80.5	5.6	57.8	6.3	56.7	12.1	70.6	4.9	61.8	6.0
1978	60.5	7.5	72.1	8.6	53.6	7.8	82.1	2.0	60.8	5.2	61.9	9.2	74.8	5.9	65.9	6.6
1979	68.5	13.2	79.6	10.4	63.0	17.5	84.5	2.9	69.2	13.8	66.0	6.6	78.7	5.2	71.1	7.9
1980	78.9	15.2	85.6	7.5	75.9	20.5	89.4	5.8	80.9	16.9	72.7	10.2	83.6	6.2	76.7	7.9
1981	87.2	10.5	93.2	8.9	83.8	10.4	95.0	6.3	92.0	13.7	81.2	11.7	88.6	6.0	84.9	10.7
1982	94.0	7.8	96.3	3.3	92.3	10.1	99.5	4.7	96.9	5.3	91.5	12.7	95.7	8.0	92.8	9.3
1983	101.2	7.7	99.8	3.6	102.6	11.2	99.3	-0.2	99.5	2.7	101.2	10.6	100.3	4.8	100.6	8.4
1984	104.8	3.6	103.9	4.1	105.1	2.4	101.3	2.0	103.6	4.1	107.4	6.1	104.1	3.8	106.7	6.1
1985	107.8	2.9	106.2	2.2	108.5	3.2	104.1	2.8	105.6	1.9	111.9	4.2	107.0	2.8	111.5	4.5
1986	109.4	1.5	107.6	1.3	111.8	3.0	102.4	-1.6	101.2	-4.2	122.3	9.3	114.2	6.7	117.0	4.9
1987	112.7	3.0	111.3	3.4	114.0	2.0	108.5	6.0	103.9	2.7	128.5	5.1	115.8	1.4	123.8	5.8
1988	116.7	3.5	116.4	4.6	117.8	3.3	105.8	-2.5	107.3	3.3	134.9	5.0	119.9	3.5	133.1	7.5
1989	122.7	5.1	124.0	6.5	122.7	4.2	111.4	5.3	113.0	5.3	143.5	6.4	127.0	5.9	141.0	5.9
1990	129.0	5.1	130.6	5.3	127.7	4.1	117.8	5.7	119.4	5.7	156.6	9.1	133.6	5.2	149.6	6.1
1991	134.2	4.0	135.4	3.7	132.5	3.8	121.9	3.5	123.1	3.1	171.7	9.6	138.6	3.7	160.1	7.0
1992	136.8	1.9	136.1	0.5	135.8	2.5	122.2	0.2	124.1	0.8	178.6	4.0	139.6	0.7	170.2	6.3
1993	-	-	-	-	-	-	-	-	-	-	-	-	-	-	-	-

Source: U.S. Department of Labor, Bureau of Labor Statistics, Division of Consumer Prices and Price Indexes. - indicates no data collected for period.

Cleveland, OH
Consumer Price Index - Urban Wage Earners
Base 1982-1984 = 100
Annual Averages

For 1914-1993. Columns headed % show percentile change in the index from the previous period for which an index is available.

Year	All Items		Food & Beverage		Housing		Apparel & Upkeep		Trans- portation		Medical Care		Entertain- ment		Other Goods & Services	
	Index	%	Index	%	Index	%	Index	%	Index	%	Index	%	Index	%	Index	%
1914	-	-	-	-	-	-	-	-	-	-	-	-	-	-	-	-
1915	8.9	-	-	-	-	-	-	-	-	-	-	-	-	-	-	-
1916	9.7	9.0	-	-	-	-	-	-	-	-	-	-	-	-	-	-
1917	11.6	19.6	-	-	-	-	-	-	-	-	-	-	-	-	-	-
1918	13.6	17.2	-	-	-	-	-	-	-	-	-	-	-	-	-	-
1919	15.9	16.9	-	-	-	-	-	-	-	-	-	-	-	-	-	-
1920	18.8	18.2	-	-	-	-	-	-	-	-	-	-	-	-	-	-
1921	17.0	-9.6	-	-	-	-	-	-	-	-	-	-	-	-	-	-
1922	15.5	-8.8	-	-	-	-	-	-	-	-	-	-	-	-	-	-
1923	16.1	3.9	-	-	-	-	-	-	-	-	-	-	-	-	-	-
1924	16.1	0.0	-	-	-	-	-	-	-	-	-	-	-	-	-	-
1925	16.4	1.9	-	-	-	-	-	-	-	-	-	-	-	-	-	-
1926	16.5	0.6	-	-	-	-	-	-	-	-	-	-	-	-	-	-
1927	16.2	-1.8	-	-	-	-	-	-	-	-	-	-	-	-	-	-
1928	16.0	-1.2	-	-	-	-	-	-	-	-	-	-	-	-	-	-
1929	15.9	-0.6	-	-	-	-	-	-	-	-	-	-	-	-	-	-
1930	15.6	-1.9	-	-	-	-	-	-	-	-	-	-	-	-	-	-
1931	14.0	-10.3	-	-	-	-	-	-	-	-	-	-	-	-	-	-
1932	12.7	-9.3	-	-	-	-	-	-	-	-	-	-	-	-	-	-
1933	12.1	-4.7	-	-	-	-	-	-	-	-	-	-	-	-	-	-
1934	12.5	3.3	-	-	-	-	-	-	-	-	-	-	-	-	-	-
1935	13.0	4.0	-	-	-	-	-	-	-	-	-	-	-	-	-	-
1936	13.2	1.5	-	-	-	-	-	-	-	-	-	-	-	-	-	-
1937	13.7	3.8	-	-	-	-	-	-	-	-	-	-	-	-	-	-
1938	13.6	-0.7	-	-	-	-	-	-	-	-	-	-	-	-	-	-
1939	13.5	-0.7	-	-	-	-	-	-	-	-	-	-	-	-	-	-
1940	13.5	0.0	-	-	-	-	-	-	-	-	-	-	-	-	-	-
1941	14.3	5.9	-	-	-	-	-	-	-	-	-	-	-	-	-	-
1942	15.9	11.2	-	-	-	-	-	-	-	-	-	-	-	-	-	-
1943	17.0	6.9	-	-	-	-	-	-	-	-	-	-	-	-	-	-
1944	17.3	1.8	-	-	-	-	-	-	-	-	-	-	-	-	-	-
1945	17.6	1.7	-	-	-	-	-	-	-	-	-	-	-	-	-	-
1946	19.0	8.0	-	-	-	-	-	-	-	-	10.4	-	-	-	-	-
1947	21.7	14.2	-	-	-	-	-	-	19.1	-	11.0	5.8	-	-	-	-
1948	23.6	8.8	-	-	-	-	-	-	22.0	15.2	11.5	4.5	-	-	-	-
1949	23.2	-1.7	-	-	-	-	-	-	23.4	6.4	11.6	0.9	-	-	-	-
1950	23.4	0.9	-	-	-	-	-	-	23.4	0.0	11.6	0.9	-	-	-	-
1951	25.3	8.1	-	-	-	-	-	-	24.9	6.4	12.4	6.9	-	-	-	-
1952	25.9	2.4	-	-	-	-	-	-	26.3	5.6	13.1	5.6	-	-	-	-
1953	26.1	0.8	-	-	-	-	42.7	-	26.6	1.1	13.6	3.8	-	-	-	-
1954	26.3	0.8	-	-	-	-	42.7	0.0	26.1	-1.9	14.3	5.1	-	-	-	-
1955	26.4	0.4	-	-	-	-	42.5	-0.5	25.9	-0.8	14.9	4.2	-	-	-	-
1956	26.9	1.9	-	-	-	-	43.4	2.1	27.0	4.2	15.8	6.0	-	-	-	-
1957	27.9	3.7	-	-	-	-	44.1	1.6	28.9	7.0	16.4	3.8	-	-	-	-
1958	28.5	2.2	-	-	-	-	44.5	0.9	29.4	1.7	16.8	2.4	-	-	-	-

[Continued]

394

Cleveland, OH
Consumer Price Index - Urban Wage Earners
Base 1982-1984 = 100
Annual Averages
[Continued]

For 1914-1993. Columns headed % show percentile change in the index from the previous period for which an index is available.

Year	All Items		Food & Beverage		Housing		Apparel & Upkeep		Trans-portation		Medical Care		Entertain-ment		Other Goods & Services	
	Index	%	Index	%	Index	%	Index	%	Index	%	Index	%	Index	%	Index	%
1959	28.6	0.4	-	-	-	-	44.8	0.7	30.4	3.4	18.4	9.5	-	-	-	-
1960	29.0	1.4	-	-	-	-	45.0	0.4	30.7	1.0	19.0	3.3	-	-	-	-
1961	29.3	1.0	-	-	-	-	45.4	0.9	31.3	2.0	20.3	6.8	-	-	-	-
1962	29.3	0.0	-	-	-	-	45.6	0.4	31.8	1.6	20.4	0.5	-	-	-	-
1963	29.7	1.4	-	-	-	-	46.3	1.5	31.9	0.3	21.5	5.4	-	-	-	-
1964	29.8	0.3	-	-	-	-	46.4	0.2	32.5	1.9	22.2	3.3	-	-	-	-
1965	30.3	1.7	-	-	-	-	46.8	0.9	33.0	1.5	22.8	2.7	-	-	-	-
1966	31.1	2.6	-	-	-	-	48.3	3.2	33.3	0.9	23.3	2.2	-	-	-	-
1967	32.0	2.9	-	-	-	-	49.8	3.1	34.3	3.0	24.7	6.0	-	-	-	-
1968	33.9	5.9	-	-	-	-	52.8	6.0	36.0	5.0	26.8	8.5	-	-	-	-
1969	35.8	5.6	-	-	-	-	55.9	5.9	37.5	4.2	30.0	11.9	-	-	-	-
1970	38.2	6.7	-	-	-	-	58.6	4.8	40.0	6.7	32.4	8.0	-	-	-	-
1971	39.3	2.9	-	-	-	-	60.5	3.2	42.7	6.8	34.6	6.8	-	-	-	-
1972	40.5	3.1	-	-	-	-	61.6	1.8	43.3	1.4	35.6	2.9	-	-	-	-
1973	42.9	5.9	-	-	-	-	64.5	4.7	44.6	3.0	37.3	4.8	-	-	-	-
1974	47.3	10.3	-	-	-	-	70.4	9.1	50.0	12.1	40.7	9.1	-	-	-	-
1975	51.5	8.9	-	-	-	-	72.2	2.6	52.7	5.4	45.3	11.3	-	-	-	-
1976	54.1	5.0	62.3	-	48.1	-	73.9	2.4	55.1	4.6	49.8	9.9	67.2	-	57.2	-
1977	57.8	6.8	65.6	5.3	51.8	7.7	78.1	5.7	58.5	6.2	55.8	12.0	70.6	5.1	60.6	5.9
1978	62.2	7.6	72.1	9.9	55.9	7.9	80.7	3.3	61.7	5.5	61.2	9.7	73.9	4.7	64.6	6.6
1979	70.6	13.5	80.4	11.5	65.3	16.8	83.6	3.6	70.6	14.4	66.5	8.7	78.2	5.8	69.8	8.0
1980	81.1	14.9	86.9	8.1	78.7	20.5	87.0	4.1	82.2	16.4	73.7	10.8	84.2	7.7	76.1	9.0
1981	89.2	10.0	94.0	8.2	86.8	10.3	93.2	7.1	92.4	12.4	81.4	10.4	89.3	6.1	84.3	10.8
1982	95.9	7.5	96.5	2.7	95.9	10.5	99.2	6.4	96.7	4.7	91.7	12.7	95.3	6.7	92.5	9.7
1983	101.1	5.4	99.9	3.5	102.4	6.8	99.3	0.1	99.6	3.0	101.1	10.3	100.1	5.0	100.7	8.9
1984	103.0	1.9	103.6	3.7	101.7	-0.7	101.5	2.2	103.7	4.1	107.1	5.9	104.6	4.5	106.8	6.1
1985	103.8	0.8	105.9	2.2	100.7	-1.0	105.0	3.4	105.6	1.8	111.5	4.1	107.4	2.7	111.2	4.1
1986	105.0	1.2	107.3	1.3	103.8	3.1	103.5	-1.4	100.1	-5.2	121.6	9.1	114.9	7.0	116.9	5.1
1987	108.0	2.9	110.9	3.4	105.7	1.8	109.2	5.5	102.1	2.0	127.9	5.2	116.0	1.0	124.7	6.7
1988	111.8	3.5	115.9	4.5	109.3	3.4	106.2	-2.7	105.4	3.2	134.1	4.8	120.6	4.0	134.8	8.1
1989	117.3	4.9	123.5	6.6	113.5	3.8	110.7	4.2	110.7	5.0	142.1	6.0	126.3	4.7	143.4	6.4
1990	123.0	4.9	130.2	5.4	117.9	3.9	117.0	5.7	116.6	5.3	154.6	8.8	130.6	3.4	150.7	5.1
1991	127.8	3.9	134.9	3.6	122.2	3.6	121.3	3.7	120.0	2.9	168.7	9.1	134.5	3.0	162.2	7.6
1992	130.3	2.0	135.7	0.6	125.4	2.6	122.4	0.9	120.8	0.7	175.6	4.1	136.2	1.3	173.3	6.8
1993	-	-	-	-	-	-	-	-	-	-	-	-	-	-	-	-

Source: U.S. Department of Labor, Bureau of Labor Statistics, Division of Consumer Prices and Price Indexes. - indicates no data collected for period.

Cleveland, OH
Consumer Price Index - All Urban Consumers
Base 1982-1984 = 100
All Items

For 1914-1993. Columns headed % show percentile change in the index from the previous period for which an index is available.

Year	Jan Index	%	Feb Index	%	Mar Index	%	Apr Index	%	May Index	%	Jun Index	%	Jul Index	%	Aug Index	%	Sep Index	%	Oct Index	%	Nov Index	%	Dec Index	%
1914	-	-	-	-	-	-	-	-	-	-	-	-	-	-	-	-	-	-	-	-	-	-	8.7	-
1915	-	-	-	-	-	-	-	-	-	-	-	-	-	-	-	-	-	-	-	-	-	-	8.8	1.1
1916	-	-	-	-	-	-	-	-	-	-	-	-	-	-	-	-	-	-	-	-	-	-	10.1	14.8
1917	-	-	-	-	-	-	-	-	-	-	-	-	-	-	-	-	-	-	-	-	-	-	12.0	18.8
1918	-	-	-	-	-	-	-	-	-	-	-	-	-	-	-	-	-	-	-	-	-	-	14.4	20.0
1919	-	-	-	-	-	-	-	-	-	-	15.1	4.9	-	-	-	-	-	-	-	-	-	-	16.9	11.9
1920	-	-	-	-	-	-	-	-	-	-	19.0	12.4	-	-	-	-	-	-	-	-	-	-	18.0	-5.3
1921	-	-	-	-	-	-	-	-	16.6	-7.8	15.1	0.7	-	-	-	-	16.2	-2.4	-	-	-	-	15.9	-1.9
1922	-	-	-	-	15.0	-5.7	-	-	-	-	15.1	0.7	-	-	-	-	14.9	-1.3	-	-	-	-	15.3	2.7
1923	-	-	-	-	15.4	0.7	-	-	-	-	15.8	2.6	-	-	-	-	16.0	1.3	-	-	-	-	15.9	-0.6
1924	-	-	-	-	15.7	-1.3	-	-	-	-	15.6	-0.6	-	-	-	-	15.7	0.6	-	-	-	-	15.7	0.0
1925	-	-	-	-	-	-	-	-	-	-	16.1	2.5	-	-	-	-	-	-	-	-	-	-	16.2	0.6
1926	-	-	-	-	-	-	-	-	-	-	16.2	0.0	-	-	-	-	-	-	-	-	-	-	16.1	-0.6
1927	-	-	-	-	-	-	-	-	-	-	16.1	0.0	-	-	-	-	-	-	-	-	-	-	15.7	-2.5
1928	-	-	-	-	-	-	-	-	-	-	15.7	0.0	-	-	-	-	-	-	-	-	-	-	15.5	-1.3
1929	-	-	-	-	-	-	-	-	-	-	15.6	0.6	-	-	-	-	-	-	-	-	-	-	15.4	-1.3
1930	-	-	-	-	-	-	-	-	-	-	15.4	0.0	-	-	-	-	-	-	-	-	-	-	14.6	-5.2
1931	-	-	-	-	-	-	-	-	-	-	13.6	-6.8	-	-	-	-	-	-	-	-	-	-	13.1	-3.7
1932	-	-	-	-	-	-	-	-	-	-	12.5	-4.6	-	-	-	-	-	-	-	-	-	-	11.8	-5.6
1933	-	-	-	-	-	-	-	-	-	-	11.6	-1.7	-	-	-	-	-	-	-	-	-	-	12.0	3.4
1934	-	-	-	-	-	-	-	-	-	-	12.2	1.7	-	-	-	-	-	-	-	-	12.2	0.0	-	-
1935	-	-	-	-	12.7	4.1	-	-	-	-	-	-	12.7	0.0	-	-	-	-	12.7	0.0	-	-	12.9	-1.5
1936	12.7	0.0	-	-	-	-	12.6	-0.8	-	-	-	-	12.9	2.4	-	-	13.1	1.6	-	-	-	-	13.4	-1.5
1937	-	-	-	-	13.1	1.6	-	-	-	-	13.4	2.3	-	-	-	-	13.6	1.5	-	-	-	-	13.2	-0.8
1938	-	-	-	-	13.2	-1.5	-	-	-	-	13.3	0.8	-	-	-	-	13.3	0.0	-	-	-	-	13.2	-0.8
1939	-	-	-	-	13.2	0.0	-	-	-	-	13.2	0.0	-	-	-	-	13.3	0.8	-	-	-	-	13.3	0.8
1940	-	-	-	-	13.2	0.0	-	-	-	-	13.3	0.8	-	-	-	-	13.4	0.8	13.3	-0.7	13.2	-0.8	13.3	0.8
1941	13.3	0.0	13.4	0.8	13.4	0.0	13.5	0.7	13.6	0.7	13.9	2.2	14.0	0.7	14.2	1.4	14.5	2.1	14.6	0.7	14.8	1.4	14.8	0.0
1942	15.0	1.4	15.0	0.0	15.3	2.0	15.4	0.7	15.5	0.6	15.6	0.6	15.6	0.0	15.5	-0.6	15.6	0.6	15.9	1.9	15.9	0.0	16.1	1.3
1943	16.1	0.0	16.2	0.6	16.4	1.2	16.5	0.6	16.7	1.2	16.9	1.2	16.7	-1.2	16.7	0.0	16.8	0.6	16.8	0.0	16.8	0.0	16.8	0.0
1944	16.7	-0.6	16.7	0.0	16.7	0.0	16.9	1.2	16.9	0.0	16.9	0.0	17.1	1.2	17.1	0.0	17.1	0.0	17.0	-0.6	17.1	0.6	16.9	-1.2
1945	17.0	0.6	17.0	0.0	17.0	0.0	17.0	0.0	17.3	1.8	17.3	0.0	17.3	0.0	17.3	0.0	17.2	-0.6	17.3	0.6	17.3	0.0	17.3	0.0
1946	17.3	0.0	17.3	0.0	17.3	0.0	17.4	0.6	17.5	0.6	17.8	1.7	18.8	5.6	19.3	2.7	19.3	0.0	19.6	1.6	20.2	3.1	20.5	1.5
1947	20.4	-0.5	20.4	0.0	20.9	2.5	20.9	0.0	20.8	-0.5	21.0	1.0	-	-	21.4	1.9	-	-	-	-	21.9	2.3	-	-
1948	-	-	22.5	2.7	-	-	-	-	22.8	1.3	-	-	-	-	23.6	3.5	-	-	-	-	23.1	-2.1	-	-
1949	-	-	22.7	-1.7	-	-	-	-	22.6	-0.4	-	-	-	-	22.6	0.0	-	-	-	-	22.4	-0.9	-	-
1950	-	-	22.2	-0.9	-	-	-	-	22.3	0.5	-	-	-	-	23.1	3.6	-	-	-	-	23.5	1.7	-	-
1951	-	-	24.3	3.4	-	-	-	-	24.6	1.2	-	-	-	-	24.7	0.4	-	-	-	-	25.1	1.6	-	-
1952	-	-	25.1	0.0	-	-	-	-	25.2	0.4	-	-	-	-	25.4	0.8	-	-	-	-	25.3	-0.4	-	-
1953	-	-	25.0	-1.2	-	-	-	-	25.3	1.2	-	-	-	-	25.6	1.2	-	-	-	-	25.7	0.4	-	-
1954	-	-	25.7	0.0	-	-	-	-	25.7	0.0	-	-	-	-	25.7	0.0	-	-	-	-	25.7	0.0	-	-
1955	-	-	25.6	-0.4	-	-	-	-	25.7	0.4	-	-	-	-	25.8	0.4	-	-	-	-	25.9	0.4	-	-
1956	-	-	25.8	-0.4	-	-	-	-	26.1	1.2	-	-	-	-	26.5	1.5	-	-	-	-	26.7	0.8	-	-
1957	-	-	26.8	0.4	-	-	-	-	27.1	1.1	-	-	-	-	27.3	0.7	-	-	-	-	27.5	0.7	-	-
1958	-	-	27.7	0.7	-	-	-	-	27.8	0.4	-	-	-	-	27.8	0.0	-	-	-	-	27.7	-0.4	-	-

[Continued]

Cleveland, OH

Consumer Price Index - All Urban Consumers
Base 1982-1984 = 100
All Items
[Continued]

For 1914-1993. Columns headed % show percentile change in the index from the previous period for which an index is available.

Year	Jan Index	%	Feb Index	%	Mar Index	%	Apr Index	%	May Index	%	Jun Index	%	Jul Index	%	Aug Index	%	Sep Index	%	Oct Index	%	Nov Index	%	Dec Index	%
1959	-	-	27.8	0.4	-	-	-	-	27.9	0.4	-	-	-	-	28.0	0.4	-	-	-	-	28.1	0.4	-	-
1960	-	-	28.1	0.0	-	-	-	-	28.3	0.7	-	-	-	-	28.4	0.4	-	-	-	-	28.5	0.4	-	-
1961	-	-	28.6	0.4	-	-	-	-	28.5	-0.3	-	-	-	-	28.6	0.4	-	-	-	-	28.5	-0.3	-	-
1962	-	-	28.5	0.0	-	-	-	-	28.6	0.4	-	-	-	-	28.7	0.3	-	-	-	-	28.7	0.0	-	-
1963	-	-	28.8	0.3	-	-	-	-	28.8	0.0	-	-	-	-	29.1	1.0	-	-	-	-	29.0	-0.3	-	-
1964	-	-	29.1	0.3	-	-	-	-	28.9	-0.7	-	-	-	-	29.1	0.7	-	-	-	-	29.3	0.7	-	-
1965	-	-	29.3	0.0	-	-	-	-	29.5	0.7	-	-	-	-	29.6	0.3	-	-	-	-	29.8	0.7	-	-
1966	-	-	29.9	0.3	-	-	-	-	30.3	1.3	-	-	-	-	30.5	0.7	-	-	-	-	30.6	0.3	-	-
1967	-	-	30.8	0.7	-	-	-	-	30.9	0.3	-	-	-	-	31.3	1.3	-	-	-	-	31.7	1.3	-	-
1968	-	-	32.5	2.5	-	-	-	-	32.9	1.2	-	-	-	-	33.2	0.9	-	-	-	-	33.7	1.5	-	-
1969	-	-	34.0	0.9	-	-	-	-	34.6	1.8	-	-	-	-	35.2	1.7	-	-	-	-	35.8	1.7	-	-
1970	-	-	36.6	2.2	-	-	-	-	37.1	1.4	-	-	-	-	37.5	1.1	-	-	-	-	37.9	1.1	-	-
1971	-	-	37.9	0.0	-	-	-	-	38.1	0.5	-	-	-	-	38.4	0.8	-	-	-	-	38.8	1.0	-	-
1972	-	-	39.3	1.3	-	-	-	-	39.4	0.3	-	-	-	-	39.4	0.0	-	-	-	-	39.9	1.3	-	-
1973	-	-	40.5	1.5	-	-	-	-	41.4	2.2	-	-	-	-	42.4	2.4	-	-	-	-	42.9	1.2	-	-
1974	-	-	44.3	3.3	-	-	-	-	45.6	2.9	-	-	-	-	46.8	2.6	-	-	-	-	47.7	1.9	-	-
1975	-	-	49.2	3.1	-	-	-	-	49.8	1.2	-	-	-	-	50.7	1.8	-	-	-	-	51.3	1.2	-	-
1976	-	-	51.5	0.4	-	-	-	-	52.1	1.2	-	-	-	-	53.2	2.1	-	-	-	-	54.0	1.5	-	-
1977	-	-	55.1	2.0	-	-	-	-	56.1	1.8	-	-	-	-	56.5	0.7	-	-	-	-	57.5	1.8	-	-
1978	-	-	58.2	1.2	-	-	59.4	2.1	-	-	59.6	0.3	-	-	60.8	2.0	-	-	62.4	2.6	-	-	64.2	2.9
1979	-	-	65.6	2.2	-	-	67.1	2.3	-	-	68.6	2.2	-	-	69.1	0.7	-	-	70.1	1.4	-	-	72.6	3.6
1980	-	-	76.0	4.7	-	-	77.2	1.6	-	-	78.0	1.0	-	-	79.2	1.5	-	-	82.6	4.3	-	-	83.2	0.7
1981	-	-	85.3	2.5	-	-	84.9	-0.5	-	-	89.0	4.8	-	-	88.8	-0.2	-	-	88.3	-0.6	-	-	87.9	-0.5
1982	-	-	89.2	1.5	-	-	89.4	0.2	-	-	92.9	3.9	-	-	97.4	4.8	-	-	98.8	1.4	-	-	99.1	0.3
1983	-	-	99.5	0.4	-	-	99.7	0.2	-	-	101.2	1.5	-	-	101.8	0.6	-	-	103.2	1.4	-	-	102.6	-0.6
1984	-	-	103.3	0.7	-	-	103.9	0.6	-	-	105.1	1.2	-	-	105.3	0.2	-	-	106.1	0.8	-	-	106.0	-0.1
1985	-	-	106.2	0.2	-	-	106.9	0.7	-	-	108.1	1.1	-	-	108.6	0.5	-	-	108.8	0.2	-	-	108.8	0.0
1986	-	-	109.3	0.5	-	-	108.3	-0.9	-	-	109.4	1.0	-	-	110.1	0.6	-	-	109.9	-0.2	110.1	0.2	109.8	-0.3
1987	110.1	0.3	-	-	111.4	1.2	-	-	111.6	0.2	-	-	112.8	1.1	-	-	114.7	1.7	-	-	114.5	-0.2	-	-
1988	113.9	-0.5	-	-	115.1	1.1	-	-	116.6	1.3	-	-	117.6	0.9	-	-	117.6	0.0	-	-	118.0	0.3	-	-
1989	118.9	0.8	-	-	121.5	2.2	-	-	122.8	1.1	-	-	124.4	1.3	-	-	123.7	-0.6	-	-	123.4	-0.2	-	-
1990	125.0	1.3	-	-	127.4	1.9	-	-	128.1	0.5	-	-	128.8	0.5	-	-	131.1	1.8	-	-	131.7	0.5	-	-
1991	131.9	0.2	-	-	133.2	1.0	-	-	134.3	0.8	-	-	133.9	-0.3	-	-	135.4	1.1	-	-	135.7	0.2	-	-
1992	136.2	0.4	-	-	136.3	0.1	-	-	136.1	-0.1	-	-	137.1	0.7	-	-	137.9	0.6	-	-	137.1	-0.6	-	-
1993	137.5	0.3	-	-	138.8	0.9	-	-	139.6	0.6	-	-	140.9	0.9	-	-	141.7	0.6	-	-	142.1	0.3	-	-

Source: U.S. Department of Labor, Bureau of Labor Statistics, Division of Consumer Prices and Price Indexes. - indicates no data collected for period.

Cleveland, OH
Consumer Price Index - Urban Wage Earners
Base 1982-1984 = 100
All Items

For 1914-1993. Columns headed % show percentile change in the index from the previous period for which an index is available.

Year	Jan Index	Jan %	Feb Index	Feb %	Mar Index	Mar %	Apr Index	Apr %	May Index	May %	Jun Index	Jun %	Jul Index	Jul %	Aug Index	Aug %	Sep Index	Sep %	Oct Index	Oct %	Nov Index	Nov %	Dec Index	Dec %
1914	-	-	-	-	-	-	-	-	-	-	-	-	-	-	-	-	-	-	-	-	-	-	8.9	-
1915	-	-	-	-	-	-	-	-	-	-	-	-	-	-	-	-	-	-	-	-	-	-	9.1	2.2
1916	-	-	-	-	-	-	-	-	-	-	-	-	-	-	-	-	-	-	-	-	-	-	10.4	14.3
1917	-	-	-	-	-	-	-	-	-	-	-	-	-	-	-	-	-	-	-	-	-	-	12.4	19.2
1918	-	-	-	-	-	-	-	-	-	-	-	-	-	-	-	-	-	-	-	-	-	-	14.8	19.4
1919	-	-	-	-	-	-	-	-	-	-	15.5	4.7	-	-	-	-	-	-	-	-	-	-	17.3	11.6
1920	-	-	-	-	-	-	-	-	-	-	19.5	12.7	-	-	-	-	-	-	-	-	-	-	18.5	-5.1
1921	-	-	-	-	-	-	-	-	17.0	-8.1	-	-	-	-	-	-	16.6	-2.4	-	-	-	-	16.3	-1.8
1922	-	-	-	-	15.4	-5.5	-	-	-	-	15.5	0.6	-	-	-	-	15.3	-1.3	-	-	-	-	15.7	2.6
1923	-	-	-	-	15.7	0.0	-	-	-	-	16.2	3.2	-	-	-	-	16.4	1.2	-	-	-	-	16.3	-0.6
1924	-	-	-	-	16.1	-1.2	-	-	-	-	16.0	-0.6	-	-	-	-	16.1	0.6	-	-	-	-	16.1	0.0
1925	-	-	-	-	-	-	-	-	-	-	16.5	2.5	-	-	-	-	-	-	-	-	-	-	16.6	0.6
1926	-	-	-	-	-	-	-	-	-	-	16.6	0.0	-	-	-	-	-	-	-	-	-	-	16.5	-0.6
1927	-	-	-	-	-	-	-	-	-	-	16.5	0.0	-	-	-	-	-	-	-	-	-	-	16.1	-2.4
1928	-	-	-	-	-	-	-	-	-	-	16.1	0.0	-	-	-	-	-	-	-	-	-	-	15.9	-1.2
1929	-	-	-	-	-	-	-	-	-	-	16.0	0.6	-	-	-	-	-	-	-	-	-	-	15.8	-1.2
1930	-	-	-	-	-	-	-	-	-	-	15.8	0.0	-	-	-	-	-	-	-	-	-	-	15.0	-5.1
1931	-	-	-	-	-	-	-	-	-	-	14.0	-6.7	-	-	-	-	-	-	-	-	-	-	13.4	-4.3
1932	-	-	-	-	-	-	-	-	-	-	12.8	-4.5	-	-	-	-	-	-	-	-	-	-	12.1	-5.5
1933	-	-	-	-	-	-	-	-	-	-	11.9	-1.7	-	-	-	-	-	-	-	-	-	-	12.3	3.4
1934	-	-	-	-	-	-	-	-	-	-	12.5	1.6	-	-	-	-	-	-	-	-	12.5	0.0	-	-
1935	-	-	-	-	13.0	4.0	-	-	-	-	-	-	13.0	0.0	-	-	-	-	13.1	0.8	-	-	-	-
1936	13.0	-0.8	-	-	-	-	13.0	0.0	-	-	-	-	13.2	1.5	-	-	13.4	1.5	-	-	-	-	13.2	-1.5
1937	-	-	-	-	13.5	2.3	-	-	-	-	13.8	2.2	-	-	-	-	14.0	1.4	-	-	-	-	13.8	-1.4
1938	-	-	-	-	13.5	-2.2	-	-	-	-	13.6	0.7	-	-	-	-	13.6	0.0	-	-	-	-	13.6	0.0
1939	-	-	-	-	13.5	-0.7	-	-	-	-	13.5	0.0	-	-	-	-	13.6	0.7	-	-	-	-	13.5	-0.7
1940	-	-	-	-	13.5	0.0	-	-	-	-	13.6	0.7	-	-	-	-	13.7	0.7	13.6	-0.7	13.5	-0.7	13.7	1.5
1941	13.7	0.0	13.7	0.0	13.8	0.7	13.9	0.7	14.0	0.7	14.2	1.4	14.3	0.7	14.6	2.1	14.8	1.4	15.0	1.4	15.1	0.7	15.2	0.7
1942	15.4	1.3	15.4	0.0	15.7	1.9	15.8	0.6	15.9	0.6	16.0	0.6	16.0	0.0	15.9	-0.6	16.0	0.6	16.3	1.9	16.4	0.6	16.5	0.6
1943	16.5	0.0	16.6	0.6	16.8	1.2	16.9	0.6	17.2	1.8	17.3	0.6	17.2	-0.6	17.2	0.0	17.2	0.0	17.2	0.0	17.2	0.0	17.2	0.0
1944	17.2	0.0	17.2	0.0	17.2	0.0	17.3	0.6	17.3	0.0	17.3	0.0	17.5	1.2	17.5	0.0	17.5	0.0	17.5	0.0	17.5	0.0	17.3	-1.1
1945	17.4	0.6	17.4	0.0	17.4	0.0	17.5	0.6	17.7	1.1	17.7	0.0	17.7	0.0	17.7	0.0	17.6	-0.6	17.7	0.6	17.7	0.0	17.8	0.6
1946	17.7	-0.6	17.7	0.0	17.7	0.0	17.8	0.6	18.0	1.1	18.2	1.1	19.3	6.0	19.7	2.1	19.8	0.5	20.1	1.5	20.7	3.0	21.0	1.4
1947	21.0	0.0	21.0	0.0	21.4	1.9	21.4	0.0	21.4	0.0	21.6	0.9	-	-	22.0	1.9	-	-	-	-	22.5	2.3	-	-
1948	-	-	23.1	2.7	-	-	-	-	23.4	1.3	-	-	-	-	24.2	3.4	-	-	-	-	23.7	-2.1	-	-
1949	-	-	23.2	-2.1	-	-	-	-	23.1	-0.4	-	-	-	-	23.2	0.4	-	-	-	-	23.0	-0.9	-	-
1950	-	-	22.8	-0.9	-	-	-	-	22.9	0.4	-	-	-	-	23.7	3.5	-	-	-	-	24.1	1.7	-	-
1951	-	-	24.9	3.3	-	-	-	-	25.2	1.2	-	-	-	-	25.3	0.4	-	-	-	-	25.7	1.6	-	-
1952	-	-	25.7	0.0	-	-	-	-	25.8	0.4	-	-	-	-	26.0	0.8	-	-	-	-	25.9	-0.4	-	-
1953	-	-	25.7	-0.8	-	-	-	-	25.9	0.8	-	-	-	-	26.3	1.5	-	-	-	-	26.4	0.4	-	-
1954	-	-	26.3	-0.4	-	-	-	-	26.3	0.0	-	-	-	-	26.3	0.0	-	-	-	-	26.3	0.0	-	-
1955	-	-	26.2	-0.4	-	-	-	-	26.3	0.4	-	-	-	-	26.5	0.8	-	-	-	-	26.5	0.0	-	-
1956	-	-	26.4	-0.4	-	-	-	-	26.8	1.5	-	-	-	-	27.2	1.5	-	-	-	-	27.4	0.7	-	-
1957	-	-	27.5	0.4	-	-	-	-	27.8	1.1	-	-	-	-	28.0	0.7	-	-	-	-	28.2	0.7	-	-
1958	-	-	28.4	0.7	-	-	-	-	28.5	0.4	-	-	-	-	28.5	0.0	-	-	-	-	28.4	-0.4	-	-

[Continued]

Cleveland, OH
Consumer Price Index - Urban Wage Earners
Base 1982-1984 = 100
All Items
[Continued]

For 1914-1993. Columns headed % show percentile change in the index from the previous period for which an index is available.

Year	Jan Index	%	Feb Index	%	Mar Index	%	Apr Index	%	May Index	%	Jun Index	%	Jul Index	%	Aug Index	%	Sep Index	%	Oct Index	%	Nov Index	%	Dec Index	%
1959	-	-	28.5	0.4	-	-	-	-	28.6	0.4	-	-	-	-	28.7	0.3	-	-	-	-	28.9	0.7	-	-
1960	-	-	28.8	-0.3	-	-	-	-	29.0	0.7	-	-	-	-	29.1	0.3	-	-	-	-	29.2	0.3	-	-
1961	-	-	29.3	0.3	-	-	-	-	29.2	-0.3	-	-	-	-	29.4	0.7	-	-	-	-	29.2	-0.7	-	-
1962	-	-	29.2	0.0	-	-	-	-	29.3	0.3	-	-	-	-	29.4	0.3	-	-	-	-	29.4	0.0	-	-
1963	-	-	29.6	0.7	-	-	-	-	29.6	0.0	-	-	-	-	29.8	0.7	-	-	-	-	29.8	0.0	-	-
1964	-	-	29.8	0.0	-	-	-	-	29.6	-0.7	-	-	-	-	29.8	0.7	-	-	-	-	30.0	0.7	-	-
1965	-	-	30.1	0.3	-	-	-	-	30.3	0.7	-	-	-	-	30.4	0.3	-	-	-	-	30.6	0.7	-	-
1966	-	-	30.6	0.0	-	-	-	-	31.1	1.6	-	-	-	-	31.2	0.3	-	-	-	-	31.4	0.6	-	-
1967	-	-	31.6	0.6	-	-	-	-	31.7	0.3	-	-	-	-	32.1	1.3	-	-	-	-	32.5	1.2	-	-
1968	-	-	33.4	2.8	-	-	-	-	33.8	1.2	-	-	-	-	34.0	0.6	-	-	-	-	34.5	1.5	-	-
1969	-	-	34.9	1.2	-	-	-	-	35.5	1.7	-	-	-	-	36.1	1.7	-	-	-	-	36.7	1.7	-	-
1970	-	-	37.5	2.2	-	-	-	-	38.1	1.6	-	-	-	-	38.4	0.8	-	-	-	-	38.8	1.0	-	-
1971	-	-	38.9	0.3	-	-	-	-	39.0	0.3	-	-	-	-	39.4	1.0	-	-	-	-	39.8	1.0	-	-
1972	-	-	40.3	1.3	-	-	-	-	40.4	0.2	-	-	-	-	40.4	0.0	-	-	-	-	40.9	1.2	-	-
1973	-	-	41.6	1.7	-	-	-	-	42.5	2.2	-	-	-	-	43.5	2.4	-	-	-	-	44.0	1.1	-	-
1974	-	-	45.5	3.4	-	-	-	-	46.8	2.9	-	-	-	-	48.0	2.6	-	-	-	-	49.0	2.1	-	-
1975	-	-	50.5	3.1	-	-	-	-	51.0	1.0	-	-	-	-	52.0	2.0	-	-	-	-	52.6	1.2	-	-
1976	-	-	52.8	0.4	-	-	-	-	53.4	1.1	-	-	-	-	54.6	2.2	-	-	-	-	55.4	1.5	-	-
1977	-	-	56.5	2.0	-	-	-	-	57.6	1.9	-	-	-	-	58.0	0.7	-	-	-	-	59.0	1.7	-	-
1978	-	-	59.7	1.2	-	-	61.0	2.2	-	-	61.5	0.8	-	-	62.7	2.0	-	-	64.2	2.4	-	-	65.9	2.6
1979	-	-	67.5	2.4	-	-	69.2	2.5	-	-	70.8	2.3	-	-	71.2	0.6	-	-	72.2	1.4	-	-	74.6	3.3
1980	-	-	78.1	4.7	-	-	79.5	1.8	-	-	80.2	0.9	-	-	81.4	1.5	-	-	84.6	3.9	-	-	85.4	0.9
1981	-	-	87.7	2.7	-	-	87.1	-0.7	-	-	90.8	4.2	-	-	90.6	-0.2	-	-	90.3	-0.3	-	-	90.0	-0.3
1982	-	-	91.2	1.3	-	-	91.4	0.2	-	-	95.0	3.9	-	-	99.4	4.6	-	-	100.5	1.1	-	-	100.8	0.3
1983	-	-	100.3	-0.5	-	-	100.9	0.6	-	-	101.3	0.4	-	-	101.6	0.3	-	-	101.5	-0.1	-	-	100.7	-0.8
1984	-	-	101.8	1.1	-	-	102.6	0.8	-	-	103.0	0.4	-	-	105.0	1.9	-	-	103.8	-1.1	-	-	102.0	-1.7
1985	-	-	102.3	0.3	-	-	103.0	0.7	-	-	104.1	1.1	-	-	104.7	0.6	-	-	104.7	0.0	-	-	104.8	0.1
1986	-	-	105.1	0.3	-	-	103.8	-1.2	-	-	105.0	1.2	-	-	105.6	0.6	-	-	105.4	-0.2	105.5	0.1	105.3	-0.2
1987	105.6	0.3	-	-	106.7	1.0	-	-	107.0	0.3	-	-	108.1	1.0	-	-	109.9	1.7	-	-	109.9	0.0	-	-
1988	109.3	-0.5	-	-	110.2	0.8	-	-	111.7	1.4	-	-	112.6	0.8	-	-	112.7	0.1	-	-	113.0	0.3	-	-
1989	113.8	0.7	-	-	116.2	2.1	-	-	117.7	1.3	-	-	118.8	0.9	-	-	118.2	-0.5	-	-	118.0	-0.2	-	-
1990	119.5	1.3	-	-	121.5	1.7	-	-	122.1	0.5	-	-	122.7	0.5	-	-	125.0	1.9	-	-	125.8	0.6	-	-
1991	125.8	0.0	-	-	126.8	0.8	-	-	127.8	0.8	-	-	127.4	-0.3	-	-	129.0	1.3	-	-	129.3	0.2	-	-
1992	129.6	0.2	-	-	129.7	0.1	-	-	129.6	-0.1	-	-	130.5	0.7	-	-	131.3	0.6	-	-	130.8	-0.4	-	-
1993	130.8	0.0	-	-	131.8	0.8	-	-	132.7	0.7	-	-	133.9	0.9	-	-	134.6	0.5	-	-	135.1	0.4	-	-

Source: U.S. Department of Labor, Bureau of Labor Statistics, Division of Consumer Prices and Price Indexes. - indicates no data collected for period.

Cleveland, OH
Consumer Price Index - All Urban Consumers
Base 1982-1984 = 100
Food and Beverages

For 1975-1993. Columns headed % show percentile change in the index from the previous period for which an index is available.

Year	Jan Index	%	Feb Index	%	Mar Index	%	Apr Index	%	May Index	%	Jun Index	%	Jul Index	%	Aug Index	%	Sep Index	%	Oct Index	%	Nov Index	%	Dec Index	%
1975	-	-	-	-	-	-	-	-	-	-	-	-	-	-	-	-	-	-	-	-	62.1	-	-	-
1976	-	-	62.1	0.0	-	-	-	-	63.0	1.4	-	-	-	-	63.2	0.3	-	-	-	-	63.7	0.8	-	-
1977	-	-	65.4	2.7	-	-	-	-	67.6	3.4	-	-	-	-	65.2	-3.6	-	-	-	-	67.4	3.4	-	-
1978	-	-	69.4	3.0	-	-	70.5	1.6	-	-	72.9	3.4	-	-	73.1	0.3	-	-	73.6	0.7	-	-	74.9	1.8
1979	-	-	77.9	4.0	-	-	79.4	1.9	-	-	79.8	0.5	-	-	80.2	0.5	-	-	80.6	0.5	-	-	81.4	1.0
1980	-	-	83.2	2.2	-	-	83.7	0.6	-	-	83.5	-0.2	-	-	86.6	3.7	-	-	89.0	2.8	-	-	89.5	0.6
1981	-	-	91.8	2.6	-	-	91.9	0.1	-	-	94.2	2.5	-	-	94.0	-0.2	-	-	94.4	0.4	-	-	94.2	-0.2
1982	-	-	95.4	1.3	-	-	95.5	0.1	-	-	96.7	1.3	-	-	96.7	0.0	-	-	97.1	0.4	-	-	97.2	0.1
1983	-	-	98.7	1.5	-	-	99.3	0.6	-	-	99.4	0.1	-	-	100.3	0.9	-	-	100.9	0.6	-	-	101.2	0.3
1984	-	-	103.6	2.4	-	-	103.2	-0.4	-	-	103.3	0.1	-	-	104.2	0.9	-	-	104.7	0.5	-	-	105.3	0.6
1985	-	-	107.0	1.6	-	-	106.2	-0.7	-	-	105.4	-0.8	-	-	106.0	0.6	-	-	106.1	0.1	-	-	106.5	0.4
1986	-	-	107.0	0.5	-	-	106.9	-0.1	-	-	106.3	-0.6	-	-	108.2	1.8	-	-	108.7	0.5	108.9	0.2	109.4	0.5
1987	110.6	1.1	-	-	110.7	0.1	-	-	110.9	0.2	-	-	110.6	-0.3	-	-	111.7	1.0	-	-	112.7	0.9	-	-
1988	113.3	0.5	-	-	114.8	1.3	-	-	114.2	-0.5	-	-	116.4	1.9	-	-	118.8	2.1	-	-	118.9	0.1	-	-
1989	121.0	1.8	-	-	121.8	0.7	-	-	123.3	1.2	-	-	124.9	1.3	-	-	125.4	0.4	-	-	125.6	0.2	-	-
1990	128.9	2.6	-	-	129.9	0.8	-	-	128.8	-0.8	-	-	131.2	1.9	-	-	131.5	0.2	-	-	131.6	0.1	-	-
1991	134.8	2.4	-	-	135.3	0.4	-	-	136.6	1.0	-	-	135.5	-0.8	-	-	134.8	-0.5	-	-	134.8	0.0	-	-
1992	136.4	1.2	-	-	136.4	0.0	-	-	136.4	0.0	-	-	134.9	-1.1	-	-	136.8	1.4	-	-	135.8	-0.7	-	-
1993	137.1	1.0	-	-	138.2	0.8	-	-	139.2	0.7	-	-	139.1	-0.1	-	-	141.5	1.7	-	-	141.9	0.3	-	-

Source: U.S. Department of Labor, Bureau of Labor Statistics, Division of Consumer Prices and Price Indexes. - indicates no data collected for period.

Cleveland, OH
Consumer Price Index - Urban Wage Earners
Base 1982-1984 = 100
Food and Beverages

For 1975-1993. Columns headed % show percentile change in the index from the previous period for which an index is available.

Year	Jan Index	%	Feb Index	%	Mar Index	%	Apr Index	%	May Index	%	Jun Index	%	Jul Index	%	Aug Index	%	Sep Index	%	Oct Index	%	Nov Index	%	Dec Index	%
1975	-	-	-	-	-	-	-	-	-	-	-	-	-	-	-	-	-	-	-	-	61.4	-	-	-
1976	-	-	61.4	0.0	-	-	-	-	62.2	1.3	-	-	-	-	62.5	0.5	-	-	-	-	62.9	0.6	-	-
1977	-	-	64.6	2.7	-	-	-	-	66.8	3.4	-	-	-	-	64.4	-3.6	-	-	-	-	66.6	3.4	-	-
1978	-	-	68.5	2.9	-	-	70.0	2.2	-	-	73.3	4.7	-	-	73.7	0.5	-	-	73.8	0.1	-	-	75.3	2.0
1979	-	-	78.4	4.1	-	-	80.3	2.4	-	-	80.8	0.6	-	-	80.9	0.1	-	-	81.2	0.4	-	-	83.0	2.2
1980	-	-	84.1	1.3	-	-	84.9	1.0	-	-	84.6	-0.4	-	-	88.1	4.1	-	-	90.1	2.3	-	-	91.5	1.6
1981	-	-	93.2	1.9	-	-	93.5	0.3	-	-	94.3	0.9	-	-	94.4	0.1	-	-	94.8	0.4	-	-	94.3	-0.5
1982	-	-	95.4	1.2	-	-	95.7	0.3	-	-	96.9	1.3	-	-	96.8	-0.1	-	-	97.4	0.6	-	-	97.6	0.2
1983	-	-	99.0	1.4	-	-	99.5	0.5	-	-	99.5	0.0	-	-	100.3	0.8	-	-	100.8	0.5	-	-	101.0	0.2
1984	-	-	103.3	2.3	-	-	102.9	-0.4	-	-	103.1	0.2	-	-	104.1	1.0	-	-	104.5	0.4	-	-	105.0	0.5
1985	-	-	106.7	1.6	-	-	106.0	-0.7	-	-	105.1	-0.8	-	-	105.8	0.7	-	-	105.9	0.1	-	-	106.2	0.3
1986	-	-	106.6	0.4	-	-	106.6	0.0	-	-	106.0	-0.6	-	-	107.9	1.8	-	-	108.3	0.4	108.6	0.3	109.0	0.4
1987	110.2	1.1	-	-	110.2	0.0	-	-	110.5	0.3	-	-	110.3	-0.2	-	-	111.4	1.0	-	-	112.3	0.8	-	-
1988	112.8	0.4	-	-	114.3	1.3	-	-	113.7	-0.5	-	-	115.9	1.9	-	-	118.3	2.1	-	-	118.4	0.1	-	-
1989	120.5	1.8	-	-	121.3	0.7	-	-	122.8	1.2	-	-	124.4	1.3	-	-	124.9	0.4	-	-	125.2	0.2	-	-
1990	128.5	2.6	-	-	129.5	0.8	-	-	128.4	-0.8	-	-	130.8	1.9	-	-	131.2	0.3	-	-	131.3	0.1	-	-
1991	134.4	2.4	-	-	134.9	0.4	-	-	136.2	1.0	-	-	135.1	-0.8	-	-	134.3	-0.6	-	-	134.3	0.0	-	-
1992	136.0	1.3	-	-	136.0	0.0	-	-	135.8	-0.1	-	-	134.3	-1.1	-	-	136.3	1.5	-	-	135.4	-0.7	-	-
1993	136.7	1.0	-	-	137.8	0.8	-	-	138.7	0.7	-	-	138.6	-0.1	-	-	141.0	1.7	-	-	141.4	0.3	-	-

Source: U.S. Department of Labor, Bureau of Labor Statistics, Division of Consumer Prices and Price Indexes. - indicates no data collected for period.

Cleveland, OH
Consumer Price Index - All Urban Consumers
Base 1982-1984 = 100
Housing

For 1975-1993. Columns headed % show percentile change in the index from the previous period for which an index is available.

Year	Jan Index	%	Feb Index	%	Mar Index	%	Apr Index	%	May Index	%	Jun Index	%	Jul Index	%	Aug Index	%	Sep Index	%	Oct Index	%	Nov Index	%	Dec Index	%
1975	-	-	-	-	-	-	-	-	-	-	-	-	-	-	-	-	-	-	-	-	45.1	-	-	-
1976	-	-	45.0	-0.2	-	-	-	-	45.2	0.4	-	-	-	-	46.8	3.5	-	-	-	-	47.4	1.3	-	-
1977	-	-	48.5	2.3	-	-	-	-	48.9	0.8	-	-	-	-	50.5	3.3	-	-	-	-	50.9	0.8	-	-
1978	-	-	51.1	0.4	-	-	52.7	3.1	-	-	51.8	-1.7	-	-	53.4	3.1	-	-	55.9	4.7	-	-	58.6	4.8
1979	-	-	59.7	1.9	-	-	61.5	3.0	-	-	63.7	3.6	-	-	63.3	-0.6	-	-	63.9	0.9	-	-	67.7	5.9
1980	-	-	72.5	7.1	-	-	73.8	1.8	-	-	75.2	1.9	-	-	75.6	0.5	-	-	80.7	6.7	-	-	80.6	-0.1
1981	-	-	82.4	2.2	-	-	80.4	-2.4	-	-	87.4	8.7	-	-	86.2	-1.4	-	-	84.1	-2.4	-	-	82.6	-1.8
1982	-	-	84.4	2.2	-	-	84.8	0.5	-	-	90.2	6.4	-	-	97.9	8.5	-	-	100.3	2.5	-	-	100.7	0.4
1983	-	-	101.1	0.4	-	-	101.0	-0.1	-	-	103.7	2.7	-	-	102.9	-0.8	-	-	104.7	1.7	-	-	102.8	-1.8
1984	-	-	102.7	-0.1	-	-	104.1	1.4	-	-	105.9	1.7	-	-	105.8	-0.1	-	-	106.9	1.0	-	-	106.0	-0.8
1985	-	-	106.3	0.3	-	-	106.3	0.0	-	-	110.4	3.9	-	-	110.6	0.2	-	-	109.4	-1.1	-	-	108.9	-0.5
1986	-	-	110.0	1.0	-	-	110.9	0.8	-	-	112.7	1.6	-	-	113.9	1.1	-	-	112.2	-1.5	112.5	0.3	111.7	-0.7
1987	111.3	-0.4	-	-	113.1	1.6	-	-	112.9	-0.2	-	-	115.1	1.9	-	-	115.8	0.6	-	-	114.8	-0.9	-	-
1988	114.5	-0.3	-	-	116.3	1.6	-	-	117.7	1.2	-	-	119.2	1.3	-	-	118.5	-0.6	-	-	119.3	0.7	-	-
1989	120.6	1.1	-	-	121.4	0.7	-	-	121.4	0.0	-	-	125.4	3.3	-	-	124.3	-0.9	-	-	122.5	-1.4	-	-
1990	123.7	1.0	-	-	125.6	1.5	-	-	126.9	1.0	-	-	128.5	1.3	-	-	130.7	1.7	-	-	129.2	-1.1	-	-
1991	129.7	0.4	-	-	131.2	1.2	-	-	132.3	0.8	-	-	132.8	0.4	-	-	133.9	0.8	-	-	133.4	-0.4	-	-
1992	136.0	1.9	-	-	134.1	-1.4	-	-	134.1	0.0	-	-	137.8	2.8	-	-	137.3	-0.4	-	-	135.1	-1.6	-	-
1993	136.7	1.2	-	-	138.5	1.3	-	-	137.3	-0.9	-	-	139.7	1.7	-	-	141.3	1.1	-	-	139.9	-1.0	-	-

Source: U.S. Department of Labor, Bureau of Labor Statistics, Division of Consumer Prices and Price Indexes. - indicates no data collected for period.

Cleveland, OH
Consumer Price Index - Urban Wage Earners
Base 1982-1984 = 100
Housing

For 1975-1993. Columns headed % show percentile change in the index from the previous period for which an index is available.

Year	Jan Index	%	Feb Index	%	Mar Index	%	Apr Index	%	May Index	%	Jun Index	%	Jul Index	%	Aug Index	%	Sep Index	%	Oct Index	%	Nov Index	%	Dec Index	%
1975	-	-	-	-	-	-	-	-	-	-	-	-	-	-	-	-	-	-	-	-	47.0	-	-	-
1976	-	-	46.9	-0.2	-	-	-	-	47.1	0.4	-	-	-	-	48.8	3.6	-	-	-	-	49.4	1.2	-	-
1977	-	-	50.6	2.4	-	-	-	-	50.9	0.6	-	-	-	-	52.6	3.3	-	-	-	-	53.1	1.0	-	-
1978	-	-	53.2	0.2	-	-	55.0	3.4	-	-	54.0	-1.8	-	-	55.7	3.1	-	-	58.3	4.7	-	-	60.9	4.5
1979	-	-	62.1	2.0	-	-	63.8	2.7	-	-	66.2	3.8	-	-	65.8	-0.6	-	-	66.3	0.8	-	-	70.2	5.9
1980	-	-	75.3	7.3	-	-	77.0	2.3	-	-	77.9	1.2	-	-	78.4	0.6	-	-	83.6	6.6	-	-	83.6	0.0
1981	-	-	85.5	2.3	-	-	83.3	-2.6	-	-	90.7	8.9	-	-	89.2	-1.7	-	-	87.2	-2.2	-	-	85.8	-1.6
1982	-	-	87.7	2.2	-	-	88.2	0.6	-	-	94.0	6.6	-	-	102.0	8.5	-	-	104.0	2.0	-	-	104.4	0.4
1983	-	-	102.9	-1.4	-	-	103.6	0.7	-	-	103.5	-0.1	-	-	102.6	-0.9	-	-	101.3	-1.3	-	-	99.3	-2.0
1984	-	-	100.3	1.0	-	-	102.0	1.7	-	-	101.6	-0.4	-	-	105.6	3.9	-	-	102.3	-3.1	-	-	98.1	-4.1
1985	-	-	98.6	0.5	-	-	98.6	0.0	-	-	102.6	4.1	-	-	102.9	0.3	-	-	101.4	-1.5	-	-	101.0	-0.4
1986	103.3	-0.2	102.1	1.1	-	-	102.8	0.7	-	-	104.7	1.8	-	-	105.8	1.1	-	-	104.2	-1.5	104.3	0.1	103.5	-0.8
1987	103.3	-0.2	-	-	104.9	1.5	-	-	104.8	-0.1	-	-	106.7	1.8	-	-	107.5	0.7	-	-	106.5	-0.9	-	-
1988	106.3	-0.2	-	-	108.0	1.6	-	-	109.2	1.1	-	-	110.5	1.2	-	-	109.9	-0.5	-	-	110.4	0.5	-	-
1989	111.6	1.1	-	-	112.2	0.5	-	-	112.4	0.2	-	-	115.7	2.9	-	-	115.1	-0.5	-	-	113.3	-1.6	-	-
1990	114.4	1.0	-	-	116.0	1.4	-	-	117.1	0.9	-	-	118.6	1.3	-	-	120.6	1.7	-	-	119.3	-1.1	-	-
1991	119.7	0.3	-	-	120.9	1.0	-	-	121.8	0.7	-	-	122.3	0.4	-	-	123.8	1.2	-	-	123.2	-0.5	-	-
1992	125.6	1.9	-	-	123.8	-1.4	-	-	123.9	0.1	-	-	127.1	2.6	-	-	126.6	-0.4	-	-	125.0	-1.3	-	-
1993	126.2	1.0	-	-	127.7	1.2	-	-	126.7	-0.8	-	-	128.8	1.7	-	-	130.1	1.0	-	-	129.3	-0.6	-	-

Source: U.S. Department of Labor, Bureau of Labor Statistics, Division of Consumer Prices and Price Indexes. - indicates no data collected for period.

Cleveland, OH
Consumer Price Index - All Urban Consumers
Base 1982-1984 = 100
Apparel and Upkeep

For 1952-1993. Columns headed % show percentile change in the index from the previous period for which an index is available.

Year	Jan Index	%	Feb Index	%	Mar Index	%	Apr Index	%	May Index	%	Jun Index	%	Jul Index	%	Aug Index	%	Sep Index	%	Oct Index	%	Nov Index	%	Dec Index	%
1952	-	-	-	-	-	-	-	-	-	-	-	-	-	-	-	-	-	-	-	-	43.7	-	-	-
1953	-	-	43.3	-0.9	-	-	-	-	44.4	2.5	-	-	-	-	44.2	-0.5	-	-	-	-	44.2	0.0	-	-
1954	-	-	44.1	-0.2	-	-	-	-	44.1	0.0	-	-	-	-	44.1	0.0	-	-	-	-	44.0	-0.2	-	-
1955	-	-	43.8	-0.5	-	-	-	-	43.8	0.0	-	-	-	-	43.7	-0.2	-	-	-	-	44.1	0.9	-	-
1956	-	-	44.2	0.2	-	-	-	-	44.6	0.9	-	-	-	-	45.0	0.9	-	-	-	-	45.3	0.7	-	-
1957	-	-	45.0	-0.7	-	-	-	-	45.4	0.9	-	-	-	-	45.5	0.2	-	-	-	-	45.8	0.7	-	-
1958	-	-	45.9	0.2	-	-	-	-	46.0	0.2	-	-	-	-	45.9	-0.2	-	-	-	-	45.9	0.0	-	-
1959	-	-	46.0	0.2	-	-	-	-	46.2	0.4	-	-	-	-	46.3	0.2	-	-	-	-	46.4	0.2	-	-
1960	-	-	46.4	0.0	-	-	-	-	46.3	-0.2	-	-	-	-	46.4	0.2	-	-	-	-	46.5	0.2	-	-
1961	-	-	46.5	0.0	-	-	-	-	46.7	0.4	-	-	-	-	46.9	0.4	-	-	-	-	47.0	0.2	-	-
1962	-	-	46.9	-0.2	-	-	-	-	47.1	0.4	-	-	-	-	46.9	-0.4	-	-	-	-	47.1	0.4	-	-
1963	-	-	47.3	0.4	-	-	-	-	47.8	1.1	-	-	-	-	48.1	0.6	-	-	-	-	47.7	-0.8	-	-
1964	-	-	47.8	0.2	-	-	-	-	48.0	0.4	-	-	-	-	47.7	-0.6	-	-	-	-	48.0	0.6	-	-
1965	-	-	47.9	-0.2	-	-	-	-	48.6	1.5	-	-	-	-	48.0	-1.2	-	-	-	-	48.5	1.0	-	-
1966	-	-	48.8	0.6	-	-	-	-	49.9	2.3	-	-	-	-	49.8	-0.2	-	-	-	-	50.4	1.2	-	-
1967	-	-	50.5	0.2	-	-	-	-	51.1	1.2	-	-	-	-	50.8	-0.6	-	-	-	-	52.7	3.7	-	-
1968	-	-	53.5	1.5	-	-	-	-	54.0	0.9	-	-	-	-	54.6	1.1	-	-	-	-	55.7	2.0	-	-
1969	-	-	56.1	0.7	-	-	-	-	57.3	2.1	-	-	-	-	57.7	0.7	-	-	-	-	59.3	2.8	-	-
1970	-	-	59.4	0.2	-	-	-	-	60.4	1.7	-	-	-	-	60.3	-0.2	-	-	-	-	61.4	1.8	-	-
1971	-	-	61.4	0.0	-	-	-	-	62.8	2.3	-	-	-	-	62.4	-0.6	-	-	-	-	63.0	1.0	-	-
1972	-	-	62.9	-0.2	-	-	-	-	63.5	1.0	-	-	-	-	63.4	-0.2	-	-	-	-	64.2	1.3	-	-
1973	-	-	64.2	0.0	-	-	-	-	65.7	2.3	-	-	-	-	66.6	1.4	-	-	-	-	69.3	4.1	-	-
1974	-	-	70.6	1.9	-	-	-	-	71.5	1.3	-	-	-	-	73.2	2.4	-	-	-	-	75.6	3.3	-	-
1975	-	-	74.0	-2.1	-	-	-	-	74.4	0.5	-	-	-	-	74.2	-0.3	-	-	-	-	74.9	0.9	-	-
1976	-	-	74.5	-0.5	-	-	-	-	75.3	1.1	-	-	-	-	76.3	1.3	-	-	-	-	78.6	3.0	-	-
1977	-	-	78.1	-0.6	-	-	-	-	79.7	2.0	-	-	-	-	81.4	2.1	-	-	-	-	82.8	1.7	-	-
1978	-	-	81.0	-2.2	-	-	80.2	-1.0	-	-	81.3	1.4	-	-	83.6	2.8	-	-	84.0	0.5	-	-	82.9	-1.3
1979	-	-	83.5	0.7	-	-	82.4	-1.3	-	-	81.4	-1.2	-	-	85.5	5.0	-	-	87.6	2.5	-	-	88.2	0.7
1980	-	-	87.7	-0.6	-	-	88.7	1.1	-	-	87.6	-1.2	-	-	90.4	3.2	-	-	91.6	1.3	-	-	91.4	-0.2
1981	-	-	93.2	2.0	-	-	96.1	3.1	-	-	94.6	-1.6	-	-	95.2	0.6	-	-	95.0	-0.2	-	-	97.3	2.4
1982	-	-	98.0	0.7	-	-	97.5	-0.5	-	-	98.4	0.9	-	-	102.1	3.8	-	-	101.6	-0.5	-	-	99.7	-1.9
1983	-	-	100.6	0.9	-	-	97.6	-3.0	-	-	98.7	1.1	-	-	99.1	0.4	-	-	99.9	0.8	-	-	99.5	-0.4
1984	-	-	101.2	1.7	-	-	98.4	-2.8	-	-	101.2	2.8	-	-	102.9	1.7	-	-	102.2	-0.7	-	-	102.8	0.6
1985	-	-	101.9	-0.9	-	-	103.2	1.3	-	-	101.5	-1.6	-	-	106.5	4.9	-	-	107.8	1.2	-	-	103.8	-3.7
1986	-	-	104.1	0.3	-	-	100.9	-3.1	-	-	99.3	-1.6	-	-	105.1	5.8	-	-	104.2	-0.9	103.1	-1.1	98.5	-4.5
1987	97.8	-0.7	-	-	105.5	7.9	-	-	104.0	-1.4	-	-	105.0	1.0	-	-	121.3	15.5	-	-	115.3	-4.9	-	-
1988	106.7	-7.5	-	-	111.0	4.0	-	-	111.8	0.7	-	-	108.0	-3.4	-	-	101.0	-6.5	-	-	100.1	-0.9	-	-
1989	91.9	-8.2	-	-	119.5	30.0	-	-	120.5	0.8	-	-	114.6	-4.9	-	-	111.2	-3.0	-	-	108.7	-2.2	-	-
1990	102.6	-5.6	-	-	128.8	25.5	-	-	127.6	-0.9	-	-	115.4	-9.6	-	-	115.5	0.1	-	-	115.0	-0.4	-	-
1991	112.8	-1.9	-	-	125.1	10.9	-	-	122.7	-1.9	-	-	115.2	-6.1	-	-	126.1	9.5	-	-	127.4	1.0	-	-
1992	121.0	-5.0	-	-	128.2	6.0	-	-	122.7	-4.3	-	-	116.8	-4.8	-	-	124.9	6.9	-	-	120.7	-3.4	-	-
1993	116.4	-3.6	-	-	119.7	2.8	-	-	126.7	5.8	-	-	127.2	0.4	-	-	129.3	1.7	-	-	128.6	-0.5	-	-

Source: U.S. Department of Labor, Bureau of Labor Statistics, Division of Consumer Prices and Price Indexes. - indicates no data collected for period.

Cleveland, OH
Consumer Price Index - Urban Wage Earners
Base 1982-1984 = 100
Apparel and Upkeep

For 1952-1993. Columns headed % show percentile change in the index from the previous period for which an index is available.

Year	Jan Index	%	Feb Index	%	Mar Index	%	Apr Index	%	May Index	%	Jun Index	%	Jul Index	%	Aug Index	%	Sep Index	%	Oct Index	%	Nov Index	%	Dec Index	%
1952	-	-	-	-	-	-	-	-	-	-	-	-	-	-	-	-	-	-	-	-	42.4	-	-	-
1953	-	-	42.0	-0.9	-	-	-	-	43.0	2.4	-	-	-	-	42.9	-0.2	-	-	-	-	42.9	0.0	-	-
1954	-	-	42.8	-0.2	-	-	-	-	42.8	0.0	-	-	-	-	42.7	-0.2	-	-	-	-	42.6	-0.2	-	-
1955	-	-	42.4	-0.5	-	-	-	-	42.5	0.2	-	-	-	-	42.4	-0.2	-	-	-	-	42.7	0.7	-	-
1956	-	-	42.9	0.5	-	-	-	-	43.2	0.7	-	-	-	-	43.6	0.9	-	-	-	-	44.0	0.9	-	-
1957	-	-	43.6	-0.9	-	-	-	-	44.0	0.9	-	-	-	-	44.1	0.2	-	-	-	-	44.4	0.7	-	-
1958	-	-	44.5	0.2	-	-	-	-	44.6	0.2	-	-	-	-	44.5	-0.2	-	-	-	-	44.5	0.0	-	-
1959	-	-	44.6	0.2	-	-	-	-	44.8	0.4	-	-	-	-	44.9	0.2	-	-	-	-	45.0	0.2	-	-
1960	-	-	45.0	0.0	-	-	-	-	44.9	-0.2	-	-	-	-	45.0	0.2	-	-	-	-	45.1	0.2	-	-
1961	-	-	45.1	0.0	-	-	-	-	45.3	0.4	-	-	-	-	45.5	0.4	-	-	-	-	45.6	0.2	-	-
1962	-	-	45.5	-0.2	-	-	-	-	45.7	0.4	-	-	-	-	45.5	-0.4	-	-	-	-	45.7	0.4	-	-
1963	-	-	45.9	0.4	-	-	-	-	46.4	1.1	-	-	-	-	46.7	0.6	-	-	-	-	46.2	-1.1	-	-
1964	-	-	46.3	0.2	-	-	-	-	46.6	0.6	-	-	-	-	46.2	-0.9	-	-	-	-	46.5	0.6	-	-
1965	-	-	46.4	-0.2	-	-	-	-	47.2	1.7	-	-	-	-	46.6	-1.3	-	-	-	-	47.1	1.1	-	-
1966	-	-	47.3	0.4	-	-	-	-	48.4	2.3	-	-	-	-	48.3	-0.2	-	-	-	-	48.9	1.2	-	-
1967	-	-	49.0	0.2	-	-	-	-	49.6	1.2	-	-	-	-	49.3	-0.6	-	-	-	-	51.1	3.7	-	-
1968	-	-	51.8	1.4	-	-	-	-	52.3	1.0	-	-	-	-	53.0	1.3	-	-	-	-	54.0	1.9	-	-
1969	-	-	54.4	0.7	-	-	-	-	55.6	2.2	-	-	-	-	56.0	0.7	-	-	-	-	57.5	2.7	-	-
1970	-	-	57.6	0.2	-	-	-	-	58.6	1.7	-	-	-	-	58.5	-0.2	-	-	-	-	59.6	1.9	-	-
1971	-	-	59.6	0.0	-	-	-	-	60.9	2.2	-	-	-	-	60.5	-0.7	-	-	-	-	61.1	1.0	-	-
1972	-	-	61.1	0.0	-	-	-	-	61.6	0.8	-	-	-	-	61.5	-0.2	-	-	-	-	62.3	1.3	-	-
1973	-	-	62.2	-0.2	-	-	-	-	63.7	2.4	-	-	-	-	64.6	1.4	-	-	-	-	67.2	4.0	-	-
1974	-	-	68.5	1.9	-	-	-	-	69.3	1.2	-	-	-	-	71.0	2.5	-	-	-	-	73.3	3.2	-	-
1975	-	-	71.8	-2.0	-	-	-	-	72.2	0.6	-	-	-	-	72.0	-0.3	-	-	-	-	72.7	1.0	-	-
1976	-	-	72.3	-0.6	-	-	-	-	73.0	1.0	-	-	-	-	74.0	1.4	-	-	-	-	76.3	3.1	-	-
1977	-	-	75.8	-0.7	-	-	-	-	77.3	2.0	-	-	-	-	79.0	2.2	-	-	-	-	80.4	1.8	-	-
1978	-	-	78.5	-2.4	-	-	79.5	1.3	-	-	79.9	0.5	-	-	81.2	1.6	-	-	82.9	2.1	-	-	83.1	0.2
1979	-	-	83.6	0.6	-	-	83.2	-0.5	-	-	81.5	-2.0	-	-	83.3	2.2	-	-	85.3	2.4	-	-	85.7	0.5
1980	-	-	85.5	-0.2	-	-	86.9	1.6	-	-	85.3	-1.8	-	-	86.7	1.6	-	-	89.1	2.8	-	-	89.9	0.9
1981	-	-	91.1	1.3	-	-	92.8	1.9	-	-	92.3	-0.5	-	-	92.3	0.0	-	-	95.3	3.3	-	-	97.5	2.3
1982	-	-	97.6	0.1	-	-	97.3	-0.3	-	-	98.3	1.0	-	-	101.8	3.6	-	-	101.3	-0.5	-	-	99.7	-1.6
1983	-	-	101.0	1.3	-	-	97.7	-3.3	-	-	98.6	0.9	-	-	99.2	0.6	-	-	100.0	0.8	-	-	99.3	-0.7
1984	-	-	101.8	2.5	-	-	98.3	-3.4	-	-	101.4	3.2	-	-	103.4	2.0	-	-	102.7	-0.7	-	-	102.1	-0.6
1985	-	-	102.6	0.5	-	-	103.9	1.3	-	-	102.2	-1.6	-	-	107.8	5.5	-	-	109.1	1.2	-	-	105.3	-3.5
1986	-	-	104.9	-0.4	-	-	102.1	-2.7	-	-	100.5	-1.6	-	-	106.4	5.9	-	-	105.8	-0.6	103.8	-1.9	99.7	-3.9
1987	98.2	-1.5	-	-	105.9	7.8	-	-	104.6	-1.2	-	-	105.8	1.1	-	-	121.8	15.1	-	-	116.6	-4.3	-	-
1988	107.3	-8.0	-	-	111.5	3.9	-	-	112.4	0.8	-	-	108.4	-3.6	-	-	101.3	-6.5	-	-	100.0	-1.3	-	-
1989	92.0	-8.0	-	-	118.5	28.8	-	-	119.8	1.1	-	-	114.0	-4.8	-	-	109.9	-3.6	-	-	107.9	-1.8	-	-
1990	102.2	-5.3	-	-	127.3	24.6	-	-	126.3	-0.8	-	-	114.2	-9.6	-	-	115.2	0.9	-	-	114.7	-0.4	-	-
1991	112.2	-2.2	-	-	124.2	10.7	-	-	121.9	-1.9	-	-	114.9	-5.7	-	-	125.7	9.4	-	-	127.1	1.1	-	-
1992	120.9	-4.9	-	-	128.4	6.2	-	-	122.9	-4.3	-	-	116.7	-5.0	-	-	125.7	7.7	-	-	121.2	-3.6	-	-
1993	116.9	-3.5	-	-	119.5	2.2	-	-	125.3	4.9	-	-	126.3	0.8	-	-	128.0	1.3	-	-	127.2	-0.6	-	-

Source: U.S. Department of Labor, Bureau of Labor Statistics, Division of Consumer Prices and Price Indexes. - indicates no data collected for period.

Cleveland, OH
Consumer Price Index - All Urban Consumers
Base 1982-1984 = 100
Transportation

For 1947-1993. Columns headed % show percentile change in the index from the previous period for which an index is available.

Year	Jan Index	%	Feb Index	%	Mar Index	%	Apr Index	%	May Index	%	Jun Index	%	Jul Index	%	Aug Index	%	Sep Index	%	Oct Index	%	Nov Index	%	Dec Index	%
1947	18.3	-	18.3	0.0	18.6	1.6	18.7	0.5	18.6	-0.5	18.6	0.0	-	-	18.9	1.6	-	-	-	-	19.5	3.2	-	-
1948	-	-	20.7	6.2	-	-	-	-	20.8	0.5	-	-	-	-	22.8	9.6	-	-	-	-	22.9	0.4	-	-
1949	-	-	23.1	0.9	-	-	-	-	23.2	0.4	-	-	-	-	23.1	-0.4	-	-	-	-	23.1	0.0	-	-
1950	-	-	22.8	-1.3	-	-	-	-	22.7	-0.4	-	-	-	-	23.4	3.1	-	-	-	-	23.5	0.4	-	-
1951	-	-	23.7	0.9	-	-	-	-	23.9	0.8	-	-	-	-	24.9	4.2	-	-	-	-	25.6	2.8	-	-
1952	-	-	26.0	1.6	-	-	-	-	26.0	0.0	-	-	-	-	26.0	0.0	-	-	-	-	26.0	0.0	-	-
1953	-	-	26.1	0.4	-	-	-	-	26.2	0.4	-	-	-	-	26.6	1.5	-	-	-	-	26.4	-0.8	-	-
1954	-	-	26.1	-1.1	-	-	-	-	26.0	-0.4	-	-	-	-	25.0	-3.8	-	-	-	-	25.9	3.6	-	-
1955	-	-	25.4	-1.9	-	-	-	-	25.0	-1.6	-	-	-	-	25.4	1.6	-	-	-	-	26.5	4.3	-	-
1956	-	-	26.0	-1.9	-	-	-	-	26.1	0.4	-	-	-	-	26.7	2.3	-	-	-	-	27.8	4.1	-	-
1957	-	-	28.1	1.1	-	-	-	-	28.1	0.0	-	-	-	-	28.6	1.8	-	-	-	-	29.4	2.8	-	-
1958	-	-	28.7	-2.4	-	-	-	-	28.9	0.7	-	-	-	-	29.0	0.3	-	-	-	-	29.4	1.4	-	-
1959	-	-	29.6	0.7	-	-	-	-	29.7	0.3	-	-	-	-	30.3	2.0	-	-	-	-	30.7	1.3	-	-
1960	-	-	30.4	-1.0	-	-	-	-	30.2	-0.7	-	-	-	-	30.1	-0.3	-	-	-	-	30.5	1.3	-	-
1961	-	-	30.5	0.0	-	-	-	-	30.6	0.3	-	-	-	-	31.3	2.3	-	-	-	-	31.4	0.3	-	-
1962	-	-	31.1	-1.0	-	-	-	-	31.4	1.0	-	-	-	-	31.5	0.3	-	-	-	-	31.5	0.0	-	-
1963	-	-	31.3	-0.6	-	-	-	-	31.3	0.0	-	-	-	-	31.6	1.0	-	-	-	-	31.9	0.9	-	-
1964	-	-	31.9	0.0	-	-	-	-	32.0	0.3	-	-	-	-	32.0	0.0	-	-	-	-	32.4	1.3	-	-
1965	-	-	32.5	0.3	-	-	-	-	32.8	0.9	-	-	-	-	32.5	-0.9	-	-	-	-	32.7	0.6	-	-
1966	-	-	32.5	-0.6	-	-	-	-	33.0	1.5	-	-	-	-	32.9	-0.3	-	-	-	-	33.2	0.9	-	-
1967	-	-	33.2	0.0	-	-	-	-	33.4	0.6	-	-	-	-	34.0	1.8	-	-	-	-	34.9	2.6	-	-
1968	-	-	35.2	0.9	-	-	-	-	35.3	0.3	-	-	-	-	35.6	0.8	-	-	-	-	36.3	2.0	-	-
1969	-	-	35.9	-1.1	-	-	-	-	37.0	3.1	-	-	-	-	37.1	0.3	-	-	-	-	38.0	2.4	-	-
1970	-	-	38.4	1.1	-	-	-	-	38.8	1.0	-	-	-	-	39.2	1.0	-	-	-	-	41.9	6.9	-	-
1971	-	-	42.1	0.5	-	-	-	-	42.3	0.5	-	-	-	-	42.4	0.2	-	-	-	-	42.1	-0.7	-	-
1972	-	-	42.4	0.7	-	-	-	-	42.8	0.9	-	-	-	-	42.9	0.2	-	-	-	-	42.9	0.0	-	-
1973	-	-	43.1	0.5	-	-	-	-	44.0	2.1	-	-	-	-	44.2	0.5	-	-	-	-	44.8	1.4	-	-
1974	-	-	47.2	5.4	-	-	-	-	49.9	5.7	-	-	-	-	50.2	0.6	-	-	-	-	50.7	1.0	-	-
1975	-	-	50.7	0.0	-	-	-	-	51.9	2.4	-	-	-	-	53.5	3.1	-	-	-	-	52.1	-2.6	-	-
1976	-	-	52.2	0.2	-	-	-	-	53.7	2.9	-	-	-	-	55.5	3.4	-	-	-	-	56.2	1.3	-	-
1977	-	-	56.4	0.4	-	-	-	-	57.9	2.7	-	-	-	-	58.0	0.2	-	-	-	-	58.7	1.2	-	-
1978	-	-	58.8	0.2	-	-	59.6	1.4	-	-	60.9	2.2	-	-	61.8	1.5	-	-	62.1	0.5	-	-	62.8	1.1
1979	-	-	64.3	2.4	-	-	66.6	3.6	-	-	68.8	3.3	-	-	71.1	3.3	-	-	72.7	2.3	-	-	74.4	2.3
1980	-	-	77.4	4.0	-	-	79.5	2.7	-	-	80.7	1.5	-	-	82.4	2.1	-	-	82.9	0.6	-	-	85.4	3.0
1981	-	-	88.4	3.5	-	-	90.1	1.9	-	-	91.4	1.4	-	-	93.4	2.2	-	-	95.3	2.0	-	-	96.2	0.9
1982	-	-	95.1	-1.1	-	-	94.2	-0.9	-	-	97.2	3.2	-	-	99.1	2.0	-	-	98.0	-1.1	-	-	98.4	0.4
1983	-	-	96.0	-2.4	-	-	97.1	1.1	-	-	98.9	1.9	-	-	101.3	2.4	-	-	102.5	1.2	-	-	102.5	0.0
1984	-	-	101.8	-0.7	-	-	102.7	0.9	-	-	104.3	1.6	-	-	103.8	-0.5	-	-	104.8	1.0	-	-	104.7	-0.1
1985	-	-	103.5	-1.1	-	-	106.0	2.4	-	-	106.1	0.1	-	-	105.4	-0.7	-	-	106.2	0.8	-	-	107.2	0.9
1986	-	-	105.0	-2.1	-	-	99.5	-5.2	-	-	101.7	2.2	-	-	99.0	-2.7	-	-	99.6	0.6	100.3	0.7	100.9	0.6
1987	102.3	1.4	-	-	101.9	-0.4	-	-	103.0	1.1	-	-	104.5	1.5	-	-	104.7	0.2	-	-	106.4	1.6	-	-
1988	105.5	-0.8	-	-	103.7	-1.7	-	-	107.6	3.8	-	-	107.8	0.2	-	-	109.1	1.2	-	-	109.4	0.3	-	-
1989	109.3	-0.1	-	-	110.5	1.1	-	-	116.1	5.1	-	-	113.8	-2.0	-	-	111.9	-1.7	-	-	114.3	2.1	-	-
1990	117.0	2.4	-	-	114.7	-2.0	-	-	116.1	1.2	-	-	116.5	0.3	-	-	122.5	5.2	-	-	128.1	4.6	-	-
1991	123.9	-3.3	-	-	121.6	-1.9	-	-	122.7	0.9	-	-	123.1	0.3	-	-	123.1	0.0	-	-	124.7	1.3	-	-

[Continued]

Cleveland, OH
Consumer Price Index - All Urban Consumers
Base 1982-1984 = 100
Transportation
[Continued]

For 1947-1993. Columns headed % show percentile change in the index from the previous period for which an index is available.

Year	Jan		Feb		Mar		Apr		May		Jun		Jul		Aug		Sep		Oct		Nov		Dec	
	Index	%	Index	%	Index	%	Index	%	Index	%	Index	%	Index	%	Index	%	Index	%	Index	%	Index	%	Index	%
1992	122.0	-2.2	-	-	123.1	0.9	-	-	124.4	1.1	-	-	124.9	0.4	-	-	123.7	-1.0	-	-	126.6	2.3	-	-
1993	122.8	-3.0	-	-	123.3	0.4	-	-	125.9	2.1	-	-	126.1	0.2	-	-	124.7	-1.1	-	-	126.5	1.4	-	-

Source: U.S. Department of Labor, Bureau of Labor Statistics, Division of Consumer Prices and Price Indexes. - indicates no data collected for period.

Cleveland, OH
Consumer Price Index - Urban Wage Earners
Base 1982-1984 = 100
Transportation

For 1947-1993. Columns headed % show percentile change in the index from the previous period for which an index is available.

Year	Jan Index	%	Feb Index	%	Mar Index	%	Apr Index	%	May Index	%	Jun Index	%	Jul Index	%	Aug Index	%	Sep Index	%	Oct Index	%	Nov Index	%	Dec Index	%
1947	18.6	-	18.6	0.0	18.8	1.1	18.9	0.5	18.8	-0.5	18.8	0.0	-	-	19.1	1.6	-	-	-	-	19.7	3.1	-	-
1948	-		20.9	6.1	-		-		21.0	0.5	-		-		23.1	10.0	-		-		23.1	0.0	-	
1949	-		23.4	1.3	-		-		23.4	0.0	-		-		23.4	0.0	-		-		23.4	0.0	-	
1950	-		23.1	-1.3	-		-		23.0	-0.4	-		-		23.7	3.0	-		-		23.8	0.4	-	
1951	-		24.0	0.8	-		-		24.2	0.8	-		-		25.2	4.1	-		-		26.0	3.2	-	
1952	-		26.3	1.2	-		-		26.3	0.0	-		-		26.3	0.0	-		-		26.4	0.4	-	
1953	-		26.5	0.4	-		-		26.5	0.0	-		-		26.9	1.5	-		-		26.7	-0.7	-	
1954	-		26.5	-0.7	-		-		26.4	-0.4	-		-		25.3	-4.2	-		-		26.2	3.6	-	
1955	-		25.7	-1.9	-		-		25.3	-1.6	-		-		25.7	1.6	-		-		26.8	4.3	-	
1956	-		26.3	-1.9	-		-		26.4	0.4	-		-		27.0	2.3	-		-		28.1	4.1	-	
1957	-		28.4	1.1	-		-		28.4	0.0	-		-		28.9	1.8	-		-		29.7	2.8	-	
1958	-		29.1	-2.0	-		-		29.2	0.3	-		-		29.3	0.3	-		-		29.8	1.7	-	
1959	-		30.0	0.7	-		-		30.0	0.0	-		-		30.7	2.3	-		-		31.1	1.3	-	
1960	-		30.7	-1.3	-		-		30.6	-0.3	-		-		30.5	-0.3	-		-		30.8	1.0	-	
1961	-		30.9	0.3	-		-		31.0	0.3	-		-		31.7	2.3	-		-		31.8	0.3	-	
1962	-		31.5	-0.9	-		-		31.8	1.0	-		-		31.9	0.3	-		-		31.9	0.0	-	
1963	-		31.7	-0.6	-		-		31.7	0.0	-		-		32.0	0.9	-		-		32.3	0.9	-	
1964	-		32.3	0.0	-		-		32.4	0.3	-		-		32.4	0.0	-		-		32.8	1.2	-	
1965	-		32.9	0.3	-		-		33.2	0.9	-		-		32.9	-0.9	-		-		33.1	0.6	-	
1966	-		32.9	-0.6	-		-		33.4	1.5	-		-		33.3	-0.3	-		-		33.6	0.9	-	
1967	-		33.6	0.0	-		-		33.8	0.6	-		-		34.4	1.8	-		-		35.4	2.9	-	
1968	-		35.6	0.6	-		-		35.7	0.3	-		-		36.0	0.8	-		-		36.7	1.9	-	
1969	-		36.4	-0.8	-		-		37.5	3.0	-		-		37.6	0.3	-		-		38.5	2.4	-	
1970	-		38.9	1.0	-		-		39.2	0.8	-		-		39.7	1.3	-		-		42.4	6.8	-	
1971	-		42.6	0.5	-		-		42.8	0.5	-		-		42.9	0.2	-		-		42.6	-0.7	-	
1972	-		42.9	0.7	-		-		43.3	0.9	-		-		43.5	0.5	-		-		43.4	-0.2	-	
1973	-		43.6	0.5	-		-		44.5	2.1	-		-		44.7	0.4	-		-		45.3	1.3	-	
1974	-		47.8	5.5	-		-		50.5	5.6	-		-		50.8	0.6	-		-		51.4	1.2	-	
1975	-		51.3	-0.2	-		-		52.6	2.5	-		-		54.2	3.0	-		-		52.8	-2.6	-	
1976	-		52.9	0.2	-		-		54.3	2.6	-		-		56.2	3.5	-		-		56.9	1.2	-	
1977	-		57.1	0.4	-		-		58.6	2.6	-		-		58.7	0.2	-		-		59.5	1.4	-	
1978	-		59.5	0.0	-		60.3	1.3	-		61.9	2.7	-		62.9	1.6	-		62.9	0.0	-		63.5	1.0
1979	-		65.5	3.1	-		68.1	4.0	-		70.5	3.5	-		72.7	3.1	-		74.4	2.3	-		75.5	1.5
1980	-		79.0	4.6	-		80.6	2.0	-		82.3	2.1	-		83.7	1.7	-		84.1	0.5	-		86.0	2.3
1981	-		89.6	4.2	-		90.9	1.5	-		91.6	0.8	-		93.7	2.3	-		95.3	1.7	-		95.9	0.6
1982	-		94.7	-1.3	-		93.6	-1.2	-		97.0	3.6	-		99.1	2.2	-		98.2	-0.9	-		98.5	0.3
1983	-		96.0	-2.5	-		97.1	1.1	-		99.2	2.2	-		101.4	2.2	-		102.5	1.1	-		102.5	0.0
1984	-		101.8	-0.7	-		102.8	1.0	-		104.5	1.7	-		104.0	-0.5	-		104.8	0.8	-		104.6	-0.2
1985	-		103.3	-1.2	-		106.1	2.7	-		106.2	0.1	-		105.4	-0.8	-		105.9	0.5	-		107.1	1.1
1986	-		104.4	-2.5	-		98.3	-5.8	-		100.7	2.4	-		97.6	-3.1	-		98.1	0.5	98.8	0.7	99.4	0.6
1987	100.6	1.2	-		100.2	-0.4	-		101.3	1.1	-		102.6	1.3	-		102.6	0.0	-		104.5	1.9	-	
1988	103.8	-0.7	-		101.9	-1.8	-		105.5	3.5	-		105.6	0.1	-		107.0	1.3	-		107.5	0.5	-	
1989	107.4	-0.1	-		108.5	1.0	-		113.7	4.8	-		111.4	-2.0	-		109.5	-1.7	-		112.1	2.4	-	
1990	114.6	2.2	-		112.2	-2.1	-		113.6	1.2	-		114.0	0.4	-		119.3	4.6	-		124.4	4.3	-	
1991	120.7	-3.0	-		118.6	-1.7	-		119.7	0.9	-		120.1	0.3	-		120.0	-0.1	-		121.4	1.2	-	

[Continued]

Cleveland, OH
Consumer Price Index - Urban Wage Earners
Base 1982-1984 = 100
Transportation
[Continued]

For 1947-1993. Columns headed % show percentile change in the index from the previous period for which an index is available.

Year	Jan Index	Jan %	Feb Index	Feb %	Mar Index	Mar %	Apr Index	Apr %	May Index	May %	Jun Index	Jun %	Jul Index	Jul %	Aug Index	Aug %	Sep Index	Sep %	Oct Index	Oct %	Nov Index	Nov %	Dec Index	Dec %
1992	118.8	-2.1	-	-	119.6	0.7	-	-	121.0	1.2	-	-	121.6	0.5	-	-	120.6	-0.8	-	-	123.1	2.1	-	-
1993	119.6	-2.8	-	-	119.7	0.1	-	-	122.4	2.3	-	-	122.8	0.3	-	-	121.7	-0.9	-	-	123.4	1.4	-	-

Source: U.S. Department of Labor, Bureau of Labor Statistics, Division of Consumer Prices and Price Indexes. - indicates no data collected for period.

Cleveland, OH

Consumer Price Index - All Urban Consumers

Base 1982-1984 = 100

Medical Care

For 1947-1993. Columns headed % show percentile change in the index from the previous period for which an index is available.

Year	Jan		Feb		Mar		Apr		May		Jun		Jul		Aug		Sep		Oct		Nov		Dec	
	Index	%	Index	%	Index	%	Index	%	Index	%	Index	%	Index	%	Index	%	Index	%	Index	%	Index	%	Index	%
1947	10.5	-	10.5	*0.0*	10.5	*0.0*	10.5	*0.0*	10.5	*0.0*	10.5	*0.0*	-	-	10.5	*0.0*	-	-	-	-	10.9	*3.8*	-	-
1948	-	-	11.0	*0.9*	-	-	-	-	11.2	*1.8*	-	-	-	-	11.2	*0.0*	-	-	-	-	11.5	*2.7*	-	-
1949	-	-	11.6	*0.9*	-	-	-	-	11.6	*0.0*	-	-	-	-	11.7	*0.9*	-	-	-	-	11.8	*0.9*	-	-
1950	-	-	11.8	*0.0*	-	-	-	-	11.8	*0.0*	-	-	-	-	11.7	*-0.8*	-	-	-	-	11.9	*1.7*	-	-
1951	-	-	12.2	*2.5*	-	-	-	-	12.6	*3.3*	-	-	-	-	12.6	*0.0*	-	-	-	-	13.2	*4.8*	-	-
1952	-	-	13.2	*0.0*	-	-	-	-	13.3	*0.8*	-	-	-	-	13.4	*0.8*	-	-	-	-	13.3	*-0.7*	-	-
1953	-	-	13.4	*0.8*	-	-	-	-	13.4	*0.0*	-	-	-	-	14.2	*6.0*	-	-	-	-	14.2	*0.0*	-	-
1954	-	-	14.4	*1.4*	-	-	-	-	14.5	*0.7*	-	-	-	-	14.5	*0.0*	-	-	-	-	14.6	*0.7*	-	-
1955	-	-	14.6	*0.0*	-	-	-	-	15.3	*4.8*	-	-	-	-	15.3	*0.0*	-	-	-	-	15.4	*0.7*	-	-
1956	-	-	15.4	*0.0*	-	-	-	-	16.3	*5.8*	-	-	-	-	16.3	*0.0*	-	-	-	-	16.3	*0.0*	-	-
1957	-	-	16.4	*0.6*	-	-	-	-	16.7	*1.8*	-	-	-	-	16.8	*0.6*	-	-	-	-	16.8	*0.0*	-	-
1958	-	-	17.0	*1.2*	-	-	-	-	17.1	*0.6*	-	-	-	-	17.1	*0.0*	-	-	-	-	17.2	*0.6*	-	-
1959	-	-	18.6	*8.1*	-	-	-	-	18.7	*0.5*	-	-	-	-	18.8	*0.5*	-	-	-	-	19.0	*1.1*	-	-
1960	-	-	19.0	*0.0*	-	-	-	-	19.3	*1.6*	-	-	-	-	19.4	*0.5*	-	-	-	-	19.4	*0.0*	-	-
1961	-	-	20.7	*6.7*	-	-	-	-	20.8	*0.5*	-	-	-	-	20.6	*-1.0*	-	-	-	-	20.7	*0.5*	-	-
1962	-	-	20.7	*0.0*	-	-	-	-	20.8	*0.5*	-	-	-	-	20.8	*0.0*	-	-	-	-	20.8	*0.0*	-	-
1963	-	-	20.8	*0.0*	-	-	-	-	22.1	*6.3*	-	-	-	-	22.2	*0.5*	-	-	-	-	22.3	*0.5*	-	-
1964	-	-	22.4	*0.4*	-	-	-	-	22.5	*0.4*	-	-	-	-	22.5	*0.0*	-	-	-	-	22.7	*0.9*	-	-
1965	-	-	23.1	*1.8*	-	-	-	-	23.2	*0.4*	-	-	-	-	23.2	*0.0*	-	-	-	-	23.3	*0.4*	-	-
1966	-	-	23.5	*0.9*	-	-	-	-	23.6	*0.4*	-	-	-	-	23.7	*0.4*	-	-	-	-	24.2	*2.1*	-	-
1967	-	-	24.4	*0.8*	-	-	-	-	25.1	*2.9*	-	-	-	-	25.4	*1.2*	-	-	-	-	25.7	*1.2*	-	-
1968	-	-	26.4	*2.7*	-	-	-	-	26.9	*1.9*	-	-	-	-	27.2	*1.1*	-	-	-	-	28.5	*4.8*	-	-
1969	-	-	29.4	*3.2*	-	-	-	-	30.3	*3.1*	-	-	-	-	31.2	*3.0*	-	-	-	-	31.4	*0.6*	-	-
1970	-	-	32.3	*2.9*	-	-	-	-	32.8	*1.5*	-	-	-	-	33.4	*1.8*	-	-	-	-	33.3	*-0.3*	-	-
1971	-	-	34.2	*2.7*	-	-	-	-	34.9	*2.0*	-	-	-	-	36.1	*3.4*	-	-	-	-	35.8	*-0.8*	-	-
1972	-	-	35.7	*-0.3*	-	-	-	-	36.0	*0.8*	-	-	-	-	36.5	*1.4*	-	-	-	-	36.8	*0.8*	-	-
1973	-	-	37.4	*1.6*	-	-	-	-	37.7	*0.8*	-	-	-	-	37.9	*0.5*	-	-	-	-	38.6	*1.8*	-	-
1974	-	-	40.2	*4.1*	-	-	-	-	40.7	*1.2*	-	-	-	-	41.9	*2.9*	-	-	-	-	42.4	*1.2*	-	-
1975	-	-	45.5	*7.3*	-	-	-	-	46.1	*1.3*	-	-	-	-	45.8	*-0.7*	-	-	-	-	46.9	*2.4*	-	-
1976	-	-	49.5	*5.5*	-	-	-	-	50.2	*1.4*	-	-	-	-	50.9	*1.4*	-	-	-	-	51.9	*2.0*	-	-
1977	-	-	55.0	*6.0*	-	-	-	-	56.4	*2.5*	-	-	-	-	57.4	*1.8*	-	-	-	-	58.3	*1.6*	-	-
1978	-	-	61.0	*4.6*	-	-	61.2	*0.3*	-	-	61.9	*1.1*	-	-	62.4	*0.8*	-	-	62.7	*0.5*	-	-	63.2	*0.8*
1979	-	-	64.7	*2.4*	-	-	65.0	*0.5*	-	-	66.0	*1.5*	-	-	66.3	*0.5*	-	-	66.8	*0.8*	-	-	68.6	*2.7*
1980	-	-	71.9	*4.8*	-	-	71.6	*-0.4*	-	-	72.1	*0.7*	-	-	73.4	*1.8*	-	-	73.9	*0.7*	-	-	74.9	*1.4*
1981	-	-	79.7	*6.4*	-	-	80.6	*1.1*	-	-	81.3	*0.9*	-	-	82.1	*1.0*	-	-	82.1	*0.0*	-	-	83.4	*1.6*
1982	-	-	87.9	*5.4*	-	-	90.8	*3.3*	-	-	91.4	*0.7*	-	-	92.5	*1.2*	-	-	94.1	*1.7*	-	-	95.0	*1.0*
1983	-	-	99.8	*5.1*	-	-	101.3	*1.5*	-	-	101.5	*0.2*	-	-	101.9	*0.4*	-	-	101.7	*-0.2*	-	-	102.7	*1.0*
1984	-	-	106.6	*3.8*	-	-	107.3	*0.7*	-	-	108.1	*0.7*	-	-	107.8	*-0.3*	-	-	107.8	*0.0*	-	-	108.1	*0.3*
1985	-	-	110.4	*2.1*	-	-	111.1	*0.6*	-	-	111.5	*0.4*	-	-	112.0	*0.4*	-	-	112.5	*0.4*	-	-	116.0	*3.1*
1986	-	-	119.0	*2.6*	-	-	119.9	*0.8*	-	-	123.5	*3.0*	-	-	124.1	*0.5*	-	-	124.4	*0.2*	124.9	*0.4*	124.8	*-0.1*
1987	127.4	*2.1*	-	-	127.7	*0.2*	-	-	128.0	*0.2*	-	-	127.7	*-0.2*	-	-	129.4	*1.3*	-	-	129.8	*0.3*	-	-
1988	132.4	*2.0*	-	-	132.9	*0.4*	-	-	133.1	*0.2*	-	-	133.8	*0.5*	-	-	137.7	*2.9*	-	-	137.5	*-0.1*	-	-
1989	140.1	*1.9*	-	-	141.1	*0.7*	-	-	141.7	*0.4*	-	-	144.3	*1.8*	-	-	144.6	*0.2*	-	-	146.6	*1.4*	-	-
1990	150.2	*2.5*	-	-	151.7	*1.0*	-	-	153.4	*1.1*	-	-	158.5	*3.3*	-	-	159.4	*0.6*	-	-	162.8	*2.1*	-	-
1991	166.0	*2.0*	-	-	168.8	*1.7*	-	-	171.4	*1.5*	-	-	171.9	*0.3*	-	-	174.2	*1.3*	-	-	175.1	*0.5*	-	-

[Continued]

Cleveland, OH
Consumer Price Index - All Urban Consumers
Base 1982-1984 = 100
Medical Care
[Continued]

For 1947-1993. Columns headed % show percentile change in the index from the previous period for which an index is available.

Year	Jan Index	%	Feb Index	%	Mar Index	%	Apr Index	%	May Index	%	Jun Index	%	Jul Index	%	Aug Index	%	Sep Index	%	Oct Index	%	Nov Index	%	Dec Index	%
1992	176.5	0.8	-	-	177.8	0.7	-	-	178.5	0.4	-	-	179.0	0.3	-	-	178.4	-0.3	-	-	179.0	0.3	-	-
1993	185.5	3.6	-	-	185.1	-0.2	-	-	186.0	0.5	-	-	188.0	1.1	-	-	188.2	0.1	-	-	188.9	0.4	-	-

Source: U.S. Department of Labor, Bureau of Labor Statistics, Division of Consumer Prices and Price Indexes. - indicates no data collected for period.

Cleveland, OH
Consumer Price Index - Urban Wage Earners
Base 1982-1984 = 100
Medical Care

For 1947-1993. Columns headed % show percentile change in the index from the previous period for which an index is available.

Year	Jan Index	%	Feb Index	%	Mar Index	%	Apr Index	%	May Index	%	Jun Index	%	Jul Index	%	Aug Index	%	Sep Index	%	Oct Index	%	Nov Index	%	Dec Index	%
1947	10.3	-	10.3	0.0	10.3	0.0	10.3	0.0	10.3	0.0	10.3	0.0	-	-	10.4	1.0	-	-	-	-	10.8	3.8	-	-
1948	-	-	10.8	0.0	-	-	-	-	11.0	1.9	-	-	-	-	11.0	0.0	-	-	-	-	11.4	3.6	-	-
1949	-	-	11.4	0.0	-	-	-	-	11.4	0.0	-	-	-	-	11.5	0.9	-	-	-	-	11.6	0.9	-	-
1950	-	-	11.6	0.0	-	-	-	-	11.6	0.0	-	-	-	-	11.5	-0.9	-	-	-	-	11.7	1.7	-	-
1951	-	-	12.0	2.6	-	-	-	-	12.4	3.3	-	-	-	-	12.4	0.0	-	-	-	-	13.0	4.8	-	-
1952	-	-	13.0	0.0	-	-	-	-	13.0	0.0	-	-	-	-	13.1	0.8	-	-	-	-	13.1	0.0	-	-
1953	-	-	13.1	0.0	-	-	-	-	13.2	0.8	-	-	-	-	13.9	5.3	-	-	-	-	14.0	0.7	-	-
1954	-	-	14.2	1.4	-	-	-	-	14.2	0.0	-	-	-	-	14.2	0.0	-	-	-	-	14.4	1.4	-	-
1955	-	-	14.4	0.0	-	-	-	-	15.0	4.2	-	-	-	-	15.0	0.0	-	-	-	-	15.2	1.3	-	-
1956	-	-	15.2	0.0	-	-	-	-	16.0	5.3	-	-	-	-	16.1	0.6	-	-	-	-	16.1	0.0	-	-
1957	-	-	16.2	0.6	-	-	-	-	16.4	1.2	-	-	-	-	16.6	1.2	-	-	-	-	16.6	0.0	-	-
1958	-	-	16.8	1.2	-	-	-	-	16.8	0.0	-	-	-	-	16.8	0.0	-	-	-	-	16.9	0.6	-	-
1959	-	-	18.3	8.3	-	-	-	-	18.4	0.5	-	-	-	-	18.5	0.5	-	-	-	-	18.7	1.1	-	-
1960	-	-	18.7	0.0	-	-	-	-	19.0	1.6	-	-	-	-	19.1	0.5	-	-	-	-	19.1	0.0	-	-
1961	-	-	20.4	6.8	-	-	-	-	20.4	0.0	-	-	-	-	20.3	-0.5	-	-	-	-	20.3	0.0	-	-
1962	-	-	20.4	0.5	-	-	-	-	20.4	0.0	-	-	-	-	20.4	0.0	-	-	-	-	20.4	0.0	-	-
1963	-	-	20.5	0.5	-	-	-	-	21.8	6.3	-	-	-	-	21.9	0.5	-	-	-	-	21.9	0.0	-	-
1964	-	-	22.0	0.5	-	-	-	-	22.1	0.5	-	-	-	-	22.1	0.0	-	-	-	-	22.3	0.9	-	-
1965	-	-	22.7	1.8	-	-	-	-	22.8	0.4	-	-	-	-	22.8	0.0	-	-	-	-	22.9	0.4	-	-
1966	-	-	23.1	0.9	-	-	-	-	23.2	0.4	-	-	-	-	23.3	0.4	-	-	-	-	23.8	2.1	-	-
1967	-	-	24.0	0.8	-	-	-	-	24.7	2.9	-	-	-	-	25.0	1.2	-	-	-	-	25.2	0.8	-	-
1968	-	-	26.0	3.2	-	-	-	-	26.5	1.9	-	-	-	-	26.7	0.8	-	-	-	-	28.1	5.2	-	-
1969	-	-	28.9	2.8	-	-	-	-	29.8	3.1	-	-	-	-	30.7	3.0	-	-	-	-	30.8	0.3	-	-
1970	-	-	31.8	3.2	-	-	-	-	32.2	1.3	-	-	-	-	32.9	2.2	-	-	-	-	32.7	-0.6	-	-
1971	-	-	33.6	2.8	-	-	-	-	34.3	2.1	-	-	-	-	35.5	3.5	-	-	-	-	35.2	-0.8	-	-
1972	-	-	35.1	-0.3	-	-	-	-	35.4	0.9	-	-	-	-	35.9	1.4	-	-	-	-	36.2	0.8	-	-
1973	-	-	36.8	1.7	-	-	-	-	37.1	0.8	-	-	-	-	37.3	0.5	-	-	-	-	38.0	1.9	-	-
1974	-	-	39.5	3.9	-	-	-	-	40.0	1.3	-	-	-	-	41.2	3.0	-	-	-	-	41.7	1.2	-	-
1975	-	-	44.8	7.4	-	-	-	-	45.4	1.3	-	-	-	-	45.1	-0.7	-	-	-	-	46.1	2.2	-	-
1976	-	-	48.7	5.6	-	-	-	-	49.3	1.2	-	-	-	-	50.0	1.4	-	-	-	-	51.0	2.0	-	-
1977	-	-	54.1	6.1	-	-	-	-	55.4	2.4	-	-	-	-	56.4	1.8	-	-	-	-	57.3	1.6	-	-
1978	-	-	60.0	4.7	-	-	60.1	0.2	-	-	61.0	1.5	-	-	61.4	0.7	-	-	62.4	1.6	-	-	63.4	1.6
1979	-	-	65.0	2.5	-	-	65.2	0.3	-	-	65.9	1.1	-	-	67.1	1.8	-	-	67.8	1.0	-	-	69.5	2.5
1980	-	-	72.6	4.5	-	-	72.7	0.1	-	-	73.6	1.2	-	-	74.5	1.2	-	-	74.5	0.0	-	-	75.6	1.5
1981	-	-	80.6	6.6	-	-	80.8	0.2	-	-	80.9	0.1	-	-	81.8	1.1	-	-	82.7	1.1	-	-	83.9	1.5
1982	-	-	88.2	5.1	-	-	91.0	3.2	-	-	91.6	0.7	-	-	92.7	1.2	-	-	94.3	1.7	-	-	95.2	1.0
1983	-	-	100.0	5.0	-	-	101.3	1.3	-	-	101.5	0.2	-	-	101.7	0.2	-	-	101.6	-0.1	-	-	102.5	0.9
1984	-	-	106.4	3.8	-	-	107.1	0.7	-	-	107.9	0.7	-	-	107.5	-0.4	-	-	107.6	0.1	-	-	107.8	0.2
1985	-	-	110.0	2.0	-	-	110.6	0.5	-	-	111.0	0.4	-	-	111.6	0.5	-	-	112.0	0.4	-	-	115.3	2.9
1986	-	-	118.4	2.7	-	-	119.3	0.8	-	-	122.8	2.9	-	-	123.4	0.5	-	-	123.7	0.2	124.2	0.4	124.1	-0.1
1987	126.7	2.1	-	-	127.0	0.2	-	-	127.4	0.3	-	-	127.1	-0.2	-	-	128.8	1.3	-	-	129.0	0.2	-	-
1988	131.6	2.0	-	-	132.1	0.4	-	-	132.4	0.2	-	-	133.1	0.5	-	-	136.8	2.8	-	-	136.6	-0.1	-	-
1989	139.1	1.8	-	-	140.0	0.6	-	-	140.6	0.4	-	-	142.8	1.6	-	-	143.1	0.2	-	-	144.9	1.3	-	-
1990	148.3	2.3	-	-	149.6	0.9	-	-	151.0	0.9	-	-	156.8	3.8	-	-	157.5	0.4	-	-	160.8	2.1	-	-
1991	163.5	1.7	-	-	165.9	1.5	-	-	168.3	1.4	-	-	168.7	0.2	-	-	171.3	1.5	-	-	172.1	0.5	-	-

[Continued]

Cleveland, OH
Consumer Price Index - Urban Wage Earners
Base 1982-1984 = 100
Medical Care
[Continued]

For 1947-1993. Columns headed % show percentile change in the index from the previous period for which an index is available.

Year	Jan Index	%	Feb Index	%	Mar Index	%	Apr Index	%	May Index	%	Jun Index	%	Jul Index	%	Aug Index	%	Sep Index	%	Oct Index	%	Nov Index	%	Dec Index	%
1992	173.5	0.8	-	-	174.6	0.6	-	-	175.6	0.6	-	-	176.2	0.3	-	-	175.6	-0.3	-	-	176.1	0.3	-	-
1993	182.2	3.5	-	-	181.9	-0.2	-	-	182.7	0.4	-	-	185.0	1.3	-	-	185.0	0.0	-	-	185.7	0.4	-	-

Source: U.S. Department of Labor, Bureau of Labor Statistics, Division of Consumer Prices and Price Indexes. - indicates no data collected for period.

Cleveland, OH
Consumer Price Index - All Urban Consumers
Base 1982-1984 = 100
Entertainment

For 1975-1993. Columns headed % show percentile change in the index from the previous period for which an index is available.

Year	Jan Index	%	Feb Index	%	Mar Index	%	Apr Index	%	May Index	%	Jun Index	%	Jul Index	%	Aug Index	%	Sep Index	%	Oct Index	%	Nov Index	%	Dec Index	%
1975	-	-	-	-	-	-	-	-	-	-	-	-	-	-	-	-	-	-	-	-	65.8	-	-	-
1976	-	-	65.9	0.2	-	-	-	-	66.6	1.1	-	-	-	-	67.6	1.5	-	-	-	-	68.9	1.9	-	-
1977	-	-	69.8	1.3	-	-	-	-	70.5	1.0	-	-	-	-	70.3	-0.3	-	-	-	-	71.8	2.1	-	-
1978	-	-	73.2	1.9	-	-	74.0	1.1	-	-	73.6	-0.5	-	-	74.3	1.0	-	-	76.7	3.2	-	-	78.2	2.0
1979	-	-	77.9	-0.4	-	-	78.5	0.8	-	-	76.4	-2.7	-	-	77.8	1.8	-	-	80.8	3.9	-	-	81.5	0.9
1980	-	-	81.9	0.5	-	-	82.5	0.7	-	-	82.2	-0.4	-	-	84.2	2.4	-	-	85.9	2.0	-	-	86.4	0.6
1981	-	-	86.8	0.5	-	-	87.9	1.3	-	-	88.2	0.3	-	-	87.4	-0.9	-	-	90.8	3.9	-	-	91.7	1.0
1982	-	-	95.2	3.8	-	-	94.7	-0.5	-	-	95.1	0.4	-	-	95.8	0.7	-	-	97.3	1.6	-	-	97.2	-0.1
1983	-	-	98.9	1.7	-	-	98.7	-0.2	-	-	98.9	0.2	-	-	99.4	0.5	-	-	103.8	4.4	-	-	103.7	-0.1
1984	-	-	104.0	0.3	-	-	104.4	0.4	-	-	103.8	-0.6	-	-	102.4	-1.3	-	-	104.3	1.9	-	-	105.8	1.4
1985	-	-	104.1	-1.6	-	-	105.8	1.6	-	-	105.0	-0.8	-	-	106.5	1.4	-	-	111.0	4.2	-	-	110.7	-0.3
1986	-	-	113.7	2.7	-	-	113.7	0.0	-	-	113.9	0.2	-	-	114.1	0.2	-	-	116.5	2.1	114.5	-1.7	115.1	0.5
1987	114.5	-0.5	-	-	115.3	0.7	-	-	116.4	1.0	-	-	116.2	-0.2	-	-	116.1	-0.1	-	-	116.0	-0.1	-	-
1988	116.5	0.4	-	-	119.5	2.6	-	-	121.8	1.9	-	-	122.8	0.8	-	-	118.8	-3.3	-	-	117.1	-1.4	-	-
1989	128.0	9.3	-	-	126.8	-0.9	-	-	120.3	-5.1	-	-	129.3	7.5	-	-	128.4	-0.7	-	-	128.6	0.2	-	-
1990	131.7	2.4	-	-	132.9	0.9	-	-	132.7	-0.2	-	-	134.9	1.7	-	-	135.2	0.2	-	-	133.4	-1.3	-	-
1991	135.7	1.7	-	-	136.6	0.7	-	-	139.2	1.9	-	-	136.5	-1.9	-	-	142.5	4.4	-	-	140.1	-1.7	-	-
1992	139.8	-0.2	-	-	142.1	1.6	-	-	137.0	-3.6	-	-	138.5	1.1	-	-	139.7	0.9	-	-	140.4	0.5	-	-
1993	141.1	0.5	-	-	140.9	-0.1	-	-	142.9	1.4	-	-	140.2	-1.9	-	-	140.1	-0.1	-	-	151.2	7.9	-	-

Source: U.S. Department of Labor, Bureau of Labor Statistics, Division of Consumer Prices and Price Indexes. - indicates no data collected for period.

Cleveland, OH
Consumer Price Index - Urban Wage Earners
Base 1982-1984 = 100
Entertainment

For 1975-1993. Columns headed % show percentile change in the index from the previous period for which an index is available.

Year	Jan Index	%	Feb Index	%	Mar Index	%	Apr Index	%	May Index	%	Jun Index	%	Jul Index	%	Aug Index	%	Sep Index	%	Oct Index	%	Nov Index	%	Dec Index	%
1975	-	-	-	-	-	-	-	-	-	-	-	-	-	-	-	-	-	-	-	-	65.7	-	-	-
1976	-	-	65.9	0.3	-	-	-	-	66.5	0.9	-	-	-	-	67.5	1.5	-	-	-	-	68.9	2.1	-	-
1977	-	-	69.7	1.2	-	-	-	-	70.5	1.1	-	-	-	-	70.2	-0.4	-	-	-	-	71.8	2.3	-	-
1978	-	-	73.2	1.9	-	-	73.9	1.0	-	-	73.0	-1.2	-	-	73.5	0.7	-	-	74.9	1.9	-	-	76.2	1.7
1979	-	-	76.7	0.7	-	-	76.8	0.1	-	-	76.2	-0.8	-	-	78.0	2.4	-	-	80.9	3.7	-	-	81.6	0.9
1980	-	-	83.1	1.8	-	-	83.4	0.4	-	-	83.3	-0.1	-	-	84.3	1.2	-	-	86.0	2.0	-	-	86.5	0.6
1981	-	-	87.4	1.0	-	-	88.6	1.4	-	-	89.3	0.8	-	-	88.7	-0.7	-	-	90.8	2.4	-	-	92.3	1.7
1982	-	-	94.8	2.7	-	-	94.4	-0.4	-	-	94.8	0.4	-	-	95.5	0.7	-	-	96.9	1.5	-	-	96.6	-0.3
1983	-	-	98.6	2.1	-	-	98.4	-0.2	-	-	98.6	0.2	-	-	99.4	0.8	-	-	103.7	4.3	-	-	103.8	0.1
1984	-	-	104.2	0.4	-	-	104.9	0.7	-	-	104.4	-0.5	-	-	103.4	-1.0	-	-	105.0	1.5	-	-	106.1	1.0
1985	-	-	105.0	-1.0	-	-	106.4	1.3	-	-	105.2	-1.1	-	-	106.8	1.5	-	-	111.4	4.3	-	-	111.2	-0.2
1986	-	-	114.4	2.9	-	-	114.4	0.0	-	-	114.6	0.2	-	-	114.7	0.1	-	-	117.3	2.3	115.1	-1.9	115.6	0.4
1987	114.6	-0.9	-	-	115.4	0.7	-	-	116.6	1.0	-	-	116.0	-0.5	-	-	116.4	0.3	-	-	116.6	0.2	-	-
1988	117.0	0.3	-	-	120.1	2.6	-	-	122.6	2.1	-	-	123.5	0.7	-	-	119.7	-3.1	-	-	118.3	-1.2	-	-
1989	127.2	7.5	-	-	126.5	-0.6	-	-	120.0	-5.1	-	-	128.4	7.0	-	-	127.8	-0.5	-	-	118.3	0.0	-	-
1990	128.6	0.6	-	-	129.8	0.9	-	-	130.0	0.2	-	-	131.9	1.5	-	-	132.0	0.1	-	-	130.1	-1.4	-	-
1991	132.5	1.8	-	-	132.7	0.2	-	-	135.0	1.7	-	-	132.4	-1.9	-	-	138.1	4.3	-	-	135.7	-1.7	-	-
1992	135.0	-0.5	-	-	138.2	2.4	-	-	133.7	-3.3	-	-	135.1	1.0	-	-	136.9	1.3	-	-	137.3	0.3	-	-
1993	137.9	0.4	-	-	136.7	-0.9	-	-	137.9	0.9	-	-	137.2	-0.5	-	-	137.3	0.1	-	-	147.7	7.6	-	-

Source: U.S. Department of Labor, Bureau of Labor Statistics, Division of Consumer Prices and Price Indexes. - indicates no data collected for period.

Cleveland, OH

Consumer Price Index - All Urban Consumers
Base 1982-1984 = 100
Other Goods and Services

For 1975-1993. Columns headed % show percentile change in the index from the previous period for which an index is available.

Year	Jan		Feb		Mar		Apr		May		Jun		Jul		Aug		Sep		Oct		Nov		Dec	
	Index	%	Index	%	Index	%	Index	%	Index	%	Index	%	Index	%	Index	%	Index	%	Index	%	Index	%	Index	%
1975	-	-	-	-	-	-	-	-	-	-	-	-	-	-	-	-	-	-	-	-	56.3	-	-	-
1976	-	-	57.2	1.6	-	-	-	-	57.4	0.3	-	-	-	-	58.5	1.9	-	-	-	-	60.2	2.9	-	-
1977	-	-	60.6	0.7	-	-	-	-	61.5	1.5	-	-	-	-	61.6	0.2	-	-	-	-	63.3	2.8	-	-
1978	-	-	64.3	1.6	-	-	64.9	0.9	-	-	65.1	0.3	-	-	65.7	0.9	-	-	67.4	2.6	-	-	69.3	2.8
1979	-	-	69.7	0.6	-	-	69.7	0.0	-	-	69.9	0.3	-	-	70.8	1.3	-	-	73.9	4.4	-	-	73.6	-0.4
1980	-	-	74.9	1.8	-	-	75.4	0.7	-	-	75.5	0.1	-	-	76.1	0.8	-	-	79.4	4.3	-	-	80.9	1.9
1981	-	-	82.7	2.2	-	-	83.3	0.7	-	-	84.6	1.6	-	-	85.3	0.8	-	-	86.8	1.8	-	-	88.2	1.6
1982	-	-	90.3	2.4	-	-	91.5	1.3	-	-	90.6	-1.0	-	-	92.2	1.8	-	-	96.4	4.6	-	-	97.8	1.5
1983	-	-	99.1	1.3	-	-	99.1	0.0	-	-	99.6	0.5	-	-	100.7	1.1	-	-	102.9	2.2	-	-	103.5	0.6
1984	-	-	104.8	1.3	-	-	104.9	0.1	-	-	105.3	0.4	-	-	107.3	1.9	-	-	109.4	2.0	-	-	109.8	0.4
1985	-	-	109.4	-0.4	-	-	109.9	0.5	-	-	110.1	0.2	-	-	112.2	1.9	-	-	114.4	2.0	-	-	114.3	-0.1
1986	-	-	115.9	1.4	-	-	115.8	-0.1	-	-	116.2	0.3	-	-	117.1	0.8	-	-	119.2	1.8	119.1	-0.1	119.5	0.3
1987	120.9	1.2	-	-	120.7	-0.2	-	-	121.7	0.8	-	-	122.8	0.9	-	-	126.7	3.2	-	-	128.0	1.0	-	-
1988	129.4	1.1	-	-	129.3	-0.1	-	-	131.5	1.7	-	-	134.4	2.2	-	-	135.2	0.6	-	-	136.7	1.1	-	-
1989	137.3	0.4	-	-	137.4	0.1	-	-	139.4	1.5	-	-	140.2	0.6	-	-	144.9	3.4	-	-	144.9	0.0	-	-
1990	145.7	0.6	-	-	147.4	1.2	-	-	148.9	1.0	-	-	148.6	-0.2	-	-	152.0	2.3	-	-	152.5	0.3	-	-
1991	154.9	1.6	-	-	156.5	1.0	-	-	157.7	0.8	-	-	159.5	1.1	-	-	163.8	2.7	-	-	165.4	1.0	-	-
1992	166.1	0.4	-	-	167.5	0.8	-	-	168.5	0.6	-	-	168.6	0.1	-	-	173.9	3.1	-	-	174.1	0.1	-	-
1993	177.0	1.7	-	-	178.3	0.7	-	-	179.3	0.6	-	-	183.4	2.3	-	-	180.8	-1.4	-	-	181.3	0.3	-	-

Source: U.S. Department of Labor, Bureau of Labor Statistics, Division of Consumer Prices and Price Indexes. - indicates no data collected for period.

Cleveland, OH
Consumer Price Index - Urban Wage Earners
Base 1982-1984 = 100
Other Goods and Services

For 1975-1993. Columns headed % show percentile change in the index from the previous period for which an index is available.

Year	Jan		Feb		Mar		Apr		May		Jun		Jul		Aug		Sep		Oct		Nov		Dec	
	Index	%	Index	%	Index	%	Index	%	Index	%	Index	%	Index	%	Index	%	Index	%	Index	%	Index	%	Index	%
1975	-	-	-	-	-	-	-	-	-	-	-	-	-	-	-	-	-	-	-	-	55.2	-	-	-
1976	-	-	56.1	1.6	-	-	-	-	56.3	0.4	-	-	-	-	57.4	2.0	-	-	-	-	59.1	3.0	-	-
1977	-	-	59.5	0.7	-	-	-	-	60.3	1.3	-	-	-	-	60.4	0.2	-	-	-	-	62.1	2.8	-	-
1978	-	-	63.1	1.6	-	-	63.2	0.2	-	-	63.9	1.1	-	-	64.8	1.4	-	-	66.6	2.8	-	-	67.6	1.5
1979	-	-	68.1	0.7	-	-	68.5	0.6	-	-	68.9	0.6	-	-	69.7	1.2	-	-	72.3	3.7	-	-	-	-
1980	-	-	74.0	2.4	-	-	74.9	1.2	-	-	75.4	0.7	-	-	76.1	0.9	-	-	78.6	3.3	-	-	79.5	1.1
1981	-	-	82.4	3.6	-	-	83.1	0.8	-	-	84.8	2.0	-	-	84.2	-0.7	-	-	85.7	1.8	-	-	87.9	2.6
1982	-	-	89.8	2.2	-	-	91.4	1.8	-	-	90.6	-0.9	-	-	91.9	1.4	-	-	95.9	4.4	-	-	97.7	1.9
1983	-	-	99.1	1.4	-	-	99.3	0.2	-	-	99.8	0.5	-	-	101.2	1.4	-	-	102.9	1.7	-	-	103.6	0.7
1984	-	-	105.3	1.6	-	-	105.5	0.2	-	-	106.0	0.5	-	-	107.4	1.3	-	-	108.9	1.4	-	-	109.3	0.4
1985	-	-	109.2	-0.1	-	-	109.7	0.5	-	-	109.9	0.2	-	-	112.0	1.9	-	-	113.9	1.7	-	-	113.8	-0.1
1986	-	-	115.6	1.6	-	-	115.5	-0.1	-	-	115.9	0.3	-	-	117.2	1.1	-	-	119.3	1.8	119.4	0.1	119.7	0.3
1987	121.3	1.3	-	-	121.2	-0.1	-	-	122.1	0.7	-	-	123.9	1.5	-	-	127.9	3.2	-	-	129.2	1.0	-	-
1988	130.8	1.2	-	-	130.6	-0.2	-	-	133.1	1.9	-	-	136.1	2.3	-	-	137.1	0.7	-	-	139.0	1.4	-	-
1989	139.7	0.5	-	-	139.7	0.0	-	-	141.9	1.6	-	-	143.0	0.8	-	-	147.2	2.9	-	-	147.3	0.1	-	-
1990	146.7	-0.4	-	-	148.5	1.2	-	-	150.4	1.3	-	-	149.4	-0.7	-	-	153.0	2.4	-	-	153.6	0.4	-	-
1991	156.5	1.9	-	-	158.4	1.2	-	-	159.5	0.7	-	-	161.6	1.3	-	-	166.2	2.8	-	-	168.2	1.2	-	-
1992	168.8	0.4	-	-	170.1	0.8	-	-	171.4	0.8	-	-	171.4	0.0	-	-	177.4	3.5	-	-	177.6	0.1	-	-
1993	181.3	2.1	-	-	181.6	0.2	-	-	182.8	0.7	-	-	187.6	2.6	-	-	184.3	-1.8	-	-	184.5	0.1	-	-

Source: U.S. Department of Labor, Bureau of Labor Statistics, Division of Consumer Prices and Price Indexes. - indicates no data collected for period.

Dallas-Fort Worth, TX
Consumer Price Index - All Urban Consumers
Base 1982-1984 = 100
Annual Averages

For 1963-1993. Columns headed % show percentile change in the index from the previous period for which an index is available.

Year	All Items		Food & Beverage		Housing		Apparel & Upkeep		Trans- portation		Medical Care		Entertain- ment		Other Goods & Services	
	Index	%	Index	%	Index	%	Index	%	Index	%	Index	%	Index	%	Index	%
1963	-	-	-	-	-	-	-	-	-	-	-	-	-	-	-	-
1964	29.5	-	-	-	-	-	45.4	-	31.3	-	24.5	-	-	-	-	-
1965	29.9	1.4	-	-	-	-	45.2	-0.4	31.6	1.0	25.0	2.0	-	-	-	-
1966	31.0	3.7	-	-	-	-	46.7	3.3	32.3	2.2	26.4	5.6	-	-	-	-
1967	31.9	2.9	-	-	-	-	48.7	4.3	33.3	3.1	28.3	7.2	-	-	-	-
1968	33.3	4.4	-	-	-	-	51.4	5.5	34.4	3.3	30.0	6.0	-	-	-	-
1969	35.5	6.6	-	-	-	-	54.8	6.6	35.6	3.5	32.4	8.0	-	-	-	-
1970	37.6	5.9	-	-	-	-	57.4	4.7	36.9	3.7	34.8	7.4	-	-	-	-
1971	38.7	2.9	-	-	-	-	57.6	0.3	39.1	6.0	36.4	4.6	-	-	-	-
1972	39.8	2.8	-	-	-	-	59.2	2.8	39.9	2.0	37.2	2.2	-	-	-	-
1973	42.1	5.8	-	-	-	-	62.6	5.7	41.1	3.0	38.7	4.0	-	-	-	-
1974	46.3	10.0	-	-	-	-	66.6	6.4	47.4	15.3	41.8	8.0	-	-	-	-
1975	50.4	8.9	-	-	-	-	68.8	3.3	52.1	9.9	46.0	10.0	-	-	-	-
1976	53.5	6.2	59.0	-	48.1	-	70.9	3.1	56.7	8.8	50.1	8.9	67.2	-	55.9	-
1977	57.4	7.3	63.7	8.0	51.7	7.5	74.8	5.5	61.0	7.6	55.2	10.2	69.5	3.4	59.5	6.4
1978	61.8	7.7	69.5	9.1	56.8	9.9	78.9	5.5	62.8	3.0	59.6	8.0	69.9	0.6	63.4	6.6
1979	69.7	12.8	78.1	12.4	65.3	15.0	83.6	6.0	71.9	14.5	62.9	5.5	73.6	5.3	68.8	8.5
1980	81.5	16.9	85.4	9.3	79.3	21.4	88.9	6.3	86.3	20.0	69.9	11.1	82.4	12.0	76.1	10.6
1981	90.8	11.4	92.4	8.2	90.1	13.6	95.0	6.9	95.5	10.7	80.3	14.9	87.2	5.8	84.0	10.4
1982	96.0	5.7	96.1	4.0	96.4	7.0	97.2	2.3	97.4	2.0	91.9	14.4	93.1	6.8	91.9	9.4
1983	99.7	3.9	99.6	3.6	99.6	3.3	99.7	2.6	99.2	1.8	101.2	10.1	99.6	7.0	100.9	9.8
1984	104.3	4.6	104.3	4.7	104.0	4.4	103.1	3.4	103.4	4.2	107.0	5.7	107.2	7.6	107.3	6.3
1985	108.2	3.7	107.1	2.7	107.3	3.2	107.7	4.5	107.2	3.7	113.9	6.4	114.0	6.3	112.5	4.8
1986	109.9	1.6	111.2	3.8	109.9	2.4	107.6	-0.1	101.1	-5.7	126.7	11.2	115.8	1.6	119.5	6.2
1987	112.9	2.7	115.9	4.2	109.5	-0.4	114.5	6.4	103.5	2.4	134.2	5.9	122.0	5.4	128.8	7.8
1988	116.1	2.8	120.1	3.6	109.8	0.3	123.1	7.5	108.0	4.3	141.9	5.7	127.3	4.3	135.2	5.0
1989	119.5	2.9	125.4	4.4	111.6	1.6	124.5	1.1	110.8	2.6	150.9	6.3	132.7	4.2	146.1	8.1
1990	125.1	4.7	131.1	4.5	114.3	2.4	137.5	10.4	117.2	5.8	161.9	7.3	137.5	3.6	156.3	7.0
1991	130.8	4.6	136.3	4.0	118.6	3.8	151.7	10.3	120.7	3.0	174.8	8.0	142.4	3.6	163.7	4.7
1992	133.9	2.4	138.3	1.5	121.8	2.7	151.3	-0.3	123.4	2.2	188.3	7.7	142.0	-0.3	170.5	4.2
1993	137.3	2.5	139.0	0.5	125.3	2.9	147.8	-2.3	128.9	4.5	196.8	4.5	144.0	1.4	180.5	5.9

Source: U.S. Department of Labor, Bureau of Labor Statistics, Division of Consumer Prices and Price Indexes. - indicates no data collected for period.

Dallas-Fort Worth, TX
Consumer Price Index - Urban Wage Earners
Base 1982-1984 = 100
Annual Averages

For 1963-1993. Columns headed % show percentile change in the index from the previous period for which an index is available.

Year	All Items		Food & Beverage		Housing		Apparel & Upkeep		Trans-portation		Medical Care		Entertain-ment		Other Goods & Services	
	Index	%	Index	%	Index	%	Index	%	Index	%	Index	%	Index	%	Index	%
1963	-	-	-	-	-	-	-	-	-	-	-	-	-	-	-	-
1964	30.0	-	-	-	-	-	47.9	-	31.3	-	24.9	-	-	-	-	-
1965	30.4	1.3	-	-	-	-	47.7	-0.4	31.6	1.0	25.4	2.0	-	-	-	-
1966	31.5	3.6	-	-	-	-	49.3	3.4	32.3	2.2	26.8	5.5	-	-	-	-
1967	32.4	2.9	-	-	-	-	51.4	4.3	33.3	3.1	28.7	7.1	-	-	-	-
1968	33.9	4.6	-	-	-	-	54.3	5.6	34.5	3.6	30.5	6.3	-	-	-	-
1969	36.1	6.5	-	-	-	-	57.9	6.6	35.6	3.2	32.9	7.9	-	-	-	-
1970	38.2	5.8	-	-	-	-	60.6	4.7	37.0	3.9	35.4	7.6	-	-	-	-
1971	39.3	2.9	-	-	-	-	60.9	0.5	39.1	5.7	37.0	4.5	-	-	-	-
1972	40.5	3.1	-	-	-	-	62.5	2.6	39.9	2.0	37.8	2.2	-	-	-	-
1973	42.8	5.7	-	-	-	-	66.1	5.8	41.1	3.0	39.3	4.0	-	-	-	-
1974	47.1	10.0	-	-	-	-	70.4	6.5	47.4	15.3	42.4	7.9	-	-	-	-
1975	51.3	8.9	-	-	-	-	72.7	3.3	52.1	9.9	46.8	10.4	-	-	-	-
1976	54.4	6.0	58.5	-	48.7	-	74.8	2.9	56.7	8.8	50.9	8.8	71.8	-	58.6	-
1977	58.4	7.4	63.2	8.0	52.4	7.6	78.9	5.5	61.0	7.6	56.1	10.2	74.3	3.5	62.4	6.5
1978	62.9	7.7	69.2	9.5	57.6	9.9	82.5	4.6	63.0	3.3	60.6	8.0	74.5	0.3	66.5	6.6
1979	70.9	12.7	77.9	12.6	66.1	14.8	87.3	5.8	72.3	14.8	65.2	7.6	76.7	3.0	71.7	7.8
1980	82.4	16.2	84.9	9.0	79.8	20.7	94.6	8.4	86.7	19.9	72.1	10.6	82.4	7.4	79.4	10.7
1981	91.5	11.0	92.2	8.6	90.5	13.4	98.9	4.5	96.4	11.2	81.2	12.6	87.6	6.3	84.4	6.3
1982	96.4	5.4	96.2	4.3	97.0	7.2	97.5	-1.4	97.6	1.2	91.7	12.9	93.6	6.8	91.6	8.5
1983	99.4	3.1	99.6	3.5	99.0	2.1	99.4	1.9	99.3	1.7	101.2	10.4	99.6	6.4	101.3	10.6
1984	104.2	4.8	104.2	4.6	104.0	5.1	103.0	3.6	103.2	3.9	107.1	5.8	106.8	7.2	107.1	5.7
1985	108.1	3.7	106.9	2.6	107.8	3.7	109.2	6.0	106.9	3.6	114.3	6.7	112.8	5.6	111.8	4.4
1986	109.4	1.2	110.8	3.6	110.3	2.3	109.3	0.1	100.5	-6.0	127.5	11.5	114.5	1.5	118.7	6.2
1987	112.6	2.9	115.6	4.3	109.8	-0.5	115.1	5.3	104.2	3.7	135.5	6.3	120.6	5.3	126.3	6.4
1988	115.8	2.8	119.7	3.5	110.1	0.3	123.1	7.0	108.5	4.1	143.5	5.9	126.0	4.5	132.6	5.0
1989	119.3	3.0	124.9	4.3	111.8	1.5	122.8	-0.2	111.8	3.0	153.2	6.8	131.6	4.4	143.3	8.1
1990	124.5	4.4	130.6	4.6	114.3	2.2	130.9	6.6	118.1	5.6	164.5	7.4	135.6	3.0	153.7	7.3
1991	129.6	4.1	135.7	3.9	118.7	3.8	138.7	6.0	121.6	3.0	177.7	8.0	140.7	3.8	161.8	5.3
1992	133.1	2.7	137.5	1.3	121.4	2.3	141.5	2.0	126.2	3.8	192.1	8.1	140.1	-0.4	168.7	4.3
1993	137.0	2.9	138.2	0.5	124.6	2.6	143.0	1.1	132.8	5.2	200.8	4.5	141.7	1.1	178.2	5.6

Source: U.S. Department of Labor, Bureau of Labor Statistics, Division of Consumer Prices and Price Indexes. - indicates no data collected for period.

Dallas-Fort Worth, TX

Consumer Price Index - All Urban Consumers
Base 1982-1984 = 100
All Items

For 1963-1993. Columns headed % show percentile change in the index from the previous period for which an index is available.

Year	Jan Index	%	Feb Index	%	Mar Index	%	Apr Index	%	May Index	%	Jun Index	%	Jul Index	%	Aug Index	%	Sep Index	%	Oct Index	%	Nov Index	%	Dec Index	%
1963	-		-		-		-		-		-		-		-		-		-		29.5	-	-	
1964	-		29.4	-0.3	-		-		29.6	0.7	-		-		29.5	-0.3	-		-		29.7	0.7	-	
1965	-		29.5	-0.7	-		-		29.8	1.0	-		-		30.0	0.7	-		-		30.3	1.0	-	
1966	-		30.5	0.7	-		-		30.9	1.3	-		-		31.1	0.6	-		-		31.4	1.0	-	
1967	-		31.6	0.6	-		-		31.7	0.3	-		-		32.1	1.3	-		-		32.2	0.3	-	
1968	-		32.5	0.9	-		-		33.2	2.2	-		-		33.5	0.9	-		-		34.0	1.5	-	
1969	-		34.4	1.2	-		-		35.2	2.3	-		-		35.7	1.4	-		-		36.5	2.2	-	
1970	-		37.0	1.4	-		-		37.5	1.4	-		-		37.8	0.8	-		-		37.9	0.3	-	
1971	-		38.2	0.8	-		-		38.4	0.5	-		-		39.1	1.8	-		-		39.0	-0.3	-	
1972	-		39.4	1.0	-		-		39.7	0.8	-		-		40.0	0.8	-		-		40.1	0.2	-	
1973	-		40.7	1.5	-		-		41.6	2.2	-		-		42.6	2.4	-		-		43.2	1.4	-	
1974	-		44.5	3.0	-		-		45.6	2.5	-		-		47.0	3.1	-		-		48.2	2.6	-	
1975	-		49.1	1.9	-		-		49.7	1.2	-		-		51.2	3.0	-		-		51.8	1.2	-	
1976	-		52.2	0.8	-		-		53.0	1.5	-		-		53.9	1.7	-		-		54.7	1.5	-	
1977	-		55.9	2.2	-		-		57.2	2.3	-		-		58.1	1.6	-		-		58.6	0.9	-	
1978	-		59.5	1.5	-		60.3	1.3	-		61.7	2.3	-		62.9	1.9	-		63.7	1.3	-		64.3	0.9
1979	-		65.6	2.0	-		67.3	2.6	-		69.3	3.0	-		71.1	2.6	-		72.7	2.3	-		74.6	2.6
1980	-		77.0	3.2	-		80.1	4.0	-		81.7	2.0	-		82.4	0.9	-		84.4	2.4	-		85.9	1.8
1981	-		87.5	1.9	-		89.1	1.8	-		91.2	2.4	-		91.9	0.8	-		93.2	1.4	-		94.1	1.0
1982	-		93.6	-0.5	-		94.7	1.2	-		97.2	2.6	-		97.0	-0.2	-		97.8	0.8	-		96.7	-1.1
1983	-		97.1	0.4	-		98.4	1.3	-		100.1	1.7	-		100.7	0.6	-		101.5	0.8	-		101.2	-0.3
1984	-		102.9	1.7	-		103.3	0.4	-		103.8	0.5	-		105.1	1.3	-		106.4	1.2	-		105.4	-0.9
1985	-		106.2	0.8	-		107.0	0.8	-		108.3	1.2	-		109.5	1.1	-		109.6	0.1	-		109.8	0.2
1986	-		110.6	0.7	-		108.8	-1.6	-		109.9	1.0	-		110.4	0.5	-		110.3	-0.1	-		109.3	-0.9
1987	-		110.9	1.5	-		112.2	1.2	-		112.9	0.6	-		113.5	0.5	-		114.9	1.2	-		113.9	-0.9
1988	-		114.0	0.1	-		115.4	1.2	-		115.6	0.2	-		117.2	1.4	-		117.9	0.6	-		117.2	-0.6
1989	-		117.5	0.3	-		118.7	1.0	-		120.0	1.1	-		120.0	0.0	-		121.4	1.2	-		120.5	-0.7
1990	-		122.2	1.4	-		122.9	0.6	-		123.8	0.7	-		126.0	1.8	-		129.5	2.8	-		128.4	-0.8
1991	-		129.4	0.8	-		129.5	0.1	-		130.1	0.5	-		131.1	0.8	-		133.6	1.9	-		132.0	-1.2
1992	-		132.4	0.3	-		132.5	0.1	-		134.2	1.3	-		134.4	0.1	-		136.1	1.3	-		134.6	-1.1
1993	-		135.4	0.6	-		137.0	1.2	-		136.2	-0.6	-		138.1	1.4	-		139.6	1.1	-		138.8	-0.6

Source: U.S. Department of Labor, Bureau of Labor Statistics, Division of Consumer Prices and Price Indexes. - indicates no data collected for period.

Dallas-Fort Worth, TX
Consumer Price Index - Urban Wage Earners
Base 1982-1984 = 100
All Items

For 1963-1993. Columns headed % show percentile change in the index from the previous period for which an index is available.

Year	Jan Index	%	Feb Index	%	Mar Index	%	Apr Index	%	May Index	%	Jun Index	%	Jul Index	%	Aug Index	%	Sep Index	%	Oct Index	%	Nov Index	%	Dec Index	%
1963	-	-	-	-	-	-	-	-	-	-	-	-	-	-	-	-	-	-	-	-	30.0	-	-	-
1964	-	-	29.9	-0.3	-	-	-	-	30.1	0.7	-	-	-	-	30.0	-0.3	-	-	-	-	30.2	0.7	-	-
1965	-	-	30.0	-0.7	-	-	-	-	30.3	1.0	-	-	-	-	30.5	0.7	-	-	-	-	30.8	1.0	-	-
1966	-	-	31.0	0.6	-	-	-	-	31.4	1.3	-	-	-	-	31.7	1.0	-	-	-	-	31.9	0.6	-	-
1967	-	-	32.1	0.6	-	-	-	-	32.2	0.3	-	-	-	-	32.7	1.6	-	-	-	-	32.7	0.0	-	-
1968	-	-	33.1	1.2	-	-	-	-	33.8	2.1	-	-	-	-	34.1	0.9	-	-	-	-	34.6	1.5	-	-
1969	-	-	35.0	1.2	-	-	-	-	35.8	2.3	-	-	-	-	36.4	1.7	-	-	-	-	37.1	1.9	-	-
1970	-	-	37.7	1.6	-	-	-	-	38.1	1.1	-	-	-	-	38.5	1.0	-	-	-	-	38.6	0.3	-	-
1971	-	-	38.8	0.5	-	-	-	-	39.0	0.5	-	-	-	-	39.8	2.1	-	-	-	-	39.7	-0.3	-	-
1972	-	-	40.1	1.0	-	-	-	-	40.4	0.7	-	-	-	-	40.7	0.7	-	-	-	-	40.8	0.2	-	-
1973	-	-	41.4	1.5	-	-	-	-	42.4	2.4	-	-	-	-	43.4	2.4	-	-	-	-	44.0	1.4	-	-
1974	-	-	45.3	3.0	-	-	-	-	46.4	2.4	-	-	-	-	47.8	3.0	-	-	-	-	49.1	2.7	-	-
1975	-	-	49.9	1.6	-	-	-	-	50.5	1.2	-	-	-	-	52.1	3.2	-	-	-	-	52.7	1.2	-	-
1976	-	-	53.1	0.8	-	-	-	-	53.9	1.5	-	-	-	-	54.8	1.7	-	-	-	-	55.7	1.6	-	-
1977	-	-	56.8	2.0	-	-	-	-	58.2	2.5	-	-	-	-	59.2	1.7	-	-	-	-	59.6	0.7	-	-
1978	-	-	60.5	1.5	-	-	61.5	1.7	-	-	62.7	2.0	-	-	64.0	2.1	-	-	64.9	1.4	-	-	65.2	0.5
1979	-	-	66.9	2.6	-	-	68.6	2.5	-	-	70.7	3.1	-	-	72.3	2.3	-	-	73.9	2.2	-	-	75.7	2.4
1980	-	-	78.1	3.2	-	-	80.9	3.6	-	-	82.5	2.0	-	-	83.5	1.2	-	-	85.3	2.2	-	-	87.0	2.0
1981	-	-	88.5	1.7	-	-	89.8	1.5	-	-	92.1	2.6	-	-	92.5	0.4	-	-	93.7	1.3	-	-	94.4	0.7
1982	-	-	94.0	-0.4	-	-	94.9	1.0	-	-	97.4	2.6	-	-	97.4	0.0	-	-	98.1	0.7	-	-	97.1	-1.0
1983	-	-	96.7	-0.4	-	-	97.8	1.1	-	-	99.3	1.5	-	-	100.2	0.9	-	-	102.1	1.9	-	-	101.7	-0.4
1984	-	-	103.0	1.3	-	-	102.6	-0.4	-	-	103.4	0.8	-	-	105.3	1.8	-	-	106.4	1.0	-	-	105.4	-0.9
1985	-	-	106.0	0.6	-	-	106.9	0.8	-	-	108.2	1.2	-	-	109.3	1.0	-	-	109.4	0.1	-	-	109.7	0.3
1986	-	-	110.4	0.6	-	-	108.3	-1.9	-	-	109.4	1.0	-	-	110.0	0.5	-	-	109.8	-0.2	-	-	108.6	-1.1
1987	-	-	110.6	1.8	-	-	111.7	1.0	-	-	112.6	0.8	-	-	113.3	0.6	-	-	114.7	1.2	-	-	113.8	-0.8
1988	-	-	113.8	0.0	-	-	114.8	0.9	-	-	115.4	0.5	-	-	117.0	1.4	-	-	117.7	0.6	-	-	117.0	-0.6
1989	-	-	117.2	0.2	-	-	118.6	1.2	-	-	120.0	1.2	-	-	119.8	-0.2	-	-	121.1	1.1	-	-	120.1	-0.8
1990	-	-	121.3	1.0	-	-	122.2	0.7	-	-	123.2	0.8	-	-	125.4	1.8	-	-	128.8	2.7	-	-	127.8	-0.8
1991	-	-	128.1	0.2	-	-	128.2	0.1	-	-	129.4	0.9	-	-	129.9	0.4	-	-	131.8	1.5	-	-	130.9	-0.7
1992	-	-	131.2	0.2	-	-	131.5	0.2	-	-	133.5	1.5	-	-	134.0	0.4	-	-	135.4	1.0	-	-	134.1	-1.0
1993	-	-	134.8	0.5	-	-	136.3	1.1	-	-	136.5	0.1	-	-	138.0	1.1	-	-	139.1	0.8	-	-	138.6	-0.4

Source: U.S. Department of Labor, Bureau of Labor Statistics, Division of Consumer Prices and Price Indexes. - indicates no data collected for period.

Dallas-Fort Worth, TX
Consumer Price Index - All Urban Consumers
Base 1982-1984 = 100
Food and Beverages

For 1975-1993. Columns headed % show percentile change in the index from the previous period for which an index is available.

Year	Jan Index	%	Feb Index	%	Mar Index	%	Apr Index	%	May Index	%	Jun Index	%	Jul Index	%	Aug Index	%	Sep Index	%	Oct Index	%	Nov Index	%	Dec Index	%
1975	-	-	-	-	-	-	-	-	-	-	-	-	-	-	-	-	-	-	-	-	58.8	-	-	-
1976	-	-	58.7	-0.2	-	-	-	-	58.6	-0.2	-	-	-	-	59.3	1.2	-	-	-	-	59.2	-0.2	-	-
1977	-	-	62.3	5.2	-	-	-	-	63.4	1.8	-	-	-	-	64.5	1.7	-	-	-	-	64.9	0.6	-	-
1978	-	-	66.5	2.5	-	-	67.5	1.5	-	-	69.6	3.1	-	-	70.4	1.1	-	-	71.6	1.7	-	-	73.8	3.1
1979	-	-	75.8	2.7	-	-	77.2	1.8	-	-	78.3	1.4	-	-	78.2	-0.1	-	-	79.6	1.8	-	-	81.4	2.3
1980	-	-	81.9	0.6	-	-	82.9	1.2	-	-	84.5	1.9	-	-	86.3	2.1	-	-	88.8	2.9	-	-	90.0	1.4
1981	-	-	91.0	1.1	-	-	92.3	1.4	-	-	92.3	0.0	-	-	92.9	0.7	-	-	93.3	0.4	-	-	93.2	-0.1
1982	-	-	94.6	1.5	-	-	95.3	0.7	-	-	96.4	1.2	-	-	96.7	0.3	-	-	96.9	0.2	-	-	97.7	0.8
1983	-	-	98.3	0.6	-	-	99.3	1.0	-	-	99.4	0.1	-	-	99.7	0.3	-	-	100.9	1.2	-	-	100.9	0.0
1984	-	-	103.5	2.6	-	-	104.2	0.7	-	-	104.1	-0.1	-	-	105.0	0.9	-	-	104.7	-0.3	-	-	105.4	0.7
1985	-	-	106.3	0.9	-	-	107.0	0.7	-	-	107.5	0.5	-	-	106.9	-0.6	-	-	107.0	0.1	-	-	109.0	1.9
1986	-	-	110.0	0.9	-	-	110.1	0.1	-	-	110.6	0.5	-	-	111.9	1.2	-	-	112.6	0.6	-	-	112.8	0.2
1987	-	-	115.6	2.5	-	-	114.5	-1.0	-	-	116.2	1.5	-	-	116.1	-0.1	-	-	117.3	1.0	-	-	116.9	-0.3
1988	-	-	117.5	0.5	-	-	118.3	0.7	-	-	119.9	1.4	-	-	120.8	0.8	-	-	122.4	1.3	-	-	123.1	0.6
1989	-	-	124.4	1.1	-	-	124.8	0.3	-	-	124.9	0.1	-	-	125.3	0.3	-	-	126.6	1.0	-	-	127.9	1.0
1990	-	-	129.6	1.3	-	-	130.7	0.8	-	-	130.5	-0.2	-	-	131.5	0.8	-	-	132.0	0.4	-	-	134.1	1.6
1991	-	-	134.7	0.4	-	-	135.5	0.6	-	-	138.2	2.0	-	-	136.6	-1.2	-	-	135.6	-0.7	-	-	138.0	1.8
1992	-	-	139.6	1.2	-	-	138.6	-0.7	-	-	137.2	-1.0	-	-	138.1	0.7	-	-	138.6	0.4	-	-	137.9	-0.5
1993	-	-	138.1	0.1	-	-	139.3	0.9	-	-	139.1	-0.1	-	-	138.3	-0.6	-	-	137.6	-0.5	-	-	142.5	3.6

Source: U.S. Department of Labor, Bureau of Labor Statistics, Division of Consumer Prices and Price Indexes. - indicates no data collected for period.

Dallas-Fort Worth, TX
Consumer Price Index - Urban Wage Earners
Base 1982-1984 = 100
Food and Beverages

For 1975-1993. Columns headed % show percentile change in the index from the previous period for which an index is available.

Year	Jan Index	%	Feb Index	%	Mar Index	%	Apr Index	%	May Index	%	Jun Index	%	Jul Index	%	Aug Index	%	Sep Index	%	Oct Index	%	Nov Index	%	Dec Index	%
1975	-	-	-	-	-	-	-	-	-	-	-	-	-	-	-	-	-	-	-	-	58.3	-	-	-
1976	-	-	58.2	-0.2	-	-	-	-	58.1	-0.2	-	-	-	-	58.8	1.2	-	-	-	-	58.7	-0.2	-	-
1977	-	-	61.8	5.3	-	-	-	-	62.9	1.8	-	-	-	-	64.0	1.7	-	-	-	-	64.4	0.6	-	-
1978	-	-	65.9	2.3	-	-	67.8	2.9	-	-	69.0	1.8	-	-	70.0	1.4	-	-	71.9	2.7	-	-	72.5	0.8
1979	-	-	75.9	4.7	-	-	77.2	1.7	-	-	78.3	1.4	-	-	77.9	-0.5	-	-	79.4	1.9	-	-	80.7	1.6
1980	-	-	81.4	0.9	-	-	82.5	1.4	-	-	83.6	1.3	-	-	86.2	3.1	-	-	88.5	2.7	-	-	89.8	1.5
1981	-	-	90.3	0.6	-	-	91.1	0.9	-	-	92.1	1.1	-	-	93.7	1.7	-	-	93.6	-0.1	-	-	93.3	-0.3
1982	-	-	94.7	1.5	-	-	95.3	0.6	-	-	96.5	1.3	-	-	96.8	0.3	-	-	97.0	0.2	-	-	97.9	0.9
1983	-	-	98.3	0.4	-	-	99.2	0.9	-	-	99.5	0.3	-	-	99.7	0.2	-	-	100.9	1.2	-	-	100.8	-0.1
1984	-	-	103.5	2.7	-	-	104.2	0.7	-	-	104.0	-0.2	-	-	104.8	0.8	-	-	104.5	-0.3	-	-	105.3	0.8
1985	-	-	106.1	0.8	-	-	106.8	0.7	-	-	107.2	0.4	-	-	106.6	-0.6	-	-	106.5	-0.1	-	-	108.8	2.2
1986	-	-	109.6	0.7	-	-	109.6	0.0	-	-	110.2	0.5	-	-	111.7	1.4	-	-	112.3	0.5	-	-	112.4	0.1
1987	-	-	115.2	2.5	-	-	114.2	-0.9	-	-	115.8	1.4	-	-	115.8	0.0	-	-	116.9	0.9	-	-	116.6	-0.3
1988	-	-	117.1	0.4	-	-	117.9	0.7	-	-	119.5	1.4	-	-	120.4	0.8	-	-	122.0	1.3	-	-	122.7	0.6
1989	-	-	123.9	1.0	-	-	124.2	0.2	-	-	124.4	0.2	-	-	124.7	0.2	-	-	126.0	1.0	-	-	127.5	1.2
1990	-	-	129.1	1.3	-	-	130.0	0.7	-	-	129.8	-0.2	-	-	131.0	0.9	-	-	131.5	0.4	-	-	133.7	1.7
1991	-	-	134.2	0.4	-	-	135.1	0.7	-	-	137.7	1.9	-	-	136.0	-1.2	-	-	135.0	-0.7	-	-	137.1	1.6
1992	-	-	138.9	1.3	-	-	137.8	-0.8	-	-	136.3	-1.1	-	-	137.1	0.6	-	-	137.8	0.5	-	-	137.1	-0.5
1993	-	-	137.5	0.3	-	-	138.6	0.8	-	-	138.4	-0.1	-	-	137.6	-0.6	-	-	137.0	-0.4	-	-	141.4	3.2

Source: U.S. Department of Labor, Bureau of Labor Statistics, Division of Consumer Prices and Price Indexes. - indicates no data collected for period.

Dallas-Fort Worth, TX
Consumer Price Index - All Urban Consumers
Base 1982-1984 = 100
Housing

For 1975-1993. Columns headed % show percentile change in the index from the previous period for which an index is available.

Year	Jan Index	%	Feb Index	%	Mar Index	%	Apr Index	%	May Index	%	Jun Index	%	Jul Index	%	Aug Index	%	Sep Index	%	Oct Index	%	Nov Index	%	Dec Index	%
1975	-	-	-	-	-	-	-	-	-	-	-	-	-	-	-	-	-	-	-	-	46.0	-	-	-
1976	-	-	47.0	2.2	-	-	-	-	47.7	1.5	-	-	-	-	48.4	1.5	-	-	-	-	49.4	2.1	-	-
1977	-	-	50.0	1.2	-	-	-	-	51.4	2.8	-	-	-	-	52.4	1.9	-	-	-	-	53.0	1.1	-	-
1978	-	-	54.3	2.5	-	-	55.3	1.8	-	-	56.7	2.5	-	-	58.2	2.6	-	-	59.0	1.4	-	-	58.9	-0.2
1979	-	-	60.4	2.5	-	-	62.0	2.6	-	-	64.8	4.5	-	-	66.9	3.2	-	-	69.3	3.6	-	-	71.3	2.9
1980	-	-	73.6	3.2	-	-	77.7	5.6	-	-	80.2	3.2	-	-	80.1	-0.1	-	-	82.7	3.2	-	-	85.0	2.8
1981	-	-	86.1	1.3	-	-	87.6	1.7	-	-	90.8	3.7	-	-	91.0	0.2	-	-	92.9	2.1	-	-	94.5	1.7
1982	-	-	92.5	-2.1	-	-	95.9	3.7	-	-	98.5	2.7	-	-	97.4	-1.1	-	-	98.4	1.0	-	-	95.8	-2.6
1983	-	-	96.7	0.9	-	-	97.9	1.2	-	-	101.3	3.5	-	-	101.0	-0.3	-	-	101.3	0.3	-	-	100.7	-0.6
1984	-	-	103.0	2.3	-	-	102.8	-0.2	-	-	104.0	1.2	-	-	105.3	1.3	-	-	106.3	0.9	-	-	103.4	-2.7
1985	-	-	105.0	1.5	-	-	105.6	0.6	-	-	107.9	2.2	-	-	110.0	1.9	-	-	109.1	-0.8	-	-	107.7	-1.3
1986	-	-	109.7	1.9	-	-	109.8	0.1	-	-	111.3	1.4	-	-	111.6	0.3	-	-	110.0	-1.4	-	-	107.1	-2.6
1987	-	-	108.0	0.8	-	-	109.1	1.0	-	-	109.7	0.5	-	-	110.5	0.7	-	-	111.4	0.8	-	-	108.9	-2.2
1988	-	-	107.9	-0.9	-	-	109.2	1.2	-	-	109.4	0.2	-	-	111.9	2.3	-	-	111.2	-0.6	-	-	109.2	-1.8
1989	-	-	110.3	1.0	-	-	109.7	-0.5	-	-	112.4	2.5	-	-	112.9	0.4	-	-	113.7	0.7	-	-	111.2	-2.2
1990	-	-	111.6	0.4	-	-	112.2	0.5	-	-	114.0	1.6	-	-	116.1	1.8	-	-	118.3	1.9	-	-	114.8	-3.0
1991	-	-	116.8	1.7	-	-	117.1	0.3	-	-	117.8	0.6	-	-	119.1	1.1	-	-	121.9	2.4	-	-	120.3	-1.3
1992	-	-	118.4	-1.6	-	-	119.0	0.5	-	-	123.9	4.1	-	-	124.9	0.8	-	-	123.2	-1.4	-	-	121.7	-1.2
1993	-	-	123.9	1.8	-	-	123.7	-0.2	-	-	123.6	-0.1	-	-	127.6	3.2	-	-	128.1	0.4	-	-	126.1	-1.6

Source: U.S. Department of Labor, Bureau of Labor Statistics, Division of Consumer Prices and Price Indexes. - indicates no data collected for period.

Dallas-Fort Worth, TX
Consumer Price Index - Urban Wage Earners
Base 1982-1984 = 100
Housing

For 1975-1993. Columns headed % show percentile change in the index from the previous period for which an index is available.

Year	Jan Index	%	Feb Index	%	Mar Index	%	Apr Index	%	May Index	%	Jun Index	%	Jul Index	%	Aug Index	%	Sep Index	%	Oct Index	%	Nov Index	%	Dec Index	%
1975	-	-	-	-	-	-	-	-	-	-	-	-	-	-	-	-	-	-	-	-	-	-	-	-
1976	-	-	47.6	2.1	-	-	-	-	48.3	1.5	-	-	-	-	49.1	1.7	-	-	-	-	46.6	-	-	-
1977	-	-	50.6	1.2	-	-	-	-	52.1	3.0	-	-	-	-	53.0	1.7	-	-	-	-	50.0	1.8	-	-
1978	-	-	55.0	2.4	-	-	56.1	2.0	-	-	57.5	2.5	-	-	59.0	2.6	-	-	-	-	53.7	1.3	-	-
1979	-	-	61.2	2.7	-	-	62.8	2.6	-	-	65.6	4.5	-	-	67.7	3.2	-	-	59.8	1.4	-	-	59.6	-0.3
1980	-	-	74.1	2.9	-	-	78.3	5.7	-	-	80.8	3.2	-	-	80.6	-0.2	-	-	70.1	3.5	-	-	72.0	2.7
1981	-	-	86.6	1.3	-	-	87.9	1.5	-	-	91.2	3.8	-	-	91.3	0.1	-	-	82.9	2.9	-	-	85.5	3.1
1982	-	-	93.1	-2.1	-	-	96.4	3.5	-	-	99.2	2.9	-	-	98.1	-1.1	-	-	93.2	2.1	-	-	95.1	2.0
1983	-	-	95.8	-0.7	-	-	96.6	0.8	-	-	99.1	2.6	-	-	99.8	0.7	-	-	99.2	1.1	-	-	96.5	-2.7
1984	-	-	103.3	1.5	-	-	101.5	-1.7	-	-	102.9	1.4	-	-	105.8	2.8	-	-	102.4	2.6	-	-	101.8	-0.6
1985	-	-	105.4	1.3	-	-	105.9	0.5	-	-	108.4	2.4	-	-	110.5	1.9	-	-	106.9	1.0	-	-	104.0	-2.7
1986	-	-	110.1	1.9	-	-	110.0	-0.1	-	-	111.8	1.6	-	-	112.1	0.3	-	-	110.3	-1.6	-	-	108.1	-1.5
1987	-	-	108.2	1.0	-	-	109.1	0.8	-	-	110.3	1.1	-	-	111.1	0.7	-	-	111.9	0.7	-	-	107.1	-2.9
1988	-	-	108.2	-0.7	-	-	109.4	1.1	-	-	110.0	0.5	-	-	112.2	2.0	-	-	111.6	-0.5	-	-	109.0	-2.6
1989	-	-	110.2	0.7	-	-	109.8	-0.4	-	-	112.7	2.6	-	-	113.2	0.4	-	-	114.0	0.7	-	-	109.4	-2.0
1990	-	-	111.3	0.0	-	-	112.2	0.8	-	-	113.9	1.5	-	-	116.1	1.9	-	-	118.7	2.2	-	-	111.3	-2.4
1991	-	-	117.1	2.4	-	-	117.1	0.0	-	-	118.0	0.8	-	-	119.4	1.2	-	-	122.1	2.3	-	-	114.4	-3.6
1992	-	-	118.6	-1.2	-	-	118.9	0.3	-	-	123.2	3.6	-	-	124.3	0.9	-	-	122.8	-1.2	-	-	120.0	-1.7
1993	-	-	123.1	1.7	-	-	122.6	-0.4	-	-	123.2	0.5	-	-	126.7	2.8	-	-	127.8	0.9	-	-	125.4	-1.9

Source: U.S. Department of Labor, Bureau of Labor Statistics, Division of Consumer Prices and Price Indexes. - indicates no data collected for period.

Dallas-Fort Worth, TX
Consumer Price Index - All Urban Consumers
Base 1982-1984 = 100
Apparel and Upkeep

For 1963-1993. Columns headed % show percentile change in the index from the previous period for which an index is available.

Year	Jan Index	Jan %	Feb Index	Feb %	Mar Index	Mar %	Apr Index	Apr %	May Index	May %	Jun Index	Jun %	Jul Index	Jul %	Aug Index	Aug %	Sep Index	Sep %	Oct Index	Oct %	Nov Index	Nov %	Dec Index	Dec %
1963	-	-	-	-	-	-	-	-	-	-	-	-	-	-	-	-	-	-	-	-	45.6	-	-	-
1964	-	-	45.6	0.0	-	-	-	-	45.5	-0.2	-	-	-	-	45.1	-0.9	-	-	-	-	45.5	0.9	-	-
1965	-	-	45.0	-1.1	-	-	-	-	45.2	0.4	-	-	-	-	44.8	-0.9	-	-	-	-	45.6	1.8	-	-
1966	-	-	45.7	0.2	-	-	-	-	46.6	2.0	-	-	-	-	46.5	-0.2	-	-	-	-	47.9	3.0	-	-
1967	-	-	48.2	0.6	-	-	-	-	48.6	0.8	-	-	-	-	48.8	0.4	-	-	-	-	49.0	0.4	-	-
1968	-	-	49.6	1.2	-	-	-	-	51.4	3.6	-	-	-	-	51.8	0.8	-	-	-	-	52.9	2.1	-	-
1969	-	-	53.3	0.8	-	-	-	-	54.6	2.4	-	-	-	-	54.8	0.4	-	-	-	-	56.7	3.5	-	-
1970	-	-	57.6	1.6	-	-	-	-	57.3	-0.5	-	-	-	-	57.7	0.7	-	-	-	-	57.1	-1.0	-	-
1971	-	-	56.9	-0.4	-	-	-	-	57.7	1.4	-	-	-	-	58.2	0.9	-	-	-	-	57.6	-1.0	-	-
1972	-	-	58.4	1.4	-	-	-	-	59.1	1.2	-	-	-	-	59.2	0.2	-	-	-	-	60.3	1.9	-	-
1973	-	-	61.1	1.3	-	-	-	-	62.4	2.1	-	-	-	-	63.1	1.1	-	-	-	-	63.9	1.3	-	-
1974	-	-	65.2	2.0	-	-	-	-	66.1	1.4	-	-	-	-	67.0	1.4	-	-	-	-	68.3	1.9	-	-
1975	-	-	68.2	-0.1	-	-	-	-	68.1	-0.1	-	-	-	-	69.3	1.8	-	-	-	-	69.6	0.4	-	-
1976	-	-	69.4	-0.3	-	-	-	-	70.7	1.9	-	-	-	-	71.0	0.4	-	-	-	-	72.2	1.7	-	-
1977	-	-	72.9	1.0	-	-	-	-	73.5	0.8	-	-	-	-	76.0	3.4	-	-	-	-	76.7	0.9	-	-
1978	-	-	77.1	0.5	-	-	78.1	1.3	-	-	78.0	-0.1	-	-	79.8	2.3	-	-	80.3	0.6	-	-	81.6	1.6
1979	-	-	81.5	-0.1	-	-	83.4	2.3	-	-	82.2	-1.4	-	-	84.5	2.8	-	-	85.2	0.8	-	-	85.6	0.5
1980	-	-	86.8	1.4	-	-	88.2	1.6	-	-	87.3	-1.0	-	-	89.7	2.7	-	-	92.6	3.2	-	-	90.1	-2.7
1981	-	-	91.6	1.7	-	-	93.1	1.6	-	-	93.5	0.4	-	-	98.0	4.8	-	-	99.5	1.5	-	-	96.2	-3.3
1982	-	-	98.6	2.5	-	-	97.6	-1.0	-	-	97.6	0.0	-	-	96.2	-1.4	-	-	96.6	0.4	-	-	96.8	0.2
1983	-	-	98.4	1.7	-	-	101.1	2.7	-	-	98.6	-2.5	-	-	99.9	1.3	-	-	100.7	0.8	-	-	100.1	-0.6
1984	-	-	103.3	3.2	-	-	102.8	-0.5	-	-	99.6	-3.1	-	-	101.0	1.4	-	-	107.0	5.9	-	-	106.8	-0.2
1985	-	-	106.2	-0.6	-	-	105.8	-0.4	-	-	106.4	0.6	-	-	108.7	2.2	-	-	110.8	1.9	-	-	108.5	-2.1
1986	-	-	107.0	-1.4	-	-	106.2	-0.7	-	-	106.6	0.4	-	-	109.2	2.4	-	-	109.7	0.5	-	-	106.5	-2.9
1987	-	-	108.2	1.6	-	-	117.5	8.6	-	-	114.9	-2.2	-	-	113.9	-0.9	-	-	118.5	4.0	-	-	116.5	-1.7
1988	-	-	117.4	0.8	-	-	125.1	6.6	-	-	120.0	-4.1	-	-	123.0	2.5	-	-	128.8	4.7	-	-	126.7	-1.6
1989	-	-	118.4	-6.6	-	-	130.0	9.8	-	-	122.8	-5.5	-	-	124.6	1.5	-	-	126.1	1.2	-	-	124.9	-1.0
1990	-	-	133.6	7.0	-	-	136.1	1.9	-	-	133.0	-2.3	-	-	137.7	3.5	-	-	146.2	6.2	-	-	142.7	-2.4
1991	-	-	149.8	5.0	-	-	154.1	2.9	-	-	146.9	-4.7	-	-	150.6	2.5	-	-	166.3	10.4	-	-	142.8	-14.1
1992	-	-	157.5	10.3	-	-	152.4	-3.2	-	-	147.6	-3.1	-	-	144.5	-2.1	-	-	157.9	9.3	-	-	149.9	-5.1
1993	-	-	144.3	-3.7	-	-	161.5	11.9	-	-	142.8	-11.6	-	-	139.7	-2.2	-	-	153.9	10.2	-	-	143.3	-6.9

Source: U.S. Department of Labor, Bureau of Labor Statistics, Division of Consumer Prices and Price Indexes. - indicates no data collected for period.

Dallas-Fort Worth, TX
Consumer Price Index - Urban Wage Earners
Base 1982-1984 = 100
Apparel and Upkeep

For 1963-1993. Columns headed % show percentile change in the index from the previous period for which an index is available.

Year	Jan Index	%	Feb Index	%	Mar Index	%	Apr Index	%	May Index	%	Jun Index	%	Jul Index	%	Aug Index	%	Sep Index	%	Oct Index	%	Nov Index	%	Dec Index	%
1963	-	-	-	-	-	-	-	-	-	-	-	-	-	-	-	-	-	-	-	-	48.1	-	-	-
1964	-	-	48.1	0.0	-	-	-	-	48.0	-0.2	-	-	-	-	47.6	-0.8	-	-	-	-	48.0	0.8	-	-
1965	-	-	47.5	-1.0	-	-	-	-	47.7	0.4	-	-	-	-	47.3	-0.8	-	-	-	-	48.1	1.7	-	-
1966	-	-	48.3	0.4	-	-	-	-	49.2	1.9	-	-	-	-	49.1	-0.2	-	-	-	-	50.6	3.1	-	-
1967	-	-	50.9	0.6	-	-	-	-	51.3	0.8	-	-	-	-	51.5	0.4	-	-	-	-	51.7	0.4	-	-
1968	-	-	52.4	1.4	-	-	-	-	54.3	3.6	-	-	-	-	54.7	0.7	-	-	-	-	55.8	2.0	-	-
1969	-	-	56.3	0.9	-	-	-	-	57.7	2.5	-	-	-	-	57.9	0.3	-	-	-	-	59.9	3.5	-	-
1970	-	-	60.8	1.5	-	-	-	-	60.5	-0.5	-	-	-	-	60.9	0.7	-	-	-	-	60.3	-1.0	-	-
1971	-	-	60.1	-0.3	-	-	-	-	60.9	1.3	-	-	-	-	61.4	0.8	-	-	-	-	60.8	-1.0	-	-
1972	-	-	61.7	1.5	-	-	-	-	62.4	1.1	-	-	-	-	62.5	0.2	-	-	-	-	63.7	1.9	-	-
1973	-	-	64.6	1.4	-	-	-	-	65.9	2.0	-	-	-	-	66.6	1.1	-	-	-	-	67.5	1.4	-	-
1974	-	-	68.8	1.9	-	-	-	-	69.8	1.5	-	-	-	-	70.7	1.3	-	-	-	-	72.1	2.0	-	-
1975	-	-	72.1	0.0	-	-	-	-	72.0	-0.1	-	-	-	-	73.1	1.5	-	-	-	-	73.5	0.5	-	-
1976	-	-	73.2	-0.4	-	-	-	-	74.7	2.0	-	-	-	-	74.9	0.3	-	-	-	-	76.3	1.9	-	-
1977	-	-	76.9	0.8	-	-	-	-	77.6	0.9	-	-	-	-	80.2	3.4	-	-	-	-	81.0	1.0	-	-
1978	-	-	81.5	0.6	-	-	80.5	-1.2	-	-	80.7	0.2	-	-	84.3	4.5	-	-	84.3	0.0	-	-	85.0	0.8
1979	-	-	85.8	0.9	-	-	86.2	0.5	-	-	85.7	-0.6	-	-	88.6	3.4	-	-	89.2	0.7	-	-	89.2	0.0
1980	-	-	90.9	1.9	-	-	93.1	2.4	-	-	94.1	1.1	-	-	96.2	2.2	-	-	97.5	1.4	-	-	98.1	0.6
1981	-	-	98.6	0.5	-	-	99.9	1.3	-	-	100.9	1.0	-	-	99.5	-1.4	-	-	98.2	-1.3	-	-	95.7	-2.5
1982	-	-	98.4	2.8	-	-	97.4	-1.0	-	-	97.3	-0.1	-	-	97.2	-0.1	-	-	97.6	0.4	-	-	97.3	-0.3
1983	-	-	98.6	1.3	-	-	100.8	2.2	-	-	98.4	-2.4	-	-	98.9	0.5	-	-	101.2	2.3	-	-	99.3	-1.9
1984	-	-	103.9	4.6	-	-	102.3	-1.5	-	-	100.1	-2.2	-	-	100.7	0.6	-	-	106.3	5.6	-	-	106.9	0.6
1985	-	-	106.3	-0.6	-	-	107.8	1.4	-	-	108.7	0.8	-	-	110.1	1.3	-	-	112.9	2.5	-	-	110.1	-2.5
1986	-	-	107.7	-2.2	-	-	107.7	0.0	-	-	107.8	0.1	-	-	111.8	3.7	-	-	111.7	-0.1	-	-	108.5	-2.9
1987	-	-	110.6	1.9	-	-	118.2	6.9	-	-	113.8	-3.7	-	-	113.3	-0.4	-	-	119.1	5.1	-	-	117.9	-1.0
1988	-	-	118.8	0.8	-	-	124.1	4.5	-	-	119.6	-3.6	-	-	122.5	2.4	-	-	129.0	5.3	-	-	127.1	-1.5
1989	-	-	118.3	-6.9	-	-	129.7	9.6	-	-	121.0	-6.7	-	-	121.1	0.1	-	-	123.6	2.1	-	-	121.9	-1.4
1990	-	-	125.9	3.3	-	-	131.1	4.1	-	-	127.4	-2.8	-	-	131.2	3.0	-	-	137.2	4.6	-	-	135.8	-1.0
1991	-	-	138.1	1.7	-	-	142.9	3.5	-	-	138.4	-3.1	-	-	134.8	-2.6	-	-	146.4	8.6	-	-	130.5	-10.9
1992	-	-	143.7	10.1	-	-	142.3	-1.0	-	-	139.2	-2.2	-	-	135.8	-2.4	-	-	148.6	9.4	-	-	142.5	-4.1
1993	-	-	139.4	-2.2	-	-	155.9	11.8	-	-	142.5	-8.6	-	-	134.8	-5.4	-	-	145.3	7.8	-	-	139.6	-3.9

Source: U.S. Department of Labor, Bureau of Labor Statistics, Division of Consumer Prices and Price Indexes. - indicates no data collected for period.

Dallas-Fort Worth, TX
Consumer Price Index - All Urban Consumers
Base 1982-1984 = 100
Transportation

For 1963-1993. Columns headed % show percentile change in the index from the previous period for which an index is available.

Year	Jan Index	%	Feb Index	%	Mar Index	%	Apr Index	%	May Index	%	Jun Index	%	Jul Index	%	Aug Index	%	Sep Index	%	Oct Index	%	Nov Index	%	Dec Index	%
1963	-	-	-		-		-		-	-	-		-		-		-		-		31.5	-	-	
1964	-		30.7	-2.5	-		-		31.9	3.9	-		-		30.6	-4.1	-		-		31.9	4.2	-	
1965	-		30.1	-5.6	-		-		31.9	6.0	-		-		32.0	0.3	-		-		32.2	0.6	-	
1966	-		31.7	-1.6	-		-		32.3	1.9	-		-		32.4	0.3	-		-		32.7	0.9	-	
1967	-		32.6	-0.3	-		-		33.1	1.5	-		-		33.8	2.1	-		-		33.6	-0.6	-	
1968	-		33.6	0.0	-		-		34.5	2.7	-		-		34.8	0.9	-		-		34.9	0.3	-	
1969	-		34.8	-0.3	-		-		35.5	2.0	-		-		35.6	0.3	-		-		36.4	2.2	-	
1970	-		35.9	-1.4	-		-		36.8	2.5	-		-		37.3	1.4	-		-		37.4	0.3	-	
1971	-		38.5	2.9	-		-		38.7	0.5	-		-		39.9	3.1	-		-		39.5	-1.0	-	
1972	-		39.2	-0.8	-		-		40.2	2.6	-		-		40.4	0.5	-		-		39.8	-1.5	-	
1973	-		39.6	-0.5	-		-		41.1	3.8	-		-		41.4	0.7	-		-		42.0	1.4	-	
1974	-		43.9	4.5	-		-		47.0	7.1	-		-		49.2	4.7	-		-		49.6	0.8	-	
1975	-		49.6	0.0	-		-		51.1	3.0	-		-		53.7	5.1	-		-		54.0	0.6	-	
1976	-		53.6	-0.7	-		-		56.1	4.7	-		-		57.7	2.9	-		-		59.2	2.6	-	
1977	-		59.4	0.3	-		-		61.5	3.5	-		-		61.7	0.3	-		-		61.3	-0.6	-	
1978	-		61.0	-0.5	-		61.4	0.7	-		62.6	2.0	-		63.4	1.3	-		64.4	1.6	-		65.0	0.9
1979	-		66.1	1.7	-		68.9	4.2	-		72.3	4.9	-		74.4	2.9	-		75.4	1.3	-		77.8	3.2
1980	-		83.3	7.1	-		86.2	3.5	-		86.6	0.5	-		87.6	1.2	-		88.1	0.6	-		88.6	0.6
1981	-		92.3	4.2	-		95.1	3.0	-		96.5	1.5	-		96.5	0.0	-		97.2	0.7	-		97.6	0.4
1982	-		97.2	-0.4	-		93.8	-3.5	-		98.0	4.5	-		99.1	1.1	-		98.4	-0.7	-		97.9	-0.5
1983	-		95.6	-2.3	-		97.3	1.8	-		99.4	2.2	-		100.6	1.2	-		102.0	1.4	-		101.5	-0.5
1984	-		100.7	-0.8	-		101.7	1.0	-		102.4	0.7	-		104.8	2.3	-		105.9	1.0	-		105.6	-0.3
1985	-		104.9	-0.7	-		106.5	1.5	-		107.6	1.0	-		108.0	0.4	-		108.6	0.6	-		108.7	0.1
1986	-		107.9	-0.7	-		99.2	-8.1	-		100.2	1.0	-		98.7	-1.5	-		99.2	0.5	-		98.7	-0.5
1987	-		101.2	2.5	-		101.0	-0.2	-		103.2	2.2	-		104.7	1.5	-		105.8	1.1	-		107.2	1.3
1988	-		107.2	0.0	-		106.6	-0.6	-		108.2	1.5	-		108.4	0.2	-		108.8	0.4	-		109.0	0.2
1989	-		108.9	-0.1	-		109.5	0.6	-		112.6	2.8	-		110.4	-2.0	-		111.9	1.4	-		112.1	0.2
1990	-		113.9	1.6	-		113.1	-0.7	-		114.1	0.9	-		116.6	2.2	-		123.6	6.0	-		125.3	1.4
1991	-		121.0	-3.4	-		118.3	-2.2	-		119.5	1.0	-		120.8	1.1	-		121.1	0.2	-		123.1	1.7
1992	-		121.3	-1.5	-		122.4	0.9	-		123.0	0.5	-		122.9	-0.1	-		126.1	2.6	-		125.6	-0.4
1993	-		125.5	-0.1	-		126.1	0.5	-		127.9	1.4	-		130.4	2.0	-		132.1	1.3	-		133.1	0.8

Source: U.S. Department of Labor, Bureau of Labor Statistics, Division of Consumer Prices and Price Indexes. - indicates no data collected for period.

Dallas-Fort Worth, TX
Consumer Price Index - Urban Wage Earners
Base 1982-1984 = 100
Transportation

For 1963-1993. Columns headed % show percentile change in the index from the previous period for which an index is available.

Year	Jan Index	%	Feb Index	%	Mar Index	%	Apr Index	%	May Index	%	Jun Index	%	Jul Index	%	Aug Index	%	Sep Index	%	Oct Index	%	Nov Index	%	Dec Index	%
1963	-	-	-	-	-	-	-	-	-	-	-	-	-	-	-	-	-	-	-	-	31.5	-	-	-
1964	-	-	30.8	-2.2	-	-	-	-	31.9	3.6	-	-	-	-	30.7	-3.8	-	-	-	-	32.0	4.2	-	-
1965	-	-	30.2	-5.6	-	-	-	-	31.9	5.6	-	-	-	-	32.1	0.6	-	-	-	-	32.2	0.3	-	-
1966	-	-	31.7	-1.6	-	-	-	-	32.3	1.9	-	-	-	-	32.4	0.3	-	-	-	-	32.8	1.2	-	-
1967	-	-	32.6	-0.6	-	-	-	-	33.1	1.5	-	-	-	-	33.9	2.4	-	-	-	-	33.6	-0.9	-	-
1968	-	-	33.7	0.3	-	-	-	-	34.5	2.4	-	-	-	-	34.8	0.9	-	-	-	-	35.0	0.6	-	-
1969	-	-	34.8	-0.6	-	-	-	-	35.6	2.3	-	-	-	-	35.6	0.0	-	-	-	-	36.4	2.2	-	-
1970	-	-	36.0	-1.1	-	-	-	-	36.9	2.5	-	-	-	-	37.3	1.1	-	-	-	-	37.5	0.5	-	-
1971	-	-	38.5	2.7	-	-	-	-	38.8	0.8	-	-	-	-	39.9	2.8	-	-	-	-	39.5	-1.0	-	-
1972	-	-	39.2	-0.8	-	-	-	-	40.2	2.6	-	-	-	-	40.4	0.5	-	-	-	-	39.9	-1.2	-	-
1973	-	-	39.6	-0.8	-	-	-	-	41.2	4.0	-	-	-	-	41.4	0.5	-	-	-	-	42.0	1.4	-	-
1974	-	-	43.9	4.5	-	-	-	-	47.0	7.1	-	-	-	-	49.3	4.9	-	-	-	-	49.7	0.8	-	-
1975	-	-	49.6	-0.2	-	-	-	-	51.1	3.0	-	-	-	-	53.7	5.1	-	-	-	-	54.0	0.6	-	-
1976	-	-	53.7	-0.6	-	-	-	-	56.1	4.5	-	-	-	-	57.7	2.9	-	-	-	-	59.2	2.6	-	-
1977	-	-	59.5	0.5	-	-	-	-	61.6	3.5	-	-	-	-	61.7	0.2	-	-	-	-	61.3	-0.6	-	-
1978	-	-	61.0	-0.5	-	-	61.5	0.8	-	-	62.7	2.0	-	-	63.7	1.6	-	-	64.6	1.4	-	-	65.3	1.1
1979	-	-	66.4	1.7	-	-	69.3	4.4	-	-	72.7	4.9	-	-	75.0	3.2	-	-	75.7	0.9	-	-	78.1	3.2
1980	-	-	83.8	7.3	-	-	86.5	3.2	-	-	86.7	0.2	-	-	87.8	1.3	-	-	88.7	1.0	-	-	89.4	0.8
1981	-	-	93.3	4.4	-	-	95.6	2.5	-	-	97.7	2.2	-	-	97.5	-0.2	-	-	98.6	1.1	-	-	98.0	-0.6
1982	-	-	97.5	-0.5	-	-	94.0	-3.6	-	-	98.2	4.5	-	-	99.3	1.1	-	-	98.6	-0.7	-	-	98.0	-0.6
1983	-	-	95.6	-2.4	-	-	97.4	1.9	-	-	99.4	2.1	-	-	100.6	1.2	-	-	102.0	1.4	-	-	101.4	-0.6
1984	-	-	100.6	-0.8	-	-	101.5	0.9	-	-	102.3	0.8	-	-	104.6	2.2	-	-	105.7	1.1	-	-	105.3	-0.4
1985	-	-	104.5	-0.8	-	-	106.2	1.6	-	-	107.3	1.0	-	-	107.6	0.3	-	-	108.3	0.7	-	-	108.4	0.1
1986	-	-	107.6	-0.7	-	-	98.7	-8.3	-	-	99.7	1.0	-	-	98.1	-1.6	-	-	98.4	0.3	-	-	97.8	-0.6
1987	-	-	101.1	3.4	-	-	101.8	0.7	-	-	104.3	2.5	-	-	106.0	1.6	-	-	106.8	0.8	-	-	107.8	0.9
1988	-	-	107.7	-0.1	-	-	106.9	-0.7	-	-	108.4	1.4	-	-	109.2	0.7	-	-	109.5	0.3	-	-	109.5	0.0
1989	-	-	109.2	-0.3	-	-	110.8	1.5	-	-	114.3	3.2	-	-	111.9	-2.1	-	-	112.9	0.9	-	-	112.6	-0.3
1990	-	-	114.4	1.6	-	-	113.5	-0.8	-	-	115.0	1.3	-	-	117.7	2.3	-	-	125.0	6.2	-	-	126.2	1.0
1991	-	-	120.9	-4.2	-	-	118.5	-2.0	-	-	120.6	1.8	-	-	122.0	1.2	-	-	122.9	0.7	-	-	124.4	1.2
1992	-	-	121.8	-2.1	-	-	123.4	1.3	-	-	126.5	2.5	-	-	127.5	0.8	-	-	129.8	1.8	-	-	129.5	-0.2
1993	-	-	128.3	-0.9	-	-	129.5	0.9	-	-	132.1	2.0	-	-	135.1	2.3	-	-	136.9	1.3	-	-	136.6	-0.2

Source: U.S. Department of Labor, Bureau of Labor Statistics, Division of Consumer Prices and Price Indexes. - indicates no data collected for period.

Dallas-Fort Worth, TX
Consumer Price Index - All Urban Consumers
Base 1982-1984 = 100
Medical Care

For 1963-1993. Columns headed % show percentile change in the index from the previous period for which an index is available.

Year	Jan Index	%	Feb Index	%	Mar Index	%	Apr Index	%	May Index	%	Jun Index	%	Jul Index	%	Aug Index	%	Sep Index	%	Oct Index	%	Nov Index	%	Dec Index	%
1963	-	-	-		-		-		-	-	-		-		-		-		-		24.1		-	-
1964	-		24.4	1.2	-		-		24.5	0.4	-		-		24.5	0.0	-		-		24.5	0.0	-	
1965	-		24.8	1.2	-		-		25.0	0.8	-		-		25.0	0.0	-		-		25.2	0.8	-	
1966	-		25.8	2.4	-		-		26.3	1.9	-		-		26.6	1.1	-		-		26.9	1.1	-	
1967	-		28.0	4.1	-		-		28.0	0.0	-		-		28.3	1.1	-		-		28.8	1.8	-	
1968	-		29.5	2.4	-		-		30.0	1.7	-		-		30.0	0.0	-		-		30.5	1.7	-	
1969	-		31.7	3.9	-		-		32.2	1.6	-		-		32.6	1.2	-		-		32.9	0.9	-	
1970	-		34.2	4.0	-		-		34.8	1.8	-		-		35.1	0.9	-		-		35.1	0.0	-	
1971	-		36.1	2.8	-		-		36.5	1.1	-		-		36.7	0.5	-		-		36.4	-0.8	-	
1972	-		36.9	1.4	-		-		37.1	0.5	-		-		37.2	0.3	-		-		37.5	0.8	-	
1973	-		38.2	1.9	-		-		38.6	1.0	-		-		38.5	-0.3	-		-		39.5	2.6	-	
1974	-		40.2	1.8	-		-		40.9	1.7	-		-		42.4	3.7	-		-		43.4	2.4	-	
1975	-		44.6	2.8	-		-		45.4	1.8	-		-		46.8	3.1	-		-		47.2	0.9	-	
1976	-		48.5	2.8	-		-		48.8	0.6	-		-		50.7	3.9	-		-		52.3	3.2	-	
1977	-		53.3	1.9	-		-		54.8	2.8	-		-		55.8	1.8	-		-		57.0	2.2	-	
1978	-		58.3	2.3	-		58.9	1.0	-		59.8	1.5	-		60.0	0.3	-		60.4	0.7	-		61.1	1.2
1979	-		61.3	0.3	-		62.2	1.5	-		62.4	0.3	-		63.5	1.8	-		63.6	0.2	-		65.2	2.5
1980	-		66.5	2.0	-		69.0	3.8	-		69.7	1.0	-		71.9	3.2	-		71.8	-0.1	-		72.4	0.8
1981	-		74.1	2.3	-		75.6	2.0	-		79.4	5.0	-		83.3	4.9	-		85.5	2.6	-		87.4	2.2
1982	-		89.2	2.1	-		90.3	1.2	-		91.6	1.4	-		92.2	0.7	-		94.2	2.2	-		96.0	1.9
1983	-		98.8	2.9	-		100.9	2.1	-		100.8	-0.1	-		102.3	1.5	-		102.3	0.0	-		104.1	1.8
1984	-		105.4	1.2	-		106.0	0.6	-		106.5	0.5	-		107.4	0.8	-		108.5	1.0	-		109.3	0.7
1985	-		110.5	1.1	-		111.3	0.7	-		112.1	0.7	-		114.7	2.3	-		116.1	1.2	-		122.1	5.2
1986	-		123.7	1.3	-		125.3	1.3	-		126.0	0.6	-		127.5	1.2	-		129.2	1.3	-		130.6	1.1
1987	-		130.3	-0.2	-		134.0	2.8	-		134.3	0.2	-		135.4	0.8	-		135.3	-0.1	-		137.9	1.9
1988	-		141.6	2.7	-		140.7	-0.6	-		140.9	0.1	-		141.6	0.5	-		142.9	0.9	-		145.7	2.0
1989	-		148.2	1.7	-		148.7	0.3	-		149.8	0.7	-		151.9	1.4	-		154.4	1.6	-		154.4	0.0
1990	-		156.4	1.3	-		156.9	0.3	-		162.1	3.3	-		163.7	1.0	-		167.3	2.2	-		168.2	0.5
1991	-		170.4	1.3	-		170.9	0.3	-		174.3	2.0	-		176.3	1.1	-		179.0	1.5	-		180.8	1.0
1992	-		182.7	1.1	-		185.7	1.6	-		187.7	1.1	-		188.9	0.6	-		193.8	2.6	-		194.1	0.2
1993	-		193.5	-0.3	-		194.0	0.3	-		196.7	1.4	-		197.9	0.6	-		199.7	0.9	-		200.6	0.5

Source: U.S. Department of Labor, Bureau of Labor Statistics, Division of Consumer Prices and Price Indexes. - indicates no data collected for period.

Dallas-Fort Worth, TX
Consumer Price Index - Urban Wage Earners
Base 1982-1984 = 100
Medical Care

For 1963-1993. Columns headed % show percentile change in the index from the previous period for which an index is available.

Year	Jan Index	%	Feb Index	%	Mar Index	%	Apr Index	%	May Index	%	Jun Index	%	Jul Index	%	Aug Index	%	Sep Index	%	Oct Index	%	Nov Index	%	Dec Index	%
1963	-		-		-		-		-		-		-		-		-		-		24.5		-	
1964	-		24.8	1.2	-		-		24.9	0.4	-		-		24.9	0.0	-		-		24.9	0.0	-	
1965	-		25.2	1.2	-		-		25.4	0.8	-		-		25.4	0.0	-		-		25.6	0.8	-	
1966	-		26.2	2.3	-		-		26.8	2.3	-		-		27.0	0.7	-		-		27.3	1.1	-	
1967	-		28.4	4.0	-		-		28.5	0.4	-		-		28.8	1.1	-		-		29.3	1.7	-	
1968	-		30.0	2.4	-		-		30.5	1.7	-		-		30.5	0.0	-		-		31.0	1.6	-	
1969	-		32.2	3.9	-		-		32.8	1.9	-		-		33.2	1.2	-		-		33.5	0.9	-	
1970	-		34.8	3.9	-		-		35.4	1.7			-		35.7	0.8	-		-		35.6	-0.3	-	
1971	-		36.7	3.1	-		-		37.1	1.1	-		-		37.3	0.5	-		-		37.0	-0.8	-	
1972	-		37.6	1.6	-		-		37.7	0.3	-		-		37.8	0.3	-		-		38.2	1.1	-	
1973	-		38.8	1.6	-		-		39.2	1.0	-		-		39.2	0.0	-		-		40.1	2.3	-	
1974	-		40.9	2.0	-		-		41.6	1.7	-		-		43.1	3.6	-		-		44.1	2.3	-	
1975	-		45.3	2.7	-		-		46.2	2.0	-		-		47.6	3.0	-		-		48.0	0.8	-	
1976	-		49.3	2.7	-		-		49.6	0.6	-		-		51.5	3.8	-		-		53.2	3.3	-	
1977	-		54.1	1.7	-		-		55.7	3.0	-		-		56.7	1.8	-		-		57.9	2.1	-	
1978	-		59.2	2.2	-		59.9	1.2	-		60.1	0.3	-		60.9	1.3	-		61.7	1.3	-		63.1	2.3
1979	-		63.1	0.0	-		64.5	2.2	-		65.1	0.9	-		66.1	1.5	-		66.0	-0.2	-		67.3	2.0
1980	-		68.2	1.3	-		70.2	2.9	-		71.1	1.3	-		74.6	4.9	-		74.5	-0.1	-		76.0	2.0
1981	-		76.8	1.1	-		77.6	1.0	-		80.4	3.6	-		83.3	3.6	-		84.8	1.8	-		87.0	2.6
1982	-		88.8	2.1	-		90.1	1.5	-		91.3	1.3	-		92.0	0.8	-		94.1	2.3	-		95.9	1.9
1983	-		98.8	3.0	-		101.0	2.2	-		100.7	-0.3	-		102.3	1.6	-		102.3	0.0	-		104.2	1.9
1984	-		105.7	1.4	-		106.1	0.4	-		106.6	0.5	-		107.6	0.9	-		108.7	1.0	-		109.6	0.8
1985	-		110.8	1.1	-		111.6	0.7	-		112.3	0.6	-		115.1	2.5	-		116.6	1.3	-		122.9	5.4
1986	-		124.5	1.3	-		126.0	1.2	-		126.8	0.6	-		128.4	1.3	-		130.1	1.3	-		131.5	1.1
1987	-		131.4	-0.1	-		135.1	2.8	-		135.5	0.3	-		136.8	1.0	-		136.8	0.0	-		139.8	2.2
1988	-		143.1	2.4	-		142.0	-0.8	-		142.4	0.3	-		143.4	0.7	-		144.4	0.7	-		148.1	2.6
1989	-		150.6	1.7	-		151.0	0.3	-		152.2	0.8	-		154.2	1.3	-		156.5	1.5	-		156.8	0.2
1990	-		158.8	1.3	-		159.3	0.3	-		164.7	3.4	-		166.6	1.2	-		170.1	2.1	-		170.8	0.4
1991	-		172.9	1.2	-		174.0	0.6	-		177.2	1.8	-		179.5	1.3	-		182.4	1.6	-		183.7	0.7
1992	-		185.7	1.1	-		189.5	2.0	-		191.9	1.3	-		193.1	0.6	-		198.1	2.6	-		198.0	-0.1
1993	-		197.2	-0.4	-		197.6	0.2	-		200.9	1.7	-		202.1	0.6	-		203.8	0.8	-		204.7	0.4

Source: U.S. Department of Labor, Bureau of Labor Statistics, Division of Consumer Prices and Price Indexes. - indicates no data collected for period.

Dallas-Fort Worth, TX
Consumer Price Index - All Urban Consumers
Base 1982-1984 = 100
Entertainment

For 1975-1993. Columns headed % show percentile change in the index from the previous period for which an index is available.

Year	Jan Index	%	Feb Index	%	Mar Index	%	Apr Index	%	May Index	%	Jun Index	%	Jul Index	%	Aug Index	%	Sep Index	%	Oct Index	%	Nov Index	%	Dec Index	%
1975	-		-		-		-		-		-		-		-		-		-		64.6	-	-	-
1976	-		65.3	1.1	-		-		67.2	2.9	-		-		67.8	0.9	-		-		68.5	1.0	-	-
1977	-		68.5	0.0	-		-		69.7	1.8	-		-		70.8	1.6	-		-		69.1	-2.4	-	-
1978	-		68.8	-0.4	-		68.4	-0.6	-		70.5	3.1	-		70.5	0.0	-		70.6	0.1	-		70.9	0.4
1979	-		71.8	1.3	-		72.3	0.7	-		72.9	0.8	-		74.1	1.6	-		75.4	1.8	-		76.5	1.5
1980	-		77.3	1.0	-		81.4	5.3	-		83.2	2.2	-		84.5	1.6	-		84.8	0.4	-		85.8	1.2
1981	-		86.4	0.7	-		86.0	-0.5	-		86.9	1.0	-		87.6	0.8	-		88.6	1.1	-		88.5	-0.1
1982	-		90.7	2.5	-		90.7	0.0	-		93.2	2.8	-		93.3	0.1	-		97.0	4.0	-		95.7	-1.3
1983	-		98.2	2.6	-		97.4	-0.8	-		98.2	0.8	-		101.2	3.1	-		102.4	1.2	-		102.1	-0.3
1984	-		104.4	2.3	-		106.2	1.7	-		106.4	0.2	-		106.8	0.4	-		110.0	3.0	-		111.9	1.7
1985	-		114.3	2.1	-		114.1	-0.2	-		112.5	-1.4	-		114.7	2.0	-		114.5	-0.2	-		115.0	0.4
1986	-		113.5	-1.3	-		114.4	0.8	-		115.7	1.1	-		115.6	-0.1	-		117.6	1.7	-		119.3	1.4
1987	-		120.8	1.3	-		121.8	0.8	-		121.8	0.0	-		122.2	0.3	-		124.8	2.1	-		121.4	-2.7
1988	-		124.0	2.1	-		128.4	3.5	-		127.9	-0.4	-		128.7	0.6	-		129.2	0.4	-		127.4	-1.4
1989	-		128.5	0.9	-		133.8	4.1	-		134.7	0.7	-		131.8	-2.2	-		134.3	1.9	-		135.3	0.7
1990	-		134.6	-0.5	-		138.4	2.8	-		137.8	-0.4	-		136.6	-0.9	-		139.8	2.3	-		138.7	-0.8
1991	-		142.4	2.7	-		142.6	0.1	-		142.5	-0.1	-		143.7	0.8	-		142.0	-1.2	-		142.1	0.1
1992	-		142.1	0.0	-		142.9	0.6	-		141.6	-0.9	-		140.9	-0.5	-		141.7	0.6	-		143.4	1.2
1993	-		144.1	0.5	-		142.6	-1.0	-		143.5	0.6	-		143.7	0.1	-		145.8	1.5	-		145.1	-0.5

Source: U.S. Department of Labor, Bureau of Labor Statistics, Division of Consumer Prices and Price Indexes. - indicates no data collected for period.

Dallas-Fort Worth, TX
Consumer Price Index - Urban Wage Earners
Base 1982-1984 = 100
Entertainment

For 1975-1993. Columns headed % show percentile change in the index from the previous period for which an index is available.

Year	Jan Index	%	Feb Index	%	Mar Index	%	Apr Index	%	May Index	%	Jun Index	%	Jul Index	%	Aug Index	%	Sep Index	%	Oct Index	%	Nov Index	%	Dec Index	%
1975	-	-	-	-	-	-	-	-	-	-	-	-	-	-	-	-	-	-	-	-	69.0	-	-	-
1976	-	-	69.8	1.2	-	-	-	-	71.8	2.9	-	-	-	-	72.5	1.0	-	-	-	-	73.3	1.1	-	-
1977	-	-	73.3	0.0	-	-	-	-	74.5	1.6	-	-	-	-	75.7	1.6	-	-	-	-	73.9	-2.4	-	-
1978	-	-	73.6	-0.4	-	-	74.3	1.0	-	-	74.8	0.7	-	-	74.5	-0.4	-	-	74.7	0.3	-	-	75.3	0.8
1979	-	-	75.7	0.5	-	-	75.9	0.3	-	-	75.4	-0.7	-	-	76.4	1.3	-	-	79.3	3.8	-	-	78.7	-0.8
1980	-	-	79.8	1.4	-	-	80.3	0.6	-	-	82.8	3.1	-	-	84.0	1.4	-	-	84.3	0.4	-	-	84.9	0.7
1981	-	-	86.4	1.8	-	-	87.1	0.8	-	-	87.4	0.3	-	-	87.9	0.6	-	-	89.0	1.3	-	-	89.1	0.1
1982	-	-	91.4	2.6	-	-	91.4	0.0	-	-	93.7	2.5	-	-	93.8	0.1	-	-	97.0	3.4	-	-	96.3	-0.7
1983	-	-	98.2	2.0	-	-	97.5	-0.7	-	-	98.2	0.7	-	-	101.1	3.0	-	-	102.1	1.0	-	-	101.7	-0.4
1984	-	-	104.2	2.5	-	-	105.9	1.6	-	-	106.5	0.6	-	-	106.5	0.0	-	-	109.4	2.7	-	-	110.5	1.0
1985	-	-	113.3	2.5	-	-	113.1	-0.2	-	-	111.1	-1.8	-	-	113.5	2.2	-	-	113.2	-0.3	-	-	113.7	0.4
1986	-	-	112.5	-1.1	-	-	113.3	0.7	-	-	114.2	0.8	-	-	114.3	0.1	-	-	116.1	1.6	-	-	117.4	1.1
1987	-	-	119.4	1.7	-	-	120.2	0.7	-	-	120.2	0.0	-	-	120.7	0.4	-	-	123.2	2.1	-	-	120.5	-2.2
1988	-	-	122.9	2.0	-	-	126.8	3.2	-	-	126.6	-0.2	-	-	127.5	0.7	-	-	127.5	0.0	-	-	126.1	-1.1
1989	-	-	127.3	1.0	-	-	132.7	4.2	-	-	133.7	0.8	-	-	130.9	-2.1	-	-	133.2	1.8	-	-	134.1	0.7
1990	-	-	133.2	-0.7	-	-	136.3	2.3	-	-	135.6	-0.5	-	-	134.8	-0.6	-	-	137.9	2.3	-	-	136.7	-0.9
1991	-	-	140.6	2.9	-	-	140.9	0.2	-	-	140.8	-0.1	-	-	142.0	0.9	-	-	140.2	-1.3	-	-	140.5	0.2
1992	-	-	140.5	0.0	-	-	141.2	0.5	-	-	139.6	-1.1	-	-	138.6	-0.7	-	-	139.6	0.7	-	-	141.3	1.2
1993	-	-	142.0	0.5	-	-	140.4	-1.1	-	-	140.7	0.2	-	-	141.0	0.2	-	-	143.7	1.9	-	-	143.0	-0.5

Source: U.S. Department of Labor, Bureau of Labor Statistics, Division of Consumer Prices and Price Indexes. - indicates no data collected for period.

Dallas-Fort Worth, TX
Consumer Price Index - All Urban Consumers
Base 1982-1984 = 100
Other Goods and Services

For 1975-1993. Columns headed % show percentile change in the index from the previous period for which an index is available.

Year	Jan Index	%	Feb Index	%	Mar Index	%	Apr Index	%	May Index	%	Jun Index	%	Jul Index	%	Aug Index	%	Sep Index	%	Oct Index	%	Nov Index	%	Dec Index	%
1975	-	-	-		-	-	-		-		-		-		-		-		-		54.4	-	-	-
1976	-		54.8	0.7	-		-		55.5	1.3	-		-		55.8	0.5	-		-		57.5	3.0	-	
1977	-		58.2	1.2	-		-		59.2	1.7	-		-		59.9	1.2	-		-		60.9	1.7	-	
1978	-		61.6	1.1	-		61.9	0.5	-		61.9	0.0	-		64.6	4.4	-		65.5	1.4	-		66.1	0.9
1979	-		67.7	2.4	-		67.7	0.0	-		67.4	-0.4	-		69.0	2.4	-		70.5	2.2	-		71.6	1.6
1980	-		74.1	3.5	-		74.6	0.7	-		75.0	0.5	-		75.1	0.1	-		79.2	5.5	-		81.2	2.5
1981	-		81.3	0.1	-		82.9	2.0	-		83.3	0.5	-		84.6	1.6	-		86.5	2.2	-		86.8	0.3
1982	-		87.9	1.3	-		89.5	1.8	-		90.7	1.3	-		92.5	2.0	-		96.1	3.9	-		97.2	1.1
1983	-		98.3	1.1	-		99.5	1.2	-		100.3	0.8	-		101.9	1.6	-		103.4	1.5	-		103.5	0.1
1984	-		104.9	1.4	-		106.2	1.2	-		107.0	0.8	-		107.2	0.2	-		109.8	2.4	-		110.1	0.3
1985	-		110.1	0.0	-		111.0	0.8	-		111.2	0.2	-		112.5	1.2	-		115.7	2.8	-		116.0	0.3
1986	-		117.0	0.9	-		116.7	-0.3	-		116.5	-0.2	-		120.7	3.6	-		122.6	1.6	-		126.3	3.0
1987	-		128.2	1.5	-		128.6	0.3	-		127.4	-0.9	-		127.3	-0.1	-		130.7	2.7	-		131.9	0.9
1988	-		131.8	-0.1	-		133.2	1.1	-		134.5	1.0	-		135.1	0.4	-		138.6	2.6	-		139.8	0.9
1989	-		143.2	2.4	-		144.9	1.2	-		144.8	-0.1	-		146.0	0.8	-		150.5	3.1	-		149.9	-0.4
1990	-		153.8	2.6	-		153.9	0.1	-		155.1	0.8	-		158.2	2.0	-		159.2	0.6	-		160.3	0.7
1991	-		160.9	0.4	-		162.1	0.7	-		164.4	1.4	-		164.7	0.2	-		164.4	-0.2	-		167.9	2.1
1992	-		170.2	1.4	-		169.5	-0.4	-		169.4	-0.1	-		168.8	-0.4	-		173.5	2.8	-		172.9	-0.3
1993	-		178.4	3.2	-		179.9	0.8	-		184.9	2.8	-		184.7	-0.1	-		177.6	-3.8	-		178.8	0.7

Source: U.S. Department of Labor, Bureau of Labor Statistics, Division of Consumer Prices and Price Indexes. - indicates no data collected for period.

Dallas-Fort Worth, TX
Consumer Price Index - Urban Wage Earners
Base 1982-1984 = 100
Other Goods and Services

For 1975-1993. Columns headed % show percentile change in the index from the previous period for which an index is available.

Year	Jan Index	%	Feb Index	%	Mar Index	%	Apr Index	%	May Index	%	Jun Index	%	Jul Index	%	Aug Index	%	Sep Index	%	Oct Index	%	Nov Index	%	Dec Index	%
1975	-		-		-		-		-		-		-		-		-		-		57.0	-	-	-
1976	-	-	57.4	0.7	-	-	-	-	58.2	1.4	-	-	-	-	58.5	0.5	-	-	-	-	60.2	2.9	-	-
1977	-	-	61.0	1.3	-	-	-	-	62.1	1.8	-	-	-	-	62.8	1.1	-	-	-	-	63.8	1.6	-	-
1978	-	-	64.5	1.1	-	-	65.4	1.4	-	-	65.6	0.3	-	-	67.8	3.4	-	-	68.2	0.6	-	-	68.6	0.6
1979	-	-	70.0	2.0	-	-	70.2	0.3	-	-	70.5	0.4	-	-	71.8	1.8	-	-	73.8	2.8	-	-	75.3	2.0
1980	-	-	77.6	3.1	-	-	78.0	0.5	-	-	78.9	1.2	-	-	79.2	0.4	-	-	82.0	3.5	-	-	83.0	1.2
1981	-	-	84.1	1.3	-	-	83.8	-0.4	-	-	84.1	0.4	-	-	83.7	-0.5	-	-	85.3	1.9	-	-	86.4	1.3
1982	-	-	87.3	1.0	-	-	89.1	2.1	-	-	90.4	1.5	-	-	92.3	2.1	-	-	95.8	3.8	-	-	97.5	1.8
1983	-	-	98.5	1.0	-	-	100.2	1.7	-	-	101.0	0.8	-	-	102.5	1.5	-	-	103.5	1.0	-	-	103.7	0.2
1984	-	-	104.8	1.1	-	-	106.1	1.2	-	-	107.1	0.9	-	-	107.3	0.2	-	-	109.3	1.9	-	-	109.6	0.3
1985	-	-	109.8	0.2	-	-	110.4	0.5	-	-	110.3	-0.1	-	-	112.1	1.6	-	-	114.6	2.2	-	-	114.9	0.3
1986	-	-	116.3	1.2	-	-	115.9	-0.3	-	-	115.5	-0.3	-	-	120.5	4.3	-	-	121.9	1.2	-	-	124.5	2.1
1987	-	-	125.8	1.0	-	-	126.3	0.4	-	-	124.9	-1.1	-	-	124.8	-0.1	-	-	127.8	2.4	-	-	129.3	1.2
1988	-	-	129.0	-0.2	-	-	130.7	1.3	-	-	132.3	1.2	-	-	132.9	0.5	-	-	135.8	2.2	-	-	137.2	1.0
1989	-	-	141.3	3.0	-	-	142.1	0.6	-	-	141.9	-0.1	-	-	143.2	0.9	-	-	147.3	2.9	-	-	146.6	-0.5
1990	-	-	150.9	2.9	-	-	151.1	0.1	-	-	152.3	0.8	-	-	155.9	2.4	-	-	156.8	0.6	-	-	158.2	0.9
1991	-	-	158.9	0.4	-	-	160.4	0.9	-	-	162.2	1.1	-	-	162.6	0.2	-	-	162.2	-0.2	-	-	166.3	2.5
1992	-	-	168.6	1.4	-	-	167.8	-0.5	-	-	167.6	-0.1	-	-	166.8	-0.5	-	-	171.5	2.8	-	-	170.8	-0.4
1993	-	-	176.4	3.3	-	-	178.0	0.9	-	-	183.0	2.8	-	-	182.9	-0.1	-	-	174.4	-4.6	-	-	175.9	0.9

Source: U.S. Department of Labor, Bureau of Labor Statistics, Division of Consumer Prices and Price Indexes. - indicates no data collected for period.

Denver-Boulder, CO
Consumer Price Index - All Urban Consumers
Base 1982-1984 = 100
Annual Averages

For 1964-1993. Columns headed % show percentile change in the index from the previous period for which an index is available.

Year	All Items		Food & Beverage		Housing		Apparel & Upkeep		Trans-portation		Medical Care		Entertain-ment		Other Goods & Services	
	Index	%	Index	%	Index	%	Index	%	Index	%	Index	%	Index	%	Index	%
1964	28.3	-	-	-	-	-	-	-	-	-	-	-	-	-	-	-
1965	28.8	1.8	-	-	-	-	-	-	-	-	-	-	-	-	-	-
1966	29.7	3.1	-	-	-	-	-	-	-	-	-	-	-	-	-	-
1967	30.0	1.0	-	-	-	-	-	-	-	-	-	-	-	-	-	-
1968	30.7	2.3	-	-	-	-	-	-	-	-	-	-	-	-	-	-
1969	32.0	4.2	-	-	-	-	-	-	-	-	-	-	-	-	-	-
1970	34.5	7.8	-	-	-	-	-	-	-	-	-	-	-	-	-	-
1971	35.9	4.1	-	-	-	-	64.3	-	37.9	-	36.5	-	-	-	-	-
1972	37.0	3.1	-	-	-	-	66.1	2.8	37.8	-0.3	37.6	3.0	-	-	-	-
1973	39.6	7.0	-	-	-	-	68.8	4.1	39.6	4.8	39.0	3.7	-	-	-	-
1974	43.9	10.9	-	-	-	-	74.3	8.0	44.0	11.1	42.6	9.2	-	-	-	-
1975	48.4	10.3	-	-	-	-	78.6	5.8	48.3	9.8	47.4	11.3	-	-	52.2	-
1976	51.1	5.6	63.8	-	44.4	-	83.1	5.7	52.4	8.5	51.0	7.6	57.8	-	52.2	-
1977	55.4	8.4	68.9	8.0	48.6	9.5	88.0	5.9	56.3	7.4	55.8	9.4	61.5	6.4	56.6	8.4
1978	60.6	9.4	74.9	8.7	54.6	12.3	90.2	2.5	59.8	6.2	60.7	8.8	66.1	7.5	60.8	7.4
1979	70.0	15.5	82.8	10.5	65.6	20.1	92.1	2.1	70.3	17.6	66.2	9.1	72.2	9.2	64.8	6.6
1980	78.4	12.0	86.1	4.0	74.7	13.9	95.6	3.8	82.4	17.2	73.7	11.3	79.7	10.4	72.2	11.4
1981	87.2	11.2	93.2	8.2	84.7	13.4	96.4	0.8	91.7	11.3	81.0	9.9	85.9	7.8	80.9	12.0
1982	95.1	9.1	96.1	3.1	94.8	11.9	101.2	5.0	96.3	5.0	91.1	12.5	94.2	9.7	89.4	10.5
1983	100.5	5.7	99.6	3.6	100.9	6.4	98.8	-2.4	100.1	3.9	100.9	10.8	101.8	8.1	101.5	13.5
1984	104.3	3.8	104.3	4.7	104.1	3.2	100.0	1.2	103.6	3.5	108.0	7.0	104.1	2.3	109.1	7.5
1985	107.1	2.7	106.1	1.7	106.8	2.6	102.6	2.6	105.9	2.2	115.1	6.6	104.4	0.3	115.5	5.9
1986	107.9	0.7	107.2	1.0	108.2	1.3	102.8	0.2	100.9	-4.7	124.0	7.7	106.7	2.2	124.1	7.4
1987	110.8	2.7	108.3	1.0	109.6	1.3	102.0	-0.8	107.9	6.9	132.1	6.5	107.9	1.1	132.7	6.9
1988	113.7	2.6	110.4	1.9	110.0	0.4	106.8	4.7	114.1	5.7	142.6	7.9	109.0	1.0	139.9	5.4
1989	115.8	1.8	115.8	4.9	107.4	-2.4	93.8	-12.2	122.3	7.2	153.4	7.6	120.5	10.6	148.6	6.2
1990	120.9	4.4	124.1	7.2	109.8	2.2	91.2	-2.8	126.8	3.7	173.4	13.0	129.3	7.3	159.6	7.4
1991	125.6	3.9	128.3	3.4	114.1	3.9	94.8	3.9	127.8	0.8	191.8	10.6	130.8	1.2	173.4	8.6
1992	130.3	3.7	128.8	0.4	118.1	3.5	94.6	-0.2	134.2	5.0	206.5	7.7	136.1	4.1	186.4	7.5
1993	135.8	4.2	131.5	2.1	124.1	5.1	95.1	0.5	141.1	5.1	217.9	5.5	141.9	4.3	191.5	2.7

Source: U.S. Department of Labor, Bureau of Labor Statistics, Division of Consumer Prices and Price Indexes. - indicates no data collected for period.

Denver-Boulder, CO
Consumer Price Index - Urban Wage Earners
Base 1982-1984 = 100
Annual Averages

For 1964-1993. Columns headed % show percentile change in the index from the previous period for which an index is available.

Year	All Items		Food & Beverage		Housing		Apparel & Upkeep		Trans- portation		Medical Care		Entertain- ment		Other Goods & Services	
	Index	%	Index	%	Index	%	Index	%	Index	%	Index	%	Index	%	Index	%
1964	28.4	-	-	-	-	-	-	-	-	-	-	-	-	-	-	-
1965	28.8	1.4	-	-	-	-	-	-	-	-	-	-	-	-	-	-
1966	29.7	3.1	-	-	-	-	-	-	-	-	-	-	-	-	-	-
1967	30.0	1.0	-	-	-	-	-	-	-	-	-	-	..	-	-	-
1968	30.8	2.7	-	-	-	-	-	-	-	-	-	-	-	-	-	-
1969	32.1	4.2	-	-	-	-	-	-	-	-	-	-	-	-	-	-
1970	34.5	7.5	-	-	-	-	-	-	-	-	-	-	-	-	-	-
1971	35.9	4.1	-	-	-	-	56.2	-	37.6	-	36.9	-	-	-	-	-
1972	37.1	3.3	-	-	-	-	57.9	3.0	37.5	-0.3	38.0	3.0	-	-	-	-
1973	39.6	6.7	-	-	-	-	60.2	4.0	39.3	4.8	39.4	3.7	-	-	-	-
1974	44.0	11.1	-	-	-	-	65.0	8.0	43.6	10.9	43.1	9.4	-	-	-	-
1975	48.5	10.2	-	-	-	-	68.8	5.8	48.0	10.1	47.8	10.9	-	-	-	-
1976	51.2	5.6	61.7	-	45.2	-	72.7	5.7	51.9	8.1	51.6	7.9	60.7	-	52.3	-
1977	55.5	8.4	66.6	7.9	49.5	9.5	77.0	5.9	55.9	7.7	56.4	9.3	64.6	6.4	56.8	8.6
1978	61.0	9.9	72.9	9.5	55.7	12.5	81.7	6.1	59.1	5.7	61.9	9.8	68.4	5.9	60.7	6.9
1979	70.9	16.2	80.3	10.2	67.5	21.2	88.3	8.1	69.8	18.1	66.4	7.3	73.2	7.0	65.6	8.1
1980	79.9	12.7	85.1	6.0	77.2	14.4	94.2	6.7	82.4	18.1	73.5	10.7	81.6	11.5	72.1	9.9
1981	88.9	11.3	92.9	9.2	87.5	13.3	95.4	1.3	91.8	11.4	81.6	11.0	87.3	7.0	80.3	11.4
1982	97.1	9.2	96.2	3.6	98.2	12.2	100.4	5.2	96.8	5.4	90.9	11.4	94.0	7.7	88.9	10.7
1983	99.8	2.8	99.6	3.5	99.5	1.3	99.0	-1.4	100.0	3.3	101.1	11.2	102.0	8.5	101.8	14.5
1984	103.2	3.4	104.2	4.6	102.3	2.8	100.6	1.6	103.3	3.3	108.0	6.8	104.0	2.0	109.3	7.4
1985	105.9	2.6	106.1	1.8	105.4	3.0	102.4	1.8	105.9	2.5	115.1	6.6	103.1	-0.9	115.4	5.6
1986	106.3	0.4	106.9	0.8	106.6	1.1	101.3	-1.1	100.6	-5.0	124.1	7.8	104.4	1.3	124.1	7.5
1987	109.1	2.6	107.9	0.9	107.7	1.0	99.6	-1.7	108.4	7.8	132.8	7.0	104.8	0.4	133.2	7.3
1988	112.0	2.7	109.9	1.9	108.0	0.3	104.4	4.8	113.6	4.8	144.3	8.7	106.2	1.3	140.5	5.5
1989	114.2	2.0	115.3	4.9	106.0	-1.9	90.9	-12.9	121.4	6.9	154.6	7.1	117.4	10.5	149.5	6.4
1990	119.1	4.3	123.3	6.9	108.1	2.0	89.6	-1.4	125.5	3.4	174.8	13.1	125.5	6.9	159.5	6.7
1991	123.4	3.6	127.7	3.6	112.0	3.6	93.5	4.4	125.7	0.2	192.8	10.3	127.5	1.6	172.4	8.1
1992	127.9	3.6	128.2	0.4	115.8	3.4	92.9	-0.6	133.5	6.2	207.9	7.8	131.7	3.3	183.9	6.7
1993	133.2	4.1	131.1	2.3	121.6	5.0	94.4	1.6	140.5	5.2	218.9	5.3	135.3	2.7	188.9	2.7

Source: U.S. Department of Labor, Bureau of Labor Statistics, Division of Consumer Prices and Price Indexes. - indicates no data collected for period.

Denver-Boulder, CO
Consumer Price Index - All Urban Consumers
Base 1982-1984 = 100
All Items

For 1964-1993. Columns headed % show percentile change in the index from the previous period for which an index is available.

Year	Jan Index	%	Feb Index	%	Mar Index	%	Apr Index	%	May Index	%	Jun Index	%	Jul Index	%	Aug Index	%	Sep Index	%	Oct Index	%	Nov Index	%	Dec Index	%
1964	28.2	-	-	-	-	-	28.0	-0.7	-	-	-	-	28.5	1.8	-	-	-	-	28.5	0.0	-	-	-	-
1965	28.5	0.0	-	-	-	-	28.6	0.4	-	-	-	-	28.9	1.0	-	-	-	-	28.9	0.0	-	-	-	-
1966	29.2	1.0	-	-	-	-	29.6	1.4	-	-	-	-	29.7	0.3	-	-	-	-	29.9	0.7	-	-	-	-
1967	29.7	-0.7	-	-	-	-	29.7	0.0	-	-	-	-	30.1	1.3	-	-	-	-	30.2	0.3	-	-	-	-
1968	30.4	0.7	-	-	-	-	30.7	1.0	-	-	-	-	30.7	0.0	-	-	-	-	30.9	0.7	-	-	-	-
1969	31.1	0.6	-	-	-	-	31.6	1.6	-	-	-	-	32.0	1.3	-	-	-	-	32.7	2.2	-	-	-	-
1970	33.0	0.9	-	-	-	-	33.9	2.7	-	-	-	-	34.9	2.9	-	-	-	-	35.2	0.9	-	-	-	-
1971	35.3	0.3	-	-	-	-	35.5	0.6	-	-	-	-	36.0	1.4	-	-	-	-	36.3	0.8	-	-	-	-
1972	36.3	0.0	-	-	-	-	36.9	1.7	-	-	-	-	37.0	0.3	-	-	-	-	37.4	1.1	-	-	-	-
1973	37.8	1.1	-	-	-	-	39.0	3.2	-	-	-	-	39.6	1.5	-	-	-	-	40.6	2.5	-	-	-	-
1974	41.5	2.2	-	-	-	-	42.7	2.9	-	-	-	-	44.1	3.3	-	-	-	-	45.6	3.4	-	-	-	-
1975	46.9	2.9	-	-	-	-	47.6	1.5	-	-	-	-	48.7	2.3	-	-	-	-	49.3	1.2	-	-	-	-
1976	49.7	0.8	-	-	-	-	50.4	1.4	-	-	-	-	51.4	2.0	-	-	-	-	51.9	1.0	-	-	-	-
1977	52.7	1.5	-	-	-	-	54.8	4.0	-	-	-	-	55.8	1.8	-	-	-	-	56.6	1.4	-	-	-	-
1978	57.7	1.9	-	-	58.5	1.4	-	-	59.5	1.7	-	-	60.7	2.0	-	-	62.1	2.3	-	-	63.4	2.1	-	-
1979	64.8	2.2	-	-	66.9	3.2	-	-	69.3	3.6	-	-	70.9	2.3	-	-	72.2	1.8	-	-	73.7	2.1	-	-
1980	74.2	0.7	-	-	76.5	3.1	-	-	77.4	1.2	-	-	78.5	1.4	-	-	80.2	2.2	-	-	81.5	1.6	-	-
1981	83.2	2.1	-	-	84.4	1.4	-	-	86.4	2.4	-	-	88.2	2.1	-	-	89.6	1.6	-	-	89.3	-0.3	-	-
1982	91.6	2.6	-	-	92.7	1.2	-	-	94.0	1.4	-	-	95.9	2.0	-	-	97.3	1.5	-	-	97.8	0.5	-	-
1983	98.2	0.4	-	-	98.8	0.6	-	-	100.4	1.6	-	-	100.7	0.3	-	-	101.8	1.1	-	-	101.9	0.1	-	-
1984	103.0	1.1	-	-	103.5	0.5	-	-	103.9	0.4	-	-	104.9	1.0	-	-	105.4	0.5	-	-	104.8	-0.6	-	-
1985	105.1	0.3	-	-	106.5	1.3	-	-	106.8	0.3	-	-	108.0	1.1	-	-	107.4	-0.6	-	-	107.8	0.4	-	-
1986	109.3	1.4	-	-	106.7	-2.4	-	-	106.8	0.1	-	-	107.5	0.7	-	-	108.8	1.2	-	-	108.3	-0.5	108.4	0.1
1987	-	-	-	-	-	-	-	-	-	-	109.9	1.4	-	-	-	-	-	-	-	-	-	-	111.6	1.5
1988	-	-	-	-	-	-	-	-	-	-	112.8	1.1	-	-	-	-	-	-	-	-	-	-	114.7	1.7
1989	-	-	-	-	-	-	-	-	-	-	115.0	0.3	-	-	-	-	-	-	-	-	-	-	116.6	1.4
1990	-	-	-	-	-	-	-	-	-	-	119.4	2.4	-	-	-	-	-	-	-	-	-	-	122.5	2.6
1991	-	-	-	-	-	-	-	-	-	-	124.8	1.9	-	-	-	-	-	-	-	-	-	-	126.4	1.3
1992	-	-	-	-	-	-	-	-	-	-	129.0	2.1	-	-	-	-	-	-	-	-	-	-	131.6	2.0
1993	-	-	-	-	-	-	-	-	-	-	134.6	2.3	-	-	-	-	-	-	-	-	-	-	-	-

Source: U.S. Department of Labor, Bureau of Labor Statistics, Division of Consumer Prices and Price Indexes. - indicates no data collected for period.

Denver-Boulder, CO
Consumer Price Index - Urban Wage Earners
Base 1982-1984 = 100
All Items

For 1964-1993. Columns headed % show percentile change in the index from the previous period for which an index is available.

Year	Jan Index	%	Feb Index	%	Mar Index	%	Apr Index	%	May Index	%	Jun Index	%	Jul Index	%	Aug Index	%	Sep Index	%	Oct Index	%	Nov Index	%	Dec Index	%
1964	28.2	-	-	-	-	-	28.1	-0.4	-	-	-	-	28.5	1.4	-	-	-	-	28.5	0.0	-	-	-	-
1965	28.6	0.4	-	-	-	-	28.6	0.0	-	-	-	-	29.0	1.4	-	-	-	-	29.0	0.0	-	-	-	-
1966	29.2	0.7	-	-	-	-	29.7	1.7	-	-	-	-	29.8	0.3	-	-	-	-	30.0	0.7	-	-	-	-
1967	29.8	-0.7	-	-	-	-	29.8	0.0	-	-	-	-	30.1	1.0	-	-	-	-	30.3	0.7	-	-	-	-
1968	30.5	0.7	-	-	-	-	30.7	0.7	-	-	-	-	30.7	0.0	-	-	-	-	31.0	1.0	-	-	-	-
1969	31.1	0.3	-	-	-	-	31.7	1.9	-	-	-	-	32.1	1.3	-	-	-	-	32.8	2.2	-	-	-	-
1970	33.1	0.9	-	-	-	-	34.0	2.7	-	-	-	-	35.0	2.9	-	-	-	-	35.3	0.9	-	-	-	-
1971	35.4	0.3	-	-	-	-	35.6	0.6	-	-	-	-	36.1	1.4	-	-	-	-	36.4	0.8	-	-	-	-
1972	36.4	0.0	-	-	-	-	36.9	1.4	-	-	-	-	37.0	0.3	-	-	-	-	37.5	1.4	-	-	-	-
1973	37.8	0.8	-	-	-	-	39.1	3.4	-	-	-	-	39.7	1.5	-	-	-	-	40.7	2.5	-	-	-	-
1974	41.6	2.2	-	-	-	-	42.8	2.9	-	-	-	-	44.2	3.3	-	-	-	-	45.6	3.2	-	-	-	-
1975	47.0	3.1	-	-	-	-	47.7	1.5	-	-	-	-	48.8	2.3	-	-	-	-	49.4	1.2	-	-	-	-
1976	49.8	0.8	-	-	-	-	50.4	1.2	-	-	-	-	51.5	2.2	-	-	-	-	52.0	1.0	-	-	-	-
1977	52.8	1.5	-	-	-	-	54.9	4.0	-	-	-	-	55.9	1.8	-	-	-	-	56.7	1.4	-	-	-	-
1978	57.8	1.9	-	-	58.8	1.7	-	-	59.9	1.9	-	-	61.0	1.8	-	-	62.5	2.5	-	-	64.0	2.4	-	-
1979	65.5	2.3	-	-	67.6	3.2	-	-	70.1	3.7	-	-	71.9	2.6	-	-	73.2	1.8	-	-	74.7	2.0	-	-
1980	75.4	0.9	-	-	77.9	3.3	-	-	78.8	1.2	-	-	79.9	1.4	-	-	81.6	2.1	-	-	83.1	1.8	-	-
1981	84.8	2.0	-	-	85.9	1.3	-	-	88.1	2.6	-	-	90.1	2.3	-	-	91.4	1.4	-	-	91.0	-0.4	-	-
1982	93.3	2.5	-	-	94.6	1.4	-	-	96.0	1.5	-	-	98.0	2.1	-	-	99.5	1.5	-	-	99.9	0.4	-	-
1983	97.3	-2.6	-	-	98.2	0.9	-	-	99.7	1.5	-	-	99.7	0.0	-	-	101.3	1.6	-	-	101.7	0.4	-	-
1984	101.0	-0.7	-	-	102.7	1.7	-	-	102.4	-0.3	-	-	104.3	1.9	-	-	104.0	-0.3	-	-	103.7	-0.3	-	-
1985	104.0	0.3	-	-	105.4	1.3	-	-	105.7	0.3	-	-	106.9	1.1	-	-	106.1	-0.7	-	-	106.4	0.3	-	-
1986	107.9	1.4	-	-	105.2	-2.5	-	-	105.2	0.0	-	-	105.9	0.7	-	-	107.3	1.3	-	-	106.7	-0.6	106.7	0.0
1987	-	-	-	-	-	-	-	-	-	-	108.3	1.5	-	-	-	-	-	-	-	-	-	-	110.0	1.6
1988	-	-	-	-	-	-	-	-	-	-	111.0	0.9	-	-	-	-	-	-	-	-	-	-	112.9	1.7
1989	-	-	-	-	-	-	-	-	-	-	113.5	0.5	-	-	-	-	-	-	-	-	-	-	114.9	1.2
1990	-	-	-	-	-	-	-	-	-	-	117.5	2.3	-	-	-	-	-	-	-	-	-	-	120.8	2.8
1991	-	-	-	-	-	-	-	-	-	-	122.7	1.6	-	-	-	-	-	-	-	-	-	-	124.2	1.2
1992	-	-	-	-	-	-	-	-	-	-	126.5	1.9	-	-	-	-	-	-	-	-	-	-	129.4	2.3
1993	-	-	-	-	-	-	-	-	-	-	132.1	2.1	-	-	-	-	-	-	-	-	-	-	-	-

Source: U.S. Department of Labor, Bureau of Labor Statistics, Division of Consumer Prices and Price Indexes. - indicates no data collected for period.

439

Denver-Boulder, CO
Consumer Price Index - All Urban Consumers
Base 1982-1984 = 100
Food and Beverages

For 1976-1993. Columns headed % show percentile change in the index from the previous period for which an index is available.

Year	Jan Index	%	Feb Index	%	Mar Index	%	Apr Index	%	May Index	%	Jun Index	%	Jul Index	%	Aug Index	%	Sep Index	%	Oct Index	%	Nov Index	%	Dec Index	%
1976	63.3	-	-		-		62.7	-0.9	-		-		64.1	2.2	-		-		64.3	0.3	-		-	
1977	65.7	2.2	-		-		69.2	5.3	-		-		70.1	1.3	-		-		68.8	-1.9	-		-	
1978	70.8	2.9	-		72.4	2.3	-		74.7	3.2	-		76.1	1.9	-		76.2	0.1	-		77.2	1.3	-	
1979	80.2	3.9	-		82.4	2.7	-		83.4	1.2	-		84.1	0.8	-		83.0	-1.3	-		83.6	0.7	-	
1980	81.9	-2.0	-		82.6	0.9	-		84.3	2.1	-		86.1	2.1	-		89.3	3.7	-		90.1	0.9	-	
1981	90.8	0.8	-		92.0	1.3	-		92.9	1.0	-		94.2	1.4	-		94.6	0.4	-		93.9	-0.7	-	
1982	94.9	1.1	-		95.6	0.7	-		95.9	0.3	-		96.5	0.6	-		96.5	0.0	-		96.7	0.2	-	
1983	97.1	0.4	-		98.2	1.1	-		100.2	2.0	-		99.8	-0.4	-		100.2	0.4	-		100.7	0.5	-	
1984	102.7	2.0	-		104.3	1.6	-		104.0	-0.3	-		104.8	0.8	-		104.9	0.1	-		104.5	-0.4	-	
1985	104.9	0.4	-		107.4	2.4	-		105.9	-1.4	-		106.9	0.9	-		105.5	-1.3	-		105.5	0.0	108.1	0.0
1986	107.8	2.2	-		107.3	-0.5	-		105.5	-1.7	108.7	0.6	106.0	0.5	-		108.5	2.4	-		108.1	-0.4	107.9	-0.7
1987	-		-		-		-		-		108.7	0.6	-		-		-		-		-		111.2	1.5
1988	-		-		-		-		-		109.6	1.6	-		-		-		-		-		116.8	1.8
1989	-		-		-		-		-		114.7	3.1	-		-		-		-		-		126.2	3.4
1990	-		-		-		-		-		122.1	4.5	-		-		-		-		-		128.4	0.1
1991	-		-		-		-		-		128.3	1.7	-		-		-		-		-		129.2	0.5
1992	-		-		-		-		-		128.5	0.1	-		-		-		-		-		-	
1993	-		-		-		-		-		131.0	1.4	-		-		-		-		-		-	

Source: U.S. Department of Labor, Bureau of Labor Statistics, Division of Consumer Prices and Price Indexes. - indicates no data collected for period.

Denver-Boulder, CO
Consumer Price Index - Urban Wage Earners
Base 1982-1984 = 100
Food and Beverages

For 1976-1993. Columns headed % show percentile change in the index from the previous period for which an index is available.

Year	Jan Index	%	Feb Index	%	Mar Index	%	Apr Index	%	May Index	%	Jun Index	%	Jul Index	%	Aug Index	%	Sep Index	%	Oct Index	%	Nov Index	%	Dec Index	%
1976	61.2	-	-	-	-	-	60.7	-0.8	-	-	-	-	62.0	2.1	-	-	-	-	62.2	0.3	-	-	-	-
1977	63.5	2.1	-	-	-	-	67.0	5.5	-	-	-	-	67.8	1.2	-	-	-	-	66.6	-1.8	-	-	-	-
1978	68.4	2.7	-	-	70.7	3.4	-	-	72.9	3.1	-	-	73.7	1.1	-	-	74.1	0.5	-	-	75.3	1.6	-	-
1979	78.0	3.6	-	-	79.5	1.9	-	-	80.3	1.0	-	-	81.4	1.4	-	-	80.3	-1.4	-	-	81.6	1.6	-	-
1980	80.8	-1.0	-	-	81.8	1.2	-	-	83.5	2.1	-	-	85.4	2.3	-	-	88.1	3.2	-	-	88.7	0.7	-	-
1981	90.1	1.6	-	-	91.5	1.6	-	-	92.1	0.7	-	-	93.9	2.0	-	-	94.1	0.2	-	-	94.2	0.1	-	-
1982	95.0	0.8	-	-	95.6	0.6	-	-	96.0	0.4	-	-	96.7	0.7	-	-	96.7	0.0	-	-	96.8	0.1	-	-
1983	97.2	0.4	-	-	98.3	1.1	-	-	100.1	1.8	-	-	99.8	-0.3	-	-	100.1	0.3	-	-	100.7	0.6	-	-
1984	102.6	1.9	-	-	104.1	1.5	-	-	103.8	-0.3	-	-	104.7	0.9	-	-	105.0	0.3	-	-	104.6	-0.4	-	-
1985	104.9	0.3	-	-	107.4	2.4	-	-	105.8	-1.5	-	-	106.8	0.9	-	-	105.5	-1.2	-	-	105.4	-0.1	-	-
1986	107.7	2.2	-	-	106.9	-0.7	-	-	105.1	-1.7	-	-	105.6	0.5	-	-	108.2	2.5	-	-	107.9	-0.3	107.8	-0.1
1987	-	-	-	-	-	-	-	-	-	-	108.3	0.5	-	-	-	-	-	-	-	-	-	-	107.5	-0.7
1988	-	-	-	-	-	-	-	-	-	-	109.1	1.5	-	-	-	-	-	-	-	-	-	-	110.8	1.6
1989	-	-	-	-	-	-	-	-	-	-	114.3	3.2	-	-	-	-	-	-	-	-	-	-	116.3	1.7
1990	-	-	-	-	-	-	-	-	-	-	121.4	4.4	-	-	-	-	-	-	-	-	-	-	125.3	3.2
1991	-	-	-	-	-	-	-	-	-	-	127.8	2.0	-	-	-	-	-	-	-	-	-	-	127.7	-0.1
1992	-	-	-	-	-	-	-	-	-	-	127.9	0.2	-	-	-	-	-	-	-	-	-	-	128.6	0.5
1993	-	-	-	-	-	-	-	-	-	-	130.6	1.6	-	-	-	-	-	-	-	-	-	-	-	-

Source: U.S. Department of Labor, Bureau of Labor Statistics, Division of Consumer Prices and Price Indexes. - indicates no data collected for period.

Denver-Boulder, CO
Consumer Price Index - All Urban Consumers
Base 1982-1984 = 100
Housing

For 1976-1993. Columns headed % show percentile change in the index from the previous period for which an index is available.

Year	Jan Index	%	Feb Index	%	Mar Index	%	Apr Index	%	May Index	%	Jun Index	%	Jul Index	%	Aug Index	%	Sep Index	%	Oct Index	%	Nov Index	%	Dec Index	%
1976	43.1	-	-	-	-	-	43.8	1.6	-	-	-	-	44.8	2.3	-	-	-	-	44.9	0.2	-	-	-	-
1977	45.6	1.6	-	-	-	-	47.9	5.0	-	-	-	-	48.8	1.9	-	-	-	-	50.3	3.1	-	-	-	-
1978	51.4	2.2	-	-	52.5	2.1	-	-	53.1	1.1	-	-	54.3	2.3	-	-	56.2	3.5	-	-	58.1	3.4	-	-
1979	59.7	2.8	-	-	61.7	3.4	-	-	64.6	4.7	-	-	66.7	3.3	-	-	68.1	2.1	-	-	70.1	2.9	-	-
1980	70.4	0.4	-	-	73.0	3.7	-	-	73.6	0.8	-	-	74.8	1.6	-	-	76.3	2.0	-	-	77.9	2.1	-	-
1981	80.1	2.8	-	-	80.7	0.7	-	-	83.7	3.7	-	-	86.2	3.0	-	-	87.9	2.0	-	-	87.0	-1.0	-	-
1982	90.3	3.8	-	-	92.0	1.9	-	-	93.8	2.0	-	-	95.9	2.2	-	-	97.7	1.9	-	-	98.1	0.4	-	-
1983	99.4	1.3	-	-	100.6	1.2	-	-	101.0	0.4	-	-	100.5	-0.5	-	-	101.7	1.2	-	-	101.0	-0.7	-	-
1984	103.2	2.2	-	-	102.7	-0.5	-	-	102.9	0.2	-	-	105.5	2.5	-	-	105.5	0.0	-	-	104.3	-1.1	-	-
1985	105.9	1.5	-	-	106.1	0.2	-	-	106.1	0.0	-	-	107.9	1.7	-	-	106.6	-1.2	-	-	107.4	0.8	108.2	0.6
1986	110.6	3.0	-	-	107.3	-3.0	-	-	107.7	0.4	109.1	0.8	108.1	0.4	-	-	108.2	0.1	-	-	107.6	-0.6	110.0	0.8
1987	-	-	-	-	-	-	-	-	-	-	110.5	0.5	-	-	-	-	-	-	-	-	-	-	109.5	-0.9
1988	-	-	-	-	-	-	-	-	-	-	107.6	-1.7	-	-	-	-	-	-	-	-	-	-	107.3	-0.3
1989	-	-	-	-	-	-	-	-	-	-	109.3	1.9	-	-	-	-	-	-	-	-	-	-	110.4	1.0
1990	-	-	-	-	-	-	-	-	-	-	113.7	3.0	-	-	-	-	-	-	-	-	-	-	114.5	0.7
1991	-	-	-	-	-	-	-	-	-	-	117.1	2.3	-	-	-	-	-	-	-	-	-	-	119.1	1.7
1992	-	-	-	-	-	-	-	-	-	-	123.0	3.3	-	-	-	-	-	-	-	-	-	-	-	-
1993	-	-	-	-	-	-	-	-	-	-	-	-	-	-	-	-	-	-	-	-	-	-	-	-

Source: U.S. Department of Labor, Bureau of Labor Statistics, Division of Consumer Prices and Price Indexes. - indicates no data collected for period.

Denver-Boulder, CO
Consumer Price Index - Urban Wage Earners
Base 1982-1984 = 100
Housing

For 1976-1993. Columns headed % show percentile change in the index from the previous period for which an index is available.

Year	Jan Index	%	Feb Index	%	Mar Index	%	Apr Index	%	May Index	%	Jun Index	%	Jul Index	%	Aug Index	%	Sep Index	%	Oct Index	%	Nov Index	%	Dec Index	%
1976	43.8	-	-	-	-	-	44.6	1.8	-	-	-	-	45.6	2.2	-	-	-	-	45.8	0.4	-	-	-	-
1977	46.4	1.3	-	-	-	-	48.8	5.2	-	-	-	-	49.7	1.8	-	-	-	-	51.2	3.0	-	-	-	-
1978	52.4	2.3	-	-	53.5	2.1	-	-	54.2	1.3	-	-	55.4	2.2	-	-	57.5	3.8	-	-	59.4	3.3	-	-
1979	61.2	3.0	-	-	63.4	3.6	-	-	66.5	4.9	-	-	68.7	3.3	-	-	70.1	2.0	-	-	72.2	3.0	-	-
1980	72.6	0.6	-	-	75.4	3.9	-	-	76.0	0.8	-	-	77.1	1.4	-	-	78.8	2.2	-	-	80.6	2.3	-	-
1981	82.8	2.7	-	-	83.2	0.5	-	-	86.6	4.1	-	-	89.1	2.9	-	-	90.8	1.9	-	-	89.8	-1.1	-	-
1982	93.3	3.9	-	-	95.3	2.1	-	-	97.2	2.0	-	-	99.5	2.4	-	-	101.4	1.9	-	-	101.6	0.2	-	-
1983	97.3	-4.2	-	-	98.6	1.3	-	-	99.6	1.0	-	-	98.8	-0.8	-	-	101.1	2.3	-	-	101.1	0.0	-	-
1984	99.7	-1.4	-	-	101.8	2.1	-	-	100.9	-0.9	-	-	104.3	3.4	-	-	103.1	-1.2	-	-	102.8	-0.3	-	-
1985	104.5	1.7	-	-	104.6	0.1	-	-	104.7	0.1	-	-	106.3	1.5	-	-	105.1	-1.1	-	-	105.9	0.8	-	-
1986	109.0	2.9	-	-	105.6	-3.1	-	-	106.1	0.5	-	-	106.6	0.5	-	-	106.7	0.1	-	-	106.1	-0.6	106.7	0.6
1987	-	-	-	-	-	-	-	-	-	-	107.4	0.7	-	-	-	-	-	-	-	-	-	-	108.1	0.7
1988	-	-	-	-	-	-	-	-	-	-	108.5	0.4	-	-	-	-	-	-	-	-	-	-	107.5	-0.9
1989	-	-	-	-	-	-	-	-	-	-	106.0	-1.4	-	-	-	-	-	-	-	-	-	-	106.0	0.0
1990	-	-	-	-	-	-	-	-	-	-	107.5	1.4	-	-	-	-	-	-	-	-	-	-	108.6	1.0
1991	-	-	-	-	-	-	-	-	-	-	111.7	2.9	-	-	-	-	-	-	-	-	-	-	112.4	0.6
1992	-	-	-	-	-	-	-	-	-	-	114.9	2.2	-	-	-	-	-	-	-	-	-	-	116.7	1.6
1993	-	-	-	-	-	-	-	-	-	-	120.6	3.3	-	-	-	-	-	-	-	-	-	-	-	-

Source: U.S. Department of Labor, Bureau of Labor Statistics, Division of Consumer Prices and Price Indexes. - indicates no data collected for period.

Denver-Boulder, CO
Consumer Price Index - All Urban Consumers
Base 1982-1984 = 100
Apparel and Upkeep

For 1971-1993. Columns headed % show percentile change in the index from the previous period for which an index is available.

Year	Jan Index	%	Feb Index	%	Mar Index	%	Apr Index	%	May Index	%	Jun Index	%	Jul Index	%	Aug Index	%	Sep Index	%	Oct Index	%	Nov Index	%	Dec Index	%
1971	62.3	-	-	-	-	-	63.5	1.9	-	-	-	-	63.3	-0.3	-	-	-	-	66.9	5.7	-	-	-	-
1972	65.3	-2.4	-	-	-	-	66.2	1.4	-	-	-	-	65.4	-1.2	-	-	-	-	67.6	3.4	-	-	-	-
1973	65.6	-3.0	-	-	-	-	68.4	4.3	-	-	-	-	68.2	-0.3	-	-	-	-	71.2	4.4	-	-	-	-
1974	71.2	0.0	-	-	-	-	73.1	2.7	-	-	-	-	74.3	1.6	-	-	-	-	77.3	4.0	-	-	-	-
1975	75.8	-1.9	-	-	-	-	77.2	1.8	-	-	-	-	78.0	1.0	-	-	-	-	82.1	5.3	-	-	-	-
1976	79.9	-2.7	-	-	-	-	82.5	3.3	-	-	-	-	82.5	0.0	-	-	-	-	86.0	4.2	-	-	-	-
1977	83.8	-2.6	-	-	-	-	87.6	4.5	-	-	-	-	87.8	0.2	-	-	-	-	91.1	3.8	-	-	-	-
1978	89.0	-2.3	-	-	86.7	-2.6	-	-	90.3	4.2	-	-	90.9	0.7	-	-	93.4	2.8	-	-	91.4	-2.1	-	-
1979	86.7	-5.1	-	-	92.2	6.3	-	-	92.3	0.1	-	-	90.2	-2.3	-	-	94.7	5.0	-	-	95.7	1.1	-	-
1980	91.3	-4.6	-	-	96.3	5.5	-	-	95.1	-1.2	-	-	94.6	-0.5	-	-	97.7	3.3	-	-	98.0	0.3	-	-
1981	94.4	-3.7	-	-	97.2	3.0	-	-	96.0	-1.2	-	-	95.0	-1.0	-	-	98.1	3.3	-	-	96.9	-1.2	-	-
1982	97.2	0.3	-	-	102.4	5.3	-	-	102.5	0.1	-	-	99.1	-3.3	-	-	102.8	3.7	-	-	103.1	0.3	-	-
1983	97.8	-5.1	-	-	100.6	2.9	-	-	98.0	-2.6	-	-	96.6	-1.4	-	-	99.6	3.1	-	-	100.6	1.0	-	-
1984	97.4	-3.2	-	-	100.3	3.0	-	-	100.4	0.1	-	-	96.6	-3.8	-	-	102.2	5.8	-	-	102.5	0.3	-	-
1985	99.1	-3.3	-	-	103.8	4.7	-	-	104.5	0.7	-	-	102.1	-2.3	-	-	103.6	1.5	-	-	102.5	-1.1	-	-
1986	98.7	-3.7	-	-	101.6	2.9	-	-	102.5	0.9	-	-	100.8	-1.7	-	-	107.1	6.3	-	-	105.5	-1.5	103.1	-2.3
1987	-	-	-	-	-	-	-	-	-	-	100.1	-2.9	-	-	-	-	-	-	-	-	-	-	104.0	3.9
1988	-	-	-	-	-	-	-	-	-	-	106.2	2.1	-	-	-	-	-	-	-	-	-	-	107.4	1.1
1989	-	-	-	-	-	-	-	-	-	-	95.5	-11.1	-	-	-	-	-	-	-	-	-	-	92.0	-3.7
1990	-	-	-	-	-	-	-	-	-	-	91.5	-0.5	-	-	-	-	-	-	-	-	-	-	91.0	-0.5
1991	-	-	-	-	-	-	-	-	-	-	94.9	4.3	-	-	-	-	-	-	-	-	-	-	94.7	-0.2
1992	-	-	-	-	-	-	-	-	-	-	93.8	-1.0	-	-	-	-	-	-	-	-	-	-	95.5	1.8
1993	-	-	-	-	-	-	-	-	-	-	96.0	0.5	-	-	-	-	-	-	-	-	-	-	-	-

Source: U.S. Department of Labor, Bureau of Labor Statistics, Division of Consumer Prices and Price Indexes. - indicates no data collected for period.

Denver-Boulder, CO
Consumer Price Index - Urban Wage Earners
Base 1982-1984 = 100
Apparel and Upkeep

For 1971-1993. Columns headed % show percentile change in the index from the previous period for which an index is available.

Year	Jan Index	%	Feb Index	%	Mar Index	%	Apr Index	%	May Index	%	Jun Index	%	Jul Index	%	Aug Index	%	Sep Index	%	Oct Index	%	Nov Index	%	Dec Index	%
1971	54.5	-	-	-	-	-	55.5	1.8	-	-	-	-	55.4	-0.2	-	-	-	-	58.6	5.8	-	-	-	-
1972	57.1	-2.6	-	-	-	-	57.9	1.4	-	-	-	-	57.2	-1.2	-	-	-	-	59.2	3.5	-	-	-	-
1973	57.3	-3.2	-	-	-	-	59.8	4.4	-	-	-	-	59.6	-0.3	-	-	-	-	62.3	4.5	-	-	-	-
1974	62.3	0.0	-	-	-	-	63.9	2.6	-	-	-	-	65.0	1.7	-	-	-	-	67.6	4.0	-	-	-	-
1975	66.3	-1.9	-	-	-	-	67.6	2.0	-	-	-	-	68.3	1.0	-	-	-	-	71.8	5.1	-	-	-	-
1976	69.9	-2.6	-	-	-	-	72.2	3.3	-	-	-	-	72.2	0.0	-	-	-	-	75.2	4.2	-	-	-	-
1977	73.3	-2.5	-	-	-	-	76.7	4.6	-	-	-	-	76.8	0.1	-	-	-	-	79.7	3.8	-	-	-	-
1978	77.9	-2.3	-	-	78.1	0.3	-	-	82.0	5.0	-	-	82.1	0.1	-	-	85.7	4.4	-	-	83.6	-2.5	-	-
1979	82.2	-1.7	-	-	86.5	5.2	-	-	87.5	1.2	-	-	87.4	-0.1	-	-	92.8	6.2	-	-	91.6	-1.3	-	-
1980	90.2	-1.5	-	-	96.4	6.9	-	-	93.6	-2.9	-	-	91.9	-1.8	-	-	96.4	4.9	-	-	96.2	-0.2	-	-
1981	92.3	-4.1	-	-	94.4	2.3	-	-	93.6	-0.8	-	-	95.4	1.9	-	-	98.7	3.5	-	-	97.0	-1.7	-	-
1982	96.6	-0.4	-	-	102.2	5.8	-	-	101.2	-1.0	-	-	97.8	-3.4	-	-	102.3	4.6	-	-	102.5	0.2	-	-
1983	97.7	-4.7	-	-	100.1	2.5	-	-	97.7	-2.4	-	-	96.7	-1.0	-	-	100.0	3.4	-	-	101.6	1.6	-	-
1984	97.9	-3.6	-	-	101.3	3.5	-	-	100.8	-0.5	-	-	97.0	-3.8	-	-	102.6	5.8	-	-	103.4	0.8	-	-
1985	100.2	-3.1	-	-	103.6	3.4	-	-	104.1	0.5	-	-	102.3	-1.7	-	-	103.1	0.8	-	-	101.6	-1.5	-	-
1986	98.2	-3.3	-	-	100.4	2.2	-	-	101.0	0.6	-	-	99.1	-1.9	-	-	105.9	6.9	-	-	103.5	-2.3	100.9	-2.5
1987	-	-	-	-	-	-	-	-	-	-	97.8	-3.1	-	-	-	-	-	-	-	-	-	-	101.5	3.8
1988	-	-	-	-	-	-	-	-	-	-	104.1	2.6	-	-	-	-	-	-	-	-	-	-	104.7	0.6
1989	-	-	-	-	-	-	-	-	-	-	92.5	-11.7	-	-	-	-	-	-	-	-	-	-	89.3	-3.5
1990	-	-	-	-	-	-	-	-	-	-	89.5	0.2	-	-	-	-	-	-	-	-	-	-	89.8	0.3
1991	-	-	-	-	-	-	-	-	-	-	93.7	4.3	-	-	-	-	-	-	-	-	-	-	93.2	-0.5
1992	-	-	-	-	-	-	-	-	-	-	91.8	-1.5	-	-	-	-	-	-	-	-	-	-	94.0	2.4
1993	-	-	-	-	-	-	-	-	-	-	95.2	1.3	-	-	-	-	-	-	-	-	-	-	-	-

Source: U.S. Department of Labor, Bureau of Labor Statistics, Division of Consumer Prices and Price Indexes. - indicates no data collected for period.

Denver-Boulder, CO
Consumer Price Index - All Urban Consumers
Base 1982-1984 = 100
Transportation

For 1971-1993. Columns headed % show percentile change in the index from the previous period for which an index is available.

Year	Jan Index	%	Feb Index	%	Mar Index	%	Apr Index	%	May Index	%	Jun Index	%	Jul Index	%	Aug Index	%	Sep Index	%	Oct Index	%	Nov Index	%	Dec Index	%
1971	38.0	-	-	-	-	-	38.0	0.0	-	-	-	-	37.8	-0.5	-	-	-	-	38.1	0.8	-	-	-	-
1972	37.1	-2.6	-	-	-	-	37.6	1.3	-	-	-	-	38.0	1.1	-	-	-	-	38.4	1.1	-	-	-	-
1973	38.0	-1.0	-	-	-	-	39.5	3.9	-	-	-	-	40.4	2.3	-	-	-	-	39.5	-2.2	-	-	-	-
1974	41.3	4.6	-	-	-	-	42.7	3.4	-	-	-	-	45.0	5.4	-	-	-	-	45.4	0.9	-	-	-	-
1975	45.9	1.1	-	-	-	-	47.0	2.4	-	-	-	-	49.3	4.9	-	-	-	-	49.8	1.0	-	-	-	-
1976	49.7	-0.2	-	-	-	-	50.8	2.2	-	-	-	-	53.2	4.7	-	-	-	-	53.9	1.3	-	-	-	-
1977	55.1	2.2	-	-	-	-	55.8	1.3	-	-	-	-	56.9	2.0	-	-	-	-	56.7	-0.4	-	-	-	-
1978	57.6	1.6	-	-	57.9	0.5	-	-	58.5	1.0	-	-	60.4	3.2	-	-	61.3	1.5	-	-	61.9	1.0	-	-
1979	63.3	2.3	-	-	65.2	3.0	-	-	68.9	5.7	-	-	71.6	3.9	-	-	73.7	2.9	-	-	75.1	1.9	-	-
1980	77.6	3.3	-	-	80.5	3.7	-	-	82.1	2.0	-	-	83.0	1.1	-	-	84.0	1.2	-	-	85.0	1.2	-	-
1981	87.0	2.4	-	-	89.7	3.1	-	-	91.1	1.6	-	-	92.7	1.8	-	-	93.5	0.9	-	-	94.7	1.3	-	-
1982	94.6	-0.1	-	-	94.0	-0.6	-	-	94.0	0.0	-	-	97.6	3.8	-	-	98.2	0.6	-	-	98.8	0.6	-	-
1983	97.0	-1.8	-	-	95.1	-2.0	-	-	99.6	4.7	-	-	101.5	1.9	-	-	102.7	1.2	-	-	103.3	0.6	-	-
1984	102.0	-1.3	-	-	102.6	0.6	-	-	104.1	1.5	-	-	103.8	-0.3	-	-	104.5	0.7	-	-	104.7	0.2	-	-
1985	102.5	-2.1	-	-	104.4	1.9	-	-	106.7	2.2	-	-	107.2	0.5	-	-	106.6	-0.6	-	-	107.2	0.6	-	-
1986	106.3	-0.8	-	-	98.8	-7.1	-	-	99.5	0.7	-	-	100.1	0.6	-	-	101.6	1.5	-	-	101.0	-0.6	100.3	-0.7
1987	-	-	-	-	-	-	-	-	-	-	105.6	5.3	-	-	-	-	-	-	-	-	-	-	110.2	4.4
1988	-	-	-	-	-	-	-	-	-	-	110.4	0.2	-	-	-	-	-	-	-	-	-	-	117.8	6.7
1989	-	-	-	-	-	-	-	-	-	-	121.6	3.2	-	-	-	-	-	-	-	-	-	-	123.0	1.2
1990	-	-	-	-	-	-	-	-	-	-	124.4	1.1	-	-	-	-	-	-	-	-	-	-	129.3	3.9
1991	-	-	-	-	-	-	-	-	-	-	126.6	-2.1	-	-	-	-	-	-	-	-	-	-	129.1	2.0
1992	-	-	-	-	-	-	-	-	-	-	131.9	2.2	-	-	-	-	-	-	-	-	-	-	136.6	3.6
1993	-	-	-	-	-	-	-	-	-	-	138.5	1.4	-	-	-	-	-	-	-	-	-	-	-	-

Source: U.S. Department of Labor, Bureau of Labor Statistics, Division of Consumer Prices and Price Indexes. - indicates no data collected for period.

Denver-Boulder, CO
Consumer Price Index - Urban Wage Earners
Base 1982-1984 = 100
Transportation

For 1971-1993. Columns headed % show percentile change in the index from the previous period for which an index is available.

Year	Jan Index	%	Feb Index	%	Mar Index	%	Apr Index	%	May Index	%	Jun Index	%	Jul Index	%	Aug Index	%	Sep Index	%	Oct Index	%	Nov Index	%	Dec Index	%
1971	37.7	-	-	-	-	-	37.7	0.0	-	-	-	-	37.5	-0.5	-	-	-	-	37.8	0.8	-	-	-	-
1972	36.8	-2.6	-	-	-	-	37.3	1.4	-	-	-	-	37.7	1.1	-	-	-	-	38.1	1.1	-	-	-	-
1973	37.7	-1.0	-	-	-	-	39.2	4.0	-	-	-	-	40.1	2.3	-	-	-	-	39.2	-2.2	-	-	-	-
1974	40.9	4.3	-	-	-	-	42.3	3.4	-	-	-	-	44.6	5.4	-	-	-	-	45.0	0.9	-	-	-	-
1975	45.6	1.3	-	-	-	-	46.6	2.2	-	-	-	-	48.9	4.9	-	-	-	-	49.4	1.0	-	-	-	-
1976	49.3	-0.2	-	-	-	-	50.4	2.2	-	-	-	-	52.8	4.8	-	-	-	-	53.5	1.3	-	-	-	-
1977	54.6	2.1	-	-	-	-	55.4	1.5	-	-	-	-	56.5	2.0	-	-	-	-	56.2	-0.5	-	-	-	-
1978	57.1	1.6	-	-	57.2	0.2	-	-	58.1	1.6	-	-	59.4	2.2	-	-	60.2	1.3	-	-	61.3	1.8	-	-
1979	62.4	1.8	-	-	64.6	3.5	-	-	68.5	6.0	-	-	71.3	4.1	-	-	73.5	3.1	-	-	74.8	1.8	-	-
1980	77.4	3.5	-	-	80.3	3.7	-	-	82.2	2.4	-	-	83.1	1.1	-	-	83.8	0.8	-	-	85.1	1.6	-	-
1981	86.8	2.0	-	-	89.6	3.2	-	-	90.9	1.5	-	-	92.7	2.0	-	-	93.8	1.2	-	-	95.1	1.4	-	-
1982	95.0	-0.1	-	-	94.7	-0.3	-	-	94.3	-0.4	-	-	98.1	4.0	-	-	98.8	0.7	-	-	99.3	0.5	-	-
1983	97.1	-2.2	-	-	95.1	-2.1	-	-	99.6	4.7	-	-	101.4	1.8	-	-	102.6	1.2	-	-	103.0	0.4	-	-
1984	101.5	-1.5	-	-	102.3	0.8	-	-	103.7	1.4	-	-	103.5	-0.2	-	-	104.2	0.7	-	-	104.3	0.1	-	-
1985	102.0	-2.2	-	-	104.0	2.0	-	-	106.7	2.6	-	-	107.3	0.6	-	-	106.8	-0.5	-	-	107.3	0.5	-	-
1986	106.3	-0.9	-	-	98.6	-7.2	-	-	99.1	0.5	-	-	99.8	0.7	-	-	101.1	1.3	-	-	100.6	-0.5	99.9	-0.7
1987	-	-	-	-	-	-	-	-	-	-	105.8	5.9	-	-	-	-	-	-	-	-	-	-	110.9	4.8
1988	-	-	-	-	-	-	-	-	-	-	110.2	-0.6	-	-	-	-	-	-	-	-	-	-	117.0	6.2
1989	-	-	-	-	-	-	-	-	-	-	120.9	3.3	-	-	-	-	-	-	-	-	-	-	121.8	0.7
1990	-	-	-	-	-	-	-	-	-	-	122.5	0.6	-	-	-	-	-	-	-	-	-	-	128.4	4.8
1991	-	-	-	-	-	-	-	-	-	-	124.3	-3.2	-	-	-	-	-	-	-	-	-	-	127.2	2.3
1992	-	-	-	-	-	-	-	-	-	-	130.3	2.4	-	-	-	-	-	-	-	-	-	-	136.8	5.0
1993	-	-	-	-	-	-	-	-	-	-	138.1	1.0	-	-	-	-	-	-	-	-	-	-	-	-

Source: U.S. Department of Labor, Bureau of Labor Statistics, Division of Consumer Prices and Price Indexes. - indicates no data collected for period.

Denver-Boulder, CO
Consumer Price Index - All Urban Consumers
Base 1982-1984 = 100
Medical Care

For 1971-1993. Columns headed % show percentile change in the index from the previous period for which an index is available.

Year	Jan Index	%	Feb Index	%	Mar Index	%	Apr Index	%	May Index	%	Jun Index	%	Jul Index	%	Aug Index	%	Sep Index	%	Oct Index	%	Nov Index	%	Dec Index	%
1971	35.4	-	-	-	-	-	36.1	2.0	-	-	-	-	37.1	2.8	-	-	-	-	36.9	-0.5	-	-	-	-
1972	37.2	0.8	-	-	-	-	37.3	0.3	-	-	-	-	37.5	0.5	-	-	-	-	38.0	1.3	-	-	-	-
1973	38.1	0.3	-	-	-	-	38.5	1.0	-	-	-	-	38.8	0.8	-	-	-	-	39.7	2.3	-	-	-	-
1974	40.7	2.5	-	-	-	-	41.2	1.2	-	-	-	-	43.2	4.9	-	-	-	-	43.7	1.2	-	-	-	-
1975	45.7	4.6	-	-	-	-	46.7	2.2	-	-	-	-	47.6	1.9	-	-	-	-	48.3	1.5	-	-	-	-
1976	49.1	1.7	-	-	-	-	50.3	2.4	-	-	-	-	51.1	1.6	-	-	-	-	52.2	2.2	-	-	-	-
1977	53.3	2.1	-	-	-	-	54.6	2.4	-	-	-	-	56.2	2.9	-	-	-	-	57.3	2.0	-	-	-	-
1978	58.9	2.8	-	-	59.5	1.0	-	-	60.3	1.3	-	-	60.4	0.2	-	-	61.4	1.7	-	-	62.5	1.8	-	-
1979	63.3	1.3	-	-	64.1	1.3	-	-	65.7	2.5	-	-	66.1	0.6	-	-	67.2	1.7	-	-	68.5	1.9	-	-
1980	71.6	4.5	-	-	72.3	1.0	-	-	73.0	1.0	-	-	73.0	0.0	-	-	74.3	1.8	-	-	76.0	2.3	-	-
1981	78.4	3.2	-	-	78.8	0.5	-	-	79.4	0.8	-	-	80.1	0.9	-	-	82.4	2.9	-	-	84.3	2.3	-	-
1982	87.5	3.8	-	-	88.2	0.8	-	-	88.9	0.8	-	-	91.8	3.3	-	-	93.2	1.5	-	-	94.5	1.4	-	-
1983	97.4	3.1	-	-	99.0	1.6	-	-	99.4	0.4	-	-	102.4	3.0	-	-	102.5	0.1	-	-	102.8	0.3	-	-
1984	106.4	3.5	-	-	107.2	0.8	-	-	107.4	0.2	-	-	108.0	0.6	-	-	108.2	0.2	-	-	109.4	1.1	-	-
1985	110.8	1.3	-	-	112.5	1.5	-	-	113.2	0.6	-	-	115.9	2.4	-	-	117.6	1.5	-	-	118.5	0.8	-	-
1986	119.9	1.2	-	-	121.2	1.1	-	-	123.2	1.7	-	-	125.7	2.0	-	-	126.4	0.6	-	-	125.7	-0.6	126.1	0.3
1987	-	-	-	-	-	-	-	-	-	-	130.8	3.7	-	-	-	-	-	-	-	-	-	-	133.3	1.9
1988	-	-	-	-	-	-	-	-	-	-	140.2	5.2	-	-	-	-	-	-	-	-	-	-	145.1	3.5
1989	-	-	-	-	-	-	-	-	-	-	150.0	3.4	-	-	-	-	-	-	-	-	-	-	156.8	4.5
1990	-	-	-	-	-	-	-	-	-	-	167.8	7.0	-	-	-	-	-	-	-	-	-	-	179.0	6.7
1991	-	-	-	-	-	-	-	-	-	-	188.3	5.2	-	-	-	-	-	-	-	-	-	-	195.3	3.7
1992	-	-	-	-	-	-	-	-	-	-	202.3	3.6	-	-	-	-	-	-	-	-	-	-	210.6	4.1
1993	-	-	-	-	-	-	-	-	-	-	216.3	2.7	-	-	-	-	-	-	-	-	-	-	-	-

Source: U.S. Department of Labor, Bureau of Labor Statistics, Division of Consumer Prices and Price Indexes. - indicates no data collected for period.

Denver-Boulder, CO
Consumer Price Index - Urban Wage Earners
Base 1982-1984 = 100
Medical Care

For 1971-1993. Columns headed % show percentile change in the index from the previous period for which an index is available.

Year	Jan Index	%	Feb Index	%	Mar Index	%	Apr Index	%	May Index	%	Jun Index	%	Jul Index	%	Aug Index	%	Sep Index	%	Oct Index	%	Nov Index	%	Dec Index	%
1971	35.8	-	-	-	-	-	36.5	2.0	-	-	-	-	37.5	2.7	-	-	-	-	37.3	-0.5	-	-	-	-
1972	37.6	0.8	-	-	-	-	37.7	0.3	-	-	-	-	37.9	0.5	-	-	-	-	38.4	1.3	-	-	-	-
1973	38.5	0.3	-	-	-	-	38.9	1.0	-	-	-	-	39.2	0.8	-	-	-	-	40.1	2.3	-	-	-	-
1974	41.1	2.5	-	-	-	-	41.7	1.5	-	-	-	-	43.7	4.8	-	-	-	-	44.1	0.9	-	-	-	-
1975	46.2	4.8	-	-	-	-	47.2	2.2	-	-	-	-	48.1	1.9	-	-	-	-	48.8	1.5	-	-	-	-
1976	49.6	1.6	-	-	-	-	50.8	2.4	-	-	-	-	51.7	1.8	-	-	-	-	52.7	1.9	-	-	-	-
1977	53.9	2.3	-	-	-	-	55.1	2.2	-	-	-	-	56.8	3.1	-	-	-	-	57.9	1.9	-	-	-	-
1978	59.5	2.8	-	-	60.3	1.3	-	-	61.4	1.8	-	-	62.1	1.1	-	-	62.9	1.3	-	-	64.0	1.7	-	-
1979	64.4	0.6	-	-	65.6	1.9	-	-	65.7	0.2	-	-	65.9	0.3	-	-	67.0	1.7	-	-	68.5	2.2	-	-
1980	70.0	2.2	-	-	71.5	2.1	-	-	72.3	1.1	-	-	73.0	1.0	-	-	75.6	3.6	-	-	76.2	0.8	-	-
1981	79.2	3.9	-	-	79.5	0.4	-	-	81.0	1.9	-	-	81.5	0.6	-	-	82.4	1.1	-	-	83.9	1.8	-	-
1982	86.9	3.6	-	-	87.8	1.0	-	-	88.6	0.9	-	-	91.6	3.4	-	-	93.1	1.6	-	-	94.5	1.5	-	-
1983	97.4	3.1	-	-	99.0	1.6	-	-	99.5	0.5	-	-	102.7	3.2	-	-	102.8	0.1	-	-	103.2	0.4	-	-
1984	106.5	3.2	-	-	107.3	0.8	-	-	107.5	0.2	-	-	108.0	0.5	-	-	108.2	0.2	-	-	109.4	1.1	-	-
1985	110.7	1.2	-	-	112.5	1.6	-	-	113.2	0.6	-	-	115.9	2.4	-	-	117.6	1.5	-	-	118.7	0.9	-	-
1986	120.0	1.1	-	-	121.2	1.0	-	-	123.3	1.7	-	-	125.9	2.1	-	-	126.6	0.6	-	-	126.1	-0.4	126.5	0.3
1987	-	-	-	-	-	-	-	-	-	-	131.3	3.8	-	-	-	-	-	-	-	-	-	-	134.4	2.4
1988	-	-	-	-	-	-	-	-	-	-	141.8	5.5	-	-	-	-	-	-	-	-	-	-	146.9	3.6
1989	-	-	-	-	-	-	-	-	-	-	151.2	2.9	-	-	-	-	-	-	-	-	-	-	157.9	4.4
1990	-	-	-	-	-	-	-	-	-	-	169.4	7.3	-	-	-	-	-	-	-	-	-	-	180.2	6.4
1991	-	-	-	-	-	-	-	-	-	-	189.4	5.1	-	-	-	-	-	-	-	-	-	-	196.3	3.6
1992	-	-	-	-	-	-	-	-	-	-	203.4	3.6	-	-	-	-	-	-	-	-	-	-	212.5	4.5
1993	-	-	-	-	-	-	-	-	-	-	217.5	2.4	-	-	-	-	-	-	-	-	-	-	-	-

Source: U.S. Department of Labor, Bureau of Labor Statistics, Division of Consumer Prices and Price Indexes. - indicates no data collected for period.

Denver-Boulder, CO
Consumer Price Index - All Urban Consumers
Base 1982-1984 = 100
Entertainment

For 1976-1993. Columns headed % show percentile change in the index from the previous period for which an index is available.

Year	Jan Index	%	Feb Index	%	Mar Index	%	Apr Index	%	May Index	%	Jun Index	%	Jul Index	%	Aug Index	%	Sep Index	%	Oct Index	%	Nov Index	%	Dec Index	%
1976	56.6	-	-	-	-	-	57.6	1.8	-	-	-	-	57.8	0.3	-	-	-	-	58.0	0.3	-	-	-	-
1977	59.4	2.4	-	-	-	-	60.8	2.4	-	-	-	-	61.8	1.6	-	-	-	-	62.6	1.3	-	-	-	-
1978	63.1	0.8	-	-	64.5	2.2	-	-	65.9	2.2	-	-	66.6	1.1	-	-	66.9	0.5	-	-	68.3	2.1	-	-
1979	69.0	1.0	-	-	71.1	3.0	-	-	71.6	0.7	-	-	72.8	1.7	-	-	73.2	0.5	-	-	73.8	0.8	-	-
1980	75.8	2.7	-	-	78.1	3.0	-	-	79.0	1.2	-	-	80.4	1.8	-	-	80.6	0.2	-	-	82.3	2.1	-	-
1981	82.9	0.7	-	-	83.9	1.2	-	-	86.4	3.0	-	-	87.1	0.8	-	-	86.5	-0.7	-	-	87.2	0.8	-	-
1982	89.5	2.6	-	-	88.1	-1.6	-	-	93.8	6.5	-	-	96.6	3.0	-	-	97.8	1.2	-	-	97.1	-0.7	-	-
1983	99.1	2.1	-	-	99.8	0.7	-	-	102.2	2.4	-	-	102.6	0.4	-	-	102.8	0.2	-	-	103.0	0.2	-	-
1984	103.5	0.5	-	-	104.8	1.3	-	-	105.7	0.9	-	-	105.7	0.0	-	-	104.8	-0.9	-	-	100.4	-4.2	-	-
1985	101.7	1.3	-	-	103.0	1.3	-	-	104.6	1.6	-	-	107.2	2.5	-	-	105.6	-1.5	-	-	103.2	-2.3	107.9	0.6
1986	105.2	1.9	-	-	105.3	0.1	-	-	105.6	0.3	-	-	107.4	1.7	-	-	108.5	1.0	-	-	107.3	-1.1	108.1	0.3
1987	-	-	-	-	-	-	-	-	-	-	107.8	-0.1	-	-	-	-	-	-	-	-	-	-	110.0	1.9
1988	-	-	-	-	-	-	-	-	-	-	107.9	-0.2	-	-	-	-	-	-	-	-	-	-	125.6	8.8
1989	-	-	-	-	-	-	-	-	-	-	115.4	4.9	-	-	-	-	-	-	-	-	-	-	131.6	3.6
1990	-	-	-	-	-	-	-	-	-	-	127.0	1.1	-	-	-	-	-	-	-	-	-	-	130.9	0.2
1991	-	-	-	-	-	-	-	-	-	-	130.7	-0.7	-	-	-	-	-	-	-	-	-	-	137.0	1.3
1992	-	-	-	-	-	-	-	-	-	-	135.2	3.3	-	-	-	-	-	-	-	-	-	-	-	-
1993	-	-	-	-	-	-	-	-	-	-	140.0	2.2	-	-	-	-	-	-	-	-	-	-	-	-

Source: U.S. Department of Labor, Bureau of Labor Statistics, Division of Consumer Prices and Price Indexes. - indicates no data collected for period.

Denver-Boulder, CO
Consumer Price Index - Urban Wage Earners
Base 1982-1984 = 100
Entertainment

For 1976-1993. Columns headed % show percentile change in the index from the previous period for which an index is available.

Year	Jan Index	%	Feb Index	%	Mar Index	%	Apr Index	%	May Index	%	Jun Index	%	Jul Index	%	Aug Index	%	Sep Index	%	Oct Index	%	Nov Index	%	Dec Index	%
1976	59.4	-	-	-	-	-	60.5	1.9	-	-	-	-	60.7	0.3	-	-	-	-	60.9	0.3	-	-	-	-
1977	62.4	2.5	-	-	-	-	63.8	2.2	-	-	-	-	64.9	1.7	-	-	-	-	65.8	1.4	-	-	-	-
1978	66.3	0.8	-	-	67.1	1.2	-	-	68.3	1.8	-	-	68.2	-0.1	-	-	68.6	0.6	-	-	70.5	2.8	-	-
1979	70.8	0.4	-	-	72.8	2.8	-	-	72.5	-0.4	-	-	73.3	1.1	-	-	73.8	0.7	-	-	74.7	1.2	-	-
1980	77.0	3.1	-	-	79.4	3.1	-	-	81.4	2.5	-	-	82.9	1.8	-	-	82.0	-1.1	-	-	85.0	3.7	-	-
1981	85.2	0.2	-	-	86.9	2.0	-	-	89.3	2.8	-	-	89.2	-0.1	-	-	86.8	-2.7	-	-	85.7	-1.3	-	-
1982	88.0	2.7	-	-	85.9	-2.4	-	-	94.5	10.0	-	-	97.3	3.0	-	-	98.4	1.1	-	-	97.4	-1.0	-	-
1983	99.4	2.1	-	-	99.9	0.5	-	-	102.3	2.4	-	-	102.9	0.6	-	-	103.0	0.1	-	-	103.2	0.2	-	-
1984	103.7	0.5	-	-	105.1	1.4	-	-	106.1	1.0	-	-	106.0	-0.1	-	-	104.9	-1.0	-	-	98.9	-5.7	-	-
1985	100.4	1.5	-	-	101.8	1.4	-	-	103.3	1.5	-	-	107.1	3.7	-	-	103.9	-3.0	-	-	101.3	-2.5	-	-
1986	103.1	1.8	-	-	103.6	0.5	-	-	103.7	0.1	-	-	105.7	1.9	-	-	105.6	-0.1	-	-	104.2	-1.3	104.9	0.7
1987	-	-	-	-	-	-	-	-	-	-	104.5	-0.4	-	-	-	-	-	-	-	-	-	-	105.1	0.6
1988	-	-	-	-	-	-	-	-	-	-	104.6	-0.5	-	-	-	-	-	-	-	-	-	-	107.8	3.1
1989	-	-	-	-	-	-	-	-	-	-	112.7	4.5	-	-	-	-	-	-	-	-	-	-	122.1	8.3
1990	-	-	-	-	-	-	-	-	-	-	123.5	1.1	-	-	-	-	-	-	-	-	-	-	127.6	3.3
1991	-	-	-	-	-	-	-	-	-	-	127.3	-0.2	-	-	-	-	-	-	-	-	-	-	127.7	0.3
1992	-	-	-	-	-	-	-	-	-	-	130.9	2.5	-	-	-	-	-	-	-	-	-	-	132.5	1.2
1993	-	-	-	-	-	-	-	-	-	-	134.2	1.3	-	-	-	-	-	-	-	-	-	-	-	-

Source: U.S. Department of Labor, Bureau of Labor Statistics, Division of Consumer Prices and Price Indexes. - indicates no data collected for period.

Denver-Boulder, CO
Consumer Price Index - All Urban Consumers
Base 1982-1984 = 100
Other Goods and Services

For 1976-1993. Columns headed % show percentile change in the index from the previous period for which an index is available.

Year	Jan Index	%	Feb Index	%	Mar Index	%	Apr Index	%	May Index	%	Jun Index	%	Jul Index	%	Aug Index	%	Sep Index	%	Oct Index	%	Nov Index	%	Dec Index	%
1976	50.6	-	-	-	-	-	51.9	2.6	-	-	-	-	52.3	0.8	-	-	-	-	52.8	1.0	-	-	-	-
1977	54.0	2.3	-	-	-	-	54.7	1.3	-	-	-	-	57.1	4.4	-	-	-	-	59.0	3.3	-	-	-	-
1978	59.8	1.4	-	-	60.5	1.2	-	-	60.2	-0.5	-	-	60.2	0.0	-	-	61.2	1.7	-	-	61.9	1.1	-	-
1979	62.7	1.3	-	-	63.7	1.6	-	-	64.0	0.5	-	-	63.3	-1.1	-	-	66.2	4.6	-	-	67.1	1.4	-	-
1980	69.1	3.0	-	-	70.5	2.0	-	-	71.1	0.9	-	-	71.1	0.0	-	-	73.9	3.9	-	-	75.4	2.0	-	-
1981	76.4	1.3	-	-	79.4	3.9	-	-	81.2	2.3	-	-	80.0	-1.5	-	-	82.4	3.0	-	-	83.6	1.5	-	-
1982	85.7	2.5	-	-	87.0	1.5	-	-	87.0	0.0	-	-	88.9	2.2	-	-	90.6	1.9	-	-	94.4	4.2	-	-
1983	96.8	2.5	-	-	98.9	2.2	-	-	99.4	0.5	-	-	101.2	1.8	-	-	103.5	2.3	-	-	106.5	2.9	-	-
1984	107.7	1.1	-	-	108.0	0.3	-	-	108.4	0.4	-	-	108.7	0.3	-	-	109.4	0.6	-	-	111.2	1.6	-	-
1985	113.2	1.8	-	-	114.1	0.8	-	-	114.7	0.5	-	-	114.1	-0.5	-	-	116.9	2.5	-	-	118.3	1.2	-	-
1986	118.8	0.4	-	-	121.7	2.4	-	-	121.2	-0.4	-	-	123.2	1.7	-	-	127.3	3.3	-	-	129.3	1.6	129.3	0.0
1987	-	-	-	-	-	-	-	-	-	-	131.1	1.4	-	-	-	-	-	-	-	-	-	-	134.2	2.4
1988	-	-	-	-	-	-	-	-	-	-	137.8	2.7	-	-	-	-	-	-	-	-	-	-	141.9	3.0
1989	-	-	-	-	-	-	-	-	-	-	145.0	2.2	-	-	-	-	-	-	-	-	-	-	152.1	4.9
1990	-	-	-	-	-	-	-	-	-	-	156.9	3.2	-	-	-	-	-	-	-	-	-	-	162.4	3.5
1991	-	-	-	-	-	-	-	-	-	-	169.2	4.2	-	-	-	-	-	-	-	-	-	-	177.6	5.0
1992	-	-	-	-	-	-	-	-	-	-	184.9	4.1	-	-	-	-	-	-	-	-	-	-	187.9	1.6
1993	-	-	-	-	-	-	-	-	-	-	190.7	1.5	-	-	-	-	-	-	-	-	-	-	-	-

Source: U.S. Department of Labor, Bureau of Labor Statistics, Division of Consumer Prices and Price Indexes. - indicates no data collected for period.

Denver-Boulder, CO
Consumer Price Index - Urban Wage Earners
Base 1982-1984 = 100
Other Goods and Services

For 1976-1993. Columns headed % show percentile change in the index from the previous period for which an index is available.

Year	Jan Index	%	Feb Index	%	Mar Index	%	Apr Index	%	May Index	%	Jun Index	%	Jul Index	%	Aug Index	%	Sep Index	%	Oct Index	%	Nov Index	%	Dec Index	%
1976	50.8	-	-	-	-	-	52.0	2.4	-	-	-	-	52.4	0.8	-	-	-	-	53.0	1.1	-	-	-	-
1977	54.1	2.1	-	-	-	-	54.9	1.5	-	-	-	-	57.2	4.2	-	-	-	-	59.1	3.3	-	-	-	-
1978	59.9	1.4	-	-	60.2	0.5	-	-	60.3	0.2	-	-	60.7	0.7	-	-	60.6	-0.2	-	-	61.8	2.0	-	-
1979	63.0	1.9	-	-	64.8	2.9	-	-	65.0	0.3	-	-	65.2	0.3	-	-	67.0	2.8	-	-	66.6	-0.6	-	-
1980	69.5	4.4	-	-	70.5	1.4	-	-	70.9	0.6	-	-	70.8	-0.1	-	-	73.0	3.1	-	-	76.1	4.2	-	-
1981	78.0	2.5	-	-	78.8	1.0	-	-	80.5	2.2	-	-	79.2	-1.6	-	-	81.3	2.7	-	-	82.3	1.2	-	-
1982	85.1	3.4	-	-	86.8	2.0	-	-	86.5	-0.3	-	-	88.5	2.3	-	-	89.9	1.6	-	-	93.8	4.3	-	-
1983	96.7	3.1	-	-	99.0	2.4	-	-	99.8	0.8	-	-	102.1	2.3	-	-	103.7	1.6	-	-	106.5	2.7	-	-
1984	108.1	1.5	-	-	108.4	0.3	-	-	108.6	0.2	-	-	109.3	0.6	-	-	109.5	0.2	-	-	110.7	1.1	-	-
1985	113.4	2.4	-	-	114.2	0.7	-	-	114.9	0.6	-	-	113.8	-1.0	-	-	116.7	2.5	-	-	117.9	1.0	-	-
1986	118.7	0.7	-	-	121.7	2.5	-	-	121.1	-0.5	-	-	123.4	1.9	-	-	127.9	3.6	-	-	129.3	1.1	129.3	0.0
1987	-	-	-	-	-	-	-	-	-	-	131.7	1.9	-	-	-	-	-	-	-	-	-	-	134.7	2.3
1988	-	-	-	-	-	-	-	-	-	-	138.3	2.7	-	-	-	-	-	-	-	-	-	-	142.7	3.2
1989	-	-	-	-	-	-	-	-	-	-	146.1	2.4	-	-	-	-	-	-	-	-	-	-	153.0	4.7
1990	-	-	-	-	-	-	-	-	-	-	156.5	2.3	-	-	-	-	-	-	-	-	-	-	162.5	3.8
1991	-	-	-	-	-	-	-	-	-	-	169.6	4.4	-	-	-	-	-	-	-	-	-	-	175.2	3.3
1992	-	-	-	-	-	-	-	-	-	-	182.3	4.1	-	-	-	-	-	-	-	-	-	-	185.5	1.8
1993	-	-	-	-	-	-	-	-	-	-	189.1	1.9	-	-	-	-	-	-	-	-	-	-	-	-

Source: U.S. Department of Labor, Bureau of Labor Statistics, Division of Consumer Prices and Price Indexes. - indicates no data collected for period.

Detroit, MI
Consumer Price Index - All Urban Consumers
Base 1982-1984 = 100
Annual Averages

For 1914-1993. Columns headed % show percentile change in the index from the previous period for which an index is available.

Year	All Items		Food & Beverage		Housing		Apparel & Upkeep		Trans- portation		Medical Care		Entertain- ment		Other Goods & Services	
	Index	%	Index	%	Index	%	Index	%	Index	%	Index	%	Index	%	Index	%
1914	-	-	-	-	-	-	-	-	-	-	-	-	-	-	-	-
1915	9.8	-	-	-	-	-	-	-	-	-	-	-	-	-	-	-
1916	10.8	10.2	-	-	-	-	-	-	-	-	-	-	-	-	-	-
1917	13.3	23.1	-	-	-	-	-	-	-	-	-	-	-	-	-	-
1918	15.7	18.0	-	-	-	-	-	-	-	-	-	-	-	-	-	-
1919	18.2	15.9	-	-	-	-	-	-	-	-	-	-	-	-	-	-
1920	21.8	19.8	-	-	-	-	-	-	-	-	-	-	-	-	-	-
1921	19.0	-12.8	-	-	-	-	-	-	-	-	-	-	-	-	-	-
1922	17.4	-8.4	-	-	-	-	-	-	-	-	-	-	-	-	-	-
1923	18.0	3.4	-	-	-	-	-	-	-	-	-	-	-	-	-	-
1924	18.0	0.0	-	-	-	-	-	-	-	-	-	-	-	-	-	-
1925	18.2	1.1	-	-	-	-	-	-	-	-	-	-	-	-	-	-
1926	18.3	0.5	-	-	-	-	-	-	-	-	-	-	-	-	-	-
1927	17.9	-2.2	-	-	-	-	-	-	-	-	-	-	-	-	-	-
1928	17.5	-2.2	-	-	-	-	-	-	-	-	-	-	-	-	-	-
1929	17.6	0.6	-	-	-	-	-	-	-	-	-	-	-	-	-	-
1930	16.9	-4.0	-	-	-	-	-	-	-	-	-	-	-	-	-	-
1931	14.8	-12.4	-	-	-	-	-	-	-	-	-	-	-	-	-	-
1932	12.8	-13.5	-	-	-	-	-	-	-	-	-	-	-	-	-	-
1933	12.1	-5.5	-	-	-	-	-	-	-	-	-	-	-	-	-	-
1934	12.8	5.8	-	-	-	-	-	-	-	-	-	-	-	-	-	-
1935	13.4	4.7	-	-	-	-	-	-	-	-	-	-	-	-	-	-
1936	13.8	3.0	-	-	-	-	-	-	-	-	-	-	-	-	-	-
1937	14.7	6.5	-	-	-	-	-	-	-	-	-	-	-	-	-	-
1938	14.4	-2.0	-	-	-	-	-	-	-	-	-	-	-	-	-	-
1939	14.0	-2.8	-	-	-	-	-	-	-	-	-	-	-	-	-	-
1940	14.1	0.7	-	-	-	-	-	-	-	-	-	-	-	-	-	-
1941	15.0	6.4	-	-	-	-	-	-	-	-	-	-	-	-	-	-
1942	16.7	11.3	-	-	-	-	-	-	-	-	-	-	-	-	-	-
1943	17.5	4.8	-	-	-	-	-	-	-	-	-	-	-	-	-	-
1944	17.8	1.7	-	-	-	-	-	-	-	-	-	-	-	-	-	-
1945	18.3	2.8	-	-	-	-	-	-	-	-	-	-	-	-	-	-
1946	19.9	8.7	-	-	-	-	-	-	-	-	-	-	-	-	-	-
1947	22.7	14.1	-	-	-	-	-	-	19.7	-	11.8	-	-	-	-	-
1948	24.5	7.9	-	-	-	-	-	-	22.2	12.7	12.3	4.2	-	-	-	-
1949	24.2	-1.2	-	-	-	-	-	-	23.4	5.4	12.6	2.4	-	-	-	-
1950	24.6	1.7	-	-	-	-	-	-	23.7	1.3	12.8	1.6	-	-	-	-
1951	26.5	7.7	-	-	-	-	-	-	24.7	4.2	13.4	4.7	-	-	-	-
1952	27.1	2.3	-	-	-	-	-	-	26.4	6.9	14.1	5.2	-	-	-	-
1953	27.6	1.8	-	-	-	-	52.1	-	27.5	4.2	14.7	4.3	-	-	-	-
1954	27.7	0.4	-	-	-	-	51.9	-0.4	26.3	-4.4	15.3	4.1	-	-	-	-
1955	27.7	0.0	-	-	-	-	51.8	-0.2	26.6	1.1	16.3	6.5	-	-	-	-
1956	28.2	1.8	-	-	-	-	52.6	1.5	27.5	3.4	17.4	6.7	-	-	-	-
1957	29.0	2.8	-	-	-	-	53.2	1.1	28.9	5.1	18.0	3.4	-	-	-	-
1958	29.4	1.4	-	-	-	-	53.0	-0.4	29.0	0.3	18.5	2.8	-	-	-	-

[Continued]

454

Detroit, MI
Consumer Price Index - All Urban Consumers
Base 1982-1984 = 100
Annual Averages
[Continued]

For 1914-1993. Columns headed % show percentile change in the index from the previous period for which an index is available.

Year	All Items		Food & Beverage		Housing		Apparel & Upkeep		Trans- portation		Medical Care		Entertain- ment		Other Goods & Services	
	Index	%	Index	%	Index	%	Index	%	Index	%	Index	%	Index	%	Index	%
1959	29.4	0.0	-	-	-	-	53.9	1.7	30.1	3.8	19.3	4.3	-	-	-	-
1960	29.7	1.0	-	-	-	-	54.4	0.9	30.2	0.3	19.6	1.6	-	-	-	-
1961	29.8	0.3	-	-	-	-	55.2	1.5	29.7	-1.7	20.6	5.1	-	-	-	-
1962	29.9	0.3	-	-	-	-	55.5	0.5	30.3	2.0	21.2	2.9	-	-	-	-
1963	30.2	1.0	-	-	-	-	56.1	1.1	30.4	0.3	22.3	5.2	-	-	-	-
1964	30.4	0.7	-	-	-	-	56.8	1.2	30.7	1.0	23.2	4.0	-	-	-	-
1965	31.2	2.6	-	-	-	-	57.7	1.6	32.0	4.2	23.8	2.6	-	-	-	-
1966	32.5	4.2	-	-	-	-	59.0	2.3	32.8	2.5	25.1	5.5	-	-	-	-
1967	33.6	3.4	-	-	-	-	60.6	2.7	33.5	2.1	26.9	7.2	-	-	-	-
1968	35.1	4.5	-	-	-	-	63.2	4.3	34.9	4.2	28.7	6.7	-	-	-	-
1969	37.2	6.0	-	-	-	-	66.0	4.4	36.0	3.2	30.8	7.3	-	-	-	-
1970	39.5	6.2	-	-	-	-	67.9	2.9	36.9	2.5	33.5	8.8	-	-	-	-
1971	40.9	3.5	-	-	-	-	70.0	3.1	38.4	4.1	36.1	7.8	-	-	-	-
1972	42.5	3.9	-	-	-	-	71.7	2.4	39.1	1.8	38.0	5.3	-	-	-	-
1973	45.2	6.4	-	-	-	-	74.1	3.3	41.5	6.1	40.0	5.3	-	-	-	-
1974	50.1	10.8	-	-	-	-	80.2	8.2	46.5	12.0	43.8	9.5	-	-	-	-
1975	53.9	7.6	-	-	-	-	83.6	4.2	50.0	7.5	50.4	15.1	-	-	-	-
1976	56.8	5.4	63.8	-	52.3	-	86.0	2.9	53.7	7.4	56.3	11.7	73.5	-	57.5	-
1977	60.7	6.9	67.6	6.0	55.8	6.7	88.9	3.4	58.6	9.1	63.2	12.3	75.7	3.0	61.3	6.6
1978	65.3	7.6	74.5	10.2	60.3	8.1	89.7	0.9	62.0	5.8	67.7	7.1	80.0	5.7	65.8	7.3
1979	73.6	12.7	82.2	10.3	70.3	16.6	89.7	0.0	70.4	13.5	73.9	9.2	82.8	3.5	70.2	6.7
1980	85.3	15.9	88.9	8.2	85.5	21.6	94.3	5.1	82.8	17.6	80.1	8.4	87.8	6.0	75.1	7.0
1981	93.2	9.3	95.8	7.8	93.4	9.2	96.4	2.2	93.8	13.3	86.1	7.5	92.3	5.1	81.8	8.9
1982	97.0	4.1	99.3	3.7	96.3	3.1	98.3	2.0	97.9	4.4	93.2	8.2	97.0	5.1	91.8	12.2
1983	99.8	2.9	99.3	0.0	100.4	4.3	101.0	2.7	98.5	0.6	98.3	5.5	101.2	4.3	102.0	11.1
1984	103.2	3.4	101.4	2.1	103.3	2.9	100.8	-0.2	103.6	5.2	108.5	10.4	101.8	0.6	106.2	4.1
1985	106.8	3.5	103.2	1.8	107.5	4.1	102.6	1.8	106.6	2.9	116.4	7.3	106.6	4.7	111.6	5.1
1986	108.3	1.4	107.3	4.0	109.8	2.1	103.3	0.7	103.2	-3.2	125.0	7.4	108.6	1.9	114.6	2.7
1987	111.7	3.1	110.5	3.0	113.0	2.9	108.0	4.5	105.3	2.0	132.9	6.3	112.1	3.2	120.4	5.1
1988	116.1	3.9	114.7	3.8	116.1	2.7	115.2	6.7	109.5	4.0	140.2	5.5	114.7	2.3	130.0	8.0
1989	122.3	5.3	120.8	5.3	121.2	4.4	122.7	6.5	117.0	6.8	147.1	4.9	120.5	5.1	137.9	6.1
1990	128.6	5.2	126.5	4.7	126.4	4.3	127.9	4.2	124.0	6.0	159.8	8.6	128.1	6.3	147.5	7.0
1991	133.1	3.5	131.1	3.6	128.6	1.7	131.8	3.0	129.3	4.3	171.0	7.0	132.7	3.6	160.7	8.9
1992	135.9	2.1	133.4	1.8	131.8	2.5	129.9	-1.4	129.9	0.5	181.6	6.2	130.7	-1.5	173.8	8.2
1993	139.6	2.7	135.2	1.3	134.4	2.0	137.9	6.2	132.5	2.0	190.9	5.1	137.7	5.4	183.5	5.6

Source: U.S. Department of Labor, Bureau of Labor Statistics, Division of Consumer Prices and Price Indexes. - indicates no data collected for period.

Detroit, MI
Consumer Price Index - Urban Wage Earners
Base 1982-1984 = 100
Annual Averages

For 1914-1993. Columns headed % show percentile change in the index from the previous period for which an index is available.

Year	All Items		Food & Beverage		Housing		Apparel & Upkeep		Trans- portation		Medical Care		Entertain- ment		Other Goods & Services	
	Index	%	Index	%	Index	%	Index	%	Index	%	Index	%	Index	%	Index	%
1914	-		-		-		-		-		-		-		-	
1915	9.8	-	-		-		-		-		-		-		-	
1916	10.9	11.2	-		-		-		-		-		-		-	
1917	13.4	22.9	-		-		-		-		-		-		-	
1918	15.8	17.9	-		-		-		-		-		-		-	
1919	18.4	16.5	-		-		-		-		-		-		-	
1920	22.0	19.6	-		-		-		-		-		-		-	-
1921	19.2	-12.7	-		-		-		-		-		-		-	
1922	17.6	-8.3	-		-		-		-		-		-		-	
1923	18.2	3.4	-		-		-		-		-		-		-	
1924	18.2	0.0	-		-		-		-		-		-		-	
1925	18.4	1.1	-		-		-		-		-		-		-	
1926	18.5	0.5	-		-		-		-		-		-		-	
1927	18.0	-2.7	-		-		-		-		-		-		-	
1928	17.7	-1.7	-		-		-		-		-		-		-	
1929	17.7	0.0	-		-		-		-		-		-		-	
1930	17.0	-4.0	-		-		-		-		-		-		-	
1931	14.9	-12.4	-		-		-		-		-		-		-	
1932	12.9	-13.4	-		-		-		-		-		-		-	
1933	12.2	-5.4	-		-		-		-		-		-		-	
1934	12.9	5.7	-		-		-		-		-		-		-	
1935	13.5	4.7	-		-		-		-		-		-		-	
1936	14.0	3.7	-		-		-		-		-		-		-	
1937	14.8	5.7	-		-		-		-		-		-		-	
1938	14.6	-1.4	-		-		-		-		-		-		-	
1939	14.2	-2.7	-		-		-		-		-		-		-	
1940	14.2	0.0	-		-		-		-		-		-		-	
1941	15.1	6.3	-		-		-		-		-		-		-	
1942	16.8	11.3	-		-		-		-		-		-		-	
1943	17.7	5.4	-		-		-		-		-		-		-	
1944	18.0	1.7	-		-		-		-		-		-		-	
1945	18.4	2.2	-		-		-		-		-		-		-	
1946	20.1	9.2	-		-		-		-		-		-		-	
1947	22.9	13.9	-		-		-		20.5	-	12.0	-	-		-	
1948	24.7	7.9	-		-		-		23.0	12.2	12.5	4.2	-		-	
1949	24.4	-1.2	-		-		-		24.3	5.7	12.8	2.4	-		-	
1950	24.8	1.6	-		-		-		24.6	1.2	13.1	2.3	-		-	
1951	26.8	8.1	-		-		-		25.6	4.1	13.6	3.8	-		-	
1952	27.4	2.2	-		-		-		27.4	7.0	14.3	5.1	-		-	
1953	27.8	1.5	-		-		53.0	-	28.5	4.0	14.9	4.2	-		-	
1954	27.9	0.4	-		-		52.9	-0.2	27.3	-4.2	15.5	4.0	-		-	
1955	27.9	0.0	-		-		52.7	-0.4	27.6	1.1	16.6	7.1	-		-	
1956	28.5	2.2	-		-		53.5	1.5	28.5	3.3	17.7	6.6	-		-	
1957	29.3	2.8	-		-		54.2	1.3	30.0	5.3	18.3	3.4	-		-	
1958	29.7	1.4	-		-		54.0	-0.4	30.1	0.3	18.9	3.3	-		-	

[Continued]

456

Detroit, MI
Consumer Price Index - Urban Wage Earners
Base 1982-1984 = 100
Annual Averages
[Continued]

For 1914-1993. Columns headed % show percentile change in the index from the previous period for which an index is available.

Year	All Items		Food & Beverage		Housing		Apparel & Upkeep		Trans-portation		Medical Care		Entertain-ment		Other Goods & Services	
	Index	%	Index	%	Index	%	Index	%	Index	%	Index	%	Index	%	Index	%
1959	29.7	0.0	-	-	-	-	54.8	1.5	31.3	4.0	19.6	3.7	-	-	-	-
1960	29.9	0.7	-	-	-	-	55.4	1.1	31.3	0.0	20.0	2.0	-	-	-	-
1961	30.1	0.7	-	-	-	-	56.2	1.4	30.8	-1.6	21.0	5.0	-	-	-	-
1962	30.2	0.3	-	-	-	-	56.5	0.5	31.5	2.3	21.6	2.9	-	-	-	-
1963	30.5	1.0	-	-	-	-	57.1	1.1	31.6	0.3	22.7	5.1	-	-	-	-
1964	30.7	0.7	-	-	-	-	57.9	1.4	31.8	0.6	23.6	4.0	-	-	-	-
1965	31.4	2.3	-	-	-	-	58.8	1.6	33.2	4.4	24.2	2.5	-	-	-	-
1966	32.8	4.5	-	-	-	-	60.1	2.2	34.0	2.4	25.6	5.8	-	-	-	-
1967	34.0	3.7	-	-	-	-	61.7	2.7	34.8	2.4	27.4	7.0	-	-	-	-
1968	35.4	4.1	-	-	-	-	64.3	4.2	36.2	4.0	29.2	6.6	-	-	-	-
1969	37.6	6.2	-	-	-	-	67.2	4.5	37.4	3.3	31.4	7.5	-	-	-	-
1970	39.9	6.1	-	-	-	-	69.1	2.8	38.2	2.1	34.1	8.6	-	-	-	-
1971	41.3	3.5	-	-	-	-	71.3	3.2	39.9	4.5	36.8	7.9	-	-	-	-
1972	42.8	3.6	-	-	-	-	73.0	2.4	40.5	1.5	38.8	5.4	-	-	-	-
1973	45.7	6.8	-	-	-	-	75.4	3.3	43.0	6.2	40.7	4.9	-	-	-	-
1974	50.6	10.7	-	-	-	-	81.7	8.4	48.3	12.3	44.6	9.6	-	-	-	-
1975	54.4	7.5	-	-	-	-	85.1	4.2	51.9	7.5	51.4	15.2	-	-	-	-
1976	57.3	5.3	63.2	-	52.5	-	87.6	2.9	55.8	7.5	57.4	11.7	77.0	-	55.5	-
1977	61.3	7.0	66.9	5.9	56.0	6.7	90.5	3.3	60.8	9.0	64.4	12.2	79.3	3.0	59.1	6.5
1978	65.9	7.5	74.2	10.9	60.3	7.7	93.7	3.5	64.1	5.4	69.1	7.3	83.1	4.8	63.0	6.6
1979	74.3	12.7	82.2	10.8	70.3	16.6	93.6	-0.1	72.7	13.4	75.8	9.7	86.0	3.5	67.3	6.8
1980	85.6	15.2	88.7	7.9	85.2	21.2	97.7	4.4	84.5	16.2	81.3	7.3	90.9	5.7	73.5	9.2
1981	92.7	8.3	95.7	7.9	92.6	8.7	97.3	-0.4	93.1	10.2	86.8	6.8	92.7	2.0	80.5	9.5
1982	96.7	4.3	99.4	3.9	95.7	3.3	98.4	1.1	97.8	5.0	93.5	7.7	97.3	5.0	91.7	13.9
1983	101.1	4.6	99.2	-0.2	103.4	8.0	100.8	2.4	98.5	0.7	98.5	5.3	101.1	3.9	102.1	11.3
1984	102.2	1.1	101.4	2.2	100.9	-2.4	100.8	0.0	103.6	5.2	108.1	9.7	101.6	0.5	106.2	4.0
1985	104.5	2.3	102.9	1.5	102.7	1.8	103.5	2.7	106.7	3.0	115.6	6.9	106.5	4.8	111.5	5.0
1986	105.8	1.2	106.9	3.9	104.9	2.1	105.5	1.9	103.2	-3.3	123.6	6.9	109.3	2.6	114.1	2.3
1987	109.1	3.1	110.2	3.1	108.0	3.0	111.3	5.5	105.5	2.2	131.3	6.2	112.9	3.3	120.0	5.2
1988	113.3	3.8	114.2	3.6	110.9	2.7	119.1	7.0	109.5	3.8	139.6	6.3	115.5	2.3	130.1	8.4
1989	119.4	5.4	120.3	5.3	115.7	4.3	125.9	5.7	117.0	6.8	146.9	5.2	121.4	5.1	137.4	5.6
1990	125.6	5.2	126.1	4.8	120.7	4.3	131.8	4.7	124.1	6.1	159.1	8.3	128.8	6.1	147.3	7.2
1991	129.8	3.3	130.7	3.6	122.8	1.7	134.9	2.4	129.2	4.1	169.7	6.7	133.4	3.6	160.3	8.8
1992	132.1	1.8	133.1	1.8	125.7	2.4	133.3	-1.2	129.7	0.4	180.0	6.1	130.8	-1.9	170.0	6.1
1993	135.4	2.5	134.8	1.3	128.1	1.9	140.6	5.5	132.4	2.1	189.3	5.2	137.9	5.4	175.8	3.4

Source: U.S. Department of Labor, Bureau of Labor Statistics, Division of Consumer Prices and Price Indexes. - indicates no data collected for period.

457

Detroit, MI
Consumer Price Index - All Urban Consumers
Base 1982-1984 = 100
All Items

For 1914-1993. Columns headed % show percentile change in the index from the previous period for which an index is available.

Year	Jan		Feb		Mar		Apr		May		Jun		Jul		Aug		Sep		Oct		Nov		Dec	
	Index	%	Index	%	Index	%	Index	%	Index	%	Index	%	Index	%	Index	%	Index	%	Index	%	Index	%	Index	%
1914	-	-	-	-	-	-	-	-	-	-	-	-	-	-	-	-	-	-	-	-	-	-	9.7	-
1915	-	-	-	-	-	-	-	-	-	-	-	-	-	-	-	-	-	-	-	-	-	-	10.1	4.1
1916	-	-	-	-	-	-	-	-	-	-	-	-	-	-	-	-	-	-	-	-	-	-	11.7	15.8
1917	-	-	-	-	-	-	-	-	-	-	-	-	-	-	-	-	-	-	-	-	-	-	14.3	22.2
1918	-	-	-	-	-	-	-	-	-	-	-	-	-	-	-	-	-	-	-	-	-	-	17.0	18.9
1919	-	-	-	-	-	-	-	-	-	-	17.8	4.7	-	-	-	-	-	-	-	-	-	-	19.9	11.8
1920	-	-	-	-	-	-	-	-	-	-	22.9	15.1	-	-	-	-	-	-	-	-	-	-	21.2	-7.4
1921	-	-	-	-	-	-	-	-	19.0	-10.4	-	-	-	-	-	-	18.5	-2.6	-	-	-	-	17.9	-3.2
1922	-	-	-	-	17.3	-3.4	-	-	-	-	17.4	0.6	-	-	-	-	17.3	-0.6	-	-	-	-	17.5	1.2
1923	-	-	-	-	17.7	1.1	-	-	-	-	18.0	1.7	-	-	-	-	18.4	2.2	-	-	-	-	18.2	-1.1
1924	-	-	-	-	18.1	-0.5	-	-	-	-	18.1	0.0	-	-	-	-	17.9	-1.1	-	-	-	-	17.9	0.0
1925	-	-	-	-	-	-	-	-	-	-	18.3	2.2	-	-	-	-	-	-	-	-	-	-	18.6	1.6
1926	-	-	-	-	-	-	-	-	-	-	18.4	-1.1	-	-	-	-	-	-	-	-	-	-	18.2	-1.1
1927	-	-	-	-	-	-	-	-	-	-	18.2	0.0	-	-	-	-	-	-	-	-	-	-	17.7	-2.7
1928	-	-	-	-	-	-	-	-	-	-	17.4	-1.7	-	-	-	-	-	-	-	-	-	-	17.4	0.0
1929	-	-	-	-	-	-	-	-	-	-	17.6	1.1	-	-	-	-	-	-	-	-	-	-	17.5	-0.6
1930	-	-	-	-	-	-	-	-	-	-	17.2	-1.7	-	-	-	-	-	-	-	-	-	-	15.9	-7.6
1931	-	-	-	-	-	-	-	-	-	-	14.8	-6.9	-	-	-	-	-	-	-	-	-	-	13.9	-6.1
1932	-	-	-	-	-	-	-	-	-	-	12.9	-7.2	-	-	-	-	-	-	-	-	-	-	12.1	-6.2
1933	-	-	-	-	-	-	-	-	-	-	11.7	-3.3	-	-	-	-	-	-	-	-	-	-	12.3	5.1
1934	-	-	-	-	-	-	-	-	-	-	12.8	4.1	-	-	-	-	-	-	-	-	12.8	0.0	-	-
1935	-	-	-	-	13.3	3.9	-	-	-	-	-	-	13.4	0.8	-	-	-	-	13.4	0.0	-	-	-	-
1936	13.6	1.5	-	-	-	-	13.6	0.0	-	-	-	-	14.0	2.9	-	-	14.1	0.7	-	-	-	-	14.0	-0.7
1937	-	-	-	-	14.4	2.9	-	-	-	-	14.8	2.8	-	-	-	-	14.9	0.7	-	-	-	-	15.0	0.7
1938	-	-	-	-	14.6	-2.7	-	-	-	-	14.5	-0.7	-	-	-	-	14.3	-1.4	-	-	-	-	14.2	-0.7
1939	-	-	-	-	14.0	-1.4	-	-	-	-	13.9	-0.7	-	-	-	-	14.1	1.4	-	-	-	-	14.0	-0.7
1940	-	-	-	-	14.1	0.7	-	-	-	-	14.2	0.7	-	-	-	-	14.1	-0.7	14.1	0.0	14.1	0.0	14.2	0.7
1941	14.2	0.0	14.3	0.7	14.4	0.7	14.6	1.4	14.6	0.0	15.0	2.7	15.0	0.0	15.1	0.7	15.4	2.0	15.7	1.9	15.8	0.6	15.9	0.6
1942	16.1	1.3	16.2	0.6	16.5	1.9	16.7	1.2	16.7	0.0	16.7	0.0	16.7	0.0	16.6	-0.6	16.7	0.6	16.9	1.2	17.0	0.6	17.1	0.6
1943	17.1	0.0	17.2	0.6	17.5	1.7	17.6	0.6	17.9	1.7	17.9	0.0	17.8	-0.6	17.5	-1.7	17.5	0.0	17.6	0.6	17.5	-0.6	17.7	1.1
1944	17.6	-0.6	17.5	-0.6	17.5	0.0	17.7	1.1	17.7	0.0	17.8	0.6	18.0	1.1	18.0	0.0	18.0	0.0	17.9	-0.6	17.9	0.0	18.0	0.6
1945	18.0	0.0	18.0	0.0	18.0	0.0	18.0	0.0	18.2	1.1	18.4	1.1	18.4	0.0	18.5	0.5	18.4	-0.5	18.4	0.0	18.5	0.5	18.5	0.0
1946	18.6	0.5	18.6	0.0	18.6	0.0	18.8	1.1	19.0	1.1	19.2	1.1	20.4	6.2	20.5	0.5	20.7	1.0	21.0	1.4	21.4	1.9	21.6	0.9
1947	21.6	0.0	21.6	0.0	22.1	2.3	22.1	0.0	22.1	0.0	22.4	1.4	22.6	0.9	23.0	1.8	23.2	0.9	23.6	1.7	23.5	-0.4	23.9	1.7
1948	24.1	0.8	23.9	-0.8	23.8	-0.4	24.3	2.1	24.5	0.8	24.7	0.8	24.9	0.8	24.9	0.0	24.8	-0.4	24.7	-0.4	24.5	-0.8	24.5	0.0
1949	24.3	-0.8	24.2	-0.4	24.2	0.0	24.2	0.0	24.3	0.4	24.3	0.0	24.1	-0.8	24.1	0.0	24.1	0.0	23.9	-0.8	24.1	0.8	24.0	-0.4
1950	23.9	-0.4	23.8	-0.4	24.0	0.8	24.0	0.0	24.2	0.8	24.4	0.8	24.6	0.8	24.7	0.4	25.0	1.2	25.2	0.8	25.3	0.4	25.5	0.8
1951	25.9	1.6	26.2	1.2	26.3	0.4	26.3	0.0	26.3	0.0	26.5	0.8	26.5	0.0	26.5	0.0	26.6	0.4	26.7	0.4	26.9	0.7	27.0	0.4
1952	27.0	0.0	26.8	-0.7	26.8	0.0	27.0	0.7	27.0	0.0	27.0	0.0	27.2	0.7	27.3	0.4	27.8	1.8	27.9	0.4	27.7	-0.7	27.7	0.0
1953	27.5	-0.4	27.3	-0.7	27.4	0.4	27.4	0.0	27.5	0.4	27.7	0.7	27.8	0.4	27.8	0.0	27.7	-0.4	27.6	-0.4	27.8	0.7	27.6	-0.7
1954	27.8	0.4	27.7	-0.4	27.7	0.0	27.7	0.0	27.8	0.4	27.8	0.0	27.9	0.4	27.7	-0.7	27.8	0.4	27.7	-0.4	27.7	0.0	27.7	0.0
1955	27.6	0.0	27.6	0.0	27.6	0.0	27.6	0.0	27.7	0.4	27.7	0.0	27.7	0.0	27.7	0.0	27.7	0.0	27.7	0.0	27.7	0.0	27.7	0.0
1956	27.6	-0.4	27.7	0.4	27.8	0.4	27.9	0.4	28.0	0.4	28.2	0.7	28.6	1.4	28.4	-0.7	28.4	0.0	28.5	0.4	28.6	0.4	28.6	0.0
1957	28.6	0.0	28.7	0.3	28.7	0.0	28.8	0.3	29.0	0.7	29.1	0.3	29.2	0.3	29.2	0.0	29.2	0.0	29.1	-0.3	29.3	0.7	29.3	0.0
1958	29.4	0.3	29.4	0.0	29.5	0.3	29.5	0.0	29.5	0.0	29.5	0.0	29.5	0.0	29.4	-0.3	29.4	0.0	29.3	-0.3	29.3	0.0	29.3	0.0

[Continued]

Detroit, MI
Consumer Price Index - All Urban Consumers
Base 1982-1984 = 100
All Items
[Continued]

For 1914-1993. Columns headed % show percentile change in the index from the previous period for which an index is available.

Year	Jan Index	%	Feb Index	%	Mar Index	%	Apr Index	%	May Index	%	Jun Index	%	Jul Index	%	Aug Index	%	Sep Index	%	Oct Index	%	Nov Index	%	Dec Index	%
1959	29.3	0.0	29.3	0.0	29.2	-0.3	29.3	0.3	29.3	0.0	29.3	0.0	29.5	0.7	29.4	-0.3	29.6	0.7	29.7	0.3	29.5	-0.7	29.5	0.0
1960	29.3	-0.7	29.4	0.3	29.4	0.0	29.5	0.3	29.5	0.0	29.7	0.7	29.9	0.7	29.8	-0.3	29.8	0.0	29.8	0.0	29.8	0.0	29.9	0.3
1961	30.0	0.3	30.0	0.0	29.9	-0.3	29.8	-0.3	29.8	0.0	29.9	0.3	29.8	-0.3	29.9	0.3	29.7	-0.7	29.8	0.3	29.7	-0.3	29.5	-0.7
1962	29.6	0.3	29.9	1.0	29.9	0.0	29.9	0.0	29.9	0.0	29.8	-0.3	29.8	0.0	29.9	0.3	30.1	0.7	30.1	0.0	30.0	-0.3	30.0	0.0
1963	30.0	0.0	30.0	0.0	30.0	0.0	29.9	-0.3	30.0	0.3	30.3	1.0	30.4	0.3	30.6	0.7	30.2	-1.3	30.3	0.3	30.4	0.3	30.3	-0.3
1964	30.4	0.3	30.2	-0.7	30.3	0.3	30.4	0.3	30.2	-0.7	30.3	0.3	30.5	0.7	30.5	0.0	30.6	0.3	30.7	0.3	30.6	-0.3	30.7	0.3
1965	30.7	0.0	30.6	-0.3	30.7	0.3	30.9	0.7	31.1	0.6	31.3	0.6	31.3	0.0	31.3	0.0	31.3	0.0	31.5	0.6	31.5	0.0	31.6	0.3
1966	31.7	0.3	31.9	0.6	32.1	0.6	32.3	0.6	32.4	0.3	32.6	0.6	32.6	0.0	32.8	0.6	32.8	0.0	33.0	0.6	33.0	0.0	33.2	0.6
1967	33.2	0.0	33.2	0.0	33.5	0.9	33.5	0.0	33.5	0.0	33.6	0.3	33.7	0.3	33.7	0.0	33.7	0.0	33.8	0.3	34.0	0.6	34.1	0.3
1968	34.1	0.0	34.3	0.6	34.6	0.9	34.7	0.3	34.8	0.3	35.1	0.9	35.2	0.3	35.3	0.3	35.5	0.6	35.6	0.3	35.8	0.6	35.9	0.3
1969	36.0	0.3	36.1	0.3	36.6	1.4	36.8	0.5	37.0	0.5	37.3	0.8	37.4	0.3	37.6	0.5	37.6	0.0	37.8	0.5	38.0	0.5	38.3	0.8
1970	38.4	0.3	38.7	0.8	39.0	0.8	39.2	0.5	39.5	0.8	39.6	0.3	39.7	0.3	39.6	-0.3	39.8	0.5	40.1	0.8	40.3	0.5	40.2	-0.2
1971	40.5	0.7	40.4	-0.2	40.4	0.0	40.4	0.0	40.7	0.7	41.0	0.7	41.0	0.0	41.3	0.7	41.3	0.0	41.3	0.0	41.5	0.5	41.6	0.2
1972	41.8	0.5	42.0	0.5	42.1	0.2	42.1	0.0	42.2	0.2	42.4	0.5	42.6	0.5	42.7	0.2	42.8	0.2	42.8	0.0	42.9	0.2	43.2	0.7
1973	43.2	0.0	43.6	0.9	44.1	1.1	44.5	0.9	44.9	0.9	45.0	0.2	45.0	0.0	46.0	2.2	46.2	0.4	46.4	0.4	46.8	0.9	47.1	0.6
1974	47.6	1.1	48.4	1.7	48.7	0.6	48.9	0.4	49.3	0.8	49.9	1.2	50.3	0.8	50.8	1.0	51.3	1.0	51.7	0.8	52.2	1.0	52.5	0.6
1975	52.3	-0.4	52.7	0.8	52.8	0.2	53.1	0.6	53.2	0.2	53.7	0.9	54.1	0.7	54.3	0.4	54.8	0.9	54.9	0.2	55.1	0.4	55.4	0.5
1976	55.7	0.5	55.8	0.2	55.7	-0.2	56.0	0.5	56.3	0.5	56.5	0.4	56.9	0.7	57.1	0.4	57.6	0.9	57.7	0.2	58.0	0.5	58.2	0.3
1977	58.5	0.5	58.9	0.7	59.5	1.0	60.2	1.2	60.3	0.2	60.9	1.0	61.4	0.8	61.4	0.0	61.5	0.2	61.6	0.2	62.1	0.8	62.0	-0.2
1978	62.2	0.3	62.4	0.3	63.4	1.6	64.0	0.9	64.7	1.1	65.4	1.1	65.5	0.2	65.9	0.6	66.5	0.9	67.6	1.7	68.0	0.6	68.0	0.0
1979	69.0	1.5	70.2	1.7	71.2	1.4	71.7	0.7	72.0	0.4	72.5	0.7	73.8	1.8	74.8	1.4	75.3	0.7	76.4	1.5	77.8	1.8	78.5	0.9
1980	79.8	1.7	80.9	1.4	81.7	1.0	83.5	2.2	83.6	0.1	86.4	3.3	85.4	-1.2	85.8	0.5	87.3	1.7	88.9	1.8	89.6	0.8	90.7	1.2
1981	90.3	-0.4	90.9	0.7	90.2	-0.8	91.6	1.6	92.6	1.1	94.4	1.9	95.2	0.8	95.4	0.2	95.6	0.2	94.7	-0.9	94.1	-0.6	93.6	-0.5
1982	94.5	1.0	93.5	-1.1	93.6	0.1	95.4	1.9	96.2	0.8	97.3	1.1	98.4	1.1	98.5	0.1	99.2	0.7	99.3	0.1	99.6	0.3	98.4	-1.2
1983	98.4	0.0	98.3	-0.1	98.4	0.1	99.2	0.8	99.2	0.0	99.8	0.6	100.4	0.6	100.5	0.1	100.7	0.2	100.3	-0.4	100.9	0.6	101.0	0.1
1984	101.4	0.4	102.0	0.6	102.3	0.3	102.8	0.5	102.8	0.0	103.0	0.2	103.5	0.5	103.6	0.1	104.8	1.2	104.9	0.1	103.9	-1.0	104.0	0.1
1985	104.6	0.6	105.5	0.9	106.1	0.6	106.2	0.1	106.3	0.1	106.6	0.3	107.0	0.4	107.0	0.0	107.8	0.7	107.6	-0.2	108.7	1.0	108.7	0.0
1986	108.7	0.0	108.6	-0.1	107.7	-0.8	107.3	-0.4	108.2	0.8	108.0	-0.2	107.1	-0.8	108.7	1.5	108.0	-0.6	109.1	1.0	109.4	0.3	109.2	-0.2
1987	-	-	110.2	0.9	-	-	111.2	0.9	-	-	111.1	-0.1	-	-	112.2	1.0	-	-	114.1	1.7	-	-	112.6	-1.3
1988	-	-	113.7	1.0	-	-	114.4	0.6	-	-	115.4	0.9	-	-	117.6	1.9	-	-	118.6	0.9	-	-	118.3	-0.3
1989	-	-	120.1	1.5	-	-	121.7	1.3	-	-	122.1	0.3	-	-	122.2	0.1	-	-	124.6	2.0	-	-	124.4	-0.2
1990	-	-	126.1	1.4	-	-	126.9	0.6	-	-	127.7	0.6	-	-	129.4	1.3	-	-	131.8	1.9	-	-	131.2	-0.5
1991	-	-	132.2	0.8	-	-	131.7	-0.4	-	-	133.5	1.4	-	-	133.2	-0.2	-	-	134.6	1.1	-	-	134.0	-0.4
1992	-	-	134.9	0.7	-	-	135.3	0.3	-	-	135.5	0.1	-	-	135.8	0.2	-	-	137.5	1.3	-	-	137.1	-0.3
1993	-	-	138.3	0.9	-	-	138.7	0.3	-	-	139.1	0.3	-	-	139.9	0.6	-	-	141.9	1.4	-	-	140.2	-1.2

Source: U.S. Department of Labor, Bureau of Labor Statistics, Division of Consumer Prices and Price Indexes. - indicates no data collected for period.

Detroit, MI
Consumer Price Index - Urban Wage Earners
Base 1982-1984 = 100
All Items

For 1914-1993. Columns headed % show percentile change in the index from the previous period for which an index is available.

Year	Jan Index	%	Feb Index	%	Mar Index	%	Apr Index	%	May Index	%	Jun Index	%	Jul Index	%	Aug Index	%	Sep Index	%	Oct Index	%	Nov Index	%	Dec Index	%
1914	-	-	-	-	-	-	-	-	-	-	-	-	-	-	-	-	-	-	-	-	-	-	9.8	-
1915	-	-	-	-	-	-	-	-	-	-	-	-	-	-	-	-	-	-	-	-	-	-	10.2	4.1
1916	-	-	-	-	-	-	-	-	-	-	-	-	-	-	-	-	-	-	-	-	-	-	11.8	15.7
1917	-	-	-	-	-	-	-	-	-	-	-	-	-	-	-	-	-	-	-	-	-	-	14.4	22.0
1918	-	-	-	-	-	-	-	-	-	-	-	-	-	-	-	-	-	-	-	-	-	-	17.2	19.4
1919	-	-	-	-	-	-	-	-	-	-	17.9	4.1	-	-	-	-	-	-	-	-	-	-	20.1	12.3
1920	-	-	-	-	-	-	-	-	-	-	23.2	15.4	-	-	-	-	-	-	-	-	-	-	21.4	-7.8
1921	-	-	-	-	-	-	-	-	19.2	-10.3	-	-	-	-	-	-	18.6	-3.1	-	-	-	-	18.1	-2.7
1922	-	-	-	-	17.5	-3.3	-	-	-	-	17.6	0.6	-	-	-	-	17.5	-0.6	-	-	-	-	17.7	1.1
1923	-	-	-	-	17.9	1.1	-	-	-	-	18.2	1.7	-	-	-	-	18.5	1.6	-	-	-	-	18.4	-0.5
1924	-	-	-	-	18.3	-0.5	-	-	-	-	18.3	0.0	-	-	-	-	18.1	-1.1	-	-	-	-	18.1	0.0
1925	-	-	-	-	-	-	-	-	-	-	18.4	1.7	-	-	-	-	-	-	-	-	-	-	18.8	2.2
1926	-	-	-	-	-	-	-	-	-	-	18.6	-1.1	-	-	-	-	-	-	-	-	-	-	18.3	-1.6
1927	-	-	-	-	-	-	-	-	-	-	18.4	0.5	-	-	-	-	-	-	-	-	-	-	17.8	-3.3
1928	-	-	-	-	-	-	-	-	-	-	17.6	-1.1	-	-	-	-	-	-	-	-	-	-	17.6	0.0
1929	-	-	-	-	-	-	-	-	-	-	17.8	1.1	-	-	-	-	-	-	-	-	-	-	17.7	-0.6
1930	-	-	-	-	-	-	-	-	-	-	17.3	-2.3	-	-	-	-	-	-	-	-	-	-	16.1	-6.9
1931	-	-	-	-	-	-	-	-	-	-	14.9	-7.5	-	-	-	-	-	-	-	-	-	-	14.0	-6.0
1932	-	-	-	-	-	-	-	-	-	-	13.0	-7.1	-	-	-	-	-	-	-	-	-	-	12.2	-6.2
1933	-	-	-	-	-	-	-	-	-	-	11.8	-3.3	-	-	-	-	-	-	-	-	-	-	12.4	5.1
1934	-	-	-	-	-	-	-	-	-	-	12.9	4.0	-	-	-	-	-	-	-	-	12.9	0.0	-	-
1935	-	-	-	-	13.4	3.9	-	-	-	-	-	-	13.5	0.7	-	-	-	-	13.5	0.0	-	-	-	-
1936	13.7	1.5	-	-	-	-	13.7	0.0	-	-	-	-	14.1	2.9	-	-	14.2	0.7	-	-	-	-	14.1	-0.7
1937	-	-	-	-	14.6	3.5	-	-	-	-	14.9	2.1	-	-	-	-	15.1	1.3	-	-	-	-	15.1	0.0
1938	-	-	-	-	14.8	-2.0	-	-	-	-	14.6	-1.4	-	-	-	-	14.4	-1.4	-	-	-	-	14.3	-0.7
1939	-	-	-	-	14.2	-0.7	-	-	-	-	14.1	-0.7	-	-	-	-	14.2	0.7	-	-	-	-	14.2	0.0
1940	-	-	-	-	14.2	0.0	-	-	-	-	14.3	0.7	-	-	-	-	14.3	0.0	14.3	0.0	14.3	0.0	14.3	0.0
1941	14.4	0.7	14.4	0.0	14.5	0.7	14.7	1.4	14.7	0.0	15.1	2.7	15.2	0.7	15.3	0.7	15.6	2.0	15.9	1.9	16.0	0.6	16.0	0.0
1942	16.3	1.9	16.4	0.6	16.6	1.2	16.8	1.2	16.9	0.6	16.8	-0.6	16.8	0.0	16.8	0.0	16.8	0.0	17.0	1.2	17.1	0.6	17.2	0.6
1943	17.2	0.0	17.4	1.2	17.6	1.1	17.8	1.1	18.1	1.7	18.0	-0.6	17.9	-0.6	17.7	-1.1	17.7	0.0	17.8	0.6	17.7	-0.6	17.8	0.6
1944	17.8	0.0	17.7	-0.6	17.7	0.0	17.8	0.6	17.9	0.6	18.0	0.6	18.2	1.1	18.1	-0.5	18.1	0.0	18.1	0.0	18.1	0.0	18.1	0.0
1945	18.1	0.0	18.1	0.0	18.1	0.0	18.2	0.6	18.4	1.1	18.6	1.1	18.6	0.0	18.7	0.5	18.6	-0.5	18.6	0.0	18.6	0.0	18.7	0.5
1946	18.8	0.5	18.8	0.0	18.8	0.0	19.0	1.1	19.1	0.5	19.4	1.6	20.5	5.7	20.7	1.0	20.8	0.5	21.2	1.9	21.6	1.9	21.8	0.9
1947	21.8	0.0	21.8	0.0	22.3	2.3	22.3	0.0	22.3	0.0	22.6	1.3	22.9	1.3	23.2	1.3	23.4	0.9	23.8	1.7	23.8	0.0	24.1	1.3
1948	24.3	0.8	24.1	-0.8	24.0	-0.4	24.5	2.1	24.7	0.8	24.9	0.8	25.1	0.8	25.1	0.0	25.0	-0.4	24.9	-0.4	24.7	-0.8	24.7	0.0
1949	24.5	-0.8	24.4	-0.4	24.4	0.0	24.4	0.0	24.5	0.4	24.5	0.0	24.3	-0.8	24.3	0.0	24.3	0.0	24.1	-0.8	24.3	0.8	24.2	-0.4
1950	24.1	-0.4	24.0	-0.4	24.2	0.8	24.2	0.0	24.4	0.8	24.7	1.2	24.9	0.8	25.0	0.4	25.2	0.8	25.4	0.8	25.5	0.4	25.7	0.8
1951	26.1	1.6	26.4	1.1	26.6	0.8	26.5	-0.4	26.6	0.4	26.8	0.8	26.8	0.0	26.8	0.0	26.8	0.0	27.0	0.7	27.2	0.7	27.2	0.0
1952	27.2	0.0	27.1	-0.4	27.1	0.0	27.2	0.4	27.2	0.0	27.3	0.4	27.5	0.7	27.6	0.4	27.5	-0.4	27.7	0.7	27.6	-0.4	27.8	0.7
1953	27.7	-0.4	27.6	-0.4	27.6	0.0	27.6	0.0	27.7	0.4	27.9	0.7	28.0	0.4	28.0	0.0	28.0	0.0	28.1	0.4	27.9	-0.7	27.9	0.0
1954	28.0	0.4	27.9	-0.4	27.9	0.0	27.9	0.0	28.0	0.4	28.1	0.4	28.1	0.0	28.0	-0.4	27.8	-0.7	27.8	0.0	28.0	0.7	27.8	-0.7
1955	27.8	0.0	27.9	0.4	27.9	0.0	27.8	-0.4	27.9	0.4	27.9	0.0	28.0	0.4	27.9	-0.4	28.0	0.4	27.9	-0.4	28.0	0.4	27.9	-0.4
1956	27.9	0.0	27.9	0.0	28.0	0.4	28.1	0.4	28.3	0.7	28.5	0.7	28.8	1.1	28.7	-0.3	28.7	0.0	28.8	0.3	28.9	0.3	28.8	-0.3
1957	28.9	0.3	29.0	0.3	29.0	0.0	29.1	0.3	29.2	0.3	29.4	0.7	29.5	0.3	29.5	0.0	29.4	-0.3	29.4	0.0	29.6	0.7	29.5	-0.3
1958	29.6	0.3	29.6	0.0	29.7	0.3	29.8	0.3	29.8	0.0	29.7	-0.3	29.8	0.3	29.6	-0.7	29.7	0.3	29.5	-0.7	29.6	0.3	29.5	-0.3

[Continued]

Detroit, MI
Consumer Price Index - Urban Wage Earners
Base 1982-1984 = 100
All Items
[Continued]

For 1914-1993. Columns headed % show percentile change in the index from the previous period for which an index is available.

Year	Jan Index	%	Feb Index	%	Mar Index	%	Apr Index	%	May Index	%	Jun Index	%	Jul Index	%	Aug Index	%	Sep Index	%	Oct Index	%	Nov Index	%	Dec Index	%
1959	29.5	0.0	29.5	0.0	29.5	0.0	29.6	0.3	29.6	0.0	29.6	0.0	29.8	0.7	29.6	-0.7	29.9	1.0	29.9	0.0	29.7	-0.7	29.7	0.0
1960	29.6	-0.3	29.7	0.3	29.7	0.0	29.7	0.0	29.8	0.3	30.0	0.7	30.2	0.7	30.1	-0.3	30.0	-0.3	30.1	0.3	30.1	0.0	30.2	0.3
1961	30.3	0.3	30.3	0.0	30.2	-0.3	30.1	-0.3	30.1	0.0	30.2	0.3	30.1	-0.3	30.2	0.3	29.9	-1.0	30.0	0.3	30.0	0.0	29.8	-0.7
1962	29.9	0.3	30.2	1.0	30.2	0.0	30.2	0.0	30.2	0.0	30.1	-0.3	30.1	0.0	30.2	0.3	30.4	0.7	30.4	0.0	30.3	-0.3	30.3	0.0
1963	30.3	0.0	30.3	0.0	30.3	0.0	30.2	-0.3	30.3	0.3	30.6	1.0	30.7	0.3	30.9	0.7	30.5	-1.3	30.6	0.3	30.7	0.3	30.6	-0.3
1964	30.7	0.3	30.5	-0.7	30.6	0.3	30.7	0.3	30.5	-0.7	30.6	0.3	30.8	0.7	30.8	0.0	30.9	0.3	31.0	0.3	30.9	-0.3	31.0	0.3
1965	31.0	0.0	30.9	-0.3	31.0	0.3	31.2	0.6	31.3	0.3	31.6	1.0	31.6	0.0	31.6	0.0	31.6	0.0	31.7	0.3	31.8	0.3	31.9	0.3
1966	32.0	0.3	32.2	0.6	32.4	0.6	32.6	0.6	32.7	0.3	32.9	0.6	32.9	0.0	33.1	0.6	33.1	0.0	33.3	0.6	33.3	0.0	33.5	0.6
1967	33.5	0.0	33.5	0.0	33.8	0.9	33.9	0.3	33.9	0.0	33.9	0.0	34.0	0.3	34.1	0.3	34.1	0.0	34.1	0.0	34.3	0.6	34.4	0.3
1968	34.5	0.3	34.7	0.6	34.9	0.6	35.0	0.3	35.1	0.3	35.4	0.9	35.5	0.3	35.7	0.6	35.8	0.3	36.0	0.6	36.1	0.3	36.2	0.3
1969	36.3	0.3	36.5	0.6	37.0	1.4	37.1	0.3	37.3	0.5	37.6	0.8	37.7	0.3	38.0	0.8	38.0	0.0	38.2	0.5	38.4	0.5	38.6	0.5
1970	38.7	0.3	39.1	1.0	39.3	0.5	39.5	0.5	39.9	1.0	40.0	0.3	40.0	0.0	40.0	0.0	40.2	0.5	40.5	0.7	40.7	0.5	40.6	-0.2
1971	40.8	0.5	40.7	-0.2	40.8	0.2	40.8	0.0	41.0	0.5	41.4	1.0	41.4	0.0	41.7	0.7	41.7	0.0	41.7	0.0	41.9	0.5	42.0	0.2
1972	42.2	0.5	42.4	0.5	42.4	0.0	42.4	0.0	42.6	0.5	42.8	0.5	43.0	0.5	43.1	0.2	43.2	0.2	43.2	0.0	43.3	0.2	43.6	0.7
1973	43.6	0.0	44.0	0.9	44.5	1.1	45.0	1.1	45.3	0.7	45.4	0.2	45.4	0.0	46.4	2.2	46.6	0.4	46.8	0.4	47.2	0.9	47.5	0.6
1974	48.0	1.1	48.8	1.7	49.2	0.8	49.4	0.4	49.7	0.6	50.4	1.4	50.7	0.6	51.2	1.0	51.7	1.0	52.2	1.0	52.7	1.0	53.0	0.6
1975	52.8	-0.4	53.1	0.6	53.3	0.4	53.5	0.4	53.7	0.4	54.2	0.9	54.6	0.7	54.8	0.4	55.3	0.9	55.4	0.2	55.6	0.4	55.9	0.5
1976	56.3	0.7	56.3	0.0	56.2	-0.2	56.5	0.5	56.8	0.5	57.0	0.4	57.4	0.7	57.6	0.3	58.2	1.0	58.2	0.0	58.6	0.7	58.8	0.3
1977	59.0	0.3	59.5	0.8	60.0	0.8	60.8	1.3	60.9	0.2	61.5	1.0	62.0	0.8	62.0	0.0	62.1	0.2	62.2	0.2	62.6	0.6	62.6	0.0
1978	62.8	0.3	63.1	0.5	63.8	1.1	64.4	0.9	65.2	1.2	66.1	1.4	66.1	0.0	66.6	0.8	67.3	1.1	68.1	1.2	68.5	0.6	68.6	0.1
1979	69.6	1.5	70.9	1.9	71.8	1.3	72.4	0.8	72.7	0.4	73.2	0.7	74.6	1.9	75.6	1.3	75.9	0.4	77.0	1.4	78.4	1.8	78.8	0.5
1980	80.3	1.9	81.5	1.5	82.3	1.0	84.2	2.3	84.5	0.4	86.9	2.8	85.6	-1.5	86.2	0.7	87.5	1.5	88.8	1.5	89.5	0.8	90.1	0.7
1981	89.8	-0.3	90.1	0.3	89.5	-0.7	91.0	1.7	92.1	1.2	93.7	1.7	94.7	1.1	94.8	0.1	95.1	0.3	94.5	-0.6	93.8	-0.7	93.4	-0.4
1982	94.3	1.0	93.3	-1.1	93.4	0.1	95.2	1.9	96.0	0.8	97.1	1.1	98.2	1.1	98.2	0.0	98.9	0.7	98.9	0.0	99.2	0.3	98.0	-1.2
1983	97.8	-0.2	97.5	-0.3	98.4	0.9	100.2	1.8	101.5	1.3	102.1	0.6	103.2	1.1	103.1	-0.1	103.4	0.3	101.5	-1.8	102.5	1.0	102.3	-0.2
1984	104.5	2.2	103.5	-1.0	102.8	-0.7	101.4	-1.4	101.3	-0.1	100.8	-0.5	101.3	0.5	101.5	0.2	102.3	0.8	102.8	0.5	101.8	-1.0	101.9	0.1
1985	102.3	0.4	103.2	0.9	103.9	0.7	104.0	0.1	104.1	0.1	104.4	0.3	104.7	0.3	104.7	0.0	105.4	0.7	105.2	-0.2	106.3	1.0	106.3	0.0
1986	106.4	0.1	106.0	-0.4	105.0	-0.9	104.6	-0.4	105.6	1.0	105.3	-0.3	104.4	-0.9	106.2	1.7	105.4	-0.8	106.5	1.0	106.9	0.4	106.6	-0.3
1987	-	-	107.5	0.8	-	-	108.6	1.0	-	-	108.6	0.0	-	-	109.6	0.9	-	-	111.3	1.6	-	-	109.8	-1.3
1988	-	-	110.9	1.0	-	-	111.9	0.9	-	-	112.7	0.7	-	-	114.6	1.7	-	-	115.6	0.9	-	-	115.7	0.1
1989	-	-	117.3	1.4	-	-	119.0	1.4	-	-	119.3	0.3	-	-	119.2	-0.1	-	-	121.5	1.9	-	-	121.4	-0.1
1990	-	-	123.2	1.5	-	-	123.9	0.6	-	-	124.7	0.6	-	-	126.5	1.4	-	-	128.7	1.7	-	-	128.1	-0.5
1991	-	-	128.9	0.6	-	-	128.3	-0.5	-	-	130.1	1.4	-	-	130.2	0.1	-	-	131.1	0.7	-	-	130.6	-0.4
1992	-	-	131.3	0.5	-	-	131.7	0.3	-	-	131.8	0.1	-	-	132.0	0.2	-	-	133.5	1.1	-	-	133.1	-0.3
1993	-	-	134.4	1.0	-	-	134.6	0.1	-	-	135.1	0.4	-	-	135.7	0.4	-	-	137.5	1.3	-	-	135.7	-1.3

Source: U.S. Department of Labor, Bureau of Labor Statistics, Division of Consumer Prices and Price Indexes. - indicates no data collected for period.

Detroit, MI
Consumer Price Index - All Urban Consumers
Base 1982-1984 = 100
Food and Beverages

For 1976-1993. Columns headed % show percentile change in the index from the previous period for which an index is available.

Year	Jan Index	%	Feb Index	%	Mar Index	%	Apr Index	%	May Index	%	Jun Index	%	Jul Index	%	Aug Index	%	Sep Index	%	Oct Index	%	Nov Index	%	Dec Index	%
1976	63.8	-	63.8	0.0	63.1	-1.1	63.5	0.6	63.9	0.6	63.9	0.0	64.3	0.6	64.0	-0.5	63.7	-0.5	63.6	-0.2	64.0	0.6	64.5	0.8
1977	64.8	0.5	65.9	1.7	65.8	-0.2	66.9	1.7	67.2	0.4	68.2	1.5	68.5	0.4	68.6	0.1	68.1	-0.7	68.4	0.4	69.2	1.2	69.2	0.0
1978	70.5	1.9	71.2	1.0	72.0	1.1	73.0	1.4	74.0	1.4	75.3	1.8	76.0	0.9	75.7	-0.4	75.9	0.3	76.2	0.4	76.8	0.8	77.6	1.0
1979	79.5	2.4	80.8	1.6	81.3	0.6	81.9	0.7	82.4	0.6	82.5	0.1	82.9	0.5	81.9	-1.2	82.4	0.6	82.9	0.6	83.3	0.5	84.2	1.1
1980	86.0	2.1	86.1	0.1	86.7	0.7	86.9	0.2	87.8	1.0	88.5	0.8	89.4	1.0	90.4	1.1	90.1	-0.3	90.6	0.6	92.1	1.7	92.8	0.8
1981	93.5	0.8	94.9	1.5	94.8	-0.1	95.1	0.3	95.3	0.2	95.4	0.1	96.1	0.7	96.1	0.0	96.6	0.5	96.7	0.1	97.3	0.6	97.4	0.1
1982	98.2	0.8	99.1	0.9	98.9	-0.2	99.1	0.2	99.3	0.2	100.1	0.8	100.2	0.1	99.5	-0.7	99.7	0.2	99.3	-0.4	99.6	0.3	99.2	-0.4
1983	99.7	0.5	100.1	0.4	100.8	0.7	100.7	-0.1	100.2	-0.5	99.9	-0.3	99.6	-0.3	99.3	-0.3	98.4	-0.9	97.1	-1.3	97.5	0.4	98.0	0.5
1984	100.2	2.2	101.1	0.9	101.1	0.0	102.1	1.0	101.6	-0.5	101.3	-0.3	102.1	0.8	101.9	-0.2	101.6	-0.3	101.0	-0.6	100.8	-0.2	101.8	1.0
1985	102.0	0.2	102.9	0.9	103.4	0.5	103.3	-0.1	103.1	-0.2	102.9	-0.2	103.1	0.2	102.5	-0.6	102.4	-0.1	103.3	0.9	104.3	1.0	104.8	0.5
1986	104.7	-0.1	105.3	0.6	105.8	0.5	105.7	-0.1	106.3	0.6	106.4	0.1	107.5	1.0	108.9	1.3	108.6	-0.3	109.3	0.6	109.5	0.2	109.2	-0.3
1987	-	-	109.7	0.5	-	-	109.4	-0.3	-	-	111.4	1.8	-	-	110.8	-0.5	-	-	111.5	0.6	-	-	110.9	-0.5
1988	-	-	112.3	1.3	-	-	113.0	0.6	-	-	114.4	1.2	-	-	115.5	1.0	-	-	116.9	1.2	-	-	117.8	0.8
1989	-	-	119.4	1.4	-	-	120.5	0.9	-	-	120.3	-0.2	-	-	121.2	0.7	-	-	121.5	0.2	-	-	123.0	1.2
1990	-	-	125.3	1.9	-	-	125.4	0.1	-	-	126.5	0.9	-	-	127.6	0.9	-	-	127.7	0.1	-	-	127.9	0.2
1991	-	-	129.0	0.9	-	-	130.3	1.0	-	-	131.6	1.0	-	-	131.6	0.0	-	-	132.6	0.8	-	-	133.0	0.3
1992	-	-	133.6	0.5	-	-	133.4	-0.1	-	-	132.9	-0.4	-	-	133.5	0.5	-	-	133.5	0.0	-	-	134.0	0.4
1993	-	-	134.1	0.1	-	-	134.2	0.1	-	-	135.1	0.7	-	-	135.8	0.5	-	-	136.8	0.7	-	-	136.1	-0.5

Source: U.S. Department of Labor, Bureau of Labor Statistics, Division of Consumer Prices and Price Indexes. - indicates no data collected for period.

Detroit, MI
Consumer Price Index - Urban Wage Earners
Base 1982-1984 = 100
Food and Beverages

For 1976-1993. Columns headed % show percentile change in the index from the previous period for which an index is available.

Year	Jan Index	%	Feb Index	%	Mar Index	%	Apr Index	%	May Index	%	Jun Index	%	Jul Index	%	Aug Index	%	Sep Index	%	Oct Index	%	Nov Index	%	Dec Index	%
1976	63.2	-	63.1	-0.2	62.5	-1.0	62.9	0.6	63.2	0.5	63.2	0.0	63.6	0.6	63.4	-0.3	63.0	-0.6	62.9	-0.2	63.3	0.6	63.9	0.9
1977	64.2	0.5	65.2	1.6	65.2	0.0	66.2	1.5	66.6	0.6	67.5	1.4	67.8	0.4	67.9	0.1	67.4	-0.7	67.7	0.4	68.5	1.2	68.5	0.0
1978	70.0	2.2	70.8	1.1	71.4	0.8	72.5	1.5	73.5	1.4	75.2	2.3	76.0	1.1	75.9	-0.1	76.0	0.1	75.7	-0.4	76.5	1.1	77.3	1.0
1979	79.2	2.5	80.5	1.6	81.5	1.2	81.8	0.4	82.2	0.5	82.4	0.2	83.2	1.0	82.0	-1.4	82.4	0.5	83.0	0.7	83.3	0.4	84.3	1.2
1980	85.8	1.8	86.0	0.2	86.6	0.7	86.7	0.1	87.6	1.0	88.3	0.8	89.1	0.9	89.9	0.9	90.0	0.1	90.5	0.6	91.5	1.1	92.2	0.8
1981	92.9	0.8	94.2	1.4	94.3	0.1	95.1	0.8	95.3	0.2	95.6	0.3	96.4	0.8	96.3	-0.1	97.0	0.7	96.9	-0.1	97.4	0.5	97.3	-0.1
1982	98.3	1.0	99.0	0.7	98.9	-0.1	99.2	0.3	99.4	0.2	100.2	0.8	100.4	0.2	99.7	-0.7	99.9	0.2	99.4	-0.5	99.6	0.2	99.1	-0.5
1983	99.7	0.6	100.1	0.4	100.8	0.7	100.7	-0.1	100.2	-0.5	99.8	-0.4	99.5	-0.3	99.2	-0.3	98.3	-0.9	97.1	-1.2	97.4	0.3	97.9	0.5
1984	100.1	2.2	101.2	1.1	101.0	-0.2	102.1	1.1	101.5	-0.6	101.3	-0.2	102.0	0.7	102.1	0.1	101.7	-0.4	100.9	-0.8	100.6	-0.3	101.9	1.3
1985	101.8	-0.1	102.8	1.0	103.2	0.4	103.0	-0.2	102.9	-0.1	102.7	-0.2	102.9	0.2	102.2	-0.7	102.1	-0.1	102.9	0.8	104.0	1.1	104.5	0.5
1986	104.4	-0.1	104.7	0.3	105.5	0.8	105.3	-0.2	106.0	0.7	106.1	0.1	107.0	0.8	108.5	1.4	108.1	-0.4	109.0	0.8	109.1	0.1	109.0	-0.1
1987	-	-	109.5	0.5	-	-	109.1	-0.4	-	-	111.1	1.8	-	-	110.5	-0.5	-	-	111.2	0.6	-	-	110.4	-0.7
1988	-	-	112.0	1.4	-	-	112.5	0.4	-	-	113.9	1.2	-	-	115.0	1.0	-	-	116.4	1.2	-	-	117.3	0.8
1989	-	-	119.0	1.4	-	-	120.1	0.9	-	-	119.9	-0.2	-	-	120.8	0.8	-	-	121.0	0.2	-	-	122.7	1.4
1990	-	-	125.0	1.9	-	-	125.0	0.0	-	-	126.1	0.9	-	-	127.2	0.9	-	-	127.2	0.0	-	-	127.4	0.2
1991	-	-	128.6	0.9	-	-	129.9	1.0	-	-	131.2	1.0	-	-	131.1	-0.1	-	-	132.3	0.9	-	-	132.7	0.3
1992	-	-	133.3	0.5	-	-	133.0	-0.2	-	-	132.6	-0.3	-	-	133.1	0.4	-	-	133.0	-0.1	-	-	133.6	0.5
1993	-	-	133.7	0.1	-	-	133.8	0.1	-	-	134.7	0.7	-	-	135.3	0.4	-	-	136.4	0.8	-	-	135.7	-0.5

Source: U.S. Department of Labor, Bureau of Labor Statistics, Division of Consumer Prices and Price Indexes. - indicates no data collected for period.

Detroit, MI
Consumer Price Index - All Urban Consumers
Base 1982-1984 = 100
Housing

For 1976-1993. Columns headed % show percentile change in the index from the previous period for which an index is available.

Year	Jan Index	%	Feb Index	%	Mar Index	%	Apr Index	%	May Index	%	Jun Index	%	Jul Index	%	Aug Index	%	Sep Index	%	Oct Index	%	Nov Index	%	Dec Index	%
1976	51.2	-	51.2	0.0	51.2	0.0	51.2	0.0	51.5	0.6	51.8	0.6	52.2	0.8	52.6	0.8	53.7	2.1	53.4	-0.6	53.7	0.6	53.9	0.4
1977	54.1	0.4	54.4	0.6	55.1	1.3	55.6	0.9	55.2	-0.7	55.7	0.9	56.6	1.6	56.2	-0.7	56.4	0.4	56.4	0.0	56.9	0.9	56.9	0.0
1978	57.1	0.4	57.1	0.0	58.4	2.3	58.8	0.7	59.4	1.0	60.3	1.5	60.0	-0.5	60.6	1.0	61.8	2.0	63.2	2.3	63.6	0.6	63.4	-0.3
1979	64.4	1.6	66.3	3.0	67.7	2.1	67.7	0.0	67.6	-0.1	68.1	0.7	70.2	3.1	71.7	2.1	72.2	0.7	74.1	2.6	76.6	3.4	77.3	0.9
1980	78.5	1.6	79.8	1.7	80.5	0.9	83.2	3.4	82.6	-0.7	88.0	6.5	86.1	-2.2	85.9	-0.2	87.7	2.1	90.4	3.1	90.5	0.1	92.8	2.5
1981	91.2	-1.7	91.0	-0.2	88.9	-2.3	91.1	2.5	92.3	1.3	96.2	4.2	96.7	0.5	97.2	0.5	97.0	-0.2	94.3	-2.8	92.7	-1.7	91.8	-1.0
1982	93.2	1.5	90.8	-2.6	91.1	0.3	95.0	4.3	95.5	0.5	96.7	1.3	98.0	1.3	98.2	0.2	99.4	1.2	99.6	0.2	100.0	0.4	98.0	-2.0
1983	98.5	0.5	98.3	-0.2	98.3	0.0	100.3	2.0	99.6	-0.7	101.5	1.9	102.1	0.6	101.5	-0.6	101.3	-0.2	101.1	-0.2	101.5	0.4	101.5	0.0
1984	101.5	0.0	101.8	0.3	102.3	0.5	102.5	0.2	102.6	0.1	103.2	0.6	103.8	0.6	103.9	0.1	105.5	1.5	105.5	0.0	102.8	-2.6	103.5	0.7
1985	105.8	2.2	106.0	0.2	106.7	0.7	106.6	-0.1	106.8	0.2	107.8	0.9	107.8	0.0	107.3	-0.5	109.2	1.8	107.5	-1.6	109.3	1.7	109.1	-0.2
1986	109.6	0.5	110.6	0.9	109.6	-0.9	109.9	0.3	110.6	0.6	109.7	-0.8	107.5	-2.0	110.8	3.1	108.8	-1.8	110.5	1.6	110.2	-0.3	110.0	-0.2
1987	-	-	112.5	2.3	-	-	112.8	0.3	-	-	112.2	-0.5	-	-	114.1	1.7	-	-	114.7	0.5	-	-	112.4	-2.0
1988	-	-	115.0	2.3	-	-	114.2	-0.7	-	-	115.4	1.1	-	-	118.6	2.8	-	-	117.9	-0.6	-	-	116.7	-1.0
1989	-	-	119.6	2.5	-	-	119.5	-0.1	-	-	120.5	0.8	-	-	121.9	1.2	-	-	124.0	1.7	-	-	123.5	-0.4
1990	-	-	123.8	0.2	-	-	125.0	1.0	-	-	126.5	1.2	-	-	127.9	1.1	-	-	128.7	0.6	-	-	127.2	-1.2
1991	-	-	129.1	1.5	-	-	125.8	-2.6	-	-	129.9	3.3	-	-	128.9	-0.8	-	-	129.8	0.7	-	-	128.8	-0.8
1992	-	-	130.7	1.5	-	-	130.7	0.0	-	-	131.9	0.9	-	-	132.5	0.5	-	-	133.3	0.6	-	-	133.0	-0.2
1993	-	-	133.4	0.3	-	-	132.1	-1.0	-	-	133.9	1.4	-	-	135.0	0.8	-	-	137.0	1.5	-	-	135.6	-1.0

Source: U.S. Department of Labor, Bureau of Labor Statistics, Division of Consumer Prices and Price Indexes. - indicates no data collected for period.

Detroit, MI
Consumer Price Index - Urban Wage Earners
Base 1982-1984 = 100
Housing

For 1976-1993. Columns headed % show percentile change in the index from the previous period for which an index is available.

Year	Jan Index	%	Feb Index	%	Mar Index	%	Apr Index	%	May Index	%	Jun Index	%	Jul Index	%	Aug Index	%	Sep Index	%	Oct Index	%	Nov Index	%	Dec Index	%
1976	51.4	-	51.4	0.0	51.3	-0.2	51.4	0.2	51.7	0.6	52.0	0.6	52.3	0.6	52.7	0.8	53.9	2.3	53.6	-0.6	53.9	0.6	54.0	0.2
1977	54.3	0.6	54.5	0.4	55.2	1.3	55.7	0.9	55.4	-0.5	55.8	0.7	56.8	1.8	56.4	-0.7	56.6	0.4	56.6	0.0	57.0	0.7	57.0	0.0
1978	57.2	0.4	57.4	0.3	58.4	1.7	58.8	0.7	59.6	1.4	60.4	1.3	60.0	-0.7	60.6	1.0	61.8	2.0	63.2	2.3	63.4	0.3	63.1	-0.5
1979	64.2	1.7	66.3	3.3	67.7	2.1	67.9	0.3	67.7	-0.3	68.1	0.6	70.2	3.1	71.8	2.3	72.3	0.7	73.8	2.1	76.4	3.5	77.1	0.9
1980	78.3	1.6	79.6	1.7	80.2	0.8	82.8	3.2	82.3	-0.6	87.7	6.6	85.6	-2.4	85.5	-0.1	87.2	2.0	89.7	2.9	90.2	0.6	92.4	2.4
1981	90.7	-1.8	90.1	-0.7	87.9	-2.4	90.2	2.6	91.6	1.6	95.1	3.8	95.9	0.8	96.3	0.4	96.1	-0.2	93.8	-2.4	92.0	-1.9	91.1	-1.0
1982	92.5	1.5	90.0	-2.7	90.4	0.4	94.4	4.4	94.9	0.5	96.1	1.3	97.5	1.5	97.6	0.1	98.8	1.2	99.0	0.2	99.5	0.5	97.4	-2.1
1983	97.1	-0.3	96.5	-0.6	98.4	2.0	102.2	3.9	104.6	2.3	106.1	1.4	107.8	1.6	107.1	-0.6	107.5	0.4	103.6	-3.6	105.0	1.4	104.7	-0.3
1984	108.9	4.0	105.2	-3.4	103.6	-1.5	99.5	-4.0	99.2	-0.3	98.3	-0.9	99.1	0.8	99.2	0.1	99.8	0.6	100.8	1.0	98.7	-2.1	99.1	0.4
1985	101.2	2.1	101.3	0.1	102.0	0.7	101.9	-0.1	102.0	0.1	102.9	0.9	103.0	0.1	102.5	-0.5	104.3	1.8	102.6	-1.6	104.4	1.8	104.3	-0.1
1986	104.7	0.4	105.5	0.8	104.7	-0.8	105.1	0.4	105.6	0.5	104.7	-0.9	102.7	-1.9	105.9	3.1	103.9	-1.9	105.6	1.6	105.3	-0.3	105.1	-0.2
1987	-	-	107.4	2.2	-	-	107.7	0.3	-	-	107.4	-0.3	-	-	109.0	1.5	-	-	109.6	0.6	-	-	107.4	-2.0
1988	-	-	109.8	2.2	-	-	109.1	-0.6	-	-	110.3	1.1	-	-	112.9	2.4	-	-	112.5	-0.4	-	-	111.7	-0.7
1989	-	-	114.2	2.2	-	-	114.1	-0.1	-	-	114.9	0.7	-	-	116.3	1.2	-	-	118.2	1.6	-	-	118.1	-0.1
1990	-	-	118.3	0.2	-	-	119.4	0.9	-	-	120.9	1.3	-	-	122.1	1.0	-	-	123.0	0.7	-	-	121.5	-1.2
1991	-	-	123.3	1.5	-	-	119.7	-2.9	-	-	123.9	3.5	-	-	123.1	-0.6	-	-	123.9	0.6	-	-	123.0	-0.7
1992	-	-	124.7	1.4	-	-	124.6	-0.1	-	-	125.9	1.0	-	-	126.3	0.3	-	-	127.1	0.6	-	-	126.9	-0.2
1993	-	-	127.2	0.2	-	-	125.9	-1.0	-	-	127.7	1.4	-	-	128.6	0.7	-	-	130.6	1.6	-	-	129.4	-0.9

Source: U.S. Department of Labor, Bureau of Labor Statistics, Division of Consumer Prices and Price Indexes. - indicates no data collected for period.

Detroit, MI
Consumer Price Index - All Urban Consumers
Base 1982-1984 = 100
Apparel and Upkeep

For 1952-1993. Columns headed % show percentile change in the index from the previous period for which an index is available.

Year	Jan Index	Jan %	Feb Index	Feb %	Mar Index	Mar %	Apr Index	Apr %	May Index	May %	Jun Index	Jun %	Jul Index	Jul %	Aug Index	Aug %	Sep Index	Sep %	Oct Index	Oct %	Nov Index	Nov %	Dec Index	Dec %
1952	-	-	-	-	-	-	-	-	-	-	-	-	-	-	-	-	-	-	-	-	-	-	51.7	-
1953	51.7	0.0	51.8	0.2	51.9	0.2	52.0	0.2	52.2	0.4	52.2	0.0	52.2	0.0	52.1	-0.2	52.1	0.0	52.3	0.4	52.2	-0.2	52.1	-0.2
1954	52.0	-0.2	52.1	0.2	51.9	-0.4	51.9	0.0	51.9	0.0	52.1	0.4	52.1	0.0	51.9	-0.4	52.1	0.4	51.9	-0.4	51.9	0.0	51.9	0.0
1955	51.9	0.0	51.9	0.0	51.9	0.0	51.7	-0.4	51.7	0.0	51.8	0.2	51.9	0.2	51.7	-0.4	51.9	0.4	51.6	-0.6	51.7	0.2	51.8	0.2
1956	51.7	-0.2	52.0	0.6	52.1	0.2	52.4	0.6	52.3	-0.2	52.3	0.0	52.5	0.4	52.9	0.8	53.3	0.8	53.3	0.0	53.2	-0.2	52.9	-0.6
1957	53.1	0.4	53.2	0.2	53.2	0.0	53.3	0.2	53.4	0.2	53.2	-0.4	53.0	-0.4	53.1	0.2	53.3	0.4	53.2	-0.2	53.3	0.2	53.2	-0.2
1958	52.7	-0.9	52.7	0.0	52.8	0.2	52.9	0.2	52.8	-0.2	52.8	0.0	52.8	0.0	52.9	0.2	53.3	0.8	53.4	0.2	53.4	0.0	53.6	0.4
1959	53.5	-0.2	53.2	-0.6	53.5	0.6	53.6	0.2	53.6	0.0	53.6	0.0	53.3	-0.6	53.7	0.8	54.6	1.7	55.0	0.7	54.5	-0.9	54.5	0.0
1960	54.1	-0.7	54.0	-0.2	53.8	-0.4	53.8	0.0	54.1	0.6	54.2	0.2	54.3	0.2	54.2	-0.2	55.1	1.7	55.1	0.0	55.1	0.0	55.0	-0.2
1961	55.4	0.7	55.5	0.2	55.3	-0.4	55.3	0.0	55.1	-0.4	55.0	-0.2	54.8	-0.4	54.9	0.2	55.2	0.5	55.5	0.5	55.3	-0.4	55.5	0.4
1962	55.1	-0.7	55.4	0.5	55.4	0.0	55.4	0.0	55.5	0.2	55.6	0.2	55.4	-0.4	55.6	0.4	55.9	0.5	55.9	0.0	55.8	-0.2	55.3	-0.9
1963	55.3	0.0	55.6	0.5	55.4	-0.4	55.7	0.5	55.7	0.0	55.9	0.4	55.8	-0.2	56.2	0.7	56.7	0.9	56.6	-0.2	56.9	0.5	56.8	-0.2
1964	56.1	-1.2	56.4	0.5	56.9	0.9	56.9	0.0	56.8	-0.2	56.8	0.0	56.8	0.0	56.8	0.0	57.2	0.7	57.3	0.2	57.2	-0.2	57.4	0.3
1965	56.8	-1.0	57.2	0.7	57.6	0.7	58.1	0.9	57.9	-0.3	58.1	0.3	57.7	-0.7	57.6	-0.2	58.1	0.9	58.1	0.0	58.1	0.0	58.3	0.3
1966	57.6	-1.2	57.9	0.5	58.4	0.9	58.8	0.7	58.8	0.0	58.8	0.0	58.4	-0.7	58.9	0.9	59.9	1.7	60.0	0.2	60.1	0.2	60.2	0.2
1967	59.9	-0.5	60.1	0.3	60.6	0.8	60.6	0.0	60.7	0.2	60.7	0.0	59.8	-1.5	60.1	0.5	61.0	1.5	61.3	0.5	61.3	0.0	61.3	0.0
1968	60.3	-1.6	61.3	1.7	62.2	1.5	62.2	0.0	63.0	1.3	63.0	0.0	62.5	-0.8	63.4	1.4	64.6	1.9	65.1	0.8	65.6	0.8	65.7	0.2
1969	64.8	-1.4	65.6	1.2	65.8	0.3	65.6	-0.3	65.7	0.2	65.7	0.0	65.0	-1.1	65.2	0.3	67.1	2.9	67.1	0.0	67.1	0.0	67.2	0.1
1970	66.0	-1.8	67.1	1.7	68.9	2.7	67.6	-1.9	67.4	-0.3	67.7	0.4	67.1	-0.9	66.8	-0.4	68.8	3.0	68.9	0.1	69.1	0.3	68.6	-0.7
1971	66.8	-2.6	69.6	4.2	70.0	0.6	69.3	-1.0	70.1	1.2	70.0	-0.1	69.6	-0.6	69.9	0.4	70.5	0.9	71.4	1.3	71.6	0.3	71.0	-0.8
1972	69.4	-2.3	70.9	2.2	70.8	-0.1	71.0	0.3	71.6	0.8	71.1	-0.7	70.8	-0.4	71.3	0.7	72.8	2.1	73.4	0.8	73.6	0.3	73.2	-0.5
1973	71.1	-2.9	72.9	2.5	73.9	1.4	74.4	0.7	74.2	-0.3	73.9	-0.4	72.2	-2.3	73.8	2.2	75.3	2.0	76.0	0.9	75.8	-0.3	75.9	0.1
1974	74.2	-2.2	76.2	2.7	77.5	1.7	78.3	1.0	78.7	0.5	79.6	1.1	79.4	-0.3	83.9	5.7	84.5	0.7	83.4	-1.3	83.7	0.4	83.1	-0.7
1975	82.0	-1.3	81.5	-0.6	83.1	2.0	82.9	-0.2	82.8	-0.1	83.6	1.0	83.6	0.0	83.7	0.1	84.5	1.0	85.1	0.7	85.1	0.0	84.9	-0.2
1976	84.6	-0.4	85.2	0.7	85.4	0.2	86.2	0.9	85.3	-1.0	85.1	-0.2	85.0	-0.1	85.9	1.1	87.1	1.4	87.8	0.8	87.6	-0.2	87.5	-0.1
1977	87.0	-0.6	87.8	0.9	88.1	0.3	88.3	0.2	88.0	-0.3	89.2	1.4	89.0	-0.2	89.4	0.4	89.7	0.3	90.0	0.3	90.4	0.4	89.9	-0.6
1978	87.0	-3.2	86.5	-0.6	87.9	1.6	89.6	1.9	91.1	1.7	91.0	-0.1	88.1	-3.2	91.1	3.4	90.3	-0.9	91.9	1.8	91.6	-0.3	90.5	-1.2
1979	87.7	-3.1	87.3	-0.5	89.5	2.5	89.5	0.0	89.9	0.4	88.1	-2.0	88.2	0.1	91.6	3.9	92.1	0.5	91.9	-0.2	91.6	-0.3	89.7	-2.1
1980	89.1	-0.7	89.7	0.7	93.4	4.1	95.5	2.2	95.0	-0.5	93.3	-1.8	93.6	0.3	94.2	0.6	97.0	3.0	96.8	-0.2	98.1	1.3	96.2	-1.9
1981	95.1	-1.1	95.6	0.5	96.8	1.3	97.6	0.8	98.4	0.8	96.5	-1.9	97.0	0.5	95.4	-1.6	96.7	1.4	97.7	1.0	96.1	-1.6	94.3	-1.9
1982	92.7	-1.7	95.2	2.7	96.2	1.1	96.5	0.3	96.5	0.0	93.4	-3.2	98.3	5.2	100.0	1.7	104.8	4.8	103.7	-1.0	103.1	-0.6	99.2	-3.8
1983	96.2	-3.0	99.2	3.1	99.0	-0.2	99.7	0.7	101.1	1.4	99.4	-1.7	99.9	0.5	103.1	3.2	105.4	2.2	104.3	-1.0	104.3	0.0	100.0	-4.1
1984	96.7	-3.3	101.9	5.4	101.6	-0.3	98.8	-2.8	99.3	0.5	99.9	0.6	100.3	0.4	99.8	-0.5	105.7	5.9	103.4	-2.2	102.3	-1.1	99.1	-3.1
1985	93.1	-6.1	99.1	6.4	100.3	1.2	100.5	0.2	101.3	0.8	100.0	-1.3	101.3	1.3	105.3	3.9	108.6	3.1	107.1	-1.4	108.8	1.6	106.0	-2.6
1986	102.0	-3.8	103.1	1.1	102.9	-0.2	102.3	-0.6	101.9	-0.4	100.2	-1.7	98.4	-1.8	103.4	5.1	106.4	2.9	106.9	0.5	106.5	-0.4	105.2	-1.2
1987	-	-	103.0	-2.1	-	-	109.8	6.6	-	-	104.6	-4.7	-	-	104.0	-0.6	-	-	116.8	12.3	-	-	111.8	-4.3
1988	-	-	108.8	-2.7	-	-	118.5	8.9	-	-	111.3	-6.1	-	-	113.2	1.7	-	-	122.8	8.5	-	-	118.5	-3.5
1989	-	-	119.6	0.9	-	-	126.2	5.5	-	-	121.1	-4.0	-	-	118.8	-1.9	-	-	128.8	8.4	-	-	122.8	-4.7
1990	-	-	126.7	3.2	-	-	131.0	3.4	-	-	122.9	-6.2	-	-	131.7	1.3	-	-	137.0	4.0	-	-	128.4	-6.3
1991	-	-	129.6	0.5	-	-	134.1	3.5	-	-	130.0	-3.1	-	-	127.8	0.3	-	-	130.1	1.8	-	-	129.0	-1.8
1992	-	-	131.7	2.6	-	-	133.4	1.3	-	-	127.4	-4.5	-	-	127.8	0.3	-	-	130.1	1.8	-	-	129.6	-0.4
1993	-	-	134.8	4.0	-	-	144.1	6.9	-	-	134.2	-6.9	-	-	138.3	3.1	-	-	144.0	4.1	-	-	133.0	-7.6

Source: U.S. Department of Labor, Bureau of Labor Statistics, Division of Consumer Prices and Price Indexes. - indicates no data collected for period.

Detroit, MI
Consumer Price Index - Urban Wage Earners
Base 1982-1984 = 100
Apparel and Upkeep

For 1952-1993. Columns headed % show percentile change in the index from the previous period for which an index is available.

Year	Jan Index	%	Feb Index	%	Mar Index	%	Apr Index	%	May Index	%	Jun Index	%	Jul Index	%	Aug Index	%	Sep Index	%	Oct Index	%	Nov Index	%	Dec Index	%
1952	-	-	-	-	-	-	-	-	-	-	-	-	-	-	-	-	-	-	-	-	-	-	52.6	-
1953	52.7	0.2	52.7	0.0	52.9	0.4	52.9	0.0	53.1	0.4	53.2	0.2	53.1	-0.2	53.1	0.0	53.1	0.0	53.2	0.2	53.1	-0.2	53.0	-0.2
1954	52.9	-0.2	53.0	0.2	52.8	-0.4	52.8	0.0	52.8	0.0	53.0	0.4	53.0	0.0	52.8	-0.4	53.0	0.4	52.9	-0.2	52.8	-0.2	52.8	0.0
1955	52.8	0.0	52.8	0.0	52.9	0.2	52.7	-0.4	52.7	0.0	52.7	0.0	52.8	0.2	52.6	-0.4	52.8	0.4	52.5	-0.6	52.6	0.2	52.7	0.2
1956	52.7	0.0	52.9	0.4	53.1	0.4	53.3	0.4	53.2	-0.2	53.2	0.0	53.4	0.4	53.9	0.9	54.3	0.7	54.2	-0.2	54.2	0.0	53.9	-0.6
1957	54.1	0.4	54.2	0.2	54.2	0.0	54.2	0.0	54.4	0.4	54.2	-0.4	53.9	-0.6	54.0	0.2	54.3	0.6	54.2	-0.2	54.3	0.2	54.2	-0.2
1958	53.7	-0.9	53.7	0.0	53.7	0.0	53.9	0.4	53.7	-0.4	53.7	0.0	53.7	0.0	53.9	0.4	54.2	0.6	54.4	0.4	54.4	0.0	54.5	0.2
1959	54.5	0.0	54.2	-0.6	54.5	0.6	54.5	0.0	54.6	0.2	54.5	-0.2	54.2	-0.6	54.7	0.9	55.6	1.6	56.0	0.7	55.5	-0.9	55.5	0.0
1960	55.0	-0.9	55.0	0.0	54.8	-0.4	54.8	0.0	55.0	0.4	55.2	0.4	55.3	0.2	55.2	-0.2	56.1	1.6	56.1	0.0	56.1	0.0	56.0	-0.2
1961	56.4	0.7	56.5	0.2	56.3	-0.4	56.3	0.0	56.1	-0.4	56.0	-0.2	55.8	-0.4	55.9	0.2	56.2	0.5	56.5	0.5	56.3	-0.4	56.5	0.4
1962	56.1	-0.7	56.4	0.5	56.4	0.0	56.4	0.0	56.5	0.2	56.6	0.2	56.4	-0.4	56.6	0.4	56.9	0.5	56.9	0.0	56.8	-0.2	56.3	-0.9
1963	56.3	0.0	56.6	0.5	56.4	-0.4	56.7	0.5	56.8	0.2	56.9	0.2	56.8	-0.2	57.2	0.7	57.7	0.9	57.6	-0.2	57.9	0.5	57.8	-0.2
1964	57.1	-1.2	57.4	0.5	57.9	0.9	57.9	0.0	57.9	0.0	57.8	-0.2	57.8	0.0	57.8	0.0	58.2	0.7	58.3	0.2	58.2	-0.2	58.4	0.3
1965	57.8	-1.0	58.2	0.7	58.7	0.9	59.1	0.7	58.9	-0.3	59.1	0.3	58.7	-0.7	58.7	0.0	59.2	0.9	59.2	0.0	59.2	0.0	59.3	0.2
1966	58.6	-1.2	58.9	0.5	59.5	1.0	59.8	0.5	59.8	0.0	59.8	0.0	59.5	-0.5	60.0	0.8	61.0	1.7	61.1	0.2	61.2	0.2	61.3	0.2
1967	61.0	-0.5	61.2	0.3	61.7	0.8	61.7	0.0	61.8	0.2	61.8	0.0	60.9	-1.5	61.1	0.3	62.1	1.6	62.4	0.5	62.4	0.0	62.4	0.0
1968	61.4	-1.6	62.4	1.6	63.3	1.4	63.3	0.0	64.1	1.3	64.2	0.2	63.7	-0.8	64.6	1.4	65.8	1.9	66.3	0.8	66.8	0.8	66.9	0.1
1969	65.9	-1.5	66.8	1.4	67.0	0.3	66.8	-0.3	66.9	0.1	66.9	0.0	66.1	-1.2	66.4	0.5	68.3	2.9	68.3	0.0	68.4	0.1	68.4	0.0
1970	67.2	-1.8	68.3	1.6	70.1	2.6	68.8	-1.9	68.7	-0.1	68.9	0.3	68.3	-0.9	68.0	-0.4	70.0	2.9	70.1	0.1	70.4	0.4	69.8	-0.9
1971	68.0	-2.6	70.8	4.1	71.3	0.7	70.6	-1.0	71.4	1.1	71.3	-0.1	70.9	-0.6	71.2	0.4	71.7	0.7	72.7	1.4	72.9	0.3	72.2	-1.0
1972	70.6	-2.2	72.2	2.3	72.1	-0.1	72.3	0.3	72.9	0.8	72.4	-0.7	72.1	-0.4	72.6	0.7	74.1	2.1	74.8	0.9	74.9	0.1	74.5	-0.5
1973	72.4	-2.8	74.2	2.5	75.2	1.3	75.7	0.7	75.6	-0.1	75.3	-0.4	73.5	-2.4	75.1	2.2	76.6	2.0	77.4	1.0	77.2	-0.3	77.2	0.0
1974	75.5	-2.2	77.5	2.6	78.9	1.8	79.7	1.0	80.1	0.5	81.0	1.1	80.9	-0.1	85.4	5.6	86.1	0.8	84.9	-1.4	85.3	0.5	84.6	-0.8
1975	83.5	-1.3	83.0	-0.6	84.6	1.9	84.4	-0.2	84.3	-0.1	85.1	0.9	85.1	0.0	85.2	0.1	86.0	0.9	86.6	0.7	86.6	0.0	86.4	-0.2
1976	86.1	-0.3	86.7	0.7	87.0	0.3	87.8	0.9	86.8	-1.1	86.7	-0.1	86.5	-0.2	87.4	1.0	88.7	1.5	89.4	0.8	89.1	-0.3	89.1	0.0
1977	88.6	-0.6	89.4	0.9	89.7	0.3	89.9	0.2	89.6	-0.3	90.8	1.3	90.6	-0.2	91.0	0.4	91.3	0.3	91.7	0.4	92.0	0.3	91.6	-0.4
1978	87.0	-5.0	87.5	0.6	87.9	0.5	90.5	3.0	93.5	3.3	95.2	1.8	92.5	-2.8	98.4	6.4	98.2	-0.2	98.0	-0.2	98.4	0.4	97.5	-0.9
1979	93.0	-4.6	92.5	-0.5	94.0	1.6	94.0	0.0	93.8	-0.2	90.8	-3.2	89.5	-1.4	95.9	7.2	96.1	0.2	95.9	-0.2	95.6	-0.3	92.0	-3.8
1980	92.4	0.4	96.6	4.5	99.4	2.9	100.4	1.0	102.6	2.2	94.1	-8.3	95.6	1.6	95.3	-0.3	96.7	1.5	100.1	3.5	100.9	0.8	97.9	-3.0
1981	97.2	-0.7	96.8	-0.4	98.6	1.9	99.4	0.8	99.4	0.0	97.7	-1.7	98.9	1.2	95.2	-3.7	97.1	2.0	97.5	0.4	95.7	-1.8	94.1	-1.7
1982	94.2	0.1	96.5	2.4	97.4	0.9	97.8	0.4	97.9	0.1	94.1	-3.9	99.1	5.3	99.5	0.4	104.3	4.8	101.4	-2.8	101.0	-0.4	97.6	-3.4
1983	95.3	-2.4	99.2	4.1	99.7	0.5	100.1	0.4	101.9	1.8	100.6	-1.3	100.4	-0.2	102.7	2.3	104.1	1.4	103.4	-0.7	103.7	0.3	98.4	-5.1
1984	95.1	-3.4	102.7	8.0	103.0	0.3	99.9	-3.0	100.3	0.4	100.5	0.2	98.8	-1.7	100.1	1.3	105.7	5.6	103.7	-1.9	101.3	-2.3	98.8	-2.5
1985	91.9	-7.0	98.6	7.3	101.2	2.6	101.4	0.2	102.2	0.8	102.0	-0.2	102.9	0.9	106.7	3.7	109.6	2.7	108.6	-0.9	110.6	1.8	106.7	-3.5
1986	105.2	-1.4	104.5	-0.7	104.0	-0.5	103.3	-0.7	102.8	-0.5	100.5	-2.2	98.3	-2.2	108.3	10.2	110.1	1.7	110.9	0.7	109.4	-1.4	108.2	-1.1
1987	-	-	105.9	-2.1	-	-	114.8	8.4	-	-	107.8	-6.1	-	-	107.6	-0.2	-	-	118.9	10.5	-	-	114.5	-3.7
1988	-	-	112.9	-1.4	-	-	123.0	8.9	-	-	115.4	-6.2	-	-	117.2	1.6	-	-	125.6	7.2	-	-	122.8	-2.2
1989	-	-	123.4	0.5	-	-	129.8	5.2	-	-	124.8	-3.9	-	-	121.1	-3.0	-	-	131.7	8.8	-	-	125.6	-4.6
1990	-	-	130.1	3.6	-	-	134.3	3.2	-	-	126.8	-5.6	-	-	133.4	5.2	-	-	135.7	1.7	-	-	132.3	-2.5
1991	-	-	132.5	0.2	-	-	135.4	2.2	-	-	131.5	-2.9	-	-	137.1	4.3	-	-	140.6	2.6	-	-	132.5	-5.8
1992	-	-	134.8	1.7	-	-	135.9	0.8	-	-	130.3	-4.1	-	-	131.3	0.8	-	-	134.0	2.1	-	-	134.0	0.0
1993	-	-	139.2	3.9	-	-	146.1	5.0	-	-	136.0	-6.9	-	-	140.4	3.2	-	-	146.9	4.6	-	-	135.7	-7.6

Source: U.S. Department of Labor, Bureau of Labor Statistics, Division of Consumer Prices and Price Indexes. - indicates no data collected for period.

Detroit, MI
Consumer Price Index - All Urban Consumers
Base 1982-1984 = 100
Transportation

For 1947-1993. Columns headed % show percentile change in the index from the previous period for which an index is available.

Year	Jan Index	%	Feb Index	%	Mar Index	%	Apr Index	%	May Index	%	Jun Index	%	Jul Index	%	Aug Index	%	Sep Index	%	Oct Index	%	Nov Index	%	Dec Index	%
1947	19.2	-	19.3	0.5	19.4	0.5	19.5	0.5	19.5	0.0	19.5	0.0	19.5	0.0	19.8	1.5	20.1	1.5	20.1	0.0	20.3	1.0	20.7	2.0
1948	20.7	0.0	20.7	0.0	20.7	0.0	21.8	5.3	21.8	0.0	22.0	0.9	22.6	2.7	23.0	1.8	23.1	0.4	23.1	0.0	23.1	0.0	23.1	0.0
1949	23.1	0.0	23.4	1.3	23.4	0.0	23.5	0.4	23.5	0.0	23.4	-0.4	23.4	0.0	23.4	0.0	23.4	0.0	23.4	0.0	23.4	0.0	23.4	0.0
1950	23.4	0.0	23.4	0.0	23.4	0.0	23.4	0.0	23.8	1.7	23.9	0.4	23.9	0.0	23.7	-0.8	23.8	0.4	23.7	-0.4	23.8	0.4	23.8	0.0
1951	23.8	0.0	23.8	0.0	24.1	1.3	24.1	0.0	24.1	0.0	24.6	2.1	24.8	0.8	24.8	0.0	25.1	1.2	25.5	1.6	25.9	1.6	25.9	0.0
1952	25.9	0.0	25.9	0.0	26.1	0.8	26.1	0.0	26.1	0.0	26.1	0.0	26.1	0.0	26.5	1.5	26.6	0.4	27.4	3.0	27.4	0.0	27.4	0.0
1953	27.4	0.0	27.4	0.0	27.3	-0.4	27.4	0.4	27.4	0.0	27.6	0.7	27.8	0.7	27.8	0.0	27.7	-0.4	27.6	-0.4	27.5	-0.4	26.7	-2.9
1954	27.3	2.2	26.5	-2.9	26.4	-0.4	26.3	-0.4	26.3	0.0	26.0	-1.1	26.1	0.4	25.7	-1.5	25.7	0.0	25.7	0.0	27.3	6.2	26.7	-2.2
1955	26.6	-0.4	26.4	-0.8	26.4	0.0	26.3	-0.4	26.3	0.0	26.7	1.5	26.6	-0.4	26.3	-1.1	26.4	0.4	26.7	1.1	27.2	1.9	27.2	0.0
1956	27.1	-0.4	27.1	0.0	27.0	-0.4	27.2	0.7	27.2	0.0	27.1	-0.4	27.5	1.5	27.6	0.4	27.5	-0.4	28.0	1.8	28.3	1.1	28.3	0.0
1957	28.6	1.1	28.5	-0.3	28.7	0.7	28.6	-0.3	28.8	0.7	28.8	0.0	28.8	0.0	28.9	0.3	28.7	-0.7	28.6	-0.3	30.0	4.9	29.7	-1.0
1958	29.3	-1.3	28.6	-2.4	28.6	0.0	28.5	-0.3	28.3	-0.7	28.7	1.4	28.7	0.0	29.2	1.7	29.3	0.3	29.2	-0.3	29.4	0.7	29.7	1.0
1959	29.8	0.3	29.5	-1.0	29.8	1.0	30.1	1.0	30.0	-0.3	29.1	-3.0	30.4	4.5	30.3	-0.3	30.7	1.3	30.7	0.0	30.5	-0.7	30.6	0.3
1960	29.9	-2.3	30.2	1.0	29.8	-1.3	29.3	-1.7	29.5	0.7	30.6	3.7	30.6	0.0	30.7	0.3	30.3	-1.3	30.4	0.3	30.4	0.0	30.0	-1.3
1961	30.2	0.7	30.1	-0.3	29.5	-2.0	29.1	-1.4	29.5	1.4	29.2	-1.0	28.9	-1.0	30.5	5.5	29.8	-2.3	30.1	1.0	30.2	0.3	28.7	-5.0
1962	29.0	1.0	30.6	5.5	30.6	0.0	31.0	1.3	29.8	-3.9	29.9	0.3	29.3	-2.0	30.3	3.4	30.8	1.7	31.0	0.6	30.4	-1.9	31.1	2.3
1963	30.6	-1.6	30.4	-0.7	30.6	0.7	29.5	-3.6	30.4	3.1	30.2	-0.7	30.3	0.3	31.4	3.6	29.7	-5.4	30.5	2.7	31.0	1.6	30.7	-1.0
1964	30.9	0.7	29.7	-3.9	30.3	2.0	30.3	0.0	29.8	-1.7	30.2	1.3	30.7	1.7	31.0	1.0	31.2	0.6	31.6	1.3	31.1	-1.6	31.3	0.6
1965	31.8	1.6	31.2	-1.9	31.1	-0.3	31.8	2.3	32.3	1.6	32.2	-0.3	32.2	0.0	32.0	-0.6	32.0	0.0	32.2	0.6	32.4	0.6	32.4	0.0
1966	32.5	0.3	32.3	-0.6	32.7	1.2	32.9	0.6	32.9	0.0	32.9	0.0	32.8	-0.3	32.9	0.3	32.6	-0.9	33.0	1.2	33.1	0.3	33.0	-0.3
1967	33.0	0.0	33.2	0.6	33.4	0.6	33.6	0.6	33.6	0.0	33.5	-0.3	33.5	0.0	33.4	-0.3	33.5	0.3	33.6	0.3	34.0	1.2	34.1	0.3
1968	34.4	0.9	34.4	0.0	34.9	1.5	34.9	0.0	35.0	0.3	35.1	0.3	35.0	-0.3	34.9	-0.3	34.8	-0.3	35.1	0.9	35.3	0.6	35.1	-0.6
1969	35.0	-0.3	35.4	1.1	36.6	3.4	36.5	-0.3	36.6	0.3	36.7	0.3	35.7	-2.7	36.7	2.8	35.6	-3.0	36.1	1.4	35.8	-0.8	36.0	0.6
1970	36.1	0.3	36.9	2.2	35.4	-4.1	36.5	3.1	37.2	1.9	36.4	-2.2	36.5	0.3	35.8	-1.9	36.0	0.6	38.7	7.5	38.9	0.5	37.8	-2.8
1971	39.5	4.5	38.1	-3.5	37.8	-0.8	38.1	0.8	38.7	1.6	38.8	0.3	37.8	-2.6	38.9	2.9	38.2	-1.8	38.2	0.0	38.6	1.0	38.4	-0.5
1972	39.1	1.8	39.2	0.3	38.8	-1.0	38.7	-0.3	38.7	0.0	39.2	1.3	39.1	-0.3	39.2	0.3	39.0	-0.5	39.2	0.5	39.2	0.0	39.6	1.0
1973	39.6	0.0	40.4	2.0	40.5	0.2	41.2	1.7	41.5	0.7	41.9	1.0	41.9	0.0	41.8	-0.2	41.5	-0.7	42.0	1.2	42.3	0.7	42.9	1.4
1974	43.4	1.2	43.9	1.2	45.2	3.0	45.9	1.5	46.3	0.9	47.1	1.7	47.5	0.8	47.6	0.2	47.8	0.4	47.9	0.2	47.9	0.0	47.9	0.0
1975	47.9	0.0	47.9	0.0	48.4	1.0	48.7	0.6	49.0	0.6	50.0	2.0	51.1	2.2	51.1	0.0	51.3	0.4	51.6	0.6	51.6	0.0	51.6	0.0
1976	51.8	0.4	51.8	0.0	51.9	0.2	52.3	0.8	53.1	1.5	53.8	1.3	54.2	0.7	54.4	0.4	54.8	0.7	55.1	0.5	55.8	1.3	55.9	0.2
1977	56.0	0.2	56.3	0.5	57.4	2.0	58.4	1.7	59.0	1.0	59.3	0.5	59.4	0.2	59.6	0.3	59.5	-0.2	59.5	0.0	59.5	0.0	59.5	0.0
1978	59.6	0.2	59.7	0.2	60.3	1.0	60.6	0.5	61.6	1.7	62.2	1.0	62.7	0.8	62.8	0.2	62.9	0.2	63.8	1.4	64.1	0.5	64.2	0.2
1979	65.3	1.7	65.8	0.8	66.3	0.8	68.0	2.6	68.9	1.3	70.3	2.0	71.5	1.7	72.5	1.4	73.1	0.8	74.0	1.2	74.4	0.5	75.3	1.2
1980	77.1	2.4	78.5	1.8	79.8	1.7	81.2	1.8	82.1	1.1	82.8	0.9	81.5	-1.6	83.2	2.1	85.2	2.4	86.4	1.4	87.9	1.7	87.7	-0.2
1981	88.9	1.4	90.0	1.2	91.1	1.2	92.0	1.0	93.1	1.2	93.3	0.2	95.4	2.3	95.4	0.0	95.4	0.0	96.8	1.5	97.1	0.3	97.0	-0.1
1982	97.4	0.4	96.2	-1.2	95.7	-0.5	95.4	-0.3	96.7	1.4	99.1	2.5	99.8	0.7	99.9	0.1	98.5	-1.4	98.6	0.1	98.6	0.0	98.4	-0.2
1983	97.3	-1.1	96.4	-0.9	96.1	-0.3	96.4	0.3	97.6	1.2	97.5	-0.1	98.7	1.2	99.6	0.9	100.2	0.6	100.3	0.1	101.2	0.9	101.0	-0.2
1984	101.1	0.1	101.4	0.3	102.0	0.6	103.1	1.1	103.6	0.5	103.5	-0.1	103.4	-0.1	103.4	0.0	104.5	1.1	106.0	1.4	106.1	0.1	105.3	-0.8
1985	104.6	-0.7	105.4	0.8	106.1	0.7	106.5	0.4	106.5	0.0	106.6	0.1	106.7	0.1	107.1	0.4	106.0	-1.0	107.2	1.1	107.9	0.7	108.3	0.4
1986	108.0	-0.3	106.0	-1.9	102.7	-3.1	101.2	-1.5	103.5	2.3	103.9	0.4	102.3	-1.5	101.7	-0.6	100.8	-0.9	102.2	1.4	103.6	1.4	103.1	-0.5
1987	-	-	102.9	-0.2	-	-	104.2	1.3	-	-	104.9	0.7	-	-	106.4	1.4	-	-	107.8	1.3	-	-	106.7	-1.0
1988	-	-	105.5	-1.1	-	-	106.8	1.2	-	-	110.3	3.3	-	-	111.3	0.9	-	-	111.7	0.4	-	-	112.8	1.0
1989	-	-	113.7	0.8	-	-	117.9	3.7	-	-	119.0	0.9	-	-	116.0	-2.5	-	-	118.4	2.1	-	-	118.3	-0.1
1990	-	-	120.5	1.9	-	-	120.2	-0.2	-	-	121.7	1.2	-	-	124.1	2.0	-	-	130.4	5.1	-	-	130.5	0.1
1991	-	-	128.3	-1.7	-	-	129.2	0.7	-	-	129.8	0.5	-	-	128.9	-0.7	-	-	129.1	0.2	-	-	130.9	1.4

[Continued]

Detroit, MI
Consumer Price Index - All Urban Consumers
Base 1982-1984 = 100
Transportation
[Continued]

For 1947-1993. Columns headed % show percentile change in the index from the previous period for which an index is available.

Year	Jan Index	%	Feb Index	%	Mar Index	%	Apr Index	%	May Index	%	Jun Index	%	Jul Index	%	Aug Index	%	Sep Index	%	Oct Index	%	Nov Index	%	Dec Index	%
1992	-	-	128.5	-1.8	-	-	130.0	1.2	-	-	130.1	0.1	-	-	128.6	-1.2	-	-	132.1	2.7	-	-	130.3	-1.4
1993	-	-	131.8	1.2	-	-	131.7	-0.1	-	-	132.7	0.8	-	-	132.7	0.0	-	-	134.4	1.3	-	-	132.6	-1.3

Source: U.S. Department of Labor, Bureau of Labor Statistics, Division of Consumer Prices and Price Indexes. - indicates no data collected for period.

Detroit, MI
Consumer Price Index - Urban Wage Earners
Base 1982-1984 = 100
Transportation

For 1947-1993. Columns headed % show percentile change in the index from the previous period for which an index is available.

Year	Jan Index	%	Feb Index	%	Mar Index	%	Apr Index	%	May Index	%	Jun Index	%	Jul Index	%	Aug Index	%	Sep Index	%	Oct Index	%	Nov Index	%	Dec Index	%
1947	19.9	-	20.0	0.5	20.1	0.5	20.2	0.5	20.2	0.0	20.2	0.0	20.2	0.0	20.5	1.5	20.9	2.0	20.9	0.0	21.1	1.0	21.5	1.9
1948	21.5	0.0	21.5	0.0	21.5	0.0	22.6	5.1	22.6	0.0	22.8	0.9	23.4	2.6	23.9	2.1	24.0	0.4	24.0	0.0	24.0	0.0	24.0	0.0
1949	24.0	0.0	24.3	1.2	24.3	0.0	24.4	0.4	24.4	0.0	24.3	-0.4	24.3	0.0	24.3	0.0	24.3	0.0	24.3	0.0	24.3	0.0	24.3	0.0
1950	24.3	0.0	24.3	0.0	24.3	0.0	24.3	0.0	24.7	1.6	24.8	0.4	24.8	0.0	24.6	-0.8	24.7	0.4	24.6	-0.4	24.7	0.4	24.7	0.0
1951	24.7	0.0	24.7	0.0	25.0	1.2	25.1	0.4	25.1	0.0	25.5	1.6	25.8	1.2	25.8	0.0	26.1	1.2	26.5	1.5	26.8	1.1	26.8	0.0
1952	26.8	0.0	26.9	0.4	27.0	0.4	27.0	0.0	27.0	0.0	27.0	0.0	27.0	0.0	27.5	1.9	27.6	0.4	28.4	2.9	28.4	0.0	28.4	0.0
1953	28.5	0.4	28.4	-0.4	28.4	0.0	28.4	0.0	28.4	0.0	28.6	0.7	28.8	0.7	28.8	0.0	28.7	-0.3	28.6	-0.3	28.5	-0.3	27.7	-2.8
1954	28.4	2.5	27.5	-3.2	27.4	-0.4	27.3	-0.4	27.3	0.0	27.0	-1.1	27.0	0.0	26.7	-1.1	26.7	0.0	26.7	0.0	28.3	6.0	27.7	-2.1
1955	27.6	-0.4	27.4	-0.7	27.4	0.0	27.3	-0.4	27.3	0.0	27.7	1.5	27.6	-0.4	27.3	-1.1	27.4	0.4	27.7	1.1	28.2	1.8	28.3	0.4
1956	28.2	-0.4	28.1	-0.4	28.1	0.0	28.2	0.4	28.3	0.4	28.2	-0.4	28.5	1.1	28.6	0.4	28.6	0.0	29.0	1.4	29.4	1.4	29.4	0.0
1957	29.7	1.0	29.6	-0.3	29.8	0.7	29.7	-0.3	29.9	0.7	29.9	0.0	29.9	0.0	30.0	0.3	29.8	-0.7	29.7	-0.3	31.1	4.7	30.8	-1.0
1958	30.5	-1.0	29.7	-2.6	29.7	0.0	29.5	-0.7	29.4	-0.3	29.8	1.4	29.8	0.0	30.3	1.7	30.4	0.3	30.3	-0.3	30.5	0.7	30.8	1.0
1959	30.9	0.3	30.6	-1.0	30.9	1.0	31.3	1.3	31.1	-0.6	30.2	-2.9	31.6	4.6	31.4	-0.6	31.8	1.3	31.8	0.0	31.6	-0.6	31.8	0.6
1960	31.0	-2.5	31.4	1.3	30.9	-1.6	30.5	-1.3	30.6	0.3	31.8	3.9	31.8	0.0	31.8	0.0	31.4	-1.3	31.5	0.3	31.5	0.0	31.1	-1.3
1961	31.4	1.0	31.2	-0.6	30.6	-1.9	30.2	-1.3	30.7	1.7	30.3	-1.3	30.0	-1.0	31.6	5.3	30.9	-2.2	31.3	1.3	31.3	0.0	29.8	-4.8
1962	30.1	1.0	31.8	5.6	31.8	0.0	32.2	1.3	30.9	-4.0	31.0	0.3	30.4	-1.9	31.5	3.6	32.0	1.6	32.2	0.6	31.6	-1.9	32.3	2.2
1963	31.8	-1.5	31.5	-0.9	31.8	1.0	30.6	-3.8	31.5	2.9	31.3	-0.6	31.4	0.3	32.5	3.5	30.8	-5.2	31.7	2.9	32.2	1.6	31.9	-0.9
1964	32.0	0.3	30.8	-3.8	31.4	1.9	31.4	0.0	30.9	-1.6	31.3	1.3	31.8	1.6	32.2	1.3	32.3	0.3	32.7	1.2	32.3	-1.2	32.4	0.3
1965	33.0	1.9	32.3	-2.1	32.2	-0.3	33.0	2.5	33.5	1.5	33.4	-0.3	33.4	0.0	33.2	-0.6	33.2	0.0	33.4	0.6	33.6	0.6	33.6	0.0
1966	33.7	0.3	33.5	-0.6	34.0	1.5	34.2	0.6	34.1	-0.3	34.1	0.0	34.0	-0.3	34.1	0.3	33.8	-0.9	34.2	1.2	34.4	0.6	34.2	-0.6
1967	34.2	0.0	34.5	0.9	34.7	0.6	34.9	0.6	34.8	-0.3	34.8	0.0	34.7	-0.3	34.7	0.0	34.7	0.0	34.9	0.6	35.3	1.1	35.4	0.3
1968	35.7	0.8	35.7	0.0	36.2	1.4	36.2	0.0	36.3	0.3	36.4	0.3	36.3	-0.3	36.2	-0.3	36.1	-0.3	36.4	0.8	36.6	0.5	36.4	-0.5
1969	36.3	-0.3	36.8	1.4	38.0	3.3	37.9	-0.3	38.0	0.3	38.1	0.3	37.0	-2.9	38.0	2.7	37.0	-2.6	37.4	1.1	37.1	-0.8	37.3	0.5
1970	37.4	0.3	38.3	2.4	36.7	-4.2	37.9	3.3	38.6	1.8	37.8	-2.1	37.8	0.0	37.2	-1.6	37.3	0.3	40.1	7.5	40.4	0.7	39.2	-3.0
1971	41.0	4.6	39.5	-3.7	39.3	-0.5	39.6	0.8	40.1	1.3	40.3	0.5	39.2	-2.7	40.4	3.1	39.7	-1.7	39.7	0.0	40.1	1.0	39.9	-0.5
1972	40.6	1.8	40.7	0.2	40.2	-1.2	40.1	-0.2	40.2	0.2	40.6	1.0	40.5	-0.2	40.7	0.5	40.5	-0.5	40.6	0.2	40.7	0.2	41.1	1.0
1973	41.1	0.0	41.9	1.9	42.0	0.2	42.7	1.7	43.1	0.9	43.4	0.7	43.5	0.2	43.4	-0.2	43.1	-0.7	43.6	1.2	43.9	0.7	44.5	1.4
1974	45.0	1.1	45.6	1.3	46.9	2.9	47.6	1.5	48.0	0.8	48.8	1.7	49.2	0.8	49.4	0.4	49.6	0.4	49.7	0.2	49.7	0.0	49.7	0.0
1975	49.7	0.0	49.7	0.0	50.3	1.2	50.5	0.4	50.8	0.6	51.9	2.2	53.0	2.1	53.0	0.0	53.2	0.4	53.5	0.6	53.5	0.0	53.5	0.0
1976	53.7	0.4	53.7	0.0	53.8	0.2	54.3	0.9	55.1	1.5	55.9	1.5	56.2	0.5	56.4	0.4	56.8	0.7	57.2	0.7	57.9	1.2	58.0	0.2
1977	58.2	0.3	58.4	0.3	59.5	1.9	60.6	1.8	61.2	1.0	61.5	0.5	61.6	0.2	61.8	0.3	61.7	-0.2	61.7	0.0	61.8	0.2	61.8	0.0
1978	61.8	0.0	62.0	0.3	62.3	0.5	62.7	0.6	63.6	1.4	64.2	0.9	64.6	0.6	64.8	0.3	64.9	0.2	65.8	1.4	66.0	0.3	66.2	0.3
1979	67.5	2.0	68.0	0.7	68.6	0.9	70.1	2.2	71.1	1.4	72.6	2.1	74.2	2.2	75.0	1.1	74.9	-0.1	76.4	2.0	76.6	0.3	77.1	0.7
1980	79.1	2.6	80.4	1.6	81.7	1.6	84.3	3.2	85.3	1.2	85.5	0.2	83.4	-2.5	85.6	2.6	87.4	2.1	86.9	-0.6	88.1	1.4	86.9	-1.4
1981	88.0	1.3	89.3	1.5	90.0	0.8	90.9	1.0	92.4	1.7	92.6	0.2	94.3	1.8	94.5	0.2	95.2	0.7	96.4	1.3	96.9	0.5	97.0	0.1
1982	97.3	0.3	96.2	-1.1	95.7	-0.5	95.3	-0.4	96.6	1.4	99.1	2.6	99.8	0.7	99.8	0.0	98.5	-1.3	98.6	0.1	98.6	0.0	98.5	-0.1
1983	97.3	-1.2	96.4	-0.9	96.1	-0.3	96.4	0.3	97.7	1.3	97.6	-0.1	98.7	1.1	99.6	0.9	100.2	0.6	100.3	0.1	101.2	0.9	101.0	-0.2
1984	101.1	0.1	101.4	0.3	102.0	0.6	103.1	1.1	103.6	0.5	103.5	-0.1	103.4	-0.1	103.4	0.0	104.5	1.1	106.0	1.4	106.0	0.0	105.3	-0.7
1985	104.6	-0.7	105.5	0.9	106.1	0.6	106.6	0.5	106.6	0.0	106.7	0.1	106.9	0.2	107.3	0.4	106.1	-1.1	107.3	1.1	108.1	0.7	108.4	0.3
1986	108.1	-0.3	106.0	-1.9	102.6	-3.2	101.1	-1.5	103.5	2.4	103.9	0.4	102.3	-1.5	101.6	-0.7	100.8	-0.8	102.1	1.3	103.5	1.4	103.0	-0.5
1987	-	-	102.9	-0.1	-	-	104.3	1.4	-	-	105.0	0.7	-	-	106.6	1.5	-	-	108.1	1.4	-	-	106.9	-1.1
1988	-	-	105.6	-1.2	-	-	107.0	1.3	-	-	110.2	3.0	-	-	111.4	1.1	-	-	111.7	0.3	-	-	112.8	1.0
1989	-	-	113.6	0.7	-	-	118.0	3.9	-	-	119.2	1.0	-	-	116.0	-2.7	-	-	118.3	2.0	-	-	118.1	-0.2
1990	-	-	120.5	2.0	-	-	120.1	-0.3	-	-	121.7	1.3	-	-	124.2	2.1	-	-	130.7	5.2	-	-	130.6	-0.1
1991	-	-	128.1	-1.9	-	-	129.0	0.7	-	-	129.7	0.5	-	-	128.8	-0.7	-	-	129.0	0.2	-	-	130.7	1.3

[Continued]

Detroit, MI
Consumer Price Index - Urban Wage Earners
Base 1982-1984 = 100
Transportation
[Continued]

For 1947-1993. Columns headed % show percentile change in the index from the previous period for which an index is available.

Year	Jan Index	%	Feb Index	%	Mar Index	%	Apr Index	%	May Index	%	Jun Index	%	Jul Index	%	Aug Index	%	Sep Index	%	Oct Index	%	Nov Index	%	Dec Index	%
1992	-	-	128.2	-1.9	-	-	129.8	1.2	-	-	129.9	0.1	-	-	128.4	-1.2	-	-	131.9	2.7	-	-	130.1	-1.4
1993	-	-	131.6	1.2	-	-	131.6	0.0	-	-	132.7	0.8	-	-	132.6	-0.1	-	-	134.3	1.3	-	-	132.4	-1.4

Source: U.S. Department of Labor, Bureau of Labor Statistics, Division of Consumer Prices and Price Indexes. - indicates no data collected for period.

Detroit, MI
Consumer Price Index - All Urban Consumers
Base 1982-1984 = 100
Medical Care

For 1947-1993. Columns headed % show percentile change in the index from the previous period for which an index is available.

Year	Jan Index	%	Feb Index	%	Mar Index	%	Apr Index	%	May Index	%	Jun Index	%	Jul Index	%	Aug Index	%	Sep Index	%	Oct Index	%	Nov Index	%	Dec Index	%
1947	11.5	-	11.6	0.9	11.7	0.9	11.7	0.0	11.8	0.9	11.8	0.0	11.8	0.0	11.8	0.0	12.0	1.7	12.0	0.0	12.0	0.0	12.0	0.0
1948	12.1	0.8	12.1	0.0	12.2	0.8	12.2	0.0	12.2	0.0	12.2	0.0	12.2	0.0	12.3	0.8	12.4	0.8	12.4	0.0	12.4	0.0	12.4	0.0
1949	12.4	0.0	12.5	0.8	12.5	0.0	12.5	0.0	12.5	0.0	12.5	0.0	12.5	0.0	12.6	0.8	12.7	0.8	12.7	0.0	12.7	0.0	12.7	0.0
1950	12.7	0.0	12.8	0.8	12.8	0.0	12.8	0.0	12.8	0.0	12.8	0.0	12.8	0.0	12.8	0.0	12.8	0.0	12.9	0.8	12.9	0.0	12.9	0.0
1951	12.9	0.0	12.9	0.0	13.0	0.8	13.0	0.0	13.0	0.0	13.5	3.8	13.6	0.7	13.6	0.0	13.6	0.0	13.6	0.0	13.6	0.0	13.8	1.5
1952	13.7	-0.7	13.7	0.0	14.0	2.2	14.0	0.0	14.0	0.0	14.1	0.7	14.1	0.0	14.1	0.0	14.2	0.7	14.3	0.7	14.3	0.0	14.3	0.0
1953	14.3	0.0	14.3	0.0	14.3	0.0	14.3	0.0	14.8	3.5	14.8	0.0	14.8	0.0	14.9	0.7	14.8	-0.7	14.9	0.7	14.9	0.0	14.9	0.0
1954	14.9	0.0	15.0	0.7	15.0	0.0	15.0	0.0	15.2	1.3	15.2	0.0	15.2	0.0	15.5	2.0	15.5	0.0	15.5	0.0	15.6	0.6	15.6	0.0
1955	15.6	0.0	16.2	3.8	16.2	0.0	16.2	0.0	16.2	0.0	16.2	0.0	16.2	0.0	16.2	0.0	16.2	0.0	16.2	0.0	16.8	3.7	16.8	0.0
1956	16.8	0.0	16.8	0.0	17.4	3.6	17.4	0.0	17.4	0.0	17.4	0.0	17.4	0.0	17.5	0.6	17.5	0.0	17.5	0.0	17.6	0.6	17.6	0.0
1957	17.7	0.6	17.9	1.1	17.9	0.0	17.9	0.0	17.9	0.0	17.9	0.0	17.9	0.0	17.9	0.0	17.9	0.0	17.9	0.0	18.5	3.4	18.5	0.0
1958	18.5	0.0	18.4	-0.5	18.5	0.5	18.5	0.0	18.5	0.0	18.5	0.0	18.5	0.0	18.6	0.5	18.6	0.0	18.6	0.0	18.7	0.5	18.7	0.0
1959	18.7	0.0	19.3	3.2	19.3	0.0	19.3	0.0	19.3	0.0	19.3	0.0	19.3	0.0	19.3	0.0	19.3	0.0	19.3	0.0	19.3	0.0	19.3	0.0
1960	19.3	0.0	19.4	0.5	19.4	0.0	19.4	0.0	19.5	0.5	19.5	0.0	19.8	1.5	19.9	0.5	19.9	0.0	19.9	0.0	19.9	0.0	19.9	0.0
1961	20.0	0.5	20.0	0.0	20.0	0.0	20.0	0.0	20.0	0.0	20.9	4.5	21.0	0.5	21.0	0.0	21.0	0.0	21.0	0.0	21.0	0.0	21.0	0.0
1962	20.9	-0.5	21.0	0.5	21.1	0.5	21.1	0.0	21.3	0.9	21.3	0.0	21.3	0.0	21.3	0.0	21.3	0.0	21.3	0.0	21.3	0.0	21.3	0.0
1963	21.3	0.0	21.4	0.5	21.4	0.0	21.4	0.0	21.5	0.5	22.9	6.5	22.9	0.0	22.9	0.0	22.9	0.0	22.9	0.0	23.0	0.4	23.0	0.0
1964	23.0	0.0	23.0	0.0	23.2	0.9	23.2	0.0	23.2	0.0	23.2	0.0	23.2	0.0	23.2	0.0	23.2	0.0	23.1	-0.4	23.3	0.9	23.3	0.0
1965	23.4	0.4	23.4	0.0	23.7	1.3	23.7	0.0	23.8	0.4	23.8	0.0	23.8	0.0	24.0	0.8	23.9	-0.4	23.9	0.0	23.9	0.0	23.9	0.0
1966	24.3	1.7	24.4	0.4	24.8	1.6	24.8	0.0	24.9	0.4	25.1	0.8	25.2	0.4	25.3	0.4	25.5	0.8	25.6	0.4	25.9	1.2	26.1	0.8
1967	26.2	0.4	26.3	0.4	26.6	1.1	26.5	-0.4	26.6	0.4	26.7	0.4	26.8	0.4	26.8	0.0	27.3	1.9	27.3	0.0	27.7	1.5	27.8	0.4
1968	28.1	1.1	28.3	0.7	28.6	1.1	28.6	0.0	28.7	0.3	28.5	-0.7	28.5	0.0	28.6	0.4	28.8	0.7	29.0	0.7	29.0	0.0	29.4	1.4
1969	29.8	1.4	30.0	0.7	30.3	1.0	30.5	0.7	30.7	0.7	30.9	0.7	31.0	0.3	31.2	0.6	31.5	1.0	31.0	-1.6	31.2	0.6	31.4	0.6
1970	31.9	1.6	32.3	1.3	32.9	1.9	33.1	0.6	33.2	0.3	33.3	0.3	33.6	0.9	34.0	1.2	34.2	0.6	34.2	0.0	34.4	0.6	34.6	0.6
1971	35.1	1.4	35.4	0.9	35.5	0.3	35.6	0.3	35.7	0.3	36.0	0.8	36.2	0.6	36.4	0.6	36.7	0.8	36.6	-0.3	36.7	0.3	37.0	0.8
1972	37.5	1.4	37.6	0.3	37.7	0.3	37.8	0.3	37.8	0.0	38.0	0.5	38.0	0.0	38.2	0.5	38.2	0.0	38.6	1.0	38.6	0.0	38.6	0.0
1973	38.7	0.3	38.8	0.3	39.4	1.5	39.5	0.3	39.7	0.5	39.8	0.3	39.9	0.3	40.0	0.3	40.4	1.0	40.8	1.0	41.2	1.0	41.2	0.0
1974	41.5	0.7	42.0	1.2	42.2	0.5	42.4	0.5	42.9	1.2	43.3	0.9	43.8	1.2	44.5	1.6	45.3	1.8	45.6	0.7	46.0	0.9	46.1	0.2
1975	47.4	2.8	48.5	2.3	48.6	0.2	49.2	1.2	49.4	0.4	49.8	0.8	50.6	1.6	51.6	2.0	52.1	1.0	52.5	0.8	52.4	-0.2	52.7	0.6
1976	54.1	2.7	54.6	0.9	54.8	0.4	55.0	0.4	55.5	0.9	55.6	0.2	57.1	2.7	57.3	0.4	57.3	0.0	57.6	0.5	58.5	1.6	58.5	0.0
1977	59.0	0.9	59.1	0.2	60.5	2.4	61.6	1.8	62.7	1.8	63.4	1.1	63.8	0.6	65.1	2.0	65.4	0.5	65.5	0.2	65.9	0.6	65.8	-0.2
1978	65.8	0.0	66.3	0.8	66.8	0.8	67.2	0.6	67.4	0.3	67.4	0.0	67.5	0.1	67.6	0.1	67.7	0.1	69.5	2.7	69.5	0.0	70.3	1.2
1979	71.7	2.0	72.1	0.6	72.2	0.1	73.0	1.1	72.6	-0.5	73.4	1.1	74.0	0.8	74.2	0.3	74.4	0.3	74.9	0.7	75.8	1.2	78.0	2.9
1980	78.1	0.1	78.2	0.1	78.6	0.5	79.3	0.9	79.4	0.1	79.7	0.4	80.4	0.9	80.0	-0.5	80.9	1.1	81.7	1.0	82.3	0.7	82.4	0.1
1981	83.2	1.0	84.4	1.4	84.7	0.4	85.2	0.6	85.8	0.7	86.0	0.2	86.3	0.3	86.3	0.0	87.1	0.9	88.0	1.0	88.1	0.1	88.3	0.2
1982	89.2	1.0	90.1	1.0	91.0	1.0	91.6	0.7	92.7	1.2	92.7	0.0	93.8	1.2	94.6	0.9	95.5	1.0	95.8	0.3	95.8	0.0	95.8	0.0
1983	96.2	0.4	96.1	-0.1	96.8	0.7	96.7	-0.1	96.5	-0.2	96.3	-0.2	97.9	1.7	98.9	1.0	98.9	0.0	99.4	0.5	101.2	1.8	105.1	3.9
1984	105.8	0.7	106.5	0.7	106.9	0.4	107.7	0.7	107.7	0.0	107.7	0.0	108.9	1.1	109.4	0.5	109.9	0.5	110.0	0.1	110.5	0.5	110.6	0.1
1985	111.4	0.7	113.1	1.5	114.2	1.0	114.5	0.3	115.2	0.6	115.2	0.0	117.1	1.6	117.7	0.5	118.7	0.8	119.2	0.4	120.1	0.8	120.3	0.2
1986	121.7	1.2	122.0	0.2	122.7	0.6	123.0	0.2	123.6	0.5	124.1	0.4	126.5	1.9	126.6	0.1	126.8	0.2	127.2	0.3	127.4	0.2	128.2	0.6
1987	-	-	130.2	1.6	-	-	131.6	1.1	-	-	132.9	1.0	-	-	134.3	1.1	-	-	134.9	0.4	-	-	135.3	0.3
1988	-	-	138.6	2.4	-	-	138.5	-0.1	-	-	137.5	-0.7	-	-	142.7	3.8	-	-	142.1	-0.4	-	-	143.8	1.2
1989	-	-	142.9	-0.6	-	-	145.0	1.5	-	-	146.2	0.8	-	-	149.5	2.3	-	-	149.9	0.3	-	-	150.8	0.6
1990	-	-	154.7	2.6	-	-	156.5	1.2	-	-	158.9	1.5	-	-	163.7	3.0	-	-	163.9	0.1	-	-	164.6	0.4
1991	-	-	168.4	2.3	-	-	167.9	-0.3	-	-	169.5	1.0	-	-	173.0	2.1	-	-	174.4	0.8	-	-	175.6	0.7

[Continued]

Detroit, MI
Consumer Price Index - All Urban Consumers
Base 1982-1984 = 100
Medical Care
[Continued]

For 1947-1993. Columns headed % show percentile change in the index from the previous period for which an index is available.

Year	Jan		Feb		Mar		Apr		May		Jun		Jul		Aug		Sep		Oct		Nov		Dec	
	Index	%	Index	%	Index	%	Index	%	Index	%	Index	%	Index	%	Index	%	Index	%	Index	%	Index	%	Index	%
1992	-	-	179.2	2.1	-	-	180.9	0.9	-	-	181.0	0.1	-	-	182.1	0.6	-	-	184.2	1.2	-	-	184.6	0.2
1993	-	-	188.6	2.2	-	-	191.3	1.4	-	-	191.0	-0.2	-	-	191.6	0.3	-	-	192.3	0.4	-	-	192.5	0.1

Source: U.S. Department of Labor, Bureau of Labor Statistics, Division of Consumer Prices and Price Indexes. - indicates no data collected for period.

Detroit, MI

Consumer Price Index - Urban Wage Earners

Base 1982-1984 = 100

Medical Care

For 1947-1993. Columns headed % show percentile change in the index from the previous period for which an index is available.

Year	Jan		Feb		Mar		Apr		May		Jun		Jul		Aug		Sep		Oct		Nov		Dec	
	Index	%	Index	%	Index	%	Index	%	Index	%	Index	%	Index	%	Index	%	Index	%	Index	%	Index	%	Index	%
1947	11.7	-	11.8	0.9	11.9	0.8	12.0	0.8	12.0	0.0	12.1	0.8	12.1	0.0	12.1	0.0	12.2	0.8	12.2	0.0	12.2	0.0	12.2	0.0
1948	12.4	1.6	12.4	0.0	12.4	0.0	12.5	0.8	12.5	0.0	12.5	0.0	12.5	0.0	12.6	0.8	12.6	0.0	12.6	0.0	12.6	0.0	12.6	0.0
1949	12.6	0.0	12.7	0.8	12.8	0.8	12.8	0.0	12.8	0.0	12.8	0.0	12.8	0.0	12.8	0.0	12.9	0.8	12.9	0.0	13.0	0.8	13.0	0.0
1950	13.0	0.0	13.0	0.0	13.0	0.0	13.0	0.0	13.0	0.0	13.1	0.8	13.1	0.0	13.1	0.0	13.1	0.0	13.1	0.0	13.2	0.8	13.2	0.0
1951	13.2	0.0	13.2	0.0	13.3	0.8	13.3	0.0	13.3	0.0	13.8	3.8	13.8	0.0	13.8	0.0	13.8	0.0	13.9	0.7	13.9	0.0	14.1	1.4
1952	14.0	-0.7	14.0	0.0	14.3	2.1	14.3	0.0	14.3	0.0	14.4	0.7	14.4	0.0	14.4	0.0	14.5	0.7	14.6	0.7	14.6	0.0	14.6	0.0
1953	14.5	-0.7	14.6	0.7	14.6	0.0	14.6	0.0	15.1	3.4	15.1	0.0	15.1	0.0	15.1	0.0	15.1	0.0	15.1	0.0	15.2	0.7	15.2	0.0
1954	15.2	0.0	15.2	0.0	15.2	0.0	15.2	0.0	15.5	2.0	15.5	0.0	15.5	0.0	15.8	1.9	15.8	0.0	15.8	0.0	15.9	0.6	15.9	0.0
1955	15.9	0.0	16.5	3.8	16.5	0.0	16.5	0.0	16.5	0.0	16.5	0.0	16.5	0.0	16.5	0.0	16.5	0.0	16.5	0.0	17.1	3.6	17.1	0.0
1956	17.1	0.0	17.1	0.0	17.7	3.5	17.7	0.0	17.7	0.0	17.8	0.6	17.8	0.0	17.9	0.6	17.9	0.0	17.8	-0.6	17.9	0.6	17.9	0.0
1957	18.0	0.6	18.3	1.7	18.3	0.0	18.3	0.0	18.2	-0.5	18.2	0.0	18.2	0.0	18.3	0.5	18.3	0.0	18.3	0.0	18.8	2.7	18.8	0.0
1958	18.8	0.0	18.8	0.0	18.8	0.0	18.8	0.0	18.8	0.0	18.9	0.5	18.9	0.0	19.0	0.5	19.0	0.0	19.0	0.0	19.1	0.5	19.1	0.0
1959	19.1	0.0	19.7	3.1	19.7	0.0	19.7	0.0	19.7	0.0	19.7	0.0	19.7	0.0	19.7	0.0	19.7	0.0	19.7	0.0	19.7	0.0	19.7	0.0
1960	19.7	0.0	19.8	0.5	19.8	0.0	19.8	0.0	19.9	0.5	19.9	0.0	20.2	1.5	20.2	0.0	20.2	0.0	20.3	0.5	20.3	0.0	20.3	0.0
1961	20.3	0.0	20.4	0.5	20.4	0.0	20.3	-0.5	20.4	0.5	21.3	4.4	21.4	0.5	21.4	0.0	21.4	0.0	21.4	0.0	21.4	0.0	21.4	0.0
1962	21.3	-0.5	21.4	0.5	21.5	0.5	21.5	0.0	21.7	0.9	21.7	0.0	21.7	0.0	21.7	0.0	21.7	0.0	21.7	0.0	21.7	0.0	21.7	0.0
1963	21.7	0.0	21.8	0.5	21.9	0.5	21.9	0.0	21.9	0.0	23.3	6.4	23.3	0.0	23.3	0.0	23.3	0.0	23.3	0.0	23.4	0.4	23.4	0.0
1964	23.4	0.0	23.5	0.4	23.6	0.4	23.6	0.0	23.6	0.0	23.6	0.0	23.6	0.0	23.7	0.4	23.6	-0.4	23.6	0.0	23.7	0.4	23.7	0.0
1965	23.9	0.8	23.9	0.0	24.1	0.8	24.2	0.4	24.2	0.0	24.3	0.4	24.3	0.0	24.5	0.8	24.4	-0.4	24.4	0.0	24.4	0.0	24.4	0.0
1966	24.8	1.6	24.9	0.4	25.3	1.6	25.3	0.0	25.4	0.4	25.6	0.8	25.6	0.0	25.7	0.4	26.0	1.2	26.1	0.4	26.4	1.1	26.6	0.8
1967	26.7	0.4	26.8	0.4	27.1	1.1	27.0	-0.4	27.1	0.4	27.3	0.7	27.3	0.0	27.3	0.0	27.8	1.8	27.9	0.4	28.2	1.1	28.4	0.7
1968	28.7	1.1	28.8	0.3	29.1	1.0	29.2	0.3	29.3	0.3	29.1	-0.7	29.1	0.0	29.1	0.0	29.3	0.7	29.6	1.0	29.6	0.0	30.0	1.4
1969	30.3	1.0	30.6	1.0	30.9	1.0	31.1	0.6	31.3	0.6	31.5	0.6	31.6	0.3	31.8	0.6	32.1	0.9	31.6	-1.6	31.8	0.6	32.0	0.6
1970	32.5	1.6	32.9	1.2	33.5	1.8	33.8	0.9	33.9	0.3	34.0	0.3	34.2	0.6	34.6	1.2	34.8	0.6	34.8	0.0	35.1	0.9	35.3	0.6
1971	35.8	1.4	36.1	0.8	36.1	0.0	36.3	0.6	36.4	0.3	36.7	0.8	36.9	0.5	37.1	0.5	37.4	0.8	37.3	-0.3	37.4	0.3	37.7	0.8
1972	38.2	1.3	38.4	0.5	38.5	0.3	38.5	0.0	38.5	0.0	38.7	0.5	38.7	0.0	38.9	0.5	38.9	0.0	39.3	1.0	39.3	0.0	39.3	0.0
1973	39.4	0.3	39.5	0.3	40.1	1.5	40.3	0.5	40.4	0.2	40.6	0.5	40.7	0.2	40.8	0.2	41.2	1.0	41.6	1.0	42.0	1.0	42.0	0.0
1974	42.3	0.7	42.8	1.2	43.0	0.5	43.2	0.5	43.7	1.2	44.1	0.9	44.6	1.1	45.4	1.8	46.1	1.5	46.5	0.9	46.9	0.9	47.0	0.2
1975	48.3	2.8	49.4	2.3	49.6	0.4	50.2	1.2	50.4	0.4	50.8	0.8	51.6	1.6	52.6	1.9	53.1	1.0	53.5	0.8	53.4	-0.2	53.7	0.6
1976	55.2	2.8	55.6	0.7	55.9	0.5	56.0	0.2	56.5	0.9	56.7	0.4	58.2	2.6	58.4	0.3	58.4	0.0	58.7	0.5	59.6	1.5	59.6	0.0
1977	60.1	0.8	60.3	0.3	61.6	2.2	62.8	1.9	63.9	1.8	64.6	1.1	65.1	0.8	66.3	1.8	66.7	0.6	66.7	0.0	67.2	0.7	67.1	-0.1
1978	67.2	0.1	67.4	0.3	67.7	0.4	68.4	1.0	68.4	0.0	68.4	0.0	68.4	0.0	68.5	0.1	69.7	1.8	71.5	2.6	71.7	0.3	71.8	0.1
1979	72.9	1.5	72.8	-0.1	73.3	0.7	75.0	2.3	75.3	0.4	75.8	0.7	76.3	0.7	76.6	0.4	76.8	0.3	77.4	0.8	78.1	0.9	79.1	1.3
1980	79.1	0.0	79.2	0.1	79.4	0.3	80.9	1.9	81.4	0.6	81.6	0.2	81.7	0.1	81.6	-0.1	82.1	0.6	82.6	0.6	82.8	0.2	83.4	0.7
1981	84.5	1.3	85.4	1.1	85.9	0.6	86.0	0.1	86.2	0.2	86.6	0.5	86.8	0.2	87.2	0.5	87.7	0.6	88.2	0.6	88.7	0.6	88.6	-0.1
1982	89.6	1.1	90.4	0.9	91.4	1.1	91.9	0.5	93.0	1.2	93.0	0.0	94.0	1.1	94.7	0.7	95.7	1.1	96.0	0.3	95.9	-0.1	95.9	0.0
1983	96.4	0.5	96.3	-0.1	96.9	0.6	96.9	0.0	96.7	-0.2	96.6	-0.1	98.2	1.7	99.0	0.8	99.0	0.0	99.6	0.6	101.2	1.6	104.8	3.6
1984	105.4	0.6	106.2	0.8	106.6	0.4	107.2	0.6	107.3	0.1	107.4	0.1	108.5	1.0	108.9	0.4	109.5	0.6	109.6	0.1	110.2	0.5	110.3	0.1
1985	111.0	0.6	112.6	1.4	113.6	0.9	113.8	0.2	114.6	0.7	114.5	-0.1	116.2	1.5	116.8	0.5	117.7	0.8	118.2	0.4	119.0	0.7	119.3	0.3
1986	120.4	0.9	120.8	0.3	121.4	0.5	121.8	0.3	122.4	0.5	122.9	0.4	125.0	1.7	125.0	0.0	125.2	0.2	125.8	0.5	125.9	0.1	126.7	0.6
1987	-	-	128.5	1.4	-	-	130.1	1.2	-	-	131.3	0.9	-	-	132.7	1.1	-	-	133.1	0.3	-	-	133.9	0.6
1988	-	-	137.7	2.8	-	-	137.7	0.0	-	-	136.5	-0.9	-	-	142.5	4.4	-	-	141.9	-0.4	-	-	143.4	1.1
1989	-	-	142.9	-0.3	-	-	144.7	1.3	-	-	145.9	0.8	-	-	149.4	2.4	-	-	149.7	0.2	-	-	150.5	0.5
1990	-	-	154.2	2.5	-	-	155.9	1.1	-	-	158.0	1.3	-	-	163.1	3.2	-	-	163.2	0.1	-	-	163.6	0.2
1991	-	-	167.7	2.5	-	-	166.8	-0.5	-	-	168.1	0.8	-	-	171.4	2.0	-	-	172.8	0.8	-	-	174.1	0.8

[Continued]

Detroit, MI
Consumer Price Index - Urban Wage Earners
Base 1982-1984 = 100
Medical Care

[Continued]

For 1947-1993. Columns headed % show percentile change in the index from the previous period for which an index is available.

Year	Jan		Feb		Mar		Apr		May		Jun		Jul		Aug		Sep		Oct		Nov		Dec	
	Index	%	Index	%	Index	%	Index	%	Index	%	Index	%	Index	%	Index	%	Index	%	Index	%	Index	%	Index	%
1992	-	-	177.6	2.0	-	-	179.3	1.0	-	-	179.5	0.1	-	-	180.4	0.5	-	-	182.7	1.3	-	-	182.9	0.1
1993	-	-	187.1	2.3	-	-	189.8	1.4	-	-	189.5	-0.2	-	-	190.0	0.3	-	-	190.7	0.4	-	-	190.7	0.0

Source: U.S. Department of Labor, Bureau of Labor Statistics, Division of Consumer Prices and Price Indexes. - indicates no data collected for period.

Detroit, MI
Consumer Price Index - All Urban Consumers
Base 1982-1984 = 100
Entertainment

For 1976-1993. Columns headed % show percentile change in the index from the previous period for which an index is available.

Year	Jan Index	%	Feb Index	%	Mar Index	%	Apr Index	%	May Index	%	Jun Index	%	Jul Index	%	Aug Index	%	Sep Index	%	Oct Index	%	Nov Index	%	Dec Index	%
1976	72.1	-	72.4	0.4	72.9	0.7	73.5	0.8	73.6	0.1	73.0	-0.8	73.2	0.3	73.0	-0.3	74.2	1.6	74.3	0.1	74.5	0.3	74.8	0.4
1977	74.9	0.1	74.9	0.0	75.1	0.3	75.0	-0.1	75.2	0.3	75.2	0.0	75.4	0.3	75.7	0.4	76.5	1.1	76.3	-0.3	76.8	0.7	77.3	0.7
1978	77.5	0.3	77.7	0.3	78.3	0.8	79.9	2.0	79.9	0.0	79.5	-0.5	80.0	0.6	81.0	1.3	81.2	0.2	81.2	0.0	81.4	0.2	82.0	0.7
1979	82.2	0.2	82.7	0.6	81.3	-1.7	83.3	2.5	84.2	1.1	84.6	0.5	83.8	-0.9	83.0	-1.0	81.4	-1.9	82.5	1.4	82.9	0.5	81.7	-1.4
1980	84.2	3.1	85.9	2.0	87.4	1.7	87.8	0.5	88.0	0.2	88.8	0.9	88.1	-0.8	87.8	-0.3	88.9	1.3	89.3	0.4	88.9	-0.4	88.9	0.0
1981	89.3	0.4	89.8	0.6	91.4	1.8	93.2	2.0	93.6	0.4	93.4	-0.2	93.4	0.0	92.5	-1.0	91.8	-0.8	93.0	1.3	92.6	-0.4	93.3	0.8
1982	93.1	-0.2	95.3	2.4	96.2	0.9	94.9	-1.4	95.5	0.6	94.9	-0.6	97.7	3.0	98.1	0.4	98.2	0.1	100.1	1.9	100.0	-0.1	100.0	0.0
1983	101.5	1.5	101.9	0.4	100.9	-1.0	100.6	-0.3	100.2	-0.4	100.9	0.7	101.2	0.3	101.8	0.6	100.8	-1.0	101.7	0.9	101.4	-0.3	101.2	-0.2
1984	101.6	0.4	101.4	-0.2	101.2	-0.2	102.2	1.0	100.2	-2.0	101.1	0.9	101.8	0.7	103.1	1.3	103.3	0.2	102.5	-0.8	101.8	-0.7	101.7	-0.1
1985	104.0	2.3	107.0	2.9	106.7	-0.3	106.3	-0.4	106.1	-0.2	105.6	-0.5	106.9	1.2	105.8	-1.0	108.5	2.6	107.0	-1.4	107.5	0.5	107.4	-0.1
1986	108.1	0.7	108.3	0.2	109.7	1.3	107.5	-2.0	106.9	-0.6	107.4	0.5	107.0	-0.4	108.6	1.5	111.1	2.3	108.1	-2.7	109.7	1.5	110.5	0.7
1987	-		110.1	-0.4	-		112.3	2.0	-		110.0	-2.0	-		113.1	2.8	-		113.6	0.4	-		114.3	0.6
1988	-		112.7	-1.4	-		113.2	0.4	-		114.1	0.8	-		115.2	1.0	-		115.8	0.5	-		118.0	1.9
1989	-		118.8	0.7	-		119.9	0.9	-		119.5	-0.3	-		119.8	0.3	-		122.5	2.3	-		124.1	1.3
1990	-		128.2	3.3	-		127.7	-0.4	-		126.8	-0.7	-		126.8	0.0	-		129.6	2.2	-		131.6	1.5
1991	-		133.0	1.1	-		135.0	1.5	-		134.6	-0.3	-		134.3	-0.2	-		129.6	-3.5	-		129.2	-0.3
1992	-		130.5	1.0	-		130.3	-0.2	-		131.0	0.5	-		130.2	-0.6	-		131.5	1.0	-		131.4	-0.1
1993	-		134.0	2.0	-		136.2	1.6	-		137.5	1.0	-		138.6	0.8	-		140.4	1.3	-		142.0	1.1

Source: U.S. Department of Labor, Bureau of Labor Statistics, Division of Consumer Prices and Price Indexes. - indicates no data collected for period.

Detroit, MI
Consumer Price Index - Urban Wage Earners
Base 1982-1984 = 100
Entertainment

For 1976-1993. Columns headed % show percentile change in the index from the previous period for which an index is available.

Year	Jan Index	%	Feb Index	%	Mar Index	%	Apr Index	%	May Index	%	Jun Index	%	Jul Index	%	Aug Index	%	Sep Index	%	Oct Index	%	Nov Index	%	Dec Index	%
1976	75.6	-	75.8	0.3	76.3	0.7	77.0	0.9	77.1	0.1	76.5	-0.8	76.7	0.3	76.5	-0.3	77.8	1.7	77.9	0.1	78.0	0.1	78.4	0.5
1977	78.4	0.0	78.5	0.1	78.6	0.1	78.5	-0.1	78.8	0.4	78.8	0.0	79.0	0.3	79.3	0.4	80.2	1.1	80.0	-0.2	80.4	0.5	81.0	0.7
1978	81.1	0.1	81.6	0.6	82.2	0.7	84.0	2.2	83.4	-0.7	82.3	-1.3	82.8	0.6	83.0	0.2	83.2	0.2	83.3	0.1	80.4	0.5	81.0	0.7
1979	85.7	0.5	86.1	0.5	84.7	-1.6	86.7	2.4	87.6	1.0	88.1	0.6	87.8	-0.3	86.3	-1.7	84.6	-2.0	84.9	0.4	85.6	0.8	84.6	-1.2
1980	86.9	2.7	88.6	2.0	91.0	2.7	91.5	0.5	91.5	0.0	92.4	1.0	92.7	0.3	91.9	-0.9	91.8	-0.1	92.3	0.5	92.0	-0.3	88.6	-3.7
1981	88.9	0.3	89.4	0.6	91.6	2.5	93.7	2.3	94.1	0.4	93.6	-0.5	94.1	0.5	93.3	-0.9	93.1	-0.2	93.4	0.3	93.2	-0.2	93.4	0.2
1982	93.2	-0.2	95.3	2.3	96.2	0.9	95.2	-1.0	95.8	0.6	95.4	-0.4	98.2	2.9	98.5	0.3	98.6	0.1	100.3	1.7	100.3	0.0	100.4	0.1
1983	101.7	1.3	102.1	0.4	100.7	-1.4	100.3	-0.4	100.0	-0.3	100.7	0.7	101.4	0.7	101.8	0.4	100.8	-1.0	101.5	0.7	101.1	-0.4	101.1	0.0
1984	101.5	0.4	101.3	-0.2	101.3	0.0	102.2	0.9	100.1	-2.1	100.7	0.6	101.5	0.8	102.8	1.3	103.0	0.2	102.3	-0.7	101.7	-0.6	101.4	-0.3
1985	103.5	2.1	106.9	3.3	106.8	-0.1	106.3	-0.5	105.7	-0.6	105.0	-0.7	106.4	1.3	105.4	-0.9	108.9	3.3	107.6	-1.2	108.1	0.5	107.9	-0.2
1986	108.7	0.7	108.8	0.1	110.3	1.4	108.0	-2.1	107.5	-0.5	107.9	0.4	107.2	-0.6	109.2	1.9	113.1	3.6	108.9	-3.7	110.3	1.3	111.3	0.9
1987	-	-	110.9	-0.4	-	-	113.3	2.2	-	-	110.6	-2.4	-	-	114.0	3.1	-	-	114.5	0.4	-	-	115.2	0.6
1988	-	-	113.8	-1.2	-	-	114.3	0.4	-	-	114.5	0.2	-	-	115.9	1.2	-	-	116.6	0.6	-	-	119.0	2.1
1989	-	-	119.9	0.8	-	-	121.1	1.0	-	-	120.5	-0.5	-	-	120.8	0.2	-	-	123.3	2.1	-	-	124.4	0.9
1990	-	-	129.0	3.7	-	-	128.3	-0.5	-	-	127.5	-0.6	-	-	127.4	-0.1	-	-	130.5	2.4	-	-	132.2	1.3
1991	-	-	133.8	1.2	-	-	136.1	1.7	-	-	135.5	-0.4	-	-	135.0	-0.4	-	-	129.9	-3.8	-	-	129.4	-0.4
1992	-	-	130.6	0.9	-	-	130.5	-0.1	-	-	131.3	0.6	-	-	130.1	-0.9	-	-	131.5	1.1	-	-	131.4	-0.1
1993	-	-	133.9	1.9	-	-	136.1	1.6	-	-	138.0	1.4	-	-	139.0	0.7	-	-	141.0	1.4	-	-	142.4	1.0

Source: U.S. Department of Labor, Bureau of Labor Statistics, Division of Consumer Prices and Price Indexes. - indicates no data collected for period.

Detroit, MI
Consumer Price Index - All Urban Consumers
Base 1982-1984 = 100
Other Goods and Services

For 1976-1993. Columns headed % show percentile change in the index from the previous period for which an index is available.

Year	Jan Index	%	Feb Index	%	Mar Index	%	Apr Index	%	May Index	%	Jun Index	%	Jul Index	%	Aug Index	%	Sep Index	%	Oct Index	%	Nov Index	%	Dec Index	%
1976	56.5	-	56.5	0.0	56.7	0.4	57.1	0.7	57.2	0.2	57.3	0.2	57.3	0.0	57.7	0.7	57.8	0.2	58.4	1.0	58.7	0.5	58.8	0.2
1977	59.2	0.7	59.4	0.3	59.6	0.3	60.8	2.0	60.9	0.2	60.9	0.0	61.4	0.8	61.5	0.2	62.3	1.3	63.2	1.4	63.4	0.3	63.5	0.2
1978	63.5	0.0	64.0	0.8	64.1	0.2	64.4	0.5	64.9	0.8	65.5	0.9	66.3	1.2	66.0	-0.5	67.5	2.3	67.7	0.3	67.7	0.0	67.7	0.0
1979	68.6	1.3	68.8	0.3	69.2	0.6	69.2	0.0	69.2	0.0	69.2	0.0	69.7	0.7	70.5	1.1	71.8	1.8	71.9	0.1	71.7	-0.3	71.9	0.3
1980	72.7	1.1	73.2	0.7	73.3	0.1	73.5	0.3	74.1	0.8	74.5	0.5	74.7	0.3	75.3	0.8	77.5	2.9	77.1	-0.5	77.5	0.5	77.7	0.3
1981	77.9	0.3	79.4	1.9	80.0	0.8	80.2	0.2	80.7	0.6	80.9	0.2	81.3	0.5	81.3	0.0	84.9	4.4	85.0	0.1	85.0	0.0	85.3	0.4
1982	85.6	0.4	86.6	1.2	87.4	0.9	87.6	0.2	90.9	3.8	91.0	0.1	91.5	0.5	91.4	-0.1	96.0	5.0	97.2	1.2	97.6	0.4	98.7	1.1
1983	100.4	1.7	100.1	-0.3	100.5	0.4	100.9	0.4	101.4	0.5	101.5	0.1	101.9	0.4	101.5	-0.4	103.6	2.1	103.6	0.0	104.1	0.5	104.5	0.4
1984	105.7	1.1	105.1	-0.6	104.9	-0.2	105.1	0.2	105.0	-0.1	105.0	0.0	105.8	0.8	106.0	0.2	108.3	2.2	108.1	-0.2	107.7	-0.4	107.8	0.1
1985	109.3	1.4	109.6	0.3	109.4	-0.2	109.8	0.4	110.5	0.6	110.8	0.3	111.8	0.9	112.0	0.2	114.3	2.1	114.4	0.1	114.0	-0.3	113.7	-0.3
1986	114.2	0.4	112.5	-1.5	112.4	-0.1	112.4	0.0	112.8	0.4	112.7	-0.1	114.4	1.5	115.6	1.0	116.6	0.9	116.6	0.0	117.6	0.9	117.3	-0.3
1987	-		117.5	0.2	-		118.2	0.6	-		119.2	0.8	-		119.7	0.4	-		124.7	4.2	-		125.0	0.2
1988	-		128.3	2.6	-		127.8	-0.4	-		128.3	0.4	-		129.8	1.2	-		134.1	3.3	-		134.4	0.2
1989	-		135.4	0.7	-		135.5	0.1	-		137.4	1.4	-		137.6	0.1	-		141.6	2.9	-		142.0	0.3
1990	-		144.0	1.4	-		143.9	-0.1	-		146.5	1.8	-		146.6	0.1	-		152.7	4.2	-		154.3	1.0
1991	-		156.2	1.2	-		157.3	0.7	-		158.3	0.6	-		159.6	0.8	-		168.3	5.5	-		167.9	-0.2
1992	-		168.8	0.5	-		168.8	0.0	-		170.4	0.9	-		175.8	3.2	-		181.8	3.4	-		180.6	-0.7
1993	-		183.7	1.7	-		183.7	0.0	-		184.1	0.2	-		181.8	-1.2	-		183.8	1.1	-		184.9	0.6

Source: U.S. Department of Labor, Bureau of Labor Statistics, Division of Consumer Prices and Price Indexes. - indicates no data collected for period.

Detroit, MI
Consumer Price Index - Urban Wage Earners
Base 1982-1984 = 100
Other Goods and Services

For 1976-1993. Columns headed % show percentile change in the index from the previous period for which an index is available.

Year	Jan Index	%	Feb Index	%	Mar Index	%	Apr Index	%	May Index	%	Jun Index	%	Jul Index	%	Aug Index	%	Sep Index	%	Oct Index	%	Nov Index	%	Dec Index	%
1976	54.5	-	54.5	0.0	54.7	0.4	55.0	0.5	55.1	0.2	55.2	0.2	55.3	0.2	55.6	0.5	55.8	0.4	56.3	0.9	56.6	0.5	56.7	0.2
1977	57.1	0.7	57.3	0.4	57.5	0.3	58.6	1.9	58.7	0.2	58.7	0.0	59.2	0.9	59.3	0.2	60.1	1.3	61.0	1.5	61.2	0.3	61.2	0.0
1978	61.5	0.5	61.8	0.5	61.4	-0.6	61.8	0.7	61.9	0.2	62.4	0.8	63.3	1.4	63.0	-0.5	64.6	2.5	64.5	-0.2	64.8	0.5	65.0	0.3
1979	66.1	1.7	66.4	0.5	66.3	-0.2	66.1	-0.3	66.1	0.0	66.1	0.0	66.5	0.6	67.7	1.8	69.0	1.9	69.2	0.3	69.0	-0.3	69.6	0.9
1980	71.2	2.3	72.0	1.1	71.8	-0.3	72.0	0.3	72.7	1.0	73.5	1.1	73.2	-0.4	73.9	1.0	75.1	1.6	75.0	-0.1	75.7	0.9	75.9	0.3
1981	76.1	0.3	78.0	2.5	77.9	-0.1	78.5	0.8	79.4	1.1	79.5	0.1	80.3	1.0	80.4	0.1	83.3	3.6	83.9	0.7	84.4	0.6	84.8	0.5
1982	85.2	0.5	86.2	1.2	87.0	0.9	87.2	0.2	91.2	4.6	91.2	0.0	91.7	0.5	91.6	-0.1	95.6	4.4	97.0	1.5	97.4	0.4	98.9	1.5
1983	100.6	1.7	100.3	-0.3	100.8	0.5	101.1	0.3	101.5	0.4	101.7	0.2	102.3	0.6	101.8	-0.5	103.5	1.7	103.5	0.0	104.0	0.5	104.4	0.4
1984	105.8	1.3	105.2	-0.6	105.0	-0.2	105.1	0.1	105.1	0.0	105.1	0.0	105.9	0.8	106.2	0.3	108.1	1.8	107.8	-0.3	107.4	-0.4	107.5	0.1
1985	109.3	1.7	109.5	0.2	109.3	-0.2	109.7	0.4	110.5	0.7	110.8	0.3	111.9	1.0	112.1	0.2	113.9	1.6	114.0	0.1	113.6	-0.4	113.2	-0.4
1986	113.8	0.5	111.9	-1.7	111.8	-0.1	111.8	0.0	112.2	0.4	112.2	0.0	114.1	1.7	115.4	1.1	115.9	0.4	115.9	0.0	117.0	0.9	116.7	-0.3
1987	-	-	116.9	0.2	-	-	118.0	0.9	-	-	119.3	1.1	-	-	120.0	0.6	-	-	123.7	3.1	-	-	124.1	0.3
1988	-	-	128.7	3.7	-	-	128.0	-0.5	-	-	128.5	0.4	-	-	130.7	1.7	-	-	133.2	1.9	-	-	133.7	0.4
1989	-	-	134.8	0.8	-	-	135.0	0.1	-	-	137.7	2.0	-	-	138.0	0.2	-	-	140.2	1.6	-	-	140.7	0.4
1990	-	-	143.5	2.0	-	-	143.6	0.1	-	-	147.1	2.4	-	-	147.2	0.1	-	-	151.6	3.0	-	-	154.0	1.6
1991	-	-	156.4	1.6	-	-	158.0	1.0	-	-	159.6	1.0	-	-	161.3	1.1	-	-	164.9	2.2	-	-	164.5	-0.2
1992	-	-	165.7	0.7	-	-	165.7	0.0	-	-	167.9	1.3	-	-	172.6	2.8	-	-	176.0	2.0	-	-	174.5	-1.0
1993	-	-	178.6	2.5	-	-	178.6	0.0	-	-	179.2	0.3	-	-	174.5	-2.6	-	-	171.2	-1.9	-	-	172.6	0.8

Source: U.S. Department of Labor, Bureau of Labor Statistics, Division of Consumer Prices and Price Indexes. - indicates no data collected for period.

Honolulu, HI
Consumer Price Index - All Urban Consumers
Base 1982-1984 = 100
Annual Averages

For 1963-1993. Columns headed % show percentile change in the index from the previous period for which an index is available.

Year	All Items		Food & Beverage		Housing		Apparel & Upkeep		Trans-portation		Medical Care		Entertain-ment		Other Goods & Services	
	Index	%	Index	%	Index	%	Index	%	Index	%	Index	%	Index	%	Index	%
1963	-	-	-	-	-	-	-	-	-	-	-	-	-	-	-	-
1964	33.7	-	-	-	-	-	46.7	-	37.7	-	25.1	-	-	-	-	-
1965	34.4	2.1	-	-	-	-	47.1	0.9	37.7	0.0	25.8	2.8	-	-	-	-
1966	35.3	2.6	-	-	-	-	47.9	1.7	37.8	0.3	26.6	3.1	-	-	-	-
1967	36.3	2.8	-	-	-	-	48.8	1.9	38.7	2.4	28.3	6.4	-	-	-	-
1968	37.7	3.9	-	-	-	-	50.7	3.9	40.1	3.6	29.9	5.7	-	-	-	-
1969	39.4	4.5	-	-	-	-	53.4	5.3	41.5	3.5	32.0	7.0	-	-	-	-
1970	41.5	5.3	-	-	-	-	56.2	5.2	43.4	4.6	33.5	4.7	-	-	-	-
1971	43.2	4.1	-	-	-	-	57.4	2.1	46.7	7.6	35.2	5.1	-	-	-	-
1972	44.6	3.2	-	-	-	-	58.9	2.6	47.6	1.9	36.0	2.3	-	-	-	-
1973	46.6	4.5	-	-	-	-	60.6	2.9	48.0	0.8	37.7	4.7	-	-	-	-
1974	51.5	10.5	-	-	-	-	65.1	7.4	52.3	9.0	41.5	10.1	-	-	-	-
1975	56.3	9.3	-	-	-	-	69.0	6.0	56.8	8.6	46.6	12.3	63.6	-	53.8	-
1976	59.1	5.0	59.7	-	59.2	-	71.6	3.8	59.5	4.8	51.5	10.5	66.3	4.2	57.5	6.9
1977	62.1	5.1	62.8	5.2	61.6	4.1	74.3	3.8	61.8	3.9	57.4	11.5	69.0	4.1	61.4	6.8
1978	66.9	7.7	69.0	9.9	66.0	7.1	78.8	6.1	66.0	6.8	62.5	8.9	72.8	5.5	66.5	8.3
1979	74.3	11.1	77.7	12.6	74.0	12.1	83.9	6.5	73.4	11.2	67.5	8.0	78.2	7.4	73.3	10.2
1980	83.0	11.7	84.2	8.4	83.2	12.4	89.8	7.0	86.6	18.0	73.1	8.3	87.2	11.5	81.5	11.2
1981	91.7	10.5	92.6	10.0	92.3	10.9	94.5	5.2	95.7	10.5	81.8	11.9	95.7	9.7	92.0	12.9
1982	97.2	6.0	96.9	4.6	98.0	6.2	98.4	4.1	99.0	3.4	91.6	12.0	100.0	4.5	101.4	10.2
1983	99.3	2.2	99.5	2.7	98.9	0.9	101.4	3.0	98.2	-0.8	101.1	10.4	104.3	4.3	106.6	5.1
1984	103.5	4.2	103.6	4.1	103.1	4.2	100.2	-1.2	102.9	4.8	107.3	6.1	111.9	7.3	112.5	5.5
1985	106.8	3.2	107.8	4.1	106.0	2.8	99.6	-0.6	104.9	1.9	113.2	5.5	113.2	1.2	119.6	6.3
1986	109.4	2.4	110.0	2.0	108.4	2.3	99.8	0.2	105.2	0.3	122.3	8.0	118.6	4.8	129.7	8.4
1987	114.9	5.0	114.1	3.7	115.0	6.1	102.5	2.7	109.7	4.3	127.9	4.6	122.9	3.6	137.1	5.7
1988	121.7	5.9	120.3	5.4	123.0	7.0	106.8	4.2	116.1	5.8	132.5	3.6	124.3	1.1	146.1	6.6
1989	128.7	5.8	128.1	6.5	131.1	6.6	104.3	-2.3	123.9	6.7	139.3	5.1	128.4	3.3	160.4	9.8
1990	138.1	7.3	137.8	7.6	141.5	7.9	107.0	2.6	131.1	5.8	154.2	10.7	134.3	4.6	175.7	9.5
1991	148.0	7.2	145.9	5.9	152.8	8.0	110.5	3.3	139.3	6.3	171.3	11.1	136.3	1.5	189.0	7.6
1992	155.1	4.8	148.5	1.8	161.7	5.8	114.2	3.3	147.4	5.8	182.6	6.6	138.3	1.5	200.1	5.9
1993	160.1	3.2	152.9	3.0	166.5	3.0	116.5	2.0	150.5	2.1	197.4	8.1				

Source: U.S. Department of Labor, Bureau of Labor Statistics, Division of Consumer Prices and Price Indexes. - indicates no data collected for period.

Honolulu, HI
Consumer Price Index - Urban Wage Earners
Base 1982-1984 = 100
Annual Averages

For 1963-1993. Columns headed % show percentile change in the index from the previous period for which an index is available.

Year	All Items		Food & Beverage		Housing		Apparel & Upkeep		Trans- portation		Medical Care		Entertain- ment		Other Goods & Services	
	Index	%	Index	%	Index	%	Index	%	Index	%	Index	%	Index	%	Index	%
1963	-	-	-	-	-	-	-	-	-	-	-	-	-	-	-	-
1964	33.3	-	-	-	-	-	45.2	-	37.8	-	24.6	-	-	-	-	-
1965	33.9	1.8	-	-	-	-	45.6	0.9	37.7	-0.3	25.3	2.8	-	-	-	-
1966	34.8	2.7	-	-	-	-	46.3	1.5	37.8	0.3	26.1	3.2	-	-	-	-
1967	35.8	2.9	-	-	-	-	47.2	1.9	38.7	2.4	27.7	6.1	-	-	-	-
1968	37.2	3.9	-	-	-	-	49.0	3.8	40.2	3.9	29.3	5.8	-	-	-	-
1969	38.8	4.3	-	-	-	-	51.7	5.5	41.5	3.2	31.3	6.8	-	-	-	-
1970	40.9	5.4	-	-	-	-	54.4	5.2	43.5	4.8	32.8	4.8	-	-	-	-
1971	42.6	4.2	-	-	-	-	55.6	2.2	46.7	7.4	34.5	5.2	-	-	-	-
1972	44.0	3.3	-	-	-	-	56.9	2.3	47.6	1.9	35.3	2.3	-	-	-	-
1973	45.9	4.3	-	-	-	-	58.6	3.0	48.0	0.8	36.9	4.5	-	-	-	-
1974	50.8	10.7	-	-	-	-	63.0	7.5	52.3	9.0	40.7	10.3	-	-	-	-
1975	55.5	9.3	-	-	-	-	66.7	5.9	56.9	8.8	45.6	12.0	-	-	-	-
1976	58.3	5.0	58.8	-	58.1	-	69.3	3.9	59.5	4.6	50.4	10.5	60.7	-	54.8	-
1977	61.2	5.0	61.9	5.3	60.4	4.0	71.9	3.8	61.9	4.0	56.2	11.5	63.2	4.1	58.5	6.8
1978	65.9	7.7	68.0	9.9	64.6	7.0	75.3	4.7	65.9	6.5	61.8	10.0	67.4	6.6	61.9	5.8
1979	73.2	11.1	76.4	12.4	72.2	11.8	79.9	6.1	73.5	11.5	66.3	7.3	73.5	9.1	66.9	8.1
1980	81.9	11.9	83.5	9.3	80.4	11.4	91.4	14.4	86.6	17.8	72.3	9.0	79.9	8.7	72.8	8.8
1981	90.5	10.5	92.3	10.5	89.0	10.7	95.3	4.3	96.2	11.1	81.9	13.3	87.4	9.4	81.1	11.4
1982	96.0	6.1	96.8	4.9	94.9	6.6	98.3	3.1	99.1	3.0	92.0	12.3	95.4	9.2	91.6	12.9
1983	99.8	4.0	99.5	2.8	100.1	5.5	101.4	3.2	98.1	-1.0	101.1	9.9	100.0	4.8	101.7	11.0
1984	104.3	4.5	103.7	4.2	104.9	4.8	100.3	-1.1	102.8	4.8	106.9	5.7	104.6	4.6	106.6	4.8
1985	107.9	3.5	108.3	4.4	108.6	3.5	99.4	-0.9	104.7	1.8	112.6	5.3	111.9	7.0	112.5	5.5
1986	110.3	2.2	110.8	2.3	111.0	2.2	100.1	0.7	104.7	0.0	121.1	7.5	113.1	1.1	119.1	5.9
1987	115.9	5.1	115.3	4.1	117.4	5.8	103.7	3.6	109.2	4.3	126.7	4.6	119.3	5.5	128.7	8.1
1988	122.8	6.0	121.7	5.6	125.5	6.9	108.2	4.3	115.7	6.0	131.4	3.7	123.6	3.6	136.4	6.0
1989	129.7	5.6	129.2	6.2	133.7	6.5	105.2	-2.8	123.7	6.9	138.3	5.3	123.5	-0.1	146.3	7.3
1990	138.9	7.1	138.6	7.3	144.3	7.9	108.1	2.8	130.2	5.3	153.3	10.8	127.9	3.6	161.9	10.7
1991	148.9	7.2	146.5	5.7	155.7	7.9	111.9	3.5	138.6	6.5	170.3	11.1	134.1	4.8	179.1	10.6
1992	155.9	4.7	149.5	2.0	164.1	5.4	115.6	3.3	146.7	5.8	182.2	7.0	136.5	1.8	193.7	8.2
1993	160.7	3.1	153.8	2.9	169.1	3.0	118.5	2.5	148.9	1.5	197.5	8.4	138.7	1.6	204.5	5.6

Source: U.S. Department of Labor, Bureau of Labor Statistics, Division of Consumer Prices and Price Indexes. - indicates no data collected for period.

Honolulu, HI

Consumer Price Index - All Urban Consumers
Base 1982-1984 = 100
All Items

For 1963-1993. Columns headed % show percentile change in the index from the previous period for which an index is available.

Year	Jan		Feb		Mar		Apr		May		Jun		Jul		Aug		Sep		Oct		Nov		Dec	
	Index	%	Index	%	Index	%	Index	%	Index	%	Index	%	Index	%	Index	%	Index	%	Index	%	Index	%	Index	%
1963	-	-	-	-	-	-	-	-	-	-	-	-	-	-	-	-	-	-	-	-	-	-	33.7	-
1964	-	-	-	-	33.9	0.6	-	-	-	-	33.6	-0.9	-	-	-	-	33.7	0.3	-	-	-	-	34.0	0.9
1965	-	-	-	-	34.2	0.6	-	-	-	-	34.2	0.0	-	-	-	-	34.4	0.6	-	-	-	-	34.9	1.5
1966	-	-	-	-	35.1	0.6	-	-	-	-	35.2	0.3	-	-	-	-	35.6	1.1	-	-	-	-	35.9	0.8
1967	-	-	-	-	35.9	0.0	-	-	-	-	36.2	0.8	-	-	-	-	36.5	0.8	-	-	-	-	37.0	1.4
1968	-	-	-	-	37.3	0.8	-	-	-	-	37.6	0.8	-	-	-	-	38.0	1.1	-	-	-	-	38.4	1.1
1969	-	-	-	-	38.9	1.3	-	-	-	-	39.3	1.0	-	-	-	-	39.8	1.3	-	-	-	-	40.3	1.3
1970	-	-	-	-	41.1	2.0	-	-	-	-	41.6	1.2	-	-	-	-	41.7	0.2	-	-	-	-	42.0	0.7
1971	-	-	-	-	42.4	1.0	-	-	-	-	43.0	1.4	-	-	-	-	44.0	2.3	-	-	-	-	44.0	0.0
1972	-	-	-	-	44.5	1.1	-	-	-	-	44.4	-0.2	-	-	-	-	44.7	0.7	-	-	-	-	45.2	1.1
1973	-	-	-	-	45.8	1.3	-	-	-	-	46.3	1.1	-	-	-	-	47.1	1.7	-	-	-	-	48.2	2.3
1974	-	-	-	-	50.0	3.7	-	-	-	-	51.3	2.6	-	-	-	-	52.9	3.1	-	-	-	-	53.9	1.9
1975	-	-	-	-	55.2	2.4	-	-	-	-	56.0	1.4	-	-	-	-	57.2	2.1	-	-	-	-	58.0	1.4
1976	-	-	-	-	58.5	0.9	-	-	-	-	59.0	0.9	-	-	-	-	59.6	1.0	-	-	-	-	60.1	0.8
1977	-	-	-	-	61.1	1.7	-	-	-	-	61.9	1.3	-	-	-	-	63.0	1.8	-	-	-	-	63.5	0.8
1978	-	-	64.7	1.9	-	-	65.9	1.9	-	-	66.8	1.4	-	-	67.4	0.9	-	-	68.6	1.8	-	-	69.5	1.3
1979	-	-	71.3	2.6	-	-	72.9	2.2	-	-	74.2	1.8	-	-	75.3	1.5	-	-	76.5	1.6	-	-	78.0	2.0
1980	-	-	80.2	2.8	-	-	82.6	3.0	-	-	82.6	0.0	-	-	83.6	1.2	-	-	85.2	1.9	-	-	85.8	0.7
1981	-	-	88.4	3.0	-	-	90.8	2.7	-	-	91.8	1.1	-	-	93.2	1.5	-	-	94.2	1.1	-	-	93.8	-0.4
1982	-	-	95.2	1.5	-	-	95.6	0.4	-	-	97.7	2.2	-	-	97.9	0.2	-	-	100.0	2.1	-	-	98.0	-2.0
1983	-	-	98.2	0.2	-	-	99.1	0.9	-	-	98.6	-0.5	-	-	99.3	0.7	-	-	100.4	1.1	-	-	101.1	0.7
1984	-	-	102.0	0.9	-	-	102.9	0.9	-	-	103.4	0.5	-	-	103.9	0.5	-	-	104.4	0.5	-	-	105.3	0.9
1985	-	-	106.3	0.9	-	-	106.3	0.0	-	-	106.6	0.3	-	-	106.9	0.3	-	-	107.4	0.5	-	-	108.4	0.9
1986	-	-	109.4	0.9	-	-	108.6	-0.7	-	-	108.7	0.1	-	-	109.5	0.7	-	-	109.8	0.3	-	-	110.9	1.0
1987	-	-	-	-	-	-	-	-	-	-	113.3	2.2	-	-	-	-	-	-	-	-	-	-	116.5	2.8
1988	-	-	-	-	-	-	-	-	-	-	120.1	3.1	-	-	-	-	-	-	-	-	-	-	123.4	2.7
1989	-	-	-	-	-	-	-	-	-	-	126.4	2.4	-	-	-	-	-	-	-	-	-	-	131.1	3.7
1990	-	-	-	-	-	-	-	-	-	-	135.5	3.4	-	-	-	-	-	-	-	-	-	-	140.8	3.9
1991	-	-	-	-	-	-	-	-	-	-	146.8	4.3	-	-	-	-	-	-	-	-	-	-	149.1	1.6
1992	-	-	-	-	-	-	-	-	-	-	153.9	3.2	-	-	-	-	-	-	-	-	-	-	156.4	1.6
1993	-	-	-	-	-	-	-	-	-	-	158.6	1.4	-	-	-	-	-	-	-	-	-	-	-	-

Source: U.S. Department of Labor, Bureau of Labor Statistics, Division of Consumer Prices and Price Indexes. - indicates no data collected for period.

Honolulu, HI
Consumer Price Index - Urban Wage Earners
Base 1982-1984 = 100
All Items

For 1963-1993. Columns headed % show percentile change in the index from the previous period for which an index is available.

Year	Jan Index	%	Feb Index	%	Mar Index	%	Apr Index	%	May Index	%	Jun Index	%	Jul Index	%	Aug Index	%	Sep Index	%	Oct Index	%	Nov Index	%	Dec Index	%
1963	-	-	-	-	-	-	-	-	-	-	-	-	-	-	-	-	-	-	-	-	-	-	33.2	-
1964	-	-	-	-	33.4	0.6	-	-	-	-	33.1	-0.9	-	-	-	-	33.3	0.6	-	-	-	-	33.5	0.6
1965	-	-	-	-	33.7	0.6	-	-	-	-	33.7	0.0	-	-	-	-	33.9	0.6	-	-	-	-	34.4	1.5
1966	-	-	-	-	34.6	0.6	-	-	-	-	34.6	0.0	-	-	-	-	35.0	1.2	-	-	-	-	35.4	1.1
1967	-	-	-	-	35.4	0.0	-	-	-	-	35.7	0.8	-	-	-	-	36.0	0.8	-	-	-	-	36.4	1.1
1968	-	-	-	-	36.8	1.1	-	-	-	-	37.0	0.5	-	-	-	-	37.4	1.1	-	-	-	-	37.8	1.1
1969	-	-	-	-	38.4	1.6	-	-	-	-	38.7	0.8	-	-	-	-	39.2	1.3	-	-	-	-	39.7	1.3
1970	-	-	-	-	40.5	2.0	-	-	-	-	40.9	1.0	-	-	-	-	41.1	0.5	-	-	-	-	41.4	0.7
1971	-	-	-	-	41.8	1.0	-	-	-	-	42.4	1.4	-	-	-	-	43.4	2.4	-	-	-	-	43.3	-0.2
1972	-	-	-	-	43.8	1.2	-	-	-	-	43.7	-0.2	-	-	-	-	44.1	0.9	-	-	-	-	44.5	0.9
1973	-	-	-	-	45.1	1.3	-	-	-	-	45.6	1.1	-	-	-	-	46.4	1.8	-	-	-	-	47.5	2.4
1974	-	-	-	-	49.3	3.8	-	-	-	-	50.5	2.4	-	-	-	-	52.1	3.2	-	-	-	-	53.2	2.1
1975	-	-	-	-	54.4	2.3	-	-	-	-	55.2	1.5	-	-	-	-	56.4	2.2	-	-	-	-	57.2	1.4
1976	-	-	-	-	57.7	0.9	-	-	-	-	58.1	0.7	-	-	-	-	58.7	1.0	-	-	-	-	59.2	0.9
1977	-	-	-	-	60.2	1.7	-	-	-	-	61.0	1.3	-	-	-	-	62.1	1.8	-	-	-	-	62.6	0.8
1978	-	-	63.5	1.4	-	-	64.9	2.2	-	-	65.9	1.5	-	-	66.6	1.1	-	-	67.5	1.4	-	-	68.4	1.3
1979	-	-	70.2	2.6	-	-	71.6	2.0	-	-	72.9	1.8	-	-	74.2	1.8	-	-	75.6	1.9	-	-	77.1	2.0
1980	-	-	79.2	2.7	-	-	81.8	3.3	-	-	81.6	-0.2	-	-	82.1	0.6	-	-	83.6	1.8	-	-	84.8	1.4
1981	-	-	87.2	2.8	-	-	89.6	2.8	-	-	90.8	1.3	-	-	91.8	1.1	-	-	92.7	1.0	-	-	92.8	0.1
1982	-	-	94.1	1.4	-	-	94.6	0.5	-	-	96.3	1.8	-	-	96.5	0.2	-	-	98.3	1.9	-	-	97.0	-1.3
1983	-	-	98.4	1.4	-	-	99.1	0.7	-	-	97.9	-1.2	-	-	99.6	1.7	-	-	102.3	2.7	-	-	103.2	0.9
1984	-	-	101.8	-1.4	-	-	103.4	1.6	-	-	104.1	0.7	-	-	105.1	1.0	-	-	105.4	0.3	-	-	106.5	1.0
1985	-	-	107.5	0.9	-	-	107.4	-0.1	-	-	107.5	0.1	-	-	107.8	0.3	-	-	108.4	0.6	-	-	109.5	1.0
1986	-	-	110.4	0.8	-	-	109.5	-0.8	-	-	109.7	0.2	-	-	110.4	0.6	-	-	110.5	0.1	-	-	111.9	1.3
1987	-	-	-	-	-	-	-	-	-	-	114.3	2.1	-	-	-	-	-	-	-	-	-	-	117.6	2.9
1988	-	-	-	-	-	-	-	-	-	-	121.1	3.0	-	-	-	-	-	-	-	-	-	-	124.5	2.8
1989	-	-	-	-	-	-	-	-	-	-	127.4	2.3	-	-	-	-	-	-	-	-	-	-	132.0	3.6
1990	-	-	-	-	-	-	-	-	-	-	136.3	3.3	-	-	-	-	-	-	-	-	-	-	141.6	3.9
1991	-	-	-	-	-	-	-	-	-	-	147.7	4.3	-	-	-	-	-	-	-	-	-	-	150.1	1.6
1992	-	-	-	-	-	-	-	-	-	-	154.6	3.0	-	-	-	-	-	-	-	-	-	-	157.2	1.7
1993	-	-	-	-	-	-	-	-	-	-	159.4	1.4	-	-	-	-	-	-	-	-	-	-	-	-

Source: U.S. Department of Labor, Bureau of Labor Statistics, Division of Consumer Prices and Price Indexes. - indicates no data collected for period.

Honolulu, HI
Consumer Price Index - All Urban Consumers
Base 1982-1984 = 100
Food and Beverages

For 1975-1993. Columns headed % show percentile change in the index from the previous period for which an index is available.

Year	Jan Index	%	Feb Index	%	Mar Index	%	Apr Index	%	May Index	%	Jun Index	%	Jul Index	%	Aug Index	%	Sep Index	%	Oct Index	%	Nov Index	%	Dec Index	%
1975	-	-	-	-	-	-	-	-	-	-	-	-	-	-	-	-	-	-	-	-	-	-	59.4	-
1976	-	-	-	-	59.5	0.2	-	-	-	-	59.6	0.2	-	-	-	-	59.5	-0.2	-	-	-	-	60.5	1.7
1977	-	-	-	-	61.8	2.1	-	-	-	-	62.6	1.3	-	-	-	-	63.8	1.9	-	-	-	-	64.4	0.9
1978	-	-	65.9	2.3	-	-	67.6	2.6	-	-	69.2	2.4	-	-	70.0	1.2	-	-	71.2	1.7	-	-	72.3	1.5
1979	-	-	74.6	3.2	-	-	76.5	2.5	-	-	78.3	2.4	-	-	78.4	0.1	-	-	79.5	1.4	-	-	80.6	1.4
1980	-	-	81.6	1.2	-	-	83.0	1.7	-	-	83.3	0.4	-	-	85.1	2.2	-	-	86.5	1.6	-	-	87.8	1.5
1981	-	-	90.8	3.4	-	-	92.2	1.5	-	-	92.7	0.5	-	-	93.5	0.9	-	-	94.2	0.7	-	-	93.8	-0.4
1982	-	-	96.1	2.5	-	-	96.2	0.1	-	-	96.9	0.7	-	-	97.3	0.4	-	-	97.7	0.4	-	-	98.3	0.6
1983	-	-	98.8	0.5	-	-	99.6	0.8	-	-	99.4	-0.2	-	-	99.8	0.4	-	-	100.0	0.2	-	-	99.6	-0.4
1984	-	-	101.4	1.8	-	-	102.2	0.8	-	-	103.6	1.4	-	-	104.5	0.9	-	-	104.6	0.1	-	-	107.3	2.6
1985	-	-	108.1	0.7	-	-	108.2	0.1	-	-	107.6	-0.6	-	-	107.5	-0.1	-	-	106.9	-0.6	-	-	108.6	1.6
1986	-	-	108.7	0.1	-	-	107.9	-0.7	-	-	110.1	2.0	-	-	109.7	-0.4	-	-	111.7	1.8	-	-	113.0	1.2
1987	-	-	-	-	-	-	-	-	-	-	113.3	0.3	-	-	-	-	-	-	-	-	-	-	115.0	1.5
1988	-	-	-	-	-	-	-	-	-	-	118.9	3.4	-	-	-	-	-	-	-	-	-	-	121.7	2.4
1989	-	-	-	-	-	-	-	-	-	-	125.6	3.2	-	-	-	-	-	-	-	-	-	-	130.6	4.0
1990	-	-	-	-	-	-	-	-	-	-	136.6	4.6	-	-	-	-	-	-	-	-	-	-	139.0	1.8
1991	-	-	-	-	-	-	-	-	-	-	146.0	5.0	-	-	-	-	-	-	-	-	-	-	145.8	-0.1
1992	-	-	-	-	-	-	-	-	-	-	148.0	1.5	-	-	-	-	-	-	-	-	-	-	149.0	0.7
1993	-	-	-	-	-	-	-	-	-	-	153.0	2.7	-	-	-	-	-	-	-	-	-	-	-	-

Source: U.S. Department of Labor, Bureau of Labor Statistics, Division of Consumer Prices and Price Indexes. - indicates no data collected for period.

Honolulu, HI
Consumer Price Index - Urban Wage Earners
Base 1982-1984 = 100
Food and Beverages

For 1975-1993. Columns headed % show percentile change in the index from the previous period for which an index is available.

Year	Jan Index	%	Feb Index	%	Mar Index	%	Apr Index	%	May Index	%	Jun Index	%	Jul Index	%	Aug Index	%	Sep Index	%	Oct Index	%	Nov Index	%	Dec Index	%
1975	-	-	-	-	-	-	-	-	-	-	-	-	-	-	-	-	-	-	-	-	-	-	58.5	-
1976	-	-	-	-	58.7	0.3	-	-	-	-	58.7	0.0	-	-	-	-	58.6	-0.2	-	-	-	-	59.6	1.7
1977	-	-	-	-	60.8	2.0	-	-	-	-	61.7	1.5	-	-	-	-	62.8	1.8	-	-	-	-	63.5	1.1
1978	-	-	64.6	1.7	-	-	66.7	3.3	-	-	68.7	3.0	-	-	69.3	0.9	-	-	69.8	0.7	-	-	70.7	1.3
1979	-	-	74.0	4.7	-	-	75.5	2.0	-	-	76.2	0.9	-	-	76.9	0.9	-	-	78.3	1.8	-	-	79.8	1.9
1980	-	-	80.8	1.3	-	-	82.3	1.9	-	-	82.6	0.4	-	-	84.0	1.7	-	-	85.6	1.9	-	-	87.6	2.3
1981	-	-	90.5	3.3	-	-	91.9	1.5	-	-	92.2	0.3	-	-	93.0	0.9	-	-	93.6	0.6	-	-	94.0	0.4
1982	-	-	96.5	2.7	-	-	96.3	-0.2	-	-	96.7	0.4	-	-	96.9	0.2	-	-	97.4	0.5	-	-	98.2	0.8
1983	-	-	98.8	0.6	-	-	99.6	0.8	-	-	99.3	-0.3	-	-	99.8	0.5	-	-	99.8	0.0	-	-	99.8	0.0
1984	-	-	101.8	2.0	-	-	102.5	0.7	-	-	103.3	0.8	-	-	104.3	1.0	-	-	104.3	0.0	-	-	108.4	3.9
1985	-	-	109.1	0.6	-	-	108.6	-0.5	-	-	107.7	-0.8	-	-	107.9	0.2	-	-	107.3	-0.6	-	-	109.2	1.8
1986	-	-	109.6	0.4	-	-	108.9	-0.6	-	-	111.0	1.9	-	-	110.1	-0.8	-	-	112.5	2.2	-	-	114.1	1.4
1987	-	-	-	-	-	-	-	-	-	-	114.4	0.3	-	-	-	-	-	-	-	-	-	-	116.2	1.6
1988	-	-	-	-	-	-	-	-	-	-	120.2	3.4	-	-	-	-	-	-	-	-	-	-	123.3	2.6
1989	-	-	-	-	-	-	-	-	-	-	126.8	2.8	-	-	-	-	-	-	-	-	-	-	131.5	3.7
1990	-	-	-	-	-	-	-	-	-	-	137.1	4.3	-	-	-	-	-	-	-	-	-	-	140.0	2.1
1991	-	-	-	-	-	-	-	-	-	-	146.6	4.7	-	-	-	-	-	-	-	-	-	-	146.5	-0.1
1992	-	-	-	-	-	-	-	-	-	-	149.0	1.7	-	-	-	-	-	-	-	-	-	-	150.0	0.7
1993	-	-	-	-	-	-	-	-	-	-	154.1	2.7	-	-	-	-	-	-	-	-	-	-	-	-

Source: U.S. Department of Labor, Bureau of Labor Statistics, Division of Consumer Prices and Price Indexes. - indicates no data collected for period.

Honolulu, HI
Consumer Price Index - All Urban Consumers
Base 1982-1984 = 100
Housing

For 1975-1993. Columns headed % show percentile change in the index from the previous period for which an index is available.

Year	Jan Index	%	Feb Index	%	Mar Index	%	Apr Index	%	May Index	%	Jun Index	%	Jul Index	%	Aug Index	%	Sep Index	%	Oct Index	%	Nov Index	%	Dec Index	%
1975	-		-		-	-	-		-		-	-	-	-	-	-	59.8	1.2	-	-	-	-	58.6	-
1976	-	-	-	-	58.6	0.0	-		-		59.1	0.9	-	-	-	-			-	-	-	-	59.7	-0.2
1977	-	-	-	-	60.7	1.7	-	-	-		61.3	1.0	-	-	-	-	62.5	2.0	-	-	-	-	62.8	0.5
1978	-	-	63.7	1.4	-	-	65.0	2.0	-		65.9	1.4	-		66.2	0.5	-	-	67.9	2.6	-	-	68.7	1.2
1979	-	-	70.9	3.2	-	-	72.8	2.7	-		73.9	1.5	-		75.1	1.6	-	-	76.3	1.6	-	-	77.7	1.8
1980	-	-	80.3	3.3	-	-	83.7	4.2	-	-	83.2	-0.6	-		83.2	0.0	-	-	85.3	2.5	-	-	85.7	0.5
1981	-	-	88.3	3.0	-	-	91.8	4.0	-	-	93.0	1.3	-		94.4	1.5	-	-	94.8	0.4	-	-	93.8	-1.1
1982	-	-	95.3	1.6	-	-	95.7	0.4	-	-	99.3	3.8	-		98.7	-0.6	-	-	102.2	3.5	-	-	97.8	-4.3
1983	-	-	98.0	0.2	-	-	99.1	1.1	-	-	97.8	-1.3	-	-	98.2	0.4	-	-	100.0	1.8	-	-	101.7	1.7
1984	-	-	101.7	0.0	-	-	102.9	1.2	-	-	103.0	0.1	-	-	103.1	0.1	-	-	104.1	1.0	-	-	104.2	0.1
1985	-	-	105.6	1.3	-	-	105.4	-0.2	-	-	106.3	0.9	-	-	105.4	-0.8	-	-	106.1	0.7	-	-	108.1	1.9
1986	-	-	108.4	0.3	-	-	108.1	-0.3	-	-	107.2	-0.8	-	-	109.4	2.1	-	-	108.3	-1.0	-	-	109.6	1.2
1987	-	-	-	-	-	-	-	-	-	-	113.4	3.5	-	-	-	-	-	-	-	-	-	-	116.5	2.7
1988	-	-	-	-	-	-	-	-	-	-	121.1	3.9	-	-	-	-	-	-	-	-	-	-	124.9	3.1
1989	-	-	-	-	-	-	-	-	-	-	128.1	2.6	-	-	-	-	-	-	-	-	-	-	134.1	4.7
1990	-	-	-	-	-	-	-	-	-	-	139.0	3.7	-	-	-	-	-	-	-	-	-	-	144.1	3.7
1991	-	-	-	-	-	-	-	-	-	-	151.3	5.0	-	-	-	-	-	-	-	-	-	-	154.3	2.0
1992	-	-	-	-	-	-	-	-	-	-	160.3	3.9	-	-	-	-	-	-	-	-	-	-	163.0	1.7
1993	-	-	-	-	-	-	-	-	-	-	164.1	0.7	-	-	-	-	-	-	-	-	-	-	-	

Source: U.S. Department of Labor, Bureau of Labor Statistics, Division of Consumer Prices and Price Indexes. - indicates no data collected for period.

Honolulu, HI
Consumer Price Index - Urban Wage Earners
Base 1982-1984 = 100
Housing

For 1975-1993. Columns headed % show percentile change in the index from the previous period for which an index is available.

Year	Jan Index	%	Feb Index	%	Mar Index	%	Apr Index	%	May Index	%	Jun Index	%	Jul Index	%	Aug Index	%	Sep Index	%	Oct Index	%	Nov Index	%	Dec Index	%
1975	-	-	-	-	-	-	-	-	-	-	-	-	-	-	-	-	-	-	-	-	-	-	57.4	-
1976	-	-	-	-	57.5	0.2	-	-	-	-	57.9	0.7	-	-	-	-	58.7	1.4	-	-	-	-	58.5	-0.3
1977	-	-	-	-	59.5	1.7	-	-	-	-	60.1	1.0	-	-	-	-	61.3	2.0	-	-	-	-	61.6	0.5
1978	-	-	62.2	1.0	-	-	63.5	2.1	-	-	64.4	1.4	-	-	65.0	0.9	-	-	66.4	2.2	-	-	67.5	1.7
1979	-	-	68.9	2.1	-	-	70.6	2.5	-	-	71.9	1.8	-	-	73.4	2.1	-	-	74.5	1.5	-	-	76.1	2.1
1980	-	-	77.7	2.1	-	-	81.5	4.9	-	-	80.8	-0.9	-	-	79.9	-1.1	-	-	81.4	1.9	-	-	82.6	1.5
1981	-	-	84.8	2.7	-	-	88.4	4.2	-	-	90.0	1.8	-	-	91.0	1.1	-	-	91.4	0.4	-	-	90.8	-0.7
1982	-	-	92.3	1.7	-	-	92.8	0.5	-	-	96.0	3.4	-	-	95.5	-0.5	-	-	98.8	3.5	-	-	95.1	-3.7
1983	-	-	98.2	3.3	-	-	99.2	1.0	-	-	96.3	-2.9	-	-	98.9	2.7	-	-	104.8	6.0	-	-	106.4	1.5
1984	-	-	101.1	-5.0	-	-	104.1	3.0	-	-	105.0	0.9	-	-	106.2	1.1	-	-	106.7	0.5	-	-	106.7	0.0
1985	-	-	108.2	1.4	-	-	108.2	0.0	-	-	108.9	0.6	-	-	107.9	-0.9	-	-	108.7	0.7	-	-	110.7	1.8
1986	-	-	111.0	0.3	-	-	110.7	-0.3	-	-	109.7	-0.9	-	-	112.2	2.3	-	-	110.5	-1.5	-	-	112.1	1.4
1987	-	-	-	-	-	-	-	-	-	-	115.9	3.4	-	-	-	-	-	-	-	-	-	-	119.0	2.7
1988	-	-	-	-	-	-	-	-	-	-	123.6	3.9	-	-	-	-	-	-	-	-	-	-	127.4	3.1
1989	-	-	-	-	-	-	-	-	-	-	130.7	2.6	-	-	-	-	-	-	-	-	-	-	136.7	4.6
1990	-	-	-	-	-	-	-	-	-	-	141.7	3.7	-	-	-	-	-	-	-	-	-	-	146.9	3.7
1991	-	-	-	-	-	-	-	-	-	-	154.3	5.0	-	-	-	-	-	-	-	-	-	-	157.1	1.8
1992	-	-	-	-	-	-	-	-	-	-	162.7	3.6	-	-	-	-	-	-	-	-	-	-	165.5	1.7
1993	-	-	-	-	-	-	-	-	-	-	166.7	0.7	-	-	-	-	-	-	-	-	-	-	-	-

Source: U.S. Department of Labor, Bureau of Labor Statistics, Division of Consumer Prices and Price Indexes. - indicates no data collected for period.

Honolulu, HI
Consumer Price Index - All Urban Consumers
Base 1982-1984 = 100
Apparel and Upkeep

For 1963-1993. Columns headed % show percentile change in the index from the previous period for which an index is available.

Year	Jan Index	%	Feb Index	%	Mar Index	%	Apr Index	%	May Index	%	Jun Index	%	Jul Index	%	Aug Index	%	Sep Index	%	Oct Index	%	Nov Index	%	Dec Index	%
1963	-	-	-	-	-	-	-	-	-	-	-	-	-	-	-	-	-	-	-	-	-	-	46.2	-
1964	-	-	-	-	46.4	0.4	-	-	-	-	46.4	0.0	-	-	-	-	47.1	1.5	-	-	-	-	47.0	-0.2
1965	-	-	-	-	46.8	-0.4	-	-	-	-	47.3	1.1	-	-	-	-	47.1	-0.4	-	-	-	-	47.4	0.6
1966	-	-	-	-	47.6	0.4	-	-	-	-	48.1	1.1	-	-	-	-	48.1	0.0	-	-	-	-	48.1	0.0
1967	-	-	-	-	48.2	0.2	-	-	-	-	48.8	1.2	-	-	-	-	49.3	1.0	-	-	-	-	49.5	0.4
1968	-	-	-	-	50.0	1.0	-	-	-	-	50.2	0.4	-	-	-	-	51.5	2.6	-	-	-	-	51.8	0.6
1969	-	-	-	-	52.5	1.4	-	-	-	-	53.5	1.9	-	-	-	-	54.0	0.9	-	-	-	-	54.4	0.7
1970	-	-	-	-	54.7	0.6	-	-	-	-	56.0	2.4	-	-	-	-	57.7	3.0	-	-	-	-	57.5	-0.3
1971	-	-	-	-	57.3	-0.3	-	-	-	-	56.9	-0.7	-	-	-	-	57.5	1.1	-	-	-	-	58.2	1.2
1972	-	-	-	-	58.8	1.0	-	-	-	-	58.8	0.0	-	-	-	-	59.1	0.5	-	-	-	-	58.9	-0.3
1973	-	-	-	-	59.9	1.7	-	-	-	-	59.8	-0.2	-	-	-	-	61.5	2.8	-	-	-	-	62.3	1.3
1974	-	-	-	-	63.6	2.1	-	-	-	-	64.7	1.7	-	-	-	-	66.6	2.9	-	-	-	-	67.2	0.9
1975	-	-	-	-	68.5	1.9	-	-	-	-	68.9	0.6	-	-	-	-	69.6	1.0	-	-	-	-	69.7	0.1
1976	-	-	-	-	70.9	1.7	-	-	-	-	71.7	1.1	-	-	-	-	72.6	1.3	-	-	-	-	72.3	-0.4
1977	-	-	-	-	73.9	2.2	-	-	-	-	73.9	0.0	-	-	-	-	74.7	1.1	-	-	-	-	75.9	1.6
1978	-	-	77.1	1.6	-	-	77.8	0.9	-	-	77.5	-0.4	-	-	80.5	3.9	-	-	80.2	-0.4	-	-	80.8	0.7
1979	-	-	83.1	2.8	-	-	82.5	-0.7	-	-	84.3	2.2	-	-	84.5	0.2	-	-	84.6	0.1	-	-	85.4	0.9
1980	-	-	88.2	3.3	-	-	88.5	0.3	-	-	88.6	0.1	-	-	91.6	3.4	-	-	92.0	0.4	-	-	91.6	-0.4
1981	-	-	93.2	1.7	-	-	93.0	-0.2	-	-	92.9	-0.1	-	-	94.6	1.8	-	-	97.5	3.1	-	-	96.8	-0.7
1982	-	-	97.4	0.6	-	-	98.2	0.8	-	-	99.0	0.8	-	-	98.1	-0.9	-	-	99.1	1.0	-	-	99.3	0.2
1983	-	-	100.4	1.1	-	-	101.9	1.5	-	-	100.4	-1.5	-	-	102.1	1.7	-	-	102.6	0.5	-	-	102.0	-0.6
1984	-	-	103.1	1.1	-	-	101.8	-1.3	-	-	101.0	-0.8	-	-	97.5	-3.5	-	-	97.7	0.2	-	-	99.2	1.5
1985	-	-	99.6	0.4	-	-	98.7	-0.9	-	-	98.4	-0.3	-	-	99.7	1.3	-	-	101.4	1.7	-	-	99.9	-1.5
1986	-	-	100.7	0.8	-	-	100.4	-0.3	-	-	96.4	-4.0	-	-	99.3	3.0	-	-	100.9	1.6	-	-	101.8	0.9
1987	-	-	-	-	-	-	-	-	-	-	101.0	-0.8	-	-	-	-	-	-	-	-	-	-	104.1	3.1
1988	-	-	-	-	-	-	-	-	-	-	105.7	1.5	-	-	-	-	-	-	-	-	-	-	108.0	2.2
1989	-	-	-	-	-	-	-	-	-	-	106.1	-1.8	-	-	-	-	-	-	-	-	-	-	102.5	-3.4
1990	-	-	-	-	-	-	-	-	-	-	106.2	3.6	-	-	-	-	-	-	-	-	-	-	107.8	1.5
1991	-	-	-	-	-	-	-	-	-	-	111.2	3.2	-	-	-	-	-	-	-	-	-	-	109.8	-1.3
1992	-	-	-	-	-	-	-	-	-	-	113.0	2.9	-	-	-	-	-	-	-	-	-	-	115.3	2.0
1993	-	-	-	-	-	-	-	-	-	-	117.3	1.7	-	-	-	-	-	-	-	-	-	-	-	-

Source: U.S. Department of Labor, Bureau of Labor Statistics, Division of Consumer Prices and Price Indexes. - indicates no data collected for period.

Honolulu, HI
Consumer Price Index - Urban Wage Earners
Base 1982-1984 = 100
Apparel and Upkeep

For 1963-1993. Columns headed % show percentile change in the index from the previous period for which an index is available.

Year	Jan		Feb		Mar		Apr		May		Jun		Jul		Aug		Sep		Oct		Nov		Dec	
	Index	%	Index	%	Index	%	Index	%	Index	%	Index	%	Index	%	Index	%	Index	%	Index	%	Index	%	Index	%
1963	-	-	-	-	-	-	-	-	-	-	-	-	-	-	-	-	-	-	-	-	-	-	44.6	-
1964	-	-	-	-	44.9	0.7	-	-	-	-	44.9	0.0	-	-	-	-	45.6	1.6	-	-	-	-	45.5	-0.2
1965	-	-	-	-	45.3	-0.4	-	-	-	-	45.8	1.1	-	-	-	-	45.5	-0.7	-	-	-	-	45.9	0.9
1966	-	-	-	-	46.0	0.2	-	-	-	-	46.5	1.1	-	-	-	-	46.5	0.0	-	-	-	-	46.5	0.0
1967	-	-	-	-	46.6	0.2	-	-	-	-	47.2	1.3	-	-	-	-	47.7	1.1	-	-	-	-	47.9	0.4
1968	-	-	-	-	48.4	1.0	-	-	-	-	48.6	0.4	-	-	-	-	49.8	2.5	-	-	-	-	50.1	0.6
1969	-	-	-	-	50.7	1.2	-	-	-	-	51.8	2.2	-	-	-	-	52.2	0.8	-	-	-	-	52.6	0.8
1970	-	-	-	-	53.0	0.8	-	-	-	-	54.2	2.3	-	-	-	-	55.8	3.0	-	-	-	-	55.6	-0.4
1971	-	-	-	-	55.5	-0.2	-	-	-	-	55.0	-0.9	-	-	-	-	55.6	1.1	-	-	-	-	56.3	1.3
1972	-	-	-	-	56.9	1.1	-	-	-	-	56.8	-0.2	-	-	-	-	57.2	0.7	-	-	-	-	57.0	-0.3
1973	-	-	-	-	58.0	1.8	-	-	-	-	57.9	-0.2	-	-	-	-	59.5	2.8	-	-	-	-	60.2	1.2
1974	-	-	-	-	61.5	2.2	-	-	-	-	62.6	1.8	-	-	-	-	64.4	2.9	-	-	-	-	65.0	0.9
1975	-	-	-	-	66.2	1.8	-	-	-	-	66.7	0.8	-	-	-	-	67.3	0.9	-	-	-	-	67.5	0.3
1976	-	-	-	-	68.5	1.5	-	-	-	-	69.3	1.2	-	-	-	-	70.2	1.3	-	-	-	-	69.9	-0.4
1977	-	-	-	-	71.5	2.3	-	-	-	-	71.5	0.0	-	-	-	-	72.2	1.0	-	-	-	-	73.5	1.8
1978	-	-	73.4	-0.1	-	-	74.4	1.4	-	-	73.9	-0.7	-	-	75.9	2.7	-	-	77.6	2.2	-	-	77.6	0.0
1979	-	-	78.9	1.7	-	-	78.0	-1.1	-	-	79.1	1.4	-	-	79.8	0.9	-	-	82.4	3.3	-	-	82.6	0.2
1980	-	-	90.8	9.9	-	-	92.3	1.7	-	-	90.2	-2.3	-	-	92.0	2.0	-	-	92.6	0.7	-	-	93.5	1.0
1981	-	-	94.8	1.4	-	-	94.7	-0.1	-	-	95.0	0.3	-	-	95.3	0.3	-	-	96.2	0.9	-	-	96.7	0.5
1982	-	-	97.1	0.4	-	-	98.0	0.9	-	-	98.8	0.8	-	-	97.9	-0.9	-	-	99.1	1.2	-	-	99.8	0.7
1983	-	-	100.5	0.7	-	-	101.8	1.3	-	-	100.3	-1.5	-	-	101.8	1.5	-	-	102.4	0.6	-	-	102.0	-0.4
1984	-	-	103.0	1.0	-	-	102.3	-0.7	-	-	100.3	-2.0	-	-	97.5	-2.8	-	-	98.5	1.0	-	-	99.6	1.1
1985	-	-	100.1	0.5	-	-	98.0	-2.1	-	-	97.6	-0.4	-	-	99.3	1.7	-	-	101.9	2.6	-	-	99.9	-2.0
1986	-	-	100.4	0.5	-	-	100.2	-0.2	-	-	97.1	-3.1	-	-	99.6	2.6	-	-	101.4	1.8	-	-	102.8	1.4
1987	-	-	-	-	-	-	-	-	-	-	102.2	-0.6	-	-	-	-	-	-	-	-	-	-	105.1	2.8
1988	-	-	-	-	-	-	-	-	-	-	106.9	1.7	-	-	-	-	-	-	-	-	-	-	109.5	2.4
1989	-	-	-	-	-	-	-	-	-	-	107.5	-1.8	-	-	-	-	-	-	-	-	-	-	103.0	-4.2
1990	-	-	-	-	-	-	-	-	-	-	107.4	4.3	-	-	-	-	-	-	-	-	-	-	108.8	1.3
1991	-	-	-	-	-	-	-	-	-	-	112.8	3.7	-	-	-	-	-	-	-	-	-	-	110.9	-1.7
1992	-	-	-	-	-	-	-	-	-	-	113.8	2.6	-	-	-	-	-	-	-	-	-	-	117.3	3.1
1993	-	-	-	-	-	-	-	-	-	-	119.4	1.8	-	-	-	-	-	-	-	-	-	-	-	-

Source: U.S. Department of Labor, Bureau of Labor Statistics, Division of Consumer Prices and Price Indexes. - indicates no data collected for period.

Honolulu, HI
Consumer Price Index - All Urban Consumers
Base 1982-1984 = 100
Transportation

For 1963-1993. Columns headed % show percentile change in the index from the previous period for which an index is available.

Year	Jan Index	%	Feb Index	%	Mar Index	%	Apr Index	%	May Index	%	Jun Index	%	Jul Index	%	Aug Index	%	Sep Index	%	Oct Index	%	Nov Index	%	Dec Index	%
1963	-	-	-	-	-	-	-	-	-	-	-	-	-	-	-	-	-	-	-	-	-	-	38.4	-
1964	-	-	-	-	38.0	-1.0	-	-	-	-	37.4	-1.6	-	-	-	-	37.4	0.0	-	-	-	-	38.0	1.6
1965	-	-	-	-	37.9	-0.3	-	-	-	-	37.5	-1.1	-	-	-	-	37.6	0.3	-	-	-	-	37.7	0.3
1966	-	-	-	-	37.5	-0.5	-	-	-	-	37.7	0.5	-	-	-	-	37.8	0.3	-	-	-	-	38.6	2.1
1967	-	-	-	-	38.4	-0.5	-	-	-	-	38.6	0.5	-	-	-	-	38.6	0.0	-	-	-	-	39.6	2.6
1968	-	-	-	-	40.1	1.3	-	-	-	-	40.0	-0.2	-	-	-	-	40.0	0.0	-	-	-	-	40.8	2.0
1969	-	-	-	-	41.7	2.2	-	-	-	-	41.5	-0.5	-	-	-	-	41.2	-0.7	-	-	-	-	42.2	2.4
1970	-	-	-	-	42.8	1.4	-	-	-	-	43.6	1.9	-	-	-	-	43.6	0.0	-	-	-	-	44.6	2.3
1971	-	-	-	-	45.7	2.5	-	-	-	-	47.7	4.4	-	-	-	-	47.2	-1.0	-	-	-	-	47.1	-0.2
1972	-	-	-	-	47.5	0.8	-	-	-	-	47.8	0.6	-	-	-	-	47.7	-0.2	-	-	-	-	47.7	0.0
1973	-	-	-	-	47.9	0.4	-	-	-	-	47.9	0.0	-	-	-	-	47.7	-0.4	-	-	-	-	48.7	2.1
1974	-	-	-	-	50.8	4.3	-	-	-	-	52.6	3.5	-	-	-	-	53.3	1.3	-	-	-	-	54.2	1.7
1975	-	-	-	-	55.2	1.8	-	-	-	-	57.1	3.4	-	-	-	-	58.1	1.8	-	-	-	-	58.0	-0.2
1976	-	-	-	-	58.7	1.2	-	-	-	-	59.3	1.0	-	-	-	-	60.0	1.2	-	-	-	-	60.9	1.5
1977	-	-	-	-	61.2	0.5	-	-	-	-	62.3	1.8	-	-	-	-	61.9	-0.6	-	-	-	-	62.6	1.1
1978	-	-	63.8	1.9	-	-	64.9	1.7	-	-	66.0	1.7	-	-	66.7	1.1	-	-	67.3	0.9	-	-	68.3	1.5
1979	-	-	68.6	0.4	-	-	70.5	2.8	-	-	72.8	3.3	-	-	74.7	2.6	-	-	76.5	2.4	-	-	79.9	4.4
1980	-	-	83.5	4.5	-	-	85.8	2.8	-	-	86.1	0.3	-	-	88.2	2.4	-	-	88.8	0.7	-	-	89.6	0.9
1981	-	-	92.5	3.2	-	-	94.7	2.4	-	-	95.9	1.3	-	-	97.1	1.3	-	-	97.6	0.5	-	-	98.3	0.7
1982	-	-	98.0	-0.3	-	-	97.6	-0.4	-	-	98.6	1.0	-	-	100.2	1.6	-	-	100.2	0.0	-	-	99.2	-1.0
1983	-	-	97.2	-2.0	-	-	96.6	-0.6	-	-	96.8	0.2	-	-	98.4	1.7	-	-	100.0	1.6	-	-	100.7	0.7
1984	-	-	101.2	0.5	-	-	101.8	0.6	-	-	103.2	1.4	-	-	104.0	0.8	-	-	103.9	-0.1	-	-	103.8	-0.1
1985	-	-	104.0	0.2	-	-	104.3	0.3	-	-	104.3	0.0	-	-	105.2	0.9	-	-	105.8	0.6	-	-	106.2	0.4
1986	-	-	108.1	1.8	-	-	104.6	-3.2	-	-	105.2	0.6	-	-	103.8	-1.3	-	-	103.5	-0.3	-	-	106.0	2.4
1987	-	-	-	-	-	-	-	-	-	-	107.3	1.2	-	-	-	-	-	-	-	-	-	-	112.1	4.5
1988	-	-	-	-	-	-	-	-	-	-	114.2	1.9	-	-	-	-	-	-	-	-	-	-	118.0	3.3
1989	-	-	-	-	-	-	-	-	-	-	121.8	3.2	-	-	-	-	-	-	-	-	-	-	126.0	3.4
1990	-	-	-	-	-	-	-	-	-	-	127.3	1.0	-	-	-	-	-	-	-	-	-	-	135.0	6.0
1991	-	-	-	-	-	-	-	-	-	-	138.1	2.3	-	-	-	-	-	-	-	-	-	-	140.4	1.7
1992	-	-	-	-	-	-	-	-	-	-	146.4	4.3	-	-	-	-	-	-	-	-	-	-	148.5	1.4
1993	-	-	-	-	-	-	-	-	-	-	149.5	0.7	-	-	-	-	-	-	-	-	-	-	-	-

Source: U.S. Department of Labor, Bureau of Labor Statistics, Division of Consumer Prices and Price Indexes. - indicates no data collected for period.

Honolulu, HI
Consumer Price Index - Urban Wage Earners
Base 1982-1984 = 100
Transportation

For 1963-1993. Columns headed % show percentile change in the index from the previous period for which an index is available.

Year	Jan Index	%	Feb Index	%	Mar Index	%	Apr Index	%	May Index	%	Jun Index	%	Jul Index	%	Aug Index	%	Sep Index	%	Oct Index	%	Nov Index	%	Dec Index	%
1963	-	-	-	-	-	-	-	-	-	-	-	-	-	-	-	-	-	-	-	-	-	-	38.5	-
1964	-	-	-	-	38.0	-1.3	-	-	-	-	37.4	-1.6	-	-	-	-	37.4	0.0	-	-	-	-	38.0	1.6
1965	-	-	-	-	37.9	-0.3	-	-	-	-	37.5	-1.1	-	-	-	-	37.6	0.3	-	-	-	-	37.7	0.3
1966	-	-	-	-	37.5	-0.5	-	-	-	-	37.8	0.8	-	-	-	-	37.8	0.0	-	-	-	-	38.6	2.1
1967	-	-	-	-	38.5	-0.3	-	-	-	-	38.6	0.3	-	-	-	-	38.7	0.3	-	-	-	-	39.7	2.6
1968	-	-	-	-	40.1	1.0	-	-	-	-	40.1	0.0	-	-	-	-	40.0	-0.2	-	-	-	-	40.9	2.3
1969	-	-	-	-	41.7	2.0	-	-	-	-	41.5	-0.5	-	-	-	-	41.2	-0.7	-	-	-	-	42.2	2.4
1970	-	-	-	-	42.8	1.4	-	-	-	-	43.6	1.9	-	-	-	-	43.6	0.0	-	-	-	-	44.6	2.3
1971	-	-	-	-	45.7	2.5	-	-	-	-	47.7	4.4	-	-	-	-	47.2	-1.0	-	-	-	-	47.1	-0.2
1972	-	-	-	-	47.6	1.1	-	-	-	-	47.8	0.4	-	-	-	-	47.7	-0.2	-	-	-	-	47.7	0.0
1973	-	-	-	-	48.0	0.6	-	-	-	-	47.9	-0.2	-	-	-	-	47.7	-0.4	-	-	-	-	48.7	2.1
1974	-	-	-	-	50.9	4.5	-	-	-	-	52.6	3.3	-	-	-	-	53.4	1.5	-	-	-	-	54.3	1.7
1975	-	-	-	-	55.3	1.8	-	-	-	-	57.2	3.4	-	-	-	-	58.2	1.7	-	-	-	-	58.0	-0.3
1976	-	-	-	-	58.7	1.2	-	-	-	-	59.3	1.0	-	-	-	-	60.1	1.3	-	-	-	-	60.9	1.3
1977	-	-	-	-	61.2	0.5	-	-	-	-	62.3	1.8	-	-	-	-	61.9	-0.6	-	-	-	-	62.6	1.1
1978	-	-	63.8	1.9	-	-	64.9	1.7	-	-	66.0	1.7	-	-	66.6	0.9	-	-	67.2	0.9	-	-	68.1	1.3
1979	-	-	68.6	0.7	-	-	70.5	2.8	-	-	73.0	3.5	-	-	75.0	2.7	-	-	76.7	2.3	-	-	79.8	4.0
1980	-	-	83.4	4.5	-	-	86.0	3.1	-	-	86.2	0.2	-	-	88.0	2.1	-	-	88.9	1.0	-	-	90.0	1.2
1981	-	-	92.9	3.2	-	-	95.3	2.6	-	-	96.5	1.3	-	-	97.7	1.2	-	-	98.4	0.7	-	-	98.9	0.5
1982	-	-	98.4	-0.5	-	-	97.9	-0.5	-	-	98.8	0.9	-	-	100.3	1.5	-	-	100.3	0.0	-	-	99.1	-1.2
1983	-	-	97.1	-2.0	-	-	96.4	-0.7	-	-	96.7	0.3	-	-	98.4	1.8	-	-	99.9	1.5	-	-	100.7	0.8
1984	-	-	101.2	0.5	-	-	101.7	0.5	-	-	103.1	1.4	-	-	103.9	0.8	-	-	103.9	0.0	-	-	103.7	-0.2
1985	-	-	103.9	0.2	-	-	104.1	0.2	-	-	104.1	0.0	-	-	105.0	0.9	-	-	105.6	0.6	-	-	106.0	0.4
1986	-	-	107.9	1.8	-	-	104.1	-3.5	-	-	104.7	0.6	-	-	103.2	-1.4	-	-	102.8	-0.4	-	-	105.1	2.2
1987	-	-	-	-	-	-	-	-	-	-	106.8	1.6	-	-	-	-	-	-	-	-	-	-	111.6	4.5
1988	-	-	-	-	-	-	-	-	-	-	113.8	2.0	-	-	-	-	-	-	-	-	-	-	117.5	3.3
1989	-	-	-	-	-	-	-	-	-	-	121.4	3.3	-	-	-	-	-	-	-	-	-	-	125.9	3.7
1990	-	-	-	-	-	-	-	-	-	-	126.7	0.6	-	-	-	-	-	-	-	-	-	-	133.8	5.6
1991	-	-	-	-	-	-	-	-	-	-	137.1	2.5	-	-	-	-	-	-	-	-	-	-	140.1	2.2
1992	-	-	-	-	-	-	-	-	-	-	145.7	4.0	-	-	-	-	-	-	-	-	-	-	147.7	1.4
1993	-	-	-	-	-	-	-	-	-	-	148.0	0.2	-	-	-	-	-	-	-	-	-	-	-	-

Source: U.S. Department of Labor, Bureau of Labor Statistics, Division of Consumer Prices and Price Indexes. - indicates no data collected for period.

Honolulu, HI
Consumer Price Index - All Urban Consumers
Base 1982-1984 = 100
Medical Care

For 1963-1993. Columns headed % show percentile change in the index from the previous period for which an index is available.

Year	Jan Index	%	Feb Index	%	Mar Index	%	Apr Index	%	May Index	%	Jun Index	%	Jul Index	%	Aug Index	%	Sep Index	%	Oct Index	%	Nov Index	%	Dec Index	%
1963	-	-	-	-	-	-	-	-	-	-	-	-	-	-	-	-	-	-	-	-	-	-	24.7	-
1964	-	-	-	-	25.0	1.2	-	-	-	-	25.1	0.4	-	-	-	-	25.2	0.4	-	-	-	-	25.3	0.4
1965	-	-	-	-	25.7	1.6	-	-	-	-	25.8	0.4	-	-	-	-	26.0	0.8	-	-	-	-	26.1	0.4
1966	-	-	-	-	26.3	0.8	-	-	-	-	26.5	0.8	-	-	-	-	26.8	1.1	-	-	-	-	27.4	2.2
1967	-	-	-	-	27.7	1.1	-	-	-	-	28.3	2.2	-	-	-	-	28.6	1.1	-	-	-	-	29.0	1.4
1968	-	-	-	-	29.3	1.0	-	-	-	-	29.8	1.7	-	-	-	-	30.3	1.7	-	-	-	-	30.7	1.3
1969	-	-	-	-	31.3	2.0	-	-	-	-	32.1	2.6	-	-	-	-	32.6	1.6	-	-	-	-	32.5	-0.3
1970	-	-	-	-	32.6	0.3	-	-	-	-	33.5	2.8	-	-	-	-	33.8	0.9	-	-	-	-	34.5	2.1
1971	-	-	-	-	35.0	1.4	-	-	-	-	35.2	0.6	-	-	-	-	35.6	1.1	-	-	-	-	35.6	0.0
1972	-	-	-	-	35.7	0.3	-	-	-	-	35.8	0.3	-	-	-	-	36.2	1.1	-	-	-	-	36.7	1.4
1973	-	-	-	-	37.1	1.1	-	-	-	-	37.5	1.1	-	-	-	-	38.0	1.3	-	-	-	-	38.7	1.8
1974	-	-	-	-	39.4	1.8	-	-	-	-	41.7	5.8	-	-	-	-	43.1	3.4	-	-	-	-	43.6	1.2
1975	-	-	-	-	45.5	4.4	-	-	-	-	46.5	2.2	-	-	-	-	47.6	2.4	-	-	-	-	48.1	1.1
1976	-	-	-	-	50.1	4.2	-	-	-	-	50.8	1.4	-	-	-	-	52.9	4.1	-	-	-	-	54.1	2.3
1977	-	-	-	-	55.6	2.8	-	-	-	-	56.7	2.0	-	-	-	-	59.3	4.6	-	-	-	-	59.7	0.7
1978	-	-	61.5	3.0	-	-	62.2	1.1	-	-	62.4	0.3	-	-	62.6	0.3	-	-	62.6	0.0	-	-	64.8	3.5
1979	-	-	66.1	2.0	-	-	66.9	1.2	-	-	67.1	0.3	-	-	68.2	1.6	-	-	68.4	0.3	-	-	69.2	1.2
1980	-	-	69.9	1.0	-	-	72.7	4.0	-	-	72.6	-0.1	-	-	74.1	2.1	-	-	75.5	1.9	-	-	75.3	-0.3
1981	-	-	76.9	2.1	-	-	79.3	3.1	-	-	81.1	2.3	-	-	84.1	3.7	-	-	85.8	2.0	-	-	86.4	0.7
1982	-	-	86.8	0.5	-	-	90.6	4.4	-	-	91.4	0.9	-	-	92.6	1.3	-	-	95.0	2.6	-	-	95.9	0.9
1983	-	-	98.6	2.8	-	-	100.4	1.8	-	-	100.6	0.2	-	-	103.3	2.7	-	-	102.5	-0.8	-	-	102.6	0.1
1984	-	-	105.2	2.5	-	-	106.9	1.6	-	-	107.0	0.1	-	-	108.5	1.4	-	-	108.6	0.1	-	-	109.3	0.6
1985	-	-	110.4	1.0	-	-	111.1	0.6	-	-	111.5	0.4	-	-	115.4	3.5	-	-	116.0	0.5	-	-	116.7	0.6
1986	-	-	120.0	2.8	-	-	120.4	0.3	-	-	121.2	0.7	-	-	124.6	2.8	-	-	125.2	0.5	-	-	124.5	-0.6
1987	-	-	-	-	-	-	-	-	-	-	126.5	1.6	-	-	-	-	-	-	-	-	-	-	129.2	2.1
1988	-	-	-	-	-	-	-	-	-	-	130.3	0.9	-	-	-	-	-	-	-	-	-	-	134.7	3.4
1989	-	-	-	-	-	-	-	-	-	-	136.0	1.0	-	-	-	-	-	-	-	-	-	-	142.7	4.9
1990	-	-	-	-	-	-	-	-	-	-	149.8	5.0	-	-	-	-	-	-	-	-	-	-	158.6	5.9
1991	-	-	-	-	-	-	-	-	-	-	168.0	5.9	-	-	-	-	-	-	-	-	-	-	174.6	3.9
1992	-	-	-	-	-	-	-	-	-	-	179.7	2.9	-	-	-	-	-	-	-	-	-	-	185.6	3.3
1993	-	-	-	-	-	-	-	-	-	-	192.8	3.9	-	-	-	-	-	-	-	-	-	-	-	-

Source: U.S. Department of Labor, Bureau of Labor Statistics, Division of Consumer Prices and Price Indexes. - indicates no data collected for period.

Honolulu, HI
Consumer Price Index - Urban Wage Earners
Base 1982-1984 = 100
Medical Care

For 1963-1993. Columns headed % show percentile change in the index from the previous period for which an index is available.

Year	Jan Index	%	Feb Index	%	Mar Index	%	Apr Index	%	May Index	%	Jun Index	%	Jul Index	%	Aug Index	%	Sep Index	%	Oct Index	%	Nov Index	%	Dec Index	%
1963	-	-	-	-	-	-	-	-	-	-	-	-	-	-	-	-	-	-	-	-	-	-	24.2	-
1964	-	-	-	-	24.5	1.2	-	-	-	-	24.5	0.0	-	-	-	-	24.7	0.8	-	-	-	-	24.8	0.4
1965	-	-	-	-	25.1	1.2	-	-	-	-	25.2	0.4	-	-	-	-	25.4	0.8	-	-	-	-	25.6	0.8
1966	-	-	-	-	25.7	0.4	-	-	-	-	26.0	1.2	-	-	-	-	26.2	0.8	-	-	-	-	26.8	2.3
1967	-	-	-	-	27.1	1.1	-	-	-	-	27.7	2.2	-	-	-	-	28.0	1.1	-	-	-	-	28.4	1.4
1968	-	-	-	-	28.7	1.1	-	-	-	-	29.2	1.7	-	-	-	-	29.7	1.7	-	-	-	-	30.1	1.3
1969	-	-	-	-	30.7	2.0	-	-	-	-	31.4	2.3	-	-	-	-	32.0	1.9	-	-	-	-	31.8	-0.6
1970	-	-	-	-	32.0	0.6	-	-	-	-	32.8	2.5	-	-	-	-	33.1	0.9	-	-	-	-	33.8	2.1
1971	-	-	-	-	34.2	1.2	-	-	-	-	34.5	0.9	-	-	-	-	34.8	0.9	-	-	-	-	34.9	0.3
1972	-	-	-	-	35.0	0.3	-	-	-	-	35.1	0.3	-	-	-	-	35.4	0.9	-	-	-	-	36.0	1.7
1973	-	-	-	-	36.3	0.8	-	-	-	-	36.7	1.1	-	-	-	-	37.3	1.6	-	-	-	-	37.9	1.6
1974	-	-	-	-	38.6	1.8	-	-	-	-	40.9	6.0	-	-	-	-	42.2	3.2	-	-	-	-	42.7	1.2
1975	-	-	-	-	44.6	4.4	-	-	-	-	45.6	2.2	-	-	-	-	46.6	2.2	-	-	-	-	47.1	1.1
1976	-	-	-	-	49.0	4.0	-	-	-	-	49.7	1.4	-	-	-	-	51.8	4.2	-	-	-	-	53.0	2.3
1977	-	-	-	-	54.4	2.6	-	-	-	-	55.5	2.0	-	-	-	-	58.1	4.7	-	-	-	-	58.5	0.7
1978	-	-	60.4	3.2	-	-	61.9	2.5	-	-	62.0	0.2	-	-	62.2	0.3	-	-	62.2	0.0	-	-	63.4	1.9
1979	-	-	64.8	2.2	-	-	65.3	0.8	-	-	66.4	1.7	-	-	66.3	-0.2	-	-	67.7	2.1	-	-	68.5	1.2
1980	-	-	68.9	0.6	-	-	71.0	3.0	-	-	71.3	0.4	-	-	73.7	3.4	-	-	75.5	2.4	-	-	75.2	-0.4
1981	-	-	76.8	2.1	-	-	78.8	2.6	-	-	81.8	3.8	-	-	84.5	3.3	-	-	85.8	1.5	-	-	86.7	1.0
1982	-	-	87.1	0.5	-	-	90.8	4.2	-	-	91.7	1.0	-	-	93.1	1.5	-	-	95.5	2.6	-	-	96.5	1.0
1983	-	-	99.0	2.6	-	-	100.5	1.5	-	-	100.6	0.1	-	-	103.1	2.5	-	-	102.3	-0.8	-	-	102.4	0.1
1984	-	-	105.0	2.5	-	-	106.6	1.5	-	-	106.7	0.1	-	-	108.0	1.2	-	-	108.0	0.0	-	-	108.7	0.6
1985	-	-	109.9	1.1	-	-	110.6	0.6	-	-	111.0	0.4	-	-	114.6	3.2	-	-	115.2	0.5	-	-	116.0	0.7
1986	-	-	119.0	2.6	-	-	119.4	0.3	-	-	120.2	0.7	-	-	123.1	2.4	-	-	123.7	0.5	-	-	123.2	-0.4
1987	-	-	-	-	-	-	-	-	-	-	125.1	1.5	-	-	-	-	-	-	-	-	-	-	128.3	2.6
1988	-	-	-	-	-	-	-	-	-	-	129.4	0.9	-	-	-	-	-	-	-	-	-	-	133.4	3.1
1989	-	-	-	-	-	-	-	-	-	-	134.8	1.0	-	-	-	-	-	-	-	-	-	-	141.9	5.3
1990	-	-	-	-	-	-	-	-	-	-	148.7	4.8	-	-	-	-	-	-	-	-	-	-	157.9	6.2
1991	-	-	-	-	-	-	-	-	-	-	166.9	5.7	-	-	-	-	-	-	-	-	-	-	173.8	4.1
1992	-	-	-	-	-	-	-	-	-	-	178.9	2.9	-	-	-	-	-	-	-	-	-	-	185.6	3.7
1993	-	-	-	-	-	-	-	-	-	-	192.6	3.8	-	-	-	-	-	-	-	-	-	-	-	-

Source: U.S. Department of Labor, Bureau of Labor Statistics, Division of Consumer Prices and Price Indexes. - indicates no data collected for period.

Honolulu, HI
Consumer Price Index - All Urban Consumers
Base 1982-1984 = 100
Entertainment

For 1975-1993. Columns headed % show percentile change in the index from the previous period for which an index is available.

Year	Jan Index	%	Feb Index	%	Mar Index	%	Apr Index	%	May Index	%	Jun Index	%	Jul Index	%	Aug Index	%	Sep Index	%	Oct Index	%	Nov Index	%	Dec Index	%
1975	-	-	-	-	-	-	-	-	-	-	-	-	-	-	-	-	-	-	-	-	-	-	61.5	-
1976	-	-	-	-	62.3	1.3	-	-	-	-	63.5	1.9	-	-	-	-	65.0	2.4	-	-	-	-	64.9	-0.2
1977	-	-	-	-	65.7	1.2	-	-	-	-	66.6	1.4	-	-	-	-	66.6	0.0	-	-	-	-	66.9	0.5
1978	-	-	67.9	1.5	-	-	68.6	1.0	-	-	69.2	0.9	-	-	69.9	1.0	-	-	69.1	-1.1	-	-	69.9	1.2
1979	-	-	70.6	1.0	-	-	71.7	1.6	-	-	73.0	1.8	-	-	73.4	0.5	-	-	74.6	1.6	-	-	74.6	0.0
1980	-	-	76.4	2.4	-	-	77.3	1.2	-	-	77.9	0.8	-	-	78.7	1.0	-	-	79.9	1.5	-	-	80.1	0.3
1981	-	-	83.7	4.5	-	-	85.2	1.8	-	-	87.2	2.3	-	-	87.4	0.2	-	-	91.0	4.1	-	-	92.0	1.1
1982	-	-	96.0	4.3	-	-	95.3	-0.7	-	-	95.5	0.2	-	-	97.1	1.7	-	-	95.7	-1.4	-	-	95.8	0.1
1983	-	-	99.5	3.9	-	-	99.6	0.1	-	-	100.5	0.9	-	-	100.7	0.2	-	-	100.5	-0.2	-	-	99.9	-0.6
1984	-	-	101.7	1.8	-	-	103.9	2.2	-	-	103.8	-0.1	-	-	105.1	1.3	-	-	104.8	-0.3	-	-	109.1	4.1
1985	-	-	109.9	0.7	-	-	111.0	1.0	-	-	112.5	1.4	-	-	113.7	1.1	-	-	113.5	-0.2	-	-	111.5	-1.8
1986	-	-	115.7	3.8	-	-	115.9	0.2	-	-	116.1	0.2	-	-	110.7	-4.7	-	-	111.1	0.4	-	-	109.3	-1.6
1987	-	-	-	-	-	-	-	-	-	-	116.3	6.4	-	-	-	-	-	-	-	-	-	-	120.9	4.0
1988	-	-	-	-	-	-	-	-	-	-	123.1	1.8	-	-	-	-	-	-	-	-	-	-	122.8	-0.2
1989	-	-	-	-	-	-	-	-	-	-	124.0	1.0	-	-	-	-	-	-	-	-	-	-	124.6	0.5
1990	-	-	-	-	-	-	-	-	-	-	125.7	0.9	-	-	-	-	-	-	-	-	-	-	131.2	4.4
1991	-	-	-	-	-	-	-	-	-	-	133.1	1.4	-	-	-	-	-	-	-	-	-	-	135.5	1.8
1992	-	-	-	-	-	-	-	-	-	-	135.7	0.1	-	-	-	-	-	-	-	-	-	-	136.8	0.8
1993	-	-	-	-	-	-	-	-	-	-	137.1	0.2	-	-	-	-	-	-	-	-	-	-	-	-

Source: U.S. Department of Labor, Bureau of Labor Statistics, Division of Consumer Prices and Price Indexes. - indicates no data collected for period.

Honolulu, HI
Consumer Price Index - Urban Wage Earners
Base 1982-1984 = 100
Entertainment

For 1975-1993. Columns headed % show percentile change in the index from the previous period for which an index is available.

Year	Jan Index	%	Feb Index	%	Mar Index	%	Apr Index	%	May Index	%	Jun Index	%	Jul Index	%	Aug Index	%	Sep Index	%	Oct Index	%	Nov Index	%	Dec Index	%
1975	-	-	-	-	-	-	-	-	-	-	-	-	-	-	-	-	-	-	-	-	-	-	58.7	-
1976	-	-	-	-	59.4	1.2	-	-	-	-	60.6	2.0	-	-	-	-	62.0	2.3	-	-	-	-	61.9	-0.2
1977	-	-	-	-	62.7	1.3	-	-	-	-	63.5	1.3	-	-	-	-	63.6	0.2	-	-	-	-	63.9	0.5
1978	-	-	66.5	4.1	-	-	66.6	0.2	-	-	67.4	1.2	-	-	68.3	1.3	-	-	68.2	-0.1	-	-	68.6	0.6
1979	-	-	70.9	3.4	-	-	71.5	0.8	-	-	72.8	1.8	-	-	75.6	3.8	-	-	75.9	0.4	-	-	75.9	0.0
1980	-	-	78.4	3.3	-	-	78.6	0.3	-	-	79.9	1.7	-	-	80.2	0.4	-	-	81.4	1.5	-	-	82.4	1.2
1981	-	-	84.1	2.1	-	-	85.8	2.0	-	-	87.3	1.7	-	-	87.3	0.0	-	-	90.7	3.9	-	-	91.5	0.9
1982	-	-	95.8	4.7	-	-	94.9	-0.9	-	-	95.1	0.2	-	-	97.0	2.0	-	-	95.3	-1.8	-	-	95.5	0.2
1983	-	-	99.6	4.3	-	-	99.5	-0.1	-	-	100.4	0.9	-	-	100.8	0.4	-	-	100.6	-0.2	-	-	100.1	-0.5
1984	-	-	102.1	2.0	-	-	104.2	2.1	-	-	104.0	-0.2	-	-	105.3	1.3	-	-	105.2	-0.1	-	-	109.0	3.6
1985	-	-	110.0	0.9	-	-	111.1	1.0	-	-	112.6	1.4	-	-	113.6	0.9	-	-	113.4	-0.2	-	-	111.5	-1.7
1986	-	-	115.2	3.3	-	-	115.5	0.3	-	-	115.8	0.3	-	-	111.0	-4.1	-	-	111.3	0.3	-	-	109.4	-1.7
1987	-	-	-	-	-	-	-	-	-	-	116.9	6.9	-	-	-	-	-	-	-	-	-	-	121.8	4.2
1988	-	-	-	-	-	-	-	-	-	-	124.2	2.0	-	-	-	-	-	-	-	-	-	-	123.0	-1.0
1989	-	-	-	-	-	-	-	-	-	-	123.3	0.2	-	-	-	-	-	-	-	-	-	-	123.8	0.4
1990	-	-	-	-	-	-	-	-	-	-	124.8	0.8	-	-	-	-	-	-	-	-	-	-	131.0	5.0
1991	-	-	-	-	-	-	-	-	-	-	132.6	1.2	-	-	-	-	-	-	-	-	-	-	135.6	2.3
1992	-	-	-	-	-	-	-	-	-	-	135.9	0.2	-	-	-	-	-	-	-	-	-	-	137.1	0.9
1993	-	-	-	-	-	-	-	-	-	-	137.6	0.4	-	-	-	-	-	-	-	-	-	-	-	-

Source: U.S. Department of Labor, Bureau of Labor Statistics, Division of Consumer Prices and Price Indexes. - indicates no data collected for period.

Honolulu, HI
Consumer Price Index - All Urban Consumers
Base 1982-1984 = 100
Other Goods and Services

For 1975-1993. Columns headed % show percentile change in the index from the previous period for which an index is available.

Year	Jan Index	%	Feb Index	%	Mar Index	%	Apr Index	%	May Index	%	Jun Index	%	Jul Index	%	Aug Index	%	Sep Index	%	Oct Index	%	Nov Index	%	Dec Index	%
1975	-	-	-	-	-	-	-	-	-	-	-	-	-	-	-	-	-	-	-	-	-	-	52.6	-
1976	-	-	-	-	53.3	1.3	-	-	-	-	53.5	0.4	-	-	-	-	54.2	1.3	-	-	-	-	55.3	2.0
1977	-	-	-	-	56.1	1.4	-	-	-	-	56.8	1.2	-	-	-	-	58.8	3.5	-	-	-	-	59.6	1.4
1978	-	-	59.9	0.5	-	-	60.3	0.7	-	-	61.1	1.3	-	-	61.9	1.3	-	-	62.9	1.6	-	-	63.1	0.3
1979	-	-	64.6	2.4	-	-	65.1	0.8	-	-	65.6	0.8	-	-	66.2	0.9	-	-	68.7	3.8	-	-	70.6	2.8
1980	-	-	71.3	1.0	-	-	70.4	-1.3	-	-	72.4	2.8	-	-	73.6	1.7	-	-	77.0	4.6	-	-	76.9	-0.1
1981	-	-	78.3	1.8	-	-	78.7	0.5	-	-	79.1	0.5	-	-	82.3	4.0	-	-	86.3	4.9	-	-	87.2	1.0
1982	-	-	87.5	0.3	-	-	90.1	3.0	-	-	91.0	1.0	-	-	91.1	0.1	-	-	96.3	5.7	-	-	99.2	3.0
1983	-	-	98.1	-1.1	-	-	101.4	3.4	-	-	102.0	0.6	-	-	101.8	-0.2	-	-	103.0	1.2	-	-	103.1	0.1
1984	-	-	104.6	1.5	-	-	104.9	0.3	-	-	105.5	0.6	-	-	107.7	2.1	-	-	109.1	1.3	-	-	109.1	0.0
1985	-	-	111.0	1.7	-	-	110.8	-0.2	-	-	111.2	0.4	-	-	113.3	1.9	-	-	114.9	1.4	-	-	115.0	0.1
1986	-	-	115.6	0.5	-	-	117.3	1.5	-	-	117.4	0.1	-	-	120.3	2.5	-	-	124.3	3.3	-	-	124.9	0.5
1987	-	-	-	-	-	-	-	-	-	-	127.0	1.7	-	-	-	-	-	-	-	-	-	-	132.4	4.3
1988	-	-	-	-	-	-	-	-	-	-	135.0	2.0	-	-	-	-	-	-	-	-	-	-	139.3	3.2
1989	-	-	-	-	-	-	-	-	-	-	142.7	2.4	-	-	-	-	-	-	-	-	-	-	149.4	4.7
1990	-	-	-	-	-	-	-	-	-	-	155.2	3.9	-	-	-	-	-	-	-	-	-	-	165.6	6.7
1991	-	-	-	-	-	-	-	-	-	-	171.9	3.8	-	-	-	-	-	-	-	-	-	-	179.6	4.5
1992	-	-	-	-	-	-	-	-	-	-	185.6	3.3	-	-	-	-	-	-	-	-	-	-	192.4	3.7
1993	-	-	-	-	-	-	-	-	-	-	197.4	2.6	-	-	-	-	-	-	-	-	-	-	-	-

Source: U.S. Department of Labor, Bureau of Labor Statistics, Division of Consumer Prices and Price Indexes. - indicates no data collected for period.

Honolulu, HI
Consumer Price Index - Urban Wage Earners
Base 1982-1984 = 100
Other Goods and Services

For 1975-1993. Columns headed % show percentile change in the index from the previous period for which an index is available.

Year	Jan Index	%	Feb Index	%	Mar Index	%	Apr Index	%	May Index	%	Jun Index	%	Jul Index	%	Aug Index	%	Sep Index	%	Oct Index	%	Nov Index	%	Dec Index	%
1975	-	-	-	-	-	-	-	-	-	-	-	-	-	-	-	-	-	-	-	-	-	-	53.5	-
1976	-	-	-	-	54.3	1.5	-	-	-	-	54.4	0.2	-	-	-	-	55.1	1.3	-	-	-	-	56.3	2.2
1977	-	-	-	-	57.1	1.4	-	-	-	-	57.8	1.2	-	-	-	-	59.8	3.5	-	-	-	-	60.6	1.3
1978	-	-	60.4	-0.3	-	-	60.8	0.7	-	-	61.3	0.8	-	-	62.4	1.8	-	-	63.5	1.8	-	-	63.6	0.2
1979	-	-	65.2	2.5	-	-	65.5	0.5	-	-	66.4	1.4	-	-	67.1	1.1	-	-	69.3	3.3	-	-	69.7	0.6
1980	-	-	70.6	1.3	-	-	70.4	-0.3	-	-	72.1	2.4	-	-	73.1	1.4	-	-	75.9	3.8	-	-	76.8	1.2
1981	-	-	77.5	0.9	-	-	78.4	1.2	-	-	79.9	1.9	-	-	80.7	1.0	-	-	86.3	6.9	-	-	86.7	0.5
1982	-	-	87.0	0.3	-	-	89.8	3.2	-	-	90.4	0.7	-	-	90.5	0.1	-	-	96.0	6.1	-	-	99.5	3.6
1983	-	-	98.5	-1.0	-	-	101.9	3.5	-	-	102.3	0.4	-	-	102.3	0.0	-	-	103.1	0.8	-	-	103.2	0.1
1984	-	-	104.7	1.5	-	-	105.1	0.4	-	-	105.5	0.4	-	-	107.8	2.2	-	-	109.1	1.2	-	-	109.0	-0.1
1985	-	-	111.2	2.0	-	-	110.9	-0.3	-	-	111.3	0.4	-	-	113.4	1.9	-	-	114.7	1.1	-	-	114.7	0.0
1986	-	-	115.5	0.7	-	-	117.0	1.3	-	-	117.1	0.1	-	-	120.2	2.6	-	-	123.2	2.5	-	-	123.9	0.6
1987	-	-	-	-	-	-	-	-	-	-	126.1	1.8	-	-	-	-	-	-	-	-	-	-	131.3	4.1
1988	-	-	-	-	-	-	-	-	-	-	134.2	2.2	-	-	-	-	-	-	-	-	-	-	138.6	3.3
1989	-	-	-	-	-	-	-	-	-	-	142.4	2.7	-	-	-	-	-	-	-	-	-	-	150.1	5.4
1990	-	-	-	-	-	-	-	-	-	-	156.8	4.5	-	-	-	-	-	-	-	-	-	-	167.1	6.6
1991	-	-	-	-	-	-	-	-	-	-	174.9	4.7	-	-	-	-	-	-	-	-	-	-	183.4	4.9
1992	-	-	-	-	-	-	-	-	-	-	190.2	3.7	-	-	-	-	-	-	-	-	-	-	197.2	3.7
1993	-	-	-	-	-	-	-	-	-	-	202.7	2.8	-	-	-	-	-	-	-	-	-	-	-	-

Source: U.S. Department of Labor, Bureau of Labor Statistics, Division of Consumer Prices and Price Indexes. - indicates no data collected for period.

Houston, TX
Consumer Price Index - All Urban Consumers
Base 1982-1984 = 100
Annual Averages

For 1914-1993. Columns headed % show percentile change in the index from the previous period for which an index is available.

Year	All Items		Food & Beverage		Housing		Apparel & Upkeep		Trans- portation		Medical Care		Entertain- ment		Other Goods & Services	
	Index	%	Index	%	Index	%	Index	%	Index	%	Index	%	Index	%	Index	%
1914	-	-	-	-	-	-	-	-	-	-	-	-	-	-	-	-
1915	9.4	-	-	-	-	-	-	-	-	-	-	-	-	-	-	-
1916	10.1	7.4	-	-	-	-	-	-	-	-	-	-	-	-	-	-
1917	12.4	22.8	-	-	-	-	-	-	-	-	-	-	-	-	-	-
1918	14.5	16.9	-	-	-	-	-	-	-	-	-	-	-	-	-	-
1919	16.9	16.6	-	-	-	-	-	-	-	-	-	-	-	-	-	-
1920	19.2	13.6	-	-	-	-	-	-	-	-	-	-	-	-	-	-
1921	17.0	-11.5	-	-	-	-	-	-	-	-	-	-	-	-	-	-
1922	15.9	-6.5	-	-	-	-	-	-	-	-	-	-	-	-	-	-
1923	15.9	0.0	-	-	-	-	-	-	-	-	-	-	-	-	-	-
1924	15.8	-0.6	-	-	-	-	-	-	-	-	-	-	-	-	-	-
1925	16.2	2.5	-	-	-	-	-	-	-	-	-	-	-	-	-	-
1926	16.0	-1.2	-	-	-	-	-	-	-	-	-	-	-	-	-	-
1927	15.7	-1.9	-	-	-	-	-	-	-	-	-	-	-	-	-	-
1928	15.6	-0.6	-	-	-	-	-	-	-	-	-	-	-	-	-	-
1929	15.7	0.6	-	-	-	-	-	-	-	-	-	-	-	-	-	-
1930	15.3	-2.5	-	-	-	-	-	-	-	-	-	-	-	-	-	-
1931	13.9	-9.2	-	-	-	-	-	-	-	-	-	-	-	-	-	-
1932	12.3	-11.5	-	-	-	-	-	-	-	-	-	-	-	-	-	-
1933	11.8	-4.1	-	-	-	-	-	-	-	-	-	-	-	-	-	-
1934	12.3	4.2	-	-	-	-	-	-	-	-	-	-	-	-	-	-
1935	12.7	3.3	-	-	-	-	-	-	-	-	-	-	-	-	-	-
1936	12.8	0.8	-	-	-	-	-	-	-	-	-	-	-	-	-	-
1937	13.3	3.9	-	-	-	-	-	-	-	-	-	-	-	-	-	-
1938	13.3	0.0	-	-	-	-	-	-	-	-	-	-	-	-	-	-
1939	13.2	-0.8	-	-	-	-	-	-	-	-	-	-	-	-	-	-
1940	13.2	0.0	-	-	-	-	-	-	-	-	-	-	-	-	-	-
1941	13.8	4.5	-	-	-	-	-	-	-	-	-	-	-	-	-	-
1942	15.2	10.1	-	-	-	-	-	-	-	-	-	-	-	-	-	-
1943	16.0	5.3	-	-	-	-	-	-	-	-	-	-	-	-	-	-
1944	16.2	1.3	-	-	-	-	-	-	-	-	-	-	-	-	-	-
1945	16.6	2.5	-	-	-	-	-	-	-	-	-	-	-	-	-	-
1946	17.9	7.8	-	-	-	-	-	-	-	-	-	-	-	-	-	-
1947	21.0	17.3	-	-	-	-	-	-	20.8	-	14.5	-	-	-	-	-
1948	22.7	8.1	-	-	-	-	-	-	23.2	11.5	14.9	2.8	-	-	-	-
1949	22.7	0.0	-	-	-	-	-	-	24.7	6.5	15.2	2.0	-	-	-	-
1950	23.4	3.1	-	-	-	-	-	-	25.7	4.0	15.6	2.6	-	-	-	-
1951	25.2	7.7	-	-	-	-	-	-	28.0	8.9	15.9	1.9	-	-	-	-
1952	25.5	1.2	-	-	-	-	-	-	28.5	1.8	16.8	5.7	-	-	-	-
1953	25.8	1.2	-	-	-	-	36.1	-	29.0	1.8	17.5	4.2	-	-	-	-
1954	25.8	0.0	-	-	-	-	36.0	-0.3	28.6	-1.4	17.7	1.1	-	-	-	-
1955	25.7	-0.4	-	-	-	-	36.0	0.0	28.3	-1.0	18.4	4.0	-	-	-	-
1956	26.1	1.6	-	-	-	-	36.7	1.9	28.9	2.1	18.9	2.7	-	-	-	-
1957	26.9	3.1	-	-	-	-	37.6	2.5	30.9	6.9	19.2	1.6	-	-	-	-
1958	27.3	1.5	-	-	-	-	38.3	1.9	31.5	1.9	19.7	2.6	-	-	-	-

[Continued]

498

Houston, TX
Consumer Price Index - All Urban Consumers
Base 1982-1984 = 100
Annual Averages
[Continued]

For 1914-1993. Columns headed % show percentile change in the index from the previous period for which an index is available.

Year	All Items		Food & Beverage		Housing		Apparel & Upkeep		Trans- portation		Medical Care		Entertain- ment		Other Goods & Services	
	Index	%	Index	%	Index	%	Index	%	Index	%	Index	%	Index	%	Index	%
1959	27.6	1.1	-	-	-	-	38.7	1.0	33.0	4.8	20.0	1.5	-	-	-	-
1960	27.8	0.7	-	-	-	-	38.7	0.0	32.9	-0.3	20.5	2.5	-	-	-	-
1961	28.0	0.7	-	-	-	-	38.9	0.5	33.1	0.6	20.8	1.5	-	-	-	-
1962	28.5	1.8	-	-	-	-	40.0	2.8	34.2	3.3	21.0	1.0	-	-	-	-
1963	28.8	1.1	-	-	-	-	40.5	1.3	33.5	-2.0	21.6	2.9	-	-	-	-
1964	29.2	1.4	-	-	-	-	40.8	0.7	34.3	2.4	22.2	2.8	-	-	-	-
1965	29.6	1.4	-	-	-	-	40.8	0.0	34.2	-0.3	22.8	2.7	-	-	-	-
1966	30.4	2.7	-	-	-	-	41.5	1.7	34.8	1.8	23.4	2.6	-	-	-	-
1967	31.2	2.6	-	-	-	-	42.2	1.7	36.0	3.4	24.9	6.4	-	-	-	-
1968	32.5	4.2	-	-	-	-	44.6	5.7	37.1	3.1	26.2	5.2	-	-	-	-
1969	34.6	6.5	-	-	-	-	48.1	7.8	38.4	3.5	28.5	8.8	-	-	-	-
1970	36.4	5.2	-	-	-	-	50.6	5.2	39.1	1.8	30.6	7.4	-	-	-	-
1971	37.7	3.6					51.5	1.8	40.8	4.3	32.4	5.9				
1972	39.0	3.4					53.1	3.1	41.4	1.5	33.7	4.0	-	-	-	-
1973	41.2	5.6					55.1	3.8	42.2	1.9	35.0	3.9				
1974	46.1	11.9	-	-	-	-	60.3	9.4	47.3	12.1	37.9	8.3				
1975	51.4	11.5	-	-	-	-	64.2	6.5	51.9	9.7	43.2	14.0	-	-	-	-
1976	55.3	7.6	58.5	-	53.0	-	68.0	5.9	56.3	8.5	48.0	11.1	61.3	-	56.3	-
1977	59.3	7.2	61.6	5.3	57.4	8.3	72.0	5.9	60.5	7.5	54.2	12.9	64.0	4.4	59.8	6.2
1978	64.9	9.4	67.8	10.1	64.4	12.2	76.9	6.8	62.8	3.8	59.4	9.6	65.7	2.7	65.5	9.5
1979	73.5	13.3	76.8	13.3	73.6	14.3	83.1	8.1	72.3	15.1	65.1	9.6	70.1	6.7	71.7	9.5
1980	82.7	12.5	83.8	9.1	82.7	12.4	89.1	7.2	85.6	18.4	72.2	10.9	79.7	13.7	79.3	10.6
1981	91.0	10.0	91.8	9.5	91.2	10.3	95.6	7.3	94.8	10.7	80.0	10.8	86.4	8.4	85.3	7.6
1982	97.3	6.9	96.4	5.0	99.8	9.4	98.4	2.9	97.7	3.1	90.7	13.4	92.8	7.4	91.8	7.6
1983	100.0	2.8	99.3	3.0	100.3	0.5	99.8	1.4	99.1	1.4	101.1	11.5	103.1	11.1	101.0	10.0
1984	102.7	2.7	104.3	5.0	99.9	-0.4	101.9	2.1	103.3	4.2	108.1	6.9	104.1	1.0	107.2	6.1
1985	104.9	2.1	105.0	0.7	100.2	0.3	104.4	2.5	106.2	2.8	116.8	8.0	111.9	7.5	112.5	4.9
1986	103.9	-1.0	107.3	2.2	98.1	-2.1	106.1	1.6	99.2	-6.6	123.5	5.7	114.5	2.3	118.6	5.4
1987	106.5	2.5	111.8	4.2	97.0	-1.1	113.6	7.1	102.5	3.3	130.4	5.6	118.5	3.5	124.8	5.2
1988	109.5	2.8	116.2	3.9	98.0	1.0	121.1	6.6	104.5	2.0	136.7	4.8	124.5	5.1	131.2	5.1
1989	114.1	4.2	121.7	4.7	100.5	2.6	123.9	2.3	109.2	4.5	148.0	8.3	133.8	7.5	138.5	5.6
1990	120.6	5.7	128.7	5.8	104.8	4.3	132.5	6.9	116.0	6.2	161.2	8.9	134.9	0.8	152.1	9.8
1991	125.1	3.7	131.6	2.3	109.5	4.5	134.8	1.7	119.6	3.1	177.7	10.2	139.6	3.5	157.7	3.7
1992	129.1	3.2	130.8	-0.6	113.2	3.4	135.8	0.7	122.9	2.8	193.6	8.9	146.4	4.9	172.1	9.1
1993	133.4	3.3	132.4	1.2	116.8	3.2	142.1	4.6	128.2	4.3	200.8	3.7	153.2	4.6	180.8	5.1

Source: U.S. Department of Labor, Bureau of Labor Statistics, Division of Consumer Prices and Price Indexes. - indicates no data collected for period.

Houston, TX
Consumer Price Index - Urban Wage Earners
Base 1982-1984 = 100
Annual Averages

For 1914-1993. Columns headed % show percentile change in the index from the previous period for which an index is available.

Year	All Items		Food & Beverage		Housing		Apparel & Upkeep		Trans-portation		Medical Care		Entertain-ment		Other Goods & Services	
	Index	%	Index	%	Index	%	Index	%	Index	%	Index	%	Index	%	Index	%
1914	-	-	-	-	-	-	-	-	-	-	-	-	-	-	-	-
1915	9.5	-	-	-	-	-	-	-	-	-	-	-	-	-	-	-
1916	10.1	6.3	-	-	-	-	-	-	-	-	-	-	-	-	-	-
1917	12.5	23.8	-	-	-	-	-	-	-	-	-	-	-	-	-	-
1918	14.5	16.0	-	-	-	-	-	-	-	-	-	-	-	-	-	-
1919	17.0	17.2	-	-	-	-	-	-	-	-	-	-	-	-	-	-
1920	19.3	13.5	-	-	-	-	-	-	-	-	-	-	-	-	-	-
1921	17.1	-11.4	-	-	-	-	-	-	-	-	-	-	-	-	-	-
1922	16.0	-6.4	-	-	-	-	-	-	-	-	-	-	-	-	-	-
1923	16.0	0.0	-	-	-	-	-	-	-	-	-	-	-	-	-	-
1924	15.9	-0.6	-	-	-	-	-	-	-	-	-	-	-	-	-	-
1925	16.2	1.9	-	-	-	-	-	-	-	-	-	-	-	-	-	-
1926	16.1	-0.6	-	-	-	-	-	-	-	-	-	-	-	-	-	-
1927	15.8	-1.9	-	-	-	-	-	-	-	-	-	-	-	-	-	-
1928	15.6	-1.3	-	-	-	-	-	-	-	-	-	-	-	-	-	-
1929	15.7	0.6	-	-	-	-	-	-	-	-	-	-	-	-	-	-
1930	15.4	-1.9	-	-	-	-	-	-	-	-	-	-	-	-	-	-
1931	13.9	-9.7	-	-	-	-	-	-	-	-	-	-	-	-	-	-
1932	12.4	-10.8	-	-	-	-	-	-	-	-	-	-	-	-	-	-
1933	11.8	-4.8	-	-	-	-	-	-	-	-	-	-	-	-	-	-
1934	12.4	5.1	-	-	-	-	-	-	-	-	-	-	-	-	-	-
1935	12.8	3.2	-	-	-	-	-	-	-	-	-	-	-	-	-	-
1936	12.9	0.8	-	-	-	-	-	-	-	-	-	-	-	-	-	-
1937	13.4	3.9	-	-	-	-	-	-	-	-	-	-	-	-	-	-
1938	13.3	-0.7	-	-	-	-	-	-	-	-	-	-	-	-	-	-
1939	13.2	-0.8	-	-	-	-	-	-	-	-	-	-	-	-	-	-
1940	13.3	0.8	-	-	-	-	-	-	-	-	-	-	-	-	-	-
1941	13.8	3.8	-	-	-	-	-	-	-	-	-	-	-	-	-	-
1942	15.3	10.9	-	-	-	-	-	-	-	-	-	-	-	-	-	-
1943	16.1	5.2	-	-	-	-	-	-	-	-	-	-	-	-	-	-
1944	16.3	1.2	-	-	-	-	-	-	-	-	-	-	-	-	-	-
1945	16.6	1.8	-	-	-	-	-	-	-	-	-	-	-	-	-	-
1946	18.0	8.4	-	-	-	-	-	-	-	-	-	-	-	-	-	-
1947	21.1	17.2	-	-	-	-	-	-	20.7	-	13.9	-	-	-	-	-
1948	22.8	8.1	-	-	-	-	-	-	23.2	12.1	14.2	2.2	-	-	-	-
1949	22.8	0.0	-	-	-	-	-	-	24.6	6.0	14.6	2.8	-	-	-	-
1950	23.5	3.1	-	-	-	-	-	-	25.6	4.1	14.9	2.1	-	-	-	-
1951	25.3	7.7	-	-	-	-	-	-	27.9	9.0	15.3	2.7	-	-	-	-
1952	25.7	1.6	-	-	-	-	-	-	28.4	1.8	16.1	5.2	-	-	-	-
1953	26.0	1.2	-	-	-	-	36.8	-	28.9	1.8	16.8	4.3	-	-	-	-
1954	25.9	-0.4	-	-	-	-	36.7	-0.3	28.5	-1.4	17.0	1.2	-	-	-	-
1955	25.8	-0.4	-	-	-	-	36.7	0.0	28.1	-1.4	17.7	4.1	-	-	-	-
1956	26.2	1.6	-	-	-	-	37.4	1.9	28.8	2.5	18.2	2.8	-	-	-	-
1957	27.0	3.1	-	-	-	-	38.3	2.4	30.8	6.9	18.4	1.1	-	-	-	-
1958	27.5	1.9	-	-	-	-	39.1	2.1	31.3	1.6	18.8	2.2	-	-	-	-

[Continued]

Houston, TX
Consumer Price Index - Urban Wage Earners
Base 1982-1984 = 100
Annual Averages
[Continued]

For 1914-1993. Columns headed % show percentile change in the index from the previous period for which an index is available.

Year	All Items		Food & Beverage		Housing		Apparel & Upkeep		Trans- portation		Medical Care		Entertain- ment		Other Goods & Services	
	Index	%	Index	%	Index	%	Index	%	Index	%	Index	%	Index	%	Index	%
1959	27.7	0.7	-	-	-	-	39.5	1.0	32.8	4.8	19.2	2.1	-	-	-	-
1960	27.9	0.7	-	-	-	-	39.4	-0.3	32.8	0.0	19.6	2.1	-	-	-	-
1961	28.1	0.7	-	-	-	-	39.6	0.5	32.9	0.3	19.9	1.5	-	-	-	-
1962	28.6	1.8	-	-	-	-	40.8	3.0	34.0	3.3	20.2	1.5	-	-	-	-
1963	28.9	1.0	-	-	-	-	41.3	1.2	33.4	-1.8	20.7	2.5	-	-	-	-
1964	29.4	1.7	-	-	-	-	41.6	0.7	34.2	2.4	21.3	2.9	-	-	-	-
1965	29.7	1.0	-	-	-	-	41.6	0.0	34.1	-0.3	21.8	2.3	-	-	-	-
1966	30.5	2.7	-	-	-	-	42.3	1.7	34.7	1.8	22.5	3.2	-	-	-	-
1967	31.3	2.6	-	-	-	-	43.0	1.7	35.9	3.5	23.9	6.2	-	-	-	-
1968	32.7	4.5	-	-	-	-	45.4	5.6	36.9	2.8	25.1	5.0	-	-	-	-
1969	34.8	6.4	-	-	-	-	49.1	8.1	38.3	3.8	27.4	9.2	-	-	-	-
1970	36.6	5.2	-	-	-	-	51.6	5.1	39.0	1.8	29.3	6.9	-	-	-	-
1971	37.9	3.6	-	-	-	-	52.5	1.7	40.6	4.1	31.0	5.8	-	-	-	-
1972	39.2	3.4	-	-	-	-	54.1	3.0	41.2	1.5	32.3	4.2	-	-	-	-
1973	41.5	5.9	-	-	-	-	56.2	3.9	42.0	1.9	33.6	4.0	-	-	-	-
1974	46.3	11.6	-	-	-	-	61.4	9.3	47.1	12.1	36.4	8.3	-	-	-	-
1975	51.7	11.7	-	-	-	-	65.5	6.7	51.7	9.8	41.4	13.7	-	-	-	-
1976	55.6	7.5	59.5	-	53.0	-	69.3	5.8	56.0	8.3	46.0	11.1	63.1	-	56.2	-
1977	59.6	7.2	62.6	5.2	57.4	8.3	73.4	5.9	60.2	7.5	51.9	12.8	65.8	4.3	59.6	6.0
1978	65.1	9.2	68.6	9.6	64.3	12.0	78.5	6.9	62.7	4.2	57.0	9.8	67.9	3.2	64.7	8.6
1979	73.4	12.7	77.0	12.2	72.7	13.1	85.3	8.7	72.1	15.0	64.7	13.5	71.6	5.4	70.6	9.1
1980	82.1	11.9	83.8	8.8	81.4	12.0	90.3	5.9	84.3	16.9	71.7	10.8	79.0	10.3	78.5	11.2
1981	90.3	10.0	91.6	9.3	90.0	10.6	96.4	6.8	93.4	10.8	79.6	11.0	85.2	7.8	84.6	7.8
1982	96.9	7.3	96.4	5.2	98.7	9.7	98.5	2.2	97.1	4.0	90.5	13.7	91.3	7.2	91.7	8.4
1983	100.1	3.3	99.4	3.1	100.4	1.7	99.8	1.3	99.0	2.0	101.2	11.8	104.0	13.9	101.0	10.1
1984	103.1	3.0	104.2	4.8	100.8	0.4	101.8	2.0	103.9	4.9	108.3	7.0	104.8	0.8	107.3	6.2
1985	104.6	1.5	104.8	0.6	100.1	-0.7	104.2	2.4	106.7	2.7	117.0	8.0	112.6	7.4	112.4	4.8
1986	103.6	-1.0	107.3	2.4	98.0	-2.1	105.7	1.4	100.3	-6.0	123.7	5.7	115.7	2.8	117.4	4.4
1987	106.4	2.7	111.7	4.1	96.5	-1.5	112.7	6.6	104.7	4.4	130.9	5.8	120.0	3.7	123.0	4.8
1988	109.7	3.1	116.1	3.9	97.5	1.0	121.1	7.5	107.1	2.3	137.7	5.2	126.3	5.2	130.4	6.0
1989	114.4	4.3	121.7	4.8	100.2	2.8	124.0	2.4	111.9	4.5	149.3	8.4	135.7	7.4	139.1	6.7
1990	120.9	5.7	128.8	5.8	104.5	4.3	132.8	7.1	118.7	6.1	162.3	8.7	136.6	0.7	152.8	9.8
1991	125.3	3.6	131.7	2.3	109.4	4.7	133.9	0.8	122.1	2.9	178.9	10.2	141.2	3.4	157.7	3.2
1992	128.9	2.9	131.0	-0.5	113.3	3.6	134.4	0.4	125.2	2.5	195.3	9.2	148.3	5.0	171.5	8.8
1993	133.0	3.2	132.6	1.2	117.2	3.4	138.9	3.3	129.4	3.4	202.9	3.9	156.2	5.3	179.6	4.7

Source: U.S. Department of Labor, Bureau of Labor Statistics, Division of Consumer Prices and Price Indexes. - indicates no data collected for period.

Houston, TX

Consumer Price Index - All Urban Consumers
Base 1982-1984 = 100
All Items

For 1914-1993. Columns headed % show percentile change in the index from the previous period for which an index is available.

Year	Jan Index	%	Feb Index	%	Mar Index	%	Apr Index	%	May Index	%	Jun Index	%	Jul Index	%	Aug Index	%	Sep Index	%	Oct Index	%	Nov Index	%	Dec Index	%
1914	-	-	-	-	-	-	-	-	-	-	-	-	-	-	-	-	-	-	-	-	-	-	9.5	-
1915	-	-	-	-	-	-	-	-	-	-	-	-	-	-	-	-	-	-	-	-	-	-	9.5	0.0
1916	-	-	-	-	-	-	-	-	-	-	-	-	-	-	-	-	-	-	-	-	-	-	10.9	14.7
1917	-	-	-	-	-	-	-	-	-	-	-	-	-	-	-	-	-	-	-	-	-	-	13.2	21.1
1918	-	-	-	-	-	-	-	-	-	-	-	-	-	-	-	-	-	-	-	-	-	-	15.9	20.5
1919	-	-	-	-	-	-	-	-	-	-	16.4	3.1	-	-	-	-	-	-	-	-	-	-	18.5	12.8
1920	-	-	-	-	-	-	-	-	-	-	19.7	6.5	-	-	-	-	-	-	-	-	-	-	18.9	-4.1
1921	-	-	-	-	-	-	-	-	16.9	-10.6	-	-	-	-	-	-	16.6	-1.8	-	-	-	-	16.4	-1.2
1922	-	-	-	-	15.9	-3.0	-	-	-	-	15.8	-0.6	-	-	-	-	15.7	-0.6	-	-	-	-	15.9	1.3
1923	-	-	-	-	15.7	-1.3	-	-	-	-	15.9	1.3	-	-	-	-	16.0	0.6	-	-	-	-	16.1	0.6
1924	-	-	-	-	15.9	-1.2	-	-	-	-	15.6	-1.9	-	-	-	-	15.8	1.3	-	-	-	-	16.0	1.3
1925	-	-	-	-	-	-	-	-	-	-	16.1	0.6	-	-	-	-	-	-	-	-	-	-	16.4	1.9
1926	-	-	-	-	-	-	-	-	-	-	16.0	-2.4	-	-	-	-	-	-	-	-	-	-	16.0	0.0
1927	-	-	-	-	-	-	-	-	-	-	15.7	-1.9	-	-	-	-	-	-	-	-	-	-	15.8	0.6
1928	-	-	-	-	-	-	-	-	-	-	15.5	-1.9	-	-	-	-	-	-	-	-	-	-	15.6	0.6
1929	-	-	-	-	-	-	-	-	-	-	15.6	0.0	-	-	-	-	-	-	-	-	-	-	15.8	1.3
1930	-	-	-	-	-	-	-	-	-	-	15.4	-2.5	-	-	-	-	-	-	-	-	-	-	14.7	-4.5
1931	-	-	-	-	-	-	-	-	-	-	13.8	-6.1	-	-	-	-	-	-	-	-	-	-	13.4	-2.9
1932	-	-	-	-	-	-	-	-	-	-	12.3	-8.2	-	-	-	-	-	-	-	-	-	-	11.7	-4.9
1933	-	-	-	-	-	-	-	-	-	-	11.6	-0.9	-	-	-	-	-	-	-	-	-	-	12.1	4.3
1934	-	-	-	-	-	-	-	-	-	-	12.2	0.8	-	-	-	-	-	-	-	-	12.6	3.3	-	-
1935	-	-	-	-	12.8	1.6	-	-	-	-	-	-	12.6	-1.6	-	-	-	-	12.7	0.8	-	-	-	-
1936	12.8	0.8	-	-	-	-	12.6	-1.6	-	-	-	-	12.9	2.4	-	-	13.0	0.8	-	-	-	-	13.0	0.0
1937	-	-	-	-	13.3	2.3	-	-	-	-	13.3	0.0	-	-	-	-	13.5	1.5	-	-	-	-	13.5	0.0
1938	-	-	-	-	13.3	-1.5	-	-	-	-	13.2	-0.8	-	-	-	-	13.3	0.8	-	-	-	-	13.3	0.0
1939	-	-	-	-	13.1	-1.5	-	-	-	-	13.1	0.0	-	-	-	-	13.3	1.5	-	-	-	-	13.2	-0.8
1940	-	-	-	-	13.2	0.0	-	-	-	-	13.2	0.0	-	-	-	-	13.2	0.0	13.3	0.8	13.3	0.0	13.3	0.0
1941	13.3	0.0	13.3	0.0	13.3	0.0	13.5	1.5	13.5	0.0	13.6	0.7	13.7	0.7	13.8	0.7	14.1	2.2	14.4	2.1	14.5	0.7	14.6	0.7
1942	14.7	0.7	14.9	1.4	15.1	1.3	15.1	0.0	15.2	0.7	15.1	-0.7	15.3	1.3	15.4	0.7	15.5	0.6	15.5	0.0	15.5	0.0	15.6	0.6
1943	15.7	0.6	15.8	0.6	16.2	2.5	16.2	0.0	16.3	0.6	16.1	-1.2	16.0	-0.6	15.9	-0.6	16.1	1.3	16.1	0.0	16.1	0.0	16.1	0.0
1944	16.1	0.0	16.1	0.0	16.0	-0.6	16.1	0.6	16.2	0.6	16.2	0.0	16.3	0.6	16.3	0.0	16.3	0.0	16.3	0.0	16.2	-0.6	16.3	0.6
1945	16.4	0.6	16.3	-0.6	16.3	0.0	16.4	0.6	16.5	0.6	16.6	0.6	16.7	0.6	16.7	0.0	16.7	0.0	16.6	-0.6	16.6	0.0	16.7	0.6
1946	16.6	-0.6	16.6	0.0	16.7	0.6	16.8	0.6	16.8	0.0	17.1	1.8	17.9	4.7	18.4	2.8	18.7	1.6	18.9	1.1	19.7	4.2	20.0	1.5
1947	20.2	1.0	20.2	0.0	20.6	2.0	20.8	1.0	20.7	-0.5	20.7	0.0	20.8	0.5	21.0	1.0	21.3	1.4	21.5	0.9	21.8	1.4	22.2	1.8
1948	22.4	0.9	22.4	0.0	22.4	0.0	22.5	0.4	22.5	0.0	22.7	0.9	22.9	0.9	23.1	0.9	23.1	0.0	23.0	-0.4	22.9	-0.4	22.9	0.0
1949	22.8	-0.4	22.5	-1.3	22.5	0.0	22.6	0.4	22.5	-0.4	22.5	0.0	22.5	0.0	22.6	0.4	22.7	0.4	22.8	0.4	23.0	0.9	23.0	0.0
1950	22.9	-0.4	22.9	0.0	23.0	0.4	22.9	-0.4	22.9	0.0	23.0	0.4	23.2	0.9	23.6	1.7	23.8	0.8	23.8	0.0	23.9	0.4	24.3	1.7
1951	24.8	2.1	25.0	0.8	25.1	0.4	25.2	0.4	25.2	0.0	25.1	-0.4	25.2	0.4	25.2	0.0	25.3	0.4	25.4	0.4	25.5	0.4	25.6	0.4
1952	25.5	-0.4	25.4	-0.4	25.4	0.0	25.4	0.0	25.4	0.0	25.4	0.0	25.5	0.4	25.6	0.4	25.5	-0.4	25.7	0.8	25.7	0.0	25.8	0.4
1953	-	-	25.7	-0.4	-	-	-	-	25.8	0.4	-	-	-	-	25.8	0.0	-	-	-	-	25.9	0.4	-	-
1954	-	-	25.9	0.0	-	-	-	-	25.8	-0.4	-	-	-	-	25.8	0.0	-	-	-	-	25.8	0.0	-	-
1955	-	-	25.6	-0.8	-	-	-	-	25.5	-0.4	-	-	-	-	25.5	0.0	-	-	-	-	25.8	1.2	-	-
1956	-	-	25.8	0.0	-	-	-	-	25.8	0.0	-	-	-	-	26.1	1.2	-	-	-	-	26.5	1.5	-	-
1957	-	-	26.7	0.8	-	-	-	-	26.8	0.4	-	-	-	-	27.0	0.7	-	-	-	-	27.1	0.4	-	-
1958	-	-	27.1	0.0	-	-	-	-	27.4	1.1	-	-	-	-	27.4	0.0	-	-	-	-	27.5	0.4	-	-

[Continued]

Houston, TX
Consumer Price Index - All Urban Consumers
Base 1982-1984 = 100
All Items
[Continued]

For 1914-1993. Columns headed % show percentile change in the index from the previous period for which an index is available.

Year	Jan Index	%	Feb Index	%	Mar Index	%	Apr Index	%	May Index	%	Jun Index	%	Jul Index	%	Aug Index	%	Sep Index	%	Oct Index	%	Nov Index	%	Dec Index	%
1959	-	-	27.4	-0.4	-	-	-	-	27.4	0.0	-	-	-	-	27.6	0.7	-	-	-	-	27.7	0.4	-	-
1960	-	-	27.8	0.4	-	-	-	-	27.7	-0.4	-	-	-	-	27.9	0.7	-	-	-	-	28.0	0.4	-	-
1961	-	-	27.7	-1.1	-	-	-	-	27.9	0.7	-	-	-	-	27.9	0.0	-	-	-	-	28.3	1.4	-	-
1962	-	-	28.5	0.7	-	-	-	-	28.5	0.0	-	-	-	-	28.5	0.0	-	-	-	-	28.5	0.0	-	-
1963	-	-	28.6	0.4	-	-	-	-	28.5	-0.3	-	-	-	-	28.9	1.4	-	-	-	-	29.1	0.7	-	-
1964	-	-	29.2	0.3	-	-	-	-	29.1	-0.3	-	-	-	-	29.2	0.3	-	-	-	-	29.2	0.0	-	-
1965	-	-	29.3	0.3	-	-	29.4	0.3	-	-	-	-	29.6	0.7	-	-	-	-	29.8	0.7	-	-	-	-
1966	30.0	0.7	-	-	-	-	30.2	0.7	-	-	-	-	30.4	0.7	-	-	-	-	30.6	0.7	-	-	-	-
1967	30.8	0.7	-	-	-	-	31.0	0.6	-	-	-	-	31.1	0.3	-	-	-	-	31.5	1.3	-	-	-	-
1968	31.8	1.0	-	-	-	-	32.1	0.9	-	-	-	-	32.5	1.2	-	-	-	-	33.0	1.5	-	-	-	-
1969	33.6	1.8	-	-	-	-	34.2	1.8	-	-	-	-	34.6	1.2	-	-	-	-	35.4	2.3	-	-	-	-
1970	35.7	0.8	-	-	-	-	36.2	1.4	-	-	-	-	36.4	0.6	-	-	-	-	36.8	1.1	-	-	-	-
1971	37.2	1.1	-	-	-	-	37.3	0.3	-	-	-	-	37.8	1.3	-	-	-	-	38.2	1.1	-	-	-	-
1972	38.4	0.5	-	-	-	-	38.9	1.3	-	-	-	-	39.0	0.3	-	-	-	-	39.4	1.0	-	-	-	-
1973	39.7	0.8	-	-	-	-	40.7	2.5	-	-	-	-	41.0	0.7	-	-	-	-	42.5	3.7	-	-	-	-
1974	43.4	2.1	-	-	-	-	44.6	2.8	-	-	-	-	46.1	3.4	-	-	-	-	48.1	4.3	-	-	-	-
1975	49.7	3.3	-	-	-	-	50.3	1.2	-	-	-	-	51.8	3.0	-	-	-	-	52.6	1.5	-	-	-	-
1976	53.7	2.1	-	-	-	-	54.3	1.1	-	-	-	-	55.2	1.7	-	-	-	-	56.7	2.7	-	-	-	-
1977	57.2	0.9	-	-	-	-	58.8	2.8	-	-	-	-	59.7	1.5	-	-	-	-	60.1	0.7	-	-	-	-
1978	61.3	2.0	-	-	-	-	63.3	3.3	-	-	64.7	2.2	-	-	65.9	1.9	-	-	67.0	1.7	-	-	68.5	2.2
1979	-	-	69.9	2.0	-	-	71.1	1.7	-	-	73.4	3.2	-	-	75.0	2.2	-	-	76.1	1.5	-	-	77.5	1.8
1980	-	-	79.8	3.0	-	-	81.3	1.9	-	-	83.1	2.2	-	-	83.7	0.7	-	-	84.9	1.4	-	-	85.7	0.9
1981	-	-	87.8	2.5	-	-	89.3	1.7	-	-	91.3	2.2	-	-	91.9	0.7	-	-	93.5	1.7	-	-	94.4	1.0
1982	-	-	94.8	0.4	-	-	95.1	0.3	-	-	97.9	2.9	-	-	99.3	1.4	-	-	99.0	-0.3	-	-	99.2	0.2
1983	-	-	98.9	-0.3	-	-	98.7	-0.2	-	-	100.2	1.5	-	-	101.0	0.8	-	-	101.1	0.1	-	-	100.0	-1.1
1984	-	-	100.9	0.9	-	-	101.5	0.6	-	-	103.0	1.5	-	-	103.5	0.5	-	-	104.3	0.8	-	-	103.9	-0.4
1985	-	-	104.0	0.1	-	-	104.5	0.5	-	-	105.3	0.8	-	-	105.4	0.1	-	-	105.3	-0.1	-	-	105.0	-0.3
1986	-	-	105.1	0.1	-	-	102.9	-2.1	-	-	103.9	1.0	-	-	103.8	-0.1	-	-	104.1	0.3	-	-	103.2	-0.9
1987	-	-	104.4	1.2	-	-	106.4	1.9	-	-	106.5	0.1	-	-	107.3	0.8	-	-	108.0	0.7	-	-	107.3	-0.6
1988	-	-	108.0	0.7	-	-	108.2	0.2	-	-	109.4	1.1	-	-	110.3	0.8	-	-	111.1	0.7	-	-	111.3	0.2
1989	-	-	112.7	1.3	-	-	113.2	0.4	-	-	114.1	0.8	-	-	114.4	0.3	-	-	115.7	1.1	-	-	115.5	-0.2
1990	-	-	118.7	2.8	-	-	118.3	-0.3	-	-	119.7	1.2	-	-	121.5	1.5	-	-	124.0	2.1	-	-	123.0	-0.8
1991	-	-	124.3	1.1	-	-	123.5	-0.6	-	-	124.9	1.1	-	-	124.8	-0.1	-	-	127.3	2.0	-	-	127.0	-0.2
1992	-	-	127.0	0.0	-	-	128.7	1.3	-	-	129.4	0.5	-	-	129.9	0.4	-	-	130.8	0.7	-	-	129.3	-1.1
1993	-	-	131.7	1.9	-	-	131.8	0.1	-	-	132.9	0.8	-	-	133.0	0.1	-	-	136.6	2.7	-	-	136.5	-0.1

Source: U.S. Department of Labor, Bureau of Labor Statistics, Division of Consumer Prices and Price Indexes. - indicates no data collected for period.

Houston, TX
Consumer Price Index - Urban Wage Earners
Base 1982-1984 = 100
All Items

For 1914-1993. Columns headed % show percentile change in the index from the previous period for which an index is available.

Year	Jan Index	Jan %	Feb Index	Feb %	Mar Index	Mar %	Apr Index	Apr %	May Index	May %	Jun Index	Jun %	Jul Index	Jul %	Aug Index	Aug %	Sep Index	Sep %	Oct Index	Oct %	Nov Index	Nov %	Dec Index	Dec %
1914																							9.6	-
1915																							9.5	-1.0
1916																							10.9	14.7
1917																							13.3	22.0
1918																							16.0	20.3
1919											16.4	2.5											18.6	13.4
1920											19.8	6.5											19.0	-4.0
1921									17.0	-10.5							16.6	-2.4					16.4	-1.2
1922					16.0	-2.4					15.9	-0.6					15.8	-0.6					16.0	1.3
1923					15.8	-1.2					15.9	0.6					16.0	0.6					16.2	1.3
1924					16.0	-1.2					15.7	-1.9					15.9	1.3					16.0	0.6
1925											16.2	1.3											16.4	1.2
1926											16.0	-2.4											16.1	0.6
1927											15.8	-1.9											15.9	0.6
1928											15.5	-2.5											15.7	1.3
1929											15.6	-0.6											15.9	1.9
1930											15.4	-3.1											14.7	-4.5
1931											13.9	-5.4											13.5	-2.9
1932											12.3	-8.9											11.7	-4.9
1933											11.7	0.0											12.1	3.4
1934											12.2	0.8									12.6	3.3		
1935					12.8	1.6							12.7	-0.8					12.7	0.0				
1936	12.8	0.8					12.7	-0.8					12.9	1.6			13.1	1.6					13.1	0.0
1937					13.3	1.5					13.3	0.0					13.6	2.3					13.5	-0.7
1938					13.4	-0.7					13.3	-0.7					13.3	0.0					13.3	0.0
1939					13.2	-0.8					13.2	0.0					13.3	0.8					13.3	0.0
1940					13.2	-0.8					13.2	0.0					13.3	0.8	13.4	0.8	13.4	0.0	13.4	0.0
1941	13.4	0.0	13.4	0.0	13.4	0.0	13.6	1.5	13.6	0.0	13.6	0.0	13.8	1.5	13.9	0.7	14.2	2.2	14.5	2.1	14.6	0.7	14.7	0.7
1942	14.8	0.7	15.0	1.4	15.2	1.3	15.2	0.0	15.3	0.7	15.2	-0.7	15.4	1.3	15.4	0.0	15.5	0.6	15.6	0.6	15.6	0.0	15.7	0.6
1943	15.7	0.0	15.9	1.3	16.2	1.9	16.3	0.6	16.3	0.0	16.2	-1.2	16.1	-0.6	16.0	-0.6	16.2	1.3	16.2	0.0	16.2	0.0	16.2	0.0
1944	16.2	0.0	16.2	0.0	16.1	-0.6	16.2	0.6	16.3	0.6	16.2	-0.6	16.4	1.2	16.4	0.0	16.4	0.0	16.4	0.0	16.3	-0.6	16.4	0.6
1945	16.4	0.0	16.4	0.0	16.4	0.0	16.5	0.6	16.6	0.6	16.7	0.6	16.8	0.6	16.8	0.0	16.8	0.0	16.7	-0.6	16.7	0.0	16.8	0.6
1946	16.7	-0.6	16.7	0.0	16.8	0.6	16.9	0.6	16.9	0.0	17.2	1.8	18.0	4.7	18.5	2.8	18.8	1.6	19.0	1.1	19.8	4.2	20.1	1.5
1947	20.3	1.0	20.3	0.0	20.7	2.0	20.9	1.0	20.8	-0.5	20.8	0.0	20.9	0.5	21.1	1.0	21.4	1.4	21.6	0.9	21.9	1.4	22.3	1.8
1948	22.5	0.9	22.5	0.0	22.5	0.0	22.7	0.9	22.7	0.0	22.8	0.4	23.0	0.9	23.2	0.9	23.2	0.0	23.2	0.0	23.0	-0.9	23.0	0.0
1949	22.9	-0.4	22.6	-1.3	22.6	0.0	22.7	0.4	22.7	0.0	22.7	0.0	22.7	0.0	22.7	0.0	22.8	0.4	22.9	0.4	23.1	0.9	23.1	0.0
1950	23.1	0.0	23.0	-0.4	23.1	0.4	23.0	-0.4	23.0	0.0	23.1	0.4	23.3	0.9	23.7	1.7	23.9	0.8	23.9	0.0	24.0	0.4	24.4	1.7
1951	25.0	2.5	25.1	0.4	25.3	0.8	25.3	0.0	25.3	0.0	25.3	0.0	25.3	0.0	25.3	0.0	25.5	0.8	25.5	0.0	25.6	0.4	25.8	0.8
1952	25.7	-0.4	25.5	-0.8	25.5	0.0	25.6	0.4	25.5	-0.4	25.6	0.4	25.6	0.0	25.8	0.8	25.7	-0.4	25.8	0.4	25.8	0.0	25.9	0.4
1953			25.8	-0.4					26.0	0.8					26.0	0.0					26.1	0.4		
1954			26.0	-0.4					25.9	-0.4					25.9	0.0					25.9	0.0		
1955			25.7	-0.8					25.7	0.0					25.7	0.0					25.9	0.8		
1956			25.9	0.0					26.0	0.4					26.3	1.2					26.6	1.1		
1957			26.8	0.8					26.9	0.4					27.1	0.7					27.2	0.4		
1958			27.2	0.0					27.5	1.1					27.5	0.0					27.6	0.4		

[Continued]

Houston, TX
Consumer Price Index - Urban Wage Earners
Base 1982-1984 = 100
All Items
[Continued]

For 1914-1993. Columns headed % show percentile change in the index from the previous period for which an index is available.

Year	Jan Index	%	Feb Index	%	Mar Index	%	Apr Index	%	May Index	%	Jun Index	%	Jul Index	%	Aug Index	%	Sep Index	%	Oct Index	%	Nov Index	%	Dec Index	%
1959	-	-	27.6	0.0	-	-	-	-	27.6	0.0	-	-	-	-	27.7	0.4	-	-	-	-	27.9	0.7	-	-
1960	-	-	27.9	0.0	-	-	-	-	27.8	-0.4	-	-	-	-	28.0	0.7	-	-	-	-	28.1	0.4	-	-
1961	-	-	27.8	-1.1	-	-	-	-	28.0	0.7	-	-	-	-	28.1	0.4	-	-	-	-	28.5	1.4	-	-
1962	-	-	28.6	0.4	-	-	-	-	28.7	0.3	-	-	-	-	28.6	-0.3	-	-	-	-	28.6	0.0	-	-
1963	-	-	28.8	0.7	-	-	-	-	28.6	-0.7	-	-	-	-	29.1	1.7	-	-	-	-	29.2	0.3	-	-
1964	-	-	29.4	0.7	-	-	-	-	29.3	-0.3	-	-	-	-	29.4	0.3	-	-	-	-	29.4	0.0	-	-
1965	-	-	29.4	0.0	-	-	29.5	0.3	-	-	-	-	29.7	0.7	-	-	-	-	29.9	0.7	-	-	-	-
1966	30.1	0.7	-	-	-	-	30.4	1.0	-	-	-	-	30.6	0.7	-	-	-	-	30.8	0.7	-	-	-	-
1967	31.0	0.6	-	-	-	-	31.1	0.3	-	-	-	-	31.3	0.6	-	-	-	-	31.6	1.0	-	-	-	-
1968	32.0	1.3	-	-	-	-	32.3	0.9	-	-	-	-	32.7	1.2	-	-	-	-	33.2	1.5	-	-	-	-
1969	33.7	1.5	-	-	-	-	34.4	2.1	-	-	-	-	34.8	1.2	-	-	-	-	35.6	2.3	-	-	-	-
1970	35.8	0.6	-	-	-	-	36.4	1.7	-	-	-	-	36.6	0.5	-	-	-	-	36.9	0.8	-	-	-	-
1971	37.4	1.4	-	-	-	-	37.4	0.0	-	-	-	-	38.0	1.6	-	-	-	-	38.4	1.1	-	-	-	-
1972	38.6	0.5	-	-	-	-	39.1	1.3	-	-	-	-	39.2	0.3	-	-	-	-	39.6	1.0	-	-	-	-
1973	39.9	0.8	-	-	-	-	40.9	2.5	-	-	-	-	41.2	0.7	-	-	-	-	42.7	3.6	-	-	-	-
1974	43.6	2.1	-	-	-	-	44.8	2.8	-	-	-	-	46.4	3.6	-	-	-	-	48.3	4.1	-	-	-	-
1975	49.9	3.3	-	-	-	-	50.6	1.4	-	-	-	-	52.0	2.8	-	-	-	-	52.9	1.7	-	-	-	-
1976	54.0	2.1	-	-	-	-	54.5	0.9	-	-	-	-	55.5	1.8	-	-	-	-	57.0	2.7	-	-	-	-
1977	57.5	0.9	-	-	-	-	59.1	2.8	-	-	-	-	60.0	1.5	-	-	-	-	60.4	0.7	-	-	-	-
1978	61.6	2.0	-	-	-	-	63.6	3.2	-	-	65.0	2.2	-	-	66.1	1.7	-	-	67.0	1.4	-	-	68.4	2.1
1979	-	-	69.9	2.2	-	-	71.3	2.0	-	-	73.5	3.1	-	-	74.9	1.9	-	-	75.8	1.2	-	-	77.1	1.7
1980	-	-	78.9	2.3	-	-	80.6	2.2	-	-	82.3	2.1	-	-	83.2	1.1	-	-	84.4	1.4	-	-	85.3	1.1
1981	-	-	87.0	2.0	-	-	88.7	2.0	-	-	90.7	2.3	-	-	91.4	0.8	-	-	92.7	1.4	-	-	93.6	1.0
1982	-	-	94.1	0.5	-	-	94.7	0.6	-	-	97.4	2.9	-	-	98.8	1.4	-	-	98.7	-0.1	-	-	99.0	0.3
1983	-	-	99.4	0.4	-	-	99.5	0.1	-	-	100.2	0.7	-	-	100.8	0.6	-	-	101.0	0.2	-	-	99.6	-1.4
1984	-	-	101.4	1.8	-	-	101.8	0.4	-	-	103.2	1.4	-	-	104.5	1.3	-	-	104.8	0.3	-	-	103.7	-1.0
1985	-	-	103.7	0.0	-	-	104.3	0.6	-	-	105.0	0.7	-	-	105.1	0.1	-	-	105.0	-0.1	-	-	104.7	-0.3
1986	-	-	104.7	0.0	-	-	102.7	-1.9	-	-	103.7	1.0	-	-	103.6	-0.1	-	-	103.9	0.3	-	-	102.9	-1.0
1987	-	-	104.3	1.4	-	-	106.1	1.7	-	-	106.4	0.3	-	-	107.1	0.7	-	-	108.1	0.9	-	-	107.4	-0.6
1988	-	-	108.1	0.7	-	-	108.1	0.0	-	-	109.4	1.2	-	-	110.6	1.1	-	-	111.4	0.7	-	-	111.4	0.0
1989	-	-	112.9	1.3	-	-	113.5	0.5	-	-	114.5	0.9	-	-	114.9	0.3	-	-	115.8	0.8	-	-	115.8	0.0
1990	-	-	118.9	2.7	-	-	118.6	-0.3	-	-	120.0	1.2	-	-	121.9	1.6	-	-	124.7	2.3	-	-	123.4	-1.0
1991	-	-	124.4	0.8	-	-	123.6	-0.6	-	-	125.2	1.3	-	-	124.9	-0.2	-	-	127.4	2.0	-	-	127.2	-0.2
1992	-	-	126.9	-0.2	-	-	128.4	1.2	-	-	129.2	0.6	-	-	129.8	0.5	-	-	130.7	0.7	-	-	129.2	-1.1
1993	-	-	131.3	1.6	-	-	131.3	0.0	-	-	132.4	0.8	-	-	132.7	0.2	-	-	136.1	2.6	-	-	136.0	-0.1

Source: U.S. Department of Labor, Bureau of Labor Statistics, Division of Consumer Prices and Price Indexes. - indicates no data collected for period.

Houston, TX

Consumer Price Index - All Urban Consumers
Base 1982-1984 = 100

Food and Beverages

For 1976-1993. Columns headed % show percentile change in the index from the previous period for which an index is available.

Year	Jan Index	%	Feb Index	%	Mar Index	%	Apr Index	%	May Index	%	Jun Index	%	Jul Index	%	Aug Index	%	Sep Index	%	Oct Index	%	Nov Index	%	Dec Index	%
1976	58.0	-	-	-	-	-	57.7	-0.5	-	-	-	-	58.9	2.1	-	-	-	-	59.0	0.2	-	-	-	-
1977	59.3	0.5	-	-	-	-	61.3	3.4	-	-	-	-	62.3	1.6	-	-	-	-	62.0	-0.5	-	-	71.7	2.4
1978	63.5	2.4	-	-	-	-	66.0	3.9	-	-	68.1	3.2	-	-	68.7	0.9	-	-	70.0	1.9	-	-	71.7	2.4
1979	-	-	74.7	4.2	-	-	75.7	1.3	-	-	77.2	2.0	-	-	77.8	0.8	-	-	78.0	0.3	-	-	79.5	1.9
1980	-	-	80.8	1.6	-	-	81.8	1.2	-	-	82.2	0.5	-	-	84.7	3.0	-	-	87.3	3.1	-	-	88.1	0.9
1981	-	-	89.9	2.0	-	-	90.9	1.1	-	-	91.7	0.9	-	-	93.2	1.6	-	-	93.3	0.1	-	-	93.3	0.0
1982	-	-	94.6	1.4	-	-	95.2	0.6	-	-	96.7	1.6	-	-	97.6	0.9	-	-	97.5	-0.1	-	-	97.8	0.3
1983	-	-	98.3	0.5	-	-	99.0	0.7	-	-	99.7	0.7	-	-	100.0	0.3	-	-	99.8	-0.2	-	-	99.7	-0.1
1984	-	-	104.0	4.3	-	-	104.2	0.2	-	-	104.3	0.1	-	-	104.6	0.3	-	-	104.6	0.0	-	-	105.4	0.8
1985	-	-	105.4	0.0	-	-	104.6	-0.8	-	-	104.6	0.0	-	-	105.0	0.4	-	-	104.6	-0.4	-	-	105.8	1.1
1986	-	-	106.4	0.6	-	-	106.3	-0.1	-	-	106.7	0.4	-	-	107.8	1.0	-	-	108.4	0.6	-	-	109.3	0.8
1987	-	-	111.4	1.9	-	-	111.2	-0.2	-	-	111.8	0.5	-	-	111.6	-0.2	-	-	113.1	1.3	-	-	112.5	-0.5
1988	-	-	113.9	1.2	-	-	114.3	0.4	-	-	114.6	0.3	-	-	117.8	2.8	-	-	119.6	1.5	-	-	118.2	-1.2
1989	-	-	121.7	3.0	-	-	121.7	0.0	-	-	121.8	0.1	-	-	121.1	-0.6	-	-	121.8	0.6	-	-	123.5	1.4
1990	-	-	127.9	3.6	-	-	127.1	-0.6	-	-	128.6	1.2	-	-	129.5	0.7	-	-	131.3	1.4	-	-	129.2	-1.6
1991	-	-	132.2	2.3	-	-	132.3	0.1	-	-	130.9	-1.1	-	-	131.4	0.4	-	-	131.7	0.2	-	-	131.5	-0.2
1992	-	-	132.7	0.9	-	-	132.2	-0.4	-	-	129.9	-1.7	-	-	129.6	-0.2	-	-	129.7	0.1	-	-	130.4	0.5
1993	-	-	132.2	1.4	-	-	128.9	-2.5	-	-	130.2	1.0	-	-	133.4	2.5	-	-	134.9	1.1	-	-	136.5	1.2

Source: U.S. Department of Labor, Bureau of Labor Statistics, Division of Consumer Prices and Price Indexes. - indicates no data collected for period.

Houston, TX
Consumer Price Index - Urban Wage Earners
Base 1982-1984 = 100
Food and Beverages

For 1976-1993. Columns headed % show percentile change in the index from the previous period for which an index is available.

Year	Jan Index	%	Feb Index	%	Mar Index	%	Apr Index	%	May Index	%	Jun Index	%	Jul Index	%	Aug Index	%	Sep Index	%	Oct Index	%	Nov Index	%	Dec Index	%
1976	59.0	-	-	-	-	-	58.7	-0.5	-	-	-	-	59.9	2.0	-	-	-	-	60.0	0.2	-	-	-	-
1977	60.3	0.5	-	-	-	-	62.3	3.3	-	-	-	-	63.3	1.6	-	-	-	-	63.1	-0.3	-	-	-	-
1978	64.6	2.4	-	-	-	-	67.1	3.9	-	-	69.3	3.3	-	-	69.4	0.1	-	-	70.4	1.4	-	-	72.0	2.3
1979	-	-	74.9	4.0	-	-	76.1	1.6	-	-	77.2	1.4	-	-	77.9	0.9	-	-	78.4	0.6	-	-	79.5	1.4
1980	-	-	80.1	0.8	-	-	81.8	2.1	-	-	82.6	1.0	-	-	84.8	2.7	-	-	87.3	2.9	-	-	88.5	1.4
1981	-	-	90.0	1.7	-	-	90.6	0.7	-	-	91.1	0.6	-	-	92.9	2.0	-	-	93.0	0.1	-	-	93.1	0.1
1982	-	-	94.6	1.6	-	-	95.3	0.7	-	-	96.7	1.5	-	-	97.6	0.9	-	-	97.6	0.0	-	-	97.9	0.3
1983	-	-	98.5	0.6	-	-	99.1	0.6	-	-	99.6	0.5	-	-	99.9	0.3	-	-	99.7	-0.2	-	-	99.7	0.0
1984	-	-	104.2	4.5	-	-	104.2	0.0	-	-	104.2	0.0	-	-	104.4	0.2	-	-	104.5	0.1	-	-	105.3	0.8
1985	-	-	105.1	-0.2	-	-	104.5	-0.6	-	-	104.5	0.0	-	-	104.8	0.3	-	-	104.5	-0.3	-	-	105.8	1.2
1986	-	-	106.3	0.5	-	-	106.4	0.1	-	-	106.7	0.3	-	-	107.7	0.9	-	-	108.5	0.7	-	-	109.3	0.7
1987	-	-	111.3	1.8	-	-	111.0	-0.3	-	-	111.6	0.5	-	-	111.4	-0.2	-	-	113.1	1.5	-	-	112.4	-0.6
1988	-	-	113.7	1.2	-	-	114.1	0.4	-	-	114.5	0.4	-	-	117.8	2.9	-	-	119.6	1.5	-	-	118.1	-1.3
1989	-	-	121.7	3.0	-	-	121.7	0.0	-	-	121.7	0.0	-	-	121.0	-0.6	-	-	121.8	0.7	-	-	123.6	1.5
1990	-	-	128.1	3.6	-	-	127.3	-0.6	-	-	128.7	1.1	-	-	129.6	0.7	-	-	131.4	1.4	-	-	129.4	-1.5
1991	-	-	132.2	2.2	-	-	132.4	0.2	-	-	130.9	-1.1	-	-	131.5	0.5	-	-	131.9	0.3	-	-	131.8	-0.1
1992	-	-	133.0	0.9	-	-	132.4	-0.5	-	-	130.0	-1.8	-	-	129.8	-0.2	-	-	129.8	0.0	-	-	130.4	0.5
1993	-	-	132.2	1.4	-	-	129.1	-2.3	-	-	130.3	0.9	-	-	133.6	2.5	-	-	135.2	1.2	-	-	136.9	1.3

Source: U.S. Department of Labor, Bureau of Labor Statistics, Division of Consumer Prices and Price Indexes. - indicates no data collected for period.

Houston, TX
Consumer Price Index - All Urban Consumers
Base 1982-1984 = 100
Housing

For 1976-1993. Columns headed % show percentile change in the index from the previous period for which an index is available.

Year	Jan Index	%	Feb Index	%	Mar Index	%	Apr Index	%	May Index	%	Jun Index	%	Jul Index	%	Aug Index	%	Sep Index	%	Oct Index	%	Nov Index	%	Dec Index	%
1976	51.2	-	-	-	-	-	52.0	1.6	-	-	-	-	52.9	1.7	-	-	-	-	54.7	3.4	-	-	-	-
1977	55.3	1.1	-	-	-	-	56.7	2.5	-	-	-	-	57.8	1.9	-	-	-	-	58.2	0.7	-	-	-	-
1978	60.0	3.1	-	-	-	-	62.3	3.8	-	-	64.2	3.0	-	-	66.0	2.8	-	-	66.9	1.4	-	-	69.0	3.1
1979	-	-	70.0	1.4	-	-	70.5	0.7	-	-	73.5	4.3	-	-	75.3	2.4	-	-	76.7	1.9	-	-	78.1	1.8
1980	-	-	79.2	1.4	-	-	80.8	2.0	-	-	84.1	4.1	-	-	84.0	-0.1	-	-	84.8	1.0	-	-	85.4	0.7
1981	-	-	86.7	1.5	-	-	88.7	2.3	-	-	91.8	3.5	-	-	92.4	0.7	-	-	94.6	2.4	-	-	95.8	1.3
1982	-	-	96.4	0.6	-	-	97.6	1.2	-	-	100.8	3.3	-	-	102.8	2.0	-	-	101.5	-1.3	-	-	100.9	-0.6
1983	-	-	99.7	-1.2	-	-	98.3	-1.4	-	-	101.2	3.0	-	-	102.2	1.0	-	-	101.4	-0.8	-	-	98.8	-2.6
1984	-	-	98.4	-0.4	-	-	99.1	0.7	-	-	101.7	2.6	-	-	100.1	-1.6	-	-	101.0	0.9	-	-	99.2	-1.8
1985	-	-	100.0	0.8	-	-	100.0	0.0	-	-	101.1	1.1	-	-	101.0	-0.1	-	-	100.4	-0.6	-	-	98.4	-2.0
1986	-	-	99.2	0.8	-	-	97.6	-1.6	-	-	98.9	1.3	-	-	98.9	0.0	-	-	98.3	-0.6	-	-	95.2	-3.2
1987	-	-	94.8	-0.4	-	-	98.3	3.7	-	-	97.5	-0.8	-	-	97.9	0.4	-	-	97.5	-0.4	-	-	95.9	-1.6
1988	-	-	96.6	0.7	-	-	97.7	1.1	-	-	98.8	1.1	-	-	98.8	0.0	-	-	98.0	-0.8	-	-	99.3	1.3
1989	-	-	100.0	0.7	-	-	99.0	-1.0	-	-	100.6	1.6	-	-	101.7	1.1	-	-	101.8	0.1	-	-	100.4	-1.4
1990	-	-	103.1	2.7	-	-	102.8	-0.3	-	-	104.7	1.8	-	-	106.6	1.8	-	-	107.2	0.6	-	-	105.8	-1.3
1991	-	-	107.6	1.7	-	-	108.0	0.4	-	-	110.2	2.0	-	-	109.8	-0.4	-	-	111.4	1.5	-	-	111.0	-0.4
1992	-	-	109.9	-1.0	-	-	112.7	2.5	-	-	114.6	1.7	-	-	113.9	-0.6	-	-	115.4	1.3	-	-	113.3	-1.8
1993	-	-	114.7	1.2	-	-	114.7	0.0	-	-	117.5	2.4	-	-	117.2	-0.3	-	-	119.0	1.5	-	-	119.3	0.3

Source: U.S. Department of Labor, Bureau of Labor Statistics, Division of Consumer Prices and Price Indexes. - indicates no data collected for period.

Houston, TX
Consumer Price Index - Urban Wage Earners
Base 1982-1984 = 100
Housing

For 1976-1993. Columns headed % show percentile change in the index from the previous period for which an index is available.

Year	Jan Index	%	Feb Index	%	Mar Index	%	Apr Index	%	May Index	%	Jun Index	%	Jul Index	%	Aug Index	%	Sep Index	%	Oct Index	%	Nov Index	%	Dec Index	%
1976	51.2	-	-	-	-	-	52.0	1.6	-	-	-	-	52.9	1.7	-	-	-	-	54.8	3.6	-	-	-	-
1977	55.3	0.9	-	-	-	-	56.7	2.5	-	-	-	-	57.9	2.1	-	-	-	-	58.3	0.7	-	-	-	-
1978	60.1	3.1	-	-	-	-	62.3	3.7	-	-	64.1	2.9	-	-	65.8	2.7	-	-	66.4	0.9	-	-	-	-
1979	-	-	69.3	1.3	-	-	69.9	0.9	-	-	72.7	4.0	-	-	74.3	2.2	-	-	75.4	1.5	-	-	68.4	3.0
1980	-	-	77.7	1.2	-	-	79.4	2.2	-	-	82.5	3.9	-	-	82.7	0.2	-	-	83.5	1.0	-	-	76.8	1.9
1981	-	-	85.2	1.2	-	-	87.5	2.7	-	-	90.7	3.7	-	-	91.3	0.7	-	-	93.3	2.2	-	-	84.2	0.8
1982	-	-	94.9	0.7	-	-	96.6	1.8	-	-	99.8	3.3	-	-	101.6	1.8	-	-	100.6	-1.0	-	-	94.2	1.0
1983	-	-	100.8	0.6	-	-	100.3	-0.5	-	-	101.0	0.7	-	-	101.3	0.3	-	-	101.0	-0.3	-	-	100.2	-0.4
1984	-	-	99.7	1.9	-	-	99.7	0.0	-	-	101.9	2.2	-	-	102.8	0.9	-	-	102.4	-0.4	-	-	97.8	-3.2
1985	-	-	100.0	1.0	-	-	99.9	-0.1	-	-	101.0	1.1	-	-	100.9	-0.1	-	-	100.3	-0.6	-	-	99.0	-3.3
1986	-	-	98.9	0.7	-	-	97.4	-1.5	-	-	98.8	1.4	-	-	98.7	-0.1	-	-	98.2	-0.5	-	-	98.2	-2.1
1987	-	-	94.5	-0.4	-	-	97.6	3.3	-	-	97.2	-0.4	-	-	97.1	-0.1	-	-	98.2	0.1	-	-	94.9	-3.4
1988	-	-	96.1	0.3	-	-	97.0	0.9	-	-	98.1	1.1	-	-	98.2	0.1	-	-	97.2	0.1	-	-	95.8	-1.4
1989	-	-	99.3	0.6	-	-	98.5	-0.8	-	-	100.3	1.8	-	-	101.6	1.3	-	-	97.6	-0.6	-	-	98.7	1.1
1990	-	-	102.2	2.0	-	-	102.4	0.2	-	-	104.5	2.1	-	-	106.4	1.8	-	-	101.4	-0.2	-	-	100.2	-1.2
1991	-	-	107.4	1.7	-	-	107.9	0.5	-	-	110.5	2.4	-	-	109.8	-0.6	-	-	107.2	0.8	-	-	105.6	-1.5
1992	-	-	109.6	-1.5	-	-	112.6	2.7	-	-	114.7	1.9	-	-	114.2	-0.4	-	-	111.1	1.2	-	-	111.3	0.2
1993	-	-	114.9	1.1	-	-	115.1	0.2	-	-	118.0	2.5	-	-	117.8	-0.2	-	-	115.7	1.3	-	-	113.6	-1.8
																	119.4	1.4					119.7	0.3

Source: U.S. Department of Labor, Bureau of Labor Statistics, Division of Consumer Prices and Price Indexes. - indicates no data collected for period.

Houston, TX
Consumer Price Index - All Urban Consumers
Base 1982-1984 = 100
Apparel and Upkeep

For 1952-1993. Columns headed % show percentile change in the index from the previous period for which an index is available.

Year	Jan Index	Jan %	Feb Index	Feb %	Mar Index	Mar %	Apr Index	Apr %	May Index	May %	Jun Index	Jun %	Jul Index	Jul %	Aug Index	Aug %	Sep Index	Sep %	Oct Index	Oct %	Nov Index	Nov %	Dec Index	Dec %
1952	-	-	-	-	-	-	-	-	-	-	-	-	-	-	35.9	-0.3	-	-	-	-	36.4	1.4	36.1	-
1953	-	-	36.0	-0.3	-	-	-	-	36.0	0.0	-	-	-	-	36.1	0.3	-	-	-	-	36.1	0.0	-	-
1954	-	-	36.0	-1.1	-	-	-	-	36.0	0.0	-	-	-	-	35.8	-0.8	-	-	-	-	36.1	0.8	-	-
1955	-	-	35.9	-0.6	-	-	-	-	36.1	0.6	-	-	-	-	36.7	1.4	-	-	-	-	37.6	2.5	-	-
1956	-	-	36.4	0.8	-	-	-	-	36.2	-0.5	-	-	-	-	37.6	0.0	-	-	-	-	38.2	1.6	-	-
1957	-	-	37.2	-1.1	-	-	-	-	37.6	1.1	-	-	-	-	38.3	-0.3	-	-	-	-	38.4	0.3	-	-
1958	-	-	38.3	0.3	-	-	-	-	38.4	0.3	-	-	-	-	38.8	0.5	-	-	-	-	38.8	0.0	-	-
1959	-	-	38.7	0.8	-	-	-	-	38.6	-0.3	-	-	-	-	38.9	0.3	-	-	-	-	38.8	-0.3	-	-
1960	-	-	38.2	-1.5	-	-	-	-	38.8	1.6	-	-	-	-	38.7	-0.3	-	-	-	-	39.6	2.3	-	-
1961	-	-	38.6	-0.5	-	-	-	-	38.8	0.5	-	-	-	-	40.2	0.5	-	-	-	-	40.3	0.2	-	-
1962	-	-	39.7	0.3	-	-	-	-	40.0	0.8	-	-	-	-	40.8	1.2	-	-	-	-	40.6	-0.5	-	-
1963	-	-	40.4	0.2	-	-	-	-	40.3	-0.2	-	-	-	-	40.7	0.0	-	-	-	-	40.7	0.0	-	-
1964	-	-	41.0	1.0	-	-	-	-	40.7	-0.7	-	-	40.8	-0.5	-	-	-	-	41.3	1.2	-	-	-	-
1965	-	-	40.2	-1.2	-	-	41.0	2.0	-	-	-	-	41.6	0.5	-	-	-	-	42.0	1.0	-	-	-	-
1966	41.0	-0.7	-	-	-	-	41.4	1.0	-	-	-	-	42.0	0.2	-	-	-	-	43.2	2.9	-	-	-	-
1967	41.2	-1.9	-	-	-	-	41.9	1.7	-	-	-	-	44.3	0.9	-	-	-	-	46.0	3.8	-	-	-	-
1968	43.1	-0.2	-	-	-	-	43.9	1.9	-	-	-	-	47.7	0.8	-	-	-	-	50.1	5.0	-	-	-	-
1969	46.5	1.1	-	-	-	-	47.3	1.7	-	-	-	-	50.1	-0.2	-	-	-	-	52.2	4.2	-	-	-	-
1970	49.7	-0.8	-	-	-	-	50.2	1.0	-	-	-	-	50.8	-1.2	-	-	-	-	52.7	3.7	-	-	-	-
1971	50.8	-2.7	-	-	-	-	51.4	1.2	-	-	-	-	52.0	-2.3	-	-	-	-	54.4	4.6	-	-	-	-
1972	52.3	-0.8	-	-	-	-	53.2	1.7	-	-	-	-	53.5	-2.9	-	-	-	-	57.3	7.1	-	-	-	-
1973	53.1	-2.4	-	-	-	-	55.1	3.8	-	-	-	-	60.5	2.0	-	-	-	-	62.2	2.8	-	-	-	-
1974	57.6	0.5	-	-	-	-	59.3	3.0	-	-	-	-	64.3	1.6	-	-	-	-	66.3	3.1	-	-	-	-
1975	61.8	-0.6	-	-	-	-	63.3	2.4	-	-	-	-	66.9	-0.7	-	-	-	-	70.4	5.2	-	-	-	-
1976	65.7	-0.9	-	-	-	-	67.4	2.6	-	-	-	-	71.6	0.0	-	-	-	-	74.0	3.4	-	-	-	-
1977	70.0	-0.6	-	-	-	-	71.6	2.3	-	-	76.6	1.2	-	-	78.0	1.8	-	-	79.9	2.4	-	-	79.7	-0.3
1978	72.8	-1.6	-	-	-	-	75.7	4.0	-	-	82.4	-0.5	-	-	83.2	1.0	-	-	85.1	2.3	-	-	86.0	1.1
1979	-	-	80.6	1.1	-	-	82.8	2.7	-	-	87.8	-0.6	-	-	89.4	1.8	-	-	91.6	2.5	-	-	90.7	-1.0
1980	-	-	88.3	2.7	-	-	88.3	0.0	-	-	87.8	-0.6	-	-	95.5	0.5	-	-	97.8	2.4	-	-	99.5	1.7
1981	-	-	93.4	3.0	-	-	94.8	1.5	-	-	95.0	0.2	-	-	95.5	0.5	-	-	97.8	2.4	-	-	98.7	0.0
1982	-	-	98.6	-0.9	-	-	98.6	0.0	-	-	97.5	-1.1	-	-	98.0	0.5	-	-	98.7	0.7	-	-	100.6	0.3
1983	-	-	101.5	2.8	-	-	100.0	-1.5	-	-	98.0	-2.0	-	-	98.8	0.8	-	-	100.3	1.5	-	-	104.0	1.4
1984	-	-	100.3	-0.3	-	-	100.8	0.5	-	-	102.1	1.3	-	-	102.1	0.0	-	-	102.6	0.5	-	-	105.5	0.6
1985	-	-	104.2	0.2	-	-	104.4	0.2	-	-	103.8	-0.6	-	-	104.2	0.4	-	-	104.9	0.7	-	-	106.1	0.4
1986	-	-	106.1	0.6	-	-	106.6	0.5	-	-	104.6	-1.9	-	-	107.6	2.9	-	-	105.7	-1.8	-	-	118.3	-0.1
1987	-	-	107.9	1.7	-	-	112.8	4.5	-	-	111.6	-1.1	-	-	115.4	3.4	-	-	118.4	2.6	-	-	119.9	-4.3
1988	-	-	121.3	2.5	-	-	117.4	-3.2	-	-	122.0	3.9	-	-	121.1	-0.7	-	-	125.3	3.5	-	-	124.9	-2.0
1989	-	-	122.7	2.3	-	-	126.7	3.3	-	-	121.0	-4.5	-	-	122.0	0.8	-	-	127.5	4.5	-	-	128.6	-4.7
1990	-	-	136.9	9.6	-	-	130.0	-5.0	-	-	133.3	2.5	-	-	132.5	-0.6	-	-	134.9	1.8	-	-	135.0	-2.7
1991	-	-	138.2	7.5	-	-	133.3	-3.5	-	-	135.3	1.5	-	-	129.7	-4.1	-	-	138.8	7.0	-	-	126.1	-8.5
1992	-	-	137.1	1.6	-	-	135.8	-0.9	-	-	134.4	-1.0	-	-	141.4	5.2	-	-	137.8	-2.5	-	-	151.3	-2.6
1993	-	-	140.4	11.3	-	-	142.4	1.4	-	-	137.8	-3.2	-	-	132.2	-4.1	-	-	155.4	17.5	-	-	-	-

Source: U.S. Department of Labor, Bureau of Labor Statistics, Division of Consumer Prices and Price Indexes. - indicates no data collected for period.

Houston, TX
Consumer Price Index - Urban Wage Earners
Base 1982-1984 = 100
Apparel and Upkeep

For 1952-1993. Columns headed % show percentile change in the index from the previous period for which an index is available.

Year	Jan Index	%	Feb Index	%	Mar Index	%	Apr Index	%	May Index	%	Jun Index	%	Jul Index	%	Aug Index	%	Sep Index	%	Oct Index	%	Nov Index	%	Dec Index	%
1952	-	-	-	-	-	-	-	-	-	-	-	-	-	-	-	-	-	-	-	-	-	-	36.8	-
1953	-	-	36.7	-0.3	-	-	-	-	36.7	0.0	-	-	-	-	36.6	-0.3	-	-	-	-	37.1	1.4	-	-
1954	-	-	36.7	-1.1	-	-	-	-	36.7	0.0	-	-	-	-	36.8	0.3	-	-	-	-	36.8	0.0	-	-
1955	-	-	36.6	-0.5	-	-	-	-	36.8	0.5	-	-	-	-	36.4	-1.1	-	-	-	-	36.8	1.1	-	-
1956	-	-	37.1	0.8	-	-	-	-	36.9	-0.5	-	-	-	-	37.4	1.4	-	-	-	-	38.3	2.4	-	-
1957	-	-	37.9	-1.0	-	-	-	-	38.3	1.1	-	-	-	-	38.3	0.0	-	-	-	-	38.9	1.6	-	-
1958	-	-	39.1	0.5	-	-	-	-	39.1	0.0	-	-	-	-	39.0	-0.3	-	-	-	-	39.2	0.5	-	-
1959	-	-	39.4	0.5	-	-	-	-	39.3	-0.3	-	-	-	-	39.5	0.5	-	-	-	-	39.5	0.0	-	-
1960	-	-	38.9	-1.5	-	-	-	-	39.5	1.5	-	-	-	-	39.6	0.3	-	-	-	-	39.5	-0.3	-	-
1961	-	-	39.4	-0.3	-	-	-	-	39.5	0.3	-	-	-	-	39.4	-0.3	-	-	-	-	40.3	2.3	-	-
1962	-	-	40.4	0.2	-	-	-	-	40.8	1.0	-	-	-	-	40.9	0.2	-	-	-	-	41.1	0.5	-	-
1963	-	-	41.2	0.2	-	-	-	-	41.1	-0.2	-	-	-	-	41.6	1.2	-	-	-	-	41.4	-0.5	-	-
1964	-	-	41.8	1.0	-	-	-	-	41.4	-1.0	-	-	-	-	41.5	0.2	-	-	-	-	41.5	0.0	-	-
1965	-	-	41.0	-1.2	-	-	41.7	1.7	-	-	-	-	41.6	-0.2	-	-	-	-	42.0	1.0	-	-	-	-
1966	41.8	-0.5	-	-	-	-	42.2	1.0	-	-	-	-	42.3	0.2	-	-	-	-	42.8	1.2	-	-	-	-
1967	42.0	-1.9	-	-	-	-	42.7	1.7	-	-	-	-	42.8	0.2	-	-	-	-	44.0	2.8	-	-	-	-
1968	43.9	-0.2	-	-	-	-	44.8	2.1	-	-	-	-	45.1	0.7	-	-	-	-	46.9	4.0	-	-	-	-
1969	47.3	0.9	-	-	-	-	48.2	1.9	-	-	-	-	48.6	0.8	-	-	-	-	51.0	4.9	-	-	-	-
1970	50.6	-0.8	-	-	-	-	51.2	1.2	-	-	-	-	51.0	-0.4	-	-	-	-	53.2	4.3	-	-	-	-
1971	51.8	-2.6	-	-	-	-	52.4	1.2	-	-	-	-	51.7	-1.3	-	-	-	-	53.7	3.9	-	-	-	-
1972	53.3	-0.7	-	-	-	-	54.3	1.9	-	-	-	-	53.0	-2.4	-	-	-	-	55.5	4.7	-	-	-	-
1973	54.1	-2.5	-	-	-	-	56.1	3.7	-	-	-	-	54.5	-2.9	-	-	-	-	58.4	7.2	-	-	-	-
1974	58.7	0.5	-	-	-	-	60.5	3.1	-	-	-	-	61.7	2.0	-	-	-	-	63.4	2.8	-	-	-	-
1975	63.0	-0.6	-	-	-	-	64.5	2.4	-	-	-	-	65.5	1.6	-	-	-	-	67.6	3.2	-	-	-	-
1976	67.0	-0.9	-	-	-	-	68.6	2.4	-	-	-	-	68.2	-0.6	-	-	-	-	71.8	5.3	-	-	-	-
1977	71.4	-0.6	-	-	-	-	72.9	2.1	-	-	-	-	72.9	0.0	-	-	-	-	75.4	3.4	-	-	-	-
1978	74.1	-1.7	-	-	-	-	77.2	4.2	-	-	78.4	1.6	-	-	79.4	1.3	-	-	81.1	2.1	-	-	81.9	1.0
1979	-	-	83.1	1.5	-	-	85.3	2.6	-	-	84.4	-1.1	-	-	85.3	1.1	-	-	87.0	2.0	-	-	88.2	1.4
1980	-	-	89.2	1.1	-	-	89.7	0.6	-	-	89.4	-0.3	-	-	90.8	1.6	-	-	91.5	0.8	-	-	92.2	0.8
1981	-	-	94.6	2.6	-	-	95.8	1.3	-	-	95.2	-0.6	-	-	96.7	1.6	-	-	98.5	1.9	-	-	99.0	0.5
1982	-	-	98.3	-0.7	-	-	98.5	0.2	-	-	97.9	-0.6	-	-	98.2	0.3	-	-	98.8	0.6	-	-	99.2	0.4
1983	-	-	101.3	2.1	-	-	100.0	-1.3	-	-	98.0	-2.0	-	-	98.8	0.8	-	-	100.3	1.5	-	-	100.8	0.5
1984	-	-	100.4	-0.4	-	-	100.4	0.0	-	-	102.0	1.6	-	-	101.9	-0.1	-	-	102.7	0.8	-	-	103.8	1.1
1985	-	-	103.8	0.0	-	-	104.1	0.3	-	-	103.8	-0.3	-	-	104.1	0.3	-	-	104.7	0.6	-	-	105.3	0.6
1986	-	-	105.8	0.5	-	-	106.3	0.5	-	-	104.5	-1.7	-	-	106.9	2.3	-	-	105.5	-1.3	-	-	105.3	-0.2
1987	-	-	107.4	2.0	-	-	111.7	4.0	-	-	110.7	-0.9	-	-	114.7	3.6	-	-	117.2	2.2	-	-	117.6	0.3
1988	-	-	120.9	2.8	-	-	117.0	-3.2	-	-	122.1	4.4	-	-	121.2	-0.7	-	-	125.6	3.6	-	-	120.5	-4.1
1989	-	-	123.1	2.2	-	-	126.7	2.9	-	-	121.9	-3.8	-	-	122.0	0.1	-	-	126.8	3.9	-	-	124.8	-1.6
1990	-	-	137.4	10.1	-	-	130.7	-4.9	-	-	133.5	2.1	-	-	133.2	-0.2	-	-	134.8	1.2	-	-	127.8	-5.2
1991	-	-	137.1	7.3	-	-	132.7	-3.2	-	-	134.7	1.5	-	-	128.2	-4.8	-	-	137.9	7.6	-	-	134.2	-2.7
1992	-	-	136.4	1.6	-	-	134.7	-1.2	-	-	133.0	-1.3	-	-	139.2	4.7	-	-	136.5	-1.9	-	-	124.6	-8.7
1993	-	-	137.3	10.2	-	-	138.7	1.0	-	-	134.1	-3.3	-	-	130.2	-2.9	-	-	151.7	16.5	-	-	147.2	-3.0

Source: U.S. Department of Labor, Bureau of Labor Statistics, Division of Consumer Prices and Price Indexes. - indicates no data collected for period.

511

Houston, TX
Consumer Price Index - All Urban Consumers
Base 1982-1984 = 100
Transportation

For 1947-1993. Columns headed % show percentile change in the index from the previous period for which an index is available.

Year	Jan Index	%	Feb Index	%	Mar Index	%	Apr Index	%	May Index	%	Jun Index	%	Jul Index	%	Aug Index	%	Sep Index	%	Oct Index	%	Nov Index	%	Dec Index	%
1947	19.9	-	20.1	1.0	20.2	0.5	20.4	1.0	20.5	0.5	20.5	0.0	20.6	0.5	20.8	1.0	21.0	1.0	21.4	1.9	21.9	2.3	22.0	0.5
1948	22.6	2.7	22.7	0.4	22.7	0.0	22.7	0.0	22.7	0.0	22.8	0.4	23.2	1.8	23.7	2.2	23.8	0.4	23.9	0.4	24.0	0.4	24.0	0.0
1949	24.0	0.0	24.3	1.2	24.3	0.0	24.4	0.4	24.4	0.0	24.3	-0.4	25.0	2.9	25.0	0.0	25.0	0.0	25.1	0.4	25.2	0.4	25.2	0.0
1950	25.3	0.4	25.3	0.0	25.3	0.0	25.3	0.0	25.5	0.8	25.5	0.0	25.6	0.4	25.7	0.4	25.7	0.0	25.7	0.0	25.7	0.0	27.2	5.8
1951	27.3	0.4	27.5	0.7	27.8	1.1	27.7	-0.4	27.7	0.0	27.9	0.7	27.9	0.0	27.9	0.0	28.2	1.1	28.2	0.0	28.6	1.4	28.6	0.0
1952	28.0	-2.1	28.4	1.4	28.4	0.0	28.4	0.0	28.4	0.0	28.4	0.0	28.4	0.0	28.4	0.0	28.4	0.0	29.2	2.8	29.2	0.0	29.2	0.0
1953	-	-	29.0	-0.7	-	-	-	-	29.0	0.0	-	-	-	-	29.1	0.3	-	-	-	-	29.0	-0.3	-	-
1954	-	-	28.7	-1.0	-	-	-	-	28.6	-0.3	-	-	-	-	28.2	-1.4	-	-	-	-	28.8	2.1	-	-
1955	-	-	28.3	-1.7	-	-	-	-	27.9	-1.4	-	-	-	-	27.8	-0.4	-	-	-	-	28.9	4.0	-	-
1956	-	-	28.7	-0.7	-	-	-	-	28.5	-0.7	-	-	-	-	28.9	1.4	-	-	-	-	29.7	2.8	-	-
1957	-	-	30.3	2.0	-	-	-	-	30.8	1.7	-	-	-	-	31.1	1.0	-	-	-	-	31.8	2.3	-	-
1958	-	-	29.0	-8.8	-	-	-	-	31.5	8.6	-	-	-	-	32.4	2.9	-	-	-	-	32.7	0.9	-	-
1959	-	-	32.5	-0.6	-	-	-	-	32.9	1.2	-	-	-	-	33.2	0.9	-	-	-	-	33.4	0.6	-	-
1960	-	-	33.7	0.9	-	-	-	-	31.4	-6.8	-	-	-	-	33.6	7.0	-	-	-	-	33.4	-0.6	-	-
1961	-	-	31.5	-5.7	-	-	-	-	33.4	6.0	-	-	-	-	32.6	-2.4	-	-	-	-	34.7	6.4	-	-
1962	-	-	34.6	-0.3	-	-	-	-	34.6	0.0	-	-	-	-	34.2	-1.2	-	-	-	-	33.2	-2.9	-	-
1963	-	-	33.9	2.1	-	-	-	-	32.4	-4.4	-	-	-	-	33.8	4.3	-	-	-	-	34.3	1.5	-	-
1964	-	-	34.0	-0.9	-	-	-	-	34.5	1.5	-	-	-	-	34.4	-0.3	-	-	-	-	34.6	0.6	-	-
1965	-	-	33.8	-2.3	-	-	34.1	0.9	-	-	-	-	34.0	-0.3	-	-	-	-	34.6	1.8	-	-	-	-
1966	34.6	0.0	-	-	-	-	34.6	0.0	-	-	-	-	35.0	1.2	-	-	-	-	35.0	0.0	-	-	-	-
1967	35.4	1.1	-	-	-	-	35.7	0.8	-	-	-	-	35.9	0.6	-	-	-	-	36.7	2.2	-	-	-	-
1968	36.7	0.0	-	-	-	-	37.0	0.8	-	-	-	-	37.0	0.0	-	-	-	-	37.3	0.8	-	-	-	-
1969	37.7	1.1	-	-	-	-	38.4	1.9	-	-	-	-	38.3	-0.3	-	-	-	-	38.8	1.3	-	-	-	-
1970	38.6	-0.5	-	-	-	-	39.0	1.0	-	-	-	-	38.9	-0.3	-	-	-	-	39.0	0.3	-	-	-	-
1971	41.3	5.9	-	-	-	-	40.8	-1.2	-	-	-	-	40.3	-1.2	-	-	-	-	40.8	1.2	-	-	-	-
1972	41.1	0.7	-	-	-	-	41.7	1.5	-	-	-	-	41.7	0.0	-	-	-	-	41.0	-1.7	-	-	-	-
1973	41.1	0.2	-	-	-	-	41.9	1.9	-	-	-	-	42.3	1.0	-	-	-	-	42.4	0.2	-	-	-	-
1974	43.9	3.5	-	-	-	-	45.9	4.6	-	-	-	-	48.0	4.6	-	-	-	-	49.6	3.3	-	-	-	-
1975	49.1	-1.0	-	-	-	-	50.4	2.6	-	-	-	-	52.9	5.0	-	-	-	-	53.4	0.9	-	-	-	-
1976	54.1	1.3	-	-	-	-	54.6	0.9	-	-	-	-	56.5	3.5	-	-	-	-	58.3	3.2	-	-	-	-
1977	58.6	0.5	-	-	-	-	60.4	3.1	-	-	-	-	61.3	1.5	-	-	-	-	60.7	-1.0	-	-	-	-
1978	61.1	0.7	-	-	-	-	61.6	0.8	-	-	62.5	1.5	-	-	63.3	1.3	-	-	64.1	1.3	-	-	65.1	1.6
1979	-	-	66.1	1.5	-	-	68.9	4.2	-	-	72.5	5.2	-	-	75.3	3.9	-	-	76.0	0.9	-	-	77.9	2.5
1980	-	-	82.8	6.3	-	-	85.4	3.1	-	-	86.1	0.8	-	-	86.6	0.6	-	-	87.0	0.5	-	-	88.2	1.4
1981	-	-	92.0	4.3	-	-	93.7	1.8	-	-	95.3	1.7	-	-	95.1	-0.2	-	-	97.0	2.0	-	-	97.9	0.9
1982	-	-	96.8	-1.1	-	-	93.9	-3.0	-	-	98.3	4.7	-	-	99.2	0.9	-	-	98.8	-0.4	-	-	99.2	0.4
1983	-	-	96.7	-2.5	-	-	97.3	0.6	-	-	98.8	1.5	-	-	99.9	1.1	-	-	101.1	1.2	-	-	100.9	-0.2
1984	-	-	100.2	-0.7	-	-	101.4	1.2	-	-	102.5	1.1	-	-	105.3	2.7	-	-	106.1	0.8	-	-	105.7	-0.4
1985	-	-	104.0	-1.6	-	-	105.7	1.6	-	-	106.9	1.1	-	-	106.8	-0.1	-	-	106.7	-0.1	-	-	107.1	0.4
1986	-	-	105.2	-1.8	-	-	97.2	-7.6	-	-	99.1	2.0	-	-	96.6	-2.5	-	-	97.7	1.1	-	-	97.3	-0.4
1987	-	-	100.3	3.1	-	-	101.3	1.0	-	-	102.8	1.5	-	-	103.9	1.1	-	-	104.3	0.4	-	-	104.2	-0.1
1988	-	-	102.9	-1.2	-	-	102.9	0.0	-	-	104.2	1.3	-	-	105.2	1.0	-	-	106.1	0.9	-	-	106.4	0.3
1989	-	-	106.9	0.5	-	-	108.5	1.5	-	-	110.3	1.7	-	-	109.1	-1.1	-	-	110.0	0.8	-	-	111.4	1.3
1990	-	-	112.8	1.3	-	-	112.5	-0.3	-	-	113.1	0.5	-	-	114.4	1.1	-	-	122.1	6.7	-	-	124.3	1.8
1991	-	-	120.1	-3.4	-	-	115.4	-3.9	-	-	118.4	2.6	-	-	118.3	-0.1	-	-	122.0	3.1	-	-	123.2	1.0

[Continued]

Houston, TX
Consumer Price Index - All Urban Consumers
Base 1982-1984 = 100
Transportation
[Continued]

For 1947-1993. Columns headed % show percentile change in the index from the previous period for which an index is available.

Year	Jan Index	%	Feb Index	%	Mar Index	%	Apr Index	%	May Index	%	Jun Index	%	Jul Index	%	Aug Index	%	Sep Index	%	Oct Index	%	Nov Index	%	Dec Index	%
1992	-	-	121.0	-1.8	-	-	122.0	0.8	-	-	123.0	0.8	-	-	123.1	0.1	-	-	124.3	1.0	-	-	124.3	0.0
1993	-	-	124.8	0.4	-	-	127.2	1.9	-	-	127.8	0.5	-	-	128.8	0.8	-	-	131.2	1.9	-	-	130.9	-0.2

Source: U.S. Department of Labor, Bureau of Labor Statistics, Division of Consumer Prices and Price Indexes. - indicates no data collected for period.

Houston, TX
Consumer Price Index - Urban Wage Earners
Base 1982-1984 = 100
Transportation

For 1947-1993. Columns headed % show percentile change in the index from the previous period for which an index is available.

Year	Jan Index	Jan %	Feb Index	Feb %	Mar Index	Mar %	Apr Index	Apr %	May Index	May %	Jun Index	Jun %	Jul Index	Jul %	Aug Index	Aug %	Sep Index	Sep %	Oct Index	Oct %	Nov Index	Nov %	Dec Index	Dec %
1947	19.8	-	20.1	1.5	20.1	0.0	20.3	1.0	20.4	0.5	20.4	0.0	20.5	0.5	20.7	1.0	21.0	1.4	21.3	1.4	21.8	2.3	21.9	0.5
1948	22.5	2.7	22.6	0.4	22.6	0.0	22.6	0.0	22.6	0.0	22.7	0.4	23.2	2.2	23.7	2.2	23.7	0.0	23.8	0.4	23.9	0.4	23.9	0.0
1949	23.9	0.0	24.2	1.3	24.2	0.0	24.3	0.4	24.3	0.0	24.2	-0.4	24.9	2.9	24.9	0.0	24.9	0.0	25.0	0.4	25.1	0.4	25.1	0.0
1950	25.2	0.4	25.2	0.0	25.2	0.0	25.2	0.0	25.4	0.8	25.4	0.0	25.5	0.4	25.6	0.4	25.6	0.0	25.6	0.0	25.6	0.0	27.1	5.9
1951	27.2	0.4	27.4	0.7	27.7	1.1	27.6	-0.4	27.6	0.0	27.8	0.7	27.8	0.0	27.8	0.0	28.1	1.1	28.1	0.0	28.5	1.4	28.5	0.0
1952	27.9	-2.1	28.2	1.1	28.2	0.0	28.2	0.0	28.2	0.0	28.2	0.0	28.2	0.0	28.2	0.0	28.3	0.4	29.0	2.5	29.0	0.0	29.0	0.0
1953	-	-	28.9	-0.3	-	-	-	-	28.9	0.0	-	-	-	-	29.0	0.3	-	-	-	-	28.9	-0.3	-	-
1954	-	-	28.6	-1.0	-	-	-	-	28.5	-0.3	-	-	-	-	28.1	-1.4	-	-	-	-	28.7	2.1	-	-
1955	-	-	28.2	-1.7	-	-	-	-	27.8	-1.4	-	-	-	-	27.7	-0.4	-	-	-	-	28.8	4.0	-	-
1956	-	-	28.6	-0.7	-	-	-	-	28.4	-0.7	-	-	-	-	28.8	1.4	-	-	-	-	29.6	2.8	-	-
1957	-	-	30.1	1.7	-	-	-	-	30.7	2.0	-	-	-	-	30.9	0.7	-	-	-	-	31.7	2.6	-	-
1958	-	-	28.9	-8.8	-	-	-	-	31.4	8.7	-	-	-	-	32.2	2.5	-	-	-	-	32.6	1.2	-	-
1959	-	-	32.4	-0.6	-	-	-	-	32.8	1.2	-	-	-	-	33.0	0.6	-	-	-	-	33.2	0.6	-	-
1960	-	-	33.6	1.2	-	-	-	-	31.3	-6.8	-	-	-	-	33.5	7.0	-	-	-	-	33.2	-0.9	-	-
1961	-	-	31.4	-5.4	-	-	-	-	33.2	5.7	-	-	-	-	32.5	-2.1	-	-	-	-	34.5	6.2	-	-
1962	-	-	34.4	-0.3	-	-	-	-	34.5	0.3	-	-	-	-	34.1	-1.2	-	-	-	-	33.0	-3.2	-	-
1963	-	-	33.8	2.4	-	-	-	-	32.3	-4.4	-	-	-	-	33.6	4.0	-	-	-	-	34.1	1.5	-	-
1964	-	-	33.9	-0.6	-	-	-	-	34.3	1.2	-	-	-	-	34.2	-0.3	-	-	-	-	34.4	0.6	-	-
1965	-	-	33.6	-2.3	-	-	34.0	1.2	-	-	-	-	33.9	-0.3	-	-	-	-	34.5	1.8	-	-	-	-
1966	34.4	-0.3	-	-	-	-	34.5	0.3	-	-	-	-	34.9	1.2	-	-	-	-	34.9	0.0	-	-	-	-
1967	35.2	0.9	-	-	-	-	35.6	1.1	-	-	-	-	35.7	0.3	-	-	-	-	36.6	2.5	-	-	-	-
1968	36.6	0.0	-	-	-	-	36.8	0.5	-	-	-	-	36.9	0.3	-	-	-	-	37.1	0.5	-	-	-	-
1969	37.5	1.1	-	-	-	-	38.3	2.1	-	-	-	-	38.2	-0.3	-	-	-	-	38.7	1.3	-	-	-	-
1970	38.5	-0.5	-	-	-	-	38.8	0.8	-	-	-	-	38.8	0.0	-	-	-	-	38.9	0.3	-	-	-	-
1971	41.1	5.7	-	-	-	-	40.6	-1.2	-	-	-	-	40.1	-1.2	-	-	-	-	40.6	1.2	-	-	-	-
1972	41.0	1.0	-	-	-	-	41.5	1.2	-	-	-	-	41.5	0.0	-	-	-	-	40.8	-1.7	-	-	-	-
1973	41.0	0.5	-	-	-	-	41.7	1.7	-	-	-	-	42.1	1.0	-	-	-	-	42.2	0.2	-	-	-	-
1974	43.8	3.8	-	-	-	-	45.7	4.3	-	-	-	-	47.8	4.6	-	-	-	-	49.4	3.3	-	-	-	-
1975	48.9	-1.0	-	-	-	-	50.2	2.7	-	-	-	-	52.7	5.0	-	-	-	-	53.2	0.9	-	-	-	-
1976	53.9	1.3	-	-	-	-	54.4	0.9	-	-	-	-	56.2	3.3	-	-	-	-	58.1	3.4	-	-	-	-
1977	58.4	0.5	-	-	-	-	60.2	3.1	-	-	-	-	61.1	1.5	-	-	-	-	60.4	-1.1	-	-	-	-
1978	60.8	0.7	-	-	-	-	61.3	0.8	-	-	62.5	2.0	-	-	63.4	1.4	-	-	64.1	1.1	-	-	65.2	1.7
1979	-	-	66.2	1.5	-	-	69.2	4.5	-	-	72.7	5.1	-	-	75.0	3.2	-	-	75.4	0.5	-	-	77.1	2.3
1980	-	-	81.5	5.7	-	-	83.9	2.9	-	-	84.8	1.1	-	-	85.2	0.5	-	-	85.8	0.7	-	-	86.9	1.3
1981	-	-	90.4	4.0	-	-	92.2	2.0	-	-	93.9	1.8	-	-	94.2	0.3	-	-	95.4	1.3	-	-	97.0	1.7
1982	-	-	95.9	-1.1	-	-	93.5	-2.5	-	-	97.8	4.6	-	-	98.7	0.9	-	-	98.3	-0.4	-	-	98.7	0.4
1983	-	-	96.5	-2.2	-	-	97.1	0.6	-	-	98.6	1.5	-	-	99.8	1.2	-	-	101.2	1.4	-	-	101.2	0.0
1984	-	-	100.6	-0.6	-	-	102.1	1.5	-	-	103.3	1.2	-	-	106.0	2.6	-	-	106.8	0.8	-	-	106.4	-0.4
1985	-	-	104.8	-1.5	-	-	106.3	1.4	-	-	107.3	0.9	-	-	107.2	-0.1	-	-	107.2	0.0	-	-	107.5	0.3
1986	-	-	105.7	-1.7	-	-	98.5	-6.8	-	-	100.1	1.6	-	-	97.9	-2.2	-	-	98.9	1.0	-	-	98.5	-0.4
1987	-	-	102.2	3.8	-	-	103.4	1.2	-	-	105.0	1.5	-	-	106.2	1.1	-	-	107.0	0.8	-	-	106.7	-0.3
1988	-	-	105.5	-1.1	-	-	105.2	-0.3	-	-	106.6	1.3	-	-	108.0	1.3	-	-	108.7	0.6	-	-	109.0	0.3
1989	-	-	109.4	0.4	-	-	111.4	1.8	-	-	113.3	1.7	-	-	112.0	-1.1	-	-	112.6	0.5	-	-	113.9	1.2
1990	-	-	115.3	1.2	-	-	115.0	-0.3	-	-	115.6	0.5	-	-	117.1	1.3	-	-	125.4	7.1	-	-	127.5	1.7
1991	-	-	122.3	-4.1	-	-	117.6	-3.8	-	-	121.0	2.9	-	-	120.8	-0.2	-	-	124.6	3.1	-	-	125.6	0.8

[Continued]

Houston, TX
Consumer Price Index - Urban Wage Earners
Base 1982-1984 = 100
Transportation
[Continued]

For 1947-1993. Columns headed % show percentile change in the index from the previous period for which an index is available.

Year	Jan Index	%	Feb Index	%	Mar Index	%	Apr Index	%	May Index	%	Jun Index	%	Jul Index	%	Aug Index	%	Sep Index	%	Oct Index	%	Nov Index	%	Dec Index	%
1992	-	-	123.0	-2.1	-	-	123.9	0.7	-	-	125.6	1.4	-	-	125.8	0.2	-	-	126.5	0.6	-	-	126.5	0.0
1993	-	-	126.1	-0.3	-	-	128.5	1.9	-	-	129.4	0.7	-	-	130.1	0.5	-	-	132.3	1.7	-	-	131.5	-0.6

Source: U.S. Department of Labor, Bureau of Labor Statistics, Division of Consumer Prices and Price Indexes. - indicates no data collected for period.

Houston, TX
Consumer Price Index - All Urban Consumers
Base 1982-1984 = 100
Medical Care

For 1947-1993. Columns headed % show percentile change in the index from the previous period for which an index is available.

Year	Jan Index	%	Feb Index	%	Mar Index	%	Apr Index	%	May Index	%	Jun Index	%	Jul Index	%	Aug Index	%	Sep Index	%	Oct Index	%	Nov Index	%	Dec Index	%
1947	14.1	-	14.2	0.7	14.2	0.0	14.3	0.7	14.5	1.4	14.6	0.7	14.5	-0.7	14.5	0.0	14.6	0.7	14.7	0.7	14.7	0.0	14.7	0.0
1948	14.7	0.0	14.7	0.0	14.9	1.4	14.8	-0.7	14.8	0.0	14.9	0.7	14.9	0.0	14.9	0.0	14.9	0.0	14.9	0.0	14.9	0.0	14.9	0.0
1949	15.1	1.3	15.1	0.0	15.1	0.0	15.1	0.0	15.2	0.7	15.3	0.7	15.3	0.0	15.3	0.0	15.3	0.0	15.3	0.0	15.2	-0.7	15.5	2.0
1950	15.5	0.0	15.5	0.0	15.5	0.0	15.5	0.0	15.5	0.0	15.5	0.0	15.5	0.0	15.6	0.6	15.6	0.0	15.6	0.0	15.6	0.0	15.6	0.0
1951	15.6	0.0	15.6	0.0	15.8	1.3	15.8	0.0	15.8	0.0	15.8	0.0	15.8	0.0	15.8	0.0	15.8	0.0	16.6	5.1	16.6	0.0	16.7	0.6
1952	16.6	-0.6	16.6	0.0	16.6	0.0	16.7	0.6	16.7	0.0	16.7	0.0	16.7	0.0	16.7	0.0	16.7	0.0	16.7	0.0	16.7	0.0	17.4	4.2
1953	-	-	17.4	0.0	-	-	-	-	17.6	1.1	-	-	-	-	17.6	0.0	-	-	-	-	17.7	0.6	-	-
1954	-	-	17.7	0.0	-	-	-	-	17.7	0.0	-	-	-	-	17.8	0.6	-	-	-	-	17.8	0.0	-	-
1955	-	-	17.8	0.0	-	-	-	-	18.5	3.9	-	-	-	-	18.5	0.0	-	-	-	-	18.9	2.2	-	-
1956	-	-	18.9	0.0	-	-	-	-	18.8	-0.5	-	-	-	-	19.0	1.1	-	-	-	-	19.1	0.5	-	-
1957	-	-	19.3	1.0	-	-	-	-	19.2	-0.5	-	-	-	-	19.1	-0.5	-	-	-	-	19.2	0.5	-	-
1958	-	-	19.6	2.1	-	-	-	-	19.6	0.0	-	-	-	-	19.6	0.0	-	-	-	-	19.8	1.0	-	-
1959	-	-	19.8	0.0	-	-	-	-	20.1	1.5	-	-	-	-	20.1	0.0	-	-	-	-	20.1	0.0	-	-
1960	-	-	20.3	1.0	-	-	-	-	20.6	1.5	-	-	-	-	20.6	0.0	-	-	-	-	20.6	0.0	-	-
1961	-	-	20.6	0.0	-	-	-	-	20.8	1.0	-	-	-	-	20.8	0.0	-	-	-	-	20.9	0.5	-	-
1962	-	-	20.9	0.0	-	-	-	-	21.0	0.5	-	-	-	-	21.0	0.0	-	-	-	-	21.2	1.0	-	-
1963	-	-	21.5	1.4	-	-	-	-	21.6	0.5	-	-	-	-	21.6	0.0	-	-	-	-	21.8	0.9	-	-
1964	-	-	22.0	0.9	-	-	-	-	22.2	0.9	-	-	-	-	22.2	0.0	-	-	-	-	22.2	0.0	-	-
1965	-	-	22.5	1.4	-	-	22.7	0.9	-	-	-	-	22.8	0.4	-	-	-	-	22.9	0.4	-	-	-	-
1966	23.0	0.4	-	-	-	-	23.1	0.4	-	-	-	-	23.3	0.9	-	-	-	-	23.9	2.6	-	-	-	-
1967	24.4	2.1	-	-	-	-	24.7	1.2	-	-	-	-	24.8	0.4	-	-	-	-	25.2	1.6	-	-	-	-
1968	25.7	2.0	-	-	-	-	25.8	0.4	-	-	-	-	26.1	1.2	-	-	-	-	26.7	2.3	-	-	-	-
1969	27.6	3.4	-	-	-	-	28.3	2.5	-	-	-	-	28.5	0.7	-	-	-	-	29.1	2.1	-	-	-	-
1970	29.8	2.4	-	-	-	-	30.5	2.3	-	-	-	-	30.6	0.3	-	-	-	-	30.8	0.7	-	-	-	-
1971	31.5	2.3	-	-	-	-	31.9	1.3	-	-	-	-	33.0	3.4	-	-	-	-	32.7	-0.9	-	-	-	-
1972	32.8	0.3	-	-	-	-	33.6	2.4	-	-	-	-	33.6	0.0	-	-	-	-	34.1	1.5	-	-	-	-
1973	34.4	0.9	-	-	-	-	34.7	0.9	-	-	-	-	34.8	0.3	-	-	-	-	35.6	2.3	-	-	-	-
1974	36.3	2.0	-	-	-	-	36.5	0.6	-	-	-	-	38.3	4.9	-	-	-	-	39.2	2.3	-	-	-	-
1975	40.6	3.6	-	-	-	-	42.0	3.4	-	-	-	-	43.6	3.8	-	-	-	-	45.0	3.2	-	-	-	-
1976	45.5	1.1	-	-	-	-	46.7	2.6	-	-	-	-	48.0	2.8	-	-	-	-	49.8	3.8	-	-	-	-
1977	51.3	3.0	-	-	-	-	53.5	4.3	-	-	-	-	54.4	1.7	-	-	-	-	55.5	2.0	-	-	-	-
1978	57.4	3.4	-	-	-	-	58.5	1.9	-	-	59.1	1.0	-	-	60.0	1.5	-	-	61.0	1.7	-	-	61.4	0.7
1979	-	-	63.0	2.6	-	-	63.9	1.4	-	-	64.5	0.9	-	-	65.3	1.2	-	-	67.6	3.5	-	-	67.9	0.4
1980	-	-	69.7	2.7	-	-	71.0	1.9	-	-	71.8	1.1	-	-	72.2	0.6	-	-	74.3	2.9	-	-	76.0	2.3
1981	-	-	76.7	0.9	-	-	77.6	1.2	-	-	80.2	3.4	-	-	80.9	0.9	-	-	82.8	2.3	-	-	84.1	1.6
1982	-	-	85.6	1.8	-	-	87.4	2.1	-	-	88.9	1.7	-	-	92.2	3.7	-	-	95.3	3.4	-	-	98.6	3.5
1983	-	-	100.2	1.6	-	-	101.7	1.5	-	-	101.4	-0.3	-	-	101.7	0.3	-	-	101.5	-0.2	-	-	100.9	-0.6
1984	-	-	104.2	3.3	-	-	105.0	0.8	-	-	108.8	3.6	-	-	109.7	0.8	-	-	111.4	1.5	-	-	112.5	1.0
1985	-	-	113.9	1.2	-	-	115.9	1.8	-	-	116.5	0.5	-	-	117.7	1.0	-	-	118.8	0.9	-	-	119.5	0.6
1986	-	-	120.8	1.1	-	-	121.8	0.8	-	-	123.5	1.4	-	-	124.5	0.8	-	-	125.6	0.9	-	-	126.4	0.6
1987	-	-	127.3	0.7	-	-	128.6	1.0	-	-	129.9	1.0	-	-	132.2	1.8	-	-	132.9	0.5	-	-	133.5	0.5
1988	-	-	134.7	0.9	-	-	135.6	0.7	-	-	136.5	0.7	-	-	136.0	-0.4	-	-	138.9	2.1	-	-	140.6	1.2
1989	-	-	144.0	2.4	-	-	145.7	1.2	-	-	148.3	1.8	-	-	149.9	1.1	-	-	151.1	0.8	-	-	152.2	0.7
1990	-	-	153.7	1.0	-	-	158.1	2.9	-	-	158.5	0.3	-	-	163.9	3.4	-	-	168.0	2.5	-	-	169.1	0.7
1991	-	-	170.4	0.8	-	-	173.8	2.0	-	-	174.9	0.6	-	-	180.3	3.1	-	-	185.1	2.7	-	-	186.0	0.5

[Continued]

Houston, TX
Consumer Price Index - All Urban Consumers
Base 1982-1984 = 100
Medical Care

[Continued]

For 1947-1993. Columns headed % show percentile change in the index from the previous period for which an index is available.

Year	Jan Index	%	Feb Index	%	Mar Index	%	Apr Index	%	May Index	%	Jun Index	%	Jul Index	%	Aug Index	%	Sep Index	%	Oct Index	%	Nov Index	%	Dec Index	%
1992	-	-	190.7	2.5	-	-	192.2	0.8	-	-	194.5	1.2	-	-	195.1	0.3	-	-	195.7	0.3	-	-	196.1	0.2
1993	-	-	200.4	2.2	-	-	201.3	0.4	-	-	200.8	-0.2	-	-	200.8	0.0	-	-	201.9	0.5	-	-	201.2	-0.3

Source: U.S. Department of Labor, Bureau of Labor Statistics, Division of Consumer Prices and Price Indexes. - indicates no data collected for period.

517

Houston, TX
Consumer Price Index - Urban Wage Earners
Base 1982-1984 = 100
Medical Care

For 1947-1993. Columns headed % show percentile change in the index from the previous period for which an index is available.

Year	Jan Index	%	Feb Index	%	Mar Index	%	Apr Index	%	May Index	%	Jun Index	%	Jul Index	%	Aug Index	%	Sep Index	%	Oct Index	%	Nov Index	%	Dec Index	%
1947	13.5	-	13.6	0.7	13.6	0.0	13.7	0.7	13.9	1.5	14.0	0.7	13.9	-0.7	13.9	0.0	14.0	0.7	14.1	0.7	14.1	0.0	14.1	0.0
1948	14.1	0.0	14.1	0.0	14.3	1.4	14.2	-0.7	14.2	0.0	14.2	0.0	14.3	0.7	14.3	0.0	14.3	0.0	14.3	0.0	14.3	0.0	14.3	0.0
1949	14.4	0.7	14.4	0.0	14.4	0.0	14.5	0.7	14.6	0.7	14.7	0.7	14.6	-0.7	14.6	0.0	14.6	0.0	14.6	0.0	14.6	0.0	14.9	2.1
1950	14.9	0.0	14.9	0.0	14.9	0.0	14.9	0.0	14.9	0.0	14.9	0.0	14.9	0.0	14.9	0.0	15.0	0.7	15.0	0.0	15.0	0.0	15.0	0.0
1951	15.0	0.0	15.0	0.0	15.1	0.7	15.1	0.0	15.1	0.0	15.1	0.0	15.1	0.0	15.1	0.0	15.1	0.0	15.9	5.3	15.9	0.0	16.0	0.6
1952	15.9	-0.6	15.9	0.0	15.9	0.0	16.0	0.6	16.0	0.0	16.0	0.0	16.0	0.0	16.0	0.0	16.0	0.0	16.0	0.0	16.0	0.0	16.7	4.4
1953	-	-	16.7	0.0	-	-	-	-	16.8	0.6	-	-	-	-	16.8	0.0	-	-	-	-	17.0	1.2	-	-
1954	-	-	17.0	0.0	-	-	-	-	17.0	0.0	-	-	-	-	17.1	0.6	-	-	-	-	17.1	0.0	-	-
1955	-	-	17.1	0.0	-	-	-	-	17.7	3.5	-	-	-	-	17.8	0.6	-	-	-	-	18.1	1.7	-	-
1956	-	-	18.2	0.6	-	-	-	-	18.0	-1.1	-	-	-	-	18.2	1.1	-	-	-	-	18.3	0.5	-	-
1957	-	-	18.5	1.1	-	-	-	-	18.4	-0.5	-	-	-	-	18.3	-0.5	-	-	-	-	18.4	0.5	-	-
1958	-	-	18.8	2.2	-	-	-	-	18.8	0.0	-	-	-	-	18.8	0.0	-	-	-	-	19.0	1.1	-	-
1959	-	-	19.0	0.0	-	-	-	-	19.3	1.6	-	-	-	-	19.2	-0.5	-	-	-	-	19.2	0.0	-	-
1960	-	-	19.4	1.0	-	-	-	-	19.7	1.5	-	-	-	-	19.7	0.0	-	-	-	-	19.8	0.5	-	-
1961	-	-	19.7	-0.5	-	-	-	-	19.9	1.0	-	-	-	-	19.9	0.0	-	-	-	-	20.0	0.5	-	-
1962	-	-	20.0	0.0	-	-	-	-	20.2	1.0	-	-	-	-	20.2	0.0	-	-	-	-	20.4	1.0	-	-
1963	-	-	20.6	1.0	-	-	-	-	20.7	0.5	-	-	-	-	20.7	0.0	-	-	-	-	20.9	1.0	-	-
1964	-	-	21.1	1.0	-	-	-	-	21.3	0.9	-	-	-	-	21.3	0.0	-	-	-	-	21.3	0.0	-	-
1965	-	-	21.6	1.4	-	-	21.8	0.9	-	-	-	-	21.9	0.5	-	-	-	-	22.0	0.5	-	-	-	-
1966	22.1	0.5	-	-	-	-	22.1	0.0	-	-	-	-	22.3	0.9	-	-	-	-	22.9	2.7	-	-	-	-
1967	23.4	2.2	-	-	-	-	23.6	0.9	-	-	-	-	23.8	0.8	-	-	-	-	24.2	1.7	-	-	-	-
1968	24.7	2.1	-	-	-	-	24.8	0.4	-	-	-	-	25.0	0.8	-	-	-	-	25.6	2.4	-	-	-	-
1969	26.4	3.1	-	-	-	-	27.1	2.7	-	-	-	-	27.3	0.7	-	-	-	-	27.9	2.2	-	-	-	-
1970	28.6	2.5	-	-	-	-	29.2	2.1	-	-	-	-	29.4	0.7	-	-	-	-	29.5	0.3	-	-	-	-
1971	30.2	2.4	-	-	-	-	30.6	1.3	-	-	-	-	31.6	3.3	-	-	-	-	31.4	-0.6	-	-	-	-
1972	31.5	0.3	-	-	-	-	32.2	2.2	-	-	-	-	32.2	0.0	-	-	-	-	32.7	1.6	-	-	-	-
1973	33.0	0.9	-	-	-	-	33.3	0.9	-	-	-	-	33.4	0.3	-	-	-	-	34.1	2.1	-	-	-	-
1974	34.8	2.1	-	-	-	-	35.0	0.6	-	-	-	-	36.7	4.9	-	-	-	-	37.6	2.5	-	-	-	-
1975	38.9	3.5	-	-	-	-	40.3	3.6	-	-	-	-	41.8	3.7	-	-	-	-	43.2	3.3	-	-	-	-
1976	43.6	0.9	-	-	-	-	44.8	2.8	-	-	-	-	46.1	2.9	-	-	-	-	47.8	3.7	-	-	-	-
1977	49.2	2.9	-	-	-	-	51.3	4.3	-	-	-	-	52.2	1.8	-	-	-	-	53.2	1.9	-	-	-	-
1978	55.0	3.4	-	-	-	-	56.1	2.0	-	-	56.3	0.4	-	-	57.8	2.7	-	-	58.4	1.0	-	-	59.0	1.0
1979	-	-	62.2	5.4	-	-	63.5	2.1	-	-	64.8	2.0	-	-	65.4	0.9	-	-	66.9	2.3	-	-	67.7	1.2
1980	-	-	68.6	1.3	-	-	70.5	2.8	-	-	70.6	0.1	-	-	72.9	3.3	-	-	74.0	1.5	-	-	75.4	1.9
1981	-	-	76.4	1.3	-	-	77.5	1.4	-	-	79.8	3.0	-	-	80.5	0.9	-	-	81.7	1.5	-	-	83.7	2.4
1982	-	-	85.3	1.9	-	-	87.1	2.1	-	-	88.6	1.7	-	-	92.1	4.0	-	-	95.3	3.5	-	-	98.8	3.7
1983	-	-	100.4	1.6	-	-	101.9	1.5	-	-	101.5	-0.4	-	-	101.7	0.2	-	-	101.3	-0.4	-	-	100.8	-0.5
1984	-	-	104.2	3.4	-	-	105.0	0.8	-	-	109.0	3.8	-	-	109.9	0.8	-	-	111.6	1.5	-	-	112.7	1.0
1985	-	-	114.2	1.3	-	-	116.2	1.8	-	-	116.8	0.5	-	-	117.9	0.9	-	-	119.0	0.9	-	-	119.6	0.5
1986	-	-	121.0	1.2	-	-	122.0	0.8	-	-	123.7	1.4	-	-	124.7	0.8	-	-	125.8	0.9	-	-	126.6	0.6
1987	-	-	127.6	0.8	-	-	129.0	1.1	-	-	130.4	1.1	-	-	132.7	1.8	-	-	133.4	0.5	-	-	134.3	0.7
1988	-	-	135.5	0.9	-	-	136.4	0.7	-	-	137.4	0.7	-	-	137.1	-0.2	-	-	140.1	2.2	-	-	141.8	1.2
1989	-	-	145.3	2.5	-	-	147.0	1.2	-	-	149.6	1.8	-	-	151.3	1.1	-	-	152.4	0.7	-	-	153.5	0.7
1990	-	-	154.7	0.8	-	-	159.3	3.0	-	-	159.5	0.1	-	-	165.0	3.4	-	-	169.2	2.5	-	-	170.3	0.7
1991	-	-	171.4	0.6	-	-	174.9	2.0	-	-	175.9	0.6	-	-	181.5	3.2	-	-	186.7	2.9	-	-	187.6	0.5

[Continued]

Houston, TX
Consumer Price Index - Urban Wage Earners
Base 1982-1984 = 100
Medical Care
[Continued]

For 1947-1993. Columns headed % show percentile change in the index from the previous period for which an index is available.

Year	Jan Index	%	Feb Index	%	Mar Index	%	Apr Index	%	May Index	%	Jun Index	%	Jul Index	%	Aug Index	%	Sep Index	%	Oct Index	%	Nov Index	%	Dec Index	%
1992	-	-	192.4	2.6	-	-	193.8	0.7	-	-	196.1	1.2	-	-	196.7	0.3	-	-	197.5	0.4	-	-	197.9	0.2
1993	-	-	202.3	2.2	-	-	203.3	0.5	-	-	202.9	-0.2	-	-	202.9	0.0	-	-	203.9	0.5	-	-	203.2	-0.3

Source: U.S. Department of Labor, Bureau of Labor Statistics, Division of Consumer Prices and Price Indexes. - indicates no data collected for period.

Houston, TX
Consumer Price Index - All Urban Consumers
Base 1982-1984 = 100
Entertainment

For 1976-1993. Columns headed % show percentile change in the index from the previous period for which an index is available.

Year	Jan Index	%	Feb Index	%	Mar Index	%	Apr Index	%	May Index	%	Jun Index	%	Jul Index	%	Aug Index	%	Sep Index	%	Oct Index	%	Nov Index	%	Dec Index	%
1976	59.9	-	-	-	-	-	60.6	1.2	-	-	-	-	61.7	1.8	-	-	-	-	61.8	0.2	-	-	-	-
1977	63.1	2.1	-	-	-	-	63.3	0.3	-	-	-	-	64.5	1.9	-	-	-	-	64.4	-0.2	-	-	-	-
1978	64.8	0.6	-	-	-	-	65.8	1.5	-	-	64.5	-2.0	-	-	65.2	1.1	-	-	66.7	2.3	-	-	67.7	1.5
1979	-	-	68.9	1.8	-	-	69.6	1.0	-	-	69.8	0.3	-	-	70.2	0.6	-	-	71.5	1.9	-	-	71.7	0.3
1980	-	-	78.4	9.3	-	-	79.2	1.0	-	-	80.2	1.3	-	-	81.2	1.2	-	-	80.8	-0.5	-	-	81.2	0.5
1981	-	-	87.3	7.5	-	-	86.5	-0.9	-	-	86.2	-0.3	-	-	86.2	0.0	-	-	86.8	0.7	-	-	86.9	0.1
1982	-	-	88.5	1.8	-	-	89.9	1.6	-	-	94.7	5.3	-	-	94.2	-0.5	-	-	95.9	1.8	-	-	95.9	0.0
1983	-	-	102.2	6.6	-	-	102.4	0.2	-	-	103.8	1.4	-	-	105.3	1.4	-	-	104.4	-0.9	-	-	102.1	-2.2
1984	-	-	102.6	0.5	-	-	102.8	0.2	-	-	101.9	-0.9	-	-	105.1	3.1	-	-	105.5	0.4	-	-	108.4	2.7
1985	-	-	109.5	1.0	-	-	112.2	2.5	-	-	113.3	1.0	-	-	113.6	0.3	-	-	111.9	-1.5	-	-	111.7	-0.2
1986	-	-	112.2	0.4	-	-	114.6	2.1	-	-	115.3	0.6	-	-	114.8	-0.4	-	-	115.4	0.5	-	-	116.0	0.5
1987	-	-	116.9	0.8	-	-	117.4	0.4	-	-	118.2	0.7	-	-	118.7	0.4	-	-	121.0	1.9	-	-	120.2	-0.7
1988	-	-	124.5	3.6	-	-	123.3	-1.0	-	-	123.6	0.2	-	-	123.4	-0.2	-	-	125.6	1.8	-	-	129.1	2.8
1989	-	-	128.4	-0.5	-	-	132.5	3.2	-	-	137.2	3.5	-	-	136.3	-0.7	-	-	135.8	-0.4	-	-	133.6	-1.6
1990	-	-	134.2	0.4	-	-	134.8	0.4	-	-	132.8	-1.5	-	-	135.8	2.3	-	-	136.1	0.2	-	-	136.2	0.1
1991	-	-	137.4	0.9	-	-	139.4	1.5	-	-	139.8	0.3	-	-	139.7	-0.1	-	-	141.2	1.1	-	-	141.2	0.0
1992	-	-	143.2	1.4	-	-	144.7	1.0	-	-	145.0	0.2	-	-	147.4	1.7	-	-	150.6	2.2	-	-	149.8	-0.5
1993	-	-	152.9	2.1	-	-	152.2	-0.5	-	-	153.4	0.8	-	-	150.8	-1.7	-	-	158.7	5.2	-	-	151.8	-4.3

Source: U.S. Department of Labor, Bureau of Labor Statistics, Division of Consumer Prices and Price Indexes. - indicates no data collected for period.

Houston, TX
Consumer Price Index - Urban Wage Earners
Base 1982-1984 = 100
Entertainment

For 1976-1993. Columns headed % show percentile change in the index from the previous period for which an index is available.

Year	Jan Index	%	Feb Index	%	Mar Index	%	Apr Index	%	May Index	%	Jun Index	%	Jul Index	%	Aug Index	%	Sep Index	%	Oct Index	%	Nov Index	%	Dec Index	%
1976	61.7	-	-	-	-	-	62.4	1.1	-	-	-	-	63.5	1.8	-	*	-	-	63.7	0.3	-	-	-	-
1977	64.9	1.9	-	-	-	-	65.2	0.5	-	-	-	-	66.4	1.8	-	-	-	-	66.3	-0.2	-	-	-	-
1978	66.7	0.6	-	-	-	-	67.7	1.5	-	-	67.0	-1.0	-	-	67.7	1.0	-	-	68.9	1.8	-	-	70.2	1.9
1979	-	-	69.9	-0.4	-	-	72.7	4.0	-	-	71.3	-1.9	-	-	71.4	0.1	-	-	72.5	1.5	-	-	72.8	0.4
1980	-	-	76.1	4.5	-	-	76.4	0.4	-	-	77.9	2.0	-	-	81.2	4.2	-	-	82.8	2.0	-	-	82.4	-0.5
1981	-	-	84.9	3.0	-	-	85.9	1.2	-	-	86.4	0.6	-	-	84.5	-2.2	-	-	85.0	0.6	-	-	85.0	0.0
1982	-	-	86.5	1.8	-	-	88.5	2.3	-	-	93.6	5.8	-	-	92.8	-0.9	-	-	94.3	1.6	-	-	94.3	0.0
1983	-	-	103.2	9.4	-	-	103.3	0.1	-	-	104.5	1.2	-	-	106.6	2.0	-	-	105.0	-1.5	-	-	103.3	-1.6
1984	-	-	103.8	0.5	-	-	103.8	0.0	-	-	101.8	-1.9	-	-	105.9	4.0	-	-	106.2	0.3	-	-	108.6	2.3
1985	-	-	109.8	1.1	-	-	112.9	2.8	-	-	113.9	0.9	-	-	114.1	0.2	-	-	113.1	-0.9	-	-	112.9	-0.2
1986	-	-	113.3	0.4	-	-	115.1	1.6	-	-	116.3	1.0	-	-	116.3	0.0	-	-	116.9	0.5	-	-	117.6	0.6
1987	-	-	118.4	0.7	-	-	118.9	0.4	-	-	119.7	0.7	-	-	120.2	0.4	-	-	122.5	1.9	-	-	121.6	-0.7
1988	-	-	126.3	3.9	-	-	124.9	-1.1	-	-	125.3	0.3	-	-	125.1	-0.2	-	-	127.5	1.9	-	-	130.9	2.7
1989	-	-	130.0	-0.7	-	-	134.3	3.3	-	-	139.3	3.7	-	-	138.3	-0.7	-	-	138.1	-0.1	-	-	135.3	-2.0
1990	-	-	135.9	0.4	-	-	136.6	0.5	-	-	134.6	-1.5	-	-	137.5	2.2	-	-	137.9	0.3	-	-	137.9	0.0
1991	-	-	139.2	0.9	-	-	141.0	1.3	-	-	141.4	0.3	-	-	141.4	0.0	-	-	142.8	1.0	-	-	142.7	-0.1
1992	-	-	144.4	1.2	-	-	146.1	1.2	-	-	146.4	0.2	-	-	149.0	1.8	-	-	153.8	3.2	-	-	152.8	-0.7
1993	-	-	155.8	2.0	-	-	155.1	-0.4	-	-	156.3	0.8	-	-	153.7	-1.7	-	-	161.9	5.3	-	-	154.7	-4.4

Source: U.S. Department of Labor, Bureau of Labor Statistics, Division of Consumer Prices and Price Indexes. - indicates no data collected for period.

Houston, TX
Consumer Price Index - All Urban Consumers
Base 1982-1984 = 100
Other Goods and Services

For 1976-1993. Columns headed % show percentile change in the index from the previous period for which an index is available.

Year	Jan Index	%	Feb Index	%	Mar Index	%	Apr Index	%	May Index	%	Jun Index	%	Jul Index	%	Aug Index	%	Sep Index	%	Oct Index	%	Nov Index	%	Dec Index	%
1976	55.4	-	-	-	-	-	56.1	1.3	-	-	-	-	56.1	0.0	-	-	-	-	56.8	1.2	-	-	-	-
1977	58.5	3.0	-	-	-	-	59.2	1.2	-	-	-	-	59.3	0.2	-	-	-	-	60.8	2.5	-	-	-	-
1978	62.6	3.0	-	-	-	-	64.0	2.2	-	-	64.6	0.9	-	-	66.1	2.3	-	-	68.0	2.9	-	-	68.7	1.0
1979	-	-	69.9	1.7	-	-	71.0	1.6	-	-	71.2	0.3	-	-	71.6	0.6	-	-	73.2	2.2	-	-	74.8	2.2
1980	-	-	76.8	2.7	-	-	78.1	1.7	-	-	78.9	1.0	-	-	79.6	0.9	-	-	81.7	2.6	-	-	82.9	1.5
1981	-	-	83.6	0.8	-	-	84.3	0.8	-	-	85.4	1.3	-	-	85.7	0.4	-	-	87.1	1.6	-	-	86.8	-0.3
1982	-	-	88.0	1.4	-	-	89.6	1.8	-	-	91.3	1.9	-	-	92.6	1.4	-	-	94.6	2.2	-	-	97.6	3.2
1983	-	-	99.8	2.3	-	-	99.6	-0.2	-	-	100.4	0.8	-	-	101.1	0.7	-	-	103.3	2.2	-	-	103.1	-0.2
1984	-	-	105.2	2.0	-	-	105.6	0.4	-	-	106.0	0.4	-	-	108.3	2.2	-	-	109.6	1.2	-	-	110.2	0.5
1985	-	-	111.0	0.7	-	-	111.1	0.1	-	-	111.5	0.4	-	-	112.1	0.5	-	-	115.2	2.8	-	-	115.2	0.0
1986	-	-	116.3	1.0	-	-	117.2	0.8	-	-	117.2	0.0	-	-	119.0	1.5	-	-	122.1	2.6	-	-	121.2	-0.7
1987	-	-	123.4	1.8	-	-	123.2	-0.2	-	-	123.6	0.3	-	-	124.3	0.6	-	-	127.8	2.8	-	-	128.1	0.2
1988	-	-	129.3	0.9	-	-	128.7	-0.5	-	-	130.1	1.1	-	-	133.1	2.3	-	-	133.6	0.4	-	-	133.5	-0.1
1989	-	-	134.5	0.7	-	-	135.0	0.4	-	-	134.4	-0.4	-	-	137.7	2.5	-	-	146.5	6.4	-	-	146.0	-0.3
1990	-	-	147.2	0.8	-	-	150.1	2.0	-	-	151.4	0.9	-	-	156.6	3.4	-	-	156.6	0.0	-	-	152.4	-2.7
1991	-	-	155.3	1.9	-	-	157.5	1.4	-	-	157.2	-0.2	-	-	159.0	1.1	-	-	160.7	1.1	-	-	157.6	-1.9
1992	-	-	161.7	2.6	-	-	168.9	4.5	-	-	172.6	2.2	-	-	176.8	2.4	-	-	178.8	1.1	-	-	179.0	0.1
1993	-	-	180.7	0.9	-	-	181.0	0.2	-	-	179.8	-0.7	-	-	179.3	-0.3	-	-	181.3	1.1	-	-	184.0	1.5

Source: U.S. Department of Labor, Bureau of Labor Statistics, Division of Consumer Prices and Price Indexes. - indicates no data collected for period.

Houston, TX
Consumer Price Index - Urban Wage Earners
Base 1982-1984 = 100
Other Goods and Services

For 1976-1993. Columns headed % show percentile change in the index from the previous period for which an index is available.

Year	Jan Index	%	Feb Index	%	Mar Index	%	Apr Index	%	May Index	%	Jun Index	%	Jul Index	%	Aug Index	%	Sep Index	%	Oct Index	%	Nov Index	%	Dec Index	%
1976	55.3	-	-	-	-	-	55.9	1.1	-	-	-	-	56.0	0.2	-	-	-	-	56.6	1.1	-	-	-	-
1977	58.3	3.0	-	-	-	-	59.0	1.2	-	-	-	-	59.1	0.2	-	-	-	-	60.7	2.7	-	-	-	-
1978	62.4	2.8	-	-	-	-	63.8	2.2	-	-	64.5	1.1	-	-	64.8	0.5	-	-	67.0	3.4	-	-	66.2	-1.2
1979	-	-	69.2	4.5	-	-	70.5	1.9	-	-	69.8	-1.0	-	-	71.1	1.9	-	-	71.6	0.7	-	-	73.1	2.1
1980	-	-	76.3	4.4	-	-	77.1	1.0	-	-	79.1	2.6	-	-	78.4	-0.9	-	-	80.8	3.1	-	-	81.1	0.4
1981	-	-	81.3	0.2	-	-	82.5	1.5	-	-	85.7	3.9	-	-	85.9	0.2	-	-	86.7	0.9	-	-	87.0	0.3
1982	-	-	88.2	1.4	-	-	89.9	1.9	-	-	90.8	1.0	-	-	92.1	1.4	-	-	94.2	2.3	-	-	97.7	3.7
1983	-	-	100.1	2.5	-	-	99.9	-0.2	-	-	100.3	0.4	-	-	101.1	0.8	-	-	103.1	2.0	-	-	102.9	-0.2
1984	-	-	105.0	2.0	-	-	105.5	0.5	-	-	106.2	0.7	-	-	108.6	2.3	-	-	109.9	1.2	-	-	110.5	0.5
1985	-	-	111.4	0.8	-	-	111.5	0.1	-	-	111.6	0.1	-	-	112.2	0.5	-	-	114.5	2.0	-	-	114.1	-0.3
1986	-	-	115.2	1.0	-	-	116.3	1.0	-	-	116.3	0.0	-	-	118.3	1.7	-	-	120.4	1.8	-	-	119.5	-0.7
1987	-	-	121.4	1.6	-	-	121.2	-0.2	-	-	121.8	0.5	-	-	122.6	0.7	-	-	126.3	3.0	-	-	126.4	0.1
1988	-	-	127.9	1.2	-	-	127.1	-0.6	-	-	128.9	1.4	-	-	133.2	3.3	-	-	133.7	0.4	-	-	133.7	0.0
1989	-	-	135.1	1.0	-	-	135.7	0.4	-	-	134.7	-0.7	-	-	139.6	3.6	-	-	146.8	5.2	-	-	146.0	-0.5
1990	-	-	147.4	1.0	-	-	150.4	2.0	-	-	151.7	0.9	-	-	158.3	4.4	-	-	158.1	-0.1	-	-	152.2	-3.7
1991	-	-	155.5	2.2	-	-	157.6	1.4	-	-	157.4	-0.1	-	-	158.6	0.8	-	-	161.3	1.7	-	-	157.0	-2.7
1992	-	-	162.3	3.4	-	-	166.7	2.7	-	-	171.7	3.0	-	-	176.3	2.7	-	-	178.8	1.4	-	-	179.0	0.1
1993	-	-	181.2	1.2	-	-	181.5	0.2	-	-	179.3	-1.2	-	-	176.4	-1.6	-	-	178.4	1.1	-	-	181.6	1.8

Source: U.S. Department of Labor, Bureau of Labor Statistics, Division of Consumer Prices and Price Indexes. - indicates no data collected for period.

Kansas City, MO-KS
Consumer Price Index - All Urban Consumers
Base 1982-1984 = 100
Annual Averages

For 1917-1993. Columns headed % show percentile change in the index from the previous period for which an index is available.

Year	All Items		Food & Beverage		Housing		Apparel & Upkeep		Trans- portation		Medical Care		Entertain- ment		Other Goods & Services	
	Index	%	Index	%	Index	%	Index	%	Index	%	Index	%	Index	%	Index	%
1917	-	-	-	-	-	-	-	-	-	-	-	-	-	-	-	-
1918	16.1	-	-	-	-	-	-	-	-	-	-	-	-	-	-	-
1919	18.5	14.9	-	-	-	-	-	-	-	-	-	-	-	-	-	-
1920	21.7	17.3	-	-	-	-	-	-	-	-	-	-	-	-	-	-
1921	19.2	-11.5	-	-	-	-	-	-	-	-	-	-	-	-	-	-
1922	17.5	-8.9	-	-	-	-	-	-	-	-	-	-	-	-	-	-
1923	17.4	-0.6	-	-	-	-	-	-	-	-	-	-	-	-	-	-
1924	17.3	-0.6	-	-	-	-	-	-	-	-	-	-	-	-	-	-
1925	17.5	1.2	-	-	-	-	-	-	-	-	-	-	-	-	-	-
1926	17.5	0.0	-	-	-	-	-	-	-	-	-	-	-	-	-	-
1927	17.0	-2.9	-	-	-	-	-	-	-	-	-	-	-	-	-	-
1928	16.7	-1.8	-	-	-	-	-	-	-	-	-	-	-	-	-	-
1929	16.8	0.6	-	-	-	-	-	-	-	-	-	-	-	-	-	-
1930	16.5	-1.8	-	-	-	-	-	-	-	-	-	-	-	-	-	-
1931	15.5	-6.1	-	-	-	-	-	-	-	-	-	-	-	-	-	-
1932	13.9	-10.3	-	-	-	-	-	-	-	-	-	-	-	-	-	-
1933	13.3	-4.3	-	-	-	-	-	-	-	-	-	-	-	-	-	-
1934	13.7	3.0	-	-	-	-	-	-	-	-	-	-	-	-	-	-
1935	14.0	2.2	-	-	-	-	-	-	-	-	-	-	-	-	-	-
1936	14.1	0.7	-	-	-	-	-	-	-	-	-	-	-	-	-	-
1937	14.6	3.5	-	-	-	-	-	-	-	-	-	-	-	-	-	-
1938	14.3	-2.1	-	-	-	-	-	-	-	-	-	-	-	-	-	-
1939	14.1	-1.4	-	-	-	-	-	-	-	-	-	-	-	-	-	-
1940	14.0	-0.7	-	-	-	-	-	-	-	-	-	-	-	-	-	-
1941	14.7	5.0	-	-	-	-	-	-	-	-	-	-	-	-	-	-
1942	16.3	10.9	-	-	-	-	-	-	-	-	-	-	-	-	-	-
1943	17.3	6.1	-	-	-	-	-	-	-	-	-	-	-	-	-	-
1944	17.6	1.7	-	-	-	-	-	-	-	-	-	-	-	-	-	-
1945	18.1	2.8	-	-	-	-	-	-	-	-	-	-	-	-	-	-
1946	19.3	6.6	-	-	-	-	-	-	-	-	-	-	-	-	-	-
1947	21.9	13.5	-	-	-	-	-	-	18.2	-	11.0	-	-	-	-	-
1948	23.6	7.8	-	-	-	-	-	-	20.2	11.0	11.9	8.2	-	-	-	-
1949	23.3	-1.3	-	-	-	-	-	-	21.5	6.4	12.2	2.5	-	-	-	-
1950	23.7	1.7	-	-	-	-	-	-	21.9	1.9	12.4	1.6	-	-	-	-
1951	25.5	7.6	-	-	-	-	-	-	23.2	5.9	13.0	4.8	-	-	-	-
1952	26.3	3.1	-	-	-	-	-	-	25.4	9.5	13.7	5.4	-	-	-	-
1953	26.4	0.4	-	-	-	-	39.2	-	26.0	2.4	14.0	2.2	-	-	-	-
1954	26.5	0.4	-	-	-	-	38.9	-0.8	25.2	-3.1	15.6	11.4	-	-	-	-
1955	26.5	0.0	-	-	-	-	38.9	0.0	25.0	-0.8	15.9	1.9	-	-	-	-
1956	26.9	1.5	-	-	-	-	39.4	1.3	25.4	1.6	16.6	4.4	-	-	-	-
1957	27.8	3.3	-	-	-	-	40.3	2.3	27.6	8.7	17.7	6.6	-	-	-	-
1958	28.5	2.5	-	-	-	-	40.4	0.2	29.1	5.4	19.0	7.3	-	-	-	-
1959	28.9	1.4	-	-	-	-	40.7	0.7	30.6	5.2	20.0	5.3	-	-	-	-
1960	29.3	1.4	-	-	-	-	41.7	2.5	30.6	0.0	20.3	1.5	-	-	-	-
1961	29.6	1.0	-	-	-	-	42.0	0.7	30.6	0.0	21.1	3.9	-	-	-	-

[Continued]

524

Kansas City, MO-KS
Consumer Price Index - All Urban Consumers
Base 1982-1984 = 100
Annual Averages
[Continued]

For 1917-1993. Columns headed % show percentile change in the index from the previous period for which an index is available.

Year	All Items		Food & Beverage		Housing		Apparel & Upkeep		Trans-portation		Medical Care		Entertain-ment		Other Goods & Services	
	Index	%	Index	%	Index	%	Index	%	Index	%	Index	%	Index	%	Index	%
1962	30.1	1.7	-	-	-	-	42.0	0.0	31.3	2.3	21.5	1.9	-	-	-	-
1963	30.4	1.0	-	-	-	-	42.6	1.4	31.3	0.0	21.7	0.9	-	-	-	-
1964	31.2	2.6	-	-	-	-	43.6	2.3	31.6	1.0	22.8	5.1	-	-	-	-
1965	32.2	3.2	-	-	-	-	44.5	2.1	33.8	7.0	24.0	5.3	-	-	-	-
1966	33.0	2.5	-	-	-	-	45.7	2.7	34.5	2.1	25.3	5.4	-	-	-	-
1967	33.7	2.1	-	-	-	-	47.3	3.5	34.7	0.6	27.2	7.5	-	-	-	-
1968	35.0	3.9	-	-	-	-	50.8	7.4	35.5	2.3	28.9	6.3	-	-	-	-
1969	36.9	5.4	-	-	-	-	54.4	7.1	37.2	4.8	30.4	5.2	-	-	-	-
1970	39.0	5.7	-	-	-	-	57.4	5.5	38.2	2.7	31.8	4.6	-	-	-	-
1971	40.6	4.1	-	-	-	-	58.9	2.6	41.0	7.3	33.8	6.3	-	-	-	-
1972	41.8	3.0	-	-	-	-	60.3	2.4	41.0	0.0	35.1	3.8	-	-	-	-
1973	43.9	5.0	-	-	-	-	61.8	2.5	42.6	3.9	36.7	4.6	-	-	-	-
1974	48.6	10.7	-	-	-	-	65.7	6.3	47.3	11.0	40.1	9.3	-	-	-	-
1975	53.2	9.5	-	-	-	-	69.0	5.0	51.5	8.9	43.6	8.7	-	-	-	-
1976	56.1	5.5	62.9	-	52.7	-	70.7	2.5	55.5	7.8	47.3	8.5	65.3	-	57.7	-
1977	60.0	7.0	67.0	6.5	56.6	7.4	77.0	8.9	59.2	6.7	51.8	9.5	68.3	4.6	61.4	6.4
1978	64.6	7.7	74.6	11.3	61.5	8.7	79.0	2.6	62.1	4.9	56.7	9.5	70.9	3.8	64.7	5.4
1979	73.8	14.2	82.6	10.7	72.1	17.2	84.3	6.7	72.3	16.4	63.7	12.3	74.2	4.7	69.9	8.0
1980	83.6	13.3	89.6	8.5	82.7	14.7	87.6	3.9	85.0	17.6	70.9	11.3	83.1	12.0	76.7	9.7
1981	90.5	8.3	95.0	6.0	89.5	8.2	92.3	5.4	93.2	9.6	79.7	12.4	90.4	8.8	84.5	10.2
1982	95.0	5.0	97.5	2.6	93.8	4.8	95.7	3.7	97.5	4.6	91.0	14.2	95.8	6.0	91.3	8.0
1983	100.5	5.8	99.2	1.7	101.2	7.9	101.8	6.4	99.5	2.1	101.1	11.1	99.9	4.3	100.6	10.2
1984	104.5	4.0	103.3	4.1	105.0	3.8	102.5	0.7	103.0	3.5	107.8	6.6	104.3	4.4	108.1	7.5
1985	107.7	3.1	106.0	2.6	107.6	2.5	105.0	2.4	106.5	3.4	111.7	3.6	107.0	2.6	115.7	7.0
1986	108.7	0.9	109.5	3.3	109.4	1.7	107.0	1.9	100.0	-6.1	117.7	5.4	111.0	3.7	125.5	8.5
1987	113.1	4.0	112.8	3.0	113.6	3.8	109.7	2.5	102.9	2.9	123.4	4.8	123.6	11.4	134.9	7.5
1988	117.4	3.8	115.8	2.7	118.3	4.1	113.1	3.1	107.2	4.2	130.8	6.0	124.2	0.5	141.6	5.0
1989	121.6	3.6	119.9	3.5	119.6	1.1	119.7	5.8	112.2	4.7	142.0	8.6	132.0	6.3	152.3	7.6
1990	126.0	3.6	127.5	6.3	121.8	1.8	116.5	-2.7	116.2	3.6	156.8	10.4	142.0	7.6	159.6	4.8
1991	131.2	4.1	130.9	2.7	125.4	3.0	124.7	7.0	119.2	2.6	173.5	10.7	149.3	5.1	175.7	10.1
1992	134.3	2.4	132.9	1.5	127.2	1.4	124.8	0.1	121.8	2.2	183.8	5.9	154.0	3.1	189.4	7.8
1993	138.1	2.8	137.7	3.6	130.4	2.5	125.3	0.4	124.7	2.4	195.6	6.4	152.5	-1.0	196.7	3.9

Source: U.S. Department of Labor, Bureau of Labor Statistics, Division of Consumer Prices and Price Indexes. - indicates no data collected for period.

Kansas City, MO-KS
Consumer Price Index - Urban Wage Earners
Base 1982-1984 = 100
Annual Averages

For 1917-1993. Columns headed % show percentile change in the index from the previous period for which an index is available.

Year	All Items		Food & Beverage		Housing		Apparel & Upkeep		Trans- portation		Medical Care		Entertain- ment		Other Goods & Services	
	Index	%	Index	%	Index	%	Index	%	Index	%	Index	%	Index	%	Index	%
1917	-	-	-	-	-	-	-	-	-	-	-	-	-	-	-	-
1918	16.3	-	-	-	-	-	-	-	-	-	-	-	-	-	-	-
1919	18.7	14.7	-	-	-	-	-	-	-	-	-	-	-	-	-	-
1920	22.0	17.6	-	-	-	-	-	-	-	-	-	-	-	-	-	-
1921	19.4	-11.8	-	-	-	-	-	-	-	-	-	-	-	-	-	-
1922	17.7	-8.8	-	-	-	-	-	-	-	-	-	-	-	-	-	-
1923	17.7	0.0	-	-	-	-	-	-	-	-	-	-	-	-	-	-
1924	17.5	-1.1	-	-	-	-	-	-	-	-	-	-	-	-	-	-
1925	17.8	1.7	-	-	-	-	-	-	-	-	-	-	-	-	-	-
1926	17.8	0.0	-	-	-	-	-	-	-	-	-	-	-	-	-	-
1927	17.2	-3.4	-	-	-	-	-	-	-	-	-	-	-	-	-	-
1928	16.9	-1.7	-	-	-	-	-	-	-	-	-	-	-	-	-	-
1929	17.0	0.6	-	-	-	-	-	-	-	-	-	-	-	-	-	-
1930	16.7	-1.8	-	-	-	-	-	-	-	-	-	-	-	-	-	-
1931	15.7	-6.0	-	-	-	-	-	-	-	-	-	-	-	-	-	-
1932	14.1	-10.2	-	-	-	-	-	-	-	-	-	-	-	-	-	-
1933	13.4	-5.0	-	-	-	-	-	-	-	-	-	-	-	-	-	-
1934	13.9	3.7	-	-	-	-	-	-	-	-	-	-	-	-	-	-
1935	14.2	2.2	-	-	-	-	-	-	-	-	-	-	-	-	-	-
1936	14.3	0.7	-	-	-	-	-	-	-	-	-	-	-	-	-	-
1937	14.8	3.5	-	-	-	-	-	-	-	-	-	-	-	-	-	-
1938	14.5	-2.0	-	-	-	-	-	-	-	-	-	-	-	-	-	-
1939	14.3	-1.4	-	-	-	-	-	-	-	-	-	-	-	-	-	-
1940	14.2	-0.7	-	-	-	-	-	-	-	-	-	-	-	-	-	-
1941	14.9	4.9	-	-	-	-	-	-	-	-	-	-	-	-	-	-
1942	16.5	10.7	-	-	-	-	-	-	-	-	-	-	-	-	-	-
1943	17.5	6.1	-	-	-	-	-	-	-	-	-	-	-	-	-	-
1944	17.8	1.7	-	-	-	-	-	-	-	-	-	-	-	-	-	-
1945	18.3	2.8	-	-	-	-	-	-	-	-	-	-	-	-	-	-
1946	19.6	7.1	-	-	-	-	-	-	-	-	-	-	-	-	-	-
1947	22.2	13.3	-	-	-	-	-	-	18.1	-	11.0	-	-	-	-	-
1948	23.9	7.7	-	-	-	-	-	-	20.1	11.0	11.9	8.2	-	-	-	-
1949	23.7	-0.8	-	-	-	-	-	-	21.3	6.0	12.2	2.5	-	-	-	-
1950	24.0	1.3	-	-	-	-	-	-	21.8	2.3	12.4	1.6	-	-	-	-
1951	25.8	7.5	-	-	-	-	-	-	23.0	5.5	13.0	4.8	-	-	-	-
1952	26.6	3.1	-	-	-	-	-	-	25.2	9.6	13.7	5.4	-	-	-	-
1953	26.7	0.4	-	-	-	-	40.5	-	25.8	2.4	14.0	2.2	-	-	-	-
1954	26.9	0.7	-	-	-	-	40.1	-1.0	25.1	-2.7	15.6	11.4	-	-	-	-
1955	26.9	0.0	-	-	-	-	40.1	0.0	24.9	-0.8	15.9	1.9	-	-	-	-
1956	27.3	1.5	-	-	-	-	40.6	1.2	25.3	1.6	16.6	4.4	-	-	-	-
1957	28.2	3.3	-	-	-	-	41.5	2.2	27.4	8.3	17.7	6.6	-	-	-	-
1958	28.8	2.1	-	-	-	-	41.6	0.2	28.9	5.5	19.0	7.3	-	-	-	-
1959	29.3	1.7	-	-	-	-	42.0	1.0	30.4	5.2	20.0	5.3	-	-	-	-
1960	29.7	1.4	-	-	-	-	43.0	2.4	30.4	0.0	20.3	1.5	-	-	-	-
1961	30.0	1.0	-	-	-	-	43.3	0.7	30.4	0.0	21.1	3.9	-	-	-	-

[Continued]

Kansas City, MO-KS
Consumer Price Index - Urban Wage Earners
Base 1982-1984 = 100
Annual Averages
[Continued]

For 1917-1993. Columns headed % show percentile change in the index from the previous period for which an index is available.

Year	All Items		Food & Beverage		Housing		Apparel & Upkeep		Trans- portation		Medical Care		Entertain- ment		Other Goods & Services	
	Index	%	Index	%	Index	%	Index	%	Index	%	Index	%	Index	%	Index	%
1962	30.5	1.7	-	-	-	-	43.3	0.0	31.1	2.3	21.5	1.9	-	-	-	-
1963	30.8	1.0	-	-	-	-	43.9	1.4	31.1	0.0	21.7	0.9	-	-	-	-
1964	31.6	2.6	-	-	-	-	45.0	2.5	31.4	1.0	22.8	5.1	-	-	-	-
1965	32.6	3.2	-	-	-	-	45.9	2.0	33.6	7.0	24.0	5.3	-	-	-	-
1966	33.4	2.5	-	-	-	-	47.1	2.6	34.3	2.1	25.3	5.4	-	-	-	-
1967	34.1	2.1	-	-	-	-	48.8	3.6	34.5	0.6	27.2	7.5	-	-	-	-
1968	35.5	4.1	-	-	-	-	52.4	7.4	35.3	2.3	28.9	6.3	-	-	-	-
1969	37.4	5.4	-	-	-	-	56.1	7.1	36.9	4.5	30.4	5.2	-	-	-	-
1970	39.5	5.6	-	-	-	-	59.2	5.5	38.0	3.0	31.8	4.6	-	-	-	-
1971	41.1	4.1	-	-	-	-	60.7	2.5	40.8	7.4	33.8	6.3	-	-	-	-
1972	42.3	2.9	-	-	-	-	62.2	2.5	40.8	0.0	35.1	3.8	-	-	-	-
1973	44.5	5.2	-	-	-	-	63.7	2.4	42.4	3.9	36.7	4.6	-	-	-	-
1974	49.2	10.6	-	-	-	-	67.8	6.4	47.0	10.8	40.1	9.3	-	-	-	-
1975	53.9	9.6	-	-	-	-	71.1	4.9	51.2	8.9	43.6	8.7	-	-	-	-
1976	56.8	5.4	63.7	-	53.8	-	72.9	2.5	55.2	7.8	47.3	8.5	61.9	-	57.9	-
1977	60.9	7.2	67.8	6.4	57.8	7.4	79.4	8.9	58.8	6.5	51.8	9.5	64.7	4.5	61.6	6.4
1978	65.5	7.6	75.0	10.6	62.9	8.8	82.1	3.4	61.7	4.9	56.4	8.9	66.8	3.2	65.1	5.7
1979	74.4	13.6	82.0	9.3	73.2	16.4	84.4	2.8	72.2	17.0	63.9	13.3	71.1	6.4	71.4	9.7
1980	84.1	13.0	89.1	8.7	83.4	13.9	87.0	3.1	85.0	17.7	71.3	11.6	82.4	15.9	78.6	10.1
1981	91.2	8.4	94.7	6.3	90.3	8.3	92.3	6.1	93.7	10.2	79.2	11.1	90.4	9.7	84.9	8.0
1982	95.7	4.9	97.5	3.0	94.9	5.1	95.8	3.8	97.5	4.1	91.0	14.9	95.6	5.8	91.2	7.4
1983	101.3	5.9	99.3	1.8	103.2	8.7	102.2	6.7	99.5	2.1	101.1	11.1	100.0	4.6	100.7	10.4
1984	103.0	1.7	103.2	3.9	102.0	-1.2	102.1	-0.1	103.1	3.6	107.9	6.7	104.4	4.4	108.0	7.2
1985	105.7	2.6	105.8	2.5	103.5	1.5	105.7	3.5	106.5	3.3	111.8	3.6	107.0	2.5	115.5	6.9
1986	106.1	0.4	109.4	3.4	105.2	1.6	106.7	0.9	99.2	-6.9	117.6	5.2	110.6	3.4	125.3	8.5
1987	110.2	3.9	112.7	3.0	109.0	3.6	110.4	3.5	101.2	2.0	123.8	5.3	122.8	11.0	134.6	7.4
1988	114.4	3.8	115.8	2.8	113.4	4.0	114.2	3.4	105.5	4.2	131.6	6.3	123.1	0.2	141.4	5.1
1989	118.5	3.6	119.8	3.5	114.8	1.2	120.3	5.3	109.9	4.2	143.0	8.7	130.5	6.0	153.1	8.3
1990	122.4	3.3	127.4	6.3	117.0	1.9	116.8	-2.9	112.6	2.5	157.6	10.2	140.4	7.6	160.1	4.6
1991	127.4	4.1	131.0	2.8	120.2	2.7	125.6	7.5	115.9	2.9	173.7	10.2	147.6	5.1	176.8	10.4
1992	130.4	2.4	132.7	1.3	121.9	1.4	125.1	-0.4	119.1	2.8	184.2	6.0	152.7	3.5	191.3	8.2
1993	134.3	3.0	137.8	3.8	125.1	2.6	126.1	0.8	122.2	2.6	196.7	6.8	152.1	-0.4	198.5	3.8

Source: U.S. Department of Labor, Bureau of Labor Statistics, Division of Consumer Prices and Price Indexes. - indicates no data collected for period.

Kansas City, MO-KS
Consumer Price Index - All Urban Consumers
Base 1982-1984 = 100
All Items

For 1917-1993. Columns headed % show percentile change in the index from the previous period for which an index is available.

Year	Jan Index	%	Feb Index	%	Mar Index	%	Apr Index	%	May Index	%	Jun Index	%	Jul Index	%	Aug Index	%	Sep Index	%	Oct Index	%	Nov Index	%	Dec Index	%
1917	-		-		-		-		-		-		-		-		-		-		-		14.8	-
1918	-		-		-		-		-		-		-		-		-		-		-		17.6	18.9
1919	-		-		-		-		-		17.7	0.6	-		-		-		-		-		20.4	15.3
1920	-		-		-		-		-		22.8	11.8	-		-		-		-		-		20.7	-9.2
1921	-		-		-		-		19.1	-7.7	-		-		-		18.7	-2.1	-		-		18.5	-1.1
1922	-		-		17.4	-5.9	-		-		17.4	0.0	-		-		17.3	-0.6	-		-		17.4	0.6
1923	-		-		17.4	0.0	-		-		17.4	0.0	-		-		17.5	0.6	-		-		17.5	0.0
1924	-		-		17.4	-0.6	-		-		17.2	-1.1	-		-		17.1	-0.6	-		-		17.3	1.2
1925	-		-		-		-		-		17.5	1.2	-		-		-		-		-		17.8	1.7
1926	-		-		-		-		-		17.7	-0.6	-		-		-		-		-		17.4	-1.7
1927	-		-		-		-		-		17.3	-0.6	-		-		-		-		-		16.7	-3.5
1928	-		-		-		-		-		16.7	0.0	-		-		-		-		-		16.7	0.0
1929	-		-		-		-		-		16.6	-0.6	-		-		-		-		-		16.8	1.2
1930	-		-		-		-		-		16.6	-1.2	-		-		-		-		-		16.1	-3.0
1931	-		-		-		-		-		15.5	-3.7	-		-		-		-		-		14.9	-3.9
1932	-		-		-		-		-		13.8	-7.4	-		-		-		-		-		13.5	-2.2
1933	-		-		-		-		-		13.2	-2.2	-		-		-		-		-		13.4	1.5
1934	-		-		-		-		-		13.6	1.5	-		-		-		-		13.8	1.5	-	-
1935	-		-		13.9	0.7	-		-		-		13.8	-0.7	-		-		-		13.9	0.7	-	-
1936	14.1	1.4	-		-		13.9	-1.4	-		-		14.1	1.4	-		14.3	1.4	-		-		14.2	-0.7
1937	-		-		14.5	2.1	-		-		14.7	1.4	-		-		14.8	0.7	-		-		14.6	-1.4
1938	-		-		14.4	-1.4	-		-		14.3	-0.7	-		-		14.3	0.0	-		-		14.2	-0.7
1939	-		-		14.1	-0.7	-		-		14.1	0.0	-		-		14.3	1.4	-		-		14.1	-1.4
1940	-		-		14.0	-0.7	-		-		14.0	0.0	-		-		13.9	-0.7	13.9	0.0	14.0	0.7	14.0	0.0
1941	14.0	0.0	14.0	0.0	14.1	0.7	14.3	1.4	14.3	0.0	14.5	1.4	14.5	0.0	14.7	1.4	15.1	2.7	15.3	1.3	15.4	0.7	15.5	0.6
1942	15.6	0.6	15.8	1.3	16.1	1.9	16.2	0.6	16.3	0.6	16.3	0.0	16.2	-0.6	16.4	1.2	16.3	-0.6	16.6	1.8	16.7	0.6	16.8	0.6
1943	16.8	0.0	16.9	0.6	17.2	1.8	17.4	1.2	17.4	0.0	17.4	0.0	17.2	-1.1	17.2	0.0	17.3	0.6	17.4	0.6	17.4	0.0	17.4	0.0
1944	17.4	0.0	17.4	0.0	17.4	0.0	17.5	0.6	17.6	0.6	17.6	0.0	17.7	0.6	17.6	-0.6	17.7	0.6	17.7	0.0	17.7	0.0	17.8	0.6
1945	17.8	0.0	17.8	0.0	17.8	0.0	17.9	0.6	18.0	0.6	18.1	0.6	18.2	0.6	18.2	0.0	18.1	-0.5	18.1	0.0	18.2	0.6	18.3	0.5
1946	18.3	0.0	18.2	-0.5	18.2	0.0	18.3	0.5	18.4	0.5	18.5	0.5	19.5	5.4	20.1	3.1	20.1	0.0	20.3	1.0	21.0	3.4	21.0	0.0
1947	21.1	0.5	21.2	0.5	21.5	1.4	21.6	0.5	21.5	-0.5	21.4	-0.5	21.5	0.5	-		-		22.6	5.1	-		-	-
1948	23.2	2.7	-		-		23.3	0.4	-		-		23.8	2.1	-		-		24.0	0.8	-		-	-
1949	23.6	-1.7	-		-		23.4	-0.8	-		-		23.3	-0.4	-		-		23.2	-0.4	-		-	-
1950	23.1	-0.4	-		-		23.3	0.9	-		-		23.8	2.1	-		-		24.1	1.3	-		-	-
1951	25.0	3.7	-		-		25.5	2.0	-		-		25.6	0.4	-		-		25.7	0.4	-		-	-
1952	26.0	1.2	-		-		26.1	0.4	-		-		26.4	1.1	-		-		26.4	0.0	-		-	-
1953	26.2	-0.8	-		-		26.2	0.0	-		-		26.4	0.8	-		-		26.5	0.4	-		-	-
1954	26.4	-0.4	-		-		26.5	0.4	-		-		26.5	0.0	-		-		26.5	0.0	-		-	-
1955	26.4	-0.4	-		-		26.4	0.0	-		-		26.6	0.8	-		-		26.6	0.0	-		-	-
1956	26.5	-0.4	-		-		26.7	0.8	-		-		27.0	1.1	-		-		27.3	1.1	-		-	-
1957	27.5	0.7	-		-		27.6	0.4	-		-		27.9	1.1	-		-		28.0	0.4	-		-	-
1958	28.1	0.4	-		-		28.4	1.1	-		-		28.6	0.7	-		-		28.7	0.3	-		-	-
1959	28.6	-0.3	-		-		28.8	0.7	-		-		28.9	0.3	-		-		29.1	0.7	-		-	-
1960	29.1	0.0	-		-		29.0	-0.3	-		-		29.3	1.0	-		-		29.4	0.3	-		-	-
1961	29.3	-0.3	-		-		29.7	1.4	-		-		29.8	0.3	-		-		29.7	-0.3	-		-	-

[Continued]

Kansas City, MO-KS
Consumer Price Index - All Urban Consumers
Base 1982-1984 = 100
All Items
[Continued]

For 1917-1993. Columns headed % show percentile change in the index from the previous period for which an index is available.

Year	Jan Index	%	Feb Index	%	Mar Index	%	Apr Index	%	May Index	%	Jun Index	%	Jul Index	%	Aug Index	%	Sep Index	%	Oct Index	%	Nov Index	%	Dec Index	%
1962	29.8	0.3	-	-	-	-	30.0	0.7	-	-	-	-	30.1	0.3	-	-	-	-	30.4	1.0	-	-	-	-
1963	30.0	-1.3	-	-	-	-	30.2	0.7	-	-	-	-	30.4	0.7	-	-	-	-	30.8	1.3	-	-	-	-
1964	30.8	0.0	-	-	-	-	30.9	0.3	-	-	-	-	31.3	1.3	-	-	-	-	31.4	0.3	-	-	-	-
1965	31.6	0.6	-	-	-	-	31.8	0.6	-	-	32.3	1.6	-	-	-	-	32.4	0.3	-	-	-	-	32.5	0.3
1966	-	-	-	-	32.7	0.6	-	-	-	-	33.0	0.9	-	-	-	-	33.2	0.6	-	-	-	-	33.3	0.3
1967	-	-	-	-	33.4	0.3	-	-	-	-	33.3	-0.3	-	-	-	-	34.1	2.4	-	-	-	-	34.1	0.0
1968	-	-	-	-	34.5	1.2	-	-	-	-	35.2	2.0	-	-	-	-	35.3	0.3	-	-	-	-	35.6	0.8
1969	-	-	-	-	36.3	2.0	-	-	-	-	37.0	1.9	-	-	-	-	37.3	0.8	-	-	-	-	37.8	1.3
1970	-	-	-	-	38.2	1.1	-	-	-	-	39.1	2.4	-	-	-	-	39.3	0.5	-	-	-	-	40.1	2.0
1971	-	-	-	-	40.1	0.0	-	-	-	-	40.6	1.2	-	-	-	-	40.9	0.7	-	-	-	-	40.9	0.0
1972	-	-	-	-	41.2	0.7	-	-	-	-	41.7	1.2	-	-	-	-	42.3	1.4	-	-	-	-	42.3	0.0
1973	-	-	-	-	42.9	1.4	-	-	-	-	43.7	1.9	-	-	-	-	44.6	2.1	-	-	-	-	45.3	1.6
1974	-	-	-	-	46.7	3.1	-	-	-	-	48.3	3.4	-	-	-	-	49.9	3.3	-	-	-	-	51.4	3.0
1975	-	-	-	-	52.1	1.4	-	-	-	-	52.9	1.5	-	-	-	-	54.0	2.1	-	-	-	-	54.9	1.7
1976	-	-	-	-	55.0	0.2	-	-	-	-	55.9	1.6	-	-	-	-	56.8	1.6	-	-	-	-	57.5	1.2
1977	-	-	-	-	58.9	2.4	-	-	-	-	60.3	2.4	-	-	-	-	60.8	0.8	-	-	-	-	61.5	1.2
1978	-	-	61.9	0.7	-	-	63.6	2.7	-	-	64.7	1.7	-	-	65.4	1.1	-	-	66.3	1.4	-	-	67.0	1.1
1979	-	-	68.9	2.8	-	-	71.2	3.3	-	-	73.9	3.8	-	-	75.6	2.3	-	-	77.4	2.4	-	-	78.7	1.7
1980	-	-	80.4	2.2	-	-	82.1	2.1	-	-	83.5	1.7	-	-	84.5	1.2	-	-	85.8	1.5	-	-	87.3	1.7
1981	-	-	88.2	1.0	-	-	89.4	1.4	-	-	91.1	1.9	-	-	91.4	0.3	-	-	91.8	0.4	-	-	92.1	0.3
1982	-	-	92.9	0.9	-	-	92.3	-0.6	-	-	94.8	2.7	-	-	96.0	1.3	-	-	97.4	1.5	-	-	97.9	0.5
1983	-	-	98.4	0.5	-	-	99.7	1.3	-	-	100.2	0.5	-	-	101.5	1.3	-	-	102.1	0.6	-	-	102.0	-0.1
1984	-	-	103.2	1.2	-	-	104.1	0.9	-	-	104.7	0.6	-	-	104.8	0.1	-	-	105.8	1.0	-	-	105.6	-0.2
1985	-	-	105.9	0.3	-	-	107.7	1.7	-	-	107.8	0.1	-	-	108.1	0.3	-	-	108.8	0.6	-	-	108.4	-0.4
1986	-	-	108.1	-0.3	-	-	108.0	-0.1	-	-	108.7	0.6	-	-	109.1	0.4	-	-	109.0	-0.1	-	-	109.3	0.3
1987	-	-	-	-	-	-	-	-	-	-	111.5	2.0	-	-	-	-	-	-	-	-	-	-	114.6	2.8
1988	-	-	-	-	-	-	-	-	-	-	116.3	1.5	-	-	-	-	-	-	-	-	-	-	118.4	1.8
1989	-	-	-	-	-	-	-	-	-	-	120.6	1.9	-	-	-	-	-	-	-	-	-	-	122.6	1.7
1990	-	-	-	-	-	-	-	-	-	-	124.3	1.4	-	-	-	-	-	-	-	-	-	-	127.7	2.7
1991	-	-	-	-	-	-	-	-	-	-	130.2	2.0	-	-	-	-	-	-	-	-	-	-	132.3	1.6
1992	-	-	-	-	-	-	-	-	-	-	133.4	0.8	-	-	-	-	-	-	-	-	-	-	135.2	1.3
1993	-	-	-	-	-	-	-	-	-	-	137.5	1.7	-	-	-	-	-	-	-	-	-	-	-	-

Source: U.S. Department of Labor, Bureau of Labor Statistics, Division of Consumer Prices and Price Indexes. - indicates no data collected for period.

Kansas City, MO-KS
Consumer Price Index - Urban Wage Earners
Base 1982-1984 = 100
All Items

For 1917-1993. Columns headed % show percentile change in the index from the previous period for which an index is available.

Year	Jan Index	%	Feb Index	%	Mar Index	%	Apr Index	%	May Index	%	Jun Index	%	Jul Index	%	Aug Index	%	Sep Index	%	Oct Index	%	Nov Index	%	Dec Index	%
1917	-	-	-	-	-	-	-	-	-	-	-	-	-	-	-	-	-	-	-	-	-	-	15.0	-
1918	-	-	-	-	-	-	-	-	-	-	-	-	-	-	-	-	-	-	-	-	-	-	17.8	18.7
1919	-	-	-	-	-	-	-	-	-	-	18.0	1.1	-	-	-	-	-	-	-	-	-	-	20.7	15.0
1920	-	-	-	-	-	-	-	-	-	-	23.1	11.6	-	-	-	-	-	-	-	-	-	-	21.0	-9.1
1921	-	-	-	-	-	-	-	-	19.4	-7.6	-	-	-	-	-	-	19.0	-2.1	-	-	-	-	18.7	-1.6
1922	-	-	-	-	17.7	-5.3	-	-	-	-	17.7	0.0	-	-	-	-	17.5	-1.1	-	-	-	-	17.6	0.6
1923	-	-	-	-	17.6	0.0	-	-	-	-	17.6	0.0	-	-	-	-	17.8	1.1	-	-	-	-	17.8	0.0
1924	-	-	-	-	17.6	-1.1	-	-	-	-	17.4	-1.1	-	-	-	-	17.4	0.0	-	-	-	-	17.5	0.6
1925	-	-	-	-	-	-	-	-	-	-	17.8	1.7	-	-	-	-	-	-	-	-	-	-	18.0	1.1
1926	-	-	-	-	-	-	-	-	-	-	17.9	-0.6	-	-	-	-	-	-	-	-	-	-	17.6	-1.7
1927	-	-	-	-	-	-	-	-	-	-	17.6	0.0	-	-	-	-	-	-	-	-	-	-	17.0	-3.4
1928	-	-	-	-	-	-	-	-	-	-	17.0	0.0	-	-	-	-	-	-	-	-	-	-	16.9	-0.6
1929	-	-	-	-	-	-	-	-	-	-	16.9	0.0	-	-	-	-	-	-	-	-	-	-	17.0	0.6
1930	-	-	-	-	-	-	-	-	-	-	16.8	-1.2	-	-	-	-	-	-	-	-	-	-	16.3	-3.0
1931	-	-	-	-	-	-	-	-	-	-	15.7	-3.7	-	-	-	-	-	-	-	-	-	-	15.1	-3.8
1932	-	-	-	-	-	-	-	-	-	-	14.0	-7.3	-	-	-	-	-	-	-	-	-	-	13.7	-2.1
1933	-	-	-	-	-	-	-	-	-	-	13.4	-2.2	-	-	-	-	-	-	-	-	-	-	13.5	0.7
1934	-	-	-	-	-	-	-	-	-	-	13.8	2.2	-	-	-	-	-	-	-	-	14.0	1.4	-	-
1935	-	-	-	-	14.1	0.7	-	-	-	-	-	-	14.0	-0.7	-	-	-	-	14.1	0.7	-	-	-	-
1936	14.3	1.4	-	-	-	-	14.1	-1.4	-	-	-	-	14.3	1.4	-	-	14.5	1.4	-	-	-	-	14.4	-0.7
1937	-	-	-	-	14.7	2.1	-	-	-	-	14.9	1.4	-	-	-	-	15.0	0.7	-	-	-	-	14.8	-1.3
1938	-	-	-	-	14.6	-1.4	-	-	-	-	14.5	-0.7	-	-	-	-	14.5	0.0	-	-	-	-	14.4	-0.7
1939	-	-	-	-	14.3	-0.7	-	-	-	-	14.3	0.0	-	-	-	-	14.5	1.4	-	-	-	-	14.3	-1.4
1940	-	-	-	-	14.2	-0.7	-	-	-	-	14.2	0.0	-	-	-	-	14.1	-0.7	14.1	0.0	14.2	0.7	14.2	0.0
1941	14.2	0.0	14.2	0.0	14.3	0.7	14.5	1.4	14.5	0.0	14.7	1.4	14.7	0.0	14.9	1.4	15.3	2.7	15.5	1.3	15.6	0.6	15.7	0.6
1942	15.8	0.6	16.0	1.3	16.3	1.9	16.4	0.6	16.5	0.6	16.5	0.0	16.5	0.0	16.6	0.6	16.6	0.0	16.8	1.2	16.9	0.6	17.0	0.6
1943	17.0	0.0	17.2	1.2	17.4	1.2	17.6	1.1	17.7	0.6	17.6	-0.6	17.4	-1.1	17.4	0.0	17.5	0.6	17.6	0.6	17.6	0.0	17.7	0.6
1944	17.6	-0.6	17.6	0.0	17.6	0.0	17.8	1.1	17.8	0.0	17.8	0.0	18.0	1.1	17.9	-0.6	18.0	0.6	17.9	-0.6	18.0	0.6	18.0	0.0
1945	18.1	0.6	18.1	0.0	18.1	0.0	18.2	0.6	18.3	0.5	18.4	0.5	18.4	0.0	18.5	0.5	18.4	-0.5	18.4	0.0	18.4	0.0	18.5	0.5
1946	18.5	0.0	18.4	-0.5	18.5	0.5	18.6	0.5	18.6	0.0	18.7	0.5	19.7	5.3	20.3	3.0	20.4	0.5	20.5	0.5	21.3	3.9	21.3	0.0
1947	21.4	0.5	21.5	0.5	21.8	1.4	21.8	0.0	21.8	0.0	21.6	-0.9	21.8	0.9	-	-	22.9	5.0	-	-	-	-	-	-
1948	23.5	2.6	-	-	-	-	23.7	0.9	-	-	-	-	24.1	1.7	-	-	-	-	24.3	0.8	-	-	-	-
1949	24.0	-1.2	-	-	-	-	23.8	-0.8	-	-	-	-	23.6	-0.8	-	-	-	-	23.5	-0.4	-	-	-	-
1950	23.4	-0.4	-	-	-	-	23.6	0.9	-	-	-	-	24.1	2.1	-	-	-	-	24.4	1.2	-	-	-	-
1951	25.4	4.1	-	-	-	-	25.8	1.6	-	-	-	-	25.9	0.4	-	-	-	-	26.0	0.4	-	-	-	-
1952	26.3	1.2	-	-	-	-	26.5	0.8	-	-	-	-	26.8	1.1	-	-	-	-	26.8	0.0	-	-	-	-
1953	26.6	-0.7	-	-	-	-	26.6	0.0	-	-	-	-	26.8	0.8	-	-	-	-	26.9	0.4	-	-	-	-
1954	26.7	-0.7	-	-	-	-	26.9	0.7	-	-	-	-	26.9	0.0	-	-	-	-	26.9	0.0	-	-	-	-
1955	26.8	-0.4	-	-	-	-	26.8	0.0	-	-	-	-	26.9	0.4	-	-	-	-	27.0	0.4	-	-	-	-
1956	26.9	-0.4	-	-	-	-	27.1	0.7	-	-	-	-	27.3	0.7	-	-	-	-	27.6	1.1	-	-	-	-
1957	27.8	0.7	-	-	-	-	28.0	0.7	-	-	-	-	28.3	1.1	-	-	-	-	28.3	0.0	-	-	-	-
1958	28.4	0.4	-	-	-	-	28.7	1.1	-	-	-	-	29.0	1.0	-	-	-	-	29.0	0.0	-	-	-	-
1959	28.9	-0.3	-	-	-	-	29.2	1.0	-	-	-	-	29.3	0.3	-	-	-	-	29.5	0.7	-	-	-	-
1960	29.5	0.0	-	-	-	-	29.4	-0.3	-	-	-	-	29.7	1.0	-	-	-	-	29.8	0.3	-	-	-	-
1961	29.7	-0.3	-	-	-	-	30.1	1.3	-	-	-	-	30.2	0.3	-	-	-	-	30.1	-0.3	-	-	-	-

[Continued]

Kansas City, MO-KS
Consumer Price Index - Urban Wage Earners
Base 1982-1984 = 100
All Items
[Continued]

For 1917-1993. Columns headed % show percentile change in the index from the previous period for which an index is available.

Year	Jan Index	%	Feb Index	%	Mar Index	%	Apr Index	%	May Index	%	Jun Index	%	Jul Index	%	Aug Index	%	Sep Index	%	Oct Index	%	Nov Index	%	Dec Index	%
1962	30.2	0.3	-	-	-	-	30.4	0.7	-	-	-	-	30.5	0.3	-	-	-	-	30.8	1.0	-	-	-	-
1963	30.4	-1.3	-	-	-	-	30.6	0.7	-	-	-	-	30.8	0.7	-	-	-	-	31.3	1.6	-	-	-	-
1964	31.2	-0.3	-	-	-	-	31.3	0.3	-	-	-	-	31.7	1.3	-	-	-	-	31.8	0.3	-	-	-	-
1965	32.0	0.6	-	-	-	-	32.2	0.6	-	-	32.8	1.9	-	-	-	-	32.9	0.3	-	-	-	-	32.9	0.0
1966	-	-	-	-	33.1	0.6	-	-	-	-	33.5	1.2	-	-	-	-	33.7	0.6	-	-	-	-	33.7	0.0
1967	-	-	-	-	33.9	0.6	-	-	-	-	33.8	-0.3	-	-	-	-	34.5	2.1	-	-	-	-	34.6	0.3
1968	-	-	-	-	35.0	1.2	-	-	-	-	35.7	2.0	-	-	-	-	35.8	0.3	-	-	-	-	36.1	0.8
1969	-	-	-	-	36.8	1.9	-	-	-	-	37.5	1.9	-	-	-	-	37.8	0.8	-	-	-	-	38.3	1.3
1970	-	-	-	-	38.7	1.0	-	-	-	-	39.7	2.6	-	-	-	-	39.8	0.3	-	-	-	-	40.6	2.0
1971	-	-	-	-	40.7	0.2	-	-	-	-	41.2	1.2	-	-	-	-	41.5	0.7	-	-	-	-	41.4	-0.2
1972	-	-	-	-	41.8	1.0	-	-	-	-	42.3	1.2	-	-	-	-	42.8	1.2	-	-	-	-	42.8	0.0
1973	-	-	-	-	43.5	1.6	-	-	-	-	44.3	1.8	-	-	-	-	45.2	2.0	-	-	-	-	45.9	1.5
1974	-	-	-	-	47.3	3.1	-	-	-	-	48.9	3.4	-	-	-	-	50.5	3.3	-	-	-	-	52.1	3.2
1975	-	-	-	-	52.8	1.3	-	-	-	-	53.7	1.7	-	-	-	-	54.7	1.9	-	-	-	-	55.6	1.6
1976	-	-	-	-	55.8	0.4	-	-	-	-	56.6	1.4	-	-	-	-	57.6	1.8	-	-	-	-	58.3	1.2
1977	-	-	-	-	59.7	2.4	-	-	-	-	61.1	2.3	-	-	-	-	61.6	0.8	-	-	-	-	62.4	1.3
1978	-	-	62.9	0.8	-	-	64.4	2.4	-	-	65.6	1.9	-	-	66.3	1.1	-	-	67.3	1.5	-	-	67.9	0.9
1979	-	-	69.7	2.7	-	-	72.0	3.3	-	-	74.5	3.5	-	-	76.1	2.1	-	-	77.8	2.2	-	-	79.3	1.9
1980	-	-	80.8	1.9	-	-	82.7	2.4	-	-	84.1	1.7	-	-	85.1	1.2	-	-	86.3	1.4	-	-	87.8	1.7
1981	-	-	88.8	1.1	-	-	90.2	1.6	-	-	91.8	1.8	-	-	92.2	0.4	-	-	92.6	0.4	-	-	92.8	0.2
1982	-	-	93.5	0.8	-	-	92.9	-0.6	-	-	95.6	2.9	-	-	96.8	1.3	-	-	98.1	1.3	-	-	98.5	0.4
1983	-	-	98.6	0.1	-	-	100.2	1.6	-	-	101.8	1.6	-	-	102.2	0.4	-	-	103.7	1.5	-	-	102.4	-1.3
1984	-	-	101.2	-1.2	-	-	102.3	1.1	-	-	102.4	0.1	-	-	103.9	1.5	-	-	105.0	1.1	-	-	103.8	-1.1
1985	-	-	103.9	0.1	-	-	105.7	1.7	-	-	106.0	0.3	-	-	106.2	0.2	-	-	106.8	0.6	-	-	106.4	-0.4
1986	-	-	105.8	-0.6	-	-	105.4	-0.4	-	-	106.3	0.9	-	-	106.5	0.2	-	-	106.2	-0.3	-	-	106.6	0.4
1987	-	-	-	-	-	-	-	-	-	-	108.6	1.9	-	-	-	-	-	-	-	-	-	-	111.7	2.9
1988	-	-	-	-	-	-	-	-	-	-	113.3	1.4	-	-	-	-	-	-	-	-	-	-	115.5	1.9
1989	-	-	-	-	-	-	-	-	-	-	117.6	1.8	-	-	-	-	-	-	-	-	-	-	119.4	1.5
1990	-	-	-	-	-	-	-	-	-	-	120.8	1.2	-	-	-	-	-	-	-	-	-	-	124.0	2.6
1991	-	-	-	-	-	-	-	-	-	-	126.2	1.8	-	-	-	-	-	-	-	-	-	-	128.5	1.8
1992	-	-	-	-	-	-	-	-	-	-	129.4	0.7	-	-	-	-	-	-	-	-	-	-	131.4	1.5
1993	-	-	-	-	-	-	-	-	-	-	133.5	1.6	-	-	-	-	-	-	-	-	-	-	-	-

Source: U.S. Department of Labor, Bureau of Labor Statistics, Division of Consumer Prices and Price Indexes. - indicates no data collected for period.

Kansas City, MO-KS
Consumer Price Index - All Urban Consumers
Base 1982-1984 = 100
Food and Beverages

For 1975-1993. Columns headed % show percentile change in the index from the previous period for which an index is available.

Year	Jan Index	%	Feb Index	%	Mar Index	%	Apr Index	%	May Index	%	Jun Index	%	Jul Index	%	Aug Index	%	Sep Index	%	Oct Index	%	Nov Index	%	Dec Index	%
1975	-		-		-		-		-		-		-		-		-		-		-		63.9	-
1976	-		-		62.7	-1.9	-		-		62.2	-0.8	-		-		63.4	1.9	-		-		63.2	-0.3
1977	-		-		65.6	3.8	-		-		67.7	3.2	-		-		68.0	0.4	-		-		68.5	0.7
1978	-		70.5	2.9	-		72.7	3.1	-		75.6	4.0	-		76.1	0.7	-		76.9	1.1	-		78.1	1.6
1979	-		81.3	4.1	-		82.3	1.2	-		82.6	0.4	-		83.1	0.6	-		83.3	0.2	-		84.9	1.9
1980	-		86.5	1.9	-		88.3	2.1	-		89.2	1.0	-		90.4	1.3	-		91.8	1.5	-		93.4	1.7
1981	-		95.0	1.7	-		95.5	0.5	-		93.5	-2.1	-		95.0	1.6	-		95.5	0.5	-		95.9	0.4
1982	-		96.9	1.0	-		96.2	-0.7	-		98.4	2.3	-		98.3	-0.1	-		98.1	-0.2	-		97.9	-0.2
1983	-		98.6	0.7	-		98.8	0.2	-		99.6	0.8	-		99.1	-0.5	-		99.8	0.7	-		99.6	-0.2
1984	-		102.6	3.0	-		103.2	0.6	-		102.6	-0.6	-		103.5	0.9	-		104.6	1.1	-		104.5	-0.1
1985	-		105.8	1.2	-		106.5	0.7	-		106.1	-0.4	-		105.7	-0.4	-		105.8	0.1	-		106.7	0.9
1986	-		107.9	1.1	-		108.6	0.6	-		109.0	0.4	-		110.8	1.7	-		110.7	-0.1	-		111.1	0.4
1987	-		-		-		-		-		112.7	1.4	-		-		-		-		-		112.9	0.2
1988	-		-		-		-		-		114.7	1.6	-		-		-		-		-		116.9	1.9
1989	-		-		-		-		-		118.8	1.6	-		-		-		-		-		120.9	1.8
1990	-		-		-		-		-		127.0	5.0	-		-		-		-		-		127.9	0.7
1991	-		-		-		-		-		131.1	2.5	-		-		-		-		-		130.8	-0.2
1992	-		-		-		-		-		130.7	-0.1	-		-		-		-		-		135.1	3.4
1993	-		-		-		-		-		137.4	1.7	-		-		-		-		-		-	-

Source: U.S. Department of Labor, Bureau of Labor Statistics, Division of Consumer Prices and Price Indexes. - indicates no data collected for period.

Kansas City, MO-KS
Consumer Price Index - Urban Wage Earners
Base 1982-1984 = 100
Food and Beverages

For 1975-1993. Columns headed % show percentile change in the index from the previous period for which an index is available.

Year	Jan		Feb		Mar		Apr		May		Jun		Jul		Aug		Sep		Oct		Nov		Dec	
	Index	%	Index	%	Index	%	Index	%	Index	%	Index	%	Index	%	Index	%	Index	%	Index	%	Index	%	Index	%
1975	-	-	-	-	-	-	-	-	-	-	-	-	-	-	-	-	-	-	-	-	-	-	64.7	-
1976	-	-	-	-	63.4	-2.0	-	-	-	-	63.0	-0.6	-	-	-	-	64.2	1.9	-	-	-	-	63.9	-0.5
1977	-	-	-	-	66.4	3.9	-	-	-	-	68.6	3.3	-	-	-	-	68.8	0.3	-	-	-	-	69.3	0.7
1978	-	-	71.0	2.5	-	-	73.0	2.8	-	-	76.1	4.2	-	-	76.5	0.5	-	-	77.2	0.9	-	-	78.6	1.8
1979	-	-	81.0	3.1	-	-	81.8	1.0	-	-	81.9	0.1	-	-	82.2	0.4	-	-	82.4	0.2	-	-	83.9	1.8
1980	-	-	85.7	2.1	-	-	87.4	2.0	-	-	88.3	1.0	-	-	90.0	1.9	-	-	91.9	2.1	-	-	93.3	1.5
1981	-	-	94.2	1.0	-	-	94.8	0.6	-	-	93.6	-1.3	-	-	94.9	1.4	-	-	95.9	1.1	-	-	95.9	0.0
1982	-	-	96.8	0.9	-	-	96.1	-0.7	-	-	98.4	2.4	-	-	98.5	0.1	-	-	98.1	-0.4	-	-	97.9	-0.2
1983	-	-	98.8	0.9	-	-	99.0	0.2	-	-	99.6	0.6	-	-	99.3	-0.3	-	-	99.8	0.5	-	-	99.6	-0.2
1984	-	-	102.5	2.9	-	-	103.1	0.6	-	-	102.5	-0.6	-	-	103.4	0.9	-	-	104.5	1.1	-	-	104.3	-0.2
1985	-	-	105.4	1.1	-	-	106.2	0.8	-	-	105.9	-0.3	-	-	105.6	-0.3	-	-	105.6	0.0	-	-	106.6	0.9
1986	-	-	107.9	1.2	-	-	108.5	0.6	-	-	108.7	0.2	-	-	110.7	1.8	-	-	110.7	0.0	-	-	111.1	0.4
1987	-	-	-	-	-	-	-	-	-	-	112.5	1.3	-	-	-	-	-	-	-	-	-	-	112.9	0.4
1988	-	-	-	-	-	-	-	-	-	-	114.7	1.6	-	-	-	-	-	-	-	-	-	-	116.9	1.9
1989	-	-	-	-	-	-	-	-	-	-	118.8	1.6	-	-	-	-	-	-	-	-	-	-	120.9	1.8
1990	-	-	-	-	-	-	-	-	-	-	126.9	5.0	-	-	-	-	-	-	-	-	-	-	127.9	0.8
1991	-	-	-	-	-	-	-	-	-	-	131.0	2.4	-	-	-	-	-	-	-	-	-	-	131.0	0.0
1992	-	-	-	-	-	-	-	-	-	-	130.4	-0.5	-	-	-	-	-	-	-	-	-	-	135.1	3.6
1993	-	-	-	-	-	-	-	-	-	-	137.3	1.6	-	-	-	-	-	-	-	-	-	-	-	-

Source: U.S. Department of Labor, Bureau of Labor Statistics, Division of Consumer Prices and Price Indexes. - indicates no data collected for period.

Kansas City, MO-KS
Consumer Price Index - All Urban Consumers
Base 1982-1984 = 100
Housing

For 1975-1993. Columns headed % show percentile change in the index from the previous period for which an index is available.

Year	Jan Index	%	Feb Index	%	Mar Index	%	Apr Index	%	May Index	%	Jun Index	%	Jul Index	%	Aug Index	%	Sep Index	%	Oct Index	%	Nov Index	%	Dec Index	%
1975	-	-	-	-	-	-	-	-	-	-	-	-	-	-	-	-	-	-	-	-	-	-	51.2	-
1976	-	-	-	-	51.6	0.8	-	-	-	-	52.5	1.7	-	-	-	-	53.4	1.7	-	-	-	-	54.4	1.9
1977	-	-	-	-	55.3	1.7	-	-	-	-	56.6	2.4	-	-	-	-	57.5	1.6	-	-	-	-	58.4	1.6
1978	-	-	58.8	0.7	-	-	60.9	3.6	-	-	61.7	1.3	-	-	62.2	0.8	-	-	63.0	1.3	-	-	63.2	0.3
1979	-	-	65.3	3.3	-	-	68.5	4.9	-	-	72.2	5.4	-	-	74.4	3.0	-	-	77.3	3.9	-	-	78.6	1.7
1980	-	-	79.3	0.9	-	-	80.6	1.6	-	-	83.0	3.0	-	-	83.8	1.0	-	-	85.2	1.7	-	-	86.6	1.6
1981	-	-	86.3	-0.3	-	-	88.0	2.0	-	-	91.5	4.0	-	-	91.0	-0.5	-	-	90.5	-0.5	-	-	90.5	0.0
1982	-	-	91.6	1.2	-	-	89.9	-1.9	-	-	93.1	3.6	-	-	94.5	1.5	-	-	97.1	2.8	-	-	98.4	1.3
1983	-	-	99.6	1.2	-	-	100.7	1.1	-	-	100.7	0.0	-	-	102.9	2.2	-	-	101.9	-1.0	-	-	102.2	0.3
1984	-	-	103.3	1.1	-	-	104.3	1.0	-	-	106.0	1.6	-	-	106.1	0.1	-	-	105.7	-0.4	-	-	105.8	0.1
1985	-	-	106.1	0.3	-	-	107.3	1.1	-	-	108.1	0.7	-	-	108.6	0.5	-	-	108.7	0.1	-	-	107.1	-1.5
1986	-	-	108.0	0.8	-	-	109.3	1.2	-	-	109.2	-0.1	-	-	111.3	1.9	-	-	109.5	-1.6	-	-	110.3	0.7
1987	-	-	-	-	-	-	-	-	-	-	112.2	1.7	-	-	-	-	-	-	-	-	-	-	114.9	2.4
1988	-	-	-	-	-	-	-	-	-	-	117.9	2.6	-	-	-	-	-	-	-	-	-	-	118.7	0.7
1989	-	-	-	-	-	-	-	-	-	-	119.6	0.8	-	-	-	-	-	-	-	-	-	-	119.7	0.1
1990	-	-	-	-	-	-	-	-	-	-	121.3	1.3	-	-	-	-	-	-	-	-	-	-	122.4	0.9
1991	-	-	-	-	-	-	-	-	-	-	124.5	1.7	-	-	-	-	-	-	-	-	-	-	126.3	1.4
1992	-	-	-	-	-	-	-	-	-	-	126.8	0.4	-	-	-	-	-	-	-	-	-	-	127.6	0.6
1993	-	-	-	-	-	-	-	-	-	-	129.3	1.3	-	-	-	-	-	-	-	-	-	-	-	-

Source: U.S. Department of Labor, Bureau of Labor Statistics, Division of Consumer Prices and Price Indexes. - indicates no data collected for period.

Kansas City, MO-KS
Consumer Price Index - Urban Wage Earners
Base 1982-1984 = 100
Housing

For 1975-1993. Columns headed % show percentile change in the index from the previous period for which an index is available.

Year	Jan Index	%	Feb Index	%	Mar Index	%	Apr Index	%	May Index	%	Jun Index	%	Jul Index	%	Aug Index	%	Sep Index	%	Oct Index	%	Nov Index	%	Dec Index	%
1975	-	-	-	-	-	-	-	-	-	-	-	-	-	-	-	-	-	-	-	-	-	-	52.2	-
1976	-	-	-	-	52.7	1.0	-	-	-	-	53.6	1.7	-	-	-	-	54.5	1.7	-	-	-	-	55.5	1.8
1977	-	-	-	-	56.4	1.6	-	-	-	-	57.8	2.5	-	-	-	-	58.7	1.6	-	-	-	-	59.6	1.5
1978	-	-	60.2	1.0	-	-	62.3	3.5	-	-	63.1	1.3	-	-	63.6	0.8	-	-	64.5	1.4	-	-	64.7	0.3
1979	-	-	66.8	3.2	-	-	69.8	4.5	-	-	73.4	5.2	-	-	75.4	2.7	-	-	78.1	3.6	-	-	79.6	1.9
1980	-	-	79.5	-0.1	-	-	81.1	2.0	-	-	83.8	3.3	-	-	84.6	1.0	-	-	85.8	1.4	-	-	87.3	1.7
1981	-	-	87.0	-0.3	-	-	88.8	2.1	-	-	92.2	3.8	-	-	91.9	-0.3	-	-	91.4	-0.5	-	-	91.4	0.0
1982	-	-	92.5	1.2	-	-	90.8	-1.8	-	-	94.2	3.7	-	-	95.7	1.6	-	-	98.2	2.6	-	-	99.8	1.6
1983	-	-	100.0	0.2	-	-	101.9	1.9	-	-	104.5	2.6	-	-	104.2	-0.3	-	-	106.0	1.7	-	-	103.4	-2.5
1984	-	-	99.3	-4.0	-	-	100.7	1.4	-	-	100.9	0.2	-	-	104.3	3.4	-	-	104.4	0.1	-	-	101.9	-2.4
1985	-	-	102.1	0.2	-	-	103.2	1.1	-	-	104.1	0.9	-	-	104.6	0.5	-	-	104.6	0.0	-	-	103.0	-1.5
1986	-	-	104.0	1.0	-	-	105.0	1.0	-	-	104.9	-0.1	-	-	107.1	2.1	-	-	105.1	-1.9	-	-	106.0	0.9
1987	-	-	-	-	-	-	-	-	-	-	107.8	1.7	-	-	-	-	-	-	-	-	-	-	110.3	2.3
1988	-	-	-	-	-	-	-	-	-	-	113.0	2.4	-	-	-	-	-	-	-	-	-	-	113.8	0.7
1989	-	-	-	-	-	-	-	-	-	-	114.8	0.9	-	-	-	-	-	-	-	-	-	-	114.8	0.0
1990	-	-	-	-	-	-	-	-	-	-	116.5	1.5	-	-	-	-	-	-	-	-	-	-	117.5	0.9
1991	-	-	-	-	-	-	-	-	-	-	119.4	1.6	-	-	-	-	-	-	-	-	-	-	121.0	1.3
1992	-	-	-	-	-	-	-	-	-	-	121.5	0.4	-	-	-	-	-	-	-	-	-	-	122.3	0.7
1993	-	-	-	-	-	-	-	-	-	-	123.9	1.3	-	-	-	-	-	-	-	-	-	-	-	-

Source: U.S. Department of Labor, Bureau of Labor Statistics, Division of Consumer Prices and Price Indexes. - indicates no data collected for period.

Kansas City, MO-KS
Consumer Price Index - All Urban Consumers
Base 1982-1984 = 100
Apparel and Upkeep

For 1952-1993. Columns headed % show percentile change in the index from the previous period for which an index is available.

Year	Jan Index	%	Feb Index	%	Mar Index	%	Apr Index	%	May Index	%	Jun Index	%	Jul Index	%	Aug Index	%	Sep Index	%	Oct Index	%	Nov Index	%	Dec Index	%
1952	-	-	-	-	-	-	-	-	-	-	-	-	-	-	-	-	-	-	39.3	-	-	-	-	-
1953	39.2	-0.3	-	-	-	-	39.2	0.0	-	-	-	-	39.4	0.5	-	-	-	-	39.3	-0.3	-	-	-	-
1954	39.0	-0.8	-	-	-	-	38.8	-0.5	-	-	-	-	38.8	0.0	-	-	-	-	39.1	0.8	-	-	-	-
1955	38.5	-1.5	-	-	-	-	38.6	0.3	-	-	-	-	38.6	0.0	-	-	-	-	39.4	2.1	-	-	-	-
1956	39.1	-0.8	-	-	-	-	39.1	0.0	-	-	-	-	39.2	0.3	-	-	-	-	39.7	1.3	-	-	-	-
1957	40.5	2.0	-	-	-	-	40.2	-0.7	-	-	-	-	39.9	-0.7	-	-	-	-	40.6	1.8	-	-	-	-
1958	40.0	-1.5	-	-	-	-	40.4	1.0	-	-	-	-	40.2	-0.5	-	-	-	-	40.8	1.5	-	-	-	-
1959	40.3	-1.2	-	-	-	-	40.5	0.5	-	-	-	-	40.5	0.0	-	-	-	-	41.4	2.2	-	-	-	-
1960	40.8	-1.4	-	-	-	-	41.6	2.0	-	-	-	-	42.0	1.0	-	-	-	-	42.2	0.5	-	-	-	-
1961	41.6	-1.4	-	-	-	-	41.9	0.7	-	-	-	-	42.1	0.5	-	-	-	-	42.5	1.0	-	-	-	-
1962	41.9	-1.4	-	-	-	-	41.8	-0.2	-	-	-	-	41.4	-1.0	-	-	-	-	43.0	3.9	-	-	-	-
1963	41.8	-2.8	-	-	-	-	42.2	1.0	-	-	-	-	42.1	-0.2	-	-	-	-	43.8	4.0	-	-	-	-
1964	43.1	-1.6	-	-	-	-	43.3	0.5	-	-	-	-	43.3	0.0	-	-	-	-	44.4	2.5	-	-	-	-
1965	43.6	-1.8	-	-	-	-	43.6	0.0	-	-	44.4	1.8	-	-	-	-	45.3	2.0	-	-	-	-	45.4	0.2
1966	-	-	-	-	45.0	-0.9	-	-	-	-	45.8	1.8	-	-	-	-	46.0	0.4	-	-	-	-	46.0	0.0
1967	-	-	-	-	46.3	0.7	-	-	-	-	46.7	0.9	-	-	-	-	48.6	4.1	-	-	-	-	48.6	0.0
1968	-	-	-	-	49.3	1.4	-	-	-	-	50.4	2.2	-	-	-	-	52.4	4.0	-	-	-	-	52.6	0.4
1969	-	-	-	-	53.1	1.0	-	-	-	-	54.2	2.1	-	-	-	-	55.6	2.6	-	-	-	-	55.8	0.4
1970	-	-	-	-	56.4	1.1	-	-	-	-	57.0	1.1	-	-	-	-	58.3	2.3	-	-	-	-	58.7	0.7
1971	-	-	-	-	58.6	-0.2	-	-	-	-	58.3	-0.5	-	-	-	-	59.8	2.6	-	-	-	-	58.9	-1.5
1972	-	-	-	-	59.7	1.4	-	-	-	-	59.9	0.3	-	-	-	-	61.5	2.7	-	-	-	-	61.1	-0.7
1973	-	-	-	-	61.2	0.2	-	-	-	-	61.6	0.7	-	-	-	-	62.6	1.6	-	-	-	-	62.3	-0.5
1974	-	-	-	-	63.6	2.1	-	-	-	-	64.9	2.0	-	-	-	-	68.2	5.1	-	-	-	-	68.3	0.1
1975	-	-	-	-	69.5	1.8	-	-	-	-	68.5	-1.4	-	-	-	-	69.5	1.5	-	-	-	-	68.3	-1.7
1976	-	-	-	-	69.5	1.8	-	-	-	-	71.0	2.2	-	-	-	-	73.2	3.1	-	-	-	-	73.0	-0.3
1977	-	-	-	-	75.9	4.0	-	-	-	-	76.3	0.5	-	-	-	-	78.8	3.3	-	-	-	-	79.0	0.3
1978	-	-	75.6	-4.3	-	-	79.2	4.8	-	-	78.1	-1.4	-	-	80.3	2.8	-	-	80.2	-0.1	-	-	81.0	1.0
1979	-	-	84.0	3.7	-	-	83.2	-1.0	-	-	83.1	-0.1	-	-	86.4	4.0	-	-	86.6	0.2	-	-	83.1	-4.0
1980	-	-	84.5	1.7	-	-	87.5	3.6	-	-	85.7	-2.1	-	-	87.9	2.6	-	-	91.1	3.6	-	-	91.1	0.0
1981	-	-	91.8	0.8	-	-	91.7	-0.1	-	-	91.1	-0.7	-	-	93.5	2.6	-	-	95.3	1.9	-	-	90.2	-5.4
1982	-	-	92.6	2.7	-	-	96.3	4.0	-	-	95.3	-1.0	-	-	97.8	2.6	-	-	96.1	-1.7	-	-	97.6	1.6
1983	-	-	98.6	1.0	-	-	102.6	4.1	-	-	101.3	-1.3	-	-	101.4	0.1	-	-	105.6	4.1	-	-	102.6	-2.8
1984	-	-	102.8	0.2	-	-	104.2	1.4	-	-	100.2	-3.8	-	-	101.9	1.7	-	-	104.0	2.1	-	-	102.0	-1.9
1985	-	-	104.8	2.7	-	-	108.1	3.1	-	-	102.8	-4.9	-	-	104.1	1.3	-	-	106.5	2.3	-	-	104.0	-2.3
1986	-	-	108.7	4.5	-	-	111.0	2.1	-	-	107.9	-2.8	-	-	106.2	-1.6	-	-	106.0	-0.2	-	-	101.4	-4.3
1987	-	-	-	-	-	-	-	-	-	-	104.8	3.4	-	-	-	-	-	-	-	-	-	-	114.6	9.4
1988	-	-	-	-	-	-	-	-	-	-	111.3	-2.9	-	-	-	-	-	-	-	-	-	-	115.0	3.3
1989	-	-	-	-	-	-	-	-	-	-	114.2	-0.7	-	-	-	-	-	-	-	-	-	-	125.1	9.5
1990	-	-	-	-	-	-	-	-	-	-	113.8	-9.0	-	-	-	-	-	-	-	-	-	-	119.3	4.8
1991	-	-	-	-	-	-	-	-	-	-	121.0	1.4	-	-	-	-	-	-	-	-	-	-	128.4	6.1
1992	-	-	-	-	-	-	-	-	-	-	125.3	-2.4	-	-	-	-	-	-	-	-	-	-	124.2	-0.9
1993	-	-	-	-	-	-	-	-	-	-	126.2	1.6	-	-	-	-	-	-	-	-	-	-	-	-

Source: U.S. Department of Labor, Bureau of Labor Statistics, Division of Consumer Prices and Price Indexes. - indicates no data collected for period.

Kansas City, MO-KS
Consumer Price Index - Urban Wage Earners
Base 1982-1984 = 100
Apparel and Upkeep

For 1952-1993. Columns headed % show percentile change in the index from the previous period for which an index is available.

Year	Jan Index	%	Feb Index	%	Mar Index	%	Apr Index	%	May Index	%	Jun Index	%	Jul Index	%	Aug Index	%	Sep Index	%	Oct Index	%	Nov Index	%	Dec Index	%
1952	-	-	-	-	-	-	-	-	-	-	-	-	-	-	-	-	-	-	40.6	-	-	-	-	-
1953	40.5	-0.2	-	-	-	-	40.4	-0.2	-	-	-	-	40.6	0.5	-	-	-	-	40.5	-0.2	-	-	-	-
1954	40.3	-0.5	-	-	-	-	40.0	-0.7	-	-	-	-	40.0	0.0	-	-	-	-	40.3	0.7	-	-	-	-
1955	39.7	-1.5	-	-	-	-	39.8	0.3	-	-	-	-	39.8	0.0	-	-	-	-	40.6	2.0	-	-	-	-
1956	40.3	-0.7	-	-	-	-	40.3	0.0	-	-	-	-	40.5	0.5	-	-	-	-	41.0	1.2	-	-	-	-
1957	41.8	2.0	-	-	-	-	41.5	-0.7	-	-	-	-	41.1	-1.0	-	-	-	-	41.9	1.9	-	-	-	-
1958	41.3	-1.4	-	-	-	-	41.6	0.7	-	-	-	-	41.5	-0.2	-	-	-	-	42.1	1.4	-	-	-	-
1959	41.5	-1.4	-	-	-	-	41.8	0.7	-	-	-	-	41.7	-0.2	-	-	-	-	42.7	2.4	-	-	-	-
1960	42.1	-1.4	-	-	-	-	42.9	1.9	-	-	-	-	43.3	0.9	-	-	-	-	43.5	0.5	-	-	-	-
1961	42.9	-1.4	-	-	-	-	43.2	0.7	-	-	-	-	43.4	0.5	-	-	-	-	43.8	0.9	-	-	-	-
1962	43.2	-1.4	-	-	-	-	43.1	-0.2	-	-	-	-	42.7	-0.9	-	-	-	-	44.3	3.7	-	-	-	-
1963	43.1	-2.7	-	-	-	-	43.5	0.9	-	-	-	-	43.4	-0.2	-	-	-	-	45.2	4.1	-	-	-	-
1964	44.4	-1.8	-	-	-	-	44.7	0.7	-	-	-	-	44.7	0.0	-	-	-	-	45.8	2.5	-	-	-	-
1965	45.0	-1.7	-	-	-	-	45.0	0.0	-	-	45.7	1.6	-	-	-	-	46.8	2.4	-	-	-	-	46.9	0.2
1966	-	-	-	-	46.4	-1.1	-	-	-	-	47.2	1.7	-	-	-	-	47.4	0.4	-	-	-	-	47.4	0.0
1967	-	-	-	-	47.7	0.6	-	-	-	-	48.1	0.8	-	-	-	-	50.1	4.2	-	-	-	-	50.1	0.0
1968	-	-	-	-	50.8	1.4	-	-	-	-	52.0	2.4	-	-	-	-	54.0	3.8	-	-	-	-	54.3	0.6
1969	-	-	-	-	54.7	0.7	-	-	-	-	55.9	2.2	-	-	-	-	57.3	2.5	-	-	-	-	57.5	0.3
1970	-	-	-	-	58.1	1.0	-	-	-	-	58.8	1.2	-	-	-	-	60.1	2.2	-	-	-	-	60.5	0.7
1971	-	-	-	-	60.4	-0.2	-	-	-	-	60.1	-0.5	-	-	-	-	61.6	2.5	-	-	-	-	60.7	-1.5
1972	-	-	-	-	61.6	1.5	-	-	-	-	61.7	0.2	-	-	-	-	63.4	2.8	-	-	-	-	63.0	-0.6
1973	-	-	-	-	63.1	0.2	-	-	-	-	63.6	0.8	-	-	-	-	64.5	1.4	-	-	-	-	64.2	-0.5
1974	-	-	-	-	65.6	2.2	-	-	-	-	66.9	2.0	-	-	-	-	70.3	5.1	-	-	-	-	70.5	0.3
1975	-	-	-	-	71.7	1.7	-	-	-	-	70.6	-1.5	-	-	-	-	71.7	1.6	-	-	-	-	70.5	-1.7
1976	-	-	-	-	71.7	1.7	-	-	-	-	73.2	2.1	-	-	-	-	75.5	3.1	-	-	-	-	75.3	-0.3
1977	-	-	-	-	78.3	4.0	-	-	-	-	78.7	0.5	-	-	-	-	81.3	3.3	-	-	-	-	81.5	0.2
1978	-	-	81.1	-0.5	-	-	82.2	1.4	-	-	79.9	-2.8	-	-	82.2	2.9	-	-	83.8	1.9	-	-	84.0	0.2
1979	-	-	84.3	0.4	-	-	84.9	0.7	-	-	82.7	-2.6	-	-	85.1	2.9	-	-	85.1	0.0	-	-	84.6	-0.6
1980	-	-	85.6	1.2	-	-	87.0	1.6	-	-	85.4	-1.8	-	-	86.5	1.3	-	-	89.7	3.7	-	-	88.8	-1.0
1981	-	-	91.6	3.2	-	-	92.8	1.3	-	-	91.7	-1.2	-	-	93.8	2.3	-	-	94.4	0.6	-	-	89.8	-4.9
1982	-	-	91.9	2.3	-	-	96.7	5.2	-	-	95.0	-1.8	-	-	98.4	3.6	-	-	96.6	-1.8	-	-	98.2	1.7
1983	-	-	98.8	0.6	-	-	102.8	4.0	-	-	101.6	-1.2	-	-	102.6	1.0	-	-	105.7	3.0	-	-	102.6	-2.9
1984	-	-	102.9	0.3	-	-	103.6	0.7	-	-	98.4	-5.0	-	-	101.2	2.8	-	-	104.2	3.0	-	-	102.1	-2.0
1985	-	-	104.5	2.4	-	-	108.5	3.8	-	-	104.1	-4.1	-	-	104.9	0.8	-	-	107.7	2.7	-	-	105.5	-2.0
1986	-	-	107.4	1.8	-	-	110.5	2.9	-	-	108.2	-2.1	-	-	106.4	-1.7	-	-	105.2	-1.1	-	-	101.8	-3.2
1987	-	-	-	-	-	-	-	-	-	-	105.6	3.7	-	-	-	-	-	-	-	-	-	-	115.3	9.2
1988	-	-	-	-	-	-	-	-	-	-	112.3	-2.6	-	-	-	-	-	-	-	-	-	-	116.2	3.5
1989	-	-	-	-	-	-	-	-	-	-	115.0	-1.0	-	-	-	-	-	-	-	-	-	-	125.6	9.2
1990	-	-	-	-	-	-	-	-	-	-	114.0	-9.2	-	-	-	-	-	-	-	-	-	-	119.6	4.9
1991	-	-	-	-	-	-	-	-	-	-	121.5	1.6	-	-	-	-	-	-	-	-	-	-	129.7	6.7
1992	-	-	-	-	-	-	-	-	-	-	125.1	-3.5	-	-	-	-	-	-	-	-	-	-	125.0	-0.1
1993	-	-	-	-	-	-	-	-	-	-	126.1	0.9	-	-	-	-	-	-	-	-	-	-	-	-

Source: U.S. Department of Labor, Bureau of Labor Statistics, Division of Consumer Prices and Price Indexes. - indicates no data collected for period.

Kansas City, MO-KS
Consumer Price Index - All Urban Consumers
Base 1982-1984 = 100
Transportation

For 1947-1993. Columns headed % show percentile change in the index from the previous period for which an index is available.

Year	Jan Index	%	Feb Index	%	Mar Index	%	Apr Index	%	May Index	%	Jun Index	%	Jul Index	%	Aug Index	%	Sep Index	%	Oct Index	%	Nov Index	%	Dec Index	%
1947	17.7	-	17.7	0.0	17.7	0.0	18.0	1.7	18.0	0.0	18.0	0.0	18.1	0.6	-	-	-	-	18.7	3.3	-	-	-	-
1948	19.5	4.3	-	-	-	-	19.6	0.5	-	-	-	-	20.1	2.6	-	-	-	-	21.1	5.0	-	-	-	-
1949	21.1	0.0	-	-	-	-	21.5	1.9	-	-	-	-	21.3	-0.9	-	-	-	-	21.6	1.4	-	-	-	-
1950	21.7	0.5	-	-	-	-	21.7	0.0	-	-	-	-	22.3	2.8	-	-	-	-	21.9	-1.8	-	-	-	-
1951	22.5	2.7	-	-	-	-	22.9	1.8	-	-	-	-	23.1	0.9	-	-	-	-	23.6	2.2	-	-	-	-
1952	23.9	1.3	-	-	-	-	25.3	5.9	-	-	-	-	25.7	1.6	-	-	-	-	26.0	1.2	-	-	-	-
1953	26.1	0.4	-	-	-	-	26.0	-0.4	-	-	-	-	26.0	0.0	-	-	-	-	26.1	0.4	-	-	-	-
1954	25.1	-3.8	-	-	-	-	25.9	3.2	-	-	-	-	25.0	-3.5	-	-	-	-	24.8	-0.8	-	-	-	-
1955	25.1	1.2	-	-	-	-	24.6	-2.0	-	-	-	-	25.1	2.0	-	-	-	-	25.4	1.2	-	-	-	-
1956	25.0	-1.6	-	-	-	-	25.5	2.0	-	-	-	-	24.5	-3.9	-	-	-	-	26.1	6.5	-	-	-	-
1957	27.1	3.8	-	-	-	-	27.4	1.1	-	-	-	-	27.6	0.7	-	-	-	-	27.7	0.4	-	-	-	-
1958	28.1	1.4	-	-	-	-	28.4	1.1	-	-	-	-	29.7	4.6	-	-	-	-	30.1	1.3	-	-	-	-
1959	29.4	-2.3	-	-	-	-	30.6	4.1	-	-	-	-	30.7	0.3	-	-	-	-	31.2	1.6	-	-	-	-
1960	30.9	-1.0	-	-	-	-	29.8	-3.6	-	-	-	-	30.9	3.7	-	-	-	-	31.0	0.3	-	-	-	-
1961	30.0	-3.2	-	-	-	-	30.8	2.7	-	-	-	-	31.0	0.6	-	-	-	-	30.3	-2.3	-	-	-	-
1962	31.0	2.3	-	-	-	-	31.7	2.3	-	-	-	-	30.6	-3.5	-	-	-	-	31.9	4.2	-	-	-	-
1963	30.6	-4.1	-	-	-	-	31.3	2.3	-	-	-	-	30.9	-1.3	-	-	-	-	32.2	4.2	-	-	-	-
1964	31.5	-2.2	-	-	-	-	31.4	-0.3	-	-	-	-	31.7	1.0	-	-	-	-	31.4	-0.9	-	-	-	-
1965	32.8	4.5	-	-	-	-	33.0	0.6	-	-	34.5	4.5	-	-	-	-	34.3	-0.6	-	-	-	-	34.1	-0.6
1966	-	-	-	-	34.1	0.0	-	-	-	-	34.7	1.8	-	-	-	-	34.6	-0.3	-	-	-	-	34.8	0.6
1967	-	-	-	-	34.9	0.3	-	-	-	-	33.6	-3.7	-	-	-	-	35.5	5.7	-	-	-	-	34.8	-2.0
1968	-	-	-	-	35.0	0.6	-	-	-	-	36.7	4.9	-	-	-	-	35.0	-4.6	-	-	-	-	35.8	2.3
1969	-	-	-	-	37.6	5.0	-	-	-	-	37.5	-0.3	-	-	-	-	36.6	-2.4	-	-	-	-	37.7	3.0
1970	-	-	-	-	36.7	-2.7	-	-	-	-	38.5	4.9	-	-	-	-	37.9	-1.6	-	-	-	-	41.1	8.4
1971	-	-	-	-	41.0	-0.2	-	-	-	-	41.7	1.7	-	-	-	-	40.9	-1.9	-	-	-	-	40.2	-1.7
1972	-	-	-	-	40.0	-0.5	-	-	-	-	41.3	3.2	-	-	-	-	41.7	1.0	-	-	-	-	41.8	0.2
1973	-	-	-	-	42.1	0.7	-	-	-	-	42.9	1.9	-	-	-	-	42.6	-0.7	-	-	-	-	43.4	1.9
1974	-	-	-	-	45.4	4.6	-	-	-	-	47.7	5.1	-	-	-	-	48.8	2.3	-	-	-	-	49.3	1.0
1975	-	-	-	-	49.5	0.4	-	-	-	-	51.1	3.2	-	-	-	-	53.1	3.9	-	-	-	-	53.7	1.1
1976	-	-	-	-	53.7	0.0	-	-	-	-	55.8	3.9	-	-	-	-	56.4	1.1	-	-	-	-	57.5	2.0
1977	-	-	-	-	58.6	1.9	-	-	-	-	59.9	2.2	-	-	-	-	59.2	-1.2	-	-	-	-	59.9	1.2
1978	-	-	59.9	0.0	-	-	60.2	0.5	-	-	62.0	3.0	-	-	62.8	1.3	-	-	64.0	1.9	-	-	65.1	1.7
1979	-	-	65.9	1.2	-	-	69.3	5.2	-	-	73.0	5.3	-	-	75.1	2.9	-	-	75.8	0.9	-	-	78.1	3.0
1980	-	-	82.0	5.0	-	-	85.0	3.7	-	-	85.1	0.1	-	-	85.7	0.7	-	-	86.3	0.7	-	-	88.2	2.2
1981	-	-	90.9	3.1	-	-	92.2	1.4	-	-	93.4	1.3	-	-	93.6	0.2	-	-	94.6	1.1	-	-	96.5	2.0
1982	-	-	95.6	-0.9	-	-	95.0	-0.6	-	-	98.7	3.9	-	-	99.3	0.6	-	-	98.9	-0.4	-	-	97.8	-1.1
1983	-	-	96.1	-1.7	-	-	97.8	1.8	-	-	99.6	1.8	-	-	100.6	1.0	-	-	102.3	1.7	-	-	101.7	-0.6
1984	-	-	101.4	-0.3	-	-	102.4	1.0	-	-	103.6	1.2	-	-	102.5	-1.1	-	-	104.6	2.0	-	-	104.3	-0.3
1985	-	-	102.9	-1.3	-	-	106.9	3.9	-	-	107.6	0.7	-	-	106.9	-0.7	-	-	107.7	0.7	-	-	107.6	-0.1
1986	-	-	102.5	-4.7	-	-	98.5	-3.9	-	-	101.7	3.2	-	-	97.7	-3.9	-	-	98.7	1.0	-	-	98.9	0.2
1987	-	-	-	-	-	-	-	-	-	-	101.0	2.1	-	-	-	-	-	-	-	-	-	-	104.7	3.7
1988	-	-	-	-	-	-	-	-	-	-	105.5	0.8	-	-	-	-	-	-	-	-	-	-	108.8	3.1
1989	-	-	-	-	-	-	-	-	-	-	112.0	2.9	-	-	-	-	-	-	-	-	-	-	112.4	0.4
1990	-	-	-	-	-	-	-	-	-	-	112.8	0.4	-	-	-	-	-	-	-	-	-	-	119.5	5.9
1991	-	-	-	-	-	-	-	-	-	-	118.5	-0.8	-	-	-	-	-	-	-	-	-	-	119.9	1.2

[Continued]

538

Kansas City, MO-KS
Consumer Price Index - All Urban Consumers
Base 1982-1984 = 100
Transportation
[Continued]

For 1947-1993. Columns headed % show percentile change in the index from the previous period for which an index is available.

Year	Jan Index	%	Feb Index	%	Mar Index	%	Apr Index	%	May Index	%	Jun Index	%	Jul Index	%	Aug Index	%	Sep Index	%	Oct Index	%	Nov Index	%	Dec Index	%
1992	-	-	-	-	-	-	-	-	-	-	120.9	0.8	-	-	-	-	-	-	-	-	-	-	122.8	1.6
1993	-	-	-	-	-	-	-	-	-	-	124.6	1.5	-	-	-	-	-	-	-	-	-	-	-	-

Source: U.S. Department of Labor, Bureau of Labor Statistics, Division of Consumer Prices and Price Indexes. - indicates no data collected for period.

Kansas City, MO-KS
Consumer Price Index - Urban Wage Earners
Base 1982-1984 = 100
Transportation

For 1947-1993. Columns headed % show percentile change in the index from the previous period for which an index is available.

Year	Jan Index	%	Feb Index	%	Mar Index	%	Apr Index	%	May Index	%	Jun Index	%	Jul Index	%	Aug Index	%	Sep Index	%	Oct Index	%	Nov Index	%	Dec Index	%
1947	17.6	-	17.6	0.0	17.6	0.0	17.9	1.7	17.9	0.0	17.9	0.0	18.0	0.6	-	-	-	-	18.5	2.8	-	-	-	-
1948	19.4	4.9	-	-	-	-	19.5	0.5	-	-	-	-	20.0	2.6	-	-	-	-	21.0	5.0	-	-	-	-
1949	21.0	0.0	-	-	-	-	21.4	1.9	-	-	-	-	21.2	-0.9	-	-	-	-	21.5	1.4	-	-	-	-
1950	21.6	0.5	-	-	-	-	21.6	0.0	-	-	-	-	22.1	2.3	-	-	-	-	21.7	-1.8	-	-	-	-
1951	22.3	2.8	-	-	-	-	22.8	2.2	-	-	-	-	23.0	0.9	-	-	-	-	23.5	2.2	-	-	-	-
1952	23.7	0.9	-	-	-	-	25.2	6.3	-	-	-	-	25.5	1.2	-	-	-	-	25.8	1.2	-	-	-	-
1953	25.9	0.4	-	-	-	-	25.8	-0.4	-	-	-	-	25.9	0.4	-	-	-	-	25.9	0.0	-	-	-	-
1954	25.0	-3.5	-	-	-	-	25.7	2.8	-	-	-	-	24.9	-3.1	-	-	-	-	24.6	-1.2	-	-	-	-
1955	25.0	1.6	-	-	-	-	24.5	-2.0	-	-	-	-	24.9	1.6	-	-	-	-	25.2	1.2	-	-	-	-
1956	24.8	-1.6	-	-	-	-	25.3	2.0	-	-	-	-	24.3	-4.0	-	-	-	-	26.0	7.0	-	-	-	-
1957	27.0	3.8	-	-	-	-	27.3	1.1	-	-	-	-	27.4	0.4	-	-	-	-	27.5	0.4	-	-	-	-
1958	27.9	1.5	-	-	-	-	28.2	1.1	-	-	-	-	29.5	4.6	-	-	-	-	29.9	1.4	-	-	-	-
1959	29.2	-2.3	-	-	-	-	30.4	4.1	-	-	-	-	30.6	0.7	-	-	-	-	31.0	1.3	-	-	-	-
1960	30.7	-1.0	-	-	-	-	29.6	-3.6	-	-	-	-	30.7	3.7	-	-	-	-	30.8	0.3	-	-	-	-
1961	29.8	-3.2	-	-	-	-	30.6	2.7	-	-	-	-	30.8	0.7	-	-	-	-	30.2	-1.9	-	-	-	-
1962	30.8	2.0	-	-	-	-	31.5	2.3	-	-	-	-	30.5	-3.2	-	-	-	-	31.7	3.9	-	-	-	-
1963	30.4	-4.1	-	-	-	-	31.2	2.6	-	-	-	-	30.7	-1.6	-	-	-	-	32.0	4.2	-	-	-	-
1964	31.3	-2.2	-	-	-	-	31.3	0.0	-	-	-	-	31.5	0.6	-	-	-	-	31.2	-1.0	-	-	-	-
1965	32.6	4.5	-	-	-	-	32.8	0.6	-	-	34.3	4.6	-	-	-	-	34.1	-0.6	-	-	-	-	33.9	-0.6
1966	-	-	-	-	33.9	0.0	-	-	-	-	34.5	1.8	-	-	-	-	34.4	-0.3	-	-	-	-	34.6	0.6
1967	-	-	-	-	34.7	0.3	-	-	-	-	33.4	-3.7	-	-	-	-	35.3	5.7	-	-	-	-	34.6	-2.0
1968	-	-	-	-	34.8	0.6	-	-	-	-	36.5	4.9	-	-	-	-	34.8	-4.7	-	-	-	-	35.6	2.3
1969	-	-	-	-	37.4	5.1	-	-	-	-	37.3	-0.3	-	-	-	-	36.4	-2.4	-	-	-	-	37.5	3.0
1970	-	-	-	-	36.5	-2.7	-	-	-	-	38.3	4.9	-	-	-	-	37.6	-1.8	-	-	-	-	40.9	8.8
1971	-	-	-	-	40.8	-0.2	-	-	-	-	41.5	1.7	-	-	-	-	40.7	-1.9	-	-	-	-	39.9	-2.0
1972	-	-	-	-	39.8	-0.3	-	-	-	-	41.0	3.0	-	-	-	-	41.4	1.0	-	-	-	-	41.5	0.2
1973	-	-	-	-	41.8	0.7	-	-	-	-	42.7	2.2	-	-	-	-	42.4	-0.7	-	-	-	-	43.1	1.7
1974	-	-	-	-	45.1	4.6	-	-	-	-	47.5	5.3	-	-	-	-	48.6	2.3	-	-	-	-	49.0	0.8
1975	-	-	-	-	49.2	0.4	-	-	-	-	50.8	3.3	-	-	-	-	52.8	3.9	-	-	-	-	53.3	0.9
1976	-	-	-	-	53.4	0.2	-	-	-	-	55.5	3.9	-	-	-	-	56.1	1.1	-	-	-	-	57.2	2.0
1977	-	-	-	-	58.2	1.7	-	-	-	-	59.6	2.4	-	-	-	-	58.8	-1.3	-	-	-	-	59.5	1.2
1978	-	-	59.4	-0.2	-	-	59.6	0.3	-	-	61.5	3.2	-	-	62.4	1.5	-	-	63.7	2.1	-	-	64.8	1.7
1979	-	-	65.6	1.2	-	-	69.2	5.5	-	-	72.9	5.3	-	-	75.1	3.0	-	-	75.8	0.9	-	-	78.2	3.2
1980	-	-	82.1	5.0	-	-	85.2	3.8	-	-	85.3	0.1	-	-	85.6	0.4	-	-	86.2	0.7	-	-	88.1	2.2
1981	-	-	91.2	3.5	-	-	92.9	1.9	-	-	94.1	1.3	-	-	94.3	0.2	-	-	95.3	1.1	-	-	96.6	1.4
1982	-	-	95.6	-1.0	-	-	94.7	-0.9	-	-	98.7	4.2	-	-	99.4	0.7	-	-	98.9	-0.5	-	-	97.8	-1.1
1983	-	-	95.9	-1.9	-	-	97.7	1.9	-	-	99.6	1.9	-	-	100.7	1.1	-	-	102.3	1.6	-	-	101.6	-0.7
1984	-	-	101.3	-0.3	-	-	102.5	1.2	-	-	103.7	1.2	-	-	102.5	-1.2	-	-	104.7	2.1	-	-	104.4	-0.3
1985	-	-	102.8	-1.5	-	-	107.0	4.1	-	-	107.8	0.7	-	-	107.0	-0.7	-	-	107.6	0.6	-	-	107.5	-0.1
1986	-	-	102.1	-5.0	-	-	97.5	-4.5	-	-	101.0	3.6	-	-	96.6	-4.4	-	-	97.7	1.1	-	-	97.8	0.1
1987	-	-	-	-	-	-	-	-	-	-	99.4	1.6	-	-	-	-	-	-	-	-	-	-	103.0	3.6
1988	-	-	-	-	-	-	-	-	-	-	104.0	1.0	-	-	-	-	-	-	-	-	-	-	107.1	3.0
1989	-	-	-	-	-	-	-	-	-	-	109.8	2.5	-	-	-	-	-	-	-	-	-	-	110.1	0.3
1990	-	-	-	-	-	-	-	-	-	-	110.0	-0.1	-	-	-	-	-	-	-	-	-	-	115.2	4.7
1991	-	-	-	-	-	-	-	-	-	-	114.9	-0.3	-	-	-	-	-	-	-	-	-	-	116.8	1.7

[Continued]

Kansas City, MO-KS
Consumer Price Index - Urban Wage Earners
Base 1982-1984 = 100
Transportation
[Continued]

For 1947-1993. Columns headed % show percentile change in the index from the previous period for which an index is available.

Year	Jan Index	%	Feb Index	%	Mar Index	%	Apr Index	%	May Index	%	Jun Index	%	Jul Index	%	Aug Index	%	Sep Index	%	Oct Index	%	Nov Index	%	Dec Index	%
1992	-	-	-	-	-	-	-	-	-	-	117.9	0.9	-	-	-	-	-	-	-	-	-	-	120.2	2.0
1993	-	-	-	-	-	-	-	-	-	-	121.8	1.3	-	-	-	-	-	-	-	-	-	-	-	-

Source: U.S. Department of Labor, Bureau of Labor Statistics, Division of Consumer Prices and Price Indexes. - indicates no data collected for period.

Kansas City, MO-KS
Consumer Price Index - All Urban Consumers
Base 1982-1984 = 100
Medical Care

For 1947-1993. Columns headed % show percentile change in the index from the previous period for which an index is available.

Year	Jan Index	%	Feb Index	%	Mar Index	%	Apr Index	%	May Index	%	Jun Index	%	Jul Index	%	Aug Index	%	Sep Index	%	Oct Index	%	Nov Index	%	Dec Index	%
1947	10.8	-	10.9	0.9	10.9	0.0	11.0	0.9	11.0	0.0	11.0	0.0	11.0	0.0	-	-	-	-	11.1	0.9	-	-	-	-
1948	11.5	3.6	-	-	-	-	11.9	3.5	-	-	-	-	11.9	0.0	-	-	-	-	12.1	1.7	-	-	-	-
1949	12.1	0.0	-	-	-	-	12.1	0.0	-	-	-	-	12.2	0.8	-	-	-	-	12.2	0.0	-	-	-	-
1950	12.2	0.0	-	-	-	-	12.3	0.8	-	-	-	-	12.3	0.0	-	-	-	-	12.7	3.3	-	-	-	-
1951	12.8	0.8	-	-	-	-	12.9	0.8	-	-	-	-	13.0	0.8	-	-	-	-	13.1	0.8	-	-	-	-
1952	13.3	1.5	-	-	-	-	13.4	0.8	-	-	-	-	13.9	3.7	-	-	-	-	13.9	0.0	-	-	-	-
1953	13.9	0.0	-	-	-	-	14.0	0.7	-	-	-	-	14.0	0.0	-	-	-	-	14.0	0.0	-	-	-	-
1954	14.0	0.0	-	-	-	-	15.8	12.9	-	-	-	-	15.9	0.6	-	-	-	-	15.9	0.0	-	-	-	-
1955	15.9	0.0	-	-	-	-	15.9	0.0	-	-	-	-	16.0	0.6	-	-	-	-	16.0	0.0	-	-	-	-
1956	16.0	0.0	-	-	-	-	16.2	1.3	-	-	-	-	16.2	0.0	-	-	-	-	17.5	8.0	-	-	-	-
1957	17.5	0.0	-	-	-	-	17.6	0.6	-	-	-	-	17.6	0.0	-	-	-	-	17.8	1.1	-	-	-	-
1958	17.9	0.6	-	-	-	-	17.9	0.0	-	-	-	-	19.9	11.2	-	-	-	-	19.9	0.0	-	-	-	-
1959	19.9	0.0	-	-	-	-	19.9	0.0	-	-	-	-	20.0	0.5	-	-	-	-	20.0	0.0	-	-	-	-
1960	20.1	0.5	-	-	-	-	20.2	0.5	-	-	-	-	20.5	1.5	-	-	-	-	20.4	-0.5	-	-	-	-
1961	20.4	0.0	-	-	-	-	21.2	3.9	-	-	-	-	21.1	-0.5	-	-	-	-	21.3	0.9	-	-	-	-
1962	21.4	0.5	-	-	-	-	21.4	0.0	-	-	-	-	21.5	0.5	-	-	-	-	21.6	0.5	-	-	-	-
1963	21.6	0.0	-	-	-	-	21.6	0.0	-	-	-	-	21.7	0.5	-	-	-	-	21.8	0.5	-	-	-	-
1964	21.8	0.0	-	-	-	-	22.0	0.9	-	-	-	-	23.5	6.8	-	-	-	-	23.5	0.0	-	-	-	-
1965	23.5	0.0	-	-	-	-	23.7	0.9	-	-	23.8	0.4	-	-	-	-	24.2	1.7	-	-	-	-	24.4	0.8
1966	-	-	-	-	25.2	3.3	-	-	-	-	25.4	0.8	-	-	-	-	25.5	0.4	-	-	-	-	25.7	0.8
1967	-	-	-	-	26.9	4.7	-	-	-	-	27.1	0.7	-	-	-	-	27.6	1.8	-	-	-	-	27.6	0.0
1968	-	-	-	-	28.7	4.0	-	-	-	-	29.0	1.0	-	-	-	-	29.1	0.3	-	-	-	-	29.6	1.7
1969	-	-	-	-	30.0	1.4	-	-	-	-	30.5	1.7	-	-	-	-	30.8	1.0	-	-	-	-	30.9	0.3
1970	-	-	-	-	31.2	1.0	-	-	-	-	31.7	1.6	-	-	-	-	32.1	1.3	-	-	-	-	32.7	1.9
1971	-	-	-	-	33.2	1.5	-	-	-	-	33.7	1.5	-	-	-	-	34.5	2.4	-	-	-	-	34.4	-0.3
1972	-	-	-	-	34.7	0.9	-	-	-	-	35.0	0.9	-	-	-	-	35.2	0.6	-	-	-	-	35.8	1.7
1973	-	-	-	-	36.4	1.7	-	-	-	-	36.5	0.3	-	-	-	-	36.7	0.5	-	-	-	-	37.7	2.7
1974	-	-	-	-	39.1	3.7	-	-	-	-	39.9	2.0	-	-	-	-	41.1	3.0	-	-	-	-	41.6	1.2
1975	-	-	-	-	43.3	4.1	-	-	-	-	43.3	0.0	-	-	-	-	44.0	1.6	-	-	-	-	44.9	2.0
1976	-	-	-	-	46.3	3.1	-	-	-	-	47.3	2.2	-	-	-	-	47.6	0.6	-	-	-	-	49.5	4.0
1977	-	-	-	-	51.1	3.2	-	-	-	-	51.7	1.2	-	-	-	-	52.5	1.5	-	-	-	-	53.3	1.5
1978	-	-	54.2	1.7	-	-	55.2	1.8	-	-	56.4	2.2	-	-	56.9	0.9	-	-	59.3	4.2	-	-	59.7	0.7
1979	-	-	61.8	3.5	-	-	62.8	1.6	-	-	63.4	1.0	-	-	63.9	0.8	-	-	65.3	2.2	-	-	66.6	2.0
1980	-	-	68.7	3.2	-	-	69.9	1.7	-	-	70.6	1.0	-	-	71.5	1.3	-	-	73.1	2.2	-	-	73.5	0.5
1981	-	-	77.7	5.7	-	-	78.2	0.6	-	-	79.0	1.0	-	-	80.2	1.5	-	-	82.5	2.9	-	-	83.2	0.8
1982	-	-	85.7	3.0	-	-	89.4	4.3	-	-	89.8	0.4	-	-	93.1	3.7	-	-	96.1	3.2	-	-	95.2	-0.9
1983	-	-	98.6	3.6	-	-	99.6	1.0	-	-	100.0	0.4	-	-	102.3	2.3	-	-	103.8	1.5	-	-	104.9	1.1
1984	-	-	107.0	2.0	-	-	108.0	0.9	-	-	107.5	-0.5	-	-	107.6	0.1	-	-	108.9	1.2	-	-	109.0	0.1
1985	-	-	109.4	0.4	-	-	109.9	0.5	-	-	111.0	1.0	-	-	113.2	2.0	-	-	113.5	0.3	-	-	114.5	0.9
1986	-	-	115.6	1.0	-	-	116.5	0.8	-	-	116.9	0.3	-	-	119.1	1.9	-	-	118.9	-0.2	-	-	120.9	1.7
1987	-	-	-	-	-	-	-	-	-	-	123.1	1.8	-	-	-	-	-	-	-	-	-	-	123.6	0.4
1988	-	-	-	-	-	-	-	-	-	-	128.8	4.2	-	-	-	-	-	-	-	-	-	-	132.9	3.2
1989	-	-	-	-	-	-	-	-	-	-	138.3	4.1	-	-	-	-	-	-	-	-	-	-	145.6	5.3
1990	-	-	-	-	-	-	-	-	-	-	152.8	4.9	-	-	-	-	-	-	-	-	-	-	160.8	5.2
1991	-	-	-	-	-	-	-	-	-	-	172.4	7.2	-	-	-	-	-	-	-	-	-	-	174.5	1.2

[Continued]

Kansas City, MO-KS
Consumer Price Index - All Urban Consumers
Base 1982-1984 = 100
Medical Care
[Continued]

For 1947-1993. Columns headed % show percentile change in the index from the previous period for which an index is available.

Year	Jan		Feb		Mar		Apr		May		Jun		Jul		Aug		Sep		Oct		Nov		Dec	
	Index	%	Index	%	Index	%	Index	%	Index	%	Index	%	Index	%	Index	%	Index	%	Index	%	Index	%	Index	%
1992	-	-	-	-	-	-	-	-	-	-	181.7	4.1	-	-	-	-	-	-	-	-	-	-	185.9	2.3
1993	-	-	-	-	-	-	-	-	-	-	195.5	5.2	-	-	-	-	-	-	-	-	-	-	-	-

Source: U.S. Department of Labor, Bureau of Labor Statistics, Division of Consumer Prices and Price Indexes. - indicates no data collected for period.

Kansas City, MO-KS
Consumer Price Index - Urban Wage Earners
Base 1982-1984 = 100
Medical Care

For 1947-1993. Columns headed % show percentile change in the index from the previous period for which an index is available.

Year	Jan Index	%	Feb Index	%	Mar Index	%	Apr Index	%	May Index	%	Jun Index	%	Jul Index	%	Aug Index	%	Sep Index	%	Oct Index	%	Nov Index	%	Dec Index	%
1947	10.8	-	10.9	0.9	10.9	0.0	11.0	0.9	11.0	0.0	11.0	0.0	11.0	0.0	-	-	-	-	11.1	0.9	-	-	-	-
1948	11.5	3.6	-	-	-	-	11.9	3.5	-	-	-	-	11.9	0.0	-	-	-	-	12.1	1.7	-	-	-	-
1949	12.1	0.0	-	-	-	-	12.1	0.0	-	-	-	-	12.2	0.8	-	-	-	-	12.2	0.0	-	-	-	-
1950	12.2	0.0	-	-	-	-	12.3	0.8	-	-	-	-	12.3	0.0	-	-	-	-	12.7	3.3	-	-	-	-
1951	12.8	0.8	-	-	-	-	12.9	0.8	-	-	-	-	13.0	0.8	-	-	-	-	13.1	0.8	-	-	-	-
1952	13.3	1.5	-	-	-	-	13.4	0.8	-	-	-	-	13.9	3.7	-	-	-	-	13.9	0.0	-	-	-	-
1953	13.9	0.0	-	-	-	-	14.0	0.7	-	-	-	-	14.0	0.0	-	-	-	-	14.0	0.0	-	-	-	-
1954	14.0	0.0	-	-	-	-	15.8	12.9	-	-	-	-	15.9	0.6	-	-	-	-	15.9	0.0	-	-	-	-
1955	15.9	0.0	-	-	-	-	15.9	0.0	-	-	-	-	16.0	0.6	-	-	-	-	16.0	0.0	-	-	-	-
1956	16.0	0.0	-	-	-	-	16.2	1.3	-	-	-	-	16.2	0.0	-	-	-	-	17.5	8.0	-	-	-	-
1957	17.5	0.0	-	-	-	-	17.6	0.6	-	-	-	-	17.6	0.0	-	-	-	-	17.8	1.1	-	-	-	-
1958	17.9	0.6	-	-	-	-	17.9	0.0	-	-	-	-	19.9	11.2	-	-	-	-	19.9	0.0	-	-	-	-
1959	19.9	0.0	-	-	-	-	19.9	0.0	-	-	-	-	20.0	0.5	-	-	-	-	20.0	0.0	-	-	-	-
1960	20.1	0.5	-	-	-	-	20.2	0.5	-	-	-	-	20.5	1.5	-	-	-	-	20.4	-0.5	-	-	-	-
1961	20.4	0.0	-	-	-	-	21.2	3.9	-	-	-	-	21.1	-0.5	-	-	-	-	21.3	0.9	-	-	-	-
1962	21.4	0.5	-	-	-	-	21.4	0.0	-	-	-	-	21.5	0.5	-	-	-	-	21.6	0.5	-	-	-	-
1963	21.6	0.0	-	-	-	-	21.6	0.0	-	-	-	-	21.7	0.5	-	-	-	-	21.8	0.5	-	-	-	-
1964	21.8	0.0	-	-	-	-	22.0	0.9	-	-	-	-	23.5	6.8	-	-	-	-	23.5	0.0	-	-	-	-
1965	23.5	0.0	-	-	-	-	23.7	0.9	-	-	23.8	0.4	-	-	-	-	24.2	1.7	-	-	-	-	24.4	0.8
1966	-	-	-	-	25.1	2.9	-	-	-	-	25.4	1.2	-	-	-	-	25.5	0.4	-	-	-	-	25.7	0.8
1967	-	-	-	-	26.9	4.7	-	-	-	-	27.1	0.7	-	-	-	-	27.6	1.8	-	-	-	-	27.6	0.0
1968	-	-	-	-	28.7	4.0	-	-	-	-	29.0	1.0	-	-	-	-	29.1	0.3	-	-	-	-	29.6	1.7
1969	-	-	-	-	30.0	1.4	-	-	-	-	30.5	1.7	-	-	-	-	30.8	1.0	-	-	-	-	30.9	0.3
1970	-	-	-	-	31.2	1.0	-	-	-	-	31.7	1.6	-	-	-	-	32.1	1.3	-	-	-	-	32.7	1.9
1971	-	-	-	-	33.2	1.5	-	-	-	-	33.6	1.2	-	-	-	-	34.5	2.7	-	-	-	-	34.4	-0.3
1972	-	-	-	-	34.7	0.9	-	-	-	-	35.0	0.9	-	-	-	-	35.2	0.6	-	-	-	-	35.8	1.7
1973	-	-	-	-	36.4	1.7	-	-	-	-	36.5	0.3	-	-	-	-	36.7	0.5	-	-	-	-	37.7	2.7
1974	-	-	-	-	39.1	3.7	-	-	-	-	39.9	2.0	-	-	-	-	41.1	3.0	-	-	-	-	41.6	1.2
1975	-	-	-	-	43.3	4.1	-	-	-	-	43.3	0.0	-	-	-	-	44.0	1.6	-	-	-	-	44.9	2.0
1976	-	-	-	-	46.3	3.1	-	-	-	-	47.3	2.2	-	-	-	-	47.6	0.6	-	-	-	-	49.5	4.0
1977	-	-	-	-	51.1	3.2	-	-	-	-	51.7	1.2	-	-	-	-	52.5	1.5	-	-	-	-	53.3	1.5
1978	-	-	54.2	1.7	-	-	55.0	1.5	-	-	56.3	2.4	-	-	56.8	0.9	-	-	58.4	2.8	-	-	59.3	1.5
1979	-	-	61.8	4.2	-	-	62.8	1.6	-	-	63.7	1.4	-	-	64.1	0.6	-	-	65.7	2.5	-	-	67.1	2.1
1980	-	-	67.8	1.0	-	-	69.9	3.1	-	-	70.2	0.4	-	-	72.8	3.7	-	-	74.2	1.9	-	-	74.7	0.7
1981	-	-	77.0	3.1	-	-	77.3	0.4	-	-	78.1	1.0	-	-	79.8	2.2	-	-	81.9	2.6	-	-	83.3	1.7
1982	-	-	85.9	3.1	-	-	89.5	4.2	-	-	89.9	0.4	-	-	93.0	3.4	-	-	95.9	3.1	-	-	95.0	-0.9
1983	-	-	98.4	3.6	-	-	99.5	1.1	-	-	100.1	0.6	-	-	102.3	2.2	-	-	103.7	1.4	-	-	104.9	1.2
1984	-	-	107.0	2.0	-	-	108.0	0.9	-	-	107.6	-0.4	-	-	107.7	0.1	-	-	109.1	1.3	-	-	109.2	0.1
1985	-	-	109.6	0.4	-	-	110.0	0.4	-	-	111.1	1.0	-	-	113.2	1.9	-	-	113.5	0.3	-	-	114.5	0.9
1986	-	-	115.6	1.0	-	-	116.4	0.7	-	-	116.8	0.3	-	-	119.0	1.9	-	-	118.8	-0.2	-	-	120.7	1.6
1987	-	-	-	-	-	-	-	-	-	-	123.4	2.2	-	-	-	-	-	-	-	-	-	-	124.2	0.6
1988	-	-	-	-	-	-	-	-	-	-	129.3	4.1	-	-	-	-	-	-	-	-	-	-	133.9	3.6
1989	-	-	-	-	-	-	-	-	-	-	139.4	4.1	-	-	-	-	-	-	-	-	-	-	146.5	5.1
1990	-	-	-	-	-	-	-	-	-	-	153.8	5.0	-	-	-	-	-	-	-	-	-	-	161.3	4.9
1991	-	-	-	-	-	-	-	-	-	-	172.7	7.1	-	-	-	-	-	-	-	-	-	-	174.7	1.2

[Continued]

Kansas City, MO-KS
Consumer Price Index - Urban Wage Earners
Base 1982-1984 = 100
Medical Care

[Continued]

For 1947-1993. Columns headed % show percentile change in the index from the previous period for which an index is available.

Year	Jan Index	%	Feb Index	%	Mar Index	%	Apr Index	%	May Index	%	Jun Index	%	Jul Index	%	Aug Index	%	Sep Index	%	Oct Index	%	Nov Index	%	Dec Index	%
1992	-	-	-	-	-	-	-	-	-	-	182.1	4.2	-	-	-	-	-	-	-	-	-	-	186.4	2.4
1993	-	-	-	-	-	-	-	-	-	-	196.7	5.5	-	-	-	-	-	-	-	-	-	-	-	-

Source: U.S. Department of Labor, Bureau of Labor Statistics, Division of Consumer Prices and Price Indexes. - indicates no data collected for period.

Kansas City, MO-KS

Consumer Price Index - All Urban Consumers
Base 1982-1984 = 100
Entertainment

For 1975-1993. Columns headed % show percentile change in the index from the previous period for which an index is available.

Year	Jan Index	%	Feb Index	%	Mar Index	%	Apr Index	%	May Index	%	Jun Index	%	Jul Index	%	Aug Index	%	Sep Index	%	Oct Index	%	Nov Index	%	Dec Index	%
1975	-	-	-	-	-	-	-	-	-	-	-	-	-	-	-	-	-	-	-	-	-	-	63.6	-
1976	-	-	-	-	64.0	0.6	-	-	-	-	65.2	1.9	-	-	-	-	66.4	1.8	-	-	-	-	66.4	0.0
1977	-	-	-	-	66.9	0.8	-	-	-	-	68.0	1.6	-	-	-	-	69.6	2.4	-	-	-	-	69.5	-0.1
1978	-	-	69.9	0.6	-	-	70.9	1.4	-	-	70.0	-1.3	-	-	71.0	1.4	-	-	72.0	1.4	-	-	72.2	0.3
1979	-	-	73.3	1.5	-	-	73.0	-0.4	-	-	73.6	0.8	-	-	74.2	0.8	-	-	76.2	2.7	-	-	76.4	0.3
1980	-	-	79.7	4.3	-	-	80.7	1.3	-	-	81.1	0.5	-	-	85.8	5.8	-	-	86.0	0.2	-	-	88.4	2.8
1981	-	-	88.9	0.6	-	-	89.1	0.2	-	-	90.2	1.2	-	-	90.4	0.2	-	-	92.0	1.8	-	-	92.7	0.8
1982	-	-	94.6	2.0	-	-	94.7	0.1	-	-	95.4	0.7	-	-	96.6	1.3	-	-	97.2	0.6	-	-	97.4	0.2
1983	-	-	99.2	1.8	-	-	98.9	-0.3	-	-	98.7	-0.2	-	-	100.9	2.2	-	-	101.3	0.4	-	-	101.7	0.4
1984	-	-	102.8	1.1	-	-	103.5	0.7	-	-	104.0	0.5	-	-	105.0	1.0	-	-	105.8	0.8	-	-	105.7	-0.1
1985	-	-	106.8	1.0	-	-	107.0	0.2	-	-	106.9	-0.1	-	-	106.9	0.0	-	-	107.6	0.7	-	-	107.0	-0.6
1986	-	-	108.1	1.0	-	-	109.3	1.1	-	-	110.4	1.0	-	-	110.6	0.2	-	-	114.4	3.4	-	-	114.8	0.3
1987	-	-	-	-	-	-	-	-	-	-	120.8	5.2	-	-	-	-	-	-	-	-	-	-	126.4	4.6
1988	-	-	-	-	-	-	-	-	-	-	123.3	-2.5	-	-	-	-	-	-	-	-	-	-	125.2	1.5
1989	-	-	-	-	-	-	-	-	-	-	129.9	3.8	-	-	-	-	-	-	-	-	-	-	134.1	3.2
1990	-	-	-	-	-	-	-	-	-	-	136.6	1.9	-	-	-	-	-	-	-	-	-	-	147.4	7.9
1991	-	-	-	-	-	-	-	-	-	-	147.3	-0.1	-	-	-	-	-	-	-	-	-	-	151.4	2.8
1992	-	-	-	-	-	-	-	-	-	-	154.5	2.0	-	-	-	-	-	-	-	-	-	-	153.5	-0.6
1993	-	-	-	-	-	-	-	-	-	-	152.4	-0.7	-	-	-	-	-	-	-	-	-	-	-	-

Source: U.S. Department of Labor, Bureau of Labor Statistics, Division of Consumer Prices and Price Indexes. - indicates no data collected for period.

Kansas City, MO-KS
Consumer Price Index - Urban Wage Earners
Base 1982-1984 = 100
Entertainment

For 1975-1993. Columns headed % show percentile change in the index from the previous period for which an index is available.

Year	Jan Index	%	Feb Index	%	Mar Index	%	Apr Index	%	May Index	%	Jun Index	%	Jul Index	%	Aug Index	%	Sep Index	%	Oct Index	%	Nov Index	%	Dec Index	%
1975	-	-	-	-	-	-	-	-	-	-	-	-	-	-	-	-	-	-	-	-	-	-	60.3	-
1976	-	-	-	-	60.7	0.7	-	-	-	-	61.8	1.8	-	-	-	-	62.9	1.8	-	-	-	-	62.9	0.0
1977	-	-	-	-	63.4	0.8	-	-	-	-	64.5	1.7	-	-	-	-	65.9	2.2	-	-	-	-	65.9	0.0
1978	-	-	66.3	0.6	-	-	66.8	0.8	-	-	66.6	-0.3	-	-	67.3	1.1	-	-	67.4	0.1	-	-	66.8	-0.9
1979	-	-	68.6	2.7	-	-	68.7	0.1	-	-	70.0	1.9	-	-	70.9	1.3	-	-	75.3	6.2	-	-	75.3	0.0
1980	-	-	78.7	4.5	-	-	80.8	2.7	-	-	81.8	1.2	-	-	85.0	3.9	-	-	84.3	-0.8	-	-	86.8	3.0
1981	-	-	87.5	0.8	-	-	90.1	3.0	-	-	90.8	0.8	-	-	91.4	0.7	-	-	91.8	0.4	-	-	92.5	0.8
1982	-	-	94.5	2.2	-	-	94.4	-0.1	-	-	95.2	0.8	-	-	96.5	1.4	-	-	97.1	0.6	-	-	97.3	0.2
1983	-	-	99.2	2.0	-	-	98.9	-0.3	-	-	98.9	0.0	-	-	100.9	2.0	-	-	101.3	0.4	-	-	101.7	0.4
1984	-	-	103.1	1.4	-	-	103.7	0.6	-	-	104.1	0.4	-	-	105.0	0.9	-	-	105.7	0.7	-	-	106.0	0.3
1985	-	-	106.9	0.8	-	-	106.9	0.0	-	-	106.9	0.0	-	-	106.8	-0.1	-	-	107.5	0.7	-	-	107.2	-0.3
1986	-	-	108.4	1.1	-	-	109.4	0.9	-	-	110.5	1.0	-	-	110.7	0.2	-	-	112.8	1.9	-	-	113.6	0.7
1987	-	-	-	-	-	-	-	-	-	-	119.9	5.5	-	-	-	-	-	-	-	-	-	-	125.7	4.8
1988	-	-	-	-	-	-	-	-	-	-	122.1	-2.9	-	-	-	-	-	-	-	-	-	-	124.1	1.6
1989	-	-	-	-	-	-	-	-	-	-	128.7	3.7	-	-	-	-	-	-	-	-	-	-	132.4	2.9
1990	-	-	-	-	-	-	-	-	-	-	134.9	1.9	-	-	-	-	-	-	-	-	-	-	145.9	8.2
1991	-	-	-	-	-	-	-	-	-	-	145.2	-0.5	-	-	-	-	-	-	-	-	-	-	150.0	3.3
1992	-	-	-	-	-	-	-	-	-	-	152.9	1.9	-	-	-	-	-	-	-	-	-	-	152.5	-0.3
1993	-	-	-	-	-	-	-	-	-	-	151.9	-0.4	-	-	-	-	-	-	-	-	-	-	-	-

Source: U.S. Department of Labor, Bureau of Labor Statistics, Division of Consumer Prices and Price Indexes. - indicates no data collected for period.

Kansas City, MO-KS
Consumer Price Index - All Urban Consumers
Base 1982-1984 = 100
Other Goods and Services

For 1975-1993. Columns headed % show percentile change in the index from the previous period for which an index is available.

Year	Jan Index	%	Feb Index	%	Mar Index	%	Apr Index	%	May Index	%	Jun Index	%	Jul Index	%	Aug Index	%	Sep Index	%	Oct Index	%	Nov Index	%	Dec Index	%
1975	-		-		-		-		-		-		-		-		-		-		-		56.2	-
1976	-		-		56.9	1.2	-		-		57.3	0.7	-		-		58.1	1.4	-		-		59.4	2.2
1977	-		-		60.1	1.2	-		-		61.0	1.5	-		-		62.6	2.6	-		-		63.0	0.6
1978	-		62.7	-0.5	-		64.2	2.4	-		63.9	-0.5	-		65.2	2.0	-		66.4	1.8	-		66.7	0.5
1979	-		67.7	1.5	-		67.9	0.3	-		69.9	2.9	-		70.4	0.7	-		71.9	2.1	-		73.2	1.8
1980	-		74.7	2.0	-		75.0	0.4	-		76.0	1.3	-		77.0	1.3	-		79.0	2.6	-		80.4	1.8
1981	-		81.6	1.5	-		81.7	0.1	-		84.2	3.1	-		85.1	1.1	-		87.9	3.3	-		88.5	0.7
1982	-		89.1	0.7	-		89.8	0.8	-		88.9	-1.0	-		90.5	1.8	-		95.5	5.5	-		95.9	0.4
1983	-		97.6	1.8	-		99.0	1.4	-		99.1	0.1	-		100.9	1.8	-		104.5	3.6	-		104.9	0.4
1984	-		105.7	0.8	-		106.4	0.7	-		107.3	0.8	-		107.7	0.4	-		111.4	3.4	-		111.9	0.4
1985	-		113.2	1.2	-		112.9	-0.3	-		112.5	-0.4	-		115.5	2.7	-		121.0	4.8	-		121.7	0.6
1986	-		122.4	0.6	-		123.0	0.5	-		123.8	0.7	-		125.5	1.4	-		129.8	3.4	-		130.3	0.4
1987	-		-		-		-		-		132.5	1.7	-		-		-		-		-		137.4	3.7
1988	-		-		-		-		-		139.5	1.5	-		-		-		-		-		143.7	3.0
1989	-		-		-		-		-		150.2	4.5	-		-		-		-		-		154.5	2.9
1990	-		-		-		-		-		157.5	1.9	-		-		-		-		-		161.8	2.7
1991	-		-		-		-		-		171.5	6.0	-		-		-		-		-		180.0	5.0
1992	-		-		-		-		-		187.8	4.3	-		-		-		-		-		191.1	1.8
1993	-		-		-		-		-		194.7	1.9	-		-		-		-		-		-	-

Source: U.S. Department of Labor, Bureau of Labor Statistics, Division of Consumer Prices and Price Indexes. - indicates no data collected for period.

Kansas City, MO-KS
Consumer Price Index - Urban Wage Earners
Base 1982-1984 = 100
Other Goods and Services

For 1975-1993. Columns headed % show percentile change in the index from the previous period for which an index is available.

Year	Jan Index	%	Feb Index	%	Mar Index	%	Apr Index	%	May Index	%	Jun Index	%	Jul Index	%	Aug Index	%	Sep Index	%	Oct Index	%	Nov Index	%	Dec Index	%
1975	-	-	-	-	-	-	-	-	-	-	-	-	-	-	-	-	-	-	-	-	-	-	56.4	-
1976	-	-	-	-	57.1	1.2	-	-	-	-	57.5	0.7	-	-	-	-	58.3	1.4	-	-	-	-	59.6	2.2
1977	-	-	-	-	60.3	1.2	-	-	-	-	61.3	1.7	-	-	-	-	62.8	2.4	-	-	-	-	63.3	0.8
1978	-	-	64.1	1.3	-	-	64.3	0.3	-	-	64.4	0.2	-	-	65.4	1.6	-	-	66.7	2.0	-	-	66.6	-0.1
1979	-	-	68.4	2.7	-	-	69.7	1.9	-	-	72.0	3.3	-	-	72.3	0.4	-	-	73.6	1.8	-	-	74.3	1.0
1980	-	-	76.5	3.0	-	-	76.4	-0.1	-	-	78.0	2.1	-	-	79.4	1.8	-	-	81.0	2.0	-	-	82.2	1.5
1981	-	-	83.2	1.2	-	-	81.5	-2.0	-	-	84.7	3.9	-	-	85.7	1.2	-	-	87.7	2.3	-	-	88.2	0.6
1982	-	-	88.8	0.7	-	-	89.8	1.1	-	-	88.7	-1.2	-	-	90.6	2.1	-	-	95.6	5.5	-	-	95.9	0.3
1983	-	-	97.5	1.7	-	-	99.3	1.8	-	-	99.3	0.0	-	-	101.5	2.2	-	-	104.3	2.8	-	-	104.7	0.4
1984	-	-	105.7	1.0	-	-	106.5	0.8	-	-	107.5	0.9	-	-	108.0	0.5	-	-	110.9	2.7	-	-	111.4	0.5
1985	-	-	113.0	1.4	-	-	112.6	-0.4	-	-	112.1	-0.4	-	-	115.8	3.3	-	-	120.6	4.1	-	-	121.3	0.6
1986	-	-	122.2	0.7	-	-	122.8	0.5	-	-	123.8	0.8	-	-	125.9	1.7	-	-	129.3	2.7	-	-	129.8	0.4
1987	-	-	-	-	-	-	-	-	-	-	132.1	1.8	-	-	-	-	-	-	-	-	-	-	137.1	3.8
1988	-	-	-	-	-	-	-	-	-	-	139.4	1.7	-	-	-	-	-	-	-	-	-	-	143.4	2.9
1989	-	-	-	-	-	-	-	-	-	-	150.9	5.2	-	-	-	-	-	-	-	-	-	-	155.4	3.0
1990	-	-	-	-	-	-	-	-	-	-	158.3	1.9	-	-	-	-	-	-	-	-	-	-	162.0	2.3
1991	-	-	-	-	-	-	-	-	-	-	172.7	6.6	-	-	-	-	-	-	-	-	-	-	180.8	4.7
1992	-	-	-	-	-	-	-	-	-	-	189.9	5.0	-	-	-	-	-	-	-	-	-	-	192.8	1.5
1993	-	-	-	-	-	-	-	-	-	-	196.8	2.1	-	-	-	-	-	-	-	-	-	-	-	-

Source: U.S. Department of Labor, Bureau of Labor Statistics, Division of Consumer Prices and Price Indexes. - indicates no data collected for period.

Los Angeles, CA
Consumer Price Index - All Urban Consumers
Base 1982-1984 = 100
Annual Averages

For 1914-1993. Columns headed % show percentile change in the index from the previous period for which an index is available.

Year	All Items		Food & Beverage		Housing		Apparel & Upkeep		Trans-portation		Medical Care		Entertain-ment		Other Goods & Services	
	Index	%	Index	%	Index	%	Index	%	Index	%	Index	%	Index	%	Index	%
1914	-	-	-	-	-	-	-	-	-	-	-	-	-	-	-	-
1915	10.0	-	-	-	-	-	-	-	-	-	-	-	-	-	-	-
1916	10.5	5.0	-	-	-	-	-	-	-	-	-	-	-	-	-	-
1917	12.1	15.2	-	-	-	-	-	-	-	-	-	-	-	-	-	-
1918	14.4	19.0	-	-	-	-	-	-	-	-	-	-	-	-	-	-
1919	17.0	18.1	-	-	-	-	-	-	-	-	-	-	-	-	-	-
1920	19.9	17.1	-	-	-	-	-	-	-	-	-	-	-	-	-	-
1921	18.6	-6.5	-	-	-	-	-	-	-	-	-	-	-	-	-	-
1922	18.1	-2.7	-	-	-	-	-	-	-	-	-	-	-	-	-	-
1923	18.3	1.1	-	-	-	-	-	-	-	-	-	-	-	-	-	-
1924	18.4	0.5	-	-	-	-	-	-	-	-	-	-	-	-	-	-
1925	18.4	0.0	-	-	-	-	-	-	-	-	-	-	-	-	-	-
1926	17.9	-2.7	-	-	-	-	-	-	-	-	-	-	-	-	-	-
1927	17.6	-1.7	-	-	-	-	-	-	-	-	-	-	-	-	-	-
1928	17.3	-1.7	-	-	-	-	-	-	-	-	-	-	-	-	-	-
1929	17.3	0.0	-	-	-	-	-	-	-	-	-	-	-	-	-	-
1930	16.7	-3.5	-	-	-	-	-	-	-	-	-	-	-	-	-	-
1931	15.1	-9.6	-	-	-	-	-	-	-	-	-	-	-	-	-	-
1932	13.6	-9.9	-	-	-	-	-	-	-	-	-	-	-	-	-	-
1933	12.8	-5.9	-	-	-	-	-	-	-	-	-	-	-	-	-	-
1934	12.9	0.8	-	-	-	-	-	-	-	-	-	-	-	-	-	-
1935	13.3	3.1	-	-	-	-	-	-	-	-	-	-	-	-	-	-
1936	13.5	1.5	-	-	-	-	-	-	-	-	-	-	-	-	-	-
1937	14.2	5.2	-	-	-	-	-	-	-	-	-	-	-	-	-	-
1938	14.0	-1.4	-	-	-	-	-	-	-	-	-	-	-	-	-	-
1939	13.9	-0.7	-	-	-	-	-	-	-	-	-	-	-	-	-	-
1940	13.9	0.0	-	-	-	-	-	-	-	-	-	-	-	-	-	-
1941	14.7	5.8	-	-	-	-	-	-	-	-	-	-	-	-	-	-
1942	16.5	12.2	-	-	-	-	-	-	-	-	-	-	-	-	-	-
1943	17.3	4.8	-	-	-	-	-	-	-	-	-	-	-	-	-	-
1944	17.6	1.7	-	-	-	-	-	-	-	-	-	-	-	-	-	-
1945	18.1	2.8	-	-	-	-	-	-	-	-	-	-	-	-	-	-
1946	19.5	7.7	-	-	-	-	-	-	-	-	-	-	-	-	-	-
1947	22.0	12.8	-	-	-	-	-	-	17.9	-	13.4	-	-	-	-	-
1948	23.6	7.3	-	-	-	-	-	-	19.8	10.6	14.2	6.0	-	-	-	-
1949	23.6	0.0	-	-	-	-	-	-	21.0	6.1	14.7	3.5	-	-	-	-
1950	23.7	0.4	-	-	-	-	-	-	20.7	-1.4	15.0	2.0	-	-	-	-
1951	25.7	8.4	-	-	-	-	-	-	21.6	4.3	15.9	6.0	-	-	-	-
1952	26.5	3.1	-	-	-	-	-	-	23.8	10.2	16.5	3.8	-	-	-	-
1953	26.7	0.8	-	-	-	-	48.7	-	24.8	4.2	16.9	2.4	-	-	-	-
1954	26.7	0.0	-	-	-	-	48.9	0.4	24.6	-0.8	17.3	2.4	-	-	-	-
1955	26.7	0.0	-	-	-	-	48.9	0.0	24.4	-0.8	17.4	0.6	-	-	-	-
1956	27.1	1.5	-	-	-	-	49.8	1.8	24.8	1.6	17.9	2.9	-	-	-	-
1957	28.0	3.3	-	-	-	-	50.9	2.2	25.8	4.0	18.4	2.8	-	-	-	-
1958	28.9	3.2	-	-	-	-	51.0	0.2	26.5	2.7	19.9	8.2	-	-	-	-

[Continued]

Los Angeles, CA
Consumer Price Index - All Urban Consumers
Base 1982-1984 = 100
Annual Averages
[Continued]

For 1914-1993. Columns headed % show percentile change in the index from the previous period for which an index is available.

Year	All Items		Food & Beverage		Housing		Apparel & Upkeep		Trans-portation		Medical Care		Entertain-ment		Other Goods & Services	
	Index	%	Index	%	Index	%	Index	%	Index	%	Index	%	Index	%	Index	%
1959	29.4	1.7	-	-	-	-	51.6	1.2	27.8	4.9	20.8	4.5	-	-	-	-
1960	30.0	2.0	-	-	-	-	52.8	2.3	28.0	0.7	21.4	2.9	-	-	-	-
1961	30.3	1.0	-	-	-	-	52.9	0.2	28.9	3.2	21.6	0.9	-	-	-	-
1962	30.7	1.3	-	-	-	-	53.0	0.2	29.9	3.5	22.3	3.2	-	-	-	-
1963	31.1	1.3	-	-	-	-	53.7	1.3	29.9	0.0	22.7	1.8	-	-	-	-
1964	31.7	1.9	-	-	-	-	54.5	1.5	31.1	4.0	23.2	2.2	-	-	-	-
1965	32.4	2.2	-	-	-	-	55.0	0.9	31.7	1.9	23.7	2.2	-	-	-	-
1966	33.0	1.9	-	-	-	-	55.9	1.6	31.9	0.6	24.6	3.8	-	-	-	-
1967	33.8	2.4	-	-	-	-	58.1	3.9	32.3	1.3	26.4	7.3	-	-	-	-
1968	35.2	4.1	-	-	-	-	61.2	5.3	33.3	3.1	27.8	5.3	-	-	-	-
1969	36.8	4.5	-	-	-	-	63.6	3.9	34.3	3.0	29.5	6.1	-	-	-	-
1970	38.7	5.2	-	-	-	-	66.5	4.6	35.4	3.2	31.6	7.1	-	-	-	-
1971	40.1	3.6	-	-	-	-	68.5	3.0	37.1	4.8	33.2	5.1	-	-	-	-
1972	41.4	3.2	-	-	-	-	69.7	1.8	38.0	2.4	33.9	2.1	-	-	-	-
1973	43.7	5.6	-	-	-	-	71.5	2.6	39.8	4.7	35.6	5.0	-	-	-	-
1974	48.2	10.3	-	-	-	-	76.7	7.3	44.5	11.8	39.0	9.6	-	-	-	-
1975	53.3	10.6	-	-	-	-	79.2	3.3	49.3	10.8	43.7	12.1	-	-	-	-
1976	56.9	6.8	60.5	-	54.4	-	80.9	2.1	54.2	9.9	49.3	12.8	70.5	-	57.3	-
1977	60.8	6.9	64.7	6.9	58.4	7.4	84.1	4.0	58.1	7.2	53.9	9.3	73.2	3.8	60.6	5.8
1978	65.3	7.4	71.6	10.7	63.2	8.2	85.8	2.0	60.6	4.3	58.6	8.7	74.4	1.6	65.1	7.4
1979	72.3	10.7	79.2	10.6	69.9	10.6	89.0	3.7	70.3	16.0	64.6	10.2	78.6	5.6	69.2	6.3
1980	83.7	15.8	85.7	8.2	83.7	19.7	98.3	10.4	82.5	17.4	72.7	12.5	85.7	9.0	76.4	10.4
1981	91.9	9.8	92.5	7.9	92.4	10.4	101.5	3.3	91.3	10.7	82.0	12.8	93.1	8.6	83.9	9.8
1982	97.3	5.9	96.8	4.6	97.8	5.8	98.9	-2.6	97.5	6.8	94.1	14.8	97.6	4.8	92.0	9.7
1983	99.1	1.8	100.1	3.4	98.3	0.5	99.7	0.8	98.8	1.3	100.7	7.0	99.8	2.3	101.2	10.0
1984	103.6	4.5	103.1	3.0	103.9	5.7	101.3	1.6	103.7	5.0	105.2	4.5	102.6	2.8	106.8	5.5
1985	108.4	4.6	105.5	2.3	109.7	5.6	105.1	3.8	107.5	3.7	112.9	7.3	106.9	4.2	115.3	8.0
1986	111.9	3.2	108.7	3.0	116.1	5.8	106.9	1.7	105.2	-2.1	120.9	7.1	109.0	2.0	122.3	6.1
1987	116.7	4.3	113.2	4.1	121.0	4.2	112.5	5.2	108.9	3.5	129.5	7.1	111.2	2.0	127.9	4.6
1988	122.1	4.6	117.2	3.5	126.6	4.6	114.3	1.6	113.8	4.5	139.6	7.8	115.4	3.8	139.9	9.4
1989	128.3	5.1	124.0	5.8	131.7	4.0	118.8	3.9	119.6	5.1	149.8	7.3	120.9	4.8	155.3	11.0
1990	135.9	5.9	130.9	5.6	139.3	5.8	126.4	6.4	126.5	5.8	163.3	9.0	125.4	3.7	166.3	7.1
1991	141.4	4.0	136.6	4.4	144.9	4.0	130.9	3.6	126.6	0.1	178.2	9.1	135.4	8.0	179.9	8.2
1992	146.5	3.6	140.9	3.1	148.6	2.6	133.2	1.8	133.0	5.1	192.4	8.0	134.1	-1.0	197.1	9.6
1993	150.3	2.6	145.1	3.0	150.4	1.2	131.6	-1.2	137.5	3.4	206.6	7.4	135.8	1.3	211.9	7.5

Source: U.S. Department of Labor, Bureau of Labor Statistics, Division of Consumer Prices and Price Indexes. - indicates no data collected for period.

Los Angeles, CA
Consumer Price Index - Urban Wage Earners
Base 1982-1984 = 100
Annual Averages

For 1914-1993. Columns headed % show percentile change in the index from the previous period for which an index is available.

Year	All Items		Food & Beverage		Housing		Apparel & Upkeep		Trans- portation		Medical Care		Entertain- ment		Other Goods & Services	
	Index	%	Index	%	Index	%	Index	%	Index	%	Index	%	Index	%	Index	%
1914	-	-	-	-	-	-	-	-	-	-	-	-	-	-	-	-
1915	9.9	-	-	-	-	-	-	-	-	-	-	-	-	-	-	-
1916	10.5	6.1	-	-	-	-	-	-	-	-	-	-	-	-	-	-
1917	12.1	15.2	-	-	-	-	-	-	-	-	-	-	-	-	-	-
1918	14.4	19.0	-	-	-	-	-	-	-	-	-	-	-	-	-	-
1919	17.0	18.1	-	-	-	-	-	-	-	-	-	-	-	-	-	-
1920	19.9	17.1	-	-	-	-	-	-	-	-	-	-	-	-	-	-
1921	18.6	-6.5	-	-	-	-	-	-	-	-	-	-	-	-	-	-
1922	18.1	-2.7	-	-	-	-	-	-	-	-	-	-	-	-	-	-
1923	18.3	1.1	-	-	-	-	-	-	-	-	-	-	-	-	-	-
1924	18.4	0.5	-	-	-	-	-	-	-	-	-	-	-	-	-	-
1925	18.4	0.0	-	-	-	-	-	-	-	-	-	-	-	-	-	-
1926	17.9	-2.7	-	-	-	-	-	-	-	-	-	-	-	-	-	-
1927	17.6	-1.7	-	-	-	-	-	-	-	-	-	-	-	-	-	-
1928	17.3	-1.7	-	-	-	-	-	-	-	-	-	-	-	-	-	-
1929	17.3	0.0	-	-	-	-	-	-	-	-	-	-	-	-	-	-
1930	16.7	-3.5	-	-	-	-	-	-	-	-	-	-	-	-	-	-
1931	15.1	-9.6	-	-	-	-	-	-	-	-	-	-	-	-	-	-
1932	13.6	-9.9	-	-	-	-	-	-	-	-	-	-	-	-	-	-
1933	12.8	-5.9	-	-	-	-	-	-	-	-	-	-	-	-	-	-
1934	12.9	0.8	-	-	-	-	-	-	-	-	-	-	-	-	-	-
1935	13.3	3.1	-	-	-	-	-	-	-	-	-	-	-	-	-	-
1936	13.5	1.5	-	-	-	-	-	-	-	-	-	-	-	-	-	-
1937	14.2	5.2	-	-	-	-	-	-	-	-	-	-	-	-	-	-
1938	14.0	-1.4	-	-	-	-	-	-	-	-	-	-	-	-	-	-
1939	13.9	-0.7	-	-	-	-	-	-	-	-	-	-	-	-	-	-
1940	13.9	0.0	-	-	-	-	-	-	-	-	-	-	-	-	-	-
1941	14.7	5.8	-	-	-	-	-	-	-	-	-	-	-	-	-	-
1942	16.5	12.2	-	-	-	-	-	-	-	-	-	-	-	-	-	-
1943	17.3	4.8	-	-	-	-	-	-	-	-	-	-	-	-	-	-
1944	17.6	1.7	-	-	-	-	-	-	-	-	-	-	-	-	-	-
1945	18.1	2.8	-	-	-	-	-	-	-	-	-	-	-	-	-	-
1946	19.5	7.7	-	-	-	-	-	-	-	-	-	-	-	-	-	-
1947	22.0	12.8	-	-	-	-	-	-	17.8	-	13.6	-	-	-	-	-
1948	23.6	7.3	-	-	-	-	-	-	19.7	10.7	14.4	5.9	-	-	-	-
1949	23.6	0.0	-	-	-	-	-	-	20.9	6.1	14.9	3.5	-	-	-	-
1950	23.7	0.4	-	-	-	-	-	-	20.6	-1.4	15.2	2.0	-	-	-	-
1951	25.7	8.4	-	-	-	-	-	-	21.5	4.4	16.1	5.9	-	-	-	-
1952	26.5	3.1	-	-	-	-	-	-	23.7	10.2	16.7	3.7	-	-	-	-
1953	26.7	0.8	-	-	-	-	48.9	-	24.6	3.8	17.2	3.0	-	-	-	-
1954	26.7	0.0	-	-	-	-	49.1	0.4	24.4	-0.8	17.5	1.7	-	-	-	-
1955	26.7	0.0	-	-	-	-	49.1	0.0	24.3	-0.4	17.6	0.6	-	-	-	-
1956	27.1	1.5	-	-	-	-	50.0	1.8	24.6	1.2	18.2	3.4	-	-	-	-
1957	28.0	3.3	-	-	-	-	51.1	2.2	25.6	4.1	18.7	2.7	-	-	-	-
1958	28.9	3.2	-	-	-	-	51.2	0.2	26.3	2.7	20.2	8.0	-	-	-	-

[Continued]

Los Angeles, CA
Consumer Price Index - Urban Wage Earners
Base 1982-1984 = 100
Annual Averages
[Continued]

For 1914-1993. Columns headed % show percentile change in the index from the previous period for which an index is available.

Year	All Items		Food & Beverage		Housing		Apparel & Upkeep		Trans- portation		Medical Care		Entertain- ment		Other Goods & Services	
	Index	%	Index	%	Index	%	Index	%	Index	%	Index	%	Index	%	Index	%
1959	29.4	1.7	-	-	-	-	51.8	1.2	27.7	5.3	21.1	4.5	-	-	-	-
1960	29.9	1.7	-	-	-	-	53.0	2.3	27.8	0.4	21.7	2.8	-	-	-	-
1961	30.3	1.3	-	-	-	-	53.1	0.2	28.7	3.2	22.0	1.4	-	-	-	-
1962	30.7	1.3	-	-	-	-	53.2	0.2	29.7	3.5	22.7	3.2	-	-	-	-
1963	31.1	1.3	-	-	-	-	53.9	1.3	29.8	0.3	23.0	1.3	-	-	-	-
1964	31.7	1.9	-	-	-	-	54.7	1.5	30.9	3.7	23.6	2.6	-	-	-	-
1965	32.4	2.2	-	-	-	-	55.2	0.9	31.6	2.3	24.0	1.7	-	-	-	-
1966	33.0	1.9	-	-	-	-	56.1	1.6	31.7	0.3	24.9	3.8	-	-	-	-
1967	33.8	2.4	-	-	-	-	58.3	3.9	32.1	1.3	26.8	7.6	-	-	-	-
1968	35.2	4.1	-	-	-	-	61.4	5.3	33.1	3.1	28.2	5.2	-	-	-	-
1969	36.8	4.5	-	-	- ·	-	63.9	4.1	34.1	3.0	29.9	6.0	-	-	-	-
1970	38.7	5.2	-	-	-	-	66.7	4.4	35.2	3.2	32.1	7.4	-	-	-	-
1971	40.1	3.6		-		-	68.8	3.1	36.9	4.8	33.7	5.0				
1972	41.4	3.2	-	-	-	-	69.9	1.6	37.8	2.4	34.5	2.4	-	-	-	-
1973	43.7	5.6		-		-	71.8	2.7	39.6	4.8	36.1	4.6	-	-	-	-
1974	48.2	10.3	-	-		-	76.9	7.1	44.2	11.6	39.5	9.4	-	-	-	-
1975	53.3	10.6	-	-	-	-	79.5	3.4	49.1	11.1	44.4	12.4	-	-	-	-
1976	56.8	6.6	59.4	-	54.5	-	81.2	2.1	53.9	9.8	50.1	12.8	77.4	-	57.0	-
1977	60.8	7.0	63.5	6.9	58.5	7.3	84.4	3.9	57.8	7.2	54.7	9.2	80.3	3.7	60.2	5.6
1978	65.1	7.1	70.0	10.2	63.3	8.2	87.1	3.2	60.3	4.3	59.0	7.9	80.2	-0.1	64.3	6.8
1979	72.8	11.8	78.0	11.4	70.6	11.5	91.5	5.1	70.5	16.9	65.3	10.7	83.4	4.0	68.6	6.7
1980	84.7	16.3	85.2	9.2	85.3	20.8	97.3	6.3	83.2	18.0	74.0	13.3	90.8	8.9	75.3	9.8
1981	93.1	9.9	92.2	8.2	94.8	11.1	100.7	3.5	92.0	10.6	83.5	12.8	94.4	4.0	82.9	10.1
1982	98.5	5.8	96.8	5.0	100.4	5.9	99.0	-1.7	97.8	6.3	94.1	12.7	97.6	3.4	91.7	10.6
1983	99.3	0.8	100.2	3.5	99.0	-1.4	99.6	0.6	98.6	0.8	100.7	7.0	99.8	2.3	101.7	10.9
1984	102.2	2.9	103.1	2.9	100.6	1.6	101.4	1.8	103.5	5.0	105.2	4.5	102.6	2.8	106.7	4.9
1985	106.5	4.2	105.4	2.2	106.2	5.6	105.0	3.6	107.0	3.4	112.9	7.3	106.6	3.9	113.7	6.6
1986	109.5	2.8	108.5	2.9	112.3	5.7	107.2	2.1	103.9	-2.9	120.7	6.9	108.4	1.7	120.7	6.2
1987	114.0	4.1	113.0	4.1	117.0	4.2	111.9	4.4	107.0	3.0	129.0	6.9	110.5	1.9	126.4	4.7
1988	119.0	4.4	117.1	3.6	122.3	4.5	114.0	1.9	111.4	4.1	139.1	7.8	114.6	3.7	137.6	8.9
1989	124.9	5.0	123.9	5.8	127.1	3.9	118.8	4.2	116.6	4.7	148.7	6.9	120.0	4.7	154.9	12.6
1990	131.9	5.6	131.0	5.7	134.1	5.5	126.1	6.1	122.2	4.8	161.5	8.6	124.4	3.7	166.1	7.2
1991	137.1	3.9	136.8	4.4	139.6	4.1	130.8	3.7	122.5	0.2	175.7	8.8	134.1	7.8	179.1	7.8
1992	142.0	3.6	141.4	3.4	143.0	2.4	133.6	2.1	128.6	5.0	190.0	8.1	134.4	0.2	194.2	8.4
1993	145.2	2.3	145.6	3.0	144.8	1.3	132.4	-0.9	132.5	3.0	203.9	7.3	136.4	1.5	204.6	5.4

Source: U.S. Department of Labor, Bureau of Labor Statistics, Division of Consumer Prices and Price Indexes. - indicates no data collected for period.

Los Angeles, CA
Consumer Price Index - All Urban Consumers
Base 1982-1984 = 100
All Items

For 1914-1993. Columns headed % show percentile change in the index from the previous period for which an index is available.

Year	Jan Index	Jan %	Feb Index	Feb %	Mar Index	Mar %	Apr Index	Apr %	May Index	May %	Jun Index	Jun %	Jul Index	Jul %	Aug Index	Aug %	Sep Index	Sep %	Oct Index	Oct %	Nov Index	Nov %	Dec Index	Dec %
1914	-	-	-	-	-	-	-	-	-	-	-	-	-	-	-	-	-	-	-	-	-	-	10.2	-
1915	-	-	-	-	-	-	-	-	-	-	-	-	-	-	-	-	-	-	-	-	-	-	10.1	-1.0
1916	-	-	-	-	-	-	-	-	-	-	-	-	-	-	-	-	-	-	-	-	-	-	11.0	8.9
1917	-	-	-	-	-	-	-	-	-	-	-	-	-	-	-	-	-	-	-	-	-	-	13.0	18.2
1918	-	-	-	-	-	-	-	-	-	-	-	-	-	-	-	-	-	-	-	-	-	-	15.8	21.5
1919	-	-	-	-	-	-	-	-	-	-	16.4	3.8	-	-	-	-	-	-	-	-	-	-	18.6	13.4
1920	-	-	-	-	-	-	-	-	-	-	20.4	9.7	-	-	-	-	-	-	-	-	-	-	19.9	-2.5
1921	-	-	-	-	-	-	-	-	18.5	-7.0	-	-	-	-	-	-	18.3	-1.1	-	-	-	-	18.4	0.5
1922	-	-	-	-	18.2	-1.1	-	-	-	-	18.1	-0.5	-	-	-	-	18.0	-0.6	-	-	-	-	18.1	0.6
1923	-	-	-	-	18.0	-0.6	-	-	-	-	18.3	1.7	-	-	-	-	18.5	1.1	-	-	-	-	18.6	0.5
1924	-	-	-	-	18.5	-0.5	-	-	-	-	18.3	-1.1	-	-	-	-	18.4	0.5	-	-	-	-	18.2	-1.1
1925	-	-	-	-	-	-	-	-	-	-	18.5	1.6	-	-	-	-	-	-	-	-	-	-	18.5	0.0
1926	-	-	-	-	-	-	-	-	-	-	17.8	-3.8	-	-	-	-	-	-	-	-	-	-	17.8	0.0
1927	-	-	-	-	-	-	-	-	-	-	17.8	0.0	-	-	-	-	-	-	-	-	-	-	17.5	-1.7
1928	-	-	-	-	-	-	-	-	-	-	17.2	-1.7	-	-	-	-	-	-	-	-	-	-	17.4	1.2
1929	-	-	-	-	-	-	-	-	-	-	17.2	-1.1	-	-	-	-	-	-	-	-	-	-	17.2	0.0
1930	-	-	-	-	-	-	-	-	-	-	16.7	-2.9	-	-	-	-	-	-	-	-	-	-	16.0	-4.2
1931	-	-	-	-	-	-	-	-	-	-	14.9	-6.9	-	-	-	-	-	-	-	-	-	-	14.6	-2.0
1932	-	-	-	-	-	-	-	-	-	-	13.6	-6.8	-	-	-	-	-	-	-	-	-	-	13.1	-3.7
1933	-	-	-	-	-	-	-	-	-	-	12.5	-4.6	-	-	-	-	-	-	-	-	-	-	13.0	4.0
1934	-	-	-	-	-	-	-	-	-	-	12.9	-0.8	-	-	-	-	-	-	-	-	13.3	3.1	-	-
1935	-	-	-	-	13.6	2.3	-	-	-	-	-	-	13.2	-2.9	-	-	-	-	13.1	-0.8	-	-	13.7	-
1936	13.4	2.3	-	-	-	-	-	-	13.2	-1.5	-	-	13.4	1.5	-	-	13.7	2.2	-	-	-	-	13.7	0.0
1937	-	-	-	-	14.3	4.4	-	-	-	-	14.2	-0.7	-	-	-	-	14.4	1.4	-	-	-	-	14.3	-0.7
1938	-	-	-	-	14.0	-2.1	-	-	-	-	14.0	0.0	-	-	-	-	14.0	0.0	-	-	-	-	14.1	0.7
1939	-	-	-	-	14.0	-0.7	-	-	-	-	13.8	-1.4	-	-	-	-	14.1	2.2	-	-	-	-	13.9	-1.4
1940	-	-	-	-	13.9	0.0	-	-	-	-	13.9	0.0	-	-	-	-	14.0	0.7	14.0	0.0	14.1	0.7	14.1	0.0
1941	14.2	0.7	14.0	-1.4	14.1	0.7	14.3	1.4	14.4	0.7	14.6	1.4	14.6	0.0	14.7	0.7	15.0	2.0	15.2	1.3	15.3	0.7	15.5	1.3
1942	15.7	1.3	15.8	0.6	16.1	1.9	16.2	0.6	16.3	0.6	16.4	0.6	16.6	1.2	16.8	1.2	16.8	0.0	17.0	1.2	17.1	0.6	17.1	0.0
1943	17.1	0.0	17.0	-0.6	17.2	1.2	17.4	1.2	17.4	0.0	17.4	0.0	17.3	-0.6	17.2	-0.6	17.3	0.6	17.4	0.6	17.5	0.6	17.5	0.0
1944	17.4	-0.6	17.4	0.0	17.4	0.0	17.4	0.0	17.6	1.1	17.5	-0.6	17.5	0.0	17.6	0.6	17.7	0.6	17.8	0.6	17.8	0.0	17.9	0.6
1945	17.9	0.0	17.8	-0.6	17.9	0.6	18.0	0.6	18.0	0.0	18.0	0.0	18.1	0.6	18.1	0.0	18.3	1.1	18.3	0.0	18.4	0.5	18.5	0.5
1946	18.4	-0.5	18.4	0.0	18.4	0.0	18.5	0.5	18.6	0.5	18.8	1.1	19.7	4.8	20.0	1.5	20.1	0.5	20.5	2.0	21.4	4.4	21.4	0.0
1947	21.5	0.5	21.6	0.5	21.7	0.5	21.8	0.5	21.8	0.0	21.7	-0.5	21.8	0.5	21.9	0.5	22.4	2.3	22.4	0.0	22.8	1.8	23.0	0.9
1948	23.3	1.3	23.4	0.4	23.3	-0.4	23.5	0.9	23.5	0.0	23.5	0.0	23.7	0.9	23.8	0.4	23.8	0.0	23.9	0.4	24.0	0.4	24.1	0.4
1949	24.1	0.0	23.9	-0.8	23.9	0.0	23.9	0.0	23.7	-0.8	23.6	-0.4	23.5	-0.4	23.4	-0.8	23.4	0.0	23.3	-0.4	23.4	0.4	23.2	-0.9
1950	23.4	0.9	23.3	-0.4	23.4	0.4	23.4	0.0	23.4	0.0	23.4	0.0	23.5	0.4	23.8	1.3	23.9	0.4	24.1	0.8	24.3	0.8	24.6	1.2
1951	25.0	1.6	25.5	2.0	25.7	0.8	25.7	0.0	25.7	0.0	25.7	0.0	25.8	0.4	25.8	0.0	25.9	0.4	25.9	0.0	26.2	1.2	26.3	0.4
1952	26.3	0.0	26.3	0.0	26.4	0.4	26.4	0.0	26.4	0.0	26.5	0.4	26.5	0.0	26.5	0.0	26.5	0.0	26.5	0.0	26.6	0.4	26.6	0.0
1953	26.6	0.0	26.5	-0.4	26.6	0.4	26.7	0.4	26.6	-0.4	26.6	0.0	26.7	0.4	26.7	0.0	26.8	0.4	26.5	-0.4	26.5	0.0	26.6	0.4
1954	27.0	1.1	26.9	-0.4	26.8	-0.4	26.7	-0.4	26.7	0.0	26.7	0.0	26.5	-0.7	26.6	0.4	26.6	0.0	26.8	0.8	26.8	0.0	26.8	0.0
1955	26.6	0.0	26.5	-0.4	26.6	0.4	26.4	-0.8	26.6	0.8	26.6	0.0	26.7	0.4	26.6	-0.4	26.8	0.4	27.3	0.4	27.5	0.7	27.6	0.4
1956	26.8	0.0	26.7	-0.4	26.8	0.4	26.8	0.0	27.0	0.7	27.1	0.4	27.2	0.4	27.1	-0.4	27.2	0.4	27.2	0.0	27.4	0.7	27.6	0.7
1957	27.6	0.0	27.8	0.7	27.8	0.0	27.8	0.0	27.9	0.4	27.9	0.0	28.0	0.4	28.0	0.0	28.2	0.7	28.2	0.0	28.4	0.7	28.4	0.0
1958	28.6	0.7	28.6	0.0	28.8	0.7	29.0	0.7	28.9	-0.3	28.9	0.0	29.0	0.3	28.9	-0.3	29.1	0.7	29.1	0.0	29.2	0.3	29.2	0.0

[Continued]

Los Angeles, CA
Consumer Price Index - All Urban Consumers
Base 1982-1984 = 100
All Items
[Continued]

For 1914-1993. Columns headed % show percentile change in the index from the previous period for which an index is available.

Year	Jan Index	%	Feb Index	%	Mar Index	%	Apr Index	%	May Index	%	Jun Index	%	Jul Index	%	Aug Index	%	Sep Index	%	Oct Index	%	Nov Index	%	Dec Index	%
1959	29.2	0.0	29.2	0.0	29.2	0.0	29.2	0.0	29.3	0.3	29.3	0.0	29.4	0.3	29.4	0.0	29.5	0.3	29.7	0.7	29.7	0.0	29.8	0.3
1960	29.8	0.0	29.7	-0.3	29.9	0.7	30.0	0.3	30.0	0.0	29.9	-0.3	29.9	0.0	29.8	-0.3	30.0	0.7	30.1	0.3	30.1	0.0	30.3	0.7
1961	30.3	0.0	30.3	0.0	30.2	-0.3	30.3	0.3	30.3	0.0	30.3	0.0	30.3	0.0	30.3	0.0	30.3	0.0	30.4	0.3	30.5	0.3	30.5	0.0
1962	30.4	-0.3	30.4	0.0	30.5	0.3	30.6	0.3	30.8	0.7	30.8	0.0	30.7	-0.3	30.7	0.0	30.9	0.7	30.9	0.0	30.8	-0.3	30.9	0.3
1963	30.9	0.0	31.0	0.3	31.0	0.0	31.1	0.3	31.0	-0.3	30.9	-0.3	31.1	0.6	31.2	0.3	31.2	0.0	31.4	0.6	31.4	0.0	31.3	-0.3
1964	31.5	0.6	31.4	-0.3	31.6	0.6	31.6	0.0	31.6	0.0	31.6	0.0	31.6	0.0	31.7	0.3	31.6	-0.3	32.0	1.3	32.0	0.0	32.1	0.3
1965	32.1	0.0	32.2	0.3	32.3	0.3	32.4	0.3	32.4	0.0	32.5	0.3	32.4	-0.3	32.1	-0.9	32.5	1.2	32.4	-0.3	32.5	0.3	32.6	0.3
1966	32.5	-0.3	32.6	0.3	32.7	0.3	32.9	0.6	32.9	0.0	33.0	0.3	33.1	0.3	33.0	-0.3	33.3	0.9	33.4	0.3	33.5	0.3	33.5	0.0
1967	33.3	-0.6	33.3	0.0	33.2	-0.3	33.5	0.9	33.6	0.3	33.7	0.3	33.8	0.3	34.1	0.9	34.3	0.6	34.2	-0.3	34.5	0.9	34.5	0.0
1968	34.7	0.6	34.7	0.0	34.9	0.6	34.9	0.0	34.8	-0.3	35.1	0.9	35.2	0.3	35.3	0.3	35.3	0.0	35.6	0.8	35.7	0.3	35.7	0.0
1969	35.9	0.6	36.0	0.3	36.5	1.4	36.5	0.0	36.5	0.0	36.8	0.8	37.0	0.5	37.1	0.3	37.3	0.5	37.4	0.3	37.4	0.0	37.7	0.8
1970	37.8	0.3	37.9	0.3	38.0	0.3	38.4	1.1	38.5	0.3	38.6	0.3	38.9	0.8	38.7	-0.5	39.2	1.3	39.3	0.3	39.3	0.0	39.5	0.5
1971	39.5	0.0	39.3	-0.5	39.6	0.8	39.5	-0.3	40.0	1.3	40.2	0.5	40.3	0.2	40.4	0.2	40.6	0.5	40.7	0.2	40.6	-0.2	40.6	0.0
1972	40.6	0.0	40.7	0.2	41.0	0.7	41.0	0.0	41.1	0.2	41.2	0.2	41.5	0.7	41.6	0.2	41.9	0.7	41.9	0.0	42.1	0.5	42.1	0.0
1973	42.2	0.2	42.5	0.7	42.8	0.7	43.0	0.5	43.1	0.2	43.5	0.9	43.7	0.5	44.3	1.4	44.4	0.2	44.8	0.9	45.2	0.9	45.4	0.4
1974	45.8	0.9	46.1	0.7	46.6	1.1	47.0	0.9	47.5	1.1	47.9	0.8	48.4	1.0	49.0	1.2	49.8	1.6	49.8	0.0	50.3	1.0	50.8	1.0
1975	51.0	0.4	51.5	1.0	52.2	1.4	52.7	1.0	53.1	0.8	53.0	-0.2	53.5	0.9	53.7	0.4	54.3	1.1	54.7	0.7	55.0	0.5	55.4	0.7
1976	55.7	0.5	55.4	-0.5	55.5	0.2	55.5	0.0	56.3	1.4	56.5	0.4	57.1	1.1	57.4	0.5	57.8	0.7	58.0	0.3	58.3	0.5	58.5	0.3
1977	59.2	1.2	59.7	0.8	59.8	0.2	60.2	0.7	60.4	0.3	60.8	0.7	61.1	0.5	61.1	0.0	61.5	0.7	61.5	0.0	61.9	0.7	62.4	0.8
1978	62.8	0.6	63.1	0.5	63.4	0.5	64.2	1.3	64.8	0.9	65.5	1.1	65.8	0.5	66.0	0.3	66.8	1.2	66.9	0.1	67.1	0.3	66.7	-0.6
1979	67.6	1.3	68.3	1.0	69.0	1.0	70.3	1.9	71.4	1.6	72.1	1.0	72.7	0.8	73.6	1.2	74.7	1.5	75.1	0.5	75.9	1.1	77.2	1.7
1980	78.7	1.9	80.4	2.2	81.7	1.6	82.8	1.3	84.3	1.8	84.7	0.5	84.2	-0.6	83.7	-0.6	84.5	1.0	85.5	1.2	86.5	1.2	87.6	1.3
1981	87.8	0.2	88.5	0.8	89.1	0.7	89.9	0.9	90.5	0.7	90.7	0.2	92.1	1.5	93.0	1.0	94.5	1.6	95.2	0.7	95.3	0.1	95.5	0.2
1982	96.7	1.3	96.6	-0.1	96.9	0.3	97.0	0.1	97.2	0.2	98.2	1.0	97.9	-0.3	97.9	0.0	97.5	-0.4	98.0	0.5	97.6	-0.4	96.6	-1.0
1983	96.7	0.1	97.1	0.4	97.2	0.1	98.0	0.8	98.8	0.8	99.4	0.6	99.7	0.3	99.9	0.2	100.3	0.4	100.5	0.2	100.4	-0.1	100.8	0.4
1984	101.2	0.4	101.6	0.4	101.8	0.2	102.5	0.7	103.4	0.9	103.4	0.0	103.5	0.1	104.5	1.0	105.0	0.5	105.5	0.5	105.5	0.0	105.3	-0.2
1985	105.9	0.6	106.3	0.4	106.5	0.2	106.9	0.4	108.0	1.0	108.1	0.1	108.8	0.6	109.6	0.7	109.6	0.0	110.4	0.7	110.0	-0.4	110.4	0.4
1986	110.6	0.2	110.5	-0.1	111.1	0.5	110.6	-0.5	111.5	0.8	112.1	0.5	112.0	-0.1	112.0	0.0	113.3	1.2	113.8	0.4	113.0	-0.7	112.7	-0.3
1987	113.4	0.6	114.7	1.1	115.5	0.7	116.0	0.4	116.8	0.7	116.5	-0.3	116.5	0.0	117.3	0.7	118.0	0.6	118.6	0.5	118.2	-0.3	118.5	0.3
1988	118.9	0.3	119.7	0.7	120.6	0.8	121.1	0.4	122.0	0.7	122.0	0.0	122.1	0.1	122.6	0.4	123.4	0.7	124.0	0.5	124.1	0.1	124.2	0.1
1989	124.6	0.3	125.5	0.7	126.2	0.6	127.2	0.8	128.3	0.9	128.7	0.3	129.0	0.2	128.9	-0.1	130.1	0.9	130.0	-0.1	130.0	0.0	130.6	0.5
1990	132.1	1.1	133.6	1.1	134.5	0.7	134.2	-0.2	134.6	0.3	135.0	0.3	135.6	0.4	136.3	0.5	137.7	1.0	138.7	0.7	138.9	0.1	139.2	0.2
1991	140.0	0.6	139.9	-0.1	139.7	-0.1	140.7	0.7	140.8	0.1	140.8	0.0	141.5	0.5	141.7	0.1	142.6	0.6	142.9	0.2	143.5	0.4	143.1	-0.3
1992	144.3	0.8	144.9	0.4	145.5	0.4	145.8	0.2	146.0	0.1	146.2	0.1	146.7	0.3	146.9	0.1	147.4	0.3	148.4	0.7	148.2	-0.1	148.2	0.0
1993	149.2	0.7	150.0	0.5	149.8	-0.1	149.9	0.1	150.1	0.1	149.7	-0.3	149.8	0.1	149.9	0.1	150.2	0.2	150.9	0.5	151.6	0.5	151.9	0.2

Source: U.S. Department of Labor, Bureau of Labor Statistics, Division of Consumer Prices and Price Indexes. - indicates no data collected for period.

Los Angeles, CA

Consumer Price Index - Urban Wage Earners
Base 1982-1984 = 100
All Items

For 1914-1993. Columns headed % show percentile change in the index from the previous period for which an index is available.

Year	Jan Index	%	Feb Index	%	Mar Index	%	Apr Index	%	May Index	%	Jun Index	%	Jul Index	%	Aug Index	%	Sep Index	%	Oct Index	%	Nov Index	%	Dec Index	%
1914	-	-	-	-	-	-	-	-	-	-	-	-	-	-	-	-	-	-	-	-	-	-	10.2	-
1915	-	-	-	-	-	-	-	-	-	-	-	-	-	-	-	-	-	-	-	-	-	-	10.0	-2.0
1916	-	-	-	-	-	-	-	-	-	-	-	-	-	-	-	-	-	-	-	-	-	-	11.0	10.0
1917	-	-	-	-	-	-	-	-	-	-	-	-	-	-	-	-	-	-	-	-	-	-	13.0	18.2
1918	-	-	-	-	-	-	-	-	-	-	-	-	-	-	-	-	-	-	-	-	-	-	15.8	21.5
1919	-	-	-	-	-	-	-	-	-	-	16.4	3.8	-	-	-	-	-	-	-	-	-	-	18.6	13.4
1920	-	-	-	-	-	-	-	-	-	-	20.4	9.7	-	-	-	-	-	-	-	-	-	-	19.9	-2.5
1921	-	-	-	-	-	-	-	-	18.5	-7.0	-	-	-	-	-	-	18.3	-1.1	-	-	-	-	18.4	0.5
1922	-	-	-	-	-	-	-	-	-	-	18.1	-0.5	-	-	-	-	18.0	-0.6	-	-	-	-	18.1	0.6
1923	-	-	-	-	18.2	-1.1	-	-	-	-	18.3	1.7	-	-	-	-	18.5	1.1	-	-	-	-	18.6	0.5
1924	-	-	-	-	18.0	-0.6	-	-	-	-	18.3	-1.1	-	-	-	-	18.4	0.5	-	-	-	-	18.2	-1.1
1925	-	-	-	-	18.5	-0.5	-	-	-	-	18.5	1.6	-	-	-	-	-	-	-	-	-	-	18.5	0.0
1926	-	-	-	-	-	-	-	-	-	-	17.8	-3.8	-	-	-	-	-	-	-	-	-	-	17.8	0.0
1927	-	-	-	-	-	-	-	-	-	-	17.8	0.0	-	-	-	-	-	-	-	-	-	-	17.5	-1.7
1928	-	-	-	-	-	-	-	-	-	-	17.2	-1.7	-	-	-	-	-	-	-	-	-	-	17.4	1.2
1929	-	-	-	-	-	-	-	-	-	-	17.2	-1.1	-	-	-	-	-	-	-	-	-	-	17.2	0.0
1930	-	-	-	-	-	-	-	-	-	-	16.7	-2.9	-	-	-	-	-	-	-	-	-	-	16.0	-4.2
1931	-	-	-	-	-	-	-	-	-	-	14.9	-6.9	-	-	-	-	-	-	-	-	-	-	14.6	-2.0
1932	-	-	-	-	-	-	-	-	-	-	13.6	-6.8	-	-	-	-	-	-	-	-	-	-	13.1	-3.7
1933	-	-	-	-	-	-	-	-	-	-	12.5	-4.6	-	-	-	-	-	-	-	-	-	-	13.0	4.0
1934	-	-	-	-	-	-	-	-	-	-	12.9	-0.8	-	-	-	-	-	-	-	-	13.3	3.1	-	-
1935	-	-	-	-	13.6	2.3	-	-	-	-	-	-	13.2	-2.9	-	-	-	-	13.1	-0.8	-	-	-	-
1936	13.4	2.3	-	-	-	-	-	-	13.2	-1.5	-	-	13.4	1.5	-	-	13.7	2.2	-	-	-	-	13.7	0.0
1937	-	-	-	-	14.3	4.4	-	-	-	-	14.2	-0.7	-	-	-	-	14.4	1.4	-	-	-	-	14.3	-0.7
1938	-	-	-	-	14.0	-2.1	-	-	-	-	14.0	0.0	-	-	-	-	14.0	0.0	-	-	-	-	14.1	0.7
1939	-	-	-	-	14.0	-0.7	-	-	-	-	13.8	-1.4	-	-	-	-	14.1	2.2	-	-	-	-	13.9	-1.4
1940	-	-	-	-	13.9	0.0	-	-	-	-	13.9	0.0	-	-	-	-	14.0	0.7	14.0	0.0	14.1	0.7	14.1	0.0
1941	14.2	0.7	14.0	-1.4	14.1	0.7	14.3	1.4	14.4	0.7	14.6	1.4	14.6	0.0	14.7	0.7	15.0	2.0	15.2	1.3	15.3	0.7	15.5	1.3
1942	15.7	1.3	15.8	0.6	16.1	1.9	16.2	0.6	16.3	0.6	16.4	0.6	16.6	1.2	16.7	0.6	16.8	0.6	17.0	1.2	17.1	0.6	17.1	0.0
1943	17.1	0.0	17.0	-0.6	17.2	1.2	17.4	1.2	17.4	0.0	17.4	0.0	17.3	-0.6	17.2	-0.6	17.7	0.6	17.8	0.6	17.8	0.0	17.9	0.6
1944	17.4	-0.6	17.4	0.0	17.4	0.0	17.4	0.0	17.6	1.1	17.5	-0.6	17.5	0.0	17.6	0.6	17.7	0.6	17.8	0.6	17.8	0.0	17.9	0.6
1945	17.9	0.0	17.8	-0.6	17.9	0.6	18.0	0.6	18.0	0.0	18.0	0.0	18.1	0.6	18.1	0.0	18.3	1.1	18.3	0.0	18.4	0.5	18.5	0.5
1946	18.4	-0.5	18.4	0.0	18.4	0.0	18.5	0.5	18.6	0.5	18.8	1.1	19.7	4.8	20.0	1.5	20.1	0.5	20.5	2.0	21.4	4.4	21.4	0.0
1947	21.5	0.5	21.6	0.5	21.7	0.5	21.8	0.5	21.8	0.0	21.7	-0.5	21.8	0.5	21.9	0.5	22.4	2.3	22.4	0.0	22.8	1.8	23.0	0.9
1948	23.2	0.9	23.3	0.4	23.2	-0.4	23.5	1.3	23.5	0.0	23.5	0.0	23.7	0.9	23.8	0.4	23.8	0.0	23.9	0.4	24.0	0.4	24.1	0.4
1949	24.1	0.0	23.9	-0.8	23.9	0.0	23.9	0.0	23.7	-0.8	23.6	-0.4	23.3	-1.3	23.3	0.0	23.3	0.0	23.3	0.0	23.3	0.0	23.2	-0.4
1950	23.4	0.9	23.3	-0.4	23.3	0.0	23.4	0.4	23.4	0.0	23.3	-0.4	23.5	0.9	23.8	1.3	23.9	0.4	24.1	0.8	24.3	0.8	24.6	1.2
1951	25.0	1.6	25.4	1.6	25.6	0.8	25.6	0.0	25.7	0.4	25.7	0.0	25.8	0.4	25.8	0.0	25.9	0.4	25.9	0.0	26.2	1.2	26.3	0.4
1952	26.3	0.0	26.3	0.0	26.4	0.4	26.4	0.0	26.4	0.0	26.5	0.4	26.5	0.0	26.5	0.0	26.5	0.0	26.5	0.0	26.6	0.4	26.6	0.0
1953	26.6	0.0	26.5	-0.4	26.6	0.4	26.7	0.4	26.6	-0.4	26.6	0.0	26.7	0.4	26.7	0.0	26.8	0.4	26.8	0.0	26.8	0.0	26.7	-0.4
1954	27.0	1.1	26.9	-0.4	26.8	-0.4	26.7	-0.4	26.7	0.0	26.7	0.0	26.5	-0.7	26.6	0.4	26.6	0.0	26.5	-0.4	26.5	0.0	26.6	0.4
1955	26.6	0.0	26.5	-0.4	26.6	0.4	26.4	-0.8	26.6	0.8	26.6	0.0	26.7	0.4	26.6	-0.4	26.8	0.8	26.8	0.0	26.8	0.0	26.8	0.0
1956	26.8	0.0	26.7	-0.4	26.8	0.4	26.8	0.0	27.0	0.7	27.1	0.4	27.2	0.4	27.1	-0.4	27.2	0.4	27.3	0.4	27.5	0.7	27.5	0.0
1957	27.6	0.4	27.8	0.7	27.8	0.0	27.8	0.0	27.9	0.4	27.9	0.0	27.9	0.0	28.0	0.4	28.2	0.7	28.2	0.0	28.4	0.7	28.4	0.0
1958	28.6	0.7	28.6	0.0	28.8	0.7	29.0	0.7	28.9	-0.3	28.9	0.0	29.0	0.3	28.9	-0.3	29.1	0.7	29.1	0.0	29.2	0.3	29.2	0.0

[Continued]

Los Angeles, CA

Consumer Price Index - Urban Wage Earners
Base 1982-1984 = 100

All Items

[Continued]

For 1914-1993. Columns headed % show percentile change in the index from the previous period for which an index is available.

Year	Jan Index	%	Feb Index	%	Mar Index	%	Apr Index	%	May Index	%	Jun Index	%	Jul Index	%	Aug Index	%	Sep Index	%	Oct Index	%	Nov Index	%	Dec Index	%
1959	29.2	0.0	29.2	0.0	29.2	0.0	29.2	0.0	29.3	0.3	29.3	0.0	29.4	0.3	29.4	0.0	29.5	0.3	29.6	0.3	29.7	0.3	29.7	0.0
1960	29.8	0.3	29.7	-0.3	29.8	0.3	30.0	0.7	29.9	-0.3	29.9	0.0	29.9	0.0	29.8	-0.3	29.9	0.3	30.1	0.7	30.1	0.0	30.3	0.7
1961	30.3	0.0	30.3	0.0	30.2	-0.3	30.3	0.3	30.3	0.0	30.3	0.0	30.3	0.0	30.3	0.0	30.3	0.0	30.4	0.3	30.5	0.3	30.5	0.0
1962	30.4	-0.3	30.4	0.0	30.5	0.3	30.6	0.3	30.8	0.7	30.8	0.0	30.7	-0.3	30.7	0.0	30.9	0.7	30.9	0.0	30.8	-0.3	30.9	0.3
1963	30.9	0.0	31.0	0.3	31.0	0.0	31.1	0.3	31.0	-0.3	30.9	-0.3	31.1	0.6	31.2	0.3	31.2	0.0	31.4	0.6	31.4	0.0	31.3	-0.3
1964	31.5	0.6	31.4	-0.3	31.6	0.6	31.6	0.0	31.6	0.0	31.6	0.0	31.6	0.0	31.7	0.3	31.6	-0.3	31.9	0.9	32.0	0.3	32.0	0.0
1965	32.1	0.3	32.2	0.3	32.3	0.3	32.4	0.3	32.4	0.0	32.5	0.3	32.4	-0.3	32.1	-0.9	32.5	1.2	32.4	-0.3	32.5	0.3	32.6	0.3
1966	32.5	-0.3	32.6	0.3	32.7	0.3	32.9	0.6	32.9	0.0	33.0	0.3	33.1	0.3	33.0	-0.3	33.3	0.9	33.4	0.3	33.5	0.3	33.5	0.0
1967	33.3	-0.6	33.3	0.0	33.2	-0.3	33.5	0.9	33.6	0.3	33.7	0.3	33.8	0.3	34.0	0.6	34.3	0.9	34.2	-0.3	34.5	0.9	34.5	0.0
1968	34.7	0.6	34.7	0.0	34.9	0.6	34.9	0.0	34.8	-0.3	35.1	0.9	35.2	0.3	35.3	0.3	35.3	0.0	35.6	0.8	35.7	0.3	35.7	0.0
1969	35.9	0.6	36.0	0.3	36.4	1.1	36.5	0.3	36.5	0.0	36.8	0.8	37.0	0.5	37.1	0.3	37.3	0.5	37.4	0.3	37.4	0.0	37.7	0.8
1970	37.8	0.3	37.9	0.3	38.0	0.3	38.4	1.1	38.5	0.3	38.5	0.0	38.9	1.0	38.6	-0.8	39.2	1.6	39.3	0.3	39.3	0.0	39.5	0.5
1971	39.5	0.0	39.3	-0.5	39.6	0.8	39.5	-0.3	40.0	1.3	40.2	0.5	40.3	0.2	40.4	0.2	40.6	0.5	40.7	0.2	40.6	-0.2	40.6	0.0
1972	40.6	0.0	40.7	0.2	41.0	0.7	41.0	0.0	41.0	0.0	41.1	0.2	41.5	1.0	41.6	0.2	41.9	0.7	41.9	0.0	42.1	0.5	42.1	0.0
1973	42.2	0.2	42.5	0.7	42.8	0.7	42.9	0.2	43.1	0.5	43.5	0.9	43.7	0.5	44.3	1.4	44.4	0.2	44.8	0.9	45.2	0.9	45.4	0.4
1974	45.7	0.7	46.1	0.9	46.6	1.1	47.0	0.9	47.5	1.1	47.8	0.6	48.4	1.3	49.0	1.2	49.7	1.4	49.8	0.2	50.3	1.0	50.8	1.0
1975	51.0	0.4	51.5	1.0	52.2	1.4	52.7	1.0	53.1	0.8	53.0	-0.2	53.5	0.9	53.7	0.4	54.3	1.1	54.6	0.6	55.0	0.7	55.4	0.7
1976	55.7	0.5	55.4	-0.5	55.5	0.2	55.5	0.0	56.3	1.4	56.5	0.4	57.1	1.1	57.4	0.5	57.8	0.7	58.0	0.3	58.2	0.3	58.5	0.5
1977	59.1	1.0	59.7	1.0	59.8	0.2	60.2	0.7	60.4	0.3	60.7	0.5	61.0	0.5	61.1	0.2	61.4	0.5	61.4	0.0	61.9	0.8	62.4	0.8
1978	62.8	0.6	63.2	0.6	63.3	0.2	63.9	0.9	64.7	1.3	65.3	0.9	65.7	0.6	65.9	0.3	66.6	1.1	66.7	0.2	66.8	0.1	66.7	-0.1
1979	67.6	1.3	68.5	1.3	69.2	1.0	70.7	2.2	71.9	1.7	72.6	1.0	73.4	1.1	74.3	1.2	75.5	1.6	75.8	0.4	76.4	0.8	77.8	1.8
1980	79.5	2.2	81.2	2.1	82.5	1.6	83.8	1.6	85.5	2.0	85.7	0.2	85.1	-0.7	84.6	-0.6	85.3	0.8	86.3	1.2	87.4	1.3	88.7	1.5
1981	88.9	0.2	89.7	0.9	90.2	0.6	91.1	1.0	91.6	0.5	91.9	0.3	93.5	1.7	94.3	0.9	95.7	1.5	96.4	0.7	96.5	0.1	96.7	0.2
1982	98.0	1.3	97.9	-0.1	98.2	0.3	98.2	0.0	98.3	0.1	99.4	1.1	99.1	-0.3	99.1	0.0	98.7	-0.4	99.1	0.4	98.7	-0.4	97.5	-1.2
1983	97.5	0.0	98.2	0.7	98.0	-0.2	98.2	0.2	98.8	0.6	98.8	0.0	99.2	0.4	99.4	0.2	100.4	1.0	101.2	0.8	100.8	-0.4	101.5	0.7
1984	100.8	-0.7	101.2	0.4	100.8	-0.4	101.1	0.3	102.6	1.5	102.7	0.1	101.6	-1.1	103.2	1.6	102.9	-0.3	102.4	-0.5	102.9	0.5	103.7	0.8
1985	104.3	0.6	104.6	0.3	104.8	0.2	105.3	0.5	106.3	0.9	106.3	0.0	106.9	0.6	107.6	0.7	107.5	-0.1	108.3	0.7	108.0	-0.3	108.3	0.3
1986	108.6	0.3	108.4	-0.2	108.8	0.4	108.3	-0.5	109.2	0.8	109.8	0.5	109.6	-0.2	109.5	-0.1	110.6	1.0	111.1	0.5	110.4	-0.6	110.1	-0.3
1987	110.8	0.6	112.1	1.2	112.8	0.6	113.3	0.4	114.1	0.7	113.8	-0.3	113.8	0.0	114.6	0.7	115.2	0.5	115.8	0.5	115.4	-0.3	115.7	0.3
1988	115.9	0.2	116.6	0.6	117.5	0.8	118.0	0.4	118.9	0.8	118.9	0.0	119.0	0.1	119.5	0.4	120.3	0.7	121.0	0.6	120.9	-0.1	121.1	0.2
1989	121.4	0.2	122.3	0.7	122.9	0.5	124.0	0.9	125.0	0.8	125.3	0.2	125.7	0.3	125.5	-0.2	126.5	0.8	126.5	0.0	126.4	-0.1	127.0	0.5
1990	128.5	1.2	129.8	1.0	130.5	0.5	130.2	-0.2	130.7	0.4	131.1	0.3	131.6	0.4	132.3	0.5	133.5	0.9	134.5	0.7	134.8	0.2	135.2	0.3
1991	135.8	0.4	135.5	-0.2	135.3	-0.1	136.3	0.7	136.5	0.1	136.4	-0.1	137.3	0.7	137.4	0.1	138.2	0.6	138.5	0.2	139.0	0.4	138.6	-0.3
1992	139.6	0.7	140.3	0.5	141.0	0.5	141.3	0.2	141.4	0.1	141.8	0.3	142.2	0.3	142.4	0.1	142.8	0.3	143.6	0.6	143.5	-0.1	143.5	0.0
1993	144.4	0.6	145.0	0.4	144.8	-0.1	144.9	0.1	145.1	0.1	144.8	-0.2	144.8	0.0	144.9	0.1	145.0	0.1	145.7	0.5	146.4	0.5	146.7	0.2

Source: U.S. Department of Labor, Bureau of Labor Statistics, Division of Consumer Prices and Price Indexes. - indicates no data collected for period.

Los Angeles, CA
Consumer Price Index - All Urban Consumers
Base 1982-1984 = 100
Food and Beverages

For 1976-1993. Columns headed % show percentile change in the index from the previous period for which an index is available.

Year	Jan Index	%	Feb Index	%	Mar Index	%	Apr Index	%	May Index	%	Jun Index	%	Jul Index	%	Aug Index	%	Sep Index	%	Oct Index	%	Nov Index	%	Dec Index	%
1976	60.6	-	59.8	-1.3	59.5	-0.5	59.5	0.0	60.2	1.2	60.4	0.3	61.0	1.0	61.0	0.0	60.6	-0.7	60.7	0.2	61.0	0.5	61.5	0.8
1977	62.3	1.3	62.9	1.0	63.3	0.6	63.9	0.9	64.3	0.6	64.9	0.9	65.2	0.5	65.4	0.3	65.5	0.2	65.7	0.3	66.1	0.6	66.6	0.8
1978	67.6	1.5	68.4	1.2	69.2	1.2	70.7	2.2	71.1	0.6	72.2	1.5	72.3	0.1	72.6	0.4	73.1	0.7	73.7	0.8	73.8	0.1	74.6	1.1
1979	75.9	1.7	77.2	1.7	77.9	0.9	79.0	1.4	79.9	1.1	79.6	-0.4	79.2	-0.5	79.1	-0.1	79.7	0.8	80.3	0.8	80.9	0.7	82.0	1.4
1980	82.5	0.6	82.4	-0.1	83.4	1.2	84.1	0.8	84.5	0.5	84.9	0.5	85.6	0.8	86.9	1.5	88.3	1.6	88.3	0.0	88.7	0.5	89.2	0.6
1981	89.7	0.6	91.3	1.8	91.9	0.7	92.2	0.3	92.3	0.1	92.4	0.1	92.7	0.3	93.4	0.8	93.4	0.0	93.5	0.1	93.1	-0.4	93.9	0.9
1982	95.0	1.2	95.4	0.4	95.7	0.3	95.8	0.1	96.5	0.7	96.7	0.2	97.6	0.9	97.5	-0.1	97.5	0.0	98.2	0.7	98.4	0.2	97.8	-0.6
1983	98.9	1.1	99.2	0.3	100.1	0.9	100.5	0.4	101.1	0.6	100.2	-0.9	100.0	-0.2	99.9	-0.1	99.9	0.0	100.4	0.5	100.1	-0.3	100.8	0.7
1984	102.3	1.5	102.6	0.3	102.9	0.3	102.6	-0.3	102.3	-0.3	102.0	-0.3	102.9	0.9	103.6	0.7	103.6	0.0	103.7	0.1	104.1	0.4	104.2	0.1
1985	105.0	0.8	105.2	0.2	104.8	-0.4	104.9	0.1	105.4	0.5	105.4	0.0	104.8	-0.6	105.2	0.4	105.5	0.3	105.9	0.4	106.8	0.8	107.9	1.0
1986	108.3	0.4	107.8	-0.5	107.8	0.0	107.7	-0.1	108.1	0.4	108.4	0.3	108.4	0.0	108.9	0.5	108.8	-0.1	109.3	0.5	110.3	0.9	110.5	0.2
1987	112.3	1.6	113.7	1.2	112.8	-0.8	112.9	0.1	113.6	0.6	113.0	-0.5	112.8	-0.2	113.2	0.4	113.4	0.2	113.6	0.2	113.3	-0.3	114.0	0.6
1988	114.6	0.5	114.8	0.2	115.4	0.5	116.0	0.5	116.2	0.2	116.2	0.0	117.8	1.4	118.8	0.8	118.8	0.0	119.1	0.3	119.1	0.0	120.0	0.8
1989	121.5	1.3	122.2	0.6	122.8	0.5	123.6	0.7	124.1	0.4	123.5	-0.5	123.6	0.1	124.1	0.4	124.6	0.4	125.2	0.5	126.1	0.7	126.8	0.6
1990	129.6	2.2	130.9	1.0	130.6	-0.2	130.1	-0.4	130.4	0.2	130.5	0.1	130.6	0.1	130.7	0.1	131.0	0.2	131.5	0.4	132.5	0.8	132.7	0.2
1991	135.9	2.4	135.6	-0.2	135.7	0.1	137.4	1.3	137.0	-0.3	137.3	0.2	136.9	-0.3	135.8	-0.8	135.6	-0.1	136.3	0.5	137.3	0.7	138.0	0.5
1992	139.4	1.0	139.5	0.1	141.1	1.1	140.9	-0.1	139.6	-0.9	140.3	0.5	140.1	-0.1	141.0	0.6	142.2	0.9	142.7	0.4	142.3	-0.3	142.2	-0.1
1993	144.2	1.4	143.4	-0.6	143.9	0.3	144.6	0.5	145.4	0.6	144.9	-0.3	144.3	-0.4	144.3	0.0	145.1	0.6	146.2	0.8	146.4	0.1	148.6	1.5

Source: U.S. Department of Labor, Bureau of Labor Statistics, Division of Consumer Prices and Price Indexes. - indicates no data collected for period.

Los Angeles, CA
Consumer Price Index - Urban Wage Earners
Base 1982-1984 = 100
Food and Beverages

For 1976-1993. Columns headed % show percentile change in the index from the previous period for which an index is available.

Year	Jan Index	%	Feb Index	%	Mar Index	%	Apr Index	%	May Index	%	Jun Index	%	Jul Index	%	Aug Index	%	Sep Index	%	Oct Index	%	Nov Index	%	Dec Index	%
1976	59.5	-	58.7	-1.3	58.4	-0.5	58.5	0.2	59.1	1.0	59.3	0.3	59.9	1.0	59.9	0.0	59.5	-0.7	59.7	0.3	59.9	0.3	60.4	0.8
1977	61.2	1.3	61.8	1.0	62.1	0.5	62.8	1.1	63.1	0.5	63.8	1.1	64.1	0.5	64.3	0.3	64.3	0.0	64.5	0.3	64.9	0.6	65.4	0.8
1978	66.5	1.7	67.4	1.4	67.7	0.4	68.9	1.8	69.6	1.0	70.4	1.1	70.7	0.4	70.9	0.3	71.4	0.7	71.8	0.6	71.7	-0.1	72.6	1.3
1979	73.9	1.8	75.3	1.9	76.6	1.7	77.5	1.2	78.1	0.8	78.4	0.4	78.3	-0.1	78.3	0.0	79.0	0.9	79.5	0.6	79.7	0.3	80.9	1.5
1980	81.3	0.5	81.4	0.1	82.3	1.1	83.5	1.5	83.9	0.5	84.3	0.5	85.1	0.9	86.4	1.5	88.0	1.9	87.9	-0.1	88.7	0.9	89.1	0.5
1981	89.6	0.6	90.8	1.3	91.5	0.8	91.8	0.3	91.5	-0.3	92.2	0.8	92.5	0.3	93.3	0.9	93.1	-0.2	92.9	-0.2	92.8	-0.1	93.7	1.0
1982	94.9	1.3	95.4	0.5	95.7	0.3	95.9	0.2	96.4	0.5	96.6	0.2	97.4	0.8	97.4	0.0	97.3	-0.1	98.1	0.8	98.3	0.2	97.8	-0.5
1983	98.9	1.1	99.3	0.4	100.2	0.9	100.6	0.4	101.2	0.6	100.3	-0.9	100.0	-0.3	100.0	0.0	99.9	-0.1	100.5	0.6	100.2	-0.3	100.9	0.7
1984	102.4	1.5	102.8	0.4	103.1	0.3	102.7	-0.4	102.3	-0.4	102.0	-0.3	102.9	0.9	103.5	0.6	103.5	0.0	103.6	0.1	103.9	0.3	104.1	0.2
1985	104.8	0.7	105.0	0.2	104.7	-0.3	104.8	0.1	105.2	0.4	105.2	0.0	104.6	-0.6	105.0	0.4	105.3	0.3	105.7	0.4	106.6	0.9	107.6	0.9
1986	108.1	0.5	107.6	-0.5	107.6	0.0	107.6	0.0	107.8	0.2	108.1	0.3	108.1	0.0	108.5	0.4	108.5	0.0	109.1	0.6	110.1	0.9	110.3	0.2
1987	112.0	1.5	113.4	1.3	112.5	-0.8	112.7	0.2	113.4	0.6	112.7	-0.6	112.6	-0.1	113.1	0.4	113.2	0.1	113.5	0.3	113.2	-0.3	113.9	0.6
1988	114.3	0.4	114.6	0.3	115.2	0.5	115.9	0.6	116.1	0.2	116.1	0.0	117.7	1.4	118.7	0.8	118.6	-0.1	119.0	0.3	119.0	0.0	119.9	0.8
1989	121.3	1.2	122.0	0.6	122.6	0.5	123.4	0.7	123.9	0.4	123.3	-0.5	123.5	0.2	124.1	0.5	124.6	0.4	125.1	0.4	126.1	0.8	126.9	0.6
1990	129.6	2.1	130.9	1.0	130.7	-0.2	130.2	-0.4	130.4	0.2	130.6	0.2	130.8	0.2	130.9	0.1	131.1	0.2	131.6	0.4	132.6	0.8	132.8	0.2
1991	136.0	2.4	135.7	-0.2	136.0	0.2	137.6	1.2	137.2	-0.3	137.5	0.2	137.2	-0.2	136.2	-0.7	135.9	-0.2	136.7	0.6	137.5	0.6	138.2	0.5
1992	139.6	1.0	139.8	0.1	141.6	1.3	141.4	-0.1	140.0	-1.0	140.7	0.5	140.6	-0.1	141.4	0.6	142.5	0.8	143.1	0.4	142.8	-0.2	142.7	-0.1
1993	144.6	1.3	143.8	-0.6	144.3	0.3	145.0	0.5	145.9	0.6	145.5	-0.3	144.8	-0.5	144.9	0.1	145.7	0.6	146.8	0.8	146.9	0.1	149.0	1.4

Source: U.S. Department of Labor, Bureau of Labor Statistics, Division of Consumer Prices and Price Indexes. - indicates no data collected for period.

Los Angeles, CA
Consumer Price Index - All Urban Consumers
Base 1982-1984 = 100
Housing

For 1976-1993. Columns headed % show percentile change in the index from the previous period for which an index is available.

Year	Jan Index	%	Feb Index	%	Mar Index	%	Apr Index	%	May Index	%	Jun Index	%	Jul Index	%	Aug Index	%	Sep Index	%	Oct Index	%	Nov Index	%	Dec Index	%
1976	53.9	-	53.2	-1.3	53.1	-0.2	52.9	-0.4	53.9	1.9	53.8	-0.2	54.4	1.1	54.7	0.6	55.4	1.3	55.7	0.5	55.7	0.0	56.0	0.5
1977	57.1	2.0	57.5	0.7	57.5	0.0	57.8	0.5	58.0	0.3	58.1	0.2	58.6	0.9	58.5	-0.2	59.1	1.0	58.8	-0.5	59.6	1.4	60.5	1.5
1978	60.9	0.7	61.2	0.5	61.4	0.3	62.2	1.3	62.9	1.1	63.5	1.0	63.8	0.5	64.0	0.3	65.1	1.7	65.0	-0.2	64.9	-0.2	63.7	-1.8
1979	64.7	1.6	65.6	1.4	66.1	0.8	67.4	2.0	68.6	1.8	69.4	1.2	70.1	1.0	71.3	1.7	72.6	1.8	73.0	0.6	74.1	1.5	75.9	2.4
1980	77.7	2.4	79.6	2.4	81.2	2.0	82.7	1.8	85.6	3.5	86.2	0.7	84.7	-1.7	83.0	-2.0	83.4	0.5	85.2	2.2	86.6	1.6	88.4	2.1
1981	88.4	0.0	88.6	0.2	88.8	0.2	89.6	0.9	90.4	0.9	90.3	-0.1	92.3	2.2	93.4	1.2	96.2	3.0	97.0	0.8	96.7	-0.3	96.7	0.0
1982	97.9	1.2	97.5	-0.4	98.3	0.8	98.4	0.1	98.3	-0.1	99.4	1.1	98.1	-1.3	98.0	-0.1	97.5	-0.5	97.8	0.3	97.0	-0.8	95.3	-1.8
1983	95.4	0.1	96.6	1.3	96.5	-0.1	97.0	0.5	97.8	0.8	98.4	0.6	98.7	0.3	99.1	0.4	100.2	1.1	100.4	0.2	100.0	-0.4	99.9	-0.1
1984	99.9	0.0	101.2	1.3	101.5	0.3	102.2	0.7	103.7	1.5	104.3	0.6	104.7	0.4	105.8	1.1	106.3	0.5	106.1	-0.2	105.6	-0.5	105.3	-0.3
1985	106.6	1.2	107.0	0.4	106.4	-0.6	106.6	0.2	109.1	2.3	108.4	-0.6	110.6	2.0	112.7	1.9	112.3	-0.4	113.5	1.1	111.7	-1.6	111.6	-0.1
1986	111.6	0.0	112.6	0.9	114.9	2.0	114.0	-0.8	115.4	1.2	115.9	0.4	116.9	0.9	117.2	0.3	120.0	2.4	120.4	0.3	117.5	-2.4	116.8	-0.6
1987	116.7	-0.1	118.3	1.4	119.5	1.0	120.4	0.8	121.6	1.0	120.7	-0.7	121.1	0.3	122.2	0.9	122.8	0.5	123.6	0.7	122.7	-0.7	122.9	0.2
1988	123.0	0.1	124.5	1.2	125.2	0.6	125.4	0.2	126.8	1.1	126.6	-0.2	126.4	-0.2	127.1	0.6	128.2	0.9	128.7	0.4	128.9	0.2	128.9	0.0
1989	128.7	-0.2	129.2	0.4	128.8	-0.3	128.6	-0.2	130.4	1.4	131.7	1.0	133.0	1.0	133.0	0.0	134.6	1.2	134.5	-0.1	134.0	-0.4	134.3	0.2
1990	135.8	1.1	136.7	0.7	138.1	1.0	137.1	-0.7	137.8	0.5	138.5	0.5	139.9	1.0	140.8	0.6	141.5	0.5	142.0	0.4	141.3	-0.5	141.5	0.1
1991	142.8	0.9	143.4	0.4	143.9	0.3	144.7	0.6	144.5	-0.1	144.4	-0.1	145.4	0.7	145.6	0.1	146.0	0.3	145.9	-0.1	146.3	0.3	146.1	-0.1
1992	147.0	0.6	147.7	0.5	147.9	0.1	147.9	0.0	148.1	0.1	148.8	0.5	149.0	0.1	149.3	0.2	149.2	-0.1	149.5	0.2	149.4	-0.1	148.9	-0.3
1993	149.9	0.7	150.8	0.6	150.0	-0.5	150.4	0.3	150.6	0.1	150.6	0.0	150.7	0.1	150.7	0.0	149.8	-0.6	150.2	0.3	150.4	0.1	151.0	0.4

Source: U.S. Department of Labor, Bureau of Labor Statistics, Division of Consumer Prices and Price Indexes. - indicates no data collected for period.

Los Angeles, CA
Consumer Price Index - Urban Wage Earners
Base 1982-1984 = 100
Housing

For 1976-1993. Columns headed % show percentile change in the index from the previous period for which an index is available.

Year	Jan Index	%	Feb Index	%	Mar Index	%	Apr Index	%	May Index	%	Jun Index	%	Jul Index	%	Aug Index	%	Sep Index	%	Oct Index	%	Nov Index	%	Dec Index	%
1976	54.0	-	53.3	-1.3	53.1	-0.4	53.0	-0.2	54.0	1.9	53.9	-0.2	54.5	1.1	54.8	0.6	55.4	1.1	55.8	0.7	55.8	0.0	56.0	0.4
1977	57.2	2.1	57.6	0.7	57.5	-0.2	57.9	0.7	58.0	0.2	58.2	0.3	58.6	0.7	58.6	0.0	59.1	0.9	58.9	-0.3	59.7	1.4	60.6	1.5
1978	61.0	0.7	61.3	0.5	61.6	0.5	62.3	1.1	62.9	1.0	63.5	1.0	63.9	0.6	64.1	0.3	65.1	1.6	64.9	-0.3	64.8	-0.2	63.8	-1.5
1979	64.9	1.7	65.9	1.5	66.5	0.9	68.0	2.3	69.4	2.1	70.1	1.0	70.8	1.0	72.3	2.1	73.7	1.9	74.0	0.4	75.1	1.5	76.9	2.4
1980	79.2	3.0	81.2	2.5	82.9	2.1	84.4	1.8	87.6	3.8	88.1	0.6	86.4	-1.9	84.6	-2.1	84.7	0.1	86.6	2.2	88.2	1.8	90.3	2.4
1981	90.3	0.0	90.4	0.1	90.7	0.3	91.7	1.1	92.5	0.9	92.4	-0.1	95.1	2.9	96.2	1.2	99.1	3.0	99.9	0.8	99.5	-0.4	99.6	0.1
1982	100.9	1.3	100.3	-0.6	101.1	0.8	101.2	0.1	101.0	-0.2	102.2	1.2	100.7	-1.5	100.6	-0.1	100.0	-0.6	100.3	0.3	99.3	-1.0	97.4	-1.9
1983	97.3	-0.1	98.9	1.6	98.4	-0.5	97.6	-0.8	97.9	0.3	97.3	-0.6	97.7	0.4	98.0	0.3	100.3	2.3	101.7	1.4	100.9	-0.8	101.4	0.5
1984	99.1	-2.3	100.2	1.1	99.2	-1.0	99.1	-0.1	101.6	2.5	102.3	0.7	100.2	-2.1	102.8	2.6	101.6	-1.2	99.2	-2.4	100.2	1.0	102.0	1.8
1985	103.2	1.2	103.6	0.4	103.0	-0.6	103.2	0.2	105.8	2.5	104.9	-0.9	107.0	2.0	109.1	2.0	108.7	-0.4	109.8	1.0	108.1	-1.5	107.9	-0.2
1986	107.9	0.0	108.9	0.9	111.2	2.1	110.3	-0.8	111.7	1.3	112.2	0.4	113.1	0.8	113.4	0.3	116.1	2.4	116.5	0.3	113.6	-2.5	113.0	-0.5
1987	112.9	-0.1	114.4	1.3	115.4	0.9	116.3	0.8	117.6	1.1	116.7	-0.8	117.1	0.3	118.2	0.9	118.7	0.4	119.4	0.6	118.6	-0.7	118.9	0.3
1988	118.9	0.0	120.1	1.0	121.0	0.7	121.1	0.1	122.5	1.2	122.3	-0.2	122.1	-0.2	122.6	0.4	123.9	1.1	124.5	0.5	124.5	0.0	124.5	0.0
1989	124.2	-0.2	124.7	0.4	124.2	-0.4	124.1	-0.1	125.8	1.4	127.0	1.0	128.4	1.1	128.3	-0.1	129.7	1.1	129.7	0.0	129.1	-0.5	129.4	0.2
1990	130.9	1.2	131.7	0.6	133.0	1.0	132.0	-0.8	132.8	0.6	133.4	0.5	134.8	1.0	135.5	0.5	136.2	0.5	136.8	0.4	136.1	-0.5	136.3	0.1
1991	137.5	0.9	138.1	0.4	138.5	0.3	139.4	0.6	139.2	-0.1	139.1	-0.1	140.1	0.7	140.2	0.1	140.7	0.4	140.7	0.0	141.0	0.2	140.7	-0.2
1992	141.4	0.5	142.2	0.6	142.4	0.1	142.4	0.0	142.5	0.1	143.2	0.5	143.3	0.1	143.6	0.2	143.5	-0.1	143.9	0.3	143.8	-0.1	143.4	-0.3
1993	144.4	0.7	145.1	0.5	144.3	-0.6	144.7	0.3	144.9	0.1	144.9	0.0	144.9	0.0	145.0	0.1	144.1	-0.6	144.5	0.3	144.9	0.3	145.4	0.3

Source: U.S. Department of Labor, Bureau of Labor Statistics, Division of Consumer Prices and Price Indexes. - indicates no data collected for period.

Los Angeles, CA
Consumer Price Index - All Urban Consumers
Base 1982-1984 = 100
Apparel and Upkeep

For 1952-1993. Columns headed % show percentile change in the index from the previous period for which an index is available.

Year	Jan Index	%	Feb Index	%	Mar Index	%	Apr Index	%	May Index	%	Jun Index	%	Jul Index	%	Aug Index	%	Sep Index	%	Oct Index	%	Nov Index	%	Dec Index	%
1952	-	-	-	-	-	-	-	-	-	-	-	-	-	-	-	-	-	-	-	-	-	-	49.2	-
1953	48.9	-0.6	48.9	0.0	48.7	-0.4	48.6	-0.2	48.6	0.0	48.5	-0.2	48.7	0.4	48.4	-0.6	48.9	1.0	48.8	-0.2	48.8	0.0	48.9	0.2
1954	48.7	-0.4	48.9	0.4	49.0	0.2	48.7	-0.6	48.5	-0.4	48.9	0.8	48.8	-0.2	48.7	-0.2	49.3	1.2	49.3	0.0	49.2	-0.2	49.2	0.0
1955	48.8	-0.8	48.9	0.2	48.7	-0.4	48.7	0.0	48.8	0.2	48.7	-0.2	48.8	0.2	48.8	0.0	49.2	0.8	49.2	0.0	49.0	-0.4	49.2	0.4
1956	49.1	-0.2	49.3	0.4	49.4	0.2	49.3	-0.2	49.8	1.0	49.8	0.0	49.9	0.2	49.8	-0.2	50.5	1.4	50.5	0.0	50.5	0.0	50.6	0.2
1957	50.4	-0.4	50.5	0.2	50.7	0.4	50.7	0.0	50.8	0.2	50.8	0.0	50.8	0.0	50.6	-0.4	51.3	1.4	51.2	-0.2	51.3	0.2	51.3	0.0
1958	51.0	-0.6	51.4	0.8	51.1	-0.6	50.9	-0.4	50.9	0.0	50.6	-0.6	50.8	0.4	50.6	-0.4	51.0	0.8	51.0	0.0	51.1	0.2	51.0	-0.2
1959	51.0	0.0	51.0	0.0	51.0	0.0	51.0	0.0	51.3	0.6	51.0	-0.6	51.6	1.2	51.4	-0.4	52.2	1.6	52.4	0.4	52.6	0.4	52.6	0.0
1960	52.5	-0.2	52.7	0.4	52.7	0.0	52.9	0.4	52.9	0.0	52.6	-0.6	52.7	0.2	52.6	-0.2	52.9	0.6	53.0	0.2	53.0	0.0	53.0	0.0
1961	52.7	-0.6	53.1	0.8	53.1	0.0	52.7	-0.8	53.0	0.6	52.7	-0.6	53.1	0.8	52.8	-0.6	53.0	0.4	52.9	-0.2	52.9	0.0	53.0	0.2
1962	52.7	-0.6	52.7	0.0	52.8	0.2	52.6	-0.4	52.7	0.2	52.7	0.0	52.8	0.2	52.5	-0.6	53.7	2.3	53.6	-0.2	53.6	0.0	53.7	0.2
1963	53.5	-0.4	53.5	0.0	53.6	0.2	53.4	-0.4	53.6	0.4	53.4	-0.4	53.5	0.2	53.6	0.2	54.1	0.9	54.1	0.0	54.1	0.0	54.5	0.7
1964	53.8	-1.3	54.3	0.9	54.4	0.2	54.5	0.2	54.5	0.0	54.6	0.2	54.6	0.0	54.4	-0.4	54.6	0.4	54.6	0.0	54.6	0.0	54.8	0.4
1965	54.6	-0.4	55.0	0.7	55.1	0.2	55.1	0.0	55.3	0.4	55.4	0.2	54.7	-1.3	54.5	-0.4	54.9	0.7	55.0	0.2	55.2	0.4	55.0	-0.4
1966	55.1	0.2	55.4	0.5	55.3	-0.2	55.5	0.4	55.9	0.7	55.9	0.0	55.7	-0.4	55.5	-0.4	56.6	2.0	56.4	-0.4	56.7	0.5	57.0	0.5
1967	56.4	-1.1	57.0	1.1	57.0	0.0	57.1	0.2	57.4	0.5	57.6	0.3	57.7	0.2	58.7	1.7	59.5	1.4	59.4	-0.2	59.6	0.3	59.6	0.0
1968	59.2	-0.7	59.8	1.0	60.4	1.0	60.4	0.0	60.6	0.3	60.8	0.3	61.2	0.7	61.2	0.0	62.2	1.6	62.5	0.5	62.5	0.0	63.0	0.8
1969	62.5	-0.8	62.9	0.6	63.1	0.3	62.7	-0.6	63.2	0.8	63.4	0.3	63.5	0.2	63.1	-0.6	64.6	2.4	64.6	0.0	64.9	0.5	65.1	0.3
1970	64.9	-0.3	65.4	0.8	65.7	0.5	66.0	0.5	66.7	1.1	66.8	0.1	66.3	-0.7	66.1	-0.3	67.2	1.7	67.2	0.0	67.7	0.7	67.9	0.3
1971	67.1	-1.2	67.5	0.6	67.7	0.3	67.7	0.0	68.8	1.6	68.9	0.1	68.9	0.0	68.5	-0.6	69.6	1.6	69.3	-0.4	69.3	0.0	69.1	-0.3
1972	68.6	-0.7	68.9	0.4	69.7	1.2	69.8	0.1	69.8	0.0	69.7	-0.1	69.2	-0.7	69.0	-0.3	70.3	1.9	70.3	0.0	70.3	0.0	70.6	0.4
1973	69.3	-1.8	69.7	0.6	71.2	2.2	71.0	-0.3	71.3	0.4	71.4	0.1	71.0	-0.6	71.6	0.8	73.0	2.0	72.6	-0.5	72.7	0.1	72.8	0.1
1974	71.8	-1.4	73.0	1.7	75.0	2.7	75.8	1.1	76.9	1.5	77.1	0.3	76.9	-0.3	78.3	1.8	79.0	0.9	78.6	-0.5	79.2	0.8	78.6	-0.8
1975	77.6	-1.3	78.0	0.5	78.0	0.0	78.5	0.6	79.1	0.8	79.4	0.4	78.6	-1.0	79.7	1.4	80.6	1.1	80.7	0.1	80.2	-0.6	80.1	-0.1
1976	79.0	-1.4	79.1	0.1	80.5	1.8	79.9	-0.7	80.7	1.0	80.5	-0.2	79.8	-0.9	81.4	2.0	82.3	1.1	82.2	-0.1	82.3	0.1	82.8	0.6
1977	82.8	0.0	83.7	1.1	84.0	0.4	83.7	-0.4	83.9	0.2	83.6	-0.4	82.7	-1.1	83.4	0.8	84.3	1.1	85.3	1.2	85.7	0.5	86.1	0.5
1978	86.2	0.1	85.0	-1.4	85.1	0.1	84.7	-0.5	85.5	0.9	85.5	0.0	85.4	-0.1	85.8	0.5	86.2	0.5	86.2	0.0	87.2	1.2	87.3	0.1
1979	85.9	-1.6	86.4	0.6	87.3	1.0	88.6	1.5	88.8	0.2	89.5	0.8	87.6	-2.1	88.0	0.5	90.7	3.1	90.5	-0.2	92.5	2.2	91.9	-0.6
1980	94.6	2.9	97.2	2.7	98.5	1.3	98.3	-0.2	97.8	-0.5	98.3	0.5	98.0	-0.3	98.4	0.4	99.0	0.6	99.7	0.7	100.1	0.4	99.7	-0.4
1981	97.7	-2.0	98.4	0.7	101.0	2.6	102.1	1.1	103.0	0.9	102.7	-0.3	101.6	-1.1	101.9	0.3	102.8	0.9	102.6	-0.2	102.8	0.2	101.5	-1.3
1982	99.9	-1.6	101.7	1.8	100.6	-1.1	99.5	-1.1	99.0	-0.5	98.6	-0.4	97.9	-0.7	97.7	-0.2	97.3	-0.4	97.9	0.6	98.8	0.9	98.1	-0.7
1983	95.3	-2.9	98.0	2.8	98.1	0.1	98.6	0.5	98.4	-0.2	99.9	1.5	99.9	0.0	101.7	1.8	102.0	0.3	101.8	-0.2	101.7	-0.1	101.2	-0.5
1984	101.3	0.1	101.2	-0.1	100.1	-1.1	100.5	0.4	100.3	-0.2	98.0	-2.3	97.7	-0.3	103.0	5.4	104.0	1.0	104.4	0.4	103.5	-0.9	102.3	-1.2
1985	99.8	-2.4	103.7	3.9	104.4	0.7	103.3	-1.1	103.5	0.2	104.3	0.8	103.0	-1.2	105.8	2.7	108.7	2.7	108.0	-0.6	108.0	0.0	108.4	0.4
1986	107.3	-1.0	106.4	-0.8	106.8	0.4	106.6	-0.2	105.9	-0.7	106.4	0.5	106.3	-0.1	105.9	-0.4	108.0	2.0	107.7	-0.3	108.4	0.6	107.3	-1.0
1987	109.6	2.1	108.8	-0.7	114.3	5.1	111.6	-2.4	112.2	0.5	113.5	1.2	110.1	-3.0	113.5	3.1	115.1	1.4	113.9	-1.0	113.1	-0.7	113.8	0.6
1988	113.2	-0.5	114.1	0.8	118.5	3.9	116.7	-1.5	117.6	0.8	115.9	-1.4	113.8	-1.8	109.7	-3.6	110.5	0.7	113.3	2.5	114.1	0.7	113.9	-0.2
1989	111.7	-1.9	114.1	2.1	122.0	6.9	122.1	0.1	122.7	0.5	120.3	-2.0	117.1	-2.7	116.8	-0.3	120.3	3.0	119.4	-0.7	119.3	-0.1	119.4	0.1
1990	119.3	-0.1	128.3	7.5	129.6	1.0	130.4	0.6	129.2	-0.9	126.3	-2.2	123.1	-2.5	122.3	-0.6	125.7	2.8	127.4	1.4	127.7	0.2	127.3	-0.3
1991	127.5	0.2	129.1	1.3	129.2	0.1	132.8	2.8	130.2	-2.0	125.2	-3.8	128.2	2.4	130.2	1.6	136.3	4.7	136.2	-0.1	136.1	-0.1	130.3	-4.3
1992	132.7	1.8	135.2	1.9	136.9	1.3	136.3	-0.4	136.0	-0.2	130.4	-4.1	130.8	0.3	132.0	0.9	131.8	-0.2	134.6	2.1	131.6	-2.2	129.5	-1.6
1993	128.9	-0.5	134.7	4.5	135.7	0.7	133.7	-1.5	129.8	-2.9	127.8	-1.5	127.4	-0.3	130.7	2.6	134.9	3.2	131.9	-2.2	133.9	1.5	130.2	-2.8

Source: U.S. Department of Labor, Bureau of Labor Statistics, Division of Consumer Prices and Price Indexes. - indicates no data collected for period.

Los Angeles, CA
Consumer Price Index - Urban Wage Earners
Base 1982-1984 = 100
Apparel and Upkeep

For 1952-1993. Columns headed % show percentile change in the index from the previous period for which an index is available.

Year	Jan Index	%	Feb Index	%	Mar Index	%	Apr Index	%	May Index	%	Jun Index	%	Jul Index	%	Aug Index	%	Sep Index	%	Oct Index	%	Nov Index	%	Dec Index	%
1952	-	-	-	-	-	-	-	-	-	-	-	-	-	-	-	-	-	-	-	-	-	-	49.4	-
1953	49.1	-0.6	49.1	0.0	48.9	-0.4	48.8	-0.2	48.8	0.0	48.7	-0.2	48.8	0.2	48.6	-0.4	49.1	1.0	49.0	-0.2	49.0	0.0	49.1	0.2
1954	48.9	-0.4	49.1	0.4	49.1	0.0	48.9	-0.4	48.7	-0.4	49.1	0.8	49.0	-0.2	48.8	-0.4	49.5	1.4	49.5	0.0	49.4	-0.2	49.4	0.0
1955	49.0	-0.8	49.1	0.2	48.9	-0.4	48.8	-0.2	49.0	0.4	48.8	-0.4	49.0	0.4	49.0	0.0	49.4	0.8	49.4	0.0	49.2	-0.4	49.4	0.4
1956	49.3	-0.2	49.5	0.4	49.5	0.0	49.5	0.0	50.0	1.0	50.0	0.0	50.1	0.2	50.0	-0.2	50.7	1.4	50.7	0.0	50.7	0.0	50.8	0.2
1957	50.6	-0.4	50.7	0.2	50.9	0.4	50.9	0.0	51.0	0.2	50.9	-0.2	51.0	0.2	50.8	-0.4	51.5	1.4	51.4	-0.2	51.5	0.2	51.5	0.0
1958	51.2	-0.6	51.6	0.8	51.3	-0.6	51.1	-0.4	51.1	0.0	50.8	-0.6	50.9	0.2	50.8	-0.2	51.2	0.8	51.2	0.0	51.3	0.2	51.2	-0.2
1959	51.2	0.0	51.2	0.0	51.2	0.0	51.2	0.0	51.5	0.6	51.2	-0.6	51.8	1.2	51.6	-0.4	52.4	1.6	52.6	0.4	52.8	0.4	52.8	0.0
1960	52.7	-0.2	52.9	0.4	52.9	0.0	53.1	0.4	53.1	0.0	52.8	-0.6	52.9	0.2	52.8	-0.2	53.1	0.6	53.2	0.2	53.2	0.0	53.2	0.0
1961	52.9	-0.6	53.3	0.8	53.3	0.0	52.9	-0.8	53.2	0.6	52.9	-0.6	53.3	0.8	53.0	-0.6	53.2	0.4	53.1	-0.2	53.1	0.0	53.2	0.2
1962	52.9	-0.6	52.9	0.0	53.0	0.2	52.8	-0.4	52.9	0.2	52.9	0.0	53.0	0.2	52.7	-0.6	53.9	2.3	53.8	-0.2	53.8	0.0	53.9	0.2
1963	53.7	-0.4	53.7	0.0	53.8	0.2	53.6	-0.4	53.8	0.4	53.6	-0.4	53.7	0.2	53.8	0.2	54.3	0.9	54.3	0.0	54.3	0.0	54.7	0.7
1964	54.0	-1.3	54.5	0.9	54.6	0.2	54.7	0.2	54.7	0.0	54.8	0.2	54.8	0.0	54.6	-0.4	54.8	0.4	54.8	0.0	54.8	0.0	55.0	0.4
1965	54.8	-0.4	55.2	0.7	55.3	0.2	55.3	0.0	55.5	0.4	55.6	0.2	54.9	-1.3	54.7	-0.4	55.1	0.7	55.2	0.2	55.4	0.4	55.2	-0.4
1966	55.3	0.2	55.6	0.5	55.5	-0.2	55.7	0.4	56.1	0.7	56.1	0.0	55.9	-0.4	55.7	-0.4	56.8	2.0	56.7	-0.2	56.9	0.4	57.2	0.5
1967	56.6	-1.0	57.2	1.1	57.2	0.0	57.4	0.3	57.6	0.3	57.8	0.3	57.9	0.2	58.9	1.7	59.7	1.4	59.6	-0.2	59.8	0.3	59.8	0.0
1968	59.4	-0.7	60.0	1.0	60.6	1.0	60.6	0.0	60.9	0.5	61.0	0.2	61.4	0.7	61.4	0.0	62.4	1.6	62.8	0.6	62.7	-0.2	63.2	0.8
1969	62.8	-0.6	63.1	0.5	63.3	0.3	63.0	-0.5	63.5	0.8	63.7	0.3	63.7	0.0	63.3	-0.6	64.9	2.5	64.9	0.0	65.2	0.5	65.3	0.2
1970	65.2	-0.2	65.6	0.6	65.9	0.5	66.2	0.5	67.0	1.2	67.1	0.1	66.6	-0.7	66.4	-0.3	67.5	1.7	67.5	0.0	67.9	0.6	68.1	0.3
1971	67.4	-1.0	67.8	0.6	68.0	0.3	68.0	0.0	69.0	1.5	69.2	0.3	69.1	-0.1	68.7	-0.6	69.8	1.6	69.6	-0.3	69.5	-0.1	69.4	-0.1
1972	68.9	-0.7	69.2	0.4	69.9	1.0	70.1	0.3	70.1	0.0	69.9	-0.3	69.4	-0.7	69.2	-0.3	70.6	2.0	70.6	0.0	70.6	0.0	70.8	0.2
1973	69.6	-1.7	69.9	0.4	71.5	2.3	71.2	-0.4	71.5	0.4	71.7	0.3	71.3	-0.6	71.9	0.8	73.3	1.9	72.9	-0.5	73.0	0.1	73.0	0.0
1974	72.0	-1.4	73.3	1.8	75.3	2.7	76.1	1.1	77.2	1.4	77.3	0.1	77.2	-0.1	78.6	1.8	79.3	0.9	78.9	-0.5	79.4	0.6	78.9	-0.6
1975	77.9	-1.3	78.3	0.5	78.3	0.0	78.7	0.5	79.4	0.9	79.7	0.4	78.9	-1.0	80.0	1.4	80.9	1.1	81.0	0.1	80.5	-0.6	80.4	-0.1
1976	79.3	-1.4	79.4	0.1	80.8	1.8	80.2	-0.7	81.0	1.0	80.8	-0.2	80.1	-0.9	81.7	2.0	82.6	1.1	82.5	-0.1	82.6	0.1	83.1	0.6
1977	83.1	0.0	84.1	1.2	84.3	0.2	84.1	-0.2	84.2	0.1	83.9	-0.4	83.0	-1.1	83.7	0.8	84.6	1.1	85.6	1.2	86.0	0.5	86.4	0.5
1978	85.5	-1.0	85.2	-0.4	85.6	0.5	85.7	0.1	86.6	1.1	87.7	1.3	86.1	-1.8	87.0	1.0	88.2	1.4	88.1	-0.1	89.7	1.8	89.5	-0.2
1979	89.1	-0.4	90.1	1.1	90.1	0.0	90.8	0.8	90.8	0.0	91.5	0.8	90.2	-1.4	91.2	1.1	93.2	2.2	93.8	0.6	93.8	0.0	93.7	-0.1
1980	95.5	1.9	96.8	1.4	98.2	1.4	97.8	-0.4	96.8	-1.0	96.9	0.1	96.7	-0.2	97.0	0.3	97.3	0.3	97.2	-0.1	98.7	1.5	99.3	0.6
1981	96.9	-2.4	98.7	1.9	99.3	0.6	100.6	1.3	101.1	0.5	100.7	-0.4	100.6	-0.1	101.8	1.2	102.4	0.6	101.9	-0.5	102.7	0.8	101.8	-0.9
1982	99.9	-1.9	101.8	1.9	100.7	-1.1	99.6	-1.1	99.1	-0.5	98.7	-0.4	98.2	-0.5	97.8	-0.4	97.6	-0.2	97.9	0.3	98.9	1.0	98.2	-0.7
1983	95.2	-3.1	97.9	2.8	97.9	0.0	98.5	0.6	98.2	-0.3	99.8	1.6	100.1	0.3	101.7	1.6	101.9	0.2	101.6	-0.3	101.5	-0.1	101.2	-0.3
1984	101.1	-0.1	101.0	-0.1	100.2	-0.8	100.8	0.6	100.3	-0.5	97.9	-2.4	97.7	-0.2	102.8	5.2	103.8	1.0	104.6	0.8	103.6	-1.0	102.2	-1.4
1985	100.0	-2.2	103.5	3.5	104.3	0.8	103.0	-1.2	103.3	0.3	104.0	0.7	102.8	-1.2	105.9	3.0	108.4	2.4	107.9	-0.5	108.0	0.1	108.6	0.6
1986	107.7	-0.8	106.8	-0.8	106.9	0.1	106.9	0.0	106.3	-0.6	106.9	0.6	106.5	-0.4	105.9	-0.6	108.2	2.2	108.1	-0.1	108.6	0.5	107.5	-1.0
1987	109.0	1.4	108.5	-0.5	113.7	4.8	111.0	-2.4	111.3	0.3	113.1	1.6	109.9	-2.8	113.1	2.9	114.4	1.1	113.3	-1.0	112.6	-0.6	113.4	0.7
1988	112.5	-0.8	113.8	1.2	116.6	2.5	115.5	-0.9	116.3	0.7	114.7	-1.4	113.1	-1.4	109.9	-2.8	111.1	1.1	114.2	2.8	115.2	0.9	115.1	-0.1
1989	112.1	-2.6	114.3	2.0	120.7	5.6	121.2	0.4	121.9	0.6	119.8	-1.7	117.2	-2.2	117.2	0.0	120.6	2.9	120.1	-0.4	120.0	-0.1	119.9	-0.1
1990	120.1	0.2	127.4	6.1	128.8	1.1	129.7	0.7	128.6	-0.8	125.7	-2.3	122.7	-2.4	122.2	-0.4	125.2	2.5	127.2	1.6	127.7	0.4	127.5	-0.2
1991	127.3	-0.2	128.6	1.0	128.8	0.2	132.8	3.1	129.9	-2.2	125.1	-3.7	128.5	2.7	130.4	1.5	135.8	4.1	135.9	0.1	136.2	0.2	130.4	-4.3
1992	132.4	1.5	135.7	2.5	137.3	1.2	136.2	-0.8	135.9	-0.2	131.2	-3.5	131.8	0.5	132.4	0.5	132.1	-0.2	135.2	2.3	132.4	-2.1	130.4	-1.5
1993	129.5	-0.7	134.9	4.2	136.2	1.0	134.1	-1.5	130.3	-2.8	128.6	-1.3	128.1	-0.4	131.7	2.8	136.0	3.3	132.8	-2.4	135.0	1.7	131.2	-2.8

Source: U.S. Department of Labor, Bureau of Labor Statistics, Division of Consumer Prices and Price Indexes. - indicates no data collected for period.

Los Angeles, CA
Consumer Price Index - All Urban Consumers
Base 1982-1984 = 100
Transportation

For 1947-1993. Columns headed % show percentile change in the index from the previous period for which an index is available.

Year	Jan Index	%	Feb Index	%	Mar Index	%	Apr Index	%	May Index	%	Jun Index	%	Jul Index	%	Aug Index	%	Sep Index	%	Oct Index	%	Nov Index	%	Dec Index	%
1947	17.3	-	17.5	1.2	17.5	0.0	17.7	1.1	17.6	-0.6	17.6	0.0	18.0	2.3	18.1	0.6	18.3	1.1	18.4	0.5	18.4	0.0	18.4	0.0
1948	19.2	4.3	19.2	0.0	19.2	0.0	19.3	0.5	19.2	-0.5	19.2	0.0	20.1	4.7	20.4	1.5	20.5	0.5	20.5	0.0	20.5	0.0	20.6	0.5
1949	20.6	0.0	21.0	1.9	20.9	-0.5	21.0	0.5	21.0	0.0	21.0	0.0	21.0	0.0	21.0	0.0	21.0	0.0	21.0	0.0	21.0	0.0	21.0	0.0
1950	21.0	0.0	20.9	-0.5	20.7	-1.0	20.5	-1.0	20.5	0.0	20.5	0.0	20.6	0.5	20.7	0.5	20.7	0.0	20.8	0.5	20.9	0.5	21.0	0.5
1951	21.0	0.0	21.3	1.4	21.5	0.9	21.5	0.0	21.5	0.0	21.5	0.0	21.6	0.5	21.6	0.0	21.8	0.9	22.0	0.9	22.3	1.4	22.3	0.0
1952	22.2	-0.4	23.5	5.9	23.5	0.0	23.5	0.0	23.7	0.9	23.7	0.0	24.2	2.1	24.2	0.0	24.2	0.0	24.2	0.0	24.4	0.8	24.4	0.0
1953	24.6	0.8	24.6	0.0	24.9	1.2	24.9	0.0	24.8	-0.4	24.8	0.0	25.0	0.8	25.1	0.4	24.9	-0.8	25.0	0.4	24.9	-0.4	24.1	-3.2
1954	25.2	4.6	25.1	-0.4	25.0	-0.4	24.9	-0.4	24.9	0.0	24.6	-1.2	23.7	-3.7	23.9	0.8	24.1	0.8	23.6	-2.1	24.7	4.7	24.7	0.0
1955	24.7	0.0	24.7	0.0	24.9	0.8	23.9	-4.0	24.2	1.3	24.0	-0.8	24.0	0.0	24.0	0.0	24.1	0.4	24.3	0.8	24.9	2.5	24.7	-0.8
1956	24.5	-0.8	24.4	-0.4	24.5	0.4	24.2	-1.2	24.6	1.7	24.6	0.0	25.0	1.6	24.7	-1.2	24.7	0.0	25.3	2.4	25.5	0.8	25.6	0.4
1957	25.5	-0.4	25.9	1.6	25.9	0.0	25.9	0.0	26.1	0.8	25.9	-0.8	25.9	0.0	25.4	-1.9	25.7	1.2	25.7	0.0	26.0	1.2	25.7	-1.2
1958	25.6	-0.4	26.0	1.6	26.0	0.0	26.2	0.8	26.3	0.4	26.2	-0.4	26.7	1.9	26.8	0.4	26.9	0.4	26.8	-0.4	27.1	1.1	27.1	0.0
1959	27.2	0.4	27.5	1.1	27.5	0.0	27.7	0.7	27.8	0.4	27.7	-0.4	27.6	-0.4	27.9	1.1	27.7	-0.7	28.3	2.2	28.5	0.7	28.5	0.0
1960	28.1	-1.4	27.9	-0.7	28.3	1.4	28.2	-0.4	28.0	-0.7	28.0	0.0	27.9	-0.4	27.8	-0.4	27.6	-0.7	27.9	1.1	27.9	0.0	28.2	1.1
1961	28.6	1.4	28.6	0.0	27.9	-2.4	27.9	0.0	28.1	0.7	29.3	4.3	29.3	0.0	29.5	0.7	29.2	-1.0	29.2	0.0	29.6	1.4	29.6	0.0
1962	29.3	-1.0	29.2	-0.3	29.3	0.3	29.6	1.0	30.0	1.4	30.2	0.7	30.1	-0.3	30.2	0.3	30.1	-0.3	30.3	0.7	30.2	-0.3	30.2	0.0
1963	29.8	-1.3	29.9	0.3	29.7	-0.7	30.0	1.0	29.8	-0.7	29.1	-2.3	29.1	0.0	30.2	3.8	30.1	-0.3	30.7	2.0	30.8	0.3	29.6	-3.9
1964	31.3	5.7	29.8	-4.8	31.0	4.0	31.1	0.3	31.0	-0.3	31.3	1.0	30.5	-2.6	31.1	2.0	30.5	-1.9	31.4	3.0	31.8	1.3	31.8	0.0
1965	31.6	-0.6	31.6	0.0	31.6	0.0	31.9	0.9	31.9	0.0	31.8	-0.3	32.0	0.6	31.1	-2.8	31.8	2.3	31.3	-1.6	32.0	2.2	32.0	0.0
1966	31.0	-3.1	31.3	1.0	31.5	0.6	31.9	1.3	31.6	-0.9	31.8	0.6	32.4	1.9	31.3	-3.4	32.3	3.2	32.5	0.6	32.7	0.6	32.2	-1.5
1967	31.6	-1.9	31.5	-0.3	31.2	-1.0	32.3	3.5	32.4	0.3	32.4	0.0	32.4	0.0	32.5	0.3	33.2	2.2	32.4	-2.4	33.5	3.4	32.3	-3.6
1968	33.3	3.1	33.3	0.0	33.6	0.9	32.9	-2.1	32.8	-0.3	33.7	2.7	33.3	-1.2	33.6	0.9	32.9	-2.1	33.6	2.1	34.0	1.2	32.8	-3.5
1969	33.6	2.4	33.6	0.0	34.6	3.0	34.3	-0.9	33.6	-2.0	34.5	2.7	34.5	0.0	34.3	-0.6	34.2	-0.3	35.0	2.3	33.8	-3.4	34.9	3.3
1970	34.4	-1.4	33.9	-1.5	33.9	0.0	35.5	4.7	35.0	-1.4	34.7	-0.9	36.0	3.7	34.7	-3.6	36.4	4.9	36.8	1.1	36.5	-0.8	37.1	1.6
1971	36.8	-0.8	36.2	-1.6	37.5	3.6	36.5	-2.7	36.8	0.8	37.1	0.8	37.1	0.0	37.5	1.1	37.5	0.0	37.9	1.1	37.3	-1.6	37.1	-0.5
1972	37.0	-0.3	36.3	-1.9	37.5	3.3	37.4	-0.3	37.8	1.1	37.3	-1.3	38.1	2.1	38.2	0.3	38.9	1.8	39.1	0.5	39.2	0.3	39.2	0.0
1973	38.8	-1.0	38.9	0.3	39.0	0.3	39.4	1.0	39.7	0.8	40.0	0.8	40.4	1.0	40.2	-0.5	39.9	-0.7	40.1	0.5	40.5	1.0	40.5	0.0
1974	41.3	2.0	41.8	1.2	42.7	2.2	43.3	1.4	44.0	1.6	44.9	2.0	45.4	1.1	45.6	0.4	45.8	0.4	45.9	0.2	46.3	0.9	46.5	0.4
1975	46.6	0.2	46.8	0.4	47.1	0.6	47.9	1.7	48.5	1.3	49.4	1.9	50.4	2.0	50.8	0.8	50.8	0.0	51.4	1.2	51.4	0.0	51.2	-0.4
1976	51.3	0.2	51.4	0.2	51.7	0.6	52.3	1.2	53.0	1.3	53.8	1.5	55.3	2.8	55.7	0.7	56.2	0.9	56.6	0.7	56.7	0.2	56.6	-0.2
1977	56.7	0.2	57.0	0.5	57.3	0.5	57.9	1.0	58.3	0.7	58.8	0.9	59.2	0.7	58.9	-0.5	58.7	-0.3	58.5	-0.3	58.2	-0.5	58.1	-0.2
1978	58.2	0.2	58.6	0.7	58.7	0.2	58.9	0.3	59.8	1.5	60.5	1.2	61.1	1.0	61.3	0.3	61.7	0.7	62.1	0.6	62.8	1.1	63.0	0.3
1979	63.4	0.6	63.9	0.8	65.0	1.7	67.4	3.7	69.1	2.5	70.3	1.7	71.8	2.1	73.4	2.2	74.3	1.2	74.4	0.1	74.7	0.4	75.8	1.5
1980	77.8	2.6	80.3	3.2	81.3	1.2	82.2	1.1	82.3	0.1	82.0	-0.4	82.3	0.4	82.8	0.6	83.9	1.3	84.2	0.4	85.0	1.0	85.4	0.5
1981	86.1	0.8	87.9	2.1	88.6	0.8	89.7	1.2	90.5	0.9	91.3	0.9	92.3	1.1	92.3	0.0	92.8	0.5	94.2	1.5	94.8	0.6	94.9	0.1
1982	97.1	2.3	96.7	-0.4	95.8	-0.9	95.5	-0.3	96.1	0.6	98.2	2.2	99.1	0.9	99.0	-0.1	98.5	-0.5	98.8	0.3	98.2	-0.6	96.8	-1.4
1983	96.4	-0.4	94.7	-1.8	94.1	-0.6	96.7	2.8	98.5	1.9	100.1	1.6	100.9	0.8	100.9	0.0	100.6	-0.3	100.4	-0.2	100.3	-0.1	102.0	1.7
1984	102.2	0.2	101.0	-1.2	101.1	0.1	103.1	2.0	104.9	1.7	104.6	-0.3	103.1	-1.4	103.4	0.3	103.4	0.0	105.6	2.1	106.1	0.5	106.1	0.0
1985	105.6	-0.5	105.2	-0.4	106.5	1.2	108.4	1.8	108.3	-0.1	108.8	0.5	108.6	-0.2	107.4	-1.1	106.7	-0.7	107.5	0.7	108.0	0.5	108.6	0.6
1986	108.9	0.3	107.2	-1.6	105.3	-1.8	104.6	-0.7	105.6	1.0	106.8	1.1	104.6	-2.1	103.2	-1.3	103.4	0.2	104.3	0.9	104.3	0.0	104.0	-0.3
1987	105.3	1.3	106.9	1.5	107.8	0.8	108.4	0.6	108.9	0.5	109.1	0.2	108.9	-0.2	109.5	0.6	109.6	0.1	110.8	1.1	110.9	0.1	110.7	-0.2
1988	111.0	0.3	110.6	-0.4	110.8	0.2	112.9	1.9	114.1	1.1	114.7	0.5	114.6	-0.1	115.5	0.8	115.4	-0.1	115.5	0.1	115.0	-0.4	115.0	0.0
1989	114.6	-0.3	116.0	1.2	117.5	1.3	121.9	3.7	122.7	0.7	122.8	0.1	121.8	-0.8	120.3	-1.2	119.1	-1.0	119.0	-0.1	119.0	0.0	120.0	0.8
1990	121.4	1.2	122.3	0.7	123.2	0.7	123.5	0.2	123.9	0.3	125.1	1.0	125.3	0.2	127.1	1.4	129.0	1.5	131.5	1.9	132.5	0.8	133.6	0.8
1991	129.9	-2.8	127.1	-2.2	124.2	-2.3	123.8	-0.3	125.8	1.6	126.2	0.3	126.2	0.0	126.4	0.2	126.4	0.0	126.6	0.2	127.4	0.6	128.6	0.9

[Continued]

Los Angeles, CA
Consumer Price Index - All Urban Consumers
Base 1982-1984 = 100
Transportation
[Continued]

For 1947-1993. Columns headed % show percentile change in the index from the previous period for which an index is available.

Year	Jan Index	%	Feb Index	%	Mar Index	%	Apr Index	%	May Index	%	Jun Index	%	Jul Index	%	Aug Index	%	Sep Index	%	Oct Index	%	Nov Index	%	Dec Index	%
1992	129.3	0.5	129.6	0.2	130.1	0.4	130.6	0.4	132.3	1.3	132.7	0.3	134.6	1.4	133.8	-0.6	134.5	0.5	135.5	0.7	136.1	0.4	137.0	0.7
1993	137.5	0.4	137.9	0.3	137.7	-0.1	136.6	-0.8	137.0	0.3	136.4	-0.4	136.9	0.4	135.9	-0.7	136.7	0.6	138.2	1.1	139.6	1.0	139.4	-0.1

Source: U.S. Department of Labor, Bureau of Labor Statistics, Division of Consumer Prices and Price Indexes. - indicates no data collected for period.

Los Angeles, CA
Consumer Price Index - Urban Wage Earners
Base 1982-1984 = 100
Transportation

For 1947-1993. Columns headed % show percentile change in the index from the previous period for which an index is available.

Year	Jan Index	%	Feb Index	%	Mar Index	%	Apr Index	%	May Index	%	Jun Index	%	Jul Index	%	Aug Index	%	Sep Index	%	Oct Index	%	Nov Index	%	Dec Index	%
1947	17.2	-	17.4	1.2	17.4	0.0	17.6	1.1	17.5	-0.6	17.5	0.0	17.9	2.3	18.0	0.6	18.2	1.1	18.3	0.5	18.3	0.0	18.3	0.0
1948	19.1	4.4	19.1	0.0	19.1	0.0	19.2	0.5	19.1	-0.5	19.1	0.0	20.0	4.7	20.3	1.5	20.3	0.0	20.3	0.0	20.3	0.0	20.5	1.0
1949	20.5	0.0	20.9	2.0	20.8	-0.5	20.9	0.5	20.9	0.0	20.9	0.0	20.9	0.0	20.9	0.0	20.9	0.0	20.9	0.0	20.9	0.0	20.9	0.0
1950	20.9	0.0	20.8	-0.5	20.6	-1.0	20.4	-1.0	20.4	0.0	20.4	0.0	20.4	0.0	20.6	1.0	20.6	0.0	20.7	0.5	20.8	0.5	20.9	0.5
1951	20.9	0.0	21.2	1.4	21.4	0.9	21.4	0.0	21.4	0.0	21.4	0.0	21.4	0.0	21.4	0.0	21.7	1.4	21.9	0.9	22.1	0.9	22.1	0.0
1952	22.1	0.0	23.4	5.9	23.4	0.0	23.4	0.0	23.6	0.9	23.6	0.0	24.0	1.7	24.0	0.0	24.1	0.4	24.1	0.0	24.3	0.8	24.3	0.0
1953	24.5	0.8	24.4	-0.4	24.8	1.6	24.7	-0.4	24.6	-0.4	24.6	0.0	24.9	1.2	24.9	0.0	24.8	-0.4	24.8	0.0	24.8	0.0	24.0	-3.2
1954	25.1	4.6	25.0	-0.4	24.8	-0.8	24.7	-0.4	24.8	0.4	24.5	-1.2	23.5	-4.1	23.8	1.3	23.9	0.4	23.5	-1.7	24.6	4.7	24.6	0.0
1955	24.6	0.0	24.6	0.0	24.8	0.8	23.8	-4.0	24.1	1.3	23.8	-1.2	23.9	0.4	23.8	-0.4	23.9	0.4	24.2	1.3	24.7	2.1	24.6	-0.4
1956	24.4	-0.8	24.2	-0.8	24.4	0.8	24.1	-1.2	24.4	1.2	24.4	0.0	24.9	2.0	24.6	-1.2	24.6	0.0	25.2	2.4	25.4	0.8	25.4	0.0
1957	25.4	0.0	25.8	1.6	25.7	-0.4	25.8	0.4	25.9	0.4	25.8	-0.4	25.7	-0.4	25.3	-1.6	25.6	1.2	25.6	0.0	25.9	1.2	25.6	-1.2
1958	25.5	-0.4	25.8	1.2	25.9	0.4	26.0	0.4	26.1	0.4	26.1	0.0	26.5	1.5	26.6	0.4	26.7	0.4	26.7	0.0	26.9	0.7	27.0	0.4
1959	27.1	0.4	27.4	1.1	27.4	0.0	27.5	0.4	27.6	0.4	27.6	0.0	27.5	-0.4	27.8	1.1	27.5	-1.1	28.1	2.2	28.3	0.7	28.3	0.0
1960	27.9	-1.4	27.7	-0.7	28.2	1.8	28.1	-0.4	27.9	-0.7	27.8	-0.4	27.8	0.0	27.7	-0.4	27.5	-0.7	27.7	0.7	27.8	0.4	28.1	1.1
1961	28.4	1.1	28.5	0.4	27.7	-2.8	27.7	0.0	28.0	1.1	29.1	3.9	29.1	0.0	29.3	0.7	29.1	-0.7	29.1	0.0	29.5	1.4	29.4	-0.3
1962	29.2	-0.7	29.0	-0.7	29.1	0.3	29.5	1.4	29.8	1.0	30.0	0.7	30.0	0.0	30.0	0.0	29.9	-0.3	30.1	0.7	30.0	-0.3	30.0	0.0
1963	29.6	-1.3	29.7	0.3	29.5	-0.7	29.9	1.4	29.6	-1.0	29.0	-2.0	29.0	0.0	30.0	3.4	30.0	0.0	30.5	1.7	30.6	0.3	29.4	-3.9
1964	31.2	6.1	29.6	-5.1	30.9	4.4	30.9	0.0	30.9	0.0	31.1	0.6	30.4	-2.3	30.9	1.6	30.3	-1.9	31.2	3.0	31.6	1.3	31.6	0.0
1965	31.5	-0.3	31.5	0.0	31.4	-0.3	31.7	1.0	31.8	0.3	31.6	-0.6	31.8	0.6	30.9	-2.8	31.6	2.3	31.2	-1.3	31.8	1.9	31.8	0.0
1966	30.8	-3.1	31.1	1.0	31.3	0.6	31.8	1.6	31.4	-1.3	31.6	0.6	32.2	1.9	31.1	-3.4	32.1	3.2	32.3	0.6	32.5	0.6	32.0	-1.5
1967	31.4	-1.9	31.3	-0.3	31.0	-1.0	32.1	3.5	32.2	0.3	32.2	0.0	32.2	0.0	32.3	0.3	33.0	2.2	32.2	-2.4	33.4	3.7	32.1	-3.9
1968	33.2	3.4	33.1	-0.3	33.4	0.9	32.7	-2.1	32.6	-0.3	33.5	2.8	33.1	-1.2	33.5	1.2	32.7	-2.4	33.4	2.1	33.8	1.2	32.6	-3.6
1969	33.5	2.8	33.5	0.0	34.5	3.0	34.1	-1.2	33.4	-2.1	34.4	3.0	34.4	0.0	34.1	-0.9	34.0	-0.3	34.8	2.4	33.6	-3.4	34.7	3.3
1970	34.2	-1.4	33.7	-1.5	33.7	0.0	35.3	4.7	34.8	-1.4	34.5	-0.9	35.8	3.8	34.5	-3.6	36.2	4.9	36.6	1.1	36.3	-0.8	36.9	1.7
1971	36.6	-0.8	36.0	-1.6	37.3	3.6	36.3	-2.7	36.6	0.8	36.9	0.8	36.9	0.0	37.2	0.8	37.3	0.3	37.7	1.1	37.1	-1.6	36.9	-0.5
1972	36.8	-0.3	36.1	-1.9	37.2	3.0	37.2	0.0	37.6	1.1	37.1	-1.3	37.9	2.2	38.0	0.3	38.7	1.8	38.9	0.5	39.0	0.3	39.0	0.0
1973	38.6	-1.0	38.7	0.3	38.8	0.3	39.2	1.0	39.5	0.8	39.8	0.8	40.1	0.8	39.9	-0.5	39.7	-0.5	39.9	0.5	40.3	1.0	40.3	0.0
1974	41.1	2.0	41.5	1.0	42.5	2.4	43.1	1.4	43.8	1.6	44.6	1.8	45.1	1.1	45.4	0.7	45.6	0.4	45.7	0.2	46.1	0.9	46.2	0.2
1975	46.3	0.2	46.5	0.4	46.9	0.9	47.7	1.7	48.2	1.0	49.1	1.9	50.1	2.0	50.5	0.8	50.5	0.0	51.1	1.2	51.1	0.0	50.9	-0.4
1976	51.0	0.2	51.2	0.4	51.4	0.4	52.0	1.2	52.7	1.3	53.5	1.5	55.0	2.8	55.4	0.7	55.9	0.9	56.3	0.7	56.4	0.2	56.3	-0.2
1977	56.4	0.2	56.7	0.5	57.0	0.5	57.6	1.1	58.0	0.7	58.5	0.9	58.9	0.7	58.6	-0.5	58.4	-0.3	58.2	-0.3	57.9	-0.5	57.8	-0.2
1978	58.0	0.3	58.0	0.0	58.3	0.5	58.7	0.7	59.5	1.4	60.3	1.3	60.9	1.0	61.2	0.5	61.5	0.5	61.9	0.7	62.7	1.3	63.0	0.5
1979	63.4	0.6	63.9	0.8	65.0	1.7	67.6	4.0	69.4	2.7	70.6	1.7	72.3	2.4	73.8	2.1	74.5	0.9	74.4	-0.1	75.0	0.8	76.1	1.5
1980	77.9	2.4	80.8	3.7	82.0	1.5	83.5	1.8	83.5	0.0	83.3	-0.2	83.3	100	83.8	0.6	84.4	0.7	84.6	0.2	85.4	0.9	85.8	0.5
1981	86.6	0.9	88.4	2.1	89.1	0.8	90.6	1.7	91.5	1.0	92.4	1.0	93.3	1.0	93.0	-0.3	93.0	0.0	94.9	2.0	95.5	0.6	95.5	0.0
1982	97.6	2.2	97.0	-0.6	96.2	-0.8	95.7	-0.5	96.3	0.6	98.7	2.5	99.6	0.9	99.6	0.0	99.0	-0.6	99.1	0.1	98.2	-0.9	96.8	-1.4
1983	96.2	-0.6	94.6	-1.7	93.9	-0.7	96.4	2.7	98.3	2.0	100.0	1.7	100.8	0.8	100.8	0.0	100.4	-0.4	100.1	-0.3	100.1	0.0	101.8	1.7
1984	101.9	0.1	100.8	-1.1	101.0	0.2	103.0	2.0	104.9	1.8	104.5	-0.4	102.9	-1.5	103.1	0.2	103.4	0.3	105.5	2.0	105.9	0.4	105.8	-0.1
1985	105.3	-0.5	104.8	-0.5	106.2	1.3	108.1	1.8	107.9	-0.2	108.4	0.5	108.2	-0.2	106.9	-1.2	106.0	-0.8	106.8	0.8	107.4	0.6	107.8	0.4
1986	108.0	0.2	106.2	-1.7	104.3	-1.8	103.5	-0.8	104.4	0.9	105.6	1.1	103.3	-2.2	101.7	-1.5	101.8	0.1	102.5	0.7	102.7	0.2	102.4	-0.3
1987	103.4	1.0	105.1	1.6	105.9	0.8	106.6	0.7	107.1	0.5	107.3	0.2	107.1	-0.2	107.6	0.5	107.6	0.0	108.9	1.2	109.0	0.1	108.8	-0.2
1988	109.0	0.2	108.7	-0.3	108.8	0.1	110.6	1.7	111.8	1.1	112.2	0.4	111.9	-0.3	112.8	0.8	112.9	0.1	113.2	0.3	112.5	-0.6	112.6	0.1
1989	112.1	-0.4	113.5	1.2	114.8	1.1	119.0	3.7	119.7	0.6	119.7	0.0	118.7	-0.8	117.1	-1.3	116.0	-0.9	115.8	-0.2	115.6	-0.2	116.7	1.0
1990	117.9	1.0	118.5	0.5	119.0	0.4	119.3	0.3	119.6	0.3	120.7	0.9	121.1	0.3	122.8	1.4	124.5	1.4	126.6	1.7	127.6	0.8	128.5	0.7
1991	125.1	-2.6	122.4	-2.2	119.8	-2.1	119.6	-0.2	121.7	1.8	122.2	0.4	122.2	0.0	122.5	0.2	122.8	0.2	123.0	0.2	123.6	0.5	124.6	0.8

[Continued]

Los Angeles, CA
Consumer Price Index - Urban Wage Earners
Base 1982-1984 = 100
Transportation
[Continued]

For 1947-1993. Columns headed % show percentile change in the index from the previous period for which an index is available.

Year	Jan		Feb		Mar		Apr		May		Jun		Jul		Aug		Sep		Oct		Nov		Dec	
	Index	%	Index	%	Index	%	Index	%	Index	%	Index	%	Index	%	Index	%	Index	%	Index	%	Index	%	Index	%
1992	125.1	0.4	125.4	0.2	125.7	0.2	126.3	0.5	128.0	1.3	128.8	0.6	129.9	0.9	129.6	-0.2	130.0	0.3	130.9	0.7	131.7	0.6	132.2	0.4
1993	132.4	0.2	132.7	0.2	132.5	-0.2	131.7	-0.6	131.9	0.2	131.7	-0.2	132.0	0.2	131.4	-0.5	131.9	0.4	133.5	1.2	134.5	0.7	134.0	-0.4

Source: U.S. Department of Labor, Bureau of Labor Statistics, Division of Consumer Prices and Price Indexes. - indicates no data collected for period.

Los Angeles, CA
Consumer Price Index - All Urban Consumers
Base 1982-1984 = 100
Medical Care

For 1947-1993. Columns headed % show percentile change in the index from the previous period for which an index is available.

Year	Jan Index	%	Feb Index	%	Mar Index	%	Apr Index	%	May Index	%	Jun Index	%	Jul Index	%	Aug Index	%	Sep Index	%	Oct Index	%	Nov Index	%	Dec Index	%
1947	13.3	-	13.3	0.0	13.3	0.0	13.4	0.8	13.3	-0.7	13.3	0.0	13.3	0.0	13.3	0.0	13.4	0.8	13.6	1.5	13.6	0.0	13.6	0.0
1948	13.7	0.7	13.7	0.0	13.7	0.0	14.0	2.2	14.0	0.0	14.1	0.7	14.4	2.1	14.4	0.0	14.5	0.7	14.6	0.7	14.6	0.0	14.6	0.0
1949	14.7	0.7	14.7	0.0	14.7	0.0	14.7	0.0	14.7	0.0	14.7	0.0	14.7	0.0	14.7	0.0	14.7	0.0	14.7	0.0	14.7	0.0	14.7	0.0
1950	14.7	0.0	14.8	0.7	14.8	0.0	14.8	0.0	14.8	0.0	14.8	0.0	14.8	0.0	14.8	0.0	15.3	3.4	15.4	0.7	15.4	0.0	15.7	1.9
1951	15.7	0.0	15.7	0.0	15.9	1.3	15.9	0.0	15.9	0.0	15.9	0.0	16.0	0.6	16.0	0.0	16.0	0.0	16.0	0.0	16.0	0.0	16.0	0.0
1952	16.1	0.6	16.1	0.0	16.1	0.0	16.1	0.0	16.1	0.0	16.7	3.7	16.7	0.0	16.7	0.0	16.7	0.0	16.7	0.0	16.7	0.0	16.7	0.0
1953	16.7	0.0	16.7	0.0	16.7	0.0	16.9	1.2	16.9	0.0	16.9	0.0	16.9	0.0	17.0	0.6	17.0	0.0	17.1	0.6	17.1	0.0	17.1	0.0
1954	17.1	0.0	17.1	0.0	17.1	0.0	17.3	1.2	17.3	0.0	17.3	0.0	17.3	0.0	17.3	0.0	17.3	0.0	17.3	0.0	17.3	0.0	17.3	0.0
1955	17.3	0.0	17.3	0.0	17.3	0.0	17.1	-1.2	17.1	0.0	17.1	0.0	17.5	2.3	17.5	0.0	17.5	0.0	17.5	0.0	17.5	0.0	17.6	0.6
1956	17.8	1.1	17.8	0.0	17.8	0.0	17.9	0.6	17.9	0.0	17.9	0.0	17.9	0.0	18.0	0.6	18.0	0.0	18.1	0.6	18.1	0.0	18.0	-0.6
1957	18.3	1.7	18.3	0.0	18.3	0.0	18.3	0.0	18.3	0.0	18.4	0.5	18.4	0.0	18.5	0.5	18.5	0.0	18.5	0.0	18.5	0.0	18.6	0.5
1958	18.9	1.6	18.9	0.0	18.9	0.0	19.3	2.1	19.3	0.0	20.3	5.2	20.3	0.0	20.4	0.5	20.4	0.0	20.5	0.5	20.5	0.0	20.5	0.0
1959	20.6	0.5	20.6	0.0	20.6	0.0	20.6	0.0	20.7	0.5	20.7	0.0	20.7	0.0	20.7	0.0	20.7	0.0	21.1	1.9	21.1	0.0	21.1	0.0
1960	21.1	0.0	21.1	0.0	21.1	0.0	21.3	0.9	21.3	0.0	21.3	0.0	21.5	0.9	21.5	0.0	21.5	0.0	21.6	0.5	21.6	0.0	21.6	0.0
1961	21.6	0.0	21.6	0.0	21.6	0.0	21.6	0.0	21.6	0.0	21.6	0.0	21.6	0.0	21.7	0.5	21.7	0.0	21.7	0.0	21.7	0.0	21.7	0.0
1962	21.7	0.0	21.7	0.0	22.3	2.8	22.4	0.4	22.4	0.0	22.4	0.0	22.5	0.4	22.4	-0.4	22.4	0.0	22.4	0.0	22.4	0.0	22.4	0.0
1963	22.5	0.4	22.5	0.0	22.5	0.0	22.6	0.4	22.7	0.4	22.7	0.0	22.7	0.0	22.7	0.0	22.7	0.0	22.9	0.9	22.9	0.0	22.9	0.0
1964	23.0	0.4	23.1	0.4	23.1	0.0	23.2	0.4	23.2	0.0	23.2	0.0	23.3	0.4	23.3	0.0	23.3	0.0	23.5	0.9	23.5	0.0	23.4	-0.4
1965	23.4	0.0	23.5	0.4	23.5	0.0	23.6	0.4	23.7	0.4	23.7	0.0	23.7	0.0	23.7	0.0	23.7	0.0	23.7	0.0	23.8	0.4	23.8	0.0
1966	23.9	0.4	24.0	0.4	24.0	0.0	24.2	0.8	24.1	-0.4	24.2	0.4	24.3	0.4	24.3	0.0	25.2	3.7	25.4	0.8	25.5	0.4	25.7	0.8
1967	25.7	0.0	25.7	0.0	25.8	0.4	26.0	0.8	26.3	1.2	26.4	0.4	26.6	0.8	26.6	0.0	26.7	0.4	26.8	0.4	26.9	0.4	27.0	0.4
1968	27.2	0.7	27.3	0.4	27.3	0.0	27.5	0.7	27.8	1.1	27.8	0.0	28.0	0.7	28.1	0.4	28.1	0.0	28.2	0.4	28.3	0.4	28.5	0.7
1969	28.6	0.4	28.8	0.7	28.9	0.3	29.3	1.4	29.4	0.3	29.5	0.3	29.6	0.3	29.8	0.7	29.9	0.3	29.8	-0.3	30.0	0.7	30.4	1.3
1970	30.4	0.0	30.7	1.0	31.0	1.0	31.6	1.9	31.8	0.6	31.8	0.0	31.9	0.3	32.0	0.3	32.0	0.0	31.9	-0.3	31.9	0.0	32.1	0.6
1971	32.1	0.0	32.2	0.3	32.4	0.6	33.2	2.5	33.4	0.6	33.5	0.3	33.6	0.3	33.6	0.0	33.7	0.3	33.4	-0.9	33.4	0.0	33.4	0.0
1972	33.5	0.3	33.6	0.3	33.6	0.0	33.7	0.3	33.7	0.0	33.8	0.3	34.1	0.9	34.1	0.0	34.2	0.3	34.4	0.6	34.3	-0.3	34.5	0.6
1973	34.6	0.3	34.7	0.3	35.0	0.9	35.2	0.6	35.3	0.3	35.4	0.3	35.6	0.6	35.8	0.6	35.9	0.3	36.6	1.9	36.6	0.0	36.6	0.0
1974	36.9	0.8	37.2	0.8	37.5	0.8	37.6	0.3	38.4	2.1	38.8	1.0	39.3	1.3	39.8	1.3	40.0	0.5	40.3	0.7	40.9	1.5	41.1	0.5
1975	41.3	0.5	42.1	1.9	42.4	0.7	42.9	1.2	43.3	0.9	43.6	0.7	43.9	0.7	44.3	0.9	44.5	0.5	44.8	0.7	45.5	1.6	46.1	1.3
1976	46.4	0.7	47.7	2.8	47.9	0.4	48.3	0.8	48.9	1.2	49.3	0.8	49.7	0.8	50.1	0.8	50.3	0.4	50.6	0.6	51.3	1.4	51.3	0.0
1977	51.6	0.6	52.4	1.6	52.6	0.4	53.0	0.8	53.2	0.4	53.6	0.8	54.1	0.9	54.5	0.7	54.9	0.7	55.3	0.7	55.5	0.4	55.6	0.2
1978	56.0	0.7	56.3	0.5	56.4	0.2	56.6	0.4	58.2	2.8	58.4	0.3	58.7	0.5	60.0	2.2	60.2	0.3	60.6	0.7	61.1	0.8	61.1	0.0
1979	62.1	1.6	62.3	0.3	62.6	0.5	62.7	0.2	63.6	1.4	64.1	0.8	65.2	1.7	65.1	-0.2	66.2	1.7	66.6	0.6	66.8	0.3	67.7	1.3
1980	68.3	0.9	70.4	3.1	70.8	0.6	72.5	2.4	72.5	0.0	72.5	0.0	73.4	1.2	73.2	-0.3	73.6	0.5	74.7	1.5	75.2	0.7	75.3	0.1
1981	76.2	1.2	77.0	1.0	77.2	0.3	77.9	0.9	78.2	0.4	78.7	0.6	84.5	7.4	85.1	0.7	85.5	0.5	85.5	0.0	88.7	3.7	89.2	0.6
1982	90.0	0.9	90.1	0.1	90.6	0.6	91.6	1.1	92.6	1.1	94.4	1.9	94.8	0.4	95.9	1.2	97.1	1.3	96.9	-0.2	97.5	0.6	97.7	0.2
1983	99.3	1.6	99.6	0.3	99.7	0.1	100.2	0.5	100.2	0.0	101.0	0.8	101.6	0.6	101.2	-0.4	101.2	0.0	101.3	0.1	101.6	0.3	101.6	0.0
1984	103.2	1.6	103.3	0.1	103.6	0.3	104.0	0.4	104.5	0.5	104.5	0.0	105.6	1.1	106.1	0.5	106.0	-0.1	107.0	0.9	107.1	0.1	107.4	0.3
1985	110.1	2.5	110.5	0.4	111.1	0.5	111.2	0.1	111.3	0.1	112.2	0.8	112.8	0.5	113.7	0.8	114.6	0.8	115.1	0.4	115.7	0.5	116.4	0.6
1986	117.0	0.5	118.1	0.9	118.9	0.7	119.4	0.4	119.7	0.3	120.2	0.4	120.7	0.4	121.7	0.8	121.9	0.2	123.0	0.9	124.5	1.2	125.3	0.6
1987	126.6	1.0	127.2	0.5	127.6	0.3	128.1	0.4	128.1	0.0	129.3	0.9	129.6	0.2	130.2	0.5	130.6	0.3	131.7	0.8	132.3	0.5	132.6	0.2
1988	135.5	2.2	136.5	0.7	137.3	0.6	137.4	0.1	137.9	0.4	139.1	0.9	139.6	0.4	140.8	0.9	141.6	0.6	143.1	1.1	143.0	-0.1	143.1	0.1
1989	145.0	1.3	145.2	0.1	146.1	0.6	147.4	0.9	148.0	0.4	149.1	0.7	150.6	1.0	151.5	0.6	152.5	0.7	152.9	0.3	154.2	0.9	154.6	0.3
1990	157.0	1.6	158.2	0.8	159.0	0.5	160.0	0.6	160.8	0.5	161.7	0.6	163.6	1.2	164.0	0.2	165.9	1.2	168.5	1.6	170.1	0.9	170.4	0.2
1991	172.9	1.5	172.9	0.0	174.7	1.0	174.9	0.1	176.1	0.7	177.6	0.9	180.1	1.4	179.9	-0.1	180.4	0.3	181.0	0.3	183.4	1.3	184.2	0.4

[Continued]

Los Angeles, CA
Consumer Price Index - All Urban Consumers
Base 1982-1984 = 100
Medical Care
[Continued]

For 1947-1993. Columns headed % show percentile change in the index from the previous period for which an index is available.

Year	Jan Index	%	Feb Index	%	Mar Index	%	Apr Index	%	May Index	%	Jun Index	%	Jul Index	%	Aug Index	%	Sep Index	%	Oct Index	%	Nov Index	%	Dec Index	%
1992	186.5	1.2	187.8	0.7	188.7	0.5	189.5	0.4	190.8	0.7	191.9	0.6	193.5	0.8	193.9	0.2	194.6	0.4	197.0	1.2	196.7	-0.2	197.9	0.6
1993	199.0	0.6	202.3	1.7	201.9	-0.2	202.6	0.3	207.2	2.3	207.0	-0.1	207.3	0.1	207.8	0.2	208.8	0.5	211.3	1.2	211.4	0.0	212.0	0.3

Source: U.S. Department of Labor, Bureau of Labor Statistics, Division of Consumer Prices and Price Indexes. - indicates no data collected for period.

Los Angeles, CA
Consumer Price Index - Urban Wage Earners
Base 1982-1984 = 100
Medical Care

For 1947-1993. Columns headed % show percentile change in the index from the previous period for which an index is available.

Year	Jan Index	%	Feb Index	%	Mar Index	%	Apr Index	%	May Index	%	Jun Index	%	Jul Index	%	Aug Index	%	Sep Index	%	Oct Index	%	Nov Index	%	Dec Index	%
1947	13.5	-	13.5	0.0	13.5	0.0	13.6	0.7	13.5	-0.7	13.5	0.0	13.5	0.0	13.5	0.0	13.6	0.7	13.8	1.5	13.8	0.0	13.8	0.0
1948	13.9	0.7	13.9	0.0	13.9	0.0	14.2	2.2	14.2	0.0	14.3	0.7	14.6	2.1	14.6	0.0	14.7	0.7	14.8	0.7	14.8	0.0	14.8	0.0
1949	14.9	0.7	14.9	0.0	14.9	0.0	14.9	0.0	14.9	0.0	14.9	0.0	14.9	0.0	14.9	0.0	15.0	0.7	15.0	0.0	15.0	0.0	15.0	0.0
1950	15.0	0.0	15.0	0.0	15.0	0.0	15.0	0.0	15.0	0.0	15.0	0.0	15.0	0.0	15.0	0.0	15.5	3.3	15.6	0.6	15.7	0.6	16.0	1.9
1951	16.0	0.0	16.0	0.0	16.2	1.3	16.2	0.0	16.2	0.0	16.2	0.0	16.2	0.0	16.2	0.0	16.2	0.0	16.2	0.0	16.2	0.0	16.2	0.0
1952	16.3	0.6	16.3	0.0	16.4	0.6	16.4	0.0	16.4	0.0	16.9	3.0	16.9	0.0	16.9	0.0	16.9	0.0	16.9	0.0	16.9	0.0	16.9	0.0
1953	16.9	0.0	16.9	0.0	16.9	0.0	17.1	1.2	17.2	0.6	17.2	0.0	17.2	0.0	17.2	0.0	17.2	0.0	17.3	0.6	17.3	0.0	17.4	0.6
1954	17.3	-0.6	17.3	0.0	17.4	0.6	17.5	0.6	17.5	0.0	17.5	0.0	17.6	0.6	17.6	0.0	17.6	0.0	17.6	0.0	17.6	0.0	17.6	0.0
1955	17.6	0.0	17.6	0.0	17.6	0.0	17.4	-1.1	17.4	0.0	17.4	0.0	17.8	2.3	17.8	0.0	17.8	0.0	17.8	0.0	17.8	0.0	17.9	0.6
1956	18.1	1.1	18.1	0.0	18.1	0.0	18.1	0.0	18.2	0.6	18.2	0.0	18.2	0.0	18.2	0.0	18.3	0.5	18.3	0.0	18.3	0.0	18.3	0.0
1957	18.5	1.1	18.5	0.0	18.5	0.0	18.6	0.5	18.6	0.0	18.6	0.0	18.7	0.5	18.7	0.0	18.7	0.0	18.7	0.0	18.8	0.5	18.9	0.5
1958	19.2	1.6	19.2	0.0	19.2	0.0	19.6	2.1	19.6	0.0	20.6	5.1	20.6	0.0	20.7	0.5	20.7	0.0	20.9	1.0	20.9	0.0	20.9	0.0
1959	20.9	0.0	20.9	0.0	20.9	0.0	20.9	0.0	21.0	0.5	21.0	0.0	21.0	0.0	21.0	0.0	21.0	0.0	21.4	1.9	21.4	0.0	21.4	0.0
1960	21.4	0.0	21.4	0.0	21.4	0.0	21.6	0.9	21.6	0.0	21.6	0.0	21.8	0.9	21.8	0.0	21.8	0.0	21.9	0.5	21.9	0.0	21.9	0.0
1961	21.9	0.0	21.9	0.0	21.9	0.0	21.9	0.0	21.9	0.0	22.0	0.5	22.0	0.0	22.0	0.0	22.1	0.5	22.1	0.0	22.1	0.0	22.1	0.0
1962	22.0	-0.5	22.0	0.0	22.7	3.2	22.8	0.4	22.8	0.0	22.8	0.0	22.8	0.0	22.8	0.0	22.8	0.0	22.8	0.0	22.8	0.0	22.8	0.0
1963	22.9	0.4	22.9	0.0	22.9	0.0	23.0	0.0	23.0	0.0	23.0	0.0	23.1	0.4	23.1	0.0	23.0	-0.4	23.2	0.9	23.2	0.0	23.2	0.0
1964	23.3	0.4	23.4	0.4	23.4	0.0	23.6	0.9	23.6	0.0	23.6	0.0	23.7	0.4	23.7	0.0	23.6	-0.4	23.8	0.8	23.8	0.0	23.8	0.0
1965	23.8	0.0	23.8	0.0	23.9	0.4	24.0	0.4	24.0	0.0	24.0	0.0	24.0	0.0	24.1	0.4	24.1	0.0	24.1	0.0	24.2	0.4	24.2	0.0
1966	24.2	0.0	24.3	0.4	24.4	0.4	24.5	0.4	24.5	0.0	24.6	0.4	24.6	0.0	24.7	0.4	25.6	3.6	25.8	0.8	25.9	0.4	26.1	0.8
1967	26.1	0.0	26.1	0.0	26.2	0.4	26.4	0.8	26.7	1.1	26.8	0.4	27.0	0.7	27.0	0.0	27.2	0.7	27.2	0.0	27.3	0.4	27.4	0.4
1968	27.6	0.7	27.7	0.4	27.7	0.0	28.0	1.1	28.2	0.7	28.2	0.0	28.4	0.7	28.5	0.4	28.5	0.0	28.6	0.4	28.7	0.3	28.9	0.7
1969	29.0	0.3	29.2	0.7	29.3	0.3	29.7	1.4	29.9	0.7	30.0	0.3	30.0	0.0	30.2	0.7	30.3	0.3	30.2	-0.3	30.4	0.7	30.8	1.3
1970	30.9	0.3	31.2	1.0	31.5	1.0	32.1	1.9	32.2	0.3	32.3	0.3	32.4	0.3	32.5	0.3	32.5	0.0	32.3	-0.6	32.4	0.0	32.5	0.3
1971	32.6	0.3	32.7	0.3	32.9	0.6	33.7	2.4	33.9	0.6	34.0	0.3	34.1	0.3	34.1	0.0	34.2	0.3	34.0	-0.6	34.0	0.0	34.0	0.0
1972	34.0	0.0	34.1	0.3	34.1	0.0	34.2	0.3	34.2	0.0	34.4	0.6	34.6	0.6	34.6	0.0	34.7	0.3	34.9	0.6	34.9	0.0	35.0	0.3
1973	35.1	0.3	35.3	0.6	35.5	0.6	35.7	0.6	35.8	0.3	35.9	0.3	36.1	0.6	36.3	0.6	36.4	0.3	37.1	1.9	37.1	0.0	37.1	0.0
1974	37.4	0.8	37.7	0.8	38.1	1.1	38.2	0.3	38.9	1.8	39.3	1.0	39.9	1.5	40.4	1.3	40.6	0.5	40.9	0.7	41.5	1.5	41.7	0.5
1975	41.9	0.5	42.7	1.9	43.0	0.7	43.5	1.2	43.9	0.9	44.2	0.7	44.5	0.7	45.0	1.1	45.2	0.4	45.5	0.7	46.2	1.5	46.8	1.3
1976	47.1	0.6	48.4	2.8	48.6	0.4	49.0	0.8	49.7	1.4	50.1	0.8	50.4	0.6	50.9	1.0	51.0	0.2	51.4	0.8	52.1	1.4	52.1	0.0
1977	52.4	0.6	53.2	1.5	53.4	0.4	53.8	0.7	54.0	0.4	54.4	0.7	54.9	0.9	55.3	0.7	55.7	0.7	56.1	0.7	56.4	0.5	56.4	0.0
1978	56.8	0.7	57.1	0.5	57.2	0.2	57.4	0.3	58.7	2.3	58.7	0.0	59.1	0.7	59.8	1.2	60.2	0.7	60.8	1.0	61.4	1.0	61.2	-0.3
1979	62.3	1.8	62.5	0.3	62.7	0.3	62.8	0.2	63.6	1.3	64.1	0.8	66.0	3.0	66.8	1.2	67.7	1.3	67.8	0.1	68.1	0.4	68.6	0.7
1980	69.3	1.0	70.4	1.6	70.6	0.3	72.6	2.8	73.9	1.8	73.7	-0.3	74.5	1.1	74.7	0.3	75.4	0.9	76.4	1.3	77.8	1.8	78.3	0.6
1981	79.0	0.9	80.7	2.2	81.0	0.4	81.5	0.6	81.9	0.5	82.8	1.1	83.7	1.1	84.3	0.7	85.3	1.2	85.2	-0.1	87.7	2.9	89.3	1.8
1982	90.0	0.8	90.2	0.2	90.8	0.7	91.8	1.1	92.8	1.1	94.5	1.8	94.9	0.4	95.9	1.1	97.0	1.1	96.7	-0.3	97.4	0.7	97.5	0.1
1983	99.2	1.7	99.4	0.2	99.7	0.3	100.2	0.5	100.3	0.1	101.1	0.8	101.6	0.5	101.2	-0.4	101.2	0.0	101.3	0.1	101.5	0.2	101.6	0.1
1984	103.1	1.5	103.2	0.1	103.6	0.4	104.1	0.5	104.6	0.5	104.6	0.0	105.5	0.9	106.1	0.6	105.8	-0.3	107.0	1.1	107.1	0.1	107.3	0.2
1985	110.0	2.5	110.5	0.5	111.1	0.5	111.2	0.1	111.4	0.2	112.2	0.7	112.8	0.5	113.7	0.8	114.5	0.7	115.0	0.4	115.7	0.6	116.4	0.6
1986	117.0	0.5	118.1	0.9	118.8	0.6	119.2	0.3	119.6	0.3	120.0	0.3	120.5	0.4	121.5	0.8	121.7	0.2	122.8	0.9	124.1	1.1	124.9	0.6
1987	126.1	1.0	126.7	0.5	127.1	0.3	127.7	0.5	127.6	-0.1	128.9	1.0	129.1	0.2	129.8	0.5	130.3	0.4	131.2	0.7	131.8	0.5	132.1	0.2
1988	135.1	2.3	136.2	0.8	137.0	0.6	136.9	-0.1	137.4	0.4	138.8	1.0	139.3	0.4	140.3	0.7	140.9	0.4	142.5	1.1	142.2	-0.2	142.3	0.1
1989	144.2	1.3	144.4	0.1	145.3	0.6	146.5	0.8	147.2	0.5	148.2	0.7	149.4	0.8	150.1	0.5	151.4	0.9	151.8	0.3	153.0	0.8	153.4	0.3
1990	155.8	1.6	156.9	0.7	157.5	0.4	158.6	0.7	159.3	0.4	160.2	0.6	161.4	0.7	161.7	0.2	163.6	1.2	166.3	1.7	168.5	1.3	168.7	0.1
1991	170.9	1.3	170.6	-0.2	172.2	0.9	172.3	0.1	173.5	0.7	175.3	1.0	177.7	1.4	177.5	-0.1	178.0	0.3	178.2	0.1	180.9	1.5	181.6	0.4

[Continued]

Los Angeles, CA
Consumer Price Index - Urban Wage Earners
Base 1982-1984 = 100
Medical Care
[Continued]

For 1947-1993. Columns headed % show percentile change in the index from the previous period for which an index is available.

Year	Jan Index	%	Feb Index	%	Mar Index	%	Apr Index	%	May Index	%	Jun Index	%	Jul Index	%	Aug Index	%	Sep Index	%	Oct Index	%	Nov Index	%	Dec Index	%
1992	183.7	1.2	185.2	0.8	186.2	0.5	186.9	0.4	188.3	0.7	189.4	0.6	191.2	1.0	191.8	0.3	192.6	0.4	194.6	1.0	194.2	-0.2	195.5	0.7
1993	196.6	0.6	199.6	1.5	199.4	-0.1	200.1	0.4	204.8	2.3	204.3	-0.2	204.7	0.2	205.1	0.2	206.0	0.4	208.5	1.2	208.3	-0.1	208.9	0.3

Source: U.S. Department of Labor, Bureau of Labor Statistics, Division of Consumer Prices and Price Indexes. - indicates no data collected for period.

Los Angeles, CA
Consumer Price Index - All Urban Consumers
Base 1982-1984 = 100
Entertainment

For 1976-1993. Columns headed % show percentile change in the index from the previous period for which an index is available.

Year	Jan Index	%	Feb Index	%	Mar Index	%	Apr Index	%	May Index	%	Jun Index	%	Jul Index	%	Aug Index	%	Sep Index	%	Oct Index	%	Nov Index	%	Dec Index	%
1976	68.9	-	69.4	0.7	69.6	0.3	70.1	0.7	70.2	0.1	70.2	0.0	71.2	1.4	70.8	-0.6	71.1	0.4	70.7	-0.6	71.8	1.6	72.0	0.3
1977	72.1	0.1	73.1	1.4	73.2	0.1	73.4	0.3	72.7	-1.0	72.8	0.1	72.9	0.1	73.6	1.0	73.5	-0.1	73.3	-0.3	73.4	0.1	75.4	2.2
1978	71.9	-2.6	73.8	2.6	74.6	1.1	76.3	2.3	76.0	-0.4	74.3	-2.2	74.6	0.4	72.6	-2.7	74.4	2.5	75.1	0.9	73.8	-1.7	75.4	2.2
1979	76.2	1.1	75.6	-0.8	77.4	2.4	77.6	0.3	78.1	0.6	78.5	0.5	79.0	0.6	79.3	0.4	79.8	0.6	79.8	0.0	80.9	1.4	81.3	0.5
1980	81.9	0.7	82.9	1.2	84.1	1.4	83.7	-0.5	84.1	0.5	84.8	0.8	85.9	1.3	87.0	1.3	88.7	2.0	88.3	-0.5	88.5	0.2	89.1	0.7
1981	91.2	2.4	91.0	-0.2	92.1	1.2	91.7	-0.4	92.7	1.1	92.1	-0.6	92.0	-0.1	94.7	2.9	95.1	0.4	94.7	-0.4	94.9	0.2	95.5	0.6
1982	96.2	0.7	96.9	0.7	98.3	1.4	99.4	1.1	99.2	-0.2	98.5	-0.7	97.5	-1.0	96.8	-0.7	96.4	-0.4	97.0	0.6	97.1	0.1	98.4	1.3
1983	98.4	0.0	100.0	1.6	101.0	1.0	99.8	-1.2	99.1	-0.7	99.4	0.3	98.7	-0.7	99.2	0.5	99.1	-0.1	100.7	1.6	100.4	-0.3	102.1	1.7
1984	101.7	-0.4	102.7	1.0	102.3	-0.4	102.3	0.0	102.1	-0.2	102.5	0.4	102.0	-0.5	102.3	0.3	103.1	0.8	103.3	0.2	103.6	0.3	103.0	-0.6
1985	104.1	1.1	104.0	-0.1	105.7	1.6	105.7	0.0	105.3	-0.4	107.9	2.5	107.7	-0.2	108.1	0.4	108.1	0.0	108.8	0.6	108.6	-0.2	108.4	-0.2
1986	108.4	0.0	108.5	0.1	108.1	-0.4	108.3	0.2	109.3	0.9	109.8	0.5	109.6	-0.2	109.5	-0.1	108.4	-1.0	108.7	0.3	109.9	1.1	109.8	-0.1
1987	110.1	0.3	110.1	0.0	109.9	-0.2	110.9	0.9	110.3	-0.5	110.8	0.5	111.4	0.5	110.9	-0.4	111.6	0.6	111.9	0.3	112.9	0.9	113.0	0.1
1988	113.1	0.1	114.0	0.8	114.3	0.3	114.9	0.5	114.9	0.0	114.7	-0.2	115.4	0.6	115.9	0.4	116.0	0.1	116.7	0.6	117.4	0.6	117.3	-0.1
1989	118.2	0.8	118.7	0.4	118.5	-0.2	119.8	1.1	120.1	0.3	120.7	0.5	121.0	0.2	121.1	0.1	123.1	1.7	122.9	-0.2	123.1	0.2	123.5	0.3
1990	122.5	-0.8	123.1	0.5	123.8	0.6	124.1	0.2	124.0	-0.1	124.0	0.0	125.5	1.2	123.6	-1.5	128.8	4.2	128.2	-0.5	128.3	0.1	128.6	0.2
1991	130.5	1.5	131.1	0.5	131.1	0.0	133.7	2.0	134.8	0.8	135.4	0.4	137.2	1.3	138.7	1.1	138.5	-0.1	140.9	1.7	139.9	-0.7	133.3	-4.7
1992	133.8	0.4	133.8	0.0	134.1	0.2	134.9	0.6	134.8	-0.1	132.9	-1.4	133.5	0.5	133.2	-0.2	134.0	0.6	134.6	0.4	134.3	-0.2	135.1	0.6
1993	135.9	0.6	135.5	-0.3	135.7	0.1	135.4	-0.2	134.1	-1.0	133.0	-0.8	133.9	0.7	135.0	0.8	136.0	0.7	137.7	1.2	138.9	0.9	138.8	-0.1

Source: U.S. Department of Labor, Bureau of Labor Statistics, Division of Consumer Prices and Price Indexes. - indicates no data collected for period.

Los Angeles, CA
Consumer Price Index - Urban Wage Earners
Base 1982-1984 = 100
Entertainment

For 1976-1993. Columns headed % show percentile change in the index from the previous period for which an index is available.

Year	Jan Index	%	Feb Index	%	Mar Index	%	Apr Index	%	May Index	%	Jun Index	%	Jul Index	%	Aug Index	%	Sep Index	%	Oct Index	%	Nov Index	%	Dec Index	%
1976	75.6	-	76.2	0.8	76.4	0.3	76.9	0.7	77.0	0.1	77.0	0.0	78.2	1.6	77.8	-0.5	78.1	0.4	77.7	-0.5	78.8	1.4	79.1	0.4
1977	79.2	0.1	80.2	1.3	80.4	0.2	80.6	0.2	79.8	-1.0	80.0	0.3	80.0	0.0	80.8	1.0	80.7	-0.1	80.5	-0.2	80.5	0.0	81.0	0.6
1978	81.5	0.6	83.3	2.2	79.2	-4.9	78.8	-0.5	80.7	2.4	79.4	-1.6	79.9	0.6	78.7	-1.5	79.6	1.1	80.1	0.6	78.9	-1.5	81.4	3.2
1979	82.0	0.7	81.3	-0.9	81.2	-0.1	81.4	0.2	83.4	2.5	84.0	0.7	85.1	1.3	81.6	-4.1	84.7	3.8	84.7	0.0	85.1	0.5	86.7	1.9
1980	87.7	1.2	88.0	0.3	88.8	0.9	89.4	0.7	89.6	0.2	90.5	1.0	90.6	0.1	90.7	0.1	93.0	2.5	93.3	0.3	94.0	0.8	94.3	0.3
1981	94.1	-0.2	94.0	-0.1	94.6	0.6	92.9	-1.8	93.7	0.9	93.6	-0.1	93.8	0.2	94.7	1.0	95.6	1.0	95.3	-0.3	95.6	0.3	95.6	0.0
1982	96.2	0.6	96.9	0.7	98.2	1.3	99.4	1.2	99.1	-0.3	98.4	-0.7	97.7	-0.7	96.9	-0.8	96.3	-0.6	96.7	0.4	96.9	0.2	98.2	1.3
1983	98.2	0.0	99.9	1.7	100.9	1.0	99.7	-1.2	99.1	-0.6	99.5	0.4	98.8	-0.7	99.3	0.5	99.1	-0.2	100.6	1.5	100.4	-0.2	101.9	1.5
1984	101.8	-0.1	102.7	0.9	102.4	-0.3	102.3	-0.1	102.1	-0.2	102.5	0.4	102.1	-0.4	102.4	0.3	103.2	0.8	103.3	0.1	103.6	0.3	103.2	-0.4
1985	104.2	1.0	104.0	-0.2	105.5	1.4	105.6	0.1	105.2	-0.4	107.5	2.2	107.3	-0.2	107.8	0.5	107.7	-0.1	108.3	0.6	108.3	0.0	107.9	-0.4
1986	108.0	0.1	108.0	0.0	107.6	-0.4	107.7	0.1	108.8	1.0	109.2	0.4	109.0	-0.2	108.9	-0.1	107.7	-1.1	108.0	0.3	109.2	1.1	109.1	-0.1
1987	109.3	0.2	109.5	0.2	109.1	-0.4	110.2	1.0	109.5	-0.6	110.2	0.6	110.6	0.4	110.5	-0.1	111.2	0.6	110.8	-0.4	111.9	1.0	112.6	0.6
1988	112.5	-0.1	112.7	0.2	113.1	0.4	113.7	0.5	114.2	0.4	114.0	-0.2	114.8	0.7	115.3	0.4	115.5	0.2	116.2	0.6	116.4	0.2	116.4	0.0
1989	117.3	0.8	118.0	0.6	117.6	-0.3	118.9	1.1	119.3	0.3	119.8	0.4	120.3	0.4	120.4	0.1	122.1	1.4	121.8	-0.2	122.1	0.2	122.6	0.4
1990	121.8	-0.7	122.3	0.4	122.8	0.4	123.3	0.4	123.3	0.0	123.4	0.1	124.5	0.9	123.8	-0.6	127.3	2.8	126.8	-0.4	126.8	0.0	127.1	0.2
1991	129.1	1.6	129.4	0.2	129.4	0.0	132.3	2.2	133.1	0.6	134.1	0.8	136.7	1.9	137.1	0.3	137.6	0.4	139.4	1.3	138.5	-0.6	132.2	-4.5
1992	132.6	0.3	132.6	0.0	133.5	0.7	134.2	0.5	134.2	0.0	134.2	0.0	134.9	0.5	134.4	-0.4	135.0	0.4	135.6	0.4	135.3	-0.2	136.2	0.7
1993	136.5	0.2	135.8	-0.5	136.6	0.6	136.3	-0.2	134.8	-1.1	134.2	-0.4	134.9	0.5	135.6	0.5	136.2	0.4	137.9	1.2	138.9	0.7	138.8	-0.1

Source: U.S. Department of Labor, Bureau of Labor Statistics, Division of Consumer Prices and Price Indexes. - indicates no data collected for period.

Los Angeles, CA
Consumer Price Index - All Urban Consumers
Base 1982-1984 = 100
Other Goods and Services

For 1976-1993. Columns headed % show percentile change in the index from the previous period for which an index is available.

Year	Jan Index	%	Feb Index	%	Mar Index	%	Apr Index	%	May Index	%	Jun Index	%	Jul Index	%	Aug Index	%	Sep Index	%	Oct Index	%	Nov Index	%	Dec Index	%
1976	55.9	-	55.9	0.0	56.5	1.1	56.6	0.2	56.8	0.4	57.3	0.9	57.4	0.2	57.4	0.0	57.8	0.7	58.3	0.9	58.9	1.0	59.2	0.5
1977	59.3	0.2	59.5	0.3	59.7	0.3	59.8	0.2	59.7	-0.2	60.1	0.7	60.3	0.3	60.3	0.0	61.5	2.0	62.1	1.0	62.0	-0.2	62.5	0.8
1978	63.4	1.4	63.6	0.3	63.4	-0.3	63.9	0.8	63.9	0.0	64.9	1.6	65.0	0.2	65.5	0.8	67.0	2.3	66.9	-0.1	66.8	-0.1	66.7	-0.1
1979	67.3	0.9	68.1	1.2	67.8	-0.4	68.5	1.0	68.0	-0.7	68.2	0.3	68.9	1.0	69.9	1.5	71.1	1.7	71.3	0.3	70.5	-1.1	71.3	1.1
1980	72.5	1.7	74.6	2.9	74.5	-0.1	75.6	1.5	76.0	0.5	76.1	0.1	76.1	0.0	76.4	0.4	78.2	2.4	78.5	0.4	78.6	0.1	79.3	0.9
1981	79.4	0.1	80.0	0.8	81.1	1.4	82.4	1.6	82.8	0.5	84.1	1.6	84.5	0.5	85.5	1.2	86.4	1.1	86.6	0.2	87.2	0.7	87.1	-0.1
1982	87.6	0.6	89.1	1.7	90.2	1.2	91.1	1.0	90.0	-1.2	90.3	0.3	91.5	1.3	92.1	0.7	92.9	0.9	94.8	2.0	97.2	2.5	97.8	0.6
1983	98.8	1.0	100.0	1.2	100.4	0.4	100.4	0.0	100.6	0.2	100.7	0.1	101.7	1.0	101.5	-0.2	102.1	0.6	102.6	0.5	102.6	0.0	102.5	-0.1
1984	103.3	0.8	103.9	0.6	103.8	-0.1	104.0	0.2	103.4	-0.6	103.3	-0.1	105.2	1.8	105.2	0.0	112.4	6.8	112.4	0.0	112.4	0.0	112.2	-0.2
1985	112.3	0.1	113.6	1.2	114.2	0.5	114.0	-0.2	113.9	-0.1	115.0	1.0	115.2	0.2	115.8	0.5	116.5	0.6	117.4	0.8	117.2	-0.2	118.1	0.8
1986	120.4	1.9	121.0	0.5	120.6	-0.3	121.4	0.7	121.7	0.2	122.3	0.5	121.2	-0.9	122.8	1.3	123.8	0.8	124.4	0.5	124.0	-0.3	123.3	-0.6
1987	124.1	0.6	124.9	0.6	125.0	0.1	125.4	0.3	126.4	0.8	126.6	0.2	126.7	0.1	127.4	0.6	131.4	3.1	131.5	0.1	132.0	0.4	133.4	1.1
1988	134.0	0.4	136.1	1.6	137.6	1.1	138.3	0.5	137.7	-0.4	138.3	0.4	139.0	0.5	139.9	0.6	143.4	2.5	144.6	0.8	144.8	0.1	145.1	0.2
1989	151.5	4.4	152.9	0.9	152.6	-0.2	152.9	0.2	152.6	-0.2	152.9	0.2	153.6	0.5	155.3	1.1	159.8	2.9	159.5	-0.2	158.8	-0.4	160.9	1.3
1990	161.6	0.4	163.3	1.1	162.5	-0.5	164.4	1.2	165.1	0.4	165.7	0.4	165.2	-0.3	165.9	0.4	169.2	2.0	170.3	0.7	170.7	0.2	171.6	0.5
1991	173.9	1.3	174.2	0.2	175.2	0.6	176.1	0.5	176.3	0.1	176.7	0.2	177.6	0.5	179.0	0.8	186.9	4.4	187.8	0.5	187.3	-0.3	188.2	0.5
1992	189.9	0.9	190.6	0.4	190.3	-0.2	195.7	2.8	195.6	-0.1	195.9	0.2	195.8	-0.1	195.8	0.0	199.3	1.8	204.3	2.5	205.6	0.6	206.4	0.4
1993	209.7	1.6	209.7	0.0	209.7	0.0	210.7	0.5	210.8	0.0	211.0	0.1	212.4	0.7	210.9	-0.7	213.2	1.1	213.3	0.0	215.4	1.0	216.2	0.4

Source: U.S. Department of Labor, Bureau of Labor Statistics, Division of Consumer Prices and Price Indexes. - indicates no data collected for period.

Los Angeles, CA
Consumer Price Index - Urban Wage Earners
Base 1982-1984 = 100
Other Goods and Services

For 1976-1993. Columns headed % show percentile change in the index from the previous period for which an index is available.

Year	Jan Index	%	Feb Index	%	Mar Index	%	Apr Index	%	May Index	%	Jun Index	%	Jul Index	%	Aug Index	%	Sep Index	%	Oct Index	%	Nov Index	%	Dec Index	%
1976	55.6	-	55.6	0.0	56.2	1.1	56.3	0.2	56.4	0.2	57.0	1.1	57.1	0.2	57.1	0.0	57.4	0.5	57.9	0.9	58.6	1.2	58.8	0.3
1977	59.0	0.3	59.1	0.2	59.3	0.3	59.4	0.2	59.4	0.0	59.7	0.5	59.9	0.3	59.9	0.0	61.1	2.0	61.7	1.0	61.6	-0.2	62.1	0.8
1978	62.7	1.0	63.2	0.8	63.4	0.3	62.9	-0.8	63.3	0.6	64.0	1.1	64.8	1.3	64.9	0.2	65.6	1.1	65.8	0.3	65.6	-0.3	65.3	-0.5
1979	66.7	2.1	67.3	0.9	67.4	0.1	67.8	0.6	68.0	0.3	68.1	0.1	68.7	0.9	69.2	0.7	69.9	1.0	70.1	0.3	69.6	-0.7	70.6	1.4
1980	72.2	2.3	73.5	1.8	73.6	0.1	74.5	1.2	75.3	1.1	74.6	-0.9	74.6	0.0	75.5	1.2	77.2	2.3	77.1	-0.1	77.3	0.3	78.6	1.7
1981	79.4	1.0	79.9	0.6	80.1	0.3	81.8	2.1	81.9	0.1	82.6	0.9	82.9	0.4	83.8	1.1	85.3	1.8	84.9	-0.5	85.7	0.9	86.3	0.7
1982	86.8	0.6	88.4	1.8	89.6	1.4	90.7	1.2	89.5	-1.3	89.9	0.4	91.1	1.3	91.8	0.8	92.5	0.8	94.6	2.3	97.1	2.6	97.8	0.7
1983	99.0	1.2	100.3	1.3	100.8	0.5	100.8	0.0	101.0	0.2	101.2	0.2	102.3	1.1	102.2	-0.1	102.8	0.6	103.2	0.4	103.3	0.1	103.0	-0.3
1984	103.9	0.9	104.6	0.7	104.5	-0.1	104.7	0.2	104.0	-0.7	103.9	-0.1	105.9	1.9	105.9	0.0	110.8	4.6	110.9	0.1	110.9	0.0	110.6	-0.3
1985	110.7	0.1	112.1	1.3	112.8	0.6	112.6	-0.2	112.5	-0.1	113.4	0.8	113.3	-0.1	114.2	0.8	114.8	0.5	115.8	0.9	115.5	-0.3	116.5	0.9
1986	118.9	2.1	119.6	0.6	119.1	-0.4	119.9	0.7	120.2	0.3	120.7	0.4	119.7	-0.8	121.4	1.4	122.1	0.6	122.7	0.5	122.4	-0.2	121.7	-0.6
1987	122.7	0.8	123.6	0.7	123.8	0.2	124.1	0.2	125.0	0.7	125.2	0.2	125.3	0.1	126.0	0.6	129.8	3.0	129.9	0.1	130.4	0.4	131.1	0.5
1988	131.9	0.6	133.6	1.3	135.1	1.1	135.9	0.6	135.1	-0.6	135.8	0.5	136.7	0.7	137.5	0.6	141.1	2.6	142.6	1.1	142.7	0.1	143.1	0.3
1989	151.0	5.5	152.7	1.1	152.4	-0.2	152.7	0.2	152.3	-0.3	152.5	0.1	153.4	0.6	155.3	1.2	159.4	2.6	159.0	-0.3	158.0	-0.6	160.5	1.6
1990	161.1	0.4	163.0	1.2	162.3	-0.4	164.3	1.2	164.9	0.4	165.8	0.5	165.3	-0.3	166.1	0.5	168.9	1.7	169.7	0.5	170.2	0.3	171.2	0.6
1991	173.7	1.5	173.8	0.1	174.8	0.6	175.6	0.5	175.9	0.2	176.5	0.3	177.6	0.6	179.3	1.0	184.8	3.1	185.4	0.3	185.2	-0.1	186.2	0.5
1992	188.1	1.0	189.1	0.5	188.5	-0.3	193.3	2.5	193.3	0.0	193.8	0.3	193.8	0.0	193.4	-0.2	195.8	1.2	199.0	1.6	200.4	0.7	201.5	0.5
1993	203.9	1.2	204.0	0.0	204.0	0.0	205.2	0.6	205.2	0.0	205.8	0.3	207.5	0.8	205.0	-1.2	202.1	-1.4	202.2	0.0	204.8	1.3	205.9	0.5

Source: U.S. Department of Labor, Bureau of Labor Statistics, Division of Consumer Prices and Price Indexes. - indicates no data collected for period.

Miami, FL
Consumer Price Index - All Urban Consumers
Base 1982-1984 = 100
Annual Averages

For 1977-1993. Columns headed % show percentile change in the index from the previous period for which an index is available.

Year	All Items		Food & Beverage		Housing		Apparel & Upkeep		Transportation		Medical Care		Entertainment		Other Goods & Services	
	Index	%	Index	%	Index	%	Index	%	Index	%	Index	%	Index	%	Index	%
1977	-	-	-	-	-	-	-	-	-	-	-	-	-	-	-	-
1978	64.8	-	69.8	-	62.9	-	77.6	-	59.6	-	61.4	-	80.2	-	63.7	-
1979	71.2	9.9	78.6	12.6	68.5	8.9	81.2	4.6	67.1	12.6	68.9	12.2	85.0	6.0	69.1	8.5
1980	81.1	13.9	84.7	7.8	80.8	18.0	87.0	7.1	78.5	17.0	75.6	9.7	89.6	5.4	76.2	10.3
1981	90.5	11.6	91.3	7.8	92.0	13.9	91.9	5.6	88.8	13.1	81.9	8.3	95.1	6.1	84.7	11.2
1982	96.7	6.9	96.8	6.0	97.8	6.3	98.2	6.9	94.8	6.8	93.8	14.5	98.4	3.5	93.1	9.9
1983	99.9	3.3	99.5	2.8	99.7	1.9	100.1	1.9	100.2	5.7	101.0	7.7	100.4	2.0	100.0	7.4
1984	103.5	3.6	103.6	4.1	102.6	2.9	101.7	1.6	105.0	4.8	105.1	4.1	101.3	0.9	106.9	6.9
1985	106.5	2.9	104.4	0.8	105.7	3.0	105.7	3.9	108.3	3.1	109.2	3.9	104.5	3.2	113.3	6.0
1986	107.9	1.3	107.1	2.6	107.0	1.2	109.0	3.1	103.7	-4.2	117.4	7.5	107.9	3.3	121.8	7.5
1987	111.8	3.6	113.0	5.5	108.7	1.6	115.6	6.1	106.6	2.8	126.6	7.8	113.7	5.4	128.3	5.3
1988	116.8	4.5	118.7	5.0	113.1	4.0	123.5	6.8	110.7	3.8	134.6	6.3	115.9	1.9	133.6	4.1
1989	121.5	4.0	125.6	5.8	116.2	2.7	131.3	6.3	114.8	3.7	140.5	4.4	117.8	1.6	139.8	4.6
1990	128.0	5.3	134.3	6.9	120.4	3.6	135.6	3.3	121.6	5.9	151.8	8.0	121.0	2.7	153.2	9.6
1991	132.3	3.4	137.7	2.5	123.7	2.7	140.4	3.5	126.0	3.6	162.8	7.2	126.4	4.5	161.5	5.4
1992	134.5	1.7	140.6	2.1	126.2	2.0	138.8	-1.1	127.8	1.4	172.3	5.8	124.6	-1.4	160.5	-0.6
1993	-	-	-	-	-	-	-	-	-	-	-	-	-	-	-	-

Source: U.S. Department of Labor, Bureau of Labor Statistics, Division of Consumer Prices and Price Indexes. - indicates no data collected for period.

Miami, FL
Consumer Price Index - Urban Wage Earners
Base 1982-1984 = 100
Annual Averages

For 1977-1993. Columns headed % show percentile change in the index from the previous period for which an index is available.

Year	All Items		Food & Beverage		Housing		Apparel & Upkeep		Trans- portation		Medical Care		Entertain- ment		Other Goods & Services	
	Index	%	Index	%	Index	%	Index	%	Index	%	Index	%	Index	%	Index	%
1977	-	-	-	-	-	-	-	-	-	-	-	-	-	-	-	-
1978	64.5	-	68.6	-	62.9	-	76.0	-	59.4	-	61.9	-	75.7	-	66.0	-
1979	71.3	10.5	78.3	14.1	68.3	8.6	80.2	5.5	67.5	13.6	67.8	9.5	81.4	7.5	71.3	-
1980	81.4	14.2	85.4	9.1	80.4	17.7	86.7	8.1	79.5	17.8	74.3	9.6	88.1	8.2	77.3	8.0
1981	90.5	11.2	91.6	7.3	92.1	14.6	91.7	5.8	89.6	12.7	79.8	7.4	94.6	7.4	84.4	8.4
1982	96.8	7.0	96.9	5.8	98.1	6.5	97.8	6.7	94.9	5.9	93.7	17.4	98.5	4.1	93.1	9.2
1983	99.9	3.2	99.5	2.7	99.6	1.5	100.0	2.2	100.3	5.7	101.3	8.1	100.5	2.0	100.1	10.3
1984	103.3	3.4	103.6	4.1	102.2	2.6	102.2	2.2	104.8	4.5	105.0	3.7	101.0	0.5	106.9	7.5
1985	106.4	3.0	104.3	0.7	106.0	3.7	106.0	3.7	107.9	3.0	108.7	3.5	105.2	4.2	112.4	6.8
1986	107.4	0.9	107.5	3.1	107.3	1.2	109.6	3.4	102.3	-5.2	116.6	7.3	108.4	3.0	120.8	5.1
1987	111.1	3.4	113.0	5.1	109.0	1.6	115.7	5.6	105.1	2.7	125.8	7.9	114.3	5.4	126.8	7.5
1988	115.9	4.3	118.5	4.9	113.4	4.0	122.8	6.1	109.0	3.7	133.1	5.8	116.2	1.7	132.6	5.0
1989	120.3	3.8	126.3	6.6	116.2	2.5	129.7	5.6	112.6	3.3	139.0	4.4	118.8	2.2	138.9	4.6
1990	126.2	4.9	134.8	6.7	120.2	3.4	133.3	2.8	118.3	5.1	150.7	8.4	122.1	2.8	151.5	4.8
1991	130.4	3.3	137.8	2.2	123.3	2.6	139.7	4.8	122.6	3.6	161.7	7.3	127.6	4.5	159.7	9.1
1992	132.6	1.7	139.7	1.4	125.7	1.9	138.3	-1.0	125.3	2.2	171.5	6.1	125.5	-1.6	157.7	5.4
1993	-	-	-	-	-	-	-	-	-	-	-	-	-	-	-	-1.3

Source: U.S. Department of Labor, Bureau of Labor Statistics, Division of Consumer Prices and Price Indexes. - indicates no data collected for period.

Miami, FL

Consumer Price Index - All Urban Consumers
Base 1982-1984 = 100

All Items

For 1977-1993. Columns headed % show percentile change in the index from the previous period for which an index is available.

Year	Jan Index	Jan %	Feb Index	Feb %	Mar Index	Mar %	Apr Index	Apr %	May Index	May %	Jun Index	Jun %	Jul Index	Jul %	Aug Index	Aug %	Sep Index	Sep %	Oct Index	Oct %	Nov Index	Nov %	Dec Index	Dec %
1977	-	-	-	-	-	-	-	-	-	-	-	-	-	-	-	-	-	-	-	-	62.0	-	-	-
1978	62.5	0.8	-	-	63.4	1.4	-	-	63.8	0.6	-	-	65.1	2.0	-	-	66.1	1.5	-	-	66.6	0.8	-	-
1979	67.6	1.5	-	-	69.0	2.1	-	-	69.8	1.2	-	-	71.8	2.9	-	-	72.8	1.4	-	-	74.1	1.8	-	-
1980	76.5	3.2	-	-	79.2	3.5	-	-	80.5	1.6	-	-	82.9	3.0	-	-	82.6	-0.4	-	-	83.1	0.6	-	-
1981	85.2	2.5	-	-	86.9	2.0	-	-	88.8	2.2	-	-	90.6	2.0	-	-	93.2	2.9	-	-	95.3	2.3	-	-
1982	96.3	1.0	-	-	96.2	-0.1	-	-	96.6	0.4	-	-	96.2	-0.4	-	-	96.8	0.6	-	-	97.3	0.5	-	-
1983	98.0	0.7	-	-	98.6	0.6	-	-	98.9	0.3	-	-	99.8	0.9	-	-	101.1	1.3	-	-	101.7	0.6	-	-
1984	102.4	0.7	-	-	102.7	0.3	-	-	103.2	0.5	-	-	103.6	0.4	-	-	104.2	0.6	-	-	104.4	0.2	-	-
1985	104.6	0.2	-	-	105.5	0.9	-	-	106.1	0.6	-	-	106.3	0.2	-	-	107.6	1.2	-	-	107.9	0.3	-	-
1986	108.3	0.4	-	-	108.3	0.0	-	-	107.3	-0.9	-	-	106.2	-1.0	-	-	108.1	1.8	-	-	109.1	0.9	-	-
1987	109.9	0.7	-	-	110.7	0.7	-	-	111.1	0.4	-	-	112.0	0.8	-	-	112.5	0.4	-	-	113.8	1.2	-	-
1988	114.5	0.6	-	-	115.1	0.5	-	-	116.2	1.0	-	-	116.8	0.5	-	-	118.8	1.7	-	-	118.3	-0.4	-	-
1989	120.0	1.4	-	-	119.8	-0.2	-	-	120.9	0.9	-	-	121.6	0.6	-	-	122.9	1.1	-	-	123.0	0.1	-	-
1990	124.6	1.3	-	-	125.1	0.4	-	-	126.4	1.0	-	-	128.7	1.8	-	-	130.1	1.1	-	-	131.2	0.8	-	-
1991	131.5	0.2	-	-	132.0	0.4	-	-	132.0	0.0	-	-	132.0	0.0	-	-	132.1	0.1	-	-	133.5	1.1	-	-
1992	133.7	0.1	-	-	134.5	0.6	-	-	133.7	-0.6	-	-	133.8	0.1	-	-	134.6	0.6	-	-	135.9	1.0	-	-
1993	137.8	1.4	-	-	139.2	1.0	-	-	139.0	-0.1	-	-	139.0	0.0	-	-	139.2	0.1	-	-	139.8	0.4	-	-

Source: U.S. Department of Labor, Bureau of Labor Statistics, Division of Consumer Prices and Price Indexes. - indicates no data collected for period.

Miami, FL
Consumer Price Index - Urban Wage Earners
Base 1982-1984 = 100
All Items

For 1977-1993. Columns headed % show percentile change in the index from the previous period for which an index is available.

Year	Jan Index	%	Feb Index	%	Mar Index	%	Apr Index	%	May Index	%	Jun Index	%	Jul Index	%	Aug Index	%	Sep Index	%	Oct Index	%	Nov Index	%	Dec Index	%
1977	-	-	-	-	-	-	-	-	-	-	-	-	-	-	-	-	-	-	-	-	61.6	-	-	-
1978	61.9	0.5	-	-	63.0	1.8	-	-	63.6	1.0	-	-	65.0	2.2	-	-	65.9	1.4	-	-	66.4	0.8	-	-
1979	67.2	1.2	-	-	69.2	3.0	-	-	70.0	1.2	-	-	72.0	2.9	-	-	73.1	1.5	-	-	74.2	1.5	-	-
1980	76.9	3.6	-	-	79.3	3.1	-	-	80.6	1.6	-	-	82.9	2.9	-	-	83.0	0.1	-	-	83.5	0.6	-	-
1981	85.4	2.3	-	-	87.2	2.1	-	-	89.1	2.2	-	-	90.7	1.8	-	-	92.9	2.4	-	-	95.2	2.5	-	-
1982	96.3	1.2	-	-	96.3	0.0	-	-	96.6	0.3	-	-	96.6	0.0	-	-	96.9	0.3	-	-	97.3	0.4	-	-
1983	98.0	0.7	-	-	98.3	0.3	-	-	99.3	1.0	-	-	100.2	0.9	-	-	101.1	0.9	-	-	101.5	0.4	-	-
1984	102.1	0.6	-	-	102.4	0.3	-	-	102.9	0.5	-	-	103.4	0.5	-	-	104.5	1.1	-	-	104.4	-0.1	-	-
1985	104.5	0.1	-	-	105.4	0.9	-	-	106.0	0.6	-	-	106.3	0.3	-	-	107.4	1.0	-	-	107.7	0.3	-	-
1986	108.1	0.4	-	-	107.8	-0.3	-	-	106.7	-1.0	-	-	105.6	-1.0	-	-	107.4	1.7	-	-	108.4	0.9	-	-
1987	109.3	0.8	-	-	109.9	0.5	-	-	110.3	0.4	-	-	111.3	0.9	-	-	111.8	0.4	-	-	113.1	1.2	-	-
1988	113.8	0.6	-	-	114.3	0.4	-	-	115.1	0.7	-	-	116.0	0.8	-	-	117.8	1.6	-	-	117.2	-0.5	-	-
1989	118.8	1.4	-	-	118.7	-0.1	-	-	120.0	1.1	-	-	120.6	0.5	-	-	121.4	0.7	-	-	121.5	0.1	-	-
1990	123.2	1.4	-	-	123.4	0.2	-	-	124.6	1.0	-	-	126.7	1.7	-	-	128.2	1.2	-	-	129.3	0.9	-	-
1991	129.8	0.4	-	-	130.1	0.2	-	-	130.2	0.1	-	-	130.2	0.0	-	-	130.2	0.0	-	-	131.4	0.9	-	-
1992	131.7	0.2	-	-	132.3	0.5	-	-	131.6	-0.5	-	-	132.0	0.3	-	-	132.8	0.6	-	-	134.2	1.1	-	-
1993	135.9	1.3	-	-	137.1	0.9	-	-	137.2	0.1	-	-	137.2	0.0	-	-	137.5	0.2	-	-	138.0	0.4	-	-

Source: U.S. Department of Labor, Bureau of Labor Statistics, Division of Consumer Prices and Price Indexes. - indicates no data collected for period.

Miami, FL
Consumer Price Index - All Urban Consumers
Base 1982-1984 = 100
Food and Beverages

For 1977-1993. Columns headed % show percentile change in the index from the previous period for which an index is available.

Year	Jan Index	%	Feb Index	%	Mar Index	%	Apr Index	%	May Index	%	Jun Index	%	Jul Index	%	Aug Index	%	Sep Index	%	Oct Index	%	Nov Index	%	Dec Index	%
1977	-	-	-	-	-	-	-	-	-	-	-	-	-	-	-	-	-	-	-	-	65.1	-	-	-
1978	65.9	1.2	-	-	67.5	2.4	-	-	69.2	2.5	-	-	71.0	2.6	-	-	71.1	0.1	-	-	72.1	1.4	-	-
1979	74.9	3.9	-	-	76.9	2.7	-	-	78.3	1.8	-	-	79.9	2.0	-	-	80.2	0.4	-	-	80.1	-0.1	-	-
1980	81.4	1.6	-	-	82.0	0.7	-	-	82.7	0.9	-	-	84.8	2.5	-	-	87.2	2.8	-	-	88.3	1.3	-	-
1981	89.4	1.2	-	-	89.6	0.2	-	-	89.8	0.2	-	-	91.1	1.4	-	-	92.8	1.9	-	-	93.9	1.2	-	-
1982	94.9	1.1	-	-	95.8	0.9	-	-	96.9	1.1	-	-	97.8	0.9	-	-	97.8	0.0	-	-	97.0	-0.8	-	-
1983	97.9	0.9	-	-	98.9	1.0	-	-	99.1	0.2	-	-	99.0	-0.1	-	-	100.2	1.2	-	-	100.8	0.6	-	-
1984	104.0	3.2	-	-	104.2	0.2	-	-	102.6	-1.5	-	-	103.2	0.6	-	-	103.5	0.3	-	-	104.3	0.8	-	-
1985	104.1	-0.2	-	-	105.2	1.1	-	-	103.5	-1.6	-	-	104.4	0.9	-	-	104.1	-0.3	-	-	104.7	0.6	-	-
1986	106.3	1.5	-	-	106.9	0.6	-	-	106.9	0.0	-	-	103.1	-3.6	-	-	108.3	5.0	-	-	110.0	1.6	-	-
1987	110.7	0.6	-	-	112.2	1.4	-	-	113.9	1.5	-	-	113.6	-0.3	-	-	113.4	-0.2	-	-	113.5	0.1	-	-
1988	114.8	1.1	-	-	116.9	1.8	-	-	117.6	0.6	-	-	118.4	0.7	-	-	121.1	2.3	-	-	121.7	0.5	-	-
1989	122.3	0.5	-	-	123.0	0.6	-	-	124.0	0.8	-	-	126.7	2.2	-	-	126.4	-0.2	-	-	128.5	1.7	-	-
1990	134.1	4.4	-	-	134.1	0.0	-	-	132.4	-1.3	-	-	134.2	1.4	-	-	134.4	0.1	-	-	136.1	1.3	-	-
1991	136.0	-0.1	-	-	137.7	1.2	-	-	137.7	0.0	-	-	138.0	0.2	-	-	138.2	0.1	-	-	138.1	-0.1	-	-
1992	138.7	0.4	-	-	140.5	1.3	-	-	138.9	-1.1	-	-	139.9	0.7	-	-	142.0	1.5	-	-	142.2	0.1	-	-
1993	144.9	1.9	-	-	145.7	0.6	-	-	146.1	0.3	-	-	145.9	-0.1	-	-	147.6	1.2	-	-	149.3	1.2	-	-

Source: U.S. Department of Labor, Bureau of Labor Statistics, Division of Consumer Prices and Price Indexes. - indicates no data collected for period.

Miami, FL
Consumer Price Index - Urban Wage Earners
Base 1982-1984 = 100
Food and Beverages

For 1977-1993. Columns headed % show percentile change in the index from the previous period for which an index is available.

Year	Jan Index	%	Feb Index	%	Mar Index	%	Apr Index	%	May Index	%	Jun Index	%	Jul Index	%	Aug Index	%	Sep Index	%	Oct Index	%	Nov Index	%	Dec Index	%
1977	-	-	-	-	-	-	-	-	-	-	-	-	-	-	-	-	-	-	-	-	63.0	-	-	-
1978	63.5	0.8	-	-	66.1	4.1	-	-	68.2	3.2	-	-	69.8	2.3	-	-	70.5	1.0	-	-	71.5	1.4	-	-
1979	73.1	2.2	-	-	77.1	5.5	-	-	78.2	1.4	-	-	79.3	1.4	-	-	79.7	0.5	-	-	80.2	0.6	-	-
1980	81.8	2.0	-	-	82.7	1.1	-	-	83.7	1.2	-	-	85.5	2.2	-	-	88.1	3.0	-	-	88.5	0.5	-	-
1981	89.5	1.1	-	-	89.8	0.3	-	-	90.0	0.2	-	-	91.8	2.0	-	-	93.8	2.2	-	-	93.6	-0.2	-	-
1982	94.7	1.2	-	-	95.6	1.0	-	-	97.0	1.5	-	-	98.2	1.2	-	-	98.2	0.0	-	-	97.0	-1.2	-	-
1983	97.8	0.8	-	-	99.0	1.2	-	-	99.2	0.2	-	-	99.2	0.0	-	-	100.2	1.0	-	-	100.5	0.3	-	-
1984	103.8	3.3	-	-	104.0	0.2	-	-	102.6	-1.3	-	-	103.1	0.5	-	-	103.6	0.5	-	-	104.3	0.7	-	-
1985	103.9	-0.4	-	-	105.1	1.2	-	-	103.4	-1.6	-	-	104.3	0.9	-	-	104.0	-0.3	-	-	104.6	0.6	-	-
1986	106.3	1.6	-	-	107.0	0.7	-	-	107.2	0.2	-	-	104.2	-2.8	-	-	108.7	4.3	-	-	110.4	1.6	-	-
1987	111.4	0.9	-	-	112.4	0.9	-	-	113.8	1.2	-	-	113.6	-0.2	-	-	113.1	-0.4	-	-	113.1	0.0	-	-
1988	114.2	1.0	-	-	116.5	2.0	-	-	116.9	0.3	-	-	118.2	1.1	-	-	121.4	2.7	-	-	121.9	0.4	-	-
1989	122.7	0.7	-	-	123.5	0.7	-	-	124.9	1.1	-	-	127.5	2.1	-	-	126.9	-0.5	-	-	128.9	1.6	-	-
1990	135.5	5.1	-	-	135.7	0.1	-	-	132.8	-2.1	-	-	134.1	1.0	-	-	134.2	0.1	-	-	136.4	1.6	-	-
1991	136.3	-0.1	-	-	138.1	1.3	-	-	138.2	0.1	-	-	138.4	0.1	-	-	138.0	-0.3	-	-	137.3	-0.5	-	-
1992	138.0	0.5	-	-	139.9	1.4	-	-	137.9	-1.4	-	-	138.7	0.6	-	-	141.2	1.8	-	-	141.0	-0.1	-	-
1993	143.7	1.9	-	-	144.8	0.8	-	-	145.2	0.3	-	-	144.5	-0.5	-	-	146.4	1.3	-	-	148.5	1.4	-	-

Source: U.S. Department of Labor, Bureau of Labor Statistics, Division of Consumer Prices and Price Indexes. - indicates no data collected for period.

Miami, FL
Consumer Price Index - All Urban Consumers
Base 1982-1984 = 100
Housing

For 1977-1993. Columns headed % show percentile change in the index from the previous period for which an index is available.

Year	Jan Index	%	Feb Index	%	Mar Index	%	Apr Index	%	May Index	%	Jun Index	%	Jul Index	%	Aug Index	%	Sep Index	%	Oct Index	%	Nov Index	%	Dec Index	%
1977	-	-	-	-	-	-	-	-	-	-	-	-	-	-	-	-	-	-	-	-	60.6	-	-	-
1978	61.0	0.7	-	-	62.0	1.6	-	-	61.7	-0.5	-	-	63.2	2.4	-	-	64.4	1.9	-	-	64.5	0.2	-	-
1979	65.1	0.9	-	-	66.4	2.0	-	-	66.3	-0.2	-	-	68.8	3.8	-	-	69.8	1.5	-	-	71.8	2.9	-	-
1980	74.7	4.0	-	-	78.8	5.5	-	-	80.6	2.3	-	-	84.4	4.7	-	-	82.1	-2.7	-	-	81.9	-0.2	-	-
1981	84.8	3.5	-	-	86.7	2.2	-	-	89.8	3.6	-	-	92.3	2.8	-	-	95.7	3.7	-	-	99.2	3.7	-	-
1982	99.9	0.7	-	-	99.2	-0.7	-	-	98.7	-0.5	-	-	95.8	-2.9	-	-	96.7	0.9	-	-	96.7	0.0	-	-
1983	98.2	1.6	-	-	99.4	1.2	-	-	98.8	-0.6	-	-	99.7	0.9	-	-	100.6	0.9	-	-	100.8	0.2	-	-
1984	101.1	0.3	-	-	101.2	0.1	-	-	102.5	1.3	-	-	102.9	0.4	-	-	103.9	1.0	-	-	103.2	-0.7	-	-
1985	103.7	0.5	-	-	104.0	0.3	-	-	105.2	1.2	-	-	105.2	0.0	-	-	107.9	2.6	-	-	107.2	-0.6	-	-
1986	106.7	-0.5	-	-	107.6	0.8	-	-	106.8	-0.7	-	-	106.0	-0.7	-	-	107.3	1.2	-	-	107.6	0.3	-	-
1987	108.1	0.5	-	-	108.0	-0.1	-	-	106.9	-1.0	-	-	108.3	1.3	-	-	109.3	0.9	-	-	110.8	1.4	-	-
1988	111.8	0.9	-	-	111.1	-0.6	-	-	112.9	1.6	-	-	113.6	0.6	-	-	114.9	1.1	-	-	113.4	-1.3	-	-
1989	115.2	1.6	-	-	115.0	-0.2	-	-	115.2	0.2	-	-	116.5	1.1	-	-	117.9	1.2	-	-	117.2	-0.6	-	-
1990	116.7	-0.4	-	-	116.1	-0.5	-	-	119.6	3.0	-	-	123.3	3.1	-	-	123.1	-0.2	-	-	122.3	-0.6	-	-
1991	122.3	0.0	-	-	122.5	0.2	-	-	123.0	0.4	-	-	124.2	1.0	-	-	123.7	-0.4	-	-	125.4	1.4	-	-
1992	126.0	0.5	-	-	126.6	0.5	-	-	126.2	-0.3	-	-	125.7	-0.4	-	-	125.1	-0.5	-	-	127.0	1.5	-	-
1993	128.5	1.2	-	-	130.3	1.4	-	-	129.8	-0.4	-	-	130.5	0.5	-	-	131.2	0.5	-	-	131.1	-0.1	-	-

Source: U.S. Department of Labor, Bureau of Labor Statistics, Division of Consumer Prices and Price Indexes. - indicates no data collected for period.

Miami, FL
Consumer Price Index - Urban Wage Earners
Base 1982-1984 = 100
Housing

For 1977-1993. Columns headed % show percentile change in the index from the previous period for which an index is available.

Year	Jan Index	%	Feb Index	%	Mar Index	%	Apr Index	%	May Index	%	Jun Index	%	Jul Index	%	Aug Index	%	Sep Index	%	Oct Index	%	Nov Index	%	Dec Index	%
1977	-	-	-	-	-	-	-	-	-	-	-	-	-	-	-	-	-	-	-	-	60.6	-	-	-
1978	60.9	0.5	-	-	62.0	1.8	-	-	61.6	-0.6	-	-	63.2	2.6	-	-	64.2	1.6	-	-	64.4	0.3	-	-
1979	65.1	1.1	-	-	66.3	1.8	-	-	66.3	0.0	-	-	68.7	3.6	-	-	69.7	1.5	-	-	71.5	2.6	-	-
1980	74.4	4.1	-	-	78.3	5.2	-	-	80.0	2.2	-	-	84.1	5.1	-	-	81.7	-2.9	-	-	81.7	0.0	-	-
1981	84.6	3.5	-	-	86.6	2.4	-	-	89.9	3.8	-	-	92.3	2.7	-	-	95.7	3.7	-	-	99.5	4.0	-	-
1982	100.4	0.9	-	-	99.7	-0.7	-	-	99.1	-0.6	-	-	96.0	-3.1	-	-	96.9	0.9	-	-	97.0	0.1	-	-
1983	97.9	0.9	-	-	98.4	0.5	-	-	99.6	1.2	-	-	100.4	0.8	-	-	100.4	0.0	-	-	100.4	0.0	-	-
1984	100.6	0.2	-	-	100.4	-0.2	-	-	101.8	1.4	-	-	102.4	0.6	-	-	104.5	2.1	-	-	103.3	-1.1	-	-
1985	103.9	0.6	-	-	104.4	0.5	-	-	105.6	1.1	-	-	105.6	0.0	-	-	108.2	2.5	-	-	107.5	-0.6	-	-
1986	107.0	-0.5	-	-	107.9	0.8	-	-	107.0	-0.8	-	-	106.1	-0.8	-	-	107.5	1.3	-	-	107.9	0.4	-	-
1987	108.4	0.5	-	-	108.3	-0.1	-	-	107.1	-1.1	-	-	108.6	1.4	-	-	109.5	0.8	-	-	111.1	1.5	-	-
1988	112.2	1.0	-	-	111.4	-0.7	-	-	113.0	1.4	-	-	113.8	0.7	-	-	115.3	1.3	-	-	113.7	-1.4	-	-
1989	115.3	1.4	-	-	114.9	-0.3	-	-	115.4	0.4	-	-	116.7	1.1	-	-	117.7	0.9	-	-	117.1	-0.5	-	-
1990	116.7	-0.3	-	-	116.0	-0.6	-	-	119.3	2.8	-	-	122.9	3.0	-	-	122.8	-0.1	-	-	122.0	-0.7	-	-
1991	122.0	0.0	-	-	122.2	0.2	-	-	122.6	0.3	-	-	123.8	1.0	-	-	123.4	-0.3	-	-	125.0	1.3	-	-
1992	125.6	0.5	-	-	126.2	0.5	-	-	125.6	-0.5	-	-	125.3	-0.2	-	-	124.6	-0.6	-	-	126.5	1.5	-	-
1993	127.9	1.1	-	-	129.6	1.3	-	-	129.3	-0.2	-	-	129.9	0.5	-	-	130.6	0.5	-	-	130.3	-0.2	-	-

Source: U.S. Department of Labor, Bureau of Labor Statistics, Division of Consumer Prices and Price Indexes. - indicates no data collected for period.

Miami, FL
Consumer Price Index - All Urban Consumers
Base 1982-1984 = 100
Apparel and Upkeep

For 1977-1993. Columns headed % show percentile change in the index from the previous period for which an index is available.

Year	Jan Index	%	Feb Index	%	Mar Index	%	Apr Index	%	May Index	%	Jun Index	%	Jul Index	%	Aug Index	%	Sep Index	%	Oct Index	%	Nov Index	%	Dec Index	%
1977	-	-	-	-	-	-	-	-	-	-	-	-	-	-	-	-	-	-	-	-	74.8	-	-	-
1978	75.6	1.1	-	-	77.2	2.1	-	-	77.1	-0.1	-	-	77.6	0.6	-	-	78.7	1.4	-	-	78.9	0.3	-	-
1979	78.7	-0.3	-	-	79.8	1.4	-	-	80.3	0.6	-	-	81.5	1.5	-	-	82.2	0.9	-	-	83.7	1.8	-	-
1980	82.3	-1.7	-	-	86.0	4.5	-	-	87.2	1.4	-	-	87.8	0.7	-	-	88.0	0.2	-	-	88.8	0.9	-	-
1981	90.9	2.4	-	-	89.8	-1.2	-	-	90.3	0.6	-	-	92.3	2.2	-	-	93.2	1.0	-	-	93.6	0.4	-	-
1982	95.7	2.2	-	-	97.6	2.0	-	-	98.3	0.7	-	-	99.4	1.1	-	-	97.0	-2.4	-	-	100.3	3.4	-	-
1983	99.0	-1.3	-	-	99.8	0.8	-	-	99.2	-0.6	-	-	100.6	1.4	-	-	99.9	-0.7	-	-	102.2	2.3	-	-
1984	99.8	-2.3	-	-	100.6	0.8	-	-	101.8	1.2	-	-	102.0	0.2	-	-	102.7	0.7	-	-	102.7	0.0	-	-
1985	101.5	-1.2	-	-	104.9	3.3	-	-	104.5	-0.4	-	-	104.7	0.2	-	-	107.5	2.7	-	-	108.8	1.2	-	-
1986	109.5	0.6	-	-	108.5	-0.9	-	-	108.6	0.1	-	-	108.5	-0.1	-	-	108.6	0.1	-	-	110.4	1.7	-	-
1987	110.5	0.1	-	-	114.8	3.9	-	-	117.1	2.0	-	-	116.3	-0.7	-	-	115.8	-0.4	-	-	117.3	1.3	-	-
1988	119.0	1.4	-	-	121.7	2.3	-	-	121.4	-0.2	-	-	122.4	0.8	-	-	126.2	3.1	-	-	127.1	0.7	-	-
1989	131.0	3.1	-	-	129.0	-1.5	-	-	129.3	0.2	-	-	125.2	-3.2	-	-	138.0	10.2	-	-	135.8	-1.6	-	-
1990	130.4	-4.0	-	-	136.6	4.8	-	-	132.1	-3.3	-	-	134.9	2.1	-	-	138.6	2.7	-	-	139.5	0.6	-	-
1991	135.6	-2.8	-	-	143.6	5.9	-	-	142.3	-0.9	-	-	137.1	-3.7	-	-	140.6	2.6	-	-	142.2	1.1	-	-
1992	140.4	-1.3	-	-	140.7	0.2	-	-	138.8	-1.4	-	-	134.2	-3.3	-	-	144.2	7.5	-	-	134.8	-6.5	-	-
1993	139.4	3.4	-	-	148.9	6.8	-	-	144.5	-3.0	-	-	139.0	-3.8	-	-	137.5	-1.1	-	-	134.1	-2.5	-	-

Source: U.S. Department of Labor, Bureau of Labor Statistics, Division of Consumer Prices and Price Indexes. - indicates no data collected for period.

Miami, FL
Consumer Price Index - Urban Wage Earners
Base 1982-1984 = 100
Apparel and Upkeep

For 1977-1993. Columns headed % show percentile change in the index from the previous period for which an index is available.

Year	Jan		Feb		Mar		Apr		May		Jun		Jul		Aug		Sep		Oct		Nov		Dec	
	Index	%	Index	%	Index	%	Index	%	Index	%	Index	%	Index	%	Index	%	Index	%	Index	%	Index	%	Index	%
1977	-	-	-		-	-	-	-	-		-		-	-	-		-		-		74.5	-	-	-
1978	74.8	0.4	-	-	74.9	0.1	-	-	75.3	0.5	-	-	76.3	1.3	-		76.7	0.5	-		77.3	0.8	-	-
1979	76.9	-0.5	-	-	79.5	3.4	-	-	79.4	-0.1	-	-	80.1	0.9	-		81.6	1.9	-		82.5	1.1	-	-
1980	82.8	0.4	-	-	84.0	1.4	-	-	85.7	2.0	-	-	86.6	1.1	-		89.2	3.0	-		90.1	1.0	-	-
1981	90.7	0.7	-	-	91.2	0.6	-	-	91.5	0.3	-	-	91.3	-0.2	-		91.5	0.2	-		93.0	1.6		
1982	95.1	2.3	-	-	97.1	2.1	-	-	97.9	0.8	-	-	99.2	1.3	-		96.5	-2.7	-		100.0	3.6	-	-
1983	98.9	-1.1	-	-	99.2	0.3	-	-	99.2	0.0	-		100.6	1.4	-		99.9	-0.7	-		101.9	2.0	-	-
1984	100.0	-1.9	-	-	100.9	0.9	-	-	102.4	1.5	-	-	102.8	0.4	-		103.4	0.6	-		103.5	0.1	-	-
1985	102.0	-1.4	-	-	105.5	3.4	-	-	104.7	-0.8	-	-	104.7	0.0	-		108.0	3.2	-		109.1	1.0	-	-
1986	110.0	0.8	-	-	109.0	-0.9	-	-	109.5	0.5	-	-	109.2	-0.3	-		109.1	-0.1	-		110.6	1.4	-	-
1987	110.8	0.2	-	-	114.9	3.7	-	-	117.1	1.9	-	-	116.1	-0.9	-		115.9	-0.2	-		117.2	1.1	-	-
1988	118.8	1.4	-	-	121.8	2.5	-	-	121.0	-0.7	-	-	122.5	1.2	-		124.5	1.6	-		125.6	0.9	-	-
1989	129.2	2.9	-	-	127.5	-1.3	-	-	127.9	0.3	-	-	123.4	-3.5	-		136.7	10.8	-		133.9	-2.0	-	-
1990	128.6	-4.0	-	-	134.3	4.4	-	-	129.6	-3.5	-	-	132.3	2.1	-		137.3	3.8	-		136.4	-0.7		
1991	134.5	-1.4	-	-	142.4	5.9	-	-	141.3	-0.8	-	-	137.2	-2.9	-		139.9	2.0	-		141.8	1.4	-	-
1992	140.5	-0.9	-	-	140.5	0.0	-	-	138.0	-1.8	-	-	132.7	-3.8	-		143.5	8.1	-		134.9	-6.0	-	-
1993	139.5	3.4	-	-	147.7	5.9	-	-	145.6	-1.4	-	-	140.1	-3.8	-		139.5	-0.4	-		134.9	-3.3	-	-

Source: U.S. Department of Labor, Bureau of Labor Statistics, Division of Consumer Prices and Price Indexes. - indicates no data collected for period.

Miami, FL
Consumer Price Index - All Urban Consumers
Base 1982-1984 = 100
Transportation

For 1977-1993. Columns headed % show percentile change in the index from the previous period for which an index is available.

Year	Jan Index	%	Feb Index	%	Mar Index	%	Apr Index	%	May Index	%	Jun Index	%	Jul Index	%	Aug Index	%	Sep Index	%	Oct Index	%	Nov Index	%	Dec Index	%
1977	-	-	-	-	-	-	-	-	-	-	-	-	-	-	-	-	-	-	-	-	58.0	-	-	-
1978	58.0	0.0	-	-	58.2	0.3	-	-	58.5	0.5	-	-	60.0	2.6	-	-	60.6	1.0	-	-	61.6	1.7	-	-
1979	62.2	1.0	-	-	63.4	1.9	-	-	66.0	4.1	-	-	68.5	3.8	-	-	69.5	1.5	-	-	70.0	0.7	-	-
1980	74.0	5.7	-	-	76.8	3.8	-	-	77.9	1.4	-	-	79.2	1.7	-	-	79.7	0.6	-	-	81.3	2.0	-	-
1981	83.0	2.1	-	-	86.8	4.6	-	-	88.4	1.8	-	-	89.8	1.6	-	-	90.5	0.8	-	-	91.8	1.4	-	-
1982	93.0	1.3	-	-	92.6	-0.4	-	-	93.4	0.9	-	-	96.1	2.9	-	-	96.0	-0.1	-	-	96.7	0.7	-	-
1983	96.9	0.2	-	-	96.6	-0.3	-	-	98.8	2.3	-	-	100.4	1.6	-	-	103.2	2.8	-	-	103.8	0.6	-	-
1984	103.1	-0.7	-	-	103.7	0.6	-	-	105.1	1.4	-	-	105.4	0.3	-	-	105.6	0.2	-	-	106.5	0.9	-	-
1985	106.1	-0.4	-	-	106.9	0.8	-	-	108.8	1.8	-	-	109.1	0.3	-	-	108.6	-0.5	-	-	109.3	0.6	-	-
1986	109.5	0.2	-	-	105.5	-3.7	-	-	102.5	-2.8	-	-	102.2	-0.3	-	-	101.4	-0.8	-	-	102.2	0.8	-	-
1987	104.0	1.8	-	-	104.8	0.8	-	-	106.2	1.3	-	-	107.0	0.8	-	-	107.3	0.3	-	-	109.3	1.9	-	-
1988	108.8	-0.5	-	-	109.0	0.2	-	-	109.8	0.7	-	-	110.7	0.8	-	-	112.2	1.4	-	-	112.3	0.1	-	-
1989	113.9	1.4	-	-	113.5	-0.4	-	-	116.3	2.5	-	-	115.9	-0.3	-	-	113.7	-1.9	-	-	114.3	0.5	-	-
1990	118.8	3.9	-	-	118.4	-0.3	-	-	119.8	1.2	-	-	119.0	-0.7	-	-	123.0	3.4	-	-	128.2	4.2	-	-
1991	129.4	0.9	-	-	126.2	-2.5	-	-	126.4	0.2	-	-	124.3	-1.7	-	-	124.4	0.1	-	-	126.3	1.5	-	-
1992	125.6	-0.6	-	-	125.5	-0.1	-	-	126.7	1.0	-	-	128.7	1.6	-	-	127.8	-0.7	-	-	131.3	2.7	-	-
1993	131.7	0.3	-	-	130.9	-0.6	-	-	131.7	0.6	-	-	132.0	0.2	-	-	130.7	-1.0	-	-	134.1	2.6	-	-

Source: U.S. Department of Labor, Bureau of Labor Statistics, Division of Consumer Prices and Price Indexes. - indicates no data collected for period.

Miami, FL
Consumer Price Index - Urban Wage Earners
Base 1982-1984 = 100
Transportation

For 1977-1993. Columns headed % show percentile change in the index from the previous period for which an index is available.

Year	Jan Index	%	Feb Index	%	Mar Index	%	Apr Index	%	May Index	%	Jun Index	%	Jul Index	%	Aug Index	%	Sep Index	%	Oct Index	%	Nov Index	%	Dec Index	%
1977	-	-	-	-	-	-	-	-	-	-	-	-	-	-	-	-	-	-	-	-	57.6	-	-	-
1978	57.6	0.0	-	-	57.7	0.2	-	-	58.4	1.2	-	-	59.8	2.4	-	-	60.5	1.2	-	-	61.2	1.2	-	-
1979	62.0	1.3	-	-	63.5	2.4	-	-	66.4	4.6	-	-	69.0	3.9	-	-	70.0	1.4	-	-	70.5	0.7	-	-
1980	75.0	6.4	-	-	77.6	3.5	-	-	79.0	1.8	-	-	80.0	1.3	-	-	81.0	1.3	-	-	82.4	1.7	-	-
1981	84.4	2.4	-	-	88.0	4.3	-	-	89.4	1.6	-	-	90.1	0.8	-	-	91.0	1.0	-	-	92.6	1.8	-	-
1982	93.5	1.0	-	-	93.0	-0.5	-	-	93.1	0.1	-	-	96.2	3.3	-	-	96.1	-0.1	-	-	96.8	0.7	-	-
1983	97.4	0.6	-	-	96.6	-0.8	-	-	98.8	2.3	-	-	100.5	1.7	-	-	103.4	2.9	-	-	103.7	0.3	-	-
1984	102.9	-0.8	-	-	103.5	0.6	-	-	104.9	1.4	-	-	105.2	0.3	-	-	105.4	0.2	-	-	106.1	0.7	-	-
1985	105.7	-0.4	-	-	106.5	0.8	-	-	108.4	1.8	-	-	108.7	0.3	-	-	108.2	-0.5	-	-	108.8	0.6	-	-
1986	109.0	0.2	-	-	104.5	-4.1	-	-	101.0	-3.3	-	-	100.6	-0.4	-	-	99.9	-0.7	-	-	100.7	0.8	-	-
1987	102.0	1.3	-	-	103.0	1.0	-	-	104.7	1.7	-	-	105.8	1.1	-	-	105.9	0.1	-	-	107.8	1.8	-	-
1988	107.4	-0.4	-	-	107.5	0.1	-	-	108.1	0.6	-	-	109.0	0.8	-	-	110.3	1.2	-	-	110.4	0.1	-	-
1989	112.0	1.4	-	-	111.6	-0.4	-	-	114.0	2.2	-	-	113.7	-0.3	-	-	111.6	-1.8	-	-	112.0	0.4	-	-
1990	115.9	3.5	-	-	115.3	-0.5	-	-	116.6	1.1	-	-	116.0	-0.5	-	-	119.7	3.2	-	-	124.1	3.7	-	-
1991	125.1	0.8	-	-	122.3	-2.2	-	-	122.9	0.5	-	-	121.3	-1.3	-	-	121.5	0.2	-	-	123.1	1.3	-	-
1992	122.3	-0.6	-	-	121.9	-0.3	-	-	123.8	1.6	-	-	126.5	2.2	-	-	126.3	-0.2	-	-	129.2	2.3	-	-
1993	129.5	0.2	-	-	128.6	-0.7	-	-	129.6	0.8	-	-	130.3	0.5	-	-	129.6	-0.5	-	-	132.3	2.1	-	-

Source: U.S. Department of Labor, Bureau of Labor Statistics, Division of Consumer Prices and Price Indexes. - indicates no data collected for period.

Miami, FL
Consumer Price Index - All Urban Consumers
Base 1982-1984 = 100
Medical Care

For 1977-1993. Columns headed % show percentile change in the index from the previous period for which an index is available.

Year	Jan Index	%	Feb Index	%	Mar Index	%	Apr Index	%	May Index	%	Jun Index	%	Jul Index	%	Aug Index	%	Sep Index	%	Oct Index	%	Nov Index	%	Dec Index	%
1977	-	-	-	-	-	-	-	-	-	-	-	-	-	-	-	-	-	-	-	-	57.9	-	-	-
1978	59.3	2.4	-	-	59.5	0.3	-	-	60.3	1.3	-	-	60.6	0.5	-	-	63.0	4.0	-	-	64.4	2.2	-	-
1979	65.2	1.2	-	-	67.4	3.4	-	-	67.5	0.1	-	-	68.4	1.3	-	-	70.5	3.1	-	-	72.3	2.6	-	-
1980	74.6	3.2	-	-	75.5	1.2	-	-	75.6	0.1	-	-	75.4	-0.3	-	-	75.8	0.5	-	-	75.7	-0.1	-	-
1981	77.8	2.8	-	-	79.1	1.7	-	-	80.2	1.4	-	-	81.6	1.7	-	-	84.6	3.7	-	-	85.6	1.2	-	-
1982	87.8	2.6	-	-	89.1	1.5	-	-	92.0	3.3	-	-	95.1	3.4	-	-	96.5	1.5	-	-	99.8	3.4	-	-
1983	99.7	-0.1	-	-	100.0	0.3	-	-	100.0	0.0	-	-	101.0	1.0	-	-	101.5	0.5	-	-	102.9	1.4	-	-
1984	103.9	1.0	-	-	105.0	1.1	-	-	105.0	0.0	-	-	105.0	0.0	-	-	104.8	-0.2	-	-	106.3	1.4	-	-
1985	107.0	0.7	-	-	108.6	1.5	-	-	108.4	-0.2	-	-	108.7	0.3	-	-	109.7	0.9	-	-	111.2	1.4	-	-
1986	113.4	2.0	-	-	115.4	1.8	-	-	115.6	0.2	-	-	116.0	0.3	-	-	120.1	3.5	-	-	121.1	0.8	-	-
1987	122.9	1.5	-	-	123.7	0.7	-	-	124.8	0.9	-	-	128.4	2.9	-	-	127.7	-0.5	-	-	130.2	2.0	-	-
1988	131.4	0.9	-	-	133.3	1.4	-	-	134.0	0.5	-	-	134.4	0.3	-	-	136.1	1.3	-	-	136.7	0.4	-	-
1989	137.9	0.9	-	-	137.9	0.0	-	-	140.5	1.9	-	-	140.9	0.3	-	-	141.7	0.6	-	-	142.6	0.6	-	-
1990	143.3	0.5	-	-	145.0	1.2	-	-	150.1	3.5	-	-	153.5	2.3	-	-	156.4	1.9	-	-	158.3	1.2	-	-
1991	159.7	0.9	-	-	160.4	0.4	-	-	161.8	0.9	-	-	163.1	0.8	-	-	162.9	-0.1	-	-	166.7	2.3	-	-
1992	169.6	1.7	-	-	171.0	0.8	-	-	171.7	0.4	-	-	171.2	-0.3	-	-	171.3	0.1	-	-	176.4	3.0	-	-
1993	179.2	1.6	-	-	180.1	0.5	-	-	182.0	1.1	-	-	183.1	0.6	-	-	183.1	0.0	-	-	182.7	-0.2	-	-

Source: U.S. Department of Labor, Bureau of Labor Statistics, Division of Consumer Prices and Price Indexes. - indicates no data collected for period.

Miami, FL
Consumer Price Index - Urban Wage Earners
Base 1982-1984 = 100
Medical Care

For 1977-1993. Columns headed % show percentile change in the index from the previous period for which an index is available.

Year	Jan Index	%	Feb Index	%	Mar Index	%	Apr Index	%	May Index	%	Jun Index	%	Jul Index	%	Aug Index	%	Sep Index	%	Oct Index	%	Nov Index	%	Dec Index	%
1977	-	-	-	-	-	-	-	-	-	-	-	-	-	-	-	-	-	-	-	-	58.2	-	-	-
1978	59.3	1.9	-	-	59.5	0.3	-	-	61.9	4.0	-	-	62.2	0.5	-	-	63.4	1.9	-	-	64.0	0.9	-	-
1979	64.7	1.1	-	-	65.5	1.2	-	-	65.8	0.5	-	-	66.8	1.5	-	-	70.4	5.4	-	-	71.4	1.4	-	-
1980	73.5	2.9	-	-	74.3	1.1	-	-	74.2	-0.1	-	-	74.0	-0.3	-	-	74.4	0.5	-	-	74.8	0.5	-	-
1981	76.0	1.6	-	-	77.1	1.4	-	-	77.5	0.5	-	-	79.5	2.6	-	-	80.7	1.5	-	-	85.4	5.8	-	-
1982	87.6	2.6	-	-	89.1	1.7	-	-	91.9	3.1	-	-	94.7	3.0	-	-	96.1	1.5	-	-	99.9	4.0	-	-
1983	100.0	0.1	-	-	100.4	0.4	-	-	100.4	0.0	-	-	101.3	0.9	-	-	101.8	0.5	-	-	103.0	1.2	-	-
1984	103.9	0.9	-	-	104.9	1.0	-	-	104.9	0.0	-	-	104.9	0.0	-	-	104.6	-0.3	-	-	106.0	1.3	-	-
1985	106.5	0.5	-	-	108.1	1.5	-	-	108.0	-0.1	-	-	108.2	0.2	-	-	109.2	0.9	-	-	110.6	1.3	-	-
1986	112.5	1.7	-	-	114.6	1.9	-	-	114.8	0.2	-	-	115.3	0.4	-	-	119.4	3.6	-	-	120.4	0.8	-	-
1987	122.2	1.5	-	-	123.0	0.7	-	-	124.2	1.0	-	-	127.6	2.7	-	-	126.9	-0.5	-	-	129.0	1.7	-	-
1988	130.4	1.1	-	-	131.8	1.1	-	-	132.6	0.6	-	-	132.8	0.2	-	-	134.5	1.3	-	-	134.8	0.2	-	-
1989	136.2	1.0	-	-	136.4	0.1	-	-	138.9	1.8	-	-	139.3	0.3	-	-	140.5	0.9	-	-	141.5	0.7	-	-
1990	142.1	0.4	-	-	143.7	1.1	-	-	149.0	3.7	-	-	152.2	2.1	-	-	155.6	2.2	-	-	157.3	1.1	-	-
1991	158.7	0.9	-	-	159.4	0.4	-	-	160.8	0.9	-	-	162.0	0.7	-	-	161.8	-0.1	-	-	165.4	2.2	-	-
1992	168.3	1.8	-	-	169.9	1.0	-	-	170.9	0.6	-	-	171.0	0.1	-	-	170.8	-0.1	-	-	175.6	2.8	-	-
1993	178.5	1.7	-	-	179.5	0.6	-	-	181.4	1.1	-	-	182.0	0.3	-	-	181.8	-0.1	-	-	181.6	-0.1	-	-

Source: U.S. Department of Labor, Bureau of Labor Statistics, Division of Consumer Prices and Price Indexes. - indicates no data collected for period.

Miami, FL
Consumer Price Index - All Urban Consumers
Base 1982-1984 = 100
Entertainment

For 1977-1993. Columns headed % show percentile change in the index from the previous period for which an index is available.

Year	Jan Index	%	Feb Index	%	Mar Index	%	Apr Index	%	May Index	%	Jun Index	%	Jul Index	%	Aug Index	%	Sep Index	%	Oct Index	%	Nov Index	%	Dec Index	%
1977	-	-	-	-	-	-	-	-	-	-	-	-	-	-	-	-	-	-	-	-	77.8	-	-	-
1978	78.2	0.5	-	-	78.0	-0.3	-	-	79.5	1.9	-	-	80.9	1.8	-	-	81.3	0.5	-	-	82.0	0.9	-	-
1979	83.2	1.5	-	-	84.4	1.4	-	-	84.9	0.6	-	-	84.8	-0.1	-	-	85.9	1.3	-	-	86.0	0.1	-	-
1980	87.3	1.5	-	-	88.1	0.9	-	-	88.3	0.2	-	-	88.7	0.5	-	-	91.6	3.3	-	-	92.3	0.8	-	-
1981	92.3	0.0	-	-	93.6	1.4	-	-	96.3	2.9	-	-	94.1	-2.3	-	-	95.6	1.6	-	-	97.8	2.3	-	-
1982	97.2	-0.6	-	-	97.5	0.3	-	-	98.1	0.6	-	-	98.3	0.2	-	-	98.7	0.4	-	-	99.9	1.2	-	-
1983	99.8	-0.1	-	-	100.7	0.9	-	-	101.0	0.3	-	-	99.4	-1.6	-	-	99.8	0.4	-	-	101.3	1.5	-	-
1984	101.2	-0.1	-	-	101.8	0.6	-	-	100.9	-0.9	-	-	101.0	0.1	-	-	100.2	-0.8	-	-	102.0	1.8	-	-
1985	102.7	0.7	-	-	103.1	0.4	-	-	104.8	1.6	-	-	104.1	-0.7	-	-	104.6	0.5	-	-	106.6	1.9	-	-
1986	107.0	0.4	-	-	108.4	1.3	-	-	106.5	-1.8	-	-	106.3	-0.2	-	-	106.8	0.5	-	-	111.2	4.1	-	-
1987	113.2	1.8	-	-	112.6	-0.5	-	-	113.2	0.5	-	-	113.5	0.3	-	-	114.4	0.8	-	-	114.9	0.4	-	-
1988	115.2	0.3	-	-	116.8	1.4	-	-	118.1	1.1	-	-	116.2	-1.6	-	-	116.8	0.5	-	-	112.0	-4.1	-	-
1989	116.0	3.6	-	-	117.0	0.9	-	-	117.6	0.5	-	-	118.0	0.3	-	-	118.5	0.4	-	-	119.0	0.4	-	-
1990	119.6	0.5	-	-	118.9	-0.6	-	-	119.3	0.3	-	-	122.3	2.5	-	-	122.1	-0.2	-	-	122.1	0.0	-	-
1991	127.3	4.3	-	-	128.8	1.2	-	-	123.1	-4.4	-	-	127.0	3.2	-	-	126.4	-0.5	-	-	126.3	-0.1	-	-
1992	126.1	-0.2	-	-	127.8	1.3	-	-	122.1	-4.5	-	-	122.4	0.2	-	-	122.4	0.0	-	-	125.6	2.6	-	-
1993	130.4	3.8	-	-	131.3	0.7	-	-	130.1	-0.9	-	-	128.2	-1.5	-	-	128.4	0.2	-	-	128.5	0.1	-	-

Source: U.S. Department of Labor, Bureau of Labor Statistics, Division of Consumer Prices and Price Indexes. - indicates no data collected for period.

Miami, FL
Consumer Price Index - Urban Wage Earners
Base 1982-1984 = 100
Entertainment

For 1977-1993. Columns headed % show percentile change in the index from the previous period for which an index is available.

Year	Jan Index	%	Feb Index	%	Mar Index	%	Apr Index	%	May Index	%	Jun Index	%	Jul Index	%	Aug Index	%	Sep Index	%	Oct Index	%	Nov Index	%	Dec Index	%
1977	-	-	-	-	-	-	-	-	-	-	-	-	-	-	-	-	-	-	-	-	73.1	-	-	-
1978	73.6	0.7	-	-	73.8	0.3	-	-	75.0	1.6	-	-	76.4	1.9	-	-	76.7	0.4	-	-	77.9	1.6	-	-
1979	77.9	0.0	-	-	80.6	3.5	-	-	81.5	1.1	-	-	81.2	-0.4	-	-	82.3	1.4	-	-	83.1	1.0	-	-
1980	84.9	2.2	-	-	86.9	2.4	-	-	86.4	-0.6	-	-	87.2	0.9	-	-	90.6	3.9	-	-	91.1	0.6	-	-
1981	91.5	0.4	-	-	92.3	0.9	-	-	95.9	3.9	-	-	93.7	-2.3	-	-	94.9	1.3	-	-	98.1	3.4	-	-
1982	97.3	-0.8	-	-	97.7	0.4	-	-	98.4	0.7	-	-	98.5	0.1	-	-	98.7	0.2	-	-	99.9	1.2	-	-
1983	99.7	-0.2	-	-	101.0	1.3	-	-	101.3	0.3	-	-	99.4	-1.9	-	-	100.0	0.6	-	-	100.9	0.9	-	-
1984	100.9	0.0	-	-	101.9	1.0	-	-	100.8	-1.1	-	-	100.5	-0.3	-	-	100.2	-0.3	-	-	101.6	1.4	-	-
1985	102.9	1.3	-	-	103.2	0.3	-	-	105.2	1.9	-	-	104.8	-0.4	-	-	106.1	1.2	-	-	107.6	1.4	-	-
1986	107.7	0.1	-	-	108.8	1.0	-	-	107.2	-1.5	-	-	107.0	-0.2	-	-	106.7	-0.3	-	-	111.8	4.8	-	-
1987	113.8	1.8	-	-	113.2	-0.5	-	-	113.6	0.4	-	-	113.9	0.3	-	-	115.2	1.1	-	-	115.5	0.3	-	-
1988	115.9	0.3	-	-	117.4	1.3	-	-	118.2	0.7	-	-	116.7	-1.3	-	-	117.0	0.3	-	-	111.9	-4.4	-	-
1989	116.9	4.5	-	-	118.0	0.9	-	-	118.5	0.4	-	-	119.0	0.4	-	-	119.5	0.4	-	-	120.0	0.4	-	-
1990	120.6	0.5	-	-	119.8	-0.7	-	-	120.1	0.3	-	-	123.6	2.9	-	-	123.6	0.0	-	-	123.2	-0.3	-	-
1991	128.5	4.3	-	-	129.6	0.9	-	-	123.8	-4.5	-	-	128.6	3.9	-	-	127.9	-0.5	-	-	127.4	-0.4	-	-
1992	127.0	-0.3	-	-	128.7	1.3	-	-	122.9	-4.5	-	-	123.7	0.7	-	-	123.6	-0.1	-	-	126.2	2.1	-	-
1993	131.0	3.8	-	-	132.3	1.0	-	-	131.2	-0.8	-	-	128.9	-1.8	-	-	129.1	0.2	-	-	128.6	-0.4	-	-

Source: U.S. Department of Labor, Bureau of Labor Statistics, Division of Consumer Prices and Price Indexes. - indicates no data collected for period.

Miami, FL
Consumer Price Index - All Urban Consumers
Base 1982-1984 = 100
Other Goods and Services

For 1977-1993. Columns headed % show percentile change in the index from the previous period for which an index is available.

Year	Jan Index	%	Feb Index	%	Mar Index	%	Apr Index	%	May Index	%	Jun Index	%	Jul Index	%	Aug Index	%	Sep Index	%	Oct Index	%	Nov Index	%	Dec Index	%
1977	-		-		-		-		-		-		-		-		-		-		61.5	-	-	-
1978	61.5	0.0	-	-	62.3	1.3	-	-	63.1	1.3	-	-	63.4	0.5	-	-	65.6	3.5	-	-	65.5	-0.2	-	-
1979	65.7	0.3	-	-	66.1	0.6	-	-	67.5	2.1	-	-	68.4	1.3	-	-	72.2	5.6	-	-	72.5	0.4	-	-
1980	74.2	2.3	-	-	74.4	0.3	-	-	74.9	0.7	-	-	75.7	1.1	-	-	78.2	3.3	-	-	78.3	0.1	-	-
1981	79.6	1.7	-	-	81.3	2.1	-	-	82.0	0.9	-	-	84.1	2.6	-	-	89.5	6.4	-	-	89.3	-0.2	-	-
1982	90.0	0.8	-	-	90.3	0.3	-	-	91.4	1.2	-	-	92.0	0.7	-	-	96.1	4.5	-	-	97.0	0.9	-	-
1983	97.5	0.5	-	-	97.1	-0.4	-	-	97.3	0.2	-	-	99.4	2.2	-	-	102.7	3.3	-	-	104.2	1.5	-	-
1984	105.4	1.2	-	-	105.7	0.3	-	-	105.8	0.1	-	-	106.5	0.7	-	-	108.2	1.6	-	-	108.8	0.6	-	-
1985	109.6	0.7	-	-	111.5	1.7	-	-	112.2	0.6	-	-	112.5	0.3	-	-	116.3	3.4	-	-	116.0	-0.3	-	-
1986	117.3	1.1	-	-	119.8	2.1	-	-	120.4	0.5	-	-	120.4	0.0	-	-	125.3	4.1	-	-	125.4	0.1	-	-
1987	125.9	0.4	-	-	126.0	0.1	-	-	126.2	0.2	-	-	128.1	1.5	-	-	131.2	2.4	-	-	131.2	0.0	-	-
1988	131.3	0.1	-	-	131.8	0.4	-	-	132.0	0.2	-	-	132.0	0.0	-	-	136.5	3.4	-	-	136.7	0.1	-	-
1989	137.6	0.7	-	-	137.6	0.0	-	-	138.4	0.6	-	-	138.4	0.0	-	-	143.1	3.4	-	-	142.4	-0.5	-	-
1990	143.7	0.9	-	-	149.9	4.3	-	-	150.2	0.2	-	-	154.1	2.6	-	-	158.8	3.0	-	-	158.2	-0.4	-	-
1991	161.0	1.8	-	-	161.9	0.6	-	-	160.9	-0.6	-	-	160.5	-0.2	-	-	162.2	1.1	-	-	162.3	0.1	-	-
1992	162.1	-0.1	-	-	162.0	-0.1	-	-	158.0	-2.5	-	-	158.0	0.0	-	-	160.4	1.5	-	-	162.4	1.2	-	-
1993	162.8	0.2	-	-	162.8	0.0	-	-	163.0	0.1	-	-	163.3	0.2	-	-	162.8	-0.3	-	-	160.3	-1.5	-	-

Source: U.S. Department of Labor, Bureau of Labor Statistics, Division of Consumer Prices and Price Indexes. - indicates no data collected for period.

Miami, FL
Consumer Price Index - Urban Wage Earners
Base 1982-1984 = 100
Other Goods and Services

For 1977-1993. Columns headed % show percentile change in the index from the previous period for which an index is available.

Year	Jan Index	%	Feb Index	%	Mar Index	%	Apr Index	%	May Index	%	Jun Index	%	Jul Index	%	Aug Index	%	Sep Index	%	Oct Index	%	Nov Index	%	Dec Index	%
1977	-	-	-	-	-	-	-	-	-	-	-	-	-	-	-	-	-	-	-	-	64.0	-	-	-
1978	63.9	-0.2	-	-	64.5	0.9	-	-	65.6	1.7	-	-	65.9	0.5	-	-	67.8	2.9	-	-	67.5	-0.4	-	-
1979	67.8	0.4	-	-	68.7	1.3	-	-	69.9	1.7	-	-	70.4	0.7	-	-	74.1	5.3	-	-	74.7	0.8	-	-
1980	76.0	1.7	-	-	75.9	-0.1	-	-	76.8	1.2	-	-	77.2	0.5	-	-	78.5	1.7	-	-	78.6	0.1	-	-
1981	80.2	2.0	-	-	81.3	1.4	-	-	82.1	1.0	-	-	83.1	1.2	-	-	88.4	6.4	-	-	88.9	0.6	-	-
1982	90.0	1.2	-	-	90.4	0.4	-	-	91.9	1.7	-	-	92.8	1.0	-	-	95.3	2.7	-	-	96.4	1.2	-	-
1983	97.1	0.7	-	-	97.1	0.0	-	-	97.4	0.3	-	-	100.3	3.0	-	-	101.8	1.5	-	-	104.5	2.7	-	-
1984	105.5	1.0	-	-	105.9	0.4	-	-	105.9	0.0	-	-	106.9	0.9	-	-	107.6	0.7	-	-	108.3	0.7	-	-
1985	109.4	1.0	-	-	110.4	0.9	-	-	111.3	0.8	-	-	111.6	0.3	-	-	115.2	3.2	-	-	114.9	-0.3	-	-
1986	116.3	1.2	-	-	119.2	2.5	-	-	119.7	0.4	-	-	119.9	0.2	-	-	123.9	3.3	-	-	123.7	-0.2	-	-
1987	124.4	0.6	-	-	124.6	0.2	-	-	124.9	0.2	-	-	126.5	1.3	-	-	129.4	2.3	-	-	129.4	0.0	-	-
1988	130.2	0.6	-	-	130.9	0.5	-	-	131.1	0.2	-	-	131.3	0.2	-	-	135.2	3.0	-	-	135.5	0.2	-	-
1989	136.6	0.8	-	-	136.6	0.0	-	-	137.8	0.9	-	-	137.8	0.0	-	-	142.0	3.0	-	-	141.1	-0.6	-	-
1990	142.6	1.1	-	-	147.9	3.7	-	-	148.3	0.3	-	-	153.8	3.7	-	-	156.5	1.8	-	-	155.7	-0.5	-	-
1991	159.5	2.4	-	-	160.8	0.8	-	-	159.4	-0.9	-	-	158.9	-0.3	-	-	159.7	0.5	-	-	159.8	0.1	-	-
1992	160.8	0.6	-	-	160.7	-0.1	-	-	154.6	-3.8	-	-	154.6	0.0	-	-	156.3	1.1	-	-	159.2	1.9	-	-
1993	160.1	0.6	-	-	160.1	0.0	-	-	160.3	0.1	-	-	160.4	0.1	-	-	158.9	-0.9	-	-	154.8	-2.6	-	-

Source: U.S. Department of Labor, Bureau of Labor Statistics, Division of Consumer Prices and Price Indexes. - indicates no data collected for period.

Milwaukee, WI
Consumer Price Index - All Urban Consumers
Base 1982-1984 = 100
Annual Averages

For 1935-1993. Columns headed % show percentile change in the index from the previous period for which an index is available.

Year	All Items		Food & Beverage		Housing		Apparel & Upkeep		Trans- portation		Medical Care		Entertain- ment		Other Goods & Services	
	Index	%	Index	%	Index	%	Index	%	Index	%	Index	%	Index	%	Index	%
1935	13.4	-	-	-	-	-	-	-	-	-	-	-	-	-	-	-
1936	13.6	1.5	-	-	-	-	-	-	-	-	-	-	-	-	-	-
1937	14.2	4.4	-	-	-	-	-	-	-	-	-	-	-	-	-	-
1938	13.8	-2.8	-	-	-	-	-	-	-	-	-	-	-	-	-	-
1939	13.5	-2.2	-	-	-	-	-	-	-	-	-	-	-	-	-	-
1940	13.5	0.0	-	-	-	-	-	-	-	-	-	-	-	-	-	-
1941	14.2	5.2	-	-			-	-	-	-	-	-	-	-	-	-
1942	15.7	10.6	-	-			-	-	-	-	-	-	-	-	-	-
1943	16.6	5.7	-	-			-	-	-	-	-	-	-	-	-	-
1944	16.9	1.8	-	-			-	-	-	-	-	-	-	-	-	-
1945	17.3	2.4	-	-			-	-	-	-	-	-	-	-	-	-
1946	18.6	7.5	-	-			-	-	-	-	-	-	-	-	-	-
1947	21.7	16.7	-	-			-	-	20.3	-	12.8	-	-	-	-	-
1948	23.4	7.8	-	-			-	-	21.9	7.9	13.6	6.3	-	-	-	-
1949	23.1	-1.3	-	-			-	-	22.8	4.1	14.2	4.4	-	-	-	-
1950	23.9	3.5	-	-			-	-	23.2	1.8	14.9	4.9	-	-	-	-
1951	26.2	9.6	-	-			-	-	24.8	6.9	16.5	10.7	-	-	-	-
1952	27.0	3.1	-	-			-	-	26.2	5.6	17.3	4.8	-	-	-	-
1953	27.1	0.4	-	-			39.6	-	27.1	3.4	17.9	3.5	-	-	-	-
1954	27.1	0.0	-	-			39.5	-0.3	26.8	-1.1	19.0	6.1	-	-	-	-
1955	27.1	0.0	-	-			39.3	-0.5	26.5	-1.1	19.5	2.6	-	-	-	-
1956	27.5	1.5	-	-			40.3	2.5	27.2	2.6	19.9	2.1	-	-	-	-
1957	28.4	3.3	-	-			40.9	1.5	28.4	4.4	21.4	7.5	-	-	-	-
1958	28.8	1.4	-	-			40.9	0.0	28.9	1.8	22.1	3.3	-	-	-	-
1959	28.8	0.0	-	-			41.3	1.0	29.8	3.1	22.5	1.8	-	-	-	-
1960	29.2	1.4	-	-			41.8	1.2	29.5	-1.0	23.1	2.7	-	-	-	-
1961	29.4	0.7	-	-			42.0	0.5	29.8	1.0	23.2	0.4	-	-	-	-
1962	29.8	1.4	-	-			42.2	0.5	30.8	3.4	23.4	0.9	-	-	-	-
1963	30.1	1.0	-	-			42.2	0.0	31.0	0.6	23.9	2.1	-	-	-	-
1964	30.4	1.0	-	-			42.8	1.4	31.1	0.3	24.4	2.1	-	-	-	-
1965	31.0	2.0	-	-			43.5	1.6	32.2	3.5	25.3	3.7	-	-	-	-
1966	31.7	2.3	-	-			44.2	1.6	32.4	0.6	26.7	5.5	-	-	-	-
1967	32.4	2.2	-	-			45.8	3.6	32.9	1.5	28.8	7.9	-	-	-	-
1968	33.5	3.4	-	-			47.7	4.1	33.2	0.9	30.4	5.6	-	-	-	-
1969	35.5	6.0	-	-			51.7	8.4	35.0	5.4	32.6	7.2	-	-	-	-
1970	37.5	5.6	-	-			55.9	8.1	36.4	4.0	34.3	5.2	-	-	-	-
1971	38.9	3.7	-	-	-	-	56.9	1.8	38.5	5.8	36.3	5.8	-	-	-	-
1972	40.1	3.1	-	-	-	-	58.1	2.1	39.2	1.8	36.9	1.7	-	-	-	-
1973	42.6	6.2	-	-	-	-	60.9	4.8	41.4	5.6	38.6	4.6	-	-	-	-
1974	46.7	9.6	-	-	-	-	64.9	6.6	46.0	11.1	42.4	9.8	-	-	-	-
1975	50.8	8.8	-	-	-	-	70.0	7.9	49.9	8.5	47.1	11.1	-	-	-	-
1976	54.1	6.5	63.4	-	47.4	-	74.2	6.0	53.5	7.2	52.6	11.7	61.8	-	59.9	-
1977	57.6	6.5	66.9	5.5	50.9	7.4	77.5	4.4	57.0	6.5	57.3	8.9	68.4	10.7	63.1	5.3
1978	62.3	8.2	73.4	9.7	55.9	9.8	78.3	1.0	60.5	6.1	61.9	8.0	72.2	5.6	66.5	5.4
1979	70.8	13.6	81.6	11.2	65.2	16.6	82.2	5.0	70.5	16.5	69.3	12.0	77.9	7.9	70.5	6.0

[Continued]

Milwaukee, WI
Consumer Price Index - All Urban Consumers
Base 1982-1984 = 100
Annual Averages
[Continued]

For 1935-1993. Columns headed % show percentile change in the index from the previous period for which an index is available.

Year	All Items		Food & Beverage		Housing		Apparel & Upkeep		Trans- portation		Medical Care		Entertain- ment		Other Goods & Services	
	Index	%	Index	%	Index	%	Index	%	Index	%	Index	%	Index	%	Index	%
1980	81.4	15.0	87.2	6.9	78.2	19.9	87.5	6.4	83.2	18.0	77.9	12.4	84.4	8.3	75.7	7.4
1981	90.7	11.4	94.9	8.8	88.3	12.9	92.3	5.5	93.5	12.4	86.7	11.3	92.1	9.1	83.2	9.9
1982	95.9	5.7	98.5	3.8	94.0	6.5	96.9	5.0	98.5	5.3	93.7	8.1	95.8	4.0	92.4	11.1
1983	100.2	4.5	99.6	1.1	100.7	7.1	101.8	5.1	99.0	0.5	100.6	7.4	100.3	4.7	100.8	9.1
1984	103.8	3.6	101.9	2.3	105.1	4.4	101.3	-0.5	102.5	3.5	105.7	5.1	103.9	3.6	106.8	6.0
1985	107.0	3.1	105.7	3.7	108.5	3.2	103.4	2.1	103.9	1.4	109.3	3.4	109.6	5.5	113.1	5.9
1986	107.4	0.4	107.9	2.1	109.5	0.9	105.1	1.6	98.7	-5.0	114.6	4.8	110.3	0.6	121.6	7.5
1987	111.5	3.8	112.0	3.8	114.3	4.4	111.4	6.0	101.5	2.8	119.3	4.1	107.7	-2.4	129.0	6.1
1988	115.9	3.9	115.8	3.4	118.4	3.6	121.0	8.6	103.1	1.6	128.4	7.6	111.3	3.3	139.0	7.8
1989	120.8	4.2	121.1	4.6	122.1	3.1	121.2	0.2	110.0	6.7	139.3	8.5	113.7	2.2	146.9	5.7
1990	126.2	4.5	128.1	5.8	126.0	3.2	126.0	4.0	115.2	4.7	150.8	8.3	118.7	4.4	156.6	6.6
1991	132.2	4.8	135.2	5.5	132.2	4.9	125.4	-0.5	119.1	3.4	159.5	5.8	124.0	4.5	169.8	8.4
1992	137.1	3.7	135.4	0.1	137.7	4.2	124.2	-1.0	123.1	3.4	174.3	9.3	130.0	4.8	182.0	7.2
1993	142.1	3.6	138.1	2.0	142.8	3.7	123.2	-0.8	128.5	4.4	185.5	6.4	133.1	2.4	194.9	7.1

Source: U.S. Department of Labor, Bureau of Labor Statistics, Division of Consumer Prices and Price Indexes. - indicates no data collected for period.

Milwaukee, WI
Consumer Price Index - Urban Wage Earners
Base 1982-1984 = 100
Annual Averages

For 1935-1993. Columns headed % show percentile change in the index from the previous period for which an index is available.

Year	All Items		Food & Beverage		Housing		Apparel & Upkeep		Trans- portation		Medical Care		Entertain- ment		Other Goods & Services	
	Index	%	Index	%	Index	%	Index	%	Index	%	Index	%	Index	%	Index	%
1935	12.9	-	-	-	-	-	-	-	-	-	-	-	-	-	-	-
1936	13.2	2.3	-	-	-	-	-	-	-	-	-	-	-	-	-	-
1937	13.7	3.8	-	-	-	-	-	-	-	-	-	-	-	-	-	-
1938	13.4	-2.2	-	-	-	-	-	-	-	-	-	-	-	-	-	-
1939	13.0	-3.0	-	-	-	-	-	-	-	-	-	-	-	-	-	-
1940	13.0	0.0	-	-	-	-	-	-	-	-	-	-	-	-	-	-
1941	13.7	5.4	-	-	-	-	-	-	-	-	-	-	-	-	-	-
1942	15.1	10.2	-	-	-	-	-	-	-	-	-	-	-	-	-	-
1943	16.0	6.0	-	-	-	-	-	-	-	-	-	-	-	-	-	-
1944	16.3	1.9	-	-	-	-	-	-	-	-	-	-	-	-	-	-
1945	16.7	2.5	-	-	-	-	-	-	-	-	-	-	-	-	-	-
1946	18.0	7.8	-	-	-	-	-	-	-	-	-	-	-	-	-	-
1947	20.9	16.1	-	-	-	-	-	-	20.5	-	13.0	-	-	-	-	-
1948	22.6	8.1	-	-	-	-	-	-	22.1	7.8	13.8	6.2	-	-	-	-
1949	22.4	-0.9	-	-	-	-	-	-	23.1	4.5	14.4	4.3	-	-	-	-
1950	23.1	3.1	-	-	-	-	-	-	23.5	1.7	15.0	4.2	-	-	-	-
1951	25.3	9.5	-	-	-	-	-	-	25.1	6.8	16.6	10.7	-	-	-	-
1952	26.1	3.2	-	-	-	-	-	-	26.5	5.6	17.5	5.4	-	-	-	-
1953	26.2	0.4	-	-	-	-	40.5	-	27.4	3.4	18.1	3.4	-	-	-	-
1954	26.2	0.0	-	-	-	-	40.4	-0.2	27.1	-1.1	19.2	6.1	-	-	-	-
1955	26.2	0.0	-	-	-	-	40.2	-0.5	26.8	-1.1	19.7	2.6	-	-	-	-
1956	26.6	1.5	-	-	-	-	41.2	2.5	27.5	2.6	20.1	2.0	-	-	-	-
1957	27.5	3.4	-	-	-	-	41.8	1.5	28.7	4.4	21.6	7.5	-	-	-	-
1958	27.8	1.1	-	-	-	-	41.8	0.0	29.2	1.7	22.3	3.2	-	-	-	-
1959	27.8	0.0	-	-	-	-	42.2	1.0	30.1	3.1	22.8	2.2	-	-	-	-
1960	28.2	1.4	-	-	-	-	42.7	1.2	29.9	-0.7	23.3	2.2	-	-	-	-
1961	28.4	0.7	-	-	-	-	43.0	0.7	30.1	0.7	23.5	0.9	-	-	-	-
1962	28.8	1.4	-	-	-	-	43.1	0.2	31.1	3.3	23.7	0.9	-	-	-	-
1963	29.1	1.0	-	-	-	-	43.1	0.0	31.3	0.6	24.2	2.1	-	-	-	-
1964	29.4	1.0	-	-	-	-	43.8	1.6	31.4	0.3	24.6	1.7	-	-	-	-
1965	30.0	2.0	-	-	-	-	44.5	1.6	32.6	3.8	25.6	4.1	-	-	-	-
1966	30.7	2.3	-	-	-	-	45.2	1.6	32.8	0.6	27.0	5.5	-	-	-	-
1967	31.3	2.0	-	-	-	-	46.8	3.5	33.2	1.2	29.1	7.8	-	-	-	-
1968	32.4	3.5	-	-	-	-	48.8	4.3	33.6	1.2	30.8	5.8	-	-	-	-
1969	34.3	5.9	-	-	-	-	52.9	8.4	35.4	5.4	32.9	6.8	-	-	-	-
1970	36.2	5.5	-	-	-	-	57.2	8.1	36.8	4.0	34.7	5.5	-	-	-	-
1971	37.6	3.9	-	-	-	-	58.2	1.7	38.9	5.7	36.7	5.8	-	-	-	-
1972	38.7	2.9	-	-	-	-	59.4	2.1	39.7	2.1	37.3	1.6	-	-	-	-
1973	41.1	6.2	-	-	-	-	62.3	4.9	41.9	5.5	39.0	4.6	-	-	-	-
1974	45.1	9.7	-	-	-	-	66.3	6.4	46.5	11.0	42.9	10.0	-	-	-	-
1975	49.1	8.9	-	-	-	-	71.5	7.8	50.4	8.4	47.6	11.0	-	-	-	-
1976	52.3	6.5	61.9	-	43.7	-	75.9	6.2	54.1	7.3	53.2	11.8	64.1	-	57.4	-
1977	55.6	6.3	65.3	5.5	46.9	7.3	79.2	4.3	57.6	6.5	58.0	9.0	70.9	10.6	60.4	5.2
1978	60.5	8.8	72.0	10.3	51.8	10.4	80.2	1.3	61.3	6.4	63.6	9.7	75.4	6.3	64.9	7.5
1979	69.2	14.4	81.1	12.6	61.3	18.3	84.6	5.5	70.9	15.7	69.9	9.9	80.2	6.4	68.9	6.2

[Continued]

596

Milwaukee, WI
Consumer Price Index - Urban Wage Earners
Base 1982-1984 = 100
Annual Averages
[Continued]

For 1935-1993. Columns headed % show percentile change in the index from the previous period for which an index is available.

Year	All Items		Food & Beverage		Housing		Apparel & Upkeep		Trans-portation		Medical Care		Entertain-ment		Other Goods & Services	
	Index	%	Index	%	Index	%	Index	%	Index	%	Index	%	Index	%	Index	%
1980	80.2	15.9	87.8	8.3	74.7	21.9	89.8	6.1	83.3	17.5	79.1	13.2	88.5	10.3	75.1	9.0
1981	89.2	11.2	95.1	8.3	84.7	13.4	95.1	5.9	93.5	12.2	87.6	10.7	94.6	6.9	82.3	9.6
1982	93.8	5.2	98.5	3.6	89.7	5.9	97.8	2.8	98.0	4.8	93.9	7.2	95.7	1.2	92.1	11.9
1983	100.0	6.6	99.7	1.2	100.3	11.8	101.6	3.9	99.1	1.1	100.2	6.7	100.0	4.5	101.0	9.7
1984	106.2	6.2	101.9	2.2	110.0	9.7	100.6	-1.0	102.9	3.8	105.9	5.7	104.3	4.3	106.9	5.8
1985	109.4	3.0	105.6	3.6	113.3	3.0	103.0	2.4	104.5	1.6	110.0	3.9	109.9	5.4	112.9	5.6
1986	109.6	0.2	107.9	2.2	114.1	0.7	105.6	2.5	99.0	-5.3	115.5	5.0	109.7	-0.2	121.1	7.3
1987	114.1	4.1	111.9	3.7	119.0	4.3	113.0	7.0	102.5	3.5	120.6	4.4	107.8	-1.7	128.4	6.0
1988	118.6	3.9	115.8	3.5	123.2	3.5	123.2	9.0	104.3	1.8	129.9	7.7	112.0	3.9	139.2	8.4
1989	123.5	4.1	120.9	4.4	126.9	3.0	123.5	0.2	110.9	6.3	141.4	8.9	115.0	2.7	147.6	6.0
1990	128.9	4.4	128.0	5.9	130.9	3.2	127.4	3.2	116.0	4.6	152.3	7.7	119.7	4.1	157.5	6.7
1991	135.0	4.7	135.1	5.5	137.2	4.8	128.1	0.5	119.3	2.8	160.7	5.5	125.4	4.8	171.6	9.0
1992	139.8	3.6	135.3	0.1	143.0	4.2	126.2	-1.5	123.9	3.9	175.3	9.1	130.9	4.4	184.3	7.4
1993	144.8	3.6	138.0	2.0	148.3	3.7	125.9	-0.2	129.5	4.5	186.2	6.2	133.6	2.1	196.6	6.7

Source: U.S. Department of Labor, Bureau of Labor Statistics, Division of Consumer Prices and Price Indexes. - indicates no data collected for period.

Milwaukee, WI
Consumer Price Index - All Urban Consumers
Base 1982-1984 = 100
All Items

For 1935-1993. Columns headed % show percentile change in the index from the previous period for which an index is available.

Year	Jan Index	%	Feb Index	%	Mar Index	%	Apr Index	%	May Index	%	Jun Index	%	Jul Index	%	Aug Index	%	Sep Index	%	Oct Index	%	Nov Index	%	Dec Index	%
1935	-	-	-	-	13.3	-	-	-	-	-	-	-	13.3	0.0	-	-	-	-	13.4	0.8	-	-	-	-
1936	13.5	0.7	-	-	-	-	13.4	-0.7	-	-	-	-	13.6	1.5	-	-	13.9	2.2	-	-	-	-	13.7	-1.4
1937	-	-	-	-	14.0	2.2	-	-	-	-	14.3	2.1	-	-	-	-	14.4	0.7	-	-	-	-	14.2	-1.4
1938	-	-	-	-	13.9	-2.1	-	-	-	-	13.9	0.0	-	-	-	-	13.7	-1.4			-	-	13.6	-0.7
1939	-	-	-	-	13.4	-1.5	-	-	-	-	13.4	0.0	-	-	-	-	13.6	1.5			-	-	13.4	-1.5
1940	-	-	-	-	13.4	0.0	-	-	-	-	13.6	1.5	-	-	-	-	13.5	-0.7	-	-	-	-	13.6	0.7
1941	-	-	-	-	13.6	0.0	-	-	-	-	14.2	4.4	-	-	-	-	14.6	2.8	-	-	-	-	15.0	2.7
1942	-	-	-	-	15.4	2.7	-	-	-	-	15.8	2.6	-	-	-	-	15.8	0.0	-	-	-	-	16.2	2.5
1943	-	-	-	-	16.5	1.9	-	-	-	-	16.8	1.8	-	-	-	-	16.6	-1.2	-	-	-	-	16.6	0.0
1944	-	-	-	-	16.6	0.0	-	-	-	-	16.9	1.8	-	-	-	-	17.0	0.6	-	-	-	-	17.0	0.0
1945	-	-	-	-	17.0	0.0	-	-	-	-	17.4	2.4	-	-	-	-	17.3	-0.6	-	-	-	-	17.4	0.6
1946	-	-	-	-	17.4	0.0	-	-	-	-	17.9	2.9	-	-	-	-	19.6	9.5	-	-	-	-	20.6	5.1
1947	-	-	-	-	21.2	2.9	-	-	-	-	21.5	1.4	-	-	21.8	1.4	-	-	-	-	22.5	3.2	-	-
1948	-	-	22.9	1.8	-	-	-	-	23.5	2.6	-	-	-	-	24.0	2.1	-	-	-	-	23.5	-2.1	-	-
1949	-	-	23.2	-1.3	-	-	-	-	23.2	0.0	-	-	-	-	23.0	-0.9	-	-	-	-	23.2	0.9	-	-
1950	-	-	23.1	-0.4	-	-	-	-	23.5	1.7	-	-	-	-	24.2	3.0	-	-	-	-	24.7	2.1	-	-
1951	-	-	25.7	4.0	-	-	-	-	26.1	1.6	-	-	-	-	26.3	0.8	-	-	-	-	26.7	1.5	27.1	-0.4
1952	-	-	26.7	0.0	-	-	-	-	27.1	1.5	-	-	-	-	27.3	0.7	-	-	-	-	27.2	-0.4	-	-
1953	-	-	26.9	-0.7	-	-	-	-	27.1	0.7	-	-	-	-	27.3	0.7	-	-	-	-	27.1	-0.7	-	-
1954	-	-	27.1	0.0	-	-	-	-	27.2	0.4	-	-	-	-	27.1	-0.4	-	-	-	-	27.1	0.0	-	-
1955	-	-	27.0	-0.4	-	-	-	-	27.0	0.0	-	-	-	-	27.1	0.4	-	-	-	-	27.2	0.4	-	-
1956	-	-	27.1	-0.4	-	-	-	-	27.3	0.7	-	-	-	-	27.7	1.5	-	-	-	-	27.8	0.4	-	-
1957	-	-	28.1	1.1	-	-	-	-	28.4	1.1	-	-	-	-	28.6	0.7	-	-	-	-	28.6	0.0	-	-
1958	-	-	28.8	0.7	-	-	-	-	28.9	0.3	-	-	-	-	28.9	0.0	-	-	-	-	28.8	-0.3	-	-
1959	-	-	28.7	-0.3	-	-	-	-	28.7	0.0	-	-	-	-	28.9	0.7	-	-	-	-	29.0	0.3	-	-
1960	-	-	28.9	-0.3	-	-	-	-	29.2	1.0	-	-	-	-	29.3	0.3	-	-	-	-	29.4	0.3	-	-
1961	-	-	29.4	0.0	-	-	-	-	29.3	-0.3	-	-	-	-	29.4	0.3	-	-	-	-	29.4	0.0	-	-
1962	-	-	29.8	1.4	-	-	-	-	29.8	0.0	-	-	-	-	29.8	0.0	-	-	-	-	29.9	0.3	-	-
1963	-	-	29.9	0.0	-	-	-	-	30.0	0.3	-	-	-	-	30.1	0.3	-	-	-	-	30.2	0.3	-	-
1964	-	-	30.2	0.0	-	-	-	-	30.3	0.3	-	-	-	-	30.5	0.7	-	-	-	-	30.6	0.3	-	-
1965	-	-	30.7	0.3	-	-	-	-	31.0	1.0	-	-	-	-	31.2	0.6	-	-	-	-	31.2	0.0	-	-
1966	-	-	31.4	0.6	-	-	-	-	31.6	0.6	-	-	-	-	32.0	1.3	-	-	-	-	32.0	0.0	-	-
1967	-	-	32.0	0.0	-	-	-	-	32.2	0.6	-	-	-	-	32.6	1.2	-	-	-	-	32.8	0.6	-	-
1968	-	-	33.0	0.6	-	-	-	-	33.3	0.9	-	-	-	-	33.7	1.2	-	-	-	-	34.0	0.9	-	-
1969	-	-	34.6	1.8	-	-	-	-	35.2	1.7	-	-	-	-	35.5	0.9	-	-	-	-	36.4	2.5	-	-
1970	-	-	36.8	1.1	-	-	-	-	37.3	1.4	-	-	-	-	37.6	0.8	-	-	-	-	38.1	1.3	-	-
1971	-	-	38.5	1.0	-	-	-	-	38.6	0.3	-	-	-	-	39.3	1.8	-	-	-	-	39.1	-0.5	-	-
1972	-	-	39.6	1.3	-	-	-	-	39.8	0.5	-	-	-	-	40.3	1.3	-	-	-	-	40.5	0.5	-	-
1973	-	-	41.1	1.5	-	-	-	-	42.1	2.4	-	-	-	-	43.1	2.4	-	-	-	-	43.9	1.9	-	-
1974	-	-	45.0	2.5	-	-	-	-	46.0	2.2	-	-	-	-	47.2	2.6	-	-	-	-	48.6	3.0	-	-
1975	-	-	49.3	1.4	-	-	-	-	50.3	2.0	-	-	-	-	51.5	2.4	-	-	-	-	52.3	1.6	-	-
1976	-	-	52.6	0.6	-	-	-	-	53.7	2.1	-	-	-	-	54.7	1.9	-	-	-	-	55.2	0.9	-	-
1977	-	-	56.2	1.8	-	-	-	-	57.6	2.5	-	-	-	-	57.9	0.5	-	-	-	-	58.8	1.6	-	-
1978	59.4	1.0	-	-	60.3	1.5	-	-	61.1	1.3	-	-	62.7	2.6	-	-	64.2	2.4	-	-	64.4	0.3	-	-
1979	64.9	0.8	-	-	67.2	3.5	-	-	70.3	4.6	-	-	72.1	2.6	-	-	73.2	1.5	-	-	74.4	1.6	-	-

[Continued]

Milwaukee, WI
Consumer Price Index - All Urban Consumers
Base 1982-1984 = 100
All Items
[Continued]

For 1935-1993. Columns headed % show percentile change in the index from the previous period for which an index is available.

Year	Jan Index	%	Feb Index	%	Mar Index	%	Apr Index	%	May Index	%	Jun Index	%	Jul Index	%	Aug Index	%	Sep Index	%	Oct Index	%	Nov Index	%	Dec Index	%
1980	76.5	2.8	-	-	78.6	2.7	-	-	81.0	3.1	-	-	81.5	0.6	-	-	83.7	2.7	-	-	84.9	1.4	-	-
1981	86.2	1.5	-	-	87.4	1.4	-	-	90.2	3.2	-	-	92.5	2.5	-	-	92.9	0.4	-	-	93.1	0.2	-	-
1982	94.3	1.3	-	-	93.7	-0.6	-	-	94.8	1.2	-	-	96.0	1.3	-	-	97.9	2.0	-	-	98.1	0.2	-	-
1983	98.7	0.6	-	-	98.7	0.0	-	-	100.0	1.3	-	-	100.3	0.3	-	-	101.6	1.3	-	-	101.2	-0.4	-	-
1984	101.7	0.5	-	-	102.6	0.9	-	-	103.8	1.2	-	-	104.0	0.2	-	-	104.9	0.9	-	-	105.0	0.1	-	-
1985	105.1	0.1	-	-	106.1	1.0	-	-	107.1	0.9	-	-	107.2	0.1	-	-	107.6	0.4	-	-	108.1	0.5	-	-
1986	108.1	0.0	-	-	106.6	-1.4	-	-	107.5	0.8	-	-	107.3	-0.2	-	-	107.8	0.5	-	-	107.1	-0.6	107.8	0.7
1987	-	-	-	-	-	-	-	-	-	-	110.1	2.1	-	-	-	-	-	-	-	-	-	-	113.0	2.6
1988	-	-	-	-	-	-	-	-	-	-	114.5	1.3	-	-	-	-	-	-	-	-	-	-	117.2	2.4
1989	-	-	-	-	-	-	-	-	-	-	120.3	2.6	-	-	-	-	-	-	-	-	-	-	121.2	0.7
1990	-	-	-	-	-	-	-	-	-	-	123.9	2.2	-	-	-	-	-	-	-	-	-	-	128.6	3.8
1991	-	-	-	-	-	-	-	-	-	-	131.0	1.9	-	-	-	-	-	-	-	-	-	-	133.5	1.9
1992	-	-	-	-	-	-	-	-	-	-	135.9	1.8	-	-	-	-	-	-	-	-	-	-	138.2	1.7
1993	-	-	-	-	-	-	-	-	-	-	140.5	1.7	-	-	-	-	-	-	-	-	-	-	-	-

Source: U.S. Department of Labor, Bureau of Labor Statistics, Division of Consumer Prices and Price Indexes. - indicates no data collected for period.

Milwaukee, WI
Consumer Price Index - Urban Wage Earners
Base 1982-1984 = 100
All Items

For 1935-1993. Columns headed % show percentile change in the index from the previous period for which an index is available.

Year	Jan Index	%	Feb Index	%	Mar Index	%	Apr Index	%	May Index	%	Jun Index	%	Jul Index	%	Aug Index	%	Sep Index	%	Oct Index	%	Nov Index	%	Dec Index	%
1935	-	-	-	-	12.9	-	-	-	-	-	-	-	12.9	0.0	-	-	-	-	13.0	0.8	-	-	-	-
1936	13.0	0.0	-	-	-	-	13.0	0.0	-	-	-	-	13.2	1.5	-	-	13.4	1.5	-	-	-	-	13.3	-0.7
1937	-	-	-	-	13.5	1.5	-	-	-	-	13.8	2.2	-	-	-	-	13.9	0.7	-	-	-	-	13.2	-1.4
1938	-	-	-	-	13.5	-1.5	-	-	-	-	13.5	0.0	-	-	-	-	13.2	-2.2	-	-	-	-	13.2	0.0
1939	-	-	-	-	13.0	-1.5	-	-	-	-	12.9	-0.8	-	-	-	-	13.1	1.6	-	-	-	-	13.0	-0.8
1940	-	-	-	-	13.0	0.0	-	-		-	13.2	1.5	-	-	-	-	13.0	-1.5	-	-	-	-	13.1	0.8
1941	-	-	-	-	13.2	0.8	-	-	-	-	13.7	3.8	-	-	-	-	14.1	2.9	-	-	-	-	14.5	2.8
1942	-	-	-	-	14.9	2.8	-	-	-	-	15.3	2.7	-	-	-	-	15.2	-0.7	-	-	-	-	15.6	2.6
1943	-	-	-	-	16.0	2.6	-	-	-	-	16.2	1.3	-	-	-	-	16.1	-0.6	-	-	-	-	16.1	0.0
1944	-	-	-	-	16.1	0.0	-	-	-	-	16.4	1.9	-	-	-	-	16.4	0.0	-	-	-	-	16.4	0.0
1945	-	-	-	-	16.4	0.0	-	-	-	-	16.8	2.4	-	-	-	-	16.7	-0.6	-	-	-	-	16.8	0.6
1946	-	-	-	-	16.8	0.0	-	-	-	-	17.3	3.0	-	-	-	-	18.9	9.2	-	-	-	-	19.9	5.3
1947	-	-	-	-	20.5	3.0	-	-		-	20.7	1.0	-	-	21.1	1.9	-	-	-	-	21.7	2.8	-	-
1948	-	-	22.1	1.8	-	-	-	-	22.7	2.7	-	-	-	-	23.1	1.8	-	-	-	-	22.7	-1.7	-	-
1949	-	-	22.4	-1.3	-	-	-	-	22.5	0.4	-	-	-	-	22.2	-1.3	-	-	-	-	22.4	0.9	-	-
1950	-	-	22.3	-0.4	-	-	-	-	22.7	1.8	-	-	-	-	23.4	3.1	-	-	-	-	23.8	1.7	-	-
1951	-	-	24.8	4.2	-	-	-	-	25.2	1.6	-	-	-	-	25.4	0.8	-	-	-	-	25.8	1.6	-	-
1952	-	-	25.8	0.0	-	-	-	-	26.2	1.6	-	-	-	-	26.3	0.4	-	-	-	-	26.2	-0.4	26.2	0.0
1953	-	-	26.0	-0.8	-	-	-	-	26.2	0.8	-	-	-	-	26.3	0.4	-	-	-	-	26.2	-0.4	-	-
1954	-	-	26.2	0.0	-	-	-	-	26.3	0.4	-	-	-	-	26.2	-0.4	-	-	-	-	26.2	0.0	-	-
1955	-	-	26.1	-0.4	-	-	-	-	26.1	0.0	-	-	-	-	26.2	0.4	-	-	-	-	26.3	0.4	-	-
1956	-	-	26.2	-0.4	-	-	-	-	26.3	0.4	-	-	-	-	26.7	1.5	-	-	-	-	26.9	0.7	-	-
1957	-	-	27.1	0.7	-	-	-	-	27.4	1.1	-	-	-	-	27.7	1.1	-	-	-	-	27.7	0.0	-	-
1958	-	-	27.8	0.4	-	-	-	-	27.9	0.4	-	-	-	-	27.9	0.0	-	-	-	-	27.8	-0.4	-	-
1959	-	-	27.7	-0.4	-	-	-	-	27.7	0.0	-	-	-	-	27.9	0.7	-	-	-	-	28.1	0.7	-	-
1960	-	-	27.9	-0.7	-	-	-	-	28.2	1.1	-	-	-	-	28.3	0.4	-	-	-	-	28.4	0.4	-	-
1961	-	-	28.4	0.0	-	-	-	-	28.3	-0.4	-	-	-	-	28.4	0.4	-	-	-	-	28.4	0.0	-	-
1962	-	-	28.8	1.4	-	-	-	-	28.8	0.0	-	-	-	-	28.7	-0.3	-	-	-	-	28.9	0.7	-	-
1963	-	-	28.9	0.0	-	-	-	-	29.0	0.3	-	-	-	-	29.1	0.3	-	-	-	-	29.2	0.3	-	-
1964	-	-	29.2	0.0	-	-	-	-	29.2	0.0	-	-	-	-	29.5	1.0	-	-	-	-	29.6	0.3	-	-
1965	-	-	29.7	0.3	-	-	-	-	30.0	1.0	-	-	-	-	30.2	0.7	-	-	-	-	30.1	-0.3	-	-
1966	-	-	30.3	0.7	-	-	-	-	30.5	0.7	-	-	-	-	30.9	1.3	-	-	-	-	30.9	0.0	-	-
1967	-	-	30.9	0.0	-	-	-	-	31.1	0.6	-	-	-	-	31.5	1.3	-	-	-	-	31.7	0.6	-	-
1968	-	-	31.9	0.6	-	-	-	-	32.1	0.6	-	-	-	-	32.5	1.2	-	-	-	-	32.9	1.2	-	-
1969	-	-	33.5	1.8	-	-	-	-	34.0	1.5	-	-	-	-	34.3	0.9	-	-	-	-	35.2	2.6	-	-
1970	-	-	35.6	1.1	-	-	-	-	36.0	1.1	-	-	-	-	36.3	0.8	-	-	-	-	36.8	1.4	-	-
1971	-	-	37.2	1.1	-	-	-	-	37.3	0.3	-	-	-	-	38.0	1.9	-	-	-	-	37.8	-0.5	-	-
1972	-	-	38.2	1.1	-	-	-	-	38.4	0.5	-	-	-	-	39.0	1.6	-	-	-	-	39.1	0.3	-	-
1973	-	-	39.7	1.5	-	-	-	-	40.7	2.5	-	-	-	-	41.7	2.5	-	-	-	-	42.4	1.7	-	-
1974	-	-	43.5	2.6	-	-	-	-	44.4	2.1	-	-	-	-	45.6	2.7	-	-	-	-	46.9	2.9	-	-
1975	-	-	47.6	1.5	-	-	-	-	48.6	2.1	-	-	-	-	49.8	2.5	-	-	-	-	50.5	1.4	-	-
1976	-	-	50.8	0.6	-	-	-	-	51.9	2.2	-	-	-	-	52.9	1.9	-	-	-	-	53.3	0.8	-	-
1977	-	-	54.3	1.9	-	-	-	-	55.7	2.6	-	-	-	-	55.9	0.4	-	-	-	-	56.8	1.6	-	-
1978	57.6	1.4	-	-	58.3	1.2	-	-	59.3	1.7	-	-	60.9	2.7	-	-	62.6	2.8	-	-	62.8	0.3	-	-
1979	63.1	0.5	-	-	65.5	3.8	-	-	68.7	4.9	-	-	70.4	2.5	-	-	71.5	1.6	-	-	72.7	1.7	-	-

[Continued]

Milwaukee, WI
Consumer Price Index - Urban Wage Earners
Base 1982-1984 = 100
All Items
[Continued]

For 1935-1993. Columns headed % show percentile change in the index from the previous period for which an index is available.

Year	Jan Index	%	Feb Index	%	Mar Index	%	Apr Index	%	May Index	%	Jun Index	%	Jul Index	%	Aug Index	%	Sep Index	%	Oct Index	%	Nov Index	%	Dec Index	%
1980	75.3	3.6	-	-	77.5	2.9	-	-	79.8	3.0	-	-	80.0	0.3	-	-	82.3	2.9	-	-	83.7	1.7	-	-
1981	85.1	1.7	-	-	85.9	0.9	-	-	88.7	3.3	-	-	91.1	2.7	-	-	91.4	0.3	-	-	91.2	-0.2	-	-
1982	92.4	1.3	-	-	91.5	-1.0	-	-	92.6	1.2	-	-	93.7	1.2	-	-	95.8	2.2	-	-	96.0	0.2	-	-
1983	94.9	-1.1	-	-	97.3	2.5	-	-	98.7	1.4	-	-	101.6	2.9	-	-	102.9	1.3	-	-	102.9	0.0	-	-
1984	102.4	-0.5	-	-	104.9	2.4	-	-	105.8	0.9	-	-	106.9	1.0	-	-	108.8	1.8	-	-	107.2	-1.5	-	-
1985	107.4	0.2	-	-	108.5	1.0	-	-	109.5	0.9	-	-	109.6	0.1	-	-	109.9	0.3	-	-	110.5	0.5	-	-
1986	110.4	-0.1	-	-	108.6	-1.6	-	-	109.7	1.0	-	-	109.5	-0.2	-	-	110.0	0.5	-	-	109.3	-0.6	110.0	0.6
1987	-	-	-	-	-	-	-	-	-	-	112.6	2.4	-	-	-	-	-	-	-	-	-	-	115.6	2.7
1988	-	-	-	-	-	-	-	-	-	-	117.2	1.4	-	-	-	-	-	-	-	-	-	-	120.1	2.5
1989	-	-	-	-	-	-	-	-	-	-	123.1	2.5	-	-	-	-	-	-	-	-	-	-	124.0	0.7
1990	-	-	-	-	-	-	-	-	-	-	126.3	1.9	-	-	-	-	-	-	-	-	-	-	131.6	4.2
1991	-	-	-	-	-	-	-	-	-	-	133.6	1.5	-	-	-	-	-	-	-	-	-	-	136.3	2.0
1992	-	-	-	-	-	-	-	-	-	-	138.4	1.5	-	-	-	-	-	-	-	-	-	-	141.2	2.0
1993	-	-	-	-	-	-	-	-	-	-	143.3	1.5	-	-	-	-	-	-	-	-	-	-	-	-

Source: U.S. Department of Labor, Bureau of Labor Statistics, Division of Consumer Prices and Price Indexes. - indicates no data collected for period.

Milwaukee, WI
Consumer Price Index - All Urban Consumers
Base 1982-1984 = 100
Food and Beverages

For 1975-1993. Columns headed % show percentile change in the index from the previous period for which an index is available.

Year	Jan Index	%	Feb Index	%	Mar Index	%	Apr Index	%	May Index	%	Jun Index	%	Jul Index	%	Aug Index	%	Sep Index	%	Oct Index	%	Nov Index	%	Dec Index	%
1975	-	-	-	-	-	-	-	-	-	-	-	-	-	-	-	-	-	-	-	-	62.1	-	-	-
1976	-	-	62.6	0.8	-	-	-	-	63.0	0.6	-	-	-	-	64.1	1.7	-	-	-	-	63.9	-0.3	-	-
1977	-	-	65.6	2.7	-	-	-	-	66.9	2.0	-	-	-	-	67.7	1.2	-	-	-	-	67.3	-0.6	-	-
1978	69.5	3.3	-	-	70.9	2.0	-	-	72.7	2.5	-	-	74.3	2.2	-	-	75.2	1.2	-	-	75.5	0.4	-	-
1979	78.0	3.3	-	-	80.3	2.9	-	-	81.7	1.7	-	-	82.1	0.5	-	-	82.3	0.2	-	-	83.7	1.7	-	-
1980	84.0	0.4	-	-	84.9	1.1	-	-	85.5	0.7	-	-	87.3	2.1	-	-	89.2	2.2	-	-	90.4	1.3	-	-
1981	91.9	1.7	-	-	94.3	2.6	-	-	94.7	0.4	-	-	95.7	1.1	-	-	95.9	0.2	-	-	95.8	-0.1	-	-
1982	96.4	0.6	-	-	97.0	0.6	-	-	98.9	2.0	-	-	99.9	1.0	-	-	99.2	-0.7	-	-	98.6	-0.6	-	-
1983	99.2	0.6	-	-	99.8	0.6	-	-	100.0	0.2	-	-	99.7	-0.3	-	-	99.6	-0.1	-	-	98.9	-0.7	-	-
1984	100.7	1.8	-	-	100.8	0.1	-	-	101.6	0.8	-	-	103.0	1.4	-	-	102.2	-0.8	-	-	102.4	0.2	-	-
1985	104.8	2.3	-	-	105.8	1.0	-	-	106.0	0.2	-	-	106.0	0.0	-	-	105.6	-0.4	-	-	105.8	0.2	-	-
1986	105.6	-0.2	-	-	106.1	0.5	-	-	107.0	0.8	-	-	108.0	0.9	-	-	109.4	1.3	-	-	110.5	1.0	110.1	-0.4
1987	-	-	-	-	-	-	-	-	-	-	112.0	1.7	-	-	-	-	-	-	-	-	-	-	111.9	-0.1
1988	-	-	-	-	-	-	-	-	-	-	114.3	2.1	-	-	-	-	-	-	-	-	-	-	117.3	2.6
1989	-	-	-	-	-	-	-	-	-	-	120.1	2.4	-	-	-	-	-	-	-	-	-	-	122.0	1.6
1990	-	-	-	-	-	-	-	-	-	-	126.2	3.4	-	-	-	-	-	-	-	-	-	-	130.0	3.0
1991	-	-	-	-	-	-	-	-	-	-	134.8	3.7	-	-	-	-	-	-	-	-	-	-	135.7	0.7
1992	-	-	-	-	-	-	-	-	-	-	135.6	-0.1	-	-	-	-	-	-	-	-	-	-	135.3	-0.2
1993	-	-	-	-	-	-	-	-	-	-	137.0	1.3	-	-	-	-	-	-	-	-	-	-	-	-

Source: U.S. Department of Labor, Bureau of Labor Statistics, Division of Consumer Prices and Price Indexes. - indicates no data collected for period.

Milwaukee, WI
Consumer Price Index - Urban Wage Earners
Base 1982-1984 = 100
Food and Beverages

For 1975-1993. Columns headed % show percentile change in the index from the previous period for which an index is available.

Year	Jan Index	%	Feb Index	%	Mar Index	%	Apr Index	%	May Index	%	Jun Index	%	Jul Index	%	Aug Index	%	Sep Index	%	Oct Index	%	Nov Index	%	Dec Index	%
1975	-	-	-	-	-	-	-	-	-	-	-	-	-	-	-	-	-	-	-	-	60.7	-	-	-
1976	-	-	61.1	0.7	-	-	-	-	61.5	0.7	-	-	-	-	62.6	1.8	-	-	-	-	62.4	-0.3	-	-
1977	-	-	64.1	2.7	-	-	-	-	65.3	1.9	-	-	-	-	66.1	1.2	-	-	-	-	65.7	-0.6	-	-
1978	67.9	3.3	-	-	69.3	2.1	-	-	71.5	3.2	-	-	72.6	1.5	-	-	73.9	1.8	-	-	74.6	0.9	-	-
1979	77.1	3.4	-	-	79.9	3.6	-	-	81.6	2.1	-	-	81.9	0.4	-	-	81.8	-0.1	-	-	82.6	1.0	-	-
1980	83.8	1.5	-	-	85.4	1.9	-	-	86.3	1.1	-	-	87.9	1.9	-	-	90.0	2.4	-	-	91.2	1.3	-	-
1981	93.1	2.1	-	-	94.5	1.5	-	-	94.3	-0.2	-	-	95.8	1.6	-	-	96.1	0.3	-	-	95.9	-0.2	-	-
1982	96.5	0.6	-	-	96.8	0.3	-	-	99.0	2.3	-	-	100.1	1.1	-	-	99.3	-0.8	-	-	98.7	-0.6	-	-
1983	99.2	0.5	-	-	99.9	0.7	-	-	100.1	0.2	-	-	99.8	-0.3	-	-	99.7	-0.1	-	-	98.9	-0.8	-	-
1984	100.6	1.7	-	-	100.6	0.0	-	-	101.5	0.9	-	-	102.9	1.4	-	-	102.2	-0.7	-	-	102.2	0.0	-	-
1985	104.7	2.4	-	-	105.8	1.1	-	-	106.0	0.2	-	-	106.0	0.0	-	-	105.5	-0.5	-	-	105.6	0.1	-	-
1986	105.6	0.0	-	-	105.9	0.3	-	-	106.9	0.9	-	-	107.9	0.9	-	-	109.4	1.4	-	-	110.4	0.9	110.1	-0.3
1987	-	-	-	-	-	-	-	-	-	-	111.9	1.6	-	-	-	-	-	-	-	-	-	-	111.8	-0.1
1988	-	-	-	-	-	-	-	-	-	-	114.4	2.3	-	-	-	-	-	-	-	-	-	-	117.1	2.4
1989	-	-	-	-	-	-	-	-	-	-	119.9	2.4	-	-	-	-	-	-	-	-	-	-	121.9	1.7
1990	-	-	-	-	-	-	-	-	-	-	126.0	3.4	-	-	-	-	-	-	-	-	-	-	130.0	3.2
1991	-	-	-	-	-	-	-	-	-	-	134.7	3.6	-	-	-	-	-	-	-	-	-	-	135.5	0.6
1992	-	-	-	-	-	-	-	-	-	-	135.4	-0.1	-	-	-	-	-	-	-	-	-	-	135.3	-0.1
1993	-	-	-	-	-	-	-	-	-	-	136.8	1.1	-	-	-	-	-	-	-	-	-	-	-	-

Source: U.S. Department of Labor, Bureau of Labor Statistics, Division of Consumer Prices and Price Indexes. - indicates no data collected for period.

Milwaukee, WI
Consumer Price Index - All Urban Consumers
Base 1982-1984 = 100
Housing

For 1975-1993. Columns headed % show percentile change in the index from the previous period for which an index is available.

Year	Jan Index	%	Feb Index	%	Mar Index	%	Apr Index	%	May Index	%	Jun Index	%	Jul Index	%	Aug Index	%	Sep Index	%	Oct Index	%	Nov Index	%	Dec Index	%
1975	-	-	-		-	-	-	-	-		-		-		-		-		-	-	45.7	-	-	-
1976	-	-	46.0	0.7	-		-	-	47.2	2.6	-		-		47.9	1.5	-		-		48.5	1.3	-	
1977	-	-	49.5	2.1	-		-	-	50.8	2.6	-		-		50.8	0.0	-		-		52.4	3.1	-	
1978	53.1	1.3	-	-	54.0	1.7	-	-	54.3	0.6	-		56.6	4.2	-		58.5	3.4	-		58.0	-0.9	-	
1979	57.6	-0.7	-	-	60.6	5.2	-	-	64.9	7.1	-		67.0	3.2	-		68.1	1.6	-		69.2	1.6	-	
1980	72.5	4.8	-	-	74.5	2.8	-	-	77.9	4.6	-		78.3	0.5	-		81.0	3.4	-		82.3	1.6	-	
1981	83.0	0.9	-	-	83.0	0.0	-	-	88.1	6.1	-		92.2	4.7	-		91.3	-1.0	-		90.2	-1.2	-	
1982	92.8	2.9	-	-	91.0	-1.9	-	-	92.4	1.5	-		92.8	0.4	-		96.9	4.4	-		97.5	0.6	-	
1983	99.2	1.7	-	-	99.4	0.2	-	-	100.6	1.2	-		101.7	1.1	-		102.1	0.4	-		100.8	-1.3	-	
1984	102.3	1.5	-	-	103.9	1.6	-	-	105.5	1.5	-		105.1	-0.4	-		106.5	1.3	-		106.1	-0.4	-	
1985	106.5	0.4	-	-	107.2	0.7	-	-	108.8	1.5	-		108.7	-0.1	-		109.7	0.9	-		109.4	-0.3	-	
1986	110.4	0.9	-	-	109.1	-1.2	-	-	110.2	1.0	-		109.8	-0.4	-		110.2	0.4	-		106.7	-3.2	109.2	2.3
1987	-	-	-		-	-	-	-	-		112.4	2.9	-		-		-		-		-		116.2	3.4
1988	-	-	-		-	-	-	-	-		117.3	0.9	-		-		-		-		-		119.5	1.9
1989	-	-	-		-	-	-	-	-		121.8	1.9	-		-		-		-		-		122.5	0.6
1990	-	-	-		-	-	-	-	-		123.6	0.9	-		-		-		-		-		128.5	4.0
1991	-	-	-		-	-	-	-	-		131.0	1.9	-		-		-		-		-		133.3	1.8
1992	-	-	-		-	-	-	-	-		136.4	2.3	-		-		-		-		-		139.1	2.0
1993	-	-	-		-	-	-	-	-		140.9	1.3	-		-		-		-		-		-	-

Source: U.S. Department of Labor, Bureau of Labor Statistics, Division of Consumer Prices and Price Indexes. - indicates no data collected for period.

Milwaukee, WI
Consumer Price Index - Urban Wage Earners
Base 1982-1984 = 100
Housing

For 1975-1993. Columns headed % show percentile change in the index from the previous period for which an index is available.

Year	Jan Index	%	Feb Index	%	Mar Index	%	Apr Index	%	May Index	%	Jun Index	%	Jul Index	%	Aug Index	%	Sep Index	%	Oct Index	%	Nov Index	%	Dec Index	%
1975	-	-	-	-	-	-	-	-	-	-	-	-	-	-	-	-	-	-	-	-	42.1	-	-	-
1976	-	-	42.5	1.0	-	-	-	-	43.5	2.4	-	-	-	-	44.2	1.6	-	-	-	-	44.7	1.1	-	-
1977	-	-	45.7	2.2	-	-	-	-	46.9	2.6	-	-	-	-	46.9	0.0	-	-	-	-	48.4	3.2	-	-
1978	49.2	1.7	-	-	49.9	1.4	-	-	50.1	0.4	-	-	52.4	4.6	-	-	54.5	4.0	-	-	54.0	-0.9	-	-
1979	53.3	-1.3	-	-	56.5	6.0	-	-	61.1	8.1	-	-	63.1	3.3	-	-	64.1	1.6	-	-	65.5	2.2	-	-
1980	69.2	5.6	-	-	71.2	2.9	-	-	74.2	4.2	-	-	74.5	0.4	-	-	77.4	3.9	-	-	79.2	2.3	-	-
1981	79.3	0.1	-	-	78.9	-0.5	-	-	84.4	7.0	-	-	88.8	5.2	-	-	88.1	-0.8	-	-	86.4	-1.9	-	-
1982	88.9	2.9	-	-	86.6	-2.6	-	-	87.9	1.5	-	-	88.1	0.2	-	-	92.6	5.1	-	-	93.2	0.6	-	-
1983	90.9	-2.5	-	-	96.2	5.8	-	-	97.7	1.6	-	-	104.1	6.6	-	-	105.0	0.9	-	-	104.8	-0.2	-	-
1984	104.0	-0.8	-	-	108.6	4.4	-	-	109.4	0.7	-	-	111.0	1.5	-	-	114.6	3.2	-	-	110.8	-3.3	-	-
1985	111.2	0.4	-	-	112.0	0.7	-	-	113.6	1.4	-	-	113.6	0.0	-	-	114.5	0.8	-	-	114.1	-0.3	-	-
1986	115.2	1.0	-	-	113.7	-1.3	-	-	115.0	1.1	-	-	114.5	-0.4	-	-	114.8	0.3	-	-	111.0	-3.3	113.8	2.5
1987	-	-	-	-	-	-	-	-	-	-	117.1	2.9	-	-	-	-	-	-	-	-	-	-	120.9	3.2
1988	-	-	-	-	-	-	-	-	-	-	122.1	1.0	-	-	-	-	-	-	-	-	-	-	124.4	1.9
1989	-	-	-	-	-	-	-	-	-	-	126.6	1.8	-	-	-	-	-	-	-	-	-	-	127.3	0.6
1990	-	-	-	-	-	-	-	-	-	-	128.4	0.9	-	-	-	-	-	-	-	-	-	-	133.4	3.9
1991	-	-	-	-	-	-	-	-	-	-	136.1	2.0	-	-	-	-	-	-	-	-	-	-	138.4	1.7
1992	-	-	-	-	-	-	-	-	-	-	141.5	2.2	-	-	-	-	-	-	-	-	-	-	144.4	2.0
1993	-	-	-	-	-	-	-	-	-	-	146.3	1.3	-	-	-	-	-	-	-	-	-	-	-	-

Source: U.S. Department of Labor, Bureau of Labor Statistics, Division of Consumer Prices and Price Indexes. - indicates no data collected for period.

Milwaukee, WI
Consumer Price Index - All Urban Consumers
Base 1982-1984 = 100
Apparel and Upkeep

For 1952-1993. Columns headed % show percentile change in the index from the previous period for which an index is available.

Year	Jan Index	%	Feb Index	%	Mar Index	%	Apr Index	%	May Index	%	Jun Index	%	Jul Index	%	Aug Index	%	Sep Index	%	Oct Index	%	Nov Index	%	Dec Index	%
1952	-	-	-	-	-	-	-	-	-	-	-	-	-	-	-	-	-	-	-	-	39.4	-	-	-
1953	-	-	39.3	-0.3	-	-	-	-	39.5	0.5	-	-	-	-	39.7	0.5	-	-	-	-	39.7	0.0	-	-
1954	-	-	39.9	0.5	-	-	-	-	39.7	-0.5	-	-	-	-	39.4	-0.8	-	-	-	-	39.2	-0.5	-	-
1955	-	-	39.1	-0.3	-	-	-	-	39.2	0.3	-	-	-	-	39.3	0.3	-	-	-	-	39.7	1.0	-	-
1956	-	-	39.9	0.5	-	-	-	-	40.1	0.5	-	-	-	-	40.5	1.0	-	-	-	-	40.6	0.2	-	-
1957	-	-	40.7	0.2	-	-	-	-	40.9	0.5	-	-	-	-	41.1	0.5	-	-	-	-	41.0	-0.2	-	-
1958	-	-	41.1	0.2	-	-	-	-	40.9	-0.5	-	-	-	-	41.0	0.2	-	-	-	-	40.9	-0.2	-	-
1959	-	-	40.7	-0.5	-	-	-	-	41.3	1.5	-	-	-	-	41.4	0.2	-	-	-	-	41.6	0.5	-	-
1960	-	-	41.7	0.2	-	-	-	-	41.9	0.5	-	-	-	-	41.8	-0.2	-	-	-	-	41.8	0.0	-	-
1961	-	-	42.1	0.7	-	-	-	-	42.1	0.0	-	-	-	-	41.7	-1.0	-	-	-	-	42.2	1.2	-	-
1962	-	-	42.1	-0.2	-	-	-	-	42.3	0.5	-	-	-	-	42.2	-0.2	-	-	-	-	42.1	-0.2	-	-
1963	-	-	41.9	-0.5	-	-	-	-	42.0	0.2	-	-	-	-	42.4	1.0	-	-	-	-	42.4	0.0	-	-
1964	-	-	42.3	-0.2	-	-	-	-	42.8	1.2	-	-	-	-	43.1	0.7	-	-	-	-	43.3	0.5	-	-
1965	-	-	43.2	-0.2	-	-	-	-	43.8	1.4	-	-	-	-	43.6	-0.5	-	-	-	-	43.3	-0.7	-	-
1966	-	-	43.6	0.7	-	-	-	-	43.9	0.7	-	-	-	-	44.3	0.9	-	-	-	-	44.8	1.1	-	-
1967	-	-	45.3	1.1	-	-	-	-	46.0	1.5	-	-	-	-	45.7	-0.7	-	-	-	-	46.4	1.5	-	-
1968	-	-	46.5	0.2	-	-	-	-	47.8	2.8	-	-	-	-	48.0	0.4	-	-	-	-	48.7	1.5	-	-
1969	-	-	49.6	1.8	-	-	-	-	51.5	3.8	-	-	-	-	51.5	0.0	-	-	-	-	54.4	5.6	-	-
1970	-	-	54.6	0.4	-	-	-	-	55.5	1.6	-	-	-	-	56.2	1.3	-	-	-	-	57.5	2.3	-	-
1971	-	-	56.7	-1.4	-	-	-	-	56.7	0.0	-	-	-	-	55.8	-1.6	-	-	-	-	58.3	4.5	-	-
1972	-	-	57.2	-1.9	-	-	-	-	58.3	1.9	-	-	-	-	57.2	-1.9	-	-	-	-	59.4	3.8	-	-
1973	-	-	59.8	0.7	-	-	-	-	60.6	1.3	-	-	-	-	60.7	0.2	-	-	-	-	62.7	3.3	-	-
1974	-	-	61.6	-1.8	-	-	-	-	64.2	4.2	-	-	-	-	65.4	1.9	-	-	-	-	68.2	4.3	-	-
1975	-	-	67.7	-0.7	-	-	-	-	69.8	3.1	-	-	-	-	69.6	-0.3	-	-	-	-	72.8	4.6	-	-
1976	-	-	71.7	-1.5	-	-	-	-	74.5	3.9	-	-	-	-	74.8	0.4	-	-	-	-	75.9	1.5	-	-
1977	-	-	75.2	-0.9	-	-	-	-	77.8	3.5	-	-	-	-	77.0	-1.0	-	-	-	-	80.1	4.0	-	-
1978	75.2	-6.1	-	-	77.6	3.2	-	-	80.0	3.1	-	-	76.7	-4.1	-	-	80.1	4.4	-	-	79.6	-0.6	-	-
1979	77.2	-3.0	-	-	81.5	5.6	-	-	80.5	-1.2	-	-	81.4	1.1	-	-	85.4	4.9	-	-	85.7	0.4	-	-
1980	83.5	-2.6	-	-	89.0	6.6	-	-	86.6	-2.7	-	-	83.7	-3.3	-	-	91.3	9.1	-	-	89.3	-2.2	-	-
1981	89.1	-0.2	-	-	91.8	3.0	-	-	89.4	-2.6	-	-	89.2	-0.2	-	-	97.0	8.7	-	-	97.2	0.2	-	-
1982	89.2	-8.2	-	-	94.8	6.3	-	-	96.4	1.7	-	-	96.9	0.5	-	-	102.2	5.5	-	-	100.1	-2.1	-	-
1983	95.6	-4.5	-	-	100.5	5.1	-	-	101.5	1.0	-	-	97.3	-4.1	-	-	108.2	11.2	-	-	107.4	-0.7	-	-
1984	98.8	-8.0	-	-	101.3	2.5	-	-	101.3	0.0	-	-	100.5	-0.8	-	-	102.4	1.9	-	-	103.5	1.1	-	-
1985	98.6	-4.7	-	-	103.6	5.1	-	-	102.5	-1.1	-	-	102.1	-0.4	-	-	106.0	3.8	-	-	106.5	0.5	-	-
1986	102.9	-3.4	-	-	107.3	4.3	-	-	106.3	-0.9	-	-	104.6	-1.6	-	-	105.3	0.7	-	-	105.0	-0.3	103.0	-1.9
1987	-	-	-	-	-	-	-	-	-	-	107.8	4.7	-	-	-	-	-	-	-	-	-	-	115.0	6.7
1988	-	-	-	-	-	-	-	-	-	-	118.1	2.7	-	-	-	-	-	-	-	-	-	-	123.9	4.9
1989	-	-	-	-	-	-	-	-	-	-	123.4	-0.4	-	-	-	-	-	-	-	-	-	-	119.1	-3.5
1990	-	-	-	-	-	-	-	-	-	-	120.7	1.3	-	-	-	-	-	-	-	-	-	-	131.4	8.9
1991	-	-	-	-	-	-	-	-	-	-	124.1	-5.6	-	-	-	-	-	-	-	-	-	-	126.7	2.1
1992	-	-	-	-	-	-	-	-	-	-	123.6	-2.4	-	-	-	-	-	-	-	-	-	-	124.7	0.9
1993	-	-	-	-	-	-	-	-	-	-	120.5	-3.4	-	-	-	-	-	-	-	-	-	-	-	-

Source: U.S. Department of Labor, Bureau of Labor Statistics, Division of Consumer Prices and Price Indexes. - indicates no data collected for period.

Milwaukee, WI
Consumer Price Index - Urban Wage Earners
Base 1982-1984 = 100
Apparel and Upkeep

For 1952-1993. Columns headed % show percentile change in the index from the previous period for which an index is available.

Year	Jan Index	Jan %	Feb Index	Feb %	Mar Index	Mar %	Apr Index	Apr %	May Index	May %	Jun Index	Jun %	Jul Index	Jul %	Aug Index	Aug %	Sep Index	Sep %	Oct Index	Oct %	Nov Index	Nov %	Dec Index	Dec %
1952	-	-	-	-	-	-	-	-	-	-	-	-	-	-	-	-	-	-	-	-	40.3	-	-	-
1953	-	-	40.2	-0.2	-	-	-	-	40.4	0.5	-	-	-	-	40.6	0.5	-	-	-	-	40.6	0.0	-	-
1954	-	-	40.8	0.5	-	-	-	-	40.6	-0.5	-	-	-	-	40.3	-0.7	-	-	-	-	40.1	-0.5	-	-
1955	-	-	40.0	-0.2	-	-	-	-	40.1	0.2	-	-	-	-	40.1	0.0	-	-	-	-	40.6	1.2	-	-
1956	-	-	40.8	0.5	-	-	-	-	41.0	0.5	-	-	-	-	41.4	1.0	-	-	-	-	41.5	0.2	-	-
1957	-	-	41.6	0.2	-	-	-	-	41.8	0.5	-	-	-	-	42.0	0.5	-	-	-	-	41.9	-0.2	-	-
1958	-	-	42.0	0.2	-	-	-	-	41.8	-0.5	-	-	-	-	41.9	0.2	-	-	-	-	41.8	-0.2	-	-
1959	-	-	41.6	-0.5	-	-	-	-	42.3	1.7	-	-	-	-	42.3	0.0	-	-	-	-	42.5	0.5	-	-
1960	-	-	42.6	0.2	-	-	-	-	42.8	0.5	-	-	-	-	42.7	-0.2	-	-	-	-	42.7	0.0	-	-
1961	-	-	43.0	0.7	-	-	-	-	43.0	0.0	-	-	-	-	42.7	-0.7	-	-	-	-	43.1	0.9	-	-
1962	-	-	43.1	0.0	-	-	-	-	43.2	0.2	-	-	-	-	43.1	-0.2	-	-	-	-	43.0	-0.2	-	-
1963	-	-	42.8	-0.5	-	-	-	-	42.9	0.2	-	-	-	-	43.4	1.2	-	-	-	-	43.4	0.0	-	-
1964	-	-	43.3	-0.2	-	-	-	-	43.8	1.2	-	-	-	-	44.0	0.5	-	-	-	-	44.2	0.5	-	-
1965	-	-	44.2	0.0	-	-	-	-	44.8	1.4	-	-	-	-	44.6	-0.4	-	-	-	-	44.3	-0.7	-	-
1966	-	-	44.6	0.7	-	-	-	-	44.9	0.7	-	-	-	-	45.3	0.9	-	-	-	-	45.8	1.1	-	-
1967	-	-	46.3	1.1	-	-	-	-	47.0	1.5	-	-	-	-	46.7	-0.6	-	-	-	-	47.4	1.5	-	-
1968	-	-	47.5	0.2	-	-	-	-	48.9	2.9	-	-	-	-	49.0	0.2	-	-	-	-	49.8	1.6	-	-
1969	-	-	50.7	1.8	-	-	-	-	52.6	3.7	-	-	-	-	52.7	0.2	-	-	-	-	55.6	5.5	-	-
1970	-	-	55.8	0.4	-	-	-	-	56.7	1.6	-	-	-	-	57.5	1.4	-	-	-	-	58.8	2.3	-	-
1971	-	-	58.0	-1.4	-	-	-	-	58.0	0.0	-	-	-	-	57.1	-1.6	-	-	-	-	59.6	4.4	-	-
1972	-	-	58.5	-1.8	-	-	-	-	59.6	1.9	-	-	-	-	58.5	-1.8	-	-	-	-	60.8	3.9	-	-
1973	-	-	61.1	0.5	-	-	-	-	62.0	1.5	-	-	-	-	62.1	0.2	-	-	-	-	64.1	3.2	-	-
1974	-	-	63.0	-1.7	-	-	-	-	65.6	4.1	-	-	-	-	66.8	1.8	-	-	-	-	69.7	4.3	-	-
1975	-	-	69.2	-0.7	-	-	-	-	71.3	3.0	-	-	-	-	71.2	-0.1	-	-	-	-	74.4	4.5	-	-
1976	-	-	73.4	-1.3	-	-	-	-	76.2	3.8	-	-	-	-	76.5	0.4	-	-	-	-	77.6	1.4	-	-
1977	-	-	76.9	-0.9	-	-	-	-	79.6	3.5	-	-	-	-	78.7	-1.1	-	-	-	-	81.9	4.1	-	-
1978	76.3	-6.8	-	-	78.0	2.2	-	-	80.1	2.7	-	-	78.3	-2.2	-	-	83.6	6.8	-	-	83.7	0.1	-	-
1979	80.2	-4.2	-	-	83.4	4.0	-	-	82.4	-1.2	-	-	82.8	0.5	-	-	88.0	6.3	-	-	89.0	1.1	-	-
1980	87.1	-2.1	-	-	90.2	3.6	-	-	89.6	-0.7	-	-	87.1	-2.8	-	-	93.1	6.9	-	-	90.3	-3.0	-	-
1981	93.4	3.4	-	-	94.9	1.6	-	-	93.4	-1.6	-	-	94.7	1.4	-	-	97.2	2.6	-	-	97.6	0.4	-	-
1982	90.3	-7.5	-	-	96.4	6.8	-	-	97.4	1.0	-	-	97.9	0.5	-	-	102.9	5.1	-	-	100.4	-2.4	-	-
1983	96.3	-4.1	-	-	101.3	5.2	-	-	101.1	-0.2	-	-	96.9	-4.2	-	-	107.2	10.6	-	-	106.4	-0.7	-	-
1984	98.8	-7.1	-	-	101.0	2.2	-	-	101.0	0.0	-	-	99.2	-1.8	-	-	101.4	2.2	-	-	102.2	0.8	-	-
1985	98.8	-3.3	-	-	103.1	4.4	-	-	102.0	-1.1	-	-	101.4	-0.6	-	-	104.8	3.4	-	-	106.7	1.8	-	-
1986	103.2	-3.3	-	-	106.7	3.4	-	-	107.0	0.3	-	-	105.6	-1.3	-	-	105.6	0.0	-	-	105.8	0.2	104.1	-1.6
1987	-	-	-	-	-	-	-	-	-	-	109.7	5.4	-	-	-	-	-	-	-	-	-	-	116.3	6.0
1988	-	-	-	-	-	-	-	-	-	-	120.5	3.6	-	-	-	-	-	-	-	-	-	-	125.9	4.5
1989	-	-	-	-	-	-	-	-	-	-	125.9	0.0	-	-	-	-	-	-	-	-	-	-	121.1	-3.8
1990	-	-	-	-	-	-	-	-	-	-	120.9	-0.2	-	-	-	-	-	-	-	-	-	-	133.8	10.7
1991	-	-	-	-	-	-	-	-	-	-	126.0	-5.8	-	-	-	-	-	-	-	-	-	-	130.3	3.4
1992	-	-	-	-	-	-	-	-	-	-	125.1	-4.0	-	-	-	-	-	-	-	-	-	-	127.4	1.8
1993	-	-	-	-	-	-	-	-	-	-	123.8	-2.8	-	-	-	-	-	-	-	-	-	-	-	-

Source: U.S. Department of Labor, Bureau of Labor Statistics, Division of Consumer Prices and Price Indexes. - indicates no data collected for period.

Milwaukee, WI
Consumer Price Index - All Urban Consumers
Base 1982-1984 = 100
Transportation

For 1946-1993. Columns headed % show percentile change in the index from the previous period for which an index is available.

Year	Jan Index	%	Feb Index	%	Mar Index	%	Apr Index	%	May Index	%	Jun Index	%	Jul Index	%	Aug Index	%	Sep Index	%	Oct Index	%	Nov Index	%	Dec Index	%
1946	-		-		-		-		-	-	-	-	-	-	-	-	-		-		19.9	-	-	-
1947	-		-		20.0	0.5	-		-	-	20.0	0.0	-	-	20.2	1.0	-		-		20.8	3.0	-	-
1948	-		21.2	1.9			-		21.3	0.5			-		22.6	6.1	-		-		22.7	0.4		
1949	-		23.0	1.3	-		-		23.1	0.4			-		22.9	-0.9	-		-		22.3	-2.6		
1950	-		22.0	-1.3	-		-		23.2	5.5			-		23.8	2.6	-		-		23.8	0.0		
1951	-		23.9	0.4			-		24.8	3.8			-		24.8	0.0	-		-		25.6	3.2		
1952	-		26.1	2.0			-		26.2	0.4			-		26.2	0.0			-		27.0	3.1		
1953	-		27.0	0.0			-		27.0	0.0			-		27.3	1.1			-		27.1	-0.7		
1954	-		26.8	-1.1			-		26.8	0.0			-		26.4	-1.5			-		27.2	3.0		
1955	-		26.5	-2.6			-		26.4	-0.4			-		26.3	-0.4			-		26.9	2.3		
1956	-		26.7	-0.7			-		26.6	-0.4			-		27.3	2.6			-		28.1	2.9		
1957	-		28.2	0.4			-		28.2	0.0			-		28.3	0.4			-		28.8	1.8		
1958	-		28.5	-1.0			-		28.4	-0.4			-		29.2	2.8			-		29.3	0.3		
1959	-		29.4	0.3			-		29.5	0.3			-		29.9	1.4			-		30.5	2.0		
1960	-		29.2	-4.3			-		29.5	1.0			-		29.8	1.0			-		29.5	-1.0		
1961	-		29.9	1.4			-		29.0	-3.0			-		30.1	3.8			-		29.9	-0.7		
1962	-		30.5	2.0			-		31.0	1.6			-		30.3	-2.3			-		31.2	3.0		
1963	-		30.5	-2.2			-		31.1	2.0			-		30.8	-1.0			-		31.5	2.3		
1964	-		30.9	-1.9			-		30.5	-1.3			-		31.3	2.6			-		31.7	1.3		
1965	-		32.1	1.3			-		32.6	1.6			-		32.1	-1.5			-		32.1	0.0		
1966	-		32.3	0.6			-		32.0	-0.9			-		32.8	2.5			-		32.7	-0.3		
1967	-		32.5	-0.6			-		32.7	0.6			-		32.8	0.3			-		33.7	2.7		
1968	-		33.6	-0.3			-		32.8	-2.4			-		32.9	0.3			-		33.6	2.1		
1969	-		35.0	4.2			-		34.8	-0.6			-		34.5	-0.9			-		35.8	3.8		
1970	-		34.9	-2.5			-		36.6	4.9			-		36.1	-1.4			-		37.8	4.7		
1971	-		38.9	2.9			-		37.8	-2.8			-		39.3	4.0			-		38.1	-3.1		
1972	-		37.9	-0.5			-		38.6	1.8			-		40.3	4.4			-		40.0	-0.7		
1973	-		40.2	0.5			-		41.6	3.5			-		41.5	-0.2			-		42.2	1.7		
1974	-		43.4	2.8			-		45.7	5.3			-		47.4	3.7			-		47.8	0.8		
1975	-		48.3	1.0			-		49.2	1.9			-		50.9	3.5			-		51.1	0.4		
1976	-		51.1	0.0			-		52.4	2.5			-		55.0	5.0			-		55.4	0.7		
1977	-		55.7	0.5			-		57.3	2.9			-		57.5	0.3			-		57.7	0.3		
1978	57.9	0.3	-		58.2	0.5	-		59.1	1.5			61.1	3.4	-		61.7	1.0	-		75.0	2.3		
1979	64.4	1.4	-		65.5	1.7	-		69.1	5.5			72.5	4.9	-		73.3	1.1	-		86.1	2.6		
1980	77.4	3.2	-		80.7	4.3	-		84.5	4.7			84.0	-0.6	-		83.9	-0.1	-		98.1	3.3		
1981	88.9	3.3	-		90.6	1.9	-		92.5	2.1			93.7	1.3	-		95.0	1.4	-		98.9	-0.2		
1982	98.2	0.1	-		97.2	-1.0	-		96.8	-0.4			100.6	3.9	-		99.1	-1.5	-		101.3	0.5		
1983	98.1	-0.8	-		95.9	-2.2	-		98.3	2.5			99.0	0.7	-		100.8	1.8	-		103.9	0.6		
1984	100.8	-0.5	-		101.3	0.5	-		102.8	1.5			102.7	-0.1	-		103.3	0.6	-		105.1	1.6		
1985	102.1	-1.7	-		103.0	0.9	-		104.7	1.7			104.6	-0.1	-		103.4	-1.1	-		98.7	1.6	98.2	-0.5
1986	104.2	-0.9	-		97.5	-6.4	-		98.8	1.3			97.7	-1.1	-		97.1	-0.6	-				103.0	2.9
1987	-		-		-		-		-		100.1	1.9	-		-		-		-				104.4	2.7
1988	-		-		-		-		-		101.7	-1.3	-		-		-		-				110.1	0.1
1989	-		-		-		-		-		110.0	5.4	-		-		-		-				117.4	4.0
1990	-		-		-		-		-		112.9	2.5	-		-		-		-					

[Continued]

Milwaukee, WI
Consumer Price Index - All Urban Consumers
Base 1982-1984 = 100
Transportation
[Continued]

For 1946-1993. Columns headed % show percentile change in the index from the previous period for which an index is available.

Year	Jan Index	%	Feb Index	%	Mar Index	%	Apr Index	%	May Index	%	Jun Index	%	Jul Index	%	Aug Index	%	Sep Index	%	Oct Index	%	Nov Index	%	Dec Index	%
1991	-	-	-	-	-	-	-	-	-	-	117.7	0.3	-	-	-	-	-	-	-	-	-	-	120.6	2.5
1992	-	-	-	-	-	-	-	-	-	-	122.1	1.2	-	-	-	-	-	-	-	-	-	-	124.1	1.6
1993	-	-	-	-	-	-	-	-	-	-	127.3	2.6	-	-	-	-	-	-	-	-	-	-	-	-

Source: U.S. Department of Labor, Bureau of Labor Statistics, Division of Consumer Prices and Price Indexes. - indicates no data collected for period.

Milwaukee, WI
Consumer Price Index - Urban Wage Earners
Base 1982-1984 = 100
Transportation

For 1946-1993. Columns headed % show percentile change in the index from the previous period for which an index is available.

Year	Jan Index	%	Feb Index	%	Mar Index	%	Apr Index	%	May Index	%	Jun Index	%	Jul Index	%	Aug Index	%	Sep Index	%	Oct Index	%	Nov Index	%	Dec Index	%
1946	-	-	-	-	-	-	-	-	-	-	-	-	-	-	-	-	-	-	-	-	20.1	-	-	-
1947	-	-	-	-	20.2	0.5	-	-	-	-	20.2	0.0	-	-	20.4	1.0	-	-	-	-	21.1	3.4	-	-
1948	-	-	21.5	1.9	-	-	-	-	21.5	0.0	-	-	-	-	22.8	6.0	-	-	-	-	22.9	0.4	-	-
1949	-	-	23.2	1.3	-	-	-	-	23.3	0.4	-	-	-	-	23.2	-0.4	-	-	-	-	22.6	-2.6	-	-
1950	-	-	22.2	-1.8	-	-	-	-	23.4	5.4	-	-	-	-	24.1	3.0	-	-	-	-	24.1	0.0	-	-
1951	-	-	24.1	0.0	-	-	-	-	25.0	3.7	-	-	-	-	25.1	0.4	-	-	-	-	25.9	3.2	-	-
1952	-	-	26.4	1.9	-	-	-	-	26.5	0.4	-	-	-	-	26.5	0.0	-	-	-	-	27.3	3.0	-	-
1953	-	-	27.3	0.0	-	-	-	-	27.3	0.0	-	-	-	-	27.6	1.1	-	-	-	-	27.4	-0.7	-	-
1954	-	-	27.1	-1.1	-	-	-	-	27.1	0.0	-	-	-	-	26.7	-1.5	-	-	-	-	27.5	3.0	-	-
1955	-	-	26.8	-2.5	-	-	-	-	26.7	-0.4	-	-	-	-	26.6	-0.4	-	-	-	-	27.2	2.3	-	-
1956	-	-	27.0	-0.7	-	-	-	-	26.9	-0.4	-	-	-	-	27.6	2.6	-	-	-	-	28.4	2.9	-	-
1957	-	-	28.6	0.7	-	-	-	-	28.6	0.0	-	-	-	-	28.7	0.3	-	-	-	-	29.1	1.4	-	-
1958	-	-	28.9	-0.7	-	-	-	-	28.7	-0.7	-	-	-	-	29.5	2.8	-	-	-	-	29.6	0.3	-	-
1959	-	-	29.7	0.3	-	-	-	-	29.8	0.3	-	-	-	-	30.3	1.7	-	-	-	-	30.8	1.7	-	-
1960	-	-	29.6	-3.9	-	-	-	-	29.8	0.7	-	-	-	-	30.1	1.0	-	-	-	-	29.9	-0.7	-	-
1961	-	-	30.2	1.0	-	-	-	-	29.4	-2.6	-	-	-	-	30.4	3.4	-	-	-	-	30.2	-0.7	-	-
1962	-	-	30.9	2.3	-	-	-	-	31.4	1.6	-	-	-	-	30.7	-2.2	-	-	-	-	31.6	2.9	-	-
1963	-	-	30.8	-2.5	-	-	-	-	31.4	1.9	-	-	-	-	31.1	-1.0	-	-	-	-	31.8	2.3	-	-
1964	-	-	31.3	-1.6	-	-	-	-	30.8	-1.6	-	-	-	-	31.6	2.6	-	-	-	-	32.0	1.3	-	-
1965	-	-	32.4	1.3	-	-	-	-	32.9	1.5	-	-	-	-	32.5	-1.2	-	-	-	-	32.5	0.0	-	-
1966	-	-	32.6	0.3	-	-	-	-	32.3	-0.9	-	-	-	-	33.1	2.5	-	-	-	-	33.1	0.0	-	-
1967	-	-	32.8	-0.9	-	-	-	-	33.0	0.6	-	-	-	-	33.1	0.3	-	-	-	-	34.0	2.7	-	-
1968	-	-	34.0	0.0	-	-	-	-	33.2	-2.4	-	-	-	-	33.3	0.3	-	-	-	-	33.9	1.8	-	-
1969	-	-	35.4	4.4	-	-	-	-	35.2	-0.6	-	-	-	-	34.9	-0.9	-	-	-	-	36.2	3.7	-	-
1970	-	-	35.2	-2.8	-	-	-	-	37.0	5.1	-	-	-	-	36.5	-1.4	-	-	-	-	38.2	4.7	-	-
1971	-	-	39.3	2.9	-	-	-	-	38.3	-2.5	-	-	-	-	39.8	3.9	-	-	-	-	38.5	-3.3	-	-
1972	-	-	38.4	-0.3	-	-	-	-	39.0	1.6	-	-	-	-	40.7	4.4	-	-	-	-	40.4	-0.7	-	-
1973	-	-	40.7	0.7	-	-	-	-	42.1	3.4	-	-	-	-	42.0	-0.2	-	-	-	-	42.7	1.7	-	-
1974	-	-	43.9	2.8	-	-	-	-	46.2	5.2	-	-	-	-	47.9	3.7	-	-	-	-	48.3	0.8	-	-
1975	-	-	48.8	1.0	-	-	-	-	49.7	1.8	-	-	-	-	51.4	3.4	-	-	-	-	51.7	0.6	-	-
1976	-	-	51.6	-0.2	-	-	-	-	53.0	2.7	-	-	-	-	55.6	4.9	-	-	-	-	56.0	0.7	-	-
1977	-	-	56.3	0.5	-	-	-	-	57.9	2.8	-	-	-	-	58.1	0.3	-	-	-	-	58.3	0.3	-	-
1978	58.6	0.5	-	-	58.9	0.5	-	-	60.2	2.2	-	-	62.1	3.2	-	-	62.7	1.0	-	-	63.7	1.6	-	-
1979	64.6	1.4	-	-	66.2	2.5	-	-	69.1	4.4	-	-	72.4	4.8	-	-	74.1	2.3	-	-	75.6	2.0	-	-
1980	78.1	3.3	-	-	81.1	3.8	-	-	84.3	3.9	-	-	83.6	-0.8	-	-	84.0	0.5	-	-	86.3	2.7	-	-
1981	88.9	3.0	-	-	91.1	2.5	-	-	92.7	1.8	-	-	93.6	1.0	-	-	94.9	1.4	-	-	97.7	3.0	-	-
1982	97.6	-0.1	-	-	96.6	-1.0	-	-	96.2	-0.4	-	-	100.2	4.2	-	-	98.9	-1.3	-	-	98.8	-0.1	-	-
1983	97.9	-0.9	-	-	95.7	-2.2	-	-	98.4	2.8	-	-	99.2	0.8	-	-	101.0	1.8	-	-	101.6	0.6	-	-
1984	101.0	-0.6	-	-	101.6	0.6	-	-	103.2	1.6	-	-	103.0	-0.2	-	-	103.7	0.7	-	-	104.3	0.6	-	-
1985	102.5	-1.7	-	-	103.5	1.0	-	-	105.3	1.7	-	-	105.2	-0.1	-	-	104.0	-1.1	-	-	105.7	1.6	-	-
1986	104.8	-0.9	-	-	97.7	-6.8	-	-	99.2	1.5	-	-	97.9	-1.3	-	-	97.6	-0.3	-	-	98.8	1.2	98.4	-0.4
1987	-	-	-	-	-	-	-	-	-	-	100.9	2.5	-	-	-	-	-	-	-	-	-	-	104.1	3.2
1988	-	-	-	-	-	-	-	-	-	-	102.9	-1.2	-	-	-	-	-	-	-	-	-	-	105.7	2.7
1989	-	-	-	-	-	-	-	-	-	-	110.9	4.9	-	-	-	-	-	-	-	-	-	-	110.8	-0.1
1990	-	-	-	-	-	-	-	-	-	-	113.3	2.3	-	-	-	-	-	-	-	-	-	-	118.7	4.8

[Continued]

610

Milwaukee, WI
Consumer Price Index - Urban Wage Earners
Base 1982-1984 = 100
Transportation
[Continued]

For 1946-1993. Columns headed % show percentile change in the index from the previous period for which an index is available.

Year	Jan		Feb		Mar		Apr		May		Jun		Jul		Aug		Sep		Oct		Nov		Dec	
	Index	%	Index	%	Index	%	Index	%	Index	%	Index	%	Index	%	Index	%	Index	%	Index	%	Index	%	Index	%
1991	-	-	-	-	-	-	-	-	-	-	117.7	-0.8	-	-	-	-	-	-	-	-	-	-	120.9	2.7
1992	-	-	-	-	-	-	-	-	-	-	122.2	1.1	-	-	-	-	-	-	-	-	-	-	125.6	2.8
1993	-	-	-	-	-	-	-	-	-	-	128.3	2.1	-	-	-	-	-	-	-	-	-	-	-	-

Source: U.S. Department of Labor, Bureau of Labor Statistics, Division of Consumer Prices and Price Indexes. - indicates no data collected for period.

Milwaukee, WI
Consumer Price Index - All Urban Consumers
Base 1982-1984 = 100
Medical Care

For 1946-1993. Columns headed % show percentile change in the index from the previous period for which an index is available.

Year	Jan Index	%	Feb Index	%	Mar Index	%	Apr Index	%	May Index	%	Jun Index	%	Jul Index	%	Aug Index	%	Sep Index	%	Oct Index	%	Nov Index	%	Dec Index	%
1946	-	-	-	-	-	-	-	-	-	-	-	-	-	-	-	-	-	-	-	-	-	-	12.3	-
1947	-	-	-	-	12.7	3.3	-	-	-	-	12.8	0.8	-	-	12.9	0.8	-	-	-	-	13.0	0.8	-	-
1948	-	-	13.3	2.3	-	-	-	-	13.4	0.8	-	-	-	-	13.6	1.5	-	-	-	-	14.1	3.7	-	-
1949	-	-	14.2	0.7	-	-	-	-	14.2	0.0	-	-	-	-	14.3	0.7	-	-	-	-	14.3	0.0	-	-
1950	-	-	14.4	0.7	-	-	-	-	14.5	0.7	-	-	-	-	15.1	4.1	-	-	-	-	15.6	3.3	-	-
1951	-	-	15.7	0.6	-	-	-	-	16.4	4.5	-	-	-	-	16.8	2.4	-	-	-	-	17.0	1.2	-	-
1952	-	-	17.1	0.6	-	-	-	-	17.3	1.2	-	-	-	-	17.5	1.2	-	-	-	-	17.5	0.0	-	-
1953	-	-	17.7	1.1	-	-	-	-	17.8	0.6	-	-	-	-	18.1	1.7	-	-	-	-	18.2	0.6	-	-
1954	-	-	18.3	0.5	-	-	-	-	19.2	4.9	-	-	-	-	19.2	0.0	-	-	-	-	19.3	0.5	-	-
1955	-	-	19.3	0.0	-	-	-	-	19.4	0.5	-	-	-	-	19.8	2.1	-	-	-	-	19.6	-1.0	-	-
1956	-	-	19.7	0.5	-	-	-	-	19.9	1.0	-	-	-	-	19.9	0.0	-	-	-	-	20.0	0.5	-	-
1957	-	-	20.4	2.0	-	-	-	-	21.6	5.9	-	-	-	-	21.6	0.0	-	-	-	-	21.9	1.4	-	-
1958	-	-	22.0	0.5	-	-	-	-	22.1	0.5	-	-	-	-	22.1	0.0	-	-	-	-	22.1	0.0	-	-
1959	-	-	22.2	0.5	-	-	-	-	22.2	0.0	-	-	-	-	22.8	2.7	-	-	-	-	23.0	0.9	-	-
1960	-	-	23.0	0.0	-	-	-	-	23.0	0.0	-	-	-	-	23.1	0.4	-	-	-	-	23.1	0.0	-	-
1961	-	-	23.1	0.0	-	-	-	-	23.2	0.4	-	-	-	-	23.3	0.4	-	-	-	-	23.3	0.0	-	-
1962	-	-	23.4	0.4	-	-	-	-	23.4	0.0	-	-	-	-	23.4	0.0	-	-	-	-	23.4	0.0	-	-
1963	-	-	23.5	0.4	-	-	-	-	24.0	2.1	-	-	-	-	24.0	0.0	-	-	-	-	24.2	0.8	-	-
1964	-	-	24.2	0.0	-	-	-	-	24.3	0.4	-	-	-	-	24.4	0.4	-	-	-	-	24.5	0.4	-	-
1965	-	-	25.1	2.4	-	-	-	-	25.2	0.4	-	-	-	-	25.3	0.4	-	-	-	-	25.6	1.2	-	-
1966	-	-	25.9	1.2	-	-	-	-	26.3	1.5	-	-	-	-	26.9	2.3	-	-	-	-	27.7	3.0	-	-
1967	-	-	28.1	1.4	-	-	-	-	28.3	0.7	-	-	-	-	29.0	2.5	-	-	-	-	29.8	2.8	-	-
1968	-	-	29.9	0.3	-	-	-	-	29.9	0.0	-	-	-	-	30.5	2.0	-	-	-	-	31.4	3.0	-	-
1969	-	-	32.0	1.9	-	-	-	-	32.4	1.3	-	-	-	-	32.8	1.2	-	-	-	-	33.0	0.6	-	-
1970	-	-	33.9	2.7	-	-	-	-	34.2	0.9	-	-	-	-	34.6	1.2	-	-	-	-	34.6	0.0	-	-
1971	-	-	35.9	3.8	-	-	-	-	36.2	0.8	-	-	-	-	36.8	1.7	-	-	-	-	36.5	-0.8	-	-
1972	-	-	36.6	0.3	-	-	-	-	36.7	0.3	-	-	-	-	36.9	0.5	-	-	-	-	37.2	0.8	-	-
1973	-	-	37.6	1.1	-	-	-	-	38.2	1.6	-	-	-	-	38.8	1.6	-	-	-	-	39.6	2.1	-	-
1974	-	-	40.5	2.3	-	-	-	-	41.9	3.5	-	-	-	-	43.4	3.6	-	-	-	-	44.0	1.4	-	-
1975	-	-	45.3	3.0	-	-	-	-	46.4	2.4	-	-	-	-	48.0	3.4	-	-	-	-	48.7	1.5	-	-
1976	-	-	50.7	4.1	-	-	-	-	52.1	2.8	-	-	-	-	53.4	2.5	-	-	-	-	54.3	1.7	-	-
1977	-	-	55.1	1.5	-	-	-	-	57.2	3.8	-	-	-	-	58.0	1.4	-	-	-	-	58.9	1.6	-	-
1978	59.7	1.4	-	-	60.9	2.0	-	-	61.4	0.8	-	-	61.9	0.8	-	-	63.0	1.8	-	-	63.2	0.3	-	-
1979	66.3	4.9	-	-	67.2	1.4	-	-	67.8	0.9	-	-	69.8	2.9	-	-	71.0	1.7	-	-	71.7	1.0	-	-
1980	73.6	2.6	-	-	75.4	2.4	-	-	75.9	0.7	-	-	78.0	2.8	-	-	80.8	3.6	-	-	81.2	0.5	-	-
1981	83.2	2.5	-	-	86.1	3.5	-	-	86.3	0.2	-	-	87.0	0.8	-	-	87.9	1.0	-	-	88.1	0.2	-	-
1982	90.1	2.3	-	-	90.4	0.3	-	-	92.5	2.3	-	-	93.4	1.0	-	-	95.4	2.1	-	-	98.0	2.7	-	-
1983	99.2	1.2	-	-	99.2	0.0	-	-	99.3	0.1	-	-	101.0	1.7	-	-	101.8	0.8	-	-	102.0	0.2	-	-
1984	104.5	2.5	-	-	104.9	0.4	-	-	105.2	0.3	-	-	106.1	0.9	-	-	106.3	0.2	-	-	106.5	0.2	-	-
1985	107.1	0.6	-	-	108.3	1.1	-	-	109.0	0.6	-	-	109.5	0.5	-	-	110.1	0.5	-	-	110.5	0.4	-	-
1986	112.1	1.4	-	-	113.1	0.9	-	-	113.8	0.6	-	-	114.9	1.0	-	-	115.3	0.3	-	-	117.0	1.5	117.0	0.0
1987	-	-	-	-	-	-	-	-	-	-	117.8	0.7	-	-	-	-	-	-	-	-	-	-	120.9	2.6
1988	-	-	-	-	-	-	-	-	-	-	127.4	5.4	-	-	-	-	-	-	-	-	-	-	129.4	1.6
1989	-	-	-	-	-	-	-	-	-	-	137.2	6.0	-	-	-	-	-	-	-	-	-	-	141.5	3.1
1990	-	-	-	-	-	-	-	-	-	-	149.5	5.7	-	-	-	-	-	-	-	-	-	-	152.1	1.7

[Continued]

Milwaukee, WI
Consumer Price Index - All Urban Consumers
Base 1982-1984 = 100
Medical Care
[Continued]

For 1946-1993. Columns headed % show percentile change in the index from the previous period for which an index is available.

Year	Jan		Feb		Mar		Apr		May		Jun		Jul		Aug		Sep		Oct		Nov		Dec	
	Index	%	Index	%	Index	%	Index	%	Index	%	Index	%	Index	%	Index	%	Index	%	Index	%	Index	%	Index	%
1991	-	-	-	-	-	-	-	-	-	-	157.3	3.4	-	-	-	-	-	-	-	-	-	-	161.8	2.9
1992	-	-	-	-	-	-	-	-	-	-	172.5	6.6	-	-	-	-	-	-	-	-	-	-	176.1	2.1
1993	-	-	-	-	-	-	-	-	-	-	183.0	3.9	-	-	-	-	-	-	-	-	-	-	-	-

Source: U.S. Department of Labor, Bureau of Labor Statistics, Division of Consumer Prices and Price Indexes. - indicates no data collected for period.

Milwaukee, WI
Consumer Price Index - Urban Wage Earners
Base 1982-1984 = 100
Medical Care

For 1946-1993. Columns headed % show percentile change in the index from the previous period for which an index is available.

Year	Jan Index	%	Feb Index	%	Mar Index	%	Apr Index	%	May Index	%	Jun Index	%	Jul Index	%	Aug Index	%	Sep Index	%	Oct Index	%	Nov Index	%	Dec Index	%
1946	-	-	-	-	-	-	-	-	-	-	-	-	-	-	-	-	-	-	-	-	-	-	12.4	-
1947	-	-	-	-	12.9	4.0	-	-	-	-	12.9	0.0	-	-	13.0	0.8	-	-	-	-	13.1	0.8	-	-
1948	-	-	13.4	2.3	-	-	-	-	13.5	0.7	-	-	-	-	13.8	2.2	-	-	-	-	14.3	3.6	-	-
1949	-	-	14.3	0.0	-	-	-	-	14.3	0.0	-	-	-	-	14.5	1.4	-	-	-	-	14.5	0.0	-	-
1950	-	-	14.5	0.0	-	-	-	-	14.7	1.4	-	-	-	-	15.3	4.1	-	-	-	-	15.7	2.6	-	-
1951	-	-	15.9	1.3	-	-	-	-	16.6	4.4	-	-	-	-	17.0	2.4	-	-	-	-	17.1	0.6	-	-
1952	-	-	17.3	1.2	-	-	-	-	17.5	1.2	-	-	-	-	17.7	1.1	-	-	-	-	17.7	0.0	-	-
1953	-	-	17.9	1.1	-	-	-	-	18.0	0.6	-	-	-	-	18.3	1.7	-	-	-	-	18.4	0.5	-	-
1954	-	-	18.5	0.5	-	-	-	-	19.4	4.9	-	-	-	-	19.4	0.0	-	-	-	-	19.5	0.5	-	-
1955	-	-	19.5	0.0	-	-	-	-	19.6	0.5	-	-	-	-	20.0	2.0	-	-	-	-	19.8	-1.0	-	-
1956	-	-	20.0	1.0	-	-	-	-	20.1	0.5	-	-	-	-	20.1	0.0	-	-	-	-	20.3	1.0	-	-
1957	-	-	20.6	1.5	-	-	-	-	21.8	5.8	-	-	-	-	21.9	0.5	-	-	-	-	22.1	0.9	-	-
1958	-	-	22.3	0.9	-	-	-	-	22.3	0.0	-	-	-	-	22.3	0.0	-	-	-	-	22.4	0.4	-	-
1959	-	-	22.4	0.0	-	-	-	-	22.5	0.4	-	-	-	-	23.1	2.7	-	-	-	-	23.2	0.4	-	-
1960	-	-	23.3	0.4	-	-	-	-	23.3	0.0	-	-	-	-	23.4	0.4	-	-	-	-	23.4	0.0	-	-
1961	-	-	23.4	0.0	-	-	-	-	23.5	0.4	-	-	-	-	23.6	0.4	-	-	-	-	23.6	0.0	-	-
1962	-	-	23.7	0.4	-	-	-	-	23.7	0.0	-	-	-	-	23.7	0.0	-	-	-	-	23.7	0.0	-	-
1963	-	-	23.8	0.4	-	-	-	-	24.2	1.7	-	-	-	-	24.3	0.4	-	-	-	-	24.5	0.8	-	-
1964	-	-	24.5	0.0	-	-	-	-	24.6	0.4	-	-	-	-	24.7	0.4	-	-	-	-	24.7	0.0	-	-
1965	-	-	25.3	2.4	-	-	-	-	25.5	0.8	-	-	-	-	25.6	0.4	-	-	-	-	25.9	1.2	-	-
1966	-	-	26.2	1.2	-	-	-	-	26.6	1.5	-	-	-	-	27.2	2.3	-	-	-	-	28.0	2.9	-	-
1967	-	-	28.4	1.4	-	-	-	-	28.6	0.7	-	-	-	-	29.3	2.4	-	-	-	-	30.2	3.1	-	-
1968	-	-	30.2	0.0	-	-	-	-	30.3	0.3	-	-	-	-	30.9	2.0	-	-	-	-	31.8	2.9	-	-
1969	-	-	32.4	1.9	-	-	-	-	32.7	0.9	-	-	-	-	33.1	1.2	-	-	-	-	33.4	0.9	-	-
1970	-	-	34.3	2.7	-	-	-	-	34.6	0.9	-	-	-	-	35.0	1.2	-	-	-	-	35.0	0.0	-	-
1971	-	-	36.3	3.7	-	-	-	-	36.6	0.8	-	-	-	-	37.2	1.6	-	-	-	-	36.9	-0.8	-	-
1972	-	-	37.0	0.3	-	-	-	-	37.1	0.3	-	-	-	-	37.3	0.5	-	-	-	-	37.6	0.8	-	-
1973	-	-	38.0	1.1	-	-	-	-	38.7	1.8	-	-	-	-	39.2	1.3	-	-	-	-	40.1	2.3	-	-
1974	-	-	40.9	2.0	-	-	-	-	42.3	3.4	-	-	-	-	43.9	3.8	-	-	-	-	44.4	1.1	-	-
1975	-	-	45.8	3.2	-	-	-	-	46.9	2.4	-	-	-	-	48.5	3.4	-	-	-	-	49.2	1.4	-	-
1976	-	-	51.3	4.3	-	-	-	-	52.7	2.7	-	-	-	-	54.0	2.5	-	-	-	-	54.9	1.7	-	-
1977	-	-	55.7	1.5	-	-	-	-	57.8	3.8	-	-	-	-	58.7	1.6	-	-	-	-	59.5	1.4	-	-
1978	61.4	3.2	-	-	62.0	1.0	-	-	63.3	2.1	-	-	63.9	0.9	-	-	64.8	1.4	-	-	64.9	0.2	-	-
1979	67.3	3.7	-	-	68.0	1.0	-	-	68.1	0.1	-	-	70.5	3.5	-	-	71.8	1.8	-	-	72.1	0.4	-	-
1980	74.5	3.3	-	-	77.2	3.6	-	-	78.1	1.2	-	-	79.4	1.7	-	-	81.3	2.4	-	-	81.9	0.7	-	-
1981	84.0	2.6	-	-	86.9	3.5	-	-	87.1	0.2	-	-	88.1	1.1	-	-	88.7	0.7	-	-	88.9	0.2	-	-
1982	91.0	2.4	-	-	91.2	0.2	-	-	92.9	1.9	-	-	93.6	0.8	-	-	95.3	1.8	-	-	97.3	2.1	-	-
1983	98.5	1.2	-	-	98.7	0.2	-	-	98.9	0.2	-	-	100.7	1.8	-	-	101.4	0.7	-	-	101.6	0.2	-	-
1984	104.4	2.8	-	-	104.9	0.5	-	-	105.3	0.4	-	-	106.6	1.2	-	-	106.7	0.1	-	-	107.0	0.3	-	-
1985	107.8	0.7	-	-	108.9	1.0	-	-	109.7	0.7	-	-	110.2	0.5	-	-	110.8	0.5	-	-	111.3	0.5	-	-
1986	113.0	1.5	-	-	114.0	0.9	-	-	114.7	0.6	-	-	115.6	0.8	-	-	116.3	0.6	-	-	117.9	1.4	118.0	0.1
1987	-	-	-	-	-	-	-	-	-	-	118.9	0.8	-	-	-	-	-	-	-	-	-	-	122.3	2.9
1988	-	-	-	-	-	-	-	-	-	-	128.8	5.3	-	-	-	-	-	-	-	-	-	-	131.0	1.7
1989	-	-	-	-	-	-	-	-	-	-	139.3	6.3	-	-	-	-	-	-	-	-	-	-	143.5	3.0
1990	-	-	-	-	-	-	-	-	-	-	151.1	5.3	-	-	-	-	-	-	-	-	-	-	153.5	1.6

[Continued]

Milwaukee, WI
Consumer Price Index - Urban Wage Earners
Base 1982-1984 = 100
Medical Care
[Continued]

For 1946-1993. Columns headed % show percentile change in the index from the previous period for which an index is available.

Year	Jan Index	%	Feb Index	%	Mar Index	%	Apr Index	%	May Index	%	Jun Index	%	Jul Index	%	Aug Index	%	Sep Index	%	Oct Index	%	Nov Index	%	Dec Index	%
1991	-	-	-	-	-	-	-	-	-	-	158.5	3.3	-	-	-	-	-	-	-	-	-	-	163.0	2.8
1992	-	-	-	-	-	-	-	-	-	-	173.6	6.5	-	-	-	-	-	-	-	-	-	-	177.0	2.0
1993	-	-	-	-	-	-	-	-	-	-	183.7	3.8	-	-	-	-	-	-	-	-	-	-	-	-

Source: U.S. Department of Labor, Bureau of Labor Statistics, Division of Consumer Prices and Price Indexes. - indicates no data collected for period.

Milwaukee, WI

Consumer Price Index - All Urban Consumers
Base 1982-1984 = 100
Entertainment

For 1975-1993. Columns headed % show percentile change in the index from the previous period for which an index is available.

Year	Jan Index	Jan %	Feb Index	Feb %	Mar Index	Mar %	Apr Index	Apr %	May Index	May %	Jun Index	Jun %	Jul Index	Jul %	Aug Index	Aug %	Sep Index	Sep %	Oct Index	Oct %	Nov Index	Nov %	Dec Index	Dec %
1975	-	-	-	-	-	-	-	-	-	-	-	-	-	-	-	-	-	-	-	-	59.6	-	-	-
1976	-	-	59.8	0.3	-	-	-	-	61.0	2.0	-	-	-	-	62.8	3.0	-	-	-	-	63.3	0.8	-	-
1977	-	-	67.1	6.0	-	-	-	-	68.5	2.1	-	-	-	-	68.7	0.3	-	-	-	-	69.6	1.3	-	-
1978	70.0	0.6	-	-	71.1	1.6	-	-	71.3	0.3	-	-	71.4	0.1	-	-	73.4	2.8	-	-	74.6	1.6	-	-
1979	75.1	0.7	-	-	75.4	0.4	-	-	77.6	2.9	-	-	78.3	0.9	-	-	79.4	1.4	-	-	79.8	0.5	-	-
1980	81.0	1.5	-	-	80.5	-0.6	-	-	84.2	4.6	-	-	84.8	0.7	-	-	86.9	2.5	-	-	86.9	0.0	-	-
1981	88.4	1.7	-	-	92.2	4.3	-	-	92.6	0.4	-	-	91.6	-1.1	-	-	93.2	1.7	-	-	92.6	-0.6	-	-
1982	96.9	4.6	-	-	96.2	-0.7	-	-	95.5	-0.7	-	-	95.4	-0.1	-	-	94.6	-0.8	-	-	96.0	1.5	-	-
1983	97.3	1.4	-	-	98.2	0.9	-	-	100.1	1.9	-	-	100.1	0.0	-	-	102.3	2.2	-	-	103.0	0.7	-	-
1984	101.0	-1.9	-	-	101.7	0.7	-	-	102.5	0.8	-	-	104.8	2.2	-	-	106.1	1.2	-	-	105.8	-0.3	-	-
1985	107.8	1.9	-	-	108.1	0.3	-	-	108.3	0.2	-	-	110.3	1.8	-	-	111.6	1.2	-	-	111.2	-0.4	-	-
1986	109.1	-1.9	-	-	110.9	1.6	-	-	110.8	-0.1	-	-	111.1	0.3	-	-	110.3	-0.7	-	-	109.5	-0.7	109.6	0.1
1987	-	-	-	-	-	-	-	-	-	-	107.9	-1.6	-	-	-	-	-	-	-	-	-	-	107.5	-0.4
1988	-	-	-	-	-	-	-	-	-	-	109.8	2.1	-	-	-	-	-	-	-	-	-	-	112.9	2.8
1989	-	-	-	-	-	-	-	-	-	-	113.1	0.2	-	-	-	-	-	-	-	-	-	-	114.3	1.1
1990	-	-	-	-	-	-	-	-	-	-	117.5	2.8	-	-	-	-	-	-	-	-	-	-	119.9	2.0
1991	-	-	-	-	-	-	-	-	-	-	122.5	2.2	-	-	-	-	-	-	-	-	-	-	125.5	2.4
1992	-	-	-	-	-	-	-	-	-	-	129.5	3.2	-	-	-	-	-	-	-	-	-	-	130.6	0.8
1993	-	-	-	-	-	-	-	-	-	-	131.4	0.6	-	-	-	-	-	-	-	-	-	-	-	-

Source: U.S. Department of Labor, Bureau of Labor Statistics, Division of Consumer Prices and Price Indexes. - indicates no data collected for period.

Milwaukee, WI
Consumer Price Index - Urban Wage Earners
Base 1982-1984 = 100
Entertainment

For 1975-1993. Columns headed % show percentile change in the index from the previous period for which an index is available.

Year	Jan Index	%	Feb Index	%	Mar Index	%	Apr Index	%	May Index	%	Jun Index	%	Jul Index	%	Aug Index	%	Sep Index	%	Oct Index	%	Nov Index	%	Dec Index	%
1975	-	-	-	-	-	-	-	-	-	-	-	-	-	-	-	-	-	-	-	-	61.8	-	-	-
1976	-	-	62.0	0.3	-	-	-	-	63.3	2.1	-	-	-	-	65.1	2.8	-	-	-	-	65.6	0.8	-	-
1977	-	-	69.5	5.9	-	-	-	-	71.0	2.2	-	-	-	-	71.2	0.3	-	-	-	-	72.1	1.3	-	-
1978	73.3	1.7	-	-	74.4	1.5	-	-	74.6	0.3	-	-	74.7	0.1	-	-	76.3	2.1	-	-	77.6	1.7	-	-
1979	78.2	0.8	-	-	78.0	-0.3	-	-	81.2	4.1	-	-	80.5	-0.9	-	-	81.8	1.6	-	-	80.4	-1.7	-	-
1980	82.9	3.1	-	-	87.5	5.5	-	-	89.3	2.1	-	-	88.5	-0.9	-	-	90.9	2.7	-	-	88.9	-2.2	-	-
1981	94.8	6.6	-	-	98.1	3.5	-	-	96.5	-1.6	-	-	92.7	-3.9	-	-	92.8	0.1	-	-	92.3	-0.5	-	-
1982	96.7	4.8	-	-	96.1	-0.6	-	-	95.8	-0.3	-	-	95.3	-0.5	-	-	94.6	-0.7	-	-	95.7	1.2	-	-
1983	97.0	1.4	-	-	98.0	1.0	-	-	99.8	1.8	-	-	99.9	0.1	-	-	101.9	2.0	-	-	102.6	0.7	-	-
1984	100.8	-1.8	-	-	102.1	1.3	-	-	103.2	1.1	-	-	105.7	2.4	-	-	106.2	0.5	-	-	105.9	-0.3	-	-
1985	107.7	1.7	-	-	108.3	0.6	-	-	108.6	0.3	-	-	110.4	1.7	-	-	112.3	1.7	-	-	112.0	-0.3	-	-
1986	108.4	-3.2	-	-	110.2	1.7	-	-	110.3	0.1	-	-	110.6	0.3	-	-	109.8	-0.7	-	-	109.1	-0.6	109.2	0.1
1987	-	-	-	-	-	-	-	-	-	-	108.0	-1.1	-	-	-	-	-	-	-	-	-	-	107.7	-0.3
1988	-	-	-	-	-	-	-	-	-	-	110.2	2.3	-	-	-	-	-	-	-	-	-	-	113.8	3.3
1989	-	-	-	-	-	-	-	-	-	-	114.6	0.7	-	-	-	-	-	-	-	-	-	-	115.5	0.8
1990	-	-	-	-	-	-	-	-	-	-	118.4	2.5	-	-	-	-	-	-	-	-	-	-	121.0	2.2
1991	-	-	-	-	-	-	-	-	-	-	124.1	2.6	-	-	-	-	-	-	-	-	-	-	126.8	2.2
1992	-	-	-	-	-	-	-	-	-	-	130.2	2.7	-	-	-	-	-	-	-	-	-	-	131.6	1.1
1993	-	-	-	-	-	-	-	-	-	-	131.7	0.1	-	-	-	-	-	-	-	-	-	-	-	-

Source: U.S. Department of Labor, Bureau of Labor Statistics, Division of Consumer Prices and Price Indexes. - indicates no data collected for period.

Milwaukee, WI
Consumer Price Index - All Urban Consumers
Base 1982-1984 = 100
Other Goods and Services

For 1975-1993. Columns headed % show percentile change in the index from the previous period for which an index is available.

Year	Jan Index	%	Feb Index	%	Mar Index	%	Apr Index	%	May Index	%	Jun Index	%	Jul Index	%	Aug Index	%	Sep Index	%	Oct Index	%	Nov Index	%	Dec Index	%
1975	-	-	-	-	-	-	-	-	-	-	-	-	-	-	-	-	-	-	-	-	58.2	-	-	-
1976	-	-	59.3	1.9	-	-	-	-	59.7	0.7	-	-	-	-	59.8	0.2	-	-	-	-	61.1	2.2	-	-
1977	-	-	61.9	1.3	-	-	-	-	62.6	1.1	-	-	-	-	63.1	0.8	-	-	-	-	64.8	2.7	-	-
1978	65.6	1.2	-	-	65.1	-0.8	-	-	65.4	0.5	-	-	65.9	0.8	-	-	67.8	2.9	-	-	68.4	0.9	-	-
1979	68.6	0.3	-	-	69.3	1.0	-	-	69.8	0.7	-	-	69.4	-0.6	-	-	71.9	3.6	-	-	72.6	1.0	-	-
1980	73.9	1.8	-	-	74.0	0.1	-	-	74.7	0.9	-	-	74.8	0.1	-	-	77.3	3.3	-	-	77.7	0.5	-	-
1981	80.2	3.2	-	-	81.2	1.2	-	-	81.9	0.9	-	-	81.9	0.0	-	-	84.9	3.7	-	-	86.9	2.4	-	-
1982	87.6	0.8	-	-	89.2	1.8	-	-	91.3	2.4	-	-	91.9	0.7	-	-	95.1	3.5	-	-	96.3	1.3	-	-
1983	99.7	3.5	-	-	100.1	0.4	-	-	100.0	-0.1	-	-	99.7	-0.3	-	-	101.5	1.8	-	-	102.7	1.2	-	-
1984	103.8	1.1	-	-	104.3	0.5	-	-	104.5	0.2	-	-	105.9	1.3	-	-	110.2	4.1	-	-	110.6	0.4	-	-
1985	110.8	0.2	-	-	111.1	0.3	-	-	111.2	0.1	-	-	111.9	0.6	-	-	114.4	2.2	-	-	117.4	2.6	-	-
1986	118.9	1.3	-	-	119.0	0.1	-	-	119.7	0.6	-	-	120.7	0.8	-	-	124.7	3.3	-	-	125.0	0.2	125.2	0.2
1987	-	-	-	-	-	-	-	-	-	-	126.3	0.9	-	-	-	-	-	-	-	-	-	-	131.8	4.4
1988	-	-	-	-	-	-	-	-	-	-	136.5	3.6	-	-	-	-	-	-	-	-	-	-	141.6	3.7
1989	-	-	-	-	-	-	-	-	-	-	145.0	2.4	-	-	-	-	-	-	-	-	-	-	148.8	2.6
1990	-	-	-	-	-	-	-	-	-	-	153.6	3.2	-	-	-	-	-	-	-	-	-	-	159.7	4.0
1991	-	-	-	-	-	-	-	-	-	-	166.6	4.3	-	-	-	-	-	-	-	-	-	-	172.9	3.8
1992	-	-	-	-	-	-	-	-	-	-	177.6	2.7	-	-	-	-	-	-	-	-	-	-	186.4	5.0
1993	-	-	-	-	-	-	-	-	-	-	194.2	4.2	-	-	-	-	-	-	-	-	-	-	-	-

Source: U.S. Department of Labor, Bureau of Labor Statistics, Division of Consumer Prices and Price Indexes. - indicates no data collected for period.

Milwaukee, WI
Consumer Price Index - Urban Wage Earners
Base 1982-1984 = 100
Other Goods and Services

For 1975-1993. Columns headed % show percentile change in the index from the previous period for which an index is available.

Year	Jan Index	%	Feb Index	%	Mar Index	%	Apr Index	%	May Index	%	Jun Index	%	Jul Index	%	Aug Index	%	Sep Index	%	Oct Index	%	Nov Index	%	Dec Index	%
1975	-	-	-	-	-	-	-	-	-	-	-	-	-	-	-	-	-	-	-	-	55.7	-	-	-
1976	-	-	56.7	1.8	-	-	-	-	57.2	0.9	-	-	-	-	57.2	0.0	-	-	-	-	58.5	2.3	-	-
1977	-	-	59.3	1.4	-	-	-	-	59.9	1.0	-	-	-	-	60.4	0.8	-	-	-	-	62.0	2.6	-	-
1978	63.2	1.9	-	-	63.9	1.1	-	-	64.1	0.3	-	-	64.5	0.6	-	-	66.3	2.8	-	-	66.6	0.5	-	-
1979	66.7	0.2	-	-	67.7	1.5	-	-	67.7	0.0	-	-	68.0	0.4	-	-	70.1	3.1	-	-	71.5	2.0	-	-
1980	73.5	2.8	-	-	73.8	0.4	-	-	74.5	0.9	-	-	74.5	0.0	-	-	76.8	3.1	-	-	76.5	-0.4	-	-
1981	78.6	2.7	-	-	79.7	1.4	-	-	80.9	1.5	-	-	81.3	0.5	-	-	84.5	3.9	-	-	86.6	2.5	-	-
1982	87.0	0.5	-	-	88.6	1.8	-	-	91.1	2.8	-	-	91.7	0.7	-	-	94.8	3.4	-	-	96.1	1.4	-	-
1983	100.0	4.1	-	-	100.3	0.3	-	-	100.2	-0.1	-	-	100.0	-0.2	-	-	101.7	1.7	-	-	102.9	1.2	-	-
1984	104.0	1.1	-	-	104.5	0.5	-	-	104.8	0.3	-	-	106.2	1.3	-	-	110.1	3.7	-	-	110.4	0.3	-	-
1985	110.6	0.2	-	-	111.0	0.4	-	-	111.0	0.0	-	-	111.8	0.7	-	-	113.8	1.8	-	-	116.9	2.7	-	-
1986	118.5	1.4	-	-	118.7	0.2	-	-	119.4	0.6	-	-	120.4	0.8	-	-	123.9	2.9	-	-	124.2	0.2	124.5	0.2
1987	-	-	-	-	-	-	-	-	-	-	125.5	0.8	-	-	-	-	-	-	-	-	-	-	131.4	4.7
1988	-	-	-	-	-	-	-	-	-	-	136.5	3.9	-	-	-	-	-	-	-	-	-	-	141.9	4.0
1989	-	-	-	-	-	-	-	-	-	-	145.6	2.6	-	-	-	-	-	-	-	-	-	-	149.6	2.7
1990	-	-	-	-	-	-	-	-	-	-	154.3	3.1	-	-	-	-	-	-	-	-	-	-	160.8	4.2
1991	-	-	-	-	-	-	-	-	-	-	168.4	4.7	-	-	-	-	-	-	-	-	-	-	174.9	3.9
1992	-	-	-	-	-	-	-	-	-	-	179.6	2.7	-	-	-	-	-	-	-	-	-	-	189.1	5.3
1993	-	-	-	-	-	-	-	-	-	-	196.7	4.0	-	-	-	-	-	-	-	-	-	-	-	-

Source: U.S. Department of Labor, Bureau of Labor Statistics, Division of Consumer Prices and Price Indexes. - indicates no data collected for period.

Minneapolis-St. Paul, MN
Consumer Price Index - All Urban Consumers
Base 1982-1984 = 100
Annual Averages

For 1917-1993. Columns headed % show percentile change in the index from the previous period for which an index is available.

Year	All Items		Food & Beverage		Housing		Apparel & Upkeep		Trans-portation		Medical Care		Entertain-ment		Other Goods & Services	
	Index	%	Index	%	Index	%	Index	%	Index	%	Index	%	Index	%	Index	%
1917	-	-	-	-	-	-	-	-	-	-	-	-	-	-	-	-
1918	14.1	-	-	-	-	-	-	-	-	-	-	-	-	-	-	-
1919	16.0	13.5	-	-	-	-	-	-	-	-	-	-	-	-	-	-
1920	18.6	16.3	-	-	-	-	-	-	-	-	-	-	-	-	-	-
1921	16.7	-10.2	-	-	-	-	-	-	-	-	-	-	-	-	-	-
1922	15.8	-5.4	-	-	-	-	-	-	-	-	-	-	-	-	-	-
1923	15.9	0.6	-	-	-	-	-	-	-	-	-	-	-	-	-	-
1924	15.8	-0.6	-	-	-	-	-	-	-	-	-	-	-	-	-	-
1925	15.9	0.6	-	-	-	-	-	-	-	-	-	-	-	-	-	-
1926	16.1	1.3	-	-	-	-	-	-	-	-	-	-	-	-	-	-
1927	15.7	-2.5	-	-	-	-	-	-	-	-	-	-	-	-	-	-
1928	15.5	-1.3	-	-	-	-	-	-	-	-	-	-	-	-	-	-
1929	15.6	0.6	-	-	-	-	-	-	-	-	-	-	-	-	-	-
1930	15.3	-1.9	-	-	-	-	-	-	-	-	-	-	-	-	-	-
1931	14.2	-7.2	-	-	-	-	-	-	-	-	-	-	-	-	-	-
1932	12.9	-9.2	-	-	-	-	-	-	-	-	-	-	-	-	-	-
1933	12.2	-5.4	-	-	-	-	-	-	-	-	-	-	-	-	-	-
1934	12.6	3.3	-	-	-	-	-	-	-	-	-	-	-	-	-	-
1935	13.0	3.2	-	-	-	-	-	-	-	-	-	-	-	-	-	-
1936	13.2	1.5	-	-	-	-	-	-	-	-	-	-	-	-	-	-
1937	13.8	4.5	-	-	-	-	-	-	-	-	-	-	-	-	-	-
1938	13.6	-1.4	-	-	-	-	-	-	-	-	-	-	-	-	-	-
1939	13.5	-0.7	-	-	-	-	-	-	-	-	-	-	-	-	-	-
1940	13.5	0.0	-	-	-	-	-	-	-	-	-	-	-	-	-	-
1941	14.2	5.2	-	-	-	-	-	-	-	-	-	-	-	-	-	-
1942	15.5	9.2	-	-	-	-	-	-	-	-	-	-	-	-	-	-
1943	16.2	4.5	-	-	-	-	-	-	-	-	-	-	-	-	-	-
1944	16.4	1.2	-	-	-	-	-	-	-	-	-	-	-	-	-	-
1945	16.7	1.8	-	-	-	-	-	-	-	-	-	-	-	-	-	-
1946	18.2	9.0	-	-	-	-	-	-	-	-	-	-	-	-	-	-
1947	21.0	15.4	-	-	-	-	-	-	21.6	-	10.7	-	-	-	-	-
1948	22.9	9.0	-	-	-	-	-	-	24.7	14.4	11.8	10.3	-	-	-	-
1949	22.7	-0.9	-	-	-	-	-	-	26.4	6.9	12.2	3.4	-	-	-	-
1950	22.9	0.9	-	-	-	-	-	-	26.5	0.4	12.6	3.3	-	-	-	-
1951	24.6	7.4	-	-	-	-	-	-	26.9	1.5	13.6	7.9	-	-	-	-
1952	25.4	3.3	-	-	-	-	-	-	28.7	6.7	14.5	6.6	-	-	-	-
1953	25.7	1.2	-	-	-	-	45.9	-	29.5	2.8	15.6	7.6	-	-	-	-
1954	25.9	0.8	-	-	-	-	45.9	0.0	29.2	-1.0	16.4	5.1	-	-	-	-
1955	25.9	0.0	-	-	-	-	45.2	-1.5	28.3	-3.1	17.0	3.7	-	-	-	-
1956	26.0	0.4	-	-	-	-	46.5	2.9	27.9	-1.4	17.3	1.8	-	-	-	-
1957	26.9	3.5	-	-	-	-	47.1	1.3	29.3	5.0	18.7	8.1	-	-	-	-
1958	27.6	2.6	-	-	-	-	47.3	0.4	30.3	3.4	21.2	13.4	-	-	-	-
1959	27.9	1.1	-	-	-	-	47.0	-0.6	31.6	4.3	22.7	7.1	-	-	-	-
1960	28.3	1.4	-	-	-	-	48.0	2.1	32.0	1.3	24.3	7.0	-	-	-	-
1961	28.6	1.1	-	-	-	-	46.9	-2.3	32.2	0.6	25.8	6.2	-	-	-	-

[Continued]

620

Minneapolis-St. Paul, MN
Consumer Price Index - All Urban Consumers
Base 1982-1984 = 100
Annual Averages
[Continued]

For 1917-1993. Columns headed % show percentile change in the index from the previous period for which an index is available.

Year	All Items		Food & Beverage		Housing		Apparel & Upkeep		Trans-portation		Medical Care		Entertain-ment		Other Goods & Services	
	Index	%	Index	%	Index	%	Index	%	Index	%	Index	%	Index	%	Index	%
1962	29.0	1.4	-	-	-	-	47.9	2.1	32.7	1.6	26.7	3.5	-	-	-	-
1963	29.4	1.4	-	-	-	-	48.8	1.9	33.2	1.5	27.0	1.1	-	-	-	-
1964	29.7	1.0	-	-	-	-	48.8	0.0	33.2	0.0	27.5	1.9	-	-	-	-
1965	30.1	1.3	-	-	-	-	49.9	2.3	33.8	1.8	27.6	0.4	-	-	-	-
1966	30.8	2.3	-	-	-	-	51.2	2.6	34.4	1.8	28.9	4.7	-	-	-	-
1967	31.8	3.2	-	-	-	-	53.0	3.5	35.6	3.5	30.4	5.2	-	-	-	-
1968	33.3	4.7	-	-	-	-	55.3	4.3	36.7	3.1	32.0	5.3	-	-	-	-
1969	35.0	5.1	-	-	-	-	58.3	5.4	37.4	1.9	33.6	5.0	-	-	-	-
1970	37.4	6.9	-	-	-	-	61.2	5.0	39.7	6.1	35.8	6.5	-	-	-	-
1971	38.7	3.5	-	-	-	-	62.6	2.3	41.1	3.5	37.7	5.3	-	-	-	-
1972	39.9	3.1	-	-	-	-	63.4	1.3	41.4	0.7	38.4	1.9	-	-	-	-
1973	42.3	6.0	-	-	-	-	66.3	4.6	43.1	4.1	40.3	4.9	-	-	-	-
1974	47.2	11.6	-	-	-	-	72.6	9.5	47.8	10.9	43.9	8.9	-	-	-	-
1975	51.2	8.5	-	-	-	-	74.0	1.9	50.9	6.5	48.6	10.7	-	-	-	-
1976	54.4	6.3	62.5	-	49.0	-	75.0	1.4	55.4	8.8	52.3	7.6	62.2	-	56.8	-
1977	58.2	7.0	65.8	5.3	53.2	8.6	78.1	4.1	59.6	7.6	56.6	8.2	65.5	5.3	60.0	5.6
1978	63.5	9.1	72.3	9.9	59.3	11.5	81.3	4.1	62.5	4.9	61.2	8.1	71.1	8.5	64.9	8.2
1979	70.8	11.5	80.9	11.9	66.3	11.8	85.5	5.2	71.8	14.9	66.2	8.2	75.1	5.6	69.3	6.8
1980	78.9	11.4	87.6	8.3	74.0	11.6	90.8	6.2	83.7	16.6	73.7	11.3	81.3	8.3	75.3	8.7
1981	88.6	12.3	92.7	5.8	85.9	16.1	94.7	4.3	93.6	11.8	80.3	9.0	93.1	14.5	83.2	10.5
1982	97.4	9.9	96.6	4.2	98.7	14.9	99.7	5.3	97.5	4.2	90.0	12.1	97.2	4.4	91.7	10.2
1983	99.5	2.2	99.5	3.0	99.3	0.6	101.5	1.8	99.3	1.8	100.3	11.4	100.2	3.1	100.7	9.8
1984	103.1	3.6	104.0	4.5	102.0	2.7	98.8	-2.7	103.2	3.9	109.7	9.4	102.6	2.4	107.6	6.9
1985	107.0	3.8	106.5	2.4	105.8	3.7	106.2	7.5	106.1	2.8	116.9	6.6	106.6	3.9	114.5	6.4
1986	108.4	1.3	109.4	2.7	107.8	1.9	107.0	0.8	100.5	-5.3	126.8	8.5	111.8	4.9	120.9	5.6
1987	111.6	3.0	113.9	4.1	109.5	1.6	109.7	2.5	102.9	2.4	133.7	5.4	116.6	4.3	128.9	6.6
1988	117.2	5.0	119.9	5.3	112.0	2.3	126.6	15.4	107.2	4.2	140.7	5.2	133.7	14.7	137.3	6.5
1989	122.0	4.1	126.6	5.6	115.8	3.4	121.5	-4.0	114.8	7.1	149.1	6.0	138.1	3.3	143.9	4.8
1990	127.0	4.1	134.6	6.3	118.5	2.3	130.5	7.4	118.5	3.2	161.5	8.3	140.5	1.7	153.0	6.3
1991	130.4	2.7	141.5	5.1	120.6	1.8	130.9	0.3	119.4	0.8	171.8	6.4	141.6	0.8	164.0	7.2
1992	135.0	3.5	144.8	2.3	124.9	3.6	141.7	8.3	121.7	1.9	182.4	6.2	145.6	2.8	171.7	4.7
1993	-	-	-	-	-	-	-	-	-	-	-	-	-	-	-	-

Source: U.S. Department of Labor, Bureau of Labor Statistics, Division of Consumer Prices and Price Indexes. - indicates no data collected for period.

Minneapolis-St. Paul, MN
Consumer Price Index - Urban Wage Earners
Base 1982-1984 = 100
Annual Averages

For 1917-1993. Columns headed % show percentile change in the index from the previous period for which an index is available.

Year	All Items		Food & Beverage		Housing		Apparel & Upkeep		Trans- portation		Medical Care		Entertain- ment		Other Goods & Services	
	Index	%	Index	%	Index	%	Index	%	Index	%	Index	%	Index	%	Index	%
1917	-		-	-	-	-	-	-	-	-	-	-	-	-	-	-
1918	14.1	-	-	-	-	-	-	-	-	-	-	-	-	-	-	-
1919	16.1	14.2	-	-	-	-	-	-	-	-	-	-	-	-	-	-
1920	18.6	15.5	-	-	-	-	-	-	-	-	-	-	-	-	-	-
1921	16.8	-9.7	-	-	-	-	-	-	-	-	-	-	-	-	-	-
1922	15.8	-6.0	-	-	-	-	-	-	-	-	-	-	-	-	-	-
1923	15.9	0.6	-	-	-	-	-	-	-	-	-	-	-	-	-	-
1924	15.8	-0.6	-	-	-	-	-	-	-	-	-	-	-	-	-	-
1925	15.9	0.6	-	-	-	-	-	-	-	-	-	-	-	-	-	-
1926	16.1	1.3	-	-	-	-	-	-	-	-	-	-	-	-	-	-
1927	15.7	-2.5	-	-	-	-	-	-	-	-	-	-	-	-	-	-
1928	15.5	-1.3	-	-	-	-	-	-	-	-	-	-	-	-	-	-
1929	15.6	0.6	-	-	-	-	-	-	-	-	-	-	-	-	-	-
1930	15.3	-1.9	-	-	-	-	-	-	-	-	-	-	-	-	-	-
1931	14.2	-7.2	-	-	-	-	-	-	-	-	-	-	-	-	-	-
1932	12.9	-9.2	-	-	-	-	-	-	-	-	-	-	-	-	-	-
1933	12.2	-5.4	-	-	-	-	-	-	-	-	-	-	-	-	-	-
1934	12.6	3.3	-	-	-	-	-	-	-	-	-	-	-	-	-	-
1935	13.0	3.2	-	-	-	-	-	-	-	-	-	-	-	-	-	-
1936	13.2	1.5	-	-	-	-	-	-	-	-	-	-	-	-	-	-
1937	13.8	4.5	-	-	-	-	-	-	-	-	-	-	-	-	-	-
1938	13.6	-1.4	-	-	-	-	-	-	-	-	-	-	-	-	-	-
1939	13.5	-0.7	-	-	-	-	-	-	-	-	-	-	-	-	-	-
1940	13.5	0.0	-	-	-	-	-	-	-	-	-	-	-	-	-	-
1941	14.2	5.2	-	-	-	-	-	-	-	-	-	-	-	-	-	-
1942	15.5	9.2	-	-	-	-	-	-	-	-	-	-	-	-	-	-
1943	16.2	4.5	-	-	-	-	-	-	-	-	-	-	-	-	-	-
1944	16.4	1.2	-	-	-	-	-	-	-	-	-	-	-	-	-	-
1945	16.7	1.8	-	-	-	-	-	-	-	-	-	-	-	-	-	-
1946	18.2	9.0	-	-	-	-	-	-	-	-	-	-	-	-	-	-
1947	21.0	15.4	-	-	-	-	-	-	21.3	-	10.8	-	-	-	-	-
1948	22.9	9.0	-	-	-	-	-	-	24.3	14.1	11.9	10.2	-	-	-	-
1949	22.7	-0.9	-	-	-	-	-	-	26.0	7.0	12.4	4.2	-	-	-	-
1950	22.9	0.9	-	-	-	-	-	-	26.1	0.4	12.8	3.2	-	-	-	-
1951	24.6	7.4	-	-	-	-	-	-	26.5	1.5	13.8	7.8	-	-	-	-
1952	25.4	3.3	-	-	-	-	-	-	28.3	6.8	14.7	6.5	-	-	-	-
1953	25.7	1.2	-	-	-	-	46.9	-	29.0	2.5	15.9	8.2	-	-	-	-
1954	25.9	0.8	-	-	-	-	47.0	0.2	28.8	-0.7	16.6	4.4	-	-	-	-
1955	25.9	0.0	-	-	-	-	46.3	-1.5	27.9	-3.1	17.2	3.6	-	-	-	-
1956	26.0	0.4	-	-	-	-	47.6	2.8	27.5	-1.4	17.5	1.7	-	-	-	-
1957	26.9	3.5	-	-	-	-	48.2	1.3	28.8	4.7	19.0	8.6	-	-	-	-
1958	27.6	2.6	-	-	-	-	48.4	0.4	29.8	3.5	21.5	13.2	-	-	-	-
1959	27.9	1.1	-	-	-	-	48.1	-0.6	31.1	4.4	23.0	7.0	-	-	-	-
1960	28.4	1.8	-	-	-	-	49.1	2.1	31.5	1.3	24.6	7.0	-	-	-	-
1961	28.6	0.7	-	-	-	-	48.0	-2.2	31.7	0.6	26.2	6.5	-	-	-	-

[Continued]

Minneapolis-St. Paul, MN
Consumer Price Index - Urban Wage Earners
Base 1982-1984 = 100
Annual Averages
[Continued]

For 1917-1993. Columns headed % show percentile change in the index from the previous period for which an index is available.

Year	All Items		Food & Beverage		Housing		Apparel & Upkeep		Trans- portation		Medical Care		Entertain- ment		Other Goods & Services	
	Index	%	Index	%	Index	%	Index	%	Index	%	Index	%	Index	%	Index	%
1962	29.0	1.4	-	-	-	-	49.0	2.1	32.2	1.6	27.1	3.4	-	-	-	-
1963	29.4	1.4	-	-	-	-	50.0	2.0	32.7	1.6	27.4	1.1	-	-	-	-
1964	29.7	1.0	-	-	-	-	50.0	0.0	32.7	0.0	27.9	1.8	-	-	-	-
1965	30.1	1.3	-	-	-	-	51.0	2.0	33.3	1.8	28.0	0.4	-	-	-	-
1966	30.8	2.3	-	-	-	-	52.3	2.5	33.9	1.8	29.3	4.6	-	-	-	-
1967	31.9	3.6	-	-	-	-	54.2	3.6	35.0	3.2	30.9	5.5	-	-	-	-
1968	33.3	4.4	-	-	-	-	56.5	4.2	36.2	3.4	32.5	5.2	-	-	-	-
1969	35.0	5.1	-	-	-	-	59.7	5.7	36.8	1.7	34.1	4.9	-	-	-	-
1970	37.4	6.9	-	-	-	-	62.5	4.7	39.1	6.3	36.3	6.5	-	-	-	-
1971	38.8	3.7	-	-	-	-	64.1	2.6	40.5	3.6	38.2	5.2	-	-	-	-
1972	40.0	3.1	-	-	-	-	64.8	1.1	40.8	0.7	38.9	1.8	-	-	-	-
1973	42.4	6.0	-	-	-	-	67.9	4.8	42.4	3.9	40.9	5.1	-	-	-	-
1974	47.3	11.6	-	-	-	-	74.3	9.4	47.1	11.1	44.5	8.8	-	-	-	-
1975	51.3	8.5	-	-	-	-	75.7	1.9	50.1	6.4	49.3	10.8	-	-	-	-
1976	54.5	6.2	63.6	-	48.2	-	76.7	1.3	54.6	9.0	53.1	7.7	63.9	-	58.5	-
1977	58.3	7.0	66.9	5.2	52.4	8.7	79.9	4.2	58.7	7.5	57.4	8.1	67.3	5.3	61.8	5.6
1978	63.7	9.3	73.3	9.6	58.6	11.8	82.9	3.8	61.6	4.9	62.0	8.0	73.1	8.6	66.7	7.9
1979	71.2	11.8	81.6	11.3	65.7	12.1	86.0	3.7	71.5	16.1	66.3	6.9	81.6	11.6	71.1	6.6
1980	79.4	11.5	88.5	8.5	73.2	11.4	91.7	6.6	83.9	17.3	72.9	10.0	88.5	8.5	76.5	7.6
1981	88.9	12.0	92.7	4.7	85.7	17.1	96.3	5.0	93.9	11.9	79.5	9.1	92.6	4.6	83.8	9.5
1982	97.5	9.7	96.5	4.1	98.9	15.4	99.5	3.3	97.7	4.0	89.5	12.6	96.5	4.2	91.8	9.5
1983	99.1	1.6	99.5	3.1	98.2	-0.7	101.4	1.9	99.4	1.7	100.2	12.0	100.6	4.2	101.0	10.0
1984	103.5	4.4	104.1	4.6	102.9	4.8	99.2	-2.2	103.0	3.6	110.4	10.2	102.9	2.3	107.2	6.1
1985	105.7	2.1	106.5	2.3	103.5	0.6	106.6	7.5	105.8	2.7	117.6	6.5	106.7	3.7	114.1	6.4
1986	106.6	0.9	109.5	2.8	105.5	1.9	106.6	0.0	99.5	-6.0	127.4	8.3	112.1	5.1	120.6	5.7
1987	109.8	3.0	113.9	4.0	106.9	1.3	108.3	1.6	102.1	2.6	134.4	5.5	116.9	4.3	129.1	7.0
1988	115.5	5.2	119.9	5.3	109.4	2.3	127.6	17.8	106.4	4.2	141.7	5.4	133.4	14.1	138.1	7.0
1989	120.1	4.0	126.6	5.6	112.9	3.2	118.8	-6.9	114.1	7.2	149.8	5.7	137.8	3.3	145.3	5.2
1990	124.8	3.9	134.7	6.4	115.5	2.3	127.2	7.1	117.5	3.0	160.9	7.4	140.2	1.7	154.2	6.1
1991	128.1	2.6	141.8	5.3	117.7	1.9	128.6	1.1	118.3	0.7	171.3	6.5	140.8	0.4	165.6	7.4
1992	132.5	3.4	144.8	2.1	121.7	3.4	139.1	8.2	121.0	2.3	182.1	6.3	144.6	2.7	173.0	4.5
1993	-	-	-	-	-	-	-	-	-	-	-	-	-	-	-	-

Source: U.S. Department of Labor, Bureau of Labor Statistics, Division of Consumer Prices and Price Indexes. - indicates no data collected for period.

Minneapolis-St. Paul, MN
Consumer Price Index - All Urban Consumers
Base 1982-1984 = 100
All Items

For 1917-1993. Columns headed % show percentile change in the index from the previous period for which an index is available.

Year	Jan Index	%	Feb Index	%	Mar Index	%	Apr Index	%	May Index	%	Jun Index	%	Jul Index	%	Aug Index	%	Sep Index	%	Oct Index	%	Nov Index	%	Dec Index	%
1917	-		-		-		-		-		-		-		-		-		-		-		13.1	-
1918	-		-		-		-		-		-		-		-		-		-		-		15.2	16.0
1919	-		-		-		-		-		15.6	2.6	-		-		-		-		-		17.5	12.2
1920	-		-		-		-		-		19.4	10.9	-		-		-		-		-		18.1	-6.7
1921	-		-		-		-		16.6	-8.3	-		-		-		16.5	-0.6	-		-		16.3	-1.2
1922	-		-		15.8	-3.1	-		-		15.9	0.6	-		-		15.5	-2.5	-		-		15.8	1.9
1923	-		-		15.8	0.0	-		-		15.8	0.0	-		-		15.9	0.6	-		-		16.0	0.6
1924	-		-		15.9	-0.6	-		-		15.7	-1.3	-		-		15.5	-1.3	-		-		15.7	1.3
1925	-		-		-		-		-		15.8	0.6	-		-		-		-		-		16.3	3.2
1926	-		-		-		-		-		16.3	0.0	-		-		-		-		-		16.0	-1.8
1927	-		-		-		-		-		16.0	0.0	-		-		-		-		-		15.6	-2.5
1928	-		-		-		-		-		15.6	0.0	-		-		-		-		-		15.5	-0.6
1929	-		-		-		-		-		15.5	0.0	-		-		-		-		-		15.7	1.3
1930	-		-		-		-		-		15.5	-1.3	-		-		-		-		-		14.9	-3.9
1931	-		-		-		-		-		14.2	-4.7	-		-		-		-		-		13.7	-3.5
1932	-		-		-		-		-		12.9	-5.8	-		-		-		-		-		12.4	-3.9
1933	-		-		-		-		-		11.9	-4.0	-		-		-		-		-		12.4	4.2
1934	-		-		-		-		-		12.6	1.6	-		-		-		-		12.6	0.0	-	
1935	-		-		12.9	2.4	-		-		-		12.9	0.0	-		-		13.0	0.8	-		-	
1936	13.1	0.8	-		-		13.0	-0.8	-		-		13.1	0.8	-		13.4	2.3	-		-		13.4	0.0
1937	-		-		13.6	1.5	-		-		13.7	0.7	-		-		13.9	1.5	-		-		13.8	-0.7
1938	-		-		13.6	-1.4	-		-		13.7	0.7	-		-		13.6	-0.7	-		-		13.5	-0.7
1939	-		-		13.4	-0.7	-		-		13.4	0.0	-		-		13.6	1.5	-		-		13.6	0.0
1940	-		-		13.5	-0.7	-		-		13.5	0.0	-		-		13.5	0.0	13.5	0.0	13.6	0.7	13.7	0.7
1941	13.6	-0.7	13.7	0.7	13.7	0.0	13.7	0.0	13.9	1.5	14.2	2.2	14.3	0.7	14.4	0.7	14.6	1.4	14.8	1.4	14.8	0.0	14.8	0.0
1942	15.0	1.4	15.1	0.7	15.3	1.3	15.4	0.7	15.5	0.6	15.5	0.0	15.6	0.6	15.6	0.0	15.7	0.6	15.8	0.6	15.9	0.6	16.0	0.6
1943	15.9	-0.6	16.0	0.6	16.2	1.3	16.2	0.0	16.3	0.6	16.3	0.0	16.2	-0.6	16.2	0.0	16.2	0.0	16.3	0.6	16.3	0.0	16.4	0.6
1944	16.2	-1.2	16.2	0.0	16.3	0.6	16.3	0.0	16.4	0.6	16.4	0.0	16.5	0.6	16.5	0.0	16.5	0.0	16.5	0.0	16.5	0.0	16.5	0.0
1945	16.5	0.0	16.5	0.0	16.5	0.0	16.5	0.0	16.6	0.6	16.7	0.6	16.7	0.0	16.7	0.0	16.8	0.6	16.8	0.0	16.9	0.6	16.9	0.0
1946	16.9	0.0	16.9	0.0	16.9	0.0	17.0	0.6	17.1	0.6	17.3	1.2	18.5	6.9	18.7	1.1	19.1	2.1	19.6	2.6	20.0	2.0	20.1	0.5
1947	19.9	-1.0	20.0	0.5	20.3	1.5	20.3	0.0	20.3	0.0	20.5	1.0	-		-		21.8	6.3	-		-		22.3	2.3
1948	-		-		22.5	0.9	-		-		23.0	2.2	-		-		23.3	1.3	-		-		22.9	-1.7
1949	-		-		22.8	-0.4	-		-		22.7	-0.4	-		-		22.7	0.0	-		-		22.5	-0.9
1950	-		-		22.4	-0.4	-		-		22.7	1.3	-		-		23.1	1.8	-		-		23.8	3.0
1951	-		-		24.5	2.9	-		-		24.6	0.4	-		-		24.5	-0.4	-		-		25.1	2.4
1952	-		-		25.2	0.4	-		-		25.5	1.2	-		-		25.5	0.0	-		-		25.4	-0.4
1953	25.4	0.0	-		-		25.5	0.4	-		-		25.7	0.8	-		-		25.9	0.8	-		-	
1954	25.9	0.0	-		-		25.8	-0.4	-		-		26.0	0.8	-		-		25.9	-0.4	-		-	
1955	25.9	0.0	-		-		26.0	0.4	-		-		26.1	0.4	-		-		25.8	-1.1	-		-	
1956	25.8	0.0	-		-		25.7	-0.4	-		-		26.1	1.6	-		-		26.1	0.0	-		-	
1957	26.5	1.5	-		-		26.6	0.4	-		-		27.0	1.5	-		-		27.1	0.4	-		-	
1958	27.3	0.7	-		-		27.5	0.7	-		-		27.7	0.7	-		-		27.6	-0.4	-		-	
1959	27.8	0.7	-		-		27.7	-0.4	-		-		27.8	0.4	-		-		28.1	1.1	-		-	
1960	28.0	-0.4	-		-		28.2	0.7	-		-		28.3	0.4	-		-		28.5	0.7	-		-	
1961	28.4	-0.4	-		-		28.6	0.7	-		-		28.7	0.3	-		-		28.7	0.0	-		-	

[Continued]

Minneapolis-St. Paul, MN
Consumer Price Index - All Urban Consumers
Base 1982-1984 = 100
All Items
[Continued]

For 1917-1993. Columns headed % show percentile change in the index from the previous period for which an index is available.

Year	Jan Index	%	Feb Index	%	Mar Index	%	Apr Index	%	May Index	%	Jun Index	%	Jul Index	%	Aug Index	%	Sep Index	%	Oct Index	%	Nov Index	%	Dec Index	%
1962	28.6	-0.3	-	-	-	-	29.0	1.4	-	-	-	-	29.0	0.0	-	-	-	-	29.1	0.3	-	-	-	-
1963	29.1	0.0	-	-	-	-	29.2	0.3	-	-	-	-	29.6	1.4	-	-	-	-	29.5	-0.3	-	-	-	-
1964	29.5	0.0	-	-	-	-	29.5	0.0	-	-	-	-	29.7	0.7	-	-	-	-	29.8	0.3	-	-	-	-
1965	29.8	0.0	-	-	-	-	29.9	0.3	-	-	-	-	30.1	0.7	-	-	-	-	30.2	0.3	-	-	-	-
1966	30.3	0.3	-	-	-	-	30.7	1.3	-	-	-	-	30.7	0.0	-	-	-	-	31.1	1.3	-	-	-	-
1967	31.1	0.0	-	-	-	-	31.3	0.6	-	-	-	-	31.7	1.3	-	-	-	-	32.5	2.5	-	-	-	-
1968	32.7	0.6	-	-	-	-	33.1	1.2	-	-	-	-	33.4	0.9	-	-	-	-	33.5	0.3	-	-	-	-
1969	33.7	0.6	-	-	-	-	34.3	1.8	-	-	-	-	35.1	2.3	-	-	-	-	35.8	2.0	-	-	-	-
1970	36.5	2.0	-	-	-	-	37.1	1.6	-	-	-	-	37.5	1.1	-	-	-	-	37.9	1.1	-	-	-	-
1971	38.2	0.8	-	-	-	-	38.3	0.3	-	-	-	-	38.8	1.3	-	-	-	-	39.3	1.3	-	-	-	-
1972	39.4	0.3	-	-	-	-	39.5	0.3	-	-	-	-	39.9	1.0	-	-	-	-	40.5	1.5	-	-	-	-
1973	40.7	0.5	-	-	-	-	41.6	2.2	-	-	-	-	42.4	1.9	-	-	-	-	43.4	2.4	-	-	-	-
1974	44.6	2.8	-	-	-	-	46.2	3.6	-	-	-	-	47.3	2.4	-	-	-	-	49.0	3.6	-	-	-	-
1975	49.7	1.4	-	-	-	-	49.9	0.4	-	-	-	-	51.5	3.2	-	-	-	-	52.5	1.9	-	-	-	-
1976	53.2	1.3	-	-	-	-	53.7	0.9	-	-	-	-	54.6	1.7	-	-	-	-	55.2	1.1	-	-	-	-
1977	56.0	1.4	-	-	-	-	57.2	2.1	-	-	-	-	58.7	2.6	-	-	-	-	59.5	1.4	-	-	-	-
1978	60.7	2.0	-	-	-	-	62.0	2.1	-	-	63.2	1.9	-	-	64.5	2.1	-	-	65.6	1.7	-	-	66.4	1.2
1979	-	-	67.4	1.5	-	-	68.7	1.9	-	-	70.7	2.9	-	-	72.2	2.1	-	-	73.6	1.9	-	-	74.5	1.2
1980	-	-	75.7	1.6	-	-	77.7	2.6	-	-	78.4	0.9	-	-	79.6	1.5	-	-	81.3	2.1	-	-	82.4	1.4
1981	-	-	82.9	0.6	-	-	84.8	2.3	-	-	87.9	3.7	-	-	91.2	3.8	-	-	92.8	1.8	-	-	95.1	2.5
1982	-	-	97.4	2.4	-	-	96.0	-1.4	-	-	96.8	0.8	-	-	99.9	3.2	-	-	97.9	-2.0	-	-	97.4	-0.5
1983	-	-	97.3	-0.1	-	-	98.5	1.2	-	-	99.5	1.0	-	-	100.6	1.1	-	-	100.8	0.2	-	-	101.0	0.2
1984	-	-	101.7	0.7	-	-	102.5	0.8	-	-	103.1	0.6	-	-	103.4	0.3	-	-	104.4	1.0	-	-	104.3	-0.1
1985	-	-	105.1	0.8	-	-	106.2	1.0	-	-	107.1	0.8	-	-	107.8	0.7	-	-	108.4	0.6	-	-	108.3	-0.1
1986	-	-	108.2	-0.1	-	-	107.7	-0.5	-	-	108.9	1.1	-	-	108.3	-0.6	-	-	108.5	0.2	108.4	-0.1	109.0	0.6
1987	-	-	-	-	-	-	-	-	-	-	109.9	0.8	-	-	-	-	-	-	-	-	-	-	113.2	3.0
1988	-	-	-	-	-	-	-	-	-	-	115.7	2.2	-	-	-	-	-	-	-	-	-	-	118.6	2.5
1989	-	-	-	-	-	-	-	-	-	-	120.3	1.4	-	-	-	-	-	-	-	-	-	-	123.8	2.9
1990	-	-	-	-	-	-	-	-	-	-	125.5	1.4	-	-	-	-	-	-	-	-	-	-	128.5	2.4
1991	-	-	-	-	-	-	-	-	-	-	129.4	0.7	-	-	-	-	-	-	-	-	-	-	131.4	1.5
1992	-	-	-	-	-	-	-	-	-	-	133.6	1.7	-	-	-	-	-	-	-	-	-	-	136.4	2.1
1993	-	-	-	-	-	-	-	-	-	-	138.5	1.5	-	-	-	-	-	-	-	-	-	-	-	-

Source: U.S. Department of Labor, Bureau of Labor Statistics, Division of Consumer Prices and Price Indexes. - indicates no data collected for period.

Minneapolis-St. Paul, MN
Consumer Price Index - Urban Wage Earners
Base 1982-1984 = 100
All Items

For 1917-1993. Columns headed % show percentile change in the index from the previous period for which an index is available.

Year	Jan Index	%	Feb Index	%	Mar Index	%	Apr Index	%	May Index	%	Jun Index	%	Jul Index	%	Aug Index	%	Sep Index	%	Oct Index	%	Nov Index	%	Dec Index	%
1917	-	-	-	-	-	-	-	-	-	-	-	-	-	-	-	-	-	-	-	-	-	-	13.2	-
1918	-	-	-	-	-	-	-	-	-	-	-	-	-	-	-	-	-	-	-	-	-	-	15.2	15.2
1919	-	-	-	-	-	-	-	-	-	-	15.6	2.6	-	-	-	-	-	-	-	-	-	-	17.5	12.2
1920	-	-	-	-	-	-	-	-	-	-	19.4	10.9	-	-	-	-	-	-	-	-	-	-	18.2	-6.2
1921	-	-	-	-	-	-	-	-	16.6	-8.8	-	-	-	-	-	-	16.5	-0.6	-	-	-	-	16.3	-1.2
1922	-	-	-	-	15.8	-3.1	-	-	-	-	15.9	0.6	-	-	-	-	15.5	-2.5	-	-	-	-	15.8	1.9
1923	-	-	-	-	15.9	0.6	-	-	-	-	15.8	-0.6	-	-	-	-	15.9	0.6	-	-	-	-	16.0	0.6
1924	-	-	-	-	15.9	-0.6	-	-	-	-	15.7	-1.3	-	-	-	-	15.5	-1.3	-	-	-	-	15.7	1.3
1925	-	-	-	-	-	-	-	-	-	-	15.8	0.6	-	-	-	-	-	-	-	-	-	-	16.3	3.2
1926	-	-	-	-	-	-	-	-	-	-	16.3	0.0	-	-	-	-	-	-	-	-	-	-	16.0	-1.8
1927	-	-	-	-	-	-	-	-	-	-	16.1	0.6	-	-	-	-	-	-	-	-	-	-	15.6	-3.1
1928	-	-	-	-	-	-	-	-	-	-	15.6	0.0	-	-	-	-	-	-	-	-	-	-	15.5	-0.6
1929	-	-	-	-	-	-	-	-	-	-	15.5	0.0	-	-	-	-	-	-	-	-	-	-	15.7	1.3
1930	-	-	-	-	-	-	-	-	-	-	15.5	-1.3	-	-	-	-	-	-	-	-	-	-	14.9	-3.9
1931	-	-	-	-	-	-	-	-	-	-	14.2	-4.7	-	-	-	-	-	-	-	-	-	-	13.8	-2.8
1932	-	-	-	-	-	-	-	-	-	-	12.9	-6.5	-	-	-	-	-	-	-	-	-	-	12.5	-3.1
1933	-	-	-	-	-	-	-	-	-	-	11.9	-4.8	-	-	-	-	-	-	-	-	-	-	12.5	5.0
1934	-	-	-	-	-	-	-	-	-	-	12.6	0.8	-	-	-	-	-	-	-	-	12.6	0.0	-	-
1935	-	-	-	-	12.9	2.4	-	-	-	-	-	-	12.9	0.0	-	-	-	-	13.0	0.8	-	-	-	-
1936	13.2	1.5	-	-	-	-	13.0	-1.5	-	-	-	-	13.2	1.5	-	-	13.4	1.5	-	-	-	-	13.4	0.0
1937	-	-	-	-	13.6	1.5	-	-	-	-	13.8	1.5	-	-	-	-	14.0	1.4	-	-	-	-	13.9	-0.7
1938	-	-	-	-	13.6	-2.2	-	-	-	-	13.7	0.7	-	-	-	-	13.6	-0.7	-	-	-	-	13.5	-0.7
1939	-	-	-	-	13.4	-0.7	-	-	-	-	13.4	0.0	-	-	-	-	13.6	1.5	-	-	-	-	13.6	0.0
1940	-	-	-	-	13.5	-0.7	-	-	-	-	13.5	0.0	-	-	-	-	13.5	0.0	13.5	0.0	13.6	0.7	13.7	0.7
1941	13.6	-0.7	13.7	0.7	13.7	0.0	13.8	0.7	13.9	0.7	14.2	2.2	14.3	0.7	14.4	0.7	14.6	1.4	14.8	1.4	14.8	0.0	14.8	0.0
1942	15.0	1.4	15.1	0.7	15.3	1.3	15.4	0.7	15.5	0.6	15.5	0.0	15.6	0.6	15.6	0.0	15.7	0.6	15.8	0.6	15.9	0.6	16.0	0.6
1943	16.0	0.0	16.1	0.6	16.2	0.6	16.2	0.0	16.3	0.6	16.3	0.0	16.2	-0.6	16.2	0.0	16.2	0.0	16.3	0.6	16.3	0.0	16.4	0.6
1944	16.2	-1.2	16.2	0.0	16.3	0.6	16.3	0.0	16.4	0.6	16.4	0.0	16.5	0.6	16.5	0.0	16.5	0.0	16.5	0.0	16.5	0.0	16.5	0.0
1945	16.5	0.0	16.5	0.0	16.5	0.0	16.5	0.0	16.6	0.6	16.7	0.6	16.8	0.6	16.8	0.0	16.8	0.0	16.8	0.0	16.9	0.6	16.9	0.0
1946	17.0	0.6	16.9	-0.6	16.9	0.0	17.0	0.6	17.1	0.6	17.4	1.8	18.5	6.3	18.7	1.1	19.1	2.1	19.6	2.6	20.0	2.0	20.1	0.5
1947	19.9	-1.0	20.0	0.5	20.4	2.0	20.3	-0.5	20.4	0.5	20.6	1.0	-	-	-	-	21.8	5.8	-	-	-	-	22.3	2.3
1948	-	-	-	-	22.6	1.3	-	-	-	-	23.0	1.8	-	-	-	-	23.4	1.7	-	-	-	-	23.0	-1.7
1949	-	-	-	-	22.8	-0.9	-	-	-	-	22.7	-0.4	-	-	-	-	22.7	0.0	-	-	-	-	22.6	-0.4
1950	-	-	-	-	22.5	-0.4	-	-	-	-	22.7	0.9	-	-	-	-	23.2	2.2	-	-	-	-	23.8	2.6
1951	-	-	-	-	24.6	3.4	-	-	-	-	24.7	0.4	-	-	-	-	24.6	-0.4	-	-	-	-	25.2	2.4
1952	-	-	-	-	25.2	0.0	-	-	-	-	25.6	1.6	-	-	-	-	25.5	-0.4	-	-	-	-	25.5	0.0
1953	25.4	-0.4	-	-	-	-	25.6	0.8	-	-	-	-	25.7	0.4	-	-	-	-	25.9	0.8	-	-	-	-
1954	25.9	0.0	-	-	-	-	25.8	-0.4	-	-	-	-	26.1	1.2	-	-	-	-	26.0	-0.4	-	-	-	-
1955	25.9	-0.4	-	-	-	-	26.0	0.4	-	-	-	-	26.1	0.4	-	-	-	-	25.9	-0.8	-	-	-	-
1956	25.8	-0.4	-	-	-	-	25.7	-0.4	-	-	-	-	26.2	1.9	-	-	-	-	26.1	-0.4	-	-	-	-
1957	26.5	1.5	-	-	-	-	26.6	0.4	-	-	-	-	27.0	1.5	-	-	-	-	27.1	0.4	-	-	-	-
1958	27.4	1.1	-	-	-	-	27.6	0.7	-	-	-	-	27.8	0.7	-	-	-	-	27.7	-0.4	-	-	-	-
1959	27.8	0.4	-	-	-	-	27.8	0.0	-	-	-	-	27.9	0.4	-	-	-	-	28.1	0.7	-	-	-	-
1960	28.0	-0.4	-	-	-	-	28.2	0.7	-	-	-	-	28.4	0.7	-	-	-	-	28.5	0.4	-	-	-	-
1961	28.4	-0.4	-	-	-	-	28.7	1.1	-	-	-	-	28.7	0.0	-	-	-	-	28.7	0.0	-	-	-	-

[Continued]

Minneapolis-St. Paul, MN
Consumer Price Index - Urban Wage Earners
Base 1982-1984 = 100
All Items
[Continued]

For 1917-1993. Columns headed % show percentile change in the index from the previous period for which an index is available.

Year	Jan Index	%	Feb Index	%	Mar Index	%	Apr Index	%	May Index	%	Jun Index	%	Jul Index	%	Aug Index	%	Sep Index	%	Oct Index	%	Nov Index	%	Dec Index	%
1962	28.7	0.0	-	-	-	-	29.0	1.0	-	-	-	-	29.1	0.3	-	-	-	-	29.1	0.0	-	-	-	-
1963	29.2	0.3	-	-	-	-	29.3	0.3	-	-	-	-	29.6	1.0	-	-	-	-	29.5	-0.3	-	-	-	-
1964	29.6	0.3	-	-	-	-	29.5	-0.3	-	-	-	-	29.7	0.7	-	-	-	-	29.9	0.7	-	-	-	-
1965	29.9	0.0	-	-	-	-	29.9	0.0	-	-	-	-	30.2	1.0	-	-	-	-	30.3	0.3	-	-	-	-
1966	30.4	0.3	-	-	-	-	30.7	1.0	-	-	-	-	30.8	0.3	-	-	-	-	31.2	1.3	-	-	-	-
1967	31.2	0.0	-	-	-	-	31.4	0.6	-	-	-	-	31.8	1.3	-	-	-	-	32.6	2.5	-	-	-	-
1968	32.8	0.6	-	-	-	-	33.1	0.9	-	-	-	-	33.5	1.2	-	-	-	-	33.5	0.0	-	-	-	-
1969	33.8	0.9	-	-	-	-	34.4	1.8	-	-	-	-	35.2	2.3	-	-	-	-	35.8	1.7	-	-	-	-
1970	36.5	2.0	-	-	-	-	37.2	1.9	-	-	-	-	37.6	1.1	-	-	-	-	38.0	1.1	-	-	-	-
1971	38.3	0.8	-	-	-	-	38.3	0.0	-	-	-	-	38.8	1.3	-	-	-	-	39.3	1.3	-	-	-	-
1972	39.4	0.3	-	-	-	-	39.6	0.5	-	-	-	-	40.0	1.0	-	-	-	-	40.5	1.3	-	-	-	-
1973	40.7	0.5	-	-	-	-	41.7	2.5	-	-	-	-	42.4	1.7	-	-	-	-	43.4	2.4	-	-	-	-
1974	44.7	3.0	-	-	-	-	46.2	3.4	-	-	-	-	47.4	2.6	-	-	-	-	49.0	3.4	-	-	-	-
1975	49.8	1.6	-	-	-	-	50.0	0.4	-	-	-	-	51.6	3.2	-	-	-	-	52.6	1.9	-	-	-	-
1976	53.2	1.1	-	-	-	-	53.7	0.9	-	-	-	-	54.7	1.9	-	-	-	-	55.2	0.9	-	-	-	-
1977	56.0	1.4	-	-	-	-	57.2	2.1	-	-	-	-	58.8	2.8	-	-	-	-	59.6	1.4	-	-	-	-
1978	60.8	2.0	-	-	-	-	62.1	2.1	-	-	63.3	1.9	-	-	64.8	2.4	-	-	65.7	1.4	-	-	66.7	1.5
1979	-	-	67.7	1.5	-	-	68.8	1.6	-	-	71.2	3.5	-	-	72.8	2.2	-	-	74.2	1.9	-	-	74.8	0.8
1980	-	-	76.3	2.0	-	-	78.3	2.6	-	-	79.1	1.0	-	-	79.8	0.9	-	-	81.8	2.5	-	-	83.0	1.5
1981	-	-	83.6	0.7	-	-	85.2	1.9	-	-	88.1	3.4	-	-	91.4	3.7	-	-	92.9	1.6	-	-	95.0	2.3
1982	-	-	97.3	2.4	-	-	96.0	-1.3	-	-	96.8	0.8	-	-	99.8	3.1	-	-	98.0	-1.8	-	-	97.5	-0.5
1983	-	-	98.5	1.0	-	-	99.5	1.0	-	-	99.3	-0.2	-	-	98.3	-1.0	-	-	99.6	1.3	-	-	99.6	0.0
1984	-	-	101.5	1.9	-	-	102.3	0.8	-	-	104.8	2.4	-	-	105.9	1.0	-	-	104.2	-1.6	-	-	103.2	-1.0
1985	-	-	103.9	0.7	-	-	104.9	1.0	-	-	105.9	1.0	-	-	106.5	0.6	-	-	107.1	0.6	-	-	107.1	0.0
1986	-	-	106.7	-0.4	-	-	105.9	-0.7	-	-	107.1	1.1	-	-	106.6	-0.5	-	-	106.6	0.0	106.6	0.0	107.0	0.4
1987	-	-	-	-	-	-	-	-	-	-	108.0	0.9	-	-	-	-	-	-	-	-	-	-	111.5	3.2
1988	-	-	-	-	-	-	-	-	-	-	114.1	2.3	-	-	-	-	-	-	-	-	-	-	116.9	2.5
1989	-	-	-	-	-	-	-	-	-	-	118.3	1.2	-	-	-	-	-	-	-	-	-	-	121.8	3.0
1990	-	-	-	-	-	-	-	-	-	-	123.1	1.1	-	-	-	-	-	-	-	-	-	-	126.4	2.7
1991	-	-	-	-	-	-	-	-	-	-	127.1	0.6	-	-	-	-	-	-	-	-	-	-	129.2	1.7
1992	-	-	-	-	-	-	-	-	-	-	131.0	1.4	-	-	-	-	-	-	-	-	-	-	133.9	2.2
1993	-	-	-	-	-	-	-	-	-	-	136.0	1.6	-	-	-	-	-	-	-	-	-	-	-	-

Source: U.S. Department of Labor, Bureau of Labor Statistics, Division of Consumer Prices and Price Indexes. - indicates no data collected for period.

Minneapolis-St. Paul, MN
Consumer Price Index - All Urban Consumers
Base 1982-1984 = 100
Food and Beverages

For 1976-1993. Columns headed % show percentile change in the index from the previous period for which an index is available.

Year	Jan Index	%	Feb Index	%	Mar Index	%	Apr Index	%	May Index	%	Jun Index	%	Jul Index	%	Aug Index	%	Sep Index	%	Oct Index	%	Nov Index	%	Dec Index	%
1976	62.4	-	-	-	-	-	62.0	-0.6	-	-	-	-	62.8	1.3	-	-	-	-	62.7	-0.2	-	-	-	-
1977	63.1	0.6	-	-	-	-	65.0	3.0	-	-	-	-	66.7	2.6	-	-	-	-	66.8	0.1	-	-	-	-
1978	67.9	1.6	-	-	-	-	70.6	4.0	-	-	72.9	3.3	-	-	73.6	1.0	-	-	74.3	1.0	-	-	75.5	1.6
1979	-	-	78.2	3.6	-	-	79.4	1.5	-	-	81.7	2.9	-	-	82.3	0.7	-	-	82.6	0.4	-	-	83.6	1.2
1980	-	-	84.4	1.0	-	-	86.0	1.9	-	-	87.6	1.9	-	-	88.6	1.1	-	-	89.9	1.5	-	-	90.7	0.9
1981	-	-	91.3	0.7	-	-	91.7	0.4	-	-	92.2	0.5	-	-	93.8	1.7	-	-	94.1	0.3	-	-	94.1	0.0
1982	-	-	94.9	0.9	-	-	95.4	0.5	-	-	96.8	1.5	-	-	97.5	0.7	-	-	97.9	0.4	-	-	97.9	0.0
1983	-	-	97.9	0.0	-	-	99.4	1.5	-	-	99.2	-0.2	-	-	99.6	0.4	-	-	100.0	0.4	-	-	101.5	1.5
1984	-	-	103.4	1.9	-	-	103.6	0.2	-	-	103.8	0.2	-	-	104.1	0.3	-	-	104.8	0.7	-	-	105.3	0.5
1985	-	-	106.5	1.1	-	-	106.3	-0.2	-	-	106.2	-0.1	-	-	106.3	0.1	-	-	106.9	0.6	-	-	107.7	0.7
1986	-	-	108.4	0.6	-	-	108.7	0.3	-	-	108.6	-0.1	-	-	109.4	0.7	-	-	110.4	0.9	111.1	0.6	112.2	1.0
1987	-	-	-	-	-	-	-	-	-	-	113.5	1.2	-	-	-	-	-	-	-	-	-	-	114.4	0.8
1988	-	-	-	-	-	-	-	-	-	-	118.5	3.6	-	-	-	-	-	-	-	-	-	-	121.4	2.4
1989	-	-	-	-	-	-	-	-	-	-	124.9	2.9	-	-	-	-	-	-	-	-	-	-	128.3	2.7
1990	-	-	-	-	-	-	-	-	-	-	133.5	4.1	-	-	-	-	-	-	-	-	-	-	135.7	1.6
1991	-	-	-	-	-	-	-	-	-	-	140.8	3.8	-	-	-	-	-	-	-	-	-	-	142.3	1.1
1992	-	-	-	-	-	-	-	-	-	-	144.4	1.5	-	-	-	-	-	-	-	-	-	-	145.1	0.5
1993	-	-	-	-	-	-	-	-	-	-	147.0	1.3	-	-	-	-	-	-	-	-	-	-	-	-

Source: U.S. Department of Labor, Bureau of Labor Statistics, Division of Consumer Prices and Price Indexes. - indicates no data collected for period.

Minneapolis-St. Paul, MN
Consumer Price Index - Urban Wage Earners
Base 1982-1984 = 100
Food and Beverages

For 1976-1993. Columns headed % show percentile change in the index from the previous period for which an index is available.

Year	Jan Index	Jan %	Feb Index	Feb %	Mar Index	Mar %	Apr Index	Apr %	May Index	May %	Jun Index	Jun %	Jul Index	Jul %	Aug Index	Aug %	Sep Index	Sep %	Oct Index	Oct %	Nov Index	Nov %	Dec Index	Dec %
1976	63.5	-	-	-	-	-	63.1	-0.6	-	-	-	-	63.9	1.3	-	-	-	-	63.8	-0.2	-	-	-	-
1977	64.2	0.6	-	-	-	-	66.1	3.0	-	-	-	-	67.9	2.7	-	-	-	-	68.0	0.1	-	-	-	-
1978	69.0	1.5	-	-	-	-	71.9	4.2	-	-	73.4	2.1	-	-	75.0	2.2	-	-	75.3	0.4	-	-	76.1	1.1
1979	-	-	79.1	3.9	-	-	79.3	0.3	-	-	82.2	3.7	-	-	83.5	1.6	-	-	83.9	0.5	-	-	83.3	-0.7
1980	-	-	85.3	2.4	-	-	86.9	1.9	-	-	88.3	1.6	-	-	89.3	1.1	-	-	91.3	2.2	-	-	91.8	0.5
1981	-	-	91.3	-0.5	-	-	91.7	0.4	-	-	92.1	0.4	-	-	94.1	2.2	-	-	94.0	-0.1	-	-	93.7	-0.3
1982	-	-	94.5	0.9	-	-	95.2	0.7	-	-	96.6	1.5	-	-	97.4	0.8	-	-	98.0	0.6	-	-	98.0	0.0
1983	-	-	97.9	-0.1	-	-	99.4	1.5	-	-	99.1	-0.3	-	-	99.6	0.5	-	-	100.1	0.5	-	-	101.6	1.5
1984	-	-	103.4	1.8	-	-	103.8	0.4	-	-	103.8	0.0	-	-	104.2	0.4	-	-	105.0	0.8	-	-	105.4	0.4
1985	-	-	106.6	1.1	-	-	106.4	-0.2	-	-	106.1	-0.3	-	-	106.2	0.1	-	-	106.8	0.6	-	-	107.6	0.7
1986	-	-	108.5	0.8	-	-	108.6	0.1	-	-	108.6	0.0	-	-	109.6	0.9	-	-	110.4	0.7	111.1	0.6	112.1	0.9
1987	-	-	-	-	-	-	-	-	-	-	113.3	1.1	-	-	-	-	-	-	-	-	-	-	114.5	1.1
1988	-	-	-	-	-	-	-	-	-	-	118.5	3.5	-	-	-	-	-	-	-	-	-	-	121.4	2.4
1989	-	-	-	-	-	-	-	-	-	-	124.8	2.8	-	-	-	-	-	-	-	-	-	-	128.4	2.9
1990	-	-	-	-	-	-	-	-	-	-	133.4	3.9	-	-	-	-	-	-	-	-	-	-	135.9	1.9
1991	-	-	-	-	-	-	-	-	-	-	140.9	3.7	-	-	-	-	-	-	-	-	-	-	142.6	1.2
1992	-	-	-	-	-	-	-	-	-	-	144.4	1.3	-	-	-	-	-	-	-	-	-	-	145.1	0.5
1993	-	-	-	-	-	-	-	-	-	-	146.8	1.2	-	-	-	-	-	-	-	-	-	-	-	-

Source: U.S. Department of Labor, Bureau of Labor Statistics, Division of Consumer Prices and Price Indexes. - indicates no data collected for period.

Minneapolis-St. Paul, MN
Consumer Price Index - All Urban Consumers
Base 1982-1984 = 100
Housing

For 1976-1993. Columns headed % show percentile change in the index from the previous period for which an index is available.

Year	Jan Index	%	Feb Index	%	Mar Index	%	Apr Index	%	May Index	%	Jun Index	%	Jul Index	%	Aug Index	%	Sep Index	%	Oct Index	%	Nov Index	%	Dec Index	%
1976	47.7	-	-	-	-	-	48.1	0.8	-	-	-	-	49.1	2.1	-	-	-	-	49.8	1.4	-	-	-	-
1977	50.8	2.0	-	-	-	-	51.6	1.6	-	-	-	-	53.7	4.1	-	-	-	-	54.9	2.2	-	-	-	-
1978	56.5	2.9	-	-	-	-	57.5	1.8	-	-	58.7	2.1	-	-	60.3	2.7	-	-	61.6	2.2	-	-	62.2	1.0
1979	-	-	63.0	1.3	-	-	64.1	1.7	-	-	65.8	2.7	-	-	67.2	2.1	-	-	69.6	3.6	-	-	70.0	0.6
1980	-	-	70.7	1.0	-	-	73.0	3.3	-	-	73.4	0.5	-	-	74.4	1.4	-	-	76.7	3.1	-	-	77.8	1.4
1981	-	-	77.5	-0.4	-	-	79.7	2.8	-	-	84.7	6.3	-	-	89.9	6.1	-	-	91.9	2.2	-	-	96.1	4.6
1982	-	-	100.3	4.4	-	-	98.1	-2.2	-	-	97.1	-1.0	-	-	102.2	5.3	-	-	98.2	-3.9	-	-	96.8	-1.4
1983	-	-	97.7	0.9	-	-	98.7	1.0	-	-	99.9	1.2	-	-	100.3	0.4	-	-	100.3	0.0	-	-	99.6	-0.7
1984	-	-	100.0	0.4	-	-	101.5	1.5	-	-	102.3	0.8	-	-	102.5	0.2	-	-	103.3	0.8	-	-	103.0	-0.3
1985	-	-	103.7	0.7	-	-	104.7	1.0	-	-	106.0	1.2	-	-	107.1	1.0	-	-	107.6	0.5	-	-	106.7	-0.8
1986	-	-	106.8	0.1	-	-	107.6	0.7	-	-	109.4	1.7	-	-	109.2	-0.2	-	-	107.2	-1.8	106.4	-0.7	107.5	1.0
1987	-	-	-	-	-	-	-	-	-	-	108.1	0.6	-	-	-	-	-	-	-	-	-	-	111.0	2.7
1988	-	-	-	-	-	-	-	-	-	-	110.8	-0.2	-	-	-	-	-	-	-	-	-	-	113.3	2.3
1989	-	-	-	-	-	-	-	-	-	-	115.0	1.5	-	-	-	-	-	-	-	-	-	-	116.6	1.4
1990	-	-	-	-	-	-	-	-	-	-	117.4	0.7	-	-	-	-	-	-	-	-	-	-	119.5	1.8
1991	-	-	-	-	-	-	-	-	-	-	120.1	0.5	-	-	-	-	-	-	-	-	-	-	121.2	0.9
1992	-	-	-	-	-	-	-	-	-	-	123.7	2.1	-	-	-	-	-	-	-	-	-	-	126.0	1.9
1993	-	-	-	-	-	-	-	-	-	-	128.0	1.6	-	-	-	-	-	-	-	-	-	-	-	-

Source: U.S. Department of Labor, Bureau of Labor Statistics, Division of Consumer Prices and Price Indexes. - indicates no data collected for period.

Minneapolis-St. Paul, MN
Consumer Price Index - Urban Wage Earners
Base 1982-1984 = 100
Housing

For 1976-1993. Columns headed % show percentile change in the index from the previous period for which an index is available.

Year	Jan Index	%	Feb Index	%	Mar Index	%	Apr Index	%	May Index	%	Jun Index	%	Jul Index	%	Aug Index	%	Sep Index	%	Oct Index	%	Nov Index	%	Dec Index	%
1976	47.0	-	-	-	-	-	47.4	0.9	-	-	-	-	48.4	2.1	-	-	-	-	49.1	1.4	-	-	-	-
1977	50.1	2.0	-	-	-	-	50.9	1.6	-	-	-	-	52.9	3.9	-	-	-	-	54.0	2.1	-	-	-	-
1978	55.7	3.1	-	-	-	-	56.6	1.6	-	-	58.1	2.7	-	-	59.9	3.1	-	-	61.0	1.8	-	-	61.7	1.1
1979	-	-	62.5	1.3	-	-	63.5	1.6	-	-	65.4	3.0	-	-	66.8	2.1	-	-	68.8	3.0	-	-	69.3	0.7
1980	-	-	70.1	1.2	-	-	72.0	2.7	-	-	72.5	0.7	-	-	73.5	1.4	-	-	76.0	3.4	-	-	77.4	1.8
1981	-	-	77.3	-0.1	-	-	79.5	2.8	-	-	84.5	6.3	-	-	89.8	6.3	-	-	91.7	2.1	-	-	96.2	4.9
1982	-	-	100.5	4.5	-	-	98.3	-2.2	-	-	97.1	-1.2	-	-	102.5	5.6	-	-	98.3	-4.1	-	-	96.8	-1.5
1983	-	-	99.8	3.1	-	-	100.7	0.9	-	-	99.2	-1.5	-	-	95.2	-4.0	-	-	97.6	2.5	-	-	96.6	-1.0
1984	-	-	99.9	3.4	-	-	101.2	1.3	-	-	105.9	4.6	-	-	107.9	1.9	-	-	103.1	-4.4	-	-	100.7	-2.3
1985	-	-	101.5	0.8	-	-	102.3	0.8	-	-	103.6	1.3	-	-	104.7	1.1	-	-	105.3	0.6	-	-	104.4	-0.9
1986	-	-	104.5	0.1	-	-	105.2	0.7	-	-	107.1	1.8	-	-	106.9	-0.2	-	-	104.7	-2.1	103.9	-0.8	104.9	1.0
1987	-	-	-	-	-	-	-	-	-	-	105.5	0.6	-	-	-	-	-	-	-	-	-	-	108.3	2.7
1988	-	-	-	-	-	-	-	-	-	-	108.2	-0.1	-	-	-	-	-	-	-	-	-	-	110.6	2.2
1989	-	-	-	-	-	-	-	-	-	-	112.1	1.4	-	-	-	-	-	-	-	-	-	-	113.6	1.3
1990	-	-	-	-	-	-	-	-	-	-	114.5	0.8	-	-	-	-	-	-	-	-	-	-	116.6	1.8
1991	-	-	-	-	-	-	-	-	-	-	117.2	0.5	-	-	-	-	-	-	-	-	-	-	118.2	0.9
1992	-	-	-	-	-	-	-	-	-	-	120.6	2.0	-	-	-	-	-	-	-	-	-	-	122.9	1.9
1993	-	-	-	-	-	-	-	-	-	-	124.9	1.6	-	-	-	-	-	-	-	-	-	-	-	-

Source: U.S. Department of Labor, Bureau of Labor Statistics, Division of Consumer Prices and Price Indexes. - indicates no data collected for period.

Minneapolis-St. Paul, MN
Consumer Price Index - All Urban Consumers
Base 1982-1984 = 100
Apparel and Upkeep

For 1952-1993. Columns headed % show percentile change in the index from the previous period for which an index is available.

Year	Jan Index	%	Feb Index	%	Mar Index	%	Apr Index	%	May Index	%	Jun Index	%	Jul Index	%	Aug Index	%	Sep Index	%	Oct Index	%	Nov Index	%	Dec Index	%
1952	-		-		-		-		-		-		-		-		-		-		-		46.0	-
1953	45.6	-0.9	-		-		45.9	0.7	-		-		45.6	-0.7	-		-		46.4	1.8	-		-	
1954	45.9	-1.1	-		-		45.9	0.0	-		-		46.0	0.2	-		-		46.1	0.2	-		-	
1955	45.2	-2.0	-		-		45.0	-0.4	-		-		44.8	-0.4	-		-		45.7	2.0	-		-	
1956	46.0	0.7	-		-		46.1	0.2	-		-		46.5	0.9	-		-		47.1	1.3	-		-	
1957	46.9	-0.4	-		-		47.2	0.6	-		-		46.9	-0.6	-		-		47.4	1.1	-		-	
1958	47.4	0.0	-		-		47.3	-0.2	-		-		47.3	0.0	-		-		47.5	0.4	-		-	
1959	47.0	-1.1	-		-		46.9	-0.2	-		-		46.9	0.0	-		-		47.1	0.4	-		-	
1960	47.3	0.4	-		-		47.8	1.1	-		-		47.9	0.2	-		-		49.0	2.3	-		-	
1961	46.8	-4.5	-		-		46.6	-0.4	-		-		46.6	0.0	-		-		47.6	2.1	-		-	
1962	47.4	-0.4	-		-		47.7	0.6	-		-		47.6	-0.2	-		-		48.8	2.5	-		-	
1963	48.6	-0.4	-		-		48.8	0.4	-		-		49.0	0.4	-		-		49.3	0.6	-		-	
1964	48.1	-2.4	-		-		48.6	1.0	-		-		48.6	0.0	-		-		49.8	2.5	-		-	
1965	49.2	-1.2	-		-		49.7	1.0	-		-		49.4	-0.6	-		-		50.7	2.6	-		-	
1966	50.3	-0.8	-		-		50.7	0.8	-		-		51.2	1.0	-		-		52.2	2.0	-		-	
1967	51.6	-1.1	-		-		52.9	2.5	-		-		52.6	-0.6	-		-		54.3	3.2	-		-	
1968	53.7	-1.1	-		-		55.2	2.8	-		-		55.1	-0.2	-		-		56.2	2.0	-		-	
1969	56.3	0.2	-		-		57.8	2.7	-		-		58.3	0.9	-		-		60.1	3.1	-		-	
1970	59.3	-1.3	-		-		60.9	2.7	-		-		60.1	-1.3	-		-		63.3	5.3	-		-	
1971	62.1	-1.9	-		-		62.8	1.1	-		-		62.2	-1.0	-		-		63.3	1.8	-		-	
1972	62.4	-1.4	-		-		63.0	1.0	-		-		62.2	-1.3	-		-		65.2	4.8	-		-	
1973	64.5	-1.1	-		-		65.4	1.4	-		-		66.1	1.1	-		-		68.1	3.0	-		-	
1974	68.4	0.4	-		-		71.0	3.8	-		-		71.1	0.1	-		-		77.5	9.0	-		-	
1975	75.8	-2.2	-		-		73.9	-2.5	-		-		73.1	-1.1	-		-		73.8	1.0	-		-	
1976	73.7	-0.1	-		-		74.5	1.1	-		-		74.0	-0.7	-		-		77.0	4.1	-		-	
1977	75.8	-1.6	-		-		77.2	1.8	-		-		78.9	2.2	-		-		79.4	0.6	-		-	
1978	78.8	-0.8	-		-		81.1	2.9	-		80.3	-1.0	-		81.8	1.9	-		82.4	0.7	-		84.2	2.2
1979	-		82.8	-1.7	-		85.5	3.3	-		84.4	-1.3	-		86.8	2.8	-		86.4	-0.5	-		88.1	2.0
1980	-		88.5	0.5	-		91.2	3.1	-		91.5	0.3	-		92.1	0.7	-		90.9	-1.3	-		91.5	0.7
1981	-		91.6	0.1	-		94.2	2.8	-		94.2	0.0	-		95.7	1.6	-		97.0	1.4	-		96.8	-0.2
1982	-		97.9	1.1	-		99.1	1.2	-		97.4	-1.7	-		101.2	3.9	-		100.9	-0.3	-		103.0	2.1
1983	-		99.7	-3.2	-		104.0	4.3	-		101.5	-2.4	-		101.6	0.1	-		100.8	-0.8	-		101.2	0.4
1984	-		98.6	-2.6	-		99.8	1.2	-		98.4	-1.4	-		96.7	-1.7	-		99.9	3.3	-		98.9	-1.0
1985	-		103.3	4.4	-		107.7	4.3	-		108.0	0.3	-		104.7	-3.1	-		107.2	2.4	-		108.7	1.4
1986	-		104.5	-3.9	-		108.9	4.2	-		106.7	-2.0	-		105.9	-0.7	-		108.7	2.6	107.3	-1.3	107.0	-0.3
1987	-		-		-		-		-		106.2	-0.7	-		-		-		-		-		113.2	6.6
1988	-		-		-		-		-		125.3	10.7	-		-		-		-		-		127.9	2.1
1989	-		-		-		-		-		114.5	-10.5	-		-		-		-		-		128.5	12.2
1990	-		-		-		-		-		125.5	-2.3	-		-		-		-		-		135.4	7.9
1991	-		-		-		-		-		126.4	-6.6	-		-		-		-		-		135.4	7.1
1992	-		-		-		-		-		137.6	1.6	-		-		-		-		-		145.9	6.0
1993	-		-		-		-		-		138.0	-5.4	-		-		-		-		-		-	

Source: U.S. Department of Labor, Bureau of Labor Statistics, Division of Consumer Prices and Price Indexes. - indicates no data collected for period.

Minneapolis-St. Paul, MN
Consumer Price Index - Urban Wage Earners
Base 1982-1984 = 100
Apparel and Upkeep

For 1952-1993. Columns headed % show percentile change in the index from the previous period for which an index is available.

Year	Jan		Feb		Mar		Apr		May		Jun		Jul		Aug		Sep		Oct		Nov		Dec	
	Index	%	Index	%	Index	%	Index	%	Index	%	Index	%	Index	%	Index	%	Index	%	Index	%	Index	%	Index	%
1952	-	-	-	-	-	-	-	-	-	-	-	-	-	-	-	-	-	-	-	-	-	-	-	-
1953	46.6	-0.9	-	-	-	-	47.0	0.9	-	-	-	-	46.6	-0.9	-	-	-	-	47.5	1.9	-	-	47.0	-
1954	47.0	-1.1	-	-	-	-	46.9	-0.2	-	-	-	-	47.0	0.2	-	-	-	-	47.1	0.2	-	-	-	-
1955	46.3	-1.7	-	-	-	-	46.0	-0.6	-	-	-	-	45.8	-0.4	-	-	-	-	46.8	2.2	-	-	-	-
1956	47.1	0.6	-	-	-	-	47.2	0.2	-	-	-	-	47.5	0.6	-	-	-	-	48.2	1.5	-	-	-	-
1957	47.9	-0.6	-	-	-	-	48.3	0.8	-	-	-	-	47.9	-0.8	-	-	-	-	48.4	1.0	-	-	-	-
1958	48.5	0.2	-	-	-	-	48.4	-0.2	-	-	-	-	48.3	-0.2	-	-	-	-	48.5	0.4	-	-	-	-
1959	48.1	-0.8	-	-	-	-	47.9	-0.4	-	-	-	-	47.9	0.0	-	-	-	-	48.2	0.6	-	-	-	-
1960	48.4	0.4	-	-	-	-	48.9	1.0	-	-	-	-	49.0	0.2	-	-	-	-	50.1	2.2	-	-	-	-
1961	47.9	-4.4	-	-	-	-	47.7	-0.4	-	-	-	-	47.7	0.0	-	-	-	-	48.7	2.1	-	-	-	-
1962	48.5	-0.4	-	-	-	-	48.8	0.6	-	-	-	-	48.7	-0.2	-	-	-	-	49.9	2.5	-	-	-	-
1963	49.7	-0.4	-	-	-	-	49.9	0.4	-	-	-	-	50.1	0.4	-	-	-	-	50.4	0.6	-	-	-	-
1964	49.2	-2.4	-	-	-	-	49.7	1.0	-	-	-	-	49.7	0.0	-	-	-	-	50.9	2.4	-	-	-	-
1965	50.3	-1.2	-	-	-	-	50.9	1.2	-	-	-	-	50.6	-0.6	-	-	-	-	51.8	2.4	-	-	-	-
1966	51.4	-0.8	-	-	-	-	51.8	0.8	-	-	-	-	52.4	1.2	-	-	-	-	53.4	1.9	-	-	-	-
1967	52.7	-1.3	-	-	-	-	54.1	2.7	-	-	-	-	53.8	-0.6	-	-	-	-	55.5	3.2	-	-	-	-
1968	54.9	-1.1	-	-	-	-	56.5	2.9	-	-	-	-	56.3	-0.4	-	-	-	-	57.4	2.0	-	-	-	-
1969	57.5	0.2	-	-	-	-	59.1	2.8	-	-	-	-	59.7	1.0	-	-	-	-	61.5	3.0	-	-	-	-
1970	60.7	-1.3	-	-	-	-	62.3	2.6	-	-	-	-	61.5	-1.3	-	-	-	-	64.8	5.4	-	-	-	-
1971	63.5	-2.0	-	-	-	-	64.3	1.3	-	-	-	-	63.6	-1.1	-	-	-	-	64.7	1.7	-	-	-	-
1972	63.8	-1.4	-	-	-	-	64.4	0.9	-	-	-	-	63.6	-1.2	-	-	-	-	66.7	4.9	-	-	-	-
1973	66.0	-1.0	-	-	-	-	66.9	1.4	-	-	-	-	67.6	1.0	-	-	-	-	69.6	3.0	-	-	-	-
1974	69.9	0.4	-	-	-	-	72.6	3.9	-	-	-	-	72.7	0.1	-	-	-	-	79.2	8.9	-	-	-	-
1975	77.5	-2.1	-	-	-	-	75.6	-2.5	-	-	-	-	74.8	-1.1	-	-	-	-	75.5	0.9	-	-	-	-
1976	75.4	-0.1	-	-	-	-	76.2	1.1	-	-	-	-	75.7	-0.7	-	-	-	-	78.7	4.0	-	-	-	-
1977	77.6	-1.4	-	-	-	-	79.0	1.8	-	-	-	-	80.7	2.2	-	-	-	-	81.3	0.7	-	-	-	-
1978	80.5	-1.0	-	-	-	-	82.9	3.0	-	-	83.1	0.2	-	-	83.0	-0.1	-	-	83.1	0.1	-	-	85.6	3.0
1979	-	-	83.0	-3.0	-	-	85.8	3.4	-	-	84.3	-1.7	-	-	87.3	3.6	-	-	87.9	0.7	-	-	88.2	0.3
1980	-	-	88.7	0.6	-	-	91.5	3.2	-	-	92.4	1.0	-	-	93.5	1.2	-	-	92.7	-0.9	-	-	92.4	-0.3
1981	-	-	94.1	1.8	-	-	95.8	1.8	-	-	96.7	0.9	-	-	97.8	1.1	-	-	98.1	0.3	-	-	96.7	-1.4
1982	-	-	97.6	0.9	-	-	99.0	1.4	-	-	97.0	-2.0	-	-	101.2	4.3	-	-	100.7	-0.5	-	-	103.3	2.6
1983	-	-	99.8	-3.4	-	-	103.9	4.1	-	-	100.9	-2.9	-	-	101.2	0.3	-	-	100.4	-0.8	-	-	101.6	1.2
1984	-	-	98.9	-2.7	-	-	100.5	1.6	-	-	98.4	-2.1	-	-	97.7	-0.7	-	-	99.8	2.1	-	-	98.8	-1.0
1985	-	-	104.0	5.3	-	-	108.0	3.8	-	-	108.6	0.6	-	-	105.2	-3.1	-	-	107.4	2.1	-	-	109.0	1.5
1986	-	-	104.3	-4.3	-	-	109.4	4.9	-	-	105.4	-3.7	-	-	105.9	0.5	-	-	108.2	2.2	106.9	-1.2	106.0	-0.8
1987	-	-	-	-	-	-	-	-	-	-	104.1	-1.8	-	-	-	-	-	-	-	-	-	-	112.6	8.2
1988	-	-	-	-	-	-	-	-	-	-	126.9	12.7	-	-	-	-	-	-	-	-	-	-	128.3	1.1
1989	-	-	-	-	-	-	-	-	-	-	112.7	-12.2	-	-	-	-	-	-	-	-	-	-	124.8	10.7
1990	-	-	-	-	-	-	-	-	-	-	121.5	-2.6	-	-	-	-	-	-	-	-	-	-	132.8	9.3
1991	-	-	-	-	-	-	-	-	-	-	123.4	-7.1	-	-	-	-	-	-	-	-	-	-	133.9	8.5
1992	-	-	-	-	-	-	-	-	-	-	135.1	0.9	-	-	-	-	-	-	-	-	-	-	143.0	5.8
1993	-	-	-	-	-	-	-	-	-	-	135.2	-5.5	-	-	-	-	-	-	-	-	-	-	-	-

Source: U.S. Department of Labor, Bureau of Labor Statistics, Division of Consumer Prices and Price Indexes. - indicates no data collected for period.

Minneapolis-St. Paul, MN
Consumer Price Index - All Urban Consumers
Base 1982-1984 = 100
Transportation

For 1947-1993. Columns headed % show percentile change in the index from the previous period for which an index is available.

Year	Jan Index	%	Feb Index	%	Mar Index	%	Apr Index	%	May Index	%	Jun Index	%	Jul Index	%	Aug Index	%	Sep Index	%	Oct Index	%	Nov Index	%	Dec Index	%
1947	20.9	-	21.0	0.5	21.1	0.5	21.1	0.0	21.3	0.9	21.3	0.0	-	-	-	-	21.9	2.8	-	-	-	-	23.3	6.4
1948	-	-	-	-	23.7	1.7	-	-	-	-	23.7	0.0	-	-	-	-	26.1	10.1	-	-	-	-	25.9	-0.8
1949	-	-	-	-	26.2	1.2	-	-	-	-	26.3	0.4	-	-	-	-	26.6	1.1	-	-	-	-	26.8	0.8
1950	-	-	-	-	26.3	-1.9	-	-	-	-	26.1	-0.8	-	-	-	-	26.7	2.3	-	-	-	-	26.8	0.4
1951	-	-	-	-	27.1	1.1	-	-	-	-	27.1	0.0	-	-	-	-	25.8	-4.8	-	-	-	-	27.8	7.8
1952	-	-	-	-	28.3	1.8	-	-	-	-	28.8	1.8	-	-	-	-	29.2	1.4	-	-	-	-	29.2	0.0
1953	29.3	0.3	-	-	-	-	29.5	0.7	-	-	-	-	29.5	0.0	-	-	-	-	29.4	-0.3	-	-	-	-
1954	29.5	0.3	-	-	-	-	29.3	-0.7	-	-	-	-	29.4	0.3	-	-	-	-	28.7	-2.4	-	-	-	-
1955	29.5	2.8	-	-	-	-	28.5	-3.4	-	-	-	-	28.8	1.1	-	-	-	-	27.1	-5.9	-	-	-	-
1956	27.6	1.8	-	-	-	-	27.0	-2.2	-	-	-	-	28.0	3.7	-	-	-	-	28.6	2.1	-	-	-	-
1957	29.3	2.4	-	-	-	-	29.4	0.3	-	-	-	-	29.4	0.0	-	-	-	-	28.8	-2.0	-	-	-	-
1958	30.1	4.5	-	-	-	-	29.6	-1.7	-	-	-	-	30.3	2.4	-	-	-	-	30.5	0.7	-	-	-	-
1959	31.7	3.9	-	-	-	-	31.5	-0.6	-	-	-	-	30.6	-2.9	-	-	-	-	32.2	5.2	-	-	-	-
1960	32.0	-0.6	-	-	-	-	31.4	-1.9	-	-	-	-	32.1	2.2	-	-	-	-	32.2	0.3	-	-	-	-
1961	32.0	-0.6	-	-	-	-	32.5	1.6	-	-	-	-	32.1	-1.2	-	-	-	-	32.2	0.3	-	-	-	-
1962	32.1	-0.3	-	-	-	-	32.9	2.5	-	-	-	-	32.4	-1.5	-	-	-	-	33.4	3.1	-	-	-	-
1963	32.6	-2.4	-	-	-	-	33.1	1.5	-	-	-	-	33.7	1.8	-	-	-	-	33.2	-1.5	-	-	-	-
1964	33.6	1.2	-	-	-	-	32.5	-3.3	-	-	-	-	33.1	1.8	-	-	-	-	33.5	1.2	-	-	-	-
1965	33.5	0.0	-	-	-	-	33.6	0.3	-	-	-	-	33.8	0.6	-	-	-	-	34.0	0.6	-	-	-	-
1966	34.1	0.3	-	-	-	-	34.2	0.3	-	-	-	-	34.4	0.6	-	-	-	-	34.7	0.9	-	-	-	-
1967	34.7	0.0	-	-	-	-	35.1	1.2	-	-	-	-	35.4	0.9	-	-	-	-	36.5	3.1	-	-	-	-
1968	36.7	0.5	-	-	-	-	36.4	-0.8	-	-	-	-	36.7	0.8	-	-	-	-	37.2	1.4	-	-	-	-
1969	36.6	-1.6	-	-	-	-	37.8	3.3	-	-	-	-	37.0	-2.1	-	-	-	-	37.6	1.6	-	-	-	-
1970	38.2	1.6	-	-	-	-	39.2	2.6	-	-	-	-	39.8	1.5	-	-	-	-	40.5	1.8	-	-	-	-
1971	41.9	3.5	-	-	-	-	40.7	-2.9	-	-	-	-	41.0	0.7	-	-	-	-	40.9	-0.2	-	-	-	-
1972	41.7	2.0	-	-	-	-	40.6	-2.6	-	-	-	-	41.4	2.0	-	-	-	-	41.9	1.2	-	-	-	-
1973	42.2	0.7	-	-	-	-	42.8	1.4	-	-	-	-	43.3	1.2	-	-	-	-	43.2	-0.2	-	-	-	-
1974	44.9	3.9	-	-	-	-	47.0	4.7	-	-	-	-	49.2	4.7	-	-	-	-	48.8	-0.8	-	-	-	-
1975	48.6	-0.4	-	-	-	-	49.2	1.2	-	-	-	-	51.6	4.9	-	-	-	-	52.5	1.7	-	-	-	-
1976	53.0	1.0	-	-	-	-	54.2	2.3	-	-	-	-	56.3	3.9	-	-	-	-	56.7	0.7	-	-	-	-
1977	57.9	2.1	-	-	-	-	59.5	2.8	-	-	-	-	60.3	1.3	-	-	-	-	60.0	-0.5	-	-	-	-
1978	60.4	0.7	-	-	-	-	60.9	0.8	-	-	62.4	2.5	-	-	63.3	1.4	-	-	63.9	0.9	-	-	64.6	1.1
1979	-	-	65.6	1.5	-	-	68.2	4.0	-	-	72.3	6.0	-	-	74.7	3.3	-	-	75.6	1.2	-	-	77.4	2.4
1980	-	-	80.4	3.9	-	-	83.2	3.5	-	-	83.9	0.8	-	-	84.2	0.4	-	-	85.9	2.0	-	-	87.3	1.6
1981	-	-	89.8	2.9	-	-	91.7	2.1	-	-	94.1	2.6	-	-	94.7	0.6	-	-	96.8	2.2	-	-	97.2	0.4
1982	-	-	96.0	-1.2	-	-	93.7	-2.4	-	-	99.2	5.9	-	-	99.3	0.1	-	-	98.7	-0.6	-	-	98.6	-0.1
1983	-	-	96.1	-2.5	-	-	96.9	0.8	-	-	99.1	2.3	-	-	101.1	2.0	-	-	101.4	0.3	-	-	101.9	0.5
1984	-	-	101.9	0.0	-	-	102.3	0.4	-	-	103.5	1.2	-	-	103.6	0.1	-	-	104.2	0.6	-	-	104.4	0.2
1985	-	-	103.4	-1.0	-	-	105.4	1.9	-	-	107.1	1.6	-	-	107.5	0.4	-	-	106.8	-0.7	-	-	107.3	0.5
1986	-	-	104.5	-2.6	-	-	98.8	-5.5	-	-	101.2	2.4	-	-	98.3	-2.9	-	-	98.9	0.6	99.3	0.4	99.0	-0.3
1987	-	-	-	-	-	-	-	-	-	-	101.2	2.2	-	-	-	-	-	-	-	-	-	-	104.5	3.3
1988	-	-	-	-	-	-	-	-	-	-	105.7	1.1	-	-	-	-	-	-	-	-	-	-	108.8	2.9
1989	-	-	-	-	-	-	-	-	-	-	112.7	3.6	-	-	-	-	-	-	-	-	-	-	116.8	3.6
1990	-	-	-	-	-	-	-	-	-	-	116.9	0.1	-	-	-	-	-	-	-	-	-	-	120.1	2.7
1991	-	-	-	-	-	-	-	-	-	-	119.3	-0.7	-	-	-	-	-	-	-	-	-	-	119.5	0.2

[Continued]

Minneapolis-St. Paul, MN
Consumer Price Index - All Urban Consumers
Base 1982-1984 = 100
Transportation
[Continued]

For 1947-1993. Columns headed % show percentile change in the index from the previous period for which an index is available.

Year	Jan		Feb		Mar		Apr		May		Jun		Jul		Aug		Sep		Oct		Nov		Dec	
	Index	%	Index	%	Index	%	Index	%	Index	%	Index	%	Index	%	Index	%	Index	%	Index	%	Index	%	Index	%
1992	-	-	-	-	-	-	-	-	-	-	119.8	0.3	-	-	-	-	-	-	-	-	-	-	123.7	3.3
1993	-	-	-	-	-	-	-	-	-	-	125.9	1.8	-	-	-	-	-	-	-	-	-	-	-	-

Source: U.S. Department of Labor, Bureau of Labor Statistics, Division of Consumer Prices and Price Indexes. - indicates no data collected for period.

Minneapolis-St. Paul, MN
Consumer Price Index - Urban Wage Earners
Base 1982-1984 = 100
Transportation

For 1947-1993. Columns headed % show percentile change in the index from the previous period for which an index is available.

Year	Jan Index	%	Feb Index	%	Mar Index	%	Apr Index	%	May Index	%	Jun Index	%	Jul Index	%	Aug Index	%	Sep Index	%	Oct Index	%	Nov Index	%	Dec Index	%
1947	20.6	-	20.6	0.0	20.7	0.5	20.8	0.5	21.0	1.0	21.0	0.0	-	-	-	-	21.5	2.4	-	-	-	-	22.9	6.5
1948	-	-	-	-	23.3	1.7	-	-	-	-	23.4	0.4	-	-	-	-	25.7	9.8	-	-	-	-	25.5	-0.8
1949	-	-	-	-	25.8	1.2	-	-	-	-	25.9	0.4	-	-	-	-	26.2	1.2	-	-	-	-	26.4	0.8
1950	-	-	-	-	25.9	-1.9	-	-	-	-	25.7	-0.8	-	-	-	-	26.3	2.3	-	-	-	-	26.4	0.4
1951	-	-	-	-	26.7	1.1	-	-	-	-	26.7	0.0	-	-	-	-	25.4	-4.9	-	-	-	-	27.4	7.9
1952	-	-	-	-	27.8	1.5	-	-	-	-	28.3	1.8	-	-	-	-	28.8	1.8	-	-	-	-	28.8	0.0
1953	28.8	0.0	-	-	-	-	29.1	1.0	-	-	-	-	29.1	0.0	-	-	-	-	28.9	-0.7	-	-	-	-
1954	29.1	0.7	-	-	-	-	28.8	-1.0	-	-	-	-	29.0	0.7	-	-	-	-	28.2	-2.8	-	-	-	-
1955	29.0	2.8	-	-	-	-	28.0	-3.4	-	-	-	-	28.3	1.1	-	-	-	-	26.7	-5.7	-	-	-	-
1956	27.2	1.9	-	-	-	-	26.6	-2.2	-	-	-	-	27.5	3.4	-	-	-	-	28.1	2.2	-	-	-	-
1957	28.8	2.5	-	-	-	-	28.9	0.3	-	-	-	-	29.0	0.3	-	-	-	-	28.3	-2.4	-	-	-	-
1958	29.6	4.6	-	-	-	-	29.2	-1.4	-	-	-	-	29.8	2.1	-	-	-	-	30.1	1.0	-	-	-	-
1959	31.3	4.0	-	-	-	-	31.1	-0.6	-	-	-	-	30.2	-2.9	-	-	-	-	31.7	5.0	-	-	-	-
1960	31.5	-0.6	-	-	-	-	30.9	-1.9	-	-	-	-	31.6	2.3	-	-	-	-	31.7	0.3	-	-	-	-
1961	31.5	-0.6	-	-	-	-	32.0	1.6	-	-	-	-	31.6	-1.2	-	-	-	-	31.7	0.3	-	-	-	-
1962	31.6	-0.3	-	-	-	-	32.4	2.5	-	-	-	-	31.9	-1.5	-	-	-	-	32.9	3.1	-	-	-	-
1963	32.1	-2.4	-	-	-	-	32.6	1.6	-	-	-	-	33.2	1.8	-	-	-	-	32.7	-1.5	-	-	-	-
1964	33.1	1.2	-	-	-	-	32.0	-3.3	-	-	-	-	32.6	1.9	-	-	-	-	32.9	0.9	-	-	-	-
1965	32.9	0.0	-	-	-	-	33.1	0.6	-	-	-	-	33.3	0.6	-	-	-	-	33.5	0.6	-	-	-	-
1966	33.5	0.0	-	-	-	-	33.7	0.6	-	-	-	-	33.9	0.6	-	-	-	-	34.2	0.9	-	-	-	-
1967	34.1	-0.3	-	-	-	-	34.5	1.2	-	-	-	-	34.9	1.2	-	-	-	-	36.0	3.2	-	-	-	-
1968	36.2	0.6	-	-	-	-	35.9	-0.8	-	-	-	-	36.1	0.6	-	-	-	-	36.6	1.4	-	-	-	-
1969	36.0	-1.6	-	-	-	-	37.2	3.3	-	-	-	-	36.5	-1.9	-	-	-	-	37.0	1.4	-	-	-	-
1970	37.6	1.6	-	-	-	-	38.6	2.7	-	-	-	-	39.2	1.6	-	-	-	-	39.8	1.5	-	-	-	-
1971	41.2	3.5	-	-	-	-	40.1	-2.7	-	-	-	-	40.3	0.5	-	-	-	-	40.3	0.0	-	-	-	-
1972	41.0	1.7	-	-	-	-	40.0	-2.4	-	-	-	-	40.7	1.7	-	-	-	-	41.2	1.2	-	-	-	-
1973	41.6	1.0	-	-	-	-	42.2	1.4	-	-	-	-	42.6	0.9	-	-	-	-	42.5	-0.2	-	-	-	-
1974	44.2	4.0	-	-	-	-	46.3	4.8	-	-	-	-	48.5	4.8	-	-	-	-	48.1	-0.8	-	-	-	-
1975	47.9	-0.4	-	-	-	-	48.5	1.3	-	-	-	-	50.8	4.7	-	-	-	-	51.7	1.8	-	-	-	-
1976	52.1	0.8	-	-	-	-	53.4	2.5	-	-	-	-	55.5	3.9	-	-	-	-	55.8	0.5	-	-	-	-
1977	57.0	2.2	-	-	-	-	58.6	2.8	-	-	-	-	59.4	1.4	-	-	-	-	59.1	-0.5	-	-	-	-
1978	59.5	0.7	-	-	-	-	60.0	0.8	-	-	61.6	2.7	-	-	62.5	1.5	-	-	63.3	1.3	-	-	64.1	1.3
1979	-	-	65.0	1.4	-	-	67.8	4.3	-	-	72.2	6.5	-	-	74.5	3.2	-	-	75.5	1.3	-	-	77.4	2.5
1980	-	-	80.5	4.0	-	-	83.3	3.5	-	-	84.2	1.1	-	-	84.2	0.0	-	-	85.9	2.0	-	-	87.6	2.0
1981	-	-	90.5	3.3	-	-	92.2	1.9	-	-	94.1	2.1	-	-	95.0	1.0	-	-	96.9	2.0	-	-	97.4	0.5
1982	-	-	96.3	-1.1	-	-	93.7	-2.7	-	-	99.4	6.1	-	-	99.4	0.0	-	-	98.8	-0.6	-	-	98.8	0.0
1983	-	-	96.1	-2.7	-	-	96.9	0.8	-	-	99.4	2.6	-	-	101.3	1.9	-	-	101.4	0.1	-	-	101.8	0.4
1984	-	-	101.7	-0.1	-	-	102.1	0.4	-	-	103.1	1.0	-	-	103.4	0.3	-	-	104.0	0.6	-	-	104.1	0.1
1985	-	-	102.8	-1.2	-	-	105.1	2.2	-	-	106.9	1.7	-	-	107.3	0.4	-	-	106.4	-0.8	-	-	107.1	0.7
1986	-	-	103.9	-3.0	-	-	97.6	-6.1	-	-	100.3	2.8	-	-	97.1	-3.2	-	-	97.7	0.6	98.1	0.4	97.8	-0.3
1987	-	-	-	-	-	-	-	-	-	-	100.4	2.7	-	-	-	-	-	-	-	-	-	-	103.9	3.5
1988	-	-	-	-	-	-	-	-	-	-	104.8	0.9	-	-	-	-	-	-	-	-	-	-	108.1	3.1
1989	-	-	-	-	-	-	-	-	-	-	112.1	3.7	-	-	-	-	-	-	-	-	-	-	116.1	3.6
1990	-	-	-	-	-	-	-	-	-	-	115.7	-0.3	-	-	-	-	-	-	-	-	-	-	119.3	3.1
1991	-	-	-	-	-	-	-	-	-	-	118.0	-1.1	-	-	-	-	-	-	-	-	-	-	118.7	0.6

[Continued]

Minneapolis-St. Paul, MN
Consumer Price Index - Urban Wage Earners
Base 1982-1984 = 100
Transportation
[Continued]

For 1947-1993. Columns headed % show percentile change in the index from the previous period for which an index is available.

Year	Jan		Feb		Mar		Apr		May		Jun		Jul		Aug		Sep		Oct		Nov		Dec	
	Index	%	Index	%	Index	%	Index	%	Index	%	Index	%	Index	%	Index	%	Index	%	Index	%	Index	%	Index	%
1992	-	-	-	-	-	-	-	-	-	-	118.8	0.1	-	-	-	-	-	-	-	-	-	-		
1993	-	-	-	-	-	-	-	-	-	-	125.3	1.7	-	-	-	-	-	-	-	-	-	-	123.2	3.7

Source: U.S. Department of Labor, Bureau of Labor Statistics, Division of Consumer Prices and Price Indexes. - indicates no data collected for period.

Minneapolis-St. Paul, MN
Consumer Price Index - All Urban Consumers
Base 1982-1984 = 100
Medical Care

For 1947-1993. Columns headed % show percentile change in the index from the previous period for which an index is available.

Year	Jan Index	%	Feb Index	%	Mar Index	%	Apr Index	%	May Index	%	Jun Index	%	Jul Index	%	Aug Index	%	Sep Index	%	Oct Index	%	Nov Index	%	Dec Index	%
1947	10.2	-	10.2	0.0	10.2	0.0	10.4	2.0	10.5	1.0	10.6	1.0	-	-	-	-	11.0	3.8	-	-	-	-	11.2	1.8
1948	-	-	-	-	11.4	1.8	-	-	-	-	11.8	3.5	-	-	-	-	11.9	0.8	-	-	-	-	12.1	1.7
1949	-	-	-	-	12.1	0.0	-	-	-	-	12.2	0.8	-	-	-	-	12.3	0.8	-	-	-	-	12.4	0.8
1950	-	-	-	-	12.4	0.0	-	-	-	-	12.4	0.0	-	-	-	-	12.8	3.2	-	-	-	-	12.9	0.8
1951	-	-	-	-	13.6	5.4	-	-	-	-	13.6	0.0	-	-	-	-	13.8	1.5	-	-	-	-	13.9	0.7
1952	-	-	-	-	14.5	4.3	-	-	-	-	14.5	0.0	-	-	-	-	14.6	0.7	-	-	-	-	14.5	-0.7
1953	14.5	0.0	-	-	-	-	15.8	9.0	-	-	-	-	15.9	0.6	-	-	-	-	15.9	0.0	-	-	-	-
1954	16.0	0.6	-	-	-	-	16.4	2.5	-	-	-	-	16.5	0.6	-	-	-	-	16.4	-0.6	-	-	-	-
1955	16.6	1.2	-	-	-	-	17.0	2.4	-	-	-	-	17.1	0.6	-	-	-	-	17.1	0.0	-	-	-	-
1956	17.2	0.6	-	-	-	-	17.2	0.0	-	-	-	-	17.3	0.6	-	-	-	-	17.3	0.0	-	-	-	-
1957	17.4	0.6	-	-	-	-	17.6	1.1	-	-	-	-	19.5	10.8	-	-	-	-	19.6	0.5	-	-	-	-
1958	19.8	1.0	-	-	-	-	20.2	2.0	-	-	-	-	21.9	8.4	-	-	-	-	22.0	0.5	-	-	-	-
1959	22.2	0.9	-	-	-	-	22.2	0.0	-	-	-	-	22.4	0.9	-	-	-	-	23.5	4.9	-	-	-	-
1960	23.5	0.0	-	-	-	-	24.1	2.6	-	-	-	-	24.7	2.5	-	-	-	-	24.4	-1.2	-	-	-	-
1961	24.4	0.0	-	-	-	-	25.4	4.1	-	-	-	-	26.4	3.9	-	-	-	-	26.5	0.4	-	-	-	-
1962	26.5	0.0	-	-	-	-	26.5	0.0	-	-	-	-	26.8	1.1	-	-	-	-	26.9	0.4	-	-	-	-
1963	27.0	0.4	-	-	-	-	27.0	0.0	-	-	-	-	27.0	0.0	-	-	-	-	27.1	0.4	-	-	-	-
1964	27.2	0.4	-	-	-	-	27.6	1.5	-	-	-	-	27.5	-0.4	-	-	-	-	27.5	0.0	-	-	-	-
1965	27.5	0.0	-	-	-	-	27.6	0.4	-	-	-	-	27.6	0.0	-	-	-	-	27.7	0.4	-	-	-	-
1966	27.9	0.7	-	-	-	-	28.6	2.5	-	-	-	-	29.0	1.4	-	-	-	-	29.4	1.4	-	-	-	-
1967	30.0	2.0	-	-	-	-	30.1	0.3	-	-	-	-	30.4	1.0	-	-	-	-	30.8	1.3	-	-	-	-
1968	31.4	1.9	-	-	-	-	31.8	1.3	-	-	-	-	32.0	0.6	-	-	-	-	32.4	1.3	-	-	-	-
1969	32.8	1.2	-	-	-	-	33.3	1.5	-	-	-	-	34.0	2.1	-	-	-	-	33.9	-0.3	-	-	-	-
1970	34.2	0.9	-	-	-	-	35.6	4.1	-	-	-	-	36.3	2.0	-	-	-	-	36.3	0.0	-	-	-	-
1971	36.9	1.7	-	-	-	-	37.5	1.6	-	-	-	-	38.1	1.6	-	-	-	-	37.9	-0.5	-	-	-	-
1972	37.9	0.0	-	-	-	-	38.0	0.3	-	-	-	-	38.3	0.8	-	-	-	-	38.8	1.3	-	-	-	-
1973	39.4	1.5	-	-	-	-	39.8	1.0	-	-	-	-	40.0	0.5	-	-	-	-	41.0	2.5	-	-	-	-
1974	42.0	2.4	-	-	-	-	42.6	1.4	-	-	-	-	43.8	2.8	-	-	-	-	45.3	3.4	-	-	-	-
1975	47.4	4.6	-	-	-	-	47.6	0.4	-	-	-	-	48.9	2.7	-	-	-	-	49.4	1.0	-	-	-	-
1976	50.5	2.2	-	-	-	-	51.4	1.8	-	-	-	-	52.4	1.9	-	-	-	-	53.5	2.1	-	-	-	-
1977	54.9	2.6	-	-	-	-	55.7	1.5	-	-	-	-	56.9	2.2	-	-	-	-	57.5	1.1	-	-	-	-
1978	59.1	2.8	-	-	-	-	60.3	2.0	-	-	60.9	1.0	-	-	62.3	2.3	-	-	62.2	-0.2	-	-	63.2	1.6
1979	-	-	65.1	3.0	-	-	64.0	-1.7	-	-	65.2	1.9	-	-	66.7	2.3	-	-	68.1	2.1	-	-	70.2	3.1
1980	-	-	72.7	3.6	-	-	72.9	0.3	-	-	73.0	0.1	-	-	74.6	2.2	-	-	74.6	0.0	-	-	75.5	1.2
1981	-	-	77.2	2.3	-	-	78.4	1.6	-	-	79.3	1.1	-	-	82.2	3.7	-	-	82.8	0.7	-	-	84.2	1.7
1982	-	-	86.5	2.7	-	-	87.7	1.4	-	-	89.0	1.5	-	-	92.0	3.4	-	-	92.9	1.0	-	-	94.3	1.5
1983	-	-	96.4	2.2	-	-	96.4	0.0	-	-	99.7	3.4	-	-	102.3	2.6	-	-	104.7	2.3	-	-	104.8	0.1
1984	-	-	107.3	2.4	-	-	107.5	0.2	-	-	109.5	1.9	-	-	110.8	1.2	-	-	112.7	1.7	-	-	112.6	-0.1
1985	-	-	114.8	2.0	-	-	115.4	0.5	-	-	116.1	0.6	-	-	117.4	1.1	-	-	119.6	1.9	-	-	120.3	0.6
1986	-	-	123.0	2.2	-	-	124.9	1.5	-	-	125.9	0.8	-	-	127.2	1.0	-	-	130.7	2.8	131.4	0.5	131.6	0.2
1987	-	-	-	-	-	-	-	-	-	-	132.3	0.5	-	-	-	-	-	-	-	-	-	-	135.2	2.2
1988	-	-	-	-	-	-	-	-	-	-	139.3	3.0	-	-	-	-	-	-	-	-	-	-	142.2	2.1
1989	-	-	-	-	-	-	-	-	-	-	146.9	3.3	-	-	-	-	-	-	-	-	-	-	151.3	3.0
1990	-	-	-	-	-	-	-	-	-	-	160.1	5.8	-	-	-	-	-	-	-	-	-	-	162.9	1.7
1991	-	-	-	-	-	-	-	-	-	-	171.2	5.1	-	-	-	-	-	-	-	-	-	-	172.4	0.7

[Continued]

Minneapolis-St. Paul, MN
Consumer Price Index - All Urban Consumers
Base 1982-1984 = 100
Medical Care
[Continued]

For 1947-1993. Columns headed % show percentile change in the index from the previous period for which an index is available.

Year	Jan Index	%	Feb Index	%	Mar Index	%	Apr Index	%	May Index	%	Jun Index	%	Jul Index	%	Aug Index	%	Sep Index	%	Oct Index	%	Nov Index	%	Dec Index	%
1992	-	-	-	-	-	-	-	-	-	-	181.2	5.1	-	-	-	-	-	-	-	-	-	-	-	-
1993	-	-	-	-	-	-	-	-	-	-	192.3	4.7	-	-	-	-	-	-	-	-	-	-	183.7	1.4

Source: U.S. Department of Labor, Bureau of Labor Statistics, Division of Consumer Prices and Price Indexes. - indicates no data collected for period.

Minneapolis-St. Paul, MN
Consumer Price Index - Urban Wage Earners
Base 1982-1984 = 100
Medical Care

For 1947-1993. Columns headed % show percentile change in the index from the previous period for which an index is available.

Year	Jan Index	%	Feb Index	%	Mar Index	%	Apr Index	%	May Index	%	Jun Index	%	Jul Index	%	Aug Index	%	Sep Index	%	Oct Index	%	Nov Index	%	Dec Index	%
1947	10.4	-	10.4	0.0	10.4	0.0	10.5	1.0	10.7	1.9	10.8	0.9	-	-	-	-	11.1	2.8	-	-	-	-	11.4	2.7
1948	-	-	-	-	11.5	0.9	-	-	-	-	12.0	4.3	-	-	-	-	12.1	0.8	-	-	-	-	12.3	1.7
1949	-	-	-	-	12.3	0.0	-	-	-	-	12.4	0.8	-	-	-	-	12.5	0.8	-	-	-	-	12.5	0.0
1950	-	-	-	-	12.6	0.8	-	-	-	-	12.6	0.0	-	-	-	-	12.9	2.4	-	-	-	-	13.1	1.6
1951	-	-	-	-	13.8	5.3	-	-	-	-	13.8	0.0	-	-	-	-	14.0	1.4	-	-	-	-	14.1	0.7
1952	-	-	-	-	14.7	4.3	-	-	-	-	14.7	0.0	-	-	-	-	14.8	0.7	-	-	-	-	14.7	-0.7
1953	14.7	0.0	-	-	-	-	16.0	8.8	-	-	-	-	16.1	0.6	-	-	-	-	16.2	0.6	-	-	-	-
1954	16.3	0.6	-	-	-	-	16.6	1.8	-	-	-	-	16.7	0.6	-	-	-	-	16.6	-0.6	-	-	-	-
1955	16.8	1.2	-	-	-	-	17.2	2.4	-	-	-	-	17.4	1.2	-	-	-	-	17.4	0.0	-	-	-	-
1956	17.4	0.0	-	-	-	-	17.4	0.0	-	-	-	-	17.5	0.6	-	-	-	-	17.5	0.0	-	-	-	-
1957	17.6	0.6	-	-	-	-	17.8	1.1	-	-	-	-	19.8	11.2	-	-	-	-	19.9	0.5	-	-	-	-
1958	20.1	1.0	-	-	-	-	20.4	1.5	-	-	-	-	22.2	8.8	-	-	-	-	22.3	0.5	-	-	-	-
1959	22.5	0.9	-	-	-	-	22.5	0.0	-	-	-	-	22.7	0.9	-	-	-	-	23.8	4.8	-	-	-	-
1960	23.8	0.0	-	-	-	-	24.5	2.9	-	-	-	-	25.0	2.0	-	-	-	-	24.8	-0.8	-	-	-	-
1961	24.7	-0.4	-	-	-	-	25.8	4.5	-	-	-	-	26.8	3.9	-	-	-	-	26.9	0.4	-	-	-	-
1962	26.9	0.0	-	-	-	-	26.9	0.0	-	-	-	-	27.1	0.7	-	-	-	-	27.3	0.7	-	-	-	-
1963	27.4	0.4	-	-	-	-	27.4	0.0	-	-	-	-	27.4	0.0	-	-	-	-	27.5	0.4	-	-	-	-
1964	27.6	0.4	-	-	-	-	27.9	1.1	-	-	-	-	27.9	0.0	-	-	-	-	27.9	0.0	-	-	-	-
1965	27.9	0.0	-	-	-	-	28.0	0.4	-	-	-	-	27.9	-0.4	-	-	-	-	28.1	0.7	-	-	-	-
1966	28.3	0.7	-	-	-	-	29.0	2.5	-	-	-	-	29.4	1.4	-	-	-	-	29.9	1.7	-	-	-	-
1967	30.4	1.7	-	-	-	-	30.6	0.7	-	-	-	-	30.8	0.7	-	-	-	-	31.2	1.3	-	-	-	-
1968	31.8	1.9	-	-	-	-	32.3	1.6	-	-	-	-	32.5	0.6	-	-	-	-	32.9	1.2	-	-	-	-
1969	33.3	1.2	-	-	-	-	33.8	1.5	-	-	-	-	34.5	2.1	-	-	-	-	34.4	-0.3	-	-	-	-
1970	34.7	0.9	-	-	-	-	36.2	4.3	-	-	-	-	36.8	1.7	-	-	-	-	36.9	0.3	-	-	-	-
1971	37.4	1.4	-	-	-	-	38.0	1.6	-	-	-	-	38.7	1.8	-	-	-	-	38.5	-0.5	-	-	-	-
1972	38.4	-0.3	-	-	-	-	38.5	0.3	-	-	-	-	38.9	1.0	-	-	-	-	39.3	1.0	-	-	-	-
1973	39.9	1.5	-	-	-	-	40.4	1.3	-	-	-	-	40.6	0.5	-	-	-	-	41.6	2.5	-	-	-	-
1974	42.6	2.4	-	-	-	-	43.2	1.4	-	-	-	-	44.5	3.0	-	-	-	-	46.0	3.4	-	-	-	-
1975	48.1	4.6	-	-	-	-	48.3	0.4	-	-	-	-	49.6	2.7	-	-	-	-	50.1	1.0	-	-	-	-
1976	51.2	2.2	-	-	-	-	52.2	2.0	-	-	-	-	53.1	1.7	-	-	-	-	54.3	2.3	-	-	-	-
1977	55.7	2.6	-	-	-	-	56.5	1.4	-	-	-	-	57.7	2.1	-	-	-	-	58.3	1.0	-	-	-	-
1978	60.0	2.9	-	-	-	-	61.2	2.0	-	-	61.9	1.1	-	-	62.8	1.5	-	-	63.3	0.8	-	-	63.7	0.6
1979	-	-	64.8	1.7	-	-	64.0	-1.2	-	-	65.1	1.7	-	-	66.1	1.5	-	-	68.6	3.8	-	-	70.7	3.1
1980	-	-	72.4	2.4	-	-	72.1	-0.4	-	-	72.1	0.0	-	-	72.9	1.1	-	-	73.8	1.2	-	-	75.1	1.8
1981	-	-	75.9	1.1	-	-	76.8	1.2	-	-	78.0	1.6	-	-	81.8	4.9	-	-	82.9	1.3	-	-	83.7	1.0
1982	-	-	86.1	2.9	-	-	87.3	1.4	-	-	88.5	1.4	-	-	91.5	3.4	-	-	92.3	0.9	-	-	93.7	1.5
1983	-	-	95.7	2.1	-	-	95.7	0.0	-	-	99.6	4.1	-	-	102.3	2.7	-	-	105.2	2.8	-	-	105.3	0.1
1984	-	-	107.8	2.4	-	-	108.0	0.2	-	-	110.2	2.0	-	-	111.5	1.2	-	-	113.4	1.7	-	-	113.3	-0.1
1985	-	-	115.5	1.9	-	-	116.0	0.4	-	-	116.7	0.6	-	-	118.1	1.2	-	-	120.3	1.9	-	-	121.1	0.7
1986	-	-	123.6	2.1	-	-	125.5	1.5	-	-	126.5	0.8	-	-	127.9	1.1	-	-	131.4	2.7	132.1	0.5	132.4	0.2
1987	-	-	-	-	-	-	-	-	-	-	132.8	0.3	-	-	-	-	-	-	-	-	-	-	136.0	2.4
1988	-	-	-	-	-	-	-	-	-	-	140.0	2.9	-	-	-	-	-	-	-	-	-	-	143.4	2.4
1989	-	-	-	-	-	-	-	-	-	-	147.8	3.1	-	-	-	-	-	-	-	-	-	-	151.8	2.7
1990	-	-	-	-	-	-	-	-	-	-	159.8	5.3	-	-	-	-	-	-	-	-	-	-	162.1	1.4
1991	-	-	-	-	-	-	-	-	-	-	170.1	4.9	-	-	-	-	-	-	-	-	-	-	172.5	1.4

[Continued]

Minneapolis-St. Paul, MN
Consumer Price Index - Urban Wage Earners
Base 1982-1984 = 100
Medical Care
[Continued]

For 1947-1993. Columns headed % show percentile change in the index from the previous period for which an index is available.

Year	Jan Index	%	Feb Index	%	Mar Index	%	Apr Index	%	May Index	%	Jun Index	%	Jul Index	%	Aug Index	%	Sep Index	%	Oct Index	%	Nov Index	%	Dec Index	%
1992	-	-	-	-	-	-	-	-	-	-	181.1	5.0	-	-	-	-	-	-	-	-	-	-	183.1	1.1
1993	-	-	-	-	-	-	-	-	-	-	191.2	4.4	-	-	-	-	-	-	-	-	-	-	-	-

Source: U.S. Department of Labor, Bureau of Labor Statistics, Division of Consumer Prices and Price Indexes. - indicates no data collected for period.

Minneapolis-St. Paul, MN

Consumer Price Index - All Urban Consumers
Base 1982-1984 = 100
Entertainment

For 1976-1993. Columns headed % show percentile change in the index from the previous period for which an index is available.

Year	Jan		Feb		Mar		Apr		May		Jun		Jul		Aug		Sep		Oct		Nov		Dec	
	Index	%	Index	%	Index	%	Index	%	Index	%	Index	%	Index	%	Index	%	Index	%	Index	%	Index	%	Index	%
1976	59.5	-	-	-	-	-	62.9	*5.7*	-	-	-	-	62.7	*-0.3*	-	-	-	-	62.4	*-0.5*	-	-	-	-
1977	63.1	*1.1*	-	-	-	-	64.7	*2.5*	-	-	-	-	63.7	*-1.5*	-	-	-	-	68.3	*7.2*	-	-	-	-
1978	69.4	*1.6*	-	-	-	-	70.1	*1.0*	-	-	70.1	*0.0*	-	-	70.3	*0.3*	-	-	73.5	*4.6*	-	-	74.2	*1.0*
1979	-	-	73.9	*-0.4*	-	-	74.1	*0.3*	-	-	76.1	*2.7*	-	-	78.0	*2.5*	-	-	74.2	*-4.9*	-	-	74.4	*0.3*
1980	-	-	75.9	*2.0*	-	-	76.9	*1.3*	-	-	78.1	*1.6*	-	-	85.7	*9.7*	-	-	86.3	*0.7*	-	-	88.4	*2.4*
1981	-	-	88.9	*0.6*	-	-	93.2	*4.8*	-	-	92.6	*-0.6*	-	-	95.1	*2.7*	-	-	95.3	*0.2*	-	-	95.3	*0.0*
1982	-	-	98.0	*2.8*	-	-	95.3	*-2.8*	-	-	98.2	*3.0*	-	-	99.3	*1.1*	-	-	96.3	*-3.0*	-	-	96.4	*0.1*
1983	-	-	97.0	*0.6*	-	-	99.4	*2.5*	-	-	98.8	*-0.6*	-	-	105.0	*6.3*	-	-	101.0	*-3.8*	-	-	101.2	*0.2*
1984	-	-	101.9	*0.7*	-	-	102.5	*0.6*	-	-	102.5	*0.0*	-	-	102.6	*0.1*	-	-	103.4	*0.8*	-	-	103.3	*-0.1*
1985	-	-	104.6	*1.3*	-	-	105.3	*0.7*	-	-	106.4	*1.0*	-	-	108.3	*1.8*	-	-	108.6	*0.3*	-	-	106.9	*-1.6*
1986	-	-	110.8	*3.6*	-	-	111.5	*0.6*	-	-	112.2	*0.6*	-	-	109.6	*-2.3*	-	-	114.6	*4.6*	114.5	*-0.1*	114.1	*-0.3*
1987	-	-	-	-	-	-	-	-	-	-	114.5	*0.4*	-	-	-	-	-	-	-	-	-	-	118.6	*3.6*
1988	-	-	-	-	-	-	-	-	-	-	131.9	*11.2*	-	-	-	-	-	-	-	-	-	-	135.5	*2.7*
1989	-	-	-	-	-	-	-	-	-	-	136.2	*0.5*	-	-	-	-	-	-	-	-	-	-	140.1	*2.9*
1990	-	-	-	-	-	-	-	-	-	-	139.7	*-0.3*	-	-	-	-	-	-	-	-	-	-	141.3	*1.1*
1991	-	-	-	-	-	-	-	-	-	-	140.4	*-0.6*	-	-	-	-	-	-	-	-	-	-	142.8	*1.7*
1992	-	-	-	-	-	-	-	-	-	-	145.0	*1.5*	-	-	-	-	-	-	-	-	-	-	146.3	*0.9*
1993	-	-	-	-	-	-	-	-	-	-	148.5	*1.5*	-	-	-	-	-	-	-	-	-	-	-	-

Source: U.S. Department of Labor, Bureau of Labor Statistics, Division of Consumer Prices and Price Indexes. - indicates no data collected for period.

Minneapolis-St. Paul, MN
Consumer Price Index - Urban Wage Earners
Base 1982-1984 = 100
Entertainment

For 1976-1993. Columns headed % show percentile change in the index from the previous period for which an index is available.

Year	Jan Index	%	Feb Index	%	Mar Index	%	Apr Index	%	May Index	%	Jun Index	%	Jul Index	%	Aug Index	%	Sep Index	%	Oct Index	%	Nov Index	%	Dec Index	%
1976	61.1	-	-	-	-	-	64.6	5.7	-	-	-	-	64.4	-0.3	-	-	-	-	64.1	-0.5	-	-	-	-
1977	64.8	1.1	-	-	-	-	66.5	2.6	-	-	-	-	65.4	-1.7	-	-	-	-	70.2	7.3	-	-	-	-
1978	71.3	1.6	-	-	-	-	72.1	1.1	-	-	69.9	-3.1	-	-	72.6	3.9	-	-	74.8	3.0	-	-	79.7	6.6
1979	-	-	78.8	-1.1	-	-	78.2	-0.8	-	-	82.2	5.1	-	-	82.8	0.7	-	-	84.4	1.9	-	-	83.9	-0.6
1980	-	-	84.7	1.0	-	-	86.9	2.6	-	-	91.0	4.7	-	-	90.6	-0.4	-	-	89.2	-1.5	-	-	90.6	1.6
1981	-	-	91.6	1.1	-	-	91.6	0.0	-	-	92.0	0.4	-	-	92.9	1.0	-	-	94.2	1.4	-	-	94.0	-0.2
1982	-	-	97.0	3.2	-	-	95.0	-2.1	-	-	97.0	2.1	-	-	97.8	0.8	-	-	96.2	-1.6	-	-	96.5	0.3
1983	-	-	97.3	0.8	-	-	100.3	3.1	-	-	99.7	-0.6	-	-	104.4	4.7	-	-	101.7	-2.6	-	-	101.7	0.0
1984	-	-	102.4	0.7	-	-	103.1	0.7	-	-	102.8	-0.3	-	-	102.8	0.0	-	-	103.5	0.7	-	-	103.3	-0.2
1985	-	-	104.8	1.5	-	-	105.3	0.5	-	-	106.6	1.2	-	-	108.5	1.8	-	-	108.8	0.3	-	-	107.7	-1.0
1986	-	-	111.1	3.2	-	-	111.6	0.5	-	-	112.4	0.7	-	-	110.3	-1.9	-	-	114.3	3.6	114.9	0.5	114.0	-0.8
1987	-	-	-	-	-	-	-	-	-	-	114.9	0.8	-	-	-	-	-	-	-	-	-	-	118.9	3.5
1988	-	-	-	-	-	-	-	-	-	-	131.6	10.7	-	-	-	-	-	-	-	-	-	-	135.3	2.8
1989	-	-	-	-	-	-	-	-	-	-	135.7	0.3	-	-	-	-	-	-	-	-	-	-	139.8	3.0
1990	-	-	-	-	-	-	-	-	-	-	139.4	-0.3	-	-	-	-	-	-	-	-	-	-	141.0	1.1
1991	-	-	-	-	-	-	-	-	-	-	139.8	-0.9	-	-	-	-	-	-	-	-	-	-	141.7	1.4
1992	-	-	-	-	-	-	-	-	-	-	144.0	1.6	-	-	-	-	-	-	-	-	-	-	145.3	0.9
1993	-	-	-	-	-	-	-	-	-	-	147.9	1.8	-	-	-	-	-	-	-	-	-	-	-	-

Source: U.S. Department of Labor, Bureau of Labor Statistics, Division of Consumer Prices and Price Indexes. - indicates no data collected for period.

Minneapolis-St. Paul, MN
Consumer Price Index - All Urban Consumers
Base 1982-1984 = 100
Other Goods and Services

For 1976-1993. Columns headed % show percentile change in the index from the previous period for which an index is available.

Year	Jan Index	%	Feb Index	%	Mar Index	%	Apr Index	%	May Index	%	Jun Index	%	Jul Index	%	Aug Index	%	Sep Index	%	Oct Index	%	Nov Index	%	Dec Index	%
1976	56.0	-	-	-	-	-	56.5	0.9	-	-	-	-	56.4	-0.2	-	-	-	-	57.5	2.0	-	-	-	-
1977	58.3	1.4	-	-	-	-	59.0	1.2	-	-	-	-	59.7	1.2	-	-	-	-	61.6	3.2	-	-	-	-
1978	62.9	2.1	-	-	-	-	63.9	1.6	-	-	64.1	0.3	-	-	65.4	2.0	-	-	66.9	2.3	-	-	67.3	0.6
1979	-	-	67.8	0.7	-	-	67.8	0.0	-	-	68.4	0.9	-	-	69.4	1.5	-	-	71.7	3.3	-	-	72.2	0.7
1980	-	-	73.5	1.8	-	-	74.0	0.7	-	-	74.4	0.5	-	-	75.4	1.3	-	-	77.6	2.9	-	-	79.0	1.8
1981	-	-	79.6	0.8	-	-	80.7	1.4	-	-	82.6	2.4	-	-	84.0	1.7	-	-	87.2	3.8	-	-	87.4	0.2
1982	-	-	89.1	1.9	-	-	90.1	1.1	-	-	90.1	0.0	-	-	90.7	0.7	-	-	95.8	5.6	-	-	97.0	1.3
1983	-	-	98.6	1.6	-	-	98.5	-0.1	-	-	99.3	0.8	-	-	100.4	1.1	-	-	104.6	4.2	-	-	104.9	0.3
1984	-	-	106.0	1.0	-	-	105.7	-0.3	-	-	106.4	0.7	-	-	107.7	1.2	-	-	110.6	2.7	-	-	110.4	-0.2
1985	-	-	112.0	1.4	-	-	112.2	0.2	-	-	112.7	0.4	-	-	115.2	2.2	-	-	118.6	3.0	-	-	118.1	-0.4
1986	-	-	119.6	1.3	-	-	119.8	0.2	-	-	119.8	0.0	-	-	120.8	0.8	-	-	123.2	2.0	123.4	0.2	123.6	0.2
1987	-	-	-	-	-	-	-	-	-	-	125.0	1.1	-	-	-	-	-	-	-	-	-	-	132.8	6.2
1988	-	-	-	-	-	-	-	-	-	-	135.0	1.7	-	-	-	-	-	-	-	-	-	-	139.5	3.3
1989	-	-	-	-	-	-	-	-	-	-	142.1	1.9	-	-	-	-	-	-	-	-	-	-	145.8	2.6
1990	-	-	-	-	-	-	-	-	-	-	150.1	2.9	-	-	-	-	-	-	-	-	-	-	156.0	3.9
1991	-	-	-	-	-	-	-	-	-	-	159.9	2.5	-	-	-	-	-	-	-	-	-	-	168.2	5.2
1992	-	-	-	-	-	-	-	-	-	-	169.1	0.5	-	-	-	-	-	-	-	-	-	-	174.4	3.1
1993	-	-	-	-	-	-	-	-	-	-	182.3	4.5	-	-	-	-	-	-	-	-	-	-	-	-

Source: U.S. Department of Labor, Bureau of Labor Statistics, Division of Consumer Prices and Price Indexes. - indicates no data collected for period.

Minneapolis-St. Paul, MN
Consumer Price Index - Urban Wage Earners
Base 1982-1984 = 100
Other Goods and Services

For 1976-1993. Columns headed % show percentile change in the index from the previous period for which an index is available.

Year	Jan Index	%	Feb Index	%	Mar Index	%	Apr Index	%	May Index	%	Jun Index	%	Jul Index	%	Aug Index	%	Sep Index	%	Oct Index	%	Nov Index	%	Dec Index	%
1976	57.7	-	-	-	-	-	58.1	0.7	-	-	-	-	58.1	0.0	-	-	-	-	59.2	1.9	-	-	-	-
1977	60.0	1.4	-	-	-	-	60.7	1.2	-	-	-	-	61.5	1.3	-	-	-	-	63.4	3.1	-	-	-	-
1978	64.8	2.2	-	-	-	-	65.8	1.5	-	-	66.3	0.8	-	-	66.9	0.9	-	-	68.2	1.9	-	-	68.8	0.9
1979	-	-	69.5	1.0	-	-	69.6	0.1	-	-	70.3	1.0	-	-	71.8	2.1	-	-	73.2	1.9	-	-	73.4	0.3
1980	-	-	74.5	1.5	-	-	75.5	1.3	-	-	76.0	0.7	-	-	76.7	0.9	-	-	78.3	2.1	-	-	80.0	2.2
1981	-	-	81.2	1.5	-	-	82.0	1.0	-	-	83.2	1.5	-	-	83.9	0.8	-	-	87.2	3.9	-	-	87.1	-0.1
1982	-	-	89.2	2.4	-	-	90.2	1.1	-	-	90.3	0.1	-	-	90.8	0.6	-	-	95.9	5.6	-	-	97.2	1.4
1983	-	-	99.1	2.0	-	-	99.0	-0.1	-	-	99.7	0.7	-	-	101.0	1.3	-	-	104.3	3.3	-	-	104.5	0.2
1984	-	-	105.8	1.2	-	-	105.5	-0.3	-	-	106.2	0.7	-	-	107.8	1.5	-	-	109.7	1.8	-	-	109.7	0.0
1985	-	-	111.6	1.7	-	-	111.7	0.1	-	-	112.3	0.5	-	-	115.4	2.8	-	-	118.2	2.4	-	-	117.7	-0.4
1986	-	-	119.4	1.4	-	-	119.5	0.1	-	-	119.6	0.1	-	-	120.8	1.0	-	-	122.7	1.6	122.9	0.2	123.1	0.2
1987	-	-	-	-	-	-	-	-	-	-	124.8	1.4	-	-	-	-	-	-	-	-	-	-	133.4	6.9
1988	-	-	-	-	-	-	-	-	-	-	135.9	1.9	-	-	-	-	-	-	-	-	-	-	140.3	3.2
1989	-	-	-	-	-	-	-	-	-	-	143.1	2.0	-	-	-	-	-	-	-	-	-	-	147.5	3.1
1990	-	-	-	-	-	-	-	-	-	-	151.2	2.5	-	-	-	-	-	-	-	-	-	-	157.3	4.0
1991	-	-	-	-	-	-	-	-	-	-	161.5	2.7	-	-	-	-	-	-	-	-	-	-	169.7	5.1
1992	-	-	-	-	-	-	-	-	-	-	170.5	0.5	-	-	-	-	-	-	-	-	-	-	175.5	2.9
1993	-	-	-	-	-	-	-	-	-	-	184.9	5.4	-	-	-	-	-	-	-	-	-	-	-	-

Source: U.S. Department of Labor, Bureau of Labor Statistics, Division of Consumer Prices and Price Indexes. - indicates no data collected for period.

New York, NY, NE NJ
Consumer Price Index - All Urban Consumers
Base 1982-1984 = 100
Annual Averages

For 1914-1993. Columns headed % show percentile change in the index from the previous period for which an index is available.

Year	All Items		Food & Beverage		Housing		Apparel & Upkeep		Trans-portation		Medical Care		Entertain-ment		Other Goods & Services	
	Index	%	Index	%	Index	%	Index	%	Index	%	Index	%	Index	%	Index	%
1914	-	-	-	-	-	-	-	-	-	-	-	-	-	-	-	-
1915	9.9	-	-	-	-	-	-	-	-	-	-	-	-	-	-	-
1916	10.6	7.1	-	-	-	-	-	-	-	-	-	-	-	-	-	-
1917	12.8	20.8	-	-	-	-	-	-	-	-	-	-	-	-	-	-
1918	15.1	18.0	-	-	-	-	-	-	-	-	-	-	-	-	-	-
1919	17.7	17.2	-	-	-	-	-	-	-	-	-	-	-	-	-	-
1920	20.2	14.1	-	-	-	-	-	-	-	-	-	-	-	-	-	-
1921	18.1	-10.4	-	-	-	-	-	-	-	-	-	-	-	-	-	-
1922	17.2	-5.0	-	-	-	-	-	-	-	-	-	-	-	-	-	-
1923	17.5	1.7	-	-	-	-	-	-	-	-	-	-	-	-	-	-
1924	17.5	0.0	-	-	-	-	-	-	-	-	-	-	-	-	-	-
1925	17.9	2.3	-	-	-	-	-	-	-	-	-	-	-	-	-	-
1926	18.1	1.1	-	-	-	-	-	-	-	-	-	-	-	-	-	-
1927	17.9	-1.1	-	-	-	-	-	-	-	-	-	-	-	-	-	-
1928	17.8	-0.6	-	-	-	-	-	-	-	-	-	-	-	-	-	-
1929	17.9	0.6	-	-	-	-	-	-	-	-	-	-	-	-	-	-
1930	17.4	-2.8	-	-	-	-	-	-	-	-	-	-	-	-	-	-
1931	16.1	-7.5	-	-	-	-	-	-	-	-	-	-	-	-	-	-
1932	14.7	-8.7	-	-	-	-	-	-	-	-	-	-	-	-	-	-
1933	13.9	-5.4	-	-	-	-	-	-	-	-	-	-	-	-	-	-
1934	14.3	2.9	-	-	-	-	-	-	-	-	-	-	-	-	-	-
1935	14.5	1.4	-	-	-	-	-	-	-	-	-	-	-	-	-	-
1936	14.5	0.0	-	-	-	-	-	-	-	-	-	-	-	-	-	-
1937	14.8	2.1	-	-	-	-	-	-	-	-	-	-	-	-	-	-
1938	14.6	-1.4	-	-	-	-	-	-	-	-	-	-	-	-	-	-
1939	14.5	-0.7	-	-	-	-	-	-	-	-	-	-	-	-	-	-
1940	14.7	1.4	-	-	-	-	-	-	-	-	-	-	-	-	-	-
1941	15.3	4.1	-	-	-	-	-	-	-	-	-	-	-	-	-	-
1942	16.7	9.2	-	-	-	-	-	-	-	-	-	-	-	-	-	-
1943	17.9	7.2	-	-	-	-	-	-	-	-	-	-	-	-	-	-
1944	18.4	2.8	-	-	-	-	-	-	-	-	-	-	-	-	-	-
1945	18.9	2.7	-	-	-	-	-	-	-	-	-	-	-	-	-	-
1946	20.7	9.5	-	-	-	-	-	-	-	-	-	-	-	-	-	-
1947	23.2	12.1	-	-	-	-	-	-	16.1	-	14.3	-	-	-	-	-
1948	24.7	6.5	-	-	-	-	-	-	18.8	16.8	15.7	9.8	-	-	-	-
1949	24.5	-0.8	-	-	-	-	-	-	21.5	14.4	16.0	1.9	-	-	-	-
1950	24.6	0.4	-	-	-	-	-	-	22.4	4.2	16.3	1.9	-	-	-	-
1951	26.5	7.7	-	-	-	-	-	-	23.5	4.9	17.0	4.3	-	-	-	-
1952	26.9	1.5	-	-	-	-	-	-	23.9	1.7	18.1	6.5	-	-	-	-
1953	27.1	0.7	-	-	-	-	44.9	-	24.5	2.5	18.6	2.8	-	-	-	-
1954	27.2	0.4	-	-	-	-	44.5	-0.9	24.9	1.6	19.0	2.2	-	-	-	-
1955	27.1	-0.4	-	-	-	-	43.9	-1.3	24.2	-2.8	19.3	1.6	-	-	-	-
1956	27.5	1.5	-	-	-	-	44.9	2.3	25.0	3.3	19.5	1.0	-	-	-	-
1957	28.4	3.3	-	-	-	-	45.7	1.8	25.9	3.6	19.8	1.5	-	-	-	-
1958	29.2	2.8	-	-	-	-	46.0	0.7	26.3	1.5	20.2	2.0	-	-	-	-

[Continued]

New York, NY, NE NJ
Consumer Price Index - All Urban Consumers
Base 1982-1984 = 100
Annual Averages
[Continued]

For 1914-1993. Columns headed % show percentile change in the index from the previous period for which an index is available.

Year	All Items		Food & Beverage		Housing		Apparel & Upkeep		Trans-portation		Medical Care		Entertain-ment		Other Goods & Services	
	Index	%	Index	%	Index	%	Index	%	Index	%	Index	%	Index	%	Index	%
1959	29.6	1.4	-	-	-	-	46.4	0.9	27.6	4.9	21.5	6.4	-	-	-	-
1960	30.2	2.0	-	-	-	-	47.3	1.9	27.7	0.4	22.2	3.3	-	-	-	-
1961	30.5	1.0	-	-	-	-	47.8	1.1	27.8	0.4	23.0	3.6	-	-	-	-
1962	30.9	1.3	-	-	-	-	48.3	1.0	28.0	0.7	23.5	2.2	-	-	-	-
1963	31.6	2.3	-	-	-	-	49.2	1.9	28.2	0.7	23.9	1.7	-	-	-	-
1964	32.1	1.6	-	-	-	-	50.0	1.6	28.3	0.4	24.4	2.1	-	-	-	-
1965	32.6	1.6	-	-	-	-	50.7	1.4	28.7	1.4	25.3	3.7	-	-	-	-
1966	33.7	3.4	-	-	-	-	51.9	2.4	29.8	3.8	26.6	5.1	-	-	-	-
1967	34.6	2.7	-	-	-	-	54.5	5.0	31.2	4.7	28.4	6.8	-	-	-	-
1968	36.1	4.3	-	-	-	-	57.6	5.7	32.0	2.6	30.3	6.7	-	-	-	-
1969	38.3	6.1	-	-	-	-	61.4	6.6	33.9	5.9	33.1	9.2	-	-	-	-
1970	41.2	7.6	-	-	-	-	64.1	4.4	38.1	12.4	35.6	7.6	-	-	-	-
1971	43.6	5.8	-	-	-	-	65.6	2.3	40.2	5.5	38.6	8.4	-	-	-	-
1972	45.5	4.4	-	-	-	-	67.0	2.1	41.5	3.2	39.8	3.1	-	-	-	-
1973	48.3	6.2	-	-	-	-	68.8	2.7	42.3	1.9	41.2	3.5	-	-	-	-
1974	53.5	10.8	-	-	-	-	74.2	7.8	45.6	7.8	45.6	10.7	-	-	-	-
1975	57.6	7.7	-	-	-	-	76.9	3.6	50.3	10.3	51.4	12.7	-	-	-	-
1976	61.0	5.9	62.7	-	59.9	-	78.9	2.6	57.5	14.3	56.8	10.5	64.5	-	58.6	-
1977	64.2	5.2	65.8	4.9	63.0	5.2	81.3	3.0	60.5	5.2	61.6	8.5	68.5	6.2	62.3	6.3
1978	67.8	5.6	71.4	8.5	66.3	5.2	85.1	4.7	62.6	3.5	65.4	6.2	72.3	5.5	65.1	4.5
1979	73.7	8.7	78.0	9.2	72.1	8.7	86.8	2.0	70.6	12.8	70.5	7.8	75.7	4.7	68.7	5.5
1980	82.1	11.4	85.1	9.1	80.8	12.1	92.7	6.8	82.5	16.9	77.3	9.6	81.5	7.7	74.1	7.9
1981	90.1	9.7	92.7	8.9	89.4	10.6	96.3	3.9	92.4	12.0	84.3	9.1	88.3	8.3	80.9	9.2
1982	95.3	5.8	97.3	5.0	95.0	6.3	97.3	1.0	95.9	3.8	91.8	8.9	95.5	8.2	89.7	10.9
1983	99.8	4.7	99.0	1.7	100.2	5.5	100.6	3.4	99.1	3.3	100.1	9.0	100.4	5.1	101.2	12.8
1984	104.8	5.0	103.7	4.7	104.8	4.6	102.0	1.4	105.0	6.0	108.1	8.0	104.0	3.6	109.0	7.7
1985	108.7	3.7	107.3	3.5	108.7	3.7	104.5	2.5	107.1	2.0	115.9	7.2	108.6	4.4	116.1	6.5
1986	112.3	3.3	112.2	4.6	112.8	3.8	104.2	-0.3	104.8	-2.1	125.6	8.4	115.1	6.0	123.6	6.5
1987	118.0	5.1	118.6	5.7	118.0	4.6	109.9	5.5	108.7	3.7	136.1	8.4	119.2	3.6	130.8	5.8
1988	123.7	4.8	124.8	5.2	125.1	6.0	107.4	-2.3	112.8	3.8	144.8	6.4	122.8	3.0	139.5	6.7
1989	130.6	5.6	132.1	5.8	131.8	5.4	114.0	6.1	116.5	3.3	155.8	7.6	129.5	5.5	151.9	8.9
1990	138.5	6.0	139.6	5.7	139.3	5.7	121.8	6.8	123.1	5.7	172.4	10.7	135.6	4.7	164.0	8.0
1991	144.8	4.5	144.3	3.4	145.7	4.6	124.5	2.2	127.9	3.9	186.6	8.2	140.8	3.8	177.2	8.0
1992	150.0	3.6	146.0	1.2	151.4	3.9	128.5	3.2	131.5	2.8	200.0	7.2	146.4	4.0	191.0	7.8
1993	154.5	3.0	149.0	2.1	155.5	2.7	129.3	0.6	137.7	4.7	209.1	4.6	149.8	2.3	200.1	4.8

Source: U.S. Department of Labor, Bureau of Labor Statistics, Division of Consumer Prices and Price Indexes. - indicates no data collected for period.

New York, NY, NE NJ
Consumer Price Index - Urban Wage Earners
Base 1982-1984 = 100
Annual Averages

For 1914-1993. Columns headed % show percentile change in the index from the previous period for which an index is available.

Year	All Items		Food & Beverage		Housing		Apparel & Upkeep		Trans- portation		Medical Care		Entertain- ment		Other Goods & Services	
	Index	%	Index	%	Index	%	Index	%	Index	%	Index	%	Index	%	Index	%
1914	-	-	-	-	-	-	-	-	-	-	-	-	-	-	-	-
1915	10.0	-	-	-	-	-	-	-	-	-	-	-	-	-	-	-
1916	10.8	8.0	-	-	-	-	-	-	-	-	-	-	-	-	-	-
1917	13.0	20.4	-	-	-	-	-	-	-	-	-	-	-	-	-	-
1918	15.3	17.7	-	-	-	-	-	-	-	-	-	-	-	-	-	-
1919	18.0	17.6	-	-	-	-	-	-	-	-	-	-	-	-	-	-
1920	20.5	13.9	-	-	-	-	-	-	-	-	-	-	-	-	-	-
1921	18.4	-10.2	-	-	-	-	-	-	-	-	-	-	-	-	-	-
1922	17.5	-4.9	-	-	-	-	-	-	-	-	-	-	-	-	-	-
1923	17.7	1.1	-	-	-	-	-	-	-	-	-	-	-	-	-	-
1924	17.7	0.0	-	-	-	-	-	-	-	-	-	-	-	-	-	-
1925	18.2	2.8	-	-	-	-	-	-	-	-	-	-	-	-	-	-
1926	18.4	1.1	-	-	-	-	-	-	-	-	-	-	-	-	-	-
1927	18.2	-1.1	-	-	-	-	-	-	-	-	-	-	-	-	-	-
1928	18.1	-0.5	-	-	-	-	-	-	-	-	-	-	-	-	-	-
1929	18.2	0.6	-	-	-	-	-	-	-	-	-	-	-	-	-	-
1930	17.7	-2.7	-	-	-	-	-	-	-	-	-	-	-	-	-	-
1931	16.4	-7.3	-	-	-	-	-	-	-	-	-	-	-	-	-	-
1932	14.9	-9.1	-	-	-	-	-	-	-	-	-	-	-	-	-	-
1933	14.1	-5.4	-	-	-	-	-	-	-	-	-	-	-	-	-	-
1934	14.5	2.8	-	-	-	-	-	-	-	-	-	-	-	-	-	-
1935	14.7	1.4	-	-	-	-	-	-	-	-	-	-	-	-	-	-
1936	14.7	0.0	-	-	-	-	-	-	-	-	-	-	-	-	-	-
1937	15.1	2.7	-	-	-	-	-	-	-	-	-	-	-	-	-	-
1938	14.8	-2.0	-	-	-	-	-	-	-	-	-	-	-	-	-	-
1939	14.7	-0.7	-	-	-	-	-	-	-	-	-	-	-	-	-	-
1940	14.9	1.4	-	-	-	-	-	-	-	-	-	-	-	-	-	-
1941	15.5	4.0	-	-	-	-	-	-	-	-	-	-	-	-	-	-
1942	17.0	9.7	-	-	-	-	-	-	-	-	-	-	-	-	-	-
1943	18.2	7.1	-	-	-	-	-	-	-	-	-	-	-	-	-	-
1944	18.7	2.7	-	-	-	-	-	-	-	-	-	-	-	-	-	-
1945	19.1	2.1	-	-	-	-	-	-	-	-	-	-	-	-	-	-
1946	21.0	9.9	-	-	-	-	-	-	-	-	-	-	-	-	-	-
1947	23.5	11.9	-	-	-	-	-	-	15.9	-	14.9	-	-	-	-	-
1948	25.1	6.8	-	-	-	-	-	-	18.6	17.0	16.3	9.4	-	-	-	-
1949	24.8	-1.2	-	-	-	-	-	-	21.3	14.5	16.7	2.5	-	-	-	-
1950	25.0	0.8	-	-	-	-	-	-	22.2	4.2	17.0	1.8	-	-	-	-
1951	26.9	7.6	-	-	-	-	-	-	23.3	5.0	17.7	4.1	-	-	-	-
1952	27.3	1.5	-	-	-	-	-	-	23.7	1.7	18.9	6.8	-	-	-	-
1953	27.5	0.7	-	-	-	-	44.8	-	24.2	2.1	19.4	2.6	-	-	-	-
1954	27.6	0.4	-	-	-	-	44.4	-0.9	24.6	1.7	19.8	2.1	-	-	-	-
1955	27.5	-0.4	-	-	-	-	43.8	-1.4	24.0	-2.4	20.1	1.5	-	-	-	-
1956	27.9	1.5	-	-	-	-	44.9	2.5	24.8	3.3	20.3	1.0	-	-	-	-
1957	28.8	3.2	-	-	-	-	45.6	1.6	25.7	3.6	20.6	1.5	-	-	-	-
1958	29.7	3.1	-	-	-	-	46.0	0.9	26.1	1.6	21.1	2.4	-	-	-	-

[Continued]

New York, NY, NE NJ
Consumer Price Index - Urban Wage Earners
Base 1982-1984 = 100
Annual Averages
[Continued]

For 1914-1993. Columns headed % show percentile change in the index from the previous period for which an index is available.

Year	All Items		Food & Beverage		Housing		Apparel & Upkeep		Trans- portation		Medical Care		Entertain- ment		Other Goods & Services	
	Index	%	Index	%	Index	%	Index	%	Index	%	Index	%	Index	%	Index	%
1959	30.1	1.3	-	-	-	-	46.3	0.7	27.3	4.6	22.4	6.2	-	-	-	-
1960	30.7	2.0	-	-	-	-	47.2	1.9	27.5	0.7	23.1	3.1	-	-	-	-
1961	30.9	0.7	-	-	-	-	47.7	1.1	27.5	0.0	24.0	3.9	-	-	-	-
1962	31.4	1.6	-	-	-	-	48.2	1.0	27.7	0.7	24.5	2.1	-	-	-	-
1963	32.1	2.2	-	-	-	-	49.2	2.1	27.9	0.7	25.0	2.0	-	-	-	-
1964	32.6	1.6	-	-	-	-	49.9	1.4	28.0	0.4	25.5	2.0	-	-	-	-
1965	33.1	1.5	-	-	-	-	50.6	1.4	28.4	1.4	26.4	3.5	-	-	-	-
1966	34.2	3.3	-	-	-	-	51.8	2.4	29.5	3.9	27.7	4.9	-	-	-	-
1967	35.1	2.6	-	-	-	-	54.4	5.0	30.9	4.7	29.6	6.9	-	-	-	-
1968	36.6	4.3	-	-	-	-	57.5	5.7	31.7	2.6	31.6	6.8	-	-	-	-
1969	38.9	6.3	-	-	-	-	61.3	6.6	33.6	6.0	34.5	9.2	-	-	-	-
1970	41.8	7.5	-	-	-	-	64.0	4.4	37.8	12.5	37.1	7.5	-	-	-	-
1971	44.2	5.7	-	-	-	-	65.5	2.3	39.8	5.3	40.2	8.4	-	-	-	-
1972	46.1	4.3	-	-	-	-	66.9	2.1	41.1	3.3	41.5	3.2	-	-	-	-
1973	49.1	6.5	-	-	-	-	68.7	2.7	41.9	1.9	43.0	3.6	-	-	-	-
1974	54.4	10.8	-	-	-	-	74.1	7.9	45.1	7.6	47.6	10.7	-	-	-	-
1975	58.5	7.5	-	-	-	-	76.7	3.5	49.8	10.4	53.6	12.6	-	-	-	-
1976	61.9	5.8	63.4	-	61.6	-	78.8	2.7	57.0	14.5	59.2	10.4	66.0	-	59.3	-
1977	65.2	5.3	66.5	4.9	64.8	5.2	81.2	3.0	59.9	5.1	64.3	8.6	70.0	6.1	63.0	6.2
1978	68.6	5.2	72.0	8.3	67.7	4.5	84.1	3.6	62.2	3.8	67.8	5.4	73.2	4.6	66.0	4.8
1979	74.7	8.9	78.7	9.3	73.6	8.7	87.3	3.8	70.3	13.0	72.5	6.9	76.7	4.8	69.6	5.5
1980	83.2	11.4	85.9	9.1	82.5	12.1	93.2	6.8	82.2	16.9	78.7	8.6	82.5	7.6	74.8	7.5
1981	91.3	9.7	92.9	8.1	91.4	10.8	96.0	3.0	92.3	12.3	86.2	9.5	89.4	8.4	80.9	8.2
1982	96.3	5.5	97.3	4.7	97.2	6.3	97.2	1.2	95.8	3.8	91.9	6.6	95.5	6.8	89.7	10.9
1983	100.1	3.9	99.1	1.8	100.9	3.8	100.6	3.5	98.9	3.2	99.9	8.7	100.5	5.2	101.6	13.3
1984	103.6	3.5	103.6	4.5	101.9	1.0	102.1	1.5	105.2	6.4	108.3	8.4	104.1	3.6	108.7	7.0
1985	107.9	4.2	107.0	3.3	107.3	5.3	104.4	2.3	107.2	1.9	116.2	7.3	108.3	4.0	115.4	6.2
1986	111.0	2.9	111.9	4.6	111.2	3.6	104.0	-0.4	104.2	-2.8	125.8	8.3	115.0	6.2	122.7	6.3
1987	116.6	5.0	118.2	5.6	116.0	4.3	110.2	6.0	108.4	4.0	136.8	8.7	120.3	4.6	129.5	5.5
1988	121.8	4.5	124.3	5.2	122.5	5.6	106.3	-3.5	112.4	3.7	145.8	6.6	123.9	3.0	137.9	6.5
1989	128.6	5.6	131.7	6.0	129.0	5.3	112.5	5.8	116.1	3.3	157.0	7.7	130.3	5.2	150.7	9.3
1990	136.3	6.0	139.4	5.8	135.9	5.3	120.1	6.8	123.1	6.0	172.0	9.6	136.2	4.5	163.6	8.6
1991	142.1	4.3	144.0	3.3	141.6	4.2	122.1	1.7	127.8	3.8	186.2	8.3	141.3	3.7	177.5	8.5
1992	146.9	3.4	145.6	1.1	146.7	3.6	125.8	3.0	131.6	3.0	200.3	7.6	146.6	3.8	191.0	7.6
1993	151.1	2.9	148.6	2.1	150.6	2.7	126.2	0.3	137.4	4.4	209.0	4.3	149.5	2.0	200.4	4.9

Source: U.S. Department of Labor, Bureau of Labor Statistics, Division of Consumer Prices and Price Indexes. - indicates no data collected for period.

New York, NY, NE NJ
Consumer Price Index - All Urban Consumers
Base 1982-1984 = 100
All Items

For 1914-1993. Columns headed % show percentile change in the index from the previous period for which an index is available.

Year	Jan Index	%	Feb Index	%	Mar Index	%	Apr Index	%	May Index	%	Jun Index	%	Jul Index	%	Aug Index	%	Sep Index	%	Oct Index	%	Nov Index	%	Dec Index	%
1914	-	-	-	-	-	-	-	-	-	-	-	-	-	-	-	-	-	-	-	-	-	-	9.9	-
1915	-	-	-	-	-	-	-	-	-	-	-	-	-	-	-	-	-	-	-	-	-	-	10.1	2.0
1916	-	-	-	-	-	-	-	-	-	-	-	-	-	-	-	-	-	-	-	-	-	-	11.3	11.9
1917	-	-	-	-	-	-	-	-	-	-	-	-	-	-	-	-	-	-	-	-	-	-	13.8	22.1
1918	-	-	-	-	-	-	-	-	-	-	-	-	-	-	-	-	-	-	-	-	-	-	16.8	21.7
1919	-	-	-	-	-	-	-	-	-	-	17.1	1.8	-	-	-	-	-	-	-	-	-	-	19.3	12.9
1920	-	-	-	-	-	-	-	-	-	-	20.9	8.3	-	-	-	-	-	-	-	-	-	-	19.5	-6.7
1921	-	-	-	-	-	-	-	-	17.9	-8.2	-	-	-	-	-	-	17.8	-0.6	-	-	-	-	17.9	0.6
1922	-	-	-	-	17.1	-4.5	-	-	-	-	17.2	0.6	-	-	-	-	17.1	-0.6	-	-	-	-	17.4	1.8
1923	-	-	-	-	17.3	-0.6	-	-	-	-	17.4	0.6	-	-	-	-	17.6	1.1	-	-	-	-	17.8	1.1
1924	-	-	-	-	17.4	-2.2	-	-	-	-	17.4	0.0	-	-	-	-	17.4	0.0	-	-	-	-	17.7	1.7
1925	-	-	-	-	-	-	-	-	-	-	17.7	0.0	-	-	-	-	-	-	-	-	-	-	18.5	4.5
1926	-	-	-	-	-	-	-	-	-	-	18.1	-2.2	-	-	-	-	-	-	-	-	-	-	18.1	0.0
1927	-	-	-	-	-	-	-	-	-	-	18.0	-0.6	-	-	-	-	-	-	-	-	-	-	18.1	0.6
1928	-	-	-	-	-	-	-	-	-	-	17.7	-2.2	-	-	-	-	-	-	-	-	-	-	17.8	0.6
1929	-	-	-	-	-	-	-	-	-	-	17.8	0.0	-	-	-	-	-	-	-	-	-	-	17.9	0.6
1930	-	-	-	-	-	-	-	-	-	-	17.4	-2.8	-	-	-	-	-	-	-	-	-	-	17.0	-2.3
1931	-	-	-	-	-	-	-	-	-	-	16.0	-5.9	-	-	-	-	-	-	-	-	-	-	15.4	-3.8
1932	-	-	-	-	-	-	-	-	-	-	14.7	-4.5	-	-	-	-	-	-	-	-	-	-	14.2	-3.4
1933	-	-	-	-	-	-	-	-	-	-	13.7	-3.5	-	-	-	-	-	-	-	-	-	-	14.0	2.2
1934	-	-	-	-	-	-	-	-	-	-	14.3	2.1	-	-	-	-	-	-	-	-	14.4	0.7	-	-
1935	-	-	-	-	14.4	0.0	-	-	-	-	-	-	14.3	-0.7	-	-	-	-	14.4	0.7	-	-	-	-
1936	14.6	1.4	-	-	-	-	14.4	-1.4	-	-	-	-	14.5	0.7	-	-	14.7	1.4	-	-	-	-	14.5	-1.4
1937	-	-	-	-	14.8	2.1	-	-	-	-	14.8	0.0	-	-	-	-	15.2	2.7	-	-	-	-	15.0	-1.3
1938	-	-	-	-	14.5	-3.3	-	-	-	-	14.5	0.0	-	-	-	-	14.6	0.7	-	-	-	-	14.6	0.0
1939	-	-	-	-	14.5	-0.7	-	-	-	-	14.3	-1.4	-	-	-	-	14.8	3.5	-	-	-	-	14.6	-1.4
1940	-	-	-	-	14.7	0.7	-	-	-	-	14.8	0.7	-	-	-	-	14.7	-0.7	14.6	-0.7	14.7	0.7	14.7	0.0
1941	14.7	0.0	14.8	0.7	14.8	0.0	14.9	0.7	15.0	0.7	15.2	1.3	15.3	0.7	15.4	0.7	15.6	1.3	15.7	0.6	15.8	0.6	15.8	0.0
1942	16.1	1.9	16.2	0.6	16.3	0.6	16.4	0.6	16.5	0.6	16.7	1.2	16.8	0.6	16.9	0.6	16.9	0.0	17.1	1.2	17.3	1.2	17.4	0.6
1943	17.5	0.6	17.5	0.0	17.8	1.7	17.9	0.6	18.1	1.1	18.1	0.0	18.1	0.0	17.9	-1.1	18.1	1.1	18.2	0.6	18.2	0.0	18.2	0.0
1944	18.2	0.0	18.1	-0.5	18.2	0.6	18.3	0.5	18.4	0.5	18.4	0.0	18.5	0.5	18.5	0.0	18.5	0.0	18.5	0.0	18.6	0.5	18.6	0.0
1945	18.6	0.0	18.6	0.0	18.5	-0.5	18.6	0.5	18.7	0.5	18.9	1.1	19.1	1.1	19.0	-0.5	18.9	-0.5	18.9	0.0	19.0	0.5	19.1	0.5
1946	19.2	0.5	19.2	0.0	19.3	0.5	19.5	1.0	19.6	0.5	19.8	1.0	21.0	6.1	21.3	1.4	21.8	2.3	22.3	2.3	22.5	0.9	22.7	0.9
1947	22.6	-0.4	22.5	-0.4	23.0	2.2	22.9	-0.4	22.7	-0.9	22.9	0.9	23.0	0.4	23.2	0.9	23.6	1.7	23.6	0.0	23.9	1.3	24.1	0.8
1948	24.4	1.2	24.3	-0.4	24.0	-1.2	24.4	1.7	24.5	0.4	24.7	0.8	25.2	2.0	25.3	0.4	25.3	0.0	25.1	-0.8	25.0	-0.4	24.7	-1.2
1949	24.7	0.0	24.3	-0.4	24.4	-1.2	24.5	0.4	24.6	0.4	24.5	-0.4	24.5	0.0	24.5	0.0	24.6	0.4	24.3	-1.2	24.3	0.0	24.2	-0.4
1950	24.0	-0.8	24.1	0.4	24.1	0.0	24.2	0.4	24.2	0.0	24.3	0.4	24.7	1.6	24.7	0.0	25.0	1.2	25.1	0.4	25.3	0.8	25.6	1.2
1951	25.9	1.2	26.3	1.5	26.3	0.0	26.3	0.0	26.5	0.8	26.3	-0.8	26.4	0.4	26.4	0.0	26.6	0.8	26.7	0.4	26.8	0.4	26.8	0.0
1952	26.8	0.0	26.7	-0.4	26.6	-0.4	26.7	0.4	26.7	0.0	27.0	0.7	27.1	0.4	27.2	0.4	27.3	0.4	27.3	0.0	27.2	-0.4	27.3	0.4
1953	26.9	-0.4	26.8	-0.4	26.8	0.0	26.8	0.0	26.8	0.0	27.2	0.0	27.3	0.4	27.3	0.0	27.2	-0.4	27.2	0.0	27.2	0.0	27.1	-0.4
1954	27.3	0.0	27.2	-0.4	27.1	-0.4	27.2	0.4	27.2	0.0	27.0	0.0	27.0	0.0	27.0	0.0	27.2	0.7	27.1	-0.4	27.2	0.4	27.0	-0.7
1955	27.1	0.0	27.2	0.4	27.1	-0.4	27.1	0.0	27.1	0.0	27.0	-0.4	27.3	0.7	27.4	0.4	27.6	0.7	27.6	0.0	27.8	0.7	27.9	0.4
1956	27.1	0.4	27.1	0.0	27.1	0.0	27.1	0.0	27.3	0.7	27.4	0.4	27.6	0.7	27.6	0.0	27.8	0.7	27.9	0.4	27.9	0.0	27.9	0.0
1957	27.9	0.0	28.0	0.4	28.0	0.0	28.2	0.7	28.3	0.4	28.4	0.4	28.6	0.7	28.6	0.0	28.5	-0.3	28.6	0.4	28.6	0.0	28.6	0.0
1958	29.0	1.4	29.0	0.0	29.2	0.7	29.2	0.0	29.2	0.0	29.2	0.0	29.2	0.0	29.2	0.0	29.3	0.3	29.3	0.0	29.4	0.3	29.3	-0.3

[Continued]

New York, NY, NE NJ
Consumer Price Index - All Urban Consumers
Base 1982-1984 = 100
All Items
[Continued]

For 1914-1993. Columns headed % show percentile change in the index from the previous period for which an index is available.

Year	Jan Index	%	Feb Index	%	Mar Index	%	Apr Index	%	May Index	%	Jun Index	%	Jul Index	%	Aug Index	%	Sep Index	%	Oct Index	%	Nov Index	%	Dec Index	%
1959	29.4	0.3	29.4	0.0	29.4	0.0	29.4	0.0	29.4	0.0	29.6	0.7	29.8	0.7	29.7	-0.3	29.8	0.3	29.9	0.3	30.0	0.3	30.0	0.0
1960	30.0	0.0	30.0	0.0	30.0	0.0	30.1	0.3	30.1	0.0	30.1	0.0	30.1	0.0	30.2	0.3	30.3	0.3	30.4	0.0	30.5	0.3	30.5	0.0
1961	30.4	-0.3	30.4	0.0	30.4	0.0	30.3	-0.3	30.3	0.0	30.3	0.0	30.5	0.7	30.5	0.0	30.6	0.3	30.6	0.0	30.6	0.0	30.6	0.0
1962	30.7	0.3	30.8	0.3	30.8	0.0	30.8	0.0	30.7	-0.3	30.8	0.3	30.9	0.3	31.0	0.3	31.2	0.6	31.2	0.0	31.1	-0.3	31.1	0.0
1963	31.2	0.3	31.3	0.3	31.3	0.0	31.4	0.3	31.3	-0.3	31.6	1.0	31.8	0.6	31.8	0.0	31.8	0.0	31.8	0.0	31.9	0.3	32.0	0.3
1964	31.9	-0.3	32.0	0.3	32.0	0.0	32.0	0.0	32.0	0.0	32.0	0.0	32.1	0.3	32.1	0.0	32.2	0.3	32.2	0.0	32.3	0.3	32.3	0.0
1965	32.2	-0.3	32.3	0.3	32.3	0.0	32.4	0.3	32.5	0.3	32.6	0.3	32.7	0.3	32.7	0.0	32.8	0.3	32.9	0.3	32.9	0.0	33.0	0.3
1966	33.0	0.0	33.2	0.6	33.4	0.6	33.5	0.3	33.5	0.0	33.5	0.0	33.8	0.9	33.9	0.3	34.1	0.6	34.2	0.3	34.2	0.0	34.2	0.0
1967	34.1	-0.3	34.3	0.6	34.3	0.0	34.3	0.0	34.4	0.3	34.5	0.3	34.6	0.3	34.7	0.3	34.8	0.3	34.9	0.3	35.0	0.3	35.1	0.3
1968	35.1	0.0	35.3	0.6	35.5	0.6	35.6	0.3	35.7	0.3	35.9	0.6	36.1	0.6	36.4	0.8	36.6	0.5	36.8	0.5	36.9	0.3	37.0	0.3
1969	37.2	0.5	37.3	0.3	37.7	1.1	37.9	0.5	38.0	0.3	38.3	0.8	38.4	0.3	38.5	0.3	38.8	0.8	39.0	0.5	39.1	0.3	39.5	1.0
1970	39.8	0.8	40.2	1.0	40.4	0.5	40.7	0.7	40.9	0.5	41.2	0.7	41.3	0.2	41.4	0.2	41.7	0.7	41.9	0.5	42.0	0.2	42.3	0.7
1971	42.4	0.2	42.7	0.7	43.0	0.7	43.1	0.2	43.3	0.5	43.6	0.7	43.9	0.7	43.9	0.0	44.0	0.2	44.1	0.2	44.1	0.0	44.3	0.5
1972	44.5	0.5	44.8	0.7	45.0	0.4	45.1	0.2	45.2	0.2	45.3	0.2	45.5	0.4	45.6	0.2	46.0	0.9	46.1	0.2	46.1	0.0	46.2	0.2
1973	46.3	0.2	46.7	0.9	47.2	1.1	47.6	0.8	47.8	0.4	48.1	0.6	48.2	0.2	49.0	1.7	49.2	0.4	49.5	0.6	50.0	1.0	50.5	1.0
1974	50.8	0.6	51.6	1.6	52.2	1.2	52.2	0.0	52.8	1.1	53.2	0.8	53.4	0.4	54.3	1.7	54.9	1.1	55.4	0.9	55.7	0.5	56.0	0.5
1975	56.0	0.0	56.5	0.9	56.5	0.0	56.6	0.2	56.8	0.4	57.1	0.5	57.6	0.9	57.9	0.5	58.6	1.2	58.8	0.3	59.3	0.9	59.6	0.5
1976	59.7	0.2	60.0	0.5	60.2	0.3	60.3	0.2	60.5	0.3	60.9	0.7	61.1	0.3	61.4	0.5	61.8	0.7	61.9	0.2	61.9	0.0	62.2	0.5
1977	62.4	0.3	63.0	1.0	63.3	0.5	63.5	0.3	63.9	0.6	64.4	0.8	64.5	0.2	64.8	0.5	64.8	0.0	64.9	0.2	65.2	0.5	65.3	0.2
1978	65.7	0.6	66.0	0.5	66.5	0.8	66.9	0.6	67.3	0.6	68.0	1.0	68.1	0.1	68.4	0.4	68.8	0.6	69.3	0.7	69.5	0.3	69.7	0.3
1979	70.2	0.7	71.0	1.1	71.4	0.6	72.1	1.0	72.8	1.0	73.5	1.0	74.0	0.7	74.5	0.7	75.4	1.2	76.1	0.9	76.6	0.7	77.1	0.7
1980	78.2	1.4	78.9	0.9	80.0	1.4	80.6	0.7	81.1	0.6	82.1	1.2	82.6	0.6	83.3	0.8	83.6	0.4	84.1	0.6	84.6	0.6	85.5	1.1
1981	86.3	0.9	87.4	1.3	87.8	0.5	88.3	0.6	88.8	0.6	89.5	0.8	90.8	1.5	91.6	0.9	93.0	1.5	92.7	-0.3	92.6	-0.1	92.7	0.1
1982	92.9	0.2	93.1	0.2	92.5	-0.6	92.8	0.3	93.7	1.0	95.7	2.1	95.9	0.2	96.3	0.4	97.1	0.8	98.4	1.3	98.1	-0.3	97.5	-0.6
1983	97.8	0.3	98.0	0.2	98.1	0.1	99.1	1.0	99.4	0.3	99.7	0.3	100.0	0.3	100.1	0.1	101.0	0.9	101.3	0.3	101.7	0.4	101.8	0.1
1984	102.8	1.0	103.4	0.6	103.7	0.3	104.1	0.4	104.1	0.0	104.3	0.2	104.8	0.5	105.5	0.7	106.2	0.7	106.1	-0.1	106.5	0.4	106.5	0.0
1985	106.7	0.2	107.3	0.6	107.5	0.2	107.9	0.4	108.1	0.2	108.3	0.2	108.4	0.1	109.2	0.7	109.6	0.4	109.8	0.2	110.7	0.8	111.0	0.3
1986	111.8	0.7	111.5	-0.3	111.5	0.0	111.2	-0.3	110.9	-0.3	111.7	0.7	112.5	0.7	112.7	0.2	113.0	0.3	113.4	0.4	113.3	-0.1	113.8	0.4
1987	114.7	0.8	115.3	0.5	115.8	0.4	116.6	0.7	117.3	0.6	117.8	0.4	117.9	0.1	118.9	0.8	119.8	0.8	120.2	0.3	120.5	0.2	120.6	0.1
1988	121.3	0.6	121.1	-0.2	121.5	0.3	122.6	0.9	122.7	0.1	123.1	0.3	123.6	0.4	124.2	0.5	126.0	1.4	126.2	0.2	125.9	-0.2	126.0	0.1
1989	127.0	0.8	127.6	0.5	128.9	1.0	129.5	0.5	130.2	0.5	130.5	0.2	130.6	0.1	130.9	0.2	132.2	1.0	132.8	0.5	133.2	0.3	133.3	0.1
1990	135.1	1.4	135.3	0.1	136.6	1.0	137.3	0.5	137.2	-0.1	137.1	-0.1	138.4	0.9	140.0	1.2	140.8	0.6	141.6	0.6	141.5	-0.1	141.6	0.1
1991	143.0	1.0	143.6	0.4	143.4	-0.1	143.7	0.2	144.0	0.2	144.6	0.4	145.2	0.4	145.4	0.1	145.8	0.3	145.7	-0.1	146.6	0.6	146.6	0.0
1992	147.3	0.5	148.0	0.5	149.1	0.7	149.2	0.1	148.9	-0.2	149.5	0.4	149.9	0.3	150.8	0.6	151.4	0.4	152.1	0.5	152.2	0.1	151.9	-0.2
1993	153.0	0.7	153.6	0.4	154.1	0.3	154.0	-0.1	153.8	-0.1	154.2	0.3	154.3	0.1	155.3	0.6	155.3	0.0	155.5	0.1	155.4	-0.1	155.6	0.1

Source: U.S. Department of Labor, Bureau of Labor Statistics, Division of Consumer Prices and Price Indexes. - indicates no data collected for period.

New York, NY, NE NJ
Consumer Price Index - Urban Wage Earners
Base 1982-1984 = 100
All Items

For 1914-1993. Columns headed % show percentile change in the index from the previous period for which an index is available.

Year	Jan Index	%	Feb Index	%	Mar Index	%	Apr Index	%	May Index	%	Jun Index	%	Jul Index	%	Aug Index	%	Sep Index	%	Oct Index	%	Nov Index	%	Dec Index	%
1914	-		-		-		-		-		-		-		-		-		-		-		10.1	-
1915	-		-		-		-		-		-		-		-		-		-		-		10.3	2.0
1916	-		-		-		-		-		-		-		-		-		-		-		11.5	11.7
1917	-		-		-		-		-		-		-		-		-		-		-		14.0	21.7
1918	-		-		-		-		-		-		-		-		-		-		-		17.1	22.1
1919	-		-		-		-		-		17.4	1.8	-		-		-		-		-		19.6	12.6
1920	-		-		-		-		-		21.2	8.2	-		-		-		-		-		19.8	-6.6
1921	-		-		-		-		18.2	-8.1	-		-		-		18.1	-0.5	-		-		18.2	0.6
1922	-		-		17.4	-4.4	-		-		17.4	0.0	-		-		17.4	0.0	-		-		17.7	1.7
1923	-		-		17.6	-0.6	-		-		17.7	0.6	-		-		17.9	1.1	-		-		18.1	1.1
1924	-		-		17.7	-2.2	-		-		17.7	0.0	-		-		17.7	0.0	-		-		18.0	1.7
1925	-		-		-		-		-		18.0	0.0	-		-		-		-		-		18.8	4.4
1926	-		-		-		-		-		18.4	-2.1	-		-		-		-		-		18.4	0.0
1927	-		-		-		-		-		18.3	-0.5	-		-		-		-		-		18.4	0.5
1928	-		-		-		-		-		18.0	-2.2	-		-		-		-		-		18.1	0.6
1929	-		-		-		-		-		18.1	0.0	-		-		-		-		-		18.2	0.6
1930	-		-		-		-		-		17.7	-2.7	-		-		-		-		-		17.2	-2.8
1931	-		-		-		-		-		16.2	-5.8	-		-		-		-		-		15.7	-3.1
1932	-		-		-		-		-		15.0	-4.5	-		-		-		-		-		14.4	-4.0
1933	-		-		-		-		-		13.9	-3.5	-		-		-		-		-		14.3	2.9
1934	-		-		-		-		-		14.5	1.4	-		-		-		-		14.6	0.7	-	
1935	-		-		14.6	0.0	-		-		-		14.5	-0.7	-		-		14.6	0.7	-		-	
1936	14.8	1.4	-		-		14.6	-1.4	-		-		14.7	0.7	-		14.9	1.4	-		-		14.7	-1.3
1937	-		-		15.0	2.0	-		-		15.0	0.0	-		-		15.4	2.7	-		-		15.2	-1.3
1938	-		-		14.8	-2.6	-		-		14.8	0.0	-		-		14.9	0.7	-		-		14.8	-0.7
1939	-		-		14.7	-0.7	-		-		14.5	-1.4	-		-		15.0	3.4	-		-		14.8	-1.3
1940	-		-		15.0	1.4	-		-		15.1	0.7	-		-		14.9	-1.3	14.8	-0.7	14.9	0.7	14.9	0.0
1941	15.0	0.7	15.0	0.0	15.0	0.0	15.1	0.7	15.2	0.7	15.5	2.0	15.5	0.0	15.6	0.6	15.8	1.3	16.0	1.3	16.1	0.6	16.1	0.0
1942	16.4	1.9	16.4	0.0	16.6	1.2	16.7	0.6	16.8	0.6	16.9	0.6	17.1	1.2	17.2	0.6	17.2	0.0	17.4	1.2	17.6	1.1	17.7	0.6
1943	17.7	0.0	17.8	0.6	18.1	1.7	18.2	0.6	18.4	1.1	18.4	0.0	18.3	-0.5	18.2	-0.5	18.4	1.1	18.4	0.0	18.5	0.5	18.5	0.0
1944	18.5	0.0	18.4	-0.5	18.5	0.5	18.6	0.5	18.6	0.0	18.6	0.0	18.8	1.1	18.8	0.0	18.8	0.0	18.8	0.0	18.9	0.5	18.9	0.0
1945	18.9	0.0	18.9	0.0	18.8	-0.5	18.9	0.5	19.0	0.5	19.2	1.1	19.4	1.0	19.2	-1.0	19.2	0.0	19.1	-0.5	19.3	1.0	19.4	0.5
1946	19.5	0.5	19.5	0.0	19.6	0.5	19.8	1.0	19.9	0.5	20.1	1.0	21.4	6.5	21.6	0.9	22.1	2.3	22.7	2.7	22.9	0.9	23.0	0.4
1947	22.9	-0.4	22.8	-0.4	23.3	2.2	23.3	0.0	23.0	-1.3	23.3	1.3	23.4	0.4	23.5	0.4	24.0	2.1	24.0	0.0	24.2	0.8	24.4	0.8
1948	24.8	1.6	24.7	-0.4	24.4	-1.2	24.8	1.6	24.9	0.4	25.1	0.8	25.6	2.0	25.7	0.4	25.7	0.0	25.5	-0.8	25.4	-0.4	25.1	-1.2
1949	25.1	0.0	24.8	-1.2	24.9	0.4	25.0	0.4	24.8	-0.8	24.8	0.0	24.9	0.4	24.8	-0.4	24.9	0.4	24.7	-0.8	24.7	0.0	24.6	-0.4
1950	24.4	-0.8	24.4	0.0	24.5	0.4	24.6	0.4	24.6	0.0	24.7	0.4	25.1	1.6	25.1	0.0	25.4	1.2	25.5	0.4	25.6	0.4	26.0	1.6
1951	26.3	1.2	26.7	1.5	26.7	0.0	26.7	0.0	26.9	0.7	26.7	-0.7	26.8	0.4	26.8	0.0	27.0	0.7	27.1	0.4	27.3	0.7	27.3	0.0
1952	27.3	0.0	27.1	-0.7	27.0	-0.4	27.1	0.4	27.1	0.0	27.1	0.0	27.5	1.5	27.5	0.0	27.5	0.0	27.5	0.0	27.6	-0.4	27.4	-0.7
1953	27.4	0.0	27.2	-0.7	27.3	0.4	27.2	-0.4	27.3	0.4	27.4	0.4	27.5	0.4	27.6	0.4	27.7	0.4	27.7	0.0	27.6	-0.4	27.5	-0.4
1954	27.7	0.0	27.6	-0.4	27.5	-0.4	27.6	0.4	27.6	0.0	27.6	0.0	27.7	0.4	27.7	0.0	27.6	-0.4	27.6	0.0	27.5	-0.4	27.4	-0.7
1955	27.5	0.0	27.6	0.4	27.5	-0.4	27.5	0.0	27.4	-0.4	27.4	0.0	27.4	0.0	27.4	0.0	27.6	0.7	27.5	-0.4	28.3	0.4	28.3	0.0
1956	27.5	0.4	27.5	0.0	27.5	0.0	27.5	0.0	27.7	0.7	27.9	0.7	28.1	0.7	28.0	-0.4	28.2	0.7	28.3	0.4	29.0	0.0	29.1	0.0
1957	28.3	0.0	28.4	0.4	28.4	0.0	28.6	0.7	28.7	0.3	28.9	0.7	29.0	0.3	29.1	0.3	29.0	-0.3	29.0	0.0	29.0	0.0	29.1	0.3
1958	29.4	1.0	29.5	0.3	29.7	0.7	29.7	0.0	29.7	0.0	29.6	-0.3	29.7	0.3	29.7	0.0	29.7	0.0	29.7	0.0	29.8	0.3	29.7	-0.3

[Continued]

New York, NY, NE NJ
Consumer Price Index - Urban Wage Earners
Base 1982-1984 = 100
All Items
[Continued]

For 1914-1993. Columns headed % show percentile change in the index from the previous period for which an index is available.

Year	Jan Index	%	Feb Index	%	Mar Index	%	Apr Index	%	May Index	%	Jun Index	%	Jul Index	%	Aug Index	%	Sep Index	%	Oct Index	%	Nov Index	%	Dec Index	%
1959	29.9	0.7	29.8	-0.3	29.8	0.0	29.9	0.3	29.9	0.0	30.0	0.3	30.2	0.7	30.1	-0.3	30.2	0.3	30.3	0.3	30.4	0.3	30.4	0.0
1960	30.4	0.0	30.5	0.3	30.5	0.0	30.6	0.3	30.6	0.0	30.6	0.0	30.6	0.0	30.7	0.3	30.7	0.0	30.9	0.7	31.0	0.3	30.9	-0.3
1961	30.9	0.0	30.9	0.0	30.9	0.0	30.8	-0.3	30.8	0.0	30.8	0.0	31.0	0.6	31.0	0.0	31.0	0.0	31.1	0.3	31.0	-0.3	31.1	0.3
1962	31.2	0.3	31.3	0.3	31.3	0.0	31.3	0.0	31.2	-0.3	31.2	0.0	31.4	0.6	31.5	0.3	31.7	0.6	31.6	-0.3	31.6	0.0	31.5	-0.3
1963	31.7	0.6	31.7	0.0	31.7	0.0	31.9	0.6	31.8	-0.3	32.1	0.9	32.2	0.3	32.2	0.0	32.2	0.0	32.3	0.3	32.4	0.3	32.5	0.3
1964	32.4	-0.3	32.5	0.3	32.5	0.0	32.5	0.0	32.5	0.0	32.5	0.0	32.6	0.3	32.6	0.0	32.7	0.3	32.7	0.0	32.8	0.3	32.8	0.0
1965	32.7	-0.3	32.8	0.3	32.8	0.0	32.9	0.3	33.0	0.3	33.1	0.3	33.2	0.3	33.2	0.0	33.3	0.3	33.4	0.3	33.4	0.0	33.5	0.3
1966	33.5	0.0	33.7	0.6	33.9	0.6	34.0	0.3	34.0	0.0	34.0	0.0	34.3	0.9	34.5	0.6	34.6	0.3	34.8	0.6	34.7	-0.3	34.7	0.0
1967	34.7	0.0	34.8	0.3	34.9	0.3	34.9	0.0	34.9	0.0	35.0	0.3	35.2	0.6	35.2	0.0	35.3	0.3	35.5	0.6	35.5	0.0	35.6	0.3
1968	35.7	0.3	35.9	0.6	36.0	0.3	36.1	0.3	36.3	0.6	36.5	0.6	36.7	0.5	36.9	0.5	37.2	0.8	37.3	0.3	37.4	0.3	37.5	0.3
1969	37.7	0.5	37.9	0.5	38.2	0.8	38.5	0.8	38.6	0.3	38.8	0.5	39.0	0.5	39.1	0.3	39.4	0.8	39.6	0.5	39.7	0.3	40.1	1.0
1970	40.4	0.7	40.8	1.0	41.1	0.7	41.3	0.5	41.5	0.5	41.8	0.7	41.9	0.2	42.1	0.5	42.3	0.5	42.6	0.7	42.7	0.2	43.0	0.7
1971	43.0	0.0	43.4	0.9	43.7	0.7	43.8	0.2	44.0	0.5	44.3	0.7	44.5	0.5	44.6	0.2	44.7	0.2	44.8	0.2	44.8	0.0	45.0	0.4
1972	45.2	0.4	45.5	0.7	45.7	0.4	45.8	0.2	45.9	0.2	46.0	0.2	46.1	0.2	46.3	0.4	46.7	0.9	46.8	0.2	46.8	0.0	47.0	0.4
1973	47.0	0.0	47.4	0.9	47.9	1.1	48.3	0.8	48.5	0.4	48.9	0.8	48.9	0.0	49.8	1.8	50.0	0.4	50.3	0.6	50.7	0.8	51.2	1.0
1974	51.6	0.8	52.4	1.6	53.0	1.1	53.0	0.0	53.6	1.1	54.0	0.7	54.3	0.6	55.1	1.5	55.8	1.3	56.3	0.9	56.5	0.4	56.8	0.5
1975	56.9	0.2	57.3	0.7	57.4	0.2	57.5	0.2	57.7	0.3	58.0	0.5	58.5	0.9	58.8	0.5	59.5	1.2	59.7	0.3	60.2	0.8	60.5	0.5
1976	60.7	0.3	60.9	0.3	61.1	0.3	61.2	0.2	61.4	0.3	61.8	0.7	62.1	0.5	62.4	0.5	62.7	0.5	62.9	0.3	62.9	0.0	63.1	0.3
1977	63.4	0.5	64.0	0.9	64.2	0.3	64.5	0.5	64.8	0.5	65.4	0.9	65.5	0.2	65.7	0.3	65.8	0.2	65.9	0.2	66.2	0.5	66.3	0.2
1978	66.7	0.6	67.0	0.4	67.4	0.6	67.7	0.4	68.0	0.4	68.7	1.0	68.8	0.1	69.1	0.4	69.4	0.4	70.0	0.9	70.2	0.3	70.6	0.6
1979	71.1	0.7	71.9	1.1	72.5	0.8	73.1	0.8	73.9	1.1	74.5	0.8	75.2	0.9	75.6	0.5	76.5	1.2	77.0	0.7	77.5	0.6	78.1	0.8
1980	79.2	1.4	80.0	1.0	81.1	1.4	81.6	0.6	82.2	0.7	83.1	1.1	83.7	0.7	84.5	1.0	84.8	0.4	85.2	0.5	85.8	0.7	86.8	1.2
1981	87.5	0.8	88.8	1.5	89.1	0.3	89.5	0.4	89.9	0.4	90.6	0.8	92.1	1.7	92.7	0.7	94.1	1.5	93.8	-0.3	93.7	-0.1	93.7	0.0
1982	94.0	0.3	94.1	0.1	93.4	-0.7	93.6	0.2	94.6	1.1	96.7	2.2	97.0	0.3	97.3	0.3	98.0	0.7	99.3	1.3	99.0	-0.3	98.4	-0.6
1983	98.6	0.2	98.2	-0.4	98.4	0.2	99.1	0.7	99.7	0.6	100.4	0.7	100.5	0.1	101.3	0.8	101.2	-0.1	101.4	0.2	100.9	-0.5	101.2	0.3
1984	101.9	0.7	102.0	0.1	101.8	-0.2	102.3	0.5	102.4	0.1	102.9	0.5	103.5	0.6	104.3	0.8	105.3	1.0	105.5	0.2	105.8	0.3	105.9	0.1
1985	106.1	0.2	106.6	0.5	106.8	0.2	107.2	0.4	107.4	0.2	107.6	0.2	107.6	0.0	108.4	0.7	108.6	0.2	108.8	0.2	109.8	0.9	110.1	0.3
1986	110.9	0.7	110.5	-0.4	110.5	0.0	110.0	-0.5	109.7	-0.3	110.4	0.6	111.2	0.7	111.4	0.2	111.5	0.1	111.9	0.4	111.9	0.0	112.4	0.4
1987	113.2	0.7	113.8	0.5	114.4	0.5	115.3	0.8	116.0	0.6	116.5	0.4	116.5	0.0	117.4	0.8	118.5	0.9	118.8	0.3	119.1	0.3	119.1	0.0
1988	119.6	0.4	119.3	-0.3	119.7	0.3	120.6	0.8	120.7	0.1	121.2	0.4	121.7	0.4	122.2	0.4	124.1	1.6	124.3	0.2	124.1	-0.2	124.1	0.0
1989	125.1	0.8	125.5	0.3	126.8	1.0	127.5	0.6	128.2	0.5	128.7	0.4	128.7	0.0	128.9	0.2	130.3	1.1	130.8	0.4	131.3	0.4	131.3	0.0
1990	133.0	1.3	133.1	0.1	134.5	1.1	135.0	0.4	134.9	-0.1	135.0	0.1	136.0	0.7	137.4	1.0	138.7	0.9	139.5	0.6	139.5	0.0	139.5	0.0
1991	140.3	0.6	140.6	0.2	140.5	-0.1	141.0	0.4	141.4	0.3	142.1	0.5	142.3	0.1	142.6	0.2	143.2	0.4	143.0	-0.1	144.0	0.7	143.9	-0.1
1992	144.4	0.3	144.8	0.3	145.8	0.7	145.9	0.1	145.8	-0.1	146.5	0.5	146.6	0.1	147.6	0.7	148.3	0.5	149.1	0.5	149.2	0.1	149.1	-0.1
1993	149.9	0.5	150.3	0.3	150.7	0.3	150.7	0.0	150.4	-0.2	150.7	0.2	150.7	0.0	151.7	0.7	151.8	0.1	152.1	0.2	152.0	-0.1	152.1	0.1

Source: U.S. Department of Labor, Bureau of Labor Statistics, Division of Consumer Prices and Price Indexes. - indicates no data collected for period.

New York, NY, NE NJ
Consumer Price Index - All Urban Consumers
Base 1982-1984 = 100
Food and Beverages

For 1976-1993. Columns headed % show percentile change in the index from the previous period for which an index is available.

Year	Jan Index	%	Feb Index	%	Mar Index	%	Apr Index	%	May Index	%	Jun Index	%	Jul Index	%	Aug Index	%	Sep Index	%	Oct Index	%	Nov Index	%	Dec Index	%
1976	62.5	-	62.3	-0.3	62.0	-0.5	62.1	0.2	62.4	0.5	62.8	0.6	63.2	0.6	63.2	0.0	63.0	-0.3	63.1	0.2	62.8	-0.5	63.2	0.6
1977	63.4	0.3	64.7	2.1	64.8	0.2	65.4	0.9	65.8	0.6	66.3	0.8	66.6	0.5	66.7	0.2	66.1	-0.9	66.2	0.2	66.8	0.9	66.8	0.0
1978	68.0	1.8	68.8	1.2	69.3	0.7	70.4	1.6	71.1	1.0	72.4	1.8	72.5	0.1	72.4	-0.1	72.4	0.0	72.8	0.6	73.3	0.7	73.6	0.4
1979	74.8	1.6	76.1	1.7	76.6	0.7	77.1	0.7	77.7	0.8	78.0	0.4	79.0	1.3	78.3	-0.9	78.9	0.8	79.5	0.8	79.6	0.1	80.3	0.9
1980	81.7	1.7	81.6	-0.1	82.6	1.2	83.3	0.8	83.6	0.4	84.2	0.7	85.1	1.1	86.6	1.8	87.3	0.8	87.6	0.3	88.4	0.9	88.7	0.3
1981	89.5	0.9	90.4	1.0	91.1	0.8	91.9	0.9	92.1	0.2	92.6	0.5	93.7	1.2	94.1	0.4	94.7	0.6	94.1	-0.6	93.8	-0.3	94.0	0.2
1982	96.0	2.1	96.8	0.8	96.9	0.1	97.0	0.1	97.3	0.3	98.6	1.3	98.3	-0.3	97.6	-0.7	97.9	0.3	97.9	0.0	96.8	-1.1	97.1	0.3
1983	97.5	0.4	98.1	0.6	98.5	0.4	98.7	0.2	98.8	0.1	98.9	0.1	98.9	0.0	99.0	0.1	99.9	0.9	99.8	-0.1	99.5	-0.3	100.3	0.8
1984	102.3	2.0	103.0	0.7	103.5	0.5	103.3	-0.2	102.9	-0.4	103.4	0.5	103.7	0.3	104.4	0.7	104.3	-0.1	104.4	0.1	104.1	-0.3	104.8	0.7
1985	105.8	1.0	106.5	0.7	106.8	0.3	107.0	0.2	106.8	-0.2	106.9	0.1	107.0	0.1	107.4	0.4	108.0	0.6	108.1	0.1	108.2	0.1	108.9	0.6
1986	110.1	1.1	109.9	-0.2	110.1	0.2	110.9	0.7	111.2	0.3	110.9	-0.3	112.8	1.7	113.6	0.7	113.5	-0.1	114.2	0.6	114.2	0.0	114.7	0.4
1987	116.3	1.4	116.5	0.2	116.8	0.3	117.2	0.3	117.8	0.5	119.2	1.2	118.9	-0.3	119.2	0.3	119.7	0.4	119.9	0.2	120.1	0.2	121.3	1.0
1988	122.5	1.0	122.7	0.2	122.5	-0.2	124.0	1.2	123.5	-0.4	124.5	0.8	125.5	0.8	126.3	0.6	126.8	0.4	126.2	-0.5	126.8	0.5	126.8	0.0
1989	129.2	1.9	130.2	0.8	130.6	0.3	131.2	0.5	132.2	0.8	132.6	0.3	133.0	0.3	133.3	0.2	133.1	-0.2	132.9	-0.2	133.4	0.4	133.7	0.2
1990	136.9	2.4	138.4	1.1	138.5	0.1	138.7	0.1	138.7	0.0	139.2	0.4	140.4	0.9	140.8	0.3	140.4	-0.3	141.1	0.5	141.1	0.0	141.2	0.1
1991	143.3	1.5	143.8	0.3	144.2	0.3	145.6	1.0	145.2	-0.3	146.1	0.6	144.6	-1.0	143.7	-0.6	143.9	0.1	143.5	-0.3	143.4	-0.1	144.1	0.5
1992	145.2	0.8	145.6	0.3	146.2	0.4	146.2	0.0	145.3	-0.6	145.8	0.3	144.9	-0.6	145.9	0.7	146.0	0.1	146.7	0.5	146.4	-0.2	147.2	0.5
1993	148.7	1.0	148.5	-0.1	148.8	0.2	149.3	0.3	149.3	0.0	147.9	-0.9	147.9	0.0	149.0	0.7	148.9	-0.1	149.1	0.1	149.9	0.5	151.0	0.7

Source: U.S. Department of Labor, Bureau of Labor Statistics, Division of Consumer Prices and Price Indexes. - indicates no data collected for period.

New York, NY, NE NJ
Consumer Price Index - Urban Wage Earners
Base 1982-1984 = 100
Food and Beverages

For 1976-1993. Columns headed % show percentile change in the index from the previous period for which an index is available.

Year	Jan Index	%	Feb Index	%	Mar Index	%	Apr Index	%	May Index	%	Jun Index	%	Jul Index	%	Aug Index	%	Sep Index	%	Oct Index	%	Nov Index	%	Dec Index	%
1976	63.2	-	63.0	-0.3	62.7	-0.5	62.8	0.2	63.1	0.5	63.5	0.6	63.9	0.6	63.9	0.0	63.7	-0.3	63.8	0.2	63.5	-0.5	63.9	0.6
1977	64.1	0.3	65.4	2.0	65.5	0.2	66.2	1.1	66.5	0.5	67.1	0.9	67.4	0.4	67.4	0.0	66.9	-0.7	66.9	0.0	67.6	1.0	67.5	-0.1
1978	68.5	1.5	69.3	1.2	70.0	1.0	70.7	1.0	71.7	1.4	73.0	1.8	72.9	-0.1	72.9	0.0	73.0	0.1	73.6	0.8	73.9	0.4	74.4	0.7
1979	75.7	1.7	77.2	2.0	77.8	0.8	78.2	0.5	78.5	0.4	78.7	0.3	79.8	1.4	79.0	-1.0	79.4	0.5	79.7	0.4	80.0	0.4	81.0	1.3
1980	82.5	1.9	82.8	0.4	83.3	0.6	84.0	0.8	84.4	0.5	85.2	0.9	85.9	0.8	87.1	1.4	87.9	0.9	88.6	0.8	89.2	0.7	89.6	0.4
1981	90.1	0.6	91.0	1.0	91.5	0.5	92.1	0.7	92.1	0.0	92.7	0.7	93.9	1.3	94.1	0.2	94.6	0.5	94.2	-0.4	94.0	-0.2	94.1	0.1
1982	96.1	2.1	96.8	0.7	96.9	0.1	96.9	0.0	97.3	0.4	98.4	1.1	98.1	-0.3	97.4	-0.7	97.7	0.3	97.5	-0.2	96.8	-0.7	97.2	0.4
1983	97.6	0.4	98.2	0.6	98.6	0.4	98.9	0.3	99.0	0.1	99.0	0.0	98.9	-0.1	99.0	0.1	100.0	1.0	99.9	-0.1	99.6	-0.3	100.5	0.9
1984	102.5	2.0	103.2	0.7	103.6	0.4	103.4	-0.2	102.9	-0.5	103.3	0.4	103.5	0.2	104.2	0.7	104.0	-0.2	104.2	0.2	104.0	-0.2	104.8	0.8
1985	105.8	1.0	106.3	0.5	106.7	0.4	106.7	0.0	106.6	-0.1	106.7	0.1	106.7	0.0	107.0	0.3	107.5	0.5	107.6	0.1	107.9	0.3	108.8	0.8
1986	110.0	1.1	109.7	-0.3	109.9	0.2	110.7	0.7	110.9	0.2	110.7	-0.2	112.5	1.6	113.2	0.6	113.2	0.0	113.9	0.6	113.9	0.0	114.5	0.5
1987	115.9	1.2	116.1	0.2	116.4	0.3	116.8	0.3	117.4	0.5	118.8	1.2	118.5	-0.3	118.8	0.3	119.2	0.3	119.5	0.3	119.6	0.1	120.8	1.0
1988	121.9	0.9	122.1	0.2	121.9	-0.2	123.4	1.2	123.0	-0.3	124.0	0.8	125.1	0.9	125.9	0.6	126.4	0.4	125.7	-0.6	126.2	0.4	126.3	0.1
1989	128.8	2.0	129.8	0.8	130.2	0.3	130.8	0.5	131.7	0.7	132.2	0.4	132.6	0.3	133.0	0.3	132.6	-0.3	132.5	-0.1	133.0	0.4	133.1	0.1
1990	136.6	2.6	138.2	1.2	138.2	0.0	138.4	0.1	138.4	0.0	139.0	0.4	140.2	0.9	140.6	0.3	140.2	-0.3	140.9	0.5	140.9	0.0	141.0	0.1
1991	143.1	1.5	143.6	0.3	143.9	0.2	145.3	1.0	144.9	-0.3	146.0	0.8	144.4	-1.1	143.5	-0.6	143.6	0.1	143.2	-0.3	143.0	-0.1	143.7	0.5
1992	144.8	0.8	145.3	0.3	145.9	0.4	145.9	0.0	144.8	-0.8	145.4	0.4	144.5	-0.6	145.5	0.7	145.6	0.1	146.3	0.5	146.1	-0.1	146.7	0.4
1993	148.3	1.1	147.9	-0.3	148.4	0.3	148.9	0.3	148.9	0.0	147.4	-1.0	147.4	0.0	148.5	0.7	148.5	0.0	148.6	0.1	149.4	0.5	150.4	0.7

Source: U.S. Department of Labor, Bureau of Labor Statistics, Division of Consumer Prices and Price Indexes. - indicates no data collected for period.

New York, NY, NE NJ
Consumer Price Index - All Urban Consumers
Base 1982-1984 = 100
Housing

For 1976-1993. Columns headed % show percentile change in the index from the previous period for which an index is available.

Year	Jan Index	%	Feb Index	%	Mar Index	%	Apr Index	%	May Index	%	Jun Index	%	Jul Index	%	Aug Index	%	Sep Index	%	Oct Index	%	Nov Index	%	Dec Index	%
1976	58.8	-	59.1	0.5	59.3	0.3	59.4	0.2	59.5	0.2	59.9	0.7	59.9	0.0	60.1	0.3	60.3	0.3	60.6	0.5	60.6	0.0	61.0	0.7
1977	61.6	1.0	61.8	0.3	62.2	0.6	62.4	0.3	62.6	0.3	63.2	1.0	63.2	0.0	63.4	0.3	63.7	0.5	63.8	0.2	63.9	0.2	64.1	0.3
1978	64.4	0.5	64.5	0.2	65.0	0.8	65.2	0.3	65.5	0.5	66.2	1.1	66.4	0.3	66.9	0.8	67.4	0.7	67.9	0.7	67.9	0.0	68.2	0.4
1979	68.7	0.7	69.2	0.7	69.4	0.3	70.1	1.0	70.9	1.1	71.8	1.3	72.2	0.6	73.0	1.1	74.1	1.5	74.7	0.8	75.4	0.9	75.9	0.7
1980	76.9	1.3	77.3	0.5	78.5	1.6	79.0	0.6	79.9	1.1	81.5	2.0	82.0	0.6	82.5	0.6	82.1	-0.5	82.5	0.5	83.1	0.7	84.7	1.9
1981	85.4	0.8	86.4	1.2	86.4	0.0	86.8	0.5	87.5	0.8	88.5	1.1	90.1	1.8	91.3	1.3	93.2	2.1	92.6	-0.6	92.3	-0.3	92.2	-0.1
1982	91.8	-0.4	91.4	-0.4	90.0	-1.5	90.8	0.9	92.7	2.1	95.9	3.5	96.0	0.1	96.7	0.7	97.3	0.6	100.0	2.8	99.7	-0.3	98.1	-1.6
1983	98.4	0.3	98.4	0.0	98.3	-0.1	99.7	1.4	100.0	0.3	100.4	0.4	100.8	0.4	100.4	-0.4	100.9	0.5	101.2	0.3	101.8	0.6	102.0	0.2
1984	102.7	0.7	103.5	0.8	103.3	-0.2	104.0	0.7	103.8	-0.2	104.1	0.3	104.9	0.8	105.5	0.6	106.4	0.9	105.8	-0.6	106.9	1.0	106.6	-0.3
1985	106.5	-0.1	107.1	0.6	106.9	-0.2	107.4	0.5	108.1	0.7	108.4	0.3	108.5	0.1	109.6	1.0	109.6	0.0	109.4	-0.2	111.2	1.6	111.5	0.3
1986	112.0	0.4	111.6	-0.4	112.2	0.5	112.0	-0.2	111.1	-0.8	112.7	1.4	113.7	0.9	113.9	0.2	113.7	-0.2	113.6	-0.1	113.1	-0.4	114.0	0.8
1987	115.2	1.1	115.6	0.3	115.4	-0.2	115.8	0.3	117.1	1.1	118.0	0.8	118.3	0.3	119.5	1.0	119.8	0.3	120.0	0.2	120.3	0.3	121.5	1.0
1988	123.2	1.4	122.8	-0.3	123.0	0.2	123.7	0.6	124.3	0.5	124.9	0.5	125.8	0.7	126.0	0.2	126.9	0.7	126.7	-0.2	126.9	0.2	127.1	0.2
1989	128.2	0.9	128.8	0.5	129.6	0.6	130.2	0.5	131.1	0.7	132.2	0.8	132.7	0.4	132.7	0.0	133.0	0.2	133.7	0.5	134.5	0.6	135.3	0.6
1990	136.3	0.7	135.8	-0.4	137.5	1.3	138.2	0.5	138.3	0.1	138.3	0.0	140.3	1.4	142.1	1.3	141.4	-0.5	141.2	-0.1	140.8	-0.3	141.1	0.2
1991	143.6	1.8	144.8	0.8	144.4	-0.3	144.2	-0.1	144.4	0.1	145.5	0.8	147.4	1.3	147.3	-0.1	146.6	-0.5	145.7	-0.6	147.2	1.0	147.4	0.1
1992	148.3	0.6	149.4	0.7	150.9	1.0	150.8	-0.1	150.2	-0.4	151.6	0.9	152.4	0.5	152.9	0.3	152.6	-0.2	152.6	0.0	152.6	0.0	152.2	-0.3
1993	153.5	0.9	153.8	0.2	154.7	0.6	154.6	-0.1	154.7	0.1	156.5	1.2	156.7	0.1	157.2	0.3	156.4	-0.5	156.2	-0.1	155.6	-0.4	156.3	0.4

Source: U.S. Department of Labor, Bureau of Labor Statistics, Division of Consumer Prices and Price Indexes. - indicates no data collected for period.

New York, NY, NE NJ
Consumer Price Index - Urban Wage Earners
Base 1982-1984 = 100
Housing

For 1976-1993. Columns headed % show percentile change in the index from the previous period for which an index is available.

Year	Jan Index	%	Feb Index	%	Mar Index	%	Apr Index	%	May Index	%	Jun Index	%	Jul Index	%	Aug Index	%	Sep Index	%	Oct Index	%	Nov Index	%	Dec Index	%
1976	60.6	-	60.9	0.5	61.0	0.2	61.1	0.2	61.2	0.2	61.7	0.8	61.7	0.0	61.8	0.2	62.1	0.5	62.4	0.5	62.4	0.0	62.8	0.6
1977	63.3	0.8	63.6	0.5	64.0	0.6	64.2	0.3	64.4	0.3	65.1	1.1	65.0	-0.2	65.3	0.5	65.5	0.3	65.6	0.2	65.7	0.2	66.0	0.5
1978	66.3	0.5	66.4	0.2	66.7	0.5	66.8	0.1	66.8	0.0	67.5	1.0	67.8	0.4	68.1	0.4	68.5	0.6	69.0	0.7	69.1	0.1	69.5	0.6
1979	70.0	0.7	70.5	0.7	70.8	0.4	71.4	0.8	72.4	1.4	73.3	1.2	73.7	0.5	74.4	0.9	75.6	1.6	76.4	1.1	77.0	0.8	77.5	0.6
1980	78.5	1.3	79.0	0.6	79.9	1.1	80.6	0.9	81.4	1.0	83.2	2.2	83.7	0.6	84.3	0.7	83.6	-0.8	84.0	0.5	84.7	0.8	86.6	2.2
1981	87.2	0.7	88.5	1.5	88.4	-0.1	88.5	0.1	89.2	0.8	90.4	1.3	92.2	2.0	93.3	1.2	95.4	2.3	94.8	-0.6	94.5	-0.3	94.3	-0.2
1982	93.9	-0.4	93.4	-0.5	91.6	-1.9	92.5	1.0	94.6	2.3	98.1	3.7	98.3	0.2	99.0	0.7	99.6	0.6	102.5	2.9	102.3	-0.2	100.5	-1.8
1983	100.6	0.1	99.1	-1.5	99.5	0.4	99.9	0.4	100.7	0.8	102.3	1.6	102.0	-0.3	103.3	1.3	101.5	-1.7	101.6	0.1	100.0	-1.6	100.5	0.5
1984	100.2	-0.3	99.8	-0.4	98.4	-1.4	99.5	1.1	99.6	0.1	100.6	1.0	101.8	1.2	102.8	1.0	104.7	1.8	104.8	0.1	105.4	0.6	105.3	-0.1
1985	105.2	-0.1	105.9	0.7	105.6	-0.3	106.1	0.5	106.7	0.6	107.1	0.4	107.0	-0.1	108.1	1.0	108.0	-0.1	108.0	0.0	109.7	1.6	110.2	0.5
1986	110.6	0.4	110.1	-0.5	110.8	0.6	110.4	-0.4	109.4	-0.9	111.1	1.6	112.0	0.8	112.2	0.2	112.0	-0.2	111.8	-0.2	111.3	-0.4	112.1	0.7
1987	113.1	0.9	113.5	0.4	113.3	-0.2	113.9	0.5	115.2	1.1	116.1	0.8	116.3	0.2	117.4	0.9	117.7	0.3	117.9	0.2	118.2	0.3	119.3	0.9
1988	120.6	1.1	120.2	-0.3	120.4	0.2	120.8	0.3	121.4	0.5	122.5	0.9	123.3	0.7	123.4	0.1	124.2	0.6	123.9	-0.2	124.3	0.3	124.5	0.2
1989	125.5	0.8	125.9	0.3	126.4	0.4	127.4	0.8	128.1	0.5	129.4	1.0	129.9	0.4	129.9	0.0	130.4	0.4	130.9	0.4	131.9	0.8	132.7	0.6
1990	133.3	0.5	132.8	-0.4	134.5	1.3	135.0	0.4	135.1	0.1	135.2	0.1	136.6	1.0	138.0	1.0	137.9	-0.1	137.8	-0.1	137.4	-0.3	137.6	0.1
1991	139.4	1.3	140.2	0.6	139.9	-0.2	140.1	0.1	140.7	0.4	141.7	0.7	143.1	1.0	142.9	-0.1	142.6	-0.2	141.8	-0.6	143.4	1.1	143.5	0.1
1992	144.0	0.3	144.8	0.6	146.0	0.8	146.1	0.1	145.8	-0.2	147.0	0.8	147.5	0.3	147.9	0.3	147.7	-0.1	147.9	0.1	148.1	0.1	148.0	-0.1
1993	149.0	0.7	149.1	0.1	149.8	0.5	149.9	0.1	149.9	0.0	151.6	1.1	151.7	0.1	152.0	0.2	151.4	-0.4	151.1	-0.2	150.6	-0.3	151.4	0.5

Source: U.S. Department of Labor, Bureau of Labor Statistics, Division of Consumer Prices and Price Indexes. - indicates no data collected for period.

New York, NY, NE NJ
Consumer Price Index - All Urban Consumers
Base 1982-1984 = 100
Apparel and Upkeep

For 1952-1993. Columns headed % show percentile change in the index from the previous period for which an index is available.

Year	Jan Index	%	Feb Index	%	Mar Index	%	Apr Index	%	May Index	%	Jun Index	%	Jul Index	%	Aug Index	%	Sep Index	%	Oct Index	%	Nov Index	%	Dec Index	%
1952	-	-	-	-	-	-	-	-	-	-	-	-	-	-	-	-	-	-	-	-	-	-	45.1	-
1953	45.0	-0.2	44.9	-0.2	45.0	0.2	44.7	-0.7	44.8	0.2	44.7	-0.2	44.6	-0.2	44.5	-0.2	45.1	1.3	45.1	0.0	45.1	0.0	45.0	-0.2
1954	44.8	-0.4	44.7	-0.2	44.6	-0.2	44.4	-0.4	44.4	0.0	44.4	0.0	44.2	-0.5	44.2	0.0	44.6	0.9	44.5	-0.2	44.6	0.2	44.3	-0.7
1955	43.8	-1.1	43.7	-0.2	43.7	0.0	43.5	-0.5	43.6	0.2	43.5	-0.2	43.3	-0.5	43.5	0.5	44.5	2.3	44.5	0.0	44.6	0.2	44.6	0.0
1956	44.2	-0.9	44.5	0.7	44.5	0.0	44.6	0.2	44.5	-0.2	44.7	0.4	44.8	0.2	44.8	0.0	45.6	1.8	45.8	0.4	45.7	-0.2	45.7	0.0
1957	45.5	-0.4	45.2	-0.7	45.7	1.1	45.4	-0.7	45.6	0.4	45.7	0.2	45.6	-0.2	45.7	0.2	46.0	0.7	46.1	0.2	46.2	0.2	46.1	-0.2
1958	46.2	0.2	46.2	0.0	46.2	0.0	45.9	-0.6	45.8	-0.2	45.8	0.0	45.8	0.0	46.0	0.4	46.3	0.7	46.1	-0.4	46.3	0.4	46.2	-0.2
1959	46.0	-0.4	46.0	0.0	46.1	0.2	46.0	-0.2	46.0	0.0	46.1	0.2	46.3	0.4	46.5	0.4	46.6	0.2	46.7	0.2	46.9	0.4	46.9	0.0
1960	46.6	-0.6	46.8	0.4	47.1	0.6	47.2	0.2	47.1	-0.2	47.1	0.0	47.0	-0.2	47.1	0.2	47.7	1.3	48.0	0.6	47.9	-0.2	48.0	0.2
1961	47.6	-0.8	47.6	0.0	47.5	-0.2	47.4	-0.2	47.3	-0.2	47.3	0.0	47.4	0.2	47.7	0.6	48.2	1.0	48.4	0.4	48.4	0.0	48.3	-0.2
1962	47.8	-1.0	47.8	0.0	48.0	0.4	47.9	-0.2	47.7	-0.4	47.9	0.4	48.0	0.2	47.8	-0.4	48.9	2.3	49.1	0.4	49.0	-0.2	48.9	-0.2
1963	48.8	-0.2	48.7	-0.2	48.7	0.0	48.8	0.2	48.5	-0.6	49.0	1.0	49.2	0.4	49.2	0.0	50.0	1.6	50.1	0.2	50.1	0.0	50.2	0.2
1964	49.2	-2.0	49.6	0.8	49.9	0.6	49.8	-0.2	50.0	0.4	49.9	-0.2	49.8	-0.2	49.6	-0.4	50.6	2.0	50.4	-0.4	50.4	0.0	50.6	0.4
1965	49.4	-2.4	50.1	1.4	50.2	0.2	50.2	0.0	50.4	0.4	50.6	0.4	50.0	-1.2	50.6	1.2	51.7	2.2	51.8	0.2	51.6	-0.4	51.4	-0.4
1966	50.3	-2.1	50.8	1.0	51.3	1.0	51.4	0.2	51.7	0.6	51.5	-0.4	51.4	-0.2	51.0	-0.8	53.0	3.9	53.4	0.8	53.3	-0.2	53.4	0.2
1967	52.4	-1.9	53.3	1.7	54.1	1.5	53.9	-0.4	54.3	0.7	54.3	0.0	54.3	0.0	54.1	-0.4	55.5	2.6	55.8	0.5	55.8	0.0	55.8	0.0
1968	54.7	-2.0	55.6	1.6	56.3	1.3	56.5	0.4	57.0	0.9	57.3	0.5	56.9	-0.7	57.5	1.1	59.4	3.3	59.6	0.3	59.9	0.5	60.0	0.2
1969	58.9	-1.8	59.4	0.8	60.8	2.4	60.8	0.0	61.2	0.7	61.3	0.2	61.1	-0.3	60.8	-0.5	62.9	3.5	63.1	0.3	63.2	0.2	63.0	-0.3
1970	61.6	-2.2	63.0	2.3	63.3	0.5	63.1	-0.3	63.5	0.6	63.8	0.5	63.0	-1.3	63.6	1.0	65.9	3.6	65.9	0.0	65.9	0.0	66.0	0.2
1971	64.2	-2.7	65.0	1.2	65.5	0.8	65.0	-0.8	65.7	1.1	65.5	-0.3	64.8	-1.1	64.8	0.0	67.0	3.4	66.9	-0.1	66.7	-0.3	66.7	0.0
1972	65.0	-2.5	66.5	2.3	67.5	1.5	67.3	-0.3	67.3	0.0	66.2	-1.6	65.5	-1.1	65.4	-0.2	68.5	4.7	68.5	0.0	68.4	-0.1	68.3	-0.1
1973	65.1	-4.7	66.3	1.8	68.4	3.2	68.5	0.1	69.0	0.7	68.6	-0.6	67.5	-1.6	68.6	1.6	70.4	2.6	70.7	0.4	71.1	0.6	71.0	-0.1
1974	68.5	-3.5	70.8	3.4	72.9	3.0	72.2	-1.0	73.3	1.5	73.3	0.0	72.3	-1.4	76.1	5.3	77.6	2.0	77.9	0.4	78.2	0.4	76.9	-1.7
1975	75.1	-2.3	77.0	2.5	77.0	0.0	76.2	-1.0	76.6	0.5	75.3	-1.7	75.1	-0.3	77.4	3.1	78.3	1.2	78.3	0.0	78.4	0.1	77.6	-1.0
1976	76.2	-1.8	77.6	1.8	77.7	0.1	77.8	0.1	77.9	0.1	77.4	-0.6	77.4	0.0	80.1	3.5	81.7	2.0	80.9	-1.0	81.3	0.5	81.3	0.0
1977	79.3	-2.5	79.4	0.1	79.5	0.1	79.4	-0.1	79.9	0.6	81.0	1.4	80.8	-0.2	82.7	2.4	83.3	0.7	83.0	-0.4	83.9	1.1	83.6	-0.4
1978	81.8	-2.2	82.2	0.5	83.7	1.8	85.6	2.3	86.2	0.7	86.5	0.3	84.0	-2.9	84.8	1.0	86.2	1.7	87.0	0.9	86.9	-0.1	86.5	-0.5
1979	83.6	-3.4	85.0	1.7	86.7	2.0	86.6	-0.1	87.5	1.0	85.9	-1.8	84.2	-2.0	86.2	2.4	88.4	2.6	88.9	0.6	88.8	-0.1	89.8	1.1
1980	88.5	-1.4	90.3	2.0	92.1	2.0	92.6	0.5	92.4	-0.2	92.3	-0.1	91.2	-1.2	91.9	0.8	94.1	2.4	95.8	1.8	95.8	0.0	95.3	-0.5
1981	93.3	-2.1	95.7	2.6	96.2	0.5	96.6	0.4	96.4	-0.2	95.9	-0.5	95.5	-0.4	96.9	1.5	98.4	1.5	97.1	-1.3	97.1	0.0	96.3	-0.8
1982	94.0	-2.4	96.5	2.7	97.7	1.2	97.5	-0.2	97.0	-0.5	97.2	0.2	97.1	-0.1	97.9	0.8	99.1	1.2	99.0	-0.1	98.2	-0.8	97.3	-0.9
1983	96.7	-0.6	97.9	1.2	99.6	1.7	100.2	0.6	101.9	1.7	100.9	-1.0	100.0	-0.9	100.9	0.9	102.9	2.0	103.2	0.3	102.3	-0.9	100.6	-1.7
1984	99.4	-1.2	99.0	-0.4	101.2	2.2	101.0	-0.2	101.9	0.9	100.3	-1.6	99.4	-0.9	103.9	4.5	104.9	1.0	105.5	0.6	105.0	-0.5	102.9	-2.0
1985	101.2	-1.7	102.8	1.6	104.5	1.7	104.6	0.1	103.6	-1.0	103.9	-0.6	102.4	-1.4	100.9	-1.5	104.3	3.4	107.2	2.8	106.3	-0.8	105.2	-0.4
1986	103.4	-1.8	102.7	-0.7	103.8	1.1	104.5	0.7	103.9	-0.6	102.4	-1.4	100.9	-1.5	104.3	3.4	107.2	2.8	106.3	-0.8	105.6	-0.7	105.2	-0.4
1987	102.7	-2.4	105.7	2.9	110.4	4.4	112.9	2.3	112.0	-0.8	108.0	-3.6	105.0	-2.8	108.8	3.6	115.2	5.9	115.6	0.3	115.4	-0.2	106.9	-7.4
1988	102.0	-4.6	100.2	-1.8	105.0	4.8	108.9	3.7	106.9	-1.8	103.6	-3.1	100.3	-3.2	102.4	2.1	116.2	13.5	119.9	3.2	112.7	-6.0	111.0	-1.5
1989	107.3	-3.3	108.1	0.7	117.4	8.6	117.0	-0.3	114.5	-2.1	110.7	-3.3	106.7	-3.6	108.7	1.9	120.8	11.1	121.7	0.7	119.8	-1.6	114.7	-4.3
1990	116.9	1.9	116.2	-0.6	122.6	5.5	126.0	2.8	122.1	-3.1	117.7	-3.6	115.1	-2.2	121.2	5.3	126.9	4.7	128.0	0.9	126.1	-1.5	122.9	-2.5
1991	121.0	-1.5	121.9	0.7	123.4	1.2	123.5	0.1	124.0	0.4	122.8	-1.0	120.6	-1.8	123.7	2.6	127.3	2.9	129.5	1.7	130.6	0.8	125.8	-3.7
1992	123.7	-1.7	123.4	-0.2	127.0	2.9	127.1	0.1	127.3	0.2	124.6	-2.1	124.5	-0.1	128.8	3.5	136.1	5.7	135.6	-0.4	134.1	-1.1	129.7	-3.3
1993	126.8	-2.2	133.8	5.5	134.2	0.3	131.7	-1.9	126.8	-3.7	124.6	-1.7	123.4	-1.0	128.5	4.1	132.4	3.0	133.0	0.5	131.4	-1.2	125.3	-4.6

Source: U.S. Department of Labor, Bureau of Labor Statistics, Division of Consumer Prices and Price Indexes. - indicates no data collected for period.

New York, NY, NE NJ
Consumer Price Index - Urban Wage Earners
Base 1982-1984 = 100
Apparel and Upkeep

For 1952-1993. Columns headed % show percentile change in the index from the previous period for which an index is available.

Year	Jan Index	%	Feb Index	%	Mar Index	%	Apr Index	%	May Index	%	Jun Index	%	Jul Index	%	Aug Index	%	Sep Index	%	Oct Index	%	Nov Index	%	Dec Index	%
1952	-	-	-	-	-	-	-	-	-	-	-	-	-	-	-	-	-	-	-	-	-	-	45.0	-
1953	45.0	0.0	44.9	-0.2	44.9	0.0	44.7	-0.4	44.7	0.0	44.7	0.0	44.5	-0.4	44.4	-0.2	45.0	1.4	45.0	0.0	45.0	0.0	44.9	-0.2
1954	44.7	-0.4	44.7	0.0	44.5	-0.4	44.4	-0.2	44.4	0.0	44.3	-0.2	44.2	-0.2	44.1	-0.2	44.5	0.9	44.4	-0.2	44.5	0.2	44.3	-0.4
1955	43.7	-1.4	43.6	-0.2	43.7	0.2	43.5	-0.5	43.5	0.0	43.4	-0.2	43.2	-0.5	43.4	0.5	44.4	2.3	44.4	0.0	44.5	0.2	44.5	0.0
1956	44.1	-0.9	44.4	0.7	44.4	0.0	44.5	0.2	44.4	-0.2	44.6	0.5	44.7	0.2	44.7	0.0	45.5	1.8	45.7	0.4	45.6	-0.2	45.6	0.0
1957	45.5	-0.2	45.1	-0.9	45.6	1.1	45.4	-0.4	45.6	0.4	45.6	0.0	45.6	0.0	45.6	0.0	45.9	0.7	46.0	0.2	46.1	0.2	46.0	-0.2
1958	46.1	0.2	46.2	0.2	46.2	0.0	45.8	-0.9	45.7	-0.2	45.7	0.0	45.7	0.0	45.9	0.4	46.2	0.7	46.1	-0.2	46.2	0.2	46.2	0.0
1959	45.9	-0.6	45.9	0.0	46.0	0.2	46.0	0.0	46.0	0.0	46.1	0.2	46.2	0.2	46.4	0.4	46.5	0.2	46.6	0.2	46.8	0.4	46.8	0.0
1960	46.5	-0.6	46.7	0.4	47.0	0.6	47.1	0.2	47.0	-0.2	47.0	0.0	46.9	-0.2	47.0	0.2	47.6	1.3	47.9	0.6	47.9	0.0	47.9	0.0
1961	47.5	-0.8	47.5	0.0	47.4	-0.2	47.3	-0.2	47.2	-0.2	47.3	0.2	47.4	0.2	47.6	0.4	48.1	1.1	48.3	0.4	48.4	0.2	48.2	-0.4
1962	47.7	-1.0	47.8	0.2	47.9	0.2	47.8	-0.2	47.6	-0.4	47.8	0.4	48.0	0.4	47.8	-0.4	48.8	2.1	49.1	0.6	48.9	-0.4	48.8	-0.2
1963	48.7	-0.2	48.6	-0.2	48.6	0.0	48.7	0.2	48.5	-0.4	48.9	0.8	49.1	0.4	49.2	0.2	49.9	1.4	50.0	0.2	50.0	0.0	50.1	0.2
1964	49.2	-1.8	49.5	0.6	49.8	0.6	49.8	0.0	49.9	0.2	49.8	-0.2	49.8	0.0	49.5	-0.6	50.5	2.0	50.4	-0.2	50.3	-0.2	50.5	0.4
1965	49.3	-2.4	50.0	1.4	50.1	0.2	50.1	0.0	50.4	0.6	50.5	0.2	49.9	-1.2	50.5	1.2	51.6	2.2	51.7	0.2	51.6	-0.2	51.3	-0.6
1966	50.3	-1.9	50.7	0.8	51.2	1.0	51.3	0.2	51.7	0.8	51.4	-0.6	51.3	-0.2	51.0	-0.6	52.9	3.7	53.3	0.8	53.2	-0.2	53.3	0.2
1967	52.3	-1.9	53.2	1.7	54.1	1.7	53.8	-0.6	54.2	0.7	54.2	0.0	54.2	0.0	54.1	-0.2	55.4	2.4	55.7	0.5	55.7	0.0	55.7	0.0
1968	54.6	-2.0	55.5	1.6	56.2	1.3	56.5	0.5	56.9	0.7	57.2	0.5	56.8	-0.7	57.4	1.1	59.3	3.3	59.5	0.3	59.8	0.5	59.9	0.2
1969	58.8	-1.8	59.3	0.9	60.8	2.5	60.8	0.0	61.1	0.5	61.2	0.2	61.0	-0.3	60.8	-0.3	62.8	3.3	63.0	0.3	63.1	0.2	62.9	-0.3
1970	61.5	-2.2	62.9	2.3	63.2	0.5	63.0	-0.3	63.4	0.6	63.7	0.5	62.9	-1.3	63.5	1.0	65.8	3.6	65.8	0.0	65.8	0.0	65.9	0.2
1971	64.1	-2.7	64.9	1.2	65.4	0.8	64.9	-0.8	65.6	1.1	65.4	-0.3	64.7	-1.1	64.7	0.0	66.9	3.4	66.8	-0.1	66.6	-0.3	66.6	0.0
1972	64.9	-2.6	66.4	2.3	67.4	1.5	67.2	-0.3	67.2	0.0	66.1	-1.6	65.4	-1.1	65.3	-0.2	68.4	4.7	68.4	0.0	68.3	-0.1	68.1	-0.3
1973	65.0	-4.6	66.2	1.8	68.3	3.2	68.4	0.1	68.9	0.7	68.5	-0.6	67.4	-1.6	68.5	1.6	70.3	2.6	70.6	0.4	71.0	0.6	70.9	-0.1
1974	68.4	-3.5	70.7	3.4	72.8	3.0	72.1	-1.0	73.2	1.5	73.2	0.0	72.2	-1.4	76.0	5.3	77.5	2.0	77.8	0.4	78.1	0.4	76.7	-1.8
1975	75.0	-2.2	76.9	2.5	76.9	0.0	76.0	-1.2	76.5	0.7	75.2	-1.7	75.0	-0.3	77.2	2.9	78.2	1.3	78.2	0.0	78.3	0.1	77.5	-1.0
1976	76.1	-1.8	77.4	1.7	77.6	0.3	77.7	0.1	77.8	0.1	77.2	-0.8	77.2	0.0	80.0	3.6	81.5	1.9	80.8	-0.9	81.2	0.5	81.1	-0.1
1977	79.1	-2.5	79.3	0.3	79.4	0.1	79.2	-0.3	79.7	0.6	80.9	1.5	80.7	-0.2	82.6	2.4	83.2	0.7	82.8	-0.5	83.8	1.2	83.5	-0.4
1978	81.7	-2.2	82.2	0.6	83.2	1.2	84.7	1.8	84.7	0.0	84.6	-0.1	83.1	-1.8	84.1	1.2	84.6	0.6	85.7	1.3	85.4	-0.4	84.8	-0.7
1979	82.9	-2.2	85.0	2.5	86.9	2.2	87.4	0.6	88.1	0.8	86.2	-2.2	85.4	-0.9	87.2	2.1	89.1	2.2	89.7	0.7	89.7	0.0	90.4	0.8
1980	88.1	-2.5	89.2	1.2	92.7	3.9	92.8	0.1	94.1	1.4	92.5	-1.7	91.6	-1.0	93.9	2.5	95.8	2.0	96.1	0.3	95.8	-0.3	95.6	-0.2
1981	94.7	-0.9	95.3	0.6	95.4	0.1	95.4	0.0	96.1	0.7	95.5	-0.6	95.3	-0.2	97.0	1.8	98.0	1.0	96.8	-1.2	96.3	-0.5	95.9	-0.4
1982	94.0	-2.0	96.4	2.6	97.6	1.2	97.6	0.0	97.0	-0.6	97.1	0.1	96.8	-0.3	97.6	0.8	98.8	1.2	98.9	0.1	97.8	-1.1	97.3	-0.5
1983	96.8	-0.5	98.0	1.2	99.5	1.5	100.3	0.8	102.1	1.8	101.0	-1.1	99.9	-1.1	100.8	0.9	102.8	2.0	103.1	0.3	102.2	-0.9	100.7	-1.5
1984	99.5	-1.2	99.3	-0.2	101.3	2.0	101.1	-0.2	101.8	0.7	100.2	-1.6	99.3	-0.9	104.0	4.7	105.2	1.2	105.6	0.4	105.1	-0.5	103.2	-1.8
1985	101.5	-1.6	102.7	1.2	104.5	1.8	104.6	0.1	103.3	-1.2	101.6	-1.6	101.0	-0.6	106.6	5.5	107.2	0.6	107.1	-0.1	107.4	0.3	105.3	-2.0
1986	103.2	-2.0	102.5	-0.7	103.4	0.9	104.2	0.8	103.4	-0.8	101.7	-1.6	100.6	-1.1	104.3	3.7	107.3	2.9	106.1	-1.1	105.8	-0.3	105.5	-0.3
1987	103.2	-2.2	105.9	2.6	111.3	5.1	114.1	2.5	113.0	-1.0	108.5	-4.0	105.1	-3.1	108.0	2.8	115.3	6.8	115.8	0.4	115.8	0.0	106.7	-7.9
1988	101.3	-5.1	98.8	-2.5	104.3	5.6	108.0	3.5	106.0	-1.9	102.3	-3.5	98.8	-3.4	100.5	1.7	115.1	14.5	118.7	3.1	111.6	-6.0	109.9	-1.5
1989	106.2	-3.4	106.4	0.2	116.2	9.2	115.6	-0.5	112.8	-2.4	109.0	-3.4	104.9	-3.8	106.8	1.8	119.6	12.0	120.3	0.6	118.8	-1.2	113.3	-4.6
1990	115.2	1.7	113.9	-1.1	121.1	6.3	124.4	2.7	120.3	-3.3	116.0	-3.6	113.2	-2.4	119.0	5.1	125.8	5.7	126.4	0.5	124.6	-1.4	121.1	-2.8
1991	119.0	-1.7	119.2	0.2	121.1	1.6	121.1	0.0	121.4	0.2	120.4	-0.8	117.7	-2.2	121.8	3.5	124.8	2.5	126.8	1.6	127.9	0.9	123.5	-3.4
1992	120.9	-2.1	119.4	-1.2	123.6	3.5	123.3	-0.2	124.3	0.8	121.7	-2.1	121.8	0.1	126.8	4.1	133.8	5.5	134.0	0.1	132.1	-1.4	127.9	-3.2
1993	124.6	-2.6	131.2	5.3	131.5	0.2	128.3	-2.4	123.1	-4.1	121.0	-1.7	119.5	-1.2	124.7	4.4	129.1	3.5	130.1	0.8	128.6	-1.2	122.1	-5.1

Source: U.S. Department of Labor, Bureau of Labor Statistics, Division of Consumer Prices and Price Indexes. - indicates no data collected for period.

New York, NY, NE NJ
Consumer Price Index - All Urban Consumers
Base 1982-1984 = 100
Transportation

For 1947-1993. Columns headed % show percentile change in the index from the previous period for which an index is available.

Year	Jan Index	%	Feb Index	%	Mar Index	%	Apr Index	%	May Index	%	Jun Index	%	Jul Index	%	Aug Index	%	Sep Index	%	Oct Index	%	Nov Index	%	Dec Index	%
1947	15.8	-	15.8	0.0	15.8	0.0	15.9	0.6	16.0	0.6	16.0	0.0	16.1	0.6	16.1	0.0	16.2	0.6	16.2	0.0	16.3	0.6	16.5	1.2
1948	16.5	0.0	16.5	0.0	16.5	0.0	16.5	0.0	16.5	0.0	16.5	0.0	20.9	26.7	21.1	1.0	21.2	0.5	21.3	0.5	21.3	0.0	21.3	0.0
1949	21.4	0.5	21.4	0.0	21.4	0.0	21.5	0.5	21.5	0.0	21.6	0.0	21.5	0.0	21.5	0.0	21.5	0.0	21.5	0.0	21.5	0.0	21.6	0.5
1950	21.6	0.0	21.6	0.0	21.6	0.0	21.6	0.0	21.6	0.0	21.6	0.0	23.1	6.9	23.2	0.4	23.2	0.0	23.2	0.0	23.3	0.4	23.3	0.0
1951	23.3	0.0	23.3	0.0	23.4	0.4	23.4	0.0	23.4	0.0	23.4	0.0	23.5	0.4	23.5	0.0	23.6	0.4	23.7	0.4	23.8	0.4	23.8	0.0
1952	23.8	0.0	23.9	0.4	23.9	0.0	23.9	0.0	23.9	0.0	23.9	0.0	23.9	0.0	23.9	0.0	24.0	0.4	24.0	0.0	24.0	0.0	24.0	0.0
1953	24.0	0.0	23.9	-0.4	23.9	0.0	23.9	0.0	23.9	0.0	24.0	0.4	24.2	0.8	25.2	4.1	25.2	0.0	25.2	0.0	25.1	-0.4	25.1	0.0
1954	25.5	1.6	25.4	-0.4	25.3	-0.4	25.2	-0.4	25.2	0.0	25.3	0.4	24.3	-4.0	24.2	-0.4	24.3	0.4	24.4	0.4	24.7	1.2	24.6	-0.4
1955	24.4	-0.8	24.4	0.0	24.4	0.0	24.3	-0.4	24.2	-0.4	24.2	0.0	23.9	-1.2	23.8	-0.4	23.8	0.0	24.0	0.8	24.6	2.5	24.3	-1.2
1956	24.5	0.8	24.7	0.8	24.6	-0.4	24.7	0.4	24.7	0.0	24.7	0.0	24.8	0.4	25.1	1.2	25.0	-0.4	25.9	3.6	25.7	-0.8	25.7	0.0
1957	25.7	0.0	25.9	0.8	25.9	0.0	26.0	0.4	26.0	0.0	26.0	0.0	25.8	-0.8	25.8	0.0	25.8	0.0	25.7	-0.4	26.3	2.3	26.2	-0.4
1958	26.2	0.0	26.1	-0.4	26.1	0.0	26.2	0.4	26.2	0.0	26.1	-0.4	26.2	0.4	26.3	0.4	26.3	0.0	26.5	0.8	27.0	1.9	27.2	0.7
1959	27.1	-0.4	27.1	0.0	27.2	0.4	27.4	0.7	27.4	0.0	27.4	0.0	27.6	0.7	27.6	0.0	27.6	0.0	28.0	1.4	28.1	0.4	28.1	0.0
1960	28.1	0.0	28.1	0.0	27.9	-0.7	27.8	-0.4	27.8	0.0	27.7	-0.4	27.6	-0.4	27.6	0.0	27.4	-0.7	27.6	0.7	27.7	0.4	27.7	0.0
1961	27.6	-0.4	27.5	-0.4	27.6	0.4	27.7	0.4	27.8	0.4	27.9	0.4	27.9	0.0	27.9	0.0	27.9	0.0	28.1	0.7	28.1	0.0	28.0	-0.4
1962	27.9	-0.4	27.8	-0.4	27.8	0.0	27.9	0.4	28.1	0.7	28.1	0.0	28.0	-0.4	28.1	0.4	28.1	0.0	28.0	-0.4	28.0	0.0	28.0	0.0
1963	28.0	0.0	27.9	-0.4	28.0	0.4	28.1	0.4	28.0	-0.4	28.3	1.1	28.3	0.0	28.3	0.0	28.3	0.0	28.4	0.4	28.6	0.7	28.5	-0.3
1964	28.4	-0.4	28.4	0.0	28.3	-0.4	28.3	0.0	28.3	0.0	28.2	-0.4	28.2	0.0	28.2	0.0	28.1	-0.4	28.2	0.4	28.5	1.1	28.6	0.4
1965	28.7	0.3	28.5	-0.7	28.6	0.4	28.6	0.0	28.5	-0.3	28.4	-0.4	28.6	0.7	28.7	0.3	28.7	0.0	28.9	0.7	28.9	0.0	28.9	0.0
1966	29.0	0.3	29.0	0.0	29.1	0.3	29.2	0.3	29.1	-0.3	29.2	0.3	30.5	4.5	30.5	0.0	30.3	-0.7	30.6	1.0	30.7	0.3	30.6	-0.3
1967	30.5	-0.3	30.7	0.7	30.8	0.3	30.9	0.3	31.0	0.3	31.0	0.0	31.2	0.6	31.4	0.6	31.3	-0.3	31.7	1.3	31.6	-0.3	31.7	0.3
1968	31.7	0.0	31.7	0.0	31.7	0.0	31.7	0.0	31.7	0.0	31.9	0.6	32.1	0.6	32.2	0.3	32.1	-0.3	32.4	0.9	32.5	0.3	32.2	-0.9
1969	33.0	2.5	33.3	0.9	33.8	1.5	33.9	0.3	33.7	-0.6	33.9	0.6	33.9	0.0	33.9	0.0	33.6	-0.9	34.2	1.8	34.2	0.0	35.1	2.6
1970	37.4	6.6	37.5	0.3	37.5	0.0	37.8	0.8	38.0	0.5	38.1	0.3	38.2	0.3	38.1	-0.3	38.1	0.0	38.6	1.3	38.9	0.8	39.1	0.5
1971	39.3	0.5	40.0	1.8	40.1	0.2	40.1	0.0	40.2	0.2	40.6	1.0	40.6	0.0	40.5	-0.2	40.1	-1.0	40.3	0.5	40.3	0.0	40.2	-0.2
1972	41.2	2.5	41.2	0.0	41.1	-0.2	41.1	0.0	41.3	0.5	41.4	0.2	41.5	0.2	41.6	0.2	41.6	0.0	41.7	0.2	41.8	0.2	41.8	0.0
1973	41.7	-0.2	41.8	0.2	41.8	0.0	42.0	0.5	42.1	0.2	42.4	0.7	42.4	0.0	42.4	0.0	42.2	-0.5	42.5	0.7	42.7	0.5	43.1	0.9
1974	43.2	0.2	43.4	0.5	43.9	1.2	44.3	0.9	45.0	1.6	45.8	1.8	46.4	1.3	46.5	0.2	46.8	0.6	47.0	0.4	47.1	0.2	47.4	0.6
1975	47.3	-0.2	47.3	0.0	47.8	1.1	48.1	0.6	48.2	0.2	48.8	1.2	49.5	1.4	49.7	0.4	53.3	7.2	53.6	0.6	54.7	2.1	55.3	1.1
1976	55.3	0.0	55.4	0.2	56.4	1.8	56.5	0.2	56.9	0.7	57.5	1.1	57.9	0.7	58.1	0.3	58.7	1.0	59.1	0.7	59.1	0.0	59.0	-0.2
1977	59.4	0.7	59.7	0.5	60.1	0.7	60.4	0.5	60.6	0.3	60.8	0.3	60.8	0.0	60.8	0.0	60.7	-0.2	60.9	0.3	61.0	0.2	61.1	0.2
1978	61.1	0.0	61.3	0.3	61.3	0.0	61.6	0.5	61.8	0.3	62.2	0.6	62.6	0.6	62.8	0.3	63.3	0.8	64.1	1.3	64.4	0.5	64.8	0.6
1979	65.1	0.5	65.7	0.9	66.4	1.1	67.7	2.0	69.0	1.9	70.6	2.3	72.2	2.3	72.9	1.0	73.6	1.0	74.1	0.7	74.7	0.8	75.4	0.9
1980	77.2	2.4	79.1	2.5	80.5	1.8	81.5	1.2	81.8	0.4	82.1	0.4	83.6	1.8	83.9	0.4	84.4	0.6	84.6	0.2	85.3	0.8	86.0	0.8
1981	87.4	1.6	89.3	2.2	90.1	0.9	90.7	0.7	91.0	0.3	91.5	0.5	93.9	2.6	94.0	0.1	94.4	0.4	94.7	0.3	95.4	0.7	95.6	0.2
1982	95.4	-0.2	95.0	-0.4	94.0	-1.1	93.3	-0.7	93.6	0.3	95.6	2.1	96.6	1.0	96.9	0.3	97.4	0.5	97.9	0.5	97.8	-0.1	97.8	0.0
1983	97.5	-0.3	96.9	-0.6	96.1	-0.8	97.8	1.8	98.1	0.3	98.7	0.6	99.2	0.5	99.9	0.7	100.5	0.6	100.9	0.4	101.6	0.7	101.5	-0.1
1984	103.3	1.8	103.5	0.2	104.1	0.6	104.5	0.4	105.0	0.5	105.1	0.1	105.5	0.4	105.5	0.0	105.5	0.0	105.8	0.3	106.1	0.3	106.1	0.0
1985	106.1	0.0	106.1	0.0	106.6	0.5	106.8	0.2	107.1	0.3	107.4	0.3	107.4	0.0	107.1	-0.3	106.8	-0.3	107.6	0.7	108.1	0.5	108.4	0.3
1986	109.5	1.0	108.5	-0.9	106.1	-2.2	103.4	-2.5	103.4	0.0	104.5	1.1	103.9	-0.6	102.9	-1.0	102.4	-0.5	104.0	1.6	104.5	0.5	104.8	0.3
1987	105.4	0.6	105.7	0.3	106.1	0.4	107.4	1.2	108.0	0.6	108.8	0.7	109.4	0.6	110.2	0.7	110.3	0.1	110.7	0.4	111.5	0.7	111.2	-0.3
1988	111.3	0.1	111.3	0.0	110.7	-0.5	111.2	0.5	111.8	0.5	112.6	0.7	113.0	0.4	113.4	0.4	113.7	0.3	114.4	0.6	114.7	0.3	114.9	0.2
1989	115.2	0.3	115.1	-0.1	115.3	0.2	116.3	0.9	117.5	1.0	117.3	-0.2	116.9	-0.3	116.4	-0.4	115.8	-0.5	116.9	0.9	117.3	0.3	117.5	0.2
1990	119.5	1.7	119.8	0.3	119.5	-0.3	119.2	-0.3	119.3	0.1	120.4	0.9	120.8	0.3	122.1	1.1	125.3	2.6	129.0	3.0	130.6	1.2	131.4	0.6
1991	129.1	-1.8	127.8	-1.0	126.6	-0.9	126.2	-0.3	127.3	0.9	127.6	0.2	127.7	0.1	127.6	-0.1	128.1	0.4	128.6	0.4	129.1	0.4	129.1	0.0

[Continued]

New York, NY, NE NJ
Consumer Price Index - All Urban Consumers
Base 1982-1984 = 100
Transportation

[Continued]

For 1947-1993. Columns headed % show percentile change in the index from the previous period for which an index is available.

Year	Jan		Feb		Mar		Apr		May		Jun		Jul		Aug		Sep		Oct		Nov		Dec	
	Index	%	Index	%	Index	%	Index	%	Index	%	Index	%	Index	%	Index	%	Index	%	Index	%	Index	%	Index	%
1992	129.5	0.3	129.7	0.2	129.9	0.2	129.6	-0.2	129.8	0.2	130.1	0.2	130.9	0.6	130.6	-0.2	130.9	0.2	134.6	2.8	135.5	0.7	136.3	0.6
1993	137.3	0.7	136.9	-0.3	136.2	-0.5	136.4	0.1	137.1	0.5	136.7	-0.3	137.1	0.3	137.2	0.1	137.1	-0.1	139.1	1.5	140.1	0.7	141.0	0.6

Source: U.S. Department of Labor, Bureau of Labor Statistics, Division of Consumer Prices and Price Indexes. - indicates no data collected for period.

New York, NY, NE NJ
Consumer Price Index - Urban Wage Earners
Base 1982-1984 = 100
Transportation

For 1947-1993. Columns headed % show percentile change in the index from the previous period for which an index is available.

Year	Jan Index	%	Feb Index	%	Mar Index	%	Apr Index	%	May Index	%	Jun Index	%	Jul Index	%	Aug Index	%	Sep Index	%	Oct Index	%	Nov Index	%	Dec Index	%
1947	15.7	-	15.7	0.0	15.7	0.0	15.8	0.6	15.8	0.0	15.9	0.6	15.9	0.0	16.0	0.6	16.1	0.6	16.1	0.0	16.1	0.0	16.3	1.2
1948	16.3	0.0	16.3	0.0	16.3	0.0	16.3	0.0	16.3	0.0	16.3	0.0	20.7	27.0	20.9	1.0	21.0	0.5	21.1	0.5	21.1	0.0	21.1	0.0
1949	21.1	0.0	21.2	0.5	21.2	0.0	21.3	0.5	21.3	0.0	21.3	0.0	21.3	0.0	21.3	0.0	21.3	0.0	21.3	0.0	21.3	0.0	21.4	0.5
1950	21.4	0.0	21.4	0.0	21.4	0.0	21.4	0.0	21.4	0.0	21.4	0.0	22.9	7.0	23.0	0.4	22.9	-0.4	22.9	0.0	23.0	0.4	23.0	0.0
1951	23.0	0.0	23.1	0.4	23.2	0.4	23.2	0.0	23.2	0.0	23.2	0.0	23.3	0.4	23.3	0.0	23.4	0.4	23.5	0.4	23.6	0.4	23.6	0.0
1952	23.6	0.0	23.7	0.4	23.7	0.0	23.7	0.0	23.7	0.0	23.7	0.0	23.7	0.0	23.7	0.0	23.8	0.4	23.8	0.0	23.8	0.0	23.7	-0.4
1953	23.8	0.4	23.7	-0.4	23.7	0.0	23.7	0.0	23.7	0.0	23.7	0.0	23.9	0.8	25.0	4.6	24.9	-0.4	25.0	0.4	24.8	-0.8	24.9	0.4
1954	25.2	1.2	25.1	-0.4	25.0	-0.4	24.9	-0.4	25.0	0.4	25.0	0.0	24.0	-4.0	24.0	0.0	24.1	0.4	24.1	0.0	24.4	1.2	24.3	-0.4
1955	24.2	-0.4	24.2	0.0	24.2	0.0	24.1	-0.4	24.0	-0.4	23.9	-0.4	23.7	-0.8	23.6	-0.4	23.6	0.0	23.8	0.8	24.4	2.5	24.1	-1.2
1956	24.3	0.8	24.4	0.4	24.4	0.0	24.4	0.0	24.5	0.4	24.4	-0.4	24.6	0.8	24.8	0.8	24.8	0.0	25.6	3.2	25.4	-0.8	25.4	0.0
1957	25.5	0.4	25.6	0.4	25.6	0.0	25.7	0.4	25.7	0.0	25.7	0.0	25.6	-0.4	25.6	0.0	25.5	-0.4	25.5	0.0	26.1	2.4	26.0	-0.4
1958	26.0	0.0	25.9	-0.4	25.8	-0.4	25.9	0.4	25.9	0.0	25.9	0.0	25.9	0.0	26.1	0.8	26.1	0.0	26.2	0.4	26.7	1.9	26.9	0.7
1959	26.9	0.0	26.9	0.0	27.0	0.4	27.2	0.7	27.2	0.0	27.2	0.0	27.3	0.4	27.4	0.4	27.3	-0.4	27.3	0.0	27.7	1.5	27.8	0.4
1960	27.8	0.0	27.8	0.0	27.6	-0.7	27.5	-0.4	27.5	0.0	27.4	-0.4	27.3	-0.4	27.3	0.0	27.2	-0.4	27.3	0.4	27.4	0.4	27.5	0.4
1961	27.3	-0.7	27.2	-0.4	27.3	0.4	27.5	0.7	27.5	0.0	27.6	0.4	27.6	0.0	27.6	0.0	27.6	0.0	27.8	0.7	27.8	0.0	27.5	-1.1
1962	27.6	0.4	27.5	-0.4	27.5	0.0	27.7	0.7	27.8	0.4	27.8	0.0	27.8	0.0	27.8	0.0	27.7	-0.4	27.8	0.4	27.9	0.4	27.7	-0.7
1963	27.7	0.0	27.7	0.0	27.7	0.0	27.8	0.4	27.7	-0.4	28.1	1.4	28.1	0.0	28.1	0.0	28.0	-0.4	27.9	-0.4	28.2	1.1	28.3	0.4
1964	28.1	-0.4	28.1	0.0	28.0	-0.4	28.0	0.0	28.0	0.0	27.9	-0.4	28.0	0.4	27.9	-0.4	27.8	-0.4	27.9	0.4	28.0	0.4	28.3	1.1
1965	28.4	0.4	28.2	-0.7	28.3	0.4	28.3	0.0	28.2	-0.4	28.1	-0.4	28.3	0.7	28.4	0.4	28.4	0.0	28.6	0.7	28.6	0.0	28.6	0.0
1966	28.7	0.3	28.7	0.0	28.8	0.3	29.0	0.7	28.9	-0.3	29.0	0.3	30.3	4.5	30.3	0.0	30.0	-1.0	30.3	1.0	30.4	0.3	30.3	-0.3
1967	30.3	0.0	30.4	0.3	30.5	0.3	30.6	0.3	30.7	0.3	30.7	0.0	30.9	0.7	31.1	0.6	31.0	-0.3	31.4	1.3	31.3	-0.3	31.4	0.3
1968	31.4	0.0	31.4	0.0	31.4	0.0	31.4	0.0	31.4	0.0	31.6	0.6	31.8	0.6	31.9	0.3	31.8	-0.3	32.1	0.9	32.2	0.3	31.9	-0.9
1969	32.7	2.5	33.0	0.9	33.5	1.5	33.6	0.3	33.4	-0.6	33.5	0.3	33.6	0.3	33.6	0.0	33.3	-0.9	33.8	1.5	33.8	0.0	34.7	2.7
1970	37.0	6.6	37.1	0.3	37.2	0.3	37.4	0.5	37.6	0.5	37.7	0.3	37.8	0.3	37.7	-0.3	37.7	0.0	38.2	1.3	38.6	1.0	38.7	0.3
1971	38.9	0.5	39.6	1.8	39.8	0.5	39.7	-0.3	39.8	0.3	40.2	1.0	40.3	0.2	40.1	-0.5	39.7	-1.0	39.9	0.5	39.9	0.0	39.8	-0.3
1972	40.8	2.5	40.8	0.0	40.7	-0.2	40.7	0.0	40.9	0.5	41.0	0.2	41.1	0.2	41.1	0.0	41.2	0.2	41.2	0.0	41.3	0.2	41.4	0.2
1973	41.3	-0.2	41.4	0.2	41.4	0.0	41.6	0.5	41.7	0.2	42.0	0.7	42.0	0.0	42.0	0.0	41.8	-0.5	42.1	0.7	42.3	0.5	42.7	0.9
1974	42.8	0.2	43.0	0.5	43.5	1.2	43.9	0.9	44.6	1.6	45.4	1.8	46.0	1.3	46.1	0.2	46.3	0.4	46.5	0.4	46.7	0.4	47.0	0.6
1975	46.9	-0.2	46.9	0.0	47.4	1.1	47.7	0.6	47.8	0.2	48.3	1.0	49.0	1.4	49.3	0.6	52.8	7.1	53.1	0.6	54.2	2.1	54.8	1.1
1976	54.8	0.0	54.9	0.2	55.8	1.6	56.0	0.4	56.4	0.7	57.0	1.1	57.3	0.5	57.5	0.3	58.1	1.0	58.6	0.9	58.6	0.0	58.5	-0.2
1977	58.8	0.5	59.1	0.5	59.5	0.7	59.8	0.5	60.0	0.3	60.2	0.3	60.2	0.0	60.2	0.0	60.1	-0.2	60.3	0.3	60.4	0.2	60.5	0.2
1978	60.5	0.0	60.7	0.3	60.8	0.2	61.1	0.5	61.4	0.5	61.9	0.8	62.3	0.6	62.6	0.5	63.0	0.6	63.6	1.0	64.0	0.6	64.4	0.6
1979	64.7	0.5	65.3	0.9	66.0	1.1	67.4	2.1	68.7	1.9	70.5	2.6	72.0	2.1	72.8	1.1	73.5	1.0	73.7	0.3	74.4	0.9	75.1	0.9
1980	77.0	2.5	78.8	2.3	80.2	1.8	81.1	1.1	81.3	0.2	81.6	0.4	83.3	2.1	83.7	0.5	84.1	0.5	84.4	0.4	85.1	0.8	85.9	0.9
1981	87.2	1.5	89.2	2.3	90.0	0.9	90.7	0.8	90.7	0.0	91.3	0.7	93.9	2.8	94.1	0.2	94.6	0.5	94.9	0.3	95.5	0.6	95.7	0.2
1982	95.5	-0.2	95.0	-0.5	94.0	-1.1	93.0	-1.1	93.4	0.4	95.5	2.2	96.7	1.3	97.0	0.3	97.3	0.3	97.8	0.5	97.5	-0.3	97.6	0.1
1983	97.3	-0.3	96.6	-0.7	95.7	-0.9	97.3	1.7	97.8	0.5	98.5	0.7	99.1	0.6	99.9	0.8	100.6	0.7	101.0	0.4	101.7	0.7	101.7	0.0
1984	103.5	1.8	103.6	0.1	104.2	0.6	104.6	0.4	105.2	0.6	105.5	0.3	105.7	0.2	105.7	0.0	105.8	0.1	106.1	0.3	106.3	0.2	106.3	0.0
1985	106.2	-0.1	106.2	0.0	106.7	0.5	107.0	0.3	107.2	0.2	107.5	0.3	107.5	0.0	107.1	-0.4	106.7	-0.4	107.5	0.7	108.1	0.6	108.3	0.2
1986	109.5	1.1	108.4	-1.0	105.8	-2.4	102.9	-2.7	102.8	-0.1	103.8	1.0	103.1	-0.7	102.1	-1.0	101.5	-0.6	103.1	1.6	103.4	0.3	103.6	0.2
1987	104.4	0.8	105.0	0.6	105.5	0.5	107.0	1.4	107.7	0.7	108.7	0.9	109.3	0.6	110.2	0.8	110.4	0.2	110.7	0.3	111.3	0.5	111.1	-0.2
1988	111.2	0.1	111.1	-0.1	110.5	-0.5	110.8	0.3	111.3	0.5	112.0	0.6	112.5	0.4	113.1	0.5	113.3	0.2	113.9	0.5	114.1	0.2	114.4	0.3
1989	114.5	0.1	114.4	-0.1	114.6	0.2	115.8	1.0	117.4	1.4	117.4	0.0	117.1	-0.3	116.5	-0.5	115.7	-0.7	116.5	0.7	116.9	0.3	116.9	0.0
1990	119.3	2.1	119.4	0.1	119.0	-0.3	118.8	-0.2	118.8	0.0	120.2	1.2	120.9	0.6	122.3	1.2	126.1	3.1	129.7	2.9	131.3	1.2	131.8	0.4
1991	129.1	-2.0	127.3	-1.4	126.0	-1.0	125.9	-0.1	127.2	1.0	127.6	0.3	127.8	0.2	127.7	-0.1	128.4	0.5	128.6	0.2	129.1	0.4	129.0	-0.1

[Continued]

New York, NY, NE NJ
Consumer Price Index - Urban Wage Earners
Base 1982-1984 = 100
Transportation
[Continued]

For 1947-1993. Columns headed % show percentile change in the index from the previous period for which an index is available.

Year	Jan Index	%	Feb Index	%	Mar Index	%	Apr Index	%	May Index	%	Jun Index	%	Jul Index	%	Aug Index	%	Sep Index	%	Oct Index	%	Nov Index	%	Dec Index	%
1992	129.5	0.4	129.4	-0.1	129.6	0.2	129.3	-0.2	129.9	0.5	130.8	0.7	131.4	0.5	131.0	-0.3	131.5	0.4	134.9	2.6	135.7	0.6	136.5	0.6
1993	137.0	0.4	136.5	-0.4	135.9	-0.4	135.8	-0.1	136.7	0.7	136.7	0.0	136.9	0.1	137.0	0.1	136.9	-0.1	139.2	1.7	139.9	0.5	140.6	0.5

Source: U.S. Department of Labor, Bureau of Labor Statistics, Division of Consumer Prices and Price Indexes. - indicates no data collected for period.

New York, NY, NE NJ
Consumer Price Index - All Urban Consumers
Base 1982-1984 = 100
Medical Care

For 1947-1993. Columns headed % show percentile change in the index from the previous period for which an index is available.

Year	Jan Index	%	Feb Index	%	Mar Index	%	Apr Index	%	May Index	%	Jun Index	%	Jul Index	%	Aug Index	%	Sep Index	%	Oct Index	%	Nov Index	%	Dec Index	%
1947	14.0	-	14.1	0.7	14.1	0.0	14.1	0.0	14.2	0.7	14.3	0.7	14.3	0.0	14.3	0.0	14.4	0.7	14.5	0.7	14.5	0.0	14.5	0.0
1948	14.8	2.1	14.9	0.7	15.0	0.7	15.6	4.0	15.6	0.0	15.6	0.0	16.0	2.6	16.0	0.0	16.1	0.6	16.1	0.0	16.1	0.0	16.1	0.0
1949	16.2	0.6	16.2	0.0	16.0	-1.2	16.0	0.0	16.0	0.0	16.0	0.0	16.0	0.0	16.0	0.0	16.0	0.0	16.0	0.0	16.0	0.0	16.2	1.3
1950	16.3	0.6	16.3	0.0	16.3	0.0	16.3	0.0	16.3	0.0	16.4	0.6	16.4	0.0	16.4	0.0	16.3	-0.6	16.4	0.6	16.4	0.0	16.4	0.0
1951	16.6	1.2	16.6	0.0	16.9	1.8	17.0	0.6	17.0	0.0	17.0	0.0	17.0	0.0	17.0	0.0	17.2	1.2	17.2	0.0	17.2	0.0	17.4	1.2
1952	17.6	1.1	17.6	0.0	17.6	0.0	17.6	0.0	17.6	0.0	18.3	4.0	18.3	0.0	18.4	0.5	18.6	1.1	18.6	0.0	18.7	0.5	18.6	-0.5
1953	18.6	0.0	18.5	-0.5	18.5	0.0	18.5	0.0	18.5	0.0	18.5	0.0	18.5	0.0	18.6	0.5	18.6	0.0	18.6	0.0	18.9	1.6	18.9	0.0
1954	18.9	0.0	18.9	0.0	18.9	0.0	19.0	0.5	19.0	0.0	19.0	0.0	19.0	0.0	19.0	0.0	19.0	0.0	19.0	0.0	19.1	0.5	19.1	0.0
1955	19.1	0.0	19.2	0.5	19.2	0.0	19.2	0.0	19.3	0.5	19.3	0.0	19.4	0.5	19.4	0.0	19.4	0.0	19.4	0.0	19.4	0.0	19.4	0.0
1956	19.4	0.0	19.4	0.0	19.4	0.0	19.4	0.0	19.4	0.0	19.4	0.0	19.4	0.0	19.6	1.0	19.6	0.0	19.6	0.0	19.6	0.0	19.6	0.0
1957	19.7	0.5	19.7	0.0	19.7	0.0	19.7	0.0	19.8	0.5	19.9	0.5	19.9	0.0	19.8	-0.5	19.8	0.0	19.8	0.0	19.9	0.5	19.9	0.0
1958	19.9	0.0	19.9	0.0	20.0	0.5	20.0	0.0	20.0	0.0	20.0	0.0	20.0	0.0	20.1	0.5	20.7	3.0	20.7	0.0	20.8	0.5	20.8	0.0
1959	20.8	0.0	21.1	1.4	21.1	0.0	21.1	0.0	21.4	1.4	21.5	0.5	21.5	0.0	21.4	-0.5	22.0	2.8	22.0	0.0	22.0	0.0	22.0	0.0
1960	22.0	0.0	22.0	0.0	22.1	0.5	22.1	0.0	22.1	0.0	22.1	0.0	22.1	0.0	22.1	0.0	22.1	0.0	22.1	0.0	22.7	2.7	22.7	0.0
1961	22.7	0.0	22.7	0.0	22.8	0.4	22.8	0.0	23.0	0.9	23.0	0.0	23.0	0.0	23.1	0.4	23.1	0.0	23.1	0.0	23.1	0.0	23.1	0.0
1962	23.1	0.0	23.3	0.9	23.4	0.4	23.4	0.0	23.5	0.4	23.5	0.0	23.5	0.0	23.6	0.4	23.6	0.0	23.5	-0.4	23.6	0.4	23.7	0.4
1963	23.7	0.0	23.9	0.8	23.9	0.0	23.9	0.0	24.0	0.4	23.9	-0.4	23.9	0.0	24.0	0.4	24.0	0.0	24.0	0.0	24.1	0.4	24.1	0.0
1964	24.2	0.4	24.3	0.4	24.3	0.0	24.4	0.4	24.4	0.0	24.4	0.0	24.4	0.0	24.6	0.8	24.4	-0.8	24.5	0.4	24.7	0.8	24.7	0.0
1965	24.9	0.8	25.1	0.8	25.2	0.4	25.2	0.0	25.2	0.0	25.4	0.8	25.4	0.0	25.3	-0.4	25.3	0.0	25.3	0.0	25.4	0.4	25.6	0.8
1966	25.7	0.4	25.8	0.4	26.0	0.8	26.1	0.4	26.3	0.8	26.7	1.5	26.8	0.4	27.0	0.7	27.0	0.0	27.2	0.7	27.3	0.4	27.3	0.0
1967	27.6	1.1	27.8	0.7	27.9	0.4	28.0	0.4	28.1	0.4	28.3	0.7	28.5	0.7	28.7	0.7	28.8	0.3	28.9	0.3	28.9	0.0	29.2	1.0
1968	29.3	0.3	29.4	0.3	29.6	0.7	29.8	0.7	29.8	0.0	30.1	1.0	30.5	1.3	30.5	0.0	30.8	1.0	31.0	0.6	31.1	0.3	31.2	0.3
1969	31.9	2.2	32.0	0.3	32.5	1.6	32.8	0.9	33.0	0.6	33.4	1.2	33.4	0.0	33.6	0.6	33.6	0.0	33.5	-0.3	33.6	0.3	33.8	0.6
1970	34.0	0.6	34.1	0.3	34.6	1.5	34.9	0.9	34.9	0.0	35.6	2.0	35.9	0.8	36.1	0.6	36.4	0.8	36.5	0.3	36.8	0.8	37.3	1.4
1971	37.6	0.8	37.8	0.5	38.2	1.1	38.2	0.0	38.4	0.5	38.5	0.3	38.8	0.8	39.0	0.5	39.0	0.0	38.9	-0.3	39.0	0.3	39.1	0.3
1972	39.4	0.8	39.4	0.0	39.4	0.0	39.5	0.3	39.6	0.3	39.8	0.5	39.8	0.0	39.9	0.3	39.9	0.0	40.1	0.5	40.3	0.5	40.6	0.7
1973	40.7	0.2	40.7	0.0	40.6	-0.2	40.6	0.0	40.9	0.7	41.0	0.2	41.0	0.0	41.1	0.2	41.3	0.5	42.0	1.7	42.1	0.2	42.3	0.5
1974	42.8	1.2	43.2	0.9	43.8	1.4	44.1	0.7	44.7	1.4	45.4	1.6	45.7	0.7	46.9	2.6	47.4	1.1	47.5	0.2	47.8	0.6	48.2	0.8
1975	48.9	1.5	49.6	1.4	50.3	1.4	50.6	0.6	51.0	0.8	51.3	0.6	51.7	0.8	51.9	0.4	52.6	1.3	52.8	0.4	52.6	-0.4	53.4	1.5
1976	54.5	2.1	55.0	0.9	55.5	0.9	55.7	0.4	55.9	0.4	56.5	1.1	57.1	1.1	57.5	0.7	57.9	0.7	57.9	0.0	58.8	1.6	58.9	0.2
1977	59.7	1.4	59.9	0.3	60.7	1.3	61.2	0.8	61.4	0.3	61.7	0.5	62.0	0.5	62.2	0.3	62.3	0.2	62.6	0.5	62.8	0.3	63.3	0.8
1978	64.1	1.3	64.5	0.6	64.6	0.2	64.8	0.3	65.5	1.1	65.5	0.0	65.5	0.0	65.5	0.0	65.7	0.3	65.7	0.0	66.7	1.5	66.3	-0.6
1979	68.1	2.7	69.0	1.3	69.2	0.3	69.7	0.7	69.8	0.1	70.1	0.4	70.2	0.1	70.5	0.4	71.1	0.9	72.2	1.5	73.0	1.1	73.5	0.7
1980	74.5	1.4	75.4	1.2	76.2	1.1	76.9	0.9	76.9	0.0	77.0	0.1	77.2	0.3	77.8	0.8	78.3	0.6	78.7	0.5	79.0	0.4	79.3	0.4
1981	80.2	1.1	80.6	0.5	81.6	1.2	82.5	1.1	82.7	0.2	84.1	1.7	85.0	1.1	85.2	0.2	86.2	1.2	87.2	1.2	87.7	0.6	88.1	0.5
1982	89.1	1.1	89.9	0.9	90.7	0.9	90.9	0.2	91.2	0.3	91.6	0.4	91.5	-0.1	91.9	0.4	92.8	1.0	93.3	0.5	94.1	0.9	94.4	0.3
1983	95.4	1.1	97.3	2.0	98.1	0.8	98.7	0.6	99.4	0.7	99.4	0.0	100.0	0.6	101.2	1.2	101.7	0.5	102.3	0.6	103.2	0.9	103.9	0.7
1984	104.7	0.8	106.1	1.3	106.7	0.6	106.7	0.0	107.3	0.6	107.2	-0.1	107.7	0.5	109.0	1.2	109.8	0.7	110.1	0.3	110.8	0.6	111.4	0.5
1985	112.0	0.5	113.8	1.6	114.3	0.4	114.6	0.3	115.4	0.7	116.2	0.7	116.7	0.4	116.8	0.1	117.2	0.3	117.5	0.3	117.8	0.3	117.7	-0.1
1986	120.0	2.0	122.2	1.8	123.7	1.2	124.2	0.4	124.6	0.3	125.1	0.4	126.0	0.7	126.4	0.3	127.8	1.1	128.7	0.7	128.7	0.0	130.3	1.2
1987	131.1	0.6	132.9	1.4	135.0	1.6	136.1	0.8	136.1	0.0	136.3	0.1	136.8	0.4	137.2	0.3	137.2	0.0	137.5	0.2	137.9	0.3	138.5	0.4
1988	139.7	0.9	141.3	1.1	142.7	1.0	143.2	0.4	144.1	0.6	144.7	0.4	146.1	1.0	145.9	-0.1	146.9	0.7	147.1	0.1	147.6	0.3	147.9	0.2
1989	149.5	1.1	151.1	1.1	152.9	1.2	153.4	0.3	154.3	0.6	155.6	0.8	156.2	0.4	157.1	0.6	157.7	0.4	159.7	1.3	160.5	0.5	161.5	0.6
1990	163.9	1.5	166.7	1.7	169.2	1.5	170.1	0.5	170.5	0.2	171.4	0.5	171.8	0.2	175.1	1.9	175.9	0.5	177.5	0.9	178.0	0.3	178.7	0.4
1991	180.8	1.2	182.8	1.1	183.9	0.6	184.2	0.2	183.9	-0.2	185.3	0.8	187.2	1.0	188.7	0.8	189.3	0.3	189.6	0.2	191.0	0.7	192.0	0.5

[Continued]

New York, NY, NE NJ
Consumer Price Index - All Urban Consumers
Base 1982-1984 = 100
Medical Care
[Continued]

For 1947-1993. Columns headed % show percentile change in the index from the previous period for which an index is available.

Year	Jan Index	%	Feb Index	%	Mar Index	%	Apr Index	%	May Index	%	Jun Index	%	Jul Index	%	Aug Index	%	Sep Index	%	Oct Index	%	Nov Index	%	Dec Index	%
1992	195.1	1.6	196.4	0.7	197.7	0.7	198.4	0.4	199.1	0.4	200.0	0.5	201.2	0.6	200.8	-0.2	201.9	0.5	202.8	0.4	203.1	0.1	203.3	0.1
1993	205.1	0.9	205.5	0.2	206.6	0.5	207.9	0.6	208.9	0.5	208.9	0.0	209.5	0.3	210.7	0.6	211.0	0.1	211.3	0.1	211.4	0.0	212.0	0.3

Source: U.S. Department of Labor, Bureau of Labor Statistics, Division of Consumer Prices and Price Indexes. - indicates no data collected for period.

New York, NY, NE NJ
Consumer Price Index - Urban Wage Earners
Base 1982-1984 = 100
Medical Care

For 1947-1993. Columns headed % show percentile change in the index from the previous period for which an index is available.

Year	Jan Index	%	Feb Index	%	Mar Index	%	Apr Index	%	May Index	%	Jun Index	%	Jul Index	%	Aug Index	%	Sep Index	%	Oct Index	%	Nov Index	%	Dec Index	%
1947	14.6	-	14.7	0.7	14.7	0.0	14.7	0.0	14.8	0.7	14.9	0.7	14.9	0.0	15.0	0.7	15.0	0.0	15.2	1.3	15.2	0.0	15.2	0.0
1948	15.5	2.0	15.5	0.0	15.6	0.6	16.3	4.5	16.3	0.0	16.3	0.0	16.7	2.5	16.7	0.0	16.8	0.6	16.8	0.0	16.8	0.0	16.8	0.0
1949	16.9	0.6	16.8	-0.6	16.7	-0.6	16.7	0.0	16.7	0.0	16.7	0.0	16.7	0.0	16.6	-0.6	16.6	0.0	16.7	0.6	16.7	0.0	16.9	1.2
1950	17.0	0.6	17.0	0.0	17.0	0.0	17.0	0.0	17.0	0.0	17.1	0.6	17.1	0.0	17.1	0.0	17.0	-0.6	17.1	0.6	17.1	0.0	17.1	0.0
1951	17.3	1.2	17.4	0.6	17.6	1.1	17.7	0.6	17.7	0.0	17.7	0.0	17.7	0.0	17.7	0.0	17.9	1.1	17.9	0.0	17.9	0.0	18.1	1.1
1952	18.3	1.1	18.4	0.5	18.4	0.0	18.4	0.0	18.4	0.0	19.1	3.8	19.1	0.0	19.2	0.5	19.4	1.0	19.4	0.0	19.5	0.5	19.4	-0.5
1953	19.4	0.0	19.3	-0.5	19.3	0.0	19.3	0.0	19.3	0.0	19.3	0.0	19.3	0.0	19.4	0.5	19.4	0.0	19.4	0.0	19.7	1.5	19.7	0.0
1954	19.7	0.0	19.7	0.0	19.7	0.0	19.8	0.5	19.8	0.0	19.8	0.0	19.8	0.0	19.8	0.0	19.8	0.0	19.8	0.0	19.9	0.5	19.9	0.0
1955	20.0	0.5	20.0	0.0	20.0	0.0	20.0	0.0	20.2	1.0	20.2	0.0	20.2	0.0	20.2	0.0	20.2	0.0	20.2	0.0	20.2	0.0	20.2	0.0
1956	20.3	0.5	20.3	0.0	20.3	0.0	20.2	-0.5	20.3	0.5	20.3	0.0	20.3	0.0	20.5	1.0	20.5	0.0	20.5	0.0	20.5	0.0	20.5	0.0
1957	20.5	0.0	20.5	0.0	20.5	0.0	20.5	0.0	20.7	1.0	20.7	0.0	20.7	0.0	20.7	0.0	20.7	0.0	20.7	0.0	20.7	0.0	20.7	0.0
1958	20.8	0.5	20.8	0.0	20.8	0.0	20.8	0.0	20.9	0.5	20.9	0.0	20.9	0.0	21.0	0.5	21.6	2.9	21.6	0.0	21.6	0.0	21.6	0.0
1959	21.7	0.5	22.0	1.4	22.0	0.0	22.0	0.0	22.4	1.8	22.4	0.0	22.4	0.0	22.4	0.0	22.9	2.2	22.9	0.0	22.9	0.0	22.9	0.0
1960	22.9	0.0	23.0	0.4	23.0	0.0	23.0	0.0	23.0	0.0	23.0	0.0	23.0	0.0	23.0	0.0	23.0	0.0	23.0	0.0	23.7	3.0	23.7	0.0
1961	23.7	0.0	23.7	0.0	23.7	0.0	23.8	0.4	24.0	0.8	24.0	0.0	24.0	0.0	24.1	0.4	24.1	0.0	24.1	0.0	24.1	0.0	24.1	0.0
1962	24.1	0.0	24.2	0.4	24.4	0.8	24.4	0.0	24.5	0.4	24.5	0.0	24.5	0.0	24.6	0.4	24.6	0.0	24.5	-0.4	24.6	0.4	24.7	0.4
1963	24.8	0.4	24.9	0.4	25.0	0.4	25.0	0.0	25.0	0.0	24.9	-0.4	24.9	0.0	25.0	0.4	25.0	0.0	25.0	0.0	25.1	0.4	25.1	0.0
1964	25.2	0.4	25.3	0.4	25.4	0.4	25.4	0.0	25.5	0.4	25.4	-0.4	25.4	0.0	25.6	0.8	25.5	-0.4	25.6	0.4	25.7	0.4	25.8	0.4
1965	26.0	0.8	26.1	0.4	26.2	0.4	26.2	0.0	26.3	0.4	26.4	0.4	26.5	0.4	26.4	-0.4	26.4	0.0	26.4	0.0	26.5	0.4	26.7	0.8
1966	26.8	0.4	26.9	0.4	27.1	0.7	27.2	0.4	27.4	0.7	27.8	1.5	28.0	0.7	28.2	0.7	28.2	0.0	28.3	0.4	28.5	0.7	28.5	0.0
1967	28.8	1.1	29.0	0.7	29.1	0.3	29.2	0.3	29.3	0.3	29.5	0.7	29.7	0.7	29.9	0.7	30.0	0.3	30.1	0.3	30.1	0.0	30.4	1.0
1968	30.6	0.7	30.6	0.0	30.9	1.0	31.0	0.3	31.1	0.3	31.4	1.0	31.8	1.3	31.8	0.0	32.1	0.9	32.3	0.6	32.4	0.3	32.5	0.3
1969	33.3	2.5	33.4	0.3	33.9	1.5	34.2	0.9	34.4	0.6	34.8	1.2	34.8	0.0	35.1	0.9	35.1	0.0	35.0	-0.3	35.0	0.0	35.3	0.9
1970	35.4	0.3	35.6	0.6	36.1	1.4	36.4	0.8	36.4	0.0	37.1	1.9	37.4	0.8	37.7	0.8	37.9	0.5	38.1	0.5	38.4	0.8	38.8	1.0
1971	39.2	1.0	39.4	0.5	39.8	1.0	39.8	0.0	40.1	0.8	40.1	0.0	40.5	1.0	40.7	0.5	40.7	0.0	40.5	-0.5	40.7	0.5	40.8	0.2
1972	41.0	0.5	41.0	0.0	41.1	0.2	41.2	0.2	41.2	0.0	41.5	0.7	41.5	0.0	41.6	0.2	41.6	0.0	41.8	0.5	42.0	0.5	42.3	0.7
1973	42.5	0.5	42.4	-0.2	42.3	-0.2	42.4	0.2	42.6	0.5	42.7	0.2	42.8	0.2	42.8	0.0	43.1	0.7	43.8	1.6	43.9	0.2	44.1	0.5
1974	44.6	1.1	45.1	1.1	45.7	1.3	46.0	0.7	46.6	1.3	47.3	1.5	47.7	0.8	48.9	2.5	49.4	1.0	49.5	0.2	49.9	0.8	50.2	0.6
1975	51.0	1.6	51.8	1.6	52.5	1.4	52.8	0.6	53.2	0.8	53.5	0.6	53.9	0.7	54.1	0.4	54.8	1.3	55.0	0.4	54.8	-0.4	55.7	1.6
1976	56.8	2.0	57.4	1.1	57.9	0.9	58.1	0.3	58.3	0.3	59.0	1.2	59.5	0.8	59.9	0.7	60.4	0.8	60.4	0.0	61.3	1.5	61.4	0.2
1977	62.3	1.5	62.4	0.2	63.3	1.4	63.8	0.8	64.0	0.3	64.3	0.5	64.7	0.6	64.8	0.2	65.0	0.3	65.3	0.5	65.5	0.3	66.0	0.8
1978	66.5	0.8	66.9	0.6	67.1	0.3	67.2	0.1	67.8	0.9	67.9	0.1	67.8	-0.1	67.9	0.1	68.0	0.1	68.3	0.4	69.1	1.2	69.5	0.6
1979	70.4	1.3	70.9	0.7	71.3	0.6	71.9	0.8	72.0	0.1	72.3	0.4	72.6	0.4	72.8	0.3	73.2	0.5	73.5	0.4	73.8	0.4	74.4	0.8
1980	75.4	1.3	76.6	1.6	77.5	1.2	78.1	0.8	78.4	0.4	78.3	-0.1	78.6	0.4	79.1	0.6	80.4	1.6	80.4	0.0	80.7	0.4	80.9	0.2
1981	82.3	1.7	82.8	0.6	84.9	2.5	85.9	1.2	86.0	0.1	86.5	0.6	87.2	0.8	87.1	-0.1	87.5	0.5	87.8	0.3	88.1	0.3	88.4	0.3
1982	89.3	1.0	90.2	1.0	91.0	0.9	91.1	0.1	91.5	0.4	91.8	0.3	91.5	-0.3	91.9	0.4	92.8	1.0	93.3	0.5	94.0	0.8	94.2	0.2
1983	95.3	1.2	97.1	1.9	97.8	0.7	98.4	0.6	99.0	0.6	99.2	0.2	99.8	0.6	101.1	1.3	101.6	0.5	102.2	0.6	103.1	0.9	103.8	0.7
1984	104.7	0.9	106.1	1.3	106.7	0.6	106.8	0.1	107.4	0.6	107.4	0.0	107.9	0.5	109.2	1.2	109.9	0.6	110.4	0.5	111.1	0.6	111.6	0.5
1985	112.4	0.7	114.1	1.5	114.6	0.4	115.0	0.3	115.8	0.7	116.5	0.6	117.1	0.5	117.2	0.1	117.6	0.3	117.9	0.3	118.2	0.3	117.8	-0.3
1986	120.3	2.1	122.5	1.8	123.8	1.1	124.4	0.5	124.9	0.4	125.2	0.2	126.2	0.8	126.6	0.3	128.0	1.1	128.8	0.6	128.7	-0.1	130.4	1.3
1987	131.1	0.5	133.1	1.5	135.4	1.7	136.7	1.0	136.7	0.0	137.1	0.3	137.6	0.4	138.1	0.4	138.2	0.1	138.5	0.2	139.3	0.6	140.0	0.5
1988	141.1	0.8	142.5	1.0	143.6	0.8	144.1	0.3	145.0	0.6	145.6	0.4	147.0	1.0	146.9	-0.1	148.1	0.8	148.3	0.1	148.8	0.3	149.1	0.2
1989	150.4	0.9	152.1	1.1	154.1	1.3	154.8	0.5	155.6	0.5	157.0	0.9	157.7	0.4	158.6	0.6	159.2	0.4	160.6	0.9	161.5	0.6	162.5	0.6
1990	164.4	1.2	166.9	1.5	169.3	1.4	170.2	0.5	170.5	0.2	171.4	0.5	172.0	0.4	174.2	1.3	174.9	0.4	176.3	0.8	176.7	0.2	177.3	0.3
1991	180.0	1.5	182.1	1.2	183.3	0.7	183.5	0.1	183.2	-0.2	184.8	0.9	186.9	1.1	188.6	0.9	189.2	0.3	189.7	0.3	191.3	0.8	192.3	0.5

[Continued]

New York, NY, NE NJ
Consumer Price Index - Urban Wage Earners
Base 1982-1984 = 100
Medical Care
[Continued]

For 1947-1993. Columns headed % show percentile change in the index from the previous period for which an index is available.

Year	Jan Index	%	Feb Index	%	Mar Index	%	Apr Index	%	May Index	%	Jun Index	%	Jul Index	%	Aug Index	%	Sep Index	%	Oct Index	%	Nov Index	%	Dec Index	%
1992	195.2	1.5	196.5	0.7	197.7	0.6	198.6	0.5	199.0	0.2	200.0	0.5	201.2	0.6	201.2	0.0	202.5	0.6	203.5	0.5	203.7	0.1	204.0	0.1
1993	205.6	0.8	205.7	0.0	206.8	0.5	208.1	0.6	208.9	0.4	208.9	0.0	209.6	0.3	210.4	0.4	210.7	0.1	211.1	0.2	211.1	0.0	211.6	0.2

Source: U.S. Department of Labor, Bureau of Labor Statistics, Division of Consumer Prices and Price Indexes. - indicates no data collected for period.

New York, NY, NE NJ
Consumer Price Index - All Urban Consumers
Base 1982-1984 = 100
Entertainment

For 1976-1993. Columns headed % show percentile change in the index from the previous period for which an index is available.

Year	Jan Index	%	Feb Index	%	Mar Index	%	Apr Index	%	May Index	%	Jun Index	%	Jul Index	%	Aug Index	%	Sep Index	%	Oct Index	%	Nov Index	%	Dec Index	%
1976	62.5	-	62.9	0.6	63.0	0.2	63.3	0.5	63.7	0.6	64.8	1.7	65.0	0.3	65.2	0.3	65.7	0.8	66.1	0.6	65.9	-0.3	66.3	0.6
1977	66.5	0.3	67.1	0.9	66.7	-0.6	66.9	0.3	67.3	0.6	69.1	2.7	69.1	0.0	69.3	0.3	70.4	1.6	70.4	0.0	69.4	-1.4	69.5	0.1
1978	69.9	0.6	71.2	1.9	71.9	1.0	72.5	0.8	72.5	0.0	72.1	-0.6	72.9	1.1	73.2	0.4	73.1	-0.1	72.8	-0.4	72.9	0.1	72.4	-0.7
1979	72.9	0.7	74.5	2.2	75.2	0.9	75.4	0.3	75.3	-0.1	75.7	0.5	75.9	0.3	76.4	0.7	76.6	0.3	76.8	0.3	77.2	0.5	77.1	-0.1
1980	78.0	1.2	79.1	1.4	81.3	2.8	81.5	0.2	81.2	-0.4	81.7	0.6	81.3	-0.5	81.9	0.7	82.4	0.6	83.0	0.7	83.0	0.0	83.4	0.5
1981	84.4	1.2	86.0	1.9	86.9	1.0	87.1	0.2	87.2	0.1	87.8	0.7	87.7	-0.1	89.6	2.2	90.5	1.0	91.3	0.9	90.7	-0.7	90.9	0.2
1982	91.0	0.1	92.3	1.4	94.1	2.0	94.1	0.0	94.2	0.1	95.0	0.8	95.5	0.5	98.0	2.6	97.5	-0.5	98.3	0.8	98.0	-0.3	97.9	-0.1
1983	98.3	0.4	99.0	0.7	100.2	1.2	99.7	-0.5	100.1	0.4	100.3	0.2	100.6	0.3	100.5	-0.1	101.1	0.6	101.8	0.7	102.0	0.2	101.6	-0.4
1984	101.8	0.2	102.2	0.4	102.4	0.2	103.1	0.7	102.9	-0.2	104.4	1.5	104.9	0.5	104.5	-0.4	105.4	0.9	105.6	0.2	105.5	-0.1	106.0	0.5
1985	105.9	-0.1	105.9	0.0	106.9	0.9	107.2	0.3	107.8	0.6	108.2	0.4	108.4	0.2	108.4	0.2	107.8	-0.6	110.4	2.4	111.2	0.7	111.4	0.2	111.8	0.4
1986	113.8	1.8	114.1	0.3	113.4	-0.6	113.6	0.2	114.1	0.4	115.4	1.1	116.1	0.6	116.3	0.2	115.9	-0.3	115.9	0.0	116.4	0.4	116.1	-0.3
1987	117.3	1.0	116.5	-0.7	117.0	0.4	117.9	0.8	117.8	-0.1	118.5	0.6	120.2	1.4	120.4	0.2	120.7	0.2	121.1	0.3	121.4	0.2	121.6	0.2
1988	122.0	0.3	122.0	0.0	120.4	-1.3	122.1	1.4	120.7	-1.1	122.3	1.3	123.6	1.1	124.1	0.4	123.0	-0.9	124.1	0.9	124.4	0.2	125.3	0.7
1989	127.6	1.8	127.0	-0.5	127.4	0.3	128.8	1.1	128.6	-0.2	127.5	-0.9	129.2	1.3	130.2	0.8	131.8	1.2	131.7	-0.1	132.4	0.5	132.3	-0.1
1990	134.2	1.4	134.5	0.2	133.2	-1.0	134.2	0.8	135.8	1.2	134.5	-1.0	136.8	1.7	134.9	-1.4	136.3	1.0	137.1	0.6	137.8	0.5	137.6	-0.1
1991	140.0	1.7	139.6	-0.3	138.6	-0.7	140.0	1.0	140.4	0.3	138.8	-1.1	140.1	0.9	140.5	0.3	142.3	1.3	142.9	0.4	142.6	-0.2	144.0	1.0
1992	144.0	0.0	145.0	0.7	144.3	-0.5	145.9	1.1	146.3	0.3	147.0	0.5	147.3	0.2	147.3	0.0	146.9	-0.3	146.2	-0.5	148.5	1.6	148.5	0.0
1993	149.4	0.6	149.0	-0.3	149.5	0.3	149.9	0.3	149.1	-0.5	149.1	0.0	148.7	-0.3	150.2	1.0	150.5	0.2	151.4	0.6	151.2	-0.1	149.8	-0.9

Source: U.S. Department of Labor, Bureau of Labor Statistics, Division of Consumer Prices and Price Indexes. - indicates no data collected for period.

New York, NY, NE NJ
Consumer Price Index - Urban Wage Earners
Base 1982-1984 = 100
Entertainment

For 1976-1993. Columns headed % show percentile change in the index from the previous period for which an index is available.

Year	Jan Index	%	Feb Index	%	Mar Index	%	Apr Index	%	May Index	%	Jun Index	%	Jul Index	%	Aug Index	%	Sep Index	%	Oct Index	%	Nov Index	%	Dec Index	%
1976	63.9	-	64.3	0.6	64.5	0.3	64.8	0.5	65.2	0.6	66.3	1.7	66.4	0.2	66.7	0.5	67.2	0.7	67.6	0.6	67.5	-0.1	67.8	0.4
1977	68.0	0.3	68.6	0.9	68.3	-0.4	68.5	0.3	68.8	0.4	70.7	2.8	70.7	0.0	70.9	0.3	72.0	1.6	72.0	0.0	71.0	-1.4	71.1	0.1
1978	71.3	0.3	73.1	2.5	73.5	0.5	73.4	-0.1	72.7	-1.0	72.4	-0.4	72.9	0.7	73.2	0.4	73.6	0.5	73.5	-0.1	73.7	0.3	74.2	0.7
1979	74.5	0.4	74.9	0.5	76.1	1.6	76.1	0.0	76.1	0.0	76.4	0.4	76.6	0.3	77.0	0.5	77.8	1.0	78.4	0.8	79.2	1.0	78.0	-1.5
1980	79.0	1.3	80.1	1.4	82.6	3.1	82.1	-0.6	81.6	-0.6	83.0	1.7	81.7	-1.6	83.1	1.7	84.6	1.8	83.5	-1.3	84.0	0.6	84.6	0.7
1981	85.8	1.4	88.3	2.9	88.8	0.6	88.9	0.1	88.9	0.0	88.9	0.0	89.3	0.4	89.9	0.7	90.4	0.6	91.2	0.9	91.0	-0.2	91.1	0.1
1982	91.3	0.2	92.5	1.3	94.1	1.7	94.1	0.0	94.3	0.2	95.0	0.7	95.9	0.9	97.9	2.1	97.5	-0.4	98.0	0.5	97.6	-0.4	97.4	-0.2
1983	98.0	0.6	99.0	1.0	100.1	1.1	99.9	-0.2	100.2	0.3	100.2	0.0	100.8	0.6	100.7	-0.1	101.1	0.4	101.8	0.7	102.0	0.2	101.5	-0.5
1984	101.9	0.4	102.2	0.3	102.5	0.3	103.2	0.7	103.1	-0.1	104.5	1.4	104.9	0.4	104.7	-0.2	105.4	0.7	105.5	0.1	105.2	-0.3	106.0	0.8
1985	105.8	-0.2	105.8	0.0	106.4	0.6	107.0	0.6	107.7	0.7	108.5	0.7	108.7	0.2	108.0	-0.6	109.8	1.7	110.7	0.8	110.9	0.2	111.0	0.1
1986	113.1	1.9	113.3	0.2	112.7	-0.5	113.1	0.4	113.8	0.6	115.4	1.4	116.1	0.6	116.5	0.3	115.8	-0.6	115.9	0.1	117.0	0.9	116.7	-0.3
1987	118.2	1.3	117.8	-0.3	118.1	0.3	119.1	0.8	118.7	-0.3	119.5	0.7	121.3	1.5	121.4	0.1	121.8	0.3	122.3	0.4	122.8	0.4	123.0	0.2
1988	123.0	0.0	123.1	0.1	121.3	-1.5	123.5	1.8	121.3	-1.8	122.9	1.3	124.4	1.2	124.6	0.2	124.0	-0.5	125.5	1.2	125.9	0.3	126.7	0.6
1989	129.1	1.9	127.9	-0.9	128.4	0.4	129.9	1.2	129.7	-0.2	128.2	-1.2	129.6	1.1	130.3	0.5	132.4	1.6	132.3	-0.1	133.1	0.6	133.0	-0.1
1990	134.7	1.3	134.9	0.1	133.5	-1.0	134.7	0.9	136.6	1.4	135.2	-1.0	137.5	1.7	135.0	-1.8	136.9	1.4	137.8	0.7	138.8	0.7	138.6	-0.1
1991	141.0	1.7	140.4	-0.4	139.4	-0.7	140.8	1.0	140.6	-0.1	138.6	-1.4	140.1	1.1	140.5	0.3	142.7	1.6	143.2	0.4	142.8	-0.3	145.0	1.5
1992	144.6	-0.3	145.4	0.6	144.6	-0.6	146.4	1.2	146.5	0.1	147.1	0.4	147.3	0.1	147.3	0.0	146.5	-0.5	145.4	-0.8	148.8	2.3	148.7	-0.1
1993	149.9	0.8	149.3	-0.4	149.8	0.3	149.5	-0.2	148.9	-0.4	148.7	-0.1	148.0	-0.5	149.9	1.3	150.2	0.2	150.8	0.4	150.5	-0.2	149.0	-1.0

Source: U.S. Department of Labor, Bureau of Labor Statistics, Division of Consumer Prices and Price Indexes. - indicates no data collected for period.

New York, NY, NE NJ
Consumer Price Index - All Urban Consumers
Base 1982-1984 = 100
Other Goods and Services

For 1976-1993. Columns headed % show percentile change in the index from the previous period for which an index is available.

Year	Jan Index	%	Feb Index	%	Mar Index	%	Apr Index	%	May Index	%	Jun Index	%	Jul Index	%	Aug Index	%	Sep Index	%	Oct Index	%	Nov Index	%	Dec Index	%
1976	56.5	-	57.3	1.4	57.7	0.7	57.9	0.3	57.9	0.0	58.2	0.5	58.4	0.3	59.0	1.0	59.6	1.0	59.8	0.3	60.1	0.5	60.1	0.0
1977	61.1	1.7	61.5	0.7	61.6	0.2	61.5	-0.2	61.7	0.3	61.9	0.3	62.0	0.2	62.1	0.2	62.7	1.0	62.9	0.3	63.9	1.6	64.0	0.2
1978	64.1	0.2	64.2	0.2	64.4	0.3	64.2	-0.3	64.2	0.0	64.4	0.3	64.9	0.8	65.0	0.2	66.4	2.2	66.4	0.0	66.7	0.5	66.7	0.0
1979	67.0	0.4	67.2	0.3	67.5	0.4	67.6	0.1	67.8	0.3	68.0	0.3	68.0	0.0	68.5	0.7	70.2	2.5	70.5	0.4	70.6	0.1	71.1	0.7
1980	71.7	0.8	72.2	0.7	72.1	-0.1	72.3	0.3	72.8	0.7	73.4	0.8	73.7	0.4	73.9	0.3	76.0	2.8	76.6	0.8	76.8	0.3	77.4	0.8
1981	78.1	0.9	78.2	0.1	78.3	0.1	78.5	0.3	79.1	0.8	79.1	0.0	79.7	0.8	79.9	0.3	84.4	5.6	84.9	0.6	85.1	0.2	85.1	0.0
1982	85.6	0.6	86.1	0.6	86.5	0.5	87.0	0.6	87.3	0.3	87.3	0.0	88.1	0.9	89.0	1.0	93.4	4.9	94.5	1.2	95.4	1.0	96.3	0.9
1983	97.1	0.8	97.3	0.2	97.6	0.3	98.9	1.3	98.7	-0.2	99.2	0.5	100.7	1.5	101.2	0.5	105.0	3.8	105.9	0.9	106.6	0.7	106.6	0.0
1984	107.0	0.4	107.1	0.1	107.0	-0.1	107.1	0.1	107.5	0.4	107.6	0.1	107.9	0.3	108.2	0.3	111.7	3.2	112.0	0.3	112.7	0.6	112.8	0.1
1985	113.6	0.7	113.7	0.1	113.9	0.2	114.3	0.4	114.4	0.1	114.6	0.2	115.2	0.5	115.4	0.2	119.0	3.1	119.4	0.3	119.7	0.3	120.3	0.5
1986	121.4	0.9	121.3	-0.1	122.0	0.6	121.9	-0.1	121.8	-0.1	121.4	-0.3	123.0	1.3	122.7	-0.2	125.9	2.6	126.9	0.8	127.3	0.3	126.9	-0.3
1987	127.9	0.8	127.9	0.0	128.6	0.5	128.8	0.2	128.9	0.1	129.4	0.4	130.1	0.5	130.0	-0.1	133.9	3.0	134.7	0.6	134.8	0.1	135.0	0.1
1988	136.6	1.2	136.9	0.2	137.5	0.4	137.6	0.1	137.4	-0.1	137.5	0.1	138.2	0.5	138.9	0.5	142.9	2.9	143.1	0.1	143.5	0.3	143.6	0.1
1989	146.3	1.9	146.6	0.2	147.0	0.3	146.9	-0.1	149.3	1.6	150.9	1.1	151.2	0.2	153.1	1.3	157.7	3.0	157.3	-0.3	157.7	0.3	158.2	0.3
1990	159.4	0.8	159.8	0.3	160.5	0.4	160.6	0.1	161.3	0.4	162.0	0.4	164.4	1.5	165.2	0.5	168.4	1.9	168.3	-0.1	168.5	0.1	169.2	0.4
1991	171.4	1.3	171.9	0.3	172.0	0.1	173.3	0.8	174.3	0.6	174.7	0.2	175.4	0.4	177.4	1.1	183.2	3.3	183.4	0.1	184.7	0.7	185.1	0.2
1992	187.3	1.2	187.6	0.2	187.6	0.0	187.9	0.2	188.6	0.4	189.0	0.2	189.5	0.3	192.5	1.6	195.4	1.5	195.3	-0.1	195.3	0.0	195.8	0.3
1993	197.4	0.8	198.3	0.5	198.8	0.3	199.3	0.3	199.1	-0.1	200.1	0.5	200.8	0.3	201.7	0.4	202.5	0.4	201.1	-0.7	201.0	-0.0	201.2	0.1

Source: U.S. Department of Labor, Bureau of Labor Statistics, Division of Consumer Prices and Price Indexes. - indicates no data collected for period.

New York, NY, NE NJ
Consumer Price Index - Urban Wage Earners
Base 1982-1984 = 100
Other Goods and Services

For 1976-1993. Columns headed % show percentile change in the index from the previous period for which an index is available.

Year	Jan Index	%	Feb Index	%	Mar Index	%	Apr Index	%	May Index	%	Jun Index	%	Jul Index	%	Aug Index	%	Sep Index	%	Oct Index	%	Nov Index	%	Dec Index	%
1976	57.2	-	58.0	1.4	58.4	0.7	58.6	0.3	58.6	0.0	58.9	0.5	59.1	0.3	59.7	1.0	60.3	1.0	60.5	0.3	60.8	0.5	60.9	0.2
1977	61.8	1.5	62.3	0.8	62.3	0.0	62.2	-0.2	62.4	0.3	62.6	0.3	62.7	0.2	62.9	0.3	63.4	0.8	63.7	0.5	64.7	1.6	64.7	0.0
1978	64.8	0.2	65.1	0.5	65.2	0.2	65.1	-0.2	65.2	0.2	65.7	0.8	66.3	0.9	66.1	-0.3	67.2	1.7	67.1	-0.1	67.5	0.6	67.2	-0.4
1979	67.8	0.9	68.3	0.7	68.6	0.4	68.6	0.0	68.6	0.0	68.7	0.1	69.2	0.7	70.0	1.2	70.9	1.3	71.3	0.6	71.5	0.3	71.9	0.6
1980	72.6	1.0	73.2	0.8	73.0	-0.3	73.3	0.4	73.8	0.7	74.1	0.4	74.4	0.4	74.9	0.7	76.5	2.1	76.9	0.5	76.9	0.0	77.5	0.8
1981	77.6	0.1	78.2	0.8	78.4	0.3	78.9	0.6	79.6	0.9	79.6	0.0	80.3	0.9	80.5	0.2	83.7	4.0	84.2	0.6	84.8	0.7	84.9	0.1
1982	85.4	0.6	86.1	0.8	86.6	0.6	87.1	0.6	87.4	0.3	87.5	0.1	88.5	1.1	89.5	1.1	92.6	3.5	94.1	1.6	95.2	1.2	96.4	1.3
1983	97.4	1.0	97.6	0.2	97.9	0.3	99.6	1.7	99.2	-0.4	99.9	0.7	101.7	1.8	102.4	0.7	104.8	2.3	105.5	0.7	106.4	0.9	106.5	0.1
1984	106.9	0.4	107.1	0.2	106.8	-0.3	107.0	0.2	107.4	0.4	107.6	0.2	108.0	0.4	108.3	0.3	110.8	2.3	111.0	0.2	111.8	0.7	111.9	0.1
1985	112.8	0.8	113.0	0.2	113.2	0.2	113.6	0.4	113.7	0.1	114.0	0.3	114.9	0.8	115.1	0.2	117.9	2.4	118.3	0.3	118.6	0.3	119.4	0.7
1986	120.8	1.2	120.7	-0.1	121.4	0.6	121.4	0.0	121.2	-0.2	120.7	-0.4	122.6	1.6	122.4	-0.2	124.4	1.6	125.4	0.8	126.0	0.5	125.5	-0.4
1987	126.7	1.0	126.8	0.1	127.2	0.3	127.4	0.2	127.5	0.1	127.9	0.3	128.6	0.5	128.7	0.1	132.4	2.9	133.2	0.6	133.4	0.2	133.6	0.1
1988	135.1	1.1	135.3	0.1	135.9	0.4	136.0	0.1	136.0	0.0	136.0	0.0	136.7	0.5	137.4	0.5	141.2	2.8	141.4	0.1	141.8	0.3	141.9	0.1
1989	144.8	2.0	145.2	0.3	145.6	0.3	145.6	0.0	148.4	1.9	150.0	1.1	150.3	0.2	152.0	1.1	156.4	2.9	156.2	-0.1	156.4	0.1	157.1	0.4
1990	158.3	0.8	158.6	0.2	159.3	0.4	159.4	0.1	160.0	0.4	160.9	0.6	164.6	2.3	165.3	0.4	168.8	2.1	168.6	-0.1	169.1	0.3	169.9	0.5
1991	171.6	1.0	171.9	0.2	172.2	0.2	173.5	0.8	174.6	0.6	175.3	0.4	175.8	0.3	178.2	1.4	183.1	2.7	183.7	0.3	184.8	0.6	185.2	0.2
1992	187.3	1.1	187.5	0.1	187.4	-0.1	188.0	0.3	188.7	0.4	189.2	0.3	189.6	0.2	193.1	1.8	195.0	1.0	195.1	0.1	195.2	0.1	195.6	0.2
1993	197.4	0.9	198.3	0.5	198.9	0.3	199.4	0.3	199.3	-0.1	200.6	0.7	201.4	0.4	202.4	0.5	203.4	0.5	201.7	-0.8	201.3	-0.2	200.8	-0.2

Source: U.S. Department of Labor, Bureau of Labor Statistics, Division of Consumer Prices and Price Indexes. - indicates no data collected for period.

Philadelphia, PA-NJ
Consumer Price Index - All Urban Consumers
Base 1982-1984 = 100
Annual Averages

For 1914-1993. Columns headed % show percentile change in the index from the previous period for which an index is available.

Year	All Items		Food & Beverage		Housing		Apparel & Upkeep		Trans- portation		Medical Care		Entertain- ment		Other Goods & Services	
	Index	%	Index	%	Index	%	Index	%	Index	%	Index	%	Index	%	Index	%
1914	-	-	-	-	-	-	-	-	-	-	-	-	-	-	-	-
1915	10.1	-	-	-	-	-	-	-	-	-	-	-	-	-	-	-
1916	10.8	6.9	-	-	-	-	-	-	-	-	-	-	-	-	-	-
1917	13.1	21.3	-	-	-	-	-	-	-	-	-	-	-	-	-	-
1918	15.5	18.3	-	-	-	-	-	-	-	-	-	-	-	-	-	-
1919	17.9	15.5	-	-	-	-	-	-	-	-	-	-	-	-	-	-
1920	20.5	14.5	-	-	-	-	-	-	-	-	-	-	-	-	-	-
1921	18.2	-11.2	-	-	-	-	-	-	-	-	-	-	-	-	-	-
1922	17.2	-5.5	-	-	-	-	-	-	-	-	-	-	-	-	-	-
1923	17.6	2.3	-	-	-	-	-	-	-	-	-	-	-	-	-	-
1924	17.7	0.6	-	-	-	-	-	-	-	-	-	-	-	-	-	-
1925	18.4	4.0	-	-	-	-	-	-	-	-	-	-	-	-	-	-
1926	18.7	1.6	-	-	-	-	-	-	-	-	-	-	-	-	-	-
1927	18.3	-2.1	-	-	-	-	-	-	-	-	-	-	-	-	-	-
1928	18.0	-1.6	-	-	-	-	-	-	-	-	-	-	-	-	-	-
1929	17.8	-1.1	-	-	-	-	-	-	-	-	-	-	-	-	-	-
1930	17.4	-2.2	-	-	-	-	-	-	-	-	-	-	-	-	-	-
1931	15.9	-8.6	-	-	-	-	-	-	-	-	-	-	-	-	-	-
1932	14.2	-10.7	-	-	-	-	-	-	-	-	-	-	-	-	-	-
1933	13.5	-4.9	-	-	-	-	-	-	-	-	-	-	-	-	-	-
1934	14.2	5.2	-	-	-	-	-	-	-	-	-	-	-	-	-	-
1935	14.3	0.7	-	-	-	-	-	-	-	-	-	-	-	-	-	-
1936	14.5	1.4	-	-	-	-	-	-	-	-	-	-	-	-	-	-
1937	14.9	2.8	-	-	-	-	-	-	-	-	-	-	-	-	-	-
1938	14.5	-2.7	-	-	-	-	-	-	-	-	-	-	-	-	-	-
1939	14.3	-1.4	-	-	-	-	-	-	-	-	-	-	-	-	-	-
1940	14.3	0.0	-	-	-	-	-	-	-	-	-	-	-	-	-	-
1941	15.0	4.9	-	-	-	-	-	-	-	-	-	-	-	-	-	-
1942	16.7	11.3	-	-	-	-	-	-	-	-	-	-	-	-	-	-
1943	17.8	6.6	-	-	-	-	-	-	-	-	-	-	-	-	-	-
1944	18.0	1.1	-	-	-	-	-	-	-	-	-	-	-	-	-	-
1945	18.5	2.8	-	-	-	-	-	-	-	-	-	-	-	-	-	-
1946	20.1	8.6	-	-	-	-	-	-	-	-	-	-	-	-	-	-
1947	23.0	14.4	-	-	-	-	-	-	16.8	-	12.4	-	-	-	-	-
1948	24.8	7.8	-	-	-	-	-	-	18.4	9.5	13.0	4.8	-	-	-	-
1949	24.5	-1.2	-	-	-	-	-	-	19.5	6.0	13.4	3.1	-	-	-	-
1950	24.7	0.8	-	-	-	-	-	-	19.5	0.0	13.6	1.5	-	-	-	-
1951	27.0	9.3	-	-	-	-	-	-	23.2	19.0	14.2	4.4	-	-	-	-
1952	27.5	1.9	-	-	-	-	-	-	24.1	3.9	15.0	5.6	-	-	-	-
1953	27.6	0.4	-	-	-	-	44.3	-	24.5	1.7	15.6	4.0	-	-	-	-
1954	27.9	1.1	-	-	-	-	44.6	0.7	25.1	2.4	16.4	5.1	-	-	-	-
1955	27.9	0.0	-	-	-	-	44.4	-0.4	24.9	-0.8	17.5	6.7	-	-	-	-
1956	28.2	1.1	-	-	-	-	44.8	0.9	24.9	0.0	17.8	1.7	-	-	-	-
1957	29.1	3.2	-	-	-	-	46.0	2.7	25.8	3.6	18.2	2.2	-	-	-	-
1958	29.7	2.1	-	-	-	-	45.6	-0.9	26.6	3.1	18.9	3.8	-	-	-	-

[Continued]

672

Philadelphia, PA-NJ
Consumer Price Index - All Urban Consumers
Base 1982-1984 = 100
Annual Averages
[Continued]

For 1914-1993. Columns headed % show percentile change in the index from the previous period for which an index is available.

Year	All Items		Food & Beverage		Housing		Apparel & Upkeep		Trans-portation		Medical Care		Entertain-ment		Other Goods & Services	
	Index	%	Index	%	Index	%	Index	%	Index	%	Index	%	Index	%	Index	%
1959	30.0	1.0	-	-	-	-	46.3	1.5	28.0	5.3	20.0	5.8	-	-	-	-
1960	30.6	2.0	-	-	-	-	48.0	3.7	28.3	1.1	20.8	4.0	-	-	-	-
1961	30.9	1.0	-	-	-	-	49.1	2.3	29.0	2.5	21.7	4.3	-	-	-	-
1962	31.2	1.0	-	-	-	-	49.6	1.0	29.2	0.7	22.6	4.1	-	-	-	-
1963	31.8	1.9	-	-	-	-	50.2	1.2	29.9	2.4	23.1	2.2	-	-	-	-
1964	32.3	1.6	-	-	-	-	50.3	0.2	30.5	2.0	23.4	1.3	-	-	-	-
1965	32.8	1.5	-	-	-	-	51.0	1.4	31.3	2.6	24.0	2.6	-	-	-	-
1966	33.7	2.7	-	-	-	-	52.9	3.7	31.8	1.6	25.1	4.6	-	-	-	-
1967	34.6	2.7	-	-	-	-	55.3	4.5	32.6	2.5	26.7	6.4	-	-	-	-
1968	36.3	4.9	-	-	-	-	58.5	5.8	34.3	5.2	28.9	8.2	-	-	-	-
1969	38.2	5.2	-	-	-	-	61.5	5.1	35.9	4.7	31.4	8.7	-	-	-	-
1970	40.8	6.8	-	-	-	-	64.1	4.2	37.9	5.6	34.0	8.3	-	-	-	-
1971	42.7	4.7		-		-	65.9	2.8	40.2	6.1	36.7	7.9	-	-	-	-
1972	44.0	3.0		-		-	66.4	0.8	40.8	1.5	38.0	3.5	-	-	-	-
1973	46.9	6.6		-		-	69.0	3.9	41.6	2.0	39.8	4.7	-	-	-	-
1974	52.5	11.9	-	-	-	-	73.1	5.9	45.9	10.3	43.4	9.0	-	-	-	-
1975	56.8	8.2	-	-	-	-	75.2	2.9	49.8	8.5	49.3	13.6	-	-	-	-
1976	59.7	5.1	62.2	-	59.1	-	77.1	2.5	54.0	8.4	53.7	8.9	68.8	-	56.0	-
1977	63.5	6.4	66.0	6.1	62.7	6.1	79.1	2.6	59.3	9.8	59.0	9.9	71.6	4.1	59.2	5.7
1978	67.3	6.0	72.4	9.7	65.7	4.8	80.9	2.3	62.5	5.4	63.2	7.1	74.0	3.4	62.4	5.4
1979	73.9	9.8	79.5	9.8	71.9	9.4	86.2	6.6	70.9	13.4	68.4	8.2	81.1	9.6	67.0	7.4
1980	83.6	13.1	86.0	8.2	83.5	16.1	94.4	9.5	83.6	17.9	75.4	10.2	84.0	3.6	73.2	9.3
1981	92.1	10.2	92.5	7.6	93.7	12.2	95.9	1.6	93.2	11.5	83.9	11.3	92.1	9.6	79.5	8.6
1982	96.6	4.9	97.7	5.6	97.6	4.2	98.8	3.0	96.1	3.1	91.7	9.3	96.4	4.7	89.5	12.6
1983	99.4	2.9	100.0	2.4	98.4	0.8	100.3	1.5	99.4	3.4	100.6	9.7	100.5	4.3	101.0	12.8
1984	104.1	4.7	102.4	2.4	104.0	5.7	100.9	0.6	104.5	5.1	107.7	7.1	103.1	2.6	109.5	8.4
1985	108.8	4.5	105.0	2.5	109.1	4.9	101.4	0.5	109.4	4.7	119.1	10.6	105.2	2.0	117.1	6.9
1986	111.5	2.5	107.8	2.7	112.9	3.5	101.3	-0.1	107.1	-2.1	126.6	6.3	109.3	3.9	126.5	8.0
1987	116.8	4.8	112.1	4.0	118.4	4.9	107.7	6.3	111.5	4.1	133.0	5.1	112.2	2.7	135.9	7.4
1988	122.4	4.8	116.0	3.5	124.8	5.4	109.9	2.0	115.6	3.7	142.2	6.9	120.8	7.7	145.1	6.8
1989	128.3	4.8	124.2	7.1	130.8	4.8	99.4	-9.6	121.5	5.1	155.3	9.2	128.6	6.5	155.4	7.1
1990	135.8	5.8	131.2	5.6	138.7	6.0	101.4	2.0	127.7	5.1	167.4	7.8	133.5	3.8	171.9	10.6
1991	142.2	4.7	135.4	3.2	145.6	5.0	103.7	2.3	132.3	3.6	183.5	9.6	138.0	3.4	185.5	7.9
1992	146.6	3.1	137.6	1.6	149.6	2.7	106.5	2.7	136.1	2.9	196.6	7.1	144.4	4.6	195.8	5.6
1993	150.2	2.5	139.7	1.5	151.9	1.5	106.0	-0.5	139.5	2.5	211.6	7.6	147.5	2.1	210.7	7.6

Source: U.S. Department of Labor, Bureau of Labor Statistics, Division of Consumer Prices and Price Indexes. - indicates no data collected for period.

Philadelphia, PA-NJ
Consumer Price Index - Urban Wage Earners
Base 1982-1984 = 100
Annual Averages

For 1914-1993. Columns headed % show percentile change in the index from the previous period for which an index is available.

Year	All Items		Food & Beverage		Housing		Apparel & Upkeep		Trans- portation		Medical Care		Entertain- ment		Other Goods & Services	
	Index	%	Index	%	Index	%	Index	%	Index	%	Index	%	Index	%	Index	%
1914	-	-	-	-	-	-	-	-	-	-	-	-	-	-	-	-
1915	10.0	-	-	-	-	-	-	-	-	-	-	-	-	-	-	-
1916	10.8	8.0	-	-	-	-	-	-	-	-	-	-	-	-	-	-
1917	13.0	20.4	-	-	-	-	-	-	-	-	-	-	-	-	-	-
1918	15.5	19.2	-	-	-	-	-	-	-	-	-	-	-	-	-	-
1919	17.8	14.8	-	-	-	-	-	-	-	-	-	-	-	-	-	-
1920	20.3	14.0	-	-	-	-	-	-	-	-	-	-	-	-	-	-
1921	18.1	-10.8	-	-	-	-	-	-	-	-	-	-	-	-	-	-
1922	17.1	-5.5	-	-	-	-	-	-	-	-	-	-	-	-	-	-
1923	17.5	2.3	-	-	-	-	-	-	-	-	-	-	-	-	-	-
1924	17.6	0.6	-	-	-	-	-	-	-	-	-	-	-	-	-	-
1925	18.3	4.0	-	-	-	-	-	-	-	-	-	-	-	-	-	-
1926	18.6	1.6	-	-	-	-	-	-	-	-	-	-	-	-	-	-
1927	18.2	-2.2	-	-	-	-	-	-	-	-	-	-	-	-	-	-
1928	17.9	-1.6	-	-	-	-	-	-	-	-	-	-	-	-	-	-
1929	17.7	-1.1	-	-	-	-	-	-	-	-	-	-	-	-	-	-
1930	17.3	-2.3	-	-	-	-	-	-	-	-	-	-	-	-	-	-
1931	15.8	-8.7	-	-	-	-	-	-	-	-	-	-	-	-	-	-
1932	14.1	-10.8	-	-	-	-	-	-	-	-	-	-	-	-	-	-
1933	13.4	-5.0	-	-	-	-	-	-	-	-	-	-	-	-	-	-
1934	14.1	5.2	-	-	-	-	-	-	-	-	-	-	-	-	-	-
1935	14.3	1.4	-	-	-	-	-	-	-	-	-	-	-	-	-	-
1936	14.5	1.4	-	-	-	-	-	-	-	-	-	-	-	-	-	-
1937	14.8	2.1	-	-	-	-	-	-	-	-	-	-	-	-	-	-
1938	14.5	-2.0	-	-	-	-	-	-	-	-	-	-	-	-	-	-
1939	14.2	-2.1	-	-	-	-	-	-	-	-	-	-	-	-	-	-
1940	14.3	0.7	-	-	-	-	-	-	-	-	-	-	-	-	-	-
1941	14.9	4.2	-	-	-	-	-	-	-	-	-	-	-	-	-	-
1942	16.6	11.4	-	-	-	-	-	-	-	-	-	-	-	-	-	-
1943	17.7	6.6	-	-	-	-	-	-	-	-	-	-	-	-	-	-
1944	17.9	1.1	-	-	-	-	-	-	-	-	-	-	-	-	-	-
1945	18.4	2.8	-	-	-	-	-	-	-	-	-	-	-	-	-	-
1946	20.0	8.7	-	-	-	-	-	-	-	-	-	-	-	-	-	-
1947	22.9	14.5	-	-	-	-	-	-	16.3	-	11.7	-	-	-	-	-
1948	24.7	7.9	-	-	-	-	-	-	17.9	9.8	12.3	5.1	-	-	-	-
1949	24.4	-1.2	-	-	-	-	-	-	19.0	6.1	12.6	2.4	-	-	-	-
1950	24.5	0.4	-	-	-	-	-	-	19.0	0.0	12.8	1.6	-	-	-	-
1951	26.8	9.4	-	-	-	-	-	-	22.5	18.4	13.4	4.7	-	-	-	-
1952	27.4	2.2	-	-	-	-	-	-	23.4	4.0	14.1	5.2	-	-	-	-
1953	27.5	0.4	-	-	-	-	51.1	-	23.8	1.7	14.7	4.3	-	-	-	-
1954	27.8	1.1	-	-	-	-	51.5	0.8	24.3	2.1	15.5	5.4	-	-	-	-
1955	27.7	-0.4	-	-	-	-	51.2	-0.6	24.1	-0.8	16.5	6.5	-	-	-	-
1956	28.1	1.4	-	-	-	-	51.7	1.0	24.2	0.4	16.8	1.8	-	-	-	-
1957	29.0	3.2	-	-	-	-	53.0	2.5	25.0	3.3	17.1	1.8	-	-	-	-
1958	29.5	1.7	-	-	-	-	52.7	-0.6	25.8	3.2	17.8	4.1	-	-	-	-

[Continued]

674

Philadelphia, PA-NJ
Consumer Price Index - Urban Wage Earners
Base 1982-1984 = 100
Annual Averages
[Continued]

For 1914-1993. Columns headed % show percentile change in the index from the previous period for which an index is available.

Year	All Items		Food & Beverage		Housing		Apparel & Upkeep		Trans-portation		Medical Care		Entertain-ment		Other Goods & Services	
	Index	%	Index	%	Index	%	Index	%	Index	%	Index	%	Index	%	Index	%
1959	29.9	1.4	-	-	-	-	53.4	1.3	27.2	5.4	18.9	6.2	-	-	-	-
1960	30.4	1.7	-	-	-	-	55.4	3.7	27.4	0.7	19.6	3.7	-	-	-	-
1961	30.8	1.3	-	-	-	-	56.7	2.3	28.2	2.9	20.5	4.6	-	-	-	-
1962	31.0	0.6	-	-	-	-	57.2	0.9	28.4	0.7	21.3	3.9	-	-	-	-
1963	31.6	1.9	-	-	-	-	58.0	1.4	29.0	2.1	21.8	2.3	-	-	-	-
1964	32.1	1.6	-	-	-	-	58.1	0.2	29.6	2.1	22.1	1.4	-	-	-	-
1965	32.6	1.6	-	-	-	-	58.9	1.4	30.4	2.7	22.7	2.7	-	-	-	-
1966	33.5	2.8	-	-	-	-	61.0	3.6	30.9	1.6	23.7	4.4	-	-	-	-
1967	34.4	2.7	-	-	-	-	63.8	4.6	31.7	2.6	25.2	6.3	-	-	-	-
1968	36.1	4.9	-	-	-	-	67.5	5.8	33.3	5.0	27.3	8.3	-	-	-	-
1969	38.0	5.3	-	-	-	-	70.9	5.0	34.9	4.8	29.6	8.4	-	-	-	-
1970	40.6	6.8	-	-	-	-	73.9	4.2	36.8	5.4	32.1	8.4	-	-	-	-
1971	42.5	4.7	-	-	-	-	76.1	3.0	39.0	6.0	34.7	8.1	-	-	-	-
1972	43.7	2.8	-	-	-	-	76.6	0.7	39.6	1.5	35.9	3.5	-	-	-	-
1973	46.6	6.6	-	-	-	-	79.6	3.9	40.4	2.0	37.6	4.7	-	-	-	-
1974	52.2	12.0	-	-	-	-	84.3	5.9	44.6	10.4	41.0	9.0	-	-	-	-
1975	56.5	8.2	-	-	-	-	86.8	3.0	48.4	8.5	46.5	13.4	-	-	-	-
1976	59.4	5.1	60.5	-	58.9	-	89.0	2.5	52.4	8.3	50.7	9.0	70.9	-	58.2	-
1977	63.2	6.4	64.3	6.3	62.6	6.3	91.3	2.6	57.6	9.9	55.7	9.9	73.8	4.1	61.5	5.7
1978	67.1	6.2	70.8	10.1	65.5	4.6	90.5	-0.9	61.3	6.4	60.2	8.1	77.3	4.7	64.7	5.2
1979	73.9	10.1	79.2	11.9	71.5	9.2	89.4	-1.2	70.1	14.4	66.6	10.6	86.3	11.6	68.4	5.7
1980	83.5	13.0	86.8	9.6	82.4	15.2	94.4	5.6	83.2	18.7	76.0	14.1	86.4	0.1	73.9	8.0
1981	91.9	10.1	93.2	7.4	92.1	11.8	96.3	2.0	93.6	12.5	83.9	10.4	94.1	8.9	80.4	8.8
1982	95.8	4.2	97.7	4.8	95.6	3.8	98.8	2.6	96.2	2.8	91.6	9.2	96.5	2.6	89.4	11.2
1983	99.7	4.1	99.9	2.3	99.3	3.9	100.2	1.4	99.4	3.3	100.6	9.8	100.6	4.2	101.2	13.2
1984	104.5	4.8	102.4	2.5	105.2	5.9	100.9	0.7	104.4	5.0	107.9	7.3	102.9	2.3	109.4	8.1
1985	109.2	4.5	105.1	2.6	110.8	5.3	100.5	-0.4	109.2	4.6	119.0	10.3	104.4	1.5	116.8	6.8
1986	111.5	2.1	107.9	2.7	114.5	3.3	99.7	-0.8	106.0	-2.9	126.3	6.1	108.2	3.6	125.9	7.8
1987	116.7	4.7	112.4	4.2	120.0	4.8	104.4	4.7	110.8	4.5	132.7	5.1	110.6	2.2	134.7	7.0
1988	122.2	4.7	116.5	3.6	126.3	5.2	106.0	1.5	115.1	3.9	141.5	6.6	118.8	7.4	144.3	7.1
1989	128.3	5.0	125.1	7.4	133.0	5.3	94.5	-10.8	121.6	5.6	154.0	8.8	126.1	6.1	153.8	6.6
1990	136.1	6.1	132.3	5.8	140.7	5.8	97.6	3.3	128.4	5.6	165.9	7.7	130.2	3.3	170.7	11.0
1991	142.2	4.5	136.5	3.2	147.5	4.8	99.0	1.4	132.8	3.4	180.9	9.0	134.7	3.5	184.3	8.0
1992	146.4	3.0	138.7	1.6	151.3	2.6	103.3	4.3	136.1	2.5	193.9	7.2	140.2	4.1	194.3	5.4
1993	150.1	2.5	140.9	1.6	153.8	1.7	104.7	1.4	139.2	2.3	208.8	7.7	142.6	1.7	208.5	7.3

Source: U.S. Department of Labor, Bureau of Labor Statistics, Division of Consumer Prices and Price Indexes. - indicates no data collected for period.

Philadelphia, PA-NJ
Consumer Price Index - All Urban Consumers
Base 1982-1984 = 100
All Items

For 1914-1993. Columns headed % show percentile change in the index from the previous period for which an index is available.

Year	Jan Index	%	Feb Index	%	Mar Index	%	Apr Index	%	May Index	%	Jun Index	%	Jul Index	%	Aug Index	%	Sep Index	%	Oct Index	%	Nov Index	%	Dec Index	%
1914	-	-	-	-	-	-	-	-	-	-	-	-	-	-	-	-	-	-	-	-	-	-	10.2	-
1915	-	-	-	-	-	-	-	-	-	-	-	-	-	-	-	-	-	-	-	-	-	-	10.3	1.0
1916	-	-	-	-	-	-	-	-	-	-	-	-	-	-	-	-	-	-	-	-	-	-	11.6	12.6
1917	-	-	-	-	-	-	-	-	-	-	-	-	-	-	-	-	-	-	-	-	-	-	14.1	21.6
1918	-	-	-	-	-	-	-	-	-	-	-	-	-	-	-	-	-	-	-	-	-	-	17.0	20.6
1919	-	-	-	-	-	-	-	-	-	-	17.5	2.9	-	-	-	-	-	-	-	-	-	-	19.2	9.7
1920	-	-	-	-	-	-	-	-	-	-	21.3	10.9	-	-	-	-	-	-	-	-	-	-	19.9	-6.6
1921	-	-	-	-	-	-	-	-	18.1	-9.0	-	-	-	-	-	-	17.9	-1.1	-	-	-	-	17.7	-1.1
1922	-	-	-	-	17.3	-2.3	-	-	-	-	17.3	0.0	-	-	-	-	16.9	-2.3	-	-	-	-	17.3	2.4
1923	-	-	-	-	17.3	0.0	-	-	-	-	17.6	1.7	-	-	-	-	17.8	1.1	-	-	-	-	17.8	0.0
1924	-	-	-	-	17.6	-1.1	-	-	-	-	17.7	0.6	-	-	-	-	17.6	-0.6	-	-	-	-	18.0	2.3
1925	-	-	-	-	-	-	-	-	-	-	18.4	2.2	-	-	-	-	-	-	-	-	-	-	18.9	2.7
1926	-	-	-	-	-	-	-	-	-	-	18.8	-0.5	-	-	-	-	-	-	-	-	-	-	18.7	-0.5
1927	-	-	-	-	-	-	-	-	-	-	18.5	-1.1	-	-	-	-	-	-	-	-	-	-	18.3	-1.1
1928	-	-	-	-	-	-	-	-	-	-	18.1	-1.1	-	-	-	-	-	-	-	-	-	-	17.8	-1.7
1929	-	-	-	-	-	-	-	-	-	-	17.8	0.0	-	-	-	-	-	-	-	-	-	-	17.9	0.6
1930	-	-	-	-	-	-	-	-	-	-	17.5	-2.2	-	-	-	-	-	-	-	-	-	-	16.8	-4.0
1931	-	-	-	-	-	-	-	-	-	-	15.9	-5.4	-	-	-	-	-	-	-	-	-	-	15.3	-3.8
1932	-	-	-	-	-	-	-	-	-	-	14.2	-7.2	-	-	-	-	-	-	-	-	-	-	13.5	-4.9
1933	-	-	-	-	-	-	-	-	-	-	13.2	-2.2	-	-	-	-	-	-	-	-	-	-	13.8	4.5
1934	-	-	-	-	-	-	-	-	-	-	14.2	2.9	-	-	-	-	-	-	-	-	14.1	-0.7	-	-
1935	-	-	-	-	14.2	0.7	-	-	-	-	-	-	14.2	0.0	-	-	-	-	14.4	1.4	-	-	14.6	0.0
1936	14.5	0.7	-	-	-	-	14.4	-0.7	-	-	-	-	14.5	0.7	-	-	14.6	0.7	-	-	-	-	14.6	0.0
1937	-	-	-	-	14.8	1.4	-	-	-	-	14.9	0.7	-	-	-	-	15.1	1.3	-	-	-	-	14.7	-2.6
1938	-	-	-	-	14.5	-1.4	-	-	-	-	14.6	0.7	-	-	-	-	14.5	-0.7	-	-	-	-	14.4	-0.7
1939	-	-	-	-	14.2	-1.4	-	-	-	-	14.2	0.0	-	-	-	-	14.5	2.1	-	-	-	-	14.3	-1.4
1940	-	-	-	-	14.3	0.0	-	-	-	-	14.4	0.7	-	-	-	-	14.3	-0.7	14.3	0.0	14.3	0.0	14.4	0.7
1941	14.4	0.0	14.4	0.0	14.5	0.7	14.6	0.7	14.7	0.7	15.0	2.0	15.0	0.0	15.2	1.3	15.5	2.0	15.7	1.3	15.7	0.0	15.8	0.6
1942	16.1	1.9	16.1	0.0	16.3	1.2	16.5	1.2	16.6	0.6	16.7	0.6	16.9	1.2	16.9	0.0	17.0	0.6	17.1	0.6	17.2	0.6	17.4	1.2
1943	17.4	0.0	17.4	0.0	17.6	1.1	18.0	2.3	18.1	0.6	18.0	-0.6	17.8	-1.1	17.8	0.0	17.8	0.0	17.9	0.6	17.9	0.0	17.9	0.0
1944	17.9	0.0	17.9	0.0	17.8	-0.6	17.9	0.6	18.0	0.6	18.1	0.6	18.1	0.0	18.2	0.6	18.2	0.0	18.1	-0.5	18.1	0.0	18.2	0.6
1945	18.3	0.5	18.4	0.5	18.3	-0.5	18.3	0.0	18.5	1.1	18.6	0.5	18.7	0.5	18.7	0.0	18.6	-0.5	18.6	0.0	18.6	0.0	18.7	0.5
1946	18.7	0.0	18.7	0.0	18.8	0.5	18.9	0.5	19.0	0.5	19.2	1.1	20.3	5.7	20.9	3.0	21.2	1.4	21.5	1.4	21.9	1.9	22.2	1.4
1947	22.1	-0.5	22.0	-0.5	22.7	3.2	22.5	-0.9	22.5	0.0	22.8	1.3	23.0	0.9	23.2	0.9	23.7	2.2	23.6	-0.4	23.8	0.8	24.2	1.7
1948	24.4	0.8	24.2	-0.8	24.0	-0.8	24.6	2.5	24.8	0.8	25.0	0.8	25.1	0.4	25.4	1.2	25.4	0.0	25.3	-0.4	25.0	-1.2	24.8	-0.8
1949	24.6	-0.8	24.5	-0.4	24.6	0.4	24.6	0.0	24.7	0.4	24.6	-0.4	24.4	-0.8	24.5	0.4	24.6	0.4	24.6	0.0	24.5	-0.4	24.3	-0.8
1950	24.1	-0.8	24.1	0.0	24.2	0.4	24.2	0.0	24.3	0.4	24.5	0.8	24.7	0.8	24.9	0.8	25.1	0.8	25.2	0.4	25.2	0.0	25.8	2.4
1951	26.3	1.9	26.9	2.3	26.9	0.0	27.0	0.4	27.0	0.0	26.9	-0.4	26.9	0.0	26.9	0.0	27.0	0.4	27.1	0.4	27.4	1.1	27.4	0.0
1952	27.4	0.0	27.1	-1.1	27.2	0.4	27.3	0.4	27.3	0.0	27.4	0.4	27.7	1.1	27.7	0.0	27.7	0.0	27.7	0.0	27.7	0.0	27.7	0.0
1953	27.6	-0.4	27.4	-0.7	27.5	0.4	27.4	-0.4	27.5	0.4	27.7	0.7	27.7	0.0	27.7	0.0	27.8	0.4	27.8	0.0	27.7	-0.4	27.7	0.0
1954	27.8	0.4	27.8	0.0	27.7	-0.4	27.8	0.4	27.8	0.0	28.0	0.7	28.1	0.4	28.0	-0.4	28.0	0.0	28.0	0.0	28.0	0.0	27.9	-0.4
1955	27.9	0.0	27.9	0.0	27.9	0.0	27.9	0.0	27.9	0.0	27.9	0.0	27.9	0.0	27.9	0.0	27.8	-0.4	27.8	0.0	27.7	-0.3	28.6	0.4
1956	27.7	0.0	27.7	0.0	27.9	0.7	28.0	0.4	28.0	0.0	28.2	0.7	28.5	1.1	28.5	0.0	28.6	0.4	28.6	0.0	28.5	-0.3	28.6	0.4
1957	28.7	0.3	28.9	0.7	28.9	0.0	28.9	0.0	28.9	0.0	29.0	0.3	29.2	0.7	29.4	0.7	29.4	0.0	29.4	0.0	29.5	0.3	29.5	0.0
1958	29.5	0.0	29.5	0.0	29.7	0.7	29.7	0.0	29.7	0.0	29.7	0.0	29.8	0.3	29.8	0.0	29.8	0.0	29.8	0.0	29.8	0.0	29.8	0.0

[Continued]

Philadelphia, PA-NJ

Consumer Price Index - All Urban Consumers
Base 1982-1984 = 100
All Items
[Continued]

For 1914-1993. Columns headed % show percentile change in the index from the previous period for which an index is available.

Year	Jan Index	%	Feb Index	%	Mar Index	%	Apr Index	%	May Index	%	Jun Index	%	Jul Index	%	Aug Index	%	Sep Index	%	Oct Index	%	Nov Index	%	Dec Index	%
1959	29.8	0.0	29.8	0.0	29.8	0.0	29.8	0.0	29.7	-0.3	29.9	0.7	30.0	0.3	30.0	0.0	30.4	1.3	30.4	0.0	30.5	0.3	30.5	0.0
1960	30.3	-0.7	30.3	0.0	30.4	0.3	30.5	0.3	30.5	0.0	30.5	0.0	30.6	0.3	30.6	0.0	30.7	0.3	30.8	0.3	30.9	0.3	30.9	0.0
1961	30.8	-0.3	30.9	0.3	30.8	-0.3	30.9	0.3	30.9	0.0	30.8	-0.3	31.0	0.6	30.9	-0.3	31.0	0.3	31.0	0.0	31.1	0.3	31.0	-0.3
1962	31.0	0.0	31.1	0.3	31.1	0.0	31.2	0.3	31.0	-0.6	31.1	0.3	31.2	0.3	31.2	0.0	31.4	0.6	31.4	0.0	31.4	0.0	31.3	-0.3
1963	31.4	0.3	31.5	0.3	31.5	0.0	31.5	0.0	31.5	0.0	31.8	1.0	31.8	0.0	31.8	0.0	31.9	0.3	32.1	0.6	32.1	0.0	32.2	0.3
1964	32.2	0.0	32.2	0.0	32.1	-0.3	32.1	0.0	32.1	0.0	32.2	0.3	32.3	0.3	32.2	-0.3	32.3	0.3	32.4	0.3	32.5	0.3	32.5	0.0
1965	32.5	0.0	32.6	0.3	32.6	0.0	32.5	-0.3	32.6	0.3	32.8	0.6	32.9	0.3	32.8	-0.3	32.8	0.0	32.9	0.3	33.0	0.3	33.1	0.3
1966	33.1	0.0	33.3	0.6	33.4	0.3	33.5	0.3	33.5	0.0	33.6	0.3	33.7	0.3	33.9	0.6	34.0	0.3	34.1	0.3	34.1	0.0	34.2	0.3
1967	34.1	-0.3	34.2	0.3	34.2	0.0	34.3	0.3	34.4	0.3	34.5	0.3	34.6	0.3	34.8	0.6	34.9	0.3	35.1	0.6	35.1	0.0	35.2	0.3
1968	35.4	0.6	35.6	0.6	35.8	0.6	35.9	0.3	36.0	0.3	36.2	0.6	36.3	0.3	36.4	0.3	36.7	0.8	36.9	0.5	37.0	0.3	37.1	0.3
1969	37.1	0.0	37.3	0.5	37.6	0.8	37.8	0.5	37.8	0.0	38.0	0.5	38.3	0.8	38.6	0.8	38.8	0.5	38.9	0.3	39.0	0.3	39.2	0.5
1970	39.4	0.5	39.8	1.0	40.1	0.8	40.2	0.2	40.5	0.7	40.6	0.2	40.7	0.2	40.9	0.5	41.4	1.2	41.7	0.7	41.9	0.5	42.0	0.2
1971	42.0	0.0	42.2	0.5	42.3	0.2	42.4	0.2	42.7	0.7	43.0	0.7	42.8	-0.5	42.8	0.0	43.1	0.7	43.3	0.5	43.2	-0.2	43.3	0.2
1972	43.2	-0.2	43.3	0.2	43.5	0.5	43.6	0.2	43.6	0.0	43.8	0.5	44.0	0.5	44.1	0.2	44.4	0.7	44.5	0.2	44.7	0.4	44.6	-0.2
1973	44.7	0.2	45.2	1.1	45.9	1.5	46.2	0.7	46.4	0.4	46.6	0.4	46.7	0.2	47.5	1.7	47.8	0.6	48.3	1.0	48.6	0.6	48.9	0.6
1974	49.4	1.0	50.2	1.6	50.9	1.4	51.3	0.8	51.7	0.8	52.2	1.0	52.5	0.6	53.1	1.1	53.9	1.5	54.4	0.9	54.9	0.9	55.1	0.4
1975	55.2	0.2	55.5	0.5	55.8	0.5	55.8	0.0	56.1	0.5	56.6	0.9	57.1	0.9	57.3	0.4	57.8	0.9	58.2	0.7	58.3	0.2	58.3	0.0
1976	58.5	0.3	58.7	0.3	58.7	0.0	58.9	0.3	59.2	0.5	59.5	0.5	59.8	0.5	59.9	0.2	60.4	0.8	60.6	0.3	60.8	0.3	60.7	-0.2
1977	61.2	0.8	61.9	1.1	62.4	0.8	63.0	1.0	63.4	0.6	63.6	0.3	64.0	0.6	64.0	0.0	64.6	0.9	64.7	0.2	64.9	0.3	64.7	-0.3
1978	64.9	0.3	65.1	0.3	65.6	0.8	66.0	0.6	66.4	0.6	67.1	1.1	67.9	1.2	68.0	0.1	68.5	0.7	68.7	0.3	69.1	0.6	69.6	0.7
1979	70.0	0.6	70.6	0.9	70.9	0.4	71.9	1.4	72.9	1.4	74.0	1.5	74.8	1.1	75.4	0.8	76.0	0.8	76.2	0.3	77.0	1.0	77.4	0.5
1980	78.6	1.6	80.0	1.8	81.2	1.5	82.2	1.2	82.9	0.9	83.9	1.2	84.5	0.7	85.2	0.8	85.6	0.5	85.8	0.2	86.3	0.6	86.7	0.5
1981	87.6	1.0	88.6	1.1	89.4	0.9	90.3	1.0	90.7	0.4	91.9	1.3	92.7	0.9	93.6	1.0	95.0	1.5	95.1	0.1	94.9	-0.2	95.2	0.3
1982	95.4	0.2	95.4	0.0	95.1	-0.3	95.2	0.1	95.2	0.0	96.8	1.7	97.3	0.5	97.4	0.1	98.0	0.6	97.5	-0.5	97.9	0.4	97.5	-0.4
1983	97.6	0.1	97.6	0.0	98.0	0.4	98.1	0.1	98.4	0.3	99.0	0.6	99.8	0.8	100.3	0.5	100.9	0.6	100.8	-0.1	101.0	0.2	101.0	0.0
1984	101.9	0.9	102.6	0.7	102.7	0.1	103.2	0.5	103.4	0.2	103.8	0.4	104.3	0.5	104.8	0.5	105.2	0.4	105.1	-0.1	105.9	0.8	105.6	-0.3
1985	106.0	0.4	107.0	0.9	107.4	0.4	108.1	0.7	108.8	0.6	108.8	0.0	109.2	0.4	109.3	0.1	109.6	0.3	109.9	0.3	110.4	0.5	110.7	0.3
1986	110.9	0.2	110.8	-0.1	110.5	-0.3	110.0	-0.5	110.4	0.4	111.4	0.9	111.8	0.4	111.8	0.0	112.8	0.9	112.4	-0.4	112.2	-0.2	112.6	0.4
1987	113.4	0.7	113.9	0.4	114.0	0.1	115.5	1.3	116.4	0.8	117.4	0.9	117.4	0.0	118.4	0.9	118.7	0.3	119.1	0.3	118.6	-0.4	118.9	0.3
1988	119.3	0.3	119.3	0.0	119.6	0.3	120.0	0.3	120.9	0.7	121.9	0.8	123.2	1.1	123.9	0.6	125.2	1.0	124.6	-0.5	125.3	0.6	125.6	0.2
1989	125.7	0.1	125.4	-0.2	126.0	0.5	126.7	0.6	127.9	0.9	128.8	0.7	129.3	0.4	129.1	-0.2	130.2	0.9	130.5	0.2	130.1	-0.3	129.9	-0.2
1990	131.2	1.0	132.2	0.8	133.6	1.1	134.3	0.5	134.6	0.2	135.1	0.4	136.3	0.9	137.3	0.7	138.2	0.7	138.8	0.4	139.1	0.2	139.4	0.2
1991	140.4	0.7	140.6	0.1	141.0	0.3	140.8	-0.1	141.3	0.4	141.8	0.4	142.4	0.4	143.3	0.6	143.8	0.3	143.1	-0.5	143.3	0.1	144.4	0.8
1992	144.4	0.0	144.2	-0.1	145.4	0.8	145.4	0.0	145.7	0.2	147.5	1.2	147.3	-0.1	148.0	0.5	148.1	0.1	148.0	-0.1	147.5	-0.3	147.5	0.0
1993	147.5	0.0	148.5	0.7	149.3	0.5	149.6	0.2	149.4	-0.1	150.5	0.7	150.7	0.1	150.6	-0.1	151.1	0.3	152.2	0.7	152.1	-0.1	151.3	-0.5

Source: U.S. Department of Labor, Bureau of Labor Statistics, Division of Consumer Prices and Price Indexes. - indicates no data collected for period.

Philadelphia, PA-NJ
Consumer Price Index - Urban Wage Earners
Base 1982-1984 = 100
All Items

For 1914-1993. Columns headed % show percentile change in the index from the previous period for which an index is available.

Year	Jan Index	%	Feb Index	%	Mar Index	%	Apr Index	%	May Index	%	Jun Index	%	Jul Index	%	Aug Index	%	Sep Index	%	Oct Index	%	Nov Index	%	Dec Index	%
1914	-	-	-	-	-	-	-	-	-	-	-	-	-	-	-	-	-	-	-	-	-	-	10.1	-
1915	-	-	-	-	-	-	-	-	-	-	-	-	-	-	-	-	-	-	-	-	-	-	10.3	2.0
1916	-	-	-	-	-	-	-	-	-	-	-	-	-	-	-	-	-	-	-	-	-	-	11.5	11.7
1917	-	-	-	-	-	-	-	-	-	-	-	-	-	-	-	-	-	-	-	-	-	-	14.0	21.7
1918	-	-	-	-	-	-	-	-	-	-	-	-	-	-	-	-	-	-	-	-	-	-	16.9	20.7
1919	-	-	-	-	-	-	-	-	-	-	17.4	3.0	-	-	-	-	-	-	-	-	-	-	19.1	9.8
1920	-	-	-	-	-	-	-	-	-	-	21.2	11.0	-	-	-	-	-	-	-	-	-	-	19.8	-6.6
1921	-	-	-	-	-	-	-	-	18.0	-9.1	-	-	-	-	-	-	17.8	-1.1	-	-	-	-	17.6	-1.1
1922	-	-	-	-	17.2	-2.3	-	-	-	-	17.2	0.0	-	-	-	-	16.8	-2.3	-	-	-	-	17.2	2.4
1923	-	-	-	-	17.2	0.0	-	-	-	-	17.5	1.7	-	-	-	-	17.7	1.1	-	-	-	-	17.7	0.0
1924	-	-	-	-	17.5	-1.1	-	-	-	-	17.6	0.6	-	-	-	-	17.5	-0.6	-	-	-	-	17.9	2.3
1925	-	-	-	-	-	-	-	-	-	-	18.3	2.2	-	-	-	-	-	-	-	-	-	-	18.8	2.7
1926	-	-	-	-	-	-	-	-	-	-	18.7	-0.5	-	-	-	-	-	-	-	-	-	-	18.6	-0.5
1927	-	-	-	-	-	-	-	-	-	-	18.4	-1.1	-	-	-	-	-	-	-	-	-	-	18.2	-1.1
1928	-	-	-	-	-	-	-	-	-	-	18.0	-1.1	-	-	-	-	-	-	-	-	-	-	17.7	-1.7
1929	-	-	-	-	-	-	-	-	-	-	17.7	0.0	-	-	-	-	-	-	-	-	-	-	17.8	0.6
1930	-	-	-	-	-	-	-	-	-	-	17.4	-2.2	-	-	-	-	-	-	-	-	-	-	16.7	-4.0
1931	-	-	-	-	-	-	-	-	-	-	15.8	-5.4	-	-	-	-	-	-	-	-	-	-	15.3	-3.2
1932	-	-	-	-	-	-	-	-	-	-	14.1	-7.8	-	-	-	-	-	-	-	-	-	-	13.5	-4.3
1933	-	-	-	-	-	-	-	-	-	-	13.2	-2.2	-	-	-	-	-	-	-	-	-	-	13.8	4.5
1934	-	-	-	-	-	-	-	-	-	-	14.1	2.2	-	-	-	-	-	-	-	-	14.0	-0.7	-	-
1935	-	-	-	-	14.1	0.7	-	-	-	-	-	-	14.1	0.0	-	-	-	-	14.3	1.4	-	-	-	-
1936	14.5	1.4	-	-	-	-	14.3	-1.4	-	-	-	-	14.5	1.4	-	-	14.6	0.7	-	-	-	-	14.5	-0.7
1937	-	-	-	-	14.7	1.4	-	-	-	-	14.8	0.7	-	-	-	-	15.0	1.4	-	-	-	-	14.7	-2.0
1938	-	-	-	-	14.5	-1.4	-	-	-	-	14.5	0.0	-	-	-	-	14.5	0.0	-	-	-	-	14.3	-1.4
1939	-	-	-	-	14.1	-1.4	-	-	-	-	14.1	0.0	-	-	-	-	14.4	2.1	-	-	-	-	14.3	-0.7
1940	-	-	-	-	14.2	-0.7	-	-	-	-	14.3	0.7	-	-	-	-	14.3	0.0	14.3	0.0	14.3	0.0	14.3	0.0
1941	14.3	0.0	14.3	0.0	14.4	0.7	14.5	0.7	14.7	1.4	14.9	1.4	14.9	0.0	15.1	1.3	15.4	2.0	15.6	1.3	15.6	0.0	15.7	0.6
1942	16.0	1.9	16.0	0.0	16.2	1.3	16.4	1.2	16.5	0.6	16.6	0.6	16.8	1.2	16.8	0.0	16.9	0.6	17.0	0.6	17.1	0.6	17.3	1.2
1943	17.3	0.0	17.3	0.0	17.5	1.2	17.9	2.3	18.0	0.6	17.9	-0.6	17.7	-1.1	17.7	0.0	17.7	0.0	17.8	0.6	17.8	0.0	17.8	0.0
1944	17.8	0.0	17.8	0.0	17.7	-0.6	17.8	0.6	17.9	0.6	18.0	0.6	18.0	0.0	18.1	0.6	18.1	0.0	18.0	-0.6	18.0	0.0	18.1	0.6
1945	18.2	0.6	18.3	0.5	18.2	-0.5	18.2	0.0	18.4	1.1	18.5	0.5	18.6	0.5	18.6	0.0	18.5	-0.5	18.5	0.0	18.5	0.0	18.6	0.5
1946	18.6	0.0	18.6	0.0	18.7	0.5	18.8	0.5	18.9	0.5	19.1	1.1	20.2	5.8	20.8	3.0	21.1	1.4	21.3	0.9	21.8	2.3	22.0	0.9
1947	22.0	0.0	21.9	-0.5	22.5	2.7	22.4	-0.4	22.4	0.0	22.7	1.3	22.9	0.9	23.1	0.9	23.6	2.2	23.4	-0.8	23.7	1.3	24.0	1.3
1948	24.3	1.2	24.1	-0.8	23.9	-0.8	24.5	2.5	24.6	0.4	24.9	1.2	25.0	0.4	25.3	1.2	25.3	0.0	25.2	-0.4	24.8	-1.6	24.7	-0.4
1949	24.5	-0.8	24.4	-0.4	24.4	0.0	24.4	0.0	24.5	0.4	24.5	0.0	24.2	-1.2	24.4	0.8	24.5	0.4	24.4	-0.4	24.4	0.0	24.2	-0.8
1950	24.0	-0.8	23.9	-0.4	24.1	0.8	24.1	0.0	24.1	0.0	24.4	1.2	24.6	0.8	24.8	0.8	25.0	0.8	25.1	0.4	25.1	0.0	25.7	2.4
1951	26.1	1.6	26.8	2.7	26.8	0.0	26.8	0.0	26.9	0.4	26.8	-0.4	26.8	0.0	26.8	0.0	26.8	0.0	27.0	0.7	27.3	1.1	27.3	0.0
1952	27.2	-0.4	27.0	-0.7	27.1	0.4	27.2	0.4	27.2	0.0	27.3	0.4	27.6	1.1	27.6	0.0	27.5	-0.4	27.5	0.0	27.5	0.0	27.6	0.4
1953	27.4	-0.4	27.3	-0.4	27.4	0.4	27.3	-0.4	27.3	0.0	27.5	0.7	27.5	0.0	27.6	0.4	27.9	0.0	27.9	0.0	27.8	-0.4	27.7	-0.4
1954	27.7	0.4	27.6	-0.4	27.6	0.0	27.6	0.0	27.7	0.4	27.8	0.4	27.9	0.4	27.8	0.0	27.6	-0.7	27.7	0.4	27.6	-0.4	27.6	0.0
1955	27.7	0.0	27.8	0.4	27.8	0.0	27.8	0.0	27.7	-0.4	27.7	0.0	27.8	0.4	28.3	1.1	28.4	0.4	28.5	0.4	28.4	-0.4	28.5	0.4
1956	27.5	-0.4	27.5	0.0	27.8	1.1	27.9	0.4	27.9	0.0	28.0	0.4	28.3	0.0	28.4	0.4	28.5	0.4	28.4	-0.4	29.3	0.0
1957	28.5	0.0	28.7	0.7	28.8	0.3	28.7	-0.3	28.8	0.3	28.8	0.0	29.1	1.0	29.2	0.3	29.3	0.3	29.3	0.0	29.3	0.0	29.3	0.0
1958	29.3	0.0	29.4	0.3	29.5	0.3	29.5	0.0	29.5	0.0	29.5	0.0	29.6	0.3	29.6	0.0	29.6	0.0	29.6	0.0	29.6	0.0	29.6	0.0

[Continued]

Philadelphia, PA-NJ
Consumer Price Index - Urban Wage Earners
Base 1982-1984 = 100
All Items
[Continued]

For 1914-1993. Columns headed % show percentile change in the index from the previous period for which an index is available.

Year	Jan Index	%	Feb Index	%	Mar Index	%	Apr Index	%	May Index	%	Jun Index	%	Jul Index	%	Aug Index	%	Sep Index	%	Oct Index	%	Nov Index	%	Dec Index	%
1959	29.6	0.0	29.6	0.0	29.6	0.0	29.7	0.3	29.6	-0.3	29.8	0.7	29.8	0.0	29.8	0.0	30.2	1.3	30.2	0.0	30.3	0.3	30.4	0.3
1960	30.1	-1.0	30.1	0.0	30.2	0.3	30.3	0.3	30.3	0.0	30.3	0.0	30.4	0.3	30.4	0.0	30.5	0.3	30.6	0.3	30.7	0.3	30.7	0.0
1961	30.7	0.0	30.7	0.0	30.6	-0.3	30.7	0.3	30.7	0.0	30.7	0.0	30.8	0.3	30.7	-0.3	30.8	0.3	30.9	0.3	30.9	0.0	30.9	0.0
1962	30.8	-0.3	31.0	0.6	31.0	0.0	31.0	0.0	30.8	-0.6	30.9	0.3	31.1	0.6	31.0	-0.3	31.3	1.0	31.2	-0.3	31.2	0.0	31.2	0.0
1963	31.2	0.0	31.3	0.3	31.4	0.3	31.4	0.0	31.3	-0.3	31.6	1.0	31.7	0.3	31.7	0.0	31.7	0.0	31.9	0.6	31.9	0.0	32.0	0.3
1964	32.0	0.0	32.1	0.3	31.9	-0.6	31.9	0.0	31.9	0.0	32.0	0.3	32.1	0.3	32.0	-0.3	32.1	0.3	32.2	0.3	32.3	0.3	32.3	0.0
1965	32.3	0.0	32.4	0.3	32.4	0.0	32.3	-0.3	32.5	0.6	32.6	0.3	32.7	0.3	32.6	-0.3	32.7	0.3	32.7	0.0	32.8	0.3	32.9	0.3
1966	32.9	0.0	33.1	0.6	33.2	0.3	33.4	0.6	33.3	-0.3	33.4	0.3	33.5	0.3	33.7	0.6	33.8	0.3	33.9	0.3	33.9	0.0	34.0	0.3
1967	33.9	-0.3	34.0	0.3	34.0	0.0	34.1	0.3	34.2	0.3	34.4	0.6	34.4	0.0	34.6	0.6	34.7	0.3	34.9	0.6	34.9	0.0	35.0	0.3
1968	35.3	0.9	35.4	0.3	35.6	0.6	35.7	0.3	35.8	0.3	36.0	0.6	36.1	0.3	36.3	0.6	36.5	0.6	36.7	0.5	36.8	0.3	36.9	0.3
1969	36.9	0.0	37.1	0.5	37.4	0.8	37.6	0.5	37.6	0.0	37.8	0.5	38.1	0.8	38.4	0.8	38.6	0.5	38.7	0.3	38.8	0.3	39.0	0.5
1970	39.2	0.5	39.6	1.0	39.9	0.8	40.0	0.3	40.2	0.5	40.4	0.5	40.5	0.2	40.7	0.5	41.2	1.2	41.5	0.7	41.7	0.5	41.8	0.2
1971	41.8	0.0	41.9	0.2	42.1	0.5	42.2	0.2	42.5	0.7	42.7	0.5	42.6	-0.2	42.6	0.0	42.9	0.7	43.0	0.2	42.9	-0.2	43.1	0.5
1972	42.9	-0.5	43.1	0.5	43.3	0.5	43.4	0.2	43.4	0.0	43.6	0.5	43.7	0.2	43.9	0.5	44.2	0.7	44.3	0.2	44.4	0.2	44.4	0.0
1973	44.4	0.0	45.0	1.4	45.6	1.3	45.9	0.7	46.2	0.7	46.4	0.4	46.4	0.0	47.2	1.7	47.5	0.6	48.0	1.1	48.4	0.8	48.7	0.6
1974	49.2	1.0	49.9	1.4	50.6	1.4	51.0	0.8	51.4	0.8	52.0	1.2	52.3	0.6	52.8	1.0	53.6	1.5	54.1	0.9	54.6	0.9	54.8	0.4
1975	54.9	0.2	55.2	0.5	55.5	0.5	55.5	0.0	55.8	0.5	56.3	0.9	56.8	0.9	57.0	0.4	57.5	0.9	57.9	0.7	58.0	0.2	58.0	0.0
1976	58.2	0.3	58.4	0.3	58.4	0.0	58.6	0.3	58.9	0.5	59.2	0.5	59.5	0.5	59.6	0.2	60.1	0.8	60.3	0.3	60.5	0.3	60.4	-0.2
1977	60.8	0.7	61.5	1.2	62.1	1.0	62.6	0.8	63.0	0.6	63.3	0.5	63.6	0.5	63.7	0.2	64.2	0.8	64.4	0.3	64.5	0.2	64.3	-0.3
1978	64.5	0.3	65.0	0.8	65.3	0.5	65.9	0.9	66.3	0.6	67.0	1.1	67.4	0.6	68.0	0.9	68.2	0.3	68.5	0.4	69.1	0.9	69.7	0.9
1979	70.2	0.7	70.9	1.0	71.2	0.4	72.0	1.1	72.8	1.1	73.8	1.4	74.7	1.2	75.1	0.5	75.8	0.9	76.2	0.5	77.0	1.0	77.3	0.4
1980	78.5	1.6	79.7	1.5	80.9	1.5	81.9	1.2	82.6	0.9	83.9	1.6	84.5	0.7	85.1	0.7	85.5	0.5	85.9	0.5	86.4	0.6	86.9	0.6
1981	88.0	1.3	88.9	1.0	89.3	0.4	90.0	0.8	90.5	0.6	91.4	1.0	92.4	1.1	93.5	1.2	94.5	1.1	94.7	0.2	94.5	-0.2	94.4	-0.1
1982	94.7	0.3	94.7	0.0	94.4	-0.3	94.5	0.1	94.6	0.1	96.1	1.6	96.7	0.6	96.6	-0.1	97.1	0.5	96.8	-0.3	97.1	0.3	96.7	-0.4
1983	97.3	0.6	97.5	0.2	98.3	0.8	98.7	0.4	98.6	-0.1	99.4	0.8	100.2	0.8	101.0	0.8	101.3	0.3	101.3	0.0	101.5	0.2	101.3	-0.2
1984	102.1	0.8	102.8	0.7	102.9	0.1	102.9	0.0	103.5	0.6	104.2	0.7	104.8	0.6	105.4	0.6	106.2	0.8	106.3	0.1	106.4	0.1	106.0	-0.4
1985	106.5	0.5	107.6	1.0	107.9	0.3	108.5	0.6	109.2	0.6	109.2	0.0	109.7	0.5	109.7	0.0	109.9	0.2	110.3	0.4	110.7	0.4	111.0	0.3
1986	111.2	0.2	111.1	-0.1	110.6	-0.5	110.1	-0.5	110.4	0.3	111.4	0.9	111.8	0.4	111.7	-0.1	112.5	0.7	112.3	-0.2	112.0	-0.3	112.5	0.4
1987	113.3	0.7	113.6	0.3	113.8	0.2	115.3	1.3	116.2	0.8	117.2	0.9	117.3	0.1	118.4	0.9	118.5	0.1	119.0	0.4	118.6	-0.3	119.0	0.3
1988	119.3	0.3	119.0	-0.3	119.5	0.4	119.8	0.3	120.8	0.8	121.8	0.8	123.1	1.1	123.6	0.4	124.9	1.1	124.4	-0.4	125.0	0.5	125.2	0.2
1989	125.5	0.2	125.4	-0.1	125.8	0.3	126.7	0.7	127.9	0.9	128.9	0.8	129.3	0.3	129.3	0.0	130.4	0.9	130.6	0.2	130.1	-0.4	130.0	-0.1
1990	131.0	0.8	132.2	0.9	133.8	1.2	134.4	0.4	134.9	0.4	135.5	0.4	136.6	0.8	137.5	0.7	138.6	0.8	139.1	0.4	139.4	0.2	139.8	0.3
1991	140.4	0.4	140.5	0.1	141.0	0.4	140.8	-0.1	141.2	0.3	141.8	0.4	142.5	0.5	143.2	0.5	143.7	0.3	142.9	-0.6	143.4	0.3	144.4	0.7
1992	144.2	-0.1	143.9	-0.2	145.0	0.8	145.1	0.1	145.5	0.3	147.4	1.3	147.3	-0.1	147.8	0.3	147.9	0.1	147.8	-0.1	147.6	-0.1	147.4	-0.1
1993	147.4	0.0	148.6	0.8	149.0	0.3	149.4	0.3	149.3	-0.1	150.4	0.7	150.6	0.1	150.4	-0.1	150.9	0.3	151.9	0.7	151.9	0.0	151.2	-0.5

Source: U.S. Department of Labor, Bureau of Labor Statistics, Division of Consumer Prices and Price Indexes. - indicates no data collected for period.

Philadelphia, PA-NJ
Consumer Price Index - All Urban Consumers
Base 1982-1984 = 100
Food and Beverages

For 1976-1993. Columns headed % show percentile change in the index from the previous period for which an index is available.

Year	Jan Index	%	Feb Index	%	Mar Index	%	Apr Index	%	May Index	%	Jun Index	%	Jul Index	%	Aug Index	%	Sep Index	%	Oct Index	%	Nov Index	%	Dec Index	%
1976	62.3	-	62.3	0.0	61.7	-1.0	61.8	0.2	62.0	0.3	62.3	0.5	62.4	0.2	62.5	0.2	62.5	0.0	62.4	-0.2	62.3	-0.2	62.2	-0.2
1977	63.1	1.4	64.7	2.5	65.3	0.9	65.8	0.8	65.9	0.2	66.3	0.6	66.7	0.6	66.3	-0.6	66.5	0.3	66.9	0.6	67.4	0.7	67.5	0.1
1978	68.3	1.2	69.3	1.5	70.1	1.2	70.6	0.7	71.6	1.4	73.5	2.7	74.1	0.8	74.0	-0.1	73.9	-0.1	73.8	-0.1	74.7	1.2	75.0	0.4
1979	76.3	1.7	77.4	1.4	78.2	1.0	78.7	0.6	79.2	0.6	79.3	0.1	80.3	1.3	80.1	-0.2	79.8	-0.4	80.9	1.4	81.3	0.5	82.0	0.9
1980	82.3	0.4	82.1	-0.2	83.0	1.1	83.9	1.1	84.8	1.1	86.2	1.7	86.7	0.6	87.5	0.9	87.9	0.5	88.6	0.8	89.3	0.8	89.6	0.3
1981	90.7	1.2	90.8	0.1	90.9	0.1	91.2	0.3	91.6	0.4	91.9	0.3	93.0	1.2	93.4	0.4	94.5	1.2	94.1	-0.4	93.9	-0.2	94.6	0.7
1982	95.5	1.0	96.7	1.3	96.7	0.0	97.7	1.0	97.4	-0.3	98.2	0.8	98.8	0.6	98.5	-0.3	98.7	0.2	98.1	-0.6	98.0	-0.1	97.8	-0.2
1983	98.3	0.5	98.8	0.5	99.1	0.3	99.7	0.6	99.9	0.2	100.7	0.8	100.4	-0.3	100.8	0.4	100.8	0.0	100.6	-0.2	100.1	-0.5	100.2	0.1
1984	101.6	1.4	102.6	1.0	102.7	0.1	102.3	-0.4	102.2	-0.1	102.4	0.2	103.2	0.8	103.6	0.4	102.2	-1.4	102.2	0.0	101.9	-0.3	101.8	-0.1
1985	103.2	1.4	104.5	1.3	104.9	0.4	104.9	0.0	104.9	0.0	104.6	-0.3	105.6	1.0	104.9	-0.7	105.6	0.7	105.8	0.2	105.3	-0.5	106.0	0.7
1986	106.1	0.1	106.0	-0.1	106.9	0.8	106.9	0.0	107.1	0.2	107.1	0.0	107.8	0.7	108.5	0.6	109.4	0.8	109.5	0.1	108.9	-0.5	109.3	0.4
1987	110.8	1.4	110.8	0.0	110.5	-0.3	111.4	0.8	111.9	0.4	112.0	0.1	112.4	0.4	112.7	0.3	112.7	0.0	113.4	0.6	113.1	-0.3	113.0	-0.1
1988	114.2	1.1	113.7	-0.4	112.7	-0.9	114.4	1.5	115.1	0.6	116.1	0.9	117.3	1.0	117.1	-0.2	117.4	0.3	118.5	0.9	117.3	-1.0	118.2	0.8
1989	119.4	1.0	120.1	0.6	121.7	1.3	122.3	0.5	123.1	0.7	125.0	1.5	125.7	0.6	125.4	-0.2	126.0	0.5	127.0	0.8	127.4	0.3	127.7	0.2
1990	128.4	0.5	130.2	1.4	130.6	0.3	130.1	-0.4	130.4	0.2	130.6	0.2	131.6	0.8	132.3	0.5	131.6	-0.5	132.5	0.7	132.5	0.0	133.6	0.8
1991	134.6	0.7	135.2	0.4	135.5	0.2	135.9	0.3	136.0	0.1	136.1	0.1	135.7	-0.3	135.2	-0.4	135.0	-0.1	135.0	0.0	135.1	0.1	135.1	0.0
1992	136.0	0.7	136.4	0.3	137.1	0.5	137.7	0.4	138.0	0.2	137.7	-0.2	138.1	0.3	137.7	-0.3	138.3	0.4	138.1	-0.1	137.6	-0.4	138.4	0.6
1993	138.6	0.1	139.0	0.3	139.4	0.3	140.4	0.7	140.9	0.4	139.5	-1.0	138.6	-0.6	138.6	0.0	140.2	1.2	139.7	-0.4	141.0	0.9	140.3	-0.5

Source: U.S. Department of Labor, Bureau of Labor Statistics, Division of Consumer Prices and Price Indexes. - indicates no data collected for period.

Philadelphia, PA-NJ
Consumer Price Index - Urban Wage Earners
Base 1982-1984 = 100
Food and Beverages

For 1976-1993. Columns headed % show percentile change in the index from the previous period for which an index is available.

Year	Jan Index	%	Feb Index	%	Mar Index	%	Apr Index	%	May Index	%	Jun Index	%	Jul Index	%	Aug Index	%	Sep Index	%	Oct Index	%	Nov Index	%	Dec Index	%
1976	60.6	-	60.6	0.0	60.0	-1.0	60.1	0.2	60.3	0.3	60.6	0.5	60.7	0.2	60.8	0.2	60.8	0.0	60.7	-0.2	60.6	-0.2	60.5	-0.2
1977	61.4	1.5	63.0	2.6	63.5	0.8	64.1	0.9	64.2	0.2	64.5	0.5	64.9	0.6	64.5	-0.6	64.7	0.3	65.1	0.6	65.6	0.8	65.7	0.2
1978	66.3	0.9	68.2	2.9	68.7	0.7	69.3	0.9	70.3	1.4	71.4	1.6	72.0	0.8	72.7	1.0	72.1	-0.8	72.1	0.0	73.1	1.4	73.3	0.3
1979	75.5	3.0	76.9	1.9	78.2	1.7	78.7	0.6	78.9	0.3	78.7	-0.3	79.6	1.1	79.5	-0.1	79.9	0.5	80.9	1.3	81.3	0.5	81.9	0.7
1980	82.1	0.2	82.1	0.0	83.5	1.7	84.7	1.4	85.6	1.1	87.6	2.3	88.1	0.6	88.9	0.9	88.8	-0.1	89.8	1.1	90.3	0.6	90.4	0.1
1981	91.4	1.1	91.6	0.2	92.1	0.5	91.9	-0.2	92.5	0.7	92.9	0.4	93.9	1.1	94.4	0.5	94.7	0.3	94.3	-0.4	93.8	-0.5	94.5	0.7
1982	95.4	1.0	96.7	1.4	96.8	0.1	97.7	0.9	97.4	-0.3	98.3	0.9	98.8	0.5	98.6	-0.2	98.8	0.2	98.0	-0.8	97.8	-0.2	97.7	-0.1
1983	98.3	0.6	98.7	0.4	99.0	0.3	99.6	0.6	99.9	0.3	100.7	0.8	100.5	-0.2	100.9	0.4	100.8	-0.1	100.6	-0.2	100.0	-0.6	100.2	0.2
1984	101.5	1.3	102.6	1.1	102.7	0.1	102.2	-0.5	102.1	-0.1	102.5	0.4	103.2	0.7	103.7	0.5	102.5	-1.2	102.4	-0.1	101.9	-0.5	101.8	-0.1
1985	103.2	1.4	104.5	1.3	105.0	0.5	104.9	-0.1	105.0	0.1	104.6	-0.4	105.7	1.1	105.0	-0.7	105.6	0.6	105.8	0.2	105.3	-0.5	106.1	0.8
1986	106.1	0.0	106.0	-0.1	106.9	0.8	107.0	0.1	107.2	0.2	107.0	-0.2	107.9	0.8	108.6	0.6	109.5	0.8	109.7	0.2	109.0	-0.6	109.4	0.4
1987	111.2	1.6	110.9	-0.3	110.5	-0.4	111.7	1.1	112.2	0.4	112.3	0.1	112.7	0.4	113.2	0.4	113.1	-0.1	113.6	0.4	113.6	0.0	113.3	-0.3
1988	114.7	1.2	114.0	-0.6	113.0	-0.9	114.6	1.4	115.5	0.8	116.6	1.0	117.8	1.0	117.6	-0.2	117.9	0.3	119.1	1.0	117.9	-1.0	118.7	0.7
1989	120.0	1.1	120.8	0.7	122.7	1.6	123.2	0.4	124.0	0.6	125.8	1.5	126.5	0.6	126.1	-0.3	126.9	0.6	128.0	0.9	128.4	0.3	128.6	0.2
1990	129.2	0.5	131.3	1.6	131.6	0.2	131.0	-0.5	131.5	0.4	131.8	0.2	133.0	0.9	133.5	0.4	132.9	-0.4	133.7	0.6	133.8	0.1	134.8	0.7
1991	135.7	0.7	136.4	0.5	136.7	0.2	136.8	0.1	137.1	0.2	137.2	0.1	137.1	-0.1	136.5	-0.4	136.1	-0.3	135.9	-0.1	136.3	0.3	136.2	-0.1
1992	137.0	0.6	137.4	0.3	138.3	0.7	138.8	0.4	139.0	0.1	138.9	-0.1	139.4	0.4	138.9	-0.4	139.5	0.4	139.4	-0.1	138.9	-0.4	139.4	0.4
1993	139.8	0.3	140.0	0.1	140.5	0.4	141.4	0.6	142.0	0.4	140.8	-0.8	140.0	-0.6	139.9	-0.1	141.7	1.3	140.8	-0.6	142.2	1.0	141.5	-0.5

Source: U.S. Department of Labor, Bureau of Labor Statistics, Division of Consumer Prices and Price Indexes. - indicates no data collected for period.

Philadelphia, PA-NJ
Consumer Price Index - All Urban Consumers
Base 1982-1984 = 100
Housing

For 1976-1993. Columns headed % show percentile change in the index from the previous period for which an index is available.

Year	Jan		Feb		Mar		Apr		May		Jun		Jul		Aug		Sep		Oct		Nov		Dec	
	Index	%	Index	%	Index	%	Index	%	Index	%	Index	%	Index	%	Index	%	Index	%	Index	%	Index	%	Index	%
1976	57.8	-	58.1	0.5	58.3	0.3	58.4	0.2	58.7	0.5	58.7	0.0	59.0	0.5	59.0	0.0	59.9	1.5	60.2	0.5	60.5	0.5	60.5	0.0
1977	60.8	0.5	61.0	0.3	61.7	1.1	62.1	0.6	62.6	0.8	62.7	0.2	63.0	0.5	63.4	0.6	64.2	1.3	64.1	-0.2	64.0	-0.2	63.5	-0.8
1978	63.7	0.3	63.8	0.2	64.2	0.6	64.4	0.3	64.5	0.2	64.8	0.5	65.8	1.5	66.3	0.8	67.1	1.2	67.5	0.6	67.8	0.4	68.3	0.7
1979	68.1	-0.3	68.2	0.1	68.1	-0.1	69.3	1.8	70.7	2.0	72.5	2.5	72.8	0.4	73.4	0.8	74.4	1.4	74.5	0.1	75.4	1.2	75.9	0.7
1980	77.6	2.2	79.3	2.2	80.5	1.5	82.1	2.0	82.9	1.0	84.7	2.2	85.3	0.7	85.5	0.2	85.8	0.4	85.7	-0.1	85.9	0.2	86.8	1.0
1981	87.7	1.0	88.8	1.3	90.2	1.6	91.7	1.7	91.8	0.1	94.0	2.4	95.2	1.3	96.5	1.4	97.8	1.3	97.4	-0.4	97.1	-0.3	96.6	-0.5
1982	97.2	0.6	96.9	-0.3	96.4	-0.5	96.0	-0.4	96.2	0.2	98.6	2.5	98.7	0.1	98.5	-0.2	99.2	0.7	97.9	-1.3	98.6	0.7	97.5	-1.1
1983	97.3	-0.2	97.3	0.0	97.4	0.1	97.1	-0.3	97.6	0.5	98.2	0.6	99.4	1.2	99.1	-0.3	99.5	0.4	98.6	-0.9	99.1	0.5	99.7	0.6
1984	100.9	1.2	102.1	1.2	102.2	0.1	102.7	0.5	103.4	0.7	104.3	0.9	104.3	0.0	104.6	0.3	105.4	0.8	105.4	0.0	106.8	1.3	105.8	-0.9
1985	106.0	0.2	107.2	1.1	107.3	0.1	108.2	0.8	109.6	1.3	109.9	0.3	110.2	0.3	110.3	0.1	109.6	-0.6	109.5	-0.1	110.6	1.0	111.5	0.8
1986	111.5	0.0	111.7	0.2	111.2	-0.4	111.5	0.3	111.7	0.2	113.8	1.9	113.7	-0.1	114.1	0.4	114.9	0.7	113.5	-1.2	113.3	-0.2	113.5	0.2
1987	113.5	0.0	114.9	1.2	115.0	0.1	116.2	1.0	118.4	1.9	120.6	1.9	120.1	-0.4	121.4	1.1	120.8	-0.5	120.7	-0.1	119.2	-1.2	120.0	0.7
1988	120.4	0.3	120.5	0.1	120.7	0.2	121.5	0.7	122.3	0.7	125.2	2.4	126.5	1.0	128.0	1.2	129.1	0.9	126.2	-2.2	128.2	1.6	128.6	0.3
1989	127.6	-0.8	127.2	-0.3	128.9	1.3	128.4	-0.4	129.5	0.9	131.3	1.4	132.4	0.8	132.7	0.2	134.2	1.1	132.9	-1.0	131.9	-0.8	132.7	0.6
1990	134.5	1.4	134.6	0.1	136.2	1.2	136.8	0.4	136.9	0.1	138.4	1.1	139.9	1.1	141.4	1.1	141.7	0.2	141.1	-0.4	141.1	0.0	141.3	0.1
1991	143.2	1.3	143.4	0.1	144.5	0.8	143.4	-0.8	144.2	0.6	146.2	1.4	147.8	1.1	148.1	0.2	147.9	-0.1	145.7	-1.5	145.0	-0.5	147.2	1.5
1992	147.9	0.5	148.0	0.1	148.5	0.3	147.3	-0.8	147.4	0.1	151.8	3.0	151.0	-0.5	152.2	0.8	151.8	-0.3	151.0	-0.5	149.1	-1.3	148.9	-0.1
1993	148.9	0.0	151.5	1.7	152.6	0.7	151.7	-0.6	150.3	-0.9	152.8	1.7	152.6	-0.1	153.1	0.3	153.2	0.1	153.1	-0.1	151.6	-1.0	151.6	0.0

Source: U.S. Department of Labor, Bureau of Labor Statistics, Division of Consumer Prices and Price Indexes. - indicates no data collected for period.

Philadelphia, PA-NJ
Consumer Price Index - Urban Wage Earners
Base 1982-1984 = 100
Housing

For 1976-1993. Columns headed % show percentile change in the index from the previous period for which an index is available.

Year	Jan Index	%	Feb Index	%	Mar Index	%	Apr Index	%	May Index	%	Jun Index	%	Jul Index	%	Aug Index	%	Sep Index	%	Oct Index	%	Nov Index	%	Dec Index	%
1976	57.6	-	58.0	0.7	58.1	0.2	58.3	0.3	58.5	0.3	58.5	0.0	58.8	0.5	58.9	0.2	59.8	1.5	60.0	0.3	60.3	0.5	60.4	0.2
1977	60.6	0.3	60.9	0.5	61.5	1.0	62.0	0.8	62.4	0.6	62.6	0.3	62.8	0.3	63.2	0.6	64.0	1.3	63.9	-0.2	63.8	-0.2	63.3	-0.8
1978	63.5	0.3	63.5	0.0	63.9	0.6	64.4	0.8	64.4	0.0	64.7	0.5	65.6	1.4	66.1	0.8	66.8	1.1	67.1	0.4	67.5	0.6	68.1	0.9
1979	67.9	-0.3	68.1	0.3	67.9	-0.3	69.0	1.6	70.1	1.6	71.7	2.3	72.3	0.8	72.9	0.8	73.8	1.2	73.9	0.1	75.0	1.5	75.3	0.4
1980	76.9	2.1	78.1	1.6	79.4	1.7	81.0	2.0	81.5	0.6	83.4	2.3	84.1	0.8	84.5	0.5	84.5	0.0	84.4	-0.1	84.9	0.6	85.7	0.9
1981	86.7	1.2	87.5	0.9	88.3	0.9	89.8	1.7	90.4	0.7	92.1	1.9	93.5	1.5	94.7	1.3	96.0	1.4	95.8	-0.2	95.3	-0.5	94.4	-0.9
1982	95.0	0.6	94.8	-0.2	94.2	-0.6	93.9	-0.3	94.1	0.2	96.6	2.7	96.6	0.0	96.4	-0.2	97.1	0.7	95.9	-1.2	96.7	0.8	95.6	-1.1
1983	96.4	0.8	97.3	0.9	98.4	1.1	98.6	0.2	97.8	-0.8	99.0	1.2	100.4	1.4	100.7	0.3	100.7	0.0	100.2	-0.5	100.9	0.7	100.9	0.0
1984	101.8	0.9	102.7	0.9	102.4	-0.3	102.1	-0.3	103.6	1.5	105.2	1.5	105.4	0.2	106.0	0.6	108.2	2.1	108.7	0.5	108.7	0.0	107.5	-1.1
1985	107.7	0.2	109.0	1.2	109.0	0.0	109.9	0.8	111.3	1.3	111.6	0.3	111.8	0.2	111.9	0.1	111.2	-0.6	111.2	0.0	112.3	1.0	113.2	0.8
1986	113.2	0.0	113.4	0.2	112.9	-0.4	113.3	0.4	113.4	0.1	115.5	1.9	115.3	-0.2	115.7	0.3	116.5	0.7	115.1	-1.2	115.0	-0.1	115.2	0.2
1987	115.2	0.0	116.4	1.0	116.5	0.1	117.5	0.9	119.8	2.0	122.2	2.0	121.7	-0.4	123.0	1.1	122.4	-0.5	122.3	-0.1	120.9	-1.1	121.9	0.8
1988	122.2	0.2	122.0	-0.2	122.2	0.2	122.9	0.6	123.8	0.7	126.8	2.4	128.2	1.1	129.5	1.0	130.7	0.9	127.8	-2.2	129.8	1.6	130.2	0.3
1989	129.6	-0.5	129.1	-0.4	130.8	1.3	130.5	-0.2	131.7	0.9	133.5	1.4	134.7	0.9	135.1	0.3	136.6	1.1	135.0	-1.2	134.1	-0.7	134.9	0.6
1990	136.5	1.2	136.7	0.1	138.3	1.2	138.8	0.4	139.0	0.1	140.7	1.2	141.9	0.9	143.2	0.9	143.8	0.4	143.0	-0.6	143.1	0.1	143.3	0.1
1991	144.7	1.0	145.0	0.2	146.1	0.8	145.2	-0.6	146.2	0.7	148.3	1.4	149.8	1.0	150.1	0.2	150.1	0.0	147.8	-1.5	147.0	-0.5	149.2	1.5
1992	149.6	0.3	149.6	0.0	150.1	0.3	149.1	-0.7	149.3	0.1	153.7	2.9	152.8	-0.6	154.0	0.8	153.6	-0.3	152.3	-0.8	150.9	-0.9	150.9	0.0
1993	150.7	-0.1	153.1	1.6	154.2	0.7	153.7	-0.3	152.3	-0.9	154.8	1.6	154.5	-0.2	155.1	0.4	155.3	0.1	154.8	-0.3	153.7	-0.7	153.7	0.0

Source: U.S. Department of Labor, Bureau of Labor Statistics, Division of Consumer Prices and Price Indexes. - indicates no data collected for period.

Philadelphia, PA-NJ
Consumer Price Index - All Urban Consumers
Base 1982-1984 = 100
Apparel and Upkeep

For 1952-1993. Columns headed % show percentile change in the index from the previous period for which an index is available.

Year	Jan Index	%	Feb Index	%	Mar Index	%	Apr Index	%	May Index	%	Jun Index	%	Jul Index	%	Aug Index	%	Sep Index	%	Oct Index	%	Nov Index	%	Dec Index	%
1952	-	-	-	-	-	-	-	-	-	-	-	-	-	-	-	-	-	-	-	-	-	-	44.2	-
1953	43.8	-0.9	44.0	0.5	44.1	0.2	43.8	-0.7	44.0	0.5	44.0	0.0	44.0	0.0	44.0	0.0	44.9	2.0	44.9	0.0	45.0	0.2	45.0	0.0
1954	44.7	-0.7	44.6	-0.2	44.5	-0.2	44.5	0.0	44.3	-0.4	44.3	0.0	44.4	0.2	44.5	0.2	44.7	0.4	44.8	0.2	44.9	0.2	44.7	-0.4
1955	44.6	-0.2	44.6	0.0	44.2	-0.9	44.1	-0.2	44.0	-0.2	44.0	0.0	43.8	-0.5	44.0	0.5	44.6	1.4	44.6	0.0	45.0	0.9	44.9	-0.2
1956	43.9	-2.2	44.3	0.9	44.4	0.2	44.4	0.0	44.4	0.0	44.4	0.0	44.9	1.1	44.9	0.0	45.9	2.2	46.0	0.2	45.9	-0.2	45.9	0.0
1957	45.4	-1.1	45.9	1.1	46.1	0.4	45.7	-0.9	45.4	-0.7	45.4	0.0	45.9	1.1	45.9	0.0	46.5	1.3	46.7	0.4	46.6	-0.2	46.2	-0.9
1958	45.2	-2.2	45.2	0.0	45.4	0.4	45.2	-0.4	45.5	0.7	45.4	-0.2	44.9	-1.1	45.1	0.4	46.5	3.1	46.4	-0.2	46.4	0.0	46.4	0.0
1959	45.3	-2.4	45.4	0.2	45.6	0.4	45.6	0.0	45.6	0.0	45.7	0.2	45.9	0.4	46.0	0.2	47.6	3.5	47.7	0.2	47.6	-0.2	47.5	-0.2
1960	46.9	-1.3	47.2	0.6	47.6	0.8	47.6	0.0	47.6	0.0	47.4	-0.4	47.6	0.4	47.6	0.0	48.9	2.7	49.2	0.6	49.2	0.0	49.4	0.4
1961	48.9	-1.0	48.8	-0.2	49.0	0.4	48.8	-0.4	48.6	-0.4	48.6	0.0	48.6	0.0	48.6	0.0	49.7	2.3	50.0	0.6	49.9	-0.2	50.0	0.2
1962	48.8	-2.4	48.9	0.2	49.0	0.2	49.2	0.4	49.2	0.0	49.3	0.2	49.2	-0.2	49.4	0.4	50.4	2.0	50.4	0.0	50.5	0.2	50.3	-0.4
1963	49.9	-0.8	49.9	0.0	50.1	0.4	50.2	0.2	50.3	0.2	50.1	-0.4	50.0	-0.2	49.8	-0.4	50.6	1.6	50.7	0.2	50.8	0.2	50.8	0.0
1964	50.1	-1.4	50.2	0.2	50.2	0.0	50.7	1.0	50.6	-0.2	51.1	1.0	51.0	-0.2	50.3	-1.4	50.6	0.6	51.0	0.8	51.1	0.2	51.1	0.0
1965	50.4	-1.4	50.6	0.4	50.7	0.2	51.2	1.0	51.1	-0.2	51.0	-0.2	50.4	-1.2	50.6	0.4	51.6	2.0	51.7	0.2	51.8	0.2	51.8	0.0
1966	51.0	-1.5	51.6	1.2	52.2	1.2	52.4	0.4	52.5	0.2	52.5	0.0	52.8	0.6	52.4	-0.8	54.1	3.2	54.0	-0.2	54.4	0.7	54.6	0.4
1967	53.5	-2.0	53.9	0.7	54.4	0.9	55.0	1.1	55.3	0.5	55.4	0.2	54.9	-0.9	55.0	0.2	56.3	2.4	56.5	0.4	56.6	0.2	56.6	0.0
1968	56.0	-1.1	56.8	1.4	57.4	1.1	57.9	0.9	58.1	0.3	58.0	-0.2	57.9	-0.2	57.9	0.0	59.8	3.3	60.5	1.2	60.4	-0.2	60.6	0.3
1969	59.6	-1.7	60.3	1.2	61.2	1.5	61.2	0.0	60.9	-0.5	60.6	-0.5	60.1	-0.8	60.6	0.8	62.8	3.6	63.1	0.5	63.3	0.3	63.2	-0.2
1970	62.7	-0.8	63.3	1.0	64.0	1.1	63.1	-1.4	63.3	0.3	63.4	0.2	62.2	-1.9	62.8	1.0	65.5	4.3	66.3	1.2	66.2	-0.2	65.5	-1.1
1971	63.9	-2.4	64.7	1.3	65.4	1.1	66.8	2.1	67.0	0.3	66.9	-0.1	65.0	-2.8	64.6	-0.6	66.9	3.6	67.2	0.4	66.7	-0.7	66.4	-0.4
1972	64.7	-2.6	64.2	-0.8	66.3	3.3	66.7	0.6	66.4	-0.4	66.4	0.0	65.1	-2.0	64.9	-0.3	67.8	4.5	68.1	0.4	67.9	-0.3	67.8	-0.1
1973	66.0	-2.7	67.8	2.7	69.2	2.1	69.4	0.3	69.4	0.0	69.3	-0.1	67.6	-2.5	67.5	-0.1	69.6	3.1	70.6	1.4	70.7	0.1	70.7	0.0
1974	68.6	-3.0	70.7	3.1	72.0	1.8	72.0	0.0	72.1	0.1	73.0	1.2	71.7	-1.8	73.3	2.2	75.2	2.6	75.8	0.8	76.6	1.1	76.0	-0.8
1975	74.2	-2.4	74.5	0.4	74.9	0.5	75.0	0.1	74.7	-0.4	74.3	-0.5	73.4	-1.2	75.2	2.5	76.1	1.2	76.1	0.0	76.8	0.9	76.6	-0.3
1976	74.8	-2.3	75.8	1.3	76.3	0.7	76.4	0.1	76.9	0.7	77.1	0.3	76.2	-1.2	76.8	0.8	78.4	2.1	78.9	0.6	79.2	0.4	78.7	-0.6
1977	77.8	-1.1	77.9	0.1	78.7	1.0	78.8	0.1	78.4	-0.5	78.3	-0.1	78.7	0.5	79.6	1.1	79.9	0.4	80.6	0.9	80.6	0.0	80.2	-0.5
1978	77.9	-2.9	76.1	-2.3	78.0	2.5	79.1	1.4	79.9	1.0	81.4	1.9	83.2	2.2	82.1	-1.3	82.4	0.4	83.6	1.5	83.9	0.4	82.7	-1.4
1979	81.9	-1.0	86.1	5.1	85.3	-0.9	85.5	0.2	85.3	-0.2	85.0	-0.4	83.9	-1.3	87.1	3.8	88.6	1.7	86.6	-2.3	89.0	2.8	89.6	0.7
1980	88.2	-1.6	92.6	5.0	96.7	4.4	96.5	-0.2	95.5	-1.0	93.4	-2.2	93.9	0.5	96.0	2.2	95.2	-0.8	96.9	1.8	95.2	-1.8	93.1	-2.2
1981	92.6	-0.5	92.6	0.0	95.4	3.0	95.4	0.0	95.1	-0.3	95.1	0.0	90.2	-5.2	97.7	8.3	100.4	2.8	100.4	0.0	98.2	-2.2	98.0	-0.2
1982	96.4	-1.6	95.7	-0.7	96.6	0.9	98.6	2.1	97.0	-1.6	98.9	2.0	97.5	-1.4	98.8	1.3	102.8	4.0	102.8	0.0	101.2	-1.6	99.3	-1.9
1983	97.6	-1.7	98.2	0.6	100.6	2.4	100.4	-0.2	98.1	-2.3	99.5	1.4	99.3	-0.2	101.8	2.5	102.7	0.9	103.7	1.0	102.4	-1.3	99.5	-2.8
1984	100.0	0.5	99.2	-0.8	99.2	0.0	100.5	1.3	99.0	-1.5	97.6	-1.4	99.0	1.4	102.4	3.4	103.8	1.4	104.3	0.5	103.1	-1.2	102.4	-0.7
1985	99.6	-2.7	100.3	0.7	101.1	0.8	103.3	2.2	102.4	-0.9	100.0	-2.3	100.0	0.0	102.7	2.7	101.9	-0.8	101.8	-0.1	103.3	1.5	100.6	-2.6
1986	100.2	-0.4	100.0	-0.2	100.4	0.4	99.7	-0.7	100.0	0.3	100.0	0.0	97.1	-2.9	100.6	3.6	102.1	1.5	104.8	2.6	104.4	-0.4	103.5	-0.9
1987	104.7	1.8	103.5	-1.1	104.3	0.8	110.6	6.0	106.6	-3.6	103.7	-2.7	102.0	-1.6	110.3	8.1	111.3	0.9	112.4	1.0	113.0	0.5	110.3	-2.4
1988	109.1	-1.1	106.9	-2.0	112.7	5.4	107.9	-4.3	109.2	1.2	104.6	-4.2	108.7	3.9	108.9	0.2	112.7	3.5	113.7	0.9	113.8	0.1	110.3	-3.1
1989	111.3	0.9	108.9	-2.2	101.0	-7.3	102.7	1.7	102.8	0.1	98.4	-4.3	96.4	-2.0	91.8	-4.8	93.4	1.7	97.8	4.7	95.8	-2.0	92.0	-4.0
1990	87.8	-4.6	94.4	7.5	101.4	7.4	107.1	5.6	108.7	1.5	102.8	-5.4	100.4	-2.3	100.7	0.3	105.9	5.2	105.1	-0.8	101.9	-3.0	100.6	-1.3
1991	103.0	2.4	103.1	0.1	106.6	3.4	105.5	-1.0	106.0	0.5	98.9	-6.7	92.8	-6.2	100.3	8.1	107.6	7.3	104.1	-3.3	108.4	4.1	108.6	0.2
1992	104.9	-3.4	100.5	-4.2	107.1	6.6	110.4	3.1	110.9	0.5	105.8	-4.6	103.6	-2.1	107.4	3.7	107.0	-0.4	107.0	0.0	108.8	1.7	104.0	-4.4
1993	103.2	-0.8	107.5	4.2	105.7	-1.7	108.8	2.9	101.0	-7.2	105.6	4.6	106.9	1.2	108.4	1.4	105.3	-2.9	111.8	6.2	108.6	-2.9	99.5	-8.4

Source: U.S. Department of Labor, Bureau of Labor Statistics, Division of Consumer Prices and Price Indexes. - indicates no data collected for period.

Philadelphia, PA-NJ
Consumer Price Index - Urban Wage Earners
Base 1982-1984 = 100
Apparel and Upkeep

For 1952-1993. Columns headed % show percentile change in the index from the previous period for which an index is available.

Year	Jan Index	%	Feb Index	%	Mar Index	%	Apr Index	%	May Index	%	Jun Index	%	Jul Index	%	Aug Index	%	Sep Index	%	Oct Index	%	Nov Index	%	Dec Index	%
1952	-	-	-	-	-	-	-	-	-	-	-	-	-	-	-	-	-	-	-	-	-	-	51.0	-
1953	50.5	-1.0	50.8	0.6	50.9	0.2	50.5	-0.8	50.8	0.6	50.8	0.0	50.8	0.0	50.8	0.0	51.8	2.0	51.8	0.0	51.9	0.2	51.9	0.0
1954	51.6	-0.6	51.5	-0.2	51.4	-0.2	51.4	0.0	51.1	-0.6	51.1	0.0	51.3	0.4	51.4	0.2	51.6	0.4	51.7	0.2	51.8	0.2	51.6	-0.4
1955	51.5	-0.2	51.5	0.0	51.0	-1.0	50.9	-0.2	50.8	-0.2	50.8	0.0	50.5	-0.6	50.8	0.6	51.5	1.4	51.5	0.0	52.0	1.0	51.8	-0.4
1956	50.7	-2.1	51.1	0.8	51.2	0.2	51.3	0.2	51.2	-0.2	51.2	0.0	51.3	0.2	51.4	0.2	52.9	2.9	52.7	-0.4	52.9	0.4	52.9	0.0
1957	52.3	-1.1	52.9	1.1	53.2	0.6	52.8	-0.8	52.3	-0.9	52.3	0.0	53.0	1.3	52.9	-0.2	53.6	1.3	53.9	0.6	53.8	-0.2	53.4	-0.7
1958	52.2	-2.2	52.2	0.0	52.3	0.2	52.2	-0.2	52.5	0.6	52.3	-0.4	51.8	-1.0	52.0	0.4	53.7	3.3	53.5	-0.4	53.6	0.2	53.5	-0.2
1959	52.3	-2.2	52.4	0.2	52.7	0.6	52.7	0.0	52.7	0.0	52.8	0.2	53.0	0.4	53.0	0.0	55.0	3.8	55.0	0.0	55.0	0.0	54.8	-0.4
1960	54.1	-1.3	54.5	0.7	54.9	0.7	54.9	0.0	54.9	0.0	54.7	-0.4	54.9	0.4	55.0	0.2	56.4	2.5	56.8	0.7	56.8	0.0	57.1	0.5
1961	56.4	-1.2	56.3	-0.2	56.6	0.5	56.3	-0.5	56.1	-0.4	56.1	0.0	56.0	-0.2	56.1	0.2	57.3	2.1	57.7	0.7	57.6	-0.2	57.7	0.2
1962	56.3	-2.4	56.4	0.2	56.6	0.4	56.8	0.4	56.8	0.0	56.9	0.2	56.8	-0.2	57.1	0.5	58.2	1.9	58.2	0.0	58.3	0.2	58.0	-0.5
1963	57.6	-0.7	57.6	0.0	57.8	0.3	57.9	0.2	57.5	-0.7	57.7	0.3	57.8	0.2	57.5	-0.5	58.3	1.4	58.7	0.7	58.6	-0.2	58.6	0.0
1964	57.8	-1.4	58.0	0.3	57.9	-0.2	58.0	0.2	57.8	-0.3	57.7	-0.2	57.4	-0.5	57.5	0.2	58.5	1.7	58.9	0.7	59.0	0.2	59.0	0.0
1965	58.2	-1.4	58.3	0.2	58.5	0.3	58.3	-0.3	58.9	1.0	58.9	0.0	58.0	-1.5	58.3	0.5	59.3	1.7	59.6	0.5	59.8	0.3	59.8	0.0
1966	58.9	-1.5	59.6	1.2	60.2	1.0	60.5	0.5	60.6	0.2	60.6	0.0	61.0	0.7	60.5	-0.8	62.4	3.1	62.4	0.0	62.8	0.6	63.1	0.5
1967	61.8	-2.1	62.2	0.6	62.8	1.0	63.5	1.1	63.8	0.5	64.0	0.3	63.3	-1.1	63.5	0.3	64.9	2.2	65.2	0.5	65.3	0.2	65.3	0.0
1968	64.6	-1.1	65.6	1.5	66.2	0.9	66.8	0.9	67.1	0.4	67.0	-0.1	66.8	-0.3	66.8	0.0	69.1	3.4	69.8	1.0	69.7	-0.1	69.9	0.3
1969	68.8	-1.6	69.6	1.2	70.7	1.6	70.6	-0.1	70.3	-0.4	70.0	-0.4	69.3	-1.0	70.0	1.0	72.5	3.6	72.8	0.4	73.1	0.4	73.0	-0.1
1970	72.3	-1.0	73.1	1.1	73.9	1.1	72.8	-1.5	73.1	0.4	73.2	0.1	71.8	-1.9	72.5	1.0	75.6	4.3	76.5	1.2	76.4	-0.1	75.6	-1.0
1971	73.8	-2.4	74.7	1.2	75.5	1.1	77.1	2.1	77.4	0.4	77.2	-0.3	75.0	-2.8	74.5	-0.7	77.2	3.6	77.5	0.4	76.9	-0.8	76.6	-0.4
1972	74.6	-2.6	74.1	-0.7	76.5	3.2	76.9	0.5	76.7	-0.3	76.6	-0.1	75.1	-2.0	74.9	-0.3	78.2	4.4	78.6	0.5	78.4	-0.3	78.2	-0.3
1973	76.2	-2.6	78.2	2.6	79.9	2.2	80.1	0.3	80.1	0.0	79.9	-0.2	78.0	-2.4	77.9	-0.1	80.4	3.2	81.5	1.4	81.6	0.1	81.6	0.0
1974	79.2	-2.9	81.6	3.0	83.1	1.8	83.1	0.0	83.2	0.1	84.2	1.2	82.8	-1.7	84.6	2.2	86.8	2.6	87.5	0.8	88.4	1.0	87.7	-0.8
1975	85.6	-2.4	86.0	0.5	86.4	0.5	86.6	0.2	86.2	-0.5	85.7	-0.6	84.7	-1.2	86.8	2.5	87.8	1.2	87.8	0.0	88.6	0.9	88.4	-0.2
1976	86.3	-2.4	87.5	1.4	88.1	0.7	88.2	0.1	88.8	0.7	88.9	0.1	87.9	-1.1	88.7	0.9	90.5	2.0	91.1	0.7	91.4	0.3	90.8	-0.7
1977	89.8	-1.1	89.9	0.1	90.8	1.0	91.0	0.2	90.5	-0.5	90.3	-0.2	90.8	0.6	91.9	1.2	92.2	0.3	93.0	0.9	93.1	0.1	92.6	-0.5
1978	89.1	-3.8	87.2	-2.1	87.5	0.3	91.4	4.5	92.2	0.9	92.6	0.4	88.2	-4.8	90.2	2.3	90.7	0.6	91.7	1.1	92.8	1.2	91.7	-1.2
1979	90.7	-1.1	90.8	0.1	89.4	-1.5	88.6	-0.9	88.6	0.0	89.2	0.7	87.2	-2.2	87.9	0.8	89.1	1.4	89.1	0.0	90.3	1.3	91.4	1.2
1980	90.5	-1.0	93.8	3.6	94.4	0.6	94.9	0.5	94.2	-0.7	93.1	-1.2	93.0	-0.1	94.6	1.7	96.6	2.1	96.9	0.3	95.9	-1.0	94.5	-1.5
1981	93.6	-1.0	95.1	1.6	94.3	-0.8	94.7	0.4	94.6	-0.1	95.3	0.7	91.4	-4.1	99.3	8.6	100.7	1.4	99.6	-1.1	99.6	0.0	96.6	-3.0
1982	96.4	-0.2	95.8	-0.6	98.1	2.4	99.5	1.4	98.3	-1.2	99.3	1.0	98.2	-1.1	97.9	-0.3	101.8	4.0	102.1	0.3	100.5	-1.6	98.1	-2.4
1983	96.3	-1.8	97.0	0.7	102.5	5.7	101.3	-1.2	99.3	-2.0	100.2	0.9	99.9	-0.3	101.0	1.1	102.3	1.3	103.0	0.7	101.4	-1.6	98.5	-2.9
1984	99.2	0.7	98.3	-0.9	100.4	2.1	100.9	0.5	98.9	-2.0	97.5	-1.4	99.6	2.2	102.7	3.1	104.4	1.7	104.3	-0.1	103.0	-1.2	101.9	-1.1
1985	99.1	-2.7	100.3	1.2	100.3	0.0	102.3	2.0	101.6	-0.7	99.8	-1.8	99.3	-0.5	100.9	1.6	100.2	-0.7	100.5	0.3	101.8	1.3	99.5	-2.3
1986	98.9	-0.6	99.3	0.4	99.7	0.4	98.7	-1.0	98.4	-0.3	96.1	-2.3	98.4	2.4	100.3	1.9	101.2	0.9	102.6	1.4	101.9	-0.7	101.3	-0.6
1987	101.5	0.2	99.5	-2.0	100.6	1.1	106.9	6.3	103.3	-3.4	100.2	-3.0	99.4	-0.8	106.7	7.3	106.9	0.2	109.8	2.7	110.0	0.2	108.3	-1.5
1988	106.1	-2.0	103.1	-2.8	110.3	7.0	104.8	-5.0	106.8	1.9	101.0	-5.4	103.9	2.9	103.4	-0.5	108.3	4.7	109.2	0.8	109.5	0.3	105.0	-4.1
1989	106.3	1.2	104.2	-2.0	95.2	-8.6	98.0	2.9	97.7	-0.3	93.2	-4.6	90.2	-3.2	87.2	-3.3	88.6	1.6	94.0	6.1	91.7	-2.4	88.0	-4.0
1990	82.6	-6.1	88.7	7.4	98.4	10.9	104.1	5.8	106.3	2.1	99.8	-6.1	96.9	-2.9	95.7	-1.2	101.3	5.9	100.2	-1.1	98.0	-2.2	99.2	1.2
1991	99.8	0.6	99.2	-0.6	102.2	3.0	101.5	-0.7	98.9	-2.6	93.1	-5.9	88.5	-4.9	95.0	7.3	101.1	6.4	98.1	-3.0	105.2	7.2	105.7	0.5
1992	101.5	-4.0	97.5	-3.9	104.1	6.8	107.7	3.5	105.9	-1.7	103.1	-2.6	101.0	-2.0	103.2	2.2	102.6	-0.6	104.0	1.4	107.4	3.3	101.9	-5.1
1993	101.4	-0.5	106.9	5.4	103.4	-3.3	107.5	4.0	99.9	-7.1	103.5	3.6	105.5	1.9	105.9	0.4	103.3	-2.5	110.7	7.2	108.4	-2.1	99.6	-8.1

Source: U.S. Department of Labor, Bureau of Labor Statistics, Division of Consumer Prices and Price Indexes. - indicates no data collected for period.

Philadelphia, PA-NJ
Consumer Price Index - All Urban Consumers
Base 1982-1984 = 100
Transportation

For 1947-1993. Columns headed % show percentile change in the index from the previous period for which an index is available.

Year	Jan Index	%	Feb Index	%	Mar Index	%	Apr Index	%	May Index	%	Jun Index	%	Jul Index	%	Aug Index	%	Sep Index	%	Oct Index	%	Nov Index	%	Dec Index	%
1947	15.6	-	15.6	0.0	16.8	7.7	16.9	0.6	16.9	0.0	16.9	0.0	16.9	0.0	17.1	1.2	17.2	0.6	17.2	0.0	17.2	0.0	17.3	0.6
1948	17.4	0.6	17.5	0.6	17.5	0.0	18.2	4.0	18.2	0.0	18.4	1.1	18.7	1.6	19.0	1.6	19.0	0.0	19.0	0.0	19.0	0.0	19.1	0.5
1949	19.2	0.5	19.3	0.5	19.3	0.0	19.3	0.0	21.1	9.3	19.4	-8.1	19.5	0.5	19.5	0.0	19.5	0.0	19.5	0.0	19.5	0.0	19.5	0.0
1950	19.5	0.0	19.5	0.0	19.5	0.0	19.4	-0.5	19.4	0.0	19.4	0.0	19.4	0.0	19.5	0.5	19.4	-0.5	19.2	-1.0	19.2	0.0	21.0	9.4
1951	21.2	1.0	23.4	10.4	23.5	0.4	23.5	0.0	23.5	0.0	23.1	-1.7	22.8	-1.3	23.0	0.9	23.0	0.0	22.8	-0.9	23.9	4.8	23.9	0.0
1952	23.9	0.0	23.2	-2.9	24.1	3.9	24.1	0.0	24.1	0.0	24.2	0.4	24.2	0.0	24.2	0.0	24.2	0.0	24.2	0.0	24.2	0.0	24.2	0.0
1953	24.3	0.4	24.2	-0.4	24.2	0.0	24.3	0.4	24.4	0.4	24.4	0.0	24.6	0.8	24.6	0.0	24.7	0.4	24.8	0.4	24.7	-0.4	24.7	0.0
1954	24.8	0.4	25.0	0.8	25.1	0.4	25.0	-0.4	25.1	0.4	25.0	-0.4	25.0	0.0	25.3	0.0	23.6	-6.7	24.1	2.1	24.7	2.5	24.5	-0.8
1955	25.1	-0.4	25.2	0.4	25.1	-0.4	25.0	-0.4	25.3	1.2	25.4	0.4	25.3	-0.4	25.0	1.2	25.0	0.0	25.1	0.4	25.6	2.0	25.7	0.4
1956	24.8	1.2	24.7	-0.4	24.8	0.4	24.6	-0.8	24.5	-0.4	24.4	-0.4	24.7	1.2	25.0	1.2	25.5	0.4	25.5	0.0	26.5	3.9	26.3	-0.8
1957	25.8	0.4	25.8	0.0	25.8	0.0	25.8	0.0	25.8	0.0	25.5	-1.2	25.4	-0.4	26.7	0.8	26.8	0.4	26.7	-0.4	27.3	2.2	27.4	0.4
1958	25.9	-1.5	25.8	-0.4	26.4	2.3	26.5	0.4	26.3	-0.8	26.3	0.0	26.5	0.8	26.7	0.8	26.8	0.4	26.7	-0.4	28.4	0.7	28.5	0.4
1959	27.6	0.7	27.4	-0.7	27.5	0.4	27.6	0.4	27.8	0.7	27.9	0.4	28.1	0.7	28.2	0.4	28.2	0.0	27.9	-0.4	28.4	1.8	28.5	0.4
1960	28.5	0.0	28.5	0.0	28.4	-0.4	28.3	-0.4	28.2	-0.4	28.1	-0.4	28.0	-0.4	28.0	0.0	27.9	-0.4	28.4	1.8	28.5	0.4	28.5	0.0
1961	28.4	-0.4	28.5	0.4	28.6	0.4	29.0	1.4	29.1	0.3	29.2	0.3	29.2	0.0	29.2	0.0	29.1	-0.3	29.4	1.0	29.3	-0.3	29.0	-1.0
1962	29.0	0.0	29.0	0.0	29.0	0.0	29.3	1.0	29.1	-0.7	29.1	0.0	29.2	0.3	29.2	0.0	29.4	0.7	29.2	-0.7	29.5	1.0	29.4	-0.3
1963	28.9	-1.7	29.7	2.8	29.8	0.3	29.9	0.3	29.9	0.0	29.9	0.0	29.9	0.0	29.9	0.0	29.9	0.0	30.2	1.0	30.3	0.3	30.3	0.0
1964	30.4	0.3	30.4	0.0	30.4	0.0	30.5	0.3	30.5	0.0	30.2	-1.0	30.5	1.0	30.5	0.0	30.3	-0.7	30.5	0.7	30.8	1.0	31.0	0.6
1965	31.1	0.3	31.4	1.0	31.3	-0.3	31.4	0.3	31.6	0.6	31.4	-0.6	31.4	0.0	31.3	-0.3	31.0	-1.0	31.4	1.3	31.4	0.0	31.4	0.0
1966	31.4	0.0	31.4	0.0	31.5	0.3	31.6	0.3	31.7	0.3	31.8	0.3	31.9	0.3	32.1	0.6	31.8	-0.9	32.1	0.9	32.1	0.0	31.9	-0.6
1967	31.9	0.0	32.0	0.3	32.4	1.3	32.4	0.0	32.4	0.0	32.5	0.3	32.7	0.6	32.8	0.3	32.7	-0.3	33.0	0.9	33.3	0.9	33.3	0.0
1968	33.9	1.8	33.9	0.0	34.0	0.3	33.9	-0.3	34.1	0.6	34.2	0.3	34.4	0.6	34.5	0.3	34.4	-0.3	34.6	0.6	34.9	0.9	34.7	-0.6
1969	34.7	0.0	35.6	2.6	36.0	1.1	36.1	0.3	35.9	-0.6	36.1	0.6	36.1	0.0	35.9	-0.6	35.6	-0.8	36.2	1.7	36.3	0.3	36.3	0.0
1970	36.2	-0.3	37.1	2.5	37.1	0.0	37.6	1.3	37.9	0.8	38.1	0.5	38.1	0.0	38.0	-0.3	37.9	-0.3	38.4	1.3	38.6	0.5	39.1	1.3
1971	39.4	0.8	39.9	1.3	39.8	-0.3	40.1	0.8	40.2	0.2	40.5	0.7	40.6	0.2	40.3	-0.7	40.0	-0.7	40.2	0.5	40.3	0.2	40.4	0.2
1972	40.5	0.2	40.3	-0.5	40.4	0.2	40.4	0.0	40.9	1.2	41.0	0.2	40.9	-0.2	41.0	0.2	41.0	0.0	40.9	-0.2	41.1	0.5	41.2	0.2
1973	41.1	-0.2	41.1	0.0	41.1	0.0	41.4	0.7	41.6	0.5	41.9	0.7	41.9	0.0	41.7	-0.5	41.4	-0.7	41.9	1.2	42.0	0.2	42.5	1.2
1974	42.9	0.9	43.4	1.2	44.3	2.1	44.6	0.7	45.3	1.6	46.1	1.8	46.7	1.3	46.9	0.4	47.2	0.6	47.4	0.4	47.8	0.8	47.9	0.2
1975	47.7	-0.4	47.9	0.4	48.3	0.8	48.6	0.6	48.9	0.6	49.8	1.8	50.4	1.2	50.6	0.4	50.8	0.4	51.3	1.0	51.8	1.0	51.8	0.0
1976	51.7	-0.2	51.7	0.0	52.3	1.2	52.9	1.1	53.5	1.1	54.2	1.3	54.7	0.9	54.9	0.4	55.1	0.4	55.4	0.5	55.6	0.4	55.6	0.0
1977	56.2	1.1	56.8	1.1	57.2	0.7	58.5	2.3	60.0	2.6	60.3	0.5	60.3	0.0	60.1	-0.3	60.6	0.8	60.6	0.0	60.6	0.0	60.5	-0.2
1978	60.7	0.3	60.7	0.0	61.1	0.7	61.4	0.5	61.9	0.8	62.7	1.3	63.1	0.6	63.2	0.2	63.2	0.0	63.0	-0.3	64.2	1.9	64.4	0.3
1979	65.0	0.9	65.4	0.6	66.2	1.2	67.6	2.1	69.3	2.5	71.5	3.2	73.1	2.2	73.7	0.8	74.1	0.5	74.1	0.0	74.7	0.8	75.8	1.5
1980	77.8	2.6	79.9	2.7	81.5	2.0	82.2	0.9	83.4	1.5	83.7	0.4	83.9	0.2	85.2	1.5	85.4	0.2	85.6	0.2	86.9	1.5	87.4	0.6
1981	88.6	1.4	90.6	2.3	91.0	0.4	91.7	0.8	92.3	0.7	92.7	0.4	93.9	1.3	93.8	-0.1	94.4	0.6	95.8	1.5	96.5	0.7	97.2	0.7
1982	96.6	-0.6	95.5	-1.1	94.8	-0.7	93.9	-0.9	94.1	0.2	95.6	1.6	97.1	1.6	96.9	-0.2	96.4	-0.5	97.0	0.6	97.1	0.1	97.5	0.4
1983	98.0	0.5	96.9	-1.1	96.4	-0.5	97.6	1.2	98.4	0.8	98.5	0.1	99.1	0.6	100.7	1.6	101.3	0.6	102.0	0.7	102.4	0.4	102.1	-0.3
1984	102.8	0.7	102.7	-0.1	103.0	0.3	103.8	0.8	104.0	0.2	104.4	0.4	104.8	0.4	105.4	0.6	105.7	0.3	105.3	-0.4	106.0	0.7	106.3	0.3
1985	106.3	0.0	107.1	0.8	107.8	0.7	108.7	0.8	109.2	0.5	109.7	0.5	109.9	0.2	110.0	0.1	110.4	0.4	111.4	0.9	111.5	0.1	111.7	0.2
1986	112.1	0.4	110.9	-1.1	108.4	-2.3	104.7	-3.4	105.8	1.1	107.1	1.2	106.9	-0.2	104.8	-2.0	105.1	0.3	106.1	1.0	106.2	0.1	107.0	0.8
1987	108.5	1.4	108.4	-0.1	108.9	0.5	110.4	1.4	110.7	0.3	111.5	0.7	112.2	0.6	112.0	-0.2	112.6	0.5	113.5	0.8	114.3	0.7	114.6	0.3
1988	114.5	-0.1	114.2	-0.3	114.5	0.3	114.2	-0.3	115.1	0.8	114.8	-0.3	115.3	0.4	115.1	-0.2	115.9	0.7	117.4	1.3	117.7	0.3	117.9	0.2
1989	118.5	0.5	118.0	-0.4	118.0	0.0	120.2	1.9	122.9	2.2	123.3	0.3	123.1	-0.2	122.3	-0.6	122.5	0.2	123.4	0.7	123.0	-0.3	123.1	0.1
1990	124.9	1.5	125.6	0.6	125.2	-0.3	125.2	0.0	125.4	0.2	125.9	0.4	125.3	-0.5	125.9	0.5	128.3	1.9	132.1	3.0	133.8	1.3	134.6	0.6
1991	132.7	-1.4	131.4	-1.0	130.2	-0.9	130.0	-0.2	130.5	0.4	131.0	0.4	132.2	0.9	132.3	0.1	132.5	0.2	134.0	1.1	135.3	1.0	135.7	0.3

[Continued]

Philadelphia, PA-NJ
Consumer Price Index - All Urban Consumers
Base 1982-1984 = 100
Transportation
[Continued]

For 1947-1993. Columns headed % show percentile change in the index from the previous period for which an index is available.

Year	Jan		Feb		Mar		Apr		May		Jun		Jul		Aug		Sep		Oct		Nov		Dec	
	Index	%	Index	%	Index	%	Index	%	Index	%	Index	%	Index	%	Index	%	Index	%	Index	%	Index	%	Index	%
1992	135.1	-0.4	134.6	-0.4	134.4	-0.1	134.8	0.3	135.0	0.1	136.0	0.7	136.6	0.4	135.9	-0.5	136.1	0.1	137.0	0.7	138.3	0.9	139.4	0.8
1993	139.2	-0.1	138.4	-0.6	138.5	0.1	137.5	-0.7	139.0	1.1	138.4	-0.4	139.4	0.7	137.4	-1.4	139.2	1.3	140.9	1.2	143.2	1.6	143.0	-0.1

Source: U.S. Department of Labor, Bureau of Labor Statistics, Division of Consumer Prices and Price Indexes. - indicates no data collected for period.

Philadelphia, PA-NJ
Consumer Price Index - Urban Wage Earners
Base 1982-1984 = 100
Transportation

For 1947-1993. Columns headed % show percentile change in the index from the previous period for which an index is available.

Year	Jan Index	%	Feb Index	%	Mar Index	%	Apr Index	%	May Index	%	Jun Index	%	Jul Index	%	Aug Index	%	Sep Index	%	Oct Index	%	Nov Index	%	Dec Index	%
1947	15.1	-	15.1	0.0	16.3	7.9	16.4	0.6	16.4	0.0	16.4	0.0	16.4	0.0	16.6	1.2	16.7	0.6	16.7	0.0	16.7	0.0	16.8	0.6
1948	16.9	0.6	17.0	0.6	17.0	0.0	17.7	4.1	17.7	0.0	17.9	1.1	18.1	1.1	18.4	1.7	18.5	0.5	18.5	0.0	18.4	-0.5	18.5	0.5
1949	18.6	0.5	18.7	0.5	18.7	0.0	18.8	0.5	20.5	9.0	18.9	-7.8	18.9	0.0	18.9	0.0	18.9	0.0	18.9	0.0	19.0	0.5	19.0	0.0
1950	19.0	0.0	19.0	0.0	19.0	0.0	18.8	-1.1	18.9	0.5	18.9	0.0	18.9	0.0	19.0	0.5	18.8	-1.1	18.6	-1.1	18.7	0.5	20.4	9.1
1951	20.6	1.0	22.8	10.7	22.9	0.4	22.9	0.0	22.9	0.0	22.4	-2.2	22.2	-0.9	22.3	0.5	22.4	0.4	22.2	-0.9	23.2	4.5	23.2	0.0
1952	23.2	0.0	22.5	-3.0	23.4	4.0	23.4	0.0	23.4	0.0	23.5	0.4	23.5	0.0	23.5	0.0	23.5	0.0	23.5	0.0	23.5	0.0	23.5	0.0
1953	23.6	0.4	23.5	-0.4	23.5	0.0	23.6	0.4	23.7	0.4	23.7	0.0	23.9	0.8	23.9	0.0	24.0	0.4	24.1	0.4	24.0	-0.4	24.0	0.0
1954	24.1	0.4	24.3	0.8	24.4	0.4	24.3	-0.4	24.3	0.0	24.3	0.0	24.2	-0.4	24.3	0.4	24.3	0.0	24.4	0.4	24.6	0.8	24.4	-0.8
1955	24.4	0.0	24.4	0.0	24.3	-0.4	24.3	0.0	24.6	1.2	24.7	0.4	24.6	-0.4	24.5	-0.4	22.9	-6.5	23.4	2.2	24.0	2.6	23.8	-0.8
1956	24.1	1.3	24.0	-0.4	24.1	0.4	23.9	-0.8	23.8	-0.4	23.7	-0.4	24.0	1.3	24.3	1.2	24.2	-0.4	24.4	0.8	24.9	2.0	25.0	0.4
1957	25.1	0.4	25.1	0.0	25.1	0.0	25.0	-0.4	25.1	0.4	24.8	-1.2	24.7	-0.4	24.7	0.0	24.8	0.4	24.7	-0.4	25.7	4.0	25.6	-0.4
1958	25.2	-1.6	25.1	-0.4	25.6	2.0	25.7	0.4	25.5	-0.8	25.6	0.4	25.8	0.8	26.0	0.8	26.0	0.0	25.9	-0.4	26.6	2.7	26.7	0.4
1959	26.8	0.4	26.6	-0.7	26.7	0.4	26.8	0.4	27.0	0.7	27.1	0.4	27.3	0.7	27.4	0.4	27.4	0.0	27.6	0.7	27.7	0.4	27.7	0.0
1960	27.7	0.0	27.7	0.0	27.6	-0.4	27.5	-0.4	27.4	-0.4	27.3	-0.4	27.2	-0.4	27.2	0.0	27.1	-0.4	27.5	1.5	27.6	0.4	27.7	0.4
1961	27.6	-0.4	27.7	0.4	27.7	0.0	28.2	1.8	28.3	0.4	28.4	0.4	28.4	0.0	28.3	-0.4	28.2	-0.4	28.5	1.1	28.5	0.0	28.1	-1.4
1962	28.2	0.4	28.2	0.0	28.1	-0.4	28.4	1.1	28.3	-0.4	28.3	0.0	28.3	0.0	28.3	0.0	28.5	0.7	28.4	-0.4	28.6	0.7	28.5	-0.3
1963	28.1	-1.4	28.9	2.8	28.9	0.0	29.0	0.3	29.0	0.0	29.0	0.0	29.1	0.3	29.0	-0.3	29.1	0.3	29.3	0.7	29.4	0.3	29.4	0.0
1964	29.5	0.3	29.5	0.0	29.5	0.0	29.6	0.3	29.6	0.0	29.3	-1.0	29.6	1.0	29.7	0.3	29.5	-0.7	29.7	0.7	29.9	0.7	30.1	0.7
1965	30.2	0.3	30.5	1.0	30.4	-0.3	30.5	0.3	30.7	0.7	30.5	-0.7	30.5	0.0	30.4	-0.3	30.1	-1.0	30.5	1.3	30.5	0.0	30.5	0.0
1966	30.5	0.0	30.5	0.0	30.6	0.3	30.7	0.3	30.7	0.0	30.9	0.7	31.0	0.3	31.2	0.6	30.9	-1.0	31.2	1.0	31.2	0.0	31.0	-0.6
1967	31.0	0.0	31.1	0.3	31.5	1.3	31.5	0.0	31.5	0.0	31.6	0.3	31.8	0.6	31.9	0.3	31.8	-0.3	32.1	0.9	32.3	0.6	32.4	0.3
1968	32.9	1.5	32.9	0.0	33.0	0.3	33.0	0.0	33.1	0.3	33.2	0.3	33.4	0.6	33.5	0.3	33.4	-0.3	33.6	0.6	33.9	0.9	33.7	-0.6
1969	33.7	0.0	34.5	2.4	35.0	1.4	35.1	0.3	34.9	-0.6	35.1	0.6	35.0	-0.3	34.9	-0.3	34.6	-0.9	35.1	1.4	35.2	0.3	35.2	0.0
1970	35.2	0.0	36.0	2.3	36.1	0.3	36.5	1.1	36.8	0.8	37.0	0.5	37.0	0.0	37.0	0.0	36.8	-0.5	37.3	1.4	37.5	0.5	38.0	1.3
1971	38.2	0.5	38.8	1.6	38.7	-0.3	38.9	0.5	39.1	0.5	39.4	0.8	39.5	0.3	39.2	-0.8	38.8	-1.0	39.1	0.8	39.2	0.3	39.3	0.3
1972	39.3	0.0	39.2	-0.3	39.3	0.3	39.3	0.0	39.7	1.0	39.8	0.3	39.7	-0.3	39.8	0.3	39.8	0.0	39.7	-0.3	40.0	0.8	40.1	0.2
1973	39.9	-0.5	39.9	0.0	39.9	0.0	40.2	0.8	40.4	0.5	40.7	0.7	40.7	0.0	40.5	-0.5	40.2	-0.7	40.7	1.2	40.8	0.2	41.3	1.2
1974	41.7	1.0	42.1	1.0	43.0	2.1	43.3	0.7	44.0	1.6	44.8	1.8	45.4	1.3	45.6	0.4	45.9	0.7	46.1	0.4	46.5	0.9	46.5	0.0
1975	46.4	-0.2	46.5	0.2	46.9	0.9	47.2	0.6	47.5	0.6	48.4	1.9	48.9	1.0	49.2	0.6	49.3	0.2	49.8	1.0	50.3	1.0	50.3	0.0
1976	50.2	-0.2	50.2	0.0	50.8	1.2	51.3	1.0	52.0	1.4	52.7	1.3	53.1	0.8	53.3	0.4	53.6	0.6	53.8	0.4	54.0	0.4	54.0	0.0
1977	54.5	0.9	55.1	1.1	55.6	0.9	56.8	2.2	58.3	2.6	58.6	0.5	58.6	0.0	58.3	-0.5	58.9	1.0	58.8	-0.2	58.8	0.0	58.8	0.0
1978	58.9	0.2	59.1	0.3	59.6	0.8	59.9	0.5	60.6	1.2	61.4	1.3	61.9	0.8	62.2	0.5	62.1	-0.2	62.4	0.5	63.4	1.6	63.6	0.3
1979	64.0	0.6	64.6	0.9	65.4	1.2	66.9	2.3	68.3	2.1	70.5	3.2	72.3	2.6	72.7	0.6	73.6	1.2	73.4	-0.3	74.3	1.2	75.2	1.2
1980	77.6	3.2	79.8	2.8	81.3	1.9	82.0	0.9	82.9	1.1	83.5	0.7	83.6	0.1	84.6	1.2	84.6	0.0	85.3	0.8	86.4	1.3	87.2	0.9
1981	88.7	1.7	91.0	2.6	91.4	0.4	91.9	0.5	92.7	0.9	93.0	0.3	94.2	1.3	94.3	0.1	94.8	0.5	96.8	2.1	97.0	0.2	97.6	0.6
1982	97.0	-0.6	95.8	-1.2	95.0	-0.8	94.1	-0.9	94.2	0.1	95.8	1.7	97.4	1.7	97.1	-0.3	96.6	-0.5	97.2	0.6	97.2	0.0	97.6	0.4
1983	98.0	0.4	96.8	-1.2	96.2	-0.6	97.5	1.4	98.3	0.8	98.5	0.2	99.2	0.7	100.7	1.5	101.3	0.6	102.0	0.7	102.3	0.3	102.0	-0.3
1984	102.6	0.6	102.6	0.0	102.9	0.3	103.7	0.8	104.0	0.3	104.3	0.3	104.6	0.3	105.2	0.6	105.6	0.4	105.1	-0.5	105.7	0.6	105.9	0.2
1985	106.1	0.2	106.8	0.7	107.5	0.7	108.4	0.8	109.0	0.6	109.5	0.5	109.7	0.2	109.8	0.1	110.1	0.3	111.1	0.9	111.2	0.1	111.3	0.1
1986	111.8	0.4	110.4	-1.3	107.6	-2.5	103.5	-3.8	104.7	1.2	106.0	1.2	105.8	-0.2	103.5	-2.2	103.8	0.3	104.6	0.8	104.7	0.1	105.6	0.9
1987	107.2	1.5	107.3	0.1	107.9	0.6	109.6	1.6	110.1	0.5	110.9	0.7	111.7	0.7	111.8	0.1	112.0	0.2	113.0	0.9	113.7	0.6	113.9	0.2
1988	113.8	-0.1	113.5	-0.3	114.0	0.4	113.8	-0.2	114.7	0.8	114.5	-0.2	115.1	0.5	115.0	-0.1	115.7	0.6	116.9	1.0	117.2	0.3	117.4	0.2
1989	118.0	0.5	117.6	-0.3	117.7	0.1	120.2	2.1	123.2	2.5	123.7	0.4	123.4	-0.2	122.9	-0.4	123.1	0.2	123.9	0.6	123.0	-0.7	123.0	0.0
1990	124.6	1.3	125.8	1.0	125.4	-0.3	125.3	-0.1	125.6	0.2	126.6	0.8	125.8	-0.6	126.8	0.8	129.7	2.3	133.9	3.2	135.2	1.0	135.6	0.3
1991	133.2	-1.8	131.4	-1.4	130.3	-0.8	130.4	0.1	130.9	0.4	131.3	0.3	133.0	1.3	133.0	0.0	133.6	0.5	134.8	0.9	135.6	0.6	135.8	0.1

[Continued]

688

Philadelphia, PA-NJ
Consumer Price Index - Urban Wage Earners
Base 1982-1984 = 100
Transportation
[Continued]

For 1947-1993. Columns headed % show percentile change in the index from the previous period for which an index is available.

Year	Jan Index	%	Feb Index	%	Mar Index	%	Apr Index	%	May Index	%	Jun Index	%	Jul Index	%	Aug Index	%	Sep Index	%	Oct Index	%	Nov Index	%	Dec Index	%
1992	135.1	-0.5	134.3	-0.6	133.7	-0.4	133.9	0.1	135.0	0.8	136.3	1.0	136.7	0.3	136.4	-0.2	136.4	0.0	137.3	0.7	138.5	0.9	139.1	0.4
1993	138.9	-0.1	138.4	-0.4	138.0	-0.3	137.0	-0.7	138.3	0.9	138.3	0.0	138.9	0.4	137.6	-0.9	138.9	0.9	140.9	1.4	142.8	1.3	142.4	-0.3

Source: U.S. Department of Labor, Bureau of Labor Statistics, Division of Consumer Prices and Price Indexes. - indicates no data collected for period.

Philadelphia, PA-NJ

Consumer Price Index - All Urban Consumers
Base 1982-1984 = 100
Medical Care

For 1947-1993. Columns headed % show percentile change in the index from the previous period for which an index is available.

Year	Jan Index	%	Feb Index	%	Mar Index	%	Apr Index	%	May Index	%	Jun Index	%	Jul Index	%	Aug Index	%	Sep Index	%	Oct Index	%	Nov Index	%	Dec Index	%
1947	12.1	-	12.1	0.0	12.2	0.8	12.4	1.6	12.5	0.8	12.5	0.0	12.5	0.0	12.5	0.0	12.5	0.0	12.6	0.8	12.6	0.0	12.7	0.8
1948	12.8	0.8	12.9	0.8	12.8	-0.8	12.9	0.8	12.9	0.0	12.9	0.0	13.0	0.8	13.0	0.0	13.0	0.0	13.0	0.0	13.2	1.5	13.2	0.0
1949	13.2	0.0	13.3	0.8	13.3	0.0	13.3	0.0	13.3	0.0	13.4	0.8	13.4	0.0	13.4	0.0	13.4	0.0	13.4	0.0	13.4	0.0	13.5	0.7
1950	13.5	0.0	13.5	0.0	13.5	0.0	13.5	0.0	13.6	0.7	13.6	0.0	13.6	0.0	13.6	0.0	13.7	0.7	13.7	0.0	13.7	0.0	13.7	0.0
1951	13.9	1.5	14.0	0.7	14.2	1.4	14.2	0.0	14.2	0.0	14.2	0.0	14.2	0.0	14.2	0.0	14.2	0.0	14.3	0.7	14.3	0.0	14.3	0.0
1952	14.3	0.0	14.3	0.0	14.5	1.4	14.5	0.0	14.5	0.0	15.2	4.8	15.2	0.0	15.2	0.0	15.5	2.0	15.5	0.0	15.5	0.0	15.5	0.0
1953	15.5	0.0	15.5	0.0	15.5	0.0	15.5	0.0	15.5	0.0	15.6	0.6	15.6	0.0	15.6	0.0	15.6	0.0	15.6	0.0	15.6	0.0	15.9	1.9
1954	15.9	0.0	16.0	0.6	16.0	0.0	16.0	0.0	16.0	0.0	16.2	1.3	16.2	0.0	16.2	0.0	17.1	5.6	17.1	0.0	17.1	0.0	17.3	1.2
1955	17.3	0.0	17.3	0.0	17.5	1.2	17.5	0.0	17.5	0.0	17.5	0.0	17.5	0.0	17.5	0.0	17.9	0.6	17.9	0.0	17.9	0.0	17.9	0.0
1956	17.6	0.0	17.6	0.0	17.8	1.1	17.8	0.0	17.8	0.0	17.8	0.0	17.8	0.0	17.8	0.0	18.2	0.0	18.2	0.0	18.2	0.0	18.5	1.6
1957	17.9	0.0	17.9	0.0	18.2	1.7	18.2	0.0	18.2	0.0	18.2	0.0	18.2	0.0	18.2	0.0	19.2	0.0	19.2	0.0	19.2	0.0	19.3	0.5
1958	18.5	0.0	18.5	0.0	18.5	0.0	18.6	0.5	18.6	0.0	18.6	0.0	19.2	3.2	19.2	0.0	19.2	0.0	20.5	0.0	20.5	0.0	20.6	0.5
1959	19.3	0.0	19.3	0.0	19.7	2.1	19.7	0.0	19.7	0.0	19.9	1.0	19.9	0.0	20.5	3.0	20.5	0.0	20.9	0.0	20.9	0.0	21.0	0.5
1960	20.6	0.0	20.6	0.0	20.8	1.0	20.8	0.0	20.8	0.0	20.9	0.5	20.9	0.0	20.9	0.0	20.9	0.0	20.9	0.0	20.9	0.0	21.0	0.5
1961	21.0	0.0	21.0	0.0	21.0	0.0	21.4	1.9	22.0	2.8	22.0	0.0	22.0	0.0	22.0	0.0	22.1	0.5	22.1	0.0	22.1	0.0	22.1	0.0
1962	22.1	0.0	22.1	0.0	22.1	0.0	22.1	0.0	22.1	0.0	22.9	3.6	22.9	0.0	22.9	0.0	22.9	0.0	22.9	0.0	22.9	0.0	22.9	0.0
1963	22.9	0.0	23.0	0.4	23.0	0.0	23.0	0.0	23.0	0.0	23.1	0.4	23.1	0.0	23.1	0.0	23.2	0.4	23.2	0.0	23.2	0.0	23.2	0.0
1964	23.3	0.4	23.3	0.0	23.3	0.0	23.3	0.0	23.3	0.0	23.3	0.0	23.5	0.9	23.4	-0.4	23.5	0.4	23.5	0.0	23.6	0.4	23.6	0.0
1965	23.6	0.0	23.6	0.0	23.8	0.8	23.8	0.0	23.9	0.4	24.1	0.8	24.2	0.4	24.2	0.0	24.3	0.4	24.3	0.0	24.3	0.0	24.4	0.4
1966	24.4	0.0	24.5	0.4	24.7	0.8	24.8	0.4	24.8	0.0	24.9	0.4	25.2	1.2	25.3	0.4	25.3	0.0	25.4	0.4	25.6	0.8	25.9	1.2
1967	26.0	0.4	26.1	0.4	26.1	0.0	26.2	0.4	26.3	0.4	26.6	1.1	26.8	0.8	26.8	0.0	27.3	1.9	27.5	0.7	27.5	0.0	27.7	0.7
1968	27.9	0.7	27.9	0.0	28.0	0.4	28.1	0.4	28.5	1.4	28.7	0.7	29.3	2.1	29.4	0.3	29.5	0.3	29.8	1.0	29.8	0.0	30.0	0.7
1969	30.1	0.3	30.2	0.3	30.6	1.3	30.7	0.3	30.9	0.7	31.1	0.6	32.1	3.2	32.2	0.3	32.4	0.6	32.1	-0.9	32.1	0.0	32.2	0.3
1970	32.5	0.9	32.7	0.6	32.9	0.6	33.1	0.6	33.3	0.6	33.4	0.3	34.6	3.6	34.9	0.9	34.9	0.0	34.8	-0.3	35.6	2.3	35.6	0.0
1971	35.8	0.6	36.0	0.6	36.0	0.0	36.1	0.3	36.2	0.3	36.7	1.4	37.4	1.9	37.4	0.0	37.5	0.3	37.2	-0.8	37.3	0.3	37.3	0.0
1972	37.3	0.0	37.5	0.5	37.5	0.0	37.6	0.3	37.6	0.0	37.7	0.3	38.0	0.8	38.3	0.8	38.3	0.0	38.6	0.8	38.6	0.0	38.7	0.3
1973	38.7	0.0	38.7	0.0	39.2	1.3	39.4	0.5	39.4	0.0	39.4	0.0	39.6	0.5	40.1	1.3	40.2	0.2	41.0	2.0	41.1	0.2	41.1	0.0
1974	41.1	0.0	41.5	1.0	41.7	0.5	41.8	0.2	42.5	1.7	43.6	2.6	44.2	1.4	44.2	0.0	44.4	0.5	45.2	1.8	45.3	0.2	45.7	0.9
1975	46.5	1.8	47.2	1.5	47.7	1.1	47.9	0.4	48.0	0.2	48.7	1.5	50.3	3.3	50.3	0.0	50.9	1.2	51.5	1.2	51.0	-1.0	51.3	0.6
1976	51.7	0.8	52.0	0.6	52.1	0.2	52.4	0.6	52.5	0.2	53.2	1.3	54.5	2.4	54.6	0.2	55.0	0.7	55.3	0.5	55.7	0.7	55.6	-0.2
1977	56.1	0.9	56.8	1.2	57.6	1.4	57.7	0.2	58.1	0.7	58.6	0.9	60.2	2.7	60.4	0.3	60.7	0.5	60.6	-0.2	60.6	0.0	60.5	-0.2
1978	61.7	2.0	62.0	0.5	62.2	0.3	63.0	1.3	61.9	-1.7	61.9	0.0	63.0	1.8	63.6	1.0	64.7	1.7	64.7	0.0	65.1	0.6	65.1	0.0
1979	65.7	0.9	66.4	1.1	66.4	0.0	66.6	0.3	66.9	0.5	67.9	1.5	69.4	2.2	69.9	0.7	69.9	0.0	70.1	0.3	70.3	0.3	71.1	1.1
1980	71.7	0.8	73.6	2.6	73.5	-0.1	73.9	0.5	73.7	-0.3	73.9	0.3	76.3	3.2	77.2	1.2	77.5	0.4	77.7	0.3	78.3	0.8	78.4	0.1
1981	80.1	2.2	81.0	1.1	81.2	0.2	81.7	0.6	81.7	0.0	82.4	0.9	85.2	3.4	86.1	1.1	86.6	0.6	86.5	-0.1	86.7	0.2	87.3	0.7
1982	89.1	2.1	89.2	0.1	89.1	-0.1	89.4	0.3	89.5	0.1	89.9	0.4	93.5	4.0	93.9	0.4	93.3	-0.6	93.6	0.3	95.0	1.5	95.3	0.3
1983	96.1	0.8	97.7	1.7	97.9	0.2	98.3	0.4	98.6	0.3	99.5	0.9	102.4	2.9	103.0	0.6	103.1	0.1	103.7	0.6	103.5	-0.2	103.6	0.1
1984	103.9	0.3	104.8	0.9	104.7	-0.1	105.6	0.9	105.6	0.0	105.9	0.3	107.5	1.5	108.4	0.8	109.0	0.6	109.3	0.3	113.4	3.8	114.0	0.5
1985	115.8	1.6	116.1	0.3	117.1	0.9	117.4	0.3	117.7	0.3	118.5	0.7	119.3	0.7	119.8	0.4	121.0	1.0	121.7	0.6	122.6	0.7	122.2	-0.3
1986	122.5	0.2	123.5	0.8	124.3	0.6	125.5	1.0	125.0	-0.4	125.5	0.4	127.6	1.7	128.3	0.5	129.0	0.5	129.2	0.2	129.2	0.0	130.0	0.6
1987	129.9	-0.1	130.3	0.3	130.7	0.3	130.6	-0.1	131.7	0.8	132.9	0.9	134.0	0.8	134.0	0.0	135.3	1.0	135.3	0.0	135.2	-0.1	136.6	1.0
1988	137.7	0.8	138.7	0.7	138.4	-0.2	139.8	1.0	140.7	0.6	140.7	0.0	143.8	2.2	143.5	-0.2	144.7	0.8	145.5	0.6	146.1	0.4	146.2	0.1
1989	146.9	0.5	147.8	0.6	148.8	0.7	151.1	1.5	152.0	0.6	155.1	2.0	156.0	0.6	155.9	-0.1	159.9	2.6	164.1	2.6	166.1	1.2	159.8	-3.8
1990	160.4	0.4	160.1	-0.2	162.1	1.2	164.2	1.3	165.2	0.6	166.2	0.6	169.2	1.8	170.4	0.7	171.0	0.4	171.5	0.3	174.3	1.6	174.6	0.2
1991	176.0	0.8	178.4	1.4	178.8	0.2	180.5	1.0	181.3	0.4	182.0	0.4	184.7	1.5	186.5	1.0	186.7	0.1	188.4	0.9	188.5	0.1	189.6	0.6

[Continued]

Philadelphia, PA-NJ
Consumer Price Index - All Urban Consumers
Base 1982-1984 = 100
Medical Care
[Continued]

For 1947-1993. Columns headed % show percentile change in the index from the previous period for which an index is available.

Year	Jan		Feb		Mar		Apr		May		Jun		Jul		Aug		Sep		Oct		Nov		Dec	
	Index	%	Index	%	Index	%	Index	%	Index	%	Index	%	Index	%	Index	%	Index	%	Index	%	Index	%	Index	%
1992	188.0	-0.8	188.7	0.4	192.1	1.8	193.0	0.5	195.6	1.3	196.4	0.4	199.4	1.5	199.5	0.1	200.4	0.5	202.0	0.8	202.0	0.0	202.2	0.1
1993	202.0	-0.1	205.0	1.5	206.3	0.6	207.3	0.5	209.7	1.2	211.2	0.7	214.7	1.7	214.2	-0.2	214.1	-0.0	218.1	1.9	217.8	-0.1	218.3	0.2

Source: U.S. Department of Labor, Bureau of Labor Statistics, Division of Consumer Prices and Price Indexes. - indicates no data collected for period.

Philadelphia, PA-NJ
Consumer Price Index - Urban Wage Earners
Base 1982-1984 = 100
Medical Care

For 1947-1993. Columns headed % show percentile change in the index from the previous period for which an index is available.

Year	Jan		Feb		Mar		Apr		May		Jun		Jul		Aug		Sep		Oct		Nov		Dec	
	Index	%	Index	%	Index	%	Index	%	Index	%	Index	%	Index	%	Index	%	Index	%	Index	%	Index	%	Index	%
1947	11.4	-	11.5	0.9	11.5	0.0	11.7	1.7	11.8	0.9	11.8	0.0	11.8	0.0	11.8	0.0	11.8	0.0	11.9	0.8	11.9	0.0	12.0	0.8
1948	12.1	0.8	12.2	0.8	12.1	-0.8	12.2	0.8	12.2	0.0	12.2	0.0	12.3	0.8	12.3	0.0	12.3	0.0	12.3	0.0	12.5	1.6	12.5	0.0
1949	12.5	0.0	12.5	0.0	12.6	0.8	12.6	0.0	12.6	0.0	12.6	0.0	12.6	0.0	12.6	0.0	12.7	0.8	12.7	0.0	12.7	0.0	12.7	0.0
1950	12.7	0.0	12.7	0.0	12.7	0.0	12.7	0.0	12.8	0.8	12.8	0.0	12.8	0.0	12.8	0.0	12.9	0.8	12.9	0.0	12.9	0.0	13.0	0.8
1951	13.2	1.5	13.2	0.0	13.4	1.5	13.4	0.0	13.4	0.0	13.4	0.0	13.4	0.0	13.4	0.0	13.4	0.0	13.5	0.7	13.5	0.0	13.5	0.0
1952	13.5	0.0	13.5	0.0	13.7	1.5	13.7	0.0	13.7	0.0	14.4	5.1	14.4	0.0	14.4	0.0	14.6	1.4	14.6	0.0	14.6	0.0	14.6	0.0
1953	14.6	0.0	14.6	0.0	14.6	0.0	14.6	0.0	14.6	0.0	14.7	0.7	14.7	0.0	14.7	0.0	14.7	0.0	14.7	0.0	14.7	0.0	15.0	2.0
1954	15.0	0.0	15.1	0.7	15.1	0.0	15.1	0.0	15.1	0.0	15.3	1.3	15.3	0.0	15.3	0.0	16.1	5.2	16.1	0.0	16.2	0.6	16.3	0.6
1955	16.3	0.0	16.3	0.0	16.5	1.2	16.5	0.0	16.5	0.0	16.5	0.0	16.5	0.0	16.5	0.0	16.5	0.0	16.5	0.0	16.5	0.0	16.6	0.6
1956	16.6	0.0	16.6	0.0	16.8	1.2	16.8	0.0	16.8	0.0	16.8	0.0	16.8	0.0	16.8	0.0	16.9	0.6	16.9	0.0	16.9	0.0	16.9	0.0
1957	16.9	0.0	16.9	0.0	17.1	1.2	17.1	0.0	17.1	0.0	17.2	0.6	17.2	0.0	17.2	0.0	17.2	0.0	17.2	0.0	17.2	0.0	17.4	1.2
1958	17.4	0.0	17.4	0.0	17.5	0.6	17.5	0.0	17.5	0.0	17.6	0.6	18.1	2.8	18.1	0.0	18.1	0.0	18.1	0.0	18.1	0.0	18.2	0.6
1959	18.3	0.5	18.3	0.0	18.6	1.6	18.6	0.0	18.6	0.0	18.8	1.1	18.8	0.0	18.8	0.0	19.3	2.7	19.4	0.5	19.4	0.0	19.4	0.0
1960	19.4	0.0	19.4	0.0	19.6	1.0	19.6	0.0	19.6	0.0	19.7	0.5	19.7	0.0	19.7	0.0	19.7	0.0	19.7	0.0	19.7	0.0	19.8	0.5
1961	19.8	0.0	19.8	0.0	19.9	0.5	20.2	1.5	20.8	3.0	20.8	0.0	20.8	0.0	20.8	0.0	20.9	0.5	20.8	-0.5	20.8	0.0	20.8	0.0
1962	20.9	0.5	20.9	0.0	20.9	0.0	20.9	0.0	20.9	0.0	21.6	3.3	21.6	0.0	21.6	0.0	21.7	0.5	21.6	-0.5	21.6	0.0	21.7	0.5
1963	21.7	0.0	21.7	0.0	21.7	0.0	21.7	0.0	21.7	0.0	21.8	0.5	21.8	0.0	21.8	0.0	21.9	0.5	21.9	0.0	21.9	0.0	21.9	0.0
1964	22.0	0.5	22.0	0.0	22.0	0.0	22.0	0.0	22.0	0.0	22.0	0.0	22.2	0.9	22.1	-0.5	22.2	0.5	22.2	0.0	22.3	0.5	22.3	0.0
1965	22.3	0.0	22.3	0.0	22.5	0.9	22.5	0.0	22.6	0.4	22.7	0.4	22.8	0.4	22.8	0.0	22.9	0.4	22.9	0.0	23.0	0.4	23.0	0.0
1966	23.1	0.4	23.1	0.0	23.3	0.9	23.4	0.4	23.4	0.0	23.5	0.4	23.8	1.3	23.9	0.4	23.9	0.0	24.0	0.4	24.2	0.8	24.5	1.2
1967	24.6	0.4	24.6	0.0	24.6	0.0	24.7	0.4	24.9	0.8	25.1	0.8	25.3	0.8	25.3	0.0	25.8	2.0	25.9	0.4	26.0	0.4	26.2	0.8
1968	26.3	0.4	26.4	0.4	26.5	0.4	26.6	0.4	26.9	1.1	27.1	0.7	27.6	1.8	27.7	0.4	27.9	0.7	28.1	0.7	28.2	0.4	28.3	0.4
1969	28.4	0.4	28.5	0.4	28.9	1.4	29.0	0.3	29.2	0.7	29.3	0.3	30.3	3.4	30.4	0.3	30.6	0.7	30.3	-1.0	30.3	0.0	30.4	0.3
1970	30.7	1.0	30.9	0.7	31.0	0.3	31.3	1.0	31.4	0.3	31.6	0.6	32.6	3.2	33.0	1.2	33.0	0.0	32.9	-0.3	33.6	2.1	33.7	0.3
1971	33.8	0.3	34.0	0.6	34.0	0.0	34.1	0.3	34.2	0.3	34.6	1.2	35.3	2.0	35.3	0.0	35.4	0.3	35.2	-0.6	35.2	0.0	35.2	0.0
1972	35.2	0.0	35.4	0.6	35.4	0.0	35.5	0.3	35.5	0.0	35.6	0.3	35.9	0.8	36.2	0.8	36.2	0.0	36.4	0.6	36.5	0.3	36.5	0.0
1973	36.6	0.3	36.6	0.0	37.0	1.1	37.2	0.5	37.2	0.0	37.2	0.0	37.4	0.5	37.8	1.1	38.0	0.5	38.7	1.8	38.8	0.3	38.8	0.0
1974	38.8	0.0	39.2	1.0	39.4	0.5	39.5	0.3	40.1	1.5	41.2	2.7	41.7	1.2	41.7	0.0	41.9	0.5	42.6	1.7	42.7	0.2	43.1	0.9
1975	43.9	1.9	44.6	1.6	45.0	0.9	45.3	0.7	45.4	0.2	46.0	1.3	47.5	3.3	47.5	0.0	48.0	1.1	48.7	1.5	48.2	-1.0	48.4	0.4
1976	48.9	1.0	49.1	0.4	49.2	0.2	49.5	0.6	49.6	0.2	50.3	1.4	51.5	2.4	51.6	0.2	51.9	0.6	52.2	0.6	52.6	0.8	52.5	-0.2
1977	53.0	1.0	53.6	1.1	54.4	1.5	54.5	0.2	54.9	0.7	55.3	0.7	56.9	2.9	57.0	0.2	57.3	0.5	57.2	-0.2	57.3	0.2	57.2	-0.2
1978	58.2	1.7	58.6	0.7	58.6	0.0	58.8	0.3	58.8	0.0	58.8	0.0	59.7	1.5	60.6	1.5	62.2	2.6	62.2	0.0	62.5	0.5	63.3	1.3
1979	63.3	0.0	63.9	0.9	64.0	0.2	64.1	0.2	64.4	0.5	66.8	3.7	67.6	1.2	67.9	0.4	68.3	0.6	69.1	1.2	69.3	0.3	69.8	0.7
1980	70.5	1.0	73.3	4.0	73.2	-0.1	73.8	0.8	74.3	0.7	74.8	0.7	77.3	3.3	78.6	1.7	78.9	0.4	79.2	0.4	79.2	0.0	79.2	0.0
1981	81.0	2.3	80.6	-0.5	80.7	0.1	81.2	0.6	81.2	0.0	81.4	0.2	84.7	4.1	86.2	1.8	87.3	1.3	87.4	0.1	87.7	0.3	87.6	-0.1
1982	89.3	1.9	89.2	-0.1	89.0	-0.2	89.4	0.4	89.6	0.2	89.8	0.2	93.1	3.7	93.7	0.6	93.1	-0.6	93.3	0.2	94.6	1.4	94.8	0.2
1983	95.8	1.1	97.7	2.0	97.8	0.1	98.2	0.4	98.5	0.3	99.7	1.2	102.4	2.7	103.0	0.6	103.1	0.1	103.6	0.5	103.5	-0.1	103.7	0.2
1984	104.0	0.3	105.1	1.1	105.0	-0.1	106.0	1.0	106.0	0.0	106.4	0.4	107.5	1.0	108.5	0.9	109.1	0.6	109.5	0.4	113.3	3.5	113.8	0.4
1985	115.9	1.8	116.2	0.3	117.2	0.9	117.3	0.1	117.7	0.3	118.5	0.7	119.1	0.5	119.6	0.4	120.8	1.0	121.7	0.7	122.6	0.7	122.1	-0.4
1986	122.3	0.2	123.3	0.8	124.1	0.6	125.4	1.0	124.8	-0.5	125.4	0.5	127.0	1.3	127.7	0.6	128.6	0.7	128.8	0.2	128.7	-0.1	129.5	0.6
1987	129.5	0.0	129.9	0.3	130.3	0.3	130.3	0.0	131.5	0.9	132.9	1.1	133.7	0.6	133.6	-0.1	134.5	0.7	134.9	0.3	134.7	-0.1	136.2	1.1
1988	137.3	0.8	138.1	0.6	137.7	-0.3	139.2	1.1	140.2	0.7	140.3	0.1	143.2	2.1	142.8	-0.3	144.1	0.9	144.7	0.4	145.3	0.4	145.3	0.0
1989	146.1	0.6	146.9	0.5	147.9	0.7	150.4	1.7	151.3	0.6	153.8	1.7	154.6	0.5	154.8	0.1	158.2	2.2	161.9	2.3	163.8	1.2	158.4	-3.3
1990	159.1	0.4	158.8	-0.2	160.8	1.3	163.0	1.4	163.9	0.6	164.9	0.6	167.6	1.6	168.7	0.7	169.3	0.4	169.7	0.2	172.3	1.5	172.5	0.1
1991	173.8	0.8	176.2	1.4	176.4	0.1	178.1	1.0	178.8	0.4	179.7	0.5	182.0	1.3	184.0	1.1	184.1	0.1	185.6	0.8	185.7	0.1	186.8	0.6

[Continued]

Philadelphia, PA-NJ
Consumer Price Index - Urban Wage Earners
Base 1982-1984 = 100
Medical Care
[Continued]

For 1947-1993. Columns headed % show percentile change in the index from the previous period for which an index is available.

Year	Jan		Feb		Mar		Apr		May		Jun		Jul		Aug		Sep		Oct		Nov		Dec	
	Index	%	Index	%	Index	%	Index	%	Index	%	Index	%	Index	%	Index	%	Index	%	Index	%	Index	%	Index	%
1992	185.5	-0.7	186.1	0.3	189.1	1.6	189.9	0.4	192.8	1.5	193.6	0.4	196.7	1.6	196.7	0.0	197.7	0.5	199.2	0.8	199.5	0.2	199.7	0.1
1993	199.4	-0.2	202.7	1.7	203.8	0.5	204.8	0.5	206.8	1.0	208.4	0.8	211.9	1.7	211.4	-0.2	211.2	-0.1	215.2	1.9	214.7	-0.2	215.3	0.3

Source: U.S. Department of Labor, Bureau of Labor Statistics, Division of Consumer Prices and Price Indexes. - indicates no data collected for period.

Philadelphia, PA-NJ
Consumer Price Index - All Urban Consumers
Base 1982-1984 = 100
Entertainment

For 1976-1993. Columns headed % show percentile change in the index from the previous period for which an index is available.

Year	Jan Index	%	Feb Index	%	Mar Index	%	Apr Index	%	May Index	%	Jun Index	%	Jul Index	%	Aug Index	%	Sep Index	%	Oct Index	%	Nov Index	%	Dec Index	%
1976	68.7	-	68.1	-0.9	67.8	-0.4	68.4	0.9	68.8	0.6	68.9	0.1	69.2	0.4	69.2	0.0	68.6	-0.9	69.0	0.6	69.2	0.3	69.8	0.9
1977	70.4	0.9	70.4	0.0	70.5	0.1	71.1	0.9	71.2	0.1	72.0	1.1	72.0	0.0	71.7	-0.4	71.9	0.3	72.4	0.7	72.8	0.6	73.2	0.5
1978	73.5	0.4	73.7	0.3	73.5	-0.3	74.2	1.0	74.3	0.1	75.6	1.7	75.1	-0.7	73.3	-2.4	73.3	0.0	73.2	-0.1	71.9	-1.8	76.6	6.5
1979	77.8	1.6	78.1	0.4	78.5	0.5	81.5	3.8	81.2	-0.4	80.3	-1.1	81.8	1.9	82.8	1.2	82.8	0.0	83.6	1.0	84.5	1.1	80.8	-4.4
1980	83.0	2.7	83.1	0.1	83.3	0.2	82.9	-0.5	83.5	0.7	83.5	0.0	83.7	0.2	84.0	0.4	84.8	1.0	85.3	0.6	85.2	-0.1	85.2	0.0
1981	87.2	2.3	88.4	1.4	88.8	0.5	90.5	1.9	91.7	1.3	93.7	2.2	93.9	0.2	92.9	-1.1	93.6	0.8	94.5	1.0	94.3	-0.2	95.9	1.7
1982	94.6	-1.4	94.9	0.3	95.7	0.8	96.3	0.6	96.8	0.5	96.3	-0.5	96.0	-0.3	97.9	2.0	96.2	-1.7	97.4	1.2	97.5	0.1	97.0	-0.5
1983	97.4	0.4	97.7	0.3	100.9	3.3	100.6	-0.3	99.0	-1.6	100.6	1.6	100.9	0.3	100.5	-0.4	100.8	0.3	101.6	0.8	103.1	1.5	102.8	-0.3
1984	101.1	-1.7	102.3	1.2	101.7	-0.6	103.4	1.7	103.2	-0.2	103.7	0.5	104.1	0.4	104.0	-0.1	103.4	-0.6	103.1	-0.3	103.3	0.2	104.2	0.9
1985	103.8	-0.4	103.9	0.1	104.9	1.0	105.1	0.2	105.7	0.6	104.5	-1.1	104.5	0.0	104.5	0.0	104.8	0.3	106.7	1.8	108.0	1.2	106.8	-1.1
1986	107.6	0.7	107.1	-0.5	107.1	0.0	108.9	1.7	108.7	-0.2	109.4	0.6	110.6	1.1	110.5	-0.1	111.2	0.6	109.8	-1.3	110.3	0.5	110.6	0.3
1987	110.9	0.3	109.5	-1.3	109.4	-0.1	111.8	2.2	112.2	0.4	112.4	0.2	112.7	0.3	112.2	-0.4	112.8	0.5	113.8	0.9	113.9	0.1	114.2	0.3
1988	114.8	0.5	116.0	1.0	116.4	0.3	116.9	0.4	119.9	2.6	121.1	1.0	121.8	0.6	122.6	0.7	124.0	1.1	125.1	0.9	124.6	-0.4	126.5	1.5
1989	125.9	-0.5	126.8	0.7	127.3	0.4	129.2	1.5	129.3	0.1	127.9	-1.1	128.3	0.3	128.6	0.2	130.3	1.3	130.3	0.0	129.7	-0.5	130.1	0.3
1990	131.9	1.4	133.4	1.1	133.0	-0.3	132.8	-0.2	133.3	0.4	132.3	-0.8	134.1	1.4	134.2	0.1	134.2	0.0	133.7	-0.4	134.5	0.6	134.1	-0.3
1991	133.2	-0.7	133.1	-0.1	135.0	1.4	139.5	3.3	139.4	-0.1	138.2	-0.9	138.9	0.5	139.3	0.3	140.3	0.7	140.9	0.4	140.0	-0.6	138.5	-1.1
1992	139.2	0.5	139.1	-0.1	142.9	2.7	144.9	1.4	145.2	0.2	146.3	0.8	146.4	0.1	145.9	-0.3	146.6	0.5	145.4	-0.8	145.7	0.2	144.6	-0.8
1993	143.2	-1.0	134.2	-6.3	140.7	4.8	150.6	7.0	149.6	-0.7	149.5	-0.1	149.5	0.0	149.7	0.1	150.3	0.4	151.1	0.5	150.6	-0.3	150.9	0.2

Source: U.S. Department of Labor, Bureau of Labor Statistics, Division of Consumer Prices and Price Indexes. - indicates no data collected for period.

Philadelphia, PA-NJ
Consumer Price Index - Urban Wage Earners
Base 1982-1984 = 100
Entertainment

For 1976-1993. Columns headed % show percentile change in the index from the previous period for which an index is available.

Year	Jan Index	%	Feb Index	%	Mar Index	%	Apr Index	%	May Index	%	Jun Index	%	Jul Index	%	Aug Index	%	Sep Index	%	Oct Index	%	Nov Index	%	Dec Index	%
1976	70.8	-	70.2	-0.8	69.9	-0.4	70.5	0.9	70.9	0.6	71.0	0.1	71.3	0.4	71.3	0.0	70.7	-0.8	71.1	0.6	71.4	0.4	72.0	0.8
1977	72.6	0.8	72.5	-0.1	72.7	0.3	73.2	0.7	73.4	0.3	74.2	1.1	74.2	0.0	73.9	-0.4	74.1	0.3	74.7	0.8	75.0	0.4	75.5	0.7
1978	75.5	0.0	75.6	0.1	75.2	-0.5	76.4	1.6	75.7	-0.9	77.7	2.6	77.7	0.0	78.1	0.5	77.9	-0.3	77.8	-0.1	75.8	-2.6	84.4	11.3
1979	85.2	0.9	85.5	0.4	85.7	0.2	86.4	0.8	86.5	0.1	84.3	-2.5	86.5	2.6	87.0	0.6	87.2	0.2	88.7	1.7	90.0	1.5	82.8	-8.0
1980	83.3	0.6	84.1	1.0	85.0	1.1	82.7	-2.7	85.1	2.9	85.3	0.2	85.6	0.4	85.3	-0.4	90.0	5.5	89.3	-0.8	90.8	1.7	90.3	-0.6
1981	92.3	2.2	93.1	0.9	93.1	0.0	93.7	0.6	91.1	-2.8	93.9	3.1	94.1	0.2	94.4	0.3	95.8	1.5	95.9	0.1	95.4	-0.5	95.9	0.5
1982	94.5	-1.5	94.8	0.3	95.4	0.6	95.8	0.4	96.3	0.5	96.1	-0.2	97.4	1.4	97.6	0.2	97.1	-0.5	97.6	0.5	97.7	0.1	97.5	-0.2
1983	97.5	0.0	97.5	0.0	100.4	3.0	100.9	0.5	100.3	-0.6	100.8	0.5	101.3	0.5	100.7	-0.6	100.6	-0.1	101.5	0.9	103.0	1.5	102.5	-0.5
1984	100.5	-2.0	101.8	1.3	102.1	0.3	102.9	0.8	102.9	0.0	103.7	0.8	104.0	0.3	104.0	0.0	103.3	-0.7	103.1	-0.2	103.3	0.2	103.6	0.3
1985	103.1	-0.5	103.2	0.1	104.0	0.8	104.2	0.2	104.6	0.4	103.3	-1.2	103.8	0.5	103.7	-0.1	104.0	0.3	105.9	1.8	106.8	0.8	105.6	-1.1
1986	106.4	0.8	106.1	-0.3	106.0	-0.1	107.9	1.8	107.7	-0.2	108.5	0.7	109.4	0.8	109.4	0.0	110.1	0.6	108.7	-1.3	109.3	0.6	109.1	-0.2
1987	109.4	0.3	107.2	-2.0	107.1	-0.1	110.4	3.1	110.6	0.2	110.7	0.1	111.5	0.7	110.7	-0.7	111.3	0.5	112.4	1.0	112.5	0.1	112.8	0.3
1988	113.4	0.5	114.3	0.8	114.7	0.3	115.2	0.4	117.8	2.3	118.9	0.9	119.7	0.7	120.6	0.8	121.7	0.9	122.8	0.9	122.0	-0.7	124.1	1.7
1989	123.6	-0.4	124.5	0.7	125.1	0.5	126.4	1.0	126.5	0.1	125.1	-1.1	125.4	0.2	126.0	0.5	127.8	1.4	127.8	0.0	127.4	-0.3	127.7	0.2
1990	129.2	1.2	130.4	0.9	130.3	-0.1	130.0	-0.2	130.3	0.2	129.0	-1.0	130.5	1.2	130.5	0.0	130.7	0.2	130.4	-0.2	131.1	0.5	130.5	-0.5
1991	129.6	-0.7	130.1	0.4	132.1	1.5	135.7	2.7	135.9	0.1	135.1	-0.6	135.8	0.5	136.0	0.1	136.3	0.2	137.2	0.7	136.6	-0.4	135.5	-0.8
1992	136.2	0.5	135.8	-0.3	139.2	2.5	140.4	0.9	140.8	0.3	141.6	0.6	141.6	0.0	141.4	-0.1	142.3	0.6	140.7	-1.1	141.5	0.6	140.4	-0.8
1993	139.3	-0.8	130.6	-6.2	136.7	4.7	145.3	6.3	144.3	-0.7	143.9	-0.3	143.9	0.0	144.2	0.2	145.0	0.6	146.1	0.8	145.4	-0.5	146.1	0.5

Source: U.S. Department of Labor, Bureau of Labor Statistics, Division of Consumer Prices and Price Indexes. - indicates no data collected for period.

Philadelphia, PA-NJ
Consumer Price Index - All Urban Consumers
Base 1982-1984 = 100
Other Goods and Services

For 1976-1993. Columns headed % show percentile change in the index from the previous period for which an index is available.

Year	Jan Index	%	Feb Index	%	Mar Index	%	Apr Index	%	May Index	%	Jun Index	%	Jul Index	%	Aug Index	%	Sep Index	%	Oct Index	%	Nov Index	%	Dec Index	%
1976	54.7	-	55.0	0.5	54.8	-0.4	55.1	0.5	55.2	0.2	55.6	0.7	56.1	0.9	56.1	0.0	56.5	0.7	57.5	1.8	57.6	0.2	57.7	0.2
1977	57.8	0.2	58.0	0.3	58.0	0.0	58.6	1.0	58.5	-0.2	58.7	0.3	58.8	0.2	58.7	-0.2	60.1	2.4	60.7	1.0	60.9	0.3	60.8	-0.2
1978	60.9	0.2	61.1	0.3	61.2	0.2	61.6	0.7	61.4	-0.3	61.8	0.7	62.3	0.8	62.1	-0.3	63.8	2.7	64.0	0.3	63.9	-0.2	64.1	0.3
1979	64.9	1.2	65.4	0.8	65.6	0.3	65.7	0.2	65.7	0.0	65.6	-0.2	66.0	0.6	66.6	0.9	69.1	3.8	69.1	0.0	70.0	1.3	70.0	0.0
1980	71.0	1.4	71.1	0.1	71.1	0.0	71.5	0.6	71.9	0.6	72.2	0.4	72.9	1.0	73.0	0.1	75.7	3.7	75.3	-0.5	76.1	1.1	76.5	0.5
1981	76.6	0.1	76.5	-0.1	76.8	0.4	76.9	0.1	77.9	1.3	78.5	0.8	78.1	-0.5	78.3	0.3	83.3	6.4	83.8	0.6	83.2	-0.7	84.8	1.9
1982	84.7	-0.1	85.2	0.6	85.1	-0.1	86.9	2.1	87.2	0.3	88.2	1.1	87.5	-0.8	88.7	1.4	93.1	5.0	94.9	1.9	95.7	0.8	96.8	1.1
1983	97.8	1.0	97.0	-0.8	98.0	1.0	97.6	-0.4	97.9	0.3	98.1	0.2	99.4	1.3	101.7	2.3	105.1	3.3	106.2	1.0	106.4	0.2	106.5	0.1
1984	107.4	0.8	107.3	-0.1	107.2	-0.1	108.1	0.8	107.7	-0.4	108.2	0.5	109.3	1.0	109.3	0.0	112.3	2.7	112.3	0.0	112.4	0.1	112.5	0.1
1985	113.8	1.2	114.8	0.9	115.0	0.2	116.0	0.9	115.5	-0.4	115.6	0.1	116.5	0.8	116.6	0.1	120.6	3.4	120.5	-0.1	120.4	-0.1	120.2	-0.2
1986	121.6	1.2	123.3	1.4	123.8	0.4	124.5	0.6	125.7	1.0	126.0	0.2	126.6	0.5	126.8	0.2	129.8	2.4	129.8	0.0	129.9	0.1	130.1	0.2
1987	133.2	2.4	133.7	0.4	133.9	0.1	134.1	0.1	134.3	0.1	134.6	0.2	135.2	0.4	135.2	0.0	138.6	2.5	139.3	0.5	139.1	-0.1	139.5	0.3
1988	140.6	0.8	142.7	1.5	142.3	-0.3	143.4	0.8	143.3	-0.1	143.5	0.1	144.1	0.4	144.5	0.3	148.5	2.8	148.8	0.2	148.8	0.0	150.4	1.1
1989	152.0	1.1	152.1	0.1	152.3	0.1	153.8	1.0	153.6	-0.1	153.9	0.2	155.5	1.0	157.7	1.4	158.1	0.3	158.0	-0.1	159.2	0.8	158.4	-0.5
1990	161.9	2.2	162.1	0.1	165.7	2.2	166.1	0.2	166.3	0.1	168.8	1.5	177.4	5.1	179.3	1.1	179.0	-0.2	178.5	-0.3	178.7	0.1	179.0	0.2
1991	182.0	1.7	185.5	1.9	182.0	-1.9	182.7	0.4	182.6	-0.1	182.6	0.0	183.5	0.5	187.5	2.2	188.2	0.4	189.2	0.5	189.7	0.3	190.4	0.4
1992	190.0	-0.2	191.4	0.7	192.5	0.6	192.8	0.2	194.0	0.6	194.9	0.5	195.3	0.2	197.2	1.0	199.5	1.2	200.6	0.6	200.3	-0.1	201.4	0.5
1993	202.6	0.6	202.7	0.0	202.9	0.1	203.1	0.1	211.8	4.3	212.5	0.3	213.3	0.4	212.6	-0.3	212.7	0.0	217.1	2.1	218.1	0.5	218.9	0.4

Source: U.S. Department of Labor, Bureau of Labor Statistics, Division of Consumer Prices and Price Indexes. - indicates no data collected for period.

Philadelphia, PA-NJ
Consumer Price Index - Urban Wage Earners
Base 1982-1984 = 100
Other Goods and Services

For 1976-1993. Columns headed % show percentile change in the index from the previous period for which an index is available.

Year	Jan Index	%	Feb Index	%	Mar Index	%	Apr Index	%	May Index	%	Jun Index	%	Jul Index	%	Aug Index	%	Sep Index	%	Oct Index	%	Nov Index	%	Dec Index	%
1976	56.8	-	57.2	0.7	57.0	-0.3	57.3	0.5	57.3	0.0	57.8	0.9	58.3	0.9	58.3	0.0	58.7	0.7	59.8	1.9	59.9	0.2	59.9	0.0
1977	60.1	0.3	60.3	0.3	60.3	0.0	60.9	1.0	60.8	-0.2	61.0	0.3	61.2	0.3	61.1	-0.2	62.5	2.3	63.1	1.0	63.3	0.3	63.2	-0.2
1978	63.4	0.3	63.6	0.3	63.6	0.0	64.0	0.6	63.8	-0.3	64.3	0.8	65.0	1.1	64.0	-1.5	65.5	2.3	66.2	1.1	66.1	-0.2	66.1	0.0
1979	66.8	1.1	67.3	0.7	67.2	-0.1	67.2	0.0	67.3	0.1	67.0	-0.4	67.5	0.7	68.0	0.7	70.1	3.1	70.0	-0.1	71.3	1.9	71.3	0.0
1980	71.9	0.8	72.0	0.1	72.0	0.0	72.2	0.3	72.8	0.8	73.4	0.8	73.4	0.0	73.8	0.5	75.9	2.8	76.1	0.3	76.6	0.7	77.2	0.8
1981	77.8	0.8	77.7	-0.1	78.1	0.5	78.3	0.3	79.2	1.1	79.0	-0.3	79.2	0.3	79.4	0.3	83.4	5.0	84.0	0.7	84.6	0.7	84.6	0.0
1982	84.5	-0.1	85.1	0.7	85.0	-0.1	86.8	2.1	87.2	0.5	88.2	1.1	87.6	-0.7	88.9	1.5	92.5	4.0	94.6	2.3	95.6	1.1	97.0	1.5
1983	98.0	1.0	97.2	-0.8	98.2	1.0	97.9	-0.3	98.0	0.1	98.3	0.3	99.9	1.6	102.6	2.7	105.3	2.6	106.0	0.7	106.2	0.2	106.3	0.1
1984	107.4	1.0	107.1	-0.3	107.3	0.2	108.2	0.8	107.8	-0.4	108.5	0.6	109.5	0.9	109.6	0.1	111.8	2.0	111.8	0.0	111.9	0.1	112.0	0.1
1985	113.6	1.4	114.5	0.8	114.7	0.2	115.9	1.0	115.5	-0.3	115.6	0.1	116.6	0.9	116.7	0.1	119.8	2.7	119.7	-0.1	119.6	-0.1	119.6	0.0
1986	121.1	1.3	122.8	1.4	123.3	0.4	124.1	0.6	125.5	1.1	125.8	0.2	126.5	0.6	126.5	0.0	128.8	1.8	128.8	0.0	128.9	0.1	129.0	0.1
1987	132.0	2.3	132.4	0.3	132.7	0.2	133.0	0.2	133.1	0.1	133.5	0.3	134.2	0.5	134.1	-0.1	137.3	2.4	138.0	0.5	137.8	-0.1	138.2	0.3
1988	139.4	0.9	141.6	1.6	141.1	-0.4	142.7	1.1	142.7	0.0	143.0	0.2	143.8	0.6	144.1	0.2	147.8	2.6	148.2	0.3	148.1	-0.1	149.5	0.9
1989	150.9	0.9	150.9	0.0	151.0	0.1	152.1	0.7	151.9	-0.1	152.6	0.5	153.9	0.9	156.0	1.4	156.4	0.3	156.3	-0.1	157.5	0.8	156.5	-0.6
1990	160.5	2.6	160.2	-0.2	163.8	2.2	164.2	0.2	164.6	0.2	167.5	1.8	177.0	5.7	178.6	0.9	178.1	-0.3	177.6	-0.3	177.9	0.2	178.2	0.2
1991	181.0	1.6	184.2	1.8	181.5	-1.5	182.2	0.4	182.1	-0.1	182.2	0.1	183.0	0.4	185.5	1.4	186.0	0.3	187.4	0.8	188.1	0.4	188.8	0.4
1992	188.5	-0.2	189.7	0.6	190.7	0.5	190.9	0.1	192.3	0.7	193.9	0.8	194.2	0.2	195.3	0.6	197.7	1.2	199.1	0.7	198.8	-0.2	200.1	0.7
1993	201.4	0.6	201.5	0.0	201.6	0.0	202.0	0.2	210.2	4.1	211.0	0.4	211.8	0.4	210.0	-0.8	209.8	-0.1	213.1	1.6	214.2	0.5	215.2	0.5

Source: U.S. Department of Labor, Bureau of Labor Statistics, Division of Consumer Prices and Price Indexes. - indicates no data collected for period.

Pittsburgh, PA
Consumer Price Index - All Urban Consumers
Base 1982-1984 = 100
Annual Averages

For 1917-1993. Columns headed % show percentile change in the index from the previous period for which an index is available.

Year	All Items		Food & Beverage		Housing		Apparel & Upkeep		Trans- portation		Medical Care		Entertain- ment		Other Goods & Services	
	Index	%	Index	%	Index	%	Index	%	Index	%	Index	%	Index	%	Index	%
1917	-	-	-	-	-	-	-	-	-	-	-	-	-	-	-	-
1918	14.8	-	-	-	-	-	-	-	-	-	-	-	-	-	-	-
1919	17.0	14.9	-	-	-	-	-	-	-	-	-	-	-	-	-	-
1920	19.5	14.7	-	-	-	-	-	-	-	-	-	-	-	-	-	-
1921	17.5	-10.3	-	-	-	-	-	-	-	-	-	-	-	-	-	-
1922	16.3	-6.9	-	-	-	-	-	-	-	-	-	-	-	-	-	-
1923	16.6	1.8	-	-	-	-	-	-	-	-	-	-	-	-	-	-
1924	16.8	1.2	-	-	-	-	-	-	-	-	-	-	-	-	-	-
1925	17.4	3.6	-	-	-	-	-	-	-	-	-	-	-	-	-	-
1926	17.5	0.6	-	-	-	-	-	-	-	-	-	-	-	-	-	-
1927	17.2	-1.7	-	-	-	-	-	-	-	-	-	-	-	-	-	-
1928	17.1	-0.6	-	-	-	-	-	-	-	-	-	-	-	-	-	-
1929	17.1	0.0	-	-	-	-	-	-	-	-	-	-	-	-	-	-
1930	16.5	-3.5	-	-	-	-	-	-	-	-	-	-	-	-	-	-
1931	15.0	-9.1	-	-	-	-	-	-	-	-	-	-	-	-	-	-
1932	13.3	-11.3	-	-	-	-	-	-	-	-	-	-	-	-	-	-
1933	12.5	-6.0	-	-	-	-	-	-	-	-	-	-	-	-	-	-
1934	12.9	3.2	-	-	-	-	-	-	-	-	-	-	-	-	-	-
1935	13.3	3.1	-	-	-	-	-	-	-	-	-	-	-	-	-	-
1936	13.5	1.5	-	-	-	-	-	-	-	-	-	-	-	-	-	-
1937	14.0	3.7	-	-	-	-	-	-	-	-	-	-	-	-	-	-
1938	13.7	-2.1	-	-	-	-	-	-	-	-	-	-	-	-	-	-
1939	13.4	-2.2	-	-	-	-	-	-	-	-	-	-	-	-	-	-
1940	13.6	1.5	-	-	-	-	-	-	-	-	-	-	-	-	-	-
1941	14.4	5.9	-	-	-	-	-	-	-	-	-	-	-	-	-	-
1942	15.8	9.7	-	-	-	-	-	-	-	-	-	-	-	-	-	-
1943	16.8	6.3	-	-	-	-	-	-	-	-	-	-	-	-	-	-
1944	17.2	2.4	-	-	-	-	-	-	-	-	-	-	-	-	-	-
1945	17.6	2.3	-	-	-	-	-	-	-	-	-	-	-	-	-	-
1946	19.1	8.5	-	-	-	-	-	-	-	-	-	-	-	-	-	-
1947	22.2	16.2	-	-	-	-	-	-	16.2	-	11.7	-	-	-	-	-
1948	23.8	7.2	-	-	-	-	-	-	17.9	10.5	12.4	6.0	-	-	-	-
1949	23.5	-1.3	-	-	-	-	-	-	18.9	5.6	12.6	1.6	-	-	-	-
1950	23.7	0.9	-	-	-	-	-	-	21.0	11.1	12.9	2.4	-	-	-	-
1951	25.6	8.0	-	-	-	-	-	-	22.8	8.6	13.5	4.7	-	-	-	-
1952	26.1	2.0	-	-	-	-	-	-	24.4	7.0	14.0	3.7	-	-	-	-
1953	26.3	0.8	-	-	-	-	42.9	-	24.7	1.2	14.7	5.0	-	-	-	-
1954	26.5	0.8	-	-	-	-	42.9	0.0	24.3	-1.6	15.4	4.8	-	-	-	-
1955	26.3	-0.8	-	-	-	-	42.2	-1.6	24.2	-0.4	15.8	2.6	-	-	-	-
1956	27.0	2.7	-	-	-	-	43.2	2.4	24.5	1.2	16.8	6.3	-	-	-	-
1957	27.8	3.0	-	-	-	-	44.4	2.8	25.7	4.9	17.7	5.4	-	-	-	-
1958	28.7	3.2	-	-	-	-	44.5	0.2	26.9	4.7	18.5	4.5	-	-	-	-
1959	29.0	1.0	-	-	-	-	44.6	0.2	28.5	5.9	19.7	6.5	-	-	-	-
1960	29.7	2.4	-	-	-	-	45.3	1.6	29.1	2.1	20.7	5.1	-	-	-	-
1961	29.9	0.7	-	-	-	-	45.6	0.7	29.2	0.3	21.4	3.4	-	-	-	-

[Continued]

Pittsburgh, PA
Consumer Price Index - All Urban Consumers
Base 1982-1984 = 100
Annual Averages
[Continued]

For 1917-1993. Columns headed % show percentile change in the index from the previous period for which an index is available.

Year	All Items		Food & Beverage		Housing		Apparel & Upkeep		Trans- portation		Medical Care		Entertain- ment		Other Goods & Services	
	Index	%	Index	%	Index	%	Index	%	Index	%	Index	%	Index	%	Index	%
1962	30.2	1.0	-	-	-	-	45.9	0.7	29.9	2.4	22.4	4.7	-	-	-	-
1963	30.5	1.0	-	-	-	-	46.9	2.2	29.9	0.0	23.0	2.7	-	-	-	-
1964	30.9	1.3	-	-	-	-	47.7	1.7	30.3	1.3	23.7	3.0	-	-	-	-
1965	31.4	1.6	-	-	-	-	48.6	1.9	30.8	1.7	24.3	2.5	-	-	-	-
1966	32.2	2.5	-	-	-	-	49.9	2.7	31.1	1.0	25.1	3.3	-	-	-	-
1967	32.8	1.9	-	-	-	-	51.2	2.6	31.6	1.6	26.9	7.2	-	-	-	-
1968	34.3	4.6	-	-	-	-	54.2	5.9	32.7	3.5	28.4	5.6	-	-	-	-
1969	36.2	5.5	-	-	-	-	57.8	6.6	34.1	4.3	30.1	6.0	-	-	-	-
1970	38.1	5.2	-	-	-	-	59.1	2.2	36.0	5.6	31.6	5.0	-	-	-	-
1971	39.8	4.5	-	-	-	-	61.2	3.6	37.9	5.3	32.9	4.1	-	-	-	-
1972	41.1	3.3	-	-	-	-	63.3	3.4	38.3	1.1	34.6	5.2	-	-	-	-
1973	43.6	6.1	-	-	-	-	65.4	3.3	39.3	2.6	36.0	4.0	-	-	-	-
1974	48.3	10.8	-	-	-	-	70.5	7.8	43.4	10.4	39.5	9.7	-	-	-	-
1975	52.4	8.5	-	-	-	-	72.5	2.8	47.0	8.3	43.7	10.6	-	-	-	-
1976	55.2	5.3	62.3	-	50.7	-	73.8	1.8	51.6	9.8	48.2	10.3	65.0	-	57.9	-
1977	58.9	6.7	66.4	6.6	54.4	7.3	75.2	1.9	56.3	9.1	53.3	10.6	68.3	5.1	61.8	6.7
1978	64.1	8.8	72.8	9.6	60.5	11.2	77.6	3.2	59.7	6.0	58.0	8.8	71.3	4.4	65.5	6.0
1979	71.2	11.1	80.0	9.9	67.9	12.2	82.6	6.4	68.5	14.7	64.2	10.7	73.7	3.4	70.3	7.3
1980	81.0	13.8	87.2	9.0	78.9	16.2	87.1	5.4	82.1	19.9	71.2	10.9	82.1	11.4	75.2	7.0
1981	89.3	10.2	93.8	7.6	86.7	9.9	93.7	7.6	93.6	14.0	79.7	11.9	90.3	10.0	82.4	9.6
1982	94.4	5.7	98.0	4.5	92.2	6.3	97.7	4.3	96.6	3.2	89.6	12.4	95.5	5.8	90.8	10.2
1983	101.1	7.1	101.1	3.2	101.7	10.3	101.2	3.6	99.8	3.3	100.9	12.6	100.4	5.1	101.0	11.2
1984	104.5	3.4	100.9	-0.2	106.1	4.3	101.2	0.0	103.6	3.8	109.6	8.6	104.1	3.7	108.2	7.1
1985	106.9	2.3	102.3	1.4	108.5	2.3	102.8	1.6	105.4	1.7	113.4	3.5	109.8	5.5	113.0	4.4
1986	108.2	1.2	105.0	2.6	111.3	2.6	100.4	-2.3	99.5	-5.6	121.2	6.9	118.7	8.1	118.0	4.4
1987	111.4	3.0	109.4	4.2	113.4	1.9	107.0	6.6	100.5	1.0	130.2	7.4	121.4	2.3	122.7	4.0
1988	114.9	3.1	111.9	2.3	115.7	2.0	114.2	6.7	102.3	1.8	138.2	6.1	127.1	4.7	132.7	8.1
1989	120.1	4.5	118.0	5.5	119.2	3.0	121.2	6.1	107.2	4.8	146.8	6.2	133.1	4.7	140.7	6.0
1990	126.2	5.1	124.3	5.3	124.8	4.7	125.0	3.1	112.1	4.6	160.6	9.4	138.8	4.3	150.4	6.9
1991	131.3	4.0	129.2	3.9	131.4	5.3	129.5	3.6	112.9	0.7	175.7	9.4	143.0	3.0	155.0	3.1
1992	136.0	3.6	132.9	2.9	135.8	3.3	133.0	2.7	115.6	2.4	185.9	5.8	145.4	1.7	168.1	8.5
1993	139.9	2.9	137.2	3.2	139.1	2.4	134.5	1.1	118.1	2.2	196.8	5.9	149.8	3.0	177.2	5.4

Source: U.S. Department of Labor, Bureau of Labor Statistics, Division of Consumer Prices and Price Indexes. - indicates no data collected for period.

Pittsburgh, PA
Consumer Price Index - Urban Wage Earners
Base 1982-1984 = 100
Annual Averages

For 1917-1993. Columns headed % show percentile change in the index from the previous period for which an index is available.

Year	All Items		Food & Beverage		Housing		Apparel & Upkeep		Trans- portation		Medical Care		Entertain- ment		Other Goods & Services	
	Index	%	Index	%	Index	%	Index	%	Index	%	Index	%	Index	%	Index	%
1917	-	-	-		-		-		-		-		-		-	
1918	15.2	-	-		-		-		-		-		-		-	
1919	17.5	15.1	-		-		-		-		-		-		-	
1920	20.0	14.3	-		-		-		-		-		-		-	
1921	17.9	-10.5	-		-		-		-		-		-		-	
1922	16.7	-6.7	-		-		-		-		-		-		-	
1923	17.1	2.4	-		-		-		-		-		-		-	
1924	17.2	0.6	-		-		-		-		-		-		-	
1925	17.8	3.5	-		-		-		-		-		-		-	
1926	18.0	1.1	-		-		-		-		-		-		-	
1927	17.7	-1.7	-		-		-		-		-		-		-	
1928	17.5	-1.1	-		-		-		-		-		-		-	
1929	17.5	0.0	-		-		-		-		-		-		-	
1930	16.9	-3.4	-		-		-		-		-		-		-	
1931	15.4	-8.9	-		-		-		-		-		-		-	
1932	13.7	-11.0	-		-		-		-		-		-		-	
1933	12.8	-6.6	-		-		-		-		-		-		-	
1934	13.3	3.9	-		-		-		-		-		-		-	
1935	13.7	3.0	-		-		-		-		-		-		-	
1936	13.9	1.5	-		-		-		-		-		-		-	
1937	14.4	3.6	-		-		-		-		-		-		-	
1938	14.1	-2.1	-		-		-		-		-		-		-	
1939	13.8	-2.1	-		-		-		-		-		-		-	
1940	14.0	1.4	-		-		-		-		-		-		-	
1941	14.7	5.0	-		-		-		-		-		-		-	
1942	16.2	10.2	-		-		-		-		-		-		-	
1943	17.3	6.8	-		-		-		-		-		-		-	
1944	17.6	1.7	-		-		-		-		-		-		-	
1945	18.1	2.8	-		-		-		-		-		-		-	
1946	19.6	8.3	-		-		-		-		11.8		-		-	
1947	22.8	16.3	-		-		-		16.0	-	12.4	5.1	-		-	
1948	24.4	7.0	-		-		-		17.7	10.6	12.7	2.4	-		-	
1949	24.1	-1.2	-		-		-		18.7	5.6	13.0	2.4	-		-	
1950	24.3	0.8	-		-		-		20.7	10.7	13.6	4.6	-		-	
1951	26.3	8.2	-		-		-		22.5	8.7	14.1	3.7	-		-	
1952	26.8	1.9	-		-		-		24.1	7.1	14.8	5.0	-		-	
1953	27.0	0.7	-		-		44.4	-	24.4	1.2	15.5	4.7	-		-	
1954	27.2	0.7	-		-		44.4	0.0	24.0	-1.6	15.9	2.6	-		-	
1955	27.0	-0.7	-		-		43.8	-1.4	23.9	-0.4	16.9	6.3	-		-	
1956	27.7	2.6	-		-		44.8	2.3	24.1	0.8	17.9	5.9	-		-	
1957	28.5	2.9	-		-		46.0	2.7	25.3	5.0	18.6	3.9	-		-	
1958	29.4	3.2	-		-		46.1	0.2	26.6	5.1	19.8	6.5	-		-	
1959	29.8	1.4	-		-		46.3	0.4	28.1	5.6	20.9	5.6	-		-	
1960	30.4	2.0	-		-		47.0	1.5	28.8	2.5	21.6	3.3	-		-	
1961	30.7	1.0	-		-		47.3	0.6	28.8	0.0						

[Continued]

Pittsburgh, PA
Consumer Price Index - Urban Wage Earners
Base 1982-1984 = 100
Annual Averages
[Continued]

For 1917-1993. Columns headed % show percentile change in the index from the previous period for which an index is available.

Year	All Items		Food & Beverage		Housing		Apparel & Upkeep		Trans- portation		Medical Care		Entertain- ment		Other Goods & Services	
	Index	%	Index	%	Index	%	Index	%	Index	%	Index	%	Index	%	Index	%
1962	31.0	1.0	-	-	-	-	47.6	0.6	29.5	2.4	22.5	4.2	-	-	-	-
1963	31.3	1.0	-	-	-	-	48.7	2.3	29.5	0.0	23.2	3.1	-	-	-	-
1964	31.7	1.3	-	-	-	-	49.4	1.4	29.9	1.4	23.9	3.0	-	-	-	-
1965	32.2	1.6	-	-	-	-	50.4	2.0	30.4	1.7	24.5	2.5	-	-	-	-
1966	33.1	2.8	-	-	-	-	51.8	2.8	30.7	1.0	25.3	3.3	-	-	-	-
1967	33.6	1.5	-	-	-	-	53.1	2.5	31.2	1.6	27.0	6.7	-	-	-	-
1968	35.2	4.8	-	-	-	-	56.2	5.8	32.3	3.5	28.5	5.6	-	-	-	-
1969	37.1	5.4	-	-	-	-	59.9	6.6	33.7	4.3	30.3	6.3	-	-	-	-
1970	39.1	5.4	-	-	-	-	61.3	2.3	35.5	5.3	31.8	5.0	-	-	-	-
1971	40.9	4.6	-	-	-	-	63.5	3.6	37.4	5.4	33.1	4.1	-	-	-	-
1972	42.1	2.9	-	-	-	-	65.6	3.3	37.8	1.1	34.8	5.1	-	-	-	-
1973	44.7	6.2	-	-	-	-	67.8	3.4	38.8	2.6	36.3	4.3	-	-	-	-
1974	49.5	10.7	-	-	-	-	73.1	7.8	42.8	10.3	39.7	9.4	-	-	-	-
1975	53.8	8.7	-	-	-	-	75.2	2.9	46.4	8.4	44.0	10.8	-	-	-	-
1976	56.6	5.2	62.2	-	53.8	-	76.5	1.7	50.9	9.7	48.5	10.2	67.2	-	57.1	-
1977	60.5	6.9	66.2	6.4	57.7	7.2	77.9	1.8	55.6	9.2	53.7	10.7	70.7	5.2	61.0	6.8
1978	65.6	8.4	72.8	10.0	64.1	11.1	78.5	0.8	59.1	6.3	57.9	7.8	73.2	3.5	64.7	6.1
1979	73.1	11.4	80.5	10.6	72.0	12.3	83.8	6.8	67.9	14.9	64.4	11.2	77.2	5.5	69.2	7.0
1980	83.4	14.1	87.4	8.6	83.9	16.5	89.4	6.7	81.4	19.9	73.3	13.8	83.6	8.3	75.2	8.7
1981	92.0	10.3	94.1	7.7	92.5	10.3	93.3	4.4	93.7	15.1	80.6	10.0	90.0	7.7	82.1	9.2
1982	97.0	5.4	98.0	4.1	98.5	6.5	97.7	4.7	96.9	3.4	89.9	11.5	95.4	6.0	89.9	9.5
1983	101.3	4.4	101.1	3.2	102.8	4.4	100.9	3.3	99.4	2.6	100.6	11.9	100.6	5.5	101.1	12.5
1984	101.6	0.3	100.9	-0.2	98.7	-4.0	101.4	0.5	103.7	4.3	109.5	8.8	104.0	3.4	108.9	7.7
1985	103.7	2.1	102.1	1.2	100.4	1.7	102.8	1.4	105.2	1.4	113.6	3.7	109.9	5.7	113.7	4.4
1986	104.2	0.5	104.7	2.5	102.9	2.5	100.0	-2.7	98.2	-6.7	121.7	7.1	118.7	8.0	118.7	4.4
1987	107.1	2.8	109.1	4.2	104.8	1.8	106.1	6.1	99.3	1.1	130.9	7.6	121.4	2.3	123.1	3.7
1988	110.4	3.1	111.9	2.6	106.9	2.0	112.6	6.1	101.7	2.4	139.4	6.5	126.5	4.2	134.3	9.1
1989	115.4	4.5	118.0	5.5	110.3	3.2	118.6	5.3	106.8	5.0	147.5	5.8	131.6	4.0	142.5	6.1
1990	121.3	5.1	124.5	5.5	115.6	4.8	122.1	3.0	111.5	4.4	161.3	9.4	137.2	4.3	153.4	7.6
1991	125.9	3.8	129.6	4.1	121.6	5.2	124.5	2.0	111.9	0.4	175.4	8.7	140.8	2.6	158.6	3.4
1992	130.1	3.3	133.1	2.7	125.5	3.2	128.0	2.8	114.7	2.5	184.1	5.0	143.0	1.6	172.6	8.8
1993	133.9	2.9	137.4	3.2	128.6	2.5	128.8	0.6	117.5	2.4	194.1	5.4	147.4	3.1	181.6	5.2

Source: U.S. Department of Labor, Bureau of Labor Statistics, Division of Consumer Prices and Price Indexes. - indicates no data collected for period.

Pittsburgh, PA
Consumer Price Index - All Urban Consumers
Base 1982-1984 = 100
All Items

For 1917-1993. Columns headed % show percentile change in the index from the previous period for which an index is available.

Year	Jan Index	%	Feb Index	%	Mar Index	%	Apr Index	%	May Index	%	Jun Index	%	Jul Index	%	Aug Index	%	Sep Index	%	Oct Index	%	Nov Index	%	Dec Index	%
1917	-	-	-	-	-	-	-	-	-	-	-	-	-	-	-	-	-	-	-	-	-	-	13.5	-
1918	-	-	-	-	-	-	-	-	-	-	-	-	-	-	-	-	-	-	-	-	-	-	16.2	20.0
1919	-	-	-	-	-	-	-	-	-	-	16.5	1.9	-	-	-	-	-	-	-	-	-	-	18.4	11.5
1920	-	-	-	-	-	-	-	-	-	-	20.4	10.9	-	-	-	-	-	-	-	-	-	-	18.9	-7.4
1921	-	-	-	-	-	-	-	-	17.5	-7.4	-	-	-	-	-	-	17.1	-2.3	-	-	-	-	16.7	-2.3
1922	-	-	-	-	16.2	-3.0	-	-	-	-	16.3	0.6	-	-	-	-	16.2	-0.6	-	-	-	-	16.4	1.2
1923	-	-	-	-	16.4	0.0	-	-	-	-	16.7	1.8	-	-	-	-	16.8	0.6	-	-	-	-	16.7	-0.6
1924	-	-	-	-	16.5	-1.2	-	-	-	-	16.8	1.8	-	-	-	-	16.9	0.6	-	-	-	-	17.0	0.6
1925	-	-	-	-	-	-	-	-	-	-	17.4	2.4	-	-	-	-	-	-	-	-	-	-	17.7	1.7
1926	-	-	-	-	-	-	-	-	-	-	17.6	-0.6	-	-	-	-	-	-	-	-	-	-	17.5	-0.6
1927	-	-	-	-	-	-	-	-	-	-	17.5	0.0	-	-	-	-	-	-	-	-	-	-	17.1	-2.3
1928	-	-	-	-	-	-	-	-	-	-	16.9	-1.2	-	-	-	-	-	-	-	-	-	-	17.1	1.2
1929	-	-	-	-	-	-	-	-	-	-	17.1	0.0	-	-	-	-	-	-	-	-	-	-	17.0	-0.6
1930	-	-	-	-	-	-	-	-	-	-	16.7	-1.8	-	-	-	-	-	-	-	-	-	-	15.9	-4.8
1931	-	-	-	-	-	-	-	-	-	-	14.9	-6.3	-	-	-	-	-	-	-	-	-	-	14.3	-4.0
1932	-	-	-	-	-	-	-	-	-	-	13.2	-7.7	-	-	-	-	-	-	-	-	-	-	12.8	-3.0
1933	-	-	-	-	-	-	-	-	-	-	12.2	-4.7	-	-	-	-	-	-	-	-	-	-	12.7	4.1
1934	-	-	-	-	-	-	-	-	-	-	13.0	2.4	-	-	-	-	-	-	-	-	13.0	0.0	-	-
1935	-	-	-	-	13.2	1.5	-	-	-	-	-	-	13.2	0.0	-	-	-	-	13.4	1.5	-	-	-	-
1936	13.4	0.0	-	-	-	-	13.3	-0.7	-	-	-	-	13.6	2.3	-	-	13.8	1.5	-	-	-	-	13.6	-1.4
1937	-	-	-	-	13.9	2.2	-	-	-	-	14.1	1.4	-	-	-	-	14.3	1.4	-	-	-	-	13.9	-2.8
1938	-	-	-	-	13.7	-1.4	-	-	-	-	13.8	0.7	-	-	-	-	13.8	0.0	-	-	-	-	13.7	-0.7
1939	-	-	-	-	13.3	-2.9	-	-	-	-	13.4	0.8	-	-	-	-	13.6	1.5	-	-	-	-	13.4	-1.5
1940	-	-	-	-	13.5	0.7	-	-	-	-	13.7	1.5	-	-	-	-	13.7	0.0	13.7	0.0	13.7	0.0	13.8	0.7
1941	13.8	0.0	13.7	-0.7	13.8	0.7	13.9	0.7	14.1	1.4	14.3	1.4	14.5	1.4	14.5	0.0	14.8	2.1	14.9	0.7	15.0	0.7	15.1	0.7
1942	15.2	0.7	15.4	1.3	15.5	0.6	15.5	0.0	15.8	1.9	15.9	0.6	15.9	0.0	15.9	0.0	16.0	0.6	16.2	1.3	16.2	0.0	16.3	0.6
1943	16.4	0.6	16.5	0.6	16.7	1.2	16.8	0.6	17.0	1.2	17.0	0.0	16.9	-0.6	16.8	-0.6	16.9	0.6	17.0	0.6	17.0	0.0	16.9	-0.6
1944	16.9	0.0	16.9	0.0	16.9	0.0	17.1	1.2	17.1	0.0	17.2	0.6	17.3	0.6	17.4	0.6	17.4	0.0	17.4	0.0	17.3	-0.6	17.4	0.6
1945	17.4	0.0	17.4	0.0	17.4	0.0	17.4	0.0	17.5	0.6	17.8	1.7	17.8	0.0	17.7	-0.6	17.7	0.0	17.7	0.0	17.7	0.0	17.8	0.6
1946	17.9	0.6	17.8	-0.6	17.9	0.6	17.9	0.0	18.0	0.6	18.3	1.7	19.4	6.0	19.8	2.1	20.1	1.5	20.3	1.0	20.9	3.0	21.1	1.0
1947	21.2	0.5	21.3	0.5	21.7	1.9	21.6	-0.5	21.7	0.5	21.9	0.9	22.2	1.4	22.4	0.9	22.9	2.2	22.8	-0.4	22.9	0.4	23.2	1.3
1948	23.5	1.3	23.1	-1.7	23.1	0.0	23.4	1.3	23.6	0.9	23.9	1.3	24.2	1.3	24.3	0.4	24.3	0.0	24.1	-0.8	23.9	-0.8	23.8	-0.4
1949	23.8	0.0	23.4	-1.7	23.5	0.4	23.5	0.0	23.5	0.0	23.6	0.4	23.4	-0.8	23.5	0.4	23.5	0.0	23.3	-0.9	23.3	0.0	23.2	-0.4
1950	23.1	-0.4	23.0	-0.4	23.0	0.0	23.1	0.4	23.3	0.9	23.4	0.4	23.5	0.4	23.9	1.7	24.2	1.3	24.3	0.4	24.3	0.0	24.5	0.8
1951	25.0	2.0	25.2	0.8	25.3	0.4	25.4	0.4	25.6	0.8	25.6	0.0	25.8	0.8	25.7	-0.4	25.9	0.8	26.0	0.4	26.1	0.4	26.1	0.0
1952	26.2	0.4	26.0	-0.8	25.9	-0.4	26.0	0.4	26.0	0.0	26.0	0.0	26.1	0.4	26.2	0.4	26.2	0.0	26.2	0.0	26.2	0.0	26.2	0.0
1953	26.1	-0.4	-	-	-	-	26.1	0.0	-	-	-	-	26.3	0.8	-	-	-	-	26.5	0.8	-	-	-	-
1954	26.5	0.0	-	-	-	-	26.5	0.0	-	-	-	-	26.7	0.8	-	-	-	-	26.4	-1.1	-	-	-	-
1955	26.3	-0.4	-	-	-	-	26.3	0.0	-	-	-	-	26.3	0.0	-	-	-	-	26.3	0.0	-	-	-	-
1956	26.3	0.0	-	-	-	-	26.6	1.1	-	-	-	-	27.1	1.9	-	-	-	-	27.3	0.7	-	-	-	-
1957	27.5	0.7	-	-	-	-	27.5	0.0	-	-	-	-	27.9	1.5	-	-	-	-	28.0	0.4	-	-	-	-
1958	28.3	1.1	-	-	-	-	28.6	1.1	-	-	-	-	28.8	0.7	-	-	-	-	28.8	0.0	-	-	-	-
1959	28.8	0.0	-	-	-	-	28.8	0.0	-	-	-	-	29.1	1.0	-	-	-	-	29.3	0.7	-	-	-	-
1960	29.3	0.0	-	-	-	-	29.6	1.0	-	-	-	-	29.8	0.7	-	-	-	-	29.8	0.0	-	-	-	-
1961	29.9	0.3	-	-	-	-	29.9	0.0	-	-	-	-	30.0	0.3	-	-	-	-	29.9	-0.3	-	-	-	-

[Continued]

Pittsburgh, PA

Consumer Price Index - All Urban Consumers
Base 1982-1984 = 100
All Items
[Continued]

For 1917-1993. Columns headed % show percentile change in the index from the previous period for which an index is available.

Year	Jan Index	%	Feb Index	%	Mar Index	%	Apr Index	%	May Index	%	Jun Index	%	Jul Index	%	Aug Index	%	Sep Index	%	Oct Index	%	Nov Index	%	Dec Index	%
1962	30.0	0.3	-	-	-	-	30.1	0.3	-	-	-	-	30.2	0.3	-	-	-	-	30.3	0.3	-	-	-	-
1963	30.3	0.0	-	-	-	-	30.3	0.0	-	-	-	-	30.7	1.3	-	-	-	-	30.6	-0.3	-	-	-	-
1964	30.7	0.3	-	-	-	-	30.8	0.3	-	-	-	-	31.0	0.6	-	-	-	-	31.0	0.0	-	-	-	-
1965	31.1	0.3	-	-	-	-	31.3	0.6	-	-	-	-	31.6	1.0	-	-	-	-	31.6	0.0	-	-	-	-
1966	31.6	0.0	-	-	-	-	32.2	1.9	-	-	-	-	32.1	-0.3	-	-	-	-	32.5	1.2	-	-	-	-
1967	32.5	0.0	-	-	-	-	32.5	0.0	-	-	-	-	32.8	0.9	-	-	-	-	32.9	0.3	-	-	-	-
1968	33.5	1.8	-	-	-	-	34.0	1.5	-	-	-	-	34.2	0.6	-	-	-	-	34.9	2.0	-	-	-	-
1969	35.3	1.1	-	-	-	-	35.9	1.7	-	-	-	-	36.4	1.4	-	-	-	-	36.6	0.5	-	-	-	-
1970	36.9	0.8	-	-	-	-	37.7	2.2	-	-	-	-	38.3	1.6	-	-	-	-	39.0	1.8	-	-	-	-
1971	39.1	0.3	-	-	-	-	39.6	1.3	-	-	-	-	39.9	0.8	-	-	-	-	40.3	1.0	-	-	-	-
1972	40.4	0.2	-	-	-	-	40.9	1.2	-	-	-	-	41.1	0.5	-	-	-	-	41.5	1.0	-	-	-	-
1973	41.7	0.5	-	-	-	-	43.0	3.1	-	-	-	-	43.5	1.2	-	-	-	-	44.8	3.0	-	-	-	-
1974	45.7	2.0	-	-	-	-	47.2	3.3	-	-	-	-	48.6	3.0	-	-	-	-	49.9	2.7	-	-	-	-
1975	50.6	1.4	-	-	-	-	51.7	2.2	-	-	-	-	53.0	2.5	-	-	-	-	53.4	0.8	-	-	-	-
1976	53.8	0.7	-	-	-	-	54.6	1.5	-	-	-	-	55.2	1.1	-	-	-	-	56.0	1.4	-	-	-	-
1977	56.7	1.3	-	-	-	-	58.4	3.0	-	-	-	-	59.2	1.4	-	-	-	-	60.1	1.5	-	-	-	-
1978	60.6	0.8	-	-	-	-	62.3	2.8	-	-	63.5	1.9	-	-	65.5	3.1	-	-	66.4	1.4	-	-	67.2	1.2
1979	-	-	68.6	2.1	-	-	69.5	1.3	-	-	70.3	1.2	-	-	71.8	2.1	-	-	74.1	3.2	-	-	75.1	1.3
1980	-	-	77.2	2.8	-	-	78.9	2.2	-	-	80.6	2.2	-	-	82.2	2.0	-	-	84.0	2.2	-	-	85.9	2.3
1981	-	-	87.0	1.3	-	-	87.1	0.1	-	-	88.9	2.1	-	-	91.0	2.4	-	-	91.0	0.0	-	-	92.3	1.4
1982	-	-	91.3	-1.1	-	-	90.2	-1.2	-	-	93.4	3.5	-	-	95.5	2.2	-	-	98.5	3.1	-	-	99.0	0.5
1983	-	-	99.9	0.9	-	-	100.0	0.1	-	-	100.1	0.1	-	-	101.7	1.6	-	-	102.8	1.1	-	-	103.0	0.2
1984	-	-	103.4	0.4	-	-	104.4	1.0	-	-	104.8	0.4	-	-	104.6	-0.2	-	-	105.2	0.6	-	-	105.6	0.4
1985	-	-	106.1	0.5	-	-	106.3	0.2	-	-	106.8	0.5	-	-	106.8	0.0	-	-	107.6	0.7	-	-	108.6	0.9
1986	-	-	108.2	-0.4	-	-	107.5	-0.6	-	-	107.7	0.2	-	-	108.2	0.5	-	-	108.7	0.5	-	-	109.1	0.4
1987	-	-	109.8	0.6	-	-	110.8	0.9	-	-	111.1	0.3	-	-	112.0	0.8	-	-	112.8	0.7	-	-	113.0	0.2
1988	-	-	113.3	0.3	-	-	114.5	1.1	-	-	114.3	-0.2	-	-	115.3	0.9	-	-	116.3	0.9	-	-	116.7	0.3
1989	-	-	117.9	1.0	-	-	119.2	1.1	-	-	120.4	1.0	-	-	120.8	0.3	-	-	121.7	0.7	-	-	121.8	0.1
1990	-	-	123.4	1.3	-	-	124.9	1.2	-	-	125.0	0.1	-	-	127.1	1.7	-	-	129.6	2.0	-	-	129.1	-0.4
1991	-	-	129.3	0.2	-	-	130.3	0.8	-	-	130.7	0.3	-	-	131.5	0.6	-	-	133.2	1.3	-	-	134.4	0.9
1992	-	-	134.3	-0.1	-	-	135.1	0.6	-	-	135.2	0.1	-	-	136.9	1.3	-	-	137.7	0.6	-	-	137.3	-0.3
1993	-	-	139.2	1.4	-	-	139.6	0.3	-	-	139.5	-0.1	-	-	140.4	0.6	-	-	140.6	0.1	-	-	141.1	0.4

Source: U.S. Department of Labor, Bureau of Labor Statistics, Division of Consumer Prices and Price Indexes. - indicates no data collected for period.

Pittsburgh, PA
Consumer Price Index - Urban Wage Earners
Base 1982-1984 = 100
All Items

For 1917-1993. Columns headed % show percentile change in the index from the previous period for which an index is available.

Year	Jan Index	%	Feb Index	%	Mar Index	%	Apr Index	%	May Index	%	Jun Index	%	Jul Index	%	Aug Index	%	Sep Index	%	Oct Index	%	Nov Index	%	Dec Index	%
	-	-	-	-	-	-	-	-	-	-	-	-	-	-	-	-	-	-	-	-	-	-	13.9	-
1917	-	-	-	-	-	-	-	-	-	-	-	-	-	-	-	-	-	-	-	-	-	-	16.6	19.4
1918	-	-	-	-	-	-	-	-	-	-	-	-	-	-	-	-	-	-	-	-	-	-	18.8	11.2
1919	-	-	-	-	-	-	-	-	-	-	16.9	1.8	-	-	-	-	-	-	-	-	-	-	19.4	-7.2
1920	-	-	-	-	-	-	-	-	-	-	20.9	11.2	-	-	-	-	-	-	-	-	-	-	17.2	-1.7
1921	-	-	-	-	-	-	-	-	17.9	-7.7	-	-	-	-	-	-	17.5	-2.2	-	-	-	-	16.8	1.2
1922	-	-	-	-	-	-	-	-	-	-	16.7	0.6	-	-	-	-	16.6	-0.6	-	-	-	-	17.2	-0.6
1923	-	-	-	-	16.6	-3.5	-	-	-	-	17.2	2.4	-	-	-	-	17.3	0.6	-	-	-	-	17.5	1.2
1924	-	-	-	-	16.8	0.0	-	-	-	-	17.3	1.8	-	-	-	-	17.3	0.0	-	-	-	-	18.2	2.2
1925	-	-	-	-	17.0	-1.2	-	-	-	-	17.8	1.7	-	-	-	-	-	-	-	-	-	-	18.0	0.0
1926	-	-	-	-	-	-	-	-	-	-	18.0	-1.1	-	-	-	-	-	-	-	-	-	-	17.6	-1.7
1927	-	-	-	-	-	-	-	-	-	-	17.9	-0.6	-	-	-	-	-	-	-	-	-	-	17.6	1.1
1928	-	-	-	-	-	-	-	-	-	-	17.4	-1.1	-	-	-	-	-	-	-	-	-	-	17.5	0.0
1929	-	-	-	-	-	-	-	-	-	-	17.5	-0.6	-	-	-	-	-	-	-	-	-	-	16.3	-4.7
1930	-	-	-	-	-	-	-	-	-	-	17.1	-2.3	-	-	-	-	-	-	-	-	-	-	14.7	-3.9
1931	-	-	-	-	-	-	-	-	-	-	15.3	-6.1	-	-	-	-	-	-	-	-	-	-	13.1	-3.7
1932	-	-	-	-	-	-	-	-	-	-	13.6	-7.5	-	-	-	-	-	-	-	-	-	-	13.0	4.0
1933	-	-	-	-	-	-	-	-	-	-	12.5	-4.6	-	-	-	-	-	-	-	-	13.3	0.0	-	-
1934	-	-	-	-	-	-	-	-	-	-	13.3	2.3	-	-	-	-	-	-	13.7	0.7	-	-	-	-
1935	-	-	-	-	13.6	2.3	-	-	-	-	-	-	13.6	0.0	-	-	14.1	0.7	-	-	-	-	14.0	-0.7
1936	13.8	0.7	-	-	-	-	-	-	13.6	-1.4	14.5	2.1	14.0	2.9	-	-	14.7	1.4	-	-	-	-	14.3	-2.7
1937	-	-	-	-	14.2	1.4	-	-	-	-	14.1	0.0	-	-	-	-	14.1	0.0	-	-	-	-	14.0	-0.7
1938	-	-	-	-	14.1	-1.4	-	-	-	-	13.8	0.7	-	-	-	-	14.0	1.4	-	-	-	-	13.8	-1.4
1939	-	-	-	-	13.7	-2.1	-	-	-	-	14.1	2.2	-	-	-	-	14.1	0.0	14.0	-0.7	14.1	0.7	14.1	0.0
1940	-	-	-	-	13.8	0.0	-	-	-	-	14.7	1.4	14.8	0.7	14.9	0.7	15.2	2.0	15.3	0.7	15.4	0.7	15.5	0.6
1941	14.1	0.0	14.1	0.0	14.2	0.7	14.3	0.7	14.5	1.4	16.2	1.9	16.3	0.0	16.3	0.0	16.4	0.6	16.6	1.2	16.6	0.0	16.7	0.6
1942	15.6	0.6	15.8	1.3	15.9	0.6	15.9	0.0	16.2	1.9	16.3	0.6	16.3	0.0	16.3	0.0	16.4	0.6	16.6	1.2	16.6	0.0	16.7	0.6
1943	16.8	0.6	16.9	0.6	17.1	1.2	17.3	1.2	17.5	1.2	17.5	0.0	17.3	-1.1	17.3	0.0	17.4	0.6	17.5	0.6	17.5	0.0	17.4	-0.6
1944	17.4	0.0	17.3	-0.6	17.3	0.0	17.5	1.2	17.5	0.0	17.7	1.1	17.7	0.0	17.8	0.6	17.8	0.0	17.8	0.0	17.7	-0.6	17.9	1.1
1945	17.9	0.0	17.9	0.0	17.8	-0.6	17.9	0.6	18.0	0.6	18.2	1.1	18.3	0.5	18.2	-0.5	18.1	-0.5	18.2	0.6	18.2	0.0	18.3	0.5
1946	18.3	0.0	18.3	0.0	18.3	0.0	18.4	0.5	18.5	0.5	18.8	1.6	19.9	5.9	20.3	2.0	20.6	1.5	20.8	1.0	21.5	3.4	21.7	0.9
1947	21.8	0.5	21.9	0.5	22.2	1.4	22.2	0.0	22.3	0.5	22.5	0.9	22.7	0.9	23.0	1.3	23.5	2.2	23.4	-0.4	23.5	0.4	23.8	1.3
1948	24.1	1.3	23.7	-1.7	23.7	0.0	24.0	1.3	24.2	0.8	24.3	0.5	24.8	1.2	24.9	0.4	24.9	0.0	24.7	-0.8	24.5	-0.8	24.4	-0.4
1949	24.4	0.0	24.0	-1.6	24.1	0.4	24.1	0.0	24.1	0.0	24.2	0.4	24.0	-0.8	24.1	0.4	24.1	0.0	23.9	-0.8	23.9	0.0	23.8	-0.4
1950	23.7	-0.4	23.6	-0.4	23.6	0.0	23.7	0.4	23.9	0.8	24.0	0.4	24.1	0.4	24.5	1.7	24.8	1.2	25.0	0.8	24.9	-0.4	25.1	0.8
1951	25.6	2.0	25.9	1.2	26.0	0.4	26.1	0.4	26.2	0.4	26.2	0.0	26.4	0.8	26.4	0.0	26.5	0.4	26.7	0.8	26.8	0.4	26.8	0.0
1952	26.8	0.0	26.7	-0.4	26.6	-0.4	26.7	0.4	26.7	0.0	26.6	-0.4	26.8	0.8	26.9	0.4	26.9	0.0	-	-	-	-	-	-
1953	26.7	-0.7	-	-	-	-	26.8	0.4	-	-	-	-	27.0	0.7	-	-	-	-	27.2	0.7	-	-	-	-
1954	27.2	0.0	-	-	-	-	27.2	0.0	-	-	-	-	27.4	0.7	-	-	-	-	27.1	-1.1	-	-	-	-
1955	27.0	-0.4	-	-	-	-	27.0	0.0	-	-	-	-	27.0	0.0	-	-	-	-	27.0	0.0	-	-	-	-
1956	27.0	0.0	-	-	-	-	27.3	1.1	-	-	-	-	27.8	1.8	-	-	-	-	28.0	0.7	-	-	-	-
1957	28.2	0.7	-	-	-	-	28.2	0.0	-	-	-	-	28.6	1.4	-	-	-	-	28.7	0.3	-	-	-	-
1958	29.1	1.4	-	-	-	-	29.4	1.0	-	-	-	-	29.6	0.7	-	-	-	-	29.6	0.0	-	-	-	-
1959	29.5	-0.3	-	-	-	-	29.6	0.3	-	-	-	-	29.8	0.7	-	-	-	-	30.1	1.0	-	-	-	-
1960	30.1	0.0	-	-	-	-	30.4	1.0	-	-	-	-	30.6	0.7	-	-	-	-	30.6	0.0	-	-	-	-
1961	30.7	0.3	-	-	-	-	30.7	0.0	-	-	-	-	30.8	0.3	-	-	-	-	30.7	-0.3	-	-	-	-

[Continued]

Pittsburgh, PA
Consumer Price Index - Urban Wage Earners
Base 1982-1984 = 100
All Items
[Continued]

For 1917-1993. Columns headed % show percentile change in the index from the previous period for which an index is available.

Year	Jan Index	Jan %	Feb Index	Feb %	Mar Index	Mar %	Apr Index	Apr %	May Index	May %	Jun Index	Jun %	Jul Index	Jul %	Aug Index	Aug %	Sep Index	Sep %	Oct Index	Oct %	Nov Index	Nov %	Dec Index	Dec %
1962	30.8	0.3	-	-	-	-	30.9	0.3	-	-	-	-	31.0	0.3	-	-	-	-	31.1	0.3	-	-	-	-
1963	31.1	0.0	-	-	-	-	31.1	0.0	-	-	-	-	31.5	1.3	-	-	-	-	31.4	-0.3	-	-	-	-
1964	31.5	0.3	-	-	-	-	31.6	0.3	-	-	-	-	31.8	0.6	-	-	-	-	31.8	0.0	-	-	-	-
1965	31.9	0.3	-	-	-	-	32.1	0.6	-	-	-	-	32.4	0.9	-	-	-	-	32.4	0.0	-	-	-	-
1966	32.4	0.0	-	-	-	-	33.1	2.2	-	-	-	-	33.0	-0.3	-	-	-	-	33.4	1.2	-	-	-	-
1967	33.3	-0.3	-	-	-	-	33.4	0.3	-	-	-	-	33.6	0.6	-	-	-	-	33.8	0.6	-	-	-	-
1968	34.4	1.8	-	-	-	-	34.9	1.5	-	-	-	-	35.1	0.6	-	-	-	-	35.8	2.0	-	-	-	-
1969	36.2	1.1	-	-	-	-	36.9	1.9	-	-	-	-	37.3	1.1	-	-	-	-	37.6	0.8	-	-	-	-
1970	37.8	0.5	-	-	-	-	38.7	2.4	-	-	-	-	39.3	1.6	-	-	-	-	40.0	1.8	-	-	-	-
1971	40.1	0.2	-	-	-	-	40.7	1.5	-	-	-	-	41.0	0.7	-	-	-	-	41.3	0.7	-	-	-	-
1972	41.4	0.2	-	-	-	-	41.9	1.2	-	-	-	-	42.2	0.7	-	-	-	-	42.5	0.7	-	-	-	-
1973	42.8	0.7	-	-	-	-	44.1	3.0	-	-	-	-	44.6	1.1	-	-	-	-	45.9	2.9	-	-	-	-
1974	46.8	2.0	-	-	-	-	48.5	3.6	-	-	-	-	49.9	2.9	-	-	-	-	51.2	2.6	-	-	-	-
1975	51.9	1.4	-	-	-	-	53.0	2.1	-	-	-	-	54.4	2.6	-	-	-	-	54.7	0.6	-	-	-	-
1976	55.2	0.9	-	-	-	-	56.0	1.4	-	-	-	-	56.7	1.3	-	-	-	-	57.5	1.4	-	-	-	-
1977	58.1	1.0	-	-	-	-	59.9	3.1	-	-	-	-	60.7	1.3	-	-	-	-	61.7	1.6	-	-	-	-
1978	62.2	0.8	-	-	-	-	63.9	2.7	-	-	65.1	1.9	-	-	66.9	2.8	-	-	67.8	1.3	-	-	68.7	1.3
1979	-	-	70.1	2.0	-	-	71.4	1.9	-	-	72.3	1.3	-	-	74.0	2.4	-	-	76.0	2.7	-	-	77.2	1.6
1980	-	-	79.3	2.7	-	-	81.4	2.6	-	-	83.0	2.0	-	-	84.5	1.8	-	-	86.6	2.5	-	-	88.4	2.1
1981	-	-	89.6	1.4	-	-	89.9	0.3	-	-	91.8	2.1	-	-	93.5	1.9	-	-	93.6	0.1	-	-	95.0	1.5
1982	-	-	94.1	-0.9	-	-	93.0	-1.2	-	-	96.1	3.3	-	-	98.1	2.1	-	-	101.0	3.0	-	-	101.4	0.4
1983	-	-	99.7	-1.7	-	-	101.1	1.4	-	-	100.7	-0.4	-	-	102.3	1.6	-	-	102.4	0.1	-	-	101.7	-0.7
1984	-	-	100.7	-1.0	-	-	101.4	0.7	-	-	101.3	-0.1	-	-	102.0	0.7	-	-	102.3	0.3	-	-	102.4	0.1
1985	-	-	102.9	0.5	-	-	103.2	0.3	-	-	103.7	0.5	-	-	103.6	-0.1	-	-	104.2	0.6	-	-	105.2	1.0
1986	-	-	104.7	-0.5	-	-	103.5	-1.1	-	-	103.7	0.2	-	-	104.0	0.3	-	-	104.4	0.4	-	-	104.8	0.4
1987	-	-	105.7	0.9	-	-	106.4	0.7	-	-	106.8	0.4	-	-	107.7	0.8	-	-	108.3	0.6	-	-	108.6	0.3
1988	-	-	108.9	0.3	-	-	110.1	1.1	-	-	110.0	-0.1	-	-	110.7	0.6	-	-	111.7	0.9	-	-	112.2	0.4
1989	-	-	113.4	1.1	-	-	114.7	1.1	-	-	115.9	1.0	-	-	116.0	0.1	-	-	116.8	0.7	-	-	117.1	0.3
1990	-	-	118.6	1.3	-	-	120.1	1.3	-	-	120.3	0.2	-	-	122.0	1.4	-	-	124.6	2.1	-	-	124.2	-0.3
1991	-	-	124.1	-0.1	-	-	124.9	0.6	-	-	125.3	0.3	-	-	125.9	0.5	-	-	127.5	1.3	-	-	128.7	0.9
1992	-	-	128.7	0.0	-	-	129.4	0.5	-	-	129.5	0.1	-	-	131.0	1.2	-	-	131.6	0.5	-	-	131.4	-0.2
1993	-	-	133.2	1.4	-	-	133.6	0.3	-	-	133.7	0.1	-	-	134.2	0.4	-	-	134.5	0.2	-	-	135.1	0.4

Source: U.S. Department of Labor, Bureau of Labor Statistics, Division of Consumer Prices and Price Indexes. - indicates no data collected for period.

Pittsburgh, PA

Consumer Price Index - All Urban Consumers
Base 1982-1984 = 100

Food and Beverages

For 1976-1993. Columns headed % show percentile change in the index from the previous period for which an index is available.

Year	Jan		Feb		Mar		Apr		May		Jun		Jul		Aug		Sep		Oct		Nov		Dec	
	Index	%	Index	%	Index	%	Index	%	Index	%	Index	%	Index	%	Index	%	Index	%	Index	%	Index	%	Index	%
1976	62.0	-	-	-	-	-	62.0	0.0	-	-	-	-	62.3	0.5	-	-	-	-	62.7	0.6	-	-	-	-
1977	62.9	0.3	-	-	-	-	66.0	4.9	-	-	-	-	67.1	1.7	-	-	-	-	67.6	0.7	-	-	-	-
1978	68.5	1.3	-	-	-	-	71.4	4.2	-	-	73.6	3.1	-	-	74.4	1.1	-	-	75.1	0.9	-	-	75.3	0.3
1979	-	-	78.5	4.2	-	-	78.8	0.4	-	-	80.0	1.5	-	-	80.4	0.5	-	-	81.7	1.6	-	-	82.6	1.1
1980	-	-	83.5	1.1	-	-	84.5	1.2	-	-	86.7	2.6	-	-	89.0	2.7	-	-	90.1	1.2	-	-	91.5	1.6
1981	-	-	92.5	1.1	-	-	93.2	0.8	-	-	93.4	0.2	-	-	94.8	1.5	-	-	95.1	0.3	-	-	94.9	-0.2
1982	-	-	96.4	1.6	-	-	96.5	0.1	-	-	98.9	2.5	-	-	97.8	-1.1	-	-	99.4	1.6	-	-	99.9	0.5
1983	-	-	100.5	0.6	-	-	101.1	0.6	-	-	101.4	0.3	-	-	-	-	-	-	101.2	0.1	-	-	101.7	0.5
1984	-	-	100.4	-1.3	-	-	101.1	0.7	-	-	101.1	0.0	-	-	101.4	0.3	-	-	100.7	-0.7	-	-	100.7	0.0
1985	-	-	102.7	2.0	-	-	102.3	-0.4	-	-	102.5	0.2	-	-	102.3	-0.2	-	-	101.9	-0.4	-	-	102.5	0.6
1986	-	-	104.0	1.5	-	-	103.8	-0.2	-	-	104.0	0.2	-	-	106.7	2.6	-	-	105.6	-1.0	-	-	107.2	1.5
1987	-	-	108.4	1.1	-	-	109.4	0.9	-	-	110.6	1.1	-	-	109.4	-1.1	-	-	109.7	0.3	-	-	109.7	0.0
1988	-	-	110.6	0.8	-	-	112.0	1.3	-	-	111.2	-0.7	-	-	113.1	1.7	-	-	112.3	-0.7	-	-	113.4	1.0
1989	-	-	116.5	2.7	-	-	117.5	0.9	-	-	118.2	0.6	-	-	119.0	0.7	-	-	118.9	-0.1	-	-	119.7	0.7
1990	-	-	122.9	2.7	-	-	123.8	0.7	-	-	124.6	0.6	-	-	125.1	0.4	-	-	125.9	0.6	-	-	124.8	-0.9
1991	-	-	128.7	3.1	-	-	129.3	0.5	-	-	129.5	0.2	-	-	128.9	-0.5	-	-	129.1	0.2	-	-	131.4	1.8
1992	-	-	132.3	0.7	-	-	131.7	-0.5	-	-	133.7	1.5	-	-	133.5	-0.1	-	-	133.3	-0.1	-	-	133.2	-0.1
1993	-	-	135.6	1.8	-	-	137.5	1.4	-	-	137.5	0.0	-	-	137.2	-0.2	-	-	137.9	0.5	-	-	139.1	0.9

Source: U.S. Department of Labor, Bureau of Labor Statistics, Division of Consumer Prices and Price Indexes. - indicates no data collected for period.

Pittsburgh, PA
Consumer Price Index - Urban Wage Earners
Base 1982-1984 = 100
Food and Beverages

For 1976-1993. Columns headed % show percentile change in the index from the previous period for which an index is available.

Year	Jan Index	%	Feb Index	%	Mar Index	%	Apr Index	%	May Index	%	Jun Index	%	Jul Index	%	Aug Index	%	Sep Index	%	Oct Index	%	Nov Index	%	Dec Index	%
1976	61.8	-	-	-	-	-	61.9	0.2	-	-	-	-	62.1	0.3	-	-	-	-	62.6	0.8	-	-	-	-
1977	62.7	0.2	-	-	-	-	65.9	5.1	-	-	-	-	66.9	1.5	-	-	-	-	67.4	0.7	-	-	-	-
1978	68.3	1.3	-	-	-	-	71.2	4.2	-	-	73.3	2.9	-	-	74.9	2.2	-	-	74.8	-0.1	-	-	75.4	0.8
1979	-	-	78.7	4.4	-	-	79.5	1.0	-	-	80.3	1.0	-	-	81.2	1.1	-	-	82.2	1.2	-	-	83.0	1.0
1980	-	-	83.7	0.8	-	-	85.5	2.2	-	-	86.6	1.3	-	-	88.8	2.5	-	-	90.1	1.5	-	-	92.1	2.2
1981	-	-	93.0	1.0	-	-	93.6	0.6	-	-	93.8	0.2	-	-	94.8	1.1	-	-	94.9	0.1	-	-	95.0	0.1
1982	-	-	96.4	1.5	-	-	96.6	0.2	-	-	99.0	2.5	-	-	97.8	-1.2	-	-	99.5	1.7	-	-	99.9	0.4
1983	-	-	100.4	0.5	-	-	101.1	0.7	-	-	101.4	0.3	-	-	101.2	-0.2	-	-	101.3	0.1	-	-	101.7	0.4
1984	-	-	100.3	-1.4	-	-	101.0	0.7	-	-	101.1	0.1	-	-	101.6	0.5	-	-	100.6	-1.0	-	-	100.6	0.0
1985	-	-	102.5	1.9	-	-	102.1	-0.4	-	-	102.4	0.3	-	-	102.1	-0.3	-	-	101.5	-0.6	-	-	102.2	0.7
1986	-	-	103.5	1.3	-	-	103.3	-0.2	-	-	103.6	0.3	-	-	106.5	2.8	-	-	105.3	-1.1	-	-	106.9	1.5
1987	-	-	108.0	1.0	-	-	109.0	0.9	-	-	110.1	1.0	-	-	109.2	-0.8	-	-	109.6	0.4	-	-	109.6	0.0
1988	-	-	110.5	0.8	-	-	111.7	1.1	-	-	111.2	-0.4	-	-	113.0	1.6	-	-	112.5	-0.4	-	-	113.6	1.0
1989	-	-	116.4	2.5	-	-	117.4	0.9	-	-	118.1	0.6	-	-	119.0	0.8	-	-	119.0	0.0	-	-	119.7	0.6
1990	-	-	122.8	2.6	-	-	124.0	1.0	-	-	124.8	0.6	-	-	125.4	0.5	-	-	126.2	0.6	-	-	125.3	-0.7
1991	-	-	129.1	3.0	-	-	129.7	0.5	-	-	129.9	0.2	-	-	129.2	-0.5	-	-	129.6	0.3	-	-	131.8	1.7
1992	-	-	132.6	0.6	-	-	132.1	-0.4	-	-	133.9	1.4	-	-	133.7	-0.1	-	-	133.4	-0.2	-	-	133.4	0.0
1993	-	-	135.7	1.7	-	-	137.7	1.5	-	-	137.7	0.0	-	-	137.6	-0.1	-	-	138.2	0.4	-	-	139.3	0.8

Source: U.S. Department of Labor, Bureau of Labor Statistics, Division of Consumer Prices and Price Indexes. - indicates no data collected for period.

Pittsburgh, PA

Consumer Price Index - All Urban Consumers
Base 1982-1984 = 100
Housing

For 1976-1993. Columns headed % show percentile change in the index from the previous period for which an index is available.

Year	Jan Index	%	Feb Index	%	Mar Index	%	Apr Index	%	May Index	%	Jun Index	%	Jul Index	%	Aug Index	%	Sep Index	%	Oct Index	%	Nov Index	%	Dec Index	%
1976	49.2	-	-	-	-	-	50.6	2.8	-	-	-	-	50.6	0.0	-	-	-	-	51.3	1.4	-	-	-	-
1977	52.6	2.5	-	-	-	-	53.7	2.1	-	-	-	-	54.2	0.9	-	-	-	-	55.7	2.8	-	-	-	-
1978	56.8	2.0	-	-	-	-	58.2	2.5	-	-	59.3	1.9	-	-	61.9	4.4	-	-	63.4	2.4	-	-	64.9	2.4
1979	-	-	65.8	1.4	-	-	66.4	0.9	-	-	66.7	0.5	-	-	67.5	1.2	-	-	71.1	5.3	-	-	72.1	1.4
1980	-	-	74.3	3.1	-	-	76.9	3.5	-	-	78.6	2.2	-	-	79.9	1.7	-	-	82.0	2.6	-	-	84.7	3.3
1981	-	-	84.5	-0.2	-	-	83.3	-1.4	-	-	86.6	4.0	-	-	89.1	2.9	-	-	87.6	-1.7	-	-	90.8	3.7
1982	-	-	87.3	-3.9	-	-	85.4	-2.2	-	-	90.9	6.4	-	-	94.1	3.5	-	-	98.8	5.0	-	-	99.2	0.4
1983	-	-	100.5	1.3	-	-	101.4	0.9	-	-	100.7	-0.7	-	-	102.3	1.6	-	-	103.0	0.7	-	-	103.2	0.2
1984	-	-	104.9	1.6	-	-	106.4	1.4	-	-	106.9	0.5	-	-	105.7	-1.1	-	-	106.4	0.7	-	-	107.4	0.9
1985	-	-	107.8	0.4	-	-	108.1	0.3	-	-	108.7	0.6	-	-	108.6	-0.1	-	-	108.2	-0.4	-	-	110.4	2.0
1986	-	-	109.9	-0.5	-	-	111.8	1.7	-	-	111.0	-0.7	-	-	111.5	0.5	-	-	112.2	0.6	-	-	111.9	-0.3
1987	-	-	113.0	1.0	-	-	112.8	-0.2	-	-	112.8	0.0	-	-	114.1	1.2	-	-	114.0	-0.1	-	-	114.7	0.6
1988	-	-	114.4	-0.3	-	-	115.8	1.2	-	-	116.7	0.8	-	-	115.6	-0.9	-	-	115.6	0.0	-	-	116.6	0.9
1989	-	-	117.8	1.0	-	-	118.0	0.2	-	-	118.8	0.7	-	-	119.7	0.8	-	-	120.8	0.9	-	-	121.2	0.3
1990	-	-	121.3	0.1	-	-	123.6	1.9	-	-	124.0	0.3	-	-	126.7	2.2	-	-	127.6	0.7	-	-	127.0	-0.5
1991	-	-	128.8	1.4	-	-	130.3	1.2	-	-	131.3	0.8	-	-	131.7	0.3	-	-	133.2	1.1	-	-	134.8	1.2
1992	-	-	134.2	-0.4	-	-	135.5	1.0	-	-	134.9	-0.4	-	-	137.7	2.1	-	-	136.6	-0.8	-	-	136.6	0.0
1993	-	-	138.7	1.5	-	-	138.0	-0.5	-	-	138.7	0.5	-	-	139.6	0.6	-	-	139.8	0.1	-	-	141.0	0.9

Source: U.S. Department of Labor, Bureau of Labor Statistics, Division of Consumer Prices and Price Indexes. - indicates no data collected for period.

Pittsburgh, PA
Consumer Price Index - Urban Wage Earners
Base 1982-1984 = 100
Housing

For 1976-1993. Columns headed % show percentile change in the index from the previous period for which an index is available.

Year	Jan Index	%	Feb Index	%	Mar Index	%	Apr Index	%	May Index	%	Jun Index	%	Jul Index	%	Aug Index	%	Sep Index	%	Oct Index	%	Nov Index	%	Dec Index	%
1976	52.2	-	-	-	-	-	53.7	2.9	-	-	-	-	53.7	0.0	-	-	-	-	54.4	1.3	-	-	-	-
1977	55.7	2.4	-	-	-	-	57.0	2.3	-	-	-	-	57.4	0.7	-	-	-	-	59.1	3.0	-	-	-	-
1978	60.2	1.9	-	-	-	-	61.7	2.5	-	-	63.1	2.3	-	-	65.3	3.5	-	-	67.1	2.8	-	-	68.5	2.1
1979	-	-	69.5	1.5	-	-	70.3	1.2	-	-	70.6	0.4	-	-	71.6	1.4	-	-	75.4	5.3	-	-	76.6	1.6
1980	-	-	79.0	3.1	-	-	81.9	3.7	-	-	83.7	2.2	-	-	85.0	1.6	-	-	87.2	2.6	-	-	90.1	3.3
1981	-	-	90.1	0.0	-	-	88.8	-1.4	-	-	92.6	4.3	-	-	94.9	2.5	-	-	93.3	-1.7	-	-	96.9	3.9
1982	-	-	93.3	-3.7	-	-	91.3	-2.1	-	-	97.2	6.5	-	-	100.6	3.5	-	-	105.3	4.7	-	-	105.7	0.4
1983	-	-	100.7	-4.7	-	-	104.9	4.2	-	-	103.0	-1.8	-	-	104.3	1.3	-	-	102.5	-1.7	-	-	100.2	-2.2
1984	-	-	98.1	-2.1	-	-	98.7	0.6	-	-	97.9	-0.8	-	-	98.7	0.8	-	-	99.0	0.3	-	-	99.4	0.4
1985	-	-	99.8	0.4	-	-	100.0	0.2	-	-	100.6	0.6	-	-	100.5	-0.1	-	-	100.2	-0.3	-	-	102.2	2.0
1986	-	-	101.9	-0.3	-	-	103.3	1.4	-	-	102.5	-0.8	-	-	103.0	0.5	-	-	103.7	0.7	-	-	103.4	-0.3
1987	-	-	104.4	1.0	-	-	104.1	-0.3	-	-	104.3	0.2	-	-	105.5	1.2	-	-	105.4	-0.1	-	-	106.0	0.6
1988	-	-	105.7	-0.3	-	-	107.0	1.2	-	-	107.8	0.7	-	-	106.8	-0.9	-	-	106.9	0.1	-	-	107.9	0.9
1989	-	-	108.9	0.9	-	-	109.1	0.2	-	-	110.2	1.0	-	-	110.8	0.5	-	-	111.7	0.8	-	-	112.3	0.5
1990	-	-	112.4	0.1	-	-	114.6	2.0	-	-	114.9	0.3	-	-	117.2	2.0	-	-	118.1	0.8	-	-	117.6	-0.4
1991	-	-	119.2	1.4	-	-	120.6	1.2	-	-	121.5	0.7	-	-	121.9	0.3	-	-	123.3	1.1	-	-	124.7	1.1
1992	-	-	124.1	-0.5	-	-	125.2	0.9	-	-	124.6	-0.5	-	-	127.2	2.1	-	-	126.3	-0.7	-	-	126.3	0.0
1993	-	-	128.2	1.5	-	-	127.6	-0.5	-	-	128.3	0.5	-	-	129.0	0.5	-	-	129.1	0.1	-	-	130.3	0.9

Source: U.S. Department of Labor, Bureau of Labor Statistics, Division of Consumer Prices and Price Indexes. - indicates no data collected for period.

Pittsburgh, PA
Consumer Price Index - All Urban Consumers
Base 1982-1984 = 100
Apparel and Upkeep

For 1952-1993. Columns headed % show percentile change in the index from the previous period for which an index is available.

Year	Jan Index	%	Feb Index	%	Mar Index	%	Apr Index	%	May Index	%	Jun Index	%	Jul Index	%	Aug Index	%	Sep Index	%	Oct Index	%	Nov Index	%	Dec Index	%
1952	-	-	-		-		-		-		-		-	-	-		-		42.4	-	-	-	-	-
1953	42.5	0.2	-		-		42.9	0.9	-		-		42.5	-0.9	-		-		43.1	1.4	-		-	
1954	43.1	0.0	-		-		42.8	-0.7	-		-		42.9	0.2	-		-		42.9	0.0	-		-	
1955	42.3	-1.4	-		-		42.5	0.5	-		-		41.9	-1.4	-		-		42.2	0.7	-		-	
1956	42.7	1.2	-		-		43.0	0.7	-		-		43.0	0.0	-		-		43.5	1.2	-		-	
1957	43.9	0.9	-		-		44.1	0.5	-		-		43.9	-0.5	-		-		45.3	3.2	-		-	
1958	44.9	-0.9	-		-		44.6	-0.7	-		-		44.2	-0.9	-		-		44.5	0.7	-		-	
1959	44.0	-1.1	-		-		44.5	1.1	-		-		44.7	0.4	-		-		45.2	1.1	-		-	
1960	44.6	-1.3	-		-		45.3	1.6	-		-		45.3	0.0	-		-		45.9	1.3	-		-	
1961	45.0	-2.0	-		-		45.2	0.4	-		-		45.5	0.7	-		-		46.3	1.8	-		-	
1962	45.5	-1.7	-		-		45.7	0.4	-		-		46.0	0.7	-		-		46.2	0.4	-		-	
1963	46.5	0.6	-		-		46.8	0.6	-		-		46.9	0.2	-		-		47.3	0.9	-		-	
1964	47.2	-0.2	-		-		47.6	0.8	-		-		47.7	0.2	-		-		48.2	1.0	-		-	
1965	47.6	-1.2	-		-		49.0	2.9	-		-		48.4	-1.2	-		-		49.3	1.9	-		-	
1966	48.2	-2.2	-		-		49.8	3.3	-		-		49.7	-0.2	-		-		51.0	2.6	-		-	
1967	50.8	-0.4	-		-		51.2	0.8	-		-		50.8	-0.8	-		-		51.8	2.0	-		-	
1968	51.4	-0.8	-		-		54.1	5.3	-		-		53.7	-0.7	-		-		56.1	4.5	-		-	
1969	55.9	-0.4	-		-		57.8	3.4	-		-		57.4	-0.7	-		-		59.5	3.7	-		-	
1970	57.2	-3.9	-		-		58.7	2.6	-		-		58.3	-0.7	-		-		61.4	5.3	-		-	
1971	59.1	-3.7	-		-		60.7	2.7	-		-		60.0	-1.2	-		-		64.0	6.7	-		-	
1972	62.4	-2.5	-		-		63.5	1.8	-		-		62.4	-1.7	-		-		64.7	3.7	-		-	
1973	63.0	-2.6	-		-		64.8	2.9	-		-		64.3	-0.8	-		-		68.1	5.9	-		-	
1974	67.3	-1.2	-		-		70.2	4.3	-		-		71.4	1.7	-		-		72.2	1.1	-		-	
1975	69.9	-3.2	-		-		72.5	3.7	-		-		71.8	-1.0	-		-		74.5	3.8	-		-	
1976	73.5	-1.3	-		-		73.2	-0.4	-		-		72.9	-0.4	-		-		75.2	3.2	-		-	
1977	74.5	-0.9	-		-		74.3	-0.3	-		-		75.4	1.5	-		-		76.9	2.0	-		-	
1978	73.3	-4.7	-		-		75.1	2.5	-		75.3	0.3	-		80.5	6.9	-		81.6	1.4	-		81.0	-0.7
1979	-		81.3	0.4	-		81.5	0.2	-		79.7	-2.2	-		83.2	4.4	-		85.5	2.8	-		85.9	0.5
1980	-		85.8	-0.1	-		86.0	0.2	-		84.0	-2.3	-		86.9	3.5	-		91.1	4.8	-		89.6	-1.6
1981	-		92.1	2.8	-		92.6	0.5	-		92.9	0.3	-		95.9	3.2	-		96.3	0.4	-		94.0	-2.4
1982	-		95.7	1.8	-		96.9	1.3	-		95.4	-1.5	-		99.0	3.8	-		101.3	2.3	-		99.0	-2.3
1983	-		103.4	4.4	-		100.9	-2.4	-		98.2	-2.7	-		101.1	3.0	-		102.8	1.7	-		101.4	-1.4
1984	-		100.4	-1.0	-		103.2	2.8	-		99.3	-3.8	-		100.3	1.0	-		102.7	2.4	-		100.9	-1.8
1985	-		104.4	3.5	-		101.2	-3.1	-		99.5	-1.7	-		100.0	0.5	-		108.8	8.8	-		104.0	-4.4
1986	-		97.7	-6.1	-		98.7	1.0	-		96.5	-2.2	-		101.9	5.6	-		104.8	2.8	-		102.4	-2.3
1987	-		101.1	-1.3	-		107.5	6.3	-		104.3	-3.0	-		108.3	3.8	-		112.4	3.8	-		110.5	-1.7
1988	-		109.7	-0.7	-		114.8	4.6	-		107.7	-6.2	-		114.7	6.5	-		122.7	7.0	-		117.3	-4.4
1989	-		116.5	-0.7	-		119.6	2.7	-		119.9	0.3	-		123.3	2.8	-		127.4	3.3	-		121.4	-4.7
1990	-		124.3	2.4	-		125.7	1.1	-		121.0	-3.7	-		125.5	3.7	-		129.1	2.9	-		125.4	-2.9
1991	-		125.9	0.4	-		131.4	4.4	-		125.0	-4.9	-		129.4	3.5	-		135.5	4.7	-		131.7	-2.8
1992	-		129.3	-1.8	-		133.2	3.0	-		127.9	-4.0	-		130.8	2.3	-		143.2	9.5	-		134.8	-5.9
1993	-		135.9	0.8	-		139.9	2.9	-		130.0	-7.1	-		140.2	7.8	-		131.4	-6.3	-		127.7	-2.8

Source: U.S. Department of Labor, Bureau of Labor Statistics, Division of Consumer Prices and Price Indexes. - indicates no data collected for period.

Pittsburgh, PA
Consumer Price Index - Urban Wage Earners
Base 1982-1984 = 100
Apparel and Upkeep

For 1952-1993. Columns headed % show percentile change in the index from the previous period for which an index is available.

Year	Jan Index	%	Feb Index	%	Mar Index	%	Apr Index	%	May Index	%	Jun Index	%	Jul Index	%	Aug Index	%	Sep Index	%	Oct Index	%	Nov Index	%	Dec Index	%
1952	-		-	-	-	-	-	-	-	-	-	-	-	-	-	-	-	-	44.0	-	-	-	-	-
1953	44.1	0.2	-	-	-	-	44.5	0.9	-	-	-	-	44.1	-0.9	-	-	-	-	44.6	1.1	-	-	-	-
1954	44.7	0.2	-	-	-	-	44.4	-0.7	-	-	-	-	44.4	0.0	-	-	-	-	44.4	0.0	-	-	-	-
1955	43.9	-1.1	-	-	-	-	44.1	0.5	-	-	-	-	43.4	-1.6	-	-	-	-	43.7	0.7	-	-	-	-
1956	44.3	1.4	-	-	-	-	44.5	0.5	-	-	-	-	44.5	0.0	-	-	-	-	45.1	1.3	-	-	-	-
1957	45.6	1.1	-	-	-	-	45.8	0.4	-	-	-	-	45.5	-0.7	-	-	-	-	46.9	3.1	-	-	-	-
1958	46.6	-0.6	-	-	-	-	46.2	-0.9	-	-	-	-	45.8	-0.9	-	-	-	-	46.2	0.9	-	-	-	-
1959	45.7	-1.1	-	-	-	-	46.1	0.9	-	-	-	-	46.3	0.4	-	-	-	-	46.9	1.3	-	-	-	-
1960	46.2	-1.5	-	-	-	-	46.9	1.5	-	-	-	-	46.9	0.0	-	-	-	-	47.6	1.5	-	-	-	-
1961	46.7	-1.9	-	-	-	-	46.9	0.4	-	-	-	-	47.2	0.6	-	-	-	-	48.0	1.7	-	-	-	-
1962	47.1	-1.9	-	-	-	-	47.4	0.6	-	-	-	-	47.7	0.6	-	-	-	-	47.9	0.4	-	-	-	-
1963	48.3	0.8	-	-	-	-	48.6	0.6	-	-	-	-	48.7	0.2	-	-	-	-	49.1	0.8	-	-	-	-
1964	48.9	-0.4	-	-	-	-	49.3	0.8	-	-	-	-	49.5	0.4	-	-	-	-	50.0	1.0	-	-	-	-
1965	49.3	-1.4	-	-	-	-	50.8	3.0	-	-	-	-	50.2	-1.2	-	-	-	-	51.1	1.8	-	-	-	-
1966	50.0	-2.2	-	-	-	-	51.7	3.4	-	-	-	-	51.6	-0.2	-	-	-	-	52.9	2.5	-	-	-	-
1967	52.7	-0.4	-	-	-	-	53.1	0.8	-	-	-	-	52.7	-0.8	-	-	-	-	53.7	1.9	-	-	-	-
1968	53.3	-0.7	-	-	-	-	56.1	5.3	-	-	-	-	55.7	-0.7	-	-	-	-	58.1	4.3	-	-	-	-
1969	58.0	-0.2	-	-	-	-	59.9	3.3	-	-	-	-	59.6	-0.5	-	-	-	-	61.7	3.5	-	-	-	-
1970	59.3	-3.9	-	-	-	-	60.8	2.5	-	-	-	-	60.5	-0.5	-	-	-	-	63.7	5.3	-	-	-	-
1971	61.3	-3.8	-	-	-	-	62.9	2.6	-	-	-	-	62.2	-1.1	-	-	-	-	66.4	6.8	-	-	-	-
1972	64.7	-2.6	-	-	-	-	65.8	1.7	-	-	-	-	64.7	-1.7	-	-	-	-	67.1	3.7	-	-	-	-
1973	65.4	-2.5	-	-	-	-	67.2	2.8	-	-	-	-	66.6	-0.9	-	-	-	-	70.7	6.2	-	-	-	-
1974	69.8	-1.3	-	-	-	-	72.8	4.3	-	-	-	-	74.0	1.6	-	-	-	-	74.9	1.2	-	-	-	-
1975	72.5	-3.2	-	-	-	-	75.2	3.7	-	-	-	-	74.4	-1.1	-	-	-	-	77.3	3.9	-	-	-	-
1976	76.2	-1.4	-	-	-	-	75.9	-0.4	-	-	-	-	75.6	-0.4	-	-	-	-	78.0	3.2	-	-	-	-
1977	77.3	-0.9	-	-	-	-	77.0	-0.4	-	-	-	-	78.2	1.6	-	-	-	-	79.7	1.9	-	-	-	-
1978	76.0	-4.6	-	-	-	-	77.8	2.4	-	-	76.5	-1.7	-	-	80.3	5.0	-	-	80.3	0.0	-	-	81.0	0.9
1979	-	-	81.4	0.5	-	-	82.9	1.8	-	-	81.5	-1.7	-	-	84.1	3.2	-	-	87.5	4.0	-	-	87.2	-0.3
1980	-	-	86.6	-0.7	-	-	86.8	0.2	-	-	85.4	-1.6	-	-	91.5	7.1	-	-	96.3	5.2	-	-	90.5	-6.0
1981	-	-	90.4	-0.1	-	-	93.1	3.0	-	-	93.1	0.0	-	-	95.5	2.6	-	-	94.9	-0.6	-	-	93.9	-1.1
1982	-	-	95.9	2.1	-	-	97.3	1.5	-	-	95.3	-2.1	-	-	98.7	3.6	-	-	101.2	2.5	-	-	99.2	-2.0
1983	-	-	102.9	3.7	-	-	100.3	-2.5	-	-	97.2	-3.1	-	-	101.1	4.0	-	-	102.9	1.8	-	-	101.5	-1.4
1984	-	-	101.5	0.0	-	-	103.2	1.7	-	-	99.1	-4.0	-	-	100.8	1.7	-	-	102.6	1.8	-	-	100.9	-1.7
1985	-	-	103.5	2.6	-	-	101.6	-1.8	-	-	100.0	-1.6	-	-	100.3	0.3	-	-	108.6	8.3	-	-	103.6	-4.6
1986	-	-	97.8	-5.6	-	-	98.6	0.8	-	-	96.4	-2.2	-	-	100.9	4.7	-	-	104.1	3.2	-	-	101.5	-2.5
1987	-	-	101.6	0.1	-	-	106.3	4.6	-	-	104.0	-2.2	-	-	107.9	3.8	-	-	110.0	1.9	-	-	108.5	-1.4
1988	-	-	108.5	0.0	-	-	113.1	4.2	-	-	108.2	-4.3	-	-	112.1	3.6	-	-	120.6	7.6	-	-	114.6	-5.0
1989	-	-	113.7	-0.8	-	-	117.8	3.6	-	-	117.7	-0.1	-	-	120.2	2.1	-	-	124.1	3.2	-	-	119.1	-4.0
1990	-	-	121.5	2.0	-	-	124.5	2.5	-	-	119.0	-4.4	-	-	120.1	0.9	-	-	125.7	4.7	-	-	122.6	-2.5
1991	-	-	122.0	-0.5	-	-	126.7	3.9	-	-	121.3	-4.3	-	-	123.2	1.6	-	-	129.3	5.0	-	-	124.9	-3.4
1992	-	-	126.8	1.5	-	-	130.1	2.6	-	-	124.0	-4.7	-	-	123.7	-0.2	-	-	135.7	9.7	-	-	128.5	-5.3
1993	-	-	130.9	1.9	-	-	135.6	3.6	-	-	125.7	-7.3	-	-	132.1	5.1	-	-	125.0	-5.4	-	-	122.3	-2.2

Source: U.S. Department of Labor, Bureau of Labor Statistics, Division of Consumer Prices and Price Indexes. - indicates no data collected for period.

Pittsburgh, PA
Consumer Price Index - All Urban Consumers
Base 1982-1984 = 100
Transportation

For 1947-1993. Columns headed % show percentile change in the index from the previous period for which an index is available.

Year	Jan Index	%	Feb Index	%	Mar Index	%	Apr Index	%	May Index	%	Jun Index	%	Jul Index	%	Aug Index	%	Sep Index	%	Oct Index	%	Nov Index	%	Dec Index	%
1947	15.9	-	15.8	-0.6	15.9	0.6	16.1	1.3	16.1	0.0	16.1	0.0	16.1	0.0	16.3	1.2	16.5	1.2	16.5	0.0	16.5	0.0	16.5	0.0
1948	17.4	5.5	17.6	1.1	17.6	0.0	17.6	0.0	17.6	0.0	17.6	0.0	18.0	2.3	18.3	1.7	18.3	0.0	18.4	0.5	18.4	0.0	18.4	0.0
1949	18.5	0.5	18.7	1.1	18.6	-0.5	18.7	0.5	18.8	0.5	18.9	0.5	18.9	0.0	18.9	0.0	18.9	0.0	18.9	0.0	18.9	0.0	20.2	6.9
1950	20.3	0.5	20.3	0.0	20.2	-0.5	20.1	-0.5	20.3	1.0	20.3	0.0	20.4	0.5	22.0	7.8	22.1	0.5	22.1	0.0	22.1	0.0	22.1	0.0
1951	22.1	0.0	22.1	0.0	22.3	0.9	22.3	0.0	22.3	0.0	22.3	0.0	22.3	0.0	22.3	0.0	23.3	4.5	23.6	1.3	24.0	1.7	24.0	0.0
1952	24.3	1.2	24.4	0.4	24.4	0.0	24.4	0.0	24.4	0.0	24.4	0.0	24.4	0.0	24.4	0.0	24.4	0.0	24.4	0.0	24.4	0.0	24.6	0.8
1953	24.6	0.0	-	-	-	-	24.6	0.0	-	-	-	-	24.9	1.2	-	-	-	-	24.9	0.0	-	-	-	-
1954	24.6	-1.2	-	-	-	-	24.5	-0.4	-	-	-	-	24.3	-0.8	-	-	-	-	23.7	-2.5	-	-	-	-
1955	24.4	3.0	-	-	-	-	24.3	-0.4	-	-	-	-	24.3	0.0	-	-	-	-	24.0	-1.2	-	-	-	-
1956	23.6	-1.7	-	-	-	-	24.0	1.7	-	-	-	-	24.1	0.4	-	-	-	-	25.4	5.4	-	-	-	-
1957	25.7	1.2	-	-	-	-	25.5	-0.8	-	-	-	-	25.4	-0.4	-	-	-	-	25.7	1.2	-	-	-	-
1958	26.4	2.7	-	-	-	-	26.3	-0.4	-	-	-	-	26.9	2.3	-	-	-	-	27.5	2.2	-	-	-	-
1959	27.8	1.1	-	-	-	-	28.0	0.7	-	-	-	-	28.6	2.1	-	-	-	-	29.1	1.7	-	-	-	-
1960	29.1	0.0	-	-	-	-	29.4	1.0	-	-	-	-	29.1	-1.0	-	-	-	-	29.0	-0.3	-	-	-	-
1961	29.0	0.0	-	-	-	-	29.3	1.0	-	-	-	-	28.9	-1.4	-	-	-	-	29.3	1.4	-	-	-	-
1962	29.7	1.4	-	-	-	-	30.0	1.0	-	-	-	-	29.9	-0.3	-	-	-	-	30.0	0.3	-	-	-	-
1963	29.7	-1.0	-	-	-	-	29.8	0.3	-	-	-	-	30.1	1.0	-	-	-	-	29.7	-1.3	-	-	-	-
1964	30.3	2.0	-	-	-	-	30.2	-0.3	-	-	-	-	30.0	-0.7	-	-	-	-	30.3	1.0	-	-	-	-
1965	30.8	1.7	-	-	-	-	30.8	0.0	-	-	-	-	30.8	0.0	-	-	-	-	30.8	0.0	-	-	-	-
1966	30.7	-0.3	-	-	-	-	30.9	0.7	-	-	-	-	31.2	1.0	-	-	-	-	31.3	0.3	-	-	-	-
1967	31.1	-0.6	-	-	-	-	31.5	1.3	-	-	-	-	31.6	0.3	-	-	-	-	31.9	0.9	-	-	-	-
1968	32.4	1.6	-	-	-	-	32.4	0.0	-	-	-	-	32.6	0.6	-	-	-	-	33.1	1.5	-	-	-	-
1969	33.1	0.0	-	-	-	-	34.3	3.6	-	-	-	-	34.2	-0.3	-	-	-	-	34.3	0.3	-	-	-	-
1970	34.3	0.0	-	-	-	-	35.7	4.1	-	-	-	-	36.3	1.7	-	-	-	-	36.5	0.6	-	-	-	-
1971	37.0	1.4	-	-	-	-	37.8	2.2	-	-	-	-	38.6	2.1	-	-	-	-	38.1	-1.3	-	-	-	-
1972	37.8	-0.8	-	-	-	-	38.1	0.8	-	-	-	-	38.5	1.0	-	-	-	-	38.6	0.3	-	-	-	-
1973	38.5	-0.3	-	-	-	-	39.0	1.3	-	-	-	-	39.5	1.3	-	-	-	-	39.6	0.3	-	-	-	-
1974	40.5	2.3	-	-	-	-	42.2	4.2	-	-	-	-	44.3	5.0	-	-	-	-	45.1	1.8	-	-	-	-
1975	44.9	-0.4	-	-	-	-	45.9	2.2	-	-	-	-	47.7	3.9	-	-	-	-	48.3	1.3	-	-	-	-
1976	48.4	0.2	-	-	-	-	50.3	3.9	-	-	-	-	52.5	4.4	-	-	-	-	53.2	1.3	-	-	-	-
1977	53.9	1.3	-	-	-	-	56.5	4.8	-	-	-	-	57.0	0.9	-	-	-	-	56.8	-0.4	-	-	-	-
1978	56.9	0.2	-	-	-	-	58.4	2.6	-	-	60.0	2.7	-	-	61.0	1.7	-	-	61.1	0.2	-	-	61.9	1.3
1979	-	-	63.0	1.8	-	-	65.3	3.7	-	-	68.0	4.1	-	-	71.3	4.9	-	-	72.4	1.5	-	-	74.0	2.2
1980	-	-	78.0	5.4	-	-	80.0	2.6	-	-	82.4	3.0	-	-	83.2	1.0	-	-	85.0	2.2	-	-	87.3	2.7
1981	-	-	90.7	3.9	-	-	92.1	1.5	-	-	93.4	1.4	-	-	94.9	1.6	-	-	96.1	1.3	-	-	96.5	0.4
1982	-	-	95.7	-0.8	-	-	93.6	-2.2	-	-	95.6	2.1	-	-	97.3	1.8	-	-	98.8	1.5	-	-	99.6	0.8
1983	-	-	97.9	-1.7	-	-	97.1	-0.8	-	-	98.4	1.3	-	-	100.7	2.3	-	-	102.4	1.7	-	-	102.8	0.4
1984	-	-	101.9	-0.9	-	-	102.7	0.8	-	-	104.3	1.6	-	-	104.0	-0.3	-	-	104.6	0.6	-	-	104.7	0.1
1985	-	-	104.0	-0.7	-	-	105.0	1.0	-	-	105.8	0.8	-	-	105.3	-0.5	-	-	106.1	0.8	-	-	107.1	0.9
1986	-	-	105.3	-1.7	-	-	98.1	-6.8	-	-	99.9	1.8	-	-	96.4	-3.5	-	-	97.2	0.8	-	-	97.7	0.5
1987	-	-	98.5	0.8	-	-	99.9	1.4	-	-	100.2	0.3	-	-	101.3	1.1	-	-	101.9	0.6	-	-	102.3	0.4
1988	-	-	100.5	-1.8	-	-	100.3	-0.2	-	-	102.2	1.9	-	-	102.3	0.1	-	-	104.4	2.1	-	-	104.7	0.3
1989	-	-	105.3	0.6	-	-	108.2	2.8	-	-	109.6	1.3	-	-	106.6	-2.7	-	-	107.1	0.5	-	-	107.3	0.2
1990	-	-	109.3	1.9	-	-	108.4	-0.8	-	-	109.2	0.7	-	-	111.4	2.0	-	-	118.8	6.6	-	-	118.7	-0.1
1991	-	-	113.0	-4.8	-	-	110.7	-2.0	-	-	111.9	1.1	-	-	112.1	0.2	-	-	113.7	1.4	-	-	114.8	1.0

[Continued]

712

Pittsburgh, PA
Consumer Price Index - All Urban Consumers
Base 1982-1984 = 100
Transportation
[Continued]

For 1947-1993. Columns headed % show percentile change in the index from the previous period for which an index is available.

Year	Jan Index	%	Feb Index	%	Mar Index	%	Apr Index	%	May Index	%	Jun Index	%	Jul Index	%	Aug Index	%	Sep Index	%	Oct Index	%	Nov Index	%	Dec Index	%
1992	-	-	113.5	-1.1	-	-	114.0	0.4	-	-	115.6	1.4	-	-	116.2	0.5	-	-	117.5	1.1	-	-	117.7	0.2
1993	-	-	117.6	-0.1	-	-	116.9	-0.6	-	-	117.5	0.5	-	-	116.5	-0.9	-	-	120.8	3.7	-	-	119.8	-0.8

Source: U.S. Department of Labor, Bureau of Labor Statistics, Division of Consumer Prices and Price Indexes. - indicates no data collected for period.

Pittsburgh, PA
Consumer Price Index - Urban Wage Earners
Base 1982-1984 = 100
Transportation

For 1947-1993. Columns headed % show percentile change in the index from the previous period for which an index is available.

Year	Jan Index	%	Feb Index	%	Mar Index	%	Apr Index	%	May Index	%	Jun Index	%	Jul Index	%	Aug Index	%	Sep Index	%	Oct Index	%	Nov Index	%	Dec Index	%
1947	15.7	-	15.6	-0.6	15.7	0.6	15.9	1.3	15.9	0.0	15.9	0.0	15.9	0.0	16.1	1.3	16.3	1.2	16.3	0.0	16.3	0.0	16.3	0.0
1948	17.2	5.5	17.3	0.6	17.3	0.0	17.3	0.0	17.3	0.0	17.4	0.6	17.8	2.3	18.1	1.7	18.1	0.0	18.2	0.6	18.1	-0.5	18.2	0.6
1949	18.3	0.5	18.4	0.5	18.4	0.0	18.5	0.5	18.6	0.5	18.7	0.5	18.7	0.0	18.7	0.0	18.7	0.0	18.7	0.0	18.7	0.0	20.0	7.0
1950	20.0	0.0	20.0	0.0	20.0	0.0	19.9	-0.5	20.0	0.5	20.1	0.5	20.1	0.0	21.7	8.0	21.8	0.5	21.8	0.0	21.8	0.0	21.8	0.0
1951	21.8	0.0	21.8	0.0	22.0	0.9	22.0	0.0	22.0	0.0	22.0	0.0	22.0	0.0	22.0	0.0	23.0	4.5	23.3	1.3	23.7	1.7	23.7	0.0
1952	24.0	1.3	24.1	0.4	24.1	0.0	24.1	0.0	24.1	0.0	24.1	0.0	24.1	0.0	24.1	0.0	24.1	0.0	24.1	0.0	24.1	0.0	24.3	0.8
1953	24.3	0.0	-	-	-	-	24.3	0.0	-	-	-	-	24.6	1.2	-	-	-	-	24.6	0.0	-	-	-	-
1954	24.3	-1.2	-	-	-	-	24.2	-0.4	-	-	-	-	24.0	-0.8	-	-	-	-	23.4	-2.5	-	-	-	-
1955	24.1	3.0	-	-	-	-	24.0	-0.4	-	-	-	-	24.0	0.0	-	-	-	-	23.7	-1.2	-	-	-	-
1956	23.3	-1.7	-	-	-	-	23.7	1.7	-	-	-	-	23.8	0.4	-	-	-	-	25.1	5.5	-	-	-	-
1957	25.4	1.2	-	-	-	-	25.2	-0.8	-	-	-	-	25.1	-0.4	-	-	-	-	25.4	1.2	-	-	-	-
1958	26.1	2.8	-	-	-	-	26.0	-0.4	-	-	-	-	26.6	2.3	-	-	-	-	27.1	1.9	-	-	-	-
1959	27.5	1.5	-	-	-	-	27.6	0.4	-	-	-	-	28.2	2.2	-	-	-	-	28.8	2.1	-	-	-	-
1960	28.8	0.0	-	-	-	-	29.0	0.7	-	-	-	-	28.8	-0.7	-	-	-	-	28.7	-0.3	-	-	-	-
1961	28.6	-0.3	-	-	-	-	28.9	1.0	-	-	-	-	28.5	-1.4	-	-	-	-	28.9	1.4	-	-	-	-
1962	29.3	1.4	-	-	-	-	29.6	1.0	-	-	-	-	29.5	-0.3	-	-	-	-	29.6	0.3	-	-	-	-
1963	29.3	-1.0	-	-	-	-	29.5	0.7	-	-	-	-	29.7	0.7	-	-	-	-	29.3	-1.3	-	-	-	-
1964	29.9	2.0	-	-	-	-	29.9	0.0	-	-	-	-	29.7	-0.7	-	-	-	-	30.0	1.0	-	-	-	-
1965	30.4	1.3	-	-	-	-	30.4	0.0	-	-	-	-	30.5	0.3	-	-	-	-	30.5	0.0	-	-	-	-
1966	30.3	-0.7	-	-	-	-	30.5	0.7	-	-	-	-	30.8	1.0	-	-	-	-	30.9	0.3	-	-	-	-
1967	30.7	-0.6	-	-	-	-	31.1	1.3	-	-	-	-	31.2	0.3	-	-	-	-	31.5	1.0	-	-	-	-
1968	32.0	1.6	-	-	-	-	32.0	0.0	-	-	-	-	32.2	0.6	-	-	-	-	32.7	1.6	-	-	-	-
1969	32.7	0.0	-	-	-	-	33.9	3.7	-	-	-	-	33.8	-0.3	-	-	-	-	33.9	0.3	-	-	-	-
1970	33.9	0.0	-	-	-	-	35.3	4.1	-	-	-	-	35.9	1.7	-	-	-	-	36.1	0.6	-	-	-	-
1971	36.5	1.1	-	-	-	-	37.3	2.2	-	-	-	-	38.1	2.1	-	-	-	-	37.6	-1.3	-	-	-	-
1972	37.3	-0.8	-	-	-	-	37.6	0.8	-	-	-	-	38.0	1.1	-	-	-	-	38.1	0.3	-	-	-	-
1973	38.0	-0.3	-	-	-	-	38.5	1.3	-	-	-	-	39.0	1.3	-	-	-	-	39.1	0.3	-	-	-	-
1974	40.0	2.3	-	-	-	-	41.7	4.2	-	-	-	-	43.7	4.8	-	-	-	-	44.5	1.8	-	-	-	-
1975	44.4	-0.2	-	-	-	-	45.3	2.0	-	-	-	-	47.1	4.0	-	-	-	-	47.7	1.3	-	-	-	-
1976	47.8	0.2	-	-	-	-	49.7	4.0	-	-	-	-	51.8	4.2	-	-	-	-	52.6	1.5	-	-	-	-
1977	53.3	1.3	-	-	-	-	55.8	4.7	-	-	-	-	56.3	0.9	-	-	-	-	56.1	-0.4	-	-	-	-
1978	56.2	0.2	-	-	-	-	57.7	2.7	-	-	59.3	2.8	-	-	60.3	1.7	-	-	60.8	0.8	-	-	61.3	0.8
1979	-	-	62.5	2.0	-	-	64.6	3.4	-	-	67.5	4.5	-	-	70.9	5.0	-	-	71.8	1.3	-	-	73.2	1.9
1980	-	-	77.4	5.7	-	-	79.4	2.6	-	-	81.8	3.0	-	-	82.0	0.2	-	-	84.7	3.3	-	-	86.9	2.6
1981	-	-	90.5	4.1	-	-	92.1	1.8	-	-	93.5	1.5	-	-	95.0	1.6	-	-	96.5	1.6	-	-	96.9	0.4
1982	-	-	96.0	-0.9	-	-	93.7	-2.4	-	-	95.7	2.1	-	-	97.9	2.3	-	-	99.1	1.2	-	-	99.6	0.5
1983	-	-	97.6	-2.0	-	-	96.6	-1.0	-	-	97.9	1.3	-	-	100.5	2.7	-	-	102.2	1.7	-	-	102.6	0.4
1984	-	-	101.7	-0.9	-	-	102.7	1.0	-	-	104.4	1.7	-	-	104.2	-0.2	-	-	104.7	0.5	-	-	104.8	0.1
1985	-	-	104.1	-0.7	-	-	105.0	0.9	-	-	105.7	0.7	-	-	105.1	-0.6	-	-	105.6	0.5	-	-	106.6	0.9
1986	-	-	104.7	-1.8	-	-	97.0	-7.4	-	-	98.5	1.5	-	-	94.8	-3.8	-	-	95.4	0.6	-	-	95.9	0.5
1987	-	-	97.0	1.1	-	-	98.5	1.5	-	-	99.1	0.6	-	-	100.4	1.3	-	-	101.0	0.6	-	-	101.4	0.4
1988	-	-	99.7	-1.7	-	-	99.7	0.0	-	-	101.5	1.8	-	-	101.7	0.2	-	-	103.9	2.2	-	-	104.1	0.2
1989	-	-	104.8	0.7	-	-	107.9	3.0	-	-	109.3	1.3	-	-	106.3	-2.7	-	-	106.7	0.4	-	-	106.8	0.1
1990	-	-	108.7	1.8	-	-	107.9	-0.7	-	-	108.8	0.8	-	-	110.8	1.8	-	-	117.9	6.4	-	-	117.7	-0.2
1991	-	-	111.8	-5.0	-	-	109.6	-2.0	-	-	111.0	1.3	-	-	111.5	0.5	-	-	113.0	1.3	-	-	113.9	0.8

[Continued]

Pittsburgh, PA
Consumer Price Index - Urban Wage Earners
Base 1982-1984 = 100
Transportation
[Continued]

For 1947-1993. Columns headed % show percentile change in the index from the previous period for which an index is available.

Year	Jan		Feb		Mar		Apr		May		Jun		Jul		Aug		Sep		Oct		Nov		Dec	
	Index	%	Index	%	Index	%	Index	%	Index	%	Index	%	Index	%	Index	%	Index	%	Index	%	Index	%	Index	%
1992	-	-	112.3	-1.4	-	-	112.9	0.5	-	-	114.7	1.6	-	-	115.4	0.6	-	-	116.9	1.3	-	-	116.9	0.0
1993	-	-	116.8	-0.1	-	-	116.2	-0.5	-	-	117.1	0.8	-	-	116.2	-0.8	-	-	120.2	3.4	-	-	119.2	-0.8

Source: U.S. Department of Labor, Bureau of Labor Statistics, Division of Consumer Prices and Price Indexes. - indicates no data collected for period.

Pittsburgh, PA
Consumer Price Index - All Urban Consumers
Base 1982-1984 = 100
Medical Care

For 1947-1993. Columns headed % show percentile change in the index from the previous period for which an index is available.

Year	Jan Index	%	Feb Index	%	Mar Index	%	Apr Index	%	May Index	%	Jun Index	%	Jul Index	%	Aug Index	%	Sep Index	%	Oct Index	%	Nov Index	%	Dec Index	%
1947	11.5	-	11.5	0.0	11.6	0.9	11.6	0.0	11.6	0.0	11.6	0.0	11.7	0.9	11.6	-0.9	11.7	0.9	11.7	0.0	11.9	1.7	11.9	0.0
1948	12.2	2.5	12.2	0.0	12.2	0.0	12.2	0.0	12.4	1.6	12.4	0.0	12.4	0.0	12.4	0.0	12.4	0.0	12.4	0.0	12.5	0.8	12.6	0.8
1949	12.6	0.0	12.6	0.0	12.6	0.0	12.6	0.0	12.6	0.0	12.6	0.0	12.6	0.0	12.6	0.0	12.6	0.0	12.6	0.0	12.6	0.0	12.7	0.8
1950	12.7	0.0	12.7	0.0	12.9	1.6	12.9	0.0	12.9	0.0	12.9	0.0	12.9	0.0	12.9	0.0	13.0	0.8	12.9	-0.8	13.0	0.8	13.0	0.0
1951	13.1	0.8	13.1	0.0	13.2	0.8	13.3	0.8	13.3	0.0	13.7	3.0	13.7	0.0	13.7	0.0	13.7	0.0	13.7	0.0	13.7	0.0	13.7	0.0
1952	13.8	0.7	13.8	0.0	13.9	0.7	13.9	0.0	13.9	0.0	13.9	0.0	13.9	0.0	13.9	0.0	14.1	1.4	14.1	0.0	14.1	0.0	14.3	1.4
1953	14.3	0.0	-	-	-	-	14.8	3.5	-	-	-	-	14.8	0.0	-	-	-	-	14.7	-0.7	-	-	-	-
1954	14.8	0.7	-	-	-	-	15.6	5.4	-	-	-	-	15.6	0.0	-	-	-	-	15.4	-1.3	-	-	-	-
1955	15.4	0.0	-	-	-	-	15.5	0.6	-	-	-	-	16.1	3.9	-	-	-	-	16.1	0.0	-	-	-	-
1956	16.1	0.0	-	-	-	-	16.5	2.5	-	-	-	-	16.5	0.0	-	-	-	-	17.5	6.1	-	-	-	-
1957	17.6	0.6	-	-	-	-	17.7	0.6	-	-	-	-	17.7	0.0	-	-	-	-	17.9	1.1	-	-	-	-
1958	18.0	0.6	-	-	-	-	18.0	0.0	-	-	-	-	18.8	4.4	-	-	-	-	18.9	0.5	-	-	-	-
1959	19.1	1.1	-	-	-	-	19.3	1.0	-	-	-	-	19.3	0.0	-	-	-	-	20.5	6.2	-	-	-	-
1960	20.6	0.5	-	-	-	-	20.7	0.5	-	-	-	-	20.7	0.0	-	-	-	-	20.8	0.5	-	-	-	-
1961	20.9	0.5	-	-	-	-	21.5	2.9	-	-	-	-	21.5	0.0	-	-	-	-	21.6	0.5	-	-	-	-
1962	21.7	0.5	-	-	-	-	21.7	0.0	-	-	-	-	22.8	5.1	-	-	-	-	23.0	0.9	-	-	-	-
1963	23.0	0.0	-	-	-	-	23.0	0.0	-	-	-	-	23.0	0.0	-	-	-	-	23.1	0.4	-	-	-	-
1964	23.2	0.4	-	-	-	-	23.6	1.7	-	-	-	-	23.9	1.3	-	-	-	-	23.9	0.0	-	-	-	-
1965	24.0	0.4	-	-	-	-	24.2	0.8	-	-	-	-	24.4	0.8	-	-	-	-	24.5	0.4	-	-	-	-
1966	24.6	0.4	-	-	-	-	24.8	0.8	-	-	-	-	25.1	1.2	-	-	-	-	25.3	0.8	-	-	-	-
1967	26.5	4.7	-	-	-	-	26.7	0.8	-	-	-	-	26.8	0.4	-	-	-	-	27.1	1.1	-	-	-	-
1968	27.5	1.5	-	-	-	-	27.7	0.7	-	-	-	-	28.5	2.9	-	-	-	-	29.1	2.1	-	-	-	-
1969	29.4	1.0	-	-	-	-	29.9	1.7	-	-	-	-	30.2	1.0	-	-	-	-	30.4	0.7	-	-	-	-
1970	30.6	0.7	-	-	-	-	31.3	2.3	-	-	-	-	31.8	1.6	-	-	-	-	32.1	0.9	-	-	-	-
1971	32.5	1.2	-	-	-	-	32.8	0.9	-	-	-	-	32.9	0.3	-	-	-	-	33.2	0.9	-	-	-	-
1972	33.6	1.2	-	-	-	-	34.2	1.8	-	-	-	-	34.9	2.0	-	-	-	-	35.0	0.3	-	-	-	-
1973	35.4	1.1	-	-	-	-	35.6	0.6	-	-	-	-	35.9	0.8	-	-	-	-	36.7	2.2	-	-	-	-
1974	37.3	1.6	-	-	-	-	38.0	1.9	-	-	-	-	40.1	5.5	-	-	-	-	40.9	2.0	-	-	-	-
1975	41.6	1.7	-	-	-	-	42.5	2.2	-	-	-	-	44.2	4.0	-	-	-	-	45.3	2.5	-	-	-	-
1976	45.8	1.1	-	-	-	-	46.4	1.3	-	-	-	-	49.1	5.8	-	-	-	-	49.9	1.6	-	-	-	-
1977	50.7	1.6	-	-	-	-	51.7	2.0	-	-	-	-	54.1	4.6	-	-	-	-	55.1	1.8	-	-	-	-
1978	55.5	0.7	-	-	-	-	56.7	2.2	-	-	57.0	0.5	-	-	59.5	4.4	-	-	59.7	0.3	-	-	60.3	1.0
1979	-	-	61.3	1.7	-	-	62.4	1.8	-	-	63.7	2.1	-	-	65.7	3.1	-	-	66.7	1.5	-	-	66.9	0.3
1980	-	-	67.9	1.5	-	-	69.1	1.8	-	-	70.8	2.5	-	-	73.4	3.7	-	-	73.4	0.0	-	-	74.2	1.1
1981	-	-	75.8	2.2	-	-	77.6	2.4	-	-	78.1	0.6	-	-	81.7	4.6	-	-	83.5	2.2	-	-	84.2	0.8
1982	-	-	85.7	1.8	-	-	86.8	1.3	-	-	87.8	1.2	-	-	92.3	5.1	-	-	93.0	0.8	-	-	94.3	1.4
1983	-	-	97.8	3.7	-	-	97.7	-0.1	-	-	99.4	1.7	-	-	102.1	2.7	-	-	105.6	3.4	-	-	105.6	0.0
1984	-	-	108.5	2.7	-	-	109.0	0.5	-	-	109.4	0.4	-	-	110.1	0.6	-	-	110.8	0.6	-	-	110.9	0.1
1985	-	-	111.4	0.5	-	-	112.1	0.6	-	-	112.3	0.2	-	-	114.0	1.5	-	-	115.0	0.9	-	-	117.0	1.7
1986	-	-	118.6	1.4	-	-	119.2	0.5	-	-	120.9	1.4	-	-	122.0	0.9	-	-	123.9	1.6	-	-	124.5	0.5
1987	-	-	125.5	0.8	-	-	127.8	1.8	-	-	130.7	2.3	-	-	132.4	1.3	-	-	133.2	0.6	-	-	134.1	0.7
1988	-	-	135.5	1.0	-	-	136.0	0.4	-	-	137.8	1.3	-	-	139.2	1.0	-	-	140.8	1.1	-	-	142.2	1.0
1989	-	-	142.3	0.1	-	-	144.0	1.2	-	-	146.3	1.6	-	-	149.2	2.0	-	-	149.9	0.5	-	-	151.3	0.9
1990	-	-	154.4	2.0	-	-	159.1	3.0	-	-	159.6	0.3	-	-	162.4	1.8	-	-	165.1	1.7	-	-	166.7	1.0
1991	-	-	168.9	1.3	-	-	171.2	1.4	-	-	175.3	2.4	-	-	179.6	2.5	-	-	181.3	0.9	-	-	182.1	0.4

[Continued]

Pittsburgh, PA
Consumer Price Index - All Urban Consumers
Base 1982-1984 = 100
Medical Care
[Continued]

For 1947-1993. Columns headed % show percentile change in the index from the previous period for which an index is available.

Year	Jan Index	%	Feb Index	%	Mar Index	%	Apr Index	%	May Index	%	Jun Index	%	Jul Index	%	Aug Index	%	Sep Index	%	Oct Index	%	Nov Index	%	Dec Index	%
1992	-	-	184.6	1.4	-	-	184.5	-0.1	-	-	182.8	-0.9	-	-	186.6	2.1	-	-	189.1	1.3	-	-	190.2	0.6
1993	-	-	194.1	2.1	-	-	194.7	0.3	-	-	197.7	1.5	-	-	198.4	0.4	-	-	199.1	0.4	-	-	199.3	0.1

Source: U.S. Department of Labor, Bureau of Labor Statistics, Division of Consumer Prices and Price Indexes. - indicates no data collected for period.

Pittsburgh, PA
Consumer Price Index - Urban Wage Earners
Base 1982-1984 = 100
Medical Care

For 1947-1993. Columns headed % show percentile change in the index from the previous period for which an index is available.

Year	Jan Index	%	Feb Index	%	Mar Index	%	Apr Index	%	May Index	%	Jun Index	%	Jul Index	%	Aug Index	%	Sep Index	%	Oct Index	%	Nov Index	%	Dec Index	%
1947	11.6	-	11.6	0.0	11.6	0.0	11.7	0.9	11.7	0.0	11.7	0.0	11.8	0.9	11.7	-0.8	11.7	0.0	11.8	0.9	11.9	0.8	11.9	0.0
1948	12.2	2.5	12.3	0.8	12.3	0.0	12.3	0.0	12.5	1.6	12.5	0.0	12.5	0.0	12.4	-0.8	12.4	0.0	12.4	0.0	12.6	1.6	12.7	0.8
1949	12.7	0.0	12.7	0.0	12.7	0.0	12.7	0.0	12.7	0.0	12.7	0.0	12.7	0.0	12.7	0.0	12.7	0.0	12.7	0.0	12.7	0.0	12.8	0.8
1950	12.8	0.0	12.8	0.0	12.9	0.8	12.9	0.0	12.9	0.0	13.0	0.8	13.0	0.0	13.0	0.0	13.1	0.8	13.0	-0.8	13.1	0.8	13.1	0.0
1951	13.2	0.8	13.2	0.0	13.3	0.8	13.4	0.8	13.4	0.0	13.8	3.0	13.8	0.0	13.8	0.0	13.8	0.0	13.8	0.0	13.8	0.0	13.8	0.0
1952	13.9	0.7	13.9	0.0	14.0	0.7	14.0	0.0	14.0	0.0	14.0	0.0	14.0	0.0	14.0	0.0	14.2	1.4	14.2	0.0	14.2	0.0	14.4	1.4
1953	14.4	0.0	-	-	-	-	14.9	3.5	-	-	-	-	14.9	0.0	-	-	-	-	14.8	-0.7	-	-	-	-
1954	14.9	0.7					15.7	5.4					15.7	0.0					15.5	-1.3				
1955	15.5	0.0					15.6	0.6					16.2	3.8					16.2	0.0				
1956	16.2	0.0					16.6	2.5					16.6	0.0					17.6	6.0				
1957	17.7	0.6					17.8	0.6					17.8	0.0					18.0	1.1				
1958	18.1	0.6					18.1	0.0					18.9	4.4					19.0	0.5				
1959	19.2	1.1					19.4	1.0					19.4	0.0					20.7	6.7				
1960	20.7	0.0					20.8	0.5					20.9	0.5					20.9	0.0				
1961	21.1	1.0	-	-	-	-	21.6	2.4	-	-	-	-	21.7	0.5	-	-	-	-	21.7	0.0	-	-	-	-
1962	21.8	0.5					21.8	0.0					22.9	5.0					23.1	0.9				
1963	23.1	0.0					23.1	0.0					23.2	0.4					23.2	0.0				
1964	23.4	0.9					23.8	1.7					24.1	1.3					24.1	0.0				
1965	24.2	0.4					24.4	0.8					24.5	0.4					24.7	0.8				
1966	24.7	0.0					24.9	0.8					25.2	1.2					25.5	1.2				
1967	26.7	4.7					26.9	0.7					27.0	0.4					27.2	0.7				
1968	27.7	1.8					27.9	0.7					28.7	2.9					29.3	2.1				
1969	29.6	1.0					30.1	1.7					30.4	1.0					30.6	0.7				
1970	30.8	0.7					31.5	2.3					32.0	1.6					32.4	1.3				
1971	32.7	0.9	-	-	-	-	33.0	0.9	-	-	-	-	33.1	0.3	-	-	-	-	33.4	0.9	-	-	-	-
1972	33.8	1.2					34.4	1.8					35.1	2.0					35.2	0.3				
1973	35.6	1.1					35.8	0.6					36.2	1.1					36.9	1.9				
1974	37.5	1.6					38.3	2.1					40.4	5.5					41.2	2.0				
1975	41.9	1.7					42.8	2.1					44.5	4.0					45.6	2.5				
1976	46.1	1.1					46.7	1.3					49.4	5.8					50.3	1.8				
1977	51.0	1.4					52.1	2.2					54.5	4.6					55.4	1.7			-	-
1978	55.9	0.9	-	-	-	-	57.1	2.1	-	-	56.8	-0.5	-	-	58.6	3.2	-	-	59.1	0.9	-	-	60.5	2.4
1979	-	-	62.0	2.5	-	-	62.7	1.1	-	-	63.4	1.1	-	-	65.5	3.3	-	-	66.6	1.7	-	-	68.4	2.7
1980	-	-	68.8	0.6	-	-	70.7	2.8	-	-	73.4	3.8	-	-	76.2	3.8	-	-	76.2	0.0	-	-	76.4	0.3
1981	-	-	77.3	1.2	-	-	78.2	1.2	-	-	78.4	0.3	-	-	82.9	5.7	-	-	84.3	1.7	-	-	84.8	0.6
1982	-	-	86.3	1.8	-	-	87.5	1.4	-	-	88.4	1.0	-	-	92.4	4.5	-	-	93.1	0.8	-	-	94.3	1.3
1983	-	-	97.6	3.5	-	-	97.5	-0.1	-	-	99.2	1.7	-	-	101.7	2.5	-	-	105.0	3.2	-	-	105.1	0.1
1984	-	-	108.4	3.1	-	-	108.9	0.5	-	-	109.4	0.5	-	-	110.0	0.5	-	-	110.8	0.7	-	-	110.9	0.1
1985	-	-	111.4	0.5	-	-	112.2	0.7	-	-	112.5	0.3	-	-	114.2	1.5	-	-	115.3	1.0	-	-	117.5	1.9
1986	-	-	119.1	1.4	-	-	119.8	0.6	-	-	121.4	1.3	-	-	122.5	0.9	-	-	124.4	1.6	-	-	125.2	0.6
1987	-	-	126.0	0.6	-	-	128.6	2.1	-	-	131.6	2.3	-	-	133.0	1.1	-	-	133.8	0.6	-	-	135.0	0.9
1988	-	-	136.6	1.2	-	-	137.3	0.5	-	-	139.1	1.3	-	-	140.3	0.9	-	-	141.7	1.0	-	-	143.3	1.1
1989	-	-	143.2	-0.1	-	-	145.0	1.3	-	-	147.2	1.5	-	-	149.7	1.7	-	-	150.1	0.3	-	-	152.0	1.3
1990	-	-	155.4	2.2	-	-	160.0	3.0	-	-	160.5	0.3	-	-	163.0	1.6	-	-	165.8	1.7	-	-	167.2	0.8
1991	-	-	169.4	1.3	-	-	171.9	1.5	-	-	174.9	1.7	-	-	178.4	2.0	-	-	180.2	1.0	-	-	181.0	0.4

[Continued]

Pittsburgh, PA
Consumer Price Index - Urban Wage Earners
Base 1982-1984 = 100
Medical Care
[Continued]

For 1947-1993. Columns headed % show percentile change in the index from the previous period for which an index is available.

Year	Jan Index	%	Feb Index	%	Mar Index	%	Apr Index	%	May Index	%	Jun Index	%	Jul Index	%	Aug Index	%	Sep Index	%	Oct Index	%	Nov Index	%	Dec Index	%
1992	-	-	183.3	1.3	-	-	183.1	-0.1	-	-	181.1	-1.1	-	-	184.2	1.7	-	-	186.9	1.5	-	-	187.8	0.5
1993	-	-	191.9	2.2	-	-	192.0	0.1	-	-	195.0	1.6	-	-	195.7	0.4	-	-	196.1	0.2	-	-	196.1	0.0

Source: U.S. Department of Labor, Bureau of Labor Statistics, Division of Consumer Prices and Price Indexes. - indicates no data collected for period.

Pittsburgh, PA

Consumer Price Index - All Urban Consumers
Base 1982-1984 = 100
Entertainment

For 1976-1993. Columns headed % show percentile change in the index from the previous period for which an index is available.

Year	Jan Index	%	Feb Index	%	Mar Index	%	Apr Index	%	May Index	%	Jun Index	%	Jul Index	%	Aug Index	%	Sep Index	%	Oct Index	%	Nov Index	%	Dec Index	%
1976	64.0	-	-	-	-	-	64.4	0.6	-	-	-	-	64.9	0.8	-	-	-	-	65.7	1.2	-	-	-	-
1977	66.7	1.5	-	-	-	-	67.5	1.2	-	-	-	-	68.6	1.6	-	-	-	-	69.4	1.2	-	-	-	-
1978	70.4	1.4	-	-	-	-	71.1	1.0	-	-	71.4	0.4	-	-	72.3	1.3	-	-	71.3	-1.4	-	-	70.9	-0.6
1979	-	-	71.6	1.0	-	-	72.9	1.8	-	-	72.9	0.0	-	-	74.6	2.3	-	-	74.4	-0.3	-	-	77.7	4.4
1980	-	-	80.0	3.0	-	-	80.4	0.5	-	-	82.0	2.0	-	-	82.7	0.9	-	-	84.9	2.7	-	-	84.5	-0.5
1981	-	-	88.9	5.2	-	-	89.5	0.7	-	-	90.8	1.5	-	-	90.0	-0.9	-	-	92.5	2.8	-	-	91.5	-1.1
1982	-	-	94.5	3.3	-	-	94.5	0.0	-	-	94.5	0.0	-	-	95.1	0.6	-	-	98.5	3.6	-	-	97.8	-0.7
1983	-	-	98.9	1.1	-	-	99.1	0.2	-	-	100.8	1.7	-	-	101.1	0.3	-	-	101.3	0.2	-	-	102.1	0.8
1984	-	-	102.5	0.4	-	-	101.8	-0.7	-	-	102.7	0.9	-	-	105.2	2.4	-	-	106.3	1.0	-	-	107.6	1.2
1985	-	-	105.4	-2.0	-	-	107.3	1.8	-	-	110.5	3.0	-	-	109.6	-0.8	-	-	113.4	3.5	-	-	114.4	0.9
1986	-	-	115.5	1.0	-	-	117.4	1.6	-	-	120.1	2.3	-	-	120.4	0.2	-	-	118.8	-1.3	-	-	122.1	2.8
1987	-	-	119.5	-2.1	-	-	120.1	0.5	-	-	119.9	-0.2	-	-	119.1	-0.7	-	-	125.5	5.4	-	-	124.9	-0.5
1988	-	-	126.6	1.4	-	-	128.0	1.1	-	-	127.8	-0.2	-	-	127.6	-0.2	-	-	125.5	-1.6	-	-	127.9	1.9
1989	-	-	127.5	-0.3	-	-	129.4	1.5	-	-	135.9	5.0	-	-	136.2	0.2	-	-	135.7	-0.4	-	-	135.8	0.1
1990	-	-	136.7	0.7	-	-	138.2	1.1	-	-	139.9	1.2	-	-	139.8	-0.1	-	-	139.1	-0.5	-	-	140.6	1.1
1991	-	-	139.5	-0.8	-	-	143.2	2.7	-	-	143.1	-0.1	-	-	144.6	1.0	-	-	144.0	-0.4	-	-	144.9	0.6
1992	-	-	146.0	0.8	-	-	145.2	-0.5	-	-	144.6	-0.4	-	-	144.9	0.2	-	-	145.6	0.5	-	-	146.9	0.9
1993	-	-	147.4	0.3	-	-	148.4	0.7	-	-	151.0	1.8	-	-	152.0	0.7	-	-	150.7	-0.9	-	-	150.3	-0.3

Source: U.S. Department of Labor, Bureau of Labor Statistics, Division of Consumer Prices and Price Indexes. - indicates no data collected for period.

Pittsburgh, PA
Consumer Price Index - Urban Wage Earners
Base 1982-1984 = 100
Entertainment

For 1976-1993. Columns headed % show percentile change in the index from the previous period for which an index is available.

Year	Jan Index	%	Feb Index	%	Mar Index	%	Apr Index	%	May Index	%	Jun Index	%	Jul Index	%	Aug Index	%	Sep Index	%	Oct Index	%	Nov Index	%	Dec Index	%
1976	66.2	-	-	-	-	-	66.7	0.8	-	-	-	-	67.2	0.7	-	-	-	-	68.0	1.2	-	-	-	-
1977	69.0	1.5	-	-	-	-	69.9	1.3	-	-	-	-	71.0	1.6	-	-	-	-	71.8	1.1	-	-	-	-
1978	72.8	1.4	-	-	-	-	73.6	1.1	-	-	72.7	-1.2	-	-	73.5	1.1	-	-	73.6	0.1	-	-	72.8	-1.1
1979	-	-	75.2	3.3	-	-	77.5	3.1	-	-	77.7	0.3	-	-	77.8	0.1	-	-	76.2	-2.1	-	-	80.7	5.9
1980	-	-	81.7	1.2	-	-	82.8	1.3	-	-	83.6	1.0	-	-	83.2	-0.5	-	-	85.5	2.8	-	-	86.3	0.9
1981	-	-	87.9	1.9	-	-	89.3	1.6	-	-	91.8	2.8	-	-	89.4	-2.6	-	-	91.4	2.2	-	-	91.5	0.1
1982	-	-	94.3	3.1	-	-	94.1	-0.2	-	-	94.3	0.2	-	-	95.1	0.8	-	-	98.3	3.4	-	-	98.0	-0.3
1983	-	-	99.2	1.2	-	-	99.4	0.2	-	-	101.1	1.7	-	-	101.3	0.2	-	-	101.5	0.2	-	-	102.4	0.9
1984	-	-	102.4	0.0	-	-	100.9	-1.5	-	-	102.6	1.7	-	-	105.3	2.6	-	-	106.2	0.9	-	-	107.6	1.3
1985	-	-	105.2	-2.2	-	-	107.4	2.1	-	-	110.8	3.2	-	-	109.9	-0.8	-	-	113.6	3.4	-	-	114.5	0.8
1986	-	-	115.6	1.0	-	-	117.4	1.6	-	-	120.2	2.4	-	-	120.5	0.2	-	-	118.7	-1.5	-	-	121.9	2.7
1987	-	-	119.9	-1.6	-	-	120.6	0.6	-	-	119.8	-0.7	-	-	119.2	-0.5	-	-	125.1	4.9	-	-	124.6	-0.4
1988	-	-	126.3	1.4	-	-	127.3	0.8	-	-	126.8	-0.4	-	-	126.6	-0.2	-	-	125.2	-1.1	-	-	127.4	1.8
1989	-	-	126.8	-0.5	-	-	128.1	1.0	-	-	134.1	4.7	-	-	134.3	0.1	-	-	134.1	-0.1	-	-	134.0	-0.1
1990	-	-	135.3	1.0	-	-	136.4	0.8	-	-	138.2	1.3	-	-	138.1	-0.1	-	-	137.5	-0.4	-	-	138.8	0.9
1991	-	-	137.5	-0.9	-	-	141.0	2.5	-	-	140.9	-0.1	-	-	142.4	1.1	-	-	141.4	-0.7	-	-	142.4	0.7
1992	-	-	143.5	0.8	-	-	142.8	-0.5	-	-	142.2	-0.4	-	-	142.4	0.1	-	-	143.0	0.4	-	-	144.4	1.0
1993	-	-	144.9	0.3	-	-	146.0	0.8	-	-	148.6	1.8	-	-	149.5	0.6	-	-	148.3	-0.8	-	-	148.1	-0.1

Source: U.S. Department of Labor, Bureau of Labor Statistics, Division of Consumer Prices and Price Indexes. - indicates no data collected for period.

Pittsburgh, PA
Consumer Price Index - All Urban Consumers
Base 1982-1984 = 100
Other Goods and Services

For 1976-1993. Columns headed % show percentile change in the index from the previous period for which an index is available.

Year	Jan Index	Jan %	Feb Index	Feb %	Mar Index	Mar %	Apr Index	Apr %	May Index	May %	Jun Index	Jun %	Jul Index	Jul %	Aug Index	Aug %	Sep Index	Sep %	Oct Index	Oct %	Nov Index	Nov %	Dec Index	Dec %
1976	56.7	-	-	-	-	-	57.2	0.9	-	-	-	-	57.8	1.0	-	-	-	-	58.7	1.6	-	-	-	-
1977	59.9	2.0	-	-	-	-	60.7	1.3	-	-	-	-	61.6	1.5	-	-	-	-	63.5	3.1	-	-	-	-
1978	64.0	0.8	-	-	-	-	64.6	0.9	-	-	64.5	-0.2	-	-	65.8	2.0	-	-	67.4	2.4	-	-	67.6	0.3
1979	-	-	68.5	1.3	-	-	68.9	0.6	-	-	69.1	0.3	-	-	70.9	2.6	-	-	72.5	2.3	-	-	72.9	0.6
1980	-	-	73.5	0.8	-	-	73.9	0.5	-	-	74.5	0.8	-	-	75.2	0.9	-	-	77.2	2.7	-	-	78.3	1.4
1981	-	-	78.9	0.8	-	-	79.5	0.8	-	-	81.0	1.9	-	-	83.1	2.6	-	-	87.0	4.7	-	-	87.3	0.3
1982	-	-	88.2	1.0	-	-	88.5	0.3	-	-	88.9	0.5	-	-	90.4	1.7	-	-	94.3	4.3	-	-	96.8	2.7
1983	-	-	98.7	2.0	-	-	98.7	0.0	-	-	98.0	-0.7	-	-	101.9	4.0	-	-	105.2	3.2	-	-	105.3	0.1
1984	-	-	107.3	1.9	-	-	106.7	-0.6	-	-	106.7	0.0	-	-	107.7	0.9	-	-	111.4	3.4	-	-	111.3	-0.1
1985	-	-	111.1	-0.2	-	-	111.3	0.2	-	-	112.1	0.7	-	-	112.9	0.7	-	-	115.7	2.5	-	-	116.2	0.4
1986	-	-	116.4	0.2	-	-	117.1	0.6	-	-	116.7	-0.3	-	-	117.7	0.9	-	-	120.4	2.3	-	-	120.7	0.2
1987	-	-	121.3	0.5	-	-	121.5	0.2	-	-	122.1	0.5	-	-	123.3	1.0	-	-	124.5	1.0	-	-	124.1	-0.3
1988	-	-	132.4	6.7	-	-	132.9	0.4	-	-	126.9	-4.5	-	-	134.0	5.6	-	-	136.4	1.8	-	-	136.6	0.1
1989	-	-	138.7	1.5	-	-	139.4	0.5	-	-	139.7	0.2	-	-	140.8	0.8	-	-	143.1	1.6	-	-	144.9	1.3
1990	-	-	147.1	1.5	-	-	149.7	1.8	-	-	148.4	-0.9	-	-	150.5	1.4	-	-	153.8	2.2	-	-	155.3	1.0
1991	-	-	151.2	-2.6	-	-	152.4	0.8	-	-	152.5	0.1	-	-	154.4	1.2	-	-	159.5	3.3	-	-	161.9	1.5
1992	-	-	165.4	2.2	-	-	166.3	0.5	-	-	167.7	0.8	-	-	170.6	1.7	-	-	169.7	-0.5	-	-	171.5	1.1
1993	-	-	176.5	2.9	-	-	177.4	0.5	-	-	178.7	0.7	-	-	178.0	-0.4	-	-	175.1	-1.6	-	-	179.3	2.4

Source: U.S. Department of Labor, Bureau of Labor Statistics, Division of Consumer Prices and Price Indexes. - indicates no data collected for period.

Pittsburgh, PA
Consumer Price Index - Urban Wage Earners
Base 1982-1984 = 100
Other Goods and Services

For 1976-1993. Columns headed % show percentile change in the index from the previous period for which an index is available.

Year	Jan Index	%	Feb Index	%	Mar Index	%	Apr Index	%	May Index	%	Jun Index	%	Jul Index	%	Aug Index	%	Sep Index	%	Oct Index	%	Nov Index	%	Dec Index	%
1976	56.0	-	-	-	-	-	56.5	0.9	-	-	-	-	57.1	1.1	-	-	-	-	58.0	1.6	-	-	-	-
1977	59.2	2.1	-	-	-	-	59.9	1.2	-	-	-	-	60.8	1.5	-	-	-	-	62.7	3.1	-	-	-	-
1978	63.2	0.8	-	-	-	-	63.8	0.9	-	-	63.7	-0.2	-	-	65.2	2.4	-	-	66.4	1.8	-	-	66.4	0.0
1979	-	-	67.2	1.2	-	-	67.7	0.7	-	-	68.5	1.2	-	-	69.7	1.8	-	-	71.2	2.2	-	-	72.3	1.5
1980	-	-	73.4	1.5	-	-	73.8	0.5	-	-	74.6	1.1	-	-	75.3	0.9	-	-	77.1	2.4	-	-	78.6	1.9
1981	-	-	79.1	0.6	-	-	79.9	1.0	-	-	81.2	1.6	-	-	82.2	1.2	-	-	85.8	4.4	-	-	86.3	0.6
1982	-	-	87.3	1.2	-	-	87.7	0.5	-	-	88.1	0.5	-	-	89.4	1.5	-	-	93.3	4.4	-	-	96.5	3.4
1983	-	-	98.5	2.1	-	-	98.6	0.1	-	-	98.0	-0.6	-	-	102.7	4.8	-	-	105.6	2.8	-	-	105.7	0.1
1984	-	-	108.2	2.4	-	-	107.6	-0.6	-	-	107.6	0.0	-	-	108.6	0.9	-	-	111.7	2.9	-	-	111.5	-0.2
1985	-	-	112.0	0.4	-	-	112.1	0.1	-	-	112.8	0.6	-	-	113.9	1.0	-	-	116.2	2.0	-	-	116.7	0.4
1986	-	-	117.0	0.3	-	-	117.8	0.7	-	-	117.5	-0.3	-	-	118.9	1.2	-	-	120.9	1.7	-	-	121.3	0.3
1987	-	-	121.8	0.4	-	-	121.9	0.1	-	-	122.5	0.5	-	-	123.4	0.7	-	-	125.3	1.5	-	-	125.0	-0.2
1988	-	-	134.1	7.3	-	-	134.4	0.2	-	-	127.9	-4.8	-	-	135.6	6.0	-	-	138.5	2.1	-	-	138.7	0.1
1989	-	-	140.6	1.4	-	-	141.1	0.4	-	-	141.4	0.2	-	-	142.2	0.6	-	-	144.9	1.9	-	-	147.2	1.6
1990	-	-	149.6	1.6	-	-	152.3	1.8	-	-	151.5	-0.5	-	-	153.7	1.5	-	-	157.4	2.4	-	-	159.0	1.0
1991	-	-	154.8	-2.6	-	-	155.7	0.6	-	-	155.9	0.1	-	-	157.8	1.2	-	-	163.3	3.5	-	-	165.9	1.6
1992	-	-	169.3	2.0	-	-	170.2	0.5	-	-	171.9	1.0	-	-	175.7	2.2	-	-	174.5	-0.7	-	-	176.5	1.1
1993	-	-	181.3	2.7	-	-	182.3	0.6	-	-	183.5	0.7	-	-	182.3	-0.7	-	-	179.0	-1.8	-	-	182.6	2.0

Source: U.S. Department of Labor, Bureau of Labor Statistics, Division of Consumer Prices and Price Indexes. - indicates no data collected for period.

Portland, OR-WA
Consumer Price Index - All Urban Consumers
Base 1982-1984 = 100
Annual Averages

For 1914-1993. Columns headed % show percentile change in the index from the previous period for which an index is available.

Year	All Items		Food & Beverage		Housing		Apparel & Upkeep		Trans- portation		Medical Care		Entertain- ment		Other Goods & Services	
	Index	%	Index	%	Index	%	Index	%	Index	%	Index	%	Index	%	Index	%
1914	10.5	-	-	-	-	-	16.5	-	-	-	-	-	-	-	-	-
1915	10.2	-2.9	-	-	-	-	16.8	1.8	-	-	-	-	-	-	-	-
1916	10.5	2.9	-	-	-	-	18.2	8.3	-	-	-	-	-	-	-	-
1917	12.3	17.1	-	-	-	-	21.7	19.2	-	-	-	-	-	-	-	-
1918	15.1	22.8	-	-	-	-	28.6	31.8	-	-	-	-	-	-	-	-
1919	17.7	17.2	-	-	-	-	36.3	26.9	-	-	-	-	-	-	-	-
1920	20.0	13.0	-	-	-	-	40.5	11.6			-	-	-	-	-	-
1921	17.3	-13.5	-	-	-	-	30.8	-24.0	-	-	-	-	-	-	-	-
1922	16.4	-5.2	-	-	-	-	25.7	-16.6	-	-	-	-	-	-	-	-
1923	16.6	1.2	-	-	-	-	26.6	3.5	-	-	-	-	-	-	-	-
1924	16.5	-0.6	-	-	-	-	26.6	0.0	-	-	-	-	-	-	-	-
1925	16.6	0.6	-	-	-	-	26.1	-1.9	-	-	-	-	-	-	-	-
1926	16.4	-1.2	-	-	-	-	25.9	-0.8	-	-	-	-	-	-	-	-
1927	16.2	-1.2	-	-	-	-	25.2	-2.7	-	-	-	-	-	-	-	-
1928	16.0	-1.2	-	-	-	-	24.9	-1.2	-	-	-	-	-	-	-	-
1929	15.8	-1.2	-	-	-	-	24.5	-1.6	-	-	-	-	-	-	-	-
1930	15.5	-1.9	-	-	-	-	23.8	-2.9	-	-	-	-	-	-	-	-
1931	14.0	-9.7	-	-	-	-	21.7	-8.8	-	-	-	-	-	-	-	-
1932	12.7	-9.3	-	-	-	-	19.2	-11.5	-	-	-	-	-	-	-	-
1933	12.1	-4.7	-	-	-	-	18.8	-2.1	-	-	-	-	-	-	-	-
1934	12.5	3.3	-	-	-	-	20.5	9.0	-	-	-	-	-	-	-	-
1935	12.9	3.2	-	-	-	-	20.5	0.0	-	-	-	-	-	-	-	-
1936	13.2	2.3	-	-	-	-	20.6	0.5	-	-	-	-	-	-	-	-
1937	13.9	5.3	-	-	-	-	21.5	4.4	-	-	-	-	-	-	-	-
1938	13.7	-1.4	-	-	-	-	21.4	-0.5	-	-	-	-	-	-	-	-
1939	13.6	-0.7	-	-	-	-	21.3	-0.5	-	-	-	-	-	-	-	-
1940	13.6	0.0	-	-	-	-	21.7	1.9	-	-	-	-	-	-	-	-
1941	14.4	5.9	-	-	-	-	22.5	3.7	-	-	-	-	-	-	-	-
1942	16.5	14.6	-	-	-	-	26.0	15.6	-	-	-	-	-	-	-	-
1943	17.5	6.1	-	-	-	-	27.6	6.2	-	-	-	-	-	-	-	-
1944	17.7	1.1	-	-	-	-	29.4	6.5	-	-	-	-	-	-	-	-
1945	18.2	2.8	-	-	-	-	30.0	2.0	-	-	-	-	-	-	-	-
1946	19.5	7.1	-	-	-	-	32.1	7.0	-	-	-	-	-	-	-	-
1947	22.1	13.3	-	-	-	-	37.9	18.1	19.8	-	14.2	-	-	-	-	-
1948	24.1	9.0	-	-	-	-	41.2	8.7	21.9	10.6	14.7	3.5	-	-	-	-
1949	23.8	-1.2	-	-	-	-	39.8	-3.4	23.6	7.8	15.0	2.0	-	-	-	-
1950	24.3	2.1	-	-	-	-	39.5	-0.8	24.0	1.7	15.4	2.7	-	-	-	-
1951	26.2	7.8	-	-	-	-	42.3	7.1	25.1	4.6	16.3	5.8	-	-	-	-
1952	26.8	2.3	-	-	-	-	41.9	-0.9	26.8	6.8	17.1	4.9	-	-	-	-
1953	26.9	0.4	-	-	-	-	41.6	-0.7	27.6	3.0	17.5	2.3	-	-	-	-
1954	26.9	0.0	-	-	-	-	41.9	0.7	26.8	-2.9	17.9	2.3	-	-	-	-
1955	26.8	-0.4	-	-	-	-	42.2	0.7	26.9	0.4	18.6	3.9	-	-	-	-
1956	27.5	2.6	-	-	-	-	43.2	2.4	26.9	0.0	19.2	3.2	-	-	-	-
1957	28.4	3.3	-	-	-	-	44.1	2.1	28.2	4.8	20.3	5.7	-	-	-	-
1958	29.0	2.1	-	-	-	-	44.2	0.2	29.8	5.7	20.6	1.5	-	-	-	-

[Continued]

724

Portland, OR-WA
Consumer Price Index - All Urban Consumers
Base 1982-1984 = 100
Annual Averages
[Continued]

For 1914-1993. Columns headed % show percentile change in the index from the previous period for which an index is available.

Year	All Items		Food & Beverage		Housing		Apparel & Upkeep		Trans-portation		Medical Care		Entertain-ment		Other Goods & Services	
	Index	%	Index	%	Index	%	Index	%	Index	%	Index	%	Index	%	Index	%
1959	29.3	1.0	-	-	-	-	44.5	0.7	31.1	4.4	20.8	1.0	-	-	-	-
1960	29.8	1.7	-	-	-	-	45.5	2.2	30.8	-1.0	21.8	4.8	-	-	-	-
1961	30.1	1.0	-	-	-	-	45.8	0.7	30.9	0.3	22.4	2.8	-	-	-	-
1962	30.2	0.3	-	-	-	-	45.5	-0.7	31.2	1.0	22.5	0.4	-	-	-	-
1963	30.8	2.0	-	-	-	-	46.3	1.8	31.5	1.0	23.0	2.2	-	-	-	-
1964	31.5	2.3	-	-	-	-	46.8	1.1	32.0	1.6	24.4	6.1	-	-	-	-
1965	32.3	2.5	-	-	-	-	48.2	3.0	32.4	1.3	25.2	3.3	-	-	-	-
1966	33.3	3.1	-	-	-	-	49.8	3.3	32.7	0.9	26.0	3.2	-	-	-	-
1967	34.2	2.7	-	-	-	-	51.0	2.4	34.1	4.3	27.7	6.5	-	-	-	-
1968	35.4	3.5	-	-	-	-	53.2	4.3	34.9	2.3	29.2	5.4	-	-	-	-
1969	37.1	4.8	-	-	-	-	56.2	5.6	36.1	3.4	30.9	5.8	-	-	-	-
1970	38.7	4.3	-	-	-	-	58.8	4.6	37.1	2.8	32.9	6.5	-	-	-	-
1971	39.7	2.6	-	-	-	-	59.5	1.2	37.3	0.5	34.2	4.0	-	-	-	-
1972	40.8	2.8	-	-	-	-	61.1	2.7	37.6	0.8	35.3	3.2	-	-	-	-
1973	43.5	6.6	-	-	-	-	65.0	6.4	38.6	2.7	37.6	6.5	-	-	-	-
1974	48.8	12.2	-	-	-	-	68.9	6.0	42.4	9.8	41.4	10.1	-	-	-	-
1975	53.5	9.6	-	-	-	-	72.9	5.8	46.8	10.4	46.0	11.1	-	-	-	-
1976	57.0	6.5	60.8	-	56.3	-	76.7	5.2	51.3	9.6	50.1	8.9	68.8	-	52.2	-
1977	61.6	8.1	64.6	6.3	61.2	8.7	82.1	7.0	56.2	9.6	55.2	10.2	71.4	3.8	56.3	7.9
1978	67.8	10.1	71.1	10.1	69.1	12.9	84.5	2.9	60.4	7.5	60.2	9.1	75.9	6.3	60.3	7.1
1979	77.0	13.6	79.8	12.2	79.7	15.3	85.7	1.4	70.6	16.9	65.9	9.5	80.7	6.3	65.5	8.6
1980	87.2	13.2	85.5	7.1	92.4	15.9	87.8	2.5	81.7	15.7	74.3	12.7	86.9	7.7	73.6	12.4
1981	95.0	8.9	92.3	8.0	100.0	8.2	92.6	5.5	91.8	12.4	83.3	12.1	90.4	4.0	82.1	11.5
1982	98.0	3.2	97.2	5.3	100.1	0.1	95.5	3.1	97.8	6.5	93.6	12.4	94.8	4.9	92.5	12.7
1983	99.1	1.1	99.7	2.6	98.6	-1.5	99.6	4.3	98.5	0.7	100.6	7.5	101.4	7.0	101.5	9.7
1984	102.8	3.7	103.2	3.5	101.2	2.6	104.9	5.3	103.6	5.2	105.8	5.2	103.8	2.4	106.0	4.4
1985	106.7	3.8	105.6	2.3	104.8	3.6	107.5	2.5	108.3	4.5	111.2	5.1	109.6	5.6	111.6	5.3
1986	108.2	1.4	108.2	2.5	106.2	1.3	100.5	-6.5	107.4	-0.8	119.1	7.1	111.2	1.5	121.0	8.4
1987	110.9	2.5	111.3	2.9	108.1	1.8	102.1	1.6	109.2	1.7	126.8	6.5	116.6	4.9	128.7	6.4
1988	114.7	3.4	112.0	0.6	111.8	3.4	111.9	9.6	110.6	1.3	138.8	9.5	120.9	3.7	136.0	5.7
1989	120.4	5.0	118.7	6.0	116.5	4.2	114.4	2.2	118.3	7.0	145.2	4.6	124.4	2.9	145.1	6.7
1990	127.4	5.8	126.1	6.2	122.6	5.2	120.7	5.5	125.5	6.1	154.4	6.3	128.6	3.4	157.9	8.8
1991	133.9	5.1	130.7	3.6	130.4	6.4	122.3	1.3	130.1	3.7	166.0	7.5	132.6	3.1	172.2	9.1
1992	139.8	4.4	131.7	0.8	138.2	6.0	124.8	2.0	134.0	3.0	176.3	6.2	139.9	5.5	183.6	6.6
1993	-	-	-	-	-	-	-	-	-	-	-	-	-	-	-	-

Source: U.S. Department of Labor, Bureau of Labor Statistics, Division of Consumer Prices and Price Indexes. - indicates no data collected for period.

Portland, OR-WA
Consumer Price Index - Urban Wage Earners
Base 1982-1984 = 100
Annual Averages

For 1914-1993. Columns headed % show percentile change in the index from the previous period for which an index is available.

Year	All Items		Food & Beverage		Housing		Apparel & Upkeep		Trans-portation		Medical Care		Entertain-ment		Other Goods & Services	
	Index	%	Index	%	Index	%	Index	%	Index	%	Index	%	Index	%	Index	%
1914	10.6	-	-	-	-	-	16.6	-	-	-	-	-	-	-	-	-
1915	10.4	-1.9	-	-	-	-	16.9	1.8	-	-	-	-	-	-	-	-
1916	10.7	2.9	-	-	-	-	18.3	8.3	-	-	-	-	-	-	-	-
1917	12.5	16.8	-	-	-	-	21.9	19.7	-	-	-	-	-	-	-	-
1918	15.3	22.4	-	-	-	-	28.8	31.5	-	-	-	-	-	-	-	-
1919	17.9	17.0	-	-	-	-	36.5	26.7	-	-	-	-	-	-	-	-
1920	20.3	13.4	-	-	-	-	40.7	11.5	-	-	-	-	-	-	-	-
1921	17.6	-13.3	-	-	-	-	31.0	-23.8	-	-	-	-	-	-	-	-
1922	16.7	-5.1	-	-	-	-	25.9	-16.5	-	-	-	-	-	-	-	-
1923	16.8	0.6	-	-	-	-	26.8	3.5	-	-	-	-	-	-	-	-
1924	16.8	0.0	-	-	-	-	26.7	-0.4	-	-	-	-	-	-	-	-
1925	16.8	0.0	-	-	-	-	26.3	-1.5	-	-	-	-	-	-	-	-
1926	16.7	-0.6	-	-	-	-	26.0	-1.1	-	-	-	-	-	-	-	-
1927	16.5	-1.2	-	-	-	-	25.4	-2.3	-	-	-	-	-	-	-	-
1928	16.2	-1.8	-	-	-	-	25.0	-1.6	-	-	-	-	-	-	-	-
1929	16.1	-0.6	-	-	-	-	24.7	-1.2	-	-	-	-	-	-	-	-
1930	15.7	-2.5	-	-	-	-	23.9	-3.2	-	-	-	-	-	-	-	-
1931	14.2	-9.6	-	-	-	-	21.9	-8.4	-	-	-	-	-	-	-	-
1932	12.9	-9.2	-	-	-	-	19.3	-11.9	-	-	-	-	-	-	-	-
1933	12.3	-4.7	-	-	-	-	18.9	-2.1	-	-	-	-	-	-	-	-
1934	12.7	3.3	-	-	-	-	20.6	9.0	-	-	-	-	-	-	-	-
1935	13.2	3.9	-	-	-	-	20.6	0.0	-	-	-	-	-	-	-	-
1936	13.4	1.5	-	-	-	-	20.7	0.5	-	-	-	-	-	-	-	-
1937	14.1	5.2	-	-	-	-	21.6	4.3	-	-	-	-	-	-	-	-
1938	13.9	-1.4	-	-	-	-	21.6	0.0	-	-	-	-	-	-	-	-
1939	13.8	-0.7	-	-	-	-	21.4	-0.9	-	-	-	-	-	-	-	-
1940	13.8	0.0	-	-	-	-	21.8	1.9	-	-	-	-	-	-	-	-
1941	14.7	6.5	-	-	-	-	22.6	3.7	-	-	-	-	-	-	-	-
1942	16.7	13.6	-	-	-	-	26.2	15.9	-	-	-	-	-	-	-	-
1943	17.8	6.6	-	-	-	-	27.8	6.1	-	-	-	-	-	-	-	-
1944	18.0	1.1	-	-	-	-	29.6	6.5	-	-	-	-	-	-	-	-
1945	18.5	2.8	-	-	-	-	30.2	2.0	-	-	-	-	-	-	-	-
1946	19.8	7.0	-	-	-	-	32.3	7.0	-	-	-	-	-	-	-	-
1947	22.4	13.1	-	-	-	-	38.2	18.3	19.7	-	15.8	-	-	-	-	-
1948	24.5	9.4	-	-	-	-	41.5	8.6	21.9	11.2	16.4	3.8	-	-	-	-
1949	24.2	-1.2	-	-	-	-	40.1	-3.4	23.6	7.8	16.7	1.8	-	-	-	-
1950	24.6	1.7	-	-	-	-	39.8	-0.7	24.0	1.7	17.2	3.0	-	-	-	-
1951	26.6	8.1	-	-	-	-	42.6	7.0	25.1	4.6	18.2	5.8	-	-	-	-
1952	27.2	2.3	-	-	-	-	42.2	-0.9	26.8	6.8	19.0	4.4	-	-	-	-
1953	27.3	0.4	-	-	-	-	41.8	-0.9	27.6	3.0	19.5	2.6	-	-	-	-
1954	27.3	0.0	-	-	-	-	42.1	0.7	26.8	-2.9	19.9	2.1	-	-	-	-
1955	27.3	0.0	-	-	-	-	42.5	1.0	26.9	0.4	20.7	4.0	-	-	-	-
1956	27.9	2.2	-	-	-	-	43.5	2.4	26.9	0.0	21.4	3.4	-	-	-	-
1957	28.8	3.2	-	-	-	-	44.3	1.8	28.2	4.8	22.6	5.6	-	-	-	-
1958	29.5	2.4	-	-	-	-	44.4	0.2	29.8	5.7	22.9	1.3	-	-	-	-

[Continued]

726

Portland, OR-WA
Consumer Price Index - Urban Wage Earners
Base 1982-1984 = 100
Annual Averages
[Continued]

For 1914-1993. Columns headed % show percentile change in the index from the previous period for which an index is available.

Year	All Items		Food & Beverage		Housing		Apparel & Upkeep		Trans-portation		Medical Care		Entertain-ment		Other Goods & Services	
	Index	%	Index	%	Index	%	Index	%	Index	%	Index	%	Index	%	Index	%
1959	29.8	1.0	-	-	-	-	44.7	0.7	31.0	4.0	23.2	1.3	-	-	-	-
1960	30.2	1.3	-	-	-	-	45.8	2.5	30.8	-0.6	24.3	4.7	-	-	-	-
1961	30.6	1.3	-	-	-	-	46.1	0.7	30.9	0.3	25.0	2.9	-	-	-	-
1962	30.7	0.3	-	-	-	-	45.8	-0.7	31.1	0.6	25.1	0.4	-	-	-	-
1963	31.3	2.0	-	-	-	-	46.6	1.7	31.5	1.3	25.7	2.4	-	-	-	-
1964	32.0	2.2	-	-	-	-	47.1	1.1	31.9	1.3	27.2	5.8	-	-	-	-
1965	32.8	2.5	-	-	-	-	48.5	3.0	32.4	1.6	28.1	3.3	-	-	-	-
1966	33.8	3.0	-	-	-	-	50.1	3.3	32.7	0.9	29.0	3.2	-	-	-	-
1967	34.7	2.7	-	-	-	-	51.3	2.4	34.1	4.3	30.9	6.6	-	-	-	-
1968	35.9	3.5	-	-	-	-	53.6	4.5	34.9	2.3	32.5	5.2	-	-	-	-
1969	37.7	5.0	-	-	-	-	56.6	5.6	36.0	3.2	34.4	5.8	-	-	-	-
1970	39.3	4.2	-	-	-	-	59.2	4.6	37.0	2.8	36.6	6.4	-	-	-	-
1971	40.3	2.5	-	-	-	-	59.9	1.2	37.3	0.8	38.1	4.1	-	-	-	-
1972	41.5	3.0	-	-	-	-	61.5	2.7	37.6	0.8	39.4	3.4	-	-	-	-
1973	44.2	6.5	-	-	-	-	65.4	6.3	38.5	2.4	41.9	6.3	-	-	-	-
1974	49.5	12.0	-	-	-	-	69.4	6.1	42.3	9.9	46.1	10.0	-	-	-	-
1975	54.3	9.7	-	-	-	-	73.4	5.8	46.8	10.6	51.2	11.1	-	-	-	-
1976	57.9	6.6	60.6	-	57.1	-	77.2	5.2	51.2	9.4	55.8	9.0	75.7	-	55.7	-
1977	62.5	7.9	64.4	6.3	62.1	8.8	82.6	7.0	56.2	9.8	61.5	10.2	78.5	3.7	60.0	7.7
1978	69.0	10.4	71.8	11.5	70.1	12.9	85.3	3.3	61.3	9.1	66.1	7.5	82.5	5.1	63.4	5.7
1979	78.3	13.5	81.0	12.8	81.1	15.7	86.9	1.9	70.7	15.3	71.8	8.6	86.9	5.3	67.6	6.6
1980	88.2	12.6	86.3	6.5	94.2	16.2	88.8	2.2	80.6	14.0	77.6	8.1	94.6	8.9	74.0	9.5
1981	95.8	8.6	92.5	7.2	102.2	8.5	93.2	5.0	91.3	13.3	83.8	8.0	91.8	-3.0	81.3	9.9
1982	98.8	3.1	97.1	5.0	101.9	-0.3	95.3	2.3	97.0	6.2	93.8	11.9	95.1	3.6	92.2	13.4
1983	99.2	0.4	99.7	2.7	98.7	-3.1	98.9	3.8	98.5	1.5	100.8	7.5	101.2	6.4	102.1	10.7
1984	102.1	2.9	103.2	3.5	99.4	0.7	105.8	7.0	104.4	6.0	105.4	4.6	103.7	2.5	105.8	3.6
1985	105.1	2.9	105.6	2.3	101.3	1.9	108.8	2.8	109.0	4.4	111.1	5.4	109.2	5.3	111.2	5.1
1986	106.0	0.9	108.0	2.3	102.6	1.3	100.4	-7.7	107.5	-1.4	118.7	6.8	110.3	1.0	120.2	8.1
1987	108.5	2.4	111.1	2.9	104.4	1.8	101.8	1.4	109.3	1.7	126.4	6.5	115.5	4.7	127.7	6.2
1988	112.0	3.2	111.9	0.7	107.8	3.3	112.0	10.0	110.7	1.3	138.3	9.4	119.6	3.5	135.7	6.3
1989	117.6	5.0	118.6	6.0	112.3	4.2	114.4	2.1	117.9	6.5	144.7	4.6	123.0	2.8	145.6	7.3
1990	124.2	5.6	125.9	6.2	118.1	5.2	120.9	5.7	124.2	5.3	153.2	5.9	127.0	3.3	158.4	8.8
1991	130.8	5.3	130.5	3.7	125.9	6.6	123.6	2.2	129.1	3.9	164.3	7.2	131.1	3.2	171.9	8.5
1992	136.6	4.4	131.7	0.9	133.7	6.2	125.1	1.2	133.1	3.1	174.9	6.5	139.2	6.2	183.0	6.5
1993	-	-	-	-	-	-	-	-	-	-	-	-	-	-	-	-

Source: U.S. Department of Labor, Bureau of Labor Statistics, Division of Consumer Prices and Price Indexes. - indicates no data collected for period.

Portland, OR-WA
Consumer Price Index - All Urban Consumers
Base 1982-1984 = 100
All Items

For 1914-1993. Columns headed % show percentile change in the index from the previous period for which an index is available.

Year	Jan Index	%	Feb Index	%	Mar Index	%	Apr Index	%	May Index	%	Jun Index	%	Jul Index	%	Aug Index	%	Sep Index	%	Oct Index	%	Nov Index	%	Dec Index	%
1914	-		-		-		-		-		-		-		-		-		-		-		10.5	-
1915	-		-		-		-		-		-		-		-		-		-		-		10.1	-3.8
1916	-		-		-		-		-		-		-		-		-		-		-		10.9	7.9
1917	-		-		-		-		-		-		-		-		-		-		-		13.2	21.1
1918	-		-		-		-		-		-		-		-		-		-		-		16.6	25.8
1919	-		-		-		-		-		17.3	4.2	-		-		-		-		-		19.0	9.8
1920	-		-		-		-		-		21.1	11.1	-		-		-		-		-		18.8	-10.9
1921	-		-		17.1	-9.0	-		-		-		-		-		17.0	-0.6	-		-		16.8	-1.2
1922	-		-		16.3	-3.0	-		-		16.2	-0.6	-		-		16.4	1.2	-		-		16.5	0.6
1923	-		-		16.4	-0.6	-		-		16.5	0.6	-		-		16.6	0.6	-		-		16.7	0.6
1924	-		-		16.6	-0.6	-		-		16.4	-1.2	-		-		16.5	0.6	-		-		16.5	0.0
1925	-		-		-		-		-		16.6	0.6	-		-		-		-		-		16.7	0.6
1926	-		-		-		-		-		16.5	-1.2	-		-		-		-		-		16.4	-0.6
1927	-		-		-		-		-		16.4	0.0	-		-		-		-		-		16.1	-1.8
1928	-		-		-		-		-		15.8	-1.9	-		-		-		-		-		15.9	0.6
1929	-		-		-		-		-		15.7	-1.3	-		-		-		-		-		15.8	0.6
1930	-		-		-		-		-		15.7	-0.6	-		-		-		-		-		14.8	-5.7
1931	-		-		-		-		-		14.1	-4.7	-		-		-		-		-		13.6	-3.5
1932	-		-		-		-		-		12.7	-6.6	-		-		-		-		-		12.4	-2.4
1933	-		-		-		-		-		11.9	-4.0	-		-		-		-		-		12.2	2.5
1934	-		-		-		-		-		12.4	1.6	-		-		-		-		12.7	2.4	-	
1935	-		-		13.0	2.4	-		-		-		12.8	-1.5	-		-		12.9	0.8	-		-	
1936	13.0	0.8	-		-		12.9	-0.8	-		-		13.2	2.3	-		13.4	1.5	-		-		13.4	0.0
1937	-		-		13.7	2.2	-		-		13.9	1.5	-		-		14.1	1.4	-		-		13.9	-1.4
1938	-		-		13.8	-0.7	-		-		13.7	-0.7	-		-		13.7	0.0	-		-		13.7	0.0
1939	-		-		13.6	-0.7	-		-		13.5	-0.7	-		-		13.7	1.5	-		-		13.6	-0.7
1940	-		-		13.4	-1.5	-		-		13.6	1.5	-		-		13.7	0.7	-		-		13.7	0.0
1941	-		-		13.8	0.7	-		-		14.3	3.6	-		-		14.9	4.2	-		-		15.3	2.7
1942	-		-		16.1	5.2	-		-		16.5	2.5	-		-		16.8	1.8	-		-		17.1	1.8
1943	-		-		17.4	1.8	-		-		17.7	1.7	-		-		17.5	-1.1	-		-		17.5	0.0
1944	-		-		17.5	0.0	-		-		17.5	0.0	-		-		17.8	1.7	-		-		18.0	1.1
1945	-		-		18.0	0.0	-		-		18.3	1.7	-		-		18.3	0.0	-		-		18.5	1.1
1946	-		-		18.4	-0.5	-		-		19.0	3.3	-		-		20.4	7.4	-		-		21.3	4.4
1947	-		-		21.7	1.9	-		-		21.8	0.5	21.9	0.5	-		-		22.5	2.7	-		-	
1948	23.6	4.9	-		-		23.8	0.8	-		-		24.4	2.5	-		-		24.4	0.0	-		-	
1949	24.1	-1.2	-		-		24.0	-0.4	-		-		23.7	-1.2	-		-		23.5	-0.8	-		-	
1950	23.6	0.4	-		-		23.7	0.4	-		-		24.1	1.7	-		-		24.8	2.9	-		-	
1951	25.6	3.2	-		-		26.2	2.3	-		-		26.4	0.8	-		-		26.4	0.0	-		-	
1952	26.8	1.5	-		-		26.7	-0.4	-		-		26.7	0.0	-		-		26.8	0.4	-		26.7	-0.4
1953	26.7	0.0	-		-		26.9	0.7	-		-		26.9	0.0	-		-		27.1	0.7	-		-	
1954	26.9	-0.7	-		-		26.8	-0.4	-		-		26.9	0.4	-		-		26.9	0.0	-		-	
1955	26.7	-0.7	-		-		26.6	-0.4	-		-		26.7	0.4	-		-		27.1	1.5	-		-	
1956	27.1	0.0	-		-		27.1	0.0	-		-		27.7	2.2	-		-		27.9	0.7	-		-	
1957	28.0	0.4	-		-		28.4	1.4	-		-		28.5	0.4	-		-		28.4	-0.4	-		-	
1958	28.8	1.4	-		-		29.2	1.4	-		-		29.1	-0.3	-		-		29.0	-0.3	-		-	

[Continued]

Portland, OR-WA
Consumer Price Index - All Urban Consumers
Base 1982-1984 = 100
All Items
[Continued]

For 1914-1993. Columns headed % show percentile change in the index from the previous period for which an index is available.

Year	Jan Index	Jan %	Feb Index	Feb %	Mar Index	Mar %	Apr Index	Apr %	May Index	May %	Jun Index	Jun %	Jul Index	Jul %	Aug Index	Aug %	Sep Index	Sep %	Oct Index	Oct %	Nov Index	Nov %	Dec Index	Dec %
1959	29.0	0.0	-		-		29.2	0.7	-		-		29.4	0.7	-		-		29.4	0.0	-		-	
1960	29.7	1.0	-		-		29.8	0.3	-		-		29.8	0.0	-		-		29.7	-0.3	-		-	
1961	30.1	1.3	-		-		29.9	-0.7	-		-		30.2	1.0	-		-		30.2	0.0	-		-	
1962	30.0	-0.7	-		-		30.0	0.0	-		-		30.3	1.0	-		-		30.4	0.3	-		-	
1963	30.5	0.3	-		-		30.7	0.7	-		-		30.9	0.7	-		-		30.9	0.0	-		-	
1964	31.1	0.6	-		-		31.4	1.0	-		-		31.6	0.6	-		-		31.7	0.3	-		-	
1965	31.8	0.3	-		-		32.1	0.9	-		-		32.5	1.2	-		-		32.6	0.3	-		-	
1966	32.6	0.0	-		-		33.1	1.5	-		-		33.4	0.9	-		-		33.7	0.9	-		-	
1967	33.9	0.6	-		-		33.9	0.0	-		-		34.2	0.9	-		-		34.5	0.9	-		-	
1968	34.6	0.3	-		-		35.0	1.2	-		-		35.4	1.1	-		-		35.8	1.1	-		-	
1969	36.2	1.1	-		-		37.0	2.2	-		-		37.1	0.3	-		-		37.6	1.3	-		-	
1970	37.8	0.5	-		-		38.6	2.1	-		-		38.8	0.5	-		-		39.1	0.8	-		-	
1971	39.2	0.3	-		-		39.2	0.0	-		-		39.7	1.3	-		-		40.1	1.0	-		-	
1972	40.3	0.5	-		-		40.4	0.2	-		-		40.9	1.2	-		-		41.2	0.7	-		-	
1973	41.6	1.0	-		-		42.8	2.9	-		-		43.4	1.4	-		-		44.7	3.0	-		-	
1974	45.7	2.2	-		-		47.5	3.9	-		-		49.1	3.4	-		-		50.6	3.1	-		-	
1975	52.1	3.0	-		-		52.7	1.2	-		-		53.7	1.9	-		-		54.4	1.3	-		-	
1976	55.4	1.8	-		-		56.2	1.4	-		-		57.4	2.1	-		-		58.0	1.0	-		-	
1977	58.9	1.6	-		-		60.7	3.1	-		-		62.0	2.1	-		-		62.8	1.3	-		-	
1978	64.2	2.2	-		65.5	2.0	-		66.7	1.8	-		68.0	1.9	-		69.4	2.1	-		70.7	1.9	-	
1979	72.3	2.3	-		73.6	1.8	-		75.4	2.4	-		77.7	3.1	-		79.3	2.1	-		80.8	1.9	-	
1980	83.6	3.5	-		86.6	3.6	-		87.9	1.5	-		86.3	-1.8	-		87.8	1.7	-		89.5	1.9	-	
1981	91.0	1.7	-		91.6	0.7	-		95.1	3.8	-		95.9	0.8	-		99.4	3.6	-		95.2	-4.2	-	
1982	98.5	3.5	-		97.9	-0.6	-		96.4	-1.5	-		99.9	3.6	-		98.4	-1.5	-		97.6	-0.8	-	
1983	97.9	0.3	-		97.2	-0.7	-		98.5	1.3	-		99.6	1.1	-		100.2	0.6	-		100.4	0.2	-	
1984	100.8	0.4	-		101.8	1.0	-		103.1	1.3	-		102.8	-0.3	-		103.3	0.5	-		104.1	0.8	-	
1985	104.8	0.7	-		105.5	0.7	-		106.0	0.5	-		106.9	0.8	-		107.6	0.7	-		108.3	0.7	-	
1986	109.7	1.3	-		107.6	-1.9	-		107.5	-0.1	-		107.5	0.0	-		108.6	1.0	-		108.6	0.0	-	
1987	-		-		-		-		-		109.9	1.2	-		-		-		-		111.9	1.8	-	
1988	-		-		-		-		-		113.6	1.5	-		-		-		-		115.9	2.0	-	
1989	-		-		-		-		-		119.3	2.9	-		-		-		-		121.6	1.9	-	
1990	-		-		-		-		-		124.9	2.7	-		-		-		-		129.8	3.9	-	
1991	-		-		-		-		-		132.8	2.3	-		-		-		-		135.1	1.7	-	
1992	-		-		-		-		-		138.8	2.7	-		-		-		-		140.9	1.5	-	
1993	-		-		-		-		-		143.6	1.9	-		-		-		-		-		-	

Source: U.S. Department of Labor, Bureau of Labor Statistics, Division of Consumer Prices and Price Indexes. - indicates no data collected for period.

Portland, OR-WA

Consumer Price Index - Urban Wage Earners
Base 1982-1984 = 100
All Items

For 1914-1993. Columns headed % show percentile change in the index from the previous period for which an index is available.

Year	Jan Index	Jan %	Feb Index	Feb %	Mar Index	Mar %	Apr Index	Apr %	May Index	May %	Jun Index	Jun %	Jul Index	Jul %	Aug Index	Aug %	Sep Index	Sep %	Oct Index	Oct %	Nov Index	Nov %	Dec Index	Dec %
1914	-	-	-	-	-	-	-	-	-	-	-	-	-	-	-	-	-	-	-	-	-	-	10.6	-
1915	-	-	-	-	-	-	-	-	-	-	-	-	-	-	-	-	-	-	-	-	-	-	10.2	-3.8
1916	-	-	-	-	-	-	-	-	-	-	-	-	-	-	-	-	-	-	-	-	-	-	11.0	7.8
1917	-	-	-	-	-	-	-	-	-	-	-	-	-	-	-	-	-	-	-	-	-	-	13.4	21.8
1918	-	-	-	-	-	-	-	-	-	-	-	-	-	-	-	-	-	-	-	-	-	-	16.9	26.1
1919	-	-	-	-	-	-	-	-	-	-	17.6	4.1	-	-	-	-	-	-	-	-	-	-	19.3	9.7
1920	-	-	-	-	-	-	-	-	-	-	21.4	10.9	-	-	-	-	-	-	-	-	-	-	19.1	-10.7
1921	-	-	-	-	17.4	-8.9	-	-	-	-	-	-	-	-	-	-	17.3	-0.6	-	-	-	-	17.1	-1.2
1922	-	-	-	-	16.5	-3.5	-	-	-	-	16.5	0.0	-	-	-	-	16.7	1.2	-	-	-	-	16.8	0.6
1923	-	-	-	-	16.7	-0.6	-	-	-	-	16.7	0.0	-	-	-	-	16.9	1.2	-	-	-	-	17.0	0.6
1924	-	-	-	-	16.8	-1.2	-	-	-	-	16.6	-1.2	-	-	-	-	16.7	0.6	-	-	-	-	16.8	0.6
1925	-	-	-	-	-	-	-	-	-	-	16.9	0.6	-	-	-	-	-	-	-	-	-	-	16.9	0.0
1926	-	-	-	-	-	-	-	-	-	-	16.7	-1.2	-	-	-	-	-	-	-	-	-	-	16.7	0.0
1927	-	-	-	-	-	-	-	-	-	-	16.7	0.0	-	-	-	-	-	-	-	-	-	-	16.4	-1.8
1928	-	-	-	-	-	-	-	-	-	-	16.1	-1.8	-	-	-	-	-	-	-	-	-	-	16.2	0.6
1929	-	-	-	-	-	-	-	-	-	-	16.0	-1.2	-	-	-	-	-	-	-	-	-	-	16.1	0.6
1930	-	-	-	-	-	-	-	-	-	-	16.0	-0.6	-	-	-	-	-	-	-	-	-	-	15.0	-6.3
1931	-	-	-	-	-	-	-	-	-	-	14.3	-4.7	-	-	-	-	-	-	-	-	-	-	13.8	-3.5
1932	-	-	-	-	-	-	-	-	-	-	12.9	-6.5	-	-	-	-	-	-	-	-	-	-	12.6	-2.3
1933	-	-	-	-	-	-	-	-	-	-	12.1	-4.0	-	-	-	-	-	-	-	-	-	-	12.4	2.5
1934	-	-	-	-	-	-	-	-	-	-	12.6	1.6	-	-	-	-	-	-	-	-	12.9	2.4	-	-
1935	-	-	-	-	13.2	2.3	-	-	-	-	-	-	13.0	-1.5	-	-	-	-	13.1	0.8	-	-	-	-
1936	13.3	1.5	-	-	-	-	13.2	-0.8	-	-	-	-	13.4	1.5	-	-	13.6	1.5	-	-	-	-	13.6	0.0
1937	-	-	-	-	13.9	2.2	-	-	-	-	14.1	1.4	-	-	-	-	14.3	1.4	-	-	-	-	14.1	-1.4
1938	-	-	-	-	14.1	0.0	-	-	-	-	13.9	-1.4	-	-	-	-	13.9	0.0	-	-	-	-	13.9	0.0
1939	-	-	-	-	13.8	-0.7	-	-	-	-	13.7	-0.7	-	-	-	-	13.9	1.5	-	-	-	-	13.8	-0.7
1940	-	-	-	-	13.6	-1.4	-	-	-	-	13.8	1.5	-	-	-	-	13.9	0.7	-	-	-	-	13.9	0.0
1941	-	-	-	-	14.1	1.4	-	-	-	-	14.5	2.8	-	-	-	-	15.2	4.8	-	-	-	-	15.5	2.0
1942	-	-	-	-	16.3	5.2	-	-	-	-	16.7	2.5	-	-	-	-	17.1	2.4	-	-	-	-	17.4	1.8
1943	-	-	-	-	17.6	1.1	-	-	-	-	17.9	1.7	-	-	-	-	17.7	-1.1	-	-	-	-	17.8	0.6
1944	-	-	-	-	17.8	0.0	-	-	-	-	17.8	0.0	-	-	-	-	18.1	1.7	-	-	-	-	18.3	1.1
1945	-	-	-	-	18.3	0.0	-	-	-	-	18.6	1.6	-	-	-	-	18.6	0.0	-	-	-	-	18.8	1.1
1946	-	-	-	-	18.7	-0.5	-	-	-	-	19.3	3.2	-	-	-	-	20.7	7.3	-	-	-	-	21.7	4.8
1947	-	-	-	-	22.0	1.4	-	-	-	-	22.2	0.9	22.2	0.0	-	-	-	-	22.9	3.2	-	-	-	-
1948	24.0	4.8	-	-	-	-	24.1	0.4	-	-	-	-	24.8	2.9	-	-	-	-	24.7	-0.4	-	-	-	-
1949	24.5	-0.8	-	-	-	-	24.4	-0.4	-	-	-	-	24.1	-1.2	-	-	-	-	23.9	-0.8	-	-	-	-
1950	23.9	0.0	-	-	-	-	24.0	0.4	-	-	-	-	24.5	2.1	-	-	-	-	25.2	2.9	-	-	-	-
1951	26.0	3.2	-	-	-	-	26.6	2.3	-	-	-	-	26.8	0.8	-	-	-	-	26.8	0.0	-	-	-	-
1952	27.2	1.5	-	-	-	-	27.2	0.0	-	-	-	-	27.2	0.0	-	-	-	-	27.2	0.0	-	-	27.2	0.0
1953	27.2	0.0	-	-	-	-	27.3	0.4	-	-	-	-	27.3	0.0	-	-	-	-	27.5	0.7	-	-	-	-
1954	27.3	-0.7	-	-	-	-	27.2	-0.4	-	-	-	-	27.3	0.4	-	-	-	-	27.3	0.0	-	-	-	-
1955	27.2	-0.4	-	-	-	-	27.1	-0.4	-	-	-	-	27.2	0.4	-	-	-	-	27.6	1.5	-	-	-	-
1956	27.6	0.0	-	-	-	-	27.6	0.0	-	-	-	-	28.1	1.8	-	-	-	-	28.3	0.7	-	-	-	-
1957	28.5	0.7	-	-	-	-	28.8	1.1	-	-	-	-	28.9	0.3	-	-	-	-	28.9	0.0	-	-	-	-
1958	29.2	1.0	-	-	-	-	29.6	1.4	-	-	-	-	29.5	-0.3	-	-	-	-	29.5	0.0	-	-	-	-

[Continued]

Portland, OR-WA
Consumer Price Index - Urban Wage Earners
Base 1982-1984 = 100
All Items
[Continued]

For 1914-1993. Columns headed % show percentile change in the index from the previous period for which an index is available.

Year	Jan Index	%	Feb Index	%	Mar Index	%	Apr Index	%	May Index	%	Jun Index	%	Jul Index	%	Aug Index	%	Sep Index	%	Oct Index	%	Nov Index	%	Dec Index	%
1959	29.4	-0.3	-	-	-	-	29.7	1.0	-	-	-	-	29.9	0.7	-	-	-	-	29.9	0.0	-	-	-	-
1960	30.2	1.0	-	-	-	-	30.2	0.0	-	-	-	-	30.2	0.0	-	-	-	-	30.2	0.0	-	-	-	-
1961	30.5	1.0	-	-	-	-	30.4	-0.3	-	-	-	-	30.6	0.7	-	-	-	-	30.7	0.3	-	-	-	-
1962	30.5	-0.7	-	-	-	-	30.5	0.0	-	-	-	-	30.8	1.0	-	-	-	-	30.9	0.3	-	-	-	-
1963	31.0	0.3	-	-	-	-	31.2	0.6	-	-	-	-	31.4	0.6	-	-	-	-	31.4	0.0	-	-	-	-
1964	31.6	0.6	-	-	-	-	31.9	0.9	-	-	-	-	32.1	0.6	-	-	-	-	32.2	0.3	-	-	-	-
1965	32.3	0.3	-	-	-	-	32.6	0.9	-	-	-	-	33.0	1.2	-	-	-	-	33.1	0.3	-	-	-	-
1966	33.1	0.0	-	-	-	-	33.7	1.8	-	-	-	-	33.9	0.6	-	-	-	-	34.2	0.9	-	-	-	-
1967	34.4	0.6	-	-	-	-	34.5	0.3	-	-	-	-	34.7	0.6	-	-	-	-	35.0	0.9	-	-	-	-
1968	35.2	0.6	-	-	-	-	35.6	1.1	-	-	-	-	35.9	0.8	-	-	-	-	36.4	1.4	-	-	-	-
1969	36.8	1.1	-	-	-	-	37.5	1.9	-	-	-	-	37.7	0.5	-	-	-	-	38.2	1.3	-	-	-	-
1970	38.4	0.5	-	-	-	-	39.2	2.1	-	-	-	-	39.4	0.5	-	-	-	-	39.7	0.8	-	-	-	-
1971	39.9	0.5	-	-	-	-	39.8	-0.3	-	-	-	-	40.3	1.3	-	-	-	-	40.7	1.0	-	-	-	-
1972	41.0	0.7	-	-	-	-	41.1	0.2	-	-	-	-	41.5	1.0	-	-	-	-	41.8	0.7	-	-	-	-
1973	42.3	1.2	-	-	-	-	43.5	2.8	-	-	-	-	44.1	1.4	-	-	-	-	45.4	2.9	-	-	-	-
1974	46.5	2.4	-	-	-	-	48.3	3.9	-	-	-	-	49.9	3.3	-	-	-	-	51.4	3.0	-	-	-	-
1975	52.9	2.9	-	-	-	-	53.5	1.1	-	-	-	-	54.5	1.9	-	-	-	-	55.2	1.3	-	-	-	-
1976	56.2	1.8	-	-	-	-	57.0	1.4	-	-	-	-	58.3	2.3	-	-	-	-	58.9	1.0	-	-	-	-
1977	59.8	1.5	-	-	-	-	61.7	3.2	-	-	-	-	63.0	2.1	-	-	-	-	63.8	1.3	-	-	-	-
1978	65.2	2.2	-	-	66.6	2.1	-	-	68.0	2.1	-	-	69.4	2.1	-	-	70.9	2.2	-	-	72.1	1.7	-	-
1979	73.6	2.1	-	-	74.9	1.8	-	-	77.0	2.8	-	-	79.1	2.7	-	-	80.7	2.0	-	-	82.1	1.7	-	-
1980	84.5	2.9	-	-	87.3	3.3	-	-	88.8	1.7	-	-	87.5	-1.5	-	-	88.6	1.3	-	-	90.5	2.1	-	-
1981	91.9	1.5	-	-	92.6	0.8	-	-	95.8	3.5	-	-	96.9	1.1	-	-	100.2	3.4	-	-	95.9	-4.3	-	-
1982	99.1	3.3	-	-	98.5	-0.6	-	-	97.0	-1.5	-	-	100.8	3.9	-	-	99.2	-1.6	-	-	98.4	-0.8	-	-
1983	97.7	-0.7	-	-	98.2	0.5	-	-	98.5	0.3	-	-	99.4	0.9	-	-	100.0	0.6	-	-	100.5	0.5	-	-
1984	100.5	0.0	-	-	101.4	0.9	-	-	103.2	1.8	-	-	102.2	-1.0	-	-	101.9	-0.3	-	-	102.6	0.7	-	-
1985	103.2	0.6	-	-	104.0	0.8	-	-	104.5	0.5	-	-	105.2	0.7	-	-	106.0	0.8	-	-	106.6	0.6	-	-
1986	107.9	1.2	-	-	105.6	-2.1	-	-	105.2	-0.4	-	-	105.3	0.1	-	-	106.3	0.9	-	-	106.2	-0.1	-	-
1987	-	-	-	-	-	-	-	-	-	-	107.5	1.2	-	-	-	-	-	-	-	-	-	-	109.5	1.9
1988	-	-	-	-	-	-	-	-	-	-	110.9	1.3	-	-	-	-	-	-	-	-	-	-	113.0	1.9
1989	-	-	-	-	-	-	-	-	-	-	116.4	3.0	-	-	-	-	-	-	-	-	-	-	118.7	2.0
1990	-	-	-	-	-	-	-	-	-	-	121.8	2.6	-	-	-	-	-	-	-	-	-	-	126.6	3.9
1991	-	-	-	-	-	-	-	-	-	-	129.6	2.4	-	-	-	-	-	-	-	-	-	-	132.1	1.9
1992	-	-	-	-	-	-	-	-	-	-	135.5	2.6	-	-	-	-	-	-	-	-	-	-	137.7	1.6
1993	-	-	-	-	-	-	-	-	-	-	140.3	1.9	-	-	-	-	-	-	-	-	-	-	-	-

Source: U.S. Department of Labor, Bureau of Labor Statistics, Division of Consumer Prices and Price Indexes. - indicates no data collected for period.

Portland, OR-WA
Consumer Price Index - All Urban Consumers
Base 1982-1984 = 100
Food and Beverages

For 1976-1993. Columns headed % show percentile change in the index from the previous period for which an index is available.

Year	Jan Index	%	Feb Index	%	Mar Index	%	Apr Index	%	May Index	%	Jun Index	%	Jul Index	%	Aug Index	%	Sep Index	%	Oct Index	%	Nov Index	%	Dec Index	%
1976	60.1	-	-	-	-	-	60.2	0.2	-	-	-	-	61.3	1.8	-	-	-	-	61.0	-0.5	-	-	-	-
1977	61.6	1.0	-	-	-	-	64.1	4.1	-	-	-	-	65.4	2.0	-	-	-	-	65.4	0.0	-	-	-	-
1978	66.7	2.0	-	-	68.3	2.4	-	-	70.6	3.4	-	-	72.5	2.7	-	-	73.0	0.7	-	-	73.3	0.4	-	-
1979	76.1	3.8	-	-	78.2	2.8	-	-	79.6	1.8	-	-	80.4	1.0	-	-	80.7	0.4	-	-	81.8	1.4	-	-
1980	82.7	1.1	-	-	84.0	1.6	-	-	84.7	0.8	-	-	85.8	1.3	-	-	86.4	0.7	-	-	87.9	1.7	-	-
1981	89.4	1.7	-	-	91.0	1.8	-	-	91.9	1.0	-	-	93.1	1.3	-	-	93.6	0.5	-	-	93.4	-0.2	-	-
1982	94.7	1.4	-	-	95.1	0.4	-	-	95.5	0.4	-	-	99.6	4.3	-	-	98.7	-0.9	-	-	98.4	-0.3	-	-
1983	98.7	0.3	-	-	99.0	0.3	-	-	99.6	0.6	-	-	100.0	0.4	-	-	100.0	0.0	-	-	100.2	0.2	-	-
1984	101.2	1.0	-	-	102.6	1.4	-	-	103.3	0.7	-	-	103.6	0.3	-	-	103.4	-0.2	-	-	104.1	0.7	-	-
1985	104.1	0.0	-	-	105.1	1.0	-	-	105.1	0.0	-	-	105.7	0.6	-	-	106.4	0.7	-	-	106.3	-0.1	-	-
1986	108.1	1.7	-	-	107.7	-0.4	-	-	107.2	-0.5	-	-	106.8	-0.4	-	-	108.9	2.0	-	-	109.6	0.6	-	-
1987	-	-	-	-	-	-	-	-	-	-	111.7	1.9	-	-	-	-	-	-	-	-	-	-	110.9	-0.7
1988	-	-	-	-	-	-	-	-	-	-	111.0	0.1	-	-	-	-	-	-	-	-	-	-	113.0	1.8
1989	-	-	-	-	-	-	-	-	-	-	118.0	4.4	-	-	-	-	-	-	-	-	-	-	119.5	1.3
1990	-	-	-	-	-	-	-	-	-	-	124.9	4.5	-	-	-	-	-	-	-	-	-	-	127.4	2.0
1991	-	-	-	-	-	-	-	-	-	-	131.4	3.1	-	-	-	-	-	-	-	-	-	-	129.9	-1.1
1992	-	-	-	-	-	-	-	-	-	-	132.1	1.7	-	-	-	-	-	-	-	-	-	-	131.3	-0.6
1993	-	-	-	-	-	-	-	-	-	-	133.8	1.9	-	-	-	-	-	-	-	-	-	-	-	-

Source: U.S. Department of Labor, Bureau of Labor Statistics, Division of Consumer Prices and Price Indexes. - indicates no data collected for period.

Portland, OR-WA
Consumer Price Index - Urban Wage Earners
Base 1982-1984 = 100
Food and Beverages

For 1976-1993. Columns headed % show percentile change in the index from the previous period for which an index is available.

Year	Jan Index	%	Feb Index	%	Mar Index	%	Apr Index	%	May Index	%	Jun Index	%	Jul Index	%	Aug Index	%	Sep Index	%	Oct Index	%	Nov Index	%	Dec Index	%
1976	59.9	-	-	-	-	-	60.1	0.3	-	-	-	-	61.1	1.7	-	-	-	-	60.8	-0.5	-	-	-	-
1977	61.5	1.2	-	-	-	-	63.9	3.9	-	-	-	-	65.2	2.0	-	-	-	-	65.2	0.0	-	-	-	-
1978	66.5	2.0	-	-	69.4	4.4	-	-	71.4	2.9	-	-	73.3	2.7	-	-	73.5	0.3	-	-	74.4	1.2	-	-
1979	77.3	3.9	-	-	79.2	2.5	-	-	81.3	2.7	-	-	81.8	0.6	-	-	82.3	0.6	-	-	82.5	0.2	-	-
1980	83.8	1.6	-	-	84.7	1.1	-	-	85.7	1.2	-	-	86.8	1.3	-	-	86.6	-0.2	-	-	88.3	2.0	-	-
1981	90.4	2.4	-	-	91.2	0.9	-	-	92.2	1.1	-	-	93.2	1.1	-	-	93.3	0.1	-	-	93.6	0.3		
1982	94.8	1.3	-	-	95.0	0.2	-	-	95.7	0.7	-	-	99.4	3.9	-	-	98.5	-0.9	-	-	98.3	-0.2		
1983	98.8	0.5	-	-	99.0	0.2	-	-	99.6	0.6	-	-	100.1	0.5	-	-	99.9	-0.2	-	-	100.3	0.4		
1984	101.2	0.9	-	-	102.5	1.3	-	-	103.3	0.8	-	-	103.7	0.4	-	-	103.4	-0.3	-	-	104.2	0.8		
1985	104.2	0.0	-	-	105.1	0.9	-	-	105.2	0.1	-	-	105.6	0.4	-	-	106.5	0.9	-	-	106.3	-0.2		
1986	108.2	1.8	-	-	107.6	-0.6	-	-	107.1	-0.5	-	-	106.4	-0.7	-	-	108.6	2.1	-	-	109.4	0.7	-	-
1987	-		-		-		-		-		111.4	1.8	-		-		-		-		-		110.8	-0.5
1988	-		-		-		-		-		110.8	0.0	-		-		-		-		-		112.9	1.9
1989	-		-		-		-		-		117.8	4.3	-		-		-		-		-		119.4	1.4
1990	-		-		-		-		-		124.6	4.4	-		-		-		-		-		127.2	2.1
1991	-		-		-		-		-		131.1	3.1	-		-		-		-		-		130.0	-0.8
1992	-		-		-		-		-		132.1	1.6	-		-		-		-		-		131.4	-0.5
1993	-		-		-		-		-		133.8	1.8	-		-		-		-		-		-	-

Source: U.S. Department of Labor, Bureau of Labor Statistics, Division of Consumer Prices and Price Indexes. - indicates no data collected for period.

Portland, OR-WA
Consumer Price Index - All Urban Consumers
Base 1982-1984 = 100
Housing

For 1976-1993. Columns headed % show percentile change in the index from the previous period for which an index is available.

Year	Jan Index	%	Feb Index	%	Mar Index	%	Apr Index	%	May Index	%	Jun Index	%	Jul Index	%	Aug Index	%	Sep Index	%	Oct Index	%	Nov Index	%	Dec Index	%
1976	54.3	-	-	-	-	-	55.5	2.2	-	-	-	-	56.6	2.0	-	-	-	-	57.4	1.4	-	-	-	-
1977	58.2	1.4	-	-	-	-	60.0	3.1	-	-	-	-	61.7	2.8	-	-	-	-	62.9	1.9	-	-	-	-
1978	64.7	2.9	-	-	66.6	2.9	-	-	67.5	1.4	-	-	69.1	2.4	-	-	70.8	2.5	-	-	73.0	3.1	-	-
1979	74.8	2.5	-	-	75.3	0.7	-	-	77.2	2.5	-	-	80.3	4.0	-	-	82.5	2.7	-	-	84.9	2.9	-	-
1980	88.4	4.1	-	-	92.5	4.6	-	-	94.3	1.9	-	-	90.6	-3.9	-	-	92.2	1.8	-	-	94.4	2.4	-	-
1981	96.0	1.7	-	-	95.1	-0.9	-	-	101.2	6.4	-	-	101.6	0.4	-	-	107.2	5.5	-	-	97.6	-9.0	-	-
1982	102.8	5.3	-	-	101.7	-1.1	-	-	97.9	-3.7	-	-	102.5	4.7	-	-	99.4	-3.0	-	-	97.8	-1.6	-	-
1983	98.2	0.4	-	-	97.3	-0.9	-	-	98.4	1.1	-	-	98.9	0.5	-	-	99.2	0.3	-	-	99.3	0.1	-	-
1984	99.9	0.6	-	-	100.5	0.6	-	-	101.3	0.8	-	-	101.0	-0.3	-	-	101.7	0.7	-	-	102.2	0.5	-	-
1985	103.5	1.3	-	-	103.7	0.2	-	-	103.8	0.1	-	-	105.6	1.7	-	-	105.2	-0.4	-	-	105.8	0.6	-	-
1986	108.1	2.2	-	-	106.0	-1.9	-	-	105.6	-0.4	-	-	104.7	-0.9	-	-	106.5	1.7	-	-	106.7	0.2	-	-
1987	-	-	-	-	-	-	-	-	-	-	107.1	0.4	-	-	-	-	-	-	-	-	-	-	109.2	2.0
1988	-	-	-	-	-	-	-	-	-	-	111.0	1.6	-	-	-	-	-	-	-	-	-	-	112.7	1.5
1989	-	-	-	-	-	-	-	-	-	-	115.1	2.1	-	-	-	-	-	-	-	-	-	-	118.0	2.5
1990	-	-	-	-	-	-	-	-	-	-	120.7	2.3	-	-	-	-	-	-	-	-	-	-	124.6	3.2
1991	-	-	-	-	-	-	-	-	-	-	128.0	2.7	-	-	-	-	-	-	-	-	-	-	132.7	3.7
1992	-	-	-	-	-	-	-	-	-	-	137.4	3.5	-	-	-	-	-	-	-	-	-	-	139.0	1.2
1993	-	-	-	-	-	-	-	-	-	-	141.6	1.9	-	-	-	-	-	-	-	-	-	-	-	-

Source: U.S. Department of Labor, Bureau of Labor Statistics, Division of Consumer Prices and Price Indexes. - indicates no data collected for period.

Portland, OR-WA
Consumer Price Index - Urban Wage Earners
Base 1982-1984 = 100
Housing

For 1976-1993. Columns headed % show percentile change in the index from the previous period for which an index is available.

Year	Jan Index	%	Feb Index	%	Mar Index	%	Apr Index	%	May Index	%	Jun Index	%	Jul Index	%	Aug Index	%	Sep Index	%	Oct Index	%	Nov Index	%	Dec Index	%
1976	55.1	-	-	-	-	-	56.3	2.2	-	-	-	-	57.4	2.0	-	-	-	-	58.2	1.4	-	-	-	-
1977	59.0	1.4	-	-	-	-	60.9	3.2	-	-	-	-	62.6	2.8	-	-	-	-	63.8	1.9	-	-	-	-
1978	65.7	3.0	-	-	67.5	2.7	-	-	68.5	1.5	-	-	70.0	2.2	-	-	72.0	2.9	-	-	74.1	2.9	-	-
1979	76.0	2.6	-	-	76.6	0.8	-	-	78.6	2.6	-	-	81.6	3.8	-	-	84.0	2.9	-	-	86.6	3.1	-	-
1980	90.4	4.4	-	-	94.4	4.4	-	-	96.4	2.1	-	-	92.2	-4.4	-	-	93.7	1.6	-	-	96.2	2.7	-	-
1981	97.8	1.7	-	-	97.3	-0.5	-	-	103.0	5.9	-	-	104.0	1.0	-	-	110.2	6.0	-	-	99.2	-10.0	-	-
1982	104.6	5.4	-	-	103.7	-0.9	-	-	99.5	-4.1	-	-	104.7	5.2	-	-	101.0	-3.5	-	-	99.4	-1.6	-	-
1983	97.8	-1.6	-	-	99.6	1.8	-	-	98.2	-1.4	-	-	98.3	0.1	-	-	98.8	0.5	-	-	99.4	0.6	-	-
1984	98.9	-0.5	-	-	99.4	0.5	-	-	101.2	1.8	-	-	99.5	-1.7	-	-	98.4	-1.1	-	-	98.8	0.4	-	-
1985	100.0	1.2	-	-	100.2	0.2	-	-	100.3	0.1	-	-	102.2	1.9	-	-	101.8	-0.4	-	-	102.2	0.4	-	-
1986	104.3	2.1	-	-	102.4	-1.8	-	-	102.0	-0.4	-	-	101.3	-0.7	-	-	103.0	1.7	-	-	103.1	0.1	-	-
1987	-	-	-	-	-	-	-	-	-	-	103.3	0.2	-	-	-	-	-	-	-	-	-	-	-	-
1988	-	-	-	-	-	-	-	-	-	-	107.0	1.6	-	-	-	-	-	-	-	-	-	-	105.3	1.9
1989	-	-	-	-	-	-	-	-	-	-	110.9	2.1	-	-	-	-	-	-	-	-	-	-	108.6	1.5
1990	-	-	-	-	-	-	-	-	-	-	116.2	2.2	-	-	-	-	-	-	-	-	-	-	113.7	2.5
1991	-	-	-	-	-	-	-	-	-	-	123.5	2.9	-	-	-	-	-	-	-	-	-	-	120.0	3.3
1992	-	-	-	-	-	-	-	-	-	-	132.9	3.7	-	-	-	-	-	-	-	-	-	-	128.2	3.8
1993	-	-	-	-	-	-	-	-	-	-	137.1	1.9	-	-	-	-	-	-	-	-	-	-	134.6	1.3

Source: U.S. Department of Labor, Bureau of Labor Statistics, Division of Consumer Prices and Price Indexes. - indicates no data collected for period.

Portland, OR-WA
Consumer Price Index - All Urban Consumers
Base 1982-1984 = 100
Apparel and Upkeep

For 1914-1993. Columns headed % show percentile change in the index from the previous period for which an index is available.

Year	Jan Index	%	Feb Index	%	Mar Index	%	Apr Index	%	May Index	%	Jun Index	%	Jul Index	%	Aug Index	%	Sep Index	%	Oct Index	%	Nov Index	%	Dec Index	%
1914	-		-		-		-		-		-		-		-		-		-		-		16.5	-
1915	-		-		-		-		-		-		-		-		-		-		-		17.1	3.6
1916	-		-		-		-		-		-		-		-		-		-		-		19.2	12.3
1917	-		-		-		-		-		-		-		-		-		-		-		23.9	24.5
1918	-		-		-		-		-		-		-		-		-		-		-		32.5	36.0
1919	-		-		-		-		-		35.6	9.5	-		-		-		-		-		40.1	12.6
1920	-		-		-		-		-		42.8	6.7	-		-		-		-		-		36.8	-14.0
1921	-		-		31.7	-13.9	-		-		-		-		-		28.2	-11.0	-		-		27.4	-2.8
1922	-		-		25.8	-5.8	-		-		25.4	-1.6	-		-		25.4	0.0	-		-		25.6	0.8
1923	-		-		26.5	3.5	-		-		26.7	0.8	-		-		26.8	0.4	-		-		26.8	0.0
1924	-		-		26.8	0.0	-		-		26.7	-0.4	-		-		26.3	-1.5	-		-		26.4	0.4
1925	-		-		-		-		-		26.1	-1.1	-		-		-		-		-		26.0	-0.4
1926	-		-		-		-		-		25.9	-0.4	-		-		-		-		-		25.5	-1.5
1927	-		-		-		-		-		25.4	-0.4	-		-		-		-		-		25.0	-1.6
1928	-		-		-		-		-		25.0	0.0	-		-		-		-		-		24.8	-0.8
1929	-		-		-		-		-		24.5	-1.2	-		-		-		-		-		24.5	0.0
1930	-		-		-		-		-		24.0	-2.0	-		-		-		-		-		22.8	-5.0
1931	-		-		-		-		-		22.0	-3.5	-		-		-		-		-		20.4	-7.3
1932	-		-		-		-		-		19.2	-5.9	-		-		-		-		-		18.2	-5.2
1933	-		-		-		-		-		18.3	0.5	-		-		-		-		-		20.1	9.8
1934	-		-		-		-		-		20.6	2.5	-		-		-		-		20.5	-0.5	-	
1935	-		-		20.5	0.0	-		-		-		20.5	0.0	-		20.6	0.0	20.5	0.0	-		-	
1936	20.6	0.5	-		-		20.7	0.5	-		-		20.6	-0.5	-		20.6	0.0	-		-		20.8	1.0
1937	-		-		21.3	2.4	-		-		21.5	0.9	-		-		21.8	1.4	-		-		21.7	-0.5
1938	-		-		21.5	-0.9	-		-		21.4	-0.5	-		-		21.4	0.0	-		-		21.3	-0.5
1939	-		-		21.2	-0.5	-		-		21.2	0.0	-		-		21.3	0.5	-		-		21.4	0.5
1940	-		-		21.7	1.4	-		-		21.7	0.0	-		-		21.7	0.0	-		-		21.7	0.0
1941	-		-		21.7	0.0	-		-		21.8	0.5	-		-		23.2	6.4	-		-		23.8	2.6
1942	-		-		25.8	8.4	-		-		26.2	1.6	-		-		26.5	1.1	-		-		26.5	0.0
1943	-		-		27.1	2.3	-		-		27.2	0.4	-		-		28.2	3.7	-		-		28.5	1.1
1944	-		-		29.1	2.1	-		-		29.5	1.4	-		-		29.8	1.0	-		-		29.8	0.0
1945	-		-		29.9	0.3	-		-		30.0	0.3	-		-		30.2	0.7	-		-		30.0	-0.7
1946	-		-		30.2	0.7	-		-		31.5	4.3	-		-		32.9	4.4	-		-		35.2	7.0
1947	-		-		37.5	6.5	-		-		37.9	1.1	37.5	-1.1	-		-		38.9	3.7	-		-	
1948	40.0	2.8	-		-		41.3	3.2	-		-		41.0	-0.7	-		-		42.3	3.2	-		-	
1949	41.1	-2.8	-		-		40.2	-2.2	-		-		39.7	-1.2	-		-		39.2	-1.3	-		-	
1950	38.7	-1.3	-		-		39.0	0.8	-		-		38.8	-0.5	-		-		40.7	4.9	-		-	
1951	41.4	1.7	-		-		42.0	1.4	-		-		42.5	1.2	-		-		42.9	0.9	-		-	
1952	42.8	-0.2	-		-		41.8	-2.3	-		-		41.6	-0.5	-		-		42.1	1.2	-		-	
1953	41.4	-1.7	-		-		41.3	-0.2	-		-		41.2	-0.2	-		-		42.4	2.9	-		-	
1954	41.8	-1.4	-		-		41.5	-0.7	-		-		41.5	0.0	-		-		42.6	2.7	-		-	
1955	42.1	-1.2	-		-		42.1	0.0	-		-		41.7	-1.0	-		-		42.8	2.6	-		-	
1956	43.1	0.7	-		-		43.0	-0.2	-		-		42.9	-0.2	-		-		43.7	1.9	-		-	
1957	43.5	-0.5	-		-		44.0	1.1	-		-		44.1	0.2	-		-		44.4	0.7	-		-	
1958	44.2	-0.5	-		-		44.3	0.2	-		-		44.2	-0.2	-		-		44.1	-0.2	-		-	

[Continued]

Portland, OR-WA
Consumer Price Index - All Urban Consumers
Base 1982-1984 = 100
Apparel and Upkeep
[Continued]

For 1914-1993. Columns headed % show percentile change in the index from the previous period for which an index is available.

Year	Jan Index	%	Feb Index	%	Mar Index	%	Apr Index	%	May Index	%	Jun Index	%	Jul Index	%	Aug Index	%	Sep Index	%	Oct Index	%	Nov Index	%	Dec Index	%
1959	44.0	-0.2	-	-	-	-	44.0	0.0	-	-	-	-	44.4	0.9	-	-	-	-	45.2	1.8	-	-	-	-
1960	45.2	0.0	-	-	-	-	45.5	0.7	-	-	-	-	45.5	0.0	-	-	-	-	45.7	0.4	-	-	-	-
1961	45.8	0.2	-	-	-	-	45.8	0.0	-	-	-	-	45.8	0.0	-	-	-	-	45.9	0.2	-	-	-	-
1962	45.3	-1.3	-	-	-	-	45.2	-0.2	-	-	-	-	45.1	-0.2	-	-	-	-	46.2	2.4	-	-	-	-
1963	46.2	0.0	-	-	-	-	46.4	0.4	-	-	-	-	46.2	-0.4	-	-	-	-	46.6	0.9	-	-	-	-
1964	45.9	-1.5	-	-	-	-	46.8	2.0	-	-	-	-	46.5	-0.6	-	-	-	-	47.6	2.4	-	-	-	-
1965	46.7	-1.9	-	-	-	-	47.5	1.7	-	-	-	-	47.9	0.8	-	-	-	-	50.0	4.4	-	-	-	-
1966	49.2	-1.6	-	-	-	-	49.7	1.0	-	-	-	-	49.8	0.2	-	-	-	-	50.3	1.0	-	-	-	-
1967	50.3	0.0	-	-	-	-	50.8	1.0	-	-	-	-	50.8	0.0	-	-	-	-	51.8	2.0	-	-	-	-
1968	51.1	-1.4	-	-	-	-	53.0	3.7	-	-	-	-	53.2	0.4	-	-	-	-	54.5	2.4	-	-	-	-
1969	54.2	-0.6	-	-	-	-	55.7	2.8	-	-	-	-	55.7	0.0	-	-	-	-	58.4	4.8	-	-	-	-
1970	57.2	-2.1	-	-	-	-	58.6	2.4	-	-	-	-	59.1	0.9	-	-	-	-	60.0	1.5	-	-	-	-
1971	58.2	-3.0	-	-	-	-	58.5	0.5	-	-	-	-	58.9	0.7	-	-	-	-	61.7	4.8	-	-	-	-
1972	60.3	-2.3	-	-	-	-	60.4	0.2	-	-	-	-	61.0	1.0	-	-	-	-	62.3	2.1	-	-	-	-
1973	61.9	-0.6	-	-	-	-	64.3	3.9	-	-	-	-	65.0	1.1	-	-	-	-	67.4	3.7	-	-	-	-
1974	66.3	-1.6	-	-	-	-	67.3	1.5	-	-	-	-	69.0	2.5	-	-	-	-	71.4	3.5	-	-	-	-
1975	71.3	-0.1	-	-	-	-	72.7	2.0	-	-	-	-	72.5	-0.3	-	-	-	-	74.6	2.9	-	-	-	-
1976	73.3	-1.7	-	-	-	-	75.5	3.0	-	-	-	-	76.9	1.9	-	-	-	-	79.2	3.0	-	-	-	-
1977	79.2	0.0	-	-	-	-	80.7	1.9	-	-	-	-	81.9	1.5	-	-	-	-	84.8	3.5	-	-	-	-
1978	84.0	-0.9	-	-	84.4	0.5	-	-	84.8	0.5	-	-	81.9	-3.4	-	-	86.0	5.0	-	-	85.6	-0.5	-	-
1979	83.9	-2.0	-	-	86.5	3.1	-	-	85.8	-0.8	-	-	84.5	-1.5	-	-	87.6	3.7	-	-	86.0	-1.8	-	-
1980	84.4	-1.9	-	-	88.3	4.6	-	-	87.3	-1.1	-	-	87.5	0.2	-	-	88.6	1.3	-	-	89.3	0.8	-	-
1981	89.6	0.3	-	-	93.1	3.9	-	-	92.2	-1.0	-	-	90.8	-1.5	-	-	94.6	4.2	-	-	94.4	-0.2	-	-
1982	92.8	-1.7	-	-	95.1	2.5	-	-	95.8	0.7	-	-	93.4	-2.5	-	-	96.6	3.4	-	-	98.2	1.7	-	-
1983	96.6	-1.6	-	-	98.2	1.7	-	-	98.8	0.6	-	-	98.8	0.0	-	-	103.4	4.7	-	-	101.4	-1.9	-	-
1984	100.0	-1.4	-	-	107.7	7.7	-	-	107.0	-0.6	-	-	101.4	-5.2	-	-	107.0	5.5	-	-	106.1	-0.8	-	-
1985	100.5	-5.3	-	-	110.6	10.0	-	-	113.6	2.7	-	-	103.3	-9.1	-	-	108.7	5.2	-	-	108.2	-0.5	-	-
1986	102.3	-5.5	-	-	100.7	-1.6	-	-	100.1	-0.6	-	-	96.1	-4.0	-	-	102.8	7.0	-	-	102.3	-0.5	-	-
1987	-	-	-	-	-	-	-	-	-	-	98.5	-3.7	-	-	-	-	-	-	-	-	-	-	-	-
1988	-	-	-	-	-	-	-	-	-	-	109.4	3.5	-	-	-	-	-	-	-	-	105.7	7.3	-	-
1989	-	-	-	-	-	-	-	-	-	-	114.5	0.0	-	-	-	-	-	-	-	-	114.5	4.7	-	-
1990	-	-	-	-	-	-	-	-	-	-	118.4	3.6	-	-	-	-	-	-	-	-	114.3	-0.2	-	-
1991	-	-	-	-	-	-	-	-	-	-	123.2	0.2	-	-	-	-	-	-	-	-	123.0	3.9	-	-
1992	-	-	-	-	-	-	-	-	-	-	124.3	2.4	-	-	-	-	-	-	-	-	121.4	-1.5	-	-
1993	-	-	-	-	-	-	-	-	-	-	124.8	-0.4	-	-	-	-	-	-	-	-	125.3	0.8	-	-

Source: U.S. Department of Labor, Bureau of Labor Statistics, Division of Consumer Prices and Price Indexes. - indicates no data collected for period.

Portland, OR-WA
Consumer Price Index - Urban Wage Earners
Base 1982-1984 = 100
Apparel and Upkeep

For 1914-1993. Columns headed % show percentile change in the index from the previous period for which an index is available.

Year	Jan Index	%	Feb Index	%	Mar Index	%	Apr Index	%	May Index	%	Jun Index	%	Jul Index	%	Aug Index	%	Sep Index	%	Oct Index	%	Nov Index	%	Dec Index	%
1914	-		-		-		-		-		-		-		-		-		-		-		16.6	-
1915	-		-		-		-		-		-		-		-		-		-		-		17.2	3.6
1916	-		-		-		-		-		-		-		-		-		-		-		19.3	12.2
1917	-		-		-		-		-		-		-		-		-		-		-		24.0	24.4
1918	-		-		-		-		-		-		-		-		-		-		-		32.7	36.3
1919	-		-		-		-		-		35.9	9.8	-		-		-		-		-		40.4	12.5
1920	-		-		-		-		-		43.1	6.7	-		-		-		-		-		37.0	-14.2
1921	-		-		31.9	-13.8	-		-		-		-		-		28.4	-11.0	-		-		27.6	-2.8
1922	-		-		25.9	-6.2	-		-		25.6	-1.2	-		-		25.6	0.0	-		-		25.8	0.8
1923	-		-		26.7	3.5	-		-		26.9	0.7	-		-		26.9	0.0	-		-		26.9	0.0
1924	-		-		27.0	0.4	-		-		26.9	-0.4	-		-		26.4	-1.9	-		-		26.5	0.4
1925	-		-		-		-		-		26.3	-0.8	-		-		-		-		-		26.1	-0.8
1926	-		-		-		-		-		26.1	0.0	-		-		-		-		-		25.7	-1.5
1927	-		-		-		-		-		25.6	-0.4	-		-		-		-		-		25.2	-1.6
1928	-		-		-		-		-		25.1	-0.4	-		-		-		-		-		24.9	-0.8
1929	-		-		-		-		-		24.7	-0.8	-		-		-		-		-		24.6	-0.4
1930	-		-		-		-		-		24.2	-1.6	-		-		-		-		-		23.0	-5.0
1931	-		-		-		-		-		22.2	-3.5	-		-		-		-		-		20.5	-7.7
1932	-		-		-		-		-		19.3	-5.9	-		-		-		-		-		18.3	-5.2
1933	-		-		-		-		-		18.4	0.5	-		-		-		-		-		20.3	10.3
1934	-		-		-		-		-		20.7	2.0	-		-		-		-		20.6	-0.5	-	-
1935	-		-		20.6	0.0	-		-		-		20.6	0.0	-		-		20.6	0.0	-		-	
1936	20.7	0.5	-		-		20.8	0.5	-		-		20.7	-0.5	-		20.7	0.0	-		-		20.9	1.0
1937	-		-		21.4	2.4	-		-		21.6	0.9	-		-		21.9	1.4	-		-		21.9	0.0
1938	-		-		21.6	-1.4	-		-		21.5	-0.5	-		-		21.5	0.0	-		-		21.5	0.0
1939	-		-		21.3	-0.9	-		-		21.3	0.0	-		-		21.4	0.5	-		-		21.5	0.5
1940	-		-		21.9	1.9	-		-		21.9	0.0	-		-		21.8	-0.5	-		-		21.8	0.0
1941	-		-		21.8	0.0	-		-		22.0	0.9	-		-		23.3	5.9	-		-		24.0	3.0
1942	-		-		26.0	8.3	-		-		26.4	1.5	-		-		26.7	1.1	-		-		26.7	0.0
1943	-		-		27.3	2.2	-		-		27.4	0.4	-		-		28.4	3.6	-		-		28.6	0.7
1944	-		-		29.3	2.4	-		-		29.7	1.4	-		-		30.0	1.0	-		-		30.0	0.0
1945	-		-		30.1	0.3	-		-		30.2	0.3	-		-		30.4	0.7	-		-		30.2	-0.7
1946	-		-		30.4	0.7	-		-		31.7	4.3	-		-		33.1	4.4	-		-		35.5	7.3
1947	-		-		37.8	6.5	-		-		38.1	0.8	37.8	-0.8	-		-		39.2	3.7	-		-	
1948	40.2	2.6	-		-		41.5	3.2	-		-		41.3	-0.5	-		-		42.5	2.9	-		-	
1949	41.3	-2.8	-		-		40.4	-2.2	-		-		39.9	-1.2	-		-		39.4	-1.3	-		-	
1950	38.9	-1.3	-		-		39.2	0.8	-		-		39.0	-0.5	-		-		41.0	5.1	-		-	
1951	41.6	1.5	-		-		42.3	1.7	-		-		42.8	1.2	-		-		43.2	0.9	-		-	
1952	43.1	-0.2	-		-		42.1	-2.3	-		-		41.8	-0.7	-		-		42.4	1.4	-		-	
1953	41.6	-1.9	-		-		41.5	-0.2	-		-		41.5	0.0	-		-		42.6	2.7	-		-	
1954	42.1	-1.2	-		-		41.8	-0.7	-		-		41.8	0.0	-		-		42.9	2.6	-		-	
1955	42.3	-1.4	-		-		42.3	0.0	-		-		42.0	-0.7	-		-		43.1	2.6	-		-	
1956	43.4	0.7	-		-		43.3	-0.2	-		-		43.2	-0.2	-		-		43.9	1.6	-		-	
1957	43.8	-0.2	-		-		44.2	0.9	-		-		44.3	0.2	-		-		44.7	0.9	-		-	
1958	44.4	-0.7	-		-		44.6	0.5	-		-		44.4	-0.4	-		-		44.4	0.0	-		-	

[Continued]

Portland, OR-WA
Consumer Price Index - Urban Wage Earners
Base 1982-1984 = 100
Apparel and Upkeep
[Continued]

For 1914-1993. Columns headed % show percentile change in the index from the previous period for which an index is available.

Year	Jan Index	%	Feb Index	%	Mar Index	%	Apr Index	%	May Index	%	Jun Index	%	Jul Index	%	Aug Index	%	Sep Index	%	Oct Index	%	Nov Index	%	Dec Index	%
1959	44.2	-0.5	-	-	-	-	44.2	0.0	-	-	-	-	44.7	1.1	-	-	-	-	45.5	1.8	-	-	-	-
1960	45.5	0.0	-	-	-	-	45.8	0.7	-	-	-	-	45.8	0.0	-	-	-	-	46.0	0.4	-	-	-	-
1961	46.1	0.2	-	-	-	-	46.1	0.0	-	-	-	-	46.1	0.0	-	-	-	-	46.2	0.2	-	-	-	-
1962	45.6	-1.3	-	-	-	-	45.5	-0.2	-	-	-	-	45.4	-0.2	-	-	-	-	46.4	2.2	-	-	-	-
1963	46.4	0.0	-	-	-	-	46.7	0.6	-	-	-	-	46.4	-0.6	-	-	-	-	46.9	1.1	-	-	-	-
1964	46.2	-1.5	-	-	-	-	47.1	1.9	-	-	-	-	46.8	-0.6	-	-	-	-	47.9	2.4	-	-	-	-
1965	47.0	-1.9	-	-	-	-	47.8	1.7	-	-	-	-	48.2	0.8	-	-	-	-	50.3	4.4	-	-	-	-
1966	49.5	-1.6	-	-	-	-	50.0	1.0	-	-	-	-	50.1	0.2	-	-	-	-	50.6	1.0	-	-	-	-
1967	50.6	0.0	-	-	-	-	51.2	1.2	-	-	-	-	51.1	-0.2	-	-	-	-	52.1	2.0	-	-	-	-
1968	51.5	-1.2	-	-	-	-	53.4	3.7	-	-	-	-	53.5	0.2	-	-	-	-	54.9	2.6	-	-	-	-
1969	54.5	-0.7	-	-	-	-	56.1	2.9	-	-	-	-	56.1	0.0	-	-	-	-	58.8	4.8	-	-	-	-
1970	57.5	-2.2	-	-	-	-	59.0	2.6	-	-	-	-	59.5	0.8	-	-	-	-	60.3	1.3	-	-	-	-
1971	58.6	-2.8	-	-	-	-	58.9	0.5	-	-	-	-	59.3	0.7	-	-	-	-	62.1	4.7	-	-	-	-
1972	60.7	-2.3	-	-	-	-	60.8	0.2	-	-	-	-	61.4	1.0	-	-	-	-	62.7	2.1	-	-	-	-
1973	62.2	-0.8	-	-	-	-	64.7	4.0	-	-	-	-	65.4	1.1	-	-	-	-	67.8	3.7	-	-	-	-
1974	66.8	-1.5	-	-	-	-	67.7	1.3	-	-	-	-	69.5	2.7	-	-	-	-	71.9	3.5	-	-	-	-
1975	71.7	-0.3	-	-	-	-	73.1	2.0	-	-	-	-	72.9	-0.3	-	-	-	-	75.0	2.9	-	-	-	-
1976	73.7	-1.7	-	-	-	-	76.0	3.1	-	-	-	-	77.3	1.7	-	-	-	-	79.7	3.1	-	-	-	-
1977	79.7	0.0	-	-	-	-	81.2	1.9	-	-	-	-	82.4	1.5	-	-	-	-	85.3	3.5	-	-	-	-
1978	84.5	-0.9	-	-	84.4	-0.1	-	-	85.9	1.8	-	-	82.8	-3.6	-	-	87.7	5.9	-	-	86.7	-1.1	-	-
1979	85.4	-1.5	-	-	84.8	-0.7	-	-	85.4	0.7	-	-	85.4	0.0	-	-	90.3	5.7	-	-	90.3	0.0	-	-
1980	85.0	-5.9	-	-	87.6	3.1	-	-	86.5	-1.3	-	-	89.0	2.9	-	-	91.1	2.4	-	-	92.1	1.1	-	-
1981	92.0	-0.1	-	-	93.5	1.6	-	-	93.8	0.3	-	-	91.0	-3.0	-	-	94.5	3.8	-	-	94.4	-0.1	-	-
1982	92.5	-2.0	-	-	95.1	2.8	-	-	96.2	1.2	-	-	93.8	-2.5	-	-	96.1	2.5	-	-	97.2	1.1	-	-
1983	95.4	-1.9	-	-	98.1	2.8	-	-	99.0	0.9	-	-	98.0	-1.0	-	-	102.3	4.4	-	-	99.8	-2.4	-	-
1984	99.7	-0.1	-	-	110.1	10.4	-	-	108.8	-1.2	-	-	102.4	-5.9	-	-	107.5	5.0	-	-	106.3	-1.1	-	-
1985	99.6	-6.3	-	-	112.8	13.3	-	-	116.3	3.1	-	-	102.8	-11.6	-	-	110.6	7.6	-	-	110.0	-0.5	-	-
1986	103.6	-5.8	-	-	100.7	-2.8	-	-	99.9	-0.8	-	-	95.6	-4.3	-	-	102.5	7.2	-	-	102.0	-0.5	-	-
1987	-	-	-	-	-	-	-	-	-	-	98.5	-3.4	-	-	-	-	-	-	-	-	-	-	105.2	6.8
1988	-	-	-	-	-	-	-	-	-	-	109.3	3.9	-	-	-	-	-	-	-	-	-	-	114.8	5.0
1989	-	-	-	-	-	-	-	-	-	-	114.7	-0.1	-	-	-	-	-	-	-	-	-	-	114.1	-0.5
1990	-	-	-	-	-	-	-	-	-	-	118.7	4.0	-	-	-	-	-	-	-	-	-	-	123.2	3.8
1991	-	-	-	-	-	-	-	-	-	-	124.6	1.1	-	-	-	-	-	-	-	-	-	-	122.6	-1.6
1992	-	-	-	-	-	-	-	-	-	-	124.6	1.6	-	-	-	-	-	-	-	-	-	-	125.6	0.8
1993	-	-	-	-	-	-	-	-	-	-	125.4	-0.2	-	-	-	-	-	-	-	-	-	-	-	-

Source: U.S. Department of Labor, Bureau of Labor Statistics, Division of Consumer Prices and Price Indexes. - indicates no data collected for period.

Portland, OR-WA
Consumer Price Index - All Urban Consumers
Base 1982-1984 = 100
Transportation

For 1947-1993. Columns headed % show percentile change in the index from the previous period for which an index is available.

Year	Jan Index	Jan %	Feb Index	Feb %	Mar Index	Mar %	Apr Index	Apr %	May Index	May %	Jun Index	Jun %	Jul Index	Jul %	Aug Index	Aug %	Sep Index	Sep %	Oct Index	Oct %	Nov Index	Nov %	Dec Index	Dec %
1947	-	-	-	-	19.5	-	-	-	-	-	19.6	0.5	19.6	0.0	-	-	-	-	20.0	2.0	-	-	-	-
1948	20.9	4.5	-	-	-	-	21.0	0.5	-	-	-	-	22.2	5.7	-	-	-	-	22.6	1.8	-	-	-	-
1949	22.9	1.3	-	-	-	-	23.2	1.3	-	-	-	-	24.0	3.4	-	-	-	-	24.0	0.0	-	-	-	-
1950	24.2	0.8	-	-	-	-	23.7	-2.1	-	-	-	-	23.8	0.4	-	-	-	-	24.2	1.7	-	-	-	-
1951	24.4	0.8	-	-	-	-	24.8	1.6	-	-	-	-	25.0	0.8	-	-	-	-	25.5	2.0	-	-	-	-
1952	26.0	2.0	-	-	-	-	26.7	2.7	-	-	-	-	26.7	0.0	-	-	-	-	27.3	2.2	-	-	-	-
1953	27.5	0.7	-	-	-	-	27.7	0.7	-	-	-	-	27.5	-0.7	-	-	-	-	27.5	0.0	-	-	-	-
1954	27.4	-0.4	-	-	-	-	27.1	-1.1	-	-	-	-	26.6	-1.8	-	-	-	-	26.4	-0.8	-	-	-	-
1955	26.9	1.9	-	-	-	-	26.7	-0.7	-	-	-	-	26.6	-0.4	-	-	-	-	27.4	3.0	-	-	-	-
1956	27.1	-1.1	-	-	-	-	26.1	-3.7	-	-	-	-	26.7	2.3	-	-	-	-	27.6	3.4	-	-	-	-
1957	27.6	0.0	-	-	-	-	28.1	1.8	-	-	-	-	28.6	1.8	-	-	-	-	28.1	-1.7	-	-	-	-
1958	29.0	3.2	-	-	-	-	29.8	2.8	-	-	-	-	30.0	0.7	-	-	-	-	30.3	1.0	-	-	-	-
1959	29.6	-2.3	-	-	-	-	31.4	6.1	-	-	-	-	30.6	-2.5	-	-	-	-	31.8	3.9	-	-	-	-
1960	31.6	-0.6	-	-	-	-	31.1	-1.6	-	-	-	-	30.6	-1.6	-	-	-	-	30.1	-1.6	-	-	-	-
1961	31.1	3.3	-	-	-	-	29.2	-6.1	-	-	-	-	31.5	7.9	-	-	-	-	31.8	1.0	-	-	-	-
1962	31.4	-1.3	-	-	-	-	30.7	-2.2	-	-	-	-	31.5	2.6	-	-	-	-	31.1	-1.3	-	-	-	-
1963	31.0	-0.3	-	-	-	-	31.6	1.9	-	-	-	-	31.5	-0.3	-	-	-	-	31.7	0.6	-	-	-	-
1964	32.0	0.9	-	-	-	-	32.1	0.3	-	-	-	-	32.2	0.3	-	-	-	-	31.5	-2.2	-	-	-	-
1965	32.4	2.9	-	-	-	-	32.5	0.3	-	-	-	-	32.7	0.6	-	-	-	-	32.2	-1.5	-	-	-	-
1966	32.1	-0.3	-	-	-	-	32.6	1.6	-	-	-	-	32.7	0.3	-	-	-	-	33.3	1.8	-	-	-	-
1967	33.1	-0.6	-	-	-	-	33.9	2.4	-	-	-	-	34.4	1.5	-	-	-	-	34.6	0.6	-	-	-	-
1968	34.7	0.3	-	-	-	-	34.7	0.0	-	-	-	-	35.0	0.9	-	-	-	-	35.0	0.0	-	-	-	-
1969	35.6	1.7	-	-	-	-	36.1	1.4	-	-	-	-	35.9	-0.6	-	-	-	-	36.3	1.1	-	-	-	-
1970	36.7	1.1	-	-	-	-	36.9	0.5	-	-	-	-	37.2	0.8	-	-	-	-	37.1	-0.3	-	-	-	-
1971	38.1	2.7	-	-	-	-	36.9	-3.1	-	-	-	-	37.3	1.1	-	-	-	-	37.3	0.0	-	-	-	-
1972	37.5	0.5	-	-	-	-	37.1	-1.1	-	-	-	-	37.4	0.8	-	-	-	-	38.1	1.9	-	-	-	-
1973	37.9	-0.5	-	-	-	-	38.2	0.8	-	-	-	-	38.7	1.3	-	-	-	-	38.8	0.3	-	-	-	-
1974	39.8	2.6	-	-	-	-	41.1	3.3	-	-	-	-	43.2	5.1	-	-	-	-	43.6	0.9	-	-	-	-
1975	45.0	3.2	-	-	-	-	45.3	0.7	-	-	-	-	47.7	5.3	-	-	-	-	48.0	0.6	-	-	-	-
1976	49.0	2.1	-	-	-	-	49.4	0.8	-	-	-	-	52.3	5.9	-	-	-	-	53.0	1.3	-	-	-	-
1977	53.6	1.1	-	-	-	-	56.4	5.2	-	-	-	-	56.6	0.4	-	-	-	-	56.7	0.2	-	-	-	-
1978	58.3	2.8	-	-	57.9	-0.7	-	-	59.5	2.8	-	-	60.9	2.4	-	-	61.9	1.6	-	-	62.8	1.5	-	-
1979	63.3	0.8	-	-	65.9	4.1	-	-	69.2	5.0	-	-	73.0	5.5	-	-	74.1	1.5	-	-	74.5	0.5	-	-
1980	77.6	4.2	-	-	79.9	3.0	-	-	80.8	1.1	-	-	81.6	1.0	-	-	83.1	1.8	-	-	85.0	2.3	-	-
1981	85.9	1.1	-	-	88.7	3.3	-	-	90.5	2.0	-	-	92.3	2.0	-	-	94.1	2.0	-	-	96.2	2.2	-	-
1982	97.9	1.8	-	-	96.1	-1.8	-	-	96.1	0.0	-	-	99.3	3.3	-	-	99.3	0.0	-	-	98.6	-0.7	-	-
1983	97.2	-1.4	-	-	94.4	-2.9	-	-	96.9	2.6	-	-	99.9	3.1	-	-	100.7	0.8	-	-	101.2	0.5	-	-
1984	100.8	-0.4	-	-	100.8	0.0	-	-	104.6	3.8	-	-	104.4	-0.2	-	-	104.2	-0.2	-	-	105.7	1.4	-	-
1985	106.6	0.9	-	-	106.2	-0.4	-	-	107.4	1.1	-	-	108.3	0.8	-	-	109.3	0.9	-	-	110.9	1.5	-	-
1986	112.5	1.4	-	-	107.3	-4.6	-	-	106.0	-1.2	-	-	108.1	2.0	-	-	106.8	-1.2	-	-	105.1	-1.6	-	-
1987	-	-	-	-	-	-	-	-	-	-	108.1	2.9	-	-	-	-	-	-	-	-	-	-	110.2	1.9
1988	-	-	-	-	-	-	-	-	-	-	109.7	-0.5	-	-	-	-	-	-	-	-	-	-	111.5	1.6
1989	-	-	-	-	-	-	-	-	-	-	117.8	5.7	-	-	-	-	-	-	-	-	-	-	118.8	0.8
1990	-	-	-	-	-	-	-	-	-	-	120.1	1.1	-	-	-	-	-	-	-	-	-	-	130.8	8.9
1991	-	-	-	-	-	-	-	-	-	-	130.0	-0.6	-	-	-	-	-	-	-	-	-	-	130.1	0.1

[Continued]

Portland, OR-WA
Consumer Price Index - All Urban Consumers
Base 1982-1984 = 100
Transportation
[Continued]

For 1947-1993. Columns headed % show percentile change in the index from the previous period for which an index is available.

Year	Jan Index	%	Feb Index	%	Mar Index	%	Apr Index	%	May Index	%	Jun Index	%	Jul Index	%	Aug Index	%	Sep Index	%	Oct Index	%	Nov Index	%	Dec Index	%
1992	-	-	-	-	-	-	-	-	-	-	131.7	1.2	-	-	-	-	-	-	-	-	-	-	136.4	3.6
1993	-	-	-	-	-	-	-	-	-	-	135.5	-0.7	-	-	-	-	-	-	-	-	-	-	-	-

Source: U.S. Department of Labor, Bureau of Labor Statistics, Division of Consumer Prices and Price Indexes. - indicates no data collected for period.

|

Portland, OR-WA
Consumer Price Index - Urban Wage Earners
Base 1982-1984 = 100
Transportation

For 1947-1993. Columns headed % show percentile change in the index from the previous period for which an index is available.

Year	Jan Index	%	Feb Index	%	Mar Index	%	Apr Index	%	May Index	%	Jun Index	%	Jul Index	%	Aug Index	%	Sep Index	%	Oct Index	%	Nov Index	%	Dec Index	%
1947	-	-	-	-	19.5	-	-	-	-	-	19.6	0.5	19.6	0.0	-	-	-	-	20.0	2.0	-	-	-	-
1948	20.9	4.5	-	-	-	-	21.0	0.5	-	-	-	-	22.2	5.7	-	-	-	-	22.6	1.8	-	-	-	-
1949	22.9	1.3	-	-	-	-	23.2	1.3	-	-	-	-	23.9	3.0	-	-	-	-	24.0	0.4	-	-	-	-
1950	24.1	0.4	-	-	-	-	23.7	-1.7	-	-	-	-	23.8	0.4	-	-	-	-	24.2	1.7	-	-	-	-
1951	24.4	0.8	-	-	-	-	24.8	1.6	-	-	-	-	25.0	0.8	-	-	-	-	25.5	2.0	-	-	-	-
1952	26.0	2.0	-	-	-	-	26.6	2.3	-	-	-	-	26.7	0.4	-	-	-	-	27.3	2.2	-	-	-	-
1953	27.4	0.4	-	-	-	-	27.7	1.1	-	-	-	-	27.5	-0.7	-	-	-	-	27.5	0.0	-	-	-	-
1954	27.3	-0.7	-	-	-	-	27.1	-0.7	-	-	-	-	26.6	-1.8	-	-	-	-	26.4	-0.8	-	-	-	-
1955	26.9	1.9	-	-	-	-	26.7	-0.7	-	-	-	-	26.6	-0.4	-	-	-	-	27.3	2.6	-	-	-	-
1956	27.1	-0.7	-	-	-	-	26.0	-4.1	-	-	-	-	26.7	2.7	-	-	-	-	27.6	3.4	-	-	-	-
1957	27.6	0.0	-	-	-	-	28.1	1.8	-	-	-	-	28.5	1.4	-	-	-	-	28.1	-1.4	-	-	-	-
1958	29.0	3.2	-	-	-	-	29.7	2.4	-	-	-	-	30.0	1.0	-	-	-	-	30.3	1.0	-	-	-	-
1959	29.6	-2.3	-	-	-	-	31.3	5.7	-	-	-	-	30.6	-2.2	-	-	-	-	31.8	3.9	-	-	-	-
1960	31.5	-0.9	-	-	-	-	31.1	-1.3	-	-	-	-	30.6	-1.6	-	-	-	-	30.0	-2.0	-	-	-	-
1961	31.1	3.7	-	-	-	-	29.2	-6.1	-	-	-	-	31.4	7.5	-	-	-	-	31.7	1.0	-	-	-	-
1962	31.4	-0.9	-	-	-	-	30.7	-2.2	-	-	-	-	31.4	2.3	-	-	-	-	31.1	-1.0	-	-	-	-
1963	31.0	-0.3	-	-	-	-	31.6	1.9	-	-	-	-	31.4	-0.6	-	-	-	-	31.6	0.6	-	-	-	-
1964	32.0	1.3	-	-	-	-	32.1	0.3	-	-	-	-	32.2	0.3	-	-	-	-	31.5	-2.2	-	-	-	-
1965	32.4	2.9	-	-	-	-	32.4	0.0	-	-	-	-	32.7	0.9	-	-	-	-	32.2	-1.5	-	-	-	-
1966	32.1	-0.3	-	-	-	-	32.6	1.6	-	-	-	-	32.7	0.3	-	-	-	-	33.2	1.5	-	-	-	-
1967	33.1	-0.3	-	-	-	-	33.8	2.1	-	-	-	-	34.3	1.5	-	-	-	-	34.6	0.9	-	-	-	-
1968	34.7	0.3	-	-	-	-	34.7	0.0	-	-	-	-	35.0	0.9	-	-	-	-	35.0	0.0	-	-	-	-
1969	35.6	1.7	-	-	-	-	36.1	1.4	-	-	-	-	35.8	-0.8	-	-	-	-	36.3	1.4	-	-	-	-
1970	36.7	1.1	-	-	-	-	36.8	0.3	-	-	-	-	37.1	0.8	-	-	-	-	37.1	0.0	-	-	-	-
1971	38.1	2.7	-	-	-	-	36.9	-3.1	-	-	-	-	37.2	0.8	-	-	-	-	37.3	0.3	-	-	-	-
1972	37.5	0.5	-	-	-	-	37.1	-1.1	-	-	-	-	37.4	0.8	-	-	-	-	38.1	1.9	-	-	-	-
1973	37.9	-0.5	-	-	-	-	38.2	0.8	-	-	-	-	38.7	1.3	-	-	-	-	38.7	0.0	-	-	-	-
1974	39.8	2.8	-	-	-	-	41.1	3.3	-	-	-	-	43.2	5.1	-	-	-	-	43.6	0.9	-	-	-	-
1975	45.0	3.2	-	-	-	-	45.2	0.4	-	-	-	-	47.6	5.3	-	-	-	-	48.0	0.8	-	-	-	-
1976	49.0	2.1	-	-	-	-	49.4	0.8	-	-	-	-	52.2	5.7	-	-	-	-	52.9	1.3	-	-	-	-
1977	53.6	1.3	-	-	-	-	56.4	5.2	-	-	-	-	56.6	0.4	-	-	-	-	56.6	0.0	-	-	-	-
1978	58.2	2.8	-	-	58.0	-0.3	-	-	60.7	4.7	-	-	62.3	2.6	-	-	63.3	1.6	-	-	63.8	0.8	-	-
1979	64.2	0.6	-	-	66.8	4.0	-	-	69.8	4.5	-	-	72.8	4.3	-	-	73.5	1.0	-	-	74.2	1.0	-	-
1980	76.3	2.8	-	-	78.5	2.9	-	-	79.8	1.7	-	-	80.8	1.3	-	-	82.1	1.6	-	-	83.9	2.2	-	-
1981	85.8	2.3	-	-	88.5	3.1	-	-	90.3	2.0	-	-	92.1	2.0	-	-	93.6	1.6	-	-	95.2	1.7	-	-
1982	96.8	1.7	-	-	95.1	-1.8	-	-	95.2	0.1	-	-	98.5	3.5	-	-	98.5	0.0	-	-	98.1	-0.4	-	-
1983	96.7	-1.4	-	-	94.0	-2.8	-	-	96.7	2.9	-	-	99.9	3.3	-	-	100.9	1.0	-	-	101.7	0.8	-	-
1984	101.4	-0.3	-	-	101.5	0.1	-	-	105.5	3.9	-	-	105.3	-0.2	-	-	105.1	-0.2	-	-	106.5	1.3	-	-
1985	107.4	0.8	-	-	107.0	-0.4	-	-	108.2	1.1	-	-	108.9	0.6	-	-	109.9	0.9	-	-	111.3	1.3	-	-
1986	112.7	1.3	-	-	107.6	-4.5	-	-	106.1	-1.4	-	-	108.0	1.8	-	-	106.8	-1.1	-	-	105.2	-1.5	-	-
1987	-	-	-	-	-	-	-	-	-	-	108.3	2.9	-	-	-	-	-	-	-	-	-	-	110.2	1.8
1988	-	-	-	-	-	-	-	-	-	-	109.9	-0.3	-	-	-	-	-	-	-	-	-	-	111.5	1.5
1989	-	-	-	-	-	-	-	-	-	-	117.4	5.3	-	-	-	-	-	-	-	-	-	-	118.3	0.8
1990	-	-	-	-	-	-	-	-	-	-	119.3	0.8	-	-	-	-	-	-	-	-	-	-	129.1	8.2
1991	-	-	-	-	-	-	-	-	-	-	128.9	-0.2	-	-	-	-	-	-	-	-	-	-	129.3	0.3

[Continued]

Portland, OR-WA
Consumer Price Index - Urban Wage Earners
Base 1982-1984 = 100
Transportation

[Continued]

For 1947-1993. Columns headed % show percentile change in the index from the previous period for which an index is available.

Year	Jan		Feb		Mar		Apr		May		Jun		Jul		Aug		Sep		Oct		Nov		Dec	
	Index	%	Index	%	Index	%	Index	%	Index	%	Index	%	Index	%	Index	%	Index	%	Index	%	Index	%	Index	%
1992	-	-	-	-	-	-	-	-	-	-	130.8	1.2	-	-	-	-	-	-	-	-	-	-	135.4	3.5
1993	-	-	-	-	-	-	-	-	-	-	135.1	-0.2	-	-	-	-	-	-	-	-	-	-		

Source: U.S. Department of Labor, Bureau of Labor Statistics, Division of Consumer Prices and Price Indexes. - indicates no data collected for period.

Portland, OR-WA
Consumer Price Index - All Urban Consumers
Base 1982-1984 = 100
Medical Care

For 1947-1993. Columns headed % show percentile change in the index from the previous period for which an index is available.

Year	Jan Index	%	Feb Index	%	Mar Index	%	Apr Index	%	May Index	%	Jun Index	%	Jul Index	%	Aug Index	%	Sep Index	%	Oct Index	%	Nov Index	%	Dec Index	%
1947	-	-	-	-	14.1	-	-	-	-	-	14.1	0.0	14.1	0.0	-	-	-	-	14.5	2.8	-	-	-	-
1948	14.6	0.7	-	-	-	-	14.6	0.0	-	-	-	-	14.8	1.4	-	-	-	-	14.8	0.0	-	-	-	-
1949	14.9	0.7	-	-	-	-	15.0	0.7	-	-	-	-	15.0	0.0	-	-	-	-	15.1	0.7	-	-	-	-
1950	15.1	0.0	-	-	-	-	15.1	0.0	-	-	-	-	15.6	3.3	-	-	-	-	15.8	1.3	-	-	-	-
1951	15.8	0.0	-	-	-	-	16.2	2.5	-	-	-	-	16.2	0.0	-	-	-	-	16.7	3.1	-	-	-	-
1952	16.8	0.6	-	-	-	-	17.0	1.2	-	-	-	-	17.2	1.2	-	-	-	-	17.2	0.0	-	-	-	-
1953	17.2	0.0	-	-	-	-	17.3	0.6	-	-	-	-	17.5	1.2	-	-	-	-	17.7	1.1	-	-	-	-
1954	17.7	0.0	-	-	-	-	17.8	0.6	-	-	-	-	17.9	0.6	-	-	-	-	18.0	0.6	-	-	-	-
1955	18.4	2.2	-	-	-	-	18.5	0.5	-	-	-	-	18.4	-0.5	-	-	-	-	18.9	2.7	-	-	-	-
1956	18.9	0.0	-	-	-	-	19.0	0.5	-	-	-	-	19.2	1.1	-	-	-	-	19.5	1.6	-	-	-	-
1957	20.0	2.6	-	-	-	-	20.2	1.0	-	-	-	-	20.3	0.5	-	-	-	-	20.4	0.5	-	-	-	-
1958	20.5	0.5	-	-	-	-	20.6	0.5	-	-	-	-	20.6	0.0	-	-	-	-	20.7	0.5	-	-	-	-
1959	20.7	0.0	-	-	-	-	20.7	0.0	-	-	-	-	20.8	0.5	-	-	-	-	20.8	0.0	-	-	-	-
1960	20.8	0.0	-	-	-	-	21.8	4.8	-	-	-	-	21.9	0.5	-	-	-	-	22.2	1.4	-	-	-	-
1961	22.2	0.0	-	-	-	-	22.4	0.9	-	-	-	-	22.6	0.9	-	-	-	-	22.5	-0.4	-	-	-	-
1962	22.3	-0.9	-	-	-	-	22.4	0.4	-	-	-	-	22.5	0.4	-	-	-	-	22.6	0.4	-	-	-	-
1963	22.8	0.9	-	-	-	-	22.8	0.0	-	-	-	-	23.0	0.9	-	-	-	-	23.4	1.7	-	-	-	-
1964	23.4	0.0	-	-	-	-	24.1	3.0	-	-	-	-	24.7	2.5	-	-	-	-	24.8	0.4	-	-	-	-
1965	24.9	0.4	-	-	-	-	25.0	0.4	-	-	-	-	25.3	1.2	-	-	-	-	25.3	0.0	-	-	-	-
1966	25.6	1.2	-	-	-	-	25.7	0.4	-	-	-	-	25.9	0.8	-	-	-	-	26.4	1.9	-	-	-	-
1967	27.1	2.7	-	-	-	-	27.2	0.4	-	-	-	-	27.7	1.8	-	-	-	-	28.2	1.8	-	-	-	-
1968	28.8	2.1	-	-	-	-	28.8	0.0	-	-	-	-	29.0	0.7	-	-	-	-	29.6	2.1	-	-	-	-
1969	30.0	1.4	-	-	-	-	30.5	1.7	-	-	-	-	31.0	1.6	-	-	-	-	31.2	0.6	-	-	-	-
1970	32.1	2.9	-	-	-	-	32.6	1.6	-	-	-	-	33.1	1.5	-	-	-	-	33.2	0.3	-	-	-	-
1971	34.1	2.7	-	-	-	-	34.2	0.3	-	-	-	-	34.2	0.0	-	-	-	-	34.1	-0.3	-	-	-	-
1972	34.6	1.5	-	-	-	-	34.9	0.9	-	-	-	-	35.3	1.1	-	-	-	-	36.0	2.0	-	-	-	-
1973	36.3	0.8	-	-	-	-	37.3	2.8	-	-	-	-	37.3	0.0	-	-	-	-	38.6	3.5	-	-	-	-
1974	39.3	1.8	-	-	-	-	40.1	2.0	-	-	-	-	42.1	5.0	-	-	-	-	42.6	1.2	-	-	-	-
1975	44.1	3.5	-	-	-	-	45.0	2.0	-	-	-	-	46.6	3.6	-	-	-	-	46.9	0.6	-	-	-	-
1976	48.7	3.8	-	-	-	-	49.0	0.6	-	-	-	-	50.3	2.7	-	-	-	-	50.9	1.2	-	-	-	-
1977	53.3	4.7	-	-	-	-	54.4	2.1	-	-	-	-	55.7	2.4	-	-	-	-	56.1	0.7	-	-	-	-
1978	57.6	2.7	-	-	59.2	2.8	-	-	59.7	0.8	-	-	60.6	1.5	-	-	61.0	0.7	-	-	61.8	1.3	-	-
1979	63.5	2.8	-	-	64.0	0.8	-	-	64.5	0.8	-	-	65.6	1.7	-	-	67.2	2.4	-	-	68.8	2.4	-	-
1980	70.6	2.6	-	-	73.0	3.4	-	-	73.7	1.0	-	-	74.0	0.4	-	-	76.1	2.8	-	-	76.6	0.7	-	-
1981	78.6	2.6	-	-	79.3	0.9	-	-	81.2	2.4	-	-	84.5	4.1	-	-	85.3	0.9	-	-	88.0	3.2	-	-
1982	89.4	1.6	-	-	91.0	1.8	-	-	92.3	1.4	-	-	94.3	2.2	-	-	95.4	1.2	-	-	96.7	1.4	-	-
1983	99.0	2.4	-	-	99.8	0.8	-	-	100.3	0.5	-	-	100.7	0.4	-	-	100.4	-0.3	-	-	102.1	1.7	-	-
1984	104.7	2.5	-	-	105.0	0.3	-	-	104.8	-0.2	-	-	105.9	1.0	-	-	106.4	0.5	-	-	107.1	0.7	-	-
1985	108.7	1.5	-	-	109.0	0.3	-	-	109.6	0.6	-	-	112.0	2.2	-	-	112.3	0.3	-	-	114.0	1.5	-	-
1986	116.0	1.8	-	-	116.9	0.8	-	-	119.4	2.1	-	-	120.1	0.6	-	-	119.7	-0.3	-	-	121.1	1.2	-	-
1987	-	-	-	-	-	-	-	-	-	-	123.7	2.1	-	-	-	-	-	-	-	-	-	-	129.8	4.9
1988	-	-	-	-	-	-	-	-	-	-	136.2	4.9	-	-	-	-	-	-	-	-	-	-	141.3	3.7
1989	-	-	-	-	-	-	-	-	-	-	143.9	1.8	-	-	-	-	-	-	-	-	-	-	146.5	1.8
1990	-	-	-	-	-	-	-	-	-	-	152.0	3.8	-	-	-	-	-	-	-	-	-	-	156.7	3.1
1991	-	-	-	-	-	-	-	-	-	-	163.5	4.3	-	-	-	-	-	-	-	-	-	-	168.4	3.0

[Continued]

Portland, OR-WA
Consumer Price Index - All Urban Consumers
Base 1982-1984 = 100
Medical Care

[Continued]

For 1947-1993. Columns headed % show percentile change in the index from the previous period for which an index is available.

Year	Jan		Feb		Mar		Apr		May		Jun		Jul		Aug		Sep		Oct		Nov		Dec	
	Index	%	Index	%	Index	%	Index	%	Index	%	Index	%	Index	%	Index	%	Index	%	Index	%	Index	%	Index	%
1992	-	-	-	-	-	-	-	-	-	-	174.5	3.6	-	-	-	-	-	-	-	-	-	-	178.2	2.1
1993	-	-	-	-	-	-	-	-	-	-	184.8	3.7	-	-	-	-	-	-	-	-	-	-	-	-

Source: U.S. Department of Labor, Bureau of Labor Statistics, Division of Consumer Prices and Price Indexes. - indicates no data collected for period.

Portland, OR-WA
Consumer Price Index - Urban Wage Earners
Base 1982-1984 = 100
Medical Care

For 1947-1993. Columns headed % show percentile change in the index from the previous period for which an index is available.

Year	Jan Index	%	Feb Index	%	Mar Index	%	Apr Index	%	May Index	%	Jun Index	%	Jul Index	%	Aug Index	%	Sep Index	%	Oct Index	%	Nov Index	%	Dec Index	%
1947	-	-	-	-	15.7	-	-	-	-	-	15.7	0.0	15.7	0.0	-	-	-	-	16.2	3.2	-	-	-	-
1948	16.2	0.0	-	-	-	-	16.3	0.6	-	-	-	-	16.5	1.2	-	-	-	-	16.5	0.0	-	-	-	-
1949	16.6	0.6	-	-	-	-	16.7	0.6	-	-	-	-	16.7	0.0	-	-	-	-	16.8	0.6	-	-	-	-
1950	16.8	0.0	-	-	-	-	16.8	0.0	-	-	-	-	17.3	3.0	-	-	-	-	17.6	1.7	-	-	-	-
1951	17.6	0.0	-	-	-	-	18.1	2.8	-	-	-	-	18.1	0.0	-	-	-	-	18.6	2.8	-	-	-	-
1952	18.7	0.5	-	-	-	-	18.9	1.1	-	-	-	-	19.1	1.1	-	-	-	-	19.1	0.0	-	-	-	-
1953	19.2	0.5	-	-	-	-	19.2	0.0	-	-	-	-	19.5	1.6	-	-	-	-	19.7	1.0	-	-	-	-
1954	19.7	0.0	-	-	-	-	19.8	0.5	-	-	-	-	19.9	0.5	-	-	-	-	20.0	0.5	-	-	-	-
1955	20.4	2.0	-	-	-	-	20.6	1.0	-	-	-	-	20.5	-0.5	-	-	-	-	21.0	2.4	-	-	-	-
1956	21.0	0.0	-	-	-	-	21.2	1.0	-	-	-	-	21.4	0.9	-	-	-	-	21.7	1.4	-	-	-	-
1957	22.3	2.8	-	-	-	-	22.5	0.9	-	-	-	-	22.7	0.9	-	-	-	-	22.7	0.0	-	-	-	-
1958	22.8	0.4	-	-	-	-	22.9	0.4	-	-	-	-	22.9	0.0	-	-	-	-	23.0	0.4	-	-	-	-
1959	23.0	0.0	-	-	-	-	23.0	0.0	-	-	-	-	23.2	0.9	-	-	-	-	23.2	0.0	-	-	-	-
1960	23.2	0.0	-	-	-	-	24.3	4.7	-	-	-	-	24.4	0.4	-	-	-	-	24.7	1.2	-	-	-	-
1961	24.7	0.0	-	-	-	-	25.0	1.2	-	-	-	-	25.2	0.8	-	-	-	-	25.1	-0.4	-	-	-	-
1962	24.8	-1.2	-	-	-	-	24.9	0.4	-	-	-	-	25.1	0.8	-	-	-	-	25.2	0.4	-	-	-	-
1963	25.4	0.8	-	-	-	-	25.4	0.0	-	-	-	-	25.6	0.8	-	-	-	-	26.0	1.6	-	-	-	-
1964	26.1	0.4	-	-	-	-	26.8	2.7	-	-	-	-	27.5	2.6	-	-	-	-	27.6	0.4	-	-	-	-
1965	27.7	0.4	-	-	-	-	27.8	0.4	-	-	-	-	28.2	1.4	-	-	-	-	28.2	0.0	-	-	-	-
1966	28.5	1.1	-	-	-	-	28.6	0.4	-	-	-	-	28.8	0.7	-	-	-	-	29.4	2.1	-	-	-	-
1967	30.2	2.7	-	-	-	-	30.3	0.3	-	-	-	-	30.9	2.0	-	-	-	-	31.4	1.6	-	-	-	-
1968	32.1	2.2	-	-	-	-	32.1	0.0	-	-	-	-	32.3	0.6	-	-	-	-	33.0	2.2	-	-	-	-
1969	33.4	1.2	-	-	-	-	34.0	1.8	-	-	-	-	34.5	1.5	-	-	-	-	34.8	0.9	-	-	-	-
1970	35.7	2.6	-	-	-	-	36.3	1.7	-	-	-	-	36.9	1.7	-	-	-	-	36.9	0.0	-	-	-	-
1971	37.9	2.7	-	-	-	-	38.1	0.5	-	-	-	-	38.1	0.0	-	-	-	-	37.9	-0.5	-	-	-	-
1972	38.6	1.8	-	-	-	-	38.8	0.5	-	-	-	-	39.4	1.5	-	-	-	-	40.0	1.5	-	-	-	-
1973	40.4	1.0	-	-	-	-	41.5	2.7	-	-	-	-	41.5	0.0	-	-	-	-	42.9	3.4	-	-	-	-
1974	43.8	2.1	-	-	-	-	44.6	1.8	-	-	-	-	46.8	4.9	-	-	-	-	47.4	1.3	-	-	-	-
1975	49.1	3.6	-	-	-	-	50.1	2.0	-	-	-	-	51.9	3.6	-	-	-	-	52.2	0.6	-	-	-	-
1976	54.2	3.8	-	-	-	-	54.5	0.6	-	-	-	-	56.0	2.8	-	-	-	-	56.6	1.1	-	-	-	-
1977	59.4	4.9	-	-	-	-	60.5	1.9	-	-	-	-	62.0	2.5	-	-	-	-	62.4	0.6	-	-	-	-
1978	64.1	2.7	-	-	65.1	1.6	-	-	65.3	0.3	-	-	66.2	1.4	-	-	66.9	1.1	-	-	68.0	1.6	-	-
1979	68.8	1.2	-	-	70.2	2.0	-	-	71.4	1.7	-	-	72.6	1.7	-	-	72.7	0.1	-	-	73.8	1.5	-	-
1980	74.8	1.4	-	-	76.0	1.6	-	-	77.7	2.2	-	-	78.2	0.6	-	-	78.7	0.6	-	-	79.2	0.6	-	-
1981	79.7	0.6	-	-	80.5	1.0	-	-	82.4	2.4	-	-	85.3	3.5	-	-	84.8	-0.6	-	-	87.9	3.7	-	-
1982	89.5	1.8	-	-	91.0	1.7	-	-	92.4	1.5	-	-	94.6	2.4	-	-	95.7	1.2	-	-	97.0	1.4	-	-
1983	99.5	2.6	-	-	100.2	0.7	-	-	100.7	0.5	-	-	100.9	0.2	-	-	100.6	-0.3	-	-	102.0	1.4	-	-
1984	104.4	2.4	-	-	104.6	0.2	-	-	104.3	-0.3	-	-	105.4	1.1	-	-	106.1	0.7	-	-	106.6	0.5	-	-
1985	108.3	1.6	-	-	108.7	0.4	-	-	109.2	0.5	-	-	111.9	2.5	-	-	112.4	0.4	-	-	114.1	1.5	-	-
1986	115.8	1.5	-	-	116.8	0.9	-	-	119.0	1.9	-	-	119.6	0.5	-	-	119.0	-0.5	-	-	120.6	1.3	-	-
1987	-	-	-	-	-	-	-	-	-	-	123.3	2.2	-	-	-	-	-	-	-	-	-	-	129.5	5.0
1988	-	-	-	-	-	-	-	-	-	-	135.7	4.8	-	-	-	-	-	-	-	-	-	-	140.9	3.8
1989	-	-	-	-	-	-	-	-	-	-	143.6	1.9	-	-	-	-	-	-	-	-	-	-	145.9	1.6
1990	-	-	-	-	-	-	-	-	-	-	151.0	3.5	-	-	-	-	-	-	-	-	-	-	155.3	2.8
1991	-	-	-	-	-	-	-	-	-	-	161.8	4.2	-	-	-	-	-	-	-	-	-	-	166.8	3.1

[Continued]

Portland, OR-WA
Consumer Price Index - Urban Wage Earners
Base 1982-1984 = 100
Medical Care
[Continued]

For 1947-1993. Columns headed % show percentile change in the index from the previous period for which an index is available.

Year	Jan		Feb		Mar		Apr		May		Jun		Jul		Aug		Sep		Oct		Nov		Dec	
	Index	%	Index	%	Index	%	Index	%	Index	%	Index	%	Index	%	Index	%	Index	%	Index	%	Index	%	Index	%
1992	-	-	-	-	-	-	-	-	-	-	173.0	3.7	-	-	-	-	-	-	-	-	-	-	176.8	2.2
1993	-	-	-	-	-	-	-	-	-	-	183.1	3.6	-	-	-	-	-	-	-	-	-	-	-	-

Source: U.S. Department of Labor, Bureau of Labor Statistics, Division of Consumer Prices and Price Indexes. - indicates no data collected for period.

Portland, OR-WA

Consumer Price Index - All Urban Consumers
Base 1982-1984 = 100

Entertainment

For 1976-1993. Columns headed % show percentile change in the index from the previous period for which an index is available.

Year	Jan Index	%	Feb Index	%	Mar Index	%	Apr Index	%	May Index	%	Jun Index	%	Jul Index	%	Aug Index	%	Sep Index	%	Oct Index	%	Nov Index	%	Dec Index	%
1976	68.4	-	-	-	-	-	68.4	0.0	-	-	-	-	68.3	-0.1	-	-	-	-	69.4	1.6	-	-	-	-
1977	70.8	2.0	-	-	-	-	71.2	0.6	-	-	-	-	70.4	-1.1	-	-	-	-	72.3	2.7	-	-	-	-
1978	72.9	0.8	-	-	74.5	2.2	-	-	75.7	1.6	-	-	76.8	1.5	-	-	76.9	0.1	-	-	77.1	0.3	-	-
1979	78.2	1.4	-	-	80.6	3.1	-	-	81.6	1.2	-	-	81.0	-0.7	-	-	80.7	-0.4	-	-	80.7	0.0	-	-
1980	83.7	3.7	-	-	87.6	4.7	-	-	87.9	0.3	-	-	87.0	-1.0	-	-	87.5	0.6	-	-	86.3	-1.4	-	-
1981	91.2	5.7	-	-	92.3	1.2	-	-	90.1	-2.4	-	-	88.9	-1.3	-	-	89.5	0.7	-	-	90.2	0.8	-	-
1982	92.9	3.0	-	-	93.6	0.8	-	-	96.4	3.0	-	-	96.6	0.2	-	-	94.7	-2.0	-	-	93.5	-1.3	-	-
1983	98.1	4.9	-	-	100.2	2.1	-	-	102.5	2.3	-	-	102.1	-0.4	-	-	102.8	0.7	-	-	101.6	-1.2	-	-
1984	102.3	0.7	-	-	103.0	0.7	-	-	104.0	1.0	-	-	103.3	-0.7	-	-	103.1	-0.2	-	-	105.9	2.7	-	-
1985	107.7	1.7	-	-	109.2	1.4	-	-	108.5	-0.6	-	-	111.3	2.6	-	-	110.8	-0.4	-	-	109.7	-1.0	-	-
1986	109.0	-0.6	-	-	107.1	-1.7	-	-	110.7	3.4	-	-	112.4	1.5	-	-	112.2	-0.2	-	-	114.3	1.9	-	-
1987	-	-	-	-	-	-	-	-	-	-	115.5	1.0	-	-	-	-	-	-	-	-	-	-	117.7	1.9
1988	-	-	-	-	-	-	-	-	-	-	119.4	1.4	-	-	-	-	-	-	-	-	-	-	122.5	2.6
1989	-	-	-	-	-	-	-	-	-	-	122.8	0.2	-	-	-	-	-	-	-	-	-	-	126.1	2.7
1990	-	-	-	-	-	-	-	-	-	-	127.5	1.1	-	-	-	-	-	-	-	-	-	-	129.8	1.8
1991	-	-	-	-	-	-	-	-	-	-	131.5	1.3	-	-	-	-	-	-	-	-	-	-	133.6	1.6
1992	-	-	-	-	-	-	-	-	-	-	138.5	3.7	-	-	-	-	-	-	-	-	-	-	141.4	2.1
1993	-	-	-	-	-	-	-	-	-	-	146.6	3.7	-	-	-	-	-	-	-	-	-	-	-	-

Source: U.S. Department of Labor, Bureau of Labor Statistics, Division of Consumer Prices and Price Indexes. - indicates no data collected for period.

Portland, OR-WA
Consumer Price Index - Urban Wage Earners
Base 1982-1984 = 100
Entertainment

For 1976-1993. Columns headed % show percentile change in the index from the previous period for which an index is available.

Year	Jan Index	%	Feb Index	%	Mar Index	%	Apr Index	%	May Index	%	Jun Index	%	Jul Index	%	Aug Index	%	Sep Index	%	Oct Index	%	Nov Index	%	Dec Index	%
1976	75.2	-	-	-	-	-	75.3	0.1	-	-	-	-	75.2	-0.1	-	-	-	-	76.3	1.5	-	-	-	-
1977	77.9	2.1	-	-	-	-	78.4	0.6	-	-	-	-	77.4	-1.3	-	-	-	-	79.5	2.7	-	-	-	-
1978	80.2	0.9	-	-	81.1	1.1	-	-	81.1	0.0	-	-	83.0	2.3	-	-	83.9	1.1	-	-	84.6	0.8	-	-
1979	84.9	0.4	-	-	85.4	0.6	-	-	88.2	3.3	-	-	86.7	-1.7	-	-	87.4	0.8	-	-	87.6	0.2	-	-
1980	88.2	0.7	-	-	94.8	7.5	-	-	96.1	1.4	-	-	96.2	0.1	-	-	96.2	0.0	-	-	94.8	-1.5	-	-
1981	93.5	-1.4	-	-	94.2	0.7	-	-	90.1	-4.4	-	-	90.5	0.4	-	-	92.0	1.7	-	-	90.8	-1.3	-	-
1982	93.4	2.9	-	-	94.1	0.7	-	-	97.6	3.7	-	-	97.4	-0.2	-	-	95.1	-2.4	-	-	92.4	-2.8	-	-
1983	97.2	5.2	-	-	99.7	2.6	-	-	102.2	2.5	-	-	102.1	-0.1	-	-	103.0	0.9	-	-	101.4	-1.6	-	-
1984	102.8	1.4	-	-	102.9	0.1	-	-	104.1	1.2	-	-	103.2	-0.9	-	-	103.0	-0.2	-	-	105.2	2.1	-	-
1985	107.0	1.7	-	-	108.4	1.3	-	-	107.8	-0.6	-	-	111.6	3.5	-	-	110.9	-0.6	-	-	109.4	-1.4	-	-
1986	108.7	-0.6	-	-	106.5	-2.0	-	-	109.6	2.9	-	-	111.6	1.8	-	-	111.2	-0.4	-	-	113.3	1.9	-	-
1987	-	-	-	-	-	-	-	-	-	-	114.5	1.1	-	-	-	-	-	-	-	-	-	-	116.6	1.8
1988	-	-	-	-	-	-	-	-	-	-	118.2	1.4	-	-	-	-	-	-	-	-	-	-	121.1	2.5
1989	-	-	-	-	-	-	-	-	-	-	121.2	0.1	-	-	-	-	-	-	-	-	-	-	124.8	3.0
1990	-	-	-	-	-	-	-	-	-	-	126.1	1.0	-	-	-	-	-	-	-	-	-	-	128.0	1.5
1991	-	-	-	-	-	-	-	-	-	-	129.8	1.4	-	-	-	-	-	-	-	-	-	-	132.4	2.0
1992	-	-	-	-	-	-	-	-	-	-	137.7	4.0	-	-	-	-	-	-	-	-	-	-	140.7	2.2
1993	-	-	-	-	-	-	-	-	-	-	146.8	4.3	-	-	-	-	-	-	-	-	-	-	-	-

Source: U.S. Department of Labor, Bureau of Labor Statistics, Division of Consumer Prices and Price Indexes. - indicates no data collected for period.

Portland, OR-WA
Consumer Price Index - All Urban Consumers
Base 1982-1984 = 100
Other Goods and Services

For 1976-1993. Columns headed % show percentile change in the index from the previous period for which an index is available.

Year	Jan Index	%	Feb Index	%	Mar Index	%	Apr Index	%	May Index	%	Jun Index	%	Jul Index	%	Aug Index	%	Sep Index	%	Oct Index	%	Nov Index	%	Dec Index	%
1976	50.4	-	-	-	-	-	51.2	1.6	-	-	-	-	52.7	2.9	-	-	-	-	53.1	0.8	-	-	-	-
1977	54.8	3.2	-	-	-	-	55.3	0.9	-	-	-	-	56.2	1.6	-	-	-	-	57.6	2.5	-	-	-	-
1978	58.3	1.2	-	-	58.5	0.3	-	-	59.3	1.4	-	-	60.2	1.5	-	-	62.1	3.2	-	-	62.2	0.2	-	-
1979	63.5	2.1	-	-	64.3	1.3	-	-	64.4	0.2	-	-	64.0	-0.6	-	-	67.0	4.7	-	-	68.1	1.6	-	-
1980	71.0	4.3	-	-	71.3	0.4	-	-	72.7	2.0	-	-	73.4	1.0	-	-	75.4	2.7	-	-	76.1	0.9	-	-
1981	78.5	3.2	-	-	79.7	1.5	-	-	80.5	1.0	-	-	81.5	1.2	-	-	84.2	3.3	-	-	85.9	2.0	-	-
1982	88.6	3.1	-	-	89.8	1.4	-	-	90.8	1.1	-	-	92.5	1.9	-	-	95.0	2.7	-	-	95.8	0.8	-	-
1983	99.3	3.7	-	-	99.0	-0.3	-	-	100.3	1.3	-	-	101.4	1.1	-	-	103.0	1.6	-	-	105.0	1.9	-	-
1984	103.8	-1.1	-	-	105.5	1.6	-	-	105.2	-0.3	-	-	105.7	0.5	-	-	107.4	1.6	-	-	106.9	-0.5	-	-
1985	108.5	1.5	-	-	109.1	0.6	-	-	108.5	-0.5	-	-	110.0	1.4	-	-	113.9	3.5	-	-	116.9	2.6	-	-
1986	118.8	1.6	-	-	119.0	0.2	-	-	120.7	1.4	-	-	121.1	0.3	-	-	121.9	0.7	-	-	122.4	0.4	-	-
1987	-	-	-	-	-	-	-	-	-	-	127.3	4.0	-	-	-	-	-	-	-	-	-	-	130.1	2.2
1988	-	-	-	-	-	-	-	-	-	-	134.7	3.5	-	-	-	-	-	-	-	-	-	-	137.3	1.9
1989	-	-	-	-	-	-	-	-	-	-	141.6	3.1	-	-	-	-	-	-	-	-	-	-	148.5	4.9
1990	-	-	-	-	-	-	-	-	-	-	155.0	4.4	-	-	-	-	-	-	-	-	-	-	160.8	3.7
1991	-	-	-	-	-	-	-	-	-	-	169.0	5.1	-	-	-	-	-	-	-	-	-	-	175.4	3.8
1992	-	-	-	-	-	-	-	-	-	-	179.8	2.5	-	-	-	-	-	-	-	-	-	-	187.5	4.3
1993	-	-	-	-	-	-	-	-	-	-	201.1	7.3	-	-	-	-	-	-	-	-	-	-	-	-

Source: U.S. Department of Labor, Bureau of Labor Statistics, Division of Consumer Prices and Price Indexes. - indicates no data collected for period.

Portland, OR-WA
Consumer Price Index - Urban Wage Earners
Base 1982-1984 = 100
Other Goods and Services

For 1976-1993. Columns headed % show percentile change in the index from the previous period for which an index is available.

Year	Jan Index	%	Feb Index	%	Mar Index	%	Apr Index	%	May Index	%	Jun Index	%	Jul Index	%	Aug Index	%	Sep Index	%	Oct Index	%	Nov Index	%	Dec Index	%
1976	53.8	-	-	-	-	-	54.6	1.5	-	-	-	-	56.2	2.9	-	-	-	-	56.6	0.7	-	-	-	-
1977	58.5	3.4	-	-	-	-	58.9	0.7	-	-	-	-	60.0	1.9	-	-	-	-	61.4	2.3	-	-	-	-
1978	62.1	1.1	-	-	62.2	0.2	-	-	62.7	0.8	-	-	63.3	1.0	-	-	64.4	1.7	-	-	64.7	0.5	-	-
1979	65.6	1.4	-	-	66.6	1.5	-	-	66.5	-0.2	-	-	66.6	0.2	-	-	68.7	3.2	-	-	69.9	1.7	-	-
1980	72.2	3.3	-	-	72.3	0.1	-	-	72.9	0.8	-	-	73.9	1.4	-	-	75.4	2.0	-	-	76.1	0.9	-	-
1981	78.0	2.5	-	-	78.7	0.9	-	-	80.3	2.0	-	-	80.9	0.7	-	-	82.7	2.2	-	-	84.7	2.4	-	-
1982	87.7	3.5	-	-	89.2	1.7	-	-	90.2	1.1	-	-	92.1	2.1	-	-	94.8	2.9	-	-	95.9	1.2	-	-
1983	100.0	4.3	-	-	99.3	-0.7	-	-	100.9	1.6	-	-	102.3	1.4	-	-	103.5	1.2	-	-	105.5	1.9	-	-
1984	104.0	-1.4	-	-	105.3	1.3	-	-	105.2	-0.1	-	-	105.8	0.6	-	-	107.1	1.2	-	-	106.1	-0.9	-	-
1985	108.1	1.9	-	-	108.8	0.6	-	-	108.1	-0.6	-	-	110.0	1.8	-	-	113.0	2.7	-	-	116.8	3.4	-	-
1986	118.6	1.5	-	-	118.1	-0.4	-	-	119.9	1.5	-	-	120.4	0.4	-	-	120.9	0.4	-	-	121.1	0.2	-	-
1987	-	-	-	-	-	-	-	-	-	-	125.9	4.0	-	-	-	-	-	-	-	-	-	-	129.5	2.9
1988	-	-	-	-	-	-	-	-	-	-	134.2	3.6	-	-	-	-	-	-	-	-	-	-	137.2	2.2
1989	-	-	-	-	-	-	-	-	-	-	141.9	3.4	-	-	-	-	-	-	-	-	-	-	149.2	5.1
1990	-	-	-	-	-	-	-	-	-	-	155.5	4.2	-	-	-	-	-	-	-	-	-	-	161.3	3.7
1991	-	-	-	-	-	-	-	-	-	-	168.4	4.4	-	-	-	-	-	-	-	-	-	-	175.5	4.2
1992	-	-	-	-	-	-	-	-	-	-	179.6	2.3	-	-	-	-	-	-	-	-	-	-	186.4	3.8
1993	-	-	-	-	-	-	-	-	-	-	199.8	7.2	-	-	-	-	-	-	-	-	-	-	-	-

Source: U.S. Department of Labor, Bureau of Labor Statistics, Division of Consumer Prices and Price Indexes. - indicates no data collected for period.

San Diego, CA
Consumer Price Index - All Urban Consumers
Base 1982-1984 = 100
Annual Averages

For 1965-1993. Columns headed % show percentile change in the index from the previous period for which an index is available.

Year	All Items		Food & Beverage		Housing		Apparel & Upkeep		Trans- portation		Medical Care		Entertain- ment		Other Goods & Services	
	Index	%	Index	%	Index	%	Index	%	Index	%	Index	%	Index	%	Index	%
1965	28.2	-	-	-	-	-	48.1	-	32.1	-	26.6	-	-	-	-	-
1966	28.7	1.8	-	-	-	-	48.7	1.2	32.1	0.0	28.0	5.3	-	-	-	-
1967	29.6	3.1	-	-	-	-	49.5	1.6	33.3	3.7	30.0	7.1	-	-	-	-
1968	30.8	4.1	-	-	-	-	52.4	5.9	34.1	2.4	30.8	2.7	-	-	-	-
1969	32.4	5.2	-	-	-	-	54.7	4.4	34.9	2.3	32.4	5.2	-	-	-	-
1970	34.1	5.2	-	-	-	-	56.8	3.8	35.9	2.9	34.5	6.5	-	-	-	-
1971	35.4	3.8	-	-	-	-	58.3	2.6	37.9	5.6	36.3	5.2	-	-	-	-
1972	36.8	4.0	-	-	-	-	60.4	3.6	39.0	2.9	37.2	2.5	-	-	-	-
1973	39.2	6.5	-	-	-	-	62.7	3.8	40.7	4.4	39.0	4.8	-	-	-	-
1974	43.5	11.0	-	-	-	-	67.9	8.3	46.1	13.3	43.2	10.8	-	-	-	-
1975	47.6	9.4	-	-	-	-	69.5	2.4	51.0	10.6	48.5	12.3	-	-	-	-
1976	50.5	6.1	59.3	-	44.3	-	71.4	2.7	54.6	7.1	53.6	10.5	62.6	-	58.0	-
1977	53.8	6.5	62.9	6.1	47.9	8.1	72.8	2.0	58.1	6.4	58.6	9.3	65.1	4.0	61.1	5.3
1978	59.2	10.0	69.7	10.8	53.8	12.3	76.9	5.6	61.2	5.3	63.6	8.5	69.3	6.5	66.2	8.3
1979	68.9	16.4	77.3	10.9	65.2	21.2	81.5	6.0	69.9	14.2	69.5	9.3	75.0	8.2	71.3	7.7
1980	79.4	15.2	84.4	9.2	76.8	17.8	87.4	7.2	82.2	17.6	76.2	9.6	83.1	10.8	77.2	8.3
1981	90.1	13.5	90.5	7.2	89.6	16.7	92.2	5.5	91.4	11.2	83.0	8.9	89.9	8.2	85.1	10.2
1982	96.2	6.8	94.8	4.8	96.3	7.5	96.5	4.7	95.7	4.7	93.1	12.2	96.1	6.9	91.5	7.5
1983	99.0	2.9	100.4	5.9	98.6	2.4	99.7	3.3	98.8	3.2	100.7	8.2	100.8	4.9	100.2	9.5
1984	104.8	5.9	104.8	4.4	104.9	6.4	103.8	4.1	105.5	6.8	106.2	5.5	103.1	2.3	108.4	8.2
1985	110.4	5.3	107.2	2.3	113.7	8.4	105.9	2.0	109.4	3.7	110.1	3.7	107.4	4.2	115.7	6.7
1986	113.5	2.8	111.2	3.7	119.2	4.8	107.3	1.3	105.6	-3.5	118.2	7.4	111.9	4.2	120.0	3.7
1987	117.5	3.5	115.8	4.1	122.2	2.5	110.2	2.7	107.6	1.9	129.4	9.5	120.9	8.0	129.8	8.2
1988	123.4	5.0	119.7	3.4	126.9	3.8	119.0	8.0	114.2	6.1	141.9	9.7	130.2	7.7	140.4	8.2
1989	130.6	5.8	127.3	6.3	131.3	3.5	120.8	1.5	124.5	9.0	158.7	11.8	138.3	6.2	158.2	12.7
1990	138.4	6.0	134.1	5.3	139.2	6.0	131.9	9.2	131.7	5.8	173.3	9.2	142.4	3.0	165.9	4.9
1991	143.4	3.6	140.3	4.6	144.1	3.5	129.6	-1.7	133.8	1.6	188.3	8.7	148.4	4.2	178.4	7.5
1992	147.4	2.8	142.5	1.6	148.2	2.8	131.2	1.2	135.9	1.6	201.6	7.1	152.1	2.5	189.1	6.0
1993	-	-	-	-	-	-	-	-	-	-	-	-	-	-	-	-

Source: U.S. Department of Labor, Bureau of Labor Statistics, Division of Consumer Prices and Price Indexes. - indicates no data collected for period.

San Diego, CA
Consumer Price Index - Urban Wage Earners
Base 1982-1984 = 100
Annual Averages

For 1965-1993. Columns headed % show percentile change in the index from the previous period for which an index is available.

Year	All Items		Food & Beverage		Housing		Apparel & Upkeep		Trans- portation		Medical Care		Entertain- ment		Other Goods & Services	
	Index	%	Index	%	Index	%	Index	%	Index	%	Index	%	Index	%	Index	%
1965	29.5	-	-	-	-	-	50.2	-	31.9	-	26.0	-	-	-	-	-
1966	30.1	2.0	-	-	-	-	50.8	1.2	31.9	0.0	27.4	5.4	-	-	-	-
1967	31.0	3.0	-	-	-	-	51.6	1.6	33.1	3.8	29.4	7.3	-	-	-	-
1968	32.3	4.2	-	-	-	-	54.7	6.0	33.9	2.4	30.1	2.4	-	-	-	-
1969	34.0	5.3	-	-	-	-	57.1	4.4	34.7	2.4	31.7	5.3	-	-	-	-
1970	35.8	5.3	-	-	-	-	59.3	3.9	35.7	2.9	33.7	6.3	-	-	-	-
1971	37.1	3.6	-	-	-	-	60.8	2.5	37.7	5.6	35.5	5.3	-	-	-	-
1972	38.6	4.0	-	-	-	-	63.1	3.8	38.8	2.9	36.4	2.5	-	-	-	-
1973	41.1	6.5	-	-	-	-	65.5	3.8	40.5	4.4	38.2	4.9	-	-	-	-
1974	45.6	10.9	-	-	-	-	70.9	8.2	45.8	13.1	42.3	10.7	-	-	-	-
1975	49.9	9.4	-	-	-	-	72.6	2.4	50.6	10.5	47.4	12.1	-	-	-	-
1976	52.9	6.0	57.9	-	48.1	-	74.6	2.8	54.2	7.1	52.4	10.5	60.8	-	59.3	-
1977	56.4	6.6	61.4	6.0	52.0	8.1	76.0	1.9	57.7	6.5	57.3	9.4	63.2	3.9	62.5	5.4
1978	61.9	9.8	67.9	10.6	58.4	12.3	77.9	2.5	61.0	5.7	62.0	8.2	67.5	6.8	67.6	8.2
1979	71.4	15.3	75.9	11.8	69.9	19.7	81.0	4.0	69.6	14.1	69.4	11.9	73.4	8.7	72.5	7.2
1980	82.1	15.0	82.9	9.2	82.4	17.9	88.5	9.3	81.2	16.7	76.2	9.8	81.8	11.4	78.5	8.3
1981	92.8	13.0	89.9	8.4	96.2	16.7	92.5	4.5	90.2	11.1	83.5	9.6	88.7	8.4	85.0	8.3
1982	99.4	7.1	94.6	5.2	103.7	7.8	96.5	4.3	95.4	5.8	93.1	11.5	96.1	8.3	91.4	7.5
1983	99.0	-0.4	100.5	6.2	98.2	-5.3	99.8	3.4	98.8	3.6	100.6	8.1	100.9	5.0	100.3	9.7
1984	101.7	2.7	104.9	4.4	98.1	-0.1	103.8	4.0	105.9	7.2	106.3	5.7	103.0	2.1	108.3	8.0
1985	104.5	2.8	107.4	2.4	100.8	2.8	106.3	2.4	109.6	3.5	110.6	4.0	107.7	4.6	115.0	6.2
1986	107.2	2.6	111.2	3.5	105.6	4.8	107.5	1.1	106.2	-3.1	118.9	7.5	113.1	5.0	118.9	3.4
1987	111.1	3.6	116.1	4.4	108.1	2.4	110.2	2.5	108.5	2.2	130.4	9.7	122.6	8.4	128.1	7.7
1988	116.5	4.9	120.0	3.4	112.0	3.6	118.8	7.8	114.7	5.7	143.9	10.4	132.4	8.0	138.3	8.0
1989	123.5	6.0	127.8	6.5	115.8	3.4	120.7	1.6	124.3	8.4	161.4	12.2	141.1	6.6	159.7	15.5
1990	130.5	5.7	134.9	5.6	122.2	5.5	131.1	8.6	131.4	5.7	175.7	8.9	145.2	2.9	167.9	5.1
1991	134.7	3.2	141.2	4.7	126.0	3.1	128.2	-2.2	133.5	1.6	190.2	8.3	150.6	3.7	179.7	7.0
1992	138.2	2.6	143.3	1.5	129.1	2.5	130.0	1.4	136.4	2.2	203.9	7.2	153.0	1.6	191.0	6.3
1993	-	-	-	-	-	-	-	-	-	-	-	-	-	-	-	-

Source: U.S. Department of Labor, Bureau of Labor Statistics, Division of Consumer Prices and Price Indexes. - indicates no data collected for period.

San Diego, CA
Consumer Price Index - All Urban Consumers
Base 1982-1984 = 100
All Items

For 1965-1993. Columns headed % show percentile change in the index from the previous period for which an index is available.

Year	Jan Index	%	Feb Index	%	Mar Index	%	Apr Index	%	May Index	%	Jun Index	%	Jul Index	%	Aug Index	%	Sep Index	%	Oct Index	%	Nov Index	%	Dec Index	%
1965	-	-	28.1	-	-	-	-	-	28.3	0.7	-	-	-	-	28.0	-1.1	-	-	-	-	28.2	0.7	-	-
1966	-	-	28.5	1.1	-	-	-	-	28.6	0.4	-	-	-	-	28.7	0.3	-	-	-	-	29.1	1.4	-	-
1967	-	-	29.2	0.3	-	-	-	-	29.3	0.3	-	-	-	-	29.8	1.7	-	-	-	-	30.0	0.7	-	-
1968	-	-	30.3	1.0	-	-	-	-	30.6	1.0	-	-	-	-	31.0	1.3	-	-	-	-	31.3	1.0	-	-
1969	-	-	31.7	1.3	-	-	-	-	32.2	1.6	-	-	-	-	32.7	1.6	-	-	-	-	32.9	0.6	-	-
1970	-	-	33.4	1.5	-	-	-	-	34.0	1.8	-	-	-	-	34.3	0.9	-	-	-	-	34.8	1.5	-	-
1971	-	-	35.0	0.6	-	-	-	-	35.3	0.9	-	-	-	-	35.6	0.8	-	-	-	-	35.7	0.3	-	-
1972	-	-	36.1	1.1	-	-	-	-	36.6	1.4	-	-	-	-	37.0	1.1	-	-	-	-	37.5	1.4	-	-
1973	-	-	37.9	1.1	-	-	-	-	38.7	2.1	-	-	-	-	39.7	2.6	-	-	-	-	40.4	1.8	-	-
1974	-	-	41.5	2.7	-	-	-	-	42.9	3.4	-	-	-	-	44.3	3.3	-	-	-	-	45.4	2.5	-	-
1975	-	-	46.5	2.4	-	-	-	-	47.0	1.1	-	-	-	-	48.1	2.3	-	-	-	-	48.8	1.5	-	-
1976	-	-	49.5	1.4	-	-	-	-	50.1	1.2	-	-	-	-	50.9	1.6	-	-	-	-	51.4	1.0	-	-
1977	-	-	52.2	1.6	-	-	-	-	53.4	2.3	-	-	-	-	54.4	1.9	-	-	-	-	55.2	1.5	-	-
1978	55.9	1.3	-	-	56.6	1.3	-	-	57.8	2.1	-	-	59.7	3.3	-	-	61.1	2.3	-	-	62.0	1.5	-	-
1979	63.5	2.4	-	-	65.5	3.1	-	-	67.5	3.1	-	-	69.8	3.4	-	-	71.1	1.9	-	-	73.3	3.1	-	-
1980	75.1	2.5	-	-	76.4	1.7	-	-	79.8	4.5	-	-	79.8	0.0	-	-	80.4	0.8	-	-	82.5	2.6	-	-
1981	85.1	3.2	-	-	86.7	1.9	-	-	88.0	1.5	-	-	90.3	2.6	-	-	92.8	2.8	-	-	95.0	2.4	-	-
1982	95.6	0.6	-	-	94.3	-1.4	-	-	97.4	3.3	-	-	99.0	1.6	-	-	96.3	-2.7	-	-	95.1	-1.2	-	-
1983	96.1	1.1	-	-	96.9	0.8	-	-	98.2	1.3	-	-	99.1	0.9	-	-	100.7	1.6	-	-	101.2	0.5	-	-
1984	102.4	1.2	-	-	103.3	0.9	-	-	104.4	1.1	-	-	103.9	-0.5	-	-	105.6	1.6	-	-	107.6	1.9	-	-
1985	107.7	0.1	-	-	109.2	1.4	-	-	110.0	0.7	-	-	110.3	0.3	-	-	111.6	1.2	-	-	112.1	0.4	-	-
1986	112.9	0.7	-	-	112.1	-0.7	-	-	113.2	1.0	-	-	113.3	0.1	-	-	114.1	0.7	-	-	114.6	0.4	-	-
1987	-	-	-	-	-	-	-	-	-	-	116.6	1.7	-	-	-	-	-	-	-	-	-	-	118.3	1.5
1988	-	-	-	-	-	-	-	-	-	-	121.9	3.0	-	-	-	-	-	-	-	-	-	-	125.0	2.5
1989	-	-	-	-	-	-	-	-	-	-	128.9	3.1	-	-	-	-	-	-	-	-	-	-	132.3	2.6
1990	-	-	-	-	-	-	-	-	-	-	136.5	3.2	-	-	-	-	-	-	-	-	-	-	140.3	2.8
1991	-	-	-	-	-	-	-	-	-	-	142.2	1.4	-	-	-	-	-	-	-	-	-	-	144.7	1.8
1992	-	-	-	-	-	-	-	-	-	-	147.0	1.6	-	-	-	-	-	-	-	-	-	-	147.7	0.5
1993	-	-	-	-	-	-	-	-	-	-	150.4	1.8	-	-	-	-	-	-	-	-	-	-	-	-

Source: U.S. Department of Labor, Bureau of Labor Statistics, Division of Consumer Prices and Price Indexes. - indicates no data collected for period.

San Diego, CA
Consumer Price Index - Urban Wage Earners
Base 1982-1984 = 100
All Items

For 1965-1993. Columns headed % show percentile change in the index from the previous period for which an index is available.

Year	Jan Index	%	Feb Index	%	Mar Index	%	Apr Index	%	May Index	%	Jun Index	%	Jul Index	%	Aug Index	%	Sep Index	%	Oct Index	%	Nov Index	%	Dec Index	%
1965	-	-	29.5	-	-	-	-	-	29.6	0.3	-	-	-	-	29.4	-0.7	-	-	-	-	29.6	0.7	-	-
1966	-	-	29.9	1.0	-	-	-	-	30.0	0.3	-	-	-	-	30.1	0.3	-	-	-	-	30.5	1.3	-	-
1967	-	-	30.6	0.3	-	-	-	-	30.7	0.3	-	-	-	-	31.3	2.0	-	-	-	-	31.4	0.3	-	-
1968	-	-	31.8	1.3	-	-	-	-	32.1	0.9	-	-	-	-	32.5	1.2	-	-	-	-	32.8	0.9	-	-
1969	-	-	33.3	1.5	-	-	-	-	33.7	1.2	-	-	-	-	34.2	1.5	-	-	-	-	34.5	0.9	-	-
1970	-	-	35.0	1.4	-	-	-	-	35.7	2.0	-	-	-	-	35.9	0.6	-	-	-	-	36.5	1.7	-	-
1971	-	-	36.7	0.5	-	-	-	-	37.1	1.1	-	-	-	-	37.4	0.8	-	-	-	-	37.5	0.3	-	-
1972	-	-	37.9	1.1	-	-	-	-	38.3	1.1	-	-	-	-	38.8	1.3	-	-	-	-	39.3	1.3	-	-
1973	-	-	39.8	1.3	-	-	-	-	40.5	1.8	-	-	-	-	41.7	3.0	-	-	-	-	42.3	1.4	-	-
1974	-	-	43.5	2.8	-	-	-	-	45.0	3.4	-	-	-	-	46.5	3.3	-	-	-	-	47.6	2.4	-	-
1975	-	-	48.7	2.3	-	-	-	-	49.2	1.0	-	-	-	-	50.4	2.4	-	-	-	-	51.1	1.4	-	-
1976	-	-	51.9	1.6	-	-	-	-	52.5	1.2	-	-	-	-	53.4	1.7	-	-	-	-	53.9	0.9	-	-
1977	-	-	54.8	1.7	-	-	-	-	56.0	2.2	-	-	-	-	57.1	2.0	-	-	-	-	57.9	1.4	-	-
1978	58.6	1.2	-	-	59.3	1.2	-	-	60.6	2.2	-	-	62.5	3.1	-	-	63.7	1.9	-	-	64.7	1.6	-	-
1979	65.9	1.9	-	-	67.8	2.9	-	-	70.1	3.4	-	-	72.3	3.1	-	-	73.7	1.9	-	-	75.9	3.0	-	-
1980	77.8	2.5	-	-	79.3	1.9	-	-	82.1	3.5	-	-	82.4	0.4	-	-	83.0	0.7	-	-	85.3	2.8	-	-
1981	87.7	2.8	-	-	89.3	1.8	-	-	90.7	1.6	-	-	93.2	2.8	-	-	95.5	2.5	-	-	97.7	2.3	-	-
1982	98.4	0.7	-	-	97.3	-1.1	-	-	100.3	3.1	-	-	102.1	1.8	-	-	99.6	-2.4	-	-	98.7	-0.9	-	-
1983	97.2	-1.5	-	-	97.8	0.6	-	-	97.6	-0.2	-	-	99.2	1.6	-	-	100.4	1.2	-	-	100.4	0.0	-	-
1984	102.1	1.7	-	-	101.2	-0.9	-	-	101.6	0.4	-	-	100.7	-0.9	-	-	102.5	1.8	-	-	102.0	-0.5	-	-
1985	102.1	0.1	-	-	103.5	1.4	-	-	104.3	0.8	-	-	104.5	0.2	-	-	105.5	1.0	-	-	106.0	0.5	-	-
1986	106.9	0.8	-	-	106.0	-0.8	-	-	107.0	0.9	-	-	107.0	0.0	-	-	107.7	0.7	-	-	108.2	0.5	-	-
1987	-	-	-	-	-	-	-	-	-	-	110.2	1.8	-	-	-	-	-	-	-	-	-	-	111.9	1.5
1988	-	-	-	-	-	-	-	-	-	-	115.1	2.9	-	-	-	-	-	-	-	-	-	-	118.0	2.5
1989	-	-	-	-	-	-	-	-	-	-	122.0	3.4	-	-	-	-	-	-	-	-	-	-	125.0	2.5
1990	-	-	-	-	-	-	-	-	-	-	128.9	3.1	-	-	-	-	-	-	-	-	-	-	132.2	2.6
1991	-	-	-	-	-	-	-	-	-	-	133.6	1.1	-	-	-	-	-	-	-	-	-	-	135.9	1.7
1992	-	-	-	-	-	-	-	-	-	-	137.9	1.5	-	-	-	-	-	-	-	-	-	-	138.6	0.5
1993	-	-	-	-	-	-	-	-	-	-	140.9	1.7	-	-	-	-	-	-	-	-	-	-	-	-

Source: U.S. Department of Labor, Bureau of Labor Statistics, Division of Consumer Prices and Price Indexes. - indicates no data collected for period.

San Diego, CA
Consumer Price Index - All Urban Consumers
Base 1982-1984 = 100
Food and Beverages

For 1975-1993. Columns headed % show percentile change in the index from the previous period for which an index is available.

Year	Jan Index	Jan %	Feb Index	Feb %	Mar Index	Mar %	Apr Index	Apr %	May Index	May %	Jun Index	Jun %	Jul Index	Jul %	Aug Index	Aug %	Sep Index	Sep %	Oct Index	Oct %	Nov Index	Nov %	Dec Index	Dec %
1975	-	-	-	-	-	-	-	-	-	-	-	-	-	-	-	-	-	-	-	-	58.9	-	-	-
1976	-	-	58.9	0.0	-	-	-	-	59.2	0.5	-	-	-	-	59.7	0.8	-	-	-	-	59.6	-0.2	-	-
1977	-	-	61.0	2.3	-	-	-	-	62.8	3.0	-	-	-	-	63.6	1.3	-	-	-	-	64.3	1.1	-	-
1978	65.8	2.3	-	-	67.3	2.3	-	-	69.8	3.7	-	-	71.0	1.7	-	-	71.3	0.4	-	-	71.0	-0.4	-	-
1979	73.6	3.7	-	-	75.6	2.7	-	-	77.4	2.4	-	-	77.5	0.1	-	-	78.4	1.2	-	-	79.4	1.3	-	-
1980	81.0	2.0	-	-	82.2	1.5	-	-	83.5	1.6	-	-	84.1	0.7	-	-	86.2	2.5	-	-	87.5	1.5	-	-
1981	88.7	1.4	-	-	89.6	1.0	-	-	89.7	0.1	-	-	90.9	1.3	-	-	91.8	1.0	-	-	91.2	-0.7	-	-
1982	93.2	2.2	-	-	93.7	0.5	-	-	94.2	0.5	-	-	95.5	1.4	-	-	95.0	-0.5	-	-	96.7	1.8	-	-
1983	96.1	-0.6	-	-	100.3	4.4	-	-	100.5	0.2	-	-	100.2	-0.3	-	-	101.0	0.8	-	-	102.1	1.1	-	-
1984	104.7	2.5	-	-	105.3	0.6	-	-	103.6	-1.6	-	-	103.9	0.3	-	-	105.1	1.2	-	-	105.6	0.5	-	-
1985	107.4	1.7	-	-	106.9	-0.5	-	-	106.9	0.0	-	-	105.9	-0.9	-	-	106.8	0.8	-	-	108.0	1.1	-	-
1986	111.2	3.0	-	-	108.9	-2.1	-	-	111.0	1.9	-	-	110.1	-0.8	-	-	111.0	0.8	-	-	113.7	2.4	-	-
1987	-	-	-	-	-	-	-	-	-	-	115.7	1.8	-	-	-	-	-	-	-	-	-	-	115.9	0.2
1988	-	-	-	-	-	-	-	-	-	-	118.5	2.2	-	-	-	-	-	-	-	-	-	-	120.9	2.0
1989	-	-	-	-	-	-	-	-	-	-	125.9	4.1	-	-	-	-	-	-	-	-	-	-	128.8	2.3
1990	-	-	-	-	-	-	-	-	-	-	134.1	4.1	-	-	-	-	-	-	-	-	-	-	134.2	0.1
1991	-	-	-	-	-	-	-	-	-	-	140.4	4.6	-	-	-	-	-	-	-	-	-	-	140.2	-0.1
1992	-	-	-	-	-	-	-	-	-	-	142.3	1.5	-	-	-	-	-	-	-	-	-	-	142.7	0.3
1993	-	-	-	-	-	-	-	-	-	-	144.5	1.3	-	-	-	-	-	-	-	-	-	-	-	-

Source: U.S. Department of Labor, Bureau of Labor Statistics, Division of Consumer Prices and Price Indexes. - indicates no data collected for period.

San Diego, CA
Consumer Price Index - Urban Wage Earners
Base 1982-1984 = 100
Food and Beverages

For 1975-1993. Columns headed % show percentile change in the index from the previous period for which an index is available.

Year	Jan Index	%	Feb Index	%	Mar Index	%	Apr Index	%	May Index	%	Jun Index	%	Jul Index	%	Aug Index	%	Sep Index	%	Oct Index	%	Nov Index	%	Dec Index	%
1975	-	-	-	-	-	-	-	-	-	-	-	-	-	-	-	-	-	-	-	-	57.4	-	-	-
1976	-	-	57.5	0.2	-	-	-	-	57.7	0.3	-	-	-	-	58.2	0.9	-	-	-	-	58.1	-0.2	-	-
1977	-	-	59.6	2.6	-	-	-	-	61.3	2.9	-	-	-	-	62.1	1.3	-	-	-	-	62.7	1.0	-	-
1978	63.9	1.9	-	-	65.4	2.3	-	-	67.9	3.8	-	-	69.3	2.1	-	-	69.7	0.6	-	-	69.4	-0.4	-	-
1979	72.0	3.7	-	-	74.2	3.1	-	-	76.0	2.4	-	-	76.5	0.7	-	-	77.1	0.8	-	-	77.9	1.0	-	-
1980	79.5	2.1	-	-	80.9	1.8	-	-	81.5	0.7	-	-	82.1	0.7	-	-	84.6	3.0	-	-	86.8	2.6	-	-
1981	87.6	0.9	-	-	88.8	1.4	-	-	89.1	0.3	-	-	90.2	1.2	-	-	91.3	1.2	-	-	90.8	-0.5	-	-
1982	92.6	2.0	-	-	93.3	0.8	-	-	93.9	0.6	-	-	95.4	1.6	-	-	94.9	-0.5	-	-	96.7	1.9	-	-
1983	96.0	-0.7	-	-	100.5	4.7	-	-	100.6	0.1	-	-	100.2	-0.4	-	-	101.0	0.8	-	-	102.3	1.3	-	-
1984	104.8	2.4	-	-	105.2	0.4	-	-	103.8	-1.3	-	-	104.0	0.2	-	-	105.4	1.3	-	-	105.8	0.4	-	-
1985	107.5	1.6	-	-	107.1	-0.4	-	-	107.2	0.1	-	-	106.2	-0.9	-	-	107.0	0.8	-	-	108.4	1.3	-	-
1986	111.4	2.8	-	-	108.9	-2.2	-	-	110.9	1.8	-	-	110.2	-0.6	-	-	111.0	0.7	-	-	114.0	2.7	-	-
1987	-	-	-	-	-	-	-	-	-	-	116.0	1.8	-	-	-	-	-	-	-	-	-	-	116.2	0.2
1988	-	-	-	-	-	-	-	-	-	-	118.8	2.2	-	-	-	-	-	-	-	-	-	-	121.3	2.1
1989	-	-	-	-	-	-	-	-	-	-	126.2	4.0	-	-	-	-	-	-	-	-	-	-	129.3	2.5
1990	-	-	-	-	-	-	-	-	-	-	134.7	4.2	-	-	-	-	-	-	-	-	-	-	135.2	0.4
1991	-	-	-	-	-	-	-	-	-	-	141.3	4.5	-	-	-	-	-	-	-	-	-	-	141.1	-0.1
1992	-	-	-	-	-	-	-	-	-	-	143.0	1.3	-	-	-	-	-	-	-	-	-	-	143.6	0.4
1993	-	-	-	-	-	-	-	-	-	-	145.1	1.0	-	-	-	-	-	-	-	-	-	-	-	-

Source: U.S. Department of Labor, Bureau of Labor Statistics, Division of Consumer Prices and Price Indexes. - indicates no data collected for period.

San Diego, CA
Consumer Price Index - All Urban Consumers
Base 1982-1984 = 100
Housing

For 1975-1993. Columns headed % show percentile change in the index from the previous period for which an index is available.

Year	Jan Index	Jan %	Feb Index	Feb %	Mar Index	Mar %	Apr Index	Apr %	May Index	May %	Jun Index	Jun %	Jul Index	Jul %	Aug Index	Aug %	Sep Index	Sep %	Oct Index	Oct %	Nov Index	Nov %	Dec Index	Dec %
1975	-	-	-	-	-	-	-	-	-	-	-	-	-	-	-	-	-	-	-	-	42.4	-	-	-
1976	-	-	43.5	2.6	-	-	-	-	43.8	0.7	-	-	-	-	44.6	1.8	-	-	-	-	45.4	1.8	-	-
1977	-	-	46.2	1.8	-	-	-	-	47.0	1.7	-	-	-	-	48.7	3.6	-	-	-	-	49.6	1.8	-	-
1978	50.3	1.4	-	-	51.0	1.4	-	-	51.9	1.8	-	-	54.1	4.2	-	-	56.1	3.7	-	-	57.3	2.1	-	-
1979	58.9	2.8	-	-	61.3	4.1	-	-	63.2	3.1	-	-	66.4	5.1	-	-	67.5	1.7	-	-	70.5	4.4	-	-
1980	72.5	2.8	-	-	72.8	0.4	-	-	77.7	6.7	-	-	77.3	-0.5	-	-	77.3	0.0	-	-	80.2	3.8	-	-
1981	83.7	4.4	-	-	85.3	1.9	-	-	86.8	1.8	-	-	89.5	3.1	-	-	92.9	3.8	-	-	96.2	3.6	-	-
1982	96.7	0.5	-	-	94.6	-2.2	-	-	99.3	5.0	-	-	100.4	1.1	-	-	95.5	-4.9	-	-	93.2	-2.4	-	-
1983	95.5	2.5	-	-	96.5	1.0	-	-	97.1	0.6	-	-	98.3	1.2	-	-	101.1	2.8	-	-	101.2	0.1	-	-
1984	101.3	0.1	-	-	103.1	1.8	-	-	104.1	1.0	-	-	103.8	-0.3	-	-	106.1	2.2	-	-	109.1	2.8	-	-
1985	108.9	-0.2	-	-	111.8	2.7	-	-	112.1	0.3	-	-	113.6	1.3	-	-	116.7	2.7	-	-	116.9	0.2	-	-
1986	117.1	0.2	-	-	117.2	0.1	-	-	118.3	0.9	-	-	119.8	1.3	-	-	120.8	0.8	-	-	121.1	0.2	-	-
1987	-	-	-	-	-	-	-	-	-	-	121.3	0.2	-	-	-	-	-	-	-	-	-	-	123.2	1.6
1988	-	-	-	-	-	-	-	-	-	-	126.1	2.4	-	-	-	-	-	-	-	-	-	-	127.6	1.2
1989	-	-	-	-	-	-	-	-	-	-	128.8	0.9	-	-	-	-	-	-	-	-	-	-	133.8	3.9
1990	-	-	-	-	-	-	-	-	-	-	136.7	2.2	-	-	-	-	-	-	-	-	-	-	141.6	3.6
1991	-	-	-	-	-	-	-	-	-	-	142.8	0.8	-	-	-	-	-	-	-	-	-	-	145.4	1.8
1992	-	-	-	-	-	-	-	-	-	-	148.2	1.9	-	-	-	-	-	-	-	-	-	-	148.3	0.1
1993	-	-	-	-	-	-	-	-	-	-	149.2	0.6	-	-	-	-	-	-	-	-	-	-	-	-

Source: U.S. Department of Labor, Bureau of Labor Statistics, Division of Consumer Prices and Price Indexes. - indicates no data collected for period.

San Diego, CA
Consumer Price Index - Urban Wage Earners
Base 1982-1984 = 100
Housing

For 1975-1993. Columns headed % show percentile change in the index from the previous period for which an index is available.

Year	Jan Index	%	Feb Index	%	Mar Index	%	Apr Index	%	May Index	%	Jun Index	%	Jul Index	%	Aug Index	%	Sep Index	%	Oct Index	%	Nov Index	%	Dec Index	%
1975	-	-	-	-	-	-	-	-	-	-	-	-	-	-	-	-	-	-	-	-	46.0	-	-	-
1976	-	-	47.2	2.6	-	-	-	-	47.6	0.8	-	-	-	-	48.4	1.7	-	-	-	-	49.3	1.9	-	-
1977	-	-	50.2	1.8	-	-	-	-	51.1	1.8	-	-	-	-	52.8	3.3	-	-	-	-	53.9	2.1	-	-
1978	54.7	1.5	-	-	55.3	1.1	-	-	56.4	2.0	-	-	58.8	4.3	-	-	60.8	3.4	-	-	62.1	2.1	-	-
1979	63.3	1.9	-	-	65.8	3.9	-	-	67.8	3.0	-	-	70.9	4.6	-	-	72.3	2.0	-	-	75.8	4.8	-	-
1980	77.9	2.8	-	-	78.2	0.4	-	-	83.1	6.3	-	-	82.9	-0.2	-	-	82.9	0.0	-	-	86.0	3.7	-	-
1981	90.0	4.7	-	-	91.5	1.7	-	-	93.0	1.6	-	-	96.2	3.4	-	-	99.6	3.5	-	-	103.3	3.7	-	-
1982	104.1	0.8	-	-	101.8	-2.2	-	-	107.0	5.1	-	-	108.1	1.0	-	-	102.7	-5.0	-	-	100.4	-2.2	-	-
1983	97.7	-2.7	-	-	97.9	0.2	-	-	95.8	-2.1	-	-	98.3	2.6	-	-	99.9	1.6	-	-	98.8	-1.1	-	-
1984	100.4	1.6	-	-	98.2	-2.2	-	-	98.1	-0.1	-	-	96.6	-1.5	-	-	99.2	2.7	-	-	96.9	-2.3	-	-
1985	96.5	-0.4	-	-	99.1	2.7	-	-	99.5	0.4	-	-	100.9	1.4	-	-	103.5	2.6	-	-	103.6	0.1	-	-
1986	103.7	0.1	-	-	103.8	0.1	-	-	104.8	1.0	-	-	106.1	1.2	-	-	107.1	0.9	-	-	107.3	0.2	-	-
1987	-	-	-	-	-	-	-	-	-	-	107.3	0.0	-	-	-	-	-	-	-	-	-	-	109.0	1.6
1988	-	-	-	-	-	-	-	-	-	-	111.3	2.1	-	-	-	-	-	-	-	-	-	-	112.6	1.2
1989	-	-	-	-	-	-	-	-	-	-	113.7	1.0	-	-	-	-	-	-	-	-	-	-	118.0	3.8
1990	-	-	-	-	-	-	-	-	-	-	120.2	1.9	-	-	-	-	-	-	-	-	-	-	124.1	3.2
1991	-	-	-	-	-	-	-	-	-	-	124.9	0.6	-	-	-	-	-	-	-	-	-	-	127.1	1.8
1992	-	-	-	-	-	-	-	-	-	-	129.2	1.7	-	-	-	-	-	-	-	-	-	-	129.1	-0.1
1993	-	-	-	-	-	-	-	-	-	-	129.8	0.5	-	-	-	-	-	-	-	-	-	-	-	-

Source: U.S. Department of Labor, Bureau of Labor Statistics, Division of Consumer Prices and Price Indexes. - indicates no data collected for period.

San Diego, CA
Consumer Price Index - All Urban Consumers
Base 1982-1984 = 100
Apparel and Upkeep

For 1965-1993. Columns headed % show percentile change in the index from the previous period for which an index is available.

Year	Jan Index	%	Feb Index	%	Mar Index	%	Apr Index	%	May Index	%	Jun Index	%	Jul Index	%	Aug Index	%	Sep Index	%	Oct Index	%	Nov Index	%	Dec Index	%
1965	-	-	48.5	-	-	-	-	-	48.4	-0.2	-	-	-	-	47.7	-1.4	-	-	-	-	47.8	0.2	-	-
1966	-	-	48.0	0.4	-	-	-	-	48.8	1.7	-	-	-	-	48.9	0.2	-	-	-	-	49.2	0.6	-	-
1967	-	-	48.8	-0.8	-	-	-	-	49.3	1.0	-	-	-	-	49.2	-0.2	-	-	-	-	50.5	2.6	-	-
1968	-	-	50.9	0.8	-	-	-	-	51.9	2.0	-	-	-	-	52.8	1.7	-	-	-	-	54.2	2.7	-	-
1969	-	-	53.9	-0.6	-	-	-	-	54.4	0.9	-	-	-	-	55.0	1.1	-	-	-	-	55.2	0.4	-	-
1970	-	-	55.8	1.1	-	-	-	-	57.2	2.5	-	-	-	-	56.8	-0.7	-	-	-	-	57.5	1.2	-	-
1971	-	-	57.5	0.0	-	-	-	-	58.4	1.6	-	-	-	-	58.5	0.2	-	-	-	-	58.7	0.3	-	-
1972	-	-	59.8	1.9	-	-	-	-	60.7	1.5	-	-	-	-	59.8	-1.5	-	-	-	-	61.4	2.7	-	-
1973	-	-	60.9	-0.8	-	-	-	-	61.7	1.3	-	-	-	-	63.3	2.6	-	-	-	-	64.7	2.2	-	-
1974	-	-	66.2	2.3	-	-	-	-	68.6	3.6	-	-	-	-	67.9	-1.0	-	-	-	-	69.1	1.8	-	-
1975	-	-	68.6	-0.7	-	-	-	-	70.3	2.5	-	-	-	-	69.2	-1.6	-	-	-	-	70.0	1.2	-	-
1976	-	-	71.0	1.4	-	-	-	-	71.5	0.7	-	-	-	-	71.9	0.6	-	-	-	-	71.5	-0.6	-	-
1977	-	-	71.1	-0.6	-	-	-	-	73.0	2.7	-	-	-	-	73.0	0.0	-	-	-	-	73.8	1.1	-	-
1978	74.0	0.3	-	-	73.8	-0.3	-	-	76.9	4.2	-	-	77.3	0.5	-	-	78.5	1.6	-	-	79.5	1.3	-	-
1979	79.2	-0.4	-	-	79.7	0.6	-	-	81.8	2.6	-	-	81.2	-0.7	-	-	82.9	2.1	-	-	82.9	0.0	-	-
1980	83.4	0.6	-	-	88.6	6.2	-	-	87.5	-1.2	-	-	86.7	-0.9	-	-	87.8	1.3	-	-	89.5	1.9	-	-
1981	87.9	-1.8	-	-	90.8	3.3	-	-	90.3	-0.6	-	-	93.5	3.5	-	-	95.0	1.6	-	-	95.0	0.0	-	-
1982	92.2	-2.9	-	-	95.1	3.1	-	-	96.4	1.4	-	-	95.9	-0.5	-	-	99.4	3.6	-	-	98.7	-0.7	-	-
1983	97.8	-0.9	-	-	97.3	-0.5	-	-	98.4	1.1	-	-	101.3	2.9	-	-	101.6	0.3	-	-	100.5	-1.1	-	-
1984	101.8	1.3	-	-	101.6	-0.2	-	-	103.8	2.2	-	-	100.6	-3.1	-	-	106.4	5.8	-	-	108.0	1.5	-	-
1985	105.1	-2.7	-	-	105.5	0.4	-	-	107.5	1.9	-	-	105.1	-2.2	-	-	106.1	1.0	-	-	106.3	0.2	-	-
1986	105.1	-1.1	-	-	108.3	3.0	-	-	108.1	-0.2	-	-	104.5	-3.3	-	-	109.0	4.3	-	-	108.2	-0.7	-	-
1987	-	-	-	-	-	-	-	-	-	-	110.1	1.8	-	-	-	-	-	-	-	-	-	-	110.3	0.2
1988	-	-	-	-	-	-	-	-	-	-	118.4	7.3	-	-	-	-	-	-	-	-	-	-	119.7	1.1
1989	-	-	-	-	-	-	-	-	-	-	123.5	3.2	-	-	-	-	-	-	-	-	-	-	118.2	-4.3
1990	-	-	-	-	-	-	-	-	-	-	133.5	12.9	-	-	-	-	-	-	-	-	-	-	130.4	-2.3
1991	-	-	-	-	-	-	-	-	-	-	127.7	-2.1	-	-	-	-	-	-	-	-	-	-	131.4	2.9
1992	-	-	-	-	-	-	-	-	-	-	131.8	0.3	-	-	-	-	-	-	-	-	-	-	130.6	-0.9
1993	-	-	-	-	-	-	-	-	-	-	142.1	8.8	-	-	-	-	-	-	-	-	-	-	-	-

Source: U.S. Department of Labor, Bureau of Labor Statistics, Division of Consumer Prices and Price Indexes. - indicates no data collected for period.

San Diego, CA
Consumer Price Index - Urban Wage Earners
Base 1982-1984 = 100
Apparel and Upkeep

For 1965-1993. Columns headed % show percentile change in the index from the previous period for which an index is available.

Year	Jan Index	%	Feb Index	%	Mar Index	%	Apr Index	%	May Index	%	Jun Index	%	Jul Index	%	Aug Index	%	Sep Index	%	Oct Index	%	Nov Index	%	Dec Index	%
1965	-		50.6	-	-	-	-	-	50.6	0.0	-	-	-	-	49.8	-1.6	-	-	-	-	49.9	0.2	-	-
1966	-		50.1	0.4	-	-	-	-	50.9	1.6	-	-	-	-	51.0	0.2	-	-	-	-	51.3	0.6	-	-
1967	-		51.0	-0.6	-	-	-	-	51.5	1.0	-	-	-	-	51.4	-0.2	-	-	-	-	52.7	2.5	-	-
1968	-		53.2	0.9	-	-	-	-	54.2	1.9	-	-	-	-	55.1	1.7	-	-	-	-	56.5	2.5	-	-
1969	-		56.2	-0.5	-	-	-	-	56.8	1.1	-	-	-	-	57.5	1.2	-	-	-	-	57.7	0.3	-	-
1970	-		58.3	1.0	-	-	-	-	59.7	2.4	-	-	-	-	59.3	-0.7	-	-	-	-	60.0	1.2	-	-
1971	-		60.0	0.0	-	-	-	-	60.9	1.5	-	-	-	-	61.0	0.2	-	-	-	-	61.2	0.3	-	-
1972	-		62.4	2.0	-	-	-	-	63.4	1.6	-	-	-	-	62.5	-1.4	-	-	-	-	64.1	2.6	-	-
1973	-		63.6	-0.8	-	-	-	-	64.4	1.3	-	-	-	-	66.0	2.5	-	-	-	-	67.5	2.3	-	-
1974	-		69.1	2.4	-	-	-	-	71.6	3.6	-	-	-	-	70.8	-1.1	-	-	-	-	72.2	2.0	-	-
1975	-		71.6	-0.8	-	-	-	-	73.4	2.5	-	-	-	-	72.2	-1.6	-	-	-	-	73.1	1.2	-	-
1976	-		74.1	1.4	-	-	-	-	74.6	0.7	-	-	-	-	75.0	0.5	-	-	-	-	74.7	-0.4	-	-
1977	-		74.2	-0.7	-	-	-	-	76.3	2.8	-	-	-	-	76.2	-0.1	-	-	-	-	77.0	1.0	-	-
1978	75.9	-1.4	-	-	76.7	1.1	-	-	77.8	1.4	-	-	78.2	0.5	-	-	79.0	1.0	-	-	79.6	0.8	-	-
1979	77.5	-2.6	-	-	77.0	-0.6	-	-	80.3	4.3	-	-	81.4	1.4	-	-	83.4	2.5	-	-	84.6	1.4	-	-
1980	84.5	-0.1	-	-	90.0	6.5	-	-	90.1	0.1	-	-	87.6	-2.8	-	-	87.9	0.3	-	-	89.6	1.9	-	-
1981	88.8	-0.9	-	-	91.1	2.6	-	-	92.5	1.5	-	-	93.2	0.8	-	-	93.9	0.8	-	-	94.6	0.7	-	-
1982	92.3	-2.4	-	-	95.0	2.9	-	-	95.9	0.9	-	-	95.8	-0.1	-	-	99.2	3.5	-	-	98.9	-0.3	-	-
1983	98.5	-0.4	-	-	97.9	-0.6	-	-	98.6	0.7	-	-	101.0	2.4	-	-	101.7	0.7	-	-	100.4	-1.3	-	-
1984	101.5	1.1	-	-	101.7	0.2	-	-	103.7	2.0	-	-	100.8	-2.8	-	-	106.2	5.4	-	-	107.8	1.5	-	-
1985	105.0	-2.6	-	-	105.8	0.8	-	-	107.8	1.9	-	-	105.5	-2.1	-	-	106.4	0.9	-	-	106.8	0.4	-	-
1986	106.4	-0.4	-	-	108.8	2.3	-	-	109.0	0.2	-	-	104.3	-4.3	-	-	107.9	3.5	-	-	108.0	0.1	-	-
1987	-	-	-	-	-	-	-	-	-	-	110.5	2.3	-	-	-	-	-	-	-	-	-	-	110.0	-0.5
1988	-	-	-	-	-	-	-	-	-	-	118.0	7.3	-	-	-	-	-	-	-	-	-	-	119.6	1.4
1989	-	-	-	-	-	-	-	-	-	-	123.5	3.3	-	-	-	-	-	-	-	-	-	-	117.8	-4.6
1990	-	-	-	-	-	-	-	-	-	-	132.6	12.6	-	-	-	-	-	-	-	-	-	-	129.5	-2.3
1991	-	-	-	-	-	-	-	-	-	-	126.4	-2.4	-	-	-	-	-	-	-	-	-	-	130.0	2.8
1992	-	-	-	-	-	-	-	-	-	-	131.0	0.8	-	-	-	-	-	-	-	-	-	-	129.1	-1.5
1993	-	-	-	-	-	-	-	-	-	-	140.6	8.9	-	-	-	-	-	-	-	-	-	-	-	-

Source: U.S. Department of Labor, Bureau of Labor Statistics, Division of Consumer Prices and Price Indexes. - indicates no data collected for period.

San Diego, CA
Consumer Price Index - All Urban Consumers
Base 1982-1984 = 100
Transportation

For 1965-1993. Columns headed % show percentile change in the index from the previous period for which an index is available.

Year	Jan Index	%	Feb Index	%	Mar Index	%	Apr Index	%	May Index	%	Jun Index	%	Jul Index	%	Aug Index	%	Sep Index	%	Oct Index	%	Nov Index	%	Dec Index	%
1965	-	-	32.0	-	-	-	-	-	32.7	2.2	-	-	-	-	32.4	-0.9	-	-	-	-	31.4	-3.1	-	-
1966	-	-	31.7	1.0	-	-	-	-	31.8	0.3	-	-	-	-	31.9	0.3	-	-	-	-	33.2	4.1	-	-
1967	-	-	33.0	-0.6	-	-	-	-	33.0	0.0	-	-	-	-	33.7	2.1	-	-	-	-	33.5	-0.6	-	-
1968	-	-	33.8	0.9	-	-	-	-	34.0	0.6	-	-	-	-	34.2	0.6	-	-	-	-	34.4	0.6	-	-
1969	-	-	34.5	0.3	-	-	-	-	35.0	1.4	-	-	-	-	35.1	0.3	-	-	-	-	35.0	-0.3	-	-
1970	-	-	34.8	-0.6	-	-	-	-	35.6	2.3	-	-	-	-	35.7	0.3	-	-	-	-	37.5	5.0	-	-
1971	-	-	36.9	-1.6	-	-	-	-	38.0	3.0	-	-	-	-	38.6	1.6	-	-	-	-	38.2	-1.0	-	-
1972	-	-	37.5	-1.8	-	-	-	-	38.8	3.5	-	-	-	-	39.7	2.3	-	-	-	-	40.2	1.3	-	-
1973	-	-	39.5	-1.7	-	-	-	-	40.6	2.8	-	-	-	-	41.2	1.5	-	-	-	-	41.3	0.2	-	-
1974	-	-	43.4	5.1	-	-	-	-	45.8	5.5	-	-	-	-	47.4	3.5	-	-	-	-	48.1	1.5	-	-
1975	-	-	48.8	1.5	-	-	-	-	50.1	2.7	-	-	-	-	52.5	4.8	-	-	-	-	52.6	0.2	-	-
1976	-	-	52.5	-0.2	-	-	-	-	53.8	2.5	-	-	-	-	55.5	3.2	-	-	-	-	56.4	1.6	-	-
1977	-	-	56.8	0.7	-	-	-	-	58.1	2.3	-	-	-	-	58.6	0.9	-	-	-	-	58.9	0.5	-	-
1978	58.8	-0.2	-	-	58.8	0.0	-	-	60.1	2.2	-	-	62.2	3.5	-	-	62.4	0.3	-	-	63.4	1.6	-	-
1979	64.1	1.1	-	-	65.2	1.7	-	-	68.9	5.7	-	-	71.2	3.3	-	-	72.9	2.4	-	-	74.2	1.8	-	-
1980	77.0	3.8	-	-	80.7	4.8	-	-	82.0	1.6	-	-	82.9	1.1	-	-	84.0	1.3	-	-	84.6	0.7	-	-
1981	86.0	1.7	-	-	88.6	3.0	-	-	90.7	2.4	-	-	92.8	2.3	-	-	93.7	1.0	-	-	94.7	1.1	-	-
1982	94.6	-0.1	-	-	93.2	-1.5	-	-	93.4	0.2	-	-	98.2	5.1	-	-	97.8	-0.4	-	-	96.6	-1.2	-	-
1983	96.2	-0.4	-	-	94.4	-1.9	-	-	98.5	4.3	-	-	100.3	1.8	-	-	100.6	0.3	-	-	101.3	0.7	-	-
1984	103.1	1.8	-	-	103.3	0.2	-	-	106.9	3.5	-	-	105.2	-1.6	-	-	105.9	0.7	-	-	107.6	1.6	-	-
1985	107.5	-0.1	-	-	108.6	1.0	-	-	111.1	2.3	-	-	110.1	-0.9	-	-	108.9	-1.1	-	-	109.3	0.4	-	-
1986	110.0	0.6	-	-	106.3	-3.4	-	-	106.6	0.3	-	-	105.3	-1.2	-	-	104.1	-1.1	-	-	102.9	-1.2	-	-
1987	-	-	-	-	-	-	-	-	-	-	106.9	3.9	-	-	-	-	-	-	-	-	-	-	108.4	1.4
1988	-	-	-	-	-	-	-	-	-	-	111.5	2.9	-	-	-	-	-	-	-	-	-	-	116.9	4.8
1989	-	-	-	-	-	-	-	-	-	-	123.4	5.6	-	-	-	-	-	-	-	-	-	-	125.6	1.8
1990	-	-	-	-	-	-	-	-	-	-	128.9	2.6	-	-	-	-	-	-	-	-	-	-	134.5	4.3
1991	-	-	-	-	-	-	-	-	-	-	132.7	-1.3	-	-	-	-	-	-	-	-	-	-	134.9	1.7
1992	-	-	-	-	-	-	-	-	-	-	135.7	0.6	-	-	-	-	-	-	-	-	-	-	136.1	0.3
1993	-	-	-	-	-	-	-	-	-	-	137.5	1.0	-	-	-	-	-	-	-	-	-	-	-	-

Source: U.S. Department of Labor, Bureau of Labor Statistics, Division of Consumer Prices and Price Indexes. - indicates no data collected for period.

San Diego, CA
Consumer Price Index - Urban Wage Earners
Base 1982-1984 = 100
Transportation

For 1965-1993. Columns headed % show percentile change in the index from the previous period for which an index is available.

Year	Jan Index	%	Feb Index	%	Mar Index	%	Apr Index	%	May Index	%	Jun Index	%	Jul Index	%	Aug Index	%	Sep Index	%	Oct Index	%	Nov Index	%	Dec Index	%
1965	-	-	31.8	-	-	-	-	-	32.5	2.2	-	-	-	-	32.1	-1.2	-	-	-	-	31.2	-2.8	-	-
1966	-	-	31.5	1.0	-	-	-	-	31.5	0.0	-	-	-	-	31.6	0.3	-	-	-	-	33.0	4.4	-	-
1967	-	-	32.8	-0.6	-	-	-	-	32.8	0.0	-	-	-	-	33.5	2.1	-	-	-	-	33.3	-0.6	-	-
1968	-	-	33.6	0.9	-	-	-	-	33.8	0.6	-	-	-	-	33.9	0.3	-	-	-	-	34.2	0.9	-	-
1969	-	-	34.3	0.3	-	-	-	-	34.8	1.5	-	-	-	-	34.9	0.3	-	-	-	-	34.7	-0.6	-	-
1970	-	-	34.6	-0.3	-	-	-	-	35.4	2.3	-	-	-	-	35.5	0.3	-	-	-	-	37.2	4.8	-	-
1971	-	-	36.6	-1.6	-	-	-	-	37.8	3.3	-	-	-	-	38.3	1.3	-	-	-	-	38.0	-0.8	-	-
1972	-	-	37.2	-2.1	-	-	-	-	38.6	3.8	-	-	-	-	39.4	2.1	-	-	-	-	39.9	1.3	-	-
1973	-	-	39.2	-1.8	-	-	-	-	40.3	2.8	-	-	-	-	40.9	1.5	-	-	-	-	41.0	0.2	-	-
1974	-	-	43.1	5.1	-	-	-	-	45.5	5.6	-	-	-	-	47.1	3.5	-	-	-	-	47.8	1.5	-	-
1975	-	-	48.4	1.3	-	-	-	-	49.8	2.9	-	-	-	-	52.1	4.6	-	-	-	-	52.2	0.2	-	-
1976	-	-	52.2	0.0	-	-	-	-	53.4	2.3	-	-	-	-	55.1	3.2	-	-	-	-	56.0	1.6	-	-
1977	-	-	56.4	0.7	-	-	-	-	57.7	2.3	-	-	-	-	58.2	0.9	-	-	-	-	58.5	0.5	-	-
1978	58.7	0.3	-	-	58.8	0.2	-	-	60.0	2.0	-	-	61.9	3.2	-	-	62.0	0.2	-	-	63.3	2.1	-	-
1979	64.0	1.1	-	-	65.1	1.7	-	-	68.8	5.7	-	-	70.9	3.1	-	-	72.6	2.4	-	-	73.5	1.2	-	-
1980	76.3	3.8	-	-	79.9	4.7	-	-	80.9	1.3	-	-	81.8	1.1	-	-	82.5	0.9	-	-	83.5	1.2	-	-
1981	84.7	1.4	-	-	87.1	2.8	-	-	89.3	2.5	-	-	91.5	2.5	-	-	92.4	1.0	-	-	93.8	1.5	-	-
1982	93.9	0.1	-	-	92.7	-1.3	-	-	93.0	0.3	-	-	98.0	5.4	-	-	97.6	-0.4	-	-	96.4	-1.2	-	-
1983	95.9	-0.5	-	-	94.4	-1.6	-	-	98.4	4.2	-	-	100.2	1.8	-	-	100.6	0.4	-	-	101.4	0.8	-	-
1984	103.3	1.9	-	-	103.6	0.3	-	-	107.1	3.4	-	-	105.8	-1.2	-	-	106.2	0.4	-	-	107.9	1.6	-	-
1985	107.9	0.0	-	-	108.8	0.8	-	-	111.3	2.3	-	-	110.4	-0.8	-	-	109.1	-1.2	-	-	109.5	0.4	-	-
1986	110.1	0.5	-	-	106.9	-2.9	-	-	107.2	0.3	-	-	105.8	-1.3	-	-	104.7	-1.0	-	-	103.5	-1.1	-	-
1987	-	-	-	-	-	-	-	-	-	-	107.5	3.9	-	-	-	-	-	-	-	-	-	-	109.5	1.9
1988	-	-	-	-	-	-	-	-	-	-	112.2	2.5	-	-	-	-	-	-	-	-	-	-	117.2	4.5
1989	-	-	-	-	-	-	-	-	-	-	123.2	5.1	-	-	-	-	-	-	-	-	-	-	125.5	1.9
1990	-	-	-	-	-	-	-	-	-	-	128.8	2.6	-	-	-	-	-	-	-	-	-	-	134.0	4.0
1991	-	-	-	-	-	-	-	-	-	-	132.1	-1.4	-	-	-	-	-	-	-	-	-	-	135.0	2.2
1992	-	-	-	-	-	-	-	-	-	-	135.6	0.4	-	-	-	-	-	-	-	-	-	-	137.2	1.2
1993	-	-	-	-	-	-	-	-	-	-	138.2	0.7	-	-	-	-	-	-	-	-	-	-	-	-

Source: U.S. Department of Labor, Bureau of Labor Statistics, Division of Consumer Prices and Price Indexes. - indicates no data collected for period.

San Diego, CA
Consumer Price Index - All Urban Consumers
Base 1982-1984 = 100
Medical Care

For 1965-1993. Columns headed % show percentile change in the index from the previous period for which an index is available.

Year	Jan Index	%	Feb Index	%	Mar Index	%	Apr Index	%	May Index	%	Jun Index	%	Jul Index	%	Aug Index	%	Sep Index	%	Oct Index	%	Nov Index	%	Dec Index	%
1965	-	-	26.4	-	-	-	-	-	26.5	0.4	-	-	-	-	26.6	0.4	-	-	-	-	26.8	0.8	-	-
1966	-	-	27.2	1.5	-	-	-	-	27.7	1.8	-	-	-	-	27.9	0.7	-	-	-	-	29.2	4.7	-	-
1967	-	-	29.4	0.7	-	-	-	-	29.9	1.7	-	-	-	-	30.2	1.0	-	-	-	-	30.5	1.0	-	-
1968	-	-	30.5	0.0	-	-	-	-	30.5	0.0	-	-	-	-	30.9	1.3	-	-	-	-	31.2	1.0	-	-
1969	-	-	31.9	2.2	-	-	-	-	32.3	1.3	-	-	-	-	32.7	1.2	-	-	-	-	32.7	0.0	-	-
1970	-	-	33.4	2.1	-	-	-	-	34.3	2.7	-	-	-	-	34.9	1.7	-	-	-	-	35.2	0.9	-	-
1971	-	-	35.6	1.1	-	-	-	-	36.3	2.0	-	-	-	-	36.8	1.4	-	-	-	-	36.6	-0.5	-	-
1972	-	-	36.7	0.3	-	-	-	-	36.8	0.3	-	-	-	-	37.2	1.1	-	-	-	-	38.0	2.2	-	-
1973	-	-	38.1	0.3	-	-	-	-	38.5	1.0	-	-	-	-	39.3	2.1	-	-	-	-	40.2	2.3	-	-
1974	-	-	41.1	2.2	-	-	-	-	42.2	2.7	-	-	-	-	44.4	5.2	-	-	-	-	45.0	1.4	-	-
1975	-	-	47.1	4.7	-	-	-	-	47.8	1.5	-	-	-	-	49.0	2.5	-	-	-	-	50.1	2.2	-	-
1976	-	-	52.0	3.8	-	-	-	-	52.8	1.5	-	-	-	-	54.3	2.8	-	-	-	-	55.3	1.8	-	-
1977	-	-	56.7	2.5	-	-	-	-	58.3	2.8	-	-	-	-	59.3	1.7	-	-	-	-	60.0	1.2	-	-
1978	61.2	2.0	-	-	62.5	2.1	-	-	62.7	0.3	-	-	63.8	1.8	-	-	64.0	0.3	-	-	65.7	2.7	-	-
1979	67.2	2.3	-	-	67.6	0.6	-	-	68.4	1.2	-	-	69.2	1.2	-	-	71.1	2.7	-	-	72.3	1.7	-	-
1980	72.7	0.6	-	-	73.8	1.5	-	-	76.2	3.3	-	-	76.5	0.4	-	-	77.1	0.8	-	-	79.1	2.6	-	-
1981	79.4	0.4	-	-	79.5	0.1	-	-	80.4	1.1	-	-	84.1	4.6	-	-	84.9	1.0	-	-	87.4	2.9	-	-
1982	88.7	1.5	-	-	89.2	0.6	-	-	90.1	1.0	-	-	93.7	4.0	-	-	95.4	1.8	-	-	98.8	3.6	-	-
1983	99.9	1.1	-	-	99.9	0.0	-	-	99.9	0.0	-	-	99.7	-0.2	-	-	101.1	1.4	-	-	102.8	1.7	-	-
1984	104.3	1.5	-	-	105.2	0.9	-	-	105.5	0.3	-	-	107.5	1.9	-	-	106.9	-0.6	-	-	107.2	0.3	-	-
1985	106.9	-0.3	-	-	108.8	1.8	-	-	109.9	1.0	-	-	110.6	0.6	-	-	110.9	0.3	-	-	112.1	1.1	-	-
1986	112.8	0.6	-	-	115.0	2.0	-	-	116.4	1.2	-	-	117.8	1.2	-	-	121.4	3.1	-	-	123.0	1.3	-	-
1987	-	-	-	-	-	-	-	-	-	-	126.9	3.2	-	-	-	-	-	-	-	-	-	-	132.0	4.0
1988	-	-	-	-	-	-	-	-	-	-	137.9	4.5	-	-	-	-	-	-	-	-	-	-	145.9	5.8
1989	-	-	-	-	-	-	-	-	-	-	153.3	5.1	-	-	-	-	-	-	-	-	-	-	164.1	7.0
1990	-	-	-	-	-	-	-	-	-	-	169.0	3.0	-	-	-	-	-	-	-	-	-	-	177.6	5.1
1991	-	-	-	-	-	-	-	-	-	-	185.7	4.6	-	-	-	-	-	-	-	-	-	-	190.9	2.8
1992	-	-	-	-	-	-	-	-	-	-	198.5	4.0	-	-	-	-	-	-	-	-	-	-	204.7	3.1
1993	-	-	-	-	-	-	-	-	-	-	211.9	3.5	-	-	-	-	-	-	-	-	-	-	-	-

Source: U.S. Department of Labor, Bureau of Labor Statistics, Division of Consumer Prices and Price Indexes. - indicates no data collected for period.

San Diego, CA
Consumer Price Index - Urban Wage Earners
Base 1982-1984 = 100
Medical Care

For 1965-1993. Columns headed % show percentile change in the index from the previous period for which an index is available.

Year	Jan Index	%	Feb Index	%	Mar Index	%	Apr Index	%	May Index	%	Jun Index	%	Jul Index	%	Aug Index	%	Sep Index	%	Oct Index	%	Nov Index	%	Dec Index	%
1965	-	-	25.8	-	-	-	-	-	26.0	0.8	-	-	-	-	26.1	0.4	-	-	-	-	26.2	0.4	-	-
1966	-	-	26.6	1.5	-	-	-	-	27.1	1.9	-	-	-	-	27.3	0.7	-	-	-	-	28.6	4.8	-	-
1967	-	-	28.8	0.7	-	-	-	-	29.2	1.4	-	-	-	-	29.6	1.4	-	-	-	-	29.9	1.0	-	-
1968	-	-	29.9	0.0	-	-	-	-	29.9	0.0	-	-	-	-	30.2	1.0	-	-	-	-	30.5	1.0	-	-
1969	-	-	31.2	2.3	-	-	-	-	31.6	1.3	-	-	-	-	32.0	1.3	-	-	-	-	32.0	0.0	-	-
1970	-	-	32.7	2.2	-	-	-	-	33.5	2.4	-	-	-	-	34.1	1.8	-	-	-	-	34.4	0.9	-	-
1971	-	-	34.9	1.5	-	-	-	-	35.5	1.7	-	-	-	-	36.0	1.4	-	-	-	-	35.8	-0.6	-	-
1972	-	-	35.9	0.3	-	-	-	-	36.0	0.3	-	-	-	-	36.4	1.1	-	-	-	-	37.1	1.9	-	-
1973	-	-	37.3	0.5	-	-	-	-	37.7	1.1	-	-	-	-	38.4	1.9	-	-	-	-	39.3	2.3	-	-
1974	-	-	40.2	2.3	-	-	-	-	41.3	2.7	-	-	-	-	43.4	5.1	-	-	-	-	44.0	1.4	-	-
1975	-	-	46.0	4.5	-	-	-	-	46.8	1.7	-	-	-	-	47.9	2.4	-	-	-	-	49.0	2.3	-	-
1976	-	-	50.9	3.9	-	-	-	-	51.6	1.4	-	-	-	-	53.1	2.9	-	-	-	-	54.1	1.9	-	-
1977	-	-	55.5	2.6	-	-	-	-	57.1	2.9	-	-	-	-	58.0	1.6	-	-	-	-	58.8	1.4	-	-
1978	60.3	2.6	-	-	60.8	0.8	-	-	61.1	0.5	-	-	62.5	2.3	-	-	62.8	0.5	-	-	63.7	1.4	-	-
1979	65.2	2.4	-	-	66.2	1.5	-	-	68.7	3.8	-	-	69.4	1.0	-	-	72.0	3.7	-	-	73.0	1.4	-	-
1980	73.8	1.1	-	-	74.4	0.8	-	-	75.1	0.9	-	-	77.0	2.5	-	-	77.6	0.8	-	-	77.9	0.4	-	-
1981	79.5	2.1	-	-	79.4	-0.1	-	-	80.1	0.9	-	-	85.4	6.6	-	-	86.5	1.3	-	-	87.9	1.6	-	-
1982	89.1	1.4	-	-	89.5	0.4	-	-	90.3	0.9	-	-	93.5	3.5	-	-	95.0	1.6	-	-	98.6	3.8	-	-
1983	99.5	0.9	-	-	99.6	0.1	-	-	99.6	0.0	-	-	99.4	-0.2	-	-	101.2	1.8	-	-	102.9	1.7	-	-
1984	104.4	1.5	-	-	105.3	0.9	-	-	105.6	0.3	-	-	107.5	1.8	-	-	107.1	-0.4	-	-	107.4	0.3	-	-
1985	107.3	-0.1	-	-	109.3	1.9	-	-	110.5	1.1	-	-	111.1	0.5	-	-	111.5	0.4	-	-	112.6	1.0	-	-
1986	113.3	0.6	-	-	115.6	2.0	-	-	117.1	1.3	-	-	118.5	1.2	-	-	122.4	3.3	-	-	123.8	1.1	-	-
1987	-	-	-	-	-	-	-	-	-	-	127.7	3.2	-	-	-	-	-	-	-	-	-	-	-	-
1988	-	-	-	-	-	-	-	-	-	-	139.5	4.8	-	-	-	-	-	-	-	-	-	-	133.1	4.2
1989	-	-	-	-	-	-	-	-	-	-	155.7	4.9	-	-	-	-	-	-	-	-	-	-	148.4	6.4
1990	-	-	-	-	-	-	-	-	-	-	171.5	2.6	-	-	-	-	-	-	-	-	-	-	167.2	7.4
1991	-	-	-	-	-	-	-	-	-	-	187.4	4.2	-	-	-	-	-	-	-	-	-	-	179.9	4.9
1992	-	-	-	-	-	-	-	-	-	-	200.8	4.0	-	-	-	-	-	-	-	-	-	-	193.0	3.0
1993	-	-	-	-	-	-	-	-	-	-	214.2	3.5	-	-	-	-	-	-	-	-	-	-	207.0	3.1

Source: U.S. Department of Labor, Bureau of Labor Statistics, Division of Consumer Prices and Price Indexes. - indicates no data collected for period.

San Diego, CA
Consumer Price Index - All Urban Consumers
Base 1982-1984 = 100
Entertainment

For 1975-1993. Columns headed % show percentile change in the index from the previous period for which an index is available.

Year	Jan Index	%	Feb Index	%	Mar Index	%	Apr Index	%	May Index	%	Jun Index	%	Jul Index	%	Aug Index	%	Sep Index	%	Oct Index	%	Nov Index	%	Dec Index	%
	-	-	-	-	-	-	-	-	-	-	-	-	-	-	-	-	-	-	-	-	60.3	-	-	-
1975	-	-	-	-	-	-	-	-	-	-	-	-	-	-	63.1	0.8	-	-	-	-	63.1	0.0	-	-
1976	-	-	61.6	2.2	-	-	-	-	62.6	1.6	-	-	-	-	65.9	1.5	-	-	-	-	66.1	0.3	-	-
1977	-	-	63.4	0.5	-	-	-	-	64.9	2.4	-	-	69.5	1.2	-	-	70.7	1.7	-	-	70.7	0.0	-	-
1978	67.1	1.5	-	-	67.8	1.0	-	-	68.7	1.3	-	-	75.5	1.6	-	-	76.0	0.7	-	-	76.5	0.7	-	-
1979	72.6	2.7	-	-	73.3	1.0	-	-	74.3	1.4	-	-	84.4	1.2	-	-	84.3	-0.1	-	-	85.1	0.9	-	-
1980	77.8	1.7	-	-	81.5	4.8	-	-	83.4	2.3	-	-	90.2	1.0	-	-	91.9	1.9	-	-	92.2	0.3	-	-
1981	86.5	1.6	-	-	87.6	1.3	-	-	89.3	1.9	-	-	96.5	1.2	-	-	96.7	0.2	-	-	98.4	1.8	-	-
1982	93.3	1.2	-	-	94.6	1.4	-	-	95.4	0.8	-	-	101.0	-0.5	-	-	101.2	0.2	-	-	101.4	0.2	-	-
1983	99.7	1.3	-	-	99.5	-0.2	-	-	101.5	2.0	-	-	102.4	-0.3	-	-	103.2	0.8	-	-	105.3	2.0	-	-
1984	101.9	0.5	-	-	102.4	0.5	-	-	102.7	0.3	-	-	108.4	1.0	-	-	108.2	-0.2	-	-	108.1	-0.1	-	-
1985	105.4	0.1	-	-	106.5	1.0	-	-	107.3	0.8	-	-	113.2	1.1	-	-	112.9	-0.3	-	-	112.7	-0.2	-	-
1986	108.7	0.6	-	-	110.5	1.7	-	-	112.0	1.4	119.6	6.1	-	-	-	-	-	-	-	-	-	-	122.2	2.2
1987	-	-	-	-	-	-	-	-	-	-	127.2	4.1	-	-	-	-	-	-	-	-	-	-	133.2	4.7
1988	-	-	-	-	-	-	-	-	-	-	138.6	4.1	-	-	-	-	-	-	-	-	-	-	138.0	-0.4
1989	-	-	-	-	-	-	-	-	-	-	141.7	2.7	-	-	-	-	-	-	-	-	-	-	143.1	1.0
1990	-	-	-	-	-	-	-	-	-	-	146.4	2.3	-	-	-	-	-	-	-	-	-	-	150.4	2.7
1991	-	-	-	-	-	-	-	-	-	-	150.6	0.1	-	-	-	-	-	-	-	-	-	-	153.6	2.0
1992	-	-	-	-	-	-	-	-	-	-	154.4	0.5	-	-	-	-	-	-	-	-	-	-	-	-
1993	-	-	-	-	-	-	-	-	-	-	-	-	-	-	-	-	-	-	-	-	-	-	-	-

Source: U.S. Department of Labor, Bureau of Labor Statistics, Division of Consumer Prices and Price Indexes. - indicates no data collected for period.

San Diego, CA
Consumer Price Index - Urban Wage Earners
Base 1982-1984 = 100
Entertainment

For 1975-1993. Columns headed % show percentile change in the index from the previous period for which an index is available.

Year	Jan Index	%	Feb Index	%	Mar Index	%	Apr Index	%	May Index	%	Jun Index	%	Jul Index	%	Aug Index	%	Sep Index	%	Oct Index	%	Nov Index	%	Dec Index	%
1975	-	-	-	-	-	-	-	-	-	-	-	-	-	-	-	-	-	-	-	-	-	-	-	-
1976	-	-	59.9	2.2	-	-	-	-	60.8	1.5	-	-	-	-	61.3	0.8	-	-	-	-	58.6	-	-	-
1977	-	-	61.6	0.5	-	-	-	-	63.0	2.3	-	-	-	-	64.0	1.6	-	-	-	-	61.3	0.0	-	-
1978	64.8	0.8	-	-	65.4	0.9	-	-	66.2	1.2	-	-	68.2	3.0	-	-	69.3	1.6	-	-	64.3	0.5	-	-
1979	70.6	1.6	-	-	71.2	0.8	-	-	73.1	2.7	-	-	73.5	0.5	-	-	74.6	1.5	-	-	69.5	0.3	-	-
1980	76.2	0.3	-	-	79.8	4.7	-	-	80.7	1.1	-	-	83.2	3.1	-	-	84.7	1.8	-	-	76.0	1.9	-	-
1981	84.2	-0.5	-	-	86.7	3.0	-	-	86.9	0.2	-	-	88.9	2.3	-	-	91.4	2.8	-	-	84.6	-0.1	-	-
1982	93.2	1.5	-	-	94.4	1.3	-	-	95.4	1.1	-	-	96.8	1.5	-	-	96.6	-0.2	-	-	91.8	0.4	-	-
1983	99.8	1.6	-	-	99.2	-0.6	-	-	101.7	2.5	-	-	101.3	-0.4	-	-	101.4	0.1	-	-	98.2	1.7	-	-
1984	101.9	0.3	-	-	102.4	0.5	-	-	102.6	0.2	-	-	102.2	-0.4	-	-	103.0	0.8	-	-	101.6	0.2	-	-
1985	105.3	0.1	-	-	106.4	1.0	-	-	107.3	0.8	-	-	108.7	1.3	-	-	108.6	-0.1	-	-	105.2	2.1	-	-
1986	109.6	0.7	-	-	111.5	1.7	-	-	113.0	1.3	-	-	114.3	1.2	-	-	114.3	0.0	-	-	108.8	0.2	-	-
1987	-	-	-	-	-	-	-	-	-	-	121.4	6.3	-	-	-	-	-	-	-	-	114.2	-0.1	-	-
1988	-	-	-	-	-	-	-	-	-	-	129.2	4.4	-	-	-	-	-	-	-	-	-	-	123.8	2.0
1989	-	-	-	-	-	-	-	-	-	-	141.5	4.4	-	-	-	-	-	-	-	-	-	-	135.6	5.0
1990	-	-	-	-	-	-	-	-	-	-	144.5	2.7	-	-	-	-	-	-	-	-	-	-	140.7	-0.6
1991	-	-	-	-	-	-	-	-	-	-	148.6	1.9	-	-	-	-	-	-	-	-	-	-	145.8	0.9
1992	-	-	-	-	-	-	-	-	-	-	151.9	-0.5	-	-	-	-	-	-	-	-	-	-	152.6	2.7
1993	-	-	-	-	-	-	-	-	-	-	154.6	0.3	-	-	-	-	-	-	-	-	-	-	154.1	1.4

Source: U.S. Department of Labor, Bureau of Labor Statistics, Division of Consumer Prices and Price Indexes. - indicates no data collected for period.

San Diego, CA
Consumer Price Index - All Urban Consumers
Base 1982-1984 = 100
Other Goods and Services

For 1975-1993. Columns headed % show percentile change in the index from the previous period for which an index is available.

Year	Jan Index	Jan %	Feb Index	Feb %	Mar Index	Mar %	Apr Index	Apr %	May Index	May %	Jun Index	Jun %	Jul Index	Jul %	Aug Index	Aug %	Sep Index	Sep %	Oct Index	Oct %	Nov Index	Nov %	Dec Index	Dec %
1975	-	-	-	-	-	-	-	-	-	-	-	-	-	-	-	-	-	-	-	-	55.4	-	-	-
1976	-	-	56.6	2.2	-	-	-	-	57.8	2.1	-	-	-	-	58.3	0.9	-	-	-	-	59.5	2.1	-	-
1977	-	-	59.7	0.3	-	-	-	-	60.5	1.3	-	-	-	-	61.5	1.7	-	-	-	-	62.7	2.0	-	-
1978	63.8	1.8	-	-	64.7	1.4	-	-	65.1	0.6	-	-	65.7	0.9	-	-	67.8	3.2	-	-	68.8	1.5	-	-
1979	69.4	0.9	-	-	70.0	0.9	-	-	70.2	0.3	-	-	70.7	0.7	-	-	72.8	3.0	-	-	73.4	0.8	-	-
1980	73.9	0.7	-	-	75.1	1.6	-	-	75.2	0.1	-	-	76.7	2.0	-	-	79.3	3.4	-	-	80.7	1.8	-	-
1981	83.0	2.9	-	-	83.1	0.1	-	-	84.4	1.6	-	-	84.3	-0.1	-	-	86.7	2.8	-	-	87.6	1.0	-	-
1982	88.9	1.5	-	-	89.6	0.8	-	-	90.2	0.7	-	-	88.6	-1.8	-	-	94.2	6.3	-	-	95.4	1.3	-	-
1983	98.0	2.7	-	-	97.1	-0.9	-	-	98.8	1.8	-	-	99.2	0.4	-	-	101.7	2.5	-	-	104.5	2.8	-	-
1984	104.9	0.4	-	-	105.0	0.1	-	-	107.6	2.5	-	-	107.1	-0.5	-	-	110.5	3.2	-	-	112.6	1.9	-	-
1985	114.2	1.4	-	-	115.1	0.8	-	-	114.6	-0.4	-	-	114.5	-0.1	-	-	117.6	2.7	-	-	117.2	-0.3	-	-
1986	118.6	1.2	-	-	119.4	0.7	-	-	119.6	0.2	-	-	118.4	-1.0	-	-	120.9	2.1	-	-	121.7	0.7	-	-
1987	-	-	-	-	-	-	-	-	-	-	127.2	4.5	-	-	-	-	-	-	-	-	-	-	132.5	4.2
1988	-	-	-	-	-	-	-	-	-	-	137.8	4.0	-	-	-	-	-	-	-	-	-	-	143.1	3.8
1989	-	-	-	-	-	-	-	-	-	-	156.4	9.3	-	-	-	-	-	-	-	-	-	-	160.1	2.4
1990	-	-	-	-	-	-	-	-	-	-	163.1	1.9	-	-	-	-	-	-	-	-	-	-	168.8	3.5
1991	-	-	-	-	-	-	-	-	-	-	175.3	3.9	-	-	-	-	-	-	-	-	-	-	181.5	3.5
1992	-	-	-	-	-	-	-	-	-	-	187.1	3.1	-	-	-	-	-	-	-	-	-	-	191.1	2.1
1993	-	-	-	-	-	-	-	-	-	-	206.8	8.2	-	-	-	-	-	-	-	-	-	-	-	-

Source: U.S. Department of Labor, Bureau of Labor Statistics, Division of Consumer Prices and Price Indexes. - indicates no data collected for period.

San Diego, CA
Consumer Price Index - Urban Wage Earners
Base 1982-1984 = 100
Other Goods and Services

For 1975-1993. Columns headed % show percentile change in the index from the previous period for which an index is available.

Year	Jan Index	%	Feb Index	%	Mar Index	%	Apr Index	%	May Index	%	Jun Index	%	Jul Index	%	Aug Index	%	Sep Index	%	Oct Index	%	Nov Index	%	Dec Index	%
1975	-	-	-	-	-	-	-	-	-	-	-	-	-	-	-	-	-	-	-	-	56.6	-	-	-
1976	-	-	57.8	2.1	-	-	-	-	59.1	2.2	-	-	-	-	59.5	0.7	-	-	-	-	60.8	2.2	-	-
1977	-	-	61.0	0.3	-	-	-	-	61.9	1.5	-	-	-	-	62.9	1.6	-	-	-	-	64.1	1.9	-	-
1978	64.7	0.9	-	-	66.9	3.4	-	-	67.1	0.3	-	-	67.1	0.0	-	-	68.6	2.2	-	-	69.5	1.3	-	-
1979	70.4	1.3	-	-	71.0	0.9	-	-	71.0	0.0	-	-	71.9	1.3	-	-	74.5	3.6	-	-	74.8	0.4	-	-
1980	76.1	1.7	-	-	77.1	1.3	-	-	76.9	-0.3	-	-	78.3	1.8	-	-	80.0	2.2	-	-	81.2	1.5	-	-
1981	82.8	2.0	-	-	82.6	-0.2	-	-	84.6	2.4	-	-	83.8	-0.9	-	-	87.0	3.8	-	-	87.6	0.7	-	-
1982	88.8	1.4	-	-	89.7	1.0	-	-	90.2	0.6	-	-	88.9	-1.4	-	-	93.4	5.1	-	-	94.9	1.6	-	-
1983	98.4	3.7	-	-	97.3	-1.1	-	-	98.9	1.6	-	-	99.6	0.7	-	-	101.5	1.9	-	-	104.5	3.0	-	-
1984	105.3	0.8	-	-	105.5	0.2	-	-	107.7	2.1	-	-	107.9	0.2	-	-	109.7	1.7	-	-	111.8	1.9	-	-
1985	113.5	1.5	-	-	114.5	0.9	-	-	114.3	-0.2	-	-	114.3	0.0	-	-	116.6	2.0	-	-	116.0	-0.5	-	-
1986	117.7	1.5	-	-	118.7	0.8	-	-	118.9	0.2	-	-	117.8	-0.9	-	-	119.0	1.0	-	-	119.9	0.8	-	-
1987	-	-	-	-	-	-	-	-	-	-	125.8	4.9	-	-	-	-	-	-	-	-	-	-	130.5	3.7
1988	-	-	-	-	-	-	-	-	-	-	135.6	3.9	-	-	-	-	-	-	-	-	-	-	141.0	4.0
1989	-	-	-	-	-	-	-	-	-	-	157.6	11.8	-	-	-	-	-	-	-	-	-	-	161.8	2.7
1990	-	-	-	-	-	-	-	-	-	-	165.1	2.0	-	-	-	-	-	-	-	-	-	-	170.7	3.4
1991	-	-	-	-	-	-	-	-	-	-	177.5	4.0	-	-	-	-	-	-	-	-	-	-	181.8	2.4
1992	-	-	-	-	-	-	-	-	-	-	189.0	4.0	-	-	-	-	-	-	-	-	-	-	193.0	2.1
1993	-	-	-	-	-	-	-	-	-	-	207.2	7.4	-	-	-	-	-	-	-	-	-	-	-	-

Source: U.S. Department of Labor, Bureau of Labor Statistics, Division of Consumer Prices and Price Indexes. - indicates no data collected for period.

San Francisco-Oakland, CA
Consumer Price Index - All Urban Consumers
Base 1982-1984 = 100
Annual Averages

For 1914-1993. Columns headed % show percentile change in the index from the previous period for which an index is available.

Year	All Items Index	%	Food & Beverage Index	%	Housing Index	%	Apparel & Upkeep Index	%	Trans-portation Index	%	Medical Care Index	%	Entertain-ment Index	%	Other Goods & Services Index	%
1914	-	-	-	-	-	-	-	-	-	-	-	-	-	-	-	-
1915	9.2	-	-	-	-	-	-	-	-	-	-	-	-	-	-	-
1916	9.5	3.3	-	-	-	-	-	-	-	-	-	-	-	-	-	-
1917	10.9	14.7	-	-	-	-	-	-	-	-	-	-	-	-	-	-
1918	12.9	18.3	-	-	-	-	-	-	-	-	-	-	-	-	-	-
1919	15.0	16.3	-	-	-	-	-	-	-	-	-	-	-	-	-	-
1920	17.0	13.3	-	-	-	-	-	-	-	-	-	-	-	-	-	-
1921	15.3	-10.0	-	-	-	-	-	-	-	-	-	-	-	-	-	-
1922	14.6	-4.6	-	-	-	-	-	-	-	-	-	-	-	-	-	-
1923	14.7	0.7	-	-	-	-	-	-	-	-	-	-	-	-	-	-
1924	14.7	0.0	-	-	-	-	-	-	-	-	-	-	-	-	-	-
1925	15.1	2.7	-	-	-	-	-	-	-	-	-	-	-	-	-	-
1926	15.0	-0.7	-	-	-	-	-	-	-	-	-	-	-	-	-	-
1927	14.9	-0.7	-	-	-	-	-	-	-	-	-	-	-	-	-	-
1928	14.8	-0.7	-	-	-	-	-	-	-	-	-	-	-	-	-	-
1929	14.9	0.7	-	-	-	-	-	-	-	-	-	-	-	-	-	-
1930	14.5	-2.7	-	-	-	-	-	-	-	-	-	-	-	-	-	-
1931	13.3	-8.3	-	-	-	-	-	-	-	-	-	-	-	-	-	-
1932	12.3	-7.5	-	-	-	-	-	-	-	-	-	-	-	-	-	-
1933	11.8	-4.1	-	-	-	-	-	-	-	-	-	-	-	-	-	-
1934	12.1	2.5	-	-	-	-	-	-	-	-	-	-	-	-	-	-
1935	12.4	2.5	-	-	-	-	-	-	-	-	-	-	-	-	-	-
1936	12.4	0.0	-	-	-	-	-	-	-	-	-	-	-	-	-	-
1937	12.8	3.2	-	-	-	-	-	-	-	-	-	-	-	-	-	-
1938	12.8	0.0	-	-	-	-	-	-	-	-	-	-	-	-	-	-
1939	12.6	-1.6	-	-	-	-	-	-	-	-	-	-	-	-	-	-
1940	12.7	0.8	-	-	-	-	-	-	-	-	-	-	-	-	-	-
1941	13.4	5.5	-	-	-	-	-	-	-	-	-	-	-	-	-	-
1942	15.0	11.9	-	-	-	-	-	-	-	-	-	-	-	-	-	-
1943	16.0	6.7	-	-	-	-	-	-	-	-	-	-	-	-	-	-
1944	16.4	2.5	-	-	-	-	-	-	-	-	-	-	-	-	-	-
1945	16.8	2.4	-	-	-	-	-	-	-	-	-	-	-	-	-	-
1946	18.2	8.3	-	-	-	-	-	-	16.4	-	13.6	-	-	-	-	-
1947	20.6	13.2	-	-	-	-	-	-	18.0	9.8	14.3	5.1	-	-	-	-
1948	22.0	6.8	-	-	-	-	-	-	19.4	7.8	14.7	2.8	-	-	-	-
1949	22.0	0.0	-	-	-	-	-	-	19.5	0.5	15.1	2.7	-	-	-	-
1950	22.0	0.0	-	-	-	-	-	-	20.8	6.7	15.8	4.6	-	-	-	-
1951	23.8	8.2	-	-	-	-	-	-	23.7	13.9	16.8	6.3	-	-	-	-
1952	24.6	3.4	-	-	-	-	-	-	25.7	8.4	17.2	2.4	-	-	-	-
1953	25.0	1.6	-	-	-	-	39.3	-	25.5	-0.8	17.5	1.7	-	-	-	-
1954	25.1	0.4	-	-	-	-	38.8	-1.3	25.1	-1.6	17.6	0.6	-	-	-	-
1955	24.9	-0.8	-	-	-	-	39.0	0.5	25.4	1.2	18.6	5.7	-	-	-	-
1956	25.5	2.4	-	-	-	-	39.8	2.1	27.1	6.7	19.6	5.4	-	-	-	-
1957	26.5	3.9	-	-	-	-	40.7	2.3	28.3	4.4	21.0	7.1	-	-	-	-
1958	27.5	3.8	-	-	-	-	41.0	0.7	-	-	-	-	-	-	-	-

[Continued]

San Francisco-Oakland, CA
Consumer Price Index - All Urban Consumers
Base 1982-1984 = 100
Annual Averages
[Continued]

For 1914-1993. Columns headed % show percentile change in the index from the previous period for which an index is available.

Year	All Items		Food & Beverage		Housing		Apparel & Upkeep		Trans-portation		Medical Care		Entertain-ment		Other Goods & Services	
	Index	%	Index	%	Index	%	Index	%	Index	%	Index	%	Index	%	Index	%
1959	28.0	1.8	-	-	-	-	41.4	1.0	29.8	5.3	21.9	4.3	-	-	-	-
1960	28.6	2.1	-	-	-	-	42.5	2.7	29.6	-0.7	22.5	2.7	-	-	-	-
1961	28.9	1.0	-	-	-	-	43.2	1.6	29.8	0.7	23.0	2.2	-	-	-	-
1962	29.4	1.7	-	-	-	-	43.8	1.4	30.4	2.0	24.1	4.8	-	-	-	-
1963	29.8	1.4	-	-	-	-	44.2	0.9	30.7	1.0	24.7	2.5	-	-	-	-
1964	30.2	1.3	-	-	-	-	44.7	1.1	31.5	2.6	25.3	2.4	-	-	-	-
1965	30.8	2.0	-	-	-	-	45.4	1.6	31.7	0.6	25.9	2.4	-	-	-	-
1966	31.6	2.6	-	-	-	-	46.5	2.4	32.0	0.9	27.3	5.4	-	-	-	-
1967	32.5	2.8	-	-	-	-	48.5	4.3	32.9	2.8	28.9	5.9	-	-	-	-
1968	34.0	4.6	-	-	-	-	51.2	5.6	33.8	2.7	30.4	5.2	-	-	-	-
1969	35.8	5.3	-	-	-	-	53.7	4.9	35.3	4.4	31.9	4.9	-	-	-	-
1970	37.7	5.3	-	-	-	-	55.3	3.0	36.7	4.0	33.6	5.3	-	-	-	-
1971	39.1	3.7	-	-	-	-	57.7	4.3	38.8	5.7	35.6	6.0	-	-	-	-
1972	40.4	3.3	-	-	-	-	59.0	2.3	39.6	2.1	36.8	3.4	-	-	-	-
1973	42.8	5.9	-	-	-	-	61.4	4.1	40.5	2.3	38.2	3.8	-	-	-	-
1974	47.0	9.8	-	-	-	-	65.9	7.3	44.8	10.6	41.5	8.6	-	-	-	-
1975	51.8	10.2	-	-	-	-	68.7	4.2	49.9	11.4	47.7	14.9	-	-	-	-
1976	54.6	5.4	59.5	-	50.5	-	70.5	2.6	54.2	8.6	52.5	10.1	64.8	-	54.3	-
1977	58.8	7.7	64.0	7.6	55.0	8.9	73.1	3.7	58.0	7.0	57.8	10.1	67.6	4.3	58.2	7.2
1978	64.3	9.4	70.7	10.5	61.6	12.0	77.2	5.6	61.4	5.9	63.3	9.5	71.8	6.2	63.4	8.9
1979	69.8	8.6	79.3	12.2	65.1	5.7	82.0	6.2	70.4	14.7	69.1	9.2	75.5	5.2	67.6	6.6
1980	80.4	15.2	85.2	7.4	77.2	18.6	88.6	8.0	83.7	18.9	76.6	10.9	84.8	12.3	72.7	7.5
1981	90.8	12.9	91.2	7.0	90.5	17.2	92.6	4.5	92.0	9.9	84.6	10.4	92.4	9.0	79.8	9.8
1982	97.6	7.5	97.1	6.5	97.8	8.1	97.6	5.4	97.2	5.7	94.2	11.3	98.4	6.5	90.7	13.7
1983	98.4	0.8	99.3	2.3	97.7	-0.1	97.8	0.2	99.1	2.0	100.7	6.9	98.7	0.3	101.2	11.6
1984	104.0	5.7	103.7	4.4	104.5	7.0	104.6	7.0	103.7	4.6	105.1	4.4	102.8	4.2	108.2	6.9
1985	108.4	4.2	105.9	2.1	111.2	6.4	103.5	-1.1	105.5	1.7	111.1	5.7	108.6	5.6	116.3	7.5
1986	111.6	3.0	109.5	3.4	117.5	5.7	101.7	-1.7	101.2	-4.1	119.7	7.7	117.4	8.1	123.2	5.9
1987	115.4	3.4	113.7	3.8	121.5	3.4	104.6	2.9	102.4	1.2	128.7	7.5	121.6	3.6	130.9	6.3
1988	120.5	4.4	120.4	5.9	126.9	4.4	102.4	-2.1	105.3	2.8	136.9	6.4	129.1	6.2	140.1	7.0
1989	126.4	4.9	128.2	6.5	132.4	4.3	104.2	1.8	109.6	4.1	147.9	8.0	133.1	3.1	152.2	8.6
1990	132.1	4.5	134.7	5.1	137.3	3.7	107.5	3.2	114.7	4.7	160.5	8.5	140.7	5.7	161.0	5.8
1991	137.9	4.4	140.3	4.2	142.7	3.9	113.1	5.2	117.1	2.1	172.9	7.7	152.4	8.3	174.5	8.4
1992	142.5	3.3	143.3	2.1	146.2	2.5	117.8	4.2	119.8	2.3	187.0	8.2	156.5	2.7	195.9	12.3
1993	146.3	2.7	146.2	2.0	149.2	2.1	118.2	0.3	123.7	3.3	199.1	6.5	162.3	3.7	207.0	5.7

Source: U.S. Department of Labor, Bureau of Labor Statistics, Division of Consumer Prices and Price Indexes. - indicates no data collected for period.

San Francisco-Oakland, CA
Consumer Price Index - Urban Wage Earners
Base 1982-1984 = 100
Annual Averages

For 1914-1993. Columns headed % show percentile change in the index from the previous period for which an index is available.

Year	All Items Index	%	Food & Beverage Index	%	Housing Index	%	Apparel & Upkeep Index	%	Trans-portation Index	%	Medical Care Index	%	Entertain-ment Index	%	Other Goods & Services Index	%
1914	-	-	-	-	-	-	-	-	-	-	-	-	-	-	-	-
1915	9.3	-	-	-	-	-	-	-	-	-	-	-	-	-	-	-
1916	9.6	3.2	-	-	-	-	-	-	-	-	-	-	-	-	-	-
1917	11.0	14.6	-	-	-	-	-	-	-	-	-	-	-	-	-	-
1918	13.0	18.2	-	-	-	-	-	-	-	-	-	-	-	-	-	-
1919	15.2	16.9	-	-	-	-	-	-	-	-	-	-	-	-	-	-
1920	17.1	12.5	-	-	-	-	-	-	-	-	-	-	-	-	-	-
1921	15.5	-9.4	-	-	-	-	-	-	-	-	-	-	-	-	-	-
1922	14.8	-4.5	-	-	-	-	-	-	-	-	-	-	-	-	-	-
1923	14.8	0.0	-	-	-	-	-	-	-	-	-	-	-	-	-	-
1924	14.8	0.0	-	-	-	-	-	-	-	-	-	-	-	-	-	-
1925	15.2	2.7	-	-	-	-	-	-	-	-	-	-	-	-	-	-
1926	15.2	0.0	-	-	-	-	-	-	-	-	-	-	-	-	-	-
1927	15.0	-1.3	-	-	-	-	-	-	-	-	-	-	-	-	-	-
1928	15.0	0.0	-	-	-	-	-	-	-	-	-	-	-	-	-	-
1929	15.0	0.0	-	-	-	-	-	-	-	-	-	-	-	-	-	-
1930	14.7	-2.0	-	-	-	-	-	-	-	-	-	-	-	-	-	-
1931	13.4	-8.8	-	-	-	-	-	-	-	-	-	-	-	-	-	-
1932	12.4	-7.5	-	-	-	-	-	-	-	-	-	-	-	-	-	-
1933	11.9	-4.0	-	-	-	-	-	-	-	-	-	-	-	-	-	-
1934	12.2	2.5	-	-	-	-	-	-	-	-	-	-	-	-	-	-
1935	12.5	2.5	-	-	-	-	-	-	-	-	-	-	-	-	-	-
1936	12.5	0.0	-	-	-	-	-	-	-	-	-	-	-	-	-	-
1937	13.0	4.0	-	-	-	-	-	-	-	-	-	-	-	-	-	-
1938	12.9	-0.8	-	-	-	-	-	-	-	-	-	-	-	-	-	-
1939	12.7	-1.6	-	-	-	-	-	-	-	-	-	-	-	-	-	-
1940	12.8	0.8	-	-	-	-	-	-	-	-	-	-	-	-	-	-
1941	13.5	5.5	-	-	-	-	-	-	-	-	-	-	-	-	-	-
1942	15.1	11.9	-	-	-	-	-	-	-	-	-	-	-	-	-	-
1943	16.1	6.6	-	-	-	-	-	-	-	-	-	-	-	-	-	-
1944	16.5	2.5	-	-	-	-	-	-	-	-	-	-	-	-	-	-
1945	17.0	3.0	-	-	-	-	-	-	-	-	-	-	-	-	-	-
1946	18.3	7.6	-	-	-	-	-	-	-	-	-	-	-	-	-	-
1947	20.8	13.7	-	-	-	-	-	-	16.0	-	13.7	-	-	-	-	-
1948	22.2	6.7	-	-	-	-	-	-	17.6	10.0	14.4	5.1	-	-	-	-
1949	22.2	0.0	-	-	-	-	-	-	19.0	8.0	14.8	2.8	-	-	-	-
1950	22.2	0.0	-	-	-	-	-	-	19.0	0.0	15.2	2.7	-	-	-	-
1951	24.0	8.1	-	-	-	-	-	-	20.3	6.8	15.9	4.6	-	-	-	-
1952	24.9	3.8	-	-	-	-	-	-	23.2	14.3	16.9	6.3	-	-	-	-
1953	25.3	1.6	-	-	-	-	40.8	-	25.1	8.2	17.4	3.0	-	-	-	-
1954	25.3	0.0	-	-	-	-	40.3	-1.2	24.9	-0.8	17.6	1.1	-	-	-	-
1955	25.2	-0.4	-	-	-	-	40.4	0.2	24.5	-1.6	17.8	1.1	-	-	-	-
1956	25.7	2.0	-	-	-	-	41.3	2.2	24.8	1.2	18.7	5.1	-	-	-	-
1957	26.8	4.3	-	-	-	-	42.2	2.2	26.4	6.5	19.7	5.3	-	-	-	-
1958	27.7	3.4	-	-	-	-	42.5	0.7	27.6	4.5	21.2	7.6	-	-	-	-

[Continued]

San Francisco-Oakland, CA
Consumer Price Index - Urban Wage Earners
Base 1982-1984 = 100
Annual Averages
[Continued]

For 1914-1993. Columns headed % show percentile change in the index from the previous period for which an index is available.

Year	All Items		Food & Beverage		Housing		Apparel & Upkeep		Trans-portation		Medical Care		Entertain-ment		Other Goods & Services	
	Index	%	Index	%	Index	%	Index	%	Index	%	Index	%	Index	%	Index	%
1959	28.3	2.2	-	-	-	-	43.0	1.2	29.1	5.4	22.0	3.8	-	-	-	-
1960	28.8	1.8	-	-	-	-	44.2	2.8	28.9	-0.7	22.7	3.2	-	-	-	-
1961	29.2	1.4	-	-	-	-	44.8	1.4	29.1	0.7	23.2	2.2	-	-	-	-
1962	29.7	1.7	-	-	-	-	45.4	1.3	29.7	2.1	24.2	4.3	-	-	-	-
1963	30.0	1.0	-	-	-	-	45.9	1.1	30.0	1.0	24.8	2.5	-	-	-	-
1964	30.5	1.7	-	-	-	-	46.4	1.1	30.8	2.7	25.4	2.4	-	-	-	-
1965	31.1	2.0	-	-	-	-	47.1	1.5	31.0	0.6	26.1	2.8	-	-	-	-
1966	31.9	2.6	-	-	-	-	48.3	2.5	31.2	0.6	27.5	5.4	-	-	-	-
1967	32.8	2.8	-	-	-	-	50.3	4.1	32.1	2.9	29.1	5.8	-	-	-	-
1968	34.3	4.6	-	-	-	-	53.2	5.8	33.0	2.8	30.6	5.2	-	-	-	-
1969	36.2	5.5	-	-	-	-	55.7	4.7	34.5	4.5	32.1	4.9	-	-	-	-
1970	38.0	5.0	-	-	-	-	57.4	3.1	35.9	4.1	33.8	5.3	-	-	-	-
1971	39.4	3.7	-	-	-	-	59.8	4.2	37.9	5.6	35.9	6.2	-	-	-	-
1972	40.8	3.6	-	-	-	-	61.2	2.3	38.6	1.8	37.0	3.1	-	-	-	-
1973	43.2	5.9	-	-	-	-	63.7	4.1	39.5	2.3	38.5	4.1	-	-	-	-
1974	47.4	9.7	-	-	-	-	68.4	7.4	43.8	10.9	41.8	8.6	-	-	-	-
1975	52.2	10.1	-	-	-	-	71.3	4.2	48.7	11.2	48.0	14.8	-	-	-	-
1976	55.2	5.7	59.1	-	51.8	-	73.1	2.5	52.9	8.6	52.9	10.2	72.6	-	54.0	-
1977	59.4	7.6	63.6	7.6	56.4	8.9	75.8	3.7	56.6	7.0	58.2	10.0	75.7	4.3	57.9	7.2
1978	64.8	9.1	70.3	10.5	63.0	11.7	78.4	3.4	60.3	6.5	63.5	9.1	81.2	7.3	61.7	6.6
1979	70.5	8.8	78.4	11.5	66.5	5.6	82.9	5.7	69.5	15.3	69.2	9.0	83.8	3.2	66.7	8.1
1980	81.2	15.2	84.9	8.3	78.9	18.6	88.8	7.1	82.3	18.4	76.9	11.1	91.7	9.4	73.1	9.6
1981	91.6	12.8	91.8	8.1	92.3	17.0	95.1	7.1	91.1	10.7	85.1	10.7	98.8	7.7	80.2	9.7
1982	98.2	7.2	97.0	5.7	100.0	8.3	98.1	3.2	96.8	6.3	94.1	10.6	100.0	1.2	91.0	13.5
1983	98.2	0.0	99.3	2.4	96.9	-3.1	97.7	-0.4	99.2	2.5	100.6	6.9	97.7	-2.3	101.1	11.1
1984	103.7	5.6	103.7	4.4	103.2	6.5	104.2	6.7	104.0	4.8	105.4	4.8	102.3	4.7	107.9	6.7
1985	107.8	4.0	105.9	2.1	109.6	6.2	103.9	-0.3	105.7	1.6	111.8	6.1	107.2	4.8	115.9	7.4
1986	110.7	2.7	109.5	3.4	115.9	5.7	102.3	-1.5	101.5	-4.0	120.5	7.8	114.1	6.4	122.5	5.7
1987	114.3	3.3	113.8	3.9	119.4	3.0	105.4	3.0	103.7	2.2	130.0	7.9	117.3	2.8	130.4	6.4
1988	119.4	4.5	120.4	5.8	124.6	4.4	104.4	-0.9	107.1	3.3	138.1	6.2	124.0	5.7	140.1	7.4
1989	125.5	5.1	128.3	6.6	129.7	4.1	107.0	2.5	111.8	4.4	149.0	7.9	130.1	4.9	154.6	10.3
1990	131.1	4.5	134.7	5.0	134.6	3.8	110.6	3.4	116.7	4.4	160.8	7.9	136.3	4.8	164.5	6.4
1991	136.3	4.0	140.4	4.2	139.7	3.8	116.2	5.1	118.6	1.6	172.1	7.0	143.5	5.3	177.8	8.1
1992	140.6	3.2	143.3	2.1	143.1	2.4	121.5	4.6	121.9	2.8	186.4	8.3	147.5	2.8	195.8	10.1
1993	144.3	2.6	146.4	2.2	146.1	2.1	122.7	1.0	125.7	3.1	197.9	6.2	151.6	2.8	204.8	4.6

Source: U.S. Department of Labor, Bureau of Labor Statistics, Division of Consumer Prices and Price Indexes. - indicates no data collected for period.

San Francisco-Oakland, CA
Consumer Price Index - All Urban Consumers
Base 1982-1984 = 100
All Items

For 1914-1993. Columns headed % show percentile change in the index from the previous period for which an index is available.

Year	Jan Index	%	Feb Index	%	Mar Index	%	Apr Index	%	May Index	%	Jun Index	%	Jul Index	%	Aug Index	%	Sep Index	%	Oct Index	%	Nov Index	%	Dec Index	%
1914	-		-		-		-		-		-		-		-		-		-		-		9.2	-
1915	-		-		-		-		-		-		-		-		-		-		-		9.2	0.0
1916	-		-		-		-		-		-		-		-		-		-		-		10.0	8.7
1917	-		-		-		-		-		-		-		-		-		-		-		11.6	16.0
1918	-		-		-		-		-		-		-		-		-		-		-		14.1	21.6
1919	-		-		-		-		-		14.7	4.3	-		-		-		-		-		16.3	10.9
1920	-		-		-		-		-		17.5	7.4	-		-		-		-		-		16.5	-5.7
1921	-		-		-		-		15.2	-7.9	-		-		-		15.0	-1.3	-		-		15.0	0.0
1922	-		-		14.7	-2.0	-		-		14.6	-0.7	-		-		14.5	-0.7	-		-		14.6	0.7
1923	-		-		14.4	-1.4	-		-		14.6	1.4	-		-		14.8	1.4	-		-		15.0	1.4
1924	-		-		14.6	-2.7	-		-		14.6	0.0	-		-		14.7	0.7	-		-		14.8	0.7
1925	-		-		-		-		-		15.1	2.0	-		-		-		-		-		15.3	1.3
1926	-		-		-		-		-		15.0	-2.0	-		-		-		-		-		15.0	0.0
1927	-		-		-		-		-		15.0	0.0	-		-		-		-		-		14.9	-0.7
1928	-		-		-		-		-		14.8	-0.7	-		-		-		-		-		15.0	1.4
1929	-		-		-		-		-		14.8	-1.3	-		-		-		-		-		14.9	0.7
1930	-		-		-		-		-		14.6	-2.0	-		-		-		-		-		14.1	-3.4
1931	-		-		-		-		-		13.3	-5.7	-		-		-		-		-		12.9	-3.0
1932	-		-		-		-		-		12.2	-5.4	-		-		-		-		-		12.0	-1.6
1933	-		-		-		-		-		11.7	-2.5	-		-		-		-		-		12.1	3.4
1934	-		-		-		-		-		12.2	0.8	-		-		-		-		12.5	2.5	-	
1935	-		-		12.6	0.8	-		-		-		12.3	-2.4	-		-		12.3	0.0	-		-	
1936	12.4	0.8	-		-		12.2	-1.6	-		-		12.4	1.6	-		12.4	0.0	-		-		12.4	0.0
1937	-		-		12.8	3.2	-		-		12.8	0.0	-		-		12.9	0.8	-		-		13.0	0.8
1938	-		-		12.8	-1.5	-		-		12.8	0.0	-		-		12.8	0.0	-		-		12.8	0.0
1939	-		-		12.7	-0.8	-		-		12.5	-1.6	-		-		12.8	2.4	-		-		12.6	-1.6
1940	-		-		12.6	0.0	-		-		12.6	0.0	-		-		12.7	0.8	12.8	0.8	12.8	0.0	12.8	0.0
1941	12.8	0.0	12.9	0.8	12.9	0.0	13.1	1.6	13.1	0.0	13.3	1.5	13.3	0.0	13.4	0.8	13.6	1.5	13.8	1.5	14.0	1.4	14.0	0.0
1942	14.3	2.1	14.4	0.7	14.6	1.4	14.8	1.4	14.8	0.0	14.9	0.7	14.9	0.0	15.1	1.3	15.2	0.7	15.3	0.7	15.6	2.0	15.6	0.0
1943	15.7	0.6	15.7	0.0	15.9	1.3	16.2	1.9	16.2	0.0	16.2	0.0	15.8	-2.5	15.7	-0.6	15.8	0.6	16.0	1.3	16.1	0.6	16.1	0.0
1944	16.1	0.0	16.0	-0.6	16.1	0.6	16.2	0.6	16.4	1.2	16.3	-0.6	16.4	0.6	16.4	0.0	16.4	0.0	16.6	1.2	16.6	0.0	16.8	1.2
1945	16.7	-0.6	16.6	-0.6	16.7	0.6	16.8	0.6	16.7	-0.6	16.8	0.6	16.9	0.6	16.8	-0.6	16.8	0.0	16.8	0.0	17.0	1.2	17.2	1.2
1946	17.0	-1.2	16.8	-1.2	16.9	0.6	16.9	0.0	17.0	0.6	17.4	2.4	18.2	4.6	18.7	2.7	19.1	2.1	19.4	1.6	20.1	3.6	20.3	1.0
1947	20.1	-1.0	20.0	-0.5	20.3	1.5	20.4	0.5	20.3	-0.5	20.1	-1.0	-		-		21.0	4.5	-		-		21.4	1.9
1948	-		-		21.7	1.4	-		-		22.0	1.4	-		-		22.4	1.8	-		-		22.4	0.0
1949	-		-		22.1	-1.3	-		-		22.0	-0.5	-		-		21.9	-0.5	-		-		21.7	-0.9
1950	-		-		21.8	0.5	-		-		21.7	-0.5	-		-		22.1	1.8	-		-		22.9	3.6
1951	-		-		23.8	3.9	-		-		23.7	-0.4	-		-		23.7	0.0	-		-		24.3	2.5
1952	-		-		24.3	0.0	-		-		24.8	2.1	-		-		24.7	-0.4	-		-		24.9	0.8
1953	-		-		24.9	0.0	-		-		25.0	0.4	-		-		25.2	0.8	-		-		25.2	0.0
1954	-		-		25.1	-0.4	-		-		25.1	0.0	-		-		25.0	-0.4	-		-		24.9	-0.4
1955	-		-		24.9	0.0	-		-		24.9	0.0	-		-		24.9	0.0	-		-		24.9	0.0
1956	-		-		25.1	0.8	-		-		25.4	1.2	-		-		25.6	0.8	-		-		26.2	2.3
1957	-		-		26.3	0.4	-		-		26.4	0.4	-		-		26.6	0.8	-		-		26.9	1.1
1958	-		-		27.3	1.5	-		-		27.6	1.1	-		-		27.6	0.0	-		-		27.6	0.0

[Continued]

San Francisco-Oakland, CA
Consumer Price Index - All Urban Consumers
Base 1982-1984 = 100
All Items
[Continued]

For 1914-1993. Columns headed % show percentile change in the index from the previous period for which an index is available.

Year	Jan Index	%	Feb Index	%	Mar Index	%	Apr Index	%	May Index	%	Jun Index	%	Jul Index	%	Aug Index	%	Sep Index	%	Oct Index	%	Nov Index	%	Dec Index	%
1959	-		-		27.8	0.7	-		-		27.9	0.4	-		-		28.2	1.1	-		-		28.4	0.7
1960	-		-		28.3	-0.4	-		-		28.5	0.7	-		-		28.7	0.7	-		-		28.9	0.7
1961	-		-		28.8	-0.3	-		-		28.8	0.0	-		-		29.0	0.7	-		-		29.1	0.3
1962	-		-		29.3	0.7	-		-		29.4	0.3	-		-		29.4	0.0	-		-		29.5	0.3
1963	-		-		29.6	0.3	-		-		29.8	0.7	-		-		29.9	0.3	-		-		30.1	0.7
1964	-		-		30.1	0.0	-		-		30.2	0.3	-		-		30.3	0.3	-		-		30.5	0.7
1965	-		-		30.7	0.7	-		-		30.9	0.7	-		-		30.8	-0.3	-		-		31.1	1.0
1966	-		-		31.4	1.0	-		-		31.5	0.3	-		-		31.8	1.0	-		-		32.0	0.6
1967	-		-		32.0	0.0	-		-		32.4	1.3	-		-		32.9	1.5	-		-		33.1	0.6
1968	-		-		33.5	1.2	-		-		34.0	1.5	-		-		34.3	0.9	-		-		34.6	0.9
1969	-		-		35.2	1.7	-		-		35.7	1.4	-		-		36.3	1.7	-		-		36.8	1.4
1970	-		-		37.2	1.1	-		-		37.6	1.1	-		-		38.0	1.1	-		-		38.5	1.3
1971	-		-		38.7	0.5	-		-		39.0	0.8	-		-		39.3	0.8	-		-		39.6	0.8
1972	-		-		39.9	0.8	-		-		40.4	1.3	-		-		40.9	1.2	-		-		41.1	0.5
1973	-		-		41.9	1.9	-		-		42.5	1.4	-		-		43.8	3.1	-		-		44.0	0.5
1974	-		-		45.3	3.0	-		-		46.8	3.3	-		-		48.2	3.0	-		-		49.5	2.7
1975	-		-		50.7	2.4	-		-		51.6	1.8	-		-		52.5	1.7	-		-		53.4	1.7
1976	-		-		53.8	0.7	-		-		54.3	0.9	-		-		55.3	1.8	-		-		56.0	1.3
1977	-		-		57.2	2.1	-		-		58.8	2.8	-		-		59.9	1.9	-		-		60.9	1.7
1978	-		61.5	1.0	-		62.7	2.0	-		64.8	3.3	-		66.6	2.8	-		66.1	-0.8	-		65.3	-1.2
1979	-		66.3	1.5	-		67.9	2.4	-		69.1	1.8	-		71.0	2.7	-		72.0	1.4	-		74.9	4.0
1980	-		78.3	4.5	-		79.2	1.1	-		80.7	1.9	-		81.6	1.1	-		81.9	0.4	-		82.9	1.2
1981	-		84.7	2.2	-		87.9	3.8	-		89.1	1.4	-		93.6	5.1	-		96.6	3.2	-		95.6	-1.0
1982	-		96.2	0.6	-		97.2	1.0	-		99.1	2.0	-		99.0	-0.1	-		98.4	-0.6	-		95.6	-2.8
1983	-		96.7	1.2	-		97.4	0.7	-		98.6	1.2	-		99.5	0.9	-		99.4	-0.1	-		100.0	0.6
1984	-		101.4	1.4	-		102.9	1.5	-		103.7	0.8	-		105.2	1.4	-		106.5	1.2	-		106.0	-0.5
1985	-		106.9	0.8	-		107.5	0.6	-		108.4	0.8	-		109.2	0.7	-		109.5	0.3	-		109.4	-0.1
1986	-		111.0	1.5	-		110.4	-0.5	-		111.9	1.4	-		112.4	0.4	-		113.1	0.6	-		111.8	-1.1
1987	112.5	0.6	113.4	0.8	113.7	0.3	114.8	1.0	115.0	0.2	115.0	0.0	115.8	0.7	116.1	0.3	116.6	0.4	117.1	0.4	117.3	0.2	117.4	0.1
1988	118.4	0.9	117.9	-0.4	119.1	1.0	118.7	-0.3	119.7	0.8	120.1	0.3	120.9	0.7	122.0	0.9	122.1	0.1	122.3	0.2	122.2	-0.1	122.6	0.3
1989	124.0	1.1	124.0	0.0	125.9	1.5	125.4	-0.4	126.3	0.7	126.2	-0.1	127.4	1.0	128.1	0.5	126.8	-1.0	127.5	0.6	127.2	-0.2	127.4	0.2
1990	128.5	0.9	129.2	0.5	130.0	0.6	130.7	0.5	130.8	0.1	131.6	0.6	132.3	0.5	133.1	0.6	134.0	0.7	134.6	0.4	134.7	0.1	135.1	0.3
1991	136.7	1.2	136.1	-0.4	136.3	0.1	135.8	-0.4	136.2	0.3	137.6	1.0	138.2	0.4	139.1	0.7	139.7	0.4	139.6	-0.1	139.8	0.1	139.8	0.0
1992	140.3	0.4	141.0	0.5	141.9	0.6	141.6	-0.2	141.9	0.2	141.9	0.0	142.2	0.2	142.7	0.4	143.7	0.7	144.3	0.4	144.2	-0.1	144.3	0.1
1993	145.1	0.6	145.5	0.3	145.7	0.1	146.8	0.8	146.9	0.1	146.1	-0.5	146.1	0.0	146.2	0.1	146.5	0.2	147.0	0.3	147.2	0.1	147.0	-0.1

Source: U.S. Department of Labor, Bureau of Labor Statistics, Division of Consumer Prices and Price Indexes. - indicates no data collected for period.

San Francisco-Oakland, CA
Consumer Price Index - Urban Wage Earners
Base 1982-1984 = 100
All Items

For 1914-1993. Columns headed % show percentile change in the index from the previous period for which an index is available.

Year	Jan Index	%	Feb Index	%	Mar Index	%	Apr Index	%	May Index	%	Jun Index	%	Jul Index	%	Aug Index	%	Sep Index	%	Oct Index	%	Nov Index	%	Dec Index	%
1914	-	-	-	-	-	-	-	-	-	-	-	-	-	-	-	-	-	-	-	-	-	-	9.3	-
1915	-	-	-	-	-	-	-	-	-	-	-	-	-	-	-	-	-	-	-	-	-	-	9.3	0.0
1916	-	-	-	-	-	-	-	-	-	-	-	-	-	-	-	-	-	-	-	-	-	-	10.0	7.5
1917	-	-	-	-	-	-	-	-	-	-	-	-	-	-	-	-	-	-	-	-	-	-	11.7	17.0
1918	-	-	-	-	-	-	-	-	-	-	-	-	-	-	-	-	-	-	-	-	-	-	14.3	22.2
1919	-	-	-	-	-	-	-	-	-	-	14.8	3.5	-	-	-	-	-	-	-	-	-	-	16.4	10.8
1920	-	-	-	-	-	-	-	-	-	-	17.7	7.9	-	-	-	-	-	-	-	-	-	-	16.7	-5.6
1921	-	-	-	-	-	-	-	-	15.3	-8.4	-	-	-	-	-	-	15.2	-0.7	-	-	-	-	15.1	-0.7
1922	-	-	-	-	14.8	-2.0	-	-	-	-	14.7	-0.7	-	-	-	-	14.6	-0.7	-	-	-	-	14.8	1.4
1923	-	-	-	-	14.6	-1.4	-	-	-	-	14.7	0.7	-	-	-	-	14.9	1.4	-	-	-	-	15.1	1.3
1924	-	-	-	-	14.7	-2.6	-	-	-	-	14.7	0.0	-	-	-	-	14.8	0.7	-	-	-	-	14.9	0.7
1925	-	-	-	-	-	-	-	-	-	-	15.3	2.7	-	-	-	-	-	-	-	-	-	-	15.4	0.7
1926	-	-	-	-	-	-	-	-	-	-	15.1	-1.9	-	-	-	-	-	-	-	-	-	-	15.1	0.0
1927	-	-	-	-	-	-	-	-	-	-	15.2	0.7	-	-	-	-	-	-	-	-	-	-	15.0	-1.3
1928	-	-	-	-	-	-	-	-	-	-	14.9	-0.7	-	-	-	-	-	-	-	-	-	-	15.1	1.3
1929	-	-	-	-	-	-	-	-	-	-	15.0	-0.7	-	-	-	-	-	-	-	-	-	-	15.0	0.0
1930	-	-	-	-	-	-	-	-	-	-	14.7	-2.0	-	-	-	-	-	-	-	-	-	-	14.2	-3.4
1931	-	-	-	-	-	-	-	-	-	-	13.4	-5.6	-	-	-	-	-	-	-	-	-	-	13.0	-3.0
1932	-	-	-	-	-	-	-	-	-	-	12.3	-5.4	-	-	-	-	-	-	-	-	-	-	12.1	-1.6
1933	-	-	-	-	-	-	-	-	-	-	11.8	-2.5	-	-	-	-	-	-	-	-	-	-	12.2	3.4
1934	-	-	-	-	-	-	-	-	-	-	12.3	0.8	-	-	-	-	-	-	-	-	12.6	2.4	-	-
1935	-	-	-	-	12.7	0.8	-	-	-	-	-	-	12.4	-2.4	-	-	-	-	12.4	0.0	-	-	-	-
1936	12.5	0.8	-	-	-	-	12.3	-1.6	-	-	-	-	12.5	1.6	-	-	12.5	0.0	-	-	-	-	12.5	0.0
1937	-	-	-	-	12.9	3.2	-	-	-	-	12.9	0.0	-	-	-	-	13.1	1.6	-	-	-	-	13.1	0.0
1938	-	-	-	-	12.9	-1.5	-	-	-	-	12.9	0.0	-	-	-	-	12.9	0.0	-	-	-	-	12.9	0.0
1939	-	-	-	-	12.8	-0.8	-	-	-	-	12.6	-1.6	-	-	-	-	12.9	2.4	-	-	-	-	12.7	-1.6
1940	-	-	-	-	12.7	0.0	-	-	-	-	12.7	0.0	-	-	-	-	12.8	0.8	12.9	0.8	12.9	0.0	12.9	0.0
1941	13.0	0.8	13.0	0.0	13.0	0.0	13.2	1.5	13.3	0.8	13.4	0.8	13.4	0.0	13.5	0.7	13.7	1.5	13.9	1.5	14.1	1.4	14.2	0.7
1942	14.5	2.1	14.5	0.0	14.7	1.4	14.9	1.4	14.9	0.0	15.0	0.7	15.0	0.0	15.2	1.3	15.4	1.3	15.5	0.6	15.7	1.3	15.8	0.6
1943	15.8	0.0	15.8	0.0	16.1	1.9	16.4	1.9	16.3	-0.6	16.4	0.6	16.0	-2.4	15.8	-1.2	16.0	1.3	16.2	1.3	16.3	0.6	16.3	0.0
1944	16.3	0.0	16.2	-0.6	16.3	0.6	16.4	0.6	16.5	0.6	16.5	0.0	16.5	0.0	16.5	0.0	16.6	0.6	16.7	0.6	16.8	0.6	16.9	0.6
1945	16.8	-0.6	16.7	-0.6	16.8	0.6	16.9	0.6	16.8	-0.6	16.9	0.6	17.0	0.6	16.9	-0.6	16.9	0.0	17.0	0.6	17.2	1.2	17.3	0.6
1946	17.1	-1.2	17.0	-0.6	17.0	0.0	17.1	0.6	17.2	0.6	17.6	2.3	18.4	4.5	18.9	2.7	19.3	2.1	19.6	1.6	20.3	3.6	20.5	1.0
1947	20.3	-1.0	20.2	-0.5	20.5	1.5	20.6	0.5	20.5	-0.5	20.3	-1.0	-	-	-	-	21.2	4.4	-	-	-	-	21.6	1.9
1948	-	-	-	-	21.9	1.4	-	-	-	-	22.2	1.4	-	-	-	-	22.6	1.8	-	-	-	-	22.6	0.0
1949	-	-	-	-	22.3	-1.3	-	-	-	-	22.2	-0.4	-	-	-	-	22.1	-0.5	-	-	-	-	21.9	-0.9
1950	-	-	-	-	22.0	0.5	-	-	-	-	21.9	-0.5	-	-	-	-	22.3	1.8	-	-	-	-	23.1	3.6
1951	-	-	-	-	24.0	3.9	-	-	-	-	23.9	-0.4	-	-	-	-	23.9	0.0	-	-	-	-	24.6	2.9
1952	-	-	-	-	24.6	0.0	-	-	-	-	25.0	1.6	-	-	-	-	24.9	-0.4	-	-	-	-	25.2	1.2
1953	-	-	-	-	25.1	-0.4	-	-	-	-	25.3	0.8	-	-	-	-	25.4	0.4	-	-	-	-	25.4	0.0
1954	-	-	-	-	25.3	-0.4	-	-	-	-	25.4	0.4	-	-	-	-	25.3	-0.4	-	-	-	-	25.2	-0.4
1955	-	-	-	-	25.2	0.0	-	-	-	-	25.1	-0.4	-	-	-	-	25.2	0.4	-	-	-	-	25.2	0.0
1956	-	-	-	-	25.4	0.8	-	-	-	-	25.6	0.8	-	-	-	-	25.9	1.2	-	-	-	-	26.4	1.9
1957	-	-	-	-	26.6	0.8	-	-	-	-	26.7	0.4	-	-	-	-	26.9	0.7	-	-	-	-	27.1	0.7
1958	-	-	-	-	27.6	1.8	-	-	-	-	27.8	0.7	-	-	-	-	27.9	0.4	-	-	-	-	27.8	-0.4

[Continued]

San Francisco-Oakland, CA
Consumer Price Index - Urban Wage Earners
Base 1982-1984 = 100
All Items
[Continued]

For 1914-1993. Columns headed % show percentile change in the index from the previous period for which an index is available.

Year	Jan Index	%	Feb Index	%	Mar Index	%	Apr Index	%	May Index	%	Jun Index	%	Jul Index	%	Aug Index	%	Sep Index	%	Oct Index	%	Nov Index	%	Dec Index	%
1959	-	-	-	-	28.1	1.1	-	-	-	-	28.2	0.4	-	-	-	-	28.4	0.7	-	-	-	-	28.7	1.1
1960	-	-	-	-	28.6	-0.3	-	-	-	-	28.8	0.7	-	-	-	-	28.9	0.3	-	-	-	-	29.1	0.7
1961	-	-	-	-	29.1	0.0	-	-	-	-	29.1	0.0	-	-	-	-	29.3	0.7	-	-	-	-	29.4	0.3
1962	-	-	-	-	29.6	0.7	-	-	-	-	29.7	0.3	-	-	-	-	29.7	0.0	-	-	-	-	29.8	0.3
1963	-	-	-	-	29.9	0.3	-	-	-	-	30.0	0.3	-	-	-	-	30.1	0.3	-	-	-	-	30.3	0.7
1964	-	-	-	-	30.3	0.0	-	-	-	-	30.5	0.7	-	-	-	-	30.6	0.3	-	-	-	-	30.8	0.7
1965	-	-	-	-	31.0	0.6	-	-	-	-	31.2	0.6	-	-	-	-	31.1	-0.3	-	-	-	-	31.4	1.0
1966	-	-	-	-	31.7	1.0	-	-	-	-	31.8	0.3	-	-	-	-	32.1	0.9	-	-	-	-	32.3	0.6
1967	-	-	-	-	32.3	0.0	-	-	-	-	32.7	1.2	-	-	-	-	33.2	1.5	-	-	-	-	33.5	0.9
1968	-	-	-	-	33.9	1.2	-	-	-	-	34.3	1.2	-	-	-	-	34.6	0.9	-	-	-	-	35.0	1.2
1969	-	-	-	-	35.6	1.7	-	-	-	-	36.1	1.4	-	-	-	-	36.6	1.4	-	-	-	-	37.1	1.4
1970	-	-	-	-	37.6	1.3	-	-	-	-	37.9	0.8	-	-	-	-	38.3	1.1	-	-	-	-	38.9	1.6
1971	-	-	-	-	39.1	0.5	-	-	-	-	39.4	0.8	-	-	-	-	39.6	0.5	-	-	-	-	39.9	0.8
1972	-	-	-	-	40.3	1.0	-	-	-	-	40.8	1.2	-	-	-	-	41.2	1.0	-	-	-	-	41.5	0.7
1973	-	-	-	-	42.3	1.9	-	-	-	-	42.9	1.4	-	-	-	-	44.2	3.0	-	-	-	-	44.4	0.5
1974	-	-	-	-	45.7	2.9	-	-	-	-	47.2	3.3	-	-	-	-	48.6	3.0	-	-	-	-	49.9	2.7
1975	-	-	-	-	51.2	2.6	-	-	-	-	52.1	1.8	-	-	-	-	53.0	1.7	-	-	-	-	53.9	1.7
1976	-	-	-	-	54.3	0.7	-	-	-	-	54.8	0.9	-	-	-	-	55.8	1.8	-	-	-	-	56.6	1.4
1977	-	-	-	-	57.8	2.1	-	-	-	-	59.3	2.6	-	-	-	-	60.4	1.9	-	-	-	-	61.5	1.8
1978	-	-	62.2	1.1	-	-	63.2	1.6	-	-	65.3	3.3	-	-	67.0	2.6	-	-	66.5	-0.7	-	-	65.8	-1.1
1979	-	-	67.1	2.0	-	-	68.7	2.4	-	-	70.2	2.2	-	-	71.8	2.3	-	-	72.5	1.0	-	-	75.2	3.7
1980	-	-	78.8	4.8	-	-	79.7	1.1	-	-	81.3	2.0	-	-	82.6	1.6	-	-	83.0	0.5	-	-	84.0	1.2
1981	-	-	85.9	2.3	-	-	89.0	3.6	-	-	90.1	1.2	-	-	94.3	4.7	-	-	97.1	3.0	-	-	96.1	-1.0
1982	-	-	96.8	0.7	-	-	97.8	1.0	-	-	99.6	1.8	-	-	99.4	-0.2	-	-	98.9	-0.5	-	-	96.4	-2.5
1983	-	-	96.5	0.1	-	-	96.8	0.3	-	-	98.1	1.3	-	-	99.0	0.9	-	-	99.0	0.0	-	-	100.5	1.5
1984	-	-	101.4	0.9	-	-	102.2	0.8	-	-	103.5	1.3	-	-	106.0	2.4	-	-	104.9	-1.0	-	-	105.6	0.7
1985	-	-	106.5	0.9	-	-	107.1	0.6	-	-	107.9	0.7	-	-	108.6	0.6	-	-	108.7	0.1	-	-	108.8	0.1
1986	-	-	110.3	1.4	-	-	109.4	-0.8	-	-	111.0	1.5	-	-	111.3	0.3	-	-	112.0	0.6	-	-	110.7	-1.2
1987	111.3	0.5	112.4	1.0	112.8	0.4	113.9	1.0	113.9	0.0	114.0	0.1	114.7	0.6	114.9	0.2	115.4	0.4	116.0	0.5	116.2	0.2	116.4	0.2
1988	117.5	0.9	117.0	-0.4	117.9	0.8	117.8	-0.1	118.7	0.8	119.0	0.3	119.7	0.6	120.5	0.7	121.1	0.5	121.3	0.2	121.1	-0.2	121.5	0.3
1989	122.8	1.1	122.9	0.1	124.6	1.4	124.8	0.2	125.7	0.7	125.6	-0.1	126.4	0.6	127.0	0.5	126.1	-0.7	126.7	0.5	126.4	-0.2	126.6	0.2
1990	127.6	0.8	128.2	0.5	129.0	0.6	129.8	0.6	129.9	0.1	130.7	0.6	131.3	0.5	132.0	0.5	132.9	0.7	133.6	0.5	133.7	0.1	133.9	0.1
1991	135.3	1.0	134.5	-0.6	134.7	0.1	134.2	-0.4	134.8	0.4	136.0	0.9	136.4	0.3	137.2	0.6	137.9	0.5	137.8	-0.1	138.1	0.2	138.2	0.1
1992	138.5	0.2	139.1	0.4	139.9	0.6	139.6	-0.2	140.1	0.4	140.3	0.1	140.4	0.1	141.0	0.4	141.8	0.6	142.3	0.4	142.3	0.0	142.3	0.0
1993	143.0	0.5	143.5	0.3	143.8	0.2	144.8	0.7	144.8	0.0	144.0	-0.6	144.1	0.1	144.0	-0.1	144.4	0.3	145.0	0.4	145.0	0.0	144.7	-0.2

Source: U.S. Department of Labor, Bureau of Labor Statistics, Division of Consumer Prices and Price Indexes. - indicates no data collected for period.

San Francisco-Oakland, CA

Consumer Price Index - All Urban Consumers
Base 1982-1984 = 100
Food and Beverages

For 1975-1993. Columns headed % show percentile change in the index from the previous period for which an index is available.

Year	Jan Index	%	Feb Index	%	Mar Index	%	Apr Index	%	May Index	%	Jun Index	%	Jul Index	%	Aug Index	%	Sep Index	%	Oct Index	%	Nov Index	%	Dec Index	%
1975	-	-	-	-	-	-	-	-	-	-	-	-	-	-	-	-	-	-	-	-	-	-	60.2	-
1976	-	-	-	-	59.1	-1.8	-	-	-	-	59.3	0.3	-	-	-	-	59.7	0.7	-	-	-	-	60.0	0.5
1977	-	-	-	-	62.5	4.2	-	-	-	-	64.6	3.4	-	-	-	-	65.0	0.6	-	-	-	-	65.9	1.4
1978	-	-	67.3	2.1	-	-	69.1	2.7	-	-	71.4	3.3	-	-	72.3	1.3	-	-	72.9	0.8	-	-	73.0	0.1
1979	-	-	76.5	4.8	-	-	78.8	3.0	-	-	79.6	1.0	-	-	79.8	0.3	-	-	81.3	1.9	-	-	81.9	0.7
1980	-	-	82.5	0.7	-	-	83.7	1.5	-	-	84.2	0.6	-	-	85.9	2.0	-	-	87.7	2.1	-	-	89.3	1.8
1981	-	-	90.1	0.9	-	-	91.0	1.0	-	-	90.1	-1.0	-	-	92.7	2.9	-	-	91.9	-0.9	-	-	92.3	0.4
1982	-	-	95.8	3.8	-	-	96.2	0.4	-	-	97.5	1.4	-	-	97.8	0.3	-	-	99.0	1.2	-	-	97.7	-1.3
1983	-	-	98.3	0.6	-	-	100.1	1.8	-	-	98.9	-1.2	-	-	98.9	0.0	-	-	99.4	0.5	-	-	100.7	1.3
1984	-	-	102.7	2.0	-	-	103.2	0.5	-	-	103.4	0.2	-	-	103.9	0.5	-	-	104.6	0.7	-	-	105.3	0.7
1985	-	-	106.1	0.8	-	-	105.8	-0.3	-	-	105.3	-0.5	-	-	106.0	0.7	-	-	105.3	-0.7	-	-	107.2	1.8
1986	-	-	107.9	0.7	-	-	108.8	0.8	-	-	109.1	0.3	-	-	110.5	1.3	-	-	111.0	0.5	-	-	110.7	-0.3
1987	112.5	1.6	111.9	-0.5	112.5	0.5	113.5	0.9	113.5	0.0	114.0	0.4	114.1	0.1	114.2	0.1	114.0	-0.2	114.0	0.0	114.1	0.1	115.8	1.5
1988	117.3	1.3	116.6	-0.6	117.8	1.0	118.5	0.6	119.4	0.8	119.9	0.4	121.2	1.1	121.6	0.3	122.8	1.0	122.8	0.0	122.6	-0.2	124.3	1.4
1989	126.1	1.4	126.8	0.6	126.9	0.1	127.0	0.1	128.2	0.9	127.8	-0.3	127.4	-0.3	128.2	0.6	129.0	0.6	130.0	0.8	130.5	0.4	131.0	0.4
1990	132.8	1.4	133.2	0.3	133.0	-0.2	133.6	0.5	133.0	-0.4	133.7	0.5	135.1	1.0	134.9	-0.1	135.7	0.6	136.5	0.6	137.2	0.5	137.1	-0.1
1991	140.0	2.1	139.1	-0.6	140.0	0.6	140.1	0.1	139.8	-0.2	140.2	0.3	139.3	-0.6	139.1	-0.1	139.8	0.5	140.1	0.2	142.4	1.6	143.6	0.8
1992	142.2	-1.0	142.9	0.5	143.1	0.1	142.8	-0.2	142.8	0.0	142.9	0.1	142.3	-0.4	144.0	1.2	143.9	-0.1	143.9	0.0	144.0	0.1	145.1	0.8
1993	146.6	1.0	146.6	0.0	146.6	0.0	146.9	0.2	146.5	-0.3	145.5	-0.7	145.8	0.2	145.1	-0.5	145.1	0.0	146.6	1.0	146.3	-0.2	147.3	0.7

Source: U.S. Department of Labor, Bureau of Labor Statistics, Division of Consumer Prices and Price Indexes. - indicates no data collected for period.

San Francisco-Oakland, CA
Consumer Price Index - Urban Wage Earners
Base 1982-1984 = 100
Food and Beverages

For 1975-1993. Columns headed % show percentile change in the index from the previous period for which an index is available.

Year	Jan Index	%	Feb Index	%	Mar Index	%	Apr Index	%	May Index	%	Jun Index	%	Jul Index	%	Aug Index	%	Sep Index	%	Oct Index	%	Nov Index	%	Dec Index	%
1975	-	-	-	-	-	-	-	-	-	-	-	-	-	-	-	-	-	-	-	-	-	-	59.8	-
1976	-	-	-	-	58.7	-1.8	-	-	-	-	58.8	0.2	-	-	-	-	59.3	0.9	-	-	-	-	59.6	0.5
1977	-	-	-	-	62.1	4.2	-	-	-	-	64.1	3.2	-	-	-	-	64.6	0.8	-	-	-	-	65.4	1.2
1978	-	-	67.0	2.4	-	-	68.7	2.5	-	-	70.9	3.2	-	-	71.9	1.4	-	-	72.3	0.6	-	-	72.7	0.6
1979	-	-	76.2	4.8	-	-	78.1	2.5	-	-	79.0	1.2	-	-	78.9	-0.1	-	-	79.9	1.3	-	-	80.5	0.8
1980	-	-	82.5	2.5	-	-	83.1	0.7	-	-	83.9	1.0	-	-	85.5	1.9	-	-	87.3	2.1	-	-	89.1	2.1
1981	-	-	90.6	1.7	-	-	92.1	1.7	-	-	91.2	-1.0	-	-	93.0	2.0	-	-	92.4	-0.6	-	-	92.4	0.0
1982	-	-	95.8	3.7	-	-	96.3	0.5	-	-	97.5	1.2	-	-	97.6	0.1	-	-	98.7	1.1	-	-	97.6	-1.1
1983	-	-	98.3	0.7	-	-	100.0	1.7	-	-	98.9	-1.1	-	-	99.0	0.1	-	-	99.5	0.5	-	-	100.9	1.4
1984	-	-	102.8	1.9	-	-	103.4	0.6	-	-	103.4	0.0	-	-	103.9	0.5	-	-	104.5	0.6	-	-	105.2	0.7
1985	-	-	106.1	0.9	-	-	105.9	-0.2	-	-	105.2	-0.7	-	-	106.0	0.8	-	-	105.3	-0.7	-	-	107.2	1.8
1986	-	-	108.0	0.7	-	-	108.8	0.7	-	-	109.0	0.2	-	-	110.5	1.4	-	-	110.8	0.3	-	-	110.7	-0.1
1987	112.6	1.7	111.9	-0.6	112.6	0.6	113.7	1.0	113.7	0.0	114.2	0.4	114.3	0.1	114.4	0.1	114.1	-0.3	114.0	-0.1	114.1	0.1	115.7	1.4
1988	117.2	1.3	116.6	-0.5	117.7	0.9	118.6	0.8	119.5	0.8	120.0	0.4	121.3	1.1	121.7	0.3	122.9	1.0	122.8	-0.1	122.6	-0.2	124.3	1.4
1989	125.9	1.3	126.9	0.8	127.0	0.1	127.2	0.2	128.4	0.9	128.0	-0.3	127.5	-0.4	128.3	0.6	129.1	0.6	130.1	0.8	130.6	0.4	131.1	0.4
1990	132.8	1.3	133.4	0.5	133.1	-0.2	133.7	0.5	133.1	-0.4	133.8	0.5	135.2	1.0	135.0	-0.1	135.8	0.6	136.6	0.6	137.2	0.4	137.2	0.0
1991	140.1	2.1	139.3	-0.6	140.2	0.6	140.3	0.1	139.9	-0.3	140.4	0.4	139.4	-0.7	139.1	-0.2	139.8	0.5	140.0	0.1	142.3	1.6	143.5	0.8
1992	142.2	-0.9	143.0	0.6	143.2	0.1	142.8	-0.3	142.7	-0.1	142.9	0.1	142.4	-0.3	144.0	1.1	143.8	-0.1	143.9	0.1	144.0	0.1	145.2	0.8
1993	146.6	1.0	146.8	0.1	146.8	0.0	147.1	0.2	146.7	-0.3	145.7	-0.7	146.0	0.2	145.3	-0.5	145.4	0.1	146.8	1.0	146.5	-0.2	147.4	0.6

Source: U.S. Department of Labor, Bureau of Labor Statistics, Division of Consumer Prices and Price Indexes. - indicates no data collected for period.

San Francisco-Oakland, CA
Consumer Price Index - All Urban Consumers
Base 1982-1984 = 100
Housing

For 1975-1993. Columns headed % show percentile change in the index from the previous period for which an index is available.

Year	Jan Index	%	Feb Index	%	Mar Index	%	Apr Index	%	May Index	%	Jun Index	%	Jul Index	%	Aug Index	%	Sep Index	%	Oct Index	%	Nov Index	%	Dec Index	%
1975	-	-	-	-	-	-	-	-	-	-	-	-	-	-	-	-	-	-	-	-	-	-	49.3	-
1976	-	-	-	-	50.0	1.4	-	-	-	-	50.4	0.8	-	-	-	-	51.4	2.0	-	-	-	-	50.9	-1.0
1977	-	-	-	-	53.1	4.3	-	-	-	-	54.8	3.2	-	-	-	-	56.5	3.1	-	-	-	-	58.2	3.0
1978	-	-	58.9	1.2	-	-	59.7	1.4	-	-	62.5	4.7	-	-	64.9	3.8	-	-	63.1	-2.8	-	-	61.0	-3.3
1979	-	-	61.7	1.1	-	-	63.0	2.1	-	-	63.9	1.4	-	-	66.4	3.9	-	-	67.0	0.9	-	-	71.4	6.6
1980	-	-	75.8	6.2	-	-	75.2	-0.8	-	-	78.1	3.9	-	-	78.6	0.6	-	-	78.2	-0.5	-	-	79.1	1.2
1981	-	-	81.1	2.5	-	-	86.2	6.3	-	-	87.7	1.7	-	-	95.2	8.6	-	-	100.1	5.1	-	-	97.3	-2.8
1982	-	-	97.4	0.1	-	-	98.5	1.1	-	-	100.2	1.7	-	-	99.5	-0.7	-	-	97.3	-2.2	-	-	92.9	-4.5
1983	-	-	95.7	3.0	-	-	96.2	0.5	-	-	97.4	1.2	-	-	99.3	2.0	-	-	99.6	0.3	-	-	99.4	-0.2
1984	-	-	100.9	1.5	-	-	102.7	1.8	-	-	103.7	1.0	-	-	106.9	3.1	-	-	108.0	1.0	-	-	106.7	-1.2
1985	-	-	108.2	1.4	-	-	109.3	1.0	-	-	111.0	1.6	-	-	113.4	2.2	-	-	114.2	0.7	-	-	112.8	-1.2
1986	-	-	115.7	2.6	-	-	115.5	-0.2	-	-	117.9	2.1	-	-	119.4	1.3	-	-	120.1	0.6	-	-	117.8	-1.9
1987	118.5	0.6	119.5	0.8	119.1	-0.3	120.4	1.1	121.2	0.7	121.2	0.0	122.7	1.2	122.9	0.2	123.3	0.3	123.7	0.3	122.6	-0.9	122.6	0.0
1988	123.7	0.9	123.8	0.1	125.6	1.5	124.2	-1.1	126.1	1.5	126.7	0.5	127.9	0.9	130.0	1.6	128.5	-1.2	128.9	0.3	128.5	-0.3	128.9	0.3
1989	130.4	1.2	130.0	-0.3	133.0	2.3	130.1	-2.2	131.3	0.9	131.6	0.2	134.4	2.1	135.0	0.4	133.0	-1.5	133.4	0.3	132.7	-0.5	133.3	0.5
1990	134.2	0.7	135.1	0.7	135.7	0.4	135.9	0.1	136.5	0.4	137.5	0.7	138.1	0.4	138.5	0.3	138.8	0.2	138.6	-0.1	139.1	0.4	139.2	0.1
1991	141.2	1.4	140.9	-0.2	141.2	0.2	140.2	-0.7	140.8	0.4	142.8	1.4	143.8	0.7	144.5	0.5	145.0	0.3	144.1	-0.6	144.1	0.0	143.7	-0.3
1992	144.7	0.7	145.3	0.4	146.6	0.9	145.5	-0.8	145.6	0.1	145.3	-0.2	146.0	0.5	145.9	-0.1	147.5	1.1	147.9	0.3	147.1	-0.5	147.3	0.1
1993	147.5	0.1	147.6	0.1	147.8	0.1	149.5	1.2	150.0	0.3	149.4	-0.4	149.1	-0.2	149.4	0.2	149.7	0.2	149.8	0.1	150.3	0.3	150.4	0.1

Source: U.S. Department of Labor, Bureau of Labor Statistics, Division of Consumer Prices and Price Indexes. - indicates no data collected for period.

San Francisco-Oakland, CA
Consumer Price Index - Urban Wage Earners
Base 1982-1984 = 100
Housing

For 1975-1993. Columns headed % show percentile change in the index from the previous period for which an index is available.

Year	Jan Index	%	Feb Index	%	Mar Index	%	Apr Index	%	May Index	%	Jun Index	%	Jul Index	%	Aug Index	%	Sep Index	%	Oct Index	%	Nov Index	%	Dec Index	%
1975	-		-		-		-		-		-		-		-		-		-		-		-	
1976	-		-		51.2	1.2	-		-		51.7	1.0	-		-		52.7	1.9	-		-		50.6	-
1977	-		-		54.4	4.4	-		-		56.2	3.3	-		-		57.9	3.0	-		-		52.1	-1.1
1978	-		60.3	1.0	-		61.1	1.3	-		63.8	4.4	-		66.3	3.9	-		64.5	-2.7	-		59.7	3.1
1979	-		63.2	1.3	-		64.4	1.9	-		65.4	1.6	-		67.7	3.5	-		68.3	0.9	-		62.4	-3.3
1980	-		77.4	6.3	-		76.9	-0.6	-		80.1	4.2	-		80.6	0.6	-		79.8	-1.0	-		72.8	6.6
1981	-		83.0	2.5	-		87.8	5.8	-		89.4	1.8	-		96.9	8.4	-		101.9	5.2	-		81.0	1.5
1982	-		99.6	0.3	-		100.7	1.1	-		102.4	1.7	-		101.5	-0.9	-		99.4	-2.1	-		99.3	-2.6
1983	-		95.5	0.5	-		95.2	-0.3	-		96.2	1.1	-		97.8	1.7	-		98.0	0.2	-		95.0	-4.4
1984	-		100.5	0.5	-		100.5	0.0	-		102.8	2.3	-		107.7	4.8	-		103.6	-3.8	-		100.0	2.0
1985	-		106.7	1.4	-		107.8	1.0	-		109.5	1.6	-		111.6	1.9	-		112.2	0.5	-		105.2	1.5
1986	-		114.1	2.7	-		113.9	-0.2	-		116.3	2.1	-		117.7	1.2	-		118.5	0.7	-		111.1	-1.0
1987	116.7	0.6	117.7	0.9	117.2	-0.4	118.5	1.1	119.0	0.4	119.0	0.0	120.4	1.2	120.5	0.1	120.9	0.3	121.4	0.4	120.5	-0.7	116.0	-2.1
1988	121.7	1.0	121.9	0.2	123.1	1.0	122.2	-0.7	123.9	1.4	124.5	0.5	125.4	0.7	127.0	1.3	126.2	-0.6	126.6	0.3	126.0	-0.5	120.5	0.0
1989	127.6	0.9	127.3	-0.2	129.8	2.0	127.8	-1.5	128.9	0.9	129.1	0.2	131.2	1.6	131.9	0.5	130.4	-1.1	131.0	0.5	130.3	-0.5	126.4	0.3
1990	131.7	0.7	132.6	0.7	133.0	0.3	133.4	0.3	134.1	0.5	135.0	0.7	135.4	0.3	135.8	0.3	136.0	0.1	136.0	0.0	136.4	0.3	130.8	0.4
1991	138.2	1.4	137.9	-0.2	138.1	0.1	137.1	-0.7	138.1	0.7	140.0	1.4	140.8	0.6	141.3	0.4	141.9	0.4	141.0	-0.6	141.2	0.1	136.3	-0.1
1992	141.6	0.6	142.1	0.4	143.2	0.8	142.2	-0.7	142.5	0.2	142.5	0.0	143.0	0.4	142.8	-0.1	144.3	1.1	144.8	0.3	144.1	-0.5	140.7	-0.4
1993	144.3	0.1	144.5	0.1	144.8	0.2	146.6	1.2	146.9	0.2	146.2	-0.5	146.0	-0.1	146.3	0.2	146.5	0.1	146.8	0.2	147.3	0.3	144.1	0.0

Source: U.S. Department of Labor, Bureau of Labor Statistics, Division of Consumer Prices and Price Indexes. - indicates no data collected for period.

San Francisco-Oakland, CA
Consumer Price Index - All Urban Consumers
Base 1982-1984 = 100
Apparel and Upkeep

For 1952-1993. Columns headed % show percentile change in the index from the previous period for which an index is available.

Year	Jan Index	%	Feb Index	%	Mar Index	%	Apr Index	%	May Index	%	Jun Index	%	Jul Index	%	Aug Index	%	Sep Index	%	Oct Index	%	Nov Index	%	Dec Index	%
1952	-	-	-	-	-	-	-	-	-	-	-	-	-	-	-	-	-	-	-	-	-	-	39.3	-
1953	-	-	-	-	39.4	0.3	-	-	-	-	38.9	-1.3	-	-	-	-	39.4	1.3	-	-	-	-	39.4	0.0
1954	-	-	-	-	38.9	-1.3	-	-	-	-	38.8	-0.3	-	-	-	-	38.8	0.0	-	-	-	-	38.4	-1.0
1955	-	-	-	-	38.8	1.0	-	-	-	-	38.8	0.0	-	-	-	-	39.3	1.3	-	-	-	-	39.3	0.0
1956	-	-	-	-	39.6	0.8	-	-	-	-	39.7	0.3	-	-	-	-	39.8	0.3	-	-	-	-	40.5	1.8
1957	-	-	-	-	40.7	0.5	-	-	-	-	40.6	-0.2	-	-	-	-	40.8	0.5	-	-	-	-	41.0	0.5
1958	-	-	-	-	41.0	0.0	-	-	-	-	40.9	-0.2	-	-	-	-	40.9	0.0	-	-	-	-	41.0	0.2
1959	-	-	-	-	41.0	0.0	-	-	-	-	41.2	0.5	-	-	-	-	41.9	1.7	-	-	-	-	42.1	0.5
1960	-	-	-	-	42.1	0.0	-	-	-	-	42.4	0.7	-	-	-	-	42.9	1.2	-	-	-	-	43.0	0.2
1961	-	-	-	-	43.0	0.0	-	-	-	-	43.2	0.5	-	-	-	-	43.2	0.0	-	-	-	-	43.4	0.5
1962	-	-	-	-	43.7	0.7	-	-	-	-	43.9	0.5	-	-	-	-	43.8	-0.2	-	-	-	-	44.0	0.5
1963	-	-	-	-	44.0	0.0	-	-	-	-	44.1	0.2	-	-	-	-	44.3	0.5	-	-	-	-	44.5	0.5
1964	-	-	-	-	44.6	0.2	-	-	-	-	44.6	0.0	-	-	-	-	44.6	0.0	-	-	-	-	44.9	0.7
1965	-	-	-	-	45.2	0.7	-	-	-	-	45.5	0.7	-	-	-	-	45.2	-0.7	-	-	-	-	45.6	0.9
1966	-	-	-	-	46.3	1.5	-	-	-	-	46.5	0.4	-	-	-	-	46.8	0.6	-	-	-	-	47.1	0.6
1967	-	-	-	-	47.7	1.3	-	-	-	-	47.8	0.2	-	-	-	-	49.5	3.6	-	-	-	-	49.7	0.4
1968	-	-	-	-	50.5	1.6	-	-	-	-	51.0	1.0	-	-	-	-	51.9	1.8	-	-	-	-	52.3	0.8
1969	-	-	-	-	53.1	1.5	-	-	-	-	53.3	0.4	-	-	-	-	54.5	2.3	-	-	-	-	54.7	0.4
1970	-	-	-	-	54.6	-0.2	-	-	-	-	54.5	-0.2	-	-	-	-	56.1	2.9	-	-	-	-	56.5	0.7
1971	-	-	-	-	57.2	1.2	-	-	-	-	57.5	0.5	-	-	-	-	58.5	1.7	-	-	-	-	58.0	-0.9
1972	-	-	-	-	58.2	0.3	-	-	-	-	58.0	-0.3	-	-	-	-	60.1	3.6	-	-	-	-	60.1	0.0
1973	-	-	-	-	60.4	0.5	-	-	-	-	61.0	1.0	-	-	-	-	62.4	2.3	-	-	-	-	62.7	0.5
1974	-	-	-	-	64.1	2.2	-	-	-	-	65.9	2.8	-	-	-	-	67.4	2.3	-	-	-	-	68.4	1.5
1975	-	-	-	-	68.4	0.0	-	-	-	-	68.1	-0.4	-	-	-	-	68.8	1.0	-	-	-	-	69.8	1.5
1976	-	-	-	-	70.5	1.0	-	-	-	-	69.8	-1.0	-	-	-	-	70.6	1.1	-	-	-	-	71.4	1.1
1977	-	-	-	-	72.6	1.7	-	-	-	-	72.7	0.1	-	-	-	-	73.7	1.4	-	-	-	-	74.1	0.5
1978	-	-	73.6	-0.7	-	-	78.3	6.4	-	-	76.5	-2.3	-	-	77.2	0.9	-	-	79.6	3.1	-	-	79.3	-0.4
1979	-	-	80.1	1.0	-	-	80.1	0.0	-	-	81.3	1.5	-	-	81.4	0.1	-	-	84.3	3.6	-	-	86.7	2.8
1980	-	-	86.9	0.2	-	-	88.3	1.6	-	-	85.4	-3.3	-	-	90.7	6.2	-	-	91.0	0.3	-	-	90.5	-0.5
1981	-	-	89.6	-1.0	-	-	91.0	1.6	-	-	92.2	1.3	-	-	94.3	2.3	-	-	93.8	-0.5	-	-	96.4	2.8
1982	-	-	97.3	0.9	-	-	97.3	0.0	-	-	97.1	-0.2	-	-	98.9	1.9	-	-	98.6	-0.3	-	-	96.4	-2.2
1983	-	-	98.8	2.5	-	-	99.1	0.3	-	-	97.8	-1.3	-	-	98.2	0.4	-	-	95.5	-2.7	-	-	98.0	2.6
1984	-	-	102.1	4.2	-	-	104.4	2.3	-	-	100.6	-3.6	-	-	107.1	6.5	-	-	109.5	2.2	-	-	105.7	-3.5
1985	-	-	108.1	2.3	-	-	105.0	-2.9	-	-	104.7	-0.3	-	-	100.6	-3.9	-	-	102.2	1.6	-	-	99.1	-3.0
1986	-	-	98.1	-1.0	-	-	103.9	5.9	-	-	100.0	-3.8	-	-	102.6	2.6	-	-	105.9	3.2	-	-	99.6	-5.9
1987	96.8	-2.8	103.1	6.5	106.6	3.4	108.6	1.9	103.7	-4.5	102.2	-1.4	100.4	-1.8	100.2	-0.2	105.1	4.9	107.4	2.2	112.2	4.5	108.4	-3.4
1988	108.9	0.5	106.3	-2.4	106.2	-0.1	105.4	-0.8	103.6	-1.7	99.7	-3.8	97.3	-2.4	95.2	-2.2	101.9	7.0	101.7	-0.2	102.7	1.0	99.5	-3.1
1989	100.6	1.1	100.2	-0.4	104.7	4.5	107.5	2.7	105.6	-1.8	103.5	-2.0	101.3	-2.1	103.1	1.8	106.9	3.7	108.2	1.2	105.5	-2.5	103.0	-2.4
1990	99.6	-3.3	104.5	4.9	107.3	2.7	108.4	1.0	106.5	-1.8	106.5	0.0	105.7	-0.8	107.6	1.8	112.2	4.3	113.2	0.9	109.2	-3.5	109.1	-0.1
1991	112.1	2.7	110.9	-1.1	112.0	1.0	114.0	1.8	111.3	-2.4	109.1	-2.0	109.2	0.1	115.6	5.9	115.8	0.2	116.6	0.7	115.8	-0.7	114.8	-0.9
1992	114.2	-0.5	117.7	3.1	121.6	3.3	119.5	-1.7	121.3	1.5	118.4	-2.4	115.4	-2.5	118.0	2.3	117.6	-0.3	117.0	-0.5	117.9	0.8	114.4	-3.0
1993	114.7	0.3	117.2	2.2	121.9	4.0	124.3	2.0	121.6	-2.2	117.1	-3.7	116.2	-0.8	115.2	-0.9	120.0	4.2	119.0	-0.8	117.3	-1.4	113.5	-3.2

Source: U.S. Department of Labor, Bureau of Labor Statistics, Division of Consumer Prices and Price Indexes. - indicates no data collected for period.

San Francisco-Oakland, CA
Consumer Price Index - Urban Wage Earners
Base 1982-1984 = 100
Apparel and Upkeep

For 1952-1993. Columns headed % show percentile change in the index from the previous period for which an index is available.

Year	Jan Index	%	Feb Index	%	Mar Index	%	Apr Index	%	May Index	%	Jun Index	%	Jul Index	%	Aug Index	%	Sep Index	%	Oct Index	%	Nov Index	%	Dec Index	%
1952	-		-		-		-		-		-		-		-		-		-		-		40.8	-
1953	-		-		40.9	0.2	-		-		40.4	-1.2	-		-		40.9	1.2	-		-		40.9	0.0
1954	-		-		40.4	-1.2	-		-		40.3	-0.2	-		-		40.2	-0.2	-		-		39.8	-1.0
1955	-		-		40.3	1.3	-		-		40.3	0.0	-		-		40.8	1.2	-		-		40.8	0.0
1956	-		-		41.1	0.7	-		-		41.2	0.2	-		-		41.3	0.2	-		-		42.0	1.7
1957	-		-		42.2	0.5	-		-		42.1	-0.2	-		-		42.3	0.5	-		-		42.5	0.5
1958	-		-		42.5	0.0	-		-		42.5	0.0	-		-		42.5	0.0	-		-		42.5	0.0
1959	-		-		42.6	0.2	-		-		42.7	0.2	-		-		43.5	1.9	-		-		43.7	0.5
1960	-		-		43.7	0.0	-		-		44.0	0.7	-		-		44.6	1.4	-		-		44.7	0.2
1961	-		-		44.6	-0.2	-		-		44.9	0.7	-		-		44.9	0.0	-		-		45.0	0.2
1962	-		-		45.3	0.7	-		-		45.5	0.4	-		-		45.5	0.0	-		-		45.7	0.4
1963	-		-		45.7	0.0	-		-		45.8	0.2	-		-		46.0	0.4	-		-		46.2	0.4
1964	-		-		46.3	0.2	-		-		46.3	0.0	-		-		46.3	0.0	-		-		46.6	0.6
1965	-		-		46.9	0.6	-		-		47.2	0.6	-		-		46.9	-0.6	-		-		47.4	1.1
1966	-		-		48.0	1.3	-		-		48.2	0.4	-		-		48.5	0.6	-		-		48.9	0.8
1967	-		-		49.5	1.2	-		-		49.6	0.2	-		-		51.4	3.6	-		-		51.5	0.2
1968	-		-		52.4	1.7	-		-		52.9	1.0	-		-		53.9	1.9	-		-		54.3	0.7
1969	-		-		55.1	1.5	-		-		55.3	0.4	-		-		56.6	2.4	-		-		56.7	0.2
1970	-		-		56.7	0.0	-		-		56.5	-0.4	-		-		58.2	3.0	-		-		58.7	0.9
1971	-		-		59.4	1.2	-		-		59.6	0.3	-		-		60.8	2.0	-		-		60.1	-1.2
1972	-		-		60.4	0.5	-		-		60.2	-0.3	-		-		62.4	3.7	-		-		62.4	0.0
1973	-		-		62.7	0.5	-		-		63.3	1.0	-		-		64.8	2.4	-		-		65.0	0.3
1974	-		-		66.5	2.3	-		-		68.4	2.9	-		-		69.9	2.2	-		-		71.0	1.6
1975	-		-		71.0	0.0	-		-		70.7	-0.4	-		-		71.4	1.0	-		-		72.4	1.4
1976	-		-		73.2	1.1	-		-		72.4	-1.1	-		-		73.3	1.2	-		-		74.1	1.1
1977	-		-		75.3	1.6	-		-		75.4	0.1	-		-		76.5	1.5	-		-		76.9	0.5
1978	-		75.1	-2.3	-		79.0	5.2	-		78.1	-1.1	-		78.8	0.9	-		80.4	2.0	-		79.9	-0.6
1979	-		81.3	1.8	-		81.8	0.6	-		83.9	2.6	-		82.6	-1.5	-		83.6	1.2	-		85.9	2.8
1980	-		86.2	0.3	-		87.2	1.2	-		85.9	-1.5	-		90.8	5.7	-		92.3	1.7	-		91.7	-0.7
1981	-		92.7	1.1	-		94.5	1.9	-		95.1	0.6	-		96.1	1.1	-		97.0	0.9	-		96.6	-0.4
1982	-		97.7	1.1	-		97.8	0.1	-		98.3	0.5	-		99.1	0.8	-		98.9	-0.2	-		97.1	-1.8
1983	-		98.5	1.4	-		98.5	0.0	-		97.6	-0.9	-		98.2	0.6	-		95.8	-2.4	-		98.0	2.3
1984	-		102.0	4.1	-		103.6	1.6	-		100.0	-3.5	-		106.6	6.6	-		109.0	2.3	-		105.9	-2.8
1985	-		107.7	1.7	-		105.3	-2.2	-		104.7	-0.6	-		101.7	-2.9	-		102.7	1.0	-		100.2	-2.4
1986	-		99.5	-0.7	-		104.5	5.0	-		100.5	-3.8	-		103.0	2.5	-		106.1	3.0	-		100.4	-5.4
1987	97.5	-2.9	103.1	5.7	106.7	3.5	109.2	2.3	104.0	-4.8	103.0	-1.0	101.2	-1.7	100.8	-0.4	105.6	4.8	109.3	3.5	113.8	4.1	110.0	-3.3
1988	110.8	0.7	108.0	-2.5	108.1	0.1	107.2	-0.8	105.2	-1.9	101.4	-3.6	99.4	-2.0	97.0	-2.4	104.4	7.6	104.1	-0.3	105.2	1.1	101.9	-3.1
1989	103.7	1.8	103.2	-0.5	107.0	3.7	110.1	2.9	108.0	-1.9	106.9	-1.0	104.8	-2.0	106.4	1.5	109.5	2.9	111.3	1.6	108.1	-2.9	105.5	-2.4
1990	103.7	-1.7	106.9	3.1	110.1	3.0	111.3	1.1	109.6	-1.5	109.7	0.1	108.9	-0.7	110.2	1.2	115.4	4.7	116.7	1.1	112.2	-3.9	112.8	0.5
1991	115.8	2.7	113.5	-2.0	114.8	1.1	117.0	1.9	114.2	-2.4	111.7	-2.2	112.1	0.4	118.6	5.8	118.9	0.3	120.2	1.1	119.3	-0.7	118.4	-0.8
1992	117.6	-0.7	120.7	2.6	124.9	3.5	122.7	-1.8	124.8	1.7	122.0	-2.2	119.2	-2.3	121.9	2.3	121.4	-0.4	120.8	-0.5	122.4	1.3	119.1	-2.7
1993	118.8	-0.3	121.4	2.2	125.2	3.1	128.7	2.8	126.0	-2.1	121.1	-3.9	120.7	-0.3	119.2	-1.2	125.6	5.4	124.9	-0.6	122.7	-1.8	118.5	-3.4

Source: U.S. Department of Labor, Bureau of Labor Statistics, Division of Consumer Prices and Price Indexes. - indicates no data collected for period.

San Francisco-Oakland, CA
Consumer Price Index - All Urban Consumers
Base 1982-1984 = 100
Transportation

For 1947-1993. Columns headed % show percentile change in the index from the previous period for which an index is available.

Year	Jan Index	%	Feb Index	%	Mar Index	%	Apr Index	%	May Index	%	Jun Index	%	Jul Index	%	Aug Index	%	Sep Index	%	Oct Index	%	Nov Index	%	Dec Index	%
1947	16.0	-	16.1	0.6	16.1	0.0	16.3	1.2	16.2	-0.6	16.2	0.0	-	-	-	-	16.7	3.1	-	-	-	-	17.0	1.8
1948	-	-	-	-	17.4	2.4	-	-	-	-	18.0	3.4	-	-	-	-	18.6	3.3	-	-	-	-	18.7	0.5
1949	-	-	-	-	19.3	3.2	-	-	-	-	19.5	1.0	-	-	-	-	19.5	0.0	-	-	-	-	19.6	0.5
1950	-	-	-	-	19.6	0.0	-	-	-	-	19.2	-2.0	-	-	-	-	19.4	1.0	-	-	-	-	19.5	0.5
1951	-	-	-	-	20.6	5.6	-	-	-	-	20.8	1.0	-	-	-	-	21.3	2.4	-	-	-	-	21.4	0.5
1952	-	-	-	-	21.6	0.9	-	-	-	-	24.1	11.6	-	-	-	-	25.2	4.6	-	-	-	-	25.2	0.0
1953	-	-	-	-	25.7	2.0	-	-	-	-	25.5	-0.8	-	-	-	-	25.8	1.2	-	-	-	-	25.9	0.4
1954	-	-	-	-	25.8	-0.4	-	-	-	-	25.7	-0.4	-	-	-	-	25.2	-1.9	-	-	-	-	25.4	0.8
1955	-	-	-	-	25.3	-0.4	-	-	-	-	24.8	-2.0	-	-	-	-	24.8	0.0	-	-	-	-	25.3	2.0
1956	-	-	-	-	25.0	-1.2	-	-	-	-	25.1	0.4	-	-	-	-	25.3	0.8	-	-	-	-	26.7	5.5
1957	-	-	-	-	27.1	1.5	-	-	-	-	26.9	-0.7	-	-	-	-	27.1	0.7	-	-	-	-	27.4	1.1
1958	-	-	-	-	28.0	2.2	-	-	-	-	28.4	1.4	-	-	-	-	28.8	1.4	-	-	-	-	28.4	-1.4
1959	-	-	-	-	29.7	4.6	-	-	-	-	29.6	-0.3	-	-	-	-	30.0	1.4	-	-	-	-	30.5	1.7
1960	-	-	-	-	29.6	-3.0	-	-	-	-	29.5	-0.3	-	-	-	-	29.3	-0.7	-	-	-	-	29.9	2.0
1961	-	-	-	-	29.6	-1.0	-	-	-	-	29.3	-1.0	-	-	-	-	30.1	2.7	-	-	-	-	30.5	1.3
1962	-	-	-	-	30.2	-1.0	-	-	-	-	30.5	1.0	-	-	-	-	30.5	0.0	-	-	-	-	30.4	-0.3
1963	-	-	-	-	30.5	0.3	-	-	-	-	30.6	0.3	-	-	-	-	30.8	0.7	-	-	-	-	31.4	1.9
1964	-	-	-	-	31.4	0.0	-	-	-	-	31.6	0.6	-	-	-	-	31.4	-0.6	-	-	-	-	31.9	1.6
1965	-	-	-	-	31.7	-0.6	-	-	-	-	31.7	0.0	-	-	-	-	31.6	-0.3	-	-	-	-	31.9	0.9
1966	-	-	-	-	31.9	0.0	-	-	-	-	31.6	-0.9	-	-	-	-	32.2	1.9	-	-	-	-	32.4	0.6
1967	-	-	-	-	32.4	0.0	-	-	-	-	32.9	1.5	-	-	-	-	33.2	0.9	-	-	-	-	33.4	0.6
1968	-	-	-	-	33.6	0.6	-	-	-	-	33.8	0.6	-	-	-	-	33.8	0.0	-	-	-	-	34.1	0.9
1969	-	-	-	-	35.0	2.6	-	-	-	-	35.3	0.9	-	-	-	-	35.4	0.3	-	-	-	-	36.1	2.0
1970	-	-	-	-	35.6	-1.4	-	-	-	-	36.5	2.5	-	-	-	-	37.0	1.4	-	-	-	-	38.6	4.3
1971	-	-	-	-	38.8	0.5	-	-	-	-	38.9	0.3	-	-	-	-	38.7	-0.5	-	-	-	-	38.6	-0.3
1972	-	-	-	-	39.0	1.0	-	-	-	-	39.5	1.3	-	-	-	-	40.1	1.5	-	-	-	-	40.2	0.2
1973	-	-	-	-	39.8	-1.0	-	-	-	-	40.7	2.3	-	-	-	-	40.6	-0.2	-	-	-	-	41.1	1.2
1974	-	-	-	-	42.6	3.6	-	-	-	-	45.0	5.6	-	-	-	-	46.5	3.3	-	-	-	-	47.3	1.7
1975	-	-	-	-	48.3	2.1	-	-	-	-	50.0	3.5	-	-	-	-	51.0	2.0	-	-	-	-	51.6	1.2
1976	-	-	-	-	52.5	1.7	-	-	-	-	53.9	2.7	-	-	-	-	55.7	3.3	-	-	-	-	56.3	1.1
1977	-	-	-	-	56.9	1.1	-	-	-	-	58.5	2.8	-	-	-	-	58.4	-0.2	-	-	-	-	59.1	1.2
1978	-	-	59.5	0.7	-	-	59.7	0.3	-	-	61.5	3.0	-	-	62.2	1.1	-	-	62.9	1.1	-	-	64.0	1.7
1979	-	-	64.7	1.1	-	-	67.4	4.2	-	-	70.5	4.6	-	-	72.9	3.4	-	-	74.3	1.9	-	-	76.0	2.3
1980	-	-	80.7	6.2	-	-	83.7	3.7	-	-	83.7	0.0	-	-	84.9	1.4	-	-	85.6	0.8	-	-	86.5	1.1
1981	-	-	88.6	2.4	-	-	90.6	2.3	-	-	92.8	2.4	-	-	93.0	0.2	-	-	94.1	1.2	-	-	94.9	0.9
1982	-	-	94.0	-0.9	-	-	94.5	0.5	-	-	98.1	3.8	-	-	99.6	1.5	-	-	99.8	0.2	-	-	98.2	-1.6
1983	-	-	96.2	-2.0	-	-	96.5	0.3	-	-	100.4	4.0	-	-	101.2	0.8	-	-	100.0	-1.2	-	-	100.8	0.8
1984	-	-	100.6	-0.2	-	-	103.2	2.6	-	-	104.9	1.6	-	-	103.8	-1.0	-	-	105.9	2.0	-	-	105.1	-0.8
1985	-	-	104.6	-0.5	-	-	105.9	1.2	-	-	106.7	0.8	-	-	105.3	-1.3	-	-	105.0	-0.3	-	-	105.5	0.5
1986	-	-	105.3	-0.2	-	-	99.8	-5.2	-	-	102.8	3.0	-	-	99.4	-3.3	-	-	99.7	0.3	-	-	98.5	-1.2
1987	99.4	0.9	100.2	0.8	101.4	1.2	101.8	0.4	102.0	0.2	102.1	0.1	102.6	0.5	103.2	0.6	103.3	0.1	103.5	0.2	104.6	1.1	104.5	-0.1
1988	104.4	-0.1	103.5	-0.9	103.4	-0.1	103.7	0.3	104.4	0.7	105.3	0.9	105.7	0.4	106.5	0.8	106.7	0.2	107.0	0.3	106.1	-0.8	106.4	0.3
1989	106.8	0.4	107.2	0.4	107.6	0.4	110.9	3.1	112.1	1.1	111.6	-0.4	111.5	-0.1	110.7	-0.7	108.7	-1.8	109.0	0.3	109.5	0.5	109.1	-0.4
1990	110.4	1.2	110.4	0.0	111.5	1.0	112.0	0.4	112.7	0.6	113.4	0.6	113.8	0.4	115.4	1.4	116.8	1.2	119.1	2.0	119.6	0.4	121.2	1.3
1991	119.5	-1.4	117.0	-2.1	115.2	-1.5	113.7	-1.3	115.9	1.9	117.6	1.5	117.7	0.1	118.4	0.6	117.5	-0.8	117.9	0.3	117.4	-0.4	117.0	-0.3

[Continued]

San Francisco-Oakland, CA
Consumer Price Index - All Urban Consumers
Base 1982-1984 = 100
Transportation
[Continued]

For 1947-1993. Columns headed % show percentile change in the index from the previous period for which an index is available.

Year	Jan Index	%	Feb Index	%	Mar Index	%	Apr Index	%	May Index	%	Jun Index	%	Jul Index	%	Aug Index	%	Sep Index	%	Oct Index	%	Nov Index	%	Dec Index	%
1992	116.6	-0.3	116.2	-0.3	116.7	0.4	117.6	0.8	119.1	1.3	120.1	0.8	121.4	1.1	121.5	0.1	120.7	-0.7	122.1	1.2	122.7	0.5	123.3	0.5
1993	125.1	1.5	124.3	-0.6	123.5	-0.6	123.1	-0.3	123.4	0.2	123.1	-0.2	123.0	-0.1	123.6	0.5	122.2	-1.1	124.4	1.8	124.7	0.2	123.5	-1.0

Source: U.S. Department of Labor, Bureau of Labor Statistics, Division of Consumer Prices and Price Indexes. - indicates no data collected for period.

San Francisco-Oakland, CA
Consumer Price Index - Urban Wage Earners
Base 1982-1984 = 100
Transportation

For 1947-1993. Columns headed % show percentile change in the index from the previous period for which an index is available.

Year	Jan Index	%	Feb Index	%	Mar Index	%	Apr Index	%	May Index	%	Jun Index	%	Jul Index	%	Aug Index	%	Sep Index	%	Oct Index	%	Nov Index	%	Dec Index	%
1947	15.7	-	15.7	0.0	15.8	0.6	15.9	0.6	15.8	-0.6	15.8	0.0	-	-	-	-	16.3	3.2	-	-	-	-	16.6	1.8
1948	-	-	-	-	17.0	2.4	-	-	-	-	17.5	2.9	-	-	-	-	18.2	4.0	-	-	-	-	18.3	0.5
1949	-	-	-	-	18.9	3.3	-	-	-	-	19.0	0.5	-	-	-	-	19.1	0.5	-	-	-	-	19.2	0.5
1950	-	-	-	-	19.2	0.0	-	-	-	-	18.8	-2.1	-	-	-	-	19.0	1.1	-	-	-	-	19.0	0.0
1951	-	-	-	-	20.1	5.8	-	-	-	-	20.3	1.0	-	-	-	-	20.8	2.5	-	-	-	-	20.9	0.5
1952	-	-	-	-	21.1	1.0	-	-	-	-	23.6	11.8	-	-	-	-	24.6	4.2	-	-	-	-	24.6	0.0
1953	-	-	-	-	25.1	2.0	-	-	-	-	24.9	-0.8	-	-	-	-	25.2	1.2	-	-	-	-	25.3	0.4
1954	-	-	-	-	25.2	-0.4	-	-	-	-	25.1	-0.4	-	-	-	-	24.6	-2.0	-	-	-	-	24.8	0.8
1955	-	-	-	-	24.7	-0.4	-	-	-	-	24.2	-2.0	-	-	-	-	24.3	0.4	-	-	-	-	24.7	1.6
1956	-	-	-	-	24.4	-1.2	-	-	-	-	24.5	0.4	-	-	-	-	24.7	0.8	-	-	-	-	26.1	5.7
1957	-	-	-	-	26.5	1.5	-	-	-	-	26.3	-0.8	-	-	-	-	26.4	0.4	-	-	-	-	26.7	1.1
1958	-	-	-	-	27.3	2.2	-	-	-	-	27.7	1.5	-	-	-	-	28.2	1.8	-	-	-	-	27.7	-1.8
1959	-	-	-	-	29.0	4.7	-	-	-	-	28.9	-0.3	-	-	-	-	29.3	1.4	-	-	-	-	29.7	1.4
1960	-	-	-	-	28.9	-2.7	-	-	-	-	28.8	-0.3	-	-	-	-	28.6	-0.7	-	-	-	-	29.2	2.1
1961	-	-	-	-	28.9	-1.0	-	-	-	-	28.6	-1.0	-	-	-	-	29.4	2.8	-	-	-	-	29.8	1.4
1962	-	-	-	-	29.4	-1.3	-	-	-	-	29.7	1.0	-	-	-	-	29.8	0.3	-	-	-	-	29.7	-0.3
1963	-	-	-	-	29.7	0.0	-	-	-	-	29.9	0.7	-	-	-	-	30.0	0.3	-	-	-	-	30.6	2.0
1964	-	-	-	-	30.6	0.0	-	-	-	-	30.9	1.0	-	-	-	-	30.7	-0.6	-	-	-	-	31.1	1.3
1965	-	-	-	-	31.0	-0.3	-	-	-	-	31.0	0.0	-	-	-	-	30.8	-0.6	-	-	-	-	31.2	1.3
1966	-	-	-	-	31.2	0.0	-	-	-	-	30.9	-1.0	-	-	-	-	31.5	1.9	-	-	-	-	31.6	0.3
1967	-	-	-	-	31.6	0.0	-	-	-	-	32.1	1.6	-	-	-	-	32.4	0.9	-	-	-	-	32.6	0.6
1968	-	-	-	-	32.8	0.6	-	-	-	-	33.0	0.6	-	-	-	-	33.0	0.0	-	-	-	-	33.3	0.9
1969	-	-	-	-	34.2	2.7	-	-	-	-	34.4	0.6	-	-	-	-	34.6	0.6	-	-	-	-	35.2	1.7
1970	-	-	-	-	34.8	-1.1	-	-	-	-	35.7	2.6	-	-	-	-	36.2	1.4	-	-	-	-	37.7	4.1
1971	-	-	-	-	37.9	0.5	-	-	-	-	38.0	0.3	-	-	-	-	37.8	-0.5	-	-	-	-	37.7	-0.3
1972	-	-	-	-	38.1	1.1	-	-	-	-	38.5	1.0	-	-	-	-	39.2	1.8	-	-	-	-	39.2	0.0
1973	-	-	-	-	38.8	-1.0	-	-	-	-	39.8	2.6	-	-	-	-	39.7	-0.3	-	-	-	-	40.1	1.0
1974	-	-	-	-	41.6	3.7	-	-	-	-	44.0	5.8	-	-	-	-	45.4	3.2	-	-	-	-	46.2	1.8
1975	-	-	-	-	47.2	2.2	-	-	-	-	48.8	3.4	-	-	-	-	49.8	2.0	-	-	-	-	50.4	1.2
1976	-	-	-	-	51.2	1.6	-	-	-	-	52.6	2.7	-	-	-	-	54.4	3.4	-	-	-	-	55.0	1.1
1977	-	-	-	-	55.6	1.1	-	-	-	-	57.1	2.7	-	-	-	-	57.0	-0.2	-	-	-	-	57.7	1.2
1978	-	-	58.1	0.7	-	-	58.4	0.5	-	-	60.3	3.3	-	-	61.2	1.5	-	-	61.9	1.1	-	-	63.0	1.8
1979	-	-	63.6	1.0	-	-	66.6	4.7	-	-	69.8	4.8	-	-	72.1	3.3	-	-	73.2	1.5	-	-	75.0	2.5
1980	-	-	79.4	5.9	-	-	81.9	3.1	-	-	81.9	0.0	-	-	83.5	2.0	-	-	84.4	1.1	-	-	85.2	0.9
1981	-	-	87.8	3.1	-	-	89.8	2.3	-	-	91.5	1.9	-	-	92.3	0.9	-	-	93.5	1.3	-	-	94.3	0.9
1982	-	-	93.4	-1.0	-	-	94.2	0.9	-	-	97.6	3.6	-	-	99.2	1.6	-	-	99.4	0.2	-	-	98.0	-1.4
1983	-	-	96.0	-2.0	-	-	96.4	0.4	-	-	100.5	4.3	-	-	101.3	0.8	-	-	100.4	-0.9	-	-	101.3	0.9
1984	-	-	101.1	-0.2	-	-	103.6	2.5	-	-	105.1	1.4	-	-	103.9	-1.1	-	-	106.0	2.0	-	-	105.3	-0.7
1985	-	-	104.8	-0.5	-	-	106.1	1.2	-	-	107.0	0.8	-	-	105.6	-1.3	-	-	105.2	-0.4	-	-	105.7	0.5
1986	-	-	105.6	-0.1	-	-	100.0	-5.3	-	-	102.9	2.9	-	-	99.7	-3.1	-	-	100.0	0.3	-	-	98.8	-1.2
1987	99.3	0.5	100.8	1.5	102.3	1.5	103.2	0.9	103.5	0.3	103.8	0.3	104.1	0.3	104.8	0.7	104.8	0.0	105.3	0.5	105.9	0.6	106.1	0.2
1988	106.1	0.0	105.5	-0.6	105.4	-0.1	105.5	0.1	106.2	0.7	107.1	0.8	107.6	0.5	108.1	0.5	108.3	0.2	108.8	0.5	108.0	-0.7	108.0	0.0
1989	108.5	0.5	108.9	0.4	109.6	0.6	113.4	3.5	114.9	1.3	114.4	-0.4	114.1	-0.3	113.3	-0.7	111.3	-1.8	111.1	-0.2	111.5	0.4	111.1	-0.4
1990	111.7	0.5	112.1	0.4	113.2	1.0	113.7	0.4	114.4	0.6	115.4	0.9	115.7	0.3	117.6	1.6	119.2	1.4	122.0	2.3	122.3	0.2	123.2	0.7
1991	121.0	-1.8	118.1	-2.4	116.2	-1.6	114.8	-1.2	117.2	2.1	118.9	1.5	119.2	0.3	119.8	0.5	119.5	-0.3	120.0	0.4	119.1	-0.8	118.9	-0.2

[Continued]

San Francisco-Oakland, CA
Consumer Price Index - Urban Wage Earners
Base 1982-1984 = 100
Transportation
[Continued]

For 1947-1993. Columns headed % show percentile change in the index from the previous period for which an index is available.

Year	Jan		Feb		Mar		Apr		May		Jun		Jul		Aug		Sep		Oct		Nov		Dec	
	Index	%	Index	%	Index	%	Index	%	Index	%	Index	%	Index	%	Index	%	Index	%	Index	%	Index	%	Index	%
1992	118.3	-0.5	118.0	-0.3	118.3	0.3	119.2	0.8	121.1	1.6	122.5	1.2	123.5	0.8	123.8	0.2	123.4	-0.3	124.3	0.7	125.0	0.6	125.3	0.2
1993	126.4	0.9	125.8	-0.5	125.2	-0.5	125.0	-0.2	125.3	0.2	125.3	0.0	125.3	0.0	125.7	0.3	125.1	-0.5	127.0	1.5	126.9	-0.1	125.6	-1.0

Source: U.S. Department of Labor, Bureau of Labor Statistics, Division of Consumer Prices and Price Indexes. - indicates no data collected for period.

San Francisco-Oakland, CA
Consumer Price Index - All Urban Consumers
Base 1982-1984 = 100
Medical Care

For 1947-1993. Columns headed % show percentile change in the index from the previous period for which an index is available.

Year	Jan Index	%	Feb Index	%	Mar Index	%	Apr Index	%	May Index	%	Jun Index	%	Jul Index	%	Aug Index	%	Sep Index	%	Oct Index	%	Nov Index	%	Dec Index	%
1947	13.3	-	13.4	0.8	13.4	0.0	13.4	0.0	13.4	0.0	13.4	0.0	-	-	-	-	13.8	3.0	-	-	-	-	13.9	0.7
1948	-	-	-	-	14.0	0.7	-	-	-	-	14.2	1.4	-	-	-	-	14.4	1.4	-	-	-	-	14.6	1.4
1949	-	-	-	-	14.7	0.7	-	-	-	-	14.7	0.0	-	-	-	-	14.8	0.7	-	-	-	-	14.8	0.0
1950	-	-	-	-	14.8	0.0	-	-	-	-	14.8	0.0	-	-	-	-	15.5	4.7	-	-	-	-	15.7	1.3
1951	-	-	-	-	15.7	0.0	-	-	-	-	15.8	0.6	-	-	-	-	15.8	0.0	-	-	-	-	16.0	1.3
1952	-	-	-	-	16.8	5.0	-	-	-	-	16.9	0.6	-	-	-	-	16.9	0.0	-	-	-	-	17.0	0.6
1953	-	-	-	-	17.0	0.0	-	-	-	-	17.2	1.2	-	-	-	-	17.4	1.2	-	-	-	-	17.4	0.0
1954	-	-	-	-	17.5	0.6	-	-	-	-	17.5	0.0	-	-	-	-	17.5	0.0	-	-	-	-	17.5	0.0
1955	-	-	-	-	17.5	0.0	-	-	-	-	17.6	0.6	-	-	-	-	17.8	1.1	-	-	-	-	17.9	0.6
1956	-	-	-	-	18.2	1.7	-	-	-	-	18.2	0.0	-	-	-	-	19.2	5.5	-	-	-	-	19.3	0.5
1957	-	-	-	-	19.3	0.0	-	-	-	-	19.5	1.0	-	-	-	-	19.6	0.5	-	-	-	-	20.0	2.0
1958	-	-	-	-	20.3	1.5	-	-	-	-	21.4	5.4	-	-	-	-	21.5	0.5	-	-	-	-	21.6	0.5
1959	-	-	-	-	21.7	0.5	-	-	-	-	22.0	1.4	-	-	-	-	22.0	0.0	-	-	-	-	22.0	0.0
1960	-	-	-	-	22.4	1.8	-	-	-	-	22.5	0.4	-	-	-	-	22.7	0.9	-	-	-	-	22.8	0.4
1961	-	-	-	-	22.9	0.4	-	-	-	-	23.0	0.4	-	-	-	-	23.1	0.4	-	-	-	-	23.2	0.4
1962	-	-	-	-	24.0	3.4	-	-	-	-	24.1	0.4	-	-	-	-	24.2	0.4	-	-	-	-	24.4	0.8
1963	-	-	-	-	24.5	0.4	-	-	-	-	24.6	0.4	-	-	-	-	24.7	0.4	-	-	-	-	24.8	0.4
1964	-	-	-	-	25.1	1.2	-	-	-	-	25.3	0.8	-	-	-	-	25.5	0.8	-	-	-	-	25.5	0.0
1965	-	-	-	-	25.8	1.2	-	-	-	-	25.9	0.4	-	-	-	-	25.9	0.0	-	-	-	-	26.3	1.5
1966	-	-	-	-	26.6	1.1	-	-	-	-	27.1	1.9	-	-	-	-	27.8	2.6	-	-	-	-	28.2	1.4
1967	-	-	-	-	28.7	1.8	-	-	-	-	28.9	0.7	-	-	-	-	29.1	0.7	-	-	-	-	29.4	1.0
1968	-	-	-	-	30.1	2.4	-	-	-	-	30.3	0.7	-	-	-	-	30.5	0.7	-	-	-	-	30.9	1.3
1969	-	-	-	-	31.4	1.6	-	-	-	-	31.7	1.0	-	-	-	-	32.2	1.6	-	-	-	-	32.5	0.9
1970	-	-	-	-	33.2	2.2	-	-	-	-	33.5	0.9	-	-	-	-	34.1	1.8	-	-	-	-	34.2	0.3
1971	-	-	-	-	35.3	3.2	-	-	-	-	35.7	1.1	-	-	-	-	36.2	1.4	-	-	-	-	35.9	-0.8
1972	-	-	-	-	36.4	1.4	-	-	-	-	36.7	0.8	-	-	-	-	37.1	1.1	-	-	-	-	37.4	0.8
1973	-	-	-	-	37.9	1.3	-	-	-	-	38.0	0.3	-	-	-	-	38.4	1.1	-	-	-	-	39.0	1.6
1974	-	-	-	-	40.1	2.8	-	-	-	-	41.2	2.7	-	-	-	-	42.7	3.6	-	-	-	-	43.5	1.9
1975	-	-	-	-	45.7	5.1	-	-	-	-	48.3	5.7	-	-	-	-	49.1	1.7	-	-	-	-	49.8	1.4
1976	-	-	-	-	51.7	3.8	-	-	-	-	52.3	1.2	-	-	-	-	53.2	1.7	-	-	-	-	54.6	2.6
1977	-	-	-	-	56.4	3.3	-	-	-	-	57.4	1.8	-	-	-	-	59.3	3.3	-	-	-	-	59.7	0.7
1978	-	-	61.0	2.2	-	-	62.6	2.6	-	-	62.6	0.0	-	-	63.7	1.8	-	-	65.5	2.8	-	-	65.9	0.6
1979	-	-	67.0	1.7	-	-	67.3	0.4	-	-	67.8	0.7	-	-	69.3	2.2	-	-	72.1	4.0	-	-	73.2	1.5
1980	-	-	74.4	1.6	-	-	76.0	2.2	-	-	76.4	0.5	-	-	76.8	0.5	-	-	78.4	2.1	-	-	78.6	0.3
1981	-	-	81.1	3.2	-	-	82.9	2.2	-	-	84.0	1.3	-	-	85.7	2.0	-	-	87.2	1.8	-	-	89.1	2.2
1982	-	-	90.8	1.9	-	-	93.1	2.5	-	-	94.3	1.3	-	-	95.2	1.0	-	-	96.3	1.2	-	-	97.6	1.3
1983	-	-	99.5	1.9	-	-	99.7	0.2	-	-	101.2	1.5	-	-	101.9	0.7	-	-	101.6	-0.3	-	-	101.7	0.1
1984	-	-	103.8	2.1	-	-	104.4	0.6	-	-	104.6	0.2	-	-	105.4	0.8	-	-	106.4	0.9	-	-	107.0	0.6
1985	-	-	107.8	0.7	-	-	108.5	0.6	-	-	110.3	1.7	-	-	113.2	2.6	-	-	113.9	0.6	-	-	115.1	1.1
1986	-	-	115.9	0.7	-	-	117.4	1.3	-	-	118.9	1.3	-	-	121.9	2.5	-	-	122.4	0.4	-	-	124.0	1.3
1987	125.1	0.9	125.2	0.1	125.8	0.5	126.6	0.6	126.4	-0.2	127.3	0.7	130.1	2.2	131.3	0.9	131.1	-0.2	131.4	0.2	132.0	0.5	132.2	0.2
1988	133.2	0.8	133.1	-0.1	133.7	0.5	134.3	0.4	134.7	0.3	136.1	1.0	137.9	1.3	138.1	0.1	139.1	0.7	140.1	0.7	140.5	0.3	141.4	0.6
1989	143.0	1.1	144.6	1.1	145.0	0.3	145.7	0.5	145.8	0.1	146.6	0.5	147.8	0.8	148.4	0.4	149.9	1.0	150.4	0.3	154.1	2.5	152.9	-0.8
1990	155.2	1.5	156.1	0.6	158.3	1.4	158.3	0.0	158.3	0.0	158.7	0.3	161.3	1.6	162.7	0.9	163.1	0.2	164.2	0.7	164.8	0.4	164.9	0.1
1991	166.6	1.0	167.8	0.7	168.7	0.5	168.7	0.0	169.0	0.2	169.7	0.4	173.2	2.1	176.6	2.0	177.9	0.7	178.2	0.2	178.9	0.4	179.4	0.3

[Continued]

San Francisco-Oakland, CA
Consumer Price Index - All Urban Consumers
Base 1982-1984 = 100
Medical Care
[Continued]

For 1947-1993. Columns headed % show percentile change in the index from the previous period for which an index is available.

Year	Jan		Feb		Mar		Apr		May		Jun		Jul		Aug		Sep		Oct		Nov		Dec	
	Index	%	Index	%	Index	%	Index	%	Index	%	Index	%	Index	%	Index	%	Index	%	Index	%	Index	%	Index	%
1992	180.1	0.4	182.2	1.2	183.1	0.5	185.3	1.2	185.2	-0.1	186.7	0.8	188.5	1.0	188.7	0.1	190.3	0.8	190.9	0.3	191.2	0.2	191.4	0.1
1993	193.1	0.9	194.9	0.9	194.7	-0.1	197.8	1.6	197.8	0.0	199.5	0.9	201.4	1.0	201.6	0.1	201.2	-0.2	202.2	0.5	202.0	-0.1	202.4	0.2

Source: U.S. Department of Labor, Bureau of Labor Statistics, Division of Consumer Prices and Price Indexes. - indicates no data collected for period.

San Francisco-Oakland, CA
Consumer Price Index - Urban Wage Earners
Base 1982-1984 = 100
Medical Care

For 1947-1993. Columns headed % show percentile change in the index from the previous period for which an index is available.

Year	Jan Index	%	Feb Index	%	Mar Index	%	Apr Index	%	May Index	%	Jun Index	%	Jul Index	%	Aug Index	%	Sep Index	%	Oct Index	%	Nov Index	%	Dec Index	%
1947	13.4	-	13.5	0.7	13.5	0.0	13.5	0.0	13.5	0.0	13.5	0.0	-	-	-	-	13.9	3.0	-	-	-	-	14.0	0.7
1948	-	-	-	-	14.1	0.7	-	-	-	-	14.3	1.4	-	-	-	-	14.5	1.4	-	-	-	-	14.7	1.4
1949	-	-	-	-	14.8	0.7	-	-	-	-	14.8	0.0	-	-	-	-	14.9	0.7	-	-	-	-	14.9	0.0
1950	-	-	-	-	14.9	0.0	-	-	-	-	14.9	0.0	-	-	-	-	15.6	4.7	-	-	-	-	15.8	1.3
1951	-	-	-	-	15.8	0.0	-	-	-	-	15.9	0.6	-	-	-	-	15.9	0.0	-	-	-	-	16.1	1.3
1952	-	-	-	-	16.9	5.0	-	-	-	-	17.0	0.6	-	-	-	-	17.0	0.0	-	-	-	-	17.1	0.6
1953	-	-	-	-	17.1	0.0	-	-	-	-	17.3	1.2	-	-	-	-	17.5	1.2	-	-	-	-	17.6	0.6
1954	-	-	-	-	17.6	0.0	-	-	-	-	17.6	0.0	-	-	-	-	17.6	0.0	-	-	-	-	17.7	0.6
1955	-	-	-	-	17.7	0.0	-	-	-	-	17.7	0.0	-	-	-	-	17.9	1.1	-	-	-	-	18.0	0.6
1956	-	-	-	-	18.3	1.7	-	-	-	-	18.3	0.0	-	-	-	-	19.4	6.0	-	-	-	-	19.4	0.0
1957	-	-	-	-	19.5	0.5	-	-	-	-	19.6	0.5	-	-	-	-	19.7	0.5	-	-	-	-	20.1	2.0
1958	-	-	-	-	20.4	1.5	-	-	-	-	21.6	5.9	-	-	-	-	21.6	0.0	-	-	-	-	21.7	0.5
1959	-	-	-	-	21.8	0.5	-	-	-	-	22.1	1.4	-	-	-	-	22.1	0.0	-	-	-	-	22.2	0.5
1960	-	-	-	-	22.5	1.4	-	-	-	-	22.7	0.9	-	-	-	-	22.8	0.4	-	-	-	-	22.9	0.4
1961	-	-	-	-	23.0	0.4	-	-	-	-	23.1	0.4	-	-	-	-	23.3	0.9	-	-	-	-	23.4	0.4
1962	-	-	-	-	24.2	3.4	-	-	-	-	24.3	0.4	-	-	-	-	24.4	0.4	-	-	-	-	24.5	0.4
1963	-	-	-	-	24.7	0.8	-	-	-	-	24.8	0.4	-	-	-	-	24.9	0.4	-	-	-	-	25.0	0.4
1964	-	-	-	-	25.2	0.8	-	-	-	-	25.4	0.8	-	-	-	-	25.7	1.2	-	-	-	-	25.7	0.0
1965	-	-	-	-	26.0	1.2	-	-	-	-	26.0	0.0	-	-	-	-	26.1	0.4	-	-	-	-	26.5	1.5
1966	-	-	-	-	26.8	1.1	-	-	-	-	27.3	1.9	-	-	-	-	28.0	2.6	-	-	-	-	28.4	1.4
1967	-	-	-	-	28.9	1.8	-	-	-	-	29.1	0.7	-	-	-	-	29.3	0.7	-	-	-	-	29.6	1.0
1968	-	-	-	-	30.3	2.4	-	-	-	-	30.5	0.7	-	-	-	-	30.7	0.7	-	-	-	-	31.1	1.3
1969	-	-	-	-	31.6	1.6	-	-	-	-	32.0	1.3	-	-	-	-	32.4	1.3	-	-	-	-	32.7	0.9
1970	-	-	-	-	33.4	2.1	-	-	-	-	33.7	0.9	-	-	-	-	34.3	1.8	-	-	-	-	34.5	0.6
1971	-	-	-	-	35.5	2.9	-	-	-	-	35.9	1.1	-	-	-	-	36.4	1.4	-	-	-	-	36.2	-0.5
1972	-	-	-	-	36.6	1.1	-	-	-	-	36.9	0.8	-	-	-	-	37.3	1.1	-	-	-	-	37.7	1.1
1973	-	-	-	-	38.2	1.3	-	-	-	-	38.3	0.3	-	-	-	-	38.6	0.8	-	-	-	-	39.3	1.8
1974	-	-	-	-	40.4	2.8	-	-	-	-	41.5	2.7	-	-	-	-	43.0	3.6	-	-	-	-	43.8	1.9
1975	-	-	-	-	46.0	5.0	-	-	-	-	48.6	5.7	-	-	-	-	49.5	1.9	-	-	-	-	50.1	1.2
1976	-	-	-	-	52.1	4.0	-	-	-	-	52.6	1.0	-	-	-	-	53.6	1.9	-	-	-	-	54.9	2.4
1977	-	-	-	-	56.8	3.5	-	-	-	-	57.8	1.8	-	-	-	-	59.7	3.3	-	-	-	-	60.1	0.7
1978	-	-	62.3	3.7	-	-	62.7	0.6	-	-	62.3	-0.6	-	-	64.4	3.4	-	-	65.0	0.9	-	-	65.8	1.2
1979	-	-	66.4	0.9	-	-	66.9	0.8	-	-	68.2	1.9	-	-	69.9	2.5	-	-	72.2	3.3	-	-	73.4	1.7
1980	-	-	74.7	1.8	-	-	75.8	1.5	-	-	76.0	0.3	-	-	77.4	1.8	-	-	79.1	2.2	-	-	80.0	1.1
1981	-	-	82.2	2.8	-	-	83.2	1.2	-	-	83.8	0.7	-	-	87.0	3.8	-	-	87.5	0.6	-	-	89.2	1.9
1982	-	-	90.9	1.9	-	-	93.1	2.4	-	-	94.3	1.3	-	-	95.0	0.7	-	-	96.0	1.1	-	-	97.1	1.1
1983	-	-	99.1	2.1	-	-	99.5	0.4	-	-	101.0	1.5	-	-	101.7	0.7	-	-	101.5	-0.2	-	-	101.7	0.2
1984	-	-	103.8	2.1	-	-	104.6	0.8	-	-	104.9	0.3	-	-	105.8	0.9	-	-	106.9	1.0	-	-	107.6	0.7
1985	-	-	108.5	0.8	-	-	109.1	0.6	-	-	110.8	1.6	-	-	113.8	2.7	-	-	114.5	0.6	-	-	115.8	1.1
1986	-	-	116.6	0.7	-	-	118.0	1.2	-	-	119.8	1.5	-	-	122.7	2.4	-	-	123.1	0.3	-	-	124.7	1.3
1987	126.0	1.0	126.3	0.2	126.9	0.5	127.7	0.6	127.7	0.0	128.7	0.8	131.5	2.2	132.6	0.8	132.4	-0.2	132.8	0.3	133.4	0.5	133.6	0.1
1988	134.4	0.6	134.4	0.0	135.0	0.4	135.6	0.4	136.0	0.3	137.3	1.0	138.9	1.2	139.3	0.3	140.0	0.5	141.5	1.1	142.0	0.4	142.5	0.4
1989	144.3	1.3	146.0	1.2	145.9	-0.1	147.0	0.8	147.1	0.1	147.9	0.5	149.1	0.8	149.4	0.2	151.0	1.1	151.5	0.3	155.1	2.4	153.6	-1.0
1990	156.1	1.6	156.8	0.4	158.9	1.3	158.8	-0.1	158.5	-0.2	158.9	0.3	161.3	1.5	163.1	1.1	163.4	0.2	164.3	0.6	164.9	0.4	164.1	-0.5
1991	166.3	1.3	167.1	0.5	168.0	0.5	168.3	0.2	168.6	0.2	169.3	0.4	172.3	1.8	175.8	2.0	177.1	0.7	176.6	-0.3	177.6	0.6	178.3	0.4

[Continued]

San Francisco-Oakland, CA
Consumer Price Index - Urban Wage Earners
Base 1982-1984 = 100
Medical Care
[Continued]

For 1947-1993. Columns headed % show percentile change in the index from the previous period for which an index is available.

Year	Jan		Feb		Mar		Apr		May		Jun		Jul		Aug		Sep		Oct		Nov		Dec	
	Index	%	Index	%	Index	%	Index	%	Index	%	Index	%	Index	%	Index	%	Index	%	Index	%	Index	%	Index	%
1992	178.6	0.2	181.4	1.6	182.2	0.4	184.7	1.4	184.4	-0.2	186.8	1.3	188.5	0.9	188.7	0.1	190.0	0.7	190.2	0.1	190.3	0.1	190.6	0.2
1993	192.2	0.8	194.2	1.0	194.0	-0.1	196.8	1.4	196.8	0.0	198.3	0.8	200.1	0.9	200.5	0.2	199.4	-0.5	201.0	0.8	200.6	-0.2	201.0	0.2

Source: U.S. Department of Labor, Bureau of Labor Statistics, Division of Consumer Prices and Price Indexes. - indicates no data collected for period.

San Francisco-Oakland, CA
Consumer Price Index - All Urban Consumers
Base 1982-1984 = 100
Entertainment

For 1975-1993. Columns headed % show percentile change in the index from the previous period for which an index is available.

Year	Jan Index	%	Feb Index	%	Mar Index	%	Apr Index	%	May Index	%	Jun Index	%	Jul Index	%	Aug Index	%	Sep Index	%	Oct Index	%	Nov Index	%	Dec Index	%
1975	-	-	-	-	-	-	-	-	-	-	-	-	-	-	-	-	-	-	-	-	-	-	62.9	-
1976	-	-	-	-	63.8	1.4	-	-	-	-	64.5	1.1	-	-	-	-	65.6	1.7	-	-	-	-	66.2	0.9
1977	-	-	-	-	66.7	0.8	-	-	-	-	67.4	1.0	-	-	-	-	68.2	1.2	-	-	-	-	68.8	0.9
1978	-	-	66.6	-3.2	-	-	70.2	5.4	-	-	71.2	1.4	-	-	73.9	3.8	-	-	75.2	1.8	-	-	75.5	0.4
1979	-	-	73.6	-2.5	-	-	76.2	3.5	-	-	76.1	-0.1	-	-	76.9	1.1	-	-	74.5	-3.1	-	-	75.7	1.6
1980	-	-	77.9	2.9	-	-	86.7	11.3	-	-	87.7	1.2	-	-	85.9	-2.1	-	-	85.8	-0.1	-	-	87.7	2.2
1981	-	-	91.5	4.3	-	-	89.6	-2.1	-	-	89.7	0.1	-	-	90.8	1.2	-	-	97.3	7.2	-	-	97.7	0.4
1982	-	-	97.0	-0.7	-	-	98.8	1.9	-	-	101.7	2.9	-	-	97.2	-4.4	-	-	98.1	0.9	-	-	98.0	-0.1
1983	-	-	97.5	-0.5	-	-	97.9	0.4	-	-	99.1	1.2	-	-	99.3	0.2	-	-	99.3	0.0	-	-	99.8	0.5
1984	-	-	101.5	1.7	-	-	101.5	0.0	-	-	102.6	1.1	-	-	103.3	0.7	-	-	103.7	0.4	-	-	106.1	2.3
1985	-	-	106.5	0.4	-	-	107.1	0.6	-	-	108.1	0.9	-	-	109.3	1.1	-	-	110.6	1.2	-	-	110.7	0.1
1986	-	-	114.9	3.8	-	-	117.1	1.9	-	-	116.7	-0.3	-	-	118.9	1.9	-	-	119.3	0.3	-	-	119.5	0.2
1987	120.1	0.5	121.2	0.9	119.3	-1.6	120.7	1.2	122.6	1.6	121.9	-0.6	120.7	-1.0	120.9	0.2	119.6	-1.1	121.8	1.8	124.8	2.5	126.0	1.0
1988	127.3	1.0	124.1	-2.5	128.9	3.9	129.1	0.2	128.6	-0.4	129.3	0.5	130.0	0.5	129.3	-0.5	131.2	1.5	128.7	-1.9	130.9	1.7	131.7	0.6
1989	133.8	1.6	133.3	-0.4	132.9	-0.3	134.4	1.1	134.3	-0.1	134.2	-0.1	135.0	0.6	137.4	1.8	130.0	-5.4	131.6	1.2	129.2	-1.8	131.5	1.8
1990	133.5	1.5	130.6	-2.2	134.8	3.2	139.8	3.7	139.9	0.1	141.3	1.0	142.6	0.9	145.4	2.0	146.0	0.4	144.6	-1.0	143.7	-0.6	145.7	1.4
1991	147.9	1.5	148.0	0.1	150.1	1.4	151.1	0.7	149.1	-1.3	152.7	2.4	154.4	1.1	154.3	-0.1	155.1	0.5	155.8	0.5	153.8	-1.3	156.0	1.4
1992	156.6	0.4	156.7	0.1	156.0	-0.4	157.5	1.0	155.4	-1.3	157.1	1.1	154.8	-1.5	155.5	0.5	155.2	-0.2	156.4	0.8	158.7	1.5	158.1	-0.4
1993	155.5	-1.6	160.9	3.5	161.3	0.2	161.7	0.2	163.5	1.1	163.1	-0.2	162.8	-0.2	163.1	0.2	162.9	-0.1	163.6	0.4	164.3	0.4	164.6	0.2

Source: U.S. Department of Labor, Bureau of Labor Statistics, Division of Consumer Prices and Price Indexes. - indicates no data collected for period.

San Francisco-Oakland, CA

Consumer Price Index - Urban Wage Earners
Base 1982-1984 = 100
Entertainment

For 1975-1993. Columns headed % show percentile change in the index from the previous period for which an index is available.

Year	Jan		Feb		Mar		Apr		May		Jun		Jul		Aug		Sep		Oct		Nov		Dec	
	Index	%	Index	%	Index	%	Index	%	Index	%	Index	%	Index	%	Index	%	Index	%	Index	%	Index	%	Index	%
1975	-	-	-	-	-	-	-	-	-	-	-	-	-	-	-	-	-	-	-	-	-	-	70.5	-
1976	-	-	-	-	71.5	1.4	-	-	-	-	72.3	1.1	-	-	-	-	73.6	1.8	-	-	-	-	74.2	0.8
1977	-	-	-	-	74.8	0.8	-	-	-	-	75.6	1.1	-	-	-	-	76.4	1.1	-	-	-	-	77.1	0.9
1978	-	-	78.7	2.1	-	-	79.7	1.3	-	-	80.7	1.3	-	-	83.2	3.1	-	-	83.2	0.0	-	-	83.0	-0.2
1979	-	-	82.9	-0.1	-	-	86.1	3.9	-	-	85.6	-0.6	-	-	86.7	1.3	-	-	80.3	-7.4	-	-	80.4	0.1
1980	-	-	81.7	1.6	-	-	92.6	13.3	-	-	92.9	0.3	-	-	94.8	2.0	-	-	96.9	2.2	-	-	95.1	-1.9
1981	-	-	97.0	2.0	-	-	95.9	-1.1	-	-	98.1	2.3	-	-	99.6	1.5	-	-	102.4	2.8	-	-	101.4	-1.0
1982	-	-	101.4	0.0	-	-	102.6	1.2	-	-	105.0	2.3	-	-	96.0	-8.6	-	-	97.0	1.0	-	-	96.9	-0.1
1983	-	-	96.3	-0.6	-	-	96.5	0.2	-	-	97.9	1.5	-	-	98.5	0.6	-	-	98.6	0.1	-	-	99.2	0.6
1984	-	-	101.1	1.9	-	-	100.8	-0.3	-	-	102.1	1.3	-	-	103.1	1.0	-	-	102.8	-0.3	-	-	105.3	2.4
1985	-	-	105.8	0.5	-	-	106.4	0.6	-	-	107.5	1.0	-	-	107.8	0.3	-	-	108.1	0.3	-	-	108.3	0.2
1986	-	-	112.6	4.0	-	-	113.9	1.2	-	-	113.5	-0.4	-	-	115.3	1.6	-	-	115.6	0.3	-	-	115.8	0.2
1987	115.8	0.0	117.4	1.4	115.6	-1.5	116.4	0.7	118.6	1.9	117.8	-0.7	116.6	-1.0	116.9	0.3	115.5	-1.2	116.7	1.0	120.0	2.8	120.8	0.7
1988	122.0	1.0	119.2	-2.3	123.4	3.5	123.8	0.3	123.6	-0.2	124.5	0.7	124.9	0.3	124.1	-0.6	125.7	1.3	123.7	-1.6	125.9	1.8	126.6	0.6
1989	128.4	1.4	128.4	0.0	129.6	0.9	130.9	1.0	130.5	-0.3	131.2	0.5	131.9	0.5	133.3	1.1	128.2	-3.8	130.1	1.5	127.5	-2.0	130.6	2.4
1990	131.9	1.0	127.7	-3.2	133.1	4.2	138.1	3.8	138.3	0.1	138.4	0.1	138.7	0.2	140.1	1.0	138.4	-1.2	136.9	-1.1	135.8	-0.8	137.9	1.5
1991	139.7	1.3	140.2	0.4	142.0	1.3	143.0	0.7	141.0	-1.4	143.9	2.1	145.1	0.8	144.5	-0.4	145.5	0.7	145.7	0.1	143.5	-1.5	147.4	2.7
1992	148.2	0.5	147.7	-0.3	146.7	-0.7	148.6	1.3	146.4	-1.5	148.1	1.2	146.1	-1.4	146.5	0.3	146.2	-0.2	147.3	0.8	149.1	1.2	148.6	-0.3
1993	146.2	-1.6	150.4	2.9	150.9	0.3	150.8	-0.1	152.5	1.1	152.0	-0.3	152.0	0.0	152.3	0.2	152.1	-0.1	152.7	0.4	152.9	0.1	154.4	1.0

Source: U.S. Department of Labor, Bureau of Labor Statistics, Division of Consumer Prices and Price Indexes. - indicates no data collected for period.

San Francisco-Oakland, CA

Consumer Price Index - All Urban Consumers
Base 1982-1984 = 100

Other Goods and Services

For 1975-1993. Columns headed % show percentile change in the index from the previous period for which an index is available.

Year	Jan Index	%	Feb Index	%	Mar Index	%	Apr Index	%	May Index	%	Jun Index	%	Jul Index	%	Aug Index	%	Sep Index	%	Oct Index	%	Nov Index	%	Dec Index	%
1975	-	-	-	-	-	-	-	-	-	-	-	-	-	-	-	-	-	-	-	-	-	-	53.0	-
1976	-	-	-	-	53.4	0.8	-	-	-	-	53.9	0.9	-	-	-	-	54.9	1.9	-	-	-	-	56.0	2.0
1977	-	-	-	-	56.8	1.4	-	-	-	-	57.8	1.8	-	-	-	-	59.6	3.1	-	-	-	-	59.9	0.5
1978	-	-	60.4	0.8	-	-	61.6	2.0	-	-	63.4	2.9	-	-	64.7	2.1	-	-	66.0	2.0	-	-	66.2	0.3
1979	-	-	66.5	0.5	-	-	66.9	0.6	-	-	66.8	-0.1	-	-	67.4	0.9	-	-	69.3	2.8	-	-	69.6	0.4
1980	-	-	70.6	1.4	-	-	71.9	1.8	-	-	71.3	-0.8	-	-	73.2	2.7	-	-	74.8	2.2	-	-	76.1	1.7
1981	-	-	77.1	1.3	-	-	77.8	0.9	-	-	79.7	2.4	-	-	79.9	0.3	-	-	82.8	3.6	-	-	83.8	1.2
1982	-	-	86.5	3.2	-	-	88.6	2.4	-	-	88.7	0.1	-	-	89.9	1.4	-	-	96.2	7.0	-	-	97.7	1.6
1983	-	-	100.0	2.4	-	-	100.2	0.2	-	-	101.3	1.1	-	-	100.5	-0.8	-	-	102.7	2.2	-	-	103.9	1.2
1984	-	-	105.6	1.6	-	-	105.9	0.3	-	-	107.6	1.6	-	-	108.0	0.4	-	-	111.6	3.3	-	-	112.4	0.7
1985	-	-	115.0	2.3	-	-	115.5	0.4	-	-	115.7	0.2	-	-	117.0	1.1	-	-	117.4	0.3	-	-	119.0	1.4
1986	-	-	122.2	2.7	-	-	122.3	0.1	-	-	123.2	0.7	-	-	122.6	-0.5	-	-	124.2	1.3	-	-	126.2	1.6
1987	127.5	1.0	128.5	0.8	128.7	0.2	129.0	0.2	128.8	-0.2	129.1	0.2	130.3	0.9	131.5	0.9	133.7	1.7	134.1	0.3	134.6	0.4	134.4	-0.1
1988	137.2	2.1	137.2	0.0	137.2	0.0	138.3	0.8	138.7	0.3	138.5	-0.1	139.1	0.4	140.6	1.1	142.1	1.1	142.6	0.4	144.3	1.2	144.9	0.4
1989	148.0	2.1	146.4	-1.1	149.5	2.1	149.6	0.1	150.4	0.5	151.5	0.7	153.3	1.2	156.2	1.9	155.0	-0.8	155.0	0.0	155.1	0.1	156.0	0.6
1990	159.2	2.1	158.6	-0.4	158.3	-0.2	160.2	1.2	159.3	-0.6	160.3	0.6	160.3	0.0	161.4	0.7	162.8	0.9	163.8	0.6	164.1	0.2	164.2	0.1
1991	165.5	0.8	170.0	2.7	169.3	-0.4	170.2	0.5	171.4	0.7	172.2	0.5	173.2	0.6	175.0	1.0	180.8	3.3	181.6	0.4	182.4	0.4	182.4	0.0
1992	190.4	4.4	191.2	0.4	191.4	0.1	192.5	0.6	192.0	-0.3	192.0	0.0	192.7	0.4	193.7	0.5	202.8	4.7	204.1	0.6	203.9	-0.1	203.7	-0.1
1993	205.9	1.1	207.3	0.7	207.1	-0.1	206.5	-0.3	207.0	0.2	205.7	-0.6	206.8	0.5	206.7	-0.0	209.6	1.4	207.1	-1.2	207.1	0.0	207.2	0.0

Source: U.S. Department of Labor, Bureau of Labor Statistics, Division of Consumer Prices and Price Indexes. - indicates no data collected for period.

San Francisco-Oakland, CA

Consumer Price Index - Urban Wage Earners
Base 1982-1984 = 100
Other Goods and Services

For 1975-1993. Columns headed % show percentile change in the index from the previous period for which an index is available.

Year	Jan		Feb		Mar		Apr		May		Jun		Jul		Aug		Sep		Oct		Nov		Dec	
	Index	%	Index	%	Index	%	Index	%	Index	%	Index	%	Index	%	Index	%	Index	%	Index	%	Index	%	Index	%
1975	-	-	-	-	-	-	-	-	-	-	-	-	-	-	-	-	-	-	-	-	-	-	52.7	-
1976	-	-	-	-	53.1	0.8	-	-	-	-	53.6	0.9	-	-	-	-	54.5	1.7	-	-	-	-	55.7	2.2
1977	-	-	-	-	56.5	1.4	-	-	-	-	57.5	1.8	-	-	-	-	59.2	3.0	-	-	-	-	59.5	0.5
1978	-	-	59.5	0.0	-	-	60.4	1.5	-	-	61.3	1.5	-	-	62.5	2.0	-	-	63.9	2.2	-	-	63.4	-0.8
1979	-	-	64.9	2.4	-	-	65.1	0.3	-	-	66.5	2.2	-	-	67.1	0.9	-	-	68.7	2.4	-	-	69.3	0.9
1980	-	-	70.3	1.4	-	-	72.0	2.4	-	-	72.9	1.3	-	-	73.5	0.8	-	-	75.2	2.3	-	-	76.7	2.0
1981	-	-	77.3	0.8	-	-	78.1	1.0	-	-	79.8	2.2	-	-	80.3	0.6	-	-	83.3	3.7	-	-	84.5	1.4
1982	-	-	87.0	3.0	-	-	88.9	2.2	-	-	89.0	0.1	-	-	90.3	1.5	-	-	96.2	6.5	-	-	97.9	1.8
1983	-	-	99.9	2.0	-	-	100.0	0.1	-	-	101.1	1.1	-	-	100.7	-0.4	-	-	102.7	2.0	-	-	103.7	1.0
1984	-	-	105.5	1.7	-	-	105.8	0.3	-	-	107.2	1.3	-	-	107.6	0.4	-	-	111.4	3.5	-	-	112.2	0.7
1985	-	-	114.7	2.2	-	-	115.3	0.5	-	-	115.2	-0.1	-	-	116.7	1.3	-	-	116.8	0.1	-	-	118.3	1.3
1986	-	-	121.5	2.7	-	-	121.5	0.0	-	-	122.5	0.8	-	-	122.1	-0.3	-	-	123.6	1.2	-	-	125.7	1.7
1987	126.7	0.8	128.0	1.0	128.4	0.3	128.6	0.2	128.2	-0.3	128.7	0.4	130.1	1.1	131.1	0.8	133.5	1.8	133.7	0.1	134.0	0.2	133.7	-0.2
1988	137.0	2.5	137.0	0.0	137.0	0.0	138.0	0.7	138.3	0.2	138.1	-0.1	138.9	0.6	140.9	1.4	142.3	1.0	142.8	0.4	144.9	1.5	145.8	0.6
1989	149.8	2.7	147.4	-1.6	151.9	3.1	151.9	0.0	152.2	0.2	153.8	1.1	156.4	1.7	159.1	1.7	157.6	-0.9	157.6	0.0	157.8	0.1	159.1	0.8
1990	162.3	2.0	161.4	-0.6	161.4	0.0	163.6	1.4	162.8	-0.5	164.2	0.9	164.2	0.0	165.2	0.6	165.8	0.4	167.4	1.0	167.8	0.2	168.0	0.1
1991	169.3	0.8	173.7	2.6	173.3	-0.2	174.3	0.6	175.4	0.6	176.0	0.3	177.1	0.6	178.6	0.8	182.4	2.1	183.6	0.7	184.7	0.6	184.7	0.0
1992	191.6	3.7	191.8	0.1	192.0	0.1	193.1	0.6	192.4	-0.4	192.4	0.0	193.5	0.6	194.4	0.5	201.2	3.5	202.6	0.7	202.4	-0.1	202.2	-0.1
1993	205.1	1.4	207.0	0.9	206.7	-0.1	205.8	-0.4	206.3	0.2	204.5	-0.9	206.1	0.8	204.9	-0.6	205.4	0.2	201.8	-1.8	201.9	0.0	202.0	0.0

Source: U.S. Department of Labor, Bureau of Labor Statistics, Division of Consumer Prices and Price Indexes. - indicates no data collected for period.

Seattle-Everett, WA
Consumer Price Index - All Urban Consumers
Base 1982-1984 = 100
Annual Averages

For 1914-1993. Columns headed % show percentile change in the index from the previous period for which an index is available.

Year	All Items		Food & Beverage		Housing		Apparel & Upkeep		Trans-portation		Medical Care		Entertain-ment		Other Goods & Services	
	Index	%	Index	%	Index	%	Index	%	Index	%	Index	%	Index	%	Index	%
1914	-	-	-	-	-	-	-	-	-	-	-	-	-	-	-	-
1915	9.0	-	-	-	-	-	-	-	-	-	-	-	-	-	-	-
1916	9.4	4.4	-	-	-	-	-	-	-	-	-	-	-	-	-	-
1917	11.0	17.0	-	-	-	-	-	-	-	-	-	-	-	-	-	-
1918	13.7	24.5	-	-	-	-	-	-	-	-	-	-	-	-	-	-
1919	16.5	20.4	-	-	-	-	-	-	-	-	-	-	-	-	-	-
1920	18.8	13.9	-	-	-	-	-	-	-	-	-	-	-	-	-	-
1921	16.7	-11.2	-	-	-	-	-	-	-	-	-	-	-	-	-	-
1922	15.6	-6.6	-	-	-	-	-	-	-	-	-	-	-	-	-	-
1923	15.5	-0.6	-	-	-	-	-	-	-	-	-	-	-	-	-	-
1924	15.5	0.0	-	-	-	-	-	-	-	-	-	-	-	-	-	-
1925	15.8	1.9	-	-	-	-	-	-	-	-	-	-	-	-	-	-
1926	15.8	0.0	-	-	-	-	-	-	-	-	-	-	-	-	-	-
1927	15.5	-1.9	-	-	-	-	-	-	-	-	-	-	-	-	-	-
1928	15.4	-0.6	-	-	-	-	-	-	-	-	-	-	-	-	-	-
1929	15.5	0.6	-	-	-	-	-	-	-	-	-	-	-	-	-	-
1930	15.2	-1.9	-	-	-	-	-	-	-	-	-	-	-	-	-	-
1931	13.8	-9.2	-	-	-	-	-	-	-	-	-	-	-	-	-	-
1932	12.6	-8.7	-	-	-	-	-	-	-	-	-	-	-	-	-	-
1933	12.0	-4.8	-	-	-	-	-	-	-	-	-	-	-	-	-	-
1934	12.3	2.5	-	-	-	-	-	-	-	-	-	-	-	-	-	-
1935	12.6	2.4	-	-	-	-	-	-	-	-	-	-	-	-	-	-
1936	12.7	0.8	-	-	-	-	-	-	-	-	-	-	-	-	-	-
1937	13.4	5.5	-	-	-	-	-	-	-	-	-	-	-	-	-	-
1938	13.2	-1.5	-	-	-	-	-	-	-	-	-	-	-	-	-	-
1939	13.2	0.0	-	-	-	-	-	-	-	-	-	-	-	-	-	-
1940	13.2	0.0	-	-	-	-	-	-	-	-	-	-	-	-	-	-
1941	14.0	6.1	-	-	-	-	-	-	-	-	-	-	-	-	-	-
1942	15.8	12.9	-	-	-	-	-	-	-	-	-	-	-	-	-	-
1943	16.7	5.7	-	-	-	-	-	-	-	-	-	-	-	-	-	-
1944	16.9	1.2	-	-	-	-	-	-	-	-	-	-	-	-	-	-
1945	17.3	2.4	-	-	-	-	-	-	-	-	-	-	-	-	-	-
1946	18.6	7.5	-	-	-	-	-	-	19.1	-	14.4	-	-	-	-	-
1947	21.1	13.4	-	-	-	-	-	-	20.8	8.9	15.1	4.9	-	-	-	-
1948	22.8	8.1	-	-	-	-	-	-	22.2	6.7	15.8	4.6	-	-	-	-
1949	22.7	-0.4	-	-	-	-	-	-	22.9	3.2	16.1	1.9	-	-	-	-
1950	23.1	1.8	-	-	-	-	-	-	24.2	5.7	17.1	6.2	-	-	-	-
1951	24.8	7.4	-	-	-	-	-	-	25.6	5.8	18.4	7.6	-	-	-	-
1952	25.5	2.8	-	-	-	-	-	-	27.4	7.0	19.0	3.3	-	-	-	-
1953	25.8	1.2	-	-	-	-	43.9	-	26.9	-1.8	19.7	3.7	-	-	-	-
1954	25.8	0.0	-	-	-	-	43.6	-0.7	26.4	-1.9	20.1	2.0	-	-	-	-
1955	25.9	0.4	-	-	-	-	43.8	0.5	26.6	0.8	20.6	2.5	-	-	-	-
1956	26.2	1.2	-	-	-	-	44.2	0.9	28.6	7.5	21.3	3.4	-	-	-	-
1957	27.3	4.2	-	-	-	-	45.1	2.0	29.7	3.8	22.3	4.7	-	-	-	-
1958	27.9	2.2	-	-	-	-	44.9	-0.4								

[Continued]

Seattle-Everett, WA
Consumer Price Index - All Urban Consumers
Base 1982-1984 = 100
Annual Averages
[Continued]

For 1914-1993. Columns headed % show percentile change in the index from the previous period for which an index is available.

Year	All Items		Food & Beverage		Housing		Apparel & Upkeep		Trans- portation		Medical Care		Entertain- ment		Other Goods & Services	
	Index	%	Index	%	Index	%	Index	%	Index	%	Index	%	Index	%	Index	%
1959	28.5	2.2	-	-	-	-	45.4	1.1	31.1	4.7	22.8	2.2	-	-	-	-
1960	28.8	1.1	-	-	-	-	46.0	1.3	30.8	-1.0	23.9	4.8	-	-	-	-
1961	29.3	1.7	-	-	-	-	46.7	1.5	31.7	2.9	24.0	0.4	-	-	-	-
1962	29.7	1.4	-	-	-	-	47.5	1.7	32.6	2.8	24.3	1.2	-	-	-	-
1963	30.2	1.7	-	-	-	-	48.2	1.5	32.5	-0.3	24.5	0.8	-	-	-	-
1964	30.6	1.3	-	-	-	-	48.7	1.0	32.6	0.3	25.0	2.0	-	-	-	-
1965	31.0	1.3	-	-	-	-	49.0	0.6	33.5	2.8	26.0	4.0	-	-	-	-
1966	31.9	2.9	-	-	-	-	50.4	2.9	34.0	1.5	27.6	6.2	-	-	-	-
1967	32.8	2.8	-	-	-	-	52.2	3.6	35.3	3.8	29.1	5.4	-	-	-	-
1968	34.1	4.0	-	-	-	-	53.7	2.9	35.9	1.7	30.8	5.8	-	-	-	-
1969	35.8	5.0	-	-	-	-	55.8	3.9	36.2	0.8	32.9	6.8	-	-	-	-
1970	37.4	4.5	-	-	-	-	58.3	4.5	37.1	2.5	34.5	4.9	-	-	-	-
1971	38.2	2.1	-	-	-	-	60.6	3.9	37.8	1.9	35.8	3.8			-	-
1972	39.3	2.9	-	-	-	-	61.4	1.3	38.6	2.1	36.5	2.0			-	-
1973	41.8	6.4	-	-	-	-	64.2	4.6	39.6	2.6	37.8	3.6			-	-
1974	46.4	11.0	-	-	-	-	68.2	6.2	44.0	11.1	41.2	9.0			-	-
1975	51.1	10.1	-	-	-	-	72.7	6.6	48.1	9.3	46.1	11.9	-	-	-	-
1976	54.0	5.7	61.3	-	50.3	-	76.9	5.8	51.8	7.7	50.9	10.4	62.2	-	50.8	-
1977	58.3	8.0	65.6	7.0	54.8	8.9	80.4	4.6	56.9	9.8	56.0	10.0	65.4	5.1	54.2	6.7
1978	63.9	9.6	71.0	8.2	61.7	12.6	82.6	2.7	61.2	7.6	62.2	11.1	68.5	4.7	57.8	6.6
1979	71.0	11.1	78.3	10.3	68.1	10.4	87.9	6.4	71.1	16.2	67.4	8.4	73.3	7.0	64.2	11.1
1980	82.7	16.5	84.5	7.9	82.7	21.4	95.0	8.1	83.1	16.9	75.8	12.5	82.0	11.9	71.5	11.4
1981	91.8	11.0	91.6	8.4	92.2	11.5	99.0	4.2	94.2	13.4	84.9	12.0	88.2	7.6	80.0	11.9
1982	97.7	6.4	98.3	7.3	98.4	6.7	99.6	0.6	98.0	4.0	93.5	10.1	93.8	6.3	91.7	14.6
1983	99.3	1.6	100.1	1.8	98.7	0.3	101.2	1.6	98.9	0.9	100.9	7.9	100.0	6.6	101.1	10.3
1984	103.0	3.7	101.6	1.5	102.8	4.2	99.2	-2.0	103.1	4.2	105.6	4.7	106.2	6.2	107.3	6.1
1985	105.6	2.5	103.2	1.6	105.5	2.6	102.5	3.3	105.0	1.8	112.2	6.3	108.5	2.2	111.9	4.3
1986	106.7	1.0	106.8	3.5	106.8	1.2	104.7	2.1	101.7	-3.1	117.6	4.8	108.6	0.1	117.1	4.6
1987	109.2	2.3	111.9	4.8	108.1	1.2	109.4	4.5	102.3	0.6	124.6	6.0	110.9	2.1	122.5	4.6
1988	112.8	3.3	114.9	2.7	111.9	3.5	115.6	5.7	103.5	1.2	132.9	6.7	115.5	4.1	127.4	4.0
1989	118.1	4.7	123.1	7.1	116.3	3.9	107.4	-7.1	109.2	5.5	141.6	6.5	126.0	9.1	135.4	6.3
1990	126.8	7.4	133.0	8.0	125.4	7.8	112.0	4.3	116.1	6.3	154.6	9.2	129.9	3.1	146.8	8.4
1991	134.1	5.8	140.6	5.7	134.0	6.9	113.4	1.3	119.9	3.3	169.4	9.6	135.9	4.6	156.5	6.6
1992	139.0	3.7	141.1	0.4	139.3	4.0	118.7	4.7	123.9	3.3	184.2	8.7	140.1	3.1	169.1	8.1
1993	142.9	2.8	142.4	0.9	143.5	3.0	115.5	-2.7	128.4	3.6	193.1	4.8	144.2	2.9	179.5	6.2

Source: U.S. Department of Labor, Bureau of Labor Statistics, Division of Consumer Prices and Price Indexes. - indicates no data collected for period.

Seattle-Everett, WA
Consumer Price Index - Urban Wage Earners
Base 1982-1984 = 100
Annual Averages

For 1914-1993. Columns headed % show percentile change in the index from the previous period for which an index is available.

Year	All Items		Food & Beverage		Housing		Apparel & Upkeep		Trans-portation		Medical Care		Entertain-ment		Other Goods & Services	
	Index	%	Index	%	Index	%	Index	%	Index	%	Index	%	Index	%	Index	%
1914	-	-	-	-	-	-	-	-	-	-	-	-	-	-	-	-
1915	9.3	-	-	-	-	-	-	-	-	-	-	-	-	-	-	-
1916	9.6	3.2	-	-	-	-	-	-	-	-	-	-	-	-	-	-
1917	11.3	17.7	-	-	-	-	-	-	-	-	-	-	-	-	-	-
1918	14.1	24.8	-	-	-	-	-	-	-	-	-	-	-	-	-	-
1919	17.0	20.6	-	-	-	-	-	-	-	-	-	-	-	-	-	-
1920	19.4	14.1	-	-	-	-	-	-	-	-	-	-	-	-	-	-
1921	17.1	-11.9	-	-	-	-	-	-	-	-	-	-	-	-	-	-
1922	16.0	-6.4	-	-	-	-	-	-	-	-	-	-	-	-	-	-
1923	15.9	-0.6	-	-	-	-	-	-	-	-	-	-	-	-	-	-
1924	15.9	0.0	-	-	-	-	-	-	-	-	-	-	-	-	-	-
1925	16.3	2.5	-	-	-	-	-	-	-	-	-	-	-	-	-	-
1926	16.3	0.0	-	-	-	-	-	-	-	-	-	-	-	-	-	-
1927	15.9	-2.5	-	-	-	-	-	-	-	-	-	-	-	-	-	-
1928	15.8	-0.6	-	-	-	-	-	-	-	-	-	-	-	-	-	-
1929	15.9	0.6	-	-	-	-	-	-	-	-	-	-	-	-	-	-
1930	15.6	-1.9	-	-	-	-	-	-	-	-	-	-	-	-	-	-
1931	14.2	-9.0	-	-	-	-	-	-	-	-	-	-	-	-	-	-
1932	12.9	-9.2	-	-	-	-	-	-	-	-	-	-	-	-	-	-
1933	12.3	-4.7	-	-	-	-	-	-	-	-	-	-	-	-	-	-
1934	12.6	2.4	-	-	-	-	-	-	-	-	-	-	-	-	-	-
1935	12.9	2.4	-	-	-	-	-	-	-	-	-	-	-	-	-	-
1936	13.1	1.6	-	-	-	-	-	-	-	-	-	-	-	-	-	-
1937	13.7	4.6	-	-	-	-	-	-	-	-	-	-	-	-	-	-
1938	13.6	-0.7	-	-	-	-	-	-	-	-	-	-	-	-	-	-
1939	13.5	-0.7	-	-	-	-	-	-	-	-	-	-	-	-	-	-
1940	13.6	0.7	-	-	-	-	-	-	-	-	-	-	-	-	-	-
1941	14.4	5.9	-	-	-	-	-	-	-	-	-	-	-	-	-	-
1942	16.2	12.5	-	-	-	-	-	-	-	-	-	-	-	-	-	-
1943	17.1	5.6	-	-	-	-	-	-	-	-	-	-	-	-	-	-
1944	17.4	1.8	-	-	-	-	-	-	-	-	-	-	-	-	-	-
1945	17.8	2.3	-	-	-	-	-	-	-	-	-	-	-	-	-	-
1946	19.2	7.9	-	-	-	-	-	-	-	-	-	-	-	-	-	-
1947	21.7	13.0	-	-	-	-	-	-	19.5	-	14.3	-	-	-	-	-
1948	23.5	8.3	-	-	-	-	-	-	21.2	8.7	15.0	4.9	-	-	-	-
1949	23.4	-0.4	-	-	-	-	-	-	22.7	7.1	15.7	4.7	-	-	-	-
1950	23.7	1.3	-	-	-	-	-	-	23.3	2.6	15.9	1.3	-	-	-	-
1951	25.5	7.6	-	-	-	-	-	-	24.7	6.0	16.9	6.3	-	-	-	-
1952	26.2	2.7	-	-	-	-	-	-	26.1	5.7	18.2	7.7	-	-	-	-
1953	26.5	1.1	-	-	-	-	44.4	-	27.9	6.9	18.9	3.8	-	-	-	-
1954	26.5	0.0	-	-	-	-	44.1	-0.7	27.4	-1.8	19.5	3.2	-	-	-	-
1955	26.6	0.4	-	-	-	-	44.3	0.5	27.0	-1.5	19.9	2.1	-	-	-	-
1956	27.0	1.5	-	-	-	-	44.7	0.9	27.1	0.4	20.4	2.5	-	-	-	-
1957	28.1	4.1	-	-	-	-	45.6	2.0	29.2	7.7	21.1	3.4	-	-	-	-
1958	28.7	2.1	-	-	-	-	45.4	-0.4	30.3	3.8	22.1	4.7	-	-	-	-

[Continued]

Seattle-Everett, WA
Consumer Price Index - Urban Wage Earners
Base 1982-1984 = 100
Annual Averages
[Continued]

For 1914-1993. Columns headed % show percentile change in the index from the previous period for which an index is available.

Year	All Items		Food & Beverage		Housing		Apparel & Upkeep		Trans- portation		Medical Care		Entertain- ment		Other Goods & Services	
	Index	%	Index	%	Index	%	Index	%	Index	%	Index	%	Index	%	Index	%
1959	29.3	2.1	-	-	-	-	45.9	1.1	31.7	4.6	22.6	2.3	-	-	-	-
1960	29.6	1.0	-	-	-	-	46.5	1.3	31.4	-0.9	23.7	4.9	-	-	-	-
1961	30.1	1.7	-	-	-	-	47.2	1.5	32.3	2.9	23.8	0.4	-	-	-	-
1962	30.5	1.3	-	-	-	-	48.0	1.7	33.3	3.1	24.1	1.3	-	-	-	-
1963	31.1	2.0	-	-	-	-	48.8	1.7	33.2	-0.3	24.3	0.8	-	-	-	-
1964	31.5	1.3	-	-	-	-	49.3	1.0	33.3	0.3	24.7	1.6	-	-	-	-
1965	31.9	1.3	-	-	-	-	49.6	0.6	34.2	2.7	25.7	4.0	-	-	-	-
1966	32.7	2.5	-	-	-	-	51.0	2.8	34.7	1.5	27.4	6.6	-	-	-	-
1967	33.7	3.1	-	-	-	-	52.8	3.5	36.0	3.7	28.8	5.1	-	-	-	-
1968	35.1	4.2	-	-	-	-	54.3	2.8	36.6	1.7	30.5	5.9	-	-	-	-
1969	36.8	4.8	-	-	-	-	56.5	4.1	36.9	0.8	32.6	6.9	-	-	-	-
1970	38.4	4.3	-	-	-	-	59.0	4.4	37.9	2.7	34.1	4.6	-	-	-	-
1971	39.2	2.1	-	-	-	-	61.3	3.9	38.6	1.8	35.4	3.8	-	-	-	-
1972	40.4	3.1	-	-	-	-	62.1	1.3	39.4	2.1	36.2	2.3	-	-	-	-
1973	43.0	6.4	-	-	-	-	65.0	4.7	40.4	2.5	37.4	3.3	-	-	-	-
1974	47.7	10.9	-	-	-	-	69.1	6.3	44.9	11.1	40.8	9.1	-	-	-	-
1975	52.5	10.1	-	-	-	-	73.5	6.4	49.1	9.4	45.7	12.0	-	-	-	-
1976	55.5	5.7	61.6	-	52.5	-	77.8	5.9	52.8	7.5	50.4	10.3	60.0	-	52.6	-
1977	59.9	7.9	65.9	7.0	57.2	9.0	81.3	4.5	58.1	10.0	55.4	9.9	63.1	5.2	56.1	6.7
1978	65.3	9.0	71.2	8.0	64.4	12.6	83.5	2.7	61.4	5.7	61.1	10.3	66.5	5.4	60.0	7.0
1979	72.4	10.9	78.3	10.0	70.9	10.1	87.9	5.3	70.8	15.3	67.4	10.3	71.4	7.4	65.2	8.7
1980	84.0	16.0	84.8	8.3	85.9	21.2	93.9	6.8	82.3	16.2	75.1	11.4	80.3	12.5	71.6	9.8
1981	93.1	10.8	92.1	8.6	95.5	11.2	97.9	4.3	93.4	13.5	84.1	12.0	87.1	8.5	79.9	11.6
1982	99.1	6.4	98.3	6.7	101.7	6.5	99.7	1.8	97.8	4.7	93.4	11.1	94.2	8.2	91.2	14.1
1983	98.9	-0.2	100.1	1.8	97.6	-4.0	100.9	1.2	98.9	1.1	100.8	7.9	100.1	6.3	101.5	11.3
1984	102.1	3.2	101.6	1.5	100.8	3.3	99.4	-1.5	103.3	4.4	105.8	5.0	105.7	5.6	107.3	5.7
1985	104.2	2.1	103.3	1.7	102.2	1.4	102.5	3.1	105.4	2.0	112.6	6.4	108.0	2.2	111.9	4.3
1986	105.0	0.8	106.6	3.2	103.3	1.1	103.7	1.2	101.8	-3.4	118.4	5.2	107.9	-0.1	117.2	4.7
1987	107.4	2.3	111.6	4.7	104.5	1.2	108.3	4.4	102.7	0.9	126.2	6.6	109.6	1.6	123.0	4.9
1988	110.9	3.3	114.6	2.7	108.0	3.3	114.1	5.4	104.6	1.9	134.7	6.7	113.4	3.5	128.0	4.1
1989	116.1	4.7	122.7	7.1	111.9	3.6	105.7	-7.4	110.2	5.4	143.4	6.5	124.2	9.5	136.3	6.5
1990	124.4	7.1	132.7	8.1	120.5	7.7	111.0	5.0	116.7	5.9	156.0	8.8	127.8	2.9	147.7	8.4
1991	131.3	5.5	140.2	5.7	128.4	6.6	112.2	1.1	120.6	3.3	170.0	9.0	132.9	4.0	157.4	6.6
1992	136.0	3.6	140.8	0.4	133.0	3.6	117.7	4.9	125.0	3.6	184.9	8.8	136.4	2.6	170.4	8.3
1993	140.0	2.9	142.5	1.2	137.0	3.0	115.0	-2.3	130.1	4.1	193.9	4.9	140.2	2.8	181.6	6.6

Source: U.S. Department of Labor, Bureau of Labor Statistics, Division of Consumer Prices and Price Indexes. - indicates no data collected for period.

Seattle-Everett, WA
Consumer Price Index - All Urban Consumers
Base 1982-1984 = 100
All Items

For 1914-1993. Columns headed % show percentile change in the index from the previous period for which an index is available.

Year	Jan Index	%	Feb Index	%	Mar Index	%	Apr Index	%	May Index	%	Jun Index	%	Jul Index	%	Aug Index	%	Sep Index	%	Oct Index	%	Nov Index	%	Dec Index	%
1914	-	-	-	-	-	-	-	-	-	-	-	-	-	-	-	-	-	-	-	-	-	-	9.2	-
1915	-	-	-	-	-	-	-	-	-	-	-	-	-	-	-	-	-	-	-	-	-	-	9.1	-1.1
1916	-	-	-	-	-	-	-	-	-	-	-	-	-	-	-	-	-	-	-	-	-	-	9.7	6.6
1917	-	-	-	-	-	-	-	-	-	-	-	-	-	-	-	-	-	-	-	-	-	-	11.8	21.6
1918	-	-	-	-	-	-	-	-	-	-	-	-	-	-	-	-	-	-	-	-	-	-	15.4	30.5
1919	-	-	-	-	-	-	-	-	-	-	16.0	3.9	-	-	-	-	-	-	-	-	-	-	18.2	13.8
1920	-	-	-	-	-	-	-	-	-	-	19.6	7.7	-	-	-	-	-	-	-	-	-	-	17.9	-8.7
1921	-	-	-	-	-	-	-	-	16.8	-6.1	-	-	-	-	-	-	16.3	-3.0	-	-	-	-	16.0	-1.8
1922	-	-	-	-	15.7	-1.9	-	-	-	-	15.6	-0.6	-	-	-	-	15.5	-0.6	-	-	-	-	15.5	0.0
1923	-	-	-	-	15.1	-2.6	-	-	-	-	15.5	2.6	-	-	-	-	15.6	0.6	-	-	-	-	15.6	0.0
1924	-	-	-	-	15.5	-0.6	-	-	-	-	15.6	0.6	-	-	-	-	15.5	-0.6	-	-	-	-	15.6	0.6
1925	-	-	-	-	-	-	-	-	-	-	16.0	2.6	-	-	-	-	-	-	-	-	-	-	16.0	0.0
1926	-	-	-	-	-	-	-	-	-	-	15.8	-1.2	-	-	-	-	-	-	-	-	-	-	15.7	-0.6
1927	-	-	-	-	-	-	-	-	-	-	15.8	0.6	-	-	-	-	-	-	-	-	-	-	15.4	-2.5
1928	-	-	-	-	-	-	-	-	-	-	15.3	-0.6	-	-	-	-	-	-	-	-	-	-	15.4	0.7
1929	-	-	-	-	-	-	-	-	-	-	15.5	0.6	-	-	-	-	-	-	-	-	-	-	15.5	0.0
1930	-	-	-	-	-	-	-	-	-	-	15.5	0.0	-	-	-	-	-	-	-	-	-	-	14.4	-7.1
1931	-	-	-	-	-	-	-	-	-	-	13.9	-3.5	-	-	-	-	-	-	-	-	-	-	13.4	-3.6
1932	-	-	-	-	-	-	-	-	-	-	12.6	-6.0	-	-	-	-	-	-	-	-	-	-	12.1	-4.0
1933	-	-	-	-	-	-	-	-	-	-	12.0	-0.8	-	-	-	-	-	-	-	-	-	-	12.1	0.8
1934	-	-	-	-	-	-	-	-	-	-	12.2	0.8	-	-	-	-	-	-	-	-	12.4	1.6	-	-
1935	-	-	-	-	12.7	2.4	-	-	-	-	-	-	12.5	-1.6	-	-	-	-	12.5	0.0	-	-	-	-
1936	12.7	1.6	-	-	-	-	12.5	-1.6	-	-	-	-	12.7	1.6	-	-	12.9	1.6	-	-	-	-	12.9	0.0
1937	-	-	-	-	13.3	3.1	-	-	-	-	13.3	0.0	-	-	-	-	13.5	1.5	-	-	-	-	13.4	-0.7
1938	-	-	-	-	13.3	-0.7	-	-	-	-	13.2	-0.8	-	-	-	-	13.2	0.0	-	-	-	-	13.2	0.0
1939	-	-	-	-	13.1	-0.8	-	-	-	-	13.1	0.0	-	-	-	-	13.3	1.5	-	-	-	-	13.1	-1.5
1940	-	-	-	-	13.2	0.8	-	-	-	-	13.2	0.0	-	-	-	-	13.2	0.0	13.2	0.0	13.2	0.0	13.3	0.8
1941	13.3	0.0	13.3	0.0	13.4	0.8	13.5	0.7	13.8	2.2	13.9	0.7	14.0	0.7	14.1	0.7	14.5	2.8	14.7	1.4	14.7	0.0	14.9	1.4
1942	15.2	2.0	15.3	0.7	15.5	1.3	15.6	0.6	15.8	1.3	15.5	-1.9	15.6	0.6	15.8	1.3	16.0	1.3	16.1	0.6	16.2	0.6	16.4	1.2
1943	16.4	0.0	16.4	0.0	16.6	1.2	16.7	0.6	16.9	1.2	16.8	-0.6	16.5	-1.8	16.4	-0.6	16.7	1.8	16.8	0.6	16.8	0.0	16.8	0.0
1944	16.8	0.0	16.7	-0.6	16.8	0.6	16.8	0.0	16.9	0.6	16.9	0.0	17.0	0.6	17.0	0.0	17.0	0.0	17.1	0.6	17.1	0.0	17.2	0.6
1945	17.2	0.0	17.1	-0.6	17.2	0.6	17.2	0.0	17.3	0.6	17.3	0.0	17.4	0.6	17.4	0.0	17.4	0.0	17.3	-0.6	17.4	0.6	17.6	1.1
1946	17.5	-0.6	17.5	0.0	17.6	0.6	17.6	0.0	17.7	0.6	17.9	1.1	18.7	4.5	19.0	1.6	19.4	2.1	19.9	2.6	20.3	2.0	20.6	1.5
1947	20.4	-1.0	20.3	-0.5	20.7	2.0	20.8	0.5	20.8	0.0	20.7	-0.5	-	-	21.2	2.4	-	-	-	-	21.8	2.8	-	-
1948	-	-	22.4	2.8	-	-	-	-	22.9	2.2	-	-	-	-	23.2	1.3	-	-	-	-	22.9	-1.3	-	-
1949	-	-	23.0	0.4	-	-	-	-	22.8	-0.9	-	-	-	-	22.5	-1.3	-	-	-	-	22.7	0.9	-	-
1950	-	-	22.6	-0.4	-	-	-	-	22.6	0.0	-	-	-	-	23.0	1.8	-	-	-	-	23.8	3.5	-	-
1951	-	-	24.5	2.9	-	-	-	-	24.9	1.6	-	-	-	-	24.8	-0.4	-	-	-	-	25.3	2.0	-	-
1952	-	-	25.4	0.4	-	-	-	-	25.5	0.4	-	-	-	-	25.5	0.0	-	-	-	-	25.7	0.8	-	-
1953	-	-	25.5	-0.8	-	-	-	-	25.8	1.2	-	-	-	-	25.9	0.4	-	-	-	-	25.8	-0.4	-	-
1954	-	-	25.8	0.0	-	-	-	-	25.8	0.0	-	-	-	-	25.8	0.0	-	-	-	-	25.7	-0.4	-	-
1955	-	-	25.8	0.4	-	-	-	-	25.9	0.4	-	-	-	-	25.9	0.0	-	-	-	-	26.1	0.8	-	-
1956	-	-	25.8	-1.1	-	-	-	-	26.0	0.8	-	-	-	-	26.4	1.5	-	-	-	-	26.7	1.1	-	-
1957	-	-	27.1	1.5	-	-	-	-	27.3	0.7	-	-	-	-	27.5	0.7	-	-	-	-	27.5	0.0	-	-
1958	-	-	27.8	1.1	-	-	-	-	28.0	0.7	-	-	-	-	28.0	0.0	-	-	-	-	28.0	0.0	-	-

[Continued]

Seattle-Everett, WA
Consumer Price Index - All Urban Consumers
Base 1982-1984 = 100
All Items
[Continued]

For 1914-1993. Columns headed % show percentile change in the index from the previous period for which an index is available.

Year	Jan Index	Jan %	Feb Index	Feb %	Mar Index	Mar %	Apr Index	Apr %	May Index	May %	Jun Index	Jun %	Jul Index	Jul %	Aug Index	Aug %	Sep Index	Sep %	Oct Index	Oct %	Nov Index	Nov %	Dec Index	Dec %
1959	-	-	28.2	0.7	-	-	-	-	28.4	0.7	-	-	-	-	28.6	0.7	-	-	-	-	28.7	0.3	-	-
1960	-	-	28.6	-0.3	-	-	-	-	28.8	0.7	-	-	-	-	28.8	0.0	-	-	-	-	29.0	0.7	-	-
1961	-	-	29.1	0.3	-	-	-	-	29.3	0.7	-	-	-	-	29.3	0.0	-	-	-	-	29.5	0.7	-	-
1962	-	-	29.6	0.3	-	-	-	-	29.7	0.3	-	-	-	-	29.8	0.3	-	-	-	-	29.9	0.3	-	-
1963	-	-	29.9	0.0	-	-	-	-	30.0	0.3	-	-	-	-	30.5	1.7	-	-	-	-	30.5	0.0	-	-
1964	-	-	30.5	0.0	-	-	-	-	30.5	0.0	-	-	-	-	30.8	1.0	-	-	-	-	30.7	-0.3	-	-
1965	-	-	30.6	-0.3	-	-	-	-	30.9	1.0	-	-	-	-	31.1	0.6	-	-	-	-	31.2	0.3	-	-
1966	-	-	31.4	0.6	-	-	-	-	31.8	1.3	-	-	-	-	32.0	0.6	-	-	-	-	32.3	0.9	-	-
1967	-	-	32.3	0.0	-	-	-	-	32.6	0.9	-	-	-	-	33.0	1.2	-	-	-	-	33.3	0.9	-	-
1968	-	-	33.6	0.9	-	-	-	-	33.8	0.6	-	-	-	-	34.4	1.8	-	-	-	-	34.8	1.2	-	-
1969	-	-	35.1	0.9	-	-	-	-	35.6	1.4	-	-	-	-	36.2	1.7	-	-	-	-	36.3	0.3	-	-
1970	-	-	36.9	1.7	-	-	-	-	37.4	1.4	-	-	-	-	37.6	0.5	-	-	-	-	37.7	0.3	-	-
1971	-	-	37.6	-0.3	-	-	-	-	37.9	0.8	-	-	-	-	38.6	1.8	-	-	-	-	38.6	0.0	-	-
1972	-	-	39.0	1.0	-	-	-	-	39.0	0.0	-	-	-	-	39.3	0.8	-	-	-	-	39.8	1.3	-	-
1973	-	-	40.4	1.5	-	-	-	-	41.4	2.5	-	-	-	-	42.3	2.2	-	-	-	-	43.1	1.9	-	-
1974	-	-	44.5	3.2	-	-	-	-	45.7	2.7	-	-	-	-	46.9	2.6	-	-	-	-	48.5	3.4	-	-
1975	-	-	49.8	2.7	-	-	-	-	50.7	1.8	-	-	-	-	51.6	1.8	-	-	-	-	52.4	1.6	-	-
1976	-	-	53.0	1.1	-	-	-	-	53.3	0.6	-	-	-	-	54.4	2.1	-	-	-	-	55.1	1.3	-	-
1977	-	-	56.2	2.0	-	-	-	-	57.8	2.8	-	-	-	-	59.1	2.2	-	-	-	-	59.9	1.4	-	-
1978	60.4	0.8	-	-	61.4	1.7	-	-	63.5	3.4	-	-	63.9	0.6	-	-	65.9	3.1	-	-	66.8	1.4	-	-
1979	66.3	-0.7	-	-	67.9	2.4	-	-	69.7	2.7	-	-	71.3	2.3	-	-	73.0	2.4	-	-	74.7	2.3	-	-
1980	77.4	3.6	-	-	80.0	3.4	-	-	81.9	2.4	-	-	83.7	2.2	-	-	84.7	1.2	-	-	86.1	1.7	-	-
1981	86.9	0.9	-	-	88.9	2.3	-	-	90.1	1.3	-	-	92.6	2.8	-	-	94.7	2.3	-	-	94.9	0.2	-	-
1982	97.1	2.3	-	-	96.2	-0.9	-	-	98.8	2.7	-	-	97.3	-1.5	-	-	99.1	1.8	-	-	97.6	-1.5	-	-
1983	97.6	0.0	-	-	97.7	0.1	-	-	98.7	1.0	-	-	99.7	1.0	-	-	100.5	0.8	-	-	100.7	0.2	-	-
1984	101.3	0.6	-	-	101.8	0.5	-	-	102.7	0.9	-	-	103.1	0.4	-	-	103.8	0.7	-	-	104.4	0.6	-	-
1985	104.8	0.4	-	-	105.4	0.6	-	-	105.3	-0.1	-	-	105.6	0.3	-	-	105.6	0.0	-	-	106.3	0.7	-	-
1986	107.3	0.9	-	-	106.6	-0.7	-	-	106.1	-0.5	-	-	106.2	0.1	-	-	107.0	0.8	-	-	106.9	-0.1	106.8	-0.1
1987	-	-	-	-	-	-	-	-	-	-	108.2	1.3	-	-	-	-	-	-	-	-	-	-	110.3	1.9
1988	-	-	-	-	-	-	-	-	-	-	111.9	1.5	-	-	-	-	-	-	-	-	-	-	113.8	1.7
1989	-	-	-	-	-	-	-	-	-	-	116.7	2.5	-	-	-	-	-	-	-	-	-	-	119.6	1.7
1990	-	-	-	-	-	-	-	-	-	-	124.2	3.8	-	-	-	-	-	-	-	-	-	-	129.4	2.5
1991	-	-	-	-	-	-	-	-	-	-	133.0	2.8	-	-	-	-	-	-	-	-	-	-	135.2	4.2
1992	-	-	-	-	-	-	-	-	-	-	137.8	1.9	-	-	-	-	-	-	-	-	-	-	140.2	1.7
1993	-	-	-	-	-	-	-	-	-	-	141.9	1.2	-	-	-	-	-	-	-	-	-	-	-	-

Source: U.S. Department of Labor, Bureau of Labor Statistics, Division of Consumer Prices and Price Indexes. - indicates no data collected for period.

Seattle-Everett, WA
Consumer Price Index - Urban Wage Earners
Base 1982-1984 = 100
All Items

For 1914-1993. Columns headed % show percentile change in the index from the previous period for which an index is available.

Year	Jan Index	%	Feb Index	%	Mar Index	%	Apr Index	%	May Index	%	Jun Index	%	Jul Index	%	Aug Index	%	Sep Index	%	Oct Index	%	Nov Index	%	Dec Index	%
1914	-		-		-		-		-		-		-		-		-		-		-		9.4	-
1915	-		-		-		-		-		-		-		-		-		-		-		9.3	-1.1
1916	-		-		-		-		-		-		-		-		-		-		-		10.0	7.5
1917	-		-		-		-		-		-		-		-		-		-		-		12.1	21.0
1918	-		-		-		-		-		-		-		-		-		-		-		15.8	30.6
1919	-		-		-		-		-		16.5	4.4	-		-		-		-		-		18.7	13.3
1920	-		-		-		-		-		20.2	8.0	-		-		-		-		-		18.4	-8.9
1921	-		-		-		-		17.2	-6.5	-		-		-		16.7	-2.9	-		-		16.4	-1.8
1922	-		-		-		-		-		16.0	-0.6	-		-		15.9	-0.6	-		-		15.9	0.0
1923	-		-		16.1	-1.8	-		-		15.9	2.6	-		-		16.1	1.3	-		-		16.0	-0.6
1924	-		-		15.5	-2.5	-		-		16.0	0.6	-		-		15.9	-0.6	-		-		16.0	0.6
1925	-		-		15.9	-0.6	-		-		16.4	2.5	-		-		-		-		-		16.5	0.6
1926	-		-		-		-		-		16.3	-1.2	-		-		-		-		-		16.1	-1.2
1927	-		-		-		-		-		16.3	1.2	-		-		-		-		-		15.8	-3.1
1928	-		-		-		-		-		15.7	-0.6	-		-		-		-		-		15.8	0.6
1929	-		-		-		-		-		15.9	0.6	-		-		-		-		-		16.0	0.6
1930	-		-		-		-		-		15.9	-0.6	-		-		-		-		-		14.8	-6.9
1931	-		-		-		-		-		14.3	-3.4	-		-		-		-		-		13.8	-3.5
1932	-		-		-		-		-		13.0	-5.8	-		-		-		-		-		12.4	-4.6
1933	-		-		-		-		-		12.3	-0.8	-		-		-		-		-		12.4	0.8
1934	-		-		-		-		-		12.5	0.8	-		-		-		-		12.8	2.4	-	-
1935	-		-		13.0	1.6	-		-		-		12.8	-1.5	-		-		12.8	0.0	-		-	-
1936	13.0	1.6	-		-		12.9	-0.8	-		-		13.0	0.8	-		13.2	1.5	-		-		13.3	0.8
1937	-		-		13.6	2.3	-		-		13.7	0.7	-		-		13.9	1.5	-		-		13.8	-0.7
1938	-		-		13.7	-0.7	-		-		13.5	-1.5	-		-		13.5	0.0	-		-		13.5	0.0
1939	-		-		13.5	0.0	-		-		13.5	0.0	-		-		13.7	1.5	-		-		13.5	-1.5
1940	-		-		13.6	0.7	-		-		13.6	0.0	-		-		13.6	0.0	13.6	0.0	13.6	0.0	13.6	0.0
1941	13.7	0.7	13.7	0.0	13.8	0.7	13.9	0.7	14.2	2.2	14.3	0.7	14.4	0.7	14.5	0.7	14.9	2.8	15.1	1.3	15.1	0.0	15.3	1.3
1942	15.6	2.0	15.7	0.6	16.0	1.9	16.1	0.6	16.2	0.6	15.9	-1.9	16.0	0.6	16.3	1.9	16.5	1.2	16.6	0.6	16.7	0.6	16.8	0.6
1943	16.9	0.6	16.9	0.0	17.0	0.6	17.2	1.2	17.4	1.2	17.2	-1.1	17.0	-1.2	16.9	-0.6	17.2	1.8	17.2	0.0	17.3	0.6	17.3	0.0
1944	17.3	0.0	17.2	-0.6	17.2	0.0	17.2	0.0	17.4	1.2	17.3	-0.6	17.4	0.6	17.4	0.0	17.5	0.6	17.6	0.6	17.5	-0.6	17.6	0.6
1945	17.6	0.0	17.6	0.0	17.7	0.6	17.7	0.0	17.8	0.6	17.8	0.0	17.8	0.0	17.9	0.6	17.8	-0.6	17.8	0.0	17.9	0.6	18.1	1.1
1946	18.0	-0.6	18.0	0.0	18.0	0.0	18.1	0.6	18.2	0.6	18.4	1.1	19.3	4.9	19.5	1.0	19.9	2.1	20.4	2.5	20.9	2.5	21.1	1.0
1947	20.9	-0.9	20.9	0.0	21.3	1.9	21.4	0.5	21.3	-0.5	21.3	0.0	-		21.8	2.3	-		-		22.4	2.8	-	-
1948	-		23.0	2.7	-		-		23.5	2.2	-		-		23.8	1.3	-		-		23.6	-0.8	-	-
1949	-		23.6	0.0	-		-		23.4	-0.8	-		-		23.2	-0.9	-		-		23.3	0.4	-	-
1950	-		23.3	0.0	-		-		23.3	0.0	-		-		23.7	1.7	-		-		24.4	3.0	-	-
1951	-		25.2	3.3	-		-		25.6	1.6	-		-		25.5	-0.4	-		-		26.0	2.0	-	-
1952	-		26.1	0.4	-		-		26.2	0.4	-		-		26.2	0.0	-		-		26.4	0.8	-	-
1953	-		26.2	-0.8	-		-		26.5	1.1	-		-		26.7	0.8	-		-		26.6	-0.4	-	-
1954	-		26.5	-0.4	-		-		26.5	0.0	-		-		26.5	0.0	-		-		26.4	-0.4	-	-
1955	-		26.5	0.4	-		-		26.7	0.8	-		-		26.6	-0.4	-		-		26.8	0.8	-	-
1956	-		26.5	-1.1	-		-		26.7	0.8	-		-		27.1	1.5	-		-		27.4	1.1	-	-
1957	-		27.9	1.8	-		-		28.0	0.4	-		-		28.2	0.7	-		-		28.3	0.4	-	-
1958	-		28.5	0.7	-		-		28.8	1.1	-		-		28.8	0.0	-		-		28.8	0.0	-	-

[Continued]

Seattle-Everett, WA
Consumer Price Index - Urban Wage Earners
Base 1982-1984 = 100
All Items
[Continued]

For 1914-1993. Columns headed % show percentile change in the index from the previous period for which an index is available.

Year	Jan Index	%	Feb Index	%	Mar Index	%	Apr Index	%	May Index	%	Jun Index	%	Jul Index	%	Aug Index	%	Sep Index	%	Oct Index	%	Nov Index	%	Dec Index	%
1959	-	-	29.0	0.7	-	-	-	-	29.2	0.7	-	-	-	-	29.4	0.7	-	-	-	-	29.5	0.3	-	-
1960	-	-	29.4	-0.3	-	-	-	-	29.6	0.7	-	-	-	-	29.6	0.0	-	-	-	-	29.8	0.7	-	-
1961	-	-	29.9	0.3	-	-	-	-	30.1	0.7	-	-	-	-	30.1	0.0	-	-	-	-	30.3	0.7	-	-
1962	-	-	30.4	0.3	-	-	-	-	30.5	0.3	-	-	-	-	30.6	0.3	-	-	-	-	30.7	0.3	-	-
1963	-	-	30.7	0.0	-	-	-	-	30.8	0.3	-	-	-	-	31.3	1.6	-	-	-	-	31.4	0.3	-	-
1964	-	-	31.4	0.0	-	-	-	-	31.3	-0.3	-	-	-	-	31.7	1.3	-	-	-	-	31.6	-0.3	-	-
1965	-	-	31.5	-0.3	-	-	-	-	31.8	1.0	-	-	-	-	32.0	0.6	-	-	-	-	32.1	0.3	-	-
1966	-	-	32.3	0.6	-	-	-	-	32.6	0.9	-	-	-	-	32.8	0.6	-	-	-	-	33.2	1.2	-	-
1967	-	-	33.2	0.0	-	-	-	-	33.5	0.9	-	-	-	-	33.9	1.2	-	-	-	-	34.2	0.9	-	-
1968	-	-	34.5	0.9	-	-	-	-	34.8	0.9	-	-	-	-	35.4	1.7	-	-	-	-	35.7	0.8	-	-
1969	-	-	36.1	1.1	-	-	-	-	36.6	1.4	-	-	-	-	37.2	1.6	-	-	-	-	37.3	0.3	-	-
1970	-	-	37.9	1.6	-	-	-	-	38.4	1.3	-	-	-	-	38.6	0.5	-	-	-	-	38.7	0.3	-	-
1971	-	-	38.6	-0.3	-	-	-	-	38.9	0.8	-	-	-	-	39.6	1.8	-	-	-	-	39.6	0.0	-	-
1972	-	-	40.1	1.3	-	-	-	-	40.1	0.0	-	-	-	-	40.4	0.7	-	-	-	-	40.9	1.2	-	-
1973	-	-	41.5	1.5	-	-	-	-	42.6	2.7	-	-	-	-	43.4	1.9	-	-	-	-	44.3	2.1	-	-
1974	-	-	45.8	3.4	-	-	-	-	47.0	2.6	-	-	-	-	48.2	2.6	-	-	-	-	49.9	3.5	-	-
1975	-	-	51.2	2.6	-	-	-	-	52.1	1.8	-	-	-	-	53.0	1.7	-	-	-	-	53.8	1.5	-	-
1976	-	-	54.5	1.3	-	-	-	-	54.8	0.6	-	-	-	-	55.9	2.0	-	-	-	-	56.6	1.3	-	-
1977	-	-	57.8	2.1	-	-	-	-	59.4	2.8	-	-	-	-	60.8	2.4	-	-	-	-	61.5	1.2	-	-
1978	62.0	0.8	-	-	63.0	1.6	-	-	64.9	3.0	-	-	65.4	0.8	-	-	67.3	2.9	-	-	68.1	1.2	-	-
1979	67.6	-0.7	-	-	69.4	2.7	-	-	71.1	2.4	-	-	72.8	2.4	-	-	74.5	2.3	-	-	76.0	2.0	-	-
1980	78.8	3.7	-	-	81.4	3.3	-	-	83.2	2.2	-	-	84.8	1.9	-	-	85.8	1.2	-	-	87.5	2.0	-	-
1981	88.4	1.0	-	-	90.3	2.1	-	-	91.5	1.3	-	-	93.7	2.4	-	-	95.9	2.3	-	-	96.3	0.4	-	-
1982	98.4	2.2	-	-	97.6	-0.8	-	-	100.2	2.7	-	-	98.8	-1.4	-	-	100.6	1.8	-	-	99.2	-1.4	-	-
1983	98.2	-1.0	-	-	98.0	-0.2	-	-	97.9	-0.1	-	-	98.5	0.6	-	-	99.7	1.2	-	-	100.1	0.4	-	-
1984	100.2	0.1	-	-	101.1	0.9	-	-	102.1	1.0	-	-	102.2	0.1	-	-	102.9	0.7	-	-	103.0	0.1	-	-
1985	103.4	0.4	-	-	104.2	0.8	-	-	104.0	-0.2	-	-	104.2	0.2	-	-	104.1	-0.1	-	-	104.8	0.7	-	-
1986	105.7	0.9	-	-	105.0	-0.7	-	-	104.3	-0.7	-	-	104.6	0.3	-	-	105.3	0.7	-	-	105.1	-0.2	105.1	0.0
1987	-	-	-	-	-	-	-	-	-	-	106.4	1.2	-	-	-	-	-	-	-	-	-	-	108.4	1.9
1988	-	-	-	-	-	-	-	-	-	-	109.9	1.4	-	-	-	-	-	-	-	-	-	-	112.0	1.9
1989	-	-	-	-	-	-	-	-	-	-	114.7	2.4	-	-	-	-	-	-	-	-	-	-	117.6	2.5
1990	-	-	-	-	-	-	-	-	-	-	122.0	3.7	-	-	-	-	-	-	-	-	-	-	126.9	4.0
1991	-	-	-	-	-	-	-	-	-	-	130.2	2.6	-	-	-	-	-	-	-	-	-	-	132.4	1.7
1992	-	-	-	-	-	-	-	-	-	-	134.8	1.8	-	-	-	-	-	-	-	-	-	-	137.2	1.8
1993	-	-	-	-	-	-	-	-	-	-	138.9	1.2	-	-	-	-	-	-	-	-	-	-	-	-

Source: U.S. Department of Labor, Bureau of Labor Statistics, Division of Consumer Prices and Price Indexes. - indicates no data collected for period.

Seattle-Everett, WA

Consumer Price Index - All Urban Consumers
Base 1982-1984 = 100
Food and Beverages

For 1975-1993. Columns headed % show percentile change in the index from the previous period for which an index is available.

Year	Jan		Feb		Mar		Apr		May		Jun		Jul		Aug		Sep		Oct		Nov		Dec	
	Index	%	Index	%	Index	%	Index	%	Index	%	Index	%	Index	%	Index	%	Index	%	Index	%	Index	%	Index	%
1975	-	-	-	-	-	-	-	-	-	-	-	-	-	-	-	-	-	-	-	-	60.8	-	-	-
1976	-	-	60.6	-0.3	-	-	-	-	60.8	0.3	-	-	-	-	61.8	1.6	-	-	-	-	61.8	0.0	-	-
1977	-	-	63.5	2.8	-	-	-	-	65.2	2.7	-	-	-	-	66.8	2.5	-	-	-	-	66.8	0.0	-	-
1978	67.1	0.4	-	-	69.2	3.1	-	-	72.5	4.8	-	-	70.9	-2.2	-	-	71.9	1.4	-	-	72.5	0.8	-	-
1979	74.1	2.2	-	-	77.5	4.6	-	-	78.8	1.7	-	-	78.8	0.0	-	-	78.5	-0.4	-	-	80.1	2.0	-	-
1980	81.4	1.6	-	-	82.5	1.4	-	-	83.6	1.3	-	-	84.4	1.0	-	-	86.4	2.4	-	-	87.2	0.9	-	-
1981	88.7	1.7	-	-	90.4	1.9	-	-	90.7	0.3	-	-	92.0	1.4	-	-	93.1	1.2	-	-	93.1	0.0	-	-
1982	95.1	2.1	-	-	94.6	-0.5	-	-	99.6	5.3	-	-	100.0	0.4	-	-	99.8	-0.2	-	-	99.5	-0.3	-	-
1983	100.0	0.5	-	-	101.5	1.5	-	-	102.4	0.9	-	-	98.9	-3.4	-	-	98.7	-0.2	-	-	99.0	0.3	-	-
1984	100.8	1.8	-	-	101.3	0.5	-	-	101.4	0.1	-	-	101.7	0.3	-	-	102.1	0.4	-	-	102.1	0.0	-	-
1985	101.7	-0.4	-	-	103.3	1.6	-	-	103.3	0.0	-	-	103.6	0.3	-	-	103.5	-0.1	-	-	103.3	-0.2	-	-
1986	104.9	1.5	-	-	105.9	1.0	-	-	107.1	1.1	-	-	106.7	-0.4	-	-	107.5	0.7	-	-	107.9	0.4	108.1	0.2
1987	-	-	-	-	-	-	-	-	-	-	111.7	3.3	-	-	-	-	-	-	-	-	-	-	112.2	0.4
1988	-	-	-	-	-	-	-	-	-	-	114.0	1.6	-	-	-	-	-	-	-	-	-	-	115.8	1.6
1989	-	-	-	-	-	-	-	-	-	-	121.7	5.1	-	-	-	-	-	-	-	-	-	-	124.4	2.2
1990	-	-	-	-	-	-	-	-	-	-	131.8	5.9	-	-	-	-	-	-	-	-	-	-	134.2	1.8
1991	-	-	-	-	-	-	-	-	-	-	141.1	5.1	-	-	-	-	-	-	-	-	-	-	140.2	-0.6
1992	-	-	-	-	-	-	-	-	-	-	141.1	0.6	-	-	-	-	-	-	-	-	-	-	141.1	0.0
1993	-	-	-	-	-	-	-	-	-	-	142.8	1.2	-	-	-	-	-	-	-	-	-	-	-	-

Source: U.S. Department of Labor, Bureau of Labor Statistics, Division of Consumer Prices and Price Indexes. - indicates no data collected for period.

Seattle-Everett, WA
Consumer Price Index - Urban Wage Earners
Base 1982-1984 = 100
Food and Beverages

For 1975-1993. Columns headed % show percentile change in the index from the previous period for which an index is available.

Year	Jan Index	%	Feb Index	%	Mar Index	%	Apr Index	%	May Index	%	Jun Index	%	Jul Index	%	Aug Index	%	Sep Index	%	Oct Index	%	Nov Index	%	Dec Index	%
1975	-		-		-		-		-		-		-		-		-		-		61.1		-	-
1976	-	-	60.9	-0.3	-		-	-	61.1	0.3	-		-		62.1	1.6	-		-		62.1	0.0	-	-
1977	-	-	63.8	2.7	-		-	-	65.5	2.7	-		-		67.1	2.4	-		-		67.1	0.0	-	-
1978	67.7	0.9	-		69.8	3.1	-		72.1	3.3	-		71.0	-1.5	-		72.3	1.8	-		72.7	0.6	-	-
1979	74.4	2.3	-		77.8	4.6	-		78.8	1.3	-		78.7	-0.1	-		79.0	0.4	-		79.3	0.4	-	-
1980	81.4	2.6	-		82.6	1.5	-		83.7	1.3	-		84.7	1.2	-		86.6	2.2	-		87.6	1.2	-	-
1981	89.6	2.3	-		91.2	1.8	-		91.5	0.3	-		92.5	1.1	-		93.5	1.1	-		93.1	-0.4	-	-
1982	95.1	2.1	-		94.7	-0.4	-		99.5	5.1	-		99.9	0.4	-		99.7	-0.2	-		99.5	-0.2	-	-
1983	100.0	0.5	-		101.6	1.6	-		102.5	0.9	-		98.9	-3.5	-		98.6	-0.3	-		99.0	0.4	-	-
1984	100.7	1.7	-		101.3	0.6	-		101.4	0.1	-		101.6	0.2	-		102.2	0.6	-		102.2	0.0	-	-
1985	101.7	-0.5	-		103.4	1.7	-		103.3	-0.1	-		103.6	0.3	-		103.7	0.1	-		103.3	-0.4	-	-
1986	104.9	1.5	-		105.8	0.9	-		106.9	1.0	-		106.6	-0.3	-		107.2	0.6	-		107.6	0.4	107.9	0.3
1987	-		-		-		-		-		111.3	3.2	-		-		-		-		-		111.8	0.4
1988	-		-		-		-		-		113.6	1.6	-		-		-		-		-		115.6	1.8
1989	-		-		-		-		-		121.3	4.9	-		-		-		-		-		124.1	2.3
1990	-		-		-		-		-		131.5	6.0	-		-		-		-		-		134.0	1.9
1991	-		-		-		-		-		140.5	4.9	-		-		-		-		-		140.0	-0.4
1992	-		-		-		-		-		140.5	0.4	-		-		-		-		-		141.0	0.4
1993	-		-		-		-		-		142.4	1.0	-		-		-		-		-		-	-

Source: U.S. Department of Labor, Bureau of Labor Statistics, Division of Consumer Prices and Price Indexes. - indicates no data collected for period.

Seattle-Everett, WA
Consumer Price Index - All Urban Consumers
Base 1982-1984 = 100
Housing

For 1975-1993. Columns headed % show percentile change in the index from the previous period for which an index is available.

Year	Jan Index	%	Feb Index	%	Mar Index	%	Apr Index	%	May Index	%	Jun Index	%	Jul Index	%	Aug Index	%	Sep Index	%	Oct Index	%	Nov Index	%	Dec Index	%
1975	-	-	-	-	-	-	-	-	-	-	-	-	-	-	-	-	-	-	-	-	48.9	-	-	-
1976	-	-	49.8	1.8	-	-	-	-	49.2	-1.2	-	-	-	-	50.7	3.0	-	-	-	-	51.5	1.6	-	-
1977	-	-	52.2	1.4	-	-	-	-	54.2	3.8	-	-	-	-	55.8	3.0	-	-	-	-	57.0	2.2	-	-
1978	57.5	0.9	-	-	58.7	2.1	-	-	60.9	3.7	-	-	61.6	1.1	-	-	64.5	4.7	-	-	65.5	1.6	-	-
1979	63.6	-2.9	-	-	64.8	1.9	-	-	66.3	2.3	-	-	68.4	3.2	-	-	70.3	2.8	-	-	72.1	2.6	-	-
1980	76.3	5.8	-	-	79.2	3.8	-	-	82.0	3.5	-	-	84.5	3.0	-	-	84.8	0.4	-	-	86.7	2.2	-	-
1981	87.2	0.6	-	-	88.8	1.8	-	-	89.8	1.1	-	-	93.1	3.7	-	-	95.9	3.0	-	-	95.7	-0.2	-	-
1982	99.0	3.4	-	-	97.7	-1.3	-	-	101.1	3.5	-	-	96.6	-4.5	-	-	99.8	3.3	-	-	97.1	-2.7	-	-
1983	97.2	0.1	-	-	97.0	-0.2	-	-	97.7	0.7	-	-	99.2	1.5	-	-	100.0	0.8	-	-	100.2	0.2	-	-
1984	100.9	0.7	-	-	101.9	1.0	-	-	102.1	0.2	-	-	102.6	0.5	-	-	103.8	1.2	-	-	104.6	0.8	-	-
1985	105.2	0.6	-	-	105.4	0.2	-	-	105.3	-0.1	-	-	105.0	-0.3	-	-	104.8	-0.2	-	-	106.5	1.6	-	-
1986	107.7	1.1	-	-	107.0	-0.6	-	-	106.2	-0.7	-	-	105.9	-0.3	-	-	107.3	1.3	-	-	107.1	-0.2	106.6	-0.5
1987	-	-	-	-	-	-	-	-	-	-	107.2	0.6	-	-	-	-	-	-	-	-	-	-	109.1	1.8
1988	-	-	-	-	-	-	-	-	-	-	111.0	1.7	-	-	-	-	-	-	-	-	-	-	112.9	1.7
1989	-	-	-	-	-	-	-	-	-	-	114.6	1.5	-	-	-	-	-	-	-	-	-	-	118.1	3.1
1990	-	-	-	-	-	-	-	-	-	-	122.0	3.3	-	-	-	-	-	-	-	-	-	-	128.9	5.7
1991	-	-	-	-	-	-	-	-	-	-	132.3	2.6	-	-	-	-	-	-	-	-	-	-	135.8	2.6
1992	-	-	-	-	-	-	-	-	-	-	138.3	1.8	-	-	-	-	-	-	-	-	-	-	140.2	1.4
1993	-	-	-	-	-	-	-	-	-	-	142.0	1.3	-	-	-	-	-	-	-	-	-	-	-	-

Source: U.S. Department of Labor, Bureau of Labor Statistics, Division of Consumer Prices and Price Indexes. - indicates no data collected for period.

Seattle-Everett, WA
Consumer Price Index - Urban Wage Earners
Base 1982-1984 = 100
Housing

For 1975-1993. Columns headed % show percentile change in the index from the previous period for which an index is available.

Year	Jan Index	%	Feb Index	%	Mar Index	%	Apr Index	%	May Index	%	Jun Index	%	Jul Index	%	Aug Index	%	Sep Index	%	Oct Index	%	Nov Index	%	Dec Index	%
1975	-	-	-	-	-	-	-	-	-	-	-	-	-	-	-	-	-	-	-	-	51.0	-	-	-
1976	-	-	51.9	1.8	-	-	-	-	51.4	-1.0	-	-	-	-	52.9	2.9	-	-	-	-	53.7	-	-	-
1977	-	-	54.5	1.5	-	-	-	-	56.6	3.9	-	-	-	-	58.3	3.0	-	-	-	-	59.5	1.5	-	-
1978	60.1	1.0	-	-	61.3	2.0	-	-	63.5	3.6	-	-	64.2	1.1	-	-	67.3	4.8	-	-	68.2	2.1	-	-
1979	66.1	-3.1	-	-	67.6	2.3	-	-	69.1	2.2	-	-	71.1	2.9	-	-	73.1	2.8	-	-	75.1	1.3	-	-
1980	79.5	5.9	-	-	82.3	3.5	-	-	85.4	3.8	-	-	87.8	2.8	-	-	88.0	0.2	-	-	90.0	2.7	-	-
1981	90.4	0.4	-	-	92.4	2.2	-	-	93.2	0.9	-	-	96.0	3.0	-	-	99.1	3.2	-	-	99.0	2.3	-	-
1982	102.3	3.3	-	-	100.9	-1.4	-	-	104.5	3.6	-	-	99.7	-4.6	-	-	103.1	3.4	-	-	100.5	-0.1	-	-
1983	98.7	-1.8	-	-	97.9	-0.8	-	-	96.1	-1.8	-	-	96.4	0.3	-	-	97.9	1.6	-	-	98.7	-2.5	-	-
1984	98.7	0.0	-	-	100.3	1.6	-	-	100.7	0.4	-	-	100.6	-0.1	-	-	101.8	1.2	-	-	101.4	0.8	-	-
1985	102.1	0.7	-	-	102.4	0.3	-	-	102.0	-0.4	-	-	101.5	-0.5	-	-	101.4	-0.1	-	-	103.0	-0.4	-	-
1986	104.1	1.1	-	-	103.5	-0.6	-	-	102.6	-0.9	-	-	102.5	-0.1	-	-	103.9	1.4	-	-	103.6	1.6	-	-
1987	-	-	-	-	-	-	-	-	-	-	103.7	0.5	-	-	-	-	-	-	-	-	-	-0.3	103.2	-0.4
1988	-	-	-	-	-	-	-	-	-	-	107.1	1.8	-	-	-	-	-	-	-	-	-	-	105.2	1.4
1989	-	-	-	-	-	-	-	-	-	-	110.3	1.3	-	-	-	-	-	-	-	-	-	-	108.9	1.7
1990	-	-	-	-	-	-	-	-	-	-	117.4	3.4	-	-	-	-	-	-	-	-	-	-	113.5	2.9
1991	-	-	-	-	-	-	-	-	-	-	126.7	2.5	-	-	-	-	-	-	-	-	-	-	123.6	5.3
1992	-	-	-	-	-	-	-	-	-	-	132.2	1.6	-	-	-	-	-	-	-	-	-	-	130.1	2.7
1993	-	-	-	-	-	-	-	-	-	-	135.7	1.4	-	-	-	-	-	-	-	-	-	-	133.8	1.2

Source: U.S. Department of Labor, Bureau of Labor Statistics, Division of Consumer Prices and Price Indexes. - indicates no data collected for period.

Seattle-Everett, WA
Consumer Price Index - All Urban Consumers
Base 1982-1984 = 100
Apparel and Upkeep

For 1952-1993. Columns headed % show percentile change in the index from the previous period for which an index is available.

Year	Jan Index	%	Feb Index	%	Mar Index	%	Apr Index	%	May Index	%	Jun Index	%	Jul Index	%	Aug Index	%	Sep Index	%	Oct Index	%	Nov Index	%	Dec Index	%
1952	-	-	-	-	-	-	-	-	-	-	-	-	-	-	-	-	-	-	-	-	43.9	-	-	-
1953	-	-	43.9	0.0	-	-	-	-	43.8	-0.2	-	-	-	-	44.1	0.7	-	-	-	-	44.0	-0.2	-	-
1954	-	-	43.5	-1.1	-	-	-	-	43.7	0.5	-	-	-	-	43.6	-0.2	-	-	-	-	43.5	-0.2	-	-
1955	-	-	43.7	0.5	-	-	-	-	43.4	-0.7	-	-	-	-	43.9	1.2	-	-	-	-	44.1	0.5	-	-
1956	-	-	43.8	-0.7	-	-	-	-	44.0	0.5	-	-	-	-	44.1	0.2	-	-	-	-	45.0	2.0	-	-
1957	-	-	44.8	-0.4	-	-	-	-	45.0	0.4	-	-	-	-	45.3	0.7	-	-	-	-	45.2	-0.2	-	-
1958	-	-	45.1	-0.2	-	-	-	-	45.1	0.0	-	-	-	-	44.8	-0.7	-	-	-	-	44.7	-0.2	-	-
1959	-	-	44.7	0.0	-	-	-	-	45.1	0.9	-	-	-	-	45.5	0.9	-	-	-	-	46.1	1.3	-	-
1960	-	-	46.0	-0.2	-	-	-	-	45.4	-1.3	-	-	-	-	45.8	0.9	-	-	-	-	46.6	1.7	-	-
1961	-	-	46.5	-0.2	-	-	-	-	46.7	0.4	-	-	-	-	46.2	-1.1	-	-	-	-	47.4	2.6	-	-
1962	-	-	47.2	-0.4	-	-	-	-	47.4	0.4	-	-	-	-	47.5	0.2	-	-	-	-	47.8	0.6	-	-
1963	-	-	48.2	0.8	-	-	-	-	47.7	-1.0	-	-	-	-	48.1	0.8	-	-	-	-	48.8	1.5	-	-
1964	-	-	48.9	0.2	-	-	-	-	49.1	0.4	-	-	-	-	48.1	-2.0	-	-	-	-	48.9	1.7	-	-
1965	-	-	48.8	-0.2	-	-	-	-	49.0	0.4	-	-	-	-	48.7	-0.6	-	-	-	-	49.7	2.1	-	-
1966	-	-	50.1	0.8	-	-	-	-	50.6	1.0	-	-	-	-	50.2	-0.8	-	-	-	-	51.0	1.6	-	-
1967	-	-	51.4	0.8	-	-	-	-	52.2	1.6	-	-	-	-	52.3	0.2	-	-	-	-	53.1	1.5	-	-
1968	-	-	52.9	-0.4	-	-	-	-	53.5	1.1	-	-	-	-	53.6	0.2	-	-	-	-	54.6	1.9	-	-
1969	-	-	54.7	0.2	-	-	-	-	55.7	1.8	-	-	-	-	55.7	0.0	-	-	-	-	57.2	2.7	-	-
1970	-	-	57.1	-0.2	-	-	-	-	58.1	1.8	-	-	-	-	58.0	-0.2	-	-	-	-	60.0	3.4	-	-
1971	-	-	59.5	-0.8	-	-	-	-	61.1	2.7	-	-	-	-	60.3	-1.3	-	-	-	-	61.4	1.8	-	-
1972	-	-	61.0	-0.7	-	-	-	-	61.0	0.0	-	-	-	-	60.8	-0.3	-	-	-	-	62.6	3.0	-	-
1973	-	-	62.9	0.5	-	-	-	-	64.3	2.2	-	-	-	-	64.1	-0.3	-	-	-	-	65.5	2.2	-	-
1974	-	-	65.8	0.5	-	-	-	-	67.5	2.6	-	-	-	-	68.6	1.6	-	-	-	-	71.1	3.6	-	-
1975	-	-	71.8	1.0	-	-	-	-	72.9	1.5	-	-	-	-	72.5	-0.5	-	-	-	-	73.4	1.2	-	-
1976	-	-	75.4	2.7	-	-	-	-	77.4	2.7	-	-	-	-	76.9	-0.6	-	-	-	-	77.9	1.3	-	-
1977	-	-	78.5	0.8	-	-	-	-	79.9	1.8	-	-	-	-	80.6	0.9	-	-	-	-	82.4	2.2	-	-
1978	81.6	-1.0	-	-	81.4	-0.2	-	-	82.8	1.7	-	-	81.5	-1.6	-	-	84.2	3.3	-	-	84.0	-0.2	-	-
1979	82.8	-1.4	-	-	86.1	4.0	-	-	87.6	1.7	-	-	86.9	-0.8	-	-	89.4	2.9	-	-	92.7	3.7	-	-
1980	90.6	-2.3	-	-	93.7	3.4	-	-	92.3	-1.5	-	-	94.5	2.4	-	-	98.8	4.6	-	-	98.5	-0.3	-	-
1981	96.8	-1.7	-	-	98.0	1.2	-	-	98.8	0.8	-	-	99.4	0.6	-	-	100.4	1.0	-	-	100.6	0.2	-	-
1982	97.7	-2.9	-	-	99.9	2.3	-	-	99.3	-0.6	-	-	97.5	-1.8	-	-	102.9	5.5	-	-	100.5	-2.3	-	-
1983	96.9	-3.6	-	-	101.6	4.9	-	-	103.1	1.5	-	-	101.6	-1.5	-	-	103.6	2.0	-	-	100.3	-3.2	-	-
1984	97.3	-3.0	-	-	100.2	3.0	-	-	98.2	-2.0	-	-	97.8	-0.4	-	-	101.6	3.9	-	-	100.4	-1.2	-	-
1985	96.9	-3.5	-	-	104.6	7.9	-	-	100.6	-3.8	-	-	100.8	0.2	-	-	107.8	6.9	-	-	108.6	0.3	105.1	-3.2
1986	99.2	-4.3	-	-	104.0	4.8	-	-	103.9	-0.1	-	-	103.9	0.0	-	-	108.3	4.2	-	-	-	-	111.9	4.6
1987	-	-	-	-	-	-	-	-	-	-	107.0	1.8	-	-	-	-	-	-	-	-	-	-	115.6	-0.1
1988	-	-	-	-	-	-	-	-	-	-	115.7	3.4	-	-	-	-	-	-	-	-	-	-	104.4	-5.4
1989	-	-	-	-	-	-	-	-	-	-	110.4	-4.5	-	-	-	-	-	-	-	-	-	-	113.6	2.9
1990	-	-	-	-	-	-	-	-	-	-	110.4	5.7	-	-	-	-	-	-	-	-	-	-	114.4	1.9
1991	-	-	-	-	-	-	-	-	-	-	112.3	-1.1	-	-	-	-	-	-	-	-	-	-	118.9	0.3
1992	-	-	-	-	-	-	-	-	-	-	118.5	3.6	-	-	-	-	-	-	-	-	-	-	-	-
1993	-	-	-	-	-	-	-	-	-	-	115.5	-2.9	-	-	-	-	-	-	-	-	-	-	-	-

Source: U.S. Department of Labor, Bureau of Labor Statistics, Division of Consumer Prices and Price Indexes. - indicates no data collected for period.

Seattle-Everett, WA
Consumer Price Index - Urban Wage Earners
Base 1982-1984 = 100
Apparel and Upkeep

For 1952-1993. Columns headed % show percentile change in the index from the previous period for which an index is available.

Year	Jan Index	%	Feb Index	%	Mar Index	%	Apr Index	%	May Index	%	Jun Index	%	Jul Index	%	Aug Index	%	Sep Index	%	Oct Index	%	Nov Index	%	Dec Index	%
1952	-	-	-	-	-	-	-	-	-	-	-	-	-	-	-	-	-	-	-	-	44.4	-	-	-
1953	-	-	44.4	0.0	-	-	-	-	44.3	-0.2	-	-	-	-	44.6	0.7	-	-	-	-	44.5	-0.2	-	-
1954	-	-	44.1	-0.9	-	-	-	-	44.2	0.2	-	-	-	-	44.1	-0.2	-	-	-	-	44.0	-0.2	-	-
1955	-	-	44.2	0.5	-	-	-	-	43.9	-0.7	-	-	-	-	44.4	1.1	-	-	-	-	44.6	0.5	-	-
1956	-	-	44.3	-0.7	-	-	-	-	44.5	0.5	-	-	-	-	44.6	0.2	-	-	-	-	45.5	2.0	-	-
1957	-	-	45.3	-0.4	-	-	-	-	45.5	0.4	-	-	-	-	45.8	0.7	-	-	-	-	45.7	-0.2	-	-
1958	-	-	45.6	-0.2	-	-	-	-	45.6	0.0	-	-	-	-	45.3	-0.7	-	-	-	-	45.2	-0.2	-	-
1959	-	-	45.3	0.2	-	-	-	-	45.6	0.7	-	-	-	-	46.1	1.1	-	-	-	-	46.6	1.1	-	-
1960	-	-	46.5	-0.2	-	-	-	-	46.0	-1.1	-	-	-	-	46.4	0.9	-	-	-	-	47.1	1.5	-	-
1961	-	-	47.0	-0.2	-	-	-	-	47.2	0.4	-	-	-	-	46.7	-1.1	-	-	-	-	47.9	2.6	-	-
1962	-	-	47.8	-0.2	-	-	-	-	48.0	0.4	-	-	-	-	48.0	0.0	-	-	-	-	48.4	0.8	-	-
1963	-	-	48.8	0.8	-	-	-	-	48.3	-1.0	-	-	-	-	48.7	0.8	-	-	-	-	49.4	1.4	-	-
1964	-	-	49.5	0.2	-	-	-	-	49.7	0.4	-	-	-	-	48.7	-2.0	-	-	-	-	49.5	1.6	-	-
1965	-	-	49.4	-0.2	-	-	-	-	49.6	0.4	-	-	-	-	49.2	-0.8	-	-	-	-	50.2	2.0	-	-
1966	-	-	50.7	1.0	-	-	-	-	51.2	1.0	-	-	-	-	50.8	-0.8	-	-	-	-	51.6	1.6	-	-
1967	-	-	52.0	0.8	-	-	-	-	52.8	1.5	-	-	-	-	52.9	0.2	-	-	-	-	53.7	1.5	-	-
1968	-	-	53.5	-0.4	-	-	-	-	54.2	1.3	-	-	-	-	54.3	0.2	-	-	-	-	55.3	1.8	-	-
1969	-	-	55.4	0.2	-	-	-	-	56.4	1.8	-	-	-	-	56.4	0.0	-	-	-	-	57.9	2.7	-	-
1970	-	-	57.8	-0.2	-	-	-	-	58.8	1.7	-	-	-	-	58.7	-0.2	-	-	-	-	60.8	3.6	-	-
1971	-	-	60.2	-1.0	-	-	-	-	61.9	2.8	-	-	-	-	61.0	-1.5	-	-	-	-	62.1	1.8	-	-
1972	-	-	61.8	-0.5	-	-	-	-	61.7	-0.2	-	-	-	-	61.5	-0.3	-	-	-	-	63.3	2.9	-	-
1973	-	-	63.7	0.6	-	-	-	-	65.1	2.2	-	-	-	-	64.9	-0.3	-	-	-	-	66.3	2.2	-	-
1974	-	-	66.6	0.5	-	-	-	-	68.3	2.6	-	-	-	-	69.4	1.6	-	-	-	-	72.0	3.7	-	-
1975	-	-	72.6	0.8	-	-	-	-	73.8	1.7	-	-	-	-	73.4	-0.5	-	-	-	-	74.3	1.2	-	-
1976	-	-	76.3	2.7	-	-	-	-	78.3	2.6	-	-	-	-	77.8	-0.6	-	-	-	-	78.8	1.3	-	-
1977	-	-	79.5	0.9	-	-	-	-	80.9	1.8	-	-	-	-	81.5	0.7	-	-	-	-	83.4	2.3	-	-
1978	82.2	-1.4	-	-	82.7	0.6	-	-	84.3	1.9	-	-	81.9	-2.8	-	-	85.5	4.4	-	-	84.7	-0.9	-	-
1979	82.1	-3.1	-	-	85.6	4.3	-	-	87.6	2.3	-	-	88.1	0.6	-	-	90.1	2.3	-	-	92.0	2.1	-	-
1980	89.8	-2.4	-	-	92.8	3.3	-	-	91.8	-1.1	-	-	94.6	3.1	-	-	96.1	1.6	-	-	97.3	1.2	-	-
1981	95.4	-2.0	-	-	98.4	3.1	-	-	97.3	-1.1	-	-	97.0	-0.3	-	-	99.3	2.4	-	-	99.7	0.4	-	-
1982	97.3	-2.4	-	-	100.1	2.9	-	-	100.1	0.0	-	-	98.1	-2.0	-	-	102.6	4.6	-	-	100.4	-2.1	-	-
1983	96.3	-4.1	-	-	101.0	4.9	-	-	102.5	1.5	-	-	101.9	-0.6	-	-	103.4	1.5	-	-	100.3	-3.0	-	-
1984	97.2	-3.1	-	-	100.5	3.4	-	-	98.2	-2.3	-	-	98.0	-0.2	-	-	101.6	3.7	-	-	100.8	-0.8	-	-
1985	96.6	-4.2	-	-	104.7	8.4	-	-	101.0	-3.5	-	-	101.5	0.5	-	-	107.9	6.3	-	-	103.1	-4.4	-	-
1986	99.0	-4.0	-	-	103.0	4.0	-	-	103.4	0.4	-	-	102.9	-0.5	-	-	106.7	3.7	-	-	107.0	0.3	103.9	-2.9
1987	-	-	-	-	-	-	-	-	-	-	105.3	1.3	-	-	-	-	-	-	-	-	-	-	111.3	5.7
1988	-	-	-	-	-	-	-	-	-	-	114.2	2.6	-	-	-	-	-	-	-	-	-	-	114.0	-0.2
1989	-	-	-	-	-	-	-	-	-	-	108.5	-4.8	-	-	-	-	-	-	-	-	-	-	103.0	-5.1
1990	-	-	-	-	-	-	-	-	-	-	109.1	5.9	-	-	-	-	-	-	-	-	-	-	112.8	3.4
1991	-	-	-	-	-	-	-	-	-	-	111.1	-1.5	-	-	-	-	-	-	-	-	-	-	113.2	1.9
1992	-	-	-	-	-	-	-	-	-	-	117.0	3.4	-	-	-	-	-	-	-	-	-	-	118.4	1.2
1993	-	-	-	-	-	-	-	-	-	-	114.3	-3.5	-	-	-	-	-	-	-	-	-	-	-	-

Source: U.S. Department of Labor, Bureau of Labor Statistics, Division of Consumer Prices and Price Indexes. - indicates no data collected for period.

Seattle-Everett, WA
Consumer Price Index - All Urban Consumers
Base 1982-1984 = 100
Transportation

For 1947-1993. Columns headed % show percentile change in the index from the previous period for which an index is available.

Year	Jan Index	%	Feb Index	%	Mar Index	%	Apr Index	%	May Index	%	Jun Index	%	Jul Index	%	Aug Index	%	Sep Index	%	Oct Index	%	Nov Index	%	Dec Index	%
1947	18.7	-	18.7	0.0	18.8	0.5	18.9	0.5	18.9	0.0	18.9	0.0	-	-	19.1	1.1	-	-	-	-	19.5	2.1	-	-
1948	-	-	20.4	4.6	-	-	-	-	20.4	0.0	-	-	-	-	21.1	3.4	-	-	-	-	21.4	1.4	-	-
1949	-	-	21.6	0.9	-	-	-	-	22.0	1.9	-	-	-	-	22.6	2.7	-	-	-	-	22.6	0.0	-	-
1950	-	-	22.8	0.9	-	-	-	-	22.3	-2.2	-	-	-	-	22.6	1.3	-	-	-	-	23.7	4.9	-	-
1951	-	-	23.8	0.4	-	-	-	-	24.0	0.8	-	-	-	-	24.2	0.8	-	-	-	-	24.8	2.5	-	-
1952	-	-	25.0	0.8	-	-	-	-	25.2	0.8	-	-	-	-	25.2	0.0	-	-	-	-	26.8	6.3	-	-
1953	-	-	26.9	0.4	-	-	-	-	27.6	2.6	-	-	-	-	27.6	0.0	-	-	-	-	27.4	-0.7	-	-
1954	-	-	27.5	0.4	-	-	-	-	26.9	-2.2	-	-	-	-	26.6	-1.1	-	-	-	-	26.7	0.4	-	-
1955	-	-	26.6	-0.4	-	-	-	-	26.2	-1.5	-	-	-	-	26.1	-0.4	-	-	-	-	26.9	3.1	-	-
1956	-	-	25.8	-4.1	-	-	-	-	25.9	0.4	-	-	-	-	26.7	3.1	-	-	-	-	27.6	3.4	-	-
1957	-	-	28.4	2.9	-	-	-	-	28.6	0.7	-	-	-	-	28.1	-1.7	-	-	-	-	29.2	3.9	-	-
1958	-	-	29.1	-0.3	-	-	-	-	29.4	1.0	-	-	-	-	30.1	2.4	-	-	-	-	29.9	-0.7	-	-
1959	-	-	30.7	2.7	-	-	-	-	30.8	0.3	-	-	-	-	32.0	3.9	-	-	-	-	31.0	-3.1	-	-
1960	-	-	30.3	-2.3	-	-	-	-	31.0	2.3	-	-	-	-	30.7	-1.0	-	-	-	-	31.0	1.0	-	-
1961	-	-	30.9	-0.3	-	-	-	-	31.4	1.6	-	-	-	-	31.8	1.3	-	-	-	-	32.6	2.5	-	-
1962	-	-	32.3	-0.9	-	-	-	-	32.5	0.6	-	-	-	-	32.6	0.3	-	-	-	-	33.0	1.2	-	-
1963	-	-	32.3	-2.1	-	-	-	-	32.2	-0.3	-	-	-	-	32.9	2.2	-	-	-	-	32.4	-1.5	-	-
1964	-	-	32.4	0.0	-	-	-	-	31.8	-1.9	-	-	-	-	33.5	5.3	-	-	-	-	32.8	-2.1	-	-
1965	-	-	32.4	-1.2	-	-	-	-	33.9	4.6	-	-	-	-	33.8	-0.3	-	-	-	-	33.8	0.0	-	-
1966	-	-	33.7	-0.3	-	-	-	-	33.4	-0.9	-	-	-	-	34.1	2.1	-	-	-	-	34.8	2.1	-	-
1967	-	-	34.6	-0.6	-	-	-	-	35.3	2.0	-	-	-	-	35.6	0.8	-	-	-	-	35.7	0.3	-	-
1968	-	-	35.7	0.0	-	-	-	-	35.6	-0.3	-	-	-	-	36.2	1.7	-	-	-	-	36.2	0.0	-	-
1969	-	-	36.3	0.3	-	-	-	-	36.0	-0.8	-	-	-	-	36.5	1.4	-	-	-	-	35.9	-1.6	-	-
1970	-	-	36.9	2.8	-	-	-	-	37.1	0.5	-	-	-	-	37.5	1.1	-	-	-	-	37.1	-1.1	-	-
1971	-	-	37.4	0.8	-	-	-	-	37.6	0.5	-	-	-	-	38.5	2.4	-	-	-	-	37.7	-2.1	-	-
1972	-	-	38.2	1.3	-	-	-	-	38.3	0.3	-	-	-	-	38.7	1.0	-	-	-	-	39.4	1.8	-	-
1973	-	-	39.0	-1.0	-	-	-	-	39.4	1.0	-	-	-	-	39.7	0.8	-	-	-	-	40.0	0.8	-	-
1974	-	-	41.3	3.2	-	-	-	-	43.6	5.6	-	-	-	-	45.4	4.1	-	-	-	-	45.8	0.9	-	-
1975	-	-	46.1	0.7	-	-	-	-	47.5	3.0	-	-	-	-	49.0	3.2	-	-	-	-	49.7	1.4	-	-
1976	-	-	49.7	0.0	-	-	-	-	51.1	2.8	-	-	-	-	52.8	3.3	-	-	-	-	53.3	0.9	-	-
1977	-	-	55.2	3.6	-	-	-	-	56.5	2.4	-	-	-	-	58.3	3.2	-	-	-	-	57.8	-0.9	-	-
1978	58.3	0.9	-	-	58.5	0.3	-	-	60.2	2.9	-	-	61.8	2.7	-	-	63.1	2.1	-	-	63.8	1.1	-	-
1979	64.5	1.1	-	-	66.0	2.3	-	-	69.6	5.5	-	-	72.5	4.2	-	-	74.7	3.0	-	-	76.1	1.9	-	-
1980	78.0	2.5	-	-	81.3	4.2	-	-	82.5	1.5	-	-	83.7	1.5	-	-	84.7	1.2	-	-	85.9	1.4	-	-
1981	86.8	1.0	-	-	91.0	4.8	-	-	93.6	2.9	-	-	96.2	2.8	-	-	97.1	0.9	-	-	97.7	0.6	-	-
1982	98.2	0.5	-	-	97.0	-1.2	-	-	96.6	-0.4	-	-	99.7	3.2	-	-	99.1	-0.6	-	-	97.8	-1.3	-	-
1983	96.4	-1.4	-	-	94.0	-2.5	-	-	96.8	3.0	-	-	100.9	4.2	-	-	102.0	1.1	-	-	102.2	0.2	-	-
1984	101.0	-1.2	-	-	99.9	-1.1	-	-	103.8	3.9	-	-	104.5	0.7	-	-	104.0	-0.5	-	-	104.4	0.4	-	-
1985	105.1	0.7	-	-	104.4	-0.7	-	-	105.0	0.6	-	-	105.5	0.5	-	-	104.5	-0.9	-	-	105.1	0.6	-	-
1986	106.5	1.3	-	-	102.9	-3.4	-	-	100.9	-1.9	-	-	100.9	0.0	-	-	100.4	-0.5	-	-	99.7	-0.7	100.4	0.7
1987	-	-	-	-	-	-	-	-	-	-	100.9	0.5	-	-	-	-	-	-	-	-	-	-	103.8	2.9
1988	-	-	-	-	-	-	-	-	-	-	102.5	-1.3	-	-	-	-	-	-	-	-	-	-	104.6	2.0
1989	-	-	-	-	-	-	-	-	-	-	107.5	2.8	-	-	-	-	-	-	-	-	-	-	110.8	3.1
1990	-	-	-	-	-	-	-	-	-	-	113.4	2.3	-	-	-	-	-	-	-	-	-	-	118.9	4.9
1991	-	-	-	-	-	-	-	-	-	-	119.3	0.3	-	-	-	-	-	-	-	-	-	-	120.6	1.1

[Continued]

Seattle-Everett, WA
Consumer Price Index - All Urban Consumers
Base 1982-1984 = 100
Transportation
[Continued]

For 1947-1993. Columns headed % show percentile change in the index from the previous period for which an index is available.

Year	Jan		Feb		Mar		Apr		May		Jun		Jul		Aug		Sep		Oct		Nov		Dec	
	Index	%	Index	%	Index	%	Index	%	Index	%	Index	%	Index	%	Index	%	Index	%	Index	%	Index	%	Index	%
1992	-	-	-	-	-	-	-	-	-	-	121.8	1.0	-	-	-	-	-	-	-	-	-	-	126.0	3.4
1993	-	-	-	-	-	-	-	-	-	-	126.6	0.5	-	-	-	-	-	-	-	-	-	-	-	-

Source: U.S. Department of Labor, Bureau of Labor Statistics, Division of Consumer Prices and Price Indexes. - indicates no data collected for period.

Seattle-Everett, WA
Consumer Price Index - Urban Wage Earners
Base 1982-1984 = 100
Transportation

For 1947-1993. Columns headed % show percentile change in the index from the previous period for which an index is available.

Year	Jan Index	%	Feb Index	%	Mar Index	%	Apr Index	%	May Index	%	Jun Index	%	Jul Index	%	Aug Index	%	Sep Index	%	Oct Index	%	Nov Index	%	Dec Index	%
1947	19.1	-	19.1	0.0	19.2	0.5	19.2	0.0	19.3	0.5	19.3	0.0	-	-	19.5	1.0	-	-	-	-	19.9	2.1	-	-
1948	-	-	20.8	4.5	-	-	-	-	20.8	0.0	-	-	-	-	21.5	3.4	-	-	-	-	21.8	1.4	-	-
1949	-	-	22.0	0.9	-	-	-	-	22.5	2.3	-	-	-	-	23.0	2.2	-	-	-	-	23.1	0.4	-	-
1950	-	-	23.3	0.9	-	-	-	-	22.8	-2.1	-	-	-	-	23.1	1.3	-	-	-	-	24.1	4.3	-	-
1951	-	-	24.3	0.8	-	-	-	-	24.5	0.8	-	-	-	-	24.6	0.4	-	-	-	-	25.3	2.8	-	-
1952	-	-	25.5	0.8	-	-	-	-	25.8	1.2	-	-	-	-	25.8	0.0	-	-	-	-	27.4	6.2	-	-
1953	-	-	27.4	0.0	-	-	-	-	28.2	2.9	-	-	-	-	28.1	-0.4	-	-	-	-	28.0	-0.4	-	-
1954	-	-	28.1	0.4	-	-	-	-	27.4	-2.5	-	-	-	-	27.1	-1.1	-	-	-	-	27.2	0.4	-	-
1955	-	-	27.1	-0.4	-	-	-	-	26.8	-1.1	-	-	-	-	26.6	-0.7	-	-	-	-	27.4	3.0	-	-
1956	-	-	26.3	-4.0	-	-	-	-	26.4	0.4	-	-	-	-	27.2	3.0	-	-	-	-	28.2	3.7	-	-
1957	-	-	29.0	2.8	-	-	-	-	29.2	0.7	-	-	-	-	28.7	-1.7	-	-	-	-	29.8	3.8	-	-
1958	-	-	29.7	-0.3	-	-	-	-	30.0	1.0	-	-	-	-	30.7	2.3	-	-	-	-	30.5	-0.7	-	-
1959	-	-	31.3	2.6	-	-	-	-	31.4	0.3	-	-	-	-	32.7	4.1	-	-	-	-	31.6	-3.4	-	-
1960	-	-	30.9	-2.2	-	-	-	-	31.6	2.3	-	-	-	-	31.3	-0.9	-	-	-	-	31.6	1.0	-	-
1961	-	-	31.5	-0.3	-	-	-	-	32.1	1.9	-	-	-	-	32.4	0.9	-	-	-	-	33.3	2.8	-	-
1962	-	-	33.0	-0.9	-	-	-	-	33.2	0.6	-	-	-	-	33.3	0.3	-	-	-	-	33.7	1.2	-	-
1963	-	-	33.0	-2.1	-	-	-	-	32.8	-0.6	-	-	-	-	33.6	2.4	-	-	-	-	33.0	-1.8	-	-
1964	-	-	33.1	0.3	-	-	-	-	32.5	-1.8	-	-	-	-	34.2	5.2	-	-	-	-	33.5	-2.0	-	-
1965	-	-	33.1	-1.2	-	-	-	-	34.6	4.5	-	-	-	-	34.5	-0.3	-	-	-	-	34.5	0.0	-	-
1966	-	-	34.4	-0.3	-	-	-	-	34.1	-0.9	-	-	-	-	34.8	2.1	-	-	-	-	35.6	2.3	-	-
1967	-	-	35.3	-0.8	-	-	-	-	36.1	2.3	-	-	-	-	36.3	0.6	-	-	-	-	36.4	0.3	-	-
1968	-	-	36.5	0.3	-	-	-	-	36.3	-0.5	-	-	-	-	36.9	1.7	-	-	-	-	37.0	0.3	-	-
1969	-	-	37.0	0.0	-	-	-	-	36.8	-0.5	-	-	-	-	37.3	1.4	-	-	-	-	36.6	-1.9	-	-
1970	-	-	37.7	3.0	-	-	-	-	37.9	0.5	-	-	-	-	38.3	1.1	-	-	-	-	37.8	-1.3	-	-
1971	-	-	38.2	1.1	-	-	-	-	38.3	0.3	-	-	-	-	39.3	2.6	-	-	-	-	38.4	-2.3	-	-
1972	-	-	39.0	1.6	-	-	-	-	39.1	0.3	-	-	-	-	39.5	1.0	-	-	-	-	40.2	1.8	-	-
1973	-	-	39.9	-0.7	-	-	-	-	40.2	0.8	-	-	-	-	40.5	0.7	-	-	-	-	40.9	1.0	-	-
1974	-	-	42.2	3.2	-	-	-	-	44.5	5.5	-	-	-	-	46.3	4.0	-	-	-	-	46.7	0.9	-	-
1975	-	-	47.1	0.9	-	-	-	-	48.5	3.0	-	-	-	-	50.1	3.3	-	-	-	-	50.7	1.2	-	-
1976	-	-	50.7	0.0	-	-	-	-	52.1	2.8	-	-	-	-	53.9	3.5	-	-	-	-	54.4	0.9	-	-
1977	-	-	56.4	3.7	-	-	-	-	57.7	2.3	-	-	-	-	59.5	3.1	-	-	-	-	59.0	-0.8	-	-
1978	59.0	0.0	-	-	59.2	0.3	-	-	60.6	2.4	-	-	62.2	2.6	-	-	62.8	1.0	-	-	63.5	1.1	-	-
1979	64.2	1.1	-	-	65.9	2.6	-	-	69.4	5.3	-	-	72.2	4.0	-	-	74.3	2.9	-	-	75.7	1.9	-	-
1980	77.2	2.0	-	-	80.9	4.8	-	-	81.9	1.2	-	-	82.7	1.0	-	-	83.8	1.3	-	-	85.3	1.8	-	-
1981	86.4	1.3	-	-	89.8	3.9	-	-	92.6	3.1	-	-	95.2	2.8	-	-	95.8	0.6	-	-	97.6	1.9	-	-
1982	98.1	0.5	-	-	96.8	-1.3	-	-	96.4	-0.4	-	-	99.5	3.2	-	-	98.8	-0.7	-	-	97.7	-1.1	-	-
1983	96.2	-1.5	-	-	93.9	-2.4	-	-	96.8	3.1	-	-	101.0	4.3	-	-	102.2	1.2	-	-	102.3	0.1	-	-
1984	101.2	-1.1	-	-	100.2	-1.0	-	-	103.9	3.7	-	-	104.5	0.6	-	-	104.1	-0.4	-	-	104.7	0.6	-	-
1985	105.4	0.7	-	-	104.7	-0.7	-	-	105.5	0.8	-	-	105.9	0.4	-	-	105.0	-0.8	-	-	105.6	0.6	-	-
1986	106.7	1.0	-	-	103.1	-3.4	-	-	101.0	-2.0	-	-	101.0	0.0	-	-	100.5	-0.5	-	-	99.8	-0.7	100.2	0.4
1987	-	-	-	-	-	-	-	-	-	-	101.1	0.9	-	-	-	-	-	-	-	-	-	-	104.2	3.1
1988	-	-	-	-	-	-	-	-	-	-	103.6	-0.6	-	-	-	-	-	-	-	-	-	-	105.7	2.0
1989	-	-	-	-	-	-	-	-	-	-	108.6	2.7	-	-	-	-	-	-	-	-	-	-	111.9	3.0
1990	-	-	-	-	-	-	-	-	-	-	113.8	1.7	-	-	-	-	-	-	-	-	-	-	119.5	5.0
1991	-	-	-	-	-	-	-	-	-	-	119.7	0.2	-	-	-	-	-	-	-	-	-	-	121.5	1.5

[Continued]

Seattle-Everett, WA
Consumer Price Index - Urban Wage Earners
Base 1982-1984 = 100
Transportation
[Continued]

For 1947-1993. Columns headed % show percentile change in the index from the previous period for which an index is available.

Year	Jan		Feb		Mar		Apr		May		Jun		Jul		Aug		Sep		Oct		Nov		Dec	
	Index	%	Index	%	Index	%	Index	%	Index	%	Index	%	Index	%	Index	%	Index	%	Index	%	Index	%	Index	%
1992	-	-	-	-	-	-	-	-	-	-	122.8	1.1	-	-	-	-	-	-	-	-	-	-	127.2	3.6
1993	-	-	-	-	-	-	-	-	-	-	127.9	0.6	-	-	-	-	-	-	-	-	-	-	-	-

Source: U.S. Department of Labor, Bureau of Labor Statistics, Division of Consumer Prices and Price Indexes. - indicates no data collected for period.

Seattle-Everett, WA
Consumer Price Index - All Urban Consumers
Base 1982-1984 = 100
Medical Care

For 1947-1993. Columns headed % show percentile change in the index from the previous period for which an index is available.

Year	Jan Index	%	Feb Index	%	Mar Index	%	Apr Index	%	May Index	%	Jun Index	%	Jul Index	%	Aug Index	%	Sep Index	%	Oct Index	%	Nov Index	%	Dec Index	%
1947	14.1	-	14.3	1.4	14.3	0.0	14.4	0.7	14.4	0.0	14.4	0.0	-	-	14.4	0.0	-	-	-	-	14.6	1.4	-	-
1948	-	-	14.7	0.7	-	-	-	-	15.0	2.0	-	-	-	-	15.3	2.0	-	-	-	-	15.6	2.0	-	-
1949	-	-	15.6	0.0	-	-	-	-	15.9	1.9	-	-	-	-	15.9	0.0	-	-	-	-	16.0	0.6	-	-
1950	-	-	16.0	0.0	-	-	-	-	16.0	0.0	-	-	-	-	16.0	0.0	-	-	-	-	16.1	0.6	-	-
1951	-	-	16.6	3.1	-	-	-	-	17.1	3.0	-	-	-	-	17.2	0.6	-	-	-	-	17.4	1.2	-	-
1952	-	-	17.8	2.3	-	-	-	-	18.3	2.8	-	-	-	-	18.7	2.2	-	-	-	-	18.7	0.0	-	-
1953	-	-	18.7	0.0	-	-	-	-	18.9	1.1	-	-	-	-	19.0	0.5	-	-	-	-	19.6	3.2	-	-
1954	-	-	19.6	0.0	-	-	-	-	19.8	1.0	-	-	-	-	19.6	-1.0	-	-	-	-	19.7	0.5	-	-
1955	-	-	19.8	0.5	-	-	-	-	19.8	0.0	-	-	-	-	19.9	0.5	-	-	-	-	21.1	6.0	-	-
1956	-	-	20.4	-3.3	-	-	-	-	20.5	0.5	-	-	-	-	20.8	1.5	-	-	-	-	20.7	-0.5	-	-
1957	-	-	20.9	1.0	-	-	-	-	21.0	0.5	-	-	-	-	21.6	2.9	-	-	-	-	21.7	0.5	-	-
1958	-	-	22.1	1.8	-	-	-	-	22.2	0.5	-	-	-	-	22.4	0.9	-	-	-	-	22.5	0.4	-	-
1959	-	-	22.6	0.4	-	-	-	-	22.6	0.0	-	-	-	-	22.9	1.3	-	-	-	-	23.3	1.7	-	-
1960	-	-	23.9	2.6	-	-	-	-	23.9	0.0	-	-	-	-	24.1	0.8	-	-	-	-	23.9	-0.8	-	-
1961	-	-	23.9	0.0	-	-	-	-	24.0	0.4	-	-	-	-	24.0	0.0	-	-	-	-	24.1	0.4	-	-
1962	-	-	24.2	0.4	-	-	-	-	24.3	0.4	-	-	-	-	24.4	0.4	-	-	-	-	24.4	0.0	-	-
1963	-	-	24.4	0.0	-	-	-	-	24.5	0.4	-	-	-	-	24.6	0.4	-	-	-	-	24.6	0.0	-	-
1964	-	-	24.6	0.0	-	-	-	-	24.9	1.2	-	-	-	-	25.1	0.8	-	-	-	-	25.2	0.4	-	-
1965	-	-	25.4	0.8	-	-	-	-	25.9	2.0	-	-	-	-	26.1	0.8	-	-	-	-	26.6	1.9	-	-
1966	-	-	26.8	0.8	-	-	-	-	27.3	1.9	-	-	-	-	27.8	1.8	-	-	-	-	28.5	2.5	-	-
1967	-	-	28.5	0.0	-	-	-	-	28.8	1.1	-	-	-	-	29.3	1.7	-	-	-	-	29.8	1.7	-	-
1968	-	-	30.1	1.0	-	-	-	-	30.6	1.7	-	-	-	-	31.1	1.6	-	-	-	-	31.5	1.3	-	-
1969	-	-	32.1	1.9	-	-	-	-	32.7	1.9	-	-	-	-	33.3	1.8	-	-	-	-	33.5	0.6	-	-
1970	-	-	34.0	1.5	-	-	-	-	34.3	0.9	-	-	-	-	34.7	1.2	-	-	-	-	34.8	0.3	-	-
1971	-	-	35.4	1.7	-	-	-	-	35.6	0.6	-	-	-	-	36.1	1.4	-	-	-	-	36.0	-0.3	-	-
1972	-	-	36.2	0.6	-	-	-	-	36.4	0.6	-	-	-	-	36.7	0.8	-	-	-	-	36.7	0.0	-	-
1973	-	-	37.2	1.4	-	-	-	-	37.4	0.5	-	-	-	-	37.9	1.3	-	-	-	-	38.6	1.8	-	-
1974	-	-	39.4	2.1	-	-	-	-	40.7	3.3	-	-	-	-	41.7	2.5	-	-	-	-	42.8	2.6	-	-
1975	-	-	44.8	4.7	-	-	-	-	45.7	2.0	-	-	-	-	46.7	2.2	-	-	-	-	47.4	1.5	-	-
1976	-	-	49.4	4.2	-	-	-	-	50.5	2.2	-	-	-	-	51.1	1.2	-	-	-	-	52.8	3.3	-	-
1977	-	-	54.6	3.4	-	-	-	-	55.5	1.6	-	-	-	-	56.4	1.6	-	-	-	-	57.3	1.6	-	-
1978	60.6	5.8	-	-	60.7	0.2	-	-	61.3	1.0	-	-	62.4	1.8	-	-	62.8	0.6	-	-	64.0	1.9	-	-
1979	64.7	1.1	-	-	66.1	2.2	-	-	66.3	0.3	-	-	67.4	1.7	-	-	68.1	1.0	-	-	69.8	2.5	-	-
1980	72.6	4.0	-	-	73.9	1.8	-	-	75.1	1.6	-	-	76.4	1.7	-	-	76.4	0.0	-	-	78.4	2.6	-	-
1981	81.2	3.6	-	-	83.2	2.5	-	-	83.8	0.7	-	-	85.3	1.8	-	-	86.1	0.9	-	-	87.5	1.6	-	-
1982	89.7	2.5	-	-	91.7	2.2	-	-	92.4	0.8	-	-	93.8	1.5	-	-	94.8	1.1	-	-	96.1	1.4	-	-
1983	99.5	3.5	-	-	101.1	1.6	-	-	100.6	-0.5	-	-	101.3	0.7	-	-	101.3	0.0	-	-	100.7	-0.6	-	-
1984	103.2	2.5	-	-	104.6	1.4	-	-	104.7	0.1	-	-	105.7	1.0	-	-	106.5	0.8	-	-	107.4	0.8	-	-
1985	109.7	2.1	-	-	111.9	2.0	-	-	112.3	0.4	-	-	113.1	0.7	-	-	113.2	0.1	-	-	112.1	-1.0	-	-
1986	113.2	1.0	-	-	116.0	2.5	-	-	116.0	0.0	-	-	118.9	2.5	-	-	119.9	0.8	-	-	119.6	-0.3	120.5	0.8
1987	-	-	-	-	-	-	-	-	-	-	122.6	1.7	-	-	-	-	-	-	-	-	-	-	126.6	3.3
1988	-	-	-	-	-	-	-	-	-	-	131.2	3.6	-	-	-	-	-	-	-	-	-	-	134.6	2.6
1989	-	-	-	-	-	-	-	-	-	-	140.6	4.5	-	-	-	-	-	-	-	-	-	-	142.6	1.4
1990	-	-	-	-	-	-	-	-	-	-	152.6	7.0	-	-	-	-	-	-	-	-	-	-	156.6	2.6
1991	-	-	-	-	-	-	-	-	-	-	166.2	6.1	-	-	-	-	-	-	-	-	-	-	172.6	3.9

[Continued]

Seattle-Everett, WA
Consumer Price Index - All Urban Consumers
Base 1982-1984 = 100
Medical Care
[Continued]

For 1947-1993. Columns headed % show percentile change in the index from the previous period for which an index is available.

Year	Jan		Feb		Mar		Apr		May		Jun		Jul		Aug		Sep		Oct		Nov		Dec	
	Index	%	Index	%	Index	%	Index	%	Index	%	Index	%	Index	%	Index	%	Index	%	Index	%	Index	%	Index	%
1992	-	-	-	-	-	-	-	-	-	-	181.2	5.0	-	-	-	-	-	-	-	-	-	-	187.1	3.3
1993	-	-	-	-	-	-	-	-	-	-	192.4	2.8	-	-	-	-	-	-	-	-	-	-	-	-

Source: U.S. Department of Labor, Bureau of Labor Statistics, Division of Consumer Prices and Price Indexes. - indicates no data collected for period.

Seattle-Everett, WA
Consumer Price Index - Urban Wage Earners
Base 1982-1984 = 100
Medical Care

For 1947-1993. Columns headed % show percentile change in the index from the previous period for which an index is available.

Year	Jan Index	%	Feb Index	%	Mar Index	%	Apr Index	%	May Index	%	Jun Index	%	Jul Index	%	Aug Index	%	Sep Index	%	Oct Index	%	Nov Index	%	Dec Index	%
1947	14.0	-	14.2	1.4	14.2	0.0	14.2	0.0	14.2	0.0	14.3	0.7	-	-	14.3	0.0	-	-	-	-	14.5	1.4	-	-
1948	-	-	14.6	0.7	-	-	-	-	14.8	1.4	-	-	-	-	15.2	2.7	-	-	-	-	15.4	1.3	-	-
1949	-	-	15.4	0.0	-	-	-	-	15.7	1.9	-	-	-	-	15.7	0.0	-	-	-	-	15.9	1.3	-	-
1950	-	-	15.9	0.0	-	-	-	-	15.9	0.0	-	-	-	-	15.9	0.0	-	-	-	-	16.0	0.6	-	-
1951	-	-	16.4	2.5	-	-	-	-	17.0	3.7	-	-	-	-	17.0	0.0	-	-	-	-	17.2	1.2	-	-
1952	-	-	17.7	2.9	-	-	-	-	18.1	2.3	-	-	-	-	18.5	2.2	-	-	-	-	18.5	0.0	-	-
1953	-	-	18.5	0.0	-	-	-	-	18.7	1.1	-	-	-	-	18.8	0.5	-	-	-	-	19.4	3.2	-	-
1954	-	-	19.4	0.0	-	-	-	-	19.6	1.0	-	-	-	-	19.4	-1.0	-	-	-	-	19.5	0.5	-	-
1955	-	-	19.6	0.5	-	-	-	-	19.6	0.0	-	-	-	-	19.7	0.5	-	-	-	-	20.9	6.1	-	-
1956	-	-	20.2	-3.3	-	-	-	-	20.3	0.5	-	-	-	-	20.6	1.5	-	-	-	-	20.5	-0.5	-	-
1957	-	-	20.7	1.0	-	-	-	-	20.8	0.5	-	-	-	-	21.4	2.9	-	-	-	-	21.5	0.5	-	-
1958	-	-	21.9	1.9	-	-	-	-	22.0	0.5	-	-	-	-	22.2	0.9	-	-	-	-	22.3	0.5	-	-
1959	-	-	22.4	0.4	-	-	-	-	22.4	0.0	-	-	-	-	22.7	1.3	-	-	-	-	23.1	1.8	-	-
1960	-	-	23.7	2.6	-	-	-	-	23.7	0.0	-	-	-	-	23.9	0.8	-	-	-	-	23.7	-0.8	-	-
1961	-	-	23.7	0.0	-	-	-	-	23.8	0.4	-	-	-	-	23.8	0.0	-	-	-	-	23.9	0.4	-	-
1962	-	-	24.0	0.4	-	-	-	-	24.1	0.4	-	-	-	-	24.1	0.0	-	-	-	-	24.2	0.4	-	-
1963	-	-	24.2	0.0	-	-	-	-	24.3	0.4	-	-	-	-	24.4	0.4	-	-	-	-	24.4	0.0	-	-
1964	-	-	24.4	0.0	-	-	-	-	24.6	0.8	-	-	-	-	24.8	0.8	-	-	-	-	25.0	0.8	-	-
1965	-	-	25.2	0.8	-	-	-	-	25.6	1.6	-	-	-	-	25.8	0.8	-	-	-	-	26.4	2.3	-	-
1966	-	-	26.6	0.8	-	-	-	-	27.0	1.5	-	-	-	-	27.5	1.9	-	-	-	-	28.3	2.9	-	-
1967	-	-	28.2	-0.4	-	-	-	-	28.5	1.1	-	-	-	-	29.1	2.1	-	-	-	-	29.5	1.4	-	-
1968	-	-	29.9	1.4	-	-	-	-	30.3	1.3	-	-	-	-	30.8	1.7	-	-	-	-	31.2	1.3	-	-
1969	-	-	31.8	1.9	-	-	-	-	32.4	1.9	-	-	-	-	33.0	1.9	-	-	-	-	33.2	0.6	-	-
1970	-	-	33.6	1.2	-	-	-	-	34.0	1.2	-	-	-	-	34.4	1.2	-	-	-	-	34.5	0.3	-	-
1971	-	-	35.0	1.4	-	-	-	-	35.3	0.9	-	-	-	-	35.8	1.4	-	-	-	-	35.7	-0.3	-	-
1972	-	-	35.9	0.6	-	-	-	-	36.1	0.6	-	-	-	-	36.4	0.8	-	-	-	-	36.3	-0.3	-	-
1973	-	-	36.9	1.7	-	-	-	-	37.1	0.5	-	-	-	-	37.6	1.3	-	-	-	-	38.3	1.9	-	-
1974	-	-	39.1	2.1	-	-	-	-	40.3	3.1	-	-	-	-	41.3	2.5	-	-	-	-	42.4	2.7	-	-
1975	-	-	44.3	4.5	-	-	-	-	45.2	2.0	-	-	-	-	46.3	2.4	-	-	-	-	47.0	1.5	-	-
1976	-	-	48.9	4.0	-	-	-	-	50.0	2.2	-	-	-	-	50.6	1.2	-	-	-	-	52.3	3.4	-	-
1977	-	-	54.0	3.3	-	-	-	-	55.0	1.9	-	-	-	-	55.8	1.5	-	-	-	-	56.8	1.8	-	-
1978	59.0	3.9	-	-	59.2	0.3	-	-	60.1	1.5	-	-	61.2	1.8	-	-	61.5	0.5	-	-	63.9	3.9	-	-
1979	64.6	1.1	-	-	65.5	1.4	-	-	66.2	1.1	-	-	67.8	2.4	-	-	68.2	0.6	-	-	69.9	2.5	-	-
1980	72.4	3.6	-	-	73.2	1.1	-	-	74.6	1.9	-	-	74.4	-0.3	-	-	76.0	2.2	-	-	78.0	2.6	-	-
1981	79.9	2.4	-	-	81.4	1.9	-	-	82.9	1.8	-	-	84.1	1.4	-	-	86.2	2.5	-	-	87.9	2.0	-	-
1982	89.8	2.2	-	-	91.7	2.1	-	-	92.4	0.8	-	-	93.8	1.5	-	-	94.5	0.7	-	-	95.9	1.5	-	-
1983	99.2	3.4	-	-	100.7	1.5	-	-	100.5	-0.2	-	-	101.3	0.8	-	-	101.2	-0.1	-	-	100.9	-0.3	-	-
1984	103.2	2.3	-	-	104.7	1.5	-	-	104.9	0.2	-	-	106.0	1.0	-	-	106.9	0.8	-	-	107.5	0.6	-	-
1985	109.9	2.2	-	-	112.2	2.1	-	-	112.5	0.3	-	-	113.3	0.7	-	-	113.6	0.3	-	-	112.8	-0.7	-	-
1986	114.0	1.1	-	-	116.9	2.5	-	-	116.8	-0.1	-	-	119.8	2.6	-	-	120.7	0.8	-	-	120.4	-0.2	121.5	0.9
1987	-	-	-	-	-	-	-	-	-	-	124.3	2.3	-	-	-	-	-	-	-	-	-	-	128.2	3.1
1988	-	-	-	-	-	-	-	-	-	-	133.0	3.7	-	-	-	-	-	-	-	-	-	-	136.5	2.6
1989	-	-	-	-	-	-	-	-	-	-	142.5	4.4	-	-	-	-	-	-	-	-	-	-	144.3	1.3
1990	-	-	-	-	-	-	-	-	-	-	154.0	6.7	-	-	-	-	-	-	-	-	-	-	157.9	2.5
1991	-	-	-	-	-	-	-	-	-	-	166.9	5.7	-	-	-	-	-	-	-	-	-	-	173.1	3.7

[Continued]

Seattle-Everett, WA
Consumer Price Index - Urban Wage Earners
Base 1982-1984 = 100
Medical Care
[Continued]

For 1947-1993. Columns headed % show percentile change in the index from the previous period for which an index is available.

Year	Jan		Feb		Mar		Apr		May		Jun		Jul		Aug		Sep		Oct		Nov		Dec	
	Index	%	Index	%	Index	%	Index	%	Index	%	Index	%	Index	%	Index	%	Index	%	Index	%	Index	%	Index	%
1992	-	-	-	-	-	-	-	-	-	-	181.9	5.1	-	-	-	-	-	-	-	-	-	-	188.0	3.4
1993	-	-	-	-	-	-	-	-	-	-	193.2	2.8	-	-	-	-	-	-	-	-	-	-	-	-

Source: U.S. Department of Labor, Bureau of Labor Statistics, Division of Consumer Prices and Price Indexes. - indicates no data collected for period.

Seattle-Everett, WA

Consumer Price Index - All Urban Consumers
Base 1982-1984 = 100
Entertainment

For 1975-1993. Columns headed % show percentile change in the index from the previous period for which an index is available.

Year	Jan Index	%	Feb Index	%	Mar Index	%	Apr Index	%	May Index	%	Jun Index	%	Jul Index	%	Aug Index	%	Sep Index	%	Oct Index	%	Nov Index	%	Dec Index	%
1975	-	-	-	-	-	-	-	-	-	-	-	-	-	-	-	-	-	-	-	-	61.1	-	-	-
1976	-	-	61.2	0.2	-	-	-	-	61.7	0.8	-	-	-	-	62.1	0.6	-	-	-	-	63.4	2.1	-	-
1977	-	-	65.2	2.8	-	-	-	-	65.1	-0.2	-	-	-	-	65.2	0.2	-	-	-	-	66.5	2.0	-	-
1978	66.6	0.2	-	-	67.2	0.9	-	-	68.4	1.8	-	-	68.9	0.7	-	-	69.0	0.1	-	-	69.9	1.3	-	-
1979	70.1	0.3	-	-	70.3	0.3	-	-	72.8	3.6	-	-	73.3	0.7	-	-	75.5	3.0	-	-	76.2	0.9	-	-
1980	77.3	1.4	-	-	79.1	2.3	-	-	80.2	1.4	-	-	81.9	2.1	-	-	84.6	3.3	-	-	86.4	2.1	-	-
1981	87.0	0.7	-	-	86.6	-0.5	-	-	87.8	1.4	-	-	87.4	-0.5	-	-	89.4	2.3	-	-	89.6	0.2	-	-
1982	91.5	2.1	-	-	90.9	-0.7	-	-	93.3	2.6	-	-	94.0	0.8	-	-	96.1	2.2	-	-	95.9	-0.2	-	-
1983	96.9	1.0	-	-	99.4	2.6	-	-	97.6	-1.8	-	-	99.7	2.2	-	-	101.6	1.9	-	-	102.5	0.9	-	-
1984	105.1	2.5	-	-	105.9	0.8	-	-	106.4	0.5	-	-	106.3	-0.1	-	-	105.2	-1.0	-	-	107.6	2.3	-	-
1985	108.0	0.4	-	-	108.1	0.1	-	-	107.6	-0.5	-	-	109.6	1.9	-	-	107.6	-1.8	-	-	109.4	1.7	-	-
1986	110.3	0.8	-	-	109.0	-1.2	-	-	107.4	-1.5	-	-	109.2	1.7	-	-	107.6	-1.5	-	-	108.6	0.9	108.6	0.0
1987	-	-	-	-	-	-	-	-	-	-	110.0	1.3	-	-	-	-	-	-	-	-	-	-	111.8	1.6
1988	-	-	-	-	-	-	-	-	-	-	113.9	1.9	-	-	-	-	-	-	-	-	-	-	117.1	2.8
1989	-	-	-	-	-	-	-	-	-	-	124.1	6.0	-	-	-	-	-	-	-	-	-	-	127.9	3.1
1990	-	-	-	-	-	-	-	-	-	-	129.1	0.9	-	-	-	-	-	-	-	-	-	-	130.8	1.3
1991	-	-	-	-	-	-	-	-	-	-	135.3	3.4	-	-	-	-	-	-	-	-	-	-	136.5	0.9
1992	-	-	-	-	-	-	-	-	-	-	138.0	1.1	-	-	-	-	-	-	-	-	-	-	142.3	3.1
1993	-	-	-	-	-	-	-	-	-	-	143.8	1.1	-	-	-	-	-	-	-	-	-	-	-	-

Source: U.S. Department of Labor, Bureau of Labor Statistics, Division of Consumer Prices and Price Indexes. - indicates no data collected for period.

Seattle-Everett, WA
Consumer Price Index - Urban Wage Earners
Base 1982-1984 = 100
Entertainment

For 1975-1993. Columns headed % show percentile change in the index from the previous period for which an index is available.

Year	Jan Index	%	Feb Index	%	Mar Index	%	Apr Index	%	May Index	%	Jun Index	%	Jul Index	%	Aug Index	%	Sep Index	%	Oct Index	%	Nov Index	%	Dec Index	%
1975	-	-	-	-	-	-	-	-	-	-	-	-	-	-	-	-	-	-	-	-	58.9	-	-	-
1976	-	-	59.1	0.3	-	-	-	-	59.5	0.7	-	-	-	-	60.0	0.8	-	-	-	-	61.2	2.0	-	-
1977	-	-	62.9	2.8	-	-	-	-	62.8	-0.2	-	-	-	-	62.9	0.2	-	-	-	-	64.2	2.1	-	-
1978	64.4	0.3	-	-	64.5	0.2	-	-	66.7	3.4	-	-	67.3	0.9	-	-	66.6	-1.0	-	-	68.3	2.6	-	-
1979	68.9	0.9	-	-	68.8	-0.1	-	-	69.9	1.6	-	-	70.5	0.9	-	-	73.5	4.3	-	-	74.9	1.9	-	-
1980	76.1	1.6	-	-	77.9	2.4	-	-	78.0	0.1	-	-	79.9	2.4	-	-	82.8	3.6	-	-	84.2	1.7	-	-
1981	87.3	3.7	-	-	83.4	-4.5	-	-	86.0	3.1	-	-	86.4	0.5	-	-	88.6	2.5	-	-	89.4	0.9	-	-
1982	91.1	1.9	-	-	91.3	0.2	-	-	93.6	2.5	-	-	94.3	0.7	-	-	97.1	3.0	-	-	96.6	-0.5	-	-
1983	96.8	0.2	-	-	100.0	3.3	-	-	96.5	-3.5	-	-	99.7	3.3	-	-	102.5	2.8	-	-	103.2	0.7	-	-
1984	104.4	1.2	-	-	105.6	1.1	-	-	106.0	0.4	-	-	105.9	-0.1	-	-	104.7	-1.1	-	-	106.7	1.9	-	-
1985	107.4	0.7	-	-	108.2	0.7	-	-	107.0	-1.1	-	-	109.5	2.3	-	-	106.5	-2.7	-	-	109.2	2.5	-	-
1986	109.7	0.5	-	-	108.7	-0.9	-	-	105.3	-3.1	-	-	108.7	3.2	-	-	107.5	-1.1	-	-	108.0	0.5	108.1	0.1
1987	-	-	-	-	-	-	-	-	-	-	109.0	0.8	-	-	-	-	-	-	-	-	-	-	110.2	1.1
1988	-	-	-	-	-	-	-	-	-	-	111.2	0.9	-	-	-	-	-	-	-	-	-	-	115.5	3.9
1989	-	-	-	-	-	-	-	-	-	-	122.1	5.7	-	-	-	-	-	-	-	-	-	-	126.3	3.4
1990	-	-	-	-	-	-	-	-	-	-	127.2	0.7	-	-	-	-	-	-	-	-	-	-	128.4	0.9
1991	-	-	-	-	-	-	-	-	-	-	133.1	3.7	-	-	-	-	-	-	-	-	-	-	132.8	-0.2
1992	-	-	-	-	-	-	-	-	-	-	135.1	1.7	-	-	-	-	-	-	-	-	-	-	137.7	1.9
1993	-	-	-	-	-	-	-	-	-	-	139.3	1.2	-	-	-	-	-	-	-	-	-	-	-	-

Source: U.S. Department of Labor, Bureau of Labor Statistics, Division of Consumer Prices and Price Indexes. - indicates no data collected for period.

Seattle-Everett, WA
Consumer Price Index - All Urban Consumers
Base 1982-1984 = 100
Other Goods and Services

For 1975-1993. Columns headed % show percentile change in the index from the previous period for which an index is available.

Year	Jan Index	%	Feb Index	%	Mar Index	%	Apr Index	%	May Index	%	Jun Index	%	Jul Index	%	Aug Index	%	Sep Index	%	Oct Index	%	Nov Index	%	Dec Index	%
1975	-	-	-	-	-	-	-	-	-	-	-	-	-	-	-	-	-	-	-	-	48.2	-	-	-
1976	-	-	49.2	2.1	-	-	-	-	50.6	2.8	-	-	-	-	50.9	0.6	-	-	-	-	52.3	2.8	-	-
1977	-	-	53.3	1.9	-	-	-	-	53.6	0.6	-	-	-	-	54.2	1.1	-	-	-	-	55.6	2.6	-	-
1978	55.8	0.4	-	-	55.9	0.2	-	-	56.6	1.3	-	-	57.3	1.2	-	-	58.9	2.8	-	-	60.9	3.4	-	-
1979	60.8	-0.2	-	-	62.5	2.8	-	-	62.4	-0.2	-	-	63.6	1.9	-	-	66.7	4.9	-	-	67.3	0.9	-	-
1980	67.9	0.9	-	-	69.9	2.9	-	-	70.9	1.4	-	-	71.2	0.4	-	-	73.6	3.4	-	-	73.9	0.4	-	-
1981	74.7	1.1	-	-	75.2	0.7	-	-	76.7	2.0	-	-	79.4	3.5	-	-	84.3	6.2	-	-	86.7	2.8	-	-
1982	88.1	1.6	-	-	89.2	1.2	-	-	90.3	1.2	-	-	91.1	0.9	-	-	92.9	2.0	-	-	96.0	3.3	-	-
1983	98.1	2.2	-	-	99.1	1.0	-	-	99.4	0.3	-	-	99.6	0.2	-	-	102.5	2.9	-	-	105.6	3.0	-	-
1984	106.4	0.8	-	-	106.5	0.1	-	-	105.9	-0.6	-	-	106.6	0.7	-	-	108.2	1.5	-	-	108.8	0.6	-	-
1985	110.6	1.7	-	-	110.5	-0.1	-	-	109.8	-0.6	-	-	111.9	1.9	-	-	112.7	0.7	-	-	114.9	2.0	-	-
1986	115.0	0.1	-	-	114.3	-0.6	-	-	117.0	2.4	-	-	117.7	0.6	-	-	118.5	0.7	-	-	118.6	0.1	119.8	1.0
1987	-	-	-	-	-	-	-	-	-	-	121.0	1.0	-	-	-	-	-	-	-	-	-	-	124.0	2.5
1988	-	-	-	-	-	-	-	-	-	-	126.5	2.0	-	-	-	-	-	-	-	-	-	-	128.2	1.3
1989	-	-	-	-	-	-	-	-	-	-	132.9	3.7	-	-	-	-	-	-	-	-	-	-	137.9	3.8
1990	-	-	-	-	-	-	-	-	-	-	144.2	4.6	-	-	-	-	-	-	-	-	-	-	149.5	3.7
1991	-	-	-	-	-	-	-	-	-	-	154.1	3.1	-	-	-	-	-	-	-	-	-	-	158.9	3.1
1992	-	-	-	-	-	-	-	-	-	-	166.0	4.5	-	-	-	-	-	-	-	-	-	-	172.1	3.7
1993	-	-	-	-	-	-	-	-	-	-	178.6	3.8	-	-	-	-	-	-	-	-	-	-	-	-

Source: U.S. Department of Labor, Bureau of Labor Statistics, Division of Consumer Prices and Price Indexes. - indicates no data collected for period.

Seattle-Everett, WA
Consumer Price Index - Urban Wage Earners
Base 1982-1984 = 100
Other Goods and Services

For 1975-1993. Columns headed % show percentile change in the index from the previous period for which an index is available.

Year	Jan Index	%	Feb Index	%	Mar Index	%	Apr Index	%	May Index	%	Jun Index	%	Jul Index	%	Aug Index	%	Sep Index	%	Oct Index	%	Nov Index	%	Dec Index	%
1975	-		-		-		-		-		-		-		-		-		-		49.9	-	-	-
1976	-	-	50.9	2.0	-		-	-	52.4	2.9	-	-	-	-	52.7	0.6	-	-	-	-	54.2	-	-	-
1977	-	-	55.1	1.7	-		-	-	55.5	0.7	-	-	-	-	56.2	1.3	-	-	-	-	57.6	2.5	-	-
1978	58.1	0.9	-	-	58.4	0.5	-	-	59.0	1.0	-	-	59.9	1.5	-	-	61.4	2.5	-	-	62.0	1.0	-	-
1979	62.5	0.8	-	-	64.1	2.6	-	-	63.7	-0.6	-	-	64.6	1.4	-	-	67.0	3.7	-	-	67.9	1.3	-	-
1980	68.6	1.0	-	-	70.1	2.2	-	-	70.5	0.6	-	-	71.1	0.9	-	-	73.4	3.2	-	-	73.9	0.7	-	-
1981	75.5	2.2	-	-	75.8	0.4	-	-	77.5	2.2	-	-	79.0	1.9	-	-	83.5	5.7	-	-	85.4	2.3	-	-
1982	87.3	2.2	-	-	88.7	1.6	-	-	89.6	1.0	-	-	90.6	1.1	-	-	92.5	2.1	-	-	96.0	3.8	-	-
1983	98.6	2.7	-	-	99.6	1.0	-	-	99.8	0.2	-	-	100.2	0.4	-	-	103.1	2.9	-	-	105.5	2.3	-	-
1984	106.5	0.9	-	-	106.5	0.0	-	-	106.1	-0.4	-	-	107.0	0.8	-	-	108.0	0.9	-	-	108.6	0.6	-	-
1985	110.6	1.8	-	-	110.6	0.0	-	-	109.8	-0.7	-	-	112.1	2.1	-	-	112.6	0.4	-	-	114.6	1.8	-	-
1986	114.7	0.1	-	-	113.9	-0.7	-	-	117.3	3.0	-	-	118.2	0.8	-	-	118.9	0.6	-	-	118.5	-0.3	119.9	1.2
1987	-	-	-	-	-	-	-	-	-	-	121.6	1.4	-	-	-	-	-	-	-	-	-	-	124.3	2.2
1988	-	-	-	-	-	-	-	-	-	-	126.8	2.0	-	-	-	-	-	-	-	-	-	-	129.1	1.8
1989	-	-	-	-	-	-	-	-	-	-	134.0	3.8	-	-	-	-	-	-	-	-	-	-	138.6	3.4
1990	-	-	-	-	-	-	-	-	-	-	145.6	5.1	-	-	-	-	-	-	-	-	-	-	149.8	2.9
1991	-	-	-	-	-	-	-	-	-	-	154.9	3.4	-	-	-	-	-	-	-	-	-	-	159.9	3.2
1992	-	-	-	-	-	-	-	-	-	-	167.2	4.6	-	-	-	-	-	-	-	-	-	-	173.5	3.8
1993	-	-	-	-	-	-	-	-	-	-	181.6	4.7	-	-	-	-	-	-	-	-	-	-	-	-

Source: U.S. Department of Labor, Bureau of Labor Statistics, Division of Consumer Prices and Price Indexes. - indicates no data collected for period.

St. Louis, MO-IL
Consumer Price Index - All Urban Consumers
Base 1982-1984 = 100
Annual Averages

For 1917-1993. Columns headed % show percentile change in the index from the previous period for which an index is available.

Year	All Items		Food & Beverage		Housing		Apparel & Upkeep		Trans- portation		Medical Care		Entertain- ment		Other Goods & Services	
	Index	%	Index	%	Index	%	Index	%	Index	%	Index	%	Index	%	Index	%
1917	-	-	-	-	-	-	-	-	-	-	-	-	-	-	-	-
1918	14.8	-	-	-	-	-	-	-	-	-	-	-	-	-	-	-
1919	16.8	13.5	-	-	-	-	-	-	-	-	-	-	-	-	-	-
1920	19.9	18.5	-	-	-	-	-	-	-	-	-	-	-	-	-	-
1921	17.4	-12.6	-	-	-	-	-	-	-	-	-	-	-	-	-	-
1922	16.3	-6.3	-	-	-	-	-	-	-	-	-	-	-	-	-	-
1923	16.7	2.5	-	-	-	-	-	-	-	-	-	-	-	-	-	-
1924	16.8	0.6	-	-	-	-	-	-	-	-	-	-	-	-	-	-
1925	17.3	3.0	-	-	-	-	-	-	-	-	-	-	-	-	-	-
1926	17.6	1.7	-	-	-	-	-	-	-	-	-	-	-	-	-	-
1927	17.3	-1.7	-	-	-	-	-	-	-	-	-	-	-	-	-	-
1928	16.9	-2.3	-	-	-	-	-	-	-	-	-	-	-	-	-	-
1929	17.1	1.2	-	-	-	-	-	-	-	-	-	-	-	-	-	-
1930	16.7	-2.3	-	-	-	-	-	-	-	-	-	-	-	-	-	-
1931	15.0	-10.2	-	-	-	-	-	-	-	-	-	-	-	-	-	-
1932	13.4	-10.7	-	-	-	-	-	-	-	-	-	-	-	-	-	-
1933	12.8	-4.5	-	-	-	-	-	-	-	-	-	-	-	-	-	-
1934	13.3	3.9	-	-	-	-	-	-	-	-	-	-	-	-	-	-
1935	13.7	3.0	-	-	-	-	-	-	-	-	-	-	-	-	-	-
1936	13.8	0.7	-	-	-	-	-	-	-	-	-	-	-	-	-	-
1937	14.3	3.6	-	-	-	-	-	-	-	-	-	-	-	-	-	-
1938	13.9	-2.8	-	-	-	-	-	-	-	-	-	-	-	-	-	-
1939	13.8	-0.7	-	-	-	-	-	-	-	-	-	-	-	-	-	-
1940	13.9	0.7	-	-	-	-	-	-	-	-	-	-	-	-	-	-
1941	14.6	5.0	-	-	-	-	-	-	-	-	-	-	-	-	-	-
1942	16.2	11.0	-	-	-	-	-	-	-	-	-	-	-	-	-	-
1943	17.0	4.9	-	-	-	-	-	-	-	-	-	-	-	-	-	-
1944	17.3	1.8	-	-	-	-	-	-	-	-	-	-	-	-	-	-
1945	17.6	1.7	-	-	-	-	-	-	-	-	-	-	-	-	-	-
1946	19.1	8.5	-	-	-	-	-	-	-	-	-	-	-	-	-	-
1947	22.2	16.2	-	-	-	-	-	-	18.2	-	13.2	-	-	-	-	-
1948	23.9	7.7	-	-	-	-	-	-	19.8	8.8	14.0	6.1	-	-	-	-
1949	23.6	-1.3	-	-	-	-	-	-	20.8	5.1	14.4	2.9	-	-	-	-
1950	23.9	1.3	-	-	-	-	-	-	21.3	2.4	14.5	0.7	-	-	-	-
1951	25.9	8.4	-	-	-	-	-	-	23.5	10.3	15.5	6.9	-	-	-	-
1952	26.7	3.1	-	-	-	-	-	-	25.8	9.8	18.0	16.1	-	-	-	-
1953	27.0	1.1	-	-	-	-	44.1	-	26.8	3.9	18.5	2.8	-	-	-	-
1954	27.1	0.4	-	-	-	-	44.0	-0.2	26.0	-3.0	18.9	2.2	-	-	-	-
1955	27.0	-0.4	-	-	-	-	44.0	0.0	26.1	0.4	19.5	3.2	-	-	-	-
1956	27.2	0.7	-	-	-	-	44.4	0.9	26.3	0.8	19.9	2.1	-	-	-	-
1957	28.1	3.3	-	-	-	-	45.0	1.4	28.0	6.5	21.5	8.0	-	-	-	-
1958	29.0	3.2	-	-	-	-	45.8	1.8	29.6	5.7	22.2	3.3	-	-	-	-
1959	29.4	1.4	-	-	-	-	46.2	0.9	31.6	6.8	23.3	5.0	-	-	-	-
1960	29.5	0.3	-	-	-	-	47.1	1.9	31.4	-0.6	23.7	1.7	-	-	-	-
1961	30.0	1.7	-	-	-	-	47.6	1.1	32.0	1.9	24.2	2.1	-	-	-	-

[Continued]

St. Louis, MO-IL
Consumer Price Index - All Urban Consumers
Base 1982-1984 = 100
Annual Averages
[Continued]

For 1917-1993. Columns headed % show percentile change in the index from the previous period for which an index is available.

Year	All Items		Food & Beverage		Housing		Apparel & Upkeep		Trans- portation		Medical Care		Entertain- ment		Other Goods & Services	
	Index	%	Index	%	Index	%	Index	%	Index	%	Index	%	Index	%	Index	%
1962	30.3	1.0	-	-	-	-	47.6	0.0	32.4	1.3	25.5	5.4	-	-	-	-
1963	30.6	1.0	-	-	-	-	48.0	0.8	32.3	-0.3	25.7	0.8	-	-	-	-
1964	31.2	2.0	-	-	-	-	48.7	1.5	32.7	1.2	25.9	0.8	-	-	-	-
1965	31.7	1.6	-	-	-	-	49.2	1.0	33.0	0.9	26.8	3.5	-	-	-	-
1966	32.7	3.2	-	-	-	-	50.7	3.0	34.0	3.0	28.2	5.2	-	-	-	-
1967	33.7	3.1	-	-	-	-	52.4	3.4	35.3	3.8	29.7	5.3	-	-	-	-
1968	35.0	3.9	-	-	-	-	55.4	5.7	36.0	2.0	31.1	4.7	-	-	-	-
1969	36.8	5.1	-	-	-	-	58.2	5.1	37.2	3.3	33.0	6.1	-	-	-	-
1970	38.8	5.4	-	-	-	-	60.4	3.8	39.4	5.9	35.2	6.7	-	-	-	-
1971	40.3	3.9			-	-	62.4	3.3	42.1	6.9	36.7	4.3	-	-	-	-
1972	41.2	2.2			-	-	63.0	1.0	42.4	0.7	37.4	1.9	-	-	-	-
1973	43.5	5.6			-	-	64.5	2.4	43.8	3.3	38.6	3.2	-	-	-	-
1974	47.9	10.1			-	-	68.0	5.4	47.4	8.2	41.8	8.3	-	-	-	-
1975	52.6	9.8	-	-	-	-	70.8	4.1	51.5	8.6	46.3	10.8	-	-	-	-
1976	55.6	5.7	62.5	-	50.5	-	74.3	4.9	56.1	8.9	50.2	8.4	66.4	-	57.2	-
1977	59.5	7.0	66.8	6.9	54.0	6.9	79.2	6.6	59.5	6.1	55.4	10.4	70.2	5.7	60.5	5.8
1978	64.5	8.4	72.7	8.8	59.4	10.0	80.2	1.3	63.5	6.7	59.6	7.6	77.5	10.4	64.6	6.8
1979	72.7	12.7	81.0	11.4	67.9	14.3	85.2	6.2	73.8	16.2	64.8	8.7	81.5	5.2	68.7	6.3
1980	82.5	13.5	87.1	7.5	79.8	17.5	91.7	7.6	85.1	15.3	72.9	12.5	88.2	8.2	74.7	8.7
1981	90.1	9.2	93.5	7.3	87.6	9.8	95.3	3.9	94.4	10.9	81.8	12.2	93.9	6.5	82.0	9.8
1982	96.6	7.2	97.1	3.9	96.6	10.3	97.6	2.4	97.8	3.6	93.4	14.2	96.3	2.6	90.6	10.5
1983	100.1	3.6	99.7	2.7	100.4	3.9	100.8	3.3	99.2	1.4	100.9	8.0	101.3	5.2	101.0	11.5
1984	103.3	3.2	103.2	3.5	102.9	2.5	101.6	0.8	102.9	3.7	105.8	4.9	102.4	1.1	108.5	7.4
1985	107.1	3.7	105.7	2.4	107.8	4.8	104.4	2.8	105.3	2.3	111.0	4.9	106.0	3.5	115.4	6.4
1986	108.6	1.4	109.7	3.8	110.4	2.4	102.7	-1.6	100.3	-4.7	120.3	8.4	110.2	4.0	122.1	5.8
1987	112.2	3.3	114.0	3.9	112.1	1.5	107.6	4.8	103.9	3.6	127.9	6.3	113.9	3.4	128.1	4.9
1988	115.7	3.1	117.7	3.2	114.9	2.5	112.5	4.6	106.0	2.0	135.6	6.0	117.9	3.5	136.8	6.8
1989	121.8	5.3	125.8	6.9	120.3	4.7	118.4	5.2	110.5	4.2	145.6	7.4	122.3	3.7	145.4	6.3
1990	128.1	5.2	134.9	7.2	124.9	3.8	120.9	2.1	117.4	6.2	159.0	9.2	124.4	1.7	153.6	5.6
1991	132.1	3.1	139.6	3.5	127.7	2.2	122.5	1.3	118.5	0.9	171.7	8.0	134.5	8.1	163.4	6.4
1992	134.7	2.0	140.1	0.4	129.7	1.6	121.7	-0.7	121.9	2.9	181.0	5.4	137.8	2.5	172.3	5.4
1993	-	-	-	-	-	-	-	-	-	-	-	-	-	-	-	-

Source: U.S. Department of Labor, Bureau of Labor Statistics, Division of Consumer Prices and Price Indexes. - indicates no data collected for period.

St. Louis, MO-IL
Consumer Price Index - Urban Wage Earners
Base 1982-1984 = 100
Annual Averages

For 1917-1993. Columns headed % show percentile change in the index from the previous period for which an index is available.

Year	All Items		Food & Beverage		Housing		Apparel & Upkeep		Trans-portation		Medical Care		Entertain-ment		Other Goods & Services	
	Index	%	Index	%	Index	%	Index	%	Index	%	Index	%	Index	%	Index	%
1917	-	-	-	-	-	-	-	-	-	-	-	-	-	-	-	-
1918	15.0	-	-	-	-	-	-	-	-	-	-	-	-	-	-	-
1919	17.0	13.3	-	-	-	-	-	-	-	-	-	-	-	-	-	-
1920	20.1	18.2	-	-	-	-	-	-	-	-	-	-	-	-	-	-
1921	17.6	-12.4	-	-	-	-	-	-	-	-	-	-	-	-	-	-
1922	16.5	-6.3	-	-	-	-	-	-	-	-	-	-	-	-	-	-
1923	16.8	1.8	-	-	-	-	-	-	-	-	-	-	-	-	-	-
1924	17.0	1.2	-	-	-	-	-	-	-	-	-	-	-	-	-	-
1925	17.5	2.9	-	-	-	-	-	-	-	-	-	-	-	-	-	-
1926	17.7	1.1	-	-	-	-	-	-	-	-	-	-	-	-	-	-
1927	17.5	-1.1	-	-	-	-	-	-	-	-	-	-	-	-	-	-
1928	17.1	-2.3	-	-	-	-	-	-	-	-	-	-	-	-	-	-
1929	17.2	0.6	-	-	-	-	-	-	-	-	-	-	-	-	-	-
1930	16.9	-1.7	-	-	-	-	-	-	-	-	-	-	-	-	-	-
1931	15.1	-10.7	-	-	-	-	-	-	-	-	-	-	-	-	-	-
1932	13.6	-9.9	-	-	-	-	-	-	-	-	-	-	-	-	-	-
1933	12.9	-5.1	-	-	-	-	-	-	-	-	-	-	-	-	-	-
1934	13.4	3.9	-	-	-	-	-	-	-	-	-	-	-	-	-	-
1935	13.8	3.0	-	-	-	-	-	-	-	-	-	-	-	-	-	-
1936	14.0	1.4	-	-	-	-	-	-	-	-	-	-	-	-	-	-
1937	14.4	2.9	-	-	-	-	-	-	-	-	-	-	-	-	-	-
1938	14.1	-2.1	-	-	-	-	-	-	-	-	-	-	-	-	-	-
1939	13.9	-1.4	-	-	-	-	-	-	-	-	-	-	-	-	-	-
1940	14.0	0.7	-	-	-	-	-	-	-	-	-	-	-	-	-	-
1941	14.7	5.0	-	-	-	-	-	-	-	-	-	-	-	-	-	-
1942	16.3	10.9	-	-	-	-	-	-	-	-	-	-	-	-	-	-
1943	17.2	5.5	-	-	-	-	-	-	-	-	-	-	-	-	-	-
1944	17.5	1.7	-	-	-	-	-	-	-	-	-	-	-	-	-	-
1945	17.8	1.7	-	-	-	-	-	-	-	-	-	-	-	-	-	-
1946	19.3	8.4	-	-	-	-	-	-	-	-	-	-	-	-	-	-
1947	22.4	16.1	-	-	-	-	-	-	18.5	-	13.1	-	-	-	-	-
1948	24.1	7.6	-	-	-	-	-	-	20.1	8.6	13.9	6.1	-	-	-	-
1949	23.8	-1.2	-	-	-	-	-	-	21.2	5.5	14.3	2.9	-	-	-	-
1950	24.1	1.3	-	-	-	-	-	-	21.7	2.4	14.4	0.7	-	-	-	-
1951	26.1	8.3	-	-	-	-	-	-	23.9	10.1	15.3	6.3	-	-	-	-
1952	27.0	3.4	-	-	-	-	-	-	26.2	9.6	17.9	17.0	-	-	-	-
1953	27.2	0.7	-	-	-	-	45.0	-	27.2	3.8	18.3	2.2	-	-	-	-
1954	27.3	0.4	-	-	-	-	44.9	-0.2	26.4	-2.9	18.7	2.2	-	-	-	-
1955	27.2	-0.4	-	-	-	-	44.8	-0.2	26.5	0.4	19.3	3.2	-	-	-	-
1956	27.5	1.1	-	-	-	-	45.3	1.1	26.7	0.8	19.7	2.1	-	-	-	-
1957	28.4	3.3	-	-	-	-	45.9	1.3	28.5	6.7	21.3	8.1	-	-	-	-
1958	29.2	2.8	-	-	-	-	46.7	1.7	30.1	5.6	22.0	3.3	-	-	-	-
1959	29.6	1.4	-	-	-	-	47.1	0.9	32.1	6.6	23.1	5.0	-	-	-	-
1960	29.8	0.7	-	-	-	-	48.0	1.9	31.9	-0.6	23.5	1.7	-	-	-	-
1961	30.3	1.7	-	-	-	-	48.5	1.0	32.5	1.9	24.0	2.1	-	-	-	-

[Continued]

824

St. Louis, MO-IL
Consumer Price Index - Urban Wage Earners
Base 1982-1984 = 100
Annual Averages
[Continued]

For 1917-1993. Columns headed % show percentile change in the index from the previous period for which an index is available.

Year	All Items		Food & Beverage		Housing		Apparel & Upkeep		Trans-portation		Medical Care		Entertain-ment		Other Goods & Services	
	Index	%	Index	%	Index	%	Index	%	Index	%	Index	%	Index	%	Index	%
1962	30.6	1.0	-	-	-	-	48.5	0.0	32.9	1.2	25.3	5.4	-	-	-	-
1963	30.9	1.0	-	-	-	-	48.9	0.8	32.8	-0.3	25.5	0.8	-	-	-	-
1964	31.5	1.9	-	-	-	-	49.6	1.4	33.2	1.2	25.6	0.4	-	-	-	-
1965	32.0	1.6	-	-	-	-	50.1	1.0	33.6	1.2	26.5	3.5	-	-	-	-
1966	33.0	3.1	-	-	-	-	51.6	3.0	34.6	3.0	28.0	5.7	-	-	-	-
1967	34.0	3.0	-	-	-	-	53.4	3.5	35.8	3.5	29.4	5.0	-	-	-	-
1968	35.3	3.8	-	-	-	-	56.5	5.8	36.6	2.2	30.8	4.8	-	-	-	-
1969	37.1	5.1	-	-	-	-	59.3	5.0	37.8	3.3	32.7	6.2				
1970	39.2	5.7	-	-	-	-	61.6	3.9	40.1	6.1	34.8	6.4	-	-	-	-
1971	40.7	3.8	-	-	-	-	63.6	3.2	42.8	6.7	36.3	4.3	-	-	-	-
1972	41.6	2.2	-	-	-	-	64.2	0.9	43.1	0.7	37.0	1.9	-	-	-	-
1973	43.9	5.5	-	-	-	-	64.2	2.3	43.1	3.2	37.0	3.2				
1974	48.3	10.0	-	-	-	-	65.7	5.5	44.5	8.3	38.2	8.4	-	-	-	-
1975	53.1	9.9	-	-	-	-	69.3	4.2	48.2	8.5	41.4	10.9	-	-	-	-
1976	56.1	5.6	62.5	-	51.0	-	72.2	4.8	52.3	9.0	45.9	8.3	72.4	-	56.8	-
1977	60.0	7.0	66.8	6.9	54.5	6.9	75.7	6.7	57.0	6.1	49.7	10.7	76.6	5.8	60.0	5.6
1978	64.7	7.8	72.5	8.5	59.9	9.9	80.8	0.1	60.5	4.3	55.0	8.2	82.3	7.4	64.2	7.0
1979	73.2	13.1	81.5	12.4	68.9	15.0	80.9	4.3	63.1	16.2	59.5	9.4	86.2	4.7	68.7	7.0
1980	83.4	13.9	87.4	7.2	81.0	17.6	84.4	7.2	73.3	16.8	65.1	12.9	93.6	8.6	75.5	9.9
1981	90.9	9.0	93.6	7.1	88.7	9.5	90.5	5.3	85.6	10.4	73.5	11.8	96.3	2.9	82.6	9.4
1982	97.1	6.8	97.1	3.7	97.8	10.3	95.3	2.3	94.5	3.5	82.2	13.6	96.5	0.2	90.6	9.7
1983	100.3	3.3	99.8	2.8	100.8	3.1	97.5	3.6	97.8	1.3	93.4	7.8	101.4	5.1	101.4	11.9
1984	102.6	2.3	103.2	3.4	101.3	0.5	101.0	0.5	99.1	4.1	100.7	5.2	102.1	0.7	108.0	6.5
1985	107.1	4.4	105.6	2.3	109.1	7.7	101.5	2.6	103.2	2.0	105.9	4.8	105.1	2.9	114.6	6.1
1986	108.2	1.0	109.8	4.0	111.9	2.6	104.1	-1.6	105.3	-5.8	111.0	7.9	109.2	3.9	121.1	5.7
1987	111.8	3.3	114.0	3.8	113.9	1.8	102.4	5.2	99.2	4.0	119.8	6.4	112.9	3.4	126.8	4.7
1988	115.4	3.2	117.8	3.3	116.6	2.4	107.7	4.5	103.2	2.5	127.5	6.0	117.1	3.7	135.7	7.0
1989	121.5	5.3	125.8	6.8	122.0	4.6	112.6	5.2	105.8	4.1	135.2	7.7	121.3	3.6	144.7	6.6
1990	127.5	4.9	134.8	7.2	126.7	3.9	118.5	2.3	110.1	4.9	145.6	8.7	123.3	1.6	153.7	6.2
1991	131.5	3.1	139.6	3.6	129.5	2.2	121.2	1.3	115.5	1.5	158.3	7.8	132.9	7.8	165.4	7.6
1992	134.3	2.1	140.2	0.4	131.9	1.9	122.8	-0.6	117.2	3.2	170.6	5.5	135.7	2.1	175.4	6.0
1993	-	-	-	-	-	-	122.1	-	121.0	-	180.0	-	-	-	-	-

Source: U.S. Department of Labor, Bureau of Labor Statistics, Division of Consumer Prices and Price Indexes. - indicates no data collected for period.

St. Louis, MO-IL

Consumer Price Index - All Urban Consumers
Base 1982-1984 = 100
All Items

For 1917-1993. Columns headed % show percentile change in the index from the previous period for which an index is available.

Year	Jan		Feb		Mar		Apr		May		Jun		Jul		Aug		Sep		Oct		Nov		Dec	
	Index	%	Index	%	Index	%	Index	%	Index	%	Index	%	Index	%	Index	%	Index	%	Index	%	Index	%	Index	%
1917	-	-	-	-	-	-	-	-	-	-	-	-	-	-	-	-	-	-	-	-	-	-	13.7	-
1918	-	-	-	-	-	-	-	-	-	-	-	-	-	-	-	-	-	-	-	-	-	-	16.0	16.8
1919	-	-	-	-	-	-	-	-	-	-	16.2	1.3	-	-	-	-	-	-	-	-	-	-	18.4	13.6
1920	-	-	-	-	-	-	-	-	-	-	21.1	14.7	-	-	-	-	-	-	-	-	-	-	18.8	-10.9
1921	-	-	-	-	-	-	-	-	17.2	-8.5	-	-	-	-	-	-	17.2	0.0	-	-	-	-	16.7	-2.9
1922	-	-	-	-	16.3	-2.4	-	-	-	-	16.5	1.2	-	-	-	-	16.2	-1.8	-	-	-	-	16.4	1.2
1923	-	-	-	-	16.5	0.6	-	-	-	-	16.6	0.6	-	-	-	-	16.9	1.8	-	-	-	-	16.8	-0.6
1924	-	-	-	-	16.7	-0.6	-	-	-	-	16.7	0.0	-	-	-	-	16.7	0.0	-	-	-	-	16.9	1.2
1925	-	-	-	-	-	-	-	-	-	-	17.3	2.4	-	-	-	-	-	-	-	-	-	-	17.7	2.3
1926	-	-	-	-	-	-	-	-	-	-	17.6	-0.6	-	-	-	-	-	-	-	-	-	-	17.6	0.0
1927	-	-	-	-	-	-	-	-	-	-	17.6	0.0	-	-	-	-	-	-	-	-	-	-	17.1	-2.8
1928	-	-	-	-	-	-	-	-	-	-	16.9	-1.2	-	-	-	-	-	-	-	-	-	-	16.9	0.0
1929	-	-	-	-	-	-	-	-	-	-	17.1	1.2	-	-	-	-	-	-	-	-	-	-	17.2	0.6
1930	-	-	-	-	-	-	-	-	-	-	16.8	-2.3	-	-	-	-	-	-	-	-	-	-	16.0	-4.8
1931	-	-	-	-	-	-	-	-	-	-	14.9	-6.9	-	-	-	-	-	-	-	-	-	-	14.2	-4.7
1932	-	-	-	-	-	-	-	-	-	-	13.4	-5.6	-	-	-	-	-	-	-	-	-	-	12.9	-3.7
1933	-	-	-	-	-	-	-	-	-	-	12.6	-2.3	-	-	-	-	-	-	-	-	-	-	12.9	2.4
1934	-	-	-	-	-	-	-	-	-	-	13.2	2.3	-	-	-	-	-	-	-	-	13.3	0.8	-	-
1935	-	-	-	-	13.6	2.3	-	-	-	-	-	-	13.7	0.7	-	-	-	-	13.7	0.0	-	-	-	-
1936	13.8	0.7	-	-	-	-	13.7	-0.7	-	-	-	-	13.9	1.5	-	-	14.1	1.4	-	-	-	-	13.9	-1.4
1937	-	-	-	-	14.2	2.2	-	-	-	-	14.3	0.7	-	-	-	-	14.5	1.4	-	-	-	-	14.3	-1.4
1938	-	-	-	-	14.0	-2.1	-	-	-	-	14.0	0.0	-	-	-	-	14.0	0.0	-	-	-	-	13.8	-1.4
1939	-	-	-	-	13.8	0.0	-	-	-	-	13.6	-1.4	-	-	-	-	14.0	2.9	-	-	-	-	13.8	-1.4
1940	-	-	-	-	13.8	0.0	-	-	-	-	13.8	0.0	-	-	-	-	13.9	0.7	13.9	0.0	13.9	0.0	14.1	1.4
1941	14.1	0.0	14.0	-0.7	14.1	0.7	14.2	0.7	14.2	0.0	14.5	2.1	14.5	0.0	14.6	0.7	15.0	2.7	15.1	0.7	15.3	1.3	15.4	0.7
1942	15.6	1.3	15.7	0.6	16.0	1.9	16.1	0.6	16.1	0.0	16.2	0.6	16.2	0.0	16.3	0.6	16.2	-0.6	16.4	1.2	16.5	0.6	16.7	1.2
1943	16.6	-0.6	16.7	0.6	16.9	1.2	17.1	1.2	17.3	1.2	17.2	-0.6	17.1	-0.6	17.1	0.0	17.1	0.0	17.1	0.0	17.1	0.0	17.1	0.0
1944	17.1	0.0	17.0	-0.6	17.1	0.6	17.2	0.6	17.3	0.6	17.3	0.0	17.5	1.2	17.4	-0.6	17.4	0.0	17.3	-0.6	17.4	0.6	17.4	0.0
1945	17.5	0.6	17.4	-0.6	17.4	0.0	17.4	0.0	17.6	1.1	17.7	0.6	17.7	0.0	17.7	0.0	17.6	-0.6	17.7	0.6	17.6	-0.6	17.9	1.7
1946	17.9	0.0	17.8	-0.6	17.9	0.6	18.0	0.6	18.0	0.0	18.3	1.7	19.5	6.6	19.9	2.1	19.9	0.0	20.4	2.5	21.0	2.9	21.1	0.5
1947	21.1	0.0	21.1	0.0	21.7	2.8	21.6	-0.5	21.5	-0.5	21.7	0.9	-	-	-	-	23.1	6.5	-	-	-	-	23.4	1.3
1948	-	-	-	-	23.4	0.0	-	-	-	-	24.0	2.6	-	-	-	-	24.4	1.7	-	-	-	-	23.9	-2.0
1949	-	-	-	-	23.6	-1.3	-	-	-	-	23.7	0.4	-	-	-	-	23.6	-0.4	-	-	-	-	23.4	-0.8
1950	-	-	-	-	23.4	0.0	-	-	-	-	23.5	0.4	-	-	-	-	24.2	3.0	-	-	-	-	24.9	2.9
1951	-	-	-	-	25.8	3.6	-	-	-	-	25.8	0.0	-	-	-	-	25.9	0.4	-	-	-	-	26.5	2.3
1952	-	-	-	-	26.5	0.0	-	-	-	-	26.8	1.1	-	-	-	-	26.8	0.0	-	-	-	-	26.7	-0.4
1953	-	-	-	-	26.6	-0.4	-	-	-	-	26.9	1.1	-	-	-	-	27.2	1.1	-	-	-	-	27.2	0.0
1954	-	-	-	-	27.2	0.0	-	-	-	-	27.3	0.4	-	-	-	-	26.9	-1.5	-	-	-	-	26.8	-0.4
1955	-	-	-	-	26.9	0.4	-	-	-	-	26.9	0.0	-	-	-	-	27.1	0.7	-	-	-	-	27.0	-0.4
1956	-	-	-	-	26.9	-0.4	-	-	-	-	27.2	1.1	-	-	-	-	27.4	0.7	-	-	-	-	27.7	1.1
1957	-	-	-	-	27.9	0.7	-	-	-	-	28.1	0.7	-	-	-	-	28.3	0.7	-	-	-	-	28.4	0.4
1958	-	-	-	-	28.9	1.8	-	-	-	-	28.9	0.0	-	-	-	-	29.1	0.7	-	-	-	-	29.2	0.3
1959	-	-	-	-	29.3	0.3	-	-	-	-	29.4	0.3	-	-	-	-	29.4	0.0	-	-	-	-	29.4	0.0
1960	-	-	-	-	29.4	0.0	-	-	-	-	29.6	0.7	-	-	-	-	29.6	0.0	-	-	-	-	29.7	0.3
1961	-	-	-	-	30.0	1.0	-	-	-	-	30.0	0.0	-	-	-	-	30.0	0.0	-	-	-	-	30.1	0.3

[Continued]

St. Louis, MO-IL
Consumer Price Index - All Urban Consumers
Base 1982-1984 = 100
All Items
[Continued]

For 1917-1993. Columns headed % show percentile change in the index from the previous period for which an index is available.

Year	Jan Index	%	Feb Index	%	Mar Index	%	Apr Index	%	May Index	%	Jun Index	%	Jul Index	%	Aug Index	%	Sep Index	%	Oct Index	%	Nov Index	%	Dec Index	%
1962	-	-	-	-	30.2	0.3	-	-	-	-	30.1	-0.3	-	-	-	-	30.4	1.0	-	-	-	-	30.6	0.7
1963	-	-	-	-	30.5	-0.3	-	-	-	-	30.4	-0.3	-	-	-	-	30.7	1.0	-	-	-	-	30.9	0.7
1964	-	-	-	-	31.0	0.3	-	-	-	-	31.0	0.0	-	-	-	-	31.3	1.0	-	-	-	-	31.4	0.3
1965	-	-	-	-	31.4	0.0	-	-	-	-	31.7	1.0	-	-	-	-	31.7	0.0	-	-	-	-	32.2	1.6
1966	-	-	-	-	32.3	0.3	-	-	-	-	32.8	1.5	-	-	-	-	33.1	0.9	-	-	-	-	33.1	0.0
1967	-	-	-	-	33.3	0.6	-	-	-	-	33.6	0.9	-	-	-	-	33.9	0.9	-	-	-	-	34.3	1.2
1968	-	-	-	-	34.6	0.9	-	-	-	-	35.0	1.2	-	-	-	-	35.4	1.1	-	-	-	-	35.6	0.6
1969	-	-	-	-	36.2	1.7	-	-	-	-	36.6	1.1	-	-	-	-	37.2	1.6	-	-	-	-	37.7	1.3
1970	-	-	-	-	38.2	1.3	-	-	-	-	38.7	1.3	-	-	-	-	39.3	1.6	-	-	-	-	39.6	0.8
1971	-	-	-	-	39.8	0.5	-	-	-	-	40.4	1.5	-	-	-	-	40.6	0.5	-	-	-	-	40.7	0.2
1972	-	-	-	-	40.7	0.0	-	-	-	-	41.0	0.7	-	-	-	-	41.6	1.5	-	-	-	-	41.6	0.0
1973	-	-	-	-	42.5	2.2	-	-	-	-	43.1	1.4	-	-	-	-	44.5	3.2	-	-	-	-	45.0	1.1
1974	-	-	-	-	46.5	3.3	-	-	-	-	47.5	2.2	-	-	-	-	49.1	3.4	-	-	-	-	50.0	1.8
1975	-	-	-	-	51.3	2.6	-	-	-	-	52.8	2.9	-	-	-	-	53.5	1.3	-	-	-	-	54.0	0.9
1976	-	-	-	-	54.8	1.5	-	-	-	-	55.6	1.5	-	-	-	-	56.3	1.3	-	-	-	-	56.6	0.5
1977	-	-	-	-	58.3	3.0	-	-	-	-	59.7	2.4	-	-	-	-	60.4	1.2	-	-	-	-	60.8	0.7
1978	-	-	-	-	61.9	1.8	-	-	63.8	3.1	-	-	65.0	1.9	-	-	66.0	1.5	-	-	67.1	1.7	-	-
1979	68.5	2.1	-	-	70.2	2.5	-	-	71.1	1.3	-	-	73.0	2.7	-	-	74.8	2.5	-	-	76.0	1.6	-	-
1980	78.3	3.0	-	-	80.2	2.4	-	-	81.4	1.5	-	-	82.5	1.4	-	-	85.0	3.0	-	-	85.4	0.5	-	-
1981	86.1	0.8	-	-	87.3	1.4	-	-	90.2	3.3	-	-	90.7	0.6	-	-	92.0	1.4	-	-	92.2	0.2	-	-
1982	93.7	1.6	-	-	94.5	0.9	-	-	96.2	1.8	-	-	97.7	1.6	-	-	99.0	1.3	-	-	97.6	-1.4	-	-
1983	98.0	0.4	-	-	98.7	0.7	-	-	99.5	0.8	-	-	100.8	1.3	-	-	101.7	0.9	-	-	100.9	-0.8	-	-
1984	101.3	0.4	-	-	101.9	0.6	-	-	102.8	0.9	-	-	103.9	1.1	-	-	104.8	0.9	-	-	104.1	-0.7	-	-
1985	105.5	1.3	-	-	105.8	0.3	-	-	106.4	0.6	-	-	107.7	1.2	-	-	108.3	0.6	-	-	108.3	0.0	-	-
1986	108.5	0.2	-	-	107.5	-0.9	-	-	107.3	-0.2	-	-	109.6	2.1	-	-	109.7	0.1	-	-	109.0	-0.6	-	-
1987	110.0	0.9	-	-	110.7	0.6	-	-	111.3	0.5	-	-	112.7	1.3	-	-	114.3	1.4	-	-	113.1	-1.0	-	-
1988	113.4	0.3	-	-	114.2	0.7	-	-	114.1	-0.1	-	-	116.0	1.7	-	-	117.3	1.1	-	-	118.3	0.9	-	-
1989	118.4	0.1	-	-	119.4	0.8	-	-	121.5	1.8	-	-	123.1	1.3	-	-	123.9	0.6	-	-	123.1	-0.6	-	-
1990	125.1	1.6	-	-	127.2	1.7	-	-	126.7	-0.4	-	-	128.0	1.0	-	-	129.9	1.5	-	-	130.4	0.4	-	-
1991	131.0	0.5	-	-	130.7	-0.2	-	-	131.3	0.5	-	-	132.7	1.1	-	-	133.5	0.6	-	-	133.2	-0.2	-	-
1992	132.5	-0.5	-	-	132.6	0.1	-	-	134.0	1.1	-	-	135.7	1.3	-	-	136.6	0.7	-	-	136.0	-0.4	-	-
1993	135.9	-0.1	-	-	136.1	0.1	-	-	136.8	0.5	-	-	138.8	1.5	-	-	138.4	-0.3	-	-	138.1	-0.2	-	-

Source: U.S. Department of Labor, Bureau of Labor Statistics, Division of Consumer Prices and Price Indexes. - indicates no data collected for period.

St. Louis, MO-IL
Consumer Price Index - Urban Wage Earners
Base 1982-1984 = 100
All Items

For 1917-1993. Columns headed % show percentile change in the index from the previous period for which an index is available.

Year	Jan Index	%	Feb Index	%	Mar Index	%	Apr Index	%	May Index	%	Jun Index	%	Jul Index	%	Aug Index	%	Sep Index	%	Oct Index	%	Nov Index	%	Dec Index	%
1917	-	-	-	-	-	-	-	-	-	-	-	-	-	-	-	-	-	-	-	-	-	-	13.9	-
1918	-	-	-	-	-	-	-	-	-	-	-	-	-	-	-	-	-	-	-	-	-	-	16.2	16.5
1919	-	-	-	-	-	-	-	-	-	-	16.4	1.2	-	-	-	-	-	-	-	-	-	-	18.6	13.4
1920	-	-	-	-	-	-	-	-	-	-	21.3	14.5	-	-	-	-	-	-	-	-	-	-	18.9	-11.3
1921	-	-	-	-	-	-	-	-	17.4	-7.9	-	-	-	-	-	-	17.4	0.0	-	-	-	-	16.9	-2.9
1922	-	-	-	-	16.5	-2.4	-	-	-	-	16.6	0.6	-	-	-	-	16.3	-1.8	-	-	-	-	16.5	1.2
1923	-	-	-	-	16.6	0.6	-	-	-	-	16.7	0.6	-	-	-	-	17.1	2.4	-	-	-	-	17.0	-0.6
1924	-	-	-	-	16.9	-0.6	-	-	-	-	16.9	0.0	-	-	-	-	16.9	0.0	-	-	-	-	17.1	1.2
1925	-	-	-	-	-	-	-	-	-	-	17.5	2.3	-	-	-	-	-	-	-	-	-	-	17.9	2.3
1926	-	-	-	-	-	-	-	-	-	-	17.8	-0.6	-	-	-	-	-	-	-	-	-	-	17.7	-0.6
1927	-	-	-	-	-	-	-	-	-	-	17.8	0.6	-	-	-	-	-	-	-	-	-	-	17.2	-3.4
1928	-	-	-	-	-	-	-	-	-	-	17.1	-0.6	-	-	-	-	-	-	-	-	-	-	17.1	0.0
1929	-	-	-	-	-	-	-	-	-	-	17.2	0.6	-	-	-	-	-	-	-	-	-	-	17.4	1.2
1930	-	-	-	-	-	-	-	-	-	-	17.0	-2.3	-	-	-	-	-	-	-	-	-	-	16.1	-5.3
1931	-	-	-	-	-	-	-	-	-	-	15.1	-6.2	-	-	-	-	-	-	-	-	-	-	14.3	-5.3
1932	-	-	-	-	-	-	-	-	-	-	13.5	-5.6	-	-	-	-	-	-	-	-	-	-	13.0	-3.7
1933	-	-	-	-	-	-	-	-	-	-	12.7	-2.3	-	-	-	-	-	-	-	-	-	-	13.1	3.1
1934	-	-	-	-	-	-	-	-	-	-	13.4	2.3	-	-	-	-	-	-	-	-	13.5	0.7	-	-
1935	-	-	-	-	13.8	2.2	-	-	-	-	-	-	13.8	0.0	-	-	-	-	13.8	0.0	-	-	-	-
1936	14.0	1.4	-	-	-	-	13.8	-1.4	-	-	-	-	14.0	1.4	-	-	14.2	1.4	-	-	-	-	14.0	-1.4
1937	-	-	-	-	14.3	2.1	-	-	-	-	14.5	1.4	-	-	-	-	14.6	0.7	-	-	-	-	14.4	-1.4
1938	-	-	-	-	14.1	-2.1	-	-	-	-	14.1	0.0	-	-	-	-	14.1	0.0	-	-	-	-	14.0	-0.7
1939	-	-	-	-	13.9	-0.7	-	-	-	-	13.7	-1.4	-	-	-	-	14.1	2.9	-	-	-	-	13.9	-1.4
1940	-	-	-	-	13.9	0.0	-	-	-	-	14.0	0.7	-	-	-	-	14.0	0.0	14.1	0.7	14.0	-0.7	14.2	1.4
1941	14.2	0.0	14.2	0.0	14.2	0.0	14.3	0.7	14.3	0.0	14.6	2.1	14.7	0.7	14.8	0.7	15.2	2.7	15.3	0.7	15.4	0.7	15.5	0.6
1942	15.7	1.3	15.9	1.3	16.1	1.3	16.2	0.6	16.2	0.0	16.4	1.2	16.3	-0.6	16.5	1.2	16.4	-0.6	16.6	1.2	16.6	0.0	16.9	1.8
1943	16.8	-0.6	16.9	0.6	17.1	1.2	17.3	1.2	17.4	0.6	17.4	0.0	17.3	-0.6	17.3	0.0	17.2	-0.6	17.3	0.6	17.3	0.0	17.3	0.0
1944	17.3	0.0	17.2	-0.6	17.2	0.0	17.4	1.2	17.4	0.0	17.5	0.6	17.7	1.1	17.6	-0.6	17.6	0.0	17.5	-0.6	17.6	0.6	17.6	0.0
1945	17.7	0.6	17.6	-0.6	17.6	0.0	17.6	0.0	17.8	1.1	17.9	0.6	17.9	0.0	17.9	0.0	17.8	-0.6	17.8	0.0	17.8	0.0	18.0	1.1
1946	18.1	0.6	18.0	-0.6	18.0	0.0	18.2	1.1	18.2	0.0	18.5	1.6	19.6	5.9	20.1	2.6	20.1	0.0	20.6	2.5	21.2	2.9	21.3	0.5
1947	21.3	0.0	21.3	0.0	21.9	2.8	21.8	-0.5	21.8	0.0	21.9	0.5	-	-	-	-	23.3	6.4	-	-	-	-	23.6	1.3
1948	-	-	-	-	23.6	0.0	-	-	-	-	24.2	2.5	-	-	-	-	24.6	1.7	-	-	-	-	24.1	-2.0
1949	-	-	-	-	23.8	-1.2	-	-	-	-	23.9	0.4	-	-	-	-	23.8	-0.4	-	-	-	-	23.6	-0.8
1950	-	-	-	-	23.6	0.0	-	-	-	-	23.7	0.4	-	-	-	-	24.4	3.0	-	-	-	-	25.1	2.9
1951	-	-	-	-	26.0	3.6	-	-	-	-	26.0	0.0	-	-	-	-	26.2	0.8	-	-	-	-	26.8	2.3
1952	-	-	-	-	26.8	0.0	-	-	-	-	27.1	1.1	-	-	-	-	27.1	0.0	-	-	-	-	27.0	-0.4
1953	-	-	-	-	26.9	-0.4	-	-	-	-	27.2	1.1	-	-	-	-	27.5	1.1	-	-	-	-	27.4	-0.4
1954	-	-	-	-	27.4	0.0	-	-	-	-	27.5	0.4	-	-	-	-	27.1	-1.5	-	-	-	-	27.1	0.0
1955	-	-	-	-	27.1	0.0	-	-	-	-	27.2	0.4	-	-	-	-	27.3	0.4	-	-	-	-	27.2	-0.4
1956	-	-	-	-	27.1	-0.4	-	-	-	-	27.4	1.1	-	-	-	-	27.7	1.1	-	-	-	-	27.9	0.7
1957	-	-	-	-	28.2	1.1	-	-	-	-	28.4	0.7	-	-	-	-	28.6	0.7	-	-	-	-	28.7	0.3
1958	-	-	-	-	29.2	1.7	-	-	-	-	29.2	0.0	-	-	-	-	29.4	0.7	-	-	-	-	29.5	0.3
1959	-	-	-	-	29.5	0.0	-	-	-	-	29.6	0.3	-	-	-	-	29.6	0.0	-	-	-	-	29.7	0.3
1960	-	-	-	-	29.6	-0.3	-	-	-	-	29.8	0.7	-	-	-	-	29.9	0.3	-	-	-	-	30.0	0.3
1961	-	-	-	-	30.3	1.0	-	-	-	-	30.3	0.0	-	-	-	-	30.3	0.0	-	-	-	-	30.4	0.3

[Continued]

St. Louis, MO-IL
Consumer Price Index - Urban Wage Earners
Base 1982-1984 = 100
All Items
[Continued]

For 1917-1993. Columns headed % show percentile change in the index from the previous period for which an index is available.

Year	Jan Index	%	Feb Index	%	Mar Index	%	Apr Index	%	May Index	%	Jun Index	%	Jul Index	%	Aug Index	%	Sep Index	%	Oct Index	%	Nov Index	%	Dec Index	%
1962	-	-	-	-	30.5	0.3	-	-	-	-	30.4	-0.3	-	-	-	-	30.7	1.0	-	-	-	-	30.9	0.7
1963	-	-	-	-	30.8	-0.3	-	-	-	-	30.7	-0.3	-	-	-	-	31.0	1.0	-	-	-	-	31.2	0.6
1964	-	-	-	-	31.3	0.3	-	-	-	-	31.3	0.0	-	-	-	-	31.6	1.0	-	-	-	-	31.7	0.3
1965	-	-	-	-	31.7	0.0	-	-	-	-	32.1	1.3	-	-	-	-	32.0	-0.3	-	-	-	-	32.5	1.6
1966	-	-	-	-	32.6	0.3	-	-	-	-	33.1	1.5	-	-	-	-	33.4	0.9	-	-	-	-	33.4	0.0
1967	-	-	-	-	33.6	0.6	-	-	-	-	33.9	0.9	-	-	-	-	34.3	1.2	-	-	-	-	34.6	0.9
1968	-	-	-	-	35.0	1.2	-	-	-	-	35.3	0.9	-	-	-	-	35.7	1.1	-	-	-	-	35.9	0.6
1969	-	-	-	-	36.5	1.7	-	-	-	-	36.9	1.1	-	-	-	-	37.6	1.9	-	-	-	-	38.0	1.1
1970	-	-	-	-	38.5	1.3	-	-	-	-	39.0	1.3	-	-	-	-	39.6	1.5	-	-	-	-	40.0	1.0
1971	-	-	-	-	40.2	0.5	-	-	-	-	40.8	1.5	-	-	-	-	41.0	0.5	-	-	-	-	41.1	0.2
1972	-	-	-	-	41.1	0.0	-	-	-	-	41.4	0.7	-	-	-	-	42.0	1.4	-	-	-	-	42.0	0.0
1973	-	-	-	-	42.9	2.1	-	-	-	-	43.5	1.4	-	-	-	-	45.0	3.4	-	-	-	-	45.5	1.1
1974	-	-	-	-	47.0	3.3	-	-	-	-	48.0	2.1	-	-	-	-	49.6	3.3	-	-	-	-	50.5	1.8
1975	-	-	-	-	51.8	2.6	-	-	-	-	53.3	2.9	-	-	-	-	54.0	1.3	-	-	-	-	54.5	0.9
1976	-	-	-	-	55.3	1.5	-	-	-	-	56.2	1.6	-	-	-	-	56.8	1.1	-	-	-	-	57.2	0.7
1977	-	-	-	-	58.9	3.0	-	-	-	-	60.3	2.4	-	-	-	-	60.9	1.0	-	-	-	-	61.4	0.8
1978	-	-	-	-	62.5	1.8	-	-	63.9	2.2	-	-	64.9	1.6	-	-	66.2	2.0	-	-	67.2	1.5	-	-
1979	68.5	1.9	-	-	70.4	2.8	-	-	71.5	1.6	-	-	73.9	3.4	-	-	75.6	2.3	-	-	76.9	1.7	-	-
1980	79.4	3.3	-	-	81.1	2.1	-	-	82.5	1.7	-	-	83.6	1.3	-	-	85.9	2.8	-	-	86.4	0.6	-	-
1981	87.0	0.7	-	-	88.2	1.4	-	-	91.2	3.4	-	-	91.5	0.3	-	-	92.8	1.4	-	-	92.8	0.0	-	-
1982	94.2	1.5	-	-	94.9	0.7	-	-	96.7	1.9	-	-	98.3	1.7	-	-	99.6	1.3	-	-	98.2	-1.4	-	-
1983	97.0	-1.2	-	-	99.7	2.8	-	-	99.9	0.2	-	-	100.8	0.9	-	-	101.7	0.9	-	-	101.7	0.0	-	-
1984	100.9	-0.8	-	-	101.1	0.2	-	-	101.1	0.0	-	-	102.4	1.3	-	-	104.7	2.2	-	-	104.4	-0.3	-	-
1985	105.5	1.1	-	-	105.7	0.2	-	-	106.4	0.7	-	-	107.6	1.1	-	-	108.3	0.7	-	-	108.3	0.0	-	-
1986	108.5	0.2	-	-	107.1	-1.3	-	-	106.8	-0.3	-	-	109.0	2.1	-	-	109.0	0.0	-	-	108.4	-0.6	-	-
1987	109.4	0.9	-	-	110.2	0.7	-	-	110.9	0.6	-	-	112.5	1.4	-	-	114.1	1.4	-	-	112.7	-1.2	-	-
1988	113.0	0.3	-	-	113.8	0.7	-	-	113.7	-0.1	-	-	115.7	1.8	-	-	117.1	1.2	-	-	117.8	0.6	-	-
1989	118.0	0.2	-	-	119.1	0.9	-	-	121.2	1.8	-	-	122.8	1.3	-	-	123.5	0.6	-	-	122.6	-0.7	-	-
1990	124.6	1.6	-	-	126.5	1.5	-	-	126.0	-0.4	-	-	127.3	1.0	-	-	129.3	1.6	-	-	129.9	0.5	-	-
1991	130.3	0.3	-	-	130.1	-0.2	-	-	130.6	0.4	-	-	132.0	1.1	-	-	133.0	0.8	-	-	132.7	-0.2	-	-
1992	132.0	-0.5	-	-	132.0	0.0	-	-	133.6	1.2	-	-	135.4	1.3	-	-	136.5	0.8	-	-	135.6	-0.7	-	-
1993	135.4	-0.1	-	-	135.5	0.1	-	-	136.4	0.7	-	-	138.3	1.4	-	-	137.6	-0.5	-	-	137.5	-0.1	-	-

Source: U.S. Department of Labor, Bureau of Labor Statistics, Division of Consumer Prices and Price Indexes. - indicates no data collected for period.

St. Louis, MO-IL
Consumer Price Index - All Urban Consumers
Base 1982-1984 = 100
Food and Beverages

For 1975-1993. Columns headed % show percentile change in the index from the previous period for which an index is available.

Year	Jan Index	%	Feb Index	%	Mar Index	%	Apr Index	%	May Index	%	Jun Index	%	Jul Index	%	Aug Index	%	Sep Index	%	Oct Index	%	Nov Index	%	Dec Index	%
1975	-	-	-	-	-	-	-	-	-	-	-	-	-	-	-	-	-	-	-	-	-	-	62.0	-
1976	-	-	-	-	61.8	-0.3	-	-	-	-	62.6	1.3	-	-	-	-	62.9	0.5	-	-	-	-	62.8	-0.2
1977	-	-	-	-	65.4	4.1	-	-	-	-	67.9	3.8	-	-	-	-	67.9	0.0	-	-	-	-	67.8	-0.1
1978	-	-	-	-	70.1	3.4	-	-	72.6	3.6	-	-	74.2	2.2	-	-	74.2	0.0	-	-	74.6	0.5	-	-
1979	77.6	4.0	-	-	79.5	2.4	-	-	81.3	2.3	-	-	82.4	1.4	-	-	82.1	-0.4	-	-	81.7	-0.5	-	-
1980	83.7	2.4	-	-	84.1	0.5	-	-	85.3	1.4	-	-	86.9	1.9	-	-	89.9	3.5	-	-	90.8	1.0	-	-
1981	91.2	0.4	-	-	92.3	1.2	-	-	92.7	0.4	-	-	94.2	1.6	-	-	94.6	0.4	-	-	94.8	0.2	-	-
1982	95.5	0.7	-	-	95.7	0.2	-	-	96.7	1.0	-	-	98.0	1.3	-	-	98.1	0.1	-	-	98.1	0.0	-	-
1983	98.2	0.1	-	-	99.5	1.3	-	-	99.8	0.3	-	-	99.7	-0.1	-	-	100.2	0.5	-	-	100.0	-0.2	-	-
1984	101.3	1.3	-	-	102.3	1.0	-	-	102.2	-0.1	-	-	103.8	1.6	-	-	104.3	0.5	-	-	104.3	0.0	-	-
1985	105.0	0.7	-	-	106.1	1.0	-	-	105.0	-1.0	-	-	105.4	0.4	-	-	106.7	1.2	-	-	105.7	-0.9	-	-
1986	107.3	1.5	-	-	107.6	0.3	-	-	108.1	0.5	-	-	110.0	1.8	-	-	111.9	1.7	-	-	112.1	0.2	-	-
1987	113.4	1.2	-	-	113.7	0.3	-	-	114.1	0.4	-	-	114.2	0.1	-	-	115.0	0.7	-	-	113.3	-1.5	-	-
1988	113.9	0.5	-	-	114.3	0.4	-	-	115.8	1.3	-	-	118.3	2.2	-	-	120.5	1.9	-	-	121.8	1.1	-	-
1989	121.3	-0.4	-	-	124.4	2.6	-	-	125.4	0.8	-	-	125.3	-0.1	-	-	127.2	1.5	-	-	128.4	0.9	-	-
1990	132.8	3.4	-	-	133.6	0.6	-	-	134.0	0.3	-	-	134.2	0.1	-	-	135.3	0.8	-	-	137.6	1.7	-	-
1991	139.8	1.6	-	-	139.1	-0.5	-	-	139.4	0.2	-	-	139.5	0.1	-	-	139.6	0.1	-	-	140.4	0.6	-	-
1992	140.5	0.1	-	-	139.2	-0.9	-	-	140.6	1.0	-	-	139.7	-0.6	-	-	139.9	0.1	-	-	140.8	0.6	-	-
1993	139.8	-0.7	-	-	138.9	-0.6	-	-	138.8	-0.1	-	-	140.0	0.9	-	-	140.9	0.6	-	-	141.1	0.1	-	-

Source: U.S. Department of Labor, Bureau of Labor Statistics, Division of Consumer Prices and Price Indexes. - indicates no data collected for period.

St. Louis, MO-IL
Consumer Price Index - Urban Wage Earners
Base 1982-1984 = 100
Food and Beverages

For 1975-1993. Columns headed % show percentile change in the index from the previous period for which an index is available.

Year	Jan Index	%	Feb Index	%	Mar Index	%	Apr Index	%	May Index	%	Jun Index	%	Jul Index	%	Aug Index	%	Sep Index	%	Oct Index	%	Nov Index	%	Dec Index	%
1975	-	-	-	-	-	-	-	-	-	-	-	-	-	-	-	-	-	-	-	-	-	-	-	-
1976	-	-	-	-	61.8	-0.3	-	-	-	-	62.6	1.3	-	-	-	-	-	-	-	-	-	-	62.0	-
1977	-	-	-	-	65.4	4.1	-	-	-	-	67.9	3.8	-	-	-	-	62.9	0.5	-	-	-	-	62.8	-0.2
1978	-	-	-	-	70.1	3.4	-	-	72.3	3.1	-	-	73.1	1.1	-	-	67.9	0.0	-	-	-	-	67.8	-0.1
1979	77.3	3.8	-	-	79.7	3.1	-	-	80.8	1.4	-	-	83.0	2.7	-	-	74.2	1.5	-	-	74.5	0.4	-	-
1980	84.7	1.9	-	-	84.5	-0.2	-	-	85.0	0.6	-	-	87.2	2.6	-	-	83.3	0.4	-	-	83.1	-0.2	-	-
1981	91.6	0.5	-	-	92.3	0.8	-	-	93.0	0.8	-	-	94.2	1.3	-	-	90.5	3.8	-	-	91.1	0.7	-	-
1982	95.3	0.4	-	-	95.7	0.4	-	-	96.6	0.9	-	-	97.9	1.3	-	-	95.0	0.8	-	-	94.9	-0.1	-	-
1983	98.3	0.2	-	-	99.6	1.3	-	-	99.9	0.3	-	-	99.8	-0.1	-	-	98.1	0.2	-	-	98.1	0.0	-	-
1984	101.2	1.1	-	-	102.3	1.1	-	-	102.2	-0.1	-	-	103.8	1.6	-	-	100.4	0.6	-	-	100.1	-0.3	-	-
1985	104.9	0.6	-	-	105.9	1.0	-	-	104.9	-0.9	-	-	105.3	0.4	-	-	104.2	0.4	-	-	104.3	0.1	-	-
1986	107.1	1.4	-	-	107.6	0.5	-	-	108.1	0.5	-	-	109.9	1.7	-	-	106.5	1.1	-	-	105.6	-0.8	-	-
1987	113.6	1.2	-	-	113.8	0.2	-	-	114.0	0.2	-	-	114.2	0.2	-	-	112.0	1.9	-	-	112.2	0.2	-	-
1988	114.0	0.4	-	-	114.5	0.4	-	-	115.7	1.0	-	-	118.3	2.2	-	-	115.1	0.8	-	-	113.5	-1.4	-	-
1989	121.2	-0.6	-	-	124.3	2.6	-	-	125.3	0.8	-	-	125.3	0.0	-	-	120.5	1.9	-	-	121.9	1.2	-	-
1990	132.6	3.1	-	-	133.6	0.8	-	-	134.1	0.4	-	-	134.3	0.1	-	-	127.3	1.6	-	-	128.6	1.0	-	-
1991	139.6	1.6	-	-	139.1	-0.4	-	-	139.3	0.1	-	-	139.5	0.1	-	-	135.3	0.7	-	-	137.4	1.6	-	-
1992	140.5	0.1	-	-	139.3	-0.9	-	-	140.6	0.9	-	-	140.0	-0.4	-	-	139.8	0.2	-	-	140.3	0.4	-	-
1993	140.0	-0.6	-	-	139.1	-0.6	-	-	139.1	0.0	-	-	140.3	0.9	-	-	140.1	0.1	-	-	140.8	0.5	-	-
																	141.1	0.6			141.3	0.1		

Source: U.S. Department of Labor, Bureau of Labor Statistics, Division of Consumer Prices and Price Indexes. - indicates no data collected for period.

St. Louis, MO-IL
Consumer Price Index - All Urban Consumers
Base 1982-1984 = 100
Housing

For 1975-1993. Columns headed % show percentile change in the index from the previous period for which an index is available.

Year	Jan Index	%	Feb Index	%	Mar Index	%	Apr Index	%	May Index	%	Jun Index	%	Jul Index	%	Aug Index	%	Sep Index	%	Oct Index	%	Nov Index	%	Dec Index	%
1975	-	-	-	-	-	-	-	-	-	-	-	-	-	-	-	-	-	-	-	-	-	-	48.7	-
1976	-	-	-	-	50.1	2.9	-	-	-	-	50.5	0.8	-	-	-	-	51.1	1.2	-	-	-	-	51.3	0.4
1977	-	-	-	-	52.8	2.9	-	-	-	-	53.9	2.1	-	-	-	-	55.1	2.2	-	-	-	-	55.7	1.1
1978	-	-	-	-	56.9	2.2	-	-	58.5	2.8	-	-	59.6	1.9	-	-	61.0	2.3	-	-	62.3	2.1	-	-
1979	63.7	2.2	-	-	65.4	2.7	-	-	65.3	-0.2	-	-	67.4	3.2	-	-	70.6	4.7	-	-	72.2	2.3	-	-
1980	75.4	4.4	-	-	77.2	2.4	-	-	78.4	1.6	-	-	79.7	1.7	-	-	83.1	4.3	-	-	82.9	-0.2	-	-
1981	82.6	-0.4	-	-	83.1	0.6	-	-	88.7	6.7	-	-	88.7	0.0	-	-	90.5	2.0	-	-	89.4	-1.2	-	-
1982	92.4	3.4	-	-	94.3	2.1	-	-	96.9	2.8	-	-	98.0	1.1	-	-	100.5	2.6	-	-	97.1	-3.4	-	-
1983	97.8	0.7	-	-	98.9	1.1	-	-	99.3	0.4	-	-	102.0	2.7	-	-	103.0	1.0	-	-	100.6	-2.3	-	-
1984	101.3	0.7	-	-	100.9	-0.4	-	-	102.7	1.8	-	-	104.4	1.7	-	-	104.8	0.4	-	-	101.9	-2.8	-	-
1985	106.2	4.2	-	-	105.2	-0.9	-	-	105.9	0.7	-	-	109.5	3.4	-	-	110.0	0.5	-	-	109.4	-0.5	-	-
1986	109.3	-0.1	-	-	108.5	-0.7	-	-	108.2	-0.3	-	-	114.2	5.5	-	-	112.9	-1.1	-	-	108.8	-3.6	-	-
1987	109.9	1.0	-	-	110.3	0.4	-	-	110.8	0.5	-	-	114.1	3.0	-	-	114.5	0.4	-	-	112.3	-1.9	-	-
1988	112.8	0.4	-	-	113.7	0.8	-	-	112.8	-0.8	-	-	115.8	2.7	-	-	116.1	0.3	-	-	117.1	0.9	-	-
1989	117.8	0.6	-	-	117.2	-0.5	-	-	118.4	1.0	-	-	122.5	3.5	-	-	124.3	1.5	-	-	120.6	-3.0	-	-
1990	121.6	0.8	-	-	124.5	2.4	-	-	123.9	-0.5	-	-	126.4	2.0	-	-	126.4	0.0	-	-	127.4	-1.6	-	-
1991	125.6	0.0	-	-	126.4	0.6	-	-	127.1	0.6	-	-	129.8	2.1	-	-	129.5	-0.2	-	-	127.4	-1.6	-	-
1992	126.5	-0.7	-	-	126.8	0.2	-	-	128.0	0.9	-	-	132.1	3.2	-	-	133.1	0.8	-	-	130.4	-2.0	-	-
1993	131.0	0.5	-	-	131.3	0.2	-	-	131.1	-0.2	-	-	135.4	3.3	-	-	135.6	0.1	-	-	132.7	-2.1	-	-

Source: U.S. Department of Labor, Bureau of Labor Statistics, Division of Consumer Prices and Price Indexes. - indicates no data collected for period.

St. Louis, MO-IL
Consumer Price Index - Urban Wage Earners
Base 1982-1984 = 100
Housing

For 1975-1993. Columns headed % show percentile change in the index from the previous period for which an index is available.

Year	Jan Index	%	Feb Index	%	Mar Index	%	Apr Index	%	May Index	%	Jun Index	%	Jul Index	%	Aug Index	%	Sep Index	%	Oct Index	%	Nov Index	%	Dec Index	%
1975	-	-	-	-	-	-	-	-	-	-	-	-	-	-	-	-	-	-	-	-	-	-	-	-
1976	-	-	-	-	50.5	2.9	-	-	-	-	51.0	1.0	-	-	-	-	51.6	1.2	-	-	-	-	49.1	-
1977	-	-	-	-	53.3	2.9	-	-	-	-	54.3	1.9	-	-	-	-	55.6	2.4	-	-	-	-	51.8	0.4
1978	-	-	-	-	57.4	2.1	-	-	58.8	2.4	-	-	60.0	2.0	-	-	61.7	2.8	-	-	63.1	2.3	56.2	1.1
1979	64.2	1.7	-	-	66.2	3.1	-	-	66.4	0.3	-	-	68.6	3.3	-	-	71.5	4.2	-	-	73.3	2.5	-	-
1980	76.5	4.4	-	-	78.4	2.5	-	-	80.0	2.0	-	-	81.2	1.5	-	-	84.1	3.6	-	-	84.1	0.0	-	-
1981	83.5	-0.7	-	-	84.0	0.6	-	-	90.1	7.3	-	-	89.8	-0.3	-	-	91.8	2.2	-	-	90.4	-1.5	-	-
1982	93.5	3.4	-	-	95.4	2.0	-	-	98.1	2.8	-	-	99.2	1.1	-	-	101.9	2.7	-	-	98.3	-3.5	-	-
1983	95.6	-2.7	-	-	101.4	6.1	-	-	100.4	-1.0	-	-	101.6	1.2	-	-	102.3	0.7	-	-	102.6	0.3	-	-
1984	100.4	-2.1	-	-	99.4	-1.0	-	-	98.5	-0.9	-	-	100.6	2.1	-	-	104.4	3.8	-	-	103.2	-1.1	-	-
1985	107.4	4.1	-	-	106.3	-1.0	-	-	107.0	0.7	-	-	110.6	3.4	-	-	111.4	0.7	-	-	110.8	-0.5	-	-
1986	110.8	0.0	-	-	110.0	-0.7	-	-	109.7	-0.3	-	-	115.6	5.4	-	-	114.4	-1.0	-	-	110.4	-3.5	-	-
1987	111.7	1.2	-	-	112.1	0.4	-	-	112.5	0.4	-	-	116.2	3.3	-	-	116.4	0.2	-	-	113.8	-2.2	-	-
1988	114.4	0.5	-	-	115.3	0.8	-	-	114.3	-0.9	-	-	117.6	2.9	-	-	117.9	0.3	-	-	118.7	0.7	-	-
1989	119.4	0.6	-	-	118.9	-0.4	-	-	120.1	1.0	-	-	124.4	3.6	-	-	126.2	1.4	-	-	122.1	-3.2	-	-
1990	123.3	1.0	-	-	126.3	2.4	-	-	125.5	-0.6	-	-	128.4	2.3	-	-	128.5	0.1	-	-	127.5	-0.8	-	-
1991	127.4	-0.1	-	-	128.1	0.5	-	-	128.8	0.5	-	-	131.7	2.3	-	-	131.6	-0.1	-	-	129.3	-1.7	-	-
1992	128.5	-0.6	-	-	128.9	0.3	-	-	130.1	0.9	-	-	134.6	3.5	-	-	135.5	0.7	-	-	132.6	-2.1	-	-
1993	133.2	0.5	-	-	133.4	0.2	-	-	133.2	-0.1	-	-	137.9	3.5	-	-	137.9	0.0	-	-	134.8	-2.2	-	-

Source: U.S. Department of Labor, Bureau of Labor Statistics, Division of Consumer Prices and Price Indexes. - indicates no data collected for period.

St. Louis, MO-IL
Consumer Price Index - All Urban Consumers
Base 1982-1984 = 100
Apparel and Upkeep

For 1952-1993. Columns headed % show percentile change in the index from the previous period for which an index is available.

Year	Jan Index	%	Feb Index	%	Mar Index	%	Apr Index	%	May Index	%	Jun Index	%	Jul Index	%	Aug Index	%	Sep Index	%	Oct Index	%	Nov Index	%	Dec Index	%
	-	-	-	-	-	-	-	-	-	-	-	-	-	-	-	-	-	-	-	-	-	-	43.8	-
1952	-	-	-	-	-	-	-	-	-	-	44.0	0.2	-	-	-	-	44.5	1.1	-	-	-	-	44.3	-0.4
1953	-	-	-	-	43.9	0.2	-	-	-	-	44.1	0.2	-	-	-	-	43.9	-0.5	-	-	-	-	43.8	-0.2
1954	-	-	-	-	44.0	-0.7	-	-	-	-	43.8	-0.5	-	-	-	-	43.9	0.2	-	-	-	-	44.1	0.5
1955	-	-	-	-	44.0	0.5	-	-	-	-	44.4	0.5	-	-	-	-	44.6	0.5	-	-	-	-	44.8	0.4
1956	-	-	-	-	44.2	0.2	-	-	-	-	44.8	-0.4	-	-	-	-	45.1	0.7	-	-	-	-	45.4	0.7
1957	-	-	-	-	45.0	0.4	-	-	-	-	45.7	-0.4	-	-	-	-	46.0	0.7	-	-	-	-	45.9	-0.2
1958	-	-	-	-	45.9	1.1	-	-	-	-	45.9	0.0	-	-	-	-	46.5	1.3	-	-	-	-	46.6	0.2
1959	-	-	-	-	45.9	0.0	-	-	-	-	46.9	0.2	-	-	-	-	47.5	1.3	-	-	-	-	47.5	0.0
1960	-	-	-	-	46.8	0.4	-	-	-	-	47.6	-0.2	-	-	-	-	47.6	0.0	-	-	-	-	47.4	-0.4
1961	-	-	-	-	47.7	0.4	-	-	-	-	47.6	0.2	-	-	-	-	47.8	0.4	-	-	-	-	47.5	-0.6
1962	-	-	-	-	47.5	0.2	-	-	-	-	48.0	0.8	-	-	-	-	48.3	0.6	-	-	-	-	48.7	0.8
1963	-	-	-	-	47.6	0.2	-	-	-	-	48.5	0.0	-	-	-	-	48.8	0.6	-	-	-	-	48.9	0.2
1964	-	-	-	-	48.5	-0.4	-	-	-	-	48.9	0.2	-	-	-	-	49.6	1.4	-	-	-	-	49.7	0.2
1965	-	-	-	-	48.8	-0.2	-	-	-	-	50.7	1.6	-	-	-	-	51.2	1.0	-	-	-	-	51.4	0.4
1966	-	-	-	-	49.9	0.4	-	-	-	-	52.2	0.2	-	-	-	-	52.6	0.8	-	-	-	-	53.4	1.5
1967	-	-	-	-	52.1	1.4	-	-	-	-	54.8	0.2	-	-	-	-	56.5	3.1	-	-	-	-	56.8	0.5
1968	-	-	-	-	54.7	2.4	-	-	-	-	57.9	0.7	-	-	-	-	58.8	1.6	-	-	-	-	59.1	0.5
1969	-	-	-	-	57.5	1.2	-	-	-	-	60.1	1.3	-	-	-	-	61.6	2.5	-	-	-	-	61.3	-0.5
1970	-	-	-	-	59.3	0.3	-	-	-	-	61.9	0.2	-	-	-	-	63.4	2.4	-	-	-	-	63.3	-0.2
1971	-	-	-	-	61.8	0.8	-	-	-	-	62.6	-0.6	-	-	-	-	63.4	1.3	-	-	-	-	63.1	-0.5
1972	-	-	-	-	63.0	-0.5	-	-	-	-	63.3	0.2	-	-	-	-	66.5	5.1	-	-	-	-	66.0	-0.8
1973	-	-	-	-	63.2	0.2	-	-	-	-	67.5	2.1	-	-	-	-	69.8	3.4	-	-	-	-	70.0	0.3
1974	-	-	-	-	66.1	0.2	-	-	-	-	70.6	0.6	-	-	-	-	71.3	1.0	-	-	-	-	72.0	1.0
1975	-	-	-	-	70.2	0.3	-	-	-	-	73.8	0.4	-	-	-	-	75.4	2.2	-	-	-	-	75.7	0.4
1976	-	-	-	-	73.5	2.1	-	-	-	-	79.0	0.3	-	-	-	-	80.0	1.3	-	-	-	-	80.9	1.1
1977	-	-	-	-	78.8	4.1	-	-	78.0	-2.0	-	-	77.9	-0.1	-	-	80.6	3.5	-	-	84.1	4.3	-	-
1978	-	-	-	-	79.6	-1.6	-	-	85.4	-2.2	-	-	81.4	-4.7	-	-	86.9	6.8	-	-	87.5	0.7	-	-
1979	81.8	-2.7	-	-	87.3	6.7	-	-	92.9	1.0	-	-	91.0	-2.0	-	-	94.4	3.7	-	-	93.2	-1.3	-	-
1980	85.4	-2.4	-	-	92.0	7.7	-	-	94.1	-2.2	-	-	95.4	1.4	-	-	97.7	2.4	-	-	95.9	-1.8	-	-
1981	91.6	-1.7	-	-	96.2	5.0	-	-	97.5	-1.7	-	-	97.6	0.1	-	-	99.4	1.8	-	-	97.1	-2.3	-	-
1982	94.1	-1.9	-	-	99.2	5.4	-	-	100.9	-2.3	-	-	100.5	-0.4	-	-	102.0	1.5	-	-	100.5	-1.5	-	-
1983	97.4	0.3	-	-	103.3	6.1	-	-	100.0	-2.4	-	-	99.8	-0.2	-	-	105.3	5.5	-	-	103.8	-1.4	-	-
1984	98.0	-2.5	-	-	102.5	4.6	-	-	107.4	0.5	-	-	104.3	-2.9	-	-	105.2	0.9	-	-	103.9	-1.2	-	-
1985	99.6	-4.0	-	-	106.9	7.3	-	-	103.2	-0.3	-	-	99.2	-3.9	-	-	104.7	5.5	-	-	106.1	1.3	-	-
1986	98.0	-5.7	-	-	103.5	5.6	-	-	107.1	0.0	-	-	100.2	-6.4	-	-	114.6	14.4	-	-	113.1	-1.3	-	-
1987	102.0	-3.9	-	-	107.1	5.0	-	-	110.6	-3.9	-	-	107.4	-2.9	-	-	116.1	8.1	-	-	116.2	0.1	-	-
1988	109.1	-3.5	-	-	115.1	5.5	-	-	121.0	1.2	-	-	118.5	-2.1	-	-	119.3	0.7	-	-	119.0	-0.3	-	-
1989	111.5	-4.0	-	-	119.6	7.3	-	-	119.2	-7.3	-	-	116.7	-2.1	-	-	121.2	3.9	-	-	121.0	-0.2	-	-
1990	118.7	-0.3	-	-	128.6	8.3	-	-	121.4	-2.6	-	-	-	-	-	-	125.8	5.6	-	-	124.6	-1.0	-	-
1991	119.1	-1.6	-	-	124.6	4.6	-	-	119.7	-2.4	-	-	119.1	-1.9	-	-	124.5	5.5	-	-	123.9	-0.5	-	-
1992	121.4	-2.6	-	-	122.6	1.0	-	-	126.0	2.6	-	-	118.0	-1.4	-	-	121.2	-1.1	-	-	123.5	1.9	-	-
1993	120.9	-2.4	-	-	122.8	1.6	-	-	-	-	-	-	122.6	-2.7	-	-	-	-	-	-	-	-	-	-

Source: U.S. Department of Labor, Bureau of Labor Statistics, Division of Consumer Prices and Price Indexes. - indicates no data collected for period.

St. Louis, MO-IL
Consumer Price Index - Urban Wage Earners
Base 1982-1984 = 100
Apparel and Upkeep

For 1952-1993. Columns headed % show percentile change in the index from the previous period for which an index is available.

Year	Jan Index	%	Feb Index	%	Mar Index	%	Apr Index	%	May Index	%	Jun Index	%	Jul Index	%	Aug Index	%	Sep Index	%	Oct Index	%	Nov Index	%	Dec Index	%
1952	-		-		-		-		-		-		-		-		-		-		-		44.6	-
1953	-		-		44.8	0.4	-		-		44.9	0.2	-		-		45.4	1.1	-		-		45.2	-0.4
1954	-		-		44.9	-0.7	-		-		44.9	0.0	-		-		44.7	-0.4	-		-		44.6	-0.2
1955	-		-		44.9	0.7	-		-		44.6	-0.7	-		-		44.8	0.4	-		-		44.9	0.2
1956	-		-		45.1	0.4	-		-		45.2	0.2	-		-		45.5	0.7	-		-		45.6	0.2
1957	-		-		45.8	0.4	-		-		45.6	-0.4	-		-		46.0	0.9	-		-		46.3	0.7
1958	-		-		46.8	1.1	-		-		46.6	-0.4	-		-		46.8	0.4	-		-		46.7	-0.2
1959	-		-		46.8	0.2	-		-		46.7	-0.2	-		-		47.4	1.5	-		-		47.5	0.2
1960	-		-		47.7	0.4	-		-		47.8	0.2	-		-		48.4	1.3	-		-		48.4	0.0
1961	-		-		48.6	0.4	-		-		48.5	-0.2	-		-		48.5	0.0	-		-		48.3	-0.4
1962	-		-		48.4	0.2	-		-		48.5	0.2	-		-		48.7	0.4	-		-		48.4	-0.6
1963	-		-		48.5	0.2	-		-		48.9	0.8	-		-		49.2	0.6	-		-		49.6	0.8
1964	-		-		49.4	-0.4	-		-		49.5	0.2	-		-		49.8	0.6	-		-		49.8	0.0
1965	-		-		49.7	-0.2	-		-		49.8	0.2	-		-		50.6	1.6	-		-		50.7	0.2
1966	-		-		50.9	0.4	-		-		51.6	1.4	-		-		52.2	1.2	-		-		52.4	0.4
1967	-		-		53.1	1.3	-		-		53.2	0.2	-		-		53.6	0.8	-		-		54.5	1.7
1968	-		-		55.7	2.2	-		-		55.8	0.2	-		-		57.6	3.2	-		-		57.8	0.3
1969	-		-		58.6	1.4	-		-		59.0	0.7	-		-		59.9	1.5	-		-		60.2	0.5
1970	-		-		60.5	0.5	-		-		61.2	1.2	-		-		62.8	2.6	-		-		62.4	-0.6
1971	-		-		63.0	1.0	-		-		63.1	0.2	-		-		64.6	2.4	-		-		64.5	-0.2
1972	-		-		64.2	-0.5	-		-		63.8	-0.6	-		-		64.6	1.3	-		-		64.4	-0.3
1973	-		-		64.4	0.0	-		-		64.5	0.2	-		-		67.8	5.1	-		-		67.3	-0.7
1974	-		-		67.3	0.0	-		-		68.8	2.2	-		-		71.1	3.3	-		-		71.4	0.4
1975	-		-		71.5	0.1	-		-		71.9	0.6	-		-		72.7	1.1	-		-		73.4	1.0
1976	-		-		74.9	2.0	-		-		75.2	0.4	-		-		76.8	2.1	-		-		77.2	0.5
1977	-		-		80.3	4.0	-		-		80.5	0.2	-		-		81.5	1.2	-		-		82.4	1.1
1978	-		-		81.1	-1.6	-		79.3	-2.2	-		79.4	0.1	-		82.1	3.4	-		82.0	-0.1	-	
1979	80.3	-2.1	-		85.3	6.2	-		84.7	-0.7	-		81.2	-4.1	-		86.6	6.7	-		87.1	0.6	-	
1980	85.6	-1.7	-		90.3	5.5	-		90.7	0.4	-		89.3	-1.5	-		93.1	4.3	-		92.3	-0.9	-	
1981	92.1	-0.2	-		97.0	5.3	-		95.2	-1.9	-		95.2	0.0	-		96.7	1.6	-		95.3	-1.4	-	
1982	93.1	-2.3	-		98.9	6.2	-		96.9	-2.0	-		97.5	0.6	-		99.4	1.9	-		98.0	-1.4	-	
1983	97.5	-0.5	-		102.8	5.4	-		101.4	-1.4	-		101.3	-0.1	-		102.5	1.2	-		100.6	-1.9	-	
1984	97.4	-3.2	-		101.1	3.8	-		98.6	-2.5	-		100.5	1.9	-		106.0	5.5	-		104.9	-1.0	-	
1985	99.9	-4.8	-		106.0	6.1	-		106.9	0.8	-		103.3	-3.4	-		105.2	1.8	-		104.1	-1.0	-	
1986	99.0	-4.9	-		102.6	3.6	-		102.1	-0.5	-		99.0	-3.0	-		105.1	6.2	-		105.9	0.8	-	
1987	101.9	-3.8	-		107.2	5.2	-		107.4	0.2	-		100.7	-6.2	-		114.5	13.7	-		112.9	-1.4	-	
1988	109.6	-2.9	-		115.3	5.2	-		110.8	-3.9	-		107.1	-3.3	-		116.4	8.7	-		116.1	-0.3	-	
1989	111.8	-3.7	-		119.4	6.8	-		120.7	1.1	-		119.0	-1.4	-		119.2	0.2	-		119.4	0.2	-	
1990	119.1	-0.3	-		129.6	8.8	-		119.2	-8.0	-		116.8	-2.0	-		121.4	3.9	-		121.0	-0.3	-	
1991	119.6	-1.2	-		125.0	4.5	-		121.4	-2.9	-		119.0	-2.0	-		126.3	6.1	-		125.2	-0.9	-	
1992	121.8	-2.7	-		123.1	1.1	-		119.9	-2.6	-		118.2	-1.4	-		125.3	6.0	-		124.7	-0.5	-	
1993	121.0	-3.0	-		123.4	2.0	-		126.3	2.4	-		122.5	-3.0	-		120.9	-1.3	-		124.3	2.8	-	

Source: U.S. Department of Labor, Bureau of Labor Statistics, Division of Consumer Prices and Price Indexes. - indicates no data collected for period.

St. Louis, MO-IL
Consumer Price Index - All Urban Consumers
Base 1982-1984 = 100
Transportation

For 1947-1993. Columns headed % show percentile change in the index from the previous period for which an index is available.

Year	Jan Index	%	Feb Index	%	Mar Index	%	Apr Index	%	May Index	%	Jun Index	%	Jul Index	%	Aug Index	%	Sep Index	%	Oct Index	%	Nov Index	%	Dec Index	%
1947	17.7	-	17.7	0.0	17.9	1.1	18.0	0.6	18.0	0.0	18.0	0.0	-	-	-	-	18.4	2.2	-	-	-	-	18.9	2.7
1948	-	-	-	-	19.2	1.6	-	-	-	-	19.6	2.1	-	-	-	-	20.4	4.1	-	-	-	-	20.4	0.0
1949	-	-	-	-	20.7	1.5	-	-	-	-	20.7	0.0	-	-	-	-	20.7	0.0	-	-	-	-	21.5	3.9
1950	-	-	-	-	21.3	-0.9	-	-	-	-	21.1	-0.9	-	-	-	-	21.4	1.4	-	-	-	-	21.6	0.9
1951	-	-	-	-	23.5	8.8	-	-	-	-	23.4	-0.4	-	-	-	-	23.7	1.3	-	-	-	-	24.3	2.5
1952	-	-	-	-	25.6	5.3	-	-	-	-	25.6	0.0	-	-	-	-	26.3	2.7	-	-	-	-	26.1	-0.8
1953	-	-	-	-	26.9	3.1	-	-	-	-	26.8	-0.4	-	-	-	-	26.8	0.0	-	-	-	-	26.7	-0.4
1954	-	-	-	-	26.7	0.0	-	-	-	-	26.7	0.0	-	-	-	-	24.5	-8.2	-	-	-	-	25.6	4.5
1955	-	-	-	-	26.4	3.1	-	-	-	-	26.4	0.0	-	-	-	-	25.7	-2.7	-	-	-	-	26.2	1.9
1956	-	-	-	-	25.9	-1.1	-	-	-	-	26.2	1.2	-	-	-	-	26.3	0.4	-	-	-	-	27.3	3.8
1957	-	-	-	-	27.6	1.1	-	-	-	-	28.0	1.4	-	-	-	-	28.3	1.1	-	-	-	-	28.6	1.1
1958	-	-	-	-	28.9	1.0	-	-	-	-	29.1	0.7	-	-	-	-	30.1	3.4	-	-	-	-	31.3	4.0
1959	-	-	-	-	31.7	1.3	-	-	-	-	31.7	0.0	-	-	-	-	31.3	-1.3	-	-	-	-	32.0	2.2
1960	-	-	-	-	31.6	-1.2	-	-	-	-	31.6	0.0	-	-	-	-	31.2	-1.3	-	-	-	-	30.6	-1.9
1961	-	-	-	-	32.0	4.6	-	-	-	-	32.2	0.6	-	-	-	-	32.0	-0.6	-	-	-	-	32.5	1.6
1962	-	-	-	-	32.1	-1.2	-	-	-	-	31.8	-0.9	-	-	-	-	32.8	3.1	-	-	-	-	33.2	1.2
1963	-	-	-	-	32.7	-1.5	-	-	-	-	31.3	-4.3	-	-	-	-	32.2	2.9	-	-	-	-	32.8	1.9
1964	-	-	-	-	32.7	-0.3	-	-	-	-	32.1	-1.8	-	-	-	-	32.9	2.5	-	-	-	-	33.3	1.2
1965	-	-	-	-	33.0	-0.9	-	-	-	-	32.9	-0.3	-	-	-	-	32.7	-0.6	-	-	-	-	33.5	2.4
1966	-	-	-	-	33.5	0.0	-	-	-	-	34.4	2.7	-	-	-	-	34.4	0.0	-	-	-	-	34.4	0.0
1967	-	-	-	-	34.8	1.2	-	-	-	-	35.2	1.1	-	-	-	-	35.7	1.4	-	-	-	-	36.0	0.8
1968	-	-	-	-	36.0	0.0	-	-	-	-	36.1	0.0	-	-	-	-	36.1	0.0	-	-	-	-	35.9	-0.6
1969	-	-	-	-	36.9	2.8	-	-	-	-	37.3	1.1	-	-	-	-	37.4	0.3	-	-	-	-	37.7	0.8
1970	-	-	-	-	37.4	-0.8	-	-	-	-	39.4	5.3	-	-	-	-	40.3	2.3	-	-	-	-	42.2	4.7
1971	-	-	-	-	41.2	-2.4	-	-	-	-	42.7	3.6	-	-	-	-	42.0	-1.6	-	-	-	-	42.6	1.4
1972	-	-	-	-	41.2	-3.3	-	-	-	-	42.3	2.7	-	-	-	-	42.9	1.4	-	-	-	-	43.3	0.9
1973	-	-	-	-	43.5	0.5	-	-	-	-	44.3	1.8	-	-	-	-	43.9	-0.9	-	-	-	-	43.6	-0.7
1974	-	-	-	-	45.5	4.4	-	-	-	-	47.9	5.3	-	-	-	-	49.0	2.3	-	-	-	-	49.2	0.4
1975	-	-	-	-	49.5	0.6	-	-	-	-	51.3	3.6	-	-	-	-	53.1	3.5	-	-	-	-	53.5	0.8
1976	-	-	-	-	54.0	0.9	-	-	-	-	56.5	4.6	-	-	-	-	57.4	1.6	-	-	-	-	58.3	1.6
1977	-	-	-	-	58.7	0.7	-	-	-	-	60.3	2.7	-	-	-	-	59.8	-0.8	-	-	-	-	60.0	0.3
1978	-	-	-	-	59.9	-0.2	-	-	63.4	5.8	-	-	64.4	1.6	-	-	65.2	1.2	-	-	66.5	2.0	-	-
1979	67.4	1.4	-	-	68.9	2.2	-	-	72.0	4.5	-	-	76.3	6.0	-	-	76.7	0.5	-	-	78.4	2.2	-	-
1980	80.9	3.2	-	-	83.3	3.0	-	-	84.8	1.8	-	-	85.5	0.8	-	-	86.0	0.6	-	-	88.1	2.4	-	-
1981	90.3	2.5	-	-	92.5	2.4	-	-	94.1	1.7	-	-	94.8	0.7	-	-	95.4	0.6	-	-	97.6	2.3	-	-
1982	96.9	-0.7	-	-	94.6	-2.4	-	-	97.1	2.6	-	-	100.0	3.0	-	-	99.2	-0.8	-	-	99.0	-0.2	-	-
1983	97.6	-1.4	-	-	95.8	-1.8	-	-	99.0	3.3	-	-	100.3	1.3	-	-	100.9	0.6	-	-	101.2	0.3	-	-
1984	100.5	-0.7	-	-	101.3	0.8	-	-	103.0	1.7	-	-	103.4	0.4	-	-	103.9	0.5	-	-	104.6	0.7	-	-
1985	103.9	-0.7	-	-	103.8	-0.1	-	-	106.0	2.1	-	-	105.8	-0.2	-	-	105.4	-0.4	-	-	106.5	1.0	-	-
1986	106.1	-0.4	-	-	100.7	-5.1	-	-	99.7	-1.0	-	-	99.3	-0.4	-	-	97.7	-1.6	-	-	99.8	2.1	-	-
1987	101.4	1.6	-	-	102.1	0.7	-	-	103.2	1.1	-	-	104.7	1.5	-	-	105.7	1.0	-	-	105.7	0.0	-	-
1988	105.2	-0.5	-	-	104.0	-1.1	-	-	105.8	1.7	-	-	106.5	0.7	-	-	106.7	0.2	-	-	107.1	0.4	-	-
1989	107.2	0.1	-	-	107.4	0.2	-	-	113.3	5.5	-	-	112.0	-1.1	-	-	109.2	-2.5	-	-	111.6	2.2	-	-
1990	115.4	3.4	-	-	114.0	-1.2	-	-	115.1	1.0	-	-	114.8	-0.3	-	-	120.9	5.3	-	-	122.6	1.4	-	-
1991	121.6	-0.8	-	-	115.8	-4.8	-	-	118.2	2.1	-	-	117.2	-0.8	-	-	118.9	1.5	-	-	120.3	1.2	-	-

[Continued]

St. Louis, MO-IL
Consumer Price Index - All Urban Consumers
Base 1982-1984 = 100
Transportation
[Continued]

For 1947-1993. Columns headed % show percentile change in the index from the previous period for which an index is available.

Year	Jan Index	%	Feb Index	%	Mar Index	%	Apr Index	%	May Index	%	Jun Index	%	Jul Index	%	Aug Index	%	Sep Index	%	Oct Index	%	Nov Index	%	Dec Index	%
1992	118.8	-1.2	-	-	119.0	0.2	-	-	122.7	3.1	-	-	122.6	-0.1	-	-	122.7	0.1	-	-	124.8	1.7	-	-
1993	122.8	-1.6	-	-	123.5	0.6	-	-	126.0	2.0	-	-	125.8	-0.2	-	-	125.1	-0.6	-	-	127.1	1.6	-	-

Source: U.S. Department of Labor, Bureau of Labor Statistics, Division of Consumer Prices and Price Indexes. - indicates no data collected for period.

St. Louis, MO-IL
Consumer Price Index - Urban Wage Earners
Base 1982-1984 = 100
Transportation

For 1947-1993. Columns headed % show percentile change in the index from the previous period for which an index is available.

Year	Jan Index	%	Feb Index	%	Mar Index	%	Apr Index	%	May Index	%	Jun Index	%	Jul Index	%	Aug Index	%	Sep Index	%	Oct Index	%	Nov Index	%	Dec Index	%
1947	18.0	-	18.0	0.0	18.2	1.1	18.3	0.5	18.3	0.0	18.2	-0.5	-	-	-	-	18.7	2.7	-	-	-	-	19.2	2.7
1948	-	-	-	-	19.5	1.6	-	-	-	-	19.9	2.1	-	-	-	-	20.7	4.0	-	-	-	-	20.7	0.0
1949	-	-	-	-	21.1	1.9	-	-	-	-	21.1	0.0	-	-	-	-	21.0	-0.5	-	-	-	-	21.9	4.3
1950	-	-	-	-	21.7	-0.9	-	-	-	-	21.4	-1.4	-	-	-	-	21.8	1.9	-	-	-	-	22.0	0.9
1951	-	-	-	-	23.8	8.2	-	-	-	-	23.8	0.0	-	-	-	-	24.1	1.3	-	-	-	-	24.7	2.5
1952	-	-	-	-	26.0	5.3	-	-	-	-	26.1	0.4	-	-	-	-	26.7	2.3	-	-	-	-	26.5	-0.7
1953	-	-	-	-	27.3	3.0	-	-	-	-	27.3	0.0	-	-	-	-	27.3	0.0	-	-	-	-	27.2	-0.4
1954	-	-	-	-	27.1	-0.4	-	-	-	-	27.1	0.0	-	-	-	-	24.9	-8.1	-	-	-	-	26.0	4.4
1955	-	-	-	-	26.9	3.5	-	-	-	-	26.9	0.0	-	-	-	-	26.1	-3.0	-	-	-	-	26.6	1.9
1956	-	-	-	-	26.3	-1.1	-	-	-	-	26.6	1.1	-	-	-	-	26.7	0.4	-	-	-	-	27.7	3.7
1957	-	-	-	-	28.0	1.1	-	-	-	-	28.5	1.8	-	-	-	-	28.8	1.1	-	-	-	-	29.1	1.0
1958	-	-	-	-	29.4	1.0	-	-	-	-	29.5	0.3	-	-	-	-	30.5	3.4	-	-	-	-	31.8	4.3
1959	-	-	-	-	32.3	1.6	-	-	-	-	32.2	-0.3	-	-	-	-	31.8	-1.2	-	-	-	-	32.5	2.2
1960	-	-	-	-	32.1	-1.2	-	-	-	-	32.1	0.0	-	-	-	-	31.7	-1.2	-	-	-	-	31.1	-1.9
1961	-	-	-	-	32.5	4.5	-	-	-	-	32.7	0.6	-	-	-	-	32.5	-0.6	-	-	-	-	33.0	1.5
1962	-	-	-	-	32.6	-1.2	-	-	-	-	32.3	-0.9	-	-	-	-	33.4	3.4	-	-	-	-	33.7	0.9
1963	-	-	-	-	33.2	-1.5	-	-	-	-	31.8	-4.2	-	-	-	-	32.7	2.8	-	-	-	-	33.3	1.8
1964	-	-	-	-	33.2	-0.3	-	-	-	-	32.6	-1.8	-	-	-	-	33.5	2.8	-	-	-	-	33.9	1.2
1965	-	-	-	-	33.5	-1.2	-	-	-	-	33.4	-0.3	-	-	-	-	33.2	-0.6	-	-	-	-	34.1	2.7
1966	-	-	-	-	34.0	-0.3	-	-	-	-	34.9	2.6	-	-	-	-	35.0	0.3	-	-	-	-	35.0	0.0
1967	-	-	-	-	35.3	0.9	-	-	-	-	35.8	1.4	-	-	-	-	36.2	1.1	-	-	-	-	36.6	1.1
1968	-	-	-	-	36.6	0.0	-	-	-	-	36.6	0.0	-	-	-	-	36.7	0.3	-	-	-	-	36.5	-0.5
1969	-	-	-	-	37.5	2.7	-	-	-	-	37.9	1.1	-	-	-	-	38.0	0.3	-	-	-	-	38.3	0.8
1970	-	-	-	-	38.0	-0.8	-	-	-	-	40.0	5.3	-	-	-	-	40.9	2.3	-	-	-	-	42.9	4.9
1971	-	-	-	-	41.8	-2.6	-	-	-	-	43.4	3.8	-	-	-	-	42.7	-1.6	-	-	-	-	43.3	1.4
1972	-	-	-	-	41.9	-3.2	-	-	-	-	43.0	2.6	-	-	-	-	43.6	1.4	-	-	-	-	44.0	0.9
1973	-	-	-	-	44.2	0.5	-	-	-	-	45.0	1.8	-	-	-	-	44.6	-0.9	-	-	-	-	44.3	-0.7
1974	-	-	-	-	46.3	4.5	-	-	-	-	48.7	5.2	-	-	-	-	49.8	2.3	-	-	-	-	50.0	0.4
1975	-	-	-	-	50.3	0.6	-	-	-	-	52.1	3.6	-	-	-	-	54.0	3.6	-	-	-	-	54.4	0.7
1976	-	-	-	-	54.9	0.9	-	-	-	-	57.4	4.6	-	-	-	-	58.3	1.6	-	-	-	-	59.3	1.7
1977	-	-	-	-	59.6	0.5	-	-	-	-	61.2	2.7	-	-	-	-	60.8	-0.7	-	-	-	-	61.0	0.3
1978	-	-	-	-	60.9	-0.2	-	-	62.2	2.1	-	-	63.4	1.9	-	-	64.3	1.4	-	-	65.3	1.6	-	-
1979	66.4	1.7	-	-	67.8	2.1	-	-	71.3	5.2	-	-	76.3	7.0	-	-	76.5	0.3	-	-	78.1	2.1	-	-
1980	81.2	4.0	-	-	83.5	2.8	-	-	85.4	2.3	-	-	86.3	1.1	-	-	86.6	0.3	-	-	88.4	2.1	-	-
1981	90.6	2.5	-	-	92.8	2.4	-	-	94.3	1.6	-	-	94.9	0.6	-	-	95.5	0.6	-	-	97.7	2.3	-	-
1982	96.9	-0.8	-	-	94.3	-2.7	-	-	96.9	2.8	-	-	100.1	3.3	-	-	99.2	-0.9	-	-	99.0	-0.2	-	-
1983	97.3	-1.7	-	-	95.3	-2.1	-	-	98.7	3.6	-	-	100.2	1.5	-	-	101.0	0.8	-	-	101.3	0.3	-	-
1984	100.5	-0.8	-	-	101.5	1.0	-	-	103.4	1.9	-	-	103.8	0.4	-	-	104.2	0.4	-	-	104.9	0.7	-	-
1985	103.8	-1.0	-	-	103.7	-0.1	-	-	106.1	2.3	-	-	105.9	-0.2	-	-	105.3	-0.6	-	-	106.3	0.9	-	-
1986	105.8	-0.5	-	-	99.9	-5.6	-	-	98.6	-1.3	-	-	98.2	-0.4	-	-	96.4	-1.8	-	-	98.3	2.0	-	-
1987	99.6	1.3	-	-	100.7	1.1	-	-	102.3	1.6	-	-	104.4	2.1	-	-	105.5	1.1	-	-	105.4	-0.1	-	-
1988	105.0	-0.4	-	-	103.9	-1.0	-	-	105.6	1.6	-	-	106.2	0.6	-	-	106.6	0.4	-	-	106.8	0.2	-	-
1989	106.9	0.1	-	-	107.4	0.5	-	-	112.9	5.1	-	-	111.7	-1.1	-	-	109.2	-2.2	-	-	111.0	1.6	-	-
1990	114.0	2.7	-	-	112.0	-1.8	-	-	113.1	1.0	-	-	113.1	0.0	-	-	118.9	5.1	-	-	120.7	1.5	-	-
1991	119.4	-1.1	-	-	114.4	-4.2	-	-	116.8	2.1	-	-	116.1	-0.6	-	-	117.9	1.6	-	-	119.2	1.1	-	-

[Continued]

St. Louis, MO-IL
Consumer Price Index - Urban Wage Earners
Base 1982-1984 = 100
Transportation
[Continued]

For 1947-1993. Columns headed % show percentile change in the index from the previous period for which an index is available.

Year	Jan		Feb		Mar		Apr		May		Jun		Jul		Aug		Sep		Oct		Nov		Dec	
	Index	%	Index	%	Index	%	Index	%	Index	%	Index	%	Index	%	Index	%	Index	%	Index	%	Index	%	Index	%
1992	117.5	-1.4	-	-	117.2	-0.3	-	-	121.3	3.5	-	-	122.1	0.7	-	-	122.4	0.2	-	-	124.2	1.5	-	-
1993	122.2	-1.6	-	-	122.3	0.1	-	-	125.2	2.4	-	-	125.5	0.2	-	-	125.0	-0.4	-	-	126.9	1.5	-	-

Source: U.S. Department of Labor, Bureau of Labor Statistics, Division of Consumer Prices and Price Indexes. - indicates no data collected for period.

St. Louis, MO-IL
Consumer Price Index - All Urban Consumers
Base 1982-1984 = 100
Medical Care

For 1947-1993. Columns headed % show percentile change in the index from the previous period for which an index is available.

Year	Jan Index	%	Feb Index	%	Mar Index	%	Apr Index	%	May Index	%	Jun Index	%	Jul Index	%	Aug Index	%	Sep Index	%	Oct Index	%	Nov Index	%	Dec Index	%
1947	12.9	-	12.9	0.0	13.0	0.8	13.0	0.0	13.0	0.0	13.0	0.0	-	-	-	-	13.4	3.1	-	-	-	-	13.7	2.2
1948	-	-	-	-	13.8	0.7	-	-	-	-	13.8	0.0	-	-	-	-	14.3	3.6	-	-	-	-	14.4	0.7
1949	-	-	-	-	14.5	0.7	-	-	-	-	14.4	-0.7	-	-	-	-	14.4	0.0	-	-	-	-	14.5	0.7
1950	-	-	-	-	14.5	0.0	-	-	-	-	14.5	0.0	-	-	-	-	14.6	0.7	-	-	-	-	14.7	0.7
1951	-	-	-	-	15.0	2.0	-	-	-	-	15.0	0.0	-	-	-	-	15.1	0.7	-	-	-	-	17.7	17.2
1952	-	-	-	-	17.8	0.6	-	-	-	-	18.1	1.7	-	-	-	-	18.1	0.0	-	-	-	-	18.3	1.1
1953	-	-	-	-	18.4	0.5	-	-	-	-	18.5	0.5	-	-	-	-	18.5	0.0	-	-	-	-	18.6	0.5
1954	-	-	-	-	18.7	0.5	-	-	-	-	18.7	0.0	-	-	-	-	18.9	1.1	-	-	-	-	19.4	2.6
1955	-	-	-	-	19.5	0.5	-	-	-	-	19.5	0.0	-	-	-	-	19.5	0.0	-	-	-	-	19.5	0.0
1956	-	-	-	-	19.5	0.0	-	-	-	-	19.5	0.0	-	-	-	-	19.9	2.1	-	-	-	-	21.2	6.5
1957	-	-	-	-	21.4	0.9	-	-	-	-	21.4	0.0	-	-	-	-	21.5	0.5	-	-	-	-	21.7	0.9
1958	-	-	-	-	22.0	1.4	-	-	-	-	22.0	0.0	-	-	-	-	22.1	0.5	-	-	-	-	23.1	4.5
1959	-	-	-	-	23.2	0.4	-	-	-	-	23.3	0.4	-	-	-	-	23.5	0.9	-	-	-	-	23.7	0.9
1960	-	-	-	-	23.7	0.0	-	-	-	-	23.6	-0.4	-	-	-	-	23.6	0.0	-	-	-	-	23.8	0.8
1961	-	-	-	-	24.0	0.8	-	-	-	-	24.0	0.0	-	-	-	-	24.2	0.8	-	-	-	-	25.3	4.5
1962	-	-	-	-	25.4	0.4	-	-	-	-	25.5	0.4	-	-	-	-	25.6	0.4	-	-	-	-	25.6	0.0
1963	-	-	-	-	25.7	0.4	-	-	-	-	25.7	0.0	-	-	-	-	25.8	0.4	-	-	-	-	25.8	0.0
1964	-	-	-	-	25.8	0.0	-	-	-	-	25.7	-0.4	-	-	-	-	25.9	0.8	-	-	-	-	26.0	0.4
1965	-	-	-	-	26.5	1.9	-	-	-	-	26.9	1.5	-	-	-	-	27.0	0.4	-	-	-	-	27.1	0.4
1966	-	-	-	-	27.6	1.8	-	-	-	-	28.2	2.2	-	-	-	-	28.7	1.8	-	-	-	-	29.1	1.4
1967	-	-	-	-	29.5	1.4	-	-	-	-	29.5	0.0	-	-	-	-	30.0	1.7	-	-	-	-	30.3	1.0
1968	-	-	-	-	30.9	2.0	-	-	-	-	30.9	0.0	-	-	-	-	31.4	1.6	-	-	-	-	31.7	1.0
1969	-	-	-	-	32.6	2.8	-	-	-	-	33.1	1.5	-	-	-	-	33.4	0.9	-	-	-	-	33.5	0.3
1970	-	-	-	-	34.7	3.6	-	-	-	-	35.3	1.7	-	-	-	-	35.6	0.8	-	-	-	-	35.7	0.3
1971	-	-	-	-	36.4	2.0	-	-	-	-	36.8	1.1	-	-	-	-	37.1	0.8	-	-	-	-	36.8	-0.8
1972	-	-	-	-	37.2	1.1	-	-	-	-	37.4	0.5	-	-	-	-	37.5	0.3	-	-	-	-	37.6	0.3
1973	-	-	-	-	38.2	1.6	-	-	-	-	38.3	0.3	-	-	-	-	38.8	1.3	-	-	-	-	39.7	2.3
1974	-	-	-	-	40.7	2.5	-	-	-	-	41.2	1.2	-	-	-	-	42.7	3.6	-	-	-	-	44.1	3.3
1975	-	-	-	-	45.2	2.5	-	-	-	-	46.2	2.2	-	-	-	-	47.4	2.6	-	-	-	-	47.5	0.2
1976	-	-	-	-	49.1	3.4	-	-	-	-	50.1	2.0	-	-	-	-	50.7	1.2	-	-	-	-	52.4	3.4
1977	-	-	-	-	54.4	3.8	-	-	-	-	55.2	1.5	-	-	-	-	56.5	2.4	-	-	-	-	57.2	1.2
1978	-	-	-	-	58.9	3.0	-	-	59.1	0.3	-	-	60.1	1.7	-	-	60.3	0.3	-	-	60.5	0.3	-	-
1979	62.4	3.1	-	-	62.5	0.2	-	-	63.5	1.6	-	-	65.6	3.3	-	-	65.7	0.2	-	-	66.8	1.7	-	-
1980	70.7	5.8	-	-	71.2	0.7	-	-	72.1	1.3	-	-	73.4	1.8	-	-	73.4	0.0	-	-	75.1	2.3	-	-
1981	77.7	3.5	-	-	79.6	2.4	-	-	81.2	2.0	-	-	81.6	0.5	-	-	83.0	1.7	-	-	84.6	1.9	-	-
1982	90.2	6.6	-	-	91.5	1.4	-	-	92.1	0.7	-	-	93.7	1.7	-	-	94.5	0.9	-	-	95.9	1.5	-	-
1983	99.9	4.2	-	-	100.0	0.1	-	-	100.0	0.0	-	-	101.2	1.2	-	-	101.1	-0.1	-	-	101.7	0.6	-	-
1984	104.6	2.9	-	-	105.1	0.5	-	-	105.3	0.2	-	-	105.6	0.3	-	-	106.2	0.6	-	-	106.8	0.6	-	-
1985	108.6	1.7	-	-	109.5	0.8	-	-	110.3	0.7	-	-	111.3	0.9	-	-	111.5	0.2	-	-	112.6	1.0	-	-
1986	117.4	4.3	-	-	118.4	0.9	-	-	119.2	0.7	-	-	121.4	1.8	-	-	121.3	-0.1	-	-	122.1	0.7	-	-
1987	124.5	2.0	-	-	126.5	1.6	-	-	127.0	0.4	-	-	128.6	1.3	-	-	129.3	0.5	-	-	129.8	0.4	-	-
1988	132.4	2.0	-	-	133.4	0.8	-	-	134.0	0.4	-	-	136.5	1.9	-	-	136.6	0.1	-	-	138.8	1.6	-	-
1989	140.5	1.2	-	-	142.3	1.3	-	-	143.7	1.0	-	-	146.9	2.2	-	-	148.4	1.0	-	-	148.9	0.3	-	-
1990	152.4	2.4	-	-	156.5	2.7	-	-	158.7	1.4	-	-	159.6	0.6	-	-	160.5	0.6	-	-	162.3	1.1	-	-
1991	168.0	3.5	-	-	169.5	0.9	-	-	170.0	0.3	-	-	172.9	1.7	-	-	173.6	0.4	-	-	174.1	0.3	-	-

[Continued]

St. Louis, MO-IL
Consumer Price Index - All Urban Consumers
Base 1982-1984 = 100
Medical Care

[Continued]

For 1947-1993. Columns headed % show percentile change in the index from the previous period for which an index is available.

Year	Jan Index	%	Feb Index	%	Mar Index	%	Apr Index	%	May Index	%	Jun Index	%	Jul Index	%	Aug Index	%	Sep Index	%	Oct Index	%	Nov Index	%	Dec Index	%
1992	177.1	1.7	-	-	178.8	1.0	-	-	179.4	0.3	-	-	182.4	1.7	-	-	183.1	0.4	-	-	182.9	-0.1	-	-
1993	186.3	1.9	-	-	188.7	1.3	-	-	190.2	0.8	-	-	192.0	0.9	-	-	194.3	1.2	-	-	195.0	0.4	-	-

Source: U.S. Department of Labor, Bureau of Labor Statistics, Division of Consumer Prices and Price Indexes. - indicates no data collected for period.

St. Louis, MO-IL
Consumer Price Index - Urban Wage Earners
Base 1982-1984 = 100
Medical Care

For 1947-1993. Columns headed % show percentile change in the index from the previous period for which an index is available.

Year	Jan Index	%	Feb Index	%	Mar Index	%	Apr Index	%	May Index	%	Jun Index	%	Jul Index	%	Aug Index	%	Sep Index	%	Oct Index	%	Nov Index	%	Dec Index	%
1947	12.8	-	12.8	0.0	12.9	0.8	12.9	0.0	12.9	0.0	12.9	0.0	-	-	-	-	13.2	2.3	-	-	-	-	13.6	3.0
1948	-	-	-	-	13.7	0.7	-	-	-	-	13.7	0.0	-	-	-	-	14.2	3.6	-	-	-	-	14.2	0.0
1949	-	-	-	-	14.3	0.7	-	-	-	-	14.3	0.0	-	-	-	-	14.3	0.0	-	-	-	-	14.3	0.0
1950	-	-	-	-	14.4	0.7	-	-	-	-	14.4	0.0	-	-	-	-	14.4	0.0	-	-	-	-	14.5	0.7
1951	-	-	-	-	14.9	2.8	-	-	-	-	14.9	0.0	-	-	-	-	14.9	0.0	-	-	-	-	17.6	18.1
1952	-	-	-	-	17.7	0.6	-	-	-	-	17.9	1.1	-	-	-	-	17.9	0.0	-	-	-	-	18.2	1.7
1953	-	-	-	-	18.2	0.0	-	-	-	-	18.3	0.5	-	-	-	-	18.3	0.0	-	-	-	-	18.4	0.5
1954	-	-	-	-	18.5	0.5	-	-	-	-	18.6	0.5	-	-	-	-	18.7	0.5	-	-	-	-	19.2	2.7
1955	-	-	-	-	19.3	0.5	-	-	-	-	19.3	0.0	-	-	-	-	19.3	0.0	-	-	-	-	19.3	0.0
1956	-	-	-	-	19.3	0.0	-	-	-	-	19.4	0.5	-	-	-	-	19.7	1.5	-	-	-	-	21.0	6.6
1957	-	-	-	-	21.3	1.4	-	-	-	-	21.3	0.0	-	-	-	-	21.3	0.0	-	-	-	-	21.5	0.9
1958	-	-	-	-	21.8	1.4	-	-	-	-	21.8	0.0	-	-	-	-	21.9	0.5	-	-	-	-	22.9	4.6
1959	-	-	-	-	23.0	0.4	-	-	-	-	23.0	0.0	-	-	-	-	23.3	1.3	-	-	-	-	23.5	0.9
1960	-	-	-	-	23.5	0.0	-	-	-	-	23.4	-0.4	-	-	-	-	23.4	0.0	-	-	-	-	23.6	0.9
1961	-	-	-	-	23.8	0.8	-	-	-	-	23.8	0.0	-	-	-	-	24.0	0.8	-	-	-	-	25.1	4.6
1962	-	-	-	-	25.1	0.0	-	-	-	-	25.3	0.8	-	-	-	-	25.3	0.0	-	-	-	-	25.3	0.0
1963	-	-	-	-	25.5	0.8	-	-	-	-	25.5	0.0	-	-	-	-	25.5	0.0	-	-	-	-	25.6	0.4
1964	-	-	-	-	25.6	0.0	-	-	-	-	25.5	-0.4	-	-	-	-	25.7	0.8	-	-	-	-	25.8	0.4
1965	-	-	-	-	26.3	1.9	-	-	-	-	26.7	1.5	-	-	-	-	26.7	0.0	-	-	-	-	26.9	0.7
1966	-	-	-	-	27.3	1.5	-	-	-	-	28.0	2.6	-	-	-	-	28.4	1.4	-	-	-	-	28.8	1.4
1967	-	-	-	-	29.2	1.4	-	-	-	-	29.2	0.0	-	-	-	-	29.7	1.7	-	-	-	-	30.0	1.0
1968	-	-	-	-	30.6	2.0	-	-	-	-	30.7	0.3	-	-	-	-	31.1	1.3	-	-	-	-	31.5	1.3
1969	-	-	-	-	32.3	2.5	-	-	-	-	32.8	1.5	-	-	-	-	33.1	0.9	-	-	-	-	33.2	0.3
1970	-	-	-	-	34.4	3.6	-	-	-	-	34.9	1.5	-	-	-	-	35.3	1.1	-	-	-	-	35.4	0.3
1971	-	-	-	-	36.0	1.7	-	-	-	-	36.4	1.1	-	-	-	-	36.8	1.1	-	-	-	-	36.5	-0.8
1972	-	-	-	-	36.8	0.8	-	-	-	-	37.1	0.8	-	-	-	-	37.1	0.0	-	-	-	-	37.3	0.5
1973	-	-	-	-	37.9	1.6	-	-	-	-	38.0	0.3	-	-	-	-	38.4	1.1	-	-	-	-	39.3	2.3
1974	-	-	-	-	40.4	2.8	-	-	-	-	40.8	1.0	-	-	-	-	42.3	3.7	-	-	-	-	43.7	3.3
1975	-	-	-	-	44.8	2.5	-	-	-	-	45.8	2.2	-	-	-	-	47.0	2.6	-	-	-	-	47.1	0.2
1976	-	-	-	-	48.6	3.2	-	-	-	-	49.6	2.1	-	-	-	-	50.2	1.2	-	-	-	-	51.9	3.4
1977	-	-	-	-	53.9	3.9	-	-	-	-	54.7	1.5	-	-	-	-	56.0	2.4	-	-	-	-	56.7	1.3
1978	-	-	-	-	58.4	3.0	-	-	59.0	1.0	-	-	59.6	1.0	-	-	60.2	1.0	-	-	61.3	1.8	-	-
1979	62.8	2.4	-	-	63.2	0.6	-	-	63.7	0.8	-	-	65.2	2.4	-	-	65.9	1.1	-	-	67.8	2.9	-	-
1980	70.9	4.6	-	-	72.3	2.0	-	-	72.6	0.4	-	-	73.7	1.5	-	-	74.0	0.4	-	-	75.8	2.4	-	-
1981	78.1	3.0	-	-	80.7	3.3	-	-	81.4	0.9	-	-	81.8	0.5	-	-	83.3	1.8	-	-	85.0	2.0	-	-
1982	90.4	6.4	-	-	91.6	1.3	-	-	92.1	0.5	-	-	93.7	1.7	-	-	94.4	0.7	-	-	95.8	1.5	-	-
1983	99.5	3.9	-	-	99.7	0.2	-	-	99.8	0.1	-	-	101.2	1.4	-	-	101.2	0.0	-	-	101.8	0.6	-	-
1984	104.6	2.8	-	-	105.1	0.5	-	-	105.3	0.2	-	-	105.7	0.4	-	-	106.4	0.7	-	-	107.0	0.6	-	-
1985	108.8	1.7	-	-	109.6	0.7	-	-	110.3	0.6	-	-	111.3	0.9	-	-	111.5	0.2	-	-	112.5	0.9	-	-
1986	117.2	4.2	-	-	118.1	0.8	-	-	118.9	0.7	-	-	121.0	1.8	-	-	120.7	-0.2	-	-	121.5	0.7	-	-
1987	123.9	2.0	-	-	126.0	1.7	-	-	126.7	0.6	-	-	128.3	1.3	-	-	129.1	0.6	-	-	129.3	0.2	-	-
1988	131.9	2.0	-	-	132.9	0.8	-	-	133.6	0.5	-	-	136.1	1.9	-	-	136.3	0.1	-	-	138.5	1.6	-	-
1989	140.4	1.4	-	-	142.2	1.3	-	-	143.6	1.0	-	-	147.1	2.4	-	-	148.6	1.0	-	-	148.8	0.1	-	-
1990	152.4	2.4	-	-	156.0	2.4	-	-	158.1	1.3	-	-	158.9	0.5	-	-	159.7	0.5	-	-	161.3	1.0	-	-
1991	167.0	3.5	-	-	168.4	0.8	-	-	169.0	0.4	-	-	171.8	1.7	-	-	172.4	0.3	-	-	172.9	0.3	-	-

[Continued]

Economic Indicators Handbook, 2nd Edition

Consumer Price Index - St. Louis

St. Louis, MO-IL
Consumer Price Index - Urban Wage Earners
Base 1982-1984 = 100
Medical Care

[Continued]

For 1947-1993. Columns headed % show percentile change in the index from the previous period for which an index is available.

Year	Jan Index	%	Feb Index	%	Mar Index	%	Apr Index	%	May Index	%	Jun Index	%	Jul Index	%	Aug Index	%	Sep Index	%	Oct Index	%	Nov Index	%	Dec Index	%
1992	175.9	1.7	-	-	177.8	1.1	-	-	178.4	0.3	-	-	181.6	1.8	-	-	182.2	0.3	-	-	182.0	-0.1	-	-
1993	185.3	1.8	-	-	187.9	1.4	-	-	189.2	0.7	-	-	190.8	0.8	-	-	193.2	1.3	-	-	193.8	0.3	-	-

Source: U.S. Department of Labor, Bureau of Labor Statistics, Division of Consumer Prices and Price Indexes. - indicates no data collected for period.

St. Louis, MO-IL

Consumer Price Index - All Urban Consumers
Base 1982-1984 = 100
Entertainment

For 1975-1993. Columns headed % show percentile change in the index from the previous period for which an index is available.

Year	Jan Index	%	Feb Index	%	Mar Index	%	Apr Index	%	May Index	%	Jun Index	%	Jul Index	%	Aug Index	%	Sep Index	%	Oct Index	%	Nov Index	%	Dec Index	%
1975	-	-	-	-	-	-	-	-	-	-	-	-	-	-	-	-	-	-	-	-	-	-	65.1	-
1976	-	-	-	-	65.4	0.5	-	-	-	-	66.5	1.7	-	-	-	-	66.8	0.5	-	-	-	-	67.5	1.0
1977	-	-	-	-	68.6	1.6	-	-	-	-	70.3	2.5	-	-	-	-	71.0	1.0	-	-	-	-	72.7	2.4
1978	-	-	-	-	75.1	3.3	-	-	76.2	1.5	-	-	78.6	3.1	-	-	79.9	1.7	-	-	80.0	0.1	-	-
1979	80.8	1.0	-	-	80.4	-0.5	-	-	80.6	0.2	-	-	80.5	-0.1	-	-	81.4	1.1	-	-	84.5	3.8	-	-
1980	83.8	-0.8	-	-	86.4	3.1	-	-	87.4	1.2	-	-	89.2	2.1	-	-	89.8	0.7	-	-	89.9	0.1	-	-
1981	93.9	4.4	-	-	94.0	0.1	-	-	94.2	0.2	-	-	91.7	-2.7	-	-	94.7	3.3	-	-	94.7	0.0	-	-
1982	95.6	1.0	-	-	96.4	0.8	-	-	93.9	-2.6	-	-	95.6	1.8	-	-	97.3	1.8	-	-	97.9	0.6	-	-
1983	99.9	2.0	-	-	101.4	1.5	-	-	101.0	-0.4	-	-	101.3	0.3	-	-	102.7	1.4	-	-	101.4	-1.3	-	-
1984	100.4	-1.0	-	-	100.8	0.4	-	-	101.9	1.1	-	-	102.0	0.1	-	-	103.0	1.0	-	-	105.1	2.0	-	-
1985	105.3	0.2	-	-	104.8	-0.5	-	-	104.5	-0.3	-	-	105.6	1.1	-	-	106.4	0.8	-	-	108.6	2.1	-	-
1986	108.4	-0.2	-	-	109.8	1.3	-	-	110.4	0.5	-	-	109.2	-1.1	-	-	110.3	1.0	-	-	111.9	1.5	-	-
1987	112.4	0.4	-	-	111.7	-0.6	-	-	112.7	0.9	-	-	114.3	1.4	-	-	115.5	1.0	-	-	116.0	0.4	-	-
1988	115.8	-0.2	-	-	117.8	1.7	-	-	116.8	-0.8	-	-	117.0	0.2	-	-	118.8	1.5	-	-	119.8	0.8	-	-
1989	120.6	0.7	-	-	121.0	0.3	-	-	122.8	1.5	-	-	123.0	0.2	-	-	123.6	0.5	-	-	123.0	-0.5	-	-
1990	120.3	-2.2	-	-	122.1	1.5	-	-	121.9	-0.2	-	-	124.3	2.0	-	-	128.4	3.3	-	-	127.7	-0.5	-	-
1991	127.5	-0.2	-	-	132.6	4.0	-	-	133.9	1.0	-	-	136.4	1.9	-	-	137.4	0.7	-	-	136.9	-0.4	-	-
1992	137.3	0.3	-	-	137.8	0.4	-	-	139.5	1.2	-	-	139.5	0.0	-	-	136.6	-2.1	-	-	135.9	-0.5	-	-
1993	137.3	1.0	-	-	137.3	0.0	-	-	135.4	-1.4	-	-	137.7	1.7	-	-	136.4	-0.9	-	-	139.5	2.3	-	-

Source: U.S. Department of Labor, Bureau of Labor Statistics, Division of Consumer Prices and Price Indexes. - indicates no data collected for period.

St. Louis, MO-IL

Consumer Price Index - Urban Wage Earners
Base 1982-1984 = 100
Entertainment

For 1975-1993. Columns headed % show percentile change in the index from the previous period for which an index is available.

Year	Jan		Feb		Mar		Apr		May		Jun		Jul		Aug		Sep		Oct		Nov		Dec	
	Index	%	Index	%	Index	%	Index	%	Index	%	Index	%	Index	%	Index	%	Index	%	Index	%	Index	%	Index	%
1975	-	-	-	-	-	-	-	-	-	-	-	-	-	-	-	-	-	-	-	-	-	-	71.0	-
1976	-	-	-	-	71.4	0.6	-	-	-	-	72.5	1.5	-	-	-	-	72.9	0.6	-	-	-	-	73.7	1.1
1977	-	-	-	-	74.8	1.5	-	-	-	-	76.7	2.5	-	-	-	-	77.5	1.0	-	-	-	-	79.3	2.3
1978	-	-	-	-	81.9	3.3	-	-	82.3	0.5	-	-	81.7	-0.7	-	-	83.1	1.7	-	-	83.4	0.4	-	-
1979	83.3	-0.1	-	-	83.2	-0.1	-	-	85.8	3.1	-	-	86.0	0.2	-	-	87.0	1.2	-	-	90.5	4.0	-	-
1980	88.6	-2.1	-	-	92.1	4.0	-	-	94.9	3.0	-	-	94.7	-0.2	-	-	95.7	1.1	-	-	93.3	-2.5	-	-
1981	98.0	5.0	-	-	97.5	-0.5	-	-	96.2	-1.3	-	-	94.5	-1.8	-	-	97.0	2.6	-	-	95.5	-1.5	-	-
1982	96.2	0.7	-	-	96.6	0.4	-	-	93.8	-2.9	-	-	95.8	2.1	-	-	97.6	1.9	-	-	98.0	0.4	-	-
1983	100.1	2.1	-	-	101.6	1.5	-	-	101.0	-0.6	-	-	101.5	0.5	-	-	102.9	1.4	-	-	101.3	-1.6	-	-
1984	100.4	-0.9	-	-	100.7	0.3	-	-	101.7	1.0	-	-	101.5	-0.2	-	-	102.3	0.8	-	-	105.0	2.6	-	-
1985	105.1	0.1	-	-	103.8	-1.2	-	-	103.7	-0.1	-	-	104.6	0.9	-	-	105.2	0.6	-	-	107.4	2.1	-	-
1986	107.3	-0.1	-	-	108.6	1.2	-	-	109.2	0.6	-	-	108.4	-0.7	-	-	109.8	1.3	-	-	111.0	1.1	-	-
1987	111.4	0.4	-	-	110.8	-0.5	-	-	111.8	0.9	-	-	113.3	1.3	-	-	114.5	1.1	-	-	114.9	0.3	-	-
1988	115.1	0.2	-	-	117.3	1.9	-	-	115.7	-1.4	-	-	116.4	0.6	-	-	117.9	1.3	-	-	118.8	0.8	-	-
1989	119.9	0.9	-	-	120.0	0.1	-	-	122.2	1.8	-	-	122.0	-0.2	-	-	122.6	0.5	-	-	121.6	-0.8	-	-
1990	118.9	-2.2	-	-	120.7	1.5	-	-	120.8	0.1	-	-	123.0	1.8	-	-	127.5	3.7	-	-	126.9	-0.5	-	-
1991	126.7	-0.2	-	-	131.5	3.8	-	-	132.2	0.5	-	-	134.5	1.7	-	-	135.7	0.9	-	-	134.9	-0.6	-	-
1992	135.1	0.1	-	-	135.8	0.5	-	-	137.4	1.2	-	-	137.4	0.0	-	-	134.8	-1.9	-	-	134.0	-0.6	-	-
1993	135.0	0.7	-	-	134.8	-0.1	-	-	133.4	-1.0	-	-	135.7	1.7	-	-	134.7	-0.7	-	-	137.9	2.4	-	-

Source: U.S. Department of Labor, Bureau of Labor Statistics, Division of Consumer Prices and Price Indexes. - indicates no data collected for period.

St. Louis, MO-IL
Consumer Price Index - All Urban Consumers
Base 1982-1984 = 100
Other Goods and Services

For 1975-1993. Columns headed % show percentile change in the index from the previous period for which an index is available.

Year	Jan Index	%	Feb Index	%	Mar Index	%	Apr Index	%	May Index	%	Jun Index	%	Jul Index	%	Aug Index	%	Sep Index	%	Oct Index	%	Nov Index	%	Dec Index	%
1975	-	-	-	-	-	-	-	-	-	-			-	-	-	-	-	-	-	-	-	-	55.7	-
1976	-	-	-	-	56.1	0.7	-	-	-	-	57.0	1.6	-	-	-	-	58.0	1.8	-	-	-	-	58.8	1.4
1977	-	-	-	-	59.2	0.7	-	-	-	-	60.1	1.5	-	-	-	-	61.4	2.2	-	-	-	-	62.6	2.0
1978	-	-	-	-	63.2	1.0	-	-	63.4	0.3	-	-	64.8	2.2	-	-	66.1	2.0	-	-	66.5	0.6	-	-
1979	66.8	0.5	-	-	67.0	0.3	-	-	67.8	1.2	-	-	68.6	1.2	-	-	70.3	2.5	-	-	70.4	0.1	-	-
1980	71.1	1.0	-	-	72.5	2.0	-	-	73.5	1.4	-	-	74.2	1.0	-	-	78.0	5.1	-	-	77.3	-0.9	-	-
1981	77.9	0.8	-	-	78.7	1.0	-	-	81.2	3.2	-	-	81.8	0.7	-	-	84.0	2.7	-	-	86.3	2.7	-	-
1982	86.7	0.5	-	-	88.3	1.8	-	-	87.6	-0.8	-	-	88.5	1.0	-	-	92.8	4.9	-	-	96.6	4.1	-	-
1983	98.3	1.8	-	-	99.7	1.4	-	-	98.8	-0.9	-	-	99.8	1.0	-	-	102.9	3.1	-	-	104.6	1.7	-	-
1984	105.8	1.1	-	-	106.2	0.4	-	-	106.5	0.3	-	-	107.5	0.9	-	-	111.5	3.7	-	-	111.6	0.1	-	-
1985	112.7	1.0	-	-	113.7	0.9	-	-	113.0	-0.6	-	-	114.6	1.4	-	-	117.0	2.1	-	-	119.5	2.1	-	-
1986	120.2	0.6	-	-	120.3	0.1	-	-	120.3	0.0	-	-	121.1	0.7	-	-	123.6	2.1	-	-	125.4	1.5	-	-
1987	126.6	1.0	-	-	125.9	-0.6	-	-	126.7	0.6	-	-	126.9	0.2	-	-	129.9	2.4	-	-	131.0	0.8	-	-
1988	133.7	2.1	-	-	135.1	1.0	-	-	134.7	-0.3	-	-	136.2	1.1	-	-	138.8	1.9	-	-	140.5	1.2	-	-
1989	141.8	0.9	-	-	143.1	0.9	-	-	143.7	0.4	-	-	145.9	1.5	-	-	146.7	0.5	-	-	149.2	1.7	-	-
1990	150.2	0.7	-	-	150.9	0.5	-	-	151.1	0.1	-	-	154.1	2.0	-	-	155.6	1.0	-	-	157.1	1.0	-	-
1991	159.7	1.7	-	-	160.6	0.6	-	-	158.1	-1.6	-	-	163.7	3.5	-	-	166.3	1.6	-	-	169.7	2.0	-	-
1992	169.9	0.1	-	-	169.9	0.0	-	-	170.9	0.6	-	-	171.6	0.4	-	-	175.0	2.0	-	-	174.8	-0.1	-	-
1993	177.4	1.5	-	-	176.6	-0.5	-	-	179.6	1.7	-	-	178.8	-0.4	-	-	170.3	-4.8	-	-	173.7	2.0	-	-

Source: U.S. Department of Labor, Bureau of Labor Statistics, Division of Consumer Prices and Price Indexes. - indicates no data collected for period.

St. Louis, MO-IL
Consumer Price Index - Urban Wage Earners
Base 1982-1984 = 100
Other Goods and Services

For 1975-1993. Columns headed % show percentile change in the index from the previous period for which an index is available.

Year	Jan Index	%	Feb Index	%	Mar Index	%	Apr Index	%	May Index	%	Jun Index	%	Jul Index	%	Aug Index	%	Sep Index	%	Oct Index	%	Nov Index	%	Dec Index	%
1975	-	-	-	-	-	-	-	-	-	-	-	-	-	-	-	-	-	-	-	-	-	-	55.3	-
1976	-	-	-	-	55.7	0.7	-	-	-	-	56.6	1.6	-	-	-	-	57.6	1.8	-	-	-	-	58.3	1.2
1977	-	-	-	-	58.8	0.9	-	-	-	-	59.7	1.5	-	-	-	-	60.9	2.0	-	-	-	-	62.1	2.0
1978	-	-	-	-	62.7	1.0	-	-	63.3	1.0	-	-	64.8	2.4	-	-	64.9	0.2	-	-	65.7	1.2	-	-
1979	67.7	3.0	-	-	67.3	-0.6	-	-	68.2	1.3	-	-	68.3	0.1	-	-	69.8	2.2	-	-	69.9	0.1	-	-
1980	71.8	2.7	-	-	73.0	1.7	-	-	74.3	1.8	-	-	74.7	0.5	-	-	78.3	4.8	-	-	78.9	0.8	-	-
1981	79.5	0.8	-	-	80.0	0.6	-	-	82.2	2.8	-	-	82.8	0.7	-	-	83.0	0.2	-	-	86.2	3.9	-	-
1982	86.4	0.2	-	-	88.5	2.4	-	-	87.8	-0.8	-	-	88.7	1.0	-	-	92.8	4.6	-	-	96.5	4.0	-	-
1983	98.6	2.2	-	-	100.5	1.9	-	-	99.3	-1.2	-	-	100.6	1.3	-	-	103.1	2.5	-	-	104.3	1.2	-	-
1984	105.8	1.4	-	-	106.0	0.2	-	-	106.2	0.2	-	-	107.5	1.2	-	-	110.5	2.8	-	-	110.5	0.0	-	-
1985	111.9	1.3	-	-	112.9	0.9	-	-	112.1	-0.7	-	-	114.2	1.9	-	-	116.4	1.9	-	-	118.5	1.8	-	-
1986	119.4	0.8	-	-	119.5	0.1	-	-	119.5	0.0	-	-	120.7	1.0	-	-	121.9	1.0	-	-	123.8	1.6	-	-
1987	125.2	1.1	-	-	124.5	-0.6	-	-	125.4	0.7	-	-	125.8	0.3	-	-	128.6	2.2	-	-	129.5	0.7	-	-
1988	132.1	2.0	-	-	133.7	1.2	-	-	133.6	-0.1	-	-	135.5	1.4	-	-	138.1	1.9	-	-	139.1	0.7	-	-
1989	141.3	1.6	-	-	142.2	0.6	-	-	143.0	0.6	-	-	145.3	1.6	-	-	145.9	0.4	-	-	148.5	1.8	-	-
1990	149.7	0.8	-	-	150.4	0.5	-	-	150.8	0.3	-	-	154.8	2.7	-	-	155.6	0.5	-	-	157.9	1.5	-	-
1991	161.4	2.2	-	-	162.8	0.9	-	-	160.1	-1.7	-	-	165.3	3.2	-	-	168.0	1.6	-	-	172.3	2.6	-	-
1992	172.5	0.1	-	-	172.5	0.0	-	-	174.6	1.2	-	-	174.7	0.1	-	-	179.0	2.5	-	-	177.0	-1.1	-	-
1993	181.1	2.3	-	-	178.7	-1.3	-	-	182.4	2.1	-	-	180.3	-1.2	-	-	165.6	-8.2	-	-	170.2	2.8	-	-

Source: U.S. Department of Labor, Bureau of Labor Statistics, Division of Consumer Prices and Price Indexes. - indicates no data collected for period.

Washington, DC-MD-VA
Consumer Price Index - All Urban Consumers
Base 1982-1984 = 100
Annual Averages

For 1914-1993. Columns headed % show percentile change in the index from the previous period for which an index is available.

Year	All Items		Food & Beverage		Housing		Apparel & Upkeep		Trans- portation		Medical Care		Entertain- ment		Other Goods & Services	
	Index	%	Index	%	Index	%	Index	%	Index	%	Index	%	Index	%	Index	%
1914	-	-	-	-	-	-	-	-	-	-	-	-	-	-	-	-
1915	10.6	-	-	-	-	-	-	-	-	-	-	-	-	-	-	-
1916	11.4	7.5	-	-	-	-	-	-	-	-	-	-	-	-	-	-
1917	13.8	21.1	-	-	-	-	-	-	-	-	-	-	-	-	-	-
1918	16.3	18.1	-	-	-	-	-	-	-	-	-	-	-	-	-	-
1919	17.8	9.2	-	-	-	-	-	-	-	-	-	-	-	-	-	-
1920	20.0	12.4	-	-	-	-	-	-	-	-	-	-	-	-	-	-
1921	17.6	-12.0	-	-	-	-	-	-	-	-	-	-	-	-	-	-
1922	16.7	-5.1	-	-	-	-	-	-	-	-	-	-	-	-	-	-
1923	16.9	1.2	-	-	-	-	-	-	-	-	-	-	-	-	-	-
1924	16.9	0.0	-	-	-	-	-	-	-	-	-	-	-	-	-	-
1925	17.3	2.4	-	-	-	-	-	-	-	-	-	-	-	-	-	-
1926	17.5	1.2	-	-	-	-	-	-	-	-	-	-	-	-	-	-
1927	17.0	-2.9	-	-	-	-	-	-	-	-	-	-	-	-	-	-
1928	16.9	-0.6	-	-	-	-	-	-	-	-	-	-	-	-	-	-
1929	16.8	-0.6	-	-	-	-	-	-	-	-	-	-	-	-	-	-
1930	16.5	-1.8	-	-	-	-	-	-	-	-	-	-	-	-	-	-
1931	15.5	-6.1	-	-	-	-	-	-	-	-	-	-	-	-	-	-
1932	14.3	-7.7	-	-	-	-	-	-	-	-	-	-	-	-	-	-
1933	13.9	-2.8	-	-	-	-	-	-	-	-	-	-	-	-	-	-
1934	14.3	2.9	-	-	-	-	-	-	-	-	-	-	-	-	-	-
1935	14.6	2.1	-	-	-	-	-	-	-	-	-	-	-	-	-	-
1936	14.7	0.7	-	-	-	-	-	-	-	-	-	-	-	-	-	-
1937	15.0	2.0	-	-	-	-	-	-	-	-	-	-	-	-	-	-
1938	14.7	-2.0	-	-	-	-	-	-	-	-	-	-	-	-	-	-
1939	14.6	-0.7	-	-	-	-	-	-	-	-	-	-	-	-	-	-
1940	14.7	0.7	-	-	-	-	-	-	-	-	-	-	-	-	-	-
1941	15.3	4.1	-	-	-	-	-	-	-	-	-	-	-	-	-	-
1942	17.0	11.1	-	-	-	-	-	-	-	-	-	-	-	-	-	-
1943	18.1	6.5	-	-	-	-	-	-	-	-	-	-	-	-	-	-
1944	18.4	1.7	-	-	-	-	-	-	-	-	-	-	-	-	-	-
1945	18.9	2.7	-	-	-	-	-	-	-	-	-	-	-	-	-	-
1946	20.6	9.0	-	-	-	-	-	-	19.1	-	12.4	-	-	-	-	-
1947	23.2	12.6	-	-	-	-	-	-	21.2	11.0	12.8	3.2	-	-	-	-
1948	24.6	6.0	-	-	-	-	-	-	22.8	7.5	13.1	2.3	-	-	-	-
1949	24.6	0.0	-	-	-	-	-	-	23.3	2.2	13.2	0.8	-	-	-	-
1950	24.9	1.2	-	-	-	-	-	-	24.2	3.9	14.0	6.1	-	-	-	-
1951	26.6	6.8	-	-	-	-	-	-	25.8	6.6	14.8	5.7	-	-	-	-
1952	27.3	2.6	-	-	-	-	-	-	26.9	4.3	15.0	1.4	-	-	-	-
1953	27.5	0.7	-	-	-	-	40.5	-	26.8	-0.4	15.0	0.0	-	-	-	-
1954	27.5	0.0	-	-	-	-	40.3	-0.5	27.2	1.5	15.3	2.0	-	-	-	-
1955	27.4	-0.4	-	-	-	-	40.0	-0.7	27.5	1.1	16.0	4.6	-	-	-	-
1956	27.7	1.1	-	-	-	-	41.1	2.8	28.9	5.1	16.8	5.0	-	-	-	-
1957	28.6	3.2	-	-	-	-	41.3	0.5	29.5	2.1	17.9	6.5	-	-	-	-
1958	29.3	2.4	-	-	-	-	41.1	-0.5								

[Continued]

Washington, DC-MD-VA
Consumer Price Index - All Urban Consumers
Base 1982-1984 = 100
Annual Averages
[Continued]

For 1914-1993. Columns headed % show percentile change in the index from the previous period for which an index is available.

Year	All Items		Food & Beverage		Housing		Apparel & Upkeep		Trans- portation		Medical Care		Entertain- ment		Other Goods & Services	
	Index	%	Index	%	Index	%	Index	%	Index	%	Index	%	Index	%	Index	%
1959	29.4	0.3	-	-	-	-	41.7	1.5	30.4	3.1	19.1	6.7	-	-	-	-
1960	29.7	1.0	-	-	-	-	42.1	1.0	30.7	1.0	19.7	3.1	-	-	-	-
1961	30.1	1.3	-	-	-	-	42.8	1.7	31.0	1.0	20.4	3.6	-	-	-	-
1962	30.4	1.0	-	-	-	-	44.1	3.0	31.3	1.0	21.5	5.4	-	-	-	-
1963	30.9	1.6	-	-	-	-	44.3	0.5	31.6	1.0	22.4	4.2	-	-	-	-
1964	31.4	1.6	-	-	-	-	44.6	0.7	32.4	2.5	23.0	2.7	-	-	-	-
1965	31.9	1.6	-	-	-	-	44.9	0.7	32.7	0.9	23.7	3.0	-	-	-	-
1966	33.0	3.4	-	-	-	-	46.4	3.3	32.9	0.6	24.9	5.1	-	-	-	-
1967	33.9	2.7	-	-	-	-	48.7	5.0	34.1	3.6	27.0	8.4	-	-	-	-
1968	35.5	4.7	-	-	-	-	52.3	7.4	35.4	3.8	29.6	9.6	-	-	-	-
1969	37.7	6.2	-	-	-	-	55.7	6.5	37.1	4.8	31.9	7.8	-	-	-	-
1970	39.8	5.6	-	-	-	-	58.2	4.5	39.7	7.0	34.3	7.5	-	-	-	-
1971	41.6	4.5	-	-	-	-	59.9	2.9	42.1	6.0	36.9	7.6	-	-	-	-
1972	43.0	3.4	-	-	-	-	60.8	1.5	42.2	0.2	37.8	2.4	-	-	-	-
1973	45.7	6.3	-	-	-	-	63.7	4.8	43.0	1.9	39.0	3.2	-	-	-	-
1974	50.8	11.2	-	-	-	-	68.5	7.5	47.6	10.7	43.5	11.5	-	-	-	-
1975	54.7	7.7	-	-	-	-	70.5	2.9	51.8	8.8	48.5	11.5	-	-	-	-
1976	58.0	6.0	62.5	-	55.2	-	72.7	3.1	55.6	7.3	53.4	10.1	68.6	-	58.4	-
1977	62.0	6.9	66.8	6.9	59.4	7.6	74.3	2.2	59.8	7.6	58.3	9.2	73.8	7.6	62.1	6.3
1978	66.7	7.6	73.4	9.9	64.6	8.8	78.0	5.0	63.4	6.0	62.2	6.7	74.9	1.5	65.6	5.6
1979	74.0	10.9	81.8	11.4	71.9	11.3	83.5	7.1	71.8	13.2	68.3	9.8	78.6	4.9	70.0	6.7
1980	82.9	12.0	88.0	7.6	81.0	12.7	90.2	8.0	84.8	18.1	74.2	8.6	84.7	7.8	75.8	8.3
1981	90.5	9.2	92.6	5.2	90.1	11.2	90.5	0.3	94.4	11.3	80.1	8.0	88.9	5.0	83.4	10.0
1982	95.5	5.5	97.2	5.0	95.4	5.9	94.7	4.6	97.0	2.8	90.6	13.1	94.1	5.8	91.3	9.5
1983	99.8	4.5	99.8	2.7	99.7	4.5	100.6	6.2	99.3	2.4	101.5	12.0	99.1	5.3	101.0	10.6
1984	104.6	4.8	103.0	3.2	104.9	5.2	104.7	4.1	103.7	4.4	107.9	6.3	106.7	7.7	107.7	6.6
1985	109.0	4.2	106.1	3.0	110.1	5.0	109.9	5.0	105.6	1.8	114.7	6.3	113.7	6.6	114.5	6.3
1986	112.2	2.9	110.1	3.8	114.8	4.3	108.7	-1.1	103.8	-1.7	122.6	6.9	116.5	2.5	121.9	6.5
1987	116.2	3.6	113.6	3.2	118.9	3.6	116.3	7.0	105.9	2.0	129.1	5.3	121.5	4.3	129.4	6.2
1988	121.0	4.1	119.2	4.9	123.4	3.8	123.1	5.8	108.1	2.1	137.8	6.7	124.8	2.7	138.4	7.0
1989	128.0	5.8	126.1	5.8	129.3	4.8	134.9	9.6	114.4	5.8	146.4	6.2	127.5	2.2	152.2	10.0
1990	135.6	5.9	133.4	5.8	136.6	5.6	139.4	3.3	120.7	5.5	162.4	10.9	135.6	6.4	165.4	8.7
1991	141.2	4.1	137.7	3.2	140.8	3.1	142.4	2.2	126.2	4.6	176.4	8.6	142.7	5.2	178.6	8.0
1992	144.7	2.5	140.9	2.3	143.9	2.2	139.6	-2.0	129.9	2.9	186.3	5.6	147.6	3.4	186.9	4.6
1993	-	-	-	-	-	-	-	-	-	-	-	-	-	-	-	-

Source: U.S. Department of Labor, Bureau of Labor Statistics, Division of Consumer Prices and Price Indexes. - indicates no data collected for period.

Washington, DC-MD-VA
Consumer Price Index - Urban Wage Earners
Base 1982-1984 = 100
Annual Averages

For 1914-1993. Columns headed % show percentile change in the index from the previous period for which an index is available.

Year	All Items		Food & Beverage		Housing		Apparel & Upkeep		Trans- portation		Medical Care		Entertain- ment		Other Goods & Services	
	Index	%	Index	%	Index	%	Index	%	Index	%	Index	%	Index	%	Index	%
1914	-	-	-	-	-	-	-	-	-	-	-	-	-	-	-	-
1915	10.5	-	-	-	-	-	-	-	-	-	-	-	-	-	-	-
1916	11.2	6.7	-	-	-	-	-	-	-	-	-	-	-	-	-	-
1917	13.6	21.4	-	-	-	-	-	-	-	-	-	-	-	-	-	-
1918	16.1	18.4	-	-	-	-	-	-	-	-	-	-	-	-	-	-
1919	17.6	9.3	-	-	-	-	-	-	-	-	-	-	-	-	-	-
1920	19.7	11.9	-	-	-	-	-	-	-	-	-	-	-	-	-	-
1921	17.4	-11.7	-	-	-	-	-	-	-	-	-	-	-	-	-	-
1922	16.4	-5.7	-	-	-	-	-	-	-	-	-	-	-	-	-	-
1923	16.7	1.8	-	-	-	-	-	-	-	-	-	-	-	-	-	-
1924	16.7	0.0	-	-	-	-	-	-	-	-	-	-	-	-	-	-
1925	17.1	2.4	-	-	-	-	-	-	-	-	-	-	-	-	-	-
1926	17.3	1.2	-	-	-	-	-	-	-	-	-	-	-	-	-	-
1927	16.8	-2.9	-	-	-	-	-	-	-	-	-	-	-	-	-	-
1928	16.7	-0.6	-	-	-	-	-	-	-	-	-	-	-	-	-	-
1929	16.6	-0.6	-	-	-	-	-	-	-	-	-	-	-	-	-	-
1930	16.3	-1.8	-	-	-	-	-	-	-	-	-	-	-	-	-	-
1931	15.3	-6.1	-	-	-	-	-	-	-	-	-	-	-	-	-	-
1932	14.1	-7.8	-	-	-	-	-	-	-	-	-	-	-	-	-	-
1933	13.7	-2.8	-	-	-	-	-	-	-	-	-	-	-	-	-	-
1934	14.1	2.9	-	-	-	-	-	-	-	-	-	-	-	-	-	-
1935	14.4	2.1	-	-	-	-	-	-	-	-	-	-	-	-	-	-
1936	14.5	0.7	-	-	-	-	-	-	-	-	-	-	-	-	-	-
1937	14.8	2.1	-	-	-	-	-	-	-	-	-	-	-	-	-	-
1938	14.5	-2.0	-	-	-	-	-	-	-	-	-	-	-	-	-	-
1939	14.4	-0.7	-	-	-	-	-	-	-	-	-	-	-	-	-	-
1940	14.5	0.7	-	-	-	-	-	-	-	-	-	-	-	-	-	-
1941	15.1	4.1	-	-	-	-	-	-	-	-	-	-	-	-	-	-
1942	16.8	11.3	-	-	-	-	-	-	-	-	-	-	-	-	-	-
1943	17.8	6.0	-	-	-	-	-	-	-	-	-	-	-	-	-	-
1944	18.1	1.7	-	-	-	-	-	-	-	-	-	-	-	-	-	-
1945	18.6	2.8	-	-	-	-	-	-	-	-	-	-	-	-	-	-
1946	20.3	9.1	-	-	-	-	-	-	-	-	-	-	-	-	-	-
1947	22.9	12.8	-	-	-	-	-	-	19.1	-	11.9	-	-	-	-	-
1948	24.3	6.1	-	-	-	-	-	-	21.1	10.5	12.3	3.4	-	-	-	-
1949	24.2	-0.4	-	-	-	-	-	-	22.7	7.6	12.5	1.6	-	-	-	-
1950	24.6	1.7	-	-	-	-	-	-	23.3	2.6	12.6	0.8	-	-	-	-
1951	26.2	6.5	-	-	-	-	-	-	24.1	3.4	13.4	6.3	-	-	-	-
1952	26.9	2.7	-	-	-	-	-	-	25.7	6.6	14.1	5.2	-	-	-	-
1953	27.1	0.7	-	-	-	-	36.4	-	26.8	4.3	14.3	1.4	-	-	-	-
1954	27.1	0.0	-	-	-	-	36.2	-0.5	26.7	-0.4	14.4	0.7	-	-	-	-
1955	27.0	-0.4	-	-	-	-	36.0	-0.6	27.1	1.5	14.6	1.4	-	-	-	-
1956	27.3	1.1	-	-	-	-	37.0	2.8	27.5	1.5	15.4	5.5	-	-	-	-
1957	28.2	3.3	-	-	-	-	37.2	0.5	28.9	5.1	16.1	4.5	-	-	-	-
1958	28.8	2.1	-	-	-	-	37.0	-0.5	29.4	1.7	17.1	6.2				

[Continued]

Washington, DC-MD-VA
Consumer Price Index - Urban Wage Earners
Base 1982-1984 = 100
Annual Averages
[Continued]

For 1914-1993. Columns headed % show percentile change in the index from the previous period for which an index is available.

Year	All Items		Food & Beverage		Housing		Apparel & Upkeep		Trans-portation		Medical Care		Entertain-ment		Other Goods & Services	
	Index	%	Index	%	Index	%	Index	%	Index	%	Index	%	Index	%	Index	%
1959	29.0	0.7	-	-	-	-	37.5	1.4	30.4	3.4	18.2	6.4	-	-	-	-
1960	29.3	1.0	-	-	-	-	37.9	1.1	30.6	0.7	18.9	3.8	-	-	-	-
1961	29.7	1.4	-	-	-	-	38.5	1.6	30.9	1.0	19.5	3.2	-	-	-	-
1962	30.0	1.0	-	-	-	-	39.7	3.1	31.3	1.3	20.6	5.6	-	-	-	-
1963	30.5	1.7	-	-	-	-	39.8	0.3	31.5	0.6	21.4	3.9	-	-	-	-
1964	31.0	1.6	-	-	-	-	40.1	0.8	32.3	2.5	22.0	2.8	-	-	-	-
1965	31.4	1.3	-	-	-	-	40.4	0.7	32.6	0.9	22.7	3.2	-	-	-	-
1966	32.5	3.5	-	-	-	-	41.8	3.5	32.9	0.9	23.8	4.8	-	-	-	-
1967	33.4	2.8	-	-	-	-	43.8	4.8	34.0	3.3	25.8	8.4	-	-	-	-
1968	35.0	4.8	-	-	-	-	47.0	7.3	35.3	3.8	28.3	9.7	-	-	-	-
1969	37.1	6.0	-	-	-	-	50.1	6.6	37.0	4.8	30.5	7.8	-	-	-	-
1970	39.3	5.9	-	-	-	-	52.4	4.6	39.6	7.0	32.8	7.5	-	-	-	-
1971	41.0	4.3	-	-	-	-	53.8	2.7	42.0	6.1	35.3	7.6	-	-	-	-
1972	42.4	3.4	-	-	-	-	54.7	1.7	42.1	0.2	36.2	2.5	-	-	-	-
1973	45.1	6.4	-	-	-	-	57.3	4.8	42.9	1.9	37.3	3.0	-	-	-	-
1974	50.1	11.1	-	-	-	-	61.6	7.5	47.5	10.7	41.6	11.5	-	-	-	-
1975	54.0	7.8	-	-	-	-	63.4	2.9	51.7	8.8	46.4	11.5	-	-	-	-
1976	57.1	5.7	61.6	-	55.7	-	65.4	3.2	55.5	7.4	51.1	10.1	58.3	-	56.3	-
1977	61.1	7.0	65.8	6.8	59.8	7.4	66.8	2.1	59.6	7.4	55.8	9.2	62.6	7.4	59.8	6.2
1978	66.2	8.3	72.4	10.0	65.8	10.0	68.3	2.2	62.8	5.4	61.1	9.5	68.4	9.3	65.4	9.4
1979	73.4	10.9	79.7	10.1	73.1	11.1	72.2	5.7	70.9	12.9	68.5	12.1	75.8	10.8	70.0	7.0
1980	82.2	12.0	85.6	7.4	81.9	12.0	80.8	11.9	83.0	17.1	74.7	9.1	82.7	9.1	76.6	9.4
1981	90.3	9.9	91.8	7.2	90.5	10.5	89.2	10.4	92.9	11.9	79.8	6.8	88.0	6.4	84.3	10.1
1982	95.8	6.1	97.3	6.0	96.2	6.3	94.1	5.5	96.6	4.0	90.3	13.2	94.5	7.4	91.3	8.3
1983	99.8	4.2	99.7	2.5	99.5	3.4	102.8	9.2	99.3	2.8	101.4	12.3	99.2	5.0	101.3	11.0
1984	104.4	4.6	103.0	3.3	104.3	4.8	103.2	0.4	104.2	4.9	108.4	6.9	106.3	7.2	107.5	6.1
1985	108.6	4.0	106.0	2.9	109.6	5.1	108.7	5.3	106.1	1.8	115.6	6.6	111.9	5.3	112.7	4.8
1986	111.0	2.2	109.9	3.7	114.3	4.3	104.0	-4.3	104.3	-1.7	123.6	6.9	112.7	0.7	119.1	5.7
1987	115.4	4.0	113.9	3.6	118.2	3.4	114.6	10.2	108.0	3.5	130.5	5.6	118.0	4.7	125.7	5.5
1988	120.3	4.2	119.3	4.7	122.6	3.7	120.8	5.4	111.2	3.0	139.5	6.9	121.8	3.2	134.6	7.1
1989	127.3	5.8	126.5	6.0	128.4	4.7	133.4	10.4	117.9	6.0	148.2	6.2	124.6	2.3	148.5	10.3
1990	134.5	5.7	133.8	5.8	135.0	5.1	137.0	2.7	124.6	5.7	163.5	10.3	132.0	5.9	160.6	8.1
1991	139.7	3.9	137.8	3.0	139.0	3.0	141.2	3.1	129.8	4.2	176.8	8.1	138.7	5.1	172.5	7.4
1992	143.0	2.4	141.0	2.3	141.7	1.9	140.0	-0.8	133.3	2.7	186.8	5.7	143.7	3.6	180.5	4.6
1993	-	-	-	-	-	-	-	-	-	-	-	-	-	-	-	-

Source: U.S. Department of Labor, Bureau of Labor Statistics, Division of Consumer Prices and Price Indexes. - indicates no data collected for period.

Washington, DC-MD-VA
Consumer Price Index - All Urban Consumers
Base 1982-1984 = 100
All Items

For 1914-1993. Columns headed % show percentile change in the index from the previous period for which an index is available.

Year	Jan Index	%	Feb Index	%	Mar Index	%	Apr Index	%	May Index	%	Jun Index	%	Jul Index	%	Aug Index	%	Sep Index	%	Oct Index	%	Nov Index	%	Dec Index	%
1914	-	-	-	-	-	-	-	-	-	-	-	-	-	-	-	-	-	-	-	-	-	-	10.7	-
1915	-	-	-	-	-	-	-	-	-	-	-	-	-	-	-	-	-	-	-	-	-	-	10.8	0.9
1916	-	-	-	-	-	-	-	-	-	-	-	-	-	-	-	-	-	-	-	-	-	-	12.0	11.1
1917	-	-	-	-	-	-	-	-	-	-	-	-	-	-	-	-	-	-	-	-	-	-	15.1	25.8
1918	-	-	-	-	-	-	-	-	-	-	-	-	-	-	-	-	-	-	-	-	-	-	17.6	16.6
1919	-	-	-	-	-	-	-	-	-	-	17.3	-1.7	-	-	-	-	-	-	-	-	-	-	18.8	8.7
1920	-	-	-	-	-	-	-	-	-	-	20.9	11.2	-	-	-	-	-	-	-	-	-	-	19.1	-8.6
1921	-	-	-	-	-	-	-	-	17.4	-8.9	-	-	-	-	-	-	17.5	0.6	-	-	-	-	17.1	-2.3
1922	-	-	-	-	16.6	-2.9	-	-	-	-	16.7	0.6	-	-	-	-	16.5	-1.2	-	-	-	-	16.7	1.2
1923	-	-	-	-	16.6	-0.6	-	-	-	-	17.0	2.4	-	-	-	-	17.2	1.2	-	-	-	-	17.0	-1.2
1924	-	-	-	-	16.8	-1.2	-	-	-	-	16.8	0.0	-	-	-	-	16.8	0.0	-	-	-	-	17.0	1.2
1925	-	-	-	-	-	-	-	-	-	-	17.3	1.8	-	-	-	-	-	-	-	-	-	-	17.6	1.7
1926	-	-	-	-	-	-	-	-	-	-	17.5	-0.6	-	-	-	-	-	-	-	-	-	-	17.4	-0.6
1927	-	-	-	-	-	-	-	-	-	-	17.1	-1.7	-	-	-	-	-	-	-	-	-	-	16.9	-1.2
1928	-	-	-	-	-	-	-	-	-	-	16.9	0.0	-	-	-	-	-	-	-	-	-	-	16.8	-0.6
1929	-	-	-	-	-	-	-	-	-	-	16.9	0.6	-	-	-	-	-	-	-	-	-	-	16.8	-0.6
1930	-	-	-	-	-	-	-	-	-	-	16.6	-1.2	-	-	-	-	-	-	-	-	-	-	16.2	-2.4
1931	-	-	-	-	-	-	-	-	-	-	15.4	-4.9	-	-	-	-	-	-	-	-	-	-	15.1	-1.9
1932	-	-	-	-	-	-	-	-	-	-	14.3	-5.3	-	-	-	-	-	-	-	-	-	-	13.9	-2.8
1933	-	-	-	-	-	-	-	-	-	-	13.7	-1.4	-	-	-	-	-	-	-	-	-	-	14.2	3.6
1934	-	-	-	-	-	-	-	-	-	-	14.3	0.7	-	-	-	-	-	-	-	-	14.5	1.4	-	-
1935	-	-	-	-	14.5	0.0	-	-	-	-	-	-	14.5	0.0	-	-	-	-	14.6	0.7	-	-	-	-
1936	14.7	0.7	-	-	-	-	14.5	-1.4	-	-	-	-	14.7	1.4	-	-	14.8	0.7	-	-	-	-	14.7	-0.7
1937	-	-	-	-	15.0	2.0	-	-	-	-	15.1	0.7	-	-	-	-	15.2	0.7	-	-	-	-	15.0	-1.3
1938	-	-	-	-	14.7	-2.0	-	-	-	-	14.7	0.0	-	-	-	-	14.7	0.0	-	-	-	-	14.7	0.0
1939	-	-	-	-	14.5	-1.4	-	-	-	-	14.5	0.0	-	-	-	-	14.7	1.4	-	-	-	-	14.5	-1.4
1940	-	-	-	-	14.7	1.4	-	-	-	-	14.7	0.0	-	-	-	-	14.7	0.0	-	-	-	-	14.7	0.0
1941	-	-	-	-	14.8	0.7	-	-	-	-	15.2	2.7	-	-	-	-	15.7	3.3	16.0	1.9	16.0	0.0	16.2	1.3
1942	16.3	0.6	16.5	1.2	16.7	1.2	16.7	0.0	16.9	1.2	17.0	0.6	17.1	0.6	17.2	0.6	17.3	0.6	17.3	0.0	17.4	0.6	17.5	0.6
1943	17.6	0.6	17.6	0.0	17.9	1.7	18.1	1.1	18.3	1.1	18.3	0.0	18.2	-0.5	18.2	0.0	18.2	0.0	18.3	0.5	18.2	-0.5	18.2	0.0
1944	18.3	0.5	18.2	-0.5	18.1	-0.5	18.2	0.6	18.3	0.5	18.4	0.5	18.4	0.0	18.5	0.5	18.5	0.0	18.5	0.0	18.6	0.5	18.6	0.0
1945	18.6	0.0	18.6	0.0	18.6	0.0	18.7	0.5	18.9	1.1	19.0	0.5	19.0	0.0	19.0	0.0	19.1	0.5	19.0	-0.5	19.1	0.5	19.2	0.5
1946	19.3	0.5	19.2	-0.5	19.4	1.0	19.4	0.0	19.4	0.0	19.8	2.1	20.8	5.1	21.1	1.4	21.4	1.4	21.8	1.9	22.2	1.8	22.5	1.4
1947	22.5	0.0	22.4	-0.4	22.9	2.2	22.9	0.0	22.9	0.0	23.1	0.9	-	-	23.5	1.7	-	-	-	-	23.9	1.7	-	-
1948	-	-	24.1	0.8	-	-	-	-	24.7	2.5	-	-	-	-	25.0	1.2	-	-	-	-	24.7	-1.2	-	-
1949	-	-	24.4	-1.2	-	-	-	-	24.6	0.8	-	-	-	-	24.7	0.4	-	-	-	-	24.8	0.4	-	-
1950	-	-	24.4	-1.6	-	-	-	-	24.5	0.4	-	-	-	-	25.1	2.4	-	-	-	-	25.5	1.6	-	-
1951	-	-	26.4	3.5	-	-	-	-	26.5	0.4	-	-	-	-	26.6	0.4	-	-	-	-	27.2	2.3	-	-
1952	-	-	27.0	-0.7	-	-	-	-	27.2	0.7	-	-	-	-	27.6	1.5	-	-	-	-	27.5	-0.4	-	-
1953	-	-	27.3	-0.7	-	-	-	-	27.4	0.4	-	-	-	-	27.6	0.7	-	-	-	-	27.6	0.0	-	-
1954	-	-	27.6	0.0	-	-	-	-	27.4	-0.7	-	-	-	-	27.6	0.7	-	-	-	-	27.4	-0.7	-	-
1955	-	-	27.3	-0.4	-	-	-	-	27.4	0.4	-	-	-	-	27.5	0.4	-	-	-	-	27.4	-0.4	-	-
1956	-	-	27.4	0.0	-	-	-	-	27.6	0.7	-	-	-	-	27.9	1.1	-	-	-	-	28.0	0.4	-	-
1957	-	-	28.4	1.4	-	-	-	-	28.3	-0.4	-	-	-	-	28.8	1.8	-	-	-	-	28.9	0.3	-	-
1958	-	-	29.1	0.7	-	-	-	-	29.3	0.7	-	-	-	-	29.3	0.0	-	-	-	-	29.3	0.0	-	-

[Continued]

Washington, DC-MD-VA
Consumer Price Index - All Urban Consumers
Base 1982-1984 = 100
All Items
[Continued]

For 1914-1993. Columns headed % show percentile change in the index from the previous period for which an index is available.

Year	Jan Index	%	Feb Index	%	Mar Index	%	Apr Index	%	May Index	%	Jun Index	%	Jul Index	%	Aug Index	%	Sep Index	%	Oct Index	%	Nov Index	%	Dec Index	%
1959	-	-	29.3	0.0	-	-	-	-	29.4	0.3	-	-	-	-	29.5	0.3	-	-	-	-	29.4	-0.3	-	-
1960	-	-	29.4	0.0	-	-	-	-	29.7	1.0	-	-	-	-	29.7	0.0	-	-	-	-	29.9	0.7	-	-
1961	-	-	30.1	0.7	-	-	-	-	30.0	-0.3	-	-	-	-	30.2	0.7	-	-	-	-	30.3	0.3	-	-
1962	-	-	30.2	-0.3	-	-	-	-	30.3	0.3	-	-	-	-	30.5	0.7	-	-	-	-	30.6	0.3	-	-
1963	-	-	30.7	0.3	-	-	-	-	30.9	0.7	-	-	-	-	31.1	0.6	-	-	-	-	31.1	0.0	-	-
1964	-	-	31.2	0.3	-	-	-	-	31.3	0.3	-	-	-	-	31.6	1.0	-	-	-	-	31.7	0.3	-	-
1965	-	-	31.6	-0.3	-	-	-	-	31.8	0.6	-	-	-	-	31.9	0.3	-	-	-	-	32.1	0.6	-	-
1966	-	-	32.6	1.6	-	-	-	-	32.8	0.6	-	-	-	-	33.2	1.2	-	-	-	-	33.3	0.3	-	-
1967	-	-	33.5	0.6	-	-	-	-	33.6	0.3	-	-	-	-	34.1	1.5	-	-	-	-	34.2	0.3	-	-
1968	-	-	34.6	1.2	-	-	-	-	35.2	1.7	-	-	-	-	35.8	1.7	-	-	-	-	36.3	1.4	-	-
1969	-	-	36.7	1.1	-	-	-	-	37.5	2.2	-	-	-	-	38.0	1.3	-	-	-	-	38.4	1.1	-	-
1970	-	-	39.1	1.8	-	-	-	-	39.7	1.5	-	-	-	-	40.1	1.0	-	-	-	-	40.4	0.7	-	-
1971	-	-	41.0	1.5	-	-	-	-	41.4	1.0	-	-	-	-	41.8	1.0	-	-	-	-	42.1	0.7	-	-
1972	-	-	42.2	0.2	-	-	-	-	42.5	0.7	-	-	-	-	43.3	1.9	-	-	-	-	43.9	1.4	-	-
1973	-	-	44.3	0.9	-	-	-	-	45.2	2.0	-	-	-	-	46.2	2.2	-	-	-	-	47.2	2.2	-	-
1974	-	-	48.8	3.4	-	-	-	-	50.0	2.5	-	-	-	-	51.7	3.4	-	-	-	-	52.9	2.3	-	-
1975	-	-	53.5	1.1	-	-	-	-	54.2	1.3	-	-	-	-	55.3	2.0	-	-	-	-	56.0	1.3	-	-
1976	-	-	56.6	1.1	-	-	-	-	57.6	1.8	-	-	-	-	58.6	1.7	-	-	-	-	59.0	0.7	-	-
1977	-	-	60.3	2.2	-	-	-	-	61.5	2.0	-	-	-	-	62.6	1.8	-	-	-	-	63.5	1.4	-	-
1978	64.3	1.3	-	-	64.7	0.6	-	-	65.8	1.7	-	-	67.0	1.8	-	-	68.0	1.5	-	-	69.1	1.6	-	-
1979	70.7	2.3	-	-	72.0	1.8	-	-	73.2	1.7	-	-	74.7	2.0	-	-	75.5	1.1	-	-	76.3	1.1	-	-
1980	78.5	2.9	-	-	80.9	3.1	-	-	81.7	1.0	-	-	83.7	2.4	-	-	84.4	0.8	-	-	85.9	1.8	-	-
1981	87.1	1.4	-	-	88.8	2.0	-	-	89.7	1.0	-	-	90.5	0.9	-	-	92.1	1.8	-	-	93.3	1.3	-	-
1982	94.2	1.0	-	-	94.4	0.2	-	-	94.3	-0.1	-	-	95.3	1.1	-	-	97.0	1.8	-	-	97.0	0.0	-	-
1983	98.0	1.0	-	-	98.0	0.0	-	-	99.2	1.2	-	-	100.6	1.4	-	-	100.7	0.1	-	-	101.2	0.5	-	-
1984	102.9	1.7	-	-	103.3	0.4	-	-	103.5	0.2	-	-	104.4	0.9	-	-	106.0	1.5	-	-	106.7	0.7	-	-
1985	106.6	-0.1	-	-	108.1	1.4	-	-	108.3	0.2	-	-	109.5	1.1	-	-	109.6	0.1	-	-	110.7	1.0	-	-
1986	112.2	1.4	-	-	111.5	-0.6	-	-	111.6	0.1	-	-	111.5	-0.1	-	-	112.6	1.0	-	-	113.1	0.4	-	-
1987	113.7	0.5	-	-	114.5	0.7	-	-	115.3	0.7	-	-	116.2	0.8	-	-	117.8	1.4	-	-	118.5	0.6	-	-
1988	118.3	-0.2	-	-	119.2	0.8	-	-	120.1	0.8	-	-	120.7	0.5	-	-	122.8	1.7	-	-	123.2	0.3	-	-
1989	124.3	0.9	-	-	126.1	1.4	-	-	127.1	0.8	-	-	127.8	0.6	-	-	130.1	1.8	-	-	130.5	0.3	-	-
1990	132.0	1.1	-	-	133.8	1.4	-	-	134.0	0.1	-	-	135.7	1.3	-	-	138.0	1.7	-	-	138.4	0.3	-	-
1991	139.1	0.5	-	-	139.3	0.1	-	-	140.9	1.1	-	-	140.9	0.0	-	-	143.3	1.7	-	-	142.6	-0.5	-	-
1992	142.9	0.2	-	-	143.0	0.1	-	-	143.2	0.1	-	-	144.8	1.1	-	-	146.0	0.8	-	-	146.9	0.6	-	-
1993	147.8	0.6	-	-	148.5	0.5	-	-	149.2	0.5	-	-	149.2	0.0	-	-	149.7	0.3	-	-	150.9	0.8	-	-

Source: U.S. Department of Labor, Bureau of Labor Statistics, Division of Consumer Prices and Price Indexes. - indicates no data collected for period.

Washington, DC-MD-VA
Consumer Price Index - Urban Wage Earners
Base 1982-1984 = 100
All Items

For 1914-1993. Columns headed % show percentile change in the index from the previous period for which an index is available.

Year	Jan Index	Jan %	Feb Index	Feb %	Mar Index	Mar %	Apr Index	Apr %	May Index	May %	Jun Index	Jun %	Jul Index	Jul %	Aug Index	Aug %	Sep Index	Sep %	Oct Index	Oct %	Nov Index	Nov %	Dec Index	Dec %
1914	-	-	-	-	-	-	-	-	-	-	-	-	-	-	-	-	-	-	-	-	-	-	10.5	-
1915	-	-	-	-	-	-	-	-	-	-	-	-	-	-	-	-	-	-	-	-	-	-	10.6	1.0
1916	-	-	-	-	-	-	-	-	-	-	-	-	-	-	-	-	-	-	-	-	-	-	11.8	11.3
1917	-	-	-	-	-	-	-	-	-	-	-	-	-	-	-	-	-	-	-	-	-	-	14.9	26.3
1918	-	-	-	-	-	-	-	-	-	-	-	-	-	-	-	-	-	-	-	-	-	-	17.3	16.1
1919	-	-	-	-	-	-	-	-	-	-	17.1	-1.2	-	-	-	-	-	-	-	-	-	-	18.5	8.2
1920	-	-	-	-	-	-	-	-	-	-	20.6	11.4	-	-	-	-	-	-	-	-	-	-	18.9	-8.3
1921	-	-	-	-	-	-	-	-	17.1	-9.5	-	-	-	-	-	-	17.3	1.2	-	-	-	-	16.9	-2.3
1922	-	-	-	-	16.4	-3.0	-	-	-	-	16.5	0.6	-	-	-	-	16.3	-1.2	-	-	-	-	16.5	1.2
1923	-	-	-	-	16.4	-0.6	-	-	-	-	16.8	2.4	-	-	-	-	16.9	0.6	-	-	-	-	16.8	-0.6
1924	-	-	-	-	16.6	-1.2	-	-	-	-	16.6	0.0	-	-	-	-	16.6	0.0	-	-	-	-	16.8	1.2
1925	-	-	-	-	-	-	-	-	-	-	17.0	1.2	-	-	-	-	-	-	-	-	-	-	17.4	2.4
1926	-	-	-	-	-	-	-	-	-	-	17.3	-0.6	-	-	-	-	-	-	-	-	-	-	17.2	-0.6
1927	-	-	-	-	-	-	-	-	-	-	16.9	-1.7	-	-	-	-	-	-	-	-	-	-	16.7	-1.2
1928	-	-	-	-	-	-	-	-	-	-	16.7	0.0	-	-	-	-	-	-	-	-	-	-	16.5	-1.2
1929	-	-	-	-	-	-	-	-	-	-	16.6	0.6	-	-	-	-	-	-	-	-	-	-	16.6	0.0
1930	-	-	-	-	-	-	-	-	-	-	16.4	-1.2	-	-	-	-	-	-	-	-	-	-	16.0	-2.4
1931	-	-	-	-	-	-	-	-	-	-	15.2	-5.0	-	-	-	-	-	-	-	-	-	-	14.9	-2.0
1932	-	-	-	-	-	-	-	-	-	-	14.1	-5.4	-	-	-	-	-	-	-	-	-	-	13.7	-2.8
1933	-	-	-	-	-	-	-	-	-	-	13.5	-1.5	-	-	-	-	-	-	-	-	-	-	14.0	3.7
1934	-	-	-	-	-	-	-	-	-	-	14.1	0.7	-	-	-	-	-	-	-	-	14.3	1.4	-	-
1935	-	-	-	-	14.3	0.0	-	-	-	-	-	-	14.3	0.0	-	-	-	-	14.4	0.7	-	-	-	-
1936	14.5	0.7	-	-	-	-	14.3	-1.4	-	-	-	-	14.5	1.4	-	-	14.6	0.7	-	-	-	-	14.5	-0.7
1937	-	-	-	-	14.8	2.1	-	-	-	-	14.9	0.7	-	-	-	-	15.0	0.7	-	-	-	-	14.8	-1.3
1938	-	-	-	-	14.5	-2.0	-	-	-	-	14.5	0.0	-	-	-	-	14.5	0.0	-	-	-	-	14.5	0.0
1939	-	-	-	-	14.3	-1.4	-	-	-	-	14.3	0.0	-	-	-	-	14.5	1.4	-	-	-	-	14.3	-1.4
1940	-	-	-	-	14.5	1.4	-	-	-	-	14.5	0.0	-	-	-	-	14.5	0.0	-	-	-	-	14.5	0.0
1941	-	-	-	-	14.6	0.7	-	-	-	-	15.0	2.7	-	-	-	-	15.5	3.3	15.7	1.3	15.8	0.6	15.9	0.6
1942	16.1	1.3	16.2	0.6	16.5	1.9	16.5	0.0	16.7	1.2	16.8	0.6	16.9	0.6	17.0	0.6	17.0	0.0	17.1	0.6	17.2	0.6	17.3	0.6
1943	17.4	0.6	17.3	-0.6	17.6	1.7	17.8	1.1	18.0	1.1	18.0	0.0	17.9	-0.6	17.9	0.0	18.0	0.6	18.1	0.6	18.0	-0.6	18.0	0.0
1944	18.0	0.0	17.9	-0.6	17.8	-0.6	17.9	0.6	18.1	1.1	18.1	0.0	18.1	0.0	18.2	0.6	18.2	0.0	18.2	0.0	18.3	0.5	18.3	0.0
1945	18.4	0.5	18.4	0.0	18.3	-0.5	18.4	0.5	18.6	1.1	18.7	0.5	18.8	0.5	18.8	0.0	18.8	0.0	18.8	0.0	18.9	0.5	18.9	0.0
1946	19.1	1.1	19.0	-0.5	19.1	0.5	19.2	0.5	19.2	0.0	19.5	1.6	20.5	5.1	20.8	1.5	21.1	1.4	21.5	1.9	21.9	1.9	22.2	1.4
1947	22.2	0.0	22.1	-0.5	22.6	2.3	22.6	0.0	22.5	-0.4	22.7	0.9	-	-	23.2	2.2	-	-	-	-	23.6	1.7	-	-
1948	-	-	23.8	0.8	-	-	-	-	24.3	2.1	-	-	-	-	24.7	1.6	-	-	-	-	24.4	-1.2	-	-
1949	-	-	24.0	-1.6	-	-	-	-	24.2	0.8	-	-	-	-	24.4	0.8	-	-	-	-	24.4	0.0	-	-
1950	-	-	24.1	-1.2	-	-	-	-	24.2	0.4	-	-	-	-	24.8	2.5	-	-	-	-	25.2	1.6	-	-
1951	-	-	26.0	3.2	-	-	-	-	26.1	0.4	-	-	-	-	26.2	0.4	-	-	-	-	26.8	2.3	-	-
1952	-	-	26.6	-0.7	-	-	-	-	26.8	0.8	-	-	-	-	27.2	1.5	-	-	-	-	27.1	-0.4	-	-
1953	-	-	26.9	-0.7	-	-	-	-	27.0	0.4	-	-	-	-	27.2	0.7	-	-	-	-	27.2	0.0	-	-
1954	-	-	27.2	0.0	-	-	-	-	27.0	-0.7	-	-	-	-	27.2	0.7	-	-	-	-	27.0	-0.7	-	-
1955	-	-	26.9	-0.4	-	-	-	-	27.0	0.4	-	-	-	-	27.1	0.4	-	-	-	-	27.0	-0.4	-	-
1956	-	-	27.0	0.0	-	-	-	-	27.2	0.7	-	-	-	-	27.5	1.1	-	-	-	-	27.6	0.4	-	-
1957	-	-	28.0	1.4	-	-	-	-	27.9	-0.4	-	-	-	-	28.3	1.4	-	-	-	-	28.4	0.4	-	-
1958	-	-	28.6	0.7	-	-	-	-	28.8	0.7	-	-	-	-	28.8	0.0	-	-	-	-	28.9	0.3	-	-

[Continued]

Washington, DC-MD-VA
Consumer Price Index - Urban Wage Earners
Base 1982-1984 = 100
All Items
[Continued]

For 1914-1993. Columns headed % show percentile change in the index from the previous period for which an index is available.

Year	Jan Index	%	Feb Index	%	Mar Index	%	Apr Index	%	May Index	%	Jun Index	%	Jul Index	%	Aug Index	%	Sep Index	%	Oct Index	%	Nov Index	%	Dec Index	%
1959	-	-	28.8	-0.3	-	-	-	-	29.0	0.7	-	-	-	-	29.0	0.0	-	-	-	-	29.0	0.0	-	-
1960	-	-	29.0	0.0	-	-	-	-	29.3	1.0	-	-	-	-	29.3	0.0	-	-	-	-	29.5	0.7	-	-
1961	-	-	29.7	0.7	-	-	-	-	29.6	-0.3	-	-	-	-	29.8	0.7	-	-	-	-	29.9	0.3	-	-
1962	-	-	29.8	-0.3	-	-	-	-	29.9	0.3	-	-	-	-	30.1	0.7	-	-	-	-	30.2	0.3	-	-
1963	-	-	30.3	0.3	-	-	-	-	30.4	0.3	-	-	-	-	30.6	0.7	-	-	-	-	30.7	0.3	-	-
1964	-	-	30.8	0.3	-	-	-	-	30.8	0.0	-	-	-	-	31.2	1.3	-	-	-	-	31.2	0.0	-	-
1965	-	-	31.2	0.0	-	-	-	-	31.4	0.6	-	-	-	-	31.4	0.0	-	-	-	-	31.7	1.0	-	-
1966	-	-	32.1	1.3	-	-	-	-	32.3	0.6	-	-	-	-	32.7	1.2	-	-	-	-	32.9	0.6	-	-
1967	-	-	33.0	0.3	-	-	-	-	33.2	0.6	-	-	-	-	33.6	1.2	-	-	-	-	33.8	0.6	-	-
1968	-	-	34.1	0.9	-	-	-	-	34.7	1.8	-	-	-	-	35.3	1.7	-	-	-	-	35.8	1.4	-	-
1969	-	-	36.2	1.1	-	-	-	-	36.9	1.9	-	-	-	-	37.5	1.6	-	-	-	-	37.8	0.8	-	-
1970	-	-	38.6	2.1	-	-	-	-	39.2	1.6	-	-	-	-	39.5	0.8	-	-	-	-	39.8	0.8	-	-
1971	-	-	40.4	1.5	-	-	-	-	40.8	1.0	-	-	-	-	41.2	1.0	-	-	-	-	41.5	0.7	-	-
1972	-	-	41.6	0.2	-	-	-	-	41.9	0.7	-	-	-	-	42.6	1.7	-	-	-	-	43.3	1.6	-	-
1973	-	-	43.6	0.7	-	-	-	-	44.5	2.1	-	-	-	-	45.5	2.2	-	-	-	-	46.5	2.2	-	-
1974	-	-	48.1	3.4	-	-	-	-	49.3	2.5	-	-	-	-	51.0	3.4	-	-	-	-	52.1	2.2	-	-
1975	-	-	52.7	1.2	-	-	-	-	53.4	1.3	-	-	-	-	54.6	2.2	-	-	-	-	55.2	1.1	-	-
1976	-	-	55.8	1.1	-	-	-	-	56.8	1.8	-	-	-	-	57.8	1.8	-	-	-	-	58.2	0.7	-	-
1977	-	-	59.4	2.1	-	-	-	-	60.7	2.2	-	-	-	-	61.7	1.6	-	-	-	-	62.6	1.5	-	-
1978	63.1	0.8	-	-	63.7	1.0	-	-	65.5	2.8	-	-	67.0	2.3	-	-	67.7	1.0	-	-	68.6	1.3	-	-
1979	69.9	1.9	-	-	71.3	2.0	-	-	72.7	2.0	-	-	74.1	1.9	-	-	74.9	1.1	-	-	75.7	1.1	-	-
1980	77.8	2.8	-	-	79.9	2.7	-	-	80.8	1.1	-	-	83.0	2.7	-	-	84.1	1.3	-	-	85.4	1.5	-	-
1981	86.6	1.4	-	-	88.2	1.8	-	-	89.4	1.4	-	-	90.6	1.3	-	-	92.1	1.7	-	-	93.3	1.3	-	-
1982	94.1	0.9	-	-	94.8	0.7	-	-	94.6	-0.2	-	-	95.6	1.1	-	-	97.5	2.0	-	-	97.4	-0.1	-	-
1983	97.9	0.5	-	-	98.4	0.5	-	-	99.4	1.0	-	-	100.3	0.9	-	-	100.6	0.3	-	-	101.2	0.6	-	-
1984	102.9	1.7	-	-	102.9	0.0	-	-	103.1	0.2	-	-	103.8	0.7	-	-	106.1	2.2	-	-	106.6	0.5	-	-
1985	106.1	-0.5	-	-	107.6	1.4	-	-	107.9	0.3	-	-	108.8	0.8	-	-	109.3	0.5	-	-	110.4	1.0	-	-
1986	111.1	0.6	-	-	110.4	-0.6	-	-	110.3	-0.1	-	-	110.3	0.0	-	-	111.7	1.3	-	-	112.2	0.4	-	-
1987	112.7	0.4	-	-	113.6	0.8	-	-	114.6	0.9	-	-	115.3	0.6	-	-	117.1	1.6	-	-	117.9	0.7	-	-
1988	117.6	-0.3	-	-	118.5	0.8	-	-	119.3	0.7	-	-	119.9	0.5	-	-	122.3	2.0	-	-	122.6	0.2	-	-
1989	123.7	0.9	-	-	125.6	1.5	-	-	126.6	0.8	-	-	127.3	0.6	-	-	129.5	1.7	-	-	129.6	0.1	-	-
1990	131.1	1.2	-	-	132.9	1.4	-	-	132.8	-0.1	-	-	134.6	1.4	-	-	136.9	1.7	-	-	137.2	0.2	-	-
1991	137.7	0.4	-	-	137.9	0.1	-	-	139.6	1.2	-	-	139.2	-0.3	-	-	141.8	1.9	-	-	141.1	-0.5	-	-
1992	141.3	0.1	-	-	141.3	0.0	-	-	141.6	0.2	-	-	143.3	1.2	-	-	144.2	0.6	-	-	145.1	0.6	-	-
1993	145.6	0.3	-	-	146.2	0.4	-	-	147.0	0.5	-	-	147.0	0.0	-	-	147.5	0.3	-	-	148.5	0.7	-	-

Source: U.S. Department of Labor, Bureau of Labor Statistics, Division of Consumer Prices and Price Indexes. - indicates no data collected for period.

Washington, DC-MD-VA
Consumer Price Index - All Urban Consumers
Base 1982-1984 = 100
Food and Beverages

For 1975-1993. Columns headed % show percentile change in the index from the previous period for which an index is available.

Year	Jan Index	%	Feb Index	%	Mar Index	%	Apr Index	%	May Index	%	Jun Index	%	Jul Index	%	Aug Index	%	Sep Index	%	Oct Index	%	Nov Index	%	Dec Index	%
1975	-	-	-	-	-	-	-	-	61.7	-	-	-	-	-	-	-	-	-	-	-	61.5	-	-	-
1976	-	-	61.5	0.0	-	-	-	-	61.7	0.3	-	-	-	-	63.5	2.9	-	-	-	-	63.0	-0.8	-	-
1977	-	-	65.1	3.3	-	-	-	-	66.4	2.0	-	-	-	-	67.5	1.7	-	-	-	-	68.3	1.2	-	-
1978	69.3	1.5	-	-	70.7	2.0	-	-	72.9	3.1	-	-	74.9	2.7	-	-	74.8	-0.1	-	-	75.4	0.8	-	-
1979	78.2	3.7	-	-	80.4	2.8	-	-	82.0	2.0	-	-	82.4	0.5	-	-	83.3	1.1	-	-	83.1	-0.2	-	-
1980	84.1	1.2	-	-	85.3	1.4	-	-	85.7	0.5	-	-	88.5	3.3	-	-	90.3	2.0	-	-	91.9	1.8	-	-
1981	93.0	1.2	-	-	93.6	0.6	-	-	90.7	-3.1	-	-	91.1	0.4	-	-	93.1	2.2	-	-	93.5	0.4	-	-
1982	95.0	1.6	-	-	96.2	1.3	-	-	97.0	0.8	-	-	97.9	0.9	-	-	98.5	0.6	-	-	97.6	-0.9	-	-
1983	98.4	0.8	-	-	99.7	1.3	-	-	100.9	1.2	-	-	100.3	-0.6	-	-	99.5	-0.8	-	-	99.2	-0.3	-	-
1984	101.8	2.6	-	-	103.4	1.6	-	-	102.5	-0.9	-	-	102.9	0.4	-	-	103.5	0.6	-	-	103.5	0.0	-	-
1985	104.2	0.7	-	-	105.7	1.4	-	-	105.9	0.2	-	-	106.0	0.1	-	-	106.4	0.4	-	-	107.3	0.8	-	-
1986	109.4	2.0	-	-	109.2	-0.2	-	-	110.9	1.6	-	-	110.5	-0.4	-	-	110.7	0.2	-	-	109.4	-1.2	-	-
1987	111.6	2.0	-	-	111.9	0.3	-	-	113.6	1.5	-	-	114.2	0.5	-	-	114.5	0.3	-	-	114.8	0.3	-	-
1988	116.0	1.0	-	-	116.7	0.6	-	-	117.9	1.0	-	-	120.5	2.2	-	-	121.3	0.7	-	-	121.1	-0.2	-	-
1989	122.7	1.3	-	-	124.4	1.4	-	-	126.5	1.7	-	-	126.4	-0.1	-	-	126.8	0.3	-	-	127.8	0.8	-	-
1990	131.7	3.1	-	-	133.3	1.2	-	-	132.8	-0.4	-	-	133.9	0.8	-	-	133.9	0.0	-	-	133.8	-0.1	-	-
1991	135.9	1.6	-	-	137.3	1.0	-	-	137.1	-0.1	-	-	137.7	0.4	-	-	138.1	0.3	-	-	139.0	0.7	-	-
1992	140.5	1.1	-	-	142.3	1.3	-	-	141.3	-0.7	-	-	140.2	-0.8	-	-	140.1	-0.1	-	-	140.9	0.6	-	-
1993	141.8	0.6	-	-	142.2	0.3	-	-	144.0	1.3	-	-	142.4	-1.1	-	-	141.9	-0.4	-	-	144.1	1.6	-	-

Source: U.S. Department of Labor, Bureau of Labor Statistics, Division of Consumer Prices and Price Indexes. - indicates no data collected for period.

Washington, DC-MD-VA
Consumer Price Index - Urban Wage Earners
Base 1982-1984 = 100
Food and Beverages

For 1975-1993. Columns headed % show percentile change in the index from the previous period for which an index is available.

Year	Jan Index	%	Feb Index	%	Mar Index	%	Apr Index	%	May Index	%	Jun Index	%	Jul Index	%	Aug Index	%	Sep Index	%	Oct Index	%	Nov Index	%	Dec Index	%
1975	-	-	-	-	-	-	-	-	-	-	-	-	-	-	-	-	-	-	-	-	60.6	-	-	-
1976	-	-	60.6	0.0	-	-	-	-	60.8	0.3	-	-	-	-	62.6	3.0	-	-	-	-	62.0	-1.0	-	-
1977	-	-	64.1	3.4	-	-	-	-	65.4	2.0	-	-	-	-	66.5	1.7	-	-	-	-	67.3	1.2	-	-
1978	68.2	1.3	-	-	69.4	1.8	-	-	72.8	4.9	-	-	74.3	2.1	-	-	73.8	-0.7	-	-	73.9	0.1	-	-
1979	76.4	3.4	-	-	78.2	2.4	-	-	80.2	2.6	-	-	80.4	0.2	-	-	81.2	1.0	-	-	80.6	-0.7	-	-
1980	81.6	1.2	-	-	82.6	1.2	-	-	82.5	-0.1	-	-	85.7	3.9	-	-	88.0	2.7	-	-	90.8	3.2	-	-
1981	91.7	1.0	-	-	92.1	0.4	-	-	89.6	-2.7	-	-	90.5	1.0	-	-	92.7	2.4	-	-	93.3	0.6	-	-
1982	95.0	1.8	-	-	96.3	1.4	-	-	97.0	0.7	-	-	98.1	1.1	-	-	98.8	0.7	-	-	97.9	-0.9	-	-
1983	98.5	0.6	-	-	99.7	1.2	-	-	100.6	0.9	-	-	100.2	-0.4	-	-	99.2	-1.0	-	-	99.0	-0.2	-	-
1984	101.9	2.9	-	-	103.3	1.4	-	-	102.5	-0.8	-	-	102.8	0.3	-	-	103.5	0.7	-	-	103.5	0.0	-	-
1985	104.0	0.5	-	-	105.7	1.6	-	-	105.9	0.2	-	-	105.9	0.0	-	-	106.3	0.4	-	-	107.2	0.8	-	-
1986	108.9	1.6	-	-	108.8	-0.1	-	-	110.5	1.6	-	-	110.2	-0.3	-	-	110.7	0.5	-	-	109.6	-1.0	-	-
1987	112.0	2.2	-	-	112.2	0.2	-	-	114.0	1.6	-	-	114.6	0.5	-	-	114.7	0.1	-	-	114.9	0.2	-	-
1988	116.2	1.1	-	-	116.9	0.6	-	-	118.1	1.0	-	-	120.6	2.1	-	-	121.4	0.7	-	-	121.2	-0.2	-	-
1989	123.0	1.5	-	-	124.7	1.4	-	-	126.7	1.6	-	-	126.6	-0.1	-	-	127.3	0.6	-	-	128.2	0.7	-	-
1990	132.2	3.1	-	-	134.3	1.6	-	-	133.1	-0.9	-	-	134.2	0.8	-	-	134.2	0.0	-	-	134.0	-0.1	-	-
1991	136.1	1.6	-	-	137.5	1.0	-	-	137.2	-0.2	-	-	137.9	0.5	-	-	138.3	0.3	-	-	138.9	0.4	-	-
1992	140.5	1.2	-	-	142.4	1.4	-	-	141.2	-0.8	-	-	140.3	-0.6	-	-	140.1	-0.1	-	-	141.0	0.6	-	-
1993	141.8	0.6	-	-	142.3	0.4	-	-	144.2	1.3	-	-	142.3	-1.3	-	-	141.9	-0.3	-	-	143.8	1.3	-	-

Source: U.S. Department of Labor, Bureau of Labor Statistics, Division of Consumer Prices and Price Indexes. - indicates no data collected for period.

Washington, DC-MD-VA

Consumer Price Index - All Urban Consumers
Base 1982-1984 = 100
Housing

For 1975-1993. Columns headed % show percentile change in the index from the previous period for which an index is available.

Year	Jan Index	%	Feb Index	%	Mar Index	%	Apr Index	%	May Index	%	Jun Index	%	Jul Index	%	Aug Index	%	Sep Index	%	Oct Index	%	Nov Index	%	Dec Index	%
1975	-	-	-	-	-	-	-	-	-	-	-	-	-	-	-	-	-	-	-	-	53.0	-	-	-
1976	-	-	53.8	1.5	-	-	-	-	54.9	2.0	-	-	-	-	55.7	1.5	-	-	-	-	56.4	1.3	-	-
1977	-	-	57.6	2.1	-	-	-	-	58.7	1.9	-	-	-	-	60.0	2.2	-	-	-	-	61.2	2.0	-	-
1978	62.2	1.6	-	-	62.4	0.3	-	-	63.4	1.6	-	-	64.6	1.9	-	-	66.0	2.2	-	-	67.0	1.5	-	-
1979	69.5	3.7	-	-	70.2	1.0	-	-	70.8	0.9	-	-	72.9	3.0	-	-	72.7	-0.3	-	-	73.6	1.2	-	-
1980	76.5	3.9	-	-	79.0	3.3	-	-	80.2	1.5	-	-	82.5	2.9	-	-	81.8	-0.8	-	-	83.9	2.6	-	-
1981	85.3	1.7	-	-	87.5	2.6	-	-	89.3	2.1	-	-	90.6	1.5	-	-	91.8	1.3	-	-	93.8	2.2	-	-
1982	94.7	1.0	-	-	94.6	-0.1	-	-	94.1	-0.5	-	-	94.7	0.6	-	-	97.0	2.4	-	-	96.6	-0.4	-	-
1983	98.2	1.7	-	-	97.8	-0.4	-	-	98.6	0.8	-	-	101.2	2.6	-	-	100.3	-0.9	-	-	101.1	0.8	-	-
1984	103.3	2.2	-	-	103.5	0.2	-	-	103.2	-0.3	-	-	104.2	1.0	-	-	106.5	2.2	-	-	107.4	0.8	-	-
1985	107.4	0.0	-	-	109.1	1.6	-	-	108.9	-0.2	-	-	111.6	2.5	-	-	110.4	-1.1	-	-	111.4	0.9	-	-
1986	114.4	2.7	-	-	114.0	-0.3	-	-	114.5	0.4	-	-	113.9	-0.5	-	-	114.7	0.7	-	-	116.3	1.4	-	-
1987	117.1	0.7	-	-	116.7	-0.3	-	-	117.7	0.9	-	-	118.8	0.9	-	-	121.0	1.9	-	-	121.0	0.0	-	-
1988	121.1	0.1	-	-	121.2	0.1	-	-	122.3	0.9	-	-	124.7	2.0	-	-	125.3	0.5	-	-	124.4	-0.7	-	-
1989	125.9	1.2	-	-	127.6	1.4	-	-	128.1	0.4	-	-	129.5	1.1	-	-	131.7	1.7	-	-	131.2	-0.4	-	-
1990	134.1	2.2	-	-	134.8	0.5	-	-	134.6	-0.1	-	-	138.4	2.8	-	-	138.8	0.3	-	-	137.7	-0.8	-	-
1991	138.2	0.4	-	-	138.9	0.5	-	-	142.0	2.2	-	-	141.8	-0.1	-	-	142.9	0.8	-	-	140.2	-1.9	-	-
1992	142.1	1.4	-	-	142.2	0.1	-	-	142.4	0.1	-	-	144.9	1.8	-	-	146.0	0.8	-	-	145.2	-0.5	-	-
1993	145.2	0.0	-	-	145.9	0.5	-	-	147.3	1.0	-	-	149.2	1.3	-	-	149.4	0.1	-	-	149.6	0.1	-	-

Source: U.S. Department of Labor, Bureau of Labor Statistics, Division of Consumer Prices and Price Indexes. - indicates no data collected for period.

Washington, DC-MD-VA
Consumer Price Index - Urban Wage Earners
Base 1982-1984 = 100
Housing

For 1975-1993. Columns headed % show percentile change in the index from the previous period for which an index is available.

Year	Jan Index	%	Feb Index	%	Mar Index	%	Apr Index	%	May Index	%	Jun Index	%	Jul Index	%	Aug Index	%	Sep Index	%	Oct Index	%	Nov Index	%	Dec Index	%
1975	-		-		-		-		-		-		-		-		-		-		53.4		-	
1976	-		54.3	1.7	-		-		55.4	2.0	-		-		56.2	1.4	-		-		56.8	1.1	-	
1977	-		58.1	2.3	-		-		59.1	1.7	-		-		60.5	2.4	-		-		61.7	2.0	-	
1978	62.6	1.5	-		62.9	0.5	-		64.6	2.7	-		66.4	2.8	-		67.8	2.1	-		68.3	0.7	-	
1979	70.5	3.2	-		71.5	1.4	-		72.2	1.0	-		73.9	2.4	-		74.0	0.1	-		74.8	1.1	-	
1980	77.5	3.6	-		79.7	2.8	-		81.2	1.9	-		83.4	2.7	-		83.0	-0.5	-		84.5	1.8	-	
1981	86.1	1.9	-		87.8	2.0	-		89.6	2.1	-		91.0	1.6	-		92.3	1.4	-		94.2	2.1	-	
1982	95.1	1.0	-		95.1	0.0	-		95.1	0.0	-		95.7	0.6	-		98.1	2.5	-		97.7	-0.4	-	
1983	98.0	0.3	-		98.6	0.6	-		98.9	0.3	-		100.0	1.1	-		99.5	-0.5	-		100.6	1.1	-	
1984	103.2	2.6	-		102.5	-0.7	-		102.6	0.1	-		103.1	0.5	-		106.4	3.2	-		106.9	0.5	-	
1985	106.6	-0.3	-		108.3	1.6	-		108.5	0.2	-		111.1	2.4	-		110.1	-0.9	-		111.2	1.0	-	
1986	113.8	2.3	-		113.5	-0.3	-		114.1	0.5	-		113.4	-0.6	-		114.2	0.7	-		115.9	1.5	-	
1987	116.7	0.7	-		116.1	-0.5	-		117.0	0.8	-		118.0	0.9	-		120.1	1.8	-		120.3	0.2	-	
1988	120.4	0.1	-		120.5	0.1	-		121.5	0.8	-		123.9	2.0	-		124.7	0.6	-		123.5	-1.0	-	
1989	125.2	1.4	-		126.9	1.4	-		127.2	0.2	-		128.7	1.2	-		130.9	1.7	-		129.8	-0.8	-	
1990	133.0	2.5	-		133.2	0.2	-		132.8	-0.3	-		136.9	3.1	-		137.3	0.3	-		135.8	-1.1	-	
1991	136.4	0.4	-		137.2	0.6	-		140.5	2.4	-		139.6	-0.6	-		141.1	1.1	-		138.5	-1.8	-	
1992	140.1	1.2	-		140.0	-0.1	-		140.3	0.2	-		142.8	1.8	-		143.4	0.4	-		142.9	-0.3	-	
1993	142.4	-0.3	-		143.1	0.5	-		144.6	1.0	-		146.7	1.5	-		146.9	0.1	-		146.9	0.0	-	

Source: U.S. Department of Labor, Bureau of Labor Statistics, Division of Consumer Prices and Price Indexes. - indicates no data collected for period.

Washington, DC-MD-VA
Consumer Price Index - All Urban Consumers
Base 1982-1984 = 100
Apparel and Upkeep

For 1952-1993. Columns headed % show percentile change in the index from the previous period for which an index is available.

Year	Jan Index	%	Feb Index	%	Mar Index	%	Apr Index	%	May Index	%	Jun Index	%	Jul Index	%	Aug Index	%	Sep Index	%	Oct Index	%	Nov Index	%	Dec Index	%
1952	-	-	-	-	-	-	-	-	-	-	-	-	-	-	-	-	-	-	-	-	40.1	-	-	-
1953	-	-	40.3	0.5	-	-	-	-	40.5	0.5	-	-	-	-	40.5	0.0	-	-	-	-	40.6	0.2	-	-
1954	-	-	40.5	-0.2	-	-	-	-	40.3	-0.5	-	-	-	-	40.0	-0.7	-	-	-	-	40.2	0.5	-	-
1955	-	-	39.8	-1.0	-	-	-	-	39.8	0.0	-	-	-	-	40.0	0.5	-	-	-	-	40.4	1.0	-	-
1956	-	-	40.7	0.7	-	-	-	-	41.1	1.0	-	-	-	-	41.2	0.2	-	-	-	-	41.2	0.0	-	-
1957	-	-	41.3	0.2	-	-	-	-	41.3	0.0	-	-	-	-	41.4	0.2	-	-	-	-	41.2	-0.5	-	-
1958	-	-	41.1	-0.2	-	-	-	-	41.1	0.0	-	-	-	-	41.2	0.2	-	-	-	-	41.2	0.0	-	-
1959	-	-	41.3	0.2	-	-	-	-	41.6	0.7	-	-	-	-	42.0	1.0	-	-	-	-	42.0	0.0	-	-
1960	-	-	41.7	-0.7	-	-	-	-	42.0	0.7	-	-	-	-	42.2	0.5	-	-	-	-	42.3	0.2	-	-
1961	-	-	42.4	0.2	-	-	-	-	42.6	0.5	-	-	-	-	42.6	0.0	-	-	-	-	43.7	2.6	-	-
1962	-	-	43.9	0.5	-	-	-	-	43.9	0.0	-	-	-	-	44.0	0.2	-	-	-	-	44.7	1.6	-	-
1963	-	-	44.2	-1.1	-	-	-	-	44.3	0.2	-	-	-	-	43.9	-0.9	-	-	-	-	44.5	1.4	-	-
1964	-	-	44.4	-0.2	-	-	-	-	44.7	0.7	-	-	-	-	44.6	-0.2	-	-	-	-	44.7	0.2	-	-
1965	-	-	44.3	-0.9	-	-	-	-	45.2	2.0	-	-	-	-	44.5	-1.5	-	-	-	-	45.3	1.8	-	-
1966	-	-	45.5	0.4	-	-	-	-	46.5	2.2	-	-	-	-	46.3	-0.4	-	-	-	-	47.5	2.6	-	-
1967	-	-	47.7	0.4	-	-	-	-	48.6	1.9	-	-	-	-	48.5	-0.2	-	-	-	-	49.7	2.5	-	-
1968	-	-	50.2	1.0	-	-	-	-	52.3	4.2	-	-	-	-	52.6	0.6	-	-	-	-	54.1	2.9	-	-
1969	-	-	54.3	0.4	-	-	-	-	55.9	2.9	-	-	-	-	55.7	-0.4	-	-	-	-	57.0	2.3	-	-
1970	-	-	57.0	0.0	-	-	-	-	58.5	2.6	-	-	-	-	58.0	-0.9	-	-	-	-	59.5	2.6	-	-
1971	-	-	58.8	-1.2	-	-	-	-	60.0	2.0	-	-	-	-	59.7	-0.5	-	-	-	-	61.1	2.3	-	-
1972	-	-	60.0	-1.8	-	-	-	-	61.0	1.7	-	-	-	-	60.3	-1.1	-	-	-	-	61.9	2.7	-	-
1973	-	-	62.2	0.5	-	-	-	-	64.1	3.1	-	-	-	-	63.7	-0.6	-	-	-	-	64.8	1.7	-	-
1974	-	-	66.3	2.3	-	-	-	-	68.2	2.9	-	-	-	-	69.2	1.5	-	-	-	-	70.5	1.9	-	-
1975	-	-	70.1	-0.6	-	-	-	-	70.5	0.6	-	-	-	-	69.9	-0.9	-	-	-	-	71.4	2.1	-	-
1976	-	-	70.6	-1.1	-	-	-	-	73.3	3.8	-	-	-	-	73.1	-0.3	-	-	-	-	73.8	1.0	-	-
1977	-	-	72.4	-1.9	-	-	-	-	74.1	2.3	-	-	-	-	74.6	0.7	-	-	-	-	75.8	1.6	-	-
1978	75.6	-0.3	-	-	76.8	1.6	-	-	78.2	1.8	-	-	76.5	-2.2	-	-	79.8	4.3	-	-	80.6	1.0	-	-
1979	77.3	-4.1	-	-	81.6	5.6	-	-	83.3	2.1	-	-	81.4	-2.3	-	-	87.2	7.1	-	-	87.7	0.6	-	-
1980	86.7	-1.1	-	-	91.5	5.5	-	-	89.9	-1.7	-	-	87.9	-2.2	-	-	91.8	4.4	-	-	93.0	1.3	-	-
1981	89.7	-3.5	-	-	89.7	0.0	-	-	90.8	1.2	-	-	87.6	-3.5	-	-	93.4	6.6	-	-	91.8	-1.7	-	-
1982	90.7	-1.2	-	-	95.5	5.3	-	-	93.7	-1.9	-	-	92.2	-1.6	-	-	96.6	4.8	-	-	97.8	1.2	-	-
1983	97.0	-0.8	-	-	100.4	3.5	-	-	102.6	2.2	-	-	103.0	0.4	-	-	100.9	-2.0	-	-	99.0	-1.9	-	-
1984	99.9	0.9	-	-	101.1	1.2	-	-	104.4	3.3	-	-	103.4	-1.0	-	-	109.8	6.2	-	-	108.6	-1.1	-	-
1985	104.8	-3.5	-	-	110.4	5.3	-	-	109.4	-0.9	-	-	106.7	-2.5	-	-	113.8	6.7	-	-	114.3	0.4	-	-
1986	106.2	-7.1	-	-	105.3	-0.8	-	-	104.4	-0.9	-	-	104.5	0.1	-	-	115.6	10.6	-	-	115.4	-0.2	-	-
1987	110.7	-4.1	-	-	113.0	2.1	-	-	115.0	1.8	-	-	112.1	-2.5	-	-	122.0	8.8	-	-	123.5	1.2	-	-
1988	116.4	-5.7	-	-	124.9	7.3	-	-	122.3	-2.1	-	-	111.6	-8.7	-	-	130.8	17.2	-	-	131.0	0.2	-	-
1989	125.0	-4.6	-	-	135.6	8.5	-	-	135.7	0.1	-	-	130.8	-3.6	-	-	142.1	8.6	-	-	139.7	-1.7	-	-
1990	128.2	-8.2	-	-	141.9	10.7	-	-	140.4	-1.1	-	-	135.0	-3.8	-	-	147.0	8.9	-	-	141.1	-4.0	-	-
1991	138.9	-1.6	-	-	138.8	-0.1	-	-	139.3	0.4	-	-	135.2	-2.9	-	-	153.3	13.4	-	-	149.9	-2.2	-	-
1992	136.5	-8.9	-	-	138.4	1.4	-	-	134.5	-2.8	-	-	136.2	1.3	-	-	145.3	6.7	-	-	144.8	-0.3	-	-
1993	145.7	0.6	-	-	150.6	3.4	-	-	146.4	-2.8	-	-	136.4	-6.8	-	-	144.3	5.8	-	-	145.2	0.6	-	-

Source: U.S. Department of Labor, Bureau of Labor Statistics, Division of Consumer Prices and Price Indexes. - indicates no data collected for period.

Washington, DC-MD-VA
Consumer Price Index - Urban Wage Earners
Base 1982-1984 = 100
Apparel and Upkeep

For 1952-1993. Columns headed % show percentile change in the index from the previous period for which an index is available.

Year	Jan Index	%	Feb Index	%	Mar Index	%	Apr Index	%	May Index	%	Jun Index	%	Jul Index	%	Aug Index	%	Sep Index	%	Oct Index	%	Nov Index	%	Dec Index	%
1952	-	-	-	-	-	-	-	-	-	-	-	-	-	-	-	-	-	-	-	-	36.0	-	-	-
1953	-	-	36.3	0.8	-	-	-	-	36.4	0.3	-	-	-	-	36.5	0.3	-	-	-	-	36.6	0.3	-	-
1954	-	-	36.4	-0.5	-	-	-	-	36.2	-0.5	-	-	-	-	35.9	-0.8	-	-	-	-	36.2	0.8	-	-
1955	-	-	35.8	-1.1	-	-	-	-	35.8	0.0	-	-	-	-	36.0	0.6	-	-	-	-	36.3	0.8	-	-
1956	-	-	36.6	0.8	-	-	-	-	37.0	1.1	-	-	-	-	37.1	0.3	-	-	-	-	37.0	-0.3	-	-
1957	-	-	37.2	0.5	-	-	-	-	37.1	-0.3	-	-	-	-	37.3	0.5	-	-	-	-	37.1	-0.5	-	-
1958	-	-	37.0	-0.3	-	-	-	-	37.0	0.0	-	-	-	-	37.0	0.0	-	-	-	-	37.1	0.3	-	-
1959	-	-	37.1	0.0	-	-	-	-	37.4	0.8	-	-	-	-	37.8	1.1	-	-	-	-	37.7	-0.3	-	-
1960	-	-	37.5	-0.5	-	-	-	-	37.8	0.8	-	-	-	-	38.0	0.5	-	-	-	-	38.1	0.3	-	-
1961	-	-	38.1	0.0	-	-	-	-	38.3	0.5	-	-	-	-	38.4	0.3	-	-	-	-	39.3	2.3	-	-
1962	-	-	39.4	0.3	-	-	-	-	39.5	0.3	-	-	-	-	39.6	0.3	-	-	-	-	40.2	1.5	-	-
1963	-	-	39.8	-1.0	-	-	-	-	39.9	0.3	-	-	-	-	39.5	-1.0	-	-	-	-	40.1	1.5	-	-
1964	-	-	39.9	-0.5	-	-	-	-	40.2	0.8	-	-	-	-	40.1	-0.2	-	-	-	-	40.2	0.2	-	-
1965	-	-	39.9	-0.7	-	-	-	-	40.7	2.0	-	-	-	-	40.1	-1.5	-	-	-	-	40.7	1.5	-	-
1966	-	-	40.9	0.5	-	-	-	-	41.8	2.2	-	-	-	-	41.7	-0.2	-	-	-	-	42.7	2.4	-	-
1967	-	-	42.9	0.5	-	-	-	-	43.7	1.9	-	-	-	-	43.6	-0.2	-	-	-	-	44.7	2.5	-	-
1968	-	-	45.1	0.9	-	-	-	-	47.0	4.2	-	-	-	-	47.3	0.6	-	-	-	-	48.6	2.7	-	-
1969	-	-	48.9	0.6	-	-	-	-	50.3	2.9	-	-	-	-	50.1	-0.4	-	-	-	-	51.3	2.4	-	-
1970	-	-	51.3	0.0	-	-	-	-	52.6	2.5	-	-	-	-	52.1	-1.0	-	-	-	-	53.5	2.7	-	-
1971	-	-	52.9	-1.1	-	-	-	-	54.0	2.1	-	-	-	-	53.7	-0.6	-	-	-	-	55.0	2.4	-	-
1972	-	-	53.9	-2.0	-	-	-	-	54.9	1.9	-	-	-	-	54.2	-1.3	-	-	-	-	55.7	2.8	-	-
1973	-	-	55.9	0.4	-	-	-	-	57.7	3.2	-	-	-	-	57.3	-0.7	-	-	-	-	58.3	1.7	-	-
1974	-	-	59.7	2.4	-	-	-	-	61.4	2.8	-	-	-	-	62.2	1.3	-	-	-	-	63.4	1.9	-	-
1975	-	-	63.0	-0.6	-	-	-	-	63.4	0.6	-	-	-	-	62.9	-0.8	-	-	-	-	64.3	2.2	-	-
1976	-	-	63.5	-1.2	-	-	-	-	65.9	3.8	-	-	-	-	65.7	-0.3	-	-	-	-	66.4	1.1	-	-
1977	-	-	65.1	-2.0	-	-	-	-	66.6	2.3	-	-	-	-	67.1	0.8	-	-	-	-	68.2	1.6	-	-
1978	65.9	-3.4	-	-	66.6	1.1	-	-	68.2	2.4	-	-	67.9	-0.4	-	-	70.2	3.4	-	-	70.9	1.0	-	-
1979	67.6	-4.7	-	-	70.4	4.1	-	-	71.4	1.4	-	-	71.4	0.0	-	-	75.3	5.5	-	-	75.5	0.3	-	-
1980	75.7	0.3	-	-	78.4	3.6	-	-	78.7	0.4	-	-	78.3	-0.5	-	-	86.5	10.5	-	-	85.3	-1.4	-	-
1981	84.1	-1.4	-	-	87.1	3.6	-	-	90.1	3.4	-	-	90.0	-0.1	-	-	93.0	3.3	-	-	90.1	-3.1	-	-
1982	88.3	-2.0	-	-	98.0	11.0	-	-	90.8	-7.3	-	-	89.0	-2.0	-	-	97.1	9.1	-	-	99.0	2.0	-	-
1983	97.7	-1.3	-	-	102.8	5.2	-	-	105.6	2.7	-	-	105.9	0.3	-	-	104.2	-1.6	-	-	99.6	-4.4	-	-
1984	100.4	0.8	-	-	99.4	-1.0	-	-	99.1	-0.3	-	-	97.5	-1.6	-	-	111.9	14.8	-	-	110.1	-1.6	-	-
1985	103.5	-6.0	-	-	109.2	5.5	-	-	106.0	-2.9	-	-	103.3	-2.5	-	-	116.1	12.4	-	-	114.7	-1.2	-	-
1986	100.8	-12.1	-	-	98.5	-2.3	-	-	96.3	-2.2	-	-	97.2	0.9	-	-	116.1	19.4	-	-	113.8	-2.0	-	-
1987	108.3	-4.8	-	-	111.1	2.6	-	-	114.0	2.6	-	-	109.1	-4.3	-	-	120.6	10.5	-	-	123.1	2.1	-	-
1988	113.8	-7.6	-	-	123.5	8.5	-	-	119.9	-2.9	-	-	107.5	-10.3	-	-	127.8	18.9	-	-	130.5	2.1	-	-
1989	123.2	-5.6	-	-	134.1	8.8	-	-	133.7	-0.3	-	-	129.5	-3.1	-	-	141.5	9.3	-	-	138.3	-2.3	-	-
1990	124.8	-9.8	-	-	139.5	11.8	-	-	138.7	-0.6	-	-	130.8	-5.7	-	-	145.1	10.9	-	-	140.7	-3.0	-	-
1991	136.2	-3.2	-	-	137.6	1.0	-	-	138.0	0.3	-	-	133.0	-3.6	-	-	152.0	14.3	-	-	150.1	-1.2	-	-
1992	137.1	-8.7	-	-	139.6	1.8	-	-	134.8	-3.4	-	-	136.9	1.6	-	-	145.4	6.2	-	-	144.9	-0.3	-	-
1993	143.7	-0.8	-	-	149.2	3.8	-	-	145.2	-2.7	-	-	135.8	-6.5	-	-	144.7	6.6	-	-	145.0	0.2	-	-

Source: U.S. Department of Labor, Bureau of Labor Statistics, Division of Consumer Prices and Price Indexes. - indicates no data collected for period.

Washington, DC-MD-VA
Consumer Price Index - All Urban Consumers
Base 1982-1984 = 100
Transportation

For 1947-1993. Columns headed % show percentile change in the index from the previous period for which an index is available.

Year	Jan Index	%	Feb Index	%	Mar Index	%	Apr Index	%	May Index	%	Jun Index	%	Jul Index	%	Aug Index	%	Sep Index	%	Oct Index	%	Nov Index	%	Dec Index	%
1947	18.0	-	18.0	0.0	18.1	0.6	18.3	1.1	19.1	4.4	19.3	1.0	-	-	19.6	1.6	-	-	-	-	19.8	1.0	-	-
1948	-	-	20.2	2.0	-	-	-	-	20.4	1.0	-	-	-	-	21.5	5.4	-	-	-	-	22.6	5.1	-	-
1949	-	-	22.7	0.4	-	-	-	-	22.8	0.4	-	-	-	-	22.8	0.0	-	-	-	-	22.9	0.4	-	-
1950	-	-	22.9	0.0	-	-	-	-	22.9	0.0	-	-	-	-	23.7	3.5	-	-	-	-	23.8	0.4	-	-
1951	-	-	23.8	0.0	-	-	-	-	24.0	0.8	-	-	-	-	24.1	0.4	-	-	-	-	24.7	2.5	-	-
1952	-	-	25.3	2.4	-	-	-	-	25.3	0.0	-	-	-	-	25.9	2.4	-	-	-	-	26.8	3.5	-	-
1953	-	-	26.7	-0.4	-	-	-	-	26.8	0.4	-	-	-	-	27.1	1.1	-	-	-	-	27.0	-0.4	-	-
1954	-	-	26.9	-0.4	-	-	-	-	26.7	-0.7	-	-	-	-	26.3	-1.5	-	-	-	-	27.2	3.4	-	-
1955	-	-	27.1	-0.4	-	-	-	-	27.0	-0.4	-	-	-	-	27.1	0.4	-	-	-	-	27.6	1.8	-	-
1956	-	-	27.4	-0.7	-	-	-	-	27.1	-1.1	-	-	-	-	27.4	1.1	-	-	-	-	28.4	3.6	-	-
1957	-	-	28.4	0.0	-	-	-	-	28.6	0.7	-	-	-	-	29.0	1.4	-	-	-	-	29.8	2.8	-	-
1958	-	-	29.0	-2.7	-	-	-	-	29.0	0.0	-	-	-	-	29.4	1.4	-	-	-	-	30.6	4.1	-	-
1959	-	-	30.2	-1.3	-	-	-	-	30.2	0.0	-	-	-	-	30.6	1.3	-	-	-	-	30.8	0.7	-	-
1960	-	-	30.7	-0.3	-	-	-	-	30.7	0.0	-	-	-	-	30.8	0.3	-	-	-	-	30.7	-0.3	-	-
1961	-	-	30.4	-1.0	-	-	-	-	30.8	1.3	-	-	-	-	31.3	1.6	-	-	-	-	31.4	0.3	-	-
1962	-	-	31.1	-1.0	-	-	-	-	31.3	0.6	-	-	-	-	31.4	0.3	-	-	-	-	31.5	0.3	-	-
1963	-	-	31.0	-1.6	-	-	-	-	31.5	1.6	-	-	-	-	31.7	0.6	-	-	-	-	32.2	1.6	-	-
1964	-	-	32.2	0.0	-	-	-	-	32.2	0.0	-	-	-	-	32.3	0.3	-	-	-	-	32.7	1.2	-	-
1965	-	-	32.7	0.0	-	-	-	-	32.7	0.0	-	-	-	-	32.5	-0.6	-	-	-	-	32.7	0.6	-	-
1966	-	-	32.6	-0.3	-	-	-	-	32.9	0.9	-	-	-	-	32.9	0.0	-	-	-	-	33.3	1.2	-	-
1967	-	-	33.3	0.0	-	-	-	-	34.1	2.4	-	-	-	-	34.3	0.6	-	-	-	-	34.7	1.2	-	-
1968	-	-	35.0	0.9	-	-	-	-	35.2	0.6	-	-	-	-	35.5	0.9	-	-	-	-	36.0	1.4	-	-
1969	-	-	36.4	1.1	-	-	-	-	36.9	1.4	-	-	-	-	37.3	1.1	-	-	-	-	38.0	1.9	-	-
1970	-	-	38.3	0.8	-	-	-	-	39.4	2.9	-	-	-	-	40.4	2.5	-	-	-	-	40.7	0.7	-	-
1971	-	-	41.8	2.7	-	-	-	-	42.5	1.7	-	-	-	-	42.3	-0.5	-	-	-	-	42.1	-0.5	-	-
1972	-	-	41.8	-0.7	-	-	-	-	42.0	0.5	-	-	-	-	42.4	1.0	-	-	-	-	42.6	0.5	-	-
1973	-	-	42.6	0.0	-	-	-	-	42.9	0.7	-	-	-	-	43.0	0.2	-	-	-	-	43.6	1.4	-	-
1974	-	-	45.1	3.4	-	-	-	-	47.1	4.4	-	-	-	-	48.8	3.6	-	-	-	-	49.4	1.2	-	-
1975	-	-	49.9	1.0	-	-	-	-	51.2	2.6	-	-	-	-	52.8	3.1	-	-	-	-	53.5	1.3	-	-
1976	-	-	53.7	0.4	-	-	-	-	55.3	3.0	-	-	-	-	56.6	2.4	-	-	-	-	56.8	0.4	-	-
1977	-	-	58.1	2.3	-	-	-	-	59.9	3.1	-	-	-	-	60.6	1.2	-	-	-	-	60.7	0.2	-	-
1978	61.0	0.5	-	-	61.3	0.5	-	-	62.3	1.6	-	-	64.0	2.7	-	-	64.5	0.8	-	-	65.9	2.2	-	-
1979	66.3	0.6	-	-	67.5	1.8	-	-	70.1	3.9	-	-	72.9	4.0	-	-	74.5	2.2	-	-	76.3	2.4	-	-
1980	79.1	3.7	-	-	82.5	4.3	-	-	83.5	1.2	-	-	85.4	2.3	-	-	87.2	2.1	-	-	88.3	1.3	-	-
1981	90.4	2.4	-	-	92.8	2.7	-	-	94.2	1.5	-	-	95.0	0.8	-	-	95.7	0.7	-	-	96.5	0.8	-	-
1982	97.1	0.6	-	-	95.2	-2.0	-	-	95.2	0.0	-	-	98.2	3.2	-	-	98.0	-0.2	-	-	98.0	0.0	-	-
1983	97.5	-0.5	-	-	96.0	-1.5	-	-	98.6	2.7	-	-	99.9	1.3	-	-	100.8	0.9	-	-	102.1	1.3	-	-
1984	102.3	0.2	-	-	102.2	-0.1	-	-	103.7	1.5	-	-	104.5	0.8	-	-	104.5	0.0	-	-	104.6	0.1	-	-
1985	104.1	-0.5	-	-	104.6	0.5	-	-	105.8	1.1	-	-	106.0	0.2	-	-	105.7	-0.3	-	-	107.0	1.2	-	-
1986	107.3	0.3	-	-	104.8	-2.3	-	-	103.2	-1.5	-	-	103.4	0.2	-	-	102.4	-1.0	-	-	102.6	0.2	-	-
1987	103.8	1.2	-	-	105.4	1.5	-	-	104.9	-0.5	-	-	107.2	2.2	-	-	106.4	-0.7	-	-	107.1	0.7	-	-
1988	106.0	-1.0	-	-	106.2	0.2	-	-	107.5	1.2	-	-	107.9	0.4	-	-	108.4	0.5	-	-	111.2	2.6	-	-
1989	112.5	1.2	-	-	112.3	-0.2	-	-	113.8	1.3	-	-	114.8	0.9	-	-	114.4	-0.3	-	-	117.0	2.3	-	-
1990	118.1	0.9	-	-	117.8	-0.3	-	-	117.9	0.1	-	-	118.7	0.7	-	-	122.3	3.0	-	-	127.1	3.9	-	-
1991	127.4	0.2	-	-	123.9	-2.7	-	-	124.8	0.7	-	-	124.7	-0.1	-	-	127.1	1.9	-	-	128.7	1.3	-	-

[Continued]

Washington, DC-MD-VA
Consumer Price Index - All Urban Consumers
Base 1982-1984 = 100
Transportation
[Continued]

For 1947-1993. Columns headed % show percentile change in the index from the previous period for which an index is available.

Year	Jan Index	%	Feb Index	%	Mar Index	%	Apr Index	%	May Index	%	Jun Index	%	Jul Index	%	Aug Index	%	Sep Index	%	Oct Index	%	Nov Index	%	Dec Index	%
1992	129.6	0.7	-	-	127.5	-1.6	-	-	129.0	1.2	-	-	130.9	1.5	-	-	127.8	-2.4	-	-	133.1	4.1	-	-
1993	135.5	1.8	-	-	134.8	-0.5	-	-	135.2	0.3	-	-	135.2	0.0	-	-	132.4	-2.1	-	-	136.3	2.9	-	-

Source: U.S. Department of Labor, Bureau of Labor Statistics, Division of Consumer Prices and Price Indexes. - indicates no data collected for period.

Washington, DC-MD-VA
Consumer Price Index - Urban Wage Earners
Base 1982-1984 = 100
Transportation

For 1947-1993. Columns headed % show percentile change in the index from the previous period for which an index is available.

Year	Jan Index	%	Feb Index	%	Mar Index	%	Apr Index	%	May Index	%	Jun Index	%	Jul Index	%	Aug Index	%	Sep Index	%	Oct Index	%	Nov Index	%	Dec Index	%
1947	18.0	-	18.0	0.0	18.0	0.0	18.3	1.7	19.1	4.4	19.2	0.5	-	-	19.6	2.1	-	-	-	-	19.8	1.0	-	-
1948	-		20.2	2.0	-		-		20.4	1.0	-		-		21.4	4.9	-		-		22.5	5.1	-	-
1949	-		22.6	0.4	-		-		22.8	0.9	-		-		22.7	-0.4	-		-		22.8	0.4	-	-
1950	-		22.9	0.4	-		-		22.9	0.0	-		-		23.6	3.1	-		-		23.7	0.4	-	-
1951	-		23.8	0.4	-		-		24.0	0.8	-		-		24.0	0.0	-		-		24.7	2.9	-	-
1952	-		25.2	2.0	-		-		25.2	0.0	-		-		25.9	2.8	-		-		26.7	3.1	-	-
1953	-		26.6	-0.4	-		-		26.7	0.4	-		-		27.0	1.1	-		-		26.9	-0.4	-	-
1954	-		26.9	0.0	-		-		26.6	-1.1	-		-		26.2	-1.5	-		-		27.1	3.4	-	-
1955	-		27.0	-0.4	-		-		27.0	0.0	-		-		27.1	0.4	-		-		27.5	1.5	-	-
1956	-		27.3	-0.7	-		-		27.0	-1.1	-		-		27.3	1.1	-		-		28.3	3.7	-	-
1957	-		28.4	0.4	-		-		28.6	0.7	-		-		28.9	1.0	-		-		29.7	2.8	-	-
1958	-		28.9	-2.7	-		-		28.9	0.0	-		-		29.3	1.4	-		-		30.5	4.1	-	-
1959	-		30.2	-1.0	-		-		30.1	-0.3	-		-		30.5	1.3	-		-		30.7	0.7	-	-
1960	-		30.6	-0.3	-		-		30.6	0.0	-		-		30.7	0.3	-		-		30.6	-0.3	-	-
1961	-		30.3	-1.0	-		-		30.7	1.3	-		-		31.3	2.0	-		-		31.3	0.0	-	-
1962	-		31.0	-1.0	-		-		31.2	0.6	-		-		31.3	0.3	-		-		31.5	0.6	-	-
1963	-		30.9	-1.9	-		-		31.4	1.6	-		-		31.6	0.6	-		-		32.1	1.6	-	-
1964	-		32.1	0.0	-		-		32.1	0.0	-		-		32.2	0.3	-		-		32.6	1.2	-	-
1965	-		32.6	0.0	-		-		32.6	0.0	-		-		32.4	-0.6	-		-		32.6	0.6	-	-
1966	-		32.5	-0.3	-		-		32.8	0.9	-		-		32.9	0.3	-		-		33.3	1.2	-	-
1967	-		33.3	0.0	-		-		34.0	2.1	-		-		34.2	0.6	-		-		34.6	1.2	-	-
1968	-		34.9	0.9	-		-		35.1	0.6	-		-		35.4	0.9	-		-		35.9	1.4	-	-
1969	-		36.3	1.1	-		-		36.8	1.4	-		-		37.2	1.1	-		-		37.9	1.9	-	-
1970	-		38.2	0.8	-		-		39.3	2.9	-		-		40.3	2.5	-		-		40.6	0.7	-	-
1971	-		41.7	2.7	-		-		42.4	1.7	-		-		42.2	-0.5	-		-		42.0	-0.5	-	-
1972	-		41.7	-0.7	-		-		41.8	0.2	-		-		42.3	1.2	-		-		42.5	0.5	-	-
1973	-		42.5	0.0	-		-		42.8	0.7	-		-		42.9	0.2	-		-		43.4	1.2	-	-
1974	-		45.0	3.7	-		-		47.0	4.4	-		-		48.7	3.6	-		-		49.3	1.2	-	-
1975	-		49.8	1.0	-		-		51.1	2.6	-		-		52.7	3.1	-		-		53.4	1.3	-	-
1976	-		53.5	0.2	-		-		55.1	3.0	-		-		56.4	2.4	-		-		56.7	0.5	-	-
1977	-		58.0	2.3	-		-		59.7	2.9	-		-		60.4	1.2	-		-		60.5	0.2	-	-
1978	60.6	0.2	-		60.8	0.3	-		62.0	2.0	-		63.3	2.1	-		63.6	0.5	-		65.5	3.0	-	-
1979	65.9	0.6	-		67.0	1.7	-		69.7	4.0	-		71.8	3.0	-		73.1	1.8	-		74.8	2.3	-	-
1980	77.8	4.0	-		80.9	4.0	-		81.5	0.7	-		84.2	3.3	-		85.3	1.3	-		86.0	0.8	-	-
1981	87.9	2.2	-		90.4	2.8	-		92.5	2.3	-		94.0	1.6	-		94.5	0.5	-		95.9	1.5	-	-
1982	96.4	0.5	-		94.8	-1.7	-		95.0	0.2	-		97.7	2.8	-		97.6	-0.1	-		97.5	-0.1	-	-
1983	97.3	-0.2	-		95.9	-1.4	-		98.4	2.6	-		99.7	1.3	-		100.8	1.1	-		102.3	1.5	-	-
1984	102.5	0.2	-		102.5	0.0	-		104.2	1.7	-		105.0	0.8	-		105.0	0.0	-		105.3	0.3	-	-
1985	104.8	-0.5	-		105.2	0.4	-		106.2	1.0	-		106.2	0.0	-		105.9	-0.3	-		107.3	1.3	-	-
1986	107.6	0.3	-		105.5	-2.0	-		103.5	-1.9	-		103.8	0.3	-		103.0	-0.8	-		103.3	0.3	-	-
1987	104.4	1.1	-		106.4	1.9	-		106.9	0.5	-		109.4	2.3	-		109.6	0.2	-		110.2	0.5	-	-
1988	108.9	-1.2	-		109.0	0.1	-		110.5	1.4	-		111.0	0.5	-		112.0	0.9	-		114.3	2.1	-	-
1989	115.6	1.1	-		115.6	0.0	-		117.5	1.6	-		118.5	0.9	-		117.9	-0.5	-		120.5	2.2	-	-
1990	121.9	1.2	-		121.3	-0.5	-		121.5	0.2	-		122.5	0.8	-		126.6	3.3	-		131.6	3.9	-	-
1991	131.4	-0.2	-		127.3	-3.1	-		128.5	0.9	-		128.5	0.0	-		130.7	1.7	-		132.4	1.3	-	-

[Continued]

Washington, DC-MD-VA
Consumer Price Index - Urban Wage Earners
Base 1982-1984 = 100
Transportation

[Continued]

For 1947-1993. Columns headed % show percentile change in the index from the previous period for which an index is available.

Year	Jan Index	%	Feb Index	%	Mar Index	%	Apr Index	%	May Index	%	Jun Index	%	Jul Index	%	Aug Index	%	Sep Index	%	Oct Index	%	Nov Index	%	Dec Index	%
1992	132.7	0.2	-	-	130.5	-1.7	-	-	132.4	1.5	-	-	134.5	1.6	-	-	131.9	-1.9	-	-	136.3	3.3	-	-
1993	138.6	1.7	-	-	137.5	-0.8	-	-	138.0	0.4	-	-	137.9	-0.1	-	-	135.6	-1.7	-	-	139.2	2.7	-	-

Source: U.S. Department of Labor, Bureau of Labor Statistics, Division of Consumer Prices and Price Indexes. - indicates no data collected for period.

Washington, DC-MD-VA
Consumer Price Index - All Urban Consumers
Base 1982-1984 = 100
Medical Care

For 1947-1993. Columns headed % show percentile change in the index from the previous period for which an index is available.

Year	Jan Index	%	Feb Index	%	Mar Index	%	Apr Index	%	May Index	%	Jun Index	%	Jul Index	%	Aug Index	%	Sep Index	%	Oct Index	%	Nov Index	%	Dec Index	%
1947	12.3	-	12.4	0.8	12.4	0.0	12.4	0.0	12.3	-0.8	12.3	0.0	-	-	12.5	1.6	-	-	-	-	12.5	0.0	-	-
1948	-	-	12.6	0.8	-	-	-	-	12.8	1.6	-	-	-	-	12.8	0.0	-	-	-	-	13.0	1.6	-	-
1949	-	-	13.1	0.8	-	-	-	-	13.1	0.0	-	-	-	-	13.1	0.0	-	-	-	-	13.1	0.0	-	-
1950	-	-	13.1	0.0	-	-	-	-	13.0	-0.8	-	-	-	-	13.2	1.5	-	-	-	-	13.3	0.8	-	-
1951	-	-	13.7	3.0	-	-	-	-	13.9	1.5	-	-	-	-	14.2	2.2	-	-	-	-	14.4	1.4	-	-
1952	-	-	14.5	0.7	-	-	-	-	14.9	2.8	-	-	-	-	14.9	0.0	-	-	-	-	14.9	0.0	-	-
1953	-	-	14.9	0.0	-	-	-	-	15.0	0.7	-	-	-	-	15.0	0.0	-	-	-	-	15.0	0.0	-	-
1954	-	-	15.0	0.0	-	-	-	-	15.0	0.0	-	-	-	-	15.1	0.7	-	-	-	-	15.2	0.7	-	-
1955	-	-	15.1	-0.7	-	-	-	-	15.1	0.0	-	-	-	-	15.1	0.0	-	-	-	-	15.7	4.0	-	-
1956	-	-	15.7	0.0	-	-	-	-	15.8	0.6	-	-	-	-	16.3	3.2	-	-	-	-	16.4	0.6	-	-
1957	-	-	16.5	0.6	-	-	-	-	16.8	1.8	-	-	-	-	16.8	0.0	-	-	-	-	17.0	1.2	-	-
1958	-	-	17.5	2.9	-	-	-	-	17.5	0.0	-	-	-	-	17.9	2.3	-	-	-	-	18.8	5.0	-	-
1959	-	-	18.9	0.5	-	-	-	-	19.2	1.6	-	-	-	-	19.0	-1.0	-	-	-	-	19.2	1.1	-	-
1960	-	-	19.6	2.1	-	-	-	-	19.7	0.5	-	-	-	-	19.7	0.0	-	-	-	-	19.9	1.0	-	-
1961	-	-	20.2	1.5	-	-	-	-	20.3	0.5	-	-	-	-	20.5	1.0	-	-	-	-	20.6	0.5	-	-
1962	-	-	21.0	1.9	-	-	-	-	21.1	0.5	-	-	-	-	21.9	3.8	-	-	-	-	22.0	0.5	-	-
1963	-	-	22.2	0.9	-	-	-	-	22.4	0.9	-	-	-	-	22.4	0.0	-	-	-	-	22.6	0.9	-	-
1964	-	-	22.8	0.9	-	-	-	-	23.0	0.9	-	-	-	-	23.0	0.0	-	-	-	-	23.2	0.9	-	-
1965	-	-	23.4	0.9	-	-	-	-	23.5	0.4	-	-	-	-	23.8	1.3	-	-	-	-	24.0	0.8	-	-
1966	-	-	24.3	1.2	-	-	-	-	24.8	2.1	-	-	-	-	25.1	1.2	-	-	-	-	25.4	1.2	-	-
1967	-	-	26.3	3.5	-	-	-	-	26.8	1.9	-	-	-	-	27.0	0.7	-	-	-	-	28.0	3.7	-	-
1968	-	-	28.8	2.9	-	-	-	-	29.4	2.1	-	-	-	-	29.7	1.0	-	-	-	-	30.3	2.0	-	-
1969	-	-	31.3	3.3	-	-	-	-	31.6	1.0	-	-	-	-	32.2	1.9	-	-	-	-	32.3	0.3	-	-
1970	-	-	33.7	4.3	-	-	-	-	34.0	0.9	-	-	-	-	34.6	1.8	-	-	-	-	35.0	1.2	-	-
1971	-	-	36.4	4.0	-	-	-	-	36.8	1.1	-	-	-	-	37.4	1.6	-	-	-	-	37.0	-1.1	-	-
1972	-	-	37.3	0.8	-	-	-	-	37.8	1.3	-	-	-	-	38.0	0.5	-	-	-	-	38.2	0.5	-	-
1973	-	-	38.4	0.5	-	-	-	-	38.6	0.5	-	-	-	-	39.1	1.3	-	-	-	-	39.9	2.0	-	-
1974	-	-	41.1	3.0	-	-	-	-	42.6	3.6	-	-	-	-	44.8	5.2	-	-	-	-	45.6	1.8	-	-
1975	-	-	47.3	3.7	-	-	-	-	48.1	1.7	-	-	-	-	48.9	1.7	-	-	-	-	49.6	1.4	-	-
1976	-	-	51.7	4.2	-	-	-	-	52.6	1.7	-	-	-	-	53.9	2.5	-	-	-	-	55.4	2.8	-	-
1977	-	-	56.7	2.3	-	-	-	-	57.9	2.1	-	-	-	-	59.1	2.1	-	-	-	-	59.6	0.8	-	-
1978	61.0	2.3	-	-	61.2	0.3	-	-	60.9	-0.5	-	-	62.3	2.3	-	-	62.6	0.5	-	-	64.2	2.6	-	-
1979	65.2	1.6	-	-	66.8	2.5	-	-	67.1	0.4	-	-	68.1	1.5	-	-	70.2	3.1	-	-	70.7	0.7	-	-
1980	71.4	1.0	-	-	72.4	1.4	-	-	74.2	2.5	-	-	74.9	0.9	-	-	75.6	0.9	-	-	75.5	-0.1	-	-
1981	77.2	2.3	-	-	78.4	1.6	-	-	78.0	-0.5	-	-	80.7	3.5	-	-	81.8	1.4	-	-	82.9	1.3	-	-
1982	84.3	1.7	-	-	87.9	4.3	-	-	88.8	1.0	-	-	90.2	1.6	-	-	93.9	4.1	-	-	94.9	1.1	-	-
1983	98.9	4.2	-	-	99.5	0.6	-	-	100.1	0.6	-	-	99.7	-0.4	-	-	103.4	3.7	-	-	105.6	2.1	-	-
1984	107.0	1.3	-	-	106.3	-0.7	-	-	107.1	0.8	-	-	107.2	0.1	-	-	108.5	1.2	-	-	110.5	1.8	-	-
1985	110.1	-0.4	-	-	112.5	2.2	-	-	113.4	0.8	-	-	115.8	2.1	-	-	116.1	0.3	-	-	117.9	1.6	-	-
1986	119.4	1.3	-	-	121.1	1.4	-	-	122.7	1.3	-	-	123.0	0.2	-	-	123.6	0.5	-	-	124.5	0.7	-	-
1987	126.0	1.2	-	-	127.5	1.2	-	-	128.6	0.9	-	-	128.3	-0.2	-	-	129.4	0.9	-	-	132.4	2.3	-	-
1988	135.1	2.0	-	-	136.4	1.0	-	-	137.3	0.7	-	-	137.9	0.4	-	-	138.0	0.1	-	-	149.6	1.6	-	-
1989	142.6	1.7	-	-	144.1	1.1	-	-	145.4	0.9	-	-	146.4	0.7	-	-	147.2	0.5	-	-	170.2	3.6	-	-
1990	155.3	3.8	-	-	157.9	1.7	-	-	160.1	1.4	-	-	162.4	1.4	-	-	164.3	1.2	-	-	178.7	1.4	-	-
1991	173.0	1.6	-	-	175.3	1.3	-	-	175.9	0.3	-	-	176.6	0.4	-	-	176.3	-0.2	-	-				

[Continued]

Washington, DC-MD-VA
Consumer Price Index - All Urban Consumers
Base 1982-1984 = 100
Medical Care

[Continued]

For 1947-1993. Columns headed % show percentile change in the index from the previous period for which an index is available.

Year	Jan Index	%	Feb Index	%	Mar Index	%	Apr Index	%	May Index	%	Jun Index	%	Jul Index	%	Aug Index	%	Sep Index	%	Oct Index	%	Nov Index	%	Dec Index	%
1992	184.1	3.0	-	-	181.9	-1.2	-	-	182.0	0.1	-	-	187.1	2.8	-	-	189.6	1.3	-	-	191.1	0.8	-	-
1993	192.6	0.8	-	-	193.6	0.5	-	-	194.3	0.4	-	-	196.1	0.9	-	-	197.0	0.5	-	-	196.8	-0.1	-	-

Source: U.S. Department of Labor, Bureau of Labor Statistics, Division of Consumer Prices and Price Indexes. - indicates no data collected for period.

Washington, DC-MD-VA
Consumer Price Index - Urban Wage Earners
Base 1982-1984 = 100
Medical Care

For 1947-1993. Columns headed % show percentile change in the index from the previous period for which an index is available.

Year	Jan Index	%	Feb Index	%	Mar Index	%	Apr Index	%	May Index	%	Jun Index	%	Jul Index	%	Aug Index	%	Sep Index	%	Oct Index	%	Nov Index	%	Dec Index	%
1947	11.8	-	11.9	0.8	11.9	0.0	11.8	-0.8	11.8	0.0	11.8	0.0	-	-	11.9	0.8	-	-	-	-	11.9	0.0	-	-
1948	-	-	12.1	1.7	-	-	-	-	12.3	1.7	-	-	-	-	12.3	0.0	-	-	-	-	12.5	1.6	-	-
1949	-	-	12.5	0.0	-	-	-	-	12.5	0.0	-	-	-	-	12.6	0.8	-	-	-	-	12.6	0.0	-	-
1950	-	-	12.6	0.0	-	-	-	-	12.4	-1.6	-	-	-	-	12.6	1.6	-	-	-	-	12.7	0.8	-	-
1951	-	-	13.1	3.1	-	-	-	-	13.3	1.5	-	-	-	-	13.6	2.3	-	-	-	-	13.8	1.5	-	-
1952	-	-	13.9	0.7	-	-	-	-	14.2	2.2	-	-	-	-	14.3	0.7	-	-	-	-	14.2	-0.7	-	-
1953	-	-	14.2	0.0	-	-	-	-	14.3	0.7	-	-	-	-	14.4	0.7	-	-	-	-	14.4	0.0	-	-
1954	-	-	14.3	-0.7	-	-	-	-	14.3	0.0	-	-	-	-	14.4	0.7	-	-	-	-	14.5	0.7	-	-
1955	-	-	14.4	-0.7	-	-	-	-	14.5	0.7	-	-	-	-	14.5	0.0	-	-	-	-	15.0	3.4	-	-
1956	-	-	15.0	0.0	-	-	-	-	15.1	0.7	-	-	-	-	15.6	3.3	-	-	-	-	15.7	0.6	-	-
1957	-	-	15.8	0.6	-	-	-	-	16.1	1.9	-	-	-	-	16.1	0.0	-	-	-	-	16.3	1.2	-	-
1958	-	-	16.7	2.5	-	-	-	-	16.7	0.0	-	-	-	-	17.1	2.4	-	-	-	-	18.0	5.3	-	-
1959	-	-	18.1	0.6	-	-	-	-	18.3	1.1	-	-	-	-	18.1	-1.1	-	-	-	-	18.4	1.7	-	-
1960	-	-	18.8	2.2	-	-	-	-	18.8	0.0	-	-	-	-	18.9	0.5	-	-	-	-	19.0	0.5	-	-
1961	-	-	19.3	1.6	-	-	-	-	19.5	1.0	-	-	-	-	19.6	0.5	-	-	-	-	19.7	0.5	-	-
1962	-	-	20.1	2.0	-	-	-	-	20.2	0.5	-	-	-	-	21.0	4.0	-	-	-	-	21.1	0.5	-	-
1963	-	-	21.2	0.5	-	-	-	-	21.5	1.4	-	-	-	-	21.5	0.0	-	-	-	-	21.6	0.5	-	-
1964	-	-	21.8	0.9	-	-	-	-	22.0	0.9	-	-	-	-	22.0	0.0	-	-	-	-	22.2	0.9	-	-
1965	-	-	22.4	0.9	-	-	-	-	22.5	0.4	-	-	-	-	22.8	1.3	-	-	-	-	22.9	0.4	-	-
1966	-	-	23.3	1.7	-	-	-	-	23.7	1.7	-	-	-	-	24.0	1.3	-	-	-	-	24.3	1.2	-	-
1967	-	-	25.1	3.3	-	-	-	-	25.6	2.0	-	-	-	-	25.9	1.2	-	-	-	-	26.8	3.5	-	-
1968	-	-	27.6	3.0	-	-	-	-	28.1	1.8	-	-	-	-	28.4	1.1	-	-	-	-	29.0	2.1	-	-
1969	-	-	29.9	3.1	-	-	-	-	30.2	1.0	-	-	-	-	30.8	2.0	-	-	-	-	30.9	0.3	-	-
1970	-	-	32.3	4.5	-	-	-	-	32.5	0.6	-	-	-	-	33.1	1.8	-	-	-	-	33.5	1.2	-	-
1971	-	-	34.8	3.9	-	-	-	-	35.2	1.1	-	-	-	-	35.8	1.7	-	-	-	-	35.4	-1.1	-	-
1972	-	-	35.7	0.8	-	-	-	-	36.1	1.1	-	-	-	-	36.3	0.6	-	-	-	-	36.5	0.6	-	-
1973	-	-	36.7	0.5	-	-	-	-	37.0	0.8	-	-	-	-	37.4	1.1	-	-	-	-	38.1	1.9	-	-
1974	-	-	39.3	3.1	-	-	-	-	40.7	3.6	-	-	-	-	42.8	5.2	-	-	-	-	43.6	1.9	-	-
1975	-	-	45.3	3.9	-	-	-	-	46.0	1.5	-	-	-	-	46.8	1.7	-	-	-	-	47.5	1.5	-	-
1976	-	-	49.5	4.2	-	-	-	-	50.3	1.6	-	-	-	-	51.5	2.4	-	-	-	-	53.0	2.9	-	-
1977	-	-	54.2	2.3	-	-	-	-	55.4	2.2	-	-	-	-	56.6	2.2	-	-	-	-	57.0	0.7	-	-
1978	58.3	2.3	-	-	59.6	2.2	-	-	60.1	0.8	-	-	61.5	2.3	-	-	62.8	2.1	-	-	63.0	0.3	-	-
1979	63.9	1.4	-	-	67.1	5.0	-	-	67.9	1.2	-	-	68.4	0.7	-	-	70.3	2.8	-	-	71.2	1.3	-	-
1980	72.2	1.4	-	-	73.1	1.2	-	-	73.6	0.7	-	-	75.5	2.6	-	-	75.8	0.4	-	-	76.7	1.2	-	-
1981	77.4	0.9	-	-	78.0	0.8	-	-	77.9	-0.1	-	-	79.9	2.6	-	-	80.7	1.0	-	-	83.1	3.0	-	-
1982	84.5	1.7	-	-	88.0	4.1	-	-	88.5	0.6	-	-	89.7	1.4	-	-	93.3	4.0	-	-	94.2	1.0	-	-
1983	98.2	4.2	-	-	99.0	0.8	-	-	99.8	0.8	-	-	99.6	-0.2	-	-	103.6	4.0	-	-	105.9	2.2	-	-
1984	107.2	1.2	-	-	106.8	-0.4	-	-	107.5	0.7	-	-	107.8	0.3	-	-	109.0	1.1	-	-	111.0	1.8	-	-
1985	110.8	-0.2	-	-	113.4	2.3	-	-	114.3	0.8	-	-	116.7	2.1	-	-	116.9	0.2	-	-	118.8	1.6	-	-
1986	120.2	1.2	-	-	122.1	1.6	-	-	123.8	1.4	-	-	124.0	0.2	-	-	124.4	0.3	-	-	125.5	0.9	-	-
1987	127.2	1.4	-	-	128.7	1.2	-	-	129.9	0.9	-	-	129.7	-0.2	-	-	131.0	1.0	-	-	134.0	2.3	-	-
1988	136.9	2.2	-	-	137.9	0.7	-	-	138.9	0.7	-	-	139.5	0.4	-	-	139.8	0.2	-	-	142.2	1.7	-	-
1989	144.5	1.6	-	-	146.1	1.1	-	-	147.4	0.9	-	-	148.3	0.6	-	-	148.9	0.4	-	-	151.2	1.5	-	-
1990	156.9	3.8	-	-	159.4	1.6	-	-	161.3	1.2	-	-	163.4	1.3	-	-	165.2	1.1	-	-	170.7	3.3	-	-
1991	173.4	1.6	-	-	175.7	1.3	-	-	176.4	0.4	-	-	177.1	0.4	-	-	176.8	-0.2	-	-	179.0	1.2	-	-

[Continued]

Washington, DC-MD-VA
Consumer Price Index - Urban Wage Earners
Base 1982-1984 = 100
Medical Care

[Continued]

For 1947-1993. Columns headed % show percentile change in the index from the previous period for which an index is available.

Year	Jan		Feb		Mar		Apr		May		Jun		Jul		Aug		Sep		Oct		Nov		Dec	
	Index	%	Index	%	Index	%	Index	%	Index	%	Index	%	Index	%	Index	%	Index	%	Index	%	Index	%	Index	%
1992	184.5	3.1	-	-	182.1	-1.3	-	-	182.3	0.1	-	-	187.5	2.9	-	-	190.3	1.5	-	-	191.7	0.7	-	-
1993	193.3	0.8	-	-	194.0	0.4	-	-	194.8	0.4	-	-	196.9	1.1	-	-	197.7	0.4	-	-	197.5	-0.1	-	-

Source: U.S. Department of Labor, Bureau of Labor Statistics, Division of Consumer Prices and Price Indexes. - indicates no data collected for period.

Washington, DC-MD-VA
Consumer Price Index - All Urban Consumers
Base 1982-1984 = 100
Entertainment

For 1975-1993. Columns headed % show percentile change in the index from the previous period for which an index is available.

Year	Jan Index	%	Feb Index	%	Mar Index	%	Apr Index	%	May Index	%	Jun Index	%	Jul Index	%	Aug Index	%	Sep Index	%	Oct Index	%	Nov Index	%	Dec Index	%
1975	-	-	-	-	-	-	-	-	-	-	-	-	-	-	-	-	-	-	-	-	66.3	-	-	-
1976	-	-	67.3	1.5	-	-	-	-	68.3	1.5	-	-	-	-	68.7	0.6	-	-	-	-	70.0	1.9	-	-
1977	-	-	72.0	2.9	-	-	-	-	73.2	1.7	-	-	-	-	74.7	2.0	-	-	-	-	75.2	0.7	-	-
1978	74.8	-0.5	-	-	74.9	0.1	-	-	74.2	-0.9	-	-	74.4	0.3	-	-	74.4	0.0	-	-	76.4	2.7	-	-
1979	76.5	0.1	-	-	77.9	1.8	-	-	78.0	0.1	-	-	78.4	0.5	-	-	79.5	1.4	-	-	79.6	0.1	-	-
1980	83.8	5.3	-	-	83.0	-1.0	-	-	82.2	-1.0	-	-	86.0	4.6	-	-	86.8	0.9	-	-	85.7	-1.3	-	-
1981	87.0	1.5	-	-	86.1	-1.0	-	-	89.1	3.5	-	-	89.0	-0.1	-	-	90.2	1.3	-	-	90.9	0.8	-	-
1982	92.3	1.5	-	-	93.7	1.5	-	-	94.1	0.4	-	-	93.9	-0.2	-	-	94.6	0.7	-	-	95.3	0.7	-	-
1983	96.0	0.7	-	-	96.2	0.2	-	-	96.5	0.3	-	-	98.1	1.7	-	-	103.7	5.7	-	-	102.8	-0.9	-	-
1984	102.1	-0.7	-	-	104.3	2.2	-	-	102.9	-1.3	-	-	108.0	5.0	-	-	108.3	0.3	-	-	112.2	3.6	-	-
1985	112.8	0.5	-	-	112.4	-0.4	-	-	112.1	-0.3	-	-	113.6	1.3	-	-	114.2	0.5	-	-	116.0	1.6	-	-
1986	116.8	0.7	-	-	116.5	-0.3	-	-	115.2	-1.1	-	-	116.6	1.2	-	-	117.8	1.0	-	-	117.0	-0.7	-	-
1987	115.2	-1.5	-	-	121.8	5.7	-	-	122.1	0.2	-	-	123.6	1.2	-	-	121.3	-1.9	-	-	122.7	1.2	-	-
1988	125.4	2.2	-	-	126.5	0.9	-	-	127.5	0.8	-	-	122.1	-4.2	-	-	124.2	1.7	-	-	123.4	-0.6	-	-
1989	125.4	1.6	-	-	125.9	0.4	-	-	126.2	0.2	-	-	127.9	1.3	-	-	130.5	2.0	-	-	128.8	-1.3	-	-
1990	127.8	-0.8	-	-	131.1	2.6	-	-	136.9	4.4	-	-	137.0	0.1	-	-	139.6	1.9	-	-	139.0	-0.4	-	-
1991	137.2	-1.3	-	-	140.7	2.6	-	-	141.4	0.5	-	-	143.4	1.4	-	-	145.4	1.4	-	-	146.4	0.7	-	-
1992	143.4	-2.0	-	-	146.4	2.1	-	-	147.7	0.9	-	-	147.4	-0.2	-	-	149.3	1.3	-	-	149.8	0.3	-	-
1993	150.6	0.5	-	-	150.1	-0.3	-	-	148.3	-1.2	-	-	149.7	0.9	-	-	153.9	2.8	-	-	152.5	-0.9	-	-

Source: U.S. Department of Labor, Bureau of Labor Statistics, Division of Consumer Prices and Price Indexes. - indicates no data collected for period.

Washington, DC-MD-VA
Consumer Price Index - Urban Wage Earners
Base 1982-1984 = 100
Entertainment

For 1975-1993. Columns headed % show percentile change in the index from the previous period for which an index is available.

Year	Jan Index	%	Feb Index	%	Mar Index	%	Apr Index	%	May Index	%	Jun Index	%	Jul Index	%	Aug Index	%	Sep Index	%	Oct Index	%	Nov Index	%	Dec Index	%
1975	-	-	-	-	-	-	-	-	-	-	-	-	-	-	-	-	-	-	-	-	56.3	-	-	-
1976	-	-	57.1	1.4	-	-	-	-	58.0	1.6	-	-	-	-	58.3	0.5	-	-	-	-	59.4	1.9	-	-
1977	-	-	61.1	2.9	-	-	-	-	62.1	1.6	-	-	-	-	63.4	2.1	-	-	-	-	63.8	0.6	-	-
1978	64.2	0.6	-	-	67.3	4.8	-	-	66.9	-0.6	-	-	69.0	3.1	-	-	69.2	0.3	-	-	71.7	3.6	-	-
1979	72.4	1.0	-	-	73.5	1.5	-	-	75.3	2.4	-	-	76.6	1.7	-	-	77.6	1.3	-	-	78.0	0.5	-	-
1980	79.3	1.7	-	-	80.3	1.3	-	-	83.3	3.7	-	-	84.2	1.1	-	-	83.6	-0.7	-	-	84.4	1.0	-	-
1981	84.2	-0.2	-	-	83.5	-0.8	-	-	86.6	3.7	-	-	89.5	3.3	-	-	90.7	1.3	-	-	91.1	0.4	-	-
1982	92.7	1.8	-	-	94.0	1.4	-	-	94.8	0.9	-	-	94.4	-0.4	-	-	95.2	0.8	-	-	95.2	0.0	-	-
1983	96.1	0.9	-	-	95.9	-0.2	-	-	96.8	0.9	-	-	98.0	1.2	-	-	103.6	5.7	-	-	103.3	-0.3	-	-
1984	102.7	-0.6	-	-	104.8	2.0	-	-	102.2	-2.5	-	-	107.4	5.1	-	-	107.6	0.2	-	-	110.6	2.8	-	-
1985	111.5	0.8	-	-	110.6	-0.8	-	-	110.2	-0.4	-	-	111.7	1.4	-	-	112.5	0.7	-	-	113.9	1.2	-	-
1986	114.8	0.8	-	-	113.9	-0.8	-	-	110.5	-3.0	-	-	111.6	1.0	-	-	114.4	2.5	-	-	113.1	-1.1	-	-
1987	110.8	-2.0	-	-	118.8	7.2	-	-	118.7	-0.1	-	-	120.0	1.1	-	-	117.3	-2.3	-	-	119.8	2.1	-	-
1988	122.0	1.8	-	-	123.1	0.9	-	-	124.0	0.7	-	-	119.1	-4.0	-	-	121.6	2.1	-	-	120.8	-0.7	-	-
1989	122.9	1.7	-	-	123.3	0.3	-	-	123.5	0.2	-	-	124.5	0.8	-	-	127.0	2.0	-	-	125.7	-1.0	-	-
1990	124.8	-0.7	-	-	127.7	2.3	-	-	133.2	4.3	-	-	133.2	0.0	-	-	135.9	2.0	-	-	135.1	-0.6	-	-
1991	133.5	-1.2	-	-	137.1	2.7	-	-	137.3	0.1	-	-	139.2	1.4	-	-	141.1	1.4	-	-	142.4	0.9	-	-
1992	139.6	-2.0	-	-	142.4	2.0	-	-	143.8	1.0	-	-	143.6	-0.1	-	-	145.5	1.3	-	-	145.8	0.2	-	-
1993	146.2	0.3	-	-	146.1	-0.1	-	-	144.6	-1.0	-	-	145.4	0.6	-	-	149.4	2.8	-	-	147.4	-1.3	-	-

Source: U.S. Department of Labor, Bureau of Labor Statistics, Division of Consumer Prices and Price Indexes. - indicates no data collected for period.

Washington, DC-MD-VA
Consumer Price Index - All Urban Consumers
Base 1982-1984 = 100
Other Goods and Services

For 1975-1993. Columns headed % show percentile change in the index from the previous period for which an index is available.

Year	Jan Index	%	Feb Index	%	Mar Index	%	Apr Index	%	May Index	%	Jun Index	%	Jul Index	%	Aug Index	%	Sep Index	%	Oct Index	%	Nov Index	%	Dec Index	%
1975	-	-	-	-	-	-	-	-	-	-	-	-	-	-	-	-	-	-	-	-	54.9	-	-	-
1976	-	-	57.3	4.4	-	-	-	-	57.7	0.7	-	-	-	-	58.6	1.6	-	-	-	-	59.9	2.2	-	-
1977	-	-	60.6	1.2	-	-	-	-	61.4	1.3	-	-	-	-	61.9	0.8	-	-	-	-	64.4	4.0	-	-
1978	63.9	-0.8	-	-	64.4	0.8	-	-	64.6	0.3	-	-	65.2	0.9	-	-	67.1	2.9	-	-	67.3	0.3	-	-
1979	68.4	1.6	-	-	69.0	0.9	-	-	69.4	0.6	-	-	69.3	-0.1	-	-	71.3	2.9	-	-	71.5	0.3	-	-
1980	73.1	2.2	-	-	73.2	0.1	-	-	74.3	1.5	-	-	75.7	1.9	-	-	78.4	3.6	-	-	78.6	0.3	-	-
1981	79.2	0.8	-	-	81.1	2.4	-	-	81.7	0.7	-	-	82.1	0.5	-	-	86.5	5.4	-	-	87.6	1.3	-	-
1982	87.7	0.1	-	-	89.1	1.6	-	-	89.3	0.2	-	-	89.5	0.2	-	-	93.3	4.2	-	-	96.1	3.0	-	-
1983	98.9	2.9	-	-	99.1	0.2	-	-	98.9	-0.2	-	-	100.8	1.9	-	-	103.0	2.2	-	-	103.6	0.6	-	-
1984	105.4	1.7	-	-	105.4	0.0	-	-	106.1	0.7	-	-	106.9	0.8	-	-	109.4	2.3	-	-	111.5	1.9	-	-
1985	112.0	0.4	-	-	112.9	0.8	-	-	113.0	0.1	-	-	113.5	0.4	-	-	116.2	2.4	-	-	117.7	1.3	-	-
1986	119.0	1.1	-	-	119.2	0.2	-	-	119.6	0.3	-	-	121.4	1.5	-	-	124.1	2.2	-	-	126.2	1.7	-	-
1987	126.9	0.6	-	-	127.4	0.4	-	-	127.7	0.2	-	-	128.2	0.4	-	-	130.8	2.0	-	-	133.4	2.0	-	-
1988	135.1	1.3	-	-	134.9	-0.1	-	-	135.4	0.4	-	-	138.8	2.5	-	-	140.3	1.1	-	-	142.9	1.9	-	-
1989	146.2	2.3	-	-	147.1	0.6	-	-	148.4	0.9	-	-	150.5	1.4	-	-	157.7	4.8	-	-	160.0	1.5	-	-
1990	160.7	0.4	-	-	162.4	1.1	-	-	162.3	-0.1	-	-	164.4	1.3	-	-	168.3	2.4	-	-	170.7	1.4	-	-
1991	174.6	2.3	-	-	175.8	0.7	-	-	177.0	0.7	-	-	180.0	1.7	-	-	181.1	0.6	-	-	181.2	0.1	-	-
1992	181.2	0.0	-	-	181.5	0.2	-	-	183.9	1.3	-	-	184.7	0.4	-	-	193.2	4.6	-	-	193.3	0.1	-	-
1993	195.1	0.9	-	-	196.2	0.6	-	-	197.7	0.8	-	-	199.5	0.9	-	-	202.6	1.6	-	-	202.7	0.0	-	-

Source: U.S. Department of Labor, Bureau of Labor Statistics, Division of Consumer Prices and Price Indexes. - indicates no data collected for period.

Washington, DC-MD-VA
Consumer Price Index - Urban Wage Earners
Base 1982-1984 = 100
Other Goods and Services

For 1975-1993. Columns headed % show percentile change in the index from the previous period for which an index is available.

Year	Jan Index	%	Feb Index	%	Mar Index	%	Apr Index	%	May Index	%	Jun Index	%	Jul Index	%	Aug Index	%	Sep Index	%	Oct Index	%	Nov Index	%	Dec Index	%
1975	-	-	-	-	-	-	-	-	-	-	-	-	-	-	-	-	-	-	-	-	52.9	-	-	-
1976	-	-	55.3	4.5	-	-	-	-	55.7	0.7	-	-	-	-	56.5	1.4	-	-	-	-	57.8	2.3	-	-
1977	-	-	58.4	1.0	-	-	-	-	59.2	1.4	-	-	-	-	59.7	0.8	-	-	-	-	62.1	4.0	-	-
1978	62.2	0.2	-	-	63.0	1.3	-	-	64.8	2.9	-	-	66.9	3.2	-	-	66.8	-0.1	-	-	67.2	0.6	-	-
1979	67.8	0.9	-	-	68.5	1.0	-	-	68.7	0.3	-	-	70.2	2.2	-	-	71.3	1.6	-	-	72.1	1.1	-	-
1980	73.7	2.2	-	-	74.4	0.9	-	-	75.5	1.5	-	-	76.9	1.9	-	-	78.1	1.6	-	-	79.3	1.5	-	-
1981	80.0	0.9	-	-	82.2	2.8	-	-	83.8	1.9	-	-	83.7	-0.1	-	-	86.6	3.5	-	-	87.6	1.2	-	-
1982	87.8	0.2	-	-	89.4	1.8	-	-	89.7	0.3	-	-	90.1	0.4	-	-	92.6	2.8	-	-	95.3	2.9	-	-
1983	98.9	3.8	-	-	99.6	0.7	-	-	99.4	-0.2	-	-	101.9	2.5	-	-	103.1	1.2	-	-	103.1	0.0	-	-
1984	105.6	2.4	-	-	105.4	-0.2	-	-	106.2	0.8	-	-	107.4	1.1	-	-	109.2	1.7	-	-	109.8	0.5	-	-
1985	110.4	0.5	-	-	111.6	1.1	-	-	111.6	0.0	-	-	112.3	0.6	-	-	114.3	1.8	-	-	114.7	0.3	-	-
1986	116.3	1.4	-	-	116.7	0.3	-	-	117.1	0.3	-	-	119.4	2.0	-	-	120.9	1.3	-	-	122.4	1.2	-	-
1987	123.4	0.8	-	-	124.1	0.6	-	-	124.5	0.3	-	-	125.0	0.4	-	-	126.9	1.5	-	-	128.5	1.3	-	-
1988	130.7	1.7	-	-	130.6	-0.1	-	-	131.3	0.5	-	-	135.4	3.1	-	-	137.3	1.4	-	-	139.6	1.7	-	-
1989	142.7	2.2	-	-	144.0	0.9	-	-	145.5	1.0	-	-	147.6	1.4	-	-	153.4	3.9	-	-	154.7	0.8	-	-
1990	155.7	0.6	-	-	157.9	1.4	-	-	157.6	-0.2	-	-	160.2	1.6	-	-	163.4	2.0	-	-	165.3	1.2	-	-
1991	169.6	2.6	-	-	170.5	0.5	-	-	171.6	0.6	-	-	174.3	1.6	-	-	174.0	-0.2	-	-	174.2	0.1	-	-
1992	174.2	0.0	-	-	174.4	0.1	-	-	178.1	2.1	-	-	178.8	0.4	-	-	186.8	4.5	-	-	187.0	0.1	-	-
1993	189.1	1.1	-	-	190.8	0.9	-	-	191.8	0.5	-	-	192.8	0.5	-	-	194.1	0.7	-	-	194.3	0.1	-	-

Source: U.S. Department of Labor, Bureau of Labor Statistics, Division of Consumer Prices and Price Indexes. - indicates no data collected for period.

CHAPTER 7

PRODUCER PRICE INDEX

PRODUCER PRICE INDEX

The Producer Price Index (PPI) is a program of the Bureau of Labor Statistics (BLS), U.S. Department of Labor. In one of its publications, BLS describes the Producer Price Index (PPI) as follows:

> The Producer Price Index . . . measures average changes in selling prices received by domestic producers for their output. Most of the information used in calculating the Producer Price Index is obtained through the systematic sampling of virtually every industry in the mining and manufacturing sectors of the economy. The PPI program (also known as the industrial price program) includes some data from other sectors as well—agriculture, fishing, forestry, services, and gas and electricity. Thus the title "Producer Price Index" refers to an entire "family" or system of indexes. (Reference 1, p. 125.)

Description of the PPI

The PPI covers nearly 500 mining and manufacturing industries and about 8,000 specific products and product categories. More than 3,000 commodity prices are included, organized by type of product and end use. Data are reported by product groupings and sub-groups as well as in large aggregates.

Important aspects of the PPI include the definition of *price*, the selection of a *sample universe*, *data collection*, and the analytical management of the collected data, including the use of *weights*. Data are expressed as an index; the base year at present (1994) is 1982, meaning that prices for 1982 are indexed at 100.

Price. Price is defined as "the net revenue accruing to a specified producing establishment from a specified kind of buyer for a specified product shipped under specified transaction terms on a specified day of the month." (Reference 1). Under this definition, companies voluntarily providing pricing information to the BLS thus report on *actual* shipments in a given month rather than average price levels. Prices exclude taxes paid but reflect discounts, low-interest financing, and other forms of incentives, rebates, and the like.

Sampling. Samples are chosen from each industry surveyed using Unemployment Insurance System data for identifying establishments—because virtually all employers are required to report to the system. Establishments are stratified, meaning that they are assigned to groups with like characteristics within an industry. Within strata, units are ordered by size. The number of units required for the sample is selected within each stratum based on employment. Selection of each establishment is then accomplished systematically with a probability of selection proportionate to its size.

Data Collection. Data are collected by companies in the sample on a voluntary basis. Within each establishment, a portion of the transactions is selected by the BLS field representative; these transactions are then priced every month. The selection of the transactions is also made systematically so that the probability of a product or commodity being selected is proportional to its relative importance to the reporting unit.

Weights. In order to create price indexes for aggregations of products, price indexes for individual products/commodities must be combined to form a composite index. This is accomplished by giving each component a weight appropriate to its importance in the aggregate as a whole. Industrial products are weighted by their proportion of total industry shipments as measured by the Standard Industrial Classification (SIC) system and reported by the *Census of Manufactures*. Commodities are weighted based on gross value of shipments data.

Base of Index. The index shows prices relative to 1982, which is defined as 100. Changes in the index are usually expressed as increases or decreases in percent, derived by the following formula:

((Current Index / Previous Index) - 1) x 100.

If the current index is 220.5 and the last index is 219.7, the formula produces a 0.36% change. This is the actual price increase from the last measured index to the current index.

This brief description hides much of the complexity of the PPI. For more details, the reader is referred to Reference 1. In summary, the methodology used is designed to present an accurate picture of price movements. The accuracy of the index is dependent on voluntary reporting; however, price definitions, sampling, and analytical factors are designed to take into account producers of all sizes operating in all kinds of markets and geographies; prices are actual, excluding taxes but including sales incentives; industrial establishments as well as products and commodities are selected to reflect, in the index, in proportion to their relative importance overall.

History of the PPI

The PPI (then called the Wholesale Price Index or WPI), was first published in 1902 and covered the 1890-1901 period. The WPI was initially an average of prices. Weighting of components was first incorporated in 1914. Major sample expansions and reclassifications took place in 1952 and 1967. In 1978, the index was renamed Producer Price Index in recognition of the fact that the meaning of the word "wholesale"—which had been understood earlier to mean goods sold in large quantities—had come to mean prices charged by wholesalers, jobbers, and distributors. The PPI is based on prices received by producers from the party that makes the first purchase, be that a distributor, a retailer, or the final consumer. The last comprehensive revision of the PPI, begun in 1978, culminated in January 1986 with the introduction of the current methods of price definition, sampling, data collection, and analysis.

Uses of the PPI

The PPI is widely used by government, industry, labor organization, and in the academic sector. It is an early measure of inflation—because producer sales predate retail sales; the latter form the backbone of the Consumer Price Index (CPI). The CPI, however, does not mirror the movements of the PPI at some lag in time. The PPI excludes imported goods, the CPI does not; the CPI includes services, the PPI largely does not. The CPI does not directly include the prices of capital equipment (industrial tooling and the like);the PPI does. Sharp swings in the prices of goods and other items may not reflect in consumer prices in the same way—because distributors and retailers absorb price rises/drops rather than cause wide price swings at the consumer level. The PPI is used in the construction of the implicit GNP deflator. In addition to the use of the index for analytical purposes in industry, it is used in contracts in price escalation clauses and in inventory valuation.

Presentation of Data

Six summary tables of the Producer Price Index are presented in Chapter 4, Other Cyclic Indicators, in the section on Prices and Productivity. In this chapter, 119 detailed PPI tables are shown. The first four tables show annual averages for 15 major product and commodity groupings and 100 subdivisions from 1926 to

1993. Thereafter, monthly data, from 1913 or a later date to 1991 are shown, first by the major group ("Farm Products") and then followed by the next level of detail provided by the PPI ("Fresh and Dried Fruits and Vegetables," "Grains," "Livestock," etc.). All tables show a 1982 base (1982 = 100). Percent changes in the index from month to month are precalculated.

Bibliography

1. U.S. Department of Labor, Bureau of Labor Statistics. *BLS Handbook of Methods*, Bulletin 2285, 1987. Washington, D.C.

Producer Price Index
Annual Averages, 1926-1934
Base 1982 = 100

Columns headed % show percentile change in the index from the previous period for which an index is available.

	1926		1927		1928		1929		1930		1931		1932		1933		1934	
	Index	%	Index	%	Index	%	Index	%	Index	%	Index	%	Index	%	Index	%	Index	%
Farm Products	25.3	-8.7	25.1	-0.8	26.7	6.4	26.4	-1.1	22.4	-15.2	16.4	-26.8	12.2	-25.6	13.0	6.6	16.5	26.9
Fresh and Dried Fruits and Vegetables	27.0	-	25.8	-4.4	25.6	-0.8	25.7	0.4	25.8	0.4	18.5	-28.3	14.3	-22.7	15.5	8.4	16.9	9.0
Grains	33.7	-	34.0	0.9	36.0	5.9	32.8	-8.9	26.4	-19.5	17.9	-32.2	13.3	-25.7	17.9	34.6	25.1	40.2
Livestock	18.8	-	18.8	0.0	20.0	6.4	20.0	0.0	16.8	-16.0	11.9	-29.2	8.9	-25.2	8.2	-7.9	9.8	19.5
Live Poultry	102.5	-	91.9	-10.3	98.5	7.2	109.0	10.7	88.4	-18.9	75.4	-14.7	60.0	-20.4	47.4	-21.0	53.3	12.4
Plant and Animal Fibers	45.0	-	44.0	-2.2	48.0	9.1	45.6	-5.0	32.3	-29.2	21.2	-34.4	15.4	-27.4	19.8	28.6	26.3	32.8
Fluid Milk	19.5	-	19.9	2.1	20.3	2.0	21.2	4.4	20.6	-2.8	18.5	-10.2	13.6	-26.5	13.2	-2.9	16.2	22.7
Eggs	67.4	-	60.5	-10.2	63.7	5.3	70.3	10.4	54.1	-23.0	41.7	-22.9	37.5	-10.1	32.9	-12.3	39.1	18.8
Hay, Hayseeds and Oilseeds	29.5	-	26.2	-11.2	28.9	10.3	30.4	5.2	27.7	-8.9	21.1	-23.8	15.4	-27.0	16.0	3.9	23.3	45.6
Farm Products n.e.c.	13.2	-	13.1	-0.8	14.8	13.0	14.4	-2.7	9.7	-32.6	6.8	-29.9	6.0	-11.8	6.6	10.0	8.2	24.2
Processed Foods and Feeds	-	-	-		-		-		-		-		-		-		-	
Cereal and Bakery Products	18.8	-	17.8	-5.3	17.6	-1.1	16.5	-6.3	15.3	-7.3	13.8	-9.8	12.5	-9.4	14.1	12.8	16.7	18.4
Meats, Poultry, and Fish	17.5	-	16.2	-7.4	18.7	15.4	19.1	2.1	17.2	-9.9	13.2	-23.3	10.2	-22.7	8.8	-13.7	11.0	25.0
Dairy Products	17.5	-	18.1	3.4	18.4	1.7	18.4	0.0	16.7	-9.2	14.3	-14.4	10.7	-25.2	10.6	-0.9	12.7	19.8
Processed Fruits and Vegetables	20.3	-	20.1	-1.0	21.5	7.0	22.4	4.2	21.0	-6.3	17.6	-16.2	15.7	-10.8	15.9	1.3	17.9	12.6
Sugar and Confectionery	19.3	-	20.7	7.3	19.5	-5.8	17.5	-10.3	16.1	-8.0	15.5	-3.7	13.8	-11.0	14.9	8.0	14.9	0.0
Beverages and Beverage Materials	-		-		-		-		-		-		-		-		-	
Fats and Oils	-		-		-		-		-		-		-		-		-	
Miscellaneous Processed Foods	-		-		-		-		-		-		-		-		-	
Prepared Animal Feeds	-		-		-		-		-		-		-		-		-	
Textile Products and Apparel	-		-		-		-		-		-		-		-		-	
Synthetic Fibers	-		-		-		-		-		-		-		-		-	
Processed Yarns and Threads	-		-		-		-		-		-		-		-		-	
Gray Fabrics	-		-		-		-		-		-		-		-		-	
Finished Fabrics	-		-		-		-		-		-		-		-		-	
Apparel & Other Fabricated Textile Products	-		-		-		-		-		-		-		-		-	
Miscellaneous Textile Products/Services	-		-		-		-		-		-		-		-		-	
Hides, Skins, Leather, and Related Products	17.1	-	18.4	7.6	20.7	12.5	18.6	-10.1	17.1	-8.1	14.7	-14.0	12.5	-15.0	13.8	10.4	14.8	7.2
Hides and Skins	20.5	-	24.6	20.0	30.4	23.6	23.0	-24.3	18.7	-18.7	12.3	-34.2	8.6	-30.1	13.6	58.1	14.0	2.9
Leather	16.2	-	17.7	9.3	20.4	15.3	18.3	-10.3	16.4	-10.4	13.9	-15.2	10.5	-24.5	11.5	9.5	12.1	5.2
Footwear	14.6	-	14.9	2.1	16.0	7.4	15.5	-3.1	14.9	-3.9	13.7	-8.1	12.6	-8.0	13.1	4.0	14.3	9.2
Leather and Related Products n.e.c.	-		-		-		-		-		-		-		-		-	

Source: U.S. Department of Labor, Bureau of Labor Statistics, Division of Industry Prices and Price Indexes. n.e.c. stands for not elsewhere classified. - indicates no data collected for period or unavailable.

Producer Price Index
Annual Averages, 1935-1943
Base 1982 = 100

Columns headed % show percentile change in the index from the previous period for which an index is available.

	1935		1936		1937		1938		1939		1940		1941		1942		1943	
	Index	%	Index	%	Index	%	Index	%	Index	%	Index	%	Index	%	Index	%	Index	%
Farm Products	19.8	20.0	20.4	3.0	21.8	6.9	17.3	-20.6	16.5	-4.6	17.1	3.6	20.8	21.6	26.7	28.4	30.9	15.7
Fresh and Dried Fruits and Vegetables	15.6	-7.7	18.4	17.9	18.9	2.7	14.2	-24.9	15.7	10.6	16.0	1.9	16.8	5.0	24.8	47.6	33.5	35.1
Grains	27.8	10.8	29.7	6.8	33.2	11.8	20.5	-38.3	19.8	-3.4	22.9	15.7	25.7	12.2	31.2	21.4	39.1	25.3
Livestock	16.8	71.4	16.8	0.0	19.2	14.3	15.5	-19.3	13.7	-11.6	13.3	-2.9	18.0	35.3	23.7	31.7	25.4	7.2
Live Poultry	71.1	33.4	70.9	-0.3	72.4	2.1	70.2	-3.0	58.5	-16.7	58.2	-0.5	74.9	28.7	86.1	15.0	97.8	13.6
Plant and Animal Fibers	25.7	-2.3	27.1	5.4	26.6	-1.8	20.4	-23.3	23.5	15.2	23.3	-0.9	29.9	28.3	38.7	29.4	40.3	4.1
Fluid Milk	17.0	4.9	17.0	0.0	16.4	-3.5	15.0	-8.5	14.2	-5.3	15.8	11.3	17.1	8.2	19.3	12.9	21.8	13.0
Eggs	50.7	29.7	48.6	-4.1	44.9	-7.6	44.1	-1.8	35.8	-18.8	38.1	6.4	50.4	32.3	64.5	28.0	76.8	19.1
Hay, Hayseeds and Oilseeds	23.0	-1.3	22.5	-2.2	26.8	19.1	22.4	-16.4	20.8	-7.1	20.5	-1.4	21.7	5.9	30.0	38.2	36.6	22.0
Farm Products n.e.c.	9.3	13.4	8.9	-4.3	10.7	20.2	8.9	-16.8	8.5	-4.5	7.7	-9.4	10.1	31.2	14.7	45.5	16.7	13.6
Processed Foods and Feeds	-		-		-		-		-		-		-		-		-	
Cereal and Bakery Products	17.7	6.0	16.2	-8.5	16.5	1.9	14.8	-10.3	14.1	-4.7	14.7	4.3	15.2	3.4	16.8	10.5	17.6	4.8
Meats, Poultry, and Fish	16.5	50.0	15.3	-7.3	17.3	13.1	14.6	-15.6	13.5	-7.5	12.8	-5.2	15.8	23.4	19.6	24.1	19.3	-1.5
Dairy Products	13.9	9.4	14.6	5.0	14.5	-0.7	12.7	-12.4	12.0	-5.5	13.5	12.5	15.2	12.6	17.4	14.5	19.4	11.5
Processed Fruits and Vegetables	17.8	-0.6	17.5	-1.7	18.2	4.0	16.3	-10.4	15.7	-3.7	15.9	1.3	18.4	15.7	21.8	18.5	22.5	3.2
Sugar and Confectionery	16.3	9.4	16.8	3.1	16.4	-2.4	14.9	-9.1	15.2	2.0	14.4	-5.3	16.7	16.0	18.5	10.8	18.6	0.5
Beverages and Beverage Materials	-		-		-		-		-		-		-		-		-	
Fats and Oils	-		-		-		-		-		-		-		-		-	
Miscellaneous Processed Foods	-		-		-		-		-		-		-		-		-	
Prepared Animal Feeds	-		-		-		-		-		-		-		-		-	
Textile Products and Apparel	-		-		-		-		-		-		-		-		-	
Synthetic Fibers	-		-		-		-		-		-		-		-		-	
Processed Yarns and Threads	-		-		-		-		-		-		-		-		-	
Gray Fabrics	-		-		-		-		-		-		-		-		-	
Finished Fabrics	-		-		-		-		-		-		-		-		-	
Apparel & Other Fabricated Textile Products	-		-		-		-		-		-		-		-		-	
Miscellaneous Textile Products/Services	-		-		-		-		-		-		-		-		-	
Hides, Skins, Leather, and Related Products	15.3	3.4	16.3	6.5	17.9	9.8	15.8	-11.7	16.3	3.2	17.2	5.5	18.4	7.0	20.1	9.2	20.1	0.0
Hides and Skins	16.4	17.1	19.3	17.7	23.2	20.2	15.1	-34.9	17.3	14.6	18.8	8.7	22.2	18.1	24.1	8.6	23.5	-2.5
Leather	13.0	7.4	13.8	6.2	15.7	13.8	13.6	-13.4	14.2	4.4	15.0	5.6	15.8	5.3	16.4	3.8	16.4	0.0
Footwear	14.3	0.0	14.6	2.1	15.3	4.8	14.9	-2.6	15.0	0.7	15.7	4.7	16.5	5.1	18.3	10.9	18.4	0.5
Leather and Related Products n.e.c.	-		-		-		-		-		-		-		-		-	

Source: U.S. Department of Labor, Bureau of Labor Statistics, Division of Industry Prices and Price Indexes. n.e.c. stands for not elsewhere classified. - indicates no data collected for period or unavailable.

Producer Price Index
Annual Averages, 1944-1952
Base 1982 = 100

Columns headed % show percentile change in the index from the previous period for which an index is available.

	1944		1945		1946		1947		1948		1949		1950		1951		1952	
	Index	%	Index	%	Index	%	Index	%	Index	%	Index	%	Index	%	Index	%	Index	%
Farm Products	31.2	1.0	32.4	3.8	37.5	15.7	45.1	20.3	48.5	7.5	41.9	-13.6	44.0	5.0	51.2	16.4	48.4	-5.5
Fresh and Dried Fruits and Vegetables	33.4	-0.3	33.7	0.9	35.7	5.9	36.0	0.8	37.4	3.9	36.3	-2.9	33.4	-8.0	35.6	6.6	44.0	23.6
Grains	42.7	9.2	43.7	2.3	52.3	19.7	71.0	35.8	67.2	-5.4	54.0	-19.6	57.5	6.5	63.6	10.6	62.9	-1.1
Livestock	24.8	-2.4	25.8	4.0	30.4	17.8	41.4	36.2	46.7	12.8	39.1	-16.3	42.7	9.2	50.8	19.0	44.1	-13.2
Live Poultry	95.3	-2.6	100.7	5.7	108.9	8.1	111.8	2.7	128.7	15.1	105.6	-17.9	96.8	-8.3	106.4	9.9	101.4	-4.7
Plant and Animal Fibers	41.0	1.7	42.9	4.6	56.9	32.6	65.7	15.5	69.7	6.1	67.1	-3.7	78.4	16.8	97.1	23.9	77.7	-20.0
Fluid Milk	22.5	3.2	22.5	0.0	27.2	20.9	30.0	10.3	34.1	13.7	27.6	-19.1	27.1	-1.8	32.1	18.5	33.5	4.4
Eggs	67.8	-11.7	73.1	7.8	70.5	-3.6	85.1	20.7	92.2	8.3	88.7	-3.8	75.3	-15.1	95.7	27.1	84.9	-11.3
Hay, Hayseeds and Oilseeds	40.5	10.7	40.3	-0.5	43.5	7.9	55.5	27.6	56.9	2.5	43.2	-24.1	46.6	7.9	53.2	14.2	51.0	-4.1
Farm Products n.e.c.	17.5	4.8	17.2	-1.7	19.7	14.5	25.3	28.4	26.3	4.0	27.3	3.8	33.6	23.1	36.4	8.3	35.9	-1.4
Processed Foods and Feeds	-	-	-	-	-	-	33.0	-	35.3	7.0	32.1	-9.1	33.2	3.4	36.9	11.1	36.4	-1.4
Cereal and Bakery Products	17.9	1.7	17.9	0.0	21.5	20.1	28.7	33.5	29.2	1.7	27.7	-5.1	28.2	1.8	30.5	8.2	30.5	0.0
Meats, Poultry, and Fish	18.5	-4.1	18.8	1.6	25.3	34.6	35.3	39.5	41.0	16.1	35.8	-12.7	37.9	5.9	43.6	15.0	40.5	-7.1
Dairy Products	19.3	-0.5	19.4	0.5	25.4	30.9	28.0	10.2	31.3	11.8	28.2	-9.9	27.7	-1.8	31.5	13.7	33.1	5.1
Processed Fruits and Vegetables	22.8	1.3	23.0	0.9	24.4	6.1	31.7	29.9	31.6	-0.3	31.4	-0.6	31.6	0.6	33.3	5.4	33.2	-0.3
Sugar and Confectionery	18.6	0.0	18.5	-0.5	22.0	18.9	28.9	31.4	29.6	2.4	27.4	-7.4	27.9	1.8	30.3	8.6	31.1	2.6
Beverages and Beverage Materials	-	-	-	-	-	-	26.6	-	27.8	4.5	28.3	1.8	30.5	7.8	32.5	6.6	33.2	2.2
Fats and Oils	-	-	-	-	-	-	-	-	-	-	-	-	-	-	-	-	-	-
Miscellaneous Processed Foods	-	-	-	-	-	-	34.8	-	36.5	4.9	40.0	9.6	43.9	9.7	45.6	3.9	44.2	-3.1
Prepared Animal Feeds	-	-	-	-	-	-	55.3	-	56.0	1.3	49.0	-12.5	48.8	-0.4	53.7	10.0	57.7	7.4
Textile Products and Apparel	-	-	-	-	-	-	50.6	-	52.8	4.3	48.3	-8.5	50.2	3.9	56.0	11.6	50.5	-9.8
Synthetic Fibers	-	-	-	-	-	-	-	-	-	-	-	-	-	-	-	-	-	-
Processed Yarns and Threads	-	-	-	-	-	-	-	-	-	-	-	-	-	-	-	-	-	-
Gray Fabrics	-	-	-	-	-	-	-	-	-	-	-	-	-	-	-	-	-	-
Finished Fabrics	-	-	-	-	-	-	-	-	-	-	-	-	-	-	-	-	-	-
Apparel & Other Fabricated Textile Products	-	-	-	-	-	-	-	-	-	-	-	-	-	-	-	-	-	-
Miscellaneous Textile Products/Services	-	-	-	-	-	-	-	-	-	-	-	-	-	-	-	-	-	-
Hides, Skins, Leather, and Related Products	19.9	-1.0	20.1	1.0	23.3	15.9	31.7	36.1	32.1	1.3	30.4	-5.3	32.9	8.2	37.7	14.6	30.5	-19.1
Hides and Skins	22.4	-4.7	23.9	6.7	30.3	26.8	47.6	57.1	44.5	-6.5	38.8	-12.8	45.0	16.0	51.9	15.3	27.5	-47.0
Leather	16.4	0.0	16.5	0.6	20.7	25.5	31.4	51.7	29.9	-4.8	27.7	-7.4	31.8	14.8	37.0	16.4	26.6	-28.1
Footwear	18.4	0.0	18.4	0.0	20.4	10.9	25.8	26.5	27.6	7.0	27.2	-1.4	28.7	5.5	32.7	13.9	30.2	-7.6
Leather and Related Products n.e.c.	-	-	-	-	-	-	35.1	-	36.0	2.6	34.3	-4.7	34.5	0.6	39.5	14.5	35.4	-10.4

Source: U.S. Department of Labor, Bureau of Labor Statistics, Division of Industry Prices and Price Indexes. n.e.c. stands for not elsewhere classified. - indicates no data collected for period or unavailable.

Producer Price Index
Annual Averages, 1953-1961
Base 1982 = 100

Columns headed % show percentile change in the index from the previous period for which an index is available.

	1953		1954		1955		1956		1957		1958		1959		1960		1961	
	Index	%	Index	%	Index	%	Index	%	Index	%	Index	%	Index	%	Index	%	Index	%
Farm Products	43.8	-9.5	43.2	-1.4	40.5	-6.3	40.0	-1.2	41.1	2.8	42.9	4.4	40.2	-6.3	40.1	-0.2	39.7	-1.0
Fresh and Dried Fruits and Vegetables	36.7	-16.6	36.3	-1.1	38.1	5.0	38.1	0.0	37.9	-0.5	41.0	8.2	37.6	-8.3	39.0	3.7	36.3	-6.9
Grains	57.8	-8.1	58.6	1.4	55.8	-4.8	55.8	0.0	53.9	-3.4	50.9	-5.6	49.5	-2.8	48.5	-2.0	49.2	1.4
Livestock	37.5	-15.0	37.0	-1.3	31.8	-14.1	30.6	-3.8	35.3	15.4	41.6	17.8	38.2	-8.2	36.6	-4.2	36.0	-1.6
Live Poultry	100.5	-0.9	81.8	-18.6	87.0	6.4	71.4	-17.9	66.4	-7.0	65.1	-2.0	59.4	-8.8	63.4	6.7	52.7	-16.9
Plant and Animal Fibers	69.8	-10.2	71.7	2.7	69.2	-3.5	69.4	0.3	70.2	1.2	68.6	-2.3	66.3	-3.4	63.6	-4.1	64.8	1.9
Fluid Milk	30.2	-9.9	27.9	-7.6	28.0	0.4	28.9	3.2	29.3	1.4	28.9	-1.4	28.9	0.0	30.0	3.8	30.2	0.7
Eggs	93.7	10.4	70.8	-24.4	76.0	7.3	72.6	-4.5	68.5	-5.6	72.5	5.8	58.1	-19.9	68.5	17.9	65.7	-4.1
Hay, Hayseeds and Oilseeds	46.8	-8.2	48.3	3.2	44.0	-8.9	42.9	-2.5	42.6	-0.7	39.9	-6.3	39.8	-0.3	38.8	-2.5	43.7	12.6
Farm Products n.e.c.	37.1	3.3	45.0	21.3	37.5	-16.7	38.6	2.9	38.0	-1.6	36.9	-2.9	34.9	-5.4	33.8	-3.2	34.1	0.9
Processed Foods and Feeds	34.8	-4.4	35.4	1.7	33.8	-4.5	33.8	0.0	34.8	3.0	36.5	4.9	35.6	-2.5	35.6	0.0	36.2	1.7
Cereal and Bakery Products	31.2	2.3	32.5	4.2	33.1	1.8	32.8	-0.9	33.3	1.5	33.6	0.9	34.0	1.2	34.7	2.1	35.4	2.0
Meats, Poultry, and Fish	34.7	-14.3	34.4	-0.9	31.7	-7.8	30.5	-3.8	34.4	12.8	39.9	16.0	36.7	-8.0	36.1	-1.6	35.3	-2.2
Dairy Products	32.3	-2.4	31.0	-4.0	31.0	0.0	31.7	2.3	32.6	2.8	32.9	0.9	33.4	1.5	34.6	3.6	35.4	2.3
Processed Fruits and Vegetables	33.1	-0.3	33.0	-0.3	33.3	0.9	34.1	2.4	32.8	-3.8	34.7	5.8	34.5	-0.6	33.8	-2.0	34.6	2.4
Sugar and Confectionery	31.3	0.6	32.2	2.9	31.6	-1.9	31.4	-0.6	32.4	3.2	33.1	2.2	32.9	-0.6	33.4	1.5	33.2	-0.6
Beverages and Beverage Materials	33.8	1.8	37.6	11.2	36.2	-3.7	37.1	2.5	37.1	0.0	36.3	-2.2	36.2	-0.3	36.1	-0.3	36.1	0.0
Fats and Oils	-		-		-		-		-		-		-		-		-	
Miscellaneous Processed Foods	43.4	-1.8	38.3	-11.8	36.9	-3.7	35.9	-2.7	35.4	-1.4	35.8	1.1	35.9	0.3	37.9	5.6	37.8	-0.3
Prepared Animal Feeds	46.9	-18.7	51.3	9.4	40.5	-21.1	38.5	-4.9	36.0	-6.5	39.8	10.6	40.2	1.0	37.2	-7.5	40.4	8.6
Textile Products and Apparel	49.3	-2.4	48.2	-2.2	48.2	0.0	48.2	0.0	48.3	0.2	47.4	-1.9	48.1	1.5	48.6	1.0	47.8	-1.6
Synthetic Fibers	-		-		-		-		-		-		-		-		-	
Processed Yarns and Threads	-		-		-		-		-		-		-		-		-	
Gray Fabrics	-		-		-		-		-		-		-		-		-	
Finished Fabrics	-		-		-		-		-		-		-		-		-	
Apparel & Other Fabricated Textile Products	-		-		-		-		-		-		-		-		-	
Miscellaneous Textile Products/Services	-		-		-		-		-		-		-		-		-	
Hides, Skins, Leather, and Related Products	31.0	1.6	29.5	-4.8	29.4	-0.3	31.2	6.1	31.2	0.0	31.6	1.3	35.9	13.6	34.6	-3.6	34.9	0.9
Hides and Skins	29.8	8.4	24.1	-19.1	24.7	2.5	25.8	4.5	24.1	-6.6	25.1	4.1	39.6	57.8	29.7	-25.0	31.9	7.4
Leather	27.7	4.1	25.3	-8.7	25.1	-0.8	27.1	8.0	26.8	-1.1	27.4	2.2	33.2	21.2	30.1	-9.3	30.9	2.7
Footwear	30.1	-0.3	30.1	0.0	30.2	0.3	32.1	6.3	32.6	1.6	32.9	0.9	34.9	6.1	35.8	2.6	35.9	0.3
Leather and Related Products n.e.c.	34.9	-1.4	34.1	-2.3	33.7	-1.2	34.6	2.7	34.4	-0.6	34.2	-0.6	38.3	12.0	37.2	-2.9	36.8	-1.1

Source: U.S. Department of Labor, Bureau of Labor Statistics, Division of Industry Prices and Price Indexes. n.e.c. stands for not elsewhere classified. - indicates no data collected for period or unavailable.

Producer Price Index
Annual Averages, 1962-1970
Base 1982 = 100

Columns headed % show percentile change in the index from the previous period for which an index is available.

	1962		1963		1964		1965		1966		1967		1968		1969		1970	
	Index	%	Index	%	Index	%	Index	%	Index	%	Index	%	Index	%	Index	%	Index	%
Farm Products	40.4	1.8	39.6	-2.0	39.0	-1.5	40.7	4.4	43.7	7.4	41.3	-5.5	42.3	2.4	45.0	6.4	45.8	1.8
Fresh and Dried Fruits and Vegetables	37.9	4.4	37.3	-1.6	40.1	7.5	39.5	-1.5	39.8	0.8	39.4	-1.0	42.0	6.6	43.4	3.3	44.0	1.4
Grains	50.8	3.3	52.4	3.1	48.4	-7.6	46.1	-4.8	50.0	8.5	47.4	-5.2	42.1	-11.2	42.8	1.7	46.8	9.3
Livestock	37.4	3.9	34.2	-8.6	32.6	-4.7	38.6	18.4	42.2	9.3	38.8	-8.1	40.2	3.6	45.4	12.9	45.3	-0.2
Live Poultry	54.3	3.0	53.9	-0.7	52.2	-3.2	55.0	5.4	58.2	5.8	52.1	-10.5	54.0	3.6	58.8	8.9	51.9	-11.7
Plant and Animal Fibers	67.3	3.9	68.7	2.1	67.2	-2.2	62.3	-7.3	56.2	-9.8	49.3	-12.3	51.5	4.5	45.9	-10.9	44.5	-3.1
Fluid Milk	29.4	-2.6	29.2	-0.7	29.6	1.4	30.1	1.7	34.2	13.6	35.4	3.5	37.5	5.9	39.2	4.5	40.8	4.1
Eggs	63.2	-3.8	62.4	-1.3	60.3	-3.4	62.1	3.0	71.6	15.3	56.0	-21.8	62.3	11.2	74.9	20.2	71.0	-5.2
Hay, Hayseeds and Oilseeds	42.9	-1.8	46.0	7.2	44.8	-2.6	46.0	2.7	50.0	8.7	47.0	-6.0	45.4	-3.4	44.5	-2.0	46.7	4.9
Farm Products n.e.c.	33.6	-1.5	32.7	-2.7	36.1	10.4	35.7	-1.1	37.1	3.9	36.4	-1.9	37.7	3.6	39.9	5.8	42.7	7.0
Processed Foods and Feeds	36.5	0.8	36.8	0.8	36.7	-0.3	38.0	3.5	40.2	5.8	39.8	-1.0	40.6	2.0	42.7	5.2	44.6	4.4
Cereal and Bakery Products	36.2	2.3	36.1	-0.3	36.3	0.6	36.7	1.1	38.8	5.7	39.4	1.5	39.8	1.0	40.5	1.8	42.4	4.7
Meats, Poultry, and Fish	36.6	3.7	34.5	-5.7	33.6	-2.6	37.3	11.0	40.8	9.4	38.8	-4.9	40.0	3.1	44.2	10.5	45.0	1.8
Dairy Products	35.2	-0.6	35.4	0.6	35.5	0.3	35.8	0.8	39.1	9.2	40.2	2.8	42.1	4.7	43.5	3.3	44.7	2.8
Processed Fruits and Vegetables	33.3	-3.8	35.3	6.0	35.6	0.8	34.7	-2.5	35.6	2.6	36.4	2.2	38.8	6.6	39.4	1.5	40.3	2.3
Sugar and Confectionery	33.5	0.9	38.9	16.1	36.7	-5.7	35.8	-2.5	36.3	1.4	37.1	2.2	38.1	2.7	40.8	7.1	42.9	5.1
Beverages and Beverage Materials	36.2	0.3	36.9	1.9	38.8	5.1	38.6	-0.5	38.7	0.3	38.9	0.5	40.0	2.8	41.3	3.2	44.0	6.5
Fats and Oils	-	-	-	-	-	-	-	-	-	-	46.5	-	44.8	-3.7	46.9	4.7	55.1	17.5
Miscellaneous Processed Foods	36.4	-3.7	37.3	2.5	38.9	4.3	40.6	4.4	40.7	0.2	40.2	-1.2	41.3	2.7	43.4	5.1	45.5	4.8
Prepared Animal Feeds	42.7	5.7	45.0	5.4	44.0	-2.2	44.9	2.0	48.9	8.9	47.3	-3.3	45.8	-3.2	45.7	-0.2	49.1	7.4
Textile Products and Apparel	48.2	0.8	48.2	0.0	48.5	0.6	48.8	0.6	48.9	0.2	48.9	0.0	50.7	3.7	51.8	2.2	52.4	1.2
Synthetic Fibers	-	-	-	-	-	-	-	-	-	-	-	-	-	-	-	-	-	-
Processed Yarns and Threads	-	-	-	-	-	-	-	-	-	-	-	-	-	-	-	-	-	-
Gray Fabrics	-	-	-	-	-	-	-	-	-	-	-	-	-	-	-	-	-	-
Finished Fabrics	-	-	-	-	-	-	-	-	-	-	-	-	-	-	-	-	-	-
Apparel & Other Fabricated Textile Products	-	-	-	-	-	-	-	-	-	-	-	-	-	-	-	-	-	-
Miscellaneous Textile Products/Services	-	-	-	-	-	-	-	-	-	-	-	-	-	-	-	-	-	-
Hides, Skins, Leather, and Related Products	35.3	1.1	34.3	-2.8	34.4	0.3	35.9	4.4	39.4	9.7	38.1	-3.3	39.3	3.1	41.5	5.6	42.0	1.2
Hides and Skins	31.4	-1.6	24.9	-20.7	25.9	4.0	32.9	27.0	41.7	26.7	27.9	-33.1	29.6	6.1	34.6	16.9	29.0	-16.2
Leather	31.6	2.3	29.7	-6.0	30.0	1.0	31.5	5.0	35.3	12.1	32.1	-9.1	32.8	2.2	34.9	6.4	34.6	-0.9
Footwear	36.3	1.1	36.2	-0.3	36.3	0.3	37.0	1.9	39.5	6.8	40.8	3.3	42.8	4.9	44.7	4.4	46.2	3.4
Leather and Related Products n.e.c.	37.2	1.1	37.1	-0.3	36.8	-0.8	37.8	2.7	40.8	7.9	40.4	-1.0	40.2	-0.5	41.8	4.0	43.0	2.9

Source: U.S. Department of Labor, Bureau of Labor Statistics, Division of Industry Prices and Price Indexes. n.e.c. stands for not elsewhere classified. - indicates no data collected for period or unavailable.

Producer Price Index
Annual Averages, 1971-1979
Base 1982 = 100

Columns headed % show percentile change in the index from the previous period for which an index is available.

	1971		1972		1973		1974		1975		1976		1977		1978		1979	
	Index	%	Index	%	Index	%	Index	%	Index	%	Index	%	Index	%	Index	%	Index	%
Farm Products	46.6	1.7	51.6	10.7	72.7	40.9	77.4	6.5	77.0	-0.5	78.8	2.3	79.4	0.8	87.7	10.5	99.6	13.6
Fresh and Dried Fruits and Vegetables	47.3	7.5	50.3	6.3	66.3	31.8	75.8	14.3	72.4	-4.5	70.3	-2.9	75.8	7.8	85.3	12.5	90.3	5.9
Grains	47.8	2.1	48.8	2.1	87.1	78.5	122.3	40.4	106.2	-13.2	97.6	-8.1	78.2	-19.9	86.5	10.6	101.8	17.7
Livestock	45.9	1.3	55.3	20.5	73.8	33.5	66.2	-10.3	72.9	10.1	67.2	-7.8	67.1	-0.1	85.4	27.3	100.9	18.1
Live Poultry	52.2	0.6	54.2	3.8	93.5	72.5	82.0	-12.3	98.9	20.6	87.0	-12.0	91.4	5.1	104.1	13.9	101.2	-2.8
Plant and Animal Fibers	45.7	2.7	57.9	26.7	97.5	68.4	95.6	-1.9	75.5	-21.0	110.3	46.1	99.7	-9.6	95.3	-4.4	103.4	8.5
Fluid Milk	42.0	2.9	43.3	3.1	51.3	18.5	61.2	19.3	63.8	4.2	71.2	11.6	71.8	0.8	77.8	8.4	88.5	13.8
Eggs	56.4	-20.6	58.0	2.8	92.7	59.8	89.9	-3.0	89.4	-0.6	100.2	12.1	90.6	-9.6	88.7	-2.1	98.8	11.4
Hay, Hayseeds and Oilseeds	51.3	9.9	55.5	8.2	103.4	86.3	107.4	3.9	94.1	-12.4	98.9	5.1	110.1	11.3	101.4	-7.9	114.8	13.2
Farm Products n.e.c.	42.1	-1.4	45.5	8.1	53.7	18.0	59.9	11.5	61.8	3.2	81.4	31.7	118.7	45.8	100.2	-15.6	105.3	5.1
Processed Foods and Feeds	45.5	2.0	48.0	5.5	58.9	22.7	68.0	15.4	72.6	6.8	70.8	-2.5	74.0	4.5	80.6	8.9	88.5	9.8
Cereal and Bakery Products	44.0	3.8	45.2	2.7	53.0	17.3	67.5	27.4	70.1	3.9	67.8	-3.3	68.3	0.7	75.0	9.8	82.9	10.5
Meats, Poultry, and Fish	45.0	0.0	50.5	12.2	65.0	28.7	63.5	-2.3	74.2	16.9	70.5	-5.0	70.7	0.3	84.3	19.2	93.9	11.4
Dairy Products	46.5	4.0	47.7	2.6	52.7	10.5	58.8	11.6	62.6	6.5	67.7	8.1	69.7	3.0	75.7	8.6	84.9	12.2
Processed Fruits and Vegetables	41.7	3.5	43.6	4.6	47.2	8.3	56.3	19.3	61.9	9.9	62.0	0.2	68.3	10.2	73.8	8.1	80.9	9.6
Sugar and Confectionery	44.3	3.3	45.1	1.8	49.1	8.9	96.0	95.5	94.3	-1.8	70.8	-24.9	65.8	-7.1	73.3	11.4	79.6	8.6
Beverages and Beverage Materials	45.2	2.7	45.9	1.5	47.4	3.3	54.8	15.6	63.2	15.3	67.5	6.8	78.3	16.0	77.9	-0.5	82.0	5.3
Fats and Oils	58.6	6.4	54.6	-6.8	75.6	38.5	120.5	59.4	104.7	-13.1	82.8	-20.9	96.5	16.5	104.7	8.5	113.1	8.0
Miscellaneous Processed Foods	45.6	0.2	46.2	1.3	49.6	7.4	63.8	28.6	71.8	12.5	70.3	-2.1	76.5	8.8	80.1	4.7	87.1	8.7
Prepared Animal Feeds	49.4	0.6	54.9	11.1	94.0	71.2	87.1	-7.3	81.5	-6.4	92.0	12.9	96.8	5.2	93.4	-3.5	103.8	11.1
Textile Products and Apparel	53.3	1.7	55.5	4.1	60.5	9.0	68.0	12.4	67.4	-0.9	72.4	7.4	75.3	4.0	78.1	3.7	82.5	5.6
Synthetic Fibers	-	-	-	-	-	-	-	-	-	-	63.2	-	66.2	4.7	67.6	2.1	73.4	8.6
Processed Yarns and Threads	-	-	-	-	-	-	-	-	-	-	71.9	-	73.0	1.5	74.0	1.4	78.9	6.6
Gray Fabrics	-	-	-	-	-	-	-	-	-	-	73.0	-	72.1	-1.2	81.6	13.2	87.5	7.2
Finished Fabrics	-	-	-	-	-	-	-	-	-	-	81.2	-	83.3	2.6	83.3	0.0	86.2	3.5
Apparel & Other Fabricated Textile Products	-	-	-	-	-	-	-	-	-	-	-	-	-	-	77.9	-	82.1	5.4
Miscellaneous Textile Products/Services	-	-	-	-	-	-	-	-	-	-	-	-	-	-	-	-	-	-
Hides, Skins, Leather, and Related Products	43.4	3.3	50.0	15.2	54.5	9.0	55.2	1.3	56.5	2.4	63.9	13.1	68.3	6.9	76.1	11.4	96.1	26.3
Hides and Skins	32.1	10.7	59.6	85.7	70.8	18.8	54.6	-22.9	48.6	-11.0	72.0	48.1	79.9	11.0	100.5	25.8	149.2	48.5
Leather	36.2	4.6	45.1	24.6	51.4	14.0	49.6	-3.5	48.7	-1.8	60.4	24.0	64.6	7.0	76.6	18.6	114.6	49.6
Footwear	47.7	3.2	50.8	6.5	53.3	4.9	57.1	7.1	60.3	5.6	64.8	7.5	68.8	6.2	74.7	8.6	89.0	19.1
Leather and Related Products n.e.c.	43.8	1.9	47.6	8.7	52.5	10.3	55.2	5.1	57.0	3.3	61.8	8.4	66.0	6.8	71.5	8.3	82.9	15.9

Source: U.S. Department of Labor, Bureau of Labor Statistics, Division of Industry Prices and Price Indexes. n.e.c. stands for not elsewhere classified. - indicates no data collected for period or unavailable.

Producer Price Index
Annual Averages, 1980-1988
Base 1982 = 100

Columns headed % show percentile change in the index from the previous period for which an index is available.

	1980 Index	%	1981 Index	%	1982 Index	%	1983 Index	%	1984 Index	%	1985 Index	%	1986 Index	%	1987 Index	%	1988 Index	%
Farm Products	102.9	3.3	105.2	2.2	100.0	-4.9	102.4	2.4	105.5	3.0	95.1	-9.9	92.9	-2.3	95.5	2.8	104.9	9.8
Fresh and Dried Fruits and Vegetables	94.1	4.2	105.4	12.0	100.0	-5.1	103.3	3.3	109.6	6.1	102.7	-6.3	103.9	1.2	106.8	2.8	108.5	1.6
Grains	113.3	11.3	117.8	4.0	100.0	-15.1	114.0	14.0	113.7	-0.3	96.1	-15.5	79.3	-17.5	71.1	-10.3	97.9	37.7
Livestock	98.0	-2.9	96.2	-1.8	100.0	4.0	94.3	-5.7	97.7	3.6	89.2	-8.7	91.8	2.9	102.0	11.1	103.3	1.3
Live Poultry	105.3	4.1	104.8	-0.5	100.0	-4.6	107.6	7.6	125.4	16.5	117.9	-6.0	129.7	10.0	101.2	-22.0	121.5	20.1
Plant and Animal Fibers	133.6	29.2	119.2	-10.8	100.0	-16.1	111.9	11.9	112.6	0.6	97.5	-13.4	88.4	-9.3	106.5	20.5	98.4	-7.6
Fluid Milk	96.0	8.5	101.7	5.9	100.0	-1.7	99.8	-0.2	98.5	-1.3	93.7	-4.9	91.0	-2.9	91.9	1.0	89.4	-2.7
Eggs	95.7	-3.1	104.7	9.4	100.0	-4.5	-	-	117.9	17.9	95.7	-18.8	99.6	4.1	87.6	-12.0	88.6	1.1
Hay, Hayseeds and Oilseeds	116.1	1.1	128.8	10.9	100.0	-22.4	116.0	16.0	120.5	3.9	96.8	-19.7	92.9	-4.0	101.4	9.1	138.4	36.5
Farm Products n.e.c.	108.9	3.4	99.7	-8.4	100.0	0.3	102.8	2.8	104.1	1.3	103.1	-1.0	96.3	-6.6	94.4	-2.0	95.4	1.1
Processed Foods and Feeds	95.9	8.4	98.9	3.1	100.0	1.1	101.8	1.8	105.4	3.5	103.5	-1.8	105.4	1.8	107.9	2.4	112.7	4.4
Cereal and Bakery Products	93.0	12.2	100.7	8.3	100.0	-0.7	102.8	2.8	106.6	3.7	110.3	3.5	111.0	0.6	112.6	1.4	123.0	9.2
Meats, Poultry, and Fish	94.4	0.5	95.6	1.3	100.0	4.6	96.7	-3.3	98.8	2.2	95.9	-2.9	100.2	4.5	104.9	4.7	106.6	1.6
Dairy Products	92.7	9.2	98.7	6.5	100.0	1.3	100.7	0.7	101.1	0.4	100.2	-0.9	99.9	-0.3	101.6	1.7	102.2	0.6
Processed Fruits and Vegetables	83.3	3.0	95.2	14.3	100.0	5.0	101.1	1.1	107.3	6.1	108.0	0.7	104.9	-2.9	108.6	3.5	113.8	4.8
Sugar and Confectionery	119.6	50.3	102.3	-14.5	100.0	-2.2	108.6	8.6	111.7	2.9	107.9	-3.4	109.7	1.7	112.7	2.7	114.7	1.8
Beverages and Beverage Materials	90.7	10.6	96.5	6.4	100.0	3.6	102.6	2.6	106.3	3.6	107.7	1.3	114.6	6.4	112.5	-1.8	114.3	1.6
Fats and Oils	105.4	-6.8	105.7	0.3	100.0	-5.4	111.0	11.0	140.1	26.2	125.5	-10.4	96.5	-23.1	97.9	1.5	117.2	19.7
Miscellaneous Processed Foods	91.4	4.9	100.6	10.1	100.0	-0.6	102.5	2.5	111.8	9.1	114.1	2.1	116.2	1.8	119.8	3.1	122.5	2.3
Prepared Animal Feeds	107.3	3.4	109.0	1.6	100.0	-8.3	108.3	8.3	104.4	-3.6	90.1	-13.7	94.6	5.0	98.5	4.1	116.0	17.8
Textile Products and Apparel	89.7	8.7	97.6	8.8	100.0	2.5	100.3	0.3	102.7	2.4	102.9	0.2	103.2	0.3	105.1	1.8	109.2	3.9
Synthetic Fibers	83.1	13.2	96.5	16.1	100.0	3.6	96.7	-3.3	98.5	1.9	95.5	-3.0	92.5	-3.1	91.8	-0.8	97.3	6.0
Processed Yarns and Threads	88.6	12.3	99.8	12.6	100.0	0.2	100.1	0.1	103.2	3.1	102.1	-1.1	101.7	-0.4	103.8	2.1	108.0	4.0
Gray Fabrics	95.0	8.6	101.0	6.3	100.0	-1.0	101.2	1.2	105.8	4.5	104.4	-1.3	103.7	-0.7	107.2	3.4	114.0	6.3
Finished Fabrics	92.9	7.8	100.5	8.2	100.0	-0.5	98.9	-1.1	101.7	2.8	101.4	-0.3	101.4	0.0	104.2	2.8	109.4	5.0
Apparel & Other Fabricated Textile Products	88.7	8.0	95.8	8.0	100.0	4.4	101.0	1.0	102.8	1.8	104.2	1.4	105.5	1.2	107.3	1.7	110.4	2.9
Miscellaneous Textile Products/Services	-	-	-	-	-	-	-	-	-	-	-	-	96.4	-	98.7	2.4	105.3	6.7
Hides, Skins, Leather, and Related Products	94.7	-1.5	99.3	4.9	100.0	0.7	103.2	3.2	109.0	5.6	108.9	-0.1	113.0	3.8	120.4	6.5	131.4	9.1
Hides and Skins	103.4	-30.7	-	-	-	-	-	-	-	-	-	-	-	-	-	-	-	-
Leather	99.8	-12.9	102.7	2.9	100.0	-2.6	106.2	6.2	119.6	12.6	113.4	-5.2	122.9	8.4	140.9	14.6	167.5	18.9
Footwear	95.2	7.0	98.3	3.3	100.0	1.7	102.1	2.1	102.7	0.6	104.8	2.0	106.9	2.0	109.4	2.3	115.1	5.2
Leather and Related Products n.e.c.	88.3	6.5	97.7	10.6	100.0	2.4	102.2	2.2	106.6	4.3	110.3	3.5	110.3	0.0	113.0	2.4	119.1	5.4

Source: U.S. Department of Labor, Bureau of Labor Statistics, Division of Industry Prices and Price Indexes. n.e.c. stands for not elsewhere classified. - indicates no data collected for period or unavailable.

Producer Price Index
Annual Averages, 1989-1993
Base 1982 = 100

Columns headed % show percentile change in the index from the previous period for which an index is available.

	1989		1990		1991		1992		1993									
	Index	%	Index	%	Index	%	Index	%	Index	%	Index	%	Index	%	Index	%	Index	%
Farm Products	110.9	5.7	112.2	1.2	105.7	-5.8	103.6	-2.0	107.0	3.3								
Fresh and Dried Fruits and Vegetables	114.6	5.6	117.5	2.5	114.7	-2.4	96.9	-15.5	106.0	9.4								
Grains	106.4	8.7	97.4	-8.5	92.0	-5.5	97.3	5.8	94.4	-3.0								
Livestock	106.1	2.7	115.6	9.0	107.9	-6.7	104.7	-3.0	107.0	2.2								
Live Poultry	128.8	6.0	118.8	-7.8	111.2	-6.4	112.6	1.3	122.0	8.3								
Plant and Animal Fibers	107.8	9.6	117.8	9.3	115.1	-2.3	89.8	-22.0	91.3	1.7								
Fluid Milk	98.8	10.5	100.8	2.0	89.5	-11.2	96.1	7.4	93.8	-2.4								
Eggs	119.6	35.0	117.6	-1.7	110.7	-5.9	94.1	-15.0	105.9	12.5								
Hay, Hayseeds and Oilseeds	137.0	-1.0	122.1	-10.9	112.1	-8.2	111.2	-0.8	126.2	13.5								
Farm Products n.e.c.	103.3	8.3	125.3	21.3	151.6	21.0	150.6	-0.7	148.6	-1.3								
Processed Foods and Feeds	117.8	4.5	121.9	3.5	121.9	0.0	122.1	0.2	124.0	1.6								
Cereal and Bakery Products	131.1	6.6	134.2	2.4	137.9	2.8	144.2	4.6	147.7	2.4								
Meats, Poultry, and Fish	111.0	4.1	119.6	7.7	116.6	-2.5	112.2	-3.8	115.4	2.9								
Dairy Products	110.6	8.2	117.2	6.0	114.6	-2.2	117.9	2.9	118.1	0.2								
Processed Fruits and Vegetables	119.9	5.4	124.7	4.0	119.6	-4.1	120.8	1.0	118.3	-2.1								
Sugar and Confectionery	120.1	4.7	123.1	2.5	128.4	4.3	127.7	-0.5	127.9	0.2								
Beverages and Beverage Materials	118.4	3.6	120.8	2.0	124.1	2.7	124.4	0.2	124.8	0.3								
Fats and Oils	112.1	-4.4	119.4	6.5	112.0	-6.2	108.8	-2.9	117.2	7.7								
Miscellaneous Processed Foods	129.4	5.6	134.2	3.7	138.3	3.1	139.2	0.7	142.4	2.3								
Prepared Animal Feeds	116.6	0.5	107.4	-7.9	106.8	-0.6	108.3	1.4	111.0	2.5								
Textile Products and Apparel	112.3	2.8	115.0	2.4	116.3	1.1	117.8	1.3	118.1	0.3								
Synthetic Fibers	104.8	7.7	106.7	1.8	105.3	-1.3	103.4	-1.8	103.8	0.4								
Processed Yarns and Threads	110.4	2.2	112.6	2.0	112.6	0.0	110.8	-1.6	107.8	-2.7								
Gray Fabrics	115.2	1.1	117.2	1.7	117.4	0.2	120.6	2.7	118.6	-1.7								
Finished Fabrics	113.6	3.8	116.0	2.1	117.5	1.3	118.8	1.1	119.5	0.6								
Apparel & Other Fabricated Textile Products	113.0	2.4	116.0	2.7	118.1	1.8	120.4	1.9	121.6	1.0								
Miscellaneous Textile Products/Services	111.8	6.2	114.0	2.0	113.5	-0.4	114.9	1.2	116.0	1.0								
Hides, Skins, Leather, and Related Products	136.3	3.7	141.7	4.0	138.9	-2.0	140.4	1.1	143.6	2.3								
Hides and Skins	212.9	-	217.9	2.3	174.2	-20.1	174.0	-0.1	184.2	5.9								
Leather	170.4	1.7	177.5	4.2	168.4	-5.1	163.7	-2.8	168.6	3.0								
Footwear	120.8	5.0	125.6	4.0	128.6	2.4	132.0	2.6	134.4	1.8								
Leather and Related Products n.e.c.	123.1	3.4	128.9	4.7	132.6	2.9	134.9	1.7	136.2	1.0								

Source: U.S. Department of Labor, Bureau of Labor Statistics, Division of Industry Prices and Price Indexes. n.e.c. stands for not elsewhere classified. - indicates no data collected for period or unavailable.

Producer Price Index
Annual Averages, 1926-1934
Base 1982 = 100

Columns headed % show percentile change in the index from the previous period for which an index is available.

	1926		1927		1928		1929		1930		1931		1932		1933		1934	
	Index	%	Index	%	Index	%	Index	%	Index	%	Index	%	Index	%	Index	%	Index	%
Fuels and Related Products and Power	10.3	-	9.1	-11.7	8.7	-4.4	8.6	-1.1	8.1	-5.8	7.0	-13.6	7.3	4.3	6.9	-5.5	7.6	10.1
Coal	8.5	-	8.4	-1.2	7.9	-6.0	7.7	-2.5	7.6	-1.3	7.3	-3.9	7.1	-2.7	7.0	-1.4	7.7	10.0
Coke Oven Products	6.0	-	5.6	-6.7	5.0	-10.7	5.0	0.0	5.0	0.0	4.9	-2.0	4.6	-6.1	4.6	0.0	5.0	8.7
Gas Fuels	-		-		-		-		-		-		-		-		-	
Electric Power	-		-		-		-		-		-		-		-		-	
Utility Natural Gas	-		-		-		-		-		-		-		-		-	
Petroleum Products, Refined	-		-		-		-		-		-		-		-		-	
Petroleum and Coal Products n.e.c.	-		-		-		-		-		-		-		16.2	-	17.0	4.9
Chemicals and Allied Products	-		-		-		-		-		-		-		-		-	
Industrial Chemicals	19.9	-	19.8	-0.5	19.6	-1.0	19.8	1.0	19.3	-2.5	17.9	-7.3	17.7	-1.1	17.3	-2.3	17.3	0.0
Paints and Allied Products	-		-		-		-		-		-		-		-		-	
Drugs and Pharmaceuticals	-		-		-		-		-		-		-		-		-	
Fats and Oils, Inedible	52.9	-	49.0	-7.4	50.5	3.1	47.1	-6.7	37.6	-20.2	25.9	-31.1	21.2	-18.1	20.9	-1.4	21.5	2.9
Agricultural Chemicals and Chemical Products	-		-		-		-		-		-		-		-		-	
Plastic Resins and Materials	-		-		-		-		-		-		-		-		-	
Chemicals and Allied Products n.e.c.	-		-		-		-		-		-		-		-		-	
Rubber and Plastic Products	47.1	-	35.7	-24.2	28.3	-20.7	24.6	-13.1	21.5	-12.6	18.3	-14.9	15.9	-13.1	16.7	5.0	19.5	16.8
Rubber and Rubber Products	-		-		-		-		-		-		-		-		-	
Plastic Products	-		-		-		-		-		-		-		-		-	
Lumber and Wood Products	9.3	-	8.8	-5.4	8.5	-3.4	8.8	3.5	8.0	-9.1	6.5	-18.8	5.6	-13.8	6.7	19.6	7.8	16.4
Lumber	8.1	-	7.6	-6.2	7.3	-3.9	7.6	4.1	6.9	-9.2	5.6	-18.8	4.8	-14.3	5.7	18.8	6.8	19.3
Millwork	10.7	-	10.7	0.0	10.7	0.0	10.8	0.9	10.2	-5.6	8.5	-16.7	8.4	-1.2	8.8	4.8	9.2	4.5
Plywood	-		-		-		-		-		-		-		-		-	
Wood Products n.e.c.	-		-		-		-		-		-		-		-		-	
Logs, Bolts, Timber and Pulpwood	-		-		-		-		-		-		-		-		-	
Prefabricated Wood Buildings & Components	-		-		-		-		-		-		-		-		-	
Treated Wood and Contract Wood Preserving	-		-		-		-		-		-		-		-		-	
Pulp, Paper, and Allied Products	-		-		-		-		-		-		-		-		-	
Pulp, Paper, and Products, ex. Building Paper	-		-		-		-		-		-		-		-		-	
Building Paper & Building Board Mill Products	-		-		-		-		-		-		-		-		-	
Publications, Printed Matter & Printing Materials	-		-		-		-		-		-		-		-		-	

Source: U.S. Department of Labor, Bureau of Labor Statistics, Division of Industry Prices and Price Indexes. n.e.c. stands for not elsewhere classified. - indicates no data collected for period or unavailable.

Producer Price Index
Annual Averages, 1935-1943
Base 1982 = 100

Columns headed % show percentile change in the index from the previous period for which an index is available.

	1935		1936		1937		1938		1939		1940		1941		1942		1943	
	Index	%	Index	%	Index	%	Index	%	Index	%	Index	%	Index	%	Index	%	Index	%
Fuels and Related Products and Power	7.6	0.0	7.9	3.9	8.0	1.3	7.9	-1.2	7.5	-5.1	7.4	-1.3	7.9	6.8	8.1	2.5	8.3	2.5
Coal	7.8	1.3	7.9	1.3	7.9	0.0	7.9	0.0	7.8	-1.3	7.8	0.0	8.3	6.4	8.7	4.8	9.2	5.7
Coke Oven Products	5.3	6.0	5.6	5.7	6.1	8.9	6.2	1.6	6.3	1.6	6.6	4.8	7.1	7.6	7.3	2.8	7.3	0.0
Gas Fuels	-	-	-	-	-	-	-	-	-	-	-	-	-	-	-	-	-	-
Electric Power	-	-	-	-	-	-	-	-	-	-	-	-	-	-	-	-	-	-
Utility Natural Gas	-	-	-	-	-	-	-	-	-	-	-	-	-	-	-	-	-	-
Petroleum Products, Refined	-	-	-	-	-	-	-	-	-	-	-	-	-	-	-	-	-	-
Petroleum and Coal Products n.e.c.	-	-	-	-	-	-	-	-	-	-	-	-	-	-	-	-	-	-
Chemicals and Allied Products	17.7	4.1	17.8	0.6	18.6	4.5	17.7	-4.8	17.6	-0.6	17.9	1.7	19.5	8.9	21.7	11.3	21.9	0.9
Industrial Chemicals	17.6	1.7	17.5	-0.6	17.5	0.0	17.2	-1.7	16.8	-2.3	16.9	0.6	17.4	3.0	19.2	10.3	19.2	0.0
Paints and Allied Products	-	-	-	-	-	-	-	-	-	-	-	-	-	-	-	-	-	-
Drugs and Pharmaceuticals	-	-	-	-	-	-	-	-	-	-	-	-	-	-	-	-	-	-
Fats and Oils, Inedible	32.7	52.1	33.5	2.4	40.7	21.5	26.2	-35.6	25.7	-1.9	23.6	-8.2	41.0	73.7	55.7	35.9	53.9	-3.2
Agricultural Chemicals and Chemical Products	-	-	-	-	-	-	-	-	-	-	-	-	-	-	-	-	-	-
Plastic Resins and Materials	-	-	-	-	-	-	-	-	-	-	-	-	-	-	-	-	-	-
Chemicals and Allied Products n.e.c.	-	-	-	-	-	-	-	-	-	-	-	-	-	-	-	-	-	-
Rubber and Plastic Products	19.6	0.5	21.1	7.7	24.9	18.0	24.4	-2.0	25.4	4.1	23.7	-6.7	25.5	7.6	29.7	16.5	30.5	2.7
Rubber and Rubber Products	-	-	-	-	-	-	-	-	-	-	-	-	-	-	-	-	-	-
Plastic Products	-	-	-	-	-	-	-	-	-	-	-	-	-	-	-	-	-	-
Lumber and Wood Products	7.5	-3.8	7.9	5.3	9.3	17.7	8.5	-8.6	8.7	2.4	9.6	10.3	11.5	19.8	12.5	8.7	13.2	5.6
Lumber	6.6	-2.9	7.0	6.1	8.1	15.7	7.1	-12.3	7.5	5.6	8.3	10.7	9.9	19.3	10.7	8.1	11.4	6.5
Millwork	9.1	-1.1	9.7	6.6	11.7	20.6	10.5	-10.3	10.3	-1.9	11.2	8.7	12.8	14.3	14.0	9.4	14.1	0.7
Plywood	-	-	-	-	-	-	-	-	-	-	-	-	-	-	-	-	-	-
Wood Products n.e.c.	-	-	-	-	-	-	-	-	-	-	-	-	-	-	-	-	-	-
Logs, Bolts, Timber and Pulpwood	-	-	-	-	-	-	-	-	-	-	-	-	-	-	-	-	-	-
Prefabricated Wood Buildings & Components	-	-	-	-	-	-	-	-	-	-	-	-	-	-	-	-	-	-
Treated Wood and Contract Wood Preserving	-	-	-	-	-	-	-	-	-	-	-	-	-	-	-	-	-	-
Pulp, Paper, and Allied Products	-	-	-	-	-	-	-	-	-	-	-	-	-	-	-	-	-	-
Pulp, Paper, and Products, ex. Building Paper	-	-	-	-	-	-	-	-	-	-	-	-	-	-	-	-	-	-
Building Paper & Building Board Mill Products	-	-	-	-	-	-	-	-	-	-	-	-	-	-	-	-	-	-
Publications, Printed Matter & Printing Materials	-	-	-	-	-	-	-	-	-	-	-	-	-	-	-	-	-	-

Source: U.S. Department of Labor, Bureau of Labor Statistics, Division of Industry Prices and Price Indexes. n.e.c. stands for not elsewhere classified. - indicates no data collected for period or unavailable.

Producer Price Index
Annual Averages, 1944-1952
Base 1982 = 100

Columns headed % show percentile change in the index from the previous period for which an index is available.

	1944		1945		1946		1947		1948		1949		1950		1951		1952	
	Index	%	Index	%	Index	%	Index	%	Index	%	Index	%	Index	%	Index	%	Index	%
Fuels and Related Products and																		
Power	8.6	3.6	8.7	1.2	9.3	6.9	11.1	19.4	13.1	18.0	12.4	-5.3	12.6	1.6	13.0	3.2	13.0	0.0
Coal	9.6	4.3	9.9	3.1	10.6	7.1	12.9	21.7	15.6	20.9	15.5	-0.6	15.6	0.6	15.9	1.9	16.0	0.6
Coke Oven Products	7.7	5.5	7.9	2.6	8.4	6.3	9.9	17.9	12.3	24.2	13.1	6.5	13.6	3.8	14.6	7.4	14.7	0.7
Gas Fuels	-	-	-	-	-	-	-	-	-	-	-	-	-	-	-	-	-	-
Electric Power	-	-	-	-	-	-	-	-	-	-	-	-	-	-	-	-	-	-
Utility Natural Gas	-	-	-	-	-	-	-	-	-	-	-	-	-	-	-	-	-	-
Petroleum Products, Refined	-	-	-	-	-	-	9.7	-	12.2	25.8	10.7	-12.3	11.2	4.7	12.1	8.0	11.9	-1.7
Petroleum and Coal Products																		
n.e.c.	-	-	-	-	-	-	-	-	-	-	-	-	-	-	-	-	-	-
Chemicals and Allied Products	22.2	1.4	22.3	0.5	24.1	8.1	32.1	33.2	32.8	2.2	30.0	-8.5	30.4	1.3	34.8	14.5	33.0	-5.2
Industrial Chemicals	19.1	-0.5	19.1	0.0	19.8	3.7	23.3	17.7	24.7	6.0	22.7	-8.1	23.8	4.8	28.4	19.3	27.1	-4.6
Paints and Allied Products	-	-	-	-	-	-	-	-	-	-	-	-	-	-	-	-	-	-
Drugs and Pharmaceuticals	-	-	-	-	-	-	57.0	-	54.7	-4.0	50.7	-7.3	50.1	-1.2	51.8	3.4	50.1	-3.3
Fats and Oils, Inedible	54.0	0.2	54.0	0.0	63.4	17.4	97.6	53.9	88.7	-9.1	43.2	-51.3	52.5	21.5	67.9	29.3	38.3	-43.6
Agricultural Chemicals and																		
Chemical Products	-	-	-	-	-	-	29.0	-	30.4	4.8	31.4	3.3	30.6	-2.5	32.5	6.2	33.1	1.8
Plastic Resins and Materials	-	-	-	-	-	-	37.4	-	37.2	-0.5	37.7	1.3	37.9	0.5	47.4	25.1	47.1	-0.6
Chemicals and Allied																		
Products n.e.c.	-	-	-	-	-	-	31.7	-	32.5	2.5	28.6	-12.0	28.5	-0.3	31.8	11.6	29.7	-6.6
Rubber and Plastic Products	30.1	-1.3	29.2	-3.0	29.3	0.3	29.2	-0.3	30.2	3.4	29.2	-3.3	35.6	21.9	43.7	22.8	39.6	-9.4
Rubber and Rubber Products	-	-	-	-	-	-	-	-	-	-	-	-	-	-	-	-	-	-
Plastic Products	-	-	-	-	-	-	-	-	-	-	-	-	-	-	-	-	-	-
Lumber and Wood Products	14.3	8.3	14.5	1.4	16.6	14.5	25.8	55.4	29.5	14.3	27.3	-7.5	31.4	15.0	34.1	8.6	33.2	-2.6
Lumber	12.4	8.8	12.5	0.8	14.4	15.2	23.0	59.7	26.1	13.5	23.9	-8.4	27.9	16.7	30.2	8.2	29.4	-2.6
Millwork	14.6	3.5	14.7	0.7	16.6	12.9	21.3	28.3	25.7	20.7	26.3	2.3	28.0	6.5	31.7	13.2	31.0	-2.2
Plywood	-	-	-	-	-	-	47.1	-	53.5	13.6	46.8	-12.5	52.3	11.8	56.6	8.2	51.6	-8.8
Wood Products n.e.c.	-	-	-	-	-	-	-	-	-	-	-	-	-	-	-	-	-	-
Logs, Bolts, Timber and																		
Pulpwood	-	-	-	-	-	-	-	-	-	-	-	-	-	-	-	-	-	-
Prefabricated Wood Buildings																		
& Components	-	-	-	-	-	-	-	-	-	-	-	-	-	-	-	-	-	-
Treated Wood and Contract																		
Wood Preserving	-	-	-	-	-	-	-	-	-	-	-	-	-	-	-	-	-	-
Pulp, Paper, and Allied Products	-	-	-	-	-	-	25.1	-	26.2	4.4	25.1	-4.2	25.7	2.4	30.5	18.7	29.7	-2.6
Pulp, Paper, and Products, ex.																		
Building Paper	-	-	-	-	-	-	26.6	-	27.7	4.1	26.5	-4.3	27.1	2.3	32.2	18.8	31.4	-2.5
Building Paper & Building																		
Board Mill Products	-	-	-	-	-	-	29.4	-	32.5	10.5	32.9	1.2	34.0	3.3	35.9	5.6	36.5	1.7
Publications, Printed Matter																		
& Printing Materials	-	-	-	-	-	-	-	-	-	-	-	-	-	-	-	-	-	-

Source: U.S. Department of Labor, Bureau of Labor Statistics, Division of Industry Prices and Price Indexes. n.e.c. stands for not elsewhere classified. - indicates no data collected for period or unavailable.

Producer Price Index
Annual Averages, 1953-1961
Base 1982 = 100

Columns headed % show percentile change in the index from the previous period for which an index is available.

	1953		1954		1955		1956		1957		1958		1959		1960		1961	
	Index	%	Index	%	Index	%	Index	%	Index	%	Index	%	Index	%	Index	%	Index	%
Fuels and Related Products and Power	13.4	3.1	13.2	-1.5	13.2	0.0	13.6	3.0	14.3	5.1	13.7	-4.2	13.7	0.0	13.9	1.5	14.0	0.7
Coal	16.6	3.8	15.6	-6.0	15.4	-1.3	16.8	9.1	18.3	8.9	18.0	-1.6	18.0	0.0	17.9	-0.6	17.7	-1.1
Coke Oven Products	15.5	5.4	15.6	0.6	15.9	1.9	17.6	10.7	19.0	8.0	19.0	0.0	19.9	4.7	20.0	0.5	20.0	0.0
Gas Fuels	-	-	-	-	-	-	-	-	-	-	7.2	-	7.8	8.3	8.2	5.1	8.4	2.4
Electric Power	-	-	-	-	-	-	-	-	-	-	24.5	-	24.6	0.4	24.9	1.2	25.0	0.4
Utility Natural Gas	-	-	-	-	-	-	-	-	-	-	-	-	-	-	-	-	-	-
Petroleum Products, Refined	12.2	2.5	11.8	-3.3	12.1	2.5	12.8	5.8	13.7	7.0	12.5	-8.8	12.4	-0.8	12.5	0.8	12.8	2.4
Petroleum and Coal Products n.e.c.	-	-	-	-	-	-	-	-	-	-	-	-	-	-	-	-	-	-
Chemicals and Allied Products	33.4	1.2	33.8	1.2	33.7	-0.3	33.9	0.6	34.6	2.1	34.9	0.9	34.8	-0.3	34.8	0.0	34.5	-0.9
Industrial Chemicals	27.7	2.2	27.7	0.0	27.9	0.7	28.6	2.5	29.1	1.7	29.1	0.0	29.2	0.3	29.3	0.3	28.6	-2.4
Paints and Allied Products	-	-	-	-	-	-	-	-	-	-	-	-	-	-	-	-	-	-
Drugs and Pharmaceuticals	50.3	0.4	50.8	1.0	50.3	-1.0	49.9	-0.8	50.6	1.4	50.9	0.6	50.5	-0.8	50.7	0.4	49.8	-1.8
Fats and Oils, Inedible	40.3	5.2	44.2	9.7	43.3	-2.0	43.0	-0.7	46.9	9.1	47.9	2.1	43.3	-9.6	37.5	-13.4	40.3	7.5
Agricultural Chemicals and Chemical Products	33.0	-0.3	33.2	0.6	33.0	-0.6	32.5	-1.5	32.6	0.3	33.2	1.8	33.3	0.3	33.7	1.2	33.8	0.3
Plastic Resins and Materials	47.1	0.0	46.8	-0.6	44.6	-4.7	40.5	-9.2	40.6	0.2	40.0	-1.5	38.3	-4.2	38.2	-0.3	36.5	-4.5
Chemicals and Allied Products n.e.c.	29.7	0.0	31.2	5.1	31.5	1.0	32.4	2.9	33.6	3.7	34.3	2.1	34.6	0.9	34.7	0.3	35.0	0.9
Rubber and Plastic Products	36.9	-6.8	37.5	1.6	42.4	13.1	43.0	1.4	42.8	-0.5	42.8	0.0	42.6	-0.5	42.7	0.2	41.1	-3.7
Rubber and Rubber Products	-	-	-	-	-	-	-	-	-	-	-	-	-	-	-	-	-	-
Plastic Products	-	-	-	-	-	-	-	-	-	-	-	-	-	-	-	-	-	-
Lumber and Wood Products	33.1	-0.3	32.5	-1.8	34.1	4.9	34.6	1.5	32.8	-5.2	32.5	-0.9	34.7	6.8	33.5	-3.5	32.0	-4.5
Lumber	29.1	-1.0	28.6	-1.7	30.4	6.3	31.1	2.3	29.2	-6.1	28.8	-1.4	31.0	7.6	29.6	-4.5	28.1	-5.1
Millwork	32.1	3.5	31.8	-0.9	31.4	-1.3	31.5	0.3	31.3	-0.6	31.2	-0.3	33.1	6.1	33.3	0.6	32.5	-2.4
Plywood	53.8	4.3	50.7	-5.8	51.9	2.4	50.0	-3.7	47.4	-5.2	47.8	0.8	49.8	4.2	47.2	-5.2	46.2	-2.1
Wood Products n.e.c.	-	-	-	-	-	-	-	-	-	-	-	-	-	-	-	-	-	-
Logs, Bolts, Timber and Pulpwood	-	-	-	-	-	-	-	-	-	-	-	-	-	-	-	-	-	-
Prefabricated Wood Buildings & Components	-	-	-	-	-	-	-	-	-	-	-	-	-	-	-	-	-	-
Treated Wood and Contract Wood Preserving	-	-	-	-	-	-	-	-	-	-	-	-	-	-	-	-	-	-
Pulp, Paper, and Allied Products	29.6	-0.3	29.6	0.0	30.4	2.7	32.4	6.6	33.0	1.9	33.4	1.2	33.7	0.9	34.0	0.9	33.0	-2.9
Pulp, Paper, and Products, ex. Building Paper	31.2	-0.6	31.2	0.0	32.0	2.6	34.1	6.6	34.8	2.1	35.2	1.1	35.4	0.6	35.8	1.1	34.7	-3.1
Building Paper & Building Board Mill Products	38.4	5.2	40.4	5.2	41.4	2.5	43.3	4.6	44.8	3.5	45.3	1.1	46.3	2.2	46.1	-0.4	45.8	-0.7
Publications, Printed Matter & Printing Materials	-	-	-	-	-	-	-	-	-	-	-	-	-	-	-	-	-	-

Source: U.S. Department of Labor, Bureau of Labor Statistics, Division of Industry Prices and Price Indexes. n.e.c. stands for not elsewhere classified. - indicates no data collected for period or unavailable.

Producer Price Index
Annual Averages, 1962-1970
Base 1982 = 100

Columns headed % show percentile change in the index from the previous period for which an index is available.

	1962		1963		1964		1965		1966		1967		1968		1969		1970	
	Index	%	Index	%	Index	%	Index	%	Index	%	Index	%	Index	%	Index	%	Index	%
Fuels and Related Products and Power	14.0	0.0	13.9	-0.7	13.5	-2.9	13.8	2.2	14.1	2.2	14.4	2.1	14.3	-0.7	14.6	2.1	15.3	4.8
Coal	17.5	-1.1	17.5	0.0	17.5	0.0	17.5	0.0	17.9	2.3	18.7	4.5	19.4	3.7	21.1	8.8	28.1	33.2
Coke Oven Products	20.0	0.0	20.0	0.0	20.6	3.0	20.8	1.0	21.2	1.9	21.7	2.4	22.4	3.2	23.6	5.4	27.6	16.9
Gas Fuels	8.4	0.0	8.7	3.6	8.5	-2.3	8.7	2.4	9.1	4.6	9.4	3.3	8.7	-7.4	8.8	1.1	9.8	11.4
Electric Power	25.1	0.4	24.9	-0.8	24.7	-0.8	24.6	-0.4	24.5	-0.4	24.6	0.4	24.8	0.8	25.0	0.8	26.1	4.4
Utility Natural Gas	-	-	-	-	-	-	-	-	-	-	-	-	-	-	-	-	-	-
Petroleum Products, Refined	12.6	-1.6	12.5	-0.8	11.9	-4.8	12.3	3.4	12.8	4.1	13.1	2.3	12.9	-1.5	13.1	1.6	13.3	1.5
Petroleum and Coal Products n.e.c.	-	-	-	-	-	-	-	-	-	-	-	-	-	-	-	-	-	-
Chemicals and Allied Products	33.9	-1.7	33.5	-1.2	33.6	0.3	33.9	0.9	34.0	0.3	34.2	0.6	34.1	-0.3	34.2	0.3	35.0	2.3
Industrial Chemicals	28.1	-1.7	27.6	-1.8	27.4	-0.7	27.7	1.1	27.9	0.7	28.4	1.8	28.6	0.7	28.4	-0.7	28.6	0.7
Paints and Allied Products	-	-	-	-	-	-	-	-	-	-	-	-	-	-	-	-	-	-
Drugs and Pharmaceuticals	48.6	-2.4	48.2	-0.8	48.1	-0.2	47.8	-0.6	47.8	0.0	47.6	-0.4	47.3	-0.6	47.6	0.6	48.2	1.3
Fats and Oils, Inedible	35.1	-12.9	37.0	5.4	44.6	20.5	51.9	16.4	47.3	-8.9	37.4	-20.9	34.0	-9.1	40.9	20.3	49.7	21.5
Agricultural Chemicals and Chemical Products	33.6	-0.6	33.1	-1.5	32.9	-0.6	33.6	2.1	33.9	0.9	34.2	0.9	32.9	-3.8	29.6	-10.0	30.3	2.4
Plastic Resins and Materials	36.3	-0.5	35.6	-1.9	35.3	-0.8	35.0	-0.8	35.3	0.9	35.3	0.0	32.4	-8.2	31.9	-1.5	32.0	0.3
Chemicals and Allied Products n.e.c.	34.9	-0.3	35.3	1.1	35.6	0.8	36.0	1.1	36.4	1.1	37.0	1.6	37.6	1.6	38.6	2.7	40.2	4.1
Rubber and Plastic Products	39.9	-2.9	40.1	0.5	39.6	-1.2	39.7	0.3	40.5	2.0	41.4	2.2	42.8	3.4	43.6	1.9	44.9	3.0
Rubber and Rubber Products	-	-	-	-	-	-	-	-	-	-	37.3	-	38.6	3.5	39.3	1.8	41.1	4.6
Plastic Products	-	-	-	-	-	-	-	-	-	-	-	-	-	-	-	-	-	-
Lumber and Wood Products	32.2	0.6	32.8	1.9	33.5	2.1	33.7	0.6	35.2	4.5	35.1	-0.3	39.8	13.4	44.0	10.6	39.9	-9.3
Lumber	28.6	1.8	29.3	2.4	29.9	2.0	30.2	1.0	32.2	6.6	32.2	0.0	37.8	17.4	42.3	11.9	36.6	-13.5
Millwork	32.5	0.0	33.2	2.2	34.6	4.2	34.4	-0.6	35.1	2.0	35.8	2.0	37.9	5.9	42.2	11.3	41.5	-1.7
Plywood	44.6	-3.5	45.1	1.1	44.6	-1.1	44.6	0.0	44.8	0.4	43.1	-3.8	49.8	15.5	52.8	6.0	46.7	-11.6
Wood Products n.e.c.	-	-	-	-	-	-	-	-	41.6	-	42.3	1.7	44.4	5.0	47.7	7.4	49.7	4.2
Logs, Bolts, Timber and Pulpwood	-	-	-	-	-	-	-	-	-	-	-	-	-	-	-	-	-	-
Prefabricated Wood Buildings & Components	-	-	-	-	-	-	-	-	-	-	-	-	-	-	-	-	-	-
Treated Wood and Contract Wood Preserving	-	-	-	-	-	-	-	-	-	-	-	-	-	-	-	-	-	-
Pulp, Paper, and Allied Products	33.4	1.2	33.1	-0.9	33.0	-0.3	33.3	0.9	34.2	2.7	34.6	1.2	35.0	1.2	36.0	2.9	37.5	4.2
Pulp, Paper, and Products, ex. Building Paper	35.2	1.4	34.9	-0.9	34.9	0.0	35.2	0.9	36.2	2.8	36.6	1.1	37.0	1.1	38.1	3.0	39.7	4.2
Building Paper & Building Board Mill Products	44.2	-3.5	43.6	-1.4	42.7	-2.1	42.1	-1.4	42.1	0.0	41.8	-0.7	42.1	0.7	44.1	4.8	42.2	-4.3
Publications, Printed Matter & Printing Materials	-	-	-	-	-	-	-	-	-	-	-	-	-	-	-	-	-	-

Source: U.S. Department of Labor, Bureau of Labor Statistics, Division of Industry Prices and Price Indexes. n.e.c. stands for not elsewhere classified. - indicates no data collected for period or unavailable.

Producer Price Index
Annual Averages, 1971-1979
Base 1982 = 100

Columns headed % show percentile change in the index from the previous period for which an index is available.

	1971		1972		1973		1974		1975		1976		1977		1978		1979	
	Index	%	Index	%	Index	%	Index	%	Index	%	Index	%	Index	%	Index	%	Index	%
Fuels and Related Products and Power	16.6	8.5	17.1	3.0	19.4	13.5	30.1	55.2	35.4	17.6	38.3	8.2	43.6	13.8	46.5	6.7	58.9	26.7
Coal	34.0	21.0	36.2	6.5	40.8	12.7	62.2	52.5	72.2	16.1	68.9	-4.6	72.8	5.7	80.4	10.4	84.3	4.9
Coke Oven Products	32.2	16.7	33.7	4.7	36.1	7.1	53.7	48.8	71.7	33.5	75.1	4.7	82.2	9.5	89.2	8.5	93.0	4.3
Gas Fuels	10.2	4.1	10.8	5.9	11.9	10.2	15.3	28.6	20.4	33.3	27.0	32.4	36.6	35.6	40.4	10.4	51.3	27.0
Electric Power	28.6	9.6	29.9	4.5	31.8	6.4	40.1	26.1	47.6	18.7	51.1	7.4	57.3	12.1	61.6	7.5	66.5	8.0
Utility Natural Gas	-	-	-	-	-	-	-	-	-	-	-	-	-	-	-	-	-	-
Petroleum Products, Refined	14.1	6.0	14.3	1.4	16.9	18.2	29.3	73.4	33.8	15.4	36.3	7.4	40.5	11.6	42.2	4.2	58.4	38.4
Petroleum and Coal Products n.e.c.	-	-	-	-	-	-	-	-	-	-	-	-	-	-	-	-	-	-
Chemicals and Allied Products	35.6	1.7	35.6	0.0	37.6	5.6	50.2	33.5	62.0	23.5	64.0	3.2	65.9	3.0	68.0	3.2	76.0	11.8
Industrial Chemicals	28.9	1.0	28.7	-0.7	29.3	2.1	43.0	46.8	58.7	36.5	62.2	6.0	63.5	2.1	64.0	0.8	74.9	17.0
Paints and Allied Products	-	-	-	-	-	-	-	-	-	-	-	-	-	-	-	-	-	-
Drugs and Pharmaceuticals	48.8	1.2	49.0	0.4	49.6	1.2	53.6	8.1	60.3	12.5	63.8	5.8	66.9	4.9	70.5	5.4	75.9	7.7
Fats and Oils, Inedible	50.0	0.6	43.4	-13.2	85.5	97.0	126.6	48.1	95.5	-24.6	93.6	-2.0	104.5	11.6	118.3	13.2	141.0	19.2
Agricultural Chemicals and Chemical Products	31.5	4.0	31.4	-0.3	33.0	5.1	47.1	42.7	69.6	47.8	64.4	-7.5	64.2	-0.3	67.8	5.6	73.3	8.1
Plastic Resins and Materials	31.3	-2.2	31.3	0.0	32.5	3.8	50.7	56.0	63.8	25.8	68.4	7.2	69.7	1.9	70.5	1.1	83.2	18.0
Chemicals and Allied Products n.e.c.	41.5	3.2	42.0	1.2	43.7	4.0	54.6	24.9	62.4	14.3	63.2	1.3	65.1	3.0	67.3	3.4	71.0	5.5
Rubber and Plastic Products	45.2	0.7	45.3	0.2	46.6	2.9	56.4	21.0	62.2	10.3	66.0	6.1	69.4	5.2	72.4	4.3	80.5	11.2
Rubber and Rubber Products	41.9	1.9	42.5	1.4	44.1	3.8	51.5	16.8	56.7	10.1	60.9	7.4	64.9	6.6	69.2	6.6	78.1	12.9
Plastic Products	-	-	-	-	-	-	-	-	-	-	-	-	-	-	-	-	83.1	-
Lumber and Wood Products	44.7	12.0	50.7	13.4	62.2	22.7	64.5	3.7	62.1	-3.7	72.2	16.3	83.0	15.0	96.9	16.7	105.5	8.9
Lumber	43.8	19.7	51.3	17.1	66.0	28.7	66.6	0.9	61.9	-7.1	75.0	21.2	89.0	18.7	103.7	16.5	114.0	9.9
Millwork	43.2	4.1	46.0	6.5	51.6	12.2	56.2	8.9	57.4	2.1	63.3	10.3	69.3	9.5	84.3	21.6	91.0	7.9
Plywood	49.4	5.8	56.3	14.0	66.9	18.8	69.4	3.7	69.4	0.0	80.6	16.1	91.4	13.4	101.5	11.1	107.9	6.3
Wood Products n.e.c.	50.3	1.2	52.8	5.0	63.4	20.1	70.5	11.2	68.5	-2.8	70.4	2.8	78.0	10.8	89.7	15.0	99.7	11.1
Logs, Bolts, Timber and Pulpwood	-	-	-	-	-	-	-	-	-	-	-	-	-	-	-	-	-	-
Prefabricated Wood Buildings & Components	-	-	-	-	-	-	-	-	-	-	-	-	-	-	-	-	-	-
Treated Wood and Contract Wood Preserving	-	-	-	-	-	-	-	-	-	-	-	-	-	-	-	-	-	-
Pulp, Paper, and Allied Products	38.1	1.6	39.3	3.1	42.3	7.6	52.5	24.1	59.0	12.4	62.1	5.3	64.6	4.0	67.7	4.8	75.9	12.1
Pulp, Paper, and Products, ex. Building Paper	40.4	1.8	41.6	3.0	44.8	7.7	55.9	24.8	62.9	12.5	66.2	5.2	68.6	3.6	71.6	4.4	80.6	12.6
Building Paper & Building Board Mill Products	42.9	1.7	44.4	3.5	47.1	6.1	51.6	9.6	53.1	2.9	57.9	9.0	65.6	13.3	78.2	19.2	76.2	-2.6
Publications, Printed Matter & Printing Materials	-	-	-	-	-	-	-	-	-	-	-	-	-	-	-	-	-	-

Source: U.S. Department of Labor, Bureau of Labor Statistics, Division of Industry Prices and Price Indexes. n.e.c. stands for not elsewhere classified. - indicates no data collected for period or unavailable.

Producer Price Index
Annual Averages, 1980-1988
Base 1982 = 100

Columns headed % show percentile change in the index from the previous period for which an index is available.

	1980		1981		1982		1983		1984		1985		1986		1987		1988	
	Index	%	Index	%	Index	%	Index	%	Index	%	Index	%	Index	%	Index	%	Index	%
Fuels and Related Products and Power	82.8	40.6	100.2	21.0	100.0	-0.2	95.9	-4.1	94.8	-1.1	91.4	-3.6	69.8	-23.6	70.2	0.6	66.7	-5.0
Coal	87.4	3.7	93.0	6.4	100.0	7.5	100.5	0.5	102.2	1.7	102.2	0.0	100.8	-1.4	97.1	-3.7	95.4	-1.8
Coke Oven Products	93.3	0.3	98.8	5.9	100.0	1.2	96.3	-3.7	94.5	-1.9	93.2	-1.4	88.0	-5.6	82.8	-5.9	84.9	2.5
Gas Fuels	71.7	39.8	88.6	23.6	100.0	12.9	108.1	8.1	104.5	-3.3	98.7	-5.6	83.2	-15.7	74.1	-10.9	71.4	-3.6
Electric Power	79.1	18.9	90.3	14.2	100.0	10.7	102.8	2.8	108.2	5.3	111.6	3.1	112.6	0.9	110.6	-1.8	111.2	0.5
Utility Natural Gas	-		-		-		-		-		-		-		-		-	
Petroleum Products, Refined	88.6	51.7	105.9	19.5	100.0	-5.6	89.9	-10.1	87.4	-2.8	83.2	-4.8	53.2	-36.1	56.8	6.8	53.9	-5.1
Petroleum and Coal Products n.e.c.	-		-		-		-		-		100.5	-	77.1	-23.3	63.7	-17.4	66.4	4.2
Chemicals and Allied Products	89.0	17.1	98.4	10.6	100.0	1.6	100.3	0.3	102.9	2.6	103.7	0.8	102.6	-1.1	106.4	3.7	116.3	9.3
Industrial Chemicals	91.9	22.7	103.1	12.2	100.0	-3.0	97.3	-2.7	96.8	-0.5	96.0	-0.8	91.5	-4.7	95.5	4.4	106.8	11.8
Paints and Allied Products	-		-		-		100.5	-	105.1	4.6	106.7	1.5	105.7	-0.9	107.4	1.6	113.1	5.3
Drugs and Pharmaceuticals	83.0	9.4	92.1	11.0	100.0	8.6	107.6	7.6	114.2	6.1	122.0	6.8	130.1	6.6	139.1	6.9	148.4	6.7
Fats and Oils, Inedible	111.6	-20.9	110.7	-0.8	100.0	-9.7	106.9	6.9	139.1	30.1	110.6	-20.5	80.1	-27.6	92.7	15.7	110.9	19.6
Agricultural Chemicals and Chemical Products	87.9	19.9	97.4	10.8	100.0	2.7	95.9	-4.1	97.4	1.6	96.2	-1.2	94.2	-2.1	96.4	2.3	104.5	8.4
Plastic Resins and Materials	98.5	18.4	102.0	3.6	100.0	-2.0	102.8	2.8	108.9	5.9	107.5	-1.3	104.4	-2.9	110.3	5.7	132.4	20.0
Chemicals and Allied Products n.e.c.	83.1	17.0	94.1	13.2	100.0	6.3	101.3	1.3	102.7	1.4	105.2	2.4	105.8	0.6	107.0	1.1	111.9	4.6
Rubber and Plastic Products	90.1	11.9	96.4	7.0	100.0	3.7	100.8	0.8	102.3	1.5	101.9	-0.4	101.9	0.0	103.0	1.1	109.3	6.1
Rubber and Rubber Products	88.7	13.6	95.7	7.9	100.0	4.5	99.3	-0.7	99.4	0.1	98.7	-0.7	98.1	-0.6	99.4	1.3	103.6	4.2
Plastic Products	91.5	10.1	97.1	6.1	100.0	3.0	102.3	2.3	105.5	3.1	105.4	-0.1	106.1	0.7	107.3	1.1	115.0	7.2
Lumber and Wood Products	101.5	-3.8	102.8	1.3	100.0	-2.7	107.9	7.9	108.0	0.1	106.6	-1.3	107.2	0.6	112.8	5.2	118.9	5.4
Lumber	104.9	-8.0	104.6	-0.3	100.0	-4.4	113.5	13.5	112.5	-0.9	109.6	-2.6	110.5	0.8	118.2	7.0	122.1	3.3
Millwork	93.2	2.4	97.8	4.9	100.0	2.2	108.2	8.2	110.2	1.8	111.7	1.4	113.7	1.8	117.7	3.5	121.9	3.6
Plywood	106.2	-1.6	105.9	-0.3	100.0	-5.6	105.2	5.2	104.1	-1.0	99.6	-4.3	101.4	1.8	102.6	1.2	103.4	0.8
Wood Products n.e.c.	101.2	1.5	101.2	0.0	100.0	-1.2	97.6	-2.4	99.3	1.7	100.1	0.8	100.9	0.8	103.7	2.8	107.2	3.4
Logs, Bolts, Timber and Pulpwood	-		-		100.0	-	96.6	-3.4	97.0	0.4	96.0	-1.0	92.3	-3.9	101.8	10.3	117.7	15.6
Prefabricated Wood Buildings & Components	-		-		-		-		-		101.4	-	104.1	2.7	105.5	1.3	108.2	2.6
Treated Wood and Contract Wood Preserving	-		-		-		-		-		-		98.0	-	98.8	0.8	102.2	3.4
Pulp, Paper, and Allied Products	86.3	13.7	94.8	9.8	100.0	5.5	103.3	3.3	110.3	6.8	113.3	2.7	116.1	2.5	121.8	4.9	130.4	7.1
Pulp, Paper, and Products, ex. Building Paper	91.7	13.8	99.1	8.1	100.0	0.9	99.3	-0.7	107.3	8.1	106.9	-0.4	107.6	0.7	114.3	6.2	124.9	9.3
Building Paper & Building Board Mill Products	86.1	13.0	96.7	12.3	100.0	3.4	104.4	4.4	108.2	3.6	107.4	-0.7	108.8	1.3	111.2	2.2	113.3	1.9
Publications, Printed Matter & Printing Materials	-		91.4		100.0	9.4	106.3	6.3	112.7	6.0	118.7	5.3	123.3	3.9	128.1	3.9	134.7	5.2

Source: U.S. Department of Labor, Bureau of Labor Statistics, Division of Industry Prices and Price Indexes. n.e.c. stands for not elsewhere classified. - indicates no data collected for period or unavailable.

Producer Price Index
Annual Averages, 1989-1993
Base 1982 = 100

Columns headed % show percentile change in the index from the previous period for which an index is available.

	1989		1990		1991		1992		1993									
	Index	%	Index	%	Index	%	Index	%	Index	%	Index	%	Index	%	Index	%	Index	%
Fuels and Related Products and Power	72.9	9.3	82.3	12.9	81.2	-1.3	80.4	-1.0	80.0	-0.5								
Coal	95.5	0.1	97.5	2.1	97.2	-0.3	95.0	-2.3	96.1	1.2								
Coke Oven Products	89.9	5.9	91.4	1.7	93.9	2.7	91.3	-2.8	89.2	-2.3								
Gas Fuels	75.3	5.5	78.4	4.1	77.0	-1.8	75.9	-1.4	78.4	3.3								
Electric Power	114.8	3.2	117.6	2.4	124.3	5.7	126.3	1.6	128.5	1.7								
Utility Natural Gas	-	-	-	-	97.2	-	98.6	1.4	104.0	5.5								
Petroleum Products, Refined	61.2	13.5	74.8	22.2	67.2	-10.2	64.7	-3.7	62.1	-4.0								
Petroleum and Coal Products n.e.c.	65.0	-2.1	67.3	3.5	63.6	-5.5	58.8	-7.5	66.4	12.9								
Chemicals and Allied Products	123.0	5.8	123.6	0.5	125.6	1.6	125.9	0.2	128.2	1.8								
Industrial Chemicals	114.8	7.5	113.2	-1.4	111.8	-1.2	109.3	-2.2	110.5	1.1								
Paints and Allied Products	122.6	8.4	128.5	4.8	131.6	2.4	131.0	-0.5	132.2	0.9								
Drugs and Pharmaceuticals	160.0	7.8	170.8	6.7	182.6	6.9	192.2	5.3	200.9	4.5								
Fats and Oils, Inedible	95.5	-13.9	88.1	-7.7	86.8	-1.5	93.0	7.1	95.7	2.9								
Agricultural Chemicals and Chemical Products	108.7	4.0	107.4	-1.2	111.7	4.0	110.3	-1.3	110.0	-0.3								
Plastic Resins and Materials	133.4	0.8	124.1	-7.0	120.0	-3.3	116.4	-3.0	117.2	0.7								
Chemicals and Allied Products n.e.c.	117.3	4.8	118.9	1.4	121.5	2.2	123.3	1.5	125.5	1.8								
Rubber and Plastic Products	112.6	3.0	113.6	0.9	115.1	1.3	115.1	0.0	116.0	0.8								
Rubber and Rubber Products	107.0	3.3	108.6	1.5	109.6	0.9	109.8	0.2	110.8	0.9								
Plastic Products	118.3	2.9	119.0	0.6	120.8	1.5	120.7	-0.1	121.6	0.7								
Lumber and Wood Products	126.7	6.6	129.7	2.4	132.1	1.9	146.6	11.0	174.0	18.7								
Lumber	125.7	2.9	124.6	-0.9	124.9	0.2	144.7	15.9	183.8	27.0								
Millwork	127.3	4.4	130.4	2.4	135.5	3.9	143.3	5.8	156.5	9.2								
Plywood	115.9	12.1	114.2	-1.5	114.3	0.1	133.3	16.6	152.7	14.6								
Wood Products n.e.c.	113.1	5.5	114.7	1.4	118.6	3.4	124.5	5.0	135.4	8.8								
Logs, Bolts, Timber and Pulpwood	131.9	12.1	142.8	8.3	144.1	0.9	164.8	14.4	211.9	28.6								
Prefabricated Wood Buildings & Components	110.7	2.3	113.1	2.2	118.2	4.5	122.8	3.9	132.4	7.8								
Treated Wood and Contract Wood Preserving	109.7	7.3	112.6	2.6	115.6	2.7	123.5	6.8	138.2	11.9								
Pulp, Paper, and Allied Products	137.8	5.7	141.2	2.5	142.9	1.2	145.2	1.6	147.3	1.4								
Pulp, Paper, and Products, ex. Building Paper	132.4	6.0	132.9	0.4	129.8	-2.3	129.2	-0.5	127.6	-1.2								
Building Paper & Building Board Mill Products	115.6	2.0	112.2	-2.9	111.8	-0.4	119.6	7.0	132.9	11.1								
Publications, Printed Matter & Printing Materials	142.1	5.5	148.4	4.4	154.8	4.3	159.6	3.1	164.9	3.3								

Source: U.S. Department of Labor, Bureau of Labor Statistics, Division of Industry Prices and Price Indexes. n.e.c. stands for not elsewhere classified. - indicates no data collected for period or unavailable.

Producer Price Index
Annual Averages, 1926-1934
Base 1982 = 100

Columns headed % show percentile change in the index from the previous period for which an index is available.

	1926		1927		1928		1929		1930		1931		1932		1933		1934	
	Index	%	Index	%	Index	%	Index	%	Index	%	Index	%	Index	%	Index	%	Index	%
Metals and Metal Products	13.7	-	12.9	-5.8	12.9	0.0	13.3	3.1	12.0	-9.8	10.8	-10.0	9.9	-8.3	10.2	3.0	11.2	9.8
Iron and Steel	11.3	-	10.6	-6.2	10.6	0.0	10.7	0.9	10.1	-5.6	9.4	-6.9	9.0	-4.3	8.9	-1.1	9.8	10.1
Nonferrous Metals	16.5	-	15.3	-7.3	15.5	1.3	17.5	12.9	13.6	-22.3	10.2	-25.0	8.2	-19.6	9.8	19.5	11.2	14.3
Metal Containers	15.2	-	15.2	0.0	14.7	-3.3	14.9	1.4	14.7	-1.3	14.1	-4.1	13.5	-4.3	12.6	-6.7	14.5	15.1
Hardware	-		-		-		-		-		-		-		-		-	
Plumbing Fixtures and Brass Fittings	26.2	-	23.4	-10.7	23.8	1.7	22.5	-5.5	21.3	-5.3	20.1	-5.6	16.4	-18.4	16.1	-1.8	16.8	4.3
Heating Equipment	-		-		-		-		-		-		-		-		-	
Fabricated Structural Metal Products	-		-		-		-		-		-		-		-		-	
Miscellaneous Metal Products	-		-		-		-		-		-		-		-		-	
Metal Treatment Services	-		-		-		-		-		-		-		-		-	
Machinery and Equipment	-		-		-		-		-		-		-		-		-	
Agricultural Machinery and Equipment	14.1	-	14.1	0.0	14.0	-0.7	13.9	-0.7	13.4	-3.6	13.0	-3.0	12.0	-7.7	11.8	-1.7	12.7	7.6
Construction Machinery and Equipment	-		-		-		-		-		-		-		-		-	
Metalworking Machinery and Equipment	-		-		-		-		-		-		-		-		-	
General Purpose Machinery and Equipment	-		-		-		-		-		-		-		-		-	
Electronic Computers and Computer Equipment	-		-		-		-		-		-		-		-		-	
Special Industry Machinery and Equipment	-		-		-		-		-		-		-		-		-	
Electrical Machinery and Equipment	-		-		-		-		-		-		-		-		-	
Miscellaneous Instruments	-		-		-		-		-		-		-		-		-	
Miscellaneous Machinery	-		-		-		-		-		-		-		-		-	
Furniture and Household Durables	28.6	-	27.9	-2.4	27.2	-2.5	27.0	-0.7	26.5	-1.9	24.4	-7.9	21.5	-11.9	21.6	0.5	23.4	8.3
Household Furniture	22.9	-	22.3	-2.6	22.1	-0.9	21.7	-1.8	21.5	-0.9	20.1	-6.5	17.1	-14.9	17.2	0.6	18.1	5.2
Commercial Furniture	-		-		-		-		-		-		-		-		-	
Floor Coverings	31.7	-	30.3	-4.4	29.7	-2.0	29.7	0.0	30.0	1.0	25.4	-15.3	22.7	-10.6	23.6	4.0	25.8	9.3
Household Appliances	-		-		-		-		-		-		-		-		-	
Home Electronic Equipment	-		-		-		-		-		-		-		-		-	
Household Durable Goods n.e.c.	-		-		-		-		-		-		-		-		-	

Source: U.S. Department of Labor, Bureau of Labor Statistics, Division of Industry Prices and Price Indexes. n.e.c. stands for not elsewhere classified. - indicates no data collected for period or unavailable.

Producer Price Index
Annual Averages, 1935-1943
Base 1982 = 100

Columns headed % show percentile change in the index from the previous period for which an index is available.

	1935		1936		1937		1938		1939		1940		1941		1942		1943	
	Index	%	Index	%	Index	%	Index	%	Index	%	Index	%	Index	%	Index	%	Index	%
Metals and Metal Products	11.2	0.0	11.4	1.8	13.1	14.9	12.6	-3.8	12.5	-0.8	12.5	0.0	12.8	2.4	13.0	1.6	12.9	-0.8
Iron and Steel	9.8	0.0	9.9	1.0	11.1	12.1	11.1	0.0	10.8	-2.7	10.7	-0.9	10.9	1.9	11.0	0.9	11.0	0.0
Nonferrous Metals	11.3	0.9	11.8	4.4	14.8	25.4	12.0	-18.9	12.9	7.5	13.4	3.9	13.9	3.7	14.1	1.4	14.2	0.7
Metal Containers	14.4	-0.7	14.5	0.7	13.5	-6.9	14.4	6.7	13.8	-4.2	13.5	-2.2	13.6	0.7	13.8	1.5	13.8	0.0
Hardware	-	-	-	-	-	-	-	-	-	-	-	-	-	-	-	-	-	-
Plumbing Fixtures and Brass Fittings	14.7	-12.5	16.8	14.3	17.1	1.8	16.9	-1.2	16.9	0.0	17.9	5.9	18.3	2.2	20.3	10.9	19.7	-3.0
Heating Equipment	-	-	-	-	-	-	-	-	-	-	-	-	-	-	-	-	-	-
Fabricated Structural Metal Products	-	-	-	-	-	-	-	-	-	-	-	-	-	-	-	-	-	-
Miscellaneous Metal Products	-	-	-	-	-	-	-	-	-	-	-	-	-	-	-	-	-	-
Metal Treatment Services	-	-	-	-	-	-	-	-	-	-	-	-	-	-	-	-	-	-
Machinery and Equipment	-	-	-	-	-	-	-	-	14.8	-	14.9	0.7	15.1	1.3	15.4	2.0	15.2	-1.3
Agricultural Machinery and Equipment	13.2	3.9	13.3	0.8	13.3	0.0	13.5	1.5	13.2	-2.2	13.1	-0.8	13.2	0.8	13.7	3.8	13.7	0.0
Construction Machinery and Equipment	-	-	-	-	-	-	-	-	9.3	-	9.5	2.2	10.0	5.3	10.3	3.0	10.3	0.0
Metalworking Machinery and Equipment	-	-	-	-	-	-	-	-	-	-	-	-	-	-	-	-	-	-
General Purpose Machinery and Equipment	-	-	-	-	-	-	-	-	13.3	-	13.3	0.0	13.6	2.3	13.7	0.7	13.4	-2.2
Electronic Computers and Computer Equipment	-	-	-	-	-	-	-	-	-	-	-	-	-	-	-	-	-	-
Special Industry Machinery and Equipment	-	-	-	-	-	-	-	-	-	-	-	-	-	-	-	-	-	-
Electrical Machinery and Equipment	-	-	-	-	-	-	-	-	19.6	-	19.5	-0.5	19.6	0.5	19.6	0.0	19.5	-0.5
Miscellaneous Instruments	-	-	-	-	-	-	-	-	-	-	-	-	-	-	-	-	-	-
Miscellaneous Machinery	-	-	-	-	-	-	-	-	-	-	-	-	-	-	-	-	-	-
Furniture and Household Durables	23.2	-0.9	23.6	1.7	26.1	10.6	25.5	-2.3	25.4	-0.4	26.0	2.4	27.6	6.2	29.9	8.3	29.7	-0.7
Household Furniture	17.7	-2.2	17.8	0.6	19.7	10.7	19.0	-3.6	18.6	-2.1	18.7	0.5	20.2	8.0	22.3	10.4	22.4	0.4
Commercial Furniture	-	-	-	-	-	-	-	-	-	-	-	-	-	-	-	-	-	-
Floor Coverings	26.2	1.6	26.3	0.4	29.5	12.2	28.2	-4.4	28.9	2.5	31.2	8.0	32.1	2.9	33.2	3.4	33.2	0.0
Household Appliances	-	-	-	-	-	-	-	-	-	-	-	-	-	-	-	-	-	-
Home Electronic Equipment	-	-	-	-	-	-	-	-	-	-	-	-	-	-	-	-	-	-
Household Durable Goods n.e.c.	-	-	-	-	-	-	-	-	-	-	-	-	-	-	-	-	-	-

Source: U.S. Department of Labor, Bureau of Labor Statistics, Division of Industry Prices and Price Indexes. n.e.c. stands for not elsewhere classified. - indicates no data collected for period or unavailable.

Producer Price Index
Annual Averages, 1944-1952
Base 1982 = 100

Columns headed % show percentile change in the index from the previous period for which an index is available.

	1944		1945		1946		1947		1948		1949		1950		1951		1952	
	Index	%	Index	%	Index	%	Index	%	Index	%	Index	%	Index	%	Index	%	Index	%
Metals and Metal Products	12.9	0.0	13.1	1.6	14.7	12.2	18.2	23.8	20.7	13.7	20.9	1.0	22.0	5.3	24.5	11.4	24.5	0.0
Iron and Steel	11.0	0.0	11.2	1.8	12.4	10.7	15.1	21.8	17.6	16.6	17.8	1.1	19.1	7.3	20.8	8.9	21.0	1.0
Nonferrous Metals	14.1	-0.7	14.1	0.0	16.3	15.6	22.4	37.4	24.8	10.7	23.1	-6.9	24.4	5.6	29.1	19.3	28.9	-0.7
Metal Containers	13.8	0.0	13.8	0.0	14.2	2.9	16.0	12.7	17.8	11.2	19.3	8.4	19.4	0.5	21.5	10.8	21.6	0.5
Hardware	-	-	-	-	-	-	17.2	-	18.7	8.7	19.6	4.8	21.1	7.7	23.3	10.4	23.2	-0.4
Plumbing Fixtures and Brass Fittings	19.0	-3.6	18.8	-1.1	20.1	6.9	24.0	19.4	26.1	8.7	26.1	0.0	27.4	5.0	31.1	13.5	29.8	-4.2
Heating Equipment	-	-	-	-	-	-	35.8	-	38.0	6.1	38.9	2.4	39.4	1.3	43.0	9.1	42.7	-0.7
Fabricated Structural Metal Products	-	-	-	-	-	-	22.6	-	23.9	5.8	23.5	-1.7	24.3	3.4	27.4	12.8	26.8	-2.2
Miscellaneous Metal Products	-	-	-	-	-	-	18.0	-	22.2	23.3	23.9	7.7	24.7	3.3	26.8	8.5	26.7	-0.4
Metal Treatment Services	-	-	-	-	-	-	-	-	-	-	-	-	-	-	-	-	-	-
Machinery and Equipment	15.1	-0.7	15.1	0.0	16.6	9.9	19.3	16.3	20.9	8.3	21.9	4.8	22.6	3.2	25.3	11.9	25.3	0.0
Agricultural Machinery and Equipment	13.7	0.0	13.8	0.7	14.8	7.2	17.1	15.5	19.2	12.3	20.5	6.8	21.0	2.4	22.8	8.6	23.0	0.9
Construction Machinery and Equipment	10.3	0.0	10.4	1.0	11.3	8.7	12.8	13.3	14.5	13.3	15.4	6.2	15.8	2.6	17.6	11.4	17.9	1.7
Metalworking Machinery and Equipment	-	-	-	-	-	-	14.3	-	15.4	7.7	16.2	5.2	17.2	6.2	19.2	11.6	19.5	1.6
General Purpose Machinery and Equipment	13.4	0.0	13.4	0.0	14.4	7.5	16.7	16.0	18.2	9.0	19.2	5.5	19.9	3.6	22.2	11.6	22.0	-0.9
Electronic Computers and Computer Equipment	-	-	-	-	-	-	-	-	-	-	-	-	-	-	-	-	-	-
Special Industry Machinery and Equipment	-	-	-	-	-	-	-	-	-	-	-	-	-	-	-	-	-	-
Electrical Machinery and Equipment	19.2	-1.5	19.3	0.5	22.0	14.0	26.9	22.3	28.1	4.5	28.8	2.5	29.8	3.5	34.1	14.4	33.6	-1.5
Miscellaneous Instruments	-	-	-	-	-	-	-	-	-	-	-	-	-	-	-	-	-	-
Miscellaneous Machinery	-	-	-	-	-	-	21.7	-	23.4	7.8	24.3	3.8	24.8	2.1	27.6	11.3	27.6	0.0
Furniture and Household Durables	30.5	2.7	30.5	0.0	32.4	6.2	37.2	14.8	39.4	5.9	40.1	1.8	40.9	2.0	44.4	8.6	43.5	-2.0
Household Furniture	23.1	3.1	23.4	1.3	25.0	6.8	29.9	19.6	32.2	7.7	31.8	-1.2	32.9	3.5	36.4	10.6	35.3	-3.0
Commercial Furniture	-	-	-	-	-	-	20.1	-	21.5	7.0	22.2	3.3	23.4	5.4	26.5	13.2	26.2	-1.1
Floor Coverings	33.2	0.0	33.1	-0.3	36.8	11.2	43.6	18.5	46.4	6.4	46.6	0.4	52.3	12.2	62.7	19.9	55.9	-10.8
Household Appliances	-	-	-	-	-	-	51.5	-	54.0	4.9	53.7	-0.6	54.0	0.6	57.3	6.1	57.0	-0.5
Home Electronic Equipment	-	-	-	-	-	-	141.0	-	146.7	4.0	151.8	3.5	141.8	-6.6	136.2	-3.9	135.9	-0.2
Household Durable Goods n.e.c.	-	-	-	-	-	-	19.5	-	20.0	2.6	20.9	4.5	21.5	2.9	23.1	7.4	23.3	0.9

Source: U.S. Department of Labor, Bureau of Labor Statistics, Division of Industry Prices and Price Indexes. n.e.c. stands for not elsewhere classified. - indicates no data collected for period or unavailable.

Producer Price Index
Annual Averages, 1953-1961
Base 1982 = 100

Columns headed % show percentile change in the index from the previous period for which an index is available.

	1953		1954		1955		1956		1957		1958		1959		1960		1961	
	Index	%	Index	%	Index	%	Index	%	Index	%	Index	%	Index	%	Index	%	Index	%
Metals and Metal Products	25.3	3.3	25.5	0.8	27.2	6.7	29.6	8.8	30.2	2.0	30.0	-0.7	30.6	2.0	30.6	0.0	30.5	-0.3
Iron and Steel	22.1	5.2	22.4	1.4	23.7	5.8	26.1	10.1	28.0	7.3	28.4	1.4	29.0	2.1	28.6	-1.4	28.7	0.3
Nonferrous Metals	29.3	1.4	29.1	-0.7	33.5	15.1	36.6	9.3	32.2	-12.0	30.0	-6.8	31.9	6.3	32.6	2.2	31.5	-3.4
Metal Containers	22.6	4.6	23.2	2.7	23.6	1.7	25.1	6.4	26.8	6.8	27.6	3.0	27.2	-1.4	27.3	0.4	27.8	1.8
Hardware	24.5	5.6	25.7	4.9	27.1	5.4	28.8	6.3	30.5	5.9	31.6	3.6	32.0	1.3	32.2	0.6	32.5	0.9
Plumbing Fixtures and Brass Fittings	29.4	-1.3	30.0	2.0	31.8	6.0	34.0	6.9	33.0	-2.9	31.4	-4.8	33.0	5.1	33.5	1.5	33.5	0.0
Heating Equipment	43.1	0.9	42.9	-0.5	43.2	0.7	44.6	3.2	45.7	2.5	45.3	-0.9	45.5	0.4	44.6	-2.0	42.9	-3.8
Fabricated Structural Metal Products	27.0	0.7	27.3	1.1	28.5	4.4	30.9	8.4	31.2	1.0	31.2	0.0	31.1	-0.3	31.4	1.0	30.8	-1.9
Miscellaneous Metal Products	26.8	0.4	26.9	0.4	27.4	1.9	28.9	5.5	31.0	7.3	31.2	0.6	31.2	0.0	31.3	0.3	32.1	2.6
Metal Treatment Services	-	-	-	-	-	-	-	-	-	-	-	-	-	-	-	-	-	-
Machinery and Equipment	25.9	2.4	26.3	1.5	27.2	3.4	29.3	7.7	31.4	7.2	32.1	2.2	32.8	2.2	33.0	0.6	33.0	0.0
Agricultural Machinery and Equipment	23.2	0.9	23.1	-0.4	23.3	0.9	24.2	3.9	25.3	4.5	26.3	4.0	27.2	3.4	27.7	1.8	28.2	1.8
Construction Machinery and Equipment	18.4	2.8	18.7	1.6	19.5	4.3	21.1	8.2	22.7	7.6	23.6	4.0	24.5	3.8	25.0	2.0	25.4	1.6
Metalworking Machinery and Equipment	19.8	1.5	20.1	1.5	21.2	5.5	23.2	9.4	24.6	6.0	25.2	2.4	25.8	2.4	26.5	2.7	26.8	1.1
General Purpose Machinery and Equipment	22.6	2.7	23.1	2.2	24.1	4.3	26.5	10.0	28.4	7.2	28.8	1.4	29.7	3.1	30.0	1.0	29.8	-0.7
Electronic Computers and Computer Equipment	-	-	-	-	-	-	-	-	-	-	-	-	-	-	-	-	-	-
Special Industry Machinery and Equipment	-	-	-	-	-	-	-	-	-	-	-	-	-	-	-	-	26.5	-
Electrical Machinery and Equipment	34.5	2.7	35.2	2.0	35.8	1.7	38.7	8.1	41.6	7.5	42.5	2.2	43.1	1.4	43.0	-0.2	42.4	-1.4
Miscellaneous Instruments	-	-	-	-	-	-	-	-	-	-	-	-	-	-	-	-	-	-
Miscellaneous Machinery	28.3	2.5	29.0	2.5	29.8	2.8	31.6	6.0	33.5	6.0	34.2	2.1	34.5	0.9	34.7	0.6	35.1	1.2
Furniture and Household Durables	44.4	2.1	44.9	1.1	45.1	0.4	46.3	2.7	47.5	2.6	47.9	0.8	48.0	0.2	47.8	-0.4	47.5	-0.6
Household Furniture	35.6	0.8	35.5	-0.3	35.6	0.3	37.2	4.5	38.3	3.0	38.5	0.5	38.8	0.8	39.2	1.0	39.6	1.0
Commercial Furniture	26.6	1.5	27.0	1.5	28.1	4.1	30.2	7.5	32.1	6.3	32.9	2.5	33.1	0.6	33.4	0.9	33.2	-0.6
Floor Coverings	56.8	1.6	56.0	-1.4	57.6	2.9	59.7	3.6	60.7	1.7	58.1	-4.3	58.3	0.3	59.3	1.7	58.6	-1.2
Household Appliances	57.5	0.9	58.1	1.0	56.7	-2.4	56.0	-1.2	56.0	0.0	55.6	-0.7	55.5	-0.2	54.0	-2.7	53.0	-1.9
Home Electronic Equipment	-	-	-	-	136.3	0.3	136.4	0.1	138.3	1.4	138.2	-0.1	135.9	-1.7	133.8	-1.5	131.0	-2.1
Household Durable Goods n.e.c.	24.2	3.9	25.0	3.3	25.9	3.6	27.3	5.4	28.7	5.1	29.8	3.8	30.2	1.3	30.8	2.0	30.8	0.0

Source: U.S. Department of Labor, Bureau of Labor Statistics, Division of Industry Prices and Price Indexes. n.e.c. stands for not elsewhere classified. - indicates no data collected for period or unavailable.

Producer Price Index
Annual Averages, 1962-1970
Base 1982 = 100

Columns headed % show percentile change in the index from the previous period for which an index is available.

	1962		1963		1964		1965		1966		1967		1968		1969		1970	
	Index	%	Index	%	Index	%	Index	%	Index	%	Index	%	Index	%	Index	%	Index	%
Metals and Metal Products	30.2	-1.0	30.3	0.3	31.1	2.6	32.0	2.9	32.8	2.5	33.2	1.2	34.0	2.4	36.0	5.9	38.7	7.5
Iron and Steel	28.3	-1.4	28.2	-0.4	28.6	1.4	28.9	1.0	29.1	0.7	29.5	1.4	30.1	2.0	31.6	5.0	34.0	7.6
Nonferrous Metals	31.1	-1.3	31.1	0.0	33.2	6.8	36.2	9.0	37.9	4.7	37.9	0.0	39.3	3.7	43.1	9.7	47.3	9.7
Metal Containers	28.2	1.4	28.5	1.1	28.7	0.7	29.3	2.1	29.9	2.0	30.4	1.7	31.6	3.9	32.5	2.8	34.3	5.5
Hardware	32.6	0.3	32.6	0.0	32.9	0.9	33.2	0.9	34.4	3.6	35.7	3.8	36.6	2.5	37.9	3.6	39.8	5.0
Plumbing Fixtures and Brass Fittings	32.5	-3.0	32.5	0.0	32.8	0.9	33.5	2.1	35.2	5.1	35.9	2.0	37.1	3.3	38.5	3.8	39.9	3.6
Heating Equipment	42.4	-1.2	42.2	-0.5	41.8	-0.9	41.7	-0.2	42.1	1.0	42.2	0.2	43.3	2.6	44.4	2.5	46.6	5.0
Fabricated Structural Metal Products	30.6	-0.6	30.6	0.0	30.9	1.0	31.5	1.9	32.4	2.9	32.8	1.2	33.5	2.1	34.7	3.6	36.7	5.8
Miscellaneous Metal Products	32.3	0.6	32.7	1.2	33.8	3.4	34.0	0.6	34.7	2.1	35.4	2.0	36.1	2.0	38.0	5.3	40.5	6.6
Metal Treatment Services	-	-	-	-	-	-	-	-	-	-	-	-	-	-	-	-	-	-
Machinery and Equipment	33.0	0.0	33.1	0.3	33.3	0.6	33.7	1.2	34.7	3.0	35.9	3.5	37.0	3.1	38.2	3.2	40.0	4.7
Agricultural Machinery and Equipment	28.8	2.1	29.2	1.4	29.6	1.4	30.2	2.0	31.1	3.0	32.1	3.2	33.4	4.0	34.9	4.5	36.4	4.3
Construction Machinery and Equipment	25.4	0.0	25.9	2.0	26.5	2.3	27.2	2.6	28.1	3.3	29.1	3.6	30.7	5.5	32.1	4.6	33.7	5.0
Metalworking Machinery and Equipment	27.2	1.5	27.3	0.4	27.8	1.8	28.6	2.9	29.9	4.5	31.2	4.3	32.4	3.8	33.7	4.0	35.6	5.6
General Purpose Machinery and Equipment	29.9	0.3	30.1	0.7	30.2	0.3	30.4	0.7	31.8	4.6	32.9	3.5	34.0	3.3	35.2	3.5	37.4	6.3
Electronic Computers and Computer Equipment	-	-	-	-	-	-	-	-	-	-	-	-	-	-	-	-	-	-
Special Industry Machinery and Equipment	26.9	1.5	27.4	1.9	27.9	1.8	28.4	1.8	29.5	3.9	30.8	4.4	32.4	5.2	33.8	4.3	35.6	5.3
Electrical Machinery and Equipment	41.8	-1.4	41.3	-1.2	41.1	-0.5	41.1	0.0	42.0	2.2	43.2	2.9	43.7	1.2	44.4	1.6	45.9	3.4
Miscellaneous Instruments	-	-	-	-	-	-	-	-	-	-	-	-	-	-	-	-	-	-
Miscellaneous Machinery	35.2	0.3	35.3	0.3	35.6	0.8	35.8	0.6	36.3	1.4	37.3	2.8	38.9	4.3	40.3	3.6	42.0	4.2
Furniture and Household Durables	47.2	-0.6	46.9	-0.6	47.1	0.4	46.8	-0.6	47.4	1.3	48.3	1.9	49.7	2.9	50.7	2.0	51.9	2.4
Household Furniture	40.0	1.0	40.3	0.7	40.6	0.7	40.9	0.7	42.0	2.7	43.5	3.6	45.2	3.9	47.2	4.4	48.6	3.0
Commercial Furniture	33.4	0.6	33.5	0.3	33.7	0.6	33.9	0.6	34.5	1.8	36.3	5.2	37.7	3.9	39.2	4.0	41.6	6.1
Floor Coverings	57.2	-2.4	57.0	-0.3	58.7	3.0	57.7	-1.7	57.2	-0.9	55.2	-3.5	55.9	1.3	55.4	-0.9	54.9	-0.9
Household Appliances	52.3	-1.3	51.1	-2.3	50.8	-0.6	49.7	-2.2	49.6	-0.2	50.2	1.2	51.1	1.8	51.7	1.2	52.9	2.3
Home Electronic Equipment	125.3	-4.4	121.8	-2.8	119.9	-1.6	117.1	-2.3	114.9	-1.9	113.6	-1.1	111.4	-1.9	107.4	-3.6	106.0	-1.3
Household Durable Goods n.e.c.	31.3	1.6	31.4	0.3	31.8	1.3	32.2	1.3	33.0	2.5	34.6	4.8	36.9	6.6	38.6	4.6	40.1	3.9

Source: U.S. Department of Labor, Bureau of Labor Statistics, Division of Industry Prices and Price Indexes. n.e.c. stands for not elsewhere classified. - indicates no data collected for period or unavailable.

Producer Price Index
Annual Averages, 1971-1979
Base 1982 = 100

Columns headed % show percentile change in the index from the previous period for which an index is available.

	1971		1972		1973		1974		1975		1976		1977		1978		1979	
	Index	%	Index	%	Index	%	Index	%	Index	%	Index	%	Index	%	Index	%	Index	%
Metals and Metal Products	39.4	1.8	40.9	3.8	44.0	7.6	57.0	29.5	61.5	7.9	65.0	5.7	69.3	6.6	75.3	8.7	86.0	14.2
Iron and Steel	35.9	5.6	37.9	5.6	40.2	6.1	52.7	31.1	59.3	12.5	63.7	7.4	68.0	6.8	74.8	10.0	83.6	11.8
Nonferrous Metals	43.5	-8.0	44.3	1.8	51.2	15.6	71.0	38.7	65.1	-8.3	68.9	5.8	74.1	7.5	78.8	6.3	99.3	26.0
Metal Containers	37.1	8.2	39.2	5.7	41.0	4.6	50.1	22.2	58.5	16.8	61.5	5.1	66.4	8.0	74.1	11.6	81.9	10.5
Hardware	41.7	4.8	42.9	2.9	44.5	3.7	50.2	12.8	58.2	15.9	61.8	6.2	66.2	7.1	71.5	8.0	78.0	9.1
Plumbing Fixtures and Brass Fittings	41.8	4.8	43.0	2.9	45.1	4.9	53.5	18.6	58.2	8.8	62.5	7.4	67.0	7.2	71.4	6.6	77.9	9.1
Heating Equipment	48.6	4.3	49.8	2.5	50.8	2.0	56.9	12.0	63.5	11.6	66.6	4.9	69.8	4.8	73.5	5.3	78.9	7.3
Fabricated Structural Metal Products	38.8	5.7	40.2	3.6	41.8	4.0	52.9	26.6	62.0	17.2	63.6	2.6	67.8	6.6	74.3	9.6	81.6	9.8
Miscellaneous Metal Products	42.1	4.0	44.0	4.5	45.9	4.3	55.7	21.4	64.1	15.1	66.2	3.3	69.5	5.0	75.1	8.1	81.9	9.1
Metal Treatment Services	-	-	-		-	-	-		-		-		-		-		-	-
Machinery and Equipment	41.4	3.5	42.3	2.2	43.7	3.3	50.0	14.4	57.9	15.8	61.3	5.9	65.2	6.4	70.3	7.8	76.7	9.1
Agricultural Machinery and Equipment	37.8	3.8	39.3	4.0	40.5	3.1	46.2	14.1	54.2	17.3	58.8	8.5	63.6	8.2	68.5	7.7	74.6	8.9
Construction Machinery and Equipment	35.4	5.0	36.6	3.4	38.0	3.8	44.3	16.6	53.8	21.4	57.8	7.4	62.1	7.4	67.7	9.0	74.5	10.0
Metalworking Machinery and Equipment	36.7	3.1	37.5	2.2	39.1	4.3	45.8	17.1	53.5	16.8	56.9	6.4	61.9	8.8	67.6	9.2	75.2	11.2
General Purpose Machinery and Equipment	39.2	4.8	40.3	2.8	41.8	3.7	49.7	18.9	58.7	18.1	62.4	6.3	66.4	6.4	71.2	7.2	77.8	9.3
Electronic Computers and Computer Equipment	-		-		-		-		-		-		-		-		-	
Special Industry Machinery and Equipment	37.2	4.5	38.0	2.2	40.0	5.3	46.4	16.0	53.8	15.9	58.0	7.8	62.3	7.4	68.6	10.1	76.0	10.8
Electrical Machinery and Equipment	47.1	2.6	47.7	1.3	48.5	1.7	54.0	11.3	60.7	12.4	63.4	4.4	66.6	5.0	71.2	6.9	77.2	8.4
Miscellaneous Instruments	-	-	-		-	-	-		-		-		-		-		-	-
Miscellaneous Machinery	43.7	4.0	44.8	2.5	46.2	3.1	52.0	12.6	60.5	16.3	64.1	6.0	67.3	5.0	72.5	7.7	77.8	7.3
Furniture and Household Durables	53.1	2.3	53.8	1.3	55.7	3.5	61.8	11.0	67.5	9.2	70.3	4.1	73.2	4.1	77.5	5.9	82.8	6.8
Household Furniture	50.0	2.9	51.0	2.0	53.5	4.9	59.4	11.0	63.6	7.1	66.8	5.0	70.6	5.7	75.5	6.9	81.0	7.3
Commercial Furniture	42.9	3.1	43.6	1.6	47.0	7.8	55.3	17.7	60.5	9.4	63.0	4.1	67.5	7.1	73.1	8.3	80.5	10.1
Floor Coverings	54.6	-0.5	54.4	-0.4	56.4	3.7	63.7	12.9	69.0	8.3	72.5	5.1	75.3	3.9	78.2	3.9	81.7	4.5
Household Appliances	54.0	2.1	54.0	0.0	54.5	0.9	59.2	8.6	66.5	12.3	69.9	5.1	72.9	4.3	76.8	5.3	80.8	5.2
Home Electronic Equipment	106.1	0.1	105.3	-0.8	104.4	-0.9	105.7	1.2	106.2	0.5	103.7	-2.4	99.6	-4.0	102.4	2.8	103.7	1.3
Household Durable Goods n.e.c.	41.8	4.2	43.4	3.8	45.1	3.9	51.4	14.0	58.3	13.4	61.9	6.2	65.7	6.1	70.2	6.8	78.9	12.4

Source: U.S. Department of Labor, Bureau of Labor Statistics, Division of Industry Prices and Price Indexes. n.e.c. stands for not elsewhere classified. - indicates no data collected for period or unavailable.

Producer Price Index
Annual Averages, 1980-1988
Base 1982 = 100

Columns headed % show percentile change in the index from the previous period for which an index is available.

	1980		1981		1982		1983		1984		1985		1986		1987		1988	
	Index	%	Index	%	Index	%	Index	%	Index	%	Index	%	Index	%	Index	%	Index	%
Metals and Metal Products	95.0	10.5	99.6	4.8	100.0	0.4	101.8	1.8	104.8	2.9	104.4	-0.4	103.2	-1.1	107.1	3.8	118.7	10.8
Iron and Steel	90.0	7.7	98.5	9.4	100.0	1.5	101.3	1.3	105.3	3.9	104.8	-0.5	101.1	-3.5	104.6	3.5	115.7	10.6
Nonferrous Metals	115.7	16.5	108.4	-6.3	100.0	-7.7	104.7	4.7	105.1	0.4	99.6	-5.2	98.5	-1.1	108.8	10.5	133.2	22.4
Metal Containers	90.9	11.0	96.1	5.7	100.0	4.1	102.1	2.1	106.5	4.3	109.0	2.3	110.2	1.1	109.5	-0.6	110.2	0.6
Hardware	85.8	10.0	93.9	9.4	100.0	6.5	103.7	3.7	105.9	2.1	109.1	3.0	109.5	0.4	109.6	0.1	113.7	3.7
Plumbing Fixtures and Brass Fittings	88.5	13.6	96.0	8.5	100.0	4.2	103.8	3.8	108.6	4.6	111.9	3.0	115.5	3.2	119.7	3.6	128.7	7.5
Heating Equipment	87.0	10.3	94.5	8.6	100.0	5.8	102.7	2.7	106.6	3.8	109.5	2.7	113.0	3.2	115.5	2.2	119.2	3.2
Fabricated Structural Metal Products	88.8	8.8	96.9	9.1	100.0	3.2	99.6	-0.4	101.9	2.3	103.2	1.3	103.6	0.4	105.4	1.7	114.3	8.4
Miscellaneous Metal Products	88.5	8.1	95.8	8.2	100.0	4.4	100.5	0.5	104.6	4.1	107.1	2.4	107.0	-0.1	107.8	0.7	112.1	4.0
Metal Treatment Services	-	-	-	-	-	-	-	-	-	-	102.4	-	104.7	2.2	106.2	1.4	109.8	3.4
Machinery and Equipment	86.0	12.1	94.4	9.8	100.0	5.9	102.7	2.7	105.1	2.3	107.2	2.0	108.8	1.5	110.4	1.5	113.2	2.5
Agricultural Machinery and Equipment	83.3	11.7	92.7	11.3	100.0	7.9	104.9	4.9	108.0	3.0	108.7	0.6	109.2	0.5	109.6	0.4	112.7	2.8
Construction Machinery and Equipment	84.2	13.0	93.3	10.8	100.0	7.2	102.3	2.3	103.8	1.5	105.4	1.5	106.7	1.2	108.9	2.1	111.8	2.7
Metalworking Machinery and Equipment	85.5	13.7	93.9	9.8	100.0	6.5	101.7	1.7	104.1	2.4	106.6	2.4	108.4	1.7	110.1	1.6	113.5	3.1
General Purpose Machinery and Equipment	87.0	11.8	95.0	9.2	100.0	5.3	101.4	1.4	103.3	1.9	105.7	2.3	107.2	1.4	108.3	1.0	112.8	4.2
Electronic Computers and Computer Equipment	-	-	-	-	-	-	-	-	-	-	-	-	-	-	-	-	-	-
Special Industry Machinery and Equipment	84.8	11.6	94.7	11.7	100.0	5.6	103.7	3.7	107.3	3.5	110.8	3.3	114.2	3.1	117.3	2.7	121.7	3.8
Electrical Machinery and Equipment	87.1	12.8	95.1	9.2	100.0	5.2	103.7	3.7	107.4	3.6	109.6	2.0	111.2	1.5	112.6	1.3	114.5	1.7
Miscellaneous Instruments	-	-	-	-	-	-	105.3	-	106.6	1.2	109.8	3.0	112.7	2.6	115.7	2.7	118.9	2.8
Miscellaneous Machinery	85.7	10.2	94.1	9.8	100.0	6.3	102.1	2.1	102.2	0.1	103.3	1.1	104.2	0.9	105.7	1.4	108.6	2.7
Furniture and Household Durables	90.7	9.5	95.9	5.7	100.0	4.3	103.4	3.4	105.7	2.2	107.1	1.3	108.2	1.0	109.9	1.6	113.1	2.9
Household Furniture	89.1	10.0	95.4	7.1	100.0	4.8	102.1	2.1	105.3	3.1	108.5	3.0	110.3	1.7	113.0	2.4	117.6	4.1
Commercial Furniture	85.7	6.5	93.5	9.1	100.0	7.0	103.9	3.9	107.8	3.8	111.9	3.8	115.3	3.0	118.6	2.9	124.2	4.7
Floor Coverings	90.0	10.2	98.7	9.7	100.0	1.3	102.4	2.4	105.6	3.1	105.6	0.0	108.3	2.6	110.7	2.2	114.7	3.6
Household Appliances	87.5	8.3	94.1	7.5	100.0	6.3	103.9	3.9	106.0	2.0	106.7	0.7	105.7	-0.9	105.6	-0.1	106.0	0.4
Home Electronic Equipment	103.8	0.1	101.3	-2.4	100.0	-1.3	97.8	-2.2	95.2	-2.7	90.8	-4.6	89.9	-1.0	88.8	-1.2	87.2	-1.8
Household Durable Goods n.e.c.	96.3	22.1	97.1	0.8	100.0	3.0	108.2	8.2	110.1	1.8	111.7	1.5	112.9	1.1	115.4	2.2	119.8	3.8

Source: U.S. Department of Labor, Bureau of Labor Statistics, Division of Industry Prices and Price Indexes. n.e.c. stands for not elsewhere classified. - indicates no data collected for period or unavailable.

Producer Price Index
Annual Averages, 1989-1993
Base 1982 = 100

Columns headed % show percentile change in the index from the previous period for which an index is available.

	1989		1990		1991		1992		1993									
	Index	%	Index	%	Index	%	Index	%	Index	%	Index	%	Index	%	Index	%	Index	%
Metals and Metal Products	124.1	4.5	122.9	-1.0	120.2	-2.2	119.2	-0.8	119.2	0.0								
Iron and Steel	119.1	2.9	117.2	-1.6	114.1	-2.6	111.5	-2.3	116.0	4.0								
Nonferrous Metals	141.5	6.2	133.8	-5.4	123.4	-7.8	120.9	-2.0	114.4	-5.4								
Metal Containers	111.5	1.2	114.0	2.2	115.5	1.3	113.9	-1.4	109.5	-3.9								
Hardware	120.4	5.9	125.9	4.6	130.2	3.4	132.7	1.9	135.2	1.9								
Plumbing Fixtures and Brass Fittings	137.7	7.0	144.3	4.8	149.7	3.7	153.1	2.3	155.8	1.8								
Heating Equipment	125.1	4.9	131.6	5.2	134.1	1.9	137.3	2.4	140.3	2.2								
Fabricated Structural Metal Products	120.3	5.2	121.8	1.2	122.4	0.5	122.1	-0.2	123.2	0.9								
Miscellaneous Metal Products	117.0	4.4	119.4	2.1	120.4	0.8	121.4	0.8	122.3	0.7								
Metal Treatment Services	114.5	4.3	116.3	1.6	117.4	0.9	118.2	0.7	119.8	1.4								
Machinery and Equipment	117.4	3.7	120.7	2.8	123.0	1.9	123.4	0.3	124.0	0.5								
Agricultural Machinery and Equipment	117.7	4.4	121.7	3.4	125.7	3.3	129.5	3.0	133.5	3.1								
Construction Machinery and Equipment	117.2	4.8	121.6	3.8	125.2	3.0	128.7	2.8	132.1	2.6								
Metalworking Machinery and Equipment	118.2	4.1	123.0	4.1	127.6	3.7	130.9	2.6	133.5	2.0								
General Purpose Machinery and Equipment	119.0	5.5	123.7	3.9	127.8	3.3	129.9	1.6	132.1	1.7								
Electronic Computers and Computer Equipment	-	-	-	-	88.9	-	73.2	-17.7	62.1	-15.2								
Special Industry Machinery and Equipment	127.0	4.4	131.5	3.5	135.9	3.3	139.5	2.6	143.6	2.9								
Electrical Machinery and Equipment	117.5	2.6	119.3	1.5	120.8	1.3	121.3	0.4	122.5	1.0								
Miscellaneous Instruments	122.5	3.0	126.7	3.4	130.3	2.8	133.7	2.6	137.8	3.1								
Miscellaneous Machinery	112.7	3.8	116.7	3.5	120.3	3.1	121.7	1.2	122.7	0.8								
Furniture and Household Durables	116.9	3.4	119.2	2.0	121.2	1.7	122.2	0.8	123.6	1.1								
Household Furniture	121.8	3.6	125.1	2.7	128.0	2.3	130.0	1.6	132.9	2.2								
Commercial Furniture	129.0	3.9	133.4	3.4	136.2	2.1	138.1	1.4	140.6	1.8								
Floor Coverings	117.6	2.5	119.0	1.2	120.4	1.2	120.3	-0.1	120.0	-0.2								
Household Appliances	108.7	2.5	110.8	1.9	111.3	0.5	111.4	0.1	113.0	1.4								
Home Electronic Equipment	86.9	-0.3	82.7	-4.8	83.2	0.6	82.0	-1.4	80.2	-2.2								
Household Durable Goods n.e.c.	127.2	6.2	130.7	2.8	134.2	2.7	136.6	1.8	137.9	1.0								

Source: U.S. Department of Labor, Bureau of Labor Statistics, Division of Industry Prices and Price Indexes. n.e.c. stands for not elsewhere classified. - indicates no data collected for period or unavailable.

Producer Price Index
Annual Averages, 1926-1934
Base 1982 = 100

Columns headed % show percentile change in the index from the previous period for which an index is available.

	1926		1927		1928		1929		1930		1931		1932		1933		1934	
	Index	%	Index	%	Index	%	Index	%	Index	%	Index	%	Index	%	Index	%	Index	%
Nonmetallic Mineral Products	16.4	-	15.7	-4.3	16.2	3.2	16.0	-1.2	15.9	-0.6	14.9	-6.3	13.9	-6.7	14.7	5.8	15.7	6.8
Glass	-		-		-		-		-		-		-		-		-	
Concrete Ingredients and Related Products	14.9	-	14.5	-2.7	16.4	13.1	16.5	0.6	16.6	0.6	15.1	-9.0	14.4	-4.6	15.6	8.3	16.6	6.4
Concrete Products	23.7	-	23.7	0.0	23.7	0.0	23.3	-1.7	23.6	1.3	22.3	-5.5	20.5	-8.1	20.9	2.0	20.9	0.0
Clay Construction Products Ex. Refractories	-		-		-		-		-		-		-		-		-	
Refractories	-		-		-		-		-		-		-		-		-	
Asphalt Felts and Coatings	21.2	-	20.0	-5.7	17.9	-10.5	15.8	-11.7	16.1	1.9	16.7	3.7	15.3	-8.4	15.7	2.6	16.9	7.6
Gypsum Products	-		-		-		-		-		-		-		-		-	
Glass Containers	-		-		-		-		-		-		-		-		-	
Nonmetallic Minerals n.e.c.	-		-		-		-		-		-		-		-		-	
Transportation Equipment	-		-		-		-		-		-		-		-		-	
Motor Vehicles and Equipment	16.7	-	16.0	-4.2	16.2	1.3	16.7	3.1	15.7	-6.0	14.9	-5.1	14.5	-2.7	13.9	-4.1	14.6	5.0
Aircraft and Aircraft Equipment	-		-		-		-		-		-		-		-		-	
Ships and Boats	-		-		-		-		-		-		-		-		-	
Railroad Equipment	-		-		-		-		-		-		-		-		-	
Transportation Equipment n.e.c.	-		-		-		-		-		-		-		-		-	
Miscellaneous Products	-		-		-		-		-		-		-		-		-	
Toys, Sporting Goods, Small Arms, Etc.	-		-		-		-		-		-		-		-		-	
Tobacco Products, Incl. Stemmed & Redried	-		-		-		-		-		-		-		-		-	
Notions	-		-		-		-		-		-		-		-		-	
Photographic Equipment and Supplies	-		-		-		-		-		-		-		-		-	
Mobile Homes	-		-		-		-		-		-		-		-		-	
Medical, Surgical & Personal Aid Devices	-		-		-		-		-		-		-		-		-	
Industrial Safety Equipment	-		-		-		-		-		-		-		-		-	
Mining Services	-		-		-		-		-		-		-		-		-	
Miscellaneous Products n.e.c.	-		-		-		-		-		-		-		-		-	

Source: U.S. Department of Labor, Bureau of Labor Statistics, Division of Industry Prices and Price Indexes. n.e.c. stands for not elsewhere classified. - indicates no data collected for period or unavailable.

Producer Price Index
Annual Averages, 1935-1943
Base 1982 = 100

Columns headed % show percentile change in the index from the previous period for which an index is available.

	1935		1936		1937		1938		1939		1940		1941		1942		1943	
	Index	%	Index	%	Index	%	Index	%	Index	%	Index	%	Index	%	Index	%	Index	%
Nonmetallic Mineral Products	15.7	0.0	15.8	0.6	16.1	1.9	15.6	-3.1	15.3	-1.9	15.3	0.0	15.7	2.6	16.3	3.8	16.4	0.6
Glass	-		-		-		-		-		-		-		-		-	
Concrete Ingredients and Related Products	16.6	0.0	16.7	0.6	16.6	-0.6	16.7	0.6	16.7	0.0	16.6	-0.6	16.8	1.2	17.3	3.0	17.3	0.0
Concrete Products	19.0	-9.1	20.2	6.3	20.3	0.5	18.7	-7.9	18.6	-0.5	16.6	-10.8	19.2	15.7	19.9	3.6	19.9	0.0
Clay Construction Products Ex. Refractories	-		-		-		-		-		-		-		-		-	
Refractories	-		-		-		-		-		-		-		-		-	
Asphalt Felts and Coatings	17.7	4.7	17.4	-1.7	19.1	9.8	15.4	-19.4	15.9	3.2	17.4	9.4	17.9	2.9	17.5	-2.2	17.5	0.0
Gypsum Products	-		-		-		-		-		-		-		-		-	
Glass Containers	-		-		-		-		-		-		-		-		-	
Nonmetallic Minerals n.e.c.	-		-		-		-		-		-		-		-		-	
Transportation Equipment	-		-		-		-		-		-		-		-		-	
Motor Vehicles and Equipment	14.0	-4.1	13.9	-0.7	14.9	7.2	15.9	6.7	15.6	-1.9	16.1	3.2	17.2	6.8	18.8	9.3	18.8	0.0
Aircraft and Aircraft Equipment	-		-		-		-		-		-		-		-		-	
Ships and Boats	-		-		-		-		-		-		-		-		-	
Railroad Equipment	-		-		-		-		-		-		-		-		-	
Transportation Equipment n.e.c.	-		-		-		-		-		-		-		-		-	
Miscellaneous Products	-		-		-		-		-		-		-		-		-	
Toys, Sporting Goods, Small Arms, Etc.	-		-		-		-		-		-		-		-		-	
Tobacco Products, Incl. Stemmed & Redried	-		-		-		-		-		-		-		-		-	
Notions	-		-		-		-		-		-		-		-		-	
Photographic Equipment and Supplies	-		-		-		-		-		-		-		-		-	
Mobile Homes	-		-		-		-		-		-		-		-		-	
Medical, Surgical & Personal Aid Devices	-		-		-		-		-		-		-		-		-	
Industrial Safety Equipment	-		-		-		-		-		-		-		-		-	
Mining Services	-		-		-		-		-		-		-		-		-	
Miscellaneous Products n.e.c.	-		-		-		-		-		-		-		-		-	

Source: U.S. Department of Labor, Bureau of Labor Statistics, Division of Industry Prices and Price Indexes. n.e.c. stands for not elsewhere classified. - indicates no data collected for period or unavailable.

Producer Price Index
Annual Averages, 1944-1952
Base 1982 = 100

Columns headed % show percentile change in the index from the previous period for which an index is available.

	1944		1945		1946		1947		1948		1949		1950		1951		1952	
	Index	%	Index	%	Index	%	Index	%	Index	%	Index	%	Index	%	Index	%	Index	%
Nonmetallic Mineral Products	16.7	1.8	17.4	4.2	18.5	6.3	20.7	11.9	22.4	8.2	23.0	2.7	23.5	2.2	25.0	6.4	25.0	0.0
Glass	-	-	-	-	-	-	30.2	-	31.8	5.3	33.4	5.0	34.1	2.1	36.3	6.5	36.3	0.0
Concrete Ingredients and Related Products	17.5	1.2	18.0	2.9	18.7	3.9	20.5	9.6	22.4	9.3	23.2	3.6	23.5	1.3	24.9	6.0	24.9	0.0
Concrete Products	19.9	0.0	19.9	0.0	21.1	6.0	23.9	13.3	25.1	5.0	25.7	2.4	26.3	2.3	28.0	6.5	28.0	0.0
Clay Construction Products Ex. Refractories	-	-	-	-	-	-	23.9	-	25.7	7.5	26.5	3.1	27.6	4.2	29.9	8.3	29.8	-0.3
Refractories	-	-	-	-	-	-	14.3	-	15.8	10.5	16.5	4.4	18.2	10.3	19.6	7.7	19.8	1.0
Asphalt Felts and Coatings	17.6	0.6	18.0	2.3	18.8	4.4	21.4	13.8	23.5	9.8	23.4	-0.4	23.1	-1.3	23.9	3.5	23.4	-2.1
Gypsum Products	-	-	-	-	-	-	27.5	-	30.0	9.1	29.7	-1.0	30.4	2.4	34.1	12.2	34.2	0.3
Glass Containers	-	-	-	-	-	-	14.7	-	16.9	15.0	19.0	12.4	19.1	0.5	20.6	7.9	21.1	2.4
Nonmetallic Minerals n.e.c.	-	-	-	-	-	-	14.9	-	16.3	9.4	16.5	1.2	17.0	3.0	17.7	4.1	17.9	1.1
Transportation Equipment	-	-	-	-	-	-	-	-	-	-	-	-	-	-	-	-	-	-
Motor Vehicles and Equipment	18.9	0.5	19.2	1.6	22.3	16.1	25.5	14.3	28.2	10.6	30.1	6.7	30.0	-0.3	31.6	5.3	33.4	5.7
Aircraft and Aircraft Equipment	-	-	-	-	-	-	-	-	-	-	-	-	-	-	-	-	-	-
Ships and Boats	-	-	-	-	-	-	-	-	-	-	-	-	-	-	-	-	-	-
Railroad Equipment	-	-	-	-	-	-	-	-	-	-	-	-	-	-	-	-	-	-
Transportation Equipment n.e.c.	-	-	-	-	-	-	-	-	-	-	-	-	-	-	-	-	-	-
Miscellaneous Products	-	-	-	-	-	-	26.6	-	27.7	4.1	28.2	1.8	28.6	1.4	30.3	5.9	30.2	-0.3
Toys, Sporting Goods, Small Arms, Etc.	-	-	-	-	-	-	35.1	-	36.7	4.6	36.7	0.0	38.7	5.4	42.0	8.5	41.0	-2.4
Tobacco Products, Incl. Stemmed & Redried	-	-	-	-	-	-	20.5	-	21.3	3.9	22.3	4.7	22.8	2.2	23.5	3.1	23.6	0.4
Notions	-	-	-	-	-	-	37.8	-	37.9	0.3	34.2	-9.8	33.7	-1.5	37.0	9.8	34.4	-7.0
Photographic Equipment and Supplies	-	-	-	-	-	-	32.2	-	35.3	9.6	36.6	3.7	36.3	-0.8	37.5	3.3	38.0	1.3
Mobile Homes	-	-	-	-	-	-	-	-	-	-	-	-	-	-	-	-	-	-
Medical, Surgical & Personal Aid Devices	-	-	-	-	-	-	-	-	-	-	-	-	-	-	-	-	-	-
Industrial Safety Equipment	-	-	-	-	-	-	-	-	-	-	-	-	-	-	-	-	-	-
Mining Services	-	-	-	-	-	-	-	-	-	-	-	-	-	-	-	-	-	-
Miscellaneous Products n.e.c.	-	-	-	-	-	-	23.2	-	23.8	2.6	23.9	0.4	24.1	0.8	25.7	6.6	25.7	0.0

Source: U.S. Department of Labor, Bureau of Labor Statistics, Division of Industry Prices and Price Indexes. n.e.c. stands for not elsewhere classified. - indicates no data collected for period or unavailable.

Producer Price Index
Annual Averages, 1953-1961
Base 1982 = 100

Columns headed % show percentile change in the index from the previous period for which an index is available.

	1953 Index	%	1954 Index	%	1955 Index	%	1956 Index	%	1957 Index	%	1958 Index	%	1959 Index	%	1960 Index	%	1961 Index	%
Nonmetallic Mineral Products	26.0	4.0	26.6	2.3	27.3	2.6	28.5	4.4	29.6	3.9	29.9	1.0	30.3	1.3	30.4	0.3	30.5	0.3
Glass	38.4	5.8	39.6	3.1	40.7	2.8	42.4	4.2	43.1	1.7	43.0	-0.2	43.0	0.0	42.1	-2.1	41.7	-1.0
Concrete Ingredients and Related Products	25.8	3.6	26.6	3.1	27.5	3.4	28.7	4.4	29.9	4.2	30.6	2.3	30.9	1.0	31.3	1.3	31.3	0.0
Concrete Products	28.7	2.5	29.2	1.7	29.5	1.0	30.6	3.7	31.4	2.6	31.9	1.6	32.3	1.3	32.6	0.9	32.6	0.0
Clay Construction Products Ex. Refractories	30.4	2.0	30.9	1.6	32.1	3.9	33.8	5.3	34.3	1.5	34.5	0.6	35.4	2.6	35.9	1.4	36.1	0.6
Refractories	21.6	9.1	22.9	6.0	24.4	6.6	25.8	5.7	27.6	7.0	28.2	2.2	29.0	2.8	29.0	0.0	28.8	-0.7
Asphalt Felts and Coatings	24.4	4.3	23.7	-2.9	24.2	2.1	25.5	5.4	27.9	9.4	25.7	-7.9	26.5	3.1	24.4	-7.9	26.3	7.8
Gypsum Products	35.2	2.9	35.5	0.9	35.5	0.0	36.9	3.9	36.9	0.0	38.4	4.1	38.7	0.8	38.7	0.0	39.4	1.8
Glass Containers	22.7	7.6	23.8	4.8	24.1	1.3	25.4	5.4	26.8	5.5	28.3	5.6	28.3	0.0	27.6	-2.5	27.4	-0.7
Nonmetallic Minerals n.e.c.	18.6	3.9	19.1	2.7	19.3	1.0	19.6	1.6	20.4	4.1	20.9	2.5	21.1	1.0	21.4	1.4	21.2	-0.9
Transportation Equipment	-	-	-	-	-	-	-	-	-	-	-	-	-	-	-	-	-	-
Motor Vehicles and Equipment	33.3	-0.3	33.4	0.3	34.3	2.7	36.3	5.8	37.9	4.4	39.0	2.9	39.9	2.3	39.3	-1.5	39.2	-0.3
Aircraft and Aircraft Equipment	-	-	-	-	-	-	-	-	-	-	-	-	-	-	-	-	-	-
Ships and Boats	-	-	-	-	-	-	-	-	-	-	-	-	-	-	-	-	-	-
Railroad Equipment	-	-	-	-	-	-	-	-	-	-	-	-	-	-	-	-	27.9	-
Transportation Equipment n.e.c.	-	-	-	-	-	-	-	-	-	-	-	-	-	-	-	-	-	-
Miscellaneous Products	31.0	2.6	31.3	1.0	31.3	0.0	31.7	1.3	32.6	2.8	33.3	2.1	33.4	0.3	33.6	0.6	33.7	0.3
Toys, Sporting Goods, Small Arms, Etc.	41.1	0.2	40.9	-0.5	41.0	0.2	42.0	2.4	42.5	1.2	43.0	1.2	42.4	-1.4	42.8	0.9	43.1	0.7
Tobacco Products, Incl. Stemmed & Redried	25.3	7.2	25.6	1.2	25.6	0.0	25.6	0.0	26.7	4.3	27.7	3.7	27.9	0.7	27.9	0.0	27.9	0.0
Notions	34.2	-0.6	34.8	1.8	33.7	-3.2	34.9	3.6	35.6	2.0	35.7	0.3	35.6	-0.3	35.5	-0.3	35.2	-0.8
Photographic Equipment and Supplies	38.3	0.8	38.7	1.0	39.1	1.0	39.8	1.8	41.5	4.3	42.6	2.7	44.0	3.3	44.4	0.9	45.0	1.4
Mobile Homes	-	-	-	-	-	-	-	-	-	-	-	-	-	-	-	-	-	-
Medical, Surgical & Personal Aid Devices	-	-	-	-	-	-	-	-	-	-	-	-	-	-	-	-	-	-
Industrial Safety Equipment	-	-	-	-	-	-	-	-	-	-	-	-	-	-	-	-	-	-
Mining Services	-	-	-	-	-	-	-	-	-	-	-	-	-	-	-	-	-	-
Miscellaneous Products n.e.c.	25.7	0.0	26.0	1.2	26.1	0.4	26.5	1.5	27.2	2.6	27.4	0.7	27.5	0.4	27.9	1.5	28.0	0.4

Source: U.S. Department of Labor, Bureau of Labor Statistics, Division of Industry Prices and Price Indexes. n.e.c. stands for not elsewhere classified. - indicates no data collected for period or unavailable.

Producer Price Index
Annual Averages, 1962-1970
Base 1982 = 100

Columns headed % show percentile change in the index from the previous period for which an index is available.

	1962		1963		1964		1965		1966		1967		1968		1969		1970	
	Index	%	Index	%	Index	%	Index	%	Index	%	Index	%	Index	%	Index	%	Index	%
Nonmetallic Mineral Products	30.5	0.0	30.3	-0.7	30.4	0.3	30.4	0.0	30.7	1.0	31.2	1.6	32.4	3.8	33.6	3.7	35.3	5.1
Glass	41.8	0.2	42.3	1.2	44.1	4.3	43.4	-1.6	43.3	-0.2	-	-	-	-	-	-	-	-
Concrete Ingredients and Related Products	31.5	0.6	31.4	-0.3	31.3	-0.3	31.5	0.6	31.6	0.3	32.3	2.2	33.3	3.1	34.4	3.3	36.3	5.5
Concrete Products	32.7	0.3	32.4	-0.9	32.1	-0.9	32.3	0.6	32.8	1.5	33.6	2.4	34.5	2.7	35.8	3.8	37.7	5.3
Clay Construction Products Ex. Refractories	36.4	0.8	36.6	0.5	36.7	0.3	37.0	0.8	37.7	1.9	38.3	1.6	39.3	2.6	40.7	3.6	42.1	3.4
Refractories	28.7	-0.3	28.6	-0.3	28.8	0.7	29.1	1.0	29.3	0.7	29.7	1.4	31.7	6.7	32.5	2.5	35.9	10.5
Asphalt Felts and Coatings	25.3	-3.8	24.0	-5.1	23.7	-1.2	24.8	4.6	25.6	3.2	25.1	-2.0	25.9	3.2	25.8	-0.4	25.8	0.0
Gypsum Products	39.9	1.3	40.0	0.3	41.1	2.8	39.5	-3.9	38.9	-1.5	39.1	0.5	40.5	3.6	40.5	0.0	38.9	-4.0
Glass Containers	26.9	-1.8	26.9	0.0	27.0	0.4	27.3	1.1	27.8	1.8	28.1	1.1	30.2	7.5	32.3	7.0	33.9	5.0
Nonmetallic Minerals n.e.c.	21.2	0.0	21.1	-0.5	21.1	0.0	21.0	-0.5	21.1	0.5	21.2	0.5	21.9	3.3	22.7	3.7	23.8	4.8
Transportation Equipment	-	-	-	-	-	-	-	-	-	-	-	-	-	-	40.4	-	41.9	3.7
Motor Vehicles and Equipment	39.2	0.0	38.9	-0.8	39.1	0.5	39.2	0.3	39.2	0.0	39.8	1.5	40.9	2.8	41.7	2.0	43.3	3.8
Aircraft and Aircraft Equipment	-	-	-	-	-	-	-	-	-	-	-	-	-	-	-	-	-	-
Ships and Boats	-	-	-	-	-	-	-	-	-	-	-	-	-	-	-	-	-	-
Railroad Equipment	28.0	0.4	28.0	0.0	28.0	0.0	28.1	0.4	28.2	0.4	28.9	2.5	29.8	3.1	31.4	5.4	33.2	5.7
Transportation Equipment n.e.c.	-	-	-	-	-	-	-	-	-	-	-	-	-	-	-	-	-	-
Miscellaneous Products	33.9	0.6	34.2	0.9	34.4	0.6	34.7	0.9	35.3	1.7	36.2	2.5	37.0	2.2	38.1	3.0	39.8	4.5
Toys, Sporting Goods, Small Arms, Etc.	43.0	-0.2	43.1	0.2	43.1	0.0	43.8	1.6	44.4	1.4	45.2	1.8	46.2	2.2	47.6	3.0	49.5	4.0
Tobacco Products, Incl. Stemmed & Redried	28.0	0.4	28.7	2.5	29.1	1.4	29.1	0.0	30.1	3.4	31.0	3.0	31.6	1.9	33.1	4.7	35.2	6.3
Notions	35.2	0.0	35.2	0.0	35.3	0.3	35.3	0.0	35.8	1.4	36.1	0.8	36.1	0.0	37.2	3.0	39.1	5.1
Photographic Equipment and Supplies	46.1	2.4	46.0	-0.2	46.3	0.7	46.7	0.9	46.5	-0.4	47.5	2.2	48.6	2.3	48.7	0.2	49.9	2.5
Mobile Homes	-	-	-	-	-	-	-	-	-	-	-	-	-	-	-	-	-	-
Medical, Surgical & Personal Aid Devices	-	-	-	-	-	-	-	-	-	-	-	-	-	-	-	-	-	-
Industrial Safety Equipment	-	-	-	-	-	-	-	-	-	-	-	-	-	-	-	-	-	-
Mining Services	-	-	-	-	-	-	-	-	-	-	-	-	-	-	-	-	-	-
Miscellaneous Products n.e.c.	28.1	0.4	28.0	-0.4	28.1	0.4	28.4	1.1	28.8	1.4	29.6	2.8	30.3	2.4	30.9	2.0	32.1	3.9

Source: U.S. Department of Labor, Bureau of Labor Statistics, Division of Industry Prices and Price Indexes. n.e.c. stands for not elsewhere classified. - indicates no data collected for period or unavailable.

Producer Price Index
Annual Averages, 1971-1979
Base 1982 = 100

Columns headed % show percentile change in the index from the previous period for which an index is available.

	1971		1972		1973		1974		1975		1976		1977		1978		1979	
	Index	%	Index	%	Index	%	Index	%	Index	%	Index	%	Index	%	Index	%	Index	%
Nonmetallic Mineral Products	38.2	8.2	39.4	3.1	40.7	3.3	47.8	17.4	54.4	13.8	58.2	7.0	62.6	7.6	69.6	11.2	77.6	11.5
Glass	-	-	-	-	-	-	-	-	-	-	-	-	-	-	-	-	-	-
Concrete Ingredients and Related Products	39.3	8.3	40.9	4.1	42.3	3.4	48.0	13.5	55.6	15.8	60.2	8.3	64.2	6.6	70.2	9.3	78.7	12.1
Concrete Products	40.5	7.4	42.2	4.2	44.2	4.7	50.9	15.2	57.3	12.6	60.5	5.6	64.4	6.4	71.9	11.6	82.0	14.0
Clay Construction Products Ex. Refractories	43.9	4.3	45.0	2.5	47.3	5.1	51.8	9.5	58.0	12.0	62.7	8.1	69.0	10.0	75.6	9.6	83.6	10.6
Refractories	37.6	4.7	38.3	1.9	40.4	5.5	42.6	5.4	49.2	15.5	54.6	11.0	59.2	8.4	64.2	8.4	70.2	9.3
Asphalt Felts and Coatings	31.5	22.1	32.9	4.4	34.0	3.3	49.2	44.7	56.7	15.2	59.8	5.5	63.5	6.2	73.3	15.4	81.7	11.5
Gypsum Products	42.7	9.8	44.8	4.9	47.2	5.4	53.7	13.8	56.2	4.7	60.3	7.3	71.7	18.9	89.5	24.8	98.5	10.1
Glass Containers	37.0	9.1	38.0	2.7	39.1	2.9	43.7	11.8	50.5	15.6	55.0	8.9	60.2	9.5	68.7	14.1	73.4	6.8
Nonmetallic Minerals n.e.c.	26.3	10.5	26.9	2.3	27.2	1.1	40.0	47.1	46.7	16.7	49.3	5.6	53.1	7.7	58.4	10.0	66.5	13.9
Transportation Equipment	44.2	5.5	45.5	2.9	46.1	1.3	50.3	9.1	56.7	12.7	60.5	6.7	64.6	6.8	69.5	7.6	75.3	8.3
Motor Vehicles and Equipment	45.7	5.5	47.0	2.8	47.4	0.9	51.4	8.4	57.6	12.1	61.2	6.3	65.2	6.5	70.0	7.4	75.8	8.3
Aircraft and Aircraft Equipment	-	-	-	-	-	-	-	-	-	-	-	-	-	-	-	-	-	-
Ships and Boats	-	-	-	-	-	-	-	-	-	-	-	-	-	-	-	-	-	-
Railroad Equipment	34.9	5.1	37.1	6.3	38.9	4.9	47.3	21.6	58.1	22.8	62.5	7.6	67.4	7.8	73.0	8.3	80.0	9.6
Transportation Equipment n.e.c.	-	-	-	-	-	-	-	-	-	-	-	-	-	-	-	-	-	-
Miscellaneous Products	40.8	2.5	41.5	1.7	43.3	4.3	48.1	11.1	53.4	11.0	55.6	4.1	59.4	6.8	66.7	12.3	75.5	13.2
Toys, Sporting Goods, Small Arms, Etc.	50.9	2.8	51.7	1.6	53.2	2.9	59.7	12.2	65.9	10.4	67.7	2.7	70.1	3.5	73.7	5.1	79.6	8.0
Tobacco Products, Incl. Stemmed & Redried	36.1	2.6	36.4	0.8	37.7	3.6	41.1	9.0	46.3	12.7	50.5	9.1	55.6	10.1	61.4	10.4	67.4	9.8
Notions	40.4	3.3	40.5	0.2	41.3	2.0	49.6	20.1	54.5	9.9	58.6	7.5	62.2	6.1	65.7	5.6	69.3	5.5
Photographic Equipment and Supplies	50.5	1.2	50.7	0.4	51.5	1.6	55.5	7.8	62.1	11.9	64.7	4.2	66.5	2.8	69.3	4.2	73.0	5.3
Mobile Homes	-	-	-	-	-	-	-	-	-	-	-	-	-	-	-	-	-	-
Medical, Surgical & Personal Aid Devices	-	-	-	-	-	-	-	-	-	-	-	-	-	-	-	-	-	-
Industrial Safety Equipment	-	-	-	-	-	-	-	-	-	-	-	-	-	-	-	-	83.3	-
Mining Services	-	-	-	-	-	-	-	-	-	-	-	-	-	-	-	-	-	-
Miscellaneous Products n.e.c.	33.3	3.7	34.3	3.0	37.1	8.2	42.0	13.2	46.0	9.5	45.2	-1.7	49.5	9.5	62.2	25.7	77.9	25.2

Source: U.S. Department of Labor, Bureau of Labor Statistics, Division of Industry Prices and Price Indexes. n.e.c. stands for not elsewhere classified. - indicates no data collected for period or unavailable.

Producer Price Index
Annual Averages, 1980-1988
Base 1982 = 100

Columns headed % show percentile change in the index from the previous period for which an index is available.

	1980		1981		1982		1983		1984		1985		1986		1987		1988	
	Index	%	Index	%	Index	%	Index	%	Index	%	Index	%	Index	%	Index	%	Index	%
Nonmetallic Mineral Products	88.4	13.9	96.7	9.4	100.0	3.4	101.6	1.6	105.4	3.7	108.6	3.0	110.0	1.3	110.0	0.0	111.2	1.1
Glass	-	-	-	-	-	-	104.0	-	105.6	1.5	104.7	-0.9	107.4	2.6	109.4	1.9	112.3	2.7
Concrete Ingredients and Related Products	88.4	12.3	95.6	8.1	100.0	4.6	101.1	1.1	105.1	4.0	108.5	3.2	109.4	0.8	110.4	0.9	112.0	1.4
Concrete Products	92.0	12.2	97.8	6.3	100.0	2.2	101.4	1.4	103.9	2.5	107.5	3.5	109.2	1.6	109.4	0.2	110.0	0.5
Clay Construction Products Ex. Refractories	88.8	6.2	95.8	7.9	100.0	4.4	106.5	6.5	110.0	3.3	113.5	3.2	118.0	4.0	121.4	2.9	124.9	2.9
Refractories	78.5	11.8	89.7	14.3	100.0	11.5	101.2	1.2	107.1	5.8	109.7	2.4	110.2	0.5	110.5	0.3	113.8	3.0
Asphalt Felts and Coatings	99.6	21.9	102.3	2.7	100.0	-2.2	96.4	-3.6	100.3	4.0	102.6	2.3	97.9	-4.6	92.4	-5.6	94.7	2.5
Gypsum Products	100.1	1.6	100.1	0.0	100.0	-0.1	111.7	11.7	135.4	21.2	132.3	-2.3	137.0	3.6	125.2	-8.6	112.9	-9.8
Glass Containers	82.3	12.1	92.5	12.4	100.0	8.1	99.1	-0.9	101.4	2.3	106.8	5.3	111.9	4.8	113.0	1.0	112.3	-0.6
Nonmetallic Minerals n.e.c.	83.6	25.7	98.3	17.6	100.0	1.7	101.8	1.8	106.0	4.1	110.5	4.2	110.2	-0.3	110.3	0.1	112.9	2.4
Transportation Equipment	82.9	10.1	94.3	13.8	100.0	6.0	102.8	2.8	105.2	2.3	107.9	2.6	110.5	2.4	112.5	1.8	114.3	1.6
Motor Vehicles and Equipment	83.1	9.6	94.6	13.8	100.0	5.7	102.2	2.2	104.1	1.9	106.4	2.2	109.1	2.5	111.7	2.4	113.1	1.3
Aircraft and Aircraft Equipment	-	-	-	-	-	-	-	-	-	-	-	-	123.8	-	123.3	-0.4	126.0	2.2
Ships and Boats	-	-	-	-	100.0	-	103.0	3.0	107.3	4.2	110.3	2.8	113.4	2.8	114.1	0.6	115.1	0.9
Railroad Equipment	90.4	13.0	97.0	7.3	100.0	3.1	101.1	1.1	102.6	1.5	104.9	2.2	105.4	0.5	104.7	-0.7	107.5	2.7
Transportation Equipment n.e.c.	-	-	-	-	-	-	-	-	-	-	-	-	100.2	-	102.0	1.8	106.1	4.0
Miscellaneous Products	93.6	24.0	96.1	2.7	100.0	4.1	104.8	4.8	107.0	2.1	109.4	2.2	111.6	2.0	114.9	3.0	120.2	4.6
Toys, Sporting Goods, Small Arms, Etc.	89.7	12.7	95.7	6.7	100.0	4.5	101.7	1.7	102.6	0.9	104.5	1.9	106.6	2.0	107.8	1.1	111.8	3.7
Tobacco Products, Incl. Stemmed & Redried	76.0	12.8	83.1	9.3	100.0	20.3	113.1	13.1	123.3	9.0	132.5	7.5	142.5	7.5	154.7	8.6	171.9	11.1
Notions	78.4	13.1	93.8	19.6	100.0	6.6	101.1	1.1	102.3	1.2	102.9	0.6	103.7	0.8	105.2	1.4	107.9	2.6
Photographic Equipment and Supplies	96.4	32.1	99.8	3.5	100.0	0.2	102.5	2.5	102.0	-0.5	102.6	0.6	104.0	1.4	105.4	1.3	107.2	1.7
Mobile Homes	-	-	96.9	-	100.0	3.2	100.9	0.9	100.9	0.0	101.7	0.8	102.8	1.1	104.3	1.5	109.3	4.8
Medical, Surgical & Personal Aid Devices	-	-	-	-	-	-	103.8	-	108.3	4.3	109.0	0.6	111.8	2.6	117.0	4.7	118.9	1.6
Industrial Safety Equipment	89.6	7.6	95.3	6.4	100.0	4.9	103.0	3.0	106.9	3.8	111.3	4.1	121.0	8.7	129.1	6.7	136.7	5.9
Mining Services	-	-	-	-	-	-	-	-	-	-	-	-	91.3	-	87.3	-4.4	90.6	3.8
Miscellaneous Products n.e.c.	107.4	37.9	102.7	-4.4	100.0	-2.6	104.0	4.0	103.6	-0.4	103.4	-0.2	104.8	1.4	108.0	3.1	111.0	2.8

Source: U.S. Department of Labor, Bureau of Labor Statistics, Division of Industry Prices and Price Indexes. n.e.c. stands for not elsewhere classified. - indicates no data collected for period or unavailable.

Producer Price Index
Annual Averages, 1989-1993
Base 1982 = 100

Columns headed % show percentile change in the index from the previous period for which an index is available.

	1989		1990		1991		1992		1993									
	Index	%	Index	%	Index	%	Index	%	Index	%	Index	%	Index	%	Index	%	Index	%
Nonmetallic Mineral Products	112.6	1.3	114.7	1.9	117.2	2.2	117.3	0.1	120.0	2.3								
Glass	113.2	0.8	113.8	0.5	114.4	0.5	115.7	1.1	117.2	1.3								
Concrete Ingredients and Related Products	113.2	1.1	115.3	1.9	118.4	2.7	119.4	0.8	123.5	3.4								
Concrete Products	111.2	1.1	113.5	2.1	116.6	2.7	117.2	0.5	120.1	2.5								
Clay Construction Products Ex. Refractories	127.0	1.7	129.9	2.3	130.2	0.2	132.0	1.4	135.1	2.3								
Refractories	119.4	4.9	122.3	2.4	125.4	2.5	126.4	0.8	127.2	0.6								
Asphalt Felts and Coatings	95.8	1.2	97.1	1.4	98.2	1.1	96.2	-2.0	96.9	0.7								
Gypsum Products	110.0	-2.6	105.2	-4.4	99.3	-5.6	99.9	0.6	108.4	8.5								
Glass Containers	115.2	2.6	120.4	4.5	125.4	4.2	125.1	-0.2	125.9	0.6								
Nonmetallic Minerals n.e.c.	114.2	1.2	116.0	1.6	118.4	2.1	116.4	-1.7	119.2	2.4								
Transportation Equipment	117.7	3.0	121.5	3.2	126.4	4.0	130.4	3.2	133.7	2.5								
Motor Vehicles and Equipment	116.2	2.7	118.2	1.7	122.1	3.3	124.9	2.3	128.0	2.5								
Aircraft and Aircraft Equipment	129.9	3.1	136.8	5.3	144.3	5.5	151.3	4.9	154.8	2.3								
Ships and Boats	120.1	4.3	125.4	4.4	130.3	3.9	137.4	5.4	143.3	4.3								
Railroad Equipment	114.0	6.0	118.6	4.0	122.2	3.0	123.7	1.2	125.2	1.2								
Transportation Equipment n.e.c.	109.8	3.5	111.6	1.6	113.6	1.8	114.7	1.0	115.6	0.8								
Miscellaneous Products	126.5	5.2	134.2	6.1	140.8	4.9	145.3	3.2	145.5	0.1								
Toys, Sporting Goods, Small Arms, Etc.	116.7	4.4	119.6	2.5	122.6	2.5	124.6	1.6	125.4	0.6								
Tobacco Products, Incl. Stemmed & Redried	194.8	13.3	221.4	13.7	249.7	12.8	275.3	10.3	260.1	-5.5								
Notions	112.4	4.2	115.8	3.0	117.9	1.8	119.3	1.2	120.4	0.9								
Photographic Equipment and Supplies	114.3	6.6	118.4	3.6	118.1	-0.3	118.6	0.4	118.6	0.0								
Mobile Homes	114.0	4.3	117.5	3.1	120.4	2.5	121.7	1.1	128.6	5.7								
Medical, Surgical & Personal Aid Devices	123.0	3.4	127.3	3.5	130.3	2.4	133.9	2.8	137.9	3.0								
Industrial Safety Equipment	144.2	5.5	149.7	3.8	157.7	5.3	163.6	3.7	166.5	1.8								
Mining Services	90.9	0.3	95.5	5.1	98.6	3.2	95.1	-3.5	99.9	5.0								
Miscellaneous Products n.e.c.	114.0	2.7	117.7	3.2	120.5	2.4	122.4	1.6	125.3	2.4								

Source: U.S. Department of Labor, Bureau of Labor Statistics, Division of Industry Prices and Price Indexes. n.e.c. stands for not elsewhere classified. - indicates no data collected for period or unavailable.

FARM PRODUCTS
Producer Price Index
Base 1982 = 100

For 1913-1993. Columns headed % show percentile change in the index from the previous period for which an index is available.

Year	Jan Index	%	Feb Index	%	Mar Index	%	Apr Index	%	May Index	%	Jun Index	%	Jul Index	%	Aug Index	%	Sep Index	%	Oct Index	%	Nov Index	%	Dec Index	%
1913	17.6	-	17.5	-0.6	17.6	0.6	17.5	-0.6	17.4	-0.6	17.6	1.1	18.1	2.8	18.2	0.6	18.8	3.3	18.8	0.0	18.9	0.5	18.5	-2.1
1914	18.4	-0.5	18.3	-0.5	18.2	-0.5	18.0	-1.1	18.0	0.0	18.1	0.6	18.0	-0.6	18.3	1.7	17.9	-2.2	17.2	-3.9	17.6	2.3	17.4	-1.1
1915	18.1	4.0	18.4	1.7	17.9	-2.7	18.2	1.7	18.2	0.0	17.7	-2.7	18.1	2.3	17.9	-1.1	17.5	-2.2	18.1	3.4	18.0	-0.6	18.4	2.2
1916	19.4	5.4	19.4	0.0	19.4	0.0	19.6	1.0	19.8	1.0	19.7	-0.5	20.3	3.0	21.7	6.9	22.6	4.1	23.7	4.9	25.3	6.8	25.0	-1.2
1917	26.2	4.8	27.2	3.8	28.6	5.1	31.6	10.5	33.6	6.3	33.8	0.6	34.0	0.6	34.6	1.8	34.3	-0.9	35.2	2.6	36.0	2.3	35.6	-1.1
1918	37.0	3.9	37.1	0.3	37.3	0.5	36.6	-1.9	35.4	-3.3	35.4	0.0	37.0	4.5	38.6	4.3	39.6	2.6	38.2	-3.5	38.0	-0.5	38.1	0.3
1919	38.9	2.1	37.5	-3.6	38.5	2.7	40.0	3.9	40.9	2.2	39.6	-3.2	41.5	4.8	41.3	-0.5	38.7	-6.3	38.5	-0.5	40.3	4.7	41.8	3.7
1920	43.0	2.9	41.2	-4.2	41.5	0.7	42.5	2.4	42.8	0.7	42.3	-1.2	40.5	-4.3	37.8	-6.7	36.4	-3.7	32.2	-11.5	30.0	-6.8	26.4	-12.0
1921	25.6	-3.0	23.4	-8.6	22.7	-3.0	20.9	-7.9	21.0	0.5	20.3	-3.3	21.8	7.4	22.5	3.2	22.7	0.9	22.7	0.0	22.1	-2.6	22.2	0.5
1922	22.2	0.0	24.0	8.1	23.6	-1.7	23.4	-0.8	23.8	1.7	23.4	-1.7	24.1	3.0	23.0	-4.6	23.3	1.3	23.8	2.1	24.7	3.8	25.0	1.2
1923	25.1	0.4	25.3	0.8	25.3	0.0	24.8	-2.0	24.4	-1.6	24.2	-0.8	23.7	-2.1	24.2	2.1	25.3	4.5	25.4	0.4	25.7	1.2	25.5	-0.8
1924	25.6	0.4	25.0	-2.3	24.2	-3.2	24.6	1.7	24.0	-2.4	23.8	-0.8	24.9	4.6	25.7	3.2	25.3	-1.6	26.0	2.8	26.2	0.8	27.3	4.2
1925	28.7	5.1	28.4	-1.0	28.5	0.4	27.1	-4.9	27.1	0.0	27.6	1.8	28.3	2.5	28.1	-0.7	27.7	-1.4	27.0	-2.5	27.3	1.1	26.6	-2.6
1926	27.1	1.9	26.5	-2.2	25.7	-3.0	26.0	1.2	25.8	-0.8	25.5	-1.2	24.9	-2.4	24.6	-1.2	25.1	2.0	24.7	-1.6	23.9	-3.2	24.0	0.4
1927	24.3	1.3	24.1	-0.8	23.8	-1.2	23.8	0.0	24.3	2.1	24.3	0.0	24.6	1.2	25.8	4.9	26.7	3.5	26.5	-0.7	26.3	-0.8	26.3	0.0
1928	26.8	1.9	26.4	-1.5	26.1	-1.1	27.1	3.8	27.7	2.2	26.9	-2.9	27.4	1.9	27.0	-1.5	27.5	1.9	26.1	-5.1	25.7	-1.5	26.2	1.9
1929	26.7	1.9	26.6	-0.4	27.1	1.9	26.5	-2.2	25.8	-2.6	26.1	1.2	27.1	3.8	27.1	0.0	26.9	-0.7	26.2	-2.6	25.5	-2.7	25.7	0.8
1930	25.5	-0.8	24.7	-3.1	23.9	-3.2	24.2	1.3	23.5	-2.9	22.5	-4.3	21.0	-6.7	21.4	1.9	21.5	0.5	20.8	-3.3	20.0	-3.8	19.0	-5.0
1931	18.4	-3.2	17.7	-3.8	17.8	0.6	17.7	-0.6	16.9	-4.5	16.5	-2.4	16.4	-0.6	16.1	-1.8	15.3	-5.0	14.8	-3.3	14.8	0.0	14.1	-4.7
1932	13.3	-5.7	12.8	-3.8	12.7	-0.8	12.4	-2.4	11.8	-4.8	11.6	-1.7	12.1	4.3	12.4	2.5	12.4	0.0	11.8	-4.8	11.8	0.0	11.1	-5.9
1933	10.8	-2.7	10.3	-4.6	10.8	4.9	11.2	3.7	12.7	13.4	13.4	5.5	15.2	13.4	14.6	-3.9	14.4	-1.4	14.1	-2.1	14.3	1.4	14.0	-2.1
1934	14.8	5.7	15.5	4.7	15.5	0.0	15.1	-2.6	15.1	0.0	16.0	6.0	16.3	1.9	17.6	8.0	18.5	5.1	17.8	-3.8	17.8	0.0	18.2	2.2
1935	19.6	7.7	20.0	2.0	19.7	-1.5	20.3	3.0	20.3	0.0	19.8	-2.5	19.5	-1.5	20.0	2.6	20.1	0.5	19.7	-2.0	19.6	-0.5	19.8	1.0
1936	19.7	-0.5	20.1	2.0	19.3	-4.0	19.4	0.5	19.0	-2.1	19.7	3.7	20.5	4.1	21.2	3.4	21.2	0.0	21.2	0.0	21.5	1.4	22.4	4.2
1937	23.1	3.1	23.1	0.0	23.8	3.0	23.3	-2.1	22.7	-2.6	22.3	-1.8	22.6	1.3	21.8	-3.5	21.7	-0.5	20.3	-6.5	19.1	-5.9	18.4	-3.7
1938	18.1	-1.6	17.6	-2.8	17.7	0.6	17.2	-2.8	17.0	-1.2	17.3	1.8	17.5	1.2	17.0	-2.9	17.2	1.2	16.8	-2.3	17.1	1.8	17.0	-0.6
1939	17.0	0.0	16.9	-0.6	16.6	-1.8	16.1	-3.0	16.1	0.0	15.7	-2.5	15.8	0.6	15.4	-2.5	17.3	12.3	16.9	-2.3	17.0	0.6	17.1	0.6
1940	17.4	1.8	17.3	-0.6	17.1	-1.2	17.5	2.3	17.1	-2.3	16.7	-2.3	16.8	0.6	16.5	-1.8	16.7	1.2	16.8	0.6	17.2	2.4	17.6	2.3
1941	18.1	2.8	17.7	-2.2	18.1	2.3	18.8	3.9	19.3	2.7	20.7	7.3	21.7	4.8	22.1	1.8	23.0	4.1	22.7	-1.3	22.9	0.9	23.9	4.4
1942	25.5	6.7	25.6	0.4	26.0	1.6	26.4	1.5	26.3	-0.4	26.3	0.0	26.6	1.1	26.8	0.8	27.2	1.5	27.5	1.1	27.9	1.5	28.7	2.9
1943	29.5	2.8	30.0	1.7	31.0	3.3	31.2	0.6	31.7	1.6	31.9	0.6	31.5	-1.3	31.2	-1.0	31.0	-0.6	30.9	-0.3	30.6	-1.0	30.7	0.3
1944	30.7	0.0	30.9	0.7	31.2	1.0	31.1	-0.3	31.0	-0.3	31.5	1.6	31.3	-0.6	30.9	-1.3	31.0	0.3	31.2	0.6	31.4	0.6	31.6	0.6
1945	31.9	0.9	32.1	0.6	32.1	0.0	32.5	1.2	32.8	0.9	32.9	0.3	32.5	-1.2	32.0	-1.5	31.4	-1.9	32.1	2.2	33.1	3.1	33.2	0.3
1946	32.7	-1.5	33.0	0.9	33.6	1.8	34.1	1.5	34.7	1.8	35.4	2.0	39.6	11.9	40.6	2.5	39.0	-3.9	41.7	6.9	42.8	2.6	42.4	-0.9
1947	41.6	-1.9	42.6	2.4	45.5	6.8	44.0	-3.3	43.6	-0.9	43.8	0.5	44.3	1.1	44.8	1.1	46.6	4.0	47.4	1.7	47.7	0.6	50.1	5.0
1948	51.2	2.2	47.7	-6.8	47.6	-0.2	48.3	1.5	49.4	2.3	50.4	2.0	50.2	-0.4	49.6	-1.2	48.8	-1.6	46.9	-3.9	46.3	-1.3	45.2	-2.4
1949	43.8	-3.1	42.0	-4.1	42.7	1.7	42.7	0.0	42.7	0.0	41.8	-2.1	41.7	-0.2	41.7	0.0	41.8	0.2	41.0	-1.9	40.9	-0.2	40.3	-1.5
1950	40.1	-0.5	41.0	2.2	41.7	1.7	41.5	-0.5	42.6	2.7	42.7	0.2	45.3	6.1	45.8	1.1	46.5	1.5	45.6	-1.9	47.1	3.3	48.8	3.6
1951	50.8	4.1	52.9	4.1	53.1	0.4	53.1	0.0	52.3	-1.5	51.5	-1.5	50.2	-2.5	49.9	-0.6	49.7	-0.4	50.4	1.4	50.6	0.4	50.3	-0.6
1952	49.7	-1.2	48.7	-2.0	48.9	0.4	49.1	0.4	48.8	-0.6	48.4	-0.8	49.8	2.9	49.7	-0.2	48.2	-3.0	47.4	-1.7	46.8	-1.3	44.8	-4.3
1953	45.0	0.4	44.2	-1.8	45.1	2.0	43.9	-2.7	44.2	0.7	43.1	-2.5	44.2	2.6	43.5	-1.6	44.3	1.8	43.0	-2.9	42.3	-1.6	42.7	0.9
1954	44.2	3.5	44.1	-0.2	44.4	0.7	44.9	1.1	44.2	-1.6	42.8	-3.2	43.4	1.4	43.3	-0.2	42.3	-2.3	42.0	-0.7	42.1	0.2	40.6	-3.6
1955	41.8	3.0	42.0	0.5	41.6	-1.0	42.5	2.2	41.2	-3.1	41.5	0.7	40.4	-2.7	39.8	-1.5	40.4	1.5	39.2	-3.0	38.0	-3.1	37.5	-1.3
1956	38.0	1.3	38.9	2.4	39.1	0.5	39.8	1.8	41.1	3.3	41.2	0.2	40.7	-1.2	40.3	-1.0	40.7	1.0	39.9	-2.0	39.7	-0.5	40.1	1.0
1957	40.4	0.7	40.1	-0.7	40.1	0.0	40.9	2.0	40.4	-1.2	41.1	1.7	41.9	1.9	42.0	0.2	41.1	-2.1	41.3	0.5	41.5	0.5	41.8	0.7

[Continued]

FARM PRODUCTS
Producer Price Index
Base 1982 = 100
[Continued]

For 1913-1993. Columns headed % show percentile change in the index from the previous period for which an index is available.

Year	Jan Index	%	Feb Index	%	Mar Index	%	Apr Index	%	May Index	%	Jun Index	%	Jul Index	%	Aug Index	%	Sep Index	%	Oct Index	%	Nov Index	%	Dec Index	%
1958	42.3	1.2	43.4	2.6	45.4	4.6	44.1	-2.9	44.5	0.9	43.2	-2.9	42.9	-0.7	42.1	-1.9	42.0	-0.2	41.7	-0.7	41.6	-0.2	40.9	-1.7
1959	41.3	1.0	41.2	-0.2	41.0	-0.5	41.8	2.0	41.0	-1.9	40.6	-1.0	39.9	-1.7	39.4	-1.3	40.1	1.8	39.1	-2.5	38.6	-1.3	38.8	0.5
1960	39.1	0.8	39.3	0.5	40.8	3.8	41.2	1.0	40.8	-1.0	40.2	-1.5	40.1	-0.2	39.1	-2.5	39.6	1.3	40.4	2.0	40.6	0.5	40.1	-1.2
1961	40.5	1.0	40.7	0.5	40.6	-0.2	40.0	-1.5	39.2	-2.0	38.5	-1.8	39.4	2.3	40.0	1.5	39.4	-1.5	39.4	0.0	39.6	0.5	39.7	0.3
1962	40.5	2.0	40.6	0.2	40.7	0.2	40.1	-1.5	39.8	-0.7	39.4	-1.0	39.9	1.3	40.4	1.3	41.6	3.0	40.8	-1.9	41.1	0.7	40.3	-1.9
1963	40.8	1.2	39.9	-2.2	39.5	-1.0	39.5	0.0	39.1	-1.0	39.3	0.5	40.1	2.0	39.9	-0.5	39.5	-1.0	39.4	-0.3	39.8	1.0	38.6	-3.0
1964	39.9	3.4	39.1	-2.0	39.4	0.8	39.1	-0.8	38.8	-0.8	38.6	-0.5	39.0	1.0	38.7	-0.8	39.6	2.3	38.8	-2.0	38.9	0.3	38.4	-1.3
1965	38.5	0.3	39.1	1.6	39.5	1.0	40.4	2.3	40.7	0.7	41.5	2.0	41.4	-0.2	41.0	-1.0	41.2	0.5	41.1	-0.2	41.5	1.0	42.6	2.7
1966	43.2	1.4	44.4	2.8	44.2	-0.5	44.0	-0.5	43.2	-1.8	43.1	-0.2	44.6	3.5	44.7	0.2	45.0	0.7	43.2	-4.0	42.4	-1.9	42.1	-0.7
1967	42.5	1.0	41.8	-1.6	41.3	-1.2	40.4	-2.2	41.7	3.2	42.4	1.7	42.5	0.2	41.1	-3.3	40.7	-1.0	40.2	-1.2	39.9	-0.7	41.0	2.8
1968	41.0	0.0	41.9	2.2	42.3	1.0	42.3	0.0	42.9	1.4	42.4	-1.2	43.0	1.4	42.0	-2.3	42.5	1.2	41.9	-1.4	42.7	1.9	42.8	0.2
1969	43.4	1.4	43.5	0.2	44.1	1.4	43.9	-0.5	45.9	4.6	46.2	0.7	46.0	-0.4	45.1	-2.0	44.9	-0.4	44.6	-0.7	46.0	3.1	46.4	0.9
1970	46.6	0.4	47.0	0.9	47.3	0.6	46.0	-2.7	45.9	-0.2	46.0	0.2	46.8	1.7	44.8	-4.3	46.3	3.3	44.5	-3.9	44.1	-0.9	44.2	0.2
1971	44.9	1.6	47.0	4.7	46.6	-0.9	46.6	0.0	47.0	0.9	47.9	1.9	46.8	-2.3	46.7	-0.2	45.6	-2.4	45.9	0.7	46.3	0.9	47.8	3.2
1972	48.6	1.7	49.8	2.5	49.4	-0.8	49.1	-0.6	50.4	2.6	51.1	1.4	52.8	3.3	52.9	0.2	53.1	0.4	51.8	-2.4	53.1	2.5	56.7	6.8
1973	59.5	4.9	62.3	4.7	66.4	6.6	66.3	-0.2	70.3	6.0	75.2	7.0	71.5	-4.9	88.0	23.1	82.7	-6.0	77.7	-6.0	75.9	-2.3	77.3	1.8
1974	83.6	8.2	84.8	1.4	81.3	-4.1	76.8	-5.5	74.6	-2.9	69.6	-6.7	74.6	7.2	78.1	4.7	75.4	-3.5	77.4	2.7	77.5	0.1	75.8	-2.2
1975	74.1	-2.2	72.1	-2.7	70.6	-2.1	73.3	3.8	76.1	3.8	76.8	0.9	79.9	4.0	79.7	-0.3	81.3	2.0	81.4	0.1	79.1	-2.8	80.0	1.1
1976	79.5	-0.6	78.7	-1.0	77.0	-2.2	79.6	3.4	79.5	-0.1	81.1	2.0	81.2	0.1	78.3	-3.6	79.2	1.1	77.0	-2.8	75.7	-1.7	79.1	4.5
1977	79.8	0.9	82.1	2.9	83.5	1.7	85.9	2.9	84.3	-1.9	79.5	-5.7	78.5	-1.3	75.0	-4.5	75.1	0.1	75.1	0.0	76.6	2.0	77.7	1.4
1978	79.3	2.1	82.1	3.5	84.2	2.6	88.2	4.8	89.0	0.9	90.6	1.8	90.7	0.1	86.8	-4.3	88.8	2.3	90.5	1.9	90.0	-0.6	91.9	2.1
1979	95.0	3.4	99.4	4.6	100.2	0.8	101.5	1.3	101.2	-0.3	100.2	-1.0	101.8	1.6	98.4	-3.3	99.5	1.1	98.9	-0.6	99.1	0.2	100.1	1.0
1980	97.6	-2.5	100.0	2.5	98.7	-1.3	94.5	-4.3	96.3	1.9	96.3	0.0	104.9	8.9	108.9	3.8	110.2	1.2	108.8	-1.3	109.3	0.5	109.5	0.2
1981	109.1	-0.4	108.3	-0.7	107.6	-0.6	108.7	1.0	107.1	-1.5	107.6	0.5	108.7	1.0	106.4	-2.1	103.6	-2.6	100.3	-3.2	97.9	-2.4	96.8	-1.1
1982	99.9	3.2	102.0	2.1	101.0	-1.0	103.4	2.4	105.8	2.3	104.3	-1.4	101.8	-2.4	99.4	-2.4	96.8	-2.6	94.6	-2.3	95.2	0.6	96.0	0.8
1983	96.2	0.2	99.3	3.2	99.6	0.3	103.4	3.8	103.3	-0.1	102.1	-1.2	100.8	-1.3	104.6	3.8	105.8	1.1	105.3	-0.5	103.6	-1.6	104.8	1.2
1984	108.7	3.7	107.9	-0.7	110.3	2.2	109.5	-0.7	107.6	-1.7	106.1	-1.4	106.7	0.6	104.5	-2.1	103.1	-1.3	99.1	-3.9	101.4	2.3	101.4	0.0
1985	100.4	-1.0	101.2	0.8	98.5	-2.7	97.7	-0.8	95.1	-2.7	94.7	-0.4	94.6	-0.1	90.0	-4.9	87.8	-2.4	90.7	3.3	95.1	4.9	95.8	0.7
1986	93.8	-2.1	91.5	-2.5	90.9	-0.7	90.2	-0.8	93.7	3.9	91.8	-2.0	94.3	2.7	93.7	-0.6	92.5	-1.3	93.8	1.4	95.0	1.3	93.8	-1.3
1987	91.1	-2.9	92.0	1.0	92.2	0.2	95.7	3.8	99.9	4.4	98.8	-1.1	97.9	-0.9	95.7	-2.2	96.1	0.4	94.9	-1.2	96.3	1.5	95.7	-0.6
1988	97.3	1.7	97.9	0.6	98.2	0.3	99.2	1.0	102.2	3.0	106.8	4.5	109.1	2.2	109.3	0.2	111.6	2.1	110.9	-0.6	107.9	-2.7	108.9	0.9
1989	112.0	2.8	110.8	-1.1	113.8	2.7	111.0	-2.5	115.1	3.7	111.8	-2.9	110.5	-1.2	109.3	-1.1	108.0	-1.2	107.8	-0.2	109.0	1.1	111.5	2.3
1990	114.9	3.0	115.7	0.7	115.3	-0.3	113.3	-1.7	113.7	0.4	113.6	-0.1	113.8	0.2	111.4	-2.1	109.2	-2.0	109.5	0.3	108.5	-0.9	107.2	-1.2
1991	106.9	-0.3	106.9	0.0	109.7	2.6	109.6	-0.1	110.4	0.7	109.1	-1.2	105.6	-3.2	102.9	-2.6	103.1	0.2	101.5	-1.6	101.6	0.1	100.6	-1.0
1992	102.8	2.2	105.5	2.6	106.4	0.9	103.2	-3.0	105.8	2.5	104.7	-1.0	102.5	-2.1	102.2	-0.3	101.6	-0.6	102.7	1.1	101.8	-0.9	103.7	1.9
1993	104.3	0.6	104.4	0.1	106.4	1.9	109.7	3.1	111.0	1.2	104.3	-6.0	105.4	1.1	106.6	1.1	106.1	-0.5	104.1	-1.9	109.3	5.0	112.4	2.8

Source: U.S. Department of Labor, Bureau of Labor Statistics, Division of Industry Prices and Price Indexes. n.e.c. stands for not elsewhere classified. - indicates no data collected for period or unavailable.

Fresh and Dried Fruits and Vegetables
Producer Price Index
Base 1982 = 100

For 1926-1993. Columns headed % show percentile change in the index from the previous period for which an index is available.

Year	Jan Index	%	Feb Index	%	Mar Index	%	Apr Index	%	May Index	%	Jun Index	%	Jul Index	%	Aug Index	%	Sep Index	%	Oct Index	%	Nov Index	%	Dec Index	%
1926	29.4	-	28.9	-1.7	28.8	-0.3	32.4	12.5	29.7	-8.3	28.0	-5.7	24.1	-13.9	22.7	-5.8	24.4	7.5	26.1	7.0	25.1	-3.8	24.2	-3.6
1927	25.4	5.0	25.0	-1.6	23.6	-5.6	24.3	3.0	28.4	16.9	28.6	0.7	25.6	-10.5	26.3	2.7	24.7	-6.1	25.0	1.2	26.8	7.2	25.7	-4.1
1928	26.4	2.7	27.5	4.2	28.6	4.0	28.6	0.0	28.3	-1.0	26.7	-5.7	25.4	-4.9	25.0	-1.6	24.6	-1.6	22.6	-8.1	22.0	-2.7	21.8	-0.9
1929	22.5	3.2	21.5	-4.4	20.9	-2.8	21.3	1.9	22.6	6.1	25.3	11.9	28.1	11.1	29.6	5.3	29.6	0.0	29.3	-1.0	28.5	-2.7	28.9	1.4
1930	27.6	-4.5	27.4	-0.7	27.1	-1.1	29.8	10.0	30.3	1.7	30.2	-0.3	25.5	-15.6	23.1	-9.4	23.8	3.0	23.8	0.0	21.4	-10.1	19.0	-11.2
1931	19.6	3.2	18.6	-5.1	18.8	1.1	19.6	4.3	19.8	1.0	20.0	1.0	19.2	-4.0	19.0	-1.0	18.3	-3.7	17.3	-5.5	16.5	-4.6	15.9	-3.6
1932	15.5	-2.5	15.4	-0.6	15.5	0.6	15.5	0.0	15.2	-1.9	15.6	2.6	14.9	-4.5	13.6	-8.7	12.7	-6.6	12.5	-1.6	12.6	0.8	12.7	0.8
1933	12.9	1.6	12.7	-1.6	13.4	5.5	14.5	8.2	14.8	2.1	16.2	9.5	20.1	24.1	18.4	-8.5	16.8	-8.7	15.4	-8.3	15.1	-1.9	15.6	3.3
1934	17.2	10.3	18.4	7.0	18.3	-0.5	17.0	-7.1	17.1	0.6	17.7	3.5	17.0	-4.0	16.3	-4.1	16.2	-0.6	16.6	2.5	15.9	-4.2	14.9	-6.3
1935	15.0	0.7	15.3	2.0	15.1	-1.3	16.5	9.3	16.2	-1.8	17.1	5.6	16.0	-6.4	14.7	-8.1	14.6	-0.7	14.3	-2.1	15.7	9.8	15.9	1.3
1936	15.5	-2.5	15.5	0.0	16.3	5.2	17.2	5.5	18.6	8.1	22.0	18.3	21.1	-4.1	19.6	-7.1	18.1	-7.7	18.8	3.9	19.1	1.6	19.3	1.0
1937	21.5	11.4	23.4	8.8	23.0	-1.7	22.0	-4.3	22.2	0.9	22.2	0.0	17.9	-19.4	16.1	-10.1	15.7	-2.5	15.1	-3.8	14.8	-2.0	13.6	-8.1
1938	13.6	0.0	13.4	-1.5	13.2	-1.5	13.5	2.3	14.1	4.4	15.3	8.5	13.8	-9.8	13.6	-1.4	14.1	3.7	13.9	-1.4	16.0	15.1	15.5	-3.1
1939	15.5	0.0	15.9	2.6	16.2	1.9	16.5	1.9	16.3	-1.2	15.8	-3.1	15.7	-0.6	14.5	-7.6	15.8	9.0	14.9	-5.7	15.2	2.0	15.8	3.9
1940	15.0	-5.1	14.4	-4.0	14.5	0.7	16.9	16.6	18.1	7.1	19.6	8.3	17.9	-8.7	16.0	-10.6	15.3	-4.4	14.6	-4.6	15.1	3.4	15.4	2.0
1941	14.9	-3.2	14.7	-1.3	15.0	2.0	15.9	6.0	15.9	0.0	18.7	17.6	17.1	-8.6	17.1	0.0	17.3	1.2	18.8	8.7	18.2	-3.2	17.9	-1.6
1942	19.0	6.1	20.9	10.0	21.7	3.8	25.0	15.2	25.3	1.2	27.9	10.3	26.3	-5.7	26.0	-1.1	25.6	-1.5	25.7	0.4	26.9	4.7	27.7	3.0
1943	27.0	-2.5	29.0	7.4	31.4	8.3	33.9	8.0	38.7	14.2	40.6	4.9	38.7	-4.7	34.7	-10.3	31.7	-8.6	31.2	-1.6	32.3	3.5	32.6	0.9
1944	32.2	-1.2	33.0	2.5	33.9	2.7	34.9	2.9	35.0	0.3	38.6	10.3	36.0	-6.7	33.6	-6.7	31.3	-6.8	30.2	-3.5	30.6	1.3	31.4	2.6
1945	30.8	-1.9	32.0	3.9	31.3	-2.2	33.8	8.0	36.4	7.7	37.5	3.0	36.0	-4.0	34.1	-5.3	31.8	-6.7	31.4	-1.3	33.9	8.0	35.6	5.0
1946	34.5	-3.1	35.2	2.0	37.0	5.1	38.6	4.3	39.3	1.8	37.8	-3.8	35.8	-5.3	32.6	-8.9	30.9	-5.2	33.3	7.8	37.1	11.4	35.4	-4.6
1947	33.7	-4.8	35.4	5.0	38.2	7.9	38.2	0.0	39.3	2.9	37.1	-5.6	33.9	-8.6	34.5	1.8	34.0	-1.4	33.5	-1.5	37.1	10.7	37.2	0.3
1948	38.7	4.0	39.6	2.3	39.5	-0.3	42.1	6.6	43.5	3.3	38.2	-12.2	36.1	-5.5	35.4	-1.9	33.8	-4.5	33.9	0.3	34.7	2.4	33.9	-2.3
1949	37.6	10.9	38.2	1.6	37.8	-1.0	40.8	7.9	42.4	3.9	36.7	-13.4	36.0	-1.9	34.1	-5.3	33.0	-3.2	31.4	-4.8	33.8	7.6	33.4	-1.2
1950	33.0	-1.2	32.5	-1.5	33.3	2.5	35.4	6.3	35.2	-0.6	32.8	-6.8	34.9	6.4	32.9	-5.7	31.5	-4.3	30.6	-2.9	34.1	11.4	35.0	2.6
1951	33.2	-5.1	35.8	7.8	32.4	-9.5	36.0	11.1	38.0	5.6	34.5	-9.2	33.2	-3.8	32.7	-1.5	33.9	3.7	35.2	3.8	39.1	11.1	43.0	10.0
1952	44.4	3.3	41.2	-7.2	45.3	10.0	46.6	2.9	47.1	1.1	45.5	-3.4	46.9	3.1	45.5	-3.0	42.3	-7.0	40.8	-3.5	41.4	1.5	41.0	-1.0
1953	39.2	-4.4	37.4	-4.6	38.7	3.5	39.1	1.0	38.5	-1.5	40.2	4.4	34.7	-13.7	35.8	3.2	35.1	-2.0	34.5	-1.7	34.5	0.0	32.8	-4.9
1954	33.3	1.5	32.8	-1.5	32.8	0.0	35.6	8.5	38.2	7.3	35.4	-7.3	40.6	14.7	39.6	-2.5	36.5	-7.8	37.3	2.2	37.8	1.3	35.4	-6.3
1955	38.5	8.8	38.0	-1.3	38.2	0.5	44.2	15.7	43.4	-1.8	38.3	-11.8	36.1	-5.7	36.4	0.8	37.3	2.5	34.0	-8.8	37.5	10.3	35.0	-6.7
1956	38.4	9.7	35.9	-6.5	38.9	8.4	37.3	-4.1	40.9	9.7	44.0	7.6	40.9	-7.0	34.7	-15.2	34.8	0.3	35.7	2.6	38.2	7.0	37.5	-1.8
1957	36.8	-1.9	35.2	-4.3	34.4	-2.3	37.7	9.6	39.9	5.8	38.5	-3.5	39.5	2.6	38.9	-1.5	36.1	-7.2	39.4	9.1	38.9	-1.3	39.6	1.8
1958	44.2	11.6	46.4	5.0	52.1	12.3	47.3	-9.2	44.6	-5.7	37.3	-16.4	38.9	4.3	35.6	-8.5	35.8	0.6	37.1	3.6	35.9	-3.2	36.3	1.1
1959	37.5	3.3	38.7	3.2	34.2	-11.6	41.7	21.9	39.1	-6.2	36.9	-5.6	36.0	-2.4	33.9	-5.8	37.7	11.2	37.4	-0.8	37.8	1.1	39.5	4.5
1960	38.4	-2.8	36.7	-4.4	38.2	4.1	40.8	6.8	42.8	4.9	40.1	-6.3	41.3	3.0	36.1	-12.6	38.3	6.1	39.9	4.2	39.3	-1.5	36.4	-7.4
1961	37.9	4.1	36.5	-3.7	38.7	6.0	36.6	-5.4	37.1	1.4	37.8	1.9	38.2	1.1	35.6	-6.8	34.7	-2.5	34.6	-0.3	34.9	0.9	33.8	-3.2
1962	37.6	11.2	40.5	7.7	41.1	1.5	38.4	-6.6	41.5	8.1	38.3	-7.7	35.8	-6.5	35.3	-1.4	36.8	4.2	37.8	2.7	37.4	-1.1	34.3	-8.3
1963	40.4	17.8	37.4	-7.4	38.4	2.7	38.6	0.5	38.7	0.3	37.7	-2.6	37.6	-0.3	35.9	-4.5	34.1	-5.0	34.6	1.5	37.3	7.8	36.8	-1.3
1964	37.2	1.1	38.0	2.2	40.7	7.1	41.1	1.0	41.7	1.5	43.9	5.3	42.3	-3.6	38.0	-10.2	39.4	3.7	38.1	-3.3	41.9	10.0	38.4	-8.4
1965	38.2	-0.5	39.8	4.2	41.8	5.0	45.6	9.1	46.0	0.9	42.3	-8.0	40.3	-4.7	33.2	-17.6	37.3	12.3	37.1	-0.5	36.5	-1.6	35.8	-1.9
1966	37.8	5.6	38.0	0.5	39.5	3.9	43.1	9.1	40.1	-7.0	38.7	-3.5	41.5	7.2	37.9	-8.7	42.8	12.9	38.0	-11.2	40.4	6.3	39.3	-2.7
1967	39.5	0.5	40.6	2.8	38.3	-5.7	38.7	1.0	40.6	4.9	44.3	9.1	41.9	-5.4	37.5	-10.5	35.8	-4.5	35.6	-0.6	39.8	11.8	40.7	2.3
1968	41.9	2.9	43.5	3.8	44.3	1.8	43.4	-2.0	47.9	10.4	41.3	-13.8	42.0	1.7	37.8	-10.0	37.9	0.3	38.7	2.1	42.7	10.3	42.8	0.2
1969	43.8	2.3	42.8	-2.3	44.1	3.0	41.9	-5.0	49.7	18.6	44.2	-11.1	40.6	-8.1	41.5	2.2	40.2	-3.1	39.3	-2.2	48.6	23.7	43.6	-10.3
1970	45.3	3.9	45.6	0.7	45.9	0.7	43.7	-4.8	48.0	9.8	47.4	-1.2	43.6	-8.0	38.6	-11.5	44.0	14.0	39.7	-9.8	42.3	6.5	43.8	3.5

[Continued]

Fresh and Dried Fruits and Vegetables
Producer Price Index
Base 1982 = 100
[Continued]

For 1926-1993. Columns headed % show percentile change in the index from the previous period for which an index is available.

Year	Jan Index	%	Feb Index	%	Mar Index	%	Apr Index	%	May Index	%	Jun Index	%	Jul Index	%	Aug Index	%	Sep Index	%	Oct Index	%	Nov Index	%	Dec Index	%
1971	45.6	4.1	46.6	2.2	49.3	5.8	47.6	-3.4	50.2	5.5	53.7	7.0	43.1	-19.7	45.7	6.0	40.9	-10.5	45.6	11.5	50.1	9.9	49.8	-0.6
1972	49.2	-1.2	50.3	2.2	44.5	-11.5	46.3	4.0	47.5	2.6	48.0	1.1	51.2	6.7	54.7	6.8	54.4	-0.5	48.4	-11.0	55.9	15.5	53.1	-5.0
1973	59.6	12.2	57.9	-2.9	62.5	7.9	69.4	11.0	73.3	5.6	77.9	6.3	74.0	-5.0	63.9	-13.6	58.7	-8.1	63.9	8.9	66.3	3.8	67.6	2.0
1974	72.7	7.5	84.6	16.4	83.0	-1.9	89.5	7.8	93.3	4.2	80.6	-13.6	73.7	-8.6	64.1	-13.0	64.3	0.3	65.5	1.9	73.7	12.5	64.5	-12.5
1975	69.0	7.0	66.6	-3.5	64.6	-3.0	72.3	11.9	72.2	-0.1	81.5	12.9	82.2	0.9	70.8	-13.9	72.0	1.7	72.2	0.3	70.5	-2.4	75.0	6.4
1976	76.8	2.4	74.6	-2.9	72.7	-2.5	76.9	5.8	70.6	-8.2	63.3	-10.3	64.9	2.5	62.8	-3.2	71.0	13.1	75.9	6.9	65.7	-13.4	68.8	4.7
1977	78.3	13.8	83.9	7.2	86.4	3.0	81.1	-6.1	79.6	-1.8	69.5	-12.7	71.8	3.3	69.6	-3.1	72.1	3.6	74.1	2.8	76.3	3.0	66.8	-12.5
1978	77.5	16.0	80.5	3.9	79.3	-1.5	89.6	13.0	86.8	-3.1	90.8	4.6	99.5	9.6	84.9	-14.7	82.0	-3.4	84.4	2.9	81.6	-3.3	87.3	7.0
1979	92.1	5.5	103.7	12.6	92.9	-10.4	94.2	1.4	90.0	-4.5	89.2	-0.9	89.4	0.2	95.3	6.6	82.1	-13.9	85.9	4.6	85.3	-0.7	83.1	-2.6
1980	86.3	3.9	87.0	0.8	86.1	-1.0	88.0	2.2	96.2	9.3	92.1	-4.3	99.4	7.9	100.1	0.7	104.9	4.8	95.0	-9.4	97.2	2.3	96.6	-0.6
1981	102.0	5.6	107.0	4.9	115.4	7.9	112.8	-2.3	108.5	-3.8	103.8	-4.3	104.7	0.9	101.7	-2.9	99.7	-2.0	98.1	-1.6	100.1	2.0	110.6	10.5
1982	114.0	3.1	114.4	0.4	101.4	-11.4	105.5	4.0	107.0	1.4	104.3	-2.5	94.3	-9.6	94.1	-0.2	87.1	-7.4	87.9	0.9	92.0	4.7	98.1	6.6
1983	89.7	-8.6	89.8	0.1	92.6	3.1	105.1	13.5	102.5	-2.5	104.2	1.7	101.8	-2.3	106.6	4.7	108.8	2.1	121.5	11.7	108.5	-10.7	108.9	0.4
1984	114.8	5.4	123.1	7.2	121.4	-1.4	104.0	-14.3	99.3	-4.5	107.9	8.7	111.1	3.0	115.8	4.2	114.4	-1.2	105.4	-7.9	99.0	-6.1	99.3	0.3
1985	102.1	2.8	114.1	11.8	109.6	-3.9	109.6	0.0	99.0	-9.7	100.2	1.2	108.7	8.5	103.0	-5.2	93.9	-8.8	92.2	-1.8	94.6	2.6	105.3	11.3
1986	101.1	-4.0	92.5	-8.5	93.5	1.1	103.8	11.0	108.1	4.1	102.8	-4.9	105.2	2.3	104.5	-0.7	105.7	1.1	113.4	7.3	109.7	-3.3	107.3	-2.2
1987	98.4	-8.3	101.9	3.6	108.3	6.3	105.1	-3.0	104.5	-0.6	110.3	5.6	112.2	1.7	99.5	-11.3	102.5	3.0	101.5	-1.0	124.1	22.3	113.8	-8.3
1988	118.2	3.9	100.5	-15.0	101.5	1.0	101.0	-0.5	101.2	0.2	100.8	-0.4	109.9	9.0	105.9	-3.6	117.4	10.9	111.3	-5.2	119.0	6.9	114.7	-3.6
1989	109.4	-4.6	123.8	13.2	118.7	-4.1	115.3	-2.9	128.9	11.8	122.3	-5.1	120.8	-1.2	109.7	-9.2	101.8	-7.2	114.3	12.3	102.9	-10.0	106.7	3.7
1990	139.1	30.4	156.9	12.8	133.3	-15.0	106.9	-19.8	103.6	-3.1	106.9	3.2	117.3	9.7	107.4	-8.4	104.0	-3.2	109.0	4.8	119.3	9.4	106.7	-10.6
1991	109.8	2.9	111.4	1.5	113.3	1.7	124.4	9.8	141.9	14.1	137.0	-3.5	124.8	-8.9	110.9	-11.1	108.1	-2.5	98.1	-9.3	108.5	10.6	88.7	-18.2
1992	99.6	12.3	106.9	7.3	104.6	-2.2	92.7	-11.4	91.3	-1.5	83.3	-8.8	85.2	2.3	95.9	12.6	89.3	-6.9	105.2	17.8	102.0	-3.0	106.3	4.2
1993	103.7	-2.4	105.2	1.4	101.6	-3.4	118.3	16.4	120.8	2.1	93.9	-22.3	97.5	3.8	99.7	2.3	101.5	1.8	94.4	-7.0	114.6	21.4	121.4	5.9

Source: U.S. Department of Labor, Bureau of Labor Statistics, Division of Industry Prices and Price Indexes. n.e.c. stands for not elsewhere classified. - indicates no data collected for period or unavailable.

Grains

Producer Price Index
Base 1982 = 100

For 1926-1993. Columns headed % show percentile change in the index from the previous period for which an index is available.

Year	Jan Index	%	Feb Index	%	Mar Index	%	Apr Index	%	May Index	%	Jun Index	%	Jul Index	%	Aug Index	%	Sep Index	%	Oct Index	%	Nov Index	%	Dec Index	%
1926	37.9	-	36.5	-3.7	34.2	-6.3	34.7	1.5	33.7	-2.9	32.9	-2.4	33.9	3.0	32.2	-5.0	32.1	-0.3	32.8	2.2	31.5	-4.0	32.6	3.5
1927	32.3	-0.9	32.1	-0.6	31.3	-2.5	31.4	0.3	35.1	11.8	36.9	5.1	36.0	-2.4	36.5	1.4	34.7	-4.9	33.4	-3.7	33.6	0.6	34.4	2.4
1928	35.2	2.3	36.5	3.7	38.3	4.9	40.9	6.8	42.8	4.6	40.4	-5.6	37.5	-7.2	32.1	-14.4	32.8	2.2	32.6	-0.6	31.8	-2.5	31.8	0.0
1929	33.1	4.1	34.4	3.9	33.2	-3.5	31.8	-4.2	29.7	-6.6	30.6	3.0	34.4	12.4	33.4	-2.9	34.2	2.4	33.4	-2.3	32.0	-4.2	32.9	2.8
1930	31.6	-4.0	30.0	-5.1	28.1	-6.3	28.4	1.1	27.7	-2.5	26.4	-4.7	24.9	-5.7	27.1	8.8	25.9	-4.4	24.3	-6.2	21.5	-11.5	21.5	0.0
1931	21.1	-1.9	20.4	-3.3	20.0	-2.0	20.1	0.5	20.1	0.0	18.9	-6.0	16.5	-12.7	15.1	-8.5	14.8	-2.0	14.9	0.7	17.3	16.1	15.8	-8.7
1932	15.7	-0.6	15.5	-1.3	14.7	-5.2	15.0	2.0	14.4	-4.0	12.7	-11.8	12.3	-3.1	12.9	4.9	12.6	-2.3	11.6	-7.9	11.1	-4.3	10.7	-3.6
1933	11.0	2.8	11.0	0.0	12.1	10.0	15.1	24.8	17.7	17.2	19.3	9.0	24.8	28.5	21.8	-12.1	21.5	-1.4	19.6	-8.8	20.6	5.1	20.4	-1.0
1934	21.4	4.9	21.3	-0.5	20.9	-1.9	19.8	-5.3	21.5	8.6	24.4	13.5	25.1	2.9	29.0	15.5	29.7	2.4	28.6	-3.7	29.3	2.4	30.8	5.1
1935	29.9	-2.9	29.4	-1.7	27.9	-5.1	29.6	6.1	28.1	-5.1	25.9	-7.8	26.4	1.9	26.7	1.1	28.1	5.2	29.1	3.6	26.2	-10.0	25.8	-1.5
1936	26.6	3.1	26.3	-1.1	25.4	-3.4	24.9	-2.0	23.8	-4.4	24.6	3.4	29.9	21.5	34.5	15.4	34.4	-0.3	34.4	0.0	34.7	0.9	36.7	5.8
1937	38.1	3.8	37.6	-1.3	38.1	1.3	40.1	5.2	38.3	-4.5	35.5	-7.3	35.4	-0.3	31.0	-12.4	31.0	0.0	25.9	-16.5	23.3	-10.0	24.1	3.4
1938	25.3	5.0	24.6	-2.8	23.2	-5.7	22.2	-4.3	21.1	-5.0	21.1	0.0	19.6	-7.1	18.0	-8.2	17.9	-0.6	17.1	-4.5	17.1	0.0	18.3	7.0
1939	19.0	3.8	18.4	-3.2	18.3	-0.5	18.6	1.6	20.1	8.1	19.6	-2.5	17.6	-10.2	17.4	-1.1	21.9	25.9	20.8	-5.0	21.6	3.8	24.2	12.0
1940	24.8	2.5	24.5	-1.2	24.8	1.2	26.0	4.8	23.9	-8.1	21.7	-9.2	20.5	-5.5	20.0	-2.4	20.8	4.0	22.0	5.8	22.8	3.6	22.5	-1.3
1941	22.8	1.3	21.7	-4.8	22.8	5.1	23.9	4.8	25.1	5.0	25.6	2.0	25.7	0.4	26.8	4.3	28.7	7.1	27.4	-4.5	28.4	3.6	30.6	7.7
1942	32.3	5.6	32.1	-0.6	31.6	-1.6	30.8	-2.5	31.1	1.0	29.9	-3.9	30.0	0.3	30.3	1.0	31.5	4.0	30.8	-2.2	31.2	1.3	33.9	8.7
1943	36.1	6.5	36.6	1.4	37.8	3.3	37.8	0.0	38.1	0.8	38.3	0.5	39.1	2.1	39.4	0.8	40.3	2.3	41.3	2.5	41.5	0.5	43.2	4.1
1944	43.6	0.9	43.6	0.0	43.6	0.0	43.6	0.0	43.7	0.2	42.8	-2.1	42.2	-1.4	41.3	-2.1	41.0	-0.7	42.2	2.9	42.0	-0.5	43.0	2.4
1945	43.6	1.4	43.7	0.2	43.7	0.0	43.9	0.5	43.5	-0.9	43.8	0.7	43.3	-1.1	42.5	-1.8	42.7	0.5	43.8	2.6	44.8	2.3	44.9	0.2
1946	45.0	0.2	45.1	0.2	46.0	2.0	46.1	0.2	49.9	8.2	51.1	2.4	61.0	19.4	56.9	-6.7	57.4	0.9	58.7	2.3	55.7	-5.1	54.9	-1.4
1947	54.8	-0.2	57.7	5.3	68.9	19.4	67.9	-1.5	69.1	1.8	69.1	0.0	67.5	-2.3	70.0	3.7	77.2	10.3	81.4	5.4	83.2	2.2	85.5	2.8
1948	86.9	1.6	74.3	-14.5	73.5	-1.1	73.5	0.0	72.1	-1.9	69.9	-3.1	63.6	-9.0	60.1	-5.5	59.3	-1.3	57.5	-3.0	57.9	0.7	57.9	0.0
1949	56.8	-1.9	53.6	-5.6	55.5	3.5	55.9	0.7	54.6	-2.3	52.4	-4.0	52.0	-0.8	51.3	-1.3	53.5	4.3	53.4	-0.2	53.7	0.6	55.0	2.4
1950	54.8	-0.4	55.2	0.7	56.7	2.7	57.9	2.1	58.9	1.7	57.4	-2.5	58.8	2.4	56.9	-3.2	56.6	-0.5	56.6	0.0	58.5	3.4	61.5	5.1
1951	63.7	3.6	65.5	2.8	64.2	-2.0	64.2	0.0	63.0	-1.9	60.7	-3.7	60.4	-0.5	61.4	1.7	61.9	0.8	64.8	4.7	66.5	2.6	67.3	1.2
1952	66.3	-1.5	65.2	-1.7	65.3	0.2	64.6	-1.1	63.3	-2.0	61.1	-3.5	60.8	-0.5	62.1	2.1	62.1	0.0	60.8	-2.1	61.8	1.6	61.5	-0.5
1953	60.6	-1.5	59.7	-1.5	60.7	1.7	60.1	-1.0	59.8	-0.5	54.0	-9.7	54.7	1.3	55.4	1.3	56.6	2.2	56.3	-0.5	57.2	1.6	58.0	1.4
1954	58.5	0.9	58.7	0.3	59.6	1.5	59.5	-0.2	58.4	-1.8	55.4	-5.1	56.4	1.8	58.4	3.5	60.0	2.7	59.5	-0.8	59.9	0.7	59.2	-1.2
1955	59.9	1.2	59.7	-0.3	59.0	-1.2	58.3	-1.2	59.2	1.5	57.9	-2.2	55.5	-4.1	50.4	-9.2	52.2	3.6	52.8	1.1	51.1	-3.2	53.0	3.7
1956	52.2	-1.5	53.1	1.7	54.1	1.9	57.3	5.9	57.9	1.0	55.7	-3.8	56.6	1.6	56.9	0.5	58.1	2.1	53.8	-7.4	56.3	4.6	56.9	1.1
1957	57.3	0.7	55.8	-2.6	56.0	0.4	55.9	-0.2	54.7	-2.1	53.7	-1.8	53.0	-1.3	52.8	-0.4	52.0	-1.5	51.6	-0.8	51.8	0.4	51.6	-0.4
1958	50.6	-1.9	51.2	1.2	52.7	2.9	54.9	4.2	54.0	-1.6	52.1	-3.5	51.1	-1.9	49.5	-3.1	48.7	-1.6	49.2	1.0	48.2	-2.0	48.7	1.0
1959	48.7	0.0	49.3	1.2	49.8	1.0	51.1	2.6	50.4	-1.4	50.1	-0.6	50.1	0.0	49.8	-0.6	48.8	-2.0	48.5	-0.6	49.0	1.0	48.7	-0.6
1960	49.5	1.6	49.1	-0.8	50.1	2.0	50.9	1.6	49.8	-2.2	49.6	-0.4	48.4	-2.4	47.6	-1.7	48.0	0.8	47.0	-2.1	45.0	-4.3	46.6	3.6
1961	48.2	3.4	48.7	1.0	49.0	0.6	47.3	-3.5	47.9	1.3	47.5	-0.8	49.8	4.8	50.0	0.4	50.0	0.0	49.9	-0.2	50.8	1.8	50.6	-0.4
1962	50.0	-1.2	49.7	-0.6	50.1	0.8	50.6	1.0	51.9	2.6	51.4	-1.0	51.0	-0.8	50.5	-1.0	50.7	0.4	50.6	-0.2	51.2	1.2	52.0	1.6
1963	52.4	0.8	53.0	1.1	53.3	0.6	54.1	1.5	52.9	-2.2	52.2	-1.3	51.2	-1.9	50.6	-1.2	52.9	4.5	52.3	-1.1	51.6	-1.3	52.3	1.4
1964	53.4	2.1	52.4	-1.9	51.0	-2.7	53.1	4.1	53.1	0.0	46.2	-13.0	44.1	-4.5	44.1	0.0	46.4	5.2	45.7	-1.5	45.2	-1.1	46.3	2.4
1965	46.5	0.4	46.6	0.2	46.6	0.0	46.9	0.6	46.8	-0.2	46.1	-1.5	45.5	-1.3	45.4	-0.2	45.9	1.1	45.6	-0.7	45.0	-1.3	46.3	2.9
1966	47.5	2.6	47.8	0.6	46.7	-2.3	46.9	0.4	48.1	2.6	48.8	1.5	53.0	8.6	54.3	2.5	53.8	-0.9	50.9	-5.4	50.4	-1.0	52.2	3.6
1967	51.8	-0.8	49.3	-4.8	51.4	4.3	50.5	-1.8	50.4	-0.2	49.4	-2.0	47.6	-3.6	44.3	-6.9	44.0	-0.7	44.5	1.1	41.8	-6.1	43.9	5.0
1968	43.7	-0.5	44.4	1.6	43.8	-1.4	43.6	-0.5	44.4	1.8	42.2	-5.0	41.2	-2.4	38.6	-6.3	39.4	2.1	40.5	2.8	42.2	4.2	41.3	-2.1
1969	42.4	2.7	42.2	-0.5	42.0	-0.5	42.7	1.7	44.6	4.4	44.0	-1.3	43.1	-2.0	42.1	-2.3	42.9	1.9	43.6	1.6	42.0	-3.7	42.6	1.4
1970	44.2	3.8	44.2	0.0	44.0	-0.5	45.1	2.5	45.5	0.9	45.9	0.9	45.9	0.0	45.9	0.0	51.7	12.6	49.4	-4.4	49.4	0.0	51.2	3.6

[Continued]

Grains

Producer Price Index
Base 1982 = 100
[Continued]

For 1926-1993. Columns headed % show percentile change in the index from the previous period for which an index is available.

Year	Jan Index	%	Feb Index	%	Mar Index	%	Apr Index	%	May Index	%	Jun Index	%	Jul Index	%	Aug Index	%	Sep Index	%	Oct Index	%	Nov Index	%	Dec Index	%
1971	52.6	2.7	53.0	0.8	51.4	-3.0	50.7	-1.4	50.8	0.2	51.9	2.2	48.6	-6.4	44.0	-9.5	42.2	-4.1	41.9	-0.7	41.6	-0.7	45.3	8.9
1972	44.6	-1.5	44.1	-1.1	44.5	0.9	45.5	2.2	46.2	1.5	44.8	-3.0	45.7	2.0	47.3	3.5	51.9	9.7	51.8	-0.2	53.9	4.1	65.3	21.2
1973	64.3	-1.5	60.8	-5.4	59.8	-1.6	62.1	3.8	71.1	14.5	84.7	19.1	74.6	-11.9	126.3	69.3	109.8	-13.1	108.6	-1.1	104.7	-3.6	117.9	12.6
1974	128.4	8.9	131.9	2.7	124.7	-5.5	101.0	-19.0	99.8	-1.2	106.3	6.5	117.2	10.3	131.7	12.4	123.0	-6.6	138.1	12.3	134.4	-2.7	130.9	-2.6
1975	121.1	-7.5	115.2	-4.9	106.0	-8.0	103.6	-2.3	101.0	-2.5	96.4	-4.6	104.0	7.9	112.7	8.4	110.4	-2.0	107.8	-2.4	98.6	-8.5	97.5	-1.1
1976	99.8	2.4	101.6	1.8	103.3	1.7	99.1	-4.1	101.2	2.1	106.7	5.4	106.4	-0.3	98.5	-7.4	97.5	-1.0	88.5	-9.2	83.2	-6.0	85.7	3.0
1977	87.7	2.3	88.1	0.5	87.0	-1.2	87.4	0.5	81.2	-7.1	74.8	-7.9	71.7	-4.1	66.6	-7.1	68.4	2.7	68.6	0.3	78.0	13.7	79.3	1.7
1978	80.2	1.1	81.0	1.0	84.8	4.7	94.2	11.1	89.7	-4.8	89.2	-0.6	87.1	-2.4	84.8	-2.6	83.9	-1.1	86.3	2.9	89.6	3.8	87.6	-2.2
1979	87.4	-0.2	89.7	2.6	91.0	1.4	94.0	3.3	99.7	6.1	103.7	4.0	117.3	13.1	108.6	-7.4	106.4	-2.0	108.6	2.1	107.5	-1.0	108.1	0.6
1980	101.8	-5.8	105.9	4.0	103.3	-2.5	99.9	-3.3	103.8	3.9	102.1	-1.6	116.1	13.7	121.6	4.7	123.6	1.6	127.7	3.3	128.5	0.6	125.7	-2.2
1981	131.7	4.8	126.8	-3.7	124.1	-2.1	125.5	1.1	122.2	-2.6	121.9	-0.2	122.0	0.1	115.1	-5.7	107.7	-6.4	107.9	0.2	107.4	-0.5	101.3	-5.7
1982	106.8	5.4	105.8	-0.9	104.7	-1.0	107.1	2.3	108.2	1.0	107.0	-1.1	100.9	-5.7	93.5	-7.3	88.8	-5.0	86.9	-2.1	94.2	8.4	95.9	1.8
1983	97.8	2.0	105.4	7.8	107.8	2.3	115.6	7.2	114.8	-0.7	114.5	-0.3	112.2	-2.0	119.4	6.4	122.3	2.4	120.3	-1.6	122.1	1.5	115.5	-5.4
1984	116.4	0.8	111.6	-4.1	119.0	6.6	124.3	4.5	121.5	-2.3	122.3	0.7	118.0	-3.5	112.3	-4.8	109.7	-2.3	103.9	-5.3	104.2	0.3	100.8	-3.3
1985	103.1	2.3	103.0	-0.1	102.5	-0.5	104.6	2.0	101.5	-3.0	100.9	-0.6	97.2	-3.7	87.8	-9.7	85.9	-2.2	83.6	-2.7	91.0	8.9	92.8	2.0
1986	91.7	-1.2	91.8	0.1	90.8	-1.1	90.7	-0.1	94.6	4.3	86.4	-8.7	72.2	-16.4	65.9	-8.7	62.9	-4.6	63.9	1.6	69.4	8.6	71.0	2.3
1987	66.8	-5.9	66.7	-0.1	67.5	1.2	71.0	5.2	79.0	11.3	74.0	-6.3	68.8	-7.0	63.4	-7.8	69.5	9.6	72.8	4.7	74.9	2.9	78.9	5.3
1988	77.5	-1.8	83.5	7.7	80.6	-3.5	82.3	2.1	82.9	0.7	103.4	24.7	111.5	7.8	109.9	-1.4	112.9	2.7	114.2	1.2	107.4	-6.0	108.9	1.4
1989	115.2	5.8	111.3	-3.4	115.1	3.4	109.8	-4.6	114.1	3.9	105.8	-7.3	105.1	-0.7	100.3	-4.6	100.1	-0.2	98.2	-1.9	101.1	3.0	101.0	-0.1
1990	100.8	-0.2	100.4	-0.4	100.2	-0.2	107.2	7.0	108.6	1.3	110.4	1.7	103.1	-6.6	92.1	-10.7	88.3	-4.1	85.8	-2.8	85.1	-0.8	87.0	2.2
1991	85.9	-1.3	88.0	2.4	94.0	6.8	94.1	0.1	92.7	-1.5	90.2	-2.7	84.3	-6.5	93.2	10.6	92.4	-0.9	94.8	2.6	96.4	1.7	97.7	1.3
1992	103.1	5.5	106.2	3.0	108.5	2.2	102.7	-5.3	103.5	0.8	105.7	2.1	95.0	-10.1	88.5	-6.8	90.6	2.4	87.8	-3.1	86.6	-1.4	89.2	3.0
1993	89.9	0.8	88.1	-2.0	89.3	1.4	93.7	4.9	91.1	-2.8	85.3	-6.4	91.2	6.9	93.9	3.0	92.2	-1.8	96.4	4.6	105.9	9.9	116.4	9.9

Source: U.S. Department of Labor, Bureau of Labor Statistics, Division of Industry Prices and Price Indexes. n.e.c. stands for not elsewhere classified. - indicates no data collected for period or unavailable.

Livestock
Producer Price Index
Base 1982 = 100

For 1926-1993. Columns headed % show percentile change in the index from the previous period for which an index is available.

Year	Jan Index	%	Feb Index	%	Mar Index	%	Apr Index	%	May Index	%	Jun Index	%	Jul Index	%	Aug Index	%	Sep Index	%	Oct Index	%	Nov Index	%	Dec Index	%
1926	-	-	-	-	-	-	-	-	-	-	-	-	-	-	-	-	-	-	-	-	-	-	-	-
1927	-	-	-	-	-	-	-	-	-	-	-	-	-	-	-	-	-	-	-	-	-	-	-	-
1928	-	-	-	-	-	-	-	-	-	-	-	-	-	-	-	-	-	-	-	-	-	-	-	-
1929	-	-	-	-	-	-	-	-	-	-	-	-	-	-	-	-	-	-	-	-	-	-	-	-
1930	-	-	-	-	-	-	-	-	-	-	-	-	-	-	-	-	-	-	-	-	-	-	-	-
1931	-	-	-	-	-	-	-	-	-	-	-	-	-	-	-	-	-	-	-	-	-	-	-	-
1932	-	-	-	-	-	-	-	-	-	-	-	-	-	-	-	-	-	-	-	-	-	-	-	-
1933	-	-	-	-	-	-	-	-	-	-	-	-	-	-	-	-	-	-	-	-	-	-	-	-
1934	-	-	-	-	-	-	-	-	-	-	-	-	-	-	-	-	-	-	-	-	-	-	-	-
1935	-	-	-	-	-	-	-	-	-	-	-	-	-	-	-	-	-	-	-	-	-	-	-	-
1936	-	-	-	-	-	-	-	-	-	-	-	-	-	-	-	-	-	-	-	-	-	-	-	-
1937	-	-	-	-	-	-	-	-	-	-	-	-	-	-	-	-	-	-	-	-	-	-	-	-
1938	-	-	-	-	-	-	-	-	-	-	-	-	-	-	-	-	-	-	-	-	-	-	-	-
1939	-	-	-	-	15.0	-	-	-	-	-	13.6	-9.3	-	-	12.8	-5.9	14.7	14.8	-	-	-	-	12.3	-16.3
1940	-	-	-	-	12.6	2.4	-	-	-	-	12.6	0.0	-	-	-	-	14.0	11.1	-	-	-	-	14.1	0.7
1941	-	-	-	-	15.7	11.3	-	-	-	-	17.9	14.0	-	-	-	-	19.4	8.4	-	-	-	-	19.0	-2.1
1942	-	-	-	-	22.2	16.8	-	-	-	-	23.7	6.8	-	-	-	-	24.3	2.5	-	-	-	-	24.4	0.4
1943	-	-	-	-	27.3	11.9	-	-	-	-	25.3	-7.3	-	-	-	-	25.3	0.0	-	-	-	-	23.4	-7.5
1944	-	-	-	-	24.8	6.0	-	-	-	-	24.6	-0.8	-	-	-	-	25.0	1.6	-	-	-	-	24.8	-0.8
1945	-	-	-	-	26.1	5.2	-	-	-	-	26.1	0.0	-	-	-	-	25.1	-3.8	-	-	-	-	25.8	2.8
1946	26.2	1.6	26.1	-0.4	26.5	1.5	26.6	0.4	26.6	0.0	27.0	1.5	31.8	17.8	34.2	7.5	28.8	-15.8	33.7	17.0	38.7	14.8	38.5	-0.5
1947	37.2	-3.4	39.6	6.5	41.6	5.1	38.6	-7.2	39.5	2.3	40.4	2.3	42.0	4.0	42.0	0.0	44.1	5.0	44.4	0.7	42.3	-4.7	45.1	6.6
1948	47.5	5.3	43.0	-9.5	42.9	-0.2	42.4	-1.2	45.7	7.8	49.7	8.8	51.9	4.4	51.8	-0.2	50.9	-1.7	47.0	-7.7	44.9	-4.5	42.7	-4.9
1949	40.4	-5.4	38.4	-5.0	40.1	4.4	39.1	-2.5	40.1	2.6	40.8	1.7	40.0	-2.0	39.3	-1.7	39.6	0.8	38.2	-3.5	36.8	-3.7	36.7	-0.3
1950	37.7	2.7	39.2	4.0	39.1	-0.3	38.8	-0.8	42.6	9.8	43.3	1.6	46.7	7.9	46.8	0.2	45.9	-1.9	43.4	-5.4	43.8	0.9	45.5	3.9
1951	49.1	7.9	52.4	6.7	53.1	1.3	53.2	0.2	51.9	-2.4	52.0	0.2	51.5	-1.0	51.4	-0.2	50.7	-1.4	50.3	-0.8	47.5	-5.6	46.8	-1.5
1952	46.0	-1.7	45.6	-0.9	45.4	-0.4	46.3	2.0	47.7	3.0	46.8	-1.9	46.9	0.2	45.9	-2.1	42.5	-7.4	40.6	-4.5	39.2	-3.4	36.9	-5.9
1953	39.4	6.8	38.7	-1.8	38.8	0.3	36.6	-5.7	38.9	6.3	37.0	-4.9	40.8	10.3	37.3	-8.6	38.6	3.5	34.9	-9.6	33.2	-4.9	36.2	9.0
1954	39.6	9.4	39.5	-0.3	39.8	0.8	41.1	3.3	40.5	-1.5	37.9	-6.4	35.8	-5.5	35.9	0.3	34.9	-2.8	33.5	-4.0	33.2	-0.9	32.2	-3.0
1955	34.0	5.6	34.2	0.6	33.0	-3.5	35.2	6.7	32.8	-6.8	35.0	6.7	33.4	-4.6	31.3	-6.3	31.5	0.6	30.3	-3.8	25.8	-14.9	24.6	-4.7
1956	26.3	6.9	28.4	8.0	28.0	-1.4	30.0	7.1	31.7	5.7	32.3	1.9	31.1	-3.7	33.0	6.1	33.2	0.6	32.0	-3.6	29.7	-7.2	31.2	5.1
1957	32.3	3.5	32.6	0.9	33.3	2.1	34.7	4.2	34.5	-0.6	36.7	6.4	38.0	3.5	38.2	0.5	36.1	-5.5	34.8	-3.6	35.1	0.9	36.9	5.1
1958	38.0	3.0	40.4	6.3	42.4	5.0	42.4	0.0	44.6	5.2	44.0	-1.3	43.4	-1.4	42.3	-2.5	41.4	-2.1	40.1	-3.1	40.7	1.5	39.7	-2.5
1959	40.5	2.0	39.5	-2.5	40.9	3.5	41.7	2.0	40.9	-1.9	40.4	-1.2	38.1	-5.7	37.5	-1.6	37.0	-1.3	35.3	-4.6	33.5	-5.1	33.0	-1.5
1960	34.5	4.5	35.5	2.9	38.1	7.3	37.9	-0.5	38.1	0.5	37.8	-0.8	37.4	-1.1	35.9	-4.0	35.1	-2.2	36.0	2.6	36.5	1.4	36.9	1.1
1961	37.6	1.9	37.6	0.0	36.8	-2.1	36.7	-0.3	34.9	-4.9	34.4	-1.4	34.4	0.0	36.8	7.0	35.9	-2.4	35.4	-1.4	35.3	-0.3	35.9	1.7
1962	37.0	3.1	36.5	-1.4	37.0	1.4	36.7	-0.8	35.6	-3.0	35.8	0.6	37.3	4.2	38.5	3.2	40.7	5.7	38.5	-5.4	38.4	-0.3	37.3	-2.9
1963	36.5	-2.1	34.2	-6.3	32.6	-4.7	33.7	3.4	33.4	-0.9	34.4	3.0	36.7	6.7	36.5	-0.5	34.3	-6.0	34.0	-0.9	33.7	-0.9	30.8	-8.6
1964	32.4	5.2	31.7	-2.2	32.2	1.6	31.6	-1.9	31.3	-0.9	31.6	1.0	33.8	7.0	34.2	1.2	35.3	3.2	33.2	-5.9	32.0	-3.6	32.0	0.0
1965	32.9	2.8	34.0	3.3	34.4	1.2	35.3	2.6	37.5	6.2	41.0	9.3	41.1	0.2	41.8	1.7	40.2	-3.8	40.5	0.7	40.8	0.7	42.9	5.1
1966	44.2	3.0	45.8	3.6	44.4	-3.1	44.0	-0.9	42.8	-2.7	42.2	-1.4	41.7	-1.2	43.0	3.1	41.9	-2.6	40.8	-2.6	37.7	-7.6	37.5	-0.5
1967	38.9	3.7	38.2	-1.8	37.3	-2.4	36.1	-3.2	39.4	9.1	40.3	2.3	41.2	2.2	40.8	-1.0	39.7	-2.7	39.1	-1.5	37.0	-5.4	37.5	1.4
1968	37.9	1.1	39.4	4.0	40.5	2.8	40.4	-0.2	40.5	0.2	40.7	0.5	42.0	3.2	40.7	-3.1	40.6	-0.2	39.9	-1.7	39.9	0.0	40.0	0.3
1969	40.7	1.7	41.9	2.9	43.2	3.1	43.7	1.2	47.2	8.0	50.0	5.9	48.6	-2.8	47.4	-2.5	45.7	-3.6	45.5	-0.4	44.7	-1.8	46.1	3.1
1970	45.0	-2.4	47.9	6.4	49.7	3.8	47.9	-3.6	46.9	-2.1	47.2	0.6	48.4	2.5	45.5	-6.0	44.1	-3.1	42.9	-2.7	39.2	-8.6	38.6	-1.5

[Continued]

Livestock
Producer Price Index
Base 1982 = 100
[Continued]

For 1926-1993. Columns headed % show percentile change in the index from the previous period for which an index is available.

Year	Jan Index	%	Feb Index	%	Mar Index	%	Apr Index	%	May Index	%	Jun Index	%	Jul Index	%	Aug Index	%	Sep Index	%	Oct Index	%	Nov Index	%	Dec Index	%
1971	39.7	2.8	46.1	16.1	44.5	-3.5	45.3	1.8	46.1	1.8	46.1	0.0	47.0	2.0	47.0	0.0	46.2	-1.7	46.9	1.5	46.9	0.0	48.4	3.2
1972	51.3	6.0	54.1	5.5	53.0	-2.0	51.9	-2.1	54.2	4.4	56.8	4.8	59.1	4.0	57.4	-2.9	56.2	-2.1	55.9	-0.5	54.1	-3.2	59.2	9.4
1973	61.8	4.4	69.0	11.7	75.4	9.3	71.4	-5.3	73.2	2.5	75.2	2.7	77.3	2.8	94.4	22.1	80.4	-14.8	72.0	-10.4	69.8	-3.1	66.3	-5.0
1974	76.5	15.4	75.6	-1.2	70.2	-7.1	65.5	-6.7	61.7	-5.8	53.5	-13.3	67.3	25.8	71.6	6.4	65.4	-8.7	64.0	-2.1	60.7	-5.2	61.9	2.0
1975	60.5	-2.3	59.0	-2.5	60.3	2.2	67.3	11.6	76.8	14.1	78.5	2.2	81.9	4.3	78.7	-3.9	81.4	3.4	80.6	-1.0	75.0	-6.9	74.3	-0.9
1976	71.6	-3.6	69.6	-2.8	66.3	-4.7	74.6	12.5	72.5	-2.8	71.8	-1.0	68.2	-5.0	64.4	-5.6	62.7	-2.6	60.5	-3.5	59.9	-1.0	64.4	7.5
1977	64.4	0.0	64.5	0.2	63.4	-1.7	65.1	2.7	69.9	7.4	66.8	-4.4	70.0	4.8	68.0	-2.9	67.0	-1.5	68.8	2.7	66.5	-3.3	70.8	6.5
1978	73.0	3.1	78.4	7.4	80.8	3.1	84.6	4.7	89.3	5.6	91.6	2.6	87.9	-4.0	84.0	-4.4	88.0	4.8	91.2	3.6	86.3	-5.4	89.3	3.5
1979	95.9	7.4	103.4	7.8	107.0	3.5	110.2	3.0	108.8	-1.3	102.4	-5.9	99.3	-3.0	93.1	-6.2	99.4	6.8	97.6	-1.8	96.3	-1.3	97.9	1.7
1980	96.1	-1.8	99.7	3.7	97.7	-2.0	89.4	-8.5	90.5	1.2	93.1	2.9	101.0	8.5	106.9	5.8	103.5	-3.2	102.0	-1.4	98.8	-3.1	97.5	-1.3
1981	94.7	-2.9	94.9	0.2	92.8	-2.2	95.7	3.1	97.6	2.0	102.0	4.5	103.4	1.4	101.6	-1.7	99.8	-1.8	94.8	-5.0	89.6	-5.5	87.3	-2.6
1982	91.8	5.2	97.4	6.1	99.1	1.7	103.8	4.7	109.7	5.7	107.6	-1.9	104.8	-2.6	104.1	-0.7	100.4	-3.6	96.4	-4.0	92.7	-3.8	92.0	-0.8
1983	94.0	2.2	97.4	3.6	97.5	0.1	101.1	3.7	100.0	-1.1	97.6	-2.4	93.3	-4.4	93.9	0.6	89.8	-4.4	89.0	-0.9	85.5	-3.9	92.4	8.1
1984	97.2	5.2	97.7	0.5	101.2	3.6	101.1	-0.1	98.8	-2.3	97.0	-1.8	100.9	4.0	98.4	-2.5	95.0	-3.5	90.7	-4.5	96.1	6.0	97.8	1.8
1985	96.0	-1.8	96.8	0.8	91.8	-5.2	89.7	-2.3	88.3	-1.6	87.9	-0.5	86.9	-1.1	82.1	-5.5	77.0	-6.2	88.2	14.5	92.8	5.2	92.8	0.0
1986	90.2	-2.8	87.7	-2.8	85.4	-2.6	82.9	-2.9	88.9	7.2	87.3	-1.8	95.1	8.9	98.1	3.2	98.2	0.1	95.9	-2.3	96.6	0.7	95.6	-1.0
1987	93.1	-2.6	95.9	3.0	96.0	0.1	104.3	8.6	109.6	5.1	109.8	0.2	107.3	-2.3	106.5	-0.7	104.1	-2.3	102.6	-1.4	96.8	-5.7	98.1	1.3
1988	99.3	1.2	105.7	6.4	106.3	0.6	107.7	1.3	111.8	3.8	106.1	-5.1	99.7	-6.0	100.6	0.9	100.7	0.1	101.8	1.1	98.3	-3.4	101.0	2.7
1989	104.5	3.5	104.6	0.1	106.8	2.1	106.4	-0.4	107.4	0.9	106.0	-1.3	104.8	-1.1	108.8	3.8	103.7	-4.7	104.6	0.9	105.6	1.0	110.5	4.6
1990	110.7	0.2	113.2	2.3	117.0	3.4	117.9	0.8	120.5	2.2	117.8	-2.2	114.7	-2.6	117.8	2.7	113.3	-3.8	116.5	2.8	113.9	-2.2	114.3	0.4
1991	112.8	-1.3	113.9	1.0	117.1	2.8	115.8	-1.1	115.2	-0.5	112.8	-2.1	110.2	-2.3	100.7	-8.6	101.1	0.4	100.9	-0.2	96.6	-4.3	97.7	1.1
1992	100.0	2.4	106.0	6.0	107.0	0.9	106.7	-0.3	108.0	1.2	105.3	-2.5	103.7	-1.5	104.2	0.5	103.4	-0.8	104.2	0.8	101.8	-2.3	106.3	4.4
1993	108.3	1.9	110.0	1.6	112.6	2.4	113.0	0.4	112.8	-0.2	109.8	-2.7	105.0	-4.4	107.1	2.0	105.7	-1.3	100.0	-5.4	100.5	0.5	99.2	-1.3

Source: U.S. Department of Labor, Bureau of Labor Statistics, Division of Industry Prices and Price Indexes. n.e.c. stands for not elsewhere classified. - indicates no data collected for period or unavailable.

Live Poultry
Producer Price Index
Base 1982 = 100

For 1926-1993. Columns headed % show percentile change in the index from the previous period for which an index is available.

Year	Jan Index	%	Feb Index	%	Mar Index	%	Apr Index	%	May Index	%	Jun Index	%	Jul Index	%	Aug Index	%	Sep Index	%	Oct Index	%	Nov Index	%	Dec Index	%
1926	-		-		-		-		-		-		-		-		-		-		-		-	
1927	-		-		-		-		-		-		-		-		-		-		-		-	
1928	-		-		-		-		-		-		-		-		-		-		-		-	
1929	-		-		-		-		-		-		-		-		-		-		-		-	
1930	-		-		-		-		-		-		-		-		-		-		-		-	
1931	-		-		-		-		-		-		-		-		-		-		-		-	
1932	-		-		-		-		-		-		-		-		-		-		-		-	
1933	-		-		-		-		-		-		-		-		-		-		-		-	
1934	-		-		-		-		-		-		-		-		-		-		-		-	
1935	-		-		-		-		-		-		-		-		-		-		-		-	
1936	-		-		-		-		-		-		-		-		-		-		-		-	
1937	-		-		-		-		-		-		-		-		-		-		-		-	
1938	-		-		-		-		-		-		-		-		-		-		-		-	
1939	-		-		67.7		-		-		55.3	-18.3	-		56.3	1.8	60.8	8.0	-		-		52.5	-13.7
1940	-		-		60.0	14.3	-		-		54.9	-8.5	-		-		59.6	8.6	-		-		58.2	-2.3
1941	-		-		72.2	24.1	-		-		77.2	6.9	-		-		76.8	-0.5	-		-		73.8	-3.9
1942	-		-		89.3	21.0	-		-		77.6	-13.1	-		-		87.0	12.1	-		-		90.9	4.5
1943	-		-		98.8	8.7	-		-		99.8	1.0	-		-		96.5	-3.3	-		-		96.2	-0.3
1944	-		-		98.8	2.7	-		-		89.2	-9.7	-		-		94.8	6.3	-		-		98.2	3.6
1945	-		-		104.0	5.9	-		-		103.0	-1.0	-		-		97.3	-5.5	-		-		98.4	1.1
1946	102.6	4.3	104.3	1.7	103.2	-1.1	108.9	5.5	108.9	0.0	108.0	-0.8	110.6	2.4	103.9	-6.1	125.7	21.0	121.0	-3.7	101.9	-15.8	107.9	5.9
1947	103.7	-3.9	103.7	0.0	115.2	11.1	115.4	0.2	116.9	1.3	111.9	-4.3	110.6	-1.2	111.9	1.2	119.5	6.8	108.2	-9.5	107.4	-0.7	117.5	9.4
1948	128.5	9.4	119.1	-7.3	131.4	10.3	135.1	2.8	131.7	-2.5	133.2	1.1	129.2	-3.0	131.0	1.4	130.3	-0.5	119.4	-8.4	123.9	3.8	131.5	6.1
1949	123.9	-5.8	116.4	-6.1	122.8	5.5	120.5	-1.9	108.3	-10.1	97.8	-9.7	98.1	0.3	102.8	4.8	97.6	-5.1	95.5	-2.2	97.9	2.5	85.0	-13.2
1950	79.5	-6.5	97.3	22.4	105.9	8.8	102.6	-3.1	95.6	-6.8	92.5	-3.2	104.9	13.4	108.0	3.0	102.5	-5.1	92.4	-9.9	89.3	-3.4	90.5	1.3
1951	100.4	10.9	111.7	11.3	120.0	7.4	120.9	0.7	114.1	-5.6	111.9	-1.9	108.6	-2.9	106.3	-2.1	102.3	-3.8	94.1	-8.0	91.0	-3.3	95.1	4.5
1952	104.5	9.9	108.5	3.8	102.9	-5.2	97.9	-4.9	89.0	-9.1	92.7	4.2	101.0	9.0	105.1	4.1	105.2	0.1	98.2	-6.7	112.7	14.8	99.1	-12.1
1953	106.2	7.2	105.3	-0.8	107.4	2.0	110.8	3.2	106.0	-4.3	94.4	-10.9	106.7	13.0	102.6	-3.8	99.4	-3.1	93.1	-6.3	91.6	-1.6	82.7	-9.7
1954	91.2	10.3	87.9	-3.6	91.8	4.4	88.4	-3.7	84.3	-4.6	83.6	-0.8	83.0	-0.7	83.3	0.4	77.9	-6.5	72.2	-7.3	70.4	-2.5	66.8	-5.1
1955	79.8	19.5	86.5	8.4	100.5	16.2	96.9	-3.6	91.1	-6.0	92.4	1.4	89.8	-2.8	91.4	1.8	89.0	-2.6	78.6	-11.7	75.4	-4.1	72.1	-4.4
1956	74.1	2.8	78.1	5.4	80.9	3.6	76.1	-5.9	77.4	1.7	72.0	-7.0	75.2	4.4	69.2	-8.0	63.7	-7.9	63.0	-1.1	63.4	0.6	64.3	1.4
1957	63.9	-0.6	68.6	7.4	70.9	3.4	67.6	-4.7	67.7	0.1	69.3	2.4	71.3	2.9	70.8	-0.7	63.7	-10.0	60.2	-5.5	61.9	2.8	60.6	-2.1
1958	68.4	12.9	69.3	1.3	73.7	6.3	65.9	-10.6	71.4	8.3	73.5	2.9	67.7	-7.9	64.0	-5.5	58.2	-9.1	53.6	-3.1	56.3	5.0	69.1	22.7
1959	62.4	12.4	63.6	1.9	63.0	-0.9	58.2	-7.6	59.0	1.4	58.7	-0.5	58.2	-0.9	54.7	-6.0	55.3	1.1	60.1	1.5	60.0	-0.2	60.8	1.3
1960	64.7	-6.4	66.1	2.2	68.4	3.5	67.8	-0.9	65.6	-3.2	64.7	-1.4	62.7	-3.1	60.1	-4.1	59.2	-1.5	60.1	1.5	60.0	-0.2	53.0	20.5
1961	64.3	5.8	67.4	4.8	63.6	-5.6	58.8	-7.5	56.9	-3.2	46.0	-19.2	46.6	1.3	46.8	0.4	41.3	-11.8	43.5	5.3	44.0	1.1	54.7	2.2
1962	56.2	6.0	57.6	2.5	56.7	-1.6	52.2	-7.9	50.6	-3.1	50.2	-0.8	53.3	6.2	54.0	1.3	57.8	7.0	54.4	-5.9	53.5	-1.7	48.8	-11.3
1963	54.6	-0.2	57.7	5.7	57.0	-1.2	57.0	0.0	53.2	-6.7	53.8	1.1	53.8	0.0	51.9	-3.5	52.1	0.4	52.2	0.2	55.0	5.4	50.7	-4.3
1964	53.9	10.5	53.2	-1.3	52.7	-0.9	52.1	-1.1	49.8	-4.4	50.7	1.8	53.8	6.1	51.7	-3.9	52.7	1.9	51.6	-2.1	53.0	2.7	55.5	2.6
1965	53.2	4.9	54.6	2.6	57.1	4.6	55.3	-3.2	53.7	-2.9	56.0	4.3	56.3	0.5	55.0	-2.3	54.3	-1.3	54.4	0.2	54.1	-0.6	49.1	-9.2
1966	58.5	5.4	60.7	3.8	64.2	5.8	60.5	-5.8	64.5	6.6	60.8	-5.7	59.9	-1.5	57.1	-4.7	55.7	-2.5	52.9	-5.0	54.1	2.3	43.4	4.1
1967	56.1	14.3	61.8	10.2	57.8	-6.5	56.6	-2.1	54.5	-3.7	54.5	0.0	56.6	3.9	49.2	-13.1	46.4	-5.7	47.0	1.3	41.7	-11.3	52.7	-5.4
1968	49.8	14.7	55.3	11.0	51.8	-6.3	51.6	-0.4	54.4	5.4	57.0	4.8	59.7	4.7	55.9	-6.4	53.9	-3.6	50.4	-6.5	55.7	10.5	55.2	0.5
1969	57.5	9.1	59.9	4.2	60.8	1.5	57.9	-4.8	62.7	8.3	61.9	-1.3	65.3	5.5	58.7	-10.1	56.5	-3.7	54.2	-4.1	54.9	1.3	41.8	-15.7
1970	60.2	9.1	55.3	-8.1	57.7	4.3	52.7	-8.7	53.2	0.9	49.5	-7.0	52.1	5.3	49.2	-5.6	51.9	5.5	48.7	-6.2	49.6	1.8	41.8	-15.7

[Continued]

Live Poultry

Producer Price Index
Base 1982 = 100
[Continued]

For 1926-1993. Columns headed % show percentile change in the index from the previous period for which an index is available.

Year	Jan Index	%	Feb Index	%	Mar Index	%	Apr Index	%	May Index	%	Jun Index	%	Jul Index	%	Aug Index	%	Sep Index	%	Oct Index	%	Nov Index	%	Dec Index	%
1971	50.1	19.9	52.0	3.8	52.1	0.2	51.8	-0.6	52.8	1.9	56.3	6.6	63.0	11.9	52.5	-16.7	53.5	1.9	48.6	-9.2	48.0	-1.2	45.4	-5.4
1972	49.1	8.1	54.9	11.8	56.1	2.2	49.1	-12.5	50.2	2.2	53.6	6.8	61.7	15.1	55.7	-9.7	58.5	5.0	54.1	-7.5	53.6	-0.9	54.0	0.7
1973	66.6	23.3	71.4	7.2	85.9	20.3	96.8	12.7	93.9	-3.0	96.1	2.3	98.7	2.7	140.5	42.4	118.0	-16.0	98.6	-16.4	80.5	-18.4	75.3	-6.5
1974	74.6	-0.9	93.7	25.6	86.6	-7.6	76.1	-12.1	76.5	0.5	69.2	-9.5	77.2	11.6	78.1	1.2	90.4	15.7	81.8	-9.5	93.2	13.9	87.2	-6.4
1975	90.5	3.8	92.1	1.8	88.6	-3.8	87.7	-1.0	92.5	5.5	99.3	7.4	114.2	15.0	105.5	-7.6	106.3	0.8	109.8	3.3	106.1	-3.4	94.5	-10.9
1976	88.1	-6.8	90.2	2.4	95.2	5.5	86.2	-9.5	90.8	5.3	91.1	0.3	95.9	5.3	93.3	-2.7	85.9	-7.9	78.4	-8.7	72.5	-7.5	75.9	4.7
1977	80.1	5.5	95.7	19.5	92.3	-3.6	95.0	2.9	95.4	0.4	95.2	-0.2	101.0	6.1	91.8	-9.1	94.7	3.2	88.8	-6.2	84.8	-4.5	82.2	-3.1
1978	88.7	7.9	98.4	10.9	97.9	-0.5	102.1	4.3	101.3	-0.8	115.5	14.0	128.5	11.3	106.7	-17.0	110.0	3.1	96.4	-12.4	100.2	3.9	103.5	3.3
1979	107.3	3.7	113.5	5.8	113.4	-0.1	109.1	-3.8	112.7	3.3	95.3	-15.4	95.8	0.5	89.6	-6.5	90.4	0.9	84.4	-6.6	101.9	20.7	101.4	-0.5
1980	101.7	0.3	96.2	-5.4	93.8	-2.5	89.6	-4.5	89.2	-0.4	86.8	-2.7	118.4	36.4	117.0	-1.2	125.6	7.4	116.2	-7.5	115.2	-0.9	114.0	-1.0
1981	111.1	-2.5	115.1	3.6	111.2	-3.4	101.8	-8.5	108.0	6.1	109.4	1.3	112.2	2.6	109.6	-2.3	102.5	-6.5	96.8	-5.6	91.2	-5.8	89.3	-2.1
1982	97.3	9.0	102.8	5.7	103.0	0.2	97.0	-5.8	100.4	3.5	108.0	7.6	110.7	2.5	98.7	-10.8	102.4	3.7	92.3	-9.9	94.6	2.5	92.7	-2.0
1983	92.3	-0.4	104.3	13.0	92.7	-11.1	89.0	-4.0	97.4	9.4	103.9	6.7	111.8	7.6	115.4	3.2	126.2	9.4	108.6	-13.9	124.3	14.5	125.7	1.1
1984	131.6	4.7	131.0	-0.5	134.6	2.7	125.5	-6.8	125.4	-0.1	118.7	-5.3	135.1	13.8	113.9	-15.7	124.9	9.7	114.3	-8.5	128.8	12.7	120.8	-6.2
1985	121.3	0.4	115.9	-4.5	112.3	-3.1	105.4	-6.1	111.8	6.1	116.5	4.2	118.6	1.8	112.6	-5.1	127.4	13.1	117.4	-7.8	132.8	13.1	122.5	-7.8
1986	110.9	-9.5	102.9	-7.2	108.9	5.8	110.1	1.1	113.7	3.3	123.3	8.4	154.6	25.4	177.2	14.6	145.7	-17.8	163.6	12.3	130.8	-20.0	114.5	-12.5
1987	110.6	-3.4	104.1	-5.9	104.0	-0.1	105.3	1.3	112.8	7.1	94.2	-16.5	102.3	8.6	111.2	8.7	100.3	-9.8	88.5	-11.8	93.9	6.1	87.7	-6.6
1988	99.1	13.0	86.9	-12.3	96.9	11.5	97.6	0.7	112.2	15.0	130.4	16.2	156.4	19.9	145.1	-7.2	142.7	-1.7	141.0	-1.2	128.0	-9.2	121.7	-4.9
1989	122.4	0.6	121.5	-0.7	138.5	14.0	138.4	-0.1	155.0	12.0	148.5	-4.2	135.5	-8.8	125.4	-7.5	134.9	7.6	109.0	-19.2	111.8	2.6	104.3	-6.7
1990	108.9	4.4	115.5	6.1	129.1	11.8	117.3	-9.1	128.2	9.3	118.5	-7.6	134.7	13.7	122.1	-9.4	128.9	5.6	110.2	-14.5	108.3	-1.7	104.2	-3.8
1991	110.4	6.0	103.1	-6.6	110.2	6.9	107.3	-2.6	113.9	6.2	112.7	-1.1	119.2	5.8	120.4	1.0	116.7	-3.1	109.1	-6.5	106.8	-2.1	105.1	-1.6
1992	106.9	1.7	102.8	-3.8	105.4	2.5	102.8	-2.5	116.1	12.9	110.7	-4.7	124.1	12.1	120.5	-2.9	111.8	-7.2	119.3	6.7	121.7	2.0	108.8	-10.6
1993	112.0	2.9	110.4	-1.4	116.1	5.2	116.5	0.3	132.3	13.6	118.9	-10.1	124.4	4.6	125.9	1.2	135.1	7.3	126.1	-6.7	127.2	0.9	118.4	-6.9

Source: U.S. Department of Labor, Bureau of Labor Statistics, Division of Industry Prices and Price Indexes. n.e.c. stands for not elsewhere classified. - indicates no data collected for period or unavailable.

Plant and Animal Fibers
Producer Price Index
Base 1982 = 100

For 1926-1993. Columns headed % show percentile change in the index from the previous period for which an index is available.

Year	Jan Index	%	Feb Index	%	Mar Index	%	Apr Index	%	May Index	%	Jun Index	%	Jul Index	%	Aug Index	%	Sep Index	%	Oct Index	%	Nov Index	%	Dec Index	%
1926	52.6	-	52.1	-1.0	48.5	-6.9	47.0	-3.1	46.4	-1.3	45.9	-1.1	46.2	0.7	48.3	4.5	43.6	-9.7	37.6	-13.8	36.4	-3.2	35.9	-1.4
1927	37.1	3.3	38.3	3.2	39.0	1.8	39.5	1.3	41.8	5.8	42.7	2.2	44.8	4.9	48.4	8.0	51.3	6.0	49.9	-2.7	48.4	-3.0	47.0	-2.9
1928	46.3	-1.5	45.6	-1.5	47.8	4.8	49.1	2.7	51.2	4.3	50.6	-1.2	50.9	0.6	46.8	-8.1	45.4	-3.0	47.1	3.7	47.5	0.8	48.2	1.5
1929	47.6	-1.2	47.7	0.2	48.9	2.5	47.2	-3.5	45.6	-3.4	45.2	-0.9	45.0	-0.4	45.4	0.9	45.6	0.4	44.7	-2.0	42.4	-5.1	41.7	-1.7
1930	41.3	-1.0	38.4	-7.0	37.3	-2.9	38.2	2.4	37.5	-1.8	33.1	-11.7	30.5	-7.9	28.7	-5.9	26.5	-7.7	25.6	-3.4	25.8	0.8	24.2	-6.2
1931	24.7	2.1	25.7	4.0	25.6	-0.4	24.2	-5.5	22.4	-7.4	22.0	-1.8	22.6	2.7	18.9	-16.4	17.5	-7.4	16.9	-3.4	17.3	2.4	16.5	-4.6
1932	16.7	1.2	16.8	0.6	16.4	-2.4	15.0	-8.5	13.7	-8.7	12.7	-7.3	13.6	7.1	16.6	22.1	17.8	7.2	15.9	-10.7	15.0	-5.7	14.3	-4.7
1933	14.5	1.4	13.9	-4.1	15.0	7.9	15.7	4.7	19.2	22.3	21.9	14.1	24.9	13.7	22.4	-10.0	22.5	0.4	22.1	-1.8	22.6	2.3	22.9	1.3
1934	24.7	7.9	26.7	8.1	26.7	0.0	26.0	-2.6	24.9	-4.2	26.2	5.2	26.7	1.9	27.4	2.6	27.0	-1.5	26.2	-3.0	26.5	1.1	26.8	1.1
1935	26.9	0.4	26.5	-1.5	24.4	-7.9	24.8	1.6	25.8	4.0	25.4	-1.6	25.7	1.2	25.1	-2.3	24.5	-2.4	27.3	-0.4	27.7	1.5	29.0	4.7
1936	26.7	-0.7	26.0	-2.6	26.1	0.4	26.2	0.4	26.0	-0.8	26.7	2.7	28.4	6.4	27.4	-3.5	27.4	0.0	27.3	-0.4	27.7	1.5	29.0	4.7
1937	29.8	2.8	29.9	0.3	31.9	6.7	31.6	-0.9	30.0	-5.1	28.9	-3.7	28.6	-1.0	24.9	-12.9	22.5	-9.6	20.8	-7.6	19.8	-4.8	20.0	1.0
1938	20.6	3.0	20.8	1.0	20.7	-0.5	20.5	-1.0	20.0	-2.4	19.8	-1.0	21.0	6.1	20.2	-3.8	19.5	-3.5	20.5	5.1	20.9	2.0	20.4	-2.4
1939	20.8	2.0	21.2	1.9	21.7	2.4	21.5	-0.9	23.1	7.4	23.5	1.7	23.3	-0.9	22.6	-3.0	24.0	6.2	25.3	5.4	26.3	4.0	29.3	11.4
1940	25.8	-11.9	25.0	-3.1	24.5	-2.0	24.0	-2.0	22.8	-5.0	23.5	3.1	22.9	-2.6	21.7	-5.2	21.7	0.0	22.0	1.4	22.8	3.6	23.0	0.9
1941	23.3	1.3	23.4	0.4	24.3	3.8	25.0	2.9	27.7	10.8	29.7	7.2	32.9	10.8	33.6	2.1	35.3	5.1	34.4	-2.5	34.1	-0.9	35.7	4.7
1942	38.7	8.4	38.7	0.0	39.5	2.1	40.4	2.3	40.3	-0.2	38.4	-4.7	39.0	1.6	37.3	-4.4	37.4	0.3	37.6	0.5	38.3	1.9	38.9	1.6
1943	40.1	3.1	40.6	1.2	41.2	1.5	41.3	0.2	41.2	-0.2	41.1	-0.2	40.7	-1.0	40.1	-1.5	40.1	0.0	39.6	-1.2	38.4	-3.0	38.5	0.3
1944	39.2	1.8	40.3	2.8	40.8	1.2	40.6	-0.5	40.7	0.2	41.5	2.0	41.7	0.5	41.1	-1.4	41.2	0.2	41.4	0.5	41.1	-0.7	41.4	0.7
1945	41.5	0.2	41.5	0.0	41.8	0.7	42.4	1.4	43.2	1.9	43.1	-0.2	42.6	-1.2	42.2	-0.9	42.4	0.5	43.5	2.6	44.9	3.2	45.3	0.9
1946	45.5	0.4	47.2	3.7	48.7	3.2	50.1	2.9	49.8	-0.6	52.1	4.6	63.1	21.1	67.5	7.0	68.7	1.8	67.7	-1.5	59.8	-11.7	61.9	3.5
1947	61.0	-1.5	62.9	3.1	65.6	4.3	66.3	1.1	67.5	1.8	69.3	2.7	70.3	1.4	65.7	-6.5	62.0	-5.6	62.7	1.1	65.9	5.1	69.5	5.5
1948	68.7	-1.2	65.7	-4.4	67.7	3.0	72.9	7.7	74.7	2.5	75.6	1.2	71.8	-5.0	67.8	-5.6	67.5	-0.4	67.1	-0.6	67.5	0.6	69.6	3.1
1949	70.7	1.6	70.6	-0.1	70.4	-0.3	70.8	0.6	69.4	-2.0	69.0	-0.6	67.1	-2.8	64.9	-3.3	63.6	-2.0	63.0	-0.9	62.0	-1.6	63.2	1.9
1950	65.0	2.8	67.4	3.7	67.1	-0.4	68.3	1.8	70.0	2.5	72.4	3.4	77.0	6.4	80.5	4.5	90.8	12.8	89.7	-1.2	94.7	5.6	98.0	3.5
1951	108.3	10.5	112.5	3.9	116.4	3.5	112.2	-3.6	107.9	-3.8	105.1	-2.6	92.6	-11.9	80.9	-12.6	77.0	-4.8	80.2	4.2	86.7	8.1	85.6	-1.3
1952	85.8	0.2	81.3	-5.2	80.2	-1.4	80.7	0.6	77.1	-4.5	80.1	3.9	77.9	-2.7	77.7	-0.3	76.5	-1.5	74.0	-3.3	72.3	-2.3	68.7	-5.0
1953	68.2	-0.7	69.3	1.6	70.6	1.9	69.8	-1.1	70.4	0.9	70.2	-0.3	70.9	1.0	70.1	-1.1	69.9	-0.3	69.6	-0.4	70.5	-2.5	70.9	0.6
1954	70.3	1.0	71.9	2.3	71.5	-0.6	71.2	-0.4	72.2	1.4	72.2	0.0	72.4	0.3	72.0	-0.6	72.5	0.7	72.3	-0.3	68.2	1.9	68.1	-0.1
1955	70.5	-0.6	70.4	-0.1	69.4	-1.4	69.3	-0.1	69.8	0.7	69.8	0.0	70.1	0.4	69.4	-1.0	68.1	-1.9	66.9	-1.8	68.2	1.9	68.1	-0.1
1956	68.7	0.9	71.4	3.9	71.2	-0.3	71.4	0.3	71.5	0.1	71.7	0.3	70.4	-1.8	66.3	-5.8	66.4	0.2	67.5	1.7	68.1	0.9	68.4	0.4
1957	69.4	1.5	70.1	1.0	70.2	0.1	70.4	0.3	70.4	0.0	70.8	0.6	70.9	0.1	70.2	-1.0	69.4	-1.1	69.7	0.4	70.7	1.4	70.0	-1.0
1958	69.8	-0.3	69.4	-0.6	68.6	-1.2	68.4	-0.3	68.6	0.3	68.7	0.1	68.7	0.0	68.7	0.0	68.0	-1.0	68.0	0.0	68.0	0.0	67.3	-1.0
1959	67.1	-0.3	66.9	-0.3	67.2	0.4	68.2	1.5	68.7	0.7	68.6	-0.1	67.5	-1.6	64.6	-4.3	64.5	-0.2	63.9	-0.9	63.9	0.0	64.6	1.1
1960	64.7	0.2	64.9	0.3	64.8	-0.2	65.0	0.3	65.2	0.3	65.3	0.2	65.1	-0.3	62.3	-4.3	62.2	-0.2	61.3	-1.4	61.3	0.0	61.3	0.0
1961	61.3	0.0	61.6	0.5	62.7	1.8	63.0	0.5	64.3	2.1	65.0	1.1	65.3	0.5	66.4	1.7	66.6	0.3	67.1	0.8	67.1	0.0	67.1	0.0
1962	67.0	-0.1	67.1	0.1	67.3	0.3	67.6	0.4	67.6	0.0	68.1	0.7	67.9	-0.3	67.3	-0.9	66.6	-1.0	66.6	0.0	66.7	0.2	67.1	0.6
1963	67.9	1.2	68.9	1.5	69.6	1.0	69.7	0.1	69.5	-0.3	69.3	-0.3	68.5	-1.2	68.1	-0.6	68.0	-0.1	68.0	0.0	68.2	0.3	69.3	1.6
1964	69.4	0.1	69.5	0.1	69.8	0.4	69.8	0.0	69.2	-0.9	69.2	0.0	68.0	-1.7	65.6	-3.5	64.5	-1.7	64.1	-0.6	64.2	0.2	63.3	-1.4
1965	63.2	-0.2	62.7	-0.8	62.6	-0.2	62.6	0.0	62.7	0.2	62.9	0.3	62.7	-0.3	61.8	-1.4	61.5	-0.5	61.5	0.0	61.4	-0.2	61.3	-0.2
1966	61.3	0.0	61.2	-0.2	61.3	0.2	61.5	0.3	61.7	0.3	61.7	0.0	61.8	0.2	49.4	-20.1	49.0	-0.8	48.8	-0.4	48.4	-0.8	48.5	0.2
1967	48.4	-0.2	48.0	-0.8	48.0	0.0	47.8	-0.4	47.8	0.0	48.4	1.3	48.4	0.0	48.8	0.8	49.5	1.4	49.5	0.0	51.2	3.4	55.2	7.8
1968	54.3	-1.6	52.3	-3.7	52.3	0.0	52.0	-0.6	51.8	-0.4	51.9	0.2	51.9	0.0	52.5	1.2	52.7	0.4	50.7	-3.8	48.7	-3.9	47.2	-3.1
1969	47.0	-0.4	46.3	-1.5	46.0	-0.6	46.0	0.0	46.3	0.7	46.3	0.0	46.3	0.0	45.7	-1.3	45.4	-0.7	45.2	-0.4	45.1	-0.2	44.9	-0.4
1970	44.6	-0.7	44.7	0.2	44.4	-0.7	44.7	0.7	44.8	0.2	44.9	0.2	45.2	0.7	45.2	0.0	44.4	-1.8	43.8	-1.4	43.3	-1.1	42.7	-1.4

[Continued]

Plant and Animal Fibers

Producer Price Index
Base 1982 = 100

[Continued]

For 1926-1993. Columns headed % show percentile change in the index from the previous period for which an index is available.

Year	Jan Index	%	Feb Index	%	Mar Index	%	Apr Index	%	May Index	%	Jun Index	%	Jul Index	%	Aug Index	%	Sep Index	%	Oct Index	%	Nov Index	%	Dec Index	%
1971	42.9	0.5	43.4	1.2	43.8	0.9	44.1	0.7	44.5	0.9	45.5	2.2	45.6	0.2	46.0	0.9	46.9	2.0	47.4	1.1	47.9	1.1	50.5	5.4
1972	54.0	6.9	55.8	3.3	56.3	0.9	60.2	6.9	64.1	6.5	62.7	-2.2	61.8	-1.4	59.4	-3.9	53.4	-10.1	52.1	-2.4	55.3	6.1	59.6	7.8
1973	66.1	10.9	69.0	4.4	75.2	9.0	76.2	1.3	84.5	10.9	87.6	3.7	91.9	4.9	112.6	22.5	132.0	17.2	131.3	-0.5	115.3	-12.2	127.8	10.8
1974	135.4	5.9	118.3	-12.6	108.1	-8.6	103.1	-4.6	96.7	-6.2	96.3	-0.4	92.6	-3.8	89.4	-3.5	83.6	-6.5	78.5	-6.1	74.3	-5.4	70.5	-5.1
1975	68.4	-3.0	66.7	-2.5	68.2	2.2	67.8	-0.6	75.5	11.4	71.7	-5.0	75.3	5.0	79.4	5.4	80.8	1.8	81.1	0.4	82.3	1.5	88.5	7.5
1976	95.3	7.7	91.9	-3.6	92.5	0.7	92.4	-0.1	99.3	7.5	116.2	17.0	132.6	14.1	116.1	-12.4	119.4	2.8	123.1	3.1	127.1	3.2	118.0	-7.2
1977	106.7	-9.6	118.3	10.9	124.4	5.2	123.0	-1.1	117.6	-4.4	97.3	-17.3	96.3	-1.0	88.8	-7.8	81.7	-8.0	82.3	0.7	80.9	-1.7	79.3	-2.0
1978	84.3	6.3	86.0	2.0	92.1	7.1	89.2	-3.1	94.5	5.9	95.1	0.6	93.6	-1.6	97.3	4.0	99.2	2.0	103.6	4.4	104.2	0.6	104.9	0.7
1979	105.3	0.4	101.1	-4.0	97.5	-3.6	97.5	0.0	102.3	4.9	108.2	5.8	102.3	-5.5	102.5	0.2	104.1	1.6	104.9	0.8	106.2	1.2	109.4	3.0
1980	117.8	7.7	132.8	12.7	125.6	-5.4	131.6	4.8	134.4	2.1	121.7	-9.4	131.6	8.1	138.4	5.2	145.5	5.1	137.2	-5.7	141.5	3.1	144.9	2.4
1981	140.0	-3.4	132.2	-5.6	133.1	0.7	135.1	1.5	127.3	-5.8	128.0	0.5	123.8	-3.3	114.6	-7.4	101.8	-11.2	104.3	2.5	97.8	-6.2	92.8	-5.1
1982	97.7	5.3	95.4	-2.4	98.3	3.0	102.2	4.0	105.5	3.2	100.1	-5.1	108.8	8.7	102.3	-6.0	97.0	-5.2	97.6	0.6	96.3	-1.3	98.8	2.6
1983	99.4	0.6	101.7	2.3	107.0	5.2	105.3	-1.6	110.3	4.7	113.2	2.6	113.5	0.3	118.6	4.5	117.6	-0.8	115.6	-1.7	120.1	3.9	120.3	0.2
1984	113.0	-6.1	114.7	1.5	123.4	7.6	124.3	0.7	127.7	2.7	124.5	-2.5	116.2	-6.7	104.2	-10.3	103.6	-0.6	100.0	-3.5	99.2	-0.8	100.1	0.9
1985	100.8	0.7	98.9	-1.9	98.8	-0.1	104.1	5.4	99.9	-4.0	98.1	-1.8	99.4	1.3	95.9	-3.5	94.2	-1.8	94.3	0.1	93.5	-0.8	91.9	-1.7
1986	96.8	5.3	97.8	1.0	101.9	4.2	103.8	1.9	106.2	2.3	108.2	1.9	108.7	0.5	46.5	-57.2	53.2	14.4	74.3	39.7	75.9	2.2	87.1	14.8
1987	94.7	8.7	93.1	-1.7	89.9	-3.4	98.4	9.5	108.7	10.5	116.1	6.8	120.1	3.4	123.4	2.7	118.5	-4.0	108.9	-8.1	105.1	-3.5	100.5	-4.4
1988	100.7	0.2	97.8	-2.9	103.2	5.5	103.6	0.4	103.7	0.1	107.6	3.8	99.4	-7.6	98.7	-0.7	89.6	-9.2	89.7	0.1	93.1	3.8	93.9	0.9
1989	95.8	2.0	94.8	-1.0	98.4	3.8	105.0	6.7	108.1	3.0	110.5	2.2	111.5	0.9	116.8	4.8	113.9	-2.5	116.9	2.6	115.3	-1.4	106.3	-7.8
1990	104.8	-1.4	108.7	3.7	114.7	5.5	118.7	3.5	121.9	2.7	125.9	3.3	129.4	2.8	125.1	-3.3	116.6	-6.8	116.4	-0.2	115.0	-1.2	116.9	1.7
1991	115.2	-1.5	126.3	9.6	129.1	2.2	134.0	3.8	139.2	3.9	130.8	-6.0	120.2	-8.1	106.7	-11.2	103.5	-3.0	96.3	-7.0	90.3	-6.2	89.7	-0.7
1992	85.4	-4.8	83.5	-2.2	84.7	1.4	89.0	5.1	93.4	4.9	96.2	3.0	102.0	6.0	96.6	-5.3	93.8	-2.9	82.8	-11.7	83.2	0.5	87.3	4.9
1993	89.5	2.5	89.5	0.0	94.2	5.3	91.5	-2.9	93.3	2.0	90.5	-3.0	90.8	0.3	88.5	-2.5	89.4	1.0	92.0	2.9	88.8	-3.5	98.1	10.5

Source: U.S. Department of Labor, Bureau of Labor Statistics, Division of Industry Prices and Price Indexes. n.e.c. stands for not elsewhere classified. - indicates no data collected for period or unavailable.

Fluid Milk
Producer Price Index
Base 1982 = 100

For 1926-1993. Columns headed % show percentile change in the index from the previous period for which an index is available.

Year	Jan Index	%	Feb Index	%	Mar Index	%	Apr Index	%	May Index	%	Jun Index	%	Jul Index	%	Aug Index	%	Sep Index	%	Oct Index	%	Nov Index	%	Dec Index	%
1926	19.6	-	19.6	0.0	19.6	0.0	19.8	1.0	19.2	-3.0	18.9	-1.6	19.1	1.1	19.3	1.0	19.9	3.1	19.8	-0.5	19.7	-0.5	19.7	0.0
1927	19.6	-0.5	19.6	0.0	19.6	0.0	19.4	-1.0	19.2	-1.0	19.2	0.0	19.4	1.0	19.4	0.0	20.9	7.7	20.9	0.0	21.0	0.5	21.0	0.0
1928	20.8	-1.0	20.8	0.0	19.4	-6.7	19.3	-0.5	19.1	-1.0	19.1	0.0	20.0	4.7	20.9	4.5	21.1	1.0	21.0	-0.5	21.0	0.0	21.0	0.0
1929	21.2	1.0	21.1	-0.5	21.1	0.0	21.1	0.0	21.1	0.0	21.4	1.4	21.1	-1.4	21.1	0.0	21.2	0.5	21.4	0.9	21.4	0.0	21.4	0.0
1930	21.1	-1.4	21.1	0.0	21.1	0.0	21.1	0.0	19.8	-6.2	19.8	0.0	19.8	0.0	20.7	4.5	21.1	1.9	21.1	0.0	21.1	0.0	19.8	-6.2
1931	18.7	-5.6	18.5	-1.1	18.5	0.0	18.5	0.0	18.5	0.0	18.9	2.2	19.2	1.6	18.8	-2.1	18.8	0.0	18.8	0.0	17.5	-6.9	17.5	0.0
1932	14.7	-16.0	13.8	-6.1	13.8	0.0	13.8	0.0	13.8	0.0	13.5	-2.2	13.5	0.0	13.5	0.0	13.5	0.0	13.5	0.0	13.5	0.0	11.9	-11.9
1933	11.5	-3.4	11.0	-4.3	10.8	-1.8	10.8	0.0	12.0	11.1	13.5	12.5	13.9	3.0	14.7	5.8	14.7	0.0	14.8	0.7	15.2	2.7	15.5	2.0
1934	15.2	-1.9	14.6	-3.9	14.4	-1.4	14.3	-0.7	15.9	11.2	16.9	6.3	17.3	2.4	17.3	0.0	17.3	0.0	17.5	1.2	17.0	-2.9	17.0	0.0
1935	17.2	1.2	17.4	1.2	17.4	0.0	17.3	-0.6	17.1	-1.2	16.9	-1.2	16.9	0.0	17.1	1.2	16.8	-1.8	16.5	-1.8	16.5	0.0	16.6	0.6
1936	16.5	-0.6	16.6	0.6	15.9	-4.2	15.8	-0.6	15.8	0.0	15.8	0.0	16.4	3.8	17.1	4.3	18.2	6.4	18.3	0.5	18.4	0.5	18.4	0.0
1937	18.4	0.0	18.5	0.5	18.5	0.0	15.1	-18.4	13.3	-11.9	13.3	0.0	14.6	9.8	15.5	6.2	16.7	7.7	16.7	0.0	17.6	5.4	17.8	1.1
1938	16.4	-7.9	15.6	-4.9	15.4	-1.3	14.8	-3.9	14.2	-4.1	14.1	-0.7	14.3	1.4	14.2	-0.7	15.2	7.0	15.2	0.0	15.3	0.7	15.4	0.7
1939	15.2	-1.3	15.1	-0.7	13.0	-13.9	10.9	-16.2	10.9	0.0	11.1	1.8	13.2	18.9	14.6	10.6	15.9	8.9	16.9	6.3	16.9	0.0	16.7	-1.2
1940	16.7	0.0	16.6	-0.6	16.5	-0.6	16.5	0.0	14.8	-10.3	14.8	0.0	15.2	2.7	15.3	0.7	15.1	-1.3	15.4	2.0	16.4	6.5	16.2	-1.2
1941	16.1	-0.6	16.0	-0.6	16.1	0.6	15.5	-3.7	14.6	-5.8	15.4	5.5	16.8	9.1	17.7	5.4	18.2	2.8	19.3	6.0	19.4	0.5	19.4	0.0
1942	19.4	0.0	19.2	-1.0	19.0	-1.0	17.9	-5.8	17.6	-1.7	17.5	-0.6	18.7	6.9	19.0	1.6	20.0	5.3	20.2	1.0	21.1	4.5	21.3	0.9
1943	21.6	1.4	21.6	0.0	21.6	0.0	21.6	0.0	21.6	0.0	21.6	0.0	21.6	0.0	21.6	0.0	21.6	0.0	21.7	0.5	22.5	3.7	22.5	0.0
1944	22.6	0.4	22.6	0.0	22.5	-0.4	22.4	-0.4	22.3	-0.4	22.3	0.0	22.3	0.0	22.4	0.4	22.5	0.4	22.5	0.0	22.5	0.0	22.6	0.4
1945	22.5	0.0	22.5	0.0	22.5	0.0	22.5	0.0	22.4	-0.4	22.4	0.0	22.4	0.0	22.4	0.0	22.4	0.0	22.4	0.0	22.5	0.4	22.6	0.4
1946	22.6	0.0	22.7	0.4	22.7	0.0	22.8	0.4	22.9	0.4	24.8	8.3	28.9	16.5	29.8	3.1	30.5	2.3	32.9	7.9	33.2	0.9	32.8	-1.2
1947	32.3	-1.5	30.6	-5.3	29.8	-2.6	28.4	-4.7	25.8	-9.2	26.1	1.2	27.4	5.0	29.6	8.0	31.0	4.7	32.0	3.2	32.8	2.5	34.0	3.7
1948	35.3	3.8	34.8	-1.4	33.6	-3.4	33.9	0.9	34.0	0.3	35.0	2.9	36.3	3.7	36.2	-0.3	34.9	-3.6	32.6	-6.6	31.5	-3.4	31.4	-0.3
1949	29.7	-5.4	28.5	-4.0	27.6	-3.2	26.7	-3.3	26.3	-1.5	26.3	0.0	26.7	1.5	27.6	3.4	27.8	0.7	27.9	0.4	28.2	1.1	27.9	-1.1
1950	27.3	-2.2	27.2	-0.4	26.9	-1.1	25.9	-3.7	25.3	-2.3	25.0	-1.2	25.8	3.2	26.7	3.5	27.6	3.4	28.4	2.9	29.1	2.5	30.1	3.4
1951	32.5	8.0	32.7	0.6	32.5	-0.6	31.5	-3.1	30.8	-2.2	30.9	0.3	31.3	1.3	31.8	·1.6	31.8	0.0	32.2	1.3	32.9	2.2	33.5	1.8
1952	33.7	0.6	33.9	0.6	33.7	-0.6	33.1	-1.8	31.9	-3.6	31.6	-0.9	32.7	3.5	33.7	3.1	34.8	3.3	35.1	0.9	34.5	-1.7	33.3	-3.5
1953	32.2	-3.3	31.5	-2.2	30.7	-2.5	29.6	-3.6	28.6	-3.4	28.5	-0.3	29.5	3.5	29.8	1.0	30.3	1.7	30.8	1.7	31.2	1.3	30.4	-2.6
1954	29.8	-2.0	29.0	-2.7	28.5	-1.7	27.0	-5.3	25.7	-4.8	25.6	-0.4	26.8	4.7	27.4	2.2	28.0	2.2	28.7	2.5	29.1	1.4	28.6	-1.7
1955	28.2	-1.4	28.1	-0.4	27.7	-1.4	27.6	-0.4	26.7	-3.3	26.6	-0.4	27.2	2.3	28.0	2.9	28.6	2.1	29.1	1.7	29.0	-0.3	28.9	-0.3
1956	28.7	-0.7	28.7	0.0	27.7	-3.5	27.5	-0.7	28.4	3.3	28.4	0.0	28.9	1.8	29.1	0.7	29.3	0.7	29.7	1.4	30.2	1.7	30.3	0.3
1957	30.0	-1.0	29.8	-0.7	29.2	-2.0	29.0	-0.7	28.2	-2.8	28.1	-0.4	28.5	1.4	29.0	1.8	29.6	2.1	30.2	2.0	30.4	0.7	30.3	-0.3
1958	30.1	-0.7	29.9	-0.7	29.2	-2.3	28.0	-4.1	27.7	-1.1	27.6	-0.4	28.1	1.8	28.6	1.8	29.3	2.4	29.4	0.3	29.5	0.3	29.4	-0.3
1959	29.2	-0.7	29.2	0.0	28.6	-2.1	28.1	-1.7	27.6	-1.8	27.5	-0.4	28.2	2.5	28.9	2.5	29.3	1.4	29.7	1.4	30.0	1.0	30.1	0.3
1960	30.3	0.7	30.3	0.0	29.9	-1.3	29.2	-2.3	28.4	-2.7	28.5	0.4	29.2	2.5	29.7	1.7	30.5	2.7	31.0	1.6	31.3	1.0	31.3	0.0
1961	30.9	-1.3	30.4	-1.6	30.2	-0.7	29.7	-1.7	29.2	-1.7	29.0	-0.7	30.0	3.4	30.1	0.3	30.4	1.0	30.7	1.0	30.8	0.3	30.6	-0.6
1962	30.6	0.0	30.4	-0.7	29.8	-2.0	28.7	-3.7	28.1	-2.1	28.2	0.4	29.0	2.8	29.3	1.0	29.5	0.7	29.8	1.0	29.7	-0.3	29.6	-0.3
1963	29.4	-0.7	29.3	-0.3	28.9	-1.4	28.5	-1.4	28.2	-1.1	28.4	0.7	29.0	2.1	29.2	0.7	29.6	1.4	29.8	0.7	30.0	0.7	30.0	0.0
1964	29.8	-0.7	29.7	-0.3	29.4	-1.0	28.9	-1.7	28.6	-1.0	28.7	0.3	29.2	1.7	29.6	1.4	30.1	1.7	30.3	0.7	30.6	1.0	30.5	-0.3
1965	30.2	-1.0	30.1	-0.3	29.1	-3.3	29.4	1.0	29.1	-1.0	29.2	0.3	29.7	1.7	30.2	1.7	30.4	0.7	30.8	1.3	31.2	1.3	31.4	0.6
1966	31.5	0.3	32.4	2.9	32.7	0.9	32.5	-0.6	32.2	-0.9	32.7	1.6	34.7	6.1	36.0	3.7	36.4	1.1	36.5	0.3	36.1	-1.1	36.0	-0.3
1967	35.8	-0.6	35.5	-0.8	34.5	-2.8	34.6	0.3	35.0	1.2	35.2	0.6	35.2	0.0	35.1	-0.3	35.9	2.3	35.9	0.0	35.9	0.0	36.1	0.6
1968	36.2	0.3	36.2	0.0	36.0	-0.6	36.7	1.9	37.5	2.2	37.6	0.3	37.9	0.8	37.9	0.0	38.1	0.5	38.4	0.8	38.4	0.0	38.4	0.0
1969	38.3	-0.3	38.5	0.5	38.5	0.0	38.8	0.8	38.9	0.3	39.1	0.5	39.2	0.3	39.2	0.0	39.5	0.8	39.7	0.5	40.0	0.8	40.8	2.0
1970	41.0	0.5	40.9	-0.2	40.6	-0.7	41.0	1.0	40.5	-1.2	40.5	0.0	40.6	0.2	40.5	-0.2	40.7	0.5	40.8	0.2	41.3	1.2	41.6	0.7

[Continued]

Fluid Milk

Producer Price Index
Base 1982 = 100
[Continued]

For 1926-1993. Columns headed % show percentile change in the index from the previous period for which an index is available.

Year	Jan Index	%	Feb Index	%	Mar Index	%	Apr Index	%	May Index	%	Jun Index	%	Jul Index	%	Aug Index	%	Sep Index	%	Oct Index	%	Nov Index	%	Dec Index	%
1971	41.6	0.0	41.7	0.2	41.9	0.5	42.1	0.5	42.0	-0.2	42.2	0.5	42.3	0.2	42.2	-0.2	42.2	0.0	42.2	0.0	42.1	-0.2	42.1	0.0
1972	42.7	1.4	42.6	-0.2	43.1	1.2	43.2	0.2	43.4	0.5	43.1	-0.7	43.2	0.2	43.2	0.0	43.5	0.7	43.8	0.7	43.7	-0.2	43.7	0.0
1973	44.8	2.5	45.5	1.6	46.1	1.3	46.2	0.2	47.0	1.7	47.2	0.4	47.2	0.0	50.8	7.6	56.2	10.6	59.6	6.0	62.7	5.2	62.7	0.0
1974	65.4	4.3	65.9	0.8	65.8	-0.2	65.3	-0.8	63.2	-3.2	58.3	-7.8	55.8	-4.3	56.0	0.4	56.4	0.7	58.8	4.3	61.8	5.1	61.2	-1.0
1975	60.9	-0.5	60.9	0.0	60.1	-1.3	59.3	-1.3	59.0	-0.5	58.6	-0.7	59.7	1.9	62.3	4.4	65.8	5.6	69.9	6.2	73.6	5.3	75.3	2.3
1976	75.2	-0.1	73.5	-2.3	71.4	-2.9	69.7	-2.4	68.7	-1.4	67.3	-2.0	68.4	1.6	71.0	3.8	72.1	1.5	73.2	1.5	72.3	-1.2	71.8	-0.7
1977	70.9	-1.3	70.2	-1.0	69.1	-1.6	70.0	1.3	70.2	0.3	70.6	0.6	71.7	1.6	72.6	1.3	73.2	0.8	74.2	1.4	74.3	0.1	74.4	0.1
1978	73.8	-0.8	74.2	0.5	74.7	0.7	75.1	0.5	75.1	0.0	75.1	0.0	76.6	2.0	78.1	2.0	80.0	2.4	82.1	2.6	83.5	1.7	85.4	2.3
1979	85.6	0.2	86.6	1.2	86.3	-0.3	85.8	-0.6	85.7	-0.1	86.3	0.7	87.7	1.6	88.5	0.9	91.5	3.4	92.3	0.9	92.9	0.7	93.5	0.6
1980	92.8	-0.7	93.4	0.6	93.1	-0.3	93.9	0.9	93.9	0.0	94.0	0.1	94.1	0.1	96.1	2.1	97.5	1.5	99.4	1.9	100.8	1.4	102.8	2.0
1981	102.1	-0.7	102.5	0.4	102.5	0.0	101.7	-0.8	100.4	-1.3	100.9	0.5	100.6	-0.3	100.9	0.3	101.7	0.8	104.2	2.5	102.0	-2.1	101.5	-0.5
1982	101.8	0.3	101.2	-0.6	100.0	-1.2	99.2	-0.8	98.7	-0.5	98.7	0.0	98.8	0.1	98.7	-0.1	99.8	1.1	100.9	1.1	101.2	0.3	101.1	-0.1
1983	100.7	-0.4	100.6	-0.1	100.1	-0.5	99.4	-0.7	99.0	-0.4	98.6	-0.4	98.7	0.1	99.7	1.0	100.7	1.0	100.6	-0.1	100.3	-0.3	99.6	-0.7
1984	98.8	-0.8	97.6	-1.2	97.1	-0.5	96.5	-0.6	96.2	-0.3	96.2	0.0	97.0	0.8	98.0	1.0	99.9	1.9	101.5	1.6	101.8	0.3	101.8	0.0
1985	100.7	-1.1	99.5	-1.2	98.5	-1.0	96.0	-2.5	93.8	-2.3	91.9	-2.0	90.7	-1.3	90.3	-0.4	90.6	0.3	90.6	0.0	91.1	0.6	90.3	-0.9
1986	90.3	0.0	90.2	-0.1	88.9	-1.4	87.9	-1.1	88.2	0.3	88.5	0.3	89.0	0.6	90.7	1.9	91.6	1.0	94.4	3.1	95.7	1.4	96.1	0.4
1987	96.1	0.0	94.6	-1.6	92.2	-2.5	90.7	-1.6	89.4	-1.4	88.1	-1.5	89.7	1.8	91.1	1.6	92.7	1.8	93.2	0.5	93.1	-0.1	91.5	-1.7
1988	90.5	-1.1	89.1	-1.5	86.7	-2.7	85.4	-1.5	85.3	-0.1	83.8	-1.8	84.9	1.3	88.1	3.8	91.2	3.5	94.3	3.4	96.5	2.3	97.0	0.5
1989	96.4	-0.6	94.7	-1.8	91.3	-3.6	90.2	-1.2	89.7	-0.6	91.0	1.4	93.7	3.0	98.1	4.7	103.1	5.1	107.6	4.4	113.1	5.1	116.2	2.7
1990	114.7	-1.3	105.1	-8.4	100.5	-4.4	98.0	-2.5	100.3	2.3	103.1	2.8	105.3	2.1	105.5	0.2	104.6	-0.9	95.4	-8.8	91.8	-3.8	85.8	-6.5
1991	84.4	-1.6	84.1	-0.4	83.1	-1.2	82.9	-0.2	83.4	0.6	85.1	2.0	88.1	3.5	91.8	4.2	94.3	2.7	98.1	4.0	99.3	1.2	99.6	0.3
1992	97.7	-1.9	93.8	-4.0	91.3	-2.7	91.7	0.4	95.3	3.9	98.0	2.8	99.6	1.6	100.1	0.5	99.5	-0.6	98.1	-1.4	95.4	-2.8	92.4	-3.1
1993	91.0	-1.5	89.1	-2.1	89.4	0.3	92.5	3.5	95.9	3.7	96.5	0.6	94.9	-1.7	92.6	-2.4	93.1	0.5	94.9	1.9	97.3	2.5	98.7	1.4

Source: U.S. Department of Labor, Bureau of Labor Statistics, Division of Industry Prices and Price Indexes. n.e.c. stands for not elsewhere classified. - indicates no data collected for period or unavailable.

Eggs
Producer Price Index
Base 1982 = 100

For 1926-1993. Columns headed % show percentile change in the index from the previous period for which an index is available.

Year	Jan Index	%	Feb Index	%	Mar Index	%	Apr Index	%	May Index	%	Jun Index	%	Jul Index	%	Aug Index	%	Sep Index	%	Oct Index	%	Nov Index	%	Dec Index	%
1926	-	-	-	-	-	-	-	-	-	-	-	-	-	-	-	-	-	-	-	-	-	-	-	-
1927	-	-	-	-	-	-	-	-	-	-	-	-	-	-	-	-	-	-	-	-	-	-	-	-
1928	-	-	-	-	-	-	-	-	-	-	-	-	-	-	-	-	-	-	-	-	-	-	-	-
1929	-	-	-	-	-	-	-	-	-	-	-	-	-	-	-	-	-	-	-	-	-	-	-	-
1930	-	-	-	-	-	-	-	-	-	-	-	-	-	-	-	-	-	-	-	-	-	-	-	-
1931	-	-	-	-	-	-	-	-	-	-	-	-	-	-	-	-	-	-	-	-	-	-	-	-
1932	-	-	-	-	-	-	-	-	-	-	-	-	-	-	-	-	-	-	-	-	-	-	-	-
1933	-	-	-	-	-	-	-	-	-	-	-	-	-	-	-	-	-	-	-	-	-	-	-	-
1934	-	-	-	-	-	-	-	-	-	-	-	-	-	-	-	-	-	-	-	-	-	-	-	-
1935	-	-	-	-	-	-	-	-	-	-	-	-	-	-	-	-	-	-	-	-	-	-	-	-
1936	-	-	-	-	-	-	-	-	-	-	-	-	-	-	-	-	-	-	-	-	-	-	-	-
1937	48.1	-	43.1	-10.4	44.3	2.8	43.3	-2.3	39.9	-7.9	39.4	-1.3	41.4	5.1	42.1	1.7	46.7	10.9	47.3	1.3	52.7	11.4	50.0	-5.1
1938	43.3	-13.4	35.1	-18.9	34.9	-0.6	35.2	0.9	39.6	12.5	39.7	0.3	42.2	6.3	44.1	4.5	50.5	14.5	52.8	4.6	57.2	8.3	54.3	-5.1
1939	38.6	-28.9	33.9	-12.2	33.2	-2.1	32.8	-1.2	31.7	-3.4	31.1	-1.9	31.8	2.3	32.0	0.6	37.3	16.6	40.9	9.7	46.8	14.4	39.3	-16.0
1940	40.7	3.6	43.4	6.6	33.2	-23.5	32.7	-1.5	32.7	0.0	31.4	-4.0	31.8	1.3	33.3	4.7	39.9	19.8	42.4	6.3	46.0	8.5	49.7	8.0
1941	37.8	-23.9	33.5	-11.4	36.1	7.8	42.5	17.7	44.5	4.7	49.3	10.8	51.8	5.1	54.1	4.4	57.7	6.7	61.0	5.7	69.4	13.8	66.7	-3.9
1942	65.0	-2.5	56.8	-12.6	54.6	-3.9	56.6	3.7	57.5	1.6	59.4	3.3	63.1	6.2	67.3	6.7	70.4	4.6	73.9	5.0	74.5	0.8	74.7	0.3
1943	74.0	-0.9	70.2	-5.1	72.9	3.8	71.6	-1.8	72.9	1.8	75.1	3.0	75.3	0.3	78.9	4.8	82.3	4.3	84.4	2.6	83.7	-0.8	80.2	-4.2
1944	72.6	-9.5	62.8	-13.5	60.2	-4.1	58.5	-2.8	57.5	-1.7	60.7	5.6	66.3	9.2	64.5	-2.7	70.3	9.0	74.5	6.0	82.4	10.6	83.8	1.7
1945	75.8	-9.5	68.2	-10.0	66.8	-2.1	67.0	0.3	67.0	0.0	68.3	1.9	69.9	2.3	74.0	5.9	67.5	-8.8	79.7	18.1	87.1	9.3	85.9	-1.4
1946	70.8	-17.6	65.8	-7.1	65.7	-0.2	64.5	-1.8	65.9	2.2	65.5	-0.6	65.3	-0.3	67.8	3.8	78.6	15.9	83.2	5.9	77.9	-6.4	75.2	-3.5
1947	76.0	1.1	74.5	-2.0	80.8	8.5	82.7	2.4	80.5	-2.7	82.0	1.9	86.6	5.6	84.5	-2.4	91.7	8.5	91.9	0.2	89.0	-3.2	100.7	13.1
1948	86.2	-14.4	83.3	-3.4	82.9	-0.5	83.3	0.5	81.9	-1.7	84.3	2.9	87.2	3.4	95.9	10.0	101.6	5.9	112.4	10.6	110.5	-1.7	96.5	-12.7
1949	85.1	-11.8	77.1	-9.4	79.8	3.5	85.6	7.3	86.0	0.5	87.2	1.4	95.2	9.2	100.6	5.7	108.7	8.1	101.2	-6.9	90.9	-10.2	67.9	-25.3
1950	58.9	-13.3	59.9	1.7	65.0	8.5	62.3	-4.2	58.5	-6.1	62.6	7.0	71.2	13.7	75.5	6.0	88.5	17.2	97.0	9.6	101.8	4.9	102.5	0.7
1951	79.9	-22.0	80.3	0.5	85.6	6.6	85.8	0.2	89.1	3.8	94.1	5.6	94.2	0.1	106.2	12.7	111.4	4.9	115.1	3.3	116.6	1.3	90.3	-22.6
1952	71.6	-20.7	65.9	-8.0	67.9	3.0	72.4	6.6	65.9	-9.0	71.8	9.0	100.1	39.4	101.2	1.1	99.8	-1.4	110.6	10.8	104.3	-5.7	88.3	-15.3
1953	83.3	-5.7	79.0	-5.2	89.2	12.9	90.9	1.9	87.5	-3.7	94.5	8.0	94.2	-0.3	100.9	7.1	108.6	7.6	112.0	3.1	99.0	-11.6	86.2	-12.9
1954	82.2	-4.6	79.5	-3.3	71.0	-10.7	69.1	-2.7	61.2	-11.4	62.8	2.6	74.8	19.1	76.6	2.4	68.5	-10.6	73.1	6.7	74.0	1.2	56.7	-23.4
1955	57.7	1.8	79.9	38.5	72.9	-8.8	69.1	-5.2	63.4	-8.2	66.0	4.1	69.8	5.8	84.6	21.2	91.3	7.9	82.1	-10.1	87.7	6.8	88.0	0.3
1956	76.2	-13.4	72.1	-5.4	75.3	4.4	70.8	-6.0	71.1	0.4	69.8	-1.8	72.8	4.3	68.9	-5.4	80.9	17.4	77.4	-4.3	70.3	-9.2	65.9	-6.3
1957	58.3	-11.5	58.8	0.9	56.6	-3.7	60.7	7.2	51.0	-16.0	54.1	6.1	67.6	25.0	70.7	4.6	80.9	14.4	91.8	13.5	88.7	-3.4	82.8	-6.7
1958	65.5	-20.9	65.8	0.5	83.0	26.1	68.4	-17.6	67.1	-1.9	66.4	-1.0	67.5	1.7	72.3	7.1	87.4	20.9	80.8	-7.6	76.7	-5.1	68.9	-10.2
1959	64.2	-6.8	61.4	-4.4	62.5	1.8	48.3	-22.7	45.3	-6.2	50.1	10.6	58.0	15.8	59.2	2.1	75.7	27.9	61.2	-19.2	56.2	-8.2	55.7	-0.9
1960	50.5	-9.3	51.8	2.6	67.3	29.9	71.1	5.6	61.7	-13.2	57.0	-7.6	58.0	1.8	67.8	16.9	75.8	11.8	87.7	15.7	95.9	9.4	77.8	-18.9
1961	66.7	-14.3	72.0	7.9	67.1	-6.8	58.9	-12.2	56.2	-4.6	56.2	0.0	67.0	19.2	71.6	6.9	67.9	-5.2	70.5	3.8	71.0	0.7	63.7	-10.3
1962	65.0	2.0	64.7	-0.5	60.3	-6.8	60.9	1.0	50.0	-17.9	53.1	6.2	57.2	7.7	65.1	13.8	73.5	12.9	68.4	-6.9	74.6	9.1	65.9	-11.7
1963	66.4	0.8	65.8	-0.9	66.3	0.8	53.9	-18.7	51.2	-5.0	52.6	2.7	58.1	10.5	63.7	9.6	71.6	12.4	65.0	-9.2	68.0	4.6	66.3	-2.5
1964	70.6	6.5	59.5	-15.7	60.1	1.0	52.8	-12.1	51.0	-3.4	58.9	15.5	58.0	-1.5	65.5	12.9	64.3	-1.8	64.9	0.9	60.8	-6.3	56.6	-6.9
1965	52.4	-7.4	50.9	-2.9	57.7	13.4	60.5	4.9	52.4	-13.4	54.4	3.8	56.2	3.3	66.4	18.1	70.3	5.9	69.8	-0.7	75.7	8.5	78.5	3.7
1966	66.3	-15.5	77.2	16.4	78.7	1.9	67.6	-14.1	57.7	-14.6	60.3	4.5	65.4	8.5	72.1	10.2	84.9	17.8	76.2	-10.2	80.9	6.2	72.4	-10.5
1967	66.4	-8.3	55.7	-16.1	60.3	8.3	51.1	-15.3	49.5	-3.1	50.5	2.0	57.1	13.1	54.5	-4.6	61.8	13.4	51.0	-17.5	53.6	5.1	60.3	12.5
1968	49.0	-18.7	53.1	8.4	53.7	1.1	54.9	2.2	48.2	-12.2	58.6	21.6	60.7	3.6	65.3	7.6	84.1	28.8	70.7	-15.9	71.4	1.0	78.2	9.5
1969	81.2	3.8	71.7	-11.7	73.6	2.6	64.6	-12.2	53.5	-17.2	57.0	6.5	77.7	36.3	66.7	-14.2	81.3	21.9	75.5	-7.1	92.8	22.9	103.4	11.4
1970	101.0	-2.3	90.9	-10.0	79.7	-12.3	63.0	-21.0	52.9	-16.0	56.6	7.0	73.8	30.4	59.5	-19.4	78.1	31.3	58.5	-25.1	65.9	12.6	71.2	8.0

[Continued]

Eggs
Producer Price Index
Base 1982 = 100
[Continued]

For 1926-1993. Columns headed % show percentile change in the index from the previous period for which an index is available.

Year	Jan Index	%	Feb Index	%	Mar Index	%	Apr Index	%	May Index	%	Jun Index	%	Jul Index	%	Aug Index	%	Sep Index	%	Oct Index	%	Nov Index	%	Dec Index	%
1971	63.4	-11.0	54.6	-13.9	56.6	3.7	58.4	3.2	51.7	-11.5	54.8	6.0	50.0	-8.8	61.6	23.2	60.3	-2.1	51.7	-14.3	49.5	-4.3	64.0	29.3
1972	51.8	-19.1	51.4	-0.8	60.3	17.3	48.8	-19.1	50.7	3.9	51.4	1.4	57.2	11.3	55.6	-2.8	64.3	15.6	55.4	-13.8	68.9	24.4	80.5	16.8
1973	88.5	9.9	72.8	-17.7	85.4	17.3	81.1	-5.0	76.7	-5.4	89.2	16.3	86.9	-2.6	117.3	35.0	107.2	-8.6	99.4	-7.3	101.4	2.0	106.6	5.1
1974	110.7	3.8	104.5	-5.6	93.9	-10.1	88.8	-5.4	70.5	-20.6	69.8	-1.0	73.8	5.7	83.7	13.4	95.0	13.5	93.9	-1.2	92.3	-1.7	101.3	9.8
1975	94.4	-6.8	90.9	-3.7	93.0	2.3	78.3	-15.8	81.4	4.0	77.1	-5.3	78.2	1.4	87.7	12.1	97.6	11.3	88.6	-9.2	98.4	11.1	107.6	9.3
1976	101.9	-5.3	99.0	-2.8	89.1	-10.0	91.0	2.1	96.0	5.5	92.8	-3.3	93.9	1.2	104.5	11.3	105.7	1.1	101.1	-4.4	107.9	6.7	119.5	10.8
1977	105.9	-11.4	109.0	2.9	97.1	-10.9	92.4	-4.8	80.8	-12.6	79.1	-2.1	87.6	10.7	90.7	3.5	91.4	0.8	77.0	-15.8	83.6	8.6	93.1	11.4
1978	81.2	-12.8	95.3	17.4	93.6	-1.8	85.2	-9.0	79.0	-7.3	71.3	-9.7	84.1	18.0	88.4	5.1	93.9	6.2	87.5	-6.8	99.6	13.8	105.7	6.1
1979	99.9	-5.5	98.9	-1.0	111.9	13.1	103.8	-7.2	91.7	-11.7	95.5	4.1	93.8	-1.8	93.3	-0.5	98.1	5.1	87.2	-11.1	100.0	14.7	111.0	11.0
1980	92.6	-16.6	84.2	-9.1	103.1	22.4	85.8	-16.8	78.6	-8.4	82.1	4.5	89.2	8.6	99.0	11.0	105.4	6.5	98.0	-7.0	108.6	10.8	121.7	12.1
1981	103.9	-14.6	103.4	-0.5	100.9	-2.4	109.8	8.8	92.3	-15.9	97.7	5.9	103.5	5.9	101.1	-2.3	108.1	6.9	108.4	0.3	117.3	8.2	109.4	-6.7
1982	104.7	-4.3	112.2	7.2	114.2	1.8	107.5	-5.9	91.9	-14.5	89.1	-3.0	96.1	7.9	96.1	0.0	97.0	0.9	99.5	2.6	96.5	-3.0	95.1	-1.5
1983	95.1	0.0	95.1	0.0	95.1	0.0	95.1	0.0	103.6	8.9	94.7	-8.6	99.2	4.8	106.0	6.9	112.0	5.7	-	-	-	-	-	-
1984	158.0	41.1	157.1	-0.6	132.0	-16.0	147.9	12.0	112.5	-23.9	99.5	-11.6	103.5	4.0	101.4	-2.0	99.4	-2.0	100.7	1.3	98.5	-2.2	104.9	6.5
1985	79.4	-24.3	90.4	13.9	93.8	3.8	98.0	4.5	84.0	-14.3	82.7	-1.5	91.8	11.0	94.5	2.9	105.4	11.5	106.9	1.4	109.2	2.2	111.9	2.5
1986	107.2	-4.2	98.5	-8.1	101.9	3.5	94.9	-6.9	90.7	-4.4	83.4	-8.0	93.6	12.2	107.1	14.4	101.3	-5.4	97.1	-4.1	110.4	13.7	108.5	-1.7
1987	99.0	-8.8	98.2	-0.8	89.7	-8.7	90.1	0.4	84.4	-6.3	80.1	-5.1	85.3	6.5	79.7	-6.6	100.6	26.2	81.1	-19.4	92.6	14.2	70.6	-23.8
1988	76.5	8.4	73.8	-3.5	79.7	8.0	73.1	-8.3	70.8	-3.1	77.1	8.9	95.7	24.1	107.0	11.8	102.1	-4.6	107.4	5.2	99.7	-7.2	100.3	0.6
1989	127.3	26.9	96.7	-24.0	135.8	40.4	110.8	-18.4	107.0	-3.4	104.8	-2.1	111.0	5.9	116.7	5.1	124.6	6.8	124.3	-0.2	134.5	8.2	141.3	5.1
1990	154.8	9.6	114.0	-26.4	128.9	13.1	127.9	-0.8	95.3	-25.5	100.4	5.4	91.6	-8.8	114.4	24.9	112.6	-1.6	121.6	8.0	125.0	2.8	124.5	-0.4
1991	140.0	12.4	110.5	-21.1	131.7	19.2	113.2	-14.0	94.6	-16.4	96.9	2.4	100.7	3.9	109.0	8.2	105.8	-2.9	105.0	-0.8	102.1	-2.8	118.7	16.3
1992	91.9	-22.6	94.1	2.4	92.8	-1.4	90.1	-2.9	86.4	-4.1	84.6	-2.1	83.9	-0.8	87.3	4.1	103.6	18.7	94.7	-8.6	112.4	18.7	107.7	-4.2
1993	102.9	-4.5	107.0	4.0	121.3	13.4	111.1	-8.4	101.6	-8.6	109.5	7.8	95.5	-12.8	110.5	15.7	93.2	-15.7	105.2	12.9	108.6	3.2	103.8	-4.4

Source: U.S. Department of Labor, Bureau of Labor Statistics, Division of Industry Prices and Price Indexes. n.e.c. stands for not elsewhere classified. - indicates no data collected for period or unavailable.

Hay, Hayseeds and Oilseeds

Producer Price Index
Base 1982 = 100

For 1926-1993. Columns headed % show percentile change in the index from the previous period for which an index is available.

Year	Jan Index	%	Feb Index	%	Mar Index	%	Apr Index	%	May Index	%	Jun Index	%	Jul Index	%	Aug Index	%	Sep Index	%	Oct Index	%	Nov Index	%	Dec Index	%
1926	30.9	-	30.1	-2.6	30.1	0.0	31.9	6.0	31.3	-1.9	27.5	-12.1	28.2	2.5	28.7	1.8	29.0	1.0	28.8	-0.7	28.7	-0.3	28.9	0.7
1927	28.9	0.0	28.6	-1.0	27.6	-3.5	27.4	-0.7	27.3	-0.4	25.1	-8.1	24.0	-4.4	24.9	3.8	24.8	-0.4	25.3	2.0	24.8	-2.0	26.0	4.8
1928	27.0	3.8	26.9	-0.4	28.3	5.2	29.6	4.6	30.5	3.0	27.4	-10.2	26.9	-1.8	27.3	1.5	28.4	4.0	30.2	6.3	31.3	3.6	32.0	2.2
1929	33.1	3.4	33.3	0.6	33.1	-0.6	32.8	-0.9	30.1	-8.2	27.0	-10.3	27.3	1.1	28.1	2.9	29.7	5.7	30.8	3.7	30.4	-1.3	29.8	-2.0
1930	29.7	-0.3	28.7	-3.4	28.2	-1.7	29.0	2.8	28.4	-2.1	25.8	-9.2	25.6	-0.8	27.9	9.0	27.5	-1.4	27.6	0.4	27.6	0.0	26.7	-3.3
1931	25.8	-3.4	24.9	-3.5	24.5	-1.6	24.6	0.4	23.1	-6.1	20.3	-12.1	19.9	-2.0	18.4	-7.5	17.9	-2.7	17.3	-3.4	17.7	2.3	18.4	4.0
1932	18.3	-0.5	17.4	-4.9	18.0	3.4	18.0	0.0	16.2	-10.0	13.9	-14.2	13.5	-2.9	13.7	1.5	13.7	0.0	14.1	2.9	14.1	0.0	13.8	-2.1
1933	13.7	-0.7	13.3	-2.9	13.7	3.0	14.2	3.6	15.6	9.9	15.3	-1.9	16.5	7.8	17.9	8.5	18.0	0.6	17.5	-2.8	17.7	1.1	18.2	2.8
1934	18.8	3.3	19.2	2.1	19.2	0.0	19.7	2.6	20.0	1.5	21.2	6.0	23.3	9.9	26.4	13.3	28.3	7.2	27.6	-2.5	27.0	-2.2	28.3	4.8
1935	28.9	2.1	28.6	-1.0	28.1	-1.7	27.3	-2.8	26.0	-4.8	23.1	-11.2	19.8	-14.3	18.0	-9.1	18.6	3.3	19.3	3.8	19.4	0.5	19.1	-1.5
1936	19.3	1.0	19.3	0.0	18.9	-2.1	20.0	5.8	19.4	-3.0	18.4	-5.2	22.0	19.6	25.0	13.6	25.8	3.2	26.2	1.6	27.3	4.2	27.9	2.2
1937	28.9	3.6	28.9	0.0	28.4	-1.7	28.7	1.1	27.1	-5.6	25.6	-5.5	24.7	-3.5	24.8	0.4	25.5	2.8	26.4	3.5	26.0	-1.5	26.5	1.9
1938	26.8	1.1	26.4	-1.5	25.6	-3.0	24.7	-3.5	23.9	-3.2	22.4	-6.3	22.1	-1.3	20.5	-7.2	18.3	-10.7	19.1	4.4	19.5	2.1	20.1	3.1
1939	21.2	5.5	20.7	-2.4	20.8	0.5	20.7	-0.5	19.9	-3.9	19.6	-1.5	19.0	-3.1	21.5	13.2	20.6	-4.2	21.6	4.9	21.7	0.5	21.9	0.9
1940	22.3	1.8	22.4	0.4	22.1	-1.3	22.0	-0.5	21.8	-0.9	19.9	-8.7	19.4	-2.5	19.7	1.5	18.8	-4.6	18.8	0.0	19.0	1.1	19.4	2.1
1941	19.9	2.6	19.9	0.0	19.7	-1.0	19.9	1.0	20.3	2.0	20.6	1.5	20.9	1.5	21.2	1.4	22.3	5.2	23.5	5.4	25.3	7.7	26.5	4.7
1942	28.1	6.0	29.2	3.9	30.5	4.5	30.9	1.3	30.5	-1.3	29.7	-2.6	29.8	0.3	29.6	-0.7	29.4	-0.7	29.7	1.0	30.4	2.4	31.6	3.9
1943	32.8	3.8	34.3	4.6	35.5	3.5	36.4	2.5	36.5	0.3	34.9	-4.4	34.8	-0.3	34.9	0.3	36.4	4.3	38.9	6.9	41.5	6.7	42.2	1.7
1944	42.1	-0.2	41.7	-1.0	41.0	-1.7	41.0	0.0	41.6	1.5	38.6	-7.2	37.9	-1.8	38.1	0.5	38.7	1.6	41.4	7.0	42.1	1.7	42.2	0.2
1945	43.2	2.4	43.8	1.4	43.5	-0.7	41.8	-3.9	39.2	-6.2	39.4	0.5	39.1	-0.8	37.6	-3.8	37.7	0.3	38.3	1.6	39.7	3.7	39.7	0.0
1946	39.8	0.3	39.6	-0.5	40.4	2.0	40.2	-0.5	40.2	0.0	40.4	0.5	41.1	1.7	41.4	0.7	42.0	1.4	46.7	11.2	54.3	16.3	55.3	1.8
1947	55.7	0.7	55.8	0.2	61.8	10.8	60.2	-2.6	51.8	-14.0	50.9	-1.7	50.9	0.0	50.3	-1.2	51.7	2.8	55.7	7.7	58.8	5.6	61.7	4.9
1948	64.3	4.2	58.6	-8.9	59.4	1.4	60.9	2.5	61.7	1.3	62.1	0.6	59.5	-4.2	53.7	-9.7	51.7	-3.7	49.2	-4.8	50.8	3.3	50.9	0.2
1949	49.3	-3.1	45.9	-6.9	45.3	-1.3	44.7	-1.3	42.2	-5.6	40.8	-3.3	41.0	0.5	45.3	10.5	41.0	-9.5	40.4	-1.5	40.8	1.0	41.7	2.2
1950	42.1	1.0	41.5	-1.4	48.3	16.4	45.0	-6.8	45.3	0.7	45.4	0.2	46.5	2.4	48.1	3.4	46.7	-2.9	45.6	-2.4	51.1	12.1	53.3	4.3
1951	55.6	4.3	57.3	3.1	57.7	0.7	57.3	-0.7	56.3	-1.7	53.2	-5.5	49.7	-6.6	48.4	-2.6	48.5	0.2	50.2	3.5	52.4	4.4	52.9	1.0
1952	52.7	-0.4	52.4	-0.6	50.3	-4.0	49.5	-1.6	49.8	0.6	51.1	2.6	52.1	2.0	51.8	-0.6	50.0	-3.5	50.1	0.2	51.1	2.0	51.0	-0.2
1953	50.4	-1.2	49.2	-2.4	50.6	2.8	49.4	-2.4	48.6	-1.6	46.5	-4.3	44.4	-4.5	44.1	-0.7	42.1	-4.5	43.7	3.8	45.6	4.3	46.5	2.0
1954	46.9	0.9	47.5	1.3	48.4	1.9	50.0	3.3	49.4	-1.2	49.8	0.8	49.2	-1.2	48.8	-0.8	45.3	-7.2	47.6	5.1	47.7	0.2	48.6	1.9
1955	48.9	0.6	48.4	-1.0	48.3	-0.2	46.6	-3.5	46.0	-1.3	45.7	-0.7	44.4	-2.8	42.3	-4.7	38.9	-8.0	39.3	1.0	39.3	0.0	40.2	2.3
1956	40.9	1.7	41.7	2.0	42.8	2.6	45.0	5.1	46.7	3.8	45.3	-3.0	41.8	-7.7	41.5	-0.7	39.7	-4.3	40.7	2.5	43.6	7.1	44.3	1.6
1957	44.9	1.4	43.9	-2.2	44.1	0.5	44.2	0.2	43.8	-0.9	43.2	-1.4	42.7	-1.2	42.2	-1.2	40.4	-4.3	40.1	-0.7	40.2	0.2	40.7	1.2
1958	41.0	0.7	41.0	0.0	41.2	0.5	41.4	0.5	41.4	0.0	41.1	-0.7	39.5	-3.9	39.3	-0.5	37.4	-4.8	38.0	1.6	38.3	0.8	38.9	1.6
1959	39.6	1.8	40.4	2.0	40.7	0.7	41.2	1.2	41.6	1.0	40.4	-2.9	38.9	-3.7	37.9	-2.6	37.9	0.0	39.1	3.2	39.6	1.3	39.6	0.0
1960	40.2	1.5	40.0	-0.5	39.8	-0.5	39.6	-0.5	39.7	0.3	38.6	-2.8	38.1	-1.3	38.2	0.3	37.5	-1.8	37.4	-0.3	37.6	0.5	38.4	2.1
1961	41.2	7.3	42.2	2.4	45.3	7.3	50.0	10.4	47.7	-4.6	43.4	-9.0	43.4	0.0	43.0	-0.9	41.5	-3.5	41.4	-0.2	42.2	1.9	42.3	0.2
1962	42.4	0.2	42.6	0.5	43.0	0.9	43.8	1.9	43.8	0.0	43.3	-1.1	42.9	-0.9	42.9	0.0	40.7	-5.1	42.0	3.2	43.5	3.6	44.1	1.4
1963	45.6	3.4	46.2	1.3	46.3	0.2	45.1	-2.6	45.8	1.6	46.3	1.1	45.3	-2.2	45.3	0.0	45.0	-0.7	46.5	3.3	47.8	2.8	46.7	-2.3
1964	47.0	0.6	46.4	-1.3	45.1	-2.8	43.8	-2.9	42.7	-2.5	42.8	0.2	43.0	0.5	43.1	0.2	44.3	2.8	45.2	2.0	47.1	4.2	47.5	0.8
1965	48.5	2.1	49.1	1.2	48.5	-1.2	48.6	0.2	47.0	-3.3	46.7	-0.6	46.3	-0.9	43.4	-6.3	42.9	-1.2	41.8	-2.6	43.7	4.5	45.1	3.2
1966	46.2	2.4	47.5	2.8	47.1	-0.8	47.6	1.1	49.0	2.9	49.9	1.8	55.1	10.4	56.7	2.9	51.4	-9.3	49.5	-3.7	50.0	1.0	50.7	1.4
1967	50.3	-0.8	49.0	-2.6	49.1	0.2	48.2	-1.8	48.0	-0.4	47.5	-1.0	47.2	-0.6	45.4	-3.8	44.4	-2.2	44.2	-0.5	44.7	1.1	45.9	2.7
1968	46.0	0.2	46.0	0.0	46.5	1.1	46.4	-0.2	46.5	0.2	46.0	-1.1	46.1	0.2	46.0	-0.2	44.6	-3.0	42.9	-3.8	43.7	1.9	44.3	1.4
1969	45.4	2.5	45.8	0.9	45.8	0.0	46.3	1.1	46.9	1.3	45.0	-4.1	45.3	0.7	43.7	-3.5	43.1	-1.4	41.2	-4.4	42.1	2.2	42.8	1.7
1970	43.8	2.3	43.3	-1.1	43.3	0.0	44.7	3.2	45.3	1.3	45.9	1.3	47.6	3.7	47.5	-0.2	48.2	1.5	50.1	3.9	50.8	1.4	50.2	-1.2

[Continued]

Hay, Hayseeds and Oilseeds
Producer Price Index
Base 1982 = 100
[Continued]

For 1926-1993. Columns headed % show percentile change in the index from the previous period for which an index is available.

Year	Jan Index	%	Feb Index	%	Mar Index	%	Apr Index	%	May Index	%	Jun Index	%	Jul Index	%	Aug Index	%	Sep Index	%	Oct Index	%	Nov Index	%	Dec Index	%
1971	51.1	1.8	51.0	-0.2	50.5	-1.0	49.2	-2.6	50.1	1.8	51.6	3.0	53.7	4.1	53.7	0.0	51.1	-4.8	50.7	-0.8	51.4	1.4	51.3	-0.2
1972	51.1	-0.4	51.8	1.4	53.7	3.7	55.7	3.7	54.9	-1.4	54.9	0.0	54.9	0.0	54.5	-0.7	55.4	1.7	54.0	-2.5	58.6	8.5	66.5	13.5
1973	67.6	1.7	83.7	23.8	88.4	5.6	87.8	-0.7	114.2	30.1	140.9	23.4	88.1	-37.5	138.0	56.6	143.1	3.7	99.2	-30.7	91.3	-8.0	98.9	8.3
1974	101.9	3.0	102.5	0.6	102.9	0.4	92.3	-10.3	91.4	-1.0	89.9	-1.6	101.5	12.9	124.4	22.6	117.1	-5.9	126.9	8.4	122.7	-3.3	115.5	-5.9
1975	109.2	-5.5	99.4	-9.0	91.6	-7.8	100.6	9.8	94.1	-6.5	89.4	-5.0	96.2	7.6	100.2	4.2	93.2	-7.0	88.6	-4.9	83.3	-6.0	83.4	0.1
1976	85.3	2.3	86.7	1.6	84.9	-2.1	84.6	-0.4	89.0	5.2	103.1	15.8	112.0	8.6	105.5	-5.8	108.9	3.2	103.4	-5.1	109.0	5.4	113.9	4.5
1977	115.1	1.1	119.6	3.9	130.6	9.2	151.5	16.0	136.2	-10.1	127.0	-6.8	97.6	-23.1	92.1	-5.6	83.8	-9.0	84.0	0.2	90.9	8.2	92.5	1.8
1978	93.3	0.9	90.0	-3.5	98.5	9.4	101.8	3.4	103.2	1.4	103.6	0.4	104.6	1.0	101.2	-3.3	99.9	-1.3	104.0	4.1	107.0	2.9	110.0	2.8
1979	112.8	2.5	115.7	2.6	117.2	1.3	116.7	-0.4	113.1	-3.1	121.4	7.3	122.2	0.7	118.4	-3.1	113.2	-4.4	110.7	-2.2	108.0	-2.4	108.2	0.2
1980	102.5	-5.3	105.6	3.0	101.5	-3.9	96.4	-5.0	97.2	0.8	97.5	0.3	118.1	21.1	122.9	4.1	131.9	7.3	133.7	1.4	140.2	4.9	145.8	4.0
1981	146.5	0.5	138.6	-5.4	136.1	-1.8	139.2	2.3	140.5	0.9	134.1	-4.6	136.3	1.6	133.6	-2.0	125.5	-6.1	108.3	-13.7	103.9	-4.1	102.8	-1.1
1982	102.6	-0.2	102.3	-0.3	100.4	-1.9	104.7	4.3	106.8	2.0	103.1	-3.5	103.4	0.3	96.1	-7.1	94.8	-1.4	91.3	-3.7	96.2	5.4	98.2	2.1
1983	99.8	1.6	102.4	2.6	102.4	0.0	106.4	3.9	106.8	0.4	100.2	-6.2	106.8	6.6	123.5	15.6	139.9	13.3	135.7	-3.0	135.2	-0.4	132.6	-1.9
1984	135.0	1.8	124.7	-7.6	132.2	6.0	132.6	0.3	139.6	5.3	128.0	-8.3	115.5	-9.8	114.0	-1.3	107.3	-5.9	103.0	-4.0	106.8	3.7	106.9	0.1
1985	106.3	-0.6	100.8	-5.2	99.6	-1.2	100.5	0.9	100.3	-0.2	99.0	-1.3	97.2	-1.8	92.5	-4.8	91.3	-1.3	86.8	-4.9	94.0	8.3	93.7	-0.3
1986	94.3	0.6	95.2	1.0	96.0	0.8	91.1	-5.1	91.4	0.3	95.2	4.2	93.7	-1.6	89.4	-4.6	89.2	-0.2	88.0	-1.3	98.4	11.8	93.5	-5.0
1987	94.0	0.5	95.6	1.7	95.4	-0.2	97.7	2.4	104.3	6.8	106.4	2.0	105.1	-1.2	101.9	-3.0	99.7	-2.2	101.0	1.3	104.9	3.9	110.7	5.5
1988	113.7	2.7	114.7	0.9	114.2	-0.4	121.8	6.7	127.8	4.9	150.3	17.6	154.3	2.7	159.2	3.2	163.5	2.7	151.0	-7.6	142.8	-5.4	147.9	3.6
1989	153.2	3.6	144.2	-5.9	149.2	3.5	142.1	-4.8	149.7	5.3	143.8	-3.9	140.3	-2.4	129.8	-7.5	128.3	-1.2	118.2	-7.9	121.0	2.4	124.2	2.6
1990	121.0	-2.6	122.4	1.2	122.0	-0.3	122.6	0.5	116.8	-4.7	118.3	1.3	124.0	4.8	118.7	-4.3	121.4	2.3	128.3	5.7	123.1	-4.1	126.2	2.5
1991	121.3	-3.9	121.9	0.5	117.9	-3.3	116.1	-1.5	110.7	-4.7	114.4	3.3	104.5	-8.7	107.8	3.2	110.3	2.3	106.1	-3.8	106.8	0.7	106.8	0.0
1992	109.2	2.2	107.8	-1.3	111.7	3.6	109.3	-2.1	117.8	7.8	121.3	3.0	111.0	-8.5	107.2	-3.4	109.3	2.0	106.8	-2.3	109.0	2.1	114.5	5.0
1993	116.6	1.8	114.9	-1.5	118.3	3.0	123.2	4.1	128.1	4.0	119.7	-6.6	134.7	12.5	129.4	-3.9	127.3	-1.6	126.1	-0.9	132.9	5.4	142.7	7.4

Source: U.S. Department of Labor, Bureau of Labor Statistics, Division of Industry Prices and Price Indexes. n.e.c. stands for not elsewhere classified. - indicates no data collected for period or unavailable.

Farm Products n.e.c.

Producer Price Index
Base 1982 = 100

For 1926-1993. Columns headed % show percentile change in the index from the previous period for which an index is available.

Year	Jan Index	%	Feb Index	%	Mar Index	%	Apr Index	%	May Index	%	Jun Index	%	Jul Index	%	Aug Index	%	Sep Index	%	Oct Index	%	Nov Index	%	Dec Index	%
1926	15.7	-	14.6	-7.0	12.8	-12.3	11.8	-7.8	12.3	4.2	12.5	1.6	12.6	0.8	12.6	0.0	12.9	2.4	12.9	0.0	13.6	5.4	14.2	4.4
1927	14.0	-1.4	12.9	-7.9	12.9	0.0	11.4	-11.6	11.0	-3.5	11.4	3.6	11.8	3.5	14.2	20.3	14.2	0.0	13.5	-4.9	13.3	-1.5	16.9	27.1
1928	18.1	7.1	16.8	-7.2	14.5	-13.7	14.4	-0.7	14.3	-0.7	12.4	-13.3	13.3	7.3	14.3	7.5	12.8	-10.5	14.3	11.7	13.3	-7.0	19.1	43.6
1929	20.3	6.3	18.0	-11.3	18.4	2.2	14.5	-21.2	14.2	-2.1	13.0	-8.5	12.8	-1.5	13.0	1.6	13.0	0.0	12.7	-2.3	11.9	-6.3	10.8	-9.2
1930	10.4	-3.7	10.2	-1.9	10.2	0.0	10.2	0.0	10.0	-2.0	9.9	-1.0	9.8	-1.0	9.6	-2.0	9.4	-2.1	9.5	1.1	8.7	-8.4	8.1	-6.9
1931	7.5	-7.4	7.3	-2.7	6.9	-5.5	6.8	-1.4	7.0	2.9	7.1	1.4	7.1	0.0	6.8	-4.2	6.6	-2.9	6.5	-1.5	6.5	0.0	6.3	-3.1
1932	5.9	-6.3	5.8	-1.7	5.8	0.0	5.9	1.7	5.9	0.0	5.8	-1.7	5.8	0.0	6.2	6.9	7.0	12.9	6.5	-7.1	6.1	-6.2	6.2	1.6
1933	6.2	0.0	6.3	1.6	6.3	0.0	6.2	-1.6	6.4	3.2	6.4	0.0	6.5	1.6	6.5	0.0	6.5	0.0	6.7	3.1	7.1	6.0	7.3	2.8
1934	7.6	4.1	7.9	3.9	7.9	0.0	7.8	-1.3	7.8	0.0	7.8	0.0	7.6	-2.6	8.0	5.3	8.5	6.3	9.2	8.2	9.4	2.2	9.4	0.0
1935	9.8	4.3	9.9	1.0	9.8	-1.0	9.7	-1.0	9.6	-1.0	9.5	-1.0	9.5	0.0	9.3	-2.1	8.9	-4.3	8.6	-3.4	8.4	-2.3	8.3	-1.2
1936	8.5	2.4	8.6	1.2	8.5	-1.2	8.4	-1.2	8.4	0.0	8.6	2.4	8.8	2.3	8.8	0.0	9.1	3.4	9.2	1.1	9.5	3.3	10.3	8.4
1937	10.9	5.8	11.1	1.8	11.0	-0.9	10.9	-0.9	10.8	-0.9	10.7	-0.9	10.7	0.0	10.8	0.9	10.7	-0.9	10.8	0.9	10.2	-5.6	9.8	-3.9
1938	9.2	-6.1	9.0	-2.2	8.9	-1.1	8.7	-2.2	8.7	0.0	8.7	0.0	8.9	2.3	9.1	2.2	9.1	0.0	9.0	-1.1	8.9	-1.1	8.8	-1.1
1939	8.8	0.0	8.9	1.1	8.7	-2.2	8.6	-1.1	8.6	0.0	8.6	0.0	8.6	0.0	8.5	-1.2	8.3	-2.4	7.8	-6.0	8.1	3.8	7.9	-2.5
1940	7.9	0.0	7.8	-1.3	7.9	1.3	7.9	0.0	7.7	-2.5	7.6	-1.3	7.5	-1.3	7.4	-1.3	7.5	1.4	7.7	2.7	7.8	1.3	8.1	3.8
1941	8.0	-1.2	8.2	2.5	8.7	6.1	9.0	3.4	9.4	4.4	9.7	3.2	9.8	1.0	10.4	6.1	11.3	8.7	11.8	4.4	12.2	3.4	13.1	7.4
1942	14.1	7.6	14.2	0.7	14.1	-0.7	14.1	0.0	14.1	0.0	14.1	0.0	14.1	0.0	14.5	2.8	15.1	4.1	15.7	4.0	15.9	1.3	16.3	2.5
1943	16.6	1.8	16.2	-2.4	16.3	0.6	16.6	1.8	16.6	0.0	16.6	0.0	16.7	0.6	16.8	0.6	17.0	1.2	16.9	-0.6	17.0	0.6	17.2	1.2
1944	17.4	1.2	17.5	0.6	17.5	0.0	17.5	0.0	17.5	0.0	17.5	0.0	17.4	-0.6	17.5	0.6	17.7	1.1	17.6	-0.6	17.7	0.6	17.7	0.0
1945	17.2	-2.8	17.1	-0.6	17.1	0.0	17.1	0.0	17.2	0.6	17.2	0.0	17.2	0.0	17.3	0.6	17.3	0.0	17.4	0.6	17.4	0.0	17.5	0.6
1946	17.8	1.7	17.7	-0.6	17.7	0.0	17.7	0.0	17.7	0.0	17.7	0.0	19.3	9.0	19.9	3.1	20.3	2.0	22.2	9.4	23.8	7.2	24.8	4.2
1947	25.4	2.4	25.1	-1.2	25.5	1.6	25.0	-2.0	24.2	-3.2	24.8	2.5	25.1	1.2	25.4	1.2	24.9	-2.0	25.7	3.2	25.9	0.8	26.2	1.2
1948	26.1	-0.4	25.9	-0.8	25.5	-1.5	25.2	-1.2	25.2	0.0	25.6	1.6	25.8	0.8	26.4	2.3	26.9	1.9	27.7	3.0	27.8	0.4	27.2	-2.2
1949	26.5	-2.6	26.0	-1.9	25.8	-0.8	25.6	-0.8	25.9	1.2	26.0	0.4	26.3	1.2	26.5	0.8	26.6	0.4	27.9	4.9	31.8	14.0	32.9	3.5
1950	32.4	-1.5	32.1	-0.9	31.3	-2.5	31.5	0.6	31.1	-1.3	32.2	3.5	34.0	5.6	35.2	3.5	36.8	4.5	35.5	-3.5	35.1	-1.1	36.0	2.6
1951	36.9	2.5	37.1	0.5	36.8	-0.8	36.8	0.0	36.7	-0.3	36.5	-0.5	36.1	-1.1	35.8	-0.8	35.7	-0.3	36.5	2.2	35.6	-2.5	36.3	2.0
1952	36.2	-0.3	36.4	0.6	36.4	0.0	35.9	-1.4	36.0	0.3	35.9	-0.3	36.3	1.1	36.2	-0.3	35.9	-0.8	35.7	-0.6	34.8	-2.5	35.4	1.7
1953	35.0	-1.1	35.3	0.9	37.5	6.2	36.0	-4.0	35.6	-1.1	35.9	0.8	37.0	3.1	37.9	2.4	39.2	3.4	38.4	-2.0	38.3	-0.3	38.9	1.6
1954	42.3	8.7	44.2	4.5	47.6	7.7	47.9	0.6	47.6	-0.6	47.7	0.2	48.3	1.3	44.4	-8.1	43.3	-2.5	42.0	-3.0	43.3	3.1	41.5	-4.2
1955	41.1	-1.0	36.7	-10.7	37.6	2.5	37.4	-0.5	36.4	-2.7	37.6	3.3	36.2	-3.7	36.4	0.6	38.4	5.5	38.2	-0.5	36.8	-3.7	36.5	-0.8
1956	36.7	0.5	38.3	4.4	37.7	-1.6	37.7	0.0	38.0	0.8	38.7	1.8	39.2	1.3	39.7	1.3	40.2	1.3	39.4	-2.0	38.7	-1.8	38.9	0.5
1957	39.1	0.5	38.9	-0.5	38.4	-1.3	38.0	-1.0	37.9	-0.3	38.3	1.1	37.6	-1.8	37.6	0.0	37.6	0.0	37.2	-1.1	37.9	1.9	37.5	-1.1
1958	37.7	0.5	37.4	-0.8	37.7	0.8	37.4	-0.8	37.3	-0.3	37.2	-0.3	36.8	-1.1	36.7	-0.3	36.1	-1.6	36.5	1.1	36.2	-0.8	35.8	-1.1
1959	35.3	-1.4	35.4	0.3	35.2	-0.6	35.1	-0.3	35.1	0.0	34.9	-0.6	34.8	-0.3	34.7	-0.3	35.0	0.9	34.6	-1.1	34.6	0.0	33.5	-3.2
1960	33.5	0.0	33.9	1.2	33.6	-0.9	33.8	0.6	33.7	-0.3	33.7	0.0	33.6	-0.3	33.0	-1.8	34.0	3.0	34.3	0.9	34.0	-0.9	34.3	0.9
1961	33.7	-1.7	34.1	1.2	34.1	0.0	34.0	-0.3	34.0	0.0	33.9	-0.3	34.0	0.3	34.0	0.0	34.5	1.5	34.2	-0.9	34.0	-0.6	34.6	1.8
1962	34.2	-1.2	34.2	0.0	34.2	0.0	34.1	-0.3	34.2	0.3	33.8	-1.2	33.8	0.0	32.9	-2.7	33.2	0.9	32.8	-1.2	33.0	0.6	32.6	-1.2
1963	32.0	-1.8	32.6	1.9	32.6	0.0	32.7	0.3	32.8	0.3	32.7	-0.3	32.6	-0.3	32.4	-0.6	32.6	0.6	33.1	1.5	33.2	0.3	33.2	0.0
1964	36.2	9.0	35.3	-2.5	36.8	4.2	36.4	-1.1	36.4	0.0	36.1	-0.8	36.0	-0.3	36.0	0.0	35.4	-1.7	36.3	2.5	36.0	-0.8	36.0	0.0
1965	34.9	-3.1	35.6	2.0	34.8	-2.2	35.0	0.6	34.7	-0.9	35.0	0.9	34.9	-0.3	36.0	3.2	36.9	2.5	36.6	-0.8	36.5	-0.3	37.9	3.8
1966	37.5	-1.1	37.4	-0.3	37.3	-0.3	37.5	0.5	37.1	-1.1	37.0	-0.3	37.1	0.3	37.5	1.1	37.4	-0.3	36.9	-1.3	36.1	-2.2	36.8	1.9
1967	36.4	-1.1	36.8	1.1	36.4	-1.1	36.3	-0.3	36.5	0.6	36.7	0.5	36.5	-0.5	36.3	-0.5	35.7	-1.7	35.6	-0.3	36.9	3.7	37.1	0.5
1968	37.2	0.3	37.0	-0.5	37.1	0.3	37.3	0.5	37.2	-0.3	37.2	0.0	37.2	0.0	37.7	1.3	38.1	1.1	38.1	0.0	39.1	2.6	39.4	0.8
1969	38.7	-1.8	38.9	0.5	39.1	0.5	38.8	-0.8	38.6	-0.5	38.8	0.5	39.1	0.8	40.0	2.3	40.7	1.7	42.7	4.9	42.4	-0.7	41.4	-2.4
1970	42.6	2.9	42.2	-0.9	42.0	-0.5	42.0	0.0	42.1	0.2	42.0	-0.2	42.6	1.4	43.3	1.6	43.4	0.2	42.8	-1.4	44.2	3.3	43.7	-1.1

[Continued]

Farm Products n.e.c.

Producer Price Index
Base 1982 = 100

[Continued]

For 1926-1993. Columns headed % show percentile change in the index from the previous period for which an index is available.

Year	Jan Index	%	Feb Index	%	Mar Index	%	Apr Index	%	May Index	%	Jun Index	%	Jul Index	%	Aug Index	%	Sep Index	%	Oct Index	%	Nov Index	%	Dec Index	%
1971	43.7	0.0	43.6	-0.2	42.3	-3.0	41.7	-1.4	41.4	-0.7	41.4	0.0	41.3	-0.2	41.8	1.2	42.1	0.7	42.1	0.0	41.2	-2.1	42.7	3.6
1972	43.0	0.7	42.5	-1.2	42.8	0.7	43.0	0.5	43.5	1.2	43.7	0.5	44.4	1.6	49.0	10.4	48.3	-1.4	48.2	-0.2	48.8	1.2	49.3	1.0
1973	49.7	0.8	51.2	3.0	52.2	2.0	51.8	-0.8	53.2	2.7	54.0	1.5	55.4	2.6	54.8	-1.1	55.8	1.8	56.3	0.9	55.6	-1.2	54.3	-2.3
1974	55.9	2.9	56.7	1.4	58.0	2.3	59.8	3.1	60.8	1.7	59.5	-2.1	58.3	-2.0	59.2	1.5	60.5	2.2	62.0	2.5	64.0	3.2	63.9	-0.2
1975	62.8	-1.7	63.6	1.3	62.3	-2.0	61.2	-1.8	60.2	-1.6	60.3	0.2	58.3	-3.3	61.2	5.0	61.9	1.1	63.7	2.9	62.8	-1.4	63.5	1.1
1976	64.8	2.0	66.0	1.9	65.6	-0.6	70.6	7.6	75.1	6.4	81.8	8.9	79.7	-2.6	82.9	4.0	92.1	11.1	93.6	1.6	98.8	5.6	105.9	7.2
1977	107.8	1.8	114.4	6.1	134.2	17.3	140.7	4.8	130.6	-7.2	124.5	-4.7	122.1	-1.9	106.4	-12.9	115.5	8.6	107.9	-6.6	110.5	2.4	110.2	-0.3
1978	103.7	-5.9	101.0	-2.6	100.1	-0.9	98.7	-1.4	98.9	0.2	99.3	0.4	97.7	-1.6	95.7	-2.0	103.3	7.9	100.7	-2.5	104.2	3.5	98.7	-5.3
1979	98.3	-0.4	92.4	-6.0	92.7	0.3	92.9	0.2	96.2	3.6	102.4	6.4	113.6	10.9	113.2	-0.4	115.1	1.7	114.2	-0.8	116.0	1.6	116.3	0.3
1980	109.7	-5.7	111.0	1.2	113.5	2.3	111.0	-2.2	113.3	2.1	112.7	-0.5	106.5	-5.5	103.0	-3.3	106.4	3.3	104.1	-2.2	108.1	3.8	107.8	-0.3
1981	107.9	0.1	107.5	-0.4	107.8	0.3	107.8	0.0	94.6	-12.2	88.4	-6.6	91.1	3.1	96.1	5.5	98.0	2.0	95.9	-2.1	99.5	3.8	102.1	2.6
1982	102.0	-0.1	99.7	-2.3	99.5	-0.2	99.9	0.4	99.8	-0.1	99.0	-0.8	96.7	-2.3	100.0	3.4	100.8	0.8	99.8	-1.0	100.7	0.9	102.1	1.4
1983	102.0	-0.1	102.4	0.4	102.1	-0.3	101.7	-0.4	102.4	0.7	103.6	1.2	102.9	-0.7	104.1	1.2	104.7	0.6	103.4	-1.2	103.3	-0.1	100.9	-2.3
1984	102.1	1.2	101.6	-0.5	101.2	-0.4	101.9	0.7	105.0	3.0	101.7	-3.1	101.1	-0.6	103.6	2.5	108.0	4.2	107.1	-0.8	108.5	1.3	107.0	-1.4
1985	105.5	-1.4	104.0	-1.4	104.1	0.1	103.4	-0.7	103.3	-0.1	103.3	0.0	103.2	-0.1	100.0	-3.1	103.0	3.0	102.9	-0.1	103.4	0.5	100.9	-2.4
1986	100.9	0.0	100.3	-0.6	99.1	-1.2	98.5	-0.6	97.9	-0.6	97.9	0.0	97.9	0.0	89.9	-8.2	94.8	5.5	91.1	-3.9	94.0	3.2	94.0	0.0
1987	93.5	-0.5	94.0	0.5	94.0	0.0	93.5	-0.5	93.5	0.0	93.5	0.0	92.0	-1.6	92.0	0.0	96.5	4.9	97.0	0.5	96.5	-0.5	96.5	0.0
1988	95.5	-1.0	95.5	0.0	95.5	0.0	91.5	-4.2	91.5	0.0	91.5	0.0	91.5	0.0	93.0	1.6	98.5	5.9	100.1	1.6	101.1	1.0	99.7	-1.4
1989	99.7	0.0	98.7	-1.0	98.7	0.0	99.2	0.5	99.2	0.0	99.2	0.0	98.7	-0.5	98.1	-0.6	101.2	3.2	114.2	12.8	114.5	0.3	117.8	2.9
1990	117.8	0.0	117.8	0.0	117.8	0.0	119.3	1.3	119.3	0.0	119.3	0.0	117.8	-1.3	117.3	-0.4	121.8	3.8	141.9	16.5	142.4	0.4	150.7	5.8
1991	151.6	0.6	151.6	0.0	151.2	-0.3	151.2	0.0	151.2	0.0	151.2	0.0	151.2	0.0	149.0	-1.5	154.3	3.6	142.7	-7.5	157.2	10.2	156.3	-0.6
1992	152.4	-2.5	152.4	0.0	169.9	11.5	140.8	-17.1	140.8	0.0	140.8	0.0	134.9	-4.2	143.7	6.5	158.2	10.1	157.3	-0.6	158.2	0.6	158.2	0.0
1993	156.3	-1.2	164.1	5.0	162.1	-1.2	145.6	-10.2	136.9	-6.0	136.9	0.0	136.9	0.0	138.8	1.4	148.5	7.0	152.4	2.6	147.6	-3.1	157.3	6.6

Source: U.S. Department of Labor, Bureau of Labor Statistics, Division of Industry Prices and Price Indexes. n.e.c. stands for not elsewhere classified. - indicates no data collected for period or unavailable.

PROCESSED FOODS AND FEEDS
Producer Price Index
Base 1982 = 100

For 1947-1993. Columns headed % show percentile change in the index from the previous period for which an index is available.

Year	Jan Index	%	Feb Index	%	Mar Index	%	Apr Index	%	May Index	%	Jun Index	%	Jul Index	%	Aug Index	%	Sep Index	%	Oct Index	%	Nov Index	%	Dec Index	%
1947	31.5	-	31.6	0.3	32.9	4.1	32.1	-2.4	31.5	-1.9	31.7	0.6	32.3	1.9	32.8	1.5	34.2	4.3	34.5	0.9	34.9	1.2	35.6	2.0
1948	36.7	3.1	35.0	-4.6	34.9	-0.3	35.4	1.4	35.7	0.8	35.9	0.6	36.1	0.6	35.8	-0.8	35.6	-0.6	34.5	-3.1	34.1	-1.2	33.6	-1.5
1949	32.9	-2.1	32.0	-2.7	32.1	0.3	32.0	-0.3	31.9	-0.3	31.9	0.0	32.1	0.6	32.5	1.2	32.2	-0.9	31.8	-1.2	31.6	-0.6	31.5	-0.3
1950	31.3	-0.6	31.5	0.6	31.7	0.6	31.7	0.0	32.4	2.2	32.4	0.0	34.2	5.6	34.7	1.5	34.9	0.6	34.1	-2.3	34.2	0.3	35.3	3.2
1951	36.4	3.1	37.2	2.2	37.0	-0.5	37.0	0.0	37.0	0.0	36.7	-0.8	36.6	-0.3	36.7	0.3	36.7	0.0	37.0	0.8	37.0	0.0	36.9	-0.3
1952	36.9	0.0	36.8	-0.3	36.6	-0.5	36.3	-0.8	36.4	0.3	36.3	-0.3	36.6	0.8	36.9	0.8	36.9	0.0	36.4	-1.4	36.0	-1.1	35.0	-2.8
1953	35.2	0.6	35.1	-0.3	34.8	-0.9	34.4	-1.1	34.8	1.2	34.2	-1.7	34.8	1.8	34.7	-0.3	35.2	1.4	34.7	-1.4	34.4	-0.9	34.9	1.5
1954	35.5	1.7	35.2	-0.8	35.4	0.6	36.0	1.7	36.2	0.6	35.4	-2.2	35.8	1.1	35.7	-0.3	35.3	-1.1	34.6	-2.0	34.7	0.3	34.6	-0.3
1955	34.7	0.3	34.5	-0.6	34.0	-1.4	34.2	0.6	33.9	-0.9	34.2	0.9	34.2	0.0	33.8	-1.2	33.6	-0.6	33.4	-0.6	32.8	-1.8	32.6	-0.6
1956	32.7	0.3	32.8	0.3	32.8	0.0	33.4	1.8	34.2	2.4	34.0	-0.6	33.8	-0.6	34.0	0.6	34.3	0.9	34.2	-0.3	34.3	0.3	34.2	-0.3
1957	34.6	1.2	34.4	-0.6	34.4	0.0	34.5	0.3	34.5	0.0	34.8	0.9	35.2	1.1	35.1	-0.3	35.0	-0.3	34.6	-1.1	34.8	0.6	35.1	0.9
1958	35.8	2.0	35.9	0.3	36.4	1.4	36.9	1.4	37.1	0.5	37.2	0.3	37.2	0.0	36.6	-1.6	36.4	-0.5	36.1	-0.8	36.1	0.0	36.3	0.6
1959	36.3	0.0	35.9	-1.1	35.8	-0.3	35.9	0.3	35.9	0.0	35.7	-0.6	35.6	-0.3	35.1	-1.4	35.4	0.9	35.2	-0.6	35.0	-0.6	34.9	-0.3
1960	35.2	0.9	35.1	-0.3	35.6	1.4	35.6	0.0	35.4	-0.6	35.5	0.3	35.8	0.8	35.5	-0.8	35.6	0.3	35.9	0.8	35.9	0.0	36.0	0.3
1961	36.5	1.4	36.6	0.3	36.5	-0.3	36.3	-0.5	36.1	-0.6	35.6	-1.4	35.9	0.8	36.0	0.3	36.0	0.0	35.9	-0.3	36.1	0.6	36.4	0.8
1962	36.7	0.8	36.6	-0.3	36.5	-0.3	36.2	-0.8	36.0	-0.6	36.0	0.0	36.5	1.4	36.6	0.3	37.3	1.9	36.7	-1.6	36.7	0.0	36.6	-0.3
1963	36.7	0.3	36.6	-0.3	36.1	-1.4	36.1	0.0	36.7	1.7	36.9	0.5	37.1	0.5	36.8	-0.8	36.9	0.3	37.2	0.8	37.2	0.0	36.7	-1.3
1964	37.3	1.6	36.8	-1.3	36.6	-0.5	36.5	-0.3	36.1	-1.1	36.3	0.6	36.6	0.8	36.5	-0.3	37.1	1.6	36.9	-0.5	36.6	-0.8	36.7	0.3
1965	37.1	1.1	37.0	-0.3	36.9	-0.3	37.1	0.5	37.3	0.5	38.3	2.7	38.5	0.5	38.5	0.0	38.5	0.0	38.5	0.0	38.9	1.0	39.3	1.0
1966	39.7	1.0	40.2	1.3	39.9	-0.7	39.7	-0.5	39.8	0.3	39.9	0.3	40.5	1.5	41.2	1.7	41.1	-0.2	40.6	-1.2	40.1	-1.2	40.2	0.2
1967	40.2	0.0	39.7	-1.2	39.4	-0.8	39.2	-0.5	39.4	0.5	40.1	1.8	40.3	0.5	39.9	-1.0	40.1	0.5	39.8	-0.7	39.5	-0.8	39.7	0.5
1968	40.0	0.8	40.3	0.7	40.2	-0.2	40.2	0.0	40.5	0.7	40.9	1.0	41.3	1.0	41.0	-0.7	41.0	0.0	40.7	-0.7	40.8	0.2	40.9	0.2
1969	41.3	1.0	41.4	0.2	41.5	0.2	41.8	0.7	42.5	1.7	43.3	1.9	43.5	0.5	43.3	-0.5	43.2	-0.2	43.3	0.2	43.3	0.0	43.7	0.9
1970	44.6	2.1	44.7	0.2	44.5	-0.4	44.5	0.0	44.2	-0.7	44.5	0.7	45.1	1.3	44.9	-0.4	45.0	0.2	44.5	-1.1	44.5	0.0	44.0	-1.1
1971	44.5	1.1	45.1	1.3	45.2	0.2	45.2	0.0	45.6	0.9	45.8	0.4	46.2	0.9	46.0	-0.4	45.7	-0.7	45.4	-0.7	45.5	0.2	46.1	1.3
1972	46.6	1.1	47.3	1.5	47.2	-0.2	46.8	-0.8	47.2	0.9	47.6	0.8	48.3	1.5	48.1	-0.4	48.5	0.8	48.5	0.0	48.9	0.8	51.5	5.3
1973	52.6	2.1	54.5	3.6	56.2	3.1	55.6	-1.1	57.7	3.8	60.3	4.5	58.3	-3.3	66.1	13.4	62.2	-5.9	60.9	-2.1	60.4	-0.8	61.9	2.5
1974	64.4	4.0	65.5	1.7	64.8	-1.1	63.3	-2.3	63.2	-0.2	62.6	-0.9	66.6	6.4	71.4	7.2	70.3	-1.5	73.0	3.8	75.4	3.3	74.8	-0.8
1975	74.1	-0.9	72.6	-2.0	70.5	-2.9	71.4	1.3	71.2	-0.3	71.5	0.4	73.4	2.7	74.1	1.0	74.0	-0.1	74.0	0.0	72.6	-1.9	72.0	-0.8
1976	71.3	-1.0	70.2	-1.5	69.9	-0.4	70.8	1.3	71.5	1.0	72.3	1.1	72.6	0.4	70.3	-3.2	70.5	0.3	69.6	-1.3	69.5	-0.1	71.2	2.4
1977	71.3	0.1	72.3	1.4	73.1	1.1	75.0	2.6	76.3	1.7	75.6	-0.9	74.4	-1.6	73.5	-1.2	73.3	-0.3	73.3	0.0	74.3	1.4	75.3	1.3
1978	76.2	1.2	77.5	1.7	78.3	1.0	79.6	1.7	80.5	1.1	81.4	1.1	81.2	-0.2	80.2	-1.2	81.7	1.9	83.1	1.7	82.8	-0.4	84.2	1.7
1979	85.6	1.7	87.1	1.8	87.7	0.7	88.4	0.8	88.3	-0.1	87.7	-0.7	88.8	1.3	87.7	-1.2	89.8	2.4	89.4	-0.4	90.3	1.0	91.2	1.0
1980	90.9	-0.3	92.7	2.0	92.1	-0.6	90.9	-1.3	92.7	2.0	93.0	0.3	96.1	3.3	99.2	3.2	99.3	0.1	101.8	2.5	102.3	0.5	100.0	-2.2
1981	100.7	0.7	99.5	-1.2	98.8	-0.7	98.4	-0.4	98.7	0.3	99.4	0.7	100.3	0.9	99.9	-0.4	99.0	-0.9	98.0	-1.0	97.2	-0.8	96.9	-0.3
1982	98.2	1.3	98.7	0.5	98.7	0.0	99.8	1.1	101.2	1.4	101.7	0.5	101.2	-0.5	100.8	-0.4	100.8	0.0	99.7	-1.1	99.5	-0.2	99.6	0.1
1983	100.1	0.5	101.3	1.2	101.2	-0.1	101.8	0.6	101.8	0.0	101.1	-0.7	101.2	0.1	101.6	0.4	103.2	1.6	102.5	-0.7	102.5	0.0	103.0	0.5
1984	104.9	1.8	104.7	-0.2	106.2	1.4	106.3	0.1	106.4	0.1	105.3	-1.0	106.3	0.9	105.3	-0.9	104.8	-0.5	104.4	-0.4	104.9	0.5	105.2	0.3
1985	105.1	-0.1	104.9	-0.2	104.3	-0.6	103.8	-0.5	103.4	-0.4	102.9	-0.5	103.3	0.4	102.3	-1.0	101.5	-0.8	102.5	1.0	103.9	1.4	104.5	0.6
1986	104.7	0.2	104.0	-0.7	103.7	-0.3	103.3	-0.4	104.3	1.0	104.7	0.4	106.1	1.3	107.2	1.0	107.0	-0.2	106.7	-0.3	106.5	-0.2	106.7	0.2
1987	106.1	-0.6	106.4	0.3	105.9	-0.5	107.2	1.2	109.1	1.8	109.0	-0.1	109.0	0.0	108.2	-0.7	108.9	0.6	108.7	-0.2	108.1	-0.6	108.2	0.1
1988	109.3	1.0	109.1	-0.2	109.6	0.5	110.1	0.5	111.2	1.0	113.5	2.1	115.0	1.3	114.5	-0.4	115.4	0.8	115.0	-0.3	114.8	-0.2	115.0	0.2
1989	116.6	1.4	116.6	0.0	117.5	0.8	117.2	-0.3	117.9	0.6	117.4	-0.4	118.1	0.6	117.9	-0.2	117.9	0.0	117.9	0.0	118.9	0.8	119.3	0.3
1990	120.2	0.8	120.0	-0.2	120.9	0.7	121.2	0.2	123.5	1.9	122.8	-0.6	123.2	0.3	123.0	-0.2	122.4	-0.5	122.2	-0.2	121.7	-0.4	121.7	0.0
1991	122.1	0.3	122.3	0.2	122.6	0.2	122.5	-0.1	122.3	-0.2	121.9	-0.3	121.6	-0.2	121.4	-0.2	121.1	-0.2	121.9	0.7	121.4	-0.4	121.4	0.0

[Continued]

PROCESSED FOODS AND FEEDS
Producer Price Index
Base 1982 = 100
[Continued]

For 1947-1993. Columns headed % show percentile change in the index from the previous period for which an index is available.

Year	Jan Index	%	Feb Index	%	Mar Index	%	Apr Index	%	May Index	%	Jun Index	%	Jul Index	%	Aug Index	%	Sep Index	%	Oct Index	%	Nov Index	%	Dec Index	%
1992	121.3	-0.1	121.7	0.3	121.8	0.1	122.0	0.2	122.5	0.4	123.0	0.4	122.4	-0.5	122.1	-0.2	122.1	0.0	121.8	-0.2	121.6	-0.2	122.4	0.7
1993	122.7	0.2	122.7	0.0	122.9	0.2	123.7	0.7	124.2	0.4	124.0	-0.2	124.3	0.2	124.3	0.0	124.3	0.0	124.6	0.2	125.0	0.3	125.5	0.4

Source: U.S. Department of Labor, Bureau of Labor Statistics, Division of Industry Prices and Price Indexes. n.e.c. stands for not elsewhere classified. - indicates no data collected for period or unavailable.

Cereal and Bakery Products
Producer Price Index
Base 1982 = 100

For 1926-1993. Columns headed % show percentile change in the index from the previous period for which an index is available.

Year	Jan Index	%	Feb Index	%	Mar Index	%	Apr Index	%	May Index	%	Jun Index	%	Jul Index	%	Aug Index	%	Sep Index	%	Oct Index	%	Nov Index	%	Dec Index	%
1926	20.1	-	19.8	-1.5	19.5	-1.5	19.3	-1.0	18.9	-2.1	19.0	0.5	18.8	-1.1	18.3	-2.7	18.1	-1.1	18.3	1.1	18.0	-1.6	17.9	-0.6
1927	17.8	-0.6	17.8	0.0	17.6	-1.1	17.6	0.0	18.2	3.4	18.3	0.5	18.2	-0.5	18.0	-1.1	17.5	-2.8	17.5	0.0	17.4	-0.6	17.4	0.0
1928	17.6	1.1	17.6	0.0	17.9	1.7	18.6	3.9	18.9	1.6	18.4	-2.6	17.9	-2.7	17.1	-4.5	17.0	-0.6	16.9	-0.6	16.7	-1.2	16.7	0.0
1929	16.7	0.0	16.9	1.2	16.4	-3.0	16.2	-1.2	15.9	-1.9	16.0	0.6	17.2	7.5	17.0	-1.2	16.9	-0.6	16.6	-1.8	16.5	-0.6	16.5	0.0
1930	16.5	0.0	16.2	-1.8	16.0	-1.2	15.9	-0.6	15.8	-0.6	15.6	-1.3	15.2	-2.6	15.1	-0.7	14.8	-2.0	14.6	-1.4	14.3	-2.1	14.3	0.0
1931	14.3	0.0	14.2	-0.7	14.0	-1.4	13.9	-0.7	14.0	0.7	13.9	-0.7	13.5	-2.9	13.4	-0.7	13.2	-1.5	13.3	0.8	13.7	3.0	13.6	-0.7
1932	13.4	-1.5	13.1	-2.2	12.8	-2.3	12.8	0.0	12.8	0.0	12.6	-1.6	12.4	-1.6	12.4	0.0	12.4	0.0	12.1	-2.4	11.8	-2.5	11.6	-1.7
1933	11.5	-0.9	11.4	-0.9	11.8	3.5	12.4	5.1	13.0	4.8	13.3	2.3	15.7	18.0	16.0	1.9	16.0	0.0	16.0	0.0	16.2	1.3	16.0	-1.2
1934	16.2	1.3	16.2	0.0	16.0	-1.2	16.0	0.0	16.4	2.5	16.7	1.8	16.7	0.0	17.1	2.4	17.3	1.2	17.1	-1.2	17.1	0.0	17.3	1.2
1935	17.3	0.0	17.3	0.0	17.3	0.0	17.5	1.2	17.4	-0.6	17.1	-1.7	17.5	2.3	17.9	2.3	18.2	1.7	18.6	2.2	18.3	-1.6	18.3	0.0
1936	17.3	-5.5	16.7	-3.5	16.2	-3.0	15.8	-2.5	15.5	-1.9	15.4	-0.6	15.9	3.2	16.5	3.8	16.5	0.0	16.5	0.0	16.2	-1.8	16.4	1.2
1937	16.6	1.2	16.8	1.2	16.9	0.6	16.9	0.0	16.7	-1.2	17.0	1.8	17.4	2.4	16.5	-5.2	16.2	-1.8	15.9	-1.9	15.3	-3.8	15.4	0.7
1938	15.6	1.3	15.6	0.0	15.2	-2.6	15.1	-0.7	14.7	-2.6	15.1	2.7	14.9	-1.3	14.5	-2.7	14.3	-1.4	14.1	-1.4	13.9	-1.4	14.1	1.4
1939	13.8	-2.1	13.7	-0.7	13.6	-0.7	13.6	0.0	13.9	2.2	14.3	2.9	13.5	-5.6	13.5	0.0	14.9	10.4	14.7	-1.3	14.7	0.0	15.2	3.4
1940	15.1	-0.7	15.5	2.6	15.5	0.0	15.6	0.6	15.2	-2.6	14.6	-3.9	14.3	-2.1	14.1	-1.4	14.3	1.4	14.5	1.4	14.1	-2.8	13.9	-1.4
1941	14.1	1.4	13.9	-1.4	14.1	1.4	14.5	2.8	14.7	1.4	15.1	2.7	15.1	0.0	15.3	1.3	16.2	5.9	16.2	0.0	16.2	0.0	16.8	3.7
1942	17.1	1.8	17.2	0.6	17.1	-0.6	17.0	-0.6	16.7	-1.8	16.4	-1.8	16.4	0.0	16.5	0.6	16.7	1.2	16.8	0.6	16.9	0.6	16.8	-0.6
1943	17.1	1.8	17.4	1.8	17.6	1.1	17.6	0.0	17.6	0.0	17.6	0.0	17.6	0.0	17.6	0.0	17.8	1.1	17.9	0.6	17.9	0.0	17.9	0.0
1944	17.9	0.0	17.9	0.0	17.9	0.0	17.9	0.0	17.9	0.0	17.9	0.0	17.9	0.0	17.8	-0.6	17.7	-0.6	17.8	0.6	17.9	0.6	17.9	0.0
1945	17.9	0.0	17.9	0.0	17.9	0.0	17.9	0.0	18.0	0.6	18.0	0.0	17.9	-0.6	17.9	0.0	17.9	0.0	17.9	0.0	18.0	0.6	18.0	0.0
1946	18.0	0.0	18.1	0.6	18.1	0.0	18.7	3.3	18.9	1.1	19.2	1.6	23.5	22.4	23.4	-0.4	24.0	2.6	24.2	0.8	25.6	5.8	26.2	2.3
1947	26.6	1.5	26.8	0.8	27.9	4.1	28.4	1.8	28.2	-0.7	27.7	-1.8	28.4	2.5	28.4	0.0	29.1	2.5	30.3	4.1	31.2	3.0	31.1	-0.3
1948	31.1	0.0	29.8	-4.2	29.6	-0.7	29.5	-0.3	29.2	-1.0	29.1	-0.3	29.2	0.3	28.8	-1.4	28.6	-0.7	28.3	-1.0	28.4	0.4	28.4	0.0
1949	28.2	-0.7	28.0	-0.7	28.0	0.0	27.9	-0.4	27.8	-0.4	27.8	0.0	27.9	0.4	27.5	-1.4	27.3	-0.7	27.3	0.0	27.3	0.0	27.3	0.0
1950	27.3	0.0	27.5	0.7	27.6	0.4	27.6	0.0	27.6	0.0	27.5	-0.4	28.4	3.3	29.0	2.1	29.1	0.3	28.8	-1.0	28.8	0.0	29.4	2.1
1951	30.3	3.1	30.7	1.3	30.5	-0.7	30.5	0.0	30.5	0.0	30.3	-0.7	30.3	0.0	30.4	0.3	30.3	-0.3	30.5	0.7	30.7	0.7	30.8	0.3
1952	30.7	-0.3	30.6	-0.3	30.7	0.3	30.6	-0.3	30.5	-0.3	30.4	-0.3	30.3	-0.3	30.3	0.0	30.3	0.0	30.3	0.0	30.5	0.7	30.5	0.0
1953	30.5	0.0	30.7	0.7	31.1	1.3	31.1	0.0	31.1	0.0	30.8	-1.0	30.9	0.3	30.9	0.0	31.6	2.3	31.9	0.9	32.1	0.6	32.0	-0.3
1954	32.0	0.0	32.2	0.6	32.1	-0.3	32.3	0.6	32.3	0.0	32.4	0.3	32.5	0.3	32.3	-0.6	32.4	0.3	32.6	0.6	33.2	1.8	33.3	0.3
1955	33.3	0.0	33.1	-0.6	33.2	0.3	33.3	0.3	33.7	1.2	33.5	-0.6	33.5	0.0	32.8	-2.1	32.6	-0.6	32.7	0.3	32.8	0.3	32.8	0.0
1956	32.8	0.0	32.9	0.3	32.9	0.0	32.9	0.0	32.9	0.0	32.9	0.0	32.7	-0.6	32.6	-0.3	32.7	0.3	32.9	0.6	33.0	0.3	32.9	-0.3
1957	33.0	0.3	33.1	0.3	33.3	0.6	33.3	0.0	33.2	-0.3	33.3	0.3	33.5	0.6	33.3	-0.6	33.3	0.0	33.5	0.6	33.5	0.0	33.7	0.6
1958	33.7	0.0	33.7	0.0	33.6	-0.3	33.8	0.6	33.6	-0.6	33.8	0.6	33.5	-0.9	33.3	-0.6	33.6	0.9	33.7	0.3	33.7	0.0	33.5	-0.6
1959	33.5	0.0	33.5	0.0	33.9	1.2	33.9	0.0	34.0	0.3	34.0	0.0	34.0	0.0	34.0	0.0	34.0	0.0	34.3	0.9	34.3	0.0	34.3	0.0
1960	34.4	0.3	34.4	0.0	34.4	0.0	34.4	0.0	34.6	0.6	34.6	0.0	34.9	0.9	34.8	-0.3	34.9	0.3	35.1	0.6	35.1	0.0	35.2	0.3
1961	35.2	0.0	35.2	0.0	35.2	0.0	35.2	0.0	35.2	0.0	35.3	0.3	35.3	0.0	35.3	0.0	35.4	0.3	35.7	0.8	35.7	0.0	35.7	0.0
1962	36.0	0.8	36.1	0.3	36.1	0.0	36.3	0.6	36.1	-0.6	36.2	0.3	36.3	0.3	36.3	0.0	36.2	-0.3	36.2	0.0	36.3	0.3	36.2	-0.3
1963	36.1	-0.3	36.5	1.1	36.3	-0.5	36.4	0.3	36.2	-0.5	36.0	-0.6	35.8	-0.6	35.7	-0.3	36.0	0.8	36.3	0.8	36.1	-0.6	36.0	-0.3
1964	36.0	0.0	36.1	0.3	35.9	-0.6	36.3	1.1	36.2	-0.3	36.3	0.3	36.5	0.6	36.4	-0.3	36.4	0.0	36.4	0.0	36.4	0.0	36.4	0.0
1965	36.4	0.0	36.3	-0.3	36.4	0.3	36.4	0.0	36.4	0.0	36.5	0.3	36.8	0.8	36.6	-0.5	36.7	0.3	36.8	0.3	37.2	1.1	37.4	0.5
1966	37.6	0.5	37.7	0.3	37.7	0.0	37.9	0.5	38.0	0.3	38.4	1.1	38.9	1.3	40.0	2.8	40.0	0.0	40.0	0.0	40.0	0.0	39.7	-0.7
1967	39.5	-0.5	39.5	0.0	39.4	-0.3	39.4	0.0	39.5	0.3	39.5	0.0	39.3	-0.5	39.3	0.0	39.3	0.0	39.3	0.0	39.4	0.3	39.4	0.0
1968	39.4	0.0	39.5	0.3	39.5	0.0	39.5	0.0	39.4	-0.3	39.4	0.0	39.8	1.0	40.2	1.0	40.0	-0.5	40.2	0.5	40.2	0.0	40.2	0.0
1969	40.2	0.0	40.2	0.0	40.2	0.0	40.2	0.0	40.2	0.0	40.3	0.2	40.4	0.2	40.5	0.2	40.6	0.2	40.8	0.5	41.0	0.5	41.1	0.2
1970	41.1	0.0	41.5	1.0	41.7	0.5	41.9	0.5	41.9	0.0	42.0	0.2	42.4	1.0	42.5	0.2	43.1	1.4	43.3	0.5	43.7	0.9	43.8	0.2

[Continued]

Cereal and Bakery Products
Producer Price Index
Base 1982 = 100
[Continued]

For 1926-1993. Columns headed % show percentile change in the index from the previous period for which an index is available.

Year	Jan Index	%	Feb Index	%	Mar Index	%	Apr Index	%	May Index	%	Jun Index	%	Jul Index	%	Aug Index	%	Sep Index	%	Oct Index	%	Nov Index	%	Dec Index	%
1971	44.0	0.5	44.0	0.0	44.1	0.2	44.1	0.0	44.1	0.0	44.1	0.0	43.9	-0.5	43.9	0.0	43.8	-0.2	43.9	0.2	43.9	0.0	44.0	0.2
1972	44.2	0.5	44.3	0.2	44.4	0.2	44.5	0.2	44.6	0.2	44.6	0.0	44.8	0.4	45.4	1.3	45.7	0.7	46.1	0.9	46.6	1.1	47.3	1.5
1973	47.7	0.8	47.6	-0.2	47.8	0.4	48.7	1.9	49.0	0.6	49.6	1.2	49.5	-0.2	53.7	8.5	58.2	8.4	59.3	1.9	61.5	3.7	63.1	2.6
1974	65.5	3.8	66.8	2.0	67.9	1.6	65.8	-3.1	65.8	0.0	65.4	-0.6	66.6	1.8	66.7	0.2	66.9	0.3	69.4	3.7	70.8	2.0	71.7	1.3
1975	71.8	0.1	72.3	0.7	71.7	-0.8	70.6	-1.5	69.4	-1.7	68.7	-1.0	69.6	1.3	69.3	-0.4	69.7	0.6	70.0	0.4	69.7	-0.4	68.8	-1.3
1976	69.0	0.3	69.1	0.1	68.8	-0.4	68.0	-1.2	68.3	0.4	68.5	0.3	68.4	-0.1	67.1	-1.9	66.9	-0.3	67.0	0.1	66.5	-0.7	66.4	-0.2
1977	66.4	0.0	67.0	0.9	67.6	0.9	67.6	0.0	67.8	0.3	67.4	-0.6	67.7	0.4	67.8	0.1	68.8	1.5	69.2	0.6	70.9	2.5	71.8	1.3
1978	72.6	1.1	72.9	0.4	73.4	0.7	74.4	1.4	74.2	-0.3	74.9	0.9	75.3	0.5	75.8	0.7	75.3	-0.7	76.2	1.2	77.3	1.4	77.5	0.3
1979	77.7	0.3	78.5	1.0	78.8	0.4	80.0	1.5	80.8	1.0	81.3	0.6	83.7	3.0	85.1	1.7	86.2	1.3	86.6	0.5	87.7	1.3	88.1	0.5
1980	88.8	0.8	90.6	2.0	91.3	0.8	91.6	0.3	92.5	1.0	91.9	-0.6	92.5	0.7	92.9	0.4	93.9	1.1	95.1	1.3	96.7	1.7	98.0	1.3
1981	99.1	1.1	99.4	0.3	99.4	0.0	100.0	0.6	101.0	1.0	101.0	0.0	101.8	0.8	101.5	-0.3	101.8	0.3	101.2	-0.6	101.1	-0.1	100.5	-0.6
1982	101.1	0.6	99.8	-1.3	99.8	0.0	99.9	0.1	99.6	-0.3	99.6	0.0	99.7	0.1	99.6	-0.1	100.1	0.5	99.7	-0.4	100.2	0.5	101.0	0.8
1983	101.4	0.4	101.2	-0.2	101.2	0.0	102.0	0.8	102.1	0.1	102.6	0.5	103.0	0.4	103.6	0.6	103.9	0.3	104.3	0.4	104.5	0.2	104.5	0.0
1984	105.1	0.6	105.3	0.2	105.4	0.1	105.7	0.3	105.9	0.2	106.9	0.9	107.3	0.4	107.1	-0.2	107.1	0.0	107.4	0.3	107.8	0.4	107.8	0.0
1985	109.0	1.1	109.4	0.4	109.5	0.1	109.9	0.4	109.6	-0.3	110.3	0.6	110.2	-0.1	110.3	0.1	110.8	0.5	111.4	0.5	111.3	-0.1	111.6	0.3
1986	111.6	0.0	111.6	0.0	111.6	0.0	111.4	-0.2	111.6	0.2	111.1	-0.4	110.7	-0.4	110.9	0.2	110.5	-0.4	110.6	0.1	110.5	-0.1	110.1	-0.4
1987	110.2	0.1	110.8	0.5	111.2	0.4	111.4	0.2	112.0	0.5	111.9	-0.1	111.9	0.0	112.6	0.6	113.0	0.4	114.5	1.3	115.3	0.7	116.7	1.2
1988	118.2	1.3	119.6	1.2	119.8	0.2	120.2	0.3	120.4	0.2	123.2	2.3	124.1	0.7	124.6	0.4	126.4	1.4	126.4	0.0	126.1	-0.2	126.5	0.3
1989	128.2	1.3	129.0	0.6	129.2	0.2	129.1	-0.1	130.8	1.3	131.2	0.3	132.1	0.7	132.9	0.6	132.8	-0.1	132.4	-0.3	132.4	0.0	133.3	0.7
1990	133.2	-0.1	133.8	0.5	133.9	0.1	134.6	0.5	135.1	0.4	134.7	-0.3	134.3	-0.3	134.2	-0.1	133.7	-0.4	134.2	0.4	134.2	0.0	134.6	0.3
1991	135.3	0.5	136.0	0.5	136.6	0.4	137.0	0.3	137.4	0.3	137.8	0.3	137.3	-0.4	138.3	0.7	138.6	0.2	139.9	0.9	140.0	0.1	141.0	0.7
1992	142.1	0.8	143.5	1.0	143.4	-0.1	143.5	0.1	144.0	0.3	145.3	0.9	144.8	-0.3	144.3	-0.3	144.6	0.2	144.9	0.2	145.1	0.1	144.7	-0.3
1993	145.7	0.7	146.5	0.5	146.1	-0.3	146.6	0.3	146.3	-0.2	146.4	0.1	146.6	0.1	147.6	0.7	147.4	-0.1	149.3	1.3	151.3	1.3	152.5	0.8

Source: U.S. Department of Labor, Bureau of Labor Statistics, Division of Industry Prices and Price Indexes. n.e.c. stands for not elsewhere classified. - indicates no data collected for period or unavailable.

Meats, Poultry, and Fish
Producer Price Index
Base 1982 = 100

For 1926-1993. Columns headed % show percentile change in the index from the previous period for which an index is available.

Year	Jan Index	%	Feb Index	%	Mar Index	%	Apr Index	%	May Index	%	Jun Index	%	Jul Index	%	Aug Index	%	Sep Index	%	Oct Index	%	Nov Index	%	Dec Index	%
1926	17.5	-	17.1	-2.3	17.2	0.6	17.4	1.2	17.5	0.6	17.9	2.3	17.7	-1.1	17.5	-1.1	17.8	1.7	17.7	-0.6	17.3	-2.3	17.2	-0.6
1927	15.6	-9.3	15.7	0.6	15.8	0.6	15.9	0.6	15.7	-1.3	15.5	-1.3	15.8	1.9	15.8	0.0	16.2	2.5	17.5	8.0	17.6	0.6	17.4	-1.1
1928	17.4	0.0	17.1	-1.7	16.6	-2.9	17.4	4.8	18.1	4.0	18.2	0.6	19.7	8.2	20.8	5.6	22.1	6.3	20.4	-7.7	19.0	-6.9	17.9	-5.8
1929	18.4	2.8	17.9	-2.7	19.0	6.1	19.5	2.6	19.5	0.0	19.5	0.0	20.4	4.6	20.3	-0.5	19.8	-2.5	18.6	-6.1	17.9	-3.8	18.1	1.1
1930	18.6	2.8	18.4	-1.1	18.2	-1.1	18.1	-0.5	17.7	-2.2	17.5	-1.1	16.0	-8.6	16.3	1.9	17.4	6.7	16.9	-2.9	16.0	-5.3	15.6	-2.5
1931	15.5	-0.6	14.6	-5.8	14.4	-1.4	14.0	-2.8	13.0	-7.1	12.5	-3.8	12.8	2.4	13.3	3.9	12.9	-3.0	12.5	-3.1	11.8	-5.6	11.1	-5.9
1932	10.8	-2.7	10.4	-3.7	10.7	2.9	10.5	-1.9	9.9	-5.7	9.8	-1.0	10.8	10.2	10.8	0.0	10.6	-1.9	9.9	-6.6	9.4	-5.1	8.6	-8.5
1933	8.7	1.2	8.8	1.1	8.9	1.1	8.8	-1.1	9.2	4.5	9.2	0.0	8.9	-3.3	8.9	0.0	9.0	1.1	8.9	-1.1	8.4	-5.6	8.0	-4.8
1934	8.5	6.3	9.4	10.6	9.9	5.3	10.0	1.0	10.5	5.0	10.9	3.8	11.1	1.8	12.2	9.9	13.4	9.8	12.2	-9.0	12.0	-1.6	12.0	0.0
1935	14.3	19.2	15.3	7.0	16.0	4.6	16.5	3.1	17.0	3.0	16.5	-2.9	16.3	-1.2	17.9	9.8	18.0	0.6	17.0	-5.6	16.5	-2.9	17.0	3.0
1936	16.6	-2.4	16.1	-3.0	15.7	-2.5	15.9	1.3	14.9	-6.3	14.9	0.0	14.8	-0.7	15.1	2.0	15.3	1.3	14.8	-3.3	14.9	0.7	15.2	2.0
1937	15.9	4.6	15.8	-0.6	16.1	1.9	16.6	3.1	16.8	1.2	17.2	2.4	18.5	7.6	19.6	5.9	19.8	1.0	18.8	-5.1	17.2	-8.5	15.5	-9.9
1938	14.4	-7.1	13.7	-4.9	14.3	4.4	14.4	0.7	14.4	0.0	14.8	2.8	15.7	6.1	15.0	-4.5	15.2	1.3	14.6	-3.9	14.3	-2.1	14.0	-2.1
1939	14.3	2.1	14.5	1.4	14.4	-0.7	14.2	-1.4	13.7	-3.5	13.2	-3.6	13.2	0.0	12.9	-2.3	14.2	10.1	13.1	-7.7	12.5	-4.6	12.0	-4.0
1940	12.2	1.7	12.0	-1.6	12.1	0.8	12.5	3.3	12.9	3.2	12.4	-3.9	12.8	3.2	13.3	3.9	13.8	3.8	13.2	-4.3	13.4	1.5	13.5	0.7
1941	14.5	7.4	14.6	0.7	14.6	0.0	15.0	2.7	15.2	1.3	15.9	4.6	16.4	3.1	17.0	3.7	17.4	2.4	16.4	-5.7	15.9	-3.0	16.7	5.0
1942	17.8	6.6	18.2	2.2	19.1	4.9	19.8	3.7	20.1	1.5	19.9	-1.0	19.8	-0.5	20.1	1.5	20.3	1.0	20.2	-0.5	19.6	-3.0	19.9	1.5
1943	20.2	1.5	20.2	0.0	20.2	0.0	20.3	0.5	20.3	0.0	19.5	-3.9	18.5	-5.1	18.5	0.0	18.5	0.0	18.6	0.5	18.6	0.0	18.5	-0.5
1944	18.5	0.0	18.5	0.0	18.5	0.0	18.6	0.5	18.6	0.0	18.5	-0.5	18.5	0.0	18.5	0.0	18.5	0.0	18.5	0.0	18.6	0.5	18.6	0.0
1945	18.6	0.0	18.6	0.0	18.8	1.1	18.9	0.5	19.0	0.5	18.9	-0.5	18.9	0.0	18.9	0.0	18.9	0.0	18.9	0.0	18.9	0.0	18.9	0.0
1946	18.9	0.0	18.9	0.0	19.2	1.6	19.3	0.5	19.3	0.0	19.3	0.0	29.7	53.9	34.6	16.5	22.9	-33.8	33.5	46.3	35.4	5.7	33.0	-6.8
1947	32.1	-2.7	32.8	2.2	34.5	5.2	33.1	-4.1	33.6	1.5	34.6	3.0	35.3	2.0	36.7	4.0	39.2	6.8	37.8	-3.6	36.4	-3.7	37.4	2.7
1948	40.3	7.8	37.8	-6.2	39.0	3.2	40.4	3.6	42.0	4.0	42.3	0.7	44.1	4.3	44.6	1.1	44.4	-0.4	41.0	-7.7	38.8	-5.4	37.7	-2.8
1949	36.6	-2.9	34.9	-4.6	36.5	4.6	36.6	0.3	36.7	0.3	36.8	0.3	36.2	-1.6	35.8	-1.1	36.8	2.8	35.3	-4.1	34.2	-3.1	33.4	-2.3
1950	33.7	0.9	34.6	2.7	34.4	-0.6	34.4	0.0	37.2	8.1	38.3	3.0	41.3	7.8	41.4	0.2	41.8	1.0	38.9	-6.9	38.8	-0.3	40.5	4.4
1951	41.9	3.5	43.9	4.8	43.8	-0.2	43.8	0.0	44.1	0.7	43.8	-0.7	43.7	-0.2	43.9	0.5	44.2	0.7	44.6	0.9	43.3	-2.9	42.4	-2.1
1952	42.4	0.0	41.4	-2.4	41.5	0.2	40.9	-1.4	41.9	2.4	41.2	-1.7	41.3	0.2	42.0	1.7	40.9	-2.6	38.9	-4.9	38.1	-2.1	35.1	-7.9
1953	37.1	5.7	36.7	-1.1	34.1	-7.1	33.3	-2.3	35.1	5.4	34.2	-2.6	36.2	5.8	35.0	-3.3	36.4	4.0	33.2	-8.8	32.2	-3.0	33.5	4.0
1954	36.0	7.5	34.7	-3.6	34.7	0.0	35.3	1.7	36.8	4.2	34.5	-6.3	35.2	2.0	34.4	-2.3	34.4	0.0	32.1	-6.7	32.2	0.3	31.8	-1.2
1955	32.7	2.8	32.5	-0.6	31.1	-4.3	32.1	3.2	32.0	-0.3	34.2	6.9	33.1	-3.2	32.2	-2.7	32.7	1.6	30.5	-6.7	29.1	-4.6	28.1	-3.4
1956	28.3	0.7	28.4	0.4	27.9	-1.8	29.7	6.5	30.7	3.4	31.1	1.3	31.3	0.6	31.8	1.6	33.4	5.0	32.0	-4.2	30.9	-3.4	30.5	-1.3
1957	31.7	3.9	31.4	-0.9	31.6	0.6	33.0	4.4	34.2	3.6	36.1	5.6	37.1	2.8	36.5	-1.6	35.8	-1.9	34.2	-4.5	35.0	2.3	35.7	2.0
1958	38.0	6.4	38.4	1.1	39.6	3.1	40.6	2.5	42.2	3.9	42.6	0.9	41.9	-1.6	40.5	-3.3	40.0	-1.2	38.7	-3.3	38.3	-1.0	37.9	-1.0
1959	38.6	1.8	37.7	-2.3	37.2	-1.3	37.7	1.3	37.9	0.5	38.1	0.5	37.1	-2.6	35.4	-4.6	37.3	5.4	35.5	-4.8	33.9	-4.5	33.8	-0.3
1960	34.6	2.4	34.8	0.6	36.6	5.2	36.1	-1.4	36.8	1.9	36.7	-0.3	37.2	1.4	36.1	-3.0	35.9	-0.6	36.6	1.9	36.1	-1.4	36.4	0.8
1961	36.8	1.1	37.2	1.1	35.9	-3.5	35.3	-1.7	34.3	-2.8	33.6	-2.0	34.6	3.0	35.4	2.3	35.3	-0.3	35.0	-0.8	34.6	-1.1	35.4	2.3
1962	36.7	3.7	36.5	-0.5	36.4	-0.3	35.3	-3.0	35.3	0.0	35.4	0.3	36.6	3.4	37.3	1.9	39.5	5.9	37.0	-6.3	37.0	0.0	36.8	-0.5
1963	36.2	-1.6	35.3	-2.5	33.9	-4.0	33.4	-1.5	34.0	1.8	34.8	2.4	35.6	2.3	35.2	-1.1	34.8	-1.1	34.5	-0.9	33.9	-1.7	32.4	-4.4
1964	33.9	4.6	32.9	-2.9	32.8	-0.3	32.7	-0.3	32.1	-1.8	33.3	3.7	34.5	3.6	34.5	0.0	35.5	2.9	34.5	-2.8	33.2	-3.8	32.8	-1.2
1965	34.0	3.7	34.0	0.0	34.2	0.6	34.6	1.2	36.1	4.3	39.0	8.0	39.3	0.8	39.3	0.0	38.9	-1.0	38.8	-0.3	39.0	0.5	40.8	4.6
1966	41.7	2.2	42.5	1.9	41.9	-1.4	41.0	-2.1	41.0	0.0	40.6	-1.0	40.7	0.2	41.1	1.0	41.5	1.0	40.0	-3.6	38.5	-3.8	38.6	0.3
1967	39.0	1.0	38.7	-0.8	37.6	-2.8	37.2	-1.1	38.4	3.2	40.0	4.2	40.6	1.5	39.7	-2.2	40.1	1.0	38.7	-3.5	37.8	-2.3	38.2	1.1
1968	39.1	2.4	39.8	1.8	39.6	-0.5	39.1	-1.3	39.5	1.0	40.6	2.8	42.0	3.4	40.6	-3.3	41.1	1.2	39.5	-3.9	39.8	0.8	39.7	-0.3
1969	41.1	3.5	41.2	0.2	41.5	0.7	42.2	1.7	44.7	5.9	46.8	4.7	47.1	0.6	46.0	-2.3	45.4	-1.3	44.5	-2.0	44.6	0.2	45.1	1.1
1970	46.6	3.3	46.2	-0.9	47.1	1.9	46.2	-1.9	45.3	-1.9	45.7	0.9	46.7	2.2	45.2	-3.2	44.7	-1.1	43.1	-3.6	42.2	-2.1	40.5	-4.0

[Continued]

Meats, Poultry, and Fish
Producer Price Index
Base 1982 = 100
[Continued]

For 1926-1993. Columns headed % show percentile change in the index from the previous period for which an index is available.

Year	Jan Index	%	Feb Index	%	Mar Index	%	Apr Index	%	May Index	%	Jun Index	%	Jul Index	%	Aug Index	%	Sep Index	%	Oct Index	%	Nov Index	%	Dec Index	%
1971	42.2	4.2	44.7	5.9	43.8	-2.0	44.0	0.5	45.2	2.7	45.3	0.2	46.4	2.4	45.7	-1.5	45.6	-0.2	45.4	-0.4	45.5	0.2	46.8	2.9
1972	48.7	4.1	50.7	4.1	49.4	-2.6	48.0	-2.8	49.2	2.5	51.0	3.7	52.7	3.3	51.3	-2.7	51.1	-0.4	50.6	-1.0	49.7	-1.8	52.9	6.4
1973	56.4	6.6	59.5	5.5	64.1	7.7	63.3	-1.2	63.1	-0.3	64.0	1.4	65.9	3.0	77.0	16.8	72.7	-5.6	66.1	-9.1	64.1	-3.0	64.0	-0.2
1974	69.0	7.8	69.8	1.2	64.3	-7.9	61.2	-4.8	59.5	-2.8	55.0	-7.6	64.9	18.0	65.9	1.5	64.3	-2.4	63.3	-1.6	62.3	-1.6	62.4	0.2
1975	64.3	3.0	63.9	-0.6	63.6	-0.5	67.7	6.4	74.0	9.3	77.5	4.7	81.4	5.0	79.4	-2.5	81.4	2.5	81.7	0.4	78.0	-4.5	76.9	-1.4
1976	75.0	-2.5	72.2	-3.7	70.1	-2.9	73.4	4.7	73.9	0.7	73.8	-0.1	71.9	-2.6	67.8	-5.7	68.4	0.9	65.4	-4.4	65.4	0.0	68.7	5.0
1977	68.6	-0.1	68.9	0.4	67.6	-1.9	67.9	0.4	71.3	5.0	71.2	-0.1	73.6	3.4	70.9	-3.7	71.0	0.1	71.7	1.0	71.2	-0.7	74.1	4.1
1978	75.2	1.5	79.8	6.1	79.5	-0.4	82.2	3.4	85.6	4.1	87.8	2.6	87.1	-0.8	83.8	-3.8	87.1	3.9	88.6	1.7	85.8	-3.2	89.0	3.7
1979	93.3	4.8	96.5	3.4	97.3	0.8	98.2	0.9	97.2	-1.0	93.7	-3.6	92.3	-1.5	87.6	-5.1	93.1	6.3	90.9	-2.4	92.9	2.2	94.3	1.5
1980	93.0	-1.4	93.0	0.0	92.9	-0.1	87.8	-5.5	87.1	-0.8	88.0	1.0	96.5	9.7	100.9	4.6	100.1	-0.8	99.4	-0.7	97.4	-2.0	96.3	-1.1
1981	96.3	0.0	94.6	-1.8	93.9	-0.7	92.8	-1.2	95.2	2.6	96.5	1.4	99.8	3.4	98.8	-1.0	98.3	-0.5	95.7	-2.6	93.2	-2.6	91.7	-1.6
1982	94.6	3.2	96.3	1.8	97.1	0.8	100.2	3.2	103.9	3.7	105.3	1.3	103.3	-1.9	101.8	-1.5	103.2	1.4	99.7	-3.4	97.7	-2.0	97.0	-0.7
1983	97.9	0.9	101.3	3.5	101.2	-0.1	100.6	-0.6	100.1	-0.5	97.1	-3.0	96.0	-1.1	94.4	-1.7	94.3	-0.1	92.0	-2.4	91.1	-1.0	94.1	3.3
1984	99.3	5.5	98.8	-0.5	102.6	3.8	101.6	-1.0	99.8	-1.8	96.1	-3.7	100.5	4.6	97.9	-2.6	96.9	-1.0	95.3	-1.7	97.2	2.0	99.4	2.3
1985	99.6	0.2	99.2	-0.4	97.0	-2.2	95.0	-2.1	94.7	-0.3	92.6	-2.2	94.4	1.9	92.9	-1.6	91.1	-1.9	94.5	3.7	99.1	4.9	100.5	1.4
1986	98.1	-2.4	95.1	-3.1	93.9	-1.3	92.4	-1.6	95.8	3.7	97.2	1.5	103.0	6.0	107.7	4.6	106.4	-1.2	105.2	-1.1	103.7	-1.4	103.6	-0.1
1987	101.9	-1.6	102.5	0.6	100.3	-2.1	104.5	4.2	109.7	5.0	108.9	-0.7	109.5	0.6	106.2	-3.0	108.0	1.7	106.1	-1.8	101.4	-4.4	99.9	-1.5
1988	103.8	3.9	102.7	-1.1	104.0	1.3	104.4	0.4	107.7	3.2	110.0	2.1	109.6	-0.4	107.8	-1.6	109.3	1.4	106.8	-2.3	106.0	-0.7	106.8	0.8
1989	109.8	2.8	109.9	0.1	111.8	1.7	111.4	-0.4	112.7	1.2	111.4	-1.2	111.6	0.2	111.3	-0.3	110.4	-0.8	109.6	-0.7	111.0	1.3	111.5	0.5
1990	114.0	2.2	114.9	0.8	116.9	1.7	118.4	1.3	124.1	4.8	121.5	-2.1	121.6	0.1	121.0	-0.5	119.5	-1.2	121.0	1.3	121.1	0.1	120.9	-0.2
1991	120.0	-0.7	119.6	-0.3	120.6	0.8	120.0	-0.5	121.0	0.8	119.1	-1.6	118.6	-0.4	114.4	-3.5	112.3	-1.8	113.3	0.9	110.9	-2.1	110.0	-0.8
1992	109.0	-0.9	110.8	1.7	112.2	1.3	113.5	1.2	113.7	0.2	113.5	-0.2	112.6	-0.8	111.8	-0.7	111.9	0.1	112.1	0.2	111.0	-1.0	113.8	2.5
1993	114.3	0.4	115.2	0.8	116.7	1.3	118.0	1.1	118.7	0.6	117.6	-0.9	115.0	-2.2	114.3	-0.6	115.0	0.6	114.3	-0.6	113.3	-0.9	112.6	-0.6

Source: U.S. Department of Labor, Bureau of Labor Statistics, Division of Industry Prices and Price Indexes. n.e.c. stands for not elsewhere classified. - indicates no data collected for period or unavailable.

Dairy Products
Producer Price Index
Base 1982 = 100

For 1926-1993. Columns headed % show percentile change in the index from the previous period for which an index is available.

Year	Jan Index	%	Feb Index	%	Mar Index	%	Apr Index	%	May Index	%	Jun Index	%	Jul Index	%	Aug Index	%	Sep Index	%	Oct Index	%	Nov Index	%	Dec Index	%
1926	17.9	-	17.7	-1.1	17.4	-1.7	17.0	-2.3	16.8	-1.2	16.6	-1.2	16.7	0.6	17.0	1.8	17.6	3.5	18.0	2.3	18.2	1.1	18.7	2.7
1927	18.4	-1.6	18.6	1.1	18.5	-0.5	18.3	-1.1	17.2	-6.0	17.0	-1.2	17.1	0.6	17.2	0.6	18.4	7.0	18.7	1.6	18.8	0.5	19.2	2.1
1928	18.8	-2.1	18.5	-1.6	18.2	-1.6	17.6	-3.3	17.4	-1.1	17.4	0.0	18.0	3.4	18.7	3.9	19.0	1.6	18.8	-1.1	19.0	1.1	19.2	1.1
1929	19.0	-1.0	19.1	0.5	19.0	-0.5	18.5	-2.6	18.2	-1.6	18.4	1.1	18.0	-2.2	18.2	1.1	18.5	1.6	18.5	0.0	18.1	-2.2	17.7	-2.2
1930	17.0	-4.0	17.0	0.0	17.2	1.2	17.3	0.6	16.1	-6.9	15.7	-2.5	16.0	1.9	17.0	6.3	17.4	2.4	17.2	-1.1	16.7	-2.9	15.5	-7.2
1931	14.6	-5.8	14.5	-0.7	14.6	0.7	14.1	-3.4	13.7	-2.8	13.7	0.0	14.1	2.9	14.3	1.4	14.7	2.8	15.0	2.0	14.1	-6.0	13.9	-1.4
1932	11.9	-14.4	11.2	-5.9	11.2	0.0	10.7	-4.5	10.4	-2.8	10.0	-3.8	10.2	2.0	10.5	2.9	10.6	1.0	10.6	0.0	10.8	1.9	10.4	-3.7
1933	9.6	-7.7	9.1	-5.2	8.9	-2.2	9.3	4.5	10.2	9.7	11.0	7.8	11.5	4.5	11.5	0.0	11.5	0.0	11.5	0.0	11.7	1.7	11.4	-2.6
1934	11.4	0.0	12.1	6.1	12.0	-0.8	11.6	-3.3	11.7	0.9	12.7	8.5	13.1	3.1	13.5	3.1	13.3	-1.5	13.5	1.5	13.7	1.5	13.9	1.5
1935	14.6	5.0	15.2	4.1	14.4	-5.3	14.8	2.8	13.6	-8.1	13.0	-4.4	12.9	-0.8	13.2	2.3	13.3	0.8	13.4	0.8	14.2	6.0	14.6	2.8
1936	14.7	0.7	14.9	1.4	14.0	-6.0	13.7	-2.1	13.1	-4.4	13.5	3.1	14.6	8.1	15.3	4.8	15.6	2.0	15.2	-2.6	15.4	1.3	15.5	0.6
1937	15.5	0.0	15.5	0.0	15.7	1.3	13.7	-12.7	12.7	-7.3	12.6	-0.8	13.3	5.6	13.9	4.5	14.8	6.5	14.9	0.7	15.5	4.0	15.7	1.3
1938	14.5	-7.6	13.7	-5.5	13.4	-2.2	12.5	-6.7	12.1	-3.2	12.0	-0.8	12.1	0.8	12.0	-0.8	12.4	3.3	12.5	0.8	12.7	1.6	12.9	1.6
1939	12.5	-3.1	12.5	0.0	11.3	-9.6	10.1	-10.6	10.2	1.0	10.5	2.9	10.4	-1.0	11.9	14.4	13.0	9.2	13.7	5.4	14.0	2.2	14.2	1.4
1940	14.3	0.7	13.9	-2.8	13.7	-1.4	13.5	-1.5	12.7	-5.9	12.6	-0.8	12.9	2.4	12.9	0.0	13.1	1.6	13.5	3.1	14.4	6.7	14.7	2.1
1941	14.0	-4.8	13.9	-0.7	14.0	0.7	14.1	0.7	14.2	0.7	14.7	3.5	15.3	4.1	15.7	2.6	16.2	3.2	16.6	2.5	16.8	1.2	16.7	-0.6
1942	16.8	0.6	16.6	-1.2	16.5	-0.6	16.4	-0.6	16.3	-0.6	16.1	-1.2	16.8	4.3	17.5	4.2	18.4	5.1	19.0	3.3	19.4	2.1	19.5	0.5
1943	19.8	1.5	19.8	0.0	19.8	0.0	19.8	0.0	19.7	-0.5	19.1	-3.0	19.0	-0.5	19.0	0.0	19.0	0.0	19.0	0.0	19.4	2.1	19.3	-0.5
1944	19.3	0.0	19.3	0.0	19.3	0.0	19.2	-0.5	19.2	0.0	19.2	0.0	19.2	0.0	19.3	0.5	19.3	0.0	19.3	0.0	19.3	0.0	19.3	0.0
1945	19.3	0.0	19.3	0.0	19.3	0.0	19.3	0.0	19.3	0.0	19.3	0.0	19.3	0.0	19.3	0.0	19.2	-0.5	19.3	0.5	19.7	2.1	19.8	0.5
1946	20.0	1.0	20.2	1.0	20.3	0.5	20.3	0.0	20.4	0.5	22.2	8.8	27.4	23.4	28.2	2.9	29.5	4.6	32.3	9.5	31.9	-1.2	31.4	-1.6
1947	28.7	-8.6	28.0	-2.4	27.4	-2.1	26.7	-2.6	26.1	-2.2	26.0	-0.4	26.9	3.5	27.8	3.3	28.5	2.5	29.3	2.8	30.3	3.4	30.9	2.0
1948	31.5	1.9	31.5	0.0	30.6	-2.9	30.9	1.0	30.8	-0.3	31.3	1.6	32.2	2.9	32.5	0.9	31.8	-2.2	31.3	-1.6	30.9	-1.3	30.5	-1.3
1949	29.8	-2.3	29.2	-2.0	28.3	-3.1	27.7	-2.1	27.3	-1.4	27.6	1.1	27.7	0.4	28.4	2.5	28.2	-0.7	28.2	0.0	28.0	-0.7	28.1	0.4
1950	27.4	-2.5	27.5	0.4	27.2	-1.1	26.9	-1.1	26.2	-2.6	26.3	0.4	27.0	2.7	27.7	2.6	28.5	2.9	28.9	1.4	29.0	0.3	29.5	1.7
1951	30.9	4.7	31.5	1.9	31.2	-1.0	30.9	-1.0	31.1	0.6	31.1	0.0	31.1	0.0	31.5	1.3	31.0	-1.6	31.7	2.3	32.4	2.2	33.0	1.9
1952	33.1	0.3	33.6	1.5	33.1	-1.5	32.7	-1.2	32.3	-1.2	32.1	-0.6	33.2	3.4	33.3	0.3	34.0	2.1	33.8	-0.6	33.7	-0.3	33.0	-2.1
1953	32.7	-0.9	32.4	-0.9	32.0	-1.2	31.7	-0.9	31.5	-0.6	31.5	0.0	32.1	1.9	32.3	0.6	32.5	0.6	32.9	1.2	33.3	1.2	32.5	-2.4
1954	31.9	-1.8	31.3	-1.9	31.0	-1.0	30.1	-2.9	29.7	-1.3	29.9	0.7	30.7	2.7	30.9	0.7	31.1	0.6	31.7	1.9	31.8	0.3	31.6	-0.6
1955	31.3	-0.9	31.3	0.0	31.3	0.0	31.2	-0.3	30.4	-2.6	30.5	0.3	30.9	1.3	31.5	1.9	30.5	-3.2	30.7	0.7	30.9	0.7	31.3	1.3
1956	31.0	-1.0	31.0	0.0	31.0	0.0	30.9	-0.3	31.5	1.9	31.5	0.0	31.5	0.0	31.8	1.0	32.0	0.6	32.4	1.3	33.1	2.2	32.9	-0.6
1957	32.8	-0.3	32.8	0.0	32.5	-0.9	32.5	0.0	32.3	-0.6	31.5	-2.5	31.6	0.3	32.2	1.9	32.8	1.9	33.2	1.2	33.4	0.6	33.5	0.3
1958	33.3	-0.6	33.3	0.0	33.1	-0.6	32.5	-1.8	32.3	-0.6	32.4	0.3	32.5	0.3	32.7	0.6	33.2	1.5	33.1	-0.3	33.1	0.0	33.1	0.0
1959	33.0	-0.3	33.0	0.0	33.0	0.0	32.7	-0.9	32.6	-0.3	32.7	0.3	33.3	1.8	33.5	0.6	33.9	1.2	34.1	0.6	34.4	0.9	34.5	0.3
1960	34.7	0.6	34.6	-0.3	34.4	-0.6	33.7	-2.0	33.5	-0.6	33.8	0.9	34.2	1.2	34.4	0.6	35.2	2.3	35.4	0.6	35.5	0.3	35.6	0.3
1961	35.4	-0.6	35.0	-1.1	35.2	0.6	35.0	-0.6	34.9	-0.3	35.0	0.3	35.1	0.3	35.3	0.6	35.6	0.8	36.1	1.4	36.1	0.0	36.3	0.6
1962	36.0	-0.8	36.0	0.0	35.6	-1.1	35.0	-1.7	34.4	-1.7	34.6	0.6	34.8	0.6	35.0	0.6	35.0	0.0	35.5	1.4	35.6	0.3	35.6	0.0
1963	35.5	-0.3	35.6	0.3	35.3	-0.8	35.2	-0.3	35.2	0.0	35.1	-0.3	35.4	0.9	35.6	0.6	35.6	0.0	35.4	-0.6	35.6	0.6	35.6	0.0
1964	35.6	0.0	35.4	-0.6	35.4	0.0	35.3	-0.3	35.1	-0.6	35.3	0.6	35.3	0.0	35.4	0.3	35.8	1.1	35.9	0.3	36.1	0.6	35.9	-0.6
1965	35.7	-0.6	35.5	-0.6	35.4	-0.3	35.4	0.0	35.2	-0.6	35.3	0.3	35.5	0.6	35.8	0.8	36.0	0.6	36.0	0.0	36.4	1.1	36.7	0.8
1966	36.6	-0.3	37.2	1.6	37.9	1.9	37.8	-0.3	37.9	0.3	38.4	1.3	39.5	2.9	40.9	3.5	40.9	0.0	41.0	0.2	40.4	-1.5	40.3	-0.2
1967	40.1	-0.5	39.9	-0.5	39.7	-0.5	39.6	-0.3	39.8	0.5	40.2	1.0	40.2	0.0	40.3	0.2	40.5	0.5	40.5	0.0	40.5	0.0	40.9	1.0
1968	40.8	-0.2	40.9	0.2	40.6	-0.7	41.5	2.2	42.5	2.4	42.4	-0.2	42.5	0.2	42.5	0.0	42.5	0.0	42.9	0.9	42.8	-0.2	43.0	0.5
1969	42.9	-0.2	42.9	0.0	43.0	0.2	43.3	0.7	43.6	0.7	43.8	0.5	43.8	0.0	43.8	0.0	44.1	0.7	43.1	-2.3	43.3	0.5	44.2	2.1
1970	44.2	0.0	44.3	0.2	43.9	-0.9	44.5	1.4	44.7	0.4	44.7	0.0	44.8	0.2	44.8	0.0	44.8	0.0	45.1	0.7	45.1	0.0	45.4	0.7

[Continued]

Dairy Products
Producer Price Index
Base 1982 = 100
[Continued]

For 1926-1993. Columns headed % show percentile change in the index from the previous period for which an index is available.

Year	Jan Index	%	Feb Index	%	Mar Index	%	Apr Index	%	May Index	%	Jun Index	%	Jul Index	%	Aug Index	%	Sep Index	%	Oct Index	%	Nov Index	%	Dec Index	%
1971	45.4	0.0	45.2	-0.4	46.2	2.2	46.4	0.4	46.7	0.6	46.7	0.0	46.7	0.0	46.8	0.2	46.8	0.0	46.8	0.0	46.7	-0.2	47.2	1.1
1972	47.1	-0.2	47.2	0.2	47.4	0.4	47.2	-0.4	47.2	0.0	46.3	-1.9	47.3	2.2	47.7	0.8	47.8	0.2	48.2	0.8	48.9	1.5	49.4	1.0
1973	49.7	0.6	49.8	0.2	51.0	2.4	51.1	0.2	50.8	-0.6	51.2	0.8	51.1	-0.2	52.8	3.3	55.1	4.4	56.1	1.8	56.2	0.2	57.2	1.8
1974	58.3	1.9	59.3	1.7	60.8	2.5	61.9	1.8	59.0	-4.7	57.4	-2.7	56.9	-0.9	57.2	0.5	58.2	1.7	58.8	1.0	59.0	0.3	59.0	0.0
1975	59.6	1.0	59.6	0.0	59.7	0.2	59.8	0.2	60.1	0.5	60.5	0.7	61.5	1.7	62.8	2.1	64.6	2.9	66.6	3.1	67.5	1.4	68.8	1.9
1976	68.2	-0.9	65.7	-3.7	67.0	2.0	67.4	0.6	67.2	-0.3	67.2	0.0	68.4	1.8	69.9	2.2	68.5	-2.0	68.2	-0.4	67.6	-0.9	67.2	-0.6
1977	67.0	-0.3	67.0	0.0	67.5	0.7	69.7	3.3	70.0	0.4	70.0	0.0	70.4	0.6	70.5	0.1	70.6	0.1	70.7	0.1	71.1	0.6	71.6	0.7
1978	71.5	-0.1	71.8	0.4	72.4	0.8	74.1	2.3	74.1	0.0	74.5	0.5	74.8	0.4	76.7	2.5	77.5	1.0	79.2	2.2	80.2	1.3	81.5	1.6
1979	81.8	0.4	81.6	-0.2	82.3	0.9	83.2	1.1	83.5	0.4	83.7	0.2	84.0	0.4	86.5	3.0	87.7	1.4	87.6	-0.1	88.1	0.6	88.3	0.2
1980	88.8	0.6	88.7	-0.1	89.6	1.0	91.4	2.0	91.8	0.4	92.2	0.4	92.4	0.2	93.5	1.2	93.9	0.4	95.6	1.8	96.5	0.9	97.4	0.9
1981	98.3	0.9	98.5	0.2	98.5	0.0	98.6	0.1	98.3	-0.3	98.5	0.2	98.5	0.0	98.5	0.0	98.6	0.1	99.2	0.6	99.2	0.0	99.3	0.1
1982	99.5	0.2	99.6	0.1	99.6	0.0	99.8	0.2	99.8	0.0	99.9	0.1	99.9	0.0	100.0	0.1	100.1	0.1	100.4	0.3	100.5	0.1	100.8	0.3
1983	100.7	-0.1	100.8	0.1	100.7	-0.1	100.8	0.1	100.8	0.0	100.6	-0.2	100.6	0.0	100.6	0.0	100.7	0.1	101.0	0.3	101.0	0.0	100.0	-1.0
1984	99.8	-0.2	99.8	0.0	100.0	0.2	100.0	0.0	100.0	0.0	100.3	0.3	101.0	0.7	100.9	-0.1	102.5	1.6	103.0	0.5	103.4	0.4	102.8	-0.6
1985	102.6	-0.2	102.1	-0.5	101.8	-0.3	101.0	-0.8	100.4	-0.6	100.2	-0.2	99.7	-0.5	99.2	-0.5	98.9	-0.3	98.8	-0.1	98.9	0.1	98.9	0.0
1986	98.8	-0.1	98.9	0.1	98.8	-0.1	98.8	0.0	99.2	0.4	99.2	0.0	99.5	0.3	100.3	0.8	100.6	0.3	101.2	0.6	101.8	0.6	102.1	0.3
1987	101.9	-0.2	101.4	-0.5	101.4	0.0	101.2	-0.2	100.9	-0.3	101.1	0.2	101.4	0.3	101.9	0.5	102.7	0.8	102.1	-0.6	102.0	-0.1	101.7	-0.3
1988	101.0	-0.7	100.5	-0.5	100.1	-0.4	100.0	-0.1	100.1	0.1	100.6	0.5	101.2	0.6	102.2	1.0	103.8	1.6	104.9	1.1	105.5	0.6	106.2	0.7
1989	107.1	0.8	106.5	-0.6	106.0	-0.5	105.6	-0.4	105.6	0.0	106.4	0.8	107.9	1.4	110.7	2.6	113.3	2.3	116.4	2.7	120.1	3.2	121.4	1.1
1990	120.5	-0.7	116.9	-3.0	116.1	-0.7	115.1	-0.9	116.6	1.3	118.0	1.2	119.5	1.3	120.2	0.6	119.0	-1.0	117.4	-1.3	114.8	-2.2	112.8	-1.7
1991	112.3	-0.4	112.0	-0.3	111.9	-0.1	111.5	-0.4	111.5	0.0	112.1	0.5	113.6	1.3	115.1	1.3	115.9	0.7	119.3	2.9	119.8	0.4	120.0	0.2
1992	118.3	-1.4	116.0	-1.9	115.0	-0.9	115.4	0.3	116.9	1.3	118.7	1.5	119.4	0.6	120.0	0.5	120.0	0.0	119.4	-0.5	118.7	-0.6	117.4	-1.1
1993	116.4	-0.9	115.4	-0.9	115.0	-0.3	117.2	1.9	118.5	1.1	119.5	0.8	119.2	-0.3	117.9	-1.1	118.3	0.3	118.8	0.4	120.3	1.3	121.0	0.6

Source: U.S. Department of Labor, Bureau of Labor Statistics, Division of Industry Prices and Price Indexes. n.e.c. stands for not elsewhere classified. - indicates no data collected for period or unavailable.

Processed Fruits and Vegetables

Producer Price Index
Base 1982 = 100

For 1926-1993. Columns headed % show percentile change in the index from the previous period for which an index is available.

Year	Jan Index	%	Feb Index	%	Mar Index	%	Apr Index	%	May Index	%	Jun Index	%	Jul Index	%	Aug Index	%	Sep Index	%	Oct Index	%	Nov Index	%	Dec Index	%
1926	20.6	-	20.5	-0.5	20.3	-1.0	20.3	0.0	20.1	-1.0	20.2	0.5	20.3	0.5	20.1	-1.0	20.3	1.0	20.5	1.0	20.4	-0.5	20.2	-1.0
1927	20.1	-0.5	20.4	1.5	20.4	0.0	20.0	-2.0	20.0	0.0	20.0	0.0	20.0	0.0	20.0	0.0	19.7	-1.5	19.6	-0.5	20.3	3.6	20.5	1.0
1928	21.4	4.4	21.5	0.5	21.7	0.9	21.8	0.5	21.8	0.0	21.8	0.0	21.6	-0.9	21.0	-2.8	21.1	0.5	21.3	0.9	21.4	0.5	21.5	0.5
1929	21.4	-0.5	21.7	1.4	21.8	0.5	22.1	1.4	22.7	2.7	23.0	1.3	23.5	2.2	22.7	-3.4	22.5	-0.9	22.4	-0.4	22.3	-0.4	22.5	0.9
1930	22.7	0.9	22.6	-0.4	22.5	-0.4	22.2	-1.3	20.7	-6.8	20.5	-1.0	20.4	-0.5	20.4	0.0	20.6	1.0	20.3	-1.5	19.6	-3.4	19.2	-2.0
1931	19.0	-1.0	19.1	0.5	18.6	-2.6	18.3	-1.6	17.7	-3.3	17.5	-1.1	17.5	0.0	17.3	-1.1	17.1	-1.2	16.8	-1.8	16.3	-3.0	16.3	0.0
1932	16.2	-0.6	16.1	-0.6	16.4	1.9	16.4	0.0	16.3	-0.6	16.1	-1.2	15.5	-3.7	15.4	-0.6	15.0	-2.6	15.2	1.3	15.1	-0.7	15.0	-0.7
1933	14.9	-0.7	14.8	-0.7	14.8	0.0	14.9	0.7	15.4	3.4	15.6	1.3	15.9	1.9	16.4	3.1	17.1	4.3	17.2	0.6	17.1	-0.6	17.1	0.0
1934	17.2	0.6	17.5	1.7	17.6	0.6	17.7	0.6	17.6	-0.6	17.6	0.0	17.8	1.1	17.5	-1.7	18.0	2.9	18.7	3.9	18.5	-1.1	18.5	0.0
1935	18.5	0.0	18.7	1.1	18.7	0.0	18.5	-1.1	18.3	-1.1	18.2	-0.5	17.9	-1.6	17.1	-4.5	17.1	0.0	16.9	-1.2	16.8	-0.6	16.8	0.0
1936	16.6	-1.2	16.6	0.0	16.9	1.8	17.1	1.2	17.1	0.0	16.9	-1.2	17.1	1.2	18.1	5.8	18.3	1.1	18.2	-0.5	18.3	0.5	18.4	0.5
1937	18.5	0.5	18.5	0.0	18.5	0.0	18.5	0.0	18.5	0.0	18.7	1.1	18.3	-2.1	17.9	-2.2	17.8	-0.6	17.7	-0.6	17.9	1.1	17.8	-0.6
1938	17.7	-0.6	17.6	-0.6	17.5	-0.6	17.2	-1.7	16.9	-1.7	16.3	-3.6	15.9	-2.5	15.3	-3.8	15.2	-0.7	15.2	0.0	15.1	-0.7	15.1	0.0
1939	15.2	0.7	15.2	0.0	15.3	0.7	15.5	1.3	15.5	0.0	15.6	0.6	15.6	0.0	15.5	-0.6	16.1	3.9	16.4	1.9	16.3	-0.6	16.2	-0.6
1940	16.1	-0.6	16.1	0.0	15.9	-1.2	15.9	0.0	15.9	0.0	16.0	0.6	16.0	0.0	15.8	-1.2	15.7	-0.6	15.7	0.0	15.7	0.0	15.7	0.0
1941	15.9	1.3	16.3	2.5	16.4	0.6	16.8	2.4	17.1	1.8	17.6	2.9	18.9	7.4	19.9	5.3	19.8	-0.5	20.4	3.0	20.7	1.5	21.0	1.4
1942	21.1	0.5	21.2	0.5	21.4	0.9	21.5	0.5	21.5	0.0	22.0	2.3	21.8	-0.9	21.8	0.0	22.0	0.9	22.5	2.3	22.5	0.0	22.5	0.0
1943	22.5	0.0	22.5	0.0	22.5	0.0	22.5	0.0	22.5	0.0	22.5	0.0	22.5	0.0	22.4	-0.4	22.4	0.0	22.5	0.4	22.5	0.0	22.5	0.0
1944	22.6	0.4	22.6	0.0	22.6	0.0	22.6	0.0	22.6	0.0	22.6	0.0	22.6	0.0	22.8	0.9	23.1	1.3	23.0	-0.4	23.0	0.0	23.1	0.4
1945	23.0	-0.4	23.0	0.0	23.0	0.0	23.0	0.0	23.1	0.4	23.1	0.0	23.1	0.0	23.1	0.0	23.1	0.0	23.0	-0.4	23.1	0.4	23.0	-0.4
1946	23.0	0.0	23.0	0.0	23.0	0.0	23.2	0.9	23.4	0.9	23.7	1.3	23.7	0.0	23.4	-1.3	23.5	0.4	23.7	0.9	29.4	24.1	29.4	0.0
1947	31.9	8.5	31.8	-0.3	31.8	0.0	31.8	0.0	32.2	1.3	31.9	-0.9	31.7	-0.6	31.3	-1.3	31.6	1.0	31.6	0.0	31.6	0.0	31.5	-0.3
1948	31.6	0.3	31.6	0.0	31.4	-0.6	31.2	-0.6	31.2	0.0	31.3	0.3	31.5	0.6	32.1	1.9	32.2	0.3	31.8	-1.2	32.0	0.6	31.8	-0.6
1949	31.7	-0.3	31.8	0.3	31.8	0.0	31.8	0.0	32.0	0.6	31.7	-0.9	31.4	-0.9	31.3	-0.3	31.3	0.0	31.3	0.0	31.1	-0.6	30.0	-3.5
1950	30.6	2.0	31.0	1.3	31.0	0.0	30.8	-0.6	30.9	0.3	31.0	0.3	31.2	0.6	32.1	2.9	32.4	0.9	32.6	0.6	32.1	-1.5	32.6	1.6
1951	33.4	2.5	33.7	0.9	33.7	0.0	33.7	0.0	33.4	-0.9	33.0	-1.2	32.7	-0.9	32.6	-0.3	33.1	1.5	33.4	0.9	33.6	0.6	33.6	0.0
1952	33.4	-0.6	33.1	-0.9	33.2	0.3	33.1	-0.3	32.9	-0.6	32.7	-0.6	32.8	0.3	33.2	1.2	33.5	0.9	33.5	0.0	33.5	0.0	33.2	-0.9
1953	33.3	0.3	33.3	0.0	33.2	-0.3	33.0	-0.6	32.9	-0.3	32.8	-0.3	33.2	1.2	33.1	-0.3	33.1	0.0	33.2	0.3	33.1	-0.3	32.8	-0.9
1954	32.8	0.0	32.6	-0.6	32.6	0.0	32.6	0.0	33.0	1.2	33.0	0.3	33.1	0.3	33.2	0.3	33.1	0.0	33.2	0.3	33.3	0.3	33.5	0.6
1955	33.1	-1.2	33.0	-0.3	33.1	0.3	33.1	0.0	32.9	-0.6	33.0	0.3	33.1	0.3	33.2	0.3	33.7	1.5	34.0	0.9	34.0	0.0	34.1	0.3
1956	34.1	0.0	34.4	0.9	34.3	-0.3	34.4	0.3	34.5	0.3	34.7	0.6	34.5	-0.6	33.9	-1.7	33.7	-0.6	33.6	-0.3	33.6	0.0	33.4	-0.6
1957	33.4	0.0	33.5	0.3	33.5	0.0	33.2	-0.9	32.7	-1.5	32.2	-1.5	32.3	0.3	32.2	-0.3	32.4	0.6	32.7	0.9	32.8	0.3	33.1	0.9
1958	33.4	0.9	33.4	0.0	33.7	0.9	34.0	0.9	34.2	0.6	34.9	2.0	35.2	0.9	35.3	0.3	35.2	-0.3	35.4	0.6	35.7	0.8	35.7	0.0
1959	35.0	-2.0	34.9	-0.3	35.2	0.9	34.9	-0.9	34.9	0.0	35.1	0.6	34.9	-0.6	34.1	-2.3	33.8	-0.9	34.0	0.6	33.6	-1.2	33.1	-1.5
1960	33.0	-0.3	33.2	0.6	33.4	0.6	33.4	0.0	33.6	0.6	33.8	0.6	33.9	0.3	33.7	-0.6	34.0	0.9	34.4	1.2	34.6	0.6	34.8	0.6
1961	35.3	1.4	35.4	0.3	35.2	-0.6	35.1	-0.3	34.4	-2.0	34.4	0.0	34.5	0.3	34.0	-1.4	33.9	-0.3	34.1	0.6	34.1	0.0	34.1	0.0
1962	33.7	-1.2	33.9	0.6	33.7	-0.6	33.7	0.0	33.5	-0.6	33.7	0.6	33.6	-0.3	33.0	-1.8	32.8	-0.6	32.8	0.0	32.7	-0.3	32.5	-0.6
1963	34.0	4.6	33.9	-0.3	34.4	1.5	35.0	1.7	35.2	0.6	35.6	1.1	35.9	0.8	35.6	-0.8	35.8	0.6	36.0	0.6	34.8	-0.3	34.7	-0.3
1964	36.4	0.3	36.5	0.3	36.5	0.0	36.5	0.0	36.1	-1.1	36.1	0.0	35.7	-1.1	34.7	-2.8	34.7	0.0	34.9	0.6	35.8	0.6	35.7	-0.3
1965	34.7	0.0	34.1	-1.7	34.2	0.3	34.3	0.3	34.1	-0.6	34.5	1.2	34.6	0.3	34.1	-1.4	34.6	1.5	35.6	2.9	36.0	0.6	36.0	0.0
1966	35.6	-0.3	35.7	0.3	35.6	-0.3	35.6	0.0	35.8	0.6	35.7	-0.3	35.5	-0.6	34.8	-2.0	35.2	1.1	35.9	2.0	36.0	0.0	36.0	0.0
1967	36.0	0.0	35.4	-1.7	35.4	0.0	35.5	0.3	35.7	0.6	36.2	1.4	36.3	0.3	36.4	0.3	36.7	0.8	37.2	1.4	38.1	2.4	38.4	0.8
1968	38.6	0.5	38.7	0.3	38.9	0.5	39.0	0.3	39.1	0.3	39.1	0.0	39.1	0.0	38.6	-1.3	38.6	0.0	38.8	0.5	38.8	0.0	38.6	-0.5
1969	38.7	0.3	39.0	0.8	39.1	0.3	39.3	0.5	39.4	0.3	39.4	0.0	39.7	0.8	39.7	0.0	39.7	0.0	39.5	-0.5	39.6	0.3	39.6	0.0
1970	39.8	0.5	39.9	0.3	39.7	-0.5	39.9	0.5	40.2	0.8	40.3	0.2	40.5	0.5	40.7	0.5	40.8	0.2	40.5	-0.7	40.7	0.5	40.5	-0.5

[Continued]

Processed Fruits and Vegetables
Producer Price Index
Base 1982 = 100
[Continued]

For 1926-1993. Columns headed % show percentile change in the index from the previous period for which an index is available.

Year	Jan Index	%	Feb Index	%	Mar Index	%	Apr Index	%	May Index	%	Jun Index	%	Jul Index	%	Aug Index	%	Sep Index	%	Oct Index	%	Nov Index	%	Dec Index	%
1971	40.6	0.2	40.7	0.2	40.9	0.5	41.2	0.7	41.5	0.7	42.1	1.4	42.3	0.5	42.3	0.0	42.2	-0.2	42.0	-0.5	42.0	0.0	42.2	0.5
1972	42.3	0.2	42.3	0.0	42.5	0.5	43.1	1.4	43.4	0.7	43.5	0.2	43.6	0.2	43.8	0.5	43.7	-0.2	44.4	1.6	45.1	1.6	45.5	0.9
1973	45.7	0.4	45.9	0.4	46.0	0.2	46.1	0.2	46.4	0.7	46.6	0.4	46.5	-0.2	47.1	1.3	47.4	0.6	49.2	3.8	49.7	1.0	50.2	1.0
1974	50.7	1.0	51.3	1.2	51.5	0.4	52.0	1.0	52.9	1.7	54.0	2.1	57.5	6.5	59.3	3.1	60.3	1.7	61.9	2.7	62.3	0.6	62.0	-0.5
1975	62.4	0.6	62.3	-0.2	61.8	-0.8	62.2	0.6	62.3	0.2	62.3	0.0	61.7	-1.0	61.4	-0.5	61.4	0.0	61.7	0.5	61.6	-0.2	61.4	-0.3
1976	61.0	-0.7	60.6	-0.7	60.6	0.0	60.8	0.3	61.2	0.7	61.5	0.5	61.8	0.5	62.3	0.8	62.7	0.6	63.5	1.3	64.0	0.8	64.0	0.0
1977	63.8	-0.3	66.6	4.4	67.1	0.8	67.5	0.6	67.7	0.3	68.4	1.0	68.6	0.3	69.4	1.2	69.6	0.3	69.4	-0.3	70.4	1.4	70.8	0.6
1978	70.8	0.0	70.9	0.1	71.3	0.6	71.6	0.4	71.9	0.4	72.4	0.7	73.0	0.8	74.1	1.5	74.7	0.8	76.6	2.5	78.8	2.9	79.6	1.0
1979	79.6	0.0	80.0	0.5	80.0	0.0	80.3	0.4	80.7	0.5	80.7	0.0	81.5	1.0	81.8	0.4	82.0	0.2	81.4	-0.7	81.0	-0.5	81.1	0.1
1980	81.2	0.1	81.4	0.2	81.5	0.1	81.9	0.5	82.1	0.2	82.8	0.9	83.7	1.1	84.1	0.5	84.3	0.2	85.2	1.1	85.5	0.4	86.2	0.8
1981	86.9	0.8	88.8	2.2	93.0	4.7	94.0	1.1	94.5	0.5	95.6	1.2	96.9	1.4	97.4	0.5	98.4	1.0	99.0	0.6	98.6	-0.4	99.0	0.4
1982	99.5	0.5	100.7	1.2	100.5	-0.2	100.3	-0.2	99.8	-0.5	100.5	0.7	100.0	-0.5	99.9	-0.1	99.4	-0.5	99.6	0.2	99.4	-0.2	100.4	1.0
1983	100.1	-0.3	99.9	-0.2	100.2	0.3	99.7	-0.5	100.3	0.6	101.0	0.7	101.0	0.0	101.4	0.4	101.5	0.1	102.4	0.9	102.3	-0.1	103.1	0.8
1984	104.8	1.6	106.7	1.8	107.6	0.8	107.5	-0.1	108.5	0.9	108.6	0.1	107.9	-0.6	107.8	-0.1	106.3	-1.4	107.8	1.4	106.5	-1.2	106.9	0.4
1985	108.1	1.1	108.1	0.0	109.3	1.1	108.8	-0.5	108.6	-0.2	109.7	1.0	109.2	-0.5	109.3	0.1	107.5	-1.6	106.9	-0.6	105.2	-1.6	105.0	-0.2
1986	104.5	-0.5	104.6	0.1	104.7	0.1	104.1	-0.6	104.3	0.2	105.4	1.1	104.5	-0.9	105.1	0.6	105.1	0.0	104.6	-0.5	105.6	1.0	106.6	0.9
1987	107.3	0.7	107.5	0.2	108.4	0.8	108.3	-0.1	108.4	0.1	109.5	1.0	108.7	-0.7	109.3	0.6	108.5	-0.7	108.4	-0.1	108.8	0.4	110.1	1.2
1988	110.9	0.7	111.4	0.5	111.8	0.4	111.5	-0.3	111.7	0.2	111.6	-0.1	113.4	1.6	115.2	1.6	115.5	0.3	116.5	0.9	117.9	1.2	118.5	0.5
1989	119.0	0.4	118.8	-0.2	119.2	0.3	119.0	-0.2	119.8	0.7	120.5	0.6	120.8	0.2	121.2	0.3	120.7	-0.4	120.0	-0.6	119.9	-0.1	120.4	0.4
1990	122.4	1.7	125.7	2.7	126.9	1.0	126.9	0.0	127.0	0.1	126.5	-0.4	126.1	-0.3	125.8	-0.2	124.9	-0.7	123.6	-1.0	120.9	-2.2	120.2	-0.6
1991	120.0	-0.2	120.2	0.2	119.8	-0.3	119.2	-0.5	119.3	0.1	119.0	-0.3	119.6	0.5	118.7	-0.8	118.6	-0.1	119.2	0.5	120.4	1.0	121.6	1.0
1992	122.1	0.4	122.4	0.2	122.3	-0.1	122.0	-0.2	122.0	0.0	121.0	-0.8	120.6	-0.3	120.5	-0.1	119.8	-0.6	119.1	-0.6	118.9	-0.2	118.4	-0.4
1993	117.5	-0.8	117.0	-0.4	116.4	-0.5	116.1	-0.3	116.7	0.5	117.6	0.8	119.0	1.2	118.7	-0.3	119.1	0.3	119.9	0.7	120.7	0.7	120.5	-0.2

Source: U.S. Department of Labor, Bureau of Labor Statistics, Division of Industry Prices and Price Indexes. n.e.c. stands for not elsewhere classified. - indicates no data collected for period or unavailable.

Sugar and Confectionery
Producer Price Index
Base 1982 = 100

For 1926-1993. Columns headed % show percentile change in the index from the previous period for which an index is available.

Year	Jan Index	%	Feb Index	%	Mar Index	%	Apr Index	%	May Index	%	Jun Index	%	Jul Index	%	Aug Index	%	Sep Index	%	Oct Index	%	Nov Index	%	Dec Index	%
1926	18.2	-	18.5	1.6	17.7	-4.3	18.3	3.4	19.0	3.8	18.8	-1.1	19.1	1.6	19.3	1.0	19.8	2.6	20.2	2.0	20.6	2.0	22.0	6.8
1927	22.0	0.0	21.4	-2.7	20.9	-2.3	20.9	0.0	21.2	1.4	21.0	-0.9	20.5	-2.4	19.8	-3.4	20.8	5.1	20.4	-1.9	20.1	-1.5	19.9	-1.0
1928	20.0	0.5	19.3	-3.5	20.1	4.1	20.4	1.5	20.5	0.5	20.4	-0.5	19.7	-3.4	19.2	-2.5	19.5	1.6	18.2	-6.7	17.8	-2.2	18.2	2.2
1929	17.7	-2.7	17.2	-2.8	17.0	-1.2	16.9	-0.6	16.9	0.0	16.8	-0.6	17.8	6.0	18.3	2.8	18.4	0.5	18.7	1.6	17.5	-6.4	17.5	0.0
1930	17.6	0.6	17.2	-2.3	16.8	-2.3	16.7	-0.6	16.0	-4.2	15.6	-2.5	15.8	1.3	15.2	-3.8	15.1	-0.7	15.5	2.6	16.1	3.9	15.7	-2.5
1931	15.8	0.6	15.5	-1.9	15.2	-1.9	15.3	0.7	14.9	-2.6	15.3	2.7	16.1	5.2	16.0	-0.6	15.6	-2.5	15.6	0.0	15.5	-0.6	14.6	-5.8
1932	14.3	-2.1	14.2	-0.7	13.5	-4.9	13.0	-3.7	12.5	-3.8	12.9	3.2	13.8	7.0	14.4	4.3	14.4	0.0	14.4	0.0	14.2	-1.4	13.8	-2.8
1933	13.1	-5.1	13.1	0.0	14.0	6.9	14.4	2.9	15.2	5.6	15.6	2.6	15.9	1.9	16.0	0.6	16.2	1.3	15.5	-4.3	15.1	-2.6	15.0	-0.7
1934	14.7	-2.0	15.3	4.1	14.9	-2.6	14.4	-3.4	13.8	-4.2	14.8	7.2	15.6	5.4	15.9	1.9	15.2	-4.4	15.1	-0.7	14.9	-1.3	14.6	-2.0
1935	14.2	-2.7	14.4	1.4	14.8	2.8	16.4	10.8	16.9	3.0	17.0	0.6	16.7	-1.8	16.7	0.0	17.0	1.8	17.5	2.9	17.2	-1.7	16.7	-2.9
1936	16.9	1.2	17.0	0.6	16.7	-1.8	17.1	2.4	17.1	0.0	17.1	0.0	16.7	-2.3	16.7	0.0	16.5	-1.2	16.0	-3.0	16.4	2.5	16.9	3.0
1937	17.4	3.0	16.9	-2.9	16.4	-3.0	16.4	0.0	16.3	-0.6	16.1	-1.2	16.3	1.2	16.3	0.0	16.8	3.1	16.0	-4.8	16.1	0.6	15.9	-1.2
1938	15.8	-0.6	15.5	-1.9	15.3	-1.3	14.8	-3.3	14.6	-1.4	14.3	-2.1	14.4	0.7	14.2	-1.4	15.0	5.6	15.3	2.0	15.0	-2.0	14.6	-2.7
1939	14.3	-2.1	14.2	-0.7	14.4	1.4	14.7	2.1	14.7	0.0	14.6	-0.7	14.5	-0.7	14.4	-0.7	18.5	28.5	17.2	-7.0	15.5	-9.9	15.2	-1.9
1940	14.6	-3.9	14.6	0.0	14.5	-0.7	14.6	0.7	14.5	-0.7	14.4	-0.7	14.3	-0.7	14.0	-2.1	14.1	0.7	14.2	0.7	14.4	1.4	14.5	0.7
1941	14.7	1.4	14.9	1.4	16.2	8.7	16.8	3.7	16.7	-0.6	16.8	0.6	16.9	0.6	17.8	5.3	17.7	-0.6	17.3	-2.3	17.3	0.0	17.4	0.6
1942	18.1	4.0	18.2	0.6	18.2	0.0	18.6	2.2	18.6	0.0	18.6	0.0	18.6	0.0	18.6	0.0	18.6	0.0	18.6	0.0	18.6	0.0	18.6	0.0
1943	18.6	0.0	18.6	0.0	18.6	0.0	18.6	0.0	18.6	0.0	18.6	0.0	18.6	0.0	18.6	0.0	18.6	0.0	18.6	0.0	18.6	0.0	18.6	0.0
1944	18.6	0.0	18.6	0.0	18.6	0.0	18.6	0.0	18.6	0.0	18.7	0.5	18.7	0.0	18.7	0.0	18.5	-1.1	18.5	0.0	18.5	0.0	18.5	0.0
1945	18.5	0.0	18.5	0.0	18.5	0.0	18.5	0.0	18.5	0.0	18.5	0.0	18.5	0.0	18.5	0.0	18.5	0.0	18.5	0.0	18.5	0.0	18.5	0.0
1946	18.5	0.0	19.5	5.4	20.2	3.6	20.2	0.0	20.2	0.0	20.2	0.0	20.7	2.5	20.8	0.5	23.5	13.0	26.1	11.1	26.6	1.9	27.2	2.3
1947	27.4	0.7	27.8	1.5	28.1	1.1	28.3	0.7	28.3	0.0	28.4	0.4	28.5	0.4	29.3	2.8	29.4	0.3	29.4	0.0	30.4	3.4	30.6	0.7
1948	30.3	-1.0	30.4	0.3	30.2	-0.7	30.1	-0.3	29.0	-3.7	28.7	-1.0	29.4	2.4	29.5	0.3	29.7	0.7	29.4	-1.0	29.6	0.7	29.2	-1.4
1949	29.4	0.7	28.7	-2.4	27.8	-3.1	27.3	-1.8	26.9	-1.5	26.9	0.0	26.7	-0.7	26.7	0.0	26.9	0.7	27.1	0.7	27.1	0.0	27.0	-0.4
1950	27.1	0.4	26.8	-1.1	26.5	-1.1	26.4	-0.4	26.7	1.1	26.9	0.7	27.7	3.0	28.6	3.2	29.7	3.8	29.6	-0.3	29.6	0.0	29.6	0.0
1951	29.6	0.0	29.6	0.0	29.6	0.0	29.5	-0.3	30.4	3.1	31.3	3.0	31.2	-0.3	30.7	-1.6	30.7	0.0	30.1	-2.0	30.2	0.3	30.1	-0.3
1952	30.1	0.0	30.2	0.3	30.5	1.0	31.2	2.3	31.1	-0.3	31.6	1.6	31.8	0.6	31.5	-0.9	31.5	0.0	31.6	0.3	31.3	-0.9	30.9	-1.3
1953	30.9	0.0	30.9	0.0	31.3	1.3	31.4	0.3	31.3	-0.3	31.4	0.3	31.4	0.0	31.5	0.3	31.4	-0.3	31.5	0.3	31.0	-1.6	31.1	0.3
1954	31.5	1.3	31.5	0.0	32.3	2.5	32.2	-0.3	32.4	0.6	32.4	0.0	32.6	0.6	32.7	0.3	32.3	-1.2	32.1	-0.6	32.1	0.0	31.9	-0.6
1955	31.9	0.0	32.2	0.9	31.7	-1.6	31.7	0.0	31.6	-0.3	31.6	0.0	31.7	0.3	31.5	-0.6	31.4	-0.3	31.5	0.3	31.4	-0.3	31.3	-0.3
1956	31.3	0.0	31.3	0.0	31.4	0.3	30.1	-4.1	31.4	4.3	31.3	-0.3	31.5	0.6	31.4	-0.3	31.5	0.3	31.7	0.6	32.0	0.9	32.1	0.3
1957	32.4	0.9	32.1	-0.9	32.1	0.0	32.1	0.0	32.3	0.6	32.5	0.6	32.7	0.6	32.6	-0.3	32.6	0.0	32.6	0.0	32.7	0.3	32.7	0.0
1958	32.8	0.3	32.7	-0.3	32.4	-0.9	32.7	0.9	33.0	0.9	33.3	0.9	33.3	0.0	33.2	-0.3	33.3	0.3	33.4	0.3	33.3	-0.3	33.5	0.6
1959	33.0	-1.5	32.6	-1.2	32.3	-0.9	32.1	-0.6	32.7	1.9	33.1	1.2	33.0	-0.3	33.0	0.0	33.3	0.9	33.6	0.9	33.4	-0.6	33.1	-0.9
1960	32.4	-2.1	32.6	0.6	32.9	0.9	33.0	0.3	33.1	0.3	33.1	0.0	33.9	2.4	33.9	0.0	34.1	0.6	33.9	-0.6	34.0	0.3	33.7	-0.9
1961	33.7	0.0	33.6	-0.3	33.4	-0.6	33.3	-0.3	33.6	0.9	33.7	0.3	33.3	-1.2	32.8	-1.5	32.7	-0.3	32.7	0.0	32.8	0.3	33.2	1.2
1962	33.2	0.0	33.4	0.6	33.4	0.0	33.6	0.6	33.5	-0.3	33.6	0.3	33.5	-0.3	33.7	0.6	33.5	-0.6	33.8	0.9	33.6	-0.6	33.7	0.3
1963	34.5	2.4	34.5	0.0	34.8	0.9	37.4	7.5	43.8	17.1	43.4	-0.9	39.5	-9.0	36.5	-7.6	36.9	1.1	41.2	11.7	43.1	4.6	41.0	-4.9
1964	42.8	4.4	40.3	-5.8	38.5	-4.5	37.9	-1.6	36.7	-3.2	35.5	-3.3	35.0	-1.4	34.9	-0.3	34.5	-1.1	34.7	0.6	34.4	-0.9	35.2	2.3
1965	36.1	2.6	36.1	0.0	35.5	-1.7	35.5	0.0	35.7	0.6	35.8	0.3	35.8	0.0	35.7	-0.3	35.7	0.0	35.9	0.6	35.8	-0.3	35.7	-0.3
1966	35.9	0.6	36.1	0.6	36.0	-0.3	35.9	-0.3	35.9	0.0	35.9	0.0	36.0	0.3	36.4	1.1	36.6	0.5	36.6	0.0	36.8	0.5	36.9	0.3
1967	37.1	0.5	37.0	-0.3	36.9	-0.3	36.7	-0.5	36.7	0.0	37.0	0.8	37.3	0.8	37.4	0.3	37.1	-0.8	37.2	0.3	37.4	0.5	37.0	-1.1
1968	37.2	0.5	37.3	0.3	37.3	0.0	37.4	0.3	37.8	1.1	38.5	1.9	38.6	0.3	38.5	-0.3	38.6	0.3	38.8	0.5	38.7	-0.3	38.9	0.5
1969	39.1	0.5	39.1	0.0	39.2	0.3	39.4	0.5	40.2	2.0	41.5	3.2	41.3	-0.5	41.7	1.0	41.8	0.2	41.9	0.2	42.0	0.2	41.7	-0.7
1970	42.3	1.4	41.9	-0.9	41.8	-0.2	42.2	1.0	42.5	0.7	42.8	0.7	43.5	1.6	43.5	0.0	43.8	0.7	44.0	0.5	43.8	-0.5	43.5	-0.7

[Continued]

Sugar and Confectionery
Producer Price Index
Base 1982 = 100
[Continued]

For 1926-1993. Columns headed % show percentile change in the index from the previous period for which an index is available.

Year	Jan Index	%	Feb Index	%	Mar Index	%	Apr Index	%	May Index	%	Jun Index	%	Jul Index	%	Aug Index	%	Sep Index	%	Oct Index	%	Nov Index	%	Dec Index	%
1971	43.7	0.5	44.2	1.1	44.5	0.7	44.2	-0.7	44.5	0.7	44.4	-0.2	44.5	0.2	44.5	0.0	44.5	0.0	43.7	-1.8	44.2	1.1	44.6	0.9
1972	44.5	-0.2	44.9	0.9	45.2	0.7	44.9	-0.7	44.8	-0.2	45.0	0.4	45.3	0.7	45.0	-0.7	45.1	0.2	45.8	1.6	45.1	-1.5	45.3	0.4
1973	45.0	-0.7	46.1	2.4	46.6	1.1	47.0	0.9	47.8	1.7	48.6	1.7	48.6	0.0	50.3	3.5	50.8	1.0	51.8	2.0	53.3	2.9	52.7	-1.1
1974	56.3	6.8	62.0	10.1	70.5	13.7	70.4	-0.1	80.0	13.6	89.3	11.6	91.5	2.5	100.3	9.6	110.5	10.2	116.9	5.8	155.7	33.2	148.8	-4.4
1975	132.8	-10.8	128.8	-3.0	112.4	-12.7	103.9	-7.6	88.8	-14.5	80.8	-9.0	84.7	4.8	90.2	6.5	81.4	-9.8	77.3	-5.0	77.0	-0.4	73.8	-4.2
1976	75.1	1.8	74.3	-1.1	76.8	3.4	75.1	-2.2	77.4	3.1	73.2	-5.4	74.6	1.9	68.6	-8.0	62.0	-9.6	65.4	5.5	63.6	-2.8	63.2	-0.6
1977	63.8	0.9	65.9	3.3	66.8	1.4	69.1	3.4	68.4	-1.0	65.4	-4.4	63.5	-2.9	66.3	4.4	64.6	-2.6	63.1	-2.3	66.2	4.9	66.4	0.3
1978	68.9	3.8	71.9	4.4	71.5	-0.6	72.7	1.7	72.8	0.1	73.1	0.4	72.6	-0.7	74.3	2.3	75.1	1.1	76.2	1.5	75.1	-1.4	75.8	0.9
1979	75.9	0.1	77.3	1.8	77.3	0.0	77.4	0.1	77.0	-0.5	78.3	1.7	80.0	2.2	80.9	1.1	80.6	-0.4	81.2	0.7	82.7	1.8	86.9	5.1
1980	87.1	0.2	106.6	22.4	98.0	-8.1	102.0	4.1	121.6	19.2	120.7	-0.7	116.3	-3.6	128.7	10.7	126.6	-1.6	150.1	18.6	151.7	1.1	126.0	-16.9
1981	127.8	1.4	119.9	-6.2	112.0	-6.6	105.5	-5.8	97.4	-7.7	101.9	4.6	98.6	-3.2	99.1	0.5	91.5	-7.7	91.5	0.0	90.5	-1.1	91.8	1.4
1982	95.2	3.7	95.4	0.2	94.6	-0.8	94.9	0.3	98.4	3.7	99.8	1.4	102.2	2.4	105.9	3.6	103.3	-2.5	102.5	-0.8	104.0	1.5	103.9	-0.1
1983	104.6	0.7	106.2	1.5	105.2	-0.9	106.6	1.3	107.5	0.8	109.8	2.1	109.9	0.1	110.8	0.8	111.3	0.5	110.5	-0.7	110.4	-0.1	110.3	-0.1
1984	111.2	0.8	111.4	0.2	111.7	0.3	111.9	0.2	112.6	0.6	112.8	0.2	113.1	0.3	112.6	-0.4	112.1	-0.4	111.2	-0.8	110.1	-1.0	109.7	-0.4
1985	108.8	-0.8	107.9	-0.8	108.5	0.6	108.8	0.3	109.2	0.4	109.2	0.0	108.9	-0.3	108.1	-0.7	107.6	-0.5	106.1	-1.4	105.8	-0.3	106.0	0.2
1986	108.0	1.9	108.4	0.4	109.2	0.7	108.8	-0.4	109.0	0.2	109.4	0.4	109.8	0.4	109.8	0.0	110.4	0.5	110.9	0.5	111.1	0.2	111.2	0.1
1987	110.8	-0.4	110.8	0.0	111.2	0.4	111.9	0.6	112.8	0.8	112.9	0.1	113.7	0.7	113.9	0.2	114.0	0.1	113.6	-0.4	113.5	-0.1	113.0	-0.4
1988	112.5	-0.4	112.8	0.3	113.0	0.2	113.3	0.3	113.1	-0.2	113.6	0.4	115.9	2.0	115.9	0.0	115.9	0.0	116.5	0.5	116.8	0.3	117.3	0.4
1989	117.8	0.4	118.3	0.4	118.6	0.3	119.2	0.5	119.6	0.3	120.7	0.9	122.0	1.1	121.3	-0.6	121.6	0.2	120.1	-1.2	120.5	0.3	121.0	0.4
1990	121.1	0.1	121.8	0.6	121.7	-0.1	122.6	0.7	122.8	0.2	123.0	0.2	123.9	0.7	123.7	-0.2	123.9	0.2	123.0	-0.7	124.8	1.5	124.7	-0.1
1991	126.3	1.3	128.4	1.7	127.8	-0.5	128.3	0.4	127.8	-0.4	127.6	-0.2	129.1	1.2	129.4	0.2	129.8	0.3	128.5	-1.0	128.6	0.1	128.8	0.2
1992	128.6	-0.2	127.7	-0.7	127.4	-0.2	127.6	0.2	127.8	0.2	127.7	-0.1	129.0	1.0	129.3	0.2	129.2	-0.1	126.0	-2.5	125.8	-0.2	125.9	0.1
1993	125.4	-0.4	124.5	-0.7	124.6	0.1	124.8	0.2	125.5	0.6	126.6	0.9	129.3	2.1	129.3	0.0	130.0	0.5	131.9	1.5	131.9	0.0	130.7	-0.9

Source: U.S. Department of Labor, Bureau of Labor Statistics, Division of Industry Prices and Price Indexes. n.e.c. stands for not elsewhere classified. - indicates no data collected for period or unavailable.

Beverages and Beverage Materials
Producer Price Index
Base 1982 = 100

For 1947-1993. Columns headed % show percentile change in the index from the previous period for which an index is available.

Year	Jan Index	%	Feb Index	%	Mar Index	%	Apr Index	%	May Index	%	Jun Index	%	Jul Index	%	Aug Index	%	Sep Index	%	Oct Index	%	Nov Index	%	Dec Index	%
1947	26.3	-	26.5	0.8	26.6	0.4	26.6	0.0	26.4	-0.8	26.2	-0.8	26.2	0.0	26.4	0.8	26.7	1.1	26.8	0.4	27.0	0.7	27.3	1.1
1948	27.5	0.7	27.7	0.7	27.7	0.0	27.7	0.0	27.7	0.0	27.8	0.4	27.8	0.0	27.8	0.0	27.8	0.0	27.8	0.0	27.9	0.4	27.9	0.0
1949	27.9	0.0	27.9	0.0	27.9	0.0	27.8	-0.4	27.8	0.0	27.8	0.0	27.8	0.0	27.8	0.0	28.0	0.7	28.1	0.4	29.7	5.7	30.2	1.7
1950	30.2	0.0	30.1	-0.3	30.1	0.0	29.7	-1.3	29.6	-0.3	29.7	0.3	30.3	2.0	30.7	1.3	31.0	1.0	31.5	1.6	31.3	-0.6	32.0	2.2
1951	32.5	1.6	32.6	0.3	32.6	0.0	32.6	0.0	32.6	0.0	32.6	0.0	32.5	-0.3	32.5	0.0	32.5	0.0	32.5	0.0	32.5	0.0	32.5	0.0
1952	32.5	0.0	33.3	2.5	33.3	0.0	33.2	-0.3	33.2	0.0	33.2	0.0	33.2	0.0	33.2	0.0	33.2	0.0	33.2	0.0	33.2	0.0	33.2	0.0
1953	33.2	0.0	33.2	0.0	33.6	1.2	33.5	-0.3	33.3	-0.6	33.3	0.0	33.8	1.5	33.8	0.0	34.0	0.6	34.5	1.5	34.6	0.3	34.6	0.0
1954	35.2	1.7	35.6	1.1	36.6	2.8	38.7	5.7	38.7	0.0	38.7	0.0	39.0	0.8	38.7	-0.8	37.6	-2.8	37.6	0.0	37.2	-1.1	37.5	0.8
1955	37.5	0.0	36.6	-2.4	36.2	-1.1	36.2	0.0	36.2	0.0	35.8	-1.1	35.8	0.0	35.9	0.3	36.1	0.6	36.4	0.8	36.1	-0.8	36.1	0.0
1956	36.1	0.0	36.4	0.8	36.9	1.4	36.7	-0.5	36.6	-0.3	36.8	0.5	37.1	0.8	37.4	0.8	37.8	1.1	37.8	0.0	38.0	0.5	37.6	-1.1
1957	37.8	0.5	37.6	-0.5	37.5	-0.3	37.2	-0.8	37.2	0.0	37.2	0.0	37.2	0.0	37.2	0.0	36.9	-0.8	36.6	-0.8	36.6	0.0	36.7	0.3
1958	36.7	0.0	36.7	0.0	36.4	-0.8	36.4	0.0	36.4	0.0	36.4	0.0	36.2	-0.5	36.1	-0.3	36.1	0.0	36.2	0.3	36.2	0.0	36.1	-0.3
1959	35.9	-0.6	35.7	-0.6	36.4	2.0	36.3	-0.3	36.3	0.0	36.3	0.0	36.3	0.0	36.2	-0.3	36.2	0.0	36.2	0.0	36.2	0.0	36.2	0.0
1960	36.2	0.0	36.2	0.0	36.2	0.0	36.2	0.0	36.2	0.0	36.2	0.0	36.1	-0.3	36.1	0.0	36.1	0.0	36.1	0.0	36.1	0.0	36.1	0.0
1961	35.9	-0.6	36.0	0.3	36.0	0.0	35.9	-0.3	35.9	0.0	35.9	0.0	36.1	0.6	36.1	0.0	36.3	0.6	36.1	-0.6	36.2	0.3	36.2	0.0
1962	36.2	0.0	36.2	0.0	36.2	0.0	36.2	0.0	36.2	0.0	36.2	0.0	36.2	0.0	36.3	0.3	36.2	-0.3	36.1	-0.3	36.1	0.0	36.0	-0.3
1963	36.0	0.0	36.0	0.0	36.0	0.0	36.2	0.6	36.3	0.3	36.8	1.4	37.4	1.6	37.5	0.3	37.5	0.0	37.5	0.0	37.7	0.5	37.9	0.5
1964	38.3	1.1	38.5	0.5	38.8	0.8	38.8	0.0	38.9	0.3	38.9	0.0	38.9	0.0	38.9	0.0	38.9	0.0	38.9	0.0	38.9	0.0	38.9	0.0
1965	38.8	-0.3	38.8	0.0	38.5	-0.8	38.6	0.3	38.6	0.0	38.6	0.0	38.6	0.0	38.6	0.0	38.6	0.0	38.6	0.0	38.6	0.0	38.7	0.3
1966	38.7	0.0	38.6	-0.3	38.6	0.0	38.6	0.0	38.6	0.0	38.8	0.5	38.9	0.3	38.9	0.0	38.6	-0.8	38.6	0.0	38.6	0.0	38.7	0.3
1967	38.7	0.0	38.7	0.0	38.6	-0.3	38.7	0.3	38.8	0.3	38.9	0.3	38.9	0.0	39.0	0.3	39.0	0.0	39.2	0.5	39.2	0.0	39.4	0.5
1968	39.4	0.0	39.7	0.8	39.8	0.3	39.9	0.3	40.0	0.3	40.0	0.0	40.0	0.0	40.1	0.3	40.2	0.2	40.4	0.5	40.4	0.0	40.4	0.0
1969	40.5	0.2	40.6	0.2	40.7	0.2	40.7	0.0	40.9	0.5	41.1	0.5	41.2	0.2	41.2	0.0	41.3	0.2	42.1	1.9	42.4	0.7	42.5	0.2
1970	42.9	0.9	43.3	0.9	43.3	0.0	43.4	0.2	44.0	1.4	44.0	0.0	44.1	0.2	44.3	0.5	44.5	0.5	44.6	0.2	44.7	0.2	44.5	-0.4
1971	44.8	0.7	44.9	0.2	44.9	0.0	45.1	0.4	45.1	0.0	45.1	0.0	45.2	0.2	45.3	0.2	45.4	0.2	45.4	0.0	45.4	0.0	45.3	-0.2
1972	45.3	0.0	45.5	0.4	45.4	-0.2	45.6	0.4	45.6	0.0	45.8	0.4	45.9	0.2	46.3	0.9	46.4	0.2	46.2	-0.4	46.5	0.6	46.6	0.2
1973	46.6	0.0	46.7	0.2	47.0	0.6	47.3	0.6	47.5	0.4	47.3	-0.4	47.1	-0.4	47.2	0.2	47.3	0.2	47.9	1.3	48.2	0.6	48.4	0.4
1974	48.9	1.0	49.1	0.4	50.3	2.4	51.5	2.4	52.4	1.7	53.9	2.9	55.9	3.7	56.9	1.8	57.5	1.1	59.4	3.3	60.1	1.2	61.6	2.5
1975	63.3	2.8	63.2	-0.2	63.1	-0.2	63.0	-0.2	62.7	-0.5	62.4	-0.5	62.1	-0.5	62.9	1.3	63.3	0.6	64.3	1.6	64.3	0.0	64.4	0.2
1976	64.3	-0.2	65.1	1.2	65.1	0.0	65.9	1.2	67.1	1.8	67.3	0.3	68.5	1.8	68.4	-0.1	68.7	0.4	69.1	0.6	69.6	0.7	71.6	2.9
1977	71.7	0.1	73.7	2.8	77.7	5.4	78.7	1.3	80.2	1.9	80.9	0.9	79.7	-1.5	80.0	0.4	79.7	-0.4	79.8	0.1	78.5	-1.6	78.4	-0.1
1978	78.7	0.4	78.4	-0.4	77.9	-0.6	77.9	0.0	77.7	-0.3	77.9	0.3	77.3	-0.8	76.6	-0.9	77.0	0.5	78.3	1.7	78.4	0.1	78.3	-0.1
1979	78.2	-0.1	78.3	0.1	78.3	0.0	78.5	0.3	79.9	1.8	81.2	1.6	83.4	2.7	84.3	1.1	84.8	0.6	85.2	0.5	86.1	1.1	86.3	0.2
1980	87.2	1.0	87.5	0.3	88.0	0.6	88.7	0.8	90.0	1.5	91.2	1.3	91.3	0.1	92.3	1.1	91.9	-0.4	93.3	1.5	93.7	0.4	93.6	-0.1
1981	94.6	1.1	95.3	0.7	95.5	0.2	95.8	0.3	96.4	0.6	96.6	0.2	96.9	0.3	97.1	0.2	97.0	-0.1	97.3	0.3	97.9	0.6	98.1	0.2
1982	98.8	0.7	99.3	0.5	99.8	0.5	99.9	0.1	99.9	0.0	99.9	0.0	100.0	0.1	100.4	0.4	100.1	-0.3	100.4	0.3	100.6	0.2	100.8	0.2
1983	101.3	0.5	101.7	0.4	102.0	0.3	102.4	0.4	102.6	0.2	102.4	-0.2	102.7	0.3	102.7	0.0	102.9	0.2	103.3	0.4	103.7	0.4	103.7	0.0
1984	104.6	0.9	105.2	0.6	105.1	-0.1	105.7	0.6	106.5	0.8	106.2	-0.3	106.6	0.4	106.9	0.3	106.9	0.0	107.5	0.6	107.4	-0.1	107.3	-0.1
1985	107.4	0.1	108.0	0.6	107.9	-0.1	107.8	-0.1	107.8	0.0	107.3	-0.5	107.5	0.2	107.1	-0.4	107.1	0.0	107.6	0.5	107.9	0.3	109.0	1.0
1986	112.9	3.6	114.5	1.4	115.0	0.4	115.9	0.8	115.9	0.0	115.5	-0.3	115.5	0.0	114.0	-1.3	113.7	-0.3	114.2	0.4	113.9	-0.3	113.8	-0.1
1987	112.6	-1.1	112.8	0.2	112.9	0.1	113.3	0.4	113.2	-0.1	113.0	-0.2	112.1	-0.8	112.3	0.2	111.6	-0.6	112.3	0.6	112.0	-0.3	112.2	0.2
1988	112.5	0.3	113.0	0.4	113.9	0.8	114.1	0.2	114.1	0.0	114.1	0.0	113.8	-0.3	114.6	0.7	114.7	0.1	115.3	0.5	115.8	0.4	115.8	0.0
1989	116.5	0.6	117.7	1.0	118.7	0.8	119.2	0.4	119.7	0.4	119.6	-0.1	119.4	-0.2	118.3	-0.9	117.1	-1.0	118.1	0.9	118.4	0.3	118.4	0.0
1990	119.7	1.1	120.7	0.8	121.5	0.7	121.5	0.0	121.0	-0.4	120.8	-0.2	120.9	0.1	120.6	-0.2	120.8	0.2	120.3	-0.4	120.5	0.2	121.1	0.5
1991	125.5	3.6	125.5	0.0	125.3	-0.2	125.5	0.2	124.3	-1.0	124.2	-0.1	123.5	-0.6	123.2	-0.2	123.1	-0.1	123.0	-0.1	123.0	0.0	123.2	0.2

[Continued]

Beverages and Beverage Materials
Producer Price Index
Base 1982 = 100
[Continued]

For 1947-1993. Columns headed % show percentile change in the index from the previous period for which an index is available.

Year	Jan Index	%	Feb Index	%	Mar Index	%	Apr Index	%	May Index	%	Jun Index	%	Jul Index	%	Aug Index	%	Sep Index	%	Oct Index	%	Nov Index	%	Dec Index	%
1992	124.8	1.3	125.2	0.3	124.5	-0.6	124.6	0.1	125.1	0.4	125.7	0.5	124.4	-1.0	124.1	-0.2	123.8	-0.2	123.4	-0.3	123.5	0.1	124.0	0.4
1993	124.5	0.4	125.4	0.7	125.4	0.0	125.2	-0.2	125.0	-0.2	124.8	-0.2	124.4	-0.3	124.5	0.1	124.5	0.0	124.8	0.2	124.5	-0.2	124.4	-0.1

Source: U.S. Department of Labor, Bureau of Labor Statistics, Division of Industry Prices and Price Indexes. n.e.c. stands for not elsewhere classified. - indicates no data collected for period or unavailable.

Fats and Oils

Producer Price Index
Base 1982 = 100

For 1967-1993. Columns headed % show percentile change in the index from the previous period for which an index is available.

Year	Jan Index	%	Feb Index	%	Mar Index	%	Apr Index	%	May Index	%	Jun Index	%	Jul Index	%	Aug Index	%	Sep Index	%	Oct Index	%	Nov Index	%	Dec Index	%
1967	48.8	-	48.3	-1.0	47.7	-1.2	47.7	0.0	47.6	-0.2	46.6	-2.1	45.3	-2.8	46.2	2.0	45.9	-0.6	44.8	-2.4	44.3	-1.1	44.3	0.0
1968	44.5	0.5	46.6	4.7	46.1	-1.1	45.4	-1.5	46.0	1.3	44.8	-2.6	44.3	-1.1	45.5	2.7	43.9	-3.5	42.3	-3.6	43.8	3.5	43.9	0.2
1969	45.1	2.7	46.6	3.3	46.6	0.0	45.8	-1.7	45.8	0.0	46.0	0.4	45.8	-0.4	45.9	0.2	45.9	0.0	48.6	5.9	50.8	4.5	49.8	-2.0
1970	49.5	-0.6	51.6	4.2	56.3	9.1	55.6	-1.2	54.4	-2.2	53.6	-1.5	53.4	-0.4	55.3	3.6	54.3	-1.8	57.5	5.9	60.7	5.6	58.2	-4.1
1971	57.7	-0.9	59.0	2.3	58.9	-0.2	56.8	-3.6	56.6	-0.4	57.3	1.2	60.2	5.1	62.9	4.5	60.3	-4.1	58.7	-2.7	58.8	0.2	56.4	-4.1
1972	55.6	-1.4	56.3	1.3	56.0	-0.5	56.3	0.5	55.4	-1.6	55.4	0.0	54.5	-1.6	53.5	-1.8	53.2	-0.6	53.2	0.0	52.7	-0.9	52.5	-0.4
1973	52.2	-0.6	57.4	10.0	63.3	10.3	64.0	1.1	68.0	6.3	73.9	8.7	74.2	0.4	103.3	39.2	84.2	-18.5	92.5	9.9	80.4	-13.1	93.7	16.5
1974	96.9	3.4	112.6	16.2	108.2	-3.9	101.3	-6.4	109.2	7.8	107.6	-1.5	119.3	10.9	145.4	21.9	128.0	-12.0	144.6	13.0	143.0	-1.1	129.9	-9.2
1975	127.9	-1.5	117.1	-8.4	110.3	-5.8	108.4	-1.7	98.7	-8.9	94.5	-4.3	108.3	14.6	113.3	4.6	103.5	-8.6	98.9	-4.4	92.0	-7.0	83.2	-9.6
1976	80.4	-3.4	79.8	-0.7	80.3	0.6	77.8	-3.1	76.8	-1.3	78.3	2.0	87.0	11.1	82.5	-5.2	89.8	8.8	85.2	-5.1	88.8	4.2	86.9	-2.1
1977	86.2	-0.8	91.4	6.0	98.3	7.5	109.8	11.7	111.1	1.2	107.1	-3.6	95.5	-10.8	92.5	-3.1	88.4	-4.4	90.2	2.0	90.9	0.8	96.6	6.3
1978	94.3	-2.4	94.5	0.2	104.9	11.0	107.0	2.0	107.9	0.8	105.7	-2.0	106.6	0.9	104.8	-1.7	111.3	6.2	108.2	-2.8	105.8	-2.2	105.8	0.0
1979	106.8	0.9	110.4	3.4	110.9	0.5	114.4	3.2	112.4	-1.7	113.2	0.7	117.7	4.0	117.0	-0.6	117.7	0.6	114.3	-2.9	112.4	-1.7	109.5	-2.6
1980	104.6	-4.5	105.2	0.6	103.5	-1.6	99.7	-3.7	98.5	-1.2	98.9	0.4	105.5	6.7	111.7	5.9	110.8	-0.8	107.4	-3.1	110.6	3.0	108.8	-1.6
1981	107.0	-1.7	106.1	-0.8	106.8	0.7	108.0	1.1	106.1	-1.8	105.7	-0.4	109.1	3.2	106.7	-2.2	104.3	-2.2	103.8	-0.5	102.9	-0.9	101.8	-1.1
1982	100.7	-1.1	100.7	0.0	99.4	-1.3	101.4	2.0	103.3	1.9	103.1	-0.2	102.9	-0.2	100.2	-2.6	98.2	-2.0	99.4	1.2	96.3	-3.1	94.3	-2.1
1983	93.8	-0.5	95.4	1.7	95.8	0.4	99.7	4.1	102.3	2.6	101.9	-0.4	103.3	1.4	114.2	10.6	141.1	23.6	130.9	-7.2	127.6	-2.5	126.3	-1.0
1984	129.4	2.5	127.0	-1.9	133.0	4.7	136.4	2.6	152.7	12.0	152.5	-0.1	145.4	-4.7	142.2	-2.2	138.8	-2.4	140.2	1.0	145.0	3.4	138.3	-4.6
1985	130.4	-5.7	132.6	1.7	135.0	1.8	140.8	4.3	137.6	-2.3	137.8	0.1	132.0	-4.2	118.4	-10.3	113.6	-4.1	110.6	-2.6	109.6	-0.9	106.8	-2.6
1986	107.3	0.5	103.8	-3.3	99.1	-4.5	97.8	-1.3	97.0	-0.8	95.5	-1.5	94.4	-1.2	92.8	-1.7	91.0	-1.9	93.4	2.6	92.9	-0.5	93.3	0.4
1987	95.3	2.1	95.8	0.5	95.6	-0.2	95.4	-0.2	99.2	4.0	97.9	-1.3	97.6	-0.3	96.4	-1.2	97.7	1.3	99.4	1.7	101.1	1.7	103.6	2.5
1988	110.6	6.8	111.1	0.5	109.3	-1.6	111.9	2.4	114.0	1.9	120.1	5.4	132.1	10.0	127.1	-3.8	122.7	-3.5	118.4	-3.5	114.3	-3.5	114.8	0.4
1989	114.1	-0.6	111.6	-2.2	114.7	2.8	113.7	-0.9	117.5	3.3	112.6	-4.2	112.5	-0.1	108.5	-3.6	108.9	0.4	108.3	-0.6	112.5	3.9	110.2	-2.0
1990	111.3	1.0	111.8	0.4	117.8	5.4	116.2	-1.4	124.6	7.2	126.0	1.1	124.6	-1.1	126.3	1.4	124.0	-1.8	118.5	-4.4	115.1	-2.9	116.9	1.6
1991	115.8	-0.9	115.8	0.0	118.2	2.1	116.9	-1.1	111.6	-4.5	110.5	-1.0	107.0	-3.2	110.8	3.6	111.2	0.4	109.8	-1.3	107.9	-1.7	108.9	0.9
1992	108.4	-0.5	108.8	0.4	111.1	2.1	108.6	-2.3	111.1	2.3	113.6	2.3	108.3	-4.7	104.2	-3.8	105.7	1.4	104.9	-0.8	108.5	3.4	111.9	3.1
1993	113.1	1.1	110.7	-2.1	111.5	0.7	112.9	1.3	113.7	0.7	111.4	-2.0	121.5	9.1	119.5	-1.6	120.0	0.4	119.3	-0.6	120.8	1.3	132.1	9.4

Source: U.S. Department of Labor, Bureau of Labor Statistics, Division of Industry Prices and Price Indexes. n.e.c. stands for not elsewhere classified. - indicates no data collected for period or unavailable.

Miscellaneous Processed Foods
Producer Price Index
Base 1982 = 100

For 1947-1993. Columns headed % show percentile change in the index from the previous period for which an index is available.

Year	Jan Index	%	Feb Index	%	Mar Index	%	Apr Index	%	May Index	%	Jun Index	%	Jul Index	%	Aug Index	%	Sep Index	%	Oct Index	%	Nov Index	%	Dec Index	%
1947	35.5	-	35.7	0.6	35.6	-0.3	34.7	-2.5	33.9	-2.3	33.7	-0.6	33.8	0.3	33.9	0.3	34.3	1.2	35.5	3.5	35.7	0.6	35.2	-1.4
1948	35.2	0.0	35.0	-0.6	34.8	-0.6	35.1	0.9	35.3	0.6	35.9	1.7	36.2	0.8	37.3	3.0	38.1	2.1	39.0	2.4	38.1	-2.3	37.9	-0.5
1949	37.2	-1.8	36.8	-1.1	38.3	4.1	38.5	0.5	38.4	-0.3	39.6	3.1	40.3	1.8	42.3	5.0	42.0	-0.7	42.6	1.4	42.3	-0.7	42.1	-0.5
1950	41.1	-2.4	42.2	2.7	42.2	0.0	41.8	-0.9	41.4	-1.0	39.5	-4.6	44.2	11.9	52.2	18.1	48.2	-7.7	44.9	-6.8	43.6	-2.9	44.7	2.5
1951	46.1	3.1	47.4	2.8	45.2	-4.6	45.6	0.9	45.8	0.4	45.5	-0.7	45.3	-0.4	45.9	1.3	46.0	0.2	45.3	-1.5	45.1	-0.4	44.3	-1.8
1952	42.5	-4.1	42.8	0.7	43.0	0.5	40.0	-7.0	41.9	4.8	43.9	4.8	47.0	7.1	46.5	-1.1	47.4	1.9	46.1	-2.7	45.3	-1.7	43.4	-4.2
1953	41.9	-3.5	42.4	1.2	44.9	5.9	44.7	-0.4	45.1	0.9	44.6	-1.1	43.5	-2.5	43.3	-0.5	43.3	0.0	43.4	0.2	40.9	-5.8	42.3	3.4
1954	41.4	-2.1	40.4	-2.4	39.5	-2.2	38.2	-3.3	37.6	-1.6	35.9	-4.5	37.6	4.7	40.7	8.2	38.4	-5.7	37.0	-3.6	36.3	-1.9	36.5	0.6
1955	36.4	-0.3	37.4	2.7	37.4	0.0	37.5	0.3	37.5	0.0	37.6	0.3	37.3	-0.8	36.9	-1.1	36.4	-1.4	36.5	0.3	36.2	-0.8	36.3	0.3
1956	36.4	0.3	36.2	-0.5	36.2	0.0	36.3	0.3	36.2	-0.3	36.2	0.0	36.0	-0.6	35.6	-1.1	35.6	0.0	35.4	-0.6	35.5	0.3	35.5	0.0
1957	35.3	-0.6	35.5	0.6	35.3	-0.6	35.3	0.0	35.4	0.3	35.4	0.0	35.4	0.0	35.2	-0.6	35.3	0.3	35.6	0.8	35.6	0.0	35.7	-0.3
1958	35.4	-0.8	35.3	-0.3	35.8	1.4	36.0	0.6	35.9	-0.3	35.9	0.0	36.0	0.3	35.8	-0.6	35.9	0.3	36.0	0.3	36.2	0.6	35.9	-0.8
1959	35.7	-0.6	36.0	0.8	35.5	-1.4	35.4	-0.3	35.6	0.6	35.4	-0.6	35.6	0.6	35.8	0.6	35.9	0.3	35.9	0.0	36.5	1.7	37.1	1.6
1960	38.5	3.8	37.7	-2.1	37.7	0.0	38.1	1.1	37.9	-0.5	38.5	1.6	38.3	-0.5	37.7	-1.6	37.6	-0.3	37.3	-0.8	38.1	2.1	37.4	-1.8
1961	38.1	1.9	37.9	-0.5	38.3	1.1	38.0	-0.8	38.1	0.3	38.3	0.5	38.1	-0.5	37.9	-0.5	37.9	0.0	37.6	-0.8	36.9	-1.9	36.6	-0.8
1962	36.5	-0.3	36.4	-0.3	36.7	0.8	36.2	-1.4	36.0	-0.6	36.4	1.1	36.1	-0.8	36.1	0.0	36.7	1.7	37.4	1.9	36.2	-3.2	35.9	-0.8
1963	35.8	-0.3	36.2	1.1	36.2	0.0	36.2	0.0	36.4	0.6	37.1	1.9	37.3	0.5	38.1	2.1	38.1	0.0	38.8	1.8	38.5	-0.8	38.4	-0.3
1964	38.4	0.0	38.1	-0.8	38.5	1.0	39.3	2.1	38.9	-1.0	38.7	-0.5	38.9	0.5	38.9	0.0	39.1	0.5	39.0	-0.3	39.4	1.0	39.7	0.8
1965	40.9	3.0	40.9	0.0	40.2	-1.7	39.9	-0.7	40.1	0.5	40.3	0.5	40.5	0.5	41.0	1.2	40.8	-0.5	40.8	0.0	40.8	0.0	40.8	0.0
1966	40.7	-0.2	40.8	0.2	40.9	0.2	40.7	-0.5	40.4	-0.7	40.2	-0.5	40.7	1.2	40.8	0.2	40.8	0.0	41.1	0.7	41.0	-0.2	40.6	-1.0
1967	40.2	-1.0	39.8	-1.0	40.0	0.5	40.4	1.0	40.2	-0.5	40.2	0.0	40.4	0.5	40.1	-0.7	40.2	0.2	40.2	0.0	40.4	0.5	40.6	0.5
1968	40.8	0.5	40.8	0.0	40.8	0.0	40.8	0.0	40.7	-0.2	40.9	0.5	41.0	0.2	41.0	0.0	41.8	2.0	42.3	1.2	42.3	0.0	42.2	-0.2
1969	42.2	0.0	42.6	0.9	42.6	0.0	42.4	-0.5	42.4	0.0	42.4	0.0	42.7	0.7	42.8	0.2	43.3	1.2	47.0	8.5	45.5	-3.2	45.2	-0.7
1970	45.2	0.0	45.5	0.7	45.4	-0.2	44.9	-1.1	44.3	-1.3	45.3	2.3	45.8	1.1	45.9	0.2	46.3	0.9	45.9	-0.9	45.5	-0.9	45.3	-0.4
1971	45.0	-0.7	45.0	0.0	45.7	1.6	46.0	0.7	45.8	-0.4	45.8	0.0	45.8	0.0	45.8	0.0	45.5	-0.7	45.4	-0.2	45.5	0.2	45.5	0.0
1972	45.7	0.4	45.8	0.2	45.7	-0.2	45.8	0.2	46.3	1.1	46.0	-0.6	46.0	0.0	45.8	-0.4	46.8	2.2	47.0	0.4	46.7	-0.6	46.6	-0.2
1973	46.9	0.6	47.2	0.6	47.8	1.3	47.7	-0.2	47.8	0.2	48.3	1.0	49.7	2.9	51.7	4.0	51.5	-0.4	52.0	1.0	52.0	0.0	52.6	1.2
1974	54.0	2.7	56.3	4.3	59.1	5.0	60.1	1.7	61.5	2.3	63.0	2.4	64.5	2.4	66.4	2.9	68.5	3.2	69.0	0.7	71.1	3.0	72.1	1.4
1975	73.2	1.5	72.9	-0.4	72.3	-0.8	72.5	0.3	72.0	-0.7	71.4	-0.8	70.8	-0.8	71.6	1.1	71.8	0.3	71.3	-0.7	70.9	-0.6	70.4	-0.7
1976	69.5	-1.3	68.8	-1.0	68.8	0.0	69.8	1.5	69.9	0.1	69.5	-0.6	69.6	0.1	69.9	0.4	70.6	1.0	71.5	1.3	71.7	0.3	73.5	2.5
1977	73.3	-0.3	74.0	1.0	74.0	0.0	74.3	0.4	77.4	4.2	77.6	0.3	78.2	0.8	78.2	0.0	78.1	-0.1	78.0	-0.1	77.2	-1.0	77.2	0.0
1978	77.8	0.8	78.1	0.4	78.8	0.9	80.2	1.8	80.6	0.5	80.4	-0.2	81.5	1.4	79.2	-2.8	79.4	0.3	80.6	1.5	82.0	1.7	82.1	0.1
1979	83.1	1.2	83.7	0.7	87.5	4.5	88.2	0.8	88.6	0.5	84.9	-4.2	85.6	0.8	87.6	2.3	88.1	0.6	88.8	0.8	89.4	0.7	89.7	0.3
1980	90.7	1.1	89.9	-0.9	90.4	0.6	90.6	0.2	90.0	-0.7	89.9	-0.1	89.9	0.0	90.1	0.2	91.2	1.2	92.8	1.8	94.6	1.9	96.7	2.2
1981	98.2	1.6	99.8	1.6	100.2	0.4	100.6	0.4	101.0	0.4	101.2	0.2	101.5	0.3	101.4	-0.1	101.8	0.4	100.5	-1.3	100.6	0.1	100.6	0.0
1982	101.0	0.4	100.9	-0.1	100.4	-0.5	100.4	0.0	99.8	-0.6	100.0	0.2	99.8	-0.2	98.9	-0.9	99.4	0.5	99.7	0.3	99.7	0.0	100.0	0.3
1983	100.1	0.1	100.3	0.2	100.0	-0.3	100.5	0.5	100.5	0.0	101.2	0.7	102.6	1.4	101.7	-0.9	104.0	2.3	105.4	1.3	106.5	1.0	107.1	0.6
1984	107.3	0.2	110.8	3.3	110.7	-0.1	111.2	0.5	111.1	-0.1	112.6	1.4	113.2	0.5	112.8	-0.4	113.1	0.3	113.1	0.0	113.0	-0.1	113.0	0.0
1985	113.2	0.2	113.2	0.0	113.2	0.0	113.5	0.3	114.1	0.5	114.1	0.0	114.5	0.4	115.1	0.5	114.5	-0.5	114.5	0.0	114.6	0.1	114.6	0.0
1986	115.4	0.7	115.1	-0.3	115.2	0.1	115.1	-0.1	115.4	0.3	115.7	0.3	116.1	0.3	116.4	0.3	116.6	0.2	117.4	0.7	117.7	0.3	118.3	0.5
1987	118.9	0.5	119.5	0.5	119.8	0.3	120.0	0.2	120.0	0.0	119.5	-0.4	119.5	0.0	119.7	0.2	119.6	-0.1	119.9	0.3	120.3	0.3	120.5	0.2
1988	119.9	-0.5	120.5	0.5	120.7	0.2	121.4	0.6	121.5	0.1	121.3	-0.2	122.7	1.2	123.4	0.6	123.8	0.3	124.3	0.4	125.1	0.6	125.3	0.2
1989	126.2	0.7	127.5	1.0	128.1	0.5	128.6	0.4	129.3	0.5	129.3	0.0	129.4	0.1	130.0	0.5	130.3	0.2	130.6	0.2	131.1	0.4	131.8	0.5
1990	131.6	-0.2	132.2	0.5	132.9	0.5	133.1	0.2	133.8	0.5	133.7	-0.1	134.1	0.3	134.8	0.5	135.0	0.1	134.8	-0.1	136.7	1.4	137.4	0.5
1991	137.6	0.1	137.9	0.2	137.8	-0.1	138.2	0.3	137.3	-0.7	137.8	0.4	137.9	0.1	139.0	0.8	138.8	-0.1	139.2	0.3	138.9	-0.2	138.8	-0.1

[Continued]

Miscellaneous Processed Foods
Producer Price Index
Base 1982 = 100
[Continued]

For 1947-1993. Columns headed % show percentile change in the index from the previous period for which an index is available.

Year	Jan		Feb		Mar		Apr		May		Jun		Jul		Aug		Sep		Oct		Nov		Dec	
	Index	%	Index	%	Index	%	Index	%	Index	%	Index	%	Index	%	Index	%	Index	%	Index	%	Index	%	Index	%
1992	139.1	0.2	139.1	0.0	138.8	-0.2	138.7	-0.1	138.7	0.0	138.4	-0.2	138.9	0.4	139.4	0.4	139.5	0.1	139.4	-0.1	140.2	0.6	140.2	0.0
1993	140.7	0.4	141.2	0.4	141.8	0.4	141.9	0.1	142.1	0.1	142.2	0.1	142.5	0.2	143.1	0.4	143.0	-0.1	143.4	0.3	143.3	-0.1	143.2	-0.1

Source: U.S. Department of Labor, Bureau of Labor Statistics, Division of Industry Prices and Price Indexes. n.e.c. stands for not elsewhere classified. - indicates no data collected for period or unavailable.

Prepared Animal Feeds
Producer Price Index
Base 1982 = 100

For 1947-1993. Columns headed % show percentile change in the index from the previous period for which an index is available.

Year	Jan Index	%	Feb Index	%	Mar Index	%	Apr Index	%	May Index	%	Jun Index	%	Jul Index	%	Aug Index	%	Sep Index	%	Oct Index	%	Nov Index	%	Dec Index	%
1947	45.3	-	42.0	-7.3	50.8	21.0	47.5	-6.5	48.7	2.5	52.8	8.4	57.3	8.5	58.4	1.9	65.4	12.0	63.8	-2.4	63.3	-0.8	67.9	7.3
1948	74.2	9.3	61.1	-17.7	60.2	-1.5	60.9	1.2	58.7	-3.6	60.3	2.7	55.4	-8.1	47.7	-13.9	48.5	1.7	44.9	-7.4	50.0	11.4	50.5	1.0
1949	49.5	-2.0	45.2	-8.7	47.4	4.9	50.5	6.5	48.7	-3.6	48.8	0.2	52.6	7.8	56.0	6.5	49.8	-11.1	47.5	-4.6	45.7	-3.8	46.5	1.8
1950	44.7	-3.9	43.8	-2.0	47.2	7.8	49.4	4.7	53.7	8.7	50.1	-6.7	56.7	13.2	49.2	-13.2	47.7	-3.0	45.5	-4.6	47.9	5.3	50.2	4.8
1951	51.4	2.4	52.7	2.5	52.9	0.4	54.4	2.8	51.7	-5.0	51.4	-0.6	52.4	1.9	51.2	-2.3	53.8	5.1	55.8	3.7	57.9	3.8	58.8	1.6
1952	60.2	2.4	60.7	0.8	58.5	-3.6	58.9	0.7	57.9	-1.7	57.7	-0.3	54.9	-4.9	58.5	6.6	57.9	-1.0	57.9	0.0	55.2	-4.7	54.6	-1.1
1953	52.3	-4.2	50.5	-3.4	50.8	0.6	47.4	-6.7	48.7	2.7	44.7	-8.2	44.2	-1.1	45.4	2.7	43.6	-4.0	43.3	-0.7	42.1	-2.8	49.3	17.1
1954	50.2	1.8	52.0	3.6	54.0	3.8	59.4	10.0	58.3	-1.9	53.8	-7.7	52.5	-2.4	50.9	-3.0	47.6	-6.5	45.1	-5.3	45.4	0.7	46.4	2.2
1955	45.3	-2.4	45.9	1.3	44.3	-3.5	42.8	-3.4	40.1	-6.3	37.8	-5.7	39.5	4.5	38.3	-3.0	38.8	1.3	39.9	2.8	36.3	-9.0	36.8	1.4
1956	37.3	1.4	36.4	-2.4	35.9	-1.4	39.8	10.9	43.7	9.8	40.6	-7.1	38.9	-4.2	38.5	-1.0	37.2	-3.4	36.4	-2.2	38.4	5.5	38.8	1.0
1957	39.8	2.6	38.9	-2.3	38.5	-1.0	38.0	-1.3	35.9	-5.5	33.9	-5.6	35.3	4.1	36.4	3.1	35.5	-2.5	33.7	-5.1	32.8	-2.7	33.2	1.2
1958	34.2	3.0	35.1	2.6	39.9	13.7	43.2	8.3	41.7	-3.5	39.2	-6.0	42.6	8.7	41.0	-3.8	38.2	-6.8	36.9	-3.4	38.8	5.1	46.2	19.1
1959	46.1	-0.2	43.9	-4.8	42.5	-3.2	44.3	4.2	40.9	-7.7	36.9	-9.8	38.6	4.6	37.8	-2.1	34.5	-8.7	37.6	9.0	39.4	4.8	39.6	0.5
1960	40.4	2.0	38.6	-4.5	39.1	1.3	40.4	3.3	36.3	-10.1	36.1	-0.6	36.0	-0.3	35.1	-2.5	36.2	3.1	35.4	-2.2	35.7	0.8	37.4	4.8
1961	39.9	6.7	39.6	-0.8	40.7	2.8	41.4	1.7	42.9	3.6	40.1	-6.5	39.9	-0.5	39.7	-0.5	39.7	0.0	38.0	-4.3	41.0	7.9	42.0	2.4
1962	42.4	1.0	41.6	-1.9	41.6	0.0	41.8	0.5	41.8	0.0	41.4	-1.0	42.9	3.6	42.6	-0.7	43.9	3.1	43.6	-0.7	44.4	1.8	44.7	0.7
1963	45.7	2.2	45.7	0.0	45.2	-1.1	43.2	-4.4	43.0	-0.5	43.3	0.7	44.9	3.7	45.5	1.3	46.0	1.1	45.5	-1.1	45.3	-0.4	46.2	2.0
1964	46.5	0.6	45.3	-2.6	44.5	-1.8	44.3	-0.4	42.7	-3.6	42.4	-0.7	42.8	0.9	42.6	-0.5	43.9	3.1	44.5	1.4	43.4	-2.5	45.0	3.7
1965	44.5	-1.1	44.2	-0.7	44.1	-0.2	44.6	1.1	43.6	-2.2	45.1	3.4	45.9	1.8	45.2	-1.5	45.1	-0.2	44.9	-0.4	46.3	3.1	45.8	-1.1
1966	47.0	2.6	48.2	2.6	46.2	-4.1	46.1	-0.2	47.6	3.3	47.9	0.6	51.2	6.9	51.6	0.8	51.1	-1.0	49.5	-3.1	49.6	0.2	51.0	2.8
1967	51.0	0.0	48.7	-4.5	48.2	-1.0	47.5	-1.5	45.9	-3.4	47.3	3.1	47.6	0.6	46.2	-2.9	47.0	1.7	46.6	-0.9	45.9	-1.5	46.2	0.7
1968	46.5	0.6	46.2	-0.6	46.0	-0.4	45.3	-1.5	45.5	0.4	46.2	1.5	46.2	0.0	45.8	-0.9	45.4	-0.9	45.4	0.0	45.3	-0.2	45.7	0.9
1969	45.7	0.0	45.4	-0.7	44.7	-1.5	45.8	2.5	44.4	-3.1	45.2	1.8	45.9	1.5	45.7	-0.4	46.1	0.9	46.4	0.7	46.2	-0.4	47.1	1.9
1970	51.0	8.3	50.9	-0.2	46.1	-9.4	46.9	1.7	46.3	-1.3	46.9	1.3	49.3	5.1	49.5	0.4	50.7	2.4	49.4	-2.6	50.0	1.2	51.7	3.4
1971	51.1	-1.2	49.7	-2.7	50.8	2.2	49.4	-2.8	49.5	0.2	50.9	2.8	50.6	-0.6	49.6	-2.0	48.0	-3.2	46.7	-2.7	47.5	1.7	49.5	4.2
1972	49.1	-0.8	49.1	0.0	51.4	4.7	51.3	-0.2	51.3	0.0	51.0	-0.6	52.5	2.9	52.9	0.8	55.8	5.5	55.1	-1.3	61.7	12.0	77.4	25.4
1973	78.7	1.7	86.4	9.8	86.3	-0.1	78.9	-8.6	100.0	26.7	122.0	22.0	93.3	-23.5	123.9	32.8	90.0	-27.4	87.3	-3.0	86.8	-0.6	95.1	9.6
1974	96.2	1.2	90.3	-6.1	85.7	-5.1	78.7	-8.2	73.4	-6.7	72.2	-1.6	73.9	2.4	102.8	39.1	87.4	-15.0	100.0	14.4	92.6	-7.4	92.1	-0.5
1975	87.8	-4.7	79.3	-9.7	75.4	-4.9	81.1	7.6	78.0	-3.8	80.0	2.6	80.2	0.3	84.0	4.7	83.9	-0.1	84.0	0.1	81.3	-3.2	82.6	1.6
1976	83.6	1.2	82.9	-0.8	82.9	0.0	82.2	-0.8	85.8	4.4	100.8	17.5	102.3	1.5	93.2	-8.9	100.1	7.4	94.6	-5.5	94.7	0.1	100.9	6.5
1977	103.6	2.7	103.6	0.0	105.0	1.4	115.0	9.5	113.3	-1.5	106.7	-5.8	89.1	-16.5	83.2	-6.6	82.7	-0.6	79.7	-3.6	91.7	15.1	88.6	-3.4
1978	92.0	3.8	88.4	-3.9	94.9	7.4	93.5	-1.5	91.7	-1.9	93.6	2.1	92.9	-0.7	89.9	-3.2	91.7	2.0	95.2	3.8	97.2	2.1	100.3	3.2
1979	100.0	-0.3	102.8	2.8	102.1	-0.7	102.0	-0.1	99.8	-2.2	104.3	4.5	111.2	6.6	102.3	-8.0	103.8	1.5	106.0	2.1	105.3	-0.7	106.5	1.1
1980	104.0	-2.3	104.0	0.0	102.5	-1.4	97.0	-5.4	98.0	1.0	97.0	-1.0	106.0	9.3	110.0	3.8	115.2	4.7	116.8	1.4	120.5	3.2	116.9	-3.0
1981	117.8	0.8	111.6	-5.3	109.4	-2.0	112.5	2.8	114.1	1.4	110.9	-2.8	109.9	-0.9	108.4	-1.4	105.5	-2.7	103.2	-2.2	101.6	-1.6	102.8	1.2
1982	102.9	0.1	101.7	-1.2	100.0	-1.7	102.4	2.4	102.9	0.5	102.4	-0.5	101.3	-1.1	98.2	-3.1	96.7	-1.5	94.6	-2.2	97.5	3.1	99.4	1.9
1983	100.2	0.8	100.5	0.3	100.5	0.0	105.5	5.0	104.8	-0.7	102.8	-1.9	104.1	1.3	110.3	6.0	118.0	7.0	117.7	-0.3	119.3	1.4	116.2	-2.6
1984	116.1	-0.1	109.4	-5.8	111.4	1.8	111.8	0.4	109.9	-1.7	106.7	-2.9	102.5	-3.9	101.3	-1.2	99.0	-2.3	95.8	-3.2	94.5	-1.4	94.1	-0.4
1985	93.7	-0.4	91.6	-2.2	89.7	-2.1	88.1	-1.8	86.3	-2.0	87.0	0.8	88.0	1.1	88.4	0.5	89.1	0.8	91.0	2.1	93.2	2.4	94.5	1.4
1986	95.6	1.2	94.1	-1.6	95.0	1.0	95.5	0.5	95.2	-0.3	95.5	0.3	94.4	-1.2	93.5	-1.0	95.7	2.4	92.5	-3.3	93.9	1.5	94.5	0.6
1987	93.8	-0.7	94.1	0.3	92.4	-1.8	93.8	1.5	98.4	4.9	99.9	1.5	99.4	-0.5	98.4	-1.0	99.9	1.5	100.3	0.4	104.8	4.5	107.3	2.4
1988	105.8	-1.4	102.9	-2.7	104.0	1.1	106.0	1.9	107.1	1.0	120.2	12.2	127.3	5.9	123.6	-2.9	125.4	1.5	125.5	0.1	123.3	-1.8	120.9	-1.9
1989	124.3	2.8	121.1	-2.6	122.0	0.7	119.0	-2.5	117.8	-1.0	114.9	-2.5	117.6	2.3	114.2	-2.9	115.3	1.0	112.3	-2.6	110.9	-1.2	110.3	-0.5
1990	110.7	0.4	106.1	-4.2	105.9	-0.2	106.2	0.3	109.1	2.7	107.4	-1.6	109.3	1.8	107.4	-1.7	107.7	0.3	108.0	0.3	105.6	-2.2	105.9	0.3
1991	104.5	-1.3	105.1	0.6	106.3	1.1	105.9	-0.4	105.8	-0.1	106.0	0.2	104.1	-1.8	107.9	3.7	109.0	1.0	108.7	-0.3	109.4	0.6	109.0	-0.4

[Continued]

Prepared Animal Feeds

Producer Price Index
Base 1982 = 100
[Continued]

For 1947-1993. Columns headed % show percentile change in the index from the previous period for which an index is available.

Year	Jan Index	%	Feb Index	%	Mar Index	%	Apr Index	%	May Index	%	Jun Index	%	Jul Index	%	Aug Index	%	Sep Index	%	Oct Index	%	Nov Index	%	Dec Index	%
1992	108.7	-0.3	108.9	0.2	109.3	0.4	107.9	-1.3	108.7	0.7	109.3	0.6	107.7	-1.5	106.9	-0.7	107.9	0.9	107.3	-0.6	107.3	0.0	109.6	2.1
1993	110.0	0.4	107.9	-1.9	107.0	-0.8	108.2	1.1	108.5	0.3	107.9	-0.6	113.2	4.9	114.9	1.5	112.8	-1.8	111.8	-0.9	113.8	1.8	116.4	2.3

Source: U.S. Department of Labor, Bureau of Labor Statistics, Division of Industry Prices and Price Indexes. n.e.c. stands for not elsewhere classified. - indicates no data collected for period or unavailable.

TEXTILE PRODUCTS AND APPAREL
Producer Price Index
Base 1982 = 100

For 1947-1993. Columns headed % show percentile change in the index from the previous period for which an index is available.

Year	Jan		Feb		Mar		Apr		May		Jun		Jul		Aug		Sep		Oct		Nov		Dec	
	Index	%	Index	%	Index	%	Index	%	Index	%	Index	%	Index	%	Index	%	Index	%	Index	%	Index	%	Index	%
1947	49.8	-	50.1	0.6	50.3	0.4	50.3	0.0	50.2	-0.2	50.0	-0.4	50.2	0.4	50.4	0.4	51.0	1.2	51.2	0.4	51.7	1.0	52.6	1.7
1948	53.2	1.1	53.5	0.6	53.4	-0.2	52.9	-0.9	53.1	0.4	52.8	-0.6	52.9	0.2	52.9	0.0	52.8	-0.2	52.6	-0.4	52.2	-0.8	52.1	-0.2
1949	51.0	-2.1	50.5	-1.0	49.8	-1.4	48.9	-1.8	47.8	-2.2	47.5	-0.6	47.3	-0.4	47.3	0.0	47.4	0.2	47.6	0.4	47.7	0.2	47.7	0.0
1950	47.7	0.0	47.8	0.2	47.7	-0.2	47.1	-1.3	47.0	-0.2	47.3	0.6	48.7	3.0	50.8	4.3	52.8	3.9	54.4	3.0	55.2	1.5	56.4	2.2
1951	58.0	2.8	58.6	1.0	58.7	0.2	58.5	-0.3	58.1	-0.7	57.2	-1.5	56.5	-1.2	54.9	-2.8	53.6	-2.4	52.6	-1.9	52.6	0.0	52.6	0.0
1952	52.3	-0.6	51.7	-1.1	50.9	-1.5	50.6	-0.6	50.3	-0.6	50.1	-0.4	50.1	0.0	50.2	0.2	50.4	0.4	50.2	-0.4	50.0	-0.4	49.8	-0.4
1953	50.1	0.6	49.9	-0.4	49.4	-1.0	49.3	-0.2	49.4	0.2	49.3	-0.2	49.4	0.2	49.4	0.0	49.1	-0.6	48.9	-0.4	48.7	-0.4	48.5	-0.4
1954	48.6	0.2	48.2	-0.8	48.1	-0.2	48.0	-0.2	48.0	0.0	48.1	0.2	48.2	0.2	48.2	0.0	48.2	0.0	48.3	0.2	48.2	-0.2	48.2	0.0
1955	48.2	0.0	48.2	0.0	48.2	0.0	48.1	-0.2	48.1	0.0	48.2	0.2	48.2	0.0	48.2	0.0	48.3	0.2	48.3	0.0	48.4	0.2	48.4	0.0
1956	48.4	0.0	48.6	0.4	48.5	-0.2	48.2	-0.6	48.1	-0.2	48.1	0.0	48.1	0.0	48.0	-0.2	48.0	0.0	48.2	0.4	48.3	0.2	48.4	0.2
1957	48.5	0.2	48.4	-0.2	48.3	-0.2	48.2	-0.2	48.3	0.2	48.3	0.0	48.3	0.0	48.3	0.0	48.3	0.0	48.2	-0.2	48.1	-0.2	48.1	0.0
1958	47.9	-0.4	47.7	-0.4	47.6	-0.2	47.5	-0.2	47.4	-0.2	47.3	-0.2	47.3	0.0	47.3	0.0	47.3	0.0	47.2	-0.2	47.2	0.0	47.3	0.2
1959	47.3	0.0	47.5	0.4	47.6	0.2	47.7	0.2	47.8	0.2	48.1	0.6	48.2	0.2	48.4	0.4	48.5	0.2	48.5	0.0	48.7	0.4	49.0	0.6
1960	48.9	-0.2	48.9	0.0	48.7	-0.4	48.7	0.0	48.7	0.0	48.7	0.0	48.7	0.0	48.6	-0.2	48.5	-0.2	48.5	0.0	48.3	-0.4	48.2	-0.2
1961	48.0	-0.4	48.0	0.0	47.8	-0.4	47.7	-0.2	47.6	-0.2	47.5	-0.2	47.6	0.2	47.7	0.2	47.8	0.2	48.0	0.4	48.0	0.0	48.1	0.2
1962	48.1	0.0	48.1	0.0	48.2	0.2	48.2	0.0	48.2	0.0	48.3	0.2	48.3	0.0	48.3	0.0	48.2	-0.2	48.2	0.0	48.2	0.0	48.2	0.0
1963	48.1	-0.2	48.1	0.0	48.0	-0.2	48.0	0.0	48.0	0.0	48.1	0.2	48.1	0.0	48.1	0.0	48.2	0.2	48.2	0.0	48.4	0.4	48.5	0.2
1964	48.5	0.0	48.5	0.0	48.5	0.0	48.4	-0.2	48.5	0.2	48.4	-0.2	48.4	0.0	48.5	0.2	48.5	0.0	48.6	0.2	48.6	0.0	48.6	0.0
1965	48.6	0.0	48.6	0.0	48.6	0.0	48.6	0.0	48.7	0.2	48.8	0.2	48.8	0.0	48.8	0.0	48.9	0.2	48.9	0.0	48.8	-0.2	48.9	0.2
1966	48.8	-0.2	48.9	0.2	48.9	0.0	49.0	0.2	49.0	0.0	49.0	0.0	49.1	0.2	49.1	0.0	49.0	-0.2	49.0	0.0	48.9	-0.2	48.8	-0.2
1967	48.9	0.2	48.9	0.0	48.8	-0.2	48.7	-0.2	48.6	-0.2	48.6	0.0	48.6	0.0	48.6	0.0	48.8	0.4	48.9	0.2	49.3	0.8	49.7	0.8
1968	50.0	0.6	50.1	0.2	50.2	0.2	50.2	0.0	50.3	0.2	50.5	0.4	50.7	0.4	50.9	0.4	51.1	0.4	51.3	0.4	51.5	0.4	51.4	-0.2
1969	51.6	0.4	51.5	-0.2	51.4	-0.2	51.4	0.0	51.4	0.0	51.7	0.6	51.9	0.4	52.1	0.4	52.1	0.0	52.2	0.2	52.3	0.2	52.2	-0.2
1970	52.4	0.4	52.3	-0.2	52.4	0.2	52.4	0.0	52.3	-0.2	52.4	0.2	52.4	0.0	52.4	0.0	52.4	0.0	52.4	0.0	52.2	-0.2	52.2	0.0
1971	52.2	0.0	52.3	0.2	52.4	0.2	52.7	0.6	52.8	0.2	53.4	1.1	53.6	0.4	53.9	0.6	53.8	-0.2	53.8	0.0	53.9	0.2	54.3	0.7
1972	54.4	0.2	54.7	0.6	54.8	0.2	55.0	0.4	55.4	0.7	55.5	0.2	55.7	0.4	55.8	0.2	55.9	0.2	56.1	0.4	56.3	0.4	56.5	0.4
1973	57.0	0.9	57.4	0.7	58.2	1.4	59.0	1.4	59.8	1.4	60.5	1.2	60.7	0.3	61.2	0.8	62.0	1.3	62.8	1.3	63.5	1.1	64.2	1.1
1974	65.4	1.9	66.1	1.1	66.5	0.6	67.2	1.1	68.0	1.2	69.3	1.9	69.5	0.3	69.6	0.1	69.5	-0.1	68.7	-1.2	68.3	-0.6	67.7	-0.9
1975	67.2	-0.7	66.7	-0.7	65.7	-1.5	65.7	0.0	66.1	0.6	66.4	0.5	66.9	0.8	67.3	0.6	67.6	0.4	69.1	2.2	70.0	1.3	70.4	0.6
1976	71.2	1.1	71.5	0.4	71.7	0.3	72.0	0.4	72.0	0.0	72.5	0.7	72.8	0.4	73.1	0.4	72.8	-0.4	73.0	0.3	73.4	0.5	73.3	-0.1
1977	73.7	0.5	74.2	0.7	74.5	0.4	75.1	0.8	75.3	0.3	75.6	0.4	75.5	-0.1	75.6	0.1	75.8	0.3	75.9	0.1	75.9	0.0	76.2	0.4
1978	76.5	0.4	76.8	0.4	76.9	0.1	77.2	0.4	77.5	0.4	77.8	0.4	78.2	0.5	78.5	0.4	78.9	0.5	79.3	0.5	79.8	0.6	80.0	0.3
1979	80.2	0.3	80.3	0.1	80.8	0.6	81.4	0.7	81.7	0.4	82.3	0.7	82.8	0.6	83.4	0.7	83.7	0.4	84.1	0.5	84.5	0.5	84.6	0.1
1980	85.7	1.3	86.3	0.7	87.6	1.5	88.6	1.1	89.0	0.5	89.4	0.4	90.3	1.0	90.7	0.4	91.2	0.6	92.0	0.9	92.7	0.8	93.1	0.4
1981	94.4	1.4	94.8	0.4	95.4	0.6	96.6	1.3	97.4	0.8	97.8	0.4	98.4	0.6	98.9	0.5	99.2	0.3	99.7	0.5	99.5	-0.2	99.4	-0.1
1982	100.2	0.8	100.5	0.3	100.2	-0.3	100.4	0.2	100.4	0.0	100.2	-0.2	99.8	-0.4	99.8	0.0	99.9	0.1	99.8	-0.1	99.7	-0.1	99.0	-0.7
1983	99.1	0.1	99.0	-0.1	99.4	0.4	99.5	0.1	99.9	0.4	100.1	0.2	100.4	0.3	100.7	0.3	100.8	0.1	101.2	0.4	101.5	0.3	101.6	0.1
1984	101.8	0.2	102.5	0.7	102.6	0.1	102.6	0.0	102.9	0.3	102.8	-0.1	102.9	0.1	102.7	-0.2	103.0	0.3	102.9	-0.1	102.7	-0.2	102.6	-0.1
1985	102.8	0.2	103.0	0.2	102.9	-0.1	103.0	0.1	102.9	-0.1	102.8	-0.1	102.7	-0.1	102.9	0.2	102.8	-0.1	102.7	-0.1	102.9	0.2	103.0	0.1
1986	103.0	0.0	103.1	0.1	103.3	0.2	103.2	-0.1	103.2	0.0	103.2	0.0	103.3	0.1	103.2	-0.1	103.2	0.0	103.2	0.0	103.3	0.1	103.4	0.1
1987	103.6	0.2	103.7	0.1	103.9	0.2	104.2	0.3	104.4	0.2	104.8	0.4	105.3	0.5	105.6	0.3	106.0	0.4	106.4	0.4	106.6	0.2	107.0	0.4
1988	107.6	0.6	108.1	0.5	108.4	0.3	108.7	0.3	108.9	0.2	109.3	0.4	109.5	0.2	109.6	0.1	109.8	0.2	110.0	0.2	110.2	0.2	110.5	0.3
1989	111.0	0.5	111.3	0.3	111.2	-0.1	111.6	0.4	111.8	0.2	112.2	0.4	112.6	0.4	112.9	0.3	113.0	0.1	113.3	0.3	113.5	0.2	113.6	0.1
1990	114.6	0.9	114.6	0.0	114.7	0.1	114.9	0.2	114.8	-0.1	115.0	0.2	115.1	0.1	115.1	0.0	115.1	0.0	115.1	0.0	115.3	0.2	115.2	-0.1
1991	115.7	0.4	115.8	0.1	115.9	0.1	116.0	0.1	116.0	0.0	116.2	0.2	116.3	0.1	116.5	0.2	116.6	0.1	116.7	0.1	116.8	0.1	116.9	0.1

[Continued]

TEXTILE PRODUCTS AND APPAREL

Producer Price Index
Base 1982 = 100
[Continued]

For 1947-1993. Columns headed % show percentile change in the index from the previous period for which an index is available.

Year	Jan Index	%	Feb Index	%	Mar Index	%	Apr Index	%	May Index	%	Jun Index	%	Jul Index	%	Aug Index	%	Sep Index	%	Oct Index	%	Nov Index	%	Dec Index	%
1992	117.4	0.4	117.6	0.2	117.7	0.1	117.8	0.1	117.7	-0.1	117.9	0.2	117.8	-0.1	117.8	0.0	118.0	0.2	118.1	0.1	118.0	-0.1	118.0	0.0
1993	118.0	0.0	117.9	-0.1	117.9	0.0	118.1	0.2	118.0	-0.1	118.0	0.0	118.2	0.2	118.3	0.1	118.2	-0.1	118.2	0.0	118.1	-0.1	117.8	-0.3

Source: U.S. Department of Labor, Bureau of Labor Statistics, Division of Industry Prices and Price Indexes. n.e.c. stands for not elsewhere classified. - indicates no data collected for period or unavailable.

Synthetic Fibers

Producer Price Index
Base 1982 = 100

For 1975-1993. Columns headed % show percentile change in the index from the previous period for which an index is available.

Year	Jan Index	%	Feb Index	%	Mar Index	%	Apr Index	%	May Index	%	Jun Index	%	Jul Index	%	Aug Index	%	Sep Index	%	Oct Index	%	Nov Index	%	Dec Index	%
1975	-	-	-	-	-	-	-	-	-	-	-	-	-	-	-	-	-	-	-	-	-	-	61.7	-
1976	62.8	1.8	63.1	0.5	63.0	-0.2	63.5	0.8	63.4	-0.2	63.2	-0.3	63.3	0.2	63.7	0.6	63.6	-0.2	62.8	-1.3	62.7	-0.2	62.7	0.0
1977	63.2	0.8	63.8	0.9	63.7	-0.2	65.7	3.1	66.1	0.6	67.4	2.0	67.2	-0.3	67.4	0.3	67.5	0.1	67.4	-0.1	67.4	0.0	67.4	0.0
1978	67.9	0.7	67.8	-0.1	67.8	0.0	67.4	-0.6	67.6	0.3	67.2	-0.6	67.2	0.0	67.3	0.1	67.3	0.0	67.5	0.3	68.2	1.0	68.2	0.0
1979	69.7	2.2	70.0	0.4	70.1	0.1	71.0	1.3	72.4	2.0	73.1	1.0	73.8	1.0	74.4	0.8	76.2	2.4	76.9	0.9	76.6	-0.4	76.9	0.4
1980	78.4	2.0	78.5	0.1	79.6	1.4	80.5	1.1	82.2	2.1	83.0	1.0	83.9	1.1	84.8	1.1	86.1	1.5	86.5	0.5	86.8	0.3	86.9	0.1
1981	90.4	4.0	90.7	0.3	91.9	1.3	93.5	1.7	96.5	3.2	97.4	0.9	98.5	1.1	99.5	1.0	99.3	-0.2	100.4	1.1	99.7	-0.7	99.6	-0.1
1982	100.5	0.9	100.7	0.2	99.5	-1.2	100.6	1.1	100.8	0.2	100.5	-0.3	99.6	-0.9	100.1	0.5	100.3	0.2	99.4	-0.9	99.5	0.1	98.5	-1.0
1983	96.7	-1.8	94.5	-2.3	95.0	0.5	94.9	-0.1	96.0	1.2	96.2	0.2	97.7	1.6	97.2	-0.5	97.5	0.3	99.1	1.6	98.3	-0.8	97.5	-0.8
1984	98.3	0.8	99.6	1.3	99.2	-0.4	99.1	-0.1	99.1	0.0	99.0	-0.1	98.8	-0.2	98.7	-0.1	98.2	-0.5	97.6	-0.6	97.2	-0.4	97.3	0.1
1985	97.2	-0.1	97.2	0.0	96.6	-0.6	97.1	0.5	96.9	-0.2	96.5	-0.4	95.4	-1.1	95.5	0.1	95.6	0.1	92.4	-3.3	92.8	0.4	93.0	0.2
1986	93.6	0.6	93.5	-0.1	93.5	0.0	92.4	-1.2	92.3	-0.1	92.1	-0.2	92.5	0.4	92.3	-0.2	92.2	-0.1	91.7	-0.5	91.7	0.0	91.6	-0.1
1987	92.1	0.5	91.4	-0.8	91.3	-0.1	90.8	-0.5	90.8	0.0	91.0	0.2	91.4	0.4	91.7	0.3	91.9	0.2	92.8	1.0	93.3	0.5	93.6	0.3
1988	94.4	0.9	94.7	0.3	95.1	0.4	96.3	1.3	97.0	0.7	96.6	-0.4	97.6	1.0	98.0	0.4	98.6	0.6	99.4	0.8	99.4	0.0	99.9	0.5
1989	100.6	0.7	101.1	0.5	101.6	0.5	104.1	2.5	105.0	0.9	106.2	1.1	106.5	0.3	106.2	-0.3	105.9	-0.3	107.1	1.1	106.7	-0.4	106.9	0.2
1990	106.9	0.0	107.3	0.4	107.4	0.1	106.6	-0.7	106.7	0.1	106.4	-0.3	107.5	1.0	107.1	-0.4	107.2	0.1	105.4	-1.7	105.8	0.4	106.0	0.2
1991	106.8	0.8	106.9	0.1	106.6	-0.3	105.5	-1.0	105.3	-0.2	105.3	0.0	105.1	-0.2	105.0	-0.1	105.0	0.0	104.2	-0.8	104.0	-0.2	103.5	-0.5
1992	103.1	-0.4	103.6	0.5	103.5	-0.1	104.2	0.7	103.4	-0.8	103.9	0.5	103.9	0.0	103.6	-0.3	103.2	-0.4	103.3	0.1	102.4	-0.9	102.5	0.1
1993	102.6	0.1	102.3	-0.3	102.4	0.1	102.8	0.4	102.9	0.1	103.5	0.6	103.8	0.3	105.1	1.3	105.5	0.4	105.4	-0.1	105.2	-0.2	104.1	-1.0

Source: U.S. Department of Labor, Bureau of Labor Statistics, Division of Industry Prices and Price Indexes. n.e.c. stands for not elsewhere classified. - indicates no data collected for period or unavailable.

Processed Yarns and Threads
Producer Price Index
Base 1982 = 100

For 1975-1993. Columns headed % show percentile change in the index from the previous period for which an index is available.

Year	Jan Index	Jan %	Feb Index	Feb %	Mar Index	Mar %	Apr Index	Apr %	May Index	May %	Jun Index	Jun %	Jul Index	Jul %	Aug Index	Aug %	Sep Index	Sep %	Oct Index	Oct %	Nov Index	Nov %	Dec Index	Dec %
1975	-	-	-	-	-	-	-	-	-	-	-	-	-	-	-	-	-	-	-	-	-	-	72.3	-
1976	73.4	1.5	73.3	-0.1	72.8	-0.7	71.8	-1.4	71.6	-0.3	72.1	0.7	73.1	1.4	72.1	-1.4	71.5	-0.8	70.9	-0.8	70.5	-0.6	70.3	-0.3
1977	70.0	-0.4	70.5	0.7	71.4	1.3	73.4	2.8	74.0	0.8	74.8	1.1	74.8	0.0	74.3	-0.7	73.8	-0.7	73.2	-0.8	72.6	-0.8	72.7	0.1
1978	72.8	0.1	73.1	0.4	73.2	0.1	73.1	-0.1	73.0	-0.1	73.5	0.7	73.7	0.3	74.0	0.4	74.7	0.9	75.2	0.7	76.2	1.3	75.7	-0.7
1979	76.2	0.7	76.2	0.0	77.4	1.6	77.2	-0.3	78.0	1.0	78.5	0.6	79.2	0.9	80.0	1.0	80.8	1.0	81.0	0.2	81.4	0.5	81.5	0.1
1980	82.8	1.6	85.3	3.0	86.3	1.2	88.3	2.3	89.8	1.7	88.8	-1.1	88.5	-0.3	89.1	0.7	89.9	0.9	90.5	0.7	91.0	0.6	92.7	1.9
1981	93.9	1.3	94.2	0.3	97.3	3.3	97.6	0.3	100.2	2.7	100.7	0.5	101.5	0.8	102.7	1.2	102.9	0.2	104.4	1.5	101.5	-2.8	101.0	-0.5
1982	100.7	-0.3	101.7	1.0	101.6	-0.1	101.6	0.0	101.9	0.3	100.8	-1.1	98.3	-2.5	98.3	0.0	98.8	0.5	98.7	-0.1	98.9	0.2	98.9	0.0
1983	97.4	-1.5	97.7	0.3	98.2	0.5	98.3	0.1	99.3	1.0	99.5	0.2	100.2	0.7	101.4	1.2	101.4	0.0	102.2	0.8	102.5	0.3	103.3	0.8
1984	102.9	-0.4	104.1	1.2	104.1	0.0	103.8	-0.3	104.3	0.5	104.0	-0.3	103.9	-0.1	102.8	-1.1	102.8	0.0	102.3	-0.5	101.8	-0.5	101.6	-0.2
1985	102.2	0.4	102.6	0.4	102.3	-0.3	102.2	-0.1	102.2	0.0	102.1	-0.1	102.2	0.1	101.9	-0.3	101.8	-0.1	101.8	0.0	101.8	0.0	101.6	-0.2
1986	101.3	-0.3	101.2	-0.1	101.3	0.1	101.9	0.6	101.7	-0.2	101.5	-0.2	101.7	0.2	102.1	0.4	102.3	0.2	101.9	-0.4	101.6	-0.3	102.1	0.5
1987	101.5	-0.6	101.3	-0.2	101.1	-0.2	101.6	0.5	102.6	1.0	103.4	0.8	104.3	0.9	104.8	0.5	105.3	0.5	106.2	0.9	106.4	0.2	106.9	0.5
1988	107.6	0.7	107.8	0.2	107.8	0.0	107.9	0.1	107.8	-0.1	108.1	0.3	108.2	0.1	108.0	-0.2	108.1	0.1	108.3	0.2	108.2	-0.1	108.5	0.3
1989	108.5	0.0	108.9	0.4	109.6	0.6	110.0	0.4	110.2	0.2	110.5	0.3	110.8	0.3	111.2	0.4	111.1	-0.1	111.2	0.0	111.2	0.0	111.4	0.2
1990	113.1	1.5	113.4	0.3	113.4	0.0	113.6	0.2	113.6	0.0	113.8	0.2	112.4	-1.2	111.3	-1.0	111.2	-0.1	111.2	0.0	112.2	0.9	112.4	0.2
1991	112.8	0.4	112.7	-0.1	112.8	0.1	112.9	0.1	112.6	-0.3	113.1	0.4	113.1	0.0	112.4	-0.6	112.1	-0.3	112.0	-0.1	112.2	0.2	112.0	-0.2
1992	111.8	-0.2	111.6	-0.2	111.7	0.1	111.7	0.0	111.6	-0.1	111.7	0.1	110.1	-1.4	110.2	0.1	109.8	-0.4	109.7	-0.1	109.8	0.1	109.6	-0.2
1993	108.5	-1.0	108.2	-0.3	108.0	-0.2	107.9	-0.1	107.7	-0.2	107.9	0.2	107.9	0.0	107.7	-0.2	107.9	0.2	107.8	-0.1	107.4	-0.4	106.7	-0.7

Source: U.S. Department of Labor, Bureau of Labor Statistics, Division of Industry Prices and Price Indexes. n.e.c. stands for not elsewhere classified. - indicates no data collected for period or unavailable.

Gray Fabrics

Producer Price Index
Base 1982 = 100

For 1975-1993. Columns headed % show percentile change in the index from the previous period for which an index is available.

Year	Jan Index	%	Feb Index	%	Mar Index	%	Apr Index	%	May Index	%	Jun Index	%	Jul Index	%	Aug Index	%	Sep Index	%	Oct Index	%	Nov Index	%	Dec Index	%
1975	-	-	-	-	-	-	-	-	-	-	-	-	-	-	-	-	-	-	-	-	-	-	68.8	-
1976	70.3	2.2	71.2	1.3	71.2	0.0	71.6	0.6	72.4	1.1	73.4	1.4	74.7	1.8	74.7	0.0	73.7	-1.3	73.9	0.3	75.1	1.6	74.1	-1.3
1977	73.0	-1.5	72.1	-1.2	71.9	-0.3	72.3	0.6	72.0	-0.4	71.9	-0.1	72.2	0.4	71.1	-1.5	70.9	-0.3	71.4	0.7	72.4	1.4	73.8	1.9
1978	75.0	1.6	75.7	0.9	77.2	2.0	78.4	1.6	80.7	2.9	81.1	0.5	82.0	1.1	83.2	1.5	85.5	2.8	87.1	1.9	87.2	0.1	86.7	-0.6
1979	86.4	-0.3	84.8	-1.9	84.7	-0.1	85.7	1.2	85.8	0.1	86.3	0.6	88.3	2.3	88.6	0.3	88.6	0.0	89.2	0.7	89.9	0.8	91.1	1.3
1980	91.3	0.2	91.1	-0.2	94.1	3.3	94.3	0.2	93.9	-0.4	92.7	-1.3	93.4	0.8	94.6	1.3	97.0	2.5	98.7	1.8	99.8	1.1	99.1	-0.7
1981	98.8	-0.3	99.1	0.3	99.6	0.5	100.9	1.3	100.4	-0.5	101.5	1.1	102.0	0.5	102.5	0.5	102.6	0.1	101.9	-0.7	101.4	-0.5	101.3	-0.1
1982	102.0	0.7	101.4	-0.6	100.9	-0.5	100.7	-0.2	100.4	-0.3	100.5	0.1	99.7	-0.8	99.5	-0.2	98.8	-0.7	98.9	0.1	98.5	-0.4	98.6	0.1
1983	99.4	0.8	99.3	-0.1	99.8	0.5	100.3	0.5	100.6	0.3	100.4	-0.2	100.6	0.2	101.0	0.4	101.4	0.4	102.9	1.5	104.2	1.3	104.6	0.4
1984	104.0	-0.6	105.2	1.2	105.4	0.2	105.3	-0.1	105.8	0.5	106.2	0.4	106.2	0.0	106.3	0.1	106.4	0.1	106.5	0.1	105.8	-0.7	106.0	0.4
1985	105.8	-0.2	105.0	-0.8	104.6	-0.4	104.4	-0.2	104.7	0.3	104.4	-0.3	104.0	-0.4	103.5	-0.5	103.5	0.0	104.0	0.5	104.2	0.2	104.3	0.1
1986	104.2	-0.1	104.1	-0.1	103.9	-0.2	104.1	0.2	103.9	-0.2	104.0	0.1	104.2	0.2	103.5	-0.7	102.9	-0.6	103.2	0.3	103.3	0.1	103.2	-0.1
1987	103.7	0.5	103.7	0.0	103.9	0.2	105.4	1.4	105.8	0.4	106.7	0.9	108.0	1.2	107.9	-0.1	109.3	1.3	110.3	0.9	110.8	0.5	111.1	0.3
1988	111.8	0.6	112.8	0.9	113.2	0.4	113.9	0.6	114.2	0.3	114.6	0.4	114.9	0.3	115.1	0.2	114.3	-0.7	114.2	-0.1	114.5	0.3	115.0	0.4
1989	115.5	0.4	113.9	-1.4	114.0	0.1	114.0	0.0	113.9	-0.1	114.5	0.5	115.5	0.9	115.7	0.2	115.8	0.1	116.5	0.6	116.5	0.0	116.7	0.2
1990	117.2	0.4	117.3	0.1	117.2	-0.1	117.3	0.1	117.2	-0.1	116.4	-0.7	117.6	1.0	117.2	-0.3	116.7	-0.4	116.8	0.1	117.5	0.6	117.8	0.3
1991	117.2	-0.5	116.7	-0.4	116.6	-0.1	116.6	0.0	116.8	0.2	116.6	-0.2	117.1	0.4	117.9	0.7	118.0	0.1	118.1	0.1	118.3	0.2	119.2	0.8
1992	119.8	0.5	120.2	0.3	120.3	0.1	120.7	0.3	121.2	0.4	121.5	0.2	121.5	0.0	121.2	-0.2	121.0	-0.2	120.5	-0.4	119.8	-0.6	120.1	0.3
1993	120.1	0.0	119.8	-0.2	119.5	-0.3	119.6	0.1	118.4	-1.0	119.0	0.5	118.8	-0.2	118.8	0.0	117.0	-1.5	118.0	0.9	116.9	-0.9	116.9	0.0

Source: U.S. Department of Labor, Bureau of Labor Statistics, Division of Industry Prices and Price Indexes. n.e.c. stands for not elsewhere classified. - indicates no data collected for period or unavailable.

Finished Fabrics

Producer Price Index
Base 1982 = 100

For 1975-1993. Columns headed % show percentile change in the index from the previous period for which an index is available.

Year	Jan Index	%	Feb Index	%	Mar Index	%	Apr Index	%	May Index	%	Jun Index	%	Jul Index	%	Aug Index	%	Sep Index	%	Oct Index	%	Nov Index	%	Dec Index	%
1975	-	-	-	-	-	-	-	-	-	-	-	-	-	-	-	-	-	-	-	-	-	-	80.3	-
1976	79.8	-0.6	80.9	1.4	81.7	1.0	82.4	0.9	81.8	-0.7	81.4	-0.5	81.1	-0.4	81.2	0.1	80.7	-0.6	80.5	-0.2	81.4	1.1	81.5	0.1
1977	80.9	-0.7	81.7	1.0	82.7	1.2	83.7	1.2	84.3	0.7	84.2	-0.1	83.9	-0.4	83.9	0.0	83.8	-0.1	83.7	-0.1	83.1	-0.7	83.2	0.1
1978	83.2	0.0	83.3	0.1	82.7	-0.7	82.8	0.1	82.9	0.1	82.8	-0.1	82.9	0.1	83.0	0.1	83.6	0.7	83.9	0.4	84.2	0.4	85.1	1.1
1979	83.1	-2.4	83.6	0.6	84.6	1.2	85.0	0.5	85.9	1.1	86.4	0.6	86.9	0.6	87.5	0.7	87.6	0.1	87.4	-0.2	88.1	0.8	88.2	0.1
1980	88.7	0.6	89.2	0.6	90.9	1.9	91.9	1.1	92.6	0.8	93.0	0.4	93.6	0.6	93.8	0.2	93.9	0.1	95.0	1.2	95.6	0.6	96.5	0.9
1981	98.1	1.7	98.7	0.6	98.9	0.2	100.3	1.4	100.9	0.6	100.8	-0.1	101.1	0.3	101.8	0.7	101.8	0.0	101.7	-0.1	101.6	-0.1	100.8	-0.8
1982	101.8	1.0	102.1	0.3	100.8	-1.3	100.6	-0.2	100.5	-0.1	99.5	-1.0	99.4	-0.1	99.8	0.4	99.3	-0.5	98.9	-0.4	98.7	-0.2	98.6	-0.1
1983	98.1	-0.5	98.2	0.1	98.3	0.1	98.9	0.6	98.6	-0.3	98.3	-0.3	98.3	0.0	99.2	0.9	99.0	-0.2	99.4	0.4	99.9	0.5	100.2	0.3
1984	100.2	0.0	101.4	1.2	101.9	0.5	101.9	0.0	102.2	0.3	102.0	-0.2	101.9	-0.1	102.1	0.2	102.2	0.1	101.8	-0.4	101.7	-0.1	101.6	-0.1
1985	101.6	0.0	102.0	0.4	102.0	0.0	102.1	0.1	101.0	-1.1	100.9	-0.1	100.8	-0.1	101.1	0.3	101.3	0.2	101.3	0.0	101.2	-0.1	101.1	-0.1
1986	101.3	0.2	101.1	-0.2	101.3	0.2	101.3	0.0	101.5	0.2	101.5	0.0	101.6	0.1	101.6	0.0	101.4	-0.2	101.3	-0.1	101.3	0.0	101.3	0.0
1987	102.7	1.4	103.0	0.3	103.1	0.1	103.4	0.3	103.7	0.3	104.0	0.3	104.0	0.0	104.6	0.6	104.7	0.1	105.5	0.8	105.9	0.4	106.2	0.3
1988	106.9	0.7	108.2	1.2	109.0	0.7	109.2	0.2	109.3	0.1	109.6	0.3	109.4	-0.2	109.4	0.0	109.9	0.5	110.1	0.2	111.0	0.8	110.8	-0.2
1989	111.7	0.8	112.1	0.4	112.6	0.4	112.9	0.3	113.5	0.5	113.8	0.3	113.9	0.1	114.1	0.2	114.2	0.1	114.6	0.4	114.9	0.3	115.0	0.1
1990	115.5	0.4	115.6	0.1	115.7	0.1	116.0	0.3	115.9	-0.1	116.0	0.1	115.8	-0.2	115.8	0.0	115.8	0.0	116.4	0.5	116.4	0.0	116.5	0.1
1991	116.7	0.2	117.1	0.3	117.3	0.2	117.4	0.1	117.5	0.1	117.4	-0.1	117.6	0.2	117.8	0.2	118.0	0.2	117.9	-0.1	118.0	0.1	117.8	-0.2
1992	118.1	0.3	118.4	0.3	118.4	0.0	118.6	0.2	118.7	0.1	119.1	0.3	118.9	-0.2	119.0	0.1	119.0	0.0	119.2	0.2	119.3	0.1	119.2	-0.1
1993	119.4	0.2	119.4	0.0	119.4	0.0	119.5	0.1	120.0	0.4	119.8	-0.2	119.6	-0.2	119.5	-0.1	119.4	-0.1	119.4	0.0	119.4	0.0	119.2	-0.2

Source: U.S. Department of Labor, Bureau of Labor Statistics, Division of Industry Prices and Price Indexes. n.e.c. stands for not elsewhere classified. - indicates no data collected for period or unavailable.

Apparel & Other Fabricated Textile Products
Producer Price Index
Base 1982 = 100

For 1977-1993. Columns headed % show percentile change in the index from the previous period for which an index is available.

Year	Jan Index	%	Feb Index	%	Mar Index	%	Apr Index	%	May Index	%	Jun Index	%	Jul Index	%	Aug Index	%	Sep Index	%	Oct Index	%	Nov Index	%	Dec Index	%
1977	-	-	-	-	-	-	-	-	-	-	-	-	-	-	-	-	-	-	-	-	-	-	76.2	-
1978	76.5	0.4	76.7	0.3	76.9	0.3	77.1	0.3	77.3	0.3	77.8	0.6	78.2	0.5	78.4	0.3	78.3	-0.1	78.6	0.4	79.1	0.6	79.4	0.4
1979	80.1	0.9	80.4	0.4	80.8	0.5	81.4	0.7	81.4	0.0	82.1	0.9	82.2	0.1	82.8	0.7	83.1	0.4	83.4	0.4	83.8	0.5	83.7	-0.1
1980	85.0	1.6	85.6	0.7	86.6	1.2	87.5	1.0	87.6	0.1	88.6	1.1	89.7	1.2	90.0	0.3	90.1	0.1	90.6	0.6	91.3	0.8	91.6	0.3
1981	92.9	1.4	93.3	0.4	93.6	0.3	94.8	1.3	95.3	0.5	95.7	0.4	96.3	0.6	96.6	0.3	97.0	0.4	97.8	0.8	98.2	0.4	98.3	0.1
1982	99.3	1.0	99.6	0.3	99.8	0.2	100.1	0.3	100.1	0.0	100.3	0.2	100.1	-0.2	100.2	0.1	100.4	0.2	100.5	0.1	100.3	-0.2	99.4	-0.9
1983	100.0	0.6	100.1	0.1	100.5	0.4	100.3	-0.2	100.8	0.5	101.2	0.4	101.4	0.2	101.5	0.1	101.6	0.1	101.5	-0.1	101.8	0.3	101.7	-0.1
1984	102.2	0.5	102.4	0.2	102.5	0.1	102.6	0.1	102.8	0.2	102.6	-0.2	102.9	0.3	102.8	-0.1	103.3	0.5	103.3	0.0	103.4	0.1	103.2	-0.2
1985	103.5	0.3	103.7	0.2	103.8	0.1	104.0	0.2	104.0	0.0	104.0	0.0	104.2	0.2	104.5	0.3	104.4	-0.1	104.5	0.1	104.8	0.3	105.0	0.2
1986	105.0	0.0	105.3	0.3	105.6	0.3	105.4	-0.2	105.5	0.1	105.5	0.0	105.6	0.1	105.5	-0.1	105.6	0.1	105.8	0.2	105.9	0.1	105.9	0.0
1987	106.0	0.1	106.2	0.2	106.5	0.3	106.7	0.2	106.7	0.0	107.0	0.3	107.4	0.4	107.7	0.3	108.0	0.3	108.1	0.1	108.1	0.0	108.6	0.5
1988	109.1	0.5	109.3	0.2	109.6	0.3	109.7	0.1	109.9	0.2	110.4	0.5	110.7	0.3	110.8	0.1	111.1	0.3	111.2	0.1	111.3	0.1	111.6	0.3
1989	112.1	0.4	112.5	0.4	112.2	-0.3	112.4	0.2	112.5	0.1	112.6	0.1	113.0	0.4	113.4	0.4	113.6	0.2	113.7	0.1	114.0	0.3	114.2	0.2
1990	115.3	1.0	115.3	0.0	115.4	0.1	115.7	0.3	115.7	0.0	116.0	0.3	116.1	0.1	116.4	0.3	116.5	0.1	116.6	0.1	116.6	0.0	116.3	-0.3
1991	116.9	0.5	117.3	0.3	117.5	0.2	117.8	0.3	117.8	0.0	118.1	0.3	118.2	0.1	118.4	0.2	118.5	0.1	118.7	0.2	118.9	0.2	119.0	0.1
1992	119.8	0.7	120.0	0.2	120.2	0.2	120.2	0.0	120.1	-0.1	120.2	0.1	120.3	0.1	120.5	0.2	120.8	0.2	121.0	0.2	121.1	0.1	121.1	0.0
1993	121.3	0.2	121.3	0.0	121.4	0.1	121.5	0.1	121.6	0.1	121.3	-0.2	121.7	0.3	121.7	0.0	121.8	0.1	121.7	-0.1	121.7	0.0	121.5	-0.2

Source: U.S. Department of Labor, Bureau of Labor Statistics, Division of Industry Prices and Price Indexes. n.e.c. stands for not elsewhere classified. - indicates no data collected for period or unavailable.

Miscellaneous Textile Products/Services
Producer Price Index
Base June 1985 = 100

For 1985-1993. Columns headed % show percentile change in the index from the previous period for which an index is available.

Year	Jan Index	%	Feb Index	%	Mar Index	%	Apr Index	%	May Index	%	Jun Index	%	Jul Index	%	Aug Index	%	Sep Index	%	Oct Index	%	Nov Index	%	Dec Index	%
1985	-	-	-	-	-	-	-	-	-	-	100.0	-	99.7	-0.3	99.3	-0.4	99.2	-0.1	99.2	0.0	99.2	0.0	97.7	-1.5
1986	97.8	0.1	98.2	0.4	98.3	0.1	96.4	-1.9	96.6	0.2	96.5	-0.1	95.4	-1.1	94.1	-1.4	94.0	-0.1	95.2	1.3	96.2	1.1	97.5	1.4
1987	97.2	-0.3	97.8	0.6	97.8	0.0	97.8	0.0	97.7	-0.1	98.1	0.4	98.5	0.4	99.2	0.7	99.8	0.6	99.8	0.0	100.1	0.3	100.7	0.6
1988	102.7	2.0	103.4	0.7	104.3	0.9	104.9	0.6	105.0	0.1	105.2	0.2	105.3	0.1	105.3	0.0	105.2	-0.1	106.2	1.0	107.8	1.5	107.9	0.1
1989	109.3	1.3	109.8	0.5	109.6	-0.2	109.4	-0.2	109.5	0.1	110.9	1.3	113.6	2.4	113.8	0.2	113.9	0.1	113.7	-0.2	113.8	0.1	113.7	-0.1
1990	113.7	0.0	113.9	0.2	114.0	0.1	113.9	-0.1	113.6	-0.3	114.0	0.4	114.0	0.0	114.1	0.1	113.9	-0.2	113.9	0.0	114.3	0.4	114.3	0.0
1991	115.9	1.4	112.6	-2.8	112.0	-0.5	111.4	-0.5	111.7	0.3	111.9	0.2	111.7	-0.2	115.2	3.1	115.1	-0.1	114.6	-0.4	115.0	0.3	114.2	-0.7
1992	114.4	0.2	114.5	0.1	114.7	0.2	114.5	-0.2	114.7	0.2	114.8	0.1	114.8	0.0	114.8	0.0	115.3	0.4	115.3	0.0	115.3	0.0	115.3	0.0
1993	115.6	0.3	115.4	-0.2	115.5	0.1	115.9	0.3	115.7	-0.2	116.0	0.3	116.1	0.1	115.9	-0.2	116.3	0.3	116.3	0.0	116.5	0.2	116.5	0.0

Source: U.S. Department of Labor, Bureau of Labor Statistics, Division of Industry Prices and Price Indexes. n.e.c. stands for not elsewhere classified. - indicates no data collected for period or unavailable.

HIDES, SKINS, LEATHER, AND RELATED PRODUCTS
Producer Price Index
Base 1982 = 100

For 1926-1993. Columns headed % show percentile change in the index from the previous period for which an index is available.

Year	Jan Index	%	Feb Index	%	Mar Index	%	Apr Index	%	May Index	%	Jun Index	%	Jul Index	%	Aug Index	%	Sep Index	%	Oct Index	%	Nov Index	%	Dec Index	%
1926	17.6	-	17.3	-1.7	17.1	-1.2	16.9	-1.2	16.9	0.0	16.9	0.0	16.9	0.0	17.0	0.6	16.9	-0.6	17.2	1.8	17.1	-0.6	17.1	0.0
1927	17.2	0.6	17.1	-0.6	17.1	0.0	17.4	1.8	17.7	1.7	18.3	3.4	19.0	3.8	19.0	0.0	19.2	1.1	19.2	0.0	19.4	1.0	19.9	2.6
1928	20.6	3.5	21.1	2.4	21.1	0.0	21.6	2.4	21.5	-0.5	21.1	-1.9	21.1	0.0	20.6	-2.4	20.6	0.0	20.0	-2.9	19.7	-1.5	19.7	0.0
1929	19.3	-2.0	18.6	-3.6	18.4	-1.1	18.4	0.0	18.2	-1.1	18.4	1.1	18.6	1.1	18.7	0.5	18.9	1.1	18.8	-0.5	18.5	-1.6	18.4	-0.5
1930	17.9	-2.7	17.7	-1.1	17.6	-0.6	17.5	-0.6	17.5	0.0	17.5	0.0	17.2	-1.7	16.9	-1.7	17.0	0.6	16.5	-2.9	16.1	-2.4	15.6	-3.1
1931	15.1	-3.2	14.8	-2.0	14.9	0.7	14.9	0.0	14.9	0.0	15.0	0.7	15.3	2.0	15.1	-1.3	14.5	-4.0	14.1	-2.8	13.9	-1.4	13.6	-2.2
1932	13.5	-0.7	13.4	-0.7	13.2	-1.5	12.8	-3.0	12.4	-3.1	12.1	-2.4	11.7	-3.3	11.9	1.7	12.3	3.4	12.4	0.8	12.2	-1.6	11.9	-2.5
1933	11.8	-0.8	11.6	-1.7	11.6	0.0	11.8	1.7	13.1	11.0	14.1	7.6	14.7	4.3	15.6	6.1	15.8	1.3	15.2	-3.8	15.1	-0.7	15.2	0.7
1934	15.3	0.7	15.3	0.0	15.1	-1.3	15.2	0.7	15.0	-1.3	14.9	-0.7	14.7	-1.3	14.3	-2.7	14.4	0.7	14.3	-0.7	14.4	0.7	14.5	0.7
1935	14.7	1.4	14.7	0.0	14.6	-0.7	14.7	0.7	15.1	2.7	15.2	0.7	15.2	0.0	15.3	0.7	15.5	1.3	16.0	3.2	16.3	1.9	16.3	0.0
1936	16.6	1.8	16.4	-1.2	16.2	-1.2	16.1	-0.6	16.0	-0.6	16.0	0.0	16.0	0.0	16.0	0.0	16.1	0.6	16.3	1.2	16.5	1.2	17.0	3.0
1937	17.4	2.4	17.5	0.6	17.7	1.1	18.2	2.8	18.2	0.0	18.2	0.0	18.2	0.0	18.4	1.1	18.4	0.0	18.2	-1.1	17.3	-4.9	16.7	-3.5
1938	16.5	-1.2	16.2	-1.8	16.0	-1.2	15.7	-1.9	15.6	-0.6	15.4	-1.3	15.6	1.3	15.7	0.6	15.7	0.0	16.0	1.9	16.1	0.6	15.9	-1.2
1939	15.9	0.0	15.7	-1.3	15.6	-0.6	15.5	-0.6	15.6	0.6	15.8	1.3	15.8	0.0	15.8	0.0	16.8	6.3	17.9	6.5	17.7	-1.1	17.7	0.0
1940	17.7	0.0	17.5	-1.1	17.4	-0.6	17.4	0.0	17.3	-0.6	16.9	-2.3	16.9	0.0	16.5	-2.4	16.8	1.8	17.1	1.8	17.5	2.3	17.5	0.0
1941	17.5	0.0	17.4	-0.6	17.5	0.6	17.7	1.1	18.2	2.8	18.4	1.1	18.7	1.6	18.8	0.5	19.0	1.1	19.2	1.1	19.5	1.6	19.6	0.5
1942	19.6	0.0	19.7	0.5	19.9	1.0	20.4	2.5	20.3	-0.5	20.2	-0.5	20.2	0.0	20.2	0.0	20.1	-0.5	20.1	0.0	20.1	0.0	20.1	0.0
1943	20.1	0.0	20.1	0.0	20.1	0.0	20.1	0.0	20.1	0.0	20.1	0.0	20.1	0.0	20.1	0.0	20.1	0.0	20.1	0.0	19.9	-1.0	20.0	0.5
1944	20.0	0.0	20.0	0.0	20.0	0.0	20.0	0.0	20.0	0.0	19.9	-0.5	19.8	-0.5	19.8	0.0	19.8	0.0	19.8	0.0	19.8	0.0	20.0	1.0
1945	20.1	0.5	20.1	0.0	20.1	0.0	20.1	0.0	20.1	0.0	20.1	0.0	20.1	0.0	20.1	0.0	20.3	1.0	20.3	0.0	20.3	0.0	20.3	0.0
1946	20.4	0.5	20.4	0.0	20.4	0.0	20.4	0.0	20.6	1.0	20.9	1.5	24.1	15.3	23.7	-1.7	24.2	2.1	24.3	0.4	29.4	21.0	30.2	2.7
1947	30.1	-0.3	30.3	0.7	30.5	0.7	30.2	-1.0	30.0	-0.7	30.2	0.7	31.0	2.6	31.9	2.9	32.2	0.9	34.0	5.6	35.2	3.5	35.0	-0.6
1948	34.2	-2.3	32.6	-4.7	31.3	-4.0	31.7	1.3	32.2	1.6	32.1	-0.3	32.4	0.9	31.9	-1.5	31.6	-0.9	31.3	-0.9	31.9	1.9	31.6	-0.9
1949	31.5	-0.3	30.7	-2.5	30.2	-1.6	30.1	-0.3	30.0	-0.3	30.0	0.0	29.7	-1.0	30.0	1.0	30.4	1.3	30.7	1.0	30.8	0.3	30.7	-0.3
1950	30.2	-1.6	30.2	0.0	30.5	1.0	30.5	0.0	30.8	1.0	31.1	1.0	32.5	4.5	33.4	2.8	34.7	3.9	35.4	2.0	36.6	3.4	38.1	4.1
1951	39.9	4.7	40.1	0.5	39.8	-0.7	39.7	-0.3	39.6	-0.3	39.1	-1.3	38.4	-1.8	37.0	-3.6	37.0	0.0	35.7	-3.5	33.6	-5.9	33.0	-1.8
1952	32.1	-2.7	31.2	-2.8	30.8	-1.3	29.5	-4.2	29.7	0.7	30.1	1.3	30.2	0.3	30.3	0.3	30.3	0.0	30.3	0.0	30.7	1.3	31.1	1.3
1953	30.5	-1.9	30.8	1.0	30.8	0.0	30.7	-0.3	31.5	2.6	31.7	0.6	31.4	-0.9	31.4	0.0	31.3	-0.3	30.5	-2.6	30.5	0.0	30.0	-1.6
1954	29.9	-0.3	29.8	-0.3	29.7	-0.3	29.7	0.0	30.1	1.3	30.0	-0.3	29.8	-0.7	29.5	-1.0	29.2	-1.0	29.0	-0.7	29.1	0.3	28.8	-1.0
1955	28.8	0.0	29.0	0.7	28.9	-0.3	29.3	1.4	29.2	-0.3	29.2	0.0	29.4	0.7	29.4	0.0	29.5	0.3	29.9	1.4	30.2	1.0	30.3	0.3
1956	30.3	0.0	30.5	0.7	30.7	0.7	31.6	2.9	31.4	-0.6	31.4	0.0	31.4	0.0	31.4	0.0	31.4	0.0	31.3	-0.3	31.3	0.0	31.1	-0.6
1957	30.9	-0.6	30.8	-0.3	30.9	0.3	31.0	0.3	31.0	0.0	31.3	1.0	31.6	1.0	31.5	-0.3	31.4	-0.3	31.4	0.0	31.4	0.0	31.2	-0.6
1958	31.2	0.0	31.3	0.3	31.2	-0.3	31.3	0.3	31.4	0.3	31.5	0.3	31.5	0.0	31.5	0.0	31.4	-0.3	31.8	1.3	32.1	0.9	32.5	1.2
1959	32.7	0.6	33.1	1.2	34.1	3.0	37.0	8.5	37.2	0.5	37.3	0.3	37.5	0.5	37.6	0.3	37.4	-0.5	36.5	-2.4	35.1	-3.8	35.3	0.6
1960	35.4	0.3	35.1	-0.8	35.1	0.0	35.2	0.3	34.9	-0.9	34.6	-0.9	34.6	0.0	34.1	-1.4	33.9	-0.6	34.1	0.6	34.1	0.0	34.2	0.3
1961	34.0	-0.6	33.9	-0.3	34.3	1.2	34.5	0.6	34.8	0.9	34.6	-0.6	34.9	0.9	35.5	1.7	35.6	0.3	35.8	0.6	35.7	-0.3	35.6	-0.3
1962	35.6	0.0	35.4	-0.6	35.3	-0.3	35.1	-0.6	35.3	0.6	35.5	0.6	35.3	-0.6	35.2	-0.3	35.3	0.3	35.3	0.0	35.3	0.0	35.1	-0.6
1963	34.8	-0.9	34.6	-0.6	34.6	0.0	34.3	-0.9	34.5	0.6	34.3	-0.6	34.3	0.0	34.1	-0.6	33.9	-0.6	34.0	0.3	34.0	0.0	33.8	-0.6
1964	33.8	0.0	33.7	-0.3	33.7	0.0	34.3	1.8	34.4	0.3	34.5	0.3	34.6	0.3	34.7	0.3	34.6	-0.3	34.8	0.6	34.7	-0.3	34.6	-0.3
1965	34.5	-0.3	34.6	0.3	34.8	0.6	35.0	0.6	35.3	0.9	35.4	0.3	35.8	1.1	36.9	3.1	36.6	-0.8	37.2	1.6	37.4	0.5	37.7	0.8
1966	38.2	1.3	38.7	1.3	39.0	0.8	39.6	1.5	40.4	2.0	40.4	0.0	40.4	0.0	39.9	-1.2	39.4	-1.3	39.0	-1.0	38.6	-1.0	38.6	0.0
1967	38.8	0.5	38.8	0.0	38.5	-0.8	38.0	-1.3	37.9	-0.3	38.0	0.3	37.9	-0.3	37.5	-1.1	37.7	0.5	37.7	0.0	38.0	0.8	38.2	0.5
1968	38.3	0.3	38.4	0.3	38.8	1.0	38.9	0.3	39.1	0.5	39.0	-0.3	39.3	0.8	39.3	0.0	39.7	1.0	40.2	1.3	40.2	0.0	40.4	0.5
1969	40.6	0.5	40.6	0.0	40.6	0.0	41.5	2.2	41.5	0.0	41.3	-0.5	41.6	0.7	41.7	0.2	42.3	1.4	42.0	-0.7	42.0	0.0	41.8	-0.5
1970	42.0	0.5	42.0	0.0	42.0	0.0	42.3	0.7	42.1	-0.5	41.8	-0.7	41.8	0.0	41.8	0.0	41.8	0.0	42.0	0.5	42.2	0.5	42.0	-0.5

[Continued]

HIDES, SKINS, LEATHER, AND RELATED PRODUCTS
Producer Price Index
Base 1982 = 100
[Continued]

For 1926-1993. Columns headed % show percentile change in the index from the previous period for which an index is available.

Year	Jan Index	%	Feb Index	%	Mar Index	%	Apr Index	%	May Index	%	Jun Index	%	Jul Index	%	Aug Index	%	Sep Index	%	Oct Index	%	Nov Index	%	Dec Index	%
1971	42.6	1.4	42.8	0.5	42.8	0.0	43.4	1.4	43.6	0.5	43.5	-0.2	43.5	0.0	43.6	0.2	43.7	0.2	43.7	0.0	43.8	0.2	44.2	0.9
1972	44.9	1.6	45.4	1.1	46.8	3.1	48.4	3.4	49.3	1.9	49.8	1.0	50.1	0.6	51.3	2.4	51.7	0.8	53.2	2.9	54.8	3.0	54.1	-1.3
1973	54.8	1.3	55.2	0.7	54.6	-1.1	55.2	1.1	54.1	-2.0	53.6	-0.9	53.8	0.4	54.4	1.1	54.7	0.6	54.7	0.0	54.5	-0.4	54.0	-0.9
1974	54.3	0.6	54.6	0.6	54.6	0.0	55.4	1.5	55.7	0.5	55.6	-0.2	55.8	0.4	55.7	-0.2	56.4	1.3	55.3	-2.0	55.0	-0.5	54.5	-0.9
1975	54.1	-0.7	54.0	-0.2	54.5	0.9	56.2	3.1	56.2	0.0	56.6	0.7	56.8	0.4	56.9	0.2	57.6	1.2	58.0	0.7	58.8	1.4	58.9	0.2
1976	60.2	2.2	61.2	1.7	62.0	1.3	63.3	2.1	64.8	2.4	64.0	-1.2	64.9	1.4	65.3	0.6	66.1	1.2	65.1	-1.5	64.6	-0.8	65.3	1.1
1977	66.8	2.3	67.3	0.7	67.7	0.6	68.5	1.2	69.3	1.2	68.3	-1.4	68.5	0.3	68.6	0.1	68.4	-0.3	68.2	-0.3	68.5	0.4	69.1	0.9
1978	70.8	2.5	71.3	0.7	71.5	0.3	73.1	2.2	73.7	0.8	74.3	0.8	75.1	1.1	78.1	4.0	80.2	2.7	81.1	1.1	82.1	1.2	82.3	0.2
1979	85.1	3.4	88.4	3.9	96.5	9.2	98.6	2.2	102.6	4.1	102.0	-0.6	99.7	-2.3	98.2	-1.5	95.6	-2.6	96.7	1.2	94.8	-2.0	94.9	0.1
1980	97.3	2.5	95.5	-1.8	94.0	-1.6	92.7	-1.4	91.6	-1.2	91.7	0.1	93.3	1.7	95.7	2.6	94.3	-1.5	95.6	1.4	97.2	1.7	97.8	0.6
1981	98.3	0.5	98.1	-0.2	99.4	1.3	100.3	0.9	100.4	0.1	99.6	-0.8	99.4	-0.2	99.5	0.1	99.6	0.1	99.0	-0.6	98.9	-0.1	99.2	0.3
1982	99.7	0.5	99.6	-0.1	99.2	-0.4	100.3	1.1	100.2	-0.1	99.7	-0.5	100.2	0.5	99.8	-0.4	100.3	0.5	100.2	-0.1	100.2	0.0	100.6	0.4
1983	101.5	0.9	100.6	-0.9	100.9	0.3	101.8	0.9	102.6	0.8	103.3	0.7	103.7	0.4	104.6	0.9	104.5	-0.1	104.2	-0.3	105.5	1.2	105.6	0.1
1984	106.3	0.7	107.9	1.5	109.2	1.2	109.2	0.0	109.9	0.6	110.5	0.5	110.0	-0.5	109.9	-0.1	109.9	0.0	109.5	-0.4	108.1	-1.3	108.0	-0.1
1985	108.0	0.0	108.0	0.0	107.5	-0.5	108.4	0.8	108.2	-0.2	108.7	0.5	108.4	-0.3	109.0	0.6	109.3	0.3	109.9	0.5	110.4	0.5	111.3	0.8
1986	111.8	0.4	112.0	0.2	111.8	-0.2	112.3	0.4	112.9	0.5	113.4	0.4	113.2	-0.2	113.1	-0.1	112.9	-0.2	113.4	0.4	114.0	0.5	114.8	0.7
1987	114.9	0.1	115.0	0.1	116.5	1.3	118.3	1.5	120.7	2.0	120.2	-0.4	121.0	0.7	121.3	0.2	123.0	1.4	124.1	0.9	124.3	0.2	125.7	1.1
1988	128.4	2.1	129.1	0.5	132.6	2.7	134.2	1.2	134.6	0.3	131.2	-2.5	130.1	-0.8	131.6	1.2	132.5	0.7	131.9	-0.5	130.4	-1.1	130.1	-0.2
1989	131.2	0.8	133.2	1.5	136.8	2.7	136.1	-0.5	134.8	-1.0	135.2	0.3	136.9	1.3	137.2	0.2	138.0	0.6	138.2	0.1	138.0	-0.1	139.5	1.1
1990	138.9	-0.4	141.7	2.0	141.6	-0.1	142.9	0.9	143.7	0.6	143.0	-0.5	142.8	-0.1	142.2	-0.4	141.4	-0.6	140.9	-0.4	140.5	-0.3	140.6	0.1
1991	140.2	-0.3	140.0	-0.1	140.4	0.3	141.1	0.5	140.4	-0.5	140.0	-0.3	138.3	-1.2	138.1	-0.1	136.6	-1.1	136.3	-0.2	137.1	0.6	137.6	0.4
1992	138.6	0.7	139.0	0.3	139.8	0.6	139.9	0.1	140.7	0.6	140.8	0.1	140.1	-0.5	140.8	0.5	140.9	0.1	141.0	0.1	140.6	-0.3	142.0	1.0
1993	143.6	1.1	142.5	-0.8	142.9	0.3	143.6	0.5	143.8	0.1	143.7	-0.1	143.5	-0.1	143.9	0.3	144.1	0.1	143.7	-0.3	143.9	0.1	144.3	0.3

Source: U.S. Department of Labor, Bureau of Labor Statistics, Division of Industry Prices and Price Indexes. n.e.c. stands for not elsewhere classified. - indicates no data collected for period or unavailable.

Hides and Skins

Producer Price Index
Base 1982 = 100

For 1926-1993. Columns headed % show percentile change in the index from the previous period for which an index is available.

Year	Jan Index	%	Feb Index	%	Mar Index	%	Apr Index	%	May Index	%	Jun Index	%	Jul Index	%	Aug Index	%	Sep Index	%	Oct Index	%	Nov Index	%	Dec Index	%
1926	23.1	-	21.3	-7.8	20.0	-6.1	18.7	-6.5	19.4	3.7	19.3	-0.5	19.9	3.1	20.6	3.5	19.6	-4.9	21.7	10.7	21.1	-2.8	21.1	0.0
1927	21.5	1.9	20.8	-3.3	20.9	0.5	22.1	5.7	23.4	5.9	25.3	8.1	27.3	7.9	26.8	-1.8	26.3	-1.9	26.2	-0.4	26.9	2.7	27.9	3.7
1928	30.9	10.8	32.4	4.9	32.2	-0.6	34.2	6.2	33.6	-1.8	31.7	-5.7	31.8	0.3	28.8	-9.4	29.0	0.7	26.6	-8.3	26.6	0.0	26.8	0.8
1929	25.4	-5.2	21.7	-14.6	22.1	1.8	22.1	0.0	21.4	-3.2	22.6	5.6	23.4	3.5	24.0	2.6	24.8	3.3	24.1	-2.8	22.3	-7.5	22.0	-1.3
1930	21.3	-3.2	20.2	-5.2	19.6	-3.0	19.6	0.0	19.8	1.0	20.2	2.0	19.2	-5.0	18.6	-3.1	19.2	3.2	17.1	-10.9	15.4	-9.9	14.1	-8.4
1931	13.2	-6.4	11.8	-10.6	12.7	7.6	12.7	0.0	12.8	0.8	13.4	4.7	14.9	11.2	14.1	-5.4	12.0	-14.9	10.2	-15.0	10.0	-2.0	10.0	0.0
1932	10.0	0.0	9.5	-5.0	9.1	-4.2	8.3	-8.8	7.3	-12.0	6.6	-9.6	6.9	4.5	8.0	15.9	9.9	23.7	10.1	2.0	9.5	-5.9	8.5	-10.5
1933	8.8	3.5	8.4	-4.5	8.5	1.2	9.4	10.6	13.8	46.8	16.6	20.3	18.1	9.0	18.7	3.3	17.2	-8.0	14.5	-15.7	14.4	-0.7	15.2	5.6
1934	15.8	3.9	16.0	1.3	15.0	-6.3	15.7	4.7	15.0	-4.5	14.3	-4.7	13.6	-4.9	11.7	-14.0	12.3	5.1	12.2	-0.8	12.9	5.7	13.8	7.0
1935	14.5	5.1	14.2	-2.1	13.6	-4.2	14.5	6.6	15.6	7.6	16.0	2.6	16.3	1.9	16.4	0.6	17.1	4.3	19.0	11.1	19.7	3.7	19.7	0.0
1936	20.6	4.6	19.8	-3.9	18.6	-6.1	18.4	-1.1	17.8	-3.3	18.2	2.2	17.9	-1.6	18.4	2.8	19.1	3.8	19.8	3.7	20.7	4.5	22.6	9.2
1937	23.7	4.9	23.5	-0.8	24.2	3.0	24.8	2.5	24.0	-3.2	23.4	-2.5	23.8	1.7	24.9	4.6	24.6	-1.2	24.0	-2.4	19.3	-19.6	17.5	-9.3
1938	16.8	-4.0	15.3	-8.9	14.2	-7.2	12.8	-9.9	13.0	1.6	12.8	-1.5	14.5	13.3	15.4	6.2	15.5	0.6	16.8	8.4	17.5	4.2	16.1	-8.0
1939	16.0	-0.6	14.9	-6.9	15.1	1.3	14.0	-7.3	14.7	5.0	15.4	4.8	15.8	2.6	15.8	0.0	19.9	25.9	23.0	15.6	21.3	-7.4	21.5	0.9
1940	21.0	-2.3	19.8	-5.7	19.3	-2.5	19.4	0.5	18.8	-3.1	16.7	-11.2	17.3	3.6	15.8	-8.7	17.2	8.9	19.2	11.6	20.7	7.8	20.3	-1.9
1941	20.2	-0.5	19.4	-4.0	20.3	4.6	21.4	5.4	22.6	5.6	23.0	1.8	23.0	0.0	22.9	-0.4	22.9	0.0	23.1	0.9	23.3	0.9	23.7	1.7
1942	23.6	-0.4	23.6	0.0	23.8	0.8	25.3	6.3	24.8	-2.0	24.2	-2.4	24.2	0.0	24.3	0.4	24.1	-0.8	23.7	-1.7	23.7	0.0	23.7	0.0
1943	23.7	0.0	23.7	0.0	23.7	0.0	23.7	0.0	23.7	0.0	23.7	0.0	23.7	0.0	23.7	0.0	23.7	0.0	23.7	0.0	22.2	-6.3	22.8	2.7
1944	23.1	1.3	22.7	-1.7	22.7	0.0	22.7	0.0	22.9	0.9	22.2	-3.1	21.9	-1.4	21.6	-1.4	21.7	0.5	22.0	1.4	21.9	-0.5	23.3	6.4
1945	23.5	0.9	23.6	0.4	23.8	0.8	23.9	0.4	23.9	0.0	24.0	0.4	24.0	0.0	24.1	0.4	24.1	0.0	24.0	-0.4	24.0	0.0	24.0	0.0
1946	24.0	0.0	24.0	0.0	24.0	0.0	24.0	0.0	24.7	2.9	24.8	0.4	34.6	39.5	31.8	-8.1	31.0	-2.5	31.3	1.0	45.2	44.4	44.2	-2.2
1947	40.6	-8.1	42.7	5.2	43.8	2.6	41.4	-5.5	39.9	-3.6	41.7	4.5	46.1	10.6	49.6	7.6	50.4	1.6	55.6	10.3	60.5	8.8	58.7	-3.0
1948	53.7	-8.5	46.8	-12.8	39.3	-16.0	42.0	6.9	45.0	7.1	44.6	-0.9	46.6	4.5	44.4	-4.7	42.9	-3.4	41.3	-3.7	44.6	8.0	43.1	-3.4
1949	43.2	0.2	38.7	-10.4	37.0	-4.4	37.2	0.5	37.2	0.0	37.7	1.3	36.0	-4.5	38.0	5.6	40.0	5.3	40.8	2.0	40.5	-0.7	38.9	-4.0
1950	37.4	-3.9	37.0	-1.1	38.4	3.8	38.1	-0.8	39.0	2.4	41.2	5.6	45.1	9.5	46.6	3.3	52.6	12.9	52.5	-0.2	54.7	4.2	57.1	4.4
1951	61.5	7.7	58.8	-4.4	58.5	-0.5	57.0	-2.6	56.8	-0.4	56.5	-0.5	54.1	-4.2	49.5	-8.5	48.6	-1.8	47.8	-1.6	38.2	-20.1	35.7	-6.5
1952	30.4	-14.8	27.8	-8.6	26.0	-6.5	21.7	-16.5	25.4	17.1	26.0	2.4	27.0	3.8	28.1	4.1	28.1	0.0	28.4	1.1	30.2	6.3	30.8	2.0
1953	27.1	-12.0	29.0	7.0	28.3	-2.4	29.0	2.5	32.6	12.4	33.3	2.1	32.0	-3.9	32.6	1.9	32.4	-0.6	28.1	-13.3	28.0	-0.4	25.2	-10.0
1954	24.8	-1.6	24.2	-2.4	24.4	0.8	24.6	0.8	27.3	11.0	26.5	-2.9	25.4	-4.2	24.4	-3.9	22.5	-7.8	21.6	-4.0	23.0	6.5	20.7	-10.0
1955	21.6	4.3	22.5	4.2	22.1	-1.8	24.8	12.2	23.2	-6.5	24.3	4.7	25.4	4.5	25.7	1.2	26.6	3.5	27.2	2.3	26.3	-3.3	26.7	1.5
1956	24.7	-7.5	25.4	2.8	25.5	0.4	27.0	5.9	25.8	-4.4	26.7	3.5	26.4	-1.1	26.4	0.0	27.6	4.5	25.2	-8.7	25.8	2.4	23.5	-8.9
1957	22.7	-3.4	21.9	-3.5	22.2	1.4	22.6	1.8	24.4	8.0	25.9	6.1	27.1	4.6	26.8	-1.1	25.4	-5.2	24.8	-2.4	23.5	-5.2	22.0	-6.4
1958	22.1	0.5	22.3	0.9	22.3	0.0	23.2	4.0	24.2	4.3	24.9	2.9	25.4	2.0	26.4	3.9	25.8	-2.3	27.0	4.7	28.4	5.2	29.0	2.1
1959	30.0	3.4	31.8	6.0	38.3	20.4	47.4	23.8	43.0	-9.3	46.6	8.4	47.0	0.9	46.6	-0.9	44.7	-4.1	38.2	-14.5	29.3	-23.3	32.2	9.9
1960	32.2	0.0	30.4	-5.6	31.4	3.3	32.1	2.2	31.8	-0.9	29.3	-7.9	29.7	1.4	27.8	-6.4	27.2	-2.2	28.0	2.9	28.7	2.5	28.3	-1.4
1961	26.9	-4.9	26.4	-1.9	30.0	13.6	29.7	-1.0	31.0	4.4	29.7	-4.2	33.3	12.1	36.2	8.7	36.0	-0.6	35.9	-0.3	34.7	-3.3	33.3	-4.0
1962	32.6	-2.1	31.2	-4.3	30.7	-1.6	30.6	-0.3	31.2	2.0	32.1	2.9	30.8	-4.0	31.1	1.0	32.8	5.5	32.2	-1.8	31.7	-1.6	30.1	-5.0
1963	28.2	-6.3	25.4	-9.9	26.1	2.8	25.1	-3.8	25.9	3.2	25.4	-1.9	24.7	-2.8	23.8	-3.6	22.9	-3.8	23.8	3.9	24.5	2.9	22.6	-7.8
1964	22.5	-0.4	21.9	-2.7	22.4	2.3	26.1	16.5	25.4	-2.7	26.7	5.1	27.4	2.6	28.4	3.6	28.3	-0.4	28.2	-0.4	26.8	-5.0	26.7	-0.4
1965	25.6	-4.1	26.7	4.3	27.3	2.2	28.5	4.4	31.3	9.8	30.5	-2.6	34.7	13.8	39.5	13.8	37.0	-6.3	37.2	0.5	37.4	0.5	39.1	4.5
1966	41.4	5.9	45.2	9.2	43.7	-3.3	44.0	0.7	48.2	9.5	47.6	-1.2	46.3	-2.7	41.8	-9.7	39.7	-5.0	35.7	-10.1	33.8	-5.3	32.3	-4.4
1967	32.6	0.9	31.9	-2.1	29.3	-8.2	26.1	-10.9	25.8	-1.1	28.4	10.1	27.7	-2.5	25.7	-7.2	27.6	7.4	25.7	-6.9	26.9	4.7	26.8	-0.4
1968	26.1	-2.6	26.8	2.7	29.7	10.8	28.3	-4.7	29.0	2.5	28.2	-2.8	30.0	6.4	30.4	1.3	31.6	3.9	31.2	-1.3	31.7	1.6	31.6	-0.3
1969	32.3	2.2	31.4	-2.8	32.3	2.9	37.2	15.2	36.3	-2.4	34.7	-4.4	36.4	4.9	36.4	0.0	38.1	4.7	34.9	-8.4	32.7	-6.3	32.2	-1.5
1970	30.4	-5.6	29.9	-1.6	29.4	-1.7	31.6	7.5	30.1	-4.7	27.8	-7.6	26.9	-3.2	27.4	1.9	27.8	1.5	28.8	3.6	30.4	5.6	28.4	-6.6

[Continued]

Hides and Skins

Producer Price Index
Base 1982 = 100
[Continued]

For 1926-1993. Columns headed % show percentile change in the index from the previous period for which an index is available.

Year	Jan Index	%	Feb Index	%	Mar Index	%	Apr Index	%	May Index	%	Jun Index	%	Jul Index	%	Aug Index	%	Sep Index	%	Oct Index	%	Nov Index	%	Dec Index	%
1971	27.6	-2.8	29.3	6.2	29.4	0.3	33.8	15.0	33.9	0.3	31.8	-6.2	31.8	0.0	31.9	0.3	32.8	2.8	32.7	-0.3	34.3	4.9	35.8	4.4
1972	37.9	5.9	41.5	9.5	48.5	16.9	52.6	8.5	55.8	6.1	56.9	2.0	59.2	4.0	67.7	14.4	68.0	0.4	75.5	11.0	80.0	6.0	71.1	-11.1
1973	76.4	7.5	76.0	-0.5	68.7	-9.6	75.3	9.6	70.7	-6.1	67.3	-4.8	68.7	2.1	72.9	6.1	71.7	-1.6	71.4	-0.4	66.8	-6.4	63.4	-5.1
1974	61.6	-2.8	61.9	0.5	56.2	-9.2	58.9	4.8	60.9	3.4	57.7	-5.3	60.1	4.2	57.0	-5.2	54.3	-4.7	44.9	-17.3	43.6	-2.9	38.1	-12.6
1975	34.8	-8.7	34.1	-2.0	38.6	13.2	48.5	25.6	47.6	-1.9	50.9	6.9	52.1	2.4	52.0	-0.2	53.6	3.1	56.0	4.5	58.3	4.1	57.2	-1.9
1976	62.6	9.4	64.0	2.2	66.8	4.4	75.4	12.9	79.7	5.7	72.8	-8.7	77.7	6.7	79.4	2.2	81.4	2.5	70.1	-13.9	64.6	-7.8	70.0	8.4
1977	77.8	11.1	78.8	1.3	79.7	1.1	85.0	6.6	87.3	2.7	80.5	-7.8	81.3	1.0	80.4	-1.1	76.5	-4.9	74.3	-2.9	76.2	2.6	81.4	6.8
1978	83.7	2.8	83.1	-0.7	82.5	-0.7	89.4	8.4	89.7	0.3	96.6	7.7	100.5	4.0	111.7	11.1	121.4	8.7	119.3	-1.7	116.2	-2.6	111.9	-3.7
1979	126.2	12.8	138.8	10.0	178.3	28.5	179.0	0.4	185.9	3.9	170.3	-8.4	157.9	-7.3	142.7	-9.6	129.7	-9.1	133.5	2.9	124.8	-6.5	123.7	-0.9
1980	130.7	5.7	112.9	-13.6	97.2	-13.9	91.6	-5.8	80.8	-11.8	88.0	8.9	99.4	13.0	111.1	11.8	99.3	-10.6	106.4	7.2	114.0	7.1	109.5	-3.9
1981	105.2	-3.9	102.4	-2.7	-		-		-		-		-		-		-		-		-		-	
1982	-		-		-		-		-		-		-		-		-		-		-		-	
1983	-		-		-		-		-		-		-		-		-		-		-		-	
1984	-		-		-		-		-		-		-		-		-		-		-		-	
1985	-		-		-		-		-		-		-		-		-		-		-		-	
1986	-		-		-		-		-		-		-		-		-		-		-		-	
1987	-		-		-		-		-		-		-		-		-		-		-		178.0	73.8
1988	-		-		-		-		-		-		-		-		-		-		-		-	
1989	181.2	1.8	190.3	5.0	228.1	19.9	222.3	-2.5	207.8	-6.5	211.2	1.6	221.3	4.8	214.3	-3.2	217.1	1.3	218.8	0.8	216.9	-0.9	225.8	4.1
1990	203.8	-9.7	227.4	11.6	220.1	-3.2	234.4	6.5	233.0	-0.6	227.8	-2.2	227.4	-0.2	217.2	-4.5	210.3	-3.2	207.2	-1.5	204.0	-1.5	202.6	-0.7
1991	196.8	-2.9	190.6	-3.2	188.1	-1.3	198.1	5.3	184.0	-7.1	174.2	-5.3	166.6	-4.4	161.4	-3.1	152.1	-5.8	154.4	1.5	160.1	3.7	163.9	2.4
1992	164.5	0.4	168.5	2.4	168.4	-0.1	175.3	4.1	180.2	2.8	174.8	-3.0	171.5	-1.9	171.7	0.1	176.8	3.0	178.2	0.8	175.2	-1.7	183.0	4.5
1993	188.1	2.8	178.1	-5.3	180.6	1.4	185.8	2.9	186.6	0.4	181.6	-2.7	185.1	1.9	178.9	-3.3	187.1	4.6	184.0	-1.7	186.3	1.3	188.4	1.1

Source: U.S. Department of Labor, Bureau of Labor Statistics, Division of Industry Prices and Price Indexes. n.e.c. stands for not elsewhere classified. - indicates no data collected for period or unavailable.

Leather
Producer Price Index
Base 1982 = 100

For 1926-1993. Columns headed % show percentile change in the index from the previous period for which an index is available.

Year	Jan Index	%	Feb Index	%	Mar Index	%	Apr Index	%	May Index	%	Jun Index	%	Jul Index	%	Aug Index	%	Sep Index	%	Oct Index	%	Nov Index	%	Dec Index	%
1926	16.4	-	16.4	0.0	16.4	0.0	16.4	0.0	16.1	-1.8	16.1	0.0	16.0	-0.6	16.0	0.0	16.1	0.6	16.1	0.0	16.1	0.0	16.1	0.0
1927	16.1	0.0	16.1	0.0	16.2	0.6	16.2	0.0	16.7	3.1	17.4	4.2	18.3	5.2	18.5	1.1	18.7	1.1	18.9	1.1	18.9	0.0	19.8	4.8
1928	20.0	1.0	20.9	4.5	20.9	0.0	21.0	0.5	21.0	0.0	20.6	-1.9	20.8	1.0	20.8	0.0	20.4	-1.9	20.1	-1.5	19.2	-4.5	19.3	0.5
1929	19.5	1.0	18.9	-3.1	18.2	-3.7	18.0	-1.1	17.9	-0.6	17.9	0.0	18.1	1.1	18.0	-0.6	18.2	1.1	18.5	1.6	18.3	-1.1	17.9	-2.2
1930	17.5	-2.2	17.4	-0.6	17.4	0.0	17.0	-2.3	16.9	-0.6	16.6	-1.8	16.2	-2.4	16.2	0.0	15.9	-1.9	15.6	-1.9	15.1	-3.2	14.8	-2.0
1931	14.7	-0.7	14.4	-2.0	14.3	-0.7	14.3	0.0	14.2	-0.7	14.2	0.0	14.5	2.1	14.6	0.7	13.5	-7.5	13.0	-3.7	12.7	-2.3	12.7	0.0
1932	12.5	-1.6	12.4	-0.8	11.9	-4.0	10.9	-8.4	9.8	-10.1	9.5	-3.1	9.7	2.1	9.7	0.0	10.2	5.2	10.4	2.0	10.0	-3.8	9.5	-5.0
1933	9.2	-3.2	8.9	-3.3	9.0	1.1	9.2	2.2	11.0	19.6	12.0	9.1	12.6	5.0	13.3	5.6	13.8	3.8	13.5	-2.2	12.8	-5.2	12.9	0.8
1934	12.9	0.0	12.9	0.0	12.9	0.0	12.7	-1.6	12.3	-3.1	12.2	-0.8	12.1	-0.8	11.5	-5.0	11.4	-0.9	11.4	0.0	11.5	0.9	11.6	0.9
1935	12.0	3.4	12.0	0.0	12.0	0.0	12.1	0.8	12.9	6.6	13.0	0.8	13.0	0.0	13.0	0.0	13.4	3.1	14.0	4.5	14.2	1.4	14.2	0.0
1936	14.1	-0.7	13.9	-1.4	13.7	-1.4	13.6	-0.7	13.6	0.0	13.5	-0.7	13.4	-0.7	13.3	-0.7	13.6	2.3	13.8	1.5	14.3	3.6	15.0	4.9
1937	15.2	1.3	15.4	1.3	15.7	1.9	16.3	3.8	16.3	0.0	16.0	-1.8	16.0	0.0	16.2	1.3	16.0	-1.2	15.7	-1.9	15.0	-4.5	14.0	-6.7
1938	14.0	0.0	13.6	-2.9	13.5	-0.7	13.3	-1.5	13.3	0.0	13.2	-0.8	13.3	0.8	13.3	0.0	13.3	0.0	13.7	3.0	14.0	2.2	13.9	-0.7
1939	13.7	-1.4	13.6	-0.7	13.4	-1.5	13.4	0.0	13.4	0.0	13.6	1.5	13.6	0.0	13.6	0.0	14.9	9.6	15.8	6.0	15.8	0.0	15.4	-2.5
1940	15.5	0.6	15.2	-1.9	15.1	-0.7	15.1	0.0	15.1	0.0	14.9	-1.3	14.8	-0.7	14.3	-3.4	14.4	0.7	14.7	2.1	15.1	2.7	15.2	0.7
1941	15.3	0.7	15.3	0.0	15.3	0.0	15.4	0.7	15.7	1.9	15.8	0.6	15.9	0.6	15.9	0.0	16.2	1.9	16.3	0.6	16.4	0.6	16.4	0.0
1942	16.4	0.0	16.4	0.0	16.4	0.0	16.4	0.0	16.4	0.0	16.4	0.0	16.4	0.0	16.4	0.0	16.4	0.0	16.4	0.0	16.4	0.0	16.4	0.0
1943	16.4	0.0	16.4	0.0	16.4	0.0	16.4	0.0	16.4	0.0	16.4	0.0	16.4	0.0	16.4	0.0	16.4	0.0	16.4	0.0	16.4	0.0	16.4	0.0
1944	16.4	0.0	16.4	0.0	16.4	0.0	16.4	0.0	16.4	0.0	16.4	0.0	16.4	0.0	16.4	0.0	16.4	0.0	16.4	0.0	16.4	0.0	16.4	0.0
1945	16.4	0.0	16.4	0.0	16.4	0.0	16.4	0.0	16.4	0.0	16.4	0.0	16.4	0.0	16.4	0.0	16.8	2.4	16.8	0.0	16.8	0.0	16.8	0.0
1946	16.8	0.0	16.8	0.0	16.8	0.0	16.8	0.0	16.8	0.0	17.9	6.5	21.5	20.1	21.6	0.5	22.4	3.7	22.4	0.0	28.8	28.6	29.9	3.8
1947	29.2	-2.3	29.5	1.0	29.8	1.0	29.6	-0.7	29.2	-1.4	29.6	1.4	30.1	1.7	30.7	2.0	31.9	3.9	35.6	11.6	36.5	2.5	35.2	-3.6
1948	33.6	-4.5	30.5	-9.2	29.2	-4.3	29.7	1.7	30.3	2.0	30.4	0.3	30.4	0.0	29.1	-4.3	28.5	-2.1	28.5	0.0	29.8	4.6	29.2	-2.0
1949	29.2	0.0	27.9	-4.5	27.4	-1.8	27.1	-1.1	27.0	-0.4	27.1	0.4	26.7	-1.5	27.2	1.9	27.8	2.2	28.5	2.5	28.5	0.0	28.4	-0.4
1950	28.1	-1.1	27.9	-0.7	28.3	1.4	28.5	0.7	28.8	1.1	29.2	1.4	32.5	11.3	33.2	2.2	34.5	3.9	35.1	1.7	36.3	3.4	38.8	6.9
1951	40.8	5.2	40.9	0.2	40.9	0.0	40.9	0.0	40.8	-0.2	39.4	-3.4	37.9	-3.8	35.2	-7.1	35.7	1.4	32.7	-8.4	29.8	-8.9	29.3	-1.7
1952	28.8	-1.7	26.6	-7.6	26.0	-2.3	25.1	-3.5	25.1	0.0	26.4	5.2	26.5	0.4	26.5	0.0	26.5	0.0	26.7	0.8	26.8	0.4	27.6	3.0
1953	27.3	-1.1	27.3	0.0	27.7	1.5	27.5	-0.7	28.9	5.1	29.1	0.7	28.5	-2.1	28.2	-1.1	28.1	-0.4	26.8	-4.6	26.8	0.0	26.3	-1.9
1954	26.1	-0.8	26.0	-0.4	25.6	-1.5	25.5	-0.4	26.0	2.0	26.0	0.0	25.7	-1.2	25.1	-2.3	24.6	-2.0	24.4	-0.8	24.3	-0.4	24.2	-0.4
1955	24.1	-0.4	24.4	1.2	24.4	0.0	24.8	1.6	25.2	1.6	24.9	-1.2	25.3	1.6	25.2	-0.4	25.3	0.4	25.6	1.2	26.0	1.6	26.2	0.8
1956	26.6	1.5	26.7	0.4	27.0	1.1	28.1	4.1	27.6	-1.8	27.2	-1.4	27.2	0.0	27.0	-0.7	27.0	0.0	27.0	0.0	26.9	-0.4	27.0	0.4
1957	26.2	-3.0	26.0	-0.8	26.3	1.2	26.3	0.0	26.3	0.0	27.0	2.7	27.4	1.5	27.2	-0.7	27.2	0.0	27.1	-0.4	27.1	0.0	27.0	-0.4
1958	26.9	-0.4	26.9	0.0	27.0	0.4	27.0	0.0	27.0	0.0	27.3	1.1	27.2	-0.4	27.2	0.0	27.1	-0.4	27.6	1.8	28.1	1.8	29.5	5.0
1959	29.5	0.0	30.0	1.7	30.7	2.3	35.7	16.3	37.0	3.6	35.7	-3.5	35.2	-1.4	34.8	-1.1	34.8	0.0	33.3	-4.3	30.8	-7.5	30.7	-0.3
1960	31.3	2.0	31.1	-0.6	30.5	-1.9	31.1	2.0	30.7	-1.3	30.6	-0.3	30.4	-0.7	29.4	-3.3	28.9	-1.7	29.1	0.7	28.8	-1.0	29.5	2.4
1961	29.0	-1.7	28.9	-0.3	29.8	3.1	30.4	2.0	30.9	1.6	30.4	-1.6	30.4	0.0	31.6	3.9	32.0	1.3	32.5	1.6	32.2	-0.9	32.2	0.0
1962	32.3	0.3	32.2	-0.3	31.9	-0.9	31.9	0.0	32.2	0.9	32.0	-0.6	31.6	-1.2	31.1	-1.6	31.0	-0.3	31.0	0.0	31.1	0.3	30.9	-0.6
1963	30.6	-1.0	30.5	-0.3	30.2	-1.0	29.9	-1.0	30.1	0.7	29.8	-1.0	29.8	0.0	29.2	-2.0	29.0	-0.7	29.0	0.0	29.0	0.0	29.0	0.0
1964	29.0	0.0	29.0	0.0	29.0	0.0	29.7	2.4	30.4	2.4	30.1	-1.0	30.5	1.3	30.4	-0.3	30.3	-0.3	30.5	0.7	30.3	-0.7	30.3	0.0
1965	30.4	0.3	30.1	-1.0	30.8	2.3	30.2	-1.9	30.4	0.7	31.3	3.0	30.8	-1.6	32.8	6.5	32.3	-1.5	32.6	0.9	33.0	1.2	33.2	0.6
1966	33.9	2.1	34.4	1.5	35.9	4.4	35.6	-0.8	36.4	2.2	36.9	1.4	36.7	-0.5	36.4	-0.8	35.5	-2.5	34.2	-3.7	33.2	-2.9	33.8	1.8
1967	34.0	0.6	33.9	-0.3	33.4	-1.5	32.9	-1.5	32.3	-1.8	32.1	-0.6	31.9	-0.6	31.1	-2.5	30.7	-1.3	30.5	-0.7	31.0	1.6	31.8	2.6
1968	31.6	-0.6	31.7	0.3	32.1	1.3	32.5	1.2	32.8	0.9	32.9	0.3	33.1	0.6	33.1	0.0	33.2	0.3	33.5	0.9	33.1	-1.2	33.7	1.8
1969	34.0	0.9	33.9	-0.3	33.9	0.0	35.6	5.0	35.4	-0.6	35.4	0.0	35.3	-0.3	35.2	-0.3	35.4	0.6	35.0	-1.1	34.8	-0.6	34.8	0.0
1970	34.8	0.0	34.1	-2.0	34.4	0.9	35.1	2.0	35.1	0.0	34.9	-0.6	34.9	0.0	34.6	-0.9	34.0	-1.7	34.4	1.2	34.5	0.3	34.5	0.0

[Continued]

Leather

Producer Price Index
Base 1982 = 100

[Continued]

For 1926-1993. Columns headed % show percentile change in the index from the previous period for which an index is available.

Year	Jan Index	%	Feb Index	%	Mar Index	%	Apr Index	%	May Index	%	Jun Index	%	Jul Index	%	Aug Index	%	Sep Index	%	Oct Index	%	Nov Index	%	Dec Index	%
1971	34.8	0.9	34.9	0.3	34.9	0.0	35.6	2.0	36.3	2.0	36.7	1.1	36.7	0.0	36.7	0.0	36.6	-0.3	36.7	0.3	36.7	0.0	37.8	3.0
1972	38.5	1.9	38.7	0.5	41.3	6.7	44.4	7.5	44.3	-0.2	44.5	0.5	44.3	-0.4	45.1	1.8	46.1	2.2	49.2	6.7	52.2	6.1	52.1	-0.2
1973	52.3	0.4	52.3	0.0	52.8	1.0	51.8	-1.9	51.3	-1.0	50.2	-2.1	50.4	0.4	50.6	0.4	52.3	3.4	51.6	-1.3	51.5	-0.2	50.1	-2.7
1974	50.0	-0.2	49.8	-0.4	50.3	1.0	50.9	1.2	51.2	0.6	50.3	-1.8	49.9	-0.8	49.6	-0.6	49.9	0.6	48.7	-2.4	47.4	-2.7	46.7	-1.5
1975	45.3	-3.0	44.6	-1.5	45.5	2.0	48.7	7.0	49.2	1.0	49.2	0.0	49.0	-0.4	48.7	-0.6	49.5	1.6	49.8	0.6	52.2	4.8	52.3	0.2
1976	53.0	1.3	55.5	4.7	57.5	3.6	59.0	2.6	65.3	10.7	61.4	-6.0	61.7	0.5	63.1	2.3	63.4	0.5	62.0	-2.2	61.5	-0.8	61.6	0.2
1977	64.1	4.1	64.7	0.9	64.7	0.0	65.6	1.4	67.7	3.2	65.0	-4.0	63.8	-1.8	64.3	0.8	64.4	0.2	63.1	-2.0	63.2	0.2	64.4	1.9
1978	67.7	5.1	68.1	0.6	69.1	1.5	69.8	1.0	69.8	0.0	69.8	0.0	72.1	3.3	80.9	12.2	86.5	6.9	86.5	0.0	89.5	3.5	89.8	0.3
1979	94.0	4.7	99.3	5.6	119.4	20.2	126.4	5.9	137.9	9.1	133.2	-3.4	123.7	-7.1	117.5	-5.0	106.0	-9.8	110.3	4.1	102.7	-6.9	104.3	1.6
1980	111.6	7.0	109.3	-2.1	99.9	-8.6	95.6	-4.3	93.3	-2.4	91.3	-2.1	93.8	2.7	100.9	7.6	95.7	-5.2	97.0	1.4	101.9	5.1	106.8	4.8
1981	106.8	0.0	99.6	-6.7	103.6	4.0	108.5	4.7	106.0	-2.3	103.1	-2.7	102.4	-0.7	100.8	-1.6	100.6	-0.2	100.7	0.1	100.0	-0.7	100.3	0.3
1982	102.5	2.2	102.0	-0.5	100.6	-1.4	99.7	-0.9	99.5	-0.2	98.8	-0.7	98.7	-0.1	97.9	-0.8	99.3	1.4	99.4	0.1	100.5	1.1	101.0	0.5
1983	101.0	0.0	100.5	-0.5	101.6	1.1	102.9	1.3	104.9	1.9	107.9	2.9	108.5	0.6	110.3	1.7	109.0	-1.2	108.1	-0.8	109.4	1.2	110.5	1.0
1984	111.2	0.6	116.3	4.6	121.4	4.4	124.2	2.3	125.5	1.0	124.6	-0.7	123.1	-1.2	121.4	-1.4	119.3	-1.7	118.6	-0.6	115.5	-2.6	113.8	-1.5
1985	115.0	1.1	113.2	-1.6	111.9	-1.1	112.5	0.5	112.6	0.1	112.1	-0.4	112.0	-0.1	112.5	0.4	113.0	0.4	114.0	0.9	115.6	1.4	116.3	0.6
1986	118.4	1.8	118.4	0.0	118.5	0.1	118.9	0.3	123.2	3.6	126.6	2.8	125.4	-0.9	125.8	0.3	124.7	-0.9	122.7	-1.6	124.2	1.2	127.8	2.9
1987	128.1	0.2	129.4	1.0	131.9	1.9	137.5	4.2	140.5	2.2	143.1	1.9	142.3	-0.6	141.0	-0.9	145.6	3.3	148.6	2.1	149.6	0.7	153.0	2.3
1988	158.0	3.3	160.1	1.3	171.1	6.9	175.1	2.3	176.4	0.7	165.0	-6.5	165.7	0.4	168.2	1.5	168.8	0.4	170.7	1.1	166.0	-2.8	164.9	-0.7
1989	166.6	1.0	169.4	1.7	170.2	0.5	168.2	-1.2	166.7	-0.9	168.0	0.8	171.4	2.0	171.5	0.1	172.5	0.6	172.9	0.2	173.0	0.1	174.0	0.6
1990	176.6	1.5	178.0	0.8	177.7	-0.2	179.5	1.0	181.2	0.9	179.6	-0.9	179.0	-0.3	177.3	-0.9	176.5	-0.5	175.4	-0.6	174.9	-0.3	174.7	-0.1
1991	174.3	-0.2	173.7	-0.3	172.6	-0.6	172.1	-0.3	172.7	0.3	171.7	-0.6	167.7	-2.3	165.8	-1.1	163.4	-1.4	161.5	-1.2	162.4	0.6	162.8	0.2
1992	161.3	-0.9	161.8	0.3	163.4	1.0	162.8	-0.4	163.9	0.7	164.0	0.1	164.7	0.4	163.7	-0.6	164.8	0.7	165.1	0.2	164.0	-0.7	165.1	0.7
1993	166.6	0.9	169.0	1.4	169.0	0.0	168.3	-0.4	169.7	0.8	168.7	-0.6	167.2	-0.9	168.7	0.9	169.0	0.2	169.1	0.1	168.6	-0.3	169.1	0.3

Source: U.S. Department of Labor, Bureau of Labor Statistics, Division of Industry Prices and Price Indexes. n.e.c. stands for not elsewhere classified. - indicates no data collected for period or unavailable.

Footwear

Producer Price Index
Base 1982 = 100

For 1926-1993. Columns headed % show percentile change in the index from the previous period for which an index is available.

Year	Jan Index	%	Feb Index	%	Mar Index	%	Apr Index	%	May Index	%	Jun Index	%	Jul Index	%	Aug Index	%	Sep Index	%	Oct Index	%	Nov Index	%	Dec Index	%
1926	14.7	-	14.7	0.0	14.7	0.0	14.7	0.0	14.7	0.0	14.7	0.0	14.5	-1.4	14.5	0.0	14.5	0.0	14.5	0.0	14.5	0.0	14.5	0.0
1927	14.5	0.0	14.5	0.0	14.5	0.0	14.5	0.0	14.6	0.7	14.7	0.7	15.0	2.0	15.1	0.7	15.4	2.0	15.4	0.0	15.5	0.6	15.6	0.6
1928	15.8	1.3	15.9	0.6	16.0	0.6	16.1	0.6	16.1	0.0	16.2	0.6	16.2	0.0	16.2	0.0	16.2	0.0	16.1	-0.6	15.9	-1.2	15.8	-0.6
1929	15.6	-1.3	15.6	0.0	15.6	0.0	15.6	0.0	15.5	-0.6	15.5	0.0	15.5	0.0	15.5	0.0	15.5	0.0	15.5	0.0	15.5	0.0	15.5	0.0
1930	15.1	-2.6	15.1	0.0	15.1	0.0	15.1	0.0	15.1	0.0	15.0	-0.7	15.0	0.0	14.7	-2.0	14.7	0.0	14.7	0.0	14.7	0.0	14.3	-2.7
1931	13.9	-2.8	13.8	-0.7	13.8	0.0	13.8	0.0	13.8	0.0	13.8	0.0	13.6	-1.4	13.6	0.0	13.6	0.0	13.6	0.0	13.5	-0.7	13.0	-3.7
1932	12.9	-0.8	12.9	0.0	12.9	0.0	12.9	0.0	12.9	0.0	12.7	-1.6	12.3	-3.1	12.3	0.0	12.3	0.0	12.3	0.0	12.3	0.0	12.2	-0.8
1933	12.2	0.0	12.1	-0.8	12.1	0.0	12.1	0.0	12.2	0.8	12.4	1.6	12.9	4.0	14.0	8.5	14.4	2.9	14.4	0.0	14.4	0.0	14.4	0.0
1934	14.4	0.0	14.4	0.0	14.4	0.0	14.4	0.0	14.4	0.0	14.4	0.0	14.3	-0.7	14.3	0.0	14.3	0.0	14.3	0.0	14.2	-0.7	14.2	0.0
1935	14.1	-0.7	14.2	0.7	14.2	0.0	14.2	0.0	14.2	0.0	14.2	0.0	14.3	0.7	14.3	0.0	14.3	0.0	14.4	0.7	14.5	0.7	14.6	0.7
1936	14.7	0.7	14.7	0.0	14.7	0.0	14.7	0.0	14.6	-0.7	14.5	-0.7	14.5	0.0	14.5	0.0	14.5	0.0	14.5	0.0	14.5	0.0	14.5	0.0
1937	14.5	0.0	14.8	2.1	14.9	0.7	15.1	1.3	15.5	2.6	15.7	1.3	15.6	-0.6	15.6	0.0	15.7	0.6	15.7	0.0	15.6	-0.6	15.4	-1.3
1938	15.3	-0.6	15.2	-0.7	15.2	0.0	15.2	0.0	14.9	-2.0	14.9	0.0	14.8	-0.7	14.7	-0.7	14.7	0.0	14.7	0.0	14.7	0.0	14.7	0.0
1939	14.8	0.7	14.7	-0.7	14.8	0.7	14.8	0.0	14.8	0.0	14.8	0.0	14.7	-0.7	14.7	0.0	14.9	1.4	15.4	3.4	15.6	1.3	15.7	0.6
1940	15.7	0.0	15.8	0.6	15.8	0.0	15.8	0.0	15.8	0.0	15.8	0.0	15.6	-1.3	15.6	0.0	15.6	0.0	15.6	0.0	15.6	0.0	15.6	0.0
1941	15.6	0.0	15.6	0.0	15.6	0.0	15.8	1.3	16.0	1.3	16.3	1.9	16.7	2.5	16.9	1.2	17.1	1.2	17.3	1.2	17.6	1.7	17.6	0.0
1942	17.7	0.6	17.8	0.6	18.1	1.7	18.5	2.2	18.5	0.0	18.4	-0.5	18.4	0.0	18.4	0.0	18.4	0.0	18.4	0.0	18.4	0.0	18.4	0.0
1943	18.4	0.0	18.4	0.0	18.4	0.0	18.4	0.0	18.4	0.0	18.4	0.0	18.4	0.0	18.4	0.0	18.4	0.0	18.4	0.0	18.4	0.0	18.4	0.0
1944	18.4	0.0	18.4	0.0	18.4	0.0	18.4	0.0	18.4	0.0	18.4	0.0	18.4	0.0	18.4	0.0	18.4	0.0	18.4	0.0	18.4	0.0	18.4	0.0
1945	18.4	0.0	18.4	0.0	18.4	0.0	18.4	0.0	18.4	0.0	18.4	0.0	18.4	0.0	18.4	0.0	18.4	0.0	18.4	0.0	18.5	0.5	18.5	0.0
1946	18.7	1.1	18.7	0.0	18.7	0.0	18.7	0.0	18.8	0.5	18.9	0.5	20.5	8.5	20.5	0.0	21.1	2.9	21.1	0.0	23.8	12.8	24.8	4.2
1947	25.3	2.0	25.3	0.0	25.3	0.0	25.4	0.4	25.6	0.8	25.6	0.0	25.7	0.4	26.0	1.2	25.8	-0.8	26.1	1.2	26.5	1.5	27.2	2.6
1948	27.4	0.7	27.4	0.0	27.6	0.7	27.8	0.7	27.6	-0.7	27.5	-0.4	27.6	0.4	27.8	0.7	27.9	0.4	27.8	-0.4	27.5	-1.1	27.5	0.0
1949	27.4	-0.4	27.4	0.0	27.4	0.0	27.3	-0.4	27.1	-0.7	27.1	0.0	27.1	0.0	27.1	0.0	27.1	0.0	27.1	0.0	27.3	0.7	27.5	0.7
1950	27.3	-0.7	27.3	0.0	27.4	0.4	27.4	0.0	27.6	0.7	27.6	0.0	27.8	0.7	28.7	3.2	29.1	1.4	30.1	3.4	31.2	3.7	32.2	3.2
1951	32.9	2.2	33.5	1.8	33.1	-1.2	33.1	0.0	33.1	0.0	33.0	-0.3	32.9	-0.3	32.8	-0.3	32.8	0.0	32.1	-2.1	31.8	-0.9	31.3	-1.6
1952	31.2	-0.3	31.2	0.0	31.2	0.0	30.4	-2.6	29.9	-1.6	29.8	-0.3	29.8	0.0	29.8	0.0	29.8	0.0	29.8	0.0	29.8	0.0	30.1	1.0
1953	30.1	0.0	30.2	0.3	30.2	0.0	30.0	-0.7	30.0	0.0	30.0	0.0	30.0	0.0	30.1	0.3	30.1	0.0	30.0	-0.3	30.1	0.3	30.1	0.0
1954	30.1	0.0	30.1	0.0	30.1	0.0	30.1	0.0	30.1	0.0	30.1	0.0	30.1	0.0	30.1	0.0	30.1	0.0	30.1	0.0	30.0	-0.3	30.0	0.0
1955	30.0	0.0	30.0	0.0	30.0	0.0	30.0	0.0	30.0	0.0	30.0	0.0	30.0	0.0	30.0	0.0	30.0	0.0	30.5	1.7	31.1	2.0	31.1	0.0
1956	31.1	0.0	31.1	0.0	31.3	0.6	32.2	2.9	32.3	0.3	32.4	0.3	32.4	0.0	32.4	0.0	32.4	0.0	32.5	0.3	32.5	0.0	32.5	0.0
1957	32.5	0.0	32.5	0.0	32.5	0.0	32.6	0.3	32.5	-0.3	32.5	0.0	32.6	0.3	32.6	0.0	32.6	0.0	32.8	0.6	32.9	0.3	32.7	-0.6
1958	32.8	0.3	32.8	0.0	32.8	0.0	32.7	-0.3	32.8	0.3	32.8	0.0	32.8	0.0	32.8	0.0	32.8	0.0	33.0	0.6	33.1	0.3	33.1	0.0
1959	33.1	0.0	33.1	0.0	33.3	0.6	34.5	3.6	34.8	0.9	35.0	0.6	35.1	0.3	35.6	1.4	35.6	0.0	35.9	0.8	36.0	0.3	36.1	0.3
1960	36.1	0.0	36.1	0.0	36.1	0.0	35.9	-0.6	35.6	-0.8	35.6	0.0	35.6	0.0	35.6	0.0	35.6	0.0	35.6	0.0	35.6	0.0	35.6	0.0
1961	35.7	0.3	35.7	0.0	35.7	0.0	35.7	0.0	35.8	0.3	35.8	0.0	35.8	0.0	35.9	0.3	36.0	0.3	36.2	0.6	36.3	0.3	36.3	0.0
1962	36.3	0.0	36.3	0.0	36.3	0.0	36.3	0.0	36.3	0.0	36.3	0.0	36.4	0.3	36.4	0.0	36.4	0.0	36.2	-0.5	36.2	0.0	36.3	0.3
1963	36.2	-0.3	36.2	0.0	36.2	0.0	36.2	0.0	36.2	0.0	36.2	0.0	36.2	0.0	36.2	0.0	36.2	0.0	36.2	0.0	36.2	0.0	36.2	0.0
1964	36.2	0.0	36.2	0.0	36.2	0.0	36.2	0.0	36.2	0.0	36.2	0.0	36.2	0.0	36.2	0.0	36.2	0.0	36.5	0.8	36.5	0.0	36.5	0.0
1965	36.5	0.0	36.5	0.0	36.5	0.0	36.7	0.5	36.7	0.0	36.7	0.0	36.8	0.3	36.9	0.3	36.9	0.0	38.0	3.0	38.0	0.0	38.0	0.0
1966	38.3	0.8	38.5	0.5	38.6	0.3	39.5	2.3	39.8	0.8	39.8	0.0	39.8	0.0	39.8	0.0	39.8	0.0	40.2	1.0	40.2	0.0	40.2	0.0
1967	40.5	0.7	40.7	0.5	40.7	0.0	40.6	-0.2	40.6	0.0	40.6	0.0	40.6	0.0	40.5	-0.2	40.7	0.5	41.3	1.5	41.3	0.0	41.6	0.7
1968	42.0	1.0	42.0	0.0	42.0	0.0	42.3	0.7	42.5	0.5	42.5	0.0	42.6	0.2	42.5	-0.2	43.1	1.4	43.9	1.9	44.0	0.2	44.0	0.0
1969	44.2	0.5	44.2	0.0	44.0	-0.5	44.1	0.2	44.2	0.2	44.2	0.0	44.4	0.5	44.5	0.2	45.3	1.8	45.6	0.7	45.8	0.4	45.7	-0.2
1970	46.1	0.9	46.4	0.7	46.4	0.0	46.2	-0.4	46.1	-0.2	46.1	0.0	46.1	0.0	46.1	0.0	46.4	0.7	46.5	0.2	46.5	0.0	46.5	0.0

[Continued]

Footwear
Producer Price Index
Base 1982 = 100
[Continued]

For 1926-1993. Columns headed % show percentile change in the index from the previous period for which an index is available.

Year	Jan Index	%	Feb Index	%	Mar Index	%	Apr Index	%	May Index	%	Jun Index	%	Jul Index	%	Aug Index	%	Sep Index	%	Oct Index	%	Nov Index	%	Dec Index	%
1971	47.5	2.2	47.5	0.0	47.5	0.0	47.6	0.2	47.7	0.2	47.7	0.0	47.7	0.0	47.7	0.0	47.7	0.0	47.7	0.0	47.7	0.0	47.8	0.2
1972	48.2	0.8	48.4	0.4	49.0	1.2	50.0	2.0	50.9	1.8	51.4	1.0	51.6	0.4	51.6	0.0	51.7	0.2	51.8	0.2	52.4	1.2	52.5	0.2
1973	52.6	0.2	53.4	1.5	53.5	0.2	53.7	0.4	52.8	-1.7	52.8	0.0	52.9	0.2	52.9	0.0	53.2	0.6	53.5	0.6	53.8	0.6	54.1	0.6
1974	54.7	1.1	55.1	0.7	55.5	0.7	56.4	1.6	56.6	0.4	56.9	0.5	57.1	0.4	57.4	0.5	58.8	2.4	58.9	0.2	59.1	0.3	59.1	0.0
1975	59.3	0.3	59.6	0.5	59.6	0.0	59.9	0.5	59.9	0.0	60.0	0.2	60.1	0.2	60.2	0.2	61.0	1.3	61.3	0.5	61.3	0.0	61.4	0.2
1976	62.1	1.1	62.8	1.1	63.2	0.6	63.8	0.9	64.0	0.3	64.8	1.3	65.6	1.2	65.8	0.3	66.3	0.8	66.4	0.2	66.5	0.2	66.8	0.5
1977	67.1	0.4	67.5	0.6	67.9	0.6	68.2	0.4	68.6	0.6	68.6	0.0	69.3	1.0	69.4	0.1	69.4	0.0	69.9	0.7	70.0	0.1	70.1	0.1
1978	70.8	1.0	71.7	1.3	71.7	0.0	73.5	2.5	73.8	0.4	73.9	0.1	74.1	0.3	75.1	1.3	75.9	1.1	77.8	2.5	78.4	0.8	79.3	1.1
1979	80.2	1.1	82.8	3.2	85.7	3.5	86.6	1.1	88.3	2.0	90.3	2.3	90.5	0.2	92.0	1.7	92.6	0.7	92.9	0.3	93.0	0.1	93.0	0.0
1980	93.5	0.5	93.1	-0.4	94.6	1.6	94.7	0.1	94.7	0.0	94.7	0.0	95.0	0.3	95.4	0.4	96.1	0.7	96.6	0.5	97.0	0.4	96.7	-0.3
1981	97.3	0.6	98.2	0.9	98.1	-0.1	98.4	0.3	98.5	0.1	98.6	0.1	98.9	0.3	99.0	0.1	99.1	0.1	97.8	-1.3	97.9	0.1	98.0	0.1
1982	97.5	-0.5	97.4	-0.1	97.9	0.5	99.9	2.0	99.8	-0.1	99.7	-0.1	101.0	1.3	101.1	0.1	101.3	0.2	101.6	0.3	101.7	0.1	101.1	-0.6
1983	102.7	1.6	101.1	-1.6	101.3	0.2	102.1	0.8	101.5	-0.6	102.0	0.5	102.0	0.0	102.4	0.4	102.7	0.3	102.6	-0.1	102.6	0.0	102.2	-0.4
1984	102.4	0.2	103.1	0.7	103.5	0.4	102.7	-0.8	102.6	-0.1	102.3	-0.3	102.1	-0.2	102.4	0.3	102.8	0.4	102.9	0.1	103.0	0.1	103.1	0.1
1985	103.2	0.1	104.5	1.3	104.2	-0.3	104.1	-0.1	103.6	-0.5	104.9	1.3	104.9	0.0	105.3	0.4	105.7	0.4	105.7	0.0	105.5	-0.2	105.5	0.0
1986	105.9	0.4	106.3	0.4	106.8	0.5	107.1	0.3	106.8	-0.3	106.4	-0.4	106.5	0.1	106.8	0.3	107.0	0.2	107.5	0.5	107.5	0.0	107.8	0.3
1987	108.0	0.2	107.5	-0.5	108.4	0.8	108.2	-0.2	108.9	0.6	107.5	-1.3	109.7	2.0	110.3	0.5	111.0	0.6	110.9	-0.1	110.6	-0.3	111.4	0.7
1988	112.7	1.2	113.7	0.9	114.0	0.3	114.1	0.1	114.2	0.1	114.8	0.5	115.5	0.6	116.0	0.4	116.2	0.2	116.4	0.2	116.9	0.4	117.2	0.3
1989	118.1	0.8	119.5	1.2	119.8	0.3	120.0	0.2	119.9	-0.1	119.9	0.0	120.4	0.4	121.8	1.2	122.3	0.4	122.5	0.2	122.5	0.0	123.1	0.5
1990	124.2	0.9	125.3	0.9	125.5	0.2	125.4	-0.1	125.8	0.3	125.5	-0.2	125.6	0.1	126.0	0.3	126.1	0.1	126.2	0.1	125.9	-0.2	126.1	0.2
1991	126.3	0.2	127.1	0.6	128.0	0.7	128.3	0.2	128.7	0.3	128.8	0.1	129.2	0.3	129.3	0.1	129.5	0.2	129.1	-0.3	129.3	0.2	129.6	0.2
1992	130.6	0.8	131.8	0.9	131.4	-0.3	131.5	0.1	131.6	0.1	131.9	0.2	132.1	0.2	132.5	0.3	132.8	0.2	132.4	-0.3	132.4	0.0	133.3	0.7
1993	133.5	0.2	133.8	0.2	133.9	0.1	134.5	0.4	134.1	-0.3	134.2	0.1	134.8	0.4	134.8	0.0	135.0	0.1	134.7	-0.2	134.7	0.0	135.0	0.2

Source: U.S. Department of Labor, Bureau of Labor Statistics, Division of Industry Prices and Price Indexes. n.e.c. stands for not elsewhere classified. - indicates no data collected for period or unavailable.

Leather and Related Products n.e.c.
Producer Price Index
Base 1982 = 100

For 1947-1993. Columns headed % show percentile change in the index from the previous period for which an index is available.

Year	Jan Index	%	Feb Index	%	Mar Index	%	Apr Index	%	May Index	%	Jun Index	%	Jul Index	%	Aug Index	%	Sep Index	%	Oct Index	%	Nov Index	%	Dec Index	%
1947	35.0	-	34.4	-1.7	34.4	0.0	34.2	-0.6	33.6	-1.8	33.5	-0.3	34.5	3.0	35.0	1.4	35.4	1.1	36.0	1.7	37.6	4.4	37.8	0.5
1948	37.7	-0.3	37.2	-1.3	36.2	-2.7	35.7	-1.4	35.8	0.3	35.9	0.3	36.1	0.6	36.0	-0.3	35.5	-1.4	35.2	-0.8	35.3	0.3	35.6	0.8
1949	35.5	-0.3	35.4	-0.3	34.8	-1.7	34.3	-1.4	34.4	0.3	34.2	-0.6	34.0	-0.6	33.9	-0.3	33.8	-0.3	33.9	0.3	33.8	-0.3	34.0	0.6
1950	33.6	-1.2	33.6	0.0	33.6	0.0	33.6	0.0	33.7	0.3	33.5	-0.6	34.0	1.5	34.8	2.4	35.2	1.1	35.7	1.4	36.1	1.1	36.9	2.2
1951	40.0	8.4	40.6	1.5	40.6	0.0	40.9	0.7	40.7	-0.5	40.5	-0.5	40.1	-1.0	39.0	-2.7	39.0	0.0	37.6	-3.6	37.2	-1.1	37.2	0.0
1952	36.6	-1.6	36.3	-0.8	35.8	-1.4	35.2	-1.7	35.3	0.3	35.4	0.3	35.3	-0.3	35.2	-0.3	35.1	-0.3	34.8	-0.9	35.0	0.6	35.3	0.9
1953	34.8	-1.4	34.8	0.0	34.8	0.0	34.9	0.3	35.1	0.6	35.3	0.6	35.0	-0.8	35.0	0.0	34.8	-0.6	34.8	0.0	34.7	-0.3	34.5	-0.6
1954	34.5	0.0	34.4	-0.3	34.3	-0.3	34.2	-0.3	34.2	0.0	34.2	0.0	34.1	-0.3	34.0	-0.3	33.9	-0.3	33.8	-0.3	33.8	0.0	33.7	-0.3
1955	33.7	0.0	33.7	0.0	33.6	-0.3	33.7	0.3	33.4	-0.9	33.4	0.0	33.9	1.5	33.9	0.0	33.8	-0.3	33.8	0.0	33.8	0.0	34.0	0.6
1956	34.3	0.9	34.5	0.6	34.5	0.0	34.8	0.9	34.8	0.0	34.8	0.0	34.7	-0.3	34.8	0.3	34.6	-0.6	34.6	0.0	34.6	0.0	34.5	-0.3
1957	34.4	-0.3	34.2	-0.6	34.4	0.6	34.4	0.0	34.2	-0.6	34.2	0.0	34.6	1.2	34.5	-0.3	34.6	0.3	34.6	0.0	34.7	0.3	34.6	-0.3
1958	34.6	0.0	34.6	0.0	34.2	-1.2	34.3	0.3	34.2	-0.3	34.2	0.0	34.2	0.0	34.0	-0.6	34.0	0.0	34.2	0.6	34.2	0.0	34.5	0.9
1959	34.8	0.9	35.4	1.7	36.3	2.5	38.7	6.6	39.5	2.1	39.4	-0.3	40.0	1.5	40.1	0.3	40.0	-0.2	39.1	-2.3	38.4	-1.8	37.9	-1.3
1960	38.0	0.3	37.7	-0.8	37.7	0.0	37.7	0.0	37.5	-0.5	37.4	-0.3	37.1	-0.8	36.8	-0.8	36.5	-0.8	36.5	0.0	36.6	0.3	36.5	-0.3
1961	36.6	0.3	36.5	-0.3	36.4	-0.3	36.6	0.5	36.7	0.3	36.7	0.0	36.6	-0.3	36.9	0.8	37.0	0.3	36.9	-0.3	37.2	0.8	37.2	0.0
1962	37.4	0.5	37.3	-0.3	37.3	0.0	36.6	-1.9	36.3	-0.8	37.4	3.0	37.5	0.3	37.1	-1.1	37.1	0.0	37.4	0.8	37.5	0.3	37.6	0.3
1963	37.4	-0.5	37.4	0.0	37.4	0.0	37.3	-0.3	37.2	-0.3	37.2	0.0	37.1	-0.3	36.9	-0.5	36.9	0.0	36.9	0.0	36.8	-0.3	36.9	0.3
1964	36.3	-1.6	36.3	0.0	36.2	-0.3	37.0	2.2	36.9	-0.3	36.8	-0.3	37.1	0.8	37.0	-0.3	36.9	-0.3	36.9	0.0	37.1	0.5	37.1	0.0
1965	36.6	-1.3	36.7	0.3	36.7	0.0	37.2	1.4	37.4	0.5	37.4	0.0	37.6	0.5	38.8	3.2	39.0	0.5	38.9	-0.3	38.9	0.0	39.3	1.0
1966	39.4	0.3	39.8	1.0	40.1	0.8	40.8	1.7	41.2	1.0	41.3	0.2	41.6	0.7	41.4	-0.5	41.1	-0.7	41.2	0.2	41.1	-0.2	40.7	-1.0
1967	41.0	0.7	41.0	0.0	40.9	-0.2	40.9	0.0	40.8	-0.2	40.4	-1.0	40.3	-0.2	40.3	0.0	40.0	-0.7	39.9	-0.2	39.9	0.0	39.8	-0.3
1968	40.0	0.5	40.0	0.0	40.1	0.3	40.1	0.0	40.1	0.0	40.1	0.0	40.2	0.2	40.2	0.0	40.2	0.0	40.5	0.7	40.5	0.0	40.6	0.2
1969	41.0	1.0	41.0	0.0	41.2	0.5	41.5	0.7	41.7	0.5	41.8	0.2	42.0	0.5	41.9	-0.2	42.1	0.5	42.2	0.2	42.4	0.5	42.3	-0.2
1970	42.6	0.7	42.7	0.2	42.8	0.2	42.8	0.0	43.1	0.7	43.1	0.0	43.2	0.2	43.2	0.0	43.2	0.0	43.2	0.0	43.2	0.0	43.2	0.0
1971	43.4	0.5	43.5	0.2	43.5	0.0	43.5	0.0	43.6	0.2	43.7	0.2	43.8	0.2	44.0	0.5	44.1	0.2	44.1	0.0	44.1	0.0	44.4	0.7
1972	44.7	0.7	44.9	0.4	45.2	0.7	46.0	1.8	46.6	1.3	47.2	1.3	47.1	-0.2	48.0	1.9	48.7	1.5	50.0	2.7	51.4	2.8	51.9	1.0
1973	52.3	0.8	52.3	0.0	52.3	0.0	52.5	0.4	52.2	-0.6	52.1	-0.2	52.2	0.2	52.8	1.1	52.7	-0.2	52.8	0.2	52.6	-0.4	52.7	0.2
1974	53.3	1.1	53.8	0.9	54.8	1.9	54.7	-0.2	54.6	-0.2	55.3	1.3	55.4	0.2	55.4	0.0	56.3	1.6	56.0	-0.5	56.0	0.0	56.5	0.9
1975	56.6	0.2	56.4	-0.4	56.2	-0.4	56.2	0.0	56.4	0.4	56.8	0.7	57.0	0.4	57.2	0.4	57.3	0.2	57.4	0.2	58.0	1.0	58.3	0.5
1976	60.3	3.4	61.0	1.2	61.1	0.2	61.2	0.2	61.5	0.5	61.5	0.0	61.6	0.2	61.7	0.2	62.7	1.6	63.0	0.5	63.0	0.0	63.1	0.2
1977	64.5	2.2	65.3	1.2	65.7	0.6	66.0	0.5	66.2	0.3	66.2	0.0	66.2	0.0	66.4	0.3	66.5	0.2	66.5	0.0	66.6	0.2	66.6	0.0
1978	68.8	3.3	68.9	0.1	69.4	0.7	69.5	0.1	71.2	2.4	71.4	0.3	71.5	0.1	72.3	1.1	72.7	0.6	72.9	0.3	74.8	2.6	74.9	0.1
1979	77.1	2.9	77.7	0.8	79.2	1.9	81.2	2.5	84.5	4.1	85.8	1.5	85.7	-0.1	85.3	-0.5	84.9	-0.5	84.8	-0.1	84.3	-0.6	84.1	-0.2
1980	86.1	2.4	86.8	0.8	88.0	1.4	87.4	-0.7	87.9	0.6	87.3	-0.7	87.9	0.7	88.4	0.6	88.5	0.1	89.7	1.4	90.0	0.3	91.1	1.2
1981	93.0	2.1	95.8	3.0	96.4	0.6	96.4	0.0	98.7	2.4	98.8	0.1	98.2	-0.6	99.1	0.9	99.0	-0.1	99.0	0.0	99.2	0.2	99.2	0.0
1982	100.1	0.9	100.3	0.2	100.3	0.0	100.3	0.0	100.3	0.0	99.3	-1.0	99.8	0.5	99.0	-0.8	100.1	1.1	99.9	-0.2	99.9	0.0	100.7	0.8
1983	101.4	0.7	101.5	0.1	101.4	-0.1	101.5	0.1	101.7	0.2	101.7	0.0	102.5	0.8	102.6	0.1	102.5	-0.1	102.5	0.0	103.4	0.9	103.3	-0.1
1984	104.0	0.7	104.0	0.0	104.0	0.0	104.3	0.3	105.0	0.7	108.3	3.1	108.0	-0.3	108.2	0.2	108.2	0.0	108.4	0.2	108.3	-0.1	107.9	-0.4
1985	109.2	1.2	109.3	0.1	110.1	0.7	110.2	0.1	110.3	0.1	110.5	0.2	110.2	-0.3	110.2	0.0	110.6	0.4	110.8	0.2	111.3	0.5	111.3	0.0
1986	111.5	0.2	111.0	-0.4	109.7	-1.2	109.5	-0.2	109.5	0.0	109.9	0.4	109.9	0.0	110.0	0.1	110.2	0.2	111.0	0.7	111.0	0.0	111.1	0.1
1987	111.5	0.4	111.4	-0.1	111.6	0.2	111.6	0.0	112.2	0.5	112.5	0.3	112.9	0.4	113.4	0.4	114.2	0.7	114.4	0.2	114.8	0.3	115.2	0.3
1988	116.6	1.2	116.8	0.2	117.1	0.3	117.7	0.5	118.2	0.4	119.5	1.1	119.9	0.3	120.0	0.1	120.6	0.5	120.6	0.0	120.7	0.1	120.9	0.2
1989	121.4	0.4	121.9	0.4	122.2	0.2	122.4	0.2	123.2	0.7	122.9	-0.2	122.9	0.0	123.7	0.7	124.4	0.6	123.9	-0.4	123.7	-0.2	124.8	0.9
1990	126.0	1.0	126.3	0.2	127.9	1.3	127.6	-0.2	129.2	1.3	129.7	0.4	129.4	-0.2	130.6	0.9	130.1	-0.4	129.6	-0.4	130.0	0.3	130.8	0.6
1991	130.8	0.0	131.3	0.4	132.4	0.8	131.9	-0.4	132.7	0.6	134.4	1.3	132.4	-1.5	134.3	1.4	132.8	-1.1	132.8	0.0	132.9	0.1	133.0	0.1

[Continued]

Leather and Related Products n.e.c.
Producer Price Index
Base 1982 = 100
[Continued]

For 1947-1993. Columns headed % show percentile change in the index from the previous period for which an index is available.

Year	Jan Index	%	Feb Index	%	Mar Index	%	Apr Index	%	May Index	%	Jun Index	%	Jul Index	%	Aug Index	%	Sep Index	%	Oct Index	%	Nov Index	%	Dec Index	%
1992	135.7	2.0	133.7	-1.5	136.2	1.9	134.0	-1.6	134.4	0.3	136.2	1.3	134.2	-1.5	136.6	1.8	134.2	-1.8	134.3	0.1	134.6	0.2	134.6	0.0
1993	137.1	1.9	135.2	-1.4	135.3	0.1	135.7	0.3	135.8	0.1	137.8	1.5	135.9	-1.4	138.3	1.8	135.8	-1.8	135.9	0.1	135.9	0.0	136.1	0.1

Source: U.S. Department of Labor, Bureau of Labor Statistics, Division of Industry Prices and Price Indexes. n.e.c. stands for not elsewhere classified. - indicates no data collected for period or unavailable.

FUELS AND RELATED PRODUCTS AND POWER
Producer Price Index
Base 1982 = 100

For 1926-1993. Columns headed % show percentile change in the index from the previous period for which an index is available.

Year	Jan Index	%	Feb Index	%	Mar Index	%	Apr Index	%	May Index	%	Jun Index	%	Jul Index	%	Aug Index	%	Sep Index	%	Oct Index	%	Nov Index	%	Dec Index	%
1926	10.2	-	10.2	0.0	10.2	0.0	10.1	-1.0	10.4	3.0	10.4	0.0	10.3	-1.0	10.4	1.0	10.4	0.0	10.4	0.0	10.5	1.0	10.2	-2.9
1927	10.1	-1.0	10.0	-1.0	9.4	-6.0	9.0	-4.3	8.9	-1.1	8.9	0.0	8.9	0.0	8.9	0.0	8.9	0.0	8.9	0.0	8.8	-1.1	8.7	-1.1
1928	8.6	-1.1	8.6	0.0	8.5	-1.2	8.6	1.2	8.6	0.0	8.7	1.2	8.7	0.0	8.9	2.3	8.9	0.0	8.9	0.0	8.9	0.0	8.8	-1.1
1929	8.7	-1.1	8.6	-1.1	8.5	-1.2	8.5	0.0	8.5	0.0	8.7	2.4	8.6	-1.1	8.5	-1.2	8.5	0.0	8.6	1.2	8.6	0.0	8.6	0.0
1930	8.4	-2.3	8.4	0.0	8.2	-2.4	8.2	0.0	8.3	1.2	8.2	-1.2	8.1	-1.2	8.0	-1.2	8.2	2.5	8.0	-2.4	7.8	-2.5	7.6	-2.6
1931	7.6	0.0	7.5	-1.3	7.0	-6.7	6.8	-2.9	6.7	-1.5	6.5	-3.0	6.5	0.0	6.9	6.2	7.0	1.4	7.0	0.0	7.2	2.9	7.0	-2.8
1932	7.0	0.0	7.0	0.0	7.0	0.0	7.2	2.9	7.3	1.4	7.4	1.4	7.5	1.4	7.4	-1.3	7.3	-1.4	7.3	0.0	7.4	1.4	7.2	-2.7
1933	6.8	-5.6	6.6	-2.9	6.5	-1.5	6.3	-3.1	6.2	-1.6	6.3	1.6	6.7	6.3	6.8	1.5	7.3	7.4	7.6	4.1	7.6	0.0	7.6	0.0
1934	7.5	-1.3	7.5	0.0	7.4	-1.3	7.4	0.0	7.5	1.4	7.5	0.0	7.6	1.3	7.7	1.3	7.7	0.0	7.7	0.0	7.7	0.0	7.6	-1.3
1935	7.5	-1.3	7.5	0.0	7.5	0.0	7.5	0.0	7.5	0.0	7.7	2.7	7.7	0.0	7.6	-1.3	7.5	-1.3	7.6	1.3	7.7	1.3	7.7	0.0
1936	7.8	1.3	7.8	0.0	7.9	1.3	7.9	0.0	7.8	-1.3	7.8	0.0	7.9	1.3	7.9	0.0	7.8	-1.3	7.9	1.3	7.9	0.0	7.9	0.0
1937	7.9	0.0	7.9	0.0	7.9	0.0	7.9	0.0	8.0	1.3	8.0	0.0	8.1	1.3	8.1	0.0	8.1	0.0	8.1	0.0	8.1	0.0	8.1	0.0
1938	8.1	0.0	8.1	0.0	8.0	-1.2	7.9	-1.2	7.9	0.0	7.9	0.0	7.9	0.0	7.9	0.0	7.9	0.0	7.8	-1.3	7.6	-2.6	7.6	0.0
1939	7.5	-1.3	7.5	0.0	7.5	0.0	7.6	1.3	7.6	0.0	7.5	-1.3	7.5	0.0	7.5	0.0	7.5	0.0	7.6	1.3	7.6	-2.6	7.6	0.0
1940	7.5	0.0	7.5	0.0	7.4	-1.3	7.4	0.0	7.4	0.0	7.4	0.0	7.3	-1.4	7.3	0.0	7.3	0.0	7.4	1.4	7.4	0.0	7.4	0.0
1941	7.4	0.0	7.4	0.0	7.4	0.0	7.5	1.4	7.8	4.0	8.0	2.6	8.1	1.3	8.2	1.2	8.2	0.0	8.2	0.0	8.1	-1.2	8.1	0.0
1942	8.1	0.0	8.0	-1.2	8.0	0.0	8.0	0.0	8.0	0.0	8.1	1.3	8.2	1.2	8.2	0.0	8.2	0.0	8.2	0.0	8.2	0.0	8.2	0.0
1943	8.2	0.0	8.2	0.0	8.3	1.2	8.3	0.0	8.3	0.0	8.4	1.2	8.4	0.0	8.4	0.0	8.4	0.0	8.4	0.0	8.4	0.0	8.5	1.2
1944	8.5	0.0	8.6	1.2	8.6	0.0	8.6	0.0	8.6	0.0	8.6	0.0	8.6	0.0	8.6	0.0	8.6	0.0	8.6	0.0	8.6	0.0	8.6	0.0
1945	8.6	0.0	8.6	0.0	8.6	0.0	8.6	0.0	8.6	0.0	8.7	1.2	8.7	0.0	8.8	1.1	8.7	-1.1	8.7	0.0	8.7	0.0	8.7	0.0
1946	8.8	1.1	8.8	0.0	8.8	0.0	8.9	1.1	8.9	0.0	9.1	2.2	9.3	2.2	9.8	5.4	9.7	-1.0	9.7	0.0	9.8	1.0	9.9	1.0
1947	10.1	2.0	10.2	1.0	10.5	2.9	10.8	2.9	10.8	0.0	10.8	0.0	11.2	3.7	11.4	1.8	11.5	0.9	11.6	0.9	11.9	2.6	12.4	4.2
1948	12.9	4.0	13.0	0.8	13.0	0.0	13.0	0.0	13.0	0.0	13.0	0.0	13.2	1.5	13.1	-0.8	13.1	0.0	13.2	0.8	13.2	0.0	13.1	-0.8
1949	13.1	0.0	12.9	-1.5	12.7	-1.6	12.4	-2.4	12.3	-0.8	12.2	-0.8	12.2	0.0	12.2	0.0	12.2	0.0	12.3	0.8	12.3	0.0	12.3	0.0
1950	12.4	0.8	12.4	0.0	12.4	0.0	12.3	-0.8	12.4	0.8	12.5	0.8	12.6	0.8	12.7	0.8	12.7	0.0	12.8	0.8	12.9	0.8	12.8	-0.8
1951	13.0	1.6	13.1	0.8	13.1	0.0	13.0	-0.8	13.0	0.0	13.0	0.0	13.0	0.0	13.0	0.0	13.0	0.0	13.0	0.0	13.0	0.0	13.1	0.8
1952	13.1	0.0	13.1	0.0	13.1	0.0	13.0	-0.8	12.9	-0.8	12.9	0.0	12.9	0.0	12.9	0.0	13.0	0.8	13.0	0.0	13.0	0.0	13.1	0.8
1953	13.1	0.0	13.2	0.8	13.2	0.0	13.1	-0.8	13.1	0.0	13.2	0.8	13.5	2.3	13.5	0.0	13.5	0.0	13.6	0.7	13.6	0.0	13.5	-0.7
1954	13.5	0.0	13.5	0.0	13.3	-1.5	13.2	-0.8	13.2	0.0	13.1	-0.8	13.0	-0.8	13.0	0.0	13.0	0.0	13.0	0.0	13.1	0.8	13.1	0.0
1955	13.2	0.8	13.3	0.8	13.2	-0.8	13.1	-0.8	13.0	-0.8	13.0	0.0	13.0	0.0	13.1	0.8	13.2	0.8	13.2	0.0	13.2	0.0	13.3	0.8
1956	13.5	1.5	13.6	0.7	13.5	-0.7	13.5	0.0	13.5	0.0	13.5	0.0	13.5	0.0	13.5	0.0	13.5	0.0	13.6	0.7	13.6	0.0	13.9	2.2
1957	14.2	2.2	14.6	2.8	14.5	-0.7	14.6	0.7	14.5	-0.7	14.3	-1.4	14.2	-0.7	14.2	0.0	14.2	0.0	14.1	-0.7	14.1	0.0	14.2	0.7
1958	14.2	0.0	13.8	-2.8	13.7	-0.7	13.5	-1.5	13.4	-0.7	13.5	0.7	13.6	0.7	13.9	2.2	13.9	0.0	13.8	-0.7	13.7	-0.7	13.8	0.7
1959	13.9	0.7	14.0	0.7	14.0	0.0	13.9	-0.7	13.8	-0.7	13.6	-1.4	13.5	-0.7	13.7	1.5	13.6	-0.7	13.6	0.0	13.6	0.0	13.6	0.0
1960	13.6	0.0	13.7	0.7	13.7	0.0	13.7	0.0	13.5	-1.5	13.7	1.5	13.9	1.5	14.1	1.4	14.2	0.7	14.2	0.0	14.2	0.0	14.2	0.0
1961	14.3	0.7	14.4	0.7	14.3	-0.7	14.1	-1.4	13.8	-2.1	13.9	0.7	14.0	0.7	14.0	0.0	13.9	-0.7	13.8	-0.7	13.9	0.7	14.0	0.7
1962	14.1	0.7	14.0	-0.7	13.8	-1.4	14.0	1.4	13.9	-0.7	13.9	0.0	13.9	0.0	13.8	-0.7	14.0	1.4	14.0	0.0	14.0	0.0	14.0	0.0
1963	14.0	0.0	14.0	0.0	14.0	0.0	14.0	0.0	14.0	0.0	14.1	0.7	14.0	-0.7	13.8	-1.4	13.8	0.0	13.8	0.0	13.6	-1.4	13.8	1.5
1964	13.8	0.0	13.8	0.0	13.5	-2.2	13.4	-0.7	13.4	0.0	13.4	0.0	13.5	0.7	13.4	-0.7	13.3	-0.7	13.5	1.5	13.6	0.7	13.7	0.7
1965	13.7	0.0	13.6	-0.7	13.6	0.0	13.6	0.0	13.7	0.7	13.7	0.0	13.7	0.0	13.8	0.7	13.8	0.0	13.8	0.0	14.0	1.4	14.0	0.0
1966	14.0	0.0	14.0	0.0	13.9	-0.7	13.9	0.0	14.0	0.7	14.1	0.7	14.1	0.0	14.2	0.7	14.2	0.0	14.3	0.7	14.3	0.0	14.3	0.0
1967	14.3	0.0	14.4	0.7	14.4	0.0	14.4	0.0	14.5	0.7	14.5	0.0	14.5	0.0	14.6	0.7	14.6	0.0	14.4	-1.4	14.3	-0.7	14.3	0.0
1968	14.2	-0.7	14.3	0.7	14.2	-0.7	14.3	0.7	14.3	0.0	14.4	0.7	14.4	0.0	14.3	-0.7	14.3	0.0	14.2	-0.7	14.2	0.0	14.2	0.0
1969	14.2	0.0	14.3	0.7	14.5	1.4	14.5	0.0	14.5	0.0	14.6	0.7	14.6	0.0	14.6	0.0	14.6	0.0	14.7	0.7	14.7	0.0	14.8	0.7
1970	14.7	-0.7	14.8	0.7	14.8	0.0	15.0	1.4	15.1	0.7	15.1	0.0	15.2	0.7	15.3	0.7	15.6	2.0	15.8	1.3	15.9	0.6	16.4	3.1

[Continued]

FUELS AND RELATED PRODUCTS AND POWER

Producer Price Index
Base 1982 = 100
[Continued]

For 1926-1993. Columns headed % show percentile change in the index from the previous period for which an index is available.

Year	Jan Index	%	Feb Index	%	Mar Index	%	Apr Index	%	May Index	%	Jun Index	%	Jul Index	%	Aug Index	%	Sep Index	%	Oct Index	%	Nov Index	%	Dec Index	%
1971	16.5	0.6	16.5	0.0	16.4	-0.6	16.4	0.0	16.6	1.2	16.6	0.0	16.7	0.6	16.8	0.6	16.8	0.0	16.7	-0.6	16.7	0.0	16.9	1.2
1972	16.7	-1.2	16.7	0.0	16.8	0.6	16.9	0.6	16.9	0.0	17.0	0.6	17.1	0.6	17.3	1.2	17.4	0.6	17.4	0.0	17.5	0.6	17.6	0.6
1973	17.6	0.0	18.2	3.4	18.4	1.1	18.6	1.1	18.9	1.6	19.2	1.6	19.4	1.0	19.5	0.5	19.8	1.5	20.1	1.5	20.8	3.5	21.9	5.3
1974	23.4	6.8	25.6	9.4	27.3	6.6	28.5	4.4	29.5	3.5	30.4	3.1	32.0	5.3	32.6	1.9	32.5	-0.3	33.0	1.5	32.8	-0.6	33.0	0.6
1975	33.5	1.5	33.5	0.0	33.6	0.3	34.1	1.5	34.4	0.9	35.0	1.7	35.6	1.7	36.4	2.2	36.8	1.1	37.0	0.5	37.1	0.3	37.2	0.3
1976	37.1	-0.3	36.9	-0.5	36.9	0.0	37.1	0.5	37.1	0.0	37.6	1.3	38.3	1.9	38.8	1.3	39.1	0.8	40.0	2.3	40.6	1.5	40.3	-0.7
1977	40.2	-0.2	41.7	3.7	42.4	1.7	43.1	1.7	43.6	1.2	43.9	0.7	44.3	0.9	44.7	0.9	44.7	0.0	44.8	0.2	44.8	0.0	45.0	0.4
1978	45.1	0.2	45.1	0.0	45.5	0.9	45.8	0.7	46.1	0.7	46.6	1.1	46.8	0.4	46.9	0.2	47.1	0.4	47.4	0.6	47.6	0.4	48.2	1.3
1979	48.8	1.2	49.4	1.2	50.6	2.4	52.2	3.2	54.5	4.4	56.8	4.2	59.4	4.6	62.4	5.1	65.6	5.1	67.6	3.0	68.8	1.8	70.4	2.3
1980	73.3	4.1	76.8	4.8	79.9	4.0	81.7	2.3	82.5	1.0	83.2	0.8	84.5	1.6	85.2	0.8	85.6	0.5	85.5	-0.1	86.6	1.3	88.8	2.5
1981	91.5	3.0	96.3	5.2	100.5	4.4	102.0	1.5	102.3	0.3	102.1	-0.2	101.7	-0.4	101.6	-0.1	101.5	-0.1	100.7	-0.8	100.7	0.0	101.3	0.6
1982	101.7	0.4	100.7	-1.0	99.5	-1.2	96.7	-2.8	95.5	-1.2	97.7	2.3	101.1	3.5	101.8	0.7	101.0	-0.8	100.8	-0.2	101.9	1.1	101.5	-0.4
1983	98.6	-2.9	96.5	-2.1	94.9	-1.7	93.0	-2.0	94.0	1.1	96.0	2.1	96.5	0.5	96.9	0.4	97.0	0.1	96.6	-0.4	95.7	-0.9	94.9	-0.8
1984	94.1	-0.8	94.6	0.5	95.0	0.4	94.4	-0.6	95.3	1.0	96.1	0.8	95.9	-0.2	94.9	-1.0	94.1	-0.8	94.4	0.3	94.5	0.1	93.6	-1.0
1985	91.9	-1.8	90.2	-1.8	90.2	0.0	91.4	1.3	93.4	2.2	92.4	-1.1	91.7	-0.8	90.5	-1.3	90.7	0.2	90.6	-0.1	91.6	1.1	92.3	0.8
1986	89.5	-3.0	81.8	-8.6	73.9	-9.7	69.6	-5.8	69.8	0.3	69.9	0.1	64.1	-8.3	63.2	-1.4	65.3	3.3	63.3	-3.1	63.3	0.0	63.4	0.2
1987	66.6	5.0	68.0	2.1	68.3	0.4	69.1	1.2	69.7	0.9	71.1	2.0	72.6	2.1	73.8	1.7	72.2	-2.2	71.1	-1.5	70.8	-0.4	69.5	-1.8
1988	67.2	-3.3	66.7	-0.7	65.9	-1.2	67.6	2.6	68.4	1.2	68.6	0.3	68.0	-0.9	67.6	-0.6	66.1	-2.2	64.5	-2.4	64.4	-0.2	65.6	1.9
1989	68.1	3.8	68.9	1.2	69.9	1.5	74.2	6.2	76.0	2.4	75.8	-0.3	75.5	-0.4	72.0	-4.6	73.9	2.6	73.7	-0.3	72.8	-1.2	73.7	1.2
1990	79.8	8.3	77.0	-3.5	74.6	-3.1	73.4	-1.6	74.1	1.0	72.8	-1.8	72.7	-0.1	82.4	13.3	91.3	10.8	101.0	10.6	97.4	-3.6	90.5	-7.1
1991	90.1	-0.4	83.0	-7.9	78.5	-5.4	78.1	-0.5	80.2	2.7	80.3	0.1	80.1	-0.2	81.3	1.5	81.4	0.1	81.3	-0.1	81.2	-0.1	79.1	-2.6
1992	76.3	-3.5	76.8	0.7	75.8	-1.3	77.1	1.7	79.7	3.4	83.2	4.4	83.3	0.1	82.8	-0.6	84.4	1.9	83.2	-1.4	82.1	-1.3	79.7	-2.9
1993	79.4	-0.4	79.2	-0.3	79.7	0.6	80.3	0.8	81.9	2.0	83.2	1.6	81.0	-2.6	80.2	-1.0	80.9	0.9	81.2	0.4	78.3	-3.6	74.4	-5.0

Source: U.S. Department of Labor, Bureau of Labor Statistics, Division of Industry Prices and Price Indexes. n.e.c. stands for not elsewhere classified. - indicates no data collected for period or unavailable.

Coal
Producer Price Index
Base 1982 = 100

For 1926-1993. Columns headed % show percentile change in the index from the previous period for which an index is available.

Year	Jan Index	%	Feb Index	%	Mar Index	%	Apr Index	%	May Index	%	Jun Index	%	Jul Index	%	Aug Index	%	Sep Index	%	Oct Index	%	Nov Index	%	Dec Index	%
1926	8.7	-	8.4	-3.4	8.3	-1.2	8.1	-2.4	8.1	0.0	8.1	0.0	8.1	0.0	8.2	1.2	8.3	1.2	8.7	4.8	9.4	8.0	8.9	-5.3
1927	8.7	-2.2	8.5	-2.3	8.4	-1.2	8.3	-1.2	8.3	0.0	8.3	0.0	8.3	0.0	8.4	1.2	8.5	1.2	8.3	-2.4	8.2	-1.2	8.2	0.0
1928	8.1	-1.2	8.1	0.0	8.0	-1.2	7.8	-2.5	7.7	-1.3	7.8	1.3	7.7	-1.3	7.8	1.3	7.8	0.0	7.9	1.3	7.9	0.0	7.8	-1.3
1929	7.9	1.3	7.9	0.0	7.8	-1.3	7.5	-3.8	7.5	0.0	7.5	0.0	7.6	1.3	7.6	0.0	7.7	1.3	7.7	0.0	7.7	0.0	7.8	1.3
1930	7.7	-1.3	7.7	0.0	7.6	-1.3	7.5	-1.3	7.4	-1.3	7.4	0.0	7.4	0.0	7.5	1.4	7.5	0.0	7.6	1.3	7.5	-1.3	7.5	0.0
1931	7.5	0.0	7.4	-1.3	7.3	-1.4	7.2	-1.4	7.2	0.0	7.2	0.0	7.2	0.0	7.3	1.4	7.3	0.0	7.3	0.0	7.3	0.0	7.3	0.0
1932	7.4	1.4	7.3	-1.4	7.2	-1.4	7.1	-1.4	7.0	-1.4	7.0	0.0	7.0	0.0	7.0	0.0	7.0	0.0	7.0	0.0	7.0	0.0	7.0	0.0
1933	7.0	0.0	6.9	-1.4	6.9	0.0	6.7	-2.9	6.6	-1.5	6.6	0.0	6.8	3.0	7.0	2.9	7.1	1.4	7.4	4.2	7.5	1.4	7.5	0.0
1934	7.5	0.0	7.5	0.0	7.5	0.0	7.6	1.3	7.6	0.0	7.6	0.0	7.7	1.3	7.8	1.3	7.8	0.0	7.8	0.0	7.8	0.0	7.8	0.0
1935	7.8	0.0	7.8	0.0	7.8	0.0	7.6	-2.6	7.6	0.0	7.6	0.0	7.7	1.3	7.7	0.0	7.8	1.3	7.9	1.3	8.0	1.3	8.0	0.0
1936	8.0	0.0	8.1	1.3	8.0	-1.2	7.8	-2.5	7.7	-1.3	7.7	0.0	7.7	0.0	7.8	1.3	7.8	0.0	7.9	1.3	7.9	0.0	7.9	0.0
1937	7.9	0.0	7.9	0.0	7.8	-1.3	7.7	-1.3	7.8	1.3	7.8	0.0	7.8	0.0	7.9	1.3	7.9	0.0	7.9	0.0	7.9	0.0	8.1	2.5
1938	8.2	1.2	8.2	0.0	7.9	-3.7	7.8	-1.3	7.7	-1.3	7.7	0.0	7.8	1.3	7.8	0.0	7.9	1.3	7.9	0.0	7.9	0.0	7.9	0.0
1939	7.9	0.0	7.9	0.0	7.9	0.0	7.8	-1.3	7.8	0.0	7.6	-2.6	7.6	0.0	7.6	0.0	7.6	0.0	7.8	2.6	7.8	0.0	7.8	0.0
1940	7.9	1.3	7.9	0.0	7.8	-1.3	7.7	-1.3	7.6	-1.3	7.7	1.3	7.7	0.0	7.7	0.0	7.8	1.3	8.0	2.6	8.0	0.0	8.1	1.3
1941	8.1	0.0	8.1	0.0	8.0	-1.2	8.0	0.0	8.2	2.5	8.3	1.2	8.4	1.2	8.5	1.2	8.6	1.2	8.6	0.0	8.6	0.0	8.6	0.0
1942	8.7	1.2	8.7	0.0	8.7	0.0	8.6	-1.1	8.7	1.2	8.7	0.0	8.7	0.0	8.8	1.1	8.8	0.0	8.8	0.0	8.8	0.0	8.9	1.1
1943	9.0	1.1	9.1	1.1	9.2	1.1	9.2	0.0	9.2	0.0	9.2	0.0	9.3	1.1	9.3	0.0	9.3	0.0	9.3	0.0	9.3	0.0	9.5	2.2
1944	9.6	1.1	9.6	0.0	9.6	0.0	9.6	0.0	9.6	0.0	9.6	0.0	9.6	0.0	9.6	0.0	9.6	0.0	9.6	0.0	9.6	0.0	9.6	0.0
1945	9.6	0.0	9.6	0.0	9.6	0.0	9.6	0.0	9.8	2.1	9.9	1.0	10.0	1.0	10.0	0.0	10.0	0.0	10.0	0.0	10.0	0.0	10.1	1.0
1946	10.1	0.0	10.1	0.0	10.1	0.0	10.1	0.0	10.1	0.0	10.6	5.0	11.0	3.8	11.1	0.9	11.1	0.0	11.1	0.0	11.1	0.0	11.2	0.9
1947	11.5	2.7	11.5	0.0	11.5	0.0	11.6	0.9	11.6	0.0	11.6	0.0	13.5	16.4	14.3	5.9	14.4	0.7	14.5	0.7	14.5	0.0	14.6	0.7
1948	14.7	0.7	14.7	0.0	14.7	0.0	14.8	0.7	15.0	1.4	15.1	0.7	16.3	7.9	16.4	0.6	16.4	0.0	16.3	-0.6	16.3	0.0	16.3	0.0
1949	16.3	0.0	16.2	-0.6	16.0	-1.2	15.4	-3.8	15.2	-1.3	15.2	0.0	15.3	0.7	15.3	0.0	15.3	0.0	15.3	0.0	15.5	1.3	15.6	0.6
1950	15.7	0.6	15.8	0.6	16.0	1.3	15.5	-3.1	15.4	-0.6	15.4	0.0	15.4	0.0	15.5	0.6	15.6	0.6	15.6	0.0	15.6	0.0	15.6	0.0
1951	15.6	0.0	16.2	3.8	16.2	0.0	15.9	-1.9	15.8	-0.6	15.9	0.6	15.7	-1.3	15.8	0.6	15.9	0.6	16.0	0.6	16.0	0.0	16.0	0.0
1952	16.0	0.0	16.0	0.0	16.0	0.0	15.4	-3.8	15.4	0.0	15.5	0.6	15.6	0.6	15.6	0.0	15.8	1.3	16.6	5.1	16.7	0.6	17.0	1.8
1953	17.1	0.6	17.0	-0.6	16.8	-1.2	16.3	-3.0	16.3	0.0	16.3	0.0	16.4	0.6	16.4	0.0	16.5	0.6	16.5	0.0	16.5	0.0	16.5	0.0
1954	16.4	-0.6	16.3	-0.6	15.8	-3.1	15.3	-3.2	15.4	0.7	15.4	0.0	15.4	0.0	15.4	0.0	15.5	0.6	15.4	-0.6	15.4	0.0	15.4	0.0
1955	15.4	0.0	15.4	0.0	15.4	0.0	15.0	-2.6	14.7	-2.0	14.8	0.7	14.9	0.7	15.0	0.7	15.9	6.0	16.0	0.6	16.0	0.0	16.1	0.6
1956	16.1	0.0	16.1	0.0	16.2	0.6	16.4	1.2	16.4	0.0	16.5	0.6	16.6	0.6	16.7	0.6	16.8	0.6	17.8	6.0	17.9	0.6	18.1	1.1
1957	18.2	0.6	18.2	0.0	18.1	-0.5	18.1	0.0	18.1	0.0	18.1	0.0	18.2	0.6	18.3	0.5	18.3	0.0	18.4	0.5	18.5	0.5	18.5	0.0
1958	18.5	0.0	18.5	0.0	18.5	0.0	17.6	-4.9	17.6	0.0	17.7	0.6	17.8	0.6	17.9	0.6	18.0	0.6	18.2	1.1	18.2	0.0	18.2	0.0
1959	18.4	1.1	18.5	0.5	18.3	-1.1	17.5	-4.4	17.4	-0.6	17.6	1.1	17.8	1.1	17.9	0.6	18.0	0.6	18.1	0.6	18.2	0.6	18.2	0.0
1960	18.2	0.0	18.2	0.0	18.2	0.0	17.5	-3.8	17.4	-0.6	17.5	0.6	17.7	1.1	17.8	0.6	18.0	1.1	18.0	0.0	18.0	0.0	18.1	0.6
1961	18.1	0.0	18.1	0.0	18.0	-0.6	17.6	-2.2	17.2	-2.3	17.3	0.6	17.4	0.6	17.5	0.6	17.6	0.6	17.7	0.6	17.8	0.6	17.9	0.6
1962	17.9	0.0	17.9	0.0	17.9	0.0	17.3	-3.4	17.1	-1.2	17.1	0.0	17.3	1.2	17.3	0.0	17.5	1.2	17.6	0.6	17.7	0.6	17.8	0.6
1963	17.8	0.0	17.8	0.0	17.8	0.0	17.2	-3.4	17.1	-0.6	17.2	0.6	17.3	0.6	17.4	0.6	17.6	1.1	17.7	0.6	17.8	0.6	17.8	0.0
1964	17.8	0.0	17.8	0.0	17.6	-1.1	17.2	-2.3	17.2	0.0	17.3	0.6	17.4	0.6	17.5	0.6	17.6	0.6	17.7	0.6	17.7	0.0	17.8	0.6
1965	17.8	0.0	17.8	0.0	17.6	-1.1	17.1	-2.8	17.1	0.0	17.1	0.0	17.2	0.6	17.3	0.6	17.5	1.2	17.6	0.6	17.7	0.6	17.7	0.0
1966	17.8	0.6	17.8	0.0	17.7	-0.6	17.2	-2.8	17.5	1.7	17.6	0.6	17.7	0.6	17.8	0.6	18.0	1.1	18.2	1.1	18.4	1.1	18.5	0.5
1967	18.5	0.0	18.5	0.0	18.5	0.0	18.6	0.5	18.6	0.0	18.6	0.0	18.6	0.0	18.8	1.1	18.8	0.0	18.9	0.5	19.0	0.5	19.0	0.0
1968	19.0	0.0	19.0	0.0	19.1	0.5	19.2	0.5	19.1	-0.5	19.1	0.0	19.2	0.5	19.2	0.0	19.2	0.0	19.9	3.6	20.2	1.5	20.4	1.0
1969	20.4	0.0	20.4	0.0	20.4	0.0	20.6	1.0	20.5	-0.5	20.7	1.0	20.9	1.0	20.9	0.0	21.0	0.5	22.0	4.8	22.4	1.8	22.5	0.4
1970	22.7	0.9	23.8	4.8	24.1	1.3	26.4	9.5	26.6	0.8	27.8	4.5	28.4	2.2	28.8	1.4	30.1	4.5	32.8	9.0	32.9	0.3	32.9	0.0

[Continued]

Coal
Producer Price Index
Base 1982 = 100
[Continued]

For 1926-1993. Columns headed % show percentile change in the index from the previous period for which an index is available.

Year	Jan Index	%	Feb Index	%	Mar Index	%	Apr Index	%	May Index	%	Jun Index	%	Jul Index	%	Aug Index	%	Sep Index	%	Oct Index	%	Nov Index	%	Dec Index	%
1971	32.9	0.0	32.9	0.0	32.9	0.0	34.4	4.6	34.2	-0.6	34.1	-0.3	34.2	0.3	34.2	0.0	34.2	0.0	34.2	0.0	34.2	0.0	36.0	5.3
1972	36.0	0.0	36.0	0.0	36.0	0.0	35.8	-0.6	35.8	0.0	35.8	0.0	35.8	0.0	35.8	0.0	35.9	0.3	36.0	0.3	37.6	4.4	38.4	2.1
1973	38.4	0.0	38.7	0.8	38.8	0.3	40.0	3.1	40.1	0.3	40.2	0.2	40.0	-0.5	40.1	0.3	41.6	3.7	41.9	0.7	44.7	6.7	45.0	0.7
1974	46.6	3.6	47.3	1.5	48.5	2.5	56.8	17.1	57.6	1.4	60.1	4.3	64.3	7.0	66.9	4.0	69.5	3.9	73.7	6.0	74.4	0.9	80.1	7.7
1975	80.2	0.1	76.6	-4.5	72.6	-5.2	72.4	-0.3	72.8	0.6	72.2	-0.8	71.5	-1.0	70.7	-1.1	69.8	-1.3	69.4	-0.6	68.2	-1.7	69.4	1.8
1976	69.2	-0.3	69.0	-0.3	68.8	-0.3	68.7	-0.1	68.7	0.0	68.6	-0.1	68.8	0.3	68.8	0.0	68.8	0.0	68.9	0.1	69.0	0.1	69.9	1.3
1977	70.3	0.6	70.6	0.4	70.8	0.3	71.0	0.3	72.3	1.8	73.0	1.0	73.5	0.7	73.7	0.3	73.9	0.3	74.5	0.8	74.9	0.5	75.2	0.4
1978	75.5	0.4	75.7	0.3	76.1	0.5	79.7	4.7	80.9	1.5	81.3	0.5	81.7	0.5	82.6	1.1	82.8	0.2	83.0	0.2	82.7	-0.4	83.0	0.4
1979	83.0	0.0	83.0	0.0	83.3	0.4	83.6	0.4	84.3	0.8	84.5	0.2	84.6	0.1	84.9	0.4	84.6	-0.4	85.0	0.5	85.1	0.1	85.8	0.8
1980	85.9	0.1	86.0	0.1	86.3	0.3	87.0	0.8	87.2	0.2	87.2	0.0	87.4	0.2	87.6	0.2	88.1	0.6	88.0	-0.1	88.9	1.0	88.9	0.0
1981	89.4	0.6	89.9	0.6	90.0	0.1	90.9	1.0	91.1	0.2	91.9	0.9	94.5	2.8	94.8	0.3	95.4	0.6	95.5	0.1	95.9	0.4	96.4	0.5
1982	98.2	1.9	99.1	0.9	99.0	-0.1	99.6	0.6	99.9	0.3	99.8	-0.1	100.6	0.8	100.8	0.2	100.7	-0.1	100.6	-0.1	100.9	0.3	100.7	-0.2
1983	100.2	-0.5	99.7	-0.5	100.7	1.0	100.6	-0.1	100.1	-0.5	99.9	-0.2	100.0	0.1	100.3	0.3	100.6	0.3	100.7	0.1	101.4	0.7	101.7	0.3
1984	101.2	-0.5	101.9	0.7	102.1	0.2	101.4	-0.7	102.4	1.0	101.8	-0.6	102.5	0.7	102.9	0.4	102.7	-0.2	102.7	0.0	102.6	-0.1	102.4	-0.2
1985	102.5	0.1	102.8	0.3	102.6	-0.2	102.4	-0.2	102.5	0.1	102.4	-0.1	102.8	0.4	102.9	0.1	102.6	-0.3	101.7	-0.9	100.6	-1.1	101.1	0.5
1986	101.3	0.2	100.9	-0.4	101.5	0.6	101.1	-0.4	100.9	-0.2	100.8	-0.1	100.9	0.1	100.7	-0.2	100.5	-0.2	100.5	0.0	100.1	-0.4	100.0	-0.1
1987	100.1	0.1	99.3	-0.8	99.0	-0.3	97.2	-1.8	96.8	-0.4	96.5	-0.3	96.1	-0.4	96.1	0.0	95.8	-0.3	96.0	0.2	96.4	0.4	95.9	-0.5
1988	95.6	-0.3	96.3	0.7	95.8	-0.5	95.5	-0.3	95.2	-0.3	95.2	0.0	95.7	0.5	95.1	-0.6	95.4	0.3	95.5	0.1	94.7	-0.8	94.6	-0.1
1989	94.1	-0.5	93.6	-0.5	93.6	0.0	94.2	0.6	94.6	0.4	94.9	0.3	96.2	1.4	96.6	0.4	96.5	-0.1	97.1	0.6	97.7	0.6	97.2	-0.5
1990	97.8	0.6	96.3	-1.5	96.4	0.1	96.7	0.3	97.7	1.0	97.9	0.2	98.0	0.1	96.9	-1.1	97.5	0.6	98.2	0.7	98.8	0.6	97.9	-0.9
1991	98.5	0.6	98.2	-0.3	97.4	-0.8	97.3	-0.1	97.1	-0.2	98.0	0.9	97.6	-0.4	96.6	-1.0	95.9	-0.7	96.6	0.0	97.1	1.3	96.3	-0.8
1992	93.7	-2.7	94.5	0.9	93.8	-0.7	94.8	1.1	95.0	0.2	96.0	1.1	95.3	-0.7	95.1	-0.2	95.1	0.0	95.7	0.6	94.8	-0.9	96.5	1.8
1993	95.6	-0.9	94.9	-0.7	94.9	0.0	94.6	-0.3	94.1	-0.5	94.1	0.0	94.4	0.3	95.5	1.2	98.9	3.6	97.9	-1.0	100.9	3.1	97.6	-3.3

Source: U.S. Department of Labor, Bureau of Labor Statistics, Division of Industry Prices and Price Indexes. n.e.c. stands for not elsewhere classified. - indicates no data collected for period or unavailable.

Coke Oven Products
Producer Price Index
Base 1982 = 100

For 1926-1993. Columns headed % show percentile change in the index from the previous period for which an index is available.

Year	Jan Index	%	Feb Index	%	Mar Index	%	Apr Index	%	May Index	%	Jun Index	%	Jul Index	%	Aug Index	%	Sep Index	%	Oct Index	%	Nov Index	%	Dec Index	%
1926	6.8	-	6.8	0.0	6.1	-10.3	5.6	-8.2	5.5	-1.8	5.6	1.8	5.6	0.0	5.6	0.0	5.7	1.8	5.7	0.0	6.3	10.5	6.1	-3.2
1927	5.8	-4.9	5.7	-1.7	5.7	0.0	5.7	0.0	5.6	-1.8	5.6	0.0	5.6	0.0	5.6	0.0	5.6	0.0	5.6	0.0	5.5	-1.8	5.5	0.0
1928	5.1	-7.3	5.0	-2.0	5.0	0.0	4.9	-2.0	5.0	2.0	5.0	0.0	5.0	0.0	5.0	0.0	5.0	0.0	5.0	0.0	5.0	0.0	5.0	0.0
1929	5.0	0.0	5.0	0.0	5.1	2.0	5.0	-2.0	5.0	0.0	5.0	0.0	5.0	0.0	5.0	0.0	5.0	0.0	5.0	0.0	5.0	0.0	5.0	0.0
1930	5.0	0.0	5.0	0.0	5.0	0.0	5.0	0.0	5.0	0.0	5.0	0.0	5.0	0.0	5.0	0.0	5.0	0.0	5.0	0.0	5.0	0.0	5.0	0.0
1931	5.0	0.0	5.0	0.0	5.0	0.0	5.0	0.0	5.0	0.0	4.9	-2.0	4.9	0.0	4.9	0.0	4.9	0.0	4.9	0.0	4.8	-2.0	4.8	0.0
1932	4.8	0.0	4.8	0.0	4.8	0.0	4.7	-2.1	4.6	-2.1	4.6	0.0	4.5	-2.2	4.6	2.2	4.6	0.0	4.6	0.0	4.5	-2.2	4.5	0.0
1933	4.5	0.0	4.5	0.0	4.5	0.0	4.5	0.0	4.5	0.0	4.5	0.0	4.5	0.0	4.6	2.2	4.7	2.2	4.9	4.3	5.0	2.0	5.0	0.0
1934	5.0	0.0	5.0	0.0	5.0	0.0	5.0	0.0	5.0	0.0	5.0	0.0	5.1	2.0	5.1	0.0	5.1	0.0	5.1	0.0	5.1	0.0	5.1	0.0
1935	5.1	0.0	5.3	3.9	5.3	0.0	5.3	0.0	5.3	0.0	5.3	0.0	5.3	0.0	5.3	0.0	5.3	0.0	5.3	0.0	5.3	0.0	5.3	0.0
1936	5.5	3.8	5.6	1.8	5.6	0.0	5.6	0.0	5.6	0.0	5.6	0.0	5.6	0.0	5.6	0.0	5.6	0.0	5.8	3.6	5.8	0.0	5.8	0.0
1937	5.8	0.0	5.8	0.0	5.8	0.0	6.1	5.2	6.2	1.6	6.2	0.0	6.2	0.0	6.2	0.0	6.2	0.0	6.2	0.0	6.3	1.6	6.3	0.0
1938	6.3	0.0	6.3	0.0	6.3	0.0	6.3	0.0	6.3	0.0	6.2	-1.6	6.2	0.0	6.2	0.0	6.2	0.0	6.2	0.0	6.2	0.0	6.2	0.0
1939	6.2	0.0	6.2	0.0	6.2	0.0	6.2	0.0	6.2	0.0	6.2	0.0	6.2	0.0	6.2	0.0	6.2	0.0	6.4	3.2	6.6	3.1	6.5	-1.5
1940	6.5	0.0	6.5	0.0	6.5	0.0	6.5	0.0	6.5	0.0	6.5	0.0	6.5	0.0	6.5	0.0	6.5	0.0	6.5	0.0	6.7	3.1	6.8	1.5
1941	6.8	0.0	6.8	0.0	6.8	0.0	6.8	0.0	7.1	4.4	7.3	2.8	7.3	0.0	7.3	0.0	7.3	0.0	7.3	0.0	7.3	0.0	7.3	0.0
1942	7.3	0.0	7.3	0.0	7.3	0.0	7.3	0.0	7.3	0.0	7.3	0.0	7.3	0.0	7.3	0.0	7.3	0.0	7.3	0.0	7.3	0.0	7.3	0.0
1943	7.3	0.0	7.3	0.0	7.3	0.0	7.3	0.0	7.3	0.0	7.3	0.0	7.3	0.0	7.3	0.0	7.3	0.0	7.3	0.0	7.4	1.4	7.4	0.0
1944	7.5	1.4	7.8	4.0	7.8	0.0	7.8	0.0	7.8	0.0	7.8	0.0	7.8	0.0	7.8	0.0	7.8	0.0	7.8	0.0	7.8	0.0	7.8	0.0
1945	7.8	0.0	7.8	0.0	7.8	0.0	7.8	0.0	7.8	0.0	7.8	0.0	7.8	0.0	8.0	2.6	8.0	0.0	8.0	0.0	8.0	0.0	8.0	0.0
1946	8.0	0.0	8.0	0.0	8.0	0.0	7.9	-1.2	7.9	0.0	7.9	0.0	8.8	11.4	8.8	0.0	8.8	0.0	8.8	0.0	8.8	0.0	8.8	0.0
1947	9.1	3.4	9.2	1.1	9.2	0.0	9.3	1.1	9.3	0.0	9.4	1.1	9.6	2.1	10.4	8.3	10.7	2.9	10.7	0.0	10.8	0.9	10.9	0.9
1948	11.3	3.7	11.4	0.9	11.4	0.0	11.5	0.9	12.1	5.2	12.4	2.5	12.6	1.6	12.9	2.4	12.9	0.0	12.9	0.0	12.9	0.0	12.9	0.0
1949	13.1	1.6	13.2	0.8	13.2	0.0	13.2	0.0	13.1	-0.8	13.1	0.0	13.1	0.0	13.1	0.0	13.1	0.0	13.1	0.0	13.1	0.0	13.1	0.0
1950	13.1	0.0	13.3	1.5	13.5	1.5	13.6	0.7	13.6	0.0	13.6	0.0	13.6	0.0	13.6	0.0	13.6	0.0	13.6	0.0	13.8	1.5	14.2	2.9	14.3	0.7
1951	14.5	1.4	14.5	0.0	14.5	0.0	14.6	0.7	14.6	0.0	14.6	0.0	14.6	0.0	14.6	0.0	14.6	0.0	14.6	0.0	14.6	0.0	14.6	0.0
1952	14.6	0.0	14.6	0.0	14.6	0.0	14.6	0.0	14.6	0.0	14.6	0.0	14.6	0.0	14.6	0.0	14.6	0.0	14.6	0.0	14.6	0.0	15.2	4.1
1953	15.5	2.0	15.5	0.0	15.5	0.0	15.5	0.0	15.5	0.0	15.5	0.0	15.5	0.0	15.5	0.0	15.5	0.0	15.6	0.6	15.6	0.0	15.6	0.0
1954	15.6	0.0	15.6	0.0	15.6	0.0	15.6	0.0	15.6	0.0	15.6	0.0	15.6	0.0	15.6	0.0	15.6	0.0	15.6	0.0	15.6	0.0	15.6	0.0
1955	15.6	0.0	15.6	0.0	15.6	0.0	15.7	0.6	15.7	0.0	15.7	0.0	15.7	0.0	16.2	3.2	16.1	-0.6	16.3	1.2	16.3	0.0	16.3	0.0
1956	17.1	4.9	17.1	0.0	17.1	0.0	17.1	0.0	17.1	0.0	17.1	0.0	17.1	0.0	18.0	5.3	18.4	2.2	18.4	0.0	18.4	0.0	18.4	0.0
1957	18.7	1.6	19.1	2.1	19.0	-0.5	19.0	0.0	19.0	0.0	19.0	0.0	19.0	0.0	19.0	0.0	19.0	0.0	19.0	0.0	19.0	0.0	19.0	0.0
1958	19.0	0.0	19.0	0.0	19.0	0.0	19.0	0.0	19.0	0.0	19.0	0.0	19.0	0.0	19.0	0.0	19.0	0.0	19.0	0.0	19.0	0.0	19.0	0.0
1959	19.2	1.1	20.0	4.2	20.0	0.0	20.0	0.0	20.0	0.0	20.0	0.0	20.0	0.0	20.0	0.0	20.0	0.0	20.0	0.0	20.0	0.0	20.0	0.0
1960	20.0	0.0	20.0	0.0	20.0	0.0	20.0	0.0	20.0	0.0	20.0	0.0	20.0	0.0	20.0	0.0	20.0	0.0	20.0	0.0	20.0	0.0	20.0	0.0
1961	20.0	0.0	20.0	0.0	20.0	0.0	20.0	0.0	20.0	0.0	20.0	0.0	20.0	0.0	20.0	0.0	20.0	0.0	20.0	0.0	20.0	0.0	20.0	0.0
1962	20.0	0.0	20.0	0.0	20.0	0.0	20.0	0.0	20.0	0.0	20.0	0.0	20.0	0.0	20.0	0.0	20.0	0.0	20.0	0.0	20.0	0.0	20.0	0.0
1963	20.0	0.0	20.0	0.0	20.0	0.0	20.0	0.0	20.0	0.0	20.0	0.0	20.0	0.0	20.0	0.0	20.0	0.0	20.0	0.0	20.0	0.0	20.0	0.0
1964	20.0	0.0	20.0	0.0	20.0	0.0	20.5	2.5	20.8	1.5	20.8	0.0	20.8	0.0	20.8	0.0	20.8	0.0	20.8	0.0	20.8	0.0	20.8	0.0
1965	20.8	0.0	20.8	0.0	20.8	0.0	20.8	0.0	20.8	0.0	20.8	0.0	20.8	0.0	20.8	0.0	20.8	0.0	20.8	0.0	20.8	0.0	20.8	0.0
1966	20.8	0.0	20.8	0.0	20.8	0.0	20.8	0.0	20.8	0.0	21.2	1.9	21.7	2.4	21.7	0.0	21.7	0.0	21.7	0.0	21.7	0.0	21.7	0.0
1967	21.7	0.0	21.7	0.0	21.7	0.0	21.7	0.0	21.7	0.0	21.7	0.0	21.7	0.0	21.7	0.0	21.7	0.0	21.7	0.0	21.7	0.0	21.7	0.0
1968	21.7	0.0	21.7	0.0	21.7	0.0	22.6	4.1	22.6	0.0	22.6	0.0	22.6	0.0	22.6	0.0	22.6	0.0	22.6	0.0	22.6	0.0	23.3	3.1
1969	23.3	0.0	23.3	0.0	23.3	0.0	23.3	0.0	23.3	0.0	23.3	0.0	23.3	0.0	23.3	0.0	23.3	0.0	24.5	5.2	24.5	0.0	24.5	0.0
1970	24.5	0.0	24.5	0.0	24.5	0.0	27.0	10.2	27.0	0.0	27.0	0.0	27.3	1.1	27.3	0.0	27.3	0.0	31.6	15.8	31.6	0.0	31.6	0.0

[Continued]

Coke Oven Products

Producer Price Index
Base 1982 = 100
[Continued]

For 1926-1993. Columns headed % show percentile change in the index from the previous period for which an index is available.

Year	Jan Index	%	Feb Index	%	Mar Index	%	Apr Index	%	May Index	%	Jun Index	%	Jul Index	%	Aug Index	%	Sep Index	%	Oct Index	%	Nov Index	%	Dec Index	%
1971	31.6	0.0	31.6	0.0	31.6	0.0	31.6	0.0	32.2	1.9	32.6	1.2	32.6	0.0	32.6	0.0	32.6	0.0	32.6	0.0	32.6	0.0	32.6	0.0
1972	32.6	0.0	33.6	3.1	33.6	0.0	33.6	0.0	33.6	0.0	33.6	0.0	33.6	0.0	33.6	0.0	33.6	0.0	34.0	1.2	34.0	0.0	34.6	1.8
1973	35.2	1.7	35.7	1.4	35.7	0.0	36.2	1.4	36.2	0.0	36.2	0.0	36.2	0.0	36.2	0.0	36.2	0.0	36.2	0.0	36.2	0.0	36.8	1.7
1974	37.7	2.4	37.6	-0.3	40.1	6.6	46.6	16.2	52.4	12.4	53.9	2.9	55.4	2.8	58.5	5.6	60.8	3.9	66.1	8.7	67.2	1.7	67.6	0.6
1975	71.6	5.9	71.6	0.0	71.6	0.0	72.0	0.6	72.0	0.0	72.0	0.0	71.4	-0.8	71.1	-0.4	71.7	0.8	71.7	0.0	71.7	0.0	71.7	0.0
1976	71.6	-0.1	74.9	4.6	75.0	0.1	75.0	0.0	75.0	0.0	75.0	0.0	75.0	0.0	75.0	0.0	75.0	0.0	75.8	1.1	75.8	0.0	78.7	3.8
1977	79.6	1.1	79.6	0.0	79.6	0.0	80.8	1.5	81.3	0.6	83.6	2.8	83.6	0.0	83.6	0.0	83.6	0.0	83.6	0.0	83.6	0.0	83.6	0.0
1978	84.1	0.6	86.8	3.2	86.8	0.0	86.8	0.0	90.7	4.5	90.7	0.0	90.7	0.0	90.7	0.0	90.7	0.0	90.7	0.0	90.7	0.0	90.7	0.0
1979	91.2	0.6	91.8	0.7	92.8	1.1	93.2	0.4	93.3	0.1	93.3	0.0	93.3	0.0	93.3	0.0	93.3	0.0	93.4	0.1	93.4	0.0	93.4	0.0
1980	93.3	-0.1	93.3	0.0	93.3	0.0	93.3	0.0	93.3	0.0	93.3	0.0	93.3	0.0	93.3	0.0	93.3	0.0	93.3	0.0	93.3	0.0	93.2	-0.1
1981	93.2	0.0	93.2	0.0	93.2	0.0	93.2	0.0	101.3	8.7	101.7	0.4	101.7	0.0	101.7	0.0	101.7	0.0	101.7	0.0	101.7	0.0	101.7	0.0
1982	101.7	0.0	101.7	0.0	101.3	-0.4	101.3	0.0	101.3	0.0	100.1	-1.2	99.7	-0.4	99.4	-0.3	99.6	0.2	98.0	-1.6	98.0	0.0	98.0	0.0
1983	97.7	-0.3	97.7	0.0	96.9	-0.8	96.9	0.0	95.0	-2.0	95.0	0.0	93.5	-1.6	98.3	5.1	98.3	0.0	98.1	-0.2	98.3	0.2	90.0	-8.4
1984	90.6	0.7	94.8	4.6	95.1	0.3	95.9	0.8	95.6	-0.3	95.8	0.2	95.7	-0.1	94.7	-1.0	94.4	-0.3	93.7	-0.7	93.7	0.0	94.2	0.5
1985	95.2	1.1	95.2	0.0	93.8	-1.5	93.2	-0.6	93.0	-0.2	93.0	0.0	92.8	-0.2	92.8	0.0	92.8	0.0	92.5	-0.3	92.5	0.0	91.8	-0.8
1986	90.2	-1.7	90.4	0.2	90.3	-0.1	89.1	-1.3	89.0	-0.1	88.1	-1.0	88.0	-0.1	87.9	-0.1	88.0	0.1	87.4	-0.7	84.0	-3.9	84.0	0.0
1987	81.9	-2.5	80.9	-1.2	82.3	1.7	83.2	1.1	84.0	1.0	82.5	-1.8	82.4	-0.1	82.5	0.1	82.3	-0.2	83.5	1.5	83.5	0.0	84.2	0.8
1988	84.3	0.1	84.6	0.4	85.0	0.5	85.0	0.0	85.0	0.0	85.0	0.0	85.0	-0.4	85.0	0.0	85.0	0.0	85.0	0.0	85.0	0.0	85.0	0.0
1989	88.8	4.5	88.9	0.1	89.1	0.2	88.5	-0.7	90.5	2.3	90.4	-0.1	90.6	0.2	90.8	0.2	90.7	-0.1	91.0	0.3	89.8	-1.3	89.8	0.0
1990	90.4	0.7	94.1	4.1	91.1	-3.2	90.9	-0.2	90.7	-0.2	90.9	0.2	90.1	-0.9	91.2	1.2	91.0	-0.2	92.7	1.9	92.3	-0.4	91.7	-0.7
1991	90.7	-1.1	93.7	3.3	94.5	0.9	95.0	0.5	94.6	-0.4	94.6	0.0	94.6	0.0	93.1	-1.6	94.1	1.1	93.9	-0.2	94.2	0.3	93.8	-0.4
1992	94.4	0.6	94.3	-0.1	92.1	-2.3	91.8	-0.3	90.9	-1.0	89.5	-1.5	90.5	1.1	90.3	-0.2	90.1	-0.2	90.1	0.0	91.1	1.1	90.9	-0.2
1993	91.3	0.4	88.6	-3.0	88.7	0.1	88.8	0.1	88.2	-0.7	88.0	-0.2	88.7	0.8	89.8	1.2	90.6	0.9	89.8	-0.9	88.5	-1.4	88.8	0.3

Source: U.S. Department of Labor, Bureau of Labor Statistics, Division of Industry Prices and Price Indexes. n.e.c. stands for not elsewhere classified. - indicates no data collected for period or unavailable.

Gas Fuels
Producer Price Index
Base 1982 = 100

For 1958-1993. Columns headed % show percentile change in the index from the previous period for which an index is available.

Year	Jan Index	%	Feb Index	%	Mar Index	%	Apr Index	%	May Index	%	Jun Index	%	Jul Index	%	Aug Index	%	Sep Index	%	Oct Index	%	Nov Index	%	Dec Index	%
1958	7.1	-	7.2	1.4	7.1	-1.4	6.9	-2.8	6.9	0.0	6.9	0.0	6.9	0.0	7.2	4.3	7.3	1.4	7.5	2.7	7.5	0.0	7.6	1.3
1959	7.9	3.9	7.9	0.0	8.0	1.3	7.7	-3.8	7.7	0.0	7.5	-2.6	7.5	0.0	7.7	2.7	8.0	3.9	7.8	-2.5	8.0	2.6	8.1	1.3
1960	8.2	1.2	8.1	-1.2	8.2	1.2	8.2	0.0	7.9	-3.7	7.9	0.0	8.1	2.5	8.2	1.2	8.5	3.7	8.5	0.0	8.5	0.0	8.5	0.0
1961	8.5	0.0	8.6	1.2	8.6	0.0	8.3	-3.5	8.4	1.2	8.1	-3.6	8.2	1.2	8.2	0.0	8.2	0.0	8.4	2.4	8.4	0.0	8.4	0.0
1962	8.3	-1.2	8.6	3.6	8.4	-2.3	8.1	-3.6	8.2	1.2	8.0	-2.4	8.4	5.0	8.3	-1.2	8.5	2.4	8.7	2.4	8.6	-1.1	8.7	1.2
1963	8.5	-2.3	9.0	5.9	9.0	0.0	8.7	-3.3	8.5	-2.3	8.5	0.0	8.5	0.0	8.5	0.0	8.6	1.2	8.6	0.0	8.6	0.0	8.8	2.3
1964	8.8	0.0	8.9	1.1	8.7	-2.2	8.5	-2.3	8.2	-3.5	8.2	0.0	8.5	3.7	8.5	0.0	8.4	-1.2	8.5	1.2	8.7	2.4	8.7	0.0
1965	8.6	-1.1	8.7	1.2	8.7	0.0	8.6	-1.1	8.6	0.0	8.7	1.2	8.6	-1.1	8.7	1.2	8.8	1.1	8.9	1.1	8.9	0.0	9.1	2.2
1966	9.0	-1.1	9.1	1.1	9.0	-1.1	9.1	1.1	9.0	-1.1	9.1	1.1	9.0	-1.1	9.1	1.1	9.1	0.0	9.2	1.1	9.2	0.0	9.3	1.1
1967	9.5	2.2	9.5	0.0	9.5	0.0	9.5	0.0	9.5	0.0	9.5	0.0	9.3	-2.1	9.4	1.1	9.4	0.0	9.4	0.0	9.4	0.0	9.4	0.0
1968	9.2	-2.1	9.4	2.2	8.9	-5.3	8.8	-1.1	8.7	-1.1	8.7	0.0	8.5	-2.3	8.5	0.0	8.5	0.0	8.5	0.0	8.5	0.0	8.6	1.2
1969	8.7	1.2	8.8	1.1	8.8	0.0	8.6	-2.3	8.6	0.0	8.6	0.0	8.6	0.0	8.7	1.2	8.7	0.0	9.1	4.6	9.1	0.0	9.3	2.2
1970	9.3	0.0	9.5	2.2	9.6	1.1	9.6	0.0	9.6	0.0	9.7	1.0	9.7	0.0	9.7	0.0	10.1	4.1	10.0	-1.0	10.1	1.0	10.3	2.0
1971	10.2	-1.0	10.3	1.0	10.4	1.0	10.1	-2.9	10.1	0.0	10.1	0.0	10.1	0.0	10.2	1.0	10.3	1.0	10.3	0.0	10.3	0.0	10.4	1.0
1972	10.4	0.0	10.4	0.0	10.5	1.0	10.6	1.0	10.7	0.9	10.6	-0.9	10.7	0.9	10.8	0.9	11.0	1.9	11.1	0.9	11.2	0.9	11.2	0.0
1973	11.2	0.0	11.2	0.0	11.2	0.0	11.3	0.9	11.4	0.9	12.1	6.1	12.1	0.0	12.3	1.7	12.5	1.6	12.6	0.8	12.5	-0.8	13.0	4.0
1974	12.9	-0.8	13.8	7.0	14.0	1.4	14.0	0.0	14.1	0.7	14.3	1.4	17.7	23.8	17.9	1.1	15.7	-12.3	15.8	0.6	16.5	4.4	16.7	1.2
1975	17.1	2.4	17.8	4.1	17.7	-0.6	19.5	10.2	20.6	5.6	20.7	0.5	21.3	2.9	21.4	0.5	21.8	1.9	21.8	0.0	22.2	1.8	23.1	4.1
1976	23.0	-0.4	23.3	1.3	24.0	3.0	25.1	4.6	25.2	0.4	26.0	3.2	26.1	0.4	27.0	3.4	27.3	1.1	31.2	14.3	34.4	10.3	31.8	-7.6
1977	30.4	-4.4	34.3	12.8	35.0	2.0	35.7	2.0	36.8	3.1	36.4	-1.1	36.9	1.4	37.8	2.4	38.2	1.1	38.3	0.3	39.0	1.8	39.8	2.1
1978	39.6	-0.5	39.4	-0.5	40.0	1.5	40.4	1.0	40.4	0.0	40.4	0.0	40.6	0.5	40.1	-1.2	40.7	1.5	40.5	-0.5	40.9	1.0	41.9	2.4
1979	42.4	1.2	43.2	1.9	44.4	2.8	45.0	1.4	47.8	6.2	49.2	2.9	51.7	5.1	54.0	4.4	56.9	5.4	58.4	2.6	60.0	2.7	62.4	4.0
1980	63.9	2.4	67.6	5.8	67.5	-0.1	68.8	1.9	70.2	2.0	70.6	0.6	71.8	1.7	72.8	1.4	74.1	1.8	75.6	2.0	77.8	2.9	79.6	2.3
1981	80.8	1.5	83.1	2.8	83.9	1.0	85.6	2.0	88.0	2.8	90.0	2.3	91.4	1.6	89.5	-2.1	92.1	2.9	91.0	-1.2	92.7	1.9	94.6	2.0
1982	93.1	-1.6	93.1	0.0	93.4	0.3	93.6	0.2	94.4	0.9	96.9	2.6	99.4	2.6	101.3	1.9	104.8	3.5	106.5	1.6	112.2	5.4	111.3	-0.8
1983	108.1	-2.9	108.8	0.6	111.2	2.2	109.0	-2.0	109.0	0.0	108.9	-0.1	108.3	-0.6	108.0	-0.3	108.1	0.1	106.4	-1.6	105.8	-0.6	105.6	-0.2
1984	105.9	0.3	105.4	-0.5	102.8	-2.5	103.9	1.1	104.1	0.2	104.6	0.5	104.7	0.1	105.3	0.6	104.1	-1.1	104.9	0.8	105.0	0.1	104.0	-1.0
1985	101.2	-2.7	100.6	-0.6	98.4	-2.2	98.9	0.5	101.7	2.8	99.7	-2.0	99.0	-0.7	96.7	-2.3	97.2	0.5	97.4	0.2	96.5	-0.9	97.1	0.6
1986	97.5	0.4	94.0	-3.6	94.2	0.2	88.6	-5.9	86.8	-2.0	85.2	-1.8	79.4	-6.8	76.3	-3.9	73.2	-4.1	74.4	1.6	74.9	0.7	73.6	-1.7
1987	73.6	0.0	73.0	-0.8	76.2	4.4	75.5	-0.9	74.4	-1.5	74.0	-0.5	74.1	0.1	74.8	0.9	75.4	0.8	73.1	-3.1	71.6	-2.1	73.8	3.1
1988	73.3	-0.7	71.7	-2.2	72.3	0.8	74.5	3.0	72.0	-3.4	69.8	-3.1	71.1	1.9	68.7	-3.4	69.0	0.4	71.7	3.9	70.5	-1.7	71.7	1.7
1989	75.2	4.9	77.3	2.8	74.0	-4.3	75.2	1.6	77.1	2.5	76.3	-1.0	76.2	-0.1	72.8	-4.5	75.4	3.6	73.7	-2.3	74.2	0.7	76.0	2.4
1990	82.5	8.6	81.8	-0.8	76.8	-6.1	74.3	-3.3	73.9	-0.5	71.8	-2.8	76.4	6.4	71.8	-6.0	76.5	6.5	80.7	5.5	85.9	6.4	88.4	2.9
1991	86.8	-1.8	80.5	-7.3	78.3	-2.7	74.6	-4.7	77.2	3.5	75.0	-2.8	73.2	-2.4	74.2	1.4	71.5	-3.6	74.3	3.9	78.4	5.5	80.6	2.8
1992	76.1	-5.6	73.7	-3.2	70.5	-4.3	70.1	-0.6	71.0	1.3	70.2	-1.1	75.9	8.1	75.3	-0.8	81.0	7.6	78.7	-2.8	86.2	9.5	82.5	-4.3
1993	82.2	-0.4	75.8	-7.8	74.0	-2.4	75.0	1.4	81.3	8.4	85.9	5.7	77.1	-10.2	75.7	-1.8	79.0	4.4	80.4	1.8	79.7	-0.9	75.2	-5.6

Source: U.S. Department of Labor, Bureau of Labor Statistics, Division of Industry Prices and Price Indexes. n.e.c. stands for not elsewhere classified. - indicates no data collected for period or unavailable.

Electric Power
Producer Price Index
Base 1982 = 100

For 1958-1993. Columns headed % show percentile change in the index from the previous period for which an index is available.

Year	Jan Index	%	Feb Index	%	Mar Index	%	Apr Index	%	May Index	%	Jun Index	%	Jul Index	%	Aug Index	%	Sep Index	%	Oct Index	%	Nov Index	%	Dec Index	%
1958	24.4	-	24.5	0.4	24.5	0.0	24.4	-0.4	24.4	0.0	24.5	0.4	24.5	0.0	24.6	0.4	24.6	0.0	24.6	0.0	24.6	0.0	24.6	0.0
1959	24.6	0.0	24.6	0.0	24.6	0.0	24.6	0.0	24.6	0.0	24.6	0.0	24.6	0.0	24.6	0.0	24.6	0.0	24.6	0.0	24.6	0.0	24.7	0.4
1960	24.7	0.0	24.9	0.8	24.9	0.0	24.9	0.0	24.8	-0.4	24.9	0.4	24.9	0.0	24.9	0.0	24.9	0.0	24.9	0.0	25.0	0.4	25.0	0.0
1961	25.0	0.0	25.0	0.0	25.0	0.0	25.0	0.0	25.0	0.0	25.0	0.0	25.0	0.0	25.0	0.0	25.0	0.0	25.0	0.0	25.1	0.4	25.0	-0.4
1962	25.0	0.0	25.2	0.8	25.2	0.0	25.2	0.0	25.1	-0.4	25.1	0.0	25.1	0.0	25.1	0.0	25.1	0.0	25.1	0.0	25.1	0.0	25.1	0.0
1963	25.0	-0.4	25.0	0.0	25.0	0.0	25.0	0.0	25.0	0.0	25.0	0.0	24.9	-0.4	24.9	0.0	24.9	0.0	24.8	-0.4	24.7	-0.4	24.7	0.0
1964	24.7	0.0	24.7	0.0	24.3	-1.6	24.7	1.6	24.7	0.0	24.6	-0.4	24.6	0.0	24.8	0.8	24.8	0.0	24.8	0.0	24.8	0.0	24.7	-0.4
1965	24.7	0.0	24.6	-0.4	24.6	0.0	24.6	0.0	24.6	0.0	24.6	0.0	24.6	0.0	24.6	0.0	24.6	0.0	24.6	0.0	24.6	0.0	24.6	0.0
1966	24.5	-0.4	24.5	0.0	24.5	0.0	24.5	0.0	24.5	0.0	24.5	0.0	24.5	0.0	24.5	0.0	24.5	0.0	24.5	0.0	24.5	0.0	24.6	0.4
1967	24.6	0.0	24.6	0.0	24.6	0.0	24.6	0.0	24.6	0.0	24.6	0.0	24.6	0.0	24.6	0.0	24.6	0.0	24.6	0.0	24.6	0.0	24.7	0.4
1968	24.7	0.0	24.7	0.0	24.7	0.0	24.7	0.0	24.7	0.0	24.7	0.0	24.9	0.8	24.9	0.0	24.9	0.0	24.9	0.0	24.9	0.0	24.9	0.0
1969	24.8	-0.4	24.8	0.0	24.9	0.4	24.9	0.0	24.9	0.0	24.9	0.0	24.9	0.0	25.1	0.8	25.3	0.8	25.3	0.0	25.3	0.0	25.3	0.0
1970	25.3	0.0	25.3	0.0	25.3	0.0	25.3	0.0	25.5	0.8	25.6	0.4	26.0	1.6	26.2	0.8	26.6	1.5	26.9	1.1	27.0	0.4	27.4	1.5
1971	27.5	0.4	27.8	1.1	28.1	1.1	28.1	0.0	28.2	0.4	28.4	0.7	28.8	1.4	29.1	1.0	29.1	0.0	29.0	-0.3	29.1	0.3	29.8	2.4
1972	29.2	-2.0	29.5	1.0	29.5	0.0	29.6	0.3	29.8	0.7	29.9	0.3	30.0	0.3	30.0	0.0	30.2	0.7	30.3	0.3	30.2	-0.3	30.2	0.0
1973	30.5	1.0	31.0	1.6	31.2	0.6	31.4	0.6	31.5	0.3	31.6	0.3	31.7	0.3	31.8	0.3	32.2	1.3	32.5	0.9	32.8	0.9	33.4	1.8
1974	33.8	1.2	35.0	3.6	36.6	4.6	37.7	3.0	39.3	4.2	40.5	3.1	41.2	1.7	42.0	1.9	42.8	1.9	43.9	2.6	44.2	0.7	44.4	0.5
1975	45.1	1.6	45.9	1.8	47.0	2.4	47.9	1.9	47.4	-1.0	46.9	-1.1	47.4	1.1	48.0	1.3	48.6	1.3	49.1	1.0	49.0	-0.2	48.6	-0.8
1976	48.8	0.4	49.0	0.4	49.6	1.2	50.3	1.4	50.4	0.2	50.8	0.8	51.7	1.8	52.5	1.5	52.8	0.6	52.4	-0.8	52.6	0.4	52.0	-1.1
1977	52.6	1.2	54.0	2.7	55.0	1.9	56.4	2.5	56.7	0.5	57.6	1.6	58.8	2.1	60.2	2.4	59.7	-0.8	59.6	-0.2	58.5	-1.8	58.3	-0.3
1978	58.9	1.0	59.7	1.4	61.5	3.0	61.7	0.3	62.2	0.8	63.2	1.6	62.7	-0.8	62.4	-0.5	62.1	-0.5	62.2	0.2	61.6	-1.0	61.7	0.2
1979	61.7	0.0	61.8	0.2	63.3	2.4	64.1	1.3	65.4	2.0	66.4	1.5	67.6	1.8	68.6	1.5	69.0	0.6	69.7	1.0	69.3	-0.6	70.6	1.9
1980	71.5	1.3	73.6	2.9	75.2	2.2	76.3	1.5	77.9	2.1	80.2	3.0	81.5	1.6	82.1	0.7	83.2	1.3	83.0	-0.2	82.1	-1.1	83.1	1.2
1981	84.0	1.1	85.2	1.4	86.4	1.4	87.4	1.2	88.7	1.5	90.2	1.7	92.2	2.2	94.9	2.9	94.4	-0.5	93.1	-1.4	93.1	0.0	94.5	1.5
1982	96.6	2.2	96.6	0.0	99.3	2.8	99.9	0.6	100.1	0.2	99.8	-0.3	102.3	2.5	102.1	-0.2	102.1	0.0	100.6	-1.5	99.6	-1.0	100.8	1.2
1983	101.1	0.3	101.1	0.0	101.2	0.1	100.7	-0.5	101.4	0.7	103.2	1.8	104.9	1.6	105.1	0.2	105.3	0.2	104.2	-1.0	103.0	-1.2	102.7	-0.3
1984	103.4	0.7	104.3	0.9	105.0	0.7	106.2	1.1	106.6	0.4	109.9	3.1	111.6	1.5	112.4	0.7	112.3	-0.1	109.6	-2.4	109.0	-0.5	108.4	-0.6
1985	109.7	1.2	109.7	0.0	110.1	0.4	110.5	0.4	110.2	-0.3	113.2	2.7	113.7	0.4	114.0	0.3	113.7	-0.3	112.0	-1.5	111.4	-0.5	111.0	-0.4
1986	112.3	1.2	113.2	0.8	112.7	-0.4	111.5	-1.1	112.1	0.5	114.0	1.7	114.8	0.7	114.8	0.0	114.8	0.0	111.0	-3.3	110.2	-0.7	109.9	-0.3
1987	108.4	-1.4	108.3	-0.1	108.7	0.4	108.0	-0.6	109.9	1.8	113.2	3.0	114.8	1.4	114.6	-0.2	114.1	-0.4	110.4	-3.2	108.1	-2.1	108.4	0.3
1988	107.8	-0.6	108.0	0.2	107.7	-0.3	107.6	-0.1	107.6	0.0	115.6	7.4	116.8	1.0	116.8	0.0	117.1	0.3	112.8	-3.7	107.8	-4.4	109.1	1.2
1989	110.6	1.4	110.8	0.2	110.9	0.1	111.1	0.2	112.6	1.4	119.3	6.0	120.8	1.3	120.7	-0.1	120.7	0.0	115.2	-4.6	111.8	-3.0	112.6	0.7
1990	113.1	0.4	113.6	0.4	113.8	0.2	113.7	-0.1	115.5	1.6	121.7	5.4	121.9	0.2	122.1	0.2	122.4	0.2	119.1	-2.7	117.6	-1.3	116.8	-0.7
1991	120.5	3.2	120.4	-0.1	120.2	-0.2	120.2	0.0	123.1	2.4	128.8	4.6	130.4	1.2	130.4	0.0	130.5	0.1	124.7	-4.4	120.2	-3.6	121.9	1.4
1992	122.2	0.2	121.8	-0.3	122.1	0.2	121.4	-0.6	124.5	2.6	131.7	5.8	132.7	0.8	132.4	-0.2	132.7	0.2	127.4	-4.0	122.8	-3.6	123.7	0.7
1993	124.2	0.4	123.9	-0.2	124.0	0.1	124.6	0.5	125.7	0.9	134.8	7.2	135.1	0.2	135.3	0.1	135.7	0.3	129.5	-4.6	124.6	-3.8	124.9	0.2

Source: U.S. Department of Labor, Bureau of Labor Statistics, Division of Industry Prices and Price Indexes. n.e.c. stands for not elsewhere classified. - indicates no data collected for period or unavailable.

Utility Natural Gas
Producer Price Index
Base Dec. 1990 = 100

For 1990-1993. Columns headed % show percentile change in the index from the previous period for which an index is available.

Year	Jan	%	Feb	%	Mar	%	Apr	%	May	%	Jun	%	Jul	%	Aug	%	Sep	%	Oct	%	Nov	%	Dec	%
1990	-	-	-	-	-	-	-	-	-	-	-	-	-	-	-	-	-	-	-	-	-	-	100.0	-
1991	101.2	1.2	99.5	-1.7	97.7	-1.8	97.1	-0.6	96.2	-0.9	95.2	-1.0	95.0	-0.2	94.7	-0.3	95.1	0.4	96.2	1.2	98.6	2.5	99.8	1.2
1992	100.1	0.3	98.0	-2.1	96.9	-1.1	96.0	-0.9	95.5	-0.5	96.0	0.5	96.1	0.1	96.9	0.8	98.3	1.4	101.2	3.0	103.7	2.5	104.2	0.5
1993	104.0	-0.2	102.8	-1.2	102.2	-0.6	101.9	-0.3	103.9	2.0	103.5	-0.4	103.2	-0.3	104.0	0.8	105.7	1.6	104.9	-0.8	105.1	0.2	106.4	1.2

Source: U.S. Department of Labor, Bureau of Labor Statistics, Division of Industry Prices and Price Indexes. n.e.c. stands for not elsewhere classified. - indicates no data collected for period or unavailable.

Petroleum Products, Refined

Producer Price Index
Base 1982 = 100

For 1947-1993. Columns headed % show percentile change in the index from the previous period for which an index is available.

Year	Jan Index	%	Feb Index	%	Mar Index	%	Apr Index	%	May Index	%	Jun Index	%	Jul Index	%	Aug Index	%	Sep Index	%	Oct Index	%	Nov Index	%	Dec Index	%
1947	8.3	-	8.4	1.2	9.0	7.1	9.6	6.7	9.6	0.0	9.7	1.0	9.9	2.1	10.1	2.0	10.1	0.0	10.2	1.0	10.7	4.9	11.3	5.6
1948	12.1	7.1	12.3	1.7	12.3	0.0	12.3	0.0	12.3	0.0	12.3	0.0	12.3	0.0	12.2	-0.8	12.1	-0.8	12.2	0.8	12.1	-0.8	11.9	-1.7
1949	11.7	-1.7	11.2	-4.3	11.0	-1.8	10.7	-2.7	10.5	-1.9	10.4	-1.0	10.3	-1.0	10.4	1.0	10.5	1.0	10.6	1.0	10.4	-1.9	10.4	0.0
1950	10.5	1.0	10.5	0.0	10.5	0.0	10.6	1.0	10.9	2.8	11.1	1.8	11.3	1.8	11.6	2.7	11.7	0.9	11.8	0.9	11.8	0.0	11.8	0.0
1951	12.0	1.7	12.0	0.0	12.1	0.8	12.1	0.0	12.0	-0.8	12.1	0.8	12.1	0.0	12.1	0.0	12.1	0.0	12.1	0.0	12.1	0.0	12.1	0.0
1952	12.1	0.0	12.0	-0.8	12.1	0.8	11.9	-1.7	12.0	0.8	11.9	-0.8	11.9	0.0	11.8	-0.8	11.8	0.0	11.8	0.0	11.7	-0.8	11.7	0.0
1953	11.7	0.0	11.6	-0.9	11.8	1.7	11.8	0.0	11.9	0.8	11.9	0.0	12.6	5.9	12.6	0.0	12.6	0.0	12.6	0.0	12.6	0.0	12.4	-1.6
1954	12.3	-0.8	12.2	-0.8	11.9	-2.5	12.0	0.8	11.9	-0.8	11.9	0.0	11.9	0.0	11.5	-3.4	11.6	0.9	11.7	0.9	11.6	-0.9	11.7	0.9
1955	11.9	0.8	11.9	0.0	12.0	0.0	11.9	-0.8	11.9	0.0	11.9	0.0	11.9	0.0	12.1	1.7	12.2	0.8	12.3	0.8	12.3	0.0	12.4	0.8
1956	12.6	1.6	12.7	0.8	12.6	-0.8	12.7	0.8	12.8	0.8	12.8	0.0	12.8	0.0	12.8	0.0	12.8	0.0	12.8	0.0	12.7	-0.8	13.1	3.1
1957	13.5	3.1	14.2	5.2	14.1	-0.7	14.1	0.0	14.0	-0.7	13.8	-1.4	13.6	-1.4	13.5	-0.7	13.5	0.0	13.4	-0.7	13.2	-1.5	13.2	0.0
1958	13.1	-0.8	12.6	-3.8	12.4	-1.6	12.2	-1.6	12.1	-0.8	12.2	0.0	12.4	1.6	12.7	2.4	12.7	0.0	12.5	-1.6	12.4	-0.8	12.4	0.0
1959	12.6	1.6	12.8	1.6	12.8	0.0	12.8	0.0	12.6	-1.6	12.2	-3.2	12.2	0.0	12.3	0.8	12.2	-0.8	12.2	0.0	12.1	-0.8	12.1	0.0
1960	12.2	0.8	12.2	0.0	12.2	0.0	12.3	0.8	12.0	-2.4	12.3	2.5	12.6	2.4	12.8	1.6	13.0	1.6	13.0	0.0	12.9	-0.8	13.0	0.8
1961	13.2	1.5	13.3	0.8	13.2	-0.8	12.8	-3.0	12.5	-2.3	12.7	1.6	12.8	0.8	12.5	-0.8	12.8	2.4	12.7	-0.8	12.7	0.0	12.7	0.0
1962	12.8	0.8	12.6	-1.6	12.2	-3.2	12.7	4.1	12.6	-0.8	12.6	0.0	12.6	0.0	12.5	-0.8	12.8	2.4	12.7	-0.8	12.1	-1.6	12.3	1.7
1963	12.6	-0.8	12.5	-0.8	12.6	0.8	12.6	0.0	12.7	0.8	12.8	0.8	12.7	-0.8	12.3	-3.1	12.3	0.0	12.3	0.0	12.1	-1.6	12.1	0.0
1964	12.4	0.8	12.2	-1.6	11.9	-2.5	11.7	-1.7	11.8	0.9	11.9	0.8	11.9	0.0	11.7	-1.7	11.5	-1.7	11.8	2.6	12.0	1.7	12.1	0.8
1965	12.2	0.8	12.1	-0.8	12.1	0.0	12.1	0.0	12.3	1.7	12.3	0.0	12.3	0.0	12.4	0.8	12.4	0.0	12.4	0.0	12.6	1.6	12.7	0.8
1966	12.6	-0.8	12.6	0.0	12.5	-0.8	12.6	0.8	12.7	0.8	12.9	1.6	12.8	-0.8	12.9	0.8	13.0	0.8	13.0	0.0	13.0	0.0	12.9	-0.8
1967	12.9	0.0	13.1	1.6	13.2	0.8	13.1	-0.8	13.3	1.5	13.3	0.0	13.3	0.0	13.4	0.8	13.4	0.0	13.0	-3.0	12.9	-0.8	12.8	-0.8
1968	12.7	-0.8	12.8	0.8	12.8	0.0	12.9	0.8	12.9	0.0	13.3	3.1	13.3	0.0	13.2	-0.8	13.0	-1.5	13.0	0.0	12.8	-1.5	12.8	0.0
1969	12.7	0.0	12.8	0.8	13.1	2.3	13.0	0.8	13.2	0.0	13.2	0.0	13.3	0.0	13.2	-0.8	13.1	-0.8	13.1	0.0	13.1	0.0	13.1	0.0
1970	13.0	-0.8	13.0	0.0	13.0	0.0	13.0	0.0	13.3	2.3	13.1	-1.5	13.2	0.8	13.3	0.8	13.3	0.0	13.3	0.0	13.5	1.5	14.2	5.2
1971	14.2	0.0	14.1	-0.7	14.0	-0.7	13.8	-1.4	14.1	2.2	14.1	0.0	14.2	0.7	14.2	0.0	14.2	0.0	14.1	-0.7	14.0	-0.7	14.0	0.0
1972	13.9	-0.7	13.9	0.0	14.0	0.7	14.0	0.0	14.1	0.7	14.3	1.4	14.3	0.0	14.5	1.4	14.6	0.7	14.6	0.0	14.7	0.7	14.7	0.0
1973	14.7	0.0	15.6	6.1	15.9	1.9	16.1	1.3	16.4	1.9	16.8	2.4	17.1	1.8	17.1	0.0	17.2	0.6	17.6	2.3	18.4	4.5	19.9	8.2
1974	21.9	10.1	24.7	12.8	27.1	9.7	28.3	4.4	29.5	4.2	30.5	3.4	31.5	3.3	32.0	1.6	31.9	-0.3	32.1	0.6	31.3	-2.5	31.3	0.0
1975	31.8	1.6	31.6	-0.6	31.8	0.6	32.0	0.6	32.3	0.9	33.1	2.5	34.0	2.7	34.9	2.6	35.3	1.1	35.5	0.6	35.8	0.8	36.1	0.8
1976	35.8	-0.8	35.8	0.0	35.4	-1.1	35.1	-0.8	35.1	0.0	35.5	1.1	36.4	2.5	36.9	1.4	37.3	1.1	37.4	0.3	37.5	0.3	37.8	0.8
1977	38.0	0.5	38.8	2.1	39.7	2.3	40.3	1.5	40.8	1.2	41.0	0.5	41.2	0.5	41.1	-0.2	41.1	0.0	41.3	0.5	41.2	-0.2	41.2	0.0
1978	41.3	0.2	41.1	-0.5	40.8	-0.7	40.9	0.2	41.3	1.0	41.8	1.2	42.2	1.0	42.5	0.7	42.8	0.7	43.3	1.2	43.6	0.7	44.4	1.8
1979	45.2	1.8	46.0	1.8	47.3	2.8	49.7	5.1	52.5	5.6	55.6	5.9	59.1	6.3	63.4	7.3	67.5	6.5	70.1	3.9	71.7	2.3	72.9	1.7
1980	76.6	5.1	81.5	6.4	86.6	6.3	89.1	2.9	89.4	0.3	89.5	0.1	91.1	1.8	91.6	0.5	91.5	-0.1	90.7	-0.9	91.6	1.0	94.2	2.8
1981	96.8	2.8	101.1	4.4	108.4	7.2	110.5	1.9	109.7	-0.7	108.8	-0.8	107.2	-1.5	106.9	-0.3	105.9	-0.9	105.4	-0.5	104.9	-0.5	104.9	0.0
1982	105.3	0.4	103.7	-1.5	101.2	-2.4	96.4	-4.7	93.7	-2.8	97.1	3.6	102.0	5.0	102.7	0.7	100.0	-2.6	99.1	-0.9	99.6	0.5	99.1	-0.5
1983	94.7	-4.4	91.0	-3.9	87.6	-3.7	84.8	-3.2	86.6	2.1	89.9	3.8	90.5	0.7	91.3	0.9	91.3	0.0	91.5	0.2	90.4	-1.2	89.1	-1.4
1984	87.1	-2.2	88.0	1.0	89.4	1.6	87.6	-2.0	89.0	1.6	89.3	0.3	88.4	-1.0	86.0	-2.7	84.9	-1.3	86.1	1.4	86.9	0.9	85.7	-1.4
1985	83.5	-2.6	80.9	-3.1	81.5	0.7	83.6	2.6	86.4	3.3	84.3	-2.4	82.8	-1.8	81.5	-1.6	81.7	0.2	82.1	0.5	84.3	2.7	85.4	1.3
1986	79.9	-6.4	68.9	-13.8	56.7	-17.7	52.0	-8.3	53.3	2.5	53.3	0.0	44.7	-16.1	44.3	-0.9	48.2	8.8	45.4	-5.8	45.5	0.2	46.4	2.0
1987	50.8	9.5	53.9	6.1	52.9	-1.9	55.4	4.7	56.1	1.3	57.7	2.9	59.3	2.8	61.5	3.7	58.9	-4.2	59.0	0.2	59.8	1.4	56.8	-5.0
1988	53.7	-5.5	52.9	-1.5	52.1	-1.5	54.4	4.4	56.4	3.7	55.4	-1.8	55.3	-0.2	55.8	0.9	52.9	-5.2	51.1	-3.4	53.5	4.7	52.9	-1.1
1989	54.4	2.8	55.0	1.1	57.1	3.8	64.9	13.7	67.7	4.3	65.6	-3.1	63.1	-3.8	58.9	-6.7	61.4	4.2	63.0	2.6	61.6	-2.2	61.9	0.5
1990	71.8	16.0	64.5	-10.2	63.3	-1.9	65.1	2.8	65.3	0.3	63.9	-2.1	62.3	-2.5	74.5	19.6	86.7	16.4	96.9	11.8	96.4	-0.5	87.0	-9.8
1991	79.1	-9.1	71.5	-9.6	64.0	-10.5	63.6	-0.6	66.4	4.4	65.4	-1.5	63.3	-3.2	66.4	4.9	67.9	2.3	66.9	-1.5	67.8	1.3	63.4	-6.5

[Continued]

Petroleum Products, Refined

Producer Price Index
Base 1982 = 100
[Continued]

For 1947-1993. Columns headed % show percentile change in the index from the previous period for which an index is available.

Year	Jan		Feb		Mar		Apr		May		Jun		Jul		Aug		Sep		Oct		Nov		Dec	
	Index	%	Index	%	Index	%	Index	%	Index	%	Index	%	Index	%	Index	%	Index	%	Index	%	Index	%	Index	%
1992	57.7	-9.0	59.7	3.5	59.2	-0.8	61.9	4.6	66.2	6.9	69.9	5.6	68.1	-2.6	67.5	-0.9	68.6	1.6	68.5	-0.1	67.0	-2.2	62.1	-7.3
1993	61.6	-0.8	62.5	1.5	63.9	2.2	65.1	1.9	66.5	2.2	64.5	-3.0	62.0	-3.9	60.3	-2.7	60.9	1.0	63.9	4.9	60.6	-5.2	53.0	-12.5

Source: U.S. Department of Labor, Bureau of Labor Statistics, Division of Industry Prices and Price Indexes. n.e.c. stands for not elsewhere classified. - indicates no data collected for period or unavailable.

Petroleum and Coal Products n.e.c.
Producer Price Index
Base Dec. 1984 = 100

For 1984-1993. Columns headed % show percentile change in the index from the previous period for which an index is available.

Year	Jan Index	%	Feb Index	%	Mar Index	%	Apr Index	%	May Index	%	Jun Index	%	Jul Index	%	Aug Index	%	Sep Index	%	Oct Index	%	Nov Index	%	Dec Index	%
1984	-	-	-	-	-	-	-	-	-	-	-	-	-	-	-	-	-	-	-	-	-	-	100.0	-
1985	100.0	0.0	99.9	-0.1	99.9	0.0	99.9	0.0	99.9	0.0	99.9	0.0	105.2	5.3	103.6	-1.5	103.1	-0.5	95.0	-7.9	100.2	5.5	99.2	-1.0
1986	95.2	-4.0	95.2	0.0	92.9	-2.4	90.8	-2.3	81.7	-10.0	78.7	-3.7	70.5	-10.4	70.8	0.4	63.4	-10.5	63.5	0.2	65.3	2.8	57.3	-12.3
1987	61.8	7.9	60.4	-2.3	63.7	5.5	63.6	-0.2	60.4	-5.0	62.4	3.3	62.8	0.6	63.7	1.4	64.6	1.4	65.6	1.5	66.0	0.6	69.9	5.9
1988	62.7	-10.3	70.8	12.9	62.6	-11.6	68.0	8.6	69.6	2.4	67.4	-3.2	69.4	3.0	69.9	0.7	68.1	-2.6	61.8	-9.3	63.7	3.1	62.7	-1.6
1989	59.1	-5.7	60.3	2.0	65.6	8.8	65.8	0.3	64.4	-2.1	63.5	-1.4	68.1	7.2	69.2	1.6	67.5	-2.5	67.1	-0.6	69.4	3.4	60.0	-13.5
1990	61.9	3.2	63.5	2.6	63.3	-0.3	64.2	1.4	67.6	5.3	68.3	1.0	66.6	-2.5	68.0	2.1	70.1	3.1	70.2	0.1	69.8	-0.6	74.2	6.3
1991	71.7	-3.4	76.3	6.4	67.0	-12.2	68.4	2.1	64.9	-5.1	68.4	5.4	61.4	-10.2	61.9	0.8	61.1	-1.3	61.9	1.3	55.9	-9.7	44.5	-20.4
1992	58.1	30.6	58.4	0.5	59.6	2.1	60.7	1.8	58.2	-4.1	54.7	-6.0	57.7	5.5	58.5	1.4	54.7	-6.5	61.1	11.7	63.1	3.3	60.5	-4.1
1993	67.0	10.7	66.8	-0.3	66.0	-1.2	69.3	5.0	68.0	-1.9	63.1	-7.2	69.0	9.4	65.8	-4.6	66.1	0.5	64.0	-3.2	67.2	5.0	64.0	-4.8

Source: U.S. Department of Labor, Bureau of Labor Statistics, Division of Industry Prices and Price Indexes. n.e.c. stands for not elsewhere classified. - indicates no data collected for period or unavailable.

CHEMICALS AND ALLIED PRODUCTS
Producer Price Index
Base 1982 = 100

For 1933-1993. Columns headed % show percentile change in the index from the previous period for which an index is available.

Year	Jan Index	%	Feb Index	%	Mar Index	%	Apr Index	%	May Index	%	Jun Index	%	Jul Index	%	Aug Index	%	Sep Index	%	Oct Index	%	Nov Index	%	Dec Index	%
1933	15.7	-	15.6	-0.6	15.7	0.6	15.7	0.0	16.0	1.9	16.2	1.3	16.6	2.5	16.7	0.6	16.6	-0.6	16.5	-0.6	16.5	0.0	16.6	0.6
1934	16.8	1.2	17.0	1.2	17.0	0.0	17.0	0.0	16.9	-0.6	16.9	0.0	16.9	0.0	16.9	0.0	17.0	0.6	17.1	0.6	17.0	-0.6	17.1	0.6
1935	17.2	0.6	17.3	0.6	17.6	1.7	17.6	0.0	17.7	0.6	17.8	0.6	17.6	-1.1	17.6	0.0	17.9	1.7	18.0	0.6	17.9	-0.6	17.9	0.0
1936	17.8	-0.6	17.7	-0.6	17.6	-0.6	17.6	0.0	17.4	-1.1	17.4	0.0	17.6	1.1	17.8	1.1	17.9	0.6	18.0	0.6	18.1	0.6	18.6	2.8
1937	18.9	1.6	19.0	0.5	19.0	0.0	19.0	0.0	18.7	-1.6	18.6	-0.5	18.7	0.5	18.6	-0.5	18.5	-0.5	18.4	-0.5	18.1	-1.6	17.9	-1.1
1938	18.1	1.1	18.1	0.0	18.0	-0.6	17.9	-0.6	17.7	-1.1	17.5	-1.1	17.5	0.0	17.6	0.6	17.6	0.0	17.6	0.0	17.6	0.0	17.5	-0.6
1939	17.5	0.0	17.4	-0.6	17.5	0.6	17.5	0.0	17.5	0.0	17.5	0.0	17.4	-0.6	17.3	-0.6	17.9	3.5	18.1	1.1	18.0	-0.6	18.1	0.6
1940	18.2	0.6	18.1	-0.5	18.1	0.0	18.3	1.1	17.9	-2.2	17.8	-0.6	17.8	0.0	17.7	-0.6	17.7	0.0	17.8	0.6	17.9	0.6	17.9	0.0
1941	18.1	1.1	18.1	0.0	18.4	1.7	18.8	2.2	19.2	2.1	19.4	1.0	19.7	1.5	19.9	1.0	20.3	2.0	20.6	1.5	20.6	0.0	20.8	1.0
1942	18.6	-10.6	21.9	17.7	22.1	0.9	22.1	0.0	22.1	0.0	22.0	-0.5	22.0	0.0	21.8	-0.9	21.9	0.5	21.9	0.0	21.8	-0.5	21.7	-0.5
1943	21.8	0.5	21.9	0.5	21.9	0.0	22.0	0.5	21.9	-0.5	21.9	0.0	21.9	0.0	22.0	0.5	22.0	0.0	22.0	0.0	22.0	0.0	22.0	0.0
1944	22.1	0.5	22.1	0.0	22.1	0.0	22.2	0.5	22.2	0.0	22.2	0.0	22.2	0.0	22.2	0.0	22.1	-0.5	22.2	0.5	22.2	0.0	22.2	0.0
1945	22.2	0.0	22.2	0.0	22.2	0.0	22.2	0.0	22.2	0.0	22.2	0.0	22.2	0.0	22.3	0.5	22.4	0.4	22.4	0.0	22.5	0.4	22.5	0.0
1946	22.5	0.0	22.5	0.0	22.5	0.0	22.5	0.0	22.6	0.4	22.6	0.0	23.5	4.0	23.3	-0.9	23.4	0.4	23.8	1.7	29.5	23.9	31.0	5.1
1947	32.1	3.5	32.4	0.9	32.9	1.5	32.8	-0.3	31.7	-3.4	31.2	-1.6	30.8	-1.3	30.5	-1.0	31.1	2.0	32.3	3.9	33.3	3.1	33.4	0.3
1948	33.8	1.2	33.3	-1.5	33.1	-0.6	33.0	-0.3	32.6	-1.2	32.8	0.6	32.9	0.3	32.7	-0.6	32.7	0.0	32.6	-0.3	32.4	-0.6	32.0	-1.2
1949	31.5	-1.6	31.1	-1.3	30.7	-1.3	30.1	-2.0	30.0	-0.3	29.9	-0.3	29.6	-1.0	29.6	0.0	29.5	-0.3	29.3	-0.7	29.3	0.0	29.2	-0.3
1950	29.2	0.0	29.1	-0.3	29.1	0.0	29.1	0.0	29.1	0.0	29.1	0.0	29.5	1.4	30.3	2.7	31.5	4.0	32.3	2.5	32.7	1.2	34.0	4.0
1951	35.2	3.5	35.6	1.1	35.4	-0.6	35.2	-0.6	35.2	0.0	34.8	-1.1	34.4	-1.1	34.3	-0.3	34.3	0.0	34.4	0.3	34.3	-0.3	34.3	0.0
1952	33.7	-1.7	33.5	-0.6	33.3	-0.6	33.1	-0.6	32.9	-0.6	32.9	0.0	32.9	0.0	32.9	0.0	32.9	0.0	32.8	-0.3	32.7	-0.3	32.6	-0.3
1953	32.7	0.3	32.7	0.0	32.9	0.6	33.4	1.5	33.4	0.0	33.4	0.0	33.6	0.6	33.6	0.0	33.7	0.3	33.7	0.0	33.9	0.6	33.9	0.0
1954	33.9	0.0	34.0	0.3	34.0	0.0	33.9	-0.3	33.9	0.0	33.8	-0.3	33.7	-0.3	33.8	0.3	33.8	0.0	33.8	0.0	33.8	0.0	33.8	0.0
1955	33.9	0.3	33.9	0.0	33.8	-0.3	33.9	0.3	33.8	-0.3	33.8	0.0	33.5	-0.9	33.5	0.0	33.5	0.0	33.7	0.6	33.7	0.0	33.7	0.0
1956	33.6	-0.3	33.6	0.0	33.7	0.3	33.8	0.3	33.8	0.0	33.9	0.3	33.9	0.0	33.9	0.0	33.9	0.0	34.0	0.3	34.2	0.6	34.2	0.0
1957	34.3	0.3	34.4	0.3	34.4	0.0	34.5	0.3	34.5	0.0	34.6	0.3	34.6	0.0	34.7	0.3	34.8	0.3	34.9	0.3	34.9	0.0	35.0	0.3
1958	35.0	0.0	35.0	0.0	35.0	0.0	35.1	0.3	35.0	-0.3	35.0	0.0	34.9	-0.3	34.8	-0.3	34.7	-0.3	34.8	0.3	34.8	0.0	34.8	0.0
1959	34.8	0.0	34.7	-0.3	34.7	0.0	34.8	0.3	34.8	0.0	34.8	0.0	34.7	-0.3	34.7	0.0	34.7	0.0	34.8	0.3	34.8	0.0	34.8	0.0
1960	34.7	-0.3	34.8	0.3	34.8	0.0	34.8	0.0	34.8	0.0	34.8	0.0	34.9	0.3	34.9	0.0	34.9	0.0	34.8	-0.3	34.8	0.0	34.8	0.0
1961	34.7	-0.3	34.8	0.3	34.8	0.0	34.8	0.0	34.7	-0.3	34.6	-0.3	34.4	-0.6	34.3	-0.3	34.2	-0.3	34.1	-0.3	34.1	0.0	34.1	0.0
1962	34.2	0.3	34.1	-0.3	34.1	0.0	34.0	-0.3	34.0	0.0	33.9	-0.3	33.8	-0.3	33.7	-0.3	33.7	0.0	33.8	0.3	33.7	-0.3	33.7	0.0
1963	33.7	0.0	33.6	-0.3	33.7	0.3	33.5	-0.6	33.5	0.0	33.5	0.0	33.4	-0.3	33.4	0.0	33.4	0.0	33.5	0.3	33.5	0.0	33.5	0.0
1964	33.5	0.0	33.5	0.0	33.6	0.3	33.6	0.0	33.6	0.0	33.6	0.0	33.6	0.0	33.6	0.0	33.6	0.0	33.7	0.3	33.8	0.3	33.8	0.0
1965	33.8	0.0	33.9	0.3	33.9	0.0	33.9	0.0	33.9	0.0	33.9	0.0	33.9	0.0	33.8	-0.3	33.8	0.0	33.9	0.3	33.9	0.0	33.9	0.0
1966	33.9	0.0	33.9	0.0	33.9	0.0	33.9	0.0	34.0	0.3	33.9	-0.3	34.0	0.3	34.0	0.0	34.1	0.3	34.0	-0.3	34.1	0.3	34.1	0.0
1967	34.2	0.3	34.2	0.0	34.2	0.0	34.3	0.3	34.3	0.0	34.2	-0.3	34.2	0.0	34.1	-0.3	34.0	-0.3	34.1	0.3	34.1	0.0	34.2	0.3
1968	34.1	-0.3	34.1	0.0	34.3	0.6	34.3	0.0	34.3	0.0	34.2	-0.3	34.1	-0.3	34.1	0.0	34.0	-0.3	34.0	0.0	34.0	0.0	34.0	0.0
1969	33.9	-0.3	34.0	0.3	34.1	0.3	34.0	-0.3	34.1	0.3	34.2	0.3	34.1	-0.3	34.3	0.6	34.4	0.3	34.3	-0.3	34.4	0.3	34.3	-0.3
1970	34.5	0.6	34.6	0.3	34.7	0.3	34.9	0.6	35.0	0.3	35.0	0.0	35.1	0.3	35.1	0.0	35.1	0.0	35.3	0.6	35.3	0.0	35.2	-0.3
1971	35.5	0.9	35.7	0.6	35.7	0.0	35.8	0.3	35.7	-0.3	35.7	0.0	35.7	0.0	35.6	-0.3	35.6	0.0	35.6	0.0	35.5	-0.3	35.4	-0.3
1972	35.4	0.0	35.4	0.0	35.4	0.0	35.6	0.6	35.7	0.3	35.7	0.0	35.6	-0.3	35.7	0.3	35.7	0.0	35.7	0.0	35.8	0.3	35.9	0.3
1973	36.0	0.3	36.1	0.3	36.5	1.1	36.8	0.8	37.4	1.6	37.8	1.1	37.9	0.3	38.0	0.3	38.1	0.3	38.6	1.3	38.8	0.5	39.6	2.1
1974	40.4	2.0	41.1	1.7	43.5	5.8	45.3	4.1	46.9	3.5	48.9	4.3	50.8	3.9	54.2	6.7	55.3	2.0	57.7	4.3	59.2	2.6	59.5	0.5
1975	60.2	1.2	60.9	1.2	62.2	2.1	62.4	0.3	62.3	-0.2	62.0	-0.5	62.1	0.2	62.3	0.3	62.3	0.0	62.4	0.2	62.6	0.3	62.7	0.2
1976	63.1	0.6	63.3	0.3	63.6	0.5	64.0	0.6	64.0	0.0	64.1	0.2	64.0	-0.2	64.3	0.5	64.5	0.3	64.5	0.0	64.5	0.0	64.4	-0.2
1977	64.6	0.3	65.0	0.6	65.4	0.6	66.0	0.9	66.4	0.6	66.4	0.0	66.2	-0.3	66.2	0.0	66.1	-0.2	66.3	0.3	66.4	0.2	66.4	0.0

[Continued]

CHEMICALS AND ALLIED PRODUCTS
Producer Price Index
Base 1982 = 100
[Continued]

For 1933-1993. Columns headed % show percentile change in the index from the previous period for which an index is available.

Year	Jan Index	%	Feb Index	%	Mar Index	%	Apr Index	%	May Index	%	Jun Index	%	Jul Index	%	Aug Index	%	Sep Index	%	Oct Index	%	Nov Index	%	Dec Index	%
1978	66.4	0.0	66.8	0.6	67.1	0.4	67.3	0.3	68.0	1.0	68.1	0.1	68.4	0.4	68.3	-0.1	68.5	0.3	69.0	0.7	69.2	0.3	69.2	0.0
1979	70.1	1.3	70.9	1.1	71.8	1.3	73.6	2.5	74.6	1.4	75.0	0.5	77.0	2.7	78.2	1.6	79.0	1.0	80.1	1.4	80.7	0.7	81.5	1.0
1980	84.2	3.3	85.1	1.1	86.5	1.6	88.9	2.8	89.8	1.0	89.9	0.1	90.1	0.2	90.5	0.4	90.1	-0.4	90.6	0.6	91.2	0.7	91.7	0.5
1981	93.9	2.4	95.0	1.2	95.9	0.9	97.8	2.0	98.7	0.9	99.4	0.7	99.7	0.3	100.3	0.6	100.4	0.1	100.1	-0.3	99.9	-0.2	99.8	-0.1
1982	100.2	0.4	100.5	0.3	100.8	0.3	100.7	-0.1	100.9	0.2	100.3	-0.6	99.7	-0.6	99.8	0.1	99.5	-0.3	99.2	-0.3	99.4	0.2	99.1	-0.3
1983	99.0	-0.1	99.4	0.4	99.2	-0.2	99.7	0.5	99.6	-0.1	99.5	-0.1	100.5	1.0	100.7	0.2	101.2	0.5	101.1	-0.1	101.4	0.3	101.9	0.5
1984	102.0	0.1	101.5	-0.5	102.7	1.2	103.3	0.6	103.6	0.3	103.4	-0.2	103.5	0.1	103.0	-0.5	103.0	0.0	103.1	0.1	103.2	0.1	102.9	-0.3
1985	103.2	0.3	103.4	0.2	103.5	0.1	103.8	0.3	103.7	-0.1	103.9	0.2	104.2	0.3	104.2	0.0	104.2	0.0	103.7	-0.5	103.5	-0.2	103.3	-0.2
1986	104.4	1.1	103.9	-0.5	104.0	0.1	102.7	-1.2	102.1	-0.6	102.1	0.0	102.1	0.0	101.6	-0.5	101.8	0.2	102.0	0.2	102.2	0.2	102.0	-0.2
1987	103.0	1.0	103.6	0.6	104.3	0.7	105.2	0.9	105.9	0.7	107.1	1.1	107.0	-0.1	107.1	0.1	107.5	0.4	108.2	0.7	108.8	0.6	109.1	0.3
1988	110.6	1.4	111.6	0.9	112.7	1.0	113.8	1.0	114.6	0.7	115.3	0.6	117.4	1.8	118.2	0.7	119.1	0.8	119.9	0.7	121.1	1.0	121.7	0.5
1989	123.7	1.6	124.3	0.5	124.5	0.2	124.9	0.3	124.9	0.0	124.1	-0.6	123.1	-0.8	121.9	-1.0	121.4	-0.4	121.4	0.0	121.0	-0.3	121.0	0.0
1990	121.2	0.2	121.7	0.4	121.8	0.1	121.9	0.1	122.3	0.3	122.2	-0.1	122.4	0.2	122.5	0.1	124.5	1.6	126.5	1.6	128.2	1.3	127.9	-0.2
1991	128.3	0.3	128.1	-0.2	126.0	-1.6	126.0	0.0	125.3	-0.6	125.0	-0.2	124.4	-0.5	124.5	0.1	124.5	0.0	124.9	0.3	124.9	0.0	125.0	0.1
1992	124.6	-0.3	124.5	-0.1	124.4	-0.1	124.8	0.3	125.2	0.3	126.0	0.6	126.4	0.3	126.7	0.2	127.0	0.2	127.1	0.1	127.5	0.3	127.0	-0.4
1993	127.6	0.5	128.1	0.4	127.8	-0.2	128.6	0.6	128.2	-0.3	128.5	0.2	128.2	-0.2	128.3	0.1	128.2	-0.1	128.3	0.1	128.5	0.2	128.0	-0.4

Source: U.S. Department of Labor, Bureau of Labor Statistics, Division of Industry Prices and Price Indexes. n.e.c. stands for not elsewhere classified. - indicates no data collected for period or unavailable.

Industrial Chemicals
Producer Price Index
Base 1982 = 100

For 1926-1993. Columns headed % show percentile change in the index from the previous period for which an index is available.

Year	Jan Index	%	Feb Index	%	Mar Index	%	Apr Index	%	May Index	%	Jun Index	%	Jul Index	%	Aug Index	%	Sep Index	%	Oct Index	%	Nov Index	%	Dec Index	%
1926	-	-	-		-		-		-		-		-		-		-		-		-		-	
1927	-		-		-		-		-		-		-		-		-		-		-		-	
1928	-		-		-		-		-		-		-		-		-		-		-		-	
1929	-		-		-		-		-		-		-		-		-		-		-		-	
1930	-		-		-		-		-		-		-		-		-		-		-		-	
1931	-		-		-		-		-		-		-		-		-		-		-		-	
1932	-		-		-		-		-		-		-		-		-		-		-		-	
1933	17.4	-	17.4	0.0	17.2	-1.1	17.2	0.0	17.3	0.6	17.3	0.0	17.2	-0.6	17.2	0.0	17.2	0.0	17.2	0.0	17.4	1.2	17.4	0.0
1934	17.4	0.0	17.4	0.0	17.4	0.0	17.3	-0.6	17.3	0.0	17.3	0.0	17.1	-1.2	17.2	0.6	17.2	0.0	17.2	0.0	17.2	0.0	17.3	0.6
1935	17.3	0.0	17.4	0.6	17.4	0.0	17.4	0.0	17.5	0.6	17.5	0.0	17.5	0.0	17.9	2.3	17.9	0.0	17.9	0.0	17.9	0.0	17.9	0.0
1936	17.8	-0.6	17.8	0.0	17.6	-1.1	17.6	0.0	17.5	-0.6	17.5	0.0	17.4	-0.6	17.3	-0.6	17.3	0.0	17.3	0.0	17.4	0.6	17.3	-0.6
1937	17.4	0.0	17.6	1.1	17.6	0.0	17.6	0.0	17.6	0.0	17.6	0.0	17.8	1.1	17.5	-1.7	17.5	0.0	17.4	-0.6	17.4	0.0	17.4	0.0
1938	17.4	0.0	17.4	0.0	17.3	-0.6	17.3	0.0	17.2	-0.6	17.2	0.0	17.2	0.0	17.1	-0.6	17.1	0.0	17.1	0.0	17.0	-0.6	17.0	0.0
1939	17.0	0.0	16.9	-0.6	16.8	-0.6	16.8	0.0	16.8	0.0	16.7	-0.6	16.7	0.0	16.7	0.0	16.8	0.6	17.0	1.2	17.0	0.0	17.0	0.0
1940	17.0	0.0	17.0	0.0	17.0	0.0	16.9	-0.6	17.0	0.6	17.0	0.0	16.9	-0.6	16.8	-0.6	16.8	0.0	16.9	0.6	17.0	0.6	17.0	0.0
1941	17.0	0.0	17.1	0.6	17.1	0.0	17.2	0.6	17.3	0.6	17.3	0.0	17.4	0.6	17.4	0.0	17.6	1.1	17.6	0.0	17.6	0.0	17.6	0.0
1942	18.9	7.4	19.2	1.6	19.2	0.0	19.2	0.0	19.2	0.0	19.2	0.0	19.2	0.0	19.2	0.0	19.2	0.0	19.2	0.0	19.2	0.0	19.1	-0.5
1943	19.3	1.0	19.3	0.0	19.2	-0.5	19.2	0.0	19.2	0.0	19.2	0.0	19.2	0.0	19.2	0.0	19.2	0.0	19.2	0.0	19.2	0.0	19.2	0.0
1944	19.2	0.0	19.2	0.0	19.2	0.0	19.2	0.0	19.2	0.0	19.2	0.0	19.2	0.0	19.2	0.0	19.1	-0.5	19.1	0.0	19.0	-0.5	19.0	0.0
1945	19.0	0.0	19.0	0.0	19.0	0.0	19.0	0.0	19.0	0.0	19.1	0.5	19.1	0.0	19.1	0.0	19.1	0.0	19.2	0.5	19.3	0.5	19.3	0.0
1946	19.3	0.0	19.3	0.0	19.3	0.0	19.3	0.0	19.5	1.0	19.5	0.0	19.6	0.5	19.6	0.0	19.6	0.0	19.7	0.5	21.2	7.6	22.2	4.7
1947	22.5	1.4	22.7	0.9	23.0	1.3	23.6	2.6	23.3	-1.3	23.4	0.4	23.2	-0.9	22.8	-1.7	23.0	0.9	23.6	2.6	24.1	2.1	24.2	0.4
1948	24.5	1.2	24.7	0.8	24.8	0.4	24.9	0.4	24.8	-0.4	24.8	0.0	25.2	1.6	24.9	-1.2	24.8	-0.4	24.9	0.4	24.4	-2.0	24.1	-1.2
1949	23.9	-0.8	23.3	-2.5	23.0	-1.3	22.6	-1.7	22.5	-0.4	22.4	-0.4	22.5	0.4	22.5	0.0	22.4	-0.4	22.3	-0.4	22.2	-0.4	22.2	0.0
1950	22.3	0.5	22.3	0.0	22.2	-0.4	22.4	0.9	22.4	0.0	22.7	1.3	23.1	1.8	23.7	2.6	24.8	4.6	26.1	5.2	26.3	0.8	27.5	4.6
1951	28.3	2.9	28.4	0.4	28.4	0.0	28.5	0.4	28.5	0.0	28.5	0.0	28.4	-0.4	28.4	0.0	28.4	0.0	28.5	0.4	28.5	0.0	28.4	-0.4
1952	27.8	-2.1	27.7	-0.4	27.5	-0.7	27.5	0.0	27.1	-1.5	27.1	0.0	27.0	-0.4	27.0	0.0	26.9	-0.4	26.8	-0.4	26.5	-1.1	26.4	-0.4
1953	26.5	0.4	26.6	0.4	26.8	0.8	27.5	2.6	27.8	1.1	28.1	1.1	28.3	0.7	28.3	0.0	28.3	0.0	28.2	-0.4	28.1	-0.4	27.9	-0.7
1954	27.9	0.0	27.9	0.0	27.8	-0.4	27.7	-0.4	27.6	-0.4	27.5	-0.4	27.6	0.4	27.7	0.4	27.7	0.0	27.7	0.0	27.7	0.0	27.7	0.0
1955	27.6	-0.4	27.7	0.4	27.7	0.0	27.8	0.4	27.7	-0.4	27.7	0.0	27.9	0.7	27.8	-0.4	27.9	0.4	28.0	0.4	28.1	0.4	28.1	0.0
1956	28.3	0.7	28.3	0.0	28.3	0.0	28.5	0.7	28.4	-0.4	28.5	0.4	28.8	1.1	28.8	0.0	28.7	-0.3	28.9	0.7	28.8	-0.3	28.8	0.0
1957	29.1	1.0	29.0	-0.3	29.0	0.0	29.1	0.3	29.1	0.0	29.2	0.3	29.1	-0.3	29.1	0.0	29.1	0.0	29.1	0.0	29.1	0.0	29.2	0.3
1958	29.2	0.0	29.1	-0.3	29.2	0.3	29.3	0.3	29.2	-0.3	29.1	-0.3	29.0	-0.3	28.9	-0.3	28.9	0.0	29.1	0.7	29.1	0.0	29.2	0.3
1959	29.2	0.0	29.2	0.0	29.1	-0.3	29.2	0.3	29.2	0.0	29.2	0.0	29.2	0.0	29.2	0.0	29.2	0.0	29.2	0.0	29.2	0.0	29.2	0.0
1960	29.0	0.0	29.3	0.3	29.3	0.0	29.3	0.0	29.4	0.3	29.4	0.0	29.4	0.0	29.4	0.0	29.3	-0.3	29.1	-0.7	29.1	0.0	29.1	0.0
1961	29.0	-0.3	29.0	0.0	29.0	0.0	29.0	0.0	28.9	-0.3	28.8	-0.3	28.5	-1.0	28.4	-0.4	28.4	0.0	28.3	-0.4	28.3	0.0	28.3	0.0
1962	28.3	0.0	28.2	-0.4	28.1	-0.4	28.1	0.0	28.1	0.0	28.0	-0.4	28.0	0.0	27.9	-0.4	27.9	0.0	28.0	0.4	27.9	-0.4	27.9	0.0
1963	28.0	0.4	27.7	-1.1	27.8	0.4	27.7	-0.4	27.7	0.0	27.7	0.0	27.6	-0.4	27.5	-0.4	27.5	0.0	27.4	-0.4	27.4	0.0	27.5	0.4
1964	27.5	0.0	27.4	-0.4	27.5	0.4	27.5	0.0	27.5	0.0	27.5	0.0	27.5	0.0	27.3	-0.7	27.3	0.0	27.5	0.7	27.4	-0.4	27.4	0.0
1965	27.5	0.4	27.6	0.4	27.5	-0.4	27.6	0.4	27.6	0.0	27.6	0.0	27.7	0.4	27.7	0.0	27.7	0.0	27.8	0.4	27.8	0.0	27.8	0.0
1966	27.7	-0.4	27.7	0.0	27.7	0.0	27.9	0.7	28.0	0.4	27.9	-0.4	27.9	0.0	27.9	0.0	27.9	0.0	27.9	0.0	28.0	0.4	28.1	0.4
1967	28.1	0.0	28.2	0.4	28.3	0.4	28.4	0.4	28.4	0.0	28.3	-0.4	28.3	0.0	28.3	0.0	28.3	0.0	28.6	1.1	28.6	0.0	28.6	0.0
1968	28.7	0.3	28.7	0.0	28.7	0.0	28.8	0.3	28.8	0.0	28.7	-0.3	28.6	-0.3	28.6	0.0	28.5	-0.3	28.5	0.0	28.5	0.0	28.5	0.0
1969	28.6	0.4	28.6	0.0	28.5	-0.3	28.2	-1.1	28.2	0.0	28.3	0.4	28.4	0.4	28.6	0.7	28.6	0.0	28.4	-0.7	28.5	0.4	28.5	0.0
1970	28.5	0.0	28.4	-0.4	28.3	-0.4	28.5	0.7	28.6	0.4	28.6	0.0	28.8	0.7	28.7	-0.3	28.7	0.0	28.8	0.3	28.8	0.0	28.7	-0.3

[Continued]

Industrial Chemicals

Producer Price Index

Base 1982 = 100

[Continued]

For 1926-1993. Columns headed % show percentile change in the index from the previous period for which an index is available.

Year	Jan		Feb		Mar		Apr		May		Jun		Jul		Aug		Sep		Oct		Nov		Dec	
	Index	%	Index	%	Index	%	Index	%	Index	%	Index	%	Index	%	Index	%	Index	%	Index	%	Index	%	Index	%
1971	28.9	0.7	28.9	0.0	29.0	0.3	28.9	-0.3	28.9	0.0	29.0	0.3	29.1	0.3	29.0	-0.3	29.1	0.3	29.1	0.0	28.8	-1.0	28.7	-0.3
1972	28.8	0.3	28.8	0.0	28.6	-0.7	28.8	0.7	28.8	0.0	28.8	0.0	28.8	0.0	28.7	-0.3	28.7	0.0	28.6	-0.3	28.6	0.0	28.6	0.0
1973	28.7	0.3	28.9	0.7	28.9	0.0	29.1	0.7	29.1	0.0	29.2	0.3	29.3	0.3	29.4	0.3	29.6	0.7	29.9	1.0	29.9	0.0	30.0	0.3
1974	30.7	2.3	31.3	2.0	34.6	10.5	37.1	7.2	39.2	5.7	41.7	6.4	44.1	5.8	47.6	7.9	49.5	4.0	51.6	4.2	53.9	4.5	55.2	2.4
1975	55.8	1.1	57.3	2.7	58.9	2.8	58.8	-0.2	59.2	0.7	58.7	-0.8	58.5	-0.3	58.8	0.5	59.1	0.5	59.3	0.3	59.7	0.7	59.9	0.3
1976	60.6	1.2	61.4	1.3	61.8	0.7	61.9	0.2	62.0	0.2	62.0	0.0	62.2	0.3	62.7	0.8	62.9	0.3	63.0	0.2	63.1	0.2	62.8	-0.5
1977	62.9	0.2	63.2	0.5	63.1	-0.2	63.4	0.5	63.6	0.3	63.6	0.0	63.7	0.2	63.7	0.0	63.6	-0.2	63.8	0.3	63.8	0.0	63.9	0.2
1978	63.6	-0.5	63.6	0.0	63.6	0.0	63.6	0.0	63.5	-0.2	63.5	0.0	63.8	0.5	64.2	0.6	64.2	0.0	64.7	0.8	64.5	-0.3	65.0	0.8
1979	66.4	2.2	67.3	1.4	68.0	1.0	70.4	3.5	72.5	3.0	73.5	1.4	76.7	4.4	78.6	2.5	79.4	1.0	81.0	2.0	81.8	1.0	82.9	1.3
1980	85.9	3.6	87.3	1.6	88.9	1.8	91.4	2.8	93.2	2.0	93.5	0.3	93.2	-0.3	93.6	0.4	92.9	-0.7	93.6	0.8	94.4	0.9	94.9	0.5
1981	97.7	3.0	99.9	2.3	100.5	0.6	102.8	2.3	104.5	1.7	104.9	0.4	105.1	0.2	105.4	0.3	105.5	0.1	104.3	-1.1	103.1	-1.2	102.9	-0.2
1982	102.9	0.0	102.7	-0.2	102.5	-0.2	101.5	-1.0	101.3	-0.2	99.6	-1.7	99.0	-0.6	99.0	0.0	98.3	-0.7	98.1	-0.2	97.9	-0.2	97.1	-0.8
1983	96.2	-0.9	96.5	0.3	96.1	-0.4	96.1	0.0	96.1	0.0	96.0	-0.1	98.4	2.5	98.6	0.2	98.0	-0.6	97.8	-0.2	98.2	0.4	99.1	0.9
1984	98.5	-0.6	95.8	-2.7	97.8	2.1	98.0	0.2	97.9	-0.1	98.0	0.1	98.0	0.0	96.7	-1.3	95.8	-0.9	95.3	-0.5	94.9	-0.4	95.0	0.1
1985	95.5	0.5	95.5	0.0	95.5	0.0	95.3	-0.2	95.5	0.2	96.3	0.8	96.4	0.1	97.5	1.1	97.1	-0.4	95.9	-1.2	95.4	-0.5	95.6	0.2
1986	96.9	1.4	95.0	-2.0	95.4	0.4	91.8	-3.8	90.2	-1.7	89.8	-0.4	89.7	-0.1	89.5	-0.2	89.9	0.4	90.2	0.3	89.8	-0.4	90.2	0.4
1987	92.0	2.0	92.8	0.9	93.7	1.0	94.1	0.4	95.2	1.2	97.8	2.7	96.3	-1.5	95.6	-0.7	95.5	-0.1	96.8	1.4	97.6	0.8	98.2	0.6
1988	99.4	1.2	100.3	0.9	102.1	1.8	103.3	1.2	104.3	1.0	105.8	1.4	108.6	2.6	109.4	0.7	110.0	0.5	111.4	1.3	112.8	1.3	114.2	1.2
1989	117.2	2.6	117.6	0.3	116.7	-0.8	117.5	0.7	117.8	0.3	115.6	-1.9	114.1	-1.3	113.4	-0.6	112.4	-0.9	112.5	0.1	111.7	-0.7	111.6	-0.1
1990	111.4	-0.2	111.3	-0.1	110.7	-0.5	110.4	-0.3	110.8	0.4	111.1	0.3	111.1	0.0	110.7	-0.4	114.9	3.8	118.4	3.0	120.1	1.4	117.8	-1.9
1991	117.5	-0.3	116.7	-0.7	113.2	-3.0	112.9	-0.3	111.9	-0.9	111.7	-0.2	109.7	-1.8	109.1	-0.5	109.7	0.5	109.7	0.0	109.7	0.0	109.9	0.2
1992	108.4	-1.4	107.3	-1.0	107.2	-0.1	107.5	0.3	107.7	0.2	109.9	2.0	110.2	0.3	110.5	0.3	111.0	0.5	110.7	-0.3	111.4	0.6	109.4	-1.8
1993	109.8	0.4	110.7	0.8	110.0	-0.6	111.9	1.7	111.1	-0.7	111.3	0.2	110.6	-0.6	110.4	-0.2	110.5	0.1	110.3	-0.2	110.4	0.1	108.8	-1.4

Source: U.S. Department of Labor, Bureau of Labor Statistics, Division of Industry Prices and Price Indexes. n.e.c. stands for not elsewhere classified. - indicates no data collected for period or unavailable.

Paints and Allied Products
Producer Price Index
Base 1982 = 100

For 1983-1993. Columns headed % show percentile change in the index from the previous period for which an index is available.

Year	Jan Index	%	Feb Index	%	Mar Index	%	Apr Index	%	May Index	%	Jun Index	%	Jul Index	%	Aug Index	%	Sep Index	%	Oct Index	%	Nov Index	%	Dec Index	%
1983	-	-	-	-	99.3	-	99.6	0.3	99.6	0.0	99.5	-0.1	99.8	0.3	100.5	0.7	101.7	1.2	101.7	0.0	101.7	0.0	101.7	0.0
1984	102.0	0.3	102.6	0.6	102.5	-0.1	104.2	1.7	105.4	1.2	105.7	0.3	106.1	0.4	106.5	0.4	106.4	-0.1	106.6	0.2	106.6	0.0	106.8	0.2
1985	106.8	0.0	106.2	-0.6	106.4	0.2	106.7	0.3	107.0	0.3	107.2	0.2	107.1	-0.1	106.9	-0.2	106.5	-0.4	106.5	0.0	106.3	-0.2	106.6	0.3
1986	106.9	0.3	106.8	-0.1	107.0	0.2	105.4	-1.5	105.3	-0.1	105.3	0.0	105.9	0.6	105.5	-0.4	105.5	0.0	104.9	-0.6	105.0	0.1	105.1	0.1
1987	105.5	0.4	105.4	-0.1	105.7	0.3	106.8	1.0	106.9	0.1	107.9	0.9	108.1	0.2	108.7	0.6	108.8	0.1	108.8	0.0	107.6	-1.1	108.4	0.7
1988	109.6	1.1	109.8	0.2	110.6	0.7	111.2	0.5	111.5	0.3	112.2	0.6	113.7	1.3	114.1	0.4	114.7	0.5	115.4	0.6	117.0	1.4	117.2	0.2
1989	119.7	2.1	121.4	1.4	121.7	0.2	123.0	1.1	123.1	0.1	124.0	0.7	124.4	0.3	122.4	-1.6	123.0	0.5	123.3	0.2	122.2	-0.9	122.4	0.2
1990	122.8	0.3	125.3	2.0	125.5	0.2	126.1	0.5	126.4	0.2	127.0	0.5	127.3	0.2	127.5	0.2	131.8	3.4	132.3	0.4	134.7	1.8	134.7	0.0
1991	135.8	0.8	136.3	0.4	130.6	-4.2	130.7	0.1	130.7	0.0	131.3	0.5	131.4	0.1	131.3	-0.1	130.1	-0.9	130.1	0.0	130.5	0.3	130.4	-0.1
1992	130.3	-0.1	130.5	0.2	130.6	0.1	130.9	0.2	131.1	0.2	131.1	0.0	131.5	0.3	131.4	-0.1	131.2	-0.2	131.3	0.1	131.3	0.0	131.3	0.0
1993	131.7	0.3	132.0	0.2	131.9	-0.1	132.5	0.5	132.3	-0.2	132.2	-0.1	132.3	0.1	132.2	-0.1	132.2	0.0	132.0	-0.2	132.5	0.4	132.4	-0.1

Source: U.S. Department of Labor, Bureau of Labor Statistics, Division of Industry Prices and Price Indexes. n.e.c. stands for not elsewhere classified. - indicates no data collected for period or unavailable.

Drugs and Pharmaceuticals
Producer Price Index
Base 1982 = 100

For 1947-1993. Columns headed % show percentile change in the index from the previous period for which an index is available.

Year	Jan Index	%	Feb Index	%	Mar Index	%	Apr Index	%	May Index	%	Jun Index	%	Jul Index	%	Aug Index	%	Sep Index	%	Oct Index	%	Nov Index	%	Dec Index	%
1947	59.3	-	59.3	0.0	58.7	-1.0	56.7	-3.4	56.8	0.2	56.5	-0.5	56.3	-0.4	55.6	-1.2	55.4	-0.4	55.6	0.4	56.5	1.6	57.5	1.8
1948	56.3	-2.1	56.3	0.0	55.4	-1.6	55.2	-0.4	55.0	-0.4	55.0	0.0	54.8	-0.4	55.3	0.9	54.6	-1.3	52.8	-3.3	52.9	0.2	52.9	0.0
1949	51.6	-2.5	51.9	0.6	51.5	-0.8	50.9	-1.2	50.9	0.0	50.9	0.0	50.5	-0.8	50.1	-0.8	50.1	0.0	50.1	0.0	50.0	-0.2	49.9	-0.2
1950	49.7	-0.4	49.5	-0.4	49.4	-0.2	49.4	0.0	49.4	0.0	49.4	0.0	49.5	0.2	50.2	1.4	50.5	0.6	50.8	0.6	51.3	1.0	51.7	0.8
1951	51.9	0.4	51.9	0.0	51.9	0.0	51.9	0.0	51.7	-0.4	51.8	0.2	51.7	-0.2	51.7	0.0	51.7	0.0	51.7	0.0	51.5	-0.4	51.6	0.2
1952	51.4	-0.4	50.6	-1.6	50.5	-0.2	50.2	-0.6	49.9	-0.6	49.9	0.0	49.9	0.0	49.9	0.0	49.9	0.0	49.8	-0.2	49.8	0.0	49.4	-0.8
1953	49.6	0.4	49.5	-0.2	49.6	0.2	50.4	1.6	50.5	0.2	50.5	0.0	50.7	0.4	50.6	-0.2	50.6	0.0	50.6	0.0	50.6	0.0	50.8	0.4
1954	50.8	0.0	50.8	0.0	50.8	0.0	50.9	0.2	50.9	0.0	50.9	0.0	50.9	0.0	50.9	0.0	50.9	0.0	50.7	-0.4	50.7	0.0	50.7	0.0
1955	50.7	0.0	50.6	-0.2	50.5	-0.2	50.5	0.0	50.5	0.0	50.4	-0.2	50.3	-0.2	50.0	-0.6	50.0	0.0	50.0	0.0	50.0	0.0	50.0	0.0
1956	50.1	0.2	49.8	-0.6	49.8	0.0	49.8	0.0	49.9	0.2	49.9	0.0	49.9	0.0	49.9	0.0	49.8	-0.2	49.8	0.0	50.0	0.4	50.1	0.2
1957	50.1	0.0	50.5	0.8	50.5	0.0	50.6	0.2	50.6	0.0	50.6	0.0	50.6	0.0	50.6	0.0	50.6	0.0	50.6	0.0	50.6	0.0	50.6	0.0
1958	50.7	0.2	50.7	0.0	50.9	0.4	50.9	0.0	51.1	0.4	51.2	0.2	51.1	-0.2	51.1	0.0	51.1	0.0	50.8	-0.6	50.5	-0.6	50.5	0.0
1959	50.5	0.0	50.5	0.0	50.3	-0.4	50.3	0.0	50.5	0.4	50.5	0.0	50.6	0.2	50.6	0.0	50.6	0.0	50.6	0.0	50.6	0.0	50.6	0.0
1960	50.6	0.0	50.6	0.0	50.6	0.0	50.7	0.2	50.9	0.4	51.1	0.4	51.1	0.0	51.1	0.0	50.7	-0.8	50.5	-0.4	50.3	-0.4	50.3	0.0
1961	50.2	-0.2	50.2	0.0	50.1	-0.2	50.1	0.0	50.0	-0.2	50.0	0.0	50.1	0.2	49.4	-1.4	49.1	-0.6	49.2	0.2	49.3	0.2	49.3	0.0
1962	49.2	-0.2	49.2	0.0	49.2	0.0	49.1	-0.2	49.1	0.0	49.1	0.0	48.2	-1.8	48.1	-0.2	48.1	0.0	48.2	0.2	48.2	0.0	48.0	-0.4
1963	48.2	0.4	48.2	0.0	48.2	0.0	48.2	0.0	48.2	0.0	48.2	0.0	48.2	0.0	48.1	-0.2	48.1	0.0	48.1	0.0	48.1	0.0	48.1	0.0
1964	48.3	0.4	48.3	0.0	48.2	-0.2	48.3	0.2	48.4	0.2	47.9	-1.0	48.0	0.2	47.9	-0.2	47.9	0.0	47.9	0.0	47.9	0.0	47.9	0.0
1965	47.8	-0.2	47.9	0.2	47.9	0.0	48.0	0.2	48.1	0.2	47.6	-1.0	47.6	0.0	47.6	0.0	47.6	0.0	47.6	0.0	47.9	0.6	47.9	0.0
1966	47.8	-0.2	47.8	0.0	47.8	0.0	47.6	-0.4	47.6	0.0	47.7	0.2	47.8	0.2	47.9	0.2	48.0	0.2	48.1	0.2	48.1	0.0	47.9	-0.4
1967	47.9	0.0	47.7	-0.4	47.8	0.2	47.6	-0.4	47.6	0.0	47.6	0.0	47.6	0.0	47.4	-0.4	47.4	0.0	47.4	0.0	47.5	0.2	47.5	0.0
1968	47.0	-1.1	47.1	0.2	47.3	0.4	47.3	0.0	47.3	0.0	47.4	0.2	47.3	-0.2	47.1	-0.4	47.0	-0.2	47.3	0.6	47.4	0.2	47.4	0.0
1969	47.4	0.0	47.4	0.0	47.4	0.0	47.5	0.2	47.6	0.2	47.5	-0.2	47.6	0.2	47.6	0.0	47.6	0.0	47.6	0.0	47.7	0.2	47.9	0.4
1970	47.8	-0.2	47.9	0.2	48.2	0.6	47.9	-0.6	48.0	0.2	48.1	0.2	48.2	0.2	48.4	0.4	48.1	-0.6	48.2	0.2	48.4	0.4	48.5	0.2
1971	48.5	0.0	48.7	0.4	48.8	0.2	48.6	-0.4	48.6	0.0	48.7	0.2	48.9	0.4	48.9	0.0	48.9	0.0	48.9	0.0	48.8	-0.2	48.8	0.0
1972	48.7	-0.2	48.7	0.0	48.8	0.2	48.8	0.0	48.9	0.2	49.1	0.4	49.1	0.0	49.2	0.2	49.1	-0.2	49.2	0.2	49.3	0.2	49.3	0.0
1973	49.3	0.0	49.3	0.0	49.4	0.2	49.4	0.0	49.5	0.2	49.7	0.4	49.7	0.0	49.7	0.0	49.8	0.2	49.8	0.0	49.9	0.2	50.0	0.2
1974	50.1	0.2	50.3	0.4	50.6	0.6	51.2	1.2	51.9	1.4	53.0	2.1	53.7	1.3	54.9	2.2	55.7	1.5	56.7	1.8	57.6	1.6	58.0	0.7
1975	58.9	1.6	59.1	0.3	59.3	0.3	59.9	1.0	59.9	0.0	60.2	0.5	60.7	0.8	60.7	0.0	60.6	-0.2	61.2	1.0	61.3	0.2	61.5	0.3
1976	62.3	1.3	62.7	0.6	62.9	0.3	63.3	0.6	63.4	0.2	64.0	0.9	64.1	0.2	64.3	0.3	64.5	0.3	64.5	0.0	64.7	0.3	64.9	0.3
1977	65.5	0.9	65.9	0.6	66.2	0.5	66.4	0.3	66.5	0.2	67.0	0.8	67.2	0.3	67.2	0.0	67.3	0.1	67.5	0.3	67.7	0.3	68.0	0.4
1978	68.6	0.9	69.0	0.6	69.2	0.3	69.6	0.6	69.8	0.3	70.3	0.7	70.7	0.6	70.9	0.3	71.2	0.4	71.5	0.4	72.4	1.3	72.9	0.7
1979	73.9	1.4	74.4	0.7	74.6	0.3	75.0	0.5	75.1	0.1	75.7	0.8	75.8	0.1	76.0	0.3	76.7	0.9	77.5	1.0	77.6	0.1	78.3	0.9
1980	79.3	1.3	79.8	0.6	80.4	0.8	82.2	2.2	82.3	0.1	83.0	0.9	83.6	0.7	83.8	0.2	84.2	0.5	84.9	0.8	86.2	1.5	86.9	0.8
1981	87.9	1.2	89.2	1.5	90.1	1.0	90.9	0.9	91.6	0.8	91.9	0.3	93.1	1.3	92.8	-0.3	94.2	1.5	94.5	0.3	94.3	-0.2	94.7	0.4
1982	96.2	1.6	97.3	1.1	98.0	0.7	99.4	1.4	99.9	0.5	99.8	-0.1	100.0	0.2	100.5	0.5	101.1	0.6	102.3	1.2	102.6	0.3	102.8	0.2
1983	104.1	1.3	105.7	1.5	106.1	0.4	107.2	1.0	107.2	0.0	107.2	0.0	108.3	1.0	108.2	-0.1	108.2	0.0	109.1	0.8	110.0	0.8	109.9	-0.1
1984	110.9	0.9	111.6	0.6	113.1	1.3	114.2	1.0	114.3	0.1	112.9	-1.2	114.5	1.4	114.6	0.1	114.1	-0.4	116.5	2.1	117.5	0.9	116.6	-0.8
1985	117.8	1.0	119.1	1.1	120.1	0.8	121.0	0.7	121.7	0.6	121.0	-0.6	123.6	2.1	122.9	-0.6	123.4	0.4	124.4	0.8	125.1	0.6	124.1	-0.8
1986	126.6	2.0	126.5	-0.1	128.0	1.2	129.2	0.9	129.6	0.3	129.8	0.2	130.3	0.4	130.7	0.3	131.5	0.6	132.5	0.8	133.2	0.5	133.2	0.0
1987	134.7	1.1	135.8	0.8	137.3	1.1	138.2	0.7	139.5	0.9	138.9	-0.4	139.2	0.2	139.5	0.2	141.0	1.1	140.0	-0.7	142.6	1.9	142.4	-0.1
1988	143.3	0.6	143.6	0.2	145.5	1.3	146.0	0.3	147.4	1.0	147.4	0.0	149.2	1.2	149.2	0.0	150.8	1.1	151.5	0.5	153.3	1.2	153.1	-0.1
1989	155.5	1.6	155.6	0.1	157.7	1.3	158.6	0.6	158.6	0.0	160.1	0.9	160.7	0.4	161.9	0.7	161.3	-0.4	162.3	0.6	163.6	0.8	164.3	0.4
1990	166.0	1.0	167.5	0.9	168.7	0.7	169.8	0.7	170.5	0.4	170.1	-0.2	171.0	0.5	171.7	0.4	171.6	-0.1	172.9	0.8	174.5	0.9	175.1	0.3
1991	176.3	0.7	178.0	1.0	178.3	0.2	181.1	1.6	181.7	0.3	182.6	0.5	184.7	1.2	185.5	0.4	184.0	-0.8	186.1	1.1	186.1	0.0	186.5	0.2

[Continued]

Drugs and Pharmaceuticals

Producer Price Index
Base 1982 = 100

[Continued]

For 1947-1993. Columns headed % show percentile change in the index from the previous period for which an index is available.

Year	Jan Index	%	Feb Index	%	Mar Index	%	Apr Index	%	May Index	%	Jun Index	%	Jul Index	%	Aug Index	%	Sep Index	%	Oct Index	%	Nov Index	%	Dec Index	%
1992	187.2	0.4	188.8	0.9	189.6	0.4	191.3	0.9	191.9	0.3	192.2	0.2	192.8	0.3	193.8	0.5	193.7	-0.1	194.8	0.6	194.6	-0.1	196.0	0.7
1993	197.9	1.0	199.1	0.6	199.2	0.1	200.5	0.7	200.3	-0.1	201.0	0.3	201.5	0.2	202.3	0.4	202.0	-0.1	202.6	0.3	202.0	-0.3	202.2	0.1

Source: U.S. Department of Labor, Bureau of Labor Statistics, Division of Industry Prices and Price Indexes. n.e.c. stands for not elsewhere classified. - indicates no data collected for period or unavailable.

Fats and Oils, Inedible
Producer Price Index
Base 1982 = 100

For 1926-1993. Columns headed % show percentile change in the index from the previous period for which an index is available.

Year	Jan Index	%	Feb Index	%	Mar Index	%	Apr Index	%	May Index	%	Jun Index	%	Jul Index	%	Aug Index	%	Sep Index	%	Oct Index	%	Nov Index	%	Dec Index	%
1926	-		-		-		-		-		-		-		-		-		-		-		-	
1927	-		-		-		-		-		-		-		-		-		-		-		-	
1928	-		-		-		-		-		-		-		-		-		-		-		-	
1929	-		-		-		-		-		-		-		-		-		-		-		-	
1930	-		-		-		-		-		-		-		-		-		-		-		-	
1931	-		-		-		-		-		-		-		-		-		-		-		-	
1932	-		-		-		-		-		-		-		-		-		-		-		-	
1933	19.3	-	18.6	-3.6	18.8	1.1	19.1	1.6	22.2	16.2	23.4	5.4	23.0	-1.7	22.7	-1.3	21.0	-7.5	20.9	-0.5	21.1	1.0	20.3	-3.8
1934	19.5	-3.9	19.9	2.1	20.2	1.5	20.1	-0.5	20.4	1.5	19.8	-2.9	20.1	1.5	21.3	6.0	23.1	8.5	24.6	6.5	23.8	-3.3	25.4	6.7
1935	29.7	16.9	33.3	12.1	36.3	9.0	34.6	-4.7	35.3	2.0	33.0	-6.5	29.5	-10.6	29.4	-0.3	31.1	5.8	33.7	8.4	33.1	-1.8	32.8	-0.9
1936	32.8	0.0	31.8	-3.0	30.3	-4.7	29.4	-3.0	26.7	-9.2	27.4	2.6	30.8	12.4	32.6	5.8	36.8	12.9	37.6	2.2	39.8	5.9	45.7	14.8
1937	51.4	12.5	50.5	-1.8	50.1	-0.8	47.8	-4.6	42.8	-10.5	40.5	-5.4	39.4	-2.7	36.9	-6.3	34.4	-6.8	33.2	-3.5	31.2	-6.0	29.7	-4.8
1938	30.4	2.4	29.4	-3.3	28.5	-3.1	26.1	-8.4	25.2	-3.4	24.6	-2.4	26.1	6.1	25.6	-1.9	25.1	-2.0	25.0	-0.4	24.6	-1.6	24.5	-0.4
1939	24.6	0.4	24.3	-1.2	25.0	2.9	24.3	-2.8	24.7	1.6	24.5	-0.8	22.9	-6.5	21.5	-6.1	28.7	33.5	30.3	5.6	29.0	-4.3	28.2	-2.8
1940	27.8	-1.4	27.0	-2.9	25.4	-5.9	24.8	-2.4	24.4	-1.6	23.9	-2.0	22.8	-4.6	20.7	-9.2	21.1	1.9	21.0	-0.5	22.4	6.7	22.4	0.0
1941	24.5	9.4	24.8	1.2	29.5	19.0	36.7	24.4	42.7	16.3	42.7	0.0	44.4	4.0	46.2	4.1	48.4	4.8	49.4	2.1	49.2	-0.4	54.0	9.8
1942	56.3	4.3	57.3	1.8	57.6	0.5	57.7	0.2	57.5	-0.3	57.4	-0.2	55.2	-3.8	53.8	-2.5	53.8	0.0	53.8	0.0	53.8	0.0	53.8	0.0
1943	53.8	0.0	53.8	0.0	53.8	0.0	53.8	0.0	54.0	0.4	54.0	0.0	54.0	0.0	54.0	0.0	54.0	0.0	54.0	0.0	54.0	0.0	54.0	0.0
1944	54.0	0.0	54.0	0.0	54.0	0.0	54.0	0.0	54.0	0.0	54.0	0.0	54.0	0.0	54.0	0.0	54.0	0.0	54.0	0.0	54.0	0.0	54.0	0.0
1945	54.0	0.0	54.0	0.0	54.0	0.0	54.0	0.0	54.0	0.0	54.0	0.0	54.0	0.0	54.0	0.0	54.0	0.0	54.0	0.0	54.0	0.0	54.0	0.0
1946	53.8	-0.4	53.9	0.2	54.1	0.4	54.1	0.0	54.1	0.0	54.1	0.0	60.4	11.6	54.3	-10.1	54.7	0.7	58.8	7.5	101.1	71.9	107.5	6.3
1947	111.5	3.7	114.9	3.0	128.8	12.1	116.8	-9.3	86.3	-26.1	67.5	-21.8	64.5	-4.4	62.6	-2.9	82.4	31.6	103.6	25.7	121.2	17.0	111.0	-8.4
1948	120.6	8.6	96.0	-20.4	100.0	4.2	96.0	-4.0	85.6	-10.8	92.6	8.2	87.4	-5.6	77.9	-10.9	80.8	3.7	77.8	-3.7	79.0	1.5	70.2	-11.1
1949	56.2	-19.9	49.8	-11.4	44.8	-10.0	39.8	-11.2	42.0	5.5	40.1	-4.5	39.2	-2.2	46.1	17.6	41.7	-9.5	39.7	-4.8	39.7	0.0	39.9	0.5
1950	42.5	6.5	41.7	-1.9	43.4	4.1	43.3	-0.2	41.8	-3.5	37.3	-10.8	44.2	18.5	53.0	19.9	66.5	25.5	65.3	-1.8	71.5	9.5	80.1	12.0
1951	88.9	11.0	94.4	6.2	87.8	-7.0	82.3	-6.3	79.3	-3.6	67.7	-14.6	53.6	-20.8	53.8	0.4	55.8	3.7	54.9	-1.6	49.9	-9.1	47.0	-5.8
1952	43.4	-7.7	39.2	-9.7	36.2	-7.7	32.6	-9.9	36.1	10.7	39.8	10.2	38.1	-4.3	36.3	-4.7	37.4	3.0	39.0	4.3	40.6	4.1	40.4	-0.5
1953	40.9	1.2	40.3	-1.5	45.1	11.9	42.7	-5.3	38.2	-10.5	35.6	-6.8	35.7	0.3	35.9	0.6	39.1	8.9	40.8	4.3	44.4	8.8	44.8	0.9
1954	46.8	4.5	48.6	3.8	46.3	-4.7	45.7	-1.3	45.4	-0.7	42.6	-6.2	39.8	-6.6	40.9	2.8	41.3	1.0	43.2	4.6	44.2	2.3	45.4	2.7
1955	47.3	4.2	46.7	-1.3	42.4	-9.2	42.2	-0.5	40.7	-3.6	41.1	1.0	42.7	3.9	41.8	-2.1	42.7	2.2	44.5	4.2	44.1	-0.9	43.3	-1.8
1956	42.5	-1.8	41.6	-2.1	42.1	1.2	44.4	5.5	46.1	3.8	42.1	-8.7	41.1	-2.4	41.1	0.0	42.4	3.2	49.5	0.4	49.9	0.8	50.0	0.2
1957	44.9	-1.1	44.4	-1.1	44.3	-0.2	44.5	0.5	45.3	1.8	46.1	1.8	46.7	1.3	48.5	3.9	49.3	1.6	47.9	1.5	49.5	3.3	47.0	-5.1
1958	48.3	-3.4	48.1	-0.4	49.1	2.1	47.6	-3.1	47.0	-1.3	47.3	0.6	47.8	1.1	47.8	0.0	47.2	-1.3	41.7	-1.0	39.9	-4.3	38.9	-2.5
1959	45.8	-2.6	45.0	-1.7	46.1	2.4	46.2	0.2	46.2	0.0	44.7	-3.2	42.3	-5.4	41.1	-2.8	42.1	2.4	41.7	-1.0	39.9	-4.3	38.9	-2.5
1960	37.6	-3.3	37.8	0.5	38.7	2.4	39.6	2.3	38.4	-3.0	36.6	-4.7	36.6	0.0	37.4	2.2	36.5	-2.4	36.6	0.3	37.4	2.2	37.1	-0.8
1961	38.4	3.5	41.8	8.9	44.1	5.5	47.5	7.7	47.0	-1.1	41.4	-11.9	39.9	-3.6	39.1	-2.0	37.3	-4.6	36.0	-3.5	35.2	-2.2	36.1	2.6
1962	38.2	5.8	35.5	-7.1	37.4	5.4	36.5	-2.4	35.5	-2.7	33.8	-4.8	33.9	0.3	33.6	-0.9	33.3	-0.9	35.3	6.0	35.0	-0.8	33.5	-4.3
1963	33.0	-1.5	33.5	1.5	34.3	2.4	35.8	4.4	36.2	1.1	37.1	2.5	37.5	1.1	37.6	0.3	37.4	-0.5	40.8	9.1	41.5	1.7	39.2	-5.5
1964	38.3	-2.3	38.3	0.0	39.5	3.1	40.2	1.8	40.8	1.5	42.9	5.1	44.2	3.0	46.7	5.7	48.9	4.7	49.6	1.4	51.9	4.6	53.8	3.7
1965	52.2	-3.0	54.5	4.4	54.7	0.4	55.8	2.0	53.7	-3.8	52.5	-2.2	50.8	-3.2	48.1	-5.3	49.9	3.7	50.7	1.6	49.1	-3.2	50.7	3.3
1966	52.1	2.8	50.7	-2.7	49.0	-3.4	47.9	-2.2	47.2	-1.5	46.8	-0.8	48.5	3.6	48.6	0.2	47.8	-1.6	43.5	-9.0	42.2	-3.0	43.8	3.8
1967	42.5	-3.0	41.0	-3.5	37.5	-8.5	39.3	4.8	38.2	-2.8	36.6	-4.2	35.5	-3.0	35.6	0.3	35.5	-0.3	36.2	2.0	35.9	-0.8	35.6	-0.8
1968	35.2	-1.1	35.3	0.3	36.8	4.2	37.2	1.1	36.1	-3.0	33.5	-7.2	31.8	-5.1	32.8	3.1	31.6	-3.7	32.2	1.9	33.8	5.0	32.2	-4.7
1969	33.3	3.4	33.9	1.8	37.0	9.1	38.6	4.3	38.4	-0.5	40.0	4.2	41.7	4.2	45.7	9.6	46.9	2.6	45.5	-3.0	46.3	1.8	42.7	-7.8
1970	43.8	2.6	43.4	-0.9	47.2	8.8	49.5	4.9	49.2	-0.6	49.8	1.2	49.6	-0.4	51.6	4.0	48.1	-6.8	54.1	12.5	56.7	4.8	53.8	-5.1

[Continued]

Fats and Oils, Inedible
Producer Price Index
Base 1982 = 100
[Continued]

For 1926-1993. Columns headed % show percentile change in the index from the previous period for which an index is available.

Year	Jan Index	%	Feb Index	%	Mar Index	%	Apr Index	%	May Index	%	Jun Index	%	Jul Index	%	Aug Index	%	Sep Index	%	Oct Index	%	Nov Index	%	Dec Index	%
1971	50.1	-6.9	53.4	6.6	54.0	1.1	53.6	-0.7	52.0	-3.0	49.4	-5.0	49.0	-0.8	50.2	2.4	49.8	-0.8	48.3	-3.0	46.9	-2.9	43.4	-7.5
1972	41.7	-3.9	41.4	-0.7	38.7	-6.5	42.0	8.5	43.4	3.3	43.4	0.0	42.4	-2.3	45.4	7.1	43.6	-4.0	43.9	0.7	46.1	5.0	48.0	4.1
1973	48.8	1.7	52.1	6.8	65.1	25.0	68.9	5.8	86.9	26.1	98.7	13.6	98.5	-0.2	102.3	3.9	104.7	2.3	102.2	-2.4	90.6	-11.4	107.1	18.2
1974	111.6	4.2	125.7	12.6	139.4	10.9	144.3	3.5	134.5	-6.8	135.3	0.6	130.1	-3.8	142.4	9.5	121.8	-14.5	122.9	0.9	112.8	-8.2	99.0	-12.2
1975	88.1	-11.0	86.7	-1.6	81.7	-5.8	97.9	19.8	93.8	-4.2	92.4	-1.5	97.5	5.5	107.0	9.7	108.5	1.4	99.0	-8.8	97.6	-1.4	96.3	-1.3
1976	92.3	-4.2	91.8	-0.5	95.9	4.5	91.2	-4.9	88.2	-3.3	91.2	3.4	97.0	6.4	93.4	-3.7	98.4	5.4	94.1	-4.4	94.1	0.0	95.3	1.3
1977	95.5	0.2	100.4	5.1	102.5	2.1	114.2	11.4	126.4	10.7	119.4	-5.5	105.6	-11.6	100.7	-4.6	92.4	-8.2	97.7	5.7	99.4	1.7	99.7	0.3
1978	98.6	-1.1	105.4	6.9	110.3	4.6	112.8	2.3	118.0	4.6	117.3	-0.6	125.7	7.2	117.2	-6.8	126.7	8.1	127.3	0.5	135.3	6.3	124.7	-7.8
1979	125.9	1.0	137.8	9.5	149.2	8.3	168.0	12.6	156.6	-6.8	140.1	-10.5	142.9	2.0	140.9	-1.4	142.3	1.0	137.4	-3.4	128.9	-6.2	122.5	-5.0
1980	121.9	-0.5	113.2	-7.1	112.3	-0.8	111.7	-0.5	110.4	-1.2	95.8	-13.2	97.4	1.7	115.2	18.3	114.0	-1.0	113.1	-0.8	115.4	2.0	118.8	2.9
1981	116.3	-2.1	108.5	-6.7	110.7	2.0	117.1	5.8	116.9	-0.2	113.5	-2.9	108.9	-4.1	114.4	5.1	106.9	-6.6	104.0	-2.7	105.8	1.7	105.0	-0.8
1982	102.1	-2.8	102.7	0.6	108.6	5.7	105.8	-2.6	108.0	2.1	107.6	-0.4	104.2	-3.2	95.2	-8.6	95.1	-0.1	90.7	-4.6	89.7	-1.1	90.2	0.6
1983	90.6	0.4	94.9	4.7	98.2	3.5	104.2	6.1	107.5	3.2	103.7	-3.5	97.7	-5.8	104.1	6.6	123.2	18.3	119.3	-3.2	120.4	0.9	119.4	-0.8
1984	125.2	4.9	130.7	4.4	137.3	5.0	143.5	4.5	149.5	4.2	155.1	3.7	141.8	-8.6	131.1	-7.5	134.6	2.7	136.7	1.6	142.3	4.1	141.1	-0.8
1985	129.7	-8.1	130.0	0.2	129.7	-0.2	130.7	0.8	124.0	-5.1	111.7	-9.9	104.8	-6.2	97.6	-6.9	92.6	-5.1	93.6	1.1	90.7	-3.1	91.9	1.3
1986	94.5	2.8	95.9	1.5	86.4	-9.9	81.6	-5.6	76.9	-5.8	71.5	-7.0	69.9	-2.2	71.2	1.9	72.2	1.4	76.9	6.5	80.2	4.3	84.1	4.9
1987	94.5	12.4	95.1	0.6	91.3	-4.0	83.0	-9.1	91.0	9.6	94.9	4.3	92.5	-2.5	93.0	0.5	95.5	2.7	94.8	-0.7	93.3	-1.6	93.4	0.1
1988	110.5	18.3	110.8	0.3	110.1	-0.6	109.6	-0.5	105.9	-3.4	115.1	8.7	123.0	6.9	122.0	-0.8	111.6	-8.5	107.2	-3.9	100.7	-6.1	103.7	3.0
1989	103.2	-0.5	102.4	-0.8	101.8	-0.6	99.1	-2.7	96.2	-2.9	99.2	3.1	94.5	-4.7	85.9	-9.1	86.8	1.0	93.9	8.2	92.2	-1.8	90.7	-1.6
1990	88.3	-2.6	94.2	6.7	90.6	-3.8	85.6	-5.5	86.8	1.4	88.5	2.0	88.4	-0.1	83.0	-6.1	82.4	-0.7	87.0	5.6	89.6	3.0	92.8	3.6
1991	96.6	4.1	89.5	-7.3	86.2	-3.7	86.5	0.3	83.5	-3.5	82.1	-1.7	80.5	-1.9	86.9	8.0	87.7	0.9	87.1	-0.7	88.3	1.4	87.0	-1.5
1992	88.9	2.2	86.5	-2.7	83.0	-4.0	84.6	1.9	87.2	3.1	91.7	5.2	94.7	3.3	98.1	3.6	99.4	1.3	98.8	-0.6	102.7	3.9	100.9	-1.8
1993	100.6	-0.3	97.5	-3.1	97.5	0.0	100.7	3.3	99.9	-0.8	96.5	-3.4	93.5	-3.1	94.7	1.3	91.2	-3.7	90.3	-1.0	91.4	1.2	95.1	4.0

Source: U.S. Department of Labor, Bureau of Labor Statistics, Division of Industry Prices and Price Indexes. n.e.c. stands for not elsewhere classified. - indicates no data collected for period or unavailable.

Agricultural Chemicals and Chemical Products
Producer Price Index
Base 1982 = 100

For 1947-1993. Columns headed % show percentile change in the index from the previous period for which an index is available.

Year	Jan Index	%	Feb Index	%	Mar Index	%	Apr Index	%	May Index	%	Jun Index	%	Jul Index	%	Aug Index	%	Sep Index	%	Oct Index	%	Nov Index	%	Dec Index	%
1947	28.3	-	28.3	0.0	28.9	2.1	29.0	0.3	29.0	0.0	28.8	-0.7	28.9	0.3	28.9	0.0	29.0	0.3	29.3	1.0	29.5	0.7	29.7	0.7
1948	29.9	0.7	29.8	-0.3	29.9	0.3	29.8	-0.3	29.7	-0.3	29.7	0.0	30.2	1.7	30.6	1.3	30.9	1.0	31.1	0.6	31.3	0.6	31.3	0.0
1949	31.6	1.0	31.5	-0.3	31.5	0.0	31.5	0.0	31.5	0.0	31.3	-0.6	31.5	0.6	31.4	-0.3	31.4	0.0	31.4	0.0	31.0	-1.3	30.9	-0.3
1950	30.8	-0.3	30.6	-0.6	30.7	0.3	30.8	0.3	30.8	0.0	30.1	-2.3	30.1	0.0	30.2	0.3	30.2	0.0	30.2	0.0	30.6	1.3	31.6	3.3
1951	32.1	1.6	32.1	0.0	32.1	0.0	32.1	0.0	32.1	0.0	31.9	-0.6	32.5	1.9	32.6	0.3	32.8	0.6	32.9	0.3	32.9	0.0	33.0	0.3
1952	33.0	0.0	33.1	0.3	33.3	0.6	33.3	0.0	33.5	0.6	32.9	-1.8	33.0	0.3	33.0	0.0	33.0	0.0	33.0	0.0	33.0	0.0	33.0	0.0
1953	32.9	-0.3	32.8	-0.3	32.8	0.0	32.9	0.3	33.0	0.3	32.7	-0.9	33.1	1.2	33.2	0.3	33.2	0.0	33.1	-0.3	33.3	0.6	33.4	0.3
1954	33.2	-0.6	33.4	0.6	33.4	0.0	33.4	0.0	33.4	0.0	33.1	-0.9	33.1	0.0	33.2	0.3	33.1	-0.3	33.0	-0.3	33.0	0.0	33.1	0.3
1955	33.2	0.3	33.2	0.0	33.2	0.0	33.1	-0.3	33.1	0.0	32.8	-0.9	32.9	0.3	33.0	0.3	32.9	-0.3	33.0	0.3	32.9	-0.3	32.9	0.0
1956	33.0	0.3	32.8	-0.6	32.8	0.0	32.8	0.0	32.3	-1.5	32.3	0.0	32.2	-0.3	32.3	0.3	32.2	-0.3	32.1	-0.3	32.3	0.6	32.3	0.0
1957	32.5	0.6	32.3	-0.6	32.3	0.0	32.5	0.6	32.4	-0.3	32.3	-0.3	32.3	0.0	32.5	0.6	32.7	0.6	32.8	0.3	32.8	0.0	33.1	0.9
1958	33.4	0.9	33.3	-0.3	33.4	0.3	33.6	0.6	33.6	0.0	33.6	0.0	33.4	-0.6	32.9	-1.5	32.8	-0.3	33.0	0.6	32.9	-0.3	32.9	0.0
1959	33.4	1.5	33.4	0.0	33.4	0.0	33.3	-0.3	33.2	-0.3	33.3	0.3	33.2	-0.3	33.0	-0.6	33.1	0.3	33.2	0.3	33.2	0.0	33.3	0.3
1960	33.4	0.3	33.5	0.3	33.5	0.0	33.5	0.0	33.5	0.0	33.5	0.0	33.7	0.6	33.7	0.0	33.8	0.3	34.0	0.6	34.0	0.0	33.9	-0.3
1961	34.0	0.3	34.0	0.0	34.0	0.0	34.0	0.0	34.0	0.0	33.8	-0.6	33.8	0.0	33.6	-0.6	33.8	0.6	33.4	-1.2	33.6	0.6	33.5	-0.3
1962	34.2	2.1	34.3	0.3	34.0	-0.9	34.0	0.0	33.9	-0.3	33.9	0.0	33.6	-0.9	33.2	-1.2	33.2	0.0	33.2	0.0	33.2	0.0	33.2	0.0
1963	33.4	0.6	33.2	-0.6	33.2	0.0	33.4	0.6	33.4	0.0	33.2	-0.6	33.1	-0.3	32.7	-1.2	32.8	0.3	32.8	0.0	32.9	0.3	32.7	-0.6
1964	32.8	0.3	32.9	0.3	32.9	0.0	32.9	0.0	32.9	0.0	32.9	0.0	33.0	0.3	32.8	-0.6	32.7	-0.3	32.8	0.3	33.0	0.6	33.0	0.0
1965	33.2	0.6	33.5	0.9	33.6	0.3	33.5	-0.3	33.5	0.0	33.6	0.3	33.7	0.3	33.6	-0.3	33.7	0.3	33.8	0.3	33.8	0.0	33.8	0.0
1966	33.8	0.0	33.9	0.3	33.9	0.0	34.1	0.6	34.2	0.3	34.0	-0.6	33.9	-0.3	33.6	-0.9	33.7	0.3	33.9	0.6	34.1	0.6	34.0	-0.3
1967	34.4	1.2	34.8	1.2	34.9	0.3	34.7	-0.6	34.7	0.0	34.7	0.0	34.2	-1.4	33.6	-1.8	33.4	-0.6	33.5	0.3	33.6	0.3	33.7	0.3
1968	32.8	-2.7	33.2	1.2	33.4	0.6	33.5	0.3	33.5	0.0	33.4	-0.3	33.4	0.0	32.7	-2.1	32.5	-0.6	32.3	-0.6	31.8	-1.5	31.8	0.0
1969	30.6	-3.8	30.4	-0.7	30.5	0.3	30.4	-0.3	30.4	0.0	30.4	0.0	29.2	-3.9	29.2	0.0	28.9	-1.0	28.5	-1.4	28.6	0.4	28.6	0.0
1970	28.9	1.0	30.2	4.5	30.4	0.7	30.5	0.3	30.3	-0.7	30.3	0.0	30.0	-1.0	30.2	0.7	30.4	0.7	30.6	0.7	30.6	0.0	30.6	0.0
1971	31.5	2.9	31.8	1.0	32.2	1.3	32.3	0.3	32.2	-0.3	32.2	0.0	31.5	-2.2	30.9	-1.9	30.9	0.0	30.9	0.0	30.9	0.0	30.9	0.0
1972	30.9	0.0	30.8	-0.3	31.0	0.6	31.5	1.6	31.5	0.0	31.6	0.3	31.4	-0.6	31.5	0.3	31.5	0.0	31.5	0.0	31.6	0.3	31.6	0.0
1973	31.8	0.6	31.8	0.0	32.0	0.6	32.3	0.9	32.4	0.3	32.5	0.3	33.1	1.8	32.8	-0.9	32.8	0.0	32.8	0.0	35.9	9.5	36.3	1.1
1974	38.4	5.8	38.7	0.8	40.4	4.4	40.4	0.0	40.4	0.0	41.1	1.7	44.8	9.0	48.6	8.5	49.7	2.3	58.3	17.3	61.9	6.2	62.3	0.6
1975	65.0	4.3	65.9	1.4	72.4	9.9	72.6	0.3	72.5	-0.1	72.2	-0.4	71.9	-0.4	70.6	-1.8	68.8	-2.5	68.4	-0.6	67.6	-1.2	67.7	0.1
1976	67.7	0.0	65.4	-3.4	65.1	-0.5	64.9	-0.3	64.9	0.0	64.3	-0.9	63.1	-1.9	63.7	1.0	63.9	0.3	63.9	0.0	63.0	-1.4	62.7	-0.5
1977	62.3	-0.6	62.9	1.0	64.0	1.7	64.6	0.9	64.5	-0.2	64.6	0.2	64.5	-0.2	64.8	0.5	65.0	0.3	65.0	0.0	64.4	-0.9	64.0	-0.6
1978	64.1	0.2	64.7	0.9	65.3	0.9	65.7	0.6	69.6	5.9	69.3	-0.4	69.1	-0.3	69.1	0.0	69.3	0.3	69.6	0.4	69.2	-0.6	69.1	-0.1
1979	69.0	-0.1	69.4	0.6	70.5	1.6	71.7	1.7	71.8	0.1	71.5	-0.4	72.2	1.0	73.6	1.9	75.0	1.9	76.7	2.3	78.5	2.3	79.6	1.4
1980	82.7	3.9	84.8	2.5	87.6	3.3	88.4	0.9	88.4	0.0	88.1	-0.3	88.5	0.5	88.9	0.5	89.1	0.2	89.1	0.0	89.3	0.2	90.0	0.8
1981	91.5	1.7	92.9	1.5	94.3	1.5	95.0	0.7	95.4	0.4	98.8	3.6	98.8	0.0	100.3	1.5	100.1	-0.2	100.2	0.1	101.1	0.9	100.8	-0.3
1982	101.5	0.7	101.9	0.4	101.6	-0.3	101.1	-0.5	100.8	-0.3	100.6	-0.2	99.7	-0.9	99.5	-0.2	99.1	-0.4	98.7	-0.4	98.0	-0.7	97.5	-0.5
1983	96.8	-0.7	96.9	0.1	97.2	0.3	96.7	-0.5	96.6	-0.1	96.0	-0.6	95.1	-0.9	94.8	-0.3	94.4	-0.4	94.5	0.1	95.9	1.5	96.4	0.5
1984	95.2	-1.2	97.7	2.6	98.5	0.8	98.6	0.1	98.1	-0.5	98.0	-0.1	97.4	-0.6	96.8	-0.6	97.4	0.6	97.6	0.2	96.6	-1.0	96.6	0.0
1985	96.7	0.1	96.3	-0.4	96.4	0.1	96.7	0.3	96.8	0.1	96.3	-0.5	96.4	0.1	96.5	0.1	96.4	-0.1	95.8	-0.6	95.7	-0.1	94.6	-1.1
1986	94.1	-0.5	95.1	1.1	95.6	0.5	95.5	-0.1	95.4	-0.1	95.7	0.3	95.1	-0.6	93.7	-1.5	93.5	-0.2	92.2	-1.4	92.4	0.2	92.2	-0.2
1987	92.1	-0.1	93.8	1.8	94.8	1.1	97.2	2.5	96.4	-0.8	96.5	0.1	96.8	0.3	97.3	0.5	97.8	0.5	97.7	-0.1	98.0	0.3	98.3	0.3
1988	101.1	2.8	103.1	2.0	104.3	1.2	104.5	0.2	103.9	-0.6	102.9	-1.0	103.4	0.5	103.8	0.4	104.4	0.6	105.5	1.1	107.6	2.0	109.2	1.5
1989	112.0	2.6	113.4	1.3	114.3	0.8	113.4	-0.8	112.2	-1.1	109.8	-2.1	106.5	-3.0	105.0	-1.4	104.7	-0.3	103.7	-1.0	104.4	0.7	104.5	0.1
1990	104.4	-0.1	105.8	1.3	105.7	-0.1	106.8	1.0	106.5	-0.3	105.3	-1.1	105.7	0.4	106.4	0.7	108.0	1.5	109.9	1.8	111.8	1.7	112.0	0.2
1991	112.0	0.0	112.3	0.3	112.3	0.0	112.2	-0.1	111.7	-0.4	111.2	-0.4	111.8	0.5	112.1	0.3	111.8	-0.3	111.5	-0.3	110.7	-0.7	110.9	0.2

[Continued]

Agricultural Chemicals and Chemical Products
Producer Price Index
Base 1982 = 100
[Continued]

For 1947-1993. Columns headed % show percentile change in the index from the previous period for which an index is available.

Year	Jan Index	%	Feb Index	%	Mar Index	%	Apr Index	%	May Index	%	Jun Index	%	Jul Index	%	Aug Index	%	Sep Index	%	Oct Index	%	Nov Index	%	Dec Index	%
1992	110.7	-0.2	110.9	0.2	111.2	0.3	111.3	0.1	111.7	0.4	111.6	-0.1	110.2	-1.3	109.3	-0.8	109.1	-0.2	109.3	0.2	109.4	0.1	109.3	-0.1
1993	110.6	1.2	110.2	-0.4	110.3	0.1	109.6	-0.6	109.3	-0.3	109.6	0.3	109.3	-0.3	107.7	-1.5	107.8	0.1	108.9	1.0	113.6	4.3	112.6	-0.9

Source: U.S. Department of Labor, Bureau of Labor Statistics, Division of Industry Prices and Price Indexes. n.e.c. stands for not elsewhere classified. - indicates no data collected for period or unavailable.

Plastic Resins and Materials
Producer Price Index
Base 1982 = 100

For 1947-1993. Columns headed % show percentile change in the index from the previous period for which an index is available.

Year	Jan Index	%	Feb Index	%	Mar Index	%	Apr Index	%	May Index	%	Jun Index	%	Jul Index	%	Aug Index	%	Sep Index	%	Oct Index	%	Nov Index	%	Dec Index	%
1947	37.3	-	37.3	0.0	37.3	0.0	37.3	0.0	37.5	0.5	37.5	0.0	37.5	0.0	37.5	0.0	37.5	0.0	37.5	0.0	37.2	-0.8	37.2	0.0
1948	37.6	1.1	37.2	-1.1	36.6	-1.6	36.6	0.0	36.6	0.0	36.6	0.0	37.5	2.5	37.4	-0.3	37.5	0.3	37.6	0.3	37.6	0.0	37.6	0.0
1949	38.1	1.3	38.1	0.0	37.6	-1.3	37.6	0.0	37.6	0.0	37.6	0.0	37.6	0.0	37.6	0.0	37.6	0.0	37.6	0.0	37.7	0.3	37.7	0.0
1950	37.5	-0.5	38.0	1.3	37.5	-1.3	37.5	0.0	37.3	-0.5	37.3	0.0	37.3	0.0	37.3	0.0	38.4	2.9	38.5	0.3	39.2	1.8	39.3	0.3
1951	45.9	16.8	46.9	2.2	47.4	1.1	47.4	0.0	47.4	0.0	47.4	0.0	47.4	0.0	47.4	0.0	47.6	0.4	47.6	0.0	47.7	0.2	47.7	0.0
1952	47.7	0.0	47.2	-1.0	47.0	-0.4	47.0	0.0	47.0	0.0	46.9	-0.2	46.9	0.0	46.9	0.0	46.9	0.0	46.9	0.0	46.9	0.0	47.0	0.2
1953	47.0	0.0	47.0	0.0	47.0	0.0	47.0	0.0	47.0	0.0	47.0	0.0	47.0	0.0	47.2	0.4	47.4	0.4	47.4	0.0	47.4	0.0	47.4	0.0
1954	47.0	-0.8	46.8	-0.4	46.8	0.0	46.8	0.0	46.8	0.0	46.8	0.0	46.8	0.0	46.8	0.0	46.8	0.0	46.8	0.0	46.5	-0.6	46.5	0.0
1955	46.3	-0.4	46.3	0.0	46.3	0.0	46.3	0.0	46.3	0.0	46.3	0.0	42.9	-7.3	42.9	0.0	42.9	0.0	42.9	0.0	42.9	0.0	42.9	0.0
1956	40.7	-5.1	40.7	0.0	40.7	0.0	40.6	-0.2	40.6	0.0	40.6	0.0	40.6	0.0	40.6	0.0	40.3	-0.7	40.3	0.0	40.3	0.0	40.4	0.2
1957	40.4	0.0	40.6	0.5	40.6	0.0	40.6	0.0	40.6	0.0	40.5	-0.2	40.5	0.0	40.7	0.5	40.7	0.0	40.7	0.0	40.5	-0.5	40.7	0.5
1958	40.7	0.0	40.7	0.0	40.5	-0.5	40.5	0.0	40.5	0.0	40.5	0.0	40.2	-0.7	39.4	-2.0	39.4	0.0	39.4	0.0	39.4	0.0	38.9	-1.3
1959	38.9	0.0	38.9	0.0	38.2	-1.8	38.2	0.0	38.2	0.0	38.2	0.0	38.2	0.0	38.2	0.0	38.2	0.0	38.2	0.0	38.2	0.0	38.2	0.0
1960	38.2	0.0	38.2	0.0	38.2	0.0	38.2	0.0	38.2	0.0	38.2	0.0	38.2	0.0	38.2	0.0	38.2	0.0	38.2	0.0	38.2	0.0	38.1	-0.3
1961	36.5	-4.2	36.5	0.0	36.5	0.0	36.5	0.0	36.5	0.0	36.5	0.0	36.4	-0.3	36.4	0.0	36.4	0.0	36.3	-0.3	36.3	0.0	36.3	0.0
1962	36.3	0.0	36.3	0.0	36.3	0.0	36.3	0.0	36.3	0.0	36.3	0.0	36.3	0.0	36.3	0.0	36.3	0.0	36.3	0.0	36.3	0.0	36.3	0.0
1963	36.3	0.0	36.3	0.0	36.3	0.0	35.3	-2.8	35.3	0.0	35.3	0.0	35.3	0.0	35.3	0.0	35.3	0.0	35.3	0.0	35.3	0.0	35.3	0.0
1964	35.3	0.0	35.3	0.0	35.3	0.0	35.3	0.0	35.3	0.0	35.3	0.0	35.3	0.0	35.3	0.0	35.3	0.0	35.3	0.0	35.0	-0.8	35.0	0.0
1965	35.0	0.0	35.0	0.0	35.0	0.0	35.0	0.0	35.0	0.0	35.0	0.0	35.0	0.0	35.0	0.0	35.0	0.0	35.0	0.0	35.0	0.0	35.0	0.0
1966	35.0	0.0	35.0	0.0	35.0	0.0	35.0	0.0	35.0	0.0	35.0	0.0	35.0	0.0	35.3	0.9	35.6	0.8	35.7	0.3	35.7	0.0	35.7	0.0
1967	35.7	0.0	35.8	0.3	35.8	0.0	35.8	0.0	36.0	0.6	35.7	-0.8	35.6	-0.3	35.5	-0.3	34.7	-2.3	34.0	-2.0	34.3	0.9	34.4	0.3
1968	34.0	-1.2	33.0	-2.9	32.8	-0.6	32.9	0.3	32.5	-1.2	32.2	-0.9	32.0	-0.6	31.9	-0.3	32.0	0.3	32.1	0.3	32.0	-0.3	31.9	-0.3
1969	31.9	0.0	32.1	0.6	32.1	0.0	32.0	-0.3	32.0	0.0	32.0	0.0	31.8	-0.6	32.0	0.6	32.1	0.3	31.7	-1.2	31.5	-0.6	31.7	0.6
1970	31.7	0.0	31.9	0.6	31.9	0.0	32.1	0.6	31.8	-0.9	31.7	-0.3	32.1	1.3	32.0	-0.3	32.1	0.3	32.3	0.6	32.0	-0.9	31.8	-0.6
1971	31.6	-0.6	31.4	-0.6	30.8	-1.9	31.1	1.0	31.1	0.0	31.0	-0.3	31.2	0.6	31.4	0.6	31.5	0.3	31.7	0.6	31.4	-0.9	31.4	0.0
1972	31.3	-0.3	31.5	0.6	31.4	-0.3	31.2	-0.6	31.3	0.3	31.0	-1.0	31.0	0.0	31.1	0.3	31.4	1.0	31.5	0.3	31.6	0.3	31.5	-0.3
1973	31.6	0.3	31.8	0.6	31.9	0.3	32.2	0.9	32.6	1.2	32.7	0.3	32.9	0.6	32.9	0.0	32.9	0.0	32.6	-0.9	32.8	0.6	32.8	0.0
1974	33.1	0.9	34.0	2.7	40.9	20.3	43.7	6.8	45.2	3.4	49.7	10.0	52.0	4.6	56.7	9.0	61.6	8.6	63.2	2.6	64.0	1.3	64.6	0.9
1975	64.6	0.0	64.3	-0.5	64.2	-0.2	64.3	0.2	62.2	-3.3	62.1	-0.2	62.5	0.6	62.6	0.2	63.2	1.0	64.9	2.7	65.2	0.5	65.8	0.9
1976	66.1	0.5	67.2	1.7	67.1	-0.1	68.4	1.9	68.5	0.1	68.9	0.6	69.7	1.2	69.6	-0.1	69.1	-0.7	69.0	-0.1	68.9	-0.1	68.8	-0.1
1977	68.3	-0.7	68.1	-0.3	68.7	0.9	69.1	0.6	69.4	0.4	69.7	0.4	70.6	1.3	70.6	0.0	70.6	0.0	70.5	-0.1	70.4	-0.1	70.1	-0.4
1978	70.1	0.0	70.0	-0.1	70.2	0.3	70.2	0.0	70.8	0.9	70.9	0.1	71.0	0.1	70.6	-0.6	70.6	0.0	70.4	-0.3	70.3	-0.1	71.0	1.0
1979	72.1	1.5	72.8	1.0	74.4	2.2	77.8	4.6	80.6	3.6	81.2	0.7	86.3	6.3	88.2	2.2	88.9	0.8	91.7	3.1	92.2	0.5	92.6	0.4
1980	95.4	3.0	96.0	0.6	96.8	0.8	101.5	4.9	101.8	0.3	101.5	-0.3	100.8	-0.7	99.3	-1.5	97.6	-1.7	97.4	-0.2	97.5	0.1	96.7	-0.8
1981	96.9	0.2	97.4	0.5	98.6	1.2	100.6	2.0	101.6	1.0	102.3	0.7	104.4	2.1	105.0	0.6	104.7	-0.3	105.7	1.0	103.4	-2.2	103.8	0.4
1982	100.9	-2.8	101.4	0.5	100.7	-0.7	100.9	0.2	99.9	-1.0	99.5	-0.4	99.1	-0.4	99.6	0.5	99.3	-0.3	99.3	0.0	99.6	0.3	99.7	0.1
1983	100.2	0.5	99.9	-0.3	99.5	-0.4	100.7	1.2	101.6	0.9	102.0	0.4	102.8	0.8	103.6	0.8	106.8	3.1	105.5	-1.2	105.1	-0.4	106.4	1.2
1984	107.7	1.2	107.6	-0.1	108.0	0.4	108.6	0.6	109.6	0.9	109.8	0.2	109.6	-0.2	109.5	-0.1	110.0	0.5	109.2	-0.7	109.0	-0.2	108.1	-0.8
1985	107.7	-0.4	108.3	0.6	108.1	-0.2	108.0	-0.1	107.8	-0.2	108.4	0.6	108.5	0.1	108.1	-0.4	107.7	-0.4	106.1	-1.5	106.0	-0.1	105.6	-0.4
1986	106.2	0.6	106.7	0.5	106.5	-0.2	104.7	-1.7	104.3	-0.4	104.2	-0.1	104.7	0.5	103.9	-0.8	102.4	-1.4	103.4	1.0	104.1	0.7	102.4	-1.6
1987	102.6	0.2	102.4	-0.2	103.2	0.8	106.3	3.0	107.0	0.7	109.7	2.5	112.8	2.8	113.1	0.3	114.2	1.0	116.8	2.3	117.4	0.5	117.7	0.3
1988	121.5	3.2	123.5	1.6	124.4	0.7	127.6	2.6	130.1	2.0	131.2	0.8	134.8	2.7	136.9	1.6	138.9	1.5	139.8	0.6	140.2	0.3	140.1	-0.1
1989	140.3	0.1	141.1	0.6	140.6	-0.4	140.7	0.1	139.8	-0.6	138.0	-1.3	135.3	-2.0	127.7	-5.6	126.1	-1.3	124.7	-1.1	123.7	-0.8	123.3	-0.3
1990	122.2	-0.9	121.6	-0.5	122.2	0.5	123.0	0.7	123.5	0.4	123.0	-0.4	122.3	-0.6	122.3	0.0	122.0	-0.2	125.9	3.2	129.1	2.5	132.1	2.3
1991	131.1	-0.8	128.7	-1.8	126.1	-2.0	122.9	-2.5	120.6	-1.9	117.0	-3.0	115.0	-1.7	114.9	-0.1	114.9	0.0	116.4	1.3	116.4	0.0	116.0	-0.3

[Continued]

Plastic Resins and Materials
Producer Price Index
Base 1982 = 100
[Continued]

For 1947-1993. Columns headed % show percentile change in the index from the previous period for which an index is available.

Year	Jan		Feb		Mar		Apr		May		Jun		Jul		Aug		Sep		Oct		Nov		Dec	
	Index	%	Index	%	Index	%	Index	%	Index	%	Index	%	Index	%	Index	%	Index	%	Index	%	Index	%	Index	%
1992	115.5	-0.4	115.6	0.1	114.2	-1.2	114.2	0.0	114.7	0.4	115.2	0.4	116.9	1.5	117.7	0.7	118.0	0.3	118.2	0.2	118.1	-0.1	118.1	0.0
1993	118.3	0.2	118.0	-0.3	117.6	-0.3	117.1	-0.4	116.3	-0.7	116.9	0.5	116.9	0.0	117.6	0.6	117.7	0.1	117.4	-0.3	116.2	-1.0	116.5	0.3

Source: U.S. Department of Labor, Bureau of Labor Statistics, Division of Industry Prices and Price Indexes. n.e.c. stands for not elsewhere classified. - indicates no data collected for period or unavailable.

Chemicals and Allied Products n.e.c.

Producer Price Index
Base 1982 = 100

For 1947-1993. Columns headed % show percentile change in the index from the previous period for which an index is available.

Year	Jan Index	%	Feb Index	%	Mar Index	%	Apr Index	%	May Index	%	Jun Index	%	Jul Index	%	Aug Index	%	Sep Index	%	Oct Index	%	Nov Index	%	Dec Index	%
1947	31.7	-	31.8	0.3	32.2	1.3	32.7	1.6	31.1	-4.9	30.8	-1.0	30.0	-2.6	30.0	0.0	30.1	0.3	32.1	6.6	33.4	4.0	34.2	2.4
1948	34.4	0.6	33.9	-1.5	33.2	-2.1	33.1	-0.3	32.2	-2.7	31.7	-1.6	32.1	1.3	32.2	0.3	32.1	-0.3	31.9	-0.6	31.8	-0.3	31.3	-1.6
1949	30.8	-1.6	30.0	-2.6	29.7	-1.0	29.0	-2.4	28.5	-1.7	28.5	0.0	28.0	-1.8	27.7	-1.1	27.8	0.4	27.8	0.0	27.8	0.0	27.7	-0.4
1950	27.3	-1.4	27.3	0.0	27.3	0.0	27.3	0.0	27.3	0.0	27.2	-0.4	27.2	0.0	28.5	4.8	29.7	4.2	30.2	1.7	30.7	1.7	32.0	4.2
1951	32.8	2.5	33.4	1.8	32.6	-2.4	32.4	-0.6	32.4	0.0	32.3	-0.3	31.7	-1.9	31.1	-1.9	30.7	-1.3	30.7	0.0	30.7	0.0	30.5	-0.7
1952	30.1	-1.3	30.1	0.0	30.1	0.0	29.7	-1.3	29.7	0.0	29.7	0.0	29.7	0.0	29.7	0.0	29.7	0.0	29.6	-0.3	29.5	-0.3	29.6	0.3
1953	29.6	0.0	29.5	-0.3	29.5	0.0	29.6	0.3	29.6	0.0	29.6	0.0	29.5	-0.3	29.5	0.0	29.4	-0.3	29.5	0.3	29.6	0.3	30.1	1.7	30.2	0.3
1954	30.4	0.7	31.0	2.0	31.4	1.3	31.4	0.0	31.4	0.0	31.3	-0.3	31.4	0.3	31.2	-0.6	31.3	0.3	31.4	0.3	31.4	0.0	31.5	0.3
1955	31.5	0.0	31.7	0.6	31.5	-0.6	31.4	-0.3	31.4	0.0	31.4	0.0	31.4	0.0	31.4	0.0	31.4	0.0	31.7	1.0	31.7	0.0	31.7	0.0
1956	31.8	0.3	31.8	0.0	31.7	-0.3	31.8	0.3	31.9	0.3	32.7	2.5	32.7	0.0	32.6	-0.3	32.6	0.0	32.8	0.6	33.0	0.6	33.0	0.0
1957	33.1	0.3	33.3	0.6	33.3	0.0	33.3	0.0	33.3	0.0	33.2	-0.3	33.5	0.9	33.5	0.0	34.1	1.8	34.1	0.0	34.1	0.0	34.2	0.3
1958	34.1	-0.3	34.1	0.0	34.1	0.0	34.4	0.9	34.4	0.0	34.4	0.0	34.4	0.0	34.4	0.0	34.5	0.3	34.4	-0.3	34.4	0.0	34.4	0.0
1959	34.6	0.6	34.5	-0.3	34.5	0.0	34.5	0.0	34.6	0.3	34.6	0.0	34.7	0.3	34.7	0.0	34.7	0.0	34.7	0.0	34.7	0.0	34.8	0.3
1960	34.6	-0.6	34.6	0.0	34.6	0.0	34.6	0.0	34.6	0.0	34.6	0.0	34.6	0.0	34.7	0.3	34.8	0.3	35.1	0.9	35.0	-0.3	35.0	0.0
1961	34.9	-0.3	35.0	0.3	35.0	0.0	35.0	0.0	35.1	0.3	35.1	0.0	35.1	0.0	34.9	-0.6	34.9	0.0	34.9	0.0	34.9	0.0	34.9	0.0
1962	34.9	0.0	34.8	-0.3	34.9	0.3	34.9	0.0	34.8	-0.3	34.9	0.3	34.9	0.0	34.8	-0.3	34.9	0.3	35.0	0.3	35.0	0.0	35.0	0.0
1963	35.1	0.3	35.1	0.0	35.2	0.3	35.3	0.3	35.3	0.0	35.3	0.0	35.3	0.0	35.4	0.3	35.4	0.0	35.5	0.3	35.5	0.0	35.5	0.0
1964	35.5	0.0	35.5	0.0	35.5	0.0	35.6	0.3	35.7	0.3	35.7	0.0	35.7	0.0	35.7	0.0	35.7	0.0	35.7	0.0	35.7	0.0	35.7	0.0
1965	35.8	0.3	35.9	0.3	35.9	0.0	35.9	0.0	35.9	0.0	35.9	0.0	35.9	0.0	36.0	0.3	36.1	0.3	36.2	0.3	36.3	0.3	36.2	-0.3
1966	36.4	0.6	36.4	0.0	36.4	0.0	36.4	0.0	36.4	0.0	36.3	-0.3	36.4	0.3	36.5	0.3	36.5	0.0	36.5	0.0	36.5	0.0	36.6	0.3
1967	36.8	0.5	36.8	0.0	36.8	0.0	37.1	0.8	37.1	0.0	37.1	0.0	37.1	0.0	37.2	0.3	37.1	-0.3	37.2	0.3	37.1	-0.3	37.1	0.0
1968	37.1	0.0	37.2	0.3	37.4	0.5	37.5	0.3	37.6	0.3	37.8	0.5	37.8	0.0	37.8	0.0	37.9	0.3	37.7	-0.5	37.7	0.0	37.7	0.0
1969	37.7	0.0	38.0	0.8	38.1	0.3	38.4	0.8	38.5	0.3	38.6	0.3	38.6	0.0	38.6	0.0	38.9	0.8	39.1	0.5	39.3	0.5	39.4	0.3
1970	39.5	0.3	39.5	0.0	39.8	0.8	39.9	0.3	40.2	0.8	40.3	0.2	40.5	0.5	40.5	0.0	40.5	0.0	40.5	0.0	40.5	0.0	40.4	-0.2
1971	41.1	1.7	41.2	0.2	41.3	0.2	41.3	0.0	41.5	0.5	41.6	0.2	41.6	0.0	41.6	0.0	41.6	0.0	41.6	0.0	41.6	0.0	41.6	0.0
1972	41.6	0.0	41.7	0.2	41.7	0.0	42.0	0.7	42.2	0.5	42.1	-0.2	41.9	-0.5	42.0	0.2	42.1	0.2	42.2	0.2	42.2	0.0	42.2	0.0
1973	42.2	0.0	42.3	0.2	42.6	0.7	43.1	1.2	43.6	1.2	43.7	0.2	43.7	0.0	43.8	0.2	43.8	0.0	44.9	2.5	45.2	0.7	46.1	2.0
1974	47.0	2.0	47.1	0.2	47.5	0.8	48.7	2.5	52.3	7.4	53.6	2.5	55.0	2.6	59.4	8.0	60.2	1.3	61.3	1.8	61.5	0.3	61.6	0.2
1975	62.8	1.9	63.1	0.5	63.1	0.0	62.2	-1.4	62.0	-0.3	62.0	0.0	61.9	-0.2	62.0	0.2	62.1	0.2	62.1	0.0	62.7	1.0	63.0	0.5
1976	63.5	0.8	63.4	-0.2	63.7	0.5	63.7	0.0	63.8	0.2	63.8	0.0	62.5	-2.0	62.6	0.2	62.7	0.2	62.9	0.3	62.9	0.0	62.7	-0.3
1977	63.8	1.8	64.2	0.6	64.6	0.6	64.9	0.5	65.1	0.3	65.2	0.2	65.1	-0.2	65.3	0.3	65.4	0.2	65.4	0.0	65.7	0.5	65.9	0.3
1978	66.1	0.3	66.8	1.1	67.1	0.4	67.2	0.1	67.3	0.1	67.5	0.3	67.6	0.1	67.1	-0.7	67.1	0.0	68.1	1.5	68.2	0.1	67.5	-1.0
1979	68.2	1.0	68.4	0.3	69.0	0.9	69.2	0.3	69.9	1.0	70.5	0.9	71.0	0.7	72.0	1.4	72.5	0.7	72.9	0.6	73.6	1.0	74.6	1.4
1980	77.5	3.9	78.2	0.9	79.6	1.8	82.6	3.8	83.2	0.7	84.0	1.0	84.6	0.7	84.8	0.2	84.8	0.0	85.5	0.8	86.0	0.6	86.7	0.8
1981	90.5	4.4	90.7	0.2	91.9	1.3	94.5	2.8	94.3	-0.2	94.9	0.6	94.3	-0.6	95.3	1.1	95.3	0.0	95.1	-0.2	96.2	1.2	96.2	0.0
1982	97.7	1.6	98.1	0.4	99.4	1.3	100.0	0.6	101.0	1.0	101.4	0.4	100.4	-1.0	100.8	0.4	100.4	-0.4	99.5	-0.9	100.8	1.3	100.7	-0.1
1983	101.0	0.3	101.6	0.6	100.7	-0.9	101.7	1.0	100.7	-1.0	100.9	0.2	101.5	0.6	101.5	0.0	101.6	0.1	101.6	0.0	101.4	-0.2	101.3	-0.1
1984	101.8	0.5	101.2	-0.6	101.9	0.7	102.6	0.7	102.6	0.0	102.1	-0.5	102.7	0.6	103.0	0.3	103.5	0.5	103.5	0.0	104.1	0.6	103.7	-0.4
1985	104.4	0.7	104.7	0.3	104.8	0.1	105.4	0.6	104.9	-0.5	105.4	0.5	105.5	0.1	105.1	-0.4	106.0	0.9	105.6	-0.4	105.5	-0.1	105.4	-0.1
1986	106.7	1.2	106.4	-0.3	105.5	-0.8	105.9	0.4	105.6	-0.3	106.0	0.4	105.8	-0.2	105.0	-0.8	105.5	0.5	105.8	0.3	105.8	0.0	105.3	-0.5
1987	105.9	0.6	106.0	0.1	106.2	0.2	106.1	-0.1	106.7	0.6	106.8	0.1	106.7	-0.1	107.4	0.7	107.7	0.3	107.9	0.2	108.2	0.3	108.1	-0.1
1988	108.6	0.5	109.3	0.6	109.4	0.1	110.1	0.6	110.6	0.5	111.0	0.4	112.5	1.4	113.4	0.8	114.2	0.7	114.1	-0.1	114.8	0.6	115.1	0.3
1989	115.7	0.5	116.1	0.3	116.8	0.6	117.1	0.3	117.3	0.2	117.6	0.3	117.7	0.1	118.0	0.3	118.0	0.0	118.1	0.1	117.6	-0.4	117.3	-0.3
1990	118.0	0.6	118.1	0.1	118.3	0.2	118.0	-0.3	118.1	0.1	118.1	0.0	118.5	0.3	118.8	0.3	119.6	0.7	119.7	0.1	120.4	0.6	120.6	0.2
1991	121.7	0.9	121.9	0.2	121.3	-0.5	121.4	0.1	121.1	-0.2	121.0	-0.1	120.9	-0.1	121.2	0.2	122.0	0.7	121.8	-0.2	122.1	0.2	122.1	0.0

[Continued]

Chemicals and Allied Products n.e.c.
Producer Price Index
Base 1982 = 100
[Continued]

For 1947-1993. Columns headed % show percentile change in the index from the previous period for which an index is available.

Year	Jan Index	%	Feb Index	%	Mar Index	%	Apr Index	%	May Index	%	Jun Index	%	Jul Index	%	Aug Index	%	Sep Index	%	Oct Index	%	Nov Index	%	Dec Index	%
1992	122.3	0.2	122.4	0.1	122.3	-0.1	122.7	0.3	123.0	0.2	123.1	0.1	123.3	0.2	123.4	0.1	123.8	0.3	124.0	0.2	124.4	0.3	124.3	-0.1
1993	124.9	0.5	125.3	0.3	125.1	-0.2	125.5	0.3	125.6	0.1	125.7	0.1	125.6	-0.1	125.6	0.0	125.6	0.0	125.5	-0.1	125.6	0.1	125.7	0.1

Source: U.S. Department of Labor, Bureau of Labor Statistics, Division of Industry Prices and Price Indexes. n.e.c. stands for not elsewhere classified. - indicates no data collected for period or unavailable.

RUBBER AND PLASTIC PRODUCTS
Producer Price Index
Base 1982 = 100

For 1926-1993. Columns headed % show percentile change in the index from the previous period for which an index is available.

Year	Jan Index	%	Feb Index	%	Mar Index	%	Apr Index	%	May Index	%	Jun Index	%	Jul Index	%	Aug Index	%	Sep Index	%	Oct Index	%	Nov Index	%	Dec Index	%
1926	59.1	-	53.7	-9.1	52.8	-1.7	51.0	-3.4	50.5	-1.0	49.4	-2.2	44.0	-10.9	42.7	-3.0	42.6	-0.2	43.0	0.9	39.1	-9.1	37.0	-5.4
1927	36.6	-1.1	36.3	-0.8	36.9	1.7	36.8	-0.3	36.9	0.3	36.0	-2.4	35.6	-1.1	35.5	-0.3	35.2	-0.8	34.3	-2.6	33.8	-1.5	34.5	2.1
1928	34.3	-0.6	32.5	-5.2	31.5	-3.1	30.1	-4.4	29.7	-1.3	27.2	-8.4	26.3	-3.3	26.3	0.0	26.1	-0.8	25.6	-1.9	25.0	-2.3	24.9	-0.4
1929	25.2	1.2	25.6	1.6	25.7	0.4	25.1	-2.3	24.9	-0.8	24.7	-0.8	24.8	0.4	24.6	-0.8	24.5	-0.4	24.2	-1.2	23.2	-4.1	23.1	-0.4
1930	22.9	-0.9	23.0	0.4	22.9	-0.4	22.8	-0.4	22.7	-0.4	21.3	-6.2	21.0	-1.4	20.6	-1.9	20.2	-1.9	20.2	0.0	20.5	1.5	20.4	-0.5
1931	19.2	-5.9	19.0	-1.0	19.0	0.0	18.7	-1.6	18.7	0.0	18.4	-1.6	18.4	0.0	18.1	-1.6	18.1	0.0	18.1	0.0	17.9	-1.1	16.1	-10.1
1932	15.7	-2.5	15.5	-1.3	15.2	-1.9	15.1	-0.7	15.1	0.0	15.2	0.7	15.4	1.3	15.6	1.3	16.5	5.8	17.1	3.6	17.1	0.0	17.1	0.0
1933	17.0	-0.6	16.2	-4.7	15.8	-2.5	14.5	-8.2	14.9	2.8	16.1	8.1	17.1	6.2	17.5	2.3	17.5	0.0	17.6	0.6	17.9	1.7	17.9	0.0
1934	18.0	0.6	18.4	2.2	18.9	2.7	19.1	1.1	19.5	2.1	19.5	0.0	19.7	1.0	20.0	1.5	19.9	-0.5	19.6	-1.5	20.3	3.6	20.3	0.0
1935	20.3	0.0	20.3	0.0	19.7	-3.0	19.6	-0.5	19.3	-1.5	19.4	0.5	19.3	-0.5	19.3	0.0	19.2	-0.5	19.5	1.6	19.6	0.5	19.6	0.0
1936	19.9	1.5	20.1	1.0	20.2	0.5	20.3	0.5	21.1	3.9	21.2	0.5	21.3	0.5	21.3	0.0	21.3	0.0	21.3	0.0	22.5	5.6	23.0	2.2
1937	23.9	3.9	24.4	2.1	25.8	5.7	26.1	1.2	25.6	-1.9	25.2	-1.6	25.0	-0.8	24.9	-0.4	24.9	0.0	24.3	-2.4	24.0	-1.2	24.0	0.0
1938	24.3	1.3	24.3	0.0	24.1	-0.8	23.7	-1.7	23.6	-0.4	23.9	1.3	24.4	2.1	24.6	0.8	24.6	0.0	24.9	1.2	25.2	1.2	25.2	0.0
1939	25.1	-0.4	25.3	0.8	25.5	0.8	25.4	-0.4	25.5	0.4	25.5	0.0	25.5	0.0	25.5	0.0	27.0	5.9	26.4	-2.2	23.5	-11.0	24.4	3.8
1940	24.2	-0.8	24.0	-0.8	24.0	0.0	23.0	-4.2	23.5	2.2	23.8	1.3	23.7	-0.4	23.3	-1.7	23.1	-0.9	23.4	1.3	23.6	0.9	24.3	3.0
1941	24.2	-0.4	24.3	0.4	24.6	1.2	24.7	0.4	24.7	0.0	24.2	-2.0	24.5	1.2	25.8	5.3	25.7	-0.4	27.3	6.2	27.9	2.2	27.9	0.0
1942	27.8	-0.4	27.8	0.0	27.8	0.0	28.4	2.2	30.5	7.4	30.5	0.0	30.5	0.0	30.5	0.0	30.5	0.0	30.5	0.0	30.5	0.0	30.5	0.0
1943	30.5	0.0	30.5	0.0	30.5	0.0	30.5	0.0	30.5	0.0	30.5	0.0	30.5	0.0	30.5	0.0	30.5	0.0	30.5	0.0	30.5	0.0	30.5	0.0
1944	30.5	0.0	30.6	0.3	30.6	0.0	30.6	0.0	29.8	-2.6	29.8	0.0	29.8	0.0	29.8	0.0	29.8	0.0	29.8	0.0	29.8	0.0	29.8	0.0
1945	29.9	0.3	29.9	0.0	29.9	0.0	29.4	-1.7	28.9	-1.7	28.9	0.0	28.9	0.0	28.9	0.0	28.9	0.0	28.9	0.0	28.9	0.0	28.9	0.0
1946	28.9	0.0	28.9	0.0	28.9	0.0	28.9	0.0	28.9	0.0	29.2	1.0	29.5	1.0	29.6	0.3	29.7	0.3	29.7	0.0	29.7	0.0	29.9	0.7
1947	30.4	1.7	30.5	0.3	30.5	0.0	30.4	-0.3	29.9	-1.6	28.4	-5.0	27.8	-2.1	27.8	0.0	28.0	0.7	28.5	1.8	29.0	1.8	29.4	1.4
1948	29.6	0.7	29.5	-0.3	29.5	0.0	29.7	0.7	29.8	0.3	29.8	0.0	30.7	3.0	30.7	0.0	30.7	0.0	30.7	0.0	30.5	-0.7	30.3	-0.7
1949	30.2	-0.3	30.0	-0.7	30.0	0.0	29.7	-1.0	29.6	-0.3	28.8	-2.7	28.4	-1.4	28.3	-0.4	28.4	0.4	28.3	-0.4	28.8	1.8	29.5	2.4
1950	29.7	0.7	29.9	0.7	29.9	0.0	30.6	2.3	31.5	2.9	32.3	2.5	34.1	5.6	38.2	12.0	39.9	4.5	41.5	4.0	44.0	6.0	44.9	2.0
1951	45.2	0.7	45.0	-0.4	45.0	0.0	44.7	-0.7	44.6	-0.2	43.8	-1.8	42.6	-2.7	42.6	0.0	42.7	0.2	42.7	0.0	42.7	0.0	42.6	-0.2
1952	42.5	-0.2	42.3	-0.5	41.9	-0.9	41.5	-1.0	41.4	-0.2	39.4	-4.8	38.4	-2.5	37.7	-1.8	37.3	-1.1	37.2	-0.3	37.3	0.3	37.7	1.1
1953	37.6	-0.3	37.2	-1.1	37.1	-0.3	36.8	-0.8	37.0	0.5	36.9	-0.3	36.8	-0.3	36.4	-1.1	36.6	0.5	36.6	0.0	36.7	0.3	36.8	0.3
1954	36.8	0.0	36.8	0.0	36.9	0.3	36.9	0.0	36.9	0.0	37.2	0.8	37.4	0.5	37.3	-0.3	37.5	0.5	37.9	1.1	38.8	2.4	38.9	0.3
1955	40.4	3.9	41.5	2.7	40.7	-1.9	40.8	0.2	40.7	-0.2	41.4	1.7	42.3	2.2	43.9	3.8	44.7	1.8	43.6	-2.5	44.4	1.8	44.5	0.2
1956	43.8	-1.6	43.4	-0.9	43.1	-0.7	42.8	-0.7	42.3	-1.2	42.2	-0.2	42.3	0.2	43.3	2.4	43.0	-0.7	43.0	0.0	43.3	0.7	43.7	0.9
1957	42.8	-2.1	42.5	-0.7	42.6	0.2	42.6	0.0	42.7	0.2	42.8	0.2	42.8	0.0	43.3	1.2	43.2	-0.2	43.1	-0.2	42.7	-0.9	43.0	0.7
1958	42.8	-0.5	42.7	-0.2	42.7	0.0	42.6	-0.2	42.4	-0.5	42.6	0.5	42.7	0.2	42.7	0.0	42.9	0.5	43.2	0.7	43.3	0.2	43.0	-0.7
1959	42.8	-0.5	42.9	0.2	43.1	0.5	43.3	0.5	43.7	0.9	43.1	-1.4	43.1	0.0	41.5	-3.7	41.8	0.7	41.8	0.0	42.6	1.9	41.9	-1.6
1960	42.3	1.0	42.7	0.9	42.7	0.0	42.7	0.0	43.2	1.2	43.3	0.2	43.3	0.0	42.9	-0.9	42.8	-0.2	42.7	-0.2	42.4	-0.7	41.6	-1.9
1961	41.2	-1.0	41.2	0.0	41.3	0.2	41.3	0.0	41.4	0.2	41.2	-0.5	41.0	-0.5	41.1	0.2	41.2	0.2	41.1	-0.2	40.9	-0.5	40.4	-1.2
1962	40.2	-0.5	40.0	-0.5	40.0	0.0	39.7	-0.7	39.9	0.5	39.8	-0.3	39.7	-0.3	39.7	0.0	39.7	0.0	39.8	0.3	40.1	0.8	40.4	0.7
1963	40.3	-0.2	40.3	0.0	40.2	-0.2	40.2	0.0	39.9	-0.7	39.8	-0.3	39.8	0.0	40.1	0.8	39.9	-0.5	40.3	1.0	40.3	0.0	40.1	-0.5
1964	40.1	0.0	40.0	-0.2	40.1	0.3	39.8	-0.7	39.6	-0.5	39.2	-1.0	39.2	0.0	39.2	0.0	39.9	0.3	39.9	0.0	40.0	0.3	39.4	0.0
1965	39.5	0.3	39.4	-0.3	39.4	0.0	39.5	0.3	39.7	0.5	39.8	0.3	39.8	0.0	39.9	0.3	39.9	0.0	40.5	-0.2	40.6	0.3	40.6	0.0
1966	40.1	0.3	40.2	0.2	40.3	0.2	40.8	1.2	40.8	0.0	40.8	0.0	40.6	-0.5	40.6	0.0	40.5	-0.2	40.4	-0.2	40.6	0.5	40.6	0.0
1967	40.9	0.7	41.0	0.2	41.0	0.0	41.0	0.0	40.9	-0.2	40.9	0.0	40.9	0.0	41.8	2.2	42.0	0.5	42.2	0.5	42.4	0.5	42.4	0.0
1968	42.4	0.0	42.5	0.2	42.5	0.0	42.5	0.0	42.6	0.2	42.7	0.2	42.9	0.5	43.1	0.5	43.1	0.0	43.2	0.2	43.2	0.0	43.3	0.2
1969	42.8	-1.2	43.0	0.5	43.1	0.2	43.3	0.5	43.2	-0.2	43.2	0.0	43.8	1.4	44.0	0.5	43.8	-0.5	44.2	0.9	44.5	0.7	44.5	0.0
1970	44.7	0.4	44.6	-0.2	44.6	0.0	44.5	-0.2	44.4	-0.2	44.4	0.0	45.0	1.4	45.2	0.4	45.2	0.0	45.2	0.0	45.2	0.0	45.2	0.0

[Continued]

RUBBER AND PLASTIC PRODUCTS
Producer Price Index
Base 1982 = 100
[Continued]

For 1926-1993. Columns headed % show percentile change in the index from the previous period for which an index is available.

Year	Jan Index	%	Feb Index	%	Mar Index	%	Apr Index	%	May Index	%	Jun Index	%	Jul Index	%	Aug Index	%	Sep Index	%	Oct Index	%	Nov Index	%	Dec Index	%
1971	44.9	-0.7	45.1	0.4	45.1	0.0	45.1	0.0	45.0	-0.2	45.0	0.0	45.3	0.7	45.5	0.4	45.4	-0.2	45.3	-0.2	45.3	0.0	45.3	0.0
1972	45.4	0.2	45.3	-0.2	45.1	-0.4	45.1	0.0	45.1	0.0	45.1	0.0	45.3	0.4	45.4	0.2	45.4	0.0	45.4	0.0	45.5	0.2	45.5	0.0
1973	45.6	0.2	45.6	0.0	45.7	0.2	45.8	0.2	46.2	0.9	46.6	0.9	46.8	0.4	46.9	0.2	46.7	-0.4	47.2	1.1	47.6	0.8	48.3	1.5
1974	48.8	1.0	49.6	1.6	51.3	3.4	53.6	4.5	55.4	3.4	56.2	1.4	57.8	2.8	59.4	2.8	60.3	1.5	61.1	1.3	61.5	0.7	61.9	0.7
1975	62.0	0.2	62.2	0.3	62.0	-0.3	61.9	-0.2	61.7	-0.3	61.6	-0.2	62.2	1.0	62.2	0.0	62.5	0.5	62.8	0.5	62.9	0.2	62.9	0.0
1976	63.1	0.3	63.9	1.3	64.4	0.8	64.9	0.8	65.1	0.3	65.1	0.0	65.6	0.8	66.7	1.7	67.9	1.8	68.2	0.4	68.3	0.1	68.2	-0.1
1977	68.2	0.0	68.0	-0.3	68.2	0.3	68.7	0.7	68.9	0.3	69.4	0.7	70.0	0.9	70.1	0.1	70.2	0.1	70.5	0.4	70.5	0.0	70.5	0.0
1978	70.5	0.0	70.5	0.0	71.0	0.7	71.6	0.8	72.0	0.6	72.3	0.4	72.5	0.3	72.8	0.4	73.2	0.5	73.8	0.8	74.3	0.7	74.4	0.1
1979	74.9	0.7	75.9	1.3	77.0	1.4	78.2	1.6	79.0	1.0	80.0	1.3	81.0	1.3	82.4	1.7	83.1	0.8	84.1	1.2	84.9	1.0	85.3	0.5
1980	86.1	0.9	87.3	1.4	88.1	0.9	88.7	0.7	89.1	0.5	90.0	1.0	90.7	0.8	91.3	0.7	92.0	0.8	92.3	0.3	92.6	0.3	92.5	-0.1
1981	93.2	0.8	93.8	0.6	94.6	0.9	95.6	1.1	96.1	0.5	96.7	0.6	96.2	-0.5	97.0	0.8	97.7	0.7	98.3	0.6	98.6	0.3	98.7	0.1
1982	98.3	-0.4	99.2	0.9	99.8	0.6	99.9	0.1	100.3	0.4	100.5	0.2	100.3	-0.2	100.5	0.2	100.5	0.0	100.4	-0.1	100.1	-0.3	100.3	0.2
1983	100.6	0.3	100.4	-0.2	100.2	-0.2	100.7	0.5	100.8	0.1	100.7	-0.1	100.8	0.1	101.0	0.2	100.8	-0.2	101.2	0.4	100.9	-0.3	101.0	0.1
1984	101.4	0.4	102.0	0.6	102.1	0.1	102.4	0.3	102.5	0.1	102.6	0.1	102.6	0.0	102.6	0.0	102.9	0.3	102.2	-0.7	102.0	-0.2	101.9	-0.1
1985	102.2	0.3	102.1	-0.1	102.1	0.0	102.2	0.1	102.1	-0.1	102.0	-0.1	101.9	-0.1	101.4	-0.5	101.5	0.1	101.6	0.1	101.7	0.1	101.9	0.2
1986	102.3	0.4	102.5	0.2	102.2	-0.3	102.2	0.0	102.0	-0.2	102.0	0.0	101.7	-0.3	102.0	0.3	101.8	-0.2	101.5	-0.3	101.3	-0.2	101.2	-0.1
1987	101.5	0.3	101.6	0.1	101.4	-0.2	101.8	0.4	102.0	0.2	102.3	0.3	102.9	0.6	103.2	0.3	103.7	0.5	104.4	0.7	105.1	0.7	105.5	0.4
1988	106.2	0.7	106.9	0.7	107.7	0.7	108.2	0.5	108.8	0.6	109.1	0.3	109.8	0.6	110.6	0.7	111.0	0.4	111.1	0.1	111.2	0.1	111.3	0.1
1989	111.9	0.5	112.2	0.3	112.7	0.4	113.0	0.3	113.0	0.0	112.8	-0.2	112.8	0.0	112.6	-0.2	112.7	0.1	112.5	-0.2	112.5	0.0	112.9	0.4
1990	113.2	0.3	112.9	-0.3	113.3	0.4	113.3	0.0	113.5	0.2	113.2	-0.3	113.1	-0.1	113.2	0.1	113.4	0.2	114.2	0.7	115.0	0.7	115.4	0.3
1991	116.0	0.5	116.0	0.0	115.8	-0.2	115.5	-0.3	115.2	-0.3	115.0	-0.2	114.8	-0.2	114.7	-0.1	114.6	-0.1	114.7	0.1	114.6	-0.1	114.7	0.1
1992	114.7	0.0	114.3	-0.3	114.3	0.0	114.6	0.3	114.9	0.3	115.0	0.1	115.2	0.2	115.3	0.1	115.5	0.2	115.7	0.2	115.8	0.1	115.7	-0.1
1993	115.7	0.0	115.7	0.0	115.6	-0.1	116.0	0.3	115.8	-0.2	115.9	0.1	115.9	0.0	116.0	0.1	116.5	0.4	116.5	0.0	116.4	-0.1	116.5	0.1

Source: U.S. Department of Labor, Bureau of Labor Statistics, Division of Industry Prices and Price Indexes. n.e.c. stands for not elsewhere classified. - indicates no data collected for period or unavailable.

Rubber and Rubber Products
Producer Price Index
Base 1982 = 100

For 1967-1993. Columns headed % show percentile change in the index from the previous period for which an index is available.

Year	Jan Index	%	Feb Index	%	Mar Index	%	Apr Index	%	May Index	%	Jun Index	%	Jul Index	%	Aug Index	%	Sep Index	%	Oct Index	%	Nov Index	%	Dec Index	%
1967	36.9	-	36.9	0.0	37.0	0.3	37.0	0.0	36.9	-0.3	36.9	0.0	36.9	0.0	37.6	1.9	37.8	0.5	38.1	0.8	38.2	0.3	38.2	0.0
1968	38.2	0.0	38.3	0.3	38.3	0.0	38.3	0.0	38.4	0.3	38.5	0.3	38.7	0.5	38.8	0.3	38.8	0.0	38.9	0.3	38.9	0.0	39.0	0.3
1969	38.5	-1.3	38.8	0.8	38.9	0.3	39.0	0.3	38.9	-0.3	38.9	0.0	39.5	1.5	39.6	0.3	39.5	-0.3	39.8	0.8	40.1	0.8	40.1	0.0
1970	40.3	0.5	40.4	0.2	40.3	-0.2	40.4	0.2	40.4	0.0	40.4	0.0	41.3	2.2	41.7	1.0	41.9	0.5	42.0	0.2	42.0	0.0	42.0	0.0
1971	41.5	-1.2	41.5	0.0	41.5	0.0	41.4	-0.2	41.4	0.0	41.5	0.2	42.3	1.9	42.5	0.5	42.4	-0.2	42.3	-0.2	42.3	0.0	42.3	0.0
1972	42.4	0.2	42.2	-0.5	42.2	0.0	42.2	0.0	42.2	0.0	42.3	0.2	42.5	0.5	42.7	0.5	42.7	0.0	42.7	0.0	42.8	0.2	42.8	0.0
1973	42.9	0.2	43.0	0.2	43.1	0.2	43.2	0.2	43.7	1.2	44.1	0.9	44.3	0.5	44.4	0.2	44.2	-0.5	44.9	1.6	45.3	0.9	46.1	1.8
1974	46.6	1.1	47.4	1.7	49.1	3.6	49.7	1.2	50.7	2.0	51.1	0.8	52.4	2.5	53.5	2.1	53.8	0.6	54.4	1.1	54.6	0.4	55.2	1.1
1975	55.5	0.5	55.9	0.7	56.0	0.2	56.1	0.2	56.1	0.0	56.1	0.0	57.2	2.0	57.2	0.0	57.3	0.2	57.5	0.3	57.7	0.3	57.8	0.2
1976	58.0	0.3	58.4	0.7	59.2	1.4	59.3	0.2	59.4	0.2	59.5	0.2	59.9	0.7	62.1	3.7	63.4	2.1	64.0	0.9	64.0	0.0	64.0	0.0
1977	63.9	-0.2	63.0	-1.4	63.2	0.3	64.2	1.6	64.2	0.0	64.6	0.6	65.3	1.1	65.5	0.3	65.8	0.5	66.2	0.6	66.2	0.0	66.3	0.2
1978	66.5	0.3	66.5	0.0	66.9	0.6	68.0	1.6	68.9	1.3	69.3	0.6	69.5	0.3	69.8	0.4	70.2	0.6	71.1	1.3	71.9	1.1	72.0	0.1
1979	72.7	1.0	73.8	1.5	74.5	0.9	75.1	0.8	75.7	0.8	76.5	1.1	78.3	2.4	80.1	2.3	81.1	1.2	82.3	1.5	83.5	1.5	83.8	0.4
1980	84.5	0.8	86.4	2.2	86.5	0.1	87.1	0.7	87.6	0.6	88.4	0.9	89.3	1.0	89.7	0.4	90.6	1.0	91.3	0.8	91.5	0.2	91.5	0.0
1981	91.9	0.4	92.8	1.0	94.1	1.4	94.5	0.4	95.0	0.5	95.9	0.9	95.1	-0.8	95.9	0.8	97.2	1.4	98.2	1.0	98.7	0.5	98.8	0.1
1982	98.0	-0.8	99.3	1.3	99.6	0.3	99.6	0.0	100.5	0.9	100.6	0.1	100.4	-0.2	100.9	0.5	100.6	-0.3	100.4	-0.2	100.0	-0.4	100.2	0.2
1983	100.7	0.5	100.2	-0.5	99.8	-0.4	99.7	-0.1	99.7	0.0	99.2	-0.5	99.0	-0.2	99.0	0.0	98.5	-0.5	98.9	0.4	98.7	-0.2	98.8	0.1
1984	99.5	0.7	99.6	0.1	99.1	-0.5	99.8	0.7	99.4	-0.4	99.5	0.1	99.5	0.0	99.9	0.4	100.1	0.2	98.9	-1.2	98.5	-0.4	98.5	0.0
1985	98.7	0.2	99.1	0.4	99.0	-0.1	98.9	-0.1	99.0	0.1	98.7	-0.3	98.9	0.2	98.5	-0.4	98.6	0.1	98.5	-0.1	98.7	0.2	98.4	-0.3
1986	98.7	0.3	99.0	0.3	98.9	-0.1	98.8	-0.1	98.6	-0.2	98.5	-0.1	97.9	-0.6	97.8	-0.1	97.6	-0.2	97.6	0.0	97.0	-0.6	97.0	0.0
1987	97.5	0.5	97.5	0.0	97.4	-0.1	98.1	0.7	98.5	0.4	99.0	0.5	100.1	1.1	100.2	0.1	100.4	0.2	100.9	0.5	101.1	0.2	101.8	0.7
1988	102.3	0.5	102.5	0.2	102.6	0.1	102.9	0.3	102.6	-0.3	103.1	0.5	103.7	0.6	104.4	0.7	104.6	0.2	104.5	-0.1	104.5	0.0	104.9	0.4
1989	105.8	0.9	106.4	0.6	106.8	0.4	107.1	0.3	107.4	0.3	107.4	0.0	107.3	-0.1	107.1	-0.2	106.9	-0.2	107.2	0.3	107.4	0.2	107.7	0.3
1990	107.9	0.2	107.6	-0.3	108.5	0.8	108.1	-0.4	108.2	0.1	108.1	-0.1	108.1	0.0	108.5	0.4	108.6	0.1	109.2	0.6	110.1	0.8	110.4	0.3
1991	110.6	0.2	110.6	0.0	110.4	-0.2	109.9	-0.5	109.8	-0.1	109.7	-0.1	109.1	-0.5	108.8	-0.3	108.6	-0.2	109.1	0.5	109.1	0.0	109.0	-0.1
1992	109.2	0.2	109.1	-0.1	109.0	-0.1	108.9	-0.1	109.0	0.1	109.8	0.7	109.8	0.0	110.0	0.2	110.3	0.3	110.3	0.0	111.0	0.6	111.0	0.0
1993	110.4	-0.5	110.3	-0.1	110.4	0.1	110.9	0.5	110.9	0.0	111.0	0.1	111.0	0.0	110.9	-0.1	111.2	0.3	111.1	-0.1	110.9	-0.2	111.0	0.1

Source: U.S. Department of Labor, Bureau of Labor Statistics, Division of Industry Prices and Price Indexes. n.e.c. stands for not elsewhere classified. - indicates no data collected for period or unavailable.

Plastic Products

Producer Price Index
Base 1982 = 100

For 1978-1993. Columns headed % show percentile change in the index from the previous period for which an index is available.

Year	Jan Index	%	Feb Index	%	Mar Index	%	Apr Index	%	May Index	%	Jun Index	%	Jul Index	%	Aug Index	%	Sep Index	%	Oct Index	%	Nov Index	%	Dec Index	%
1978	-	-	-	-	-	-	-	-	-	-	75.6	-	75.7	0.1	76.1	0.5	76.6	0.7	76.7	0.1	77.0	0.4	77.1	0.1
1979	77.3	0.3	78.2	1.2	79.9	2.2	81.6	2.1	82.7	1.3	83.9	1.5	84.0	0.1	84.8	1.0	85.4	0.7	86.1	0.8	86.4	0.3	87.0	0.7
1980	87.9	1.0	88.2	0.3	89.9	1.9	90.4	0.6	90.7	0.3	91.8	1.2	92.2	0.4	93.1	1.0	93.5	0.4	93.4	-0.1	93.7	0.3	93.6	-0.1
1981	94.5	1.0	94.9	0.4	95.2	0.3	96.9	1.8	97.2	0.3	97.6	0.4	97.3	-0.3	98.1	0.8	98.2	0.1	98.5	0.3	98.5	0.0	98.7	0.2
1982	98.6	-0.1	99.0	0.4	100.0	1.0	100.3	0.3	100.1	-0.2	100.4	0.3	100.1	-0.3	100.2	0.1	100.3	0.1	100.3	0.0	100.3	0.0	100.5	0.2
1983	100.6	0.1	100.6	0.0	100.7	0.1	101.7	1.0	101.9	0.2	102.4	0.5	102.8	0.4	103.1	0.3	103.2	0.1	103.8	0.6	103.3	-0.5	103.4	0.1
1984	103.5	0.1	104.6	1.1	105.4	0.8	105.4	0.0	106.0	0.6	105.9	-0.1	106.0	0.1	105.6	-0.4	105.9	0.3	105.9	0.0	105.8	-0.1	105.7	-0.1
1985	106.1	0.4	105.4	-0.7	105.6	0.2	105.9	0.3	105.6	-0.3	105.7	0.1	105.2	-0.5	104.7	-0.5	104.8	0.1	105.0	0.2	105.1	0.1	105.8	0.7
1986	106.3	0.5	106.5	0.2	106.0	-0.5	106.0	0.0	105.9	-0.1	105.9	0.0	105.9	0.0	106.7	0.8	106.5	-0.2	105.9	-0.6	106.0	0.1	105.8	-0.2
1987	106.1	0.3	106.1	0.0	106.0	-0.1	106.1	0.1	106.2	0.1	106.4	0.2	106.7	0.3	107.3	0.6	107.9	0.6	108.7	0.7	109.6	0.8	109.9	0.3
1988	110.8	0.8	111.7	0.8	112.9	1.1	113.5	0.5	114.6	1.0	114.9	0.3	115.6	0.6	116.5	0.8	117.0	0.4	117.3	0.3	117.4	0.1	117.4	0.0
1989	117.8	0.3	118.0	0.2	118.5	0.4	118.8	0.3	118.7	-0.1	118.4	-0.3	118.4	0.0	118.2	-0.2	118.5	0.3	117.9	-0.5	117.9	0.0	118.3	0.3
1990	118.7	0.3	118.4	-0.3	118.5	0.1	118.7	0.2	119.0	0.3	118.6	-0.3	118.4	-0.2	118.4	0.0	118.7	0.3	119.5	0.7	120.3	0.7	120.8	0.4
1991	121.6	0.7	121.6	0.0	121.5	-0.1	121.2	-0.2	120.8	-0.3	120.6	-0.2	120.6	0.0	120.6	0.0	120.6	0.0	120.3	-0.2	120.3	0.0	120.5	0.2
1992	120.4	-0.1	119.8	-0.5	119.9	0.1	120.4	0.4	120.7	0.2	120.5	-0.2	120.8	0.2	120.9	0.1	121.1	0.2	121.3	0.2	121.3	0.0	121.0	-0.2
1993	121.3	0.2	121.3	0.0	121.2	-0.1	121.5	0.2	121.3	-0.2	121.3	0.0	121.3	0.0	121.5	0.2	122.1	0.5	122.2	0.1	122.2	0.0	122.3	0.1

Source: U.S. Department of Labor, Bureau of Labor Statistics, Division of Industry Prices and Price Indexes. n.e.c. stands for not elsewhere classified. - indicates no data collected for period or unavailable.

LUMBER AND WOOD PRODUCTS
Producer Price Index
Base 1982 = 100

For 1926-1993. Columns headed % show percentile change in the index from the previous period for which an index is available.

Year	Jan Index	%	Feb Index	%	Mar Index	%	Apr Index	%	May Index	%	Jun Index	%	Jul Index	%	Aug Index	%	Sep Index	%	Oct Index	%	Nov Index	%	Dec Index	%
1926	9.6	-	9.5	-1.0	9.5	0.0	9.4	-1.1	9.3	-1.1	9.2	-1.1	9.2	0.0	9.2	0.0	9.2	0.0	9.1	-1.1	9.3	2.2	9.2	-1.1
1927	9.0	-2.2	9.0	0.0	8.9	-1.1	8.9	0.0	8.9	0.0	8.9	0.0	8.8	-1.1	8.7	-1.1	8.6	-1.1	8.6	0.0	8.5	-1.2	8.4	-1.2
1928	8.4	0.0	8.4	0.0	8.4	0.0	8.3	-1.2	8.3	0.0	8.3	0.0	8.4	1.2	8.5	1.2	8.6	1.2	8.6	0.0	8.7	1.2	8.8	1.1
1929	8.7	-1.1	8.9	2.3	9.0	1.1	8.9	-1.1	8.8	-1.1	8.8	0.0	8.7	-1.1	8.8	1.1	8.9	1.1	8.9	0.0	8.6	-3.4	8.6	0.0
1930	8.6	0.0	8.6	0.0	8.6	0.0	8.6	0.0	8.4	-2.3	8.1	-3.6	7.8	-3.7	7.7	-1.3	7.7	0.0	7.5	-2.6	7.5	0.0	7.3	-2.7
1931	7.2	-1.4	6.9	-4.2	7.0	1.4	6.8	-2.9	6.6	-2.9	6.5	-1.5	6.4	-1.5	6.3	-1.6	6.3	0.0	6.1	-3.2	6.2	1.6	6.2	0.0
1932	6.2	0.0	6.0	-3.2	5.9	-1.7	5.8	-1.7	5.7	-1.7	5.5	-3.5	5.5	0.0	5.3	-3.6	5.4	1.9	5.4	0.0	5.4	0.0	5.4	0.0
1933	5.3	-1.9	5.4	1.9	5.5	1.9	5.5	0.0	5.7	3.6	6.4	12.3	7.1	10.9	7.4	4.2	7.7	4.1	7.9	2.6	8.1	2.5	8.1	0.0
1934	8.1	0.0	8.1	0.0	8.0	-1.2	8.1	1.3	8.0	-1.2	8.0	0.0	7.8	-2.5	7.6	-2.6	7.6	0.0	7.6	0.0	7.5	-1.3	7.5	0.0
1935	7.4	-1.3	7.5	1.4	7.4	-1.3	7.4	0.0	7.4	0.0	7.5	1.4	7.6	1.3	7.7	1.3	7.7	0.0	7.7	0.0	7.7	0.0	7.6	-1.3
1936	7.7	1.3	7.7	0.0	7.7	0.0	7.8	1.3	7.8	0.0	7.7	-1.3	7.8	1.3	7.8	0.0	8.0	2.6	8.0	0.0	8.1	1.3	8.4	3.7
1937	8.7	3.6	9.2	5.7	9.5	3.3	9.6	1.1	9.7	1.0	9.7	0.0	9.5	-2.1	9.4	-1.1	9.3	-1.1	9.2	-1.1	8.9	-3.3	8.9	0.0
1938	8.7	-2.2	8.6	-1.1	8.6	0.0	8.6	0.0	8.3	-3.5	8.3	0.0	8.3	0.0	8.4	1.2	8.5	1.2	8.4	-1.2	8.4	0.0	8.5	1.2
1939	8.6	1.2	8.6	0.0	8.6	0.0	8.5	-1.2	8.5	0.0	8.5	0.0	8.6	1.2	8.6	0.0	8.7	1.2	9.1	4.6	9.2	1.1	9.1	-1.1
1940	9.1	0.0	9.1	0.0	9.1	0.0	9.0	-1.1	9.0	0.0	9.0	0.0	9.0	0.0	9.3	3.3	10.1	8.6	10.7	5.9	11.0	2.8	11.1	0.9
1941	11.1	0.0	11.0	-0.9	11.0	0.0	11.0	0.0	11.0	0.0	11.0	0.0	11.4	3.6	11.9	4.4	12.0	0.8	12.2	1.7	12.1	-0.8	12.2	0.8
1942	12.4	1.6	12.5	0.8	12.5	0.0	12.4	-0.8	12.4	0.0	12.4	0.0	12.5	0.8	12.5	0.0	12.5	0.0	12.5	0.0	12.6	0.8	12.7	0.8
1943	12.7	0.0	12.8	0.8	12.8	0.0	12.8	0.0	12.9	0.8	13.0	0.8	13.1	0.8	13.5	3.1	13.7	1.5	13.7	0.0	13.8	0.7	13.8	0.0
1944	13.8	0.0	13.9	0.7	14.1	1.4	14.3	1.4	14.4	0.7	14.4	0.0	14.4	0.0	14.4	0.0	14.4	0.0	14.4	0.0	14.4	0.0	14.4	0.0
1945	14.4	0.0	14.4	0.0	14.4	0.0	14.4	0.0	14.4	0.0	14.4	0.0	14.5	0.7	14.5	0.0	14.5	0.0	14.5	0.0	14.5	0.0	14.6	0.7
1946	14.7	0.7	14.9	1.4	15.5	4.0	15.9	2.6	16.1	1.3	16.4	1.9	16.5	0.6	16.5	0.0	16.6	0.6	16.8	1.2	17.9	6.5	20.9	16.8
1947	23.4	12.0	23.9	2.1	24.7	3.3	25.4	2.8	25.5	0.4	25.4	-0.4	25.5	0.4	26.0	2.0	26.6	2.3	27.0	1.5	27.7	2.6	28.2	1.8
1948	28.7	1.8	28.9	0.7	29.2	1.0	29.3	0.3	29.6	1.0	29.8	0.7	30.0	0.7	30.2	0.7	30.1	-0.3	29.7	-1.3	29.5	-0.7	29.0	-1.7
1949	28.7	-1.0	28.3	-1.4	28.1	-0.7	27.8	-1.1	27.4	-1.4	27.0	-1.5	26.6	-1.5	26.3	-1.1	26.4	0.4	26.7	1.1	27.0	1.1	27.3	1.1
1950	27.7	1.5	28.3	2.2	28.9	2.1	29.3	1.4	30.3	3.4	30.9	2.0	31.7	2.6	33.1	4.4	34.3	3.6	34.0	-0.9	33.8	-0.6	33.9	0.3
1951	34.6	2.1	34.8	0.6	34.9	0.3	34.9	0.0	34.8	-0.3	34.3	-1.4	34.1	-0.6	33.7	-1.2	33.5	-0.6	33.5	0.0	33.4	-0.3	33.2	-0.6
1952	33.1	-0.3	33.2	0.3	33.2	0.0	33.3	0.3	33.3	0.0	33.1	-0.6	33.2	0.3	33.2	0.0	33.2	0.0	33.1	-0.3	33.0	-0.3	33.0	0.0
1953	33.2	0.6	33.4	0.6	33.5	0.3	33.7	0.6	33.6	-0.3	33.5	-0.3	33.4	-0.3	33.2	-0.6	32.8	-1.2	32.6	-0.6	32.3	-0.9	32.3	0.0
1954	32.2	-0.3	32.2	0.0	32.2	0.0	32.0	-0.6	32.0	0.0	32.1	0.3	32.8	2.2	32.8	0.0	32.9	0.3	33.0	0.3	33.0	0.0	33.1	0.3
1955	33.2	0.3	33.4	0.6	33.5	0.3	33.8	0.9	34.1	0.9	34.1	0.0	34.2	0.3	34.5	0.9	34.7	0.6	34.6	-0.3	34.5	-0.3	34.5	0.0
1956	34.8	0.9	34.9	0.3	35.3	1.1	35.4	0.3	35.3	-0.3	35.1	-0.6	34.9	-0.6	34.5	-1.1	34.1	-1.2	33.6	-1.5	33.5	-0.3	33.4	-0.3
1957	33.5	0.3	33.3	-0.6	33.1	-0.6	33.2	0.3	33.0	-0.6	33.0	0.0	32.9	-0.3	32.7	-0.6	32.5	-0.6	32.3	-0.6	32.2	-0.3	32.1	-0.3
1958	32.1	0.0	31.9	-0.6	31.8	-0.3	31.9	0.3	32.0	0.3	32.1	0.3	32.2	0.3	32.7	1.6	33.2	1.5	33.3	0.3	33.1	-0.6	33.0	-0.3
1959	33.2	0.6	33.8	1.8	34.2	1.2	34.8	1.8	35.3	1.4	35.5	0.6	35.4	-0.3	35.4	0.0	35.1	-0.8	34.8	-0.9	34.3	-1.4	34.4	0.3
1960	34.5	0.3	34.4	-0.3	34.3	-0.3	34.2	-0.3	34.1	-0.3	33.8	-0.9	33.5	-0.9	32.9	-1.8	32.8	-0.3	32.5	-0.9	32.2	-0.9	32.2	0.0
1961	31.9	-0.9	31.6	-0.9	31.8	0.6	32.5	2.2	32.4	-0.3	32.5	0.3	32.3	-0.6	32.0	-0.9	31.9	-0.3	31.6	-0.9	31.6	0.0	31.5	-0.3
1962	31.5	0.0	31.7	0.6	32.1	1.3	32.2	0.3	32.3	0.3	32.4	0.3	32.5	0.3	32.5	0.0	32.3	-0.6	32.2	-0.3	32.1	-0.3	31.9	-0.6
1963	32.0	0.3	32.0	0.0	32.2	0.6	32.3	0.3	32.5	0.6	32.8	0.9	33.9	3.4	34.2	0.9	33.3	-2.6	33.0	-0.9	33.0	0.0	33.0	0.0
1964	33.0	0.0	33.3	0.9	33.6	0.9	33.9	0.9	33.9	0.0	33.8	-0.3	33.7	-0.3	33.6	-0.3	33.5	-0.3	33.4	-0.3	33.2	-0.6	33.1	-0.3
1965	33.6	1.5	33.6	0.0	33.5	-0.3	33.5	0.0	33.5	0.0	33.4	-0.3	33.5	0.3	33.9	1.2	34.0	0.3	33.9	-0.3	33.9	0.0	34.0	0.3
1966	34.2	0.6	34.6	1.2	35.2	1.7	36.1	2.6	36.5	1.1	35.9	-1.6	35.5	-1.1	35.4	-0.3	35.3	-0.3	34.9	-1.1	34.3	-1.7	34.1	-0.6
1967	34.2	0.3	34.6	1.2	34.5	-0.3	34.7	0.6	34.7	0.0	34.9	0.6	35.1	0.6	35.4	0.9	36.2	2.3	35.7	-1.4	35.5	-0.6	35.9	1.1
1968	36.2	0.8	37.2	2.8	38.0	2.2	38.6	1.6	39.0	1.0	39.1	0.3	39.7	1.5	40.1	1.0	40.9	2.0	41.7	2.0	42.3	1.4	44.5	5.2
1969	45.9	3.1	48.2	5.0	49.8	3.3	47.8	-4.0	45.9	-4.0	43.3	-5.7	41.8	-3.5	41.3	-1.2	41.1	-0.5	40.9	-0.5	41.3	1.0	40.8	-1.2
1970	40.5	-0.7	40.0	-1.2	39.7	-0.7	40.0	0.8	40.3	0.7	40.0	-0.7	39.9	-0.2	40.1	0.5	40.1	0.0	39.7	-1.0	39.3	-1.0	39.0	-0.8

[Continued]

LUMBER AND WOOD PRODUCTS

Producer Price Index
Base 1982 = 100
[Continued]

For 1926-1993. Columns headed % show percentile change in the index from the previous period for which an index is available.

Year	Jan Index	%	Feb Index	%	Mar Index	%	Apr Index	%	May Index	%	Jun Index	%	Jul Index	%	Aug Index	%	Sep Index	%	Oct Index	%	Nov Index	%	Dec Index	%
1971	39.4	1.0	41.2	4.6	43.4	5.3	43.9	1.2	44.0	0.2	44.4	0.9	46.0	3.6	47.5	3.3	47.3	-0.4	46.4	-1.9	46.2	-0.4	46.7	1.1
1972	47.4	1.5	48.4	2.1	49.0	1.2	49.6	1.2	50.1	1.0	50.6	1.0	51.3	1.4	52.0	1.4	52.1	0.2	52.4	0.6	52.5	0.2	52.6	0.2
1973	53.0	0.8	56.5	6.6	60.8	7.6	63.9	5.1	65.6	2.7	64.3	-2.0	62.4	-3.0	62.8	0.6	63.9	1.8	63.3	-0.9	64.9	2.5	65.4	0.8
1974	64.5	-1.4	64.6	0.2	67.2	4.0	70.3	4.6	69.5	-1.1	67.5	-2.9	66.2	-1.9	64.5	-2.6	63.4	-1.7	59.5	-6.2	58.2	-2.2	58.1	-0.2
1975	57.9	-0.3	59.5	2.8	59.6	0.2	61.4	3.0	64.3	4.7	63.6	-1.1	63.1	-0.8	63.1	0.0	63.2	0.2	62.9	-0.5	62.6	-0.5	64.3	2.7
1976	67.0	4.2	68.9	2.8	71.1	3.2	71.4	0.4	71.1	-0.4	70.2	-1.3	71.5	1.9	72.9	2.0	74.7	2.5	75.0	0.4	75.3	0.4	77.3	2.7
1977	78.2	1.2	78.8	0.8	80.4	2.0	80.7	0.4	80.6	-0.1	80.3	-0.4	82.7	3.0	85.3	3.1	88.8	4.1	87.0	-2.0	85.5	-1.7	87.5	2.3
1978	90.0	2.9	92.6	2.9	93.5	1.0	94.7	1.3	96.0	1.4	97.8	1.9	97.4	-0.4	98.9	1.5	99.3	0.4	99.8	0.5	101.9	2.1	101.4	-0.5
1979	101.9	0.5	103.2	1.3	105.5	2.2	107.1	1.5	106.4	-0.7	105.3	-1.0	105.4	0.1	107.0	1.5	108.8	1.7	108.5	-0.3	105.0	-3.2	101.9	-3.0
1980	101.9	0.0	103.5	1.6	103.6	0.1	96.8	-6.6	95.5	-1.3	98.3	2.9	101.6	3.4	104.0	2.4	102.6	-1.3	101.5	-1.1	103.0	1.5	105.2	2.1
1981	104.1	-1.0	103.5	-0.6	103.4	-0.1	105.1	1.6	104.8	-0.3	104.7	-0.1	104.1	-0.6	103.4	-0.7	101.6	-1.7	99.8	-1.8	99.1	-0.7	100.2	1.1
1982	100.3	0.1	100.2	-0.1	100.2	0.0	100.6	0.4	99.9	-0.7	101.5	1.6	101.4	-0.1	99.8	-1.6	99.4	-0.4	98.1	-1.3	98.3	0.2	100.3	2.0
1983	103.0	2.7	106.4	3.3	107.4	0.9	107.9	0.5	108.2	0.3	110.6	2.2	110.5	-0.1	110.3	-0.2	107.3	-2.7	107.3	0.0	107.1	-0.2	108.4	1.2
1984	108.6	0.2	110.9	2.1	111.3	0.4	110.7	-0.5	108.3	-2.2	107.9	-0.4	106.9	-0.9	107.0	0.1	106.5	-0.5	105.5	-0.9	105.7	0.2	106.4	0.7
1985	106.9	0.5	106.5	-0.4	106.4	-0.1	105.9	-0.5	107.7	1.7	110.0	2.1	108.9	-1.0	107.3	-1.5	105.5	-1.7	105.2	-0.3	104.3	-0.9	104.7	0.4
1986	105.0	0.3	104.3	-0.7	105.8	1.4	108.4	2.5	108.2	-0.2	107.5	-0.6	107.8	0.3	107.9	0.1	108.4	0.5	107.9	-0.5	108.0	0.1	107.8	-0.2
1987	108.1	0.3	109.4	1.2	110.6	1.1	110.7	0.1	110.7	0.0	111.4	0.6	112.4	0.9	113.7	1.2	116.2	2.2	116.1	-0.1	116.9	0.7	117.1	0.2
1988	117.8	0.6	118.4	0.5	118.9	0.4	119.2	0.3	119.1	-0.1	119.3	0.2	120.0	0.6	118.8	-1.0	118.9	0.1	118.7	-0.2	118.8	0.1	119.0	0.2
1989	120.1	0.9	122.0	1.6	123.2	1.0	125.2	1.6	126.5	1.0	127.4	0.7	128.9	1.2	129.0	0.1	129.0	0.0	130.9	1.5	130.0	-0.7	128.5	-1.2
1990	129.0	0.4	129.7	0.5	130.5	0.6	132.4	1.5	132.0	-0.3	130.7	-1.0	131.3	0.5	130.2	-0.8	129.3	-0.7	127.5	-1.4	126.9	-0.5	126.8	-0.1
1991	127.6	0.6	127.2	-0.3	127.8	0.5	129.2	1.1	132.3	2.4	136.2	2.9	136.9	0.5	133.3	-2.6	133.4	0.1	133.2	-0.1	133.4	0.2	134.6	0.9
1992	137.6	2.2	142.9	3.9	145.7	2.0	147.5	1.2	147.6	0.1	146.3	-0.9	145.3	-0.7	145.4	0.1	148.7	2.3	148.7	0.0	149.5	0.5	154.4	3.3
1993	160.2	3.8	169.3	5.7	176.9	4.5	181.2	2.4	179.8	-0.8	174.1	-3.2	171.7	-1.4	171.1	-0.3	173.0	1.1	173.1	0.1	177.0	2.3	180.9	2.2

Source: U.S. Department of Labor, Bureau of Labor Statistics, Division of Industry Prices and Price Indexes. n.e.c. stands for not elsewhere classified. - indicates no data collected for period or unavailable.

Lumber
Producer Price Index
Base 1982 = 100

For 1926-1993. Columns headed % show percentile change in the index from the previous period for which an index is available.

Year	Jan Index	%	Feb Index	%	Mar Index	%	Apr Index	%	May Index	%	Jun Index	%	Jul Index	%	Aug Index	%	Sep Index	%	Oct Index	%	Nov Index	%	Dec Index	%
1926	8.3	-	8.3	0.0	8.3	0.0	8.2	-1.2	8.1	-1.2	8.0	-1.2	8.0	0.0	7.9	-1.2	7.9	0.0	7.9	0.0	8.1	2.5	8.0	-1.2
1927	7.9	-1.2	7.8	-1.3	7.7	-1.3	7.7	0.0	7.7	0.0	7.7	0.0	7.6	-1.3	7.5	-1.3	7.4	-1.3	7.4	0.0	7.3	-1.4	7.2	-1.4
1928	7.2	0.0	7.2	0.0	7.2	0.0	7.1	-1.4	7.1	0.0	7.2	1.4	7.2	0.0	7.3	1.4	7.4	1.4	7.5	1.4	7.5	0.0	7.6	1.3
1929	7.5	-1.3	7.7	2.7	7.8	1.3	7.7	-1.3	7.6	-1.3	7.6	0.0	7.5	-1.3	7.5	0.0	7.7	2.7	7.8	1.3	7.4	-5.1	7.4	0.0
1930	7.5	1.4	7.4	-1.3	7.4	0.0	7.4	0.0	7.2	-2.7	6.9	-4.2	6.8	-1.4	6.6	-2.9	6.6	0.0	6.4	-3.0	6.5	1.6	6.3	-3.1
1931	6.2	-1.6	6.0	-3.2	6.0	0.0	6.0	0.0	5.6	-6.7	5.6	0.0	5.4	-3.6	5.4	0.0	5.4	0.0	5.3	-1.9	5.3	0.0	5.3	0.0
1932	5.3	0.0	5.1	-3.8	5.0	-2.0	4.8	-4.0	4.8	0.0	4.7	-2.1	4.6	-2.1	4.5	-2.2	4.5	0.0	4.6	2.2	4.6	0.0	4.6	0.0
1933	4.5	-2.2	4.5	0.0	4.7	4.4	4.7	0.0	4.8	2.1	5.5	14.6	6.1	10.9	6.4	4.9	6.6	3.1	6.8	3.0	7.0	2.9	7.1	1.4
1934	7.1	0.0	7.1	0.0	7.0	-1.4	7.1	1.4	7.0	-1.4	7.0	0.0	6.9	-1.4	6.6	-4.3	6.7	1.5	6.6	-1.5	6.6	0.0	6.6	0.0
1935	6.4	-3.0	6.4	0.0	6.3	-1.6	6.3	0.0	6.5	3.2	6.7	3.1	6.9	3.0	6.9	0.0	6.8	-1.4	6.7	-1.5	6.6	-1.5	6.7	1.5
1936	6.8	1.5	6.8	0.0	7.0	2.9	7.1	1.4	7.1	0.0	7.1	0.0	7.0	-1.4	7.0	0.0	7.0	0.0	7.1	1.4	7.1	0.0	7.4	4.2
1937	7.8	5.4	8.3	6.4	8.6	3.6	8.6	0.0	8.5	-1.2	8.3	-2.4	8.1	-2.4	8.0	-1.2	8.0	0.0	7.8	-2.5	7.5	-3.8	7.2	-4.0
1938	7.1	-1.4	7.1	0.0	7.1	0.0	7.0	-1.4	7.0	0.0	6.8	-2.9	6.8	0.0	7.0	2.9	7.1	1.4	7.1	0.0	7.2	1.4	7.4	2.8
1939	7.4	0.0	7.4	0.0	7.4	0.0	7.4	0.0	7.3	-1.4	7.2	-1.4	7.2	0.0	7.3	1.4	7.6	4.1	8.0	5.3	8.1	1.3	8.0	-1.2
1940	8.0	0.0	7.9	-1.2	7.9	0.0	7.8	-1.3	7.8	0.0	7.7	-1.3	7.7	0.0	7.9	2.6	8.7	10.1	9.3	6.9	9.5	2.2	9.6	1.1
1941	9.6	0.0	9.5	-1.0	9.4	-1.1	9.4	0.0	9.4	0.0	9.5	1.1	9.9	4.2	10.3	4.0	10.5	1.9	10.5	0.0	10.4	-1.0	10.5	1.0
1942	10.6	1.0	10.7	0.9	10.7	0.0	10.7	0.0	10.6	-0.9	10.6	0.0	10.7	0.9	10.7	0.0	10.7	0.0	10.5	-1.9	10.9	3.8	10.9	0.0
1943	10.9	0.0	11.0	0.9	11.0	0.0	11.0	0.0	11.2	1.8	11.2	0.0	11.3	0.9	11.7	3.5	11.8	0.9	11.9	0.8	12.0	0.8	12.0	0.0
1944	12.0	0.0	12.1	0.8	12.2	0.8	12.5	2.5	12.5	0.0	12.5	0.0	12.5	0.0	12.5	0.0	12.5	0.0	12.5	0.0	12.5	0.0	12.5	0.0
1945	12.5	0.0	12.5	0.0	12.5	0.0	12.5	0.0	12.5	0.0	12.5	0.0	12.5	0.0	12.5	0.0	12.5	0.0	12.5	0.0	12.5	0.0	12.8	2.4
1946	12.8	0.0	12.9	0.8	13.6	5.4	13.9	2.2	14.0	0.7	14.2	1.4	14.4	1.4	14.4	0.0	14.4	0.0	14.4	0.0	15.5	7.6	18.4	18.7
1947	20.6	12.0	21.1	2.4	22.0	4.3	22.7	3.2	22.7	0.0	22.6	-0.4	22.8	0.9	23.2	1.8	23.9	3.0	24.2	1.3	24.9	2.9	25.4	2.0
1948	25.6	0.8	25.8	0.8	26.0	0.8	26.0	0.0	26.4	1.5	26.4	0.0	26.5	0.4	26.7	0.8	26.5	-0.7	26.2	-1.1	25.8	-1.5	25.5	-1.2
1949	25.2	-1.2	24.9	-1.2	24.7	-0.8	24.4	-1.2	24.0	-1.6	23.6	-1.7	23.3	-1.3	22.9	-1.7	23.0	0.4	23.3	1.3	23.6	1.3	23.9	1.3
1950	24.3	1.7	24.9	2.5	25.5	2.4	25.9	1.6	27.0	4.2	27.6	2.2	28.4	2.9	29.6	4.2	30.7	3.7	30.2	-1.6	30.1	-0.3	30.2	0.3
1951	30.6	1.3	30.8	0.7	30.9	0.3	30.9	0.0	30.8	-0.3	30.3	-1.6	30.0	-1.0	29.7	-1.0	29.5	-0.7	29.5	0.0	29.5	0.0	29.4	-0.3
1952	29.3	-0.3	29.4	0.3	29.4	0.0	29.6	0.7	29.5	-0.3	29.3	-0.7	29.4	0.3	29.3	-0.3	29.1	-0.7	28.9	-0.7	28.6	-1.0	28.4	-0.7
1953	29.3	0.3	29.3	0.0	29.5	0.7	29.7	0.7	29.5	-0.7	29.4	-0.3	29.3	-0.3	29.1	-0.7	28.9	-0.7	28.6	-1.0	28.4	-0.7	28.4	0.0
1954	28.3	-0.4	28.2	-0.4	28.2	0.0	28.1	-0.4	28.1	0.0	28.2	0.4	28.9	2.5	28.9	0.0	29.0	0.3	29.2	0.7	29.2	0.0	29.2	0.0
1955	29.3	0.3	29.6	1.0	29.7	0.3	30.0	1.0	30.3	1.0	30.4	0.3	30.5	0.3	30.9	1.3	31.0	0.3	31.0	0.0	30.9	-0.3	30.8	-0.3
1956	31.2	1.3	31.3	0.3	31.7	1.3	31.9	0.6	31.9	0.0	31.6	-0.9	31.4	-0.6	31.0	-1.3	30.6	-1.3	30.2	-1.3	30.1	-0.3	29.9	-0.7
1957	30.0	0.3	29.8	-0.7	29.6	-0.7	29.6	0.0	29.6	0.0	29.4	-0.7	29.3	-0.3	29.2	-0.3	28.9	-1.0	28.7	-0.7	28.6	-0.3	28.4	-0.7
1958	28.5	0.4	28.3	-0.7	28.3	0.0	28.3	0.0	28.5	0.7	28.5	0.0	28.5	0.0	29.1	2.1	29.5	1.4	29.5	0.0	29.3	-0.7	29.3	0.0
1959	29.5	0.7	30.1	2.0	30.6	1.7	30.9	1.0	31.5	1.9	31.8	1.0	31.7	-0.3	31.8	0.3	31.6	-0.6	31.2	-1.3	30.7	-1.6	30.8	0.3
1960	30.8	0.0	30.8	0.0	30.7	-0.3	30.7	0.0	30.5	-0.7	30.1	-1.3	29.7	-1.3	29.1	-2.0	28.8	-1.0	28.4	-1.4	28.1	-1.1	28.1	0.0
1961	27.9	-0.7	27.7	-0.7	27.9	0.7	28.4	1.8	28.5	0.4	28.5	0.0	28.5	0.0	28.5	0.0	28.2	-1.1	28.1	-0.4	27.9	-0.7	27.8	-0.4
1962	27.9	0.4	28.2	1.1	28.4	0.7	28.7	1.1	28.9	0.7	29.0	0.3	29.1	0.3	29.0	-0.3	28.9	-0.3	28.7	-0.7	28.6	-0.3	28.4	-0.7
1963	28.5	0.4	28.5	0.0	28.7	0.7	29.0	1.0	29.2	0.7	29.4	0.7	30.3	3.1	30.5	0.7	29.9	-2.0	29.5	-1.3	29.5	0.0	29.4	-0.3
1964	29.4	0.0	29.8	1.4	30.1	1.0	30.3	0.7	30.3	0.0	30.2	-0.3	30.1	-0.3	30.0	-0.3	29.9	-0.3	29.8	-0.3	29.4	-1.3	29.4	0.0
1965	29.9	1.7	30.1	0.7	30.1	0.0	30.0	-0.3	30.0	0.0	30.0	0.0	30.1	0.3	30.4	1.0	30.6	0.7	30.6	0.0	30.6	0.0	30.7	0.3
1966	31.0	1.0	31.3	1.0	31.8	1.6	32.9	3.5	33.6	2.1	33.2	-1.2	32.8	-1.2	32.7	-0.3	32.5	-0.6	32.0	-1.5	31.3	-2.2	31.0	-1.0
1967	31.0	0.0	31.3	1.0	31.5	0.6	31.6	0.3	31.8	0.6	32.0	0.6	32.1	0.3	32.6	1.6	33.3	2.1	33.0	-0.9	32.8	-0.6	33.2	1.2
1968	33.9	2.1	34.8	2.7	35.7	2.6	36.7	2.8	37.2	1.4	37.1	-0.3	37.9	2.2	38.5	1.6	39.0	1.3	39.6	1.5	40.4	2.0	42.2	4.5
1969	43.9	4.0	46.3	5.5	48.9	5.6	49.0	0.2	46.3	-5.5	42.3	-8.6	39.6	-6.4	38.9	-1.8	38.5	-1.0	38.0	-1.3	38.4	1.1	38.1	-0.8
1970	37.7	-1.0	36.9	-2.1	36.5	-1.1	36.7	0.5	36.9	0.5	36.5	-1.1	36.2	-0.8	36.5	0.8	36.8	0.8	36.6	-0.5	36.1	-1.4	35.7	-1.1

[Continued]

Lumber
Producer Price Index
Base 1982 = 100
[Continued]

For 1926-1993. Columns headed % show percentile change in the index from the previous period for which an index is available.

Year	Jan Index	%	Feb Index	%	Mar Index	%	Apr Index	%	May Index	%	Jun Index	%	Jul Index	%	Aug Index	%	Sep Index	%	Oct Index	%	Nov Index	%	Dec Index	%
1971	36.4	2.0	38.7	6.3	41.5	7.2	42.5	2.4	42.9	0.9	43.5	1.4	46.1	6.0	47.6	3.3	47.5	-0.2	46.1	-2.9	45.8	-0.7	46.4	1.3
1972	47.3	1.9	48.4	2.3	49.0	1.2	49.9	1.8	50.5	1.2	51.2	1.4	52.0	1.6	52.8	1.5	53.1	0.6	53.5	0.8	53.7	0.4	54.0	0.6
1973	54.4	0.7	58.7	7.9	63.0	7.3	66.7	5.9	69.3	3.9	69.1	-0.3	67.4	-2.5	67.8	0.6	69.8	2.9	69.0	-1.1	67.9	-1.6	69.1	1.8
1974	68.6	-0.7	68.4	-0.3	71.2	4.1	74.3	4.4	73.1	-1.6	70.9	-3.0	68.9	-2.8	66.5	-3.5	64.2	-3.5	59.1	-7.9	57.3	-3.0	57.0	-0.5
1975	56.8	-0.4	58.3	2.6	58.7	0.7	60.9	3.7	64.6	6.1	64.2	-0.6	63.3	-1.4	63.7	0.6	63.3	-0.6	63.1	-0.3	62.1	-1.6	64.4	3.7
1976	67.6	5.0	70.7	4.6	74.1	4.8	74.2	0.1	73.1	-1.5	72.2	-1.2	74.4	3.0	76.0	2.2	78.6	3.4	79.0	0.5	78.6	-0.5	81.1	3.2
1977	83.0	2.3	83.5	0.6	85.7	2.6	86.5	0.9	86.3	-0.2	85.2	-1.3	88.8	4.2	92.1	3.7	97.1	5.4	94.1	-3.1	91.6	-2.7	93.6	2.2
1978	96.7	3.3	99.3	2.7	100.5	1.2	101.9	1.4	101.8	-0.1	103.2	1.4	102.7	-0.5	105.1	2.3	106.9	1.7	107.6	0.7	110.0	2.2	109.1	-0.8
1979	108.3	-0.7	109.4	1.0	112.8	3.1	114.3	1.3	114.2	-0.1	114.2	0.0	114.2	0.0	117.5	2.9	120.3	2.4	119.2	-0.9	114.4	-4.0	109.2	-4.5
1980	108.2	-0.9	109.9	1.6	109.6	-0.3	99.8	-8.9	97.0	-2.8	100.7	3.8	105.3	4.6	107.4	2.0	105.6	-1.7	103.2	-2.3	104.6	1.4	107.1	2.4
1981	106.6	-0.5	105.2	-1.3	104.9	-0.3	107.4	2.4	108.2	0.7	108.0	-0.2	107.0	-0.9	106.2	-0.7	103.0	-3.0	100.3	-2.6	98.7	-1.6	99.7	1.0
1982	99.7	0.0	99.1	-0.6	99.2	0.1	100.5	1.3	99.9	-0.6	101.6	1.7	102.7	1.1	100.3	-2.3	99.8	-0.5	98.3	-1.5	98.2	-0.1	100.6	2.4
1983	105.2	4.6	110.9	5.4	112.4	1.4	114.0	1.4	115.4	1.2	120.0	4.0	120.1	0.1	118.0	-1.7	111.5	-5.5	110.9	-0.5	110.3	-0.5	113.0	2.4
1984	113.5	0.4	117.4	3.4	119.2	1.5	118.9	-0.3	114.4	-3.8	112.8	-1.4	110.2	-2.3	110.1	-0.1	108.8	-1.2	107.6	-1.1	108.3	0.7	109.2	0.8
1985	110.4	1.1	110.4	0.0	110.7	0.3	109.4	-1.2	112.4	2.7	116.8	3.9	114.1	-2.3	110.0	-3.6	107.0	-2.7	105.3	-1.6	103.8	-1.4	104.8	1.0
1986	106.0	1.1	105.7	-0.3	108.3	2.5	113.3	4.6	113.0	-0.3	110.4	-2.3	111.1	0.6	111.3	0.2	112.9	1.4	111.1	-1.6	112.0	0.8	111.3	-0.6
1987	111.9	0.5	114.4	2.2	116.0	1.4	116.8	0.7	116.9	0.1	117.9	0.9	119.7	1.5	120.2	0.4	123.3	2.6	120.5	-2.3	120.4	-0.1	120.3	-0.1
1988	120.8	0.4	121.5	0.6	123.0	1.2	123.9	0.7	123.8	-0.1	124.4	0.5	125.1	0.6	123.2	-1.5	120.9	-1.9	120.0	-0.7	119.9	-0.1	118.8	-0.9
1989	119.8	0.8	122.3	2.1	123.4	0.9	126.5	2.5	128.5	1.6	128.7	0.2	130.0	1.0	128.8	-0.9	127.0	-1.4	127.3	0.2	123.2	-3.2	123.1	-0.1
1990	124.5	1.1	125.8	1.0	127.4	1.3	129.3	1.5	128.0	-1.0	125.9	-1.6	126.5	0.5	124.8	-1.3	123.5	-1.0	120.5	-2.4	119.4	-0.9	119.3	-0.1
1991	120.0	0.6	118.8	-1.0	119.6	0.7	121.6	1.7	125.2	3.0	132.7	6.0	133.2	0.4	125.1	-6.1	125.0	-0.1	124.5	-0.4	125.4	0.7	128.2	2.2
1992	132.3	3.2	140.9	6.5	146.4	3.9	148.6	1.5	148.7	0.1	144.1	-3.1	142.8	-0.9	142.0	-0.6	144.8	2.0	143.8	-0.7	146.9	2.2	155.5	5.9
1993	164.6	5.9	181.1	10.0	196.4	8.4	197.3	0.5	189.0	-4.2	178.7	-5.4	172.9	-3.2	175.9	1.7	180.6	2.7	182.1	0.8	189.5	4.1	197.2	4.1

Source: U.S. Department of Labor, Bureau of Labor Statistics, Division of Industry Prices and Price Indexes. n.e.c. stands for not elsewhere classified. - indicates no data collected for period or unavailable.

Millwork
Producer Price Index
Base 1982 = 100

For 1926-1993. Columns headed % show percentile change in the index from the previous period for which an index is available.

Year	Jan Index	%	Feb Index	%	Mar Index	%	Apr Index	%	May Index	%	Jun Index	%	Jul Index	%	Aug Index	%	Sep Index	%	Oct Index	%	Nov Index	%	Dec Index	%
1926	10.7	-	10.7	0.0	10.7	0.0	10.7	0.0	10.7	0.0	10.7	0.0	10.7	0.0	10.7	0.0	10.7	0.0	10.7	0.0	10.7	0.0	10.7	0.0
1927	10.7	0.0	10.7	0.0	10.7	0.0	10.7	0.0	10.7	0.0	10.7	0.0	10.7	0.0	10.7	0.0	10.7	0.0	10.7	0.0	10.7	0.0	10.7	0.0
1928	10.7	0.0	10.7	0.0	10.7	0.0	10.7	0.0	10.7	0.0	10.7	0.0	10.7	0.0	10.7	0.0	10.7	0.0	10.7	0.0	10.7	0.0	10.7	0.0
1929	10.8	0.9	10.8	0.0	10.8	0.0	10.8	0.0	10.8	0.0	10.8	0.0	10.7	-0.9	10.7	0.0	10.7	0.0	10.7	0.0	10.7	0.0	10.7	0.0
1930	10.7	0.0	10.7	0.0	10.7	0.0	10.7	0.0	10.6	-0.9	10.6	0.0	9.9	-6.6	9.9	0.0	9.9	0.0	9.4	-5.1	9.4	0.0	9.1	-3.2
1931	8.9	-2.2	8.7	-2.2	8.7	0.0	8.7	0.0	8.7	0.0	8.7	0.0	8.7	0.0	8.7	0.0	8.4	-3.4	8.1	-3.6	8.1	0.0	8.1	0.0
1932	8.7	7.4	8.7	0.0	8.7	0.0	8.7	0.0	8.7	0.0	8.7	0.0	8.3	-4.6	8.3	0.0	8.3	0.0	7.8	-6.0	7.8	0.0	7.8	0.0
1933	7.8	0.0	7.8	0.0	8.3	6.4	8.3	0.0	8.3	0.0	8.4	1.2	8.9	6.0	9.7	9.0	9.7	0.0	9.7	0.0	9.7	0.0	9.5	-2.1
1934	9.5	0.0	9.5	0.0	9.5	0.0	9.6	1.1	9.7	1.0	9.7	0.0	9.2	-5.2	8.7	-5.4	8.7	0.0	8.7	0.0	8.7	0.0	8.7	0.0
1935	8.7	0.0	8.7	0.0	8.7	0.0	8.7	0.0	8.7	0.0	8.7	0.0	8.9	2.3	9.6	7.9	9.6	0.0	9.6	0.0	9.6	0.0	9.6	0.0
1936	9.6	0.0	9.6	0.0	9.6	0.0	9.6	0.0	9.6	0.0	9.8	2.1	9.8	0.0	9.8	0.0	9.8	0.0	9.8	0.0	9.8	0.0	10.1	3.1
1937	10.2	1.0	10.7	4.9	10.7	0.0	10.7	0.0	12.7	18.7	12.7	0.0	12.3	-3.1	12.1	-1.6	12.1	0.0	12.1	0.0	12.0	-0.8	11.9	-0.8
1938	11.1	-6.7	11.1	0.0	11.1	0.0	11.1	0.0	10.2	-8.1	10.2	0.0	10.1	-1.0	10.1	0.0	10.1	0.0	10.2	1.0	10.2	0.0	10.2	0.0
1939	10.2	0.0	10.2	0.0	10.2	0.0	10.2	0.0	10.2	0.0	10.2	0.0	10.2	0.0	10.2	0.0	10.2	0.0	10.2	0.0	10.7	4.9	10.7	0.0
1940	10.7	0.0	10.7	0.0	10.7	0.0	10.7	0.0	10.7	0.0	11.3	5.6	11.5	1.8	11.5	0.0	11.5	0.0	11.5	0.0	12.1	5.2	12.1	0.0
1941	12.1	0.0	12.1	0.0	12.2	0.8	12.3	0.8	12.5	1.6	12.5	0.0	12.6	0.8	12.8	1.6	12.8	0.0	13.9	8.6	14.0	0.7	14.0	0.0
1942	14.0	0.0	14.0	0.0	14.0	0.0	14.0	0.0	14.0	0.0	14.0	0.0	14.0	0.0	14.0	0.0	14.0	0.0	14.0	0.0	14.0	0.0	14.0	0.0
1943	14.0	0.0	14.0	0.0	14.0	0.0	14.0	0.0	14.0	0.0	14.0	0.0	14.0	0.0	14.0	0.0	14.0	0.0	14.4	2.9	14.4	0.0	14.4	0.0
1944	14.4	0.0	14.4	0.0	14.4	0.0	14.4	0.0	14.7	2.1	14.7	0.0	14.7	0.0	14.7	0.0	14.7	0.0	14.7	0.0	14.7	0.0	14.7	0.0
1945	14.7	0.0	14.7	0.0	14.7	0.0	14.7	0.0	14.7	0.0	14.7	0.0	14.7	0.0	14.7	0.0	14.7	0.0	14.7	0.0	14.7	0.0	14.7	0.0
1946	14.7	0.0	14.7	0.0	14.7	0.0	14.7	0.0	17.0	15.6	17.0	0.0	17.0	0.0	17.0	0.0	17.5	2.9	18.3	4.6	18.4	0.5	18.4	0.0
1947	19.5	6.0	19.9	2.1	20.1	1.0	20.3	1.0	20.6	1.5	21.0	1.9	21.4	1.9	21.6	0.9	22.2	2.8	22.8	2.7	23.0	0.9	23.0	0.0
1948	23.7	3.0	23.9	0.8	24.7	3.3	24.8	0.4	24.8	0.0	25.5	2.8	26.4	3.5	26.7	1.1	26.8	0.4	26.8	0.0	26.8	0.0	26.8	0.0
1949	26.6	-0.7	26.6	0.0	26.5	-0.4	26.4	-0.4	26.4	0.0	26.3	-0.4	26.2	-0.4	26.1	-0.4	26.0	-0.4	26.0	0.0	26.0	0.0	26.1	0.4
1950	26.4	1.1	26.6	0.8	26.6	0.0	26.8	0.8	26.9	0.4	27.1	0.7	27.6	1.8	28.4	2.9	29.5	3.9	29.8	1.0	29.9	0.3	29.9	0.0
1951	31.5	5.4	32.0	1.6	31.9	-0.3	32.0	0.3	32.0	0.0	31.9	-0.3	31.8	-0.3	31.6	-0.6	31.6	0.0	31.6	0.0	31.5	-0.3	31.4	-0.3
1952	31.0	-1.3	30.8	-0.6	30.9	0.3	30.8	-0.3	30.8	0.0	30.8	0.0	30.9	0.3	31.0	0.3	31.0	0.0	31.1	0.3	31.1	0.0	31.3	0.6
1953	31.5	0.6	32.1	1.9	32.1	0.0	32.2	0.3	32.2	0.0	32.2	0.0	32.1	-0.3	32.1	0.0	32.1	0.0	32.0	-0.3	32.0	0.0	32.0	0.0
1954	32.0	0.0	32.0	0.0	32.0	0.0	31.9	-0.3	31.9	0.0	31.9	0.0	31.9	0.0	31.6	-0.9	31.7	0.3	31.7	0.0	31.7	0.0	31.8	0.3
1955	31.8	0.0	31.5	-0.9	31.4	-0.3	31.5	0.3	31.5	0.0	31.3	-0.6	31.3	0.0	31.3	0.0	31.2	-0.3	31.2	0.0	31.2	0.0	31.4	0.6
1956	31.5	0.3	31.5	0.0	31.5	0.0	31.5	0.0	31.5	0.0	31.6	0.3	31.6	0.0	31.6	0.0	31.5	-0.3	31.4	-0.3	31.3	-0.3	31.3	0.0
1957	31.4	0.3	31.4	0.0	31.4	0.0	31.3	-0.3	31.3	0.0	31.3	0.0	31.3	0.0	31.3	0.0	31.3	0.0	31.3	0.0	31.2	-0.3	31.1	-0.3
1958	31.1	0.0	31.1	0.0	31.1	0.0	31.1	0.0	31.0	-0.3	31.0	0.0	31.0	0.0	30.9	-0.3	31.1	0.6	31.8	2.3	31.8	0.0	31.8	0.0
1959	31.7	-0.3	31.7	0.0	31.7	0.0	33.0	4.1	33.5	1.5	33.5	0.0	33.6	0.3	33.8	0.6	33.8	0.0	33.8	0.0	33.7	-0.3	33.6	-0.3
1960	33.6	0.0	33.6	0.0	33.6	0.0	33.4	-0.6	33.4	0.0	33.4	0.0	33.5	0.3	33.3	-0.6	33.0	-0.9	33.0	0.0	33.1	0.3	33.0	-0.3
1961	33.1	0.3	32.9	-0.6	32.9	0.0	32.9	0.0	32.5	-1.2	32.7	0.6	32.2	-1.5	31.9	-0.9	32.3	1.3	32.3	0.0	32.2	-0.3	32.2	0.0
1962	32.2	0.0	32.1	-0.3	32.2	0.3	32.3	0.3	32.5	0.6	32.5	0.0	32.6	0.3	32.7	0.3	32.6	-0.3	32.6	0.0	32.6	0.0	32.6	0.0
1963	32.6	0.0	32.6	0.0	32.7	0.3	32.7	0.0	32.7	0.0	32.9	0.6	33.2	0.9	33.5	0.9	33.7	0.6	33.9	0.6	33.9	0.0	33.9	0.0
1964	34.0	0.3	34.1	0.3	34.2	0.3	34.7	1.5	34.8	0.3	34.8	0.0	34.8	0.0	34.8	0.0	34.8	0.0	34.8	0.0	34.8	0.0	34.8	0.0
1965	34.4	-1.1	34.3	-0.3	34.3	0.0	34.3	0.0	34.4	0.3	34.4	0.0	34.4	0.0	34.4	0.0	34.4	0.0	34.4	0.0	34.4	0.0	34.4	0.0
1966	34.4	0.0	34.6	0.6	34.9	0.9	35.0	0.3	35.2	0.6	35.3	0.3	35.3	0.0	35.4	0.3	35.4	0.0	35.4	0.0	35.2	-0.6	35.2	0.0
1967	35.2	0.0	35.5	0.9	35.5	0.0	35.6	0.3	35.6	0.0	35.6	0.0	35.8	0.6	35.9	0.3	36.1	0.6	36.2	0.3	36.2	0.0	36.3	0.3
1968	36.4	0.3	36.6	0.5	36.9	0.8	37.2	0.8	37.6	1.1	37.8	0.5	37.8	0.0	38.0	0.5	38.5	1.3	38.8	0.8	39.2	1.0	39.5	0.8
1969	39.9	1.0	40.5	1.5	41.1	1.5	42.2	2.7	42.6	0.9	43.4	1.9	43.3	-0.2	43.1	-0.5	42.9	-0.5	42.7	-0.5	42.5	-0.5	42.0	-1.2
1970	41.9	-0.2	41.7	-0.5	41.7	0.0	41.7	0.0	41.8	0.2	41.8	0.0	41.8	0.0	41.8	0.0	41.4	-1.0	40.9	-1.2	40.9	0.0	40.8	-0.2

[Continued]

Millwork
Producer Price Index
Base 1982 = 100
[Continued]

For 1926-1993. Columns headed % show percentile change in the index from the previous period for which an index is available.

Year	Jan Index	%	Feb Index	%	Mar Index	%	Apr Index	%	May Index	%	Jun Index	%	Jul Index	%	Aug Index	%	Sep Index	%	Oct Index	%	Nov Index	%	Dec Index	%
1971	40.9	0.2	41.3	1.0	41.6	0.7	42.5	2.2	43.1	1.4	43.7	1.4	44.0	0.7	44.4	0.9	44.3	-0.2	44.3	0.0	44.3	0.0	44.5	0.5
1972	44.7	0.4	44.9	0.4	45.0	0.2	45.3	0.7	45.7	0.9	46.0	0.7	46.4	0.9	46.5	0.2	46.6	0.2	46.8	0.4	46.8	0.0	46.8	0.0
1973	47.0	0.4	47.7	1.5	48.3	1.3	50.5	4.6	52.4	3.8	52.9	1.0	53.1	0.4	53.1	0.0	53.3	0.4	53.5	0.4	53.5	0.0	53.8	0.6
1974	54.2	0.7	54.3	0.2	54.9	1.1	56.1	2.2	57.5	2.5	58.4	1.6	57.9	-0.9	57.7	-0.3	57.5	-0.3	56.2	-2.3	55.0	-2.1	54.9	-0.2
1975	55.1	0.4	55.5	0.7	55.5	0.0	56.0	0.9	57.4	2.5	57.9	0.9	58.3	0.7	58.4	0.2	58.5	0.2	58.7	0.3	58.7	0.0	59.0	0.5
1976	59.8	1.4	60.5	1.2	61.7	2.0	62.7	1.6	63.6	1.4	63.7	0.2	63.5	-0.3	63.8	0.5	64.5	1.1	65.0	0.8	65.5	0.8	65.5	0.0
1977	65.7	0.3	66.6	1.4	67.4	1.2	68.2	1.2	68.5	0.4	68.9	0.6	68.8	-0.1	69.7	1.3	70.8	1.6	71.8	1.4	72.5	1.0	73.1	0.8
1978	74.9	2.5	78.5	4.8	80.8	2.9	83.7	3.6	86.1	2.9	87.7	1.9	88.3	0.7	86.5	-2.0	86.0	-0.6	85.8	-0.2	86.4	0.7	86.5	0.1
1979	87.5	1.2	90.0	2.9	92.3	2.6	95.2	3.1	93.6	-1.7	92.7	-1.0	90.4	-2.5	89.3	-1.2	89.8	0.6	91.5	1.9	90.3	-1.3	89.6	-0.8
1980	90.9	1.5	92.3	1.5	93.8	1.6	92.2	-1.7	90.1	-2.3	90.5	0.4	91.6	1.2	93.2	1.7	94.6	1.5	94.7	0.1	96.6	2.0	97.8	1.2
1981	97.9	0.1	98.0	0.1	98.7	0.7	99.0	0.3	98.4	-0.6	97.4	-1.0	97.9	0.5	97.5	-0.4	97.1	-0.4	97.1	0.0	97.3	0.2	97.9	0.6
1982	99.2	1.3	99.7	0.5	98.9	-0.8	99.0	0.1	98.9	-0.1	100.4	1.5	101.0	0.6	100.3	-0.7	100.0	-0.3	99.7	-0.3	100.3	0.6	102.5	2.2
1983	105.1	2.5	107.5	2.3	108.8	1.2	108.4	-0.4	107.0	-1.3	105.5	-1.4	106.0	0.5	109.7	3.5	109.5	-0.2	110.0	0.5	110.2	0.2	110.4	0.2
1984	110.4	0.0	110.5	0.1	110.9	0.4	109.9	-0.9	108.9	-0.9	109.2	0.3	109.8	0.5	109.9	0.1	110.0	0.1	109.9	-0.1	110.8	0.8	111.5	0.6
1985	111.9	0.4	111.5	-0.4	111.0	-0.4	110.8	-0.2	111.1	0.3	111.6	0.5	112.2	0.5	112.3	0.1	112.3	0.0	112.0	-0.3	111.9	-0.1	111.8	-0.1
1986	111.6	-0.2	111.7	0.1	112.1	0.4	112.8	0.6	113.3	0.4	114.4	1.0	114.8	0.3	115.1	0.3	115.1	0.0	114.5	-0.5	114.2	-0.3	114.2	0.0
1987	114.7	0.4	115.0	0.3	116.1	1.0	116.9	0.7	117.4	0.4	118.1	0.6	118.5	0.3	118.8	0.3	118.9	0.1	119.3	0.3	119.4	0.1	119.5	0.1
1988	119.7	0.2	120.3	0.5	120.8	0.4	121.2	0.3	121.6	0.3	121.9	0.2	122.4	0.4	122.5	0.1	122.7	0.2	123.3	0.5	122.9	-0.3	123.0	0.1
1989	123.5	0.4	125.1	1.3	126.3	1.0	127.4	0.9	128.0	0.5	128.3	0.2	127.9	-0.3	128.0	0.1	127.9	-0.1	128.2	0.2	128.3	0.1	128.7	0.3
1990	128.9	0.2	129.5	0.5	130.0	0.4	130.6	0.5	130.9	0.2	130.4	-0.4	130.5	0.1	130.5	0.0	130.6	0.1	130.5	-0.1	130.8	0.2	131.0	0.2
1991	131.5	0.4	131.6	0.1	131.9	0.2	133.6	1.3	134.3	0.5	135.8	1.1	136.9	0.8	137.6	0.5	137.6	0.0	138.0	0.3	138.1	0.1	139.3	0.9
1992	140.3	0.7	142.2	1.4	142.9	0.5	144.0	0.8	144.0	0.0	144.0	0.0	143.3	-0.5	142.3	-0.7	143.3	0.7	143.6	0.2	143.7	0.1	145.7	1.4
1993	148.0	1.6	151.8	2.6	155.9	2.7	158.8	1.9	158.2	-0.4	156.6	-1.0	155.7	-0.6	156.1	0.3	158.5	1.5	159.2	0.4	159.3	0.1	160.2	0.6

Source: U.S. Department of Labor, Bureau of Labor Statistics, Division of Industry Prices and Price Indexes. n.e.c. stands for not elsewhere classified. - indicates no data collected for period or unavailable.

Plywood
Producer Price Index
Base 1982 = 100

For 1947-1993. Columns headed % show percentile change in the index from the previous period for which an index is available.

Year	Jan Index	%	Feb Index	%	Mar Index	%	Apr Index	%	May Index	%	Jun Index	%	Jul Index	%	Aug Index	%	Sep Index	%	Oct Index	%	Nov Index	%	Dec Index	%
1947	47.9	-	48.2	0.6	48.2	0.0	48.6	0.8	48.7	0.2	48.7	0.0	45.7	-6.2	45.7	0.0	45.7	0.0	45.7	0.0	45.8	0.2	46.9	2.4
1948	51.8	10.4	51.8	0.0	52.1	0.6	52.2	0.2	53.0	1.5	53.9	1.7	54.6	1.3	54.8	0.4	54.8	0.0	54.8	0.0	54.8	0.0	54.3	-0.9
1949	49.6	-8.7	49.0	-1.2	49.0	0.0	48.7	-0.6	47.0	-3.5	45.1	-4.0	44.5	-1.3	45.2	1.6	45.0	-0.4	45.5	1.1	46.1	1.3	47.0	2.0
1950	48.3	2.8	49.2	1.9	49.5	0.6	49.5	0.0	49.6	0.2	50.0	0.8	51.1	2.2	54.3	6.3	56.0	3.1	56.7	1.3	56.7	0.0	57.4	1.2
1951	57.7	0.5	57.9	0.3	57.9	0.0	57.9	0.0	57.9	0.0	57.9	0.0	57.5	-0.7	57.5	0.0	56.5	-1.7	56.2	-0.5	53.8	-4.3	50.5	-6.1
1952	51.2	1.4	51.5	0.6	51.9	0.8	51.9	0.0	51.9	0.0	52.0	0.2	52.0	0.0	52.1	0.2	52.1	0.0	52.2	0.2	50.3	-3.6	50.3	0.0
1953	53.4	6.2	54.5	2.1	55.1	1.1	55.1	0.0	55.3	0.4	55.3	0.0	55.4	0.2	55.3	-0.2	52.5	-5.1	51.5	-1.9	50.7	-1.6	51.1	0.8
1954	50.9	-0.4	51.6	1.4	50.6	-1.9	49.5	-2.2	49.8	0.6	49.0	-1.6	50.7	3.5	51.8	2.2	50.7	-2.1	51.3	1.2	51.3	0.0	51.3	0.0
1955	51.5	0.4	51.5	0.0	51.5	0.0	51.5	0.0	51.9	0.8	51.9	0.0	52.0	0.2	52.0	0.0	52.2	0.4	52.2	0.0	52.1	-0.2	52.0	-0.2
1956	52.8	1.5	52.8	0.0	52.8	0.0	52.6	-0.4	50.5	-4.0	49.6	-1.8	50.8	2.4	48.8	-3.9	48.8	0.0	47.2	-3.3	46.6	-1.3	46.5	-0.2
1957	47.7	2.6	47.4	-0.6	47.3	-0.2	47.5	0.4	47.6	0.2	48.0	0.8	47.6	-0.8	46.8	-1.7	46.6	-0.4	47.6	2.1	47.4	-0.4	47.0	-0.8
1958	47.0	0.0	46.0	-2.1	45.7	-0.7	46.4	1.5	45.4	-2.2	46.7	2.9	48.3	3.4	49.2	1.9	50.1	1.8	50.5	0.8	49.2	-2.6	48.7	-1.0
1959	49.0	0.6	51.0	4.1	51.1	0.2	52.4	2.5	52.4	0.0	51.7	-1.3	50.3	-2.7	49.6	-1.4	47.5	-4.2	47.4	-0.2	46.4	-2.1	47.8	3.0
1960	48.3	1.0	47.7	-1.2	47.1	-1.3	47.2	0.2	47.0	-0.4	47.0	0.0	47.0	0.0	46.6	-0.9	47.4	1.7	47.7	0.6	47.2	-1.0	46.7	-1.1
1961	45.1	-3.4	44.6	-1.1	45.2	1.3	48.7	7.7	47.8	-1.8	47.8	0.0	47.8	0.0	46.8	-2.1	46.1	-1.5	44.7	-3.0	45.0	0.7	44.8	-0.4
1962	44.5	-0.7	44.8	0.7	45.5	1.6	45.5	0.0	44.5	-2.2	44.8	0.7	44.6	-0.4	44.5	-0.2	44.5	0.0	44.4	-0.2	44.2	-0.5	43.6	-1.4
1963	43.7	0.2	43.7	0.0	44.0	0.7	43.9	-0.2	43.9	0.0	44.7	1.8	48.7	8.9	50.3	3.3	44.7	-11.1	44.6	-0.2	44.7	0.2	44.6	-0.2
1964	44.0	-1.3	44.5	1.1	45.7	2.7	45.8	0.2	45.5	-0.7	44.7	-1.8	44.6	-0.2	44.3	-0.7	44.3	0.0	44.0	-0.7	43.8	-0.5	43.6	-0.5
1965	45.6	4.6	44.9	-1.5	44.5	-0.9	44.4	-0.2	44.1	-0.7	43.7	-0.9	43.9	0.5	45.7	4.1	45.1	-1.3	44.2	-2.0	44.3	0.2	44.5	0.5
1966	45.4	2.0	45.4	0.0	47.2	4.0	49.5	4.9	48.4	-2.2	44.5	-8.1	44.2	-0.7	43.5	-1.6	43.1	-0.9	42.6	-1.2	42.0	-1.4	42.2	0.5
1967	42.2	0.0	43.1	2.1	42.3	-1.9	42.4	0.2	42.3	-0.2	42.3	0.0	43.2	2.1	43.9	1.6	46.2	5.2	43.4	-6.1	42.4	-2.3	43.6	2.8
1968	43.4	-0.5	45.7	5.3	47.0	2.8	47.0	0.0	47.0	0.0	47.4	0.9	48.9	3.2	49.2	0.6	51.5	4.7	54.0	4.9	54.4	0.7	62.3	14.5
1969	65.2	4.7	70.7	8.4	71.0	0.4	53.6	-24.5	50.0	-6.7	45.5	-9.0	45.4	-0.2	45.2	-0.4	45.6	0.9	46.4	1.8	48.1	3.7	46.8	-2.7
1970	45.9	-1.9	46.4	1.1	45.5	-1.9	47.0	3.3	47.9	1.9	47.4	-1.0	47.6	0.4	48.0	0.8	47.7	-0.6	46.5	-2.5	45.5	-2.2	45.1	-0.9
1971	45.2	0.2	48.4	7.1	51.8	7.0	49.9	-3.7	47.6	-4.6	47.5	-0.2	48.1	1.3	51.9	7.9	51.2	-1.3	49.9	-2.5	50.0	0.2	50.8	1.6
1972	51.8	2.0	53.9	4.1	55.5	3.0	55.5	0.0	56.1	1.1	56.7	1.1	57.3	1.1	58.5	2.1	58.0	-0.9	58.0	0.0	57.4	-1.0	57.0	-0.7
1973	57.8	1.4	64.4	11.4	76.2	18.3	78.6	3.1	76.6	-2.5	66.7	-12.9	59.4	-10.9	60.3	1.5	59.5	-1.3	58.0	-2.5	73.2	26.2	71.5	-2.3
1974	66.7	-6.7	68.0	1.9	73.6	8.2	81.5	10.7	77.3	-5.2	70.2	-9.2	69.4	-1.1	66.9	-3.6	68.1	1.8	63.4	-6.9	63.7	0.5	64.2	0.8
1975	63.1	-1.7	67.9	7.6	67.5	-0.6	71.1	5.3	74.4	4.6	69.9	-6.0	69.4	-0.7	68.3	-1.6	69.8	2.2	68.6	-1.7	70.2	2.3	73.1	4.1
1976	77.9	6.6	79.2	1.7	79.8	0.8	79.7	-0.1	78.8	-1.1	76.1	-3.4	78.0	2.5	80.8	3.6	82.5	2.1	82.0	-0.6	83.8	2.2	88.4	5.5
1977	88.2	-0.2	88.2	0.0	89.6	1.6	87.3	-2.6	86.2	-1.3	87.3	1.3	91.3	4.6	94.7	3.7	99.3	4.9	95.5	-3.8	92.0	-3.7	97.3	5.8
1978	99.9	2.7	100.5	0.6	97.5	-3.0	94.9	-2.7	98.4	3.7	101.7	3.4	99.7	-2.0	104.5	4.8	102.6	-1.8	103.5	0.9	107.7	4.1	107.3	-0.4
1979	110.9	3.4	110.8	-0.1	109.7	-1.0	108.7	-0.9	107.4	-1.2	102.8	-4.3	107.6	4.7	109.6	1.9	111.1	1.4	109.4	-1.5	104.3	-4.7	102.5	-1.7
1980	102.6	0.1	104.9	2.2	103.4	-1.4	94.7	-8.4	99.4	5.0	104.1	4.7	108.9	4.6	114.6	5.2	108.8	-5.1	109.0	0.2	110.6	1.5	113.5	2.6
1981	108.2	-4.7	108.2	0.0	107.2	-0.9	110.3	2.9	107.0	-3.0	108.4	1.3	106.7	-1.6	105.8	-0.8	103.8	-1.9	100.9	-2.8	100.6	-0.3	103.3	2.7
1982	102.3	-1.0	101.3	-1.0	101.9	0.6	100.8	-1.1	99.3	-1.5	103.0	3.7	100.1	-2.8	98.7	-1.4	98.4	-0.3	96.5	-1.9	98.2	1.8	99.6	1.4
1983	101.4	1.8	103.2	1.8	102.9	-0.3	103.1	0.2	103.9	0.8	110.1	6.0	108.8	-1.2	106.1	-2.5	104.3	-1.7	106.2	1.8	105.4	-0.8	106.5	1.0
1984	106.9	0.4	107.5	0.6	107.1	-0.4	104.9	-2.1	101.4	-3.3	101.8	0.4	102.2	0.4	106.0	3.7	104.9	-1.0	103.4	-1.4	101.2	-2.1	101.6	0.4
1985	100.9	-0.7	97.6	-3.3	96.3	-1.3	96.0	-0.3	100.1	4.3	102.2	2.1	102.0	-0.2	102.4	0.4	99.2	-3.1	100.8	1.6	99.0	-1.8	99.4	0.4
1986	98.9	-0.5	98.5	-0.4	100.6	2.1	105.3	4.7	103.3	-1.9	101.5	-1.7	101.6	0.1	101.3	-0.3	101.6	0.3	101.9	0.3	101.3	-0.6	100.6	-0.7
1987	100.5	-0.1	102.3	1.8	103.4	1.1	101.1	-2.2	99.3	-1.8	98.8	-0.5	100.3	1.5	102.8	2.5	107.4	4.5	104.6	-2.6	105.9	1.2	104.2	-1.6
1988	105.3	1.1	104.4	-0.9	103.4	-1.0	102.1	-1.3	100.3	-1.8	102.2	1.9	105.3	3.0	100.3	-4.7	106.3	6.0	103.1	-3.0	103.6	0.5	104.7	1.1
1989	105.9	1.1	109.9	3.8	111.1	1.1	111.3	0.2	113.4	1.9	113.4	0.0	118.4	4.4	115.2	-2.7	118.5	2.9	127.6	7.7	128.7	0.9	116.9	-9.2
1990	114.3	-2.2	115.8	1.3	116.1	0.3	125.3	7.9	122.7	-2.1	115.8	-5.6	117.6	1.6	112.6	-4.3	111.3	-1.2	106.8	-4.0	105.7	-1.0	106.7	0.9
1991	104.0	-2.5	102.7	-1.2	105.4	2.6	106.9	1.4	118.9	11.2	129.3	8.7	130.0	0.5	114.4	-12.0	116.2	1.6	112.6	-3.1	114.3	1.5	116.4	1.8

[Continued]

Plywood
Producer Price Index
Base 1982 = 100
[Continued]

For 1947-1993. Columns headed % show percentile change in the index from the previous period for which an index is available.

Year	Jan		Feb		Mar		Apr		May		Jun		Jul		Aug		Sep		Oct		Nov		Dec	
	Index	%	Index	%	Index	%	Index	%	Index	%	Index	%	Index	%	Index	%	Index	%	Index	%	Index	%	Index	%
1992	119.5	2.7	132.2	10.6	135.3	2.3	132.2	-2.3	130.1	-1.6	128.8	-1.0	125.2	-2.8	128.8	2.9	143.5	11.4	140.3	-2.2	138.0	-1.6	145.8	5.7
1993	154.9	6.2	164.8	6.4	168.9	2.5	158.7	-6.0	148.5	-6.4	144.0	-3.0	143.3	-0.5	146.4	2.2	149.5	2.1	147.8	-1.1	151.0	2.2	155.0	2.6

Source: U.S. Department of Labor, Bureau of Labor Statistics, Division of Industry Prices and Price Indexes. n.e.c. stands for not elsewhere classified. - indicates no data collected for period or unavailable.

Wood Products n.e.c.
Producer Price Index
Base 1982 = 100

For 1966-1993. Columns headed % show percentile change in the index from the previous period for which an index is available.

Year	Jan Index	%	Feb Index	%	Mar Index	%	Apr Index	%	May Index	%	Jun Index	%	Jul Index	%	Aug Index	%	Sep Index	%	Oct Index	%	Nov Index	%	Dec Index	%
1966	-	-	-	-	-	-	-	-	-	-	-	-	-	-	-	-	-	-	-	-	-	-	41.6	-
1967	42.4	1.9	42.4	0.0	42.4	0.0	42.4	0.0	42.4	0.0	42.4	0.0	42.4	0.0	42.3	-0.2	42.1	-0.5	42.2	0.2	42.2	0.0	42.2	0.0
1968	42.5	0.7	44.0	3.5	44.0	0.0	44.1	0.2	44.2	0.2	44.2	0.0	44.3	0.2	44.3	0.0	44.7	0.9	44.8	0.2	45.4	1.3	45.9	1.1
1969	46.0	0.2	46.2	0.4	46.7	1.1	46.8	0.2	47.6	1.7	47.8	0.4	48.0	0.4	48.5	1.0	48.4	-0.2	48.5	0.2	48.5	0.0	49.2	1.4
1970	49.7	1.0	49.7	0.0	49.7	0.0	49.6	-0.2	49.6	0.0	49.6	0.0	49.7	0.2	49.7	0.0	49.6	-0.2	49.6	0.0	49.6	0.0	49.9	0.6
1971	49.9	0.0	50.0	0.2	50.1	0.2	50.5	0.8	50.5	0.0	50.4	-0.2	50.4	0.0	50.4	0.0	50.4	0.0	50.4	0.0	50.4	0.0	50.4	0.0
1972	50.6	0.4	50.8	0.4	50.9	0.2	51.3	0.8	51.9	1.2	52.2	0.6	53.2	1.9	53.7	0.9	54.0	0.6	54.3	0.6	55.1	1.5	55.2	0.2
1973	56.4	2.2	57.2	1.4	59.7	4.4	62.4	4.5	63.4	1.6	64.3	1.4	64.7	0.6	64.9	0.3	66.0	1.7	67.0	1.5	67.3	0.4	67.4	0.1
1974	67.4	0.0	68.5	1.6	69.2	1.0	69.5	0.4	70.8	1.9	71.3	0.7	71.6	0.4	71.8	0.3	72.1	0.4	71.7	-0.6	71.3	-0.6	71.1	-0.3
1975	70.4	-1.0	70.2	-0.3	69.5	-1.0	68.9	-0.9	68.7	-0.3	68.4	-0.4	68.0	-0.6	68.1	0.1	68.0	-0.1	67.8	-0.3	67.7	-0.1	66.9	-1.2
1976	67.8	1.3	68.7	1.3	68.9	0.3	69.2	0.4	69.3	0.1	70.0	1.0	70.3	0.4	70.4	0.1	71.9	2.1	72.1	0.3	72.5	0.6	73.0	0.7
1977	73.4	0.5	74.7	1.8	75.8	1.5	76.7	1.2	78.1	1.8	78.5	0.5	78.6	0.1	79.0	0.5	80.3	1.6	80.3	0.0	80.4	0.1	80.9	0.6
1978	82.4	1.9	84.3	2.3	85.6	1.5	86.7	1.3	88.4	2.0	90.6	2.5	92.0	1.5	92.0	0.0	92.8	0.9	93.4	0.6	93.8	0.4	94.0	0.2
1979	94.5	0.5	95.8	1.4	98.3	2.6	99.7	1.4	100.9	1.2	101.0	0.1	100.6	-0.4	100.5	-0.1	100.8	0.3	100.7	-0.1	101.6	0.9	101.8	0.2
1980	102.6	0.8	103.0	0.4	102.9	-0.1	102.3	-0.6	101.9	-0.4	101.1	-0.8	100.3	-0.8	100.0	-0.3	100.3	0.3	100.2	-0.1	100.2	0.0	100.0	-0.2
1981	101.0	1.0	100.8	-0.2	100.3	-0.5	100.9	0.6	100.9	0.0	101.5	0.6	101.9	0.4	101.5	-0.4	101.8	0.3	101.6	-0.2	101.3	-0.3	101.4	0.1
1982	100.9	-0.5	101.1	0.2	101.0	-0.1	100.7	-0.3	100.5	-0.2	99.9	-0.6	99.9	0.0	99.8	-0.1	99.8	0.0	99.8	0.0	98.7	-1.1	97.9	-0.8
1983	98.2	0.3	98.7	0.5	98.1	-0.6	97.7	-0.4	97.9	0.2	97.2	-0.7	97.3	0.1	97.1	-0.2	97.1	0.0	97.2	0.1	97.3	0.1	97.6	0.3
1984	97.4	-0.2	97.7	0.3	98.2	0.5	98.8	0.6	99.4	0.6	99.5	0.1	99.6	0.1	100.1	0.5	99.9	-0.2	100.2	0.3	100.2	0.0	100.8	0.6
1985	100.7	-0.1	100.7	0.0	101.0	0.3	101.2	0.2	100.1	-1.1	99.9	-0.2	99.9	0.0	99.7	-0.2	99.6	-0.1	99.7	0.1	99.5	-0.2	99.5	0.0
1986	99.7	0.2	99.6	-0.1	99.6	0.0	99.6	0.0	99.8	0.2	100.8	1.0	101.4	0.6	101.0	-0.4	101.1	0.1	102.0	0.9	102.7	0.7	102.9	0.2
1987	103.0	0.1	102.9	-0.1	103.0	0.1	103.2	0.2	103.3	0.1	103.5	0.2	103.5	0.0	103.8	0.3	104.1	0.3	104.6	0.5	104.6	0.0	105.0	0.4
1988	105.4	0.4	105.8	0.4	106.2	0.4	106.5	0.3	106.5	0.0	107.1	0.6	107.5	0.4	107.7	0.2	107.9	0.2	108.3	0.4	108.6	0.3	108.3	-0.3
1989	108.5	0.2	109.4	0.8	110.2	0.7	111.4	1.1	112.4	0.9	113.7	1.2	114.2	0.4	115.6	1.2	116.2	0.5	115.1	-0.9	115.2	0.1	114.9	-0.3
1990	114.6	-0.3	114.4	-0.2	114.1	-0.3	114.4	0.3	114.5	0.1	114.9	0.3	114.8	-0.1	115.1	0.3	115.0	-0.1	115.3	0.3	114.9	-0.3	114.8	-0.1
1991	115.4	0.5	116.1	0.6	117.0	0.8	117.9	0.8	118.3	0.3	119.1	0.7	120.4	1.1	119.3	-0.9	120.5	1.0	119.7	-0.7	119.9	0.2	119.9	0.0
1992	119.9	0.0	119.8	-0.1	121.7	1.6	122.4	0.6	125.1	2.2	125.6	0.4	125.4	-0.2	125.4	0.0	126.0	0.5	126.8	0.6	127.7	0.7	127.6	-0.1
1993	129.7	1.6	131.4	1.3	133.6	1.7	135.1	1.1	137.1	1.5	136.2	-0.7	136.4	0.1	135.6	-0.6	137.6	1.5	136.7	-0.7	136.8	0.1	138.6	1.3

Source: U.S. Department of Labor, Bureau of Labor Statistics, Division of Industry Prices and Price Indexes. n.e.c. stands for not elsewhere classified. - indicates no data collected for period or unavailable.

Logs, Bolts, Timber and Pulpwood
Producer Price Index
Base 1982 = 100

For 1981-1993. Columns headed % show percentile change in the index from the previous period for which an index is available.

Year	Jan Index	%	Feb Index	%	Mar Index	%	Apr Index	%	May Index	%	Jun Index	%	Jul Index	%	Aug Index	%	Sep Index	%	Oct Index	%	Nov Index	%	Dec Index	%
1981	-	-	-	-	-	-	-	-	-	-	-	-	-	-	-	-	-	-	-	-	-	-	103.1	-
1982	102.0	-1.1	103.3	1.3	104.4	1.1	104.8	0.4	103.3	-1.4	102.7	-0.6	99.8	-2.8	98.6	-1.2	97.1	-1.5	94.4	-2.8	93.7	-0.7	95.9	2.3
1983	94.8	-1.1	96.0	1.3	96.9	0.9	96.6	-0.3	96.2	-0.4	96.9	0.7	96.5	-0.4	97.3	0.8	97.9	0.6	96.2	-1.7	97.1	0.9	96.5	-0.6
1984	95.9	-0.6	100.8	5.1	96.9	-3.9	97.9	1.0	100.2	2.3	100.5	0.3	99.1	-1.4	94.7	-4.4	96.5	1.9	93.4	-3.2	93.7	0.3	93.8	0.1
1985	94.4	0.6	96.5	2.2	96.8	0.3	97.3	0.5	97.2	-0.1	97.5	0.3	96.5	-1.0	95.5	-1.0	94.4	-1.2	95.4	1.1	95.3	-0.1	95.3	0.0
1986	94.5	-0.8	90.6	-4.1	91.6	1.1	91.9	0.3	92.4	0.5	92.9	0.5	91.8	-1.2	92.3	0.5	92.0	-0.3	92.4	0.4	92.2	-0.2	92.6	0.4
1987	93.2	0.6	94.8	1.7	96.2	1.5	95.9	-0.3	96.0	0.1	97.3	1.4	98.5	1.2	102.1	3.7	107.2	5.0	111.0	3.5	114.0	2.7	115.6	1.4
1988	117.3	1.5	118.2	0.8	118.6	0.3	119.1	0.4	118.9	-0.2	117.5	-1.2	117.3	-0.2	116.6	-0.6	116.4	-0.2	116.8	0.3	117.4	0.5	118.7	1.1
1989	120.8	1.8	122.2	1.2	123.6	1.1	127.2	2.9	128.2	0.8	131.1	2.3	133.7	2.0	137.2	2.6	137.3	0.1	140.7	2.5	140.8	0.1	140.4	-0.3
1990	142.1	1.2	142.1	0.0	143.3	0.8	143.7	0.3	144.2	0.3	144.8	0.4	146.1	0.9	145.2	-0.6	143.3	-1.3	140.9	-1.7	139.5	-1.0	138.6	-0.6
1991	141.9	2.4	142.1	0.1	141.0	-0.8	141.6	0.4	144.3	1.9	144.0	-0.2	144.4	0.3	146.3	1.3	145.4	-0.6	147.5	1.4	145.8	-1.2	145.4	-0.3
1992	151.6	4.3	155.8	2.8	158.8	1.9	164.1	3.3	164.9	0.5	165.1	0.1	165.1	0.0	165.9	0.5	168.1	1.3	170.7	1.5	171.4	0.4	176.4	2.9
1993	183.2	3.9	193.8	5.8	200.9	3.7	222.6	10.8	233.5	4.9	224.9	-3.7	222.5	-1.1	212.6	-4.4	209.0	-1.7	207.4	-0.8	213.6	3.0	218.4	2.2

Source: U.S. Department of Labor, Bureau of Labor Statistics, Division of Industry Prices and Price Indexes. n.e.c. stands for not elsewhere classified. - indicates no data collected for period or unavailable.

Prefabricated Wood Buildings & Components
Producer Price Index
Base Dec. 1984 = 100

For 1984-1993. Columns headed % show percentile change in the index from the previous period for which an index is available.

Year	Jan Index	%	Feb Index	%	Mar Index	%	Apr Index	%	May Index	%	Jun Index	%	Jul Index	%	Aug Index	%	Sep Index	%	Oct Index	%	Nov Index	%	Dec Index	%
1984	-	-	-	-	-	-	-	-	-	-	-	-	-	-	-	-	-	-	-	-	-	-	100.0	-
1985	100.4	0.4	100.2	-0.2	100.6	0.4	100.7	0.1	101.1	0.4	101.6	0.5	101.9	0.3	102.1	0.2	102.2	0.1	102.2	0.0	102.1	-0.1	102.1	0.0
1986	102.7	0.6	103.1	0.4	103.3	0.2	104.1	0.8	104.4	0.3	104.4	0.0	104.3	-0.1	104.4	0.1	104.7	0.3	104.7	0.0	104.7	0.0	104.8	0.1
1987	104.8	0.0	104.9	0.1	104.5	-0.4	105.4	0.9	105.5	0.1	105.2	-0.3	105.7	0.5	105.8	0.1	105.8	0.0	105.8	0.0	106.1	0.3	106.1	0.0
1988	106.2	0.1	107.3	1.0	107.8	0.5	107.9	0.1	107.6	-0.3	108.1	0.5	108.5	0.4	108.5	0.0	108.5	0.0	109.2	0.6	109.2	0.0	109.2	0.0
1989	109.8	0.5	109.8	0.0	110.5	0.6	110.7	0.2	110.7	0.0	110.7	0.0	111.0	0.3	111.0	0.0	111.0	0.0	111.0	0.0	110.8	-0.2	111.0	0.2
1990	111.3	0.3	111.8	0.4	111.6	-0.2	111.9	0.3	112.8	0.8	113.1	0.3	113.2	0.1	113.8	0.5	113.9	0.1	114.7	0.7	114.7	0.0	114.7	0.0
1991	115.7	0.9	115.7	0.0	115.9	0.2	117.2	1.1	117.5	0.3	119.6	1.8	119.7	0.1	120.1	0.3	120.2	0.1	119.0	-1.0	118.9	-0.1	118.9	0.0
1992	119.3	0.3	120.3	0.8	120.6	0.2	122.8	1.8	122.9	0.1	123.0	0.1	122.9	-0.1	123.1	0.2	123.2	0.1	124.5	1.1	125.2	0.6	125.4	0.2
1993	125.7	0.2	128.3	2.1	130.1	1.4	132.1	1.5	134.7	2.0	134.4	-0.2	134.0	-0.3	133.2	-0.6	133.2	0.0	134.5	1.0	134.9	0.3	133.7	-0.9

Source: U.S. Department of Labor, Bureau of Labor Statistics, Division of Industry Prices and Price Indexes. n.e.c. stands for not elsewhere classified. - indicates no data collected for period or unavailable.

Treated Wood and Contract Wood Preserving
Producer Price Index
Base June 1985 = 100

For 1985-1993. Columns headed % show percentile change in the index from the previous period for which an index is available.

Year	Jan Index	%	Feb Index	%	Mar Index	%	Apr Index	%	May Index	%	Jun Index	%	Jul Index	%	Aug Index	%	Sep Index	%	Oct Index	%	Nov Index	%	Dec Index	%
1985	-	-	-	-	-	-	-	-	-	-	100.0	-	99.5	-0.5	99.0	-0.5	99.0	0.0	98.9	-0.1	98.9	0.0	98.8	-0.1
1986	98.8	0.0	98.3	-0.5	98.9	0.6	98.1	-0.8	98.2	0.1	98.0	-0.2	97.7	-0.3	97.8	0.1	97.6	-0.2	97.7	0.1	97.3	-0.4	97.4	0.1
1987	97.0	-0.4	97.7	0.7	98.0	0.3	98.5	0.5	98.9	0.4	100.0	1.1	99.4	-0.6	99.5	0.1	99.4	-0.1	98.9	-0.5	98.9	0.0	99.1	0.2
1988	100.0	0.9	100.9	0.9	100.9	0.0	101.0	0.1	101.4	0.4	102.2	0.8	102.6	0.4	102.1	-0.5	101.8	-0.3	103.9	2.1	104.6	0.7	104.8	0.2
1989	106.6	1.7	107.9	1.2	108.3	0.4	108.9	0.6	110.6	1.6	110.9	0.3	111.2	0.3	111.1	-0.1	110.9	-0.2	110.1	-0.7	109.9	-0.2	110.0	0.1
1990	110.3	0.3	111.7	1.3	111.9	0.2	112.3	0.4	113.3	0.9	113.2	-0.1	113.5	0.3	113.6	0.1	112.7	-0.8	112.0	-0.6	113.3	1.2	113.3	0.0
1991	113.5	0.2	113.4	-0.1	114.4	0.9	114.8	0.3	114.6	-0.2	118.9	3.8	119.6	0.6	115.5	-3.4	115.3	-0.2	115.0	-0.3	115.9	0.8	116.7	0.7
1992	118.9	1.9	122.6	3.1	123.2	0.5	123.4	0.2	124.0	0.5	122.4	-1.3	122.2	-0.2	123.2	0.8	125.5	1.9	124.3	-1.0	124.4	0.1	127.6	2.6
1993	131.1	2.7	135.9	3.7	141.7	4.3	142.4	0.5	138.3	-2.9	132.4	-4.3	132.1	-0.2	134.3	1.7	136.7	1.8	139.3	1.9	146.5	5.2	147.4	0.6

Source: U.S. Department of Labor, Bureau of Labor Statistics, Division of Industry Prices and Price Indexes. n.e.c. stands for not elsewhere classified. - indicates no data collected for period or unavailable.

PULP, PAPER, AND ALLIED PRODUCTS
Producer Price Index
Base 1982 = 100

For 1947-1993. Columns headed % show percentile change in the index from the previous period for which an index is available.

Year	Jan Index	%	Feb Index	%	Mar Index	%	Apr Index	%	May Index	%	Jun Index	%	Jul Index	%	Aug Index	%	Sep Index	%	Oct Index	%	Nov Index	%	Dec Index	%
1947	24.5	-	24.7	0.8	24.8	0.4	25.1	1.2	25.1	0.0	25.1	0.0	25.1	0.0	25.2	0.4	25.3	0.4	25.5	0.8	25.5	0.0	25.8	1.2
1948	26.0	0.8	26.3	1.2	26.2	-0.4	26.1	-0.4	26.1	0.0	26.1	0.0	26.2	0.4	26.3	0.4	26.4	0.4	26.4	0.0	26.3	-0.4	26.3	0.0
1949	26.3	0.0	26.2	-0.4	26.0	-0.8	25.7	-1.2	25.3	-1.6	24.8	-2.0	24.5	-1.2	24.4	-0.4	24.5	0.4	24.5	0.0	24.6	0.4	24.6	0.0
1950	24.6	0.0	24.5	-0.4	24.5	0.0	24.5	0.0	24.4	-0.4	24.5	0.4	24.9	1.6	25.9	4.0	26.4	1.9	27.4	3.8	28.0	2.2	29.2	4.3
1951	30.6	4.8	30.7	0.3	30.7	0.0	30.5	-0.7	30.5	0.0	30.6	0.3	30.6	0.0	30.5	-0.3	30.4	-0.3	30.3	-0.3	30.2	-0.3	30.2	0.0
1952	30.1	-0.3	30.2	0.3	30.0	-0.7	29.9	-0.3	29.8	-0.3	29.7	-0.3	29.4	-1.0	29.5	0.3	29.5	0.0	29.4	-0.3	29.4	0.0	29.5	0.3
1953	29.5	0.0	29.4	-0.3	29.3	-0.3	29.4	0.3	29.4	0.0	29.5	0.3	29.5	0.0	29.6	0.3	29.8	0.7	30.0	0.7	29.9	-0.3	29.8	-0.3
1954	29.8	0.0	29.8	0.0	29.7	-0.3	29.6	-0.3	29.5	-0.3	29.5	0.0	29.6	0.3	29.6	0.0	29.6	0.0	29.6	0.0	29.6	0.0	29.5	-0.3
1955	29.6	0.3	29.7	0.3	29.8	0.3	29.9	0.3	30.0	0.3	30.2	0.7	30.3	0.3	30.5	0.7	30.7	0.7	31.3	2.0	31.4	0.3	31.5	0.3
1956	31.8	1.0	32.0	0.6	32.3	0.9	32.5	0.6	32.4	-0.3	32.5	0.3	32.5	0.0	32.6	0.3	32.6	0.0	32.7	0.3	32.6	-0.3	32.6	0.0
1957	32.8	0.6	32.8	0.0	32.8	0.0	32.8	0.0	32.9	0.3	32.9	0.0	33.0	0.3	33.1	0.3	33.2	0.3	33.4	0.6	33.4	0.0	33.4	0.0
1958	33.3	-0.3	33.3	0.0	33.3	0.0	33.3	0.0	33.3	0.0	33.3	0.0	33.4	0.3	33.4	0.0	33.6	0.6	33.6	0.0	33.6	0.0	33.5	-0.3
1959	33.5	0.0	33.6	0.3	33.6	0.0	33.7	0.3	33.6	-0.3	33.7	0.3	33.7	0.0	33.7	0.0	33.7	0.0	33.8	0.3	33.7	-0.3	33.7	0.0
1960	34.1	1.2	33.9	-0.6	33.9	0.0	33.9	0.0	34.0	0.3	34.0	0.0	34.0	0.0	33.9	-0.3	33.9	0.0	34.0	0.3	33.9	-0.3	33.7	-0.6
1961	33.7	0.0	33.7	0.0	33.5	-0.6	33.4	-0.3	32.1	-3.9	32.2	0.3	32.2	0.0	32.2	0.0	33.0	2.5	33.3	0.9	33.1	-0.6	33.3	0.6
1962	33.3	0.0	33.3	0.0	33.7	1.2	33.8	0.3	33.6	-0.6	33.5	-0.3	33.4	-0.3	33.3	-0.3	33.2	-0.3	33.1	-0.3	33.1	0.0	33.0	-0.3
1963	33.0	0.0	33.1	0.3	33.0	-0.3	33.0	0.0	33.1	0.3	33.2	0.3	33.0	-0.6	33.1	0.3	33.1	0.0	33.2	0.3	33.2	0.0	33.2	0.0
1964	33.3	0.3	33.3	0.0	33.1	-0.6	33.1	0.0	32.9	-0.6	32.9	0.0	32.9	0.0	32.9	0.0	32.9	0.0	33.1	0.6	33.0	-0.3	33.0	0.0
1965	33.0	0.0	33.0	0.0	33.2	0.6	33.3	0.3	33.4	0.3	33.4	0.0	33.3	-0.3	33.3	0.0	33.4	0.3	33.5	0.3	33.6	0.3	33.7	0.3
1966	33.8	0.3	33.8	0.0	34.0	0.6	34.2	0.6	34.3	0.3	34.4	0.3	34.4	0.0	34.4	0.0	34.4	0.0	34.4	0.0	34.4	0.0	34.4	0.0
1967	34.4	0.0	34.4	0.0	34.5	0.3	34.6	0.3	34.6	0.0	34.6	0.0	34.7	0.3	34.6	-0.3	34.6	0.0	34.7	0.3	34.8	0.3	34.9	0.3
1968	34.9	0.0	35.1	0.6	35.1	0.0	35.1	0.0	35.1	0.0	34.9	-0.6	35.0	0.3	34.9	-0.3	35.0	0.3	35.1	0.3	35.1	0.0	35.1	0.0
1969	35.4	0.9	35.6	0.6	35.8	0.6	35.9	0.3	36.0	0.3	36.0	0.0	36.0	0.0	36.2	0.6	36.3	0.3	36.4	0.3	36.5	0.3	36.6	0.3
1970	37.2	1.6	37.3	0.3	37.4	0.3	37.5	0.3	37.4	-0.3	37.4	0.0	37.5	0.3	37.4	-0.3	37.5	0.3	37.7	0.5	37.7	0.0	37.6	-0.3
1971	37.8	0.5	37.8	0.0	37.9	0.3	38.0	0.3	38.1	0.3	38.2	0.3	38.3	0.3	38.3	0.0	38.3	0.0	38.3	0.0	38.3	0.0	38.4	0.3
1972	38.4	0.0	38.7	0.8	38.9	0.5	39.1	0.5	39.2	0.3	39.3	0.3	39.4	0.3	39.5	0.3	39.6	0.3	39.7	0.3	39.8	0.3	39.9	0.3
1973	40.1	0.5	40.4	0.7	41.0	1.5	41.5	1.2	41.8	0.7	42.3	1.2	42.4	0.2	42.7	0.7	43.1	0.9	43.6	1.2	44.2	1.4	44.6	0.9
1974	45.6	2.2	46.0	0.9	47.5	3.3	50.0	5.3	50.8	1.6	51.1	0.6	53.1	3.9	56.4	6.2	56.9	0.9	57.5	1.1	57.8	0.5	57.9	0.2
1975	58.8	1.6	58.8	0.0	58.9	0.2	58.8	-0.2	58.8	0.0	58.8	0.0	58.9	0.2	58.9	0.0	59.0	0.2	59.2	0.3	59.3	0.2	59.9	1.0
1976	60.5	1.0	60.9	0.7	61.3	0.7	61.9	1.0	62.1	0.3	62.2	0.2	62.5	0.5	62.7	0.3	62.9	0.3	62.9	0.0	62.9	0.0	63.0	0.2
1977	63.4	0.6	63.4	0.0	63.6	0.3	64.2	0.9	64.5	0.5	64.9	0.6	65.0	0.2	65.1	0.2	65.2	0.2	65.3	0.2	65.2	-0.2	65.0	-0.3
1978	65.1	0.2	65.3	0.3	65.7	0.6	66.5	1.2	66.9	0.6	67.0	0.1	67.7	1.0	67.8	0.1	68.9	1.6	70.1	1.7	70.6	0.7	71.1	0.7
1979	71.7	0.8	72.3	0.8	73.5	1.7	74.5	1.4	74.9	0.5	75.0	0.1	75.6	0.8	77.0	1.9	77.2	0.3	78.8	2.1	79.5	0.9	80.3	1.0
1980	82.2	2.4	82.8	0.7	84.0	1.4	85.8	2.1	86.3	0.6	87.0	0.8	87.2	0.2	87.4	0.2	87.5	0.1	88.1	0.7	88.3	0.2	88.9	0.7
1981	91.6	3.0	92.5	1.0	93.2	0.8	94.0	0.9	94.3	0.3	94.5	0.2	95.2	0.7	95.6	0.4	96.2	0.6	96.7	0.5	97.1	0.4	97.3	0.2
1982	98.9	1.6	99.2	0.3	99.5	0.3	99.9	0.4	100.3	0.4	100.3	0.0	100.1	-0.2	100.2	0.1	100.2	0.0	100.4	0.2	100.4	0.0	100.6	0.2
1983	101.7	1.1	101.9	0.2	102.1	0.2	102.3	0.2	102.5	0.2	102.9	0.4	103.2	0.3	103.5	0.3	103.9	0.4	104.7	0.8	105.2	0.5	105.3	0.1
1984	107.0	1.6	108.1	1.0	108.8	0.6	109.5	0.6	110.1	0.5	110.3	0.2	110.8	0.5	111.3	0.5	111.5	0.2	111.9	0.4	112.2	0.3	112.3	0.1
1985	113.3	0.9	113.5	0.2	113.5	0.0	113.5	0.0	113.4	-0.1	113.3	-0.1	113.2	-0.1	113.2	0.0	113.1	-0.1	113.3	0.2	113.4	0.1	113.4	0.0
1986	114.5	1.0	114.7	0.2	114.7	0.0	115.3	0.5	115.6	0.3	115.8	0.2	116.1	0.3	116.5	0.3	117.0	0.4	117.6	0.5	117.9	0.3	118.1	0.2
1987	119.5	1.2	120.3	0.7	120.6	0.2	120.9	0.2	121.0	0.1	121.2	0.2	121.6	0.3	122.2	0.5	122.9	0.6	123.8	0.7	123.9	0.1	124.2	0.2
1988	126.6	1.9	127.3	0.6	128.0	0.5	128.9	0.7	129.6	0.5	130.0	0.3	131.0	0.8	131.3	0.2	132.1	0.6	132.8	0.5	133.1	0.2	133.5	0.3
1989	135.1	1.2	136.3	0.9	136.9	0.4	137.4	0.4	137.8	0.3	137.9	0.1	138.0	0.1	138.4	0.3	138.6	0.1	139.1	0.4	139.3	0.1	139.2	-0.1
1990	140.3	0.8	140.5	0.1	140.7	0.1	140.9	0.1	141.1	0.1	141.0	-0.1	141.1	0.1	141.1	0.0	141.3	0.1	142.0	0.5	142.3	0.2	142.3	0.0
1991	143.6	0.9	143.8	0.1	143.7	-0.1	143.2	-0.3	143.0	-0.1	142.7	-0.2	142.3	-0.3	142.2	-0.1	142.3	0.1	142.6	0.2	142.8	0.1	142.7	-0.1

[Continued]

PULP, PAPER, AND ALLIED PRODUCTS
Producer Price Index
Base 1982 = 100
[Continued]

For 1947-1993. Columns headed % show percentile change in the index from the previous period for which an index is available.

Year	Jan Index	%	Feb Index	%	Mar Index	%	Apr Index	%	May Index	%	Jun Index	%	Jul Index	%	Aug Index	%	Sep Index	%	Oct Index	%	Nov Index	%	Dec Index	%
1992	144.1	1.0	144.2	0.1	144.4	0.1	144.9	0.3	145.2	0.2	145.1	-0.1	145.2	0.1	145.4	0.1	145.8	0.3	146.1	0.2	145.9	-0.1	145.9	0.0
1993	147.0	0.8	147.1	0.1	147.3	0.1	147.7	0.3	147.7	0.0	147.1	-0.4	147.1	0.0	147.1	0.0	147.2	0.1	147.4	0.1	147.4	0.0	147.6	0.1

Source: U.S. Department of Labor, Bureau of Labor Statistics, Division of Industry Prices and Price Indexes. n.e.c. stands for not elsewhere classified. - indicates no data collected for period or unavailable.

Pulp, Paper, and Products, ex. Building Paper

Producer Price Index
Base 1982 = 100

For 1947-1993. Columns headed % show percentile change in the index from the previous period for which an index is available.

Year	Jan Index	%	Feb Index	%	Mar Index	%	Apr Index	%	May Index	%	Jun Index	%	Jul Index	%	Aug Index	%	Sep Index	%	Oct Index	%	Nov Index	%	Dec Index	%
1947	25.8	-	26.0	0.8	26.2	0.8	26.6	1.5	26.5	-0.4	26.5	0.0	26.5	0.0	26.7	0.8	26.8	0.4	26.9	0.4	26.9	0.0	27.3	1.5
1948	27.5	0.7	27.7	0.7	27.7	0.0	27.6	-0.4	27.6	0.0	27.6	0.0	27.7	0.4	27.8	0.4	27.8	0.0	27.8	0.0	27.8	0.0	27.7	-0.4
1949	27.7	0.0	27.6	-0.4	27.5	-0.4	27.1	-1.5	26.6	-1.8	26.1	-1.9	25.8	-1.1	25.7	-0.4	25.8	0.4	25.8	0.0	25.9	0.4	25.9	0.0
1950	25.9	0.0	25.8	-0.4	25.8	0.0	25.8	0.0	25.7	-0.4	25.7	0.0	26.2	1.9	27.3	4.2	27.8	1.8	28.8	3.6	29.6	2.8	30.8	4.1
1951	32.4	5.2	32.5	0.3	32.4	-0.3	32.2	-0.6	32.2	0.0	32.4	0.6	32.4	0.0	32.2	-0.6	32.1	-0.3	32.0	-0.3	31.9	-0.3	31.9	0.0
1952	31.8	-0.3	31.8	0.0	31.7	-0.3	31.6	-0.3	31.5	-0.3	31.4	-0.3	31.0	-1.3	31.1	0.3	31.1	0.0	31.1	0.0	31.0	-0.3	31.1	0.3
1953	31.1	0.0	31.0	-0.3	30.9	-0.3	31.0	0.3	31.0	0.0	31.1	0.3	31.1	0.0	31.2	0.3	31.4	0.6	31.6	0.6	31.5	-0.3	31.4	-0.3
1954	31.4	0.0	31.4	0.0	31.3	-0.3	31.2	-0.3	31.1	-0.3	31.1	0.0	31.2	0.3	31.2	0.0	31.2	0.0	31.2	0.0	31.1	-0.3	31.1	0.0
1955	31.2	0.3	31.3	0.3	31.3	0.0	31.5	0.6	31.6	0.3	31.8	0.6	32.0	0.6	32.1	0.3	32.4	0.9	32.9	1.5	33.1	0.6	33.2	0.3
1956	33.5	0.9	33.7	0.6	34.1	1.2	34.2	0.3	34.2	0.0	34.2	0.0	34.3	0.3	34.4	0.3	34.3	-0.3	34.4	0.3	34.3	-0.3	34.4	0.3
1957	34.5	0.3	34.5	0.0	34.6	0.3	34.5	-0.3	34.6	0.3	34.6	0.0	34.7	0.3	34.9	0.6	35.0	0.3	35.1	0.3	35.2	0.3	35.2	0.0
1958	35.1	-0.3	35.1	0.0	35.0	-0.3	35.0	0.0	35.0	0.0	35.0	0.0	35.1	0.3	35.2	0.3	35.3	0.3	35.4	0.3	35.4	0.0	35.0	-1.1
1959	35.3	0.9	35.3	0.0	35.4	0.3	35.5	0.3	35.4	-0.3	35.5	0.3	35.5	0.0	35.5	0.0	35.5	0.0	35.5	0.0	35.5	0.0	35.5	0.0
1960	35.9	1.1	35.7	-0.6	35.7	0.0	35.7	0.0	35.8	0.3	35.8	0.0	35.9	0.3	35.7	-0.6	35.7	0.0	35.8	0.3	35.7	-0.3	35.5	-0.6
1961	35.5	0.0	35.4	-0.3	35.3	-0.3	35.1	-0.6	33.8	-3.7	33.9	0.3	33.8	-0.3	33.8	0.0	34.7	2.7	35.0	0.9	34.8	-0.6	35.0	0.6
1962	35.1	0.3	35.1	0.0	35.5	1.1	35.7	0.6	35.5	-0.6	35.4	-0.3	35.2	-0.6	35.1	-0.3	35.0	-0.3	34.9	-0.3	34.8	-0.3	34.8	0.0
1963	34.8	0.0	34.9	0.3	34.8	-0.3	34.8	0.0	34.8	0.0	35.0	0.6	34.8	-0.6	34.8	0.0	34.8	0.0	35.0	0.6	35.0	0.0	35.0	0.0
1964	35.1	0.3	35.2	0.3	35.0	-0.6	34.9	-0.3	34.7	-0.6	34.7	0.0	34.7	0.0	34.7	0.0	34.7	0.0	34.9	0.6	34.8	-0.3	34.8	0.0
1965	34.8	0.0	34.9	0.3	35.1	0.6	35.2	0.3	35.2	0.0	35.2	0.0	35.2	0.0	35.2	0.0	35.2	0.0	35.4	0.6	35.5	0.3	35.5	0.0
1966	35.7	0.6	35.7	0.0	35.9	0.6	36.1	0.6	36.2	0.3	36.3	0.3	36.4	0.3	36.4	0.0	36.4	0.0	36.3	-0.3	36.3	0.0	36.3	0.0
1967	36.3	0.0	36.4	0.3	36.5	0.3	36.6	0.3	36.6	0.0	36.6	0.0	36.7	0.3	36.6	-0.3	36.6	0.0	36.7	0.3	36.9	0.5	36.9	0.0
1968	37.0	0.3	37.1	0.3	37.0	-0.3	37.0	0.0	37.1	0.3	36.9	-0.5	37.0	0.3	36.9	-0.3	37.0	0.3	37.0	0.0	37.0	0.0	37.0	0.0
1969	37.4	1.1	37.6	0.5	37.8	0.5	37.9	0.3	37.9	0.0	38.0	0.3	38.1	0.3	38.3	0.5	38.4	0.3	38.5	0.3	38.7	0.5	38.7	0.0
1970	39.4	1.8	39.5	0.3	39.6	0.3	39.7	0.3	39.6	-0.3	39.6	0.0	39.7	0.3	39.7	0.0	39.7	0.0	39.9	0.5	39.9	0.0	39.9	0.0
1971	40.1	0.5	40.0	-0.2	40.1	0.3	40.2	0.2	40.3	0.2	40.5	0.5	40.6	0.2	40.6	0.0	40.6	0.0	40.6	0.0	40.6	0.0	40.6	0.0
1972	40.7	0.2	41.0	0.7	41.2	0.5	41.4	0.5	41.5	0.2	41.6	0.2	41.7	0.2	41.9	0.5	41.9	0.0	42.1	0.5	42.2	0.2	42.3	0.2
1973	42.5	0.5	42.8	0.7	43.4	1.4	44.0	1.4	44.3	0.7	44.8	1.1	44.9	0.2	45.3	0.9	45.7	0.9	46.2	1.1	46.8	1.3	47.2	0.9
1974	48.4	2.5	48.8	0.8	50.4	3.3	53.1	5.4	53.9	1.5	54.3	0.7	56.5	4.1	60.1	6.4	60.6	0.8	61.3	1.2	61.7	0.7	61.8	0.2
1975	62.7	1.5	62.8	0.2	62.8	0.0	62.7	-0.2	62.7	0.0	62.7	0.0	62.8	0.2	62.8	0.0	62.9	0.2	63.1	0.3	63.2	0.2	63.9	1.1
1976	64.6	1.1	64.9	0.5	65.3	0.6	65.9	0.9	66.2	0.5	66.2	0.0	66.6	0.6	66.7	0.2	67.0	0.4	67.0	0.0	66.9	-0.1	67.0	0.1
1977	67.4	0.6	67.5	0.1	67.7	0.3	68.3	0.9	68.6	0.4	69.0	0.6	69.1	0.1	69.0	-0.1	69.1	0.1	69.2	0.1	69.1	-0.1	68.8	-0.4
1978	68.9	0.1	69.0	0.1	69.3	0.4	70.2	1.3	70.6	0.6	70.7	0.1	71.5	1.1	71.7	0.3	72.9	1.7	74.2	1.8	74.8	0.8	75.3	0.7
1979	76.0	0.9	76.7	0.9	78.0	1.7	79.0	1.3	79.5	0.6	79.7	0.3	80.4	0.9	81.9	1.9	82.1	0.2	83.8	2.1	84.6	1.0	85.4	0.9
1980	87.5	2.5	88.1	0.7	89.3	1.4	91.3	2.2	91.7	0.4	92.4	0.8	92.6	0.2	92.9	0.3	93.0	0.1	93.6	0.6	93.8	0.2	94.4	0.6
1981	95.5	1.2	96.8	1.4	97.7	0.9	98.3	0.6	98.8	0.5	99.3	0.5	99.6	0.3	100.2	0.6	100.6	0.4	100.9	0.3	100.9	0.0	100.9	0.0
1982	101.0	0.1	101.3	0.3	101.3	0.0	100.8	-0.5	100.6	-0.2	100.3	-0.3	99.8	-0.5	99.6	-0.2	99.4	-0.2	98.9	-0.5	98.6	-0.3	98.4	-0.2
1983	98.4	0.0	98.4	0.0	98.4	0.0	98.3	-0.1	98.3	0.0	98.5	0.2	98.9	0.4	99.2	0.3	100.0	0.8	100.7	0.7	101.4	0.7	101.5	0.1
1984	102.8	1.3	104.3	1.5	105.5	1.2	106.7	1.1	107.1	0.4	107.4	0.3	108.2	0.7	108.5	0.3	108.9	0.4	109.6	0.6	109.7	0.1	109.4	-0.3
1985	109.1	-0.3	108.7	-0.4	108.2	-0.5	107.8	-0.4	107.4	-0.4	107.0	-0.4	106.3	-0.7	106.0	-0.3	105.7	-0.3	105.6	-0.1	105.4	-0.2	105.4	0.0
1986	105.4	0.0	105.5	0.1	105.9	0.4	106.3	0.4	106.7	0.4	106.9	0.2	107.6	0.7	108.2	0.6	108.7	0.5	109.3	0.6	109.8	0.5	110.0	0.2
1987	111.3	1.2	112.4	1.0	112.6	0.2	113.2	0.5	113.1	-0.1	113.4	0.3	114.0	0.5	114.8	0.7	115.7	0.8	116.7	0.9	117.1	0.3	117.6	0.4
1988	119.9	2.0	120.5	0.5	121.6	0.9	123.1	1.2	124.1	0.8	124.6	0.4	125.8	1.0	126.4	0.5	127.6	0.9	128.1	0.4	128.3	0.2	128.5	0.2
1989	129.5	0.8	131.1	1.2	131.8	0.5	132.4	0.5	132.9	0.4	132.8	-0.1	132.5	-0.2	132.8	0.2	132.8	0.0	133.6	0.6	133.6	0.0	133.4	-0.1
1990	133.4	0.0	133.3	-0.1	133.2	-0.1	133.4	0.2	133.1	-0.2	132.8	-0.2	132.6	-0.2	132.5	-0.1	132.3	-0.2	132.7	0.3	132.8	0.1	132.8	0.0
1991	132.6	-0.2	132.4	-0.2	131.8	-0.5	130.8	-0.8	129.8	-0.8	129.1	-0.5	128.6	-0.4	128.1	-0.4	128.5	0.3	128.4	-0.1	128.6	0.2	128.5	-0.1

[Continued]

Pulp, Paper, and Products, ex. Building Paper
Producer Price Index
Base 1982 = 100
[Continued]

For 1947-1993. Columns headed % show percentile change in the index from the previous period for which an index is available.

Year	Jan Index	%	Feb Index	%	Mar Index	%	Apr Index	%	May Index	%	Jun Index	%	Jul Index	%	Aug Index	%	Sep Index	%	Oct Index	%	Nov Index	%	Dec Index	%
1992	128.5	0.0	128.6	0.1	128.6	0.0	129.4	0.6	129.5	0.1	129.4	-0.1	129.4	0.0	129.4	0.0	129.9	0.4	129.6	-0.2	129.2	-0.3	128.8	-0.3
1993	128.3	-0.4	128.0	-0.2	128.2	0.2	128.3	0.1	128.2	-0.1	128.0	-0.2	127.5	-0.4	127.0	-0.4	126.7	-0.2	126.9	0.2	126.9	0.0	126.9	0.0

Source: U.S. Department of Labor, Bureau of Labor Statistics, Division of Industry Prices and Price Indexes. n.e.c. stands for not elsewhere classified. - indicates no data collected for period or unavailable.

Building Paper & Building Board Mill Products
Producer Price Index
Base 1982 = 100

For 1947-1993. Columns headed % show percentile change in the index from the previous period for which an index is available.

Year	Jan Index	%	Feb Index	%	Mar Index	%	Apr Index	%	May Index	%	Jun Index	%	Jul Index	%	Aug Index	%	Sep Index	%	Oct Index	%	Nov Index	%	Dec Index	%
1947	29.0	-	29.0	0.0	29.1	0.3	29.1	0.0	29.1	0.0	29.1	0.0	29.1	0.0	29.0	-0.3	29.0	0.0	29.5	1.7	30.9	4.7	30.9	0.0
1948	31.1	0.6	31.4	1.0	31.4	0.0	31.4	0.0	31.8	1.3	33.1	4.1	33.4	0.9	33.4	0.0	33.4	0.0	33.4	0.0	33.4	0.0	33.4	0.0
1949	33.3	-0.3	33.2	-0.3	33.2	0.0	33.2	0.0	32.9	-0.9	32.8	-0.3	32.8	0.0	32.8	0.0	32.8	0.0	32.8	0.0	32.8	0.0	32.8	0.0
1950	32.8	0.0	32.8	0.0	32.8	0.0	32.8	0.0	32.8	0.0	33.6	2.4	34.4	2.4	34.4	0.0	34.7	0.9	35.6	2.6	35.6	0.0	35.9	0.8
1951	35.9	0.0	35.9	0.0	35.9	0.0	35.9	0.0	35.9	0.0	35.9	0.0	35.9	0.0	35.9	0.0	35.9	0.0	35.9	0.0	35.9	0.0	35.9	0.0
1952	35.9	0.0	35.9	0.0	35.9	0.0	36.0	0.3	36.6	1.7	36.6	0.0	36.6	0.0	36.6	0.0	36.6	0.0	36.6	0.0	37.3	1.9	37.3	0.0
1953	37.3	0.0	37.3	0.0	37.3	0.0	37.3	0.0	38.9	4.3	38.9	0.0	38.9	0.0	38.9	0.0	38.9	0.0	38.9	0.0	38.9	0.0	38.9	0.0
1954	40.4	3.9	40.4	0.0	40.4	0.0	40.4	0.0	40.4	0.0	40.4	0.0	40.4	0.0	40.3	-0.2	40.3	0.0	40.3	0.0	40.3	0.0	40.3	0.0
1955	40.3	0.0	40.9	1.5	41.0	0.2	41.0	0.0	41.0	0.0	41.0	0.0	41.0	0.0	41.9	2.2	41.9	0.0	42.2	0.7	42.2	0.0	42.2	0.0
1956	42.2	0.0	42.2	0.0	42.2	0.0	43.7	3.6	43.7	0.0	43.7	0.0	43.7	0.0	43.7	0.0	43.7	0.0	43.7	0.0	43.7	0.0	43.7	0.0
1957	44.6	2.1	44.6	0.0	44.6	0.0	44.8	0.4	44.8	0.0	44.8	0.0	44.8	0.0	44.8	0.0	44.8	0.0	44.8	0.0	44.8	0.0	44.8	0.0
1958	44.8	0.0	44.8	0.0	45.1	0.7	45.6	1.1	45.6	0.0	45.6	0.0	45.3	-0.7	45.3	0.0	45.3	0.0	45.3	0.0	45.3	0.0	45.4	0.2
1959	45.5	0.2	45.6	0.2	45.6	0.0	45.8	0.4	46.4	1.3	46.4	0.0	46.6	0.4	46.7	0.2	46.7	0.0	46.7	0.0	46.7	0.0	46.7	0.0
1960	46.7	0.0	46.7	0.0	46.3	-0.9	45.9	-0.9	45.9	0.0	45.9	0.0	45.6	-0.7	46.0	0.9	45.9	-0.2	46.1	0.4	46.0	-0.2	46.0	0.0
1961	46.0	0.0	46.2	0.4	46.1	-0.2	45.9	-0.4	45.7	-0.4	45.8	0.2	45.8	0.0	45.8	0.0	45.8	0.0	45.8	0.0	45.5	-0.7	45.3	-0.4
1962	44.8	-1.1	44.7	-0.2	44.6	-0.2	44.5	-0.2	44.4	-0.2	43.4	-2.3	43.8	0.9	44.1	0.7	44.1	0.0	43.7	-0.9	43.8	0.2	43.6	-0.5
1963	43.3	-0.7	43.3	0.0	42.7	-1.4	43.3	1.4	43.6	0.7	44.2	1.4	44.2	0.0	44.2	0.0	44.3	0.2	43.9	-0.9	43.1	-1.8	43.2	0.2
1964	43.2	0.0	43.0	-0.5	42.5	-1.2	42.4	-0.2	42.8	0.9	42.8	0.0	42.8	0.0	42.7	-0.2	42.8	0.2	42.8	0.0	42.6	-0.5	42.3	-0.7
1965	42.3	0.0	41.8	-1.2	41.8	0.0	41.8	0.0	42.0	0.5	42.0	0.0	42.3	0.7	42.3	0.0	42.3	0.0	42.5	0.5	42.3	-0.5	42.0	-0.7
1966	42.0	0.0	42.0	0.0	42.0	0.0	42.0	0.0	42.0	0.0	42.0	0.0	42.1	0.2	42.2	0.2	42.1	-0.2	42.3	0.5	42.3	0.0	42.1	-0.5
1967	42.0	-0.2	42.2	0.5	41.9	-0.7	41.9	0.0	41.7	-0.5	41.5	-0.5	41.5	0.0	41.3	-0.5	41.5	0.5	41.8	0.7	41.8	0.0	41.7	-0.2
1968	41.7	0.0	41.6	-0.2	41.7	0.2	41.8	0.2	41.9	0.2	41.8	-0.2	41.8	0.0	42.3	1.2	42.4	0.2	42.5	0.2	42.6	0.2	43.0	0.9
1969	44.2	2.8	44.6	0.9	45.2	1.3	45.6	0.9	45.8	0.4	45.1	-1.5	43.5	-3.5	43.2	-0.7	43.2	0.0	42.9	-0.7	42.9	0.0	42.7	-0.5
1970	42.3	-0.9	42.2	-0.2	42.1	-0.2	42.4	0.7	42.3	-0.2	42.3	0.0	42.2	-0.2	42.1	-0.2	42.0	-0.2	42.0	0.0	42.0	0.0	41.8	-0.5
1971	41.7	-0.2	41.7	0.0	42.2	1.2	42.5	0.7	42.9	0.9	43.2	0.7	43.2	0.0	43.5	0.7	43.5	0.0	43.6	0.2	43.6	0.0	43.6	0.0
1972	43.7	0.2	43.7	0.0	44.1	0.9	44.3	0.5	44.5	0.5	44.5	0.0	44.6	0.2	44.7	0.2	44.8	0.2	44.8	0.0	44.8	0.0	44.8	0.0
1973	44.7	-0.2	45.1	0.9	45.3	0.4	45.6	0.7	46.3	1.5	46.7	0.9	46.8	0.2	47.1	0.6	48.4	2.8	49.2	1.7	49.6	0.8	50.2	1.2
1974	50.8	1.2	50.9	0.2	51.5	1.2	51.6	0.2	52.4	1.6	52.2	-0.4	51.9	-0.6	52.2	0.6	52.3	0.2	51.8	-1.0	50.5	-2.5	50.6	0.2
1975	51.8	2.4	51.9	0.2	51.6	-0.6	51.5	-0.2	52.5	1.9	52.7	0.4	53.2	0.9	53.3	0.2	53.8	0.9	54.8	1.9	54.9	0.2	55.0	0.2
1976	54.8	-0.4	55.6	1.5	57.2	2.9	56.9	-0.5	56.9	0.0	58.3	2.5	59.0	1.2	58.7	-0.5	59.2	0.9	58.9	-0.5	59.4	0.8	60.2	1.3
1977	60.6	0.7	60.3	-0.5	60.9	1.0	62.1	2.0	63.2	1.8	64.2	1.6	65.9	2.6	67.8	2.9	69.6	2.7	70.5	1.3	70.3	-0.3	71.3	1.4
1978	73.1	2.5	75.2	2.9	77.9	3.6	78.8	1.2	79.7	1.1	80.3	0.8	80.6	0.4	79.3	-1.6	78.1	-1.5	79.1	1.3	78.8	-0.4	77.9	-1.1
1979	76.9	-1.3	76.7	-0.3	76.2	-0.7	76.6	0.5	76.5	-0.1	75.5	-1.3	74.3	-1.6	74.8	0.7	76.3	2.0	76.6	0.4	76.7	0.1	77.1	0.5
1980	77.7	0.8	80.0	3.0	83.0	3.8	84.0	1.2	86.4	2.9	87.2	0.9	88.4	1.4	87.8	-0.7	87.8	0.0	88.8	1.1	90.4	1.8	91.7	1.4
1981	91.7	0.0	94.3	2.8	95.2	1.0	97.1	2.0	99.1	2.1	99.1	0.0	98.3	-0.8	97.8	-0.5	97.8	0.0	97.4	-0.4	96.9	-0.5	96.2	-0.7
1982	97.6	1.5	96.6	-1.0	100.1	3.6	98.7	-1.4	100.3	1.6	100.2	-0.1	100.1	-0.1	102.1	2.0	101.6	-0.5	101.1	-0.5	100.6	-0.5	101.1	0.5
1983	100.7	-0.4	100.8	0.1	102.0	1.2	103.1	1.1	104.1	1.0	106.8	2.6	107.0	0.2	105.3	-1.6	105.5	0.2	106.3	0.8	106.4	0.1	104.6	-1.7
1984	105.2	0.6	106.5	1.2	108.0	1.4	111.0	2.8	110.7	-0.3	110.7	0.0	109.8	-0.8	108.5	-1.2	108.3	-0.2	107.6	-0.6	105.9	-1.6	105.8	-0.1
1985	106.6	0.8	107.0	0.4	107.0	0.0	107.5	0.5	108.0	0.5	108.5	0.5	108.5	0.0	108.0	-0.5	108.6	0.6	106.5	-1.9	106.4	-0.1	105.9	-0.5
1986	105.8	-0.1	106.4	0.6	107.4	0.9	108.9	1.4	109.6	0.6	109.6	0.0	109.5	-0.1	109.5	0.0	109.7	0.2	110.7	0.9	109.7	-0.9	109.4	-0.3
1987	109.6	0.2	109.3	-0.3	109.2	-0.1	109.1	-0.1	109.8	0.6	110.2	0.4	111.1	0.8	112.2	1.0	113.2	0.9	113.8	0.5	113.4	-0.4	113.7	0.3
1988	113.7	0.0	114.0	0.3	113.1	-0.8	113.3	0.2	113.4	0.1	114.2	0.7	113.9	-0.3	112.7	-1.1	112.5	-0.2	112.5	0.0	112.7	0.2	113.3	0.5
1989	112.9	-0.4	113.8	0.8	114.2	0.4	115.1	0.8	115.5	0.3	115.8	0.3	116.4	0.5	116.2	-0.2	116.3	0.1	116.6	0.3	117.0	0.3	116.9	-0.1
1990	116.6	-0.3	116.0	-0.5	115.5	-0.4	113.7	-1.6	113.4	-0.3	111.9	-1.3	111.2	-0.6	110.3	-0.8	109.8	-0.5	109.4	-0.4	109.1	-0.3	108.9	-0.2
1991	109.3	0.4	109.8	0.5	111.3	1.4	112.7	1.3	113.5	0.7	113.4	-0.1	114.6	1.1	112.8	-1.6	112.2	-0.5	110.9	-1.2	110.6	-0.3	110.9	0.3

[Continued]

Building Paper & Building Board Mill Products
Producer Price Index
Base 1982 = 100
[Continued]

For 1947-1993. Columns headed % show percentile change in the index from the previous period for which an index is available.

Year	Jan Index	%	Feb Index	%	Mar Index	%	Apr Index	%	May Index	%	Jun Index	%	Jul Index	%	Aug Index	%	Sep Index	%	Oct Index	%	Nov Index	%	Dec Index	%
1992	112.5	1.4	117.1	4.1	119.2	1.8	118.5	-0.6	119.1	0.5	118.9	-0.2	118.8	-0.1	120.0	1.0	123.7	3.1	123.5	-0.2	121.8	-1.4	121.7	-0.1
1993	124.9	2.6	129.0	3.3	133.9	3.8	135.4	1.1	133.8	-1.2	132.0	-1.3	131.2	-0.6	131.6	0.3	135.4	2.9	134.3	-0.8	135.1	0.6	138.1	2.2

Source: U.S. Department of Labor, Bureau of Labor Statistics, Division of Industry Prices and Price Indexes. n.e.c. stands for not elsewhere classified. - indicates no data collected for period or unavailable.

Publications, Printed Matter & Printing Materials
Producer Price Index
Base 1982 = 100

For 1980-1993. Columns headed % show percentile change in the index from the previous period for which an index is available.

Year	Jan Index	%	Feb Index	%	Mar Index	%	Apr Index	%	May Index	%	Jun Index	%	Jul Index	%	Aug Index	%	Sep Index	%	Oct Index	%	Nov Index	%	Dec Index	%
1980	-	-	-	-	-	-	-	-	-	-	-	-	-	-	-	-	-	-	-	-	-	-	84.5	-
1981	88.5	4.7	89.1	0.7	89.5	0.4	90.5	1.1	90.5	0.0	90.6	0.1	91.6	1.1	91.8	0.2	92.7	1.0	93.3	0.6	94.1	0.9	94.5	0.4
1982	97.2	2.9	97.5	0.3	98.2	0.7	99.3	1.1	100.1	0.8	100.2	0.1	100.4	0.2	100.6	0.2	100.9	0.3	101.5	0.6	101.7	0.2	102.4	0.7
1983	104.4	2.0	104.7	0.3	105.1	0.4	105.5	0.4	105.8	0.3	106.2	0.4	106.4	0.2	106.8	0.4	106.9	0.1	107.8	0.8	108.1	0.3	108.3	0.2
1984	110.5	2.0	111.1	0.5	111.4	0.3	111.8	0.4	112.3	0.4	112.6	0.3	112.8	0.2	113.6	0.7	113.7	0.1	113.9	0.2	114.4	0.4	114.7	0.3
1985	116.8	1.8	117.4	0.5	118.0	0.5	118.2	0.2	118.3	0.1	118.5	0.2	118.8	0.3	119.2	0.3	119.2	0.0	119.8	0.5	120.0	0.2	120.0	0.0
1986	122.0	1.7	122.2	0.2	122.1	-0.1	122.7	0.5	122.9	0.2	123.0	0.1	123.2	0.2	123.4	0.2	123.9	0.4	124.4	0.4	124.7	0.2	124.8	0.1
1987	126.4	1.3	127.0	0.5	127.3	0.2	127.4	0.1	127.6	0.2	127.8	0.2	128.0	0.2	128.4	0.3	128.8	0.3	129.5	0.5	129.4	-0.1	129.6	0.2
1988	132.2	2.0	132.8	0.5	133.3	0.4	133.6	0.2	134.0	0.3	134.3	0.2	135.1	0.6	135.2	0.1	135.6	0.3	136.5	0.7	136.9	0.3	137.3	0.3
1989	139.7	1.7	140.5	0.6	140.9	0.3	141.3	0.3	141.5	0.1	142.0	0.4	142.4	0.3	142.9	0.4	143.3	0.3	143.5	0.1	143.8	0.2	143.9	0.1
1990	146.0	1.5	146.6	0.4	147.0	0.3	147.4	0.3	148.0	0.4	148.0	0.0	148.4	0.3	148.7	0.2	149.3	0.4	150.2	0.6	150.7	0.3	150.9	0.1
1991	153.5	1.7	154.1	0.4	154.5	0.3	154.4	-0.1	154.9	0.3	155.0	0.1	154.7	-0.2	155.0	0.2	154.9	-0.1	155.5	0.4	155.8	0.2	155.7	-0.1
1992	158.4	1.7	158.3	-0.1	158.7	0.3	159.0	0.2	159.4	0.3	159.2	-0.1	159.5	0.2	159.8	0.2	160.1	0.2	161.0	0.6	161.0	0.0	161.3	0.2
1993	163.8	1.5	164.3	0.3	164.3	0.0	164.8	0.3	164.9	0.1	164.2	-0.4	164.5	0.2	165.1	0.4	165.5	0.2	165.7	0.1	165.7	0.0	165.9	0.1

Source: U.S. Department of Labor, Bureau of Labor Statistics, Division of Industry Prices and Price Indexes. n.e.c. stands for not elsewhere classified. - indicates no data collected for period or unavailable.

METALS AND METAL PRODUCTS
Producer Price Index
Base 1982 = 100

For 1926-1993. Columns headed % show percentile change in the index from the previous period for which an index is available.

Year	Jan Index	%	Feb Index	%	Mar Index	%	Apr Index	%	May Index	%	Jun Index	%	Jul Index	%	Aug Index	%	Sep Index	%	Oct Index	%	Nov Index	%	Dec Index	%
1926	13.9	-	13.8	-0.7	13.8	0.0	13.7	-0.7	13.6	-0.7	13.6	0.0	13.6	0.0	13.7	0.7	13.8	0.7	13.8	0.0	13.7	-0.7	13.7	0.0
1927	13.2	-3.6	13.0	-1.5	13.0	0.0	13.0	0.0	12.9	-0.8	12.8	-0.8	12.8	0.0	12.9	0.8	12.8	-0.8	12.7	-0.8	12.7	0.0	12.7	0.0
1928	12.7	0.0	12.8	0.8	12.8	0.0	12.8	0.0	12.8	0.0	12.8	0.0	12.8	0.0	12.8	0.0	12.9	0.8	13.0	0.8	13.1	0.8	13.1	0.0
1929	13.2	0.8	13.3	0.8	13.7	3.0	13.6	-0.7	13.4	-1.5	13.4	0.0	13.3	-0.7	13.3	0.0	13.3	0.0	13.3	0.0	13.2	-0.8	13.1	-0.8
1930	12.9	-1.5	12.8	-0.8	12.8	0.0	12.5	-2.3	12.2	-2.4	11.9	-2.5	11.7	-1.7	11.6	-0.9	11.6	0.0	11.4	-1.7	11.4	0.0	11.4	0.0
1931	11.2	-1.8	11.2	0.0	11.2	0.0	11.1	-0.9	10.9	-1.8	10.8	-0.9	10.7	-0.9	10.6	-0.9	10.6	0.0	10.4	-1.9	10.4	0.0	10.3	-1.0
1932	10.2	-1.0	10.0	-2.0	9.9	-1.0	9.9	0.0	9.9	0.0	9.9	0.0	9.6	-3.0	9.8	2.1	10.0	2.0	10.1	1.0	9.9	-2.0	9.8	-1.0
1933	9.7	-1.0	9.5	-2.1	9.5	0.0	9.5	0.0	9.7	2.1	10.0	3.1	10.3	3.0	10.4	1.0	10.6	1.9	10.8	1.9	10.7	-0.9	10.9	1.9
1934	10.9	0.0	11.1	1.8	11.2	0.9	11.3	0.9	11.6	2.7	11.4	-1.7	11.2	-1.8	11.2	0.0	11.2	0.0	11.1	-0.9	11.1	0.0	11.1	0.0
1935	11.1	0.0	11.1	0.0	11.1	0.0	11.1	0.0	11.2	0.9	11.2	0.0	11.2	0.0	11.2	0.0	11.2	0.0	11.1	-0.9	11.1	0.0	11.1	0.0
1936	11.3	0.0	11.3	0.0	11.2	-0.9	11.2	0.0	11.2	0.0	11.2	0.0	11.4	1.8	11.4	0.0	11.5	0.9	11.6	0.9	11.7	0.9	12.0	2.6
1937	12.3	2.5	12.4	0.8	13.4	8.1	13.5	0.7	13.3	-1.5	13.3	0.0	13.3	0.0	13.4	0.8	13.3	-0.7	13.1	-1.5	12.8	-2.3	12.7	-0.8
1938	12.8	0.8	12.6	-1.6	12.6	0.0	12.7	0.8	12.8	0.8	12.6	-1.6	12.4	-1.6	12.5	0.8	12.5	0.0	12.5	0.0	12.6	0.8	12.5	-0.8
1939	12.5	0.0	12.5	0.0	12.5	0.0	12.4	-0.8	12.3	-0.8	12.3	0.0	12.3	0.0	12.3	0.0	12.6	2.4	12.7	0.8	12.7	0.0	12.7	0.0
1940	12.7	0.0	12.6	-0.8	12.6	0.0	12.4	-1.6	12.4	0.0	12.4	0.0	12.4	0.0	12.4	0.0	12.5	0.8	12.6	0.8	12.6	0.0	12.6	0.0
1941	12.6	0.0	12.6	0.0	12.7	0.8	12.7	0.0	12.7	0.0	12.8	0.8	12.8	0.0	12.8	0.0	12.8	0.0	12.8	0.0	12.9	0.8	12.9	0.0
1942	12.9	0.0	12.9	0.0	13.0	0.8	13.0	0.0	13.0	0.0	13.0	0.0	12.9	-0.8	12.9	0.0	13.0	0.8	13.0	0.0	13.0	0.0	12.9	-0.8
1943	12.9	0.0	12.9	0.0	12.9	0.0	12.9	0.0	12.9	0.0	13.0	0.8	12.9	-0.8	12.9	0.0	12.9	0.0	12.9	0.0	12.9	0.0	12.9	0.0
1944	12.9	0.0	12.9	0.0	13.0	0.8	13.0	0.0	12.9	-0.8	12.9	0.0	12.9	0.0	12.9	0.0	12.9	0.0	12.9	0.0	12.9	0.0	12.9	0.0
1945	13.0	0.8	13.0	0.0	13.0	0.0	13.0	0.0	13.0	0.0	13.1	0.8	13.1	0.0	13.1	0.0	13.2	0.8	13.2	0.0	13.3	0.8	13.3	0.0
1946	13.3	0.0	13.5	1.5	13.9	3.0	14.0	0.7	14.1	0.7	14.7	4.3	15.0	2.0	15.1	0.7	15.1	0.0	15.2	0.7	15.7	3.3	16.4	4.5
1947	17.5	6.7	17.6	0.6	17.9	1.7	18.0	0.6	17.8	-1.1	17.9	0.6	18.1	1.1	18.5	2.2	18.6	0.5	18.7	0.5	18.8	0.5	18.9	0.5
1948	19.3	2.1	19.5	1.0	19.7	1.0	20.1	2.0	20.0	-0.5	20.1	0.5	20.5	2.0	21.6	5.4	21.8	0.9	21.9	0.5	22.0	0.5	22.1	0.5
1949	22.2	0.5	21.9	-1.4	21.7	-0.9	21.1	-2.8	20.6	-2.4	20.3	-1.5	20.3	0.0	20.4	0.5	20.5	0.5	20.5	0.0	20.6	0.5	20.6	0.0
1950	20.8	1.0	20.9	0.5	20.9	0.0	21.0	0.5	21.3	1.4	21.7	1.9	21.8	0.5	22.1	1.4	22.6	2.3	23.1	2.2	23.5	1.7	24.3	3.4
1951	24.7	1.6	24.7	0.0	24.6	-0.4	24.6	0.0	24.6	0.0	24.4	-0.8	24.4	0.0	24.3	-0.4	24.3	0.0	24.4	0.4	24.4	0.0	24.4	0.0
1952	24.4	0.0	24.4	0.0	24.4	0.0	24.4	0.0	24.3	-0.4	24.1	-0.8	24.3	0.8	24.7	1.6	24.8	0.4	24.7	-0.4	24.7	0.0	24.7	0.0
1953	24.7	0.0	24.8	0.4	25.0	0.8	24.9	-0.4	25.0	0.4	25.3	1.2	25.8	2.0	25.8	0.0	25.6	-0.8	25.5	-0.4	25.5	0.0	25.4	-0.4
1954	25.4	0.0	25.2	-0.8	25.2	0.0	25.3	0.4	25.3	0.0	25.3	0.0	25.5	0.8	25.6	0.4	25.7	0.4	25.9	0.8	25.9	0.0	25.9	0.0
1955	25.9	0.0	26.2	1.2	26.3	0.4	26.5	0.8	26.4	-0.4	26.4	0.0	27.3	3.4	27.8	1.8	28.3	1.8	28.4	0.4	28.5	0.4	28.7	0.7
1956	28.9	0.7	28.9	0.0	29.2	1.0	29.4	0.7	29.2	-0.7	29.1	-0.3	28.9	-0.7	29.9	3.5	30.3	1.3	30.3	0.0	30.3	0.0	30.4	0.3
1957	30.3	-0.3	30.2	-0.3	30.1	-0.3	29.9	-0.7	29.9	0.0	30.0	0.3	30.4	1.3	30.5	0.3	30.3	-0.7	30.1	-0.7	30.0	-0.3	30.0	0.0
1958	29.9	-0.3	29.9	0.0	29.9	0.0	29.6	-1.0	29.6	0.0	29.6	0.0	29.6	0.0	30.1	1.7	30.2	0.3	30.3	0.3	30.5	0.7	30.5	0.0
1959	30.5	0.0	30.6	0.3	30.6	0.0	30.5	-0.3	30.5	0.0	30.6	0.3	30.4	-0.7	30.5	0.3	30.6	0.3	30.8	0.7	31.1	1.0	30.9	-0.6
1960	31.0	0.3	30.9	-0.3	30.8	-0.3	30.8	0.0	30.7	-0.3	30.6	-0.3	30.6	0.0	30.6	0.0	30.6	0.0	30.5	-0.3	30.4	-0.3	30.3	-0.3
1961	30.3	0.0	30.4	0.3	30.4	0.0	30.4	0.0	30.5	0.3	30.5	0.0	30.5	0.0	30.6	0.3	30.6	0.0	30.5	-0.3	30.4	-0.3	30.4	0.0
1962	30.5	0.3	30.4	-0.3	30.4	0.0	30.3	-0.3	30.3	0.0	30.2	-0.3	30.2	0.0	30.2	0.0	30.2	0.0	30.1	-0.3	30.0	-0.3	30.0	0.0
1963	30.1	0.3	30.1	0.0	30.1	0.0	30.1	0.0	30.2	0.3	30.2	0.0	30.2	0.0	30.3	0.3	30.3	0.0	30.5	0.7	30.6	0.3	30.6	0.0
1964	30.8	0.7	30.8	0.0	30.9	0.3	30.9	0.0	30.9	0.0	30.9	0.0	31.0	0.3	31.2	0.6	31.2	0.0	31.4	0.6	31.6	0.6	31.7	0.3
1965	31.6	-0.3	31.6	0.0	31.7	0.3	31.8	0.3	32.0	0.6	32.0	0.0	32.0	0.0	32.1	0.3	32.1	0.0	32.2	0.3	32.3	0.3	32.3	0.0
1966	32.4	0.3	32.5	0.3	32.7	0.6	32.7	0.0	32.8	0.3	32.9	0.3	32.9	0.0	32.8	-0.3	32.8	0.0	32.9	0.3	33.0	0.3	33.0	0.0
1967	33.1	0.3	33.2	0.3	33.1	-0.3	33.0	-0.3	33.0	0.0	33.0	0.0	33.0	0.0	33.0	0.0	33.2	0.6	33.3	0.3	33.6	0.9	33.7	0.3
1968	34.0	0.9	34.3	0.9	34.4	0.3	34.2	-0.6	33.8	-1.2	33.8	0.0	33.7	-0.3	33.7	0.0	33.9	0.6	34.0	0.3	34.0	0.0	34.1	0.3
1969	34.6	1.5	34.8	0.6	35.0	0.6	35.2	0.6	35.5	0.9	35.7	0.6	35.9	0.6	36.4	1.4	36.8	1.1	37.0	0.5	37.1	0.3	37.5	1.1
1970	37.8	0.8	38.2	1.1	38.4	0.5	38.7	0.8	38.9	0.5	39.1	0.5	39.0	-0.3	38.9	-0.3	38.9	0.0	39.0	0.3	38.7	-0.8	38.5	-0.5

[Continued]

METALS AND METAL PRODUCTS
Producer Price Index
Base 1982 = 100
[Continued]

For 1926-1993. Columns headed % show percentile change in the index from the previous period for which an index is available.

Year	Jan Index	%	Feb Index	%	Mar Index	%	Apr Index	%	May Index	%	Jun Index	%	Jul Index	%	Aug Index	%	Sep Index	%	Oct Index	%	Nov Index	%	Dec Index	%
1971	38.6	0.3	38.5	-0.3	38.5	0.0	38.9	1.0	39.1	0.5	39.2	0.3	39.5	0.8	40.1	1.5	40.1	0.0	40.0	-0.2	40.0	0.0	39.9	-0.2
1972	40.3	1.0	40.6	0.7	40.9	0.7	40.9	0.0	41.0	0.2	41.0	0.0	40.9	-0.2	41.0	0.2	41.1	0.2	41.1	0.0	41.2	0.2	41.2	0.0
1973	41.6	1.0	42.1	1.2	42.8	1.7	43.3	1.2	43.7	0.9	43.9	0.5	44.0	0.2	44.3	0.7	44.5	0.5	45.1	1.3	45.9	1.8	47.0	2.4
1974	48.1	2.3	49.1	2.1	51.3	4.5	53.4	4.1	55.9	4.7	57.7	3.2	59.8	3.6	61.5	2.8	62.0	0.8	62.0	0.0	61.9	-0.2	61.2	-1.1
1975	61.5	0.5	61.8	0.5	61.7	-0.2	61.6	-0.2	61.4	-0.3	61.2	-0.3	60.8	-0.7	61.1	0.5	61.5	0.7	62.1	1.0	62.0	-0.2	62.0	0.0
1976	62.3	0.5	62.7	0.6	63.2	0.8	64.0	1.3	64.4	0.6	65.2	1.2	65.9	1.1	66.2	0.5	66.3	0.2	66.3	0.0	66.3	0.0	66.6	0.5
1977	67.0	0.6	67.4	0.6	68.5	1.6	69.0	0.7	69.1	0.1	68.9	-0.3	69.8	1.3	70.2	0.6	70.5	0.4	70.2	-0.4	70.3	0.1	70.7	0.6
1978	71.4	1.0	72.6	1.7	73.3	1.0	74.2	1.2	74.5	0.4	74.9	0.5	75.4	0.7	76.6	1.6	76.7	0.1	77.6	1.2	78.1	0.6	78.5	0.5
1979	80.2	2.2	82.0	2.2	83.5	1.8	84.9	1.7	84.9	0.0	85.6	0.8	86.5	1.1	86.8	0.3	87.4	0.7	89.4	2.3	89.9	0.6	90.7	0.9
1980	94.3	4.0	95.8	1.6	95.1	-0.7	94.3	-0.8	93.4	-1.0	93.5	0.1	93.7	0.2	94.5	0.9	95.3	0.8	96.8	1.6	96.5	-0.3	96.4	-0.1
1981	97.5	1.1	97.5	0.0	98.3	0.8	99.1	0.8	99.2	0.1	98.9	-0.3	100.1	1.2	100.8	0.7	101.1	0.3	101.2	0.1	100.9	-0.3	100.5	-0.4
1982	101.0	0.5	100.9	-0.1	100.4	-0.5	100.5	0.1	100.4	-0.1	99.2	-1.2	99.3	0.1	99.2	-0.1	100.0	0.8	100.0	0.0	99.6	-0.4	99.4	-0.2
1983	99.6	0.2	101.0	1.4	100.9	-0.1	101.0	0.1	101.5	0.5	101.5	0.0	101.9	0.4	102.2	0.3	103.0	0.8	103.1	0.1	103.1	0.0	103.4	0.3
1984	103.7	0.3	104.4	0.7	105.0	0.6	105.4	0.4	105.2	-0.2	105.2	0.0	104.8	-0.4	104.8	0.0	104.7	-0.1	104.8	0.1	104.9	0.1	104.6	-0.3
1985	104.4	-0.2	104.6	0.2	104.6	0.0	105.0	0.4	104.9	-0.1	104.4	-0.5	104.3	-0.1	104.3	0.0	104.2	-0.1	104.2	0.0	103.9	-0.3	103.9	0.0
1986	103.1	-0.8	103.2	0.1	103.2	0.0	103.1	-0.1	103.0	-0.1	103.0	0.0	102.9	-0.1	103.1	0.2	103.3	0.2	103.4	0.1	103.4	0.0	103.3	-0.1
1987	103.7	0.4	103.8	0.1	104.0	0.2	104.4	0.4	105.2	0.8	105.8	0.6	106.7	0.9	107.7	0.9	108.8	1.0	110.8	1.8	111.7	0.8	112.9	1.1
1988	114.4	1.3	114.7	0.3	115.4	0.6	116.9	1.3	117.4	0.4	118.0	0.5	119.2	1.0	119.8	0.5	120.2	0.3	121.4	1.0	122.8	1.2	124.0	1.0
1989	125.3	1.0	125.1	-0.2	125.6	0.4	125.6	0.0	125.2	-0.3	124.0	-1.0	123.0	-0.8	123.0	0.0	123.7	0.6	123.9	0.2	122.8	-0.9	121.7	-0.9
1990	121.7	0.0	120.9	-0.7	122.0	0.9	122.9	0.7	123.1	0.2	122.6	-0.4	122.9	0.2	124.2	1.1	124.6	0.3	124.5	-0.1	123.3	-1.0	122.4	-0.7
1991	122.4	0.0	121.9	-0.4	121.5	-0.3	121.3	-0.2	120.5	-0.7	119.7	-0.7	119.6	-0.1	119.5	-0.1	119.5	0.0	119.3	-0.2	118.9	-0.3	118.7	-0.2
1992	118.2	-0.4	118.9	0.6	119.4	0.4	119.6	0.2	119.5	-0.1	119.6	0.1	120.0	0.3	120.2	0.2	119.6	-0.5	118.8	-0.7	118.2	-0.5	118.5	0.3
1993	118.9	0.3	119.2	0.3	119.0	-0.2	118.7	-0.3	118.4	-0.3	118.9	0.4	119.5	0.5	119.5	0.0	119.5	0.0	119.4	-0.1	119.5	0.1	120.2	0.6

Source: U.S. Department of Labor, Bureau of Labor Statistics, Division of Industry Prices and Price Indexes. n.e.c. stands for not elsewhere classified. - indicates no data collected for period or unavailable.

Iron and Steel

Producer Price Index

Base 1982 = 100

For 1926-1993. Columns headed % show percentile change in the index from the previous period for which an index is available.

Year	Jan Index	%	Feb Index	%	Mar Index	%	Apr Index	%	May Index	%	Jun Index	%	Jul Index	%	Aug Index	%	Sep Index	%	Oct Index	%	Nov Index	%	Dec Index	%
1926	11.4	-	11.4	0.0	11.4	0.0	11.3	-0.9	11.3	0.0	11.2	-0.9	11.2	0.0	11.2	0.0	11.3	0.9	11.3	0.0	11.3	0.0	11.2	-0.9
1927	10.9	-2.7	10.7	-1.8	10.7	0.0	10.7	0.0	10.7	0.0	10.7	0.0	10.6	-0.9	10.6	0.0	10.6	0.0	10.5	-0.9	10.5	0.0	10.4	-1.0
1928	10.5	1.0	10.6	1.0	10.6	0.0	10.6	0.0	10.6	0.0	10.5	-0.9	10.5	0.0	10.5	0.0	10.5	0.0	10.6	1.0	10.6	0.0	10.7	0.9
1929	10.7	0.0	10.7	0.0	10.7	0.0	10.8	0.9	10.8	0.0	10.8	0.0	10.8	0.0	10.7	-0.9	10.7	0.0	10.7	0.0	10.6	-0.9	10.6	0.0
1930	10.4	-1.9	10.3	-1.0	10.3	0.0	10.2	-1.0	10.2	0.0	10.1	-1.0	10.0	-1.0	9.9	-1.0	9.9	0.0	9.9	0.0	9.8	-1.0	9.8	0.0
1931	9.6	-2.0	9.7	1.0	9.6	-1.0	9.5	-1.0	9.5	0.0	9.4	-1.1	9.4	0.0	9.3	-1.1	9.3	0.0	9.2	-1.1	9.2	0.0	9.1	-1.1
1932	9.0	-1.1	9.0	0.0	9.0	0.0	9.1	1.1	9.0	-1.1	9.0	0.0	8.7	-3.3	8.9	2.3	9.0	1.1	9.1	1.1	9.0	-1.1	8.9	-1.1
1933	8.8	-1.1	8.7	-1.1	8.6	-1.1	8.6	0.0	8.5	-1.2	8.6	1.2	8.8	2.3	8.9	1.1	9.1	2.2	9.3	2.2	9.2	-1.1	9.4	2.2
1934	9.4	0.0	9.7	3.2	9.8	1.0	9.9	1.0	10.2	3.0	10.0	-2.0	9.8	-2.0	9.8	0.0	9.8	0.0	9.7	-1.0	9.7	0.0	9.7	0.0
1935	9.7	0.0	9.7	0.0	9.7	0.0	9.7	0.0	9.8	1.0	9.9	1.0	9.8	-1.0	9.9	1.0	9.8	-1.0	9.8	0.0	9.8	0.0	9.8	0.0
1936	9.9	1.0	9.8	-1.0	9.8	0.0	9.8	0.0	9.7	-1.0	9.7	0.0	9.9	2.1	9.9	0.0	10.0	1.0	10.1	1.0	10.1	0.0	10.2	1.0
1937	10.4	2.0	10.4	0.0	11.0	5.8	11.2	1.8	11.2	0.0	11.2	0.0	11.3	0.9	11.3	0.0	11.3	0.0	11.2	-0.9	11.2	0.0	11.2	0.0
1938	11.2	0.0	11.2	0.0	11.2	0.0	11.3	0.9	11.5	1.8	11.4	-0.9	11.0	-3.5	11.0	0.0	11.0	0.0	10.9	-0.9	11.0	0.9	10.9	-0.9
1939	10.9	0.0	10.9	0.0	10.9	0.0	10.9	0.0	10.8	-0.9	10.7	-0.9	10.7	0.0	10.7	0.0	10.8	0.9	10.9	0.9	10.9	0.0	10.9	0.0
1940	10.9	0.0	10.9	0.0	10.9	0.0	10.6	-2.8	10.6	0.0	10.6	0.0	10.7	0.9	10.7	0.0	10.7	0.0	10.7	0.0	10.8	0.9	10.8	0.0
1941	10.8	0.0	10.8	0.0	10.8	0.0	10.8	0.0	10.9	0.9	10.9	0.0	10.9	0.0	11.0	0.9	11.0	0.0	11.0	0.0	11.0	0.0	11.0	0.0
1942	11.0	0.0	11.0	0.0	11.0	0.0	11.0	0.0	11.0	0.0	11.0	0.0	11.0	0.0	11.0	0.0	11.0	0.0	11.0	0.0	11.0	0.0	11.0	0.0
1943	11.0	0.0	11.0	0.0	11.0	0.0	11.0	0.0	11.0	0.0	11.0	0.0	11.0	0.0	11.0	0.0	11.0	0.0	11.0	0.0	11.0	0.0	11.0	0.0
1944	11.0	0.0	11.0	0.0	11.0	0.0	11.0	0.0	11.0	0.0	11.0	0.0	11.0	0.0	11.0	0.0	11.0	0.0	11.0	0.0	11.0	0.0	11.0	0.0
1945	11.1	0.9	11.1	0.0	11.1	0.0	11.1	0.0	11.1	0.0	11.2	0.9	11.2	0.0	11.2	0.0	11.2	0.0	11.3	0.9	11.3	0.0	11.4	0.9
1946	11.4	0.0	11.7	2.6	12.1	3.4	12.1	0.0	12.2	0.8	12.4	1.6	12.6	1.6	12.8	1.6	12.8	0.0	12.8	0.0	12.9	0.8	13.3	3.1
1947	14.4	8.3	14.5	0.7	14.7	1.4	14.7	0.0	14.4	-2.0	14.5	0.7	14.9	2.8	15.8	6.0	15.7	-0.6	15.9	1.3	15.9	0.0	16.0	0.6
1948	16.5	3.1	16.7	1.2	16.8	0.6	16.9	0.6	16.8	-0.6	16.8	0.0	17.2	2.4	18.5	7.6	18.5	0.0	18.6	0.5	18.7	0.5	18.8	0.5
1949	18.8	0.0	18.4	-2.1	18.3	-0.5	17.7	-3.3	17.4	-1.7	17.4	0.0	17.3	-0.6	17.4	0.0	17.7	1.7	17.8	0.6	17.9	0.6	18.1	1.1
1950	18.3	1.1	18.5	1.1	18.5	0.0	18.5	0.0	18.7	1.1	19.1	2.1	19.0	-0.5	19.2	1.1	19.3	0.5	19.4	0.5	19.6	1.0	20.6	5.1
1951	21.0	1.9	20.8	-1.0	20.7	-0.5	20.7	0.0	20.7	0.0	20.7	0.0	20.7	0.0	20.7	0.0	20.7	0.0	20.7	0.0	20.7	0.0	20.7	0.0
1952	20.7	0.0	20.8	0.5	20.8	0.0	20.7	-0.5	20.7	0.0	20.6	-0.5	20.6	0.0	21.4	3.9	21.5	0.5	21.4	-0.5	21.4	0.0	21.4	0.0
1953	21.4	0.0	21.5	0.5	21.5	0.0	21.5	0.0	21.7	0.9	22.0	1.4	22.9	4.1	22.9	0.0	22.7	-0.9	22.5	-0.9	22.5	0.0	22.4	-0.4
1954	22.2	-0.9	22.1	-0.5	22.0	-0.5	22.1	0.5	22.2	0.5	22.2	0.0	22.5	1.4	22.5	0.0	22.6	0.4	22.7	0.4	22.8	0.4	22.7	-0.4
1955	22.9	0.9	22.9	0.0	22.9	0.0	23.0	0.4	22.8	-0.9	22.9	0.4	24.1	5.2	24.4	1.2	24.4	0.0	24.5	0.4	24.6	0.4	24.8	0.8
1956	25.2	1.6	25.1	-0.4	25.2	0.4	25.4	0.8	25.4	0.0	25.2	-0.8	25.2	0.0	26.8	6.3	27.2	1.5	27.1	-0.4	27.4	1.1	27.5	0.4
1957	27.7	0.7	27.6	-0.4	27.6	0.0	27.3	-1.1	27.5	0.7	27.9	1.5	28.7	2.9	28.8	0.3	28.7	-0.3	28.3	-1.4	28.1	-0.7	28.1	0.0
1958	28.1	0.0	28.3	0.7	28.2	-0.4	28.1	-0.4	28.0	-0.4	28.1	0.4	28.1	0.0	28.9	2.8	28.9	0.0	28.9	0.0	29.0	0.3	28.9	-0.3
1959	29.0	0.3	29.1	0.3	29.0	-0.3	28.8	-0.7	28.7	-0.3	28.9	0.7	28.9	0.0	29.0	0.3	29.1	0.3	29.1	0.0	29.2	0.3	29.0	-0.7
1960	29.1	0.3	28.9	-0.7	28.7	-0.7	28.7	0.0	28.7	0.0	28.6	-0.3	28.6	0.0	28.6	0.0	28.6	0.0	28.4	-0.7	28.4	0.0	28.4	0.0
1961	28.5	0.4	28.6	0.4	28.7	0.3	28.8	0.3	28.7	-0.3	28.7	0.0	28.6	-0.3	28.7	0.3	28.8	0.3	28.7	-0.3	28.5	-0.7	28.5	0.0
1962	28.6	0.4	28.6	0.0	28.4	-0.7	28.3	-0.4	28.3	0.0	28.2	-0.4	28.2	0.0	28.2	0.0	28.2	0.0	28.1	-0.4	28.0	-0.4	28.1	0.4
1963	28.1	0.0	28.1	0.0	28.0	-0.4	28.1	0.4	28.3	0.7	28.2	-0.4	28.2	0.0	28.2	0.0	28.2	0.0	28.4	0.7	28.4	0.0	28.5	0.4
1964	28.5	0.0	28.5	0.0	28.5	0.0	28.5	0.0	28.6	0.4	28.6	0.0	28.7	0.3	28.8	0.3	28.6	-0.7	28.7	0.3	28.7	0.0	28.8	0.3
1965	28.9	0.3	28.8	-0.3	28.8	0.0	28.9	0.3	28.9	0.0	28.8	-0.3	28.9	0.3	28.9	0.0	28.8	-0.3	28.8	0.0	28.8	0.0	29.0	0.7
1966	29.1	0.3	29.1	0.0	29.1	0.0	29.1	0.0	29.0	-0.3	29.1	0.3	29.1	0.0	29.2	0.3	29.2	0.0	29.2	0.0	29.3	0.3	29.3	0.0
1967	29.4	0.3	29.4	0.0	29.5	0.3	29.4	-0.3	29.4	0.0	29.4	0.0	29.4	0.0	29.4	0.0	29.6	0.7	29.6	0.0	29.7	0.3	29.8	0.3
1968	30.1	1.0	30.1	0.0	30.0	-0.3	29.9	-0.3	29.9	0.0	29.9	0.0	29.9	0.0	29.9	0.0	30.4	1.7	30.4	0.0	30.2	-0.7	30.2	0.0
1969	30.6	1.3	30.7	0.3	30.9	0.7	31.0	0.3	31.3	1.0	31.4	0.3	31.6	0.6	32.1	1.6	32.2	0.3	32.4	0.6	32.4	0.0	32.5	0.3
1970	32.7	0.6	33.3	1.8	33.5	0.6	33.4	-0.3	33.9	1.5	34.3	1.2	34.3	0.0	34.2	-0.3	34.4	0.6	34.6	0.6	34.3	-0.9	34.3	0.0

[Continued]

Iron and Steel
Producer Price Index
Base 1982 = 100
[Continued]

For 1926-1993. Columns headed % show percentile change in the index from the previous period for which an index is available.

Year	Jan Index	%	Feb Index	%	Mar Index	%	Apr Index	%	May Index	%	Jun Index	%	Jul Index	%	Aug Index	%	Sep Index	%	Oct Index	%	Nov Index	%	Dec Index	%
1971	34.6	0.9	34.8	0.6	34.8	0.0	34.9	0.3	35.4	1.4	35.5	0.3	36.0	1.4	37.0	2.8	37.1	0.3	37.1	0.0	37.0	-0.3	37.0	0.0
1972	37.4	1.1	37.8	1.1	37.9	0.3	37.8	-0.3	37.8	0.0	37.8	0.0	37.8	0.0	37.9	0.3	38.0	0.3	38.0	0.0	38.1	0.3	38.2	0.3
1973	38.9	1.8	39.2	0.8	39.3	0.3	39.5	0.5	39.9	1.0	40.1	0.5	40.1	0.0	40.1	0.0	40.3	0.5	40.9	1.5	41.8	2.2	42.0	0.5
1974	42.7	1.7	43.9	2.8	46.5	5.9	48.6	4.5	49.9	2.7	52.5	5.2	56.2	7.0	57.7	2.7	58.4	1.2	58.7	0.5	58.9	0.3	58.0	-1.5
1975	58.8	1.4	59.1	0.5	59.2	0.2	59.3	0.2	59.2	-0.2	58.8	-0.7	58.2	-1.0	58.5	0.5	59.1	1.0	60.4	2.2	60.2	-0.3	60.3	0.2
1976	60.8	0.8	61.8	1.6	62.4	1.0	62.9	0.8	62.9	0.0	64.4	2.4	64.9	0.8	64.9	0.0	64.5	-0.6	64.5	0.0	64.6	0.2	65.7	1.7
1977	66.1	0.6	66.3	0.3	67.1	1.2	67.3	0.3	67.2	-0.1	66.9	-0.4	68.5	2.4	68.8	0.4	69.6	1.2	69.1	-0.7	68.9	-0.3	69.5	0.9
1978	70.2	1.0	72.2	2.8	73.0	1.1	74.3	1.8	74.3	0.0	74.5	0.3	74.9	0.5	76.3	1.9	76.3	0.0	76.7	0.5	77.2	0.7	77.6	0.5
1979	80.3	3.5	81.1	1.0	82.6	1.8	82.6	0.0	82.4	-0.2	83.5	1.3	84.6	1.3	84.4	-0.2	84.2	-0.2	85.3	1.3	86.1	0.9	86.4	0.3
1980	87.7	1.5	88.6	1.0	89.0	0.5	90.6	1.8	89.9	-0.8	89.5	-0.4	88.7	-0.9	89.3	0.7	89.8	0.6	91.6	2.0	92.2	0.7	93.3	1.2
1981	95.3	2.1	95.3	0.0	96.8	1.6	97.6	0.8	97.5	-0.1	97.4	-0.1	99.9	2.6	100.3	0.4	100.2	-0.1	100.7	0.5	100.3	-0.4	100.3	0.0
1982	101.2	0.9	101.1	-0.1	101.0	-0.1	101.1	0.1	100.7	-0.4	99.8	-0.9	99.5	-0.3	99.4	-0.1	99.3	-0.1	99.6	0.3	99.1	-0.5	98.2	-0.9
1983	98.3	0.1	100.3	2.0	100.8	0.5	100.7	-0.1	100.6	-0.1	100.7	0.1	100.9	0.2	101.2	0.3	102.7	1.5	102.8	0.1	103.1	0.3	103.5	0.4
1984	104.4	0.9	105.1	0.7	105.1	0.0	105.1	0.0	105.4	0.3	105.3	-0.1	105.4	0.1	105.4	0.0	105.6	0.2	105.7	0.1	105.5	-0.2	105.3	-0.2
1985	105.3	0.0	105.4	0.1	105.5	0.1	105.4	-0.1	105.0	-0.4	104.6	-0.4	104.5	-0.1	104.6	0.1	104.6	0.0	104.5	-0.1	104.1	-0.4	104.1	0.0
1986	101.0	-3.0	101.1	0.1	100.8	-0.3	101.0	0.2	101.2	0.2	101.1	-0.1	101.1	0.0	101.2	0.1	101.4	0.2	101.4	0.0	101.3	-0.1	101.3	0.0
1987	102.0	0.7	102.3	0.3	101.9	-0.4	101.9	0.0	102.2	0.3	102.5	0.3	103.1	0.6	103.7	0.6	105.4	1.6	109.5	3.9	110.4	0.8	109.9	-0.5
1988	110.9	0.9	113.0	1.9	113.6	0.5	114.8	1.1	115.0	0.2	114.9	-0.1	117.0	1.8	118.0	0.9	117.4	-0.5	118.3	0.8	117.6	-0.6	117.6	0.0
1989	119.7	1.8	120.6	0.8	120.7	0.1	120.8	0.1	120.6	-0.2	119.8	-0.7	119.0	-0.7	118.4	-0.5	118.1	-0.3	117.8	-0.3	116.9	-0.8	116.5	-0.3
1990	116.7	0.2	116.2	-0.4	116.5	0.3	117.1	0.5	117.9	0.7	117.4	-0.4	117.5	0.1	118.2	0.6	117.9	-0.3	117.5	-0.3	116.9	-0.5	116.8	-0.1
1991	117.0	0.2	116.6	-0.3	115.8	-0.7	115.4	-0.3	114.5	-0.8	113.5	-0.9	113.3	-0.2	113.0	-0.3	112.8	-0.2	112.4	-0.4	112.3	-0.1	112.3	0.0
1992	112.1	-0.2	112.3	0.2	112.7	0.4	112.3	-0.4	112.2	-0.1	111.4	-0.7	111.4	0.0	111.2	-0.2	111.0	-0.2	110.3	-0.6	110.1	-0.2	110.6	0.5
1993	111.9	1.2	113.1	1.1	113.4	0.3	113.5	0.1	114.2	0.6	115.6	1.2	116.5	0.8	116.7	0.2	117.2	0.4	119.1	1.6	119.9	0.7	120.9	0.8

Source: U.S. Department of Labor, Bureau of Labor Statistics, Division of Industry Prices and Price Indexes. n.e.c. stands for not elsewhere classified. - indicates no data collected for period or unavailable.

Nonferrous Metals
Producer Price Index
Base 1982 = 100

For 1926-1993. Columns headed % show percentile change in the index from the previous period for which an index is available.

Year	Jan Index	%	Feb Index	%	Mar Index	%	Apr Index	%	May Index	%	Jun Index	%	Jul Index	%	Aug Index	%	Sep Index	%	Oct Index	%	Nov Index	%	Dec Index	%
1926	16.8	-	16.8	0.0	16.6	-1.2	16.2	-2.4	16.0	-1.2	16.1	0.6	16.5	2.5	16.8	1.8	16.8	0.0	16.6	-1.2	16.4	-1.2	16.0	-2.4
1927	15.7	-1.9	15.5	-1.3	15.8	1.9	15.5	-1.9	15.2	-1.9	15.0	-1.3	14.9	-0.7	15.4	3.4	15.1	-1.9	15.0	-0.7	15.1	0.7	15.4	2.0
1928	15.3	-0.6	15.1	-1.3	15.0	-0.7	15.2	1.3	15.3	0.7	15.4	0.7	15.4	0.0	15.4	0.0	15.6	1.3	15.9	1.9	16.2	1.9	16.2	0.0
1929	16.7	3.1	17.4	4.2	19.3	10.9	18.6	-3.6	17.4	-6.5	17.4	0.0	17.4	0.0	17.4	0.0	17.3	-0.6	17.3	0.0	17.0	-1.7	16.8	-1.2
1930	16.7	-0.6	16.7	0.0	16.4	-1.8	15.1	-7.9	13.5	-10.6	13.2	-2.2	12.4	-6.1	12.3	-0.8	12.1	-1.6	11.5	-5.0	11.6	0.9	11.8	1.7
1931	11.5	-2.5	11.3	-1.7	11.4	0.9	11.1	-2.6	10.4	-6.3	10.1	-2.9	10.1	0.0	9.9	-2.0	9.7	-2.0	9.1	-6.2	9.0	-1.1	8.9	-1.1
1932	9.1	2.2	8.7	-4.4	8.3	-4.6	8.1	-2.4	7.9	-2.5	7.9	0.0	7.7	-2.5	8.0	3.9	8.5	6.3	8.3	-2.4	8.1	-2.4	7.9	-2.5
1933	7.7	-2.5	7.6	-1.3	7.9	3.9	8.1	2.5	9.3	14.8	10.4	11.8	11.2	7.7	11.2	0.0	11.3	0.9	11.0	-2.7	11.2	1.8	11.0	-1.8
1934	10.9	-0.9	10.8	-0.9	10.9	0.9	11.2	2.8	11.2	0.0	11.3	0.9	11.3	0.0	11.3	0.0	11.3	0.0	11.2	-0.9	11.2	0.0	11.1	-0.9
1935	11.2	0.9	11.1	-0.9	11.1	0.0	11.2	0.9	11.4	1.8	11.4	0.0	10.9	-4.4	11.0	0.9	11.3	2.7	11.7	3.5	11.8	0.9	11.6	-1.7
1936	11.5	-0.9	11.5	0.0	11.5	0.0	11.6	0.9	11.7	0.9	11.5	-1.7	11.6	0.9	11.7	0.9	11.8	0.9	11.8	0.0	12.4	5.1	13.0	4.8
1937	14.0	7.7	14.8	5.7	16.7	12.8	16.0	-4.2	15.1	-5.6	15.1	0.0	15.3	1.3	15.4	0.7	15.3	-0.6	14.1	-7.8	12.9	-8.5	12.4	-3.9
1938	12.4	0.0	11.9	-4.0	11.8	-0.8	11.7	-0.8	11.3	-3.4	11.1	-1.8	11.8	6.3	12.0	1.7	12.1	0.8	12.6	4.1	12.8	1.6	12.7	-0.8
1939	12.6	-0.8	12.6	0.0	12.6	0.0	12.3	-2.4	12.1	-1.6	12.0	-0.8	12.1	0.8	12.3	1.7	14.0	13.8	14.1	0.7	14.0	-0.7	13.9	-0.7
1940	13.6	-2.2	13.0	-4.4	13.2	1.5	13.0	-1.5	13.2	1.5	13.4	1.5	13.4	0.0	13.0	-3.0	13.3	2.3	13.8	3.8	13.8	0.0	13.7	-0.7
1941	13.8	0.7	13.8	0.0	13.9	0.7	13.9	0.0	13.9	0.0	13.9	0.0	14.0	0.7	13.9	-0.7	13.9	0.0	13.9	0.0	14.0	0.7	14.0	0.0
1942	14.1	0.7	14.1	0.0	14.1	0.0	14.1	0.0	14.1	0.0	14.1	0.0	14.1	0.0	14.1	0.0	14.2	0.7	14.2	0.0	14.2	0.0	14.2	0.0
1943	14.2	0.0	14.2	0.0	14.2	0.0	14.2	0.0	14.2	0.0	14.2	0.0	14.2	0.0	14.2	0.0	14.2	0.0	14.2	0.0	14.2	0.0	14.2	0.0
1944	14.1	-0.7	14.1	0.0	14.1	0.0	14.1	0.0	14.1	0.0	14.1	0.0	14.1	0.0	14.1	0.0	14.1	0.0	14.1	0.0	14.1	0.0	14.1	0.0
1945	14.1	0.0	14.2	0.7	14.1	-0.7	14.1	0.0	14.1	0.0	14.1	0.0	14.1	0.0	14.1	0.0	14.1	0.0	14.1	0.0	14.1	0.0	14.1	0.0
1946	14.1	0.0	14.1	0.0	14.2	0.7	14.4	1.4	14.6	1.4	16.4	12.3	16.9	3.0	16.7	-1.2	16.7	0.0	16.8	0.6	19.5	16.1	21.3	9.2
1947	21.5	0.9	21.7	0.9	22.6	4.1	22.8	0.9	22.8	0.0	22.7	-0.4	22.5	-0.9	22.5	0.0	22.5	0.0	22.5	0.0	22.5	0.0	22.8	1.3
1948	23.0	0.9	23.2	0.9	23.2	0.0	23.6	1.7	23.6	0.0	23.9	1.3	24.6	2.9	26.1	6.1	26.1	0.0	26.3	0.8	27.0	2.7	27.1	0.4
1949	27.0	-0.4	26.8	-0.7	26.1	-2.6	24.4	-6.5	22.4	-8.2	21.2	-5.4	21.4	0.9	21.9	2.3	21.9	0.0	21.5	-1.8	21.7	0.9	21.4	-1.4
1950	21.4	0.0	21.3	-0.5	21.2	-0.5	21.4	0.9	22.4	4.7	23.9	6.7	24.1	0.8	24.9	3.3	26.4	6.0	27.9	5.7	28.9	3.6	29.1	0.7
1951	29.6	1.7	29.7	0.3	29.4	-1.0	29.5	0.3	29.4	-0.3	28.9	-1.7	28.5	-1.4	28.5	0.0	28.6	0.4	29.1	1.7	29.1	0.0	29.1	0.0
1952	29.1	0.0	29.3	0.7	29.3	0.0	29.3	0.0	28.6	-2.4	28.1	-1.7	29.1	3.6	29.2	0.3	29.2	0.0	28.8	-1.4	28.8	0.0	28.7	-0.3
1953	28.8	0.3	29.2	1.4	30.8	5.5	30.1	-2.3	29.7	-1.3	29.9	0.7	29.7	-0.7	29.2	-1.7	28.8	-1.4	28.6	-0.7	28.7	0.3	28.6	-0.3
1954	28.5	-0.3	28.1	-1.4	28.4	1.1	28.9	1.8	29.0	0.3	29.0	0.0	29.1	0.3	29.3	0.7	29.6	1.0	29.9	1.0	29.9	0.0	29.9	0.0
1955	30.0	0.3	31.4	4.7	31.5	0.3	32.4	2.9	32.3	-0.3	32.3	0.0	32.7	1.2	34.0	4.0	36.2	6.5	36.1	-0.3	36.1	0.0	36.6	1.4
1956	36.8	0.5	36.9	0.3	38.0	3.0	38.3	0.8	37.5	-2.1	37.1	-1.1	35.8	-3.5	36.5	2.0	36.3	-0.5	36.2	-0.3	35.1	-3.0	35.1	0.0
1957	34.9	-0.6	34.1	-2.3	33.6	-1.5	33.4	-0.6	32.8	-1.8	32.4	-1.2	31.5	-2.8	31.6	0.3	30.9	-2.2	30.5	-1.3	30.7	0.7	30.6	-0.3
1958	30.2	-1.3	30.0	-0.7	29.8	-0.7	29.1	-2.3	29.1	0.0	29.3	0.7	29.3	0.0	29.6	1.0	29.9	1.0	30.7	2.7	31.4	2.3	31.3	-0.3
1959	31.3	0.0	31.5	0.6	31.9	1.3	31.6	-0.9	31.9	0.9	31.9	0.0	31.4	-1.6	31.4	0.0	31.9	1.6	32.2	0.9	33.1	2.8	33.0	-0.3
1960	33.5	1.5	33.5	0.0	33.0	-1.5	32.9	-0.3	32.9	0.0	32.6	-0.9	32.5	-0.3	32.5	0.0	32.5	0.0	32.2	-0.9	31.8	-1.2	31.4	-1.3
1961	31.0	-1.3	31.0	0.0	31.0	0.0	31.1	0.3	31.5	1.3	31.7	0.6	31.9	0.6	31.9	0.0	32.0	0.3	31.7	-0.9	31.4	-0.9	31.6	0.6
1962	31.5	-0.3	31.5	0.0	31.4	-0.3	31.3	-0.3	31.3	0.0	31.1	-0.6	31.1	0.0	31.1	0.0	31.0	-0.3	30.7	-1.0	30.8	0.3	30.7	-0.3
1963	30.8	0.3	30.8	0.0	30.8	0.0	30.8	0.0	31.0	0.6	31.0	0.0	31.1	0.3	31.2	0.3	31.3	0.3	31.3	0.0	31.4	0.3	31.7	1.0
1964	31.8	0.3	31.9	0.3	32.2	0.9	32.6	1.2	32.6	0.0	32.6	0.0	32.8	0.6	33.2	1.2	33.6	1.2	34.6	3.0	35.1	1.4	35.5	1.1
1965	35.0	-1.4	35.1	0.3	35.2	0.3	35.6	1.1	36.2	1.7	36.5	0.8	36.2	-0.8	36.6	1.1	36.7	0.3	36.8	0.3	37.3	1.4	36.8	-1.3
1966	37.1	0.8	37.5	1.1	37.9	1.1	38.3	1.1	38.4	0.3	38.7	0.8	38.6	-0.3	37.8	-2.1	37.6	-0.5	37.7	0.3	38.0	0.8	37.8	-0.5
1967	38.2	1.1	38.4	0.5	38.0	-1.0	37.7	-0.8	37.3	-1.1	37.3	0.0	37.2	-0.3	37.3	0.3	37.5	0.5	38.0	1.3	39.0	2.6	39.5	1.3
1968	40.0	1.3	41.1	2.8	41.8	1.7	40.9	-2.2	38.8	-5.1	38.7	-0.3	38.3	-1.0	38.1	-0.5	38.0	-0.3	38.2	0.5	38.3	0.3	38.7	1.0
1969	39.8	2.8	40.4	1.5	40.7	0.7	41.5	2.0	42.0	1.2	42.5	1.2	42.6	0.2	43.7	2.6	45.0	3.0	45.4	0.9	45.9	1.1	47.0	2.4
1970	48.0	2.1	48.0	0.0	48.2	0.4	49.3	2.3	49.3	0.0	48.6	-1.4	47.8	-1.6	47.2	-1.3	46.4	-1.7	46.1	-0.6	45.0	-2.4	44.0	-2.2

[Continued]

Nonferrous Metals

Producer Price Index
Base 1982 = 100
[Continued]

For 1926-1993. Columns headed % show percentile change in the index from the previous period for which an index is available.

Year	Jan Index	%	Feb Index	%	Mar Index	%	Apr Index	%	May Index	%	Jun Index	%	Jul Index	%	Aug Index	%	Sep Index	%	Oct Index	%	Nov Index	%	Dec Index	%
1971	43.3	-1.6	42.8	-1.2	42.6	-0.5	44.0	3.3	43.9	-0.2	43.6	-0.7	43.7	0.2	43.9	0.5	43.7	-0.5	43.6	-0.2	43.5	-0.2	43.1	-0.9
1972	43.4	0.7	43.6	0.5	44.5	2.1	44.6	0.2	44.7	0.2	44.6	-0.2	44.3	-0.7	44.3	0.0	44.5	0.5	44.5	0.0	44.5	0.0	44.5	0.0
1973	44.7	0.4	45.9	2.7	48.7	6.1	49.8	2.3	50.5	1.4	51.2	1.4	51.5	0.6	52.3	1.6	52.6	0.6	53.4	1.5	55.0	3.0	59.0	7.3
1974	61.1	3.6	62.6	2.5	66.9	6.9	70.8	5.8	76.0	7.3	76.0	0.0	75.3	-0.9	76.0	0.9	74.7	-1.7	72.4	-3.1	71.0	-1.9	69.0	-2.8
1975	67.8	-1.7	66.8	-1.5	66.0	-1.2	65.3	-1.1	64.9	-0.6	64.2	-1.1	63.6	-0.9	64.2	0.9	64.8	0.9	64.8	0.0	64.5	-0.5	64.3	-0.3
1976	64.1	-0.3	64.4	0.5	65.2	1.2	67.4	3.4	68.9	2.2	69.5	0.9	71.0	2.2	71.3	0.4	72.0	1.0	71.5	-0.7	71.1	-0.6	70.2	-1.3
1977	70.7	0.7	71.9	1.7	74.3	3.3	75.9	2.2	76.2	0.4	74.8	-1.8	75.1	0.4	75.3	0.3	74.0	-1.7	73.4	-0.8	73.7	0.4	74.0	0.4
1978	75.1	1.5	75.8	0.9	76.3	0.7	77.0	0.9	77.1	0.1	77.9	1.0	78.1	0.3	80.1	2.6	80.2	0.1	82.4	2.7	82.8	0.5	83.1	0.4
1979	84.8	2.0	90.7	7.0	93.6	3.2	98.5	5.2	98.0	-0.5	98.5	0.5	99.5	1.0	99.8	0.3	102.2	2.4	107.4	5.1	107.8	0.4	110.7	2.7
1980	123.8	11.8	128.1	3.5	121.9	-4.8	113.2	-7.1	109.9	-2.9	109.6	-0.3	111.0	1.3	113.2	2.0	114.6	1.2	117.4	2.4	114.6	-2.4	111.3	-2.9
1981	110.8	-0.4	109.0	-1.6	108.7	-0.3	109.4	0.6	109.1	-0.3	107.9	-1.1	107.3	-0.6	109.0	1.6	109.8	0.7	108.3	-1.4	106.6	-1.6	105.1	-1.4
1982	104.1	-1.0	103.8	-0.3	101.4	-2.3	100.9	-0.5	100.0	-0.9	96.1	-3.9	97.3	1.2	97.0	-0.3	100.6	3.7	99.7	-0.9	99.3	-0.4	99.8	0.5
1983	101.3	1.5	104.6	3.3	102.6	-1.9	103.1	0.5	105.3	2.1	104.6	-0.7	105.6	1.0	106.1	0.5	107.0	0.8	106.0	-0.9	104.9	-1.0	105.5	0.6
1984	105.0	-0.5	106.3	1.2	108.6	2.2	109.7	1.0	107.8	-1.7	107.3	-0.5	105.1	-2.1	104.4	-0.7	103.1	-1.2	101.2	-1.8	102.2	1.0	100.9	-1.3
1985	99.9	-1.0	100.5	0.6	99.6	-0.9	101.8	2.2	101.7	-0.1	100.0	-1.7	99.2	-0.8	99.2	0.0	98.7	-0.5	99.0	0.3	98.9	-0.1	98.5	-0.4
1986	98.5	0.9	98.6	0.1	99.3	0.7	98.5	-0.8	97.9	-0.6	98.2	0.3	97.6	-0.6	98.2	0.6	98.7	0.5	99.0	0.3	98.9	-0.1	124.1	4.7
1987	99.1	0.6	99.1	0.0	100.2	1.1	101.8	1.6	104.6	2.8	106.0	1.3	109.1	2.9	112.0	2.7	114.2	2.0	116.7	2.2	118.5	1.5	148.3	3.0
1988	127.5	2.7	124.8	-2.1	125.7	0.7	128.9	2.5	129.3	0.3	131.7	1.9	132.8	0.8	132.9	0.1	134.8	1.4	137.8	2.2	144.0	4.5	131.9	-3.4
1989	149.9	1.1	147.1	-1.9	148.2	0.7	147.2	-0.7	144.6	-1.8	140.1	-3.1	136.3	-2.7	136.9	0.4	139.0	3.1	139.2	0.1	134.8	-3.2	130.6	-3.1
1990	130.9	-0.8	127.9	-2.3	131.8	3.0	134.5	2.0	134.0	-0.4	132.1	-1.4	133.2	0.8	137.3	3.1	139.0	1.2	139.2	0.1	134.8	-3.2	130.6	-3.1
1991	129.6	-0.8	128.1	-1.2	127.2	-0.7	126.5	-0.6	124.2	-1.8	121.6	-2.1	120.9	-0.6	121.2	0.2	121.3	0.1	121.1	-0.2	120.2	-0.7	118.9	-1.1
1992	117.1	-1.5	119.4	2.0	121.0	1.3	121.5	0.4	121.6	0.1	122.8	1.0	124.0	1.0	125.2	1.0	122.9	-1.8	120.0	-2.4	117.6	-2.0	117.9	0.3
1993	119.1	1.0	118.8	-0.3	117.5	-1.1	115.7	-1.5	113.2	-2.2	113.5	0.3	114.6	1.0	114.7	0.1	113.5	-1.0	111.0	-2.2	110.2	-0.7	111.4	1.1

Source: U.S. Department of Labor, Bureau of Labor Statistics, Division of Industry Prices and Price Indexes. n.e.c. stands for not elsewhere classified. - indicates no data collected for period or unavailable.

Metal Containers
Producer Price Index
Base 1982 = 100

For 1926-1993. Columns headed % show percentile change in the index from the previous period for which an index is available.

Year	Jan Index	%	Feb Index	%	Mar Index	%	Apr Index	%	May Index	%	Jun Index	%	Jul Index	%	Aug Index	%	Sep Index	%	Oct Index	%	Nov Index	%	Dec Index	%
1926	15.2	-	15.2	0.0	15.2	0.0	15.2	0.0	15.2	0.0	15.2	0.0	15.2	0.0	15.2	0.0	15.2	0.0	15.2	0.0	15.2	0.0	15.2	0.0
1927	15.2	0.0	15.2	0.0	15.2	0.0	15.2	0.0	15.2	0.0	15.2	0.0	15.2	0.0	15.2	0.0	15.2	0.0	15.2	0.0	15.2	0.0	15.2	0.0
1928	14.7	-3.3	14.7	0.0	14.7	0.0	14.7	0.0	14.7	0.0	14.7	0.0	14.7	0.0	14.7	0.0	14.7	0.0	14.7	0.0	14.7	0.0	14.7	0.0
1929	14.9	1.4	14.9	0.0	14.9	0.0	14.9	0.0	14.9	0.0	14.9	0.0	14.9	0.0	14.9	0.0	14.9	0.0	14.9	0.0	14.9	0.0	14.9	0.0
1930	14.7	-1.3	14.7	0.0	14.7	0.0	14.7	0.0	14.7	0.0	14.7	0.0	14.7	0.0	14.7	0.0	14.6	-0.7	14.6	0.0	14.6	0.0	14.6	0.0
1931	14.2	-2.7	14.2	0.0	14.1	-0.7	14.1	0.0	14.1	0.0	14.1	0.0	14.0	-0.7	14.0	0.0	14.0	0.0	14.0	0.0	14.0	0.0	14.0	0.0
1932	13.5	-3.6	13.5	0.0	13.5	0.0	13.5	0.0	13.5	0.0	13.5	0.0	13.5	0.0	13.5	0.0	13.5	0.0	13.5	0.0	13.5	0.0	13.5	0.0
1933	12.6	-6.7	12.6	0.0	12.6	0.0	12.6	0.0	12.6	0.0	12.6	0.0	12.6	0.0	12.6	0.0	12.6	0.0	12.7	0.8	12.7	0.0	12.7	0.0
1934	14.4	13.4	14.4	0.0	14.4	0.0	14.5	0.7	14.5	0.0	14.5	0.0	14.5	0.0	14.5	0.0	14.5	0.0	14.5	0.0	14.5	0.0	14.5	0.0
1935	14.4	-0.7	14.4	0.0	14.4	0.0	14.4	0.0	14.4	0.0	14.4	0.0	14.4	0.0	14.4	0.0	14.4	0.0	14.4	0.0	14.4	0.0	14.4	0.0
1936	14.4	0.0	14.4	0.0	14.4	0.0	14.4	0.0	14.4	0.0	14.4	0.0	14.4	0.0	14.4	0.0	14.4	0.0	14.6	1.4	14.6	0.0	14.6	0.0
1937	13.4	-8.2	13.4	0.0	13.4	0.0	13.5	0.7	13.5	0.0	13.5	0.0	13.5	0.0	13.5	0.0	13.5	0.0	13.5	0.0	13.5	0.0	13.5	0.0
1938	14.4	6.7	14.4	0.0	14.4	0.0	14.4	0.0	14.4	0.0	14.4	0.0	14.4	0.0	14.4	0.0	14.4	0.0	14.4	0.0	14.4	0.0	14.4	0.0
1939	13.8	-4.2	13.8	0.0	13.8	0.0	13.8	0.0	13.8	0.0	13.8	0.0	13.8	0.0	13.8	0.0	13.8	0.0	13.8	0.0	13.8	0.0	13.8	0.0
1940	13.5	-2.2	13.5	0.0	13.5	0.0	13.5	0.0	13.5	0.0	13.5	0.0	13.5	0.0	13.5	0.0	13.5	0.0	13.5	0.0	13.5	0.0	13.5	0.0
1941	13.5	0.0	13.5	0.0	13.5	0.0	13.5	0.0	13.5	0.0	13.5	0.0	13.6	0.7	13.6	0.0	13.6	0.0	13.6	0.0	13.6	0.0	13.6	0.0
1942	13.8	1.5	13.8	0.0	13.8	0.0	13.8	0.0	13.8	0.0	13.8	0.0	13.8	0.0	13.8	0.0	13.8	0.0	13.8	0.0	13.8	0.0	13.8	0.0
1943	13.8	0.0	13.8	0.0	13.8	0.0	13.8	0.0	13.8	0.0	13.8	0.0	13.8	0.0	13.8	0.0	13.8	0.0	13.8	0.0	13.8	0.0	13.8	0.0
1944	13.8	0.0	13.8	0.0	13.8	0.0	13.8	0.0	13.8	0.0	13.8	0.0	13.8	0.0	13.8	0.0	13.8	0.0	13.8	0.0	13.8	0.0	13.8	0.0
1945	13.8	0.0	13.8	0.0	13.8	0.0	13.8	0.0	13.8	0.0	13.8	0.0	13.8	0.0	13.8	0.0	13.8	0.0	13.8	0.0	13.8	0.0	13.8	0.0
1946	13.8	0.0	13.8	0.0	13.8	0.0	13.8	0.0	14.3	3.6	14.3	0.0	14.3	0.0	14.3	0.0	14.3	0.0	14.3	0.0	14.3	0.0	14.3	0.0
1947	15.9	11.2	15.9	0.0	15.9	0.0	15.9	0.0	15.9	0.0	15.9	0.0	15.9	0.0	16.3	2.5	16.3	0.0	16.3	0.0	16.3	0.0	16.3	0.0
1948	17.8	9.2	17.8	0.0	17.8	0.0	17.8	0.0	17.7	-0.6	17.7	0.0	17.8	0.6	17.9	0.6	17.9	0.0	17.9	0.0	17.9	0.0	17.9	0.0
1949	19.3	7.8	19.3	0.0	19.3	0.0	19.3	0.0	19.3	0.0	19.3	0.0	19.3	0.0	19.3	0.0	19.3	0.0	19.3	0.0	19.3	0.0	19.3	0.0
1950	19.4	0.5	19.4	0.0	19.3	-0.5	19.3	0.0	19.3	0.0	19.3	0.0	19.3	0.0	19.3	0.0	19.3	0.0	19.3	0.0	19.3	0.0	19.6	1.6
1951	21.5	9.7	21.5	0.0	21.5	0.0	21.5	0.0	21.5	0.0	21.5	0.0	21.5	0.0	21.5	0.0	21.5	0.0	21.5	0.0	21.5	0.0	21.5	0.0
1952	21.4	-0.5	21.4	0.0	21.4	0.0	21.4	0.0	21.4	0.0	21.4	0.0	21.4	0.0	21.4	0.0	22.0	2.8	22.2	0.9	22.2	0.0	22.2	0.0
1953	22.2	0.0	22.2	0.0	22.2	0.0	22.4	0.9	22.4	0.0	22.4	0.0	22.8	1.8	22.8	0.0	22.8	0.0	22.8	0.0	22.8	0.0	22.8	0.0
1954	23.0	0.9	23.0	0.0	23.0	0.0	23.0	0.0	23.0	0.0	23.0	0.0	23.1	0.4	23.2	0.4	23.2	0.0	23.2	0.0	23.3	0.4	23.3	0.0
1955	23.3	0.0	23.3	0.0	23.3	0.0	23.3	0.0	23.3	0.0	23.3	0.0	23.3	0.0	23.5	0.9	23.5	0.0	23.5	0.0	24.4	3.8	24.4	0.0
1956	24.4	0.0	24.4	0.0	24.4	0.0	24.4	0.0	25.0	2.5	25.0	0.0	25.0	0.0	25.1	0.4	25.4	1.2	25.4	0.0	26.1	2.8	26.1	0.0
1957	26.1	0.0	26.1	0.0	26.2	0.4	26.2	0.0	27.0	3.1	27.0	0.0	27.0	0.0	27.1	0.4	27.1	0.0	27.1	0.0	27.1	0.0	27.1	0.0
1958	27.1	0.0	27.1	0.0	27.6	1.8	27.6	0.0	27.6	0.0	27.6	0.0	27.6	0.0	27.6	0.0	27.7	0.4	27.7	0.0	27.7	0.0	28.3	2.2
1959	27.7	-2.1	27.7	0.0	27.7	0.0	27.1	-2.2	27.1	0.0	27.1	0.0	27.1	0.0	27.1	0.0	27.1	0.0	27.1	0.0	27.1	0.0	27.1	0.0
1960	27.1	0.0	27.4	1.1	27.4	0.0	27.4	0.0	27.4	0.0	27.2	-0.7	27.2	0.0	27.2	0.0	27.2	0.0	27.2	0.0	27.2	0.0	27.2	0.0
1961	27.8	2.2	27.8	0.0	27.8	0.0	27.8	0.0	27.8	0.0	27.8	0.0	27.8	0.0	27.8	0.0	27.8	0.0	27.8	0.0	27.8	0.0	27.8	0.0
1962	28.2	1.4	28.2	0.0	28.2	0.0	28.2	0.0	28.2	0.0	28.2	0.0	28.2	0.0	28.2	0.0	28.2	0.0	28.2	0.0	28.2	0.0	28.2	0.0
1963	28.4	0.7	28.4	0.0	28.4	0.0	28.4	0.0	28.5	0.4	28.5	0.0	28.6	0.4	28.6	0.0	28.5	-0.3	28.5	0.0	28.5	0.0	28.5	0.0
1964	28.5	0.0	28.7	0.7	28.7	0.0	28.7	0.0	28.7	0.0	28.7	0.0	28.7	0.0	28.7	0.0	28.7	0.0	28.7	0.0	28.7	0.0	28.7	0.0
1965	28.8	0.3	28.8	0.0	28.8	0.0	28.8	0.0	29.5	2.4	29.5	0.0	29.5	0.0	29.5	0.0	29.5	0.0	29.5	0.0	29.5	0.0	29.9	1.4
1966	29.9	0.0	29.9	0.0	29.9	0.0	29.9	0.0	30.0	0.3	30.0	0.0	30.0	0.0	30.0	0.0	30.0	0.0	30.0	0.0	30.0	0.0	30.0	0.0
1967	30.3	1.0	30.3	0.0	30.3	0.0	30.4	0.3	30.4	0.0	30.4	0.0	30.4	0.0	30.4	0.0	30.4	0.0	30.4	0.0	30.7	1.0	30.7	0.0
1968	30.7	0.0	30.8	0.3	30.8	0.0	31.8	3.2	31.8	0.0	31.8	0.0	31.8	0.0	31.8	0.0	31.8	0.0	31.9	0.3	31.9	0.0	31.8	-0.3
1969	31.8	0.0	32.4	1.9	32.4	0.0	32.5	0.3	32.5	0.0	32.5	0.0	32.5	0.0	32.5	0.0	32.7	0.6	32.8	0.3	32.8	0.0	32.8	0.0
1970	32.8	0.0	34.0	3.7	34.0	0.0	34.0	0.0	34.0	0.0	34.0	0.0	34.3	0.9	34.3	0.0	34.3	0.0	35.2	2.6	35.2	0.0	35.2	0.0

[Continued]

Metal Containers
Producer Price Index
Base 1982 = 100
[Continued]

For 1926-1993. Columns headed % show percentile change in the index from the previous period for which an index is available.

Year	Jan Index	%	Feb Index	%	Mar Index	%	Apr Index	%	May Index	%	Jun Index	%	Jul Index	%	Aug Index	%	Sep Index	%	Oct Index	%	Nov Index	%	Dec Index	%
1971	35.2	0.0	35.2	0.0	35.2	0.0	37.5	6.5	37.5	0.0	37.5	0.0	37.5	0.0	37.8	0.8	37.8	0.0	37.8	0.0	37.8	0.0	37.8	0.0
1972	37.8	0.0	38.7	2.4	38.7	0.0	38.7	0.0	38.8	0.3	39.2	1.0	39.5	0.8	39.8	0.8	39.9	0.3	39.9	0.0	39.9	0.0	39.9	0.0
1973	39.9	0.0	39.8	-0.3	41.3	3.8	41.3	0.0	41.3	0.0	41.3	0.0	41.3	0.0	41.3	0.0	41.3	0.0	41.0	-0.7	41.0	0.0	41.0	0.0
1974	42.2	2.9	42.3	0.2	42.5	0.5	44.7	5.2	46.3	3.6	50.3	8.6	52.0	3.4	56.1	7.9	56.2	0.2	56.4	0.4	56.4	0.0	56.4	0.0
1975	56.4	0.0	60.0	6.4	59.6	-0.7	59.6	0.0	58.2	-2.3	58.2	0.0	58.2	0.0	58.1	-0.2	58.2	0.2	58.2	0.0	58.4	0.3	58.7	0.5
1976	58.6	-0.2	58.7	0.2	61.9	5.5	61.9	0.0	61.9	0.0	61.9	0.0	62.3	0.6	62.2	-0.2	62.2	0.0	62.2	0.0	62.3	0.2	62.3	0.0
1977	62.3	0.0	62.3	0.0	66.0	5.9	66.1	0.2	66.0	-0.2	66.0	0.0	66.2	0.3	66.4	0.3	68.5	3.2	69.0	0.7	69.1	0.1	69.1	0.0
1978	69.2	0.1	71.1	2.7	72.1	1.4	72.1	0.0	73.9	2.5	74.0	0.1	74.3	0.4	75.0	0.9	74.9	-0.1	77.5	3.5	77.5	0.0	77.4	-0.1
1979	78.2	1.0	78.2	0.0	80.5	2.9	82.2	2.1	81.7	-0.6	81.4	-0.4	81.3	-0.1	81.7	0.5	81.8	0.1	85.2	4.2	85.5	0.4	85.5	0.0
1980	86.2	0.8	86.6	0.5	87.8	1.4	91.6	4.3	92.1	0.5	92.1	0.0	92.2	0.1	92.3	0.1	92.3	0.0	92.7	0.4	92.3	-0.4	92.3	0.0
1981	94.8	2.7	95.5	0.7	95.6	0.1	95.6	0.0	95.6	0.0	95.6	0.0	96.0	0.4	97.0	1.0	97.0	0.0	96.9	-0.1	96.8	-0.1	96.4	-0.4
1982	98.7	2.4	99.3	0.6	99.6	0.3	100.5	0.9	100.5	0.0	100.4	-0.1	100.5	0.1	100.1	-0.4	100.1	0.0	100.3	0.2	100.1	-0.2	99.9	-0.2
1983	99.8	-0.1	100.8	1.0	100.9	0.1	101.0	0.1	102.6	1.6	102.7	0.1	102.4	-0.3	102.5	0.1	103.0	0.5	103.0	0.0	102.9	-0.1	103.6	0.7
1984	104.7	1.1	104.9	0.2	105.1	0.2	105.1	0.0	105.9	0.8	105.9	0.0	105.9	0.0	107.2	1.2	107.2	0.0	108.8	1.5	108.8	0.0	108.7	-0.1
1985	108.8	0.1	109.0	0.2	108.9	-0.1	108.9	0.0	109.0	0.1	109.0	0.0	109.0	0.0	108.9	-0.1	108.9	0.0	108.9	0.0	109.0	0.1	109.9	0.8
1986	110.2	0.3	110.1	-0.1	110.2	0.1	110.1	-0.1	110.0	-0.1	109.7	0.1	110.3	0.3	110.4	0.1	110.4	0.0	110.4	0.0	110.4	0.0	108.0	-1.6
1987	109.9	-0.5	110.0	0.1	109.8	-0.2	109.8	0.0	109.6	-0.2	109.7	0.1	109.0	-0.6	109.1	0.1	109.8	0.6	109.6	-0.2	109.8	0.2	110.1	-0.8
1988	108.3	0.3	108.9	0.6	109.5	0.6	110.1	0.5	110.4	0.3	110.3	-0.1	110.1	-0.2	110.9	0.7	111.3	0.4	111.1	-0.2	111.0	-0.1	110.1	-0.8
1989	110.1	0.0	109.7	-0.4	109.7	0.0	110.3	0.5	111.3	0.9	111.5	0.2	112.5	0.9	112.0	-0.4	112.2	0.2	113.0	0.7	113.1	0.1	112.6	-0.4
1990	113.6	0.9	113.5	-0.1	113.8	0.3	113.8	0.0	114.2	0.4	114.1	-0.1	114.2	0.1	114.1	-0.1	114.2	0.1	114.1	-0.1	114.1	0.0	113.9	-0.2
1991	114.7	0.7	114.9	0.2	114.6	-0.3	114.7	0.1	114.9	0.2	114.9	0.0	114.9	0.0	116.1	1.0	116.3	0.2	116.2	-0.1	116.4	0.2	116.3	-0.1
1992	113.8	-2.1	114.3	0.4	113.9	-0.3	114.0	0.1	113.8	-0.2	114.0	0.2	113.9	-0.1	113.7	-0.2	113.9	0.2	113.9	0.0	113.9	0.0	114.0	0.1
1993	109.9	-3.6	110.2	0.3	109.5	-0.6	109.2	-0.3	109.1	-0.1	109.1	0.0	109.2	0.1	108.8	-0.4	108.8	0.0	109.7	0.8	109.9	0.2	110.7	0.7

Source: U.S. Department of Labor, Bureau of Labor Statistics, Division of Industry Prices and Price Indexes. n.e.c. stands for not elsewhere classified. - indicates no data collected for period or unavailable.

Hardware
Producer Price Index
Base 1982 = 100

For 1947-1993. Columns headed % show percentile change in the index from the previous period for which an index is available.

Year	Jan Index	%	Feb Index	%	Mar Index	%	Apr Index	%	May Index	%	Jun Index	%	Jul Index	%	Aug Index	%	Sep Index	%	Oct Index	%	Nov Index	%	Dec Index	%
1947	16.7	-	16.9	1.2	16.9	0.0	16.9	0.0	17.0	0.6	17.0	0.0	17.1	0.6	17.2	0.6	17.4	1.2	17.6	1.1	17.7	0.6	17.7	0.0
1948	17.7	0.0	17.8	0.6	17.9	0.6	17.9	0.0	18.2	1.7	18.3	0.5	18.3	0.0	19.1	4.4	19.7	3.1	19.8	0.5	19.9	0.5	19.9	0.0
1949	19.9	0.0	19.9	0.0	19.9	0.0	19.7	-1.0	19.7	0.0	19.7	0.0	19.7	0.0	19.7	0.0	19.5	-1.0	19.2	-1.5	19.2	0.0	19.2	0.0
1950	19.6	2.1	20.1	2.6	20.2	0.5	20.3	0.5	20.5	1.0	20.6	0.5	20.9	1.5	21.4	2.4	21.8	1.9	22.2	1.8	22.9	3.2	23.2	1.3
1951	23.3	0.4	23.3	0.0	23.3	0.0	23.3	0.0	23.3	0.0	23.3	0.0	23.3	0.0	23.3	0.0	23.3	0.0	23.3	0.0	23.3	0.0	23.3	0.0
1952	23.3	0.0	23.3	0.0	23.4	0.4	23.4	0.0	23.4	0.0	22.9	-2.1	22.9	0.0	22.9	0.0	22.9	0.0	23.2	1.3	23.2	0.0	23.3	0.4
1953	23.3	0.0	23.3	0.0	23.3	0.0	23.7	1.7	24.7	4.2	24.9	0.8	24.9	0.0	25.1	0.8	25.3	0.8	25.4	0.4	25.4	0.0	25.4	0.0
1954	25.4	0.0	25.5	0.4	25.5	0.0	25.6	0.4	25.5	-0.4	25.5	0.0	25.5	0.0	25.7	0.8	26.0	1.2	26.2	0.8	26.3	0.4	26.3	0.0
1955	26.4	0.4	26.5	0.4	26.7	0.8	26.7	0.0	26.7	0.0	26.7	0.0	26.8	0.4	27.0	0.7	27.3	1.1	28.0	2.6	28.0	0.0	28.0	0.0
1956	28.0	0.0	28.0	0.0	28.3	1.1	28.5	0.7	28.5	0.0	28.6	0.4	28.7	0.3	29.3	2.1	29.3	0.0	29.5	0.7	29.6	0.3	29.6	0.0
1957	29.9	1.0	29.9	0.0	30.0	0.3	30.2	0.7	30.4	0.7	30.4	0.0	30.4	0.0	30.7	1.0	30.9	0.7	30.9	0.0	30.9	0.0	31.1	0.6
1958	31.2	0.3	31.2	0.0	31.2	0.0	31.3	0.3	31.6	1.0	31.8	0.6	31.8	0.0	31.8	0.0	31.8	0.0	31.8	0.0	31.9	0.3	31.9	0.0
1959	31.9	0.0	32.0	0.3	32.0	0.0	32.0	0.0	32.0	0.0	32.0	0.0	32.0	0.0	32.0	0.0	32.0	0.0	32.0	0.0	32.0	0.0	32.0	0.0
1960	32.1	0.3	32.1	0.0	32.1	0.0	32.2	0.3	32.2	0.0	32.3	0.3	32.3	0.0	32.3	0.0	32.3	0.0	32.3	0.0	32.3	0.0	32.3	0.0
1961	32.3	0.0	32.4	0.3	32.4	0.0	32.4	0.0	32.6	0.6	32.6	0.0	32.6	0.0	32.6	0.0	32.7	0.3	32.7	0.0	32.7	0.0	32.7	0.0
1962	32.8	0.3	32.7	-0.3	32.7	0.0	32.6	-0.3	32.6	0.0	32.7	0.3	32.5	-0.6	32.5	0.0	32.5	0.0	32.5	0.0	32.5	0.0	32.5	0.0
1963	32.5	0.0	32.6	0.3	32.6	0.0	32.6	0.0	32.6	0.0	32.6	0.0	32.6	0.0	32.6	0.0	32.7	0.3	32.7	0.0	32.7	0.0	32.7	0.0
1964	32.8	0.3	32.8	0.0	32.9	0.3	32.9	0.0	32.9	0.0	32.9	0.0	32.9	0.0	32.9	0.0	32.9	0.0	32.9	0.0	32.9	0.0	32.9	0.0
1965	32.9	0.0	32.9	0.0	33.0	0.3	33.0	0.0	33.2	0.6	33.2	0.0	33.3	0.3	33.4	0.3	33.4	0.0	33.5	0.3	33.5	0.0	33.6	0.3
1966	33.6	0.0	33.7	0.3	34.0	0.9	34.0	0.0	34.4	1.2	34.4	0.0	34.4	0.0	34.5	0.3	34.6	0.3	34.8	0.6	35.0	0.6	35.1	0.3
1967	35.0	-0.3	35.0	0.0	35.3	0.9	35.3	0.0	35.4	0.3	35.4	0.0	35.7	0.8	36.1	1.1	36.1	0.0	36.2	0.3	36.3	0.3	36.4	0.3
1968	36.4	0.0	36.6	0.5	36.5	-0.3	36.5	0.0	36.6	0.3	36.6	0.0	36.6	0.0	36.6	0.0	36.7	0.3	36.8	0.3	36.8	0.0	37.1	0.8
1969	37.3	0.5	37.4	0.3	37.5	0.3	37.5	0.0	37.6	0.3	37.6	0.0	37.8	0.5	37.8	0.0	37.9	0.3	38.4	1.3	38.6	0.5	38.6	0.0
1970	39.0	1.0	39.1	0.3	39.2	0.3	39.3	0.3	39.4	0.3	39.5	0.3	39.7	0.5	39.9	0.5	40.1	0.5	40.3	0.5	41.0	1.7	41.1	0.2
1971	41.2	0.2	41.3	0.2	41.3	0.0	41.3	0.0	41.3	0.0	41.4	0.2	41.7	0.7	42.0	0.7	42.0	0.0	42.0	0.0	42.1	0.2	42.2	0.2
1972	42.3	0.2	42.5	0.5	42.5	0.0	42.7	0.5	42.9	0.5	43.0	0.2	43.0	0.0	43.1	0.2	43.1	0.0	43.2	0.2	43.3	0.2	43.3	0.0
1973	43.4	0.2	43.5	0.2	43.6	0.2	43.8	0.5	44.0	0.5	44.3	0.7	44.4	0.2	44.4	0.0	45.2	1.8	45.6	0.9	45.7	0.2	46.1	0.9
1974	46.5	0.9	46.7	0.4	46.9	0.4	47.1	0.4	48.4	2.8	49.3	1.9	49.9	1.2	51.0	2.2	52.5	2.9	53.9	2.7	55.0	2.0	55.5	0.9
1975	56.0	0.9	56.5	0.9	57.7	2.1	57.7	0.0	58.1	0.7	58.2	0.2	58.3	0.2	58.4	0.2	58.6	0.3	59.3	1.2	59.5	0.3	59.6	0.2
1976	60.2	1.0	60.5	0.5	60.7	0.3	60.9	0.3	61.5	1.0	61.7	0.3	61.8	0.2	61.9	0.2	62.2	0.5	62.6	0.6	63.2	1.0	63.9	1.1
1977	64.8	1.4	65.1	0.5	65.4	0.5	65.5	0.2	65.6	0.2	65.9	0.5	66.7	1.2	66.7	0.0	66.9	0.3	66.7	-0.3	67.1	0.6	67.6	0.7
1978	69.0	2.1	69.2	0.3	69.4	0.3	70.2	1.2	70.7	0.7	70.8	0.1	71.5	1.0	71.9	0.6	72.2	0.4	73.5	1.8	74.4	1.2	75.2	1.1
1979	75.5	0.4	76.1	0.8	76.4	0.4	77.0	0.8	77.4	0.5	77.5	0.1	78.0	0.6	78.5	0.6	79.0	0.6	79.9	1.1	80.5	0.8	80.7	0.2
1980	81.4	0.9	82.2	1.0	82.6	0.5	84.7	2.5	85.1	0.5	85.8	0.8	86.6	0.9	86.8	0.2	87.7	1.0	88.0	0.3	89.1	1.3	89.8	0.8
1981	90.8	1.1	92.1	1.4	92.3	0.2	92.2	-0.1	92.6	0.4	92.6	0.0	94.1	1.6	94.7	0.6	95.6	1.0	96.2	0.6	96.9	0.7	97.1	0.2
1982	97.8	0.7	98.0	0.2	99.3	1.3	99.4	0.1	99.5	0.1	100.0	0.5	100.3	0.3	100.8	0.5	100.9	0.1	101.0	0.1	101.0	0.0	102.0	1.0
1983	102.5	0.5	102.7	0.2	102.8	0.1	103.0	0.2	103.0	0.0	104.0	1.0	104.2	0.2	104.3	0.1	104.4	0.1	104.5	0.1	104.6	0.1	104.7	0.1
1984	104.7	0.0	104.9	0.2	105.1	0.2	105.1	0.0	105.4	0.3	105.7	0.3	106.0	0.3	106.3	0.3	106.7	0.4	107.0	0.3	107.0	0.0	107.4	0.4
1985	108.0	0.6	108.2	0.2	108.8	0.6	109.1	0.3	109.1	0.0	109.1	0.0	109.2	0.1	109.4	0.2	109.4	0.0	109.6	0.2	109.7	0.1	109.9	0.2
1986	110.8	0.8	110.9	0.1	109.1	-1.6	109.2	0.1	109.3	0.1	109.3	0.0	109.4	0.1	109.5	0.1	109.2	-0.3	109.4	0.2	108.7	-0.6	108.9	0.2
1987	108.5	-0.4	108.9	0.4	109.0	0.1	109.2	0.2	109.6	0.4	109.8	0.2	109.6	-0.2	109.7	0.1	109.8	0.1	110.1	0.3	110.2	0.1	111.0	0.7
1988	111.5	0.5	111.9	0.4	112.2	0.3	112.8	0.5	113.0	0.2	112.9	-0.1	113.6	0.6	114.0	0.4	114.3	0.3	115.6	1.1	116.1	0.4	116.7	0.5
1989	117.3	0.5	118.4	0.9	119.1	0.6	119.2	0.1	119.7	0.4	119.9	0.2	120.5	0.5	120.7	0.2	121.2	0.4	122.3	0.9	122.8	0.4	123.2	0.3
1990	124.0	0.6	124.8	0.6	125.0	0.2	125.5	0.4	125.6	0.1	125.7	0.1	126.0	0.2	126.2	0.2	126.5	0.2	126.9	0.3	127.0	0.1	127.7	0.6
1991	129.4	1.3	129.7	0.2	129.9	0.2	129.9	0.0	130.0	0.1	130.1	0.1	130.1	0.0	130.2	0.1	130.3	0.1	130.7	0.3	130.6	-0.1	131.2	0.5

[Continued]

Hardware
Producer Price Index
Base 1982 = 100
[Continued]

For 1947-1993. Columns headed % show percentile change in the index from the previous period for which an index is available.

Year	Jan		Feb		Mar		Apr		May		Jun		Jul		Aug		Sep		Oct		Nov		Dec	
	Index	%	Index	%	Index	%	Index	%	Index	%	Index	%	Index	%	Index	%	Index	%	Index	%	Index	%	Index	%
1992	131.6	0.3	132.0	0.3	132.2	0.2	132.5	0.2	132.6	0.1	132.6	0.0	132.8	0.2	133.0	0.2	133.1	0.1	133.2	0.1	133.5	0.2	133.8	0.2
1993	134.1	0.2	134.3	0.1	134.6	0.2	134.8	0.1	134.8	0.0	135.2	0.3	135.3	0.1	135.5	0.1	135.6	0.1	135.8	0.1	135.6	-0.1	136.3	0.5

Source: U.S. Department of Labor, Bureau of Labor Statistics, Division of Industry Prices and Price Indexes. n.e.c. stands for not elsewhere classified. - indicates no data collected for period or unavailable.

Plumbing Fixtures and Brass Fittings
Producer Price Index
Base 1982 = 100

For 1926-1993. Columns headed % show percentile change in the index from the previous period for which an index is available.

Year	Jan Index	%	Feb Index	%	Mar Index	%	Apr Index	%	May Index	%	Jun Index	%	Jul Index	%	Aug Index	%	Sep Index	%	Oct Index	%	Nov Index	%	Dec Index	%
1926	26.4	-	26.4	0.0	26.4	0.0	26.4	0.0	26.3	-0.4	25.9	-1.5	25.8	-0.4	26.0	0.8	26.2	0.8	26.2	0.0	26.1	-0.4	26.2	0.4
1927	26.2	0.0	25.5	-2.7	23.5	-7.8	23.5	0.0	23.1	-1.7	22.8	-1.3	22.8	0.0	22.8	0.0	22.9	0.4	22.9	0.0	22.9	0.0	22.7	-0.9
1928	22.7	0.0	22.7	0.0	23.4	3.1	23.5	0.4	23.6	0.4	24.3	3.0	24.3	0.0	24.3	0.0	24.3	0.0	24.3	0.0	24.4	0.4	24.4	0.0
1929	24.1	-1.2	22.4	-7.1	22.4	0.0	22.6	0.9	22.6	0.0	22.6	0.0	22.1	-2.2	22.5	1.8	22.5	0.0	22.1	-1.8	22.1	0.0	22.1	0.0
1930	22.1	0.0	22.7	2.7	23.0	1.3	24.1	4.8	24.1	0.0	20.8	-13.7	19.9	-4.3	19.9	0.0	19.8	-0.5	19.8	0.0	19.7	-0.5	20.5	4.1
1931	20.6	0.5	20.2	-1.9	20.2	0.0	20.2	0.0	20.2	0.0	20.2	0.0	20.2	0.0	20.2	0.0	20.0	-1.0	20.1	0.5	20.0	-0.5	19.3	-3.5
1932	16.4	-15.0	16.2	-1.2	15.6	-3.7	15.6	0.0	15.6	0.0	16.6	6.4	16.8	1.2	16.8	0.0	16.8	0.0	16.8	0.0	16.8	0.0	16.8	0.0
1933	14.5	-13.7	12.8	-11.7	12.8	0.0	12.8	0.0	13.8	7.8	16.2	17.4	16.7	3.1	16.9	1.2	19.1	13.0	19.1	0.0	19.1	0.0	19.0	-0.5
1934	19.0	0.0	18.8	-1.1	18.8	0.0	18.8	0.0	17.9	-4.8	16.9	-5.6	16.9	0.0	17.0	0.6	15.5	-8.8	14.0	-9.7	13.9	-0.7	13.9	0.0
1935	13.9	0.0	14.0	0.7	14.1	0.7	14.0	-0.7	14.0	0.0	14.0	0.0	14.9	6.4	15.5	4.0	15.5	0.0	15.5	0.0	15.5	0.0	15.5	0.0
1936	15.8	1.9	16.9	7.0	16.9	0.0	16.9	0.0	16.9	0.0	16.9	0.0	16.9	0.0	16.9	0.0	16.9	0.0	16.9	0.0	16.9	0.0	16.9	0.0
1937	16.9	0.0	16.9	0.0	17.0	0.6	17.2	1.2	17.2	0.0	17.2	0.0	17.2	0.0	17.2	0.0	17.2	0.0	17.2	0.0	17.2	0.0	17.2	0.0
1938	17.1	-0.6	17.1	0.0	17.0	-0.6	17.0	0.0	17.0	0.0	17.0	0.0	17.0	0.0	17.0	0.0	16.6	-2.4	16.6	0.0	16.6	0.0	16.6	0.0
1939	16.6	0.0	16.9	1.8	16.9	0.0	16.9	0.0	16.9	0.0	16.9	0.0	16.9	0.0	16.9	0.0	16.9	0.0	16.9	0.0	16.9	0.0	16.9	0.0
1940	17.0	0.6	17.2	1.2	18.1	5.2	18.1	0.0	18.1	0.0	18.1	0.0	18.1	0.0	18.1	0.0	18.1	0.0	18.1	0.0	18.1	0.0	18.1	0.0
1941	18.1	0.0	18.1	0.0	18.0	-0.6	18.0	0.0	18.0	0.0	18.0	0.0	18.1	0.6	18.3	1.1	18.5	1.1	18.6	0.5	18.7	0.5	19.2	2.7
1942	21.2	10.4	21.1	-0.5	20.5	-2.8	20.6	0.5	20.6	0.0	20.6	0.0	19.8	-3.9	19.8	0.0	19.8	0.0	19.8	0.0	19.8	0.0	19.8	0.0
1943	19.8	0.0	19.8	0.0	19.8	0.0	19.8	0.0	19.8	0.0	19.8	0.0	19.8	0.0	19.8	0.0	19.7	-0.5	19.7	0.0	19.7	0.0	19.7	0.0
1944	19.7	0.0	19.7	0.0	19.7	0.0	19.7	0.0	18.6	-5.6	18.6	0.0	18.6	0.0	18.6	0.0	18.6	0.0	18.6	0.0	18.6	0.0	18.6	0.0
1945	18.6	0.0	18.6	0.0	18.6	0.0	18.7	0.5	18.7	0.0	18.7	0.0	18.7	0.0	18.9	1.1	19.1	1.1	19.1	0.0	19.1	0.0	19.1	0.0
1946	19.1	0.0	19.1	0.0	19.6	2.6	19.9	1.5	19.9	0.0	19.8	-0.5	19.8	0.0	20.0	1.0	20.4	2.0	20.4	0.0	20.4	0.0	22.8	11.8
1947	22.9	0.4	23.6	3.1	23.8	0.8	23.8	0.0	23.8	0.0	23.8	0.0	23.9	0.4	24.1	0.8	24.6	2.1	24.6	0.0	24.7	0.4	24.7	0.0
1948	25.2	2.0	25.7	2.0	25.7	0.0	25.7	0.0	25.7	0.0	25.7	0.0	25.8	0.4	26.6	3.1	26.7	0.4	26.7	0.0	26.7	0.0	26.6	-0.4
1949	26.5	-0.4	26.3	-0.8	26.2	-0.4	26.2	0.0	25.9	-1.1	25.9	0.0	25.9	0.0	25.9	0.0	25.9	0.0	25.9	0.0	25.9	0.0	25.8	-0.4
1950	25.8	0.0	25.8	0.0	25.8	0.0	25.9	0.4	26.2	1.2	26.2	0.0	26.2	0.0	27.8	6.1	28.1	1.1	29.6	5.3	30.8	4.1	31.3	1.6
1951	31.3	0.0	31.3	0.0	31.3	0.0	31.3	0.0	31.3	0.0	31.2	-0.3	31.1	-0.3	31.0	-0.3	30.9	-0.3	30.8	-0.3	30.8	0.0	30.7	-0.3
1952	29.6	-3.6	29.6	0.0	29.6	0.0	29.5	-0.3	29.4	-0.3	29.9	1.7	30.0	0.3	30.0	0.0	30.0	0.0	30.0	0.0	30.0	0.0	30.0	0.0
1953	28.8	-4.0	29.0	0.7	29.0	0.0	28.9	-0.3	28.9	0.0	28.8	-0.3	29.5	2.4	30.1	2.0	30.1	0.0	30.1	-0.3	30.0	0.0	30.0	0.0
1954	30.0	0.0	30.0	0.0	30.0	0.0	30.0	0.0	30.0	0.0	30.1	0.3	30.1	0.0	30.1	0.0	30.1	0.0	30.1	0.0	30.1	0.0	30.1	0.0
1955	30.1	0.0	30.1	0.0	31.2	3.7	31.3	0.3	31.3	0.0	31.3	0.0	31.3	0.0	32.5	3.8	32.5	0.0	32.8	0.9	33.8	3.0	33.8	0.0
1956	33.8	0.0	33.8	0.0	33.8	0.0	34.0	0.6	34.3	0.9	34.0	-0.9	34.0	0.0	34.0	0.0	34.0	0.0	34.0	0.0	34.0	0.0	34.0	0.0
1957	33.8	-0.6	33.8	0.0	33.5	-0.9	33.4	-0.3	33.0	-1.2	32.8	-0.6	32.8	0.0	32.7	-0.3	32.7	0.0	32.6	-0.3	32.6	0.0	32.6	0.0
1958	32.3	-0.9	31.9	-1.2	31.6	-0.9	31.4	-0.6	31.1	-1.0	31.1	0.0	30.4	-2.3	30.4	0.0	31.4	3.3	31.6	0.6	31.6	0.0	31.6	0.0
1959	31.7	0.3	31.9	0.6	32.8	2.8	32.9	0.3	33.2	0.9	33.2	0.0	33.2	0.0	33.2	0.0	33.2	0.0	33.2	0.0	33.6	1.2	33.8	0.6
1960	34.0	0.6	34.0	0.0	34.0	0.0	33.5	-1.5	33.7	0.6	33.3	-1.2	33.3	0.0	33.3	0.0	33.3	0.0	33.1	-0.6	33.1	0.0	33.1	0.0
1961	33.2	0.3	33.2	0.0	33.2	0.0	33.2	0.0	33.3	0.3	33.5	0.6	33.6	0.3	33.8	0.6	33.8	0.0	33.9	0.3	33.9	0.0	33.8	-0.3
1962	33.8	0.0	33.8	0.0	33.7	-0.3	33.7	0.0	33.7	0.0	32.0	-5.0	31.5	-1.6	31.4	-0.3	31.4	0.0	31.5	0.3	31.6	0.3	31.6	0.0
1963	31.6	0.0	32.8	3.8	32.8	0.0	32.7	-0.3	32.7	0.0	32.6	-0.3	32.5	-0.3	32.5	0.0	32.5	0.0	32.5	0.0	32.5	0.0	32.5	0.0
1964	32.4	-0.3	32.4	0.0	32.3	-0.3	32.3	0.0	32.3	0.0	32.3	0.0	32.6	0.9	33.1	1.5	33.1	0.0	33.4	0.9	33.4	0.0	33.4	0.0
1965	33.3	-0.3	33.3	0.0	33.3	0.0	33.3	0.0	33.3	0.0	33.3	0.0	33.6	0.9	33.6	0.0	33.6	0.0	33.6	0.0	33.7	0.3	34.1	1.2
1966	34.0	-0.3	34.1	0.3	34.3	0.6	34.8	1.5	35.0	0.6	35.2	0.6	35.7	1.4	35.7	0.0	35.9	0.6	35.9	0.0	35.9	0.0	35.9	0.0
1967	35.9	0.0	36.0	0.3	36.0	0.0	36.0	0.0	36.0	0.0	36.0	0.0	35.7	-0.8	35.7	0.0	35.7	0.0	35.7	0.0	35.7	0.0	35.9	0.6
1968	36.0	0.3	37.0	2.8	37.1	0.3	37.2	0.3	37.2	0.0	37.0	-0.5	37.0	0.0	37.1	0.3	37.1	0.0	37.2	0.3	37.4	0.5	37.4	0.0
1969	37.6	0.5	37.7	0.3	37.8	0.3	37.8	0.0	38.0	0.5	38.3	0.8	38.8	1.3	38.8	0.0	39.1	0.8	39.2	0.3	39.6	1.0	39.4	-0.5
1970	39.2	-0.5	39.2	0.0	39.2	0.0	40.0	2.0	39.6	-1.0	39.8	0.5	40.0	0.5	39.8	-0.5	40.6	2.0	40.5	-0.2	40.4	-0.2	40.6	0.5

[Continued]

Plumbing Fixtures and Brass Fittings
Producer Price Index
Base 1982 = 100
[Continued]

For 1926-1993. Columns headed % show percentile change in the index from the previous period for which an index is available.

Year	Jan Index	%	Feb Index	%	Mar Index	%	Apr Index	%	May Index	%	Jun Index	%	Jul Index	%	Aug Index	%	Sep Index	%	Oct Index	%	Nov Index	%	Dec Index	%
1971	40.7	0.2	40.7	0.0	40.7	0.0	41.3	1.5	41.6	0.7	42.0	1.0	42.3	0.7	42.4	0.2	42.4	0.0	42.4	0.0	42.4	0.0	42.5	0.2
1972	42.4	-0.2	42.6	0.5	42.6	0.0	42.7	0.2	42.7	0.0	42.9	0.5	43.0	0.2	43.1	0.2	43.2	0.2	43.3	0.2	43.3	0.0	43.3	0.0
1973	43.4	0.2	43.6	0.5	44.2	1.4	44.8	1.4	45.1	0.7	45.3	0.4	45.3	0.0	45.4	0.2	45.6	0.4	45.8	0.4	46.3	1.1	46.7	0.9
1974	47.9	2.6	48.3	0.8	48.8	1.0	50.5	3.5	52.2	3.4	53.1	1.7	54.6	2.8	56.6	3.7	57.2	1.1	57.4	0.3	57.7	0.5	57.9	0.3
1975	58.3	0.7	58.4	0.2	58.7	0.5	58.3	-0.7	58.1	-0.3	58.0	-0.2	57.7	-0.5	57.6	-0.2	57.8	0.3	58.6	1.4	58.7	0.2	58.7	0.0
1976	59.0	0.5	60.4	2.4	60.5	0.2	60.9	0.7	61.4	0.8	62.8	2.3	63.8	1.6	63.8	0.0	64.2	0.6	64.2	0.0	64.3	0.2	64.3	0.0
1977	64.4	0.2	64.5	0.2	65.4	1.4	65.6	0.3	66.4	1.2	66.8	0.6	67.9	1.6	68.1	0.3	68.5	0.6	68.5	0.0	68.6	0.1	68.9	0.4
1978	69.0	0.1	69.9	1.3	70.3	0.6	70.9	0.9	71.1	0.3	71.4	0.4	71.7	0.4	72.2	0.7	72.4	0.3	72.6	0.3	72.6	0.0	73.1	0.7
1979	73.3	0.3	74.6	1.8	75.2	0.8	76.1	1.2	76.7	0.8	77.8	1.4	78.8	1.3	79.8	1.3	80.0	0.3	80.2	0.3	80.9	0.9	81.3	0.5
1980	83.5	2.7	84.9	1.7	87.0	2.5	87.5	0.6	88.8	1.5	89.2	0.5	89.6	0.4	89.9	0.3	89.9	0.0	89.9	0.0	90.5	0.7	91.5	1.1
1981	92.1	0.7	93.0	1.0	93.1	0.1	95.2	2.3	95.5	0.3	96.5	1.0	97.2	0.7	97.3	0.1	97.4	0.1	97.9	0.5	98.0	0.1	98.3	0.3
1982	98.5	0.2	99.2	0.7	100.2	1.0	100.6	0.4	100.8	0.2	101.4	0.6	101.6	0.2	98.5	-3.1	99.4	0.9	99.7	0.3	99.9	0.2	100.2	0.3
1983	100.7	0.5	101.7	1.0	102.5	0.8	103.2	0.7	103.7	0.5	104.3	0.6	104.2	-0.1	104.1	-0.1	104.9	0.8	105.0	0.1	105.5	0.5	105.5	0.0
1984	105.5	0.0	106.3	0.8	107.6	1.2	108.2	0.6	108.2	0.0	108.5	0.3	108.6	0.1	109.3	0.6	109.2	-0.1	109.9	0.6	110.9	0.9	111.0	0.1
1985	109.9	-1.0	110.1	0.2	110.4	0.3	111.7	1.2	112.1	0.4	112.3	0.2	112.3	0.0	112.4	0.1	112.6	0.2	113.0	0.4	113.0	0.0	112.9	-0.1
1986	113.0	0.1	113.5	0.4	115.7	1.9	115.8	0.1	115.9	0.1	116.3	0.3	116.2	-0.1	115.9	-0.3	116.1	0.2	115.9	-0.2	115.8	-0.1	115.6	-0.2
1987	116.2	0.5	118.4	1.9	118.3	-0.1	118.7	0.3	120.0	1.1	120.1	0.1	120.2	0.1	120.5	0.2	120.6	0.1	120.9	0.2	121.2	0.2	121.7	0.4
1988	121.9	0.2	123.6	1.4	127.6	3.2	127.9	0.2	128.4	0.4	128.7	0.2	129.0	0.2	130.6	1.2	130.8	0.2	131.6	0.6	131.8	0.2	132.2	0.3
1989	133.8	1.2	135.6	1.3	135.8	0.1	136.7	0.7	137.5	0.6	137.7	0.1	138.0	0.2	138.7	0.5	139.5	0.6	139.5	0.0	139.9	0.3	139.9	0.0
1990	141.2	0.9	141.9	0.5	142.7	0.6	143.5	0.6	144.0	0.3	144.1	0.1	144.3	0.1	144.5	0.1	145.9	1.0	146.3	0.3	146.5	0.1	146.6	0.1
1991	146.5	-0.1	149.0	1.7	149.4	0.3	150.0	0.4	150.1	0.1	150.1	0.0	150.3	0.1	150.3	0.0	150.0	-0.2	150.2	0.1	150.3	0.1	150.5	0.1
1992	150.7	0.1	151.0	0.2	152.1	0.7	153.4	0.9	153.7	0.2	153.9	0.1	154.1	0.1	154.2	0.1	152.9	-0.8	153.8	0.6	153.5	-0.2	153.8	0.2
1993	153.7	-0.1	153.3	-0.3	155.2	1.2	156.2	0.6	156.3	0.1	156.5	0.1	155.9	-0.4	156.5	0.4	156.6	0.1	156.6	0.0	156.7	0.1	156.6	-0.1

Source: U.S. Department of Labor, Bureau of Labor Statistics, Division of Industry Prices and Price Indexes. n.e.c. stands for not elsewhere classified. - indicates no data collected for period or unavailable.

Heating Equipment
Producer Price Index
Base 1982 = 100

For 1947-1993. Columns headed % show percentile change in the index from the previous period for which an index is available.

Year	Jan Index	%	Feb Index	%	Mar Index	%	Apr Index	%	May Index	%	Jun Index	%	Jul Index	%	Aug Index	%	Sep Index	%	Oct Index	%	Nov Index	%	Dec Index	%
1947	35.3	-	35.3	0.0	35.3	0.0	35.3	0.0	35.4	0.3	35.2	-0.6	35.5	0.9	35.7	0.6	36.3	1.7	36.5	0.6	36.6	0.3	36.7	0.3
1948	36.6	-0.3	36.8	0.5	36.8	0.0	37.0	0.5	37.1	0.3	37.1	0.0	37.2	0.3	38.6	3.8	39.7	2.8	39.7	0.0	39.7	0.0	39.7	0.0
1949	39.7	0.0	39.7	0.0	39.4	-0.8	39.3	-0.3	39.2	-0.3	38.9	-0.8	38.6	-0.8	38.5	-0.3	38.4	-0.3	38.4	0.0	38.3	-0.3	38.3	0.0
1950	38.2	-0.3	38.3	0.3	38.3	0.0	38.3	0.0	38.4	0.3	38.3	-0.3	38.6	0.8	39.6	2.6	40.3	1.8	41.2	2.2	41.5	0.7	42.4	2.2
1951	43.0	1.4	43.1	0.2	43.1	0.0	43.1	0.0	43.1	0.0	43.0	-0.2	42.9	-0.2	43.0	0.2	43.0	0.0	43.0	0.0	42.9	-0.2	43.0	0.2
1952	42.8	-0.5	42.8	0.0	42.8	0.0	42.7	-0.2	42.7	0.0	42.6	-0.2	42.7	0.2	42.7	0.0	42.7	0.0	42.7	0.0	42.7	0.0	42.7	0.0
1953	42.7	0.0	42.7	0.0	42.7	0.0	42.7	0.0	42.9	0.5	43.0	0.2	43.2	0.5	43.4	0.5	43.5	0.2	43.5	0.0	43.5	0.0	43.4	-0.2
1954	43.3	-0.2	43.1	-0.5	42.9	-0.5	43.0	0.2	42.7	-0.7	42.7	0.0	42.8	0.2	42.8	0.0	42.8	0.0	42.9	0.2	42.9	0.0	42.9	0.0
1955	42.7	-0.5	42.7	0.0	42.7	0.0	42.7	0.0	42.6	-0.2	42.6	0.0	42.7	0.2	43.5	1.9	44.0	1.1	44.0	0.0	44.1	0.2	44.0	-0.2
1956	44.0	0.0	44.0	0.0	44.0	0.0	44.0	0.0	44.0	0.0	44.1	0.2	44.3	0.5	44.7	0.9	45.4	1.6	45.7	0.7	45.8	0.2	45.8	0.0
1957	46.0	0.4	46.0	0.0	45.5	-1.1	45.5	0.0	45.4	-0.2	45.6	0.4	46.0	0.9	45.7	-0.7	45.7	0.0	45.7	0.0	45.7	0.0	45.5	-0.4
1958	45.4	-0.2	45.3	-0.2	45.1	-0.4	45.1	0.0	45.1	0.0	45.2	0.2	45.3	0.2	45.3	0.0	45.4	0.2	45.4	0.0	45.4	0.0	45.5	0.2
1959	45.5	0.0	45.6	0.2	45.5	-0.2	45.5	0.0	45.5	0.0	45.5	0.0	45.5	0.0	45.4	-0.2	45.4	0.0	45.4	0.0	45.4	0.0	45.4	0.0
1960	45.2	-0.4	44.9	-0.7	44.9	0.0	44.9	0.0	44.9	0.0	44.9	0.0	44.3	-1.3	44.4	0.2	44.6	0.5	44.6	0.0	44.3	-0.7	43.6	-1.6
1961	42.9	-1.6	42.9	0.0	42.7	-0.5	43.0	0.7	43.1	0.2	43.1	0.0	43.1	0.0	43.2	0.2	43.0	-0.5	42.9	-0.2	42.7	-0.5	42.9	0.5
1962	42.7	-0.5	42.7	0.0	42.6	-0.2	42.6	0.0	42.3	-0.7	42.2	-0.2	42.2	0.0	42.2	0.0	42.1	-0.2	42.2	0.2	42.2	0.0	42.4	0.5
1963	42.1	-0.7	42.0	-0.2	42.1	0.2	42.2	0.2	42.3	0.2	42.4	0.2	42.4	0.0	42.3	-0.2	42.3	0.0	42.3	0.0	42.2	-0.2	42.2	0.0
1964	41.8	-0.9	41.7	-0.2	41.9	0.5	41.9	0.0	41.8	-0.2	42.0	0.5	41.8	-0.5	41.7	-0.2	41.7	0.0	41.7	0.0	41.8	0.2	41.9	0.2
1965	41.5	-1.0	41.6	0.2	41.7	0.2	41.8	0.2	41.7	-0.2	41.8	0.2	41.7	-0.2	41.8	0.2	41.8	0.0	41.8	0.0	41.7	-0.2	41.7	0.0
1966	41.6	-0.2	41.7	0.2	41.7	0.0	41.9	0.5	41.9	0.0	42.1	0.5	42.2	0.2	42.1	-0.2	42.2	0.2	42.4	0.5	42.5	0.2	42.5	0.0
1967	42.1	-0.9	41.8	-0.7	41.9	0.2	41.9	0.0	41.9	0.0	42.2	0.7	42.2	0.0	42.1	-0.2	42.2	0.2	42.3	0.2	42.5	0.5	42.6	0.2
1968	42.5	-0.2	42.7	0.5	42.9	0.5	43.1	0.5	43.3	0.5	43.4	0.2	43.5	0.2	43.5	0.0	43.5	0.0	43.5	0.0	43.6	0.2	43.8	0.5
1969	43.7	-0.2	43.8	0.2	43.9	0.2	44.1	0.5	44.1	0.0	44.3	0.5	44.4	0.2	44.5	0.2	44.6	0.2	44.9	0.7	45.4	1.1	45.4	0.0
1970	45.4	0.0	45.5	0.2	45.7	0.4	46.1	0.9	46.2	0.2	46.6	0.9	47.0	0.9	47.0	0.0	47.1	0.2	47.4	0.6	47.6	0.4	47.7	0.2
1971	47.8	0.2	48.1	0.6	48.1	0.0	48.3	0.4	48.6	0.6	48.5	-0.2	48.8	0.6	49.0	0.4	49.0	0.0	49.0	0.0	49.0	0.0	49.0	0.0
1972	48.9	-0.2	49.0	0.2	49.3	0.6	49.7	0.8	49.8	0.2	50.0	0.4	50.2	0.4	50.2	0.0	50.3	0.2	50.2	-0.2	50.3	0.2	50.2	-0.2
1973	50.1	-0.2	50.3	0.4	50.4	0.2	50.8	0.8	50.7	-0.2	50.9	0.4	51.0	0.2	50.9	-0.2	50.9	0.0	50.9	0.0	51.0	0.2	51.3	0.6
1974	51.8	1.0	52.1	0.6	52.5	0.8	53.8	2.5	54.8	1.9	56.0	2.2	57.8	3.2	59.0	2.1	59.6	1.0	61.1	2.5	62.0	1.5	62.6	1.0
1975	62.5	-0.2	62.8	0.5	63.0	0.3	63.1	0.2	63.3	0.3	63.5	0.3	63.3	-0.3	63.4	0.2	63.4	0.0	64.1	1.1	64.5	0.6	65.4	1.4
1976	65.5	0.2	65.5	0.0	65.4	-0.2	65.7	0.5	66.1	0.6	66.2	0.2	66.8	0.9	67.2	0.6	67.6	0.6	67.5	-0.1	67.8	0.4	68.2	0.6
1977	68.7	0.7	68.8	0.1	69.0	0.3	68.9	-0.1	69.1	0.3	69.4	0.4	69.7	0.4	70.0	0.4	70.3	0.4	70.8	0.7	70.9	0.1	71.4	0.7
1978	72.2	1.1	72.0	-0.3	72.2	0.3	72.8	0.8	73.1	0.4	73.3	0.3	73.5	0.3	74.3	1.1	74.2	-0.1	74.6	0.5	74.7	0.1	75.5	1.1
1979	75.9	0.5	76.3	0.5	77.3	1.3	77.5	0.3	78.3	1.0	78.1	-0.3	78.4	0.4	79.3	1.1	80.7	1.8	81.0	0.4	81.4	0.5	82.4	1.2
1980	84.1	2.1	85.4	1.5	85.4	0.0	86.1	0.8	86.0	-0.1	86.4	0.5	86.9	0.6	87.7	0.9	88.0	0.3	88.8	0.9	89.4	0.7	90.2	0.9
1981	91.3	1.2	91.7	0.4	92.5	0.9	92.7	0.2	93.7	1.1	94.2	0.5	95.4	1.3	96.1	0.7	96.3	0.2	96.5	0.2	96.5	0.0	96.9	0.4
1982	98.4	1.5	98.3	-0.1	99.3	1.0	99.5	0.2	100.0	0.5	100.5	0.5	100.7	0.2	100.5	-0.2	100.8	0.3	100.5	-0.3	100.7	0.2	100.9	0.2
1983	101.5	0.6	101.5	0.0	101.6	0.1	102.2	0.6	102.3	0.1	102.4	0.1	103.2	0.8	103.3	0.1	104.0	0.7	103.4	-0.6	103.5	0.1	103.6	0.1
1984	104.2	0.6	104.6	0.4	104.8	0.2	105.5	0.7	106.4	0.9	106.5	0.1	107.6	1.0	107.7	0.1	107.8	0.1	107.9	0.1	107.9	0.0	108.1	0.2
1985	108.0	-0.1	108.5	0.5	108.6	0.1	108.7	0.1	109.4	0.6	109.5	0.1	109.6	0.1	110.0	0.4	110.3	0.3	110.2	-0.1	110.3	0.1	110.5	0.2
1986	111.6	1.0	111.7	0.1	111.6	-0.1	112.5	0.8	112.3	-0.2	113.0	0.6	113.1	0.1	113.5	0.4	113.4	-0.1	114.3	0.8	114.4	0.1	114.5	0.1
1987	115.3	0.7	115.4	0.1	115.7	0.3	115.6	-0.1	115.6	0.0	115.1	-0.4	115.5	0.3	115.6	0.1	115.5	-0.1	115.7	0.2	117.1	1.2	114.1	-2.6
1988	115.9	1.6	118.4	2.2	118.4	0.0	118.5	0.1	118.8	0.3	118.5	-0.3	119.9	1.2	120.1	0.2	120.0	-0.1	120.5	0.4	120.8	0.2	121.0	0.2
1989	121.8	0.7	123.2	1.1	123.7	0.4	124.6	0.7	124.7	0.1	124.3	-0.3	124.8	0.4	125.1	0.2	126.9	1.4	126.9	0.0	127.3	0.3	127.6	0.2
1990	129.9	1.8	130.8	0.7	130.9	0.1	130.7	-0.2	130.7	0.0	130.6	-0.1	131.7	0.8	131.8	0.1	132.0	0.2	133.3	1.0	133.3	0.0	133.3	0.0
1991	134.0	0.5	134.3	0.2	134.1	-0.1	133.2	-0.7	133.5	0.2	133.5	0.0	134.1	0.4	134.4	0.2	134.0	-0.3	134.8	0.6	134.8	0.0	134.6	-0.1

[Continued]

Heating Equipment
Producer Price Index
Base 1982 = 100
[Continued]

For 1947-1993. Columns headed % show percentile change in the index from the previous period for which an index is available.

Year	Jan Index	%	Feb Index	%	Mar Index	%	Apr Index	%	May Index	%	Jun Index	%	Jul Index	%	Aug Index	%	Sep Index	%	Oct Index	%	Nov Index	%	Dec Index	%
1992	136.2	1.2	136.6	0.3	137.2	0.4	137.1	-0.1	137.6	0.4	137.4	-0.1	137.6	0.1	137.4	-0.1	137.3	-0.1	137.6	0.2	137.0	-0.4	138.1	0.8
1993	139.2	0.8	139.3	0.1	139.4	0.1	140.6	0.9	140.7	0.1	141.2	0.4	140.9	-0.2	140.7	-0.1	140.2	-0.4	140.4	0.1	140.7	0.2	140.7	0.0

Source: U.S. Department of Labor, Bureau of Labor Statistics, Division of Industry Prices and Price Indexes. n.e.c. stands for not elsewhere classified. - indicates no data collected for period or unavailable.

Fabricated Structural Metal Products
Producer Price Index
Base 1982 = 100

For 1947-1993. Columns headed % show percentile change in the index from the previous period for which an index is available.

Year	Jan Index	%	Feb Index	%	Mar Index	%	Apr Index	%	May Index	%	Jun Index	%	Jul Index	%	Aug Index	%	Sep Index	%	Oct Index	%	Nov Index	%	Dec Index	%
1947	22.2	-	22.2	0.0	22.4	0.9	22.4	0.0	22.3	-0.4	22.3	0.0	22.3	0.0	22.3	0.0	22.9	2.7	23.0	0.4	23.1	0.4	23.1	0.0
1948	23.2	0.4	23.2	0.0	23.3	0.4	23.4	0.4	23.2	-0.9	23.2	0.0	23.4	0.9	24.5	4.7	24.7	0.8	24.7	0.0	24.7	0.0	24.7	0.0
1949	24.6	-0.4	24.5	-0.4	24.4	-0.4	24.0	-1.6	23.7	-1.2	23.4	-1.3	23.4	0.0	22.8	-2.6	22.7	-0.4	22.7	0.0	22.8	0.4	22.9	0.4
1950	23.0	0.4	23.4	1.7	23.4	0.0	23.3	-0.4	23.3	0.0	23.3	0.0	23.9	2.6	24.2	1.3	24.6	1.7	25.7	4.5	26.0	1.2	27.2	4.6
1951	27.6	1.5	27.8	0.7	27.7	-0.4	27.7	0.0	27.7	0.0	27.7	0.0	27.3	-1.4	27.1	-0.7	27.1	0.0	27.0	-0.4	27.0	0.0	27.0	0.0
1952	27.0	0.0	26.9	-0.4	26.9	0.0	26.9	0.0	26.9	0.0	26.9	0.0	26.9	0.0	26.9	0.0	26.9	0.0	26.6	-1.1	26.6	0.0	26.5	-0.4
1953	26.5	0.0	26.5	0.0	26.5	0.0	26.5	0.0	26.5	0.0	26.7	0.8	27.4	2.6	27.5	0.4	27.5	0.0	27.4	-0.4	27.4	0.0	27.3	-0.4
1954	27.4	0.4	27.2	-0.7	27.2	0.0	27.2	0.0	27.1	-0.4	27.0	-0.4	27.0	0.0	27.4	1.5	27.5	0.4	27.5	0.0	27.4	-0.4	27.5	0.4
1955	27.5	0.0	27.5	0.0	27.5	0.0	27.6	0.4	27.7	0.4	27.7	0.0	28.8	4.0	29.5	2.4	29.6	0.3	29.7	0.3	29.7	0.0	29.8	0.3
1956	30.0	0.7	30.0	0.0	30.2	0.7	30.6	1.3	30.1	-1.6	30.1	0.0	30.2	0.3	31.3	3.6	31.9	1.9	31.9	0.0	32.0	0.3	32.0	0.0
1957	31.2	-2.5	31.1	-0.3	31.1	0.0	30.9	-0.6	30.8	-0.3	30.7	-0.3	31.3	2.0	31.6	1.0	31.4	-0.6	31.4	0.0	31.4	0.0	31.4	0.0
1958	31.4	0.0	31.4	0.0	31.3	-0.3	31.3	0.0	31.3	0.0	31.2	-0.3	31.0	-0.6	31.1	0.3	31.0	-0.3	31.1	0.3	31.2	0.3	31.2	0.0
1959	31.2	0.0	31.2	0.0	30.8	-1.3	30.8	0.0	30.8	0.0	30.8	0.0	30.8	0.0	30.8	0.0	31.3	1.6	31.3	0.0	31.6	1.0	31.6	0.0
1960	31.6	0.0	31.6	0.0	31.7	0.3	31.5	-0.6	31.4	-0.3	31.4	0.0	31.4	0.0	31.4	0.0	31.3	-0.3	31.2	-0.3	31.2	0.0	31.2	0.0
1961	31.1	-0.3	31.1	0.0	30.9	-0.6	30.9	0.0	30.8	-0.3	30.8	0.0	30.8	0.0	30.8	0.0	30.7	-0.3	30.7	0.0	30.7	0.0	30.7	0.0
1962	30.6	-0.3	30.6	0.0	30.6	0.0	30.6	0.0	30.6	0.0	30.6	0.0	30.6	0.0	30.6	0.0	30.6	0.0	30.6	0.0	30.6	0.0	30.6	0.0
1963	30.6	0.0	30.5	-0.3	30.5	0.0	30.4	-0.3	30.5	0.3	30.6	0.3	30.6	0.0	30.6	0.0	30.7	0.3	30.7	0.0	30.8	0.3	30.8	0.0
1964	30.8	0.0	30.9	0.3	30.7	-0.6	30.8	0.3	30.7	-0.3	30.9	0.7	30.9	0.0	31.0	0.3	31.0	0.0	31.0	0.0	31.1	0.3	31.2	0.3
1965	31.3	0.3	31.2	-0.3	31.3	0.3	31.4	0.3	31.5	0.3	31.5	0.0	31.6	0.3	31.7	0.3	31.7	0.0	31.7	0.0	31.8	0.3	31.8	0.0
1966	31.9	0.3	32.0	0.3	32.1	0.3	32.3	0.6	32.3	0.0	32.4	0.3	32.5	0.3	32.5	0.0	32.5	0.0	32.6	0.3	32.6	0.0	32.7	0.3
1967	32.6	-0.3	32.6	0.0	32.6	0.0	32.7	0.3	32.7	0.0	32.7	0.0	32.8	0.3	32.9	0.3	32.9	0.0	33.0	0.3	33.0	0.0	33.0	0.0
1968	33.1	0.3	33.1	0.0	33.3	0.6	33.3	0.0	33.2	-0.3	33.5	0.9	33.5	0.0	33.7	0.6	33.8	0.3	33.9	0.3	33.9	0.0	34.0	0.3
1969	34.0	0.0	34.1	0.3	34.1	0.0	34.3	0.6	34.5	0.6	34.8	0.9	34.9	0.3	35.1	0.6	35.2	0.3	35.3	0.3	35.4	0.3	35.4	0.0
1970	35.6	0.6	35.8	0.6	36.2	1.1	36.3	0.3	36.5	0.6	36.8	0.8	37.1	0.8	37.2	0.3	37.3	0.3	37.3	0.0	37.3	0.0	37.5	0.5
1971	37.7	0.5	37.9	0.5	38.2	0.8	38.3	0.3	38.4	0.3	38.6	0.5	38.8	0.5	39.5	1.8	39.4	-0.3	39.4	0.0	39.4	0.0	39.4	0.0
1972	39.9	1.3	40.0	0.3	40.1	0.3	40.1	0.0	40.0	-0.2	40.1	0.3	40.1	0.0	40.2	0.2	40.2	0.0	40.4	0.5	40.4	0.0	40.5	0.2
1973	40.8	0.7	40.9	0.2	41.0	0.2	41.2	0.5	41.6	1.0	41.6	0.0	41.7	0.2	41.9	0.5	42.2	0.7	42.5	0.7	42.9	0.9	43.2	0.7
1974	44.4	2.8	44.9	1.1	46.0	2.4	47.2	2.6	49.8	5.5	52.1	4.6	54.2	4.0	57.5	6.1	59.0	2.6	59.7	1.2	59.9	0.3	60.0	0.2
1975	60.8	1.3	62.2	2.3	62.3	0.2	61.8	-0.8	61.9	0.2	61.9	0.0	61.8	-0.2	62.0	0.3	62.1	0.2	62.4	0.5	62.3	-0.2	62.6	0.5
1976	62.5	-0.2	62.4	-0.2	62.6	0.3	62.5	-0.2	62.6	0.2	63.0	0.6	63.5	0.8	64.1	0.9	64.6	0.8	64.8	0.3	65.0	0.3	65.3	0.5
1977	65.4	0.2	65.7	0.5	66.2	0.8	66.6	0.6	67.0	0.6	67.2	0.3	68.2	1.5	68.9	1.0	69.5	0.9	69.5	0.0	69.6	0.1	70.0	0.6
1978	70.4	0.6	71.8	2.0	72.6	1.1	73.7	1.5	73.9	0.3	74.1	0.3	74.8	0.9	75.5	0.9	75.7	0.3	76.0	0.4	76.2	0.3	76.6	0.5
1979	78.2	2.1	78.9	0.9	79.2	0.4	80.0	1.0	81.0	1.3	81.4	0.5	82.2	1.0	82.7	0.6	83.2	0.6	84.1	1.1	84.2	0.1	84.5	0.4
1980	84.9	0.5	85.2	0.4	87.0	2.1	88.3	1.5	88.5	0.2	88.6	0.1	89.3	0.8	89.6	0.3	89.9	0.3	90.9	1.1	91.2	0.3	91.6	0.4
1981	92.9	1.4	93.6	0.8	95.0	1.5	96.1	1.2	96.4	0.3	96.8	0.4	97.7	0.9	98.2	0.5	98.4	0.2	99.3	0.9	99.5	0.2	99.4	-0.1
1982	99.6	0.2	99.7	0.1	99.9	0.2	100.1	0.2	100.0	-0.1	100.2	0.2	99.7	-0.5	99.8	0.1	100.5	0.7	100.4	-0.1	100.2	-0.2	100.0	-0.2
1983	99.6	-0.4	99.4	-0.2	99.6	0.2	99.2	-0.4	99.1	-0.1	99.1	0.0	99.2	0.1	99.4	0.2	99.8	0.4	99.8	0.0	100.2	0.4	100.4	0.2
1984	100.6	0.2	100.7	0.1	101.2	0.5	101.5	0.3	101.9	0.4	102.1	0.2	102.3	0.2	102.4	0.1	102.4	0.0	102.9	0.5	102.6	-0.3	102.8	0.2
1985	102.9	0.1	102.9	0.0	103.2	0.3	103.2	0.0	103.2	0.0	103.2	0.0	103.2	0.0	103.4	0.2	103.3	-0.1	103.5	0.2	103.3	-0.2	103.3	0.0
1986	103.3	0.0	103.5	0.2	103.4	-0.1	103.4	0.0	103.3	-0.1	103.5	0.2	103.5	0.0	103.7	0.2	103.7	0.0	103.6	-0.1	104.1	0.5	103.8	-0.3
1987	103.6	-0.2	103.8	0.2	104.0	0.2	104.2	0.2	104.4	0.2	104.9	0.5	105.2	0.3	105.6	0.4	106.1	0.5	107.0	0.8	107.8	0.7	108.6	0.7
1988	110.2	1.5	110.8	0.5	111.7	0.8	112.9	1.1	113.8	0.8	114.4	0.5	115.4	0.9	115.8	0.3	116.2	0.3	116.5	0.3	116.8	0.3	117.4	0.5
1989	118.2	0.7	118.9	0.6	119.4	0.4	119.8	0.3	120.5	0.6	120.5	0.0	120.7	0.2	120.8	0.1	120.9	0.1	121.0	0.1	121.2	0.2	121.1	-0.1
1990	121.1	0.0	121.2	0.1	121.3	0.1	121.4	0.1	121.9	0.4	122.0	0.1	122.0	0.0	122.1	0.1	122.1	0.0	122.2	0.1	122.1	-0.1	122.4	0.2
1991	122.7	0.2	122.5	-0.2	122.5	0.0	122.9	0.3	122.7	-0.2	122.6	-0.1	122.5	-0.1	122.6	0.1	122.5	-0.1	122.0	-0.4	121.7	-0.2	121.7	0.0

[Continued]

Fabricated Structural Metal Products
Producer Price Index
Base 1982 = 100
[Continued]

For 1947-1993. Columns headed % show percentile change in the index from the previous period for which an index is available.

Year	Jan Index	%	Feb Index	%	Mar Index	%	Apr Index	%	May Index	%	Jun Index	%	Jul Index	%	Aug Index	%	Sep Index	%	Oct Index	%	Nov Index	%	Dec Index	%
1992	122.0	0.2	121.8	-0.2	122.0	0.2	122.2	0.2	122.0	-0.2	122.0	0.0	122.2	0.2	122.3	0.1	122.1	-0.2	122.2	0.1	122.2	0.0	122.2	0.0
1993	121.8	-0.3	122.1	0.2	122.4	0.2	122.7	0.2	122.9	0.2	123.1	0.2	123.4	0.2	123.6	0.2	123.8	0.2	124.0	0.2	124.4	0.3	124.8	0.3

Source: U.S. Department of Labor, Bureau of Labor Statistics, Division of Industry Prices and Price Indexes. n.e.c. stands for not elsewhere classified. - indicates no data collected for period or unavailable.

Miscellaneous Metal Products

Producer Price Index
Base 1982 = 100

For 1947-1993. Columns headed % show percentile change in the index from the previous period for which an index is available.

Year	Jan Index	%	Feb Index	%	Mar Index	%	Apr Index	%	May Index	%	Jun Index	%	Jul Index	%	Aug Index	%	Sep Index	%	Oct Index	%	Nov Index	%	Dec Index	%
1947	17.4	-	17.4	0.0	17.7	1.7	17.9	1.1	17.9	0.0	18.0	0.6	18.1	0.6	18.2	0.6	18.2	0.0	18.5	1.6	18.6	0.5	18.6	0.0
1948	18.6	0.0	18.9	1.6	20.0	5.8	22.5	12.5	22.5	0.0	22.6	0.4	22.6	0.0	23.6	4.4	23.8	0.8	23.8	0.0	23.9	0.4	23.9	0.0
1949	23.9	0.0	23.9	0.0	23.9	0.0	24.0	0.4	24.0	0.0	23.9	-0.4	23.9	0.0	23.8	-0.4	23.8	0.0	23.8	0.0	23.7	-0.4	23.6	-0.4
1950	24.0	1.7	24.1	0.4	24.2	0.4	24.2	0.0	24.2	0.0	24.2	0.0	24.3	0.4	24.4	0.4	25.1	2.9	25.7	2.4	25.8	0.4	26.4	2.3
1951	26.9	1.9	26.9	0.0	26.9	0.0	26.9	0.0	26.9	0.0	26.9	0.0	26.9	0.0	26.8	-0.4	26.6	-0.7	26.6	0.0	26.6	0.0	26.6	0.0
1952	26.6	0.0	26.6	0.0	26.6	0.0	26.6	0.0	26.6	0.0	26.6	0.0	26.6	0.0	26.6	0.0	26.8	0.8	26.9	0.4	26.9	0.0	27.0	0.4
1953	27.0	0.0	27.1	0.4	26.1	-3.7	26.2	0.4	26.5	1.1	26.5	0.0	26.8	1.1	27.0	0.7	27.1	0.4	27.2	0.4	27.2	0.0	27.2	0.0
1954	27.2	0.0	27.0	-0.7	27.0	0.0	26.8	-0.7	26.8	0.0	26.8	0.0	26.8	0.0	26.9	0.4	26.9	0.0	26.9	0.0	27.0	0.4	26.9	-0.4
1955	26.9	0.0	26.9	0.0	26.9	0.0	26.9	0.0	26.9	0.0	26.9	0.0	27.1	0.7	27.7	2.2	27.9	0.7	28.1	0.7	28.2	0.4	28.3	0.4
1956	28.3	0.0	28.3	0.0	28.4	0.4	28.3	-0.4	28.3	0.0	28.3	0.0	28.3	0.0	28.5	0.7	29.3	2.8	30.2	3.1	30.2	0.0	30.2	0.0
1957	30.2	0.0	30.4	0.7	30.5	0.3	30.6	0.3	30.6	0.0	30.6	0.0	31.1	1.6	31.3	0.6	31.5	0.6	31.5	0.0	31.4	-0.3	31.6	0.6
1958	31.4	-0.6	31.3	-0.3	31.3	0.0	31.2	-0.3	31.2	0.0	31.0	-0.6	31.0	0.0	31.1	0.3	31.1	0.0	31.1	0.0	31.0	-0.3	31.0	0.0
1959	31.1	0.3	31.2	0.3	31.2	0.0	31.2	0.0	31.2	0.0	31.2	0.0	31.1	-0.3	31.0	-0.3	31.2	0.6	31.3	0.3	31.5	0.6	31.3	-0.6
1960	31.3	0.0	31.3	0.0	31.2	-0.3	31.2	0.0	31.2	0.0	31.2	0.0	31.2	0.0	31.2	0.0	31.2	0.0	31.2	0.0	31.3	0.3	31.7	1.3
1961	32.0	0.9	32.0	0.0	32.0	0.0	32.1	0.3	32.1	0.0	32.0	-0.3	31.9	-0.3	32.2	0.9	32.2	0.0	32.2	0.0	32.1	-0.3	32.1	0.0
1962	32.1	0.0	32.1	0.0	32.4	0.9	32.5	0.3	32.4	-0.3	32.3	-0.3	32.3	0.0	32.3	0.0	32.3	0.0	32.3	0.0	32.3	0.0	32.3	0.0
1963	32.2	-0.3	32.2	0.0	32.2	0.0	32.3	0.3	32.3	0.0	32.6	0.9	32.7	0.3	32.7	0.0	32.7	0.0	33.3	1.8	33.3	0.0	33.6	0.9
1964	34.0	1.2	34.0	0.0	33.9	-0.3	33.9	0.0	33.6	-0.9	33.7	0.3	33.6	-0.3	33.6	0.0	33.6	0.0	33.6	0.0	33.6	0.0	33.7	0.3
1965	33.7	0.0	33.9	0.6	33.9	0.0	34.0	0.3	34.0	0.0	34.0	0.0	33.9	-0.3	34.2	0.9	34.2	0.0	34.1	-0.3	34.1	0.0	34.1	0.0
1966	34.2	0.3	34.4	0.6	34.5	0.3	34.5	0.0	34.5	0.0	34.6	0.3	34.6	0.0	34.9	0.9	35.0	0.3	35.0	0.0	35.2	0.6	35.2	0.0
1967	35.3	0.3	35.3	0.0	35.3	0.0	35.3	0.0	35.3	0.0	35.3	0.0	35.4	0.3	35.5	0.3	35.5	0.0	35.5	0.0	35.5	0.0	35.6	0.3
1968	35.7	0.3	35.9	0.6	35.9	0.0	35.9	0.0	35.9	0.0	35.9	0.0	36.0	0.3	36.0	0.0	36.3	0.8	36.6	0.8	36.6	0.0	36.8	0.5
1969	37.2	1.1	37.4	0.5	37.5	0.3	37.5	0.0	37.5	0.0	37.6	0.3	38.0	1.1	38.5	1.3	38.7	0.5	38.7	0.0	38.7	0.0	38.8	0.3
1970	38.9	0.3	39.0	0.3	39.6	1.5	39.6	0.0	39.9	0.8	40.6	1.8	40.8	0.5	40.9	0.2	41.5	1.5	41.6	0.2	41.7	0.2	41.7	0.0
1971	41.6	-0.2	41.7	0.2	41.7	0.0	41.8	0.2	41.8	0.0	42.0	0.5	42.3	0.7	42.4	0.2	42.4	0.0	42.3	-0.2	42.3	0.0	42.8	1.2
1972	43.0	0.5	43.6	1.4	44.0	0.9	44.0	0.0	44.0	0.0	44.1	0.2	44.0	-0.2	44.2	0.5	44.2	0.0	44.2	0.0	44.2	0.0	44.2	0.0
1973	44.4	0.5	44.5	0.2	44.8	0.7	45.1	0.7	45.4	0.7	45.6	0.4	45.7	0.2	46.4	1.5	46.5	0.2	46.8	0.6	47.4	1.3	47.7	0.6
1974	48.5	1.7	49.1	1.2	49.5	0.8	50.7	2.4	53.2	4.9	54.6	2.6	57.1	4.6	59.0	3.3	60.5	2.5	61.7	2.0	62.2	0.8	62.6	0.6
1975	63.1	0.8	63.3	0.3	63.7	0.6	63.8	0.2	63.5	-0.5	64.3	1.3	64.5	0.3	64.5	0.0	64.5	0.0	64.6	0.2	64.7	0.2	64.7	0.0
1976	65.0	0.5	65.0	0.0	64.9	-0.2	65.2	0.5	65.5	0.5	65.7	0.3	66.3	0.9	67.0	1.1	67.2	0.3	67.4	0.3	67.7	0.4	67.5	-0.3
1977	67.8	0.4	68.0	0.3	68.1	0.1	68.1	0.0	68.3	0.3	68.9	0.9	69.7	1.2	70.2	0.7	70.8	0.9	71.0	0.3	71.4	0.6	71.6	0.3
1978	71.8	0.3	72.2	0.6	72.8	0.8	73.3	0.7	73.9	0.8	74.8	1.2	75.6	1.1	76.4	1.1	77.0	0.8	77.3	0.4	77.9	0.8	78.2	0.4
1979	78.6	0.5	79.1	0.6	79.8	0.9	80.4	0.8	80.9	0.6	81.5	0.7	82.1	0.7	83.4	1.6	83.8	0.5	84.5	0.8	84.5	0.0	84.7	0.2
1980	85.2	0.6	85.6	0.5	86.5	1.1	87.2	0.8	87.4	0.2	88.7	1.5	88.9	0.2	89.7	0.9	90.3	0.7	90.8	0.6	91.0	0.2	91.2	0.2
1981	92.3	1.2	93.2	1.0	93.8	0.6	94.6	0.9	95.5	1.0	95.4	-0.1	96.3	0.9	96.7	0.4	96.9	0.2	97.8	0.9	98.5	0.7	98.6	0.1
1982	99.6	1.0	98.7	-0.9	98.8	0.1	99.1	0.3	100.8	1.7	100.6	-0.2	100.3	-0.3	100.4	0.1	100.5	0.1	100.6	0.1	100.4	-0.2	100.3	-0.1
1983	98.9	-1.4	98.8	-0.1	99.3	0.5	99.4	0.1	99.5	0.1	100.4	0.9	100.5	0.1	100.6	0.1	100.7	0.1	102.3	1.6	102.6	0.3	102.6	0.0
1984	102.8	0.2	103.1	0.3	103.5	0.4	103.8	0.3	103.9	0.1	104.2	0.3	104.2	0.0	104.5	0.3	104.8	0.3	106.8	1.9	106.8	0.0	106.9	0.1
1985	106.9	0.0	107.0	0.1	107.0	0.0	107.0	0.0	107.0	0.0	107.2	0.2	107.3	0.1	107.2	-0.1	107.1	-0.1	107.0	-0.1	107.1	0.1	107.0	-0.1
1986	107.1	0.1	107.2	0.1	107.2	0.0	107.2	0.0	106.8	-0.4	106.8	0.0	106.6	-0.2	106.7	0.1	106.9	0.2	107.1	0.2	107.2	0.1	107.3	0.1
1987	107.5	0.2	107.6	0.1	107.6	0.0	107.5	-0.1	107.5	0.0	107.6	0.1	107.8	0.2	107.7	-0.1	107.7	0.0	108.2	0.5	108.4	0.2	108.8	0.4
1988	109.2	0.4	109.7	0.5	110.3	0.5	111.3	0.9	112.0	0.6	111.9	-0.1	112.3	0.4	113.1	0.7	113.4	0.3	113.8	0.4	114.2	0.4	114.5	0.3
1989	115.3	0.7	115.7	0.3	115.9	0.2	116.5	0.5	116.9	0.3	117.0	0.1	117.1	0.1	117.6	0.4	117.7	0.1	117.8	0.1	118.0	0.2	118.3	0.3
1990	118.6	0.3	118.8	0.2	118.9	0.1	119.1	0.2	119.2	0.1	119.4	0.2	119.3	-0.1	119.6	0.3	119.9	0.3	119.8	-0.1	119.9	0.1	119.8	-0.1
1991	120.1	0.3	120.1	0.0	120.2	0.1	120.1	-0.1	120.4	0.2	120.6	0.2	120.9	0.2	120.7	-0.2	120.7	0.0	120.6	-0.1	120.4	-0.2	120.6	0.2

[Continued]

Miscellaneous Metal Products
Producer Price Index
Base 1982 = 100
[Continued]

For 1947-1993. Columns headed % show percentile change in the index from the previous period for which an index is available.

Year	Jan		Feb		Mar		Apr		May		Jun		Jul		Aug		Sep		Oct		Nov		Dec	
	Index	%	Index	%	Index	%	Index	%	Index	%	Index	%	Index	%	Index	%	Index	%	Index	%	Index	%	Index	%
1992	120.9	0.2	121.0	0.1	121.1	0.1	121.2	0.1	121.2	0.0	121.2	0.0	121.3	0.1	121.3	0.0	121.5	0.2	121.9	0.3	121.9	0.0	121.9	0.0
1993	121.8	-0.1	122.0	0.2	122.0	0.0	122.2	0.2	122.3	0.1	122.3	0.0	122.5	0.2	122.3	-0.2	122.6	0.2	122.4	-0.2	122.5	0.1	122.6	0.1

Source: U.S. Department of Labor, Bureau of Labor Statistics, Division of Industry Prices and Price Indexes. n.e.c. stands for not elsewhere classified. - indicates no data collected for period or unavailable.

Metal Treatment Services
Producer Price Index
Base Dec. 1984 = 100

For 1984-1993. Columns headed % show percentile change in the index from the previous period for which an index is available.

Year	Jan Index	%	Feb Index	%	Mar Index	%	Apr Index	%	May Index	%	Jun Index	%	Jul Index	%	Aug Index	%	Sep Index	%	Oct Index	%	Nov Index	%	Dec Index	%
1984	-	-	-	-	-	-	-	-	-	-	-	-	-	-	-	-	-	-	-	-	-	-	100.0	-
1985	100.4	0.4	100.9	0.5	100.8	-0.1	101.4	0.6	102.2	0.8	102.2	0.0	102.7	0.5	103.4	0.7	103.4	0.0	103.4	0.0	103.8	0.4	104.0	0.2
1986	104.5	0.5	104.2	-0.3	104.3	0.1	104.4	0.1	104.4	0.0	104.5	0.1	104.7	0.2	104.9	0.2	105.0	0.1	105.1	0.1	105.2	0.1	105.1	-0.1
1987	105.5	0.4	105.6	0.1	105.7	0.1	105.8	0.1	106.1	0.3	106.1	0.0	106.0	-0.1	106.5	0.5	106.2	-0.3	106.7	0.5	106.8	0.1	107.4	0.6
1988	107.5	0.1	107.7	0.2	107.8	0.1	108.7	0.8	108.3	-0.4	109.1	0.7	110.0	0.8	110.3	0.3	111.8	1.4	112.1	0.3	112.2	0.1	112.6	0.4
1989	113.3	0.6	113.6	0.3	114.0	0.4	114.6	0.5	114.6	0.0	114.7	0.1	114.6	-0.1	114.7	0.1	114.9	0.2	115.0	0.1	115.0	0.0	115.2	0.2
1990	115.5	0.3	115.6	0.1	115.7	0.1	115.7	0.0	115.8	0.1	115.9	0.1	116.7	0.7	116.8	0.1	116.9	0.1	117.1	0.2	116.9	-0.2	116.9	0.0
1991	117.5	0.5	117.6	0.1	117.5	-0.1	117.4	-0.1	117.3	-0.1	117.3	0.0	117.3	0.0	117.3	0.0	117.3	0.0	117.7	0.3	117.7	0.0	117.5	-0.2
1992	117.7	0.2	117.8	0.1	117.9	0.1	118.0	0.1	118.1	0.1	118.1	0.0	118.3	0.2	118.4	0.1	118.5	0.1	118.5	0.0	118.5	0.0	118.7	0.2
1993	119.1	0.3	119.3	0.2	119.4	0.1	119.6	0.2	119.6	0.0	119.7	0.1	119.9	0.2	120.1	0.2	120.1	0.0	120.2	0.1	120.3	0.1	120.3	0.0

Source: U.S. Department of Labor, Bureau of Labor Statistics, Division of Industry Prices and Price Indexes. n.e.c. stands for not elsewhere classified. - indicates no data collected for period or unavailable.

MACHINERY AND EQUIPMENT
Producer Price Index
Base 1982 = 100

For 1939-1993. Columns headed % show percentile change in the index from the previous period for which an index is available.

Year	Jan Index	%	Feb Index	%	Mar Index	%	Apr Index	%	May Index	%	Jun Index	%	Jul Index	%	Aug Index	%	Sep Index	%	Oct Index	%	Nov Index	%	Dec Index	%
1939	14.9	-	14.9	0.0	14.9	0.0	14.8	-0.7	14.8	0.0	14.8	0.0	14.8	0.0	14.8	0.0	14.8	0.0	14.8	0.0	14.8	0.0	14.8	0.0
1940	14.9	0.7	14.9	0.0	14.9	0.0	14.9	0.0	14.8	-0.7	14.9	0.7	14.9	0.0	14.9	0.0	14.9	0.0	14.9	0.0	14.9	0.0	14.9	0.0
1941	14.9	0.0	15.0	0.7	15.0	0.0	15.0	0.0	15.0	0.0	15.1	0.7	15.1	0.0	15.1	0.0	15.2	0.7	15.2	0.0	15.4	1.3	15.4	0.0
1942	15.4	0.0	15.4	0.0	15.4	0.0	15.4	0.0	15.4	0.0	15.4	0.0	15.4	0.0	15.3	-0.6	15.2	-0.7	15.2	0.0	15.2	0.0	15.2	0.0
1943	15.2	0.0	15.2	0.0	15.2	0.0	15.2	0.0	15.2	0.0	15.2	0.0	15.2	0.0	15.2	0.0	15.2	0.0	15.2	0.0	15.2	0.0	15.1	-0.7
1944	15.2	0.7	15.2	0.0	15.2	0.0	15.2	0.0	15.2	0.0	15.1	-0.7	15.1	0.0	15.1	0.0	15.1	0.0	15.1	0.0	15.1	0.0	15.1	0.0
1945	15.1	0.0	15.1	0.0	15.1	0.0	15.1	0.0	15.1	0.0	15.2	0.7	15.2	0.0	15.2	0.0	15.2	0.0	15.2	0.0	15.2	0.0	15.2	0.0
1946	15.3	0.7	15.4	0.7	15.4	0.0	15.6	1.3	16.3	4.5	16.6	1.8	16.9	1.8	17.1	1.2	17.4	1.8	17.5	0.6	17.9	2.3	18.4	2.8
1947	18.6	1.1	18.7	0.5	18.7	0.0	18.8	0.5	19.2	2.1	19.3	0.5	19.3	0.0	19.4	0.5	19.6	1.0	19.7	0.5	19.9	1.0	19.9	0.0
1948	20.1	1.0	20.1	0.0	20.2	0.5	20.2	0.0	20.2	0.0	20.4	1.0	20.7	1.5	21.2	2.4	21.6	1.9	21.8	0.9	21.9	0.5	22.0	0.5
1949	22.0	0.0	22.1	0.5	22.0	-0.5	22.0	0.0	21.9	-0.5	21.8	-0.5	21.8	0.0	21.8	0.0	21.8	0.0	21.7	-0.5	21.7	0.0	21.7	0.0
1950	21.7	0.0	21.7	0.0	21.7	0.0	21.8	0.5	21.8	0.0	22.0	0.9	22.2	0.9	22.8	2.7	23.2	1.8	23.6	1.7	23.9	1.3	24.8	3.8
1951	25.2	1.6	25.3	0.4	25.3	0.0	25.3	0.0	25.3	0.0	25.3	0.0	25.3	0.0	25.3	0.0	25.3	0.0	25.4	0.4	25.4	0.0	25.4	0.0
1952	25.4	0.0	25.4	0.0	25.4	0.0	25.4	0.0	25.4	0.0	25.3	-0.4	25.3	0.0	25.3	0.0	25.3	0.0	25.3	0.0	25.3	0.0	25.3	0.0
1953	25.3	0.0	25.3	0.0	25.4	0.4	25.6	0.8	25.7	0.4	25.9	0.8	26.0	0.4	26.2	0.8	26.3	0.4	26.3	0.0	26.3	0.0	26.3	0.0
1954	26.3	0.0	26.4	0.4	26.4	0.0	26.3	-0.4	26.3	0.0	26.3	0.0	26.3	0.0	26.3	0.0	26.3	0.0	26.3	0.0	26.4	0.4	26.4	0.0
1955	26.5	0.4	26.6	0.4	26.6	0.0	26.6	0.0	26.7	0.4	26.8	0.4	27.0	0.7	27.3	1.1	27.8	1.8	27.9	0.4	28.1	0.7	28.2	0.4
1956	28.3	0.4	28.4	0.4	28.5	0.4	28.8	1.1	29.1	1.0	29.1	0.0	29.2	0.3	29.4	0.7	30.0	2.0	30.3	1.0	30.6	1.0	30.7	0.3
1957	30.9	0.7	31.0	0.3	31.1	0.3	31.1	0.0	31.2	0.3	31.2	0.0	31.4	0.6	31.5	0.3	31.7	0.6	31.9	0.6	32.0	0.3	32.0	0.0
1958	32.1	0.3	32.0	-0.3	32.0	0.0	32.1	0.3	32.1	0.0	32.1	0.0	32.1	0.0	32.1	0.0	32.1	0.0	32.1	0.0	32.2	0.3	32.3	0.3
1959	32.4	0.3	32.4	0.0	32.5	0.3	32.5	0.0	32.6	0.3	32.7	0.3	32.9	0.6	33.0	0.3	33.0	0.0	33.0	0.0	33.1	0.3	33.1	0.0
1960	33.1	0.0	33.1	0.0	33.1	0.0	33.1	0.0	33.0	-0.3	33.0	0.0	33.0	0.0	33.0	0.0	33.0	0.0	33.0	0.0	33.0	0.0	33.0	0.0
1961	33.1	0.3	33.1	0.0	33.1	0.0	33.0	-0.3	33.0	0.0	33.0	0.0	33.0	0.0	32.9	-0.3	32.9	0.0	33.0	0.3	33.0	0.0	33.0	0.0
1962	33.0	0.0	33.0	0.0	33.1	0.3	33.1	0.0	33.1	0.0	33.0	-0.3	33.0	0.0	33.0	0.0	33.0	0.0	33.0	0.0	33.0	0.0	33.0	0.0
1963	33.0	0.0	33.0	0.0	32.9	-0.3	33.0	0.3	33.0	0.0	33.1	0.3	33.0	-0.3	33.0	0.0	33.1	0.3	33.1	0.0	33.2	0.3	33.3	0.3
1964	33.2	-0.3	33.3	0.3	33.3	0.0	33.4	0.3	33.4	0.0	33.3	-0.3	33.3	0.0	33.3	0.0	33.3	0.0	33.3	0.0	33.4	0.3	33.4	0.0
1965	33.5	0.3	33.5	0.0	33.5	0.0	33.6	0.3	33.6	0.0	33.7	0.3	33.6	-0.3	33.7	0.3	33.7	0.0	33.8	0.3	33.9	0.3	33.9	0.0
1966	34.0	0.3	34.2	0.6	34.3	0.3	34.4	0.3	34.6	0.6	34.7	0.3	34.8	0.3	34.8	0.0	34.9	0.3	35.1	0.6	35.4	0.9	35.5	0.3
1967	35.7	0.6	35.7	0.0	35.7	0.0	35.8	0.3	35.8	0.0	35.8	0.0	35.8	0.0	35.9	0.3	35.9	0.0	36.0	0.3	36.2	0.6	36.3	0.3
1968	36.6	0.8	36.7	0.3	36.7	0.0	36.9	0.5	37.0	0.3	37.0	0.0	37.1	0.3	37.1	0.0	37.2	0.3	37.3	0.3	37.4	0.3	37.5	0.3
1969	37.6	0.3	37.7	0.3	37.8	0.3	37.9	0.3	38.0	0.3	38.1	0.3	38.2	0.3	38.2	0.0	38.5	0.8	38.7	0.5	38.9	0.5	39.1	0.5
1970	39.4	0.8	39.4	0.0	39.5	0.3	39.6	0.3	39.7	0.3	39.8	0.3	40.0	0.5	40.0	0.0	40.2	0.5	40.4	0.5	40.6	0.5	40.8	0.5
1971	41.0	0.5	41.1	0.2	41.2	0.2	41.3	0.2	41.4	0.2	41.4	0.0	41.6	0.5	41.7	0.2	41.6	-0.2	41.6	0.0	41.6	0.0	41.7	0.2
1972	41.8	0.2	42.0	0.5	42.1	0.2	42.2	0.2	42.3	0.2	42.4	0.2	42.4	0.0	42.4	0.0	42.4	0.0	42.5	0.2	42.5	0.0	42.5	0.0
1973	42.6	0.2	42.8	0.5	43.0	0.5	43.3	0.7	43.6	0.7	43.7	0.2	43.8	0.2	43.9	0.2	44.0	0.2	44.2	0.5	44.4	0.5	44.7	0.7
1974	45.2	1.1	45.6	0.9	46.3	1.5	46.9	1.3	48.1	2.6	49.2	2.3	50.3	2.2	51.8	3.0	52.7	1.7	53.8	2.1	54.8	1.9	55.2	0.7
1975	56.2	1.8	56.6	0.7	57.0	0.7	57.3	0.5	57.5	0.3	57.7	0.3	58.0	0.5	58.2	0.3	58.5	0.5	58.9	0.7	59.3	0.7	59.5	0.3
1976	60.0	0.8	60.2	0.3	60.4	0.3	60.7	0.5	60.9	0.3	61.1	0.3	61.4	0.5	61.6	0.3	62.0	0.6	62.4	0.6	62.6	0.3	62.9	0.5
1977	63.4	0.8	63.7	0.5	63.9	0.3	64.2	0.5	64.6	0.6	64.8	0.3	65.2	0.6	65.6	0.6	65.9	0.5	66.6	1.1	67.0	0.6	67.3	0.4
1978	67.9	0.9	68.3	0.6	68.7	0.6	69.1	0.6	69.6	0.7	70.1	0.7	70.5	0.6	70.9	0.6	71.3	0.6	71.9	0.8	72.7	1.1	73.1	0.6
1979	73.6	0.7	74.1	0.7	74.6	0.7	75.2	0.8	75.8	0.8	76.2	0.5	77.0	1.0	77.5	0.6	78.1	0.8	78.9	1.0	79.4	0.6	80.1	0.9
1980	81.6	1.9	82.6	1.2	83.4	1.0	84.8	1.7	85.2	0.5	85.8	0.7	86.6	0.9	87.0	0.5	87.8	0.9	88.5	0.8	89.1	0.7	89.6	0.6
1981	90.9	1.5	91.6	0.8	92.4	0.9	93.1	0.8	93.5	0.4	94.0	0.5	95.0	1.1	95.5	0.5	96.2	0.7	96.6	0.4	97.0	0.4	97.6	0.6
1982	98.3	0.7	98.8	0.5	99.1	0.3	99.6	0.5	99.8	0.2	99.9	0.1	100.3	0.4	100.4	0.1	100.5	0.1	100.8	0.3	101.1	0.3	101.3	0.2
1983	101.6	0.3	102.0	0.4	102.1	0.1	102.4	0.3	102.6	0.2	102.7	0.1	103.1	0.4	103.1	0.0	103.3	0.2	103.2	-0.1	103.3	0.1	103.6	0.3

[Continued]

MACHINERY AND EQUIPMENT
Producer Price Index
Base 1982 = 100
[Continued]

For 1939-1993. Columns headed % show percentile change in the index from the previous period for which an index is available.

Year	Jan Index	%	Feb Index	%	Mar Index	%	Apr Index	%	May Index	%	Jun Index	%	Jul Index	%	Aug Index	%	Sep Index	%	Oct Index	%	Nov Index	%	Dec Index	%
1984	103.9	0.3	104.1	0.2	104.4	0.3	104.8	0.4	105.0	0.2	105.2	0.2	105.5	0.3	105.5	0.0	105.6	0.1	105.8	0.2	105.9	0.1	106.0	0.1
1985	106.5	0.5	106.8	0.3	106.8	0.0	106.9	0.1	107.1	0.2	107.2	0.1	107.3	0.1	107.5	0.2	107.6	0.1	107.6	0.0	107.7	0.1	107.8	0.1
1986	108.0	0.2	108.2	0.2	108.3	0.1	108.6	0.3	108.6	0.0	108.7	0.1	109.0	0.3	109.1	0.1	109.1	0.0	109.2	0.1	109.4	0.2	109.5	0.1
1987	109.8	0.3	109.9	0.1	110.0	0.1	110.0	0.0	110.2	0.2	110.1	-0.1	110.4	0.3	110.6	0.2	110.6	0.0	110.9	0.3	111.0	0.1	111.3	0.3
1988	111.9	0.5	112.2	0.3	112.3	0.1	112.5	0.2	112.9	0.4	112.9	0.0	113.2	0.3	113.6	0.4	113.9	0.3	114.2	0.3	114.5	0.3	114.8	0.3
1989	115.6	0.7	116.0	0.3	116.3	0.3	116.5	0.2	116.9	0.3	117.3	0.3	117.8	0.4	118.0	0.2	118.2	0.2	118.5	0.3	118.7	0.2	118.9	0.2
1990	119.6	0.6	119.7	0.1	120.0	0.3	120.2	0.2	120.4	0.2	120.5	0.1	120.8	0.2	120.9	0.1	121.2	0.2	121.4	0.2	121.7	0.2	122.0	0.2
1991	122.6	0.5	122.9	0.2	123.0	0.1	123.1	0.1	123.1	0.0	123.1	0.0	123.0	-0.1	123.0	0.0	123.0	0.0	123.0	0.0	123.1	0.1	123.2	0.1
1992	123.3	0.1	123.5	0.2	123.6	0.1	123.4	-0.2	123.4	0.0	123.2	-0.2	123.1	-0.1	123.2	0.1	123.2	0.0	123.3	0.1	123.4	0.1	123.5	0.1
1993	123.9	0.3	123.9	0.0	123.9	0.0	124.0	0.1	123.9	-0.1	124.0	0.1	124.0	0.0	124.0	0.0	124.1	0.1	124.1	0.0	124.1	0.0	124.2	0.1

Source: U.S. Department of Labor, Bureau of Labor Statistics, Division of Industry Prices and Price Indexes. n.e.c. stands for not elsewhere classified. - indicates no data collected for period or unavailable.

Agricultural Machinery and Equipment
Producer Price Index
Base 1982 = 100

For 1926-1993. Columns headed % show percentile change in the index from the previous period for which an index is available.

Year	Jan Index	%	Feb Index	%	Mar Index	%	Apr Index	%	May Index	%	Jun Index	%	Jul Index	%	Aug Index	%	Sep Index	%	Oct Index	%	Nov Index	%	Dec Index	%
1926	14.1	-	14.1	0.0	14.1	0.0	14.1	0.0	14.1	0.0	14.1	0.0	14.1	0.0	14.1	0.0	14.1	0.0	14.1	0.0	14.1	0.0	14.1	0.0
1927	14.1	0.0	14.1	0.0	14.1	0.0	14.1	0.0	14.1	0.0	14.1	0.0	14.1	0.0	14.1	0.0	14.1	0.0	14.0	-0.7	14.0	0.0	14.0	0.0
1928	14.0	0.0	14.0	0.0	14.0	0.0	14.0	0.0	14.0	0.0	14.0	0.0	14.0	0.0	14.0	0.0	14.0	0.0	14.0	0.0	14.0	0.0	14.0	0.0
1929	14.0	0.0	14.0	0.0	14.0	0.0	14.0	0.0	14.0	0.0	14.0	0.0	14.0	0.0	14.0	0.0	14.0	0.0	13.8	-1.4	13.8	0.0	13.7	-0.7
1930	13.7	0.0	13.7	0.0	13.5	-1.5	13.3	-1.5	13.3	0.0	13.3	0.0	13.3	0.0	13.3	0.0	13.3	0.0	13.3	0.0	13.3	0.0	13.3	0.0
1931	13.3	0.0	13.3	0.0	13.3	0.0	13.3	0.0	13.3	0.0	13.3	0.0	13.3	0.0	13.3	0.0	13.3	0.0	12.1	-9.0	12.1	0.0	12.1	0.0
1932	12.1	0.0	12.0	-0.8	12.0	0.0	12.0	0.0	12.0	0.0	12.0	0.0	12.0	0.0	12.0	0.0	12.0	0.0	12.0	0.0	12.0	0.0	11.9	-0.8
1933	11.9	0.0	11.7	-1.7	11.7	0.0	11.7	0.0	11.7	0.0	11.7	0.0	11.7	0.0	11.7	0.0	11.7	0.0	11.8	0.9	11.8	0.0	12.0	1.7
1934	12.0	0.0	12.0	0.0	12.0	0.0	12.0	0.0	12.9	7.5	12.9	0.0	13.0	0.8	13.0	0.0	13.0	0.0	13.0	0.0	13.0	0.0	13.1	0.8
1935	13.1	0.0	13.2	0.8	13.2	0.0	13.2	0.0	13.2	0.0	13.2	0.0	13.2	0.0	13.2	0.0	13.2	0.0	13.2	0.0	13.3	0.8	13.3	0.0
1936	13.3	0.0	13.4	0.8	13.3	-0.7	13.3	0.0	13.3	0.0	13.3	0.0	13.3	0.0	13.3	0.0	13.3	0.0	13.3	0.0	13.1	-1.5	13.1	0.0
1937	13.1	0.0	13.1	0.0	13.1	0.0	13.0	-0.8	13.2	1.5	13.3	0.8	13.3	0.0	13.3	0.0	13.3	0.0	13.3	0.0	13.6	2.3	13.6	0.0
1938	13.6	0.0	13.6	0.0	13.6	0.0	13.6	0.0	13.6	0.0	13.6	0.0	13.6	0.0	13.5	-0.7	13.5	0.0	13.5	0.0	13.2	-2.2	13.2	0.0
1939	13.2	0.0	13.1	-0.8	13.1	0.0	13.2	0.8	13.2	0.0	13.2	0.0	13.2	0.0	13.2	0.0	13.2	0.0	13.2	0.0	13.2	0.0	13.2	0.0
1940	13.2	0.0	13.2	0.0	13.2	0.0	13.2	0.0	13.1	-0.8	13.1	0.0	13.0	-0.8	13.0	0.0	13.1	0.8	13.1	0.0	13.1	0.0	13.1	0.0
1941	13.1	0.0	13.1	0.0	13.1	0.0	13.0	-0.8	13.1	0.8	13.1	0.0	13.1	0.0	13.1	0.0	13.2	0.8	13.2	0.0	13.6	3.0	13.6	0.0
1942	13.6	0.0	13.7	0.7	13.7	0.0	13.7	0.0	13.7	0.0	13.7	0.0	13.7	0.0	13.7	0.0	13.7	0.0	13.7	0.0	13.7	0.0	13.7	0.0
1943	13.7	0.0	13.7	0.0	13.7	0.0	13.7	0.0	13.7	0.0	13.7	0.0	13.7	0.0	13.7	0.0	13.7	0.0	13.7	0.0	13.7	0.0	13.7	0.0
1944	13.7	0.0	13.7	0.0	13.7	0.0	13.7	0.0	13.7	0.0	13.7	0.0	13.7	0.0	13.8	0.7	13.8	0.0	13.8	0.0	13.8	0.0	13.8	0.0
1945	13.8	0.0	13.8	0.0	13.8	0.0	13.8	0.0	13.8	0.0	13.8	0.0	13.8	0.0	13.8	0.0	13.8	0.0	13.8	0.0	13.9	0.7	13.9	0.0
1946	13.8	-0.7	13.8	0.0	13.8	0.0	13.9	0.7	14.4	3.6	14.8	2.8	14.8	0.0	15.2	2.7	15.3	0.7	15.3	0.0	15.8	3.3	16.7	5.7
1947	16.8	0.6	16.8	0.0	16.8	0.0	16.8	0.0	16.9	0.6	16.9	0.0	16.9	0.0	17.0	0.6	17.1	0.6	17.3	1.2	17.7	2.3	18.1	2.3
1948	18.2	0.6	18.3	0.5	18.4	0.5	18.5	0.5	18.6	0.5	18.8	1.1	19.1	1.6	19.3	1.0	20.0	3.6	20.3	1.5	20.5	1.0	20.5	0.0
1949	20.5	0.0	20.5	0.0	20.5	0.0	20.5	0.0	20.5	0.0	20.5	0.0	20.5	0.0	20.5	0.0	20.5	0.0	20.5	0.0	20.4	-0.5	20.4	0.0
1950	20.4	0.0	20.4	0.0	20.4	0.0	20.5	0.5	20.5	0.0	20.5	0.0	20.5	0.0	20.8	1.5	21.4	2.9	21.7	1.4	21.9	0.9	22.4	2.3
1951	22.4	0.0	22.8	1.8	22.8	0.0	22.8	0.0	22.8	0.0	22.8	0.0	22.8	0.0	22.8	0.0	22.8	0.0	22.8	0.0	22.8	0.0	22.8	0.0
1952	23.0	0.9	23.0	0.0	23.0	0.0	23.0	0.0	23.0	0.0	23.0	0.0	23.0	0.0	23.0	0.0	23.0	0.0	23.0	0.0	23.0	0.0	23.0	0.0
1953	23.0	0.0	23.0	0.0	23.1	0.4	23.2	0.4	23.2	0.0	23.2	0.0	23.2	0.0	23.2	0.0	23.2	0.0	23.2	0.0	23.2	0.0	23.2	0.0
1954	23.2	0.0	23.3	0.4	23.2	-0.4	23.2	0.0	23.2	0.0	23.2	0.0	23.2	0.0	23.1	-0.4	23.1	0.0	23.1	0.0	23.0	-0.4	23.0	0.0
1955	23.0	0.0	23.0	0.0	23.0	0.0	23.0	0.0	23.0	0.0	23.0	0.0	23.0	0.0	23.2	0.9	23.9	3.0	24.0	0.4	23.9	-0.4	23.9	0.0
1956	24.0	0.4	24.0	0.0	23.9	-0.4	23.9	0.0	23.9	0.0	24.0	0.4	24.0	0.0	24.0	0.0	24.1	0.4	24.5	1.7	24.8	1.2	24.8	0.0
1957	24.9	0.4	25.0	0.4	25.0	0.0	25.0	0.0	25.0	0.0	25.0	0.0	25.0	0.0	25.1	0.4	25.3	0.8	25.8	2.0	26.0	0.8	26.2	0.8
1958	26.2	0.0	26.2	0.0	26.2	0.0	26.2	0.0	26.2	0.0	26.2	0.0	26.2	0.0	26.1	-0.4	26.3	0.8	26.4	0.4	26.9	1.9	27.1	0.7
1959	27.1	0.0	27.1	0.0	27.1	0.0	27.1	0.0	27.2	0.4	27.2	0.0	27.2	0.0	27.2	0.0	27.2	0.0	27.2	0.0	27.3	0.4	27.3	0.0
1960	27.3	0.0	27.5	0.7	27.5	0.0	27.6	0.4	27.6	0.0	27.6	0.0	27.6	0.0	27.7	0.4	27.7	0.0	27.8	0.4	28.1	1.1	28.0	-0.4
1961	28.1	0.4	28.1	0.0	28.1	0.0	28.2	0.4	28.2	0.0	28.2	0.0	28.2	0.0	28.2	0.0	28.2	0.0	28.2	0.0	28.3	0.4	28.5	0.7
1962	28.6	0.4	28.7	0.3	28.7	0.0	28.7	0.0	28.7	0.0	28.8	0.3	28.8	0.0	28.7	-0.3	28.7	0.0	28.8	0.3	28.8	0.0	28.9	0.3
1963	29.1	0.7	29.1	0.0	29.2	0.3	29.1	-0.3	29.1	0.0	29.2	0.3	29.1	-0.3	29.1	0.0	29.1	0.0	29.2	0.3	29.3	0.3	29.4	0.3
1964	29.4	0.0	29.5	0.3	29.6	0.3	29.6	0.0	29.6	0.0	29.6	0.0	29.6	0.0	29.7	0.3	29.7	0.0	29.6	-0.3	29.9	1.0	30.0	0.3
1965	30.0	0.0	30.1	0.3	30.1	0.0	30.1	0.0	30.1	0.0	30.1	0.0	30.2	0.3	30.2	0.0	30.2	0.0	30.2	0.0	30.7	1.7	30.7	0.0
1966	30.8	0.3	30.9	0.3	31.0	0.3	31.0	0.0	31.1	0.3	31.1	0.0	31.1	0.0	31.1	0.0	31.1	0.0	31.1	0.0	31.6	1.6	31.7	0.3
1967	31.9	0.6	32.0	0.3	32.0	0.0	32.0	0.0	32.0	0.0	32.0	0.0	32.1	0.3	32.1	0.0	32.1	0.0	32.1	0.0	32.7	1.9	32.9	0.6
1968	33.0	0.3	33.1	0.3	33.1	0.0	33.1	0.0	33.1	0.0	33.2	0.3	33.3	0.3	33.4	0.3	33.5	0.3	33.7	0.6	34.0	0.9	34.2	0.6
1969	34.5	0.9	34.6	0.3	34.6	0.0	34.6	0.0	34.6	0.0	34.7	0.3	34.8	0.3	34.8	0.0	34.9	0.3	35.1	0.6	35.6	1.4	35.8	0.6
1970	35.9	0.3	36.1	0.6	36.1	0.0	36.1	0.0	36.2	0.3	36.1	-0.3	36.2	0.3	36.2	0.0	36.4	0.6	36.6	0.5	37.4	2.2	37.5	0.3

[Continued]

Agricultural Machinery and Equipment
Producer Price Index
Base 1982 = 100
[Continued]

For 1926-1993. Columns headed % show percentile change in the index from the previous period for which an index is available.

Year	Jan Index	%	Feb Index	%	Mar Index	%	Apr Index	%	May Index	%	Jun Index	%	Jul Index	%	Aug Index	%	Sep Index	%	Oct Index	%	Nov Index	%	Dec Index	%
1971	37.5	0.0	37.5	0.0	37.5	0.0	37.6	0.3	37.6	0.0	37.7	0.3	37.8	0.3	37.9	0.3	37.9	0.0	37.9	0.0	37.9	0.0	38.2	0.8
1972	38.5	0.8	39.1	1.6	39.2	0.3	39.3	0.3	39.3	0.0	39.4	0.3	39.4	0.0	39.5	0.3	39.4	-0.3	39.4	0.0	39.5	0.3	39.5	0.0
1973	39.7	0.5	40.0	0.8	40.1	0.3	40.1	0.0	40.2	0.2	40.3	0.2	40.3	0.0	40.4	0.2	40.4	0.0	41.0	1.5	41.4	1.0	41.6	0.5
1974	42.1	1.2	42.2	0.2	42.6	0.9	42.9	0.7	44.3	3.3	45.3	2.3	46.3	2.2	47.6	2.8	48.9	2.7	49.8	1.8	51.3	3.0	51.5	0.4
1975	52.6	2.1	52.8	0.4	53.4	1.1	53.6	0.4	53.8	0.4	53.9	0.2	54.2	0.6	54.3	0.2	54.4	0.2	55.1	1.3	56.0	1.6	56.3	0.5
1976	56.9	1.1	57.2	0.5	57.6	0.7	57.8	0.3	58.2	0.7	58.5	0.5	58.8	0.5	59.1	0.5	59.7	1.0	59.9	0.3	60.7	1.3	61.3	1.0
1977	61.8	0.8	62.2	0.6	62.5	0.5	62.6	0.2	62.8	0.3	63.0	0.3	63.2	0.3	63.8	0.9	64.4	0.9	64.7	0.5	66.0	2.0	66.3	0.5
1978	66.4	0.2	66.8	0.6	66.9	0.1	67.2	0.4	67.4	0.3	67.8	0.6	68.2	0.6	68.8	0.9	70.0	1.7	70.3	0.4	70.9	0.9	71.3	0.6
1979	71.6	0.4	72.0	0.6	72.3	0.4	72.8	0.7	73.4	0.8	73.7	0.4	74.3	0.8	75.0	0.9	76.3	1.7	77.1	1.0	78.2	1.4	78.5	0.4
1980	79.8	1.7	80.3	0.6	81.0	0.9	81.8	1.0	82.4	0.7	82.7	0.4	83.1	0.5	83.5	0.5	84.8	1.6	85.3	0.6	87.3	2.3	87.7	0.5
1981	88.8	1.3	89.5	0.8	90.0	0.6	90.8	0.9	91.8	1.1	92.2	0.4	92.6	0.4	93.3	0.8	94.1	0.9	95.0	1.0	96.7	1.8	97.3	0.6
1982	97.4	0.1	97.9	0.5	98.5	0.6	98.6	0.1	99.1	0.5	99.6	0.5	100.0	0.4	100.4	0.4	101.0	0.6	102.1	1.1	102.5	0.4	103.1	0.6
1983	103.6	0.5	103.9	0.3	104.0	0.1	104.1	0.1	104.9	0.8	104.9	0.0	105.1	0.2	105.2	0.1	105.6	0.4	105.4	-0.2	105.6	0.2	106.1	0.5
1984	106.4	0.3	106.5	0.1	107.0	0.5	107.9	0.8	108.7	0.7	108.6	-0.1	108.9	0.3	108.9	0.0	108.4	-0.5	108.4	0.0	108.3	-0.1	108.5	0.2
1985	108.8	0.3	108.7	-0.1	108.8	0.1	108.7	-0.1	108.8	0.1	108.9	0.1	108.9	0.0	108.7	-0.2	108.4	-0.3	108.5	0.1	108.6	0.1	108.7	0.1
1986	108.8	0.1	108.8	0.0	109.0	0.2	109.1	0.1	109.1	0.0	109.2	0.1	109.3	0.1	109.4	0.1	109.3	-0.1	109.6	0.3	109.7	0.1	109.6	-0.1
1987	108.9	-0.6	109.0	0.1	109.1	0.1	109.6	0.5	109.9	0.3	109.9	0.0	110.0	0.1	109.8	-0.2	109.7	-0.1	109.8	0.1	109.9	0.1	109.9	0.0
1988	111.4	1.4	111.5	0.1	112.2	0.6	112.3	0.1	112.5	0.2	111.8	-0.6	112.4	0.5	113.2	0.7	113.3	0.1	113.3	0.0	114.0	0.6	114.2	0.2
1989	114.2	0.0	116.5	2.0	116.5	0.0	116.9	0.3	117.7	0.7	117.6	-0.1	117.9	0.3	118.3	0.3	118.7	0.3	118.5	-0.2	119.5	0.8	120.1	0.5
1990	120.4	0.2	120.5	0.1	120.7	0.2	121.2	0.4	121.3	0.1	121.4	0.1	121.5	0.1	122.3	0.7	122.6	0.2	122.3	-0.2	122.8	0.4	123.4	0.5
1991	123.7	0.2	124.4	0.6	124.7	0.2	124.9	0.2	125.1	0.2	125.4	0.2	125.6	0.2	126.2	0.5	126.5	0.2	126.6	0.1	127.7	0.9	127.7	0.0
1992	127.9	0.2	128.3	0.3	128.5	0.2	128.7	0.2	128.7	0.0	128.8	0.1	128.9	0.1	129.1	0.2	131.3	1.7	131.4	0.1	131.4	0.0	131.5	0.1
1993	131.7	0.2	132.1	0.3	132.3	0.2	133.1	0.6	133.5	0.3	133.6	0.1	133.6	0.0	133.7	0.1	134.0	0.2	134.5	0.4	134.4	-0.1	135.3	0.7

Source: U.S. Department of Labor, Bureau of Labor Statistics, Division of Industry Prices and Price Indexes. n.e.c. stands for not elsewhere classified. - indicates no data collected for period or unavailable.

Construction Machinery and Equipment
Producer Price Index
Base 1982 = 100

For 1939-1993. Columns headed % show percentile change in the index from the previous period for which an index is available.

Year	Jan Index	%	Feb Index	%	Mar Index	%	Apr Index	%	May Index	%	Jun Index	%	Jul Index	%	Aug Index	%	Sep Index	%	Oct Index	%	Nov Index	%	Dec Index	%
1939	-	-	-	-	-	-	-	-	-	-	-	-	-	-	9.3	-	9.3	0.0	9.3	0.0	9.4	1.1	9.4	0.0
1940	9.4	0.0	9.4	0.0	9.4	0.0	9.4	0.0	9.4	0.0	9.4	0.0	9.5	1.1	9.5	0.0	9.5	0.0	9.5	0.0	9.5	0.0	9.5	0.0
1941	9.6	1.1	9.7	1.0	9.7	0.0	9.8	1.0	9.8	0.0	9.9	1.0	9.9	0.0	10.1	2.0	10.2	1.0	10.3	1.0	10.3	0.0	10.3	0.0
1942	10.3	0.0	10.3	0.0	10.3	0.0	10.3	0.0	10.3	0.0	10.3	0.0	10.3	0.0	10.3	0.0	10.3	0.0	10.3	0.0	10.3	0.0	10.3	0.0
1943	10.3	0.0	10.3	0.0	10.3	0.0	10.3	0.0	10.3	0.0	10.3	0.0	10.3	0.0	10.3	0.0	10.3	0.0	10.3	0.0	10.3	0.0	10.3	0.0
1944	10.3	0.0	10.3	0.0	10.3	0.0	10.3	0.0	10.3	0.0	10.3	0.0	10.3	0.0	10.3	0.0	10.3	0.0	10.3	0.0	10.3	0.0	10.4	1.0
1945	10.4	0.0	10.4	0.0	10.4	0.0	10.4	0.0	10.4	0.0	10.4	0.0	10.4	0.0	10.4	0.0	10.4	0.0	10.5	1.0	10.6	1.0	10.6	0.0
1946	10.6	0.0	10.7	0.9	10.7	0.0	11.0	2.8	11.2	1.8	11.4	1.8	11.4	0.0	11.4	0.0	11.5	0.9	11.7	1.7	11.7	0.0	12.0	2.6
1947	12.3	2.5	12.4	0.8	12.4	0.0	12.4	0.0	12.6	1.6	12.7	0.8	12.9	1.6	12.9	0.0	13.0	0.8	13.1	0.8	13.3	1.5	13.5	1.5
1948	13.6	0.7	13.7	0.7	13.8	0.7	13.9	0.7	13.9	0.0	14.2	2.2	14.4	1.4	14.8	2.8	15.2	2.7	15.4	1.3	15.4	0.0	15.5	0.6
1949	15.5	0.0	15.5	0.0	15.4	-0.6	15.4	0.0	15.4	0.0	15.4	0.0	15.4	0.0	15.4	0.0	15.4	0.0	15.4	0.0	15.4	0.0	15.4	0.0
1950	15.4	0.0	15.4	0.0	15.4	0.0	15.4	0.0	15.4	0.0	15.4	0.0	15.5	0.6	16.0	3.2	16.3	1.9	16.5	1.2	16.5	0.0	17.3	4.8
1951	17.5	1.2	17.6	0.6	17.6	0.0	17.6	0.0	17.6	0.0	17.6	0.0	17.6	0.0	17.6	0.0	17.6	0.0	17.6	0.0	17.6	0.0	17.6	0.0
1952	17.7	0.6	17.8	0.6	17.8	0.0	17.8	0.0	17.8	0.0	17.9	0.6	17.9	0.0	17.8	-0.6	17.9	0.6	17.9	0.0	18.0	0.6	18.0	0.0
1953	18.0	0.0	18.0	0.0	18.1	0.6	18.3	1.1	18.3	0.0	18.4	0.5	18.6	1.1	18.6	0.0	18.6	0.0	18.6	0.0	18.6	0.0	18.6	0.0
1954	18.7	0.5	18.7	0.0	18.7	0.0	18.7	0.0	18.7	0.0	18.7	0.0	18.7	0.0	18.7	0.0	18.7	0.0	18.7	0.0	18.7	0.0	18.9	1.1
1955	19.0	0.5	19.0	0.0	19.0	0.0	19.1	0.5	19.1	0.0	19.2	0.5	19.2	0.0	19.7	2.6	20.0	1.5	20.2	1.0	20.2	0.0	20.3	0.5
1956	20.4	0.5	20.4	0.0	20.4	0.0	20.6	1.0	20.8	1.0	20.8	0.0	21.0	1.0	21.3	1.4	21.5	0.9	22.0	2.3	22.1	0.5	22.2	0.5
1957	22.2	0.0	22.2	0.0	22.2	0.0	22.4	0.9	22.4	0.0	22.4	0.0	22.4	0.0	22.9	2.2	23.1	0.9	23.4	1.3	23.5	0.4	23.5	0.0
1958	23.5	0.0	23.5	0.0	23.5	0.0	23.5	0.0	23.5	0.0	23.5	0.0	23.5	0.0	23.5	0.0	23.6	0.4	23.7	0.4	23.9	0.8	24.2	1.3
1959	24.3	0.4	24.4	0.4	24.4	0.0	24.4	0.0	24.4	0.0	24.4	0.0	24.4	0.0	24.5	0.4	24.5	0.0	24.5	0.0	24.6	0.4	24.6	0.0
1960	24.7	0.4	24.7	0.0	24.8	0.4	24.9	0.4	24.9	0.0	24.9	0.0	25.0	0.4	25.1	0.4	25.1	0.0	25.1	0.0	25.2	0.4	25.2	0.0
1961	25.3	0.4	25.4	0.4	25.4	0.0	25.4	0.0	25.4	0.0	25.4	0.0	25.4	0.0	25.4	0.0	25.4	0.0	25.4	0.0	25.4	0.0	25.4	0.0
1962	25.4	0.0	25.4	0.0	25.4	0.0	25.4	0.0	25.4	0.0	25.4	0.0	25.4	0.0	25.4	0.0	25.4	0.0	25.5	0.4	25.5	0.0	25.6	0.4
1963	25.6	0.0	25.6	0.0	25.7	0.4	25.7	0.0	25.8	0.4	25.9	0.4	25.9	0.0	26.0	0.4	26.0	0.0	26.1	0.4	26.2	0.4	26.3	0.4
1964	26.4	0.4	26.4	0.0	26.4	0.0	26.5	0.4	26.5	0.0	26.5	0.0	26.5	0.0	26.5	0.0	26.5	0.0	26.5	0.0	26.8	1.1	26.8	0.0
1965	26.9	0.4	27.0	0.4	27.0	0.0	27.1	0.4	27.2	0.4	27.2	0.0	27.2	0.0	27.3	0.4	27.3	0.0	27.3	0.0	27.5	0.7	27.5	0.0
1966	27.6	0.4	27.7	0.4	27.8	0.4	28.0	0.7	28.1	0.4	28.1	0.0	28.1	0.0	28.1	0.0	28.2	0.4	28.3	0.4	28.5	0.7	28.6	0.4
1967	28.6	0.0	28.7	0.3	28.8	0.3	28.8	0.0	28.9	0.3	28.9	0.0	29.0	0.3	29.0	0.0	29.0	0.0	29.4	1.4	29.7	1.0	29.9	0.7
1968	30.2	1.0	30.3	0.3	30.4	0.3	30.5	0.3	30.6	0.3	30.6	0.0	30.6	0.0	30.6	0.0	30.9	1.0	31.1	0.6	31.4	1.0	31.4	0.0
1969	31.6	0.6	31.7	0.3	31.8	0.3	31.8	0.0	31.8	0.0	31.9	0.3	32.0	0.3	32.0	0.0	32.3	0.9	32.7	1.2	32.9	0.6	33.1	0.6
1970	33.1	0.0	33.2	0.3	33.2	0.0	33.2	0.0	33.4	0.6	33.4	0.0	33.4	0.0	33.6	0.6	33.7	0.3	34.4	2.1	34.7	0.9	35.0	0.9
1971	35.1	0.3	35.2	0.3	35.2	0.0	35.3	0.3	35.3	0.0	35.3	0.0	35.5	0.6	35.5	0.0	35.5	0.0	35.5	0.0	35.5	0.0	35.9	1.1
1972	36.1	0.6	36.3	0.6	36.3	0.0	36.5	0.6	36.5	0.0	36.6	0.3	36.6	0.0	36.7	0.3	36.7	0.0	36.7	0.0	36.7	0.0	36.7	0.0
1973	36.8	0.3	37.0	0.5	37.4	1.1	37.9	1.3	38.1	0.5	38.2	0.3	38.2	0.0	38.2	0.0	38.2	0.0	38.5	0.8	38.6	0.3	39.0	1.0
1974	39.4	1.0	39.8	1.0	40.3	1.3	40.7	1.0	42.2	3.7	43.3	2.6	44.0	1.6	46.9	6.6	47.5	1.3	48.6	2.3	49.1	1.0	49.4	0.6
1975	51.6	4.5	52.4	1.6	52.9	1.0	53.5	1.1	53.5	0.0	53.6	0.2	53.8	0.4	53.9	0.2	54.5	1.1	54.8	0.6	55.6	1.5	56.0	0.7
1976	56.2	0.4	56.6	0.7	56.7	0.2	56.8	0.2	57.1	0.5	57.5	0.7	58.1	1.0	58.3	0.3	58.4	0.2	58.9	0.9	59.5	1.0	59.9	0.7
1977	60.2	0.5	60.5	0.5	60.6	0.2	61.1	0.8	61.6	0.8	61.7	0.2	62.2	0.8	62.6	0.6	62.4	-0.3	63.2	1.3	64.2	1.6	64.9	1.1
1978	65.0	0.2	65.4	0.6	65.6	0.3	66.4	1.2	67.0	0.9	67.2	0.3	67.7	0.7	68.2	0.7	68.9	1.0	69.9	1.5	70.5	0.9	70.9	0.6
1979	71.4	0.7	72.1	1.0	72.3	0.3	73.2	1.2	73.8	0.8	73.9	0.1	74.7	1.1	75.2	0.7	75.3	0.1	76.7	1.9	77.2	0.7	78.2	1.3
1980	80.3	2.7	80.9	0.7	81.3	0.5	82.6	1.6	83.1	0.6	83.6	0.6	84.8	1.4	85.3	0.6	86.0	0.8	87.0	1.2	87.3	0.3	87.6	0.3
1981	88.9	1.5	90.1	1.3	90.9	0.9	92.2	1.4	92.6	0.4	93.1	0.5	94.2	1.2	94.5	0.3	94.9	0.4	95.5	0.6	95.9	0.4	96.5	0.6
1982	98.0	1.6	98.3	0.3	98.6	0.3	99.3	0.7	99.9	0.6	100.0	0.1	100.6	0.6	100.8	0.2	101.1	0.3	101.1	0.0	101.2	0.1	101.2	0.0
1983	101.3	0.1	101.6	0.3	101.7	0.1	102.0	0.3	102.4	0.4	102.5	0.1	102.6	0.1	102.6	0.0	102.8	0.2	102.8	0.0	102.9	0.1	102.8	-0.1

[Continued]

Construction Machinery and Equipment
Producer Price Index
Base 1982 = 100
[Continued]

For 1939-1993. Columns headed % show percentile change in the index from the previous period for which an index is available.

Year	Jan Index	%	Feb Index	%	Mar Index	%	Apr Index	%	May Index	%	Jun Index	%	Jul Index	%	Aug Index	%	Sep Index	%	Oct Index	%	Nov Index	%	Dec Index	%
1984	103.0	0.2	103.5	0.5	103.3	-0.2	104.0	0.7	104.0	0.0	104.1	0.1	104.2	0.1	103.8	-0.4	103.9	0.1	104.0	0.1	104.0	0.0	104.0	0.0
1985	105.3	1.3	105.6	0.3	105.4	-0.2	105.2	-0.2	105.2	0.0	105.3	0.1	105.3	0.0	105.4	0.1	105.5	0.1	105.6	0.1	105.7	0.1	105.7	0.0
1986	106.2	0.5	106.3	0.1	106.3	0.0	106.4	0.1	106.5	0.1	106.7	0.2	106.7	0.0	106.7	0.0	106.7	0.0	106.7	0.0	107.5	0.7	107.5	0.0
1987	107.7	0.2	107.9	0.2	108.4	0.5	108.5	0.1	109.2	0.6	109.2	0.0	109.1	-0.1	109.2	0.1	109.3	0.1	109.4	0.1	109.5	0.1	109.7	0.2
1988	110.6	0.8	111.0	0.4	111.0	0.0	111.1	0.1	111.1	0.0	111.2	0.1	111.9	0.6	112.3	0.4	112.3	0.0	112.3	0.0	113.0	0.6	113.2	0.2
1989	115.1	1.7	115.3	0.2	115.8	0.4	116.1	0.3	116.3	0.2	117.6	1.1	117.9	0.3	118.2	0.3	118.3	0.1	118.2	-0.1	118.5	0.3	118.6	0.1
1990	119.7	0.9	120.5	0.7	120.5	0.0	120.5	0.0	120.8	0.2	121.3	0.4	122.4	0.9	122.7	0.2	122.5	-0.2	122.6	0.1	122.8	0.2	123.1	0.2
1991	123.7	0.5	124.2	0.4	124.4	0.2	124.5	0.1	124.6	0.1	124.7	0.1	125.7	0.8	125.8	0.1	125.8	0.0	125.8	0.0	126.3	0.4	126.6	0.2
1992	126.8	0.2	127.3	0.4	127.4	0.1	127.7	0.2	127.7	0.0	128.2	0.4	129.4	0.9	129.6	0.2	129.7	0.1	129.8	0.1	130.2	0.3	130.5	0.2
1993	131.6	0.8	132.3	0.5	132.3	0.0	132.0	-0.2	132.1	0.1	132.2	0.1	132.2	0.0	132.3	0.1	132.2	-0.1	131.7	-0.4	131.9	0.2	132.1	0.2

Source: U.S. Department of Labor, Bureau of Labor Statistics, Division of Industry Prices and Price Indexes. n.e.c. stands for not elsewhere classified. - indicates no data collected for period or unavailable.

Metalworking Machinery and Equipment
Producer Price Index
Base 1982 = 100

For 1947-1993. Columns headed % show percentile change in the index from the previous period for which an index is available.

Year	Jan Index	%	Feb Index	%	Mar Index	%	Apr Index	%	May Index	%	Jun Index	%	Jul Index	%	Aug Index	%	Sep Index	%	Oct Index	%	Nov Index	%	Dec Index	%
1947	13.9	-	13.9	0.0	13.9	0.0	14.0	0.7	14.2	1.4	14.3	0.7	14.3	0.0	14.5	1.4	14.5	0.0	14.7	1.4	14.8	0.7	14.8	0.0
1948	15.0	1.4	15.0	0.0	15.0	0.0	15.1	0.7	15.1	0.0	15.1	0.0	15.2	0.7	15.6	2.6	15.9	1.9	16.0	0.6	16.0	0.0	16.1	0.6
1949	16.2	0.6	16.2	0.0	16.2	0.0	16.2	0.0	16.2	0.0	16.2	0.0	16.2	0.0	16.1	-0.6	16.1	0.0	16.1	0.0	16.1	0.0	16.1	0.0
1950	16.3	1.2	16.3	0.0	16.3	0.0	16.6	1.8	16.7	0.6	16.7	0.0	16.9	1.2	17.4	3.0	17.7	1.7	17.9	1.1	18.2	1.7	18.8	3.3
1951	19.1	1.6	19.1	0.0	19.1	0.0	19.1	0.0	19.1	0.0	19.0	-0.5	19.0	0.0	19.0	0.0	19.2	1.1	19.4	1.0	19.5	0.5	19.6	0.5
1952	19.5	-0.5	19.5	0.0	19.5	0.0	19.5	0.0	19.5	0.0	19.5	0.0	19.5	0.0	19.5	0.0	19.5	0.0	19.5	0.0	19.5	0.0	19.5	0.0
1953	19.5	0.0	19.5	0.0	19.5	0.0	19.6	0.5	19.7	0.5	19.8	0.5	19.9	0.5	19.9	0.0	20.0	0.5	20.0	0.0	20.0	0.0	20.0	0.0
1954	20.0	0.0	20.1	0.5	20.1	0.0	20.0	-0.5	20.0	0.0	20.0	0.0	20.0	0.0	20.1	0.5	20.1	0.0	20.2	0.5	20.2	0.0	20.2	0.0
1955	20.3	0.5	20.4	0.5	20.4	0.0	20.5	0.5	20.8	1.5	21.2	1.9	21.5	1.4	21.6	0.5	21.7	0.5	21.8	0.5	21.9	0.5	22.0	0.5
1956	22.2	0.9	22.3	0.5	22.6	1.3	22.8	0.9	22.9	0.4	23.0	0.4	23.0	0.0	23.2	0.9	23.7	2.2	24.0	1.3	24.0	0.0	24.1	0.4
1957	24.1	0.0	24.2	0.4	24.3	0.4	24.3	0.0	24.3	0.0	24.3	0.0	24.5	0.8	24.6	0.4	24.8	0.8	25.1	1.2	25.2	0.4	25.2	0.0
1958	25.2	0.0	25.2	0.0	25.2	0.0	25.2	0.0	25.1	-0.4	25.1	0.0	25.1	0.0	25.1	0.0	25.1	0.0	25.2	0.4	25.2	0.0	25.2	0.0
1959	25.3	0.4	25.4	0.4	25.6	0.8	25.6	0.0	25.6	0.0	25.7	0.4	25.7	0.0	26.0	1.2	26.1	0.4	26.1	0.0	26.1	0.0	26.1	0.0
1960	26.1	0.0	26.2	0.4	26.3	0.4	26.3	0.0	26.4	0.4	26.5	0.4	26.5	0.0	26.5	0.0	26.6	0.4	26.7	0.4	26.8	0.4	26.8	0.0
1961	26.8	0.0	26.8	0.0	26.8	0.0	26.6	-0.7	26.6	0.0	26.6	0.0	26.6	0.0	26.6	0.0	26.7	0.4	26.8	0.4	26.9	0.4	27.0	0.4
1962	27.1	0.4	27.1	0.0	27.2	0.4	27.2	0.0	27.2	0.0	27.3	0.4	27.3	0.0	27.4	0.4	27.4	0.0	27.4	0.0	27.4	0.0	27.2	-0.4
1963	27.2	0.0	27.2	0.0	27.2	0.0	27.2	0.0	27.2	0.0	27.3	0.4	27.3	0.0	27.4	0.4	27.4	0.0	27.4	0.0	27.4	0.0	27.5	0.4
1964	27.5	0.0	27.5	0.0	27.5	0.0	27.6	0.4	27.7	0.4	27.8	0.4	28.0	0.7	28.0	0.0	28.0	0.0	28.1	0.4	28.1	0.0	28.1	0.0
1965	28.3	0.7	28.4	0.4	28.4	0.0	28.4	0.0	28.5	0.4	28.5	0.0	28.5	0.0	28.7	0.7	28.8	0.3	28.9	0.3	28.9	0.0	29.0	0.3
1966	29.1	0.3	29.3	0.7	29.4	0.3	29.4	0.0	29.7	1.0	29.9	0.7	29.9	0.0	30.1	0.7	30.3	0.7	30.5	0.7	30.6	0.3	30.7	0.3
1967	30.7	0.0	30.8	0.3	30.9	0.3	30.9	0.0	31.1	0.6	31.1	0.0	31.2	0.3	31.3	0.3	31.3	0.0	31.4	0.3	31.6	0.6	31.7	0.3
1968	31.8	0.3	31.9	0.3	32.0	0.3	32.2	0.6	32.3	0.3	32.3	0.0	32.5	0.6	32.6	0.3	32.7	0.3	32.7	0.0	32.8	0.3	32.9	0.3
1969	33.0	0.3	33.1	0.3	33.1	0.0	33.2	0.3	33.3	0.3	33.3	0.0	33.6	0.9	33.7	0.3	33.9	0.6	34.1	0.6	34.5	1.2	34.8	0.9
1970	35.1	0.9	35.2	0.3	35.3	0.3	35.3	0.0	35.7	1.1	35.8	0.3	35.9	0.3	35.5	-1.1	35.6	0.3	35.7	0.3	35.8	0.3	35.9	0.3
1971	36.0	0.3	36.2	0.6	36.2	0.0	36.4	0.6	36.6	0.5	36.8	0.5	36.9	0.3	37.0	0.3	37.0	0.0	37.0	0.0	37.0	0.0	37.0	0.0
1972	36.9	-0.3	37.1	0.5	37.2	0.3	37.3	0.3	37.4	0.3	37.4	0.0	37.5	0.3	37.6	0.3	37.7	0.3	37.8	0.3	37.8	0.0	37.8	0.0
1973	38.0	0.5	38.1	0.3	38.5	1.0	38.8	0.8	39.0	0.5	39.2	0.5	39.2	0.0	39.2	0.0	39.5	0.8	39.7	0.5	39.9	0.5	40.2	0.8
1974	40.9	1.7	41.2	0.7	41.8	1.5	42.6	1.9	43.9	3.1	45.1	2.7	46.5	3.1	47.6	2.4	48.6	2.1	49.8	2.5	50.4	1.2	50.8	0.8
1975	51.4	1.2	52.1	1.4	52.6	1.0	52.9	0.6	53.0	0.2	53.6	1.1	53.8	0.4	53.9	0.2	53.9	0.0	54.6	1.3	54.9	0.5	55.1	0.4
1976	55.5	0.7	55.7	0.4	55.9	0.4	56.3	0.7	56.5	0.4	56.7	0.4	56.9	0.4	57.2	0.5	57.5	0.5	57.9	0.7	58.4	0.9	58.8	0.7
1977	59.5	1.2	60.0	0.8	60.4	0.7	60.7	0.5	61.0	0.5	61.7	1.1	62.1	0.6	62.6	0.8	62.9	0.5	63.4	0.8	63.9	0.8	64.2	0.5
1978	64.9	1.1	65.3	0.6	65.7	0.6	66.1	0.6	66.7	0.9	67.2	0.7	67.5	0.4	68.0	0.7	68.7	1.0	69.7	1.5	70.5	1.1	71.1	0.9
1979	71.8	1.0	72.3	0.7	72.6	0.4	73.3	1.0	74.1	1.1	74.5	0.5	75.2	0.9	75.9	0.9	76.8	1.2	77.8	1.3	78.6	1.0	79.3	0.9
1980	80.7	1.8	81.6	1.1	82.3	0.9	84.2	2.3	85.0	1.0	85.8	0.9	86.6	0.9	86.9	0.3	87.3	0.5	88.0	0.8	88.5	0.6	89.0	0.6
1981	90.3	1.5	90.9	0.7	91.9	1.1	93.1	1.3	93.5	0.4	93.9	0.4	94.4	0.5	94.6	0.2	95.1	0.5	95.5	0.4	95.9	0.4	97.5	1.7
1982	98.4	0.9	98.9	0.5	99.0	0.1	99.6	0.6	99.9	0.3	100.1	0.2	100.5	0.4	100.6	0.1	100.7	0.1	100.7	0.0	100.8	0.1	100.8	0.0
1983	101.0	0.2	101.3	0.3	101.4	0.1	101.7	0.3	101.8	0.1	101.9	0.1	101.8	-0.1	101.7	-0.1	101.8	0.1	101.9	0.1	102.0	0.1	102.4	0.4
1984	102.6	0.2	102.9	0.3	103.0	0.1	103.6	0.6	103.9	0.3	103.9	0.0	104.1	0.2	104.3	0.2	104.6	0.3	105.0	0.4	105.4	0.4	105.5	0.1
1985	105.5	0.0	105.8	0.3	106.0	0.2	106.2	0.2	106.3	0.1	106.5	0.2	106.6	0.1	107.1	0.5	107.1	0.0	107.2	0.1	107.2	0.0	107.2	0.0
1986	107.6	0.4	107.8	0.2	107.9	0.1	108.1	0.2	108.2	0.1	108.5	0.3	108.7	0.2	108.7	0.0	108.7	0.0	108.9	0.2	109.0	0.1	109.2	0.2
1987	109.3	0.1	109.4	0.1	109.6	0.2	109.8	0.2	109.9	0.1	109.8	-0.1	110.3	0.5	110.3	0.0	110.5	0.2	110.6	0.1	110.8	0.2	111.0	0.2
1988	111.4	0.4	111.7	0.3	112.4	0.6	112.7	0.3	113.0	0.3	113.2	0.2	113.6	0.4	114.2	0.5	114.5	0.3	114.7	0.2	115.0	0.3	115.3	0.3
1989	116.0	0.6	116.4	0.3	116.9	0.4	117.4	0.4	117.8	0.3	118.1	0.3	118.5	0.3	118.8	0.3	119.0	0.2	119.3	0.3	119.9	0.5	120.1	0.2
1990	120.7	0.5	121.4	0.6	122.2	0.7	122.4	0.2	122.7	0.2	122.8	0.1	122.9	0.1	123.1	0.2	123.6	0.4	124.3	0.6	124.6	0.2	124.8	0.2
1991	126.4	1.3	126.7	0.2	127.1	0.3	127.2	0.1	127.3	0.1	127.8	0.4	128.0	0.2	128.0	0.0	128.1	0.1	128.2	0.1	128.4	0.2	128.5	0.1

[Continued]

Metalworking Machinery and Equipment
Producer Price Index
Base 1982 = 100
[Continued]

For 1947-1993. Columns headed % show percentile change in the index from the previous period for which an index is available.

Year	Jan Index	%	Feb Index	%	Mar Index	%	Apr Index	%	May Index	%	Jun Index	%	Jul Index	%	Aug Index	%	Sep Index	%	Oct Index	%	Nov Index	%	Dec Index	%
1992	129.4	0.7	129.7	0.2	130.2	0.4	130.6	0.3	130.8	0.2	130.8	0.0	131.0	0.2	131.5	0.4	131.6	0.1	131.7	0.1	131.6	-0.1	131.7	0.1
1993	132.4	0.5	132.5	0.1	133.0	0.4	132.8	-0.2	133.0	0.2	133.3	0.2	133.7	0.3	133.8	0.1	134.3	0.4	134.2	-0.1	134.3	0.1	134.3	0.0

Source: U.S. Department of Labor, Bureau of Labor Statistics, Division of Industry Prices and Price Indexes. n.e.c. stands for not elsewhere classified. - indicates no data collected for period or unavailable.

General Purpose Machinery and Equipment
Producer Price Index
Base 1982 = 100

For 1939-1993. Columns headed % show percentile change in the index from the previous period for which an index is available.

Year	Jan Index	%	Feb Index	%	Mar Index	%	Apr Index	%	May Index	%	Jun Index	%	Jul Index	%	Aug Index	%	Sep Index	%	Oct Index	%	Nov Index	%	Dec Index	%
1939	13.4	-	13.3	-0.7	13.3	0.0	13.3	0.0	13.3	0.0	13.3	0.0	13.3	0.0	13.3	0.0	13.3	0.0	13.3	0.0	13.3	0.0	13.3	0.0
1940	13.3	0.0	13.3	0.0	13.3	0.0	13.3	0.0	13.3	0.0	13.3	0.0	13.3	0.0	13.3	0.0	13.3	0.0	13.3	0.0	13.3	0.0	13.3	0.0
1941	13.4	0.8	13.4	0.0	13.4	0.0	13.4	0.0	13.4	0.0	13.6	1.5	13.6	0.0	13.7	0.7	13.7	0.0	13.7	0.0	13.7	0.0	13.8	0.7
1942	13.9	0.7	13.8	-0.7	13.8	0.0	13.8	0.0	13.8	0.0	13.8	0.0	13.8	0.0	13.6	-1.4	13.6	0.0	13.6	0.0	13.5	-0.7	13.5	0.0
1943	13.5	0.0	13.5	0.0	13.5	0.0	13.5	0.0	13.4	-0.7	13.4	0.0	13.4	0.0	13.4	0.0	13.4	0.0	13.4	0.0	13.4	0.0	13.4	0.0
1944	13.4	0.0	13.4	0.0	13.4	0.0	13.4	0.0	13.4	0.0	13.4	0.0	13.4	0.0	13.4	0.0	13.4	0.0	13.4	0.0	13.4	0.0	13.4	0.0
1945	13.4	0.0	13.4	0.0	13.4	0.0	13.4	0.0	13.4	0.0	13.4	0.0	13.4	0.0	13.4	0.0	13.4	0.0	13.4	0.0	13.4	0.0	13.4	0.0
1946	13.4	0.0	13.5	0.7	13.5	0.0	13.5	0.0	13.8	2.2	14.0	1.4	14.4	2.9	14.7	2.1	15.2	3.4	15.3	0.7	15.6	2.0	16.0	2.6
1947	16.2	1.3	16.3	0.6	16.3	0.0	16.3	0.0	16.4	0.6	16.6	1.2	16.6	0.0	16.7	0.6	17.0	1.8	17.2	1.2	17.2	0.0	17.3	0.6
1948	17.4	0.6	17.4	0.0	17.5	0.6	17.5	0.0	17.6	0.6	17.6	0.0	17.9	1.7	18.5	3.4	18.8	1.6	19.1	1.6	19.1	0.0	19.1	0.0
1949	19.2	0.5	19.3	0.5	19.2	-0.5	19.2	0.0	19.2	0.0	19.2	0.0	19.1	-0.5	19.1	0.0	19.1	0.0	19.1	0.0	19.1	0.0	19.1	0.0
1950	19.0	-0.5	19.1	0.5	19.1	0.0	19.2	0.5	19.2	0.0	19.2	0.0	19.5	1.6	20.0	2.6	20.4	2.0	20.7	1.5	21.0	1.4	21.9	4.3
1951	22.2	1.4	22.2	0.0	22.2	0.0	22.2	0.0	22.2	0.0	22.2	0.0	22.2	0.0	22.2	0.0	22.2	0.0	22.3	0.5	22.3	0.0	22.2	-0.4
1952	22.2	0.0	22.2	0.0	22.1	-0.5	22.1	0.0	22.1	0.0	22.0	-0.5	22.0	0.0	22.0	0.0	22.0	0.0	21.9	-0.5	21.9	0.0	21.9	0.0
1953	21.9	0.0	21.9	0.0	22.0	0.5	22.2	0.9	22.3	0.5	22.5	0.9	22.6	0.4	22.8	0.9	23.0	0.9	23.1	0.4	23.1	0.0	23.1	0.0
1954	23.1	0.0	23.1	0.0	23.1	0.0	23.1	0.0	23.1	0.0	23.1	0.0	23.0	-0.4	23.0	0.0	23.1	0.4	23.1	0.0	23.1	0.0	23.1	0.0
1955	23.1	0.0	23.5	1.7	23.5	0.0	23.6	0.4	23.6	0.0	23.7	0.4	23.8	0.4	24.2	1.7	24.6	1.7	24.9	1.2	25.3	1.6	25.5	0.8
1956	25.5	0.0	25.5	0.0	25.7	0.8	25.9	0.8	26.3	1.5	26.2	-0.4	26.3	0.4	26.8	1.9	27.3	1.9	27.5	0.7	27.7	0.7	27.8	0.4
1957	28.0	0.7	28.0	0.0	28.1	0.4	28.1	0.0	28.1	0.0	28.2	0.4	28.3	0.4	28.4	0.4	28.5	0.4	28.7	0.7	28.9	0.7	28.9	0.0
1958	28.9	0.0	28.7	-0.7	28.7	0.0	28.7	0.0	28.7	0.0	28.8	0.3	28.7	-0.3	28.6	-0.3	28.7	0.3	28.8	0.3	29.1	1.0	29.2	0.3
1959	29.3	0.3	29.5	0.7	29.4	-0.3	29.3	-0.3	29.3	0.0	29.8	1.7	29.9	0.3	29.9	0.0	30.0	0.3	30.1	0.3	30.1	0.0	30.2	0.3
1960	30.1	-0.3	30.2	0.3	30.1	-0.3	30.2	0.3	30.1	-0.3	29.9	-0.7	29.9	0.0	29.9	0.0	30.0	0.3	29.9	-0.3	29.9	0.0	29.9	0.0
1961	29.9	0.0	29.9	0.0	29.9	0.0	29.8	-0.3	29.8	0.0	29.9	0.3	29.8	-0.3	29.7	-0.3	29.7	0.0	29.6	-0.3	29.7	0.3	29.7	0.0
1962	29.8	0.3	29.8	0.0	29.9	0.3	29.9	0.0	29.9	0.0	29.9	0.0	29.8	-0.3	29.9	0.3	30.0	0.3	30.0	0.0	30.0	0.0	30.1	0.3
1963	30.1	0.0	30.0	-0.3	29.9	-0.3	29.9	0.0	29.9	0.0	30.0	0.3	30.0	0.0	30.0	0.0	30.1	0.3	30.2	0.3	30.2	0.0	30.3	0.3
1964	30.3	0.0	30.3	0.0	30.4	0.3	30.3	-0.3	30.4	0.3	30.3	-0.3	30.2	-0.3	30.0	-0.7	30.0	0.0	30.3	1.0	30.3	0.0	30.4	0.3
1965	30.1	-1.0	30.2	0.3	30.2	0.0	30.2	0.0	30.3	0.3	30.3	0.0	30.3	0.0	30.5	0.7	30.6	0.3	30.8	0.7	30.9	0.3	30.9	0.0
1966	30.9	0.0	30.9	0.0	31.1	0.6	31.4	1.0	31.6	0.6	31.8	0.6	31.8	0.0	32.0	0.6	32.2	0.6	32.4	0.6	32.5	0.3	32.5	0.0
1967	32.7	0.6	32.8	0.3	32.8	0.0	32.8	0.0	32.8	0.0	32.7	-0.3	32.8	0.3	32.9	0.3	33.0	0.3	33.1	0.3	33.2	0.3	33.3	0.3
1968	33.4	0.3	33.6	0.6	33.7	0.3	33.8	0.3	33.9	0.3	34.0	0.3	34.0	0.0	34.1	0.3	34.2	0.3	34.3	0.3	34.2	-0.3	34.3	0.3
1969	34.4	0.3	34.5	0.3	34.7	0.6	34.8	0.3	34.9	0.3	35.1	0.6	35.2	0.3	35.3	0.3	35.6	0.8	35.8	0.6	35.9	0.3	36.2	0.8
1970	36.6	1.1	36.6	0.0	36.8	0.5	36.9	0.3	37.1	0.5	37.1	0.0	37.5	1.1	37.6	0.3	37.8	0.5	38.1	0.8	38.2	0.3	38.5	0.8
1971	38.5	0.0	38.6	0.3	38.8	0.5	39.0	0.5	39.2	0.5	39.3	0.3	39.5	0.5	39.6	0.3	39.6	0.0	39.6	0.0	39.6	0.0	39.7	0.3
1972	39.7	0.0	39.9	0.5	40.0	0.3	40.1	0.3	40.2	0.2	40.4	0.5	40.4	0.0	40.4	0.0	40.5	0.2	40.5	0.0	40.6	0.2	40.6	0.0
1973	40.7	0.2	40.9	0.5	41.1	0.5	41.3	0.5	41.6	0.7	41.8	0.5	41.9	0.2	41.9	0.0	42.0	0.2	42.2	0.5	42.9	1.7	43.0	0.2
1974	43.6	1.4	44.0	0.9	44.7	1.6	45.9	2.7	47.5	3.5	49.1	3.4	50.5	2.9	52.0	3.0	53.2	2.3	54.7	2.8	55.6	1.6	56.2	1.1
1975	56.8	1.1	57.2	0.7	57.5	0.5	57.9	0.7	58.4	0.9	58.6	0.3	59.1	0.9	59.3	0.3	59.6	0.5	59.8	0.3	60.1	0.5	60.4	0.5
1976	60.7	0.5	61.0	0.5	61.2	0.3	61.6	0.7	62.0	0.6	62.5	0.8	62.6	0.2	62.8	0.3	63.3	0.8	63.7	0.6	63.7	0.0	64.0	0.5
1977	64.4	0.6	64.7	0.5	65.0	0.5	65.2	0.3	65.9	1.1	66.4	0.8	66.7	0.5	67.0	0.4	67.3	0.4	67.6	0.4	68.0	0.6	68.2	0.3
1978	68.7	0.7	69.1	0.6	69.5	0.6	69.9	0.6	70.5	0.9	71.0	0.7	71.5	0.7	71.8	0.4	72.3	0.7	72.9	0.8	73.6	1.0	74.0	0.5
1979	74.5	0.7	74.9	0.5	75.8	1.2	76.5	0.9	77.0	0.7	77.3	0.4	78.0	0.9	78.4	0.5	79.0	0.8	79.9	1.1	80.3	0.5	81.4	1.4
1980	82.6	1.5	83.3	0.8	84.4	1.3	85.9	1.8	86.4	0.6	87.1	0.8	87.5	0.5	87.8	0.3	88.8	1.1	89.6	0.9	90.2	0.7	90.7	0.6
1981	91.6	1.0	92.2	0.7	92.9	0.8	93.5	0.6	94.1	0.6	94.4	0.3	95.6	1.3	96.1	0.5	96.7	0.6	97.1	0.4	97.4	0.3	98.0	0.6
1982	98.7	0.7	99.1	0.4	99.3	0.2	99.8	0.5	99.9	0.1	99.8	-0.1	100.3	0.5	100.3	0.0	100.3	0.0	100.6	0.3	100.8	0.2	101.0	0.2
1983	101.1	0.1	101.3	0.2	101.2	-0.1	101.4	0.2	101.5	0.1	101.5	0.0	101.5	0.0	101.3	-0.2	101.4	0.1	101.3	-0.1	101.5	0.2	101.9	0.4

[Continued]

General Purpose Machinery and Equipment
Producer Price Index
Base 1982 = 100
[Continued]

For 1939-1993. Columns headed % show percentile change in the index from the previous period for which an index is available.

Year	Jan Index	%	Feb Index	%	Mar Index	%	Apr Index	%	May Index	%	Jun Index	%	Jul Index	%	Aug Index	%	Sep Index	%	Oct Index	%	Nov Index	%	Dec Index	%
1984	102.2	0.3	102.3	0.1	102.5	0.2	103.0	0.5	103.0	0.0	103.3	0.3	103.7	0.4	103.8	0.1	103.9	0.1	103.9	0.0	104.1	0.2	104.2	0.1
1985	104.7	0.5	104.9	0.2	105.2	0.3	105.4	0.2	105.7	0.3	105.8	0.1	106.0	0.2	106.1	0.1	106.0	-0.1	106.1	0.1	106.2	0.1	106.2	0.0
1986	106.4	0.2	106.7	0.3	106.9	0.2	107.2	0.3	107.2	0.0	107.2	0.0	107.3	0.1	107.4	0.1	107.4	0.0	107.5	0.1	107.5	0.0	107.6	0.1
1987	107.8	0.2	107.8	0.0	107.9	0.1	107.9	0.0	108.0	0.1	108.1	0.1	108.2	0.1	108.3	0.1	108.6	0.3	108.6	0.0	108.9	0.3	109.4	0.5
1988	110.2	0.7	110.7	0.5	111.3	0.5	111.7	0.4	112.0	0.3	112.3	0.3	112.9	0.5	113.3	0.4	113.9	0.5	114.3	0.4	115.1	0.7	115.8	0.6
1989	116.6	0.7	117.0	0.3	117.7	0.6	118.0	0.3	118.6	0.5	119.1	0.4	119.3	0.2	119.6	0.3	120.2	0.5	120.5	0.2	120.7	0.2	121.0	0.2
1990	121.8	0.7	122.3	0.4	122.9	0.5	123.0	0.1	123.3	0.2	123.5	0.2	123.8	0.2	124.1	0.2	124.3	0.2	124.7	0.3	124.8	0.1	125.4	0.5
1991	126.3	0.7	126.9	0.5	127.2	0.2	127.3	0.1	127.7	0.3	128.0	0.2	128.0	0.0	128.1	0.1	128.2	0.1	128.4	0.2	128.5	0.1	128.6	0.1
1992	129.2	0.5	129.4	0.2	129.7	0.2	130.0	0.2	130.1	0.1	129.5	-0.5	129.8	0.2	130.0	0.2	130.2	0.2	130.2	0.0	130.3	0.1	130.3	0.0
1993	131.2	0.7	131.4	0.2	131.5	0.1	131.7	0.2	131.8	0.1	132.1	0.2	132.3	0.2	132.6	0.2	132.4	-0.2	132.7	0.2	132.9	0.2	133.1	0.2

Source: U.S. Department of Labor, Bureau of Labor Statistics, Division of Industry Prices and Price Indexes. n.e.c. stands for not elsewhere classified. - indicates no data collected for period or unavailable.

Electronic Computers and Computer Equipment
Producer Price Index
Base Dec. 1990 = 100

For 1990-1993. Columns headed % show percentile change in the index from the previous period for which an index is available.

Year	Jan Index	%	Feb Index	%	Mar Index	%	Apr Index	%	May Index	%	Jun Index	%	Jul Index	%	Aug Index	%	Sep Index	%	Oct Index	%	Nov Index	%	Dec Index	%
1990	-	-	-	-	-	-	-	-	-	-	-	-	-	-	-	-	-	-	-	-	-	-	100.0	-
1991	97.9	-2.1	97.2	-0.7	96.2	-1.0	95.7	-0.5	93.1	-2.7	89.7	-3.7	86.1	-4.0	83.5	-3.0	83.2	-0.4	82.0	-1.4	81.6	-0.5	80.6	-1.2
1992	79.7	-1.1	78.9	-1.0	77.7	-1.5	75.7	-2.6	75.0	-0.9	73.1	-2.5	71.1	-2.7	70.8	-0.4	69.7	-1.6	68.9	-1.1	68.8	-0.1	68.6	-0.3
1993	67.6	-1.5	66.1	-2.2	64.9	-1.8	63.5	-2.2	62.9	-0.9	62.0	-1.4	61.3	-1.1	60.3	-1.6	60.5	0.3	59.1	-2.3	58.4	-1.2	58.2	-0.3

Source: U.S. Department of Labor, Bureau of Labor Statistics, Division of Industry Prices and Price Indexes. n.e.c. stands for not elsewhere classified. - indicates no data collected for period or unavailable.

Special Industry Machinery and Equipment
Producer Price Index
Base 1982 = 100

For 1961-1993. Columns headed % show percentile change in the index from the previous period for which an index is available.

Year	Jan Index	%	Feb Index	%	Mar Index	%	Apr Index	%	May Index	%	Jun Index	%	Jul Index	%	Aug Index	%	Sep Index	%	Oct Index	%	Nov Index	%	Dec Index	%
1961	26.4	-	26.4	0.0	26.4	0.0	26.4	0.0	26.5	0.4	26.5	0.0	26.5	0.0	26.5	0.0	26.5	0.0	26.5	0.0	26.5	0.0	26.6	0.4
1962	26.7	0.4	26.8	0.4	26.8	0.0	26.8	0.0	26.8	0.0	26.8	0.0	26.9	0.4	26.9	0.0	26.9	0.0	26.9	0.0	27.0	0.4	27.1	0.4
1963	27.1	0.0	27.2	0.4	27.2	0.0	27.4	0.7	27.4	0.0	27.4	0.0	27.4	0.0	27.5	0.4	27.6	0.4	27.6	0.0	27.6	0.0	27.7	0.4
1964	27.7	0.0	27.7	0.0	27.9	0.7	27.9	0.0	27.9	0.0	27.9	0.0	27.9	0.0	27.9	0.0	27.9	0.0	27.9	0.0	28.1	0.7	28.1	0.0
1965	28.3	0.7	28.3	0.0	28.4	0.4	28.4	0.0	28.4	0.0	28.4	0.0	28.4	0.0	28.4	0.0	28.5	0.4	28.5	0.0	28.7	0.7	28.7	0.0
1966	28.8	0.3	28.8	0.0	29.0	0.7	29.0	0.0	29.2	0.7	29.5	1.0	29.6	0.3	29.7	0.3	29.8	0.3	30.0	0.7	30.1	0.3	30.1	0.0
1967	30.4	1.0	30.5	0.3	30.5	0.0	30.5	0.0	30.7	0.7	30.7	0.0	30.7	0.0	30.8	0.3	30.8	0.0	31.2	1.3	31.2	0.0	31.4	0.6
1968	31.8	1.3	31.8	0.0	31.8	0.0	32.2	1.3	32.3	0.3	32.4	0.3	32.5	0.3	32.5	0.0	32.6	0.3	32.7	0.3	32.9	0.6	32.9	0.0
1969	33.0	0.3	33.3	0.9	33.4	0.3	33.5	0.3	33.6	0.3	33.7	0.3	34.0	0.9	34.0	0.0	34.1	0.3	34.2	0.3	34.4	0.6	34.9	1.5
1970	35.1	0.6	35.1	0.0	35.2	0.3	35.2	0.0	35.3	0.3	35.4	0.3	35.6	0.6	35.6	0.0	35.8	0.6	36.1	0.8	36.1	0.0	36.4	0.8
1971	36.7	0.8	36.8	0.3	36.8	0.0	36.9	0.3	37.0	0.3	37.2	0.5	37.4	0.5	37.4	0.0	37.5	0.3	37.5	0.0	37.5	0.0	37.5	0.0
1972	37.7	0.5	37.9	0.5	37.8	-0.3	37.9	0.3	38.0	0.3	38.1	0.3	38.1	0.0	38.1	0.0	38.1	0.0	38.2	0.3	38.3	0.3	38.3	0.0
1973	38.4	0.3	38.9	1.3	39.1	0.5	39.5	1.0	39.7	0.5	40.0	0.8	40.0	0.0	40.5	1.3	40.8	0.7	40.9	0.2	41.0	0.2	41.5	1.2
1974	41.8	0.7	42.5	1.7	43.6	2.6	44.1	1.1	45.2	2.5	45.8	1.3	46.2	0.9	48.0	3.9	48.8	1.7	49.8	2.0	50.4	1.2	51.0	1.2
1975	51.8	1.6	52.2	0.8	53.1	1.7	53.3	0.4	53.3	0.0	53.6	0.6	54.0	0.7	54.3	0.6	54.3	0.0	54.9	1.1	55.2	0.5	55.7	0.9
1976	56.3	1.1	56.5	0.4	56.8	0.5	57.5	1.2	57.5	0.0	57.8	0.5	58.3	0.9	58.4	0.2	58.7	0.5	59.0	0.5	59.0	0.0	59.6	1.0
1977	60.1	0.8	60.4	0.5	60.7	0.5	61.2	0.8	61.7	0.8	62.1	0.6	62.4	0.5	62.7	0.5	62.8	0.2	64.4	2.5	64.6	0.3	65.1	0.8
1978	65.7	0.9	65.9	0.3	66.6	1.1	67.1	0.8	67.4	0.4	68.3	1.3	68.7	0.6	69.2	0.7	69.8	0.9	70.8	1.4	71.6	1.1	71.9	0.4
1979	72.7	1.1	72.9	0.3	73.5	0.8	74.9	1.9	75.4	0.7	75.7	0.4	76.8	1.5	77.2	0.5	77.2	0.0	78.1	1.2	78.4	0.4	78.8	0.5
1980	80.1	1.6	80.9	1.0	81.6	0.9	83.6	2.5	84.0	0.5	84.4	0.5	85.1	0.8	85.2	0.1	87.0	2.1	88.0	1.1	88.5	0.6	89.5	1.1
1981	90.9	1.6	92.0	1.2	92.6	0.7	93.3	0.8	94.5	1.3	95.0	0.5	95.6	0.6	95.4	-0.2	96.2	0.8	96.8	0.6	96.9	0.1	97.3	0.4
1982	98.6	1.3	98.6	0.0	98.8	0.2	99.3	0.5	99.6	0.3	100.0	0.4	100.6	0.6	100.5	-0.1	100.5	0.0	100.8	0.3	101.2	0.4	101.5	0.3
1983	102.1	0.6	102.3	0.2	102.6	0.3	102.9	0.3	103.3	0.4	103.5	0.2	103.9	0.4	104.3	0.4	104.5	0.2	104.7	0.2	104.9	0.2	105.2	0.3
1984	105.2	0.0	105.5	0.3	106.0	0.5	106.7	0.7	107.1	0.4	107.2	0.1	108.2	0.9	108.5	0.3	108.0	-0.5	108.1	0.1	108.2	0.1	108.4	0.2
1985	109.4	0.9	109.8	0.4	110.0	0.2	110.2	0.2	110.4	0.2	110.7	0.3	111.0	0.3	111.2	0.2	111.4	0.2	111.5	0.1	111.8	0.3	112.2	0.4
1986	112.6	0.4	112.9	0.3	113.0	0.1	113.3	0.3	113.6	0.3	114.2	0.5	114.4	0.2	114.8	0.3	115.2	0.3	115.2	0.0	115.4	0.2	115.8	0.3
1987	116.2	0.3	116.6	0.3	116.7	0.1	116.8	0.1	117.0	0.2	117.0	0.0	117.3	0.3	117.3	0.0	117.5	0.2	118.1	0.5	118.4	0.3	118.8	0.3
1988	119.3	0.4	119.8	0.4	120.1	0.3	120.7	0.5	121.0	0.2	121.5	0.4	122.0	0.4	122.3	0.2	122.6	0.2	123.2	0.5	123.9	0.6	124.1	0.2
1989	124.7	0.5	125.4	0.6	125.7	0.2	126.2	0.4	126.7	0.4	127.1	0.3	127.3	0.2	127.6	0.2	127.9	0.2	128.1	0.2	128.3	0.2	128.6	0.2
1990	129.2	0.5	129.8	0.5	130.1	0.2	131.0	0.7	131.2	0.2	131.5	0.2	131.8	0.2	131.9	0.1	132.4	0.4	132.7	0.2	133.1	0.3	133.4	0.2
1991	134.7	1.0	134.9	0.1	135.2	0.2	135.6	0.3	136.0	0.3	136.1	0.1	136.1	0.0	136.1	0.0	136.4	0.2	136.7	0.2	136.8	0.1	136.9	0.1
1992	137.6	0.5	138.1	0.4	138.3	0.1	138.8	0.4	139.2	0.3	139.3	0.1	139.4	0.1	139.5	0.1	140.5	0.7	140.7	0.1	141.0	0.2	141.2	0.1
1993	141.9	0.5	142.6	0.5	143.0	0.3	143.3	0.2	143.4	0.1	143.7	0.2	143.9	0.1	143.9	0.0	144.0	0.1	144.5	0.3	144.6	0.1	144.7	0.1

Source: U.S. Department of Labor, Bureau of Labor Statistics, Division of Industry Prices and Price Indexes. n.e.c. stands for not elsewhere classified. - indicates no data collected for period or unavailable.

Electrical Machinery and Equipment

Producer Price Index
Base 1982 = 100

For 1939-1993. Columns headed % show percentile change in the index from the previous period for which an index is available.

Year	Jan Index	%	Feb Index	%	Mar Index	%	Apr Index	%	May Index	%	Jun Index	%	Jul Index	%	Aug Index	%	Sep Index	%	Oct Index	%	Nov Index	%	Dec Index	%
1939	19.6	-	19.6	0.0	19.6	0.0	19.6	0.0	19.6	0.0	19.6	0.0	19.5	-0.5	19.5	0.0	19.5	0.0	19.5	0.0	19.5	0.0	19.5	0.0
1940	19.5	0.0	19.5	0.0	19.5	0.0	19.5	0.0	19.5	0.0	19.5	0.0	19.5	0.0	19.5	0.0	19.6	0.5	19.7	0.5	19.7	0.0	19.8	0.5	19.8	0.0
1941	19.5	0.0	19.5	0.0	19.5	0.0	19.5	0.0	19.5	0.0	19.5	0.0	19.6	0.0	19.6	0.0	19.6	0.0	19.6	0.0	19.5	-0.5	19.5	0.0
1942	19.8	0.0	19.8	0.0	19.7	-0.5	19.6	-0.5	19.6	0.0	19.6	0.0	19.6	0.0	19.6	0.0	19.6	0.0	19.6	0.0	19.5	-0.5	19.5	0.0
1943	19.5	0.0	19.5	0.0	19.5	0.0	19.5	0.0	19.5	0.0	19.5	0.0	19.5	0.0	19.4	-0.5	19.4	0.0	19.4	0.0	19.4	0.0	19.4	0.0
1944	19.4	0.0	19.4	0.0	19.4	0.0	19.4	0.0	19.4	0.0	19.1	-1.5	19.0	-0.5	19.0	0.0	19.0	0.0	19.0	0.0	19.0	0.0	19.0	0.0
1945	19.0	0.0	19.0	0.0	19.0	0.0	19.0	0.0	19.2	1.1	19.3	0.5	19.3	0.0	19:3	0.0	19.3	0.0	19.4	0.5	19.5	0.5	19.5	0.0
1946	19.6	0.5	19.6	0.0	19.6	0.0	20.5	4.6	21.9	6.8	22.3	1.8	22.5	0.9	22.6	0.4	22.8	0.9	23.3	2.2	24.4	4.7	25.3	3.7
1947	25.5	0.8	25.6	0.4	25.7	0.4	26.0	1.2	27.3	5.0	27.5	0.7	27.4	-0.4	27.5	0.4	27.6	0.4	27.5	-0.4	27.5	0.0	27.6	0.4
1948	27.4	-0.7	27.3	-0.4	27.3	0.0	27.3	0.0	27.2	-0.4	27.3	0.4	27.9	2.2	28.8	3.2	29.1	1.0	29.2	0.3	29.4	0.7	29.5	0.3
1949	29.7	0.7	29.8	0.3	29.8	0.0	29.2	-2.0	28.8	-1.4	28.5	-1.0	28.4	-0.4	28.4	0.0	28.4	0.0	28.4	0.0	28.4	0.0	28.4	0.0
1950	28.2	-0.7	28.0	-0.7	28.1	0.4	28.1	0.0	28.1	0.0	28.5	1.4	29.1	2.1	30.4	4.5	30.9	1.6	31.9	3.2	32.0	0.3	33.5	4.7
1951	34.0	1.5	34.0	0.0	34.0	0.0	34.0	0.0	34.0	0.0	34.0	0.0	34.2	0.6	34.1	-0.3	34.1	0.0	34.0	-0.3	34.1	0.3	34.0	-0.3
1952	33.9	-0.3	34.0	0.3	33.9	-0.3	33.8	-0.3	33.8	0.0	33.5	-0.9	33.5	0.0	33.5	0.0	33.4	-0.3	33.3	-0.3	33.4	0.3	33.4	0.0
1953	33.4	0.0	33.4	0.0	33.5	0.3	33.9	1.2	34.2	0.9	34.7	1.5	34.9	0.6	35.1	0.6	35.2	0.3	35.3	0.3	35.4	0.3	35.4	0.0
1954	35.4	0.0	35.4	0.0	35.4	0.0	35.3	-0.3	35.2	-0.3	35.2	0.0	35.2	0.0	35.1	-0.3	35.1	0.0	35.0	-0.3	35.4	1.1	35.4	0.0
1955	35.4	0.0	35.4	0.0	35.3	-0.3	35.3	0.0	35.3	0.0	35.3	0.0	35.4	0.3	35.7	0.8	36.5	2.2	36.5	0.0	36.7	0.5	36.9	0.5
1956	37.0	0.3	37.2	0.5	37.3	0.3	37.9	1.6	38.3	1.1	38.4	0.3	38.4	0.0	38.6	0.5	39.6	2.6	40.0	1.0	40.6	1.5	40.6	0.0
1957	40.8	0.5	41.1	0.7	41.2	0.2	41.3	0.2	41.4	0.2	41.4	0.0	41.8	1.0	41.8	0.0	42.2	1.0	42.1	-0.2	42.2	0.2	42.2	0.0
1958	42.2	0.0	42.2	0.0	42.2	0.0	42.4	0.5	42.5	0.2	42.6	0.2	42.6	0.0	42.7	0.2	42.7	0.0	42.7	0.0	42.5	-0.5	42.5	0.0
1959	42.5	0.0	42.5	0.0	42.7	0.5	42.7	0.0	43.0	0.7	43.0	0.0	43.5	1.2	43.4	-0.2	43.5	0.2	43.6	0.2	43.6	0.0	43.4	-0.5
1960	43.5	0.2	43.5	0.0	43.5	0.0	43.3	-0.5	42.8	-1.2	42.8	0.0	42.9	0.2	42.8	-0.2	42.7	-0.2	42.6	-0.2	42.6	0.0	42.6	0.0
1961	42.9	0.7	42.9	0.0	42.9	0.0	42.4	-1.2	42.4	0.0	42.4	0.0	42.4	0.0	42.0	-0.9	42.0	0.0	42.2	0.5	42.2	0.0	42.1	-0.2
1962	41.9	-0.5	41.9	0.0	41.9	0.0	41.8	-0.2	41.8	0.0	41.8	0.0	41.6	-0.5	41.6	0.0	41.8	0.5	41.8	0.0	41.6	-0.5	41.6	0.0
1963	41.5	-0.2	41.5	0.0	41.1	-1.0	41.2	0.2	41.4	0.5	41.5	0.2	41.2	-0.7	41.2	0.0	41.2	0.0	41.3	0.2	41.4	0.2	41.5	0.2
1964	41.0	-1.2	41.1	0.2	41.2	0.2	41.5	0.7	41.5	0.0	40.9	-1.4	40.9	0.0	41.0	0.2	40.9	-0.2	40.9	0.0	40.9	0.0	40.9	0.0
1965	41.0	0.2	41.1	0.2	41.1	0.0	41.2	0.2	41.2	0.0	41.1	-0.2	42.0	0.2	41.0	-0.5	41.0	0.0	41.0	0.0	40.9	-0.2	41.0	0.2
1966	41.2	0.5	41.5	0.7	41.7	0.5	41.8	0.2	42.0	0.5	41.9	-0.2	42.0	0.2	42.0	0.0	42.1	0.2	42.2	0.2	42.7	1.2	43.1	0.9
1967	43.2	0.2	43.2	0.0	43.2	0.0	43.2	0.0	43.2	0.0	43.2	0.0	43.2	0.0	43.1	-0.2	43.1	0.0	43.0	-0.2	43.1	0.2	43.4	0.7
1968	43.5	0.2	43.6	0.2	43.6	0.0	43.6	0.0	43.7	0.2	43.7	0.0	43.7	0.0	43.7	0.0	43.9	0.5	43.9	0.0	44.0	0.2	43.9	-0.2
1969	43.9	0.0	44.2	0.7	44.2	0.0	44.2	0.0	44.3	0.2	44.4	0.2	44.4	0.0	44.4	0.0	44.7	0.7	44.8	0.2	45.0	0.4	45.1	0.2
1970	45.3	0.4	45.2	-0.2	45.4	0.4	45.5	0.2	45.6	0.2	45.9	0.7	46.1	0.4	46.2	0.2	46.4	0.4	46.4	0.0	46.6	0.4	46.7	0.2
1971	46.9	0.4	47.1	0.4	47.2	0.2	47.1	-0.2	47.1	0.0	47.1	0.0	47.2	0.2	47.3	0.2	47.2	-0.2	47.2	0.0	47.1	-0.2	47.1	0.0
1972	47.3	0.4	47.5	0.4	47.6	0.2	47.6	0.0	47.7	0.2	47.8	0.2	47.8	0.0	47.8	0.0	47.7	-0.2	47.7	0.0	47.8	0.2	47.8	0.0
1973	47.9	0.2	47.9	0.0	48.1	0.4	48.2	0.2	48.5	0.6	48.7	0.4	48.7	0.0	48.7	0.0	48.7	0.0	48.8	0.2	48.9	0.2	49.2	0.6
1974	49.7	1.0	50.0	0.6	50.5	1.0	51.2	1.4	52.1	1.8	53.3	2.3	54.5	2.3	55.5	1.8	56.3	1.4	57.2	1.6	58.5	2.3	59.0	0.9
1975	59.6	1.0	59.9	0.5	60.1	0.3	60.2	0.2	60.5	0.5	60.6	0.2	60.8	0.3	60.9	0.2	61.2	0.5	61.5	0.5	61.8	0.5	61.8	0.0
1976	62.3	0.8	62.5	0.3	62.6	0.2	62.7	0.2	62.8	0.2	63.1	0.5	63.2	0.2	63.3	0.2	64.0	1.1	64.4	0.6	64.6	0.3	64.8	0.3
1977	65.1	0.5	65.4	0.5	65.6	0.3	65.7	0.2	66.0	0.5	66.1	0.2	66.5	0.6	66.7	0.3	67.2	0.7	67.9	1.0	68.2	0.4	68.2	0.0
1978	69.1	1.3	69.4	0.4	69.9	0.7	70.3	0.6	70.6	0.4	71.1	0.7	71.4	0.4	71.6	0.3	71.9	0.4	72.3	0.6	73.2	1.2	73.6	0.5
1979	73.9	0.4	74.6	0.9	75.1	0.7	75.6	0.7	76.2	0.8	76.7	0.7	77.7	1.3	78.2	0.6	78.8	0.8	79.6	1.0	79.8	0.3	80.6	1.0
1980	82.3	2.1	83.9	1.9	84.9	1.2	85.9	1.2	86.3	0.5	87.1	0.9	88.0	1.0	88.5	0.6	89.0	0.6	89.4	0.4	89.6	0.2	90.2	0.7
1981	91.5	1.4	92.3	0.9	93.3	1.1	93.9	0.6	93.9	0.0	94.7	0.9	95.5	0.8	96.2	0.7	96.8	0.6	97.3	0.5	97.6	0.3	98.0	0.4
1982	98.8	0.8	99.1	0.3	99.5	0.4	100.0	0.5	99.9	-0.1	100.0	0.1	100.0	0.0	100.1	0.1	100.1	0.0	100.5	0.4	100.9	0.4	101.2	0.3
1983	101.6	0.4	102.4	0.8	102.6	0.2	102.9	0.3	103.0	0.1	103.1	0.1	104.4	1.3	104.4	0.0	104.9	0.5	104.8	-0.1	104.9	0.1	105.3	0.4

[Continued]

Electrical Machinery and Equipment
Producer Price Index
Base 1982 = 100
[Continued]

For 1939-1993. Columns headed % show percentile change in the index from the previous period for which an index is available.

Year	Jan		Feb		Mar		Apr		May		Jun		Jul		Aug		Sep		Oct		Nov		Dec	
	Index	%	Index	%	Index	%	Index	%	Index	%	Index	%	Index	%	Index	%	Index	%	Index	%	Index	%	Index	%
1984	105.7	0.4	106.1	0.4	106.5	0.4	107.0	0.5	107.1	0.1	107.6	0.5	107.7	0.1	107.7	0.0	107.9	0.2	108.3	0.4	108.6	0.3	108.7	0.1
1985	109.3	0.6	109.6	0.3	109.6	0.0	109.3	-0.3	109.5	0.2	109.4	-0.1	109.6	0.2	109.7	0.1	109.8	0.1	109.9	0.1	109.8	-0.1	110.0	0.2
1986	110.3	0.3	110.6	0.3	110.8	0.2	111.0	0.2	111.0	0.0	110.9	-0.1	111.5	0.5	111.5	0.0	111.7	0.2	111.7	0.0	111.8	0.1	111.9	0.1
1987	112.3	0.4	112.4	0.1	112.3	-0.1	112.2	-0.1	112.3	0.1	112.2	-0.1	112.7	0.4	112.9	0.2	112.7	-0.2	113.1	0.4	113.2	0.1	113.4	0.2
1988	113.7	0.3	114.1	0.4	113.7	-0.4	113.8	0.1	114.4	0.5	114.2	-0.2	114.4	0.2	114.7	0.3	114.8	0.1	115.1	0.3	115.2	0.1	115.4	0.2
1989	116.2	0.7	116.6	0.3	116.7	0.1	116.8	0.1	117.0	0.2	117.5	0.4	117.9	0.3	118.0	0.1	117.9	-0.1	118.4	0.4	118.3	-0.1	118.4	0.1
1990	118.9	0.4	118.6	-0.3	118.9	0.3	119.0	0.1	119.0	0.0	119.2	0.2	119.5	0.3	119.4	-0.1	119.5	0.1	119.6	0.1	119.8	0.2	119.9	0.1
1991	120.5	0.5	120.6	0.1	120.7	0.1	120.9	0.2	120.7	-0.2	120.8	0.1	120.9	0.1	120.9	0.0	120.8	-0.1	120.8	0.0	120.9	0.1	120.9	0.0
1992	120.9	0.0	121.2	0.2	121.4	0.2	121.2	-0.2	121.3	0.1	121.2	-0.1	121.2	0.0	121.2	0.0	121.2	0.0	121.4	0.2	121.6	0.2	121.7	0.1
1993	122.0	0.2	122.2	0.2	122.2	0.0	122.6	0.3	122.4	-0.2	122.4	0.0	122.4	0.0	122.5	0.1	122.6	0.1	122.7	0.1	122.8	0.1	122.9	0.1

Source: U.S. Department of Labor, Bureau of Labor Statistics, Division of Industry Prices and Price Indexes. n.e.c. stands for not elsewhere classified. - indicates no data collected for period or unavailable.

Miscellaneous Instruments

Producer Price Index
Base 1982 = 100

For 1983-1993. Columns headed % show percentile change in the index from the previous period for which an index is available.

Year	Jan Index	%	Feb Index	%	Mar Index	%	Apr Index	%	May Index	%	Jun Index	%	Jul Index	%	Aug Index	%	Sep Index	%	Oct Index	%	Nov Index	%	Dec Index	%
1983	-	-	-	-	106.9	-	106.3	-0.6	105.9	-0.4	104.7	-1.1	104.6	-0.1	104.7	0.1	105.0	0.3	105.1	0.1	104.9	-0.2	104.6	-0.3
1984	104.9	0.3	105.4	0.5	105.6	0.2	105.0	-0.6	105.2	0.2	105.7	0.5	106.5	0.8	108.1	1.5	108.4	0.3	108.3	-0.1	108.0	-0.3	108.8	0.7
1985	109.4	0.6	109.5	0.1	109.0	-0.5	108.3	-0.6	108.8	0.5	109.6	0.7	110.5	0.8	110.1	-0.4	110.4	0.3	110.6	0.2	110.9	0.3	110.8	-0.1
1986	111.4	0.5	111.7	0.3	111.4	-0.3	111.7	0.3	111.9	0.2	112.3	0.4	113.2	0.8	113.7	0.4	113.7	0.0	113.9	0.2	114.0	0.1	114.2	0.2
1987	114.8	0.5	115.3	0.4	115.3	0.0	115.4	0.1	115.5	0.1	115.1	-0.3	115.7	0.5	115.9	0.2	116.1	0.2	116.3	0.2	116.4	0.1	116.8	0.3
1988	117.6	0.7	118.2	0.5	118.9	0.6	118.6	-0.3	118.6	0.0	118.6	0.0	118.9	0.3	119.2	0.3	119.2	0.0	119.3	0.1	119.9	0.5	119.9	0.0
1989	121.0	0.9	121.4	0.3	121.5	0.1	121.9	0.3	122.1	0.2	122.4	0.2	122.8	0.3	123.1	0.2	123.2	0.1	123.1	-0.1	123.4	0.2	123.9	0.4
1990	125.0	0.9	125.5	0.4	125.9	0.3	126.1	0.2	126.5	0.3	126.2	-0.2	126.9	0.6	127.1	0.2	127.2	0.1	127.5	0.2	128.1	0.5	128.3	0.2
1991	129.1	0.6	129.5	0.3	129.5	0.0	129.8	0.2	129.7	-0.1	129.9	0.2	130.5	0.5	130.6	0.1	130.8	0.2	131.4	0.5	131.3	-0.1	131.5	0.2
1992	132.4	0.7	132.6	0.2	132.6	0.0	132.9	0.2	132.9	0.0	133.4	0.4	134.0	0.4	134.2	0.1	134.4	0.1	135.0	0.4	135.1	0.1	135.2	0.1
1993	136.7	1.1	136.8	0.1	136.9	0.1	137.5	0.4	137.5	0.0	137.8	0.2	138.2	0.3	138.3	0.1	138.4	0.1	138.6	0.1	138.4	-0.1	138.5	0.1

Source: U.S. Department of Labor, Bureau of Labor Statistics, Division of Industry Prices and Price Indexes. n.e.c. stands for not elsewhere classified. - indicates no data collected for period or unavailable.

Miscellaneous Machinery
Producer Price Index
Base 1982 = 100

For 1947-1993. Columns headed % show percentile change in the index from the previous period for which an index is available.

Year	Jan Index	%	Feb Index	%	Mar Index	%	Apr Index	%	May Index	%	Jun Index	%	Jul Index	%	Aug Index	%	Sep Index	%	Oct Index	%	Nov Index	%	Dec Index	%
1947	21.2	-	21.3	0.5	21.4	0.5	21.4	0.0	21.5	0.5	21.6	0.5	21.6	0.0	21.7	0.5	21.8	0.5	22.0	0.9	22.2	0.9	22.4	0.9
1948	22.5	0.4	22.6	0.4	22.7	0.4	22.8	0.4	22.8	0.0	22.9	0.4	23.4	2.2	23.8	1.7	24.0	0.8	24.2	0.8	24.3	0.4	24.3	0.0
1949	24.3	0.0	24.3	0.0	24.3	0.0	24.3	0.0	24.3	0.0	24.3	0.0	24.3	0.0	24.3	0.0	24.3	0.0	24.3	0.0	24.3	0.0	24.2	-0.4
1950	24.2	0.0	24.3	0.4	24.3	0.0	24.3	0.0	24.3	0.0	24.3	0.0	24.4	0.4	24.9	2.0	25.2	1.2	25.5	1.2	25.8	1.2	26.5	2.7
1951	27.5	3.8	27.5	0.0	27.5	0.0	27.5	0.0	27.5	0.0	27.5	0.0	27.6	0.4	27.6	0.0	27.6	0.0	27.6	0.0	27.6	0.0	27.8	0.7
1952	27.8	0.0	27.8	0.0	27.6	-0.7	27.6	0.0	27.5	-0.4	27.5	0.0	27.5	0.0	27.5	0.0	27.5	0.0	27.6	0.4	27.6	0.0	27.6	0.0
1953	27.6	0.0	27.8	0.7	27.8	0.0	27.8	0.0	28.2	1.4	28.3	0.4	28.5	0.7	28.7	0.7	28.7	0.0	28.7	0.0	28.7	0.0	28.8	0.3
1954	28.8	0.0	28.8	0.0	28.9	0.3	28.9	0.0	28.9	0.0	29.0	0.3	29.0	0.0	29.0	0.0	29.1	0.3	29.1	0.0	29.1	0.0	29.1	0.0
1955	29.2	0.3	29.2	0.0	29.3	0.3	29.3	0.0	29.4	0.3	29.4	0.0	29.4	0.0	30.1	2.4	30.5	1.3	30.7	0.7	30.8	0.3	30.8	0.0
1956	30.8	0.0	30.9	0.3	31.0	0.3	31.0	0.0	31.2	0.6	31.3	0.3	31.6	1.0	31.7	0.3	32.1	1.3	32.5	1.2	32.8	0.9	32.9	0.3
1957	32.9	0.0	33.0	0.3	33.1	0.3	33.2	0.3	33.2	0.0	33.2	0.0	33.4	0.6	33.8	1.2	34.0	0.6	34.1	0.3	34.2	0.3	34.3	0.3
1958	34.4	0.3	34.4	0.0	34.4	0.0	34.4	0.0	34.1	-0.9	34.1	0.0	34.1	0.0	34.1	0.0	34.1	0.0	34.1	0.0	34.2	0.3	34.3	0.3
1959	34.3	0.0	34.4	0.3	34.5	0.3	34.5	0.0	34.5	0.0	34.5	0.0	34.5	0.0	34.6	0.3	34.5	-0.3	34.6	0.3	34.6	0.0	34.6	0.0
1960	34.6	0.0	34.6	0.0	34.7	0.3	34.7	0.0	34.7	0.0	34.7	0.0	34.7	0.0	34.7	0.0	34.7	0.0	34.7	0.0	34.8	0.3	34.9	0.3
1961	34.9	0.0	34.9	0.0	34.9	0.0	35.0	0.3	35.0	0.0	35.0	0.0	35.1	0.3	35.1	0.0	35.1	0.0	35.0	-0.3	35.0	0.0	35.1	0.3
1962	35.1	0.0	35.1	0.0	35.2	0.3	35.1	-0.3	35.1	0.0	35.2	0.3	35.2	0.0	35.3	0.3	35.2	-0.3	35.2	0.0	35.2	0.0	35.2	0.0
1963	35.2	0.0	35.2	0.0	35.4	0.6	35.2	-0.6	35.2	0.0	35.2	0.0	35.2	0.0	35.2	0.0	35.3	0.3	35.3	0.0	35.4	0.3	35.4	0.0
1964	35.5	0.3	35.5	0.0	35.6	0.3	35.6	0.0	35.6	0.0	35.6	0.0	35.7	0.3	35.7	0.0	35.8	0.3	35.8	0.0	35.8	0.0	35.5	-0.8
1965	35.8	0.8	35.8	0.0	35.8	0.0	35.9	0.3	35.9	0.0	36.0	0.3	35.8	-0.6	35.8	0.0	35.8	0.0	35.8	0.0	35.9	0.3	35.9	0.0
1966	35.9	0.0	36.0	0.3	36.1	0.3	36.0	-0.3	36.1	0.3	36.1	0.0	36.3	0.6	36.3	0.0	36.4	0.3	36.6	0.5	36.7	0.3	36.8	0.3
1967	37.0	0.5	37.1	0.3	37.1	0.0	37.1	0.0	37.1	0.0	37.2	0.3	37.2	0.0	37.2	0.0	37.3	0.3	37.4	0.3	37.6	0.5	37.7	0.3
1968	38.2	1.3	38.4	0.5	38.5	0.3	38.6	0.3	38.9	0.8	38.9	0.0	38.9	0.0	38.9	0.0	39.0	0.3	39.3	0.8	39.3	0.0	39.4	0.3
1969	39.5	0.3	39.6	0.3	39.7	0.3	39.9	0.5	40.1	0.5	40.1	0.0	40.3	0.5	40.4	0.2	40.6	0.5	40.8	0.5	41.0	0.5	41.2	0.5
1970	41.3	0.2	41.4	0.2	41.6	0.5	41.9	0.7	41.8	-0.2	41.9	0.2	41.9	0.0	41.9	0.0	42.3	1.0	42.5	0.5	42.7	0.5	43.1	0.9
1971	43.3	0.5	43.3	0.0	43.4	0.2	43.7	0.7	43.8	0.2	43.7	-0.2	43.8	0.2	44.0	0.5	43.9	-0.2	43.9	0.0	43.9	0.0	44.0	0.2
1972	44.1	0.2	44.3	0.5	44.3	0.0	44.6	0.7	44.8	0.4	45.0	0.4	45.0	0.0	45.0	0.0	45.0	0.0	45.1	0.2	45.0	-0.2	45.1	0.2
1973	45.1	0.0	45.3	0.4	45.6	0.7	45.9	0.7	46.4	1.1	46.4	0.0	46.4	0.0	46.5	0.2	46.6	0.2	46.6	0.0	46.8	0.4	47.0	0.4
1974	47.6	1.3	47.9	0.6	48.7	1.7	49.3	1.2	50.0	1.4	51.0	2.0	52.0	2.0	53.5	2.9	54.0	0.9	55.7	3.1	56.9	2.2	57.1	0.4
1975	58.9	3.2	59.1	0.3	59.0	-0.2	59.7	1.2	60.2	0.8	60.2	0.0	60.3	0.2	60.8	0.8	61.5	1.2	61.8	0.5	62.1	0.5	62.2	0.2
1976	62.9	1.1	63.2	0.5	63.5	0.5	63.7	0.3	63.7	0.0	63.8	0.2	64.2	0.6	64.1	-0.2	64.4	0.5	65.0	0.9	65.0	0.0	65.2	0.3
1977	65.6	0.6	65.9	0.5	66.1	0.3	66.3	0.3	66.8	0.8	67.0	0.3	67.3	0.4	67.8	0.7	68.3	0.7	68.6	0.4	69.0	0.6	69.3	0.4
1978	70.1	1.2	70.5	0.6	71.2	1.0	71.4	0.3	71.8	0.6	72.3	0.7	72.9	0.8	73.3	0.5	73.6	0.4	73.9	0.4	74.6	0.9	74.7	0.1
1979	75.5	1.1	75.8	0.4	76.0	0.3	76.5	0.7	77.1	0.8	77.3	0.3	78.1	1.0	78.1	0.0	79.0	1.2	79.6	0.8	80.1	0.6	80.6	0.6
1980	82.1	1.9	82.4	0.4	83.2	1.0	84.7	1.8	84.7	0.0	85.0	0.4	86.1	1.3	86.5	0.5	87.0	0.6	88.1	1.3	88.9	0.9	89.3	0.4
1981	90.7	1.6	91.3	0.7	92.0	0.8	92.6	0.7	92.7	0.1	93.2	0.5	94.7	1.6	95.4	0.7	96.3	0.9	96.5	0.2	96.8	0.3	97.0	0.2
1982	97.4	0.4	98.4	1.0	98.7	0.3	99.2	0.5	99.8	0.6	100.1	0.3	100.4	0.3	100.9	0.5	101.1	0.2	101.2	0.1	101.4	0.2	101.5	0.1
1983	101.7	0.2	101.6	-0.1	102.0	0.4	102.1	0.1	102.6	0.5	102.5	-0.1	102.5	0.0	102.6	0.1	102.3	-0.3	101.8	-0.5	102.0	0.2	102.0	0.0
1984	102.7	0.7	102.2	-0.5	102.3	0.1	102.3	0.0	102.0	-0.3	102.1	0.1	102.2	0.1	102.1	-0.1	102.3	0.2	102.2	-0.1	102.4	0.2	102.3	-0.1
1985	102.5	0.2	102.6	0.1	102.6	0.0	103.1	0.5	103.0	-0.1	103.5	0.5	103.5	0.0	103.6	0.1	103.7	0.1	103.6	-0.1	103.7	0.1	103.7	0.0
1986	103.8	0.1	103.7	-0.1	103.8	0.1	104.2	0.4	104.3	0.1	104.3	0.0	104.3	0.0	104.3	0.0	104.0	-0.3	104.2	0.2	104.3	0.1	104.6	0.3
1987	105.1	0.5	105.2	0.1	105.4	0.2	105.5	0.1	105.6	0.1	105.4	-0.2	105.3	-0.1	105.9	0.6	105.9	0.0	106.1	0.2	106.6	0.5	106.9	0.3
1988	107.5	0.6	107.5	0.0	107.7	0.2	107.9	0.2	108.0	0.1	108.1	0.1	108.5	0.4	109.1	0.6	109.5	0.4	109.5	0.0	109.7	0.2	110.2	0.5
1989	110.7	0.5	110.8	0.1	111.1	0.3	111.3	0.2	111.7	0.4	112.2	0.4	113.1	0.8	113.5	0.4	114.2	0.6	114.4	0.2	114.6	0.2	114.7	0.1
1990	115.7	0.9	115.7	0.0	115.9	0.2	116.0	0.1	116.1	0.1	116.2	0.1	116.3	0.1	116.8	0.4	117.5	0.6	117.6	0.1	118.4	0.7	118.3	-0.1
1991	119.1	0.7	119.4	0.3	119.8	0.3	119.8	0.0	120.0	0.2	120.1	0.1	120.4	0.2	120.8	0.3	121.0	0.2	120.9	-0.1	121.0	0.1	121.2	0.2

[Continued]

Miscellaneous Machinery

Producer Price Index
Base 1982 = 100
[Continued]

For 1947-1993. Columns headed % show percentile change in the index from the previous period for which an index is available.

Year	Jan		Feb		Mar		Apr		May		Jun		Jul		Aug		Sep		Oct		Nov		Dec	
	Index	%	Index	%	Index	%	Index	%	Index	%	Index	%	Index	%	Index	%	Index	%	Index	%	Index	%	Index	%
1992	121.5	0.2	121.5	0.0	121.4	-0.1	121.3	-0.1	121.5	0.2	121.6	0.1	121.7	0.1	121.9	0.2	121.9	0.0	121.9	0.0	122.0	0.1	122.0	0.0
1993	122.3	0.2	122.4	0.1	122.5	0.1	122.4	-0.1	122.5	0.1	122.4	-0.1	122.6	0.2	122.9	0.2	123.1	0.2	123.2	0.1	123.1	-0.1	123.1	0.0

Source: U.S. Department of Labor, Bureau of Labor Statistics, Division of Industry Prices and Price Indexes. n.e.c. stands for not elsewhere classified. - indicates no data collected for period or unavailable.

FURNITURE AND HOUSEHOLD DURABLES

Producer Price Index
Base 1982 = 100

For 1926-1993. Columns headed % show percentile change in the index from the previous period for which an index is available.

Year	Jan Index	%	Feb Index	%	Mar Index	%	Apr Index	%	May Index	%	Jun Index	%	Jul Index	%	Aug Index	%	Sep Index	%	Oct Index	%	Nov Index	%	Dec Index	%
1926	28.8	-	28.8	0.0	28.8	0.0	28.7	-0.3	28.6	-0.3	28.6	0.0	28.6	0.0	28.6	0.0	28.5	-0.3	28.5	0.0	28.5	0.0	28.2	-1.1
1927	28.0	-0.7	28.0	0.0	27.9	-0.4	27.9	0.0	27.9	0.0	28.0	0.4	27.9	-0.4	27.9	0.0	27.6	-1.1	27.8	0.7	27.9	0.4	27.9	0.0
1928	27.6	-1.1	27.6	0.0	27.4	-0.7	27.3	-0.4	27.4	0.4	27.1	-1.1	27.1	0.0	27.1	0.0	27.1	0.0	26.9	-0.7	26.9	0.0	26.9	0.0
1929	26.9	0.0	26.8	-0.4	26.8	0.0	26.9	0.4	26.9	0.0	27.1	0.7	27.0	-0.4	27.0	0.0	27.0	0.0	27.1	0.4	27.1	0.0	27.1	0.0
1930	26.8	-1.1	26.8	0.0	26.8	0.0	26.8	0.0	26.8	0.0	26.8	0.0	26.6	-0.7	26.6	0.0	26.4	-0.8	26.4	0.0	26.2	-0.8	25.4	-3.1
1931	25.4	0.0	25.4	0.0	25.3	-0.4	25.3	0.0	24.9	-1.6	24.8	-0.4	24.6	-0.8	24.4	-0.8	23.7	-2.9	23.2	-2.1	23.2	0.0	22.5	-3.0
1932	22.3	-0.9	22.2	-0.4	22.1	-0.5	21.9	-0.9	21.4	-2.3	21.4	0.0	21.2	-0.9	21.2	0.0	21.1	-0.5	21.2	0.5	21.2	0.0	21.2	0.0
1933	20.8	-1.9	20.6	-1.0	20.6	0.0	20.5	-0.5	20.6	0.5	21.0	1.9	21.4	1.9	21.8	1.9	22.3	2.3	23.0	3.1	23.0	0.0	23.0	0.0
1934	23.1	0.4	23.2	0.4	23.3	0.4	23.4	0.4	23.6	0.9	23.6	0.0	23.5	-0.4	23.5	0.0	23.6	0.4	23.5	-0.4	23.4	-0.4	23.4	0.0
1935	23.2	-0.9	23.2	0.0	23.3	0.4	23.2	-0.4	23.3	0.4	23.2	-0.4	23.2	0.0	23.2	0.0	23.2	0.0	23.2	0.0	23.2	0.0	23.2	0.0
1936	23.5	1.3	23.5	0.0	23.5	0.0	23.5	0.0	23.5	0.0	23.5	0.0	23.4	-0.4	23.5	0.4	23.6	0.4	23.7	0.4	23.8	0.4	24.1	1.3
1937	25.4	5.4	25.7	1.2	25.8	0.4	25.9	0.4	26.1	0.8	26.1	0.0	26.4	1.1	26.6	0.8	26.6	0.0	26.6	0.0	26.4	-0.8	26.2	-0.8
1938	25.8	-1.5	25.8	0.0	25.8	0.0	25.7	-0.4	25.7	0.0	25.7	0.0	25.4	-1.2	25.4	0.0	25.3	-0.4	25.2	-0.4	25.2	0.0	25.3	0.4
1939	25.2	-0.4	25.2	0.0	25.2	0.0	25.2	0.0	25.2	0.0	25.3	0.4	25.3	0.0	25.3	0.0	25.5	0.8	25.9	1.6	25.9	0.0	25.9	0.0
1940	25.8	-0.4	25.9	0.4	25.9	0.0	26.0	0.4	26.0	0.0	26.0	0.0	26.0	0.0	26.0	0.0	26.0	0.0	26.0	0.0	26.0	0.0	26.1	0.4
1941	26.1	0.0	26.1	0.0	26.4	1.1	26.6	0.8	26.8	0.8	27.4	2.2	27.8	1.5	28.0	0.7	28.5	1.8	29.1	2.1	29.3	0.7	29.6	1.0
1942	29.8	0.7	29.8	0.0	29.8	0.0	29.9	0.3	29.9	0.0	29.9	0.0	29.9	0.0	29.9	0.0	29.9	0.0	29.9	0.0	29.9	0.0	29.9	0.0
1943	29.7	-0.7	29.7	0.0	29.7	0.0	29.7	0.0	29.7	0.0	29.7	0.0	29.7	0.0	29.7	0.0	29.7	0.0	29.7	0.0	29.7	0.0	29.7	0.0
1944	30.5	2.7	30.4	-0.3	30.4	0.0	30.4	0.0	30.4	0.0	30.4	0.0	30.5	0.3	30.5	0.0	30.5	0.0	30.5	0.0	30.5	0.0	30.5	0.0
1945	30.5	0.0	30.5	0.0	30.5	0.0	30.5	0.0	30.5	0.0	30.5	0.0	30.5	0.0	30.5	0.0	30.5	0.0	30.5	0.0	30.5	0.0	30.5	0.0
1946	30.8	1.0	30.9	0.3	31.0	0.3	31.2	0.6	31.6	1.3	32.2	1.9	32.4	0.6	32.5	0.3	32.9	1.2	33.2	0.9	34.2	3.0	35.9	5.0
1947	36.5	1.7	36.6	0.3	36.6	0.0	36.8	0.5	36.8	0.0	36.9	0.3	37.2	0.8	37.3	0.3	37.5	0.5	37.8	0.8	37.9	0.3	38.1	0.5
1948	38.4	0.8	38.4	0.0	38.5	0.3	38.8	0.8	38.8	0.0	38.9	0.3	39.2	0.8	39.5	0.8	40.0	1.3	40.8	2.0	40.9	0.2	40.9	0.0
1949	40.7	-0.5	40.7	0.0	40.6	-0.2	40.5	-0.2	40.3	-0.5	40.2	-0.2	39.8	-1.0	39.7	-0.3	39.6	-0.3	39.5	-0.3	39.6	0.3	39.7	0.3
1950	39.7	0.0	39.8	0.3	39.8	0.0	39.9	0.3	40.1	0.5	40.1	0.0	40.3	0.5	40.8	1.2	41.6	2.0	42.6	2.4	43.1	1.2	43.6	1.2
1951	44.4	1.8	44.6	0.5	44.7	0.2	44.9	0.4	44.8	-0.2	44.7	-0.2	44.5	-0.4	44.1	-0.9	44.0	-0.2	43.9	-0.2	43.8	-0.2	43.8	0.0
1952	43.7	-0.2	43.7	0.0	43.5	-0.5	43.6	0.2	43.4	-0.5	43.4	0.0	43.4	0.0	43.3	-0.2	43.5	0.5	43.5	0.0	43.6	0.2	43.7	0.2
1953	43.8	0.2	43.9	0.2	44.0	0.2	44.3	0.7	44.4	0.2	44.5	0.2	44.6	0.2	44.6	0.0	44.7	0.2	44.6	-0.2	44.7	0.2	44.7	0.0
1954	44.8	0.2	44.7	-0.2	44.7	0.0	44.9	0.4	44.9	0.0	44.9	0.0	44.8	-0.2	44.8	0.0	44.8	0.0	44.9	0.2	44.9	0.0	45.0	0.2
1955	44.9	-0.2	44.9	0.0	44.7	-0.4	44.7	0.0	44.7	0.0	44.8	0.2	44.9	0.2	45.1	0.4	45.3	0.4	45.5	0.4	45.6	0.2	45.6	0.0
1956	45.9	0.7	46.0	0.2	46.0	0.0	45.9	-0.2	45.9	0.0	46.0	0.2	46.0	0.0	46.3	0.7	46.5	0.4	47.0	1.1	47.1	0.2	47.1	0.0
1957	47.4	0.6	47.4	0.0	47.4	0.0	47.2	-0.4	47.3	0.2	47.3	0.0	47.5	0.4	47.6	0.2	47.5	-0.2	47.6	0.2	47.7	0.2	48.0	0.6
1958	48.1	0.2	48.0	-0.2	48.0	0.0	48.0	0.0	47.9	-0.2	47.8	-0.2	47.9	0.2	47.8	-0.2	47.8	0.0	47.8	0.0	47.7	-0.2	47.7	0.0
1959	47.9	0.4	47.9	0.0	48.0	0.2	48.0	0.0	48.0	0.0	48.0	0.0	48.1	0.2	48.0	-0.2	48.0	0.0	47.9	-0.2	47.9	0.0	47.9	0.0
1960	48.0	0.2	48.0	0.0	48.1	0.2	48.0	-0.2	47.9	-0.2	47.8	-0.2	47.8	0.0	47.8	0.0	47.7	-0.2	47.7	0.0	47.6	-0.2	47.6	0.0
1961	47.5	-0.2	47.5	0.0	47.5	0.0	47.6	0.2	47.6	0.0	47.6	0.0	47.5	-0.2	47.5	0.0	47.5	0.0	47.5	0.0	47.5	0.0	47.5	0.0
1962	47.5	0.0	47.4	-0.2	47.3	-0.2	47.3	0.0	47.3	0.0	47.3	0.0	47.2	-0.2	47.2	0.0	47.1	-0.2	47.1	0.0	47.1	0.0	47.0	-0.2
1963	47.0	0.0	46.9	-0.2	46.9	0.0	46.9	0.0	46.8	-0.2	46.9	0.2	46.8	-0.2	46.9	0.2	46.9	0.0	46.9	0.0	46.9	0.0	46.8	-0.2
1964	47.0	0.4	47.1	0.2	47.1	0.0	47.1	0.0	47.1	0.0	47.1	0.0	47.1	0.0	47.1	0.0	47.1	0.0	47.1	0.0	47.1	0.0	47.0	-0.2
1965	47.0	0.0	46.9	-0.2	47.0	0.2	46.8	-0.4	46.8	0.0	46.8	0.0	46.7	-0.2	46.7	0.0	46.7	0.0	46.7	0.0	46.8	0.2	46.9	0.2
1966	47.0	0.2	47.0	0.0	47.0	0.0	47.1	0.2	47.3	0.4	47.3	0.0	47.3	0.0	47.4	0.2	47.4	0.0	47.6	0.4	47.9	0.6	48.0	0.2
1967	48.0	0.0	48.0	0.0	48.0	0.0	48.1	0.2	48.2	0.2	48.2	0.0	48.2	0.0	48.3	0.2	48.4	0.2	48.6	0.4	48.8	0.4	48.9	0.2
1968	49.2	0.6	49.4	0.4	49.5	0.2	49.6	0.2	49.7	0.2	49.6	-0.2	49.7	0.2	49.8	0.2	49.8	0.0	49.9	0.2	49.9	0.0	50.1	0.4
1969	50.4	0.6	50.4	0.0	50.5	0.2	50.5	0.0	50.5	0.0	50.5	0.0	50.6	0.2	50.7	0.2	50.8	0.2	50.9	0.2	51.0	0.2	51.2	0.4
1970	51.4	0.4	51.6	0.4	51.6	0.0	51.8	0.4	51.7	-0.2	51.8	0.2	52.0	0.4	52.0	0.0	52.1	0.2	52.2	0.2	52.4	0.4	52.5	0.2

[Continued]

Producer Price Index - Furniture and Household Durables   *Economic Indicators Handbook, 2nd Edition*

FURNITURE AND HOUSEHOLD DURABLES
Producer Price Index
Base 1982 = 100
[Continued]

For 1926-1993. Columns headed % show percentile change in the index from the previous period for which an index is available.

Year	Jan Index	%	Feb Index	%	Mar Index	%	Apr Index	%	May Index	%	Jun Index	%	Jul Index	%	Aug Index	%	Sep Index	%	Oct Index	%	Nov Index	%	Dec Index	%
1971	52.8	0.6	53.0	0.4	53.0	0.0	53.0	0.0	53.1	0.2	53.1	0.0	53.3	0.4	53.3	0.0	53.3	0.0	53.3	0.0	53.2	-0.2	53.2	0.0
1972	53.3	0.2	53.5	0.4	53.6	0.2	53.6	0.0	53.7	0.2	53.7	0.0	53.8	0.2	54.0	0.4	54.1	0.2	54.1	0.0	54.3	0.4	54.3	0.0
1973	54.4	0.2	54.6	0.4	54.8	0.4	55.1	0.5	55.6	0.9	55.7	0.2	55.7	0.0	56.0	0.5	56.1	0.2	56.3	0.4	56.6	0.5	56.8	0.4
1974	57.5	1.2	58.1	1.0	58.6	0.9	59.4	1.4	60.2	1.3	60.9	1.2	62.0	1.8	62.7	1.1	64.2	2.4	65.5	2.0	66.2	1.1	66.5	0.5
1975	67.1	0.9	67.2	0.1	66.9	-0.4	66.9	0.0	67.0	0.1	67.2	0.3	67.3	0.1	67.6	0.4	67.7	0.1	68.2	0.7	68.4	0.3	68.6	0.3
1976	69.3	1.0	69.4	0.1	69.6	0.3	69.8	0.3	70.0	0.3	70.2	0.3	70.4	0.3	70.6	0.3	70.9	0.4	71.1	0.3	71.3	0.3	71.5	0.3
1977	71.9	0.6	72.1	0.3	72.3	0.3	72.5	0.3	72.8	0.4	73.2	0.5	73.2	0.0	73.7	0.7	73.8	0.1	74.0	0.3	74.3	0.4	74.5	0.3
1978	75.6	1.5	75.7	0.1	76.2	0.7	76.5	0.4	76.9	0.5	77.1	0.3	78.0	1.2	78.2	0.3	78.3	0.1	78.7	0.5	79.0	0.4	79.5	0.6
1979	80.5	1.3	81.1	0.7	81.3	0.2	81.5	0.2	82.0	0.6	82.2	0.2	82.5	0.4	82.9	0.5	83.5	0.7	84.6	1.3	85.2	0.7	86.0	0.9
1980	88.6	3.0	89.7	1.2	89.7	0.0	89.1	-0.7	89.6	0.6	90.1	0.6	90.8	0.8	91.3	0.6	91.6	0.3	92.2	0.7	92.5	0.3	93.3	0.9
1981	93.7	0.4	94.3	0.6	94.6	0.3	94.9	0.3	95.4	0.5	95.3	-0.1	96.4	1.2	96.4	0.0	97.1	0.7	97.3	0.2	97.6	0.3	98.1	0.5
1982	98.3	0.2	98.9	0.6	99.3	0.4	99.6	0.3	99.8	0.2	100.0	0.2	100.0	0.0	100.5	0.5	100.7	0.2	101.0	0.3	100.9	-0.1	101.1	0.2
1983	101.8	0.7	102.7	0.9	102.6	-0.1	102.8	0.2	103.2	0.4	103.4	0.2	103.8	0.4	103.9	0.1	104.1	0.2	104.0	-0.1	104.2	0.2	104.2	0.0
1984	104.7	0.5	105.0	0.3	105.1	0.1	105.4	0.3	105.9	0.5	105.9	0.0	105.9	0.0	105.9	0.0	105.8	-0.1	105.9	0.1	106.3	0.4	106.3	0.0
1985	106.4	0.1	106.7	0.3	106.8	0.1	107.1	0.3	107.1	0.0	107.1	0.0	107.3	0.2	107.3	0.0	107.2	-0.1	107.2	0.0	107.4	0.2	107.5	0.1
1986	107.6	0.1	107.7	0.1	107.9	0.2	108.1	0.2	108.3	0.2	108.4	0.1	108.3	-0.1	108.4	0.1	108.3	-0.1	108.5	0.2	108.7	0.2	108.7	0.0
1987	109.0	0.3	109.1	0.1	109.2	0.1	109.6	0.4	109.8	0.2	109.9	0.1	110.0	0.1	110.3	0.3	110.3	0.0	110.5	0.2	110.7	0.2	110.9	0.2
1988	111.6	0.6	111.9	0.3	112.3	0.4	112.5	0.2	112.8	0.3	112.7	-0.1	113.1	0.4	113.4	0.3	113.7	0.3	113.9	0.2	114.3	0.4	114.5	0.2
1989	115.0	0.4	115.3	0.3	115.7	0.3	116.2	0.4	116.5	0.3	117.0	0.4	117.5	0.4	117.9	0.3	117.9	0.0	117.7	-0.2	117.8	0.1	117.9	0.1
1990	118.4	0.4	118.7	0.3	118.7	0.0	119.0	0.3	119.0	0.0	119.2	0.2	119.1	-0.1	119.2	0.1	119.3	0.1	119.5	0.2	119.8	0.3	120.0	0.2
1991	120.6	0.5	120.9	0.2	121.0	0.1	121.2	0.2	121.2	0.0	121.2	0.0	121.2	0.0	121.2	0.0	121.2	0.0	121.4	0.2	121.4	0.0	121.5	0.1
1992	121.8	0.2	121.8	0.0	121.9	0.1	122.0	0.1	122.1	0.1	122.2	0.1	122.2	0.0	122.2	0.0	122.4	0.2	122.3	-0.1	122.6	0.2	122.6	0.0
1993	122.6	0.0	122.9	0.2	123.0	0.1	123.2	0.2	123.4	0.2	123.6	0.2	123.8	0.2	124.0	0.2	124.0	0.0	124.2	0.2	124.4	0.2	124.5	0.1

Source: U.S. Department of Labor, Bureau of Labor Statistics, Division of Industry Prices and Price Indexes. n.e.c. stands for not elsewhere classified. - indicates no data collected for period or unavailable.

Household Furniture
Producer Price Index
Base 1982 = 100

For 1926-1993. Columns headed % show percentile change in the index from the previous period for which an index is available.

Year	Jan Index	%	Feb Index	%	Mar Index	%	Apr Index	%	May Index	%	Jun Index	%	Jul Index	%	Aug Index	%	Sep Index	%	Oct Index	%	Nov Index	%	Dec Index	%
1926	23.2	-	23.1	-0.4	23.1	0.0	23.0	-0.4	22.9	-0.4	22.8	-0.4	22.8	0.0	22.8	0.0	22.8	0.0	22.8	0.0	22.8	0.0	22.8	0.0
1927	22.4	-1.8	22.4	0.0	22.4	0.0	22.4	0.0	22.4	0.0	22.4	0.0	22.4	0.0	22.4	0.0	22.4	0.0	22.2	-0.9	22.3	0.5	22.2	-0.4
1928	22.3	0.5	22.3	0.0	22.2	-0.4	22.2	0.0	22.2	0.0	22.2	0.0	22.2	0.0	22.2	0.0	22.2	0.0	21.8	-1.8	21.8	0.0	21.8	0.0
1929	21.6	-0.9	21.6	0.0	21.6	0.0	21.6	0.0	21.6	0.0	21.8	0.9	21.8	0.0	21.8	0.0	21.8	0.0	21.5	-1.4	21.8	1.4	21.8	0.0
1930	21.7	-0.5	21.7	0.0	21.7	0.0	21.7	0.0	21.7	0.0	21.6	-0.5	21.5	-0.5	21.5	0.0	21.4	-0.5	21.4	0.0	21.4	0.0	21.1	-1.4
1931	21.1	0.0	21.1	0.0	21.1	0.0	21.1	0.0	20.7	-1.9	20.5	-1.0	20.4	-0.5	20.3	-0.5	19.4	-4.4	18.8	-3.1	18.8	0.0	18.4	-2.1
1932	18.2	-1.1	18.2	0.0	18.1	-0.5	17.7	-2.2	17.0	-4.0	16.9	-0.6	16.7	-1.2	16.6	-0.6	16.7	0.6	16.7	0.0	16.7	0.0	16.6	-0.6
1933	16.5	-0.6	16.4	-0.6	16.4	0.0	16.4	0.0	16.4	0.0	16.8	2.4	17.1	1.8	17.5	2.3	17.9	2.3	18.2	1.7	18.2	0.0	18.1	-0.5
1934	18.1	0.0	18.1	0.0	18.2	0.6	18.3	0.5	18.3	0.0	18.1	-1.1	18.0	-0.6	18.1	0.6	18.1	0.0	18.1	0.0	18.0	-0.6	17.9	-0.6
1935	17.9	0.0	17.7	-1.1	17.7	0.0	17.7	0.0	17.7	0.0	17.7	0.0	17.6	-0.6	17.6	0.0	17.6	0.0	17.6	0.0	17.7	0.6	17.7	0.0
1936	17.8	0.6	17.8	0.0	17.8	0.0	17.8	0.0	17.8	0.0	17.7	-0.6	17.7	0.0	17.7	0.0	17.8	0.6	17.9	0.6	18.1	1.1	18.2	0.6
1937	19.2	5.5	19.4	1.0	19.4	0.0	19.6	1.0	19.7	0.5	19.8	0.5	19.8	0.0	19.9	0.5	19.9	0.0	19.9	0.0	19.7	-1.0	19.7	0.0
1938	19.1	-3.0	19.1	0.0	19.1	0.0	19.1	0.0	19.1	0.0	19.1	0.0	18.8	-1.6	18.8	0.0	18.8	0.0	18.8	0.0	18.7	-0.5	18.7	0.0
1939	18.4	-1.6	18.4	0.0	18.4	0.0	18.5	0.5	18.5	0.0	18.5	0.0	18.5	0.0	18.5	0.0	18.6	0.5	18.7	0.5	18.8	0.5	18.8	0.0
1940	18.7	-0.5	18.7	0.0	18.7	0.0	18.7	0.0	18.7	0.0	18.7	0.0	18.7	0.0	18.7	0.0	18.7	0.0	18.7	0.0	18.7	0.0	18.8	0.5
1941	18.9	0.5	18.9	0.0	19.0	0.5	19.1	0.5	19.3	1.0	19.9	3.1	20.4	2.5	20.5	0.5	21.1	2.9	21.6	2.4	21.9	1.4	22.1	0.9
1942	22.3	0.9	22.3	0.0	22.3	0.0	22.3	0.0	22.3	0.0	22.3	0.0	22.3	0.0	22.3	0.0	22.3	0.0	22.3	0.0	22.3	0.0	22.3	0.0
1943	22.4	0.4	22.4	0.0	22.4	0.0	22.4	0.0	22.4	0.0	22.4	0.0	22.4	0.0	22.4	0.0	22.4	0.0	22.4	0.0	22.4	0.0	22.6	0.9
1944	22.9	1.3	23.1	0.9	23.1	0.0	23.1	0.0	23.1	0.0	23.1	0.0	23.1	0.0	23.1	0.0	23.1	0.0	23.1	0.0	23.2	0.4	23.2	0.0
1945	23.2	0.0	23.2	0.0	23.2	0.0	23.2	0.0	23.2	0.0	23.5	1.3	23.5	0.0	23.5	0.0	23.5	0.0	23.5	0.0	23.5	0.0	23.5	0.0
1946	23.9	1.7	24.0	0.4	24.0	0.0	24.1	0.4	24.5	1.7	24.8	1.2	24.9	0.4	25.2	1.2	25.4	0.8	25.8	1.6	26.3	1.9	26.9	2.3
1947	29.4	9.3	29.4	0.0	29.4	0.0	29.5	0.3	29.5	0.0	29.5	0.0	29.7	0.7	29.9	0.7	30.3	1.3	30.7	1.3	30.8	0.3	31.1	1.0
1948	31.9	2.6	31.9	0.0	31.9	0.0	32.0	0.3	31.9	-0.3	32.0	0.3	32.0	0.0	32.3	0.9	32.5	0.6	32.5	0.0	32.5	0.0	32.5	0.0
1949	32.3	-0.6	32.3	0.0	32.3	0.0	32.3	0.0	32.0	-0.9	31.9	-0.3	31.2	-2.2	31.3	0.3	31.3	0.0	31.3	0.0	31.3	0.0	31.4	0.3
1950	31.5	0.3	31.5	0.0	31.5	0.0	31.6	0.3	31.6	0.0	31.8	0.6	32.2	1.3	33.2	3.1	34.2	3.0	34.8	1.8	35.2	1.1	35.9	2.0
1951	36.7	2.2	36.8	0.3	36.8	0.0	36.8	0.0	36.7	-0.3	36.5	-0.5	36.2	-0.8	36.2	0.0	36.2	0.0	36.1	-0.3	36.2	0.3	36.0	-0.6
1952	35.5	-1.4	35.5	0.0	35.5	0.0	35.5	0.0	35.4	-0.3	35.2	-0.6	35.2	0.0	35.2	0.0	35.2	0.0	35.2	0.0	35.3	0.3	35.3	0.0
1953	35.4	0.3	35.5	0.0	35.5	0.0	35.6	0.3	35.6	0.0	35.7	0.3	35.6	-0.3	35.6	0.0	35.7	0.3	35.7	0.0	35.7	0.0	35.7	0.0
1954	35.7	0.0	35.6	-0.3	35.6	0.0	35.5	-0.3	35.5	0.0	35.4	-0.3	35.3	-0.3	35.3	0.0	35.3	0.0	35.3	0.0	35.3	0.0	35.3	0.0
1955	35.2	-0.3	35.2	0.0	35.2	0.0	35.3	0.3	35.4	0.3	35.3	-0.3	35.4	0.3	35.8	1.1	36.0	0.6	36.2	0.6	36.4	0.6	36.5	0.3
1956	36.7	0.5	36.7	0.0	36.8	0.3	36.9	0.3	36.9	0.0	36.9	0.0	37.3	1.1	37.4	0.3	37.6	0.5	37.8	0.5	37.9	0.3	37.9	0.0
1957	38.2	0.8	38.2	0.0	38.2	0.0	38.3	0.3	38.3	0.0	38.3	0.0	38.4	0.3	38.5	0.3	38.3	-0.5	38.3	0.0	38.4	0.3	38.4	0.0
1958	38.5	0.3	38.6	0.3	38.4	-0.5	38.4	0.0	38.4	0.0	38.3	-0.3	38.3	0.0	38.3	0.0	38.4	0.3	38.5	0.3	38.7	0.5	38.8	0.3
1959	38.8	0.0	38.8	0.0	38.8	0.0	38.6	-0.5	38.7	0.3	38.8	0.3	38.9	0.3	38.9	0.0	38.8	-0.3	38.9	0.3	38.9	0.0	38.9	0.0
1960	39.0	0.3	39.1	0.3	39.1	0.0	39.1	0.0	39.1	0.0	39.1	0.0	39.1	0.0	39.1	0.0	39.1	0.0	39.3	0.5	39.3	0.0	39.3	0.0
1961	39.5	0.5	39.5	0.0	39.5	0.0	39.5	0.0	39.6	0.3	39.6	0.0	39.6	0.0	39.6	0.0	39.6	0.0	39.7	0.3	39.9	0.5	39.8	-0.3
1962	39.9	0.3	39.9	0.0	39.9	0.0	39.9	0.0	40.0	0.3	40.0	0.0	40.1	0.3	40.1	0.0	40.0	-0.2	40.1	0.3	40.1	0.0	40.2	0.2
1963	40.3	0.2	40.3	0.0	40.3	0.0	40.2	-0.2	40.2	0.0	40.3	0.2	40.3	0.0	40.3	0.0	40.4	0.2	40.4	0.0	40.4	0.0	40.3	-0.2
1964	40.5	0.5	40.5	0.0	40.5	0.0	40.6	0.2	40.6	0.0	40.5	-0.2	40.6	0.2	40.6	0.0	40.6	0.0	40.6	0.0	40.7	0.2	40.7	0.0
1965	40.9	0.5	40.9	0.0	40.9	0.0	40.9	0.0	40.9	0.0	40.8	-0.2	40.8	0.0	40.9	0.2	40.9	0.0	41.0	0.2	41.1	0.2	41.1	0.0
1966	41.2	0.2	41.3	0.2	41.3	0.0	41.7	1.0	42.0	0.7	42.0	0.0	42.0	0.0	42.2	0.5	42.3	0.2	42.5	0.5	43.0	1.2	43.1	0.2
1967	43.1	0.0	43.2	0.2	43.3	0.2	43.3	0.0	43.3	0.0	43.3	0.0	43.4	0.2	43.6	0.5	43.6	0.0	43.7	0.2	44.0	0.7	44.0	0.0
1968	44.4	0.9	44.6	0.5	44.7	0.2	44.8	0.2	45.1	0.7	45.2	0.2	45.3	0.2	45.3	0.0	45.4	0.2	45.7	0.7	45.9	0.4	46.0	0.2
1969	46.6	1.3	46.7	0.2	46.8	0.2	46.8	0.0	47.0	0.4	47.1	0.2	47.4	0.6	47.4	0.0	47.5	0.2	47.6	0.2	47.7	0.2	47.6	-0.2
1970	47.9	0.6	48.3	0.8	48.4	0.2	48.4	0.0	48.6	0.4	48.6	0.0	48.7	0.2	48.8	0.2	48.8	0.0	48.8	0.0	48.9	0.2	49.0	0.2

[Continued]

Household Furniture

Producer Price Index
Base 1982 = 100
[Continued]

For 1926-1993. Columns headed % show percentile change in the index from the previous period for which an index is available.

Year	Jan Index	%	Feb Index	%	Mar Index	%	Apr Index	%	May Index	%	Jun Index	%	Jul Index	%	Aug Index	%	Sep Index	%	Oct Index	%	Nov Index	%	Dec Index	%
1971	49.2	0.4	49.7	1.0	49.7	0.0	49.7	0.0	50.1	0.8	50.1	0.0	50.2	0.2	50.3	0.2	50.3	0.0	50.3	0.0	50.0	-0.6	50.0	0.0
1972	50.5	1.0	50.8	0.6	50.8	0.0	50.9	0.2	51.0	0.2	51.0	0.0	51.1	0.2	51.3	0.4	51.2	-0.2	51.2	0.0	51.4	0.4	51.6	0.4
1973	51.8	0.4	51.9	0.2	52.2	0.6	53.0	1.5	53.2	0.4	53.6	0.8	53.6	0.0	53.8	0.4	54.1	0.6	54.5	0.7	55.1	1.1	55.3	0.4
1974	56.1	1.4	56.5	0.7	56.7	0.4	57.8	1.9	58.7	1.6	58.9	0.3	59.5	1.0	60.0	0.8	60.9	1.5	62.1	2.0	62.9	1.3	62.9	0.0
1975	63.3	0.6	63.3	0.0	63.2	-0.2	63.3	0.2	63.2	-0.2	63.2	0.0	63.3	0.2	63.3	0.0	63.6	0.5	64.3	1.1	64.6	0.5	65.1	0.8
1976	65.6	0.8	65.5	-0.2	65.6	0.2	65.8	0.3	66.1	0.5	66.6	0.8	66.8	0.3	66.9	0.1	67.4	0.7	68.1	1.0	68.5	0.6	69.0	0.7
1977	69.1	0.1	69.1	0.0	69.5	0.6	69.9	0.6	70.1	0.3	70.6	0.7	70.9	0.4	71.0	0.1	71.1	0.1	71.4	0.4	71.8	0.6	72.4	0.8
1978	73.2	1.1	73.4	0.3	73.7	0.4	73.9	0.3	74.3	0.5	75.0	0.9	76.0	1.3	76.4	0.5	76.6	0.3	77.4	1.0	77.8	0.5	78.0	0.3
1979	78.8	1.0	78.9	0.1	79.1	0.3	79.5	0.5	80.4	1.1	80.6	0.2	80.8	0.2	81.0	0.2	82.0	1.2	82.7	0.9	84.0	1.6	84.8	1.0
1980	85.9	1.3	86.4	0.6	86.6	0.2	87.2	0.7	88.3	1.3	88.8	0.6	89.8	1.1	90.5	0.8	90.7	0.2	91.3	0.7	91.8	0.5	92.3	0.5
1981	92.6	0.3	93.0	0.4	93.3	0.3	94.2	1.0	94.1	-0.1	95.1	1.1	95.7	0.6	96.0	0.3	96.7	0.7	96.9	0.2	97.9	1.0	98.6	0.7
1982	99.0	0.4	98.9	-0.1	99.0	0.1	99.9	0.9	100.1	0.2	100.2	0.1	100.1	-0.1	100.2	0.1	100.4	0.2	100.6	0.2	100.7	0.1	100.9	0.2
1983	100.9	0.0	101.2	0.3	100.6	-0.6	100.8	0.2	102.0	1.2	102.2	0.2	102.4	0.2	102.8	0.4	102.9	0.1	103.1	0.2	103.3	0.2	103.2	-0.1
1984	103.5	0.3	104.0	0.5	104.4	0.4	104.8	0.4	105.1	0.3	105.4	0.3	105.4	0.0	105.6	0.2	105.9	0.3	106.3	0.4	106.6	0.3	106.8	0.2
1985	107.4	0.6	107.7	0.3	107.7	0.0	108.3	0.6	108.8	0.5	109.0	0.2	108.7	-0.3	108.8	0.1	108.8	0.0	108.7	-0.1	108.9	0.2	109.0	0.1
1986	109.3	0.3	109.8	0.5	110.0	0.2	109.8	-0.2	110.3	0.5	110.2	-0.1	110.1	-0.1	110.6	0.5	110.4	-0.2	110.7	0.3	110.8	0.1	111.0	0.2
1987	111.2	0.2	111.7	0.4	112.0	0.3	112.5	0.4	112.8	0.3	112.8	0.0	112.8	0.0	113.1	0.3	113.6	0.4	113.6	0.0	114.2	0.5	115.2	0.9
1988	115.8	0.5	116.2	0.3	116.8	0.5	117.0	0.2	117.2	0.2	117.4	0.2	117.8	0.3	118.1	0.3	118.1	0.0	118.6	0.4	119.0	0.3	119.5	0.4
1989	119.6	0.1	120.2	0.5	120.7	0.4	121.3	0.5	121.6	0.2	121.7	0.1	121.9	0.2	122.3	0.3	122.5	0.2	123.1	0.5	123.4	0.2	123.5	0.1
1990	123.6	0.1	123.9	0.2	124.0	0.1	124.4	0.3	124.9	0.4	125.1	0.2	125.2	0.1	125.3	0.1	125.5	0.2	126.0	0.4	126.5	0.4	126.6	0.1
1991	126.9	0.2	127.3	0.3	127.7	0.3	127.8	0.1	127.9	0.1	127.9	0.0	128.0	0.1	128.1	0.1	128.3	0.2	128.7	0.3	128.9	0.2	128.9	0.0
1992	129.2	0.2	129.4	0.2	129.6	0.2	129.7	0.1	129.7	0.0	129.9	0.2	130.0	0.1	130.1	0.1	130.4	0.2	130.5	0.1	130.9	0.3	131.0	0.1
1993	131.2	0.2	131.6	0.3	131.7	0.1	132.2	0.4	132.6	0.3	133.0	0.3	133.2	0.2	133.3	0.1	133.8	0.4	133.9	0.1	134.2	0.2	134.4	0.1

Source: U.S. Department of Labor, Bureau of Labor Statistics, Division of Industry Prices and Price Indexes. n.e.c. stands for not elsewhere classified. - indicates no data collected for period or unavailable.

Commercial Furniture
Producer Price Index
Base 1982 = 100

For 1947-1993. Columns headed % show percentile change in the index from the previous period for which an index is available.

Year	Jan Index	%	Feb Index	%	Mar Index	%	Apr Index	%	May Index	%	Jun Index	%	Jul Index	%	Aug Index	%	Sep Index	%	Oct Index	%	Nov Index	%	Dec Index	%
1947	19.5	-	19.5	0.0	19.6	0.5	20.1	2.6	20.3	1.0	20.3	0.0	20.3	0.0	20.3	0.0	20.4	0.5	20.5	0.5	20.5	0.0	20.7	1.0
1948	20.9	1.0	21.0	0.5	21.1	0.5	21.1	0.0	21.1	0.0	21.1	0.0	21.2	0.5	21.9	3.3	22.0	0.5	22.3	1.4	22.3	0.0	22.3	0.0
1949	22.3	0.0	22.3	0.0	22.3	0.0	22.3	0.0	22.2	-0.4	22.2	0.0	22.2	0.0	22.2	0.0	22.2	0.0	22.2	0.0	22.2	0.0	22.2	0.0
1950	22.2	0.0	22.2	0.0	22.2	0.0	22.2	0.0	22.5	1.4	22.6	0.4	23.0	1.8	23.7	3.0	23.8	0.4	24.5	2.9	25.4	3.7	26.0	2.4
1951	26.6	2.3	26.6	0.0	26.6	0.0	26.6	0.0	26.6	0.0	26.6	0.0	26.6	0.0	26.6	0.0	26.6	0.0	26.4	-0.8	26.1	-1.1	26.1	0.0
1952	26.1	0.0	26.1	0.0	26.2	0.4	26.2	0.0	26.2	0.0	26.2	0.0	26.2	0.0	26.1	-0.4	26.1	0.0	26.2	0.4	26.2	0.0	26.2	0.0
1953	26.2	0.0	26.2	0.0	26.2	0.0	26.2	0.0	26.5	1.1	26.8	1.1	26.8	0.0	26.8	0.0	26.8	0.0	26.8	0.0	26.9	0.4	26.9	0.0
1954	26.9	0.0	26.9	0.0	26.9	0.0	26.9	0.0	26.9	0.0	26.9	0.0	26.9	0.0	26.9	0.0	26.9	0.0	27.1	0.7	27.4	1.1	27.4	0.0
1955	27.4	0.0	27.4	0.0	27.4	0.0	27.4	0.0	27.4	0.0	27.6	0.7	27.7	0.4	28.6	3.2	29.0	1.4	29.2	0.7	29.2	0.0	29.2	0.0
1956	29.3	0.3	29.5	0.7	29.5	0.0	29.5	0.0	29.5	0.0	29.5	0.0	29.6	0.3	31.1	5.1	31.3	0.6	31.3	0.0	31.3	0.0	31.3	0.0
1957	31.3	0.0	31.3	0.0	31.3	0.0	31.4	0.3	31.4	0.0	31.4	0.0	32.7	4.1	32.7	0.0	32.7	0.0	32.7	0.0	32.8	0.3	32.8	0.0
1958	32.8	0.0	32.8	0.0	32.8	0.0	32.8	0.0	32.8	0.0	32.8	0.0	33.0	0.6	33.0	0.0	33.0	0.0	33.0	0.0	33.0	0.0	33.0	0.0
1959	33.0	0.0	33.0	0.0	33.0	0.0	33.0	0.0	33.0	0.0	33.0	0.0	33.1	0.3	33.1	0.0	33.1	0.0	33.1	0.0	33.1	0.0	33.1	0.0
1960	33.2	0.3	33.2	0.0	33.4	0.6	33.4	0.0	33.4	0.0	33.4	0.0	33.5	0.3	33.5	0.0	33.5	0.0	33.5	0.0	33.5	0.0	33.5	0.0
1961	33.2	-0.9	33.2	0.0	33.2	0.0	33.2	0.0	33.2	0.0	33.2	0.0	33.2	0.0	33.2	0.0	33.4	0.6	33.4	0.0	33.4	0.0	33.4	0.0
1962	33.4	0.0	33.4	0.0	33.4	0.0	33.4	0.0	33.4	0.0	33.4	0.0	33.5	0.3	33.5	0.0	33.5	0.0	33.5	0.0	33.5	0.0	33.4	-0.3
1963	33.4	0.0	33.4	0.0	33.4	0.0	33.4	0.0	33.4	0.0	33.6	0.6	33.6	0.0	33.7	0.3	33.7	0.0	33.7	0.0	33.7	0.0	33.7	0.0
1964	33.7	0.0	33.7	0.0	33.7	0.0	33.7	0.0	33.7	0.0	33.7	0.0	33.7	0.0	33.7	0.0	33.7	0.0	33.7	0.0	33.7	0.0	33.8	0.3
1965	33.8	0.0	33.8	0.0	33.8	0.0	33.8	0.0	33.9	0.3	33.9	0.0	33.9	0.0	33.9	0.0	33.9	0.0	33.9	0.0	34.0	0.3	34.0	0.0
1966	34.0	0.0	34.0	0.0	34.0	0.0	34.0	0.0	34.4	1.2	34.4	0.0	34.6	0.6	34.6	0.0	34.6	0.0	35.1	1.4	35.3	0.6	35.5	0.6
1967	35.5	0.0	35.7	0.6	35.7	0.0	35.7	0.0	36.6	2.5	36.6	0.0	36.6	0.0	36.6	0.0	36.6	0.0	36.6	0.0	36.7	0.3	36.8	0.3
1968	37.1	0.8	37.1	0.0	37.2	0.3	37.4	0.5	37.6	0.5	37.8	0.5	37.9	0.3	37.9	0.0	37.9	0.0	38.1	0.5	38.1	0.0	38.2	0.3
1969	38.2	0.0	38.3	0.3	38.5	0.5	38.5	0.0	38.9	1.0	39.0	0.3	39.1	0.3	39.1	0.0	39.8	1.8	40.0	0.5	40.5	1.3	40.5	0.0
1970	40.7	0.5	40.7	0.0	40.9	0.5	40.9	0.0	40.9	0.0	41.7	2.0	41.7	0.0	42.0	0.7	42.0	0.0	42.1	0.2	42.7	1.4	42.7	0.0
1971	42.7	0.0	42.9	0.5	42.9	0.0	42.9	0.0	42.9	0.0	42.9	0.0	42.9	0.0	42.9	0.0	42.9	0.0	42.9	0.0	42.9	0.0	42.9	0.0
1972	42.9	0.0	42.9	0.0	43.1	0.5	43.3	0.5	43.3	0.0	43.4	0.2	43.5	0.2	43.5	0.0	44.0	1.1	44.2	0.5	44.8	1.4	44.8	0.0
1973	44.9	0.2	44.9	0.0	44.9	0.0	44.9	0.0	47.4	5.6	47.4	0.0	47.4	0.0	48.0	1.3	48.2	0.4	48.5	0.6	48.6	0.2	48.6	0.0
1974	49.5	1.9	50.5	2.0	51.0	1.0	51.4	0.8	52.3	1.8	53.5	2.3	55.5	3.7	56.7	2.2	60.4	6.5	60.6	0.3	61.3	1.2	61.3	0.0
1975	60.5	-1.3	60.4	-0.2	60.3	-0.2	60.3	0.0	60.3	0.0	60.3	0.0	60.3	0.0	60.8	0.8	60.8	0.0	61.3	0.8	60.6	-1.1	60.6	0.0
1976	60.9	0.5	61.5	1.0	61.6	0.2	62.5	1.5	63.0	0.8	63.3	0.5	63.5	0.3	63.7	0.3	63.7	0.0	64.0	0.5	64.0	0.0	64.0	0.0
1977	64.3	0.5	64.7	0.6	64.9	0.3	66.5	2.5	67.1	0.9	67.8	1.0	66.9	-1.3	69.3	3.6	69.2	-0.1	69.2	0.0	69.8	0.9	69.8	0.0
1978	70.7	1.3	70.8	0.1	72.2	2.0	72.8	0.8	72.8	0.0	72.8	0.0	73.7	1.2	74.0	0.4	73.9	-0.1	74.2	0.4	74.4	0.3	75.2	1.1
1979	77.8	3.5	80.3	3.2	80.3	0.0	80.5	0.2	80.5	0.0	80.5	0.0	80.8	0.4	80.8	0.0	80.8	0.0	81.1	0.4	81.1	0.0	81.7	0.7
1980	82.4	0.9	84.0	1.9	84.5	0.6	84.8	0.4	84.9	0.1	85.5	0.7	86.1	0.7	86.1	0.0	86.3	0.2	87.6	1.5	87.9	0.3	88.0	0.1
1981	89.6	1.8	91.3	1.9	92.0	0.8	92.4	0.4	93.5	1.2	93.6	0.1	93.9	0.3	94.1	0.2	94.9	0.9	95.2	0.3	95.6	0.4	95.8	0.2
1982	96.8	1.0	98.4	1.7	99.3	0.9	99.5	0.2	99.9	0.4	100.2	0.3	100.7	0.5	100.9	0.2	101.0	0.1	101.0	0.0	101.1	0.1	101.1	0.0
1983	102.0	0.9	102.4	0.4	103.5	1.1	103.9	0.4	103.8	-0.1	104.1	0.3	104.3	0.2	104.0	-0.3	104.3	0.3	104.3	0.0	105.2	0.9	105.1	-0.1
1984	106.5	1.3	107.0	0.5	107.0	0.0	107.5	0.5	107.9	0.4	107.8	-0.1	108.2	0.4	108.3	0.1	108.0	-0.3	107.9	-0.1	109.1	1.1	108.8	-0.3
1985	109.0	0.2	109.9	0.8	110.2	0.3	111.2	0.9	111.4	0.2	111.7	0.3	112.5	0.7	112.9	0.4	113.1	0.2	112.9	-0.2	113.9	0.9	113.9	0.0
1986	114.2	0.3	114.2	0.0	114.2	0.0	114.9	0.6	114.9	0.0	115.3	0.3	115.5	0.2	115.4	-0.1	115.5	0.1	116.2	0.6	116.7	0.4	116.5	-0.2
1987	116.9	0.3	117.1	0.2	117.5	0.3	118.2	0.6	118.4	0.2	118.6	0.2	118.6	0.0	118.9	0.3	119.1	0.2	119.7	0.5	119.9	0.2	120.0	0.1
1988	121.2	1.0	121.4	0.2	122.7	1.1	123.5	0.7	123.8	0.2	123.8	0.0	125.0	1.0	125.2	0.2	125.8	0.5	125.7	-0.1	125.9	0.2	126.5	0.5
1989	126.9	0.3	126.9	0.0	127.4	0.4	127.7	0.2	128.2	0.4	128.6	0.3	129.3	0.5	130.1	0.6	130.8	0.5	130.6	-0.2	130.8	0.2	130.8	0.0
1990	131.8	0.8	132.4	0.5	132.4	0.0	132.7	0.2	133.2	0.4	133.4	0.2	133.5	0.1	133.7	0.1	133.9	0.1	134.3	0.3	134.6	0.2	135.4	0.6
1991	135.9	0.4	136.4	0.4	135.9	-0.4	135.8	-0.1	136.1	0.2	136.1	0.0	136.2	0.1	136.2	0.0	136.3	0.1	136.5	0.1	136.6	0.1	136.6	0.0

[Continued]

Commercial Furniture
Producer Price Index
Base 1982 = 100
[Continued]

For 1947-1993. Columns headed % show percentile change in the index from the previous period for which an index is available.

Year	Jan		Feb		Mar		Apr		May		Jun		Jul		Aug		Sep		Oct		Nov		Dec	
	Index	%	Index	%	Index	%	Index	%	Index	%	Index	%	Index	%	Index	%	Index	%	Index	%	Index	%	Index	%
1992	137.0	0.3	137.2	0.1	137.3	0.1	137.9	0.4	138.0	0.1	138.1	0.1	137.8	-0.2	138.2	0.3	138.5	0.2	138.5	0.0	139.1	0.4	139.3	0.1
1993	139.2	-0.1	139.8	0.4	139.6	-0.1	140.1	0.4	140.3	0.1	140.5	0.1	140.8	0.2	141.0	0.1	141.1	0.1	141.1	0.0	141.7	0.4	142.5	0.6

Source: U.S. Department of Labor, Bureau of Labor Statistics, Division of Industry Prices and Price Indexes. n.e.c. stands for not elsewhere classified. - indicates no data collected for period or unavailable.

Floor Coverings
Producer Price Index
Base 1982 = 100

For 1926-1993. Columns headed % show percentile change in the index from the previous period for which an index is available.

Year	Jan Index	%	Feb Index	%	Mar Index	%	Apr Index	%	May Index	%	Jun Index	%	Jul Index	%	Aug Index	%	Sep Index	%	Oct Index	%	Nov Index	%	Dec Index	%
1926	31.9	-	31.9	0.0	31.9	0.0	31.9	0.0	31.9	0.0	31.7	-0.6	31.7	0.0	31.7	0.0	31.7	0.0	31.7	0.0	31.7	0.0	30.3	-4.4
1927	30.3	0.0	30.3	0.0	30.1	-0.7	30.1	0.0	30.1	0.0	30.3	0.7	30.3	0.0	30.3	0.0	30.3	0.0	30.3	0.0	30.3	0.0	30.4	0.3
1928	30.4	0.0	30.4	0.0	30.4	0.0	30.4	0.0	30.4	0.0	29.1	-4.3	29.1	0.0	29.1	0.0	29.1	0.0	29.1	0.0	29.4	1.0	29.4	0.0
1929	29.4	0.0	29.4	0.0	29.4	0.0	29.4	0.0	29.4	0.0	29.4	0.0	29.7	1.0	29.7	0.0	29.7	0.0	30.2	1.7	30.2	0.0	30.3	0.3
1930	30.6	1.0	30.6	0.0	30.6	0.0	30.6	0.0	30.6	0.0	30.6	0.0	30.6	0.0	30.6	0.0	29.9	-2.3	29.9	0.0	29.9	0.0	25.6	-14.4
1931	25.6	0.0	25.6	0.0	25.6	0.0	25.6	0.0	25.6	0.0	25.6	0.0	25.6	0.0	25.6	0.0	25.6	0.0	25.6	0.0	25.6	0.0	22.7	-11.3
1932	22.7	0.0	22.7	0.0	22.7	0.0	22.7	0.0	22.9	0.9	23.0	0.4	22.8	-0.9	22.7	-0.4	22.7	0.0	22.7	0.0	22.7	0.0	22.7	0.0
1933	22.7	0.0	22.7	0.0	22.7	0.0	22.7	0.0	22.7	0.0	23.2	2.2	23.5	1.3	24.0	2.1	24.3	1.3	24.7	1.6	24.7	0.0	24.7	0.0
1934	24.7	0.0	24.7	0.0	24.7	0.0	24.7	0.0	25.4	2.8	26.7	5.1	26.7	0.0	26.7	0.0	26.7	0.0	26.1	-2.2	26.1	0.0	26.1	0.0
1935	26.2	0.4	26.2	0.0	26.2	0.0	26.2	0.0	26.2	0.0	26.2	0.0	26.2	0.0	26.2	0.0	26.2	0.0	26.2	0.0	26.2	0.0	26.2	0.0
1936	26.3	0.4	26.3	0.0	26.3	0.0	26.3	0.0	26.3	0.0	26.4	0.4	26.0	-1.5	26.0	0.0	26.1	0.4	26.3	0.8	26.3	0.0	27.1	3.0
1937	27.4	1.1	28.9	5.5	28.9	0.0	28.9	0.0	28.9	0.0	28.9	0.0	29.8	3.1	30.7	3.0	30.7	0.0	30.7	0.0	30.7	0.0	29.6	-3.6
1938	29.1	-1.7	29.1	0.0	28.7	-1.4	28.4	-1.0	28.4	0.0	28.4	0.0	28.2	-0.7	28.2	0.0	27.9	-1.1	27.0	-3.2	27.3	1.1	27.9	2.2
1939	28.1	0.7	28.1	0.0	28.1	0.0	28.1	0.0	28.1	0.0	28.1	0.0	28.0	-0.4	28.0	0.0	29.5	5.4	30.9	4.7	31.1	0.6	31.1	0.0
1940	30.8	-1.0	30.8	0.0	30.8	0.0	31.2	1.3	31.3	0.3	31.3	0.0	31.3	0.0	31.3	0.0	31.3	0.0	31.3	0.0	31.3	0.0	31.3	0.0
1941	31.3	0.0	31.3	0.0	31.5	0.6	32.0	1.6	32.2	0.6	32.5	0.9	32.5	0.0	32.5	0.0	32.5	0.0	32.5	0.0	32.5	0.0	32.5	0.0
1942	33.1	1.8	33.2	0.3	33.2	0.0	33.2	0.0	33.2	0.0	33.2	0.0	33.2	0.0	33.2	0.0	33.2	0.0	33.2	0.0	33.2	0.0	33.2	0.0
1943	33.2	0.0	33.2	0.0	33.2	0.0	33.2	0.0	33.2	0.0	33.2	0.0	33.2	0.0	33.2	0.0	33.2	0.0	33.2	0.0	33.2	0.0	33.2	0.0
1944	33.2	0.0	33.2	0.0	33.2	0.0	33.2	0.0	33.2	0.0	33.2	0.0	33.2	0.0	33.2	0.0	33.2	0.0	33.2	0.0	33.2	0.0	33.2	0.0
1945	33.1	-0.3	33.1	0.0	33.1	0.0	33.1	0.0	33.1	0.0	33.1	0.0	33.1	0.0	33.1	0.0	33.1	0.0	33.1	0.0	33.1	0.0	33.1	0.0
1946	34.3	3.6	34.8	1.5	35.3	1.4	36.3	2.8	37.0	1.9	37.0	0.0	37.0	0.0	37.0	0.0	37.3	0.8	37.4	0.3	39.0	4.3	39.9	2.3
1947	42.7	7.0	42.7	0.0	42.8	0.2	42.9	0.2	42.9	0.0	43.1	0.5	44.0	2.1	44.0	0.0	44.1	0.2	44.1	0.0	44.1	0.0	45.3	2.7
1948	45.5	0.4	45.6	0.2	45.6	0.0	45.6	0.0	45.6	0.0	46.2	1.3	46.5	0.6	46.6	0.2	47.2	1.3	47.4	0.4	47.4	0.0	47.4	0.0
1949	47.8	0.8	47.9	0.2	48.0	0.2	47.3	-1.5	47.3	0.0	46.5	-1.7	45.6	-1.9	45.6	0.0	45.5	-0.2	45.6	0.2	46.0	0.9	46.8	1.7
1950	47.4	1.3	48.2	1.7	48.4	0.4	48.5	0.2	49.6	2.3	49.6	0.0	50.4	1.6	53.9	6.9	55.3	2.6	57.9	4.7	58.3	0.7	60.3	3.4
1951	63.0	4.5	64.0	1.6	66.6	4.1	68.0	2.1	68.0	0.0	66.9	-1.6	64.8	-3.1	60.8	-6.2	58.4	-3.9	57.7	-1.2	57.1	-1.0	57.5	0.7
1952	57.5	0.0	57.6	0.2	57.4	-0.3	57.7	0.5	55.0	-4.7	54.2	-1.5	54.2	0.0	54.1	-0.2	55.7	3.0	55.7	0.0	55.7	0.0	55.9	0.4
1953	56.5	1.1	56.5	0.0	56.5	0.0	56.5	0.0	56.9	0.7	56.8	-0.2	57.0	0.4	57.0	0.0	57.0	0.0	57.0	0.0	56.9	-0.2	56.8	-0.2
1954	55.8	-1.8	55.7	-0.2	55.8	0.2	55.8	0.0	55.8	0.0	55.8	0.0	55.9	0.2	56.2	0.5	56.6	0.7	56.4	-0.4	56.4	0.0	56.4	0.0
1955	56.5	0.2	56.6	0.2	56.6	0.0	56.9	0.5	56.9	0.0	57.5	1.1	57.7	0.3	57.7	0.0	58.3	1.0	58.6	0.5	58.6	0.0	58.8	0.3
1956	59.4	1.0	59.4	0.0	59.4	0.0	59.4	0.0	59.4	0.0	59.4	0.0	59.8	0.7	59.8	0.0	60.1	0.5	60.0	-0.2	60.1	0.2	60.1	0.0
1957	61.4	2.2	61.1	-0.5	61.1	0.0	60.9	-0.3	60.9	0.0	60.9	0.0	60.3	-1.0	60.3	0.0	60.3	0.0	60.3	0.0	60.3	0.0	60.3	0.0
1958	59.8	-0.8	59.1	-1.2	58.8	-0.5	58.5	-0.5	58.5	0.0	58.2	-0.5	57.7	-0.9	57.7	0.0	57.5	-0.3	57.4	-0.2	57.4	0.0	57.4	0.0
1959	57.4	0.0	57.5	0.2	57.9	0.7	58.1	0.3	58.1	0.0	58.3	0.3	58.5	0.3	58.5	0.0	58.7	0.3	58.8	0.2	58.8	0.0	58.7	-0.2
1960	59.0	0.5	59.0	0.0	59.5	0.8	59.5	0.0	59.5	0.0	59.5	0.0	59.5	0.0	59.5	0.0	59.4	-0.2	59.4	0.0	59.3	-0.2	59.3	0.0
1961	58.6	-1.2	58.5	-0.2	58.5	0.0	58.5	0.0	58.5	0.0	58.5	0.0	58.8	0.5	58.8	0.0	58.8	0.0	58.7	-0.2	58.7	0.0	58.6	-0.2
1962	58.4	-0.3	57.2	-2.1	57.2	0.0	57.2	0.0	57.2	0.0	57.2	0.0	57.1	-0.2	57.1	0.0	57.1	0.0	57.1	0.0	57.1	0.0	56.9	-0.4
1963	56.8	-0.2	56.6	-0.4	56.7	0.2	56.6	-0.2	56.5	-0.2	56.6	0.2	57.0	0.7	57.0	0.0	57.1	0.2	57.5	0.7	57.8	0.5	57.9	0.2
1964	59.1	2.1	59.1	0.0	59.1	0.0	59.1	0.0	58.9	-0.3	58.2	-1.2	58.5	0.5	58.5	0.0	58.5	0.0	58.5	0.0	58.5	0.0	58.5	0.0
1965	57.9	-1.0	57.9	0.0	57.8	-0.2	57.7	-0.2	57.7	0.0	57.7	0.0	57.7	0.0	57.6	-0.2	57.6	0.0	57.5	-0.2	57.5	0.0	57.6	0.2
1966	57.7	0.2	57.7	0.0	57.6	-0.2	57.6	0.0	57.6	0.0	57.4	-0.3	57.1	-0.5	57.0	-0.2	57.0	0.0	57.0	0.0	57.0	0.0	56.8	-0.4
1967	55.5	-2.3	55.0	-0.9	55.2	0.4	54.9	-0.5	54.9	0.0	54.9	0.0	54.5	-0.7	54.5	0.0	55.0	0.9	55.9	1.6	55.9	0.0	56.1	0.4
1968	56.1	0.0	56.0	-0.2	56.0	0.0	56.0	0.0	56.0	0.0	55.7	-0.5	55.8	0.2	56.0	0.4	55.9	-0.2	55.9	0.0	55.9	1.0	55.9	0.0
1969	56.3	0.7	56.4	0.2	56.3	-0.2	56.0	-0.5	55.8	-0.4	55.3	-0.9	54.9	-0.7	54.9	0.0	54.9	0.0	54.9	0.0	54.9	0.0	54.9	0.0
1970	55.1	0.4	55.1	0.0	55.0	-0.2	55.0	0.0	54.7	-0.5	54.5	-0.4	54.9	0.7	54.7	-0.4	54.7	0.0	54.9	0.4	54.9	0.0	55.0	0.2

[Continued]

Floor Coverings

Producer Price Index
Base 1982 = 100
[Continued]

For 1926-1993. Columns headed % show percentile change in the index from the previous period for which an index is available.

Year	Jan Index	%	Feb Index	%	Mar Index	%	Apr Index	%	May Index	%	Jun Index	%	Jul Index	%	Aug Index	%	Sep Index	%	Oct Index	%	Nov Index	%	Dec Index	%
1971	55.7	1.3	55.5	-0.4	55.4	-0.2	55.2	-0.4	55.2	0.0	54.2	-1.8	54.2	0.0	53.9	-0.6	53.9	0.0	53.9	0.0	53.9	0.0	54.1	0.4
1972	54.2	0.2	54.2	0.0	54.2	0.0	54.2	0.0	54.2	0.0	54.4	0.4	54.5	0.2	54.5	0.0	54.7	0.4	54.7	0.0	54.7	0.0	54.7	0.0
1973	55.0	0.5	55.7	1.3	55.8	0.2	56.1	0.5	56.6	0.9	56.7	0.2	56.7	0.0	56.7	0.0	56.6	-0.2	57.1	0.9	57.1	0.0	57.2	0.2
1974	58.6	2.4	59.0	0.7	59.4	0.7	61.0	2.7	61.4	0.7	63.2	2.9	64.0	1.3	65.8	2.8	67.6	2.7	68.1	0.7	68.2	0.1	68.6	0.6
1975	68.4	-0.3	68.2	-0.3	68.2	0.0	68.1	-0.1	67.9	-0.3	67.9	0.0	68.4	0.7	69.9	2.2	70.0	0.1	70.0	0.0	70.0	0.0	70.2	0.3
1976	72.1	2.7	72.4	0.4	72.4	0.0	72.4	0.0	72.4	0.0	72.5	0.1	72.5	0.0	72.6	0.1	72.6	0.0	72.6	0.0	72.6	0.0	72.8	0.3
1977	74.8	2.7	74.8	0.0	74.8	0.0	74.8	0.0	74.8	0.0	75.0	0.3	75.2	0.3	75.4	0.3	75.4	0.0	75.7	0.4	76.3	0.8	76.4	0.1
1978	77.2	1.0	77.2	0.0	77.3	0.1	78.2	1.2	78.3	0.1	78.6	0.4	78.7	0.1	78.7	0.0	78.6	-0.1	78.4	-0.3	78.4	0.0	78.5	0.1
1979	79.1	0.8	79.3	0.3	79.5	0.3	79.7	0.3	80.6	1.1	80.9	0.4	82.3	1.7	82.8	0.6	83.0	0.2	84.0	1.2	84.4	0.5	84.4	0.0
1980	87.8	4.0	87.5	-0.3	88.8	1.5	89.5	0.8	89.4	-0.1	89.5	0.1	90.1	0.7	90.4	0.3	90.5	0.1	90.7	0.2	91.4	0.8	94.2	3.1
1981	95.1	1.0	94.9	-0.2	96.1	1.3	96.8	0.7	99.1	2.4	99.8	0.7	100.9	1.1	100.4	-0.5	100.3	-0.1	99.9	-0.4	100.6	0.7	100.2	-0.4
1982	99.5	-0.7	99.7	0.2	99.7	0.0	100.0	0.3	100.1	0.1	100.4	0.3	100.0	-0.4	99.9	-0.1	100.2	0.3	100.2	0.0	100.1	-0.1	100.2	0.1
1983	100.6	0.4	100.5	-0.1	100.4	-0.1	100.6	0.2	100.5	-0.1	100.2	-0.3	103.0	2.8	104.3	1.3	104.6	0.3	104.6	0.0	104.5	-0.1	104.5	0.0
1984	103.9	-0.6	104.0	0.1	103.9	-0.1	103.9	0.0	105.8	1.8	106.4	0.6	106.4	0.0	106.3	-0.1	106.3	0.0	106.5	0.2	106.5	0.0	106.7	0.2
1985	106.9	0.2	106.2	-0.7	106.4	0.2	106.5	0.1	105.7	-0.8	104.8	-0.9	105.2	0.4	104.9	-0.3	105.2	0.3	104.9	-0.3	105.2	0.3	105.3	0.1
1986	107.4	2.0	107.7	0.3	107.7	0.0	107.8	0.1	108.1	0.3	108.6	0.5	108.1	-0.5	108.3	0.2	108.4	0.1	109.0	0.6	109.3	0.3	109.2	-0.1
1987	109.9	0.6	109.8	-0.1	109.2	-0.5	109.4	0.2	109.9	0.5	110.2	0.3	111.1	0.8	111.5	0.4	111.6	0.1	112.0	0.4	111.9	-0.1	111.6	-0.3
1988	112.7	1.0	113.1	0.4	112.9	-0.2	113.6	0.6	114.0	0.4	113.8	-0.2	114.7	0.8	115.4	0.6	116.0	0.5	116.5	0.4	117.1	0.5	117.0	-0.1
1989	117.5	0.4	116.7	-0.7	117.3	0.5	117.3	0.0	116.9	-0.3	117.9	0.9	118.6	0.6	119.0	0.3	117.5	-1.3	117.0	-0.4	117.4	0.3	117.7	0.3
1990	117.7	0.0	118.3	0.5	119.3	0.8	119.5	0.2	119.6	0.1	119.4	-0.2	119.4	0.0	119.2	-0.2	118.8	-0.3	118.6	-0.2	119.1	0.4	119.5	0.3
1991	120.3	0.7	121.4	0.9	120.9	-0.4	120.7	-0.2	120.5	-0.2	120.1	-0.3	120.1	0.0	120.1	0.0	119.9	-0.2	120.2	0.3	120.4	0.2	120.3	-0.1
1992	120.1	-0.2	120.1	0.0	119.5	-0.5	119.7	0.2	120.4	0.6	120.8	0.3	121.0	0.2	120.7	-0.2	120.5	-0.2	120.5	0.0	120.2	-0.2	120.2	0.0
1993	119.4	-0.7	119.5	0.1	119.5	0.0	119.4	-0.1	119.2	-0.2	119.1	-0.1	120.0	0.8	120.8	0.7	120.3	-0.4	120.9	0.5	120.9	0.0	120.6	-0.2

Source: U.S. Department of Labor, Bureau of Labor Statistics, Division of Industry Prices and Price Indexes. n.e.c. stands for not elsewhere classified. - indicates no data collected for period or unavailable.

Household Appliances
Producer Price Index
Base 1982 = 100

For 1947-1993. Columns headed % show percentile change in the index from the previous period for which an index is available.

Year	Jan Index	%	Feb Index	%	Mar Index	%	Apr Index	%	May Index	%	Jun Index	%	Jul Index	%	Aug Index	%	Sep Index	%	Oct Index	%	Nov Index	%	Dec Index	%
1947	50.3	-	50.4	0.2	50.5	0.2	50.6	0.2	50.8	0.4	51.1	0.6	51.5	0.8	51.7	0.4	52.3	1.2	52.7	0.8	52.9	0.4	53.2	0.6
1948	53.1	-0.2	53.1	0.0	53.1	0.0	53.2	0.2	53.0	-0.4	53.1	0.2	54.0	1.7	54.3	0.6	54.7	0.7	55.4	1.3	55.5	0.2	55.5	0.0
1949	54.6	-1.6	54.6	0.0	54.4	-0.4	54.1	-0.6	53.7	-0.7	53.5	-0.4	53.4	-0.2	53.2	-0.4	53.2	0.0	53.1	-0.2	53.1	0.0	53.1	0.0
1950	53.1	0.0	53.0	-0.2	53.0	0.0	53.2	0.4	53.2	0.0	53.1	-0.2	53.2	0.2	53.8	1.1	54.7	1.7	55.5	1.5	56.0	0.9	56.7	1.3
1951	57.1	0.7	57.3	0.4	57.3	0.0	57.3	0.0	57.3	0.0	57.4	0.2	57.1	-0.5	57.1	0.0	57.3	0.4	57.3	0.0	57.3	0.0	57.4	0.2
1952	57.3	-0.2	57.3	0.0	57.0	-0.5	57.2	0.4	56.9	-0.5	56.7	-0.4	56.7	0.0	56.7	0.0	56.9	0.4	56.9	0.0	56.9	0.0	57.0	0.2
1953	57.0	0.0	57.0	0.0	57.3	0.5	57.3	0.0	57.4	0.2	57.4	0.0	57.8	0.7	57.8	0.0	57.9	0.2	57.9	0.0	57.9	0.0	57.9	0.0
1954	58.1	0.3	58.2	0.2	58.1	-0.2	58.3	0.3	58.3	0.0	58.3	0.0	58.2	-0.2	58.2	0.0	58.0	-0.3	58.1	0.2	57.9	-0.3	58.0	0.2
1955	57.7	-0.5	57.6	-0.2	56.9	-1.2	56.9	0.0	56.5	-0.7	56.5	0.0	56.5	0.0	56.6	0.2	56.4	-0.4	56.3	-0.2	56.4	0.2	56.2	-0.4
1956	56.0	-0.4	56.1	0.2	55.9	-0.4	55.8	-0.2	55.8	0.0	55.8	0.0	55.4	-0.7	55.8	0.7	56.0	0.4	56.5	0.9	56.5	0.0	56.2	-0.5
1957	56.5	0.5	56.7	0.4	56.7	0.0	55.9	-1.4	55.8	-0.2	55.8	0.0	55.7	-0.2	55.6	-0.2	55.5	-0.2	55.9	0.7	55.8	-0.2	55.9	0.2
1958	55.9	0.0	55.9	0.0	55.9	0.0	55.9	0.0	55.7	-0.4	55.7	0.0	55.7	0.0	55.6	-0.2	55.2	-0.7	55.3	0.2	55.1	-0.4	55.1	0.0
1959	55.8	1.3	55.8	0.0	55.8	0.0	55.8	0.0	55.8	0.0	55.8	0.0	55.4	-0.7	55.4	0.0	55.4	0.0	55.2	-0.4	55.3	0.2	55.0	-0.5
1960	54.8	-0.4	54.8	0.0	54.7	-0.2	54.7	0.0	54.2	-0.9	53.9	-0.6	53.9	0.0	53.6	-0.6	53.5	-0.2	53.5	0.0	53.4	-0.2	53.3	-0.2
1961	53.2	-0.2	53.2	0.0	53.1	-0.2	53.1	0.0	53.0	-0.2	52.9	-0.2	52.9	0.0	52.9	0.0	52.9	0.0	53.0	0.2	52.9	-0.2	52.8	-0.2
1962	52.9	0.2	52.9	0.0	52.8	-0.2	52.7	-0.2	52.5	-0.4	52.5	0.0	52.3	-0.4	52.0	-0.6	51.9	-0.2	51.8	-0.2	51.8	0.0	51.8	0.0
1963	51.4	-0.8	51.4	0.0	51.4	0.0	51.3	-0.2	51.2	-0.2	51.2	0.0	51.1	-0.2	51.1	0.0	50.9	-0.4	50.8	-0.2	50.8	0.0	50.7	-0.2
1964	50.9	0.4	51.1	0.4	51.1	0.0	51.0	-0.2	51.0	0.0	50.8	-0.4	50.8	0.0	50.8	0.0	50.7	-0.2	50.8	0.2	50.5	-0.6	50.4	-0.2
1965	50.2	-0.4	50.1	-0.2	50.1	0.0	49.8	-0.6	49.7	-0.2	49.8	0.2	49.7	-0.2	49.3	-0.8	49.3	0.0	49.3	0.0	49.3	0.0	49.4	0.2
1966	49.6	0.4	49.6	0.0	49.6	0.0	49.7	0.2	49.8	0.2	49.8	0.0	49.6	-0.4	49.4	-0.4	49.4	0.0	49.5	0.2	49.7	0.4	49.7	0.0
1967	49.9	0.4	50.0	0.2	50.0	0.0	50.1	0.2	50.0	-0.2	50.2	0.4	50.3	0.2	50.2	-0.2	50.3	0.2	50.4	0.2	50.6	0.4	50.6	0.0
1968	50.7	0.2	50.9	0.4	51.1	0.4	51.2	0.2	51.1	-0.2	51.0	-0.2	51.2	0.4	51.3	0.2	51.3	0.0	51.4	0.2	51.2	-0.4	51.3	0.2
1969	51.4	0.2	51.6	0.4	51.6	0.0	51.6	0.0	51.6	0.0	51.6	0.0	51.6	0.0	51.6	0.0	51.8	0.4	51.9	0.2	51.9	0.0	52.1	0.4
1970	52.7	1.2	52.6	-0.2	52.6	0.0	52.8	0.4	52.7	-0.2	52.7	0.0	52.8	0.2	52.9	0.2	52.9	0.0	53.2	0.6	53.3	0.2	53.3	0.0
1971	53.8	0.9	53.9	0.2	54.0	0.2	53.9	-0.2	53.9	0.0	53.9	0.0	54.1	0.4	54.2	0.2	54.2	0.0	54.2	0.0	54.1	-0.2	54.1	0.0
1972	53.7	-0.7	54.0	0.6	53.9	-0.2	54.0	0.2	53.9	-0.2	53.8	-0.2	53.9	0.2	54.1	0.4	54.3	0.4	54.2	-0.2	54.2	0.0	54.2	0.0
1973	54.1	-0.2	54.3	0.4	54.4	0.2	54.4	0.0	54.2	-0.4	53.9	-0.6	54.1	0.4	54.7	1.1	54.7	0.0	54.8	0.2	55.0	0.4	55.2	0.4
1974	55.9	1.3	56.1	0.4	56.5	0.7	56.9	0.7	57.3	0.7	58.0	1.2	58.6	1.0	59.4	1.4	60.7	2.2	62.8	3.5	63.7	1.4	64.6	1.4
1975	65.3	1.1	65.6	0.5	65.3	-0.5	65.6	0.5	65.8	0.3	66.4	0.9	66.4	0.0	66.5	0.2	67.1	0.9	67.4	0.4	68.0	0.9	68.2	0.3
1976	68.5	0.4	69.0	0.7	69.5	0.7	69.7	0.3	69.7	0.0	69.9	0.3	70.2	0.4	70.3	0.1	70.4	0.1	70.5	0.1	70.6	0.1	70.8	0.3
1977	71.0	0.3	71.4	0.6	71.8	0.6	72.0	0.3	72.0	0.0	72.7	1.0	73.2	0.7	73.6	0.5	74.1	0.7	74.2	0.1	74.3	0.1	74.3	0.0
1978	75.1	1.1	75.2	0.1	75.9	0.9	76.5	0.8	76.6	0.1	76.7	0.1	77.1	0.5	77.4	0.4	77.4	0.0	77.6	0.3	78.2	0.8	78.2	0.0
1979	78.9	0.9	79.5	0.8	79.8	0.4	79.7	-0.1	80.0	0.4	80.4	0.5	80.9	0.6	81.5	0.7	81.7	0.2	82.0	0.4	82.6	0.7	83.0	0.5
1980	83.6	0.7	84.8	1.4	85.3	0.6	85.9	0.7	87.0	1.3	88.1	1.3	88.3	0.2	88.5	0.2	89.0	0.6	89.2	0.2	89.6	0.4	90.1	0.6
1981	91.5	1.6	92.2	0.8	92.5	0.3	93.0	0.5	93.2	0.2	93.5	0.3	94.8	1.4	95.0	0.2	95.5	0.5	95.8	0.3	95.9	0.1	96.1	0.2
1982	97.1	1.0	98.1	1.0	99.1	1.0	99.3	0.2	99.9	0.6	100.2	0.3	100.6	0.4	101.0	0.4	101.1	0.1	101.1	0.0	101.1	0.0	101.3	0.2
1983	102.4	1.1	102.9	0.5	103.0	0.1	103.6	0.6	104.2	0.6	104.2	0.0	104.4	0.2	104.3	-0.1	104.5	0.2	104.3	-0.2	104.5	0.2	104.7	0.2
1984	105.4	0.7	105.8	0.4	106.0	0.2	105.9	-0.1	105.9	0.0	106.1	0.2	106.2	0.1	106.5	0.3	106.3	-0.2	106.0	-0.3	106.0	0.0	106.1	0.1
1985	106.1	0.0	106.1	0.0	106.3	0.2	106.5	0.2	106.7	0.2	106.8	0.1	107.1	0.3	107.2	0.1	107.0	-0.2	107.0	0.0	106.9	-0.1	106.6	-0.3
1986	105.5	-1.0	105.6	0.1	105.8	0.2	106.1	0.3	106.4	0.3	105.9	-0.5	105.9	0.0	105.6	-0.3	105.5	-0.1	105.4	-0.1	105.2	-0.2	105.0	-0.2
1987	105.2	0.2	105.3	0.1	105.6	0.3	105.7	0.1	105.8	0.1	105.8	0.0	106.0	0.2	105.8	-0.2	105.5	-0.3	105.4	-0.1	105.7	0.3	105.2	-0.5
1988	105.5	0.3	106.0	0.5	106.2	0.2	106.2	0.0	106.3	0.1	106.1	-0.2	105.6	-0.5	105.6	0.0	105.8	0.2	106.0	0.2	106.5	0.5	106.2	-0.3
1989	107.0	0.8	107.3	0.3	107.6	0.3	107.7	0.1	108.1	0.4	108.5	0.4	109.2	0.6	109.3	0.1	109.7	0.4	110.0	0.3	110.0	0.0	110.1	0.1
1990	110.5	0.4	110.6	0.1	110.7	0.1	110.9	0.2	110.4	-0.5	111.0	0.5	110.7	-0.3	110.8	0.1	110.9	0.1	110.9	0.0	111.0	0.1	110.9	-0.1
1991	111.6	0.6	111.3	-0.3	111.3	0.0	111.4	0.1	111.5	0.1	111.3	-0.2	111.3	0.0	111.4	0.1	111.3	-0.1	111.3	0.0	111.2	-0.1	111.0	-0.2

[Continued]

Household Appliances
Producer Price Index
Base 1982 = 100
[Continued]

For 1947-1993. Columns headed % show percentile change in the index from the previous period for which an index is available.

Year	Jan		Feb		Mar		Apr		May		Jun		Jul		Aug		Sep		Oct		Nov		Dec	
	Index	%	Index	%	Index	%	Index	%	Index	%	Index	%	Index	%	Index	%	Index	%	Index	%	Index	%	Index	%
1992	111.2	0.2	111.1	-0.1	111.1	0.0	111.4	0.3	111.3	-0.1	111.2	-0.1	111.2	0.0	111.2	0.0	111.3	0.1	111.6	0.3	112.3	0.6	111.8	-0.4
1993	112.0	0.2	112.3	0.3	112.5	0.2	112.8	0.3	113.0	0.2	113.4	0.4	113.4	0.0	113.4	0.0	113.5	0.1	113.5	0.0	113.6	0.1	113.0	-0.5

Source: U.S. Department of Labor, Bureau of Labor Statistics, Division of Industry Prices and Price Indexes. n.e.c. stands for not elsewhere classified. - indicates no data collected for period or unavailable.

Home Electronic Equipment

Producer Price Index
Base 1982 = 100

For 1947-1993. Columns headed % show percentile change in the index from the previous period for which an index is available.

Year	Jan Index	%	Feb Index	%	Mar Index	%	Apr Index	%	May Index	%	Jun Index	%	Jul Index	%	Aug Index	%	Sep Index	%	Oct Index	%	Nov Index	%	Dec Index	%
1947	140.1	-	140.5	0.3	140.5	0.0	140.5	0.0	140.5	0.0	140.5	0.0	140.5	0.0	140.8	0.2	142.3	1.1	142.3	0.0	142.3	0.0	142.3	0.0
1948	142.1	-0.1	142.1	0.0	142.1	0.0	141.6	-0.4	141.6	0.0	143.8	1.6	143.8	0.0	143.8	0.0	152.6	6.1	155.5	1.9	155.5	0.0	155.3	-0.1
1949	154.6	-0.5	154.6	0.0	154.6	0.0	154.4	-0.1	154.4	0.0	154.2	-0.1	153.5	-0.5	149.9	-2.3	149.9	0.0	146.9	-2.0	146.9	0.0	146.7	-0.1
1950	146.2	-0.3	146.7	0.3	146.7	0.0	146.7	0.0	146.7	0.0	146.4	-0.2	141.8	-3.1	131.4	-7.3	134.9	2.7	139.1	3.1	139.0	-0.1	136.4	-1.9
1951	135.7	-0.5	135.7	0.0	135.7	0.0	135.7	0.0	135.7	0.0	135.7	0.0	137.1	1.0	136.5	-0.4	136.2	-0.2	136.3	0.1	136.3	0.0	136.3	0.0
1952	136.4	0.1	136.4	0.0	132.8	-2.6	132.8	0.0	132.8	0.0	137.3	3.4	137.3	0.0	137.2	-0.1	137.2	0.0	137.2	0.0	137.3	0.1	137.3	0.0
1953	-	-	-	-	-	-	-	-	-	-	-	-	-	-	-	-	-	-	-	-	-	-	-	-
1954	-	-	-	-	-	-	-	-	-	-	-	-	-	-	-	-	-	-	-	-	-	-	-	-
1955	137.0	-0.2	136.5	-0.4	136.4	-0.1	136.4	0.0	136.6	0.1	136.5	-0.1	136.4	-0.1	134.9	-1.1	135.7	0.6	135.8	0.1	135.9	0.1	136.4	0.4
1956	136.4	0.0	136.6	0.1	136.6	0.0	135.9	-0.5	135.7	-0.1	135.2	-0.4	136.2	0.7	136.5	0.2	137.2	0.5	137.0	-0.1	137.0	0.0	136.6	-0.3
1957	137.0	0.3	137.0	0.0	136.4	-0.4	136.4	0.0	136.4	0.0	136.8	0.3	138.9	1.5	140.1	0.9	140.1	0.0	140.1	0.0	140.1	0.0	140.4	0.2
1958	139.7	-0.5	138.8	-0.6	138.8	0.0	138.8	0.0	138.2	-0.4	137.2	-0.7	139.1	1.4	139.0	-0.1	139.0	0.0	139.0	0.0	135.8	-2.3	135.6	-0.1
1959	136.5	0.7	136.5	0.0	135.9	-0.4	135.9	0.0	135.9	0.0	136.2	0.2	138.2	1.5	136.6	-1.2	135.8	-0.6	134.9	-0.7	134.5	-0.3	134.6	0.1
1960	134.3	-0.2	134.5	0.1	134.5	0.0	134.3	-0.1	134.3	0.0	133.9	-0.3	133.9	0.0	133.5	-0.3	133.5	0.0	132.5	-0.7	132.5	0.0	133.7	0.9
1961	133.1	-0.4	132.5	-0.5	132.8	0.2	132.8	0.0	131.6	-0.9	131.8	0.2	131.8	0.0	129.9	-1.4	129.3	-0.5	128.8	-0.4	129.0	0.2	129.0	0.0
1962	127.1	-1.5	126.1	-0.8	125.7	-0.3	125.4	-0.2	126.8	1.1	124.9	-1.5	124.8	-0.1	124.8	0.0	124.7	-0.1	124.7	0.0	124.2	-0.4	124.2	0.0
1963	123.9	-0.2	123.9	0.0	122.9	-0.8	122.9	0.0	122.2	-0.6	122.2	0.0	120.6	-1.3	120.6	0.0	120.7	0.1	120.7	0.0	120.7	0.0	120.0	-0.6
1964	119.9	-0.1	119.9	0.0	119.9	0.0	120.0	0.1	120.0	0.0	120.0	0.0	120.0	0.0	120.0	0.0	120.0	0.0	120.0	0.0	119.9	-0.1	119.0	-0.8
1965	118.8	-0.2	118.1	-0.6	118.1	0.0	118.1	0.0	118.1	0.0	118.1	0.0	116.3	-1.5	116.1	-0.2	116.1	0.0	116.2	0.1	116.2	0.0	116.2	0.0
1966	115.4	-0.7	115.3	-0.1	114.8	-0.4	114.8	0.0	114.8	0.0	114.8	0.0	114.8	0.0	114.2	-0.5	114.5	0.3	115.3	0.7	115.3	0.0	115.3	0.0
1967	114.9	-0.3	114.5	-0.3	114.5	0.0	114.5	0.0	114.0	-0.4	112.8	-1.1	112.4	-0.4	112.4	0.0	112.2	-0.2	113.4	1.1	113.6	0.2	112.9	-0.6
1968	112.9	0.0	113.0	0.1	112.7	-0.3	112.3	-0.4	112.4	0.1	111.2	-1.1	110.9	-0.3	110.9	0.0	110.8	-0.1	110.3	-0.5	109.7	-0.5	109.7	0.0
1969	108.2	-1.4	108.2	0.0	108.1	-0.1	107.8	-0.3	107.2	-0.6	107.0	-0.2	107.0	0.0	107.0	0.0	107.0	0.0	107.0	0.0	106.6	-0.4	106.6	0.0
1970	105.8	-0.8	105.8	0.0	105.8	0.0	105.8	0.0	105.6	-0.2	105.5	-0.1	105.8	0.3	106.0	0.2	106.2	0.2	106.4	0.2	107.0	0.6	106.5	-0.5
1971	106.6	0.1	106.3	-0.3	106.2	-0.1	106.1	-0.1	106.1	0.0	106.2	0.1	106.3	0.1	105.9	-0.4	105.8	-0.1	105.8	0.0	105.8	0.0	105.8	0.0
1972	105.9	0.1	105.5	-0.4	105.6	0.1	105.4	-0.2	105.5	0.1	105.2	-0.3	104.9	-0.3	104.9	0.0	105.5	0.6	105.5	0.0	105.0	-0.5	104.8	-0.2
1973	104.9	0.1	104.9	0.0	104.7	-0.2	104.7	0.0	104.7	0.0	104.0	-0.7	104.0	0.0	104.4	0.4	103.9	-0.5	103.9	0.0	103.9	0.0	103.4	-0.5
1974	103.7	0.3	103.8	0.1	104.7	0.9	104.7	0.0	105.0	0.3	105.7	0.7	106.3	0.6	106.3	0.0	106.8	0.5	106.8	0.0	107.3	0.5	107.5	0.2
1975	108.3	0.7	108.6	0.3	108.4	-0.2	104.4	-3.7	104.4	0.0	105.6	1.1	105.9	0.3	107.4	1.4	105.4	-1.9	105.4	0.0	105.4	0.0	105.4	0.0
1976	104.8	-0.6	104.1	-0.7	103.7	-0.4	103.7	0.0	103.7	0.0	103.6	-0.1	103.6	0.0	103.6	0.0	103.6	0.0	103.6	0.0	103.3	-0.3	103.2	-0.1
1977	101.8	-1.4	101.5	-0.3	101.5	0.0	100.2	-1.3	100.3	0.1	100.4	0.1	98.6	-1.8	98.6	0.0	98.1	-0.5	97.9	-0.2	98.3	0.4	98.2	-0.1
1978	101.0	2.9	100.7	-0.3	101.1	0.4	100.7	-0.4	102.2	1.5	100.5	-1.7	103.2	2.7	103.1	-0.1	104.0	0.9	103.7	-0.3	103.9	0.2	104.9	1.0
1979	104.7	-0.2	104.8	0.1	104.8	0.0	104.8	0.0	105.0	0.2	105.4	0.4	102.4	-2.8	102.4	0.0	102.5	0.1	102.5	0.0	102.6	0.1	102.8	0.2
1980	103.3	0.5	103.5	0.2	103.6	0.1	103.8	0.2	104.5	0.7	104.3	-0.2	104.1	-0.2	103.7	-0.4	104.1	0.4	103.9	-0.2	103.6	-0.3	103.4	-0.2
1981	103.4	0.0	103.7	0.3	103.7	0.0	103.3	-0.4	103.1	-0.2	98.4	-4.6	99.3	0.9	99.4	0.1	99.7	0.3	100.0	0.3	99.9	-0.1	101.8	1.9
1982	101.4	-0.4	101.7	0.3	101.2	-0.5	99.8	-1.4	100.0	0.2	100.4	0.4	99.1	-1.3	99.9	0.8	99.2	-0.7	99.7	0.5	98.8	-0.9	98.9	0.1
1983	99.2	0.3	98.8	-0.4	98.8	0.0	98.3	-0.5	98.1	-0.2	98.2	0.1	97.6	-0.6	97.1	-0.5	97.4	0.3	97.4	0.0	96.7	-0.7	95.9	-0.8
1984	95.9	0.0	95.5	-0.4	95.4	-0.1	96.4	1.0	96.0	-0.4	95.3	-0.7	95.6	0.3	95.2	-0.4	94.3	-0.9	94.4	0.1	94.3	-0.1	93.9	-0.4
1985	91.8	-2.2	93.0	1.3	92.0	-1.1	91.8	-0.2	90.8	-1.1	90.1	-0.8	90.9	0.9	90.4	-0.6	89.7	-0.8	89.4	-0.3	89.4	0.0	90.3	1.0
1986	89.8	-0.6	89.8	0.0	89.8	0.0	89.8	0.0	89.8	0.0	90.5	0.8	90.1	-0.4	89.9	-0.2	89.9	0.0	89.9	0.0	89.9	0.0	89.9	0.0
1987	89.1	-0.9	88.5	-0.7	88.9	0.5	89.1	0.2	88.9	-0.2	88.8	-0.1	88.7	-0.1	89.0	0.3	88.9	-0.1	88.7	-0.2	88.7	0.0	88.7	0.0
1988	88.5	-0.2	89.0	0.6	88.2	-0.9	87.1	-1.2	87.2	0.1	86.3	-1.0	86.7	0.5	86.6	-0.1	86.7	0.1	86.6	-0.1	86.8	0.2	86.7	-0.1
1989	88.0	1.5	88.0	0.0	88.0	0.0	88.3	0.3	88.3	0.0	88.4	0.1	88.4	0.0	88.0	-0.5	87.5	-0.6	83.2	-4.9	83.2	0.0	83.0	-0.2
1990	83.0	0.0	82.9	-0.1	82.8	-0.1	82.7	-0.1	82.6	-0.1	82.6	0.0	82.6	0.0	82.6	0.0	82.6	0.0	82.6	0.0	82.7	0.1	82.8	0.1	82.8	0.0
1991	82.9	0.1	83.1	0.2	83.1	0.0	83.1	0.0	83.5	0.5	83.6	0.1	83.5	-0.1	83.0	-0.6	83.0	0.0	83.1	0.1	83.0	-0.1	83.0	0.0

[Continued]

Home Electronic Equipment
Producer Price Index
Base 1982 = 100
[Continued]

For 1947-1993. Columns headed % show percentile change in the index from the previous period for which an index is available.

Year	Jan		Feb		Mar		Apr		May		Jun		Jul		Aug		Sep		Oct		Nov		Dec	
	Index	%	Index	%	Index	%	Index	%	Index	%	Index	%	Index	%	Index	%	Index	%	Index	%	Index	%	Index	%
1992	83.0	0.0	82.8	-0.2	82.8	0.0	82.6	-0.2	82.3	-0.4	81.9	-0.5	81.9	0.0	81.9	0.0	81.6	-0.4	81.0	-0.7	80.8	-0.2	80.8	0.0
1993	80.6	-0.2	80.7	0.1	80.5	-0.2	80.4	-0.1	80.2	-0.2	79.9	-0.4	80.0	0.1	79.8	-0.2	79.8	0.0	80.3	0.6	79.9	-0.5	79.9	0.0

Source: U.S. Department of Labor, Bureau of Labor Statistics, Division of Industry Prices and Price Indexes. n.e.c. stands for not elsewhere classified. - indicates no data collected for period or unavailable.

Household Durable Goods n.e.c.
Producer Price Index
Base 1982 = 100

For 1947-1993. Columns headed % show percentile change in the index from the previous period for which an index is available.

Year	Jan Index	%	Feb Index	%	Mar Index	%	Apr Index	%	May Index	%	Jun Index	%	Jul Index	%	Aug Index	%	Sep Index	%	Oct Index	%	Nov Index	%	Dec Index	%
1947	19.5	-	19.4	-0.5	19.5	0.5	19.5	0.0	19.5	0.0	19.5	0.0	19.4	-0.5	19.4	0.0	19.5	0.5	19.5	0.0	19.5	0.0	19.6	0.5
1948	19.5	-0.5	19.5	0.0	19.5	0.0	19.5	0.0	19.6	0.5	19.6	0.0	19.9	1.5	20.2	1.5	20.2	0.0	20.5	1.5	20.8	1.5	21.0	1.0
1949	21.1	0.5	21.1	0.0	21.1	0.0	21.1	0.0	21.0	-0.5	21.0	0.0	20.9	-0.5	20.9	0.0	20.8	-0.5	20.8	0.0	20.8	0.0	20.8	0.0
1950	21.0	1.0	21.0	0.0	21.0	0.0	21.0	0.0	21.0	0.0	21.1	0.5	21.2	0.5	21.4	0.9	21.7	1.4	22.0	1.4	22.3	1.4	22.7	1.8
1951	23.0	1.3	23.1	0.4	23.1	0.0	23.1	0.0	23.1	0.0	23.1	0.0	23.1	0.0	23.1	0.0	23.2	0.4	23.2	0.0	23.2	0.0	23.2	0.0
1952	23.2	0.0	23.2	0.0	23.2	0.0	23.3	0.4	23.2	-0.4	23.2	0.0	23.3	0.4	23.3	0.0	23.3	0.0	23.3	0.0	23.3	0.0	23.4	0.4
1953	23.8	1.7	24.0	0.8	24.0	0.0	24.0	0.0	24.0	0.0	24.0	0.0	24.4	1.7	24.4	0.0	24.4	0.0	24.5	0.4	24.7	0.8	24.8	0.4
1954	24.9	0.4	24.9	0.0	24.9	0.0	25.0	0.4	25.0	0.0	25.0	0.0	25.0	0.0	25.0	0.0	25.0	0.0	25.2	0.8	25.3	0.4	25.3	0.0
1955	25.4	0.4	25.4	0.0	25.4	0.0	25.4	0.0	25.4	0.0	25.5	0.4	25.8	1.2	26.1	1.2	26.1	0.0	26.4	1.1	26.5	0.4	26.7	0.8
1956	26.9	0.7	27.1	0.7	27.1	0.0	27.0	-0.4	27.1	0.4	27.1	0.0	27.1	0.0	27.2	0.4	27.3	0.4	27.8	1.8	27.8	0.0	28.3	1.8
1957	28.3	0.0	28.4	0.4	28.4	0.0	28.4	0.0	28.6	0.7	28.7	0.3	28.7	0.0	28.7	0.0	28.8	0.3	28.9	0.3	29.0	0.3	29.3	1.0
1958	29.8	1.7	29.8	0.0	29.8	0.0	29.8	0.0	29.8	0.0	29.9	0.3	29.8	-0.3	29.7	-0.3	29.8	0.3	29.8	0.0	29.8	0.0	30.0	0.7
1959	30.0	0.0	30.1	0.3	30.1	0.0	30.1	0.0	30.2	0.3	30.2	0.0	30.3	0.3	30.2	-0.3	30.2	0.0	30.2	0.0	30.2	0.0	30.2	0.0
1960	30.7	1.7	30.8	0.3	30.8	0.0	30.8	0.0	30.8	0.0	30.8	0.0	30.9	0.3	30.9	0.0	30.9	0.0	30.9	0.0	30.9	0.0	30.9	0.0
1961	30.8	-0.3	30.7	-0.3	30.7	0.0	30.7	0.0	30.8	0.3	30.8	0.0	30.8	0.0	30.8	0.0	30.8	0.0	30.8	0.0	30.9	0.3	31.0	0.3
1962	31.3	1.0	31.2	-0.3	31.4	0.6	31.4	0.0	31.4	0.0	31.4	0.0	31.3	-0.3	31.2	-0.3	31.4	0.6	31.2	-0.6	31.2	0.0	31.2	0.0
1963	31.2	0.0	31.2	0.0	31.2	0.0	31.4	0.6	31.3	-0.3	31.5	0.6	31.6	0.3	31.5	-0.3	31.6	0.3	31.6	0.0	31.6	0.0	31.5	-0.3
1964	31.7	0.6	31.7	0.0	31.7	0.0	31.7	0.0	31.8	0.3	31.8	0.0	31.8	0.0	31.8	0.0	31.8	0.0	31.8	0.0	31.8	0.0	32.0	0.6
1965	32.2	0.6	32.2	0.0	32.2	0.0	32.2	0.0	32.2	0.0	32.2	0.0	32.2	0.0	32.1	-0.3	32.2	0.3	32.2	0.0	32.2	0.0	32.2	0.0
1966	32.5	0.9	32.6	0.3	32.6	0.0	32.6	0.0	32.6	0.0	32.6	0.0	33.1	1.5	33.1	0.0	33.3	0.6	33.6	0.9	33.6	0.0	33.7	0.3
1967	33.9	0.6	33.9	0.0	34.0	0.3	34.2	0.6	34.3	0.3	34.3	0.0	34.5	0.6	34.9	1.2	35.0	0.3	35.2	0.6	35.2	0.0	35.3	0.3
1968	36.5	3.4	36.6	0.3	36.7	0.3	36.8	0.3	36.7	-0.3	36.7	0.0	36.9	0.5	37.0	0.3	37.1	0.3	37.1	0.0	37.2	0.3	37.9	1.9
1969	38.1	0.5	38.2	0.3	38.3	0.3	38.4	0.3	38.4	0.0	38.5	0.3	38.7	0.5	38.7	0.0	38.8	0.3	38.9	0.3	38.8	-0.3	39.5	1.8
1970	39.5	0.0	39.9	1.0	39.8	-0.3	40.1	0.8	40.0	-0.2	40.1	0.3	40.1	0.0	40.1	0.0	40.4	0.7	40.3	-0.2	40.4	0.2	40.6	0.5
1971	41.2	1.5	41.4	0.5	41.4	0.0	41.5	0.2	41.5	0.0	41.5	0.0	42.1	1.4	42.2	0.2	42.2	0.0	42.1	-0.2	42.1	0.0	42.2	0.2
1972	42.3	0.2	42.9	1.4	43.0	0.2	43.0	0.0	43.2	0.5	43.4	0.5	43.7	0.7	43.8	0.2	43.9	0.2	43.9	0.0	43.9	0.0	43.9	0.0
1973	43.9	0.0	44.3	0.9	44.6	0.7	45.0	0.9	45.2	0.4	45.3	0.2	45.2	-0.2	45.2	0.0	45.1	-0.2	45.4	0.7	45.6	0.4	45.9	0.7
1974	46.3	0.9	47.2	1.9	48.1	1.9	49.2	2.3	50.2	2.0	50.8	1.2	52.3	3.0	52.6	0.6	53.3	1.3	55.1	3.4	55.5	0.7	56.1	1.1
1975	57.7	2.9	58.1	0.7	57.4	-1.2	58.1	1.2	58.1	0.0	58.1	0.0	58.1	0.0	58.0	-0.2	58.1	0.2	58.7	1.0	59.1	0.7	59.4	0.5
1976	60.6	2.0	60.9	0.5	61.0	0.2	61.1	0.2	61.4	0.5	61.4	0.0	61.7	0.5	62.1	0.6	62.9	1.3	62.9	0.0	63.2	0.5	63.4	0.3
1977	64.8	2.2	65.0	0.3	65.1	0.2	64.9	-0.3	65.5	0.9	65.6	0.2	65.9	0.5	66.1	0.3	66.1	0.0	66.3	0.3	66.5	0.3	66.9	0.6
1978	68.5	2.4	68.5	0.0	68.4	-0.1	68.4	0.0	69.3	1.3	69.9	0.9	70.9	1.4	70.7	-0.3	70.7	0.0	71.9	1.7	72.1	0.3	73.4	1.8
1979	74.7	1.8	74.9	0.3	75.3	0.5	75.6	0.4	75.9	0.4	76.3	0.5	77.3	1.3	78.3	1.3	79.8	1.9	84.9	6.4	85.8	1.1	87.9	2.4
1980	99.3	13.0	102.1	2.8	99.6	-2.4	92.4	-7.2	91.8	-0.6	92.1	0.3	93.8	1.8	95.4	1.7	95.5	0.1	97.4	2.0	97.2	-0.2	98.7	1.5
1981	96.4	-2.3	97.0	0.6	96.1	-0.9	95.2	-0.9	95.6	0.4	95.5	-0.1	97.5	2.1	97.1	-0.4	98.8	1.8	98.8	0.0	98.6	-0.2	98.9	0.3
1982	98.0	-0.9	98.1	0.1	98.5	0.4	98.8	0.3	98.7	-0.1	98.9	0.2	98.6	-0.3	100.9	2.3	101.4	0.5	102.5	1.1	102.7	0.2	103.1	0.4
1983	104.7	1.6	108.8	3.9	108.1	-0.6	107.8	-0.3	108.1	0.3	108.6	0.5	108.8	0.2	108.5	-0.3	108.7	0.2	108.5	-0.2	108.9	0.4	108.9	0.0
1984	109.9	0.9	109.5	-0.4	109.5	0.0	110.3	0.7	111.2	0.8	110.6	-0.5	110.1	-0.5	109.5	-0.5	109.5	0.0	109.8	0.3	110.8	0.9	110.8	0.0
1985	111.5	0.6	111.5	0.0	112.0	0.4	111.9	-0.1	111.7	-0.2	111.9	0.2	111.5	-0.4	111.4	-0.1	111.2	-0.2	111.9	0.6	111.8	-0.1	112.0	0.2
1986	112.6	0.5	112.1	-0.4	112.3	0.2	112.6	0.3	112.6	0.0	112.9	0.3	113.0	0.1	112.9	-0.1	113.1	0.2	113.1	0.0	113.3	0.2	113.6	0.3
1987	114.6	0.9	114.5	-0.1	114.7	0.2	114.7	0.0	115.2	0.4	115.3	0.1	115.6	0.3	115.8	0.2	115.8	0.0	116.2	0.3	116.3	0.1	116.6	0.3
1988	117.8	1.0	118.1	0.3	118.4	0.3	118.8	0.3	119.4	0.5	119.3	-0.1	119.8	0.4	120.5	0.6	120.9	0.3	121.2	0.2	121.4	0.2	121.8	0.3
1989	122.7	0.7	123.5	0.7	124.1	0.5	126.2	1.7	126.7	0.4	127.9	0.9	128.5	0.5	129.0	0.4	129.2	0.2	129.7	0.4	129.6	-0.1	129.7	0.1
1990	130.9	0.9	131.5	0.5	130.5	-0.8	131.1	0.5	130.7	-0.3	130.9	0.2	130.0	-0.7	130.4	0.3	130.7	0.2	130.8	0.1	130.7	-0.1	130.7	0.0
1991	132.1	1.1	132.6	0.4	133.5	0.7	134.6	0.8	134.5	-0.1	134.6	0.1	134.8	0.1	134.8	0.0	134.7	-0.1	134.7	0.0	134.8	0.1	135.2	0.3

[Continued]

Household Durable Goods n.e.c.
Producer Price Index
Base 1982 = 100
[Continued]

For 1947-1993. Columns headed % show percentile change in the index from the previous period for which an index is available.

Year	Jan Index	%	Feb Index	%	Mar Index	%	Apr Index	%	May Index	%	Jun Index	%	Jul Index	%	Aug Index	%	Sep Index	%	Oct Index	%	Nov Index	%	Dec Index	%
1992	136.1	0.7	136.6	0.4	137.2	0.4	136.1	-0.8	136.2	0.1	136.5	0.2	136.5	0.0	136.7	0.1	136.9	0.1	136.6	-0.2	136.5	-0.1	136.7	0.1
1993	137.3	0.4	137.4	0.1	137.8	0.3	137.9	0.1	137.8	-0.1	137.8	0.0	137.8	0.0	138.0	0.1	137.8	-0.1	138.2	0.3	138.3	0.1	138.8	0.4

Source: U.S. Department of Labor, Bureau of Labor Statistics, Division of Industry Prices and Price Indexes. n.e.c. stands for not elsewhere classified. - indicates no data collected for period or unavailable.

NONMETALLIC MINERAL PRODUCTS
Producer Price Index
Base 1982 = 100

For 1926-1993. Columns headed % show percentile change in the index from the previous period for which an index is available.

Year	Jan Index	%	Feb Index	%	Mar Index	%	Apr Index	%	May Index	%	Jun Index	%	Jul Index	%	Aug Index	%	Sep Index	%	Oct Index	%	Nov Index	%	Dec Index	%
1926	16.4	-	16.4	0.0	16.5	0.6	16.5	0.0	16.4	-0.6	16.4	0.0	16.4	0.0	16.3	-0.6	16.2	-0.6	16.4	1.2	16.4	0.0	16.4	0.0
1927	16.1	-1.8	15.9	-1.2	15.8	-0.6	15.8	0.0	15.8	0.0	15.8	0.0	15.8	0.0	15.7	-0.6	15.6	-0.6	15.6	0.0	15.3	-1.9	15.4	0.7
1928	15.5	0.6	15.4	-0.6	15.2	-1.3	16.0	5.3	16.3	1.9	16.6	1.8	16.6	0.0	16.6	0.0	16.6	0.0	16.6	0.0	16.6	0.0	16.3	-1.8
1929	16.1	-1.2	16.1	0.0	16.0	-0.6	16.1	0.6	16.1	0.0	16.0	-0.6	16.1	0.6	16.0	-0.6	15.8	-1.2	15.7	-0.6	15.8	0.6	16.1	1.9
1930	16.1	0.0	16.1	0.0	16.1	0.0	16.1	0.0	16.0	-0.6	15.7	-1.9	15.8	0.6	15.8	0.0	15.8	0.0	15.9	0.6	16.0	0.6	15.8	-1.2
1931	15.6	-1.3	15.6	0.0	15.3	-1.9	15.1	-1.3	15.0	-0.7	14.9	-0.7	14.5	-2.7	14.6	0.7	14.6	0.0	14.6	0.0	14.5	-0.7	14.3	-1.4
1932	14.1	-1.4	14.0	-0.7	14.0	0.0	13.9	-0.7	13.5	-2.9	13.4	-0.7	13.7	2.2	13.8	0.7	14.1	2.2	14.1	0.0	14.2	0.7	14.3	0.7
1933	14.2	-0.7	14.1	-0.7	14.1	0.0	14.1	0.0	14.2	0.7	14.4	1.4	14.8	2.8	15.1	2.0	15.2	0.7	15.5	2.0	15.6	0.6	15.6	0.0
1934	15.8	1.3	15.8	0.0	15.7	-0.6	15.6	-0.6	15.6	0.0	15.8	1.3	15.8	0.0	15.7	-0.6	15.7	0.0	15.7	0.0	15.7	0.0	15.7	0.0
1935	15.8	0.6	15.7	-0.6	15.7	0.0	15.7	0.0	15.8	0.6	15.8	0.0	15.8	0.0	15.7	-0.6	15.7	0.0	15.7	0.0	15.7	0.0	15.6	-0.6
1936	15.6	0.0	15.6	0.0	15.6	0.0	15.7	0.6	15.8	0.6	15.8	0.0	15.8	0.0	15.8	0.0	15.8	0.0	15.8	0.0	15.9	0.6	16.0	0.6
1937	16.0	0.0	16.1	0.6	16.1	0.0	16.2	0.6	16.3	0.6	16.2	-0.6	16.3	0.6	16.3	0.0	16.1	-1.2	16.1	0.0	16.0	-0.6	15.8	-1.2
1938	15.8	0.0	15.8	0.0	15.6	-1.3	15.6	0.0	15.6	0.0	15.6	0.0	15.7	0.6	15.6	-0.6	15.6	0.0	15.7	0.6	15.3	-2.5	15.4	0.7
1939	15.3	-0.6	15.3	0.0	15.3	0.0	15.4	0.7	15.3	-0.6	15.3	0.0	15.3	0.0	15.2	-0.7	15.3	0.7	15.3	0.0	15.3	0.0	15.4	0.7
1940	15.4	0.0	15.4	0.0	15.4	0.0	15.3	-0.6	15.3	0.0	15.3	0.0	15.3	0.0	15.3	0.0	15.3	0.0	15.3	0.0	15.3	0.0	15.3	0.0
1941	15.4	0.7	15.4	0.0	15.4	0.0	15.4	0.0	15.5	0.6	15.6	0.6	15.6	0.0	15.8	1.3	15.8	0.0	16.0	1.3	16.3	1.9	16.2	-0.6
1942	16.2	0.0	16.2	0.0	16.3	0.6	16.3	0.0	16.3	0.0	16.3	0.0	16.3	0.0	16.3	0.0	16.3	0.0	16.3	0.0	16.3	0.0	16.3	0.0
1943	16.3	0.0	16.3	0.0	16.3	0.0	16.3	0.0	16.3	0.0	16.3	0.0	16.3	0.0	16.3	0.0	16.5	1.2	16.5	0.0	16.5	0.0	16.5	0.0
1944	16.5	0.0	16.5	0.0	16.5	0.0	16.5	0.0	16.6	0.6	16.6	0.0	16.7	0.6	16.7	0.0	16.8	0.6	17.0	1.2	17.0	0.0	17.0	0.0
1945	17.2	1.2	17.3	0.6	17.3	0.0	17.3	0.0	17.3	0.0	17.3	0.0	17.4	0.6	17.4	0.0	17.5	0.6	17.6	0.6	17.7	0.6	17.7	0.0
1946	17.9	1.1	17.9	0.0	18.0	0.6	18.1	0.6	18.2	0.6	18.3	0.5	18.5	1.1	18.8	1.6	18.9	0.5	19.0	0.5	19.2	1.1	19.5	1.6
1947	20.0	2.6	20.1	0.5	20.4	1.5	20.6	1.0	20.6	0.0	20.6	0.0	20.7	0.5	20.7	0.0	20.8	0.5	21.0	1.0	21.2	1.0	21.4	0.9
1948	21.8	1.9	21.9	0.5	21.9	0.0	22.0	0.5	22.0	0.0	22.1	0.5	22.6	2.3	22.8	0.9	22.8	0.0	22.9	0.4	22.9	0.0	22.9	0.0
1949	23.0	0.4	23.0	0.0	23.0	0.0	23.0	0.0	23.0	0.0	23.0	0.0	22.9	-0.4	23.0	0.4	23.0	0.0	23.0	0.0	23.0	0.0	23.0	0.0
1950	23.1	0.4	23.1	0.0	23.2	0.4	23.2	0.0	23.1	-0.4	23.2	0.4	23.2	0.0	23.4	0.9	23.6	0.9	24.1	2.1	24.4	1.2	24.6	0.8
1951	25.0	1.6	25.0	0.0	25.0	0.0	25.0	0.0	25.0	0.0	25.0	0.0	25.0	0.0	25.0	0.0	25.0	0.0	25.0	0.0	25.0	0.0	24.8	-0.8
1952	24.9	0.4	24.9	0.0	24.9	0.0	24.8	-0.4	24.9	0.4	25.0	0.4	25.0	0.0	25.0	0.0	25.0	0.0	25.2	0.8	25.2	0.0	25.2	0.0
1953	25.2	0.0	25.2	0.0	25.3	0.4	25.7	1.6	25.8	0.4	26.0	0.8	26.3	1.2	26.3	0.0	26.5	0.8	26.5	0.0	26.6	0.4	26.6	0.0
1954	26.6	0.0	26.6	0.0	26.6	0.0	26.6	0.0	26.3	-1.1	26.2	-0.4	26.5	1.1	26.5	0.0	26.8	1.1	26.8	0.0	26.8	0.0	26.8	0.0
1955	26.9	0.4	26.8	-0.4	26.8	0.0	26.9	0.4	27.1	0.7	27.2	0.4	27.6	1.5	27.8	0.7	27.8	0.0	27.9	0.4	27.5	-1.4	27.6	0.4
1956	28.0	1.4	28.0	0.0	28.1	0.4	28.3	0.7	28.3	0.0	28.4	0.4	28.7	1.1	28.8	0.3	28.9	0.3	28.9	0.0	28.9	0.0	28.9	0.0
1957	29.0	0.3	29.2	0.7	29.3	0.3	29.6	1.0	29.7	0.3	29.7	0.0	29.8	0.3	29.8	0.0	29.8	0.0	29.8	0.0	29.8	0.0	29.9	0.3
1958	30.0	0.3	30.0	0.0	29.8	-0.7	29.8	0.0	29.8	0.0	29.8	0.0	29.8	0.0	29.8	0.0	30.1	1.0	30.1	0.0	30.1	0.0	30.1	0.0
1959	30.2	0.3	30.3	0.3	30.3	0.0	30.4	0.3	30.4	0.0	30.2	-0.7	30.3	0.3	30.2	-0.3	30.3	0.3	30.3	0.0	30.3	0.0	30.3	0.0
1960	30.4	0.3	30.4	0.0	30.4	0.0	30.4	0.0	30.3	-0.3	30.3	0.0	30.3	0.0	30.3	0.0	30.4	0.3	30.4	0.0	30.3	-0.3	30.3	0.0
1961	30.5	0.7	30.4	-0.3	30.5	0.3	30.5	0.0	30.5	0.0	30.4	-0.3	30.4	0.0	30.5	0.3	30.5	0.0	30.6	0.3	30.5	-0.3	30.4	-0.3
1962	30.5	0.3	30.6	0.3	30.6	0.0	30.7	0.3	30.6	-0.3	30.5	-0.3	30.4	-0.3	30.4	0.0	30.4	0.0	30.4	0.0	30.4	0.0	30.4	0.0
1963	30.4	0.0	30.4	0.0	30.4	0.0	30.4	0.0	30.3	-0.3	30.3	0.0	30.2	-0.3	30.2	0.0	30.3	0.3	30.3	0.0	30.3	0.0	30.3	0.0
1964	30.3	0.0	30.3	0.0	30.3	0.0	30.3	0.0	30.3	0.0	30.4	0.3	30.4	0.0	30.4	0.0	30.5	0.3	30.5	0.0	30.5	0.0	30.4	-0.3
1965	30.4	0.0	30.5	0.3	30.5	0.0	30.5	0.0	30.5	0.0	30.5	0.0	30.5	0.0	30.4	-0.3	30.4	0.0	30.4	0.0	30.4	0.0	30.4	0.0
1966	30.5	0.3	30.6	0.3	30.6	0.0	30.6	0.0	30.6	0.0	30.7	0.3	30.7	0.0	30.8	0.3	30.8	0.0	30.9	0.3	30.9	0.0	30.9	0.0
1967	31.1	0.6	31.1	0.0	31.1	0.0	31.2	0.3	31.0	-0.6	31.1	0.3	31.2	0.3	31.3	0.3	31.3	0.0	31.4	0.3	31.5	0.3	31.6	0.3
1968	31.9	0.9	32.0	0.3	32.2	0.6	32.2	0.0	32.3	0.3	32.4	0.3	32.5	0.3	32.5	0.0	32.5	0.0	32.6	0.3	32.7	0.3	32.7	0.0
1969	33.1	1.2	33.3	0.6	33.3	0.0	33.5	0.6	33.6	0.3	33.6	0.0	33.7	0.3	33.7	0.0	33.8	0.3	33.9	0.3	33.9	0.0	34.1	0.6
1970	34.8	2.1	34.9	0.3	34.9	0.0	35.3	1.1	35.1	-0.6	35.1	0.0	35.2	0.3	35.3	0.3	35.3	0.0	35.5	0.6	35.8	0.8	36.0	0.6

[Continued]

NONMETALLIC MINERAL PRODUCTS
Producer Price Index
Base 1982 = 100
[Continued]

For 1926-1993. Columns headed % show percentile change in the index from the previous period for which an index is available.

Year	Jan Index	%	Feb Index	%	Mar Index	%	Apr Index	%	May Index	%	Jun Index	%	Jul Index	%	Aug Index	%	Sep Index	%	Oct Index	%	Nov Index	%	Dec Index	%
1971	37.1	3.1	37.2	0.3	37.8	1.6	38.0	0.5	38.1	0.3	38.3	0.5	38.5	0.5	38.7	0.5	38.7	0.0	38.7	0.0	38.7	0.0	38.8	0.3
1972	38.8	0.0	38.9	0.3	39.0	0.3	39.2	0.5	39.3	0.3	39.3	0.0	39.4	0.3	39.6	0.5	39.6	0.0	39.7	0.3	39.8	0.3	39.8	0.0
1973	40.0	0.5	40.1	0.3	40.3	0.5	40.6	0.7	40.7	0.2	40.9	0.5	40.6	-0.7	40.6	0.0	40.6	0.0	40.9	0.7	41.1	0.5	41.4	0.7
1974	43.3	4.6	44.4	2.5	45.0	1.4	45.8	1.8	47.1	2.8	47.6	1.1	48.8	2.5	49.2	0.8	49.9	1.4	50.7	1.6	51.0	0.6	51.3	0.6
1975	52.6	2.5	53.2	1.1	53.4	0.4	54.0	1.1	54.1	0.2	54.1	0.0	54.6	0.9	54.9	0.5	55.0	0.2	55.3	0.5	55.5	0.4	55.6	0.2
1976	56.6	1.8	56.7	0.2	57.1	0.7	57.9	1.4	58.1	0.3	58.2	0.2	58.5	0.5	58.7	0.3	58.9	0.3	59.1	0.3	59.2	0.2	59.2	0.0
1977	60.1	1.5	60.5	0.7	60.9	0.7	62.0	1.8	62.2	0.3	62.6	0.6	63.0	0.6	63.3	0.5	63.8	0.8	64.1	0.5	64.2	0.2	64.5	0.5
1978	66.5	3.1	67.2	1.1	67.4	0.3	68.2	1.2	68.5	0.4	69.3	1.2	70.2	1.3	71.0	1.1	71.3	0.4	71.6	0.4	71.8	0.3	72.2	0.6
1979	74.4	3.0	75.1	0.9	75.2	0.1	76.0	1.1	76.7	0.9	77.1	0.5	77.9	1.0	78.1	0.3	79.5	1.8	80.0	0.6	80.4	0.5	81.1	0.9
1980	83.8	3.3	85.6	2.1	86.4	0.9	88.6	2.5	88.7	0.1	88.5	-0.2	88.9	0.5	89.3	0.4	89.6	0.3	90.1	0.6	90.2	0.1	90.9	0.8
1981	92.6	1.9	93.1	0.5	94.0	1.0	97.0	3.2	97.4	0.4	97.9	0.5	98.2	0.3	98.1	-0.1	97.8	-0.3	97.8	0.0	98.0	0.2	97.9	-0.1
1982	98.6	0.7	99.6	1.0	99.9	0.3	100.0	0.1	100.3	0.3	100.2	-0.1	100.3	0.1	100.1	-0.2	100.3	0.2	100.3	0.0	100.3	0.0	100.1	-0.2
1983	100.4	0.3	100.7	0.3	100.6	-0.1	101.2	0.6	101.2	0.0	101.4	0.2	101.5	0.1	101.9	0.4	102.2	0.3	102.4	0.2	102.7	0.3	102.7	0.0
1984	103.1	0.4	103.7	0.6	104.1	0.4	104.9	0.8	105.4	0.5	105.6	0.2	106.1	0.5	106.4	0.3	106.3	-0.1	106.2	-0.1	106.0	-0.2	106.2	0.2
1985	106.7	0.5	107.0	0.3	107.4	0.4	107.9	0.5	108.7	0.7	109.1	0.4	109.2	0.1	109.4	0.2	109.3	-0.1	109.5	0.2	109.5	0.0	109.6	0.1
1986	110.1	0.5	110.0	-0.1	110.1	0.1	110.2	0.1	110.4	0.2	110.2	-0.2	110.2	0.0	109.9	-0.3	109.7	-0.2	109.7	0.0	109.7	0.0	109.3	-0.4
1987	109.3	0.0	109.6	0.3	109.7	0.1	109.9	0.2	109.9	0.0	110.1	0.2	110.1	0.0	109.9	-0.2	110.0	0.1	110.4	0.4	110.5	0.1	110.4	-0.1
1988	110.8	0.4	110.9	0.1	110.9	0.0	111.0	0.1	111.2	0.2	111.3	0.1	111.1	-0.2	111.1	0.0	111.3	0.2	111.4	0.1	111.5	0.1	111.7	0.2
1989	111.8	0.1	111.8	0.0	112.0	0.2	112.6	0.5	112.7	0.1	112.8	0.1	112.8	0.0	112.8	0.0	112.9	0.1	113.0	0.1	113.1	0.1	113.2	0.1
1990	113.8	0.5	113.9	0.1	114.2	0.3	114.3	0.1	114.5	0.2	114.6	0.1	114.6	0.0	114.7	0.1	115.0	0.3	115.3	0.3	115.8	0.4	115.8	0.0
1991	116.9	0.9	117.2	0.3	117.4	0.2	117.3	-0.1	117.3	0.0	117.3	0.0	117.2	-0.1	117.1	-0.1	117.2	0.1	117.4	0.2	117.2	-0.2	117.1	-0.1
1992	117.2	0.1	117.1	-0.1	117.3	0.2	116.9	-0.3	116.9	0.0	117.0	0.1	117.1	0.1	117.4	0.3	117.4	0.0	117.4	0.0	117.7	0.3	117.8	0.1
1993	118.4	0.5	118.6	0.2	118.9	0.3	119.6	0.6	119.7	0.1	120.0	0.3	120.2	0.2	120.5	0.2	120.7	0.2	121.3	0.5	121.4	0.1	121.3	-0.1

Source: U.S. Department of Labor, Bureau of Labor Statistics, Division of Industry Prices and Price Indexes. n.e.c. stands for not elsewhere classified. - indicates no data collected for period or unavailable.

Glass
Producer Price Index
Base 1982 = 100

For 1947-1993. Columns headed % show percentile change in the index from the previous period for which an index is available.

Year	Jan Index	%	Feb Index	%	Mar Index	%	Apr Index	%	May Index	%	Jun Index	%	Jul Index	%	Aug Index	%	Sep Index	%	Oct Index	%	Nov Index	%	Dec Index	%
1947	28.9	-	28.9	0.0	30.0	3.8	30.5	1.7	30.5	0.0	30.5	0.0	30.5	0.0	30.5	0.0	30.5	0.0	30.5	0.0	30.5	0.0	30.5	0.0
1948	30.7	0.7	30.5	-0.7	30.5	0.0	30.7	0.7	30.5	-0.7	30.5	0.0	31.8	4.3	33.1	4.1	33.1	0.0	33.3	0.6	33.5	0.6	33.5	0.0
1949	33.5	0.0	33.5	0.0	33.4	-0.3	33.3	-0.3	33.3	0.0	33.3	0.0	33.3	0.0	33.3	0.0	33.3	0.0	33.3	0.0	33.3	0.0	33.3	0.0
1950	33.3	0.0	33.1	-0.6	33.9	2.4	34.0	0.3	33.6	-1.2	33.6	0.0	33.6	0.0	33.6	0.0	33.6	0.0	35.0	4.2	36.3	3.7	36.3	0.0
1951	36.3	0.0	36.3	0.0	36.3	0.0	36.3	0.0	36.3	0.0	36.3	0.0	36.3	0.0	36.3	0.0	36.3	0.0	36.3	0.0	36.3	0.0	36.3	0.0
1952	36.3	0.0	36.3	0.0	36.3	0.0	36.3	0.0	36.3	0.0	36.3	0.0	36.3	0.0	36.3	0.0	36.3	0.0	36.3	0.0	36.3	0.0	36.3	0.0
1953	36.3	0.0	36.3	0.0	37.0	1.9	37.0	0.0	37.0	0.0	39.1	5.7	39.6	1.3	39.6	0.0	39.6	0.0	39.6	0.0	39.6	0.0	39.6	0.0
1954	39.6	0.0	39.6	0.0	39.6	0.0	39.6	0.0	39.6	0.0	39.6	0.0	39.6	0.0	39.6	0.0	39.4	-0.5	39.4	0.0	39.4	0.0	39.4	0.0
1955	39.4	0.0	39.4	0.0	39.4	0.0	39.7	0.8	39.7	0.0	40.1	1.0	41.7	4.0	41.7	0.0	41.7	0.0	42.3	1.4	41.7	-1.4	41.7	0.0
1956	41.7	0.0	41.7	0.0	41.7	0.0	41.7	0.0	41.7	0.0	41.9	0.5	42.9	2.4	43.1	0.5	43.1	0.0	43.1	0.0	43.1	0.0	43.1	0.0
1957	43.1	0.0	43.1	0.0	43.1	0.0	43.1	0.0	43.1	0.0	43.1	0.0	43.1	0.0	43.1	0.0	43.1	0.0	43.1	0.0	43.1	0.0	43.1	0.0
1958	43.1	0.0	43.1	0.0	43.1	0.0	43.1	0.0	43.1	0.0	43.1	0.0	43.1	0.0	43.0	-0.2	42.9	-0.2	42.9	0.0	42.9	0.0	42.9	0.0
1959	42.9	0.0	42.9	0.0	42.9	0.0	42.9	0.0	42.9	0.0	43.0	0.2	43.0	0.0	43.0	0.0	43.0	0.0	43.0	0.0	43.0	0.0	43.0	0.0
1960	43.0	0.0	43.0	0.0	43.0	0.0	43.0	0.0	41.4	-3.7	41.4	0.0	41.4	0.0	41.4	0.0	42.0	1.4	42.0	0.0	42.0	0.0	42.0	0.0
1961	42.0	0.0	42.0	0.0	42.0	0.0	42.0	0.0	42.0	0.0	41.4	-1.4	41.4	0.0	41.4	0.0	41.4	0.0	41.4	0.0	41.4	0.0	41.4	0.0
1962	41.4	0.0	41.4	0.0	41.4	0.0	42.1	1.7	42.2	0.2	42.2	0.0	42.2	0.0	41.6	-1.4	41.6	0.0	41.6	0.0	41.6	0.0	41.6	0.0
1963	41.6	0.0	41.6	0.0	41.6	0.0	41.6	0.0	41.6	0.0	41.6	0.0	41.6	0.0	42.6	2.4	43.0	0.9	43.8	1.9	43.5	-0.7	43.5	0.0
1964	43.5	0.0	43.5	0.0	43.8	0.7	44.2	0.9	44.1	-0.2	44.1	0.0	44.1	0.0	44.4	0.7	44.4	0.0	44.4	0.0	44.4	0.0	43.9	-1.1
1965	43.9	0.0	43.8	-0.2	43.8	0.0	43.8	0.0	43.8	0.0	43.8	0.0	43.1	-1.6	43.1	0.0	43.0	-0.2	43.0	0.0	43.0	0.0	43.0	0.0
1966	43.0	0.0	43.0	0.0	42.7	-0.7	42.9	0.5	43.1	0.5	43.1	0.0	43.2	0.2	42.9	-0.7	43.3	0.9	43.9	1.4	44.5	1.4	44.5	0.0
1967	-	-	-	-	-	-	-	-	-	-	-	-	-	-	-	-	-	-	-	-	-	-	-	-
1968	-	-	-	-	-	-	-	-	-	-	-	-	-	-	-	-	-	-	-	-	-	-	-	-
1969	-	-	-	-	-	-	-	-	-	-	-	-	-	-	-	-	-	-	-	-	-	-	-	-
1970	-	-	-	-	-	-	-	-	-	-	-	-	-	-	-	-	-	-	-	-	-	-	-	-
1971	-	-	-	-	-	-	-	-	-	-	-	-	-	-	-	-	-	-	-	-	-	-	-	-
1972	-	-	-	-	-	-	-	-	-	-	-	-	-	-	-	-	-	-	-	-	-	-	-	-
1973	-	-	-	-	-	-	-	-	-	-	-	-	-	-	-	-	-	-	-	-	-	-	-	-
1974	-	-	-	-	-	-	-	-	-	-	-	-	-	-	-	-	-	-	-	-	-	-	-	-
1975	-	-	-	-	-	-	-	-	-	-	-	-	-	-	-	-	-	-	-	-	-	-	-	-
1976	-	-	-	-	-	-	-	-	-	-	-	-	-	-	-	-	-	-	-	-	-	-	-	-
1977	-	-	-	-	-	-	-	-	-	-	-	-	-	-	-	-	-	-	-	-	-	-	-	-
1978	-	-	-	-	-	-	-	-	-	-	-	-	-	-	-	-	-	-	-	-	-	-	-	-
1979	-	-	-	-	-	-	-	-	-	-	-	-	-	-	-	-	-	-	-	-	-	-	-	-
1980	-	-	-	-	-	-	-	-	-	-	-	-	-	-	-	-	-	-	-	-	-	-	-	-
1981	-	-	-	-	-	-	-	-	-	-	-	-	-	-	-	-	-	-	-	-	-	-	-	-
1982	-	-	-	-	-	-	-	-	-	-	-	-	-	-	-	-	-	-	-	-	-	-	-	-
1983	-	-	-	-	103.7	133.0	103.7	0.0	103.7	0.0	103.7	0.0	103.7	0.0	103.7	0.0	103.8	0.1	104.5	0.7	104.8	0.3	104.7	-0.1
1984	107.0	2.2	107.1	0.1	106.8	-0.3	107.1	0.3	105.9	-1.1	106.0	0.1	106.0	0.0	103.9	-2.0	104.2	0.3	104.3	0.1	104.1	-0.2	104.2	0.1
1985	103.4	-0.8	103.3	-0.1	103.3	0.0	103.8	0.5	104.6	0.8	104.5	-0.1	105.1	0.6	105.4	0.3	105.2	-0.2	105.8	0.6	106.0	0.2	106.2	0.2
1986	106.8	0.6	106.8	0.0	106.8	0.0	107.0	0.2	106.9	-0.1	106.9	0.0	108.1	1.1	107.8	-0.3	107.8	0.0	107.8	0.0	108.1	0.3	108.2	0.1
1987	108.2	0.0	108.3	0.1	109.1	0.7	109.2	0.1	109.0	-0.2	109.5	0.5	109.7	0.2	109.8	0.1	109.6	-0.2	110.1	0.5	110.0	-0.1	110.7	0.6
1988	110.8	0.1	111.2	0.4	111.7	0.4	111.9	0.2	112.3	0.4	111.9	-0.4	112.3	0.4	112.7	0.4	113.1	0.4	113.0	-0.1	113.2	0.2	113.9	0.6
1989	113.4	-0.4	113.1	-0.3	112.6	-0.4	112.8	0.2	113.7	0.8	113.2	-0.4	113.3	0.1	113.0	-0.3	113.2	0.2	113.5	0.3	113.2	-0.3	113.7	0.4
1990	114.8	1.0	114.5	-0.3	114.3	-0.2	114.0	-0.3	114.1	0.1	113.9	-0.2	113.6	-0.3	113.2	-0.4	113.3	0.1	113.4	0.1	113.4	0.0	113.3	-0.1
1991	113.9	0.5	113.9	0.0	114.4	0.4	114.2	-0.2	114.3	0.1	113.7	-0.5	113.4	-0.3	114.0	0.5	115.0	0.9	115.8	0.7	115.2	-0.5	115.1	-0.1

[Continued]

Glass
Producer Price Index
Base 1982 = 100
[Continued]

For 1947-1993. Columns headed % show percentile change in the index from the previous period for which an index is available.

Year	Jan		Feb		Mar		Apr		May		Jun		Jul		Aug		Sep		Oct		Nov		Dec	
	Index	%	Index	%	Index	%	Index	%	Index	%	Index	%	Index	%	Index	%	Index	%	Index	%	Index	%	Index	%
1992	115.4	0.3	114.8	-0.5	114.9	0.1	115.3	0.3	115.3	0.0	115.2	-0.1	115.2	0.0	116.6	1.2	116.4	-0.2	116.0	-0.3	116.1	0.1	117.1	0.9
1993	116.3	-0.7	116.8	0.4	116.6	-0.2	116.9	0.3	117.0	0.1	117.1	0.1	117.0	-0.1	117.4	0.3	117.1	-0.3	117.7	0.5	118.5	0.7	117.3	-1.0

Source: U.S. Department of Labor, Bureau of Labor Statistics, Division of Industry Prices and Price Indexes. n.e.c. stands for not elsewhere classified. - indicates no data collected for period or unavailable.

Concrete Ingredients and Related Products
Producer Price Index
Base 1982 = 100

For 1926-1993. Columns headed % show percentile change in the index from the previous period for which an index is available.

Year	Jan Index	%	Feb Index	%	Mar Index	%	Apr Index	%	May Index	%	Jun Index	%	Jul Index	%	Aug Index	%	Sep Index	%	Oct Index	%	Nov Index	%	Dec Index	%
1926	15.0	-	15.0	0.0	15.0	0.0	14.9	-0.7	14.9	0.0	14.9	0.0	14.9	0.0	14.8	-0.7	14.8	0.0	14.9	0.7	14.9	0.0	15.0	0.7
1927	14.9	-0.7	14.6	-2.0	14.6	0.0	14.6	0.0	14.6	0.0	14.6	0.0	14.6	0.0	14.4	-1.4	14.4	0.0	14.4	0.0	14.4	0.0	14.5	0.7
1928	14.6	0.7	14.6	0.0	14.5	-0.7	16.5	13.8	17.1	3.6	17.1	0.0	17.0	-0.6	17.1	0.6	16.9	-1.2	16.8	-0.6	16.9	0.6	17.0	0.6
1929	17.0	0.0	17.0	0.0	16.7	-1.8	16.6	-0.6	16.6	0.0	16.6	0.0	16.6	0.0	16.4	-1.2	15.8	-3.7	15.7	-0.6	15.9	1.3	16.4	3.1
1930	16.5	0.6	16.7	1.2	16.6	-0.6	16.6	0.0	16.6	0.0	16.2	-2.4	16.6	2.5	16.6	0.0	16.6	0.0	16.6	0.0	16.6	0.0	16.5	-0.6
1931	16.5	0.0	16.2	-1.8	15.9	-1.9	15.6	-1.9	15.4	-1.3	15.2	-1.3	14.4	-5.3	14.6	1.4	14.6	0.0	14.5	-0.7	14.5	0.0	14.2	-2.1
1932	13.9	-2.1	13.9	0.0	13.9	0.0	13.7	-1.4	13.6	-0.7	13.8	1.5	14.7	6.5	14.8	0.7	14.8	0.0	14.8	0.0	14.9	0.7	15.1	1.3
1933	15.1	0.0	15.2	0.7	15.2	0.0	15.2	0.0	15.2	0.0	15.2	0.0	15.8	3.9	16.1	1.9	16.1	0.0	16.2	0.6	16.2	0.0	16.3	0.6
1934	16.6	1.8	16.7	0.6	16.6	-0.6	16.2	-2.4	16.2	0.0	16.6	2.5	16.6	0.0	16.6	0.0	16.6	0.0	16.6	0.0	16.6	0.0	16.6	0.0
1935	16.6	0.0	16.6	0.0	16.6	0.0	16.7	0.6	16.6	-0.6	16.6	0.0	16.6	0.0	16.6	0.0	16.6	0.0	16.6	0.0	16.7	0.6	16.7	0.0
1936	16.6	-0.6	16.7	0.6	16.6	-0.6	16.6	0.0	16.7	0.6	16.7	0.0	16.7	0.0	16.7	0.0	16.7	0.0	16.7	0.0	16.7	0.0	16.7	0.0
1937	16.7	0.0	16.6	-0.6	16.6	0.0	16.6	0.0	16.6	0.0	16.6	0.0	16.7	0.6	16.7	0.0	16.3	-2.4	16.7	2.5	16.7	0.0	16.7	0.0
1938	16.7	0.0	16.7	0.0	16.7	0.0	16.7	0.0	16.7	0.0	16.6	-0.6	16.8	1.2	16.7	-0.6	16.6	-0.6	16.7	0.6	16.9	1.2	16.9	0.0
1939	16.7	-1.2	16.7	0.0	16.7	0.0	16.7	0.0	16.7	0.0	16.7	0.0	16.7	0.0	16.7	0.0	16.7	0.0	16.7	0.0	16.7	0.0	16.7	0.0
1940	16.7	0.0	16.7	0.0	16.7	0.0	16.6	-0.6	16.6	0.0	16.6	0.0	16.6	0.0	16.6	0.0	16.6	0.0	16.6	0.0	16.6	0.0	16.6	0.0
1941	16.6	0.0	16.6	0.0	16.6	0.0	16.6	0.0	16.7	0.6	16.7	0.0	16.8	0.6	16.8	0.0	16.9	0.6	16.9	0.0	17.0	0.6	17.1	0.6
1942	17.1	0.0	17.2	0.6	17.2	0.0	17.3	0.6	17.3	0.0	17.3	0.0	17.3	0.0	17.3	0.0	17.3	0.0	17.3	0.0	17.3	0.0	17.3	0.0
1943	17.3	0.0	17.3	0.0	17.3	0.0	17.3	0.0	17.3	0.0	17.2	-0.6	17.2	0.0	17.3	0.6	17.3	0.0	17.2	-0.6	17.2	0.0	17.2	0.0
1944	17.2	0.0	17.2	0.0	17.2	0.0	17.3	0.6	17.6	1.7	17.6	0.0	17.6	0.0	17.6	0.0	17.6	0.0	17.7	0.6	17.7	0.0	17.7	0.0
1945	17.7	0.0	17.9	1.1	17.9	0.0	17.9	0.0	17.9	0.0	17.9	0.0	17.9	0.0	17.9	0.0	18.0	0.6	18.1	0.6	18.1	0.0	18.1	0.0
1946	18.4	1.7	18.4	0.0	18.5	0.5	18.5	0.0	18.5	0.0	18.6	0.5	18.7	0.5	18.9	1.1	19.0	0.5	19.0	0.0	19.1	0.5	19.2	0.5
1947	19.6	2.1	19.9	1.5	20.0	0.5	20.2	1.0	20.2	0.0	20.3	0.5	20.4	0.5	20.7	1.5	20.9	1.0	21.0	0.5	21.1	0.5	21.1	0.0
1948	21.7	2.8	21.9	0.9	22.0	0.5	22.1	0.5	22.1	0.0	22.2	0.5	22.7	2.3	22.7	0.0	22.8	0.4	22.8	0.0	22.9	0.4	23.0	0.4
1949	23.1	0.4	23.2	0.4	23.2	0.0	23.2	0.0	23.2	0.0	23.2	0.0	23.1	-0.4	23.1	0.0	23.1	0.0	23.2	0.4	23.2	0.0	23.2	0.0
1950	23.3	0.4	23.3	0.0	23.3	0.0	23.3	0.0	23.3	0.0	23.3	0.0	23.3	0.0	23.4	0.4	23.5	0.4	23.9	1.7	24.0	0.4	24.1	0.4
1951	24.9	3.3	24.9	0.0	24.9	0.0	24.9	0.0	24.9	0.0	24.9	0.0	24.9	0.0	24.9	0.0	24.9	0.0	24.9	0.0	24.9	0.0	24.9	0.0
1952	24.9	0.0	24.9	0.0	24.9	0.0	24.9	0.0	24.9	0.0	24.9	0.0	24.9	0.0	24.9	0.0	24.9	0.0	24.9	0.0	24.9	0.0	24.9	0.0
1953	24.9	0.0	24.9	0.0	25.0	0.4	25.9	3.6	26.0	0.4	26.0	0.0	26.0	0.0	26.1	0.4	26.3	0.8	26.3	0.0	26.3	0.0	26.3	0.0
1954	26.4	0.4	26.4	0.0	26.4	0.0	26.4	0.0	26.4	0.0	26.5	0.4	26.9	1.5	26.9	0.0	26.9	0.0	26.9	0.0	26.9	0.0	26.9	0.0
1955	27.1	0.7	27.3	0.7	27.3	0.0	27.5	0.7	27.5	0.0	27.5	0.0	27.5	0.0	27.6	0.4	27.6	0.0	27.6	0.0	27.6	0.0	27.7	0.4
1956	28.6	3.2	28.6	0.0	28.6	0.0	28.6	0.0	28.6	0.0	28.7	0.3	28.7	0.0	28.7	0.0	28.7	0.0	29.0	1.0	29.0	0.0	29.0	0.0
1957	29.6	2.1	29.7	0.3	29.7	0.0	29.8	0.3	29.8	0.0	29.9	0.3	30.0	0.3	30.0	0.0	30.1	0.3	30.1	0.0	30.1	0.0	30.1	0.0
1958	30.6	1.7	30.6	0.0	30.5	-0.3	30.6	0.3	30.6	0.0	30.6	0.0	30.6	0.0	30.6	0.0	30.6	0.0	30.6	0.0	30.6	0.0	30.6	0.0
1959	30.9	1.0	30.9	0.0	30.9	0.0	30.9	0.0	30.9	0.0	30.8	-0.3	30.9	0.3	30.9	0.0	30.9	0.0	30.9	0.0	30.9	0.0	30.9	0.0
1960	31.3	1.3	31.3	0.0	31.3	0.0	31.3	0.0	31.3	0.0	31.3	0.0	31.3	0.0	31.3	0.0	31.3	0.0	31.3	0.0	31.3	0.0	31.3	0.0
1961	31.3	0.0	31.3	0.0	31.4	0.3	31.4	0.0	31.4	0.0	31.4	0.0	31.4	0.0	31.4	0.0	31.4	0.0	31.4	0.0	31.2	-0.6	31.0	-0.6
1962	31.3	1.0	31.4	0.3	31.4	0.0	31.4	0.0	31.5	0.3	31.5	0.0	31.5	0.0	31.5	0.0	31.5	0.0	31.5	0.0	31.5	0.0	31.5	0.0
1963	31.3	-0.6	31.4	0.3	31.4	0.0	31.4	0.0	31.4	0.0	31.5	0.3	31.5	0.0	31.4	-0.3	31.4	0.0	31.4	0.0	31.4	0.0	31.4	0.0
1964	31.3	-0.3	31.3	0.0	31.3	0.0	31.3	0.0	31.3	0.0	31.3	0.0	31.3	0.0	31.3	0.0	31.3	0.0	31.3	0.0	31.4	0.3	31.4	0.0
1965	31.5	0.3	31.5	0.0	31.5	0.0	31.5	0.0	31.5	0.0	31.4	-0.3	31.4	0.0	31.5	0.3	31.5	0.0	31.5	0.0	31.5	0.0	31.5	0.0
1966	31.6	0.3	31.6	0.0	31.6	0.0	31.6	0.0	31.6	0.0	31.6	0.0	31.6	0.0	31.6	0.0	31.6	0.0	31.8	0.6	31.7	-0.3	31.8	0.3
1967	32.2	1.3	32.2	0.0	32.2	0.0	32.3	0.3	32.2	-0.3	32.2	0.0	32.2	0.0	32.3	0.3	32.3	0.0	32.4	0.3	32.4	0.0	32.5	0.3
1968	32.9	1.2	33.1	0.6	33.1	0.0	33.2	0.3	33.2	0.0	33.3	0.3	33.4	0.3	33.4	0.0	33.4	0.0	33.4	0.0	33.6	0.6	33.6	0.0
1969	34.3	2.1	34.2	-0.3	34.3	0.3	34.3	0.0	34.3	0.0	34.4	0.3	34.5	0.3	34.5	0.0	34.6	0.3	34.6	0.0	34.6	0.0	34.6	0.0
1970	35.9	3.8	36.1	0.6	36.1	0.0	37.1	2.8	36.2	-2.4	36.3	0.3	36.3	0.0	36.3	0.0	36.4	0.3	36.4	0.0	36.4	0.0	36.4	0.0

[Continued]

Concrete Ingredients and Related Products
Producer Price Index
Base 1982 = 100
[Continued]

For 1926-1993. Columns headed % show percentile change in the index from the previous period for which an index is available.

Year	Jan Index	%	Feb Index	%	Mar Index	%	Apr Index	%	May Index	%	Jun Index	%	Jul Index	%	Aug Index	%	Sep Index	%	Oct Index	%	Nov Index	%	Dec Index	%
1971	37.7	3.6	37.8	0.3	38.9	2.9	39.0	0.3	39.1	0.3	39.2	0.3	39.8	1.5	40.0	0.5	40.1	0.3	40.1	0.0	40.1	0.0	40.1	0.0
1972	40.1	0.0	40.2	0.2	40.2	0.0	40.8	1.5	40.9	0.2	40.9	0.0	40.9	0.0	41.3	1.0	41.4	0.2	41.4	0.0	41.4	0.0	41.4	0.0
1973	41.6	0.5	41.7	0.2	41.9	0.5	42.5	1.4	42.4	-0.2	42.5	0.2	42.5	0.0	42.5	0.0	42.5	0.0	42.6	0.2	42.6	0.0	42.6	0.0
1974	44.8	5.2	45.1	0.7	45.3	0.4	46.2	2.0	46.9	1.5	47.1	0.4	49.5	5.1	49.7	0.4	49.8	0.2	50.2	0.8	50.4	0.4	50.5	0.2
1975	53.9	6.7	54.4	0.9	54.7	0.6	55.3	1.1	55.5	0.4	55.6	0.2	56.1	0.9	56.1	0.0	56.5	0.7	56.4	-0.2	56.4	0.0	56.4	0.0
1976	58.2	3.2	58.4	0.3	58.6	0.3	60.3	2.9	60.4	0.2	60.5	0.2	60.9	0.7	60.9	0.0	61.0	0.2	61.1	0.2	61.0	-0.2	61.1	0.2
1977	62.6	2.5	62.7	0.2	63.0	0.5	64.0	1.6	64.4	0.6	64.5	0.2	64.7	0.3	64.8	0.2	64.9	0.2	64.9	0.0	65.0	0.2	65.0	0.0
1978	67.7	4.2	68.0	0.4	68.4	0.6	69.9	2.2	70.0	0.1	70.2	0.3	70.7	0.7	71.0	0.4	71.3	0.4	71.6	0.4	72.1	0.7	72.1	0.0
1979	76.1	5.5	76.9	1.1	77.4	0.7	78.1	0.9	78.2	0.1	78.5	0.4	79.1	0.8	79.3	0.3	79.6	0.4	80.1	0.6	80.5	0.5	81.0	0.6
1980	85.5	5.6	86.0	0.6	86.3	0.3	87.7	1.6	87.9	0.2	88.1	0.2	89.0	1.0	89.9	1.0	90.0	0.1	90.0	0.0	90.1	0.1	90.2	0.1
1981	93.5	3.7	94.0	0.5	94.4	0.4	96.0	1.7	96.0	0.0	96.0	0.0	96.1	0.1	96.1	0.0	96.3	0.2	96.3	0.0	96.3	0.0	96.4	0.1
1982	98.8	2.5	99.5	0.7	99.9	0.4	99.8	-0.1	100.8	1.0	100.9	0.1	100.6	-0.3	100.4	-0.2	100.3	-0.1	100.0	-0.3	100.0	0.0	98.9	-1.1
1983	99.1	0.2	100.0	0.9	99.5	-0.5	100.9	1.4	101.2	0.3	101.4	0.2	101.3	-0.1	102.1	0.8	102.3	0.2	102.2	-0.1	101.6	-0.6	101.5	-0.1
1984	101.8	0.3	103.2	1.4	104.6	1.4	104.6	0.0	105.8	1.1	105.4	-0.4	105.5	0.1	106.0	0.5	105.9	-0.1	105.7	-0.2	106.0	0.3	106.3	0.3
1985	106.8	0.5	107.6	0.7	108.2	0.6	108.5	0.3	109.3	0.7	109.3	0.0	108.9	-0.4	109.1	0.2	108.7	-0.4	108.6	-0.1	108.1	-0.5	108.4	0.3
1986	109.4	0.9	109.4	0.0	109.7	0.3	110.1	0.4	109.7	-0.4	109.5	-0.2	109.4	-0.1	109.3	-0.1	109.4	0.1	109.5	0.1	109.5	0.0	108.2	-1.2
1987	109.1	0.8	109.6	0.5	110.1	0.5	110.4	0.3	110.7	0.3	110.8	0.1	110.8	0.0	110.8	0.0	110.8	0.0	110.8	0.0	110.8	0.0	110.6	-0.2
1988	111.3	0.6	111.6	0.3	111.6	0.0	112.3	0.6	112.6	0.3	112.3	-0.3	112.1	-0.2	112.2	0.1	112.0	-0.2	111.9	-0.1	111.9	0.0	111.9	0.0
1989	112.3	0.4	112.3	0.0	112.3	0.0	113.1	0.7	113.3	0.2	113.3	0.0	113.3	0.0	113.2	-0.1	113.7	0.4	113.8	0.1	113.6	-0.2	113.6	0.0
1990	113.9	0.3	114.3	0.4	114.8	0.4	115.2	0.3	115.5	0.3	115.5	0.0	115.3	-0.2	115.5	0.2	115.8	0.3	115.8	0.0	116.0	0.2	115.9	-0.1
1991	117.1	1.0	118.3	1.0	118.3	0.0	118.6	0.3	118.8	0.2	118.9	0.1	118.7	-0.2	118.8	0.1	118.5	-0.3	118.5	0.0	118.3	-0.2	118.2	-0.1
1992	118.8	0.5	118.8	0.0	119.4	0.5	119.3	-0.1	119.4	0.1	119.4	0.0	119.4	0.0	119.5	0.1	119.4	-0.1	119.6	0.2	119.7	0.1	119.9	0.2
1993	120.9	0.8	121.1	0.2	121.4	0.2	123.2	1.5	123.2	0.0	123.5	0.2	123.7	0.2	123.8	0.1	124.4	0.5	125.5	0.9	125.3	-0.2	125.5	0.2

Source: U.S. Department of Labor, Bureau of Labor Statistics, Division of Industry Prices and Price Indexes. n.e.c. stands for not elsewhere classified. - indicates no data collected for period or unavailable.

Concrete Products

Producer Price Index
Base 1982 = 100

For 1926-1993. Columns headed % show percentile change in the index from the previous period for which an index is available.

Year	Jan Index	%	Feb Index	%	Mar Index	%	Apr Index	%	May Index	%	Jun Index	%	Jul Index	%	Aug Index	%	Sep Index	%	Oct Index	%	Nov Index	%	Dec Index	%
1926	23.7	-	23.7	0.0	23.7	0.0	23.7	0.0	23.7	0.0	23.7	0.0	23.7	0.0	23.7	0.0	23.7	0.0	23.7	0.0	23.7	0.0	23.7	0.0
1927	23.7	0.0	23.7	0.0	23.7	0.0	23.7	0.0	23.7	0.0	23.7	0.0	23.7	0.0	23.7	0.0	23.7	0.0	23.7	0.0	23.7	0.0	23.7	0.0
1928	23.7	0.0	23.7	0.0	23.7	0.0	23.7	0.0	23.7	0.0	23.7	0.0	23.7	0.0	23.7	0.0	23.7	0.0	23.7	0.0	23.7	0.0	23.7	0.0
1929	23.7	0.0	23.7	0.0	23.7	0.0	23.7	0.0	23.7	0.0	23.7	0.0	23.0	-3.0	23.0	0.0	23.0	0.0	23.0	0.0	23.0	0.0	23.0	0.0
1930	23.0	0.0	23.0	0.0	23.0	0.0	23.0	0.0	22.6	-1.7	22.6	0.0	23.0	1.8	23.7	3.0	25.0	5.5	25.0	0.0	25.0	0.0	25.0	0.0
1931	24.6	-1.6	23.2	-5.7	22.6	-2.6	22.6	0.0	22.6	0.0	22.6	0.0	22.5	-0.4	21.3	-5.3	21.3	0.0	21.3	0.0	21.3	0.0	21.3	0.0
1932	21.3	0.0	21.2	-0.5	21.2	0.0	20.0	-5.7	20.0	0.0	20.0	0.0	20.0	0.0	20.0	0.0	20.0	0.0	20.9	4.5	20.9	0.0	20.9	0.0
1933	20.9	0.0	20.9	0.0	20.9	0.0	20.9	0.0	20.9	0.0	20.9	0.0	20.9	0.0	20.9	0.0	20.9	0.0	20.9	0.0	20.9	0.0	20.9	0.0
1934	20.9	0.0	20.9	0.0	20.9	0.0	20.9	0.0	20.9	0.0	20.9	0.0	20.9	0.0	20.9	0.0	20.9	0.0	20.9	0.0	20.9	0.0	20.9	0.0
1935	20.9	0.0	20.9	0.0	19.7	-5.7	18.6	-5.6	18.6	0.0	18.6	0.0	18.6	0.0	18.6	0.0	18.6	0.0	18.6	0.0	18.6	0.0	18.6	0.0
1936	20.9	12.4	20.9	0.0	20.9	0.0	20.9	0.0	20.9	0.0	20.9	0.0	20.9	0.0	20.9	0.0	20.4	-2.4	18.6	-8.8	18.6	0.0	18.6	0.0
1937	18.6	0.0	18.6	0.0	18.6	0.0	21.2	14.0	21.2	0.0	21.2	0.0	21.2	0.0	21.2	0.0	21.2	0.0	21.2	0.0	21.2	0.0	19.2	-9.4
1938	18.6	-3.1	18.6	0.0	18.6	0.0	18.6	0.0	18.6	0.0	18.6	0.0	18.6	0.0	18.6	0.0	18.6	0.0	18.6	0.0	18.6	0.0	19.9	7.0
1939	21.2	6.5	21.2	0.0	21.2	0.0	21.2	0.0	18.0	-15.1	15.9	-11.7	15.9	0.0	15.9	0.0	17.2	8.2	18.6	8.1	18.6	0.0	18.6	0.0
1940	18.6	0.0	18.6	0.0	16.6	-10.8	15.9	-4.2	15.9	0.0	15.9	0.0	15.9	0.0	15.9	0.0	15.9	0.0	15.9	0.0	15.9	0.0	18.0	13.2
1941	18.6	3.3	18.6	0.0	18.6	0.0	18.6	0.0	18.6	0.0	18.9	1.6	19.9	5.3	19.9	0.0	19.9	0.0	19.9	0.0	19.9	0.0	19.9	0.0
1942	19.9	0.0	19.9	0.0	19.9	0.0	19.9	0.0	19.9	0.0	19.9	0.0	19.9	0.0	19.9	0.0	19.9	0.0	19.9	0.0	19.9	0.0	19.9	0.0
1943	19.9	0.0	19.9	0.0	19.9	0.0	19.9	0.0	19.9	0.0	19.9	0.0	19.9	0.0	19.9	0.0	19.9	0.0	19.9	0.0	19.9	0.0	19.9	0.0
1944	19.9	0.0	19.9	0.0	19.9	0.0	19.9	0.0	19.9	0.0	19.9	0.0	19.9	0.0	19.9	0.0	19.9	0.0	19.9	0.0	19.9	0.0	19.9	0.0
1945	19.9	0.0	19.9	0.0	19.9	0.0	19.9	0.0	19.9	0.0	19.9	0.0	19.9	0.0	19.9	0.0	19.9	0.0	19.9	0.0	19.9	0.0	19.9	0.0
1946	19.9	0.0	19.9	0.0	19.9	0.0	19.9	0.0	20.2	1.5	21.2	5.0	22.0	3.8	21.2	-3.6	21.2	0.0	21.2	0.0	22.5	6.1	23.9	6.2
1947	23.9	0.0	23.9	0.0	23.9	0.0	23.9	0.0	23.9	0.0	23.9	0.0	24.0	0.4	23.8	-0.8	23.6	-0.8	24.0	1.7	24.2	0.8	24.2	0.0
1948	24.7	2.1	24.8	0.4	24.8	0.0	24.8	0.0	24.8	0.0	24.8	0.0	25.0	0.8	25.4	1.6	25.4	0.0	25.4	0.0	25.4	0.0	25.4	0.0
1949	25.4	0.0	25.4	0.0	25.6	0.8	25.6	0.0	25.6	0.0	25.6	0.0	25.6	0.0	25.8	0.8	25.8	0.0	25.8	0.0	25.8	0.0	25.8	0.0
1950	25.8	0.0	25.8	0.0	25.8	0.0	25.8	0.0	25.9	0.4	26.0	0.4	26.0	0.0	26.2	0.8	26.6	1.5	27.0	1.5	27.0	0.0	27.2	0.7
1951	27.9	2.6	28.0	0.4	28.0	0.0	28.0	0.0	28.0	0.0	28.0	0.0	28.0	0.0	28.0	0.0	28.0	0.0	28.0	0.0	28.0	0.0	28.0	0.0
1952	28.0	0.0	28.0	0.0	28.0	0.0	28.0	0.0	28.0	0.0	28.0	0.0	28.0	0.0	28.0	0.0	28.0	0.0	28.0	0.0	28.0	0.0	28.0	0.0
1953	28.1	0.4	28.1	0.0	28.1	0.0	28.4	1.1	28.7	1.1	28.7	0.0	28.8	0.3	28.9	0.3	29.2	1.0	29.2	0.0	29.2	0.0	29.1	-0.3
1954	29.1	0.0	29.2	0.3	29.2	0.0	29.2	0.0	29.2	0.0	29.2	0.0	29.3	0.3	29.3	0.0	29.3	0.0	29.3	0.0	29.2	-0.3	29.2	0.0
1955	29.0	-0.7	29.1	0.3	29.4	1.0	29.4	0.0	29.4	0.0	29.4	0.0	29.4	0.0	29.5	0.3	29.8	1.0	29.9	0.3	29.9	0.0	29.9	0.0
1956	30.2	1.0	30.2	0.0	30.2	0.0	30.3	0.3	30.3	0.0	30.3	0.0	30.6	1.0	30.7	0.3	31.1	1.3	31.1	0.0	31.2	0.3	31.2	0.0
1957	31.3	0.3	31.3	0.0	31.3	0.0	31.5	0.6	31.5	0.0	31.5	0.0	31.4	-0.3	31.4	0.0	31.4	0.0	31.5	0.3	31.5	0.0	31.6	0.3
1958	31.8	0.6	31.8	0.0	31.8	0.0	31.8	0.0	31.9	0.3	31.9	0.0	32.0	0.3	31.9	-0.3	31.8	-0.3	31.9	0.3	31.9	0.0	32.0	0.3
1959	32.0	0.0	32.1	0.3	32.2	0.3	32.2	0.0	32.3	0.3	32.3	0.0	32.3	0.0	32.3	0.0	32.4	0.3	32.4	0.0	32.4	0.0	32.4	0.0
1960	32.5	0.3	32.6	0.3	32.6	0.0	32.6	0.0	32.7	0.3	32.6	-0.3	32.6	0.0	32.6	0.0	32.6	0.0	32.6	0.0	32.6	0.0	32.6	0.0
1961	32.6	0.0	32.6	0.0	32.6	0.0	32.6	0.0	32.6	0.0	32.6	0.0	32.6	0.0	32.6	0.0	32.7	0.3	32.7	0.0	32.6	-0.3	32.6	0.0
1962	32.6	0.0	32.7	0.3	32.7	0.0	32.7	0.0	32.6	-0.3	32.6	0.0	32.7	0.3	32.7	0.0	32.7	0.0	32.7	0.0	32.7	0.0	32.6	-0.3
1963	32.6	0.0	32.6	0.0	32.6	0.0	32.6	0.0	32.5	-0.3	32.5	0.0	32.2	-0.9	32.2	0.0	32.3	0.3	32.3	0.0	32.3	0.0	32.3	0.0
1964	32.2	-0.3	32.2	0.0	32.1	-0.3	32.0	-0.3	32.0	0.0	32.1	0.3	32.1	0.0	32.1	0.0	32.2	0.3	32.2	0.0	32.2	0.0	32.2	0.0
1965	32.3	0.3	32.2	-0.3	32.2	0.0	32.3	0.3	32.3	0.0	32.4	0.3	32.4	0.0	32.3	-0.3	32.4	0.3	32.4	0.0	32.4	0.0	32.4	0.0
1966	32.5	0.3	32.5	0.0	32.6	0.3	32.7	0.3	32.7	0.0	32.8	0.3	32.8	0.0	32.9	0.3	33.0	0.3	33.0	0.0	33.0	0.0	33.1	0.3
1967	33.3	0.6	33.4	0.3	33.4	0.0	33.5	0.3	33.5	0.0	33.6	0.3	33.6	0.0	33.7	0.3	33.7	0.0	33.7	0.0	33.7	0.0	33.7	0.0
1968	33.9	0.6	34.0	0.3	34.1	0.3	34.3	0.6	34.3	0.0	34.5	0.6	34.5	0.0	34.6	0.3	34.6	0.0	34.8	0.6	34.8	0.0	34.9	0.3
1969	35.3	1.1	35.4	0.3	35.5	0.3	35.6	0.3	35.6	0.0	35.6	0.0	35.8	0.6	35.9	0.3	36.1	0.6	36.2	0.3	36.2	0.0	36.4	0.6
1970	37.0	1.6	37.1	0.3	37.3	0.5	37.3	0.0	37.4	0.3	37.6	0.5	37.7	0.3	37.8	0.3	38.1	0.8	38.1	0.0	38.2	0.3	38.4	0.5

[Continued]

Concrete Products
Producer Price Index
Base 1982 = 100
[Continued]

For 1926-1993. Columns headed % show percentile change in the index from the previous period for which an index is available.

Year	Jan Index	%	Feb Index	%	Mar Index	%	Apr Index	%	May Index	%	Jun Index	%	Jul Index	%	Aug Index	%	Sep Index	%	Oct Index	%	Nov Index	%	Dec Index	%
1971	39.3	2.3	39.5	0.5	39.8	0.8	40.1	0.8	40.1	0.0	40.3	0.5	40.8	1.2	41.2	1.0	41.1	-0.2	41.1	0.0	41.1	0.0	41.3	0.5
1972	41.4	0.2	41.6	0.5	41.8	0.5	42.0	0.5	42.0	0.0	42.1	0.2	42.3	0.5	42.3	0.0	42.4	0.2	42.7	0.7	42.7	0.0	42.8	0.2
1973	43.1	0.7	43.3	0.5	43.5	0.5	43.9	0.9	44.1	0.5	44.4	0.7	44.4	0.0	44.4	0.0	44.5	0.2	44.9	0.9	45.0	0.2	45.2	0.4
1974	47.0	4.0	47.8	1.7	48.6	1.7	48.8	0.4	49.6	1.6	50.3	1.4	52.1	3.6	52.5	0.8	52.8	0.6	53.6	1.5	53.9	0.6	54.3	0.7
1975	56.1	3.3	56.4	0.5	56.8	0.7	57.0	0.4	57.1	0.2	57.2	0.2	57.5	0.5	57.5	0.0	57.5	0.0	57.8	0.5	57.9	0.2	58.1	0.3
1976	59.6	2.6	59.8	0.3	59.8	0.0	59.9	0.2	60.2	0.5	60.3	0.2	60.8	0.8	60.9	0.2	60.9	0.0	60.9	0.0	61.2	0.5	61.5	0.5
1977	62.9	2.3	63.1	0.3	63.2	0.2	63.8	0.9	64.0	0.3	64.1	0.2	64.7	0.9	65.0	0.5	65.1	0.2	65.5	0.6	65.6	0.2	65.7	0.2
1978	68.1	3.7	68.9	1.2	69.2	0.4	69.8	0.9	70.4	0.9	71.1	1.0	72.0	1.3	73.8	2.5	74.4	0.8	74.6	0.3	74.8	0.3	75.3	0.7
1979	79.1	5.0	79.4	0.4	79.8	0.5	80.7	1.1	81.1	0.5	81.8	0.9	82.3	0.6	82.7	0.5	83.5	1.0	84.0	0.6	84.1	0.1	85.0	1.1
1980	89.1	4.8	89.6	0.6	90.3	0.8	91.6	1.4	92.4	0.9	92.6	0.2	92.6	0.0	92.7	0.1	93.1	0.4	93.2	0.1	93.3	0.1	93.2	-0.1
1981	96.1	3.1	96.2	0.1	96.3	0.1	97.3	1.0	97.8	0.5	98.5	0.7	98.5	0.0	98.5	0.0	98.4	-0.1	98.5	0.1	98.5	0.0	98.6	0.1
1982	99.2	0.6	99.3	0.1	99.5	0.2	100.0	0.5	100.1	0.1	100.2	0.1	100.3	0.1	100.4	0.1	100.3	-0.1	100.3	0.0	100.1	-0.2	100.2	0.1
1983	100.5	0.3	100.8	0.3	100.9	0.1	101.1	0.2	101.1	0.0	101.3	0.2	101.5	0.2	101.7	0.2	101.9	0.2	101.9	0.0	102.1	0.2	102.2	0.1
1984	102.4	0.2	102.7	0.3	102.8	0.1	103.7	0.9	103.9	0.2	104.1	0.2	104.3	0.2	104.5	0.2	104.7	0.2	104.8	0.1	104.7	-0.1	104.8	0.1
1985	105.6	0.8	105.6	0.0	106.0	0.4	106.3	0.3	107.5	1.1	107.9	0.4	107.9	0.0	108.4	0.5	108.5	0.1	108.4	-0.1	108.6	0.2	108.8	0.2
1986	109.1	0.3	109.1	0.0	109.1	0.0	109.6	0.5	109.6	0.0	109.3	-0.3	109.4	0.1	109.2	-0.2	109.1	-0.1	108.9	-0.2	108.9	0.0	109.1	0.2
1987	109.4	0.3	109.4	0.0	109.2	-0.2	109.3	0.1	109.4	0.1	109.3	-0.1	109.4	0.1	109.3	-0.1	109.4	0.1	109.4	0.0	109.6	0.2	109.4	-0.2
1988	109.7	0.3	109.8	0.1	109.8	0.0	109.7	-0.1	109.9	0.2	110.1	0.2	110.1	0.0	110.1	0.0	109.9	-0.2	109.9	0.0	110.2	0.3	110.3	0.1
1989	110.4	0.1	110.7	0.3	110.7	0.0	110.7	0.0	110.8	0.1	111.2	0.4	111.4	0.2	111.7	0.3	111.6	-0.1	111.6	0.0	111.6	0.0	111.9	0.3
1990	112.1	0.2	112.2	0.1	112.8	0.5	112.6	-0.2	113.1	0.4	113.3	0.2	113.7	0.4	113.9	0.2	114.2	0.3	114.2	0.0	114.8	0.5	115.0	0.2
1991	116.0	0.9	116.2	0.2	116.5	0.3	116.3	-0.2	116.5	0.2	116.9	0.3	117.0	0.1	116.9	-0.1	116.7	-0.2	116.7	0.0	116.7	0.0	116.9	0.2
1992	117.1	0.2	117.2	0.1	117.2	0.0	116.9	-0.3	117.1	0.2	117.0	-0.1	117.1	0.1	117.3	0.2	117.1	-0.2	117.2	0.1	117.7	0.4	118.0	0.3
1993	118.7	0.6	118.9	0.2	119.2	0.3	119.5	0.3	119.7	0.2	120.0	0.3	120.2	0.2	120.3	0.1	120.5	0.2	121.2	0.6	121.4	0.2	121.7	0.2

Source: U.S. Department of Labor, Bureau of Labor Statistics, Division of Industry Prices and Price Indexes. n.e.c. stands for not elsewhere classified. - indicates no data collected for period or unavailable.

Clay Construction Products Ex. Refractories
Producer Price Index
Base 1982 = 100

For 1947-1993. Columns headed % show percentile change in the index from the previous period for which an index is available.

Year	Jan Index	%	Feb Index	%	Mar Index	%	Apr Index	%	May Index	%	Jun Index	%	Jul Index	%	Aug Index	%	Sep Index	%	Oct Index	%	Nov Index	%	Dec Index	%
1947	23.5	-	23.5	0.0	23.6	0.4	23.6	0.0	23.7	0.4	23.7	0.0	23.7	0.0	24.0	1.3	24.2	0.8	24.3	0.4	24.5	0.8	24.5	0.0
1948	24.9	1.6	25.1	0.8	25.2	0.4	25.3	0.4	25.5	0.8	25.7	0.8	25.9	0.8	26.0	0.4	26.1	0.4	26.3	0.8	26.3	0.0	26.3	0.0
1949	26.5	0.8	26.5	0.0	26.5	0.0	26.5	0.0	26.5	0.0	26.5	0.0	26.5	0.0	26.4	-0.4	26.3	-0.4	26.3	0.0	26.4	0.4	26.4	0.0
1950	26.5	0.4	26.6	0.4	26.7	0.4	26.7	0.0	27.0	1.1	27.2	0.7	27.6	1.5	28.1	1.8	28.4	1.1	28.7	1.1	28.9	0.7	29.4	1.7
1951	29.8	1.4	29.9	0.3	29.9	0.0	29.9	0.0	29.9	0.0	29.9	0.0	29.9	0.0	29.9	0.0	29.9	0.0	29.9	0.0	29.9	0.0	29.9	0.0
1952	29.9	0.0	29.9	0.0	29.9	0.0	29.8	-0.3	29.9	0.3	29.9	0.0	29.8	-0.3	29.8	0.0	29.8	0.0	29.8	0.0	29.8	0.0	29.8	0.0
1953	29.8	0.0	29.8	0.0	29.9	0.3	30.1	0.7	30.1	0.0	30.3	0.7	30.4	0.3	30.6	0.7	30.8	0.7	30.8	0.0	30.8	0.0	30.8	0.0
1954	30.8	0.0	30.8	0.0	30.8	0.0	30.8	0.0	30.8	0.0	30.8	0.0	30.8	0.0	30.9	0.3	31.0	0.3	31.0	0.0	31.0	0.0	31.0	0.0
1955	31.2	0.6	31.3	0.3	31.5	0.6	31.6	0.3	31.7	0.3	31.9	0.6	32.0	0.3	32.3	0.9	32.8	1.5	33.0	0.6	33.0	0.0	33.1	0.3
1956	33.4	0.9	33.5	0.3	33.6	0.3	33.7	0.3	33.7	0.0	33.9	0.6	33.9	0.0	33.9	0.0	33.9	0.0	33.9	0.0	34.1	0.6	34.1	0.0
1957	34.2	0.3	34.2	0.0	34.3	0.3	34.3	0.0	34.3	0.0	34.4	0.3	34.4	0.0	34.3	-0.3	34.3	0.0	34.3	0.0	34.3	0.0	34.4	0.3
1958	34.5	0.3	34.5	0.0	34.5	0.0	34.5	0.0	34.5	0.0	34.5	0.0	34.5	0.0	34.5	0.0	34.6	0.3	34.6	0.0	34.7	0.3	34.9	0.6
1959	35.0	0.3	35.2	0.6	35.2	0.0	35.2	0.0	35.3	0.3	35.4	0.3	35.5	0.3	35.5	0.0	35.5	0.0	35.5	0.0	35.5	0.0	35.6	0.3
1960	35.8	0.6	35.9	0.3	35.9	0.0	35.9	0.0	35.9	0.0	35.9	0.0	35.9	0.0	36.0	0.3	36.1	0.3	36.1	0.0	36.1	0.0	36.1	0.0
1961	36.0	-0.3	36.0	0.0	36.0	0.0	36.0	0.0	36.1	0.3	36.1	0.0	36.1	0.0	36.2	0.3	36.2	0.0	36.3	0.3	36.3	0.0	36.3	0.0
1962	36.3	0.0	36.4	0.3	36.4	0.0	36.5	0.3	36.5	0.0	36.5	0.0	36.5	0.0	36.5	0.0	36.5	0.0	36.4	-0.3	36.4	0.0	36.4	0.0
1963	36.5	0.3	36.5	0.0	36.5	0.0	36.6	0.3	36.7	0.3	36.7	0.0	36.7	0.0	36.7	0.0	36.6	-0.3	36.6	0.0	36.7	0.3	36.7	0.0
1964	36.5	-0.5	36.7	0.5	36.7	0.0	36.8	0.3	36.8	0.0	36.7	-0.3	36.7	0.0	36.7	0.0	36.8	0.3	36.8	0.0	36.8	0.0	36.9	0.3
1965	36.9	0.0	36.9	0.0	36.9	0.0	36.9	0.0	36.9	0.0	36.9	0.0	36.9	0.0	37.1	0.5	37.2	0.3	37.2	0.0	37.2	0.0	37.3	0.3
1966	37.3	0.0	37.4	0.3	37.5	0.3	37.5	0.0	37.5	0.0	37.7	0.5	37.7	0.0	37.8	0.3	37.8	0.0	37.8	0.0	38.0	0.5	37.9	-0.3
1967	38.0	0.3	38.0	0.0	38.1	0.3	38.1	0.0	38.2	0.3	38.2	0.0	38.5	0.8	38.5	0.0	38.6	0.3	38.6	0.0	38.6	0.0	38.8	0.5
1968	38.9	0.3	38.9	0.0	39.0	0.3	39.0	0.0	39.2	0.5	39.0	-0.5	39.1	0.3	39.6	1.3	39.6	0.0	39.7	0.3	40.1	1.0	40.1	0.0
1969	40.3	0.5	40.3	0.0	40.3	0.0	40.6	0.7	40.6	0.0	40.6	0.0	40.6	0.0	40.7	0.2	40.9	0.5	41.0	0.2	41.2	0.5	41.2	0.0
1970	41.5	0.7	41.5	0.0	41.7	0.5	42.0	0.7	42.1	0.2	42.1	0.0	42.2	0.2	42.2	0.0	42.4	0.5	42.5	0.2	42.5	0.0	42.6	0.2
1971	43.0	0.9	43.5	1.2	43.8	0.7	44.0	0.5	44.0	0.0	44.1	0.2	44.1	0.0	44.3	0.5	44.0	-0.7	44.0	0.0	44.0	0.0	44.3	0.7
1972	44.0	-0.7	44.5	1.1	44.6	0.2	44.9	0.7	45.0	0.2	45.0	0.0	45.1	0.2	45.1	0.0	45.1	0.0	45.4	0.7	45.5	0.2	45.6	0.2
1973	46.1	1.1	46.6	1.1	46.9	0.6	47.2	0.6	47.4	0.4	47.5	0.2	47.5	0.0	47.5	0.0	47.5	0.0	47.8	0.6	47.8	0.0	47.9	0.2
1974	48.8	1.9	49.2	0.8	50.1	1.8	50.4	0.6	50.9	1.0	51.4	1.0	51.9	1.0	52.6	1.3	53.4	1.5	54.2	1.5	54.2	0.0	54.9	1.3
1975	55.7	1.5	56.3	1.1	56.3	0.0	57.0	1.2	57.2	0.4	57.9	1.2	58.0	0.2	58.4	0.7	59.1	1.2	59.7	1.0	59.9	0.3	59.9	0.0
1976	61.0	1.8	61.4	0.7	61.6	0.3	61.9	0.5	62.0	0.2	62.2	0.3	62.5	0.5	63.2	1.1	63.7	0.8	63.7	0.0	64.5	1.3	64.7	0.3
1977	65.2	0.8	64.6	-0.9	65.4	1.2	68.1	4.1	68.5	0.6	69.1	0.9	70.5	2.0	70.8	0.4	71.2	0.6	72.0	1.1	71.0	-1.4	71.2	0.3
1978	72.7	2.1	73.0	0.4	73.9	1.2	74.3	0.5	74.5	0.3	75.0	0.7	75.4	0.5	75.8	0.5	77.6	2.4	77.6	0.0	78.4	1.0	79.2	1.0
1979	80.4	1.5	80.8	0.5	81.6	1.0	82.4	1.0	82.7	0.4	83.0	0.4	84.5	1.8	85.3	0.9	85.8	0.6	84.8	-1.2	84.8	0.0	86.9	2.5
1980	88.0	1.3	88.6	0.7	88.7	0.1	90.1	1.6	88.2	-2.1	88.2	0.0	88.2	0.0	88.1	-0.1	88.2	0.1	89.5	1.5	89.6	0.1	89.6	0.0
1981	91.8	2.5	92.0	0.2	93.8	2.0	94.3	0.5	95.9	1.7	96.1	0.2	96.2	0.1	96.2	0.0	97.9	1.8	98.2	0.3	98.4	0.2	98.7	0.3
1982	98.7	0.0	98.8	0.1	98.8	0.0	99.0	0.2	99.2	0.2	99.3	0.1	99.4	0.1	101.2	1.8	101.2	0.0	101.2	0.0	101.5	0.3	101.5	0.0
1983	101.6	0.1	101.3	-0.3	103.8	2.5	105.7	1.8	106.5	0.8	107.9	1.3	108.3	0.4	108.3	0.0	108.3	0.0	108.7	0.4	108.9	0.2	109.0	0.1
1984	109.0	0.0	108.8	-0.2	109.0	0.2	109.3	0.3	109.5	0.2	109.8	0.3	109.8	0.0	110.5	0.6	111.0	0.5	111.0	0.0	111.0	0.0	111.1	0.1
1985	111.7	0.5	111.8	0.1	111.9	0.1	112.1	0.2	112.3	0.2	113.9	1.4	113.8	-0.1	114.2	0.4	114.5	0.3	114.7	0.2	114.9	0.2	115.8	0.8
1986	116.8	0.9	115.5	-1.1	116.8	1.1	117.6	0.7	117.7	0.1	118.3	0.5	119.2	0.8	119.0	-0.2	118.9	-0.1	119.6	0.6	118.6	-0.8	118.3	-0.3
1987	119.6	1.1	119.5	-0.1	119.8	0.3	120.9	0.9	121.4	0.4	121.8	0.3	121.5	-0.2	122.4	0.7	122.2	-0.2	122.5	0.2	122.7	0.2	122.7	0.0
1988	123.1	0.3	124.0	0.7	124.0	0.0	123.7	-0.2	124.4	0.6	125.4	0.8	125.9	0.4	125.1	-0.6	125.2	0.1	125.5	0.2	125.7	0.2	126.2	0.4
1989	126.1	-0.1	125.6	-0.4	126.3	0.6	126.5	0.2	125.7	-0.6	126.9	1.0	126.8	-0.1	127.5	0.6	127.7	0.2	127.9	0.2	128.2	0.2	128.6	0.3
1990	128.5	-0.1	128.6	0.1	129.4	0.6	129.4	0.0	129.6	0.2	130.0	0.3	130.5	0.4	130.4	-0.1	130.4	0.0	130.5	0.1	130.2	-0.2	130.7	0.4
1991	129.5	-0.9	129.7	0.2	129.9	0.2	130.4	0.4	130.6	0.2	130.2	-0.3	130.1	-0.1	130.0	-0.1	130.3	0.2	130.4	0.1	130.3	-0.1	130.4	0.1

[Continued]

Clay Construction Products Ex. Refractories
Producer Price Index
Base 1982 = 100
[Continued]

For 1947-1993. Columns headed % show percentile change in the index from the previous period for which an index is available.

Year	Jan Index	%	Feb Index	%	Mar Index	%	Apr Index	%	May Index	%	Jun Index	%	Jul Index	%	Aug Index	%	Sep Index	%	Oct Index	%	Nov Index	%	Dec Index	%
1992	130.3	-0.1	130.7	0.3	131.2	0.4	131.0	-0.2	132.0	0.8	132.4	0.3	132.5	0.1	132.7	0.2	132.6	-0.1	132.8	0.2	132.9	0.1	132.8	-0.1
1993	133.4	0.5	134.1	0.5	134.0	-0.1	134.7	0.5	134.9	0.1	135.3	0.3	135.5	0.1	135.8	0.2	135.8	0.0	136.0	0.1	136.1	0.1	135.9	-0.1

Source: U.S. Department of Labor, Bureau of Labor Statistics, Division of Industry Prices and Price Indexes. n.e.c. stands for not elsewhere classified. - indicates no data collected for period or unavailable.

Refractories

Producer Price Index
Base 1982 = 100

For 1947-1993. Columns headed % show percentile change in the index from the previous period for which an index is available.

Year	Jan Index	%	Feb Index	%	Mar Index	%	Apr Index	%	May Index	%	Jun Index	%	Jul Index	%	Aug Index	%	Sep Index	%	Oct Index	%	Nov Index	%	Dec Index	%
1947	13.4	-	13.4	0.0	13.4	0.0	14.5	8.2	14.5	0.0	14.5	0.0	14.5	0.0	14.5	0.0	14.5	0.0	14.5	0.0	15.0	3.4	15.1	0.7
1948	15.1	0.0	15.1	0.0	15.1	0.0	15.1	0.0	15.1	0.0	15.1	0.0	16.1	6.6	16.5	2.5	16.5	0.0	16.5	0.0	16.5	0.0	16.5	0.0
1949	16.5	0.0	16.5	0.0	16.5	0.0	16.5	0.0	16.5	0.0	16.5	0.0	16.5	0.0	16.5	0.0	16.5	0.0	16.5	0.0	16.5	0.0	16.5	0.0
1950	17.6	6.7	17.8	1.1	17.8	0.0	17.8	0.0	17.8	0.0	17.8	0.0	17.8	0.0	17.8	0.0	17.8	0.0	19.1	7.3	19.6	2.6	19.6	0.0
1951	19.6	0.0	19.6	0.0	19.6	0.0	19.6	0.0	19.6	0.0	19.6	0.0	19.6	0.0	19.6	0.0	19.6	0.0	19.6	0.0	19.6	0.0	19.6	0.0
1952	19.6	0.0	19.6	0.0	19.6	0.0	19.6	0.0	19.6	0.0	19.6	0.0	19.6	0.0	19.6	0.0	19.6	0.0	20.5	4.6	20.5	0.0	20.5	0.0
1953	20.5	0.0	20.5	0.0	20.5	0.0	20.5	0.0	20.5	0.0	20.5	0.0	22.5	9.8	22.5	0.0	22.5	0.0	22.5	0.0	22.5	0.0	22.5	0.0
1954	22.5	0.0	22.5	0.0	22.5	0.0	22.5	0.0	22.5	0.0	22.5	0.0	22.5	0.0	22.5	0.0	23.6	4.9	23.6	0.0	23.6	0.0	23.6	0.0
1955	23.6	0.0	23.6	0.0	23.6	0.0	23.6	0.0	23.6	0.0	23.6	0.0	24.9	5.5	25.2	1.2	25.2	0.0	25.2	0.0	25.2	0.0	25.2	0.0
1956	25.2	0.0	25.2	0.0	25.2	0.0	25.2	0.0	25.2	0.0	25.2	0.0	26.2	4.0	26.5	1.1	26.5	0.0	26.5	0.0	26.5	0.0	26.5	0.0
1957	26.5	0.0	26.5	0.0	26.5	0.0	27.9	5.3	27.9	0.0	27.9	0.0	27.9	0.0	27.9	0.0	27.9	0.0	27.9	0.0	27.9	0.0	27.9	0.0
1958	27.9	0.0	27.9	0.0	27.9	0.0	27.9	0.0	27.9	0.0	27.9	0.0	27.9	0.0	27.9	0.0	29.0	3.9	29.0	0.0	29.0	0.0	29.0	0.0
1959	29.0	0.0	29.0	0.0	29.0	0.0	29.0	0.0	29.0	0.0	29.0	0.0	29.0	0.0	29.0	0.0	29.0	0.0	29.0	0.0	29.0	0.0	29.0	0.0
1960	29.0	0.0	29.0	0.0	29.0	0.0	29.0	0.0	29.0	0.0	29.0	0.0	29.0	0.0	29.0	0.0	29.0	0.0	29.0	0.0	29.0	0.0	29.0	0.0
1961	29.0	0.0	29.0	0.0	29.0	0.0	29.0	0.0	28.7	-1.0	28.7	0.0	28.7	0.0	28.7	0.0	28.7	0.0	28.7	0.0	28.7	0.0	28.7	0.0
1962	28.7	0.0	28.7	0.0	28.7	0.0	28.7	0.0	28.7	0.0	28.7	0.0	28.7	0.0	28.7	0.0	28.7	0.0	28.7	0.0	28.7	0.0	28.7	0.0
1963	28.7	0.0	28.7	0.0	28.7	0.0	28.7	0.0	28.7	0.0	28.7	0.0	28.4	-1.0	28.4	0.0	28.4	0.0	28.4	0.0	28.4	0.0	28.4	0.0
1964	28.4	0.0	28.4	0.0	28.4	0.0	28.9	1.8	28.9	0.0	28.9	0.0	28.9	0.0	28.9	0.0	28.9	0.0	29.0	0.3	29.1	0.3	29.1	0.0
1965	29.1	0.0	29.1	0.0	29.1	0.0	29.1	0.0	29.1	0.0	29.1	0.0	29.1	0.0	29.1	0.0	29.1	0.0	29.1	0.0	29.1	0.0	29.1	0.0
1966	29.1	0.0	29.1	0.0	29.1	0.0	29.2	0.3	29.4	0.7	29.4	0.0	29.4	0.0	29.4	0.0	29.4	0.0	29.4	0.0	29.4	0.0	29.4	0.0
1967	29.6	0.7	29.6	0.0	29.6	0.0	29.6	0.0	29.6	0.0	29.6	0.0	29.6	0.0	29.6	0.0	29.6	0.0	29.6	0.0	29.9	1.0	29.9	0.0
1968	30.1	0.7	31.7	5.3	31.8	0.3	31.8	0.0	31.8	0.0	31.8	0.0	31.8	0.0	31.8	0.0	31.8	0.0	31.8	0.0	31.8	0.0	31.8	0.0
1969	31.8	0.0	31.8	0.0	31.8	0.0	32.1	0.9	32.1	0.0	32.1	0.0	32.1	0.0	33.0	2.8	33.1	0.3	33.1	0.0	33.1	0.0	34.1	3.0
1970	34.9	2.3	35.3	1.1	35.4	0.3	35.6	0.6	35.6	0.0	35.5	-0.3	35.6	0.3	35.6	0.0	35.6	0.0	35.6	0.0	37.6	5.6	37.6	0.0
1971	37.6	0.0	37.6	0.0	37.6	0.0	37.6	0.0	37.6	0.0	37.7	0.3	37.7	0.0	37.7	0.0	37.7	0.0	37.7	0.0	37.7	0.0	37.7	0.0
1972	37.7	0.0	37.7	0.0	37.7	0.0	37.7	0.0	37.7	0.0	37.7	0.0	37.7	0.0	38.5	2.1	39.2	1.8	39.2	0.0	39.2	0.0	39.2	0.0
1973	40.4	3.1	40.4	0.0	40.4	0.0	40.4	0.0	40.4	0.0	40.4	0.0	40.4	0.0	40.4	0.0	40.4	0.0	40.4	0.0	40.4	0.0	40.4	0.0
1974	40.4	0.0	40.4	0.0	40.4	0.0	40.4	0.0	40.4	0.0	40.4	0.0	40.9	1.2	40.9	0.0	45.5	11.2	46.6	2.4	46.8	0.4	47.6	1.7
1975	47.8	0.4	48.4	1.3	48.5	0.2	48.5	0.0	48.6	0.2	48.6	0.0	48.6	0.0	48.6	0.0	48.7	0.2	48.7	0.0	52.5	7.8	53.3	1.5
1976	53.3	0.0	53.3	0.0	53.4	0.2	53.5	0.2	53.5	0.0	53.5	0.0	53.6	0.2	53.8	0.4	56.0	4.1	56.7	1.3	57.2	0.9	57.2	0.0
1977	57.3	0.2	57.3	0.0	57.3	0.0	57.3	0.0	57.6	0.5	58.3	1.2	58.5	0.3	58.9	0.7	61.4	4.2	61.8	0.7	62.1	0.5	62.1	0.0
1978	62.2	0.2	62.3	0.2	62.3	0.0	62.4	0.2	62.5	0.2	62.5	0.0	63.2	1.1	66.0	4.4	66.4	0.6	66.9	0.8	67.1	0.3	67.1	0.0
1979	67.5	0.6	67.6	0.1	67.7	0.1	67.8	0.1	67.8	0.0	69.0	1.8	71.4	3.5	71.7	0.4	71.9	0.3	72.6	1.0	73.4	1.1	73.6	0.3
1980	73.7	0.1	74.5	1.1	75.3	1.1	77.6	3.1	78.4	1.0	78.9	0.6	79.7	1.0	80.3	0.8	80.3	0.0	81.1	1.0	81.1	0.0	81.1	0.0
1981	83.8	3.3	87.1	3.9	87.9	0.9	87.9	0.0	90.2	2.6	91.1	1.0	91.1	0.0	91.1	0.0	91.1	0.0	91.3	0.2	91.6	0.3	92.4	0.9
1982	94.0	1.7	99.4	5.7	100.1	0.7	100.5	0.4	100.7	0.2	101.0	0.3	101.0	0.0	101.1	0.1	101.1	0.0	101.1	0.0	100.0	-1.1	100.0	0.0
1983	100.2	0.2	100.2	0.0	100.2	0.0	100.3	0.1	100.3	0.0	99.9	-0.4	100.3	0.4	100.7	0.4	100.9	0.2	102.3	1.4	104.8	2.4	104.8	0.0
1984	105.0	0.2	105.6	0.6	107.1	1.4	107.3	0.2	107.3	0.0	107.3	0.0	107.3	0.0	107.3	0.0	107.3	0.0	107.3	0.0	108.4	1.0	108.4	0.0
1985	108.6	0.2	108.6	0.0	108.9	0.3	109.5	0.6	110.1	0.5	110.1	0.0	110.1	0.0	110.1	0.0	110.1	0.0	110.1	0.0	110.1	0.0	110.2	0.1
1986	110.2	0.0	110.2	0.0	110.2	0.0	110.3	0.1	110.5	0.2	110.5	0.0	110.5	0.0	110.5	0.0	110.4	-0.1	109.9	-0.5	109.3	-0.5	109.7	0.4
1987	109.9	0.2	109.9	0.0	109.9	0.0	110.0	0.1	110.0	0.0	110.4	0.4	110.6	0.2	110.8	0.2	110.9	0.1	110.9	0.0	111.1	0.2	111.9	0.7
1988	112.6	0.6	112.6	0.0	112.5	-0.1	113.5	0.9	113.7	0.2	113.8	0.1	113.8	0.0	113.8	0.0	114.1	0.3	115.1	0.9	115.2	0.1	115.4	0.2
1989	118.1	2.3	119.0	0.8	119.2	0.2	119.6	0.3	119.6	0.0	119.6	0.0	119.8	0.2	119.3	-0.4	119.4	0.1	119.6	0.2	119.6	0.0	119.6	0.0
1990	120.3	0.6	120.9	0.5	121.5	0.5	122.0	0.4	122.1	0.1	122.8	0.6	122.8	0.0	122.9	0.1	122.7	-0.2	122.8	0.1	123.4	0.5	123.4	0.0
1991	124.7	1.1	125.1	0.3	125.3	0.2	125.4	0.1	125.8	0.3	125.3	-0.4	125.3	0.0	125.4	0.1	125.5	0.1	125.5	0.0	125.5	0.0	125.9	0.3

[Continued]

Refractories

Producer Price Index
Base 1982 = 100
[Continued]

For 1947-1993. Columns headed % show percentile change in the index from the previous period for which an index is available.

Year	Jan Index	%	Feb Index	%	Mar Index	%	Apr Index	%	May Index	%	Jun Index	%	Jul Index	%	Aug Index	%	Sep Index	%	Oct Index	%	Nov Index	%	Dec Index	%
1992	126.1	0.2	125.6	-0.4	126.8	1.0	126.7	-0.1	126.7	0.0	126.8	0.1	126.3	-0.4	127.6	1.0	126.3	-1.0	126.3	0.0	125.2	-0.9	125.8	0.5
1993	126.1	0.2	126.1	0.0	126.5	0.3	126.5	0.0	127.2	0.6	127.4	0.2	127.7	0.2	127.9	0.2	127.6	-0.2	127.9	0.2	127.4	-0.4	127.8	0.3

Source: U.S. Department of Labor, Bureau of Labor Statistics, Division of Industry Prices and Price Indexes. n.e.c. stands for not elsewhere classified. - indicates no data collected for period or unavailable.

Asphalt Felts and Coatings
Producer Price Index
Base 1982 = 100

For 1926-1993. Columns headed % show percentile change in the index from the previous period for which an index is available.

Year	Jan Index	%	Feb Index	%	Mar Index	%	Apr Index	%	May Index	%	Jun Index	%	Jul Index	%	Aug Index	%	Sep Index	%	Oct Index	%	Nov Index	%	Dec Index	%
1926	20.6	-	20.5	-0.5	20.8	1.5	21.0	1.0	21.2	1.0	21.3	0.5	21.4	0.5	21.4	0.0	21.4	0.0	21.4	0.0	21.4	0.0	21.3	-0.5
1927	20.8	-2.3	20.8	0.0	20.5	-1.4	20.1	-2.0	20.3	1.0	20.3	0.0	20.2	-0.5	20.3	0.5	20.3	0.0	20.3	0.0	17.7	-12.8	17.8	0.6
1928	18.0	1.1	17.6	-2.2	15.6	-11.4	15.8	1.3	15.8	0.0	18.9	19.6	19.2	1.6	19.2	0.0	19.3	0.5	19.4	0.5	19.4	0.0	15.9	-18.0
1929	14.4	-9.4	14.3	-0.7	14.3	0.0	15.4	7.7	16.1	4.5	16.2	0.6	16.4	1.2	16.4	0.0	16.4	0.0	16.4	0.0	16.4	0.0	16.4	0.0
1930	15.6	-4.9	15.6	0.0	15.6	0.0	15.6	0.0	15.6	0.0	15.6	0.0	15.6	0.0	15.8	1.3	16.4	3.8	17.3	5.5	17.3	0.0	17.3	0.0
1931	16.7	-3.5	16.7	0.0	16.7	0.0	16.7	0.0	16.7	0.0	16.7	0.0	16.7	0.0	16.7	0.0	16.7	0.0	16.7	0.0	16.7	0.0	16.7	0.0
1932	15.8	-5.4	15.3	-3.2	15.5	1.3	15.6	0.6	15.3	-1.9	14.3	-6.5	13.2	-7.7	13.6	3.0	15.1	11.0	16.1	6.6	17.0	5.6	16.9	-0.6
1933	15.7	-7.1	13.7	-12.7	13.8	0.7	13.9	0.7	15.1	8.6	15.8	4.6	16.0	1.3	16.4	2.5	16.5	0.6	16.9	2.4	17.1	1.2	17.1	0.0
1934	17.2	0.6	16.2	-5.8	15.2	-6.2	15.4	1.3	16.2	5.2	16.6	2.5	17.0	2.4	17.5	2.9	17.7	1.1	17.7	0.0	17.7	0.0	17.8	0.6
1935	17.9	0.6	17.8	-0.6	17.7	-0.6	17.7	0.0	18.0	1.7	18.1	0.6	18.0	-0.6	17.5	-2.8	17.5	0.0	17.7	1.1	17.8	0.6	16.7	-6.2
1936	16.5	-1.2	16.4	-0.6	16.4	0.0	17.2	4.9	17.5	1.7	17.5	0.0	17.5	0.0	17.6	0.6	17.7	0.6	18.3	3.4	18.4	0.5	18.4	0.0
1937	18.5	0.5	18.7	1.1	19.3	3.2	19.3	0.0	19.8	2.6	20.0	1.0	20.0	0.0	20.0	0.0	19.6	-2.0	19.1	-2.6	18.3	-4.2	16.3	-10.9
1938	16.1	-1.2	15.9	-1.2	15.0	-5.7	15.2	1.3	15.3	0.7	15.3	0.0	15.3	0.0	15.3	0.0	15.3	0.0	15.3	0.0	15.3	0.0	15.3	0.0
1939	15.5	1.3	15.5	0.0	15.5	0.0	15.6	0.6	15.9	1.9	15.9	0.0	15.9	0.0	16.0	0.6	16.2	1.3	16.3	0.6	16.3	0.0	16.6	1.8
1940	17.0	2.4	17.0	0.0	17.5	2.9	17.8	1.7	17.8	0.0	17.8	0.0	17.7	-0.6	17.4	-1.7	17.3	-0.6	17.1	-1.2	17.1	0.0	17.1	0.0
1941	17.2	0.6	17.2	0.0	16.9	-1.7	16.7	-1.2	17.0	1.8	17.5	2.9	18.0	2.9	18.5	2.8	18.8	1.6	19.5	3.7	19.5	0.0	18.3	-6.2
1942	17.5	-4.4	17.5	0.0	17.5	0.0	17.5	0.0	17.5	0.0	17.5	0.0	17.5	0.0	17.5	0.0	17.5	0.0	17.5	0.0	17.5	0.0	17.5	0.0
1943	17.5	0.0	17.5	0.0	17.5	0.0	17.5	0.0	17.5	0.0	17.5	0.0	17.5	0.0	17.5	0.0	17.5	0.0	17.5	0.0	17.5	0.0	17.5	0.0
1944	17.5	0.0	17.5	0.0	17.5	0.0	17.5	0.0	17.5	0.0	17.5	0.0	17.5	0.0	17.6	0.6	17.9	1.7	18.0	0.6	18.0	0.0	18.0	0.0
1945	18.0	0.0	18.0	0.0	18.0	0.0	18.0	0.0	18.0	0.0	18.0	0.0	18.0	0.0	18.0	0.0	18.0	0.0	18.0	0.0	18.0	0.0	18.0	0.0
1946	18.0	0.0	18.0	0.0	18.0	0.0	18.0	0.0	18.5	2.8	18.9	2.2	19.0	0.5	19.1	0.5	19.1	0.0	19.2	0.5	19.3	0.5	20.7	7.3
1947	20.5	-1.0	20.6	0.5	21.4	3.9	21.6	0.9	21.6	0.0	21.6	0.0	21.6	0.0	21.5	-0.5	21.5	0.0	21.5	0.0	21.5	0.0	22.6	5.1
1948	23.2	2.7	23.2	0.0	23.2	0.0	23.2	0.0	23.2	0.0	23.2	0.0	23.6	1.7	24.2	2.5	23.6	-2.5	23.6	0.0	23.6	0.0	23.6	0.0
1949	23.6	0.0	23.6	0.0	23.6	0.0	23.6	0.0	23.6	0.0	23.6	0.0	23.4	-0.8	23.4	0.0	23.4	0.0	23.2	-0.9	23.2	0.0	23.2	0.0
1950	23.2	0.0	23.2	0.0	23.2	0.0	22.9	-1.3	22.5	-1.7	22.5	0.0	22.5	0.0	22.9	1.8	22.9	0.0	23.2	1.3	24.0	3.4	24.0	0.0
1951	24.0	0.0	24.0	0.0	24.0	0.0	24.0	0.0	24.0	0.0	24.0	0.0	24.0	0.0	24.0	0.0	24.0	0.0	24.0	0.0	24.0	0.0	22.5	-6.3
1952	22.5	0.0	22.5	0.0	22.5	0.0	22.5	0.0	22.5	0.0	24.2	7.6	24.2	0.0	24.2	0.0	24.2	0.0	24.2	0.0	24.2	0.0	24.2	0.0
1953	24.2	0.0	24.2	0.0	24.2	0.0	24.2	0.0	24.2	0.0	24.2	0.0	24.1	-0.4	24.1	0.0	25.0	3.7	25.1	0.4	25.1	0.0	25.1	0.0
1954	25.1	0.0	25.1	0.0	25.1	0.0	24.7	-1.6	21.9	-11.3	21.5	-1.8	22.5	4.7	22.5	0.0	23.7	5.3	24.2	2.1	24.2	0.0	24.2	0.0
1955	24.2	0.0	22.9	-5.4	22.5	-1.7	22.5	0.0	24.1	7.1	24.3	0.8	25.3	4.1	26.1	3.2	26.1	0.0	26.1	0.0	23.0	-11.9	23.0	0.0
1956	22.7	-1.3	22.7	0.0	24.3	7.0	25.5	4.9	25.5	0.0	25.5	0.0	26.9	5.5	26.8	-0.4	26.8	0.0	26.8	0.0	26.1	-2.6	26.1	0.0
1957	25.4	-2.7	26.3	3.5	26.9	2.3	27.7	3.0	28.7	3.6	28.7	0.0	28.7	0.0	28.7	0.0	28.4	-1.0	28.4	0.0	28.4	0.0	28.4	0.0
1958	28.4	0.0	28.4	0.0	24.4	-14.1	24.4	0.0	24.2	-0.8	23.5	-2.9	23.5	0.0	23.5	0.0	27.0	14.9	27.0	0.0	27.0	0.0	27.0	0.0
1959	27.0	0.0	27.3	1.1	27.2	-0.4	28.8	5.9	28.8	0.0	25.9	-10.1	25.5	-1.5	25.5	0.0	25.3	-0.8	25.3	0.0	25.9	2.4	25.9	0.0
1960	25.9	0.0	24.5	-5.4	24.5	0.0	24.3	-0.8	24.3	0.0	24.3	0.0	24.3	0.0	24.3	0.0	24.3	0.0	24.3	0.0	24.3	0.0	24.3	0.0
1961	26.0	7.0	26.0	0.0	26.0	0.0	26.0	0.0	25.8	-0.8	25.8	0.0	26.0	0.8	26.0	0.0	26.0	0.0	27.5	5.8	27.5	0.0	27.5	0.0
1962	27.3	-0.7	27.1	-0.7	27.1	0.0	27.1	0.0	26.4	-2.6	25.5	-3.4	23.9	-6.3	23.9	0.0	23.9	0.0	23.9	0.0	23.9	0.0	23.9	0.0
1963	23.9	0.0	25.1	5.0	25.1	0.0	25.1	0.0	24.7	-1.6	23.8	-3.6	23.5	-1.3	23.5	0.0	23.5	0.0	23.3	-0.9	23.3	0.0	23.3	0.0
1964	23.3	0.0	23.3	0.0	23.1	-0.9	23.1	0.0	23.1	0.0	23.1	0.0	23.7	2.6	24.3	2.5	24.3	0.0	24.3	0.0	24.3	0.0	24.3	0.0
1965	24.3	0.0	24.3	0.0	24.5	0.8	24.6	0.4	24.6	0.0	24.6	0.0	24.6	0.0	24.6	0.0	25.4	3.3	25.3	-0.4	25.3	0.0	25.3	0.0
1966	25.3	0.0	25.3	0.0	25.3	0.0	25.3	0.0	25.2	-0.4	25.2	0.0	26.1	3.6	26.1	0.0	26.1	0.0	26.1	0.0	26.1	0.0	25.6	-1.9
1967	25.6	0.0	25.3	-1.2	25.3	0.0	25.3	0.0	23.6	-6.7	23.6	0.0	24.4	3.4	24.4	0.0	25.3	3.7	25.3	0.0	26.5	4.7	26.5	0.0
1968	26.6	0.4	26.2	-1.5	26.2	0.0	26.1	-0.4	26.1	0.0	25.8	-1.1	26.1	1.2	26.1	0.0	25.4	-2.7	25.4	0.0	25.4	0.0	25.4	0.0
1969	25.4	0.0	26.1	2.8	26.0	-0.4	26.0	0.0	25.6	-1.5	26.3	2.7	26.6	1.1	25.1	-5.6	25.1	0.0	25.1	0.0	25.1	0.0	27.1	8.0
1970	27.2	0.4	26.9	-1.1	26.1	-3.0	25.4	-2.7	25.4	0.0	24.5	-3.5	24.3	-0.8	24.9	2.5	25.4	2.0	25.6	0.8	26.5	3.5	26.9	1.5

[Continued]

Asphalt Felts and Coatings
Producer Price Index
Base 1982 = 100
[Continued]

For 1926-1993. Columns headed % show percentile change in the index from the previous period for which an index is available.

Year	Jan Index	%	Feb Index	%	Mar Index	%	Apr Index	%	May Index	%	Jun Index	%	Jul Index	%	Aug Index	%	Sep Index	%	Oct Index	%	Nov Index	%	Dec Index	%
1971	27.3	1.5	27.3	0.0	31.0	13.6	31.0	0.0	31.0	0.0	32.8	5.8	32.9	0.3	32.9	0.0	32.9	0.0	32.9	0.0	32.9	0.0	32.9	0.0
1972	32.9	0.0	32.9	0.0	32.9	0.0	32.9	0.0	32.9	0.0	32.9	0.0	32.9	0.0	32.9	0.0	32.9	0.0	32.9	0.0	32.9	0.0	32.9	0.0
1973	32.9	0.0	32.9	0.0	32.9	0.0	33.7	2.4	34.3	1.8	34.3	0.0	34.2	-0.3	34.2	0.0	34.2	0.0	34.3	0.3	35.1	2.3	35.1	0.0
1974	37.7	7.4	40.1	6.4	43.0	7.2	48.2	12.1	50.2	4.1	50.8	1.2	51.8	2.0	52.9	2.1	52.9	0.0	54.1	2.3	54.3	0.4	54.3	0.0
1975	54.3	0.0	54.7	0.7	54.7	0.0	57.2	4.6	57.2	0.0	57.2	0.0	57.5	0.5	56.9	-1.0	57.4	0.9	58.1	1.2	57.5	-1.0	57.5	0.0
1976	57.5	0.0	57.6	0.2	59.3	3.0	60.1	1.3	59.6	-0.8	59.6	0.0	59.6	0.0	62.1	4.2	61.6	-0.8	61.7	0.2	60.1	-2.6	58.9	-2.0
1977	57.9	-1.7	57.9	0.0	61.0	5.4	61.0	0.0	61.0	0.0	61.8	1.3	63.6	2.9	63.6	0.0	67.0	5.3	69.1	3.1	69.1	0.0	69.1	0.0
1978	69.6	0.7	69.6	0.0	69.7	0.1	72.2	3.6	72.2	0.0	72.6	0.6	74.2	2.2	74.7	0.7	74.8	0.1	76.6	2.4	76.6	0.0	76.6	0.0
1979	77.0	0.5	79.8	3.6	76.1	-4.6	79.4	4.3	79.8	0.5	81.1	1.6	82.4	1.6	81.8	-0.7	83.6	2.2	84.7	1.3	87.2	3.0	87.0	-0.2
1980	89.5	2.9	93.5	4.5	97.6	4.4	102.6	5.1	100.7	-1.9	100.6	-0.1	103.9	3.3	103.2	-0.7	102.4	-0.8	102.5	0.1	99.7	-2.7	99.1	-0.6
1981	99.1	0.0	97.8	-1.3	98.0	0.2	104.4	6.5	102.3	-2.0	107.6	5.2	105.9	-1.6	105.6	-0.3	100.8	-4.5	101.1	0.3	103.0	1.9	101.8	-1.2
1982	100.7	-1.1	100.5	-0.2	99.0	-1.5	97.1	-1.9	96.8	-0.3	99.5	2.8	100.4	0.9	100.4	0.0	103.8	3.4	102.1	-1.6	100.2	-1.9	99.6	-0.6
1983	98.8	-0.8	95.5	-3.3	94.0	-1.6	96.4	2.6	95.4	-1.0	95.3	-0.1	96.7	1.5	96.2	-0.5	97.2	1.0	97.4	0.2	97.3	-0.1	96.4	-0.9
1984	96.6	0.2	98.5	2.0	96.8	-1.7	99.4	2.7	100.1	0.7	99.0	-1.1	99.0	0.0	102.5	3.5	102.4	-0.1	102.7	0.3	102.9	0.2	103.4	0.5
1985	102.8	-0.6	102.3	-0.5	101.9	-0.4	103.4	1.5	103.6	0.2	103.0	-0.6	103.0	0.0	102.5	-0.5	102.1	-0.4	101.7	-0.4	102.7	1.0	102.2	-0.5
1986	101.8	-0.4	101.8	0.0	100.6	-1.2	99.3	-1.3	99.3	0.0	97.3	-2.0	97.1	-0.2	97.3	0.2	96.6	-0.7	95.6	-1.0	94.6	-1.0	94.0	-0.6
1987	91.8	-2.3	91.5	-0.3	90.8	-0.8	91.4	0.7	91.3	-0.1	90.9	-0.4	90.6	-0.3	92.8	2.4	93.4	0.6	94.4	1.1	94.9	0.5	94.8	-0.1
1988	93.8	-1.1	92.7	-1.2	93.4	0.8	92.7	-0.7	93.1	0.4	94.6	1.6	95.8	1.3	95.6	-0.2	96.3	0.7	97.1	0.8	96.0	-1.1	95.4	-0.6
1989	95.0	-0.4	94.9	-0.1	94.2	-0.7	96.0	1.9	95.7	-0.3	95.9	0.2	95.8	-0.1	95.7	-0.1	96.2	0.5	96.6	0.4	96.7	0.1	97.1	0.4
1990	97.1	0.0	95.8	-1.3	95.7	-0.1	96.0	0.3	95.6	-0.4	94.9	-0.7	94.3	-0.6	95.9	1.7	96.5	0.6	100.4	4.0	101.5	1.1	101.7	0.2
1991	100.5	-1.2	100.0	-0.5	100.4	0.4	99.3	-1.1	97.9	-1.4	98.4	0.5	98.4	0.0	97.0	-1.4	97.2	0.2	97.1	-0.1	96.5	-0.6	96.0	-0.5
1992	96.0	0.0	95.6	-0.4	95.4	-0.2	95.1	-0.3	95.6	0.5	95.9	0.3	96.3	0.4	96.2	-0.1	96.0	-0.2	97.1	1.1	98.1	1.0	97.8	-0.3
1993	98.2	0.4	97.3	-0.9	97.6	0.3	96.9	-0.7	96.7	-0.2	96.8	0.1	97.0	0.2	97.1	0.1	96.6	-0.5	96.4	-0.2	96.1	-0.3	96.0	-0.1

Source: U.S. Department of Labor, Bureau of Labor Statistics, Division of Industry Prices and Price Indexes. n.e.c. stands for not elsewhere classified. - indicates no data collected for period or unavailable.

Gypsum Products
Producer Price Index
Base 1982 = 100

For 1947-1993. Columns headed % show percentile change in the index from the previous period for which an index is available.

Year	Jan Index	%	Feb Index	%	Mar Index	%	Apr Index	%	May Index	%	Jun Index	%	Jul Index	%	Aug Index	%	Sep Index	%	Oct Index	%	Nov Index	%	Dec Index	%
1947	26.9	-	26.9	0.0	26.9	0.0	26.9	0.0	26.9	0.0	26.9	0.0	26.9	0.0	26.9	0.0	26.9	0.0	28.6	6.3	29.4	2.8	29.4	0.0
1948	29.4	0.0	29.4	0.0	29.4	0.0	29.6	0.7	30.2	2.0	30.2	0.0	30.2	0.0	30.2	0.0	30.2	0.0	30.2	0.0	30.2	0.0	30.1	-0.3
1949	29.8	-1.0	29.7	-0.3	29.7	0.0	29.7	0.0	29.7	0.0	29.7	0.0	29.7	0.0	29.7	0.0	29.7	0.0	29.7	0.0	29.7	0.0	29.7	0.0
1950	29.7	0.0	29.7	0.0	29.7	0.0	29.7	0.0	29.7	0.0	29.7	0.0	29.7	0.0	30.4	2.4	31.1	2.3	31.1	0.0	31.1	0.0	32.9	5.8
1951	34.1	3.6	34.1	0.0	34.1	0.0	34.1	0.0	34.1	0.0	34.1	0.0	34.1	0.0	34.1	0.0	34.1	0.0	34.1	0.0	34.2	0.3	34.2	0.0
1952	34.2	0.0	34.2	0.0	34.2	0.0	34.2	0.0	34.2	0.0	34.2	0.0	34.2	0.0	34.2	0.0	34.2	0.0	34.2	0.0	34.2	0.0	34.2	0.0
1953	34.2	0.0	34.2	0.0	34.4	0.6	35.5	3.2	35.5	0.0	35.5	0.0	35.5	0.0	35.5	0.0	35.5	0.0	35.5	0.0	35.5	0.0	35.5	0.0
1954	35.5	0.0	35.5	0.0	35.5	0.0	35.5	0.0	35.5	0.0	35.5	0.0	35.5	0.0	35.5	0.0	35.5	0.0	35.5	0.0	35.5	0.0	35.5	0.0
1955	35.5	0.0	35.5	0.0	35.5	0.0	35.5	0.0	35.5	0.0	35.5	0.0	35.5	0.0	35.5	0.0	35.5	0.0	35.5	0.0	35.5	0.0	35.5	0.0
1956	36.9	3.9	36.9	0.0	36.9	0.0	36.9	0.0	36.9	0.0	36.9	0.0	36.9	0.0	36.9	0.0	36.9	0.0	36.9	0.0	36.9	0.0	36.9	0.0
1957	36.9	0.0	36.9	0.0	36.9	0.0	36.9	0.0	36.9	0.0	36.9	0.0	36.9	0.0	36.9	0.0	36.9	0.0	36.9	0.0	36.9	0.0	36.9	0.0
1958	36.9	0.0	36.9	0.0	38.7	4.9	38.7	0.0	38.7	0.0	38.7	0.0	38.7	0.0	38.7	0.0	38.7	0.0	38.7	0.0	38.7	0.0	38.7	0.0
1959	38.7	0.0	38.7	0.0	38.7	0.0	38.7	0.0	38.7	0.0	38.7	0.0	38.7	0.0	38.7	0.0	38.7	0.0	38.7	0.0	38.7	0.0	38.7	0.0
1960	38.7	0.0	38.7	0.0	38.7	0.0	38.7	0.0	38.7	0.0	38.7	0.0	38.7	0.0	38.7	0.0	38.7	0.0	38.7	0.0	38.7	0.0	38.7	0.0
1961	39.1	1.0	39.1	0.0	39.1	0.0	39.1	0.0	39.1	0.0	39.1	0.0	39.1	0.0	39.9	2.0	39.9	0.0	39.9	0.0	39.9	0.0	39.9	0.0
1962	39.9	0.0	39.9	0.0	39.9	0.0	39.9	0.0	39.9	0.0	39.9	0.0	39.9	0.0	39.9	0.0	39.9	0.0	39.9	0.0	39.9	0.0	39.9	0.0
1963	39.9	0.0	39.9	0.0	39.9	0.0	39.9	0.0	39.9	0.0	39.9	0.0	39.9	0.0	40.2	0.8	40.3	0.2	40.3	0.0	40.3	0.0	40.3	0.0
1964	40.3	0.0	41.2	2.2	41.2	0.0	41.2	0.0	41.2	0.0	41.2	0.0	41.2	0.0	41.2	0.0	41.2	0.0	41.2	0.0	41.2	0.0	40.5	-1.7
1965	40.5	0.0	40.9	1.0	41.2	0.7	41.1	-0.2	41.1	0.0	40.9	-0.5	40.1	-2.0	38.2	-4.7	38.0	-0.5	37.6	-1.1	37.5	-0.3	37.0	-1.3
1966	38.5	4.1	38.5	0.0	38.5	0.0	38.5	0.0	38.8	0.8	39.0	0.5	39.0	0.0	39.0	0.0	39.0	0.0	39.0	0.0	39.3	0.8	39.3	0.0
1967	39.4	0.3	39.4	0.0	38.9	-1.3	38.9	0.0	38.9	0.0	38.4	-1.3	38.3	-0.3	38.3	0.0	38.3	0.0	40.1	4.7	40.1	0.0	40.1	0.0
1968	40.1	0.0	40.5	1.0	40.5	0.0	40.5	0.0	40.5	0.0	40.5	0.0	40.5	0.0	40.5	0.0	40.5	0.0	40.3	-0.5	40.3	0.0	40.3	0.0
1969	40.3	0.0	40.3	0.0	40.3	0.0	40.3	0.0	41.7	3.5	40.2	-3.6	40.2	0.0	39.6	-1.5	40.2	1.5	40.9	1.7	41.6	1.7	39.5	-5.0
1970	40.7	3.0	41.2	1.2	40.6	-1.5	40.1	-1.2	39.5	-1.5	38.3	-3.0	38.1	-0.5	38.7	1.6	37.7	-2.6	37.9	0.5	37.5	-1.1	37.1	-1.1
1971	38.0	2.4	39.4	3.7	40.4	2.5	41.4	2.5	42.6	2.9	43.4	1.9	44.0	1.4	44.7	1.6	45.0	0.7	44.7	-0.7	44.1	-1.3	44.8	1.6
1972	44.3	-1.1	44.1	-0.5	45.0	2.0	44.9	-0.2	44.3	-1.3	44.5	0.5	45.2	1.6	45.4	0.4	45.0	-0.9	45.1	0.2	44.9	-0.4	44.9	0.0
1973	45.8	2.0	45.2	-1.3	46.1	2.0	46.7	1.3	47.0	0.6	48.5	3.2	48.0	-1.0	47.8	-0.4	47.6	-0.4	47.8	0.4	47.7	-0.2	48.1	0.8
1974	49.9	3.7	50.8	1.8	50.6	-0.4	51.8	2.4	52.1	0.6	53.7	3.1	54.2	0.9	55.8	3.0	56.9	2.0	56.5	-0.7	56.2	-0.5	56.4	0.4
1975	56.1	-0.5	56.1	0.0	56.9	1.4	56.2	-1.2	56.0	-0.4	56.0	0.0	55.0	-1.8	55.9	1.6	56.2	0.5	56.7	0.9	57.4	1.2	56.4	-1.7
1976	58.7	4.1	58.0	-1.2	58.7	1.2	58.9	0.3	60.0	1.9	59.9	-0.2	59.9	0.0	60.6	1.2	61.6	1.7	62.1	0.8	62.5	0.6	62.5	0.0
1977	62.8	0.5	63.5	1.1	64.1	0.9	67.2	4.8	68.7	2.2	73.1	6.4	72.9	-0.3	74.1	1.6	75.6	2.0	78.7	4.1	79.4	0.9	80.0	0.8
1978	81.9	2.4	84.3	2.9	84.8	0.6	86.4	1.9	89.1	3.1	89.9	0.9	91.4	1.7	92.1	0.8	92.2	0.1	92.5	0.3	94.5	2.2	94.8	0.3
1979	96.7	2.0	97.9	1.2	98.0	0.1	98.5	0.5	97.2	-1.3	98.2	1.0	98.3	0.1	98.5	0.2	99.6	1.1	99.7	0.1	100.1	0.4	99.6	-0.5
1980	99.7	0.1	102.4	2.7	104.5	2.1	103.1	-1.3	100.2	-2.8	100.4	0.2	98.9	-1.5	98.4	-0.5	98.3	-0.1	97.5	-0.8	98.9	1.4	98.7	-0.2
1981	101.4	2.7	100.5	-0.9	100.6	0.1	100.3	-0.3	102.0	1.7	101.8	-0.2	101.4	-0.4	99.7	-1.7	98.8	-0.9	98.6	-0.2	98.2	-0.4	97.5	-0.7
1982	97.8	0.3	99.6	1.8	101.8	2.2	102.8	1.0	101.3	-1.5	100.1	-1.2	99.9	-0.2	99.2	-0.7	99.2	0.0	99.6	0.4	99.6	0.0	99.2	-0.4
1983	102.7	3.5	104.4	1.7	103.9	-0.5	106.2	2.2	107.7	1.4	106.9	-0.7	107.8	0.8	113.0	4.8	116.3	2.9	122.2	5.1	123.1	0.7	126.0	2.4
1984	128.3	1.8	132.6	3.4	132.6	0.0	137.9	4.0	140.9	2.2	140.7	-0.1	140.5	-0.1	140.4	-0.1	138.8	-1.1	132.4	-4.6	130.6	-1.4	129.1	-1.1
1985	128.3	-0.6	134.5	4.8	131.4	-2.3	130.2	-0.9	130.1	-0.1	132.0	1.5	132.2	0.2	132.1	-0.1	129.4	-2.0	132.7	2.6	135.9	2.4	139.2	2.4
1986	140.7	1.1	141.4	0.5	137.4	-2.8	135.2	-1.6	140.7	4.1	138.3	-1.7	136.5	-1.3	134.3	-1.6	133.2	-0.8	134.0	0.6	137.0	2.2	135.7	-0.9
1987	133.9	-1.3	131.8	-1.6	127.1	-3.6	127.2	0.1	129.5	1.8	128.0	-1.2	124.0	-3.1	119.5	-3.6	118.8	-0.6	119.8	0.8	120.8	0.8	121.5	0.6
1988	120.9	-0.5	116.7	-3.5	113.3	-2.9	111.7	-1.4	112.7	0.9	110.4	-2.0	108.6	-1.6	108.0	-0.6	110.6	2.4	113.6	2.7	114.6	0.9	113.9	-0.6
1989	111.3	-2.3	110.8	-0.4	110.1	-0.6	110.3	0.2	110.6	0.3	110.4	-0.2	109.8	-0.5	107.9	-1.7	108.9	0.9	109.5	0.6	111.5	1.8	109.4	-1.9
1990	106.9	-2.3	106.0	-0.8	106.3	0.3	106.8	0.5	107.0	0.2	106.2	-0.7	105.4	-0.8	102.4	-2.8	104.0	1.6	103.4	-0.6	104.5	1.1	103.3	-1.1
1991	102.8	-0.5	105.4	2.5	104.8	-0.6	101.4	-3.2	100.3	-1.1	97.0	-3.3	96.0	-1.0	95.0	-1.0	97.5	2.6	98.2	0.7	96.8	-1.4	96.9	0.1

[Continued]

Gypsum Products
Producer Price Index
Base 1982 = 100
[Continued]

For 1947-1993. Columns headed % show percentile change in the index from the previous period for which an index is available.

Year	Jan Index	%	Feb Index	%	Mar Index	%	Apr Index	%	May Index	%	Jun Index	%	Jul Index	%	Aug Index	%	Sep Index	%	Oct Index	%	Nov Index	%	Dec Index	%
1992	94.8	-2.2	92.8	-2.1	96.0	3.4	96.6	0.6	100.5	4.0	100.4	-0.1	100.4	0.0	103.0	2.6	105.4	2.3	104.1	-1.2	104.0	-0.1	101.2	-2.7
1993	99.4	-1.8	102.0	2.6	103.4	1.4	108.8	5.2	108.2	-0.6	107.6	-0.6	106.7	-0.8	110.2	3.3	114.3	3.7	112.1	-1.9	113.8	1.5	114.1	0.3

Source: U.S. Department of Labor, Bureau of Labor Statistics, Division of Industry Prices and Price Indexes. n.e.c. stands for not elsewhere classified. - indicates no data collected for period or unavailable.

Glass Containers
Producer Price Index
Base 1982 = 100

For 1947-1993. Columns headed % show percentile change in the index from the previous period for which an index is available.

Year	Jan Index	%	Feb Index	%	Mar Index	%	Apr Index	%	May Index	%	Jun Index	%	Jul Index	%	Aug Index	%	Sep Index	%	Oct Index	%	Nov Index	%	Dec Index	%
1947	14.1	-	14.5	2.8	14.5	0.0	14.5	0.0	14.5	0.0	14.5	0.0	14.9	2.8	14.9	0.0	14.9	0.0	14.9	0.0	14.9	0.0	14.9	0.0
1948	14.9	0.0	14.9	0.0	14.9	0.0	16.9	13.4	16.9	0.0	16.9	0.0	16.9	0.0	16.9	0.0	16.9	0.0	19.2	13.6	19.2	0.0	19.2	0.0
1949	19.2	0.0	19.2	0.0	19.2	0.0	19.2	0.0	19.2	0.0	19.0	-1.0	19.0	0.0	19.0	0.0	19.0	0.0	19.0	0.0	19.0	0.0	19.0	0.0
1950	18.7	-1.6	18.7	0.0	18.7	0.0	18.7	0.0	18.7	0.0	18.7	0.0	18.7	0.0	18.7	0.0	18.7	0.0	20.0	7.0	20.0	0.0	20.0	0.0
1951	20.6	3.0	20.6	0.0	20.6	0.0	20.6	0.0	20.6	0.0	20.6	0.0	20.6	0.0	20.6	0.0	20.6	0.0	20.6	0.0	20.6	0.0	20.6	0.0
1952	20.6	0.0	20.6	0.0	20.6	0.0	20.6	0.0	21.4	3.9	21.4	0.0	21.4	0.0	21.4	0.0	21.4	0.0	21.4	0.0	21.4	0.0	21.4	0.0
1953	21.4	0.0	21.4	0.0	21.4	0.0	23.2	8.4	23.2	0.0	23.2	0.0	23.2	0.0	23.2	0.0	23.2	0.0	23.0	-0.9	23.0	0.0	23.0	0.0
1954	23.0	0.0	23.0	0.0	23.0	0.0	24.1	4.8	24.1	0.0	24.1	0.0	24.1	0.0	24.1	0.0	24.1	0.0	24.1	0.0	24.1	0.0	24.1	0.0
1955	24.1	0.0	24.1	0.0	24.1	0.0	24.1	0.0	24.1	0.0	24.1	0.0	24.1	0.0	24.1	0.0	24.3	0.8	24.3	0.0	24.3	0.0	24.3	0.0
1956	24.9	2.5	24.9	0.0	24.9	0.0	24.9	0.0	24.9	0.0	24.9	0.0	24.9	0.0	24.9	0.0	24.9	0.0	26.7	7.2	26.7	0.0	26.7	0.0
1957	26.7	0.0	26.7	0.0	26.7	0.0	26.7	0.0	26.7	0.0	26.7	0.0	26.7	0.0	26.7	0.0	26.7	0.0	26.7	0.0	26.9	0.7	28.3	5.2
1958	28.3	0.0	28.3	0.0	28.3	0.0	28.3	0.0	28.3	0.0	28.3	0.0	28.3	0.0	28.3	0.0	28.3	0.0	28.3	0.0	28.3	0.0	28.3	0.0
1959	28.3	0.0	28.3	0.0	28.3	0.0	28.3	0.0	28.3	0.0	28.3	0.0	28.3	0.0	28.3	0.0	28.3	0.0	28.3	0.0	28.3	0.0	28.3	0.0
1960	28.2	-0.4	28.2	0.0	28.2	0.0	27.5	-2.5	27.5	0.0	27.5	0.0	27.5	0.0	27.5	0.0	27.5	0.0	27.0	-1.8	27.0	0.0	27.0	0.0
1961	27.0	0.0	27.0	0.0	27.0	0.0	27.8	3.0	27.8	0.0	27.8	0.0	27.4	-1.4	27.4	0.0	27.4	0.0	27.4	0.0	27.4	0.0	26.9	-1.8
1962	26.9	0.0	26.9	0.0	26.9	0.0	26.9	0.0	26.9	0.0	26.9	0.0	26.9	0.0	26.9	0.0	26.9	0.0	26.9	0.0	26.9	0.0	26.9	0.0
1963	26.9	0.0	26.9	0.0	26.9	0.0	26.9	0.0	26.9	0.0	26.8	-0.4	26.8	0.0	26.8	0.0	26.8	0.0	26.8	0.0	26.8	0.0	26.8	0.0
1964	26.8	0.0	26.8	0.0	26.8	0.0	27.1	1.1	27.1	0.0	27.1	0.0	27.1	0.0	27.1	0.0	27.1	0.0	27.1	0.0	27.1	0.0	27.1	0.0
1965	27.1	0.0	27.1	0.0	27.1	0.0	27.1	0.0	27.1	0.0	27.2	0.4	27.2	0.0	27.3	0.4	27.3	0.0	27.3	0.0	27.8	1.8	27.8	0.0
1966	27.8	0.0	27.9	0.4	27.8	-0.4	27.6	-0.7	27.6	0.0	27.6	0.0	27.6	0.0	27.6	0.0	27.6	0.0	28.1	1.8	28.1	0.0	28.1	0.0
1967	28.1	0.0	28.1	0.0	28.1	0.0	28.1	0.0	28.1	0.0	28.1	0.0	28.1	0.0	28.1	0.0	28.1	0.0	28.1	0.0	28.1	0.0	28.1	0.0
1968	29.3	4.3	29.6	1.0	29.6	0.0	29.6	0.0	30.5	3.0	30.5	0.0	30.5	0.0	30.5	0.0	30.5	0.0	30.7	0.7	30.7	0.0	30.7	0.0
1969	32.3	5.2	32.3	0.0	32.3	0.0	32.3	0.0	32.3	0.0	32.3	0.0	32.3	0.0	32.3	0.0	32.3	0.0	32.3	0.0	32.3	0.0	32.3	0.0
1970	33.6	4.0	33.6	0.0	33.6	0.0	33.6	0.0	33.6	0.0	33.6	0.0	33.6	0.0	33.6	0.0	33.6	0.0	33.6	0.0	35.0	4.2	35.0	0.0
1971	37.1	6.0	37.0	-0.3	37.0	0.0	37.0	0.0	37.0	0.0	37.0	0.0	37.0	0.0	37.0	0.0	37.0	0.0	37.0	0.0	37.0	0.0	37.0	0.0
1972	37.0	0.0	37.0	0.0	37.0	0.0	38.3	3.5	38.3	0.0	38.3	0.0	38.4	0.3	38.4	0.0	38.4	0.0	38.4	0.0	38.4	0.0	38.4	0.0
1973	38.4	0.0	38.4	0.0	38.4	0.0	38.5	0.3	38.5	0.0	39.8	3.4	38.6	-3.0	38.6	0.0	38.6	0.0	40.4	4.7	40.4	0.0	40.4	0.0
1974	40.4	0.0	40.4	0.0	41.0	1.5	41.3	0.7	44.2	7.0	44.3	0.2	44.3	0.0	44.3	0.0	44.3	0.0	46.7	5.4	46.7	0.0	46.7	0.0
1975	46.7	0.0	49.8	6.6	49.8	0.0	49.8	0.0	49.8	0.0	49.8	0.0	49.8	0.0	52.3	5.0	52.2	-0.2	52.2	0.0	52.2	0.0	52.2	0.0
1976	52.1	-0.2	52.1	0.0	52.1	0.0	55.3	6.1	55.5	0.4	55.5	0.0	55.5	0.0	55.5	0.0	55.5	0.0	56.8	2.3	56.8	0.0	56.8	0.0
1977	56.8	0.0	56.8	0.0	56.8	0.0	61.3	7.9	61.3	0.0	61.3	0.0	61.3	0.0	61.3	0.0	61.3	0.0	61.5	0.3	61.5	0.0	61.5	0.0
1978	66.5	8.1	66.5	0.0	66.5	0.0	66.5	0.0	66.5	0.0	70.0	5.3	70.0	0.0	70.5	0.7	70.5	0.0	70.5	0.0	70.5	0.0	70.5	0.0
1979	70.5	0.0	70.5	0.0	70.5	0.0	70.5	0.0	74.6	5.8	74.6	0.0	74.6	0.0	74.6	0.0	74.6	0.0	74.6	0.0	74.6	0.0	77.1	3.4
1980	77.1	0.0	77.1	0.0	77.1	0.0	82.8	7.4	82.8	0.0	82.8	0.0	82.8	0.0	82.8	0.0	82.8	0.0	86.1	4.0	86.1	0.0	87.6	1.7
1981	87.6	0.0	87.6	0.0	87.6	0.0	91.9	4.9	94.3	2.6	94.3	0.0	94.4	0.1	94.4	0.0	94.4	0.0	94.4	0.0	94.4	0.0	94.4	0.0
1982	94.3	-0.1	99.1	5.1	100.1	1.0	100.7	0.6	100.7	0.0	100.7	0.0	100.7	0.0	100.7	0.0	100.9	0.2	100.8	-0.1	100.6	-0.2	100.6	0.0
1983	100.3	-0.3	100.1	-0.2	99.6	-0.5	99.4	-0.2	99.0	-0.4	98.9	-0.1	98.9	0.0	98.8	-0.1	98.8	0.0	98.5	-0.3	98.5	0.0	98.6	0.1
1984	98.6	0.0	98.6	0.0	98.9	0.3	100.7	1.8	101.8	1.1	102.7	0.9	103.0	0.3	103.0	0.0	102.5	-0.5	102.6	0.1	102.4	-0.2	102.4	0.0
1985	102.3	-0.1	102.5	0.2	105.2	2.6	105.3	0.1	105.9	0.6	107.4	1.4	108.8	1.3	108.9	0.1	108.8	-0.1	109.2	0.4	108.8	-0.4	108.8	0.0
1986	109.5	0.6	109.5	0.0	111.0	1.4	111.1	0.1	112.2	1.0	112.6	0.4	112.8	0.2	113.1	0.3	113.1	0.0	112.7	-0.4	112.7	0.0	112.5	-0.2
1987	112.5	0.0	113.4	0.8	113.7	0.3	113.8	0.1	113.2	-0.5	113.3	0.1	113.0	-0.3	112.9	-0.1	112.9	0.0	112.7	-0.2	112.5	-0.2	112.5	0.0
1988	112.3	-0.2	112.2	-0.1	112.2	0.0	112.1	-0.1	112.1	0.0	112.2	0.1	112.2	0.0	112.5	0.3	112.3	-0.2	112.3	0.0	112.3	0.0	112.3	0.0
1989	112.3	0.0	112.3	0.0	113.8	1.3	116.9	2.7	116.4	-0.4	115.9	-0.4	115.9	0.0	115.9	0.0	115.7	-0.2	115.7	0.0	115.7	0.0	115.7	0.0
1990	118.9	2.8	119.5	0.5	120.0	0.4	120.2	0.2	120.4	0.2	120.7	0.2	120.7	0.0	120.7	0.0	121.0	0.2	121.0	0.0	121.0	0.0	121.0	0.0
1991	124.8	3.1	124.9	0.1	125.0	0.1	125.3	0.2	125.6	0.2	125.6	0.0	125.6	0.0	125.5	-0.1	125.7	0.2	125.7	0.0	125.7	0.0	125.7	0.0

[Continued]

Glass Containers
Producer Price Index
Base 1982 = 100
[Continued]

For 1947-1993. Columns headed % show percentile change in the index from the previous period for which an index is available.

Year	Jan Index	%	Feb Index	%	Mar Index	%	Apr Index	%	May Index	%	Jun Index	%	Jul Index	%	Aug Index	%	Sep Index	%	Oct Index	%	Nov Index	%	Dec Index	%
1992	125.5	-0.2	125.5	0.0	125.4	-0.1	125.3	-0.1	125.0	-0.2	125.1	0.1	125.1	0.0	125.0	-0.1	124.9	-0.1	124.9	0.0	124.7	-0.2	124.7	0.0
1993	124.5	-0.2	124.9	0.3	125.0	0.1	124.9	-0.1	125.4	0.4	126.0	0.5	126.4	0.3	126.5	0.1	127.1	0.5	126.7	-0.3	126.6	-0.1	126.6	0.0

Source: U.S. Department of Labor, Bureau of Labor Statistics, Division of Industry Prices and Price Indexes. n.e.c. stands for not elsewhere classified. - indicates no data collected for period or unavailable.

Nonmetallic Minerals n.e.c.
Producer Price Index
Base 1982 = 100

For 1947-1993. Columns headed % show percentile change in the index from the previous period for which an index is available.

Year	Jan Index	%	Feb Index	%	Mar Index	%	Apr Index	%	May Index	%	Jun Index	%	Jul Index	%	Aug Index	%	Sep Index	%	Oct Index	%	Nov Index	%	Dec Index	%
1947	14.4	-	14.6	1.4	14.7	0.7	14.8	0.7	14.9	0.7	14.9	0.0	14.9	0.0	14.9	0.0	15.0	0.7	15.0	0.0	15.5	3.3	15.7	1.3
1948	15.9	1.3	16.0	0.6	16.0	0.0	16.1	0.6	16.1	0.0	16.3	1.2	16.6	1.8	16.6	0.0	16.6	0.0	16.6	0.0	16.5	-0.6	16.7	1.2
1949	16.6	-0.6	16.6	0.0	16.6	0.0	16.6	0.0	16.6	0.0	16.6	0.0	16.5	-0.6	16.4	-0.6	16.4	0.0	16.3	-0.6	16.3	0.0	16.3	0.0
1950	16.3	0.0	16.7	2.5	16.8	0.6	16.8	0.0	16.8	0.0	16.8	0.0	16.9	0.6	17.1	1.2	17.3	1.2	17.3	0.0	17.4	0.6	17.7	1.7
1951	17.7	0.0	17.7	0.0	17.7	0.0	17.7	0.0	17.7	0.0	17.7	0.0	17.7	0.0	17.7	0.0	17.7	0.0	17.7	0.0	17.7	0.0	17.7	0.0
1952	17.7	0.0	17.7	0.0	17.7	0.0	17.8	0.6	17.8	0.0	17.8	0.0	17.8	0.0	17.8	0.0	17.8	0.0	17.9	0.6	18.3	2.2	18.4	0.5
1953	18.4	0.0	18.4	0.0	18.4	0.0	18.4	0.0	18.4	0.0	18.5	0.5	18.7	1.1	18.8	0.5	18.8	0.0	18.8	0.0	18.9	0.5	18.9	0.0
1954	19.1	1.1	19.1	0.0	19.1	0.0	19.1	0.0	19.1	0.0	19.1	0.0	19.1	0.0	19.2	0.5	19.2	0.0	19.2	0.0	19.0	-1.0	19.0	0.0
1955	19.0	0.0	19.0	0.0	19.0	0.0	19.0	0.0	19.3	1.6	19.5	1.0	19.5	0.0	19.5	0.0	19.6	0.5	19.6	0.0	19.4	-1.0	19.4	0.0
1956	19.4	0.0	19.6	1.0	19.5	-0.5	19.6	0.5	19.6	0.0	19.6	0.0	19.7	0.5	19.7	0.0	19.7	0.0	19.8	0.5	19.8	0.0	19.8	0.0
1957	19.8	0.0	20.1	1.5	20.3	1.0	20.4	0.5	20.4	0.0	20.4	0.0	20.4	0.0	20.5	0.5	20.5	0.0	20.5	0.0	20.5	0.0	20.9	2.0
1958	20.9	0.0	20.9	0.0	20.9	0.0	20.9	0.0	20.9	0.0	20.9	0.0	20.9	0.0	20.9	0.0	20.9	0.0	20.9	0.0	20.9	0.0	20.9	0.0
1959	20.9	0.0	21.0	0.5	21.1	0.5	21.1	0.0	21.1	0.0	21.1	0.0	21.1	0.0	21.1	0.0	21.1	0.0	21.1	0.0	21.1	0.0	21.1	0.0
1960	21.1	0.0	21.3	0.9	21.3	0.0	21.4	0.5	21.4	0.0	21.4	0.0	21.4	0.0	21.4	0.0	21.4	0.0	21.5	0.5	21.3	-0.9	21.3	0.0
1961	21.3	0.0	21.2	-0.5	21.3	0.5	21.3	0.0	21.3	0.0	21.3	0.0	21.3	0.0	21.3	0.0	21.2	-0.5	21.2	0.0	21.2	0.0	21.1	-0.5
1962	21.1	0.0	21.4	1.4	21.4	0.0	21.4	0.0	21.2	-0.9	21.2	0.0	21.1	-0.5	21.1	0.0	21.1	0.0	21.2	0.5	21.3	0.5	21.3	0.0
1963	21.2	-0.5	21.1	-0.5	21.1	0.0	21.1	0.0	21.1	0.0	21.0	-0.5	21.0	0.0	20.9	-0.5	21.0	0.5	21.1	0.5	21.1	0.0	21.1	0.0
1964	21.0	-0.5	21.0	0.0	21.0	0.0	21.0	0.0	21.0	0.0	21.1	0.5	21.2	0.5	21.2	0.0	21.1	-0.5	21.1	0.0	21.1	0.0	21.0	-0.5
1965	21.0	0.0	21.0	0.0	21.1	0.5	21.1	0.0	21.1	0.0	21.1	0.0	21.1	0.0	21.1	0.0	21.0	-0.5	21.0	0.0	21.0	0.0	21.0	0.0
1966	21.2	1.0	21.1	-0.5	21.2	0.5	21.2	0.0	21.1	-0.5	21.0	-0.5	21.1	0.5	21.2	0.5	21.2	0.0	21.2	0.0	21.0	-0.9	21.0	0.0
1967	21.1	0.5	21.1	0.0	21.3	0.9	21.2	-0.5	21.2	0.0	21.2	0.0	21.2	0.0	21.2	0.0	21.1	-0.5	21.2	0.5	21.2	0.0	21.3	0.5
1968	21.6	1.4	21.6	0.0	21.6	0.0	21.6	0.0	21.6	0.0	21.9	1.4	22.0	0.5	22.0	0.0	22.0	0.0	22.2	0.9	22.2	0.0	22.2	0.0
1969	22.3	0.5	22.4	0.4	22.4	0.0	22.7	1.3	22.7	0.0	22.7	0.0	22.7	0.0	22.7	0.0	22.8	0.4	23.0	0.9	23.0	0.0	23.0	0.0
1970	23.0	0.0	23.1	0.4	23.4	1.3	23.6	0.9	23.6	0.0	23.6	0.0	23.7	0.4	23.8	0.4	23.8	0.0	24.4	2.5	24.4	0.0	24.9	2.0
1971	25.6	2.8	25.7	0.4	25.7	0.0	25.9	0.8	26.5	2.3	26.5	0.0	26.6	0.4	26.6	0.0	26.6	0.0	26.6	0.0	26.6	0.0	26.6	0.0
1972	26.6	0.0	26.7	0.4	26.8	0.4	26.8	0.0	27.2	1.5	27.0	-0.7	26.9	-0.4	26.9	0.0	27.0	0.4	27.0	0.0	27.0	0.0	27.0	0.0
1973	27.1	0.4	27.1	0.0	27.2	0.4	27.2	0.0	27.4	0.7	27.5	0.4	27.1	-1.5	27.1	0.0	27.0	-0.4	27.0	0.0	27.1	0.4	27.9	3.0
1974	31.9	14.3	35.4	11.0	36.2	2.3	37.5	3.6	40.1	6.9	40.4	0.7	41.4	2.5	42.0	1.4	42.8	1.9	43.1	0.7	44.4	3.0	44.5	0.2
1975	45.2	1.6	45.3	0.2	45.3	0.0	46.4	2.4	46.4	0.0	46.6	0.4	47.3	1.5	47.4	0.2	47.3	-0.2	47.7	0.8	47.6	-0.2	47.7	0.2
1976	48.5	1.7	48.5	0.0	49.3	1.6	49.0	-0.6	49.2	0.4	49.2	0.0	49.3	0.2	49.2	-0.2	49.7	1.0	49.8	0.2	49.8	0.0	49.8	0.0
1977	51.0	2.4	51.2	0.4	52.0	1.6	52.5	1.0	52.5	0.0	53.1	1.1	53.3	0.4	53.8	0.9	54.6	1.5	54.3	-0.5	54.3	0.0	54.5	0.4
1978	55.3	1.5	56.7	2.5	56.9	0.4	57.0	0.2	57.2	0.4	58.1	1.6	59.9	3.1	59.8	-0.2	59.8	0.0	60.0	0.3	60.1	0.2	60.1	0.0
1979	61.2	1.8	62.3	1.8	62.4	0.2	63.6	1.9	64.2	0.9	64.0	-0.3	65.8	2.8	65.7	-0.2	71.2	8.4	72.3	1.5	72.5	0.3	72.5	0.0
1980	74.6	2.9	80.9	8.4	82.0	1.4	84.7	3.3	84.9	0.2	83.7	-1.4	84.1	0.5	84.2	0.1	84.9	0.8	85.4	0.6	85.5	0.1	88.8	3.9
1981	88.7	-0.1	90.0	1.5	93.6	4.0	101.5	8.4	101.2	-0.3	101.1	-0.1	100.9	-0.2	100.7	-0.2	100.5	-0.2	100.3	-0.2	100.4	0.1	100.6	0.2
1982	100.6	0.0	101.5	0.9	101.6	0.1	101.5	-0.1	99.9	-1.6	98.6	-1.3	98.9	0.3	98.8	-0.1	99.1	0.3	99.7	0.6	99.9	0.2	99.8	-0.1
1983	99.9	0.1	100.9	1.0	101.0	0.1	101.5	0.5	101.4	-0.1	101.6	0.2	101.7	0.1	102.1	0.4	102.3	0.2	102.4	0.1	103.3	0.9	103.2	-0.1
1984	103.1	-0.1	103.4	0.3	104.0	0.6	104.1	0.1	104.9	0.8	105.8	0.9	107.5	1.6	108.4	0.8	108.0	-0.4	107.9	-0.1	107.2	-0.6	107.5	0.3
1985	109.0	1.4	109.0	0.0	109.0	0.0	110.0	0.9	110.9	0.8	111.0	0.1	111.0	0.0	111.1	0.1	111.1	0.0	111.5	0.4	111.0	-0.4	110.9	-0.1
1986	111.1	0.2	110.9	-0.2	110.8	-0.1	110.6	-0.2	111.0	0.4	111.0	0.0	110.4	-0.5	109.5	-0.8	109.3	-0.2	109.6	0.3	109.4	-0.2	109.0	-0.4
1987	108.6	-0.4	109.1	0.5	109.6	0.5	109.8	0.2	109.6	-0.2	110.3	0.6	110.9	0.5	110.1	-0.7	110.6	0.5	111.8	1.1	111.9	0.1	111.3	-0.5
1988	112.5	1.1	112.8	0.3	112.9	0.1	113.1	0.2	113.2	0.1	113.4	0.2	112.4	-0.9	112.3	-0.1	112.7	0.4	112.8	0.1	113.0	0.2	113.2	0.2
1989	113.6	0.4	113.5	-0.1	113.9	0.4	114.3	0.4	114.1	-0.2	114.2	0.1	114.5	0.3	114.4	-0.1	114.4	0.0	114.3	-0.1	114.5	0.2	114.7	0.2
1990	115.2	0.4	115.4	0.2	115.4	0.0	115.5	0.1	115.5	0.0	115.6	0.1	115.6	0.0	115.8	0.2	116.5	0.6	116.6	0.1	117.6	0.9	117.7	0.1
1991	118.5	0.7	118.4	-0.1	118.3	-0.1	118.5	0.2	118.6	0.1	118.5	-0.1	118.4	-0.1	118.4	0.0	118.4	0.0	118.5	0.1	118.5	0.0	118.1	-0.3

[Continued]

Nonmetallic Minerals n.e.c.
Producer Price Index
Base 1982 = 100
[Continued]

For 1947-1993. Columns headed % show percentile change in the index from the previous period for which an index is available.

Year	Jan Index	%	Feb Index	%	Mar Index	%	Apr Index	%	May Index	%	Jun Index	%	Jul Index	%	Aug Index	%	Sep Index	%	Oct Index	%	Nov Index	%	Dec Index	%
1992	117.8	-0.3	118.0	0.2	117.8	-0.2	116.1	-1.4	115.0	-0.9	115.5	0.4	115.8	0.3	116.0	0.2	116.0	0.0	116.0	0.0	116.2	0.2	116.3	0.1
1993	117.6	1.1	117.8	0.2	118.0	0.2	118.5	0.4	118.7	0.2	119.2	0.4	119.7	0.4	119.8	0.1	119.8	0.0	120.8	0.8	120.3	-0.4	119.9	-0.3

Source: U.S. Department of Labor, Bureau of Labor Statistics, Division of Industry Prices and Price Indexes. n.e.c. stands for not elsewhere classified. - indicates no data collected for period or unavailable.

TRANSPORTATION EQUIPMENT
Producer Price Index
Base 1982 = 100

For 1969-1993. Columns headed % show percentile change in the index from the previous period for which an index is available.

Year	Jan Index	%	Feb Index	%	Mar Index	%	Apr Index	%	May Index	%	Jun Index	%	Jul Index	%	Aug Index	%	Sep Index	%	Oct Index	%	Nov Index	%	Dec Index	%
1969	40.1	-	40.1	0.0	40.1	0.0	40.1	0.0	40.1	0.0	40.2	0.2	40.2	0.0	40.1	-0.2	40.1	0.0	41.0	2.2	41.2	0.5	41.2	0.0
1970	41.3	0.2	41.2	-0.2	41.4	0.5	41.3	-0.2	41.4	0.2	41.4	0.0	41.4	0.0	41.5	0.2	41.5	0.0	43.3	4.3	43.5	0.5	43.5	0.0
1971	43.7	0.5	43.9	0.5	44.0	0.2	44.0	0.0	44.1	0.2	44.1	0.0	44.3	0.5	44.3	0.0	43.9	-0.9	44.4	1.1	44.4	0.0	45.2	1.8
1972	45.4	0.4	45.5	0.2	45.5	0.0	45.6	0.2	45.6	0.0	45.7	0.2	45.7	0.0	45.7	0.0	45.7	0.0	45.2	-1.1	45.3	0.2	45.7	0.9
1973	45.7	0.0	45.7	0.0	45.9	0.4	46.0	0.2	46.1	0.2	46.0	-0.2	46.1	0.2	46.1	0.0	45.9	-0.4	46.4	1.1	46.5	0.2	47.0	1.1
1974	47.5	1.1	47.6	0.2	47.7	0.2	47.8	0.2	48.6	1.7	49.2	1.2	50.1	1.8	50.8	1.4	51.1	0.6	53.8	5.3	54.1	0.6	54.9	1.5
1975	54.9	0.0	55.4	0.9	55.9	0.9	56.0	0.2	56.0	0.0	56.1	0.2	56.1	0.0	56.3	0.4	56.5	0.4	58.7	3.9	59.0	0.5	59.1	0.2
1976	59.6	0.8	59.6	0.0	59.7	0.2	59.7	0.0	59.7	0.0	59.8	0.2	59.8	0.0	60.2	0.7	60.5	0.5	62.5	3.3	62.6	0.2	62.9	0.5
1977	62.9	0.0	63.0	0.2	63.4	0.6	63.6	0.3	63.7	0.2	63.9	0.3	63.9	0.0	64.4	0.8	64.7	0.5	67.2	3.9	67.3	0.1	67.4	0.1
1978	67.7	0.4	67.9	0.3	67.9	0.0	68.3	0.6	68.9	0.9	69.1	0.3	69.2	0.1	69.3	0.1	69.5	0.3	71.8	3.3	72.1	0.4	72.3	0.3
1979	73.2	1.2	73.5	0.4	73.6	0.1	74.8	1.6	75.0	0.3	75.1	0.1	75.4	0.4	74.5	-1.2	74.8	0.4	77.8	4.0	78.0	0.3	78.3	0.4
1980	79.6	1.7	79.4	-0.3	79.6	0.3	81.4	2.3	81.1	-0.4	81.4	0.4	82.6	1.5	83.6	1.2	81.9	-2.0	87.1	6.3	87.2	0.1	89.8	3.0
1981	91.1	1.4	91.8	0.8	91.4	-0.4	92.9	1.6	93.6	0.8	93.8	0.2	94.1	0.3	94.5	0.4	92.8	-1.8	97.9	5.5	98.7	0.8	98.9	0.2
1982	99.6	0.7	98.2	-1.4	98.2	0.0	98.4	0.2	99.1	0.7	99.8	0.7	100.1	0.3	100.4	0.3	97.9	-2.5	102.5	4.7	102.6	0.1	103.1	0.5
1983	102.7	-0.4	102.5	-0.2	102.2	-0.3	102.4	0.2	102.5	0.1	102.6	0.1	102.6	0.0	102.9	0.3	100.3	-2.5	104.4	4.1	104.4	0.0	104.4	0.0
1984	104.8	0.4	105.0	0.2	105.1	0.1	105.2	0.1	105.1	-0.1	105.0	-0.1	105.1	0.1	105.0	-0.1	103.2	-1.7	106.1	2.8	106.4	0.3	106.2	-0.2
1985	106.9	0.7	107.4	0.5	107.2	-0.2	107.4	0.2	107.8	0.4	107.9	0.1	108.1	0.2	108.1	0.0	104.1	-3.7	110.2	5.9	110.2	0.0	109.8	-0.4
1986	109.5	-0.3	109.7	0.2	109.5	-0.2	110.3	0.7	110.2	-0.1	110.3	0.1	110.4	0.1	110.0	-0.4	107.5	-2.3	113.2	5.3	113.1	-0.1	112.8	-0.3
1987	113.1	0.3	112.1	-0.9	112.4	0.3	113.0	0.5	112.4	-0.5	112.3	-0.1	112.2	-0.1	111.9	-0.3	110.9	-0.9	113.8	2.6	113.5	-0.3	112.5	-0.9
1988	113.2	0.6	113.2	0.0	113.1	-0.1	113.5	0.4	113.7	0.2	114.0	0.3	113.9	-0.1	114.0	0.1	113.2	-0.7	116.6	3.0	116.3	-0.3	116.3	0.0
1989	116.8	0.4	117.1	0.3	116.8	-0.3	116.4	-0.3	117.2	0.7	117.6	0.3	116.9	-0.6	117.1	0.2	116.6	-0.4	120.0	2.9	120.0	0.0	119.8	-0.2
1990	119.7	-0.1	120.2	0.4	120.3	0.1	120.5	0.2	120.4	-0.1	121.0	0.5	121.2	0.2	121.1	-0.1	121.0	-0.1	124.0	2.5	124.2	0.2	124.2	0.0
1991	125.2	0.8	125.7	0.4	125.7	0.0	125.5	-0.2	125.6	0.1	125.6	0.0	125.7	0.1	126.0	0.2	125.2	-0.6	129.1	3.1	128.9	-0.2	129.0	0.1
1992	129.8	0.6	129.7	-0.1	130.0	0.2	130.2	0.2	130.2	0.0	130.1	-0.1	130.2	0.1	130.0	-0.2	128.5	-1.2	132.3	3.0	132.2	-0.1	132.1	-0.1
1993	132.7	0.5	133.1	0.3	133.3	0.2	133.4	0.1	133.3	-0.1	133.3	0.0	133.6	0.2	133.5	-0.1	131.6	-1.4	135.3	2.8	135.3	0.0	135.5	0.1

Source: U.S. Department of Labor, Bureau of Labor Statistics, Division of Industry Prices and Price Indexes. n.e.c. stands for not elsewhere classified. - indicates no data collected for period or unavailable.

Motor Vehicles and Equipment
Producer Price Index
Base 1982 = 100

For 1926-1993. Columns headed % show percentile change in the index from the previous period for which an index is available.

Year	Jan Index	%	Feb Index	%	Mar Index	%	Apr Index	%	May Index	%	Jun Index	%	Jul Index	%	Aug Index	%	Sep Index	%	Oct Index	%	Nov Index	%	Dec Index	%
1926	-	-	-	-	-	-	-	-	-	-	-	-	-	-	-	-	-	-	-	-	-	-	-	-
1927	-	-	-	-	-	-	-	-	-	-	-	-	-	-	-	-	-	-	-	-	-	-	-	-
1928	-	-	-	-	-	-	-	-	-	-	-	-	-	-	-	-	-	-	-	-	-	-	-	-
1929	-	-	-	-	-	-	-	-	-	-	-	-	-	-	-	-	-	-	-	-	-	-	-	-
1930	-	-	-	-	-	-	-	-	-	-	-	-	-	-	-	-	-	-	-	-	-	-	-	-
1931	-	-	-	-	-	-	-	-	-	-	-	-	-	-	-	-	-	-	-	-	-	-	-	-
1932	-	-	-	-	-	-	-	-	-	-	-	-	-	-	-	-	-	-	-	-	-	-	-	-
1933	-	-	-	-	-	-	-	-	-	-	-	-	-	-	-	-	-	-	-	-	-	-	-	-
1934	-	-	-	-	-	-	-	-	-	-	-	-	-	-	-	-	-	-	-	-	-	-	-	-
1935	-	-	-	-	-	-	-	-	-	-	-	-	-	-	-	-	-	-	-	-	-	-	-	-
1936	-	-	-	-	-	-	-	-	-	-	-	-	-	-	-	-	-	-	-	-	-	-	-	-
1937	14.4	-	14.4	0.0	14.4	0.0	14.5	0.7	14.5	0.0	14.5	0.0	14.5	0.0	15.0	3.4	15.2	1.3	15.4	1.3	15.9	3.2	15.9	0.0
1938	15.9	0.0	15.9	0.0	15.9	0.0	15.9	0.0	16.0	0.6	16.0	0.0	16.0	0.0	16.0	0.0	16.0	0.0	15.8	-1.2	15.6	-1.3	15.6	0.0
1939	15.6	0.0	15.6	0.0	15.6	0.0	15.6	0.0	15.5	-0.6	15.5	0.0	15.5	0.0	15.4	-0.6	15.4	0.0	15.6	1.3	15.8	1.3	15.8	0.0
1940	15.8	0.0	15.8	0.0	15.8	0.0	15.8	0.0	15.8	0.0	15.8	0.0	15.9	0.6	15.9	0.0	16.0	0.6	16.7	4.4	16.7	0.0	16.7	0.0
1941	16.7	0.0	16.6	-0.6	16.6	0.0	16.7	0.6	16.7	0.0	16.7	0.0	16.8	0.6	16.8	0.0	16.8	0.0	18.7	11.3	18.7	0.0	18.7	0.0
1942	18.7	0.0	18.7	0.0	18.8	0.5	18.8	0.0	18.8	0.0	18.8	0.0	18.8	0.0	18.8	0.0	18.8	0.0	18.8	0.0	18.8	0.0	18.8	0.0
1943	18.8	0.0	18.8	0.0	18.8	0.0	18.8	0.0	18.8	0.0	18.8	0.0	18.8	0.0	18.8	0.0	18.8	0.0	18.8	0.0	18.8	0.0	18.8	0.0
1944	18.8	0.0	18.8	0.0	18.8	0.0	18.8	0.0	18.8	0.0	18.9	0.5	18.9	0.0	18.9	0.0	18.9	0.0	18.9	0.0	19.0	0.5	19.0	0.0
1945	19.0	0.0	19.0	0.0	19.1	0.5	19.1	0.0	19.2	0.5	19.3	0.5	19.3	0.0	19.3	0.0	19.3	0.0	19.3	0.0	19.5	1.0	19.5	0.0
1946	19.7	1.0	20.1	2.0	20.4	1.5	20.9	2.5	21.9	4.8	22.6	3.2	22.6	0.0	23.1	2.2	23.4	1.3	23.6	0.9	24.3	3.0	24.8	2.1
1947	24.9	0.4	24.9	0.0	24.9	0.0	24.8	-0.4	24.9	0.4	25.0	0.4	25.0	0.0	25.9	3.6	26.4	1.9	26.4	0.0	26.5	0.4	26.6	0.4
1948	26.8	0.8	26.7	-0.4	26.7	0.0	26.7	0.0	26.8	0.4	27.8	3.7	28.5	2.5	29.4	3.2	29.6	0.7	29.6	0.0	29.7	0.3	29.9	0.7
1949	30.0	0.3	30.3	1.0	30.4	0.3	30.2	-0.7	30.1	-0.3	30.0	-0.3	30.1	0.3	30.1	0.0	30.1	0.0	30.1	0.0	30.1	0.0	30.1	0.0
1950	30.0	-0.3	29.9	-0.3	29.8	-0.3	29.8	0.0	29.9	0.3	29.9	0.0	29.9	0.0	29.9	0.0	30.1	0.7	30.1	0.0	30.1	0.0	30.4	1.0
1951	30.5	0.3	30.6	0.3	31.4	2.6	31.4	0.0	31.4	0.0	31.4	0.0	31.4	0.0	31.6	0.6	31.9	0.9	32.4	1.6	32.5	0.3	32.6	0.3
1952	32.7	0.3	33.5	2.4	33.5	0.0	33.5	0.0	33.5	0.0	33.5	0.0	33.5	0.0	33.5	0.0	33.5	0.0	33.5	0.0	33.5	0.0	33.5	0.0
1953	33.5	0.0	33.5	0.0	33.5	0.0	33.2	-0.9	33.2	0.0	33.2	0.0	33.2	0.0	33.2	0.0	33.2	0.0	33.2	0.0	33.2	0.0	33.2	0.0
1954	33.2	0.0	33.2	0.0	33.2	0.0	33.2	0.0	33.2	0.0	33.2	0.0	33.2	0.0	33.2	0.0	33.2	0.0	33.2	0.0	33.8	1.8	34.0	0.6
1955	34.0	0.0	34.0	0.0	34.0	0.0	34.1	0.3	34.1	0.0	34.1	0.0	34.1	0.0	34.1	0.0	34.1	0.0	34.9	2.3	35.3	1.1	35.4	0.3
1956	35.4	0.0	35.6	0.6	36.1	1.4	36.1	0.0	36.1	0.0	36.1	0.0	36.1	0.0	36.1	0.0	36.2	0.3	36.6	1.1	37.5	2.5	37.5	0.0
1957	37.5	0.0	37.6	0.3	37.6	0.0	37.7	0.3	37.7	0.0	37.7	0.0	37.7	0.0	37.7	0.0	37.7	0.0	37.9	0.5	38.8	2.4	38.9	0.3
1958	38.9	0.0	38.9	0.0	38.9	0.0	38.9	0.0	38.9	0.0	38.9	0.0	38.9	0.0	38.9	0.0	38.9	0.0	39.0	0.3	39.9	2.3	40.0	0.3
1959	40.0	0.0	40.0	0.0	40.0	0.0	40.0	0.0	40.0	0.0	40.0	0.0	40.0	0.0	40.0	0.0	40.0	0.0	39.6	-1.0	39.6	0.0	39.6	0.0
1960	39.6	0.0	39.6	0.0	39.6	0.0	39.6	0.0	39.6	0.0	39.6	0.0	39.6	0.0	39.6	0.0	37.9	-4.3	39.2	3.4	39.2	0.0	39.3	0.3
1961	39.4	0.3	39.2	-0.5	39.2	0.0	39.2	0.0	39.2	0.0	39.2	0.0	39.2	0.0	39.2	0.0	39.2	0.0	39.2	0.0	39.2	0.0	39.2	0.0
1962	39.2	0.0	39.1	-0.3	39.1	0.0	39.1	0.0	39.1	0.0	39.4	0.8	39.4	0.0	39.4	0.0	39.4	0.0	39.2	-0.5	39.2	0.0	39.2	0.0
1963	39.2	0.0	39.2	0.0	39.2	0.0	39.0	-0.5	38.9	-0.3	38.7	-0.5	38.9	0.5	38.8	-0.3	38.7	-0.3	38.9	0.5	38.9	0.0	38.9	0.0
1964	38.9	0.0	38.9	0.0	38.9	0.0	38.9	0.0	39.4	1.3	39.3	-0.3	39.3	0.0	39.2	-0.3	39.1	-0.3	39.2	0.3	39.2	0.0	39.2	0.0
1965	39.2	0.0	39.3	0.3	39.2	-0.3	39.2	0.0	39.2	0.0	39.2	0.0	39.2	0.0	39.2	0.0	39.1	-0.3	39.1	0.0	39.1	0.0	39.1	0.0
1966	39.1	0.0	39.1	0.0	39.0	-0.3	39.0	0.0	39.3	0.8	39.2	-0.3	39.2	0.0	39.1	-0.3	39.0	-0.3	39.6	1.5	39.6	0.0	39.6	0.0
1967	39.6	0.0	39.6	0.0	39.6	0.0	39.6	0.0	39.4	-0.5	39.5	0.3	39.4	-0.3	39.6	0.5	39.6	0.0	40.6	2.5	40.6	0.0	40.6	0.0
1968	40.7	0.2	40.7	0.0	40.7	0.0	40.7	0.0	40.6	-0.2	40.8	0.5	40.7	-0.2	40.7	0.0	40.7	0.0	41.6	2.2	41.6	0.0	41.6	0.0
1969	41.5	-0.2	41.5	0.0	41.4	-0.2	41.5	0.2	41.5	0.0	41.6	0.2	41.5	-0.2	41.4	-0.2	41.4	0.0	42.3	2.2	42.5	0.5	42.5	0.0
1970	42.5	0.0	42.5	0.0	42.7	0.5	42.5	-0.5	42.7	0.5	42.7	0.0	42.7	0.0	42.7	0.0	42.8	0.2	44.9	4.9	45.0	0.2	45.0	0.0

[Continued]

Motor Vehicles and Equipment
Producer Price Index
Base 1982 = 100
[Continued]

For 1926-1993. Columns headed % show percentile change in the index from the previous period for which an index is available.

Year	Jan Index	%	Feb Index	%	Mar Index	%	Apr Index	%	May Index	%	Jun Index	%	Jul Index	%	Aug Index	%	Sep Index	%	Oct Index	%	Nov Index	%	Dec Index	%
1971	45.2	0.4	45.4	0.4	45.5	0.2	45.6	0.2	45.6	0.0	45.7	0.2	45.8	0.2	45.8	0.0	45.3	-1.1	46.0	1.5	46.0	0.0	46.9	2.0
1972	46.9	0.0	47.0	0.2	46.9	-0.2	47.0	0.2	47.0	0.0	47.2	0.4	47.1	-0.2	47.1	0.0	47.1	0.0	46.5	-1.3	46.6	0.2	47.1	1.1
1973	47.0	-0.2	47.1	0.2	47.2	0.2	47.4	0.4	47.4	0.0	47.3	-0.2	47.4	0.2	47.4	0.0	47.1	-0.6	47.7	1.3	47.8	0.2	48.3	1.0
1974	48.9	1.2	49.0	0.2	49.0	0.0	49.1	0.2	49.7	1.2	50.2	1.0	51.1	1.8	51.8	1.4	52.0	0.4	55.0	5.8	55.3	0.5	56.0	1.3
1975	55.8	-0.4	56.3	0.9	56.9	1.1	56.9	0.0	56.9	0.0	57.0	0.2	56.9	-0.2	57.1	0.4	57.3	0.4	59.7	4.2	59.9	0.3	60.0	0.2
1976	60.2	0.3	60.2	0.0	60.4	0.3	60.4	0.0	60.3	-0.2	60.4	0.2	60.4	0.0	60.8	0.7	61.1	0.5	63.3	3.6	63.4	0.2	63.5	0.2
1977	63.4	-0.2	63.5	0.2	64.0	0.8	64.1	0.2	64.3	0.3	64.4	0.2	64.4	0.0	64.9	0.8	65.2	0.5	68.0	4.3	67.9	-0.1	68.0	0.1
1978	68.2	0.3	68.4	0.3	68.4	0.0	68.8	0.6	69.5	1.0	69.7	0.3	69.8	0.1	70.0	0.3	70.0	0.0	72.4	3.4	72.6	0.3	72.8	0.3
1979	73.6	1.1	74.0	0.5	74.1	0.1	75.4	1.8	75.6	0.3	75.7	0.1	76.0	0.4	74.7	-1.7	75.0	0.4	78.4	4.5	78.6	0.3	78.9	0.4
1980	79.9	1.3	79.6	-0.4	79.9	0.4	81.8	2.4	81.4	-0.5	81.7	0.4	83.0	1.6	84.2	1.4	81.8	-2.9	86.9	6.2	87.0	0.1	90.0	3.4
1981	91.1	1.2	91.9	0.9	91.4	-0.5	93.1	1.9	93.9	0.9	94.2	0.3	94.5	0.3	94.9	0.4	92.7	-2.3	98.6	6.4	99.1	0.5	99.3	0.2
1982	99.8	0.5	98.2	-1.6	98.2	0.0	98.4	0.2	99.2	0.8	99.9	0.7	100.3	0.4	100.6	0.3	97.4	-3.2	102.6	5.3	102.6	0.0	102.7	0.1
1983	102.3	-0.4	102.0	-0.3	101.7	-0.3	101.8	0.1	102.0	0.2	102.1	0.1	102.1	0.0	102.2	0.1	99.2	-2.9	103.7	4.5	103.7	0.0	103.7	0.0
1984	103.9	0.2	104.0	0.1	104.1	0.1	104.2	0.1	104.1	-0.1	103.9	-0.2	104.0	0.1	103.9	-0.1	101.6	-2.2	105.0	3.3	105.2	0.2	104.9	-0.3
1985	105.5	0.6	106.1	0.6	105.9	-0.2	106.0	0.1	106.4	0.4	106.5	0.1	106.5	0.0	106.5	0.0	101.4	-4.8	108.8	7.3	108.8	0.0	108.2	-0.6
1986	107.6	-0.6	107.8	0.2	107.5	-0.3	108.6	1.0	108.5	-0.1	108.7	0.2	108.8	0.1	108.3	-0.5	105.2	-2.9	113.1	7.5	113.0	-0.1	112.5	-0.4
1987	112.6	0.1	110.9	-1.5	111.1	0.2	112.3	1.1	111.8	-0.4	111.5	-0.3	111.4	-0.1	110.8	-0.5	108.9	-1.7	114.2	4.9	113.3	-0.8	111.8	-1.3
1988	112.0	0.2	111.9	-0.1	111.8	-0.1	112.0	0.2	112.3	0.3	112.4	0.1	112.6	0.2	112.8	0.2	110.9	-1.7	116.9	5.4	116.1	-0.7	116.0	-0.1
1989	116.2	0.2	116.5	0.3	115.5	-0.9	114.8	-0.6	115.6	0.7	115.9	0.3	114.5	-1.2	114.5	0.0	113.8	-0.6	119.6	5.1	118.8	-0.7	118.6	-0.2
1990	117.2	-1.2	117.3	0.1	117.0	-0.3	116.9	-0.1	116.6	-0.3	117.6	0.9	117.8	0.2	117.2	-0.5	116.7	-0.4	121.6	4.2	121.5	-0.1	121.5	0.0
1991	121.9	0.3	122.4	0.4	122.2	-0.2	121.5	-0.6	120.7	-0.7	120.6	-0.1	120.5	-0.1	120.6	0.1	119.2	-1.2	125.8	5.5	125.4	-0.3	124.9	-0.4
1992	124.8	-0.1	124.6	-0.2	124.9	0.2	124.8	-0.1	124.7	-0.1	124.3	-0.3	124.4	0.1	123.9	-0.4	121.3	-2.1	127.1	4.8	127.1	0.0	126.9	-0.2
1993	127.1	0.2	127.8	0.6	127.8	0.0	127.7	-0.1	127.6	-0.1	127.7	0.1	127.8	0.1	127.7	-0.1	125.0	-2.1	129.7	3.8	129.9	0.2	130.0	0.1

Source: U.S. Department of Labor, Bureau of Labor Statistics, Division of Industry Prices and Price Indexes. n.e.c. stands for not elsewhere classified. - indicates no data collected for period or unavailable.

Aircraft and Aircraft Equipment
Producer Price Index
Base 1982 = 100

For 1985-1993. Columns headed % show percentile change in the index from the previous period for which an index is available.

Year	Jan		Feb		Mar		Apr		May		Jun		Jul		Aug		Sep		Oct		Nov		Dec	
	Index	%	Index	%	Index	%	Index	%	Index	%	Index	%	Index	%	Index	%	Index	%	Index	%	Index	%	Index	%
1985	-	-	-	-	-	-	-	-	-	-	-	-	-	-	-	-	370.5	-	375.0	1.2	374.6	-0.1	374.8	0.1
1986	124.1	-66.9	124.4	0.2	124.4	0.0	124.6	0.2	124.3	-0.2	124.3	0.0	124.5	0.2	124.6	0.1	122.6	-1.6	122.8	0.2	122.8	0.0	122.7	-0.1
1987	123.5	0.7	123.5	0.0	123.9	0.3	123.9	0.0	122.8	-0.9	122.9	0.1	122.9	0.0	122.9	0.0	123.1	0.2	123.1	0.0	123.4	0.2	123.3	-0.1
1988	125.1	1.5	125.2	0.1	125.3	0.1	126.2	0.7	126.0	-0.2	126.7	0.6	125.8	-0.7	126.0	0.2	126.4	0.3	126.3	-0.1	126.6	0.2	126.7	0.1
1989	127.9	0.9	128.1	0.2	128.9	0.6	129.3	0.3	129.4	0.1	129.6	0.2	129.9	0.2	130.4	0.4	130.4	0.0	130.7	0.2	132.0	1.0	132.2	0.2
1990	134.3	1.6	134.9	0.4	135.4	0.4	136.1	0.5	136.3	0.1	136.4	0.1	136.7	0.2	137.5	0.6	137.6	0.1	138.4	0.6	138.9	0.4	139.1	0.1
1991	141.7	1.9	142.0	0.2	142.3	0.2	142.8	0.4	144.2	1.0	144.3	0.1	144.7	0.3	145.5	0.6	145.6	0.1	146.0	0.3	146.2	0.1	146.4	0.1
1992	149.5	2.1	149.7	0.1	149.9	0.1	150.6	0.5	150.9	0.2	151.4	0.3	151.4	0.0	152.0	0.4	152.5	0.3	152.8	0.2	152.5	-0.2	152.6	0.1
1993	153.5	0.6	153.5	0.0	153.9	0.3	154.6	0.5	154.7	0.1	154.0	-0.5	154.7	0.5	155.1	0.3	154.2	-0.6	156.5	1.5	156.1	-0.3	156.4	0.2

Source: U.S. Department of Labor, Bureau of Labor Statistics, Division of Industry Prices and Price Indexes. n.e.c. stands for not elsewhere classified. - indicates no data collected for period or unavailable.

Ships and Boats
Producer Price Index
Base 1982 = 100

For 1981-1993. Columns headed % show percentile change in the index from the previous period for which an index is available.

Year	Jan Index	%	Feb Index	%	Mar Index	%	Apr Index	%	May Index	%	Jun Index	%	Jul Index	%	Aug Index	%	Sep Index	%	Oct Index	%	Nov Index	%	Dec Index	%
1981	-	-	-	-	-	-	-	-	-	-	-	-	-	-	-	-	-	-	-	-	-	-	97.5	-
1982	98.1	0.6	98.9	0.8	99.2	0.3	99.7	0.5	99.8	0.1	100.3	0.5	100.1	-0.2	100.4	0.3	100.6	0.2	100.9	0.3	101.0	0.1	100.9	-0.1
1983	101.0	0.1	101.4	0.4	101.5	0.1	102.4	0.9	102.7	0.3	102.9	0.2	103.1	0.2	103.2	0.1	104.1	0.9	104.5	0.4	104.4	-0.1	105.2	0.8
1984	106.1	0.9	106.3	0.2	106.5	0.2	106.6	0.1	108.1	1.4	108.0	-0.1	108.6	0.6	108.0	-0.6	107.0	-0.9	107.3	0.3	107.6	0.3	108.1	0.5
1985	108.6	0.5	109.0	0.4	109.1	0.1	110.0	0.8	110.0	0.0	110.0	0.0	109.7	-0.3	110.4	0.6	110.5	0.1	111.6	1.0	112.0	0.4	112.4	0.4
1986	113.2	0.7	113.2	0.0	113.3	0.1	113.4	0.1	113.6	0.2	113.6	0.0	113.5	-0.1	113.4	-0.1	113.4	0.0	113.6	0.2	113.6	0.0	113.6	0.0
1987	113.8	0.2	113.9	0.1	114.0	0.1	114.1	0.1	114.1	0.0	114.1	0.0	114.1	0.0	114.1	0.0	114.2	0.1	114.2	0.0	114.2	0.0	114.3	0.1
1988	114.4	0.1	114.5	0.1	114.1	-0.3	114.1	0.0	114.2	0.1	114.2	0.0	114.5	0.3	114.6	0.1	116.5	1.7	116.3	-0.2	116.8	0.4	116.7	-0.1
1989	116.9	0.2	117.2	0.3	117.2	0.0	114.8	-2.0	119.9	4.4	122.1	1.8	122.4	0.2	124.0	1.3	122.1	-1.5	122.0	-0.1	122.1	0.1	120.6	-1.2
1990	120.9	0.2	123.5	2.2	125.0	1.2	125.1	0.1	125.1	0.0	125.2	0.1	125.3	0.1	125.9	0.5	127.0	0.9	127.4	0.3	127.2	-0.2	127.3	0.1
1991	127.5	0.2	127.7	0.2	128.7	0.8	128.7	0.0	130.6	1.5	130.6	0.0	130.8	0.2	130.8	0.0	130.8	0.0	131.3	0.4	131.3	0.0	134.9	2.7
1992	135.0	0.1	135.2	0.1	137.2	1.5	137.8	0.4	137.9	0.1	137.9	0.0	137.9	0.0	137.6	-0.2	137.9	0.2	137.9	0.0	138.0	0.1	138.1	0.1
1993	142.5	3.2	142.9	0.3	143.1	0.1	143.5	0.3	143.5	0.0	143.5	0.0	143.5	0.0	143.1	-0.3	143.5	0.3	143.6	0.1	143.5	-0.1	143.5	0.0

Source: U.S. Department of Labor, Bureau of Labor Statistics, Division of Industry Prices and Price Indexes. n.e.c. stands for not elsewhere classified. - indicates no data collected for period or unavailable.

Railroad Equipment
Producer Price Index
Base 1982 = 100

For 1961-1993. Columns headed % show percentile change in the index from the previous period for which an index is available.

Year	Jan Index	%	Feb Index	%	Mar Index	%	Apr Index	%	May Index	%	Jun Index	%	Jul Index	%	Aug Index	%	Sep Index	%	Oct Index	%	Nov Index	%	Dec Index	%
1961	27.9	-	27.9	0.0	27.9	0.0	27.9	0.0	27.9	0.0	27.9	0.0	27.9	0.0	27.9	0.0	27.9	0.0	28.0	0.4	28.0	0.0	28.0	0.0
1962	28.0	0.0	28.0	0.0	28.0	0.0	28.0	0.0	28.0	0.0	28.0	0.0	28.0	0.0	28.0	0.0	28.0	0.0	28.0	0.0	28.0	0.0	28.0	0.0
1963	28.0	0.0	28.0	0.0	28.0	0.0	28.0	0.0	28.0	0.0	28.0	0.0	28.0	0.0	28.0	0.0	28.0	0.0	28.0	0.0	28.0	0.0	28.0	0.0
1964	28.0	0.0	28.0	0.0	28.0	0.0	27.9	-0.4	27.9	0.0	27.9	0.0	28.0	0.4	28.0	0.0	28.0	0.0	28.0	0.0	28.0	0.0	28.0	0.0
1965	28.0	0.0	28.0	0.0	28.0	0.0	28.0	0.0	28.0	0.0	28.1	0.4	28.1	0.0	28.1	0.0	28.1	0.0	28.1	0.0	28.1	0.0	28.1	0.0
1966	28.1	0.0	28.1	0.0	28.1	0.0	28.1	0.0	28.1	0.0	28.1	0.0	28.1	0.0	28.1	0.0	28.1	0.0	28.1	0.0	28.1	0.0	28.6	1.8
1967	28.7	0.3	28.7	0.0	28.7	0.0	28.7	0.0	28.7	0.0	28.7	0.0	28.7	0.0	28.7	0.0	28.7	0.0	29.2	1.7	29.3	0.3	29.3	0.0
1968	29.4	0.3	29.4	0.0	29.4	0.0	29.4	0.0	29.4	0.0	29.4	0.0	29.8	1.4	29.9	0.3	29.9	0.0	30.3	1.3	30.3	0.0	30.3	0.0
1969	30.3	0.0	30.3	0.0	30.8	1.7	30.8	0.0	31.0	0.6	31.2	0.6	31.9	2.2	32.0	0.3	32.0	0.0	32.2	0.6	32.2	0.0	32.3	0.3
1970	32.7	1.2	32.8	0.3	33.0	0.6	33.1	0.3	33.1	0.0	33.2	0.3	33.2	0.0	33.2	0.0	33.3	0.3	33.5	0.6	33.5	0.0	33.7	0.6
1971	34.3	1.8	34.3	0.0	34.5	0.6	34.5	0.0	34.7	0.6	34.8	0.3	35.2	1.1	35.3	0.3	35.3	0.0	35.3	0.0	35.3	0.0	35.3	0.0
1972	35.7	1.1	35.8	0.3	36.7	2.5	37.1	1.1	37.4	0.8	37.4	0.0	37.6	0.5	37.6	0.0	37.6	0.0	37.6	0.0	37.6	0.0	37.8	0.5
1973	38.0	0.5	38.2	0.5	38.3	0.3	38.5	0.5	38.8	0.8	38.9	0.3	38.9	0.0	39.0	0.3	39.3	0.8	39.3	0.0	39.4	0.3	40.0	1.5
1974	40.5	1.3	40.7	0.5	41.8	2.7	42.9	2.6	44.4	3.5	47.2	6.3	48.5	2.8	50.4	3.9	51.4	2.0	52.2	1.6	53.1	1.7	54.2	2.1
1975	56.7	4.6	56.9	0.4	57.2	0.5	57.2	0.0	57.6	0.7	57.5	-0.2	58.4	1.6	58.2	-0.3	58.4	0.3	59.1	1.2	59.7	1.0	60.0	0.5
1976	60.4	0.7	61.2	1.3	61.2	0.0	61.7	0.8	61.7	0.0	62.2	0.8	62.6	0.6	63.2	1.0	63.2	0.0	64.3	1.7	64.3	0.0	64.4	0.2
1977	65.8	2.2	65.8	0.0	66.4	0.9	66.7	0.5	66.7	0.0	66.9	0.3	67.6	1.0	67.9	0.4	67.9	0.0	68.9	1.5	68.9	0.0	69.2	0.4
1978	70.3	1.6	70.6	0.4	70.6	0.0	72.2	2.3	72.4	0.3	72.4	0.0	73.2	1.1	73.4	0.3	74.1	1.0	75.1	1.3	75.5	0.5	75.6	0.1
1979	76.9	1.7	77.4	0.7	77.6	0.3	78.4	1.0	78.4	0.0	79.3	1.1	81.0	2.1	81.1	0.1	81.3	0.2	82.6	1.6	83.2	0.7	83.4	0.2
1980	85.9	3.0	86.4	0.6	87.2	0.9	89.4	2.5	89.6	0.2	90.1	0.6	91.3	1.3	91.8	0.5	92.4	0.7	93.3	1.0	93.4	0.1	93.5	0.1
1981	96.0	2.7	96.0	0.0	96.4	0.4	96.9	0.5	95.6	-1.3	95.7	0.1	97.6	2.0	97.8	0.2	97.8	0.0	97.8	0.0	98.5	0.7	98.2	-0.3
1982	99.8	1.6	99.8	0.0	99.9	0.1	99.1	-0.8	98.9	-0.2	98.9	0.0	98.9	0.0	100.4	1.5	100.4	0.0	101.2	0.8	101.2	0.0	101.2	0.0
1983	101.3	0.1	101.2	-0.1	101.1	-0.1	101.0	-0.1	101.1	0.1	101.0	-0.1	101.4	0.4	101.3	-0.1	101.2	-0.1	100.6	-0.6	100.6	0.0	101.2	0.6
1984	101.5	0.3	101.5	0.0	101.6	0.1	102.3	0.7	102.3	0.0	102.3	0.0	102.9	0.6	103.2	0.3	103.2	0.0	103.6	0.4	103.6	0.0	103.6	0.0
1985	103.9	0.3	104.4	0.5	104.7	0.3	104.8	0.1	104.6	-0.2	105.0	0.4	105.1	0.1	105.2	0.1	105.2	0.0	105.2	0.0	105.1	-0.1	105.2	0.1
1986	105.9	0.7	105.5	-0.4	105.6	0.1	105.6	0.0	105.3	-0.3	105.3	0.0	106.1	0.8	104.9	-1.1	105.2	0.3	105.2	0.0	105.2	0.0	105.3	0.1
1987	105.2	-0.1	104.6	-0.6	104.7	0.1	104.6	-0.1	104.5	-0.1	104.4	-0.1	104.7	0.3	104.8	0.1	104.8	0.0	104.6	-0.2	105.0	0.4	105.0	0.0
1988	105.3	0.3	104.8	-0.5	105.5	0.7	106.2	0.7	107.0	0.7	108.1	1.0	108.2	0.1	108.6	0.4	108.8	0.2	108.8	0.0	109.0	0.2	110.2	1.1
1989	111.8	1.5	112.2	0.4	112.2	0.0	114.2	1.8	114.2	0.0	114.3	0.1	114.6	0.3	114.6	0.0	114.7	0.1	114.8	0.1	114.9	0.1	115.6	0.6
1990	116.3	0.6	117.5	1.0	117.4	-0.1	117.6	0.2	117.7	0.1	118.5	0.7	118.5	0.0	118.5	0.0	119.9	1.2	119.9	0.0	120.9	0.8	120.9	0.0
1991	122.0	0.9	121.9	-0.1	122.2	0.2	122.1	-0.1	122.2	0.1	122.2	0.0	122.6	0.3	122.8	0.2	122.8	0.0	122.3	-0.4	121.9	-0.3	121.8	-0.1
1992	122.5	0.6	123.2	0.6	123.6	0.3	123.6	0.0	123.7	0.1	123.9	0.2	124.0	0.1	123.9	-0.1	124.2	0.2	124.2	0.0	123.8	-0.3	123.3	-0.4
1993	123.6	0.2	124.2	0.5	124.3	0.1	124.5	0.2	124.5	0.0	124.6	0.1	125.0	0.3	125.8	0.6	126.1	0.2	125.9	-0.2	125.7	-0.2	127.6	1.5

Source: U.S. Department of Labor, Bureau of Labor Statistics, Division of Industry Prices and Price Indexes. n.e.c. stands for not elsewhere classified. - indicates no data collected for period or unavailable.

Transportation Equipment n.e.c.
Producer Price Index
Base June 1985 = 100

For 1985-1993. Columns headed % show percentile change in the index from the previous period for which an index is available.

Year	Jan Index	%	Feb Index	%	Mar Index	%	Apr Index	%	May Index	%	Jun Index	%	Jul Index	%	Aug Index	%	Sep Index	%	Oct Index	%	Nov Index	%	Dec Index	%
1985	-	-	-	-	-	-	-	-	-	-	100.0	-	100.0	0.0	99.5	-0.5	99.3	-0.2	99.3	0.0	99.3	0.0	99.3	0.0
1986	99.0	-0.3	99.4	0.4	100.1	0.7	100.0	-0.1	99.9	-0.1	100.0	0.1	100.1	0.1	100.6	0.5	100.2	-0.4	100.3	0.1	101.1	0.8	101.1	0.0
1987	101.1	0.0	101.2	0.1	101.2	0.0	101.2	0.0	101.6	0.4	101.8	0.2	102.0	0.2	102.1	0.1	102.8	0.7	103.2	0.4	103.1	-0.1	103.1	0.0
1988	103.3	0.2	103.9	0.6	104.0	0.1	105.4	1.3	105.4	0.0	105.3	-0.1	106.5	1.1	106.6	0.1	108.0	1.3	108.0	0.0	108.3	0.3	108.2	-0.1
1989	108.7	0.5	109.0	0.3	109.1	0.1	109.4	0.3	109.4	0.0	109.2	-0.2	109.4	0.2	109.7	0.3	110.3	0.5	110.9	0.5	111.1	0.2	111.2	0.1
1990	111.2	0.0	111.2	0.0	111.0	-0.2	111.7	0.6	111.7	0.0	111.7	0.0	111.8	0.1	111.8	0.0	111.8	0.0	111.7	-0.1	112.0	0.3	111.8	-0.2
1991	112.4	0.5	112.6	0.2	113.1	0.4	113.3	0.2	113.7	0.4	113.8	0.1	113.8	0.0	113.9	0.1	114.3	0.4	114.2	-0.1	114.2	0.0	114.2	0.0
1992	114.8	0.5	114.9	0.1	114.7	-0.2	114.7	0.0	114.7	0.0	114.8	0.1	114.6	-0.2	114.6	0.0	114.6	0.0	114.8	0.2	114.8	0.0	114.8	0.0
1993	115.0	0.2	115.5	0.4	115.4	-0.1	115.5	0.1	115.5	0.0	115.5	0.0	115.6	0.1	115.8	0.2	115.6	-0.2	115.2	-0.3	116.0	0.7	116.3	0.3

Source: U.S. Department of Labor, Bureau of Labor Statistics, Division of Industry Prices and Price Indexes. n.e.c. stands for not elsewhere classified. - indicates no data collected for period or unavailable.

MISCELLANEOUS PRODUCTS
Producer Price Index
Base 1982 = 100

For 1947-1993. Columns headed % show percentile change in the index from the previous period for which an index is available.

Year	Jan Index	%	Feb Index	%	Mar Index	%	Apr Index	%	May Index	%	Jun Index	%	Jul Index	%	Aug Index	%	Sep Index	%	Oct Index	%	Nov Index	%	Dec Index	%
1947	26.5	-	26.5	0.0	26.5	0.0	26.6	0.4	26.7	0.4	26.6	-0.4	26.4	-0.8	26.6	0.8	26.6	0.0	26.6	0.0	26.8	0.8	26.8	0.0
1948	27.0	0.7	27.1	0.4	27.2	0.4	27.2	0.0	27.3	0.4	27.3	0.0	27.3	0.0	28.2	3.3	28.3	0.4	28.3	0.0	28.4	0.4	28.5	0.4
1949	28.5	0.0	28.5	0.0	28.5	0.0	28.2	-1.1	28.2	0.0	28.1	-0.4	28.1	0.0	28.0	-0.4	28.0	0.0	28.0	0.0	28.1	0.4	28.2	0.4
1950	28.1	-0.4	28.1	0.0	28.1	0.0	28.1	0.0	28.1	0.0	28.1	0.0	28.2	0.4	29.0	2.8	29.2	0.7	29.4	0.7	29.6	0.7	29.9	1.0
1951	30.3	1.3	30.3	0.0	30.3	0.0	30.4	0.3	30.4	0.0	30.3	-0.3	30.4	0.3	30.4	0.0	30.4	0.0	30.4	0.0	30.3	-0.3	30.3	0.0
1952	30.3	0.0	30.3	0.0	30.2	-0.3	30.2	0.0	30.2	0.0	30.1	-0.3	30.1	0.0	30.1	0.0	30.1	0.0	30.1	0.0	30.1	0.0	30.1	0.0
1953	30.1	0.0	30.1	0.0	31.1	3.3	31.1	0.0	31.1	0.0	31.1	0.0	31.1	0.0	31.1	0.0	31.1	0.0	31.1	0.0	31.1	0.0	31.1	0.0
1954	31.1	0.0	31.1	0.0	31.1	0.0	31.3	0.6	31.2	-0.3	31.3	0.3	31.3	0.0	31.3	0.0	31.3	0.0	31.3	0.0	31.3	0.0	31.3	0.0
1955	31.2	-0.3	31.1	-0.3	31.1	0.0	31.2	0.3	31.2	0.0	31.2	0.0	31.2	0.0	31.3	0.3	31.3	0.0	31.3	0.0	31.4	0.3	31.5	0.3
1956	31.6	0.3	31.6	0.0	31.6	0.0	31.7	0.3	31.7	0.0	31.7	0.0	31.7	0.0	31.7	0.0	31.8	0.3	31.8	0.0	31.9	0.3	31.9	0.0
1957	32.1	0.6	32.2	0.3	32.2	0.0	32.2	0.0	32.2	0.0	32.2	0.0	33.0	2.5	33.0	0.0	33.1	0.3	33.1	0.0	33.2	0.3	33.2	0.0
1958	33.2	0.0	33.2	0.0	33.2	0.0	33.2	0.0	33.2	0.0	33.4	0.6	33.3	-0.3	33.4	0.3	33.3	-0.3	33.3	0.0	33.3	0.0	33.3	0.0
1959	33.3	0.0	33.3	0.0	33.4	0.3	33.4	0.0	33.4	0.0	33.4	0.0	33.4	0.0	33.4	0.0	33.4	0.0	33.4	0.0	33.4	0.0	33.5	0.3
1960	33.6	0.3	33.6	0.0	33.6	0.0	33.6	0.0	33.6	0.0	33.6	0.0	33.6	0.0	33.7	0.3	33.7	0.0	33.7	0.0	33.7	0.0	33.7	0.0
1961	33.7	0.0	33.7	0.0	33.7	0.0	33.7	0.0	33.7	0.0	33.7	0.0	33.7	0.0	33.8	0.3	33.8	0.0	33.9	0.3	33.9	0.0	33.9	0.0
1962	33.8	-0.3	33.9	0.3	33.9	0.0	33.9	0.0	33.9	0.0	33.9	0.0	33.9	0.0	33.9	0.0	33.9	0.0	34.0	0.3	34.0	0.0	34.0	0.0
1963	34.0	0.0	34.0	0.0	33.9	-0.3	33.9	0.0	34.1	0.6	34.3	0.6	34.3	0.0	34.3	0.0	34.3	0.0	34.4	0.3	34.4	0.0	34.4	0.0
1964	34.4	0.0	34.4	0.0	34.4	0.0	34.4	0.0	34.4	0.0	34.4	0.0	34.4	0.0	34.5	0.3	34.5	0.0	34.5	0.0	34.5	0.0	34.5	0.0
1965	34.5	0.0	34.5	0.0	34.5	0.0	34.7	0.6	34.8	0.3	34.6	-0.6	34.8	0.6	34.8	0.0	34.8	0.0	34.8	0.0	34.8	0.0	34.8	0.0
1966	34.9	0.3	34.9	0.0	35.2	0.9	35.3	0.3	35.3	0.0	35.4	0.3	35.4	0.0	35.4	0.0	35.4	0.0	35.5	0.3	35.6	0.3	35.6	0.0
1967	35.7	0.3	35.7	0.0	35.7	0.0	35.7	0.0	35.8	0.3	36.3	1.4	36.4	0.3	36.4	0.0	36.5	0.3	36.6	0.3	36.6	0.0	36.7	0.3
1968	36.7	0.0	36.8	0.3	36.8	0.0	36.9	0.3	36.9	0.0	36.9	0.0	36.9	0.0	37.0	0.3	37.0	0.0	37.1	0.3	37.3	0.5	37.3	0.0
1969	37.3	0.0	37.3	0.0	37.3	0.0	37.4	0.3	37.4	0.0	38.2	2.1	38.4	0.5	38.5	0.3	38.6	0.3	38.7	0.3	38.7	0.0	38.7	0.0
1970	38.9	0.5	39.0	0.3	39.1	0.3	39.0	-0.3	39.2	0.5	40.1	2.3	40.2	0.2	40.2	0.0	40.3	0.2	40.3	0.0	40.3	0.0	40.4	0.2
1971	40.6	0.5	40.7	0.2	40.7	0.0	40.7	0.0	40.8	0.2	40.8	0.0	40.9	0.2	41.0	0.2	41.0	0.0	41.0	0.0	41.0	0.0	41.0	0.0
1972	41.1	0.2	41.2	0.2	41.3	0.2	41.3	0.0	41.3	0.0	41.3	0.0	41.6	0.7	41.6	0.0	41.7	0.2	41.6	-0.2	41.6	0.0	41.6	0.0
1973	41.9	0.7	42.4	1.2	42.7	0.7	42.9	0.5	43.2	0.7	43.5	0.7	43.7	0.5	43.8	0.2	43.8	0.0	43.8	0.0	43.9	0.2	44.0	0.2
1974	44.7	1.6	45.1	0.9	45.5	0.9	46.4	2.0	48.2	3.9	48.6	0.8	48.9	0.6	49.0	0.2	49.3	0.6	49.6	0.6	50.9	2.6	51.5	1.2
1975	52.6	2.1	52.9	0.6	53.1	0.4	53.3	0.4	53.3	0.0	53.4	0.2	53.4	0.0	53.4	0.0	53.6	0.4	53.4	-0.4	53.8	0.7	54.7	1.7
1976	54.9	0.4	55.1	0.4	55.2	0.2	55.2	0.0	55.2	0.0	55.8	1.1	55.6	-0.4	55.5	-0.2	55.7	0.4	55.7	0.0	56.4	1.3	56.8	0.7
1977	57.9	1.9	58.1	0.3	58.2	0.2	58.8	1.0	59.0	0.3	59.1	0.2	59.3	0.3	59.4	0.2	60.1	1.2	60.9	1.3	61.1	0.3	61.4	0.5
1978	62.1	1.1	62.0	-0.2	62.4	0.6	65.6	5.1	66.1	0.8	66.7	0.9	68.6	2.8	69.2	0.9	69.8	0.9	69.0	-1.1	68.4	-0.9	70.0	2.3
1979	71.5	2.1	72.3	1.1	72.6	0.4	72.9	0.4	73.6	1.0	74.2	0.8	74.9	0.9	75.6	0.9	77.1	2.0	79.2	2.7	80.1	1.1	82.3	2.7
1980	87.9	6.8	95.1	8.2	92.6	-2.6	91.4	-1.3	91.0	-0.4	93.3	2.5	94.6	1.4	94.1	-0.5	95.9	1.9	96.2	0.3	95.4	-0.8	96.0	0.6
1981	95.6	-0.4	95.8	0.2	95.5	-0.3	96.2	0.7	96.5	0.3	96.3	-0.2	95.2	-1.1	95.0	-0.2	96.6	1.7	97.1	0.5	96.8	-0.3	96.8	0.0
1982	97.1	0.3	98.9	1.9	98.7	-0.2	98.8	0.1	98.5	-0.3	98.2	-0.3	98.9	0.7	98.4	-0.5	101.1	2.7	103.3	2.2	103.1	-0.2	105.0	1.8
1983	103.3	-1.6	104.4	1.1	104.0	-0.4	104.0	0.0	103.8	-0.2	104.2	0.4	105.5	1.2	105.6	0.1	105.4	-0.2	105.5	0.1	105.5	0.0	105.9	0.4
1984	106.5	0.6	106.7	0.2	106.7	0.0	106.6	-0.1	106.4	-0.2	107.0	0.6	107.5	0.5	107.9	0.4	107.3	-0.6	107.2	-0.1	107.2	0.0	107.3	0.1
1985	108.2	0.8	108.8	0.6	108.7	-0.1	109.1	0.4	109.0	-0.1	109.0	0.0	109.8	0.7	109.8	0.0	109.9	0.1	110.0	0.1	110.1	0.1	109.9	-0.2
1986	111.2	1.2	111.0	-0.2	111.1	0.1	111.2	0.1	111.1	-0.1	111.0	-0.1	111.9	0.8	112.0	0.1	112.1	0.1	112.3	0.2	112.4	0.1	112.2	-0.2
1987	113.1	0.8	113.1	0.0	113.3	0.2	113.9	0.5	114.0	0.1	114.0	0.0	115.1	1.0	115.5	0.3	115.8	0.3	116.2	0.3	116.7	0.4	117.7	0.9
1988	118.7	0.8	119.2	0.4	119.1	-0.1	119.4	0.3	119.4	0.0	119.4	0.0	120.9	1.3	120.7	-0.2	120.7	0.0	121.1	0.3	121.2	0.1	122.6	1.2
1989	124.0	1.1	124.2	0.2	124.5	0.2	124.6	0.1	125.2	0.5	126.7	1.2	127.2	0.4	127.4	0.2	127.6	0.2	128.2	0.5	128.4	0.2	130.0	1.2
1990	131.2	0.9	131.9	0.5	132.0	0.1	132.3	0.2	133.2	0.7	134.4	0.9	134.6	0.1	134.9	0.2	135.3	0.3	135.9	0.4	136.9	0.7	138.2	0.9
1991	139.1	0.7	138.9	-0.1	139.4	0.4	140.0	0.4	140.1	0.1	140.9	0.6	141.8	0.6	141.7	-0.1	141.5	-0.1	141.4	-0.1	141.8	0.3	143.4	1.1

[Continued]

MISCELLANEOUS PRODUCTS
Producer Price Index
Base 1982 = 100
[Continued]

For 1947-1993. Columns headed % show percentile change in the index from the previous period for which an index is available.

Year	Jan Index	%	Feb Index	%	Mar Index	%	Apr Index	%	May Index	%	Jun Index	%	Jul Index	%	Aug Index	%	Sep Index	%	Oct Index	%	Nov Index	%	Dec Index	%
1992	143.9	0.3	143.9	0.0	144.0	0.1	144.8	0.6	146.4	1.1	146.2	-0.1	146.3	0.1	143.8	-1.7	145.3	1.0	145.5	0.1	145.8	0.2	147.3	1.0
1993	148.6	0.9	149.4	0.5	149.4	0.0	150.4	0.7	150.7	0.2	149.6	-0.7	149.6	0.0	138.9	-7.2	139.3	0.3	139.2	-0.1	139.5	0.2	141.0	1.1

Source: U.S. Department of Labor, Bureau of Labor Statistics, Division of Industry Prices and Price Indexes. n.e.c. stands for not elsewhere classified. - indicates no data collected for period or unavailable.

Toys, Sporting Goods, Small Arms, Etc.
Producer Price Index
Base 1982 = 100

For 1947-1993. Columns headed % show percentile change in the index from the previous period for which an index is available.

Year	Jan Index	%	Feb Index	%	Mar Index	%	Apr Index	%	May Index	%	Jun Index	%	Jul Index	%	Aug Index	%	Sep Index	%	Oct Index	%	Nov Index	%	Dec Index	%
1947	34.8	-	34.8	0.0	34.9	0.3	35.1	0.6	35.1	0.0	35.1	0.0	35.3	0.6	35.3	0.0	35.1	-0.6	35.1	0.0	35.1	0.0	35.3	0.6
1948	36.0	2.0	36.1	0.3	36.3	0.6	36.5	0.6	36.6	0.3	36.6	0.0	36.6	0.0	37.0	1.1	37.0	0.0	37.0	0.0	37.1	0.3	37.1	0.0
1949	36.6	-1.3	36.8	0.5	36.9	0.3	36.9	0.0	36.8	-0.3	36.8	0.0	36.6	-0.5	36.5	-0.3	36.4	-0.3	36.5	0.3	36.9	1.1	36.9	0.0
1950	37.6	1.9	37.7	0.3	37.7	0.0	37.8	0.3	37.8	0.0	37.9	0.3	38.2	0.8	38.5	0.8	39.6	2.9	40.1	1.3	40.2	0.2	41.0	2.0
1951	41.8	2.0	42.0	0.5	42.2	0.5	42.2	0.0	42.2	0.0	42.2	0.0	42.1	-0.2	42.1	0.0	42.0	-0.2	42.0	0.0	41.7	-0.7	41.7	0.0
1952	41.5	-0.5	41.4	-0.2	41.1	-0.7	41.0	-0.2	41.0	0.0	41.0	0.0	41.0	0.0	40.9	-0.2	40.9	0.0	40.9	0.0	40.9	0.0	40.9	0.0
1953	40.8	-0.2	40.8	0.0	40.8	0.0	41.1	0.7	41.3	0.5	41.2	-0.2	41.2	0.0	41.2	0.0	41.2	0.0	41.2	0.0	41.2	0.0	40.9	-0.7
1954	40.9	0.0	40.9	0.0	40.9	0.0	41.0	0.2	41.0	0.0	41.0	0.0	41.0	0.0	41.0	0.0	40.8	-0.5	40.8	0.0	40.8	0.0	40.8	0.0
1955	40.9	0.2	40.9	0.0	40.9	0.0	40.9	0.0	40.9	0.0	40.9	0.0	40.9	0.0	41.0	0.2	41.0	0.0	41.1	0.2	41.3	0.5	41.6	0.7
1956	41.9	0.7	41.9	0.0	41.8	-0.2	41.9	0.2	41.9	0.0	41.9	0.0	41.8	-0.2	42.0	0.5	42.2	0.5	42.2	0.0	42.2	0.0	42.3	0.2
1957	42.4	0.2	42.4	0.0	42.4	0.0	42.4	0.0	42.4	0.0	42.4	0.0	42.4	0.0	42.6	0.5	42.7	0.2	42.6	-0.2	42.6	0.0	42.6	0.0
1958	43.2	1.4	43.2	0.0	43.1	-0.2	43.1	0.0	43.1	0.0	43.1	0.0	43.1	0.0	43.1	0.0	42.9	-0.5	42.9	0.0	42.9	0.0	42.9	0.0
1959	42.6	-0.7	42.6	0.0	42.4	-0.5	42.3	-0.2	42.3	0.0	42.3	0.0	42.4	0.2	42.5	0.2	42.5	0.0	42.5	0.0	42.5	0.0	42.6	0.2
1960	42.5	-0.2	42.6	0.2	42.6	0.0	42.8	0.5	42.8	0.0	42.8	0.0	42.9	0.2	42.9	0.0	42.9	0.0	42.9	0.0	42.9	0.0	42.9	0.0
1961	42.8	-0.2	42.8	0.0	43.0	0.5	43.0	0.0	43.0	0.0	43.0	0.0	43.0	0.0	43.3	0.7	43.2	-0.2	43.4	0.5	43.4	0.0	43.1	-0.7
1962	42.9	-0.5	42.8	-0.2	42.9	0.2	42.9	0.0	42.9	0.0	43.0	0.2	43.1	0.2	43.1	0.0	43.2	0.2	43.2	0.0	43.2	0.0	43.2	0.0
1963	43.2	0.0	43.2	0.0	42.9	-0.7	43.0	0.2	43.0	0.0	43.0	0.0	43.1	0.2	43.2	0.2	43.2	0.0	43.2	0.0	43.1	-0.2	43.2	0.2
1964	43.1	-0.2	43.1	0.0	43.2	0.2	43.0	-0.5	43.0	0.0	43.1	0.2	43.1	0.0	43.1	0.0	43.2	0.2	43.2	0.0	43.2	0.0	43.2	0.0
1965	43.6	0.9	43.6	0.0	43.6	0.0	43.7	0.2	43.8	0.2	43.8	0.0	43.9	0.2	43.8	-0.2	44.0	0.5	44.0	0.0	44.0	0.0	44.0	0.0
1966	44.0	0.0	44.1	0.2	44.1	0.0	44.3	0.5	44.3	0.0	44.3	0.0	44.6	0.7	44.8	0.4	44.8	0.0	44.8	0.0	44.8	0.0	44.8	0.0
1967	45.0	0.4	45.0	0.0	44.9	-0.2	45.0	0.2	45.0	0.0	45.1	0.2	45.2	0.2	45.2	0.0	45.3	0.2	45.4	0.2	45.4	0.0	45.4	0.0
1968	45.6	0.4	45.5	-0.2	46.1	1.3	46.1	0.0	46.2	0.2	46.2	0.0	46.3	0.2	46.4	0.2	46.5	0.2	46.5	0.0	46.6	0.2	46.6	0.0
1969	47.1	1.1	47.1	0.0	47.2	0.2	47.2	0.0	47.3	0.2	47.3	0.0	47.5	0.4	47.8	0.6	47.9	0.2	48.0	0.2	48.1	0.2	48.2	0.2
1970	48.9	1.5	49.0	0.2	49.6	1.2	49.1	-1.0	49.4	0.6	49.4	0.0	49.5	0.2	49.6	0.2	49.9	0.6	49.9	0.0	49.9	0.0	50.0	0.2
1971	50.8	1.6	50.8	0.0	51.0	0.4	50.8	-0.4	50.8	0.0	51.0	0.4	51.0	0.0	50.9	-0.2	50.9	0.0	50.9	0.0	51.0	0.2	51.0	0.0
1972	51.3	0.6	51.5	0.4	51.7	0.4	51.5	-0.4	51.5	0.0	51.6	0.2	51.7	0.2	51.7	0.0	51.8	0.2	51.9	0.2	51.9	0.0	52.0	0.2
1973	52.5	1.0	52.6	0.2	52.9	0.6	52.9	0.0	53.0	0.2	53.1	0.2	53.1	0.0	53.2	0.2	53.4	0.4	53.8	0.7	54.1	0.6	54.2	0.2
1974	56.2	3.7	57.0	1.4	57.5	0.9	57.8	0.5	58.4	1.0	59.0	1.0	59.6	1.0	61.3	2.9	61.8	0.8	62.4	1.0	63.0	1.0	63.0	0.0
1975	65.4	3.8	65.9	0.8	66.0	0.2	65.8	-0.3	65.8	0.0	65.9	0.2	65.9	0.0	65.9	0.0	65.9	0.0	66.1	0.3	66.3	0.3	66.3	0.0
1976	66.9	0.9	67.1	0.3	67.5	0.6	67.4	-0.1	67.6	0.3	67.9	0.4	68.0	0.1	67.9	-0.1	68.1	0.3	68.1	0.0	68.2	0.1	68.2	0.0
1977	69.4	1.8	69.6	0.3	69.8	0.3	69.7	-0.1	69.8	0.1	69.9	0.1	70.1	0.3	70.3	0.3	70.2	-0.1	70.7	0.7	70.8	0.1	70.9	0.1
1978	72.1	1.7	72.9	1.1	73.3	0.5	73.5	0.3	73.3	-0.3	73.7	0.5	73.7	0.0	74.0	0.4	74.1	0.1	74.5	0.5	74.6	0.1	74.4	-0.3
1979	76.9	3.4	77.2	0.4	77.5	0.4	78.2	0.9	78.7	0.6	78.9	0.3	79.9	1.3	80.2	0.4	81.2	1.2	81.8	0.7	81.8	0.0	82.6	1.0
1980	86.2	4.4	87.4	1.4	87.8	0.5	88.2	0.5	88.5	0.3	89.2	0.8	90.4	1.3	90.9	0.6	91.4	0.6	91.5	0.1	91.6	0.1	92.9	1.4
1981	94.1	1.3	95.1	1.1	95.3	0.2	95.4	0.1	95.4	0.0	95.4	0.0	96.3	0.9	96.0	-0.3	96.5	0.5	96.2	-0.3	96.1	-0.1	96.3	0.2
1982	98.6	2.4	99.4	0.8	99.6	0.2	99.8	0.2	100.2	0.4	100.2	0.0	100.3	0.1	100.9	0.6	100.1	-0.8	99.9	-0.2	100.0	0.1	101.0	1.0
1983	100.6	-0.4	101.7	1.1	101.9	0.2	102.2	0.3	102.1	-0.1	102.0	-0.1	101.3	-0.7	101.4	0.1	101.5	0.1	102.0	0.5	101.7	-0.3	101.7	0.0
1984	102.7	1.0	102.9	0.2	102.8	-0.1	102.3	-0.5	102.4	0.1	102.3	-0.1	102.3	0.0	102.3	0.0	102.5	0.2	102.7	0.2	102.8	0.1	102.8	0.0
1985	103.0	0.2	104.3	1.3	104.5	0.2	104.4	-0.1	104.4	0.0	104.3	-0.1	104.2	-0.1	104.2	0.0	104.4	0.2	105.7	1.2	105.9	0.2	105.2	-0.7
1986	105.7	0.5	106.1	0.4	106.3	0.2	106.4	0.1	106.5	0.1	106.6	0.1	106.8	0.2	106.9	0.1	106.8	-0.1	107.1	0.3	107.1	0.0	106.6	-0.5
1987	106.5	-0.1	107.3	0.8	107.1	-0.2	107.4	0.3	107.4	0.0	107.6	0.2	107.7	0.1	107.7	0.0	108.3	0.6	108.6	0.3	108.8	0.2	109.0	0.2
1988	110.1	1.0	110.9	0.7	111.0	0.1	111.1	0.1	111.2	0.1	111.5	0.3	112.0	0.4	112.2	0.2	112.3	0.1	112.7	0.4	112.9	0.2	113.2	0.3
1989	114.7	1.3	115.5	0.7	115.9	0.3	116.0	0.1	116.2	0.2	116.7	0.4	116.9	0.2	117.4	0.4	117.6	0.2	118.0	0.3	117.7	-0.3	118.1	0.3
1990	118.5	0.3	119.1	0.5	119.1	0.0	119.2	0.1	119.3	0.1	119.4	0.1	119.3	-0.1	119.6	0.3	119.5	-0.1	120.8	1.1	120.6	-0.2	120.8	0.2
1991	121.3	0.4	121.6	0.2	121.9	0.2	122.0	0.1	122.2	0.2	122.6	0.3	122.7	0.1	123.1	0.3	123.2	0.1	123.6	0.3	123.3	-0.2	123.2	-0.1

[Continued]

Toys, Sporting Goods, Small Arms, Etc.
Producer Price Index
Base 1982 = 100
[Continued]

For 1947-1993. Columns headed % show percentile change in the index from the previous period for which an index is available.

Year	Jan		Feb		Mar		Apr		May		Jun		Jul		Aug		Sep		Oct		Nov		Dec	
	Index	%	Index	%	Index	%	Index	%	Index	%	Index	%	Index	%	Index	%	Index	%	Index	%	Index	%	Index	%
1992	123.8	0.5	124.1	0.2	123.9	-0.2	124.0	0.1	124.4	0.3	124.6	0.2	124.6	0.0	124.7	0.1	125.9	1.0	125.9	0.0	124.6	-1.0	124.2	-0.3
1993	125.0	0.6	125.2	0.2	125.1	-0.1	125.2	0.1	125.3	0.1	125.3	0.0	125.3	0.0	125.9	0.5	125.5	-0.3	125.7	0.2	125.7	0.0	126.1	0.3

Source: U.S. Department of Labor, Bureau of Labor Statistics, Division of Industry Prices and Price Indexes. n.e.c. stands for not elsewhere classified. - indicates no data collected for period or unavailable.

Tobacco Products, Incl. Stemmed & Redried
Producer Price Index
Base 1982 = 100

For 1947-1993. Columns headed % show percentile change in the index from the previous period for which an index is available.

Year	Jan Index	%	Feb Index	%	Mar Index	%	Apr Index	%	May Index	%	Jun Index	%	Jul Index	%	Aug Index	%	Sep Index	%	Oct Index	%	Nov Index	%	Dec Index	%
1947	20.4	-	20.4	0.0	20.4	0.0	20.5	0.5	20.5	0.0	20.5	0.0	20.5	0.0	20.5	0.0	20.5	0.0	20.5	0.0	20.5	0.0	20.5	0.0
1948	20.5	0.0	20.5	0.0	20.5	0.0	20.5	0.0	20.5	0.0	20.5	0.0	20.6	0.5	22.3	8.3	22.3	0.0	22.3	0.0	22.3	0.0	22.3	0.0
1949	22.3	0.0	22.3	0.0	22.3	0.0	22.3	0.0	22.3	0.0	22.3	0.0	22.3	0.0	22.4	0.4	22.4	0.0	22.4	0.0	22.4	0.0	22.4	0.0
1950	22.4	0.0	22.4	0.0	22.4	0.0	22.4	0.0	22.4	0.0	22.4	0.0	22.4	0.0	23.3	4.0	23.3	0.0	23.4	0.4	23.4	0.0	23.4	0.0
1951	23.4	0.0	23.4	0.0	23.4	0.0	23.4	0.0	23.4	0.0	23.4	0.0	23.4	0.0	23.4	0.0	23.4	0.0	23.4	0.0	23.6	0.9	23.6	0.0
1952	23.6	0.0	23.6	0.0	23.6	0.0	23.6	0.0	23.6	0.0	23.6	0.0	23.6	0.0	23.6	0.0	23.6	0.0	23.6	0.0	23.6	0.0	23.6	0.0
1953	23.7	0.4	23.7	0.0	25.6	8.0	25.6	0.0	25.6	0.0	25.6	0.0	25.6	0.0	25.6	0.0	25.6	0.0	25.6	0.0	25.6	0.0	25.6	0.0
1954	25.6	0.0	25.6	0.0	25.6	0.0	25.6	0.0	25.6	0.0	25.6	0.0	25.6	0.0	25.6	0.0	25.6	0.0	25.6	0.0	25.6	0.0	25.6	0.0
1955	25.6	0.0	25.6	0.0	25.6	0.0	25.6	0.0	25.6	0.0	25.6	0.0	25.6	0.0	25.6	0.0	25.6	0.0	25.6	0.0	25.6	0.0	25.6	0.0
1956	25.6	0.0	25.6	0.0	25.6	0.0	25.6	0.0	25.6	0.0	25.6	0.0	25.6	0.0	25.6	0.0	25.6	0.0	25.6	0.0	25.6	0.0	25.7	0.4
1957	25.7	0.0	25.7	0.0	25.7	0.0	25.7	0.0	25.8	0.4	25.8	0.0	27.7	7.4	27.7	0.0	27.7	0.0	27.7	0.0	27.7	0.0	27.7	0.0
1958	27.7	0.0	27.7	0.0	27.7	0.0	27.7	0.0	27.7	0.0	27.7	0.0	27.7	0.0	27.7	0.0	27.7	0.0	27.7	0.0	27.7	0.0	27.7	0.0
1959	27.7	0.0	27.8	0.4	27.9	0.4	27.9	0.0	27.9	0.0	27.9	0.0	27.9	0.0	27.9	0.0	27.9	0.0	27.9	0.0	27.9	0.0	27.9	0.0
1960	27.9	0.0	27.9	0.0	27.9	0.0	27.9	0.0	27.9	0.0	27.9	0.0	27.9	0.0	27.9	0.0	27.9	0.0	27.9	0.0	27.9	0.0	27.9	0.0
1961	27.9	0.0	27.9	0.0	27.9	0.0	27.9	0.0	27.9	0.0	27.9	0.0	27.9	0.0	27.9	0.0	27.9	0.0	27.9	0.0	27.9	0.0	27.9	0.0
1962	27.9	0.0	27.9	0.0	27.9	0.0	27.9	0.0	27.9	0.0	27.9	0.0	27.9	0.0	27.9	0.0	28.0	0.4	28.0	0.0	28.0	0.0	28.0	0.0
1963	28.0	0.0	28.0	0.0	28.0	0.0	28.0	0.0	28.7	2.5	29.0	1.0	29.0	0.0	29.0	0.0	29.0	0.0	29.0	0.0	29.0	0.0	29.0	0.0
1964	29.0	0.0	29.0	0.0	29.1	0.3	29.1	0.0	29.1	0.0	29.1	0.0	29.1	0.0	29.1	0.0	29.1	0.0	29.1	0.0	29.1	0.0	29.1	0.0
1965	29.1	0.0	29.1	0.0	29.1	0.0	29.2	0.3	29.4	0.7	29.1	-1.0	29.1	0.0	29.1	0.0	29.1	0.0	29.1	0.0	29.1	0.0	29.1	0.0
1966	29.2	0.3	29.2	0.0	30.1	3.1	30.2	0.3	30.2	0.0	30.2	0.0	30.2	0.0	30.2	0.0	30.2	0.0	30.2	0.0	30.2	0.0	30.2	0.0
1967	30.2	0.0	30.2	0.0	30.2	0.0	30.2	0.0	30.2	0.0	31.5	4.3	31.5	0.0	31.5	0.0	31.5	0.0	31.5	0.0	31.5	0.0	31.5	0.0
1968	31.5	0.0	31.5	0.0	31.5	0.0	31.5	0.0	31.5	0.0	31.5	0.0	31.5	0.0	31.5	0.0	31.5	0.0	31.6	0.3	32.0	1.3	32.0	0.0
1969	32.0	0.0	32.0	0.0	32.0	0.0	32.1	0.3	32.1	0.0	33.8	5.3	33.9	0.3	33.9	0.0	34.0	0.3	34.0	0.0	34.0	0.0	34.0	0.0
1970	34.0	0.0	34.0	0.0	34.0	0.0	34.0	0.0	34.0	0.0	36.3	6.8	36.0	-0.8	35.9	-0.3	35.9	0.0	35.9	0.0	35.9	0.0	35.9	0.0
1971	36.0	0.3	36.1	0.3	36.1	0.0	36.1	0.0	36.1	0.0	36.1	0.0	36.1	0.0	36.1	0.0	36.1	0.0	36.1	0.0	36.1	0.0	36.1	0.0
1972	36.3	0.6	36.3	0.0	36.3	0.0	36.3	0.0	36.4	0.3	36.4	0.0	36.4	0.0	36.4	0.0	36.4	0.0	36.4	0.0	36.4	0.0	36.4	0.0
1973	36.4	0.0	37.5	3.0	37.7	0.5	37.7	0.0	37.9	0.5	37.9	0.0	37.9	0.0	37.9	0.0	37.9	0.0	38.0	0.3	38.0	0.0	38.1	0.3
1974	38.1	0.0	38.2	0.3	38.2	0.0	38.3	0.3	41.2	7.6	41.7	1.2	41.7	0.0	41.9	0.5	41.9	0.0	41.9	0.0	44.8	6.9	45.4	1.3
1975	45.6	0.4	45.8	0.4	45.9	0.2	46.0	0.2	46.0	0.0	46.0	0.0	46.0	0.0	46.0	0.0	46.1	0.2	46.2	0.2	46.8	1.3	49.2	5.1
1976	49.2	0.0	49.2	0.0	49.3	0.2	50.2	1.8	50.1	-0.2	50.1	0.0	50.1	0.0	50.1	0.0	50.2	0.2	50.3	0.2	53.3	6.0	53.3	0.0
1977	54.1	1.5	54.1	0.0	54.1	0.0	54.2	0.2	54.2	0.0	54.3	0.2	54.4	0.2	54.4	0.0	57.8	6.3	58.7	1.6	58.7	0.0	58.8	0.2
1978	59.0	0.3	59.2	0.3	59.2	0.0	59.3	0.2	59.3	0.0	61.3	3.4	63.6	3.8	63.6	0.0	63.6	0.0	63.1	-0.8	63.1	0.0	63.1	0.0
1979	66.1	4.8	66.1	0.0	66.2	0.2	66.4	0.3	66.4	0.0	66.4	0.0	66.5	0.2	68.5	3.0	68.7	0.3	68.8	0.1	68.8	0.0	70.1	1.9
1980	73.2	4.4	73.4	0.3	73.5	0.1	73.7	0.3	76.7	4.1	76.8	0.1	76.8	0.0	76.8	0.0	76.8	0.0	77.2	0.5	78.8	2.1	78.9	0.1
1981	78.9	0.0	79.3	0.5	79.3	0.0	83.2	4.9	83.2	0.0	83.2	0.0	83.2	0.0	83.2	0.0	85.0	2.2	86.1	1.3	86.1	0.0	86.1	0.0
1982	86.1	0.0	94.9	10.2	94.9	0.0	94.9	0.0	95.0	0.1	95.0	0.0	96.4	1.5	96.4	0.0	101.9	5.7	113.1	11.0	112.8	-0.3	118.5	5.1
1983	110.2	-7.0	110.3	0.1	109.5	-0.7	109.6	0.1	109.5	-0.1	109.0	-0.5	115.6	6.1	116.6	0.9	116.6	0.0	116.6	0.0	116.7	0.1	116.7	0.0
1984	120.5	3.3	120.8	0.2	120.8	0.0	120.8	0.0	120.9	0.1	123.9	2.5	126.5	2.1	125.9	-0.5	125.9	0.0	124.5	-1.1	124.6	0.1	124.7	0.1
1985	130.0	4.3	130.2	0.2	130.2	0.0	130.2	0.0	130.2	0.0	130.2	0.0	134.9	3.6	134.9	0.0	134.9	0.0	134.7	-0.1	134.8	0.1	134.8	0.0
1986	139.6	3.6	139.7	0.1	139.8	0.1	139.7	-0.1	139.8	0.1	139.8	0.0	145.2	3.9	145.2	0.0	145.2	0.0	145.2	0.0	145.2	0.0	145.2	0.0
1987	150.8	3.9	150.8	0.0	150.8	0.0	150.9	0.1	150.9	0.0	150.9	0.0	157.5	4.4	157.6	0.1	157.6	0.0	157.5	-0.1	157.6	0.1	163.3	3.6
1988	166.6	2.0	166.7	0.1	166.7	0.0	166.8	0.1	166.8	0.0	166.8	0.0	175.4	5.2	175.4	0.0	175.4	0.0	175.6	0.1	175.5	-0.1	184.7	5.2
1989	187.2	1.4	187.3	0.1	187.3	0.0	187.3	0.0	187.4	0.1	196.8	5.0	197.9	0.6	198.1	0.1	198.1	0.0	200.4	1.2	200.4	0.0	209.6	4.6
1990	212.3	1.3	212.8	0.2	212.8	0.0	212.8	0.0	217.4	2.2	224.1	3.1	224.3	0.1	224.3	0.0	225.0	0.3	224.9	-0.0	230.4	2.4	236.1	2.5
1991	237.4	0.6	237.4	0.0	239.6	0.9	243.3	1.5	243.4	0.0	249.1	2.3	254.4	2.1	255.0	0.2	254.9	-0.0	255.0	0.0	259.8	1.9	267.2	2.8

[Continued]

Tobacco Products, Incl. Stemmed & Redried
Producer Price Index
Base 1982 = 100
[Continued]

For 1947-1993. Columns headed % show percentile change in the index from the previous period for which an index is available.

Year	Jan Index	%	Feb Index	%	Mar Index	%	Apr Index	%	May Index	%	Jun Index	%	Jul Index	%	Aug Index	%	Sep Index	%	Oct Index	%	Nov Index	%	Dec Index	%
1992	268.1	0.3	268.2	0.0	268.2	0.0	273.7	2.1	283.2	3.5	283.2	0.0	283.4	0.1	265.9	-6.2	274.1	3.1	274.2	0.0	276.5	0.8	285.1	3.1
1993	291.8	2.4	292.2	0.1	292.2	0.0	296.2	1.4	296.9	0.2	289.2	-2.6	287.2	-0.7	213.3	-25.7	213.5	0.1	214.0	0.2	213.5	-0.2	221.2	3.6

Source: U.S. Department of Labor, Bureau of Labor Statistics, Division of Industry Prices and Price Indexes. n.e.c. stands for not elsewhere classified. - indicates no data collected for period or unavailable.

Notions

Producer Price Index
Base 1982 = 100

For 1947-1993. Columns headed % show percentile change in the index from the previous period for which an index is available.

Year	Jan Index	%	Feb Index	%	Mar Index	%	Apr Index	%	May Index	%	Jun Index	%	Jul Index	%	Aug Index	%	Sep Index	%	Oct Index	%	Nov Index	%	Dec Index	%
1947	37.9	-	37.9	0.0	37.9	0.0	37.9	0.0	37.9	0.0	37.9	0.0	37.9	0.0	37.9	0.0	37.6	-0.8	37.5	-0.3	37.5	0.0	37.5	0.0
1948	37.9	1.1	37.9	0.0	37.9	0.0	37.9	0.0	37.9	0.0	37.9	0.0	38.0	0.3	38.0	0.0	38.3	0.8	37.8	-1.3	37.8	0.0	37.5	-0.8
1949	37.5	0.0	37.5	0.0	37.1	-1.1	33.4	-10.0	33.0	-1.2	33.0	0.0	33.0	0.0	33.0	0.0	33.0	0.0	33.0	0.0	33.0	0.0	33.0	0.0
1950	33.0	0.0	33.0	0.0	33.0	0.0	33.0	0.0	32.5	-1.5	32.5	0.0	32.3	-0.6	33.6	4.0	34.6	3.0	34.9	0.9	35.8	2.6	36.1	0.8
1951	36.4	0.8	37.1	1.9	37.1	0.0	37.1	0.0	37.1	0.0	37.1	0.0	37.1	0.0	37.1	0.0	37.1	0.0	37.1	0.0	37.1	0.0	37.1	0.0
1952	36.7	-1.1	36.7	0.0	36.0	-1.9	35.2	-2.2	33.5	-4.8	33.5	0.0	33.5	0.0	33.2	-0.9	33.2	0.0	33.3	0.3	33.4	0.3	34.0	1.8
1953	34.0	0.0	34.0	0.0	34.5	1.5	34.1	-1.2	34.1	0.0	34.1	0.0	34.1	0.0	34.2	0.3	34.2	0.0	34.2	0.0	34.2	0.0	34.2	0.0
1954	34.2	0.0	34.2	0.0	34.2	0.0	34.2	0.0	34.2	0.0	35.2	2.9	35.2	0.0	35.2	0.0	35.1	-0.3	35.1	0.0	35.1	0.0	35.1	0.0
1955	35.1	0.0	33.8	-3.7	33.8	0.0	33.8	0.0	34.0	0.6	34.0	0.0	33.3	-2.1	33.3	0.0	33.3	0.0	33.3	0.0	33.3	0.0	33.3	0.0
1956	33.9	1.8	33.9	0.0	34.4	1.5	34.9	1.5	35.0	0.3	35.0	0.0	35.0	0.0	35.1	0.3	35.3	0.6	35.3	0.0	35.3	0.0	35.3	0.0
1957	35.4	0.3	35.4	0.0	35.4	0.0	35.6	0.6	35.6	0.0	35.6	0.0	35.6	0.0	35.6	0.0	35.6	0.0	35.6	0.0	35.8	0.6	36.0	0.6
1958	35.6	-1.1	35.7	0.3	35.7	0.0	35.7	0.0	35.7	0.0	35.7	0.0	35.7	0.0	35.7	0.0	35.7	0.0	35.7	0.0	35.7	0.0	35.7	0.0
1959	35.7	0.0	35.7	0.0	35.7	0.0	35.7	0.0	35.7	0.0	35.7	0.0	35.7	0.0	35.2	-1.4	35.2	0.0	35.7	1.4	35.7	0.0	35.7	0.0
1960	35.7	0.0	35.7	0.0	35.7	0.0	35.6	-0.3	35.3	-0.8	35.3	0.0	35.6	0.8	35.6	0.0	35.3	-0.8	35.3	0.0	35.3	0.0	35.3	0.0
1961	35.3	0.0	35.3	0.0	35.3	0.0	35.3	0.0	35.2	-0.3	35.2	0.0	35.2	0.0	35.2	0.0	35.2	0.0	35.2	0.0	35.2	0.0	35.2	0.0
1962	35.2	0.0	35.2	0.0	35.2	0.0	35.2	0.0	35.2	0.0	35.2	0.0	35.2	0.0	35.2	0.0	35.2	0.0	35.2	0.0	35.2	0.0	35.2	0.0
1963	35.2	0.0	35.2	0.0	35.2	0.0	35.2	0.0	35.2	0.0	35.2	0.0	35.2	0.0	35.2	0.0	35.3	0.3	35.3	0.0	35.3	0.0	35.3	0.0
1964	35.3	0.0	35.3	0.0	35.3	0.0	35.3	0.0	35.3	0.0	35.3	0.0	35.3	0.0	35.3	0.0	35.3	0.0	35.3	0.0	35.3	0.0	35.3	0.0
1965	35.3	0.0	35.3	0.0	35.3	0.0	35.3	0.0	35.3	0.0	35.3	0.0	35.3	0.0	35.3	0.0	35.3	0.0	35.3	0.0	35.3	0.0	35.3	0.0
1966	35.3	0.0	35.6	0.8	35.6	0.0	35.6	0.0	35.9	0.8	36.3	1.1	35.9	-1.1	35.9	0.0	35.9	0.0	35.9	0.0	35.9	0.0	35.9	0.0
1967	35.9	0.0	35.9	0.0	35.9	0.0	35.9	0.0	35.9	0.0	35.9	0.0	35.9	0.0	35.9	0.0	35.9	0.0	35.7	-0.6	37.0	3.6	37.0	0.0
1968	37.0	0.0	38.2	3.2	35.7	-6.5	35.7	0.0	35.7	0.0	35.7	0.0	35.7	0.0	35.8	0.3	35.8	0.0	36.0	0.6	36.0	0.0	36.0	0.0
1969	36.0	0.0	36.0	0.0	36.0	0.0	36.0	0.0	36.5	1.4	36.7	0.5	36.7	0.0	38.3	4.4	38.3	0.0	38.3	0.0	38.3	0.0	38.3	0.0
1970	38.3	0.0	39.0	1.8	39.0	0.0	38.8	-0.5	39.0	0.5	39.1	0.3	39.2	0.3	39.2	0.0	39.5	0.8	39.5	0.0	39.5	0.0	39.7	0.5
1971	40.4	1.8	40.4	0.0	40.4	0.0	40.4	0.0	40.4	0.0	40.4	0.0	40.4	0.0	40.4	0.0	40.4	0.0	40.4	0.0	40.4	0.0	40.4	0.0
1972	40.3	-0.2	40.3	0.0	40.3	0.0	40.3	0.0	40.3	0.0	40.3	0.0	40.3	0.0	40.3	0.0	40.8	1.2	40.8	0.0	40.8	0.0	40.8	0.0
1973	40.8	0.0	40.8	0.0	40.8	0.0	40.8	0.0	41.4	1.5	41.4	0.0	40.8	-1.4	41.0	0.5	41.0	0.0	41.7	1.7	42.3	1.4	42.6	0.7
1974	42.9	0.7	42.9	0.0	44.0	2.6	45.5	3.4	49.5	8.8	50.9	2.8	51.9	2.0	52.5	1.2	53.8	2.5	53.8	0.0	53.8	0.0	53.8	0.0
1975	54.2	0.7	54.2	0.0	54.2	0.0	54.2	0.0	54.2	0.0	54.2	0.0	54.2	0.0	54.2	0.0	54.2	0.0	54.7	0.9	55.7	1.8	56.5	1.4
1976	56.5	0.0	56.5	0.0	57.1	1.1	57.4	0.5	58.4	1.7	59.4	1.7	59.4	0.0	59.7	0.5	59.7	0.0	59.7	0.0	59.7	0.0	59.8	0.2
1977	61.3	2.5	62.3	1.6	62.3	0.0	62.3	0.0	62.3	0.0	62.3	0.0	62.3	0.0	62.4	0.2	62.4	0.0	62.4	0.0	62.4	0.0	62.4	0.0
1978	65.3	4.6	65.3	0.0	65.5	0.3	65.5	0.0	65.5	0.0	65.5	0.0	65.5	0.0	65.6	0.2	66.2	0.9	66.2	0.0	66.2	0.0	66.2	0.0
1979	67.9	2.6	67.9	0.0	68.7	1.2	68.7	0.0	68.8	0.1	68.8	0.0	69.3	0.7	69.3	0.0	69.3	0.0	70.6	1.9	70.7	0.1	71.0	0.4
1980	73.3	3.2	73.4	0.1	74.8	1.9	78.3	4.7	78.4	0.1	78.4	0.0	80.0	2.0	80.8	1.0	80.8	0.0	80.9	0.1	80.9	0.0	81.2	0.4
1981	82.0	1.0	89.3	8.9	89.3	0.0	89.7	0.4	96.7	7.8	96.7	0.0	96.6	-0.1	96.7	0.1	96.7	0.0	97.4	0.7	97.4	0.0	97.4	0.0
1982	97.6	0.2	97.6	0.0	98.0	0.4	98.0	0.0	101.1	3.2	101.1	0.0	101.1	0.0	101.1	0.0	101.1	0.0	101.1	0.0	101.0	-0.1	101.0	0.0
1983	101.3	0.3	101.3	0.0	101.3	0.0	101.2	-0.1	101.2	0.0	101.2	0.0	101.2	0.0	101.0	-0.2	101.0	0.0	101.0	0.0	100.9	-0.1	101.1	0.2
1984	101.6	0.5	101.9	0.3	101.9	0.0	102.2	0.3	102.5	0.3	102.5	0.0	102.5	0.0	102.5	0.0	102.5	0.0	102.3	-0.2	102.3	0.0	102.4	0.1
1985	102.4	0.0	102.6	0.2	102.6	0.0	103.1	0.5	103.1	0.0	103.1	0.0	103.1	0.0	103.0	-0.1	103.0	0.0	103.0	0.0	103.0	0.0	102.9	-0.1
1986	103.0	0.1	103.8	0.8	103.6	-0.2	103.8	0.2	103.9	0.1	103.8	-0.1	103.8	0.0	103.8	0.0	103.7	-0.1	103.7	0.0	103.9	0.2	103.9	0.0
1987	103.6	-0.3	104.8	1.2	105.0	0.2	105.0	0.0	105.1	0.1	105.2	0.1	105.5	0.3	105.7	0.2	105.7	0.0	105.8	0.1	105.5	-0.3	105.9	0.4
1988	106.3	0.4	106.6	0.3	106.5	-0.1	107.4	0.8	107.4	0.0	108.1	0.7	108.2	0.1	108.5	0.3	108.9	0.4	108.9	0.0	109.1	0.2	109.2	0.1
1989	109.9	0.6	110.6	0.6	111.1	0.5	111.5	0.4	112.0	0.4	112.2	0.2	112.1	-0.1	112.1	0.0	113.8	1.5	114.7	0.8	114.6	-0.1	114.7	0.1
1990	114.9	0.2	115.2	0.3	115.3	0.1	115.4	0.1	115.3	-0.1	115.7	0.3	115.7	0.0	115.7	0.0	115.9	0.2	116.5	0.5	116.5	0.0	116.9	0.3
1991	117.0	0.1	116.8	-0.2	116.9	0.1	116.9	0.0	117.5	0.5	118.2	0.6	118.4	0.2	118.7	0.3	118.5	-0.2	118.1	-0.3	118.2	0.1	119.1	0.8

[Continued]

Notions

Producer Price Index
Base 1982 = 100
[Continued]

For 1947-1993. Columns headed % show percentile change in the index from the previous period for which an index is available.

Year	Jan		Feb		Mar		Apr		May		Jun		Jul		Aug		Sep		Oct		Nov		Dec	
	Index	%	Index	%	Index	%	Index	%	Index	%	Index	%	Index	%	Index	%	Index	%	Index	%	Index	%	Index	%
1992	119.1	0.0	119.1	0.0	119.1	0.0	119.0	-0.1	119.3	0.3	119.4	0.1	119.6	0.2	119.0	-0.5	118.7	-0.3	119.4	0.6	120.1	0.6	119.3	-0.7
1993	119.6	0.3	120.4	0.7	119.8	-0.5	120.1	0.3	120.4	0.2	120.6	0.2	120.5	-0.1	120.4	-0.1	120.4	0.0	120.9	0.4	120.7	-0.2	120.7	0.0

Source: U.S. Department of Labor, Bureau of Labor Statistics, Division of Industry Prices and Price Indexes. n.e.c. stands for not elsewhere classified. - indicates no data collected for period or unavailable.

Photographic Equipment and Supplies
Producer Price Index
Base 1982 = 100

For 1947-1993. Columns headed % show percentile change in the index from the previous period for which an index is available.

Year	Jan Index	%	Feb Index	%	Mar Index	%	Apr Index	%	May Index	%	Jun Index	%	Jul Index	%	Aug Index	%	Sep Index	%	Oct Index	%	Nov Index	%	Dec Index	%
1947	31.5	-	31.5	0.0	31.6	0.3	31.6	0.0	31.8	0.6	31.9	0.3	31.9	0.0	32.9	3.1	32.9	0.0	32.9	0.0	33.0	0.3	33.4	1.2
1948	34.4	3.0	34.6	0.6	34.7	0.3	34.8	0.3	34.9	0.3	35.0	0.3	35.0	0.0	35.3	0.9	35.5	0.6	35.8	0.8	36.4	1.7	36.7	0.8
1949	36.7	0.0	37.5	2.2	37.1	-1.1	37.0	-0.3	36.7	-0.8	36.5	-0.5	36.5	0.0	36.5	0.0	36.5	0.0	36.3	-0.5	36.3	0.0	36.3	0.0
1950	36.3	0.0	36.2	-0.3	35.9	-0.8	35.9	0.0	36.0	0.3	36.0	0.0	36.0	0.0	36.0	0.0	36.4	1.1	36.9	1.4	36.9	0.0	37.1	0.5
1951	37.2	0.3	37.2	0.0	37.2	0.0	37.2	0.0	37.2	0.0	37.2	0.0	37.8	1.6	37.8	0.0	37.8	0.0	37.8	0.0	37.9	0.3	37.9	0.0
1952	37.7	-0.5	38.0	0.8	38.0	0.0	38.0	0.0	38.0	0.0	38.0	0.0	38.0	0.0	38.0	0.0	38.0	0.0	38.0	0.0	38.0	0.0	38.0	0.0
1953	38.0	0.0	38.0	0.0	38.1	0.3	38.1	0.0	38.2	0.3	38.4	0.5	38.4	0.0	38.3	-0.3	38.5	0.5	38.5	0.0	38.5	0.0	38.5	0.0
1954	38.5	0.0	38.5	0.0	38.5	0.0	38.7	0.5	38.7	0.0	38.7	0.0	38.8	0.3	38.7	-0.3	38.7	0.0	38.7	0.0	38.7	0.0	38.7	0.0
1955	38.6	-0.3	38.6	0.0	38.7	0.3	39.0	0.8	39.0	0.0	39.0	0.0	39.2	0.5	39.3	0.3	39.3	0.0	39.4	0.3	39.5	0.3	39.5	0.0
1956	39.6	0.3	39.7	0.3	39.7	0.0	39.6	-0.3	39.6	0.0	39.8	0.5	39.8	0.0	39.8	0.0	39.8	0.0	39.8	0.0	40.5	1.8	40.5	0.0
1957	41.1	1.5	41.1	0.0	41.2	0.2	41.3	0.2	41.3	0.0	41.3	0.0	41.3	0.0	41.8	1.2	42.2	1.0	42.2	0.0	42.2	0.0	42.3	0.2
1958	42.3	0.0	42.4	0.2	42.4	0.0	42.4	0.0	42.4	0.0	42.8	0.9	42.8	0.0	42.7	-0.2	42.7	0.0	42.7	0.0	42.8	0.2	42.8	0.0
1959	43.3	1.2	43.3	0.0	44.0	1.6	44.1	0.2	44.1	0.0	44.1	0.0	44.1	0.0	44.2	0.2	44.3	0.2	44.3	0.0	44.3	0.0	44.3	0.0
1960	44.2	-0.2	44.2	0.0	44.2	0.0	44.2	0.0	44.2	0.0	44.2	0.0	44.2	0.0	44.4	0.5	44.4	0.0	44.6	0.5	44.9	0.7	44.9	0.0
1961	44.8	-0.2	44.9	0.2	44.8	-0.2	44.8	0.0	44.5	-0.7	44.4	-0.2	44.5	0.2	45.0	1.1	45.2	0.4	45.4	0.4	45.5	0.2	45.7	0.4
1962	45.7	0.0	46.0	0.7	46.0	0.0	45.9	-0.2	46.0	0.2	46.1	0.2	46.1	0.0	46.2	0.2	46.1	-0.2	46.1	0.0	46.1	0.0	46.1	0.0
1963	46.2	0.2	46.2	0.0	45.9	-0.6	45.9	0.0	46.0	0.2	46.1	0.2	46.2	0.2	45.9	-0.6	45.8	-0.2	45.9	0.2	45.9	0.0	46.1	0.4
1964	46.2	0.2	46.2	0.0	46.2	0.0	46.2	0.0	46.2	0.0	46.2	0.0	46.3	0.2	46.3	0.0	46.3	0.0	46.5	0.4	46.5	0.0	46.5	0.0
1965	46.5	0.0	46.5	0.0	46.6	0.2	46.8	0.4	46.8	0.0	46.7	-0.2	46.7	0.0	46.7	0.0	46.7	0.0	46.7	0.0	46.7	0.0	46.7	0.0
1966	46.6	-0.2	46.6	0.0	46.6	0.0	46.5	-0.2	46.5	0.0	46.5	0.0	46.5	0.0	46.4	-0.2	46.3	-0.2	46.3	0.0	46.9	1.3	47.0	0.2
1967	47.1	0.2	47.1	0.0	47.1	0.0	47.1	0.0	47.1	0.0	47.1	0.0	47.1	0.0	47.6	1.1	47.7	0.2	48.6	1.9	48.6	0.0	48.6	0.0
1968	48.0	-1.2	48.6	1.3	48.6	0.0	48.6	0.0	49.0	0.8	49.0	0.0	48.5	-1.0	48.5	0.0	48.5	0.0	48.6	0.2	48.6	0.0	48.6	0.0
1969	48.4	-0.4	48.4	0.0	48.1	-0.6	48.2	0.2	48.4	0.4	48.4	0.0	48.7	0.6	48.7	0.0	49.0	0.6	49.1	0.2	49.2	0.2	49.3	0.2
1970	49.4	0.2	49.5	0.2	49.5	0.0	49.7	0.4	49.7	0.0	49.5	-0.4	50.1	1.2	50.2	0.2	50.1	-0.2	50.1	0.0	50.2	0.2	50.2	0.0
1971	50.3	0.2	50.4	0.2	50.4	0.0	50.4	0.0	50.4	0.0	50.5	0.2	50.6	0.2	50.6	0.0	50.6	0.0	50.6	0.0	50.6	0.0	50.6	0.0
1972	50.6	0.0	50.7	0.2	50.8	0.2	50.5	-0.6	50.5	0.0	50.5	0.0	50.5	0.0	50.8	0.6	50.8	0.0	50.8	0.0	50.8	0.0	50.8	0.0
1973	51.0	0.4	51.1	0.2	51.6	1.0	51.5	-0.2	51.4	-0.2	51.5	0.2	51.6	0.2	51.6	0.0	51.6	0.0	51.6	0.0	51.7	0.2	51.9	0.4
1974	51.9	0.0	52.3	0.8	52.5	0.4	52.6	0.2	55.6	5.7	55.6	0.0	56.4	1.4	56.4	0.0	57.4	1.8	57.6	0.3	58.0	0.7	59.9	3.3
1975	60.3	0.7	60.5	0.3	61.1	1.0	61.8	1.1	61.9	0.2	62.2	0.5	62.3	0.2	62.4	0.2	62.8	0.6	63.4	1.0	63.5	0.2	62.7	-1.3
1976	63.2	0.8	64.0	1.3	64.1	0.2	64.2	0.2	64.2	0.0	65.2	1.6	65.1	-0.2	65.1	0.0	65.1	0.0	65.1	0.0	65.2	0.2	66.2	1.5
1977	65.7	-0.8	65.8	0.2	65.8	0.0	65.6	-0.3	66.5	1.4	66.7	0.3	67.1	0.6	67.0	-0.1	66.8	-0.3	66.9	0.1	66.9	0.0	67.2	0.4
1978	67.6	0.6	67.8	0.3	67.8	0.0	68.7	1.3	68.8	0.1	69.4	0.9	69.4	0.0	69.6	0.3	70.2	0.9	70.7	0.7	70.7	0.0	70.7	0.0
1979	71.4	1.0	71.4	0.0	71.4	0.0	71.3	-0.1	71.6	0.4	72.1	0.7	72.2	0.1	72.3	0.1	73.3	1.4	74.8	2.0	76.6	2.4	78.1	2.0
1980	78.9	1.0	103.9	31.7	104.1	0.2	100.9	-3.1	94.9	-5.9	95.9	1.1	95.8	-0.1	95.5	-0.3	95.5	0.0	95.4	-0.1	98.2	2.9	98.2	0.0
1981	98.6	0.4	99.6	1.0	100.4	0.8	100.9	0.5	101.0	0.1	101.0	0.0	100.5	-0.5	98.4	-2.1	99.2	0.8	99.3	0.1	99.4	0.1	99.4	0.0
1982	99.8	0.4	100.0	0.2	100.8	0.8	101.8	1.0	100.1	-1.7	100.0	-0.1	99.3	-0.7	99.3	0.0	99.8	0.5	99.7	-0.1	99.7	0.0	99.8	0.1
1983	99.8	0.0	100.7	0.9	102.9	2.2	103.0	0.1	103.0	0.0	102.9	-0.1	102.9	0.0	102.9	0.0	102.9	0.0	103.0	0.1	103.0	0.0	103.0	0.0
1984	103.1	0.1	103.6	0.5	101.1	-2.4	101.5	0.4	101.5	0.0	101.5	0.0	101.6	0.1	102.4	0.8	102.4	0.0	102.5	0.1	101.2	-1.3	101.3	0.1
1985	101.5	0.2	101.6	0.1	102.6	1.0	102.6	0.0	102.5	-0.1	102.6	0.1	102.5	-0.1	102.5	0.0	103.0	0.5	103.0	0.0	103.1	0.1	103.2	0.1
1986	103.2	0.0	103.2	0.0	103.9	0.7	103.8	-0.1	104.7	0.9	104.1	-0.6	104.1	0.0	104.1	0.0	104.1	0.0	104.2	0.1	104.2	0.0	104.1	-0.1
1987	104.2	0.1	104.4	0.2	104.3	-0.1	105.4	1.1	105.6	0.2	105.7	0.1	105.7	0.0	105.7	0.0	105.9	0.2	106.1	0.2	106.1	0.0	105.8	-0.3
1988	105.8	0.0	105.8	0.0	105.8	0.0	106.5	0.7	106.5	0.0	107.1	0.6	107.1	0.0	107.3	0.2	107.3	0.0	108.9	1.5	109.1	0.2	108.7	-0.4
1989	111.8	2.9	111.9	0.1	112.7	0.7	113.1	0.4	114.4	1.1	114.4	0.0	114.4	0.0	114.5	0.1	115.8	1.1	116.2	0.3	116.2	0.0	116.2	0.0
1990	117.5	1.1	117.8	0.3	117.8	0.0	117.8	0.0	117.9	0.1	117.9	0.0	118.9	0.8	118.8	-0.1	119.0	0.2	118.9	-0.1	118.9	0.0	119.5	0.5
1991	119.6	0.1	117.6	-1.7	117.7	0.1	118.0	0.3	117.9	-0.1	117.9	0.0	117.9	0.0	117.9	0.0	117.9	0.0	118.3	0.3	118.4	0.1	118.5	0.1

[Continued]

Photographic Equipment and Supplies
Producer Price Index
Base 1982 = 100
[Continued]

For 1947-1993. Columns headed % show percentile change in the index from the previous period for which an index is available.

Year	Jan		Feb		Mar		Apr		May		Jun		Jul		Aug		Sep		Oct		Nov		Dec	
	Index	%	Index	%	Index	%	Index	%	Index	%	Index	%	Index	%	Index	%	Index	%	Index	%	Index	%	Index	%
1992	118.6	0.1	118.7	0.1	118.2	-0.4	118.2	0.0	118.4	0.2	118.7	0.3	118.7	0.0	118.7	0.0	118.9	0.2	118.8	-0.1	118.9	0.1	118.9	0.0
1993	117.7	-1.0	117.8	0.1	117.8	0.0	117.9	0.1	117.9	0.0	117.9	0.0	118.3	0.3	118.8	0.4	119.6	0.7	119.4	-0.2	119.9	0.4	120.2	0.3

Source: U.S. Department of Labor, Bureau of Labor Statistics, Division of Industry Prices and Price Indexes. n.e.c. stands for not elsewhere classified. - indicates no data collected for period or unavailable.

Mobile Homes
Producer Price Index
Base 1982 = 100

For 1981-1993. Columns headed % show percentile change in the index from the previous period for which an index is available.

Year	Jan Index	%	Feb Index	%	Mar Index	%	Apr Index	%	May Index	%	Jun Index	%	Jul Index	%	Aug Index	%	Sep Index	%	Oct Index	%	Nov Index	%	Dec Index	%
1981	94.5	-	94.6	0.1	95.8	1.3	96.2	0.4	96.3	0.1	96.4	0.1	97.7	1.3	97.8	0.1	98.0	0.2	98.3	0.3	98.4	0.1	98.4	0.0
1982	98.5	0.1	98.6	0.1	100.0	1.4	100.2	0.2	100.4	0.2	100.3	-0.1	100.5	0.2	100.6	0.1	100.6	0.0	100.5	-0.1	99.9	-0.6	99.9	0.0
1983	100.0	0.1	99.9	-0.1	100.6	0.7	100.3	-0.3	100.3	0.0	100.8	0.5	101.0	0.2	101.2	0.2	101.5	0.3	101.8	0.3	101.9	0.1	102.0	0.1
1984	100.1	-1.9	100.3	0.2	100.4	0.1	101.2	0.8	101.1	-0.1	100.5	-0.6	100.7	0.2	100.8	0.1	101.1	0.3	101.1	0.0	101.6	0.5	101.5	-0.1
1985	101.5	0.0	101.6	0.1	101.5	-0.1	101.5	0.0	101.5	0.0	101.8	0.3	101.7	-0.1	101.8	0.1	102.0	0.2	101.8	-0.2	101.9	0.1	101.9	0.0
1986	102.2	0.3	100.9	-1.3	101.1	0.2	102.8	1.7	102.9	0.1	103.1	0.2	103.1	0.0	103.2	0.1	103.2	0.0	103.3	0.1	103.5	0.2	103.6	0.1
1987	103.7	0.1	103.7	0.0	103.7	0.0	103.5	-0.2	104.0	0.5	104.0	0.0	104.4	0.4	103.9	-0.5	104.7	0.8	105.0	0.3	105.1	0.1	106.2	1.0
1988	106.5	0.3	107.0	0.5	107.7	0.7	108.2	0.5	108.9	0.6	109.3	0.4	109.8	0.5	109.9	0.1	110.4	0.5	110.7	0.3	111.6	0.8	111.4	-0.2
1989	111.6	0.2	111.9	0.3	112.1	0.2	112.5	0.4	113.9	1.2	113.9	0.0	114.3	0.4	114.8	0.4	115.2	0.3	115.5	0.3	115.8	0.3	115.9	0.1
1990	115.9	0.0	116.2	0.3	116.2	0.0	116.4	0.2	116.9	0.4	117.5	0.5	117.7	0.2	118.0	0.3	118.2	0.2	118.4	0.2	119.3	0.8	119.3	0.0
1991	119.3	0.0	119.5	0.2	119.5	0.0	119.6	0.1	120.1	0.4	120.4	0.2	120.8	0.3	121.1	0.2	121.0	-0.1	121.0	0.0	121.2	0.2	121.2	0.0
1992	120.4	-0.7	120.4	0.0	120.4	0.0	120.9	0.4	121.3	0.3	121.4	0.1	121.7	0.2	122.0	0.2	122.1	0.1	123.0	0.7	123.5	0.4	123.5	0.0
1993	123.5	0.0	124.6	0.9	125.5	0.7	126.6	0.9	127.3	0.6	127.6	0.2	129.2	1.3	129.2	0.0	131.2	1.5	131.2	0.0	133.6	1.8	133.4	-0.1

Source: U.S. Department of Labor, Bureau of Labor Statistics, Division of Industry Prices and Price Indexes. n.e.c. stands for not elsewhere classified. - indicates no data collected for period or unavailable.

Medical, Surgical & Personal Aid Devices
Producer Price Index
Base 1982 = 100

For 1982-1993. Columns headed % show percentile change in the index from the previous period for which an index is available.

Year	Jan Index	%	Feb Index	%	Mar Index	%	Apr Index	%	May Index	%	Jun Index	%	Jul Index	%	Aug Index	%	Sep Index	%	Oct Index	%	Nov Index	%	Dec Index	%
1982	-	-	-	-	-	-	-	-	-	-	-	-	100.5	-	100.5	0.0	101.4	0.9	101.6	0.2	101.6	0.0	101.6	0.0
1983	102.7	1.1	101.7	-1.0	102.6	0.9	102.4	-0.2	102.6	0.2	102.8	0.2	104.4	1.6	104.7	0.3	104.5	-0.2	105.2	0.7	105.9	0.7	105.9	0.0
1984	107.6	1.6	107.7	0.1	107.8	0.1	108.3	0.5	108.2	-0.1	108.2	0.0	108.4	0.2	108.9	0.5	108.4	-0.5	108.6	0.2	108.7	0.1	108.7	0.0
1985	109.4	0.6	109.2	-0.2	109.3	0.1	109.2	-0.1	109.2	0.0	109.2	0.0	108.7	-0.5	108.7	0.0	108.7	0.0	108.9	0.2	108.9	0.0	109.0	0.1
1986	110.4	1.3	110.5	0.1	110.8	0.3	111.0	0.2	111.0	0.0	111.2	0.2	111.5	0.3	111.6	0.1	111.8	0.2	112.4	0.5	114.7	2.0	114.3	-0.3
1987	114.1	-0.2	114.2	0.1	114.6	0.4	117.8	2.8	117.6	-0.2	117.8	0.2	117.6	-0.2	117.9	0.3	117.7	-0.2	117.8	0.1	118.4	0.5	118.2	-0.2
1988	119.1	0.8	119.2	0.1	119.4	0.2	119.5	0.1	119.8	0.3	117.8	-1.7	118.0	0.2	118.1	0.1	118.1	0.0	119.3	1.0	119.4	0.1	119.4	0.0
1989	121.2	1.5	121.5	0.2	121.8	0.2	122.1	0.2	123.1	0.8	123.1	0.0	122.9	-0.2	123.0	0.1	123.8	0.7	124.4	0.5	124.5	0.1	124.8	0.2
1990	125.9	0.9	126.0	0.1	126.3	0.2	126.9	0.5	127.2	0.2	127.3	0.1	127.4	0.1	127.8	0.3	128.0	0.2	128.4	0.3	128.3	-0.1	128.5	0.2
1991	129.3	0.6	129.5	0.2	129.7	0.2	130.0	0.2	130.0	0.0	130.2	0.2	130.4	0.2	130.6	0.2	131.2	0.5	130.9	-0.2	131.1	0.2	130.9	-0.2
1992	132.4	1.1	132.8	0.3	133.5	0.5	133.6	0.1	133.8	0.1	133.9	0.1	133.5	-0.3	134.4	0.7	134.3	-0.1	134.8	0.4	134.7	-0.1	134.6	-0.1
1993	136.0	1.0	137.5	1.1	137.9	0.3	137.8	-0.1	138.5	0.5	137.9	-0.4	137.5	-0.3	138.3	0.6	138.5	0.1	138.2	-0.2	138.2	0.0	138.5	0.2

Source: U.S. Department of Labor, Bureau of Labor Statistics, Division of Industry Prices and Price Indexes. n.e.c. stands for not elsewhere classified. - indicates no data collected for period or unavailable.

Industrial Safety Equipment
Producer Price Index
Base 1982 = 100

For 1978-1993. Columns headed % show percentile change in the index from the previous period for which an index is available.

Year	Jan Index	%	Feb Index	%	Mar Index	%	Apr Index	%	May Index	%	Jun Index	%	Jul Index	%	Aug Index	%	Sep Index	%	Oct Index	%	Nov Index	%	Dec Index	%
1978	-	-	-	-	-	-	-	-	-	-	77.3	-	77.5	0.3	77.5	0.0	77.8	0.4	78.5	0.9	79.0	0.6	79.6	0.8
1979	80.2	0.8	81.0	1.0	81.6	0.7	82.5	1.1	82.9	0.5	83.1	0.2	83.7	0.7	83.9	0.2	84.2	0.4	84.5	0.4	86.3	2.1	86.1	-0.2
1980	87.4	1.5	88.2	0.9	88.6	0.5	89.0	0.5	89.5	0.6	89.9	0.4	90.2	0.3	90.2	0.0	90.2	0.0	90.5	0.3	90.5	0.0	91.1	0.7
1981	93.0	2.1	94.4	1.5	94.7	0.3	95.0	0.3	94.9	-0.1	94.9	0.0	95.7	0.8	96.1	0.4	96.1	0.0	96.3	0.2	96.4	0.1	96.6	0.2
1982	98.1	1.6	99.2	1.1	99.6	0.4	99.6	0.0	99.8	0.2	100.2	0.4	100.2	0.0	100.6	0.4	100.5	-0.1	100.7	0.2	100.7	0.0	100.7	0.0
1983	101.9	1.2	102.0	0.1	102.5	0.5	102.9	0.4	102.9	0.0	103.0	0.1	103.6	0.6	103.6	0.0	103.6	0.0	103.2	-0.4	103.2	0.0	104.2	1.0
1984	103.6	-0.6	103.6	0.0	103.6	0.0	103.6	0.0	103.8	0.2	109.5	5.5	108.1	-1.3	110.1	1.9	109.2	-0.8	109.2	0.0	109.0	-0.2	109.8	0.7
1985	111.1	1.2	111.2	0.1	111.0	-0.2	111.2	0.2	111.1	-0.1	110.9	-0.2	110.9	0.0	110.7	-0.2	111.1	0.4	111.1	0.0	112.1	0.9	113.4	1.2
1986	117.5	3.6	117.6	0.1	118.1	0.4	120.8	2.3	120.7	-0.1	120.7	0.0	120.8	0.1	121.7	0.7	121.9	0.2	123.2	1.1	124.4	1.0	125.0	0.5
1987	125.1	0.1	128.0	2.3	128.0	0.0	128.4	0.3	127.9	-0.4	128.7	0.6	129.3	0.5	130.0	0.5	130.2	0.2	130.9	0.5	131.0	0.1	131.1	0.1
1988	132.0	0.7	132.1	0.1	133.8	1.3	136.5	2.0	136.5	0.0	136.7	0.1	137.6	0.7	137.7	0.1	137.7	0.0	137.8	0.1	140.9	2.2	140.9	0.0
1989	140.9	0.0	140.9	0.0	142.0	0.8	144.6	1.8	144.6	0.0	144.8	0.1	144.9	0.1	144.9	0.0	144.8	-0.1	146.1	0.9	145.9	-0.1	146.0	0.1
1990	146.1	0.1	146.1	0.0	146.1	0.0	149.5	2.3	150.2	0.5	150.7	0.3	150.4	-0.2	150.4	0.0	151.0	0.4	151.5	0.3	151.2	-0.2	152.7	1.0
1991	154.6	1.2	153.7	-0.6	156.4	1.8	157.0	0.4	156.7	-0.2	156.9	0.1	158.5	1.0	159.9	0.9	159.8	-0.1	161.1	0.8	158.8	-1.4	159.5	0.4
1992	159.7	0.1	159.8	0.1	160.0	0.1	163.1	1.9	163.7	0.4	163.6	-0.1	166.3	1.7	166.3	0.0	165.5	-0.5	165.5	0.0	164.8	-0.4	164.7	-0.1
1993	165.0	0.2	166.0	0.6	165.3	-0.4	165.0	-0.2	165.5	0.3	166.0	0.3	166.1	0.1	166.7	0.4	166.9	0.1	166.8	-0.1	169.2	1.4	169.2	0.0

Source: U.S. Department of Labor, Bureau of Labor Statistics, Division of Industry Prices and Price Indexes. n.e.c. stands for not elsewhere classified. - indicates no data collected for period or unavailable.

Mining Services
Producer Price Index
Base June 1985 = 100

For 1985-1993. Columns headed % show percentile change in the index from the previous period for which an index is available.

Year	Jan Index	%	Feb Index	%	Mar Index	%	Apr Index	%	May Index	%	Jun Index	%	Jul Index	%	Aug Index	%	Sep Index	%	Oct Index	%	Nov Index	%	Dec Index	%
1985	-	-	-	-	-	-	-	-	-	-	100.0	-	99.6	-0.4	99.6	0.0	99.6	0.0	99.5	-0.1	99.2	-0.3	99.0	-0.2
1986	98.8	-0.2	97.0	-1.8	95.9	-1.1	93.7	-2.3	91.7	-2.1	90.7	-1.1	89.6	-1.2	88.8	-0.9	88.7	-0.1	87.6	-1.2	86.9	-0.8	86.7	-0.2
1987	86.5	-0.2	86.2	-0.3	86.4	0.2	86.5	0.1	86.5	0.0	86.3	-0.2	86.5	0.2	87.2	0.8	87.8	0.7	88.5	0.8	89.5	1.1	90.0	0.6
1988	90.6	0.7	91.6	1.1	91.1	-0.5	91.2	0.1	91.0	-0.2	91.0	0.0	90.9	-0.1	90.0	-1.0	89.9	-0.1	89.8	-0.1	89.8	0.0	89.8	0.0
1989	90.4	0.7	90.3	-0.1	90.3	0.0	90.0	-0.3	90.5	0.6	90.7	0.2	91.3	0.7	91.6	0.3	91.2	-0.4	91.4	0.2	91.7	0.3	91.9	0.2
1990	92.8	1.0	93.8	1.1	93.8	0.0	94.4	0.6	94.7	0.3	95.0	0.3	95.0	0.0	95.7	0.7	96.4	0.7	97.4	1.0	97.8	0.4	98.7	0.9
1991	99.6	0.9	99.6	0.0	99.8	0.2	99.5	-0.3	99.6	0.1	99.2	-0.4	99.0	-0.2	98.3	-0.7	97.9	-0.4	97.0	-0.9	96.3	-0.7	97.5	1.2
1992	97.0	-0.5	96.6	-0.4	96.8	0.2	95.6	-1.2	95.7	0.1	93.7	-2.1	94.2	0.5	93.3	-1.0	94.0	0.8	94.3	0.3	94.7	0.4	95.8	1.2
1993	96.3	0.5	98.4	2.2	98.3	-0.1	99.2	0.9	99.2	0.0	99.8	0.6	100.4	0.6	100.5	0.1	101.3	0.8	100.8	-0.5	101.4	0.6	102.7	1.3

Source: U.S. Department of Labor, Bureau of Labor Statistics, Division of Industry Prices and Price Indexes. n.e.c. stands for not elsewhere classified. - indicates no data collected for period or unavailable.

Miscellaneous Products n.e.c.
Producer Price Index
Base 1982 = 100

For 1947-1993. Columns headed % show percentile change in the index from the previous period for which an index is available.

Year	Jan Index	%	Feb Index	%	Mar Index	%	Apr Index	%	May Index	%	Jun Index	%	Jul Index	%	Aug Index	%	Sep Index	%	Oct Index	%	Nov Index	%	Dec Index	%
1947	23.2	-	23.2	0.0	23.2	0.0	23.4	0.9	23.4	0.0	23.1	-1.3	22.9	-0.9	22.9	0.0	23.0	0.4	23.2	0.9	23.4	0.9	23.4	0.0
1948	23.5	0.4	23.7	0.9	23.7	0.0	23.7	0.0	23.7	0.0	23.8	0.4	23.8	0.0	23.9	0.4	23.9	0.0	23.9	0.0	24.0	0.4	24.2	0.8
1949	24.2	0.0	24.2	0.0	24.2	0.0	23.8	-1.7	23.9	0.4	23.9	0.0	23.7	-0.8	23.7	0.0	23.7	0.0	23.7	0.0	23.9	0.8	23.9	0.0
1950	23.6	-1.3	23.6	0.0	23.6	0.0	23.7	0.4	23.7	0.0	23.6	-0.4	23.7	0.4	24.3	2.5	24.2	-0.4	24.6	1.7	24.7	0.4	25.2	2.0
1951	25.7	2.0	25.7	0.0	25.7	0.0	25.7	0.0	25.7	0.0	25.7	0.0	25.7	0.0	25.7	0.0	25.7	0.0	25.7	0.0	25.7	0.0	25.7	0.0
1952	25.7	0.0	25.7	0.0	25.7	0.0	25.7	0.0	25.7	0.0	25.7	0.0	25.7	0.0	25.7	0.0	25.7	0.0	25.7	0.0	25.7	0.0	25.7	0.0
1953	25.7	0.0	25.7	0.0	25.8	0.4	25.8	0.0	25.7	-0.4	25.7	0.0	25.7	0.0	25.7	0.0	25.7	0.0	25.7	0.0	25.7	0.0	25.7	0.0
1954	25.7	0.0	25.8	0.4	25.9	0.4	26.0	0.4	25.9	-0.4	26.0	0.4	26.0	0.0	26.0	0.0	26.0	0.0	26.1	0.4	26.1	0.0	26.1	0.0
1955	26.0	-0.4	26.0	0.0	26.0	0.0	26.0	0.0	26.0	0.0	26.0	0.0	26.1	0.4	26.2	0.4	26.2	0.0	26.2	0.0	26.3	0.4	26.4	0.4
1956	26.4	0.0	26.4	0.0	26.4	0.0	26.5	0.4	26.5	0.0	26.5	0.0	26.5	0.0	26.5	0.0	26.6	0.4	26.6	0.0	26.7	0.4	26.7	0.0
1957	27.0	1.1	27.1	0.4	27.1	0.0	27.1	0.0	27.1	0.0	27.0	-0.4	27.1	0.4	27.1	0.0	27.2	0.4	27.3	0.4	27.3	0.0	27.3	0.0
1958	27.2	-0.4	27.3	0.4	27.3	0.0	27.3	0.0	27.3	0.0	27.5	0.7	27.4	-0.4	27.4	0.0	27.4	0.0	27.4	0.0	27.4	0.0	27.5	0.4
1959	27.5	0.0	27.5	0.0	27.5	0.0	27.5	0.0	27.5	0.0	27.4	-0.4	27.4	0.0	27.5	0.4	27.5	0.0	27.5	0.0	27.5	0.0	27.7	0.7
1960	27.9	0.7	27.9	0.0	27.9	0.0	27.9	0.0	28.0	0.4	27.9	-0.4	28.0	0.4	28.0	0.0	28.0	0.0	28.0	0.0	27.9	-0.4	28.0	0.4
1961	28.1	0.4	28.1	0.0	28.0	-0.4	27.9	-0.4	28.0	0.4	28.0	0.0	28.0	0.0	28.1	0.4	28.1	0.0	28.1	0.0	28.1	0.0	28.1	0.0
1962	28.0	-0.4	28.0	0.0	28.0	0.0	28.1	0.4	28.1	0.0	28.1	0.0	28.1	0.0	28.1	0.0	28.1	0.0	28.1	0.0	28.2	0.4	28.1	-0.4
1963	28.1	0.0	28.1	0.0	28.1	0.0	28.0	-0.4	28.0	0.0	28.0	0.0	28.0	0.0	28.0	0.0	28.0	0.0	28.0	0.0	28.0	0.0	28.0	0.0
1964	28.1	0.4	28.0	-0.4	28.1	0.4	28.1	0.0	28.1	0.0	28.0	-0.4	28.2	0.7	28.2	0.0	28.2	0.0	28.2	0.0	28.2	0.0	28.2	0.0
1965	28.1	-0.4	28.1	0.0	28.1	0.0	28.1	0.0	28.1	0.0	28.3	0.7	28.6	1.1	28.6	0.0	28.6	0.0	28.6	0.0	28.6	0.0	28.6	0.0
1966	28.7	0.3	28.7	0.0	28.6	-0.3	28.7	0.3	28.7	0.0	28.7	0.0	28.8	0.3	28.9	0.3	28.9	0.0	28.9	0.0	29.0	0.3	29.0	0.0
1967	29.3	1.0	29.3	0.0	29.4	0.3	29.4	0.0	29.5	0.3	29.6	0.3	29.7	0.3	29.7	0.0	29.7	0.0	29.7	0.0	29.8	0.3	29.9	0.3
1968	30.1	0.7	30.1	0.0	30.1	0.0	30.2	0.3	30.2	0.0	30.2	0.0	30.3	0.3	30.4	0.3	30.5	0.3	30.6	0.3	30.6	0.0	30.6	0.0
1969	30.4	-0.7	30.4	0.0	30.5	0.3	30.5	0.0	30.6	0.3	30.9	1.0	31.2	1.0	31.2	0.0	31.3	0.3	31.4	0.3	31.4	0.0	31.4	0.0
1970	31.5	0.3	31.5	0.0	31.5	0.0	31.5	0.0	32.0	1.6	32.1	0.3	32.5	1.2	32.5	0.0	32.6	0.3	32.6	0.0	32.7	0.3	32.7	0.0
1971	32.9	0.6	33.0	0.3	32.9	-0.3	33.1	0.6	33.2	0.3	33.3	0.3	33.5	0.6	33.5	0.0	33.5	0.0	33.5	0.0	33.5	0.0	33.5	0.0
1972	33.7	0.6	33.8	0.3	33.8	0.0	34.0	0.6	34.0	0.0	34.1	0.3	34.7	1.8	34.8	0.3	34.8	0.0	34.6	-0.6	34.5	-0.3	34.6	0.3
1973	35.1	1.4	35.2	0.3	35.4	0.6	36.1	2.0	36.9	2.2	37.6	1.9	38.3	1.9	38.3	0.0	38.3	0.0	37.8	-1.3	37.9	0.3	38.0	0.3
1974	39.0	2.6	39.4	1.0	40.3	2.3	42.4	5.2	42.7	0.7	42.9	0.5	43.1	0.5	42.2	-2.1	42.5	0.7	42.9	0.9	43.1	0.5	43.6	1.2
1975	45.3	3.9	45.8	1.1	46.0	0.4	46.1	0.2	46.2	0.2	46.2	0.0	46.3	0.2	46.3	0.0	46.6	0.6	45.5	-2.4	45.5	0.0	45.8	0.7
1976	46.0	0.4	45.9	-0.2	45.9	0.0	45.0	-2.0	45.0	0.0	45.7	1.6	45.0	-1.5	44.6	-0.9	44.7	0.2	44.8	0.2	44.8	0.0	45.1	0.7
1977	47.4	5.1	47.6	0.4	47.9	0.6	49.4	3.1	49.4	0.0	49.4	0.0	49.4	0.0	49.5	0.2	49.6	0.2	51.2	3.2	51.5	0.6	51.7	0.4
1978	52.5	1.5	51.5	-1.9	52.5	1.9	61.0	16.2	62.3	2.1	62.4	0.2	66.9	7.2	68.1	1.8	69.3	1.8	66.6	-3.9	64.6	-3.0	69.4	7.4
1979	70.3	1.3	72.1	2.6	72.6	0.7	72.7	0.1	74.1	1.9	75.6	2.0	76.8	1.6	77.3	0.7	80.5	4.1	85.2	5.8	86.7	1.8	91.3	5.3
1980	103.9	13.8	111.8	7.6	103.8	-7.2	100.8	-2.9	100.6	-0.2	106.5	5.9	109.6	2.9	107.8	-1.6	112.9	4.7	113.3	0.4	108.5	-4.2	109.5	0.9
1981	107.4	-1.9	105.9	-1.4	103.8	-2.0	103.2	-0.6	103.3	0.1	102.6	-0.7	98.5	-4.0	98.9	0.4	102.1	3.2	103.0	0.9	101.9	-1.1	101.8	-0.1
1982	101.2	-0.6	100.8	-0.4	98.9	-1.9	98.7	-0.2	97.9	-0.8	97.1	-0.8	98.6	1.5	96.7	-1.9	102.0	5.5	102.0	0.0	102.0	0.0	103.9	1.9
1983	103.7	-0.2	106.4	2.6	103.6	-2.6	103.6	0.0	103.2	-0.4	104.5	1.3	104.5	0.0	104.3	-0.2	103.3	-1.0	103.2	-0.1	103.2	0.0	104.4	1.2
1984	103.7	-0.7	103.6	-0.1	104.7	1.1	104.0	-0.7	103.6	-0.4	103.5	-0.1	103.5	0.0	104.4	0.9	102.6	-1.7	103.0	0.4	103.4	0.4	103.5	0.1
1985	102.6	-0.9	103.7	1.1	103.0	-0.7	104.2	1.2	103.9	-0.3	103.7	-0.2	103.5	-0.2	103.4	-0.1	103.3	-0.1	103.4	0.1	103.5	0.1	103.1	-0.4
1986	103.7	0.6	103.9	0.2	104.2	0.3	104.4	0.2	104.5	0.1	104.5	0.0	104.6	0.1	105.1	0.5	105.5	0.4	106.1	0.6	106.0	-0.1	105.8	-0.2
1987	106.4	0.6	106.5	0.1	106.8	0.3	107.2	0.4	107.6	0.4	107.9	0.3	108.1	0.2	108.5	0.4	108.5	0.0	109.0	0.5	109.4	0.4	109.5	0.1
1988	110.0	0.5	109.8	-0.2	109.9	0.1	110.3	0.4	110.6	0.3	110.9	0.3	111.4	0.5	111.6	0.2	111.7	0.1	111.6	-0.1	111.9	0.3	112.1	0.2
1989	112.6	0.4	112.9	0.3	113.3	0.4	113.6	0.3	113.8	0.2	113.9	0.1	114.2	0.3	114.5	0.3	114.6	0.1	114.7	0.1	115.0	0.3	115.4	0.3
1990	116.5	1.0	117.0	0.4	117.4	0.3	117.2	-0.2	117.3	0.1	117.6	0.3	117.6	0.0	118.1	0.4	118.1	0.0	118.5	0.3	118.6	0.1	118.5	-0.1
1991	119.7	1.0	119.8	0.1	120.2	0.3	120.4	0.2	120.5	0.1	120.8	0.2	120.9	0.1	120.6	-0.2	120.4	-0.2	120.6	0.2	120.7	0.1	120.9	0.2

[Continued]

Miscellaneous Products n.e.c.
Producer Price Index
Base 1982 = 100
[Continued]

For 1947-1993. Columns headed % show percentile change in the index from the previous period for which an index is available.

Year	Jan Index	%	Feb Index	%	Mar Index	%	Apr Index	%	May Index	%	Jun Index	%	Jul Index	%	Aug Index	%	Sep Index	%	Oct Index	%	Nov Index	%	Dec Index	%
1992	121.6	0.6	121.6	0.0	121.7	0.1	122.2	0.4	122.3	0.1	122.4	0.1	122.5	0.1	122.7	0.2	122.6	-0.1	122.8	0.2	123.1	0.2	123.5	0.3
1993	123.9	0.3	124.2	0.2	124.2	0.0	124.9	0.6	125.3	0.3	125.3	0.0	125.8	0.4	126.0	0.2	126.0	0.0	125.8	-0.2	126.3	0.4	126.3	0.0

Source: U.S. Department of Labor, Bureau of Labor Statistics, Division of Industry Prices and Price Indexes. n.e.c. stands for not elsewhere classified. - indicates no data collected for period or unavailable.

CHAPTER 8

SELECTED STOCK MARKET PRICE INDEXES

SELECTED STOCK MARKET PRICE INDEXES

This chapter presents stock market index data for the American Stock Exchange, the NASDAQ Stock Market, and the New York Stock Exchange. The Standard & Poors composite index, used by the Bureau of Economic Analysis (Department of Commerce) as a component of the composite index of leading indicators, is shown in Chapter 3.

General Concepts

Stock indexes measure the value of stocks traded on exchanges or in the over-the-counter (OTC) market.

Index Weightings. All the indexes presented here are so-called "market-value weighted" indexes, also called "capitalization-weighted" indexes. This means that the contribution of any one stock to the index is weighted by the stock's overall value—its price multiplied by the number of its shares outstanding.

A stock (Stock A) with a price of $100 per share and 50,000 shares outstanding has a capitalization of $5 million; another stock (Stock B), with a price of $50 and 30,000 shares outstanding has a capitalization of $1.5 million. If only these two stocks were present in a market, the total market would be valued at $6.5 million. Stock A's contribution to index changes would be 77% ($5 million as a percent of $6.5 million); Stock B's contribution would be 23%. Since prices and the number of shares outstanding are constantly changing—and the number of stocks traded is large—any one stock's contribution to an index is continuously in flux and relatively small.

Indexes are calculated so that the distorting effect of stock splits, mergers, and similar changes in corporate capitalization are eliminated.

Alternatives to the market-value weighted indexes are price-weighted indexes (none is shown in *EIH*). In these indexes, for example, in the American Stock Exchange's Major Market Index and the Dow Jones Industrial Average, high-priced stocks have a greater influence on the index than low-priced issues.

Market-value weighted indexes reflect overall market performance; price-weighted indexes tend to reflect the performance of important, leading stocks.

Index Basing. Index values are expressed in relation to a base—the value of the market on a given date. The *base index* may be any value but is 50 or 100 for the data shown here. Index values are calculated using the following formula:

(Market Today / Base Period Market) x Base Index

We can apply this formula to a situation where the base period market was $1,000, today's market is $1,050, and the base index is 100. The new index will be 105 (1,050 / 1,000 x 100). If a different base index is used, 50, for example, the same formula and values would yield a new index of 52.5.

The total market values ("market today" and "base period market") are obtained by adding, for each period, the capital value of all stocks: each stock's price multiplied by the number of shares of that stock outstanding. This, in effect, produces a market-value weighting of each stock.

Analytical Uses

The most common use of stock market indexes is to measure the performance of a given market or, by combining various indexes, measuring the performance of stocks as a whole. Investors can use stock market indexes to measure how well their portfolios are doing. The indexes included in this chapter are all broad composites; therefore, portfolios that under-perform these indexes may be overdue for review. Stock markets are sensitive indicators of anticipated economic conditions; the sustained rise or fall of composite indexes, therefore, can be used to forecast the future—the future as it is seen by all those buying and selling stocks.

Presentation

The composite indexes for the American, the NASDAQ, and the New York stock exchanges are presented for 1984-1991 side by side in the first table. All other tables are specific to one of these three stock markets.

American Stock Exchange. The AMEX Market Value Index is a broadly-based index reflecting the prices of more than 800 stocks. It is based on AMEX market value as of July 29, 1983, which was defined as 50. Unlike other stock indexes, this index includes the value of stock dividends paid. Two tables highlight the AMEX index; the first shows annual high, low, and close indexes for the 1969-1991 period; the second shows the Market Value Index and its sub-indexes for 1980 to 1991 by quarter, each item of data being the closing value of the quarter.

NASDAQ Stock Market. NASDAQ stands for the National Association of Security Dealers Automated Quotation System; NASDAQ reports the prices of more than 5,000 stocks traded over-the-counter (OTC); this is a relatively small subset of the more than 40 million OTC stock issues traded. The base period for the NASDAQ Price Index is February 5, 1971; the base index is 100. Two tables are included for the NASDAQ index; the first shows high, low, and close data for the 1971 to 1991 period; the second shows quarterly data for 1980 through 1991. In addition to the composite index, data for six sub-indexes are also included.

New York Stock Exchange. The New York Stock Exchange (NYSE) is the largest U.S. stock exchange, and the NYSE Composite Index reflects the share prices of more than 1,600 stocks traded on the exchange. The index base period is December 31, 1965 and the base index is 50. A single table summarizes the NYSE's performance. It shows annual high, low, and close data from 1966 through 1991. Like the AMEX and NASDAQ markets, the NYSE's composite index is also subdivided into specialized indexes (Industrials, Transportation, Utilities, and Financials). Data showing sub-indexes were not received in time for inclusion.

Bibliography

1. Berlin, Howard M. *The Handbook of Financial Market Indexes, Averages, and Indicators*. Dow Jones-Irwin, Homewood, IL, 1990.

2. Downes, John and Jordan Elliot Goodman. *Dictionary of Finance and Investment Terms*. Barron's, New York, 1991.

AMEX, NASD, and NYSE Indexes
1984-1993

For 1984-1993. Index is the closing value at month end. Columns headed % show percentile change in each index from the previous period. The acronyms AMEX, NASD, and NYSE stand for American Stock Exchange, National Association of Securities Dealers (over the counter market), and New York Stock Exchange.

Year	Month	AMEX Index	%	NASD Index	%	NYSE Index	%
1984	JAN	216.91	-2.7	268.43	-3.7	94.32	-0.9
	FEB	210.22	-3.1	252.57	-5.9	90.44	-4.1
	MAR	211.34	0.5	250.78	-0.7	91.67	1.4
	APR	210.42	-0.4	247.44	-1.3	91.98	0.3
	MAY	198.63	-5.6	232.82	-5.9	86.71	-5.7
	JUN	200.08	0.7	239.65	2.9	88.38	1.9
	JUL	188.67	-5.7	229.70	-4.2	86.73	-1.9
	AUG	215.41	14.2	254.64	10.9	95.86	10.5
	SEP	215.45	0.0	249.94	-1.8	95.77	-0.1
	OCT	208.18	-3.4	247.03	-1.2	95.74	-0.0
	NOV	204.27	-1.9	242.53	-1.8	94.30	-1.5
	DEC	204.26	-0.0	247.35	2.0	96.38	2.2
1985	JAN	224.07	9.7	278.70	12.7	103.75	7.6
	FEB	227.43	1.5	284.17	2.0	104.93	1.1
	MAR	229.59	0.9	279.20	-1.7	104.60	-0.3
	APR	227.44	-0.9	280.56	0.5	104.12	-0.5
	MAY	231.69	1.9	290.80	3.6	109.63	5.3
	JUN	230.89	-0.3	296.20	1.9	111.11	1.3
	JUL	233.92	1.3	301.29	1.7	110.47	-0.6
	AUG	234.25	0.1	297.31	-1.3	109.47	-0.9
	SEP	222.31	-5.1	280.33	-5.7	105.19	-3.9
	OCT	228.61	2.8	292.54	4.4	109.65	4.2
	NOV	242.26	6.0	313.95	7.3	116.55	6.3
	DEC	246.13	1.6	324.93	3.5	121.58	4.3
1986	JAN	243.87	-0.9	335.77	3.3	122.13	0.5
	FEB	257.35	5.5	359.53	7.1	130.74	7.0
	MAR	270.03	4.9	374.72	4.2	137.71	5.3
	APR	268.97	-0.4	383.24	2.3	135.75	-1.4
	MAY	282.60	5.1	400.16	4.4	142.06	4.6
	JUN	284.20	0.6	405.51	1.3	143.96	1.3
	JUL	261.56	-8.0	371.37	-8.4	135.89	-5.6
	AUG	273.85	4.7	382.86	3.1	145.32	6.9
	SEP	260.69	-4.8	350.67	-8.4	133.44	-8.2
	OCT	265.59	1.9	360.77	2.9	140.42	5.2
	NOV	264.81	-0.3	359.57	-0.3	142.57	1.5
	DEC	263.27	-0.6	348.83	-3.0	138.58	-2.8
1987	JAN	300.47	14.1	392.06	12.4	156.11	12.6
	FEB	321.76	7.1	424.97	8.4	162.01	3.8
	MAR	332.66	3.4	430.05	1.2	165.89	2.4
	APR	325.19	-2.2	417.81	-2.8	162.86	-1.8
	MAY	326.39	0.4	416.54	-0.3	163.48	0.4
	JUN	338.13	3.6	424.67	2.0	171.07	4.6
	JUL	358.03	5.9	434.93	2.4	178.63	4.4
	AUG	361.35	0.9	454.97	4.6	184.45	3.3
	SEP	358.45	-0.8	444.29	-2.3	180.24	-2.3
	OCT	260.36	-27.4	323.30	-27.2	140.80	-21.9
	NOV	242.39	-6.9	305.16	-5.6	129.69	-7.9
	DEC	260.35	7.4	330.47	8.3	138.23	6.6

[Continued]

1117

AMEX, NASD, and NYSE Indexes
1984-1993

[Continued]

Year	Month	AMEX Index	AMEX %	NASD Index	NASD %	NYSE Index	NYSE %
1988	JAN	269.10	3.4	344.66	4.3	144.13	4.3
	FEB	288.46	7.2	366.94	6.5	150.46	4.4
	MAR	296.43	2.8	374.64	2.1	146.60	-2.6
	APR	303.14	2.3	379.23	1.2	147.87	0.9
	MAY	294.19	-3.0	370.34	-2.3	148.04	0.1
	JUN	309.25	5.1	394.66	6.6	154.47	4.3
	JUL	306.18	-1.0	387.33	-1.9	153.35	-0.7
	AUG	294.80	-3.7	376.55	-2.8	148.29	-3.3
	SEP	301.63	2.3	387.71	3.0	153.57	3.6
	OCT	300.95	-0.2	382.46	-1.4	156.94	2.2
	NOV	294.36	-2.2	371.45	-2.9	153.90	-1.9
	DEC	306.01	4.0	381.38	2.7	156.26	1.5
1989	JAN	323.02	5.6	401.30	5.2	166.63	6.6
	FEB	322.47	-0.2	399.71	-0.4	162.49	-2.5
	MAR	328.31	1.8	406.73	1.8	165.63	1.9
	APR	345.08	5.1	427.55	5.1	173.13	4.5
	MAY	356.66	3.4	446.17	4.4	178.85	3.3
	JUN	358.97	0.6	435.29	-2.4	177.90	-0.5
	JUL	376.56	4.9	453.84	4.3	192.41	8.2
	AUG	382.19	1.5	469.33	3.4	195.27	1.5
	SEP	388.76	1.7	472.92	0.8	193.97	-0.7
	OCT	370.58	-4.7	455.63	-3.7	188.24	-3.0
	NOV	373.84	0.9	456.09	0.1	191.30	1.6
	DEC	378.00	1.1	454.82	-0.3	195.04	2.0
1990	JAN	350.07	-7.4	415.81	-8.6	181.50	-6.9
	FEB	352.90	0.8	425.83	2.4	183.07	0.9
	MAR	361.75	2.5	435.54	2.3	186.84	2.1
	APR	343.10	-5.2	420.07	-3.6	181.49	-2.9
	MAY	363.06	5.8	458.97	9.3	196.94	8.5
	JUN	361.21	-0.5	462.29	0.7	195.48	-0.7
	JUL	353.60	-2.1	438.24	-5.2	194.60	-0.5
	AUG	323.39	-8.5	381.21	-13.0	176.97	-9.1
	SEP	307.72	-4.8	344.51	-9.6	167.85	-5.2
	OCT	287.79	-6.5	329.84	-4.3	166.17	-1.0
	NOV	301.79	4.9	359.06	8.9	176.06	6.0
	DEC	308.11	2.1	373.84	4.1	180.49	2.5
1991	JAN	317.54	3.1	414.20	10.8	187.59	3.9
	FEB	346.13	9.0	453.05	9.4	200.70	7.0
	MAR	359.20	3.8	482.30	6.5	205.30	2.3
	APR	360.76	0.4	484.72	0.5	205.37	0.0
	MAY	371.99	3.1	506.11	4.4	212.99	3.7
	JUN	358.12	-3.7	475.92	-6.0	203.47	-4.5
	JUL	388.28	8.4	502.04	5.5	212.34	4.4
	AUG	372.13	-4.2	525.68	4.7	216.69	2.0
	SEP	374.58	0.7	526.88	0.2	213.34	-1.5
	OCT	387.31	3.4	542.98	3.1	216.54	1.5
	NOV	370.68	-4.3	523.90	-3.5	207.75	-4.1
	DEC	395.05	6.6	586.34	11.9	229.44	10.4

[Continued]

AMEX, NASD, and NYSE Indexes
1984-1993
[Continued]

Year	Month	AMEX Index	AMEX %	NASD Index	NASD %	NYSE Index	NYSE %
1992	JAN	411.37	4.1	620.21	5.8	226.20	-1.4
	FEB	416.09	1.1	633.47	2.1	228.21	0.9
	MAR	395.04	-5.1	603.77	-4.7	223.25	-2.2
	APR	380.90	-3.6	578.68	-4.2	228.30	2.3
	MAY	394.90	3.7	585.31	1.1	228.87	0.2
	JUN	379.28	-4.0	563.60	-3.7	224.33	-2.0
	JUL	388.85	2.5	580.83	3.1	233.15	3.9
	AUG	380.78	-2.1	563.12	-3.0	228.03	-2.2
	SEP	376.72	-1.1	583.27	3.6	229.46	0.6
	OCT	381.72	1.3	605.17	3.8	230.57	0.5
	NOV	395.11	3.5	652.73	7.9	237.45	3.0
	DEC	399.23	1.0	676.95	3.7	240.21	1.2
1993	JAN	411.08	3.0	696.34	2.9	241.92	0.7
	FEB	406.84	-1.0	670.77	-3.7	244.08	0.9
	MAR	423.43	4.1	690.13	2.9	249.42	2.2
	APR	420.96	-0.6	661.42	-4.2	243.46	-2.4
	MAY	438.22	4.1	700.53	5.9	248.60	2.1
	JUN	434.24	-0.9	703.95	0.5	249.10	0.2
	JUL	437.00	0.6	704.70	0.1	248.49	-0.2
	AUG	458.60	4.9	742.84	5.4	256.88	3.4
	SEP	460.39	0.4	762.78	2.7	255.23	-0.6
	OCT	481.44	4.6	779.26	2.2	259.38	1.6
	NOV	460.03	-4.4	754.39	-3.2	254.79	-1.8
	DEC	477.15	3.7	776.80	3.0	259.08	1.7

Source: American Stock Exchange, private communication, for 1984-1991 and from the exchanges for later years.

American Stock Exchange Market Value Index
Yearly High, Low, and Close
1969-1993

For 1969 through December 31, 1993. Dates indicate the date of high and low values reached in the year. Close is the last day of the year. Percent change is from previous year-end.

Year	High		Low		Close	% Change
	Index	Date	Index	Date	Index	
1969	84.50	1/2	57.23	7/29	60.01	
1970	62.77	1/5	36.10	5/26	49.21	-18.0
1971	60.86	4/28	49.09	1/4	58.49	18.9
1972	69.18	4/30	58.55	1/3	64.53	10.3
1973	65.06	1/2	42.61	12/24	45.17	-30.0
1974	51.01	3/14	29.13	12/9	30.16	-33.2
1975	48.43	7/15	31.10	1/2	41.74	38.4
1976	54.92	12/31	42.16	1/2	54.92	31.6
1977	63.95	12/30	54.81	1/12	63.95	16.4
1978	88.44	9/13	59.87	1/11	75.28	17.7
1979	123.54	12/31	76.02	1/2	123.54	64.1
1980	185.38	11/28	107.85	3/27	174.50	41.2
1981	190.18	8/13	138.38	9/25	160.32	-8.1
1982	170.93	11/11	118.65	8/12	170.30	6.2
1983	249.03	7/26	169.61	1/3	223.01	31.0
1984	227.73	1/16	187.16	7/25	204.26	-8.4
1985	246.13	12/31	202.06	1/8	246.13	20.5
1986	285.19	6/25	240.30	2/4	263.27	7.0
1987	365.01	8/13	231.90	12/4	260.35	-1.1
1988	309.59	7/5	262.76	1/12	306.01	17.5
1989	397.03	10/10	305.24	1/3	378.00	23.5
1990	382.45	1/5	287.79	10/31	308.11	-18.5
1991	393.01	11/11	368.51	10/9	395.05	28.2
1992	418.99	2/12	364.85	10/9	399.23	7.7
1993	484.28	11/2	395.84	1/8	477.15	19.5

Source: American Stock Exchange, private communication.

American Stock Exchange Market Value Index
Quarterly Index and Sub-Indices

For 1980-1993 by Quarters. QTR stands for Quarter. MVI stands for Market Value Index.

QTR	Year	MVI	High Tech	Capital Goods	Consumer Goods	Services	Retail	Financials	Natural Resources	Housing, Constr., & Land
1	1980	116.52	155.94	111.47	69.37	115.58	98.33	93.74	129.69	95.65
2		146.81	175.24	127.44	80.55	145.54	113.08	113.76	172.95	119.20
3		165.78	254.94	147.45	103.90	173.14	131.88	135.77	178.76	142.85
4		174.50	316.74	158.66	118.35	189.03	126.55	143.93	177.80	145.93
1	1981	180.30	326.82	171.10	121.85	209.31	150.25	148.71	178.08	162.68
2		187.32	331.55	169.80	129.21	208.79	172.49	157.94	187.72	176.33
3		146.43	246.97	139.17	106.89	166.36	144.13	138.09	143.51	142.83
4		160.32	282.99	138.64	120.52	201.84	148.61	156.59	154.25	160.54
1	1982	130.06	247.33	116.40	117.06	191.02	145.78	153.81	112.19	137.17
2		125.40	246.12	115.08	116.94	199.25	162.72	151.48	101.18	137.11
3		141.59	294.16	121.71	132.79	222.22	190.77	168.52	115.47	158.10
4		170.30	426.62	143.92	166.10	287.16	242.20	214.39	119.37	249.39
1	1983	194.54	509.06	175.34	197.48	331.50	319.77	256.17	124.18	302.43
2		242.32	626.55	213.16	230.00	418.77	396.43	296.59	162.98	370.53
3		230.28	542.32	199.64	216.92	380.04	397.06	287.66	165.52	328.55
4		223.01	525.00	211.90	213.48	359.20	410.36	290.32	157.50	312.55
1	1984	211.34	421.50	196.45	195.92	356.41	378.47	294.33	157.53	304.48
2		200.08	404.96	190.39	190.47	362.42	404.01	299.35	140.14	282.72
3		215.45	402.27	210.07	207.47	384.28	458.05	325.85	155.40	300.47
4		204.26	374.87	202.84	195.49	403.65	465.89	351.54	135.60	305.48
1	1985	229.59	364.57	227.06	222.20	485.59	610.38	402.00	152.97	335.43
2		230.89	342.11	234.60	237.62	532.33	675.23	417.38	144.95	341.12
3		222.31	317.00	226.68	233.25	474.24	626.42	402.27	147.07	326.47
4		246.13	383.81	260.29	274.30	537.77	746.10	455.40	146.30	373.50
1	1986	270.03	417.26	299.49	332.93	654.23	877.42	538.73	128.63	456.82
2		284.20	423.69	314.92	379.02	747.81	975.06	586.47	120.16	442.97
3		260.69	384.57	264.95	341.27	656.11	794.23	504.62	127.11	398.50
4		263.27	349.26	273.28	335.83	662.25	769.80	478.49	137.94	390.10
1	1987	332.66	462.04	334.28	401.48	809.73	872.02	504.78	193.60	492.05
2		338.13	463.30	342.48	404.63	875.89	899.07	469.46	202.98	466.87
3		356.45	516.60	365.11	409.52	904.95	928.01	455.69	227.02	472.23
4		260.35	364.91	264.87	304.83	626.67	655.04	355.34	176.97	335.02
1	1988	296.43	378.96	300.67	357.99	718.63	772.42	382.89	200.20	377.01
2		309.25	423.65	332.08	374.30	709.98	885.87	396.24	201.52	414.99
3		301.63	375.48	315.42	368.91	701.25	982.95	386.82	190.88	435.53
4		306.01	368.83	321.55	393.07	710.63	949.31	378.49	202.21	429.99
1	1989	328.31	362.73	349.91	429.92	765.84	1050.22	378.37	221.40	452.81
2		358.97	378.65	377.86	466.48	909.00	1156.33	403.24	229.49	490.99
3		388.76	393.23	417.19	507.83	1002.04	1306.77	422.06	247.90	519.91
4		378.00	376.69	401.37	504.76	930.78	1193.34	407.45	258.52	446.11
1	1990	361.75	371.80	395.42	452.50	868.48	1178.63	400.54	253.99	416.85
2		361.21	390.96	413.50	459.92	890.36	1300.56	398.11	237.46	378.69
3		307.72	291.90	326.76	358.86	654.05	869.09	360.10	250.01	300.78
4		308.11	332.10	335.31	396.80	732.38	1000.70	351.31	215.22	230.58

[Continued]

1121

American Stock Exchange Market Value Index
Quarterly Index and Sub-Indices
[Continued]

For 1980-1993 by Quarters. QTR stands for Quarter. MVI stands for Market Value Index.

QTR	Year	MVI	High Tech	Capital Goods	Consumer Goods	Services	Retail	Financials	Natural Resources	Housing, Constr., & Land
1	1991	359.20	454.92	396.58	515.93	852.89	1236.86	414.45	215.62	334.59
2		372.13	456.03	411.13	561.44	921.42	1225.14	435.31	219.56	286.58
3		374.58	466.42	411.43	579.21	931.05	1321.73	433.63	216.53	266.30
4		395.05	573.19	405.53	701.82	1034.14	1268.93	446.83	187.79	279.46
1	1992	395.04	543.87	438.78	740.29	1041.79	1293.46	484.44	172.89	341.48
2		379.28	422.20	399.87	537.19	872.35	1250.37	428.80	209.97	321.49
3		376.72	437.36	389.25	753.19	969.20	1107.57	471.52	187.71	282.47
4		399.23	486.10	410.73	805.70	1123.98	1334.84	500.65	164.56	344.25
1	1993	406.84	475.04	428.48	764.08	1111.29	1341.62	542.96	177.85	382.94
2		434.24	481.79	428.75	783.84	1196.67	1411.12	513.10	213.24	390.64
3		460.39	519.22	489.52	811.94	1386.74	1366.93	542.91	205.84	425.04
4		477.15	539.76	508.03	864.99	1468.54	1465.48	537.99	203.63	504.49

Source: American Stock Exchange, private communication.

NASDAQ Composite Index
Yearly High, Low, and Close
1971-1993

For 1971 through 1993. Dates indicate the date of high and low values reached in the year. Close is the last day of the year. Percent change is from previous year-end. The NASDAQ index began on February 5, 1971.

Year	High		Low		Close	% Change
	Index	Date	Index	Date	Index	
1971	114.12	12/31	99.68	2/22	114.12	-
1972	135.15	12/8	113.65	1/3	133.73	17.2
1973	136.84	1/11	88.67	12/24	92.19	-31.1
1974	96.53	3/15	54.87	10/3	59.82	-35.1
1975	88.00	7/15	60.70	1/2	77.62	29.8
1976	97.88	12/31	78.06	1/2	97.88	26.1
1977	105.05	12/30	93.66	4/5	105.05	7.3
1978	139.25	9/13	99.09	1/11	117.98	12.3
1979	152.29	10/5	117.84	1/2	151.14	28.1
1980	208.15	11/28	124.09	3/27	202.34	33.9
1981	223.47	5/29	175.03	9/28	195.84	-3.2
1982	240.70	12/8	159.14	8/13	232.41	18.7
1983	328.91	6/24	230.59	1/3	278.60	19.9
1984	287.90	1/6	225.30	7/25	247.35	-11.2
1985	325.22	12/31	245.91	1/2	325.22	31.5
1986	411.16	7/3	323.01	1/9	348.83	7.3
1987	455.26	8/26	291.88	10/28	330.47	-5.3
1988	396.11	7/5	331.97	1/12	381.38	15.4
1989	485.73	10/9	378.56	1/3	454.82	19.3
1990	469.60	7/16	325.44	10/16	373.84	-17.8
1991	586.34	12/31	355.75	1/14	586.34	56.8
1992	676.95	12/31	547.84	6/26	676.95	15.5
1993	787.42	10/15	645.87	4/26	776.80	14.7

Source: The NASDAQ Stock Market, Historical Data Services.

NASDAQ Stock Market Index
Quarterly Index and Sub-Indices

For 1980-1993 by Quarters. QTR stands for Quarter. Data show closing index for each period.

QTR	Year	Composite Index	Industrials	Banks	Insurance	Financials	Trans-portation	Utilities
1	1980	131.00	155.70	93.29	133.26	109.84	105.28	110.74
2		157.78	185.74	108.34	158.94	136.35	125.10	134.37
3		187.76	233.90	114.87	176.90	148.74	160.17	151.00
4		202.34	261.36	118.39	166.81	154.07	164.19	165.70
1	1981	210.18	264.85	126.96	184.80	168.44	171.81	165.71
2		215.75	265.68	138.92	198.44	178.53	193.04	177.73
3		180.03	212.22	128.86	177.56	160.41	166.15	158.68
4		195.84	229.29	143.13	194.31	176.20	167.77	181.67
1	1982	175.65	199.05	136.66	188.09	165.00	148.10	175.40
2		171.30	196.33	130.61	172.49	158.52	151.46	196.24
3		187.65	213.35	134.16	201.84	177.31	172.50	213.82
4		232.41	273.58	156.37	226.40	207.50	195.48	286.23
1	1983	270.80	323.52	169.58	259.19	235.16	230.82	332.64
2		318.70	392.90	186.70	268.63	269.96	259.46	366.09
3		296.65	353.52	201.06	262.89	280.58	277.99	287.37
4		278.60	323.68	203.75	257.63	277.53	280.80	269.39
1	1984	250.78	283.34	204.09	254.19	270.20	228.19	210.02
2		239.65	270.65	194.48	244.26	258.28	203.71	208.76
3		249.94	275.16	209.23	271.59	281.23	224.99	219.24
4		247.35	260.73	229.77	283.11	298.62	239.29	238.66
1	1985	279.20	297.37	253.43	326.29	330.37	255.54	262.27
2		296.20	303.82	290.49	350.14	377.06	261.79	299.05
3		280.33	284.39	296.10	329.77	365.53	256.52	264.53
4		325.22	330.17	349.36	382.07	423.49	291.59	301.57
1	1986	374.72	375.91	403.25	455.06	499.73	340.56	338.61
2		405.51	409.96	450.45	452.72	543.95	362.92	351.86
3		350.67	344.16	403.70	425.20	482.84	322.95	316.43
4		348.83	349.33	412.53	404.14	460.64	348.84	316.09
1	1987	430.05	454.21	506.19	446.17	527.82	398.87	374.91
2		424.67	450.71	475.48	433.04	511.97	406.13	392.39
3		444.29	475.25	489.82	457.39	520.74	418.38	427.01
4		330.47	338.94	390.66	351.06	406.96	319.21	355.30
1	1988	374.64	383.67	448.77	397.65	456.39	373.51	411.97
2		394.66	411.48	455.91	398.36	468.43	374.07	443.71
3		387.71	388.19	456.94	435.45	473.20	390.74	473.22
4		381.38	378.95	435.31	429.14	459.34	395.81	501.13
1	1989	406.73	398.63	458.57	470.56	487.75	412.84	579.02
2		435.29	421.71	466.03	505.05	513.14	421.25	694.45
3		472.92	458.97	478.84	533.63	559.54	476.97	754.15
4		454.82	447.99	391.02	546.01	505.64	498.20	737.20
1	1990	435.54	450.51	366.25	502.65	466.36	476.70	611.24
2		462.29	499.01	335.71	506.31	446.61	488.28	647.56
3		344.51	368.46	249.25	406.56	340.34	389.31	462.98
4		373.84	406.05	254.91	451.84	359.13	417.07	483.01
1	1991	482.30	545.03	310.15	548.98	437.31	509.21	563.91
2		475.92	527.10	327.30	534.39	472.42	513.80	543.97
3		526.88	590.19	343.52	534.10	521.94	530.73	602.11
4		586.34	668.95	350.56	601.09	560.79	571.39	629.53

[Continued]

NASDAQ Stock Market Index
Quarterly Index and Sub-Indices
[Continued]

QTR	Year	Composite Index	Industrials	Banks	Insurance	Financials	Trans-portation	Utilities
1	1992	603.77	676.05	396.32	617.46	621.85	604.09	641.65
2		563.60	601.65	442.93	623.26	666.02	551.92	622.57
3		583.27	620.85	462.50	705.60	687.31	567.47	635.39
4		676.95	724.94	532.93	803.91	788.81	634.10	734.20
1	1993	690.13	713.55	627.47	861.30	860.92	672.01	810.13
2		703.95	729.52	607.88	853.02	834.96	673.48	917.04
3		762.78	780.13	698.81	946.00	907.00	701.78	1067.47
4		776.80	805.84	689.43	920.59	892.64	746.26	1063.50

Source: The NASDAQ Stock Market, Historical Data Services.

New York Stock Exchange Composite Index
Yearly High, Low, and Close
1966-1993

For 1966 through 1993. Dates indicate the date of high and low values reached in the year. Close is the last day of the year. Percent change is from previous year-end.

Year	High		Low		Close	% Change
	Index	Date	Index	Date	Index	
1966	51.06	9/2	39.37	7/10	43.72	-12.6
1967	54.16	9/10	43.74	3/1	53.83	23.1
1968	61.27	29/11	48.70	5/3	58.90	9.4
1969	59.32	14/5	49.31	29/7	51.53	-12.5
1970	52.36	5/1	37.69	26/5	50.23	-2.5
1971	57.76	28/4	49.60	23/11	56.43	12.3
1972	65.14	11/12	56.23	3/1	64.48	14.3
1973	65.48	11/1	49.05	5/12	51.82	-19.6
1974	53.37	13/3	32.89	3/10	36.13	-30.3
1975	51.24	15/7	37.06	2/1	47.64	31.9
1976	57.88	31/12	48.04	2/1	57.88	21.5
1977	57.69	3/1	49.78	2/11	52.50	-9.3
1978	60.38	11/9	48.37	6/3	53.62	2.1
1979	63.39	5/10	53.88	27/2	61.95	15.5
1980	81.02	28/11	55.30	27/3	77.86	25.7
1981	79.14	6/1	64.96	25/9	71.11	-8.7
1982	82.35	9/11	58.80	12/8	81.03	14.0
1983	99.63	10/10	79.79	3/1	95.18	17.5
1984	98.12	6/11	85.13	24/7	96.38	1.3
1985	121.90	16/12	94.60	4/1	121.58	26.1
1986	145.75	4/9	117.75	22/1	138.58	14.0
1987	187.99	25/8	125.91	4/12	138.23	-0.3
1988	159.42	21/10	136.72	20/1	156.26	13.0
1989	199.34	9/10	154.98	3/1	195.04	24.8
1990	201.13	16/7	162.20	11/10	180.49	-7.5
1991	229.44	31/12	170.97	9/1	229.44	27.1
1992	242.08	18/12	217.92	8/4	240.21	4.7
1993	260.67	29/12	236.21	8/1	259.08	7.9

Source: New York Stock Exchange Data Services.

KEYWORD INDEX

The *Keyword Index* is an alphabetical arrangement of the topics covered in the text and tables of *Economic Indicators Handbook*, 2nd edition. The table of contents (page v) provides an alternative means of locating tables. The primary reference numbers that follow subject index terms are page numbers. Cities cited in this index are metropolitan statistical areas (MSAs).

Boston, MA consumer price index
— all items, pp. 300, 302
— annual averages, pp. 296, 298
— apparel and upkeep, pp. 308-309
— entertainment, pp. 318-319
— food and beverages, pp. 304-305
— housing, pp. 306-307
— medical care, pp. 314, 316
— other goods and services, pp. 320-321
— transportation, pp. 310, 312
Boulder, CO *See:* Denver-Boulder, CO consumer price index
Bridges
— and fixed investment, p. 26
— government expenditures, p. 53
Brokerage services
— personal expenditures, p. 16
Brokers commissions
— fixed investment, p. 26
Buffalo, NY consumer price index
— all items, pp. 324-325
— annual averages, pp. 322-323
— apparel and upkeep, pp. 330-331
— entertainment, pp. 336-337
— food and beverages, pp. 326-327
— housing, pp. 328-329
— medical care, pp. 334-335
— other goods and services, pp. 338-339
— transportation, pp. 332-333
Building paper & building board mill products, p. 1016
Building permits
— issuance of, p. 71
Buildings
— expenditures, p. 26
— fixed investment, p. 26
Bureau of Economic Affairs, p. 16
Bureau of Economic Analysis (BEA), pp. xxiv, xxvii, 3, 11-12, 26-27, 46, 53, 72, 87, 95
   See also: United States Department of Commerce
Bureau of Labor Statistics (BLS), pp. xxviii, 72, 87, 95
   See also: United States Department of Labor
Business cycle indicators, pp. xxiii-xxiv, xxvi, 67, 111
— history of, p. 67
Business cycles
— and coincident to lagging ratio, p. 106
— and fixed capital investment, p. 123
— and GDP, p. 12
— and lagging indicators, p. 94
— and retail sales, p. 120
— and unemployment, p. 112
Business debt, p. 138
Business expenditures
— plant and equipment, p. 123
Business incorporations, p. 123

Business inventories, p. 3
— changes in, pp. 26, 129
Business saving, p. 152
Cable television
— personal expenditures, p. 16
Capacity utilization rate, p. 115
Capital consumption allowances, p. 152
Capital equipment
— fixed investment, p. 26
Capital goods
— business expenditures, p. 123
— expenditures, p. 26
— future spending, pp. 70, 123
— net exports, p. 26
Capital goods investment
— and GDP, p. 12
Capital investment, p. 26
— fixed, cyclic indicators, p. 111
— indicators, p. 123
Cattle hides
— and sensitive materials price index, p. 131
Cereal and bakery products, p. 934
Checking accounts, p. 71
Chemicals and allied products, pp. 981, 994
Chicago, IL-NW IN consumer price index
— all items, pp. 344, 346
— annual averages, pp. 340, 342
— apparel and upkeep, pp. 352-353
— entertainment, pp. 362-363
— food and beverages, pp. 348-349
— housing, pp. 350-351
— medical care, pp. 358, 360
— other goods and services, pp. 364-365
— transportation, pp. 354, 356
Cincinnati, OH-KY-IN consumer price index
— all items, pp. 370, 372
— annual averages, pp. 366, 368
— apparel and upkeep, pp. 378-379
— entertainment, pp. 388-389
— food and beverages, pp. 374-375
— housing, pp. 376-377
— medical care, pp. 384, 386
— other goods and services, pp. 390-391
— transportation, pp. 380, 382
Clay construction products ex. refractories, p. 1077
Cleveland, OH consumer price index
— all items, pp. 396, 398
— annual averages, pp. 392, 394
— apparel and upkeep, pp. 404-405
— entertainment, pp. 414-415
— food and beverages, pp. 400-401
— housing, pp. 402-403
— medical care, pp. 410, 412
— other goods and services, pp. 416-417

Numbers following p. or pp. are page references.

Numbers following p. or pp. are page references.

Numbers following p. or pp. are page references.

Numbers following p. or pp. are page references.

Numbers following p. or pp. are page references.

Numbers following p. or pp. are page references.

Numbers following p. or pp. are page references.

Numbers following p. or pp. are page references.

Numbers following p. or pp. are page references.

Numbers following p. or pp. are page references.